Mergent's

HANDBOOK OF COMMON STOCKS

2017-2018 Winter Common

INTRODUCTION

Mergent's Handbook of Common Stocks provides quick and easy access to basic financial and business information on more than 900 stocks that are included in the Russell 1000, S&P 500, S&P 400 and Mergent's Dividend Achievers. The Tab Section provides one-line information on New York Stock Exchange companies.

The price charts, statistics, and analyses are presented in a format that provides the investor with the necessary perspective for acting on investment advice or suggestions. It also affords investors the opportunity to make investment decisions on their own.

Statistics and analyses are revised quarterly. Every effort is made to secure the most current operating results and dividend information available. In the case of year-end results, preliminary results are shown and analyzed as they are received. Full statistical presentations of annual report information are shown in the following edition. The schedule below describes the publication dates and company reporting periods usually covered in each edition.

The Winter Edition (published in January) covers quarterly reports and preliminary annual reports through September 30.

The Spring Edition (published in April) covers quarterly reports and preliminary annual reports through December 31.

The Summer Edition (published in July) covers quarterly reports and preliminary annual reports through March 31.

The Fall Edition (published in October) covers quarterly reports and preliminary annual reports through June 30.

Note: For various reasons, some companies may not report in time to meet our publication deadlines. Company reports received close to press time are shown in the Addenda. The remainder of late reports are published and analyzed in the next edition of the Handbook.

The special section on these opening pages contains a number of features, including a guide on how to use this book, a classification of companies by their major line of business based on their NAIC code, outstanding stock price movements by company, plus long-term charts on popular stock market averages. The Addenda provide the latest developments available just prior to publication but after the company reports have been completed.

TABLE OF CONTENTS

Page

HOW TO USE THIS BOOK.. 4a

SPECIAL FEATURES

ADDENDA

COMPANY REPORTS

HOW TO USE THIS BOOK

The presentation of historical data and analytical comments provides the answers to four basic questions for each company:

1. What does the company do?
(See G.)
2. How has it done in the past?
(See B, J.)
3. How is it doing now?
(See C, D, H.)
4. How will it fare in the future?
(See I.)

A. CAPSULE STOCK INFORMATION shows where the stock is traded and its symbol, a recent price and price/earnings ratio, plus the yield afforded by the indicated dividend based on a recent price. The indicated dividend is the current annualized dividend based on the most recent price. Some companies are designated as Dividend Achievers. Dividend Achievers have, by *Mergent's* criteria, increased their cash dividend payments for at least ten consecutive years, adjusting for splits. The number of years of consecutive increases is given for each Dividend Achiever.

B. LONG-TERM PRICE CHART illustrates the pattern of monthly stock price movements, fully adjusted for stock dividends and splits. The chart points out the degree of volatility in the price movement of the company's stock and what its long-term trend has been. It also shows how it has performed long-term relative to an initial investment in the S&P 500 Index equal to the price of the company's stock at the beginning of the period shown in the price chart. It indicates areas of price support and resistance, plus other technical points to be considered by the investor. The bars at the base of the long-term price chart indicate the monthly trading volume. Monthly trading volume offers the individual an opportunity to recognize at what periods stock accumulation occurs and what percent of a company's outstanding shares are traded.

PRICE SCORES – Above each company's price/volume chart are its *Mergent's Price Scores*. These are basic measures of the stock's performance. Each stock is measured against the New York Stock Exchange Composite Index.

A score of 100 indicates that the stock did as well as the New York Stock Exchange Composite Index during the time period. A score of less than 100 means that the stock did not do as well; a score of more than 100 means that the stock outperformed the NYSE Composite Index. All stock prices are adjusted for splits and stock dividends. The time periods measured for each company conclude with the date of the recent price shown in the top line of each company's profile.

The *7 YEAR PRICE SCORE* mirrors the common stock's price growth over the previous seven years. The higher the price score, the better the relative performance. It is based on the ratio of the latest 12-month average price to the current seven-year average. This ratio is then indexed against the same ratio for the market as a whole (the New York Stock Exchange Composite Index), which is taken as 100.

The *12 MONTH PRICE SCORE* is a similar measurement but for a shorter period of time. It is based on the ratio of the latest two-month average price to the current 12-month average. As was done for the Long-Term Price Score, this ratio is also indexed to the same ratio for the market as a whole.

C. INTERIM EARNINGS (Per Share) – Figures are reported after the effect of extraordinary items, discontinued operations and cumulative effects of accounting changes. Each figure is for the quarterly period indicated. These figures are essentially as reported by the company, although all figures are adjusted for all stock dividends and splits.

4a

ILLUSTRATIVE INC.

Exchange **A**	Symbol	Price	52Wk Range	Yield	P/E	Div Achiever
NYS	A00	$136.31 (12/31/2017)	136.31-77.08	0.94	17.45	22 Years

*7 Year Price Score 124.21 *NYSE Composite Index=100 *12 Month Price Score 113.32

Interim Earnings (Per Share)

Qtr.	Mar	Jun	Sep	Dec
2014	0.71	0.28	0.93	(0.22)
2015	0.40	0.46	0.58	1.56
2016	2.02	(2.78)	1.13	5.31
2017	0.45	0.92	...	...

Interim Dividends (Per Share)

Amt	Decl	Ex	Rec	Pay
0.305Q	11/03/2016	12/13/2016	12/15/2016	01/02/2017
0.32Q	02/23/2017	03/13/2017	03/15/2017	04/03/2017
0.32Q	05/11/2017	06/13/2017	06/15/2017	07/03/2017
0.32Q	07/10/2017	09/14/2017	09/15/2017	10/02/2017

Indicated Div: $1.28 (Div. Reinv. Plan)

Valuation Analysis   Institutional Holding

Forecast EPS	$4.38 (12/31/2017)	No of Institutions 687
Market Cap	$15.0 Billion	Shares
Book Value	$3.8 Billion	111,805,624
Price/Book	4.00	% Held
Price/Sales	5.35	68.76

Business Summary: Specialty Chemicals (MIC: 8.3.2 SIC: 2821 NAIC: 325211) **G**

Illustrative is a developer, manufacturer and marketer of chemicals across a range of end markets including, among others, the petroleum refining, consumer electronics, energy storage, construction, automotive, lubricants, and pharmaceuticals. Co.'s segments include: Lithium and Advanced Materials, which consisted of Lithium and Performance Catalyst Solutions; Bromine Specialties, which includes products used in fire safety solutions and other specialty chemicals applications; and Refining Solutions, which consisted of two main product lines: Clean Fuels Technologies composed of hydroprocessing catalysts, and Heavy Oil Upgrading composed of fluidized catalytic cracking catalysts and additives.

Recent Developments: For the quarter ended Dec. 31, 2017, income from continuing operations increased 18.9% to US$113.7 million from US$95.6 million in the year-earlier quarter. Net income amounted to US$113.7 million versus a net loss of US$302.8 million in the year-earlier quarter. Revenues were US$737.3 million, up 10.1% from US$669.3 million the year before. Operating income was US$139.1 million versus US$123.5 million in the prior-year quarter, an increase of 12.6%. Direct operating expenses rose 10.4% to US$465.2 million from US$421.2 million in the comparable period the year before. Indirect operating expenses increased 6.8% to US$133.0 million from US$124.6 million in the equivalent prior-year period. **H**

Prospects: Our evaluation of Illustrative Inc. as of Oct. 15, 2017 is the result of our systematic analysis on three basic characteristics: earnings strength, relative valuation, and recent stock price movement. The company has enjoyed a very positive trend in earnings per share over the past 5 quarters and while recent estimates for the company have been raised by analysts, A00 has posted better than expected results. Based on operating earnings yield, the company is about fairly valued when compared to all of the companies in our coverage universe. Share price changes over the past year indicates that ALB will perform well over the near term.

Financial Data
(US$ in Thousands)

	6 Mos	3 Mos	12/31/2016	12/31/2015	12/31/2014	12/31/2013	12/31/2012	12/31/2011
Earnings Per Share	7.81	4.11	5.68	3.00	1.69	4.90	3.47	4.77
Cash Flow Per Share	3.85	5.74	6.51	3.24	6.26	5.16	5.47	5.38
Tang Book Value Per Share	15.91	15.19	16.89	N.M.	13.74	15.68	16.45	13.37
Dividends Per Share	1.250	1.235	1.220	1.160	1.100	0.960	0.800	0.670
Dividend Payout %	16.01	30.05	21.48	38.67	65.09	19.59	23.05	14.05
Income Statement								
Total Revenue	1,459,321	722,063	2,677,203	3,651,335	2,445,548	2,616,416	2,745,420	2,869,005
EBITDA	352,523	167,040	759,245	671,609	352,437	675,286	495,693	671,797
Depn & Amortn	94,192	45,070	178,800	180,700	97,900	99,300	88,300	83,600
Income Before Taxes	175,228	53,457	515,264	358,187	213,179	544,427	374,593	550,623
Income Taxes	35,101	11,971	96,263	29,122	18,484	136,322	82,533	130,014
Net Income	154,546	51,213	643,675	334,906	133,316	413,171	311,536	436,280
Average Shares	112,105	113,289	113,239	111,556	79,102	84,322	89,884	91,522
Balance Sheet								
Current Assets	2,204,448	2,390,254	3,306,618	1,831,003	3,348,850	1,482,915	1,407,313	1,355,620
Total Assets	7,291,989	7,366,468	8,161,207	9,615,014	5,223,103	3,584,797	3,437,291	3,203,824
Current Liabilities	983,662	1,207,947	1,140,103	1,616,685	1,139,886	436,363	385,009	401,178
Long-Term Obligations	1,421,468	1,398,386	2,121,718	3,174,674	2,223,035	1,054,310	686,588	749,257
Total Liabilities	3,531,159	3,728,799	4,366,145	6,360,622	3,863,638	1,957,436	1,603,693	1,612,547
Stockholders' Equity	3,760,830	3,637,669	3,795,062	3,254,392	1,359,465	1,627,361	1,833,598	1,591,277
Shares Outstanding	110,391	110,752	112,523	112,219	78,030	80,052	88,899	88,841
Statistical Record								
Return on Assets %	10.66	5.55	7.22	4.51	3.03	11.77	9.36	13.91
Return on Equity %	25.58	13.00	18.21	14.52	8.93	23.88	18.14	29.01
EBITDA Margin %	24.16	23.13	28.36	18.39	14.41	25.81	18.06	23.42
Net Margin %	10.59	7.09	24.04	9.17	5.45	15.79	11.35	15.21
Asset Turnover	0.34	0.33	0.30	0.49	0.56	0.75	0.82	0.91
Current Ratio	2.24	1.98	2.90	1.13	2.94	3.40	3.66	3.38
Debt to Equity	0.38	0.38	0.56	0.98	1.64	0.65	0.37	0.47
Price Range	115.40-75.72	106.21-63.93	91.80-47.71	64.38-41.78	72.62-53.16	69.55-57.75	67.70-51.56	71.11-39.00
P/E Ratio	14.78-9.70	25.84-15.55	16.16-8.40	21.46-13.93	42.97-31.46	14.19-11.79	19.51-14.86	14.91-8.18
Average Yield %	1.34	1.47	1.65	2.16	1.71	1.50	1.34	1.17

Address: 4 the street 700, Charlotte, NC 28209 Telephone: 900-000-0000 **K**	Web Site: www..com Officers: Jim W.- Chairman Luther - President, President (frmr), Chief Executive Officer, Principal Financial Officer, Principal Executive Officer	Auditors: PricewaterhouseCoopers LLP Investor Contact: 225-388 Transfer Agents: Wells Fargo Bank, N.A. Shareowner Services, St. Paul, MN

HOW TO USE THIS BOOK

D. INTERIM DIVIDENDS (Per Share) – The cash dividends are the actual dollar amounts declared by the company. No adjustments have been made for stock dividends and splits. **Ex-Dividend Date**: a stockholder must purchase the stock prior to this date in order to be entitled to the dividend. The **Record Date** indicates the date on which the shareholder had to have been a holder of record in order to qualify for the dividend. The **Payable Date** indicates the date the company paid or intends to pay the dividend. The cash amount shown in the first column is followed by a letter (example "Q" for quarterly) to indicate the frequency of the dividend. A notation of "Dividend payment suspended" indicates that dividend payments have been suspended within the most recent ten years.
Indicated Dividend This is the annualized amount (fully adjusted for splits) of the latest regular cash dividend. Companies with Dividend Reinvestment Plans are indicated here.

E. VALUATION ANALYSIS is a tool for evaluating a company's stock. Included are: Forecast Earnings Per Share (EPS), Market Capitalization, Book Value, Price/Book and Price/Sales.

F. INSTITUTIONAL HOLDINGS – indicates the number of investment companies, insurance companies, mutual funds, bank trust and college endowment funds holding the stock and the total number of shares held as last reported.

G. BUSINESS SUMMARY explains what a company does in terms of the products or services it sells, its markets, and the position the company occupies in its industry. For a quick reference, included are the Company's Standard Industrial Classification (SIC), North American Industry Classification (NAIC) and Mergent's Industry Classification (MIC).

H. RECENT DEVELOPMENTS – This section captures what has happened in the most recent quarter for which results are available. It provides recently released sales, earnings and expense figures.

I. PROSPECTS – This section focuses on what is anticipated for the immediate future, as well as the outlook for the next few years, based on analysis by Mergent.

J. FINANCIAL DATA (fully adjusted for stock dividends and splits) is provided for at least the past seven fiscal years preceded by the most recent three-, six- and nine-month results if available.
Fiscal Years are the annual financial reporting periods as determined by each company. Annual prices and dividends are displayed based on the Company's fiscal year.

Per Share Data:
The Earnings Per Share figure is based on a trailing 12-month period. Earnings per share, and all per share figures, are adjusted for subsequent stock dividends and splits.
Cash Flow Per Share represents the annualized cash flow from operating activities (or for quarters, TTM cash flow from operating activities) divided by the average shares outstanding.
Tangible Book Value Per Share is calculated as stockholders equity (the value of common shares, paid-in capital and retained earnings) minus preferred stock and intangibles such as goodwill, patents and excess acquisition costs, divided by shares outstanding. It demonstrates the underlying cash value of each common share if the company were to be liquidated as of that date.

Dividends Per Share is the total of cash payments made per share to shareholders for the trailing 12-month period.

HOW TO USE THIS BOOK

Dividend Payout % is the proportion of earnings available for common stock that is paid to common shareholders in the form of cash dividends. It is significant because it indicates what percentage of earnings is being reinvested in the business for internal growth.

EDITOR'S NOTE: TTM net income is net income for the last 365 days (normally four reported quarters) ended on the quarterly balance sheet date. Where that last 365 days does not exactly equate to the last four reported quarters the net income for any included partial quarter is adjusted on a pro-rata basis.

INCOME STATEMENT, BALANCE SHEET AND STATISTICAL RECORD

Includes pertinent earnings and balance sheet information essential to analyzing a corporation's performance. The comparisons provide the necessary historical perspective to intelligently review the various operating and financial trends. Generic definitions follow.

Income Statement:
Total Revenues consists of all revenues from operations.

EBITDA represents earnings before, interest, taxes, depreciation and amortization, and special items.

Depreciation and Amortization includes all non-cash charges such as depletion and amortization as well as depreciation.

Income Before Taxes is the remaining income *after* deducting all costs, expenses, property charges, interest etc. but *before* deducting income taxes.

Income Taxes includes the amount charged against earnings to provide for current and deferred income taxes.

Net Income consists of all revenues less all expenses (operating and non-operating), and is presented before preference and common dividends.

Average Shares Outstanding is the weighted average number of shares including common equivalent shares outstanding during the year, as reported by the corporation and fully adjusted for all stock dividends and splits. The use of *average shares* minimizes the distortion in *earnings per share* which could result from issuance of a large amount of stock or the company's purchase of a large amount of its own stock during the year.

Balance Sheet:
Current Assets includes the short-term assets expected to be realized or consumed within one year. Normally includes cash and cash equivalents, short term investments, receivables, prepayments and inventories.

Total Assets represents all of the assets of the company, including tangible and intangible, and current and non-current.

Current Liabilities are all of the obligations of the company normally expected to be paid within one year. Includes bank overdrafts, short-term debt, payables and accruals.

Long-Term Obligations are the total long-term debts (due beyond one year) reported by the company, including bonds, capital lease obligations, notes, mortgages, debentures, etc.

Total Liabilities represents all liabilities of the company, whether current or non-current.

Stockholders' Equity is the sum of all capital stock accounts – paid in capital (including additional premium), retained earnings, and all other capital balances.

Shares Outstanding is the number of shares outstanding as of the date of the company's quarterly/annual report, exclusive of treasury stock and adjusted for subsequent stock dividends and splits.

Statistical Record:
Return on Assets % represents the ratio of annualized net income (or for Mos, TTM net income) to average total assets. This ratio

HOW TO USE THIS BOOK

represents how effectively assets are being used to produce a profit.

Return on Equity % is the ratio of annualized net income (or for Mos, TTM net income) to average stockholders' equity, expressed as a percentage. This ratio illustrates how effectively the investment of the stockholders is being utilized to earn a profit.

EBITDA Margin % represents earnings before interest, taxes, depreciation and amortization as a percentage of total revenue.

Net Margin % is net income expressed as a percentage of total revenues.

Asset Turnover is annualized total revenue (or for Mos, TTM total revenue) divided by average total assets. A measure of efficiency for the use of assets.

Current Ratio represents current assets divided by current liabilities. The higher the figure the better the company is able to meet its current liabilities out of its current assets. A key measure of liquidity for industrial companies.

Debt to Equity is the ratio of long-term obligations to stockholders' equity.

Price Ranges are based on each Company's fiscal year. Where actual stock sales did not take place, a range of lowest bid and highest asked prices is shown.

Price/Earnings Ratio is shown as a range. The figures are calculated by dividing the stock's highest price for the year and its lowest price by the year's earnings per share. Growth stocks tend to command higher P/Es than cyclical stocks.

Average Yield % is the ratio of annual dividends to the real average of the prices over the fiscal year.

EDITOR'S NOTE: In order to preserve the historical relationships between prices, earnings and dividends, figures are not restated to reflect subsequent events. Figures are presented in U.S. dollars unless otherwise indicated.

K. ADDITIONAL INFORMATION on each stock includes the officers of the company, investor relations contact, address, telephone number, web site and transfer agents.

OTHER DEFINITIONS

Factors Pertaining Especially to Real Estate Investment Trusts

Property Income is income from property rental and other associated activities.

Non-Property Income includes interest income and other income not from property activities.

Factors Pertaining Especially to Utilities

PPE Turnover represents annualized total revenue (or for Mos, TTM total revenue) divided by average net property, plant and equipment.

Factors Pertaining Especially to Banks

Interest Income is all interest income, including income from loans and leases, securities and deposits.

Interest Expense is all interest expense, including from loans and leases, securities and deposits.

Net Interest Income is interest income less interest expense. This figure is presented before provision for losses.

Provision for Losses represents the amount charged against earnings to increase the provision made for losses on loans and leases.

Non-Interest Income is any income that is not interest-related. Such income could include trading revenue and gains on the sale of assets.

Non-Interest Expense is all expenses that are not interest-related, including employment costs, office costs, marketing costs, etc.

Net Loans & Leases includes all loans and leases net of provisions for losses. May include commercial, agricultural, real estate, consumer and foreign loans.

Total Deposits are all time and demand deposits entrusted to a bank.

Net Interest Margin % is net interest income before provisions expressed as a

HOW TO USE THIS BOOK

percentage of total interest income. A key measure of bank profitability.

Efficiency Ratio % is non-interest expense expressed as a percentage of total revenue.

Loans to Deposits are net loans and leases divided by total deposits. A key measure of bank liquidity.

Factors Pertaining Especially to Insurance Companies

Premium Income is the amount of insurance premiums received from policyholders. This is the primary revenue source for insurance companies.

Benefits and Claims represents the payments made to policyholders under the terms of insurance contracts.

Loss Ratio % is benefits and claims expressed as a percentage of premium income. A key ratio of insurance company profitability.

ABBREVIATIONS AND SYMBOLS

A...Annual
ASE.............…......American Stock Exchange
().................................….........Deficit
(Div. Reinv. Plan)..Dividend Reinvest Plan offered
E...Extra
M......................................…..Monthly
N/A...........................….....Not Applicable
N.M...........................…......Not Meaningful
NMS....…............. National Market Systems
NYS....…..........New York Stock Exchange
Q.......................................Quarterly
S..:................................Semi-Annual
Sp............…..................Special Dividend
U.....................…....Frequency Unknown

FORDS TOP 50 EARNINGS MOMENTUM

Name	Symbol	12 Mo	6 Mo	Cur Mo	Momentum	Percentile
AMPCO-PITTSBURGH	AP	17.2	-26.9	-21.4	71.7	94
ANTHERA PHARM	ANTH	-92.9	-89.5	1.2	-64.1	8
BALL CORP	BLL	23.2	10.1	3.4	-20	30
CAL MAINE FOODS	CALM	-8.7	-16.1	-6.2	-10.6	40
CHIASMA	CHMA	-46.6	-33	-1.3	-44.5	14
CHURCHILL DOWNS	CHDN	49.7	19.8	7.4	-7.8	43
CIDARA THERAPEUT	CDTX	-24.7	-32.6	8.9	-65.5	8
CONIFER	CNFR	8.6	-2	0	-9.4	41
DXC TECHNOLOGY	DXC	65.4	26.9	-1.4	37.1	84
DATAWATCH	DWCH	75.2	58.9	9.9	20.9	73
DIANA SHIPPING	DSX	84	15	-1.8	83.9	96
EMCORE	EMKR	147.2	27.3	8.7	74.5	95
EMERGENT BIO	EBS	29	2	3.4	-13.9	36
ENERGY FOCUS	EFOI	-56.3	-46.6	25.3	21.6	74
EVERTEC	EVTC	14.5	-6.2	2.1	-18.3	32
HERON THERAPEUT	HRTX	-20.7	3.4	-0.7	-31.8	21
HOUSTON WIRE	HWCC	-0.4	-23.5	-21.2	66.4	93
INTL FCSTONE	INTL	48.9	-6.4	8.9	-1.4	51
JUNIPER NETWORKS	JNPR	31.5	-2.6	-4.7	26.3	77
KB HOME	KBH	61.7	40.3	7	4.1	57
KFORCE INC	KFRC	19.2	-17.1	4.9	3.7	56
LSI INDUSTRIES	LYTS	-14	-6.5	3.3	-34.7	19
MERCER INTL	MERC	46.1	5.1	-2.2	39	85
MICRON TECH	MU	158.9	35.9	6.4	110.9	98
MICROSOFT	MSFT	42.9	9.4	-1.1	21.1	73
NATL OILWELL VAR	NOV	0.3	-18.6	-3.3	8.9	62
NOKIA CORP	NOK	23.6	27.9	-1.6	-5.4	46
NORFOLK SOUTHERN	NSC	49.4	8.8	-2.7	31.7	81
ONCOMED PHARMA	OMED	-69.9	-56.4	-7.6	-1.6	51
PATTERSON-UTI	PTEN	3.1	-26.4	-7.4	20.1	72
PHILLIPS 66	PSX	4.7	-8.2	4	-30.2	22
PROTEON THERAPEU	PRTO	-79.9	-30.8	8	-106.9	3
Q2 HOLDINGS	QTWO	39.6	25	-8.9	45.7	87
SCHLUMBERGER	SLB	-12.9	-23.5	-6.7	3.8	56
SCORPIO TANKERS	STNG	-4.2	-12.3	7.4	-41.5	16
SPECTRA EN PTNRS	SEP	-5.5	-5.9	-1.2	23.4	27
STERICYCLE	SRCL	-22.1	0.1	-6.3	-16.7	33
U S SILICA	SLCA	11.5	-41.1	-7.8	39.7	85
VALERO ENERGY	VLO	30.7	-3.8	7	-9.9	41
WAYFAIR	W	93.8	107.6	15.8	-63.6	8
ACCELERATE DIAGN	AXDX	88.8	25	-3.5	61.5	92
ARISTA NETWORKS	ANET	150.8	56.2	4.3	103.5	97
ARTISAN PARTNERS	APAM	13.2	-0.5	6	-35.2	19
ATLANTICA YIELD	ABY	30.9	9	3.7	0.7	53
BERKSHIRE HILLS	BHLB	37.8	-5.8	-5.3	36.3	83
BLUE BIRD CORP	BLBD	42.1	2.1	-7	45.8	87
BLUE HILLS BANCP	BHBK	23.3	-6.4	-3.3	11.6	64
BLUEBIRD BIO	BLUE	191.5	64.8	35.8	51.7	89
CBOE HOLDINGS	CBOE	41.6	22.1	3.9	-2.5	50
CABELA'S	CAB	25.3	-6.1	9.2	-46.4	13
AVERAGE DATA		27.3	1	0.4	6.7	55
FORD UNIV AVGS		26.3	3.7	1.8	0	51
S&P 500 AVERAGES	SP500	20.9	6.6	0.1	0.6	52
FORD 1000 AVGS	F1000	21.5	6.6	0.2	0.7	53

SHORT-TERM PRICE SCORES: COMPANY RANKINGS

25 Highest	SHORT TERM PRICE SCORE	LONG TERM PRICE SCORE	52 WEEK HIGH	52 WEEK LOW	RECENT PRICE
Square Inc	149.4 ...		48.86	13.81	34.67
Xerox Corp	139.5	183.6	33.95	6.88	29.15
Kemper Corp. (DE)	133.9	105.4	70.45	36.70	68.90
HollyFrontier Corp	132.6	66.7	51.63	23.90	51.22
Arista Networks Inc	130.9	...	243.55	88.23	235.58
CalAtlantic Group Inc	128.8	89.4	57.10	33.10	56.39
Michael Kors Holdings Ltd	126.5	...	64.03	33.05	62.95
NVR Inc.	126.5	149.5	3,525.73	1,649.99	3,508.22
Dana Inc	126.4	102.5	33.04	17.57	32.01
XPO Logistics, Inc.	126.1	157.3	92.17	42.71	91.59
KB HOME	125.7	113.9	32.25	16.11	31.95
Horton (DR) Inc	125.2	120.2	51.45	27.56	51.07
NRG Energy Inc	124.7	75.0	29.49	12.30	28.48
Westlake Chemical Corp	124.3	110.4	106.53	57.29	106.53
PBF Energy Inc	123.8	...	35.59	19.32	35.45
Thor Industries, Inc.	122.4	152.0	155.25	89.41	150.72
PulteGroup Inc	122.1	114.9	34.44	18.46	33.25
Polaris Industries Inc.	121.4	77.2	133.70	78.82	123.99
Boeing Co. (The)	120.8	136.2	297.90	156.97	294.91
TRI Pointe Group Inc	120.6	...	18.44	11.37	17.92
Navistar International Corp.	120.5	80.5	45.30	22.89	42.88
Red Hat Inc	119.8	119.3	129.44	70.12	120.10
Owens Corning	119.7	124.2	92.75	51.66	91.94
AbbVie Inc	119.6	...	98.21	60.00	96.71
Caterpillar Inc.	119.5	95.5	158.42	91.39	157.58
25 Lowest					
Genesis Healthcare Inc	37.7	28.6	4.69	0.69	0.76
Rite Aid Corp	49.6	61.2	8.70	1.43	1.97
Envision Healthcare Corp	54.1	...	72.48	24.79	34.56
Pandora Media Inc	55.3	...	13.58	4.49	4.82
Avon Products, Inc.	56.4	21.8	5.93	1.87	2.15
Community Health Systems, Inc.	56.5	23.4	10.32	3.99	4.26
3D Systems Corp. (DE)	58.1	43.6	23.31	8.12	8.64
Nabors Industries Ltd	58.7	48.9	18.19	5.48	6.83
Penney (J.C.) Co.,Inc.	58.7	25.2	8.47	2.37	3.16
NACCO Industries Inc	59.5	97.0	88.85	31.90	37.65
Owens & Minor, Inc.	60.2	72.2	36.95	18.10	18.88
Tahoe Resources Inc.	61.4	36.8	11.18	4.18	4.79
Intrexon Corp	62.5	...	26.25	11.33	11.52
Veritiv Corp	63.0	...	62.25	22.70	28.90
Now Inc	64.2	...	22.67	9.88	11.03
TreeHouse Foods Inc	65.2	81.0	89.94	41.87	49.46
Dean Foods Co.	65.7	78.5	21.91	9.09	11.56
SCANA Corp	66.5	88.0	73.28	37.39	39.78
General Electric Co	66.8	82.9	31.70	17.36	17.45
Under Armour Inc	67.1	60.4	30.71	11.61	14.43
Newell Brands Inc	67.7	110.0	54.85	27.97	30.90
CenturyLink Inc	67.8	52.0	27.31	13.62	16.68
Vista Outdoor Inc	68.0	...	39.34	13.25	14.57
Dick's Sporting Goods, Inc	68.4	66.2	55.33	24.39	28.74
Diebold Nixdorf Inc	69.4	61.3	31.60	16.15	16.35

Ranking by Total Revenues

Based on most recent fiscal year-end figures.

Rank	Company Name	Revenues ($Mill)	Rank	Company Name	Revenues ($Mill)
1.	Wal-Mart Stores Inc	485,873.0	26.	Philip Morris International	74,953.0
2.	Exxon Mobil Corp	226,094.0	27.	Johnson & Johnson	71,890.0
3.	Berkshire Hathaway Inc	223,604.0	28.	Target Corp	69,495.0
4.	McKesson Corp	198,533.0	29.	Procter & Gamble Co.	65,058.0
5.	UnitedHealth Group Inc	184,840.0	30.	Lowe's Companies Inc	65,017.0
6.	CVS Health Corporation	177,526.0	31.	MetLife Inc	63,476.0
7.	General Motors Co	166,380.0	32.	Marathon Petroleum Corp.	63,364.0
8.	AT&T Inc	163,786.0	33.	Aetna Inc.	63,155.0
9.	AmerisourceBergen Corp.	153,143.8	34.	Archer Daniels Midland Co.	62,346.0
10.	Ford Motor Co. (DE)	151,800.0	35.	Dell Technologies Inc	61,642.0
11.	Cardinal Health, Inc.	129,976.0	36.	United Parcel Service Inc	60,906.0
12.	Verizon Communications	125,980.0	37.	FedEx Corp	60,319.0
13.	General Electric Co	123,693.0	38.	Prudential Financial, Inc.	58,779.0
14.	Kroger Co (The)	115,337.0	39.	United Technologies Corp	57,244.0
15.	Chevron Corporation	114,472.0	40.	Sysco Corp	55,371.1
16.	JPMorgan Chase & Co	105,486.0	41.	Disney (Walt) Co.	55,137.0
17.	Home Depot Inc	94,595.0	42.	Humana Inc.	54,379.0
18.	Boeing Co. (The)	94,571.0	43.	Pfizer Inc	52,824.0
19.	Wells Fargo & Co.	94,176.0	44.	American Intl. Group Inc	52,367.0
20.	Bank of America Corp.	93,662.0	45.	HP Inc	52,056.0
21.	Phillips 66	85,777.0	46.	Lockheed Martin Corp	47,248.0
22.	Anthem Inc	84,863.0	47.	Bunge Ltd.	42,679.0
23.	Citigroup Inc	82,386.0	48.	Coca-Cola Co	41,863.0
24.	Intl. Bus. Machines Corp	79,919.0	49.	HCA Healthcare Inc	41,490.0
25.	Valero Energy Corp	75,659.0	50.	Centene Corp	40,607.0

Ranking by Net Income

Based on most recent fiscal year-end figures.

Rank	Company Name	Net Income ($Mill)	Rank	Company Name	Net Income ($Mill)
1.	JPMorgan Chase & Co	24,733.0	26.	AbbVie Inc	5,953.0
2.	Berkshire Hathaway Inc	24,074.0	27.	US Bancorp (DE)	5,888.0
3.	Wells Fargo & Co.	21,938.0	28.	American Express Co.	5,408.0
4.	Bank of America Corp.	17,906.0	29.	CVS Health Corporation	5,317.0
5.	Johnson & Johnson	16,540.0	30.	Lockheed Martin Corp	5,302.0
6.	Procter & Gamble Co	15,326.0	31.	McKesson Corp	5,070.0
7.	Allergan PLC	14,973.4	32.	United Technologies Corp	5,055.0
8.	Citigroup Inc	14,912.0	33.	3M Co	5,050.0
9.	Altria Group Inc	14,239.0	34.	Baxter International Inc	4,965.0
10.	Wal-Mart Stores Inc	13,643.0	35.	Boeing Co. (The)	4,895.0
11.	Verizon Communications	13,127.0	36.	Honeywell International	4,809.0
12.	AT&T Inc	12,976.0	37.	McDonald's Corp	4,686.5
13.	Intl. Bus. Machines Corp	11,872.0	38.	Ford Motor Co. (DE)	4,596.0
14.	General Motors Co	9,427.0	39.	Bristol-Myers Squibb Co.	4,457.0
15.	Oracle Corp	9,335.0	40.	Delta Air Lines Inc (DE)	4,373.0
16.	Disney (Walt) Co.	8,980.0	41.	Prudential Financial, Inc.	4,368.0
17.	General Electric Co	8,831.0	42.	Equity Residential	4,292.2
18.	Home Depot Inc	7,957.0	43.	NIKE Inc	4,240.0
19.	Exxon Mobil Corp	7,840.0	44.	Union Pacific Corp	4,233.0
20.	Pfizer Inc	7,215.0	45.	Chubb Ltd	4,135.0
21.	UnitedHealth Group Inc	7,017.0	46.	Mastercard Inc	4,059.0
22.	Philip Morris International	6,967.0	47.	Medtronic PLC	4,028.0
23.	Visa Inc	6,699.0	48.	Time Warner Inc	3,926.0
24.	Coca-Cola Co (The)	6,527.0	49.	Merck & Co Inc	3,920.0
25.	Morgan Stanley	5,979.0	50.	PNC Financial Services Grp	3,903.0

Ranking by Total Assets

Based on most recent fiscal year-end figures.

Rank	Company Name	Assets ($Mill)	Rank	Company Name	Assets ($Mill)
1.	JPMorgan Chase & Co	2,490,972.0	26.	BB&T Corp.	219,276.0
2.	Bank of America Corp.	2,187,702.0	27.	Voya Financial Inc	214,235.1
3.	Wells Fargo & Co.	1,930,115.0	28.	SunTrust Banks, Inc.	204,875.0
4.	Citigroup Inc	1,792,077.0	29.	Wal-Mart Stores Inc	198,825.0
5.	MetLife Inc	898,764.0	30.	Pfizer Inc	171,615.0
6.	Morgan Stanley	814,949.0	31.	Ally Financial Inc	163,728.0
7.	Prudential Financial, Inc.	783,962.0	32.	Chubb Ltd	159,786.0
8.	Berkshire Hathaway Inc	620,854.0	33.	American Express Co.	158,893.0
9.	American Intl. Group Inc	498,264.0	34.	Johnson & Johnson	141,208.0
10.	US Bancorp (DE)	445,964.0	35.	Ameriprise Financial Inc	139,821.0
11.	AT&T Inc	403,821.0	36.	KeyCorp	136,453.0
12.	PNC Financial Services Grp	366,380.0	37.	Oracle Corp	134,991.0
13.	General Electric Co	365,183.0	38.	Duke Energy Corp	132,761.0
14.	Capital One Financial Corp	357,033.0	39.	AFLAC Inc	129,819.0
15.	Bank of New York Mellon	333,469.0	40.	Allergan PLC	128,986.3
16.	Exxon Mobil Corp	330,314.0	41.	Regions Financial Corp	125,968.0
17.	Lincoln National Corp.	261,627.0	42.	M & T Bank Corp	123,449.2
18.	Chevron Corporation	260,078.0	43.	UnitedHealth Group Inc	122,810.0
19.	Verizon Communications	244,180.0	44.	Procter & Gamble Co	120,406.0
20.	State Street Corp.	242,698.0	45.	Dell Technologies Inc	118,206.0
21.	Ford Motor Co. (DE)	237,951.0	46.	Intl. Bus. Machines Corp	117,470.0
22.	Hartford Financial Services	223,432.0	47.	Exelon Corp	114,904.0
23.	Schwab (Charles) Corp	223,383.0	48.	Southern Company	109,697.0
24.	General Motors Co	221,690.0	49.	Allstate Corp.	108,610.0
25.	BlackRock Inc	220,177.0	50.	Genworth Financial, Inc.	104,658.0

Ranking by Market Capitalization

Based on most recent fiscal year-end figures and closing prices at 12/31/2017

Rank	Company Name	Market Cap ($Mill)	Rank	Company Name	Market Cap ($Mill)
1.	Johnson & Johnson	375,360.6	26.	3M Co	140,188.3
2.	JPMorgan Chase & Co	371,052.5	27.	McDonald's Corp	137,211.6
3.	Exxon Mobil Corp	354,391.6	28.	Altria Group Inc	136,263.8
4.	Bank of America Corp.	307,911.7	29.	Honeywell International	116,833.1
5.	Wells Fargo & Co.	298,754.9	30.	Medtronic PLC	109,295.0
6.	Wal-Mart Stores Inc	292,535.2	31.	Union Pacific Corp	105,559.3
7.	AT&T Inc	238,684.3	32.	United Technologies Corp	101,873.6
8.	Chevron Corporation	237,782.6	33.	Bristol-Myers Squibb Co.	100,297.0
9.	Procter & Gamble Co	231,629.8	34.	Abbott Laboratories	99,336.1
10.	Home Depot Inc	221,323.4	35.	Accenture plc	98,368.0
11.	Citigroup Inc	216,205.9	36.	Morgan Stanley	94,860.5
12.	Verizon Communications	215,924.8	37.	Caterpillar Inc.	93,749.6
13.	Pfizer Inc	215,896.8	38.	Schlumberger Ltd	93,263.2
14.	UnitedHealth Group Inc	213,640.6	39.	Lilly (Eli) & Co	92,998.5
15.	Visa Inc	206,771.1	40.	Lockheed Martin Corp	92,056.0
16.	Oracle Corp	195,720.4	41.	US Bancorp (DE)	88,915.5
17.	Coca-Cola Co (The)	195,479.4	42.	American Express Co.	86,200.7
18.	Boeing Co. (The)	175,642.1	43.	BlackRock Inc	82,364.2
19.	Philip Morris International	164,095.9	44.	United Parcel Service Inc	81,862.9
20.	Disney (Walt) Co. (The)	162,373.7	45.	NIKE Inc	81,182.1
21.	Mastercard Inc	157,959.7	46.	Lowe's Companies Inc	77,117.9
22.	AbbVie Inc	154,390.7	47.	Thermo Fisher Scientific	76,141.0
23.	Merck & Co Inc	153,304.1	48.	Salesforce.Com Inc	73,840.7
24.	General Electric Co	151,327.9	49.	NextEra Energy Inc	73,471.4
25.	Intl. Bus. Machines Corp	142,034.9	50.	CVS Health Corporation	73,442.0

Ranking by Current Yield

Based on closing prices at 12/31/2017

Rank	Company Name	Yield %	Rank	Company Name	Yield %
1.	Allergan PLC	33.62	26.	Medical Properties Trust Inc	6.97
2.	Washington Prime Group	14.04	27.	Energy Transfer Equity LP	6.84
3.	CenturyLink Inc	12.95	28.	Pitney Bowes Inc	6.71
4.	New Residential Investment	11.19	29.	EPR Properties	6.60
5.	NGL Energy Partners LP	11.10	30.	Enterprise Products Partners	6.41
6.	Global Partners LP	11.08	31.	LaSalle Hotel Properties	6.41
7.	Chimera Investment Corp	10.82	32.	Iron Mountain Inc (New)	6.23
8.	Buckeye Partners LP	10.19	33.	OUTFRONT Media Inc	6.21
9.	MFA Financial, Inc.	10.10	34.	Kimco Realty Corp	6.17
10.	Annaly Capital Management	10.09	35.	SCANA Corp	6.16
11.	Omega Healthcare Investors	9.59	36.	Apple Hospitality REIT Inc	6.12
12.	Colony NorthStar Inc	9.47	37.	Macy's Inc	5.99
13.	Genesis Energy L.P.	9.13	38.	Brixmor Property Group Inc	5.89
14.	Starwood Property Trust Inc.	8.99	39.	W.P. Carey Inc	5.86
15.	Barnes & Noble Inc	8.96	40.	ONEOK Inc	5.76
16.	Macquarie Infrastructure	8.85	41.	HCP Inc	5.67
17.	DDR Corp	8.48	42.	Welltower Inc	5.46
18.	GameStop Corp	8.47	43.	Owens & Minor, Inc.	5.46
19.	Spirit Realty Capital Inc	8.39	44.	Ventas Inc	5.27
20.	AmeriGas Partners LP	8.22	45.	N.Y. Community Bancorp	5.22
21.	TC PipeLines, LP	7.53	46.	Magellan Midstream Partner	5.19
22.	Targa Resources Corp	7.52	47.	Becton, Dickinson & Co	5.18
23.	CoreCivic Inc	7.47	48.	Tanger Factory Outlet Center	5.17
24.	Vector Group Ltd	7.15	49.	AT&T Inc	5.14
25.	VEREIT Inc	7.06	50.	PPL Corp	5.11

Ranking by Return on Equity

Based on most recent fiscal year-end figures.

Rank	Company Name	Return on Equity %	Rank	Company Name	Return on Equity %
1.	Energy Transfer Equity	3,006.91	26.	Hershey Company	80.51
2.	Energizer Holdings Inc	731.40	27.	Armstrong World Industries	80.25
3.	Hilton Grand Vacations	549.31	28.	Mettler-Toledo Intl, Inc.	75.50
4.	S&P Global Inc	497.69	29.	Wyndham Worldwide Corp	73.24
5.	Lennox International Inc	399.19	30.	Intl. Bus. Machines Corp	72.84
6.	Herbalife Ltd	363.15	31.	Tenneco Inc	70.91
7.	Pitney Bowes Inc	246.60	32.	Mastercard Inc	69.29
8.	United Parcel Service Inc	238.03	33.	Dana Inc	67.72
9.	Lockheed Martin Corp	229.49	34.	Verizon Communications	67.22
10.	Crown Holdings Inc	193.98	35.	Zoetis Inc	64.09
11.	McDonald's Corp	191.40	36.	Owens-Illinois, Inc.	57.90
12.	Altria Group Inc	181.47	37.	Baxter International Inc	57.79
13.	Clorox Co (The)	167.10	38.	United Rentals Inc	56.63
14.	CSRA Inc	154.52	39.	Asbury Automotive Group	56.12
15.	Home Depot Inc	149.85	40.	Campbell Soup Co.	56.10
16.	Tempur Sealy Intl, Inc.	146.58	41.	NewMarket Corp	55.76
17.	Taubman Centers, Inc.	143.06	42.	Berry Global Group Inc	55.44
18.	AbbVie Inc	138.37	43.	Aptiv PLC	53.91
19.	Boeing Co. (The)	136.51	44.	TJX Companies, Inc.	52.27
20.	ONEOK Inc	133.86	45.	Booz Allen Hamilton Hldg	51.42
21.	Tupperware Brands Corp	117.70	46.	McKesson Corp	50.65
22.	BWX Technologies inc	87.82	47.	Omnicom Group, Inc.	49.65
23.	Ciena Corp	86.95	48.	FactSet Research Systems	47.96
24.	Sealed Air Corp	85.34	49.	Toro Company (The)	45.88
25.	Sherwin-Williams Co	82.26	50.	3M Co	45.77

Ranking by High P/E Ratio

Based on closing prices at 12/31/2017

Rank	Company Name	P/E Ratio	Rank	Company Name	P/E Ratio
1.	Salesforce.Com Inc	10,223.00	26.	Healthcare Trust Of America	120.16
2.	Ashland Global Holdings	7,120.00	27.	Brandywine Realty Trust	113.69
3.	EOG Resources, Inc.	5,395.50	28.	Caterpillar Inc.	108.68
4.	Live Nation Entertainment	1,419.00	29.	Tennant Co.	106.84
5.	Clean Harbors Inc	774.29	30.	Occidental Petroleum Corp	103.75
6.	Knowles Corp	733.00	31.	Ralph Lauren Corp	103.69
7.	Edgewell Personal Care	593.90	32.	American Campus Commun.	100.07
8.	FMC Corp.	591.63	33.	Zayo Group Holdings Inc	99.46
9.	ABM Industries, Inc.	538.86	34.	SL Green Realty Corp	97.99
10.	Parsley Energy Inc	420.57	35.	Spirit Realty Capital Inc	95.33
11.	QEP Resources Inc	319.00	36.	Mack Cali Realty Corp	93.74
12.	Bio-Rad Laboratories Inc	302.11	37.	Digital Realty Trust Inc	92.60
13.	EQT Corp	299.58	38.	Crown Castle International	91.74
14.	Guidewire Software Inc	275.04	39.	Howard Hughes Corp	90.53
15.	Markel Corp (Holding Co)	253.14	40.	Southern Company (The)	89.06
16.	Newmont Mining Corp	250.13	41.	AK Steel Holding Corp.	80.86
17.	Pioneer Natural Resources	233.58	42.	World Fuel Services Corp.	80.40
18.	Halliburton Company	195.48	43.	Hudson Pacific Properties	79.65
19.	GoDaddy Inc	193.38	44.	Deckers Outdoor Corp.	79.46
20.	Great Plains Energy Inc	169.68	45.	Teradata Corp (DE)	78.49
21.	Post Holdings Inc	158.46	46.	Douglas Emmett Inc	77.47
22.	Alexandria Real Estate Eq	146.73	47.	Olin Corp.	77.35
23.	Univar Inc	134.61	48.	Regency Centers Corp	76.02
24.	Navistar International Corp.	134.00	49.	XPO Logistics, Inc.	75.69
25.	Sun Communities Inc	128.86	50.	CBS Corp	75.64

Ranking by Low P/E Ratio

Based on closing prices at 12/31/2017

Rank	Company Name	P/E Ratio	Rank	Company Name	P/E Ratio
1.	Ciena Corp	2.78	26.	Dick's Sporting Goods, Inc	10.61
2.	Annaly Capital Management	4.57	27.	MFA Financial, Inc.	10.70
3.	Genworth Financial, Inc.	4.64	28.	United Rentals Inc	10.93
4.	Assured Guaranty Ltd	4.87	29.	Lear Corp.	11.02
5.	GameStop Corp	5.28	30.	Macy's Inc	11.15
6.	Chimera Investment Corp	5.69	31.	Delta Air Lines Inc (DE)	11.18
7.	New Residential Investment	5.73	32.	Penske Automotive Group	11.23
8.	NACCO Industries Inc	5.82	33.	Group 1 Automotive, Inc.	11.27
9.	White Mountains Insur. Grp	6.18	34.	Ford Motor Co. (DE)	11.35
10.	Duke Realty Corp	6.53	35.	Prudential Financial, Inc.	11.51
11.	Dana Inc	6.74	36.	Foot Locker, Inc.	11.81
12.	Southwestern Energy Co	6.89	37.	Alaska Air Group, Inc.	11.82
13.	McKesson Corp	7.61	38.	Newell Brands Inc	11.93
14.	Molson Coors Brewing Co.	7.86	39.	Lincoln National Corp.	11.94
15.	Asbury Automotive Group	8.38	40.	Sonic Automotive, Inc.	11.98
16.	Washington Prime Group	8.38	41.	Air Products & Chemicals	12.02
17.	Altria Group Inc	8.95	42.	Sally Beauty Holdings Inc	12.03
18.	Cooper Tire & Rubber Co.	9.11	43.	USG Corp	12.24
19.	Sealed Air Corp	9.39	44.	Eaton Corp plc	12.40
20.	DST Systems Inc (DE)	9.48	45.	HCA Healthcare Inc	12.53
21.	Avnet Inc	9.83	46.	Becton, Dickinson & Co	12.59
22.	Santander Consumer USA	10.01	47.	SCANA Corp	12.63
23.	PG&E Corp (Holding Co)	10.26	48.	Louisiana-Pacific Corp	12.69
24.	American Eq Inves Life Hdg	10.42	49.	AFLAC Inc	12.74
25.	United Continental Holdings	10.58	50.	Intl. Bus. Machines Corp	12.83

CLASSIFICATION BY INDUSTRY

Accommodation and Food Services
Accommodation
  Choice Hotels International, Inc.
  Extended Stay America Inc
  Hilton Grand Vacations
  Host Hotels & Resorts Inc.
  Hyatt Hotels Corp.
  Park Place Entertainment Corp.
  Wyndham Worldwide Corp.

Food Services and Drinking Places
  Brinker International, Inc.
  Chipotle Mexican Grill Inc
*Darden Restaurants, Inc.
*McDonald's Corporation
  Ruby Tuesday, Inc.
*Yum! Brands, Inc.

Administrative & Support and Waste Management & Remediation Services
Administrative and Support Services
*Equifax Inc.
*ManpowerGroup
  Mid Atlantic Medical Services
  Robert Half International, Inc.
*Rollins, Inc.

Waste Management and Remediation Services
  Clean Harbors, Inc.
  Republic Services, Inc.
*Waste Management, Inc.

Arts, Entertainment, and Recreation
*Carnival Corp.
*Disney (Walt) Company (The)
  GTECH Holdings Corp.
  Las Vegas Sands Corp.
  Live Nation Entertainment, Inc.
  MGM Resorts International
  Royal Caribbean Cruises Ltd.
  Six Flags Entertainment Corp
  Vail Resorts Inc
  Vista Outdoor Inc

Construction
  ABM Industries Incorporated
*Boston Properties, Inc.
  CalAtlantic Group Inc
  Chicago Bridge & Iron Co., N.V.
  Dycom Industries, Inc.
  Eagle Materials Inc.
  EMCOR Group, Inc.
  Fortune Brands Home & Security, Inc.
*Granite Construction Inc.
  Horton (D.R.) Inc.
  Jacobs Engineering Group Inc.
  KB Home
  KBR Inc.
  Lennar Corporation
  Martin Marietta Materials, Inc.
*MDU Resources Group, Inc.

NVR Inc.
Owens Corning
Pulte Homes, Inc.
Quanta Services, Inc.
Toll Brothers, Inc.
TRI Pointe Group Inc.a

Educational Services
  DeVry Education Group Inc.
  Graham Holdings Co.

Electric Power Generation
  Calpine Corp.
  Covanta Holding Corp.
  NRG Energy, Inc.
  Ormat Technologies Inc

Finance and Insurance
Commercial Banking
  Ally Financial Inc
  Associated Banc-Corp
*BancorpSouth, Inc.
*Bank of America Corporation
*Bank of Hawaii Corporation
*Bank of New York Mellon Corp.
  BankUnited Inc.
*BB&T Corporation
*Comerica, Inc.
*Community Bank System, Inc.
  Cullen/Frost Bankers, Inc.
  First Data Corp.
*First Horizon National Corporation
  First Republic Bank (San Francisco, CA)
  HRG Group
*Hudson United Bancorp
*J.P. Morgan Chase & Co.
*KeyCorp
*M&T Bank Corporation
*North Fork Bancorporation, Inc.
*PNC Financial Services Group
  Prosperity Bancshares Inc.
*Regions Financial Corp.
*State Street Corporation
*SunTrust Banks, Inc.
  Synchrony Financial
*Synovus Financial Corporation
*TCF Financial Corp.
  TransUnion
*U.S. Bancorp
*Valley National Bancorp
*Wells Fargo & Company
*Wilmington Trust Corporation

Direct Health and Medical Insurance Carriers
*AFLAC Incorporated
  Cigna Corp.
  Humana Inc.
  Pacificare Health Systems, Inc.

Reinsurance Group of America
UnitedHealth Group Inc.
Universal American Corp.
*UnumProvident Corporation
WellCare Health Plans Inc.

Direct Life Insurance Carriers

American Equity Investment Life Holding Co.
Assurant Inc.
*Genworth Financial Inc. (Holding Co)
*Lincoln National Corporation
Primerica Inc.
Principal Financial Group, Inc.
*Protective Life Corporation
Prudential Financial, Inc.
*Torchmark Corporation
Voya Financial Inc.

Direct Property and Casualty Insurance Carriers
Allied World Assurance Company Holdings AG
Allmerica Financial Corporation
*Allstate Corporation (The)
*American Financial Group, Inc.
American International Group
Aspen Insurance Holdings Ltd
Berkley (W.R.) Corporation
Berkshire Hathaway Inc.
CNA Financial Corporation
Everest Re Group Ltd
Hanover Insurance Group Inc.
*Kemper Corp.
Leucadia National Corporation
Loews Corporation
Markel Corporation
Mercury General Corporation
ProAssurance Corp.
Progressive Corporation (The)
RenaissanceRe Holdings Ltd
*RLI Corp.
*The St Paul Travelers Companies Inc.
White Mountains Insurance Group, Ltd
XL Capital Ltd

Direct Title Insurance Carriers
Alleghany Corporation
*CoreLogic Inc.
Fidelity National Financial Inc.
First American Financial Corp

Insurance Agencies and Brokerages
Aetna, Inc.
Anthem Inc.
Brown & Brown, Inc.
Centene Corp
Gallagher (Arthur J.) & Company
*Hartford Financial Services Group
Metlife, Inc.
Molina Healthcare Inc.

Mortgage and Nonmortgage Loan Brokers
Community Bancorp, Inc.
Nondepository Credit Intermediation
*American Express Company

Ameriprise Financial Inc.
*Capital One Financial Corp.
Discover Financial Services
Invesco Ltd
Lazard Ltd
*Morgan Stanley

Real Estate Investment Trusts
Alexandria Real Estate Equities, Inc.
American Campus Communities Inc.
American Homes 4 Rent
American Tower Corp
AMB Property Corporation
*Annaly Capital Management Inc.
Apartment Investment & Management Co
Apple Hospitality REIT Inc.
AvalonBay Communities, Inc.
*Brandywine Realty Trust
*Brixmor Property Group Inc
Camden Property Trust
Care Capital Properties Inc.
*Chimera Investment Corp.
Columbia Property Trust Inc
Corporate Office Properties Trust
*Crown Castle International Corp.
CubeSmart
*DCT Industrial Trust Inc.
*DDR Corp
Digital Realty Trust Inc.
Douglas Emmett Inc.
*Duke Realty Corporation
*Education Realty Trust Inc.
Empire State Realty Trust Inc
*Equity Commonwealth
Equity Lifestyle Properties Inc
*Equity Residential Prop. Trust
*EPR Properties
*Essex Property Trust, Inc.
Extra Space Storage Inc
*Federal Realty Investment Trust
General Growth Properties Inc.
*HCP, Inc.
*Healthcare Realty Trust, Inc.
Healthcare Trust of America Inc
*Highwoods Properties, Inc.
*Kilroy Realty Corp.
*Kimco Realty Corp.
LaSalle Hotel Properties
*Liberty Property Trust
*Macerich Company (The)
*Mack-Cali Realty Corporation
Medical Properties Trust Inc.
MFA Financial, Inc.
*Mid-America Apartment Communities Inc
National Health Investors, Inc.
*National Retail Properties Inc.
*Omega Healthcare Investors, Inc.
OUTFRONT Media Inc
Paramount Group Inc
Piedmont Office Realty Trust Inc
*ProLogis
Public Storage, Inc.
Realty Income Corp.

*Regency Centers Corporation
Retail Properties of America, Inc
*Shurgard Storage Centers, Inc.
*Simon Property Group, Inc.
SL Green Realty Corp.
Spirit Reality Capital
Starwood Hotels & Resorts
Sun Communities, Inc.
*Tanger Factory Outlet Centers, Inc.
*Taubman Centers, Inc.
*UDR Inc.
*Universal Health Realty Inc. Trust
*Urban Edge Properties
*Urstadt Biddle Properties Inc.
*Ventas, Inc.
*Vornado Realty Trust
Washington Prime Group
*Weingarten Realty Investors
*Welltower Inc.

Reinsurance Carriers
*Marsh & McLennan Cos. Inc.
*Old Republic International Corp.

Savings Institutions
*Sovereign Bancorp, Inc.
*Webster Financial Corp.

*Securities, Commodity Contracts, and Other
Financial Investments and Related Activities*
Affiliated Managers Group Inc.
Assured Guaranty Ltd
Broadridge Financial Solutions Inc.
*Citigroup Inc.
CME Group Inc.
Eaton Vance Corporation
Federated Investors, Inc.
*Franklin Resources, Inc.
Goldman Sachs Group, Inc.
IntercontinentalExchange Inc.
Janus Capital Group, Inc.
Legg Mason, Inc.
Raymond James Financial, Inc.
*Waddell & Reed Financial, Inc.
Westwood Holdings Group, Inc.

Other Financial Vehicles
BlackRock, Inc.

Health Care and Social Assistance
Brookdale Senior Living Inc.
Community Health Systems, Inc.
DaVita Inc.
Genesis Healthcare Inc.
HCA Holdings Inc.
Health Management Associates
HealthSouth Corp
Kindred Healthcare, Inc.
Laboratory Corp. of America
Mednax, Inc.
*Tenet Healthcare Corporation
Universal Health Services, Inc.

Information
*Cable Networks, Program Distribution and
Internet Service Providers*
Time Warner Inc.

*Information Services and Data Processing
Services*
Alliance Data Systems Corp.
Arista Networks Inc
Black Knight Financial Services Inc.
Concord EFS, Inc.
DST Systems, Inc.
Dun & Bradstreet Corp. (The)
Fair Isaac Corporation
FactSet Research Systems Inc.
FleetCor Technologies Inc.
GoDaddy Inc.
Green Dot Corp
*Hewlett Packard Enterprise Co
Lender Processing Services Inc.
MasterCard Inc.
Nielsen Holdings PLC
NCR Corporation
Square Inc
*Thomson Reuters Corp
Total System Services, Inc.
Vantiv Inc.
VeriFone Systems
Visa Inc.
Western Union Co.

Motion Picture and Sound Recording Industries
Cinemark Holdings Inc
DreamWorks Animation SKG Inc.
News Corp.
Regal Entertainment Group

Publishing Industries
3D Systems Corp.
Guidewire Software Inc
Meredith Corporation
Monster Worldwide Inc.
MSCI Inc.
*New York Times Company
Oracle Corp.
*Reader's Digest Association, Inc.
ServiceNow Inc
Solera Holdings Inc.
Time Inc.
Tyler Technologies, Inc.
Veeva Systems
Veritiv Corp
VMWARE, Inc.
Wiley (John) & Sons Inc.

Radio and Television Broadcasting
Cable One Inc
Dolby Laboratories Inc.
Pandora Media Inc
Tegna Inc
Westwood One, Inc.

Telecommunications
*AT&T Inc

*CenturyLink, Inc.
*Citizens Communications Co.
Fidelity National Information Services Inc.
Keysight Technology
Level 3 Communications, Inc.
Neustar Inc.
Qwest Communications International
Sprint Nextel Corporation
Sprint Corp
*Telephone and Data Systems, Inc.
United States Cellular Corp.
*Verizon Communications Inc.
Zayo Group Holdings Inc

Manufacturing
Beverage and Tobacco Product Manufacturing
*Altria Group, Inc.
Boston Beer Co., Inc.
*Brown-Forman Corporation
*Coca-Cola Company (The)
Constellation Brands, Inc.
Dr Pepper Snapple Group Inc
Molson Coors Brewing Company
*PepsiCo Inc.
*Philip Morris International Inc.
*Reynolds American Inc.
*Vector Group Inc.

Chemical Manufacturing
*3M Company
*Air Products & Chemicals, Inc.
*Albemarle Corporation
Alberto-Culver Company
*Avon Products, Inc.
*Cabot Corporation
Celanese Corp.
CF Industries Holdings Inc.
Charles River Laboratories Int.
Chemours Co
Chemtura Corp.
*Church & Dwight Company, Inc.
*Clorox Company (The)
*Colgate-Palmolive Company
Compass Minerals International Inc.
*Dow Chemical Company
*du Pont (E.I.) de Nemours & Co.
*Eastman Chemical Company
*Ecolab, Inc.
*Fuller (H.B.) Company
Grace (W.R.) Co.
Huntsman Corp.
IMC Global, Inc.
*International Flavors & Fragrances
Monsanto Co.
*Olin Corporation
Platform Specialty Products Corp
*PPG Industries, Inc.
*Praxair, Inc.
*Procter & Gamble Company
Rockwood Holdings Inc.
*Rohm & Haas Company
*RPM International Inc.
Scotts Company (The)
*Sherwin-Williams Company

Stepan Co.
Westlake Chemical Corp.
Univar Inc.
Versum Materials
*Valspar Corporation (The)

Computer and Electronic Product Manufacturing
Advanced Micro Devices, Inc.
Agilent Technologies, Inc.
*Allegheny Technologies Inc.
*Ametek, Inc.
Ciena Corp.
*Corning Incorporated
*Emerson Electric Co.
Esterline Technologies Corp
Fitbit Inc
Global Payments Inc.
Harman International Industries
Juniper Networks Inc.
*Harris Corporation
*HP Inc
Knowles Corp
*International Business Machines
Jabil Circuit, Inc.
L-3 Communications Holdings
Mettler-Toledo International Inc.
Micron Technology, Inc.
*Motorola Solutions Inc.
Plantronics, Inc.
*Raytheon Company
*Rockwell Collins, Inc.
Teradyne, Inc.
Teradata Corp.
Thermo Fisher Scientific Inc.
TE Connectivity Ltd
Vishay Intertechnology, Inc.
Waters Corporation

*Electrical Equipment, Appliance, and Component
Manufacturing*
Acuity Brands Inc.
Amphenol Corp.
Anixter International Inc.
Belden Inc.
*Eaton Corporation
Edgewell Personal Care Co.
Energizer Holdings Inc
Enersys
*General Electric Company
*Hubbell, Inc.
Manitowoc Foodservice Inc
Regal Beloit Corp.
*Rockwell Automation
*Smith (A.O.) Corporation
Spectrum Brands Holdings Inc
*Whirlpool Corporation

Fabricated Metal Product Manufacturing
*Badger Meter, Inc.
*Ball Corporation
*Crane Co.
Crown Holdings, Inc.
Danaher Corporation

Greif Inc.
Orbital ATK Inc
*Parker-Hannifin Corp.
Shaw Group Inc. (The)
*Snap-On Incorporated
*Stanley Works
*Timken Company (The)
Valmont Industries, Inc.

Food Manufacturing
*Archer Daniels Midland Co.
Bunge Ltd
*Campbell Soup Company
*ConAgra Brands, Inc.
Corn Products International Inc.
Dean Foods Company
*Flowers Foods, Inc.
*General Mills, Inc.
*Hershey Foods Corporation
Hillshire Brands Co
*Hormel Foods Corporation
*Kellogg Company
Lamb Weston
*McCormick & Company, Inc.
Mead Johnson Nutrition Co.
Pinnacle Foods Inc.
Post Holdings Inc
Ralcorp Holdings Inc.
*Sensient Technologies Corp.
*Smucker (J.M.) Company
Tootsie Roll Industries, Inc.
TreeHouse Foods Inc
*Tyson Foods, Inc.
Whitewave Foods Co.

Furniture and Related Product Manufacturing
HNI Corporation
Leggett & Platt, Incorporated
*Masco Corporation
Tempur Sealy International Inc.
Steelcase Inc.

Machinery Manufacturing
AGCO Corporation
*Brunswick Corporation
BWX Technologies Inc.
*Caterpillar Inc.
Colfax Corp
*Cummins Inc.
*Curtiss-Wright Corp.
*Deere & Company
*Diebold Nixdorf Inc.
*Donaldson Company, Inc.
*Dover Corporation
Flowserve Corporation
FMC Corporation
Gardner Denver, Inc.
*Graco Inc.
*IDEX Corporation
Ingersoll-Rand Plc
ITT Inc
*Kennametal Inc.
Lindsay Corp
Lennox International Inc.
Pentair Ltd

Roper Technologies Inc.
Terex Corporation
*Tennant Company
*Toro Co. (The)
Varian Medical Systems, Inc.
Watsco Inc.
*Xerox Corporation
Xylem Inc.
*York International Corporation

Medical Equipment and Supplies Manufacturing
Advanced Medical Optics Inc.
Alere Inc.
*Bard (C.R.), Inc.
*Baxter International Inc.
*Becton, Dickinson and Company
Bio-Rad Laboratories, Inc.
Boston Scientific Corporation
CareFusion Corp
Cooper Companies, Inc.
Covidien Plc
Globus Medical
Halyard Health Inc
Hill-Rom Holdings, Inc.
*Medtronic PLC
Mine Safety Appliances Company
ResMed Inc.
Steris plc
Stryker Corporation
*Teleflex Inc.
Zimmer Biomet Holdings, Inc.

Nonmetallic Mineral Product Manufacturing
Brink's Company (The)
Minerals Technologies Inc.
Oil-Dri Corp. of America
Owens-Illinois, Inc.
USG Corporation

Paper and Wood Product Manufacturing
*Avery Dennison Corporation
*Bemis Company, Inc.
*Boise Cascade Corporation
Domtar Corp.
Graphic Packaging Holding Co.
*International Paper Company
*Kimberly-Clark Corporation
*Louisiana-Pacific Corporation
Packaging Corp. of America
*Rayonier Inc.
*Sonoco Products Company
Tenneco Inc.

Petroleum and Coal Products Manufacturing
*Chevron Corp.
*ConocoPhillips
*Exxon Mobil Corporation
*Hess Corp.
HollyFrontier Corp
*Marathon Petroleum Corp
Murphy Oil Corporation
NGL Energy
PBF Energy, Inc.
Phillips 66
Tesoro Corporation

Valero Energy Corporation
Western Refining Inc.

Pharmaceutical Preparation Manufacturing
*Abbott Laboratories
AbbVie Inc.
*Allergan, Inc.
AmerisourceBergen Corporation
Ashland Global
*Bristol-Myers Squibb Company
Catalent Inc
Edwards Lifesciences Corp.
Genentech, Inc.
*Johnson & Johnson
*Lilly (Eli) & Company
*Merck & Co., Inc.
*Pfizer Inc.
Prestige Brands Holdings Inc.
Zoetis Inc.

Plastics and Rubber Products Manufacturing
AptarGroup Inc.
Armstrong World Industry Inc.
Berry Plastics Group Inc.
*Carlisle Companies Incorporated
Hexcel Corp
*Illinois Tool Works, Incorporated
*Myers Industries, Inc.
*Newell Brands Inc.
PolyOne Corp.d
Sealed Air Corporation
Tupperware Brands Corporation
*West Pharmaceutical Services

Primary Metal Manufacturing
*AK Steel Holding Corporation
*Arconic Inc.
Carpenter Technology Corp.
Commercial Metals Co.
*Nucor Corporation
*United States Steel Corporation
*Worthington Industries, Inc.

Printing and Related Support Activities
Deluxe Corporation

Textiles, Apparel, and Leather Manufacturing
Coach, Inc.
Kate Spade & Co.
Michael Kors Holdings Ltd
Mohawk Industries, Inc.
*NIKE, Inc.
PVH Corp.
Ralph Lauren Corp
Under Armour Inc.
*VF Corporation

Transportation Equipment Manufacturing
Allison Transmission Holdings Inc
Autoliv, Inc.
*Boeing Company (The)
*BorgWarner Inc.
Dana Corp
Delphi Automotive Plc
*Ford Motor Company
General Dynamics Corporation

General Motors Co.
*Harley-Davidson, Inc.
*Honeywell International Inc.
Huntington Ingalls Industries Inc
Lear Corp.
*Lockheed Martin Corporation
*Meritor Inc.
*Modine Manufacturing Company
Navistar International Inc.
*Oshkosh Corp.
*Polaris Industries Inc.
Sequa Corporation
Spirit AeroSystems Holdings Inc.
Teledyne Technologies
*Textron Inc.
Thor Industries, Inc.
Transdigm Group Inc.
Trinity Industries, Inc.
*United Technologies Corp.
Visteon Corp.
WABCO Holdings Inc.
Wabtec Corp.

Other Manufacturing
*Brady Corporation
Coty, Inc.
*Estee Lauder Companies, Inc.
Fortive
Macquaire Infrastructure

Mining
Activities Support for Mining
*Baker Hughes Inc.
Diamond Offshore Drilling, Inc.
Dril-Quip, Inc.
Ensco plc
Frank's International N.V.
EOG Resources, Inc.
Halliburton Company
Helmerich & Payne, Inc.
*Marathon Oil Corporation
Noble Corp
Now Inc.
Oceaneering International, Inc.
Oil States International, Inc.
Pride International, Inc.
Rowan Companies Plc
RPC, Inc.
Schlumberger Ltd.
Superior Energy Services, Inc.
Transocean Ltd

Mining (except Oil and Gas)
*Arch Coal, Inc.
CONSOL Energy Inc.
Freeport-McMoRan Inc.
*Massey Energy Co.
Mosaic Co. (The)
Newmont Mining Corporation
*Southern Copper Corp.
Tahoe Resources Inc.
*Vulcan Materials Company

Oil and Gas Extraction
AmeriGas Partners LP

*Anadarko Petroleum Corp.
*Apache Corporation
Cabot Oil & Gas Corp.
Chesapeake Energy Corp.
Cimarex Energy Co.
Concho Resources Inc
Continental Resources Inc.
Delek US Holdings
Denbury Resources, Inc.
Devon Energy Corporation
*Kerr-McGee Corporation
Kosmos Energy Ltd
Laredo Petroleum, Inc.
Nabors Industries Ltd.
Newfield Exploration Co.
Noble Corp.
Noble Energy, Inc.
*Occidental Petroleum Corp.
Pioneer Natural Resources Co.
QEP Resources Inc
Range Resources Corp.
St. Mary Land & Exploration Co.
Southwestern Energy Company
Ultra Petroleum Corp
Whiting Petroleum Corp.
WPX Energy, Inc.

Other Services
Aramark
Clear Channel Outdoor Holdings
CoreCivic Inc.
CSRA Inc
Genpact Ltd
Hillenbrand Inc.
Leidos Holdings Inc.
Northwestern Corp
Palo Alto Networks, Inc
Red Hat Inc.
*Regis Corporation
Reliance Steel & Aluminum Co.
Salesforce.Com Inc.
Science Applications International Corp
Service Corporation International
ServiceMaster Global Holdings, Inc
StoneMor Partners LP
Tableau Software Inc
Twitter Inc
*Universal Corporation
Valassis Communications, Inc.
Workday Inc.
Wex Inc.
WestRock Co
Yelp Inc.

Professional, Scientific, and Technical Services
Accenture Ltd
AECOM Technology Corp.
Agere Systems Inc.
*Block (H & R), Inc.
Booz Allen Hamilton Holding Corp.
Convergys Corporation

Covance Inc.
Fluor Corporation
FTI Consulting Inc.
Gartner Group, Inc.
*Interpublic Group of Companies
Korn/Ferry International
Moody's Corporation
*Omnicom Group, Inc.
*PerkinElmer, Inc.
Quest Diagnostics, Incorporated
Quintiles IMS Holdings Inc.
*S&P Global Inc
Synnex Corp.

Real Estate and Rental and Leasing
Real Estate
Alexander & Baldwin Inc.
CBRE Group Inc.
Colony Northstar
Howard Hughes Corp
Jones Lang LaSalle Inc.
Realogy Holdings Corp
Store Capital
*W.P. Carey & Co. LLC

Rental and Leasing Services
Air Lease Corp
United Rentals, Inc.

Retail Trade
*Building Material and Garden Equipment and
Supplies Dealers*
*Home Depot (The), Inc.
*Lowe's Companies, Inc.
Wesco International, Inc.

Clothing and Clothing Accessories Stores
American Eagle Outfitters, Inc.
Burlington Stores Inc.
Carter's Inc
Chico's FAS, Inc.
Deckers Outdoor Corp..
*Foot Locker, Inc.
Gap, Inc. (The)
Nordstrom, Inc.
Payless ShoeSource Inc.
*Tiffany & Co.
TJX Companies, Inc. (The)

Furniture and Consumer Electronics
Aaron's, Inc.
Best Buy Co., Inc.
GameStop Corp.
*RadioShack Corporation
Williams-Sonoma, Inc.

General Merchandise Stores
Big Lots, Inc.
Dillard's, Inc.
Dollar General Corp.
Kohl's Corporation
Macys Inc.
Penney (J.C.) Company, Inc.
*Target Corporation
*Wal-Mart Stores, Inc.

Grocery Stores
Kroger Company (The)
*Ruddick Corporation
Safeway Inc.

Health and Personal Care Stores
*CVS Health Corp
*Rite Aid Corporation
*Walgreen Co.

Motor Vehicle and Parts Dealers
Advance Auto Parts, Inc.
Asbury Automotive Group, Inc.
AutoNation, Inc.
AutoZone, Inc.
Carmax Inc.
Group 1 Automotive, Inc.
KAR Auction Services Inc.
Lithia Motors, Inc
Penske Automotive Group Inc.
Sonic Automotive, Inc.

Sporting Goods, Hobby, Book, and Music Stores and other
Barnes & Noble, Inc.
Cabelas Inc.
CST Brands Inc.
Dick's Sporting Goods, Inc.
Murphy USA Inc.
Sally Beauty Holdings Inc.
Signet Jewelers Ltd.
*Sotheby's Holdings, Inc.

Transportation and Warehousing
AirTran Holdings, Inc.
Alaska Air Group, Inc.
*Atmos Energy Corporation
*Buckeye Partners, L.P.
Delta Air Lines, Inc.
*Energy Transfer Equity L P
*Enterprise Products Partners L.P.
*FedEx Corporation
*GATX Corporation
Genesee & Wyoming Inc.
Genesis Energy L.P.
Global Partners LP
Iron Mountain Incorporated
Kansas City Southern
Kinder Morgan Inc.
Kirby Corp.
Magellan Midstream Partners LP
*Norfolk Southern Corporation
*OGE Energy Corp.
*Oneok Inc.
Plains All American Pipeline, L.P.
*Ryder System, Inc.
Southwest Airlines Co.
Targa Resources Corp
TC PipeLines, LP
*Union Pacific Corp.
United Parcel Service, Inc.
Western Gas Resources, Inc.
Williams Companies, Inc. (The)
XPO Logistics, Inc.

Utilities
Utilities - Electric
AES Corporation (The)
*Alliant Energy Corporation
*Ameren Corporation
*American Electric Power Co.
*Avista Corp.
*Black Hills Corporation
*CenterPoint Energy, Inc.
*Cleco Corp.
*CMS Energy Corporation
*Consolidated Edison, Inc.
*Dominion Resources, Inc.
*DTE Energy Co.
*Duke Energy Corporation
*Edison International
*Entergy Corporation
*Eversource Energy
*Exelon Corporation
*FirstEnergy Corporation
*Great Plains Energy Incorporated
*Hawaiian Electric Industries, Inc.
*Idacorp, Inc.
*NextEra Energy Inc.
New Jersey Resources Corp.
*NiSource, Inc.
*PG&E Corporation
*Pinnacle West Capital Corp.
*PNM Resources, Inc.
*PPL Corporation
*Puget Energy, Inc.
RRI Energy, Inc.
*SCANA Corporation
*Southern Company (The)
*WEC Energy Group Inc.
*Westar Energy, Inc.
*Xcel Energy, Inc.

Utilities - Natural Gas
*Chesapeake Utilities Corp.
Antero Resources Corp

*Energen Corporation
*Equitable Resources, Inc.
*National Fuel Gas Company
Northwest Natural Gas Co.
One Gas, Inc.
Oneok Partners LP
Rice Energy Inc.
*Sempra Energy
South Jersey Industries, Inc
*Southwest Gas Corporation.
*Spire Inc.
*UGI Corporation
*Vectren Corporation
*WGL Holdings, Inc.

Utilities - Water
*American States Water Co.
American Water Works Co., Inc.
*Aqua America, Inc.
*California Water Service Group
SJW Group

Wholesale Trade

Wholesale Trade, Durable Goods
  Arrow Electronics, Inc.
*Avnet, Inc.
  Ceridian Corporation
*Genuine Parts Company
  Grainger (W.W.), Inc.
  Hughes Supply, Inc.
  MSC Industrial Direct Co., Inc.
  National-Oilwell, Inc.
*Owens & Minor, Inc.
*Pitney Bowes Inc.
*Weyerhaeuser Company
  World Fuel Services Corp.

Wholesale Trade, Nondurable Goods
  Cardinal Health, Inc.
*Crompton Corporation
*Dominos Pizza Inc.
  Herbalife Ltd.
*McKesson Corporation
  Nu Skin Enterprises, Inc.
  Performance Food Group Inc.
*Supervalu Inc.
*Sysco Corporation
  US Foods Holding Corp

* Designates companies offering dividend reinvestment plans.

DOW JONES INDUSTRIAL AVERAGE
PRICES - EARNINGS - DIVIDENDS

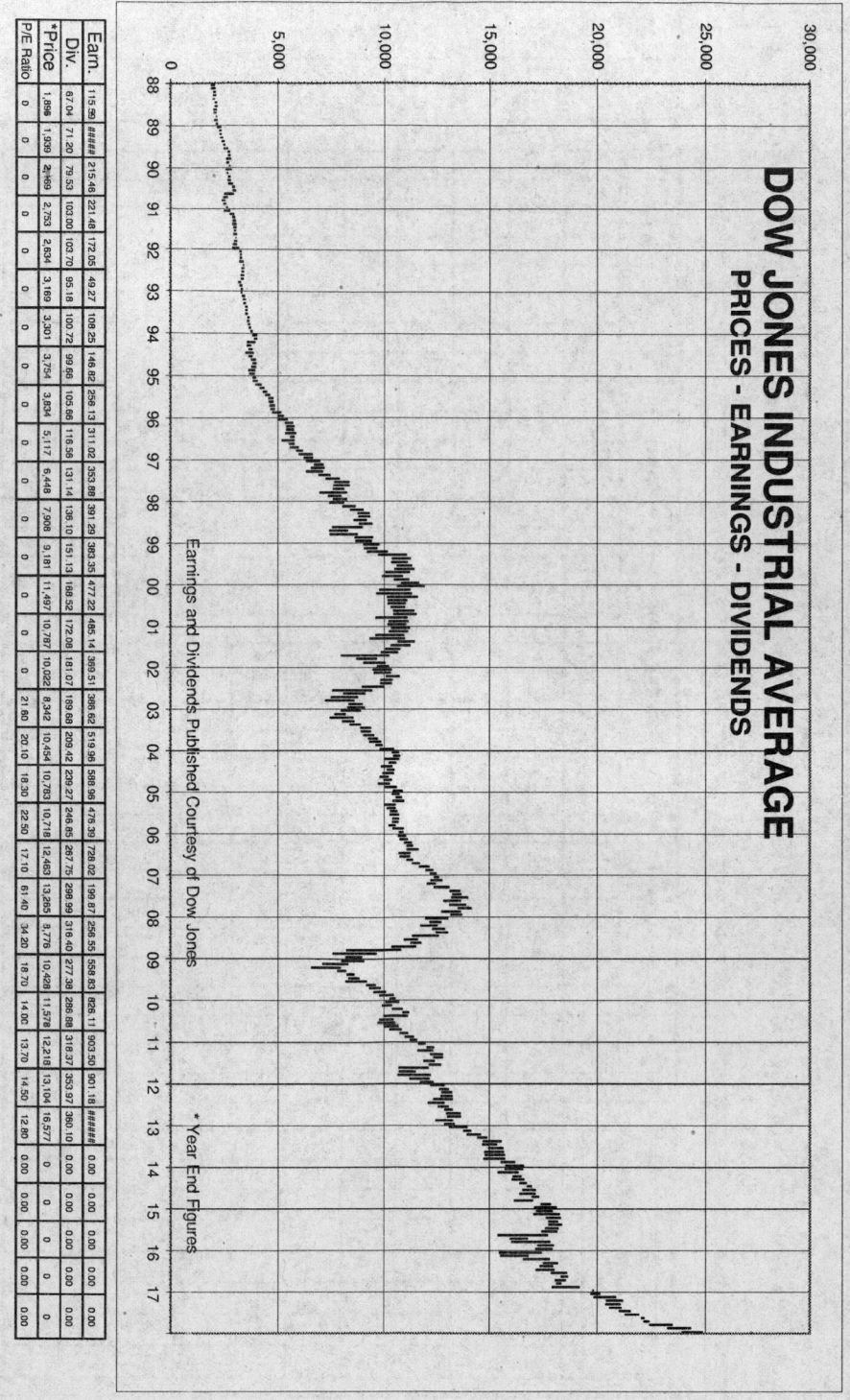

Earnings and Dividends Published Courtesy of Dow Jones

* Year End Figures

Year	Earn.	Div.	*Price	P/E Ratio
88	115.99	67.04	1,898	0
89	####	71.20	1,939	0
90	215.46	79.53	2,469	0
91	221.48	103.00	2,753	0
92	172.05	103.70	2,634	0
93	49.27	95.18	3,169	0
94	108.25	100.72	3,301	0
95	146.82	105.66	3,754	0
96	256.13	116.56	5,117	0
97	311.02	131.14	6,448	0
98	353.88	136.10	7,908	0
99	391.29	151.13	9,181	0
00	383.35	169.52	11,497	0
01	477.22	172.08	10,787	0
02	485.14	181.07	10,022	0
03	369.51	189.68	8,342	0
04	386.62	209.42	10,454	0
05	519.96	239.27	10,783	0
06	588.96	246.85	10,718	0
07	476.39	287.75	12,463	0
08	738.02	298.99	13,265	0
09	190.87	316.40	8,776	0
10	256.55	277.38	10,428	0
11	558.83	286.68	11,578	0
12	826.11	318.37	12,218	0
13	903.50	353.97	13,104	0
14	901.18	360.10	16,577	0
15	####	0.00	0.00	0.00
16	0.00	0.00	0.00	0.00
17	0.00	0.00	0.00	0.00

25a

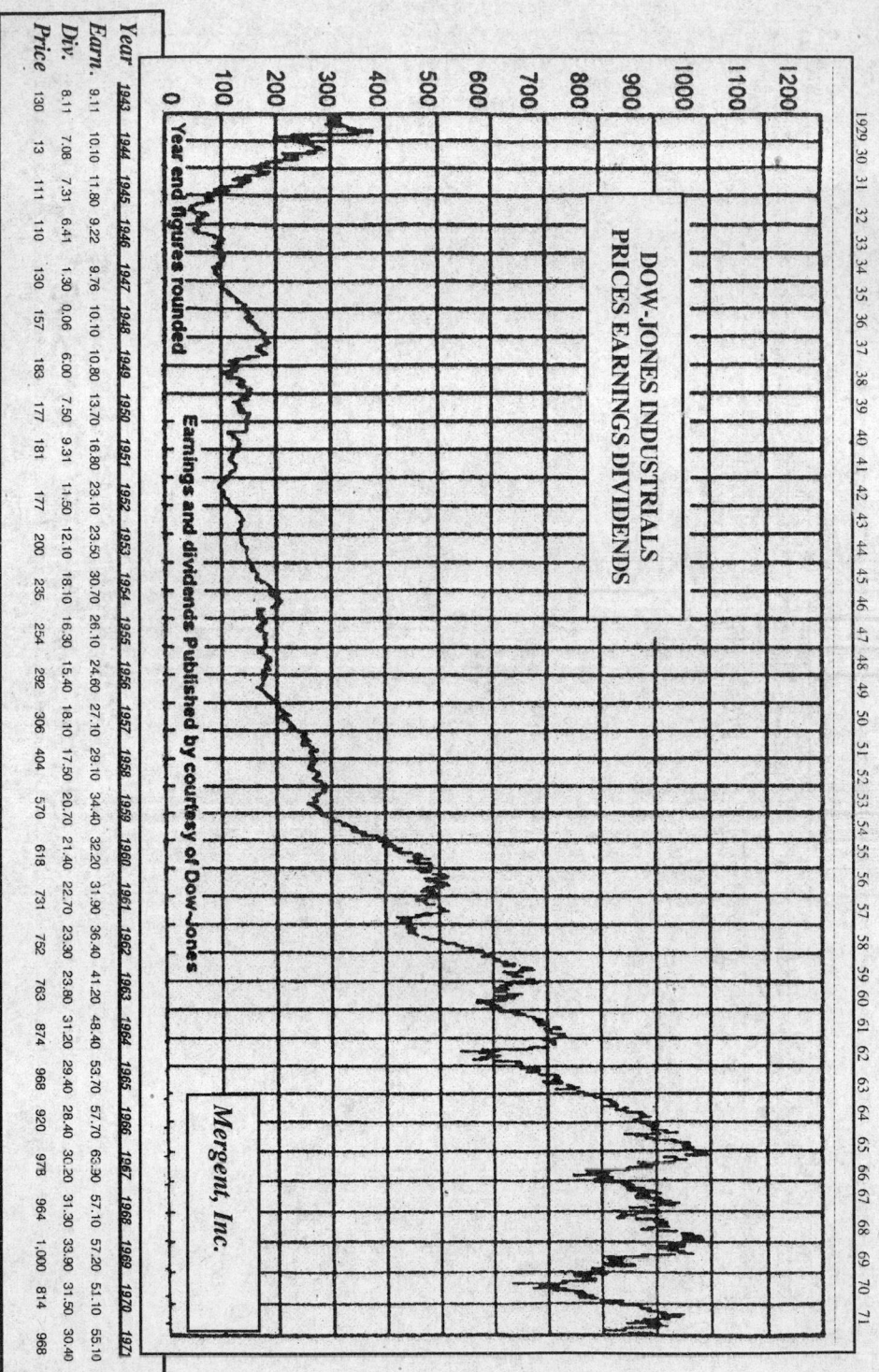

DOW-JONES INDUSTRIALS
PRICES EARNINGS DIVIDENDS

Mergent, Inc.

Year end figures rounded

Earnings and dividends published by courtesy of Dow-Jones

Year	Earn.	Div.	Price
1943	9.11	8.11	130
1944	10.10	7.08	13
1945	11.80	7.31	111
1946	9.22	6.41	110
1947	9.76	1.30	130
1948	10.10	0.06	157
1949	10.80	6.00	183
1950	13.70	7.50	177
1951	16.80	9.31	181
1952	23.10	11.50	177
1953	23.50	12.10	200
1954	30.70	18.10	235
1955	26.10	16.30	254
1956	24.60	15.40	292
1957	27.10	18.10	306
1958	29.10	17.50	404
1959	34.40	20.70	570
1960	32.20	21.40	618
1961	31.90	22.70	731
1962	36.40	23.30	752
1963	41.20	23.80	763
1964	48.40	31.20	874
1965	53.70	29.40	968
1966	57.70	28.40	920
1967	63.90	30.20	978
1968	57.10	31.30	964
1969	57.20	33.90	1,000
1970	51.10	31.50	814
1971	55.10	30.40	968

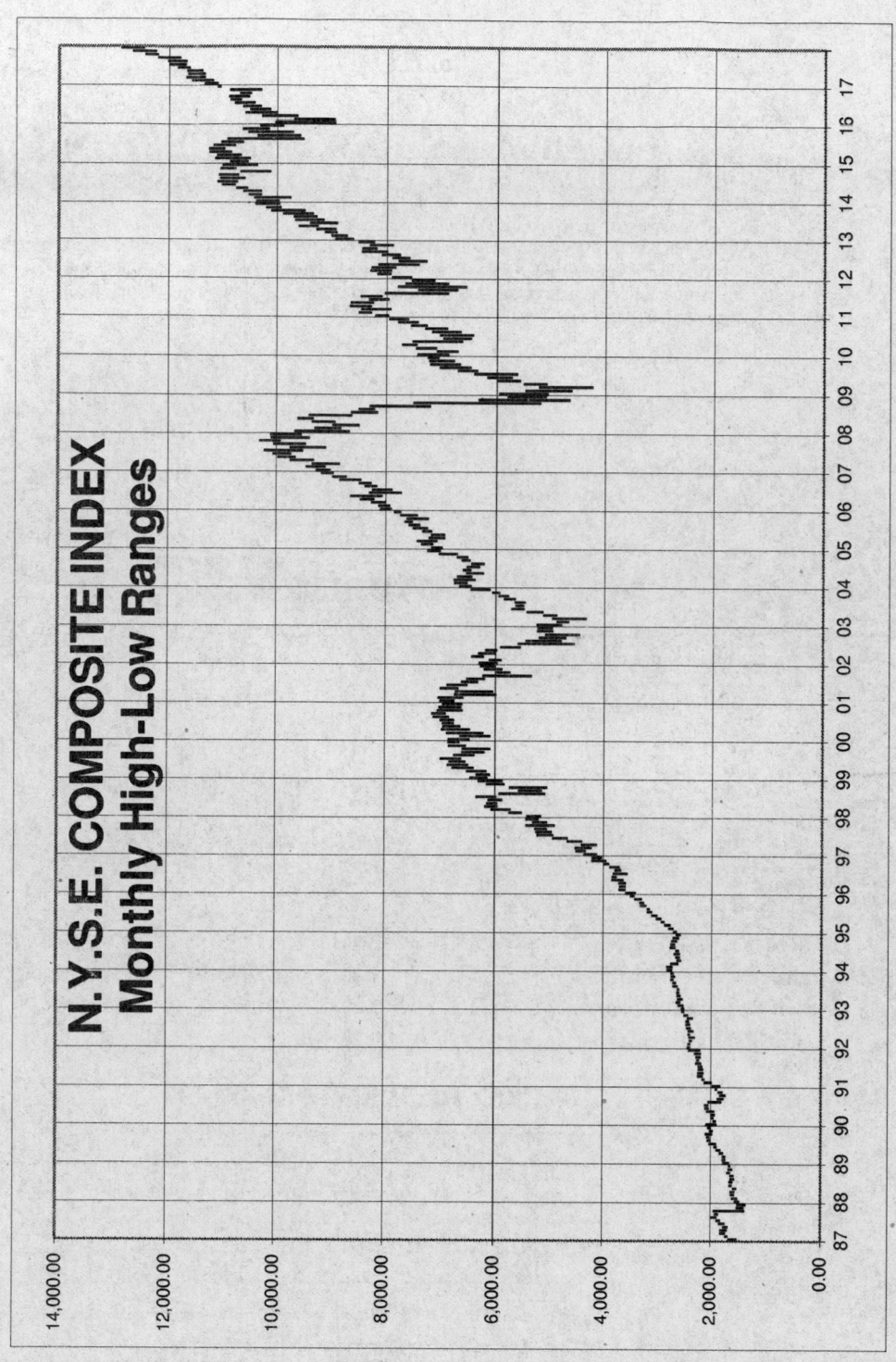

N.Y.S.E. COMPOSITE INDEX
Monthly High-Low Ranges

27a

ADDENDA

COMPANIES ADDED AND DROPPED

Companies are removed for various reasons such as mergers, acquisitions, bankruptcies and lack of investor interest. Added are companies that have recently been included in the Russell 1000, S&P 500, S&P 400 or Mergent's Dividend Achievers, as well as any companies previously covered in Mergent's Handbook of Nasdaq Stocks that have migrated to the New York Stock Exchange.

DROPPED

PEPSICO INC.   VISTEON CORP
PRINCIPAL FINANCIAL GROUP INC   XCEL ENERGY INC

ADDITIONS

Alcoa Corporation   FNB Corp.

Brinks Co. (The)   Spirit Airlines

RECENT DIVIDEND STOCK CHANGES

Company	Amount	Ex-Div Date	Date of Record	Payable Date
Bank of Hawaii Corp	25%	1/18/2018	1/3/2018	1/17/2018
Bristol-Myers Squibb Co.	25%	3/1/2018	2/7/2018	2/28/2018
Gorman-Rupp Company	3-for-1	12/28/2017	12/18/2017	12/27/2017
Regal Entertainment Group	1-for-4	11/9/2017	...	...

RECENT DIVIDEND DECREASES

General Electric Co	0.12	Q	12/26/2017
Genesis Energy L.P.	0.50	Q	10/30/2017
Mosaic Co (The)	0.03	Q	12/6/2017
Santander Consumer USA Holdings Inc	0.03	Q	11/6/2017
SJW Group	0.17	Q	11/28/2017

ADDENDA

RECENT DIVIDEND INCREASES

Company Increased	Amount		Date	Company Increased	Amount		Date
				Duke Realty Corp	0.85	Q	11/30/2017
Aaron's Inc	0.03	Q	12/12/2017	Eastman Chemical Co	0.56	Q	12/15/2017
Accenture plc	1.33	Q	10/18/2017	Eaton Vance Corp	0.31	Q	10/30/2017
AFLAC Inc	0.45	Q	11/14/2017	Ecolab Inc	0.41	Q	12/18/2017
Agilent Technologies, Inc.	0.15	Q	12/29/2017	Edison International	0.61	Q	12/28/2017
Air Lease Corp	0.10	Q	12/13/2017	Emerson Electric Co.	0.49	Q	11/16/2017
Alexandria Real Estate Equities Inc	0.90	Q	12/28/2017	Energizer Holdings Inc (New)	0.29	Q	11/29/2017
Ameren Corp	0.46	Q	12/12/2017	Energy Transfer Equity LP	0.30	Q	11/6/2017
American Electric Power Company,	0.62	Q	11/9/2017	Entergy Corp	0.89	Q	11/8/2017
American Equity Investment Life	0.26	Q	11/28/2017	Enterprise Products Partners L.P.	0.42	Q	10/30/2017
American Express Co.	0.35	Q	10/5/2017	Everest Re Group Ltd	1.30	Q	11/28/2017
American Financial Group Inc	2.00	Q	11/16/2017	Franklin Resources, Inc.	0.23	Q	12/22/2017
American Tower Corp (New)	0.70	Q	12/27/2017	Gorman-Rupp Company (The)	0.13	Q	11/14/2017
AmerisourceBergen Corp.	0.38	Q	11/17/2017	Group 1 Automotive, Inc.	0.25	Q	11/30/2017
Aramark	0.11	Q	11/24/2017	Hanover Insurance Group Inc	0.54	Q	12/14/2017
Associated Banc-Corp	0.14	Q	11/30/2017	Hartford Financial Services Group	0.25	Q	11/30/2017
Assurant Inc	0.56	Q	11/24/2017	Honeywell International Inc	0.75	Q	11/16/2017
Atmos Energy Corp.	0.49	Q	11/24/2017	Horton (DR) Inc	0.13	Q	11/30/2017
Becton, Dickinson & Co	0.75	Q	12/7/2017	Host Hotels & Resorts Inc	0.20	Q	12/28/2017
Berkley (WR) Corp	0.50	Q	11/29/2017	HP Inc	0.14	Q	12/12/2017
Black Hills Corporation	0.48	Q	11/16/2017	Hubbell Inc.	0.77	Q	11/29/2017
BorgWarner Inc	0.17	Q	11/30/2017	Huntington Ingalls Industries, Inc.	0.72	Q	11/22/2017
Boston Properties Inc	0.80	Q	12/28/2017	Idacorp Inc	0.59	Q	11/3/2017
Brady Corp	0.21	Q	10/6/2017	International Paper Co	0.48	Q	11/14/2017
Brown & Brown, Inc.	0.15	Q	10/26/2017	Iron Mountain Inc (New)	0.59	Q	12/14/2017
Brown-Forman Corp	0.20	Q	12/6/2017	Jones Lang LaSalle Inc	0.37	Q	11/15/2017
Brunswick Corp.	0.19	Q	11/20/2017	JPMorgan Chase & Co	0.56	Q	10/5/2017
Carnival Corp	0.45	Q	11/22/2017	KAR Auction Services Inc.	0.35	Q	12/19/2017
Crown Castle International Corp	1.05	Q	12/14/2017	KeyCorp	0.11	Q	11/27/2017
CubeSmart	0.30	Q	12/29/2017	Kimco Realty Corp	0.28	Q	12/29/2017
DCT Industrial Trust Inc	0.36	Q	12/21/2017	Lauder (Estee) Cos., Inc. (The)	0.38	Q	11/29/2017
Disney (Walt) Co. (The)	0.84	Q	12/8/2017	Lockheed Martin Corp	2.00	Q	11/30/2017
Dolby Laboratories Inc	0.16	Q	11/3/2017	Macerich Co (The)	0.74	Q	11/9/2017
Dominion Energy Inc (New)	0.77	Q	11/30/2017	Macquarie Infrastructure Corp	1.42	Q	11/10/2017
Douglas Emmett Inc	0.25	Q	12/28/2017	Magellan Midstream Partners LP	0.91	Q	11/1/2017
DTE Energy Co	0.88	Q	12/15/2017	Masco Corp.	0.11	Q	10/12/2017

ADDENDA

McCormick & Co Inc	0.52	Q	12/28/2017					
McDonald's Corp	1.01	Q	11/30/2017	Six Flags Entertainment Corp	0.70	Q	11/29/2017
MDU Resources Group Inc	0.20	Q	12/13/2017	SL Green Realty Corp	0.81	Q	12/29/2017
Merck & Co Inc	0.48	Q	12/14/2017	Snap-On, Inc.	0.82	Q	11/16/2017
Mercury General Corp.	0.63	Q	12/13/2017	South Jersey Industries, Inc.	0.28	Q	12/8/2017
Motorola Solutions Inc.	0.52	Q	12/14/2017	Southern Copper Corp	0.25	Q	11/7/2017
MSC Industrial Direct Co Inc	0.48	Q	11/13/2017	Spire Inc	0.56	Q	12/8/2017
NIKE Inc	0.20	Q	12/1/2017	Stepan Co.	0.23	Q	11/29/2017
Northwest Natural Gas Co.	0.47	Q	10/30/2017	Stryker Corp	0.47	Q	12/28/2017
Nucor Corp.	0.38	Q	12/28/2017	Synnex Corp	0.30	Q	10/12/2017
OGE Energy Corp.	0.33	Q	10/6/2017	Toro Company (The)	0.20	Q	12/21/2017
Omega Healthcare Investors, Inc.	0.65	Q	10/30/2017	Tyson Foods Inc	0.30	Q	11/30/2017
Omnicom Group, Inc.	0.60	Q	12/18/2017	Union Pacific Corp	0.67	Q	11/29/2017
Oshkosh Corp (New)	0.24	Q	11/15/2017	Universal Health Realty Income Tr	0.67	Q	12/15/2017
Owens Corning	0.21	Q	12/29/2017	Valvoline Inc	0.07	Q	11/30/2017
Penske Automotive Group Inc	0.33	Q	11/9/2017	Vector Group Ltd	0.40	Q	12/19/2017
Piedmont Office Realty Trust Inc	0.50	Q	12/22/2017	Vectren Corp	0.45	Q	11/14/2017
Pinnacle West Capital Corp	0.70	Q	10/31/2017	Ventas Inc	0.79	Q	12/29/2017
PolyOne Corp.	0.18	Q	12/14/2017	Verizon Communications Inc	0.59	Q	10/6/2017
ProAssurance Corp	4.69	Q	12/20/2017	VF Corp.	0.46	Q	12/7/2017
Prosperity Bancshares Inc.	0.36	Q	12/14/2017	Visa Inc	0.20	Q	11/16/2017
Realty Income Corp	0.21	Q	12/29/2017	Vishay Intertechnology, Inc.	0.07	Q	12/6/2017
RLI Corp.	1.75	Q	11/29/2017	W.P. Carey Inc	1.01	Q	12/28/2017
Rockwell Automation, Inc.	0.84	Q	11/10/2017	Weingarten Realty Investors	0.75	Q	12/22/2017
Rollins, Inc.	0.12	Q	11/9/2017	West Pharmaceutical Services, Inc.	0.14	Q	10/17/2017
RPM International Inc (DE)	0.32	Q	10/13/2017	WestRock Co	0.43	Q	11/9/2017
Sensient Technologies Corp.	0.33	Q	11/3/2017	Westwood Holdings Group, Inc.	0.68	Q	12/7/2017
Simon Property Group, Inc.	1.85	Q	11/15/2017	Weyerhaeuser Co	0.32	Q	11/30/2017

RECENT AND PENDING NAME CHANGES

Old	New
Alexander & Baldwin Inc (New)	Alexander & Baldwin Inc (REIT)
BancorpSouth Inc	BancorpSouth Bank (Tupelo, MS)
Coach Inc	Tapestry Inc
CONSOL Energy Inc	CNX Resources Corp
Delphi Automotive PLC	Aptiv PLC
HealthSouth Corp	Encompass Health Corp
Quintiles IMS Holdings Inc	IQVIA Holdings Inc
Vantiv Inc	Worldpay Inc

The 2017 Dividend Achievers

Companies listed below qualified for the 2017-2018 Winter Edition of Mergent's Dividend Achievers Also shown are total numbers of consecutive years of dividend growth.

Company Name	Years of Growth	Company Name	Years of Growth
3M Co	58	Digital Realty Trust, Inc.	12
Aaron's, Inc.	13	Dominion Energy Inc.	13
Abbott Laboratories	43	Donaldson Co. Inc.	21
ABM Industries, Inc.	52	Dover Corp	61
AFLAC Inc.	34	Duke Energy Corp	12
Air Products & Chemicals, Inc.	34	Eaton Vance Corp	35
Albemarle Corp.	22	Ecolab, Inc.	24
Alliant Energy Corp.	13	Edison International	12
Altria Group Inc	51	Emerson Electric Co.	60
American Equity Investment Life Holding Co	13	Enbridge Energy Partners LP	10
American Financial Group Inc	11	Energy Transfer Equity LP	10
American States Water Co.	63	Enterprise Products Partners L.P.	18
AmeriGas Partners, L.P.	12	Equity Lifestyle Properties Inc	12
Ameriprise Financial Inc	11	Erie Indemnity Co.	21
AmerisourceBergen Corp.	12	Essex Property Trust, Inc.	22
Amtrust Financial	10	Eversource Energy	17
Analog Devices, Inc.	13	Exxon Mobil Corp.	34
AptarGroup Inc.	23	FactSet Research Systems Inc.	17
Aqua America Inc	25	Federal Realty Investment Trust (MD)	49
Archer Daniels Midland Co.	42	FedEx Corp	13
Assurant Inc	12	Flowers Foods, Inc.	13
AT&T Inc	32	Franklin Resources, Inc.	27
Atlantic Tele-Network, Inc.	17	Fuller (H.B.) Company	49
Atmos Energy Corp.	29	General Dynamics Corp.	25
Atrion Corp.	13	General Mills, Inc.	13
Automatic Data Processing Inc.	41	Genesis Energy L.P.	13
Avista Corp.	14	Genuine Parts Co.	60
Badger Meter, Inc.	24	Gorman-Rupp Co. (The)	44
Becton, Dickinson and Co.	44	Graco Inc.	17
Bemis Co Inc	33	Grainger (W.W.) Inc.	45
Berkley (W. R.) Corp.	15	Hanover Insurance Group Inc	11
Best Buy Inc	13	Harris Corp.	15
Black Hills Corporation	45	Hasbro, Inc.	13
Brady Corp.	32	Helmerich & Payne, Inc.	40
Brown & Brown, Inc.	23	Holly Energy Partners LP	12
Brown-Forman Corp.	32	Hormel Foods Corp.	50
Buckeye Partners, L.P.	21	Illinois Tool Works, Inc.	54
California Water Service Group (DE)	49	International Business Machines Corp.	21
Cardinal Health, Inc.	20	International Flavors & Fragrances Inc.	14
Carlisle Companies Inc.	40	ITT Corporation	14
Caterpillar Inc.	23	Johnson & Johnson	52
CenterPoint Energy, Inc	11	Kellogg Co	12
Chesapeake Utilities Corp.	13	Kimberly-Clark Corp.	42
Chevron Corporation	29	Kroger Co	10
Church & Dwight Co., Inc.	20	Leggett & Platt, Inc.	45
Clorox Co.	40	Lindsay Corp	14
Coca-Cola Co (The)	54	Lockheed Martin Corp.	14
Colgate-Palmolive Co.	54	Lowe's Companies Inc	55
Community Bank System, Inc.	25	Magellan Midstream Partners LP	15
Compass Minerals International Inc	12	McCormick & Co., Inc.	30
Consolidated Edison, Inc.	42	McDonald's Corp.	40
CSX Corp.	12	MDU Resources Group Inc.	26
Cullen/Frost Bankers, Inc.	23	Mercury General Corp.	30
Cummins, Inc.	11	Meredith Corp.	23
CVS Health Corporation	13	Monsanto Co.	15

Company Name	Years of Growth	Company Name	Years of Growth
MSA Safety Inc	46	Southern Company (The)	15
MSC Industrial Direct Co., Inc.	13	Southwest Gas Holdings	10
Nacco Industries	10	Spire Inc.	13
National Fuel Gas Co. (NJ)	45	Stanley Black & Decker, Inc.	49
National Health Investors, Inc.	14	Stepan Co.	49
National Healthcare Corp.	11	Stryker Corp.	24
National Retail Properties Inc	27	Sunoco Logistics Partners L.P.	14
New Jersey Resources Corp	21	Sysco Corp.	40
Newmarket Corp	10	Tanger Factory Outlet Centers, Inc.	23
NextEra Energy Inc	21	Target Corp	45
NIKE, Inc	15	TC PipeLines, LP	17
Northrop Grumman Corp	13	Telephone & Data Systems, Inc.	42
Northwest Natural Gas Co.	61	Tennant Co.	44
Northwestern Corp.	11	Texas Instruments Inc.	13
NU Skin Enterprises, Inc.	15	The Gap, Inc.	12
Nucor Corp.	44	Tiffany & Co.	14
Occidental Petroleum Corp	14	TJX Companies, Inc.	20
OGE Energy	10	Tompkins Financial Corp	20
Oil-Dri Corp. of America	14	Tootsie Roll Industries Inc	53
Old Republic International Corp.	35	Torchmark Corp.	11
Omega Healthcare Investors, Inc.	14	Toro Co. (The)	13
Oneok Inc.	14	TransMontaigne Partners L.P.	11
Owens & Minor, Inc.	19	Travelers Companies Inc (The)	11
Polaris Industries Inc.	21	UGI Corp.	29
Portland General Electric	10	Union Pacific	10
PPG Industries, Inc.	45	United Bankshares, Inc.	35
PPL Corp	17	United Technologies Corp.	23
Praxair, Inc.	24	Universal Corp.	46
Procter & Gamble Co.	63	Universal Health Realty Income Trust	29
Prosperity Bancshares Inc.	17	Urstadt Biddle Properties Inc	18
Raytheon Co.	12	Vector Group Ltd	18
Realty Income Corp.	22	Vectren Corp	41
Regal Beloit Corp	12	Verizon Communications Inc	12
Republic Services, Inc.	13	VF Corp.	44
RLI Corp.	40	W.P. Carey Inc	18
Robert Half International Inc.	12	Walgreens Boots Alliance Inc	41
Rollins, Inc.	14	Wal-Mart Stores, Inc.	41
Roper Industries, Inc	24	Waste Management, Inc. (DE)	13
RPM International Inc (DE)	43	WEC Energy Group Inc	13
Ryder System, Inc.	12	Welltower Inc	13
SCANA Corp	16	West Pharmaceutical Services, Inc.	24
Sensient Technologies Corp.	11	Westar Energy Inc	13
Sherwin-Williams Co.	37	Westlake Chemical Corp	12
SJW Corp.	49	Westwood Holdings Group, Inc.	14
Smith (A.O.) Corp	24	WGL Holdings, Inc.	40
Smucker (J.M.) Co.	19	Wiley (John) & Sons Inc.	23
Sonoco Products Co.	33	Williams Sonoma Inc	10
South Jersey Industries, Inc.	17	Yum! Brands, Inc.	12

AARON'S INC

Exchange	Symbol	Price	52Wk Range	Yield	P/E	Div Achiever
NYS	AAN	$39.85 (12/29/2017)	47.54-26.92	0.30	20.97	13 Years

*7 Year Price Score 98.25 *NYSE Composite Index=100 *12 Month Price Score 95.85

Interim Earnings (Per Share)

Qtr.	Mar	Jun	Sep	Dec
2014	0.53	0.12	0.13	0.31
2015	0.68	0.56	0.33	0.30
2016	0.68	0.53	0.40	0.30
2017	0.74	0.51	0.35	...

Interim Dividends (Per Share)

Amt	Decl	Ex	Rec	Pay
0.028Q	02/27/2017	03/13/2017	03/15/2017	04/03/2017
0.028Q	05/17/2017	06/23/2017	06/27/2017	07/03/2017
0.028Q	08/15/2017	09/14/2017	09/15/2017	10/02/2017
0.03Q	11/08/2017	12/12/2017	12/13/2017	01/02/2018

Indicated Div: $0.12

Valuation Analysis

	Institutional Holding	
Forecast EPS	$2.45 (01/17/2018)	No of Institutions 354
Market Cap	$2.8 Billion	Shares 89,391,472
Book Value	$1.6 Billion	% Held
Price/Book	1.79	N/A
Price/Sales	0.86	

Business Summary: Retail - Furniture & Home Furnishings (MIC: 2.1.6 SIC: 5712 NAIC: 442110)

Aaron's is an omnichannel provider of lease-purchase solutions. Co. is engaged in the sales and lease ownership and specialty retailing of furniture, consumer electronics, home appliances and accessories through its more than 1,860 Company-operated and franchised stores in 47 states and Canada as well as its e-commerce platform, Aarons.com. Co.'s stores carry brands such as Samsung®, Frigidaire®, Hewlett-Packard®, LG®, Whirlpool®, Simmons®, Philips®, Ashley® and Magnavox®. As of Dec 31 2016, Co. had 1,864 Aaron's stores, comprised of 1,165 Company-operated stores in 28 states, the District of Columbia and Canada, and 699 independently-owned franchised stores in 46 states and Canada.

Recent Developments: For the quarter ended Sep 30 2017, net income decreased 14.0% to US$25.3 million from US$29.5 million in the year-earlier quarter. Revenues were US$838.9 million, up 9.1% from US$769.0 million the year before. Operating income was US$42.7 million versus US$50.8 million in the prior-year quarter, a decrease of 16.0%. Direct operating expenses declined 14.4% to US$55.1 million from US$64.4 million in the comparable period the year before. Indirect operating expenses increased 13.4% to US$741.1 million from US$653.8 million in the equivalent prior-year period.

Prospects: Our evaluation of Aaron's Inc as of Jan. 14, 2018 is the result of our systematic analysis on three basic characteristics: earnings strength, relative valuation, and recent stock price movement. The company has generated a negative trend in earnings per share over the past 5 quarters and while recent estimates for the company have been mixed, AAN has posted results that fell short of analysts expectations. Based on operating earnings yield, the company is undervalued when compared to all of the companies in our coverage universe. Share price changes over the past year indicates that AAN will perform poorly over the near term.

Financial Data

(US$ in Thousands)	9 Mos	6 Mos	3 Mos	12/31/2016	12/31/2015	12/31/2014	12/31/2013	12/31/2012
Earnings Per Share	1.90	1.95	1.97	1.91	1.86	1.08	1.58	2.25
Cash Flow Per Share	2.62	3.63	5.26	6.42	2.30	(0.68)	4.07	0.79
Tang Book Value Per Share	10.04	11.02	10.37	9.90	7.59	5.45	12.30	11.83
Dividends Per Share	0.110	0.108	0.105	0.102	0.094	0.086	0.072	0.062
Dividend Payout %	5.79	5.51	5.33	5.37	5.05	7.96	4.56	2.76
Income Statement								
Total Revenue	2,499,081	1,660,198	844,554	3,207,716	3,179,756	2,725,239	2,234,631	2,222,588
EBITDA	1,266,189	857,029	449,462	292,713	286,274	191,698	240,875	332,806
Depn & Amortn	1,072,972	707,396	361,998	53,600	52,000	53,700	53,300	53,100
Income Before Taxes	178,839	139,618	82,623	218,422	213,120	121,704	184,960	276,855
Income Taxes	63,863	49,983	29,323	79,139	77,411	43,471	64,294	103,812
Net Income	114,976	89,635	53,300	139,283	135,709	78,233	120,666	173,043
Average Shares	72,095	71,697	72,386	73,013	73,043	72,723	76,390	76,826
Balance Sheet								
Current Assets	1,374,678	1,445,382	1,531,786	1,630,070	1,617,652	1,409,286	1,353,167	1,342,110
Total Assets	2,595,004	2,548,130	2,624,484	2,615,736	2,658,875	2,456,844	1,827,176	1,812,929
Current Liabilities	648,357	604,944	639,575	360,193	374,326	358,690	317,551	271,554
Long-Term Obligations	372,691	401,113	484,716	497,829	610,450	606,082	142,704	141,528
Total Liabilities	1,021,048	1,006,057	1,124,291	1,134,138	1,292,257	1,233,323	687,213	676,803
Stockholders' Equity	1,573,956	1,542,073	1,500,193	1,481,598	1,366,618	1,223,521	1,139,963	1,136,126
Shares Outstanding	70,760	70,722	70,643	71,448	72,600	72,488	72,956	75,720
Statistical Record								
Return on Assets %	5.31	5.53	5.52	5.27	5.31	3.65	6.63	9.73
Return on Equity %	9.01	9.38	9.79	9.75	10.48	6.62	10.60	16.34
EBITDA Margin %	50.67	51.62	53.22	9.13	9.00	7.03	10.78	14.97
Net Margin %	4.60	5.40	6.31	4.34	4.27	2.87	5.40	7.79
Asset Turnover	1.28	1.27	1.24	1.21	1.24	1.27	1.23	1.25
Current Ratio	2.12	2.39	2.40	4.53	4.32	3.93	4.26	4.94
Debt to Equity	0.24	0.26	0.32	0.34	0.45	0.50	0.13	0.12
Price Range	47.54-22.63	40.12-21.89	33.97-21.10	33.97-20.33	40.46-21.74	35.90-23.27	30.60-26.68	31.16-24.83
P/E Ratio	25.02-11.91	20.57-11.23	17.24-10.71	17.79-10.64	21.75-11.69	33.24-21.55	19.37-16.89	13.85-11.04
Average Yield %	0.33	0.37	0.39	0.41	0.29	0.30	0.25	0.22

Address: 400 Galleria Parkway S.E., Suite 300, Atlanta, GA 30339-3182 Telephone: 678-402-3000	Web Site: www.aarons.com Officers: Ray M. Robinson - Chairman R. Charles Loudermilk - Chairman Emeritus, Chairman, Chief Executive Officer	Auditors: Ernst & Young LLP Investor Contact: 678-402-3116 Transfer Agents: Computershare Investor Services, Canton, MA

ABBVIE INC

Exchange	Symbol	Price	52Wk Range	Yield	P/E
NYS	ABBV	$96.71 (12/29/2017)	98.21-60.00	2.94	23.53

*7 Year Price Score N/A *NYSE Composite Index=100 *12 Month Price Score 119.63

Interim Earnings (Per Share)

Qtr.	Mar	Jun	Sep	Dec
2014	0.61	0.68	0.31	(0.50)
2015	0.63	0.83	0.74	0.92
2016	0.83	0.98	0.97	0.85
2017	1.06	1.19	1.01	...

Interim Dividends (Per Share)

Amt	Decl	Ex	Rec	Pay
0.64Q	02/16/2017	04/11/2017	04/13/2017	05/15/2017
0.64Q	06/22/2017	07/12/2017	07/14/2017	08/15/2017
0.64Q	09/08/2017	10/12/2017	10/13/2017	11/15/2017
0.71Q	10/27/2017	01/11/2018	01/12/2018	02/15/2018

Indicated Div: $2.84 (Div. Reinv. Plan)

Valuation Analysis

Forecast EPS	$5.54 (01/18/2018)	Institutional Holding	
		No of Institutions	2101
Market Cap	$154.4 Billion	Shares	
Book Value	$6.7 Billion		1,255,921,664
Price/Book	23.08	% Held	67.34
Price/Sales	5.66		

Business Summary: Pharmaceuticals (MIC: 4.1.1 SIC: 2834 NAIC: 325412)

AbbVie is a research-based biopharmaceutical company. Co.'s portfolio of products includes a line of therapies that addresses serious diseases such as: HUMIRA (adalimumab) to treat autoimmune diseases; oncology products such as IMBRUVICA (ibrutinib) and Venclexta (venetoclax); virology products such as VIEKIRA PAK for the treatment of hepatitis C and Norvir (ritonavir) for the treatment of human immunodeficiency virus-1 infection; metabolic and hormone products that target conditions such as testosterone deficiency; endocrinology products such as Lupron (leuprolide acetate) for the palliative treatment of advanced prostate cancer, treatment of endometriosis and central precocious puberty.

Recent Developments: For the quarter ended Sep 30 2017, net income increased 2.1% to US$1.63 billion from US$1.60 billion in the year-earlier quarter. Revenues were US$7.00 billion, up 8.8% from US$6.43 billion the year before. Operating income was US$2.71 billion versus US$2.36 billion in the prior-year quarter, an increase of 14.6%. Direct operating expenses rose 7.4% to US$1.62 billion from US$1.50 billion in the comparable period the year before. Indirect operating expenses increased 4.2% to US$2.67 billion from US$2.57 billion in the equivalent prior-year period.

Prospects: Our evaluation of AbbVie Inc. as of Jan. 14, 2018 is the result of our systematic analysis on three basic characteristics: earnings strength, relative valuation, and recent stock price movement. The company has enjoyed a very positive trend in earnings per share over the past 5 quarters. However, while recent estimates for the company have been lowered by analysts, ABBV has posted better than expected results. Based on operating earnings yield, the company is undervalued when compared to all of the companies in our coverage universe. Share price changes over the past year indicates that ABBV will perform very well over the near term.

Financial Data

(US$ in Thousands)	9 Mos	6 Mos	3 Mos	12/31/2016	12/31/2015	12/31/2014	12/31/2013	12/31/2012
Earnings Per Share	4.11	4.07	3.86	3.63	3.13	1.10	2.56	3.35
Cash Flow Per Share	5.58	4.45	4.39	4.33	4.64	2.23	3.94	4.01
Dividends Per Share	2.490	2.420	2.350	2.280	2.020	1.660	1.600	...
Dividend Payout %	60.58	59.46	60.88	62.81	64.54	150.91	62.50	...
Income Statement								
Total Revenue	20,477,000	13,482,000	6,538,000	25,638,000	22,859,000	19,960,000	18,790,000	18,380,000
EBITDA	8,418,000	5,692,000	2,707,000	10,038,000	8,167,000	3,546,000	6,507,000	6,959,000
Depn & Amortn	1,132,000	753,000	374,000	1,189,000	836,000	786,000	897,000	1,150,000
Income Before Taxes	6,534,000	4,439,000	2,086,000	7,884,000	6,645,000	2,369,000	5,332,000	5,725,000
Income Taxes	1,277,000	813,000	375,000	1,931,000	1,501,000	595,000	1,204,000	450,000
Net Income	5,257,000	3,626,000	1,711,000	5,953,000	5,144,000	1,774,000	4,128,000	5,275,000
Average Shares	1,603,000	1,600,000	1,603,000	1,631,000	1,637,000	1,610,000	1,604,000	1,577,000
Balance Sheet								
Current Assets	18,930,000	16,962,000	15,547,000	16,187,000	16,314,000	16,088,000	17,848,000	15,354,000
Total Assets	68,840,000	66,994,000	65,664,000	66,099,000	53,050,000	27,547,000	29,198,000	27,008,000
Current Liabilities	13,033,000	12,259,000	8,844,000	9,781,000	10,894,000	11,400,000	6,879,000	6,776,000
Long-Term Obligations	33,974,000	33,817,000	36,526,000	36,440,000	29,240,000	10,565,000	14,292,000	14,630,000
Total Liabilities	62,153,000	60,985,000	60,666,000	61,463,000	49,105,000	25,805,000	24,706,000	23,645,000
Stockholders' Equity	6,687,000	6,009,000	4,998,000	4,636,000	3,945,000	1,742,000	4,492,000	3,363,000
Shares Outstanding	1,596,123	1,593,720	1,591,365	1,592,512	1,609,892	1,591,389	1,587,360	1,577,334
Statistical Record								
Return on Assets %	9.82	9.86	10.57	9.97	12.76	6.25	14.69	22.55
Return on Equity %	101.06	113.57	130.90	138.37	180.90	56.91	105.11	67.50
EBITDA Margin %	41.11	42.22	41.40	39.15	35.73	17.77	34.63	37.86
Net Margin %	25.67	26.90	26.17	23.22	22.50	8.89	21.97	28.70
Asset Turnover	0.40	0.40	0.44	0.43	0.57	0.70	0.67	0.79
Current Ratio	1.45	1.38	1.76	1.65	1.50	1.41	2.59	2.27
Debt to Equity	5.08	5.63	7.31	7.86	7.41	6.06	3.18	4.35
Price Range	89.22-55.78	73.18-55.78	67.39-55.78	67.39-51.18	71.23-48.27	69.71-46.46	54.32-33.71	...
P/E Ratio	21.71-13.57	17.98-13.71	17.46-14.45	18.56-14.10	22.76-15.42	63.37-42.24	21.22-13.17	...
Average Yield %	3.73	3.78	3.78	3.77	3.76	3.25	2.99	3.66

Address: 1 North Waukegan Road, North Chicago, IL 60064-6400
Telephone: 847-932-7900

Web Site: www.abbvie.com
Officers: Richard A. Gonzalez - Chairman, Chief Executive Officer Laura J. Schumacher - Executive Vice President, Corporate Secretary, General Counsel

Auditors: Ernst & Young LLP
Investor Contact: 847-932-7900
Transfer Agents: Computershare Trust Company, N.A., Canton, MA

ABBOTT LABORATORIES

Exchange	Symbol	Price	52Wk Range	Yield	P/E	Div Achiever
NYS	ABT	$57.07 (12/29/2017)	57.47-39.05	1.96	44.59	43 Years

*7 Year Price Score 99.98 *NYSE Composite Index=100 *12 Month Price Score 108.03

Interim Earnings (Per Share)

Qtr.	Mar	Jun	Sep	Dec
2014	0.24	0.30	0.36	0.59
2015	1.51	0.52	0.38	0.51
2016	0.21	0.41	(0.22)	0.54
2017	0.24	0.16	0.34	...

Interim Dividends (Per Share)

Amt	Decl	Ex	Rec	Pay
0.265Q	02/17/2017	04/11/2017	04/14/2017	05/15/2017
0.265Q	06/09/2017	07/12/2017	07/14/2017	08/15/2017
0.265Q	09/14/2017	10/12/2017	10/13/2017	11/15/2017
0.28Q	12/15/2017	01/11/2018	01/12/2018	02/15/2018

Indicated Div: $1.12 (Div. Reinv. Plan)

Valuation Analysis / **Institutional Holding**

Forecast EPS	$2.49 (01/18/2018)	No of Institutions 2245
Market Cap	$99.3 Billion	Shares 1,517,959,040
Book Value	$32.0 Billion	% Held
Price/Book	3.10	63.62
Price/Sales	3.95	

Business Summary: Medical Instruments & Equipment (MIC: 4.3.1 SIC: 2834 NAIC: 325412)

Abbott Laboratories is engaged in the discovery, development, manufacture, and sale of a line of health care products. Co. has four reportable segments: Established Pharmaceutical Products, which sells a line of branded generic pharmaceutical products internationally; Nutritional Products, which sells adult and pediatric nutritional products; Diagnostic Products, which sells diagnostic systems and tests for blood banks, hospitals, commercial laboratories and alternate-care testing sites; and Vascular Products, which sells coronary, endovascular, structural heart, vessel closure and other medical device products. Non-reportable segments include the Diabetes Care and Medical Optics segments.

Recent Developments: For the quarter ended Sep 30 2017, income from continuing operations was US$561.0 million compared with a loss of US$357.0 million in the year-earlier quarter. Net income amounted to US$603 million versus a net loss of US$329.0 million in the year-earlier quarter. Revenues were US$6.83 billion, up 28.8% from US$5.30 billion the year before. Operating income was US$810.0 million versus US$897.0 million in the prior-year quarter, a decrease of 9.7%. Direct operating expenses rose 25.0% to US$2.86 billion from US$2.29 billion in the comparable period the year before. Indirect operating expenses increased 49.2% to US$3.16 billion from US$2.12 billion in the equivalent prior-year period.

Prospects: Our evaluation of Abbott Laboratories as of Jan. 14, 2018 is the result of our systematic analysis on three basic characteristics: earnings strength, relative valuation, and recent stock price movement. The company has produced a positive trend in earnings per share over the past 5 quarters and while recent estimates for the company have remained steady, ABT has posted better than expected results. Based on operating earnings yield, the company is about fairly valued when compared to all of the companies in our coverage universe. Share price changes over the past year indicates that ABT will perform well over the near term.

Financial Data

(US$ in Thousands)	9 Mos	6 Mos	3 Mos	12/31/2016	12/31/2015	12/31/2014	12/31/2013	12/31/2012
Earnings Per Share	0.34	0.16	0.24	0.94	2.92	1.49	1.62	3.72
Cash Flow Per Share	4.56	3.11	1.35	2.16	1.98	2.42	2.13	5.90
Tang Book Value Per Share	N.M.	N.M.	N.M.	5.65	4.08	3.49	6.24	1.50
Dividends Per Share	0.265	0.265	0.265	1.040	0.960	0.880	0.560	2.010
Dividend Payout %	77.94	165.63	110.42	110.64	32.88	59.06	34.57	54.03
Income Statement								
Total Revenue	6,829,000	6,637,000	6,335,000	20,853,000	20,405,000	20,247,000	21,848,000	39,873,910
EBITDA	1,565,000	1,125,000	1,714,000	3,098,000	4,713,000	4,139,000	4,330,000	9,674,326
Depn & Amortn	757,000	647,000	774,000	1,353,000	1,472,000	1,548,000	1,719,000	2,898,534
Income Before Taxes	626,000	295,000	736,000	1,413,000	3,183,000	2,518,000	2,521,000	6,262,614
Income Taxes	65,000	25,000	350,000	350,000	577,000	797,000	138,000	299,694
Net Income	603,000	283,000	419,000	1,400,000	4,423,000	2,284,000	2,576,000	5,962,920
Average Shares	1,754,156	1,748,883	1,735,195	1,483,000	1,506,000	1,527,000	1,574,000	1,591,838
Balance Sheet								
Current Assets	21,377,000	19,983,000	19,329,000	26,776,000	14,155,000	15,261,000	19,247,000	31,322,583
Total Assets	72,248,000	71,151,000	70,887,000	52,666,000	41,247,000	41,275,000	42,953,000	67,234,944
Current Liabilities	7,935,000	6,803,000	6,646,000	6,660,000	9,186,000	10,532,000	9,507,000	13,280,176
Long-Term Obligations	23,310,000	23,810,000	23,764,000	20,681,000	5,871,000	3,408,000	3,388,000	18,085,302
Total Liabilities	40,216,000	39,549,000	39,525,000	32,128,000	20,036,000	19,749,000	17,782,000	40,513,983
Stockholders' Equity	32,032,000	31,602,000	31,362,000	20,538,000	21,211,000	21,526,000	25,171,000	26,720,961
Shares Outstanding	1,740,600	1,737,443	1,735,272	1,472,869	1,472,665	1,508,035	1,548,098	1,576,667
Statistical Record								
Return on Assets %	3.34	1.60	2.75	2.97	10.72	5.42	4.68	9.33
Return on Equity %	7.52	3.61	6.55	6.69	20.70	9.78	9.93	23.25
EBITDA Margin %	22.92	16.95	27.06	14.86	23.10	20.44	19.82	24.26
Net Margin %	8.83	4.26	6.61	6.71	21.68	11.28	11.79	14.95
Asset Turnover	0.38	0.37	0.42	0.44	0.49	0.48	0.40	0.62
Current Ratio	2.69	2.94	2.91	4.02	1.54	1.45	2.02	2.36
Debt to Equity	0.73	0.75	0.76	1.01	0.28	0.16	0.13	0.68
Price Range	53.64-37.60	49.27-37.60	45.72-36.95	45.29-36.34	51.20-39.06	46.37-35.85	38.71-31.34	34.51-25.91
P/E Ratio	157.76-110.59	307.94-235.00	190.50-153.96	48.18-38.66	17.53-13.38	31.12-24.06	23.90-19.35	9.28-6.96
Average Yield %	0.59	0.62	0.64	2.57	2.07	2.15	1.73	6.66

Address: 100 Abbott Park Road, Abbott Park, IL 60064-6400	**Web Site:** www.abbott.com	**Auditors:** Ernst & Young LLP
Telephone: 224-667-6100	**Officers:** Miles D. White - Chairman, Chief Executive Officer Brian B. Yoor - Executive Vice President, Chief Financial Officer, Senior Vice President	**Investor Contact:** 847-937-7300 **Transfer Agents:** Computershare Trust Company, NA, Providence, RI

3

ABM INDUSTRIES, INC.

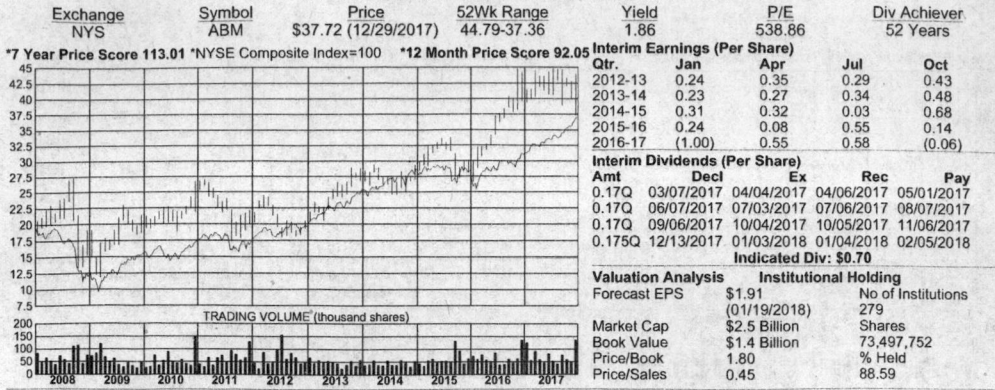

Exchange	Symbol	Price	52Wk Range	Yield	P/E	Div Achiever
NYS	ABM	$37.72 (12/29/2017)	44.79-37.36	1.86	538.86	52 Years

*7 Year Price Score 113.01 *NYSE Composite Index=100 *12 Month Price Score 92.05

Interim Earnings (Per Share)

Qtr.	Jan	Apr	Jul	Oct
2012-13	0.24	0.35	0.29	0.43
2013-14	0.23	0.27	0.34	0.48
2014-15	0.31	0.32	0.03	0.68
2015-16	0.24	0.08	0.55	0.14
2016-17	(1.00)	0.55	0.58	(0.06)

Interim Dividends (Per Share)

Amt	Decl	Ex	Rec	Pay
0.17Q	03/07/2017	04/04/2017	04/06/2017	05/01/2017
0.17Q	06/07/2017	07/03/2017	07/06/2017	08/07/2017
0.17Q	09/06/2017	10/04/2017	10/05/2017	11/06/2017
0.175Q	12/13/2017	01/03/2018	01/04/2018	02/05/2018

Indicated Div: $0.70

Valuation Analysis / **Institutional Holding**

Forecast EPS	$1.91	No of Institutions	279
	(01/19/2018)		
Market Cap	$2.5 Billion	Shares	73,497,752
Book Value	$1.4 Billion	% Held	88.59
Price/Book	1.80		
Price/Sales	0.45		

Business Summary: Sanitation Services (MIC: 7.5.3 SIC: 7349 NAIC: 561720)

ABM Industries is a provider of integrated facility solutions. Co.'s segments are: Janitorial, which provides a range of cleaning services; Facility Services, which provides onsite mechanical engineering and technical services and solutions for facilities and infrastructure systems; Parking, which provides parking and transportation services; Building and Energy Solutions, which provides energy solutions, electrical, heating, ventilation and air conditioning, lighting, and other maintenance and repair services; and Other, which provides facility solutions to airlines and airports related to access control, aircraft cabin cleaning, certain shuttle bus operations, and passenger assistance.

Recent Developments: For the year ended Oct 31 2017, income from continuing operations increased 25.4% to US$78.1 million from US$62.3 million a year earlier. Net income decreased 93.4% to US$3.8 million from US$57.2 million in the prior year. Revenues were US$5.45 billion, up 6.0% from US$5.14 billion the year before. Operating income was US$101.9 million versus US$54.7 million in the prior year, an increase of 86.3%. Indirect operating expenses increased 5.1% to US$5.35 billion from US$5.09 billion in the equivalent prior-year period.

Prospects: Our evaluation of ABM Industries Inc. as of Jan. 14, 2018 is the result of our systematic analysis on three basic characteristics: earnings strength, relative valuation, and recent stock price movement. The company has generated a negative trend in earnings per share over the past 5 quarters. However, while recent estimates for the company have been lowered by analysts, ABM has posted results that fell short of analysts expectations. Based on operating earnings yield, the company is undervalued when compared to all of the companies in our coverage universe. Share price changes over the past year indicates that ABM will perform very well over the near term.

Financial Data

(US$ in Thousands)	10/31/2017	10/31/2016	10/31/2015	10/31/2014	10/31/2013	10/31/2012	10/31/2011	10/31/2010
Earnings Per Share	0.07	1.01	1.33	1.32	1.30	1.14	1.27	1.23
Cash Flow Per Share	0.10	1.48	2.56	2.15	2.47	2.78	3.01	2.88
Tang Book Value Per Share	N.M.	N.M.	0.51	N.M.	N.M.	N.M.	N.M.	1.51
Dividends Per Share	0.680	0.660	0.640	0.620	0.600	0.580	0.560	0.540
Dividend Payout %	971.43	65.35	48.12	46.97	46.15	50.88	44.09	43.90
Income Statement								
Total Revenue	5,453,600	5,144,700	4,897,800	5,032,800	4,809,281	4,300,265	4,246,842	3,495,747
EBITDA	172,000	112,300	130,600	185,900	179,378	147,111	170,216	144,976
Depn & Amortn	70,100	57,600	57,000	57,300	60,353	50,864	52,648	36,264
Income Before Taxes	82,700	44,300	63,400	117,900	106,133	86,254	101,763	104,073
Income Taxes	8,800	(10,400)	18,300	48,800	39,552	29,931	36,980	40,203
Net Income	3,800	57,200	76,300	75,600	72,900	62,582	68,504	64,121
Average Shares	58,300	56,900	57,400	57,100	56,067	54,914	54,103	52,908
Balance Sheet								
Current Assets	1,235,500	993,700	947,200	927,200	864,632	767,427	733,757	608,756
Total Assets	3,812,600	2,281,200	2,149,800	2,192,900	2,119,236	1,869,251	1,879,598	1,548,670
Current Liabilities	757,800	599,200	568,200	526,400	508,524	473,910	443,196	333,851
Long-Term Obligations	1,161,300	268,300	158,000	319,800	314,870	215,000	300,000	140,500
Total Liabilities	2,436,900	1,307,200	1,142,300	1,224,100	1,201,729	1,018,853	1,083,712	809,645
Stockholders' Equity	1,375,700	974,000	1,007,500	968,800	917,507	850,398	795,886	739,025
Shares Outstanding	65,502	55,599	56,105	55,691	55,477	54,393	53,333	52,635
Statistical Record								
Return on Assets %	0.12	2.57	3.51	3.51	3.66	3.33	4.00	4.18
Return on Equity %	0.32	5.76	7.72	8.02	8.25	7.58	8.93	8.99
EBITDA Margin %	3.15	2.18	2.67	3.69	3.73	3.42	4.01	4.15
Net Margin %	0.07	1.11	1.56	1.50	1.52	1.46	1.61	1.83
Asset Turnover	1.79	2.32	2.26	2.33	2.41	2.29	2.48	2.28
Current Ratio	1.63	1.66	1.67	1.76	1.70	1.62	1.66	1.82
Debt to Equity	0.84	0.28	0.16	0.33	0.34	0.25	0.38	0.19
Price Range	44.79-38.22	40.42-26.58	33.80-26.70	29.43-24.57	28.99-18.27	24.50-17.95	27.00-17.29	22.77-18.35
P/E Ratio	639.86-546.00	40.02-26.32	25.41-20.08	22.30-18.61	22.30-14.05	21.49-15.75	21.26-13.61	18.51-14.92
Average Yield %	1.62	1.97	2.10	2.29	2.59	2.79	2.41	2.59

Address: One Liberty Plaza, 7th Floor, New York, NY 10006	Web Site: www.abm.com	Auditors: KPMG LLP
Telephone: 212-297-0200	Officers: Scott B. Salmirs - President, Chief Executive Officer, Executive Vice President Scott Giacobbe - Chief Operating Officer, Executive Vice President, Division Officer	Investor Contact: 212-297-0200
		Transfer Agents: Computershare, Providence, RI

ACCENTURE PLC

Exchange	Symbol	Price	52Wk Range	Yield	P/E
NYS	ACN	$153.09 (12/29/2017)	154.20-113.21	1.74	27.10

*7 Year Price Score 114.98 *NYSE Composite Index=100 *12 Month Price Score 108.26

TRADING VOLUME (thousand shares)

Interim Earnings (Per Share)

Qtr.	Nov	Feb	May	Aug
2014-15	1.29	1.08	1.24	1.15
2015-16	1.28	-2.08	1.41	1.68
2016-17	1.58	1.33	1.05	1.48
2017-18	1.79	...	...	...

Interim Dividends (Per Share)

Amt	Decl	Ex	Rec	Pay
1.10S	03/24/2016	04/13/2016	04/15/2016	05/13/2016
1.21S	09/29/2016	10/19/2016	10/21/2016	11/15/2016
1.21S	03/23/2017	04/11/2017	04/13/2017	05/15/2017
1.33S	09/28/2017	10/18/2017	10/19/2017	11/15/2017

Indicated Div: $2.66

Valuation Analysis

		Institutional Holding	
Forecast EPS	N/A	No of Institutions	1390
Market Cap	$97.3 Billion	Shares	552,272,960
Book Value	$9.1 Billion	% Held	72.38
Price/Book	10.69		
Price/Sales	2.57		

Business Summary: Business Services (MIC: 7.5.2 SIC: 7389 NAIC: 561499)

Accenture is a services company. Co.'s operating groups are: Communications, Media and Technology, which serves communications, media, high tech, software and platform companies; Financial Services, which serves the banking, capital markets and insurance industries; Health and Public Service, which serves healthcare payers and providers, government departments and agencies, public service organizations, educational institutions and non-profit organizations; Products, which serves a set of interconnected consumer-relevant industries such as consumer goods and retail; and Resources, which serves the chemicals, energy, forest products, metals and mining, utilities and related industries.

Recent Developments: For the quarter ended Nov 30 2017, net income increased 12.2% to US$1.19 billion from US$1.06 billion in the year-earlier quarter. Revenues were US$10.05 billion, up 11.6% from US$9.01 billion the year before. Operating income was US$1.49 billion versus US$1.33 billion in the prior-year quarter, an increase of 11.6%. Direct operating expenses rose 11.6% to US$7.00 billion from US$6.28 billion in the comparable period the year before. Indirect operating expenses increased 12.0% to US$1.57 billion from US$1.40 billion in the equivalent prior-year period.

Prospects: Our evaluation of Accenture PLC as of July 19, 2015 is the result of our systematic analysis on three basic characteristics: earnings strength, relative valuation, and recent stock price movement. The company has managed to produce a neutral trend in earnings per share over the past 5 quarters and while recent estimates for the company have been raised by analysts, ACN has posted better than expected results. Based on operating earnings yield, the company is about fairly valued when compared to all of the companies in our coverage universe. Share price changes over the past year indicates that ACN will perform in line with the market over the near term.

Financial Data

(US$ in Thousands)	3 Mos	08/31/2017	08/31/2016	08/31/2015	08/31/2014	08/31/2013	08/31/2012	08/31/2011
Earnings Per Share	5.65	5.44	6.45	4.76	4.52	4.93	3.84	3.40
Cash Flow Per Share	7.95	8.02	7.30	6.53	5.50	5.12	6.60	5.33
Tang Book Value Per Share	6.33	6.21	6.14	4.93	5.08	4.71	4.33	3.98
Dividends Per Share	2.540	2.420	2.200	2.040	1.860	1.620	1.350	0.900
Dividend Payout %	44.96	44.49	34.11	42.86	41.15	32.86	35.16	26.47
Income Statement								
Total Revenue	10,054,493	36,765,478	34,797,661	32,914,424	31,874,678	30,394,285	29,777,985	27,352,914
EBITDA	1,720,028	4,956,454	6,318,398	5,037,040	4,611,862	4,645,433	4,194,677	3,783,488
Depn & Amortn	232,633	362,817	729,052	645,923	326,910	324,997	317,992	297,549
Income Before Taxes	1,494,124	4,616,032	5,603,572	4,410,530	4,297,701	4,339,294	3,904,174	3,512,022
Income Taxes	305,582	981,100	1,253,969	1,136,741	1,121,743	784,775	1,079,241	958,782
Net Income	1,123,660	3,445,149	4,111,892	3,053,581	2,941,498	3,281,878	2,553,510	2,277,677
Average Shares	656,671	660,463	667,770	678,757	692,389	712,763	726,416	742,184
Balance Sheet								
Current Assets	12,303,841	12,097,289	11,976,222	11,579,394	11,904,442	11,844,178	12,587,931	11,471,183
Total Assets	22,974,153	22,689,890	20,609,004	18,266,058	17,930,452	16,867,049	16,665,415	15,731,510
Current Liabilities	9,863,026	9,824,279	8,878,924	8,532,199	8,158,079	8,160,990	8,109,205	7,906,589
Long-Term Obligations	22,226	22,163	24,457	25,587	26,403	25,600	22	...
Total Liabilities	13,872,023	13,740,413	13,053,742	12,132,333	12,198,417	11,906,863	12,519,582	11,852,559
Stockholders' Equity	9,102,130	8,949,477	7,555,262	6,133,725	5,732,035	4,960,186	4,145,833	3,878,951
Shares Outstanding	635,318	636,088	642,590	650,036	656,556	666,355	676,750	690,799
Statistical Record								
Return on Assets %	16.42	15.91	21.10	16.87	16.91	19.57	15.72	15.95
Return on Equity %	43.15	41.75	59.91	51.47	55.02	72.08	63.47	67.84
EBITDA Margin %	17.11	13.48	18.16	15.30	14.47	15.28	14.09	13.83
Net Margin %	11.18	9.37	11.82	9.28	9.23	10.80	8.58	8.33
Asset Turnover	1.74	1.70	1.79	1.82	1.83	1.81	1.83	1.92
Current Ratio	1.25	1.23	1.35	1.36	1.46	1.45	1.55	1.45
Debt to Equity	N.M.	N.M.	N.M.	N.M.	N.M.	0.01	N.M.	...
Price Range	148.04-113.21	130.76-109.80	119.65-92.29	105.20-75.85	85.40-70.28	83.09-61.06	65.89-49.82	63.44-36.60
P/E Ratio	26.20-20.04	24.04-20.18	18.55-14.31	22.10-15.93	18.89-15.55	16.85-12.39	17.16-12.97	18.66-10.76
Average Yield %	1.94	2.00	2.03	2.26	2.35	2.22	2.32	1.76

Address: 1 Grand Canal Square, Grand Canal Harbour, Dublin, 2	Web Site: www.accenture.com	Auditors: KPMG LLP
Telephone: 164-620-00	Officers: Pierre Nanterme - Chairman, Chief Executive Officer Johan G. (Jo) Deblaere - Chief Operating Officer, Region Officer	Investor Contact: 353-140-78203 Transfer Agents: Computershare, Canton, MA

ACUITY BRANDS INC (HOLDING COMPANY)

Exchange	**Symbol**	**Price**	**52Wk Range**	**Yield**	**P/E**
NYS	AYI	$176.00 (12/29/2017)	239.93-156.39	0.30	24.21

*7 Year Price Score 109.91 *NYSE Composite Index=100 *12 Month Price Score 83.93

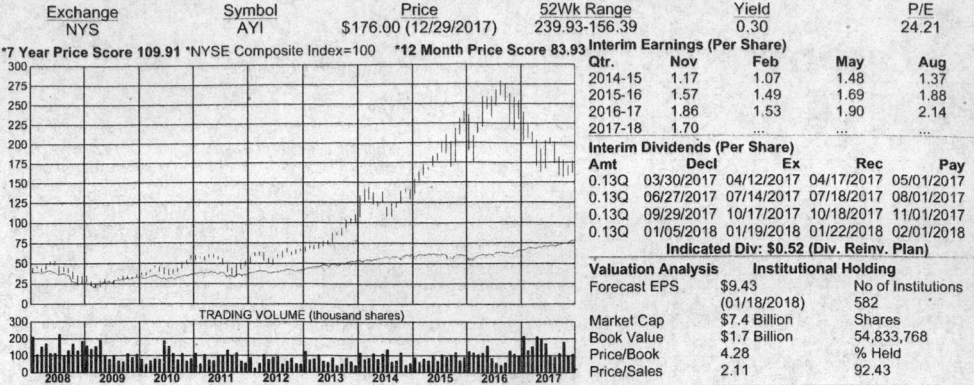

Interim Earnings (Per Share)

Qtr.	Nov	Feb	May	Aug
2014-15	1.17	1.07	1.48	1.37
2015-16	1.57	1.49	1.69	1.88
2016-17	1.86	1.53	1.90	2.14
2017-18	1.70	...	...	...

Interim Dividends (Per Share)

Amt	Decl	Ex	Rec	Pay
0.13Q	03/30/2017	04/12/2017	04/17/2017	05/01/2017
0.13Q	06/27/2017	07/14/2017	07/18/2017	08/01/2017
0.13Q	09/29/2017	10/17/2017	10/18/2017	11/01/2017
0.13Q	01/05/2018	01/19/2018	01/22/2018	02/01/2018

Indicated Div: $0.52 (Div. Reinv. Plan)

Valuation Analysis / Institutional Holding

Valuation Analysis		Institutional Holding	
Forecast EPS	$9.43 (01/18/2018)	No of Institutions	582
Market Cap	$7.4 Billion	Shares	54,833,768
Book Value	$1.7 Billion	% Held	92.43
Price/Book	4.28		
Price/Sales	2.11		

Business Summary: Electrical Equipment (MIC: 7.3.1 SIC: 3648 NAIC: 335129)

Acuity Brands is a provider of lighting and building management solutions and services for commercial, institutional, industrial, infrastructure, and residential applications throughout North America and select international markets. Co.'s lighting and building management solutions include devices such as luminaires, lighting controls, power supplies, prismatic skylights, and drivers, as well as integrated systems designed to optimize energy efficiency and comfort for various indoor and outdoor applications. Co.'s solutions portfolio also includes software and services to provide a host of other economic benefits resulting from data analytics that enables the Internet of Things.

Recent Developments: For the quarter ended Nov 30 2017, net income decreased 12.5% to US$71.5 million from US$81.7 million in the year-earlier quarter. Revenues were US$842.8 million, down 1.0% from US$851.2 million the year before. Operating income was US$118.6 million versus US$126.6 million in the prior-year quarter, a decrease of 6.3%. Direct operating expenses rose 0.2% to US$492.6 million from US$491.6 million in the comparable period the year before. Indirect operating expenses decreased 0.6% to US$231.6 million from US$233.0 million in the equivalent prior-year period.

Prospects: Our evaluation of Acuity Brands Inc. as of Jan. 14, 2018 is the result of our systematic analysis on three basic characteristics: earnings strength, relative valuation, and recent stock price movement. The company has produced a positive trend in earnings per share over the past 5 quarters and while recent estimates for the company have been raised by analysts, AYI has posted results that fell short of analysts expectations. Based on operating earnings yield, the company is undervalued when compared to all of the companies in our coverage universe. Share price changes over the past year indicates that AYI will perform in line with the market over the near term.

Financial Data
(US$ in Thousands)

	3 Mos	08/31/2017	08/31/2016	08/31/2015	08/31/2014	08/31/2013	08/31/2012	08/31/2011
Earnings Per Share	7.27	7.43	6.63	5.09	4.05	2.95	2.72	2.42
Cash Flow Per Share	9.96	7.34	7.93	6.70	5.45	3.14	4.15	3.82
Tang Book Value Per Share	9.29	7.54	7.54	13.16	8.40	4.18	1.06	N.M.
Dividends Per Share	0.520	0.520	0.520	0.520	0.520	0.520	0.520	0.520
Dividend Payout %	7.15	7.00	7.84	10.22	12.84	17.63	19.12	21.49
Income Statement								
Total Revenue	842,800	3,505,100	3,291,300	2,706,700	2,393,500	2,089,100	1,933,700	1,795,700
EBITDA	138,000	571,700	517,700	409,500	329,600	253,300	237,200	216,300
Depn & Amortn	19,000	46,600	40,900	34,400	31,800	29,000	27,500	28,800
Income Before Taxes	110,900	492,600	444,600	343,600	265,700	193,100	179,000	157,600
Income Taxes	39,400	170,900	153,800	121,500	89,900	65,700	62,700	52,100
Net Income	71,500	321,700	290,800	222,100	175,800	127,400	116,300	105,500
Average Shares	42,100	43,300	43,800	43,400	43,000	42,500	41,900	42,800
Balance Sheet								
Current Assets	1,323,800	1,245,600	1,322,900	1,436,500	1,186,700	913,500	779,000	630,500
Total Assets	2,961,400	2,899,600	2,948,000	2,429,600	2,168,100	1,903,800	1,736,900	1,597,400
Current Liabilities	594,900	600,900	672,500	520,900	470,500	386,200	364,800	331,400
Long-Term Obligations	356,500	356,500	355,000	352,400	353,600	353,600	353,500	353,400
Total Liabilities	1,235,300	1,234,000	1,288,200	1,069,600	1,004,600	910,300	902,900	840,400
Stockholders' Equity	1,726,100	1,665,600	1,659,800	1,360,000	1,163,500	993,500	834,000	757,000
Shares Outstanding	41,944	41,871	43,736	43,305	42,862	42,486	41,789	41,488
Statistical Record								
Return on Assets %	10.52	11.00	10.79	9.66	8.63	7.00	6.96	6.80
Return on Equity %	18.03	19.35	19.21	17.60	16.30	13.94	14.58	14.54
EBITDA Margin %	16.37	16.31	15.73	15.13	13.77	12.12	12.27	12.05
Net Margin %	8.48	9.18	8.84	8.21	7.34	6.10	6.01	5.88
Asset Turnover	1.18	1.20	1.22	1.18	1.18	1.15	1.16	1.16
Current Ratio	2.23	2.07	1.97	2.76	2.52	2.37	2.14	1.90
Debt to Equity	0.21	0.21	0.21	0.26	0.30	0.36	0.42	0.47
Price Range	254.26-156.39	275.12-162.78	279.15-169.87	211.15-117.71	143.65-84.43	88.34-59.86	64.98-33.97	60.96-38.74
P/E Ratio	34.97-21.51	37.03-21.91	42.10-25.62	41.48-23.13	35.47-20.85	29.95-20.29	23.89-12.49	25.19-16.01
Average Yield %	0.27	0.25	0.23	0.32	0.44	0.72	0.97	0.98

Address: 1170 Peachtree Street, N.E., Suite 2300, Atlanta, GA 30309-7676 **Telephone:** 404-853-1400 **Fax:** 404-853-1300	**Web Site:** www.acuitybrands.com **Officers:** Vernon J. Nagel - Chairman, President, Chief Executive Officer Richard K. Reece - Executive Vice President, Chief Financial Officer

Auditors: Ernst & Young LLP
Investor Contact: 404-853-1400
Transfer Agents: Computershare
Shareowner Services, Pittsburgh, PA

ADTALEM GLOBAL EDUCATION INC

Exchange	Symbol	Price	52Wk Range	Yield	P/E
NYS	ATGE	$42.05 (12/29/2017)	45.85-31.35	N/A	24.45

*7 Year Price Score 81.86 *NYSE Composite Index=100 *12 Month Price Score 107.18

Interim Earnings (Per Share)

Qtr.	Sep	Dec	Mar	Jun
2014-15	0.31	0.65	0.72	0.46
2015-16	0.08	(0.79)	0.81	(0.16)
2016-17	0.39	0.23	0.62	0.67
2017-18	0.20	...	...	...

Interim Dividends (Per Share)

Amt	Decl	Ex	Rec	Pay
0.18S	05/14/2015	06/03/2015	06/05/2015	06/26/2015
0.18S	11/05/2015	12/02/2015	12/04/2015	12/23/2015
0.18S	05/16/2016	06/01/2016	06/03/2016	06/24/2016
0.18S	11/14/2016	11/30/2016	12/02/2016	12/22/2016

Valuation Analysis

		Institutional Holding	
Forecast EPS	$2.80 (01/09/2018)	No of Institutions	368
Market Cap	$2.6 Billion	Shares	73,971,776
Book Value	$1.7 Billion	% Held	94.03
Price/Book	1.55		
Price/Sales	1.44		

Business Summary: Educational Services (MIC: 2.2.2 SIC: 8221 NAIC: 611310)

Adtalem Global Education is a provider of educational services. Co.'s institutions and companies provide a range of programs in healthcare, technology, business, accounting, finance and law. Co. conducts its operations through four segments. The Medical and Healthcare segment includes the operations of its Chamberlain University, and Medical and Veterinary Schools. The Professional Education segment includes the operations of Becker Professional Education. The Technology and Business segment includes the operations of Adtalem Education of Brazil. The U.S. Traditional Postsecondary segment includes the operations of its DeVry University and Carrington College.

Recent Developments: For the quarter ended Sep 30 2017, net income decreased 48.6% to US$12.9 million from US$25.1 million in the year-earlier quarter. Revenues were US$421.0 million, down 6.4% from US$449.9 million the year before. Operating income was US$14.4 million versus US$33.1 million in the prior-year quarter, a decrease of 56.4%. Direct operating expenses declined 1.0% to US$248.1 million from US$250.7 million in the comparable period the year before. Indirect operating expenses decreased 4.6% to US$158.5 million from US$166.1 million in the equivalent prior-year period.

Prospects: Our evaluation of Adtalem Global Education Inc. as of Jan. 14, 2018 is the result of our systematic analysis on three basic characteristics: earnings strength, relative valuation, and recent stock price movement. The company has generated a negative trend in earnings per share over the past 5 quarters and while recent estimates for the company have remained steady, ATGE has posted results that fell short of analysts expectations. Based on operating earnings yield, the company is undervalued when compared to all of the companies in our coverage universe. Share price changes over the past year indicates that ATGE will perform in line with the market over the near term.

Financial Data
(US$ in Thousands)

	3 Mos	06/30/2017	06/30/2016	06/30/2015	06/30/2014	06/30/2013	06/30/2012	06/30/2011
Earnings Per Share	1.72	1.91	(0.05)	2.14	2.07	1.65	2.09	4.68
Cash Flow Per Share	3.51	3.59	3.61	3.15	4.14	4.07	4.12	5.84
Tang Book Value Per Share	6.20	6.48	10.41	11.14	11.29	9.63	8.05	9.77
Dividends Per Share	0.180	0.180	0.360	0.360	0.340	0.340	0.300	0.240
Dividend Payout %	10.47	9.42	...	16.82	16.43	20.61	14.35	5.13
Income Statement								
Total Revenue	421,025	1,809,800	1,843,537	1,909,943	1,923,371	1,964,375	2,089,781	2,182,371
EBITDA	34,081	210,801	67,257	241,918	264,007	250,039	285,081	552,208
Depn & Amortn	19,645	72,188	79,400	85,008	82,739	83,111	77,149	58,033
Income Before Taxes	14,638	134,394	(17,298)	153,660	179,367	164,969	206,138	494,432
Income Taxes	1,678	10,420	(14,542)	18,537	27,699	39,227	63,757	163,602
Net Income	12,785	122,283	(3,166)	139,899	134,032	106,786	141,565	330,403
Average Shares	63,432	64,019	64,371	65,277	64,853	64,611	67,705	70,620
Balance Sheet								
Current Assets	541,626	471,207	518,105	601,057	577,091	442,164	401,114	624,650
Total Assets	2,383,596	2,314,035	2,096,996	2,074,193	1,997,636	1,857,018	1,838,616	1,850,503
Current Liabilities	450,518	377,327	361,836	321,909	316,812	316,217	315,209	316,431
Long-Term Obligations	135,000	125,000	...	...	...	...	...	...
Total Liabilities	725,557	644,996	514,909	489,383	464,243	459,862	482,223	460,987
Stockholders' Equity	1,658,039	1,669,039	1,582,087	1,584,810	1,533,393	1,397,156	1,356,393	1,389,516
Shares Outstanding	61,194	62,371	62,549	63,623	63,624	62,946	64,722	68,635
Statistical Record								
Return on Assets %	4.67	5.54	N.M.	6.87	6.95	5.78	7.65	19.00
Return on Equity %	6.74	7.52	N.M.	8.97	9.15	7.76	10.28	25.72
EBITDA Margin %	8.09	11.65	3.65	12.67	13.73	12.73	13.64	25.30
Net Margin %	3.04	6.76	N.M.	7.32	6.97	5.44	6.77	15.14
Asset Turnover	0.76	0.82	0.88	0.94	1.00	1.06	1.13	1.25
Current Ratio	1.20	1.25	1.43	1.87	1.82	1.40	1.27	1.97
Debt to Equity	0.08	0.07	...	...	...	...	...	...
Price Range	40.65-22.23	40.65-17.84	32.02-15.84	49.18-29.98	45.99-28.32	34.03-18.35	66.55-26.58	61.86-37.50
P/E Ratio	23.63-12.92	21.28-9.34	...	22.98-14.01	22.22-13.68	20.62-11.12	31.84-12.72	13.22-8.01
Average Yield %	0.55	0.60	1.58	0.89	0.93	1.29	0.77	0.48

Address: 3005 Highland Parkway, Downers Grove, IL 60515 **Telephone:** 630-515-7700	**Web Site:** www.devryeducationgroup.com **Officers:** Lisa W. Wardell - President, Chief Executive Officer Patrick J. Unzicker - Senior Vice President, Vice President, Chief Financial Officer, Chief Accounting Officer, Treasurer, Controller	**Auditors:** PricewaterhouseCoopers LLP **Investor Contact:** 630-353-3800 **Transfer Agents:** Computershare Investor Services, L.L.C.

ADVANCE AUTO PARTS INC

Exchange	Symbol	Price	52Wk Range	Yield	P/E
NYS	AAP	$99.69 (12/29/2017)	174.79-79.38	0.24	20.90

*7 Year Price Score 84.78 ***NYSE Composite Index=100** ***12 Month Price Score 72.80**

Interim Earnings (Per Share)

Qtr.	Apr	Jul	Sep	Jan
2015	2.00	2.03	1.63	0.74
2016	2.14	1.38	1.53	0.84
2017	1.46	1.17	1.30	...

Interim Dividends (Per Share)

Amt	Decl	Ex	Rec	Pay
0.06Q	02/15/2017	03/22/2017	03/24/2017	04/07/2017
0.06Q	05/16/2017	06/21/2017	06/23/2017	07/07/2017
0.06Q	08/10/2017	09/21/2017	09/22/2017	10/06/2017
0.06Q	11/07/2017	12/21/2017	12/22/2017	01/05/2018

Indicated Div: $0.24

Valuation Analysis **Institutional Holding**

Forecast EPS	$5.24 (01/18/2018)	No of Institutions 663
Market Cap	$7.4 Billion	Shares
Book Value	$3.2 Billion	92,518,208
Price/Book	2.28	% Held
Price/Sales	0.78	92.92

Business Summary: Retail - Automotive (MIC: 2.1.4 SIC: 5531 NAIC: 441310)

Advance Auto Parts is an automotive aftermarket parts provider in North America, serving both professional installers and do-it-yourself customers as well as independently-owned operators. Co.'s stores and branches provide a selection of brand name, original equipment manufacturer and private label automotive replacement parts, accessories, batteries, and maintenance items for domestic and imported cars, vans, sport utility vehicles and light and heavy duty trucks. As of Dec 31 2016, Co. operated 5,062 total stores and 127 branches primarily under the trade names Advance Auto Parts, Autopart International, Carquest and Worldpac.

Recent Developments: For the quarter ended Oct 7 2017, net income decreased 15.7% to US$96.0 million from US$113.8 million in the year-earlier quarter. Revenues were US$2.18 billion, down 3.0% from US$2.25 billion the year before. Operating income was US$156.6 million versus US$193.8 million in the prior-year quarter, a decrease of 19.2%. Direct operating expenses declined 2.1% to US$1.23 billion from US$1.26 billion in the comparable period the year before. Indirect operating expenses decreased 0.4% to US$791.1 million from US$794.4 million in the equivalent prior-year period.

Prospects: Our evaluation of Advance Auto Parts Inc. as of Jan. 14, 2018 is the result of our systematic analysis on three basic characteristics: earnings strength, relative valuation, and recent stock price movement. The company has produced a positive trend in earnings per share over the past 5 quarters and while recent estimates for the company have been raised by analysts, AAP has posted better than expected results. Based on operating earnings yield, the company is undervalued when compared to all of the companies in our coverage universe. Share price changes over the past year indicates that AAP will perform very poorly over the near term.

Financial Data
(US$ in Thousands)

	9 Mos	6 Mos	3 Mos	12/31/2016	01/02/2016	01/03/2015	12/28/2013	12/29/2012
Earnings Per Share	4.77	5.00	5.51	6.20	6.40	6.71	5.32	5.22
Cash Flow Per Share	6.67	7.79	6.24	6.83	9.45	9.56	7.50	9.40
Tang Book Value Per Share	22.03	20.52	19.04	17.42	10.69	3.55	17.39	15.06
Dividends Per Share	0.240	0.240	0.240	0.240	0.240	0.240	0.240	0.240
Dividend Payout %	5.03	4.80	4.36	3.87	3.75	3.58	4.51	4.60
Income Statement								
Total Revenue	7,336,798	5,154,565	2,890,838	9,567,679	9,737,018	9,843,861	6,493,814	6,205,003
EBITDA	684,540	469,673	262,023	1,014,726	1,042,024	1,089,842	862,837	843,824
Depn & Amortn	192,753	135,200	77,430	215,981	223,728	235,040	199,821	185,909
Income Before Taxes	446,122	302,122	166,163	738,835	752,888	781,394	626,398	624,074
Income Taxes	155,117	107,113	58,203	279,213	279,490	287,569	234,640	236,404
Net Income	291,005	195,009	107,960	459,622	473,398	493,825	391,758	387,670
Average Shares	74,106	74,093	74,093	73,856	73,733	73,414	73,414	74,062
Balance Sheet								
Current Assets	5,367,952	5,326,215	5,306,693	5,172,764	4,940,746	4,741,040	3,989,384	3,184,200
Total Assets	8,468,224	8,437,413	8,428,657	8,315,033	8,134,565	7,962,358	5,564,774	4,613,814
Current Liabilities	3,537,409	3,598,327	3,659,631	3,676,046	3,797,477	3,743,066	2,764,785	2,559,638
Long-Term Obligations	1,044,008	1,043,690	1,073,372	1,042,949	1,213,161	1,636,311	1,052,668	604,461
Total Liabilities	5,237,437	5,309,136	5,404,982	5,398,841	5,673,917	5,959,446	4,048,569	3,403,120
Stockholders' Equity	3,230,787	3,128,277	3,023,675	2,916,192	2,460,648	2,002,912	1,516,205	1,210,694
Shares Outstanding	73,898	73,862	73,844	73,749	73,314	73,074	72,840	73,383
Statistical Record								
Return on Assets %	4.19	4.40	4.85	5.60	5.90	7.18	7.72	9.40
Return on Equity %	11.61	12.63	14.46	17.14	21.27	27.61	28.81	37.77
EBITDA Margin %	9.33	9.11	9.06	10.61	10.70	11.07	13.29	13.60
Net Margin %	3.97	3.78	3.73	4.80	4.86	5.02	6.03	6.25
Asset Turnover	1.12	1.12	1.12	1.17	1.21	1.43	1.28	1.50
Current Ratio	1.52	1.48	1.45	1.41	1.30	1.27	1.44	1.24
Debt to Equity	0.32	0.33	0.35	0.36	0.49	0.82	0.69	0.50
Price Range	176.78-87.08	176.78-100.25	176.78-136.19	176.78-136.19	200.38-143.00	161.22-109.63	110.28-71.76	92.37-65.59
P/E Ratio	37.06-18.26	35.36-20.05	32.08-24.72	28.51-21.97	31.31-22.34	24.03-16.34	20.73-13.49	17.70-12.57
Average Yield %	0.17	0.16	0.15	0.15	0.15	0.15	0.18	0.32

Address: 5008 Airport Road, Roanoke, VA 24012	**Web Site:** www.AdvanceAutoParts.com
Telephone: 540-362-4911	**Officers:** Thomas R. Greco - Chief Executive Officer, Robert B. Cushing - Executive Vice President
Auditors: Deloitte & Touche LLP	**Investor Contact:** 540-561-6444
Transfer Agents: BNY Mellon Shareowner Services, Pittsburgh, PA	

AECOM

Exchange	Symbol	Price	52Wk Range	Yield	P/E
NYS	ACM	$37.15 (12/29/2017)	39.13-30.47	N/A	17.44

*7 Year Price Score 93.91   *NYSE Composite Index=100   *12 Month Price Score 99.43

Interim Earnings (Per Share)

Qtr.	Dec	Mar	Jun	Sep
2012-13	0.36	0.53	0.70	0.77
2013-14	0.58	0.41	0.70	0.64
2014-15	(0.73)	0.00	(0.11)	0.01
2015-16	(0.13)	0.27	0.43	0.05
2016-17	0.30	0.65	0.64	0.55

Interim Dividends (Per Share)

No Dividends Paid

Valuation Analysis

Forecast EPS	$2.70	
	(01/17/2018)	
Market Cap	$5.9 Billion	
Book Value	$4.0 Billion	
Price/Book	1.46	
Price/Sales	0.32	

Institutional Holding

No of Institutions 415
Shares 149,433,744
% Held 60.98

Business Summary: Construction Services (MIC: 7.5.4 SIC: 8711 NAIC: 541330)

AECOM is a firm positioned to design, build, finance and operate infrastructure assets for governments, businesses and organizations. Co.'s business segments are: Design and Consulting Services, which include of planning, consulting, architectural and engineering design services to commercial and government clients; Construction Services including construction, program and construction management services; Management Services, which include program and facilities management and maintenance, training, logistics, and systems integration and information technology services; and AECOM Capital, which invests in and develops real estate, public-private partnership and infrastructure projects.

Recent Developments: For the year ended Sep 30 2017, net income increased 157.8% to US$421.5 million from US$163.5 million in the prior year. Revenues were US$18.20 billion, up 4.6% from US$17.41 billion the year before. Operating income was US$653.9 million versus US$375.5 million in the prior year, an increase of 74.1%. Direct operating expenses rose 4.5% to US$17.52 billion from US$16.77 billion in the comparable period the year before. Indirect operating expenses decreased 88.8% to US$29.9 million from US$267.3 million in the equivalent prior-year period.

Prospects: Our evaluation of AECOM as of Jan. 14, 2018 is the result of our systematic analysis on three basic characteristics: earnings strength, relative valuation, and recent stock price movement. The company has managed to produce a neutral trend in earnings per share over the past 5 quarters. However, while recent estimates for the company have been mixed, ACM has posted better than expected results. Based on operating earnings yield, the company is undervalued when compared to all of the companies in our coverage universe. Share price changes over the past year indicates that ACM will perform in line with the market over the near term.

Financial Data

(US$ in Thousands)	09/30/2017	09/30/2016	09/30/2015	09/30/2014	09/30/2013	09/30/2012	09/30/2011	09/30/2010
Earnings Per Share	2.13	0.62	(1.04)	2.33	2.35	(0.52)	2.33	2.05
Cash Flow Per Share	4.47	5.25	5.11	3.71	4.06	3.86	1.12	1.39
Tang Book Value Per Share	N.M.	N.M.	N.M.	1.64	1.32	2.78	1.19	2.52
Income Statement								
Total Revenue	18,203,402	17,410,825	17,989,880	8,356,783	8,153,495	8,218,180	8,037,374	6,545,791
EBITDA	676,010	451,385	233,182	366,806	426,892	91,029	452,972	389,358
Depn & Amortn	157,100	171,700	191,300	69,100	70,700	77,100	73,200	59,300
Income Before Taxes	287,600	21,523	(257,745)	256,864	311,455	(31,167)	339,361	320,130
Income Taxes	7,706	(37,917)	(80,237)	82,024	92,578	74,416	100,090	91,696
Net Income	339,390	96,109	(154,845)	229,854	239,243	(58,567)	275,800	236,887
Average Shares	159,135	156,073	149,605	98,657	101,942	111,875	118,345	115,463
Balance Sheet								
Current Assets	6,682,222	6,000,771	6,246,085	3,434,113	3,131,602	3,147,293	2,990,066	2,946,499
Total Assets	14,396,956	13,726,745	14,014,298	6,123,377	5,665,623	5,664,568	5,789,328	5,242,909
Current Liabilities	5,578,379	5,304,756	4,836,052	2,455,769	2,053,549	2,078,402	1,814,446	1,852,260
Long-Term Obligations	3,702,109	3,758,966	4,446,527	939,565	1,089,060	907,141	1,144,723	914,686
Total Liabilities	10,400,830	10,359,824	10,606,550	3,936,860	3,644,180	3,495,104	3,449,617	3,152,897
Stockholders' Equity	3,996,126	3,366,921	3,407,748	2,186,517	2,021,443	2,169,464	2,339,711	2,090,012
Shares Outstanding	157,529	153,901	151,263	96,715	96,016	107,041	113,248	115,316
Statistical Record								
Return on Assets %	2.41	0.69	N.M.	3.90	4.22	N.M.	5.00	5.25
Return on Equity %	9.22	2.83	N.M.	10.92	11.42	N.M.	12.45	12.40
EBITDA Margin %	3.71	2.59	1.30	4.39	5.24	1.11	5.64	5.95
Net Margin %	1.86	0.55	N.M.	2.75	2.93	N.M.	3.43	3.62
Asset Turnover	1.29	1.25	1.79	1.42	1.44	1.43	1.46	1.45
Current Ratio	1.20	1.13	1.29	1.40	1.52	1.51	1.65	1.59
Debt to Equity	0.93	1.12	1.30	0.43	0.54	0.42	0.49	0.44
Price Range	40.13-26.92	36.17-23.15	35.36-24.92	38.13-27.47	35.20-18.87	24.06-14.91	29.93-17.67	30.73-22.02
P/E Ratio	18.84-12.64	58.34-37.34	...	16.36-11.79	14.98-8.03	...	12.85-7.58	14.99-10.74

Address: 1999 Avenue of the Stars, Suite 2600, Los Angeles, CA 90067 **Telephone:** 213-593-8000	**Web Site:** www.aecom.com **Officers:** Michael S. Burke - Chairman, President, Chief Executive Officer Daniel R. Tishman - Vice-Chairman	**Auditors:** Ernst & Young LLP **Investor Contact:** 212-973-2982 **Transfer Agents:** Computershare Investor Services, LLC, Canton, MA

9

AES CORP.

Exchange	Symbol	Price	52Wk Range	Yield	P/E
NYS	AES	$10.83 (12/29/2017)	11.95-10.23	4.80	N/A

*7 Year Price Score 71.65 *NYSE Composite Index=100 *12 Month Price Score 89.67

TRADING VOLUME (thousand shares)

Interim Earnings (Per Share)

Qtr.	Mar	Jun	Sep	Dec
2014	(0.08)	0.18	0.67	0.28
2015	0.20	0.10	0.26	(0.12)
2016	0.19	(0.73)	0.26	(1.43)
2017	(0.04)	0.08	0.23	...

Interim Dividends (Per Share)

Amt	Decl	Ex	Rec	Pay
0.12Q	04/13/2017	04/27/2017	05/01/2017	05/15/2017
0.12Q	07/17/2017	08/01/2017	08/03/2017	08/17/2017
0.12Q	10/13/2017	10/31/2017	11/01/2017	11/15/2017
0.13Q	12/11/2017	01/31/2018	02/01/2018	02/15/2018

Indicated Div: $0.52

Valuation Analysis / Institutional Holding

Forecast EPS	$1.02	No of Institutions
	(01/26/2018)	727
Market Cap	$7.2 Billion	Shares
Book Value	$4.2 Billion	769,337,216
Price/Book	1.72	% Held
Price/Sales	0.51	75.99

Business Summary: Electric Utilities (MIC: 3.1.1 SIC: 4911 NAIC: 221121)

AES is a holding company. Through its subsidiaries and affiliates, Co. operates a portfolio of electricity generation and distribution businesses. Co. has two lines of business: generation, where Co. owns and/or operates power plants to generate and sell power to customers, such as utilities, industrial users, and other intermediaries; and utilities, where Co. owns and/or operates utilities to generate or purchase, distribute, transmit and sell electricity to end-user customers in the residential, commercial, industrial and governmental sectors within a defined service area. In certain circumstances, Co.'s utilities also generate and sell electricity on the wholesale market.

Recent Developments: For the quarter ended Sep 30 2017, income from continuing operations increased 13.5% to US$261.0 million from US$230.0 million in the year-earlier quarter. Net income increased 14.0% to US$261.0 million from US$229.0 million in the year-earlier quarter. Revenues were US$3.63 billion, up 2.5% from US$3.54 billion the year before. Direct operating expenses rose 2.3% to US$2.92 billion from US$2.85 billion in the comparable period the year before. Indirect operating expenses increased 67.5% to, US$67.0 million from US$40.0 million in the equivalent prior-year period.

Prospects: Our evaluation of AES Corp. as of Jan. 21, 2018 is the result of our systematic analysis on three basic characteristics: earnings strength, relative valuation, and recent stock price movement. The company has generated a negative trend in earnings per share over the past 5 quarters and while recent estimates for the company have been mixed, AES has posted results that fell short of analysts expectations. Based on operating earnings yield, the company is undervalued when compared to all of the companies in our coverage universe. Share price changes over the past year indicates that AES will perform very poorly over the near term.

Financial Data

(US$ in Millions)	9 Mos	6 Mos	3 Mos	12/31/2016	12/31/2015	12/31/2014	12/31/2013	12/31/2012
Earnings Per Share	(1.16)	(1.13)	(1.94)	(1.71)	0.44	1.06	0.15	(1.21)
Cash Flow Per Share	3.62	3.74	4.47	4.36	3.11	2.49	3.65	3.83
Tang Book Value Per Share	3.82	3.42	3.42	3.13	3.47	3.71	3.44	2.98
Dividends Per Share	0.470	0.460	0.450	0.440	0.400	0.200	0.160	0.040
Dividend Payout %	...	...	...	...	90.91	18.87	106.67	...
Income Statement								
Total Revenue	10,594	6,962	3,492	13,586	14,963	17,146	15,891	18,141
EBITDA	2,373	1,471	702	2,209	3,138	3,886	3,448	2,788
Depn & Amortn	884	581	291	1,105	1,104	1,204	1,193	1,251
Income Before Taxes	746	399	160	137	1,122	1,576	1,048	314
Income Taxes	270	160	69	(188)	465	419	343	708
Net Income	181	29	(24)	(1,130)	306	769	114	(912)
Average Shares	663	662	659	662	689	724	748	755
Balance Sheet								
Current Assets	6,660	6,318	6,401	6,411	6,866	7,826	7,739	8,465
Total Assets	38,834	36,469	36,508	36,119	36,850	38,966	40,411	41,830
Current Liabilities	6,736	6,411	5,243	5,272	6,950	6,997	7,653	8,319
Long-Term Obligations	19,776	18,195	19,197	19,160	18,278	18,725	18,869	18,519
Total Liabilities	34,681	32,657	32,743	32,543	33,163	34,616	36,003	37,183
Stockholders' Equity	4,153	3,812	3,765	3,576	3,687	4,350	4,408	4,647
Shares Outstanding	660	660	660	659	666	703	722	744
Statistical Record								
Return on Assets %	N.M.	N.M.	N.M.	N.M.	0.81	1.94	0.28	N.M.
Return on Equity %	N.M.	N.M.	N.M.	N.M.	7.61	17.56	2.52	N.M.
EBITDA Margin %	22.40	21.13	20.10	16.26	20.97	22.66	21.70	15.37
Net Margin %	1.71	0.42	N.M.	N.M.	2.05	4.49	0.72	N.M.
Asset Turnover	0.37	0.38	0.38	0.37	0.39	0.43	0.39	0.42
Current Ratio	0.99	0.99	1.22	1.22	0.99	1.12	1.01	1.02
Debt to Equity	4.76	4.77	5.10	5.36	4.96	4.30	4.28	3.99
Price Range	12.85-10.68	13.26-11.00	13.26-10.73	13.26-8.54	13.94-8.83	15.57-12.79	15.31-10.70	13.80-9.72
P/E Ratio	...	...	...	...	31.68-20.07	14.69-12.07	102.07-71.33	...
Average Yield %	4.10	3.90	3.84	3.97	3.33	1.42	1.25	0.34

Address: 4300 Wilson Boulevard, Arlington, VA 22203 Telephone: 703-522-1315 Fax: 703-528-4510	Web Site: www.aes.com Officers: Charles O. Rossotti - Chairman Andres R. Gluski - Chief Executive Officer, Executive Vice President, Chief Operating Officer	Auditors: Ernst & Young LLP Investor Contact: 703-682-6451 Transfer Agents: Computershare Investor Services, Canton, MA

AETNA INC.

Exchange	Symbol	Price	52Wk Range	Yield	P/E
NYS	AET	$180.39 (12/29/2017)	182.73-116.71	1.11	33.41

*7 Year Price Score 137.83 *NYSE Composite Index=100 *12 Month Price Score 112.63

Interim Earnings (Per Share)

Qtr.	Mar	Jun	Sep	Dec
2014	1.82	1.52	1.67	0.67
2015	2.20	2.08	1.59	0.91
2016	2.06	2.23	1.70	0.39
2017	(1.11)	3.60	2.52	...

Interim Dividends (Per Share)

Amt	Decl	Ex	Rec	Pay
0.50Q	02/17/2017	04/11/2017	04/13/2017	04/28/2017
0.50Q	05/19/2017	07/11/2017	07/13/2017	07/28/2017
0.50Q	09/29/2017	10/11/2017	10/12/2017	10/27/2017
0.50Q	12/03/2017	01/10/2018	01/11/2018	01/26/2018

Indicated Div: $2.00

Valuation Analysis — **Institutional Holding**

Forecast EPS	$9.77 (01/18/2018)	No of Institutions 1247
Market Cap	$58.8 Billion	Shares
Book Value	$15.6 Billion	374,548,512
Price/Book	3.77	% Held
Price/Sales	0.96	89.26

TRADING VOLUME (thousand shares)

Business Summary: Life & Health (MIC: 5.2.2 SIC: 6324 NAIC: 524114)

Aetna is a health care benefits company. Co. conducts its operations in three business segments: Health Care, which provides medical, pharmacy benefit management services, dental, behavioral health and vision plans provided on both an insured basis and an employer-funded basis and businesses products and services that complement its medical products; Group Insurance, which primarily includes group life insurance and group disability products and long-term care products; and Large Case Pensions, which manages a variety of retirement products (including pension and annuity products) primarily for tax-qualified pension plans.

Recent Developments: For the quarter ended Sep 30 2017, net income increased 42.0% to US$848.0 million from US$597.0 million in the year-earlier quarter. Revenues were US$14.99 billion, down 5.0% from US$15.78 billion the year before. Net premiums earned were US$13.27 billion versus US$14.07 billion in the prior-year quarter, a decrease of 5.7%. Net investment income rose 6.4% to US$233.0 million from US$219.0 million a year ago.

Prospects: Our evaluation of Aetna Inc. as of Jan. 14, 2018 is the result of our systematic analysis on three basic characteristics: earnings strength, relative valuation, and recent stock price movement. The company has generated a negative trend in earnings per share over the past 5 quarters and while recent estimates for the company have been mixed, AET has posted better than expected results. Based on operating earnings yield, the company is undervalued when compared to all of the companies in our coverage universe. Share price changes over the past year indicates that AET will perform very well over the near term.

Financial Data
(US$ in Thousands)

	9 Mos	6 Mos	3 Mos	12/31/2016	12/31/2015	12/31/2014	12/31/2013	12/31/2012
Earnings Per Share	5.40	4.58	3.21	6.41	6.78	5.68	5.33	4.81
Cash Flow Per Share	4.01	6.62	8.25	10.56	11.07	9.49	6.41	5.34
Tang Book Value Per Share	11.12	10.37	6.76	16.50	10.84	5.49	4.70	10.30
Dividends Per Share	1.500	1.250	1.000	1.000	1.000	0.900	0.800	0.700
Dividend Payout %	27.78	27.29	31.15	15.60	14.75	15.85	15.01	14.55
Income Statement								
Premium Income	40,810,000	27,538,000	13,763,000	56,298,000	53,788,800	51,748,500	41,836,600	31,715,400
Total Revenue	45,682,000	30,688,000	15,165,000	63,155,000	60,336,500	58,003,200	47,294,600	36,595,900
Benefits & Claims	1,632,000	1,084,000	545,000	2,101,000	2,120,600	2,165,000	2,350,400	2,949,500
Income Before Taxes	2,466,000	1,192,000	(628,000)	3,991,000	4,235,600	3,499,900	2,940,500	2,545,400
Income Taxes	815,000	389,000	(249,000)	1,735,000	1,841,000	1,454,700	1,028,600	887,500
Net Income	1,660,000	822,000	(381,000)	2,271,000	2,390,200	2,040,800	1,913,600	1,657,900
Average Shares	332,000	334,500	343,800	354,300	352,600	359,100	359,200	345,000
Balance Sheet								
Total Assets	57,383,000	56,714,000	56,351,000	69,146,000	53,424,100	53,402,100	49,871,800	41,494,500
Total Liabilities	41,800,000	41,310,000	42,090,000	51,265,000	37,309,800	38,919,500	35,846,300	31,088,700
Stockholders' Equity	15,583,000	15,404,000	14,261,000	17,881,000	16,114,300	14,482,600	14,025,500	10,405,800
Shares Outstanding	326,100	332,100	331,700	351,700	349,500	349,800	362,200	327,600
Statistical Record								
Return on Assets %	2.78	2.46	2.04	3.70	4.47	3.95	4.19	4.13
Return on Equity %	10.63	9.45	7.42	13.32	15.62	14.32	15.67	16.11
Loss Ratio %	4.00	3.94	3.96	3.73	3.94	4.18	5.62	9.30
Net Margin %	3.63	2.68	(2.51)	3.60	3.96	3.52	4.05	4.53
Price Range	163.21-105.20	152.98-105.20	134.90-105.20	134.90-94.31	132.60-87.60	90.84-65.15	68.93-44.38	50.23-35.30
P/E Ratio	30.22-19.48	33.40-22.97	42.02-32.77	21.05-14.71	19.56-12.92	15.99-11.47	12.93-8.33	10.44-7.34
Average Yield %	1.11	0.99	0.84	0.87	0.92	1.15	1.35	1.65

Address: 151 Farmington Avenue, Hartford, CT 06156
Telephone: 860-273-0123

Web Site: www.aetna.com
Officers: Mark T. Bertolini - Chairman, President, Chief Executive Officer Karen S. Rohan - President, Executive Vice President

Auditors: KPMG LLP
Investor Contact: 860-273-2402
Transfer Agents: Computershare Trust Company, N.A, Providence, RI

AFFILIATED MANAGERS GROUP INC.

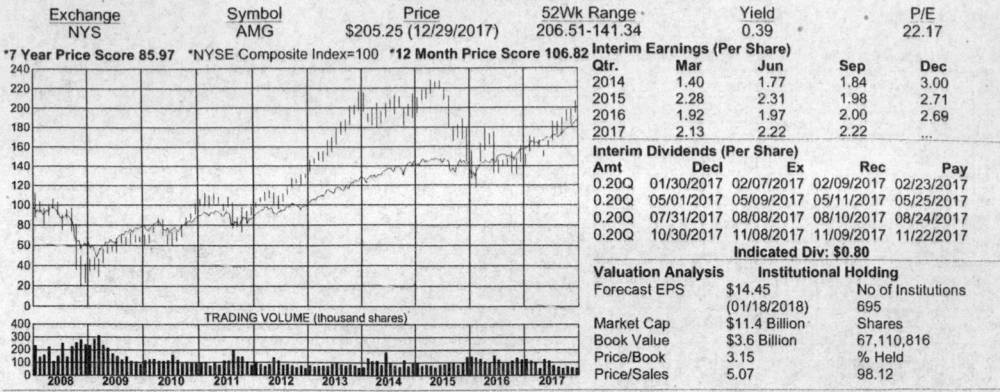

Exchange	Symbol	Price	52Wk Range	Yield	P/E
NYS	AMG	$205.25 (12/29/2017)	206.51-141.34	0.39	22.17

*7 Year Price Score 85.97   *NYSE Composite Index=100   *12 Month Price Score 106.82

Interim Earnings (Per Share)

Qtr.	Mar	Jun	Sep	Dec
2014	1.40	1.77	1.84	3.00
2015	2.28	2.31	1.98	2.71
2016	1.92	1.97	2.00	2.69
2017	2.13	2.22	2.22	...

Interim Dividends (Per Share)

Amt	Decl	Ex	Rec	Pay
0.20Q	01/30/2017	02/07/2017	02/09/2017	02/23/2017
0.20Q	05/01/2017	05/09/2017	05/11/2017	05/25/2017
0.20Q	07/31/2017	08/08/2017	08/10/2017	08/24/2017
0.20Q	10/30/2017	11/08/2017	11/09/2017	11/22/2017

Indicated Div: $0.80

Valuation Analysis

		Institutional Holding	
Forecast EPS	$14.45 (01/18/2018)	No of Institutions	695
Market Cap	$11.4 Billion	Shares	67,110,816
Book Value	$3.6 Billion	% Held	98.12
Price/Book	3.15		
Price/Sales	5.07		

TRADING VOLUME (thousand shares)

Business Summary: Wealth Management (MIC: 5.5.2 SIC: 6282 NAIC: 523920)

Affiliated Managers Group is a global asset management company with equity investments in boutique investment management firms (Affiliates). Co.'s Affiliates provide investment management services globally to institutional, retail and high net worth clients. In addition, Co. provides centralized assistance to its Affiliates in strategic matters, marketing, distribution, product development and operations. Co. operates in three business segments representing its three principal distribution channels: Institutional, Mutual Fund and High Net Worth.

Recent Developments: For the quarter ended Sep 30 2017, net income increased 23.3% to US$216.8 million from US$175.9 million in the year-earlier quarter. Revenues were US$585.7 million, up 7.5% from US$544.7 million the year before. Operating income was US$218.8 million versus US$171.0 million in the prior-year quarter, an increase of 28.0%. Indirect operating expenses decreased 1.8% to US$366.9 million from US$373.7 million in the equivalent prior-year period.

Prospects: Our evaluation of Affiliated Managers Group Inc. as of Jan. 14, 2018 is the result of our systematic analysis on three basic characteristics: earnings strength, relative valuation, and recent stock price movement. The company has produced a positive trend in earnings per share over the past 5 quarters and while recent estimates for the company have been raised by analysts, AMG has posted better than expected results. Based on operating earnings yield, the company is undervalued when compared to all of the companies in our coverage universe. Share price changes over the past year indicates that AMG will perform very well over the near term.

Financial Data
(US$ in Thousands)

	9 Mos	6 Mos	3 Mos	12/31/2016	12/31/2015	12/31/2014	12/31/2013	12/31/2012
Earnings Per Share	9.26	9.04	8.79	8.57	9.28	8.01	6.55	3.28
Cash Flow Per Share	20.52	20.08	19.82	18.91	22.19	25.31	18.02	12.21
Dividends Per Share	0.600	0.400	0.200	...	...	...	...	...
Dividend Payout %	6.48	4.42	2.28	...	...	...	...	...
Income Statement								
Total Revenue	1,700,900	1,115,200	544,300	2,194,600	2,484,500	2,510,900	2,188,800	1,805,500
EBITDA	709,400	452,900	213,100	873,600	992,600	977,600	817,100	644,700
Depn & Amortn	68,400	46,200	23,000	134,500	142,300	139,100	142,200	222,300
Income Before Taxes	571,500	359,300	167,400	645,800	801,700	731,800	555,900	365,500
Income Taxes	188,200	122,200	59,700	235,600	256,900	227,900	194,100	83,800
Net Income	374,200	248,800	122,500	472,800	516,000	452,100	360,500	174,000
Average Shares	58,300	58,700	59,200	57,000	57,200	58,400	56,700	53,000
Balance Sheet								
Current Assets	1,115,000	1,060,300	1,006,900	1,084,000	1,304,200	1,316,300	1,210,200	912,300
Total Assets	8,701,400	8,632,300	8,590,100	8,749,100	7,784,800	7,698,100	6,318,800	6,187,100
Current Liabilities	698,300	618,300	541,600	729,300	729,400	808,300	514,700	375,800
Long-Term Obligations	1,913,600	2,032,400	2,026,000	1,808,000	1,589,600	1,591,800	865,000	1,630,600
Total Liabilities	5,073,900	5,032,300	5,005,200	5,129,500	4,947,700	5,071,100	4,184,600	4,102,900
Stockholders' Equity	3,627,500	3,600,000	3,584,900	3,619,600	2,837,100	2,627,000	2,134,200	2,084,200
Shares Outstanding	55,600	58,500	58,500	58,500	55,800	54,600	53,900	53,900
Statistical Record								
Return on Assets %	6.18	6.12	5.88	5.70	6.67	6.45	5.77	3.04
Return on Equity %	15.44	15.64	15.21	14.61	18.89	18.99	17.09	8.79
EBITDA Margin %	41.71	40.61	39.15	39.81	39.95	38.93	37.33	35.71
Net Margin %	22.00	22.31	22.51	21.54	20.77	18.01	16.47	9.64
Asset Turnover	0.26	0.27	0.26	0.26	0.32	0.36	0.35	0.32
Current Ratio	1.60	1.71	1.86	1.49	1.79	1.63	2.35	2.43
Debt to Equity	0.53	0.56	0.57	0.50	0.56	0.61	0.41	0.78
Price Range	189.83-131.57	170.91-131.57	179.01-131.57	179.01-117.80	228.02-144.01	216.88-179.30	216.88-130.15	132.30-96.00
P/E Ratio	20.50-14.21	18.91-14.55	20.37-14.97	20.89-13.75	24.57-15.52	27.08-22.38	33.11-19.87	40.34-29.27
Average Yield %	0.37	0.26	0.13	...	...	...	...	...

Address: 777 South Flagler Drive, West Palm Beach, FL 33401
Telephone: 800-345-1100

Web Site: www.amg.com
Officers: Sean M. Healey - Chairman, Chief Executive Officer John Kingston - Vice-Chairman, Executive Vice President, General Counsel, Secretary

Auditors: PricewaterhouseCoopers LLP
Investor Contact: 617-747-3300
Transfer Agents: American Stock Transfer & Trust Company, New York, NY

AFLAC INC

Exchange	Symbol	Price	52Wk Range	Yield	P/E	Div Achiever
NYS	AFL	$87.78 (12/29/2017)	89.26-67.14	2.05	12.74	34 Years

*7 Year Price Score 101.55 *NYSE Composite Index=100 *12 Month Price Score 105.01

TRADING VOLUME (thousand shares)

Interim Earnings (Per Share)

Qtr.	Mar	Jun	Sep	Dec
2014	1.60	1.78	1.56	1.57
2015	1.51	1.32	1.32	1.71
2016	1.74	1.32	1.53	1.83
2017	1.47	1.79	1.80	...

Interim Dividends (Per Share)

Amt	Decl	Ex	Rec	Pay
0.43Q	01/31/2017	02/13/2017	02/15/2017	03/01/2017
0.43Q	04/27/2017	05/22/2017	05/24/2017	06/01/2017
0.43Q	07/27/2017	08/21/2017	08/23/2017	09/01/2017
0.45Q	10/25/2017	11/14/2017	11/15/2017	12/01/2017

Indicated Div: $1.80 (Div. Reinv. Plan)

Valuation Analysis | **Institutional Holding**

Forecast EPS	$6.75	No of Institutions
	(01/18/2018)	1315
Market Cap	$34.6 Billion	Shares
Book Value	$22.0 Billion	336,716,608
Price/Book	1.57	% Held
Price/Sales	1.56	56.32

Business Summary: Life & Health (MIC: 5.2.2 SIC: 6311 NAIC: 524113)

Aflac Incorporated is a holding company. Co. sells supplemental health and life insurance, which is marketed and administered via its subsidiary, American Family Life Assurance Company of Columbus (Aflac). Aflac operates in the U.S. (Aflac U.S.), which designs the U.S. insurance products to provide supplemental coverage for people having medical or insurance coverage; and as a branch in Japan (Aflac Japan), which provides insurance products to help consumers pay for medical and nonmedical costs that are not reimbursed under Japan's national health insurance system. Aflac U.S. also provides group products via Continental American Insurance Company (CAIC), branded as Aflac Group Insurance.

Recent Developments: For the quarter ended Sep 30 2017, net income increased 13.8% to US$716.0 million from US$629.0 million in the year-earlier quarter. Revenues were US$5.51 billion, down 3.7% from US$5.72 billion the year before. Net premiums earned were US$4.65 billion versus US$5.02 billion in the prior-year quarter, a decrease of 7.4%. Net investment income fell 3.7% to US$811.0 million from US$842.0 million a year ago.

Prospects: Our evaluation of AFLAC Inc. as of Jan. 14, 2018 is the result of our systematic analysis on three basic characteristics: earnings strength, relative valuation, and recent stock price movement. The company has managed to produce a neutral trend in earnings per share over the past 5 quarters. However, while recent estimates for the company have been mixed, AFL has posted better than expected results. Based on operating earnings yield, the company is undervalued when compared to all of the companies in our coverage universe. Share price changes over the past year indicates that AFL will perform very well over the near term.

Financial Data

(US$ in Thousands)	9 Mos	6 Mos	3 Mos	12/31/2016	12/31/2015	12/31/2014	12/31/2013	12/31/2012
Earnings Per Share	6.89	6.62	6.15	6.42	5.85	6.50	6.76	6.11
Cash Flow Per Share	16.38	15.89	15.99	14.51	15.73	14.52	22.71	31.94
Tang Book Value Per Share	55.80	54.30	51.11	50.47	41.73	41.47	31.82	34.16
Dividends Per Share	1.720	1.700	1.680	1.660	1.580	1.500	1.420	1.340
Dividend Payout %	24.96	25.68	27.32	25.86	27.01	23.08	21.01	21.93
Income Statement								
Premium Income	13,951,000	9,303,000	4,638,000	19,225,000	17,570,000	19,072,000	20,135,000	22,148,000
Total Revenue	16,243,000	10,737,000	5,309,000	22,559,000	20,872,000	22,728,000	23,939,000	25,364,000
Benefits & Claims	9,174,000	6,091,000	3,052,000	12,919,000	11,746,000	12,937,000	13,813,000	15,330,000
Income Before Taxes	3,019,000	1,944,000	898,000	4,067,000	3,862,000	4,491,000	4,816,000	4,302,000
Income Taxes	998,000	639,000	306,000	1,408,000	1,329,000	1,540,000	1,658,000	1,436,000
Net Income	2,021,000	1,305,000	592,000	2,659,000	2,533,000	2,951,000	3,158,000	2,866,000
Average Shares	397,381	399,348	404,069	413,921	433,172	454,000	467,408	469,287
Balance Sheet								
Total Assets	136,083,000	135,394,000	133,650,000	129,819,000	118,296,000	119,767,000	121,307,000	131,094,000
Total Liabilities	114,106,000	113,891,000	113,310,000	109,337,000	100,588,000	101,420,000	106,687,000	115,116,000
Stockholders' Equity	21,977,000	21,503,000	20,340,000	20,482,000	17,708,000	18,347,000	14,620,000	15,978,000
Shares Outstanding	393,875	395,999	398,002	405,810	424,380	442,445	459,413	467,786
Statistical Record								
Return on Assets %	1.98	1.94	1.93	2.14	2.13	2.45	2.50	2.30
Return on Equity %	12.39	12.19	12.49	13.89	14.05	17.90	20.64	19.39
Loss Ratio %	65.76	65.47	65.80	67.20	66.85	67.83	68.60	69.22
Net Margin %	12.44	12.15	11.15	11.79	12.14	12.98	13.19	11.30
Price Range	84.26-67.14	79.26-67.14	74.28-63.00	74.28-55.55	65.99-55.23	66.80-55.80	67.48-48.65	54.70-38.45
P/E Ratio	12.23-9.74	11.97-10.14	12.08-10.24	11.57-8.65	11.28-9.44	10.28-8.58	9.98-7.20	8.95-6.29
Average Yield %	2.32	2.35	2.38	2.45	2.56	2.44	2.45	2.90

Address: 1932 Wynnton Road,	Web Site: www.aflac.com	Auditors: KPMG LLP
Columbus, GA 31999	Officers: Daniel P. Amos - Chairman, Chief	Investor Contact: 706-596-3264
Telephone: 706-323-3431	Executive Officer Kriss Cloninger - President, Chief	Transfer Agents: Aflac Incorporated
Fax: 706-596-3488	Financial Officer, Treasurer	Shareholder Services, Columbus, GA

AGCO CORP.

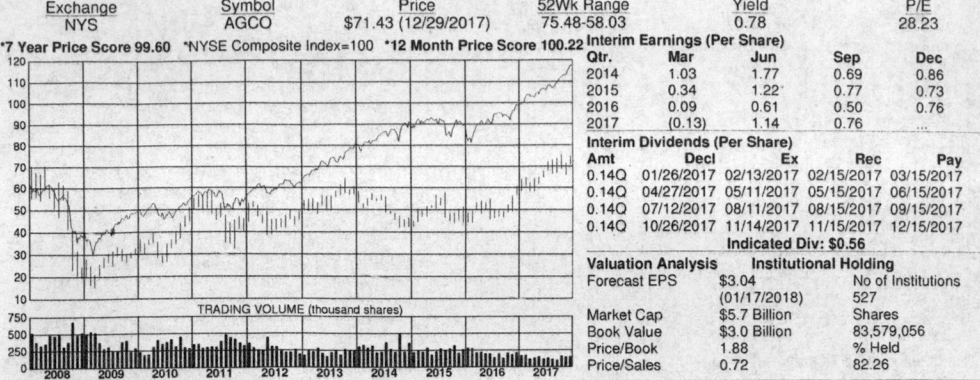

Exchange	Symbol	Price	52Wk Range	Yield	P/E
NYS	AGCO	$71.43 (12/29/2017)	75.48-58.03	0.78	28.23

*7 Year Price Score 99.60   *NYSE Composite Index=100   *12 Month Price Score 100.22

Interim Earnings (Per Share)

Qtr.	Mar	Jun	Sep	Dec
2014	1.03	1.77	0.69	0.86
2015	0.34	1.22	0.77	0.73
2016	0.09	0.61	0.50	0.76
2017	(0.13)	1.14	0.76	...

Interim Dividends (Per Share)

Amt	Decl	Ex	Rec	Pay
0.14Q	01/26/2017	02/13/2017	02/15/2017	03/15/2017
0.14Q	04/27/2017	05/11/2017	05/15/2017	06/15/2017
0.14Q	07/12/2017	08/11/2017	08/15/2017	09/15/2017
0.14Q	10/26/2017	11/14/2017	11/15/2017	12/15/2017

Indicated Div: $0.56

Valuation Analysis

Forecast EPS	$3.04	
	(01/17/2018)	
	Institutional Holding	
	No of Institutions	527
Market Cap	$5.7 Billion	Shares
Book Value	$3.0 Billion	83,579,056
Price/Book	1.88	% Held
Price/Sales	0.72	82.26

TRADING VOLUME (thousand shares)

Business Summary: Industrial Machinery & Equipment (MIC: 7.2.1 SIC: 3523 NAIC: 333111)

AGCO is a manufacturer and distributor of agricultural equipment and related replacement parts. Co. sells a range of agricultural equipment, including tractors, combines, hay tools, sprayers, forage equipment, seeding and tillage equipment, implements, and grain storage and protein production systems. Co. distributes its products through a combination of over 3,000 independent dealers and distributors as well as Co. utilizes associates and licensees to provide a distribution channel for its products. In addition, Co. provides retail financing through its finance joint ventures with Cooperatieve Centrale Raiffeisen-Boerenleenbank B.A.

Recent Developments: For the quarter ended Sep 30 2017, net income increased 54.3% to US$60.8 million from US$39.4 million in the year-earlier quarter. Revenues were US$1.99 billion, up 12.8% from US$1.76 billion the year before. Operating income was US$97.0 million versus US$59.0 million in the prior-year quarter, an increase of 64.4%. Direct operating expenses rose 10.6% to US$1.56 billion from US$1.41 billion in the comparable period the year before. Indirect operating expenses increased 12.6% to US$331.6 million from US$294.5 million in the equivalent prior-year period.

Prospects: Our evaluation of AGCO Corp. as of Jan. 14, 2018 is the result of our systematic analysis on three basic characteristics: earnings strength, relative valuation, and recent stock price movement. The company has produced a positive trend in earnings per share over the past 5 quarters. However, while recent estimates for the company have been mixed, AGCO has posted better than expected results. Based on operating earnings yield, the company is undervalued when compared to all of the companies in our coverage universe. Share price changes over the past year indicates that AGCO will perform well over the near term.

Financial Data

(US$ in Thousands)	9 Mos	6 Mos	3 Mos	12/31/2016	12/31/2015	12/31/2014	12/31/2013	12/31/2012
Earnings Per Share	2.53	2.27	1.74	1.96	3.06	4.36	6.01	5.30
Cash Flow Per Share	5.88	4.63	5.87	4.53	6.03	4.69	8.19	6.84
Tang Book Value Per Share	10.81	11.18	10.40	9.97	14.51	19.09	23.27	17.20
Dividends Per Share	0.550	0.540	0.530	0.520	0.480	0.440	0.400	...
Dividend Payout %	21.74	23.79	30.46	26.53	15.69	10.09	6.66	...
Income Statement								
Total Revenue	5,779,100	3,792,800	1,627,600	7,410,500	7,467,300	9,723,700	10,786,900	9,962,200
EBITDA	419,100	269,700	70,500	531,600	584,900	877,800	1,120,000	888,300
Depn & Amortn	207,200	136,400	67,900	274,600	260,100	280,400	259,400	229,900
Income Before Taxes	178,300	111,300	(8,100)	204,900	279,400	539,000	802,600	600,800
Income Taxes	64,900	48,000	11,100	92,200	72,500	187,700	258,500	137,900
Net Income	142,100	81,400	(10,100)	160,100	266,400	410,400	597,200	522,100
Average Shares	80,200	80,100	79,500	81,700	87,100	94,200	99,400	98,600
Balance Sheet								
Current Assets	3,839,200	3,590,400	3,359,500	3,165,700	2,898,300	3,527,900	4,517,100	3,954,700
Total Assets	8,174,400	7,692,500	7,394,600	7,168,400	6,501,300	7,395,900	8,438,800	7,721,800
Current Liabilities	2,547,800	2,359,200	2,165,200	2,144,900	2,185,400	2,216,900	2,812,000	2,464,800
Long-Term Obligations	1,950,300	1,772,100	1,780,500	1,610,000	928,800	997,600	938,500	1,035,600
Total Liabilities	5,146,200	4,785,000	4,583,400	4,392,300	3,663,000	3,947,400	4,428,600	4,257,100
Stockholders' Equity	3,028,200	2,907,500	2,811,200	2,776,100	2,838,300	3,448,500	4,010,200	3,464,700
Shares Outstanding	79,549	79,502	79,475	79,465	83,814	89,146	97,362	96,815
Statistical Record								
Return on Assets %	2.60	2.49	1.98	2.34	3.83	5.18	7.39	6.95
Return on Equity %	6.89	6.29	5.00	5.69	8.47	11.00	15.98	16.12
EBITDA Margin %	7.25	7.11	4.33	7.17	7.83	9.03	10.38	8.92
Net Margin %	2.46	2.15	N.M.	2.16	3.57	4.22	5.54	5.24
Asset Turnover	1.00	1.04	1.04	1.08	1.07	1.23	1.33	1.33
Current Ratio	1.51	1.52	1.55	1.48	1.33	1.59	1.61	1.60
Debt to Equity	0.64	0.61	0.63	0.58	0.33	0.29	0.23	0.30
Price Range	73.77-48.89	67.80-46.22	64.74-45.51	60.66-44.02	57.87-42.72	59.19-42.08	64.42-48.02	53.73-38.56
P/E Ratio	29.16-19.32	29.87-20.36	37.21-26.16	30.95-22.46	18.91-13.96	13.58-9.65	10.72-7.99	10.14-7.28
Average Yield %	0.88	0.95	0.99	1.03	0.98	0.87	0.72	...

Address: 4205 River Green Parkway, Duluth, GA 30096	**Web Site:** www.agcocorp.com	**Auditors:** KPMG LLP
Telephone: 770-813-9200	**Officers:** Martin H. Richenhagen - Chairman, President, Chief Executive Officer Andrew H. Beck - Senior Vice President, Chief Financial Officer	**Investor Contact:** 770-232-8229
		Transfer Agents: Computershare Trust Company, N.A., Canton, MA

AGILENT TECHNOLOGIES, INC.

Exchange	Symbol	Price	52Wk Range	Yield	P/E
NYS	A	$66.97 (12/29/2017)	70.59-46.49	0.89	31.89

*7 Year Price Score 118.31 ***NYSE Composite Index=100** ***12 Month Price Score 108.01**

Interim Earnings (Per Share)

Qtr.	Jan	Apr	Jul	Oct
2012-13	0.51	0.48	0.49	0.63
2013-14	0.58	0.41	0.43	0.07
2014-15	0.21	0.25	0.31	0.43
2015-16	0.37	0.28	0.38	0.38
2016-17	0.52	0.50	0.54	0.54

Interim Dividends (Per Share)

Amt	Decl	Ex	Rec	Pay
0.132Q	03/15/2017	03/31/2017	04/04/2017	04/26/2017
0.132Q	05/17/2017	06/29/2017	07/03/2017	07/26/2017
0.132Q	09/20/2017	10/02/2017	10/03/2017	10/25/2017
0.149Q	11/15/2017	12/29/2017	01/02/2018	01/24/2018

Indicated Div: $0.60

Valuation Analysis

		Institutional Holding	
Forecast EPS	$2.57		No of Institutions
	(01/18/2018)		906
Market Cap	$21.6 Billion	Shares	
Book Value	$4.8 Billion		348,495,520
Price/Book	4.46	% Held	
Price/Sales	4.82		78.76

Business Summary: Medical Instruments & Equipment (MIC: 4.3.1 SIC: 3826 NAIC: 334516)

Agilent Technologies engages in life sciences, diagnostics and applied chemical markets, providing application focused solutions including instruments, software, services and consumables. Co.'s life sciences and applied markets business provides solutions including instruments and software to identify, quantify and analyze the physical and biological properties of substances and products, and interrogate samples at the molecular level. The diagnostics and genomics business includes genomics, nucleic acid contract manufacturing and the pathology, companion diagnostics and reagent partnership businesses. The CrossLab business spans the entire lab with its consumables and services portfolio.

Recent Developments: For the year ended Oct 31 2017, income from continuing operations increased 48.1% to US$684.0 million from US$462.0 million a year earlier. Net income increased 48.1% to US$684.0 million from US$462.0 million in the prior year. Revenues were US$4.47 billion, up 6.4% from US$4.20 billion the year before. Operating income was US$841.0 million versus US$615.0 million in the prior year, an increase of 36.7%. Direct operating expenses rose 2.9% to US$2.06 billion from US$2.01 billion in the comparable period the year before. Indirect operating expenses decreased 0.9% to US$1.57 billion from US$1.58 billion in the equivalent prior-year period.

Prospects: Our evaluation of Agilent Technologies Inc. as of Jan. 14, 2018 is the result of our systematic analysis on three basic characteristics: earnings strength, relative valuation, and recent stock price movement. The company has managed to produce a neutral trend in earnings per share over the past 5 quarters and while recent estimates for the company have remained steady, A has posted better than expected results. Based on operating earnings yield, the company is about fairly valued when compared to all of the companies in our coverage universe. Share price changes over the past year indicates that A will perform well over the near term.

Financial Data
(US$ in Millions)

	10/31/2017	10/31/2016	10/31/2015	10/31/2014	10/31/2013	10/31/2012	10/31/2011	10/31/2010
Earnings Per Share	2.10	1.40	1.20	1.49	2.10	3.27	2.85	1.94
Cash Flow Per Share	2.76	2.43	1.47	2.14	3.38	3.52	3.63	2.07
Tang Book Value Per Share	5.79	4.07	4.09	5.17	3.98	3.09	6.67	3.69
Dividends Per Share	0.528	0.460	0.400	0.528	0.460	0.300	...	...
Dividend Payout %	25.14	32.86	33.33	35.44	21.90	9.17	...	...
Income Statement								
Total Revenue	4,472	4,202	4,038	6,981	6,782	6,858	6,615	5,444
EBITDA	954	700	637	944	1,140	1,306	1,246	892
Depn & Amortn	94	95	98	194	181	171	142	124
Income Before Taxes	803	544	480	646	859	1,043	1,032	692
Income Taxes	119	82	42	142	135	(110)	20	8
Net Income	684	462	401	504	724	1,153	1,012	684
Average Shares	326	329	335	338	345	353	355	353
Balance Sheet								
Current Assets	4,169	3,635	3,686	5,500	4,983	4,629	5,569	6,169
Total Assets	8,426	7,802	7,479	10,831	10,686	10,536	9,057	9,696
Current Liabilities	1,263	945	976	1,702	1,602	1,893	1,837	3,083
Long-Term Obligations	1,801	1,912	1,655	2,762	2,699	2,112	1,932	2,190
Total Liabilities	3,595	3,559	3,312	5,533	5,400	5,354	4,749	6,468
Stockholders' Equity	4,831	4,243	4,167	5,298	5,286	5,182	4,308	3,228
Shares Outstanding	322	323	331	334	332	346	346	346
Statistical Record								
Return on Assets %	8.43	6.03	4.38	4.68	6.82	11.74	10.79	7.90
Return on Equity %	15.08	10.96	8.47	9.52	13.83	24.23	26.86	23.86
EBITDA Margin %	21.33	16.66	15.78	13.52	16.81	19.04	18.84	16.39
Net Margin %	15.30	10.99	9.93	7.22	10.68	16.81	15.30	12.56
Asset Turnover	0.55	0.55	0.44	0.65	0.64	0.70	0.71	0.63
Current Ratio	3.30	3.85	3.78	3.23	3.11	2.45	3.03	2.00
Debt to Equity	0.37	0.45	0.40	0.52	0.51	0.41	0.45	0.68
Price Range	68.03-43.21	48.44-34.80	43.55-33.37	43.57-35.79	37.89-25.56	32.79-23.55	37.60-21.02	26.62-17.90
P/E Ratio	32.40-20.58	34.60-24.86	36.29-27.81	29.24-24.02	18.04-12.17	10.03-7.20	13.19-7.38	13.72-9.23
Average Yield %	0.95	1.08	1.01	1.31	1.46	1.06	...	...

Address: 5301 Stevens Creek Blvd., Santa Clara, CA 95051 Telephone: 408-345-8886	Web Site: www.investor.agilent.com Officers: Michael R. McMullen - President, Chief Executive Officer, Senior Vice President, Division Officer Didier Hirsch - Senior Vice President, Chief Financial Officer, Chief Accounting Officer	Auditors: PricewaterhouseCoopers LLP Investor Contact: 408-345-8948 Transfer Agents: ComputerShare Investor Services, Chicago, IL

AIR LEASE CORP

Exchange	Symbol	Price	52Wk Range	Yield	P/E
NYS	AL	$48.09 (12/29/2017)	48.31-34.64	0.83	13.78

*7 Year Price Score N/A *NYSE Composite Index=100 *12 Month Price Score 105.15

Interim Earnings (Per Share)

Qtr.	Mar	Jun	Sep	Dec
2014	0.57	0.58	0.58	0.65
2015	0.19	0.70	0.71	0.74
2016	0.85	0.84	0.86	0.89
2017	0.78	0.92	0.90	...

Interim Dividends (Per Share)

Amt	Decl	Ex	Rec	Pay
0.075Q	02/23/2017	03/16/2017	03/20/2017	04/07/2017
0.075Q	05/04/2017	06/12/2017	06/14/2017	07/11/2017
0.075Q	08/03/2017	09/12/2017	09/13/2017	10/06/2017
0.10Q	11/09/2017	12/13/2017	12/14/2017	01/04/2018

Indicated Div: $0.40

Valuation Analysis

		Institutional Holding	
Forecast EPS	$3.43	No of Institutions	
	(01/16/2018)	318	
Market Cap	$5.0 Billion	Shares	
Book Value	$3.7 Billion	103,676,696	
Price/Book	1.36	% Held	
Price/Sales	3.34	86.20	

TRADING VOLUME (thousand shares)

Business Summary: Miscellaneous Transportation Services (MIC: 7.4.5 SIC: 7359 NAIC: 532420)

Air Lease is an aircraft leasing company. Co. is principally engaged in purchasing new commercial jet transport aircraft directly from aircraft manufacturers, such as The Boeing Company and Airbus S.A.S., and leasing those aircraft to airlines. In addition to Co.'s leasing activities, Co. sells aircraft from its operating lease portfolio to third parties, including other leasing companies, financial services companies and airlines. Co. also provides fleet management services to investors and owners of aircraft portfolios. As of Dec 31 2016, Co. owned 237 aircraft, comprised of 188 single-aisle narrowbody jet aircraft and 49 twin-aisle widebody jet aircraft.

Recent Developments: For the quarter ended Sep 30 2017, net income increased 6.3% to US$99.2 million from US$93.3 million in the year-earlier quarter. Revenues were US$376.8 million, up 6.1% from US$355.1 million the year before. Indirect operating expenses increased 5.8% to US$222.6 million from US$210.5 million in the equivalent prior-year period.

Prospects: Our evaluation of Air Lease Corp as of Jan. 14, 2018 is the result of our systematic analysis on three basic characteristics: earnings strength, relative valuation, and recent stock price movement. The company has managed to produce a neutral trend in earnings per share over the past 5 quarters. However, while recent estimates for the company have been mixed, AL has posted better than expected results. Based on operating earnings yield, the company is undervalued when compared to all of the companies in our coverage universe. Share price changes over the past year indicates that AL will perform in line with the market over the near term.

Financial Data

(US$ in Thousands)	9 Mos	6 Mos	3 Mos	12/31/2016	12/31/2015	12/31/2014	12/31/2013	12/31/2012
Earnings Per Share	3.49	3.45	3.37	3.44	2.34	2.38	1.80	1.28
Cash Flow Per Share	9.79	9.82	9.83	9.90	8.19	7.53	6.44	4.85
Tang Book Value Per Share	35.41	34.47	33.53	32.89	29.44	27.07	24.78	23.04
Dividends Per Share	0.300	0.275	0.250	0.225	0.170	0.130	0.105	...
Dividend Payout %	8.60	7.97	7.42	6.54	7.26	5.46	5.83	...
Income Statement								
Total Revenue	1,117,909	741,144	360,187	1,419,055	1,222,840	1,050,493	858,675	655,746
EBITDA	1,060,185	701,081	342,834	1,319,121	1,056,857	952,023	765,849	567,605
Depn & Amortn	400,340	265,828	132,901	452,682	397,760	336,657	280,037	216,219
Income Before Taxes	443,866	289,747	133,878	580,238	392,953	394,776	293,442	203,973
Income Taxes	158,816	103,885	48,941	205,313	139,562	138,778	103,031	72,054
Net Income	285,050	185,862	84,937	374,925	253,391	255,998	190,411	131,919
Average Shares	111,709	111,564	111,429	110,798	110,628	110,192	108,963	107,656
Balance Sheet								
Current Assets	245,430	261,949	174,088	1,581,478	1,244,238	1,434,891	1,432,504	901,114
Total Assets	14,901,647	14,861,397	14,477,040	13,975,616	12,355,098	10,774,784	9,332,604	7,353,624
Current Liabilities	232,399	274,353	223,374	1,113,110	1,069,313	889,124	701,070	502,392
Long-Term Obligations	9,237,320	9,303,312	9,102,989	8,713,874	7,712,421	6,714,362	5,853,317	4,384,732
Total Liabilities	11,246,064	11,303,193	11,017,808	10,593,429	9,335,186	8,002,722	6,809,170	5,021,003
Stockholders' Equity	3,655,583	3,558,204	3,459,232	3,382,187	3,019,912	2,772,062	2,523,434	2,332,621
Shares Outstanding	103,239	103,211	103,163	102,844	102,582	102,392	101,822	101,247
Statistical Record								
Return on Assets %	2.67	2.67	2.69	2.84	2.19	2.55	2.28	2.10
Return on Equity %	11.00	11.14	11.18	11.68	8.75	9.67	7.84	5.84
EBITDA Margin %	94.84	94.59	95.18	92.96	86.43	90.63	89.19	86.56
Net Margin %	25.50	25.08	23.58	26.42	20.72	24.37	22.17	20.12
Asset Turnover	0.10	0.10	0.11	0.11	0.11	0.10	0.10	0.10
Current Ratio	1.06	0.95	0.78	1.42	1.16	1.61	2.04	1.79
Debt to Equity	2.53	2.61	2.63	2.58	2.55	2.42	2.32	1.88
Price Range	42.74-28.21	40.12-25.63	40.12-24.93	37.02-22.73	40.21-29.83	42.44-30.27	33.29-21.50	25.58-18.62
P/E Ratio	12.25-8.08	11.63-7.43	11.91-7.40	10.76-6.61	17.18-12.75	17.83-12.72	18.49-11.94	19.98-14.55
Average Yield %	0.81	0.81	0.78	0.75	0.48	0.36	0.38	...

Address: 2000 Avenue of the Stars, Suite 1000N, Los Angeles, CA 90067
Telephone: 310-553-0555

Web Site: www.airleasecorp.com
Officers: Steven F. Udvar-Házy - Chairman, Chief Executive Officer John L. Plueger - President, Chief Operating Officer, Chief Executive Officer

Auditors: KPMG LLP
Investor Contact: 310-553-0555
Transfer Agents: American Stock Transfer & Trust Company, LLC, Seattle, WA

AIR PRODUCTS & CHEMICALS INC

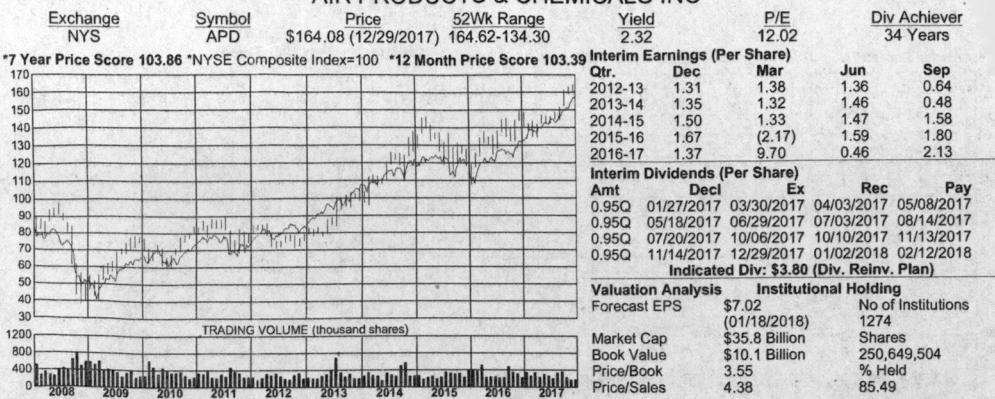

*7 Year Price Score 103.86 *NYSE Composite Index=100 *12 Month Price Score 103.39

Interim Earnings (Per Share)

Qtr.	Dec	Mar	Jun	Sep
2012-13	1.31	1.38	1.36	0.64
2013-14	1.35	1.32	1.46	0.48
2014-15	1.50	1.33	1.47	1.58
2015-16	1.67	(2.17)	1.59	1.80
2016-17	1.37	9.70	0.46	2.13

Interim Dividends (Per Share)

Amt	Decl	Ex	Rec	Pay
0.95Q	01/27/2017	03/30/2017	04/03/2017	05/08/2017
0.95Q	05/18/2017	06/29/2017	07/03/2017	08/14/2017
0.95Q	07/20/2017	10/06/2017	10/10/2017	11/13/2017
0.95Q	11/14/2017	12/29/2017	01/02/2018	02/12/2018

Indicated Div: $3.80 (Div. Reinv. Plan)

Valuation Analysis

		Institutional Holding	
Forecast EPS	$7.02 (01/18/2018)	No of Institutions	1274
Market Cap	$35.8 Billion	Shares	250,649,504
Book Value	$10.1 Billion	% Held	
Price/Book	3.55	85.49	
Price/Sales	4.38		

Business Summary: Specialty Chemicals (MIC: 8.3.2 SIC: 2813 NAIC: 325120)

Air Products and Chemicals serves energy, electronics, chemicals, metals, and manufacturing customers with solutions that include gases, equipment, and services. Co.'s Industrial Gases business produces atmospheric gases (oxygen, nitrogen, argon, and rare gases); process gases (hydrogen, helium, carbon dioxide, carbon monoxide, syngas, and specialty gases); and equipment for the production or processing of gases, such as air separation units and non-cryogenic generators. Co.'s industrial gases equipment business designs and manufactures equipment for air separation, hydrocarbon recovery and purification, natural gas liquefaction, and liquid helium and liquid hydrogen transport and storage.

Recent Developments: For the year ended Sep 30 2017, income from continuing operations increased 3.0% to US$1.16 billion from US$1.12 billion a year earlier. Net income increased 356.7% to US$3.02 billion from US$661.5 million in the prior year. Revenues were US$8.19 billion, up 9.1% from US$7.50 billion the year before. Operating income was US$1.43 billion versus US$1.53 billion in the prior year, a decrease of 6.7%. Direct operating expenses rose 11.1% to US$5.75 billion from US$5.18 billion in the comparable period the year before. Indirect operating expenses increased 26.2% to US$1.01 billion from US$797.4 million in the equivalent prior-year period.

Prospects: Our evaluation of Air Products & Chemicals Inc. as of Jan. 14, 2018 is the result of our systematic analysis on three basic characteristics: earnings strength, relative valuation, and recent stock price movement. The company has produced a positive trend in earnings per share over the past 5 quarters and while recent estimates for the company have been raised by analysts, APD has posted better than expected results. Based on operating earnings yield, the company is about fairly valued when compared to all of the companies in our coverage universe. Share price changes over the past year indicates that APD will perform in line with the market over the near term.

Financial Data
(US$ in Thousands)

	09/30/2017	09/30/2016	09/30/2015	09/30/2014	09/30/2013	09/30/2012	09/30/2011	09/30/2010
Earnings Per Share	13.65	2.89	5.88	4.61	4.68	5.44	5.63	4.74
Cash Flow Per Share	11.62	12.48	11.34	10.28	7.41	8.33	8.23	7.17
Tang Book Value Per Share	41.20	25.04	26.05	25.82	22.12	19.38	22.09	20.33
Dividends Per Share	3.620	2.530	3.200	3.020	2.770	2.500	2.230	1.920
Dividend Payout %	26.52	87.54	54.42	65.51	59.19	45.96	39.61	40.51
Income Statement								
Total Revenue	8,187,600	9,524,400	9,894,900	10,439,000	10,180,400	9,611,700	10,082,000	9,026,000
EBITDA	2,298,300	2,985,900	2,560,400	2,233,600	2,182,700	2,094,200	2,473,000	2,231,700
Depn & Amortn	843,200	893,000	900,400	914,800	864,700	817,200	856,500	846,100
Income Before Taxes	1,336,000	1,983,600	1,561,100	1,203,100	1,182,600	1,158,700	1,506,700	1,267,100
Income Taxes	260,900	586,500	415,900	366,000	307,900	287,300	408,400	339,500
Net Income	3,000,400	631,100	1,277,900	991,700	994,200	1,167,300	1,224,200	1,029,100
Average Shares	218,000	218,300	217,300	215,200	212,300	214,700	217,600	217,100
Balance Sheet								
Current Assets	5,876,700	4,317,300	2,910,800	3,294,800	3,439,100	3,415,800	3,189,800	3,033,800
Total Assets	18,467,200	18,055,300	17,438,100	17,779,100	17,850,100	16,941,800	14,290,700	13,505,900
Current Liabilities	2,489,000	3,283,300	3,648,100	2,963,000	3,227,600	2,689,900	2,342,000	2,244,100
Long-Term Obligations	3,402,400	4,918,100	3,949,100	4,824,500	5,056,300	4,584,200	3,927,500	3,659,800
Total Liabilities	8,381,000	10,975,700	10,189,100	10,413,300	10,808,000	10,464,600	8,494,900	7,959,000
Stockholders' Equity	10,086,200	7,079,600	7,249,000	7,365,800	7,042,100	6,477,200	5,795,800	5,546,900
Shares Outstanding	218,346	217,350	215,359	213,538	211,179	212,475	210,185	213,802
Statistical Record								
Return on Assets %	16.43	3.55	7.26	5.57	5.72	7.45	8.81	7.76
Return on Equity %	34.96	8.78	17.49	13.77	14.71	18.97	21.59	19.91
EBITDA Margin %	28.07	31.35	25.88	21.40	21.44	21.79	24.53	24.73
Net Margin %	36.65	6.63	12.91	9.50	9.77	12.14	12.14	11.40
Asset Turnover	0.45	0.54	0.56	0.59	0.59	0.61	0.73	0.68
Current Ratio	2.36	1.31	0.80	1.11	1.07	1.27	1.36	1.35
Debt to Equity	0.34	0.69	0.54	0.65	0.72	0.71	0.68	0.66
Price Range	151.53-132.26	145.52-107.53	146.19-110.04	126.03-94.84	101.71-71.27	85.68-68.29	90.41-69.15	78.31-59.92
P/E Ratio	11.10-9.69	50.35-37.21	24.86-18.71	27.34-20.57	21.73-15.23	15.75-12.55	16.06-12.28	16.52-12.64
Average Yield %	2.54	1.95	2.43	2.74	3.30	3.20	2.74	2.74

Address: 7201 Hamilton Boulevard, Allentown, PA 18195-1501 Telephone: 610-481-4911 Fax: 610-481-5900	Web Site: www.airproducts.com Officers: Seifollah (Seifi) Ghasemi - Chairman, President, Chief Executive Officer M. Scott Crocco - Chief Financial Officer, Executive Vice President, Senior Vice President, Vice President, Controller, Principal Accounting Officer	Auditors: KPMG LLP Investor Contact: 610-481-7461 Transfer Agents: Broadridge Corporate Issuer Solutions, Inc., Brentwood, NY

AK STEEL HOLDING CORP.

Exchange	Symbol	Price	52Wk Range	Yield	P/E
NYS	AKS	$5.66 (12/29/2017)	11.11-4.14	N/A	80.86

7 Year Price Score 77.90 *NYSE Composite Index=100   *12 Month Price Score 71.69

Interim Earnings (Per Share)

Qtr.	Mar	Jun	Sep	Dec
2014	(0.63)	(0.13)	(0.05)	0.14
2015	(1.72)	(0.36)	0.04	(0.81)
2016	(0.08)	0.08	0.21	(0.29)
2017	0.19	0.19	(0.02)	...

Interim Dividends (Per Share)
No Dividends Paid

Valuation Analysis | Institutional Holding

Forecast EPS	$0.25 (01/18/2018)	No of Institutions 405
Market Cap	$1.8 Billion	Shares
Book Value	N/A	252,404,944
Price/Book	N/A	% Held
Price/Sales	0.30	71.70

TRADING VOLUME (thousand shares)

Business Summary: Non-Precious Metals (MIC: 8.2.2 SIC: 3312 NAIC: 331111)

AK Steel Holding is a producer of flat-rolled carbon, stainless and electrical steels and tubular products through its subsidiary, AK Steel Corporation. Co.'s operations produce flat-rolled carbon to automotive manufacturers, stainless steels to manufacturers and their suppliers in the automotive industry and to manufacturers of food handling, chemical processing, pollution control, medical as well as health equipment, and electrical steels to manufacturers of power transmission and distribution transformers; in sheet and strip form, and carbon and stainless steel that Co. finishes into welded steel tubing. Co. also produces metallurgical coal through its AK Coal Resources, Inc. subsidiary.

Recent Developments: For the quarter ended Sep 30 2017, net income decreased 83.6% to US$11.3 million from US$68.9 million in the year-earlier quarter. Revenues were US$1.49 billion, up 2.8% from US$1.45 billion the year before. Operating income was US$37.8 million versus US$130.8 million in the prior-year quarter, a decrease of 71.1%. Direct operating expenses rose 12.8% to US$1.35 billion from US$1.19 billion in the comparable period the year before. Indirect operating expenses decreased 14.5% to US$109.5 million from US$128.0 million in the equivalent prior-year period.

Prospects: Our evaluation of AK Steel Holding Corp. as of Jan. 14, 2018 is the result of our systematic analysis on three basic characteristics: earnings strength, relative valuation, and recent stock price movement. The company has suffered a very negative trend in earnings per share over the past 5 quarters and while recent estimates for the company have been mixed, AKS has posted results that fell short of analysts expectations. Based on operating earnings yield, the company is about fairly valued when compared to all of the companies in our coverage universe. Share price changes over the past year indicates that AKS will perform very poorly over the near term.

Financial Data

(US$ in Thousands)	9 Mos	6 Mos	3 Mos	12/31/2016	12/31/2015	12/31/2014	12/31/2013	12/31/2012
Earnings Per Share	0.07	0.30	0.19	(0.03)	(2.86)	(0.65)	(0.34)	(9.06)
Cash Flow Per Share	0.54	0.75	0.65	1.32	1.13	(2.18)	(0.81)	(2.39)
Dividends Per Share	...	...	...	...	...	...	...	0.100
Income Statement								
Total Revenue	4,584,900	3,090,600	1,533,400	5,882,500	6,692,900	6,505,700	5,570,400	5,933,700
EBITDA	426,700	332,500	167,000	441,900	6,200	320,200	324,500	70,100
Depn & Amortn	186,100	121,900	62,300	216,600	216,000	201,900	190,100	192,000
Income Before Taxes	125,500	133,000	65,300	61,400	(382,800)	(26,400)	7,000	(208,600)
Income Taxes	(40,900)	(22,100)	(13,400)	3,200	63,400	7,700	(10,400)	790,000
Net Income	117,900	123,700	62,500	(7,800)	(509,000)	(96,900)	(46,800)	(1,027,300)
Average Shares	314,300	319,000	325,600	230,000	177,200	148,100	135,800	113,000
Balance Sheet								
Current Assets	1,932,400	1,854,400	1,923,700	1,823,700	1,806,200	2,025,700	1,273,200	1,442,700
Total Assets	4,459,300	4,005,600	4,104,400	4,036,000	4,084,400	4,858,500	3,605,700	3,903,100
Current Liabilities	1,004,400	927,000	1,037,900	865,300	1,042,600	1,125,200	831,400	812,400
Long-Term Obligations	2,098,200	1,689,700	1,684,500	1,816,600	2,354,100	2,452,500	1,506,200	1,411,200
Total Liabilities	4,636,000	4,172,400	4,333,600	4,308,200	5,062,000	5,351,000	3,826,700	4,408,400
Stockholders' Equity	(176,700)	(166,800)	(229,200)	(272,200)	(977,600)	(492,500)	(221,000)	(505,300)
Shares Outstanding	314,848	314,817	314,785	314,160	177,893	177,215	136,380	135,944
Statistical Record								
Return on Assets %	1.32	2.83	1.69	N.M.	N.M.	N.M.	N.M.	N.M.
EBITDA Margin %	9.31	10.76	10.89	7.51	0.09	4.92	5.83	1.18
Net Margin %	2.57	4.00	4.08	N.M.	N.M.	N.M.	N.M.	N.M.
Asset Turnover	1.43	1.50	1.46	1.44	1.50	1.54	1.48	1.42
Current Ratio	1.92	2.00	1.85	2.11	1.73	1.80	1.53	1.78
Price Range	11.11-4.51	11.11-4.06	11.11-3.40	10.95-1.83	5.97-2.04	11.19-5.20	8.20-2.82	10.04-3.57
P/E Ratio	158.71-64.43	37.03-13.53	58.47-17.89	...	...	...	...	...
Average Yield %	...	...	...	...	...	...	...	1.60

Address: 9227 Centre Pointe Drive, West Chester, OH 45069 **Telephone:** 513-425-5000 **Fax:** 513-425-5220	**Web Site:** www.aksteel.com **Officers:** Roger K. Newport - Executive Vice President, Senior Vice President, Vice President, Vice President, Chief Financial Officer, Chief Executive Officer Jaime Vasquez - Vice President, Chief Financial Officer	**Auditors:** Ernst & Young LLP **Investor Contact:** 513-425-5270 **Transfer Agents:** Computershare Investor Services, LLC, Canton, MA

ALASKA AIR GROUP, INC.

Exchange	Symbol	Price	52Wk Range	Yield	P/E
NYS	ALK	$73.51 (12/29/2017)	100.24-61.68	1.63	11.82

*7 Year Price Score 135.25 *NYSE Composite Index=100 *12 Month Price Score 77.02

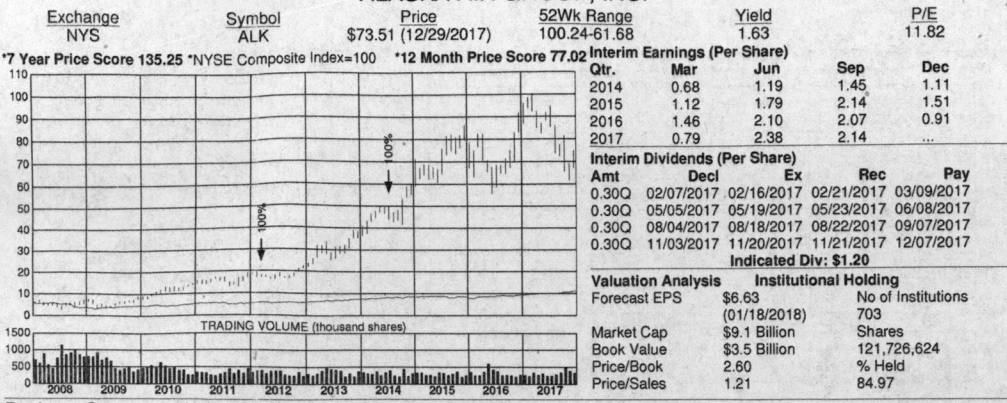

Interim Earnings (Per Share)

Qtr.	Mar	Jun	Sep	Dec
2014	0.68	1.19	1.45	1.11
2015	1.12	1.79	2.14	1.51
2016	1.46	2.10	2.07	0.91
2017	0.79	2.38	2.14	...

Interim Dividends (Per Share)

Amt	Decl	Ex	Rec	Pay
0.30Q	02/07/2017	02/16/2017	02/21/2017	03/09/2017
0.30Q	05/05/2017	05/19/2017	05/23/2017	06/08/2017
0.30Q	08/04/2017	08/18/2017	08/22/2017	09/07/2017
0.30Q	11/03/2017	11/20/2017	11/21/2017	12/07/2017

Indicated Div: $1.20

Valuation Analysis

		Institutional Holding	
Forecast EPS	$6.63 (01/18/2018)	No of Institutions	703
Market Cap	$9.1 Billion	Shares	121,726,624
Book Value	$3.5 Billion	% Held	84.97
Price/Book	2.60		
Price/Sales	1.21		

Business Summary: Airlines/Air Freight (MIC: 7.4.4 SIC: 4512 NAIC: 481111)

Alaska Air Group is a holding company. Co.'s Alaska Airlines, Inc. (Alaska) and Virgin America Inc. subsidiaries operate fleets of passenger jets (mainline operations). Alaska also contracts with Co.'s Horizon Air Industries, Inc (Horizon) subsidiary, SkyWest Airlines, Inc. and Peninsula Airways, Inc. for regional capacity. Horizon operates a fleet of turboprop aircraft and sells its capacity to Alaska under a capacity purchase arrangement. Co.'s mainline operations provide passenger service from the western U.S. throughout the contiguous U.S., Alaska, Hawaii, Canada, Mexico, Costa Rica and Cuba; and regional operations carry passengers mainly in Washington, Oregon, Idaho and California.

Recent Developments: For the quarter ended Sep 30 2017, net income increased 3.9% to US$266.0 million from US$256.0 million in the year-earlier quarter. Revenues were US$2.12 billion, up 35.4% from US$1.57 billion the year before. Operating income was US$439.0 million versus US$400.0 million in the prior-year quarter, an increase of 9.8%. Direct operating expenses rose 54.4% to US$806.0 million from US$522.0 million in the comparable period the year before. Indirect operating expenses increased 35.9% to US$875.0 million from US$644.0 million in the equivalent prior-year period.

Prospects: Our evaluation of Alaska Air Group Inc. as of Jan. 14, 2018 is the result of our systematic analysis on three basic characteristics: earnings strength, relative valuation, and recent stock price movement. The company has generated a negative trend in earnings per share over the past 5 quarters. However, while recent estimates for the company have been mixed, ALK has posted results that fell short of analysts expectations. Based on operating earnings yield, the company is undervalued when compared to all of the companies in our coverage universe. Share price changes over the past year indicates that ALK will perform poorly over the near term.

Financial Data (US$ in Thousands)	9 Mos	6 Mos	3 Mos	12/31/2016	12/31/2015	12/31/2014	12/31/2013	12/31/2012
Earnings Per Share	6.22	6.15	5.87	6.54	6.56	4.42	3.58	2.20
Cash Flow Per Share	12.45	12.71	10.78	11.19	12.34	7.60	7.01	5.31
Tang Book Value Per Share	11.52	9.61	7.54	6.92	19.26	16.18	14.76	10.10
Dividends Per Share	1.175	1.150	1.125	1.100	0.800	0.500	0.200	...
Dividend Payout %	18.89	18.70	19.17	16.82	12.20	11.31	5.59	...
Income Statement								
Total Revenue	5,971,000	3,851,000	1,749,000	5,931,000	5,598,000	5,368,000	5,156,000	4,657,000
EBITDA	1,372,000	838,000	256,000	1,711,000	1,619,000	1,276,000	1,103,000	805,000
Depn & Amortn	275,000	180,000	90,000	363,000	320,000	294,000	270,000	264,000
Income Before Taxes	1,058,000	631,000	152,000	1,345,000	1,312,000	975,000	816,000	514,000
Income Taxes	397,000	236,000	53,000	531,000	464,000	370,000	308,000	198,000
Net Income	661,000	395,000	99,000	814,000	848,000	605,000	508,000	316,000
Average Shares	124,220	124,332	124,299	124,389	129,372	136,801	141,878	143,568
Balance Sheet								
Current Assets	2,214,000	2,425,000	2,213,000	2,050,000	1,663,000	1,756,000	1,762,000	1,737,000
Total Assets	10,739,000	10,720,000	10,302,000	9,962,000	6,533,000	6,181,000	5,838,000	5,505,000
Current Liabilities	2,765,000	2,974,000	2,835,000	2,535,000	1,806,000	1,671,000	1,580,000	1,501,000
Long-Term Obligations	2,367,000	2,469,000	2,531,000	2,645,000	571,000	686,000	754,000	871,000
Total Liabilities	7,248,000	7,456,000	7,288,000	7,031,000	4,122,000	4,054,000	3,809,000	4,084,000
Stockholders' Equity	3,491,000	3,264,000	3,014,000	2,931,000	2,411,000	2,127,000	2,029,000	1,421,000
Shares Outstanding	123,387	123,520	123,729	123,328	125,175	131,481	137,491	140,753
Statistical Record								
Return on Assets %	7.97	8.62	8.51	9.84	13.34	10.07	8.96	5.89
Return on Equity %	24.39	25.97	26.66	30.39	37.37	29.11	29.45	24.30
EBITDA Margin %	22.98	21.76	14.64	28.85	28.92	23.77	21.39	17.29
Net Margin %	11.07	10.26	5.66	13.72	15.15	11.27	9.85	6.79
Asset Turnover	0.77	0.78	0.74	0.72	0.88	0.89	0.91	0.87
Current Ratio	0.80	0.82	0.78	0.81	0.92	1.05	1.12	1.16
Debt to Equity	0.68	0.76	0.84	0.90	0.24	0.32	0.37	0.61
Price Range	100.24-65.86	100.24-58.29	100.24-55.66	91.56-55.66	86.33-58.77	59.77-36.59	39.09-21.55	22.46-16.10
P/E Ratio	16.12-10.59	16.30-9.48	17.08-9.48	14.00-8.51	13.16-8.96	13.52-8.28	10.92-6.02	10.21-7.32
Average Yield %	1.37	1.41	1.46	1.53	1.12	1.06	0.66	...

Address: 19300 International Boulevard, Seattle, WA 98188 Telephone: 206-392-5040	Web Site: www.alaskaair.com Officers: Bradley D. Tilden - Chairman, Chief Executive Officer Brandon S. Pedersen - Vice President, Chief Financial Officer, Controller	Auditors: KPMG LLP Investor Contact: 206-392-5260 Transfer Agents: Computershare Trust Company N.A., Providence, RI

19

ALBEMARLE CORP.

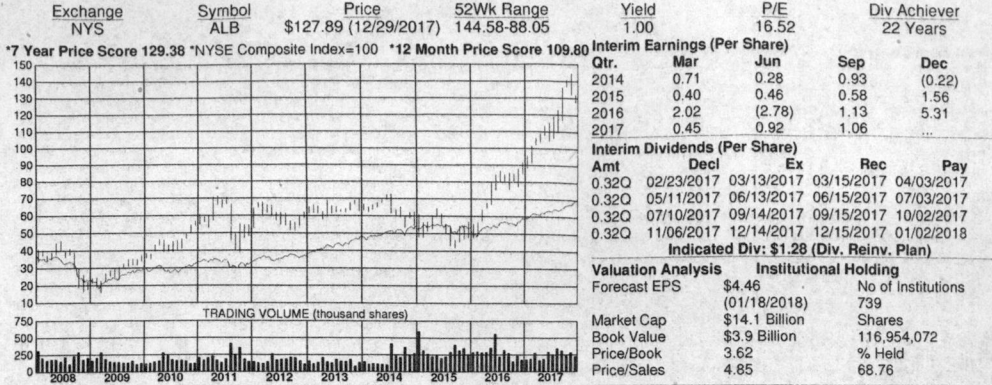

Exchange	Symbol	Price	52Wk Range	Yield	P/E	Div Achiever
NYS	ALB	$127.89 (12/29/2017)	144.58-88.05	1.00	16.52	22 Years

*7 Year Price Score 129.38 *NYSE Composite Index=100 *12 Month Price Score 109.80

Interim Earnings (Per Share)

Qtr.	Mar	Jun	Sep	Dec
2014	0.71	0.28	0.93	(0.22)
2015	0.40	0.46	0.58	1.56
2016	2.02	(2.78)	1.13	5.31
2017	0.45	0.92	1.06	...

Interim Dividends (Per Share)

Amt	Decl	Ex	Rec	Pay
0.32Q	02/23/2017	03/13/2017	03/15/2017	04/03/2017
0.32Q	05/11/2017	06/13/2017	06/15/2017	07/03/2017
0.32Q	07/10/2017	09/14/2017	09/15/2017	10/02/2017
0.32Q	11/06/2017	12/14/2017	12/15/2017	01/02/2018

Indicated Div: $1.28 (Div. Reinv. Plan)

TRADING VOLUME (thousand shares)

Valuation Analysis		Institutional Holding	
Forecast EPS	$4.46 (01/18/2018)	No of Institutions	739
Market Cap	$14.1 Billion	Shares	116,954,072
Book Value	$3.9 Billion	% Held	68.76
Price/Book	3.62		
Price/Sales	4.85		

Business Summary: Specialty Chemicals (MIC: 8.3.2 SIC: 2821 NAIC: 325211)

Albemarle is a developer, manufacturer and marketer of chemicals across a range of end markets including, among others, the petroleum refining, consumer electronics, energy storage, construction, automotive, lubricants, and pharmaceuticals. Co.'s segments include: Lithium and Advanced Materials, which consisted of Lithium and Performance Catalyst Solutions; Bromine Specialties, which includes products used in fire safety solutions and other specialty chemicals applications; and Refining Solutions, which consisted of two main product lines: Clean Fuels Technologies composed of hydroprocessing catalysts, and Heavy Oil Upgrading composed of fluidized catalytic cracking catalysts and additives.

Recent Developments: For the quarter ended Sep 30 2017, income from continuing operations increased 13.7% to US$130.2 million from US$114.5 million in the year-earlier quarter. Net income decreased 5.4% to US$130.2 million from US$137.7 million in the year-earlier quarter. Revenues were US$754.9 million, up 15.4% from US$654.0 million the year before. Operating income was US$148.4 million versus US$124.9 million in the prior-year quarter, an increase of 18.8%. Direct operating expenses rose 15.4% to US$479.1 million from US$415.0 million in the comparable period the year before. Indirect operating expenses increased 11.6% to US$127.3 million from US$114.1 million in the equivalent prior-year period.

Prospects: Our evaluation of Albemarle Corp. as of Jan. 14, 2018 is the result of our systematic analysis on three basic characteristics: earnings strength, relative valuation, and recent stock price movement. The company has enjoyed a very positive trend in earnings per share over the past 5 quarters. However, while recent estimates for the company have been mixed, ALB has posted better than expected results. Based on operating earnings yield, the company is about fairly valued when compared to all of the companies in our coverage universe. Share price changes over the past year indicates that ALB will perform very well over the near term.

Financial Data

(US$ in Thousands)	9 Mos	6 Mos	3 Mos	12/31/2016	12/31/2015	12/31/2014	12/31/2013	12/31/2012
Earnings Per Share	7.74	7.81	4.11	5.68	3.00	1.69	4.90	3.47
Cash Flow Per Share	3.22	3.85	5.74	6.51	3.24	6.26	5.16	5.47
Tang Book Value Per Share	16.89	15.91	15.19	16.89	N.M.	13.74	15.68	16.45
Dividends Per Share	1.265	1.250	1.235	1.220	1.160	1.100	0.960	0.800
Dividend Payout %	16.34	16.01	30.05	21.48	38.67	65.09	19.59	23.05
Income Statement								
Total Revenue	2,214,187	1,459,321	722,063	2,677,293	3,651,335	2,445,548	2,616,416	2,745,420
EBITDA	547,854	352,523	167,040	759,245	671,609	352,437	675,286	495,693
Depn & Amortn	144,087	94,192	45,070	178,800	180,700	97,900	99,300	88,300
Income Before Taxes	304,872	175,228	53,457	515,264	358,187	213,179	544,427	374,593
Income Taxes	53,596	35,101	11,971	96,263	29,122	18,484	136,322	82,533
Net Income	273,216	154,546	51,213	643,675	334,906	133,316	413,171	311,536
Average Shares	111,975	112,105	113,289	113,239	111,556	79,102	84,322	89,884
Balance Sheet								
Current Assets	2,327,324	2,204,448	2,390,254	3,306,618	1,831,003	3,348,850	1,482,915	1,407,313
Total Assets	7,523,300	7,291,989	7,366,468	8,161,207	9,615,014	5,223,103	3,584,797	3,437,291
Current Liabilities	1,103,017	983,662	1,207,947	1,140,103	1,616,685	1,139,886	436,363	385,009
Long-Term Obligations	1,407,171	1,421,468	1,398,386	2,121,718	3,174,674	2,223,035	1,054,310	686,588
Total Liabilities	3,624,481	3,531,159	3,728,799	4,366,145	6,360,622	3,863,638	1,957,436	1,603,693
Stockholders' Equity	3,898,819	3,760,830	3,637,669	3,795,062	3,254,392	1,359,465	1,627,361	1,833,598
Shares Outstanding	110,495	110,391	110,752	112,523	112,219	78,030	80,052	88,899
Statistical Record								
Return on Assets %	10.35	10.66	5.55	7.22	4.51	3.03	11.77	9.36
Return on Equity %	24.32	25.58	13.00	18.21	14.52	8.93	23.88	18.14
EBITDA Margin %	24.74	24.16	23.13	28.36	18.39	14.41	25.81	18.06
Net Margin %	12.34	10.59	7.09	24.04	9.17	5.45	15.79	11.35
Asset Turnover	0.34	0.34	0.33	0.30	0.49	0.56	0.75	0.82
Current Ratio	2.11	2.24	1.98	2.90	1.13	2.94	3.40	3.66
Debt to Equity	0.36	0.38	0.38	0.56	0.98	1.64	0.65	0.37
Price Range	136.31-77.08	115.40-75.72	106.21-63.93	91.80-47.71	64.38-41.78	72.62-53.16	69.55-57.75	67.70-51.56
P/E Ratio	17.61-9.96	14.78-9.70	25.84-15.55	16.16-8.40	21.46-13.93	42.97-31.46	14.19-11.79	19.51-14.86
Average Yield %	1.24	1.34	1.47	1.65	2.16	1.71	1.50	1.34

Address: 4350 Congress Street, Suite 700, Charlotte, NC 28209
Telephone: 980-299-5700

Web Site: www.albemarle.com
Officers: Luther C. Kissam - Chairman, President, President (frmr), Chief Executive Officer, Principal Financial Officer, Principal Executive Officer Scott A. Tozier - Executive Vice President, Senior Vice President, Chief Financial Officer, Chief Risk Officer, Principal Accounting Officer

Auditors: PricewaterhouseCoopers LLP
Investor Contact: 225-388-8011
Transfer Agents: Wells Fargo Bank, N.A. Shareowner Services, St. Paul, MN

ALCOA CORPORATION

Exchange	Symbol	Price	52Wk Range	Yield	P/E
NYS	AA	$53.87 (12/29/2017)	54.14-28.83	N/A	37.15

*7 Year Price Score N/A   *NYSE Composite Index=100   *12 Month Price Score 112.16

TRADING VOLUME (thousand shares)

Interim Earnings (Per Share)

Qtr.	Mar	Jun	Sep	Dec
2016	(1.15)	(0.29)	(0.04)	(0.76)
2017	1.21	0.40	0.60	...

Interim Dividends (Per Share)

No Dividends Paid

Valuation Analysis		Institutional Holding	
Forecast EPS	$3.71	No of Institutions	
	(01/26/2018)	N/A	
Market Cap	$10.0 Billion	Shares	
Book Value	$5.9 Billion	N/A	
Price/Book	1.70	% Held	
Price/Sales	0.90	N/A	

Business Summary: Metal Products (MIC: 8.2.3 SIC: 3353 NAIC: 331315)

Alcoa is a vertically integrated aluminum company which comprised of bauxite mining, alumina refining, aluminum production (smelting, casting, and rolling), and energy generation. As of Dec 31 2016, Co. had 43 operating locations in 10 countries around the world, primarily in Australia, Brazil, Canada, Europe, and the U.S.

Recent Developments: For the quarter ended Sep 30 2017, net income increased to US$169.0 million from US$10.0 million in the year-earlier quarter. Revenues were US$2.96 billion, up 27.3% from US$2.33 billion the year before. Direct operating expenses rose 20.0% to US$2.36 billion from US$1.97 billion in the comparable period the year before. Indirect operating expenses increased 21.6% to US$315.0 million from US$259.0 million in the equivalent prior-year period.

Prospects: Our evaluation of Alcoa Corporation as of Jan. 21, 2018 is the result of our systematic analysis on three basic characteristics: earnings strength, relative valuation, and recent stock price movement. The company has suffered a very negative trend in earnings per share over the past 5 quarters and while recent estimates for the company have been raised by analysts, AA has posted results that fell short of analysts expectations. Based on operating earnings yield, the company is undervalued when compared to all of the companies in our coverage universe. Share price changes over the past year indicates that AA will perform in line with the market over the near term.

Financial Data
(US$ in Thousands)

	9 Mos	6 Mos	3 Mos	12/31/2016	12/31/2015	12/31/2014	12/31/2013
Earnings Per Share	1.45	0.81	0.12	(2.19)	...	...	...
Cash Flow Per Share	5.45	2.80	0.66	(1.69)	...	...	...
Tang Book Value Per Share	31.68	32.30	31.89	30.91	...	...	...
Income Statement							
Total Revenue	8,478,000	5,514,000	2,655,000	9,318,000	11,199,000	13,147,000	12,573,000
EBITDA	1,584,000	1,075,000	623,000	799,000	713,000	1,200,000	(1,416,000)
Depn & Amortn	564,000	369,000	179,000	718,000	780,000	954,000	1,026,000
Income Before Taxes	943,000	655,000	418,000	(162,000)	(337,000)	(63,000)	(2,747,000)
Income Taxes	328,000	209,000	110,000	184,000	402,000	284,000	123,000
Net Income	413,000	300,000	225,000	(400,000)	(863,000)	(256,000)	(2,909,000)
Average Shares	187,000	186,000	186,000	183,000	...	...	...
Balance Sheet							
Current Assets	3,804,000	3,583,000	3,404,000	3,181,000	2,566,000	2,917,000	...
Total Assets	17,254,000	16,929,000	17,076,000	16,741,000	16,413,000	18,680,000	...
Current Liabilities	2,766,000	2,608,000	2,623,000	2,821,000	2,404,000	2,735,000	...
Long-Term Obligations	1,384,000	1,418,000	1,431,000	1,424,000	207,000	313,000	...
Total Liabilities	11,392,000	10,975,000	11,200,000	11,087,000	6,971,000	8,081,000	...
Stockholders' Equity	5,862,000	5,954,000	5,876,000	5,654,000	9,442,000	10,599,000	...
Shares Outstanding	185,022	184,339	184,240	182,930	...	...	...
Statistical Record							
Return on Assets %	1.59	...	...	N.M.	N.M.	...	...
Return on Equity %	4.27	...	...	N.M.	N.M.	...	...
EBITDA Margin %	18.68	19.50	23.47	8.57	6.37	9.13	N.M.
Net Margin %	4.87	5.44	8.47	N.M.	N.M.	N.M.	N.M.
Asset Turnover	0.64	...	...	0.56	0.64	...	...
Current Ratio	1.38	1.37	1.30	1.13	1.07	1.07	...
Debt to Equity	0.24	0.24	0.24	0.25	0.02	0.03	...
Price Range	47.50-22.91	38.56-22.91	38.56-22.91	32.05-22.91	...	...	...
P/E Ratio	32.76-15.80	47.60-28.28	321.33-190.92	...	...	...	...

Address: 201 Isabella Street, Pittsburgh, PA 15212-5858 Telephone: 412-315-2900	Web Site: www.alcoa.com Officers: Roy C. Harvey - President, Chief Executive Officer William F. Oplinger - Executive Vice President, Chief Financial Officer	Auditors: PricewaterhouseCoopers LLP Transfer Agents: Computershare Trust Company, N.A.

ALEXANDER & BALDWIN INC (REIT)

Exchange	Symbol	Price	52Wk Range	Yield	P/E
NYS	ALEX	$27.74 (12/29/2017)	46.87-27.62	N/A	74.97

*7 Year Price Score N/A   *NYSE Composite Index=100   *12 Month Price Score 73.78

Interim Earnings (Per Share)

Qtr.	Mar	Jun	Sep	Dec
2014	0.68	0.19	0.21	0.18
2015	0.51	0.20	0.11	(0.28)
2016	(0.15)	(0.01)	(0.03)	0.01
2017	0.14	0.09	0.13	...

Interim Dividends (Per Share)

Amt	Decl	Ex	Rec	Pay
15.92Sp	11/16/2017	11/28/2017	11/29/2017	01/23/2018

Valuation Analysis		Institutional Holding	
Forecast EPS	$0.50 (01/17/2018)	No of Institutions	N/A
Market Cap	$1.4 Billion	Shares	
Book Value	$1.2 Billion		N/A
Price/Book	1.12	% Held	N/A
Price/Sales	4.01		N/A

TRADING VOLUME (thousand shares)

Business Summary: REITs (MIC: 5.3.1 SIC: 6798 NAIC: 525930)

Alexander & Baldwin is a Hawaii real estate company. Co. operates in three segments: Commercial Real Estate, which owns, operates and manages retail, industrial and office properties in Hawaii and on the Mainland, and leases urban land in Hawaii to third-party lessees; Land Operations, which engages in planning, zoning, financing, constructing, purchasing, managing, selling, and investing in real property, renewable energy and diversified agribusiness activities; and Materials and Construction, which includes asphalt paving as prime contractor and subcontractor, imports and sells liquid asphalt, and manufactures and sells precast concrete products.

Recent Developments: For the quarter ended Sep 30 2017, income from continuing operations decreased 39.3% to US$7.4 million from US$12.2 million in the year-earlier quarter. Net income amounted to US$6.6 million versus a net loss of US$1.4 million in the year-earlier quarter. Revenues were US$111.5 million, up 8.4% from US$102.9 million the year before. Revenues from property income rose 11.2% to US$56.5 million from US$50.8 million in the corresponding quarter a year earlier.

Prospects: Our evaluation of Alexander & Baldwin Inc. (REIT) as of Jan. 14, 2018 is the result of our systematic analysis on three basic characteristics: earnings strength, relative valuation, and recent stock price movement. The company has suffered a very negative trend in earnings per share over the past 5 quarters. However, while recent estimates for the company have been mixed, ALEX has posted better than expected results. Based on operating earnings yield, the company is overvalued when compared to all of the companies in our coverage universe. Share price changes over the past year indicates that ALEX will perform well over the near term.

Financial Data
(US$ in Thousands)

	9 Mos	6 Mos	3 Mos	12/31/2016	12/31/2015	12/31/2014	12/31/2013	12/31/2012
Earnings Per Share	0.37	0.21	0.11	(0.18)	0.54	1.25	0.82	0.48
Cash Flow Per Share	0.36	1.32	1.94	2.26	2.63	0.80	(0.86)	0.26
Tang Book Value Per Share	21.71	21.56	21.52	21.71	22.06	21.26	20.42	21.31
Dividends Per Share	0.280	0.270	0.260	0.250	...	...	...	...
Dividend Payout %	75.68	128.57	236.36	...	...	...	...	...
Income Statement								
Total Revenue	302,800	191,300	93,200	387,500	570,500	560,000	365,200	296,700
EBITDA	68,600	42,500	9,000	165,200	117,000	106,700	81,700	66,400
Depn & Amortn	31,400	21,000	...	106,100	43,800	55,000	41,700	35,100
Income Before Taxes	22,400	11,300	3,800	35,300	47,600	28,800	23,600	16,500
Income Taxes	6,400	2,700	(800)	2,600	16,500	(1,400)	8,500	(1,200)
Net Income	16,700	10,600	6,300	(10,200)	29,600	61,400	36,900	20,500
Average Shares	49,600	49,600	49,600	49,400	49,300	49,300	45,100	42,900
Balance Sheet								
Current Assets	239,800	159,000	130,600	138,300	152,500	175,900	171,400	63,400
Total Assets	2,208,300	2,177,000	2,160,600	2,156,300	2,243,500	2,329,900	2,285,200	1,437,300
Current Liabilities	129,600	128,200	130,900	165,100	184,700	183,000	218,200	69,600
Long-Term Obligations	584,200	530,800	511,200	472,700	497,800	631,500	605,500	220,000
Total Liabilities	989,400	963,600	950,000	936,200	1,008,300	1,126,000	1,119,300	522,900
Stockholders' Equity	1,218,900	1,213,400	1,210,600	1,220,100	1,235,200	1,203,900	1,165,900	914,400
Shares Outstanding	49,200	49,200	49,100	49,000	48,900	48,800	48,600	42,900
Statistical Record								
Return on Assets %	0.75	0.39	0.16	N.M.	1.29	2.66	1.98	...
Return on Equity %	1.37	0.71	0.30	N.M.	2.43	5.18	3.55	...
EBITDA Margin %	22.66	22.22	9.66	42.63	20.51	19.05	22.37	22.38
Net Margin %	5.52	5.54	6.76	N.M.	5.19	10.96	10.10	6.91
Asset Turnover	0.15	0.17	0.17	0.18	0.25	0.24	0.20	...
Current Ratio	1.85	1.24	1.00	0.84	0.83	0.96	0.79	0.91
Debt to Equity	0.48	0.44	0.42	0.39	0.40	0.52	0.52	0.24
Price Range	46.58-37.08	46.58-35.25	46.10-34.43	46.09-29.30	43.52-33.34	44.56-34.74	45.92-29.21	34.25-25.30
P/E Ratio	125.89-100.22	221.81-167.86	419.09-313.00	...	80.59-61.74	35.65-27.79	56.00-35.62	71.35-52.71
Average Yield %	0.65	0.64	0.64	0.66	...	...	...	...

Address: 822 Bishop Street, Honolulu, HI 96813 Telephone: 808-525-6611	Web Site: www.alexanderbaldwin.com Officers: Stanley M. Kuriyama - Chairman, President, Chief Executive Officer Christopher J. Benjamin - President, Chief Executive Officer, Chief Operating Officer	Auditors: Deloitte & Touche LLP Transfer Agents: Computershare Shareowner Services LLC

22

ALEXANDRIA REAL ESTATE EQUITIES INC

Exchange	Symbol	Price	52Wk Range	Yield	P/E
NYS	ARE	$130.59 (12/29/2017)	134.03-108.18	2.76	146.73

*7 Year Price Score 108.40 *NYSE Composite Index=100 *12 Month Price Score 101.63

Interim Earnings (Per Share)

Qtr.	Mar	Jun	Sep	Dec
2014	0.46	0.39	0.39	(0.23)
2015	0.25	0.44	0.46	0.49
2016	(0.05)	(1.72)	0.07	(0.30)
2017	0.29	0.35	0.55	...

Interim Dividends (Per Share)

Amt	Decl	Ex	Rec	Pay
0.83Q	03/06/2017	03/29/2017	03/31/2017	04/17/2017
0.86Q	06/05/2017	06/28/2017	06/30/2017	07/17/2017
0.86Q	09/06/2017	09/28/2017	09/29/2017	10/16/2017
0.90Q	12/04/2017	12/28/2017	12/29/2017	01/15/2018

Indicated Div: $3.60

Valuation Analysis		Institutional Holding	
Forecast EPS	$1.61 (01/18/2018)	No of Institutions	499
Market Cap	$12.5 Billion	Shares	116,189,392
Book Value	$5.4 Billion	% Held	98.01
Price/Book	2.31		
Price/Sales	11.59		

Business Summary: REITs (MIC: 5.3.1 SIC: 6798 NAIC: 525930)

Alexandria Real Estate Equities is an urban office Real Estate Investment Trust focused on collaborative life science and technology campuses in AAA innovation cluster locations. Co. is engaged in the business of providing space for lease to the life science and technology industries. Co. has market presence in key locations, including Greater Boston, San Francisco, New York City, San Diego, Seattle, Maryland, and Research Triangle Park. As of Dec 31 2016, Co. had 199 properties in North America containing of operating properties and development and redevelopment of new Class A properties (under construction or pre-construction), of which 44.0% were single-tenant properties.

Recent Developments: For the quarter ended Sep 30 2017, net income increased 108.5% to US$59.5 million from US$28.6 million in the year-earlier quarter. Revenues were US$285.4 million, up 23.9% from US$230.4 million the year before. Revenues from property income rose 25.7% to US$283.1 million from US$225.3 million in the corresponding quarter a year earlier.

Prospects: Our evaluation of Alexandria Real Estate Equities Inc. as of Jan. 14, 2018 is the result of our systematic analysis on three basic characteristics: earnings strength, relative valuation, and recent stock price movement. The company has enjoyed a very positive trend in earnings per share over the past 5 quarters. Because the company lacks sufficient analyst estimate data, we place greater weight on the historical EPS trend as the measure of earnings strength. Based on operating earnings yield, the company is overvalued when compared to all of the companies in our coverage universe. Share price changes over the past year indicates that ARE will perform very well over the near term.

Financial Data

(US$ in Thousands)	9 Mos	6 Mos	3 Mos	12/31/2016	12/31/2015	12/31/2014	12/31/2013	12/31/2012
Earnings Per Share	0.89	0.41	(1.66)	(1.99)	1.63	1.01	1.60	1.09
Cash Flow Per Share	4.94	4.90	4.52	5.14	4.79	4.70	4.60	4.90
Tang Book Value Per Share	55.71	55.19	54.27	53.37	49.73	48.43	49.69	48.41
Dividends Per Share	3.380	3.320	3.260	3.230	3.050	2.880	2.610	2.090
Dividend Payout %	379.78	809.76	...	...	187.12	285.15	163.13	191.74
Income Statement								
Total Revenue	829,306	543,936	270,877	921,706	843,474	726,877	631,151	586,073
EBITDA	217,526	143,406	73,648	376,287	516,121	410,164	400,404	369,778
Depn & Amortn	(8,203)	(5,846)	(3,060)	319,039	265,802	232,277	197,927	199,148
Income Before Taxes	133,166	87,720	46,924	(49,705)	144,506	98,588	134,525	101,446
Net Income	129,705	75,932	41,711	(65,901)	144,217	101,574	136,217	102,126
Average Shares	93,296	90,745	88,200	76,103	71,528	71,169	68,038	62,160
Balance Sheet								
Current Assets	156,174	153,272	179,508	151,110	164,455	123,443	95,323	189,367
Total Assets	11,545,323	11,245,667	10,868,626	10,354,888	8,911,120	8,136,036	7,529,764	7,150,116
Current Liabilities	823,472	815,791	861,613	808,585	651,361	547,899	489,762	465,109
Long-Term Obligations	4,817,040	4,775,385	4,430,686	4,164,025	3,965,795	3,678,579	3,061,061	3,181,949
Total Liabilities	6,138,353	6,088,503	5,916,195	5,459,092	4,936,033	4,307,597	3,612,975	3,708,265
Stockholders' Equity	5,406,970	5,157,164	4,952,431	4,895,796	3,975,087	3,828,439	3,916,789	3,441,851
Shares Outstanding	95,717	92,100	89,884	87,665	72,548	71,463	71,172	63,244
Statistical Record								
Return on Assets %	1.39	1.13	N.M.	N.M.	1.69	1.30	1.86	1.48
Return on Equity %	3.11	2.52	N.M.	N.M.	3.70	2.62	3.70	2.99
EBITDA Margin %	26.23	26.36	27.19	40.83	61.19	56.43	63.44	63.09
Net Margin %	15.64	13.96	15.40	N.M.	17.10	13.97	21.58	17.43
Asset Turnover	0.10	0.10	0.10	0.10	0.10	0.09	0.09	0.09
Current Ratio	0.19	0.19	0.21	0.19	0.25	0.23	0.19	0.41
Debt to Equity	0.89	0.93	0.89	0.85	1.00	0.96	0.78	0.92
Price Range	122.09-101.92	121.60-101.27	120.47-89.79	114.52-71.65	102.42-83.40	90.19-63.62	78.09-61.02	76.65-64.75
P/E Ratio	137.18-114.52	296.59-247.00	...	...	62.83-51.17	89.30-62.99	48.81-38.14	70.32-59.40
Average Yield %	2.96	2.98	3.07	3.28	3.30	3.75	3.83	2.91

Address: 385 East Colorado Boulevard, Suite 299, Pasadena, CA 91101 Telephone: 626-578-0777	Web Site: www.are.com Officers: Joel S. Marcus - Chairman, President, Chief Executive Officer Dean A. Shigenaga - Executive Vice President, Chief Financial Officer, Treasurer	Auditors: Ernst & Young LLP Investor Contact: 626-396-4828 Transfer Agents: American Stock Transfer & Trust Company, LLC, Brooklyn, NY

ALLEGHANY CORP.

Exchange	Symbol	Price	52Wk Range	Yield	P/E
NYS	Y	$596.09 (12/29/2017)	656.22-523.19	N/A	N/A

*7 Year Price Score 106.55 *NYSE Composite Index=100 *12 Month Price Score 91.33

TRADING VOLUME (thousand shares)

Interim Earnings (Per Share)

Qtr.	Mar	Jun	Sep	Dec
2014	12.28	9.06	11.40	8.66
2015	7.82	11.40	6.07	9.83
2016	9.96	4.99	10.09	4.51
2017	9.67	6.60	(20.90)	...

Interim Dividends (Per Share)

No Dividends Paid

Valuation Analysis | Institutional Holding

Forecast EPS	$-0.75	No of Institutions
	(01/17/2018)	454
Market Cap	$9.2 Billion	Shares
Book Value	$8.2 Billion	16,081,190
Price/Book	1.12	% Held
Price/Sales	1.48	79.84

Business Summary: General Insurance (MIC: 5.2.1 SIC: 6331 NAIC: 524126)

Alleghany is an insurance holding company. Through its Alleghany Insurance Holdings LLC subsidiary, Co. is engaged in the property and casualty insurance business. Co. sources, executes, manages and monitors certain private capital investments through its subsidiary, Alleghany Capital Corporation (Alleghany Capital). Alleghany Capital's investments include: Stranded Oil Resources Corporation; Bourn & Koch, Inc.; R.C. Tway Company, LLC; IPS-Integrated Project Services, LLC; and Jazwares, LLC. Co. has two segments: reinsurance, which consists of property and casualty reinsurance operations; and insurance, which consists of property and casualty insurance operations.

Recent Developments: For the quarter ended Sep 30 2017, net loss amounted to US$309.9 million versus net income of US$158.8 million in the year-earlier quarter. Revenues were US$1.67 billion, up 3.3% from US$1.61 billion the year before. Net premiums earned were US$1.24 billion versus US$1.25 billion in the prior-year quarter, a decrease of 1.1%. Net investment income fell 13.2% to US$104.7 million from US$120.6 million a year ago.

Prospects: Our evaluation of Alleghany Corp. as of Jan. 14, 2018 is the result of our systematic analysis on three basic characteristics: earnings strength, relative valuation, and recent stock price movement. The company has generated a negative trend in earnings per share over the past 5 quarters. Because the company lacks sufficient analyst estimate data, we place greater weight on the historical EPS trend as the measure of earnings strength. Based on operating earnings yield, the company is undervalued when compared to all of the companies in our coverage universe. Share price changes over the past year indicates that Y will perform poorly over the near term.

Financial Data

(US$ in Thousands)	9 Mos	6 Mos	3 Mos	12/31/2016	12/31/2015	12/31/2014	12/31/2013	12/31/2012
Earnings Per Share	(0.12)	30.87	29.26	29.59	35.13	41.40	37.44	45.48
Cash Flow Per Share	41.86	43.79	46.12	51.23	20.54	22.72	34.78	32.02
Tang Book Value Per Share	480.55	495.79	488.06	472.17	463.26	450.23	399.42	366.57
Income Statement								
Premium Income	3,692,838	2,453,117	1,209,188	4,975,777	4,230,286	4,410,647	4,239,216	3,733,005
Total Revenue	4,753,853	3,086,370	1,532,452	6,131,019	4,999,478	5,231,809	4,971,654	4,753,212
Benefits & Claims	2,926,039	1,434,191	699,305	2,917,166	2,339,790	2,494,565	2,479,353	2,630,170
Income Before Taxes	(174,296)	348,030	207,910	647,805	757,368	931,909	855,236	719,276
Income Taxes	(116,368)	96,011	58,550	187,141	195,173	251,777	225,882	17,032
Net Income	(63,170)	250,987	149,176	456,921	560,315	679,239	628,421	702,244
Average Shares	15,458	15,419	15,420	15,442	15,879	16,405	16,786	15,441
Balance Sheet								
Total Assets	25,714,235	24,529,488	23,939,141	23,756,591	22,846,333	23,489,436	23,361,088	22,807,967
Total Liabilities	17,513,212	16,094,234	15,754,292	15,816,646	15,291,626	16,016,008	16,437,331	16,404,180
Stockholders' Equity	8,201,023	8,435,254	8,184,849	7,939,945	7,554,707	7,473,428	6,923,757	6,403,787
Shares Outstanding	15,403	15,419	15,418	15,410	15,544	16,054	16,766	16,890
Statistical Record								
Return on Assets %	0.03	1.97	1.92	1.96	2.42	2.90	2.72	4.78
Return on Equity %	0.08	5.83	5.66	5.88	7.46	9.44	9.43	15.01
Loss Ratio %	79.24	58.46	57.83	58.63	55.31	56.56	58.49	70.46
Net Margin %	(1.33)	8.13	9.73	7.45	11.21	12.98	12.64	14.77
Price Range	656.22-512.10	656.22-512.10	656.22-487.39	616.13-450.94	515.25-440.61	482.00-363.60	417.39-335.42	355.46-284.25
P/E Ratio		21.26-16.59	22.43-16.66	20.82-15.24	14.67-12.54	11.64-8.78	11.15-8.96	7.82-6.25

Address: 1411 Broadway, 34th Floor, New York, NY 10018 **Telephone:** 212-752-1356	**Web Site:** www.alleghany.com **Officers:** John J. Burns - Chairman Weston M. Hicks - President, Chief Executive Officer	**Auditors:** Ernst & Young LLP **Transfer Agents:** Computershare Trust Company, N.A., Providence, RI

24

ALLEGHENY TECHNOLOGIES, INC

Exchange	Symbol	Price	52Wk Range	Yield	P/E
NYS	ATI	$24.14 (12/29/2017)	25.84-14.89	N/A	N/A

*7 Year Price Score 50.23 ***NYSE Composite Index=100** ***12 Month Price Score 110.22**

TRADING VOLUME (thousand shares)

Interim Earnings (Per Share)

Qtr.	Mar	Jun	Sep	Dec
2014	(0.19)	(0.03)	(0.01)	0.20
2015	0.09	(0.15)	(1.35)	(2.12)
2016	(0.94)	(0.18)	(4.95)	0.10
2017	0.16	0.09	(1.12)	...

Interim Dividends (Per Share)

Dividend Payment Suspended

Valuation Analysis		Institutional Holding	
Forecast EPS	$0.34	No of Institutions	
	(01/17/2018)	436	
Market Cap	$2.6 Billion	Shares	
Book Value	N/A	149,533,840	
Price/Book	N/A	% Held	
Price/Sales	N/A	77.28	

Business Summary: Non-Precious Metals (MIC: 8.2.2 SIC: 3317 NAIC: 331210)

Allegheny Technologies is a manufacturer of specialty materials and complex components. Co.'s business segments are High Performance Materials and Components, which produces, converts and distributes materials, including titanium and titanium-based alloys, nickel- and cobalt-based alloys and superalloys; zirconium and related alloys; and Flat Rolled Products, which produces, converts and distributes stainless steel, nickel-based alloys, specialty alloys, and titanium and titanium-based alloys, in a variety of product forms including plate, sheet, engineered strip, and Precision Rolled Strip® products.

Recent Developments: For the quarter ended Sep 30 2017, net loss amounted to US$119.4 million versus a net loss of US$527.2 million in the year-earlier quarter. Revenues were US$869.1 million, up 12.8% from US$770.5 million the year before. Operating loss was US$87.3 million versus a loss of US$498.9 million in the prior-year quarter. Direct operating expenses rose 7.7% to US$775.8 million from US$720.3 million in the comparable period the year before. Indirect operating expenses decreased 67.1% to US$180.6 million from US$549.1 million in the equivalent prior-year period.

Prospects: Our evaluation of Allegheny Technologies Inc. as of Jan. 14, 2018 is the result of our systematic analysis on three basic characteristics: earnings strength, relative valuation, and recent stock price movement. The company has suffered a very negative trend in earnings per share over the past 5 quarters and while recent estimates for the company have remained steady, ATI has posted results that fell short of analysts expectations. Based on operating earnings yield, the company is overvalued when compared to all of the companies in our coverage universe. Share price changes over the past year indicates that ATI will perform poorly over the near term.

Financial Data

(US$ in Thousands)	9 Mos	6 Mos	3 Mos	12/31/2016	12/31/2015	12/31/2014	12/31/2013	12/31/2012
Earnings Per Share	(1.12)	0.09	0.16	(5.97)	(3.53)	(0.03)	1.44	1.43
Cash Flow Per Share	1.17	...	(4.16)	(0.41)	1.22	0.52	3.45	4.02
Tang Book Value Per Share	7.49	7.07	6.91	6.55	13.11	16.72	20.06	16.20
Dividends Per Share	...	...	...	0.240	0.620	0.720	0.720	0.720
Dividend Payout %	...	...	...	...	...	...	50.00	50.35
Income Statement								
Total Revenue	869,100	880,200	865,900	3,134,600	3,719,600	4,223,400	4,043,500	5,031,500
EBITDA	(47,000)	45,800	96,900	(439,700)	(177,900)	286,800	91,000	509,600
Depn & Amortn	40,100	...	40,300	170,300	189,900	176,600	180,600	194,000
Income Before Taxes	(121,300)	11,300	23,100	(734,000)	(478,000)	1,500	(154,800)	244,000
Income Taxes	(1,900)	...	2,000	(106,900)	(112,100)	(8,700)	(63,600)	76,200
Net Income	(121,200)	10,100	17,500	(640,900)	(377,900)	(2,600)	154,000	158,400
Average Shares	107,700	128,300	128,200	107,300	107,300	107,100	106,800	116,600
Balance Sheet								
Current Assets	1,804,100	1,800,100	1,762,600	1,766,500	1,867,600	2,482,100	2,950,800	2,510,600
Total Assets	5,075,100	5,186,300	5,154,400	5,170,000	5,751,700	6,582,600	6,898,500	6,247,800
Current Liabilities	673,600	701,000	795,600	708,700	686,500	959,900	1,211,000	871,500
Long-Term Obligations	1,877,700	1,876,600	1,772,500	1,771,900	1,491,800	1,509,100	1,527,400	1,463,000
Total Liabilities	3,727,300	3,772,800	3,760,200	3,814,800	3,668,900	3,984,200	4,004,300	3,768,200
Stockholders' Equity	1,347,800	1,413,500	1,394,200	1,355,200	2,082,800	2,598,400	2,894,200	2,479,600
Shares Outstanding	108,863	108,879	108,824	108,925	109,174	108,710	107,983	107,398
Statistical Record								
Return on Assets %	N.M.	0.78	1.37	N.M.	N.M.	N.M.	2.34	2.57
Return on Equity %	N.M.	2.89	5.16	N.M.	N.M.	N.M.	5.73	6.38
EBITDA Margin %	N.M.	5.20	11.19	N.M.	N.M.	6.79	2.25	10.13
Net Margin %	N.M.	1.15	2.02	N.M.	N.M.	N.M.	3.81	3.15
Asset Turnover	0.67	0.68	0.68	0.57	0.60	0.63	0.62	0.82
Current Ratio	2.68	2.57	2.22	2.49	2.72	2.59	2.44	2.88
Debt to Equity	1.39	1.33	1.27	1.31	0.72	0.58	0.53	0.59
Price Range	23.90-13.16	22.28-12.69	22.28-11.23	18.94-7.62	37.45-10.46	46.23-29.86	35.64-26.00	51.62-25.61
P/E Ratio	...	247.56-141.00	139.25-70.19	...	...	...	24.75-18.06	36.10-17.91
Average Yield %	...	...	...	1.61	2.52	1.92	2.39	2.06

Address: 1000 Six PPG Place, Pittsburgh, PA 15222-5479	**Web Site:** www.atimetals.com	**Auditors:** Ernst & Young LLP
Telephone: 412-394-2800	**Officers:** Richard J. Harshman - Chairman, President, Chief Executive Officer L. Patrick Hassey - Chairman, Outgoing Chief Executive Officer	**Investor Contact:** 412-394-3004
		Transfer Agents: Computershare

ALLERGAN PLC

Exchange	Symbol	Price	52Wk Range	Yield	P/E
NYS	AGN PRA	$163.58 (12/29/2017)	256.15-163.58	33.62	N/A

*7 Year Price Score 97.28   *NYSE Composite Index=100   *12 Month Price Score 73.89

Interim Earnings (Per Share)

Qtr.	Mar	Jun	Sep	Dec
2014	0.55	0.28	(3.95)	(3.03)
2015	(1.85)	(0.80)	13.29	(2.20)
2016	0.47	(1.44)	38.58	0.74
2017	(7.86)	(2.37)	(12.07)	---

Interim Dividends (Per Share)

Amt	Decl	Ex	Rec	Pay
13.75Q	04/19/2017	08/11/2017	08/15/2017	09/01/2017
13.75Q	04/19/2017	05/11/2017	05/15/2017	06/01/2017
13.75Q	10/31/2017	11/14/2017	11/15/2017	12/01/2017
13.75Q	10/31/2017	02/14/2018	02/15/2018	03/01/2018

Indicated Div: $55.00

Valuation Analysis		Institutional Holding	
Forecast EPS	N/A	No of Institutions	1310
Market Cap	$54.4 Billion	Shares	300,812,000
Book Value	$71.2 Billion	% Held	
Price/Book	0.76	N/A	
Price/Sales	3.51		

Business Summary: Pharmaceuticals (MIC: 4.1.1 SIC: 2834 NAIC: 325412)

Allergan is a specialty pharmaceutical company engaged in the development, manufacturing, marketing, and distribution of brand name pharmaceutical products, medical aesthetics, biosimilar and over-the-counter pharmaceutical products. Co. has three operating segments: U.S. Specialized Therapeutics, which provides branded products within the U.S., including medical aesthetics, medical dermatology, eye care, neurosciences and urology therapeutic products; U.S. General Medicine, which includes Central Nervous System, gastrointestinal women's health, and anti-infectives products within the U.S.; and International, which provides a range of branded and aesthetics products outside of the U.S.

Recent Developments: For the quarter ended Sep 30 2017, loss from continuing operations was US$3.95 billion compared with a loss of US$380.1 million in the year-earlier quarter. Net loss amounted to US$3.95 billion versus net income of US$15.22 billion in the year-earlier quarter. Revenues were US$4.03 billion, up 11.4% from US$3.62 billion the year before. Operating loss was US$4.02 billion versus a loss of US$266.4 million in the prior-year quarter. Direct operating expenses rose 26.9% to US$586.5 million from US$462.2 million in the comparable period the year before. Indirect operating expenses increased 118.0% to US$7.47 billion from US$3.43 billion in the equivalent prior-year period.

Prospects: Our evaluation of Allergan PLC as of Aug. 2, 2015 is the result of our systematic analysis on three basic characteristics: earnings strength, relative valuation, and recent stock price movement. The company has managed to produce a neutral trend in earnings per share over the past 5 quarters. However, while recent estimates for the company have been lowered by analysts, AGN has posted better than expected results. Based on operating earnings yield, the company is about fairly valued when compared to all of the companies in our coverage universe. Share price changes over the past year indicates that AGN will perform in line with the market over the near term.

Financial Data
(US$ in Thousands)

	9 Mos	6 Mos	3 Mos	12/31/2016	12/31/2015	12/31/2014	12/31/2013	12/31/2012
Earnings Per Share	(21.56)	29.09	30.02	38.18	10.01	(7.42)	(5.27)	0.76
Cash Flow Per Share	11.22	3.51	2.78	3.69	12.32	10.21	8.53	5.28
Dividends Per Share	55.000	55.000	55.000	55.000	41.097	10.21	8.53	5.28
Dividend Payout %	...	189.07	183.21	144.05	410.56	10.21	8.53	5.28
Income Statement								
Total Revenue	11,614,600	7,580,300	3,572,900	14,570,600	15,071,000	13,062,300	8,677,600	5,914,900
EBITDA	(3,653,400)	(188,600)	(1,016,600)	(1,452,600)	(3,119,700)	(1,078,300)	(207,400)	455,500
Depn & Amortn	5,543,900	3,676,100	1,812,200	153,700	128,600	230,900	202,000	97,500
Income Before Taxes	(9,976,600)	(4,389,900)	(3,093,200)	(2,832,000)	(4,430,200)	(1,712,100)	(644,400)	243,800
Income Taxes	(2,752,100)	(1,113,300)	(532,100)	(1,897,000)	(1,561,900)	(81,900)	112,700	146,800
Net Income	(7,246,800)	(3,291,100)	(2,565,200)	14,973,400	3,915,200	(1,630,500)	(750,400)	97,300
Average Shares	333,500	335,200	335,100	384,600	367,800	219,700	142,300	128,400
Balance Sheet								
Current Assets	10,112,800	10,433,200	13,700,700	17,857,900	8,615,400	6,881,700	4,434,700	3,879,700
Total Assets	118,992,800	124,734,800	126,836,900	128,986,300	135,840,700	52,529,100	22,725,900	14,103,500
Current Liabilities	8,559,800	8,638,300	10,391,600	7,874,700	8,328,300	5,018,600	3,294,900	2,710,600
Long-Term Obligations	26,539,100	26,443,300	26,223,000	29,970,800	40,293,400	14,846,300	8,517,400	6,257,100
Total Liabilities	47,833,400	49,514,400	51,648,500	52,793,600	59,249,300	24,198,000	13,193,800	10,269,700
Stockholders' Equity	71,159,400	75,220,400	75,188,400	76,192,700	76,591,400	28,331,100	9,532,100	3,833,800
Shares Outstanding	332,600	334,100	335,600	334,900	394,500	247,600	174,200	127,700
Statistical Record								
Return on Assets %	N.M.	9.27	9.24	11.28	4.16	N.M.	N.M.	0.93
Return on Equity %	N.M.	15.71	15.92	19.55	7.46	N.M.	N.M.	2.62
EBITDA Margin %	N.M.	N.M.	N.M.	N.M.	N.M.	N.M.	N.M.	7.70
Net Margin %	N.M.	N.M.	N.M.	102.76	25.98	N.M.	N.M.	1.64
Asset Turnover	0.12	0.12	0.11	0.11	0.16	0.35	0.47	0.57
Current Ratio	1.18	1.21	1.32	2.27	1.03	1.37	1.35	1.43
Debt to Equity	0.37	0.35	0.35	0.39	0.53	0.52	0.89	1.63
Price Range	256.15-188.47	260.24-188.47	277.55-188.47	312.50-188.47	339.50-252.10	270.61-167.93	168.00-83.10	90.85-55.89
P/E Ratio	...	8.95-6.48	9.25-6.28	8.18-4.94	33.92-25.18	...	...	119.54-73.54
Average Yield %	24.74	24.52	23.60	21.96	13.89	...	...	...

Address: Clonshaugh Business and Technology Park, Coolock, 07054 Telephone: 862-261-7000	Web Site: www.allergan.com Officers: Brenton L. Saunders - Chairman, President, Chief Executive Officer Maria Teresa Hilado - Executive Vice President, Chief Financial Officer, Chief Financial Officer	Auditors: PricewaterhouseCoopers LLP Investor Contact: 862-261-7488 Transfer Agents: American Stock Transfer and Trust Company, New York, NY

ALLIANCE DATA SYSTEMS CORP.

Exchange	Symbol	Price	52Wk Range	Yield	P/E
NYS	ADS	$253.48 (12/29/2017)	264.57-210.43	0.82	26.77

*7 Year Price Score 92.14 *NYSE Composite Index=100 *12 Month Price Score 93.47

TRADING VOLUME (thousand shares)

Interim Earnings (Per Share)

Qtr.	Mar	Jun	Sep	Dec
2014	2.08	2.19	2.74	0.89
2015	2.32	2.11	2.08	2.34
2016	2.35	1.24	3.55	0.22
2017	2.58	2.47	4.20	...

Interim Dividends (Per Share)

Amt	Decl	Ex	Rec	Pay
0.52Q	01/26/2017	02/13/2017	02/15/2017	03/17/2017
0.52Q	04/20/2017	05/11/2017	05/15/2017	06/19/2017
0.52Q	07/20/2017	08/10/2017	08/14/2017	09/19/2017
0.52Q	10/10/2017	11/13/2017	11/14/2017	12/19/2017

Indicated Div: $2.08

Valuation Analysis / Institutional Holding

Forecast EPS	$18.10	No of Institutions
(01/18/2018)		729
Market Cap	$14.0 Billion	Shares
Book Value	$1.6 Billion	66,716,504
Price/Book	8.80	% Held
Price/Sales	1.88	104.99

Business Summary: Business Services (MIC: 7.5.2 SIC: 7389 NAIC: 561499)
Alliance Data Systems is a provider of data-driven marketing and loyalty solutions. Co. provides a portfolio of outsourced marketing solutions, including customer loyalty programs, database marketing services, end-to-end marketing services, analytics and creative services, direct marketing services and private label and co-brand retail credit card programs. Co. focuses on facilitating and managing interactions between its clients and their customers through all consumer marketing channels, including in-store, online, email, social media, mobile, direct mail and telephone. Co.'s products and services are reported under three segments: LoyaltyOne®, Epsilon and Card Services.

Recent Developments: For the quarter ended Sep 30 2017, net income increased 12.4% to US$233.2 million from US$207.5 million in the year-earlier quarter. Revenues were US$1.91 billion, up 1.4% from US$1.89 billion the year before. Operating income was US$478.9 million versus US$421.0 million in the prior-year quarter, an increase of 13.8%. Direct operating expenses rose 2.0% to US$1.07 billion from US$1.05 billion in the comparable period the year before. Indirect operating expenses decreased 12.4% to US$367.0 million from US$419.0 million in the equivalent prior-year period.

Prospects: Our evaluation of Alliance Data Systems Corp. as of Jan. 14, 2018 is the result of our systematic analysis on three basic characteristics: earnings strength, relative valuation, and recent stock price movement. The company has produced a positive trend in earnings per share over the past 5 quarters. However, while recent estimates for the company have been mixed, ADS has posted better than expected results. Based on operating earnings yield, the company is undervalued when compared to all of the companies in our coverage universe. Share price changes over the past year indicates that ADS will perform very poorly over the near term.

Financial Data
(US$ in Thousands)

	9 Mos	6 Mos	3 Mos	12/31/2016	12/31/2015	12/31/2014	12/31/2013	12/31/2012
Earnings Per Share	9.47	8.82	7.59	7.34	8.85	7.87	7.42	6.58
Cash Flow Per Share	45.83	43.02	41.11	35.54	27.57	23.84	20.40	22.62
Dividends Per Share	2.080	1.560	1.040	0.520	...	...	...	...
Dividend Payout %	21.96	17.69	13.70	7.08	...	...	...	...
Income Statement								
Total Revenue	5,613,200	3,700,800	1,879,000	7,138,100	6,439,746	5,302,940	4,319,063	3,641,390
EBITDA	1,215,100	725,000	486,700	1,708,200	1,698,049	1,368,994	1,284,440	1,114,038
Depn & Amortn	32,300	21,200	134,300	442,700	436,189	270,527	185,528	139,674
Income Before Taxes	774,800	441,100	227,200	837,000	931,676	837,941	793,412	682,904
Income Taxes	257,400	157,000	80,800	319,400	326,248	321,801	297,242	260,648
Net Income	517,400	284,100	146,400	515,800	596,541	506,293	496,170	422,256
Average Shares	55,600	55,800	56,700	58,900	62,301	62,445	66,866	64,143
Balance Sheet								
Current Assets	21,969,300	19,839,100	18,783,000	19,589,300	16,250,417	13,814,776	10,400,842	9,132,143
Total Assets	27,894,100	25,728,300	24,642,700	25,514,100	22,421,830	20,263,977	13,244,257	12,000,139
Current Liabilities	10,392,400	8,804,600	9,004,400	9,229,500	6,405,559	6,305,483	4,512,498	5,032,777
Long-Term Obligations	5,704,100	5,882,300	5,445,000	10,103,300	10,136,018	8,134,248	2,435,792	2,051,570
Total Liabilities	26,300,500	24,303,500	23,279,200	23,855,900	20,411,800	17,867,597	12,388,496	11,471,652
Stockholders' Equity	1,593,600	1,424,800	1,363,500	1,658,200	2,010,030	2,396,380	855,761	528,487
Shares Outstanding	55,300	55,500	55,800	57,400	60,877	63,812	51,550	49,603
Statistical Record								
Return on Assets %	2.05	2.07	2.15	2.15	2.80	3.02	3.93	4.01
Return on Equity %	31.26	31.84	32.54	28.05	27.08	31.14	71.69	119.55
EBITDA Margin %	21.65	19.59	25.90	23.93	26.37	25.82	29.74	30.59
Net Margin %	9.22	7.68	7.79	7.23	9.26	9.55	11.49	11.60
Asset Turnover	0.29	0.31	0.31	0.30	0.30	0.32	0.34	0.35
Current Ratio	2.11	2.25	2.09	2.12	2.54	2.19	2.30	1.81
Debt to Equity	3.58	4.13	3.99	6.09	5.04	3.39	2.85	3.88
Price Range	264.57-199.80	263.01-193.68	249.00-186.40	276.57-177.12	309.91-247.05	294.27-233.67	262.93-144.76	148.02-100.94
P/E Ratio	27.94-21.10	29.82-21.96	32.81-24.56	37.68-24.13	35.02-27.92	37.39-29.69	35.44-19.51	22.50-15.34
Average Yield %	0.89	0.68	0.47	0.24	...	...	...	...

Address: 7500 Dallas Parkway, Suite 700, Plano, TX 75024 Telephone: 214-494-3000	Web Site: www.alliancedata.com Officers: Edward J. Heffernan - President, Chief Executive Officer Bryan J. Kennedy - Executive Vice President, Division Officer	Auditors: Deloitte & Touche LLP Investor Contact: 212-850-5721 Transfer Agents: ComputerShare Investor Services, Providence, RI

ALLIANT ENERGY CORP

Exchange	Symbol	Price	52Wk Range	Yield	P/E	Div Achiever
NYS	LNT	$42.61 (12/29/2017)	45.18-36.86	3.14	22.91	13 Years

*7 Year Price Score 109.79 *NYSE Composite Index=100 *12 Month Price Score 100.98

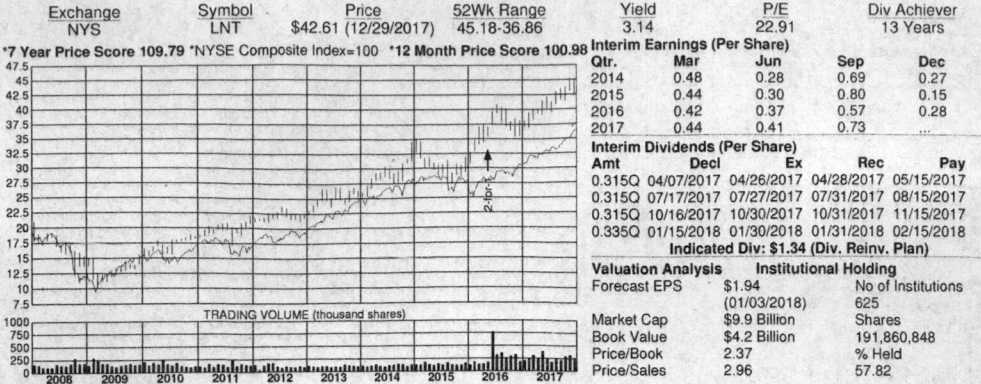

Interim Earnings (Per Share)

Qtr.	Mar	Jun	Sep	Dec
2014	0.48	0.28	0.69	0.27
2015	0.44	0.30	0.80	0.15
2016	0.42	0.37	0.57	0.28
2017	0.44	0.41	0.73	...

Interim Dividends (Per Share)

Amt	Decl	Ex	Rec	Pay
0.315Q	04/07/2017	04/26/2017	04/28/2017	05/15/2017
0.315Q	07/17/2017	07/27/2017	07/31/2017	08/15/2017
0.315Q	10/16/2017	10/30/2017	10/31/2017	11/15/2017
0.335Q	01/15/2018	01/30/2018	01/31/2018	02/15/2018

Indicated Div: $1.34 (Div. Reinv. Plan)

Valuation Analysis / **Institutional Holding**

Forecast EPS	$1.94 (01/03/2018)	No of Institutions	625
Market Cap	$9.9 Billion	Shares	191,860,848
Book Value	$4.2 Billion	% Held	57.82
Price/Book	2.37		
Price/Sales	2.96		

Business Summary: Electric Utilities (MIC: 3.1.1 SIC: 4931 NAIC: 221122)

Alliant Energy is a public utility holding company. Through its subsidiaries, Co. principally generates and distributes electricity and distributes and transports natural gas to retail customers in select markets in Iowa and Wisconsin, and sells electricity to wholesale customers in Wisconsin. At Dec 31 2016, Co. supplied electric and natural gas service to approximately 960,000 electric and approximately 410,000 natural gas customers in the Midwest. Co.'s non-utility operations consist of its non-regulated generation, transportation, and other non-regulated investments including an interest in American Transmission Company LLC, a transmission-only utility operating in the Midwest.

Recent Developments: For the quarter ended Sep 30 2017, income from continuing operations increased 30.4% to US$171.4 million from US$131.4 million in the year-earlier quarter. Net income increased 30.8% to US$171.4 million from US$131.0 million in the year-earlier quarter. Revenues were US$906.9 million, down 1.9% from US$924.6 million the year before. Operating income was US$231.5 million versus US$162.6 million in the prior-year quarter, an increase of 42.4%. Direct operating expenses declined 3.3% to US$527.7 million from US$545.6 million in the comparable period the year before. Indirect operating expenses decreased 31.7% to US$147.7 million from US$216.4 million in the equivalent prior-year period.

Prospects: Our evaluation of Alliant Energy Corp. as of Jan. 14, 2018 is the result of our systematic analysis on three basic characteristics: earnings strength, relative valuation, and recent stock price movement. The company has managed to produce a neutral trend in earnings per share over the past 5 quarters. However, while recent estimates for the company have been mixed, LNT has posted results that fell short of analysts expectations. Based on operating earnings yield, the company is undervalued when compared to all of the companies in our coverage universe. Share price changes over the past year indicates that LNT will perform very well over the near term.

Financial Data

(US$ in Thousands)	9 Mos	6 Mos	3 Mos	12/31/2016	12/31/2015	12/31/2014	12/31/2013	12/31/2012
Earnings Per Share	1.86	1.70	1.66	1.64	1.68	1.73	1.62	1.45
Cash Flow Per Share	4.71	3.72	4.24	3.77	3.87	4.02	3.30	3.79
Tang Book Value Per Share	17.97	17.53	17.10	16.96	16.41	15.50	14.79	14.39
Dividends Per Share	1.239	1.218	1.196	1.175	1.100	1.020	0.940	0.900
Dividend Payout %	66.60	71.62	72.06	71.65	65.48	58.96	58.20	62.28
Income Statement								
Total Revenue	2,526,100	1,619,200	853,900	3,320,000	3,253,600	3,350,300	3,276,800	3,094,500
EBITDA	903,100	541,300	266,900	1,006,300	1,027,600	1,020,700	975,800	929,500
Depn & Amortn	342,700	222,000	107,000	406,800	413,700	442,300	411,100	387,900
Income Before Taxes	401,800	214,400	107,700	403,800	427,500	399,600	392,300	388,900
Income Taxes	64,900	38,800	17,600	59,400	70,400	44,300	53,900	89,400
Net Income	371,200	199,800	103,000	381,700	388,400	393,300	376,200	335,700
Average Shares	231,000	229,000	227,600	227,100	225,400	221,600	221,600	221,536
Balance Sheet								
Current Assets	751,500	814,700	749,800	877,100	826,800	1,043,100	1,011,200	994,300
Total Assets	14,114,900	13,743,400	13,464,900	13,373,800	12,495,200	12,085,900	11,112,400	10,785,500
Current Liabilities	1,470,100	1,208,200	1,165,000	1,162,000	1,359,300	1,214,700	1,433,300	1,020,000
Long-Term Obligations	4,255,100	4,354,300	4,316,100	4,315,600	3,522,200	3,606,700	2,977,800	3,136,600
Total Liabilities	9,960,700	9,693,000	9,568,000	9,511,800	8,771,100	8,647,200	7,831,000	7,590,600
Stockholders' Equity	4,154,200	4,050,400	3,896,900	3,862,000	3,724,100	3,438,700	3,281,400	3,194,900
Shares Outstanding	231,204	231,062	227,823	227,673	226,918	221,871	221,887	221,974
Statistical Record								
Return on Assets %	3.22	3.00	2.97	2.94	3.16	3.39	3.44	3.27
Return on Equity %	10.89	10.10	10.07	10.04	10.84	11.71	11.62	10.68
EBITDA Margin %	35.75	33.43	31.26	30.31	31.58	30.47	29.78	30.04
Net Margin %	14.69	12.34	12.06	11.50	11.94	11.74	11.48	10.85
Asset Turnover	0.24	0.25	0.26	0.26	0.26	0.29	0.30	0.30
Current Ratio	0.51	0.67	0.64	0.75	0.61	0.86	0.71	0.97
Debt to Equity	1.02	1.08	1.11	1.12	0.95	1.05	0.91	0.98
Price Range	43.60-35.36	42.18-35.36	40.87-34.39	40.87-30.79	35.16-27.27	34.66-25.25	26.97-21.95	23.75-21.05
P/E Ratio	23.44-19.01	24.81-20.80	24.62-20.72	24.92-18.77	20.93-16.24	20.03-14.59	16.65-13.55	16.38-14.52
Average Yield %	3.15	3.14	3.16	3.20	3.60	3.54	3.75	4.07

Address: 4902 N. Biltmore Lane, Madison, WI 53718
Telephone: 608-458-3311
Fax: 608-458-4824

Web Site: www.alliantenergy.com
Officers: Patricia L. Kampling - Chairman, President, Chief Executive Officer, Chief Operating Officer
Robert J. Durian - Chief Financial Officer, Vice President, Treasurer, Chief Accounting Officer, Controller

Auditors: Deloitte & Touche LLP
Investor Contact: 608-458-3956
Transfer Agents: Wells Fargo Shareowner Services, Mendota Heights, MN

ALLISON TRANSMISSION HOLDINGS INC

Exchange	Symbol	Price	52Wk Range	Yield	P/E
NYS	ALSN	$43.07 (12/29/2017)	44.08-32.81	1.39	19.06

*7 Year Price Score N/A   *NYSE Composite Index=100   *12 Month Price Score 104.73

Interim Earnings (Per Share)

Qtr.	Mar	Jun	Sep	Dec
2014	0.28	0.31	0.38	0.28
2015	0.38	0.30	0.27	0.08
2016	0.28	0.36	0.27	0.36
2017	0.52	0.63	0.75	...

Interim Dividends (Per Share)

Amt	Decl	Ex	Rec	Pay
0.15Q	02/23/2017	03/02/2017	03/06/2017	03/15/2017
0.15Q	05/11/2017	05/18/2017	05/22/2017	05/26/2017
0.15Q	08/10/2017	08/17/2017	08/21/2017	08/31/2017
0.15Q	11/08/2017	11/17/2017	11/20/2017	11/30/2017

Indicated Div: $0.60

Valuation Analysis

		Institutional Holding	
Forecast EPS	$2.50 (01/12/2018)	No of Institutions	371
Market Cap	$6.1 Billion	Shares	248,471,088
Book Value	$555.0 Million	% Held	78.83
Price/Book	11.08		
Price/Sales	2.87		

Business Summary: Auto Parts (MIC: 1.8.2 SIC: 3714 NAIC: 336350)

Allison Transmission Holdings is a manufacturer of fully-automatic transmissions for medium- and heavy-duty commercial vehicles and medium- and heavy-tactical U.S. defense vehicles. Co.'s transmissions are used in a variety of applications, including on-highway trucks (distribution, refuse, construction, fire and emergency), buses (primarily school, transit and hybrid-transit), motorhomes, off-highway vehicles and equipment (primarily energy, mining and construction) and defense vehicles (wheeled and tracked). Co. also sells branded replacement parts, support equipment and other products necessary to service the installed base of vehicles utilizing Co.'s transmissions.

Recent Developments: For the quarter ended Sep 30 2017, net income increased 146.7% to US$111.0 million from US$45.0 million in the year-earlier quarter. Revenues were US$595.0 million, up 37.1% from US$434.0 million the year before. Operating income was US$198.0 million versus US$104.0 million in the prior-year quarter, an increase of 90.4%. Direct operating expenses rose 27.4% to US$293.0 million from US$230.0 million in the comparable period the year before. Indirect operating expenses increased 4.0% to US$104.0 million from US$100.0 million in the equivalent prior-year period.

Prospects: Our evaluation of Allison Transmission Holding as of Jan. 14, 2018 is the result of our systematic analysis on three basic characteristics: earnings strength, relative valuation, and recent stock price movement. The company has managed to produce a neutral trend in earnings per share over the past 5 quarters. However, while recent estimates for the company have been mixed, ALSN has posted better than expected results. Based on operating earnings yield, the company is undervalued when compared to all of the companies in our coverage universe. Share price changes over the past year indicates that ALSN will perform in line with the market over the near term.

Financial Data

(US$ in Thousands)	9 Mos	6 Mos	3 Mos	12/31/2016	12/31/2015	12/31/2014	12/31/2013	12/31/2012
Earnings Per Share	2.26	1.78	1.51	1.27	1.03	1.25	0.88	2.76
Cash Flow Per Share	4.57	3.84	3.70	3.51	3.30	3.10	2.46	2.73
Dividends Per Share	0.600	0.600	0.600	0.600	0.600	0.510	0.420	0.180
Dividend Payout %	26.55	33.71	39.74	47.24	58.25	40.80	47.73	6.52
Income Statement								
Total Revenue	1,674,000	1,079,000	499,000	1,840,200	1,985,800	2,127,400	1,926,800	2,141,800
EBITDA	652,000	412,000	194,000	618,100	588,700	699,100	603,000	619,900
Depn & Amortn	131,000	87,000	42,000	175,900	185,400	192,600	204,000	252,500
Income Before Taxes	443,000	273,000	127,000	341,300	288,800	368,100	266,100	216,200
Income Taxes	154,000	95,000	44,000	126,400	106,500	139,500	100,700	(298,000)
Net Income	289,000	178,000	83,000	214,900	182,300	228,600	165,400	514,200
Average Shares	147,000	152,000	158,800	168,800	177,200	182,300	187,900	186,200
Balance Sheet								
Current Assets	665,000	527,000	537,000	547,600	616,800	758,000	606,900	490,300
Total Assets	4,261,000	4,142,000	4,179,000	4,218,600	4,408,400	4,804,200	4,812,600	4,866,000
Current Liabilities	444,000	397,000	378,000	342,200	304,600	345,900	387,200	377,800
Long-Term Obligations	2,536,000	2,348,000	2,390,000	2,146,800	2,352,700	2,502,600	2,660,400	2,801,300
Total Liabilities	3,706,000	3,446,000	3,442,000	3,138,300	3,219,800	3,406,400	3,373,800	3,509,100
Stockholders' Equity	555,000	696,000	737,000	1,080,300	1,188,600	1,397,800	1,438,800	1,356,900
Shares Outstanding	142,735	163,795	152,003	163,795	171,157	179,488	183,376	184,084
Statistical Record								
Return on Assets %	8.24	6.60	5.79	4.97	3.96	4.75	3.42	10.20
Return on Equity %	41.90	30.54	26.00	18.89	14.10	16.12	11.83	47.08
EBITDA Margin %	38.95	38.18	38.88	33.59	29.65	32.86	31.30	28.94
Net Margin %	17.26	16.50	16.63	11.68	9.18	10.75	8.58	24.01
Asset Turnover	0.50	0.46	0.44	0.43	0.43	0.44	0.40	0.42
Current Ratio	1.50	1.33	1.42	1.60	2.02	2.19	1.57	1.30
Debt to Equity	4.57	3.37	3.24	1.99	1.98	1.79	1.85	2.06
Price Range	39.05-27.40	39.05-26.90	38.02-26.00	35.02-21.58	33.90-24.64	34.38-26.46	28.04-20.42	25.02-16.21
P/E Ratio	17.28-12.12	21.94-15.11	25.18-17.22	27.57-16.99	32.91-23.92	27.50-21.17	31.86-23.20	9.07-5.87
Average Yield %	1.71	1.82	1.96	2.15	2.02	1.68	1.76	0.91

Address: One Allison Way, Indianapolis, IN 46222 **Telephone:** 317-242-5000	**Web Site:** www.allisontransmission.com **Officers:** Lawrence E. (Larry) Dewey - Chairman, President, Chief Executive Officer David S. Graziosi - President, Chief Executive Officer, Executive Vice President, Chief Financial Officer, Treasurer, Assistant Secretary	**Auditors:** PricewaterhouseCoopers LLP **Transfer Agents:** American Stock Transfer & Trust Company, LLC, Brooklyn, NY

ALLSTATE CORP.

Exchange	Symbol	Price	52Wk Range	Yield	P/E
NYS	ALL	$104.71 (12/29/2017)	104.91-73.09	1.41	14.58

*7 Year Price Score 121.97 *NYSE Composite Index=100 *12 Month Price Score 108.46

Interim Earnings (Per Share)

Qtr.	Mar	Jun	Sep	Dec
2014	1.30	1.39	1.74	1.85
2015	1.53	0.79	1.54	1.18
2016	0.57	0.54	1.31	2.16
2017	1.79	1.49	1.74	...

Interim Dividends (Per Share)

Amt	Decl	Ex	Rec	Pay
0.37Q	02/10/2017	02/24/2017	02/28/2017	04/03/2017
0.37Q	05/25/2017	06/05/2017	06/05/2017	07/03/2017
0.37Q	07/11/2017	08/29/2017	08/31/2017	10/02/2017
0.37Q	11/16/2017	11/29/2017	11/30/2017	01/02/2018

Indicated Div: $1.48 (Div. Reinv. Plan)

Valuation Analysis	Institutional Holding	
Forecast EPS	$6.08	No of Institutions
	(01/18/2018)	1286
Market Cap	$37.7 Billion	Shares
Book Value	$22.1 Billion	373,579,488
Price/Book	1.70	% Held
Price/Sales	0.99	68.27

Business Summary: General Insurance (MIC: 5.2.1 SIC: 6331 NAIC: 524126)

Allstate is a holding company. Through its subsidiaries, Co. provides property-liability insurance and the life insurance, retirement and investment products. Co. has four segments: Allstate Protection, which sells private passenger auto, homeowners, and other property-liability insurance products; Allstate Financial, which sells life insurance and voluntary accident and health insurance products; Discontinued Lines and Coverages, which includes results from property-liability insurance coverage that Co. no longer write and results for certain commercial and other businesses in run-off; and Corporate and Other, which includes holding company activities and certain non-insurance operations.

Recent Developments: For the quarter ended Sep 30 2017, net income increased 28.1% to US$666.0 million from US$520.0 million in the year-earlier quarter. Revenues were US$9.66 billion, up 4.8% from US$9.22 billion the year before. Net premiums earned were US$8.71 billion versus US$8.44 billion in the prior-year quarter, an increase of 3.2%. Net investment income rose 12.7% to US$843.0 million from US$748.0 million a year ago.

Prospects: Our evaluation of Allstate Corp. as of Jan. 14, 2018 is the result of our systematic analysis on three basic characteristics: earnings strength, relative valuation, and recent stock price movement. The company has generated a negative trend in earnings per share over the past 5 quarters. However, while recent estimates for the company have been mixed, ALL has posted better than expected results. Based on operating earnings yield, the company is undervalued when compared to all of the companies in our coverage universe. Share price changes over the past year indicates that ALL will perform very well over the near term.

Financial Data
(US$ in Millions)

	9 Mos	6 Mos	3 Mos	12/31/2016	12/31/2015	12/31/2014	12/31/2013	12/31/2012
Earnings Per Share	7.18	6.75	5.90	4.67	5.05	6.27	4.81	4.68
Cash Flow Per Share	12.36	10.95	11.31	10.68	9.02	7.50	9.13	6.22
Tang Book Value Per Share	50.18	48.33	46.90	48.11	44.78	46.27	43.33	40.38
Dividends Per Share	1.440	1.400	1.360	1.320	1.200	1.120	1.000	0.880
Dividend Payout %	20.06	20.74	23.05	28.27	23.76	17.86	20.79	18.80
Income Statement								
Premium Income	25,875	17,161	8,552	33,582	32,467	31,086	29,970	28,978
Total Revenue	28,681	19,021	9,434	36,534	35,653	35,239	34,507	33,315
Benefits & Claims	1,416	960	474	24,078	22,837	21,193	19,828	20,302
Income Before Taxes	2,834	1,863	1,012	2,754	3,282	4,236	3,396	3,306
Income Taxes	894	589	317	877	1,111	1,386	1,116	1,000
Net Income	1,940	1,274	695	1,877	2,171	2,850	2,280	2,306
Average Shares	367	369	371	377	406	438	470	493
Balance Sheet								
Total Assets	113,632	110,865	110,243	108,610	104,656	108,533	123,520	126,947
Total Liabilities	91,513	89,364	89,085	88,037	84,631	86,229	102,040	106,367
Stockholders' Equity	22,119	21,501	21,158	20,573	20,025	22,304	21,480	20,580
Shares Outstanding	360	361	365	366	381	418	449	479
Statistical Record								
Return on Assets %	2.50	2.41	2.15	1.76	2.04	2.46	1.82	1.82
Return on Equity %	12.91	12.53	11.21	9.22	10.26	13.02	10.84	11.72
Loss Ratio %	5.47	5.59	5.54	71.70	70.34	68.18	66.16	70.06
Net Margin %	6.76	6.70	7.37	5.14	6.09	8.09	6.61	6.92
Price Range	94.70-66.72	89.82-66.72	82.89-64.95	74.58-57.70	72.58-56.99	71.00-49.55	54.71-40.17	42.62-27.56
P/E Ratio	13.19-9.29	13.31-9.88	14.05-11.01	15.97-12.36	14.37-11.29	11.32-7.90	11.37-8.35	9.11-5.89
Average Yield %	1.77	1.85	1.91	1.96	1.82	1.89	2.02	2.47

Address: 2775 Sanders Road, Northbrook, IL 60062 Telephone: 847-402-5000	Web Site: www.allstate.com Officers: Thomas J. Wilson - Chairman, President, Chief Executive Officer Steven E. Shebik - Vice-Chairman, Executive Vice President, Chief Financial Officer	Auditors: Deloitte & Touche LLP Investor Contact: 800-416-8803 Transfer Agents: Wells Fargo Bank, N.A. Shareowner Services, St. Paul, MN

ALLY FINANCIAL INC

Exchange	Symbol	Price	52Wk Range	Yield	P/E
NYS	ALLY	$29.16 (12/29/2017)	29.41-18.22	1.78	13.50

*7 Year Price Score N/A   *NYSE Composite Index=100   *12 Month Price Score 114.19

Interim Earnings (Per Share)

Qtr.	Mar	Jun	Sep	Dec
2014	0.33	0.54	0.74	0.23
2015	1.06	(2.22)	0.47	(1.98)
2016	0.49	0.71	0.43	0.52
2017	0.46	0.55	0.63	...

Interim Dividends (Per Share)

Amt	Decl	Ex	Rec	Pay
0.08Q	04/18/2017	04/27/2017	05/01/2017	05/15/2017
0.12Q	07/19/2017	07/28/2017	08/01/2017	08/15/2017
0.12Q	10/11/2017	10/31/2017	11/01/2017	11/15/2017
0.13Q	01/11/2010	01/31/2018	02/01/2018	02/15/2018

Indicated Div: $0.52

Valuation Analysis

		Institutional Holding	
Forecast EPS	$2.31 (01/18/2018)	No of Institutions	434
Market Cap	$12.9 Billion	Shares	482,985,216
Book Value	$13.6 Billion	% Held	
Price/Book	0.95	N/A	
Price/Sales	1.31		

Business Summary: Credit & Lending (MIC: 5.4.1 SIC: 6141 NAIC: 522291)

Ally Financial is a financial holding company. Co.'s Dealer Financial Services includes its Automotive Finance and Insurance segments, providing a range of financial services and insurance products to automotive dealerships and their retail customers. Co.'s banking subsidiary, Ally Bank, acquires deposits directly from customers through direct banking via the internet, telephone, mobile, and mail channels. Ally Bank's products include checking, savings, and certificates of deposit, Popmoney person-to-person transfer services, eCheck remote deposit capture and mobile banking. At Dec 31 2016, Co. had total assets of $163.73 billion and total deposits of $79.02 billion.

Recent Developments: For the quarter ended Sep 30 2017, income from continuing operations increased 7.3% to US$280.0 million from US$261.0 million in the year-earlier quarter. Net income increased 34.9% to US$282.0 million from US$209.0 million in the year-earlier quarter. Net interest income decreased 3.6% to US$1.35 billion from US$1.40 billion in the year-earlier quarter. Provision for loan losses was US$314.0 million versus US$258.0 million in the prior-year quarter, an increase of 21.7%. Non-interest income fell 1.8% to US$381.0 million from US$388.0 million, while non-interest expense declined 10.3% to US$1.03 billion.

Prospects: Our evaluation of Ally Financial Inc as of Jan. 14, 2018 is the result of our systematic analysis on three basic characteristics: earnings strength, relative valuation, and recent stock price movement. The company has enjoyed a very positive trend in earnings per share over the past 5 quarters and while recent estimates for the company have been mixed, ALLY has posted better than expected results. Based on operating earnings yield, the company is undervalued when compared to all of the companies in our coverage universe. Share price changes over the past year indicates that ALLY will perform well over the near term.

Financial Data (US$ in Millions)	9 Mos	6 Mos	3 Mos	12/31/2016	12/31/2015	12/31/2014	12/31/2013	12/31/2012
Earnings Per Share	2.16	1.96	2.12	2.15	(2.66)	1.83	(1.64)	0.95
Cash Flow Per Share	9.69	9.21	9.77	9.47	10.55	7.07	5.95	12.20
Tang Book Value Per Share	30.04	29.26	28.40	28.00	26.44	29.46	27.00	29.03
Dividends Per Share	0.360	0.320	0.240	0.160	...	...	...	...
Dividend Payout %	16.67	16.33	11.32	7.44	...	...	...	...
Income Statement								
Total Revenue	7,391	4,922	2,446	9,835	9,539	9,667	9,577	10,497
Income Before Taxes	1,097	702	326	1,581	1,393	1,246	357	(755)
Income Taxes	350	235	113	470	496	321	(59)	(1,284)
Net Income	748	466	214	1,067	1,289	1,150	361	1,196
Average Shares	451	458	466	482	482	481	420	412
Balance Sheet								
Total Assets	164,013	164,345	162,101	163,728	158,581	151,828	151,167	182,347
Total Liabilities	150,440	150,872	148,736	150,411	145,142	136,429	136,959	162,449
Stockholders' Equity	13,573	13,473	13,365	13,317	13,439	15,399	14,208	19,898
Shares Outstanding	443	452	462	467	481	480	479	412
Statistical Record								
Return on Assets %	0.62	0.57	0.65	0.66	0.83	0.76	0.22	0.65
Return on Equity %	7.32	6.82	7.58	7.95	8.94	7.77	2.12	6.07
Net Margin %	10.12	9.47	8.75	10.85	13.51	11.90	3.77	11.39
Asset Turnover	0.06	0.06	0.06	0.06	0.06	0.06	0.06	0.06
Price Range	24.26-16.84	23.48-15.73	23.48-14.90	20.40-14.90	23.88-18.33	27.90-20.12	...	...
P/E Ratio	11.23-7.80	11.98-8.03	11.08-7.03	9.49-6.93	...	15.25-10.99	...	...
Average Yield %	1.75	1.63	1.26	0.88	...	...	...	...

Address: Ally Detroit Center, 500 Woodward Avenue, Floor 10, Detroit, MI 48226
Telephone: 866-710-4623

Web Site: www.ally.com
Officers: Franklin W. Hobbs - Chairman Jeffrey J. Brown - Chief Executive Officer, Senior Executive Vice President, Division Officer

Auditors: Deloitte & Touche LLP
Investor Contact: 866-710-4623
Transfer Agents: Computershare Limited

ALTRIA GROUP INC

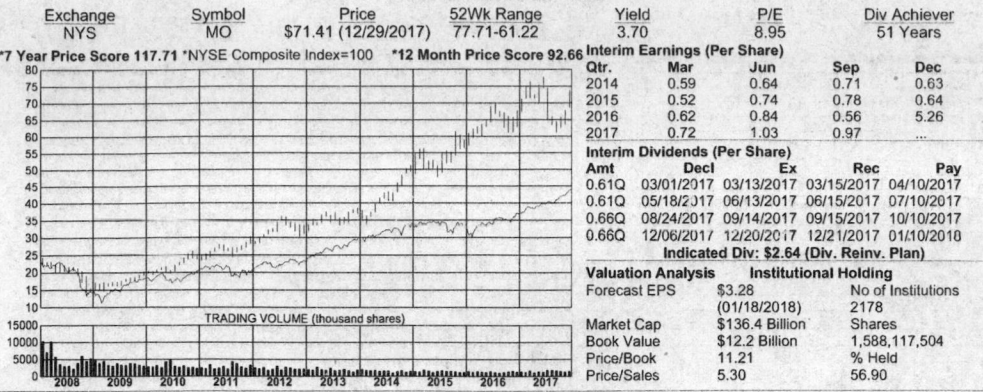

Exchange	Symbol	Price	52Wk Range	Yield	P/E	Div Achiever
NYS	MO	$71.41 (12/29/2017)	77.71-61.22	3.70	8.95	51 Years

*7 Year Price Score 117.71 *NYSE Composite Index=100 *12 Month Price Score 92.66

Interim Earnings (Per Share)

Qtr.	Mar	Jun	Sep	Dec
2014	0.59	0.64	0.71	0.63
2015	0.52	0.74	0.78	0.64
2016	0.62	0.84	0.56	5.26
2017	0.72	1.03	0.97	...

Interim Dividends (Per Share)

Amt	Decl	Ex	Rec	Pay
0.61Q	03/01/2017	03/13/2017	03/15/2017	04/10/2017
0.61Q	05/18/2017	06/13/2017	06/15/2017	07/10/2017
0.66Q	08/24/2017	09/14/2017	09/15/2017	10/10/2017
0.66Q	12/06/2017	12/20/2017	12/21/2017	01/10/2018

Indicated Div: $2.64 (Div. Reinv. Plan)

Valuation Analysis — **Institutional Holding**

Forecast EPS	$3.28	No of Institutions
(01/18/2018)		2178
Market Cap	$136.4 Billion	Shares
Book Value	$12.2 Billion	1,588,117,504
Price/Book	11.21	% Held
Price/Sales	5.30	56.90

TRADING VOLUME (thousand shares)

Business Summary: Tobacco Products (MIC: 1.3.1 SIC: 2111 NAIC: 312221)

Altria Group is a holding company. Co.'s subsidiaries include: Philip Morris USA Inc., which is engaged in the manufacture and sale of cigarettes; John Middleton Co., which is engaged in the manufacture and sale of machine-made cigars and pipe tobacco; and UST LLC, which through its subsidiaries, including U.S. Smokeless Tobacco Company LLC and Ste. Michelle Wine Estates Ltd., is engaged in the manufacture and sale of smokeless tobacco products and wine. Co.'s other operating companies included Nu Mark LLC, a subsidiary that is engaged in the manufacture and sale of tobacco products, and Philip Morris Capital Corporation, a subsidiary that maintains a portfolio of finance assets.

Recent Developments: For the quarter ended Sep 30 2017, net income increased 70.7% to US$1.87 billion from US$1.09 billion in the year-earlier quarter. Revenues were US$6.73 billion, down 2.5% from US$6.91 billion the year before. Operating income was US$2.61 billion versus US$2.38 billion in the prior-year quarter, an increase of 9.4%. Direct operating expenses declined 5.6% to US$3.55 billion from US$3.76 billion in the comparable period the year before. Indirect operating expenses decreased 25.0% to US$576.0 million from US$768.0 million in the equivalent prior-year period.

Prospects: Our evaluation of Altria Group Inc. as of Jan. 14, 2018 is the result of our systematic analysis on three basic characteristics: earnings strength, relative valuation, and recent stock price movement. The company has managed to produce a neutral trend in earnings per share over the past 5 quarters. However, while recent estimates for the company have been mixed, MO has posted better than expected results. Based on operating earnings yield, the company is undervalued when compared to all of the companies in our coverage universe. Share price changes over the past year indicates that MO will perform in line with the market over the near term.

Financial Data

(US$ in Thousands)	9 Mos	6 Mos	3 Mos	12/31/2016	12/31/2015	12/31/2014	12/31/2013	12/31/2012
Earnings Per Share	7.98	7.57	7.38	7.28	2.67	2.56	2.26	2.06
Cash Flow Per Share	2.33	2.43	1.94	1.94	2.96	2.36	2.19	1.92
Dividends Per Share	2.490	2.440	2.395	2.350	2.170	2.000	1.840	1.700
Dividend Payout %	31.20	32.23	32.45	32.28	81.27	78.13	81.42	82.52
Income Statement								
Total Revenue	19,475,000	12,746,000	6,083,000	25,744,000	25,434,000	24,522,000	24,466,000	24,618,000
EBITDA	7,993,000	5,298,000	2,299,000	21,987,000	8,342,000	7,764,000	7,212,000	6,604,000
Depn & Amortn	155,000	104,000	52,000	183,000	204,000	188,000	212,000	225,000
Income Before Taxes	7,313,000	4,838,000	2,068,000	21,057,000	7,321,000	6,768,000	5,951,000	5,253,000
Income Taxes	2,386,000	1,609,000	689,000	7,608,000	2,835,000	2,704,000	2,407,000	2,294,000
Net Income	5,256,000	3,390,000	1,401,000	14,239,000	5,241,000	5,070,000	4,535,000	4,180,000
Average Shares	1,915,000	1,928,000	1,939,000	1,952,000	1,961,000	1,978,000	1,999,000	2,024,000
Balance Sheet								
Current Assets	5,156,000	4,611,000	7,626,000	7,260,000	6,086,000	6,878,000	6,590,000	6,315,000
Total Assets	44,160,000	43,726,000	46,175,000	45,932,000	32,535,000	34,475,000	34,859,000	35,329,000
Current Liabilities	6,662,000	5,582,000	8,300,000	7,375,000	7,078,000	7,673,000	7,058,000	8,251,000
Long-Term Obligations	13,890,000	13,887,000	13,884,000	13,881,000	12,915,000	13,693,000	13,992,000	12,419,000
Total Liabilities	31,994,000	31,308,000	33,915,000	33,162,000	29,655,000	31,461,000	30,740,000	32,161,000
Stockholders' Equity	12,166,000	12,418,000	12,260,000	12,770,000	2,880,000	3,014,000	4,119,000	3,168,000
Shares Outstanding	1,909,620	1,920,792	1,935,145	1,943,272	1,960,059	1,971,474	1,993,479	2,009,740
Statistical Record								
Return on Assets %	40.29	39.33	35.95	36.19	15.64	14.62	12.92	11.53
Return on Equity %	205.59	189.73	192.24	181.47	177.84	142.16	124.47	121.75
EBITDA Margin %	41.04	41.57	37.79	85.41	32.80	31.66	29.48	26.83
Net Margin %	26.99	26.60	23.03	55.31	20.61	20.68	18.54	16.98
Asset Turnover	0.67	0.69	0.64	0.65	0.76	0.71	0.70	0.68
Current Ratio	0.77	0.83	0.92	0.98	0.86	0.90	0.93	0.77
Debt to Equity	1.14	1.12	1.13	1.09	4.48	4.54	3.40	3.92
Price Range	77.71-61.19	77.71-61.19	76.45-60.18	69.87-57.20	61.53-47.54	51.27-34.00	38.57-31.44	36.16-28.14
P/E Ratio	9.74-7.67	10.27-8.08	10.36-8.15	9.60-7.86	23.04-17.81	20.03-13.28	17.07-13.91	17.55-13.66
Average Yield %	3.60	3.53	3.59	3.68	4.03	4.75	5	5.26

Address: 6601 West Broad Street, Richmond, VA 23230 Telephone: 804-274-2200	Web Site: www.altria.com Officers: Martin J. Barrington - Chairman, President, Chief Executive Officer, Vice-Chairman William F. Gifford - Executive Vice President, Chief Financial Officer	Auditors: PricewaterhouseCoopers LLP Investor Contact: 804-484-8222 Transfer Agents: Computershare Trust Company, N.A., Providence, RI

AMEREN CORP

Exchange	Symbol	Price	52Wk Range	Yield	P/E
NYS	AEE	$58.99 (12/29/2017)	64.54-51.69	3.10	23.50

*7 Year Price Score 109.61 *NYSE Composite Index=100 *12 Month Price Score 102.68

Interim Earnings (Per Share)

Qtr.	Mar	Jun	Sep	Dec
2014	0.40	0.61	1.20	0.20
2015	0.45	0.61	1.41	0.12
2016	0.43	0.61	1.52	0.12
2017	0.42	0.79	1.18	...

Interim Dividends (Per Share)

Amt	Decl	Ex	Rec	Pay
0.44Q	02/10/2017	03/10/2017	03/14/2017	03/31/2017
0.44Q	04/28/2017	06/12/2017	06/14/2017	06/30/2017
0.44Q	08/11/2017	09/12/2017	09/13/2017	09/29/2017
0.458Q	10/13/2017	12/12/2017	12/13/2017	12/29/2017

Indicated Div: $1.83 (Div. Reinv. Plan)

Valuation Analysis		Institutional Holding	
Forecast EPS	$2.80 (01/17/2018)	No of Institutions	725
Market Cap	$14.3 Billion	Shares	211,538,368
Book Value	$7.3 Billion	% Held	62.59
Price/Book	1.95		
Price/Sales	2.33		

Business Summary: Electric Utilities (MIC: 3.1.1 SIC: 4931 NAIC: 221111)

Ameren is a public utility holding company. Through its subsidiary, Union Electric Company, doing business as Ameren Missouri, Co. operates a rate-regulated electric generation, transmission, and distribution business and a rate-regulated natural gas distribution business in Missouri. Through its subsidiary, Ameren Illinois Company, doing business as Ameren Illinois, Co. operates rate-regulated electric transmission, electric distribution, and natural gas distribution businesses in Illinois. As of Dec 31 2016, Ameren Missouri and Ameren Illinois supplied electric service to 1.2 million customers each, and natural gas service to 100,000 customers and 800,000 customers, respectively.

Recent Developments: For the quarter ended Sep 30 2017, net income decreased 21.8% to US$290.0 million from US$371.0 million in the year-earlier quarter. Revenues were US$1.72 billion, down 7.3% from US$1.86 billion the year before. Operating income was US$581.0 million versus US$691.0 million in the prior-year quarter, a decrease of 15.9%. Direct operating expenses declined 4.2% to US$917.0 million from US$957.0 million in the comparable period the year before. Indirect operating expenses increased 6.6% to US$225.0 million from US$211.0 million in the equivalent prior-year period.

Prospects: Our evaluation of Ameren Corp. as of Jan. 14, 2018 is the result of our systematic analysis on three basic characteristics: earnings strength, relative valuation, and recent stock price movement. The company has managed to produce a neutral trend in earnings per share over the past 5 quarters. However, while recent estimates for the company have been mixed, AEE has posted results that fell short of analysts expectations. Based on operating earnings yield, the company is undervalued when compared to all of the companies in our coverage universe. Share price changes over the past year indicates that AEE will perform very well over the near term.

Financial Data

(US$ in Thousands)	9 Mos	6 Mos	3 Mos	12/31/2016	12/31/2015	12/31/2014	12/31/2013	12/31/2012
Earnings Per Share	2.51	2.85	2.67	2.68	2.59	2.40	1.18	(4.01)
Cash Flow Per Share	9.10	9.16	8.68	8.73	8.31	6.39	6.98	6.95
Tang Book Value Per Share	28.58	27.81	27.42	27.58	26.94	25.98	25.19	25.51
Dividends Per Share	1.760	1.745	1.730	1.715	1.655	1.610	1.600	1.600
Dividend Payout %	70.12	61.23	64.79	63.99	63.90	67.08	135.59	...
Income Statement								
Total Revenue	4,775,000	3,052,000	1,514,000	6,076,000	6,098,000	6,053,000	5,838,000	6,828,000
EBITDA	1,974,000	1,141,000	498,000	2,328,000	2,158,000	2,087,000	1,958,000	(397,000)
Depn & Amortn	740,000	492,000	247,000	945,000	896,000	813,000	761,000	842,000
Income Before Taxes	964,000	469,000	161,000	1,041,000	948,000	970,000	829,000	(1,654,000)
Income Taxes	376,000	171,000	57,000	382,000	363,000	377,000	311,000	(680,000)
Net Income	583,000	295,000	102,000	653,000	630,000	586,000	289,000	(974,000)
Average Shares	242,600	242,600	242,600	243,400	243,600	244,400	244,500	242,600
Balance Sheet								
Current Assets	1,581,000	1,571,000	1,450,000	1,593,000	1,917,000	2,046,000	1,972,000	2,369,000
Total Assets	25,617,000	25,254,000	24,811,000	24,699,000	23,640,000	22,676,000	21,042,000	21,835,000
Current Liabilities	2,581,000	2,765,000	2,762,000	2,674,000	2,093,000	2,249,000	2,461,000	1,698,000
Long-Term Obligations	6,922,000	6,821,000	6,597,000	6,595,000	6,880,000	6,120,000	5,504,000	6,626,000
Total Liabilities	18,272,000	18,096,000	17,747,000	17,596,000	16,694,000	15,963,000	14,498,000	15,219,000
Stockholders' Equity	7,345,000	7,158,000	7,064,000	7,103,000	6,946,000	6,713,000	6,544,000	6,616,000
Shares Outstanding	242,600	242,600	242,600	242,600	242,600	242,600	242,600	242,600
Statistical Record								
Return on Assets %	2.47	2.84	2.70	2.69	2.72	2.68	1.35	N.M.
Return on Equity %	8.46	9.89	9.33	9.27	9.22	8.84	4.39	N.M.
EBITDA Margin %	41.34	37.39	32.89	38.31	35.39	34.48	33.54	N.M.
Net Margin %	12.21	9.67	6.74	10.75	10.33	9.68	4.95	N.M.
Asset Turnover	0.25	0.26	0.26	0.25	0.26	0.28	0.27	0.30
Current Ratio	0.61	0.57	0.52	0.60	0.92	0.91	0.80	1.40
Debt to Equity	0.94	0.95	0.93	0.93	0.99	0.91	0.84	1.00
Price Range	60.91-46.88	57.17-46.88	56.19-46.47	53.77-42.13	46.54-37.51	47.92-35.40	37.03-30.72	34.71-28.55
P/E Ratio	24.27-18.68	20.06-16.45	21.04-17.40	20.06-15.72	17.97-14.48	19.97-14.75	31.38-26.03	...
Average Yield %	3.25	3.33	3.41	3.50	3.96	4.02	4.62	4.96

Address: 1901 Chouteau Avenue, St. Louis, MO 63103 Telephone: 314-621-3222	Web Site: www.ameren.com Officers: Warner L. Baxter - Chairman, President, Chief Executive Officer Martin J. Lyons - Executive Vice President, Senior Vice President, Chief Financial Officer	Auditors: PricewaterhouseCoopers LLP Transfer Agents: Ameren Services Company, St. Louis, MO

AMERICAN CAMPUS COMMUNITIES INC

Exchange	Symbol	Price	52Wk Range	Yield	P/E
NYS	ACC	$41.03 (12/29/2017)	51.43-40.23	4.29	100.07

*7 Year Price Score 87.31 *NYSE Composite Index=100 *12 Month Price Score 85.25

Interim Earnings (Per Share)

Qtr.	Mar	Jun	Sep	Dec
2014	0.27	0.12	(0.06)	0.25
2015	0.62	0.14	0.01	0.25
2016	0.36	0.14	0.07	0.19
2017	0.25	(0.02)	(0.01)	...

Interim Dividends (Per Share)

Amt	Decl	Ex	Rec	Pay
0.42Q	01/25/2017	02/02/2017	02/06/2017	02/17/2017
0.44Q	05/03/2017	05/11/2017	05/15/2017	05/26/2017
0.44Q	08/02/2017	08/10/2017	08/14/2017	08/25/2017
0.44Q	11/01/2017	11/10/2017	11/13/2017	11/27/2017

Indicated Div: $1.76

Valuation Analysis / Institutional Holding

Valuation Analysis		Institutional Holding	
Forecast EPS	$0.61	No of Institutions	430
	(01/16/2018)		
Market Cap	$5.6 Billion	Shares	167,386,064
Book Value	$3.5 Billion	% Held	100.00
Price/Book	1.60		
Price/Sales	7.24		

TRADING VOLUME (thousand shares)

Business Summary: REITs (MIC: 5.3.1 SIC: 6798 NAIC: 525930)

American Campus Communities is a real estate investment trust. Through American Campus Communities Operating Partnership L.P., Co. owns, manages and develops student housing properties. Co. focuses on the acquisition, design, financing, development, construction management, leasing and management of student housing properties. Co. has four reportable segments: Wholly-Owned Properties, On-Campus Participating Properties, Development Services and Property Management Services. As of Dec 31 2016, Co.'s property portfolio contained 154 properties, with 121 owned off-campus student housing properties, 28 American Campus Equity properties, and five on-campus participating properties.

Recent Developments:
For the quarter ended Sep 30 2017, revenues were US$196.9 million, up 0.3% from US$196.4 million the year before. Revenues from property income fell 1.1% to US$190.4 million from US$192.5 million in the corresponding quarter a year earlier.

Prospects:
Our evaluation of American Campus Communities Inc. as of Jan. 14, 2018 is the result of our systematic analysis on three basic characteristics: earnings strength, relative valuation, and recent stock price movement. The company has produced a positive trend in earnings per share over the past 5 quarters. However, while recent estimates for the company have been mixed, ACC has posted results that fell short of analysts expectations. Based on operating earnings yield, the company is overvalued when compared to all of the companies in our coverage universe. Share price changes over the past year indicates that ACC will perform well over the near term.

Financial Data
(US$ in Thousands)

	9 Mos	6 Mos	3 Mos	12/31/2016	12/31/2015	12/31/2014	12/31/2013	12/31/2012
Earnings Per Share	0.41	0.49	0.65	0.75	1.02	0.58	0.98	0.65
Cash Flow Per Share	2.28	2.12	2.34	2.38	2.33	2.47	2.35	2.39
Tang Book Value Per Share	25.67	26.07	26.09	26.05	24.66	24.35	25.05	25.30
Dividends Per Share	1.720	1.700	1.680	1.660	1.580	1.500	1.418	1.350
Dividend Payout %	419.51	346.94	258.46	221.33	154.90	258.62	144.64	207.69
Income Statement								
Total Revenue	568,884	371,946	192,938	786,361	753,381	733,915	657,462	491,290
EBITDA	76,389	59,595	48,420	175,879	206,371	151,286	137,179	118,644
Depn & Amortn	(2,383)	(1,602)	(799)	900	3,700	2,400	13,700	6,800
Income Before Taxes	31,354	32,320	34,706	101,773	119,303	62,692	48,456	57,027
Income Taxes	791	524	257	1,150	1,242	1,308	1,020	725
Net Income	29,976	31,288	34,050	99,061	115,991	62,839	104,644	56,636
Average Shares	136,421	134,614	133,986	130,018	114,032	105,711	105,382	85,309
Balance Sheet								
Current Assets	57,696	61,242	66,297	55,385	68,809	67,144	83,440	72,366
Total Assets	6,686,891	6,224,973	5,987,966	5,865,913	6,025,947	5,834,748	5,598,040	5,118,962
Current Liabilities	79,612	62,547	48,510	76,614	71,988	70,629	65,088	56,046
Long-Term Obligations	2,766,285	2,360,034	2,208,321	2,125,297	2,967,980	2,972,719	2,744,387	2,221,105
Total Liabilities	3,186,798	2,670,973	2,500,188	2,420,928	3,255,751	3,225,194	2,973,139	2,470,581
Stockholders' Equity	3,500,093	3,554,000	3,487,778	3,444,985	2,770,196	2,609,554	2,624,901	2,648,381
Shares Outstanding	136,362	136,316	133,668	132,225	112,350	107,175	104,782	104,665
Statistical Record								
Return on Assets %	0.85	1.06	1.42	1.66	1.96	1.10	1.95	1.39
Return on Equity %	1.59	1.90	2.52	3.18	4.31	2.40	3.97	2.81
EBITDA Margin %	13.43	16.02	25.10	22.37	27.39	20.61	20.86	24.15
Net Margin %	5.27	8.41	17.65	12.60	15.40	8.56	15.92	11.53
Asset Turnover	0.12	0.12	0.13	0.13	0.13	0.13	0.12	0.12
Current Ratio	0.72	0.98	1.37	0.72	0.96	0.95	1.28	1.29
Debt to Equity	0.79	0.66	0.63	0.62	1.07	1.14	1.05	0.84
Price Range	52.11-44.14	54.55-45.03	54.55-43.84	54.55-39.33	44.84-32.26	41.88-32.21	47.88-31.80	47.69-40.86
P/E Ratio	127.10-107.66	111.33-91.90	83.92-67.45	72.73-52.44	43.96-31.63	72.21-55.53	48.86-32.45	73.37-62.86
Average Yield %	3.58	3.47	3.44	3.50	3.98	3.95	3.55	3.04

Address: 12700 Hill Country Blvd., Suite T-200, Austin, TX 78738 Telephone: 512-732-1000	Web Site: www.americancampus.com Officers: Edward Lowenthal - Chairman James C. Hopke - President, Chief Operating Officer, Executive Vice President, Executive Vice President, Executive Vice President (frmr)	Auditors: Ernst & Young LLP Investor Contact: 512-732-1041 Transfer Agents: Wells Fargo Bank N.A., Mendota Heights, MN

34

AMERICAN EAGLE OUTFITTERS, INC.

Exchange	Symbol	Price	52Wk Range	Yield	P/E
NYS	AEO	$18.80 (12/29/2017)	19.37-10.62	2.66	20.43

*7 Year Price Score 68.71   *NYSE Composite Index=100   *12 Month Price Score 110.14

Interim Earnings (Per Share)
Qtr.	Apr	Jul	Oct	Jan
2014-15	0.02	0.03	0.05	0.32
2015-16	0.15	0.17	0.38	0.42
2016-17	0.22	0.23	0.41	0.30
2017-18	0.14	0.12	0.36	...

Interim Dividends (Per Share)
Amt	Decl	Ex	Rec	Pay
0.125Q	03/08/2017	04/05/2017	04/07/2017	04/21/2017
0.125Q	05/23/2017	07/05/2017	07/07/2017	07/21/2017
0.125Q	09/07/2017	10/05/2017	10/06/2017	10/20/2017
0.125Q	12/05/2017	12/14/2017	12/15/2017	12/29/2017

Indicated Div: $0.50

Valuation Analysis / Institutional Holding
Forecast EPS	$1.16 (01/18/2018)	No of Institutions	503
Market Cap	$3.3 Billion	Shares	209,670,320
Book Value	$1.2 Billion	% Held	73.96
Price/Book	2.86		
Price/Sales	0.91		

Business Summary: Retail - Apparel and Accessories (MIC: 2.1.5 SIC: 5651 NAIC: 448140)

American Eagle Outfitters is a multi-brand retailer. Co. operates over 1,000 retail stores and online at www.ae.com and www.aerie.com. Co. provides a range of assortment of apparel and accessories for men and women under the American Eagle Outfitters brand, and intimates, apparel and personal care products for women under the Aerie brand. Co. operates stores in the U.S., Canada, Mexico, Hong Kong, China and the U.K. Co. also has license agreements with third-parties to operate American Eagle Outfitters and Aerie stores throughout Asia, Europe, Latin America and the Middle East. As of Jan 28 2017, Co. operated 943 American Eagle Outfitters stores and 102 Aerie stand-alone stores.

Recent Developments: For the quarter ended Oct 28 2017, net income decreased 15.9% to US$63.7 million from US$75.8 million in the year-earlier quarter. Revenues were US$960.4 million, up 2.1% from US$940.6 million the year before. Operating income was US$110.9 million versus US$118.3 million in the prior-year quarter, a decrease of 6.2%. Direct operating expenses rose 4.0% to US$585.5 million from US$562.8 million in the comparable period the year before. Indirect operating expenses increased 1.7% to US$264.0 million from US$259.5 million in the equivalent prior-year period.

Prospects: Our evaluation of American Eagle Outfitters Inc. as of Jan. 14, 2018 is the result of our systematic analysis on three basic characteristics: earnings strength, relative valuation, and recent stock price movement. The company has enjoyed a very positive trend in earnings per share over the past 5 quarters and while recent estimates for the company have been mixed, AEO has posted results that fell short of analysts expectations. Based on operating earnings yield, the company is undervalued when compared to all of the companies in our coverage universe. Share price changes over the past year indicates that AEO will perform very poorly over the near term.

Financial Data
(US$ in Thousands)

	9 Mos	6 Mos	3 Mos	01/28/2017	01/30/2016	01/31/2015	02/01/2014	02/02/2013
Earnings Per Share	0.92	0.97	1.08	1.16	1.11	0.42	0.43	1.16
Cash Flow Per Share	1.98	1.79	1.93	2.02	1.76	1.75	1.20	2.51
Tang Book Value Per Share	6.22	6.00	5.96	6.27	5.45	5.55	5.71	6.08
Dividends Per Share	0.500	0.500	0.500	0.500	0.500	0.500	0.375	2.050
Dividend Payout %	54.35	51.55	46.30	43.10	45.05	119.05	87.21	176.72
Income Statement								
Total Revenue	2,566,826	1,606,393	761,836	3,609,865	3,521,848	3,282,867	3,305,802	3,475,802
EBITDA	292,573	151,219	78,245	487,906	462,487	292,031	258,838	524,794
Depn & Amortn	125,370	81,697	40,893	152,644	140,616	132,529	116,761	122,756
Income Before Taxes	167,203	69,522	37,352	335,262	321,871	159,502	142,077	402,038
Income Taxes	56,997	23,050	12,116	122,813	108,580	70,715	59,094	137,940
Net Income	110,206	46,472	25,236	212,449	218,138	80,322	82,983	232,108
Average Shares	179,132	178,788	181,678	183,835	196,237	195,135	194,475	200,665
Balance Sheet								
Current Assets	930,212	817,185	763,672	901,229	723,375	890,513	923,560	1,141,800
Total Assets	1,801,780	1,686,323	1,633,193	1,782,660	1,612,246	1,696,908	1,694,164	1,756,053
Current Liabilities	552,840	471,982	420,591	493,783	463,682	459,093	415,478	435,902
Total Liabilities	638,581	562,024	515,320	578,091	560,870	557,162	527,986	534,866
Stockholders' Equity	1,163,199	1,124,299	1,117,873	1,204,569	1,051,376	1,139,746	1,166,178	1,221,187
Shares Outstanding	177,084	176,965	176,965	181,886	180,135	194,516	193,149	192,604
Statistical Record								
Return on Assets %	9.10	10.47	12.21	12.55	13.22	4.75	4.82	12.32
Return on Equity %	14.12	15.90	17.97	18.89	19.97	6.99	6.97	17.31
EBITDA Margin %	11.40	9.41	10.27	13.52	13.13	8.90	7.83	15.10
Net Margin %	4.29	2.89	3.31	5.89	6.19	2.45	2.51	6.68
Asset Turnover	2.02	2.16	2.24	2.13	2.13	1.94	1.92	1.85
Current Ratio	1.68	1.73	1.82	1.83	1.56	1.94	2.22	2.62
Price Range	18.91-10.62	19.37-10.85	19.37-13.08	19.37-13.12	18.35-13.24	14.85-10.28	22.55-12.77	23.80-13.58
P/E Ratio	20.55-11.54	19.97-11.19	17.94-12.11	16.70-11.31	16.53-11.93	35.36-24.48	52.44-29.70	20.52-11.71
Average Yield %	3.60	3.28	3.10	3.05	3.08	3.93	2.18	10.52

Address: 77 Hot Metal Street, Pittsburgh, PA 15203-2329 Telephone: 412-432-3300	Web Site: www.ae.com Officers: Jay L. Schottenstein - Executive Chairman, Chairman, Chief Executive Officer, Interim Chief Executive Officer James H. Keefer - Vice President, Chief Accounting Officer, Controller	Auditors: Ernst & Young LLP Investor Contact: 412-432-3300 Transfer Agents: Computershare Trust Company, N.A., Providence, RI

AMERICAN ELECTRIC POWER COMPANY, INC.

Exchange	Symbol	Price	52Wk Range	Yield	P/E
NYS	AEP	$73.57 (12/29/2017)	77.63-62.12	3.37	19.26

*7 Year Price Score 104.03 *NYSE Composite Index=100 *12 Month Price Score 101.58

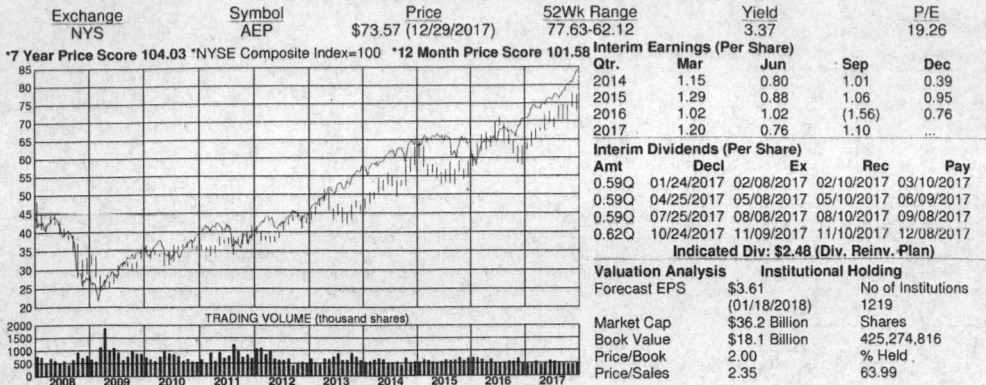

Interim Earnings (Per Share)

Qtr.	Mar	Jun	Sep	Dec
2014	1.15	0.80	1.01	0.39
2015	1.29	0.88	1.06	0.95
2016	1.02	1.02	(1.56)	0.76
2017	1.20	0.76	1.10	...

Interim Dividends (Per Share)

Amt	Decl	Ex	Rec	Pay
0.59Q	01/24/2017	02/08/2017	02/10/2017	03/10/2017
0.59Q	04/25/2017	05/08/2017	05/10/2017	06/09/2017
0.59Q	07/25/2017	08/08/2017	08/10/2017	09/08/2017
0.62Q	10/24/2017	11/09/2017	11/10/2017	12/08/2017

Indicated Div: $2.48 (Div. Reinv. Plan)

Valuation Analysis | **Institutional Holding**

Forecast EPS	$3.61	No of Institutions
(01/18/2018)		1219
Market Cap	$36.2 Billion	Shares
Book Value	$18.1 Billion	425,274,816
Price/Book	2.00	% Held
Price/Sales	2.35	63.99

Business Summary: Electric Utilities (MIC: 3.1.1 SIC: 4911 NAIC: 221122)

American Electric Power Company is a public utility holding company. The public utility subsidiaries of Co. provide electric service, consisting of generation, transmission and distribution, on an integrated basis to their retail customers. The service areas of Co.'s public utility subsidiaries cover portions of the states of Arkansas, Indiana, Kentucky, Louisiana, Michigan, Ohio, Oklahoma, Tennessee, Texas, Virginia and West Virginia. Transmission networks are interconnected with distribution facilities in the territories served.

Recent Developments: For the quarter ended Sep 30 2017, income from continuing operations was US$556.7 million compared with a loss of US$764.2 million in the year-earlier quarter. Net income amounted to US$556.7 million versus a net loss of US$764.2 million in the year-earlier quarter. Revenues were US$4.10 billion, down 11.8% from US$4.65 billion the year before. Operating income was US$986.5 million versus a loss of US$1.13 billion in the prior-year quarter. Direct operating expenses declined 14.1% to US$2.33 billion from US$2.71 billion in the comparable period the year before. Indirect operating expenses decreased 74.3% to US$788.6 million from US$3.07 billion in the equivalent prior-year period.

Prospects: Our evaluation of American Electric Power Company Inc. as of Jan. 14, 2018 is the result of our systematic analysis on three basic characteristics: earnings strength, relative valuation, and recent stock price movement. The company has produced a positive trend in earnings per share over the past 5 quarters and while recent estimates for the company have been mixed, AEP has posted results that fell short of analysts expectations. Based on operating earnings yield, the company is undervalued when compared to all of the companies in our coverage universe. Share price changes over the past year indicates that AEP will perform very well over the near term.

Financial Data

(US$ in Thousands)	9 Mos	6 Mos	3 Mos	12/31/2016	12/31/2015	12/31/2014	12/31/2013	12/31/2012
Earnings Per Share	3.82	1.16	1.42	1.24	4.17	3.34	3.04	2.60
Cash Flow Per Share	8.59	9.18	9.21	9.18	9.68	9.44	8.44	7.83
Tang Book Value Per Share	36.65	36.14	35.87	35.27	36.33	34.18	32.79	31.19
Dividends Per Share	2.360	2.330	2.300	2.270	2.150	2.030	1.950	1.880
Dividend Payout %	61.78	200.86	161.97	183.06	51.56	60.78	64.14	72.31
Income Statement								
Total Revenue	11,614,500	7,509,800	3,933,300	16,380,100	16,453,200	17,020,000	15,357,000	14,945,000
EBITDA	3,021,900	1,967,200	1,159,300	3,443,700	5,651,500	5,448,000	4,890,000	4,728,000
Depn & Amortn	104,800	71,600	35,100	2,090,900	2,154,700	2,073,000	1,874,000	1,918,000
Income Before Taxes	2,261,800	1,461,200	910,400	475,600	2,622,900	2,490,000	2,110,000	1,822,000
Income Taxes	797,800	533,800	343,200	(73,700)	919,600	942,000	684,000	604,000
Net Income	1,511,900	967,200	592,200	610,900	2,047,100	1,634,000	1,480,000	1,259,000
Average Shares	492,986	492,642	492,031	491,662	490,574	488,899	487,040	485,084
Balance Sheet								
Current Assets	4,067,800	3,809,100	3,616,400	6,033,900	4,072,400	4,478,000	4,310,000	4,589,000
Total Assets	63,964,900	62,739,100	61,728,300	63,467,700	61,683,100	59,633,000	56,414,000	54,367,000
Current Liabilities	7,322,000	8,392,200	7,914,500	9,498,000	7,108,500	7,967,000	6,112,000	6,823,000
Long-Term Obligations	18,362,400	16,796,900	16,722,200	17,378,400	17,740,900	16,181,000	16,828,000	15,586,000
Total Liabilities	45,886,500	44,909,500	44,039,600	46,070,700	43,791,400	42,813,000	40,329,000	39,130,000
Stockholders' Equity	18,078,400	17,829,600	17,688,700	17,397,000	17,891,700	16,820,000	16,085,000	15,237,000
Shares Outstanding	491,842	491,837	491,712	491,711	491,052	489,402	487,777	485,668
Statistical Record								
Return on Assets %	3.01	0.91	1.13	0.97	3.37	2.82	2.67	2.36
Return on Equity %	10.65	3.17	3.92	3.45	11.79	9.93	9.45	8.40
EBITDA Margin %	26.02	26.20	29.47	21.02	34.35	32.01	31.84	31.64
Net Margin %	13.02	12.88	15.06	3.73	12.44	9.60	9.64	8.42
Asset Turnover	0.25	0.25	0.26	0.26	0.27	0.29	0.28	0.28
Current Ratio	0.56	0.45	0.46	0.64	0.57	0.56	0.71	0.67
Debt to Equity	1.02	0.94	0.95	1.00	0.99	0.96	1.05	1.02
Price Range	74.55-58.16	72.67-58.16	71.27-58.16	71.27-57.64	64.57-52.54	62.91-46.08	51.43-41.92	45.27-37.22
P/E Ratio	19.52-15.23	62.65-50.14	50.19-40.96	57.48-46.48	15.48-12.60	18.84-13.80	16.92-13.79	17.41-14.32
Average Yield %	3.53	3.54	3.55	3.54	3.79	3.84	4.24	4.59

Address: 1 Riverside Plaza, Columbus, OH 43215-2373	**Web Site:** www.aep.com	**Auditors:** Deloitte & Touche LLP
Telephone: 614-716-1000	**Officers:** Nicholas K. Akins - Chairman, President, Chief Executive Officer Brian X. Tierney - Executive Vice President, Chief Financial Officer	**Investor Contact:** 614-716-2819
Fax: 614-223-1823		**Transfer Agents:** Computershare Trust Company, N.A., Providence, RI

AMERICAN EQUITY INVESTMENT LIFE HOLDING CO

Exchange	Symbol	Price	52Wk Range	Yield	P/E	Div Achiever
NYS	AEL	$30.73 (12/29/2017)	32.22-22.34	0.85	10.42	13 Years

*7 Year Price Score 108.10 *NYSE Composite Index=100 *12 Month Price Score 108.83

Interim Earnings (Per Share)

Qtr.	Mar	Jun	Sep	Dec
2014	(0.13)	0.46	0.85	0.39
2015	0.07	1.05	1.19	0.39
2016	(0.55)	0.18	(0.09)	1.42
2017	0.60	0.30	0.63	...

Interim Dividends (Per Share)

Amt	Decl	Ex	Rec	Pay
0.20A	11/21/2014	11/26/2014	12/01/2014	12/15/2014
0.22A	11/19/2015	11/25/2015	11/30/2015	12/14/2015
0.24A	11/17/2016	12/01/2016	12/05/2016	12/20/2016
0.26A	11/16/2017	11/28/2017	11/29/2017	12/12/2017

Indicated Div: $0.26

Valuation Analysis

		Institutional Holding	
Forecast EPS	$3.01	No of Institutions	330
	(01/18/2018)		
Market Cap	$2.7 Billion	Shares	102,024,656
Book Value	$2.8 Billion	% Held	
Price/Book	0.99	% Held	105.63
Price/Sales	0.83		

TRADING VOLUME (thousand shares)

Business Summary: Life & Health (MIC: 5.2.2 SIC: 6311 NAIC: 524113)

American Equity Investment Life Holding is a holding company. Co. is engaged in the development and sale of fixed index and fixed rate annuity products. Co. issues fixed annuity and life insurance products through its wholly-owned life insurance subsidiaries, American Equity Investment Life Insurance Company, American Equity Investment Life Insurance Company of New York, and Eagle Life Insurance Company. Co.'s life insurance products include ordinary and term, universal life and other interest-sensitive life insurance products. Co. was licensed to sell its products in 50 states and the District of Columbia at Dec 31 2016.

Recent Developments: For the quarter ended Sep 30 2017, net income amounted to US$57.0 million versus a net loss of US$7.4 million in the year-earlier quarter. Revenues were US$906.0 million, up 43.8% from US$630.1 million the year before. Net premiums earned were US$60.5 million versus US$60.4 million in the prior-year quarter, an increase of 0.2%. Net investment income rose 7.9% to US$500.2 million from US$463.6 million a year ago.

Prospects: Our evaluation of American Equity Investment Life Holding Co as of Jan. 14, 2018 is the result of our systematic analysis on three basic characteristics: earnings strength, relative valuation, and recent stock price movement. The company has managed to produce a neutral trend in earnings per share over the past 5 quarters and while recent estimates for the company have been mixed, AEL has posted better than expected results. Based on operating earnings yield, the company is undervalued when compared to all of the companies in our coverage universe. Share price changes over the past year indicates that AEL will perform well over the near term.

Financial Data

(US$ in Thousands)	9 Mos	6 Mos	3 Mos	12/31/2016	12/31/2015	12/31/2014	12/31/2013	12/31/2012
Earnings Per Share	2.95	2.23	2.11	0.97	2.72	1.58	3.38	0.89
Cash Flow Per Share	19.47	20.51	19.97	16.63	6.40	9.51	13.16	12.77
Tang Book Value Per Share	31.06	29.88	27.49	26.04	23.90	28.13	19.63	27.86
Dividends Per Share	0.240	0.240	0.240	0.240	0.220	0.200	0.180	0.150
Dividend Payout %	8.14	10.76	11.37	24.74	8.09	12.66	5.33	16.85
Income Statement								
Total Revenue	2,652,382	1,746,429	927,301	2,220,282	1,518,937	2,168,973	2,610,692	1,588,558
Income Before Taxes	208,533	121,744	81,477	130,247	337,314	196,064	389,332	85,989
Income Taxes	70,691	40,859	27,538	47,004	117,484	70,041	136,049	28,191
Net Income	137,842	80,885	53,939	83,243	219,830	126,023	253,283	57,798
Average Shares	90,420	90,112	89,975	85,605	80,961	79,893	75,040	65,675
Balance Sheet								
Total Assets	60,379,715	59,635,590	57,548,610	56,053,472	49,041,163	43,989,734	39,621,499	35,133,478
Total Liabilities	57,617,048	56,984,182	55,112,379	53,761,877	47,096,628	41,849,858	38,236,812	33,413,241
Stockholders' Equity	2,762,667	2,651,408	2,436,231	2,291,595	1,944,535	2,139,876	1,384,687	1,720,237
Shares Outstanding	88,933	88,741	88,630	88,001	81,354	76,062	70,535	61,750
Statistical Record								
Return on Assets %	0.45	0.34	0.33	0.16	0.47	0.30	0.68	0.17
Return on Equity %	9.28	7.38	7.79	3.92	10.76	7.15	16.31	3.68
Net Margin %	5.20	4.63	5.82	3.75	14.47	5.81	9.70	3.64
Asset Turnover	0.06	0.05	0.05	0.04	0.03	0.05	0.07	0.05
Price Range	29.29-15.71	27.67-13.54	27.67-12.88	24.03-12.81	29.67-22.76	29.46-20.43	26.38-12.21	12.95-10.05
P/E Ratio	9.93-5.33	12.41-6.07	13.11-6.10	24.77-13.21	10.91-8.37	18.65-12.93	7.80-3.61	14.55-11.29
Average Yield %	0.99	1.12	1.26	1.41	0.83	0.83	1.01	1.30

Address: 6000 Westown Parkway, West Des Moines, IA 50266
Telephone: 515-221-0002
Web Site: www.american-equity.com
Officers: David J. Noble - Chairman John M. Matovina - Vice-Chairman, President, Chief Executive Officer, Chief Financial Officer, Treasurer
Auditors: KPMG LLP
Investor Contact: 515-221-0002
Transfer Agents: Computershare Trust Company, N.A., Providence, RI

AMERICAN EXPRESS CO.

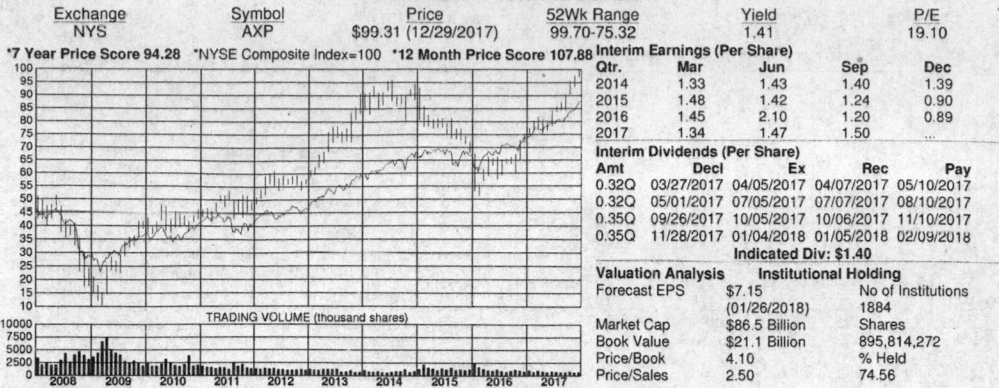

Exchange	Symbol	Price	52Wk Range	Yield	P/E
NYS	AXP	$99.31 (12/29/2017)	99.70-75.32	1.41	19.10

*7 Year Price Score 94.28 ***NYSE Composite Index=100** ***12 Month Price Score 107.88**

Interim Earnings (Per Share)

Qtr.	Mar	Jun	Sep	Dec
2014	1.33	1.43	1.40	1.39
2015	1.48	1.42	1.24	0.90
2016	1.45	2.10	1.20	0.89
2017	1.34	1.47	1.50	...

Interim Dividends (Per Share)

Amt	Decl	Ex	Rec	Pay
0.32Q	03/27/2017	04/05/2017	04/07/2017	05/10/2017
0.32Q	05/01/2017	07/05/2017	07/07/2017	08/10/2017
0.35Q	09/26/2017	10/05/2017	10/06/2017	11/10/2017
0.35Q	11/28/2017	01/04/2018	01/05/2018	02/09/2018

Indicated Div: $1.40

Valuation Analysis

		Institutional Holding	
Forecast EPS	$7.15	No of Institutions	
	(01/26/2018)	1884	
Market Cap	$86.5 Billion	Shares	
Book Value	$21.1 Billion	895,814,272	
Price/Book	4.10	% Held	
Price/Sales	2.50	74.56	

TRADING VOLUME (thousand shares)

Business Summary: Credit & Lending (MIC: 5.4.1 SIC: 6153 NAIC: 522210)

American Express, together with its subsidiaries, Co. is a global services company that provides charge and credit card products and travel-related services to consumers and businesses around the world. Co.'s range of products and services includes: charge card, credit card and other payment and financing products; network services; merchant acquisition and processing, servicing and settlement, and point-of-sale marketing and information products and services for merchants; other fee services, including fraud prevention services and the design and operation of customer loyalty programs; expense management products and services; travel-related services; and stored value/prepaid products.

Recent Developments: For the quarter ended Sep 30 2017, net income increased 18.7% to US$1.36 billion from US$1.14 billion in the year-earlier quarter. Net interest income increased 25.6% to US$1.68 billion from US$1.33 billion in the year-earlier quarter. Provision for loan losses was US$769.0 million versus US$504.0 million in the prior-year quarter, an increase of 52.6%. Non-interest income rose 5.0% to US$6.76 billion from US$6.44 billion, while non-interest expense advanced 5.5% to US$5.84 billion.

Prospects: Our evaluation of American Express Co. as of Jan. 21, 2018 is the result of our systematic analysis on three basic characteristics: earnings strength, relative valuation, and recent stock price movement. The company has produced a positive trend in earnings per share over the past 5 quarters and while recent estimates for the company have been raised by analysts, AXP has posted better than expected results. Based on operating earnings yield, the company is undervalued when compared to all of the companies in our coverage universe. Share price changes over the past year indicates that AXP will perform well over the near term.

Financial Data
(US$ in Thousands)

	9 Mos	6 Mos	3 Mos	12/31/2016	12/31/2015	12/31/2014	12/31/2013	12/31/2012
Earnings Per Share	5.20	4.90	5.53	5.65	5.05	5.56	4.88	3.89
Cash Flow Per Share	13.58	10.53	7.69	8.79	10.98	10.52	7.90	6.22
Tang Book Value Per Share	24.21	23.93	23.39	18.48	17.68	16.42	14.55	13.31
Dividends Per Share	1.280	0.960	1.220	1.190	1.100	0.980	0.860	0.780
Dividend Payout %	24.62	19.59	22.06	21.06	21.78	17.63	17.62	20.05
Income Statement								
Total Revenue	26,164,000	17,161,000	8,332,000	33,823,000	34,441,000	35,999,000	34,932,000	33,808,000
Income Before Taxes	5,593,000	3,766,000	1,817,000	8,096,000	7,938,000	8,991,000	7,888,000	6,451,000
Income Taxes	1,660,000	1,189,000	580,000	2,688,000	2,775,000	3,106,000	2,529,000	1,969,000
Net Income	3,933,000	2,577,000	1,237,000	5,408,000	5,163,000	5,885,000	5,359,000	4,482,000
Average Shares	881,000	893,000	903,000	935,000	1,003,000	1,051,000	1,089,000	1,141,000
Balance Sheet								
Total Assets	168,577,000	166,997,000	161,385,000	158,893,000	161,184,000	159,103,000	153,375,000	153,140,000
Total Liabilities	147,492,000	145,822,000	140,450,000	138,392,000	140,511,000	138,430,000	133,879,000	134,254,000
Stockholders' Equity	21,085,000	21,175,000	20,935,000	20,501,000	20,673,000	20,673,000	19,496,000	18,886,000
Shares Outstanding	871,000	885,000	895,000	904,000	969,000	1,023,000	1,064,000	1,105,000
Statistical Record								
Return on Assets %	2.96	2.78	3.26	3.37	3.22	3.77	3.50	2.92
Return on Equity %	22.60	21.70	25.05	26.20	24.97	29.30	27.92	23.72
Net Margin %	15.03	15.02	14.85	15.99	14.99	16.35	15.34	13.26
Asset Turnover	0.21	0.21	0.21	0.21	0.22	0.23	0.23	0.22
Price Range	90.46-59.90	84.24-59.15	81.92-57.67	75.32-51.11	93.04-67.87	95.84-80.24	90.73-57.48	61.05-48.24
P/E Ratio	17.40-11.52	17.19-12.07	14.81-10.43	13.33-9.05	18.42-13.44	17.24-14.43	18.59-11.78	15.69-12.40
Average Yield %	1.64	1.32	1.78	1.86	1.41	1.09	1.18	1.39

Address: 200 Vesey Street, New York, NY 10285
Telephone: 212-640-2000
Fax: 212-640-0404

Web Site: www.americanexpress.com
Officers: Kenneth I. (Ken) Chenault - Chairman, Chief Executive Officer Stephen J. Squeri - Vice-Chairman, Division Officer

Auditors: PricewaterhouseCoopers LLP
Transfer Agents: Computershare Shareowner Services LLC, Canton, MA

AMERICAN FINANCIAL GROUP INC

Exchange	Symbol	Price	52Wk Range	Yield	P/E	Div Achiever
NYS	AFG	$108.54 (12/29/2017)	109.06-85.86	1.29	13.90	11 Years

*7 Year Price Score 128.98 *NYSE Composite Index=100 *12 Month Price Score 100.22

Interim Earnings (Per Share)

Qtr.	Mar	Jun	Sep	Dec
2014	1.13	1.15	1.28	1.41
2015	0.21	1.57	0.71	1.45
2016	1.14	0.62	1.23	4.35
2017	1.72	1.61	0.13	...

Interim Dividends (Per Share)

Amt	Decl	Ex	Rec	Pay
0.313Q	07/03/2017	07/12/2017	07/14/2017	07/25/2017
0.35Q	10/02/2017	10/12/2017	10/13/2017	10/25/2017
2.00Sp	11/06/2017	11/16/2017	11/17/2017	11/27/2017
0.35Q	01/02/2018	01/11/2018	01/15/2018	01/25/2018

Indicated Div: $1.40 (Div. Reinv. Plan)

Valuation Analysis / Institutional Holding

Valuation Analysis		Institutional Holding	
Forecast EPS	$6.04 (01/17/2018)	No of Institutions	503
Market Cap	$9.6 Billion	Shares	71,627,720
Book Value	$5.4 Billion	% Held	
Price/Book	1.78		53.28
Price/Sales	1.41		

Business Summary: General Insurance (MIC: 5.2.1 SIC: 6331 NAIC: 524126)

American Financial Group is a holding company. Co.'s segments include Property and Casualty Insurance, which includes Property and Transportation (inland and ocean marine, agricultural-related, and commercial automobile), Specialty Casualty (executive and professional liability, umbrella and excess liability, excess and surplus, general liability, targeted programs, and workers' compensation), and Specialty Financial (fidelity and surety, and lease and loan services); Annuity, which sells fixed and fixed-indexed annuities in the retail, financial institutions and education markets; and other, which includes commercial real estate operations.

Recent Developments: For the quarter ended Sep 30 2017, net income decreased 90.3% to US$11.0 million from US$113.0 million in the year-earlier quarter. Revenues were US$1.84 billion, up 7.6% from US$1.71 billion the year before. Net premiums earned were US$1.27 billion versus US$1.17 billion in the prior-year quarter, an increase of 9.3%.

Prospects: Our evaluation of American Financial Group Inc. as of Jan. 14, 2018 is the result of our systematic analysis on three basic characteristics: earnings strength, relative valuation, and recent stock price movement. The company has generated a negative trend in earnings per share over the past 5 quarters and while recent estimates for the company have been mixed, AFG has posted better than expected results. Based on operating earnings yield, the company is undervalued when compared to all of the companies in our coverage universe. Share price changes over the past year indicates that AFG will perform well over the near term.

Financial Data
(US$ in Thousands)

	9 Mos	6 Mos	3 Mos	12/31/2016	12/31/2015	12/31/2014	12/31/2013	12/31/2012
Earnings Per Share	7.81	8.91	7.92	7.33	3.94	4.97	5.16	5.09
Cash Flow Per Share	16.69	14.78	8.47	13.20	15.49	13.73	8.51	8.65
Tang Book Value Per Share	58.80	58.10	56.99	54.27	50.22	53.34	49.31	49.37
Dividends Per Share	3.750	3.717	2.185	2.152	2.030	1.910	1.805	0.970
Dividend Payout %	48.02	41.72	27.59	29.37	51.52	38.43	34.98	19.06
Income Statement								
Premium Income	3,371,000	2,098,000	1,028,000	4,352,000	4,328,000	3,986,000	3,318,000	3,165,000
Total Revenue	5,057,000	3,222,000	1,576,000	6,498,000	6,145,000	5,713,000	5,092,000	5,062,000
Benefits & Claims	2,895,000	1,679,000	814,000	3,595,000	3,558,000	3,306,000	2,731,000	2,779,000
Income Before Taxes	457,000	428,000	223,000	787,000	565,000	626,000	689,000	537,000
Income Taxes	146,000	128,000	68,000	119,000	195,000	220,000	236,000	135,000
Net Income	309,000	298,000	153,000	649,000	352,000	452,000	471,000	488,000
Average Shares	90,000	89,800	89,300	88,500	89,400	91,000	91,200	95,900
Balance Sheet								
Total Assets	60,163,000	58,618,000	57,464,000	55,072,000	49,859,000	47,535,000	42,087,000	39,171,000
Total Liabilities	54,784,000	53,306,000	52,273,000	50,156,000	45,267,000	42,656,000	37,488,000	34,593,000
Stockholders' Equity	5,379,000	5,312,000	5,191,000	4,916,000	4,592,000	4,879,000	4,599,000	4,578,000
Shares Outstanding	88,092	88,007	87,591	86,924	87,474	87,708	89,513	88,979
Statistical Record								
Return on Assets %	1.21	1.42	1.29	1.23	0.72	1.01	1.16	1.29
Return on Equity %	13.17	15.36	14.10	13.61	7.43	9.54	10.26	10.67
Loss Ratio %	85.88	80.03	79.18	82.61	82.21	82.94	82.31	87.80
Net Margin %	6.11	9.25	9.71	9.99	5.73	7.91	9.25	9.64
Price Range	105.28-73.93	102.43-71.70	96.40-67.22	88.12-65.14	75.17-58.04	62.36-52.93	58.16-39.52	40.25-36.58
P/E Ratio	13.48-9.47	11.50-8.05	12.17-8.49	12.02-8.89	19.08-14.73	12.55-10.65	11.27-7.66	7.91-7.19
Average Yield %	4.04	4.33	2.77	2.93	3.03	3.28	3.60	2.54

Address: 301 East Fourth Street, Cincinnati, OH 45202 **Telephone:** 513-579-2121	**Web Site:** www.afginc.com **Officers:** Carl H. Lindner - Co-President, Co-Chief Executive Officer S. Craig Lindner - Co-President, Co-Chief Executive Officer	**Auditors:** Ernst & Young LLP **Investor Contact:** 513-579-6739 **Transfer Agents:** American Stock Transfer & Trust Company, New York, NY

AMERICAN HOMES 4 RENT

Exchange	Symbol	Price	52Wk Range	Yield	P/E
NYS	AMH	$21.84 (12/29/2017)	23.77-20.34	0.92	N/A

'7 Year Price Score N/A   ***NYSE Composite Index=100**   ***12 Month Price Score 91.98**

Interim Earnings (Per Share)

Qtr.	Mar	Jun	Sep	Dec
2014	(0.07)	(0.07)	(0.11)	(0.09)
2015	(0.08)	(0.08)	(0.14)	(0.10)
2016	(0.02)	(0.04)	(0.09)	0.01
2017	(0.01)	0.00	0.01	...

Interim Dividends (Per Share)

Amt	Decl	Ex	Rec	Pay
0.05Q	02/23/2017	03/13/2017	03/15/2017	03/31/2017
0.05Q	05/04/2017	06/13/2017	06/15/2017	06/30/2017
0.05Q	08/03/2017	09/14/2017	09/15/2017	09/29/2017
0.05Q	11/02/2017	12/29/2017	01/02/2018	01/05/2018

Indicated Div: $0.20

Valuation Analysis / Institutional Holding

Forecast EPS	$0.04 (01/16/2018)	No of Institutions	N/A
Market Cap	$6.0 Billion	Shares	N/A
Book Value	$5.1 Billion	% Held	N/A
Price/Book	1.17		N/A
Price/Sales	6.34		

TRADING VOLUME (thousand shares)

Business Summary: REITs (MIC: 5.3.1 SIC: 6798 NAIC: 525930)

American Homes 4 Rent is a real estate investment trust which engaged in acquiring, renovating, leasing and operating single-family homes as rental properties. As of Dec 31 2016, Co. owned 48,422 single-family properties in 22 states, including 1,119 properties held for sale.

Recent Developments: For the quarter ended Sep 30 2017, net income amounted to US$19.1 million versus a net loss of US$167,000 in the year-earlier quarter. Revenues were US$246.8 million, up 4.6% from US$236.1 million the year before. Revenues from property income rose 6.8% to US$246.4 million from US$230.8 million in the corresponding quarter a year earlier.

Prospects: Our evaluation of American Homes 4 Rent as of Jan. 14, 2018 is the result of our systematic analysis on three basic characteristics: earnings strength, relative valuation, and recent stock price movement. The company has managed to produce a neutral trend in earnings per share over the past 5 quarters and while recent estimates for the company have been mixed, AMH has posted better than expected results. Based on operating earnings yield, the company is overvalued when compared to all of the companies in our coverage universe. Share price changes over the past year indicates that AMH will perform well over the near term.

Financial Data
(US$ in Thousands)

	9 Mos	6 Mos	3 Mos	12/31/2016	12/31/2015	12/31/2014	12/31/2013	12/31/2012
Earnings Per Share	...	...	(0.13)	(0.14)	(0.40)	(0.34)	(0.36)	(1.42)
Cash Flow Per Share	1.44	1.37	1.36	1.19	0.96	0.82	0.13	(0.90)
Tang Book Value Per Share	18.21	17.57	17.05	16.73	15.10	15.74	15.17	23.40
Dividends Per Share	0.200	0.200	0.200	0.200	0.200	0.200	0.050	...
Income Statement								
Total Revenue	717,598	470,762	233,754	878,889	630,576	398,874	139,032	4,540
EBITDA	350,641	231,067	115,787	401,447	265,196	152,305	51,283	(8,125)
Depn & Amortn	217,809	143,924	72,102	260,154	223,731	165,516	70,987	2,111
Income Before Taxes	45,959	26,862	11,796	10,446	(47,948)	(33,092)	(20,074)	(10,236)
Net Income	45,981	27,193	12,097	6,695	(62,301)	(48,057)	(32,311)	(10,236)
Average Shares	289,153	258,900	244,391	234,010	210,600	196,348	123,592	7,225
Balance Sheet								
Current Assets	398,550	215,111	649,580	250,241	168,968	185,985	175,419	397,198
Total Assets	8,509,876	8,146,307	8,490,605	8,107,210	6,807,786	6,227,351	4,224,144	921,458
Current Liabilities	263,745	314,990	199,693	568,751	291,591	486,723	573,485	16,294
Long-Term Obligations	2,339,235	2,342,703	2,944,096	2,600,839	2,580,962	1,571,034	...	...
Total Liabilities	3,406,287	3,473,250	3,960,613	3,914,274	3,548,441	2,777,250	1,289,200	16,784
Stockholders' Equity	5,103,589	4,673,057	4,529,992	4,192,936	3,259,345	3,450,101	2,934,944	904,674
Shares Outstanding	274,240	259,125	258,890	243,375	207,870	211,473	185,504	38,664
Statistical Record								
Return on Assets %	0.75	0.44	0.21	0.09	N.M.	N.M.	N.M.	N.M.
Return on Equity %	1.35	0.81	0.43	0.18	N.M.	N.M.	N.M.	N.M.
EBITDA Margin %	48.86	49.08	49.53	45.68	42.06	38.18	36.89	N.M.
Net Margin %	6.41	5.78	5.18	0.76	N.M.	N.M.	N.M.	N.M.
Asset Turnover	0.11	0.11	0.11	0.12	0.10	0.08	0.05	0.01
Current Ratio	1.51	0.68	3.25	0.44	0.58	0.38	0.31	24.38
Debt to Equity	0.46	0.50	0.65	0.62	0.79	0.46	...	...
Price Range	23.77-19.74	23.77-19.74	23.77-15.62	22.84-13.21	17.48-15.30	18.51-15.87	16.90-15.22	...
Average Yield %	0.91	0.91	0.98	1.07	1.21	1.16	0.31	...

Address: 30601 Agoura Road, Suite 200, Agoura Hills, CA 91301 **Telephone:** 805-413-5300	**Web Site:** www.americanhomes4rent.com **Officers:** David P. Singelyn - Chief Executive Officer, Interim Chief Financial Officer David Goldberg - Executive Vice President	**Auditors:** Ernst & Young LLP **Transfer Agents:** American Stock Transfer & Trust Company, LLC

AMERICAN INTERNATIONAL GROUP INC

Exchange	Symbol	Price	52Wk Range	Yield	P/E
NYS	AIG	$59.58 (12/29/2017)	67.20-58.11	N/A	N/A

*7 Year Price Score 101.61 *NYSE Composite Index=100 *12 Month Price Score 91.21

Interim Earnings (Per Share)

Qtr.	Mar	Jun	Sep	Dec
2014	1.09	2.10	1.52	0.49
2015	1.78	1.32	(0.18)	(1.32)
2016	(0.16)	1.68	0.42	(2.70)
2017	1.18	1.19	(1.91)	...

Interim Dividends (Per Share)

Amt	Decl	Ex	Rec	Pay
0.32Q	02/14/2017	03/13/2017	03/15/2017	03/29/2017
0.32Q	05/03/2017	06/12/2017	06/14/2017	06/28/2017
0.32Q	08/02/2017	09/14/2017	09/15/2017	09/29/2017
0.32Q	11/02/2017	12/07/2017	12/08/2017	12/22/2017

Indicated Div: $1.28 (Div. Reinv. Plan)

Valuation Analysis		Institutional Holding	
Forecast EPS	$2.49	No of Institutions	
	(01/18/2018)	1384	
Market Cap	$53.6 Billion	Shares	
Book Value	$72.5 Billion	1,003,703,168	
Price/Book	0.74	% Held	
Price/Sales	1.07	N/A	

Business Summary: General Insurance (MIC: 5.2.1 SIC: 6331 NAIC: 524126)

American International Group is a holding company. Co.'s business operations consist of Commercial Insurance, Consumer Insurance, Other Operations, and a Legacy Portfolio. Commercial Insurance consists of Liability and Financial Lines and Property and Special Risks. Consumer Insurance consists of Group Retirement, Individual Retirement, Life Insurance and Personal Insurance. Other Operations include Institutional Markets, which consists of stable value wrap products, structured settlement and terminal funding annuities, corporate- and bank-owned life insurance and guaranteed investment contracts. Co.'s Legacy Portfolio includes its Legacy Property and Casualty Run-Off Insurance Lines.

Recent Developments: For the quarter ended Sep 30 2017, loss from continuing operations was US$1.71 billion compared with income of US$433.0 million in the year-earlier quarter. Net loss amounted to US$1.71 billion versus net income of US$436.0 million in the year-earlier quarter. Revenues were US$11.75 billion, down 8.6% from US$12.85 billion the year before. Net premiums earned were US$8.06 billion versus US$8.58 billion in the prior-year quarter, a decrease of 6.0%. Net investment income fell 20.0% to US$456.0 million from US$570.0 million a year ago.

Prospects: Our evaluation of American International Group Inc. as of Jan. 14, 2018 is the result of our systematic analysis on three basic characteristics: earnings strength, relative valuation, and recent stock price movement. The company has managed to produce a neutral trend in earnings per share over the past 5 quarters. However, while recent estimates for the company have been mixed, AIG has posted results that fell short of analysts expectations. Based on operating earnings yield, the company is about fairly valued when compared to all of the companies in our coverage universe. Share price changes over the past year indicates that AIG will perform in line with the market over the near term.

Financial Data
(US$ in Thousands)

	9 Mos	6 Mos	3 Mos	12/31/2016	12/31/2015	12/31/2014	12/31/2013	12/31/2012
Earnings Per Share	(2.24)	0.09	0.58	(0.78)	1.65	5.20	6.13	2.04
Cash Flow Per Share	(9.43)	(8.07)	(7.15)	2.18	2.21	3.51	3.98	2.17
Tang Book Value Per Share	80.62	81.62	78.59	76.66	75.10	77.69	68.62	66.38
Dividends Per Share	1.280	1.280	1.280	1.280	0.810	0.500	0.200	...
Dividend Payout %	...	1,422.22	220.69	...	49.09	9.62	3.26	...
Income Statement								
Premium Income	23,459,000	15,396,000	7,782,000	34,393,000	36,655,000	37,254,000	37,350,000	38,011,000
Total Revenue	36,885,000	25,134,000	12,632,000	52,367,000	58,327,000	64,406,000	68,678,000	65,656,000
Benefits & Claims	22,653,000	12,331,000	6,047,000	32,437,000	31,345,000	28,281,000	29,503,000	31,977,000
Income Before Taxes	591,000	3,394,000	1,727,000	(74,000)	3,281,000	10,501,000	9,368,000	9,322,000
Income Taxes	(18,000)	1,073,000	516,000	185,000	1,059,000	2,927,000	360,000	1,570,000
Net Income	576,000	2,315,000	1,185,000	(849,000)	2,196,000	7,529,000	9,085,000	3,438,000
Average Shares	908,667	948,248	1,005,315	1,091,085	1,334,464	1,447,553	1,481,206	1,687,226
Balance Sheet								
Total Assets	503,073,000	499,762,000	500,162,000	498,264,000	496,943,000	515,581,000	541,329,000	548,633,000
Total Liabilities	430,605,000	426,030,000	426,093,000	421,964,000	407,285,000	408,683,000	440,859,000	450,631,000
Stockholders' Equity	72,468,000	73,732,000	74,069,000	76,300,000	89,658,000	106,898,000	100,470,000	98,002,000
Shares Outstanding	898,880	903,392	942,480	995,335	1,193,916	1,375,926	1,464,063	1,476,321
Statistical Record								
Return on Assets %	N.M.	N.M.	0.10	N.M.	0.43	1.42	1.67	0.62
Return on Equity %	N.M.	N.M.	0.64	N.M.	2.23	7.26	9.15	3.38
Loss Ratio %	96.56	80.09	77.70	94.31	85.51	75.91	78.99	84.13
Net Margin %	1.56	9.21	9.38	(1.62)	3.76	11.69	13.23	5.24
Price Range	67.20-57.38	67.20-51.21	67.20-48.79	66.70-48.79	64.54-48.87	56.51-46.88	52.30-34.84	37.21-23.54
P/E Ratio	...	746.67-569.00	115.86-84.12	...	39.12-29.62	10.87-9.02	8.53-5.68	18.24-11.54
Average Yield %	2.04	2.08	2.14	2.23	1.38	0.95	0.45	...

Address: 175 Water Street, New York, NY 10038
Telephone: 212-770-7000

Web Site: www.aig.com
Officers: Douglas M. Steenland - Chairman Brian Duperreault - President, Chief Executive Officer

Auditors: PricewaterhouseCoopers LLP
Transfer Agents: Wells Fargo Bank, N.A. Shareowner Services, St. Paul, MN

AMERICAN STATES WATER CO

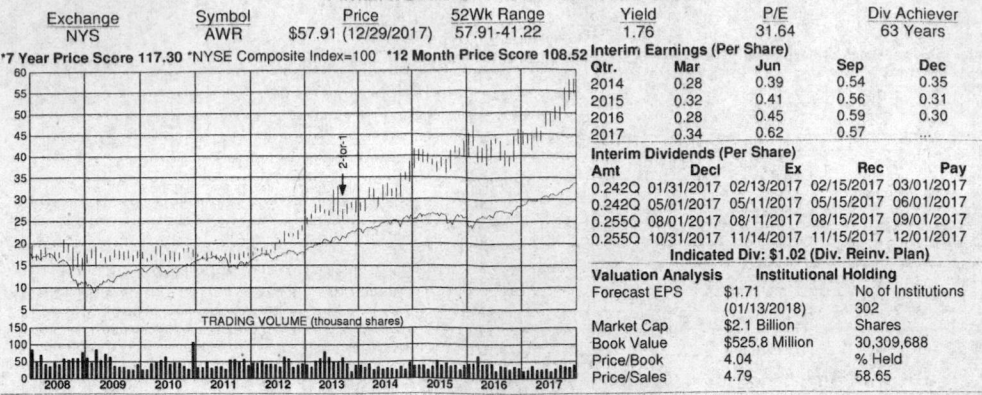

Exchange	Symbol	Price	52Wk Range	Yield	P/E	Div Achiever
NYS	AWR	$57.91 (12/29/2017)	57.91-41.22	1.76	31.64	63 Years

*7 Year Price Score 117.30 *NYSE Composite Index=100 *12 Month Price Score 108.52

Interim Earnings (Per Share)

Qtr.	Mar	Jun	Sep	Dec
2014	0.28	0.39	0.54	0.35
2015	0.32	0.41	0.56	0.31
2016	0.28	0.45	0.59	0.30
2017	0.34	0.62	0.57	

Interim Dividends (Per Share)

Amt	Decl	Ex	Rec	Pay
0.242Q	01/31/2017	02/13/2017	02/15/2017	03/01/2017
0.242Q	05/01/2017	05/11/2017	05/15/2017	06/01/2017
0.255Q	08/01/2017	08/11/2017	08/15/2017	09/01/2017
0.255Q	10/31/2017	11/14/2017	11/15/2017	12/01/2017

Indicated Div: $1.02 (Div. Reinv. Plan)

Valuation Analysis

		Institutional Holding	
Forecast EPS	$1.71	No of Institutions	
	(01/13/2018)	302	
Market Cap	$2.1 Billion	Shares	
Book Value	$525.8 Million	30,309,688	
Price/Book	4.04	% Held	
Price/Sales	4.79	58.65	

Business Summary: Water Utilities (MIC: 3.2.1 SIC: 4941 NAIC: 221310)

American States Water is a holding company. Co. is the parent company of Golden State Water Company (GSWC) and American States Utility Services, Inc. (ASUS) and its subsidiaries. Co. has three reportable segments: water, electric and contracted services. Within the segments, Co. has two principal business units, water and electric service utility operations, conducted through GSWC, and contracted services conducted through ASUS and its subsidiaries. GSWC is a public utility company engaged principally in the purchase, production, distribution and sale of water in 10 counties in the State of California. At Dec 31 2016, GSWC served 261,002 water customers and 23,940 electric customers.

Recent Developments: For the quarter ended Sep 30 2017, net income decreased 2.9% to US$21.0 million from US$21.6 million in the year-earlier quarter. Revenues were US$124.4 million, up 0.5% from US$123.8 million the year before. Operating income was US$38.6 million versus US$39.6 million in the prior-year quarter, a decrease of 2.7%. Direct operating expenses declined 1.3% to US$54.2 million from US$54.9 million in the comparable period the year before. Indirect operating expenses increased 8.1% to US$31.6 million from US$29.3 million in the equivalent prior-year period.

Prospects: Our evaluation of American States Water Co. as of Jan. 14, 2018 is the result of our systematic analysis on three basic characteristics: earnings strength, relative valuation, and recent stock price movement. The company has managed to produce a neutral trend in earnings per share over the past 5 quarters and while recent estimates for the company have been mixed, AWR has posted results that fell short of analysts expectations. Based on operating earnings yield, the company is about fairly valued when compared to all of the companies in our coverage universe. Share price changes over the past year indicates that AWR will perform well over the near term.

Financial Data

(US$ in Thousands)	9 Mos	6 Mos	3 Mos	12/31/2016	12/31/2015	12/31/2014	12/31/2013	12/31/2012
Earnings Per Share	1.83	1.85	1.68	1.62	1.60	1.57	1.61	1.41
Cash Flow Per Share	3.81	3.38	2.66	2.65	2.54	4.22	3.51	2.66
Tang Book Value Per Share	14.31	13.97	13.57	13.49	12.73	13.21	12.69	11.79
Dividends Per Share	0.981	0.950	0.932	0.914	0.874	0.831	0.760	0.635
Dividend Payout %	53.61	51.35	55.48	56.42	54.63	52.93	47.20	45.04
Income Statement								
Total Revenue	336,423	212,005	98,810	436,087	458,641	465,791	472,077	466,908
EBITDA	135,940	87,057	34,946	154,822	161,519	161,547	161,144	154,759
Depn & Amortn	29,365	19,450	9,744	39,109	42,674	41,751	40,967	43,234
Income Before Taxes	90,169	56,655	19,556	94,478	98,215	99,106	98,469	90,093
Income Taxes	33,670	21,162	6,855	34,735	37,731	38,048	35,783	35,945
Net Income	56,499	35,493	12,701	59,743	60,484	61,058	62,686	54,148
Average Shares	36,856	36,825	36,782	36,750	37,614	38,880	38,869	38,262
Balance Sheet								
Current Assets	146,663	149,536	192,079	166,875	132,697	209,451	191,617	184,033
Total Assets	1,486,486	1,462,653	1,480,268	1,470,493	1,348,600	1,378,298	1,310,183	1,280,943
Current Liabilities	151,869	140,454	178,673	177,944	123,507	99,290	100,906	93,697
Long-Term Obligations	320,949	320,969	320,985	325,252	325,541	325,798	326,079	332,463
Total Liabilities	960,674	949,628	982,324	976,196	882,655	871,497	817,779	826,364
Stockholders' Equity	525,812	513,025	497,944	494,297	465,945	506,801	492,404	454,579
Shares Outstanding	36,679	36,644	36,616	36,571	36,501	38,286	38,720	38,474
Statistical Record								
Return on Assets %	4.63	4.76	4.37	4.23	4.44	4.54	4.84	4.29
Return on Equity %	13.32	13.81	12.91	12.41	12.44	12.22	13.24	12.51
EBITDA Margin %	40.41	41.06	35.37	35.50	35.22	34.68	34.14	33.15
Net Margin %	16.79	16.74	12.85	13.70	13.19	13.11	13.28	11.60
Asset Turnover	0.30	0.31	0.31	0.31	0.34	0.35	0.36	0.37
Current Ratio	0.97	1.06	1.08	0.94	1.07	2.11	1.90	1.96
Debt to Equity	0.61	0.63	0.64	0.66	0.70	0.64	0.66	0.73
Price Range	51.53-37.62	49.94-37.62	46.18-37.62	47.18-37.62	43.57-36.00	38.71-27.15	32.86-23.99	23.99-17.15
P/E Ratio	28.16-20.56	26.99-20.34	27.49-22.39	29.12-23.22	27.23-22.50	24.66-17.29	20.41-14.90	17.01-12.16
Average Yield %	2.17	2.20	2.23	2.23	2.21	2.21	2.64	3.16

Address: 630 E. Foothill Boulevard, San Dimas, CA 91773-1212 **Telephone:** 909-394-3600	**Web Site:** www.aswater.com **Officers:** Lloyd E. Ross - Chairman Robert J. Sprowls - President, Chief Executive Officer	**Auditors:** PricewaterhouseCoopers LLP **Investor Contact:** 909-394-3600 **Transfer Agents:** Computershare Shareowner Services, Jersey City, NJ

AMERICAN TOWER CORP

Exchange	Symbol	Price	52Wk Range	Yield	P/E
NYS	AMT	$142.67 (12/29/2017)	152.72-103.01	1.96	54.25

*7 Year Price Score 114.76 *NYSE Composite Index=100 *12 Month Price Score 104.45

Interim Earnings (Per Share)

Qtr.	Mar	Jun	Sep	Dec
2014	0.51	0.58	0.50	0.42
2015	0.45	0.30	0.18	0.49
2016	0.58	0.37	0.55	0.47
2017	0.67	0.80	0.69	...

Interim Dividends (Per Share)

Amt	Decl	Ex	Rec	Pay
0.62Q	03/09/2017	04/10/2017	04/12/2017	04/28/2017
0.64Q	06/01/2017	06/15/2017	06/19/2017	07/14/2017
0.66Q	09/12/2017	09/28/2017	09/29/2017	10/17/2017
0.70Q	12/07/2017	12/27/2017	12/28/2017	01/16/2018

Indicated Div: $2.80

Valuation Analysis — **Institutional Holding**

Forecast EPS	$2.89 (01/18/2018)	No of Institutions 1286
Market Cap	$61.2 Billion	Shares 483,867,232
Book Value	$6.5 Billion	% Held
Price/Book	9.40	N/A
Price/Sales	9.42	

Business Summary: REITs (MIC: 5.3.1 SIC: 6798 NAIC: 525930)

American Tower is a holding company. Through its subsidiaries, Co. is a real estate investment trusts and independent owner, operator and developer of multitenant communications real estate. Co.'s property operations lease space on communications sites to wireless service providers, radio and television broadcast companies, wireless data providers, government agencies and municipalities and tenants in a number of other industries. Co.'s services operations provides tower-related services, including site acquisition, zoning and permitting and structural analysis services, which support its site leasing business, including through the addition of new tenants and equipment on its sites.

Recent Developments: For the quarter ended Sep 30 2017, net income increased 26.9% to US$334.7 million from US$263.7 million in the year-earlier quarter. Revenues were US$1.68 billion, up 11.0% from US$1.51 billion the year before.

Prospects: Our evaluation of Americann Tower REIT, Inc. as of Jan. 14, 2018 is the result of our systematic analysis on three basic characteristics: earnings strength, relative valuation, and recent stock price movement. The company has managed to produce a neutral trend in earnings per share over the past 5 quarters. However, while recent estimates for the company have been mixed, AMT has posted results that fell short of analysts expectations. Based on operating earnings yield, the company is overvalued when compared to all of the companies in our coverage universe. Share price changes over the past year indicates that AMT will perform very well over the near term.

Financial Data
(US$ in Thousands)

	9 Mos	6 Mos	3 Mos	12/31/2016	12/31/2015	12/31/2014	12/31/2013	12/31/2012
Earnings Per Share	2.63	2.49	2.06	1.98	1.41	2.00	1.38	1.60
Cash Flow Per Share	6.66	6.72	6.61	6.34	5.21	5.39	4.05	3.57
Dividends Per Share	2.500	2.390	2.170	2.170	1.810	1.400	1.100	0.900
Dividend Payout %	95.06	95.98	105.34	109.60	128.37	70.00	79.71	56.25
Income Statement								
Total Revenue	4,959,438	3,278,672	1,616,238	5,785,668	4,771,516	4,100,048	3,361,407	2,875,960
EBITDA	2,889,361	1,911,153	926,381	2,565,307	2,059,623	1,973,189	1,451,704	1,492,921
Depn & Amortn	1,249,849	817,495	421,140	758,900	661,400	551,800	483,600	411,900
Income Before Taxes	1,114,739	746,643	334,173	1,125,860	829,962	865,704	541,749	701,294
Income Taxes	84,155	50,743	26,763	155,501	157,955	62,505	59,541	107,304
Net Income	1,000,399	683,131	316,080	956,425	685,074	824,910	551,333	637,283
Average Shares	432,831	430,487	430,199	429,283	423,015	400,086	399,146	399,287
Balance Sheet								
Current Assets	1,963,574	1,802,759	1,711,187	1,689,870	996,468	947,968	952,656	829,528
Total Assets	32,319,326	32,138,210	32,057,389	30,879,150	26,904,272	21,331,545	20,272,571	14,089,129
Current Liabilities	2,260,236	3,278,911	3,209,058	1,631,269	1,200,029	1,929,692	924,758	632,178
Long-Term Obligations	18,581,381	17,509,937	17,182,754	18,294,659	17,068,807	13,711,084	14,408,146	8,693,345
Total Liabilities	25,801,199	25,655,501	25,204,915	24,115,255	20,252,593	17,377,985	16,738,406	10,516,028
Stockholders' Equity	6,518,127	6,482,709	6,852,474	6,763,895	6,651,679	3,953,560	3,534,165	3,573,101
Shares Outstanding	429,243	429,174	426,247	427,102	423,885	396,698	394,864	395,091
Statistical Record								
Return on Assets %	3.91	3.74	3.37	3.30	2.84	3.97	3.21	4.83
Return on Equity %	18.59	17.76	14.47	14.22	12.92	22.03	15.51	18.53
EBITDA Margin %	58.26	58.29	57.32	44.34	43.16	48.13	43.19	51.91
Net Margin %	20.17	20.84	19.56	16.53	14.36	20.12	16.40	22.16
Asset Turnover	0.21	0.20	0.21	0.20	0.20	0.20	0.20	0.22
Current Ratio	0.87	0.55	0.53	1.04	0.83	0.49	1.03	1.31
Debt to Equity	2.85	2.70	2.51	2.70	2.57	3.47	4.08	2.43
Price Range	148.05-100.85	135.75-100.85	121.54-100.85	117.84-83.66	104.06-87.01	105.01-78.83	84.64-68.36	77.27-58.81
P/E Ratio	56.29-38.35	54.52-40.50	59.00-48.96	59.52-42.25	73.80-61.71	52.51-39.41	61.33-49.54	48.29-36.76
Average Yield %	2.06	2.07	1.98	2.05	1.89	1.55	1.44	1.32

Address: 116 Huntington Avenue, Boston, MA 02116 **Telephone:** 617-375-7500	**Web Site:** www.americantower.com **Officers:** James D. (Jim) Taiclet - Chairman, President, Chief Executive Officer Thomas A. Bartlett - Executive Vice President, Chief Financial Officer, Treasurer	**Auditors:** Deloitte & Touche LLP **Investor Contact:** 617-375-7500 **Transfer Agents:** Computershare

AMERICAN WATER WORKS CO, INC.

Exchange	Symbol	Price	52Wk Range	Yield	P/E
NYS	AWK	$91.49 (12/29/2017)	92.25-70.57	1.81	31.01

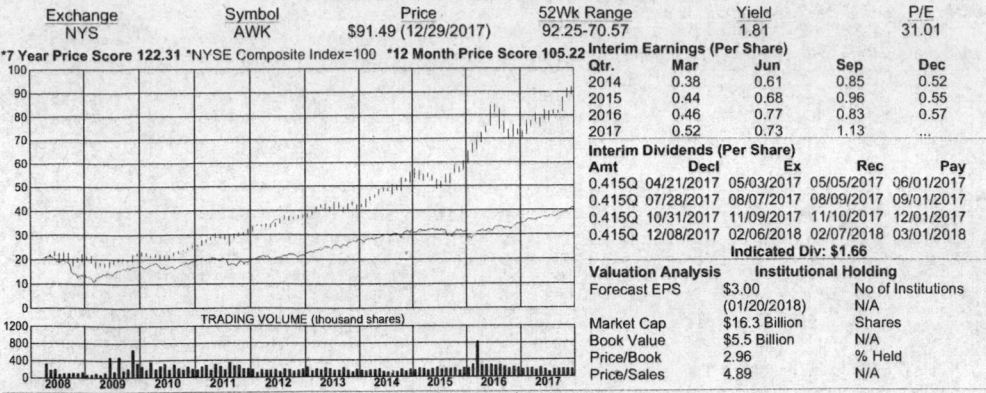

*7 Year Price Score 122.31 *NYSE Composite Index=100 *12 Month Price Score 105.22

Interim Earnings (Per Share)

Qtr.	Mar	Jun	Sep	Dec
2014	0.38	0.61	0.85	0.52
2015	0.44	0.68	0.96	0.55
2016	0.46	0.77	0.83	0.57
2017	0.52	0.73	1.13	...

Interim Dividends (Per Share)

Amt	Decl	Ex	Rec	Pay
0.415Q	04/21/2017	05/03/2017	05/05/2017	06/01/2017
0.415Q	07/28/2017	08/07/2017	08/09/2017	09/01/2017
0.415Q	10/31/2017	11/09/2017	11/10/2017	12/01/2017
0.415Q	12/08/2017	02/06/2018	02/07/2018	03/01/2018

Indicated Div: $1.66

Valuation Analysis

		Institutional Holding	
Forecast EPS	$3.00	No of Institutions	
	(01/20/2018)	N/A	
Market Cap	$16.3 Billion	Shares	
Book Value	$5.5 Billion	N/A	
Price/Book	2.96	% Held	
Price/Sales	4.89	N/A	

TRADING VOLUME (thousand shares)

Business Summary: Water Utilities (MIC: 3.2.1 SIC: 4941 NAIC: 221310)

American Water Works Company is a holding company. Through its subsidiaries, Co. is a water and wastewater utility company. Co.'s Regulated Businesses provide water and wastewater services as public utilities. Co.'s Market-Based Businesses consists of four segments including Military Services Group, which operates and maintains water and wastewater systems for military bases; Contract Operations Group, which operates and maintains water and wastewater facilities for municipalities, the food and beverage industry; Homeowner Services Group, which provides warranty-type services for homeowners; and Keystone, which provides services for natural gas exploration and production companies.

Recent Developments: For the quarter ended Sep 30 2017, net income increased 37.2% to US$203.0 million from US$148.0 million in the year-earlier quarter. Revenues were US$936.0 million, up 0.6% from US$930.0 million the year before. Operating income was US$430.0 million versus US$319.0 million in the prior-year quarter, an increase of 34.8%. Direct operating expenses declined 25.0% to US$324.0 million from US$432.0 million in the comparable period the year before. Indirect operating expenses increased 1.7% to US$182.0 million from US$179.0 million in the equivalent prior-year period.

Prospects: Our evaluation of American Water Works Co. Inc. as of Jan. 21, 2018 is the result of our systematic analysis on three basic characteristics: earnings strength, relative valuation, and recent stock price movement. The company has produced a positive trend in earnings per share over the past 5 quarters. However, while recent estimates for the company have been mixed, AWK has posted results that were in line with analysts expectations. Based on operating earnings yield, the company is about fairly valued when compared to all of the companies in our coverage universe. Share price changes over the past year indicates that AWK will perform very well over the near term.

Financial Data

(US$ in Thousands)	9 Mos	6 Mos	3 Mos	12/31/2016	12/31/2015	12/31/2014	12/31/2013	12/31/2012
Earnings Per Share	2.95	2.65	2.69	2.62	2.64	2.35	2.06	2.01
Cash Flow Per Share	7.51	7.20	7.34	7.15	6.59	6.13	5.04	5.40
Tang Book Value Per Share	23.24	22.50	22.18	21.75	21.02	20.66	19.73	18.28
Dividends Per Share	1.580	1.540	1.500	1.465	1.330	1.210	0.840	1.210
Dividend Payout %	53.56	58.11	55.76	55.92	50.38	51.49	40.78	60.20
Income Statement								
Total Revenue	2,536,000	1,600,000	756,000	3,302,000	3,159,000	3,011,328	2,901,858	2,876,889
EBITDA	1,612,000	928,000	418,000	1,530,000	1,495,000	1,349,306	1,232,271	1,233,328
Depn & Amortn	642,000	387,000	188,000	435,000	405,000	356,952	337,653	314,639
Income Before Taxes	711,000	371,000	145,000	770,000	782,000	709,814	605,470	631,258
Income Taxes	284,000	147,000	52,000	302,000	306,000	279,973	236,206	257,008
Net Income	427,000	224,000	93,000	468,000	476,000	423,108	369,264	358,070
Average Shares	179,000	179,000	179,000	179,000	180,000	179,806	179,056	177,671
Balance Sheet								
Current Assets	860,000	808,000	767,000	784,000	657,000	661,369	550,390	499,447
Total Assets	19,361,000	18,966,000	18,610,000	18,482,000	17,241,000	16,130,956	15,069,533	14,718,976
Current Liabilities	1,747,000	2,661,000	2,418,000	2,392,000	1,533,000	1,240,998	1,235,533	994,832
Long-Term Obligations	6,672,000	5,650,000	5,744,000	5,744,000	5,749,000	5,862,000	5,432,744	5,212,881	5,190,509
Total Liabilities	13,843,000	13,582,000	13,323,000	13,264,000	12,192,000	11,215,365	10,341,729	10,273,988
Stockholders' Equity	5,518,000	5,384,000	5,287,000	5,218,000	5,049,000	4,915,591	4,727,804	4,444,988
Shares Outstanding	178,373	178,278	177,729	178,096	178,282	179,462	178,379	176,988
Statistical Record								
Return on Assets %	2.83	2.58	2.66	2.61	2.85	2.71	2.48	2.42
Return on Equity %	9.82	8.98	9.24	9.09	9.55	8.78	8.05	8.22
EBITDA Margin %	63.56	58.00	55.29	46.34	47.33	44.81	42.46	42.87
Net Margin %	16.84	14.00	12.30	14.17	15.07	14.05	12.73	12.45
Asset Turnover	0.18	0.18	0.18	0.18	0.19	0.19	0.19	0.19
Current Ratio	0.49	0.30	0.32	0.33	0.43	0.53	0.45	0.50
Debt to Equity	1.21	1.05	1.09	1.10	1.16	1.11	1.10	1.17
Price Range	82.92-70.49	84.76-70.49	84.76-68.26	84.76-59.44	60.61-48.63	55.86-41.16	43.50-37.13	38.35-31.38
P/E Ratio	28.11-23.89	31.98-26.60	31.51-25.38	32.35-22.69	22.96-18.42	23.77-17.51	21.12-18.02	19.08-15.61
Average Yield %	2.06	2.03	2.01	2.02	2.45	2.53	2.05	3.43

Address: 1025 Laurel Oak Road, Voorhees, NJ 08043
Telephone: 856-346-8200

Web Site: www.amwater.com
Officers: George MacKenzie - Chairman Susan N. Story - President, Chief Executive Officer, Senior Vice President, Chief Financial Officer

Auditors: PricewaterhouseCoopers LLP
Investor Contact: 856-566-4005
Transfer Agents: American Stock Transfer & Trust Company, Brooklyn, NY

AMERIGAS PARTNERS LP

Exchange	Symbol	Price	52Wk Range	Yield	P/E	Div Achiever
NYS	APU	$46.23 (12/29/2017)	49.87-42.09	8.22	36.98	12 Years

*7 Year Price Score 79.94   *NYSE Composite Index=100   *12 Month Price Score 93.89

Interim Earnings (Per Share)

Qtr.	Dec	Mar	Jun	Sep
2012-13	0.93	1.56	(0.43)	(0.56)
2013-14	1.14	1.71	(0.47)	(0.22)
2014-15	(0.49)	2.17	(0.37)	(0.62)
2015-16	0.77	1.74	(0.46)	(1.03)
2016-17	0.87	1.14	(0.62)	(0.31)

Interim Dividends (Per Share)

Amt	Decl	Ex	Rec	Pay
0.94Q	01/23/2017	02/08/2017	02/10/2017	02/17/2017
0.95Q	04/24/2017	05/08/2017	05/10/2017	05/18/2017
0.95Q	07/24/2017	08/08/2017	08/10/2017	08/18/2017
0.95Q	10/26/2017	11/09/2017	11/10/2017	11/17/2017

Indicated Div: $3.80

Valuation Analysis

		Institutional Holding	
Forecast EPS	$2.74 (01/18/2018)	No of Institutions	314
Market Cap	$4.3 Billion	Shares	27,320,476
Book Value	N/A	% Held	29.71
Price/Book	N/A		
Price/Sales	1.75		

Business Summary: Gas Utilities (MIC: 3.3.1 SIC: 5989 NAIC: 454312)

AmeriGas Partners is a holding company and it conducts its business principally through its subsidiary, AmeriGas Propane, L.P. Co. is a retail propane distributor. As of Sep 30 2017, Co. served about 1,900,000 residential, commercial, industrial, agricultural, wholesale and motor fuel customers in all 50 states from about 1,900 propane distribution locations. AmeriGas Propane, Inc. is Co.'s general partner and is engaged in managing Co.'s operations. In addition to distributing propane, Co. sells, installs and services propane appliances. As part of its overall transportation and distribution infrastructure, Co. operates as an interstate carrier throughout the continental U.S.

Recent Developments: For the year ended Sep 30 2017, net income decreased 21.5% to US$165.9 million from US$211.2 million in the prior year. Revenues were US$2.45 billion, up 6.1% from US$2.31 billion the year before. Operating income was US$387.9 million versus US$422.6 million in the prior year, a decrease of 8.2%. Direct operating expenses rose 21.7% to US$971.9 million from US$798.7 million in the comparable period the year before. Indirect operating expenses were unchanged at US$1.09 billion versus the equivalent prior-year period.

Prospects: Our evaluation of AmeriGas Partners, L.P. as of Jan. 14, 2018 is the result of our systematic analysis on three basic characteristics: earnings strength, relative valuation, and recent stock price movement. The company has generated a negative trend in earnings per share over the past 5 quarters and while recent estimates for the company have been raised by analysts, APU has posted better than expected results. Based on operating earnings yield, the company is about fairly valued when compared to all of the companies in our coverage universe. Share price changes over the past year indicates that APU will perform poorly over the near term.

Financial Data
(US$ in Thousands)

	09/30/2017	09/30/2016	09/30/2015	09/30/2014	09/30/2013	09/30/2012	09/30/2011	09/30/2010
Earnings Per Share	1.25	1.77	1.91	2.82	2.14	(0.11)	2.30	2.80
Cash Flow Per Share	3.84	4.54	5.64	5.17	3.83	4.22	3.31	3.83
Dividends Per Share	3.780	3.720	3.600	3.440	3.280	3.103	2.890	2.750
Dividend Payout %	302.40	210.17	188.48	121.99	153.27	...	125.65	98.21
Income Statement								
Total Revenue	2,453,495	2,311,817	2,885,322	3,712,935	3,166,543	2,921,616	2,537,959	2,320,342
EBITDA	475,870	520,520	532,913	616,653	551,500	291,468	287,809	315,544
Depn & Amortn	147,741	146,805	152,204	154,020	159,306	134,225	82,977	79,679
Income Before Taxes	167,903	209,620	217,867	297,052	226,762	14,602	141,314	170,759
Income Taxes	2,034	(1,573)	2,898	2,611	1,671	1,931	390	3,265
Net Income	162,059	206,984	211,211	289,893	221,222	11,025	138,523	165,213
Average Shares	93,050	93,023	92,977	92,946	92,910	81,433	57,170	57,123
Balance Sheet								
Current Assets	413,774	344,448	366,361	505,908	500,692	523,368	393,819	325,858
Total Assets	4,059,261	4,057,770	4,141,712	4,364,058	4,409,846	4,517,331	1,795,735	1,696,219
Current Liabilities	581,532	588,455	546,294	617,514	616,974	670,845	450,993	460,262
Long-Term Obligations	2,563,832	2,325,334	2,273,817	2,280,145	2,288,097	2,297,363	928,858	771,279
Total Liabilities	3,311,362	3,073,549	2,977,496	3,041,544	3,024,743	3,088,223	1,457,079	1,315,371
Shares Outstanding	92,958	92,923	92,889	92,867	92,824	92,801	57,124	57,088
Statistical Record								
Return on Assets %	3.99	5.03	4.97	6.61	4.96	0.35	7.93	9.85
EBITDA Margin %	19.40	22.52	18.47	16.61	17.42	9.98	11.34	13.60
Net Margin %	6.61	8.95	7.32	7.81	6.99	0.38	5.46	7.12
Asset Turnover	0.60	0.56	0.68	0.85	0.71	0.92	1.45	1.38
Current Ratio	0.71	0.59	0.67	0.82	0.81	0.78	0.87	0.71
Price Range	49.87-42.09	49.89-32.21	52.55-39.73	48.30-41.18	50.00-37.76	46.21-37.19	51.41-38.06	46.30-34.79
P/E Ratio	39.90-33.67	28.19-18.20	27.51-20.80	17.13-14.60	23.36-17.64	...	22.35-16.55	16.54-12.43
Average Yield %	8.30	8.76	7.65	7.76	7.52	7.36	6.26	6.77

Address: 460 North Gulph Road, King of Prussia, PA 19406 **Telephone:** 610-337-7000	**Web Site:** www.amerigas.com **Officers:** John L. Walsh - Executive Chairman, Vice-Chairman, Holding/Parent Company Officer Jerry E. Sheridan - President, Chief Executive Officer, Vice President, Chief Operating Officer	**Auditors:** Ernst & Young LLP **Investor Contact:** 610-337-7000ext.10 **Transfer Agents:** ComputerShare Investor Services, Providence, RI

AMERIPRISE FINANCIAL INC

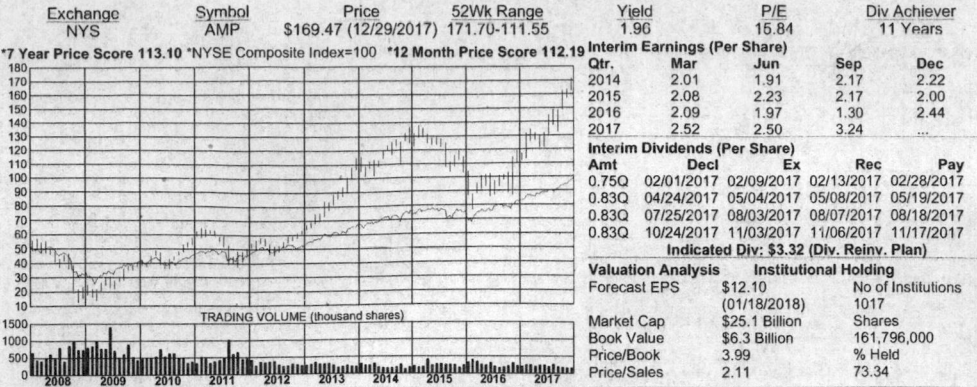

Exchange	Symbol	Price	52Wk Range	Yield	P/E	Div Achiever
NYS	AMP	$169.47 (12/29/2017)	171.70-111.55	1.96	15.84	11 Years

*7 Year Price Score 113.10 *NYSE Composite Index=100 *12 Month Price Score 112.19

Interim Earnings (Per Share)

Qtr.	Mar	Jun	Sep	Dec
2014	2.01	1.91	2.17	2.22
2015	2.08	2.23	2.17	2.00
2016	2.09	1.97	1.30	2.44
2017	2.52	2.50	3.24	...

Interim Dividends (Per Share)

Amt	Decl	Ex	Rec	Pay
0.75Q	02/01/2017	02/09/2017	02/13/2017	02/28/2017
0.83Q	04/24/2017	05/04/2017	05/08/2017	05/19/2017
0.83Q	07/25/2017	08/03/2017	08/07/2017	08/18/2017
0.83Q	10/24/2017	11/03/2017	11/06/2017	11/17/2017

Indicated Div: $3.32 (Div. Reinv. Plan)

Valuation Analysis

		Institutional Holding	
Forecast EPS	$12.10	No of Institutions	
	(01/18/2018)	1017	
Market Cap	$25.1 Billion	Shares	
Book Value	$6.3 Billion	161,796,000	
Price/Book	3.99	% Held	
Price/Sales	2.11	73.34	

Business Summary: Wealth Management (MIC: 5.5.2 SIC: 6282 NAIC: 523930)

Ameriprise Financial is a holding company. Co. provides a range of products and services to individual and institutional clients. Co.'s segments include Advice & Wealth Management, which provides financial planning and advice, as well as brokerage services, primarily to retail clients through Co.'s advisors; Asset Management, which provides investment management and advice and investment products to institutional clients; Annuities, which provides variable and fixed annuity products; Protection, which provides a range of products to address the protection and risk management needs of Co.'s retail clients including life, DI and property casualty insurance; and Corporate & Other.

Recent Developments: For the quarter ended Sep 30 2017, net income increased 134.0% to US$503.0 million from US$215.0 million in the year-earlier quarter. Revenues were US$2.98 billion, down 0.6% from US$3.00 billion the year before. Direct operating expenses declined 21.7% to US$1.55 billion from US$1.98 billion in the comparable period the year before. Indirect operating expenses increased 2.8% to US$805.0 million from US$783.0 million in the equivalent prior-year period.

Prospects: Our evaluation of Ameriprise Financial Inc. as of Jan. 14, 2018 is the result of our systematic analysis on three basic characteristics: earnings strength, relative valuation, and recent stock price movement. The company has managed to produce a neutral trend in earnings per share over the past 5 quarters and while recent estimates for the company have been raised by analysts, AMP has posted better than expected results. Based on operating earnings yield, the company is undervalued when compared to all of the companies in our coverage universe. Share price changes over the past year indicates that AMP will perform well over the near term.

Financial Data

(US$ in Millions)	9 Mos	6 Mos	3 Mos	12/31/2016	12/31/2015	12/31/2014	12/31/2013	12/31/2012
Earnings Per Share	10.70	8.76	8.23	7.81	8.48	8.30	6.44	4.62
Cash Flow Per Share	9.44	8.78	8.61	11.82	14.16	12.52	6.71	6.86
Tang Book Value Per Share	42.50	41.58	40.70	40.66	42.20	44.37	42.64	44.58
Dividends Per Share	3.160	3.080	3.000	2.920	2.590	2.260	2.010	1.430
Dividend Payout %	29.53	35.16	36.45	37.39	30.54	27.23	31.21	30.95
Income Statement								
Total Revenue	8,867	5,886	2,901	11,696	12,170	12,268	11,199	10,217
EBITDA	1,944	1,209	588	1,982	2,679	3,019	2,395	1,666
Depn & Amortn	176	121	63	149	150	144	144	152
Income Before Taxes	1,614	986	475	1,592	2,142	2,547	1,970	1,238
Income Taxes	315	190	72	278	455	545	492	335
Net Income	1,299	796	403	1,314	1,562	1,619	1,334	1,029
Average Shares	155	157	160	168	184	195	207	222
Balance Sheet								
Current Assets	2,504	2,563	2,177	7,796	8,133	8,055	7,661	7,265
Total Assets	145,486	143,144	140,857	139,821	145,342	148,810	144,576	134,729
Current Liabilities	12,356	12,000	11,986	11,963	10,440	9,387	8,991	8,351
Long-Term Obligations	5,169	5,216	5,252	5,236	10,246	9,929	8,456	7,384
Total Liabilities	139,181	136,894	134,630	133,529	138,125	140,686	136,384	125,637
Stockholders' Equity	6,305	6,250	6,227	6,292	7,217	8,124	8,192	9,092
Shares Outstanding	148	150	152	154	171	183	192	203
Statistical Record								
Return on Assets %	1.18	0.99	0.96	0.92	1.06	1.10	0.96	0.76
Return on Equity %	25.94	21.16	20.32	19.40	20.36	19.85	15.44	10.61
EBITDA Margin %	21.92	20.54	20.27	16.95	22.01	24.61	21.39	16.31
Net Margin %	14.65	13.52	13.89	11.23	12.83	13.20	11.91	10.07
Asset Turnover	0.08	0.08	0.08	0.08	0.08	0.08	0.08	0.08
Current Ratio	0.20	0.21	0.18	0.65	0.78	0.86	0.85	0.87
Debt to Equity	0.82	0.83	0.84	0.83	1.42	1.22	1.03	0.81
Price Range	148.80-86.76	134.60-86.76	134.60-85.52	118.90-76.27	137.81-103.08	136.76-101.47	115.05-62.63	63.52-45.46
P/E Ratio	13.91-8.11	15.37-9.90	16.35-10.39	15.22-9.77	16.25-12.16	16.48-12.23	17.86-9.73	13.75-9.84
Average Yield %	2.55	2.72	2.84	3.00	2.12	1.92	2.38	2.61

Address: 1099 Ameriprise Financial Center, Minneapolis, MN 55474
Telephone: 612-671-3131

Web Site: www.ameriprise.com
Officers: James M. Cracchiolo - Chairman, Chief Executive Officer Walter Stanley Berman - Executive Vice President, Chief Financial Officer

Auditors: PricewaterhouseCoopers LLP
Investor Contact: 612-671-2080
Transfer Agents: Computershare Trust Company, N.A, Providence, RI

AMERISOURCEBERGEN CORP.

Exchange	Symbol	Price	52Wk Range	Yield	P/E	Div Achiever
NYS	ABC	$91.82 (12/29/2017)	96.38-73.23	1.66	55.99	12 Years

*7 Year Price Score 98.10 *NYSE Composite Index=100 *12 Month Price Score 91.73

Interim Earnings (Per Share)

Qtr.	Dec	Mar	Jun	Sep
2012-13	0.71	0.19	0.71	0.21
2013-14	0.17	0.76	(0.06)	0.30
2014-15	(0.91)	(2.33)	0.89	1.65
2015-16	1.46	2.68	1.56	0.63
2016-17	1.11	1.86	0.23	(1.56)

Interim Dividends (Per Share)

Amt	Decl	Ex	Rec	Pay
0.365Q	02/09/2017	02/16/2017	02/21/2017	03/06/2017
0.365Q	05/09/2017	05/18/2017	05/22/2017	06/05/2017
0.365Q	08/10/2017	08/17/2017	08/21/2017	09/05/2017
0.38Q	11/09/2017	11/17/2017	11/20/2017	12/04/2017

Indicated Div: $1.52

Valuation Analysis

		Institutional Holding	
Forecast EPS	$6.12	No of Institutions	
	(01/18/2018)	1009	
Market Cap	$20.0 Billion	Shares	
Book Value	$2.1 Billion	200,403,696	
Price/Book	9.70	% Held	
Price/Sales	0.13	73.27	

Business Summary: Pharmaceuticals (MIC: 4.1.1 SIC: 5122 NAIC: 424210)

AmerisourceBergen is a pharmaceutical sourcing and distribution services company. Co.'s operations are comprised of the Pharmaceutical Distribution segment and Other. The Pharmaceutical Distribution segment includes: Co.'s AmerisourceBergen Drug Corporation subsidiary, which distributes brand-name and generic pharmaceuticals, over-the-counter healthcare products, home healthcare supplies and equipment, outsourced compounded sterile preparations, and related services to a variety of healthcare providers; and Co.'s AmerisourceBergen Specialty Group Inc. subsidiary, which provides pharmaceutical distribution and additional services to physicians who focus on a variety of disease states.

Recent Developments: For the year ended Sep 30 2017, net income decreased 74.5% to US$364.5 million from US$1.43 billion in the prior year. Revenues were US$153.14 billion, up 4.3% from US$146.85 billion the year before. Operating income was US$1.06 billion versus US$1.53 billion in the prior year, a decrease of 30.5%. Direct operating expenses rose 4.2% to US$148.60 billion from US$142.58 billion in the comparable period the year before. Indirect operating expenses increased 26.9% to US$3.49 billion from US$2.75 billion in the equivalent prior-year period.

Prospects: Our evaluation of AmerisourceBergen Corp. as of Jan. 14, 2018 is the result of our systematic analysis on three basic characteristics: earnings strength, relative valuation, and recent stock price movement. The company has generated a negative trend in earnings per share over the past 5 quarters and while recent estimates for the company have been raised by analysts, ABC has posted better than expected results. Based on operating earnings yield, the company is undervalued when compared to all of the companies in our coverage universe. Share price changes over the past year indicates that ABC will perform very poorly over the near term.

Financial Data

(US$ in Thousands)	09/30/2017	09/30/2016	09/30/2015	09/30/2014	09/30/2013	09/30/2012	09/30/2011	09/30/2010
Earnings Per Share	1.64	6.32	(0.62)	1.17	1.84	2.80	2.54	2.22
Cash Flow Per Share	6.89	14.94	18.00	6.44	3.41	5.15	4.29	3.93
Tang Book Value Per Share	N.M.	N.M.	N.M.	N.M.	N.M.	N.M.	0.01	0.39
Dividends Per Share	1.460	1.360	1.160	0.940	0.840	0.520	0.430	0.320
Dividend Payout %	89.02	21.52	...	80.34	45.65	18.57	16.93	14.41
Income Statement								
Total Revenue	153,143,826	146,849,686	135,961,803	119,569,127	87,959,167	79,489,596	80,217,558	77,953,979
EBITDA	1,325,492	1,763,360	561,085	912,379	1,037,045	1,377,084	1,312,105	1,183,016
Depn & Amortn	262,420	232,538	187,935	162,089	138,690	118,529	104,743	82,753
Income Before Taxes	917,887	1,390,910	274,149	673,428	824,458	1,163,131	1,130,641	1,027,769
Income Taxes	553,403	(37,019)	409,036	389,398	331,023	454,945	424,017	391,021
Net Income	364,484	1,427,929	(134,887)	276,484	433,707	718,986	706,624	636,748
Average Shares	221,602	225,959	217,786	235,405	235,345	256,903	277,417	287,246
Balance Sheet								
Current Assets	24,303,299	22,851,847	20,334,488	16,800,205	14,393,651	10,987,151	11,217,623	10,748,350
Total Assets	35,316,470	33,656,200	27,736,157	21,532,183	18,918,638	15,444,126	14,982,671	14,434,843
Current Liabilities	26,818,165	25,281,308	22,700,765	17,250,160	14,870,635	11,214,482	10,855,120	9,906,344
Long-Term Obligations	3,781,569	3,870,244	3,493,048	1,995,632	1,396,606	1,446,770	972,863	1,343,158
Total Liabilities	33,252,009	31,526,796	27,102,637	19,575,284	16,598,893	12,987,414	12,115,813	11,480,546
Stockholders' Equity	2,064,461	2,129,404	633,520	1,956,899	2,319,745	2,456,712	2,866,858	2,954,297
Shares Outstanding	217,993	220,050	206,891	221,908	229,994	235,394	260,991	277,521
Statistical Record								
Return on Assets %	1.06	4.64	N.M.	1.37	2.52	4.71	4.80	4.55
Return on Equity %	17.38	103.08	N.M.	12.93	18.16	26.94	24.28	22.46
EBITDA Margin %	0.87	1.20	0.41	0.76	1.18	1.73	1.64	1.52
Net Margin %	0.24	0.97	N.M.	0.23	0.49	0.90	0.88	0.82
Asset Turnover	4.44	4.77	5.52	5.91	5.12	5.21	5.45	5.57
Current Ratio	0.91	0.90	0.90	0.97	0.97	0.98	1.03	1.08
Debt to Equity	1.83	1.82	5.51	1.02	0.60	0.59	0.34	0.45
Price Range	96.38-69.03	105.02-73.66	115.48-75.02	78.33-61.10	62.23-38.99	42.08-35.57	43.09-30.66	32.88-21.62
P/E Ratio	58.77-42.09	16.62-11.66	...	66.95-52.22	33.82-21.19	15.03-12.70	16.96-12.07	14.81-9.74
Average Yield %	1.72	1.54	1.15	1.15	1.34	1.67	1.15	1.14

Address: 1300 Morris Drive, Chesterbrook, PA 19087-5594 Telephone: 610-727-7000 Fax: 610-647-0141	Web Site: www.amerisourcebergen.com Officers: Steven H. Collis - President, Chief Executive Officer Tim G. Guttman - Chief Financial Officer, Executive Vice President, Senior Vice President, Vice President, Acting Chief Financial Officer, Controller	Auditors: Ernst & Young LLP Investor Contact: 610-727-7199 Transfer Agents: ComputerShare, College Station, TX

AMETEK INC

Exchange	Symbol	Price	52Wk Range	Yield	P/E
NYS	AME	$72.47 (12/29/2017)	72.87-49.18	0.50	30.45

*7 Year Price Score 105.00 *NYSE Composite Index=100 *12 Month Price Score 109.47

Interim Earnings (Per Share)

Qtr.	Mar	Jun	Sep	Dec
2014	0.57	0.61	0.57	0.62
2015	0.59	0.64	0.65	0.58
2016	0.57	0.59	0.56	0.47
2017	0.60	0.65	0.66	...

Interim Dividends (Per Share)

Amt	Decl	Ex	Rec	Pay
0.09Q	02/13/2017	03/15/2017	03/17/2017	03/31/2017
0.09Q	05/10/2017	06/14/2017	06/16/2017	06/30/2017
0.09Q	08/04/2017	09/14/2017	09/15/2017	09/29/2017
0.09Q	11/10/2017	12/05/2017	12/06/2017	12/20/2017

Indicated Div: $0.36 (Div. Reinv. Plan)

Valuation Analysis

		Institutional Holding	
Forecast EPS	$2.58	No of Institutions	
	(01/13/2018)	712	
Market Cap	$16.7 Billion	Shares	
Book Value	$3.8 Billion	234,778,656	
Price/Book	4.45	% Held	
Price/Sales	4.06	84.69	

TRADING VOLUME (thousand shares)

Business Summary: Electrical Equipment (MIC: 7.3.1 SIC: 3629 NAIC: 335999)

AMETEK is a manufacturer of electronic instruments and electromechanical devices with operations in North America, Europe, Asia and South America. Co.'s products are marketed and sold through two operating groups: the Electronic Instruments Group, which is engaged in the design and manufacture of instruments for the process, power and industrial, and aerospace markets; and the Electromechanical Group, which supplies precision motion control solutions, thermal management systems, specialty metals and electrical interconnects. Co.'s end markets include aerospace and defense, medical, automation, mass transit, petrochemical and other industrial markets.

Recent Developments: For the quarter ended Sep 30 2017, net income increased 17.5% to US$153.5 million from US$130.7 million in the year-earlier quarter. Revenues were US$1.08 billion, up 14.8% from US$945.0 million the year before. Operating income was US$232.8 million versus US$201.1 million in the prior-year quarter, an increase of 15.8%. Direct operating expenses rose 14.1% to US$719.7 million from US$630.7 million in the comparable period the year before. Indirect operating expenses increased 16.9% to US$132.3 million from US$113.2 million in the equivalent prior-year period.

Prospects: Our evaluation of Ametek Inc. as of Jan. 14, 2018 is the result of our systematic analysis on three basic characteristics: earnings strength, relative valuation, and recent stock price movement. The company has enjoyed a very positive trend in earnings per share over the past 5 quarters and while recent estimates for the company have remained steady, AME has posted better than expected results. Based on operating earnings yield, the company is about fairly valued when compared to all of the companies in our coverage universe. Share price changes over the past year indicates that AME will perform well over the near term.

Financial Data

(US$ in Thousands)	9 Mos	6 Mos	3 Mos	12/31/2016	12/31/2015	12/31/2014	12/31/2013	12/31/2012
Earnings Per Share	2.38	2.28	2.22	2.19	2.45	2.37	2.10	1.88
Cash Flow Per Share	3.59	3.29	3.26	3.25	2.80	2.96	2.71	2.53
Dividends Per Share	0.360	0.360	0.360	0.360	0.360	0.330	0.240	0.220
Dividend Payout %	15.13	15.79	16.22	16.44	14.69	13.92	11.43	11.70
Income Statement								
Total Revenue	3,157,085	2,072,286	1,007,682	3,840,087	3,974,295	4,021,964	3,594,136	3,334,213
EBITDA	803,986	530,229	258,479	967,123	966,882	948,484	855,605	791,624
Depn & Amortn	131,005	86,384	42,541	179,716	68,707	63,724	57,238	53,677
Income Before Taxes	599,204	394,671	191,422	693,103	806,380	804,832	724,795	662,475
Income Taxes	156,266	105,370	52,496	180,945	215,521	220,372	207,796	203,343
Net Income	442,938	289,407	138,926	512,158	590,859	584,460	516,999	459,132
Average Shares	232,253	231,588	231,004	233,730	241,586	247,102	246,065	243,986
Balance Sheet								
Current Assets	2,024,483	1,789,273	1,787,443	1,928,190	1,619,613	1,578,604	1,369,129	1,164,743
Total Assets	7,783,301	7,535,013	7,298,810	7,100,674	6,664,530	6,420,963	5,877,902	5,190,056
Current Liabilities	1,270,341	995,146	1,016,798	924,441	1,025,172	936,144	874,545	879,969
Long-Term Obligations	1,920,879	2,128,838	2,076,577	2,062,644	1,556,045	1,427,825	1,141,750	1,133,121
Total Liabilities	4,017,146	3,942,817	3,894,575	3,844,161	3,409,904	3,181,402	2,741,781	2,654,905
Stockholders' Equity	3,766,155	3,592,196	3,404,235	3,256,513	3,254,626	3,239,561	3,136,121	2,535,151
Shares Outstanding	231,117	230,795	230,108	229,378	235,515	241,335	245,006	243,395
Statistical Record								
Return on Assets %	7.48	7.30	7.23	7.42	9.03	9.50	9.34	9.63
Return on Equity %	15.46	15.23	15.43	15.69	18.20	18.33	18.23	19.96
EBITDA Margin %	25.47	25.59	25.65	25.18	24.33	23.58	23.81	23.74
Net Margin %	14.03	13.97	13.79	13.34	14.87	14.53	14.38	13.77
Asset Turnover	0.56	0.55	0.55	0.56	0.61	0.65	0.65	0.70
Current Ratio	1.59	1.80	1.76	2.09	1.58	1.69	1.57	1.32
Debt to Equity	0.51	0.59	0.61	0.63	0.48	0.44	0.36	0.45
Price Range	66.40-44.10	62.86-44.10	55.31-43.88	53.59-43.88	57.50-47.90	54.20-46.12	52.67-37.57	38.02-28.17
P/E Ratio	27.90-18.53	27.57-19.34	24.91-19.77	24.47-20.04	23.47-19.55	22.87-19.46	25.08-17.89	20.22-14.98
Average Yield %	0.65	0.70	0.74	0.75	0.67	0.64	0.54	0.65

Address: 1100 Cassatt Road, Berwyn, PA 19312-1177 **Telephone:** 610-647-2121 **Fax:** 610-647-0211	**Web Site:** www.ametek.com **Officers:** David A. Zapico - Chairman, Chief Executive Officer, Chief Operating Officer, Executive Vice President, Division Officer William J. Burke - Executive Vice President, Chief Financial Officer, Senior Vice President, Comptroller, Treasurer	**Auditors:** Ernst & Young LLP **Transfer Agents:** American Stock Transfer & Trust Co., New York, NY

48

AMPHENOL CORP.

Exchange	Symbol	Price	52Wk Range	Yield	P/E
NYS	APH	$87.80 (12/29/2017)	91.04-66.60	0.87	27.96

*7 Year Price Score 127.23 *NYSE Composite Index=100 **12 Month Price Score 108.54

TRADING VOLUME (thousand shares)

Interim Earnings (Per Share)

Qtr.	Mar	Jun	Sep	Dec
2014	0.49	0.56	0.57	0.61
2015	0.57	0.56	0.65	0.63
2016	0.50	0.65	0.71	0.75
2017	0.71	0.80	0.88	...

Interim Dividends (Per Share)

Amt	Decl	Ex	Rec	Pay
0.16Q	02/02/2017	03/16/2017	03/20/2017	04/11/2017
0.16Q	05/04/2017	06/15/2017	06/19/2017	07/11/2017
0.19Q	07/26/2017	09/15/2017	09/18/2017	10/11/2017
0.19Q	11/01/2017	12/15/2017	12/18/2017	01/10/2018

Indicated Div: $0.76

Valuation Analysis / Institutional Holding

Forecast EPS	$3.21 (01/16/2018)	No of Institutions	810
Market Cap	$26.8 Billion	Shares	351,222,400
Book Value	$4.1 Billion	% Held	93.08
Price/Book	6.59		
Price/Sales	3.99		

Business Summary: Electrical Equipment (MIC: 7.3.1 SIC: 3678 NAIC: 334417)

Amphenol is engaged in designing, manufacturing and marketing electrical, electronic and fiber optic connectors, interconnect systems, antennas, sensors and sensor-based products and coaxial and high-speed specialty cable. Co. has two reportable business segments: Interconnect Products and Assemblies, which designs, manufacturers and markets a range of connector and connector systems, antennas and sensors used in a range of applications; and Cable Products and Solutions, which primarily designs, manufacturers and markets cable, other products and components for use primarily in the broadband communications and information technology markets as well as certain applications in other markets.

Recent Developments:
For the quarter ended Sep 30 2017, net income increased 23.4% to US$280.3 million from US$227.1 million in the year-earlier quarter. Revenues were US$1.84 billion, up 12.5% from US$1.64 billion the year before. Operating income was US$377.9 million versus US$326.3 million in the prior-year quarter, an increase of 15.8%. Direct operating expenses rose 12.4% to US$1.23 billion from US$1.10 billion in the comparable period the year before. Indirect operating expenses increased 8.2% to US$228.2 million from US$211.0 million in the equivalent prior-year period.

Prospects:
Our evaluation of Amphenol Corp. as of Jan. 14, 2018 is the result of our systematic analysis on three basic characteristics: earnings strength, relative valuation, and recent stock price movement. The company has managed to produce a neutral trend in earnings per share over the past 5 quarters and while recent estimates for the company have been mixed, APH has posted better than expected results. Based on operating earnings yield, the company is about fairly valued when compared to all of the companies in our coverage universe. Share price changes over the past year indicates that APH will perform well over the near term.

Financial Data

(US$ in Thousands)	9 Mos	6 Mos	3 Mos	12/31/2016	12/31/2015	12/31/2014	12/31/2013	12/31/2012
Earnings Per Share	3.14	2.97	2.82	2.61	2.41	2.21	1.96	1.70
Cash Flow Per Share	3.49	3.79	3.66	3.49	3.33	2.81	2.42	2.08
Tang Book Value Per Share	0.32	N.M.	N.M.	N.M.	1.77	0.94	9.04	1.56
Dividends Per Share	0.670	0.620	0.600	0.580	0.530	0.450	0.305	0.210
Dividend Payout %	21.34	20.88	21.28	22.22	21.99	20.36	15.56	12.39
Income Statement								
Total Revenue	5,067,400	3,226,600	1,560,100	6,286,400	5,568,700	5,345,500	4,614,669	4,292,065
EBITDA	1,209,600	768,800	371,800	1,419,200	1,274,300	1,200,800	1,031,708	948,721
Depn & Amortn	168,500	110,600	54,100	217,000	171,600	168,100	136,482	121,779
Income Before Taxes	973,800	615,500	298,400	1,141,100	1,052,800	972,500	846,645	778,841
Income Taxes	212,700	134,600	71,100	308,500	280,500	257,300	207,896	219,333
Net Income	753,900	476,400	224,900	822,900	763,500	709,100	635,672	555,317
Average Shares	315,700	316,100	316,400	315,200	316,500	320,430	324,548	327,894
Balance Sheet								
Current Assets	4,352,900	3,992,400	3,722,400	3,591,200	3,850,000	3,504,100	3,157,567	2,706,915
Total Assets	9,608,800	9,172,900	8,707,400	8,498,700	7,458,400	7,027,000	6,168,028	5,215,463
Current Liabilities	1,433,700	1,713,900	1,583,300	1,635,200	1,008,400	1,045,600	1,609,878	888,514
Long-Term Obligations	3,559,700	3,020,600	2,862,100	2,635,500	2,813,200	2,672,300	1,431,437	1,606,204
Total Liabilities	5,541,600	5,298,000	5,003,200	4,823,800	4,219,900	4,119,600	3,308,519	2,785,504
Stockholders' Equity	4,067,200	3,874,900	3,704,200	3,674,900	3,238,500	2,907,400	2,859,509	2,429,959
Shares Outstanding	305,339	305,444	305,400	308,300	308,000	309,884	316,412	319,715
Statistical Record								
Return on Assets %	11.01	10.88	10.74	10.29	10.54	10.75	11.17	11.47
Return on Equity %	25.45	25.27	25.14	23.74	24.85	24.59	24.04	24.07
EBITDA Margin %	23.87	23.83	23.83	22.58	22.88	22.46	22.36	22.10
Net Margin %	14.88	14.76	14.42	13.09	13.71	13.27	13.78	12.94
Asset Turnover	0.75	0.76	0.77	0.79	0.77	0.81	0.81	0.89
Current Ratio	3.04	2.33	2.35	2.20	3.82	3.35	1.96	3.05
Debt to Equity	0.88	0.78	0.77	0.72	0.87	0.92	0.50	0.66
Price Range	84.64-63.05	76.18-55.97	71.89-55.08	68.83-45.42	60.20-49.06	55.45-42.34	44.59-32.35	32.51-22.91
P/E Ratio	26.96-20.08	25.65-18.85	25.49-19.53	26.37-17.40	24.98-20.36	25.09-19.16	22.75-16.51	19.12-13.48
Average Yield %	0.93	0.92	0.95	0.98	0.96	0.93	0.79	0.73

Address: 358 Hall Avenue, Wallingford, CT 06492 **Telephone:** 203-265-8900 **Fax:** 203-265-8746	**Web Site:** www.amphenol.com **Officers:** Martin H. Loeffler - Chairman, Executive Chairman Richard Adam Norwitt - President, Chief Executive Officer	**Auditors:** Deloitte & Touche LLP **Transfer Agents:** Computershare Trust Company, N.A., Providence, RI

ANADARKO PETROLEUM CORP

Exchange	Symbol	Price	52Wk Range	Yield	P/E
NYS	APC	$53.64 (12/29/2017)	71.74-40.52	0.37	N/A

*7 Year Price Score 57.30   *NYSE Composite Index=100   *12 Month Price Score 88.07

Interim Earnings (Per Share)

Qtr.	Mar	Jun	Sep	Dec
2014	(5.30)	0.45	2.12	(0.78)
2015	(6.45)	0.12	(4.41)	(2.45)
2016	(2.03)	(1.36)	(1.61)	(0.90)
2017	(0.58)	(0.76)	(1.27)	...

Interim Dividends (Per Share)

Amt	Decl	Ex	Rec	Pay
0.05Q	02/09/2017	03/06/2017	03/08/2017	03/22/2017
0.05Q	05/10/2017	06/12/2017	06/14/2017	06/28/2017
0.05Q	08/02/2017	09/12/2017	09/13/2017	09/27/2017
0.05Q	11/15/2017	12/12/2017	12/13/2017	12/27/2017

Indicated Div: $0.20 (Div. Reinv. Plan)

Valuation Analysis / Institutional Holding

Forecast EPS	$-2.18	No of Institutions	
	(01/18/2018)	1252	
Market Cap	$29.6 Billion	Shares	
Book Value	$10.8 Billion	634,564,608	
Price/Book	2.75	% Held	
Price/Sales	2.61	84.90	

Business Summary: Production & Extraction (MIC: 9.1.1 SIC: 1311 NAIC: 211111)

Anadarko Petroleum is an independent exploration and production company. Co. is engaged in the exploration, development, production, and marketing of oil, natural gas, and natural gas liquids (NGLs), and in the marketing of liquefied natural gas. In addition, Co. engages in the gathering, processing, treating, and transporting of oil, natural gas, and NGLs. Co. also participates in the hard-minerals business through royalty arrangements. As of Dec 31 2016, Co.'s proved reserves consisted of 1.72 billion barrels of oil equivalent, of which 4.42 trillion cubic feet were natural gas, 702.0 million barrels were oil and condensate and 283.0 million barrels were NGLs.

Recent Developments:
For the quarter ended Sep 30 2017, net loss amounted to US$641.0 million versus a net loss of US$747.0 million in the year-earlier quarter. Revenues were US$2.50 billion, up 31.9% from US$1.89 billion the year before. Operating loss was US$775.0 million versus a loss of US$793.0 million in the prior-year quarter. Direct operating expenses rose 55.0% to US$1.63 billion from US$1.05 billion in the comparable period the year before. Indirect operating expenses increased 0.5% to US$1.65 billion from US$1.64 billion in the equivalent prior-year period.

Prospects:
Our evaluation of Anadarko Petroleum Corp. as of Jan. 14, 2018 is the result of our systematic analysis on three basic characteristics: earnings strength, relative valuation, and recent stock price movement. The company has managed to produce a neutral trend in earnings per share over the past 5 quarters. Because the company lacks sufficient analyst estimate data, we place greater weight on the historical EPS trend as the measure of earnings strength. Based on operating earnings yield, the company is overvalued when compared to all of the companies in our coverage universe. Share price changes over the past year indicates that APC will perform very poorly over the near term.

Financial Data
(US$ in Thousands)

	9 Mos	6 Mos	3 Mos	12/31/2016	12/31/2015	12/31/2014	12/31/2013	12/31/2012
Earnings Per Share	(3.51)	(3.85)	(4.45)	(5.90)	(13.18)	(3.47)	1.58	4.74
Cash Flow Per Share	6.77	7.04	7.73	5.73	(3.69)	16.73	17.71	16.63
Tang Book Value Per Share	9.25	10.42	11.08	11.44	12.76	25.97	32.15	29.87
Dividends Per Share	0.200	0.200	0.200	0.200	1.080	0.990	0.540	0.360
Dividend Payout %	...	...	...	...	...	...	34.18	7.59
Income Statement								
Total Revenue	8,979,000	6,483,000	3,767,000	7,869,000	8,698,000	18,470,000	14,581,000	13,411,000
EBITDA	2,299,000	2,052,000	1,160,000	1,362,000	(4,261,000)	5,376,000	6,719,000	8,271,000
Depn & Amortn	3,235,000	2,152,000	1,115,000	4,301,000	4,603,000	4,550,000	3,927,000	3,964,000
Income Before Taxes	(1,616,000)	(550,000)	(178,000)	(3,829,000)	(9,689,000)	54,000	2,106,000	3,565,000
Income Taxes	(366,000)	59,000	97,000	(1,021,000)	(2,877,000)	1,617,000	1,165,000	1,120,000
Net Income	(1,432,000)	(733,000)	(318,000)	(3,071,000)	(6,692,000)	(1,750,000)	801,000	2,391,000
Average Shares	553,000	552,000	551,000	522,000	508,000	506,000	505,000	502,000
Balance Sheet								
Current Assets	7,473,000	7,984,000	7,707,000	5,266,000	3,982,000	11,221,000	7,108,000	6,795,000
Total Assets	43,128,000	44,348,000	44,693,000	45,564,000	46,414,000	61,689,000	55,781,000	52,589,000
Current Liabilities	3,683,000	3,154,000	3,762,000	3,328,000	4,181,000	10,234,000	5,703,000	3,994,000
Long-Term Obligations	15,424,000	15,436,000	15,284,000	15,281,000	15,718,000	15,092,000	13,065,000	13,269,000
Total Liabilities	32,346,000	32,876,000	32,837,000	33,352,000	33,595,000	41,964,000	33,924,000	31,960,000
Stockholders' Equity	10,782,000	11,472,000	11,856,000	12,212,000	12,819,000	19,725,000	21,857,000	20,629,000
Shares Outstanding	552,600	552,500	551,900	551,200	508,300	506,600	503,700	500,500
Statistical Record								
Return on Assets %	N.M.	N.M.	N.M.	N.M.	N.M.	N.M.	1.48	4.57
Return on Equity %	N.M.	N.M.	N.M.	N.M.	N.M.	N.M.	3.77	12.31
EBITDA Margin %	25.60	31.65	30.79	17.31	N.M.	29.11	46.08	61.67
Net Margin %	N.M.	N.M.	N.M.	N.M.	N.M.	N.M.	5.49	17.83
Asset Turnover	0.26	0.24	0.22	0.17	0.16	0.31	0.27	0.26
Current Ratio	2.03	2.53	2.05	1.58	0.95	1.10	1.25	1.70
Debt to Equity	1.43	1.35	1.29	1.25	1.23	0.77	0.60	0.64
Price Range	72.69-40.52	72.69-43.79	72.69-44.10	72.69-30.54	94.54-45.67	112.69-72.01	97.76-74.31	88.05-57.12
P/E Ratio	...	...	...	...	...	...	61.87-47.03	18.58-12.05
Average Yield %	0.35	0.33	0.34	0.38	1.44	1.04	0.62	0.49

Address: 1201 Lake Robbins Drive, The Woodlands, TX 77380-1046
Telephone: 832-636-1000

Web Site: www.anadarko.com
Officers: R. A. Walker - Chairman, President, Chief Executive Officer, Chief Operating Officer Robert G. Gwin - Executive Vice President, Senior Vice President, Chief Financial Officer

Auditors: KPMG LLP
Investor Contact: 855-820-6605
Transfer Agents: BNYMellon Shareowner Services, Jersey City, NJ

ANDEAVOR

Exchange	Symbol	Price	52Wk Range	Yield	P/E
NYS	ANDV	$114.34 (12/29/2017)	115.36-75.49	2.06	23.15

*7 Year Price Score 117.08 ***NYSE Composite Index=100** ***12 Month Price Score 109.80**

Interim Earnings (Per Share)

Qtr.	Mar	Jun	Sep	Dec
2014	0.58	1.70	3.05	1.14
2015	1.15	4.59	6.13	0.54
2016	0.57	3.47	1.42	0.67
2017	0.42	0.31	3.54	...

Interim Dividends (Per Share)

Amt	Decl	Ex	Rec	Pay
0.55Q	02/03/2017	02/24/2017	02/28/2017	03/15/2017
0.55Q	05/04/2017	05/17/2017	05/19/2017	06/15/2017
0.59Q	08/07/2017	08/29/2017	08/31/2017	09/15/2017
0.59Q	11/08/2017	11/29/2017	11/30/2017	12/15/2017

Indicated Div: $2.36

Valuation Analysis | **Institutional Holding**

Forecast EPS	$6.86	No of Institutions
	(01/18/2018)	796
Market Cap	$17.8 Billion	Shares
Book Value	$9.1 Billion	152,017,856
Price/Book	1.96	% Held
Price/Sales	0.58	78.82

Business Summary: Refining & Marketing (MIC: 9.1.2 SIC: 2911 NAIC: 324110)

Andeavor is a petroleum refining, logistics and marketing company. Co.'s business is organized into three segments: refining, which refines crude oil and other feedstocks into transportation fuels, such as gasoline and gasoline blendstocks, jet fuel and diesel fuel, as well as other products; logistics, which is comprised of Tesoro Logistics LP's assets and operations, including certain crude oil and natural gas gathering assets, natural gas and natural gas liquids processing assets, and crude oil and refined products terminalling, transportation and storage assets acquired from Co. and third parties; and marketing, which sells transportation fuels through branded and unbranded channels.

Recent Developments: For the quarter ended Sep 30 2017, income from continuing operations increased 193.6% to US$593.0 million from US$202.0 million in the year-earlier quarter. Net income increased 199.0% to US$601.0 million from US$201.0 million in the year-earlier quarter. Revenues were US$9.84 billion, up 50.3% from US$6.54 billion the year before. Operating income was US$954.0 million versus US$360.0 million in the prior-year quarter, an increase of 165.0%. Direct operating expenses rose 44.6% to US$7.54 billion from US$5.22 billion in the comparable period the year before. Indirect operating expenses increased 38.5% to US$1.34 billion from US$968.0 million in the equivalent prior-year period.

Prospects: Our evaluation of Andeavor as of Jan. 14, 2018 is the result of our systematic analysis on three basic characteristics: earnings strength, relative valuation, and recent stock price movement. The company has enjoyed a very positive trend in earnings per share over the past 5 quarters. However, while recent estimates for the company have been mixed, ANDV has posted results that fell short of analysts expectations. Based on operating earnings yield, the company is undervalued when compared to all of the companies in our coverage universe. Share price changes over the past year indicates that ANDV will perform well over the near term.

Financial Data

(US$ in Thousands)	9 Mos	6 Mos	3 Mos	12/31/2016	12/31/2015	12/31/2014	12/31/2013	12/31/2012
Earnings Per Share	4.94	2.82	5.98	6.12	12.36	6.44	3.00	5.25
Cash Flow Per Share	8.33	11.06	10.42	10.97	17.30	10.61	6.36	11.34
Tang Book Value Per Share	26.67	25.57	34.69	34.20	31.94	24.30	30.33	28.96
Dividends Per Share	2.240	2.200	2.150	2.100	1.850	1.100	0.900	0.270
Dividend Payout %	45.34	78.01	35.95	34.31	14.97	17.08	30.00	5.14
Income Statement								
Total Revenue	24,323,000	14,487,000	6,638,000	24,582,000	28,711,000	40,633,000	37,601,000	32,974,000
EBITDA	1,392,000	434,000	423,000	2,075,000	3,331,000	2,052,000	1,140,000	1,671,000
Depn & Amortn	15,000	10,000	226,000	537,000	491,000	363,000	322,000	295,000
Income Before Taxes	1,104,000	248,000	108,000	1,264,000	2,623,000	1,454,000	669,000	1,212,000
Income Taxes	351,000	77,000	21,000	427,000	936,000	547,000	246,000	442,000
Net Income	649,000	90,000	50,000	734,000	1,540,000	843,000	412,000	743,000
Average Shares	157,800	131,700	118,100	119,900	124,600	130,800	137,300	141,500
Balance Sheet								
Current Assets	6,545,000	6,035,000	6,261,000	7,414,000	4,307,000	5,074,000	5,326,000	4,636,000
Total Assets	27,886,000	27,029,000	20,069,000	20,398,000	16,332,000	16,584,000	13,389,000	10,702,000
Current Liabilities	4,451,000	4,153,000	3,053,000	3,554,000	2,530,000	3,466,000	3,408,000	2,881,000
Long-Term Obligations	7,633,000	7,164,000	6,178,000	6,468,000	4,067,000	4,254,000	2,823,000	1,587,000
Total Liabilities	18,781,000	18,151,000	14,583,000	14,933,000	11,119,000	12,130,000	9,087,000	6,451,000
Stockholders' Equity	9,105,000	8,878,000	5,486,000	5,465,000	5,213,000	4,454,000	4,302,000	4,251,000
Shares Outstanding	155,994	158,558	117,396	116,899	119,393	124,960	131,804	138,162
Statistical Record								
Return on Assets %	3.17	1.51	3.96	3.99	9.36	5.63	3.42	7.20
Return on Equity %	9.96	4.68	13.35	13.71	31.86	19.26	9.63	18.71
EBITDA Margin %	5.72	3.00	6.37	8.44	11.60	5.05	3.03	5.07
Net Margin %	2.67	0.62	0.75	2.99	5.36	2.07	1.10	2.25
Asset Turnover	1.35	1.24	1.45	1.33	1.74	2.71	3.12	3.19
Current Ratio	1.47	1.45	2.05	2.09	1.70	1.46	1.56	1.61
Debt to Equity	0.84	0.81	1.13	1.18	0.78	0.96	0.66	0.37
Price Range	105.28-75.49	94.45-70.01	92.00-70.01	107.10-68.64	118.24-66.67	78.55-47.47	64.90-40.22	44.73-21.55
P/E Ratio	21.31-15.28	33.49-24.83	15.38-11.71	17.50-11.22	9.57-5.39	12.20-7.37	21.63-13.41	8.52-4.10
Average Yield %	2.55	2.67	2.65	2.57	1.97	1.84	1.72	0.86

Address: 19100 Ridgewood Pkwy., San Antonio, TX 78259-1828
Telephone: 210-626-6000

Web Site: www.tsocorp.com
Officers: Gregory J. (Greg) Goff - Chairman, President, Chief Executive Officer Keith M. Casey - Executive Vice President, Executive Vice President (frmr)

Auditors: Ernst & Young LLP
Transfer Agents: American Stock Transfer & Trust Company, New York, NY

ANIXTER INTERNATIONAL INC

Exchange	Symbol	Price	52Wk Range	Yield	P/E
NYS	AXE	$76.00 (12/29/2017)	88.00-63.15	N/A	17.72

*7 Year Price Score 84.93   *NYSE Composite Index=100   *12 Month Price Score 84.67

TRADING VOLUME (thousand shares)

Interim Earnings (Per Share)

Qtr.	Mar	Jun	Sep	Dec
2014	1.43	1.61	1.57	1.23
2015	0.57	2.14	0.97	0.13
2016	0.68	0.61	1.21	1.09
2017	0.91	1.18	1.11	...

Interim Dividends (Per Share)

Dividend Payment Suspended

Valuation Analysis | **Institutional Holding**

Forecast EPS	$5.05	No of Institutions
	(01/25/2018)	312
Market Cap	$2.6 Billion	Shares
Book Value	$1.5 Billion	40,430,540
Price/Book	1.75	% Held
Price/Sales	0.33	77.41

Business Summary: Electrical Equipment (MIC: 7.3.1 SIC: 5063 NAIC: 423610)

Anixter International is engaged in the distribution of network and security solutions, electrical and electronic solutions, and utility power solutions through Anixter Inc. and its subsidiaries. The Network and Security Solutions segment supplies products and customized supply chain solutions. The Electrical and Electronic Solutions segment supplies wire and cable, control, lighting and electrical bulk products and customized supply chain solutions. The Utility Power Solutions segment supplies electrical transmission and distribution products, power plant maintenance, repair and operations supplies and smart-grid products, and arranges materials management and procurement outsourcing.

Recent Developments: For the quarter ended Sep 29 2017, income from continuing operations decreased 6.7% to US$37.6 million from US$40.3 million in the year-earlier quarter. Net income decreased 6.9% to US$37.6 million from US$40.4 million in the year-earlier quarter. Revenues were US$2.02 billion, up 3.1% from US$1.96 billion the year before. Operating income was US$81.0 million versus US$87.3 million in the prior-year quarter, a decrease of 7.2%. Direct operating expenses rose 3.8% to US$1.62 billion from US$1.56 billion in the comparable period the year before. Indirect operating expenses increased 2.2% to US$316.2 million from US$309.4 million in the equivalent prior-year period.

Prospects: Our evaluation of Anixter International Inc. as of Jan. 21, 2018 is the result of our systematic analysis on three basic characteristics: earnings strength, relative valuation, and recent stock price movement. The company has generated a negative trend in earnings per share over the past 5 quarters and while recent estimates for the company have been raised by analysts, AXE has posted results that fell short of analysts expectations. Based on operating earnings yield, the company is undervalued when compared to all of the companies in our coverage universe. Share price changes over the past year indicates that AXE will perform poorly over the near term.

Financial Data
(US$ in Thousands)

	9 Mos	6 Mos	3 Mos	12/30/2016	01/01/2016	01/02/2015	01/03/2014	12/28/2012
Earnings Per Share	4.29	4.39	3.82	3.59	3.81	5.84	6.04	3.69
Cash Flow Per Share	4.48	7.93	7.92	8.37	2.78	3.17	10.03	4.30
Tang Book Value Per Share	8.41	6.69	5.01	3.36	N.M.	16.62	20.86	19.30
Dividends Per Share	...	...	...	...	...	...	5.000	4.500
Dividend Payout %	...	...	...	...	...	...	82.78	121.95
Income Statement								
Total Revenue	5,913,600	3,897,200	1,895,800	7,622,800	6,190,500	6,445,500	6,226,500	6,253,100
EBITDA	282,000	183,700	85,300	341,700	294,300	378,600	373,500	301,400
Depn & Amortn	50,200	33,200	16,500	65,500	47,600	35,700	30,100	32,500
Income Before Taxes	176,100	113,700	49,900	197,500	182,900	294,800	296,000	209,200
Income Taxes	67,500	42,700	19,000	76,400	86,000	100,000	95,600	84,600
Net Income	108,600	71,000	30,900	120,500	127,600	194,800	200,500	124,800
Average Shares	34,000	34,000	33,900	33,600	33,400	33,300	33,200	33,800
Balance Sheet								
Current Assets	2,837,500	2,796,700	2,637,400	2,688,500	2,727,800	2,589,800	2,275,700	2,450,100
Total Assets	4,252,500	4,203,900	4,040,200	4,093,600	4,142,000	3,586,500	2,860,800	3,089,600
Current Liabilities	1,371,700	1,318,400	1,202,800	1,263,900	1,156,200	1,030,500	902,400	967,300
Long-Term Obligations	1,270,100	1,331,200	1,337,600	1,378,800	1,642,900	1,207,700	836,000	982,200
Total Liabilities	2,796,200	2,807,500	2,697,600	2,801,400	2,962,600	2,453,500	1,833,400	2,119,700
Stockholders' Equity	1,456,300	1,396,400	1,342,600	1,292,200	1,179,400	1,133,000	1,027,400	969,900
Shares Outstanding	33,620	33,595	33,574	33,437	33,278	33,141	32,853	32,537
Statistical Record								
Return on Assets %	3.46	3.55	3.17	2.93	3.31	6.06	6.63	4.10
Return on Equity %	10.61	11.20	10.02	9.78	11.07	18.08	19.75	12.73
EBITDA Margin %	4.77	4.71	4.50	4.48	4.75	5.87	6.00	4.82
Net Margin %	1.84	1.82	1.63	1.58	2.06	3.02	3.22	2.00
Asset Turnover	1.86	1.86	1.90	1.86	1.61	2.00	2.06	2.05
Current Ratio	2.07	2.12	2.19	2.13	2.36	2.51	2.52	2.53
Debt to Equity	0.87	0.95	1.00	1.07	1.39	1.07	0.81	1.01
Price Range	86.10-59.83	85.75-51.91	85.75-49.90	83.65-38.29	88.18-56.66	107.51-76.57	92.36-62.64	73.37-49.76
P/E Ratio	20.07-13.95	19.53-11.82	22.45-13.06	23.30-10.67	23.14-14.87	18.41-13.11	15.29-10.37	19.88-13.49
Average Yield %	...	...	...	...	...	...	...	7.30

Address: 2301 Patriot Blvd., Glenview, IL 60026	**Web Site:** www.anixter.com	**Auditors:** Ernst & Young LLP
Telephone: 224-521-8000	**Officers:** Samuel Zell - Chairman Robert J. Eck - President, Chief Executive Officer	**Investor Contact:** 224-521-8895
		Transfer Agents: Wells Fargo Shareowner Services, Mendota Heights, MN

ANNALY CAPITAL MANAGEMENT INC

Exchange	Symbol	Price	52Wk Range	Yield	P/E
NYS	NLY	$11.89 (12/29/2017)	12.66-10.08	10.09	4.57

*7 Year Price Score 70.56 *NYSE Composite Index=100 *12 Month Price Score 95.30

Interim Earnings (Per Share)

Qtr.	Mar	Jun	Sep	Dec
2014	(0.23)	(0.37)	0.35	(0.71)
2015	(0.52)	0.93	(0.68)	0.69
2016	(0.96)	(0.32)	0.70	1.89
2017	0.41	(0.01)	0.31	...

Interim Dividends (Per Share)

Amt	Decl	Ex	Rec	Pay
0.30Q	03/16/2017	03/29/2017	03/31/2017	04/28/2017
0.30Q	06/15/2017	06/28/2017	06/30/2017	07/31/2017
0.30Q	09/14/2017	09/28/2017	00/29/2017	10/31/2017
0.30Q	12/14/2017	12/28/2017	12/29/2017	01/31/2018

Indicated Div: $1.20 (Div. Reinv. Plan)

Valuation Analysis

Forecast EPS	$1.21
	(11/12/2017)
Market Cap	$12.9 Billion
Book Value	$14.1 Billion
Price/Book	0.91
Price/Sales	3.43

Institutional Holding

No of Institutions	804
Shares	816,225,664
% Held	51.34

Business Summary: REITs (MIC: 5.3.1 SIC: 6798 NAIC: 525930)

Annaly Capital Management is a real estate finance company. Co. owns a portfolio of real estate related investments, such as collateralized mortgage obligations, Agency debentures, and mortgage servicing rights. Co.'s investment groups are comprised of agency, which invests in agency mortgage-backed securities and related derivatives; residential credit, which invests in non-agency mortgage-backed assets within securitized products and residential mortgage loan markets; commercial real estate, which invests in commercial mortgage loans, securities, and other commercial real estate investments; and middle market lending, which provides customized debt financing to middle-market businesses.

Recent Developments: For the quarter ended Sep 30 2017, net income decreased 49.7% to US$367.3 million from US$730.9 million in the year-earlier quarter. Revenues were US$694.6 million, down 30.6% from US$1.00 billion the year before.

Prospects: Our evaluation of Annaly Capital Management Inc. as of Jan. 21, 2018 is the result of our systematic analysis on three basic characteristics: earnings strength, relative valuation, and recent stock price movement. The company has generated a negative trend in earnings per share over the past 5 quarters and while recent estimates for the company have remained steady, NLY has posted better than expected results. Based on operating earnings yield, the company is undervalued when compared to all of the companies in our coverage universe. Share price changes over the past year indicates that NLY will perform very well over the near term.

Financial Data

(US$ in Thousands)	9 Mos	6 Mos	3 Mos	12/31/2016	12/31/2015	12/31/2014	12/31/2013	12/31/2012
Earnings Per Share	2.60	2.99	2.68	1.39	0.42	(0.96)	3.74	1.71
Cash Flow Per Share	10.23	4.84	7.03	7.05	(3.34)	6.47	(13.61)	7.83
Tang Book Value Per Share	11.33	11.09	11.13	10.41	11.62	13.00	12.03	15.78
Dividends Per Share	2.977	3.169	3.169	3.169	3.169	3.169	3.469	4.019
Dividend Payout %	114.51	105.98	118.24	227.97	754.46	...	92.75	235.01
Income Statement								
Interest Income	1,747,703	1,125,153	587,727	2,210,951	2,170,697	2,632,647	2,918,562	3,259,145
Interest Expense	689,643	420,706	198,425	657,752	471,596	512,659	624,714	667,172
Net Interest Income	1,058,060	704,447	389,302	1,553,199	1,699,101	2,119,988	2,293,848	2,591,973
Non-Interest Income	(68,929)	(141,018)	105,911	128,348	(1,035,068)	(2,747,604)	1,676,144	(584,602)
Non-Interest Expense	164,867	107,851	53,828	250,356	200,240	209,338	232,081	235,559
Income Before Taxes	824,264	455,578	441,385	1,431,191	463,793	(836,954)	3,737,911	1,771,812
Income Taxes	2,019	648	977	(1,595)	(1,954)	5,325	8,213	35,912
Net Income	822,682	455,135	440,511	1,433,756	466,556	(842,083)	3,729,698	1,735,900
Average Shares	1,073,040	1,019,000	1,019,307	970,102	947,276	947,539	995,557	1,005,755
Balance Sheet								
Net Loans & Leases	895,919	779,685	682,416	456,714	278,600	...	...	...
Total Assets	97,574,181	84,976,578	84,658,957	87,905,046	75,190,893	88,355,367	81,922,460	133,452,295
Total Liabilities	83,425,423	72,374,064	72,018,931	75,336,866	63,294,919	75,026,876	69,517,405	117,527,851
Stockholders' Equity	14,148,758	12,602,514	12,640,026	12,568,180	11,895,974	13,328,491	12,405,055	15,924,444
Shares Outstanding	1,088,083	1,019,027	1,018,971	1,018,913	935,929	947,643	947,432	947,213
Statistical Record								
Return on Assets %	2.90	3.73	3.38	1.75	0.57	N.M.	3.46	1.42
Return on Equity %	19.50	25.13	22.58	11.69	3.70	N.M.	26.33	10.92
Net Interest Margin %	56.80	58.64	66.24	70.25	78.27	80.53	78.60	79.53
Efficiency Ratio %	8.21	18.60	7.76	10.70	17.63	...	5.05	8.81
Price Range	12.66-9.89	12.66-9.89	11.31-9.89	11.25-8.69	11.04-9.06	11.92-9.97	16.13-9.74	17.75-14.01
P/E Ratio	4.87-3.80	4.23-3.31	4.22-3.69	8.09-6.25	26.29-21.57	...	4.31-2.60	10.38-8.19
Average Yield %	26.56	29.18	29.98	30.57	31.33	28.13	26.57	24.68

Address: 1211 Avenue of the Americas, New York, NY 10036 **Telephone:** 212-696-0100 **Fax:** 212-696-9809	**Web Site:** www.annaly.com **Officers:** Wellington J. Denahan-Norris - Chairman, Vice-Chairman, Chief Executive Officer, Co-Chief Executive Officer, Chief Operating Officer Kevin G. Keyes - President, Chief Executive Officer, Chief Strategy Officer, Managing Director	**Auditors:** Ernst & Young LLP **Investor Contact:** 888-826-6259 **Transfer Agents:** Computershare Shareowner Services LLC, Jersey City, NJ

ANTHEM INC

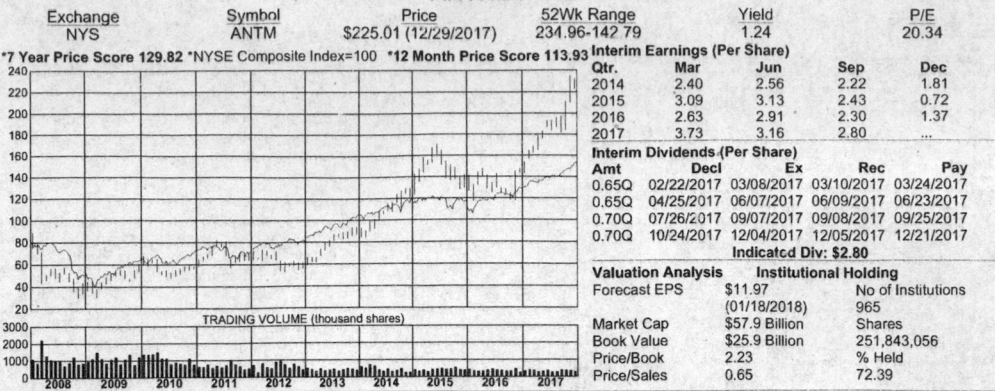

Exchange	Symbol	Price	52Wk Range	Yield	P/E
NYS	ANTM	$225.01 (12/29/2017)	234.96-142 79	1.24	20.34

*7 Year Price Score 129.82 *NYSE Composite Index=100 *12 Month Price Score 113.93

Interim Earnings (Per Share)

Qtr.	Mar	Jun	Sep	Dec
2014	2.40	2.56	2.22	1.81
2015	3.09	3.13	2.43	0.72
2016	2.63	2.91	2.30	1.37
2017	3.73	3.16	2.80	...

Interim Dividends (Per Share)

Amt	Decl	Ex	Rec	Pay
0.65Q	02/22/2017	03/08/2017	03/10/2017	03/24/2017
0.65Q	04/25/2017	06/07/2017	06/09/2017	06/23/2017
0.70Q	07/26/2017	09/07/2017	09/08/2017	09/25/2017
0.70Q	10/24/2017	12/04/2017	12/05/2017	12/21/2017

Indicated Div: $2.80

Valuation Analysis

Forecast EPS	$11.97 (01/18/2018)
Market Cap	$57.9 Billion
Book Value	$25.9 Billion
Price/Book	2.23
Price/Sales	0.65

Institutional Holding

No of Institutions	965
Shares	251,843,056
% Held	72.39

Business Summary: Life & Health (MIC: 5.2.2 SIC: 6324 NAIC: 524114)

Anthem is an insurance holding company. Co. provides network-based managed care plans to large and small employer, individual, Medicaid and Medicare markets. Co.'s managed care plans include preferred provider organizations, health maintenance organizations, point-of-service plans, indemnity plans and other hybrid plans, and hospital only and limited benefit products. In addition, Co. provides managed care services to self-funded customers, including claims processing. Co. also provides other insurance products and services such as dental, vision, life and disability insurance benefits, as well as services to the federal government in connection with the Federal Employee Program.

Recent Developments: For the quarter ended Sep 30 2017, net income increased 20.9% to US$746.9 million from US$617.8 million in the year-earlier quarter. Revenues were US$22.43 billion, up 4.8% from US$21.40 billion the year before. Net premiums earned were US$20.80 billion versus US$19.79 billion in the prior-year quarter, an increase of 5.1%. Net investment income rose 9.6% to US$220.2 million from US$200.9 million a year ago.

Prospects: Our evaluation of Anthem Inc. as of Jan. 14, 2018 is the result of our systematic analysis on three basic characteristics: earnings strength, relative valuation, and recent stock price movement. The company has generated a negative trend in earnings per share over the past 5 quarters and while recent estimates for the company have been raised by analysts, ANTM has posted better than expected results. Based on operating earnings yield, the company is undervalued when compared to all of the companies in our coverage universe. Share price changes over the past year indicates that ANTM will perform well over the near term.

Financial Data
(US$ in Thousands)

	9 Mos	6 Mos	3 Mos	12/31/2016	12/31/2015	12/31/2014	12/31/2013	12/31/2012
Earnings Per Share	11.06	10.56	10.31	9.21	9.38	8.99	8.20	8.18
Cash Flow Per Share	22.11	16.32	17.35	12.16	15.65	12.21	10.23	8.51
Tang Book Value Per Share	2.02	3.76	2.29	N.M.	N.M.	N.M.	N.M.	N.M.
Dividends Per Share	2.650	2.600	2.600	2.600	2.500	1.750	1.500	1.150
Dividend Payout %	23.96	24.62	25.22	28.23	26.65	19.47	18.29	14.06
Income Statement								
Total Revenue	67,359,100	44,933,100	22,525,900	84,863,000	79,156,500	73,874,100	71,023,500	61,711,700
Income Before Taxes	3,839,600	2,720,700	1,515,000	4,555,400	4,631,000	4,368,100	3,840,200	3,865,500
Income Taxes	1,227,500	855,500	505,100	2,085,600	2,071,000	1,808,000	1,205,900	1,210,000
Net Income	2,612,100	1,865,200	1,009,900	2,469,800	2,560,000	2,569,700	2,489,700	2,655,500
Average Shares	267,000	270,800	270,400	268,100	272,900	285,900	303,800	324,800
Balance Sheet								
Total Assets	68,309,900	68,237,600	68,943,500	65,083,100	61,717,800	62,065,000	59,574,500	58,955,400
Total Liabilities	42,361,600	41,805,900	42,851,600	39,982,700	38,673,700	37,813,700	34,809,300	35,152,700
Stockholders' Equity	25,948,300	26,431,700	26,091,900	25,100,400	23,044,100	24,251,300	24,765,200	23,802,700
Shares Outstanding	257,404	263,095	265,074	263,747	261,238	268,109	293,273	304,715
Statistical Record								
Return on Assets %	4.49	4.31	4.18	3.88	4.14	4.23	4.20	4.77
Return on Equity %	11.76	11.26	11.19	10.23	10.83	10.49	10.25	11.25
Net Margin %	3.88	4.15	4.48	2.91	3.23	3.48	3.51	4.30
Price Range	197.43-117.42	193.36-117.42	169.20-117.42	147.66-117.22	171.04-123.26	129.16-84.25	93.92-58.93	73.80-52.93
P/E Ratio	17.85-10.62	18.31-11.12	16.41-11.39	16.03-12.73	18.23-13.14	14.37-9.37	11.45-7.19	9.02-6.47
Average Yield %	1.60	1.73	1.86	1.95	1.70	1.62	1.91	1.82

Address: 120 Monument Circle, Indianapolis, IN 46204-4903 **Telephone:** 317-488-6000	**Web Site:** www.antheminc.com **Officers:** Joseph R. Swedish - Chairman, President, Chief Executive Officer Gail Koziara Boudreaux - President, Chief Executive Officer	**Auditors:** Ernst & Young LLP **Investor Contact:** 212-476-1473 **Transfer Agents:** EquiServe Trust Company, N.A., Providence, RI

54

ANTERO RESOURCES CORP

Exchange	Symbol	Price	52Wk Range	Yield	P/E
NYS	AR	$19.00 (12/29/2017)	26.16-17.65	N/A	N/A

*7 Year Price Score N/A *NYSE Composite Index=100 *12 Month Price Score 83.90

Interim Earnings (Per Share)

Qtr.	Mar	Jun	Sep	Dec
2014	(0.36)	(0.16)	0.78	2.31
2015	1.49	(0.52)	1.93	0.56
2016	(0.02)	(2.12)	0.77	(1.62)
2017	0.85	(0.02)	(0.43)	...

Interim Dividends (Per Share)

No Dividends Paid

Valuation Analysis **Institutional Holding**

Forecast EPS	$0.26	No of Institutions
	(01/18/2018)	355
Market Cap	$6.0 Billion	Shares
Book Value	$7.7 Billion	522,653,632
Price/Book	0.78	% Held
Price/Sales	2.15	101.26

TRADING VOLUME (thousand shares)

Business Summary: Production & Extraction (MIC: 9.1.1 SIC: 1311 NAIC: 211111)

Antero Resources is an independent oil and natural gas company engaged in the exploration, development and acquisition of natural gas, natural gas liquids (NGLs), and oil properties located in the Appalachian Basin. Co. operates in the following industry segments: the exploration, development and production of natural gas, NGLs, and oil; gathering and compression; water handling and treatment; and marketing of excess firm transportation capacity. As of Dec 31 2016, Co.'s estimated proved reserves were 15.40 trillion cubic feet equivalent, consisting of 9.40 trillion cubic feet of natural gas, 404.0 million barrels (MMBbl) of NGLs and 38.0 MMBbl of oil.

Recent Developments: For the quarter ended Sep 30 2017, net loss amounted to US$90.0 million versus net income of US$268.2 million in the year-earlier quarter. Revenues were US$647.9 million, down 42.0% from US$1.12 billion the year before. Operating loss was US$72.1 million versus an income of US$467.3 million in the prior-year quarter. Direct operating expenses rose 7.5% to US$407.5 million from US$378.9 million in the comparable period the year before. Indirect operating expenses increased 15.6% to US$312.4 million from US$270.2 million in the equivalent prior-year period.

Prospects: Our evaluation of Antero Resources Corp as of Jan. 14, 2018 is the result of our systematic analysis on three basic characteristics: earnings strength, relative valuation, and recent stock price movement. The company has generated a negative trend in earnings per share over the past 5 quarters. However, while recent estimates for the company have been mixed, AR has posted results that fell short of analysts expectations. Based on operating earnings yield, the company is overvalued when compared to all of the companies in our coverage universe. Share price changes over the past year indicates that AR will perform very poorly over the near term.

Financial Data
(US$ in Thousands)

	9 Mos	6 Mos	3 Mos	12/31/2016	12/31/2015	12/31/2014	12/31/2013	12/31/2012
Earnings Per Share	(1.22)	(0.02)	(2.12)	(2.88)	3.43	2.57	(0.07)	(1.10)
Cash Flow Per Share	6.43	4.15	4.11	4.20	3.67	3.81	2.06	1.27
Tang Book Value Per Share	24.27	24.29	24.25	19.89	21.42	16.73	13.73	...
Income Statement								
Total Revenue	2,633,848	1,985,968	1,195,579	1,744,525	3,954,858	2,720,632	1,313,134	735,718
EBITDA	1,165,857	1,030,283	704,709	(983,857)	1,797,986	1,758,515	533,581	636,238
Depn & Amortn	612,823	405,197	203,366	8,900	7,700	479,167	234,941	192,223
Income Before Taxes	347,723	489,834	434,673	(1,246,309)	1,555,886	1,119,297	162,023	346,505
Income Taxes	105,087	150,165	131,346	(496,376)	575,890	445,672	186,210	121,229
Net Income	128,201	263,264	268,396	(848,816)	941,364	673,587	(18,930)	(285,069)
Average Shares	315,463	315,401	315,769	294,945	274,143	262,068	260,100	260,100
Balance Sheet								
Current Assets	610,953	735,883	503,698	402,587	1,248,236	1,252,160	333,564	274,606
Total Assets	14,849,214	15,442,221	14,888,654	14,255,550	14,155,224	11,573,495	6,613,581	3,618,793
Current Liabilities	717,676	693,060	723,436	817,388	707,270	1,155,105	622,229	376,296
Long-Term Obligations	4,510,521	5,291,973	4,775,302	4,703,973	4,708,513	4,362,550	2,078,999	1,444,058
Total Liabilities	7,193,543	7,780,761	7,249,955	7,992,925	8,220,832	7,189,702	3,014,921	1,945,056
Stockholders' Equity	7,655,671	7,661,460	7,638,699	6,262,625	5,934,392	4,383,793	3,598,660	1,673,737
Shares Outstanding	315,470	315,448	315,006	314,877	277,035	262,071	262,049	...
Statistical Record								
Return on Assets %	N.M.	0.11	N.M.	N.M.	7.32	7.41	N.M.	N.M.
Return on Equity %	N.M.	0.23	N.M.	N.M.	18.25	16.88	N.M.	N.M.
EBITDA Margin %	44.26	51.88	58.94	N.M.	45.46	64.64	40.63	86.48
Net Margin %	4.87	13.26	22.45	N.M.	23.80	24.76	N.M.	N.M.
Asset Turnover	0.19	0.22	0.15	0.12	0.31	0.30	0.26	0.20
Current Ratio	0.85	1.06	0.70	0.49	1.76	1.08	0.54	0.73
Debt to Equity	0.59	0.69	0.63	0.75	0.79	1.00	0.58	0.86
Price Range	27.82-18.49	28.04-19.68	30.10-22.26	30.10-19.77	45.65-19.12	67.41-38.60	63.44-52.01	...
P/E Ratio	...	...	...	...	13.31-5.57	26.23-15.02	...	...

Address: 1615 Wynkoop Street, Denver, CO 80202 **Telephone:** 303-357-7310	**Web Site:** www.anteroresources.com **Officers:** Paul M. Rady - Chairman, Chief Executive Officer Michael N. Kennedy - Senior Vice President	**Auditors:** KPMG LLP **Transfer Agents:** American Stock Transfer & Trust Company, LLC

APACHE CORP

Exchange	Symbol	Price	52Wk Range	Yield	P/E
NYS	APA	$42.22 (12/29/2017)	63.78-38.37	2.37	24.40

*7 Year Price Score 50.19 *NYSE Composite Index=100 *12 Month Price Score 82.76

Interim Earnings (Per Share)

Qtr.	Mar	Jun	Sep	Dec
2014	0.60	1.31	(3.50)	(12.54)
2015	(12.34)	(14.83)	(14.95)	(19.08)
2016	(1.29)	(0.65)	(1.60)	(0.49)
2017	0.56	1.50	0.16	

Interim Dividends (Per Share)

Amt	Decl	Ex	Rec	Pay
0.25Q	02/13/2017	04/19/2017	04/21/2017	05/22/2017
0.25Q	05/12/2017	07/19/2017	07/21/2017	08/22/2017
0.25Q	09/13/2017	10/20/2017	10/23/2017	11/22/2017
0.25Q	12/14/2017	01/19/2018	01/22/2018	02/22/2018

Indicated Div: $1.00 (Div. Reinv. Plan)

Valuation Analysis		Institutional Holding	
Forecast EPS	$0.12	No of Institutions	
	(01/18/2018)	1189	
Market Cap	$16.1 Billion	Shares	
Book Value	$7.0 Billion	447,944,896	
Price/Book	2.29	% Held	
Price/Sales	2.56	85.01	

Business Summary: Production & Extraction (MIC: 9.1.1 SIC: 1311 NAIC: 211111)

Apache is an independent energy company that explores for, develops, and produces natural gas, crude oil, and natural gas liquids. As of Dec 31 2016, Co. had exploration and production interests in four geographic areas: the U.S., Canada, Egypt, and offshore the U.K. in the North Sea. Co. also has exploration interests in Suriname. As of Dec 31 2016, Co. had total estimated proved reserves of 1.31 billion barrels of oil equivalent, which consisited of 642.3 million barrels of crude oil, 192.4 million barrels of natural gas liquids, and 2.90 trillion cubic feet of natural gas.

Recent Developments: For the quarter ended Sep 30 2017, net income amounted to US$105.0 million versus a net loss of US$559.0 million in the year-earlier quarter. Revenues were US$1.58 billion, up 9.5% from US$1.44 billion the year before. Direct operating expenses declined 8.3% to US$397.0 million from US$433.0 million in the comparable period the year before. Indirect operating expenses decreased 43.2% to US$1.09 billion from US$1.91 billion in the equivalent prior-year period.

Prospects: Our evaluation of Apache Corp. as of Jan. 14, 2018 is the result of our systematic analysis on three basic characteristics: earnings strength, relative valuation, and recent stock price movement. The company has managed to produce a neutral trend in earnings per share over the past 5 quarters and while recent estimates for the company have been raised by analysts, APA has posted better than expected results. Based on operating earnings yield, the company is overvalued when compared to all of the companies in our coverage universe. Share price changes over the past year indicates that APA will perform very poorly over the near term.

Financial Data

(US$ in Thousands)	9 Mos	6 Mos	3 Mos	12/31/2016	12/31/2015	12/31/2014	12/31/2013	12/31/2012
Earnings Per Share	1.73	(0.03)	(2.18)	(3.71)	(61.20)	(14.06)	5.50	4.92
Cash Flow Per Share	6.71	6.96	6.87	6.39	7.89	22.03	24.90	21.80
Tang Book Value Per Share	18.40	18.11	16.78	16.44	6.79	68.66	80.92	73.58
Dividends Per Share	1.000	1.000	1.000	1.000	1.000	0.950	0.770	0.660
Dividend Payout %	57.80	...	...	...	...	...	14.00	13.41
Income Statement								
Total Revenue	4,837,000	3,262,000	1,878,000	5,354,000	6,366,000	13,851,000	16,054,000	17,078,000
EBITDA	2,646,000	1,893,000	1,213,000	1,352,000	1,406,000	7,382,000	11,106,000	12,151,000
Depn & Amortn	1,707,000	1,148,000	576,000	2,618,000	29,372,000	10,158,000	6,700,000	7,109,000
Income Before Taxes	640,000	547,000	538,000	(1,682,000)	(28,226,000)	(2,906,000)	4,216,000	4,877,000
Income Taxes	(345,000)	(333,000)	271,000	(442,000)	(5,469,000)	1,637,000	1,928,000	2,876,000
Net Income	848,000	785,000	213,000	(1,405,000)	(23,119,000)	(5,403,000)	2,232,000	2,001,000
Average Shares	381,000	381,000	380,000	379,000	378,000	384,000	406,000	391,000
Balance Sheet								
Current Assets	3,769,000	4,647,000	3,426,000	3,241,000	3,752,000	6,415,000	6,366,000	4,962,000
Total Assets	21,835,000	22,602,000	22,610,000	22,519,000	18,842,000	55,952,000	61,637,000	60,737,000
Current Liabilities	2,465,000	2,873,000	1,898,000	1,843,000	1,841,000	3,664,000	4,700,000	5,536,000
Long-Term Obligations	7,933,000	8,329,000	8,327,000	8,544,000	8,777,000	11,245,000	9,672,000	11,355,000
Total Liabilities	14,824,000	15,703,000	16,225,000	16,281,000	16,276,000	30,015,000	28,241,000	29,406,000
Stockholders' Equity	7,011,000	6,899,000	6,385,000	6,238,000	2,566,000	25,937,000	33,396,000	31,331,000
Shares Outstanding	380,937	380,928	380,434	379,439	378,034	376,504	395,772	391,640
Statistical Record								
Return on Assets %	2.96	N.M.	N.M.	N.M.	N.M.	N.M.	3.65	3.54
Return on Equity %	9.88	N.M.	N.M.	N.M.	N.M	N.M.	6.90	6.62
EBITDA Margin %	54.70	58.03	64.59	25.25	22.09	53.30	69.18	71.15
Net Margin %	17.53	24.06	11.34	N.M.	N.M.	N.M.	13.90	11.72
Asset Turnover	0.28	0.26	0.31	0.26	0.17	0.24	0.26	0.30
Current Ratio	1.53	1.62	1.81	1.76	2.04	1.75	1.35	0.90
Debt to Equity	1.13	1.21	1.30	1.37	3.42	0.43	0.29	0.36
Price Range	67.35-38.37	67.35-45.63	67.35-46.82	67.35-34.38	71.40-36.20	103.48-55.20	94.42-68.84	111.57-75 07
P/E Ratio	38.93-22.18	...	...	...	...	...	17.17-12.52	22.68-15.26
Average Yield %	1.88	1.79	1.75	1.87	1.84	1.11	0.93	0.74

Address: One Post Oak Central, 2000 Post Oak Boulevard, Suite 100, Houston, TX 77056-4400 Telephone: 713-296-6000	Web Site: www.apachecorp.com Officers: John J. Christmann - President, Chief Executive Officer, Vice President, Region Officer Stephen J. Riney - Executive Vice President, Chief Financial Officer	Auditors: Ernst & Young LLP Investor Contact: 281-302-2286 Transfer Agents: Wells Fargo Bank, N.A., South St. Paul, MN

APARTMENT INVESTMENT & MANAGEMENT CO

Exchange	Symbol	Price	52Wk Range	Yield	P/E
NYS	AIV	$43.71 (12/29/2017)	46.53-42.42	3.29	33.37

*7 Year Price Score 102.53 *NYSE Composite Index=100 *12 Month Price Score 93.73

Interim Earnings (Per Share)

Qtr.	Mar	Jun	Sep	Dec
2014	0.44	0.51	0.85	0.25
2015	0.58	0.39	0.12	0.43
2016	0.15	1.41	0.07	1.03
2017	0.07	0.10	0.11	...

Interim Dividends (Per Share)

Amt	Decl	Ex	Rec	Pay
0.36Q	01/31/2017	02/15/2017	02/17/2017	02/28/2017
0.36Q	04/25/2017	05/17/2017	05/19/2017	05/31/2017
0.36Q	07/26/2017	08/16/2017	08/10/2017	08/31/2017
0.36Q	10/25/2017	11/16/2017	11/17/2017	11/30/2017

Indicated Div: $1.44

Valuation Analysis

		Institutional Holding	
Forecast EPS	$0.38	No of Institutions	
	(01/18/2018)	485	
Market Cap	$6.9 Billion	Shares	
Book Value	$1.5 Billion	206,009,360	
Price/Book	4.72	% Held	
Price/Sales	6.87	99.78	

Business Summary: REITs (MIC: 5.3.1 SIC: 6798 NAIC: 525930)

Apartment Investment and Management is a self-administered and self-managed real estate investment trust. Co. is focused on the ownership, management, redevelopment and limited development of apartment communities. Co., through its wholly-owned subsidiaries, AIMCO-GP, Inc. and AIMCO-LP Trust, owns a majority of the ownership interests in AIMCO Properties, L.P. (the Aimco Operating Partnership). Co. conducts all of its business through the Aimco Operating Partnership. As of Dec 31 2016, Co.'s real estate portfolio consisted of 189 apartment communities with 46,311 apartment homes. Co.'s reportable segments are conventional and affordable real estate operations.

Recent Developments: For the quarter ended Sep 30 2017, income from continuing operations increased 44.0% to US$22.4 million from US$15.5 million in the year-earlier quarter. Net income decreased 26.3% to US$22.1 million from US$30.0 million in the year-earlier quarter. Revenues were US$254.6 million, up 2.3% from US$248.9 million the year before.

Prospects: Our evaluation of Apartment Investment & Management Co. as of Jan. 14, 2018 is the result of our systematic analysis on three basic characteristics: earnings strength, relative valuation, and recent stock price movement. The company has enjoyed a very positive trend in earnings per share over the past 5 quarters. Because the company lacks sufficient analyst estimate data, we place greater weight on the historical EPS trend as the measure of earnings strength. Based on operating earnings yield, the company is overvalued when compared to all of the companies in our coverage universe. Share price changes over the past year indicates that AIV will perform well over the near term.

Financial Data

(US$ in Thousands)	9 Mos	6 Mos	3 Mos	12/31/2016	12/31/2015	12/31/2014	12/31/2013	12/31/2012
Earnings Per Share	1.31	1.27	2.58	2.67	1.52	2.06	1.40	0.61
Cash Flow Per Share	2.47	2.41	2.38	2.41	2.32	2.21	2.24	2.35
Tang Book Value Per Share	8.46	8.72	9.95	10.64	9.36	7.11	6.16	5.82
Dividends Per Share	1.410	1.380	1.350	1.320	1.180	1.040	0.960	0.760
Dividend Payout %	107.63	108.66	52.33	49.44	77.63	50.49	68.57	124.59
Income Statement								
Total Revenue	750,208	495,573	246,481	995,854	981,310	984,363	974,053	1,033,197
EBITDA	453,138	294,483	145,422	590,993	568,089	547,943	549,525	576,113
Depn & Amortn	268,836	176,323	87,168	338,126	311,487	286,422	296,825	350,692
Income Before Taxes	45,131	27,624	12,564	64,275	63,866	47,428	31,711	(11,427)
Income Taxes	(14,878)	(10,008)	(4,985)	(25,208)	(27,524)	(20,047)	(1,959)	(929)
Net Income	51,385	31,750	13,698	430,410	248,710	309,249	207,290	132,456
Average Shares	156,835	156,715	156,754	156,391	155,570	146,002	145,532	134,479
Balance Sheet								
Current Assets	133,596	133,381	138,623	131,150	137,745	120,416	185,933	368,189
Total Assets	6,169,338	6,199,202	6,187,440	6,232,818	6,144,194	6,097,028	6,079,413	6,401,380
Current Liabilities	...	...	...	36,677	36,123	41,919	43,161	30,747
Long-Term Obligations	4,390,522	4,341,573	3,971,036	3,884,632	3,873,160	4,135,139	4,388,185	4,688,447
Total Liabilities	4,715,152	4,704,700	4,499,304	4,438,915	4,521,803	4,869,293	5,111,956	5,485,955
Stockholders' Equity	1,454,186	1,494,502	1,688,136	1,793,903	1,622,391	1,227,735	967,457	915,425
Shares Outstanding	157,023	157,022	157,022	156,888	156,326	146,403	145,917	145,563
Statistical Record								
Return on Assets %	3.46	3.39	6.78	6.94	4.06	5.08	3.32	1.99
Return on Equity %	13.76	12.96	25.40	25.13	17.45	28.18	22.02	14.49
EBITDA Margin %	60.40	59.42	59.00	59.35	57.89	55.66	56.42	55.76
Net Margin %	6.85	6.41	5.56	43.22	25.34	31.42	21.28	12.82
Asset Turnover	0.16	0.16	0.16	0.16	0.16	0.16	0.16	0.16
Current Ratio	...	...	...	3.58	3.81	2.87	4.31	11.97
Debt to Equity	3.02	2.91	2.35	2.17	2.39	3.37	4.54	5.12
Price Range	46.53-39.88	47.59-39.88	47.59-39.57	47.59-35.45	41.19-34.85	38.32-25.72	33.20-25.00	28.27-22.40
P/E Ratio	35.52-30.44	37.47-31.40	18.45-15.34	17.82-13.28	27.10-22.93	18.60-12.49	23.71-17.86	46.34-36.72
Average Yield %	3.20	3.13	3.10	3.14	3.07	3.22	3.32	2.92

Address: 4582 South Ulster Street, Suite 1100, Denver, CO 80237	Web Site: www.aimco.com	Auditors: Ernst & Young LLP
Telephone: 303-757-8101	Officers: Terry Considine - Chairman, Chief Executive Officer Paul L. Beldin - Executive Vice President, Chief Financial Officer, Senior Vice President, Chief Accounting Officer	**Investor Contact:** 303-691-4350
Fax: 303-759-3226		**Transfer Agents:** Computershare Trust Company, N.A., Providence, RI

APPLE HOSPITALITY REIT INC

Exchange	Symbol	Price	52Wk Range	Yield	P/E
NYS	APLE	$19.61 (12/29/2017)	20.64-17.59	6.12	19.42

*7 Year Price Score N/A   *NYSE Composite Index=100   *12 Month Price Score 95.88

Interim Earnings (Per Share)

Qtr.	Mar	Jun	Sep	Dec
2014	(0.76)	0.24	0.18	0.14
2015	0.24	0.24	0.27	(0.09)
2016	0.20	0.31	0.07	0.19
2017	0.15	0.39	0.28	...

Interim Dividends (Per Share)

Amt	Decl	Ex	Rec	Pay
0.10M	09/22/2017	10/03/2017	10/04/2017	10/16/2017
0.10M	10/19/2017	11/02/2017	11/03/2017	11/15/2017
0.10M	11/20/2017	12/01/2017	12/04/2017	12/18/2017
0.10M	12/20/2017	01/02/2018	01/03/2018	01/16/2018

Indicated Div: $1.20

Valuation Analysis

Forecast EPS	$1.00 (01/13/2018)	
Market Cap	$4.4 Billion	
Book Value	$3.5 Billion	
Price/Book	1.25	
Price/Sales	3.55	

Institutional Holding

No of Institutions	229
Shares	134,446,144
% Held	N/A

TRADING VOLUME (thousand shares)

Business Summary: REITs (MIC: 5.3.1 SIC: 6798 NAIC: 525930)

Apple Hospitality REIT is a real estate investment trust (REIT) that invests in real estate, primarily in the lodging sector, in the U.S. As of Dec 31 2016, Co. owned 235 hotels with an aggregate of 30,073 rooms located in urban, suburban and developing markets throughout 33 states. All of Co.'s hotels operate under Marriott or Hilton brands. The hotels are operated and managed under separate management agreements with 22 hotel management companies, none of which are affiliated with Co. Co. has wholly-owned taxable REIT subsidiaries, which lease all of Co.'s hotels from wholly-owned qualified REIT subsidiaries.

Recent Developments: For the quarter ended Sep 30 2017, net income increased 358.8% to US$62.8 million from US$13.7 million in the year-earlier quarter. Revenues were US$324.9 million, up 17.5% from US$276.5 million the year before. Revenues from property income rose 18.4% to US$302.3 million from US$255.3 million in the corresponding quarter a year earlier.

Prospects: Our evaluation of Apple Hospitality REIT Inc as of Jan. 14, 2018 is the result of our systematic analysis on three basic characteristics: earnings strength, relative valuation, and recent stock price movement. The company has managed to produce a neutral trend in earnings per share over the past 5 quarters and while recent estimates for the company have remained steady, APLE has posted results that fell short of analysts expectations. Based on operating earnings yield, the company is undervalued when compared to all of the companies in our coverage universe. Share price changes over the past year indicates that APLE will perform in line with the market over the near term.

Financial Data

(US$ in Thousands)	9 Mos	6 Mos	3 Mos	12/31/2016	12/31/2015	12/31/2014	12/31/2013	12/31/2012
Earnings Per Share	1.01	0.80	0.72	0.76	0.65	0.04	1.26	0.82
Cash Flow Per Share	1.68	1.58	1.43	1.73	1.56	1.47	1.51	1.35
Tang Book Value Per Share	15.71	15.73	15.64	15.78	15.18	16.13	14.35	14.74
Dividends Per Share	1.100	1.200	1.200	1.200	0.800	...	...	...
Dividend Payout %	108.91	150.00	166.67	157.89	123.08	...	...	...
Income Statement								
Total Revenue	949,555	624,629	292,925	1,041,025	898,314	803,896	387,991	365,586
EBITDA	352,867	233,706	90,099	333,272	278,767	145,437	146,611	129,343
Depn & Amortn	131,770	87,660	43,767	148,163	127,449	113,112	54,827	52,748
Income Before Taxes	185,507	122,480	34,615	145,083	118,186	8,802	83,338	69,850
Income Taxes	712	509	250	431	898	1,969	1,422	1,166
Net Income	184,795	121,971	34,365	144,652	117,288	6,833	115,222	75,476
Average Shares	223,057	223,052	223,047	190,856	180,261	171,488	91,308	91,111
Balance Sheet								
Current Assets	...	...	...	29,425	22,651	32,526	27,518	18,949
Total Assets	4,913,887	4,904,574	4,974,923	4,979,883	3,722,775	3,779,749	1,491,281	1,526,017
Current Liabilities	104,467	88,685	84,237	124,856	77,614	55,555	16,919	13,101
Long-Term Obligations	1,305,471	1,308,317	1,402,840	1,337,963	998,103	709,570	162,551	166,783
Total Liabilities	1,409,938	1,397,002	1,487,077	1,462,819	1,075,717	765,125	179,470	179,884
Stockholders' Equity	3,503,949	3,507,572	3,487,846	3,517,064	2,647,058	3,014,624	1,311,811	1,346,133
Shares Outstanding	223,060	223,055	223,049	222,938	174,368	186,910	91,392	91,309
Statistical Record								
Return on Assets %	4.56	4.11	3.32	3.32	3.13	0.26	7.64	...
Return on Equity %	6.43	5.78	4.72	4.68	4.14	0.32	8.67	...
EBITDA Margin %	37.16	37.42	30.76	32.01	31.03	18.09	37.79	35.38
Net Margin %	19.46	19.53	11.73	13.90	13.06	0.85	29.70	20.65
Asset Turnover	0.25	0.27	0.26	0.24	0.24	0.31	0.26	...
Current Ratio	...	...	...	0.24	0.29	0.59	1.63	1.45
Debt to Equity	0.37	0.37	0.40	0.38	0.38	0.24	0.12	0.12
Price Range	20.64-17.45	20.64-17.45	20.64-17.45	20.59-17.26	20.68-16.38	...	...	...
P/E Ratio	20.44-17.28	25.80-21.81	28.67-24.24	27.09-22.71	31.82-25.20	...	...	...
Average Yield %	5.82	6.26	6.28	6.32	4.23	...	...	...

Address: 814 East Main Street, Richmond, VA 23219 Telephone: 804-344-8121	Web Site: www.applehospitalityreit.com Officers: Glade M. Knight - Executive Chairman, Chief Executive Officer Justin G. Knight - President, Chief Executive Officer	Auditors: Ernst & Young LLP

58

APTARGROUP INC.

Exchange	Symbol	Price	52Wk Range	Yield	P/E	Div Achiever
NYS	ATR	$86.28 (12/29/2017)	90.09-71.64	1.48	25.23	23 Years

*7 Year Price Score 100.19 *NYSE Composite Index=100 *12 Month Price Score 99.87

Interim Earnings (Per Share)

Qtr.	Mar	Jun	Sep	Dec
2014	0.71	0.79	0.73	0.64
2015	0.70	0.90	0.83	0.68
2016	0.67	0.91	0.82	0.77
2017	0.81	1.01	0.83	...

Interim Dividends (Per Share)

Amt	Decl	Ex	Rec	Pay
0.32Q	01/19/2017	01/30/2017	02/01/2017	02/22/2017
0.32Q	04/20/2017	05/01/2017	05/03/2017	05/24/2017
0.32Q	07/13/2017	07/24/2017	07/26/2017	08/10/2017
0.32Q	10/19/2017	10/31/2017	11/01/2017	11/22/2017

Indicated Div: $1.28

Valuation Analysis

		Institutional Holding	
Forecast EPS	$3.35	No of Institutions	455
	(01/17/2018)		
Market Cap	$5.4 Billion	Shares	81,092,960
Book Value	$1.3 Billion	% Held	84.18
Price/Book	4.07		
Price/Sales	2.26		

Business Summary: Plastics (MIC: 8.4.2 SIC: 3089 NAIC: 326199)

AptarGroup is a provider of a range of packaging, dispensing and sealing solutions, primarily for the beauty, personal care, home care, prescription drug, consumer health care, injectables, food and beverage markets. While Co. provides a range of dispensing and sealing solutions, its primary products are: dispensing pumps, which dispense a spray or lotion from non-pressurized containers; closures, which are plastic caps which allow a product to be dispensed without removing the cap; aerosol valves, which dispense product from pressurized containers; and elastomeric primary packaging components, which include stoppers for infusion, antibiotic, lyophilization and diagnostic vials.

Recent Developments: For the quarter ended Sep 30 2017, net income increased 0.8% to US$53.5 million from US$53.1 million in the year-earlier quarter. Revenues were US$624.3 million, up 5.9% from US$589.7 million the year before. Operating income was US$80.4 million versus US$82.3 million in the prior-year quarter, a decrease of 2.3%. Direct operating expenses rose 7.1% to US$408.1 million from US$381.0 million in the comparable period the year before. Indirect operating expenses increased 7.5% to US$135.8 million from US$126.4 million in the equivalent prior-year period.

Prospects: Our evaluation of AptarGroup Inc. as of Jan. 14, 2018 is the result of our systematic analysis on three basic characteristics: earnings strength, relative valuation, and recent stock price movement. The company has managed to produce a neutral trend in earnings per share over the past 5 quarters and while recent estimates for the company have remained steady, ATR has posted better than expected results. Based on operating earnings yield, the company is about fairly valued when compared to all of the companies in our coverage universe. Share price changes over the past year indicates that ATR will perform well over the near term.

Financial Data

(US$ in Thousands)	9 Mos	6 Mos	3 Mos	12/31/2016	12/31/2015	12/31/2014	12/31/2013	12/31/2012
Earnings Per Share	3.42	3.41	3.31	3.17	3.09	2.85	2.52	2.38
Cash Flow Per Share	6.20	6.23	5.71	5.20	5.19	4.84	4.32	4.71
Tang Book Value Per Share	12.61	12.52	11.78	10.81	12.89	11.85	16.38	14.81
Dividends Per Share	1.280	1.260	1.240	1.220	1.140	1.090	1.000	0.880
Dividend Payout %	37.43	36.95	37.46	38.49	36.89	38.25	39.68	36.97
Income Statement								
Total Revenue	1,843,388	1,219,062	601,316	2,330,934	2,317,149	2,597,809	2,520,013	2,331,036
EBITDA	356,989	238,692	114,791	458,767	458,955	451,343	427,470	391,629
Depn & Amortn	114,660	74,573	37,331	145,485	134,647	146,893	144,923	133,845
Income Before Taxes	218,708	149,118	69,528	280,688	295,289	288,218	265,266	241,830
Income Taxes	48,043	32,054	17,675	74,893	95,276	94,677	92,457	78,953
Net Income	170,517	116,994	51,820	205,590	199,348	191,658	171,994	162,612
Average Shares	64,821	64,828	64,234	64,849	64,492	67,292	68,208	68,395
Balance Sheet								
Current Assets	1,941,395	1,244,469	1,156,734	1,270,170	1,294,994	1,213,938	1,198,411	1,038,933
Total Assets	3,408,854	2,663,864	2,523,639	2,606,785	2,438,726	2,437,190	2,497,762	2,324,412
Current Liabilities	705,037	479,060	412,931	542,955	411,900	604,738	542,821	455,323
Long-Term Obligations	1,271,530	770,648	771,291	772,737	762,524	588,892	354,814	352,860
Total Liabilities	2,087,340	1,354,987	1,283,301	1,432,835	1,289,315	1,333,783	1,018,005	944,522
Stockholders' Equity	1,321,514	1,308,877	1,240,338	1,173,950	1,149,411	1,103,407	1,479,757	1,379,890
Shares Outstanding	62,300	62,600	62,500	62,146	62,516	61,931	65,384	65,928
Statistical Record								
Return on Assets %	7.22	8.27	8.21	8.13	8.18	7.77	7.13	7.23
Return on Equity %	16.88	17.11	17.03	17.65	17.70	14.84	12.03	12.15
EBITDA Margin %	19.37	19.58	19.09	19.68	19.81	17.37	16.96	16.80
Net Margin %	9.25	9.60	8.62	8.82	8.60	7.38	6.83	6.98
Asset Turnover	0.78	0.88	0.90	0.92	0.95	1.05	1.05	1.04
Current Ratio	2.75	2.60	2.80	2.34	3.14	2.01	2.21	2.28
Debt to Equity	0.96	0.59	0.62	0.66	0.66	0.53	0.24	0.26
Price Range	90.09-70.62	87.14-70.62	80.46-70.62	80.46-66.70	75.72-61.38	68.38-56.18	67.81-47.72	55.26-45.80
P/E Ratio	26.34-20.65	25.55-20.71	24.31-21.34	25.38-21.04	24.50-19.86	23.99-19.71	26.91-18.94	23.22-19.24
Average Yield %	1.62	1.63	1.63	1.61	1.71	1.69	1.72	1.71

Address: 475 West Terra Cotta Avenue, Suite E, Crystal Lake, IL 60014	**Web Site:** www.aptar.com	**Auditors:** PricewaterhouseCoopers LLP
Telephone: 815-477-0424	**Officers:** King W. Harris - Chairman Stephan B. Tanda - President, Chief Executive Officer	**Investor Contact:** 815-477-0424
Fax: 815-477-0481		**Transfer Agents:** Wells Fargo Shareowner Services, South St. Paul, MN

APTIV PLC

Exchange	Symbol	Price	52Wk Range	Yield	P/E
NYS	APTV	$84.83 (12/29/2017)	88.77-56.57	1.04	16.54

*7 Year Price Score N/A   *NYSE Composite Index=100   *12 Month Price Score 108.51

Interim Earnings (Per Share)

Qtr.	Mar	Jun	Sep	Dec
2014	1.04	1.26	1.02	1.16
2015	0.72	2.23	1.42	0.70
2016	1.53	0.94	1.07	1.03
2017	1.24	1.38	1.48	...

Interim Dividends (Per Share)

Amt	Decl	Ex	Rec	Pay
0.29Q	04/27/2017	05/08/2017	0510/2017	05/24/2017
0.29Q	07/27/2017	08/07/2017	08/09/2017	08/23/2017
0.29Q	10/26/2017	11/07/2017	11/08/2017	11/22/2017
0.22Q	12/07/2017	02/02/2018	02/05/2018	02/14/2018

Indicated Div: $0.88

Valuation Analysis		Institutional Holding	
Forecast EPS	N/A	No of Institutions	721
Market Cap	$22.6 Billion	Shares	274,531,360
Book Value	$3.2 Billion	% Held	90.19
Price/Book	7.04		
Price/Sales	1.31		

TRADING VOLUME (thousand shares)

Business Summary: Auto Parts (MIC: 1.8.2 SIC: 3714 NAIC: 336399)

Aptiv is a vehicle components manufacturer and provides electrical and electronic, powertrain, and safety technology solutions to the global automotive and commercial vehicle markets. Co. has three segments: Electrical / Electronic Architecture, which provides electrical and electronic architectures such as connectors, electrical centers and distribution systems; Powertrain Systems, which provides products for engine management systems and products; and Electronics and Safety, which provides a range of electronic and safety equipment and software in the areas of controls, security, infotainment, communications and safety systems.

Recent Developments: For the quarter ended Sep 30 2017, income from continuing operations increased 35.0% to US$413.0 million from US$306.0 million in the year-earlier quarter. Net income increased 35.0% to US$413.0 million from US$306.0 million in the year-earlier quarter. Revenues were US$4.33 billion, up 5.9% from US$4.09 billion the year before. Operating income was US$511.0 million versus US$463.0 million in the prior-year quarter, an increase of 10.4%. Direct operating expenses rose 6.1% to US$3.45 billion from US$3.25 billion in the comparable period the year before. Indirect operating expenses decreased 0.8% to US$372.0 million from US$375.0 million in the equivalent prior-year period.

Prospects: Our evaluation of Delphi Automotive PLC as of July 26, 2015 is the result of our systematic analysis on three basic characteristics: earnings strength, relative valuation, and recent stock price movement. The company has managed to produce a neutral trend in earnings per share over the past 5 quarters. However, while recent estimates for the company have been lowered by analysts, DLPH has posted better than expected results. Based on operating earnings yield, the company is undervalued when compared to all of the companies in our coverage universe. Share price changes over the past year indicates that DLPH will perform very well over the near term.

Financial Data

(US$ in Millions)	9 Mos	6 Mos	3 Mos	12/31/2016	12/31/2015	12/31/2014	12/31/2013	12/31/2012
Earnings Per Share	5.13	4.72	4.28	4.59	5.06	4.48	3.89	3.33
Cash Flow Per Share	6.47	7.43	7.29	7.09	5.97	7.11	5.63	4.56
Tang Book Value Per Share	1.20	0.13	N.M.	N.M.	N.M.	3.80	5.52	3.39
Dividends Per Share	1.160	1.160	1.160	1.160	1.000	1.000	...	...
Dividend Payout %	22.61	24.58	27.10	25.27	19.76	22.32	...	...
Income Statement								
Total Revenue	12,943	8,610	4,292	16,661	15,165	17,023	16,463	15,519
EBITDA	1,953	1,268	611	2,150	2,077	2,316	2,088	1,866
Depn & Amortn	544	359	177	570	447	486	436	402
Income Before Taxes	1,309	843	402	1,425	1,508	1,705	1,523	1,345
Income Taxes	183	123	61	242	263	282	256	212
Net Income	1,099	704	335	1,257	1,450	1,351	1,212	1,077
Average Shares	267	268	269	273	286	301	311	323
Balance Sheet								
Current Assets	6,710	5,849	5,487	5,419	5,121	5,224	5,752	5,227
Total Assets	14,166	13,056	12,497	12,292	11,973	10,746	11,047	10,176
Current Liabilities	4,143	4,170	4,092	4,148	3,927	3,889	3,894	3,659
Long-Term Obligations	4,884	4,059	3,991	3,959	3,956	2,417	2,351	2,324
Total Liabilities	10,963	10,161	9,918	9,891	9,723	8,236	8,136	7,831
Stockholders' Equity	3,203	2,895	2,579	2,401	2,250	2,510	2,911	2,345
Shares Outstanding	265	266	267	269	278	291	306	315
Statistical Record								
Return on Assets %	10.50	10.22	9.50	10.33	12.76	12.40	11.42	11.13
Return on Equity %	47.96	48.45	48.18	53.91	60.92	49.84	46.12	53.26
EBITDA Margin %	15.09	14.73	14.24	12.90	13.70	13.61	12.68	12.02
Net Margin %	8.49	8.18	7.81	7.54	9.56	7.94	7.36	6.94
Asset Turnover	1.31	1.36	1.38	1.37	1.34	1.56	1.55	1.60
Current Ratio	1.62	1.40	1.34	1.31	1.30	1.34	1.48	1.43
Debt to Equity	1.52	1.40	1.55	1.65	1.76	0.96	0.81	0.99
Price Range	86.65-52.96	74.70-50.41	68.92-49.47	71.81-47.75	74.68-55.77	62.10-48.83	50.36-31.51	32.04-18.54
P/E Ratio	16.89-10.32	15.83-10.68	16.10-11.56	15.64-10.40	14.76-11.02	13.86-10.90	12.95-8.10	9.62-5.57
Average Yield %	1.73	1.89	1.98	2.03	1.49	1.77	...	...

Address: Courteney Road, Hoath Way, Gillingham, ME8 0RU Telephone: 163-423-4422	Web Site: www.delphi.com Officers: Rajiv L. Gupta - Chairman Kevin P. Clark - President, Chief Executive Officer, Chief Operating Officer, Chief Financial Officer, Executive Vice President, Senior Vice President	Auditors: Ernst & Young LLP Investor Contact: 248-813-2494 Transfer Agents: Computershare Trust Company, N.A., Providence

AQUA AMERICA INC

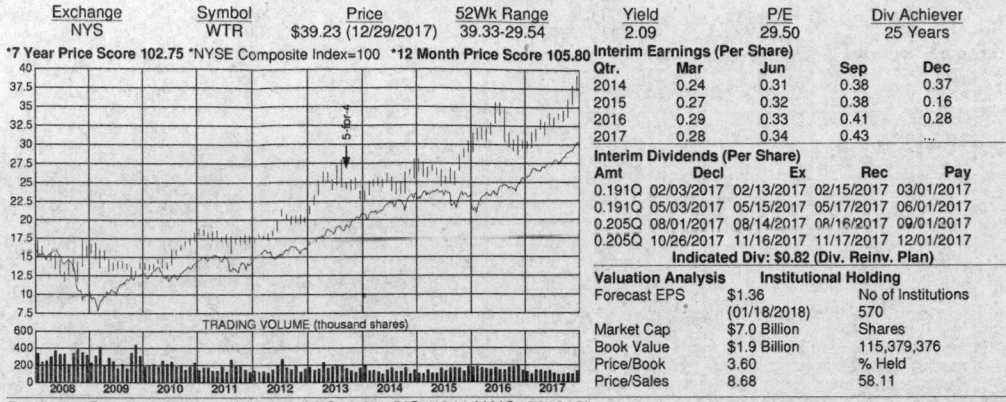

Exchange	Symbol	Price	52Wk Range	Yield	P/E	Div Achiever
NYS	WTR	$39.23 (12/29/2017)	39.33-29.54	2.09	29.50	25 Years

*7 Year Price Score 102.75 *NYSE Composite Index=100 *12 Month Price Score 105.80

Interim Earnings (Per Share)

Qtr.	Mar	Jun	Sep	Dec
2014	0.24	0.31	0.38	0.37
2015	0.27	0.32	0.38	0.16
2016	0.29	0.33	0.41	0.28
2017	0.28	0.34	0.43	...

Interim Dividends (Per Share)

Amt	Decl	Ex	Rec	Pay
0.191Q	02/03/2017	02/13/2017	02/15/2017	03/01/2017
0.191Q	05/03/2017	05/15/2017	05/17/2017	06/01/2017
0.205Q	08/01/2017	08/14/2017	08/16/2017	09/01/2017
0.205Q	10/26/2017	11/16/2017	11/17/2017	12/01/2017

Indicated Div: $0.82 (Div. Reinv. Plan)

Valuation Analysis

		Institutional Holding	
Forecast EPS	$1.36	No of Institutions	
	(01/18/2018)	570	
Market Cap	$7.0 Billion	Shares	
Book Value	$1.9 Billion	115,379,376	
Price/Book	3.60	% Held	
Price/Sales	8.68	58.11	

Business Summary: Water Utilities (MIC: 3.2.1 SIC: 4941 NAIC: 221310)

Aqua America is the holding company for regulated utilities providing water or wastewater services in Pennsylvania, Ohio, Texas, Illinois, North Carolina, New Jersey, Indiana, and Virginia. As of Dec 31 2016, Co.'s Aqua Pennsylvania, Inc. subsidiary service territory is located in the suburban areas north and west of the City of Philadelphia and in 27 other counties in Pennsylvania. Co.'s Aqua Resources, Inc. subsidiary provides water and wastewater service through operating and maintenance contracts with municipal authorities and other parties. Co.'s Aqua Infrastructure, LLC subsidiary provides non-utility raw water supply services for firms in the natural gas drilling industry.

Recent Developments: For the quarter ended Sep 30 2017, net income increased 4.2% to US$76.2 million from US$73.2 million in the year-earlier quarter. Revenues were US$215.0 million, down 5.1% from US$226.6 million the year before. Operating income was US$97.5 million versus US$97.8 million in the prior-year quarter, a decrease of 0.3%. Direct operating expenses declined 14.8% to US$68.0 million from US$79.8 million in the comparable period the year before. Indirect operating expenses increased 1.1% to US$49.5 million from US$49.0 million in the equivalent prior-year period.

Prospects: Our evaluation of Aqua America Inc. as of Jan. 14, 2018 is the result of our systematic analysis on three basic characteristics: earnings strength, relative valuation, and recent stock price movement. The company has enjoyed a very positive trend in earnings per share over the past 5 quarters and while recent estimates for the company have remained steady, WTR has posted results that fell short of analysts expectations. Based on operating earnings yield, the company is about fairly valued when compared to all of the companies in our coverage universe. Share price changes over the past year indicates that WTR will perform very well over the near term.

Financial Data

(US$ in Thousands)	9 Mos	6 Mos	3 Mos	12/31/2016	12/31/2015	12/31/2014	12/31/2013	12/31/2012
Earnings Per Share	1.33	1.31	1.30	1.32	1.14	1.31	1.25	1.12
Cash Flow Per Share	2.19	2.11	2.15	2.23	2.10	2.06	2.09	2.11
Tang Book Value Per Share	10.67	10.44	10.28	10.19	9.58	9.19	8.52	7.75
Dividends Per Share	0.779	0.765	0.752	0.739	0.686	0.634	0.622	0.536
Dividend Payout %	58.54	58.41	57.84	55.95	60.18	48.40	49.76	47.86
Income Statement								
Total Revenue	606,213	391,205	187,787	819,875	814,204	779,903	768,643	757,760
EBITDA	364,394	228,687	107,195	465,765	453,755	442,543	426,922	438,516
Depn & Amortn	101,508	67,244	33,837	130,987	125,290	123,054	119,258	111,767
Income Before Taxes	197,762	118,730	52,032	254,184	251,929	243,092	230,348	248,992
Income Taxes	11,899	8,499	2,930	20,978	14,962	25,219	22,690	66,881
Net Income	186,265	110,040	49,072	234,182	201,790	233,239	221,300	196,563
Average Shares	178,124	178,045	177,969	177,846	177,517	177,763	176,814	174,917
Balance Sheet								
Current Assets	138,342	138,091	122,463	128,650	128,370	152,522	171,669	260,894
Total Assets	6,545,381	6,383,699	6,235,595	6,158,991	5,741,038	5,406,752	5,051,817	4,858,517
Current Liabilities	252,950	332,547	277,600	301,536	193,199	225,335	266,910	274,164
Long-Term Obligations	1,952,473	1,822,581	1,797,511	1,737,605	1,743,612	1,560,655	1,468,583	1,543,954
Total Liabilities	4,607,116	4,487,169	4,368,368	4,308,923	4,015,108	3,751,409	3,516,982	3,472,813
Stockholders' Equity	1,938,265	1,896,530	1,867,227	1,850,068	1,725,930	1,655,343	1,534,835	1,385,704
Shares Outstanding	177,684	177,651	177,583	177,394	176,544	176,753	176,750	175,209
Statistical Record								
Return on Assets %	3.75	3.78	3.84	3.93	3.62	4.46	4.47	4.26
Return on Equity %	12.51	12.63	12.76	13.06	11.94	14.62	15.15	14.87
EBITDA Margin %	60.11	58.46	57.08	56.81	55.73	56.74	55.54	57.87
Net Margin %	30.73	28.13	26.13	28.56	24.78	29.91	28.79	25.94
Asset Turnover	0.13	0.13	0.14	0.14	0.15	0.15	0.16	0.16
Current Ratio	0.55	0.42	0.44	0.43	0.66	0.68	0.64	0.95
Debt to Equity	1.01	0.96	0.96	0.94	1.01	0.94	0.96	1.11
Price Range	34.62-28.67	35.66-28.67	35.66-28.67	35.66-28.67	30.51-24.49	28.05-22.59	27.99-20.34	21.48-16.94
P/E Ratio	26.03-21.56	27.22-21.89	27.43-22.05	27.02-21.72	26.76-21.48	21.41-17.24	22.39-16.27	19.18-15.13
Average Yield %	2.46	2.43	2.40	2.35	2.56	2.55	2.54	2.80

Address: 762 W. Lancaster Avenue, Bryn Mawr, PA 19010-3489 Telephone: 610-527-8000	Web Site: www.aquaamerica.com Officers: Nicholas DeBenedictis - Chairman, President, Senior Advisor, President, Chief Executive Officer, Senior Advisor, Chief Executive Officer Christopher H. Franklin - President, Chief Executive Officer, Executive Vice President, Chief Executive Officer, Senior Vice President, Executive Vice President, Region Officer, Senior Vice President, Region Officer, Division Officer, Division Officer	Auditors: PricewaterhouseCoopers LLP Investor Contact: 610-645-1191 Transfer Agents: Computershare Trust Company, N.A., Providence, RI

ARAMARK

Exchange	Symbol	Price	52Wk Range	Yield	P/E
NYS	ARMK	$42.74 (12/29/2017)	43.75-33.08	0.98	28.68

*7 Year Price Score N/A   *NYSE Composite Index=100   *12 Month Price Score 102.40

Interim Earnings (Per Share)

Qtr.	Dec	Mar	Jun	Sep
2012-13	0.20	(0.20)	0.13	0.18
2013-14	0.21	0.05	0.19	0.18
2014-15	0.35	0.24	0.14	0.23
2015-16	0.38	0.27	0.18	0.34
2016-17	0.50	0.28	0.26	0.45

Interim Dividends (Per Share)

Amt	Decl	Ex	Rec	Pay
0.103Q	02/01/2017	02/13/2017	02/15/2017	03/01/2017
0.103Q	05/03/2017	05/15/2017	05/17/2017	06/06/2017
0.103Q	08/02/2017	08/14/2017	08/16/2017	09/05/2017
0.105Q	11/14/2017	11/24/2017	11/27/2017	12/07/2017

Indicated Div: $0.42

Valuation Analysis

Forecast EPS	$2.15
	(01/17/2018)
Market Cap	$10.5 Billion
Book Value	$2.5 Billion
Price/Book	4.27
Price/Sales	0.72

Institutional Holding

No of Institutions	382
Shares	257,426,176
% Held	72.38

Business Summary: Hotels, Restaurants & Travel (MIC: 2.2.1 SIC: 5812 NAIC: 722110)

Aramark is a provider of food, facilities and uniform services to education, healthcare, business and industry, and sports, leisure and corrections clients. Co.'s business segments are: Food and Support Services (FSS) North America and FSS International, manage interrelated services-including food, hospitality and facility services-for school districts, colleges and universities, healthcare facilities, businesses, sports, entertainment and recreational venues, conference and convention centers, national and state parks and correctional institutions; and Uniform and Career Apparel, which provides uniforms and other garments and work clothes and ancillary items such as mats and shop towels.

Recent Developments: For the year ended Sep 29 2017, net income increased 29.8% to US$374.2 million from US$288.2 million in the prior year. Revenues were US$14.60 billion, up 1.3% from US$14.42 billion the year before. Operating income was US$808.1 million versus US$746.3 million in the prior year, an increase of 8.3%. Direct operating expenses rose 0.8% to US$12.99 billion from US$12.89 billion in the comparable period the year before. Indirect operating expenses increased 3.6% to US$807.4 million from US$779.1 million in the equivalent prior-year period.

Prospects: Our evaluation of Aramark as of Jan. 14, 2018 is the result of our systematic analysis on three basic characteristics: earnings strength, relative valuation, and recent stock price movement. The company has generated a negative trend in earnings per share over the past 5 quarters. However, while recent estimates for the company have been mixed, ARMK has posted results that fell short of analysts' expectations. Based on operating earnings yield, the company is about fairly valued when compared to all of the companies in our coverage universe. Share price changes over the past year indicates that ARMK will perform well over the near term.

Financial Data

(US$ in Thousands)	09/29/2017	09/30/2016	10/02/2015	10/03/2014	09/27/2013	09/28/2012	09/30/2011
Earnings Per Share	1.49	1.16	0.96	0.63	0.33	0.49	0.40
Cash Flow Per Share	4.32	3.34	2.88	1.73	3.46	3.41	1.49
Dividends Per Share	0.412	0.380	0.345	0.225	...	...	...
Dividend Payout %	27.65	32.76	35.94	35.71	...	...	...
Income Statement							
Total Revenue	14,604,412	14,415,829	14,329,135	14,832,913	13,945,657	13,505,426	13,082,377
EBITDA	1,038,595	975,609	849,925	799,681	748,924	815,174	777,956
Depn & Amortn	237,900	234,800	226,600	239,900	239,100	236,600	234,500
Income Before Taxes	520,642	430,931	341,996	229,677	90,629	124,968	95,969
Income Taxes	146,455	142,699	105,020	80,218	19,233	18,066	(734)
Net Income	373,923	287,806	235,946	148,956	69,356	103,551	83,846
Average Shares	251,557	248,763	246,616	237,451	209,370	209,707	209,999
Balance Sheet							
Current Assets	2,653,139	2,492,571	2,379,123	2,464,976	2,287,165	2,185,501	...
Total Assets	11,006,229	10,582,072	10,224,050	10,455,693	10,267,106	10,487,354	...
Current Liabilities	2,368,095	2,184,745	2,180,988	2,378,873	2,389,253	2,163,674	...
Long-Term Obligations	5,190,331	5,223,514	5,212,290	5,355,789	5,758,229	5,971,305	...
Total Liabilities	8,547,168	8,421,066	8,340,691	8,737,657	9,363,399	9,554,337	...
Stockholders' Equity	2,459,061	2,161,006	1,883,359	1,718,036	903,707	933,017	...
Shares Outstanding	245,593	244,713	239,917	233,910	201,798	202,573	...
Statistical Record							
Return on Assets %	3.47	2.77	2.29	1.41	0.67	...	...
Return on Equity %	16.23	14.27	13.14	11.18	7.57	...	...
EBITDA Margin %	7.11	6.77	5.93	5.39	5.37	6.04	5.95
Net Margin %	2.56	2.00	1.65	1.00	0.50	0.77	0.64
Asset Turnover	1.36	1.39	1.39	1.41	1.35	...	...
Current Ratio	1.12	1.14	1.09	1.04	0.96	1.01	...
Debt to Equity	2.11	2.42	2.77	3.12	6.37	6.40	...
Price Range	41.48-33.08	38.21-29.57	33.49-25.35	29.89-22.70	...	...	...
P/E Ratio	27.84-22.20	32.94-25.49	34.89-26.41	47.44-36.03	...	...	...
Average Yield %	1.10	1.14	1.12	0.84	...	...	...

Address: Aramark Tower, 1101 Market Street, Philadelphia, PA 19107 **Telephone:** 215-238-3000	**Web Site:** www.aramark.com **Officers:** Joseph Neubauer - Chairman Eric J. Foss - President, Chief Executive Officer	**Auditors:** KPMG LLP **Transfer Agents:** Computershare Trust Company, N.A.

ARCHER DANIELS MIDLAND CO.

Exchange	Symbol	Price	52Wk Range	Yield	P/E	Div Acheiver
NYS	ADM	$40.08 (12/29/2017)	46.97-38.96	3.19	18.82	42 Years

*7 Year Price Score 86.77   *NYSE Composite Index=100   *12 Month Price Score 88.48

Interim Earnings (Per Share)

Qtr.	Mar	Jun	Sep	Dec
2014	0.40	0.81	1.14	1.08
2015	0.77	0.62	0.41	1.18
2016	0.39	0.48	0.58	0.72
2017	0.59	0.48	0.34	...

Interim Dividends (Per Share)

Amt	Decl	Ex	Rec	Pay
0.32Q	02/07/2017	02/16/2017	02/21/2017	03/14/2017
0.32Q	05/04/2017	05/16/2017	05/18/2017	06/08/2017
0.32Q	08/03/2017	08/15/2017	08/17/2017	09/07/2017
0.32Q	11/02/2017	11/15/2017	11/16/2017	12/07/2017

Indicated Div: $1.28 (Div. Reinv. Plan)

Valuation Analysis — **Institutional Holding**

Forecast EPS	$2.31	No of Institutions
	(01/24/2018)	1066
Market Cap	$22.4 Billion	Shares
Book Value	$17.6 Billion	586,332,032
Price/Book	1.28	% Held
Price/Sales	0.37	69.52

Business Summary: Food (MIC: 1.2.1 SIC: 2041 NAIC: 311211)

Archer Daniels Midland is principally engaged in procuring, transporting, storing, processing, and merchandising agricultural commodities and products. Co. has four segments: Agricultural Services, which buy, store, clean, and transport agricultural commodities and resells these commodities primarily as food and feed ingredients and as raw materials; Corn Processing, which is engaged in corn wet milling and dry milling activities; Oilseeds Processing, which is engaged in the origination, merchandising, crushing, and further processing of oilseeds; and Wild Flavors and Specialty Ingredients, which engages in the manufacturing, sales, and distribution of specialty products.

Recent Developments: For the quarter ended Sep 30 2017, net income decreased 43.3% to US$195.0 million from US$344.0 million in the year-earlier quarter. Revenues were US$14.83 billion, down 6.3% from US$15.83 billion the year before. Direct operating expenses declined 4.9% to US$14.02 billion from US$14.74 billion in the comparable period the year before. Indirect operating expenses increased 5.0% to US$585.0 million from US$557.0 million in the equivalent prior-year period.

Prospects: Our evaluation of Archer Daniels Midland Co. as of Jan. 21, 2018 is the result of our systematic analysis on three basic characteristics: earnings strength, relative valuation, and recent stock price movement. The company has generated a negative trend in earnings per share over the past 5 quarters. However, while recent estimates for the company have been mixed, ADM has posted results that fell short of analysts expectations. Based on operating earnings yield, the company is undervalued when compared to all of the companies in our coverage universe. Share price changes over the past year indicates that ADM will perform poorly over the near term.

Financial Data

(US$ in Thousands)	9 Mos	6 Mos	3 Mos	12/31/2016	12/31/2015	12/31/2014	12/31/2013	12/31/2012
Earnings Per Share	2.13	2.37	2.37	2.16	2.98	3.43	2.02	1.05
Cash Flow Per Share	4.37	5.53	3.23	2.50	4.01	7.60	7.91	7.45
Tang Book Value Per Share	24.38	24.06	23.45	23.51	23.88	25.58	29.43	27.87
Dividends Per Share	1.260	1.240	1.220	1.200	1.120	0.960	0.760	0.350
Dividend Payout %	59.15	52.32	51.48	55.56	37.58	27.99	37.62	33.33
Income Statement								
Total Revenue	44,758,000	29,931,000	14,988,000	62,346,000	67,702,000	81,201,000	89,804,000	46,729,000
EBITDA	1,594,000	1,131,000	569,000	2,518,000	2,930,000	3,853,000	2,751,000	1,331,000
Depn & Amortn	684,000	452,000	225,000	787,000	799,000	850,000	827,000	435,000
Income Before Taxes	739,000	560,000	286,000	1,530,000	1,894,000	2,758,000	1,613,000	742,000
Income Taxes	256,000	226,000	118,000	534,000	438,000	877,000	670,000	303,000
Net Income	807,000	615,000	339,000	1,279,000	1,849,000	2,248,000	1,342,000	692,000
Average Shares	569,000	574,000	579,000	591,000	621,000	656,000	663,000	661,000
Balance Sheet								
Current Assets	19,140,000	18,201,000	20,486,000	21,045,000	21,829,000	26,028,000	28,530,000	29,762,000
Total Assets	38,969,000	37,817,000	39,630,000	39,769,000	40,157,000	44,027,000	43,752,000	45,136,000
Current Liabilities	11,873,000	11,421,000	13,602,000	13,173,000	13,505,000	15,602,000	15,658,000	16,993,000
Long-Term Obligations	6,595,000	6,056,000	5,956,000	6,504,000	5,779,000	5,558,000	5,347,000	6,456,000
Total Liabilities	21,399,000	20,406,000	22,509,000	22,596,000	22,258,000	24,452,000	23,596,000	26,216,000
Stockholders' Equity	17,570,000	17,411,000	17,121,000	17,173,000	17,899,000	19,575,000	20,156,000	18,920,000
Shares Outstanding	559,000	563,000	569,000	573,000	595,000	637,000	659,000	659,000
Statistical Record								
Return on Assets %	3.12	3.54	3.50	3.19	4.39	5.12	3.02	3.14
Return on Equity %	7.01	7.87	7.93	7.27	9.87	11.32	6.87	7.28
EBITDA Margin %	3.56	3.78	3.80	4.04	4.33	4.75	3.06	2.85
Net Margin %	1.80	2.05	2.26	2.05	2.73	2.77	1.49	1.48
Asset Turnover	1.55	1.60	1.59	1.56	1.61	1.85	2.02	2.12
Current Ratio	1.61	1.59	1.51	1.60	1.62	1.67	1.82	1.75
Debt to Equity	0.38	0.35	0.35	0.38	0.32	0.28	0.27	0.34
Price Range	47.72-40.29	47.72-40.63	47.72-35.11	47.72-30.51	53.17-34.18	53.71-38.23	43.79-27.39	33.50-24.48
P/E Ratio	22.40-18.92	20.14-17.14	20.14-14.81	22.09-14.12	17.84-11.47	15.66-11.15	21.68-13.56	31.90-23.31
Average Yield %	2.89	2.83	2.84	2.96	2.44	2.08	2.15	1.21

Address: 77 West Wacker Drive, Suite 4600, Chicago, IL 60601
Telephone: 312-634-8100

Web Site: www.adm.com
Officers: Juan R. Luciano - Chairman, President, Chief Executive Officer, Executive Vice President, Chief Operating Officer Ray G. Young - Executive Vice President, Senior Vice President, Chief Financial Officer

Auditors: Ernst & Young LLP
Investor Contact: 217-424-5656
Transfer Agents: Hickory Point Bank & Trust, fsb, Decatur, IL

ARCONIC INC

Exchange	Symbol	Price	52Wk Range	Yield	P/E
NYS	ARNC	$27.25 (12/29/2017)	30.55-19.19	0.88	N/A

*7 Year Price Score 78.82 *NYSE Composite Index=100 *12 Month Price Score 92.73

Interim Earnings (Per Share)

Qtr.	Mar	Jun	Sep	Dec
2014	(0.48)	0.36	0.36	0.36
2015	0.42	0.30	0.06	(1.71)
2016	0.00	0.27	0.33	(2.91)
2017	0.65	0.43	0.22	...

Interim Dividends (Per Share)

Amt	Decl	Ex	Rec	Pay
0.06Q	01/13/2017	02/01/2017	02/03/2017	02/25/2017
0.06Q	02/23/2017	05/03/2017	05/05/2017	05/25/2017
0.06Q	07/24/2017	08/02/2017	08/04/2017	08/25/2017
0.06Q	09/19/2017	11/02/2017	11/03/2017	11/25/2017

Indicated Div: $0.24

Valuation Analysis

Forecast EPS	$1.15 (01/17/2018)	
Market Cap	$13.1 Billion	
Book Value	$5.9 Billion	
Price/Book	2.21	
Price/Sales	1.98	

Institutional Holding

No of Institutions	1325
Shares	639,782,464
% Held	72.19

TRADING VOLUME (thousand shares)

Business Summary: Non-Precious Metals (MIC: 8.2.2 SIC: 3334 NAIC: 331312)

Arconic is engaged in lightweight metals engineering and manufacturing. Co.'s operations consist of three reportable segments: Global Rolled Products, which produces a range of aluminum sheet and plate products for the aerospace, automotive, commercial transportation, brazing and industrial markets; Engineered Products and Solutions, which develops and manufactures products for the aerospace (commercial and defense), commercial transportation, and power generation end markets; as well as Transportation and Construction Solutions, which produces products that are used mostly in the nonresidential building and construction and commercial transportation end markets.

Recent Developments: For the quarter ended Sep 30 2017, net income decreased 36.0% to US$119.0 million from US$186.0 million in the year-earlier quarter. Revenues were US$3.24 billion, up 3.1% from US$3.14 billion the year before. Operating income was US$271.0 million versus US$237.0 million in the prior-year quarter, an increase of 14.3%. Direct operating expenses rose 4.9% to US$2.63 billion from US$2.50 billion in the comparable period the year before. Indirect operating expenses decreased 14.8% to US$339.0 million from US$398.0 million in the equivalent prior-year period.

Prospects: Our evaluation of Arconic Inc. as of Jan. 14, 2018 is the result of our systematic analysis on three basic characteristics: earnings strength, relative valuation, and recent stock price movement. The company has enjoyed a very positive trend in earnings per share over the past 5 quarters and while recent estimates for the company have been mixed, ARNC has posted results that fell short of analysts' expectations. Based on operating earnings yield, the company is about fairly valued when compared to all of the companies in our coverage universe. Share price changes over the past year indicates that ARNC will perform very poorly over the near term.

Financial Data
(US$ in Thousands)

	9 Mos	6 Mos	3 Mos	12/31/2016	12/31/2015	12/31/2014	12/31/2013	12/31/2012
Earnings Per Share	(1.61)	(1.50)	(1.66)	(2.31)	(0.93)	0.63	(6.42)	0.54
Cash Flow Per Share	1.70	2.01	2.27	1.98	3.77	4.32	4.42	4.20
Tang Book Value Per Share	1.34	1.06	0.58	N.M.	12.43	15.45	18.83	21.27
Dividends Per Share	0.270	0.210	0.150	0.090	...	...	0.360	0.360
Dividend Payout %	...	...	...	...	...	...	...	66.67
Income Statement								
Total Revenue	9,689,000	6,453,000	3,192,000	12,394,000	22,534,000	23,906,000	23,032,000	23,700,000
EBITDA	1,733,000	1,321,000	732,000	2,022,000	2,099,000	2,415,000	114,000	2,273,000
Depn & Amortn	410,000	270,000	133,000	1,132,000	1,280,000	1,372,000	1,422,000	1,462,000
Income Before Taxes	925,000	753,000	484,000	407,000	337,000	589,000	(1,748,000)	352,000
Income Taxes	272,000	219,000	162,000	1,476,000	445,000	320,000	428,000	162,000
Net Income	653,000	534,000	322,000	(941,000)	(322,000)	268,000	(2,285,000)	191,000
Average Shares	462,000	462,000	499,000	438,000	419,666	393,333	356,666	358,666
Balance Sheet								
Current Assets	6,148,000	6,033,000	6,710,000	5,892,000	7,953,000	8,269,000	6,969,000	7,700,000
Total Assets	19,237,000	19,106,000	20,157,000	20,038,000	36,528,000	37,399,000	35,742,000	40,179,000
Current Liabilities	2,677,000	2,658,000	2,587,000	2,749,000	5,211,000	5,541,000	6,105,000	5,942,000
Long-Term Obligations	6,802,000	6,796,000	8,046,000	8,044,000	9,044,000	8,769,000	7,607,000	8,311,000
Total Liabilities	13,289,000	13,366,000	14,675,000	14,923,000	24,482,000	25,093,000	25,149,000	26,980,000
Stockholders' Equity	5,948,000	5,740,000	5,482,000	5,115,000	12,046,000	12,306,000	10,593,000	13,199,000
Shares Outstanding	481,324	441,030	440,826	438,519	436,720	405,554	357,003	355,737
Statistical Record								
Return on Assets %	N.M.	N.M.	N.M.	N.M.	N.M.	0.73	N.M.	0.47
Return on Equity %	N.M.	N.M.	N.M.	N.M.	N.M.	2.34	N.M.	1.41
EBITDA Margin %	17.89	20.47	22.93	16.31	9.31	10.10	0.49	9.59
Net Margin %	6.74	8.28	10.09	N.M.	N.M.	1.12	N.M.	0.81
Asset Turnover	0.23	0.31	0.38	0.44	0.61	0.65	0.61	0.59
Current Ratio	2.30	2.27	2.59	2.14	1.53	1.49	1.14	1.30
Debt to Equity	1.14	1.18	1.47	1.57	0.75	0.71	0.72	0.63
Price Range	30.55-17.34	30.55-17.34	30.55-17.34	25.49-15.19	38.47-17.62	39.66-22.76	24.09-17.35	24.25-18.07
P/E Ratio	...	...	...	...	...	62.95-36.13	...	44.90-33.47
Average Yield %	1.11	0.88	0.66	0.43	...	...	1.86	1.75

Address: 390 Park Avenue, New York, NY 10022-4608	**Web Site:** www.arconic.com	**Auditors:** PricewaterhouseCoopers LLP
Telephone: 212-836-2732	**Officers:** John C. Plant - Chairman Charles P. (Chip) Blankenship - Chief Executive Officer	**Investor Contact:** 212-836-2674
		Transfer Agents: Computershares

ARISTA NETWORKS INC

Exchange	Symbol	Price	52Wk Range	Yield	P/E
NYS	ANET	$235.58 (12/29/2017)	243.55-88.23	N/A	48.67

*7 Year Price Score N/A   *NYSE Composite Index=100   *12 Month Price Score 130.86

Interim Earnings (Per Share)

Qtr.	Mar	Jun	Sep	Dec
2014	0.20	0.34	0.30	0.44
2015	0.34	0.33	0.39	0.60
2016	0.48	0.53	0.69	0.79
2017	1.07	1.30	1.68	...

Interim Dividends (Per Share)

No Dividends Paid

Valuation Analysis		Institutional Holding	
Forecast EPS	$5.28	No of Institutions	
	(01/18/2018)	394	
Market Cap	$17.2 Billion	Shares	
Book Value	$1.5 Billion	44,638,988	
Price/Book	11.29	% Held	
Price/Sales	11.43	N/A	

TRADING VOLUME (thousand shares)

Business Summary: Computer Hardware & Equipment (MIC: 6.2.1 SIC: 5045 NAIC: 423430)

Arista Networks is a supplier of cloud networking solutions that use software to address the needs of large-scale Internet companies, cloud service providers and data centers. Co.'s cloud networking solutions consist of its Extensible Operating System (EOS), a set of network applications and its Ethernet switching and routing platforms. EOS supports cloud and virtualization solutions, including VMware NSX, Microsoft System Center, OpenStack and other cloud management frameworks. Co. also co-authored the VXLAN protocol specification with VMware. Co.'s EOS+ is a software platform for network programmability and automation, provides an advanced level of programmability.

Recent Developments: For the quarter ended Sep 30 2017, net income increased 160.9% to US$133.7 million from US$51.3 million in the year-earlier quarter. Revenues were US$437.6 million, up 50.8% from US$290.3 million the year before. Operating income was US$140.8 million versus US$63.0 million in the prior-year quarter, an increase of 123.5%. Direct operating expenses rose 51.2% to US$157.0 million from US$103.8 million in the comparable period the year before. Indirect operating expenses increased 13.3% to US$139.8 million from US$123.4 million in the equivalent prior-year period.

Prospects: Our evaluation of Arista Networks Inc as of Jan. 14, 2018 is the result of our systematic analysis on three basic characteristics: earnings strength, relative valuation, and recent stock price movement. The company has produced a positive trend in earnings per share over the past 5 quarters and while recent estimates for the company have been mixed, ANET has posted better than expected results. Based on operating earnings yield, the company is overvalued when compared to all of the companies in our coverage universe. Share price changes over the past year indicates that ANET will perform very well over the near term.

Financial Data
(US$ in Thousands)

	9 Mos	6 Mos	3 Mos	12/31/2016	12/31/2015	12/31/2014	12/31/2013	12/31/2012
Earnings Per Share	4.84	3.85	3.08	2.50	1.67	1.29	0.72	0.39
Cash Flow Per Share	6.90	3.44	3.14	1.91	3.04	2.36	1.27	1.06
Tang Book Value Per Share	20.87	18.74	17.08	15.64	11.57	8.48	2.25	0.43
Income Statement								
Total Revenue	1,178,319	740,686	335,475	1,129,167	837,591	584,106	361,224	193,408
EBITDA	336,270	202,749	79,573	264,761	162,561	135,513	71,148	41,697
Depn & Amortn	1,106	10,553	5,130	19,400	13,400	10,000	5,000	1,800
Income Before Taxes	333,125	190,858	73,728	242,225	146,009	121,508	58,275	32,975
Income Taxes	13,757	5,212	(9,233)	58,036	24,907	34,658	15,815	11,626
Net Income	319,368	185,646	82,961	184,189	121,102	86,850	42,460	21,349
Average Shares	79,322	78,756	77,516	73,222	71,411	54,590	30,051	24,901
Balance Sheet								
Current Assets	2,075,539	1,949,189	1,736,825	1,526,126	974,328	679,479	285,523	177,172
Total Assets	2,301,710	2,162,940	1,939,598	1,729,007	1,159,890	811,023	364,520	220,168
Current Liabilities	567,547	610,797	532,513	459,553	235,011	144,373	209,344	46,364
Long-Term Obligations	...	...	...	...	...	...	...	97,673
Total Liabilities	777,158	805,191	711,224	621,187	371,738	255,365	286,788	201,258
Stockholders' Equity	1,524,552	1,357,749	1,228,374	1,107,820	788,152	555,658	77,732	18,910
Shares Outstanding	73,067	72,450	71,904	70,811	68,132	65,528	31,927	30,305
Statistical Record								
Return on Assets %	19.79	16.91	14.73	12.72	12.29	14.78	14.52	...
Return on Equity %	29.82	26.00	22.32	19.38	18.02	27.42	87.87	...
EBITDA Margin %	28.54	27.37	23.72	23.45	19.41	23.20	19.70	21.56
Net Margin %	27.10	25.06	24.73	16.31	14.46	14.87	11.75	11.04
Asset Turnover	0.79	0.78	0.78	0.78	0.85	0.99	1.24	...
Current Ratio	3.66	3.19	3.26	3.32	4.15	4.71	1.36	3.82
Debt to Equity	...	...	...	...	...	...	...	5.17
Price Range	191.05-80.45	161.62-63.45	133.97-60.93	98.00-53.00	87.68-56.71	93.31-55.00	...	...
P/E Ratio	39.47-16.62	41.98-16.48	43.50-19.78	39.20-21.20	52.50-33.96	72.33-42.64	...	...

Address: 5453 Great America Parkway,	Web Site: www.arista.com	Auditors: Ernst & Young LLP
Santa Clara, CA 95054	Officers: Andy Bechtolsheim - Chairman, Chief	Transfer Agents: Computershare Trust
Telephone: 408-547-5500	Development Officer, Interim Chief Financial Officer,	Company, N.A., Canton, MA
	Principal Financial Officer Andreas Bechtolsheim -	
	Executive Officer	

ARMSTRONG WORLD INDUSTRIES INC

Exchange	Symbol	Price	52Wk Range	Yield	P/E
NYS	AWI	$60.55 (12/29/2017)	60.55-38.80	N/A	22.10

*7 Year Price Score 86.25 *NYSE Composite Index=100 *12 Month Price Score 112.61

Interim Earnings (Per Share)

Qtr.	Mar	Jun	Sep	Dec
2014	0.30	0.34	0.57	(0.07)
2015	0.83	0.53	0.57	(0.24)
2016	(0.18)	0.30	1.26	0.49
2017	0.56	0.77	0.92	...

Interim Dividends (Per Share)

Dividend Payment Suspended

Valuation Analysis | **Institutional Holding**

Forecast EPS	$2.83	No of Institutions	
	(01/24/2018)	246	
Market Cap	$3.2 Billion	Shares	
Book Value	$366.2 Million	68,750,136	
Price/Book	8.73	% Held	
Price/Sales	2.47	81.62	

Business Summary: Construction Materials (MIC: 8.5.1 SIC: 5039 NAIC: 327993)

Armstrong World Industries designs, manufactures and sells ceiling systems (primarily mineral fiber, fiberglass wool and metal) for use in the construction and renovation of residential, commercial and institutional buildings. Co. has three segments: Americas (including Canada); Europe, Middle East and Africa (including Russia); and Pacific Rim. Each of Co.'s segments produce suspended fiber and metal ceilings for use in commercial and institutional settings in addition to sourcing complimentary ceiling products. Each segment also includes Co.'s Worthington Armstrong Venture joint venture, which manufactures suspension system (grid) products that are invoiced by both Co. and WAVE.

Recent Developments: For the quarter ended Sep 30 2017, income from continuing operations decreased 22.2% to US$43.5 million from US$55.9 million in the year-earlier quarter. Net income decreased 30.0% to US$49.4 million from US$70.6 million in the year-earlier quarter. Revenues were US$351.9 million, up 5.1% from US$334.9 million the year before. Operating income was US$69.0 million versus US$71.0 million in the prior-year quarter, a decrease of 2.8%. Direct operating expenses rose 7.0% to US$241.0 million from US$225.2 million in the comparable period the year before. Indirect operating expenses increased 8.3% to US$41.9 million from US$38.7 million in the equivalent prior-year period.

Prospects: Our evaluation of Armstrong World Industries Inc. as of Jan. 21, 2018 is the result of our systematic analysis on three basic characteristics: earnings strength, relative valuation, and recent stock price movement. The company has produced a positive trend in earnings per share over the past 5 quarters. However, while recent estimates for the company have been mixed, AWI has posted results that fell short of analysts expectations. Based on operating earnings yield, the company is undervalued when compared to all of the companies in our coverage universe. Share price changes over the past year indicates that AWI will perform very well over the near term.

Financial Data

(US$ in Thousands)	9 Mos	6 Mos	3 Mos	12/31/2016	12/31/2015	12/31/2014	12/31/2013	12/31/2012
Earnings Per Share	2.74	3.08	2.61	1.87	1.68	1.14	1.60	2.19
Cash Flow Per Share	2.96	2.76	2.31	3.53	3.67	3.80	3.70	3.72
Tang Book Value Per Share	N.M.	N.M.	N.M.	N.M.	5.04	2.68	2.76	3.25
Dividends Per Share	...	...	...	...	...	...	...	8.550
Dividend Payout %	...	...	...	...	...	...	...	390.41
Income Statement								
Total Revenue	998,100	646,200	315,400	1,234,500	2,420,000	2,515,300	2,719,900	2,618,900
EBITDA	225,200	144,500	49,900	207,600	219,200	293,000	287,100	327,900
Depn & Amortn	62,900	38,600	3,600	89,200	118,300	129,400	109,000	112,700
Income Before Taxes	134,800	87,500	37,100	71,200	57,800	120,100	112,500	164,600
Income Taxes	70,900	53,200	24,600	50,400	71,300	83,200	71,400	76,100
Net Income	121,100	71,700	30,400	104,700	94,200	63,800	94,100	131,300
Average Shares	53,500	53,700	54,500	55,700	55,900	55,400	58,400	59,500
Balance Sheet								
Current Assets	407,800	362,000	353,500	406,200	880,800	811,500	884,000	1,019,900
Total Assets	1,829,700	1,784,300	1,757,800	1,758,000	2,691,900	2,606,200	2,916,600	2,854,300
Current Liabilities	205,900	215,900	221,100	224,100	436,300	388,100	410,900	384,700
Long-Term Obligations	825,300	832,900	840,500	848,600	950,900	1,003,000	1,042,600	1,038,000
Total Liabilities	1,463,500	1,487,000	1,486,600	1,491,600	1,923,100	1,957,100	2,243,400	2,135,200
Stockholders' Equity	366,200	297,300	271,200	266,400	768,800	649,100	673,200	719,100
Shares Outstanding	52,792	52,880	53,316	54,428	55,359	55,126	54,406	58,934
Statistical Record								
Return on Assets %	8.32	9.73	6.62	18.67	3.56	2.31	3.26	4.48
Return on Equity %	47.40	67.80	27.84	80.25	13.29	9.65	13.52	14.16
EBITDA Margin %	22.56	22.36	15.82	16.82	9.06	11.65	10.56	12.52
Net Margin %	12.13	11.10	9.64	8.48	3.89	2.54	3.46	5.01
Asset Turnover	0.73	0.73	0.58	2.20	0.91	0.91	0.94	0.89
Current Ratio	1.98	1.68	1.60	1.81	2.02	2.09	2.15	2.65
Debt to Equity	2.25	2.80	3.10	3.19	1.24	1.55	1.55	1.44
Price Range	51.90-36.65	47.65-36.65	47.65-36.53	45.51-31.45	51.99-38.75	53.19-39.27	49.93-40.06	50.38-33.50
P/E Ratio	18.94-13.38	15.47-11.90	18.26-14.00	24.34-16.82	30.95-23.06	46.65-34.44	31.20-25.04	23.00-15.29
Average Yield %	...	...	...	...	...	...	...	20.81

Address: 2500 Columbia Avenue, Lancaster, PA 17603 **Telephone:** 717-397-0611	**Web Site:** www.armstrong.com **Officers:** James J. O'Connor - Chairman Victor D. Grizzle - President, Chief Executive Officer, Executive Vice President, Division Officer	**Auditors:** KPMG LLP **Investor Contact:** 717-396-6354 **Transfer Agents:** American Stock Transfer & Trust Company, New York, NY

ARROW ELECTRONICS, INC.

Exchange	Symbol	Price	52Wk Range	Yield	P/E
NYS	ARW	$80.41 (12/29/2017)	83.96-69.97	N/A	14.16

*7 Year Price Score 113.06 *NYSE Composite Index=100 *12 Month Price Score 97.32

Interim Earnings (Per Share)

Qtr.	Mar	Jun	Sep	Dec
2014	1.06	1.27	1.47	1.18
2015	1.09	1.28	1.15	1.68
2016	1.14	1.45	1.28	1.81
2017	1.26	1.11	1.50	...

Interim Dividends (Per Share)

No Dividends Paid

Valuation Analysis		Institutional Holding	
Forecast EPS	$7.35	No of Institutions	536
	(01/05/2018)		
Market Cap	$7.1 Billion	Shares	
Book Value	$4.9 Billion		111,061,376
Price/Book	1.45	% Held	
Price/Sales	0.28		83.57

Business Summary: Electrical Equipment (MIC: 7.3.1 SIC: 3679 NAIC: 334419)

Arrow Electronics is a provider of products, services, and solutions to industrial and commercial users of electronic components and enterprise computing solutions. Co. has two business segments: the global components business, which markets and distributes electronic components to original equipment manufacturers and contract manufacturers, and provides a range of capabilities throughout the life cycle of technology products and services; and the global enterprise computing solutions business, which provides computing solutions and services, including datacenter, cloud, security, and analytics solutions to value-added resellers.

Recent Developments: For the quarter ended Sep 30 2017, net income increased 15.0% to US$135.5 million from US$117.8 million in the year-earlier quarter. Revenues were US$6.95 billion, up 17.1% from US$5.94 billion the year before. Operating income was US$236.0 million versus US$198.7 million in the prior-year quarter, an increase of 18.8%. Direct operating expenses rose 18.4% to US$6.11 billion from US$5.16 billion in the comparable period the year before. Indirect operating expenses increased 5.7% to US$607.4 million from US$574.5 million in the equivalent prior-year period.

Prospects: Our evaluation of Arrow Electronics Inc. as of Jan. 14, 2018 is the result of our systematic analysis on three basic characteristics: earnings strength, relative valuation, and recent stock price movement. The company has enjoyed a very positive trend in earnings per share over the past 5 quarters and while recent estimates for the company have remained steady, ARW has posted better than expected results. Based on operating earnings yield, the company is undervalued when compared to all of the companies in our coverage universe. Share price changes over the past year indicates that ARW will perform in line with the market over the near term.

Financial Data

(US$ in Thousands)	9 Mos	6 Mos	3 Mos	12/31/2016	12/31/2015	12/31/2014	12/31/2013	12/31/2012
Earnings Per Share	5.68	5.46	5.80	5.68	5.20	4.98	3.85	4.56
Cash Flow Per Share	2.51	1.25	4.16	3.90	6.92	6.82	4.39	6.16
Tang Book Value Per Share	23.89	22.01	20.08	18.94	15.22	18.24	17.16	17.52
Income Statement								
Total Revenue	19,178,638	12,224,898	5,759,552	23,825,261	23,282,020	22,768,674	21,357,285	20,405,128
EBITDA	614,042	384,926	203,297	1,057,559	1,023,575	989,978	857,287	954,019
Depn & Amortn	30,301	21,391	11,575	199,020	203,028	197,978	168,064	149,896
Income Before Taxes	463,562	283,104	153,649	707,824	685,146	676,015	574,790	702,247
Income Taxes	114,998	68,799	39,224	190,674	191,697	184,943	182,343	203,642
Net Income	348,077	213,447	113,768	522,750	497,726	498,045	399,420	506,332
Average Shares	89,540	89,837	90,541	92,033	95,686	99,947	103,699	111,077
Balance Sheet								
Current Assets	11,039,168	10,223,162	9,484,503	10,316,721	9,186,471	9,032,607	8,585,770	7,715,301
Total Assets	15,056,966	14,200,025	13,419,375	14,206,366	13,021,930	12,442,856	12,060,883	10,785,687
Current Liabilities	6,978,997	6,439,430	6,033,288	6,689,222	6,056,152	5,838,021	5,301,946	4,910,211
Long-Term Obligations	2,802,960	2,642,043	2,459,849	2,696,334	2,380,575	2,075,453	2,226,132	1,587,478
Total Liabilities	10,177,898	9,493,350	8,903,363	9,792,928	8,879,487	8,288,886	7,880,651	6,802,465
Stockholders' Equity	4,879,068	4,706,675	4,516,012	4,413,438	4,142,443	4,153,970	4,180,232	3,983,222
Shares Outstanding	87,961	88,259	88,905	88,913	90,923	95,895	99,936	106,001
Statistical Record								
Return on Assets %	3.64	3.65	4.12	3.83	3.91	4.07	3.50	4.90
Return on Equity %	11.02	10.89	12.00	12.19	12.00	11.95	9.79	13.20
EBITDA Margin %	3.20	3.15	3.53	4.44	4.40	4.35	4.01	4.68
Net Margin %	1.81	1.75	1.98	2.19	2.14	2.19	1.87	2.48
Asset Turnover	1.82	1.81	1.87	1.75	1.83	1.86	1.87	1.97
Current Ratio	1.58	1.59	1.57	1.54	1.52	1.55	1.62	1.57
Debt to Equity	0.57	0.56	0.54	0.61	0.57	0.50	0.53	0.40
Price Range	83.85-59.25	79.81-59.25	75.37-59.06	72.44-46.66	64.67-50.79	62.71-46.42	54.25-36.47	42.63-31.02
P/E Ratio	14.76-10.43	14.62-10.85	12.99-10.18	12.75-8.21	12.44-9.77	12.59-9.32	14.09-9.47	9.35-6.80

Address: 9201 East Dry Creek Road, Centennial, CO 80112 Telephone: 303-824-4000	Web Site: www.arrow.com Officers: Michael J. Long - Chairman, President, Chief Executive Officer, Chief Operating Officer Paul J. Reilly - Executive Vice President, Chief Financial Officer, Interim Chief Accounting Officer	Auditors: Ernst & Young LLP Investor Contact: 303-824-4000 Transfer Agents: Wells Fargo Shareowner Services, South St. Paul, MN

ASBURY AUTOMOTIVE GROUP INC

Exchange	Symbol	Price	52Wk Range	Yield	P/E
NYS	ABG	$64.00 (12/29/2017)	69.45-50.15	N/A	8.38

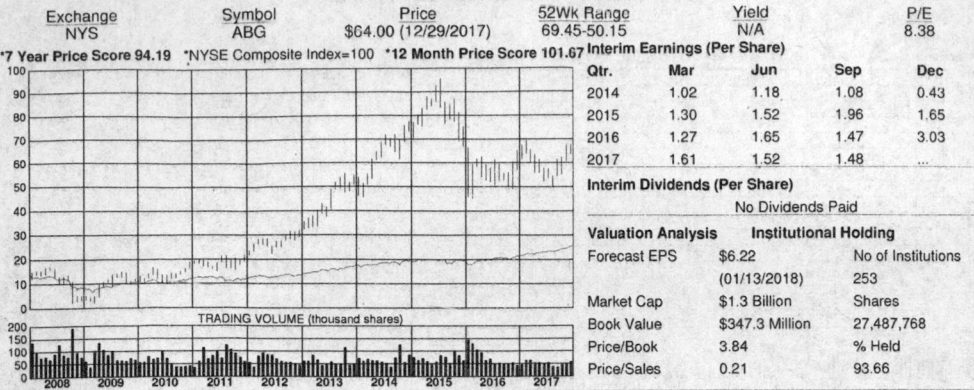

*7 Year Price Score 94.19 *NYSE Composite Index=100 *12 Month Price Score 101.67

Interim Earnings (Per Share)

Qtr.	Mar	Jun	Sep	Dec
2014	1.02	1.18	1.08	0.43
2015	1.30	1.52	1.96	1.65
2016	1.27	1.65	1.47	3.03
2017	1.61	1.52	1.48	...

Interim Dividends (Per Share)

No Dividends Paid

Valuation Analysis   **Institutional Holding**

Forecast EPS	$6.22	No of Institutions
	(01/13/2018)	253
Market Cap	$1.3 Billion	Shares
Book Value	$347.3 Million	27,487,768
Price/Book	3.84	% Held
Price/Sales	0.21	93.66

Business Summary: Retail - Automotive (MIC: 2.1.4 SIC: 5599 NAIC: 441229)

Asbury Automotive Group is an automotive retailer with store operations conducted by its subsidiaries. As of Dec 31 2016, Co. owned and operated 93 new vehicle franchises, representing 28 brands of automobiles at 77 dealership locations, and 23 collision centers, as well as two stand-alone used vehicle stores in Florida. Co.'s stores provide a range of automotive products and services, including new and used vehicles; parts and service, including vehicle repair and maintenance services, replacement parts, and collision repair services; and finance and insurance products, including arranging vehicle financing through third parties and aftermarket products, such as extended service contracts.

Recent Developments: For the quarter ended Sep 30 2017, net income decreased 5.2% to US$30.7 million from US$32.4 million in the year-earlier quarter. Revenues were US$1.60 billion, down 4.8% from US$1.68 billion the year before. Operating income was US$69.7 million versus US$70.7 million in the prior-year quarter, a decrease of 1.4%. Direct operating expenses declined 5.3% to US$1.34 billion from US$1.42 billion in the comparable period the year before. Indirect operating expenses decreased 2.3% to US$190.6 million from US$195.0 million in the equivalent prior-year period.

Prospects: Our evaluation of Asbury Automotive Group Inc. as of Jan. 14, 2018 is the result of our systematic analysis on three basic characteristics: earnings strength, relative valuation, and recent stock price movement. The company has managed to produce a neutral trend in earnings per share over the past 5 quarters and while recent estimates for the company have been mixed, ABG has posted results that fell short of analysts expectations. Based on operating earnings yield, the company is undervalued when compared to all of the companies in our coverage universe. Share price changes over the past year indicates that ABG will perform very poorly over the near term.

Financial Data
(US$ in Thousands)	9 Mos	6 Mos	3 Mos	12/31/2016	12/31/2015	12/31/2014	12/31/2013	12/31/2012
Earnings Per Share	7.64	7.63	7.76	7.40	6.41	3.71	3.51	2.61
Cash Flow Per Share	11.38	9.18	9.31	6.31	5.91	2.82	1.65	(0.66)
Tang Book Value Per Share	6.33	4.91	3.91	4.85	5.47	10.25	12.92	10.84
Income Statement								
Total Revenue	4,785,600	3,183,500	1,551,700	6,527,800	6,588,300	5,867,700	5,334,900	4,640,300
EBITDA	230,400	155,200	78,200	374,000	366,000	262,700	243,600	208,100
Depn & Amortn	16,800	11,300	5,900	30,700	29,500	26,400	24,300	22,600
Income Before Taxes	154,700	104,600	53,100	267,800	273,400	183,000	165,300	133,300
Income Taxes	58,100	38,700	19,100	100,600	104,000	71,000	64,200	50,000
Net Income	96,600	65,900	34,000	167,200	169,200	111,600	109,100	82,200
Average Shares	20,800	21,000	21,100	22,600	26,400	30,100	31,100	31,500
Balance Sheet								
Current Assets	1,220,700	1,318,000	1,348,600	1,332,400	1,343,000	1,276,700	1,108,600	986,400
Total Assets	2,269,800	2,367,000	2,399,700	2,336,100	2,305,900	2,192,000	1,888,600	1,661,400
Current Liabilities	980,400	1,103,200	1,153,400	1,104,900	1,007,800	1,041,100	834,200	779,800
Long-Term Obligations	901,400	905,200	908,900	912,700	940,400	678,700	543,300	461,400
Total Liabilities	1,922,500	2,048,900	2,101,500	2,056,400	1,991,400	1,747,100	1,398,000	1,258,600
Stockholders' Equity	347,300	318,100	298,200	279,700	314,500	444,900	490,600	402,800
Shares Outstanding	20,819	20,900	21,151	21,253	24,810	28,523	30,765	31,316
Statistical Record								
Return on Assets %	7.12	6.98	7.19	7.18	7.52	5.47	6.15	5.32
Return on Equity %	54.30	61.52	63.04	56.12	44.56	23.86	24.42	22.48
EBITDA Margin %	4.81	4.88	5.04	5.73	5.56	4.48	4.57	4.48
Net Margin %	2.02	2.07	2.19	2.56	2.57	1.90	2.05	1.77
Asset Turnover	2.81	2.76	2.76	2.80	2.93	2.38	3.01	3.00
Current Ratio	1.25	1.19	1.17	1.21	1.33	1.23	1.33	1.26
Debt to Equity	2.60	2.85	3.05	3.26	2.99	1.53	1.11	1.15
Price Range	69.45-48.85	69.45-48.85	69.45-48.85	67.44-45.07	95.54-66.76	77.56-45.42	55.61-32.03	32.03-21.50
P/E Ratio	9.09-6.39	9.10-6.40	8.95-6.30	9.11-6.09	14.90-10.41	20.91-12.24	15.84-9.13	12.27-8.24

Address: 2905 Premiere Parkway N.W., Suite 300, Duluth, GA 30097	Web Site: www.asburyauto.com	Auditors: Ernst & Young LLP
Telephone: 770-418-8200	Officers: Thomas C. (Tom) DeLoach - Chairman	Investor Contact: 770-418-8210
	Craig T. Monaghan - Vice-Chairman, President, Chief Executive Officer	Transfer Agents: Computershare Trust Company, N.A.

ASHLAND GLOBAL HOLDINGS INC

Exchange	Symbol	Price	52Wk Range	Yield	P/E
NYS	ASH	$71.20 (12/29/2017)	73.98-53.39	1.26	7120.00

*7 Year Price Score 106.32 *NYSE Composite Index=100 *12 Month Price Score 104.39

Interim Earnings (Per Share)

Qtr.	Dec	Mar	Jun	Sep
2015-16	1.35	1.38	1.13	(4.33)
2016-17	(0.01)	1.47	(0.54)	(0.92)

Interim Dividends (Per Share)

Amt	Decl	Ex	Rec	Pay
0.39Q	01/25/2017	02/27/2017	03/01/2017	03/15/2017
0.225Q	05/17/2017	05/30/2017	06/01/2017	06/15/2017
0.225Q	07/19/2017	08/30/2017	09/01/2017	09/15/2017
0.225Q	11/15/2017	11/30/2017	12/01/2017	12/15/2017

Indicated Div: $0.90

Valuation Analysis		Institutional Holding	
Forecast EPS	$3.35	No of Institutions	
	(01/24/2018)	N/A	
Market Cap	$4.4 Billion	Shares	
Book Value	$3.4 Billion	N/A	
Price/Book	1.30	% Held	
Price/Sales	1.35	N/A	

Business Summary: Specialty Chemicals (MIC: 8.3.2 SIC: 5169 NAIC: 325199)

Ashland Global Holdings is engaged in providing specialty chemical solutions to customers in a range of consumer and industrial markets. Co. has three segments: Specialty Ingredients, which include various end use markets, such as the oral care, hair care, skin care, home care, pharmaceutical, nutrition, adhesives, coatings, construction, energy, and performance specialties; Composites, which manufactures and sells a range of unsaturated polyester and vinyl ester resins, gelcoats and additives for the reinforced plastics industry; and Intermediates and Solvents, which produces related derivatives used as chemical intermediates and as specialty process solvents in a range of applications.

Recent Developments: For the year ended Sep 30 2017, loss from continuing operations was US$105.0 million compared with a loss of US$283.0 million a year earlier. Net income was unchanged at US$28.0 million versus US$28.0 million the prior year. Revenues were US$3.26 billion, up 8.0% from US$3.02 billion the year before. Operating income was US$142.0 million versus a loss of US$127.0 million in the prior year. Direct operating expenses rose 10.2% to US$2.37 billion from US$2.15 billion in the comparable period the year before. Indirect operating expenses decreased 24.9% to US$746.0 million from US$993.0 million in the equivalent prior-year period.

Prospects: Our evaluation of Ashland Global Holdings Inc. as of Jan. 21, 2018 is the result of our systematic analysis on three basic characteristics: earnings strength, relative valuation, and recent stock price movement. The company has generated a negative trend in earnings per share over the past 5 quarters and while recent estimates for the company have remained steady, ASH has posted better than expected results. Based on operating earnings yield, the company is about fairly valued when compared to all of the companies in our coverage universe. Share price changes over the past year indicates that ASH will perform well over the near term.

Financial Data

(US$ in Millions)	09/30/2017	09/30/2016	09/30/2015	09/30/2014
Earnings Per Share	0.01	(0.46)	4.48	3.00
Cash Flow Per Share	4.11	11.13	1.31	7.53
Dividends Per Share	1.230	1.560	1.460	1.360
Dividend Payout %	12,300.00	...	32.59	45.33
Income Statement				
Total Revenue	3,260	4,948	5,387	6,121
EBITDA	342	552	569	343
Depn & Amortn	219	260	263	304
Income Before Taxes	(105)	108	146	(118)
Income Taxes	7	133	(22)	(188)
Net Income	1	(29)	309	233
Average Shares	62	64	69	78
Balance Sheet				
Current Assets	1,903	2,866	3,093	...
Total Assets	8,618	9,697	10,054	...
Current Liabilities	968	1,216	1,442	...
Long-Term Obligations	2,584	3,055	3,348	...
Total Liabilities	5,212	6,350	7,017	...
Stockholders' Equity	3,406	3,347	3,037	...
Shares Outstanding	62	62	67	...
Statistical Record				
Return on Assets %	0.01	N.M.	...	...
Return on Equity %	0.03	N.M.	...	...
EBITDA Margin %	10.49	11.16	10.56	5.60
Net Margin %	0.03	N.M.	5.74	3.81
Asset Turnover	0.36	0.50	...	...
Current Ratio	1.97	2.36	2.14	...
Debt to Equity	0.76	0.91	1.10	...
Price Range	67.45-52.62	60.33-43.67	64.35-47.16	53.51-41.63
P/E Ratio	N.M.	...	14.36-10.53	17.84-13.88
Average Yield %	2.05	2.92	2.53	2.81

Address: 50 E. RiverCenter Boulevard, Covington, KY 41011 **Telephone:** 859-815-3333	**Web Site:** www.ashland.com **Officers:** William A. Wulfsohn - Chairman, Chief Executive Officer J. Kevin Willis - Senior Vice President, Chief Financial Officer	**Auditors:** Ernst & Young LLP **Transfer Agents:** Wells Fargo Shareowner Services, Mendota Heights, MN

ASPEN INSURANCE HOLDINGS LTD

Exchange	Symbol	Price	52Wk Range	Yield	P/E
NYS	AHL	$40.60 (12/29/2017)	57.70-36.45	2.36	N/A

*7 Year Price Score 95.65   *NYSE Composite Index=100   *12 Month Price Score 80.15

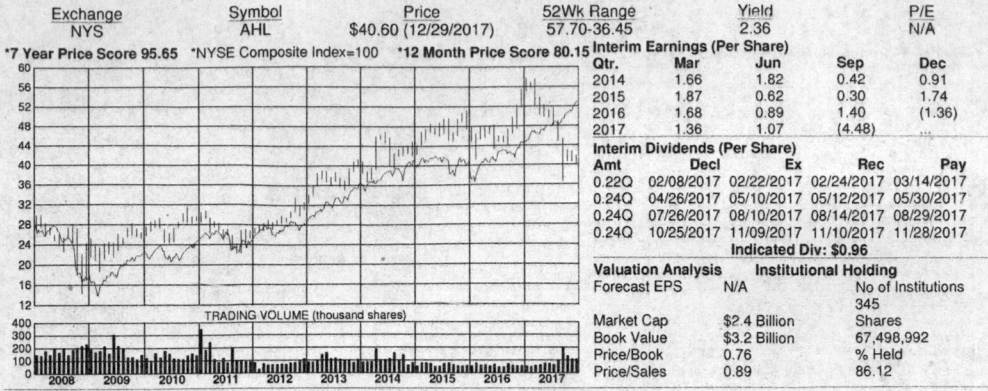

Interim Earnings (Per Share)

Qtr.	Mar	Jun	Sep	Dec
2014	1.66	1.82	0.42	0.91
2015	1.87	0.62	0.30	1.74
2016	1.68	0.89	1.40	(1.36)
2017	1.36	1.07	(4.48)	...

Interim Dividends (Per Share)

Amt	Decl	Ex	Rec	Pay
0.22Q	02/08/2017	02/22/2017	02/24/2017	03/14/2017
0.24Q	04/26/2017	05/10/2017	05/12/2017	05/30/2017
0.24Q	07/26/2017	08/10/2017	08/14/2017	08/29/2017
0.24Q	10/25/2017	11/09/2017	11/10/2017	11/28/2017

Indicated Div: $0.96

Valuation Analysis		Institutional Holding	
Forecast EPS	N/A	No of Institutions	345
Market Cap	$2.4 Billion	Shares	67,498,992
Book Value	$3.2 Billion	% Held	86.12
Price/Book	0.76		
Price/Sales	0.89		

TRADING VOLUME (thousand shares)

Business Summary: General Insurance (MIC: 5.2.1 SIC: 6331 NAIC: 524126)

Aspen Insurance Holdings is a holding company. Co. underwrites specialty insurance and reinsurance through its subsidiaries in Bermuda, the U.S. and the U.K. Co. has two segments: reinsurance, which consists of property catastrophe reinsurance, other property reinsurance (risk excess, pro rata and facultative), casualty reinsurance (U.S. treaty, international treaty and global facultative) and specialty reinsurance (credit and surety, agriculture insurance and reinsurance, marine, aviation, terrorism, engineering and other specialty lines), and insurance, which consists of property and casualty insurance, marine, aviation and energy insurance and financial and professional lines insurance.

Recent Developments: For the quarter ended Sep 30 2017, net loss amounted to US$253.8 million versus net income of US$95.6 million in the year-earlier quarter. Revenues were US$726.6 million, down 3.8% from US$755.6 million the year before. Net premiums earned were US$652.5 million versus US$681.0 million in the prior-year quarter, a decrease of 4.2%. Net investment income was unchanged at US$46.4 million versus a year ago.

Prospects: Our evaluation of Aspen Insurance Holdings Ltd. as of July 19, 2015 is the result of our systematic analysis on three basic characteristics: earnings strength, relative valuation, and recent stock price movement. The company has managed to produce a neutral trend in earnings per share over the past 5 quarters. However, while recent estimates for the company have been lowered by analysts, AHL has posted better than expected results. Based on operating earnings yield, the company is undervalued when compared to all of the companies in our coverage universe. Share price changes over the past year indicates that AHL will perform in line with the market over the near term.

Financial Data
(US$ in Thousands)

	9 Mos	6 Mos	3 Mos	12/31/2016	12/31/2015	12/31/2014	12/31/2013	12/31/2012
Earnings Per Share	(3.41)	2.47	2.29	2.61	4.54	4.82	4.14	3.38
Cash Flow Per Share	2.03	1.78	5.15	7.47	9.37	9.41	8.47	6.96
Tang Book Value Per Share	51.89	59.15	58.55	59.68	55.82	54.83	50.06	49.03
Income Statement								
Premium Income	1,795,600	1,143,100	581,100	2,637,300	2,473,300	2,405,300	2,171,800	2,083,500
Total Revenue	2,072,200	1,345,600	683,600	2,938,500	2,753,400	2,646,400	2,423,300	2,329,400
Benefits & Claims	1,450,500	674,300	328,200	...	...	...	...	...
Income Before Taxes	(86,700)	176,300	99,300	209,500	337,500	367,900	342,700	295,400
Income Taxes	(5,200)	4,000	2,800	6,100	14,400	12,100	13,400	15,000
Net Income	(82,300)	172,100	96,400	203,300	322,300	355,000	329,800	280,600
Average Shares	59,759	61,022	61,196	61,860	62,687	65,872	69,417	73,689
Balance Sheet								
Total Assets	13,051,600	12,516,500	12,247,800	12,090,100	11,048,800	10,716,300	10,230,500	10,310,600
Total Liabilities	9,890,900	8,897,200	8,654,900	8,443,200	7,630,200	7,297,500	6,930,600	6,822,400
Stockholders' Equity	3,160,700	3,619,300	3,592,900	3,646,900	3,418,600	3,418,800	3,299,900	3,488,200
Shares Outstanding	59,407	59,844	59,988	59,774	60,918	62,017	65,546	70,753
Statistical Record								
Return on Assets %	N.M.	1.62	1.56	1.75	2.96	3.39	3.21	2.83
Return on Equity %	N.M.	5.43	5.18	5.74	9.43	10.57	9.72	8.40
Loss Ratio %	80.78	58.99	56.48	...	...	...	...	...
Net Margin %	(3.97)	12.79	14.10	6.92	11.71	13.41	13.61	12.05
Price Range	57.70-36.45	57.70-44.08	57.70-43.27	55.50-41.07	51.19-42.32	46.94-36.63	41.31-32.08	33.58-26.17
P/E Ratio	...	23.36-17.85	25.20-18.90	21.26-15.74	11.28-9.32	9.74-7.60	9.98-7.75	9.93-7.74

Address: 141 Front Street, Hamilton, HM 19
Telephone: 441-295-8201

Web Site: www.aspen.bm
Officers: Glyn Jones - Chairman Christopher O'Kane - Chief Executive Officer

Auditors: KPMG LLP
Investor Contact: 646-502-1076
Transfer Agents: Computershare Investor Services, Jersey City, NJ

ASSOCIATED BANC-CORP

Exchange	Symbol	Price	52Wk Range	Yield	P/E
NYS	ASB	$25.40 (12/29/2017)	26.50-21.25	2.20	17.40

*7 Year Price Score 110.71 *NYSE Composite Index=100 *12 Month Price Score 97.03

Interim Earnings (Per Share)

Qtr.	Mar	Jun	Sep	Dec
2014	0.27	0.28	0.31	0.31
2015	0.30	0.31	0.31	0.27
2016	0.27	0.31	0.34	0.34
2017	0.35	0.36	0.41	...

Interim Dividends (Per Share)

Amt	Decl	Ex	Rec	Pay
0.12Q	02/07/2017	02/27/2017	03/01/2017	03/15/2017
0.12Q	04/25/2017	05/30/2017	06/01/2017	06/15/2017
0.12Q	07/25/2017	08/30/2017	09/01/2017	09/15/2017
0.14Q	10/24/2017	11/30/2017	12/01/2017	12/15/2017

Indicated Div: $0.56 (Div. Reinv. Plan)

Valuation Analysis **Institutional Holding**

Forecast EPS	$1.50	No of Institutions	
	(01/18/2018)	347	
Market Cap	$3.9 Billion	Shares	
Book Value	$3.2 Billion	138,201,376	
Price/Book	1.21	% Held	
Price/Sales	3.23	73.45	

Business Summary: Banking (MIC: 5.1.1 SIC: 6022 NAIC: 522110)

Associated Banc is a bank holding company. Through banking and various nonbanking subsidiaries, Co. provides banking and nonbanking products and services. Co. has three segments: Corporate and Commercial Specialty, which provides lending solutions such as commercial loans, deposit and cash management solutions; Community, Consumer, and Business, which includes lending solutions such as residential mortgages, deposit and transactional solutions; and Risk Management and Shared Services, which includes corporate risk management, credit administration, treasury, finance, operations and technology functions. At Dec 31 2016, Co. had total assets of $29.14 billion and deposits of $21.89 billion.

Recent Developments: For the quarter ended Sep 30 2017, net income increased 20.8% to US$65.0 million from US$53.8 million in the year-earlier quarter. Net interest income increased 6.5% to US$190.1 million from US$178.5 million in the year-earlier quarter. Provision for loan losses was US$5.0 million versus US$21.0 million in the prior-year quarter, a decrease of 76.2%. Non-interest income fell 9.8% to US$85.9 million from US$95.2 million, while non-interest expense advanced 1.2% to US$177.4 million.

Prospects: Our evaluation of Associated Banc-Corp. as of Jan. 14, 2018 is the result of our systematic analysis on three basic characteristics: earnings strength, relative valuation, and recent stock price movement. The company has managed to produce a neutral trend in earnings per share over the past 5 quarters and while recent estimates for the company have been mixed, ASB has posted better than expected results. Based on operating earnings yield, the company is undervalued when compared to all of the companies in our coverage universe. Share price changes over the past year indicates that ASB will perform poorly over the near term.

Financial Data

(US$ in Thousands)	9 Mos	6 Mos	3 Mos	12/31/2016	12/31/2015	12/31/2014	12/31/2013	12/31/2012
Earnings Per Share	1.46	1.39	1.34	1.26	1.19	1.16	1.10	1.00
Cash Flow Per Share	3.57	5.42	5.15	4.22	2.02	1.35	2.94	2.03
Tang Book Value Per Share	13.13	12.91	12.60	12.38	11.70	11.51	11.12	11.06
Dividends Per Share	0.480	0.470	0.460	0.450	0.410	0.370	0.330	0.230
Dividend Payout %	32.88	33.81	34.33	35.71	34.45	31.90	30.00	23.00
Income Statement								
Interest Income	656,283	424,389	206,789	791,568	753,662	736,745	708,983	718,284
Interest Expense	102,068	60,296	26,515	84,295	77,384	55,778	63,440	92,292
Net Interest Income	554,215	364,093	180,274	707,273	676,278	680,967	645,543	625,992
Provision for Losses	26,000	21,000	9,000	70,000	37,500	16,000	10,000	3,000
Non-Interest Income	248,136	162,241	79,831	352,883	328,409	290,319	313,099	313,290
Non-Interest Expense	527,434	350,007	173,691	702,560	697,399	679,241	680,749	681,823
Income Before Taxes	248,917	155,327	77,414	287,596	269,788	276,045	267,893	254,459
Income Taxes	69,663	41,074	21,144	87,322	81,487	85,536	79,201	75,486
Net Income	179,254	114,253	56,270	200,274	188,301	190,509	188,692	178,973
Average Shares	152,968	154,302	153,869	149,961	150,603	158,254	165,802	172,357
Balance Sheet								
Net Loans & Leases	20,777,691	20,548,360	19,901,963	19,896,865	18,564,994	17,482,479	15,692,684	15,375,023
Total Assets	30,064,547	29,769,025	29,109,857	29,139,315	27,715,021	26,821,774	24,226,920	23,487,735
Total Deposits	22,333,451	21,618,180	21,828,035	21,888,448	21,007,665	18,763,504	17,267,167	16,939,865
Total Liabilities	26,860,946	26,577,523	25,965,063	26,048,003	24,777,775	24,021,523	21,335,630	20,551,336
Stockholders' Equity	3,203,601	3,191,502	3,144,794	3,091,312	2,937,246	2,800,251	2,891,290	2,936,399
Shares Outstanding	152,317	153,848	153,733	152,120	151,239	151,541	164,138	170,239
Statistical Record								
Return on Assets %	0.79	0.76	0.75	0.70	0.69	0.75	0.79	0.79
Return on Equity %	7.43	7.17	6.99	6.63	6.56	6.69	6.48	6.15
Net Interest Margin %	81.99	84.48	87.18	89.35	89.73	92.43	91.05	87.15
Efficiency Ratio %	55.83	58.77	60.60	61.39	64.45	66.13	66.60	66.10
Loans to Deposits	0.93	0.95	0.91	0.91	0.88	0.93	0.91	0.91
Price Range	26.50-19.05	26.50-16.49	26.50-15.84	25.15-15.48	20.84-16.62	19.36-15.58	17.60-13.12	14.63-11.43
P/E Ratio	18.15-13.05	19.06-11.86	19.78-11.82	19.96-12.29	17.51-13.97	16.69-13.43	16.00-11.93	14.63-11.43
Average Yield %	2.02	2.08	2.20	2.36	2.26	2.16	2.08	1.77

Address: 433 Main Street, Green Bay, WI 54301 **Telephone:** 920-491-7500	**Web Site:** www.associatedbank.com **Officers:** William R. Hutchinson - Chairman Tammy C. Stadler - Executive Vice President, Corporate Controller, Principal Accounting Officer	**Auditors:** KPMG LLP **Investor Contact:** 920-491-7059 **Transfer Agents:** Wells Fargo Shareowner Services, Saint Paul, MN

ASSURANT INC

Exchange	Symbol	Price	52Wk Range	Yield	P/E	Div Achiever
NYS	AIZ	$100.84 (12/29/2017)	106.27-87.74	2.22	23.40	12 Years

*7 Year Price Score 121.11 *NYSE Composite Index=100 *12 Month Price Score 95.41

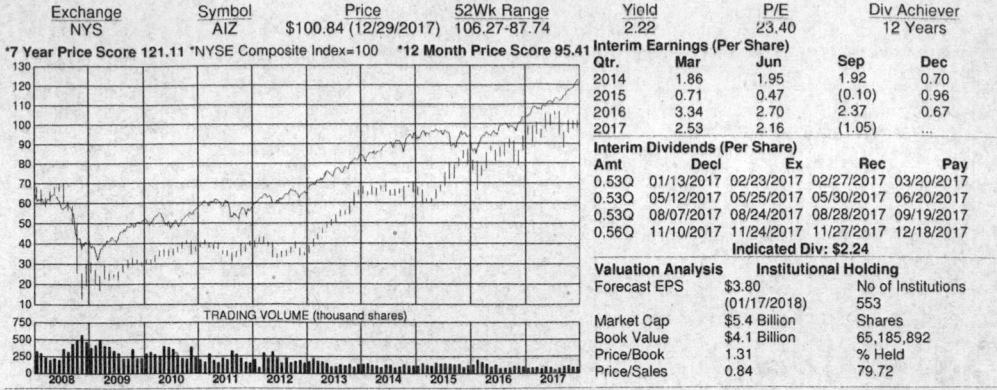

Interim Earnings (Per Share)

Qtr.	Mar	Jun	Sep	Dec
2014	1.86	1.95	1.92	0.70
2015	0.71	0.47	(0.10)	0.96
2016	3.34	2.70	2.37	0.67
2017	2.53	2.16	(1.05)	...

Interim Dividends (Per Share)

Amt	Decl	Ex	Rec	Pay
0.53Q	01/13/2017	02/23/2017	02/27/2017	03/20/2017
0.53Q	05/12/2017	05/25/2017	05/30/2017	06/20/2017
0.53Q	08/07/2017	08/24/2017	08/28/2017	09/19/2017
0.56Q	11/10/2017	11/24/2017	11/27/2017	12/18/2017

Indicated Div: $2.24

Valuation Analysis	Institutional Holding	
Forecast EPS	$3.80	No of Institutions
(01/17/2018)		553
Market Cap	$5.4 Billion	Shares
Book Value	$4.1 Billion	65,185,892
Price/Book	1.31	% Held
Price/Sales	0.84	79.72

Business Summary: Life & Health (MIC: 5.2.2 SIC: 6321 NAIC: 524114)

Assurant is a holding company. Co. is a provider risk management solutions in the housing and lifestyle markets, protecting where consumers live and the goods they buy. Through its operating subsidiaries, Co. provides mobile device protection products and services; extended service contracts and related services for consumer electronics and appliances; vehicle protection services; pre-funded funeral insurance; credit insurance; lender-placed homeowners insurance; manufactured housing and flood insurance; renters insurance and related products; and field services, valuation services and other property risk management services.

Recent Developments: For the quarter ended Sep 30 2017, net loss amounted to US$57.3 million versus net income of US$144.4 million in the year-earlier quarter. Revenues were US$1.59 billion, down 13.5% from US$1.83 billion the year before. Net premiums earned were US$1.07 billion versus US$1.22 billion in the prior-year quarter, a decrease of 11.7%. Net investment income rose 6.3% to US$132.6 million from US$124.8 million a year ago.

Prospects: Our evaluation of Assurant Inc. as of Jan. 14, 2018 is the result of our systematic analysis on three basic characteristics: earnings strength, relative valuation, and recent stock price movement. The company has generated a negative trend in earnings per share over the past 5 quarters and while recent estimates for the company have been mixed, AIZ has posted better than expected results. Based on operating earnings yield, the company is undervalued when compared to all of the companies in our coverage universe. Share price changes over the past year indicates that AIZ will perform well over the near term.

Financial Data (US$ in Thousands)	9 Mos	6 Mos	3 Mos	12/31/2016	12/31/2015	12/31/2014	12/31/2013	12/31/2012
Earnings Per Share	4.31	7.73	8.27	9.13	2.05	6.44	6.30	5.67
Cash Flow Per Share	9.98	7.89	8.86	2.19	3.73	5.46	13.41	8.04
Tang Book Value Per Share	53.71	55.02	52.78	54.11	51.83	57.12	51.43	54.43
Dividends Per Share	2.120	2.090	2.060	2.030	1.370	1.060	0.960	0.810
Dividend Payout %	49.19	27.04	24.91	22.23	66.83	16.46	15.24	14.29
Income Statement								
Total Revenue	4,738,400	3,152,000	1,551,500	7,531,780	10,325,494	10,381,653	9,047,657	8,508,270
Income Before Taxes	286,200	393,800	215,100	848,588	201,181	744,137	789,699	757,751
Income Taxes	79,500	129,800	71,300	283,238	59,626	273,230	300,792	274,046
Net Income	206,700	264,000	143,800	565,350	141,555	470,907	488,907	483,705
Average Shares	54,524	55,509	56,756	61,934	69,017	73,152	77,654	85,307
Balance Sheet								
Total Assets	32,405,200	30,058,900	29,567,700	29,709,128	30,043,128	31,562,466	29,714,689	28,946,607
Total Liabilities	28,267,000	25,834,300	25,408,900	25,611,028	25,519,161	26,381,159	24,881,210	23,761,241
Stockholders' Equity	4,138,200	4,224,600	4,158,800	4,098,100	4,523,967	5,181,307	4,833,479	5,185,366
Shares Outstanding	53,796	54,064	55,029	55,941	65,850	69,299	71,828	78,664
Statistical Record								
Return on Assets %	0.76	1.47	1.63	1.89	0.46	1.54	1.67	1.72
Return on Equity %	5.51	9.96	11.21	13.08	2.92	9.40	9.76	9.45
Net Margin %	4.36	8.38	9.27	7.51	1.37	4.54	5.40	5.69
Asset Turnover	0.21	0.23	0.23	0.25	0.34	0.34	0.31	0.30
Price Range	106.27-78.72	105.30-78.72	100.85-77.09	93.74-66.23	86.81-59.86	69.52-60.81	66.37-34.70	43.35-32.57
P/E Ratio	24.66-18.26	13.62-10.18	12.19-9.32	10.27-7.25	42.35-29.20	10.80-9.44	10.53-5.51	7.65-5.74
Average Yield %	2.21	2.25	2.32	2.42	1.92	1.60	1.88	2.18

Address: 28 Liberty Street, 41st Floor, New York, NY 10005
Telephone: 212-859-7000

Web Site: www.assurant.com
Officers: Alan B. Colberg - President, Chief Executive Officer, Executive Vice President Carey S. Roberts - Executive Vice President, Chief Legal Officer, Secretary

Auditors: PricewaterhouseCoopers LLP
Investor Contact: 212-859-7197
Transfer Agents: Computershare, Providence, RI

ASSURED GUARANTY LTD

Exchange	Symbol	Price	52Wk Range	Yield	P/E
NYS	AGO	$33.87 (12/29/2017)	45.38-33.65	1.68	4.87

*7 Year Price Score 129.85 *NYSE Composite Index=100 *12 Month Price Score 85.75

Interim Earnings (Per Share)

Qtr.	Mar	Jun	Sep	Dec
2014	0.23	0.89	2.09	3.13
2015	1.28	1.96	0.88	2.95
2016	0.43	1.09	3.60	1.50
2017	2.49	1.24	1.72	...

Interim Dividends (Per Share)

Amt	Decl	Ex	Rec	Pay
0.142Q	02/22/2017	03/06/2017	03/08/2017	03/22/2017
0.142Q	05/03/2017	05/15/2017	05/17/2017	05/31/2017
0.142Q	08/02/2017	08/14/2017	08/16/2017	08/30/2017
0.142Q	11/01/2017	11/14/2017	11/15/2017	11/29/2017

Indicated Div: $0.57

Valuation Analysis   **Institutional Holding**

Forecast EPS	N/A	No of Institutions
		410
Market Cap	$4.0 Billion	Shares
Book Value	$6.9 Billion	143,373,696
Price/Book	0.58	% Held
Price/Sales	2.07	91.20

Business Summary: General Insurance (MIC: 5.2.1 SIC: 6351 NAIC: 524298)

Assured Guaranty is a Bermuda-based holding company that provides, through its operating subsidiaries, credit protection products and international public finance including infrastructure and structured finance markets. Co. markets its financial guaranty insurance directly to issuers and underwriters of public finance and structured finance securities as well as to investors in such obligations. Co. guarantees obligations issued principally in the U.S. and the U.K, and also guarantees obligations issued in other countries and regions. Co.'s financial guaranty direct and assumed businesses provide credit protection on public finance, infrastructure and structured finance obligations.

Recent Developments: For the quarter ended Sep 30 2017, net income decreased 56.6% to US$208.0 million from US$479.0 million in the year-earlier quarter. Revenues were US$623.0 million, up 10.1% from US$566.0 million the year before. Net premiums earned were US$186.0 million versus US$231.0 million in the prior-year quarter, a decrease of 19.5%. Net investment income rose 5.3% to US$99.0 million from US$94.0 million a year ago.

Prospects: Our evaluation of Assured Guaranty Ltd. as of Sep. 17, 2017 is the result of our systematic analysis on three basic characteristics: earnings strength, relative valuation, and recent stock price movement. The company has suffered a very negative trend in earnings per share over the past 5 quarters and while recent estimates for the company have been mixed, AGO has posted better than expected results. Based on operating earnings yield, the company is undervalued when compared to all of the companies in our coverage universe. Share price changes over the past year indicates that AGO will perform very well over the near term.

Financial Data
(US$ in Thousands)

	9 Mos	6 Mos	3 Mos	12/31/2016	12/31/2015	12/31/2014	12/31/2013	12/31/2012
Earnings Per Share	6.95	8.83	8.68	6.56	7.08	6.26	4.30	0.57
Cash Flow Per Share	3.40	0.86	0.41	(1.06)	(0.35)	3.34	1.31	(0.87)
Tang Book Value Per Share	58.32	56.41	53.95	50.82	43.96	36.37	28.08	25.74
Dividends Per Share	0.558	0.545	0.532	0.520	0.480	0.440	0.400	0.360
Dividend Payout %	8.02	6.17	6.13	7.93	6.78	7.03	9.30	63.16
Income Statement								
Total Revenue	1,458,000	835,000	527,000	1,677,000	2,207,000	1,994,000	1,608,000	973,000
Income Before Taxes	835,000	522,000	372,000	1,017,000	1,431,000	1,531,000	1,142,000	132,000
Income Taxes	157,000	52,000	55,000	136,000	375,000	443,000	334,000	22,000
Net Income	678,000	470,000	317,000	881,000	1,056,000	1,088,000	808,000	110,000
Average Shares	120,700	122,700	127,100	134,100	149,000	173,600	187,600	190,700
Balance Sheet								
Total Assets	14,649,000	14,655,000	14,675,000	14,151,000	14,544,000	14,925,000	16,287,000	17,242,000
Total Liabilities	7,771,000	7,905,000	8,038,000	7,647,000	8,481,000	9,167,000	11,172,000	12,248,000
Stockholders' Equity	6,878,000	6,750,000	6,637,000	6,504,000	6,063,000	5,758,000	5,115,000	4,994,000
Shares Outstanding	117,937	119,668	123,028	127,988	137,928	158,306	182,177	194,003
Statistical Record								
Return on Assets %	5.97	7.97	7.82	6.12	7.17	6.97	4.82	0.62
Return on Equity %	12.95	17.63	17.87	13.98	17.87	20.01	15.99	2.26
Net Margin %	46.50	56.29	60.15	52.53	47.85	54.56	50.25	11.31
Asset Turnover	0.13	0.13	0.13	0.12	0.15	0.13	0.10	0.05
Price Range	45.38-27.61	42.38-24.90	42.38-23.51	38.86-22.04	29.52-23.62	26.65-20.73	24.65-14.23	18.98-11.26
P/E Ratio	6.53-3.97	4.80-2.82	4.88-2.71	5.92-3.36	4.17-3.34	4.26-3.31	5.73-3.31	33.30-19.75
Average Yield %	1.44	1.57	1.70	1.87	1.82	1.84	1.93	2.53

Address: 30 Woodbourne Avenue, Hamilton, HM 08	**Web Site:** www.assuredguaranty.com	**Auditors:** PricewaterhouseCoopers LLP
Telephone: 441-279-5700	**Officers:** Robin Monro-Davies - Chairman Dominic J. Frederico - President, Chief Executive Officer	**Investor Contact:** 441-279-5700
Fax: 441-279-5701		**Transfer Agents:** Mellon Investor Services LLC

AT&T INC

Exchange	Symbol	Price	52Wk Range	Yield	P/E	Div Achiever
NYS	T	$38.88 (12/29/2017)	43.02-32.86	5.14	18.69	32 Years

*7 Year Price Score 86.38 *NYSE Composite Index=100 *12 Month Price Score 88.04

Interim Earnings (Per Share)

Qtr.	Mar	Jun	Sep	Dec
2014	0.70	0.68	0.58	(0.76)
2015	0.61	0.58	0.50	0.66
2016	0.61	0.55	0.54	0.40
2017	0.56	0.63	0.49	...

Interim Dividends (Per Share)

Amt	Decl	Ex	Rec	Pay
0.49Q	03/31/2017	04/06/2017	04/10/2017	05/01/2017
0.49Q	06/30/2017	07/06/2017	07/10/2017	08/01/2017
0.49Q	09/29/2017	10/06/2017	10/10/2017	11/01/2017
0.50Q	12/15/2017	01/09/2018	01/10/2018	02/01/2018

Indicated Div: $2.00 (Div. Reinv. Plan)

Valuation Analysis / Institutional Holding

Forecast EPS	$2.92	No of Institutions
(01/18/2018)		2720
Market Cap	$238.7 Billion	Shares
Book Value	$125.0 Billion	4,221,453,568
Price/Book	1.91	% Held
Price/Sales	1.49	N/A

Business Summary: Services (MIC: 6.1.2 SIC: 4813 NAIC: 517110)

AT&T is a holding company. Co.'s subsidiaries and affiliates operate in the communications and digital entertainment services industry, providing services and equipment that deliver voice, video and broadband services domestically and internationally. The services and products that Co. offer vary by market, and include: wireless communications, data/broadband and internet services, digital video services, local and long-distance telephone services, telecommunications equipment, managed networking, and wholesale services. Co. also owns and operates regional TV sports networks and a network dedicated to game-related programming as well as internet interactive game playing.

Recent Developments: For the quarter ended Sep 30 2017, net income decreased 8.6% to US$3.12 billion from US$3.42 billion in the year-earlier quarter. Revenues were US$39.67 billion, down 3.0% from US$40.89 billion the year before. Operating income was US$6.40 billion versus US$6.41 billion in the prior-year quarter, a decrease of 0.1%. Direct operating expenses rose 0.1% to US$18.91 billion from US$18.89 billion in the comparable period the year before. Indirect operating expenses decreased 7.9% to US$14.36 billion from US$15.59 billion in the equivalent prior-year period.

Prospects: Our evaluation of AT&T Inc. as of Jan. 14, 2018 is the result of our systematic analysis on three basic characteristics: earnings strength, relative valuation, and recent stock price movement. The company has managed to produce a neutral trend in earnings per share over the past 5 quarters and while recent estimates for the company have been mixed, T has posted results that fell short of analysts expectations. Based on operating earnings yield, the company is undervalued when compared to all of the companies in our coverage universe. Share price changes over the past year indicates that T will perform in line with the market over the near term.

Financial Data

(US$ in Thousands)	9 Mos	6 Mos	3 Mos	12/31/2016	12/31/2015	12/31/2014	12/31/2013	12/31/2012
Earnings Per Share	2.08	2.13	2.05	2.10	2.37	1.19	3.39	1.25
Cash Flow Per Share	6.40	6.37	6.59	6.36	6.38	6.02	6.48	6.73
Dividends Per Share	1.950	1.940	1.930	1.920	1.880	1.840	1.800	1.760
Dividend Payout %	93.75	91.08	94.15	91.43	79.32	154.62	53.10	140.80
Income Statement								
Total Revenue	118,870,000	79,202,000	39,365,000	163,786,000	146,801,000	132,447,000	128,752,000	127,434,000
EBITDA	39,260,000	26,569,000	12,971,000	45,285,000	44,022,000	31,171,000	48,797,000	30,064,000
Depn & Amortn	18,316,000	12,274,000	6,127,000	20,661,000	19,289,000	17,773,000	17,722,000	16,933,000
Income Before Taxes	16,570,000	11,607,000	5,551,000	19,714,000	20,613,000	9,785,000	27,135,000	9,687,000
Income Taxes	5,711,000	3,860,000	1,804,000	6,479,000	7,005,000	3,442,000	9,224,000	2,900,000
Net Income	10,413,000	7,384,000	3,469,000	12,976,000	13,345,000	6,224,000	18,249,000	7,264,000
Average Shares	6,181,999	6,183,999	6,185,999	6,188,999	5,645,999	5,220,999	5,384,999	5,820,999
Balance Sheet								
Current Assets	76,357,000	53,547,000	45,727,000	38,369,000	35,992,000	32,028,000	23,196,000	22,706,000
Total Assets	443,865,000	420,795,000	411,903,000	403,821,000	402,672,000	292,829,000	277,787,000	272,315,000
Current Liabilities	47,693,000	48,012,000	50,690,000	50,576,000	47,816,000	37,282,000	34,995,000	31,787,000
Long-Term Obligations	154,728,000	132,824,000	120,568,000	113,681,000	118,515,000	76,011,000	69,290,000	66,358,000
Total Liabilities	318,905,000	296,070,000	288,062,000	280,686,000	280,001,000	206,459,000	186,799,000	179,953,000
Stockholders' Equity	124,960,000	124,725,000	123,841,000	123,135,000	122,671,000	86,370,000	90,988,000	92,362,000
Shares Outstanding	6,139,333	6,139,781	6,147,489	6,138,993	6,144,939	5,186,912	5,226,315	5,581,394
Statistical Record								
Return on Assets %	3.03	3.20	3.10	3.21	3.84	2.18	6.63	2.67
Return on Equity %	10.34	10.60	10.23	10.53	12.77	7.02	19.91	7.32
EBITDA Margin %	33.03	33.55	32.95	27.65	29.99	23.53	37.90	23.59
Net Margin %	8.76	9.32	8.81	7.92	9.09	4.70	14.17	5.70
Asset Turnover	0.38	0.39	0.40	0.41	0.42	0.46	0.47	0.47
Current Ratio	1.60	1.12	0.90	0.76	0.75	0.86	0.66	0.71
Debt to Equity	1.24	1.06	0.97	0.92	0.97	0.88	0.76	0.72
Price Range	43.02-35.59	43.47-36.13	43.47-36.13	43.47-33.51	36.18-31.80	36.74-31.86	39.00-33.11	38.34-29.16
P/E Ratio	20.68-17.11	20.41-16.96	21.20-17.62	20.70-15.96	15.27-13.42	30.87-26.77	11.50-9.77	30.67-23.33
Average Yield %	4.96	4.80	4.77	4.89	5.56	5.32	5.08	5.20

Address: 208 S. Akard St., Dallas, TX 75202	Web Site: www.att.com	Auditors: Ernst & Young LLP
Telephone: 210-821-4105	Officers: Randall L. Stephenson - Chairman, President, Chief Executive Officer, Senior Executive Vice President, Chief Financial Officer, Chief Operating Officer John Joseph Stephens - Senior Executive Vice President, Chief Financial Officer	Investor Contact: 210-351-2058 Transfer Agents: Computershare Trust Company, N.A, Providence, RI

ATMOS ENERGY CORP.

Exchange	Symbol	Price	52Wk Range	Yield	P/E	Div Achiever
NYS	ATO	$85.89 (12/29/2017)	92.29-73.21	2.26	23.03	29 Years

*7 Year Price Score 122.41 *NYSE Composite Index=100 *12 Month Price Score 100.84

Interim Earnings (Per Share)

Qtr.	Dec	Mar	Jun	Sep
2012-13	0.88	1.27	0.42	0.07
2013-14	0.95	1.38	0.45	0.18
2014-15	0.96	1.35	0.55	0.23
2015-16	1.00	1.38	0.69	0.32
2016-17	1.19	1.55	0.67	0.33

Interim Dividends (Per Share)

Amt	Decl	Ex	Rec	Pay
0.45Q	02/07/2017	02/23/2017	02/27/2017	03/13/2017
0.45Q	05/03/2017	05/18/2017	05/22/2017	06/05/2017
0.45Q	08/02/2017	08/17/2017	08/21/2017	09/05/2017
0.485Q	11/08/2017	11/24/2017	11/27/2017	12/11/2017

Indicated Div: $1.94 (Div. Reinv. Plan)

Valuation Analysis

Institutional Holding	
Forecast EPS	$3.82 (01/18/2018)
Market Cap	$9.1 Billion
Book Value	$3.9 Billion
Price/Book	2.34
Price/Sales	3.30

No of Institutions 551
Shares 96,031,032
% Held 71.55

TRADING VOLUME (thousand shares)

Business Summary: Gas Utilities (MIC: 3.3.1 SIC: 4924 NAIC: 221210)

Atmos Energy is engaged in the regulated natural gas distribution and pipeline and storage businesses. Co. operates in the following segments: distribution, which is primarily comprised of its regulated natural gas distribution and related sales operations in eight states and storage assets located in Kentucky and Tennessee; and pipeline and storage, which is comprised primarily of the pipeline and storage operations of its Atmos Pipeline-Texas division and its natural gas transmission operations in Louisiana. As of Sep 30 2017, Co. delivered natural gas to over 3.0 million residential, commercial, public authority and industrial customers in eight states located primarily in the South.

Recent Developments: For the year ended Sep 30 2017, income from continuing operations increased 10.8% to US$382.7 million from US$345.5 million a year earlier. Net income increased 13.2% to US$396.4 million from US$350.1 million in the prior year. Revenues were US$2.76 billion, up 12.4% from US$2.45 billion the year before. Operating income was US$727.5 million versus US$657.2 million in the prior year, an increase of 10.7%. Direct operating expenses rose 24.0% to US$925.5 million from US$746.2 million in the comparable period the year before. Indirect operating expenses increased 5.3% to US$1.11 billion from US$1.05 billion in the equivalent prior-year period.

Prospects: Our evaluation of Atmos Energy Corp. as of Jan. 14, 2018 is the result of our systematic analysis on three basic characteristics: earnings strength, relative valuation, and recent stock price movement. The company has managed to produce a neutral trend in earnings per share over the past 5 quarters. However, while recent estimates for the company have been mixed, ATO has posted results that fell short of analysts expectations. Based on operating earnings yield, the company is undervalued when compared to all of the companies in our coverage universe. Share price changes over the past year indicates that ATO will perform very well over the near term.

Financial Data
(US$ in Thousands)

	09/30/2017	09/30/2016	09/30/2015	09/30/2014	09/30/2013	09/30/2012	09/30/2011	09/30/2010
Earnings Per Share	3.73	3.38	3.09	2.96	2.64	2.37	2.27	2.20
Cash Flow Per Share	8.17	7.66	8.21	7.58	6.77	6.49	6.46	7.91
Tang Book Value Per Share	29.86	26.17	24.16	23.35	20.29	17.93	16.78	15.95
Dividends Per Share	1.800	1.680	1.560	1.480	1.400	1.380	1.360	1.340
Dividend Payout %	48.26	49.70	50.49	50.00	53.03	58.23	59.91	60.91
Income Statement								
Total Revenue	2,759,735	3,349,949	4,142,136	4,940,916	3,886,257	3,438,483	4,347,634	4,789,690
EBITDA	1,043,909	959,521	903,011	861,070	739,289	678,173	696,781	706,230
Depn & Amortn	319,633	293,096	276,005	254,956	237,607	246,577	233,383	217,133
Income Before Taxes	604,094	550,477	510,765	476,819	373,297	290,422	312,573	334,626
Income Taxes	221,383	200,373	195,690	187,002	142,599	98,226	113,689	128,787
Net Income	396,421	350,104	315,075	289,817	243,194	216,717	207,601	205,839
Average Shares	106,100	103,524	101,892	97,608	91,711	91,172	90,652	92,422
Balance Sheet								
Current Assets	539,646	681,686	630,985	775,840	683,266	827,962	1,010,953	875,192
Total Assets	10,749,596	10,010,889	9,092,945	8,594,704	7,940,401	7,495,675	7,282,871	6,763,791
Current Liabilities	1,013,443	1,788,281	1,154,823	910,650	978,486	1,275,954	867,598	1,166,079
Long-Term Obligations	3,067,045	2,188,779	2,455,388	2,455,986	2,455,671	1,956,305	2,206,117	1,809,551
Total Liabilities	6,850,930	6,547,830	5,898,148	5,508,472	5,359,992	5,136,432	5,027,450	4,585,443
Stockholders' Equity	3,898,666	3,463,059	3,194,797	3,086,232	2,580,409	2,359,243	2,255,421	2,178,348
Shares Outstanding	106,104	103,930	101,478	100,388	90,640	90,239	90,296	90,164
Statistical Record								
Return on Assets %	3.82	3.66	3.56	3.51	3.15	2.92	2.96	3.14
Return on Equity %	10.77	10.49	10.03	10.23	9.85	9.37	9.36	9.45
EBITDA Margin %	37.83	28.64	21.80	17.43	19.02	19.72	16.03	14.74
Net Margin %	14.36	10.45	7.61	5.87	6.26	6.30	4.78	4.30
Asset Turnover	0.27	0.35	0.47	0.60	0.50	0.46	0.62	0.73
Current Ratio	0.53	0.38	0.55	0.85	0.70	0.65	1.17	0.75
Debt to Equity	0.79	0.63	0.77	0.80	0.95	0.83	0.98	0.83
Price Range	88.69-68.96	81.32-57.82	58.81-47.35	53.40-41.08	45.19-33.20	36.94-30.60	34.98-28.87	30.06-26.41
P/E Ratio	23.78-18.49	24.06-17.11	19.03-15.32	18.04-13.88	17.12-12.58	15.59-12.91	15.41-12.72	13.66-12.00
Average Yield %	2.27	2.39	2.89	3.11	3.52	4.11	4.20	4.70

Address: Three Lincoln Centre, Suite 1800, 5430 LBJ Freeway, Dallas, TX 75240	Web Site: www.atmosenergy.com	Auditors: Ernst & Young LLP
Telephone: 972-934-9227	Officers: Kim R. Cocklin - Executive Chairman, President, Chief Executive Officer Michael E. Haefner - President, Chief Executive Officer, Chief Operating Officer, Executive Vice President, Senior Vice President	Investor Contact: 972-855-3729
Fax: 972-855-3075		Transfer Agents: American Stock Transfer & Trust Company, New York, NY

AUTOLIV INC.

Exchange	Symbol	Price	52Wk Range	Yield	P/E
NYS	ALV	$127.08 (12/29/2017)	129.61-96.27	1.89	21.87

*7 Year Price Score 96.42   *NYSE Composite Index=100   *12 Month Price Score 104.74

Interim Earnings (Per Share)

Qtr.	Mar	Jun	Sep	Dec
2014	1.38	0.89	1.16	1.63
2015	0.40	1.55	1.12	2.10
2016	1.51	1.68	1.56	1.68
2017	1.62	1.47	1.04	...

Interim Dividends (Per Share)

Amt	Decl	Ex	Rec	Pay
0.60Q	02/20/2017	05/15/2017	05/17/2017	06/01/2017
0.60Q	05/09/2017	08/21/2017	08/23/2017	09/07/2017
0.60Q	08/14/2017	11/21/2017	11/22/2017	12/07/2017
0.60Q	12/12/2017	02/21/2018	02/22/2018	03/08/2018

Indicated Div: $2.40

Valuation Analysis   **Institutional Holding**

Forecast EPS	$6.29 (01/18/2018)	No of Institutions 393
Market Cap	$11.1 Billion	Shares 41,348,660
Book Value	$4.0 Billion	% Held 31.61
Price/Book	2.79	
Price/Sales	1.08	

Business Summary: Auto Parts (MIC: 1.8.2 SIC: 3714 NAIC: 336399)

Autoliv is a holding company. Through its subsidiaries, Co. is a supplier of automotive safety systems with a range of product offerings, including passive safety systems and active safety systems that are sold within its two operating segments: Passive Safety and Electronics. Passive safety products include modules and components for passenger and driver-side airbags, side-impact airbag protection systems, seatbelts, steering wheels, inflator technologies, whiplash protection systems and child seats, and components for such systems as well as passive safety electronic products such as restraint electronics and crash sensors. Active safety products include camera-based vision systems.

Recent Developments: For the quarter ended Sep 30 2017, net income decreased 34.9% to US$88.2 million from US$135.5 million in the year-earlier quarter. Revenues were US$2.50 billion, up 1.6% from US$2.46 billion the year before. Operating income was US$158.7 million versus US$191.1 million in the prior-year quarter, a decrease of 17.0%. Direct operating expenses rose 1.5% to US$2.00 billion from US$1.97 billion in the comparable period the year before. Indirect operating expenses increased 13.6% to US$345.6 million from US$304.2 million in the equivalent prior-year period.

Prospects: Our evaluation of Autoliv Inc. as of Jan. 14, 2018 is the result of our systematic analysis on three basic characteristics: earnings strength, relative valuation, and recent stock price movement. The company has generated a negative trend in earnings per share over the past 5 quarters and while recent estimates for the company have been mixed, ALV has posted better than expected results. Based on operating earnings yield, the company is undervalued when compared to all of the companies in our coverage universe. Share price changes over the past year indicates that ALV will perform in line with the market over the near term.

Financial Data (US$ in Thousands)	9 Mos	6 Mos	3 Mos	12/31/2016	12/31/2015	12/31/2014	12/31/2013	12/31/2012
Earnings Per Share	5.81	6.33	6.54	6.42	5.17	5.06	5.07	5.08
Cash Flow Per Share	9.67	10.17	9.25	9.82	8.51	7.74	8.77	7.34
Tang Book Value Per Share	21.67	20.51	20.13	18.07	18.86	19.90	24.30	21.48
Dividends Per Share	2.360	2.340	2.320	2.300	2.220	2.120	2.000	1.890
Dividend Payout %	40.62	36.97	35.47	35.83	42.94	41.90	39.45	37.20
Income Statement								
Total Revenue	7,653,400	5,153,000	2,608,100	10,073,600	9,169,600	9,240,500	8,803,400	8,266,700
EBITDA	612,600	448,400	229,900	1,242,100	1,052,400	1,024,100	1,041,700	972,000
Depn & Amortn	38,000	29,200	21,800	383,000	319,000	305,400	286,000	273,200
Income Before Taxes	533,600	391,700	193,900	801,200	671,000	660,100	726,700	660,500
Income Taxes	158,500	114,200	52,300	242,200	218,200	198,000	244,100	183,000
Net Income	364,500	273,700	143,900	567,100	456,800	467,800	485,800	483,100
Average Shares	87,200	88,100	88,500	88,400	88,400	92,400	95,900	95,100
Balance Sheet								
Current Assets	4,122,400	4,047,500	4,329,000	4,140,900	4,038,300	4,136,200	3,700,400	3,289,200
Total Assets	8,585,200	8,443,700	8,517,500	8,234,400	7,525,500	7,442,900	6,983,000	6,570,300
Current Liabilities	2,666,000	2,622,600	2,701,300	2,597,600	2,226,400	2,138,600	2,428,500	1,849,800
Long-Term Obligations	1,322,600	1,323,100	1,323,700	1,323,600	1,499,400	1,521,200	279,100	562,900
Total Liabilities	4,626,600	4,584,400	4,663,800	4,557,200	4,069,900	4,015,800	3,001,700	2,811,700
Stockholders' Equity	3,958,600	3,859,700	3,853,700	3,677,200	3,455,600	3,427,100	3,981,300	3,758,600
Shares Outstanding	86,953	86,913	88,300	88,230	88,107	88,726	94,396	95,500
Statistical Record								
Return on Assets %	6.07	6.70	6.94	7.18	6.10	6.49	7.17	7.59
Return on Equity %	13.27	14.84	15.50	15.86	13.27	12.63	12.55	13.59
EBITDA Margin %	8.00	8.70	8.81	12.33	11.48	11.08	11.83	11.76
Net Margin %	4.76	5.31	5.52	5.63	4.98	5.06	5.52	5.84
Asset Turnover	1.21	1.22	1.23	1.27	1.23	1.28	1.30	1.30
Current Ratio	1.55	1.54	1.60	1.59	1.81	1.93	1.52	1.78
Debt to Equity	0.33	0.34	0.34	0.36	0.43	0.44	0.07	0.15
Price Range	127.15-94.29	116.39-94.29	125.77-94.29	125.77-94.29	130.81-96.57	108.03-86.27	94.41-64.13	69.05-51.89
P/E Ratio	21.88-16.23	18.39-14.90	19.23-14.42	19.59-14.69	25.30-18.68	21.35-17.05	18.62-12.65	13.59-10.21
Average Yield %	2.20	2.22	2.13	2.10	1.94	2.14	2.53	3.10

Address: Klarabergsviadukten 70, Section B,7th Floor, Box 70381, Stockholm, SE-107 24 Telephone: 858-720-600	Web Site: www.autoliv.com Officers: Jan Carlson - Interim Chairman, President, Chief Executive Officer Mats Backman - Chief Financial Officer, Division Officer	Auditors: Ernst & Young AB Investor Contact: 248-223-8107 Transfer Agents: Computershare Trust Company, N.A., Providence, RI

AUTONATION, INC.

Exchange	Symbol	Price	52Wk Range	Yield	P/E
NYS	AN	$51.33 (12/29/2017)	56.25-38.72	N/A	12.96

*7 Year Price Score 76.16 *NYSE Composite Index=100 *12 Month Price Score 108.33

Interim Earnings (Per Share)

Qtr.	Mar	Jun	Sep	Dec
2014	0.78	0.83	0.90	1.01
2015	0.97	1.00	1.04	0.88
2016	0.89	1.08	1.05	1.13
2017	0.97	0.86	1.00	...

Interim Dividends (Per Share)

No Dividends Paid

Valuation Analysis

	Institutional Holding	
Forecast EPS	$3.77	No of Institutions
(01/26/2018)		442
Market Cap	$4.7 Billion	Shares
Book Value	$2.2 Billion	94,928,240
Price/Book	2.13	% Held
Price/Sales	0.22	51.31

TRADING VOLUME (thousand shares)

Business Summary: Retail - Automotive (MIC: 2.1.4 SIC: 5511 NAIC: 441110)

AutoNation, through its subsidiaries, is an automotive retailer. Co. provides a range of automotive products and services, including new vehicles, used vehicles, parts and service, which includes automotive repair and maintenance services as well as wholesale parts and collision businesses, and automotive finance and insurance products, which include vehicle service and other protection products, as well as the arranging of financing for vehicle purchases through third-party finance sources. As of Dec 31 2016, Co. owned and operated 371 new vehicle franchises from 260 stores located in the U.S. As of Dec 31 2016, Co. had three reportable segments: Domestic, Import, and Premium Luxury.

Recent Developments: For the quarter ended Sep 30 2017, income from continuing operations decreased 9.5% to US$97.6 million from US$107.8 million in the year-earlier quarter. Net income decreased 9.1% to US$97.5 million from US$107.3 million in the year-earlier quarter. Revenues were US$5.43 billion, down 2.4% from US$5.57 billion the year before. Operating income was US$211.2 million versus US$219.0 million in the prior-year quarter, a decrease of 3.6%. Direct operating expenses declined 3.1% to US$4.59 billion from US$4.73 billion in the comparable period the year before. Indirect operating expenses increased 2.8% to US$634.7 million from US$617.4 million in the equivalent prior-year period.

Prospects: Our evaluation of AutoNation Inc. as of Jan. 21, 2018 is the result of our systematic analysis on three basic characteristics: earnings strength, relative valuation, and recent stock price movement. The company has managed to produce a neutral trend in earnings per share over the past 5 quarters. However, while recent estimates for the company have been mixed, AN has posted better than expected results. Based on operating earnings yield, the company is undervalued when compared to all of the companies in our coverage universe. Share price changes over the past year indicates that AN will perform very poorly over the near term.

Financial Data

(US$ in Thousands)	9 Mos	6 Mos	3 Mos	12/31/2016	12/31/2015	12/31/2014	12/31/2013	12/31/2012
Earnings Per Share	3.96	4.01	4.23	4.15	3.89	3.52	3.04	2.52
Cash Flow Per Share	5.08	5.20	4.98	4.99	4.50	4.14	3.99	2.55
Tang Book Value Per Share	0.60	3.54	3.14	1.99	4.65	3.55	3.86	1.32
Income Statement								
Total Revenue	15,851,100	10,418,700	5,139,400	21,609,000	20,862,000	19,108,800	17,517,600	15,668,800
EBITDA	624,700	410,500	211,100	1,042,000	1,003,900	934,700	846,900	741,800
Depn & Amortn	4,200	2,800	1,400	148,800	132,100	112,600	101,000	92,900
Income Before Taxes	462,600	304,700	159,800	702,300	722,700	682,300	604,400	516,800
Income Taxes	179,100	118,800	61,600	270,600	279,000	262,500	228,600	199,500
Net Income	283,300	185,800	98,100	430,500	442,600	418,700	374,900	316,400
Average Shares	97,700	101,500	101,600	103,800	113,900	118,900	123,300	125,800
Balance Sheet								
Current Assets	4,450,100	4,646,200	4,676,800	4,714,800	4,711,400	3,999,200	3,830,000	3,361,100
Total Assets	9,954,800	10,149,700	10,092,700	10,060,000	9,558,300	8,399,700	7,914,100	7,203,000
Current Liabilities	6,128,100	6,108,500	5,722,500	5,829,200	5,169,100	3,882,600	3,751,800	3,201,700
Long-Term Obligations	1,295,500	1,216,100	1,615,800	1,611,100	1,753,700	2,103,400	1,809,800	2,066,300
Total Liabilities	7,754,600	7,651,100	7,658,500	7,749,700	7,209,000	6,327,600	5,852,400	5,514,500
Stockholders' Equity	2,200,500	2,498,600	2,434,200	2,310,300	2,349,300	2,072,100	2,061,700	1,688,500
Shares Outstanding	91,244	100,437	101,292	100,652	110,804	113,313	120,915	120,856
Statistical Record								
Return on Assets %	4.06	4.10	4.31	4.38	4.93	5.13	4.96	4.71
Return on Equity %	18.03	17.54	19.13	18.43	20.02	20.26	19.99	17.61
EBITDA Margin %	3.94	3.94	4.11	4.82	4.81	4.89	4.83	4.73
Net Margin %	1.79	1.78	1.91	1.99	2.12	2.19	2.14	2.02
Asset Turnover	2.17	2.15	2.15	2.20	2.32	2.34	2.32	2.33
Current Ratio	0.73	0.76	0.82	0.81	0.91	1.03	1.02	1.05
Debt to Equity	0.59	0.49	0.66	0.70	0.75	1.02	0.88	1.22
Price Range	53.12-38.72	53.35-38.90	53.35-40.26	59.66-40.26	66.20-56.12	61.23-46.84	54.10-39.59	48.45-32.54
P/E Ratio	13.41-9.78	13.30-9.70	12.61-9.52	14.38-9.70	17.02-14.43	17.39-13.31	17.80-13.02	19.23-12.91

Address: 200 S.W. 1st Avenue, Fort Lauderdale, FL 33301 Telephone: 954-769-6000	Web Site: www.autonation.com Officers: Michael J. (Mike) Jackson - Chairman, President, Chief Executive Officer Marc K. Cannon - Executive Vice President, Chief Marketing Officer	Auditors: KPMG LLP Investor Contact: 954-769-7342 Transfer Agents: Computershare Trust Company, N.A.

AUTOZONE, INC.

Exchange	Symbol	Price	52Wk Range	Yield	P/E
NYS	AZO	$711.37 (12/29/2017)	793.68-493.15	N/A	15.90

*7 Year Price Score 94.60   *NYSE Composite Index=100   *12 Month Price Score 98.01

TRADING VOLUME (thousand shares)

Interim Earnings (Per Share)

Qtr.	Nov	Feb	Apr	Aug
2014-15	7.27	6.51	9.57	12.70
2015-16	8.29	7.43	10.77	14.24
2016-17	9.36	8.08	11.44	15.21
2017-18	10.00	...	...	...

Interim Dividends (Per Share)

No Dividends Paid

Valuation Analysis   Institutional Holding

Forecast EPS	$47.73	No of Institutions
	(01/24/2018)	812
Market Cap	$19.4 Billion	Shares
Book Value	N/A	32,676,692
Price/Book	N/A	% Held
Price/Sales	1.76	71.72

Business Summary: Retail - Automotive (MIC: 2.1.4 SIC: 5531 NAIC: 441310)

AutoZone is a retailer and a distributor of automotive replacement parts and accessories. At Aug 26 2017, Co. operated 5,465 stores in the U.S., including Puerto Rico; 524 stores in Mexico; 14 stores in Brazil; and 26 Interamerican Motor Corporation branches. Each AutoZone store carries a product line for cars, sport utility vehicles, vans and light trucks, including new and remanufactured automotive hard parts, maintenance items, accessories and non-automotive products. Co. also has commercial programs in AutoZone stores in Mexico and Brazil. Co. also sells the AALLDATA brand automotive diagnostic and repair software through www.alldata.com and www.alldatadiy.com.

Recent Developments: For the quarter ended Nov 18 2017, net income increased 1.0% to US$281.0 million from US$278.1 million in the year-earlier quarter. Revenues were US$2.59 billion, up 4.9% from US$2.47 billion the year before. Operating income was US$468.8 million versus US$458.9 million in the prior-year quarter, an increase of 2.1%. Direct operating expenses rose 4.9% to US$1.22 billion from US$1.17 billion in the comparable period the year before. Indirect operating expenses increased 6.5% to US$897.1 million from US$842.6 million in the equivalent prior-year period.

Prospects: Our evaluation of AutoZone Inc. as of Jan. 21, 2018 is the result of our systematic analysis on three basic characteristics: earnings strength, relative valuation, and recent stock price movement. The company has managed to produce a neutral trend in earnings per share over the past 5 quarters and while recent estimates for the company have been raised by analysts, AZO has posted better than expected results. Based on operating earnings yield, the company is undervalued when compared to all of the companies in our coverage universe. Share price changes over the past year indicates that AZO will perform very poorly over the near term.

Financial Data

(US$ in Thousands)	3 Mos	08/26/2017	08/27/2016	08/29/2015	08/30/2014	08/31/2013	08/25/2012	08/27/2011
Earnings Per Share	44.73	44.07	40.70	36.03	31.57	27.79	23.48	19.47
Cash Flow Per Share	62.56	55.40	52.92	48.46	40.43	38.73	31.72	30.38
Income Statement								
Total Revenue	2,589,131	10,888,676	10,635,676	10,187,340	9,475,313	9,147,530	8,603,863	8,072,973
EBITDA	470,753	2,411,489	2,365,772	2,229,200	2,088,346	2,008,588	1,848,788	1,699,974
Depn & Amortn	1,999	331,420	305,377	276,149	258,123	235,490	219,897	205,171
Income Before Taxes	429,865	1,925,489	1,912,714	1,802,612	1,662,714	1,587,683	1,452,986	1,324,246
Income Taxes	148,862	644,620	671,707	642,371	592,970	571,203	522,613	475,272
Net Income	281,003	1,280,869	1,241,007	1,160,241	1,069,744	1,016,480	930,373	848,974
Average Shares	28,096	29,065	30,488	32,206	33,882	36,581	39,625	43,603
Balance Sheet								
Current Assets	4,717,192	4,611,255	4,239,573	3,970,294	3,580,612	3,278,013	2,978,946	2,792,425
Total Assets	9,397,084	9,259,781	8,599,787	8,102,349	7,517,858	6,892,089	6,265,639	5,869,602
Current Liabilities	5,067,640	4,766,301	4,690,320	4,712,873	4,541,094	4,169,150	3,655,592	3,430,896
Long-Term Obligations	4,982,984	5,081,238	4,924,119	4,624,876	4,162,890	4,013,267	3,718,302	3,317,600
Total Liabilities	10,922,183	10,688,158	10,387,325	9,803,739	9,139,715	8,579,408	7,813,664	7,123,834
Stockholders' Equity	(1,525,099)	(1,428,377)	(1,787,538)	(1,701,390)	(1,621,857)	(1,687,319)	(1,548,025)	(1,254,232)
Shares Outstanding	27,262	27,833	29,118	30,659	32,304	34,293	37,028	40,109
Statistical Record								
Return on Assets %	14.15	14.38	14.90	14.90	14.89	15.20	15.38	14.88
EBITDA Margin %	18.18	22.15	22.24	21.88	22.04	21.96	21.49	21.06
Net Margin %	10.85	11.76	11.67	11.39	11.29	11.11	10.81	10.52
Asset Turnover	1.21	1.22	1.28	1.31	1.32	1.37	1.42	1.42
Current Ratio	0.93	0.97	0.90	0.84	0.79	0.79	0.81	0.81
Price Range	809.87-493.15	809.87-493.15	815.98-695.46	750.13-501.78	543.84-411.89	448.58-344.99	397.13-307.00	304.10-209.78
P/E Ratio	18.11-11.03	18.38-11.19	20.05-17.09	20.82-13.93	17.23-13.05	16.14-12.41	16.91-13.07	15.62-10.77

Address: 123 South Front Street, Memphis, TN 38103 **Telephone:** 901-495-6500	**Web Site:** www.autozone.com **Officers:** William C. Rhodes - Chairman, President, Chief Executive Officer William T. Giles - Executive Vice President, Chief Financial Officer	**Auditors:** Ernst & Young LLP **Transfer Agents:** ComputerShare Investor Services, Providence, RI

AVALONBAY COMMUNITIES, INC.

Exchange	Symbol	Price	52Wk Range	Yield	P/E
NYS	AVB	$178.41 (12/29/2017)	199.10-169.61	3.18	27.88

*7 Year Price Score 94.61 *NYSE Composite Index=100 *12 Month Price Score 92.95

Interim Earnings (Per Share)

Qtr.	Mar	Jun	Sep	Dec
2014	1.09	1.21	1.83	1.07
2015	1.56	1.29	1.53	1.12
2016	1.73	1.44	2.59	1.76
2017	1.72	1.20	1.72	...

Interim Dividends (Per Share)

Amt	Decl	Ex	Rec	Pay
1.42Q	02/01/2017	03/29/2017	03/31/2017	04/17/2017
1.42Q	05/18/2017	06/28/2017	06/30/2017	07/17/2017
1.42Q	09/14/2017	09/28/2017	09/29/2017	10/16/2017
1.42Q	11/09/2017	12/28/2017	12/29/2017	01/16/2018

Indicated Div: $5.68 (Div. Reinv. Plan)

Valuation Analysis

		Institutional Holding	
Forecast EPS	$5.80	No of Institutions	683
	(01/18/2018)		
Market Cap	$24.6 Billion	Shares	162,438,848
Book Value	$10.3 Billion	% Held	96.22
Price/Book	2.38		
Price/Sales	11.61		

Business Summary: REITs (MIC: 5.3.1 SIC: 6798 NAIC: 525930)

AvalonBay Communities is a real estate investment trust. Co. focuses on the development, redevelopment, acquisition, ownership and operation of multifamily communities primarily in New England, the New York/New Jersey metro area, the Mid-Atlantic, the Pacific Northwest, and Northern and Southern California. At Jan 31 2017, Co. owned or held a direct or indirect ownership interest in 259 operating apartment communities containing 75,038 apartment homes in 10 states and the District of Columbia; 27 communities under development; and rights to develop an additional 25 communities. Co. operates its apartment communities under three core brands Avalon, AVA and Eaves by Avalon.

Recent Developments: For the quarter ended Sep 30 2017, net income decreased 33.2% to US$238.2 million from US$356.3 million in the year-earlier quarter. Revenues were US$550.5 million, up 6.6% from US$516.2 million the year before.

Prospects: Our evaluation of AvalonBay Communities Inc. as of Jan. 14, 2018 is the result of our systematic analysis on three basic characteristics: earnings strength, relative valuation, and recent stock price movement. The company has enjoyed a very positive trend in earnings per share over the past 5 quarters. Because the company lacks sufficient analyst estimate data, we place greater weight on the historical EPS trend as the measure of earnings strength. Based on operating earnings yield, the company is about fairly valued when compared to all of the companies in our coverage universe. Share price changes over the past year indicates that AVB will perform very well over the near term.

Financial Data
(US$ in Thousands)

	9 Mos	6 Mos	3 Mos	12/31/2016	12/31/2015	12/31/2014	12/31/2013	12/31/2012
Earnings Per Share	6.40	7.27	7.51	7.52	5.51	5.21	2.78	4.32
Cash Flow Per Share	8.78	8.43	8.46	8.33	7.91	6.79	5.71	5.54
Tang Book Value Per Share	74.84	74.47	74.51	74.07	71.83	68.51	66.42	59.76
Dividends Per Share	5.610	5.540	5.470	5.400	5.000	4.640	4.280	3.880
Dividend Payout %	87.66	76.20	72.84	71.81	90.74	89.06	153.96	89.81
Income Statement								
Total Revenue	1,603,337	1,052,837	522,326	2,045,255	1,856,028	1,685,061	1,462,921	1,038,660
EBITDA	1,156,532	771,768	410,569	1,687,995	1,327,114	1,143,050	815,098	640,856
Depn & Amortn	440,504	289,137	142,145	531,434	477,923	442,682	573,715	260,094
Income Before Taxes	568,890	383,234	219,129	969,051	673,576	519,750	68,981	243,842
Income Taxes	102	78	20	305	1,861	9,368	...	...
Net Income	639,348	401,100	235,875	1,034,002	742,038	683,567	353,141	423,869
Average Shares	138,307	138,173	137,531	137,461	134,593	131,237	127,265	98,025
Balance Sheet								
Current Assets	217,111	293,153	368,720	362,048	535,405	634,702	406,694	2,808,399
Total Assets	18,177,837	17,943,745	17,978,421	17,867,271	16,931,305	16,176,723	15,328,143	11,160,078
Current Liabilities	396,022	384,670	403,655	280,727	264,474	244,027	227,314	182,648
Long-Term Obligations	7,128,030	6,991,759	7,005,729	7,030,880	6,456,948	6,525,852	6,145,391	3,851,033
Total Liabilities	7,844,024	7,661,333	7,711,799	7,695,855	7,090,779	7,130,318	6,732,011	4,322,863
Stockholders' Equity	10,333,813	10,282,412	10,266,622	10,171,416	9,840,526	9,046,405	8,596,132	6,837,215
Shares Outstanding	138,086	138,083	137,786	137,330	137,002	132,050	129,416	114,403
Statistical Record								
Return on Assets %	4.93	5.66	5.89	5.93	4.48	4.34	2.67	4.30
Return on Equity %	8.66	9.93	10.26	10.31	7.86	7.75	4.58	7.53
EBITDA Margin %	72.13	73.30	78.60	82.53	71.50	67.83	55.72	61.70
Net Margin %	39.88	38.10	45.16	50.56	39.98	40.57	24.14	40.81
Asset Turnover	0.12	0.12	0.12	0.12	0.11	0.11	0.11	0.11
Current Ratio	0.55	0.76	0.91	1.29	2.02	2.60	1.79	15.38
Debt to Equity	0.69	0.68	0.68	0.69	0.66	0.72	0.71	0.56
Price Range	199.10-159.75	199.10-159.75	191.00-159.75	191.00-159.75	185.54-159.08	169.20-117.53	141.46-116.86	151.00-124.26
P/E Ratio	31.11-24.96	27.39-21.97	25.43-21.27	25.40-21.24	33.67-28.87	32.48-22.56	50.88-42.04	34.95-28.76
Average Yield %	3.09	3.08	3.09	3.06	2.91	3.26	3.30	2.81

Address: Ballston Tower, 671 N. Glebe Road, Suite 800, Arlington, VA 22203	**Web Site:** www.avalonbay.com	**Auditors:** Ernst & Young LLP
Telephone: 703-329-6300	**Officers:** Timothy J. Naughton - Chairman, President, Chief Executive Officer Leo S. Horey - Executive Vice President, Chief Administrative Officer	**Investor Contact:** 703-317-4681
Fax: 703-329-9130		**Transfer Agents:** Computershare, Pittsburgh, PA

AVANGRID INC

Exchange	Symbol	Price	52Wk Range	Yield	P/E
NYS	AGR	$50.58 (12/29/2017)	53.07-37.80	3.42	23.42

*7 Year Price Score N/A   *NYSE Composite Index=100   *12 Month Price Score 106.75

Interim Earnings (Per Share)

Qtr.	Mar	Jun	Sep	Dec
2015	0.42	0.04	0.20	0.35
2016	0.69	0.33	0.35	0.68
2017	0.77	0.39	0.32	...

Interim Dividends (Per Share)

Amt	Decl	Ex	Rec	Pay
0.432Q	02/16/2017	03/08/2017	03/10/2017	04/03/2017
0.432Q	04/20/2017	06/07/2017	06/09/2017	07/03/2017
0.432Q	07/06/2017	09/07/2017	09/08/2017	10/02/2017
0.432Q	12/01/2017	12/08/2017	12/11/2017	01/02/2018

Indicated Div: $1.73

Valuation Analysis

		Institutional Holding	
Forecast EPS	$2.25	No of Institutions	
	(01/18/2018)	260	
Market Cap	$15.6 Billion	Shares	
Book Value	$15.2 Billion	44,865,004	
Price/Book	1.03	% Held	
Price/Sales	2.64	N/A	

Business Summary: Electric Utilities (MIC: 3.1.1 SIC: 4911 NAIC: 221122)

AVANGRID is an energy services holding company. Through its subsidiaries, Co. is engaged in the regulated energy distribution, renewable energy generation and gas storage and trading businesses. Co. has three segments: Networks, which include electric transmission and distribution and natural gas distribution, transportation and sales; Renewables, which has activities relating to renewable energy, mainly wind energy generation and trading related with such activities; and Gas, which include gas trading and storage businesses. Networks delivered electricity to about 2.2 million electric utility customers and natural gas to about 992,000 natural gas public utility customers as of Dec 31 2016.

Recent Developments: For the quarter ended Sep 30 2017, net income decreased 8.3% to US$100.0 million from US$109.0 million in the year-earlier quarter. Revenues were US$1.34 billion, down 5.4% from US$1.42 billion the year before. Operating income was US$189.0 million versus US$217.0 million in the prior-year quarter, a decrease of 12.9%. Direct operating expenses declined 6.4% to US$810.0 million from US$865.0 million in the comparable period the year before. Indirect operating expenses increased 1.8% to US$342.0 million from US$336.0 million in the equivalent prior-year period.

Prospects: Our evaluation of Avangrid Inc as of Jan. 14, 2018 is the result of our systematic analysis on three basic characteristics: earnings strength, relative valuation, and recent stock price movement. The company has generated a negative trend in earnings per share over the past 5 quarters and while recent estimates for the company have been raised by analysts, AGR has posted better than expected results. Based on operating earnings yield, the company is undervalued when compared to all of the companies in our coverage universe. Share price changes over the past year indicates that AGR will perform very well over the near term.

Financial Data

(US$ in Thousands)	9 Mos	6 Mos	3 Mos	12/31/2016	12/31/2015	12/31/2014	12/31/2013	12/31/2012
Earnings Per Share	2.16	2.19	2.13	2.04	1.05	1.70	(0.30)	1.00
Cash Flow Per Share	5.39	5.10	5.19	5.03	5.35	5.48	4.84	2.98
Tang Book Value Per Share	37.39	37.45	37.47	37.05	36.85	43.25	41.38	...
Dividends Per Share	1.728	1.728	1.728	1.728	...	...	...	...
Dividend Payout %	80.00	78.90	81.13	84.71	...	...	...	...
Income Statement								
Total Revenue	4,430,000	3,089,000	1,758,000	6,018,000	4,367,000	4,594,000	4,313,000	4,055,000
EBITDA	888,000	673,000	435,000	2,056,000	1,209,000	1,512,000	752,000	849,000
Depn & Amortn	43,000	31,000	24,000	779,000	641,000	563,000	545,000	484,000
Income Before Taxes	635,000	503,000	340,000	1,009,000	301,000	706,000	(38,000)	49,000
Income Taxes	179,000	147,000	103,000	379,000	34,000	282,000	26,000	(121,000)
Net Income	458,000	359,000	239,000	630,000	267,000	424,000	(65,000)	243,000
Average Shares	309,801	309,826	309,837	309,817	254,605	243,000	243,000	243,000
Balance Sheet								
Current Assets	2,021,000	1,932,000	2,098,000	2,252,000	2,474,000	2,299,000	2,012,000	...
Total Assets	31,921,000	31,485,000	31,396,000	31,309,000	30,743,000	24,252,000	23,209,000	...
Current Liabilities	2,934,000	2,472,000	2,588,000	2,712,000	2,035,000	1,773,000	1,630,000	...
Long-Term Obligations	4,767,000	4,773,000	4,507,000	4,510,000	4,530,000	2,516,000	2,696,000	...
Total Liabilities	16,719,000	16,258,000	16,157,000	16,200,000	15,690,000	11,812,000	11,194,000	...
Stockholders' Equity	15,202,000	15,227,000	15,239,000	15,109,000	15,053,000	12,440,000	12,015,000	...
Shares Outstanding	309,005	309,005	309,069	308,993	308,864	243,000	243,000	243,000
Statistical Record								
Return on Assets %	2.13	2.18	2.12	2.03	0.97	1.79	...	...
Return on Equity %	4.40	4.46	4.33	4.17	1.94	3.47	...	...
EBITDA Margin %	20.05	21.79	24.74	34.16	27.68	32.91	17.44	20.94
Net Margin %	10.34	11.62	13.59	10.47	6.11	9.23	N.M.	5.99
Asset Turnover	0.19	0.19	0.20	0.19	0.16	0.19	...	...
Current Ratio	0.69	0.78	0.81	0.83	1.22	1.30	1.23	...
Debt to Equity	0.31	0.31	0.30	0.30	0.30	0.20	0.22	...
Price Range	48.93-35.62	46.49-35.62	46.49-35.62	46.49-35.62	38.40-33.26	...	...	...
P/E Ratio	22.65-16.49	21.23-16.26	21.83-16.72	22.79-17.46	36.57-31.68	...	...	...
Average Yield %	4.07	4.13	4.22	4.26	...	...	...	...

Address: 180 Marsh Hill Road, Orange, CT 06477
Telephone: 207-688-6000

Web Site: www.avangrid.com
Officers: Ignacio Sánchez Galán - Chairman James P. Torgerson - Chief Executive Officer

Auditors: KPMG US, LLP
Transfer Agents: Broadridge Corporate Issuer Solutions, Inc., Philadelphia, PA

AVERY DENNISON CORP

Exchange	Symbol	Price	52Wk Range	Yield	P/E
NYS	AVY	$114.86 (12/29/2017)	117.10-70.14	1.57	25.64

*7 Year Price Score 131.37 *NYSE Composite Index=100 *12 Month Price Score 116.14

Interim Earnings (Per Share)

Qtr.	Mar	Jun	Sep	Dec
2014	0.73	0.44	0.68	0.76
2015	0.77	0.68	0.88	0.61
2016	0.98	0.88	0.98	0.69
2017	1.25	1.34	1.20	...

Interim Dividends (Per Share)

Amt	Decl	Ex	Rec	Pay
0.41Q	02/01/2017	02/27/2017	03/01/2017	03/15/2017
0.45Q	04/27/2017	06/05/2017	06/07/2017	06/21/2017
0.45Q	07/27/2017	09/01/2017	09/06/2017	09/20/2017
0.45Q	10/27/2017	12/05/2017	12/06/2017	12/20/2017

Indicated Div: $1.80 (Div. Reinv. Plan)

Valuation Analysis

		Institutional Holding	
Forecast EPS	$4.93	No of Institutions	
	(01/11/2018)	728	
Market Cap	$10.1 Billion	Shares	
Book Value	$1.1 Billion	103,637,984	
Price/Book	8.91	% Held	
Price/Sales	1.57	75.65	

Business Summary: Containers & Packaging (MIC: 8.1.3 SIC: 2672 NAIC: 322222)

Avery Dennison operates in three reportable segments: Label and Graphic Materials, which manufactures and sells Fasson®-, JAC®-, and Avery Dennison®-brand pressure-sensitive label and packaging materials, Avery Dennison®- and Mactac®-brand graphics, and Avery Dennison®-brand reflective products; Retail Branding and Information Solutions, which designs, manufactures and sells a range of branding and information solutions; as well as Industrial and Healthcare Materials, which manufactures and sells Fasson®-brand and Avery Dennison®-brand tapes and fasteners, Vancive®,,¢-brand medical pressure-sensitive adhesive based materials and products, and performance polymers.

Recent Developments: For the quarter ended Sep 30 2017, net income increased 21.5% to US$108.3 million from US$89.1 million in the year-earlier quarter. Revenues were US$1.68 billion, up 11.3% from US$1.51 billion the year before. Direct operating expenses rose 12.5% to US$1.23 billion from US$1.09 billion in the comparable period the year before. Indirect operating expenses increased 5.2% to US$304.8 million from US$289.6 million in the equivalent prior-year period.

Prospects: Our evaluation of Avery Dennison Corp. as of Jan. 14, 2018 is the result of our systematic analysis on three basic characteristics: earnings strength, relative valuation, and recent stock price movement. The company has enjoyed a very positive trend in earnings per share over the past 5 quarters and while recent estimates for the company have been mixed, AVY has posted better than expected results. Based on operating earnings yield, the company is about fairly valued when compared to all of the companies in our coverage universe. Share price changes over the past year indicates that AVY will perform very well over the near term.

Financial Data

(US$ in Thousands)	9 Mos	6 Mos	3 Mos	12/31/2016	01/02/2016	01/03/2015	12/28/2013	12/29/2012
Earnings Per Share	4.48	4.26	3.80	3.54	2.95	2.60	2.16	2.08
Cash Flow Per Share	6.93	6.19	6.87	6.59	5.22	3.92	3.26	5.02
Tang Book Value Per Share	N.M.	N.M.	1.18	0.74	2.60	3.07	6.71	6.92
Dividends Per Share	1.720	1.680	1.640	1.600	1.460	1.340	1.140	1.080
Dividend Payout %	38.39	39.44	43.16	45.20	49.49	51.54	52.78	51.92
Income Statement								
Total Revenue	4,878,500	3,199,000	1,572,100	6,086,500	5,966,900	6,330,300	6,140,000	6,035,600
EBITDA	616,700	409,100	197,200	654,500	594,600	563,200	557,700	478,400
Depn & Amortn	134,800	90,800	44,600	117,500	125,200	135,500	135,600	150,100
Income Before Taxes	432,200	285,400	135,900	477,100	408,900	364,400	363,100	255,500
Income Taxes	90,800	52,300	23,700	156,400	134,500	113,300	118,800	86,400
Net Income	341,400	233,100	112,200	320,700	274,300	248,900	215,800	215,400
Average Shares	89,900	89,900	90,000	90,700	92,900	95,700	100,100	103,500
Balance Sheet								
Current Assets	2,283,300	2,209,800	2,184,600	1,904,800	1,775,400	1,921,300	2,091,800	2,411,700
Total Assets	5,270,000	5,091,800	4,765,900	4,396,400	4,133,700	4,360,200	4,610,600	5,105,300
Current Liabilities	2,023,300	1,972,400	1,759,300	2,004,300	1,459,100	1,597,800	1,554,100	2,074,500
Long-Term Obligations	1,298,400	1,276,300	1,250,200	713,400	963,600	945,300	950,600	702,200
Total Liabilities	4,135,100	4,022,000	3,751,300	3,470,900	3,168,000	3,293,700	3,118,400	3,524,400
Stockholders' Equity	1,134,900	1,069,800	1,014,600	925,500	965,700	1,066,500	1,492,200	1,580,900
Shares Outstanding	88,080	88,390	88,714	88,308	89,967	90,458	96,178	99,915
Statistical Record								
Return on Assets %	8.17	8.19	7.62	7.54	6.48	5.46	4.45	4.29
Return on Equity %	37.06	37.92	34.63	34.01	27.07	19.14	14.08	13.34
EBITDA Margin %	12.64	12.79	12.54	10.75	9.96	8.90	9.08	7.93
Net Margin %	7.00	7.29	7.14	5.27	4.60	3.93	3.51	3.57
Asset Turnover	1.30	1.33	1.37	1.43	1.41	1.39	1.27	1.20
Current Ratio	1.13	1.12	1.24	0.95	1.22	1.20	1.35	1.16
Debt to Equity	1.14	1.19	1.23	0.77	1.00	0.89	0.64	0.44
Price Range	99.93-68.61	88.78-68.61	81.85-68.61	78.84-58.16	66.18-51.07	52.67-41.28	50.65-34.92	34.97-26.38
P/E Ratio	22.31-15.31	20.84-16.11	21.54-18.06	22.27-16.43	22.43-17.31	20.26-15.88	23.45-16.17	16.81-12.68
Average Yield %	2.10	2.17	2.18	2.22	2.49	2.74	2.63	3.54

Address: 207 Goode Avenue, Glendale, CA 91203 Telephone: 626-304-2000	Web Site: www.averydennison.com Officers: Mitchell R. Butier - President, Chief Executive Officer, Senior Vice President, Chief Financial Officer, Chief Operating Officer Anne Hill - Senior Vice President, Chief Human Resources Officer	Auditors: PricewaterhouseCoopers LLP Investor Contact: 626-304-2000 Transfer Agents: Broadridge Corporate Issuer Solutions, Inc., Brentwood, NY

AVISTA CORP

Exchange	Symbol	Price	52Wk Range	Yield	P/E	Div Achiever
NYS	AVA	$51.49 (12/29/2017)	52.74-37.94	2.78	25.87	14 Years

*7 Year Price Score 109.51 *NYSE Composite Index=100 *12 Month Price Score 106.79

Interim Earnings (Per Share)

Qtr.	Mar	Jun	Sep	Dec
2014	0.81	1.67	0.16	0.51
2015	0.74	0.40	0.21	0.62
2016	0.89	0.43	0.19	0.62
2017	0.96	0.34	0.07	...

Interim Dividends (Per Share)

Amt	Decl	Ex	Rec	Pay
0.357Q	02/03/2017	02/22/2017	02/24/2017	03/15/2017
0.357Q	05/11/2017	05/23/2017	05/25/2017	06/15/2017
0.357Q	08/17/2017	08/29/2017	08/31/2017	09/15/2017
0.357Q	11/21/2017	11/30/2017	12/01/2017	12/15/2017

Indicated Div: $1.43 (Div. Reinv. Plan)

Valuation Analysis — **Institutional Holding**

Forecast EPS	$1.88	No of Institutions	
	(01/03/2018)	360	
Market Cap	$3.3 Billion	Shares	
Book Value	$1.7 Billion	66,399,952	
Price/Book	1.99	% Held	
Price/Sales	2.29	69.19	

Business Summary: Electric Utilities (MIC: 3.1.1 SIC: 4931 NAIC: 221121)

Avista is a holding company. Through its subsidiaries, Co. operates two segments: Avista Utilities, which generates, transmits and distributes electricity and distributes natural gas, serving electric and gas customers in eastern Washington and northern Idaho and natural gas customers in parts of Oregon; and Alaska Electric Light and Power Co. (AEL&P), which provides electric services in Juneau, AK. Co. also has other businesses, including sheet metal fabrication, venture fund investments and real estate investments. As of Dec 31 2016, Avista Utilities supplied retail electric and natural gas services to 377,000 and 340,000 customers, respectively, while AEL&P served about 17,000 customers.

Recent Developments: For the quarter ended Sep 30 2017, net income decreased 63.6% to US$4.5 million from US$12.3 million in the year-earlier quarter. Revenues were US$297.1 million, down 2.1% from US$303.3 million the year before. Operating income was US$31.0 million versus US$39.6 million in the prior-year quarter, a decrease of 21.6%. Direct operating expenses rose 1.0% to US$259.3 million from US$256.8 million in the comparable period the year before. Indirect operating expenses decreased 3.1% to US$6.7 million from US$6.9 million in the equivalent prior-year period.

Prospects: Our evaluation of Avista Corp. as of Jan. 14, 2018 is the result of our systematic analysis on three basic characteristics: earnings strength, relative valuation, and recent stock price movement. The company has generated a negative trend in earnings per share over the past 5 quarters and while recent estimates for the company have remained steady, AVA has posted results that fell short of analysts expectations. Based on operating earnings yield, the company is about fairly valued when compared to all of the companies in our coverage universe. Share price changes over the past year indicates that AVA will perform very well over the near term.

Financial Data

(US$ in Thousands)	9 Mos	6 Mos	3 Mos	12/31/2016	12/31/2015	12/31/2014	12/31/2013	12/31/2012
Earnings Per Share	1.99	2.11	2.20	2.15	1.97	3.10	1.85	1.32
Cash Flow Per Share	6.39	6.69	6.25	5.63	6.03	4.34	4.05	5.35
Tang Book Value Per Share	25.04	25.30	25.29	24.79	23.61	22.91	19.68	19.01
Dividends Per Share	1.415	1.400	1.385	1.370	1.320	1.270	1.220	1.160
Dividend Payout %	71.11	66.35	62.95	63.72	67.01	40.97	65.95	87.88
Income Statement								
Total Revenue	1,048,067	750,971	436,470	1,442,483	1,484,776	1,472,562	1,618,505	1,547,002
EBITDA	221,817	185,458	123,004	499,131	450,490	404,802	391,648	343,932
Depn & Amortn	12,694	9,218	4,517	202,381	188,677	142,075	141,458	149,849
Income Before Taxes	139,865	130,254	95,481	215,402	185,619	192,106	175,524	120,061
Income Taxes	51,548	46,395	33,344	78,086	67,449	72,240	63,230	41,261
Net Income	88,338	83,887	62,116	137,228	123,227	192,041	111,077	78,210
Average Shares	64,892	64,553	64,469	63,920	62,708	61,887	59,997	59,201
Balance Sheet								
Current Assets	316,634	320,736	357,292	351,341	306,046	395,347	549,679	505,794
Total Assets	5,452,232	5,373,004	5,340,359	5,309,755	4,906,649	4,712,331	4,361,923	4,313,179
Current Liabilities	673,251	682,114	366,825	407,528	474,680	385,269	625,340	576,149
Long-Term Obligations	1,543,336	1,454,611	1,729,660	1,730,264	1,531,658	1,543,609	1,371,403	1,301,752
Total Liabilities	3,781,905	3,685,831	3,654,683	3,661,028	3,378,023	3,228,660	3,063,657	3,053,702
Stockholders' Equity	1,670,327	1,687,173	1,685,676	1,648,727	1,528,626	1,483,671	1,298,266	1,259,477
Shares Outstanding	64,414	64,408	64,386	64,187	62,312	62,243	60,076	59,812
Statistical Record								
Return on Assets %	2.41	2.61	2.75	2.68	2.56	4.23	2.56	1.83
Return on Equity %	7.79	8.24	8.65	8.61	8.18	13.81	8.69	6.38
EBITDA Margin %	21.16	24.70	28.18	34.60	30.34	27.49	24.20	22.23
Net Margin %	8.43	11.17	14.23	9.51	8.30	13.04	6.86	5.06
Asset Turnover	0.27	0.28	0.28	0.28	0.31	0.32	0.37	0.36
Current Ratio	0.47	0.47	0.97	0.86	0.64	1.03	0.88	0.88
Debt to Equity	0.92	0.86	1.03	1.05	1.00	1.04	1.06	1.03
Price Range	52.74-37.94	44.97-37.94	44.97-37.94	44.97-34.67	38.30-29.93	37.27-27.73	29.15-24.11	27.86-23.07
P/E Ratio	26.50-19.07	21.31-17.98	20.44-17.25	20.92-16.13	19.44-15.19	12.02-8.95	15.76-13.03	21.11-17.48
Average Yield %	3.30	3.41	3.39	3.39	3.96	4.01	4.51	4.55

Address: 1411 East Mission Avenue,	Web Site: www.avistacorp.com	Auditors: Deloitte & Touche LLP
Spokane, WA 99202-2600	Officers: Scott L. Morris - Chairman, President, Chief	Investor Contact: 509-489-0500
Telephone: 509-489-0500	Executive Officer Mark T. Thies - Senior Vice	Transfer Agents: Computershare,
Fax: 509-482-4361	President, Chief Financial Officer, Treasurer	Pittsburgh, PA

AVNET INC

Exchange	Symbol	Price	52Wk Range	Yield	P/E
NYS	AVT	$39.62 (12/29/2017)	47.61-35.93	1.82	9.83

*7 Year Price Score 83.03 *NYSE Composite Index=100 *12 Month Price Score 92.28

Interim Earnings (Per Share)

Qtr.	Sep	Dec	Mar	Jun
2014-15	0.91	1.18	0.88	1.15
2015-16	0.96	1.16	0.94	0.75
2016-17	0.53	0.79	2.10	0.67
2017-18	0.47	...	...	...

Interim Dividends (Per Share)

Amt	Decl	Ex	Rec	Pay
0.18Q	02/28/2017	03/10/2017	03/14/2017	03/28/2017
0.18Q	05/11/2017	06/02/2017	06/06/2017	06/19/2017
0.10Q	08/11/2017	09/01/2017	09/06/2017	09/15/2017
0.18Q	11/10/2017	12/05/2017	12/06/2017	12/19/2017

Indicated Div: $0.72

Valuation Analysis / **Institutional Holding**

Forecast EPS	$3.38	No of Institutions	
	(01/13/2018)	528	
Market Cap	$4.8 Billion	Shares	
Book Value	$5.2 Billion	157,928,608	
Price/Book	0.92	% Held	
Price/Sales	0.27	87.28	

Business Summary: Electrical Equipment (MIC: 7.3.1 SIC: 5065 NAIC: 423690)

Avnet, together with its consolidated subsidiaries, is a distributor of electronic components. Co. distributes electronic components, as received from its suppliers or through a customized integrated solution, and provides assembly and other services. Co. has two primary operating groups: Electronic Components (EC) and Premier Farnell (PF). EC markets and sells semiconductors, electronic components, including interconnect, passive and electromechanical devices, and other integrated components from electronic component manufacturers. PF globally distributes a portfolio of electronic components primarily to support design engineers, maintenance and test engineers, makers and entrepreneurs.

Recent Developments: For the quarter ended Sep 30 2017, income from continuing operations decreased 15.2% to US$58.2 million from US$68.6 million in the year-earlier quarter. Net income decreased 15.3% to US$58.3 million from US$68.8 million in the year-earlier quarter. Revenues were US$4.66 billion, up 11.7% from US$4.17 billion the year before. Operating income was US$70.0 million versus US$131.0 million in the prior-year quarter, a decrease of 46.6%. Direct operating expenses rose 11.0% to US$4.05 billion from US$3.65 billion in the comparable period the year before. Indirect operating expenses increased 37.5% to US$542.6 million from US$394.5 million in the equivalent prior-year period.

Prospects: Our evaluation of Avnet Inc. as of Jan. 14, 2018 is the result of our systematic analysis on three basic characteristics: earnings strength, relative valuation, and recent stock price movement. The company has managed to produce a neutral trend in earnings per share over the past 5 quarters. However, while recent estimates for the company have been mixed, AVT has posted better than expected results. Based on operating earnings yield, the company is undervalued when compared to all of the companies in our coverage universe. Share price changes over the past year indicates that AVT will perform poorly over the near term.

Financial Data

(US$ in Thousands)	3 Mos	07/01/2017	07/02/2016	06/27/2015	06/28/2014	06/29/2013	06/30/2012	07/02/2011
Earnings Per Share	4.03	4.08	3.80	4.12	3.89	3.21	3.79	4.34
Cash Flow Per Share	(4.05)	(2.91)	1.69	4.28	1.73	5.06	3.60	1.83
Tang Book Value Per Share	31.14	30.52	26.16	24.41	24.29	22.09	19.68	20.75
Dividends Per Share	0.710	0.700	0.680	0.640	0.600	...	...	...
Dividend Payout %	17.62	17.16	17.89	15.53	15.42	...	...	...
Income Statement								
Total Revenue	4,660,943	17,439,963	26,219,279	27,924,657	27,499,654	25,458,924	25,707,522	26,534,413
EBITDA	149,303	518,495	867,964	904,230	898,450	745,221	952,286	1,020,934
Depn & Amortn	63,769	101,400	98,400	95,600	92,500	88,303	70,645	57,516
Income Before Taxes	61,474	310,404	670,509	712,965	701,127	549,265	790,782	870,966
Income Taxes	3,292	47,053	163,978	141,052	155,523	99,192	223,763	201,897
Net Income	58,303	525,278	506,531	571,913	545,604	450,073	567,019	669,069
Average Shares	123,984	128,651	133,173	138,791	140,119	140,003	149,553	154,337
Balance Sheet								
Current Assets	7,545,687	7,533,808	9,003,973	8,642,073	8,954,199	8,356,878	8,254,439	8,227,207
Total Assets	9,773,158	9,699,589	11,239,805	10,799,953	11,255,517	10,474,680	10,167,866	9,905,569
Current Liabilities	2,711,703	2,453,771	4,942,493	4,272,296	4,978,826	4,821,444	4,798,652	4,477,728
Long-Term Obligations	1,495,139	1,729,212	1,339,204	1,646,501	1,213,814	1,206,993	1,271,985	1,273,509
Total Liabilities	4,529,055	4,517,521	6,548,519	6,114,932	6,365,324	6,185,555	6,262,134	5,849,499
Stockholders' Equity	5,244,103	5,182,068	4,691,286	4,685,021	4,890,193	4,289,125	3,905,732	4,056,070
Shares Outstanding	121,235	123,080	127,350	135,464	138,248	137,088	142,548	152,797
Statistical Record								
Return on Assets %	4.94	5.03	4.52	5.20	5.04	4.37	5.66	7.59
Return on Equity %	10.26	10.67	10.63	11.98	11.92	11.01	14.28	18.99
EBITDA Margin %	3.20	2.97	3.31	3.24	3.27	2.93	3.70	3.85
Net Margin %	1.25	3.01	1.93	2.05	1.98	1.77	2.21	2.52
Asset Turnover	1.73	1.67	2.34	2.54	2.54	2.47	2.57	3.01
Current Ratio	2.78	3.07	1.82	2.02	1.80	1.73	1.72	1.84
Debt to Equity	0.29	0.33	0.29	0.35	0.25	0.28	0.33	0.31
Price Range	48.84-35.93	48.84-35.96	46.95-37.78	47.12-36.54	47.50-33.97	36.86-27.01	36.83-24.19	37.81-22.86
P/E Ratio	12.12-8.92	11.97-8.81	12.36-9.94	11.44-8.87	12.21-8.73	11.48-8.41	9.72-6.38	8.71-5.27
Average Yield %	1.68	1.64	1.61	1.47	1.44	...	...	...

Address: 2211 South 47th Street, Phoenix, AZ 85034 **Telephone:** 480-643-2000	**Web Site:** www.avnet.com **Officers:** William J. Amelio - Chief Executive Officer, Interim Chief Executive Officer Gerard W. Fay - Senior Vice President, Chief Logistics and Global Operations Officer, Division Officer	**Auditors:** KPMG LLP **Investor Contact:** 480-643-7053 **Transfer Agents:** American Stock Transfer & Trust Company, Brooklyn, NY

AVON PRODUCTS, INC.

Exchange	Symbol	Price	52Wk Range	Yield	P/E
NYS	AVP	$2.15 (12/29/2017)	5.93-1.87	N/A	N/A

*7 Year Price Score 21.81 *NYSE Composite Index=100 *12 Month Price Score 56.39

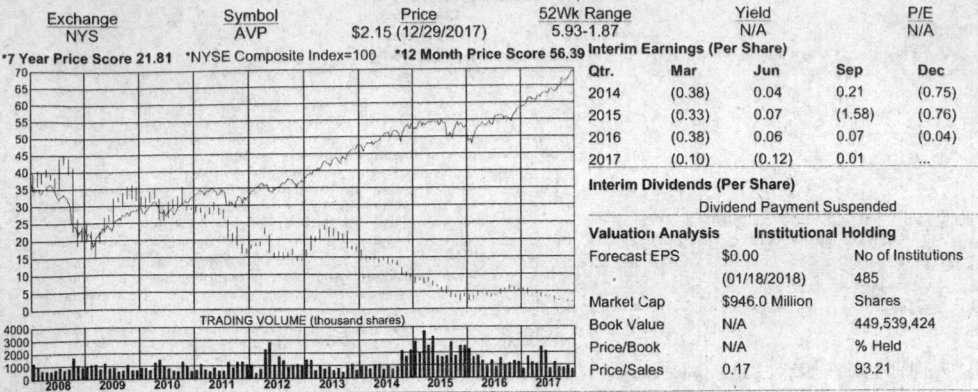

Interim Earnings (Per Share)

Qtr.	Mar	Jun	Sep	Dec
2014	(0.38)	0.04	0.21	(0.75)
2015	(0.33)	0.07	(1.58)	(0.76)
2016	(0.38)	0.06	0.07	(0.04)
2017	(0.10)	(0.12)	0.01	...

Interim Dividends (Per Share)

Dividend Payment Suspended

Valuation Analysis

		Institutional Holding	
Forecast EPS	$0.00	No of Institutions	
	(01/18/2018)	485	
Market Cap	$946.0 Million	Shares	
Book Value	N/A	449,539,424	
Price/Book	N/A	% Held	
Price/Sales	0.17	93.21	

Business Summary: Household & Personal Products (MIC: 1.7.1 SIC: 2844 NAIC: 446120)

Avon Products is a manufacturer and marketer of beauty and related products. Co.'s product categories are Beauty and Fashion and Home. Beauty consists of skincare (which includes personal care), fragrance and color (cosmetics). Fashion and Home consists of fashion jewelry, watches, apparel, footwear, accessories, gift and decorative products, housewares, entertainment and leisure products, children's products and nutritional products. Co.'s business is conducted primarily in one channel, direct selling. Co.'s reportable segments are based on geographic operations in four regions: Europe, Middle East and Africa; South Latin America; North Latin America; and Asia Pacific.

Recent Developments: For the quarter ended Sep 30 2017, income from continuing operations decreased 67.2% to US$11.9 million from US$36.3 million in the year-earlier quarter. Net income decreased 66.6% to US$11.9 million from US$35.6 million in the year-earlier quarter. Revenues were US$1.42 billion, up 0.6% from US$1.41 billion the year before. Operating income was US$83.0 million versus US$112.0 million in the prior-year quarter, a decrease of 25.9%. Direct operating expenses declined 0.2% to US$550.0 million from US$550.9 million in the comparable period the year before. Indirect operating expenses increased 5.2% to US$784.8 million from US$745.9 million in the equivalent prior-year period.

Prospects: Our evaluation of Avon Products Inc. as of Jan. 14, 2018 is the result of our systematic analysis on three basic characteristics: earnings strength, relative valuation, and recent stock price movement. The company has enjoyed a very positive trend in earnings per share over the past 5 quarters. Because the company lacks sufficient analyst estimate data, we place greater weight on the historical EPS trend as the measure of earnings strength. Based on operating earnings yield, the company is overvalued when compared to all of the companies in our coverage universe. Share price changes over the past year indicates that AVP will perform very poorly over the near term.

Financial Data

(US$ in Thousands)	9 Mos	6 Mos	3 Mos	12/31/2016	12/31/2015	12/31/2014	12/31/2013	12/31/2012
Earnings Per Share	(0.25)	(0.19)	(0.01)	(0.29)	(2.60)	(0.88)	(0.13)	(0.10)
Cash Flow Per Share	0.61	0.61	0.55	0.29	0.21	0.83	1.25	1.28
Tang Book Value Per Share	...	...	...	...	...	N.M.	1.55	1.13
Dividends Per Share	...	...	...	...	0.240	0.240	0.240	0.750
Income Statement								
Total Revenue	4,146,800	2,729,000	1,333,100	5,717,700	6,160,500	8,851,400	9,955,000	10,717,100
EBITDA	209,500	101,200	51,300	235,300	224,700	401,800	422,100	470,200
Depn & Amortn	85,600	56,700	27,600	83,300	94,000	141,300	164,800	162,400
Income Before Taxes	29,100	(18,900)	(6,700)	31,200	22,700	164,200	162,600	218,600
Income Taxes	99,500	63,400	29,800	124,600	819,200	549,100	163,600	256,800
Net Income	(69,500)	(82,000)	(36,500)	(107,600)	(1,148,900)	(388,600)	(56,400)	(42,500)
Average Shares	440,000	439,900	438,600	437,000	435,200	434,500	433,400	431,900
Balance Sheet								
Current Assets	2,092,500	2,015,200	1,948,900	1,992,300	2,341,100	2,964,500	3,479,100	3,928,900
Total Assets	3,516,600	3,467,500	3,426,200	3,418,900	3,879,500	5,496,800	6,492,300	7,382,500
Current Liabilities	1,471,500	1,487,500	1,450,900	1,485,700	2,195,100	2,047,200	2,240,500	2,704,600
Long-Term Obligations	1,873,000	1,873,800	1,874,900	1,875,800	2,159,600	2,463,900	2,532,700	2,623,900
Total Liabilities	3,875,200	3,864,500	3,796,300	3,822,200	4,949,800	5,207,000	5,382,200	6,165,400
Stockholders' Equity	(358,600)	(397,000)	(370,100)	(403,300)	(1,070,300)	289,800	1,110,100	1,217,100
Shares Outstanding	439,997	439,949	439,847	437,600	435,500	434,700	433,900	432,200
Statistical Record								
Return on Assets %	N.M.	N.M.	0.62	N.M.	N.M.	N.M.	N.M.	N.M.
EBITDA Margin %	5.05	3.71	3.85	4.12	3.65	4.54	4.24	4.39
Asset Turnover	1.54	1.61	1.63	1.56	1.31	1.48	1.43	1.41
Current Ratio	1.42	1.35	1.34	1.34	1.07	1.45	1.55	1.45
Debt to Equity	...	...	...	...	...	8.50	2.28	2.16
Price Range	6.89-2.33	6.89-3.35	6.89-3.53	6.89-2.38	9.39-2.50	17.22-9.11	24.20-14.36	23.52-13.80
Average Yield %	...	...	...	...	3.93	1.78	1.19	4.42

Address: Building 6, Chiswick Park, London, W4 5HR **Telephone:** 160-423-2425	**Web Site:** www.avon.com **Officers:** Sherilyn S. McCoy - Chief Executive Officer Jonathan Myers - Chief Operating Officer, Executive Vice President	**Auditors:** PricewaterhouseCoopers LLP, U.K. **Investor Contact:** 212-282-5320 **Transfer Agents:** Computershare Investor Services, Canton, MA

BADGER METER INC

Exchange	Symbol	Price	52Wk Range	Yield	P/E	Div Achiever
NYS	BMI	$47.80 (12/29/2017)	51.60-34.60	1.09	41.93	24 Years

*7 Year Price Score 118.73 *NYSE Composite Index=100 *12 Month Price Score 103.74

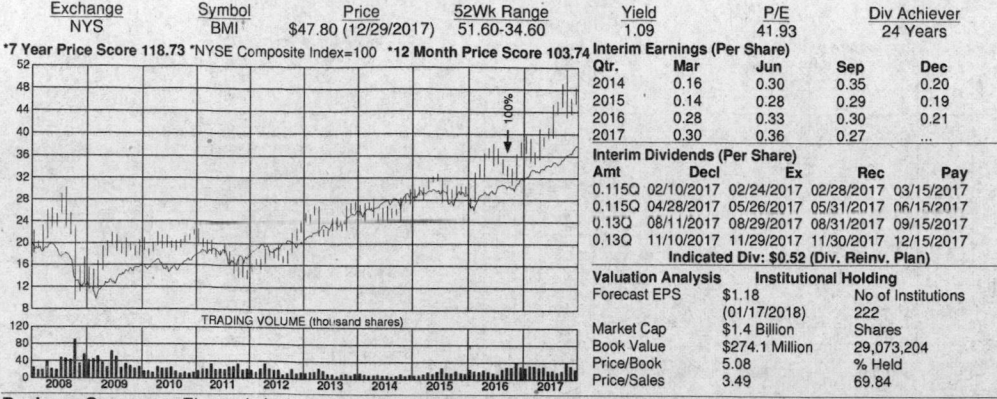

Interim Earnings (Per Share)

Qtr.	Mar	Jun	Sep	Dec
2014	0.16	0.30	0.35	0.20
2015	0.14	0.28	0.29	0.19
2016	0.28	0.33	0.30	0.21
2017	0.30	0.36	0.27	...

Interim Dividends (Per Share)

Amt	Decl	Ex	Rec	Pay
0.115Q	02/10/2017	02/24/2017	02/28/2017	03/15/2017
0.115Q	04/28/2017	05/26/2017	05/31/2017	06/15/2017
0.13Q	08/11/2017	08/29/2017	08/31/2017	09/15/2017
0.13Q	11/10/2017	11/29/2017	11/30/2017	12/15/2017

Indicated Div: $0.52 (Div. Reinv. Plan)

Valuation Analysis   **Institutional Holding**

Forecast EPS	$1.18 (01/17/2018)	No of Institutions	222
Market Cap	$1.4 Billion	Shares	29,073,204
Book Value	$274.1 Million	% Held	69.84
Price/Book	5.08		
Price/Sales	3.49		

Business Summary: Electronic Instruments & Related Products (MIC: 6.2.3 SIC: 3824 NAIC: 334514)

Badger Meter is a manufacturer and marketer of products incorporating flow measurement, control and communication solutions. Co.'s product lines fall into two categories: sales of water meters and related technologies to municipal water utilities (municipal water), which includes mechanical and ultrasonic (electronic) water meters and related technologies and services used by municipal water utilities; and sales of meters to various industries for water and other fluids (flow instrumentation), which includes meters and valves sold worldwide to measure and control materials flowing through a pipe or pipeline including water, air, steam, oil, and other liquids and gases.

Recent Developments: For the quarter ended Sep 30 2017, net income decreased 9.3% to US$8.0 million from US$8.8 million in the year-earlier quarter. Revenues were US$100.0 million, up 3.9% from US$96.3 million the year before. Operating income was US$12.4 million versus US$13.9 million in the prior-year quarter, a decrease of 11.0%. Direct operating expenses rose 9.3% to US$63.0 million from US$57.6 million in the comparable period the year before. Indirect operating expenses decreased 0.3% to US$24.6 million from US$24.7 million in the equivalent prior-year period.

Prospects: Our evaluation of Badger Meter Inc. as of Jan. 14, 2018 is the result of our systematic analysis on three basic characteristics: earnings strength, relative valuation, and recent stock price movement. The company has generated a negative trend in earnings per share over the past 5 quarters. However, while recent estimates for the company have been mixed, BMI has posted results that fell short of analysts expectations. Based on operating earnings yield, the company is overvalued when compared to all of the companies in our coverage universe. Share price changes over the past year indicates that BMI will perform well over the near term.

Financial Data
(US$ in Thousands)

	9 Mos	6 Mos	3 Mos	12/31/2016	12/31/2015	12/31/2014	12/31/2013	12/31/2012
Earnings Per Share	1.14	1.17	1.14	1.11	0.90	1.03	0.85	0.97
Cash Flow Per Share	2.14	2.27	1.75	1.94	1.25	1.25	1.21	1.21
Tang Book Value Per Share	5.33	5.09	5.54	5.32	4.37	3.63	3.28	2.69
Dividends Per Share	0.475	0.460	0.445	0.430	0.390	0.370	0.350	0.330
Dividend Payout %	41.67	39.32	39.21	38.74	43.33	35.92	41.18	33.85
Income Statement								
Total Revenue	305,790	205,782	101,606	393,761	377,698	364,768	334,122	319,660
EBITDA	60,639	42,051	19,332	61,480	52,362	54,938	47,619	52,056
Depn & Amortn	18,168	11,991	5,863	10,715	9,993	8,891	8,512	7,587
Income Before Taxes	41,904	29,735	13,291	49,844	41,152	44,912	38,009	43,471
Income Taxes	14,566	10,372	4,542	17,549	15,214	15,234	13,392	15,439
Net Income	27,338	19,363	8,749	32,295	25,938	29,678	24,617	28,032
Average Shares	29,118	29,097	29,082	29,050	28,894	28,756	28,880	28,798
Balance Sheet								
Current Assets	163,256	156,499	152,202	151,012	149,328	141,105	127,163	121,374
Total Assets	386,093	378,746	353,570	349,699	355,480	341,158	316,058	290,453
Current Liabilities	92,494	90,272	75,504	75,838	104,544	107,075	98,041	94,080
Total Liabilities	111,963	109,340	92,710	93,490	123,205	126,827	119,495	119,206
Stockholders' Equity	274,130	269,406	260,860	256,209	232,275	214,331	196,563	171,247
Shares Outstanding	29,112	29,113	29,114	29,118	29,049	28,922	28,823	28,628
Statistical Record								
Return on Assets %	9.00	9.31	9.31	9.13	7.45	9.03	8.12	10.98
Return on Equity %	12.70	13.30	13.24	13.19	11.62	14.45	13.39	15.95
EBITDA Margin %	19.83	20.43	19.03	15.61	13.86	15.06	14.25	16.28
Net Margin %	8.94	9.41	8.61	8.20	6.87	8.14	7.37	8.77
Asset Turnover	1.07	1.07	1.11	1.11	1.08	1.11	1.10	1.25
Current Ratio	1.77	1.73	2.02	1.99	1.43	1.32	1.30	1.29
Price Range	49.10-30.70	41.20-30.70	39.65-30.70	38.55-26.61	32.79-27.66	30.02-23.79	27.68-21.27	24.14-14.84
P/E Ratio	43.07-26.93	35.21-26.24	34.78-26.93	34.73-23.97	36.43-30.73	29.15-23.10	32.56-25.02	24.88-15.30
Average Yield %	1.23	1.27	1.25	1.26	1.30	1.41	1.43	1.78

Address: 4545 W. Brown Deer Road, Milwaukee, WI 53223
Telephone: 414-355-0400

Web Site: www.badgermeter.com
Officers: Richard A. Meeusen - Chairman, President, Chief Executive Officer Richard E. Johnson - Senior Vice President, Chief Financial Officer, Treasurer

Auditors: Ernst & Young LLP
Investor Contact: 414-371-5702
Transfer Agents: American Stock Transfer & Trust Company, LLC, New York, NY

BALL CORP

Exchange	Symbol	Price	52Wk Range	Yield	P/E
NYS	BLL	$37.85 (12/29/2017)	42.93-35.77	1.06	51.15

*7 Year Price Score 107.14 *NYSE Composite Index=100 *12 Month Price Score 95.30

Interim Earnings (Per Share)

Qtr.	Mar	Jun	Sep	Dec
2014	0.33	0.54	0.52	0.27
2015	0.07	0.56	0.16	0.20
2016	(0.45)	1.17	0.00	0.14
2017	0.19	0.28	0.13	...

Interim Dividends (Per Share)

Amt	Decl	Ex	Rec	Pay
0.10Q	04/26/2017	05/30/2017	06/01/2017	06/15/2017
100%	04/26/2017	05/17/2017	05/08/2017	05/16/2017
0.10Q	07/26/2017	08/30/2017	09/01/2017	09/15/2017
0.10Q	10/25/2017	11/30/2017	12/01/2017	12/15/2017

Indicated Div: $0.40 (Div. Reinv. Plan)

Valuation Analysis **Institutional Holding**

Forecast EPS	$1.95 (01/18/2018)	No of Institutions 672
Market Cap	$13.2 Billion	Shares
Book Value	$3.5 Billion	341,274,976
Price/Book	3.75	% Held
Price/Sales	1.24	65.15

TRADING VOLUME (thousand shares)

Business Summary: Metal Products (MIC: 8.2.3 SIC: 3411 NAIC: 332431)

Ball is a supplier of metal packaging to the beverage, food, personal care and household products industries. Co.'s segments include: beverage packaging, North and Central America; beverage packaging, South America; beverage packaging, Europe, all of which is engaged in manufacturing and sells metal beverage containers; food and aerosol packaging, which manufacture and sell steel food, aerosol, paint and general line containers, as well as extruded aluminum aerosol containers and aluminum slugs; and aerospace, which manufacture and sell aerospace and other related products and the provision of services used in the defense, civil space and commercial space industries.

Recent Developments: For the quarter ended Sep 30 2017, net income increased 50.0% to US$51.0 million from US$34.0 million in the year-earlier quarter. Revenues were US$2.91 billion, up 5.7% from US$2.75 billion the year before. Operating income was US$124.0 million versus US$132.0 million in the prior-year quarter, a decrease of 6.1%. Direct operating expenses rose 2.8% to US$2.34 billion from US$2.28 billion in the comparable period the year before. Indirect operating expenses increased 29.3% to US$446.0 million from US$345.0 million in the equivalent prior-year period.

Prospects: Our evaluation of Ball Corp. as of Jan. 14, 2018 is the result of our systematic analysis on three basic characteristics: earnings strength, relative valuation, and recent stock price movement. The company has produced a positive trend in earnings per share over the past 5 quarters and while recent estimates for the company have remained steady, BLL has posted results that fell short of analysts expectations. Based on operating earnings yield, the company is undervalued when compared to all of the companies in our coverage universe. Share price changes over the past year indicates that BLL will perform well over the near term.

Financial Data

(US$ in Thousands)	9 Mos	6 Mos	3 Mos	12/31/2016	12/31/2015	12/31/2014	12/31/2013	12/31/2012
Earnings Per Share	0.74	...	...	0.81	1.00	1.65	1.37	1.27
Cash Flow Per Share	3.92	1.20	0.52	0.61	3.67	3.66	2.87	2.75
Dividends Per Share	0.330	0.295	0.260	0.260	0.260	0.260	0.260	0.200
Dividend Payout %	44.59	...	...	31.90	26.13	15.76	19.05	15.69
Income Statement								
Total Revenue	8,236,000	5,328,000	2,473,000	9,061,000	7,997,000	8,570,000	8,468,100	8,735,700
EBITDA	836,000	599,000	259,000	812,000	852,500	1,078,100	1,056,700	1,038,800
Depn & Amortn	373,000	260,000	107,000	349,000	247,300	239,500	261,300	248,300
Income Before Taxes	246,000	196,000	84,000	125,000	345,500	645,600	583,600	595,600
Income Taxes	48,000	44,000	22,000	(126,000)	47,000	149,900	149,600	165,000
Net Income	215,000	167,000	68,000	263,000	280,900	470,000	406,800	403,500
Average Shares	358,556	358,979	357,934	322,884	281,968	284,860	298,446	316,168
Balance Sheet								
Current Assets	3,930,000	3,765,000	3,907,000	3,653,000	2,184,000	2,313,500	2,465,700	2,339,400
Total Assets	17,003,000	16,721,000	16,644,000	16,173,000	9,777,000	7,571,000	7,819,800	7,507,100
Current Liabilities	3,778,000	3,350,000	3,018,000	2,969,000	2,141,000	2,006,800	1,927,400	1,685,800
Long-Term Obligations	7,104,000	7,226,000	7,476,000	7,310,000	5,054,200	2,993,800	3,182,500	3,085,300
Total Liabilities	13,474,000	13,117,000	13,025,000	12,738,000	8,525,700	6,537,900	6,619,900	6,392,500
Stockholders' Equity	3,529,000	3,604,000	3,619,000	3,435,000	1,251,300	1,033,100	1,199,900	1,114,600
Shares Outstanding	349,851	350,148	350,840	349,730	284,578	273,932	284,236	299,458
Statistical Record								
Return on Assets %	1.57	1.05	3.44	2.02	3.24	6.11	5.31	5.44
Return on Equity %	7.40	6.00	19.59	11.19	24.59	42.10	35.15	34.49
EBITDA Margin %	10.15	11.24	10.47	8.96	10.66	12.58	12.48	11.89
Net Margin %	2.61	3.13	2.75	2.90	3.51	5.48	4.80	4.62
Asset Turnover	0.63	0.51	0.73	0.70	0.92	1.11	1.10	1.18
Current Ratio	1.04	1.12	1.29	1.23	1.02	1.15	1.28	1.39
Debt to Equity	2.01	2.00	2.07	2.13	4.04	2.90	2.65	2.77
Price Range	42.92-35.77	42.52-34.88	41.01-34.17	41.01-31.95	38.58-30.25	35.08-24.14	25.90-20.77	22.73-18.13
P/E Ratio	58.00-48.33	...	...	50.63-39.44	38.58-30.25	21.26-14.63	18.90-15.16	17.90-14.27
Average Yield %	0.84	0.77	0.69	0.71	0.75	0.81	1.13	0.96

Address: 10 Longs Peak Drive, P.O. Box 5000, Broomfield, CO 80021-2510 **Telephone:** 303-469-3131	**Web Site:** www.ball.com **Officers:** John A. Hayes - Chairman, President, Chief Executive Officer Scott C. Morrison - Senior Vice President, Chief Financial Officer, Treasurer	**Auditors:** PricewaterhouseCoopers LLP **Investor Contact:** 303-460-3537 **Transfer Agents:** Computershare, Providence, RI

BANCORPSOUTH BANK (TUPELO, MS)

Exchange	Symbol	Price	52Wk Range	Yield	P/E
NYS	BXS	$31.45 (12/29/2017)	34.20-27.55	1.78	18.95

*7 Year Price Score 115.28 *NYSE Composite Index=100 *12 Month Price Score 99.72

Interim Earnings (Per Share)

Qtr.	Mar	Jun	Sep	Dec
2014	0.30	0.32	0.30	0.29
2015	0.33	0.41	0.36	0.23
2016	0.24	0.37	0.40	0.41
2017	0.41	0.41	0.43	...

Interim Dividends (Per Share)

Amt	Decl	Ex	Rec	Pay
0.14Q	10/25/2017	12/14/2017	12/15/2017	01/02/2018

Indicated Div: $0.56 (Div. Reinv. Plan)

Valuation Analysis

Forecast EPS	$1.66
	(01/18/2018)
Market Cap	$2.8 Billion
Book Value	$1.7 Billion
Price/Book	1.67
Price/Sales	3.63

Institutional Holding

No of Institutions	259
Shares	75,026,296
% Held	75.95

Business Summary: Banking (MIC: 5.1.1 SIC: 6022 NAIC: 522110)

BancorpSouth is a financial holding company. Through its subsidiary, BancorpSouth Bank, Co. provides financial services to individuals and small-to-medium size businesses. Co. has three segments: Community Banking, which provides deposit products, commercial loans and consumer loans; Insurance Agencies, which serves as agents in the sale of commercial lines of insurance and lines of property and casualty, life, health and employee benefits products and services; and General Corporate and Other, which includes mortgage banking, trust services, credit card activities, investment services and others. At Dec 31 2016, Co. had total assets of $14.72 billion and total deposits of $11.69 billion.

Recent Developments: For the quarter ended Sep 30 2017, net income increased 4.5% to US$39.5 million from US$37.8 million in the year-earlier quarter. Net interest income increased 5.2% to US$120.6 million from US$114.6 million in the year-earlier quarter. Non-interest income fell 5.3% to US$66.0 million from US$69.7 million, while non-interest expense declined 1.1% to US$126.9 million.

Prospects: Our evaluation of BancorpSouth Bank as of Jan. 14, 2018 is the result of our systematic analysis on three basic characteristics: earnings strength, relative valuation, and recent stock price movement. The company has managed to produce a neutral trend in earnings per share over the past 5 quarters. However, while recent estimates for the company have been mixed, BXS has posted better than expected results. Based on operating earnings yield, the company is undervalued when compared to all of the companies in our coverage universe. Share price changes over the past year indicates that BXS will perform poorly over the near term.

Financial Data

(US$ in Thousands)	9 Mos	6 Mos	3 Mos	12/31/2016	12/31/2015	12/31/2014	12/31/2013	12/31/2012
Earnings Per Share	1.66	1.63	1.59	1.41	1.33	1.21	0.99	0.90
Cash Flow Per Share	2.47	1.98	1.90	1.52	1.39	1.48	2.14	1.42
Tang Book Value Per Share	15.29	15.06	14.95	14.95	14.27	13.40	12.60	12.43
Dividends Per Share	0.520	0.510	0.480	0.450	0.350	0.250	0.120	0.040
Dividend Payout %	31.33	31.29	30.19	31.91	26.32	20.66	12.12	4.44
Income Statement								
Interest Income	380,715	249,781	122,926	483,179	464,378	450,257	449,507	486,424
Interest Expense	28,065	17,692	8,315	29,727	28,696	33,595	50,558	71,833
Net Interest Income	352,650	232,089	114,611	453,452	435,682	416,662	398,949	414,591
Provision for Losses	2,500	2,000	1,000	4,000	(13,000)	...	7,500	28,000
Non-Interest Income	204,959	138,999	70,869	279,030	277,968	269,146	275,066	280,149
Non-Interest Expense	381,565	254,662	127,109	532,038	539,911	518,406	534,849	549,193
Income Before Taxes	173,544	114,426	57,371	196,444	186,739	167,402	131,666	117,547
Income Taxes	58,034	38,444	19,278	63,716	59,248	50,652	37,551	33,252
Net Income	115,510	75,982	38,093	132,728	127,491	116,750	94,115	84,295
Average Shares	91,100	91,531	93,829	94,455	96,124	96,302	95,332	93,864
Balance Sheet								
Net Loans & Leases	11,074,366	11,081,900	10,838,098	10,855,182	10,404,227	9,711,508	8,874,372	8,601,661
Total Assets	14,760,394	14,843,130	14,866,054	14,724,388	13,798,662	13,326,369	13,029,733	13,397,198
Total Deposits	11,775,988	11,938,296	12,042,845	11,688,141	11,331,161	10,972,339	10,773,836	11,088,146
Total Liabilities	13,059,892	13,151,298	13,163,665	13,000,505	12,143,218	11,720,310	11,516,603	11,948,146
Stockholders' Equity	1,700,502	1,691,832	1,702,389	1,723,883	1,655,444	1,606,059	1,513,130	1,449,052
Shares Outstanding	90,329	91,022	92,344	93,696	94,162	96,254	95,231	94,437
Statistical Record								
Return on Assets %	1.04	1.05	1.03	0.93	0.94	0.89	0.71	0.64
Return on Equity %	8.95	8.90	8.77	7.83	7.82	7.49	6.35	6.20
Net Interest Margin %	92.08	92.61	93.24	93.85	93.82	92.54	88.75	85.23
Efficiency Ratio %	64.45	65.42	65.59	69.80	72.73	72.06	73.82	71.64
Loans to Deposits	0.94	0.93	0.90	0.92	0.92	0.89	0.82	0.78
Price Range	32.30-22.42	32.30-21.42	32.30-20.34	31.60-18.96	26.93-19.76	25.90-19.62	25.45-14.28	15.57-10.89
P/E Ratio	19.46-13.51	19.82-13.14	20.31-12.79	22.41-13.45	20.25-14.86	21.40-16.21	25.71-14.42	17.30-12.10
Average Yield %	1.77	1.84	1.85	1.91	1.45	1.09	0.65	0.29

Address: One Mississippi Plaza, 201 South Spring Street, Tupelo, MS 38804
Telephone: 662-680-2000

Web Site: www.bancorpsouth.com
Officers: James D. Rollins - Chairman, Chief Executive Officer Chris A. Bagley - President, Chief Operating Officer, Interim Chief Financial Officer, Treasurer

Auditors: KPMG LLP
Investor Contact: 662-680-2000
Transfer Agents: Computershare, Canton, MA

BANK OF AMERICA CORP.

Exchange	Symbol	Price	52Wk Range	Yield	P/E
NYS	BAC	$29.52 (12/29/2017)	29.88-22.05	1.63	16.87

*7 Year Price Score 128.73 *NYSE Composite Index=100 *12 Month Price Score 107.51

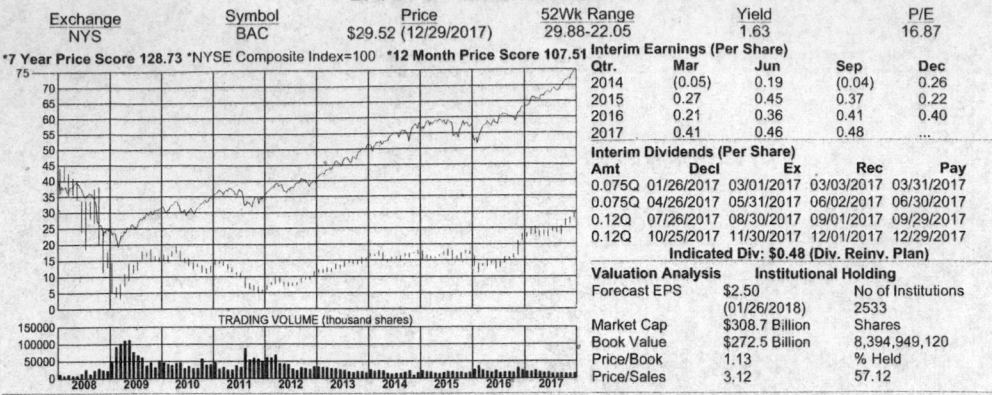

Interim Earnings (Per Share)

Qtr.	Mar	Jun	Sep	Dec
2014	(0.05)	0.19	(0.04)	0.26
2015	0.27	0.45	0.37	0.22
2016	0.21	0.36	0.41	0.40
2017	0.41	0.46	0.48	...

Interim Dividends (Per Share)

Amt	Decl	Ex	Rec	Pay
0.075Q	01/26/2017	03/01/2017	03/03/2017	03/31/2017
0.075Q	04/26/2017	05/31/2017	06/02/2017	06/30/2017
0.12Q	07/26/2017	08/30/2017	09/01/2017	09/29/2017
0.12Q	10/25/2017	11/30/2017	12/01/2017	12/29/2017

Indicated Div: $0.48 (Div. Reinv. Plan)

Valuation Analysis		Institutional Holding	
Forecast EPS	$2.50	No of Institutions	
	(01/26/2018)	2533	
Market Cap	$308.7 Billion	Shares	
Book Value	$272.5 Billion	8,394,949,120	
Price/Book	1.13	% Held	
Price/Sales	3.12	57.12	

Business Summary: Banking (MIC: 5.1.1 SIC: 6021 NAIC: 522110)

Bank of America is a bank and financial holding company. Through its banking and various nonbanking subsidiaries throughout the U.S. and in international markets, Co. serves individual consumers, small- and middle-market businesses, institutional investors, corporations and governments with a range of banking, investing, asset management and other financial and risk management products and services. Co. provides its services and products through four segments: Consumer Banking, Global Wealth & Investment Management, Global Banking and Global Markets. As of Dec 31 2016, Co. had total assets of $2.19 trillion and total deposits of $1.26 trillion.

Recent Developments: For the quarter ended Sep 30 2017, net income increased 12.8% to US$5.59 billion from US$4.96 billion in the year-earlier quarter. Net interest income increased 9.4% to US$11.16 billion from US$10.20 billion in the year-earlier quarter. Provision for loan losses was US$834.0 million versus US$850.0 million in the prior-year quarter, a decrease of 1.9%. Non-interest income fell 6.6% to US$10.68 billion from US$11.43 billion, while non-interest expense declined 2.5% to US$13.14 billion.

Prospects: Our evaluation of Bank of America Corp. as of Jan. 21, 2018 is the result of our systematic analysis on three basic characteristics: earnings strength, relative valuation, and recent stock price movement. The company has enjoyed a very positive trend in earnings per share over the past 5 quarters and while recent estimates for the company have been raised by analysts, BAC has posted better than expected results. Based on operating earnings yield, the company is undervalued when compared to all of the companies in our coverage universe. Share price changes over the past year indicates that BAC will perform in line with the market over the near term.

Financial Data

(US$ in Millions)	9 Mos	6 Mos	3 Mos	12/31/2016	12/31/2015	12/31/2014	12/31/2013	12/31/2012
Earnings Per Share	1.75	1.68	1.58	1.50	1.31	0.36	0.90	0.25
Cash Flow Per Share	0.89	(1.08)	(0.53)	1.78	2.65	2.54	8.65	(1.29)
Tang Book Value Per Share	16.86	17.38	16.90	16.61	15.16	13.91	13.11	12.59
Dividends Per Share	0.345	0.300	0.275	0.250	0.200	0.120	0.040	0.040
Dividend Payout %	19.71	17.86	17.41	16.67	15.27	33.33	4.44	16.00
Income Statement								
Interest Income	42,513	27,856	13,710	51,057	49,800	50,886	55,020	57,400
Interest Expense	9,308	5,812	2,652	9,961	10,549	10,934	12,755	16,744
Net Interest Income	33,205	22,044	11,058	41,096	39,251	39,952	42,265	40,656
Provision for Losses	2,395	1,561	835	3,597	3,161	2,275	3,556	8,169
Non-Interest Income	33,711	23,033	11,190	42,605	43,256	44,295	46,677	42,678
Non-Interest Expense	41,713	28,574	14,848	54,951	57,192	75,117	69,214	72,093
Income Before Taxes	22,808	14,942	6,565	25,153	22,154	6,855	16,172	3,072
Income Taxes	7,096	4,817	1,709	7,247	6,266	2,022	4,741	(1,116)
Net Income	15,712	10,125	4,856	17,906	15,888	4,833	11,431	4,188
Average Shares	10,725	10,823	10,915	11,036	11,215	10,584	11,492	10,841
Balance Sheet								
Net Loans & Leases	929,667	911,673	909,881	904,512	898,220	879,808	922,167	903,053
Total Assets	2,283,896	2,254,529	2,247,701	2,187,702	2,144,316	2,104,534	2,102,273	2,209,974
Total Deposits	1,284,417	1,262,980	1,272,141	1,260,934	1,197,259	1,118,936	1,119,271	1,105,261
Total Liabilities	2,011,437	1,983,542	1,979,548	1,920,862	1,888,111	1,861,063	1,869,588	1,973,018
Stockholders' Equity	272,459	270,987	268,153	266,840	256,205	243,471	232,685	236,956
Shares Outstanding	10,457	9,878	9,974	10,052	10,380	10,516	10,591	10,779
Statistical Record								
Return on Assets %	0.91	0.89	0.85	0.82	0.75	0.23	0.53	0.19
Return on Equity %	7.52	7.35	7.06	6.83	6.36	2.03	4.87	1.79
Net Interest Margin %	76.15	77.66	80.66	80.49	78.82	78.51	76.82	70.83
Efficiency Ratio %	51.86	52.81	59.63	58.67	61.46	78.92	68.06	72.04
Loans to Deposits	0.72	0.72	0.72	0.72	0.75	0.79	0.82	0.82
Price Range	25.50-15.63	25.50-12.74	25.50-12.18	23.16-11.16	18.45-15.15	18.13-14.51	15.88-11.03	11.61-5.80
P/E Ratio	14.57-8.93	15.18-7.58	16.14-7.71	15.44-7.44	14.08-11.56	50.36-40.31	17.64-12.26	46.44-23.20
Average Yield %	1.53	1.48	1.54	1.62	1.21	0.73	0.30	0.47

Address: Bank of America Corporate Center, 100 N. Tryon Street, Charlotte, NC 28255	Web Site: www.bankofamerica.com	Auditors: PricewaterhouseCoopers LLP
Telephone: 704-386-5681	Officers: Brian T. Moynihan - Chairman, President, Chief Executive Officer, Division Officer Paul M. Donofrio - Chief Financial Officer, Executive Officer	Investor Contact: 800-521-3984 Transfer Agents: Computershare Trust Company, N.A., Providence, RI

BANK OF HAWAII CORP

Exchange	Symbol	Price	52Wk Range	Yield	P/E
NYS	BOH	$85.70 (12/29/2017)	90.36-75.00	2.43	19.70

*7 Year Price Score 108.57 *NYSE Composite Index=100 *12 Month Price Score 95.69

Interim Earnings (Per Share)

Qtr.	Mar	Jun	Sep	Dec
2014	0.87	0.94	0.95	0.94
2015	0.97	0.95	0.79	0.99
2016	1.16	1.03	1.02	1.02
2017	1.20	1.05	1.08	...

Interim Dividends (Per Share)

Amt	Decl	Ex	Rec	Pay
0.50Q	04/21/2017	05/26/2017	05/31/2017	06/14/2017
0.52Q	07/24/2017	08/29/2017	08/31/2017	09/15/2017
0.52Q	10/20/2017	11/29/2017	11/30/2017	12/14/2017
0.52Q	01/19/2018	02/27/2018	02/28/2018	03/14/2018

Indicated Div: $2.08 (Div. Reinv. Plan)

Valuation Analysis		Institutional Holding	
Forecast EPS	$5.28	No of Institutions	
	(01/27/2018)	403	
Market Cap	$3.6 Billion	Shares	
Book Value	$1.2 Billion	46,155,816	
Price/Book	2.97	% Held	
Price/Sales	5.36	64.19	

Business Summary: Banking (MIC: 5.1.1 SIC: 6022 NAIC: 522110)

Bank of Hawaii is a bank holding company. Through its subsidiary, Bank of Hawaii, Co. provides financial products and services to customers in Hawaii, Guam, and other Pacific Islands. Co. has four segments: Retail Banking, which provides loan and lease, deposit, and retail insurance products; Commercial Banking, which provides corporate banking, commercial real estate loans, commercial lease financing, and deposit products; Investment Services, which includes trust services and investment management; and Treasury and Other, which consists of corporate asset and liability management activities. As of Dec 31 2016, Co. had total assets of $16.49 billion and total deposits of $14.32 billion.

Recent Developments: For the quarter ended Sep 30 2017, net income increased 5.5% to US$45.9 million from US$43.5 million in the year-earlier quarter. Net interest income increased 11.9% to US$116.3 million from US$103.9 million in the year-earlier quarter. Provision for loan losses was US$4.0 million versus US$2.5 million in the prior-year quarter, an increase of 60.0%. Non-interest income fell 11.9% to US$42.4 million from US$48.1 million, while non-interest expense advanced 1.2% to US$88.6 million.

Prospects: Our evaluation of Bank of Hawaii Corp. as of Jan. 21, 2018 is the result of our systematic analysis on three basic characteristics: earnings strength, relative valuation, and recent stock price movement. The company has managed to produce a neutral trend in earnings per share over the past 5 quarters. However, while recent estimates for the company have been mixed, BOH has posted better than expected results. Based on operating earnings yield, the company is undervalued when compared to all of the companies in our coverage universe. Share price changes over the past year indicates that BOH will perform in line with the market over the near term.

Financial Data

(US$ in Thousands)	9 Mos	6 Mos	3 Mos	12/31/2016	12/31/2015	12/31/2014	12/31/2013	12/31/2012
Earnings Per Share	4.35	4.29	4.27	4.23	3.70	3.69	3.38	3.67
Cash Flow Per Share	6.39	7.75	5.32	5.30	5.41	4.77	5.45	4.92
Tang Book Value Per Share	27.57	27.14	26.61	25.95	24.53	22.84	21.41	21.56
Dividends Per Share	2.000	1.960	1.940	1.890	1.800	1.800	1.800	1.800
Dividend Payout %	45.98	45.69	45.43	44.68	48.65	48.78	53.25	49.05
Income Statement								
Interest Income	372,181	243,420	119,852	457,900	432,110	417,633	398,505	420,489
Interest Expense	33,713	21,269	9,980	40,321	38,023	37,977	39,598	43,218
Net Interest Income	338,468	222,151	109,872	417,579	394,087	379,656	358,907	377,271
Provision for Losses	12,650	8,650	4,400	4,750	1,000	(4,864)	...	979
Non-Interest Income	143,562	101,152	55,916	197,343	186,219	180,017	186,223	200,286
Non-Interest Expense	265,355	176,757	88,568	350,578	348,104	326,899	330,969	334,288
Income Before Taxes	204,025	137,896	72,820	259,594	231,202	237,638	214,161	242,290
Income Taxes	62,306	42,058	21,644	78,133	70,498	74,596	63,659	76,214
Net Income	141,719	95,838	51,176	181,461	160,704	163,042	150,502	166,076
Average Shares	42,565	42,658	42,749	42,879	43,454	44,125	44,572	45,249
Balance Sheet								
Net Loans & Leases	9,476,827	9,301,614	9,029,644	8,908,011	7,780,913	6,794,037	5,986,368	5,747,038
Total Assets	17,268,302	16,981,292	16,664,215	16,492,367	15,455,016	14,787,208	14,084,280	13,728,372
Total Deposits	15,048,160	14,784,649	14,476,533	14,320,240	13,251,103	12,633,089	11,914,656	11,529,482
Total Liabilities	16,040,409	15,767,535	15,471,078	15,330,830	14,338,756	13,732,122	13,072,304	12,706,707
Stockholders' Equity	1,227,893	1,213,757	1,193,137	1,161,537	1,116,260	1,055,086	1,011,976	1,021,665
Shares Outstanding	42,513	42,655	42,736	42,635	43,282	43,724	44,490	44,754
Statistical Record								
Return on Assets %	1.11	1.11	1.13	1.13	1.06	1.13	1.08	1.20
Return on Equity %	15.49	15.42	15.65	15.89	14.80	15.78	14.80	16.36
Net Interest Margin %	90.34	90.86	91.67	91.19	91.20	90.91	90.06	89.72
Efficiency Ratio %	51.76	52.24	50.39	53.50	56.30	54.70	56.60	53.85
Loans to Deposits	0.63	0.63	0.62	0.62	0.59	0.54	0.50	0.50
Price Range	90.36-71.94	90.36-66.16	90.36-65.12	89.31-55.26	69.22-54.53	61.52-53.53	59.67-44.05	49.60-42.04
P/E Ratio	20.77-16.54	21.06-15.42	21.16-15.25	21.11-13.06	18.71-14.74	16.67-14.51	17.65-13.03	13.51-11.46
Average Yield %	2.44	2.48	2.55	2.67	2.85	3.12	3.44	3.90

Address: 130 Merchant Street, Honolulu, HI 96813 Telephone: 888-643-3888	Web Site: www.boh.com Officers: Peter S. Ho - Chairman, President, Chief Executive Officer, Chief Banking Officer Wayne Y. Hamano - Vice-Chairman, Chief Commercial Officer	Auditors: Ernst & Young LLP Investor Contact: 808-694-8430 Transfer Agents: Computershare Investor Services, LLC, Canton, MA

BANK OF NEW YORK MELLON CORP

Exchange	Symbol	Price	52Wk Range	Yield	P/E
NYS	BK	$53.86 (12/29/2017)	54.97-43.87	1.78	15.75

*7 Year Price Score 111.50 *NYSE Composite Index=100 *12 Month Price Score 101.00

Interim Earnings (Per Share)

Qtr.	Mar	Jun	Sep	Dec
2014	0.57	0.48	0.93	0.18
2015	0.67	0.73	0.74	0.58
2016	0.73	0.75	0.90	0.77
2017	0.83	0.88	0.94	...

Interim Dividends (Per Share)

Amt	Decl	Ex	Rec	Pay
0.19Q	04/20/2017	04/28/2017	05/02/2017	05/12/2017
0.24Q	07/20/2017	07/28/2017	08/01/2017	08/11/2017
0.24Q	10/19/2017	10/30/2017	10/31/2017	11/09/2017
0.24Q	01/18/2018	01/29/2018	01/30/2018	02/09/2018

Indicated Div: $0.96 (Div. Reinv. Plan)

Valuation Analysis

		Institutional Holding	
Forecast EPS	$3.55	No of Institutions	
	(01/18/2018)	1330	
Market Cap	$55.2 Billion	Shares	
Book Value	$40.5 Billion	972,952,128	
Price/Book	1.36	% Held	
Price/Sales	3.36	77.60	

Business Summary: Banking (MIC: 5.1.1 SIC: 6022 NAIC: 522110)

Bank of New York Mellon is global investments company. Co. divides its businesses into two principal segments, Investment Management and Investment Services. Co. also has an Other segment which includes the leasing portfolio, corporate treasury activities, derivatives and other trading, corporate and bank-owned life insurance and renewable energy investments, and business exits. Co.'s two principal banking subsidiaries are: The Bank of New York Mellon, which houses Co.'s Investment Services businesses and BNY Mellon, National Association which houses Co.'s Wealth Management business. As of Dec 31 2016, Co. had total assets of $333.47 billion and deposits of $221.49 billion.

Recent Developments: For the quarter ended Sep 30 2017, net income increased 2.7% to US$1.02 billion from US$993.0 million in the year-earlier quarter. Net interest income increased 8.4% to US$839.0 million from US$774.0 million in the year-earlier quarter. Credit for loan losses was US$6.0 million versus US$19.0 million in the prior-year quarter, a decrease of 68.4%. Non-interest income rose 0.3% to US$3.18 billion from US$3.17 billion, while non-interest expense advanced 0.4% to US$2.65 billion.

Prospects: Our evaluation of Bank of New York Mellon Corp. as of Jan. 14, 2018 is the result of our systematic analysis on three basic characteristics: earnings strength, relative valuation, and recent stock price movement. The company has managed to produce a neutral trend in earnings per share over the past 5 quarters and while recent estimates for the company have been raised by analysts, BK has posted better than expected results. Based on operating earnings yield, the company is undervalued when compared to all of the companies in our coverage universe. Share price changes over the past year indicates that BK will perform in line with the market over the near term.

Financial Data

(US$ in Thousands)	9 Mos	6 Mos	3 Mos	12/31/2016	12/31/2015	12/31/2014	12/31/2013	12/31/2012
Earnings Per Share	0.94	0.88	0.83	3.15	2.71	2.15	1.74	2.03
Cash Flow Per Share	19.95	(2.41)	(4.80)	5.84	3.74	3.97	(0.56)	1.38
Tang Book Value Per Share	14.12	13.54	12.73	12.32	11.67	11.22	10.67	9.77
Dividends Per Share	0.240	0.190	0.190	0.720	0.680	0.660	0.580	0.520
Dividend Payout %	25.53	21.59	22.89	22.86	25.09	30.70	33.33	25.62
Income Statement								
Total Revenue	4,328,000	4,182,000	4,011,000	15,674,000	15,494,000	16,046,000	15,326,000	15,249,000
Income Before Taxes	1,368,000	1,308,000	1,206,000	4,725,000	4,235,000	3,563,000	3,712,000	3,302,000
Income Taxes	348,000	332,000	269,000	1,177,000	1,013,000	912,000	1,520,000	779,000
Net Income	1,018,000	975,000	922,000	3,547,000	3,158,000	2,567,000	2,111,000	2,445,000
Average Shares	1,041,138	1,041,879	1,047,746	1,072,013	1,112,511	1,137,480	1,154,441	1,178,430
Balance Sheet								
Total Assets	354,397,000	354,815,000	337,536,000	333,469,000	393,780,000	385,303,000	374,310,000	358,990,000
Total Liabilities	313,874,000	314,841,000	298,398,000	294,658,000	355,743,000	347,862,000	336,789,000	322,559,000
Stockholders' Equity	40,523,000	39,974,000	39,138,000	38,811,000	38,037,000	37,441,000	37,521,000	36,431,000
Shares Outstanding	1,024,022	1,033,156	1,039,877	1,047,488	1,085,342	1,118,227	1,142,249	1,163,490
Statistical Record								
Return on Assets %	1.14	1.13	1.11	0.97	0.81	0.68	0.58	0.71
Return on Equity %	10.03	9.89	9.59	9.21	8.37	6.85	5.71	6.98
Net Margin %	23.52	23.31	22.99	22.63	20.38	16.00	13.77	16.03
Asset Turnover	0.05	0.05	0.05	0.04	0.04	0.04	0.04	0.04
Price Range	54.04-39.09	51.02-37.13	49.17-35.49	49.17-32.74	45.26-35.66	41.53-30.91	34.94-25.70	26.20-19.51
P/E Ratio	57.49-41.59	57.98-42.19	59.24-42.76	15.61-10.39	16.70-13.16	19.32-14.38	20.08-14.77	12.91-9.61
Average Yield %	0.50	0.42	0.44	1.79	1.65	1.81	1.94	2.30

| **Address:** 225 Liberty Street, New York, NY 10286
Telephone: 212-495-1784 | **Web Site:** www.bnymellon.com
Officers: Charles W. Scharf - Chairman, Chief Executive Officer Thomas P. (Todd) Gibbons - Vice-Chairman, Chief Financial Officer, Senior Executive Vice President, Division Officer | **Auditors:** KPMG LLP
Investor Contact: 412-234-4633
Transfer Agents: Computershare Shareowner Services LLC, Jersey City, NJ |

BANKUNITED INC.

Exchange	Symbol	Price	52Wk Range	Yield	P/E
NYS	BKU	$40.72 (12/29/2017)	40.90-30.50	2.06	17.11

*7 Year Price Score 92.08 *NYSE Composite Index=100 *12 Month Price Score 98.33

Interim Earnings (Per Share)

Qtr.	Mar	Jun	Sep	Dec
2014	0.53	0.46	0.51	0.45
2015	0.44	0.43	0.95	0.52
2016	0.51	0.52	0.47	0.59
2017	0.57	0.60	0.62	...

Interim Dividends (Per Share)

Amt	Decl	Ex	Rec	Pay
0.21Q	03/30/2017	04/11/2017	04/13/2017	04/28/2017
0.21Q	06/29/2017	07/12/2017	07/14/2017	07/31/2017
0.21Q	09/25/2017	10/13/2017	10/16/2017	10/31/2017
0.21Q	12/27/2017	01/11/2018	01/12/2018	01/31/2018

Indicated Div: $0.84

Valuation Analysis

		Institutional Holding	
Forecast EPS	$2.40 (01/18/2018)	No of Institutions	316
Market Cap	$4.3 Billion	Shares	128,491,136
Book Value	$2.6 Billion	% Held	93.04
Price/Book	1.66		
Price/Sales	3.32		

TRADING VOLUME (thousand shares)

Business Summary: Banking (MIC: 5.1.1 SIC: 6035 NAIC: 522120)

BankUnited is a bank holding company. Through its subsidiary, BankUnited, National Association, Co. provides banking services to individual and corporate customers. Co.'s lending products include small business loans, commercial real estate loans, equipment loans and leases, term loans, formula-based loans, municipal and non-profit loans and leases, commercial and mortgage warehouse lines of credit, letters of credit and consumer loans. Co.'s deposit products including checking accounts, money market deposit accounts, savings accounts and certificates of deposit. As of Dec 31 2016, Co. had total assets of $27.89 billion and total deposits of $19.49 billion.

Recent Developments: For the quarter ended Sep 30 2017, net income increased 33.3% to US$67.8 million from US$50.8 million in the year-earlier quarter. Net interest income increased 8.8% to US$241.3 million from US$221.7 million in the year-earlier quarter. Provision for loan losses was US$37.9 million versus US$24.4 million in the prior-year quarter, an increase of 55.1%. Non-interest income rose 112.7% to US$53.3 million from US$25.1 million, while non-interest expense advanced 5.9% to US$156.7 million.

Prospects: Our evaluation of BankUnited Inc as of Jan. 14, 2018 is the result of our systematic analysis on three basic characteristics: earnings strength, relative valuation, and recent stock price movement. The company has managed to produce a neutral trend in earnings per share over the past 5 quarters and while recent estimates for the company have been raised by analysts, BKU has posted better than expected results. Based on operating earnings yield, the company is undervalued when compared to all of the companies in our coverage universe. Share price changes over the past year indicates that BKU will perform poorly over the near term.

Financial Data
(US$ in Thousands)

	9 Mos	6 Mos	3 Mos	12/31/2016	12/31/2015	12/31/2014	12/31/2013	12/31/2012
Earnings Per Share	2.38	2.23	2.15	2.09	2.35	1.95	2.01	2.05
Cash Flow Per Share	2.95	2.77	2.72	2.98	2.13	(0.50)	(0.68)	(3.74)
Tang Book Value Per Share	23.83	23.44	22.98	22.47	20.90	19.52	18.41	18.28
Dividends Per Share	0.840	0.840	0.840	0.840	0.630	1.050	0.630	0.720
Dividend Payout %	35.29	37.67	39.07	40.19	26.81	53.85	31.34	35.12
Income Statement								
Total Revenue	1,003,179	640,410	311,682	1,165,634	983,040	867,909	769,927	810,103
Income Before Taxes	285,539	185,508	90,080	335,444	296,893	293,250	318,002	344,865
Income Taxes	89,060	56,808	27,787	109,703	45,233	89,035	109,066	133,605
Net Income	196,479	128,700	62,293	225,741	251,660	204,215	208,936	211,260
Average Shares	106,073	106,138	105,377	103,656	102,972	100,595	99,751	93,828
Balance Sheet								
Total Assets	29,554,831	28,993,736	27,988,731	27,880,151	23,883,467	19,210,529	15,046,649	12,375,953
Total Liabilities	26,931,342	26,412,916	25,455,717	25,461,722	21,639,569	17,157,995	13,117,951	10,569,273
Stockholders' Equity	2,623,489	2,580,820	2,533,014	2,418,429	2,243,898	2,052,534	1,928,698	1,806,680
Shares Outstanding	106,821	106,800	106,839	104,166	103,626	101,656	101,013	95,006
Statistical Record								
Return on Assets %	0.91	0.88	0.88	0.87	1.17	1.19	1.52	1.78
Return on Equity %	10.40	9.89	9.72	9.66	11.71	10.26	11.19	12.61
Net Margin %	19.59	20.10	19.99	19.37	25.60	23.53	27.14	26.08
Asset Turnover	0.05	0.04	0.05	0.04	0.05	0.05	0.06	0.07
Price Range	40.84-28.52	40.84-28.52	40.84-28.13	38.22-28.13	39.34-26.74	35.38-27.66	33.22-24.44	26.15-22.04
P/E Ratio	17.16-11.98	18.31-12.79	19.00-13.08	18.29-13.46	16.74-11.38	18.14-14.18	16.53-12.16	12.76-10.75
Average Yield %	2.41	2.46	2.49	2.57	1.82	3.30	2.23	3.00

Address: 14817 Oak Lane, Miami Lakes, FL 33016
Telephone: 305-569-2000

Web Site: www.bankunited.com
Officers: John Adam Kanas - Chairman, President, Chief Executive Officer Rajinder P. Singh - President, Chief Executive Officer, Chief Operating Officer

Auditors: KPMG LLP
Investor Contact: 305-569-2000
Transfer Agents: Registrar and Transfer Company

BARNES & NOBLE INC

Exchange	Symbol	Price	52Wk Range	Yield	P/E
NYS	BKS	$6.70 (12/29/2017)	11.45-6.50	8.96	N/A

*7 Year Price Score 58.21 ***NYSE Composite Index=100** ***12 Month Price Score 80.51**

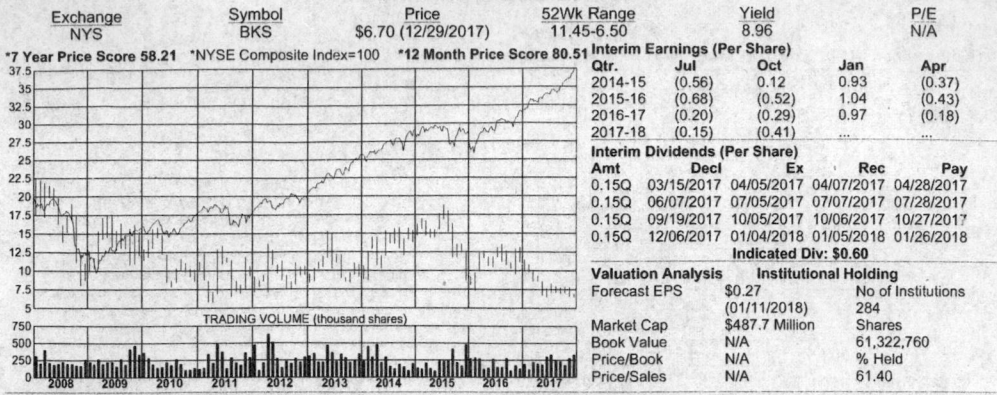

Interim Earnings (Per Share)

Qtr.	Jul	Oct	Jan	Apr
2014-15	(0.56)	0.12	0.93	(0.37)
2015-16	(0.68)	(0.52)	1.04	(0.43)
2016-17	(0.20)	(0.29)	0.97	(0.18)
2017-18	(0.15)	(0.41)		

Interim Dividends (Per Share)

Amt	Decl	Ex	Rec	Pay
0.15Q	03/15/2017	04/05/2017	04/07/2017	04/28/2017
0.15Q	06/07/2017	07/05/2017	07/07/2017	07/28/2017
0.15Q	09/19/2017	10/05/2017	10/06/2017	10/27/2017
0.15Q	12/06/2017	01/04/2018	01/05/2018	01/26/2018

Indicated Div: $0.60

Valuation Analysis		Institutional Holding	
Forecast EPS	$0.27	No of Institutions	
	(01/11/2018)	284	
Market Cap	$487.7 Million	Shares	
Book Value	N.A	61,322,760	
Price/Book	N.A	% Held	
Price/Sales	N.A	61.40	

Business Summary: Retail - Specialty (MIC: 2.1.3 SIC: 5942 NAIC: 451211)

Barnes & Noble is engaged in the sale of trade books, mass market paperbacks, children's books, eBooks and other digital content, NOOK® and related accessories, bargain books, magazines, gifts, cafe products and services, educational toys & games, music and movies. Co.'s operating segments are: B&N Retail, which provides trade book titles, a cafe, and departments providing juvenile, toys & games, DVDs, music & vinyl, gift, and magazine products, among others; and NOOK, which includes its digital business that provides eBooks, digital newsstand and sales of NOOK® devices and accessories. At Apr 29 2017, Co. operated 633 bookstores in 50 states, an eCommerce site, and a digital bookstore.

Recent Developments: For the quarter ended Oct 28 2017, net loss amounted to US$30.1 million versus a net loss of US$20.4 million in the year-earlier quarter. Revenues were US$791.1 million, down 7.9% from US$858.5 million the year before. Operating loss was US$52.2 million versus a loss of US$29.3 million in the prior-year quarter. Direct operating expenses declined 6.8% to US$562.4 million from US$603.2 million in the comparable period the year before. Indirect operating expenses decreased 1.3% to US$280.9 million from US$284.6 million in the equivalent prior-year period.

Prospects: Our evaluation of Barnes & Noble Inc. as of Jan. 14, 2018 is the result of our systematic analysis on three basic characteristics: earnings strength, relative valuation, and recent stock price movement. The company has suffered a very negative trend in earnings per share over the past 5 quarters. However, while recent estimates for the company have been lowered by analysts, BKS has posted results that fell short of analysts expectations. Based on operating earnings yield, the company is undervalued when compared to all of the companies in our coverage universe. Share price changes over the past year indicates that BKS will perform very well over the near term.

Financial Data
(US$ in Thousands)

	6 Mos	3 Mos	04/29/2017	04/30/2016	05/02/2015	05/03/2014	04/27/2013	04/28/2012
Earnings Per Share	(0.41)	(0.15)	0.30	(0.49)	0.21	(1.12)	(3.02)	(1.41)
Cash Flow Per Share	...	0.71	2.02	2.71	0.92	5.34	2.02	(0.42)
Tang Book Value Per Share	N.M.	0.53	0.78	1.11	2.94	N.M.	N.M.	N.M.
Dividends Per Share	0.150	0.150	0.600	0.600	...	...	...	...
Dividend Payout %	...	...	200.00	...	...	...	...	...
Income Statement								
Total Revenue	791,117	853,316	3,894,558	4,163,844	6,069,497	6,381,357	6,839,005	7,129,199
EBITDA	(25,033)	11,673	171,413	149,506	312,635	256,956	12,600	176,745
Depn & Amortn	27,199	26,885	117,105	134,850	179,462	222,764	232,604	238,048
Income Before Taxes	(54,910)	(17,252)	46,799	5,886	115,283	4,685	(255,349)	(96,607)
Income Taxes	...	(6,474)	24,776	(8,814)	78,687	51,953	(97,543)	(27,740)
Net Income	(30,094)	(10,778)	22,023	(24,446)	36,596	(47,268)	(157,806)	(68,867)
Average Shares	72,597	72,453	72,328	72,542	60,928	58,971	58,247	57,337
Balance Sheet								
Current Assets	1,403,551	1,136,966	1,128,012	1,178,390	1,729,315	1,980,438	2,047,135	1,997,793
Total Assets	2,202,688	1,935,358	1,932,921	2,012,782	3,229,505	3,537,449	3,732,536	3,765,249
Current Liabilities	1,264,742	1,114,591	1,108,267	1,193,871	1,447,259	1,721,645	1,715,470	1,827,280
Long-Term Obligations	242,833	84,100	64,900	47,200	...	...	77,000	324,200
Total Liabilities	1,686,515	1,379,575	1,358,610	1,409,272	2,040,147	2,878,753	3,018,793	3,017,592
Stockholders' Equity	516,173	555,783	574,311	603,510	1,189,358	658,696	713,743	747,657
Shares Outstanding	72,646	72,534	72,436	73,287	63,274	59,176	58,706	57,654
Statistical Record								
EBITDA Margin %	N.M.	1.37	4.40	3.59	5.15	4.03	0.18	2.48
Net Margin %	N.M.	N.M.	0.57	N.M.	0.60	N.M.	N.M.	N.M.
Current Ratio	1.11	1.02	1.02	0.99	1.19	1.15	1.19	1.09
Debt to Equity	0.47	0.15	0.11	0.08	...	...	0.11	0.43
Price Range	13.15-6.50	13.52-6.50	13.52-8.50	18.77-7.33	16.98-10.26	15.27-8.40	13.59-7.40	13.37-6.54
P/E Ratio	...	...	45.07-28.33	...	80.85-48.88	...	...	...
Average Yield %	1.68	1.51	3.44	4.59	...	...	...	...

Address: 122 Fifth Avenue, New York, NY 10011	Web Site: www.barnesandnoble.com	Auditors: Ernst & Young LLP
Telephone: 212-633-3300	Officers: Demos Parneros - Chief Operating Officer, Chief Executive Officer Allen W. Lindstrom - Vice President, Chief Financial Officer, Acting Chief Financial Officer, Corporate Controller	Investor Contact: 212-633-3489 Transfer Agents: Computershare, Jersey City, NJ

BAXTER INTERNATIONAL INC

Exchange	Symbol	Price	52Wk Range	Yield	P/E
NYS	BAX	$64.64 (12/29/2017)	66.05-44.44	0.99	34.38

*7 Year Price Score 114.61 *NYSE Composite Index=100 *12 Month Price Score 105.22

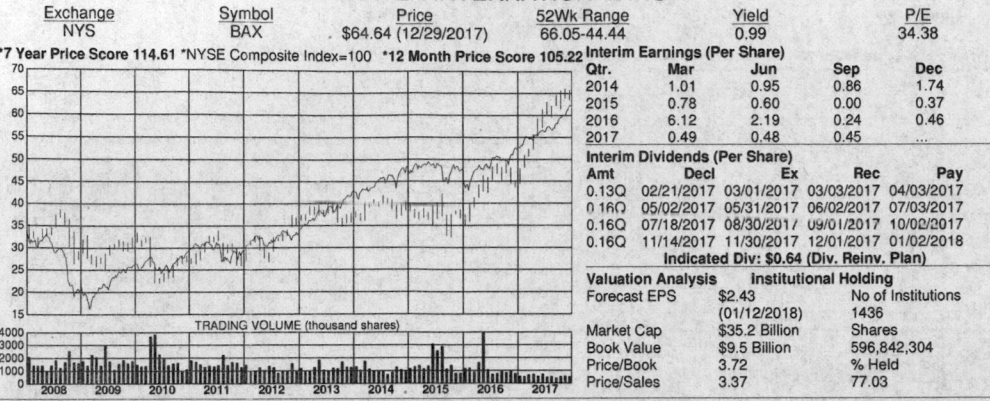

Interim Earnings (Per Share)

Qtr.	Mar	Jun	Sep	Dec
2014	1.01	0.95	0.86	1.74
2015	0.78	0.60	0.00	0.37
2016	6.12	2.19	0.24	0.46
2017	0.49	0.48	0.45	...

Interim Dividends (Per Share)

Amt	Decl	Ex	Rec	Pay
0.13Q	02/21/2017	03/01/2017	03/03/2017	04/03/2017
0.16Q	05/02/2017	05/31/2017	06/02/2017	07/03/2017
0.16Q	07/18/2017	08/30/2017	09/01/2017	10/02/2017
0.16Q	11/14/2017	11/30/2017	12/01/2017	01/02/2018

Indicated Div: $0.64 (Div. Reinv. Plan)

Valuation Analysis — **Institutional Holding**

Forecast EPS	$2.43	No of Institutions
	(01/12/2018)	1436
Market Cap	$35.2 Billion	Shares
Book Value	$9.5 Billion	596,842,304
Price/Book	3.72	% Held
Price/Sales	3.37	77.03

Business Summary: Medical Instruments & Equipment (MIC: 4.3.1 SIC: 3841 NAIC: 339112)

Baxter International provides a portfolio of renal and hospital products, including acute and chronic dialysis; sterile intravenous solutions; infusion systems and devices; parenteral nutrition therapies; premixed and oncolytic injectables; biosurgery products and anesthetics; drug reconstitution systems; and pharmacy automation, software and services. These products are used by hospitals, kidney dialysis centers, nursing homes, rehabilitation centers, doctors' offices and by patients at home under physician supervision. As of Dec 31 2016, Co. manufactured products in about 20 countries and sells them in about 100 countries. Co. operates in two segments: Hospital Products and Renal.

Recent Developments: For the quarter ended Sep 30 2017, income from continuing operations increased 95.3% to US$248.0 million from US$127.0 million in the year-earlier quarter. Net income increased 93.1% to US$251.0 million from US$130.0 million in the year-earlier quarter. Revenues were US$2.71 billion, up 5.8% from US$2.56 billion the year before. Operating income was US$292.0 million versus US$186.0 million in the prior-year quarter, an increase of 57.0%. Direct operating expenses rose 6.2% to US$1.58 billion from US$1.49 billion in the comparable period the year before. Indirect operating expenses decreased 5.5% to US$836.0 million from US$885.0 million in the equivalent prior-year period.

Prospects: Our evaluation of Baxter International Inc. as of Jan. 14, 2018 is the result of our systematic analysis on three basic characteristics: earnings strength, relative valuation, and recent stock price movement. The company has managed to produce a neutral trend in earnings per share over the past 5 quarters and while recent estimates for the company have been mixed, BAX has posted better than expected results. Based on operating earnings yield, the company is about fairly valued when compared to all of the companies in our coverage universe. Share price changes over the past year indicates that BAX will perform well over the near term.

Financial Data
(US$ in Millions)	9 Mos	6 Mos	3 Mos	12/31/2016	12/31/2015	12/31/2014	12/31/2013	12/31/2012
Earnings Per Share	1.88	1.67	3.38	9.01	1.76	4.56	3.66	4.18
Cash Flow Per Share	3.74	3.55	4.02	3.02	3.02	5.93	5.89	5.62
Tang Book Value Per Share	9.14	9.77	9.14	8.50	8.78	4.00	3.62	6.63
Dividends Per Share	0.580	0.550	0.520	0.505	1.270	2.050	1.920	1.570
Dividend Payout %	30.85	32.93	15.38	5.60	72.16	44.96	52.46	37.56
Income Statement								
Total Revenue	7,787	5,080	2,475	10,163	9,968	16,671	15,259	14,190
EBITDA	1,527	1,039	536	5,820	1,313	3,589	3,445	3,661
Depn & Amortn	562	378	194	800	759	1,005	823	712
Income Before Taxes	924	634	328	4,954	428	2,439	2,494	2,862
Income Taxes	139	97	55	(12)	35	493	537	563
Net Income	788	537	272	4,965	968	2,497	2,012	2,326
Average Shares	557	555	551	551	549	547	549	556
Balance Sheet								
Current Assets	7,448	7,704	6,633	6,574	11,796	10,351	10,004	9,260
Total Assets	17,541	16,963	15,659	15,546	20,975	25,917	25,869	20,390
Current Liabilities	2,662	2,558	2,438	2,744	5,750	6,042	5,906	4,759
Long-Term Obligations	3,495	3,454	2,784	2,779	3,935	7,606	8,126	5,580
Total Liabilities	8,075	7,788	6,973	7,256	12,129	17,797	17,406	13,452
Stockholders' Equity	9,466	9,175	8,686	8,290	8,846	8,120	8,463	6,938
Shares Outstanding	544	544	542	539	547	542	543	546
Statistical Record								
Return on Assets %	6.19	5.52	11.25	27.12	4.13	9.64	8.70	11.76
Return on Equity %	11.37	10.29	20.98	57.79	11.41	30.12	26.13	34.31
EBITDA Margin %	19.61	20.45	21.66	57.27	13.17	21.53	22.58	25.80
Net Margin %	10.12	10.57	10.99	48.85	9.71	14.98	13.19	16.39
Asset Turnover	0.63	0.62	0.62	0.56	0.43	0.64	0.66	0.72
Current Ratio	2.80	3.01	2.72	2.40	2.05	1.71	1.69	1.95
Debt to Equity	0.37	0.38	0.32	0.34	0.44	0.94	0.96	0.80
Price Range	64.61-43.63	61.38-43.63	52.30-41.08	49.16-34.76	42.13-32.27	41.83-36.12	40.43-34.71	37.38-26.64
P/E Ratio	34.37-23.21	36.75-26.13	15.47-12.15	5.46-3.86	23.94-18.34	9.17-7.92	11.05-9.48	8.94-6.37
Average Yield %	1.08	1.10	1.12	1.15	3.39		5.22	5.10	4.98

Address: One Baxter Parkway, Deerfield, IL 60015
Telephone: 224-948-2000
Fax: 847-948-2964

Web Site: www.baxter.com
Officers: Jose E. Almeida - Chairman, President, Chief Executive Officer James K. Saccaro - Corporate Vice-President, Chief Financial Officer

Auditors: PricewaterhouseCoopers LLP
Transfer Agents: Computershare Trust Company, N.A., Providence, RI

BB&T CORP.

Exchange	Symbol	Price	52Wk Range	Yield	P/E
NYS	BBT	$49.72 (12/29/2017)	50.45-41.65	2.65	N/A

*7 Year Price Score 102.17 *NYSE Composite Index=100 *12 Month Price Score 99.56

Interim Earnings (Per Share)

Qtr.	Mar	Jun	Sep	Dec
2014	0.69	0.58	0.71	0.76
2015	0.67	0.62	0.64	0.64
2016	0.67	0.66	0.73	0.72
2017	0.46	0.77	0.74	...

Interim Dividends (Per Share)

Amt	Decl	Ex	Rec	Pay
0.30Q	01/24/2017	02/08/2017	02/10/2017	03/01/2017
0.30Q	04/25/2017	05/10/2017	05/12/2017	06/01/2017
0.33Q	07/25/2017	08/09/2017	08/11/2017	09/01/2017
0.33Q	10/23/2017	11/09/2017	11/10/2017	12/01/2017

Indicated Div: $1.32 (Div. Reinv. Plan)

Valuation Analysis | **Institutional Holding**

Forecast EPS	$2.76 (01/18/2018)	No of Institutions	1195
Market Cap	$39.2 Billion	Shares	
Book Value	N/A		601,546,112
Price/Book	N/A	% Held	
Price/Sales	N/A		60.61

Business Summary: Banking (MIC: 5.1.1 SIC: 6021 NAIC: 522110)

BB&T is a financial holding company. Through its subsidiary, Branch Banking and Trust Company, Co. provides loans and lease financing, including insurance premium financing, permanent commercial real estate financing, loan servicing for third-party investors, direct consumer finance loans to individuals, credit card lending, automobile financing, factoring and equipment financing. Co. also markets other services, including deposits; discount and brokerage, annuities and mutual funds; and life insurance, property and casualty insurance, health insurance and commercial general liability insurance. At Dec 31 2016, Co. had total assets of $219.28 billion and total deposits of $160.23 billion.

Recent Developments: For the quarter ended Sep 30 2017, net income increased 0.9% to US$648.0 million from US$642.0 million in the year-earlier quarter. Net interest income increased 2.3% to US$1.65 billion from US$1.61 billion in the year-earlier quarter. Provision for loan losses was US$126.0 million versus US$148.0 million in the prior-year quarter, a decrease of 14.9%. Non-interest income rose 0.2% to US$1.17 billion from US$1.16 billion, while non-interest expense advanced 2.0% to US$1.75 billion.

Prospects: Our evaluation of BB&T Corp. as of Jan. 14, 2018 is the result of our systematic analysis on three basic characteristics: earnings strength, relative valuation, and recent stock price movement. The company has enjoyed a very positive trend in earnings per share over the past 5 quarters. However, while recent estimates for the company have been mixed, BBT has posted results that fell short of analysts expectations. Based on operating earnings yield, the company is undervalued when compared to all of the companies in our coverage universe. Share price changes over the past year indicates that BBT will perform poorly over the near term.

Financial Data

(US$ in Thousands)	9 Mos	6 Mos	3 Mos	12/31/2016	12/31/2015	12/31/2014	12/31/2013	12/31/2012
Earnings Per Share	0.74	0.77	0.46	2.77	2.56	2.75	2.19	2.70
Cash Flow Per Share	7.35	...	0.79	3.31	3.90	4.54	7.59	5.28
Tang Book Value Per Share	19.46	19.55	19.03	18.88	18.70	-18.76	16.59	15.63
Dividends Per Share	0.330	0.300	0.300	1.150	1.050	0.950	1.120	0.760
Dividend Payout %	44.59	38.96	65.22	41.52	41.02	34.55	51.14	28.15
Income Statement								
Interest Income	1,877,000	1,824,000	1,775,000	7,066,000	6,327,000	6,142,000	6,507,000	6,917,000
Interest Expense	230,000	189,000	166,000	745,000	735,000	768,000	891,000	1,060,000
Net Interest Income	1,647,000	1,635,000	1,609,000	6,321,000	5,592,000	5,374,000	5,616,000	5,857,000
Provision for Losses	126,000	135,000	148,000	572,000	428,000	251,000	592,000	1,057,000
Non-Interest Income	1,166,000	1,220,000	1,171,000	4,472,000	4,019,000	3,784,000	3,937,000	3,820,000
Non-Interest Expense	1,745,000	1,742,000	1,710,000	6,721,000	6,266,000	5,921,000	5,837,000	5,828,000
Income Before Taxes	942,000	978,000	530,000	3,500,000	2,917,000	2,986,000	3,124,000	2,792,000
Income Taxes	294,000	...	104,000	1,058,000	794,000	760,000	1,395,000	764,000
Net Income	640,000	675,000	421,000	2,426,000	2,084,000	2,151,000	1,679,000	1,979,000
Average Shares	806,124	819,389	822,719	814,916	757,765	728,372	714,363	708,877
Balance Sheet								
Net Loans & Leases	142,533,000	143,631,000	142,409,000	143,549,000	135,526,000	119,833,000	115,407,000	116,346,000
Total Assets	220,340,000	221,192,000	220,501,000	219,276,000	209,947,000	186,814,000	183,010,000	183,872,000
Total Deposits	156,135,000	156,968,000	161,333,000	160,234,000	149,124,000	129,040,000	127,475,000	133,075,000
Total Liabilities	190,530,000	190,885,000	190,476,000	189,395,000	182,641,000	162,476,000	160,251,000	162,714,000
Stockholders' Equity	29,810,000	30,307,000	30,025,000	29,881,000	27,306,000	24,338,000	22,759,000	21,158,000
Shares Outstanding	788,921	808,093	811,700	809,475	780,337	720,698	706,620	699,728
Statistical Record								
Net Interest Margin %	87.75	89.64	90.65	89.46	88.38	87.50	86.31	84.68
Efficiency Ratio %	57.34	57.23	58.04	58.25	60.56	59.65	55.89	54.28
Loans to Deposits	0.91	0.92	0.88	0.90	0.91	0.93	0.91	0.87
Price Range	49.70-37.43	49.70-34.22	49.70-32.44	47.71-30.28	41.60-34.78	40.77-35.20	37.32-29.11	33.99-25.79
P/E Ratio	67.16-50.58	64.55-44.44	108.04-70.52	17.22-10.93	16.25-13.59	14 83-12.80	17.04-13.29	12.59-9.55
Average Yield %	0.74	0.71	0.74	3.11	2.74	2.50	3.39	2.51

Address: 200 West Second Street, Winston-Salem, NC 27101	Web Site: www.bbt.com	Auditors: PricewaterhouseCoopers LLP
Telephone: 336-733-2000	Officers: Kelly S. King - Chairman, President, Chief Executive Officer, Chief Operating Officer, President (frmr) Christopher L. Henson - President, Chief Operating Officer	Investor Contact: 336-733-3021
Fax: 336-671-2399		Transfer Agents: Computershare Trust Company, N.A., Providence, RI

94

BECTON, DICKINSON & CO

Exchange	Symbol	Price	52Wk Range	Yield	P/E	Div Achiever
NYS	BDX	$214.06 (12/29/2017)	228.21-164.80	1.40	46.53	44 Years

*7 Year Price Score 121.58 *NYSE Composite Index=100 *12 Month Price Score 106.30

Interim Earnings (Per Share)

Qtr.	Dec	Mar	Jun	Sep
2012-13	3.13	1.39	1.52	0.45
2013-14	1.37	1.45	1.65	1.52
2014-15	1.20	1.08	0.30	0.83
2015-16	1.06	1.56	1.80	0.08
2016-17	2.58	1.58	(0.75)	1.24

Interim Dividends (Per Share)

Amt	Decl	Ex	Rec	Pay
0.73Q	01/23/2017	03/08/2017	03/10/2017	03/31/2017
0.73Q	05/23/2017	06/07/2017	06/09/2017	06/30/2017
0.73Q	07/25/2017	09/07/2017	09/08/2017	09/29/2017
0.75Q	11/20/2017	12/07/2017	12/08/2017	12/29/2017

Indicated Div: $3.00 (Div. Reinv. Plan)

Valuation Analysis

		Institutional Holding	
Forecast EPS	$10.85	No of Institutions	
	(01/16/2018)	1483	
Market Cap	$48.8 Billion	Shares	
Book Value	$12.9 Billion	249,336,224	
Price/Book	3.77	% Held	
Price/Sales	4.03	77.82	

Business Summary: Medical Instruments & Equipment (MIC: 4.3.1 SIC: 3841 NAIC: 339112)

Becton, Dickinson and Company is a medical technology company engaged in the development, manufacture and sale of a range of medical supplies, devices, laboratory equipment and diagnostic products. Co.'s operations consist of two business segments: BD Medical and BD Life Sciences. BD Medical segment produces an array of medical technologies and devices that are used to help improve healthcare delivery in a range of settings. BD Life Sciences segment provides products for the safe collection and transport of diagnostics specimens, and instruments and reagent systems to detect a range of infectious diseases, healthcare-associated infections and cancers.

Recent Developments: For the year ended Sep 30 2017, net income increased 12.7% to US$1.10 billion from US$976.0 million in the prior year. Revenues were US$12.09 billion, down 3.1% from US$12.48 billion the year before. Operating income was US$1.48 billion versus US$1.43 billion in the prior year, an increase of 3.4%. Direct operating expenses declined 5.3% to US$6.15 billion from US$6.49 billion in the comparable period the year before. Indirect operating expenses decreased 2.1% to US$4.46 billion from US$4.56 billion in the equivalent prior-year period.

Prospects: Our evaluation of Becton, Dickinson and Co. as of Jan. 14, 2018 is the result of our systematic analysis on three basic characteristics: earnings strength, relative valuation, and recent stock price movement. The company has managed to produce a neutral trend in earnings per share over the past 5 quarters and while recent estimates for the company have been raised by analysts, BDX has posted better than expected results. Based on operating earnings yield, the company is about fairly valued when compared to all of the companies in our coverage universe. Share price changes over the past year indicates that BDX will perform in line with the market over the near term.

Financial Data
(US$ in Thousands)

	09/30/2017	09/30/2016	09/30/2015	09/30/2014	09/30/2013	09/30/2012	09/30/2011	09/30/2010
Earnings Per Share	4.60	4.49	3.35	5.99	6.49	5.59	5.62	5.49
Cash Flow Per Share	11.65	12.00	8.54	9.03	8.80	8.22	7.74	7.08
Tang Book Value Per Share	N.M.	N.M.	N.M.	14.79	14.07	9.65	12.67	16.87
Dividends Per Share	2.920	2.640	2.400	2.180	1.980	1.800	1.640	1.480
Dividend Payout %	63.48	58.80	71.64	36.39	30.51	32.20	29.18	26.96
Income Statement								
Total Revenue	12,093,000	12,483,000	10,282,000	8,446,000	8,054,000	7,708,382	7,828,904	7,372,333
EBITDA	2,509,000	2,555,000	1,986,000	2,173,000	1,809,000	2,067,671	2,261,162	2,179,407
Depn & Amortn	1,088,000	1,114,000	891,000	562,000	546,000	510,938	504,089	502,113
Income Before Taxes	976,000	1,074,000	739,000	1,522,000	1,165,000	1,472,408	1,716,263	1,661,160
Income Taxes	(124,000)	97,000	44,000	337,000	236,000	362,880	451,411	484,820
Net Income	1,100,000	976,000	695,000	1,185,000	1,293,000	1,169,927	1,270,994	1,317,610
Average Shares	223,588	217,536	207,509	197,709	199,193	209,181	226,280	240,136
Balance Sheet								
Current Assets	18,633,000	6,367,000	6,045,000	6,131,000	5,873,000	5,322,071	4,668,331	4,505,250
Total Assets	37,734,000	25,586,000	26,820,000	12,447,000	12,149,000	11,360,909	10,430,428	9,650,694
Current Liabilities	3,342,000	4,400,000	4,386,000	2,235,000	2,130,000	1,978,055	1,823,228	1,671,673
Long-Term Obligations	18,664,000	10,550,000	11,370,000	3,769,000	3,763,000	3,761,112	2,484,665	1,495,357
Total Liabilities	24,783,000	17,953,000	19,656,000	7,396,000	7,106,000	7,225,020	5,602,253	4,216,114
Stockholders' Equity	12,948,000	7,633,000	7,164,000	5,053,000	5,043,000	4,135,889	4,828,175	5,434,580
Shares Outstanding	227,942	213,291	210,695	191,892	193,999	196,911	214,818	229,816
Statistical Record								
Return on Assets %	3.47	3.71	3.54	9.64	11.00	10.71	12.66	13.90
Return on Equity %	10.69	13.16	11.38	23.47	28.17	26.03	24.77	24.91
EBITDA Margin %	20.75	20.47	19.32	25.73	22.46	26.82	28.88	29.56
Net Margin %	9.10	7.82	6.76	14.03	16.05	15.18	16.23	17.87
Asset Turnover	0.38	0.48	0.52	0.69	0.69	0.71	0.78	0.78
Current Ratio	5.58	1.45	1.38	2.74	2.76	2.69	2.56	2.70
Debt to Equity	1.44	1.38	1.59	0.75	0.75	0.91	0.51	0.28
Price Range	205.63-162.80	181.55-132.19	153.86-113.60	120.33-98.33	104.50-74.63	79.91-70.65	89.74-73.25	80.14-66.60
P/E Ratio	44.70-35.39	40.43-29.44	45.93-33.91	20.09-16.42	16.10-11.50	14.30-12.64	15.97-13.03	14.60-12.13
Average Yield %	1.59	1.67	1.72	1.93	2.18	2.39	2.01	2.01

Address: 1 Becton Drive, Franklin Lakes, NJ 07417-1880 Telephone: 201-847-6800	Web Site: www.bd.com Officers: Vincent A. Forlenza - Chairman, President, Chief Executive Officer, Chief Operating Officer Thomas E. Polen - President, Executive Vice President, Division Officer	Auditors: Ernst & Young LLP Investor Contact: 180-028-46845 Transfer Agents: Computershare Trust Company, N.A., Canton, MA

BELDEN INC

Exchange	Symbol	Price	52Wk Range	Yield	P/E
NYS	BDC	$77.17 (12/29/2017)	86.29-64.68	0.26	52.86

*7 Year Price Score 101.76 *NYSE Composite Index=100 *12 Month Price Score 102.48

Interim Earnings (Per Share)

Qtr.	Mar	Jun	Sep	Dec
2014	0.56	0.00	0.77	0.37
2015	(0.46)	0.50	0.34	1.16
2016	0.39	0.98	0.68	0.60
2017	0.40	0.64	(0.18)	...

Interim Dividends (Per Share)

Amt	Decl	Ex	Rec	Pay
0.05Q	02/23/2017	03/14/2017	03/16/2017	04/05/2017
0.05Q	05/25/2017	06/13/2017	06/15/2017	07/06/2017
0.05Q	08/21/2017	09/14/2017	09/15/2017	10/04/2017
0.05Q	11/30/2017	12/14/2017	12/15/2017	01/04/2018

Indicated Div: $0.20

Valuation Analysis

		Institutional Holding	
Forecast EPS	$5.50	No of Institutions	
	(01/23/2018)	341	
Market Cap	$3.3 Billion	Shares	
Book Value	$1.4 Billion	63,559,204	
Price/Book	2.26	% Held	
Price/Sales	1.36	92.61	

Business Summary: Electrical Equipment (MIC: 7.3.1 SIC: 3357 NAIC: 335921)

Belden is a signal transmission solutions company. Co. has five segments: Broadcast Solutions, which provides production, distribution, and connectivity systems for television broadcast, cable, satellite, and Internet Protocol television industries; Enterprise Connectivity Solutions, which provides network infrastructure solutions; Industrial Connectivity Solutions, which provides networking components and connectivity products; Industrial IT Solutions, which provides networking systems for markets such as discrete manufacturing, process, including oil and gas, energy and transportation; and Network Security Solutions, which provides software and services that protect against cyberattacks.

Recent Developments: For the quarter ended Oct 1 2017, net income decreased 97.4% to US$945,000 from US$36.1 million in the year-earlier quarter. Revenues were US$621.7 million, up 3.4% from US$601.1 million the year before. Operating income was US$60.8 million versus US$62.0 million in the prior-year quarter, a decrease of 1.9%. Direct operating expenses rose 7.5% to US$381.9 million from US$355.1 million in the comparable period the year before. Indirect operating expenses decreased 2.7% to US$179.0 million from US$184.0 million in the equivalent prior-year period.

Prospects: Our evaluation of Belden Inc. as of Jan. 21, 2018 is the result of our systematic analysis on three basic characteristics: earnings strength, relative valuation, and recent stock price movement. The company has enjoyed a very positive trend in earnings per share over the past 5 quarters and while recent estimates for the company have been mixed, BDC has posted better than expected results. Based on operating earnings yield, the company is undervalued when compared to all of the companies in our coverage universe. Share price changes over the past year indicates that BDC will perform poorly over the near term.

Financial Data

(US$ in Thousands)	9 Mos	6 Mos	3 Mos	12/31/2016	12/31/2015	12/31/2014	12/31/2013	12/31/2012
Earnings Per Share	1.46	2.32	2.66	2.65	1.54	1.69	2.31	4.23
Cash Flow Per Share	6.43	6.84	6.87	7.46	5.58	4.48	3.75	3.08
Dividends Per Share	0.200	0.200	0.200	0.200	0.200	0.200	0.200	0.200
Dividend Payout %	13.70	8.62	7.52	7.55	12.99	11.83	8.66	4.73
Income Statement								
Total Revenue	1,783,759	1,162,014	551,381	2,356,672	2,309,222	2,308,265	2,069,193	1,840,739
EBITDA	234,712	186,653	86,406	367,096	289,174	261,290	285,131	104,235
Depn & Amortn	112,544	73,682	35,069	145,585	150,391	102,126	94,403	57,892
Income Before Taxes	55,744	65,932	27,831	126,461	38,170	77,591	118,127	(4,662)
Income Taxes	(6,673)	4,460	2,250	(1,185)	(26,568)	7,114	22,315	(38,194)
Net Income	62,691	61,664	25,687	128,003	66,204	74,449	103,313	194,490
Average Shares	42,256	42,832	42,675	42,557	42,953	43,997	44,737	45,942
Balance Sheet								
Current Assets	1,266,134	1,416,851	1,478,423	1,478,952	843,164	1,414,150	1,195,498	959,582
Total Assets	3,704,848	3,862,670	3,787,641	3,806,803	3,315,841	3,262,827	2,751,753	2,584,583
Current Liabilities	560,634	537,691	521,710	570,279	549,263	525,359	401,566	452,482
Long-Term Obligations	1,530,077	1,679,382	1,641,929	1,620,161	1,750,521	1,765,422	1,364,536	1,135,527
Total Liabilities	2,263,186	2,384,331	2,322,361	2,346,490	2,491,742	2,455,641	1,915,212	1,772,723
Stockholders' Equity	1,441,662	1,478,339	1,465,280	1,460,313	824,099	807,186	836,541	811,860
Shares Outstanding	42,160	42,299	42,271	42,180	41,981	42,464	43,455	44,168
Statistical Record								
Return on Assets %	2.57	3.69	3.91	3.58	2.01	2.48	3.87	8.87
Return on Equity %	6.78	11.12	11.91	11.18	8.12	9.06	12.53	25.75
EBITDA Margin %	13.16	16.06	15.67	15.58	12.52	11.32	13.78	5.66
Net Margin %	3.51	5.31	4.66	5.43	2.87	3.23	4.99	10.57
Asset Turnover	0.64	0.67	0.68	0.66	0.70	0.77	0.78	0.84
Current Ratio	2.26	2.64	2.83	2.59	1.54	2.69	2.98	2.12
Debt to Equity	1.06	1.14	1.12	1.11	2.12	2.19	1.63	1.40
Price Range	81.15-60.41	80.48-58.07	80.48-56.30	80.48-37.15	95.14-45.10	80.96-58.56	71.30-44.99	44.99-30.24
P/E Ratio	55.58-41.38	34.69-25.03	30.26-21.17	30.37-14.02	61.78-29.29	47.91-34.65	30.87-19.48	10.64-7.15
Average Yield %	0.27	0.28	0.29	0.32	0.28	0.28	0.35	0.55

Address: 1 North Brentwood Boulevard, 15th Floor, St. Louis, MO 63105 **Telephone:** 314-854-8000 **Fax:** 314-854-8001	**Web Site:** www.belden.com **Officers:** John S. Stroup - Chairman, President, Chief Executive Officer Ross Rosenberg - Senior Vice President	**Auditors:** Ernst & Young LLP **Investor Contact:** 314-854-8054 **Transfer Agents:** American Stock Transfer & Trust Company, Brooklyn, NY

BEMIS CO INC

Exchange	Symbol	Price	52Wk Range	Yield	P/E	Div Achiever
NYS	BMS	$47.79 (12/29/2017)	51.65-40.96	2.51	22.76	33 Years

*7 Year Price Score 89.62   *NYSE Composite Index=100   *12 Month Price Score 93.93

Interim Earnings (Per Share)

Qtr.	Mar	Jun	Sep	Dec
2014	0.48	0.65	0.17	0.59
2015	0.55	0.67	0.64	0.58
2016	0.59	0.53	0.72	0.64
2017	0.55	0.30	0.61	...

Interim Dividends (Per Share)

Amt	Decl	Ex	Rec	Pay
0.30Q	02/09/2017	02/16/2017	02/21/2017	03/01/2017
0.30Q	05/04/2017	05/15/2017	05/17/2017	06/01/2017
0.30Q	08/03/2017	08/15/2017	08/17/2017	09/01/2017
0.30Q	11/02/2017	11/14/2017	11/15/2017	12/01/2017

Indicated Div: $1.20 (Div. Reinv. Plan)

Valuation Analysis   **Institutional Holding**

Forecast EPS	$2.36	No of Institutions	
	(01/11/2018)	512	
Market Cap	$4.3 Billion	Shares	
Book Value	$1.3 Billion	97,655,576	
Price/Book	3.40	% Held	
Price/Sales	1.08	70.14	

Business Summary: Containers & Packaging (MIC: 8.1.3 SIC: 2671 NAIC: 322221)

Bemis Co is a manufacturer of packaging products. The majority of Co.'s products are sold to customers in the food industry. The U.S. Packaging segment represents all food, consumer, and industrial products packaging-related manufacturing operations located in the U.S. This segment manufactures multilayer polymer, blown and cast film structures which are then converted to produce packaging for processed and fresh meat, dairy, liquids, and frozen foods. The Global Packaging segment includes all packaging-related manufacturing operations located outside of the U.S. as well as global medical device and pharmaceutical packaging-related manufacturing operations.

Recent Developments: For the quarter ended Sep 30 2017, net income decreased 19.0% to US$55.6 million from US$68.6 million in the year-earlier quarter. Revenues were US$1.04 billion, up 0.8% from US$1.03 billion the year before. Operating income was US$98.0 million versus US$116.2 million in the prior-year quarter, a decrease of 15.7%. Direct operating expenses rose 3.1% to US$827.4 million from US$802.4 million in the comparable period the year before. Indirect operating expenses increased 1.0% to US$109.7 million from US$108.6 million in the equivalent prior-year period.

Prospects: Our evaluation of Bemis Co Inc. as of Jan. 14, 2018 is the result of our systematic analysis on three basic characteristics: earnings strength, relative valuation, and recent stock price movement. The company has managed to produce a neutral trend in earnings per share over the past 5 quarters and while recent estimates for the company have been mixed, BMS has posted better than expected results. Based on operating earnings yield, the company is undervalued when compared to all of the companies in our coverage universe. Share price changes over the past year indicates that BMS will perform in line with the market over the near term.

Financial Data

(US$ in Thousands)	9 Mos	6 Mos	3 Mos	12/31/2016	12/31/2015	12/31/2014	12/31/2013	12/31/2012
Earnings Per Share	2.10	2.21	2.44	2.48	2.44	1.89	2.04	1.66
Cash Flow Per Share	4.27	5.27	5.19	4.63	5.71	2.48	3.63	4.07
Tang Book Value Per Share	0.91	0.86	0.79	0.82	1.14	3.07	4.34	3.93
Dividends Per Share	1.190	1.180	1.170	1.160	1.120	1.080	1.040	1.000
Dividend Payout %	56.67	53.39	47.95	46.77	45.90	57.14	50.98	60.24
Income Statement								
Total Revenue	3,042,600	2,007,500	995,400	4,004,400	4,071,400	4,343,500	5,029,800	5,139,200
EBITDA	373,600	232,400	132,100	557,200	559,800	594,500	578,800	555,200
Depn & Amortn	127,500	85,000	41,800	146,100	144,220	170,000	190,300	205,700
Income Before Taxes	197,400	115,400	74,300	350,900	363,900	363,700	320,300	278,600
Income Taxes	62,700	36,300	23,200	114,700	122,000	124,600	107,700	104,800
Net Income	134,700	79,100	51,100	236,200	239,300	191,100	212,600	173,800
Average Shares	91,200	92,300	92,800	95,100	97,900	101,200	103,900	103,900
Balance Sheet								
Current Assets	1,264,900	1,240,200	1,196,000	1,165,500	1,119,000	1,287,800	1,504,500	1,525,000
Total Assets	3,876,700	3,830,300	3,778,800	3,715,700	3,489,800	3,615,100	4,110,200	4,185,700
Current Liabilities	703,700	695,100	625,500	576,100	589,100	481,400	601,900	643,000
Long-Term Obligations	1,530,600	1,516,800	1,536,700	1,527,800	1,353,900	1,315,900	1,421,400	1,417,600
Total Liabilities	2,600,800	2,565,600	2,517,000	2,456,000	2,282,400	2,182,100	2,425,400	2,544,800
Stockholders' Equity	1,275,900	1,264,700	1,261,800	1,259,700	1,207,400	1,433,000	1,684,800	1,640,900
Shares Outstanding	90,800	92,000	92,000	92,700	95,100	98,200	101,900	103,200
Statistical Record								
Return on Assets %	5.12	5.48	6.29	6.54	6.74	4.95	5.13	4.08
Return on Equity %	15.26	16.25	18.53	19.10	18.13	12.26	12.79	10.76
EBITDA Margin %	12.28	11.58	13.27	13.91	13.75	13.69	11.51	10.80
Net Margin %	4.43	3.94	5.13	5.90	5.88	4.40	4.23	3.38
Asset Turnover	1.06	1.06	1.10	1.11	1.15	1.12	1.21	1.21
Current Ratio	1.80	1.78	1.91	2.02	1.90	2.68	2.50	2.37
Debt to Equity	1.20	1.20	1.22	1.21	1.12	0.92	0.84	0.86
Price Range	51.65-40.96	53.09-43.75	53.74-47.70	54.08-43.25	49.33-39.17	46.08-37.17	42.23-33.46	33.79-29.78
P/E Ratio	24.60-19.50	24.02-19.80	22.02-19.55	21.81-17.44	20.22-16.05	24.38-19.67	20.70-16.40	20.36-17.94
Average Yield %	2.52	2.41	2.33	2.33	2.48	2.70	2.66	3.17

Address: One Neenah Center, 4th Floor, P.O. Box 669, Neenah, WI 54957-0669 **Telephone:** 920-527-5000	**Web Site:** www.bemis.com **Officers:** Timothy M. Manganello - Chairman William F. Austen - President, Chief Executive Officer, Executive Vice President, Vice President, Chief Operating Officer, Division Officer	**Auditors:** PricewaterhouseCoopers LLP **Investor Contact:** 920-727-4100 **Transfer Agents:** Wells Fargo Bank, N.A., South St. Paul, MN

BERKLEY (WR) CORP

Exchange	Symbol	Price	52Wk Range	Yield	P/E	Div Achiever
NYS	WRB	$71.65 (12/29/2017)	72.98-62.54	0.78	16.86	15 Years

*7 Year Price Score 112.16 *NYSE Composite Index=100 *12 Month Price Score 95.14

Interim Earnings (Per Share)

Qtr.	Mar	Jun	Sep	Dec
2014	1.25	1.35	1.42	0.84
2015	0.89	0.95	1.18	0.85
2016	0.93	0.85	1.72	1.18
2017	0.96	0.85	1.26	...

Interim Dividends (Per Share)

Amt	Decl	Ex	Rec	Pay
0.50Q	05/16/2017	06/13/2017	06/15/2017	07/05/2017
0.14Q	08/08/2017	09/19/2017	09/20/2017	10/04/2017
0.14Q	11/13/2017	11/29/2017	11/30/2017	12/14/2017
0.50Q	11/13/2017	11/29/2017	11/30/2017	12/14/2017

Indicated Div: $0.56

Valuation Analysis

		Institutional Holding	
Forecast EPS	$2.42	No of Institutions	
	(01/18/2018)	525	
Market Cap	$8.7 Billion	Shares	
Book Value	$5.4 Billion	121,571,320	
Price/Book	1.61	% Held	
Price/Sales	1.13	63.86	

Business Summary: General Insurance (MIC: 5.2.1 SIC: 6331 NAIC: 524126)

W. R. Berkley is an insurance holding company. Co. operates in two segments of the property casualty insurance business: Insurance, which includes commercial insurance business, including excess and surplus lines and admitted lines, throughout the U.S., as well as insurance business in the U.K., Continental Europe, South America, Canada, Mexico, Scandinavia, Asia and Australia; and Reinsurance, which provides reinsurance business on a facultative and treaty basis in the U.S., U.K., Continental Europe, Australia, the Asia-Pacific region and South Africa. Co. also invests in equity securities, merger arbitrage securities, investment funds, private equity, loans and real estate related assets.

Recent Developments: For the quarter ended Sep 30 2017, net income decreased 26.2% to US$162.8 million from US$220.7 million in the year-earlier quarter. Revenues were US$2.03 billion, up 0.6% from US$2.02 billion the year before. Net premiums earned were US$1.58 billion versus US$1.59 billion in the prior-year quarter, a decrease of 0.3%. Net investment income fell 2.2% to US$142.5 million from US$145.7 million a year ago.

Prospects: Our evaluation of Berkley (W. R.) Corp. as of Jan. 14, 2018 is the result of our systematic analysis on three basic characteristics: earnings strength, relative valuation, and recent stock price movement. The company has generated a negative trend in earnings per share over the past 5 quarters and while recent estimates for the company have been mixed, WRB has posted better than expected results. Based on operating earnings yield, the company is about fairly valued when compared to all of the companies in our coverage universe. Share price changes over the past year indicates that WRB will perform well over the near term.

Financial Data

(US$ in Thousands)	9 Mos	6 Mos	3 Mos	12/31/2016	12/31/2015	12/31/2014	12/31/2013	12/31/2012
Earnings Per Share	4.25	4.71	4.71	4.68	3.87	4.86	3.55	3.56
Cash Flow Per Share	5.12	5.91	6.42	6.90	7.10	5.75	6.06	4.91
Tang Book Value Per Share	43.17	42.40	41.54	40.45	36.06	35.02	31.96	31.01
Dividends Per Share	1.540	2.030	1.520	1.510	0.470	1.430	0.390	1.350
Dividend Payout %	36.24	43.10	32.27	32.26	12.14	29.42	10.99	37.92
Income Statement								
Premium Income	4,720,244	3,138,744	1,570,042	6,293,348	6,040,609	5,744,418	5,226,537	4,673,516
Total Revenue	5,749,808	3,718,467	1,870,418	7,654,184	7,206,457	7,128,928	6,408,534	5,823,554
Benefits & Claims	3,025,475	1,944,302	979,603	3,845,800	3,656,270	3,490,567	3,197,024	2,948,479
Income Before Taxes	571,370	345,258	184,297	896,438	732,030	952,196	698,888	701,928
Income Taxes	174,305	111,011	59,623	292,953	227,923	302,593	193,587	191,285
Net Income	394,505	232,451	123,447	601,916	503,694	648,884	499,925	510,592
Average Shares	128,944	128,601	128,453	128,552	130,188	133,652	140,742	143,314
Balance Sheet								
Total Assets	24,336,076	23,993,491	23,547,414	23,364,844	21,730,967	21,716,691	20,551,796	20,155,896
Total Liabilities	18,905,540	18,706,973	18,367,808	18,317,636	17,130,721	17,126,746	16,215,761	15,849,679
Stockholders' Equity	5,430,536	5,286,518	5,179,606	5,047,208	4,600,246	4,589,945	4,336,035	4,306,217
Shares Outstanding	121,769	121,271	121,218	121,193	123,307	126,748	132,233	136,017
Statistical Record								
Return on Assets %	2.30	2.58	2.65	2.66	2.32	3.07	2.46	2.64
Return on Equity %	10.57	11.89	12.20	12.44	10.96	14.54	11.57	12.25
Loss Ratio %	64.10	61.95	62.39	61.11	60.53	60.76	61.17	63.09
Net Margin %	6.86	6.25	6.60	7.86	6.99	9.10	7.80	8.77
Price Range	72.98-55.83	72.98-55.83	72.98-54.97	66.75-47.95	58.41-48.40	53.96-37.93	45.39-37.74	40.21-33.85
P/E Ratio	17.17-13.14	15.49-11.85	15.49-11.67	14.26-10.25	15.09-12.51	11.10-7.80	12.79-10.63	11.29-9.51
Average Yield %	2.32	3.17	2.66	2.66	0.89	3.13	0.92	3.60

Address: 475 Steamboat Road, Greenwich, CT 06830 Telephone: 203-629-3000	Web Site: www.wrberkley.com Officers: William R. Berkley - Executive Chairman, Chairman, Chief Executive Officer W. Robert Berkley - President, Chief Executive Officer, Chief Operating Officer	Auditors: KPMG LLP Investor Contact: 203-629-3040 Transfer Agents: Wells Fargo Bank, N.A., Mendota Heights, MN

BERKSHIRE HATHAWAY INC

Exchange	Symbol	Price	52Wk Range	Yield	P/E
NYS	BRK B	$297600 (12/29/2017)	299360.00-238100.00	N/A	26.20

*7 Year Price Score 111.39 *NYSE Composite Index=100 *12 Month Price Score 103.53

TRADING VOLUME (thousand shares)

Interim Earnings (Per Share)

Qtr.	Mar	Jun	Sep	Dec
2014	2862.00	3889.00	2811.00	2530.00
2015	3143.00	2442.00	5737.00	3333.00
2016	3401.00	3042.00	4379.00	3823.00
2017	2469.00	2592.00	2473.00	...

Interim Dividends (Per Share)

No Dividends Paid

Valuation Analysis — **Institutional Holding**

Valuation Analysis		Institutional Holding	
Forecast EPS	$9379.00	No of Institutions	
	(01/17/2018)	2484	
Market Cap	$489.5 Billion	Shares	
Book Value	$308.3 Billion	1,064,545,728	
Price/Book	1.59	% Held	
Price/Sales	2.03	15.99	

Business Summary: General Insurance (MIC: 5.2.1 SIC: 6331 NAIC: 524126)

Berkshire Hathaway is a holding company. Co.'s subsidiaries are engaged in several business activities which include: underwriting private passenger automobile insurance; operation of a railroad system in North America; regulated electric and gas utility; manufacturing of products including industrial, consumer and building products; wholesale distribution of groceries and non-food items; provider of services including aviation pilot training, electronic components distribution and retailing businesses, including automotive dealerships; and manufactured housing and related consumer financing, transportation equipment, manufacturing and leasing, and furniture leasing.

Recent Developments: For the quarter ended Sep 30 2017, net income decreased 42.7% to US$4.20 billion from US$7.33 billion in the year-earlier quarter. Revenues were US$60.53 billion, up 2.9% from US$58.84 billion the year before. Net premiums earned were US$13.35 billion versus US$11.36 billion in the prior-year quarter, an increase of 17.5%.

Prospects: Our evaluation of Berkshire Hathaway Inc. as of Aug. 27, 2017 is the result of our systematic analysis on three basic characteristics: earnings strength, relative valuation, and recent stock price movement. The company has produced a positive trend in earnings per share over the past 5 quarters. However, while recent estimates for the company have been lowered by analysts, BRK.B has posted results that fell short of analysts expectations. Based on operating earnings yield, the company is about fairly valued when compared to all of the companies in our coverage universe. Share price changes over the past year indicates that BRK.B will perform poorly over the near term.

Financial Data
(US$ in Thousands)

	9 Mos	6 Mos	3 Mos	12/31/2016	12/31/2015	12/31/2014	12/31/2013	12/31/2012
Earnings Per Share	11,357.00	13,263.00	13,713.00	14,645.00	14,656.00	12,092.00	11,850.00	8,977.00
Cash Flow Per Share	27,276.83	26,663.95	26,367.27	19,738.16	19,164.63	19,477.25	16,855.55	12,652.36
Tang Book Value Per Share	118,210.07	142,374.45	109,104.02	103,406.82	111,777.28	109,230.64	100,294.17	81,027.67
Income Statement								
Premium Income	47,469,000	34,120,000	21,753,000	45,881,000	41,294,000	41,253,000	36,684,000	34,545,000
Total Revenue	183,230,000	122,705,000	65,187,000	223,604,000	210,821,000	194,673,000	182,150,000	162,463,000
Benefits & Claims	43,153,000	29,803,000	19,793,000	36,037,000	31,940,000	31,587,000	26,347,000	25,227,000
Income Before Taxes	16,647,000	11,269,000	5,449,000	32,744,000	34,946,000	28,105,000	28,796,000	22,236,000
Income Taxes	4,750,000	3,323,000	1,549,000	9,240,000	10,532,000	7,935,000	8,951,000	6,924,000
Net Income	12,389,000	8,322,000	4,060,000	24,074,000	24,083,000	19,872,000	19,476,000	14,824,000
Average Shares	1,644	1,644	1,644	1,643	1,643	1,643	1,643	1,651
Balance Sheet								
Total Assets	681,554,000	665,590,000	654,451,000	620,854,000	552,257,000	526,186,000	484,931,000	427,452,000
Total Liabilities	373,276,000	364,931,000	361,600,000	337,853,000	296,707,000	286,016,000	263,041,000	239,805,000
Stockholders' Equity	308,278,000	300,659,000	292,851,000	283,001,000	255,550,000	240,170,000	221,890,000	187,647,000
Shares Outstanding	1,644	1,315	1,644	1,644	1,643	1,642	1,643	1,642
Statistical Record								
Return on Assets %	2.91	3.47	3.63	4.09	4.47	3.93	4.27	3.61
Return on Equity %	6.47	7.74	8.18	8.92	9.72	8.60	9.51	8.39
Loss Ratio %	90.91	87.35	90.99	78.54	77.35	76.57	71.82	73.03
Net Margin %	6.76	6.78	6.23	10.77	11.42	10.21	10.69	9.12
Price Range	275630-214520	266013-212501	266013-208000	249711-187001	226680-192200	229300-164075	178275-134060	135936-114500
P/E Ratio	24.27-18.89	20.06-16.02	19.40-15.17	17.05-12.77	15.47-13.11	18.96-13.57	15.04-11.31	15.14-12.75

Address: 3555 Farnam Street, Omaha, NE 68131 Telephone: 402-346-1400	Web Site: www.berkshirehathaway.com Officers: Warren E. Buffett - Chairman, Chief Executive Officer Charles T. Munger - Vice-Chairman	Auditors: Deloitte & Touche LLP Transfer Agents: Wells Fargo Bank, N.A., St. Paul, MN

BERRY GLOBAL GROUP INC

Exchange	Symbol	Price	52Wk Range	Yield	P/E
NYS	BERY	$58.67 (12/29/2017)	60.79-47.50	N/A	22.92

*7 Year Price Score N/A   *NYSE Composite Index=100   *12 Month Price Score 101.54

TRADING VOLUME (thousand shares)

Interim Earnings (Per Share)

Qtr.	Dec	Mar	Jun	Sep
2012-13	(0.09)	0.01	0.33	0.22
2013-14	0.05	0.10	0.12	0.24
2014-15	0.11	0.31	(0.11)	0.39
2015-16	0.03	0.47	0.76	0.61
2016-17	0.40	0.54	0.79	0.81

Interim Dividends (Per Share)

No Dividends Paid

Valuation Analysis

	Institutional Holding	
Forecast EPS	$3.45	No of Institutions
	(01/18/2018)	421
Market Cap	$7.7 Billion	Shares
Book Value	$1.0 Billion	134,691,344
Price/Book	7.59	% Held
Price/Sales	1.08	99.29

Business Summary: Plastics (MIC: 8.4.2 SIC: 3089 NAIC: 326199)

Berry Global Group is a provider of plastic consumer packaging, nonwoven specialty materials and engineered materials. Co. operates in three operating segments: Health, Hygiene & Specialties, which consists of nonwoven specialty materials used in hygiene, infection prevention, personal care, industrial, construction, and filtration applications; Consumer Packaging, which consists of containers, foodservice items, closures, overcaps, bottles, prescription vials, tubes, and printed films; and Engineered Materials, which consists of pipeline corrosion protection solutions, tapes and adhesives, polyethylene based film products, can liners, and specialty coated and laminated products.

Recent Developments: For the year ended Sep 30 2017, net income increased 44.1% to US$340.0 million from US$236.0 million in the prior year. Revenues were US$7.10 billion, up 9.3% from US$6.49 billion the year before. Operating income was US$732.0 million versus US$581.0 million in the prior year, an increase of 26.0%. Direct operating expenses rose 9.4% to US$5.69 billion from US$5.20 billion in the comparable period the year before. Indirect operating expenses decreased 4.8% to US$672.0 million from US$706.0 million in the equivalent prior-year period.

Prospects: Our evaluation of Berry Global Group Inc. as of Jan. 14, 2018 is the result of our systematic analysis on three basic characteristics: earnings strength, relative valuation, and recent stock price movement. The company has managed to produce a neutral trend in earnings per share over the past 5 quarters and while recent estimates for the company have been raised by analysts, BERY has posted better than expected results. Based on operating earnings yield, the company is undervalued when compared to all of the companies in our coverage universe. Share price changes over the past year indicates that BERY will perform well over the near term.

Financial Data
(US$ in Millions)

	09/30/2017	10/01/2016	09/26/2015	09/27/2014	09/28/2013	09/29/2012	10/01/2011	10/02/2010
Earnings Per Share	2.56	1.89	0.70	0.51	0.48	0.02	(3.55)	(1.34)
Cash Flow Per Share	7.66	6.98	5.36	4.55	4.10	5.76	3.90	1.30
Income Statement								
Total Revenue	7,095	6,489	4,881	4,958	4,647	4,756	4,561	4,257
EBITDA	1,239	1,124	663	646	670	687	325	468
Depn & Amortn	521	525	350	358	341	355	344	317
Income Before Taxes	449	305	122	67	85	4	(346)	(162)
Income Taxes	109	72	36	4	28	2	(47)	(49)
Net Income	340	236	86	62	57	2	(299)	(113)
Average Shares	132	125	123	121	119	86	84	84
Balance Sheet								
Current Assets	2,004	1,792	1,383	1,432	1,337	1,233	1,255	1,315
Total Assets	8,476	7,653	5,028	5,268	5,135	5,106	5,217	5,344
Current Liabilities	1,134	1,031	705	767	684	646	684	662
Long-Term Obligations	5,608	5,712	3,648	3,860	3,875	4,431	4,581	4,397
Total Liabilities	7,464	7,435	5,096	5,385	5,334	5,561	5,671	5,474
Stockholders' Equity	1,012	218	(68)	(117)	(199)	(455)	(454)	(130)
Shares Outstanding	130	122	119	117	115	83	83	84
Statistical Record								
Return on Assets %	4.23	3.66	1.68	1.20	1.12	0.04	N.M.	...
Return on Equity %	55.44	309.58	...	...	...	...	...	...
EBITDA Margin %	17.46	17.32	13.58	13.03	14.42	14.41	7.13	10.99
Net Margin %	4.79	3.64	1.76	1.25	1.23	0.04	N.M.	N.M.
Asset Turnover	0.88	1.01	0.95	0.96	0.91	0.93	0.87	...
Current Ratio	1.77	1.74	1.96	1.87	1.95	1.91	1.83	1.99
Debt to Equity	5.54	26.20	...	...	...	...	...	...
Price Range	58.77-42.81	45.97-28.42	36.80-23.14	26.21-18.12	24.99-13.48	...	...	...
P/E Ratio	22.96-16.72	24.32-15.04	52.57-33.06	51.39-35.53	52.06-28.08	...	...	...

Address: 101 Oakley Street, Evansville, IN 47710	Web Site: www.berryplastics.com	Auditors: Ernst & Young LLP
Telephone: 812-424-2904	Officers: Jonathan D. Rich - Chairman, Chief Executive Officer Thomas E. Salmon - President, Chief Operating Officer, Division Officer, Chief Executive Officer	Investor Contact: 812-.30-6.2964 Transfer Agents: Computershare Trust Company, N.A.

BEST BUY INC

Exchange	Symbol	Price	52Wk Range	Yield	P/E	Div Achiever
NYS	BBY	$68.47 (12/29/2017)	68.47-42.14	1.99	N/A	13 Years

*7 Year Price Score 126.89 *NYSE Composite Index=100 *12 Month Price Score 106.50

Interim Earnings (Per Share)

Qtr.	Apr	Jul	Oct	Jan
2014-15	1.31	0.42	0.30	1.47
2015-16	0.36	0.46	0.36	1.38
2016-17	0.70	0.61	0.61	1.89
2017-18	0.60	0.67	0.78	...

Interim Dividends (Per Share)

Amt	Decl	Ex	Rec	Pay
0.34Q	03/01/2017	03/20/2017	03/22/2017	04/12/2017
0.34Q	05/26/2017	06/13/2017	06/15/2017	07/06/2017
0.34Q	08/30/2017	09/18/2017	09/19/2017	10/10/2017
0.34Q	11/17/2017	12/06/2017	12/07/2017	12/28/2017

Indicated Div: $1.36 (Div. Reinv. Plan)

Valuation Analysis / **Institutional Holding**

Forecast EPS	$4.02 (01/18/2018)	No of Institutions 856
Market Cap	$20.0 Billion	Shares 304,533,888
Book Value	N/A	% Held 70.92
Price/Book	N/A	
Price/Sales	N/A	

Business Summary: Retail - Appliances and Electronics (MIC: 2.1.7 SIC: 5731 NAIC: 443112)

Best Buy is a provider of technology products, services and solutions. Co. provides these products and services to the customers who visit its stores, engage with Geek Squad agents or use its websites or mobile applications. Co. has two reportable segments: Domestic and International. Co.'s Domestic and International segments have offerings in six categories: Consumer Electronics, Computing and Mobile Phones, Entertainment, Appliances, Services and Other. As of Jan 28 2017, Co. had approximately 1,200 large-format and 400 small-format stores throughout its Domestic and International segments.

Recent Developments: For the quarter ended Oct 28 2017, income from continuing operations increased 24.0% to US$238.0 million from US$192.0 million in the year-earlier quarter. Net income increased 23.2% to US$239.0 million from US$194.0 million in the year-earlier quarter. Revenues were US$9.32 billion, up 4.2% from US$8.95 billion the year before. Operating income was US$350.0 million versus US$312.0 million in the prior-year quarter, an increase of 12.2%. Direct operating expenses rose 4.4% to US$7.04 billion from US$6.74 billion in the comparable period the year before. Indirect operating expenses increased 2.1% to US$1.93 billion from US$1.89 billion in the equivalent prior-year period.

Prospects: Our evaluation of Best Buy Inc. as of Jan. 14, 2018 is the result of our systematic analysis on three basic characteristics: earnings strength, relative valuation, and recent stock price movement. The company has managed to produce a neutral trend in earnings per share over the past 5 quarters and while recent estimates for the company have been raised by analysts, BBY has posted results that were in line with analysts expectations. Based on operating earnings yield, the company is undervalued when compared to all of the companies in our coverage universe. Share price changes over the past year indicates that BBY will perform poorly over the near term.

Financial Data

(US$ in Thousands)	9 Mos	6 Mos	3 Mos	01/28/2017	01/30/2016	01/31/2015	02/01/2014	02/02/2013
Earnings Per Share	0.78	0.67	0.60	3.81	2.56	3.49	1.53	(1.30)
Cash Flow Per Share	6.85	...	3.15	8.01	3.83	5.55	3.21	4.66
Tang Book Value Per Share	12.59	13.07	13.31	13.77	12.15	12.84	9.98	6.50
Dividends Per Share	0.340	0.340	0.340	1.570	1.430	0.720	0.680	0.660
Dividend Payout %	43.59	50.75	56.67	41.21	55.86	20.63	44.44	...
Income Statement								
Total Revenue	9,320,000	8,940,000	8,528,000	39,403,000	39,528,000	40,339,000	42,410,000	45,085,000
EBITDA	533,000	499,000	472,000	2,542,000	2,047,000	2,133,000	1,903,000	758,000
Depn & Amortn	171,000	171,000	161,000	654,000	657,000	656,000	716,000	832,000
Income Before Taxes	342,000	310,000	292,000	1,816,000	1,310,000	1,387,000	1,087,000	(186,000)
Income Taxes	104,000	...	104,000	609,000	503,000	141,000	398,000	231,000
Net Income	239,000	209,000	188,000	1,228,000	897,000	1,233,000	532,000	(441,000)
Average Shares	305,400	310,800	315,000	322,600	350,700	353,600	347,600	338,600
Balance Sheet								
Current Assets	11,405,000	10,078,000	9,656,000	10,516,000	9,886,000	11,729,000	10,485,000	12,047,000
Total Assets	14,785,000	13,444,000	12,955,000	13,856,000	13,519,000	15,256,000	14,013,000	16,787,000
Current Liabilities	9,152,000	7,105,000	6,470,000	7,122,000	6,925,000	7,777,000	7,436,000	10,810,000
Long-Term Obligations	784,000	1,310,000	1,302,000	1,321,000	1,339,000	1,580,000	1,612,000	1,153,000
Total Liabilities	10,633,000	9,097,000	8,456,000	9,147,000	9,141,000	10,261,000	10,027,000	13,726,000
Stockholders' Equity	4,152,000	4,347,000	4,499,000	4,709,000	4,378,000	4,995,000	3,986,000	3,061,000
Shares Outstanding	296,000	300,000	306,000	311,108	323,779	351,468	346,751	338,276
Statistical Record								
EBITDA Margin %	5.72	5.58	5.53	6.45	5.18	5.29	4.49	1.68
Net Margin %	2.56	2.34	2.20	3.12	2.27	3.06	1.25	N.M.
Current Ratio	1.25	1.42	1.49	1.48	1.43	1.51	1.41	1.11
Debt to Equity	0.19	0.30	0.29	0.28	0.31	0.32	0.40	0.38
Price Range	62.47-37.99	61.25-32.59	52.35-29.17	49.31-26.93	41.77-25.87	39.91-22.78	44.33-15.12	27.51-11.29
P/E Ratio	80.09-48.71	91.42-48.64	87.25-48.62	12.94-7.07	16.32-10.11	11.44-6.53	28.97-9.88	...
Average Yield %	0.67	0.74	0.86	4.36	4.13	2.35	2.20	3.58

Address: 7601 Penn Avenue South, Richfield, MN 55423 **Telephone:** 612-291-1000	**Web Site:** www.bestbuy.com **Officers:** Hubert Joly - Chairman, President, Chief Executive Officer Richard M. Schulze - Chairman Emeritus, Chairman	**Auditors:** Deloitte & Touche LLP **Investor Contact:** 612-291-1000 **Transfer Agents:** Computershare, Providence, RI

BIG LOTS, INC.

Exchange	Symbol	Price	52Wk Range	Yield	P/E
NYS	BIG	$56.15 (12/29/2017)	59.55-46.45	1.78	14.47

*7 Year Price Score 95.77 *NYSE Composite Index=100 *12 Month Price Score 103.56

Interim Earnings (Per Share)

Qtr.	Apr	Jul	Oct	Jan
2014-15	0.06	0.36	(0.06)	1.71
2015-16	0.60	0.34	(0.03)	1.86
2016-17	0.79	0.50	0.03	1.96
2017-18	1.15	0.67	0.10	...

Interim Dividends (Per Share)

Amt	Decl	Ex	Rec	Pay
0.25Q	02/28/2017	03/15/2017	03/17/2017	03/31/2017
0.25Q	05/25/2017	06/07/2017	06/09/2017	06/23/2017
0.25Q	08/24/2017	09/07/2017	09/08/2017	09/22/2017
0.25Q	11/29/2017	12/14/2017	12/15/2017	12/29/2017

Indicated Div: $1.00

Valuation Analysis

Forecast EPS	$4.26
	(01/17/2018)
Market Cap	$2.3 Billion
Book Value	$565.7 Million
Price/Book	4.15
Price/Sales	0.45

Institutional Holding

No of Institutions	504
Shares	70,376,288
% Held	87.56

TRADING VOLUME (thousand shares)

Business Summary: Retail - General Merchandise/Department Stores (MIC: 2.1.1 SIC: 5331 NAIC: 452990)

Big Lots is a retailer. At Jan 28 2017, Co. operated a total of 1,432 stores. Co.'s merchandising categories are Furniture (upholstery, mattress, and case goods departments), Seasonal (lawn and garden, and other holiday departments), Soft Home (home decor, frames, bedding, utility bedding, bath, window, textile, and area rugs departments), Food (beverage and grocery, candy and snacks, and specialty foods departments), Consumables (health and beauty, plastics, chemical, and pet departments), Hard Home (small appliances, table top, stationery, and home maintenance departments), and Electronics, Toys, and Accessories (electronics, jewelry, hosiery, toys, and infant accessories departments).

Recent Developments: For the quarter ended Oct 28 2017, net income increased 217.7% to US$4.4 million from US$1.4 million in the year-earlier quarter. Revenues were US$1.11 billion, unchanged from the year before. Operating income was US$5.8 million versus US$2.0 million in the prior-year quarter, an increase of 189.8%. Direct operating expenses rose 0.6% to US$667.2 million from US$663.5 million in the comparable period the year before. Indirect operating expenses decreased 0.5% to US$437.8 million from US$440.0 million in the equivalent prior-year period.

Prospects: Our evaluation of Big Lots Inc. as of Jan. 14, 2018 is the result of our systematic analysis on three basic characteristics: earnings strength, relative valuation, and recent stock price movement. The company has generated a negative trend in earnings per share over the past 5 quarters and while recent estimates for the company have been raised by analysts, BIG has posted better than expected results. Based on operating earnings yield, the company is undervalued when compared to all of the companies in our coverage universe. Share price changes over the past year indicates that BIG will perform in line with the market over the near term.

Financial Data

(US$ in Thousands)	9 Mos	6 Mos	3 Mos	01/28/2017	01/30/2016	01/31/2015	02/01/2014	02/02/2013
Earnings Per Share	3.88	3.81	3.64	3.32	2.80	2.06	2.16	2.93
Cash Flow Per Share	7.09	6.96	7.19	6.90	6.80	5.81	3.46	4.62
Tang Book Value Per Share	13.52	13.86	14.82	14.70	14.67	14.92	15.66	13.00
Dividends Per Share	0.960	0.920	0.880	0.840	0.760	0.510	...	...
Dividend Payout %	24.74	24.15	24.18	25.30	27.14	24.76	...	...
Income Statement								
Total Revenue	3,628,912	2,518,088	1,296,787	5,200,439	5,190,582	5,177,078	5,301,912	5,400,119
EBITDA	221,284	185,567	107,786	369,732	353,233	344,188	304,326	404,805
Depn & Amortn	87,489	57,981	28,595	120,400	122,700	119,700	115,100	106,300
Income Before Taxes	129,090	124,958	78,182	244,241	226,850	221,900	185,887	294,313
Income Taxes	44,086	44,326	26,670	91,458	83,842	85,239	61,118	117,148
Net Income	85,004	80,632	51,512	152,828	142,873	114,276	125,295	177,121
Average Shares	42,524	43,564	44,728	45,974	50,964	55,552	57,958	60,476
Balance Sheet								
Current Assets	1,214,990	974,393	990,135	994,379	994,432	1,038,429	1,121,061	1,090,630
Total Assets	1,846,109	1,591,464	1,599,715	1,607,707	1,640,370	1,635,891	1,739,599	1,753,626
Current Liabilities	731,776	600,194	652,311	678,595	678,448	587,829	577,447	629,634
Long-Term Obligations	371,900	226,600	115,700	106,400	62,300	62,100	77,000	171,200
Total Liabilities	1,280,445	1,006,526	945,810	957,077	919,900	846,341	838,172	995,484
Stockholders' Equity	565,664	584,938	653,905	650,630	720,470	789,550	901,427	758,142
Shares Outstanding	41,842	42,205	44,114	44,259	49,101	52,912	57,548	57,269
Statistical Record								
Return on Assets %	9.48	10.70	10.33	9.44	8.75	6.79	7.19	10.27
Return on Equity %	31.53	30.50	26.01	22.35	18.98	13.55	15.14	22.04
EBITDA Margin %	6.10	7.37	8.31	7.11	6.81	6.65	5.74	7.50
Net Margin %	2.34	3.20	3.97	2.94	2.75	2.21	2.36	3.28
Asset Turnover	2.82	3.24	3.23	3.21	3.18	3.08	3.04	3.13
Current Ratio	1.66	1.62	1.52	1.47	1.47	1.77	1.94	1.73
Debt to Equity	0.66	0.39	0.18	0.16	0.09	0.08	0.09	0.23
Price Range	56.02-42.87	56.02-42.69	56.02-41.86	56.02-36.19	50.96-35.88	50.80-25.71	38.96-26.79	46.81-26.86
P/E Ratio	14.44-11.05	14.70-11.20	15.39-11.50	16.87-10.90	18.20-12.81	24.66-12.48	18.04-12.40	15.98-9.17
Average Yield %	1.92	1.86	1.77	1.75	1.68	1.22	...	...

Address: 300 Phillipi Road, P.O. Box 28512, Columbus, OH 43228-5311
Telephone: 614-278-6800
Fax: 614-278-6666

Web Site: www.biglots.com
Officers: David J. Campisi - President, Chief Executive Officer Lisa M. Bachmann - Executive Vice President, Senior Vice President, Chief Operating Officer, Chief Information Officer, Chief Merchandising Officer

Auditors: Deloitte & Touche LLP
Investor Contact: 614-278-6622
Transfer Agents: Computershare Investor Services, Canton, MA

BIO-RAD LABORATORIES INC

Exchange	Symbol	Price	52Wk Range	Yield	P/E
NYS	BIO	$238.67 (12/29/2017)	271.30-182.91	N/A	302.11

*7 Year Price Score 125.92 *NYSE Composite Index=100 *12 Month Price Score 106.76

TRADING VOLUME (thousand shares)

Interim Earnings (Per Share)

Qtr.	Mar	Jun	Sep	Dec
2014	0.23	1.09	0.39	1.34
2015	0.61	0.97	0.59	1.68
2016	0.42	0.61	0.62	(0.70)
2017	0.41	0.17	0.91	...

Interim Dividends (Per Share)

No Dividends Paid

Valuation Analysis	Institutional Holding	
Forecast EPS	$2.70	No of Institutions
	(11/01/2017)	383
Market Cap	$7.1 Billion	Shares
Book Value	$2.8 Billion	22,694,156
Price/Book	2.49	% Held
Price/Sales	3.36	61.43

Business Summary: Biotechnology (MIC: 4.1.2 SIC: 3826 NAIC: 334516)

Bio-Rad Laboratories is a manufacturer and distributor of its own life science research and clinical diagnostics products. Co. has two primary segments: Life Science, which is engaged in developing, manufacturing and marketing a range of reagents, apparatus and laboratory instruments used for biological research; and Clinical Diagnostics, which designs, manufactures, sells and supports test systems, informatics systems, test kits and quality controls that serve clinical laboratories in the diagnostics market. Co. sells its products and services to a diverse client base comprised of scientific research, healthcare, education and government customers.

Recent Developments: For the quarter ended Sep 30 2017, net income increased 48.8% to US$27.4 million from US$18.4 million in the year-earlier quarter. Revenues were US$535.0 million, up 5.2% from US$508.7 million the year before. Operating income was US$46.4 million versus US$28.1 million in the prior-year quarter, an increase of 65.1%. Direct operating expenses rose 0.5% to US$230.5 million from US$229.3 million in the comparable period the year before. Indirect operating expenses increased 2.7% to US$258.1 million from US$251.4 million in the equivalent prior-year period.

Prospects: Our evaluation of Bio-Rad Laboratories Inc. as of Jan. 14, 2018 is the result of our systematic analysis on three basic characteristics: earnings strength, relative valuation, and recent stock price movement. The company has managed to produce a neutral trend in earnings per share over the past 5 quarters and while recent estimates for the company have remained steady, BIO has posted better than expected results. Based on operating earnings yield, the company is overvalued when compared to all of the companies in our coverage universe. Share price changes over the past year indicates that BIO will perform very well over the near term.

Financial Data (US$ in Thousands)	9 Mos	6 Mos	3 Mos	12/31/2016	12/31/2015	12/31/2014	12/31/2013	12/31/2012
Earnings Per Share	0.79	0.50	0.94	0.95	3.85	3.05	2.69	5.72
Cash Flow Per Share	4.37	5.16	5.67	7.33	6.38	9.46	6.14	9.83
Tang Book Value Per Share	72.12	70.76	67.58	65.86	60.64	49.21	48.75	44.04
Income Statement								
Total Revenue	1,539,720	1,004,717	500,051	2,068,172	2,019,441	2,175,044	2,132,694	2,069,235
EBITDA	168,281	89,666	57,750	191,702	289,239	290,088	307,456	393,043
Depn & Amortn	106,051	70,688	33,662	142,900	131,800	149,900	147,200	130,400
Income Before Taxes	60,122	21,267	20,147	41,560	145,847	131,557	112,385	222,931
Income Taxes	15,281	3,819	7,734	13,435	32,754	42,712	34,574	59,084
Net Income	44,841	17,448	12,413	28,125	113,093	88,845	77,790	163,778
Average Shares	30,052	30,006	29,911	29,646	29,409	29,133	28,906	28,642
Balance Sheet								
Current Assets	1,892,451	1,826,528	1,732,571	1,844,524	1,777,596	1,716,367	1,747,856	1,929,932
Total Assets	4,185,728	4,143,459	3,952,769	3,850,504	3,711,542	3,341,278	3,388,790	3,436,753
Current Liabilities	466,456	455,110	407,504	471,322	441,351	446,761	487,472	469,920
Long-Term Obligations	434,475	434,386	434,289	434,186	435,707	435,710	435,615	732,414
Total Liabilities	1,337,281	1,332,462	1,245,303	1,263,745	1,221,039	1,156,123	1,202,068	1,426,018
Stockholders' Equity	2,848,447	2,810,997	2,707,466	2,586,759	2,490,503	2,185,155	2,186,722	2,010,735
Shares Outstanding	29,763	29,620	29,605	29,576	29,359	29,069	28,776	28,481
Statistical Record								
Return on Assets %	0.59	0.38	0.73	0.74	3.21	2.64	2.28	5.00
Return on Equity %	0.87	0.56	1.08	1.10	4.84	4.06	3.71	8.70
EBITDA Margin %	10.93	8.92	11.55	9.27	14.32	13.34	14.42	18.99
Net Margin %	2.91	1.74	2.48	1.36	5.60	4.08	3.65	7.91
Asset Turnover	0.51	0.52	0.54	0.55	0.57	0.65	0.62	0.63
Current Ratio	4.06	4.01	4.25	3.91	4.03	3.84	3.59	4.11
Debt to Equity	0.15	0.15	0.16	0.17	0.17	0.20	0.20	0.36
Price Range	242.28-155.52	229.26-141.34	207.83-135.03	183.46-123.93	151.93-113.77	133.73-106.48	126.00-105.05	114.25-92.30
P/E Ratio	306.68-196.86	458.52-282.68	221.10-143.65	193.12-130.45	39.46-29.55	43.85-34.91	46.84-39.05	19.97-16.14

Address: 1000 Alfred Nobel Drive, Hercules, CA 94547 Telephone: 510-724-7000	Web Site: www.bio-rad.com Officers: Norman D. Schwartz - Chairman, President, Chief Executive Officer Michael Crowley - Executive Vice President	Auditors: KPMG LLP Investor Contact: 510-741-6104 Transfer Agents: Computershare, Canton, MA

BLACK HILLS CORPORATION

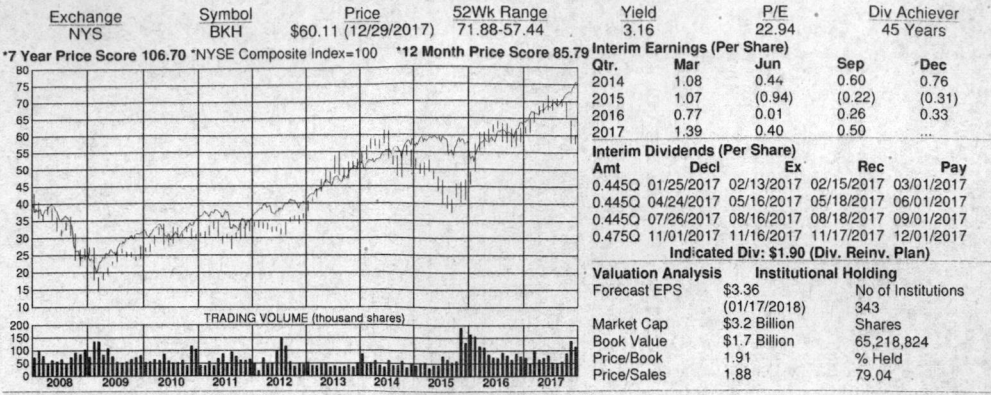

Exchange	Symbol	Price	52Wk Range	Yield	P/E	Div Achiever
NYS	BKH	$60.11 (12/29/2017)	71.88-57.44	3.16	22.94	45 Years

*7 Year Price Score 106.70 *NYSE Composite Index=100 *12 Month Price Score 85.79

Interim Earnings (Per Share)

Qtr.	Mar	Jun	Sep	Dec
2014	1.08	0.44	0.60	0.76
2015	1.07	(0.94)	(0.22)	(0.31)
2016	0.77	0.01	0.26	0.33
2017	1.39	0.40	0.50	

Interim Dividends (Per Share)

Amt	Decl	Ex	Rec	Pay
0.445Q	01/25/2017	02/13/2017	02/15/2017	03/01/2017
0.445Q	04/24/2017	05/16/2017	05/18/2017	06/01/2017
0.445Q	07/26/2017	08/16/2017	08/18/2017	09/01/2017
0.475Q	11/01/2017	11/16/2017	11/17/2017	12/01/2017

Indicated Div: $1.90 (Div. Reinv. Plan)

Valuation Analysis

		Institutional Holding
Forecast EPS	$3.36	No of Institutions
	(01/17/2018)	343
Market Cap	$3.2 Billion	Shares
Book Value	$1.7 Billion	65,218,824
Price/Book	1.91	% Held
Price/Sales	1.88	79.04

Business Summary: Electric Utilities (MIC: 3.1.1 SIC: 4911 NAIC: 221121)

Black Hills is a holding company. Through its subsidiaries, Co. has the following segments: Electric Utilities, which generates, transmits and distributes electricity in South Dakota, Wyoming, Colorado and Montana; Gas Utilities, which serves natural gas utility customers in Arkansas, Colorado, Iowa, Nebraska, Kansas and Wyoming; Power Generation, which produces electric power from its generating plants and sells the electric capacity and energy primarily to Co.'s utilities; Mining, which produces and sells the coal to electric generation facilities; and Oil and Gas, which engages in the exploration, development and production of crude oil and natural gas, in the Rocky Mountain region.

Recent Developments: For the quarter ended Sep 30 2017, net income increased 76.7% to US$31.6 million from US$17.9 million in the year-earlier quarter. Revenues were US$342.1 million, up 2.5% from US$333.8 million the year before. Operating income was US$78.5 million versus US$58.4 million in the prior-year quarter, an increase of 34.4%. Direct operating expenses rose 2.9% to US$200.9 million from US$195.3 million in the comparable period the year before. Indirect operating expenses decreased 21.7% to US$62.7 million from US$80.1 million in the equivalent prior-year period.

Prospects: Our evaluation of Black Hills Corp. as of Jan. 14, 2018 is the result of our systematic analysis on three basic characteristics: earnings strength, relative valuation, and recent stock price movement. The company has generated a negative trend in earnings per share over the past 5 quarters. However, while recent estimates for the company have been mixed, BKH has posted results that fell short of analysts' expectations. Based on operating earnings yield, the company is undervalued when compared to all of the companies in our coverage universe. Share price changes over the past year indicates that BKH will perform very well over the near term.

Financial Data

(US$ in Thousands)	9 Mos	6 Mos	3 Mos	12/31/2016	12/31/2015	12/31/2014	12/31/2013	12/31/2012
Earnings Per Share	2.62	2.38	1.99	1.37	(0.71)	2.89	2.59	1.85
Cash Flow Per Share	7.80	6.77	6.19	6.16	9.45	7.29	7.35	7.21
Tang Book Value Per Share	7.02	6.90	6.86	5.75	21.54	22.82	21.37	19.80
Dividends Per Share	1.755	1.730	1.705	1.680	1.620	1.560	1.520	1.480
Dividend Payout %	66.98	72.69	85.68	122.63	...	53.98	58.69	80.00
Income Statement								
Total Revenue	1,244,119	901,981	554,003	1,572,974	1,304,605	1,393,570	1,275,852	1,173,884
EBITDA	303,119	221,641	149,591	419,042	193,413	412,428	434,978	408,195
Depn & Amortn	6,212	4,138	1,690	195,223	161,734	150,210	147,980	160,187
Income Before Taxes	194,617	149,214	113,501	93,106	(49,522)	194,177	177,540	136,895
Income Taxes	57,562	43,757	33,355	10,475	(22,160)	65,395	61,608	48,400
Net Income	126,381	98,718	76,523	72,970	(32,111)	128,781	114,962	81,528
Average Shares	55,432	55,384	54,932	53,271	45,288	44,598	44,419	44,073
Balance Sheet								
Current Assets	385,018	359,256	401,402	466,814	822,151	454,036	345,288	405,106
Total Assets	6,551,177	6,489,092	6,475,849	6,515,444	4,655,501	4,279,806	3,875,178	3,729,471
Current Liabilities	554,270	438,865	391,542	527,932	422,029	651,281	378,394	734,889
Long-Term Obligations	3,109,864	3,160,302	3,210,730	3,211,189	1,866,866	1,267,589	1,396,948	938,877
Total Liabilities	4,868,373	4,812,853	4,801,533	4,900,805	3,189,634	2,903,782	2,567,430	2,496,962
Stockholders' Equity	1,682,804	1,676,239	1,674,316	1,614,639	1,465,867	1,376,024	1,307,748	1,232,509
Shares Outstanding	53,483	53,474	53,460	53,382	51,192	44,671	44,499	44,206
Statistical Record								
Return on Assets %	2.22	2.03	1.71	1.30	N.M.	3.16	3.02	2.07
Return on Equity %	8.79	8.09	6.94	4.72	N.M.	9.60	9.05	6.66
EBITDA Margin %	24.36	24.57	27.00	26.64	14.83	29.60	34.09	34.77
Net Margin %	10.16	10.94	13.81	4.64	N.M.	9.24	9.01	6.95
Asset Turnover	0.26	0.26	0.26	0.28	0.29	0.34	0.34	0.30
Current Ratio	0.69	0.82	1.03	0.88	1.95	0.70	0.91	0.55
Debt to Equity	1.85	1.89	1.92	1.99	1.27	0.92	1.07	0.76
Price Range	71.88-56.61	71.88-56.61	66.65-56.55	64.08-45.57	53.12-37.29	61.39-47.48	54.82-36.34	36.95-30.67
P/E Ratio	27.44-21.61	30.20-23.79	33.49-28.42	46.77-33.26	...	21.24-16.43	21.17-14.03	19.97-16.58
Average Yield %	2.69	2.74	2.79	2.87	3.54	2.84	3.21	4.40

Address: 625 Ninth Street, Rapid City, SD 57701	**Web Site:** www.blackhillscorp.com	**Auditors:** Deloitte & Touche LLP
Telephone: 605-721-1700	**Officers:** David R. Emery - Chairman, President, Chief Executive Officer Linden R. Evans - President, Chief Operating Officer, Division Officer	**Investor Contact:** 605-721-1171
		Transfer Agents: Wells Fargo Shareowner Services, St. Paul, MN

BLACKROCK INC

Exchange	Symbol	Price	52Wk Range	Yield	P/E
NYS	BLK	$513.71 (12/29/2017)	518.86-371.64	2.24	24.06

*7 Year Price Score 112.10 *NYSE Composite Index=100 *12 Month Price Score 110.40

TRADING VOLUME (thousand shares)

Interim Earnings (Per Share)

Qtr.	Mar	Jun	Sep	Dec
2014	4.40	4.72	5.37	4.77
2015	4.84	4.84	5.00	5.11
2016	3.92	4.73	5.26	5.12
2017	5.23	5.22	5.78	...

Interim Dividends (Per Share)

Amt	Decl	Ex	Rec	Pay
2.50Q	05/25/2017	06/01/2017	06/05/2017	06/23/2017
2.50Q	07/20/2017	08/31/2017	09/05/2017	09/22/2017
2.50Q	11/16/2017	12/01/2017	12/04/2017	12/21/2017
2.88Q	01/11/2018	03/06/2018	03/07/2018	03/22/2018

Indicated Div: $11.52

Valuation Analysis / Institutional Holding

Forecast EPS	$28.77 (01/18/2018)	No of Institutions 1337
Market Cap	$82.5 Billion	Shares 156,006,128
Book Value	$30.0 Billion	% Held
Price/Book	2.74	74.23
Price/Sales	6.92	

Business Summary: Finance Intermediaries & Services (MIC: 5.5.1 SIC: 6211 NAIC: 523120)

BlackRock is an investment management firm. Co.'s products include single- and multi-asset portfolios investing in equities, fixed income, alternatives and money market instruments. Products are provided directly and via intermediaries in a variety of vehicles, including open-end and closed-end mutual funds, iShares® exchange-traded funds, collective investment funds and other pooled investment vehicles. Co. also provides its BlackRock Solutions® investment and risk management technology platform, Aladdin®, risk analytics, advisory and technology services and solutions to institutional and wealth management investors. As of Dec 31 2016, Co. had $5.15 trillion of assets under management.

Recent Developments: For the quarter ended Sep 30 2017, net income increased 9.4% to US$959.0 million from US$877.0 million in the year-earlier quarter. Revenues were US$3.23 billion, up 14.0% from US$2.84 billion the year before. Operating income was US$1.39 billion versus US$1.21 billion in the prior-year quarter, an increase of 15.3%. Indirect operating expenses increased 13.0% to US$1.84 billion from US$1.63 billion in the equivalent prior-year period.

Prospects: Our evaluation of BlackRock Inc. as of Jan. 14, 2018 is the result of our systematic analysis on three basic characteristics: earnings strength, relative valuation, and recent stock price movement. The company has enjoyed a very positive trend in earnings per share over the past 5 quarters. Because the company lacks sufficient analyst estimate data, we place greater weight on the historical EPS trend as the measure of earnings strength. Based on operating earnings yield, the company is about fairly valued when compared to all of the companies in our coverage universe. Share price changes over the past year indicates that BLK will perform well over the near term.

Financial Data
(US$ in Thousands)

	9 Mos	6 Mos	3 Mos	12/31/2016	12/31/2015	12/31/2014	12/31/2013	12/31/2012
Earnings Per Share	21.35	20.83	20.34	19.04	19.79	19.25	16.87	13.79
Cash Flow Per Share	22.72	20.87	15.51	13.06	18.05	18.31	21.40	12.77
Dividends Per Share	9.790	9.580	9.370	9.160	8.720	7.720	6.720	6.000
Dividend Payout %	45.85	45.99	46.07	48.11	44.06	40.10	39.83	43.51
Income Statement								
Total Revenue	9,022,000	5,789,000	2,824,000	11,155,000	11,401,000	11,081,000	10,180,000	9,337,000
EBITDA	3,988,000	2,526,000	1,203,000	4,888,000	5,049,000	4,901,000	4,473,000	3,971,000
Depn & Amortn	77,000	50,000	5,000	223,000	243,000	274,000	289,000	286,000
Income Before Taxes	3,787,000	2,383,000	1,140,000	4,460,000	4,602,000	4,395,000	3,973,000	3,470,000
Income Taxes	1,090,000	645,000	269,000	1,290,000	1,250,000	1,131,000	1,022,000	1,030,000
Net Income	2,666,000	1,719,000	862,000	3,172,000	3,345,000	3,294,000	2,932,000	2,458,000
Average Shares	163,773	164,149	164,856	166,579	169,038	171,112	173,828	178,017
Balance Sheet								
Current Assets	9,348,000	8,492,000	8,930,000	8,441,000	8,320,000	7,843,000	6,637,000	6,856,000
Total Assets	220,567,000	217,488,000	230,586,000	220,177,000	225,261,000	239,808,000	219,873,000	200,451,000
Current Liabilities	3,266,000	2,660,000	2,769,000	2,974,000	3,039,000	2,900,000	2,831,000	2,716,000
Long-Term Obligations	5,000,000	4,970,000	5,619,000	4,915,000	4,930,000	4,938,000	4,939,000	5,687,000
Total Liabilities	190,525,000	187,933,000	201,430,000	191,079,000	196,758,000	212,442,000	193,413,000	175,048,000
Stockholders' Equity	30,042,000	29,555,000	29,156,000	29,098,000	28,503,000	27,366,000	26,460,000	25,403,000
Shares Outstanding	160,528	161,137	161,798	161,534	163,461	164,786	166,589	168,875
Statistical Record								
Return on Assets %	1.57	1.57	1.49	1.42	1.44	1.43	1.40	1.29
Return on Equity %	11.93	11.85	11.74	10.98	11.97	12.24	11.31	9.72
EBITDA Margin %	44.20	43.63	42.60	43.82	44.29	44.23	43.94	42.53
Net Margin %	29.55	29.69	30.52	28.44	29.34	29.73	28.80	26.33
Asset Turnover	0.05	0.05	0.05	0.05	0.05	0.05	0.05	0.05
Current Ratio	2.86	3.19	3.22	2.84	2.74	2.70	2.34	2.52
Debt to Equity	0.17	0.17	0.19	0.17	0.17	0.18	0.19	0.22
Price Range	447.09-338.61	428.38-335.11	398.45-319.54	398.45-289.72	380.33-293.52	364.40-286.39	316.47-206.71	209.29-163.37
P/E Ratio	20.94-15.86	20.57-16.09	19.59-15.71	20.93-15.22	19.22-14.83	18.93-14.88	18.76-12.25	15.18-11.85
Average Yield %	2.49	2.54	2.56	2.62	2.51	2.42	2.49	3.24

Address: 55 East 52nd Street, New York, NY 10055 Telephone: 212-810-5300	Web Site: www.blackrock.com Officers: Laurence D. Fink - Chairman, Chief Executive Officer Robert S. (Rob) Kapito - President	Auditors: Deloitte & Touche LLP Transfer Agents: Computershare, Jersey City, NJ

BLOCK (H & R), INC.

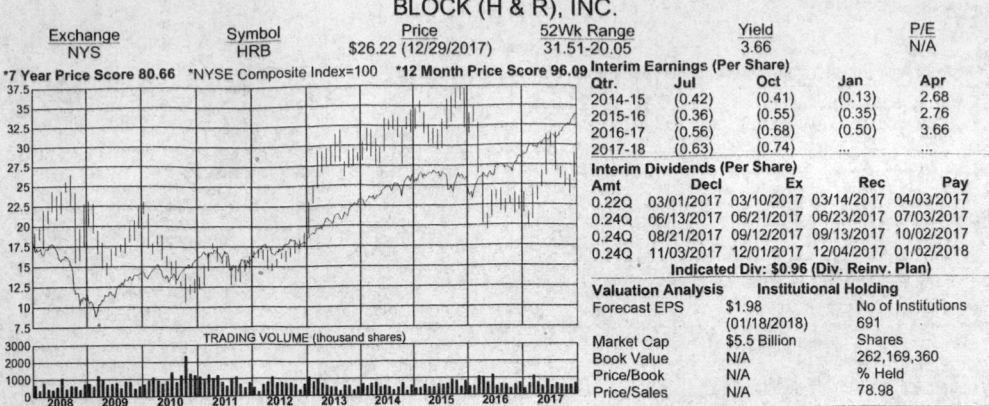

Exchange	Symbol	Price	52Wk Range	Yield	P/E
NYS	HRB	$26.22 (12/29/2017)	31.51-20.05	3.66	N/A

*7 Year Price Score 80.66   *NYSE Composite Index=100   *12 Month Price Score 96.09

Interim Earnings (Per Share)

Qtr.	Jul	Oct	Jan	Apr
2014-15	(0.42)	(0.41)	(0.13)	2.68
2015-16	(0.36)	(0.55)	(0.35)	2.76
2016-17	(0.56)	(0.68)	(0.50)	3.66
2017-18	(0.63)	(0.74)		

Interim Dividends (Per Share)

Amt	Decl	Ex	Rec	Pay
0.22Q	03/01/2017	03/10/2017	03/14/2017	04/03/2017
0.24Q	06/13/2017	06/21/2017	06/23/2017	07/03/2017
0.24Q	08/21/2017	09/12/2017	09/13/2017	10/02/2017
0.24Q	11/03/2017	12/01/2017	12/04/2017	01/02/2018

Indicated Div: $0.96 (Div. Reinv. Plan)

Valuation Analysis

		Institutional Holding	
Forecast EPS	$1.98	No of Institutions	
	(01/18/2018)	691	
Market Cap	$5.5 Billion	Shares	
Book Value	N/A		262,169,360
Price/Book	N/A	% Held	
Price/Sales	N/A		78.98

TRADING VOLUME (thousand shares)

Business Summary: Miscellaneous Consumer Services (MIC: 2.2.3 SIC: 7291 NAIC: 541213)

H&R Block and its subsidiaries are engaged in providing assisted and do-it-yourself tax return preparations solutions through multiple channels (including in-person, online and mobile applications, and desktop software) and distribute Co.'s financial products and services to the public in the U.S., Canada, Australia, and their respective territories. In addition to its tax services and products, Co. also provides additional services, including refund transfers, H&R Block Emerald Advance® lines of credit, H&R Block Emerald Prepaid MasterCard®, peace of Mind® Extended Service Plan, Tax Identity Shield®, Refund Advance Loans and, for Co.'s Canadian clients, an Instant Cash Back® refund option.

Recent Developments: For the quarter ended Oct 31 2017, loss from continuing operations was US$148.3 million compared with a loss of US$143.4 million in the year-earlier quarter. Net loss amounted to US$153.6 million versus a net loss of US$146.2 million in the year-earlier quarter. Revenues were US$140.9 million, up 7.3% from US$131.3 million the year before. Direct operating expenses rose 6.3% to US$240.0 million from US$225.7 million in the comparable period the year before. Indirect operating expenses increased 2.8% to US$116.8 million from US$113.7 million in the equivalent prior-year period.

Prospects: Our evaluation of Block (H & R) Inc. as of Jan. 14, 2018 is the result of our systematic analysis on three basic characteristics: earnings strength, relative valuation, and recent stock price movement. The company has suffered a very negative trend in earnings per share over the past 5 quarters and while recent estimates for the company have remained steady, HRB has posted better than expected results. Based on operating earnings yield, the company is undervalued when compared to all of the companies in our coverage universe. Share price changes over the past year indicates that HRB will perform well over the near term.

Financial Data
(US$ in Thousands)

	6 Mos	3 Mos	04/30/2017	04/30/2016	04/30/2015	04/30/2014	04/30/2013	04/30/2012
Earnings Per Share	(0.74)	(0.63)	1.91	1.49	1.71	1.72	1.58	0.89
Cash Flow Per Share	...	(7.81)	2.58	2.13	2.28	2.96	1.82	1.21
Tang Book Value Per Share	...	...	...	N.M.	3.48	2.79	2.00	2.17
Dividends Per Share	0.240	0.240	0.880	0.800	0.800	0.800	0.800	0.700
Dividend Payout %	...	...	46.07	53.69	46.78	46.51	50.63	78.65
Income Statement								
Total Revenue	140,854	137,802	3,036,314	3,038,153	3,078,658	3,024,295	2,905,943	2,893,771
EBITDA	(171,519)	(141,706)	821,608	730,693	889,351	851,816	770,211	645,370
Depn & Amortn	44,792	43,598	103,200	100,800	101,300	84,700	68,200	69,300
Income Before Taxes	(236,265)	(205,219)	629,287	569,479	742,805	767,116	702,011	576,070
Income Taxes	...	(77,401)	208,370	185,926	256,061	267,019	236,853	230,102
Net Income	(153,566)	(130,567)	408,945	374,267	473,663	475,157	433,948	265,932
Average Shares	209,065	207,935	214,095	250,818	277,136	276,027	274,359	298,601
Balance Sheet								
Current Assets	444,616	833,940	1,346,039	1,222,298	2,951,301	3,114,006	2,462,343	2,500,994
Total Assets	1,716,561	2,132,248	2,694,108	2,857,775	4,515,420	4,693,529	4,537,779	4,649,567
Current Liabilities	393,177	562,506	939,280	1,039,605	1,878,289	2,313,116	2,012,205	2,526,428
Long-Term Obligations	1,493,828	1,493,422	1,493,017	1,501,925	505,298	505,837	905,958	409,115
Total Liabilities	2,129,334	2,346,576	2,754,991	2,834,672	2,682,471	3,136,980	3,274,232	3,323,675
Stockholders' Equity	(412,773)	(214,328)	(60,883)	23,103	1,832,949	1,556,549	1,263,547	1,325,892
Shares Outstanding	209,068	209,057	207,171	220,517	275,275	274,228	272,635	292,119
Statistical Record								
EBITDA Margin %	N.M.	N.M.	27.06	24.05	28.89	28.17	26.50	22.30
Net Margin %	N.M.	N.M.	13.47	12.32	15.39	15.71	14.93	9.19
Current Ratio	1.13	1.48	1.43	1.18	1.57	1.35	1.22	0.99
Debt to Equity	...	...	...	65.01	0.28	0.32	0.72	0.31
Price Range	31.51-20.05	31.51-20.05	24.79-19.46	37.40-20.24	35.64-27.64	32.19-26.05	29.42-14.47	17.48-12.73
P/E Ratio	...	...	12.98-10.19	25.10-13.58	20.84-16.16	18.72-15.15	18.62-9.16	19.64-14.30
Average Yield %	0.95	0.99	3.88	2.47	2.48	2.76	4.11	4.51

Address: One H&R Block Way, Kansas City, MO 64105 **Telephone:** 816-854-3000	**Web Site:** www.hrblock.com **Officers:** Robert A. Gerard - Chairman Jeffrey J. Jones - President, Chief Executive Officer, Chief Executive Officer - Designate	**Auditors:** Deloitte & Touche LLP **Transfer Agents:** Wells Fargo Shareowner Services, St. Paul, MN

BOEING CO. (THE)

Exchange	Symbol	Price	52Wk Range	Yield	P/E
NYS	BA	$294.91 (12/29/2017)	297.90-156.97	2.32	27.16

*7 Year Price Score 136.24 *NYSE Composite Index=100 *12 Month Price Score 120.76

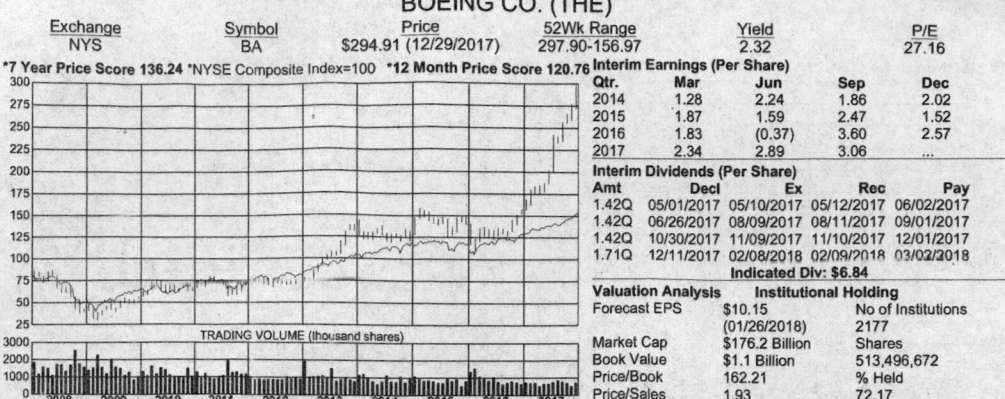

Interim Earnings (Per Share)

Qtr.	Mar	Jun	Sep	Dec
2014	1.28	2.24	1.86	2.02
2015	1.87	1.59	2.47	1.52
2016	1.83	(0.37)	3.60	2.57
2017	2.34	2.89	3.06	...

Interim Dividends (Per Share)

Amt	Decl	Ex	Rec	Pay
1.42Q	05/01/2017	05/10/2017	05/12/2017	06/02/2017
1.42Q	06/26/2017	08/09/2017	08/11/2017	09/01/2017
1.42Q	10/30/2017	11/09/2017	11/10/2017	12/01/2017
1.71Q	12/11/2017	02/08/2018	02/09/2018	03/02/2018

Indicated Div: $6.84

Valuation Analysis		Institutional Holding	
Forecast EPS	$10.15	No of Institutions	
	(01/26/2018)	2177	
Market Cap	$176.2 Billion	Shares	
Book Value	$1.1 Billion	513,496,672	
Price/Book	162.21	% Held	
Price/Sales	1.93	72.17	

Business Summary: Aerospace (MIC: 7.1.1 SIC: 3721 NAIC: 336411)

Boeing is an aerospace firm. Co. has five segments: Commercial Airplanes; Defense, Space and Security (BDS), which is comprised of the Boeing Military Aircraft (BMA), Network and Space Systems (N&SS) and Global Services and Support (GSS) segments; and Boeing Capital (BCC). Commercial Airplanes segment provides commercial jet aircraft and provides related support services. N&SS provides defense and intelligence systems and intelligence systems. GS&S segment provides support solutions. BCC segment facilitates, arranges, structures and provides selective financing solutions for Co.'s Boeing customers.

Recent Developments: For the quarter ended Sep 30 2017, net income decreased 18.7% to US$1.85 billion from US$2.28 billion in the year-earlier quarter. Revenues were US$24.31 billion, up 1.7% from US$23.90 billion the year before. Operating income was US$2.69 billion versus US$2.28 billion in the prior-year quarter, an increase of 17.8%. Direct operating expenses rose 0.4% to US$19.99 billion from US$19.90 billion in the comparable period the year before. Indirect operating expenses decreased 4.6% to US$1.63 billion from US$1.71 billion in the equivalent prior-year period.

Prospects: Our evaluation of Boeing Co. as of Jan. 21, 2018 is the result of our systematic analysis on three basic characteristics: earnings strength, relative valuation, and recent stock price movement. The company has generated a negative trend in earnings per share over the past 5 quarters and while recent estimates for the company have been mixed, BA has posted better than expected results. Based on operating earnings yield, the company is about fairly valued when compared to all of the companies in our coverage universe. Share price changes over the past year indicates that BA will perform very well over the near term.

Financial Data

(US$ in Millions)	9 Mos	6 Mos	3 Mos	12/31/2016	12/31/2015	12/31/2014	12/31/2013	12/31/2012
Earnings Per Share	10.86	11.40	8.14	7.61	7.44	7.38	5.96	5.11
Cash Flow Per Share	22.21	21.73	18.52	16.48	13.63	12.17	10.78	9.91
Tang Book Value Per Share	N.M.	...	N.M.	N.M.	N.M.	0.96	9.07	N.M.
Dividends Per Share	5.350	5.020	4.690	4.360	3.640	2.920	1.940	1.760
Dividend Payout %	49.26	44.04	57.62	57.29	48.92	39.57	32.55	34.44
Income Statement								
Total Revenue	68,024	43,715	20,976	94,571	96,114	90,762	86,623	81,698
EBITDA	8,660	5,453	2,436	6,989	8,513	8,597	7,742	7,353
Depn & Amortn	1,487	965	471	1,418	1,357	1,414	1,338	1,248
Income Before Taxes	6,906	4,308	1,878	5,265	6,881	6,850	6,018	5,642
Income Taxes	2,010	1,216	508	673	1,979	1,691	1,646	2,007
Net Income	5,065	3,212	1,451	4,895	5,176	5,446	4,585	3,900
Average Shares	605	608	620	642	695	736	767	761
Balance Sheet								
Current Assets	64,142	62,831	62,367	62,488	68,234	67,785	65,074	57,309
Total Assets	91,007	90,036	89,673	89,997	94,408	99,198	92,663	88,896
Current Liabilities	54,409	52,909	49,781	50,134	50,412	56,717	51,486	44,982
Long-Term Obligations	9,780	10,055	10,432	9,568	8,730	8,141	8,072	8,973
Total Liabilities	89,921	92,073	89,578	89,180	88,073	90,533	77,788	83,029
Stockholders' Equity	1,086	(2,037)	95	817	6,335	8,665	14,875	5,867
Shares Outstanding	597	593	605	617	666	706	747	755
Statistical Record								
Return on Assets %	7.44	7.93	5.66	5.29	5.35	5.68	5.05	4.61
Return on Equity %	421.80	...	247.80	136.51	69.01	46.27	44.21	82.91
EBITDA Margin %	12.73	12.47	11.61	7.39	8.86	9.47	8.94	9.00
Net Margin %	7.45	7.35	6.92	5.18	5.39	6.00	5.29	4.77
Asset Turnover	1.01	1.01	1.03	1.02	0.99	0.95	0.95	0.96
Current Ratio	1.18	1.19	1.25	1.25	1.35	1.20	1.26	1.27
Debt to Equity	9.01	...	109.81	11.71	1.38	0.94	0.54	1.53
Price Range	256.45-131.74	202.23-126.70	183.91-122.70	157.81-108.44	158.31-125.49	144.37-118.34	138.36-73.65	77.27-67.24
P/E Ratio	23.61-12.13	17.74-11.11	22.59-15.07	20.74-14.25	21.28-16.87	19.56-16.04	23.21-12.36	15.12-13.16
Average Yield %	2.91	3.17	3.25	3.27	2.54	2.27	1.88	2.40

Address: 100 North Riverside Plaza, Chicago, IL 60606-1596 Telephone: 312-544-2000	Web Site: www.boeing.com Officers: Dennis A. Muilenburg - Chairman, Vice-Chairman, President, Chief Executive Officer, Chief Operating Officer, Executive Vice President, Division Officer Raymond L. Conner - Executive Vice President, Division Officer, Vice-Chairman	Auditors: Deloitte & Touche LLP Transfer Agents: Computershare Trust Company, N.A., Providence, RI

BOOZ ALLEN HAMILTON HOLDING CORP.

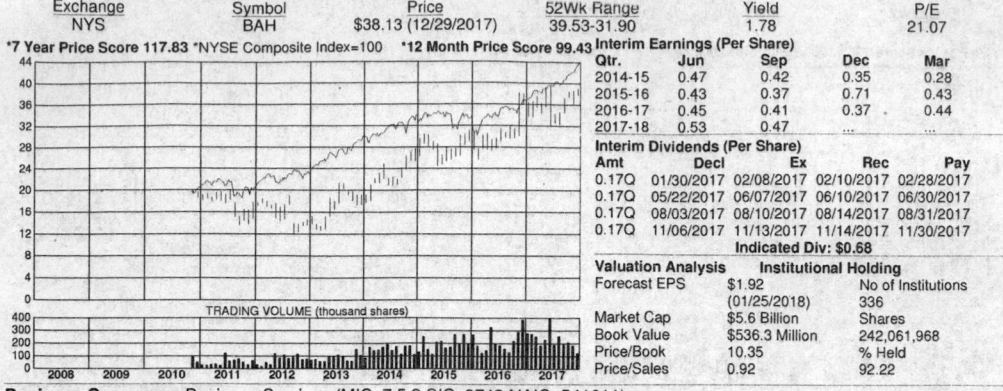

Exchange	Symbol	Price	52Wk Range	Yield	P/E
NYS	BAH	$38.13 (12/29/2017)	39.53-31.90	1.78	21.07

*7 Year Price Score 117.83 *NYSE Composite Index=100 *12 Month Price Score 99.43

Interim Earnings (Per Share)

Qtr.	Jun	Sep	Dec	Mar
2014-15	0.47	0.42	0.35	0.28
2015-16	0.43	0.37	0.71	0.43
2016-17	0.45	0.41	0.37	0.44
2017-18	0.53	0.47	...	...

Interim Dividends (Per Share)

Amt	Decl	Ex	Rec	Pay
0.17Q	01/30/2017	02/08/2017	02/10/2017	02/28/2017
0.17Q	05/22/2017	06/07/2017	06/10/2017	06/30/2017
0.17Q	08/03/2017	08/10/2017	08/14/2017	08/31/2017
0.17Q	11/06/2017	11/13/2017	11/14/2017	11/30/2017

Indicated Div: $0.68

Valuation Analysis   **Institutional Holding**

Forecast EPS	$1.92	No of Institutions	
	(01/25/2018)	336	
Market Cap	$5.6 Billion	Shares	
Book Value	$536.3 Million	242,061,968	
Price/Book	10.35	% Held	
Price/Sales	0.92	92.22	

Business Summary: Business Services (MIC: 7.5.2 SIC: 8742 NAIC: 541611)

Booz Allen Hamilton Holding is a holding company. Co. provides management and technology, consulting, and engineering services to the U.S. and international governments, corporations, and non-profit organizations. Co.'s services include: Consulting, which focuses on develop solutions for specific domains, human capital, and operations; Analytics, which include decision analysts' capabilities, and data scientists; Digital Solutions, which include Software Developers and Systems Architects; Engineering, which include engineers that provide prototyping, reverse engineering, and Networks and Information Technology Infrastructure; and Cyber, which focuses on prevention against cyber attacks.

Recent Developments: For the quarter ended Sep 30 2017, net income increased 12.9% to US$70.9 million from US$62.8 million in the year-earlier quarter. Revenues were US$1.54 billion, up 10.6% from US$1.39 billion the year before. Operating income was US$126.5 million versus US$117.7 million in the prior-year quarter, an increase of 7.5%. Direct operating expenses rose 10.9% to US$1.18 billion from US$1.07 billion in the comparable period the year before. Indirect operating expenses increased 10.5% to US$231.1 million from US$209.1 million in the equivalent prior-year period.

Prospects: Our evaluation of Booz Allen Hamilton Holding as of Jan. 21, 2018 is the result of our systematic analysis on three basic characteristics: earnings strength, relative valuation, and recent stock price movement. The company has managed to produce a neutral trend in earnings per share over the past 5 quarters and while recent estimates for the company have been raised by analysts, BAH has posted better than expected results. Based on operating earnings yield, the company is undervalued when compared to all of the companies in our coverage universe. Share price changes over the past year indicates that BAH will perform in line with the market over the near term.

Financial Data

(US$ in Thousands)	6 Mos	3 Mos	03/31/2017	03/31/2016	03/31/2015	03/31/2014	03/31/2013	03/31/2012
Earnings Per Share	1.81	1.75	1.67	1.94	1.52	1.54	1.45	1.70
Cash Flow Per Share	2.33	2.54	2.58	1.70	2.13	2.35	3.46	2.76
Dividends Per Share	0.660	0.640	0.620	0.540	1.460	2.400	8.360	0.090
Dividend Payout %	36.46	36.57	37.13	27.84	96.05	155.84	576.55	5.29
Income Statement								
Total Revenue	3,035,655	1,493,570	5,804,284	5,405,738	5,274,770	5,478,693	5,758,059	5,859,218
EBITDA	269,907	141,514	520,498	500,377	510,450	516,417	497,895	450,752
Depn & Amortn	2,633	1,289	46,300	50,100	52,700	57,600	59,300	58,800
Income Before Taxes	227,569	121,478	411,900	379,462	385,918	380,787	368,311	343,874
Income Taxes	77,116	41,938	159,410	85,368	153,349	148,599	149,253	103,919
Net Income	150,453	79,540	252,490	294,094	232,569	232,188	219,058	239,955
Average Shares	148,887	149,868	150,274	149,719	150,375	148,681	144,854	140,812
Balance Sheet								
Current Assets	1,449,277	1,506,976	1,294,480	1,189,771	1,163,208	1,255,977	1,424,352	1,657,663
Total Assets	3,529,635	3,575,525	3,373,105	3,010,171	2,877,493	2,940,818	3,177,528	3,314,791
Current Liabilities	969,507	945,267	1,101,401	939,913	848,994	917,104	964,646	914,446
Long-Term Obligations	1,783,897	1,798,655	1,470,174	1,484,448	1,569,272	1,585,231	1,659,611	922,925
Total Liabilities	2,993,352	2,976,498	2,799,514	2,601,683	2,690,995	2,769,182	2,950,735	2,129,606
Stockholders' Equity	536,283	599,027	573,591	408,488	186,498	171,636	226,793	1,185,185
Shares Outstanding	145,591	148,676	148,887	147,992	149,089	149,295	146,206	142,552
Statistical Record								
Return on Assets %	8.22	7.99	7.91	9.96	7.99	7.59	6.75	7.55
Return on Equity %	51.74	49.79	51.42	98.59	129.88	116.55	31.03	22.87
EBITDA Margin %	8.89	9.47	8.97	9.26	9.68	9.43	8.65	7.69
Net Margin %	4.96	5.33	4.35	5.44	4.41	4.24	3.80	4.10
Asset Turnover	1.82	1.78	1.82	1.83	1.81	1.79	1.77	1.84
Current Ratio	1.49	1.59	1.18	1.27	1.37	1.37	1.48	1.81
Debt to Equity	3.33	3.00	2.56	3.63	8.41	9.24	7.32	0.78
Price Range	39.53-29.69	39.53-29.14	38.20-27.24	31.13-24.45	30.46-20.82	22.16-12.90	19.06-11.90	19.87-13.52
P/E Ratio	21.84-16.40	22.59-16.65	22.87-16.31	16.05-12.60	20.04-13.70	14.39-8.38	13.14-8.21	11.69-7.95
Average Yield %	1.89		1.93	1.94	5.87	13.04	56.23	0.52

Address: 8283 Greensboro Drive, McLean, VA 22102 Telephone: 703-902-5000	Web Site: www.boozallen.com Officers: Ralph W. Shrader - Chairman, President, Chief Executive Officer Horacio D. Rozanski - President, Executive Vice President, Chief Operating Officer, Chief Executive Officer	Auditors: Ernst & Young LLP Investor Contact: 703-377-5332 Transfer Agents: Computershare, Jersey City, NJ

BORGWARNER INC

Exchange	Symbol	Price	52Wk Range	Yield	P/E
NYS	BWA	$51.09 (12/29/2017)	55.68-37.99	1.33	35.73

*7 Year Price Score 81.08 *NYSE Composite Index=100 *12 Month Price Score 110.52

Interim Earnings (Per Share)

Qtr.	Mar	Jun	Sep	Dec
2014	0.69	0.83	0.73	0.61
2015	0.79	0.65	0.70	0.56
2016	0.75	0.76	0.39	(1.35)
2017	0.89	1.01	0.88	...

Interim Dividends (Per Share)

Amt	Decl	Ex	Rec	Pay
0.14Q	02/09/2017	02/27/2017	03/01/2017	03/15/2017
0.14Q	04/27/2017	05/30/2017	06/01/2017	06/15/2017
0.14Q	07/27/2017	08/30/2017	09/01/2017	09/15/2017
0.17Q	11/09/2017	11/30/2017	12/01/2017	12/15/2017

Indicated Div: $0.68

Valuation Analysis

		Institutional Holding	
Forecast EPS	$3.83	No of Institutions	766
	(01/18/2018)	Shares	234,344,736
Market Cap	$10.8 Billion		
Book Value	$3.8 Billion	% Held	89.36
Price/Book	2.82		
Price/Sales	1.14		

Business Summary: Auto Parts (MIC: 1.8.2 SIC: 3714 NAIC: 336350)

Borg Warner is a supplier of technology solutions for combustion, hybrid and electric vehicles. These products are manufactured and sold primarily to original equipment manufacturers (OEMs) of light vehicles. Co.'s products are also sold to other OEMs of commercial vehicles and off-highway vehicles. Co.'s products fall into two reporting segments: Engine and Drivetrain. The Engine segment's products include turbochargers, timing systems, emissions systems, thermal systems, thermostats, diesel cold start and gasoline ignition technology. The Drivetrain segment's products include friction, mechanical and controls products, torque management, and rotating electrical components.

Recent Developments: For the quarter ended Sep 30 2017, net income increased 109.0% to US$194.6 million from US$93.1 million in the year-earlier quarter. Revenues were US$2.42 billion, up 9.1% from US$2.21 billion the year before. Operating income was US$275.9 million versus US$150.3 million in the prior-year quarter, an increase of 83.6%. Direct operating expenses rose 8.6% to US$1.89 billion from US$1.74 billion in the comparable period the year before. Indirect operating expenses decreased 23.1% to US$246.8 million from US$320.8 million in the equivalent prior-year period.

Prospects: Our evaluation of Borg Warner Inc. as of Jan. 14, 2018 is the result of our systematic analysis on three basic characteristics: earnings strength, relative valuation, and recent stock price movement. The company has enjoyed a very positive trend in earnings per share over the past 5 quarters and while recent estimates for the company have been mixed, BWA has posted better than expected results. Based on operating earnings yield, the company is undervalued when compared to all of the companies in our coverage universe. Share price changes over the past year indicates that BWA will perform well over the near term.

Financial Data

(US$ in Thousands)	9 Mos	6 Mos	3 Mos	12/31/2016	12/31/2015	12/31/2014	12/31/2013	12/31/2012
Earnings Per Share	1.43	0.94	0.69	0.55	2.70	2.86	2.70	2.09
Cash Flow Per Share	5.08	5.09	5.02	4.82	3.87	3.53	3.14	3.89
Tang Book Value Per Share	6.80	6.74	5.84	4.96	5.71	9.98	9.63	7.33
Dividends Per Share	0.560	0.550	0.540	0.530	0.520	0.510	0.250	...
Dividend Payout %	39.16	58.51	78.26	96.36	19.26	17.83	9.26	...
Income Statement								
Total Revenue	7,212,900	4,796,700	2,407,000	9,071,000	8,023,200	8,305,100	7,436,600	7,183,200
EBITDA	1,170,100	789,300	390,000	617,300	1,259,900	1,294,100	1,154,600	1,046,800
Depn & Amortn	302,000	197,100	97,300	391,400	320,200	330,400	299,400	293,900
Income Before Taxes	818,700	559,100	276,200	147,600	886,800	932,800	825,800	718,200
Income Taxes	241,900	162,500	86,300	30,300	280,400	292,600	218,300	238,600
Net Income	586,100	401,200	189,200	118,500	609,700	655,800	624,300	500,900
Average Shares	211,013	211,478	212,236	215,328	225,648	228,924	231,337	242,754
Balance Sheet								
Current Assets	3,401,100	3,193,200	3,107,300	2,911,600	3,135,300	2,970,800	2,798,500	2,472,800
Total Assets	9,816,200	9,288,500	9,083,700	8,834,700	8,841,500	7,228,000	6,917,000	6,400,800
Current Liabilities	2,381,200	2,106,100	2,151,200	2,091,800	2,357,300	2,168,200	1,623,900	1,603,100
Long-Term Obligations	2,091,900	2,077,900	2,040,300	2,043,600	2,124,600	716,300	1,021,000	823,800
Total Liabilities	5,990,500	5,676,500	5,680,300	5,616,400	5,287,800	3,611,800	3,356,400	3,318,200
Stockholders' Equity	3,825,700	3,612,000	3,403,400	3,218,300	3,553,700	3,616,200	3,560,600	3,082,600
Shares Outstanding	210,838	211,062	212,219	212,262	219,324	226,430	227,932	231,145
Statistical Record								
Return on Assets %	3.11	2.09	1.59	1.34	7.59	9.27	9.38	8.08
Return on Equity %	7.77	5.24	4.05	3.49	17.01	18.28	18.80	18.26
EBITDA Margin %	16.22	16.46	16.20	6.81	15.70	15.58	15.53	14.57
Net Margin %	8.13	8.36	7.86	1.31	7.60	7.90	8.39	6.97
Asset Turnover	1.01	1.01	1.02	1.02	1.00	1.17	1.12	1.16
Current Ratio	1.43	1.52	1.44	1.39	1.33	1.37	1.72	1.54
Debt to Equity	0.55	0.58	0.60	0.63	0.60	0.20	0.29	0.27
Price Range	51.23-33.64	44.36-28.52	43.95-27.69	43.23-27.69	63.01-38.89	67.38-50.24	55.96-35.42	43.52-30.27
P/E Ratio	35.83-23.52	47.19-30.34	63.70-40.13	78.60-50.35	23.34-14.40	23.56-17.57	20.73-13.12	20.83-14.48
Average Yield %	1.35	1.44	1.48	1.53	1.00	0.86	0.56	...

Address: 3850 Hamlin Road, Auburn Hills, MI 48326	Web Site: www.borgwarner.com	Auditors: PricewaterhouseCoopers LLP
Telephone: 248-754-9200	Officers: James R. Verrier - President, Chief Executive Officer, Vice President, Chief Operating Officer Ronald T. Hundzinski - Executive Vice President, Chief Financial Officer, Vice President, Treasurer, Controller	Investor Contact: 248-754-0881
		Transfer Agents: BNY Mellon Shareowner Services, Jersey City, NJ

BOSTON BEER CO INC (THE)

Exchange	Symbol	Price	52Wk Range	Yield	P/E
NYS	SAM	$191.10 (12/29/2017)	194.60-129.90	N/A	26.11

*7 Year Price Score 71.88   *NYSE Composite Index=100   *12 Month Price Score 109.18

TRADING VOLUME (thousand shares)

Interim Earnings (Per Share)

Qtr.	Mar	Jun	Sep	Dec
2014	0.62	1.88	2.79	1.40
2015	1.00	2.18	2.85	1.23
2016	0.53	2.06	2.48	1.74
2017	0.45	2.35	2.78	...

Interim Dividends (Per Share)

No Dividends Paid

Valuation Analysis

		Institutional Holding	
Forecast EPS	$6.45	No of Institutions	
	(01/18/2018)	322	
Market Cap	$2.2 Billion	Shares	
Book Value	$414.3 Million	12,470,596	
Price/Book	5.42	% Held	
Price/Sales	2.56	59.65	

Business Summary: Beverages (MIC: 1.2.2 SIC: 2082 NAIC: 312120)

Boston Beer Company is engaged in the business of selling alcohol beverages throughout the U.S. and in selected international markets. Co. consists of two operating segments that each produce and sell alcohol beverages. The first is the Boston Beer Company operating segment comprised of Co.'s Samuel Adams®, Twisted Tea® and Angry Orchard® brands. The second is the A&S Brewing Collaborative operating segment which is comprised of The Traveler Beer Company, Coney Island Brewing Company, Angel City Brewing Company and Concrete Beach Brewing Company. Co. produces malt beverages, hard cider and hard seltzer at Co.-owned breweries and under contract arrangements at other brewery locations.

Recent Developments: For the quarter ended Sep 30 2017, net income increased 6.8% to US$33.7 million from US$31.5 million in the year-earlier quarter. Revenues were US$247.0 million, down 2.5% from US$253.4 million the year before. Direct operating expenses declined 3.6% to US$115.5 million from US$119.8 million in the comparable period the year before. Indirect operating expenses decreased 4.0% to US$80.0 million from US$83.3 million in the equivalent prior-year period.

Prospects: Our evaluation of Boston Beer Co. Inc. as of Jan. 14, 2018 is the result of our systematic analysis on three basic characteristics: earnings strength, relative valuation, and recent stock price movement. The company has generated a negative trend in earnings per share over the past 5 quarters and while recent estimates for the company have been raised by analysts, SAM has posted better than expected results. Based on operating earnings yield, the company is about fairly valued when compared to all of the companies in our coverage universe. Share price changes over the past year indicates that SAM will perform in line with the market over the near term.

Financial Data

(US$ in Thousands)	9 Mos	6 Mos	3 Mos	12/31/2016	12/26/2015	12/27/2014	12/28/2013	12/29/2012
Earnings Per Share	7.32	7.02	6.73	6.79	7.25	6.69	5.18	4.39
Cash Flow Per Share	12.96	13.69	11.52	12.10	12.89	10.92	7.85	7.47
Tang Book Value Per Share	34.95	34.75	34.98	35.81	35.87	33.09	23.41	18.93
Income Statement								
Total Revenue	656,672	409,625	161,695	906,446	959,934	903,007	739,053	580,222
EBITDA	139,437	74,989	16,680	186,253	198,354	180,373	138,210	115,686
Depn & Amortn	38,372	25,616	12,724	49,300	43,400	34,800	25,700	20,200
Income Before Taxes	101,446	49,543	4,040	137,121	155,010	145,594	112,541	95,517
Income Taxes	32,927	14,707	(1,671)	49,772	56,596	54,851	42,149	36,050
Net Income	68,519	34,836	5,711	87,349	98,414	90,743	70,392	59,467
Average Shares	12,037	12,344	12,516	12,796	13,520	13,484	13,504	13,435
Balance Sheet								
Current Assets	179,143	190,714	166,073	201,238	223,603	207,462	164,278	162,342
Total Assets	587,114	601,507	586,955	623,297	645,400	605,161	444,075	359,484
Current Liabilities	109,394	112,805	84,478	101,519	111,160	110,170	104,377	88,894
Long-Term Obligations	...	...	...	411	471	528	584	566
Total Liabilities	172,825	179,843	151,544	176,715	184,179	169,021	141,990	114,393
Stockholders' Equity	414,289	421,664	435,411	446,582	461,221	436,140	302,085	245,091
Shares Outstanding	11,748	12,027	12,343	12,368	12,756	13,069	12,747	12,811
Statistical Record								
Return on Assets %	14.93	14.85	14.40	13.55	15.78	17.34	17.57	18.87
Return on Equity %	20.98	21.23	19.76	18.93	21.99	24.65	25.80	27.75
EBITDA Margin %	21.23	18.31	10.32	20.55	20.66	19.97	18.70	19.94
Net Margin %	10.43	8.50	3.53	9.64	10.25	10.05	9.52	10.25
Asset Turnover	1.44	1.48	1.47	1.41	1.54	1.73	1.84	1.84
Current Ratio	1.64	1.69	1.97	1.98	2.01	1.88	1.57	1.83
Price Range	178.00-129.90	192.05-129.90	192.05-144.65	204.25-146.42	323.99-197.05	297.78-203.81	259.25-134.45	139.24-94.52
P/E Ratio	24.32-17.75	27.36-18.50	28.54-21.49	30.08-21.56	44.69-27.18	44.51-30.46	50.05-25.96	31.72-21.53

Address: One Design Center Place, Suite 850, Boston, MA 02210 **Telephone:** 617-368-5000 **Fax:** 617-368-5500	**Web Site:** www.bostonbeer.com **Officers:** C. James Koch - Chairman Martin F. Roper - President, Chief Executive Officer	**Auditors:** Deloitte & Touche LLP **Investor Contact:** 617-368-5060 **Transfer Agents:** Computershare Shareowner Services LLC, Jersey City, NJ

BOSTON PROPERTIES INC

Exchange	Symbol	Price	52Wk Range	Yield	P/E
NYS	BXP	$130.03 (12/29/2017)	139.88-117.70	2.46	40.51

*7 Year Price Score 85.37 *NYSE Composite Index=100 *12 Month Price Score 93.50

Interim Earnings (Per Share)

Qtr.	Mar	Jun	Sep	Dec
2014	0.35	0.50	0.83	1.14
2015	1.11	0.52	1.20	0.91
2016	1.18	0.63	0.50	0.95
2017	0.63	0.87	0.76	...

Interim Dividends (Per Share)

Amt	Decl	Ex	Rec	Pay
0.75Q	03/16/2017	03/29/2017	03/31/2017	04/28/2017
0.75Q	06/16/2017	06/28/2017	06/30/2017	07/31/2017
0.75Q	09/15/2017	09/28/2017	09/29/2017	10/31/2017
0.80Q	12/18/2017	12/28/2017	12/29/2017	01/30/2018

Indicated Div: $3.20

Valuation Analysis

		Institutional Holding	
Forecast EPS	$2.95 (01/16/2018)	No of Institutions	655
Market Cap	$20.1 Billion	Shares	187,393,216
Book Value	$5.8 Billion	% Held	100.28
Price/Book	3.44		
Price/Sales	7.77		

Business Summary: REITs (MIC: 5.3.1 SIC: 6798 NAIC: 525930)

Boston Properties is a self-administered and self-managed real estate investment trust, with substantial in-house capabilities and resources in acquisitions, development, financing, capital markets, construction management, property management, marketing, leasing, accounting, risk management, tax and legal services. At Dec 31 2016, Co. owned or had interests in 174 commercial real estate properties, including eight properties under construction/redevelopment. As of Dec 31 2016, Co.'s properties consisted of: 164 office properties, one hotel, five retail properties, and four residential properties (including two under construction).

Recent Developments: For the quarter ended Sep 30 2017, net income increased 106.6% to US$147.7 million from US$71.5 million in the year-earlier quarter. Revenues were US$657.7 million, up 5.2% from US$625.2 million the year before. Revenues from property income rose 4.5% to US$633.8 million from US$606.5 million in the corresponding quarter a year earlier.

Prospects: Our evaluation of Boston Properties Inc. as of Jan. 14, 2018 is the result of our systematic analysis on three basic characteristics: earnings strength, relative valuation, and recent stock price movement. The company has enjoyed a very positive trend in earnings per share over the past 5 quarters. Because the company lacks sufficient analyst estimate data, we place greater weight on the historical EPS trend as the measure of earnings strength. Based on operating earnings yield, the company is overvalued when compared to all of the companies in our coverage universe. Share price changes over the past year indicates that BXP will perform well over the near term.

Financial Data
(US$ in Thousands)

	9 Mos	6 Mos	3 Mos	12/31/2016	12/31/2015	12/31/2014	12/31/2013	12/31/2012
Earnings Per Share	3.21	2.95	2.71	3.26	3.73	2.83	4.86	1.92
Cash Flow Per Share	5.74	5.35	6.07	6.73	5.21	4.54	5.11	4.27
Tang Book Value Per Share	36.45	36.38	36.24	36.32	35.87	35.90	36.56	34.35
Dividends Per Share	3.000	2.900	2.800	2.700	3.850	7.100	4.850	2.300
Dividend Payout %	93.46	98.31	103.32	82.82	103.22	250.88	99.79	119.79
Income Statement								
Total Revenue	1,946,847	1,289,135	632,228	2,550,820	2,490,821	2,396,998	2,135,539	1,876,267
EBITDA	1,159,002	776,065	366,472	1,588,549	1,472,991	1,429,565	1,640,851	1,112,752
Depn & Amortn	463,288	311,124	159,205	694,403	639,542	628,573	565,397	454,044
Income Before Taxes	416,452	276,382	112,347	481,297	401,253	345,249	628,574	245,144
Net Income	355,961	236,014	99,708	512,785	583,106	443,611	749,811	289,650
Average Shares	154,483	154,331	154,214	153,977	153,844	153,308	152,521	150,711
Balance Sheet								
Current Assets	1,491,999	1,448,489	1,239,319	1,311,774	1,650,256	2,988,994	3,133,405	2,152,220
Total Assets	19,308,518	19,281,762	18,966,627	18,851,643	18,379,456	19,886,767	20,162,251	15,462,321
Current Liabilities	554,974	519,163	710,855	672,765	792,415	1,289,267	867,235	382,051
Long-Term Obligations	10,234,624	10,236,639	9,886,845	9,796,133	9,216,513	10,086,984	11,521,508	8,912,369
Total Liabilities	13,483,300	13,467,388	13,191,094	13,065,348	12,670,021	14,189,469	14,369,786	10,254,380
Stockholders' Equity	5,825,218	5,814,374	5,775,533	5,786,295	5,709,435	5,697,298	5,792,465	5,207,941
Shares Outstanding	154,322	154,307	153,849	153,790	153,579	153,113	152,983	151,601
Statistical Record								
Return on Assets %	2.66	2.43	2.24	2.75	3.05	2.22	4.21	1.91
Return on Equity %	8.76	8.06	7.43	8.90	10.22	7.72	13.63	5.70
EBITDA Margin %	59.53	60.20	57.97	62.28	59.14	59.64	76.84	59.31
Net Margin %	18.28	18.31	15.77	20.10	23.41	18.51	35.11	15.44
Asset Turnover	0.14	0.13	0.13	0.14	0.13	0.12	0.12	0.12
Current Ratio	2.69	2.79	1.74	1.95	2.08	2.32	3.61	5.63
Debt to Equity	1.76	1.76	1.71	1.69	1.61	1.77	1.99	1.71
Price Range	139.88-114.07	143.61-114.07	143.61-114.07	143.61-108.18	144.74-108.65	136.28-100.37	114.59-98.27	116.07-97.49
P/E Ratio	43.58-35.54	48.68-38.67	52.99-42.09	44.05-33.18	38.80-29.13	48.16-35.47	23.58-20.22	60.45-50.78
Average Yield %	2.38	2.22	2.24	2.12	2.99	6.00	4.58	2.16

Address: Prudential Center, 800 Boylston Street, Suite 1900, Boston, MA 02199-8103 **Telephone:** 617-236-3300	**Web Site:** www.bostonproperties.com **Officers:** Mortimer B. Zuckerman - Chairman Emeritus, Chairman, Executive Chairman, Chief Executive Officer Douglas T. Linde - President	**Auditors:** PricewaterhouseCoopers LLP **Investor Contact:** 617-236-3322 **Transfer Agents:** Computershare Trust Company, N.A., Providence, RI

BOSTON SCIENTIFIC CORP.

Exchange	Symbol	Price	52Wk Range	Yield	P/E
NYS	BSX	$24.79 (12/29/2017)	29.80-21.88	N/A	40.64

*7 Year Price Score 145.04 *NYSE Composite Index=100 *12 Month Price Score 94.46

Interim Earnings (Per Share)

Qtr.	Mar	Jun	Sep	Dec
2014	0.10	0.00	0.03	(0.22)
2015	0.00	0.08	(0.15)	(0.11)
2016	0.15	(0.15)	0.17	0.09
2017	0.21	0.11	0.20	...

Interim Dividends (Per Share)

No Dividends Paid

Valuation Analysis | **Institutional Holding**

Forecast EPS	$1.26	No of Institutions
	(01/26/2018)	833
Market Cap	$34.0 Billion	Shares
Book Value	$7.6 Billion	1,475,348,480
Price/Book	4.48	% Held
Price/Sales	3.85	79.73

Business Summary: Medical Instruments & Equipment (MIC: 4.3.1 SIC: 3841 NAIC: 339112)

Boston Scientific is a developer, manufacturer and marketer of medical devices. Co.'s products include: drug-eluting coronary stent systems, coronary therapies, and structural heart therapy for Interventional Cardiology; stents, peripheral embolization devices and vena cava filters for Peripheral Interventions; a range of implantable devices that monitor the heart for Cardiac Rhythm Management; steerable radio frequency ablation catheters for Electrophysiology; devices for gastroenterology and interventional bronchoscopy for Endoscopy; devices to treat urological and pelvic conditions for Urology and Public Health; and Precision SpectraTM Spinal Cord Stimulator Systems for Neuromodulation

Recent Developments: For the quarter ended Sep 30 2017, net income increased 24.1% to US$283.0 million from US$228.0 million in the year-earlier quarter. Revenues were US$2.22 billion, up 5.6% from US$2.11 billion the year before. Operating income was US$377.0 million versus US$348.0 million in the prior-year quarter, an increase of 8.3%. Direct operating expenses rose 7.2% to US$637.0 million from US$594.0 million in the comparable period the year before. Indirect operating expenses increased 3.9% to US$1.21 billion from US$1.16 billion in the equivalent prior-year period.

Prospects: Our evaluation of Boston Scientific Corp. as of Jan. 21, 2018 is the result of our systematic analysis on three basic characteristics: earnings strength, relative valuation, and recent stock price movement. The company has produced a positive trend in earnings per share over the past 5 quarters and while recent estimates for the company have been mixed, BSX has posted better than expected results. Based on operating earnings yield, the company is undervalued when compared to all of the companies in our coverage universe. Share price changes over the past year indicates that BSX will perform in line with the market over the near term.

Financial Data

(US$ in Thousands)	9 Mos	6 Mos	3 Mos	12/31/2016	12/31/2015	12/31/2014	12/31/2013	12/31/2012
Earnings Per Share	0.61	0.58	0.32	0.25	(0.18)	(0.09)	(0.09)	(2.89)
Cash Flow Per Share	0.74	0.54	0.71	0.71	0.45	0.96	0.81	0.89
Income Statement								
Total Revenue	6,640,000	4,418,000	2,160,000	8,386,000	7,477,000	7,380,000	7,143,000	7,249,000
EBITDA	1,072,000	637,000	424,000	675,000	(97,000)	(11,000)	374,000	(3,563,000)
Depn & Amortn	198,000	127,000	63,000	270,000	274,000	287,000	279,000	288,000
Income Before Taxes	706,000	396,000	305,000	177,000	(650,000)	(509,000)	(223,000)	(4,107,000)
Income Taxes	(13,000)	(40,000)	15,000	(170,000)	(411,000)	(390,000)	(102,000)	(39,000)
Net Income	719,000	436,000	290,000	347,000	(239,000)	(119,000)	(121,000)	(4,068,000)
Average Shares	1,394,100	1,391,100	1,390,200	1,377,200	1,341,200	1,324,300	1,341,200	1,406,700
Balance Sheet								
Current Assets	3,478,000	3,222,000	3,026,000	3,239,000	3,471,000	3,606,000	3,011,000	3,022,000
Total Assets	18,636,000	18,382,000	17,943,000	18,096,000	18,133,000	17,042,000	16,571,000	17,154,000
Current Liabilities	4,828,000	4,300,000	3,490,000	3,587,000	2,430,000	2,846,000	1,824,000	1,772,000
Long-Term Obligations	4,416,000	4,817,000	5,509,000	5,420,000	5,674,000	3,859,000	4,237,000	4,252,000
Total Liabilities	11,048,000	11,147,000	10,890,000	11,363,000	11,813,000	10,585,000	10,032,000	10,284,000
Stockholders' Equity	7,588,000	7,235,000	7,053,000	6,733,000	6,320,000	6,457,000	6,539,000	6,870,000
Shares Outstanding	1,372,735	1,370,464	1,369,082	1,362,104	1,346,647	1,327,451	1,322,296	1,355,711
Statistical Record								
Return on Assets %	4.64	4.35	2.44	1.91	N.M.	N.M.	N.M.	N.M.
Return on Equity %	11.98	11.71	6.44	5.30	N.M.	N.M.	N.M.	N.M.
EBITDA Margin %	16.14	14.42	19.63	8.05	N.M.	N.M.	5.24	N.M.
Net Margin %	10.83	9.87	13.43	4.14	N.M.	N.M.	N.M.	N.M.
Asset Turnover	0.49	0.48	0.48	0.46	0.43	0.44	0.42	0.38
Current Ratio	0.72	0.75	0.87	0.90	1.43	1.27	1.65	1.71
Debt to Equity	0.58	0.67	0.78	0.80	0.90	0.60	0.65	0.62
Price Range	29.17-20.09	28.25-20.09	25.41-18.81	24.48-16.07	18.94-13.22	13.98-11.37	12.38-5.73	6.36-4.97
P/E Ratio	47.82-32.93	48.71-34.64	79.41-58.78	97.92-64.28	...	...	...	...

Address: 300 Boston Scientific Way, Marlborough, MA 01752-1234 **Telephone:** 508-683-4000	**Web Site:** www.bostonscientific.com **Officers:** Michael F. Mahoney - Chairman, President, Chief Executive Officer Daniel J. Brennan - Chief Financial Officer, Executive Vice President	**Auditors:** Ernst & Young LLP **Investor Contact:** 508-650-8023 **Transfer Agents:** Computershare Shareowner Services, Providence, RI

BRADY CORP

Exchange	Symbol	Price	52Wk Range	Yield	P/E	Div Achiever
NYS	BRC	$37.90 (12/29/2017)	39.80-31.95	2.19	20.05	32 Years

*7 Year Price Score 94.41   *NYSE Composite Index=100   *12 Month Price Score 98.55

Interim Earnings (Per Share)

Qtr.	Oct	Jan	Apr	Jul
2014-15	0.26	0.23	0.34	(0.77)
2015-16	0.37	0.30	0.42	0.50
2016-17	0.44	0.49	0.43	0.48
2017-18	0.49	...	...	...

Interim Dividends (Per Share)

Amt	Decl	Ex	Rec	Pay
0.205Q	02/22/2017	04/05/2017	04/07/2017	04/28/2017
0.205Q	05/24/2017	07/06/2017	07/10/2017	07/31/2017
0.207Q	09/06/2017	10/06/2017	10/10/2017	10/31/2017
0.207Q	11/14/2017	01/09/2018	01/10/2018	01/31/2018

Indicated Div: $0.83 (Div. Reinv. Plan)

Valuation Analysis

	Institutional Holding	
Forecast EPS	$1.95	No of Institutions
	(01/03/2018)	261
Market Cap	$2.0 Billion	Shares
Book Value	$712.7 Million	50,297,044
Price/Book	2.74	% Held
Price/Sales	1.74	76.05

Business Summary: Printing (MIC: 7.5.5 SIC: 3999 NAIC: 339950)

Brady is a manufacturer and supplier of identification solutions and workplace safety products that identify and protect premises, products and people. Co. has two segments: Identification Solutions, which includes industrial and healthcare identification products in several categories, including facility identification and protection, product identification, wire identification, people identification, patient identification, and custom wristbands; and Workplace Safety, which includes workplace safety and compliance products in several categories, including safety and compliance signs, tags, and labels, informational and architectural signage, asset tracking labels, and first aid products.

Recent Developments: For the quarter ended Oct 31 2017, net income increased 14.6% to US$25.8 million from US$22.6 million in the year-earlier quarter. Revenues were US$290.2 million, up 3.6% from US$280.2 million the year before. Operating income was US$35.4 million versus US$33.2 million in the prior-year quarter, an increase of 6.6%. Direct operating expenses rose 3.1% to US$144.1 million from US$139.8 million in the comparable period the year before. Indirect operating expenses increased 3.3% to US$110.7 million from US$107.2 million in the equivalent prior-year period.

Prospects: Our evaluation of Brady Corp. as of Jan. 14, 2018 is the result of our systematic analysis on three basic characteristics: earnings strength, relative valuation, and recent stock price movement. The company has managed to produce a neutral trend in earnings per share over the past 5 quarters and while recent estimates for the company have remained steady, BRC has posted better than expected results. Based on operating earnings yield, the company is undervalued when compared to all of the companies in our coverage universe. Share price changes over the past year indicates that BRC will perform well over the near term.

Financial Data (US$ in Thousands)	3 Mos	07/31/2017	07/31/2016	07/31/2015	07/31/2014	07/31/2013	07/31/2012	07/31/2011
Earnings Per Share	1.89	1.84	1.58	0.06	(0.89)	(3.02)	(0.35)	2.04
Cash Flow Per Share	2.81	2.82	2.74	1.82	1.80	2.80	2.75	3.18
Tang Book Value Per Share	4.42	4.08	2.26	1.67	2.48	1.09	4.82	5.00
Dividends Per Share	0.823	0.820	0.810	0.800	0.780	0.760	0.740	0.720
Dividend Payout %	43.52	44.57	51.27	1,333.33	...	...	...	35.29
Income Statement								
Total Revenue	290,151	1,113,316	1,120,625	1,171,731	1,225,034	1,152,109	1,324,269	1,339,597
EBITDA	42,191	152,326	140,544	63,506	(12,082)	(33,380)	85,827	215,009
Depn & Amortn	6,564	20,190	23,375	27,355	26,727	48,725	43,987	48,827
Income Before Taxes	34,764	126,632	109,345	24,995	(53,109)	(98,746)	22,750	144,058
Income Taxes	8,928	30,987	29,235	20,093	(4,963)	42,070	40,661	35,406
Net Income	25,836	95,645	80,110	2,987	(45,968)	(154,535)	(17,911)	108,652
Average Shares	52,383	51,956	50,769	51,383	51,866	51,330	52,453	53,133
Balance Sheet								
Current Assets	423,642	407,814	407,424	408,582	463,842	512,490	650,854	758,287
Total Assets	1,057,613	1,050,223	1,043,964	1,062,897	1,253,665	1,438,683	1,607,719	1,861,505
Current Liabilities	193,785	187,198	166,727	209,247	291,945	323,497	267,018	301,881
Long-Term Obligations	93,810	104,536	211,982	200,774	159,296	201,150	254,944	331,914
Total Liabilities	344,942	350,083	440,366	475,209	520,589	607,886	598,366	705,313
Stockholders' Equity	712,671	700,140	603,598	587,688	733,076	830,797	1,009,353	1,156,192
Shares Outstanding	51,559	51,353	50,459	51,319	51,322	52,173	51,554	53,132
Statistical Record								
Return on Assets %	9.39	9.13	7.58	0.26	N.M.	N.M.	N.M.	6.02
Return on Equity %	14.91	14.67	13.41	0.45	N.M.	N.M.	N.M.	10.05
EBITDA Margin %	14.54	13.68	12.54	5.42	N.M.	N.M.	6.48	16.05
Net Margin %	8.90	8.59	7.15	0.25	N.M.	N.M.	N.M.	8.11
Asset Turnover	1.07	1.06	1.06	1.01	0.91	0.76	0.76	0.74
Current Ratio	2.19	2.18	2.44	1.95	1.59	1.58	2.44	2.51
Debt to Equity	0.13	0.15	0.35	0.34	0.22	0.24	0.25	0.29
Price Range	39.80-31.95	39.80-31.86	32.64-19.52	28.91-21.19	35.54-24.26	36.33-26.34	34.40-24.73	38.49-25.35
P/E Ratio	21.06-16.90	21.63-17.32	20.66-12.35	481.83-353.17	...	...	...	18.87-12.43
Average Yield %	2.25	2.27	3.20	3.12	2.69	2.38	2.49	2.23

Address: 6555 West Good Hope Road, Milwaukee, WI 53223 **Telephone:** 414-358-6600	**Web Site:** www.bradycorp.com **Officers:** J. Michael Nauman - President, Chief Executive Officer Thomas J. Felmer - Interim President, Interim Chief Executive Officer, Senior Vice President, Chief Financial Officer, Division Officer	**Auditors:** DELOITTE & TOUCHE LLP **Investor Contact:** 414-438-6940 **Transfer Agents:** Wells Fargo Bank Minnesota, N.A., St. Paul, MN

BRANDYWINE REALTY TRUST

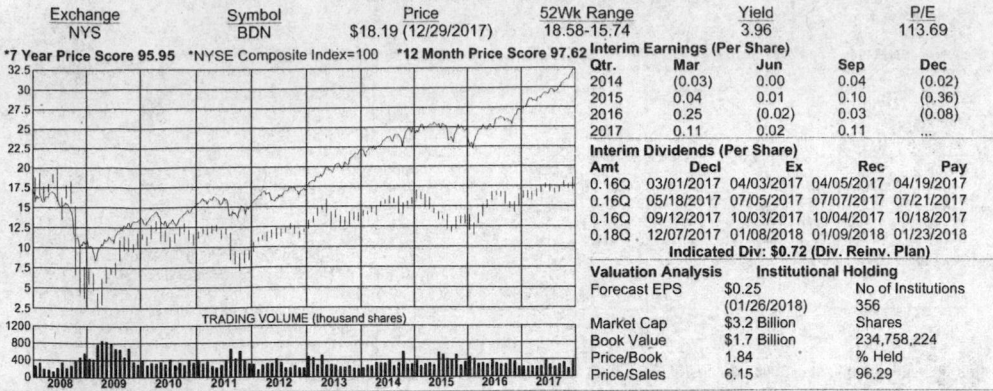

Exchange	Symbol	Price	52Wk Range	Yield	P/E
NYS	BDN	$18.19 (12/29/2017)	18.58-15.74	3.96	113.69

*7 Year Price Score 95.95   *NYSE Composite Index=100   *12 Month Price Score 97.62

Interim Earnings (Per Share)

Qtr.	Mar	Jun	Sep	Dec
2014	(0.03)	0.00	0.04	(0.02)
2015	0.04	0.01	0.10	(0.36)
2016	0.25	(0.02)	0.03	(0.08)
2017	0.11	0.02	0.11	

Interim Dividends (Per Share)

Amt	Decl	Ex	Rec	Pay
0.16Q	03/01/2017	04/03/2017	04/05/2017	04/19/2017
0.16Q	05/18/2017	07/05/2017	07/07/2017	07/21/2017
0.16Q	09/12/2017	10/03/2017	10/04/2017	10/18/2017
0.18Q	12/07/2017	01/08/2018	01/09/2018	01/23/2018

Indicated Div: $0.72 (Div. Reinv. Plan)

Valuation Analysis   Institutional Holding

Forecast EPS	$0.25	No of Institutions
	(01/26/2018)	356
Market Cap	$3.2 Billion	Shares
Book Value	$1.7 Billion	234,758,224
Price/Book	1.84	% Held
Price/Sales	6.15	96.29

Business Summary: REITs (MIC: 5.3.1 SIC: 6798 NAIC: 525930)

Brandywine Realty Trust is a self-administered and self-managed real estate investment trust that provides leasing, property management, development, redevelopment, acquisition and other tenant-related services for a portfolio of office, residential, retail and mixed-use properties. As of Dec 31 2016, Co. owned 113 properties (the Properties) and economic interests in 14 unconsolidated real estate ventures (the Real Estate Ventures). The Properties and the properties owned by the Real Estate Ventures are located in or near Philadelphia, PA; Metropolitan Washington, D.C.; Southern New Jersey; Richmond, VA; Wilmington, DE; Austin, TX and Concord, CA.

Recent Developments: For the quarter ended Sep 30 2017, net income increased 141.6% to US$19.0 million from US$7.9 million in the year-earlier quarter. Revenues were US$128.4 million, down 1.0% from US$129.7 million the year before. Revenues from property income fell 1.4% to US$126.9 million from US$128.7 million in the corresponding quarter a year earlier.

Prospects: Our evaluation of Brandywine Realty Trust as of Jan. 21, 2018 is the result of our systematic analysis on three basic characteristics: earnings strength, relative valuation, and recent stock price movement. The company has enjoyed a very positive trend in earnings per share over the past 5 quarters. Because the company lacks sufficient analyst estimate data, we place greater weight on the historical EPS trend as the measure of earnings strength. Based on operating earnings yield, the company is overvalued when compared to all of the companies in our coverage universe. Share price changes over the past year indicates that BDN will perform well over the near term.

Financial Data

(US$ in Thousands)	9 Mos	6 Mos	3 Mos	12/31/2016	12/31/2015	12/31/2014	12/31/2013	12/31/2012
Earnings Per Share	0.16	0.08	0.04	0.19	(0.21)	...	0.23	(0.06)
Cash Flow Per Share	1.28	1.29	1.30	0.98	1.10	1.14	1.20	1.09
Tang Book Value Per Share	9.54	9.59	10.32	10.24	10.43	11.39	11.28	11.72
Dividends Per Share	0.640	0.640	0.480	0.620	0.600	0.600	0.600	0.600
Dividend Payout %	400.00	800.00	1,200.00	326.32	...	...	260.87	...
Income Statement								
Total Revenue	387,149	258,711	130,920	525,463	602,631	596,982	562,210	559,833
EBITDA	119,932	74,933	46,479	330,475	305,294	344,407	367,574	310,238
Depn & Amortn	4,917	3,885	2,782	191,624	219,936	210,946	205,715	206,148
Income Before Taxes	52,370	28,633	22,019	52,004	(29,929)	6,814	35,318	(32,895)
Income Taxes	(1,032)	...	...	...	...	...	...	...
Net Income	47,631	28,755	21,102	40,191	(30,401)	6,975	42,777	6,595
Average Shares	176,835	176,756	176,201	176,010	178,162	166,202	154,414	143,257
Balance Sheet								
Current Assets	206,165	209,471	399,572	355,989	218,912	410,310	406,891	139,213
Total Assets	3,855,419	3,872,449	4,101,862	4,099,213	4,554,511	4,859,173	4,765,095	4,506,709
Current Liabilities	140,804	128,280	145,126	165,056	158,518	184,369	180,912	178,178
Long-Term Obligations	1,889,640	1,912,172	2,012,671	2,013,112	2,384,717	2,451,308	2,595,381	2,465,330
Total Liabilities	2,121,703	2,131,629	2,239,385	2,232,869	2,620,586	2,718,346	2,864,875	2,754,431
Stockholders' Equity	1,733,716	1,740,820	1,862,477	1,866,344	1,933,925	2,140,827	1,900,220	1,752,278
Shares Outstanding	175,477	175,389	174,265	175,140	174,688	179,293	156,731	143,538
Statistical Record								
Return on Assets %	0.88	0.60	0.36	0.93	N.M.	0.14	0.92	0.15
Return on Equity %	1.95	1.33	0.81	2.11	N.M.	0.35	2.34	0.36
EBITDA Margin %	30.98	28.96	35.50	62.89	50.66	57.69	65.38	55.42
Net Margin %	12.30	11.11	16.12	7.65	N.M.	1.17	7.61	1.18
Asset Turnover	0.13	0.13	0.12	0.12	0.13	0.12	0.12	0.12
Current Ratio	1.46	1.63	2.75	2.16	1.38	2.23	2.25	0.78
Debt to Equity	1.09	1.10	1.08	1.08	1.23	1.15	1.37	1.41
Price Range	17.80-14.21	17.80-14.21	16.89-13.72	16.87-11.29	17.00-11.72	16.29-13.77	15.94-12.18	12.88-9.40
P/E Ratio	111.25-88.81	222.50-177.63	422.25-343.00	88.79-59.42	...	N.M.	69.30-52.96	...
Average Yield %	3.89	3.93	3.04	4.15	4.23	4.00	4.36	5.17

Address: 2929 Walnut Street, Suite 1700, Philadelphia, PA 19104 **Telephone:** 610-325-5600	**Web Site:** www.brandywinerealty.com **Officers:** Gerard H. Sweeney - President, Chief Executive Officer Thomas E. Wirth - Executive Vice President, Chief Financial Officer, Principal Accounting Officer	**Auditors:** PricewaterhouseCoopers LLP **Investor Contact:** 610-832-7702 **Transfer Agents:** Computershare, Providence, RI

114

BRIGHT HORIZONS FAMILY SOLUTIONS, INC

Exchange	Symbol	Price	52Wk Range	Yield	P/E
NYS	BFAM	$94.00 (12/29/2017)	94.71-68.01	N/A	46.77

7 Year Price Score N/A   **NYSE Composite Index=100**   **12 Month Price Score 107.65**

Interim Earnings (Per Share)

Qtr.	Mar	Jun	Sep	Dec
2014	0.24	0.32	0.23	0.28
2015	0.35	0.43	0.33	0.39
2016	0.40	0.50	0.37	0.28
2017	0.68	0.54	0.51	...

Interim Dividends (Per Share)

No Dividends Paid

Valuation Analysis / Institutional Holding

Valuation Analysis		Institutional Holding	
Forecast EPS	$2.65	No of Institutions	
	(01/09/2018)	N/A	
Market Cap	$5.5 Billion	Shares	
Book Value	$774.5 Million	N/A	
Price/Book	7.15	% Held	
Price/Sales	3.26	N/A	

TRADING VOLUME (thousand shares)

Business Summary: Services (MIC: 6.1.2 SIC: 8351 NAIC: 624410)

Bright Horizons Family Solutions is a provider of child care, early education, back-up dependent care and educational advisory services. Co. provides services under contracts with employers. Co.'s service offerings include center-based full service child care and early education, back-up dependent care, and educational advisory services. Co.'s center-based child care services have two models: a profit and loss model; and a cost-plus model. Co. also provides back-up dependent care services through its full-service centers, its back-up centers, as well as through its Back-Up Care Advantage program. Co.'s educational advisory services consist of its EdAssist and College Coach services.

Recent Developments: For the quarter ended Sep 30 2017, net income increased 38.2% to US$31.1 million from US$22.5 million in the year-earlier quarter. Revenues were US$433.3 million, up 12.9% from US$383.9 million the year before. Operating income was US$45.0 million versus US$44.7 million in the prior-year quarter, an increase of 0.6%. Direct operating expenses rose 12.9% to US$330.1 million from US$292.5 million in the comparable period the year before. Indirect operating expenses increased 24.5% to US$58.2 million from US$46.8 million in the equivalent prior-year period.

Prospects: Our evaluation of Bright Horizons Family Solutions Inc as of Jan. 14, 2018 is the result of our systematic analysis on three basic characteristics: earnings strength, relative valuation, and recent stock price movement. The company has generated a negative trend in earnings per share over the past 5 quarters and while recent estimates for the company have been mixed, BFAM has posted better than expected results. Based on operating earnings yield, the company is about fairly valued when compared to all of the companies in our coverage universe. Share price changes over the past year indicates that BFAM will perform well over the near term.

Financial Data
(US$ in Thousands)

	9 Mos	6 Mos	3 Mos	12/31/2016	12/31/2015	12/31/2014	12/31/2013	12/31/2012
Earnings Per Share	2.01	1.87	1.83	1.55	1.50	1.07	0.20	(12.62)
Cash Flow Per Share	4.24	3.96	3.95	3.59	2.80	2.66	2.55	17.61
Income Statement								
Total Revenue	1,301,026	867,710	422,164	1,569,841	1,458,445	1,352,999	1,218,776	1,070,938
EBITDA	154,496	109,091	51,843	271,363	260,291	224,319	118,127	129,864
Depn & Amortn	1,323	881	439	85,242	78,689	77,399	72,775	34,400
Income Before Taxes	120,921	86,782	40,630	143,197	140,156	112,314	4,811	11,752
Income Taxes	15,402	12,368	(744)	48,437	46,229	40,279	(7,533)	3,243
Net Income	105,519	74,414	41,374	94,760	93,927	72,035	12,623	8,162
Average Shares	60,088	60,379	60,903	60,594	62,360	67,244	64,509	6,058
Balance Sheet								
Current Assets	195,786	167,906	166,465	154,399	152,713	223,158	165,170	136,017
Total Assets	2,463,150	2,418,372	2,376,458	2,359,017	2,150,541	2,141,076	2,102,670	1,913,632
Current Liabilities	398,441	397,126	356,112	387,580	305,343	279,423	255,088	201,893
Long-Term Obligations	1,048,643	1,050,889	1,051,761	1,054,009	905,661	911,627	756,323	904,607
Total Liabilities	1,688,637	1,696,335	1,650,407	1,671,150	1,422,933	1,390,117	1,213,533	1,313,418
Stockholders' Equity	774,513	722,037	726,051	687,867	727,608	750,959	889,137	600,214
Shares Outstanding	58,886	58,765	59,416	58,910	60,008	61,534	65,302	7,389
Statistical Record								
Return on Assets %	5.34	5.04	4.93	4.19	4.38	3.39	0.63	0.44
Return on Equity %	16.66	16.29	15.32	13.35	12.71	8.78	1.70	1.40
EBITDA Margin %	11.87	12.57	12.28	17.29	17.85	16.58	9.69	12.13
Net Margin %	8.11	8.58	9.80	6.04	6.44	5.32	1.04	0.76
Asset Turnover	0.74	0.73	0.71	0.69	0.68	0.64	0.61	0.58
Current Ratio	0.49	0.42	0.47	0.40	0.50	0.80	0.65	0.67
Debt to Equity	1.35	1.46	1.45	1.53	1.24	1.21	0.85	1.51
Price Range	86.21-62.74	80.76-62.74	72.49-62.74	72.30-60.59	68.58-44.22	47.14-35.94	38.15-27.50	...
P/E Ratio	42.89-31.21	43.19-33.55	39.61-34.28	46.65-39.09	45.72-29.48	44.06-33.59	190.75-137.50	...

Address: 200 Talcott Avenue South, Watertown, MA 02472 Telephone: 617-673-8000	Web Site: www.brighthorizons.com Officers: David H. Lissy - Executive Chairman, Chief Executive Officer Linda A. Mason - Chairman	Auditors: Deloitte & Touche LLP Transfer Agents: Wells Fargo Shareowner Services SM, St. Paul, MN

BRINKER INTERNATIONAL, INC.

Exchange	Symbol	Price	52Wk Range	Yield	P/E
NYS	EAT	$38.84 (12/29/2017)	49.17-29.89	3.91	14.07

*7 Year Price Score 73.64   *NYSE Composite Index=100   ***12 Month Price Score 88.43**

Interim Earnings (Per Share)

Qtr.	Sep	Dec	Mar	Jun
2014-15	0.49	0.64	1.02	0.91
2015-16	0.54	0.80	1.00	1.09
2016-17	0.42	0.69	0.86	1.01
2017-18	0.20	...	...	...

Interim Dividends (Per Share)

Amt	Decl	Ex	Rec	Pay
0.34Q	02/09/2017	03/08/2017	03/10/2017	03/30/2017
0.34Q	05/25/2017	06/08/2017	06/12/2017	06/29/2017
0.38Q	08/10/2017	09/07/2017	09/08/2017	09/28/2017
0.38Q	11/16/2017	12/07/2017	12/08/2017	12/28/2017

Indicated Div: $1.52

Valuation Analysis

		Institutional Holding	
Forecast EPS	$3.26	No of Institutions	
	(01/18/2018)	438	
Market Cap	$1.8 Billion	Shares	
Book Value	N/A	71,135,424	
Price/Book	N/A	% Held	
Price/Sales	0.59	83.03	

Business Summary: Hotels, Restaurants & Travel (MIC: 2.2.1 SIC: 5812 NAIC: 722110)

Brinker International owns, develops, operates and franchises the Chili's® Grill & Bar (Chili's) and Maggiano's Little Italy® (Maggiano's) restaurant brands. Co.'s Chili's restaurant menu features American food and Fresh Mex and Fresh Tex offerings, including burgers, ribs and fajitas, as well as margaritas. Co.'s Maggiano's restaurant features lunch and dinner menu in the form of appetizers and entrees with pasta, chicken, seafood, veal, steaks and desserts, including a selection of cocktails and wines. As of June 28 2017, Co.'s system of Co.-owned and franchised restaurants included 1,674 restaurants located in 49 states and Washington, D.C. Co. also has restaurants in other countries.

Recent Developments: For the quarter ended Sep 27 2017, net income decreased 57.5% to US$9.9 million from US$23.2 million in the year-earlier quarter. Revenues were US$739.4 million, down 2.5% from US$758.5 million the year before. Operating income was US$28.6 million versus US$41.5 million in the prior-year quarter, a decrease of 31.1%. Direct operating expenses declined 2.0% to US$626.8 million from US$639.5 million in the comparable period the year before. Indirect operating expenses increased 8.4% to US$84.0 million from US$77.5 million in the equivalent prior-year period.

Prospects: Our evaluation of Brinker International Inc. as of Jan. 14, 2018 is the result of our systematic analysis on three basic characteristics: earnings strength, relative valuation, and recent stock price movement. The company has produced a positive trend in earnings per share over the past 5 quarters and while recent estimates for the company have been raised by analysts, EAT has posted results that fell short of analysts expectations. Based on operating earnings yield, the company is undervalued when compared to all of the companies in our coverage universe. Share price changes over the past year indicates that EAT will perform very poorly over the near term.

Financial Data
(US$ in Thousands)

	3 Mos	06/28/2017	06/29/2016	06/24/2015	06/25/2014	06/26/2013	06/27/2012	06/29/2011
Earnings Per Share	2.76	2.94	3.42	3.05	2.26	2.20	1.87	1.53
Cash Flow Per Share	6.15	6.20	6.71	5.86	5.45	4.06	3.87	2.87
Tang Book Value Per Share	...	...	...	...	N.M.	0.11	2.48	3.80
Dividends Per Share	1.400	1.360	1.280	1.120	0.960	0.800	0.640	0.560
Dividend Payout %	50.72	46.26	37.43	36.72	42.48	36.36	34.22	36.60
Income Statement								
Total Revenue	739,390	3,150,837	3,257,489	3,002,278	2,905,452	2,846,098	2,820,722	2,761,386
EBITDA	29,516	260,043	475,329	458,525	380,460	390,914	360,663	340,087
Depn & Amortn	483	1,988	156,368	145,242	136,081	131,481	125,054	128,447
Income Before Taxes	15,149	208,508	286,387	284,277	216,288	230,315	208,809	183,329
Income Taxes	5,272	57,685	85,642	87,583	62,249	66,956	57,577	42,269
Net Income	9,877	150,823	200,745	196,694	154,039	163,359	151,232	141,060
Average Shares	48,732	51,250	58,684	64,404	68,152	74,158	80,664	92,320
Balance Sheet								
Current Assets	140,876	154,392	176,774	189,717	210,854	198,591	194,846	221,360
Total Assets	1,368,625	1,413,700	1,472,716	1,435,873	1,490,604	1,452,603	1,436,072	1,484,568
Current Liabilities	414,362	446,428	432,443	418,475	466,110	390,211	401,749	405,601
Long-Term Obligations	1,353,659	1,319,829	1,113,949	970,825	832,302	780,121	587,890	502,572
Total Liabilities	1,907,653	1,907,381	1,685,815	1,514,333	1,427,510	1,303,246	1,126,199	1,045,658
Stockholders' Equity	(539,028)	(493,681)	(213,099)	(78,460)	63,094	149,357	309,873	438,910
Shares Outstanding	47,233	48,440	55,420	60,585	64,558	67,444	74,342	82,938
Statistical Record								
Return on Assets %	9.72	10.48	13.58	13.48	10.50	11.34	10.38	8.48
Return on Equity %	...	...	...	...	145.41	71.34	40.51	24.23
EBITDA Margin %	3.99	8.25	14.59	15.27	13.09	13.74	12.79	12.32
Net Margin %	1.34	4.79	6.16	6.55	5.30	5.74	5.36	5.11
Asset Turnover	2.22	2.19	2.20	2.06	1.98	1.98	1.94	1.66
Current Ratio	0.34	0.35	0.41	0.45	0.45	0.51	0.48	0.55
Debt to Equity	...	...	...	...	13.19	5.22	1.90	1.15
Price Range	55.19-29.89	55.19-36.93	59.90-43.42	63.12-44.16	55.00-38.19	41.60-28.71	32.69-20.01	26.03-14.12
P/E Ratio	20.00-10.83	18.77-12.56	17.51-12.70	20.70-14.48	24.34-16.90	18.91-13.05	17.48-10.70	17.01-9.23
Average Yield %	3.25	2.89	2.60	2.04	2.08	2.32	2.46	2.67

Address: 6820 LBJ Freeway, Dallas, TX 75240	Web Site: www.brinker.com	Auditors: KPMG LLP
Telephone: 972-980-9917	Officers: Joseph M. DePinto - Chairman Wyman T. Roberts - President, Chief Executive Officer	Investor Contact: 972-980-9917
		Transfer Agents: Computershare, Canton, MA

BRINKS CO (THE)

Exchange	Symbol	Price	52Wk Range	Yield	P/E
NYS	BCO	$78.70 (12/29/2017)	87.00-41.30	0.76	49.81

*7 Year Price Score 153.69 *NYSE Composite Index=100 ***12 Month Price Score 112.07**

TRADING VOLUME (thousand shares)

Interim Earnings (Per Share)

Qtr.	Mar	Jun	Sep	Dec
2014	(1.20)	0.03	0.41	(0.96)
2015	(0.06)	(0.26)	0.15	(0.07)
2016	(0.06)	0.01	0.48	0.25
2017	0.67	0.28	0.38	...

Interim Dividends (Per Share)

Amt	Decl	Ex	Rec	Pay
0.15Q	05/08/2017	05/16/2017	05/18/2017	06/01/2017
0.15Q	07/13/2017	07/25/2017	07/27/2017	09/01/2017
0.15Q	10/17/2017	11/10/2017	11/13/2017	12/01/2017
0.15Q	01/15/2018	02/07/2018	02/08/2018	03/01/2018

Indicated Div: $0.60

Valuation Analysis / Institutional Holding

Forecast EPS	$3.01	No of Institutions
	(01/17/2018)	398
Market Cap	$4.0 Billion	Shares
Book Value	$458.4 Million	58,066,024
Price/Book	8.67	% Held
Price/Sales	1.22	105.25

Business Summary: Business Services (MIC: 7.5.2 SIC: 4731 NAIC: 488510)

Brink's is a provider of logistics and security solutions including cash-in-transit, Automated teller machine (ATM) replenishment and maintenance, cash management services, including vault outsourcing, money processing, and intelligent safe services, international transportation of valuables, and payment services. Co.'s primary services include: Cash-in-Transit Services, which include the transportation of: cash between businesses and financial institutions; ATM Services, which provides customers who own and operate ATMs a variety of service options; and Cash Management Services, which include money processing and other cash management services.

Recent Developments: For the quarter ended Sep 30 2017, income from continuing operations decreased 18.5% to US$21.1 million from US$25.9 million in the year-earlier quarter. Net income decreased 18.5% to US$21.1 million from US$25.9 million in the year-earlier quarter. Revenues were US$849.5 million, up 12.4% from US$755.8 million the year before. Operating income was US$66.4 million versus US$59.7 million in the prior-year quarter, an increase of 11.2%. Direct operating expenses rose 12.1% to US$666.4 million from US$594.4 million in the comparable period the year before. Indirect operating expenses increased 14.7% to US$116.7 million from US$101.7 million in the equivalent prior-year period.

Prospects: Our evaluation of Brink's Co as of Jan. 14, 2018 is the result of our systematic analysis on three basic characteristics: earnings strength, relative valuation, and recent stock price movement. The company has generated a negative trend in earnings per share over the past 5 quarters. However, while recent estimates for the company have been mixed, BCO has posted better than expected results. Based on operating earnings yield, the company is about fairly valued when compared to all of the companies in our coverage universe. Share price changes over the past year indicates that BCO will perform very well over the near term.

Financial Data

(US$ in Thousands)	9 Mos	6 Mos	3 Mos	12/31/2016	12/31/2015	12/31/2014	12/31/2013	12/31/2012
Earnings Per Share	1.58	1.68	1.41	0.68	(0.24)	(1.71)	1.16	1.83
Cash Flow Per Share	4.47	5.04	4.60	3.34	4.24	2.88	4.14	5.16
Tang Book Value Per Share	N.M.	2.98	3.53	2.64	2.13	3.67	8.42	4.22
Dividends Per Share	0.500	0.450	0.400	0.400	0.400	0.400	0.400	0.400
Dividend Payout %	31.65	26.79	28.37	58.82	...	...	34.48	21.86
Income Statement								
Total Revenue	2,443,800	1,594,300	788,400	3,020,600	3,061,400	3,562,300	3,942,200	3,842,100
EBITDA	245,600	164,000	93,100	167,500	81,100	(27,400)	345,300	342,000
Depn & Amortn	106,400	68,500	33,900	23,200	24,900	5,500	181,400	174,600
Income Before Taxes	123,100	85,700	54,800	126,500	40,600	(53,300)	141,500	148,500
Income Taxes	48,100	31,700	14,400	78,500	66,500	36,700	52,000	26,900
Net Income	68,800	48,900	34,700	34,500	(11,900)	(83,900)	56,800	88,900
Average Shares	51,900	51,600	51,500	50,600	49,300	49,000	49,000	48,600
Balance Sheet								
Current Assets	1,141,300	1,015,300	968,800	843,700	777,700	907,600	1,102,700	995,500
Total Assets	2,698,400	2,289,000	2,162,900	1,994,800	1,946,700	2,192,200	2,498,000	2,553,900
Current Liabilities	940,900	843,100	759,500	753,800	641,800	728,400	798,600	743,000
Long-Term Obligations	574,400	362,800	338,300	247,600	358,100	373,300	330,500	335,600
Total Liabilities	2,240,000	1,865,700	1,766,100	1,657,700	1,628,800	1,758,200	1,804,100	2,052,100
Stockholders' Equity	458,400	423,300	396,800	337,100	317,900	434,000	693,900	501,800
Shares Outstanding	50,500	50,400	50,400	50,000	48,900	48,600	48,400	47,800
Statistical Record								
Return on Assets %	3.46	4.03	3.48	1.75	N.M.	N.M.	2.25	3.57
Return on Equity %	19.60	22.56	19.78	10.51	N.M.	N.M.	9.50	19.49
EBITDA Margin %	10.05	10.29	11.81	5.55	2.65	N.M.	8.76	8.90
Net Margin %	2.82	3.07	4.40	1.14	N.M.	N.M.	1.44	2.31
Asset Turnover	1.38	1.47	1.49	1.53	1.48	1.52	1.56	1.54
Current Ratio	1.21	1.20	1.28	1.12	1.21	1.21	1.38	1.34
Debt to Equity	1.25	0.86	0.85	0.73	1.13	0.86	0.48	0.67
Price Range	84.25-36.63	67.50-27.71	54.35-27.00	45.10-26.04	33.54-22.41	35.57-20.10	34.44-24.37	29.62-21.05
P/E Ratio	53.32-23.18	40.18-16.49	38.55-19.15	66.32-38.29	...	...	29.69-21.01	16.19-11.50
Average Yield %	0.88	0.98	1.04	1.19	1.39	1.49	1.41	1.61

Address: 1801 Bayberry Court, Richmond, VA 23226-8100
Telephone: 804-289-9600
Fax: 804-289-9770

Web Site: www.brinks.com
Officers: Douglas A. Pertz - President, Chief Executive Officer Ronald J. Domanico - Executive Vice President, Chief Financial Officer

Auditors: Deloitte & Touche LLP
Investor Contact: 804-289-9708
Transfer Agents: Computershare, Providence, RI

BRISTOL-MYERS SQUIBB CO.

Exchange	Symbol	Price	52Wk Range	Yield	P/E
NYS	BMY	$61.28 (12/29/2017)	65.35-46.82	2.61	24.13

*7 Year Price Score 91.26 ***NYSE Composite Index=100** ***12 Month Price Score 102.00**

Interim Earnings (Per Share)

Qtr.	Mar	Jun	Sep	Dec
2014	0.56	0.20	0.43	0.01
2015	0.71	(0.08)	0.42	(0.12)
2016	0.71	0.70	0.72	0.53
2017	0.94	0.56	0.51	...

Interim Dividends (Per Share)

Amt	Decl	Ex	Rec	Pay
0.39Q	03/02/2017	04/05/2017	04/07/2017	05/01/2017
0.39Q	06/13/2017	07/05/2017	07/07/2017	08/01/2017
0.39Q	09/13/2017	10/05/2017	10/06/2017	11/01/2017
0.40Q	.12/07/2017	01/04/2018	01/05/2018	02/01/2018

Indicated Div: $1.60

Valuation Analysis | **Institutional Holding**

Forecast EPS	$3.00	No of Institutions
(01/26/2018)		2237
Market Cap	$100.3 Billion	Shares
Book Value	$14.8 Billion	1,406,830,592
Price/Book	6.78	% Held
Price/Sales	4.88	67.12

TRADING VOLUME (thousand shares)

Business Summary: Pharmaceuticals (MIC: 4.1.1 SIC: 2834 NAIC: 325412)

Bristol-Myers Squibb is engaged in the discovery, development, licensing, manufacturing, marketing, distribution and sale of biopharmaceutical products. Co. has products in the following therapeutic classes: oncology; cardiovascular; immunoscience; and virology, including human immunodeficiency virus (HIV) infection. Co.'s products include: Empliciti, a humanized monoclonal antibody for the treatment of multiple myeloma; Yervoy, a monoclonal antibody for the treatment of patients with unresectable or metastatic melanoma; Baraclude, an oral antiviral agent for the treatment of chronic hepatitis B; and Reyataz is a protease inhibitor for the treatment of HIV.

Recent Developments: For the quarter ended Sep 30 2017, net income decreased 29.5% to US$856.0 million from US$1.22 billion in the year-earlier quarter. Revenues were US$5.25 billion, up 6.7% from US$4.92 billion the year before. Direct operating expenses rose 20.5% to US$1.57 billion from US$1.31 billion in the comparable period the year before. Indirect operating expenses increased 17.9% to US$2.69 billion from US$2.28 billion in the equivalent prior-year period.

Prospects: Our evaluation of Bristol-Myers Squibb Co. as of Jan. 21, 2018 is the result of our systematic analysis on three basic characteristics: earnings strength, relative valuation, and recent stock price movement. The company has generated a negative trend in earnings per share over the past 5 quarters. However, while recent estimates for the company have been mixed, BMY has posted results that fell short of analysts expectations. Based on operating earnings yield, the company is undervalued when compared to all of the companies in our coverage universe. Share price changes over the past year indicates that BMY will perform well over the near term.

Financial Data

(US$ in Millions)	9 Mos	6 Mos	3 Mos	12/31/2016	12/31/2015	12/31/2014	12/31/2013	12/31/2012
Earnings Per Share	2.54	2.75	2.89	2.65	0.93	1.20	1.54	1.16
Cash Flow Per Share	3.41	3.21	2.47	1.70	1.10	1.90	2.16	4.14
Tang Book Value Per Share	4.10	4.02	3.80	4.76	3.57	3.66	3.48	N.M.
Dividends Per Share	1.550	1.160	1.150	1.140	1.490	1.450	1.760	1.360
Dividend Payout %	61.02	42.18	39.79	43.02	160.22	120.83	114.29	117.24
Income Statement								
Total Revenue	15,327	10,073	4,929	19,427	16,560	15,879	16,385	17,621
EBITDA	5,170	3,765	2,200	6,530	2,761	3,127	3,543	2,798
Depn & Amortn	651	456	218	448	500	543	453	382
Income Before Taxes	4,374	3,212	1,937	5,915	2,077	2,381	2,891	2,340
Income Taxes	1,129	802	429	1,408	446	352	311	(161)
Net Income	3,335	2,490	1,574	4,457	1,565	2,004	2,563	1,960
Average Shares	1,645	1,650	1,671	1,680	1,679	1,670	1,662	1,688
Balance Sheet								
Current Assets	15,048	14,324	13,615	13,704	10,415	14,608	18,916	9,521
Total Assets	33,977	33,409	32,937	33,707	31,748	33,749	38,592	35,897
Current Liabilities	9,438	9,017	8,494	8,841	8,017	8,461	12,440	8,279
Long-Term Obligations	6,982	6,911	7,237	5,716	6,550	7,242	7,981	6,568
Total Liabilities	19,194	18,710	18,521	17,530	17,482	18,897	23,438	22,274
Stockholders' Equity	14,783	14,699	14,416	16,177	14,266	14,852	15,154	13,623
Shares Outstanding	1,636	1,639	1,647	1,664	1,669	1,661	1,649	1,630
Statistical Record								
Return on Assets %	12.49	13.85	14.92	13.58	4.78	5.54	6.88	5.68
Return on Equity %	27.83	30.97	33.58	29.20	10.75	13.36	17.81	13.22
EBITDA Margin %	33.73	37.38	44.63	33.61	16.67	19.69	21.62	15.88
Net Margin %	21.76	24.72	31.93	22.94	9.45	12.62	15.64	11.12
Asset Turnover	0.61	0.61	0.62	0.59	0.51	0.44	0.44	0.51
Current Ratio	1.59	1.59	1.60	1.55	1.30	1.73	1.52	1.15
Debt to Equity	0.47	0.47	0.50	0.35	0.46	0.49	0.53	0.48
Price Range	63.74-46.82	76.77-46.82	76.77-46.82	76.77-49.23	70.71-57.30	61.30-46.59	53.84-32.59	36.15-30.81
P/E Ratio	25.09-18.43	27.92-17.03	26.56-16.20	28.97-18.58	76.03-61.61	51.08-38.83	34.96-21.16	31.16-26.56
Average Yield %	2.79	2.03	1.88	1.80	2.31	2.78	4.02	4.08

Address: 345 Park Avenue, New York, NY 10154	Web Site: www.bms.com	Auditors: Deloitte & Touche LLP
Telephone: 212-546-4000	Officers: Giovanni Caforio - Chairman, Chief Executive Officer, Executive Vice President, Chief	Investor Contact: 609-252-4611
Fax: 212-546-4020	Commercial Officer, Chief Operating Officer, Division Officer Sandra Leung - Executive Vice President, Senior Vice President, General Counsel, Corporate Secretary	Transfer Agents: Wells Fargo Shareowner Services, Mendota Heights, MN

BRIXMOR PROPERTY GROUP INC

Exchange	Symbol	Price	52Wk Range	Yield	P/E
NYS	BRX	$18.66 (12/29/2017)	25.29-17.47	5.89	17.77

*7 Year Price Score N/A   *NYSE Composite Index=100   *12 Month Price Score 85.11

Interim Earnings (Per Share)

Qtr.	Mar	Jun	Sep	Dec
2014	0.07	0.10	0.11	0.08
2015	0.10	0.18	0.18	0.19
2016	0.20	0.21	0.19	0.30
2017	0.23	0.25	0.27	

Interim Dividends (Per Share)

Amt	Decl	Ex	Rec	Pay
0.26Q	02/13/2017	04/03/2017	04/05/2017	04/17/2017
0.26Q	05/01/2017	07/03/2017	07/06/2017	07/17/2017
0.26Q	07/31/2017	10/04/2017	10/05/2017	10/16/2017
0.275Q	10/30/2017	01/03/2018	01/04/2018	01/17/2018

Indicated Div: $1.10 (Div. Reinv. Plan)

Valuation Analysis

		Institutional Holding	
Forecast EPS	$0.94	No of Institutions	
	(01/24/2018)	347	
Market Cap	$5.7 Billion	Shares	
Book Value	$2.9 Billion	335,185,280	
Price/Book	1.95	% Held	
Price/Sales	4.42	100.79	

Business Summary: REITs (MIC: 5.3.1 SIC: 6798 NAIC: 525930)

Brixmor Property Group is an internally-managed real estate investment trust. Brixmor Operating Partnership LP and subsidiaries (Operating Partnership) is the entity through which Co. conducts substantially all of its operations and owns substantially all of its assets. Co. is engaged in the ownership, management, leasing, acquisition, disposition and redevelopment of retail shopping centers through the Operating Partnership. As of Dec 31 2016, Co.'s portfolio was comprised of 512 shopping centers, including 511 wholly owned shopping centers and one shopping center held through an unconsolidated joint venture; and had one land parcel under development.

Recent Developments: For the quarter ended Sep 30 2017, net income increased 44.2% to US$83.4 million from US$57.8 million in the year-earlier quarter. Revenues were US$314.5 million, down 1.3% from US$318.6 million the year before. Revenues from property income fell 0.5% to US$246.6 million from US$247.9 million in the corresponding quarter a year earlier.

Prospects: Our evaluation of Brixmor Property Group Inc as of Jan. 21, 2018 is the result of our systematic analysis on three basic characteristics: earnings strength, relative valuation, and recent stock price movement. The company has generated a negative trend in earnings per share over the past 5 quarters and while recent estimates for the company have remained steady, BRX has posted better than expected results. Based on operating earnings yield, the company is undervalued when compared to all of the companies in our coverage universe. Share price changes over the past year indicates that BRX will perform in line with the market over the near term.

Financial Data

(US$ in Thousands)	9 Mos	6 Mos	3 Mos	12/31/2016	12/31/2015	12/31/2014	12/31/2013	12/31/2012
Earnings Per Share	1.05	0.97	0.93	0.91	0.65	0.36	(0.50)	...
Cash Flow Per Share	1.87	1.90	1.84	1.88	1.79	1.97	1.76	...
Tang Book Value Per Share	9.58	9.56	9.58	9.60	9.59	9.79	10.29	23.04
Dividends Per Share	1.025	1.010	0.995	0.980	0.900	0.727	...	...
Dividend Payout %	97.62	104.12	106.99	107.69	138.46	201.94	...	...
Income Statement								
Total Revenue	963,120	648,624	325,806	1,275,772	1,265,980	1,236,599	1,174,697	1,125,797
EBITDA	373,786	244,816	119,446	526,064	482,117	402,055	287,090	323,882
Depn & Amortn	(22,100)	(14,943)	(7,680)	22,270	40,343	29,264	41,921	91,519
Income Before Taxes	225,536	146,743	71,468	277,665	197,077	110,581	(101,995)	(152,879)
Net Income	230,397	147,017	71,579	275,628	193,720	89,002	(93,534)	(122,567)
Average Shares	305,176	305,115	304,795	305,060	305,017	244,588	188,993	...
Balance Sheet								
Current Assets	505,031	473,060	413,453	403,872	400,625	410,941	473,399	445,320
Total Assets	9,196,220	9,297,074	9,359,098	9,319,685	9,498,007	9,702,402	10,171,916	9,603,729
Current Liabilities	561,191	561,378	512,647	553,636	603,439	679,102	709,529	632,112
Long-Term Obligations	5,713,688	5,819,948	5,924,834	5,838,889	5,974,266	6,042,997	5,981,289	6,499,356
Total Liabilities	6,274,879	6,381,326	6,438,129	6,396,801	6,628,224	6,798,692	7,807,981	7,860,767
Stockholders' Equity	2,921,341	2,915,748	2,920,969	2,922,884	2,869,783	2,903,710	2,363,935	1,742,962
Shares Outstanding	304,937	304,935	304,893	304,343	299,138	296,552	229,689	75,649
Statistical Record								
Return on Assets %	3.50	3.18	3.05	2.92	2.02	0.90	N.M.	N.M.
Return on Equity %	11.15	10.30	9.93	9.49	6.71	3.38	N.M.	N.M.
EBITDA Margin %	38.81	37.74	36.66	41.23	38.08	32.51	24.44	28.77
Net Margin %	23.92	22.67	21.97	21.60	15.30	7.20	N.M.	N.M.
Asset Turnover	0.14	0.14	0.14	0.14	0.13	0.12	0.12	0.11
Current Ratio	0.90	0.84	0.81	0.73	0.66	0.61	0.67	0.70
Debt to Equity	1.96	2.00	2.03	2.00	2.08	2.08	2.53	3.73
Price Range	27.79-17.58	28.96-17.58	28.96-20.80	28.96-21.10	27.39-22.23	25.24-20.13	20.94-19.66	...
P/E Ratio	26.47-16.74	29.86-18.12	31.14-22.37	31.82-23.19	42.14-34.20	70.11-55.92	...	...
Average Yield %	4.73	4.23	3.91	3.80	3.62	3.23	...	...

Address: 450 Lexington Avenue, New York, NY 10017
Telephone: 212-869-3000

Web Site: www.brixmor.com
Officers: John G. Schreiber - Chairman James M. Taylor - President, Chief Executive Officer

Auditors: Deloitte & Touche LLP
Transfer Agents: Computershare Trust Company, N.A., Canton, MA

BROADRIDGE FINANCIAL SOLUTIONS INC

Exchange	Symbol	Price	52Wk Range	Yield	P/E
NYS	BR	$90.58 (12/29/2017)	91.61-65.74	1.61	31.78

*7 Year Price Score 136.01 *NYSE Composite Index=100 *12 Month Price Score 110.64

Interim Earnings (Per Share)

Qtr.	Sep	Dec	Mar	Jun
2014-15	0.26	0.28	0.43	1.35
2015-16	0.28	0.33	0.52	1.40
2016-17	0.28	0.25	0.63	1.55
2017-18	0.42	...	...	...

Interim Dividends (Per Share)

Amt	Decl	Ex	Rec	Pay
0.33Q	02/02/2017	03/10/2017	03/14/2017	04/03/2017
0.33Q	05/05/2017	06/13/2017	06/15/2017	07/03/2017
0.365Q	08/09/2017	09/14/2017	09/15/2017	10/03/2017
0.365Q	11/16/2017	12/14/2017	12/15/2017	01/03/2018

Indicated Div: $1.46

Valuation Analysis — **Institutional Holding**

Forecast EPS	$3.74	No of Institutions
	(01/16/2018)	702
Market Cap	$10.6 Billion	Shares
Book Value	$1.0.Billion	139,433,008
Price/Book	10.17	% Held
Price/Sales	2.53	82.92

Business Summary: Finance Intermediaries & Services (MIC: 5.5.1 SIC: 7389 NAIC: 523999)

Broadridge Financial Solutions provides investor communications and technology solutions to banks, broker-dealers, mutual funds and corporate issuers. Co.'s businesses operate in two business segments: Investor Communication Solutions, which involves the processing and distribution of proxy materials to investors in equity securities and mutual funds, as well as the facilitation of related vote processing; and Global Technology and Operations, which provides a suite of computerized real-time transaction processing services that automate the securities transaction lifecycle, from desktop productivity tools, data aggregation, performance reporting, and portfolio management.

Recent Developments: For the quarter ended Sep 30 2017, net income increased 48.1% to US$49.9 million from US$33.7 million in the year-earlier quarter. Revenues were US$924.8 million, up 3.3% from US$895.3 million the year before. Operating income was US$84.4 million versus US$66.0 million in the prior-year quarter, an increase of 27.9%. Direct operating expenses rose 1.2% to US$726.6 million from US$717.9 million in the comparable period the year before. Indirect operating expenses increased 2.2% to US$113.8 million from US$111.3 million in the equivalent prior-year period.

Prospects: Our evaluation of Broadridge Financial Solutions Inc. as of Jan. 14, 2018 is the result of our systematic analysis on three basic characteristics: earnings strength, relative valuation, and recent stock price movement. The company has managed to produce a neutral trend in earnings per share over the past 5 quarters. However, while recent estimates for the company have been mixed, BR has posted better than expected results. Based on operating earnings yield, the company is about fairly valued when compared to all of the companies in our coverage universe. Share price changes over the past year indicates that BR will perform well over the near term.

Financial Data

(US$ in Thousands)	3 Mos	06/30/2017	06/30/2016	06/30/2015	06/30/2014	06/30/2013	06/30/2012	06/30/2011
Earnings Per Share	2.85	2.70	2.53	2.32	2.12	1.69	0.97	1.32
Cash Flow Per Share	4.38	4.37	3.69	3.60	3.24	2.22	2.34	1.53
Dividends Per Share	1.355	1.320	1.200	1.080	0.840	0.720	0.640	0.600
Dividend Payout %	47.54	48.89	47.43	46.55	39.62	42.60	65.98	45.45
Income Statement								
Total Revenue	924,800	4,142,600	2,897,000	2,694,200	2,558,000	2,430,800	2,303,500	2,166,900
EBITDA	114,200	662,100	570,300	530,300	475,500	392,400	270,900	313,500
Depn & Amortn	30,500	126,100	70,500	63,300	58,100	57,000	58,500	36,100
Income Before Taxes	74,300	493,300	474,000	444,400	395,500	323,200	200,900	269,700
Income Taxes	24,400	161,400	161,400	151,800	132,500	111,100	75,900	97,900
Net Income	49,900	326,800	307,500	287,100	263,000	212,100	123,600	169,600
Average Shares	119,800	120,800	121,600	124,000	124,100	125,400	127,500	128,300
Balance Sheet								
Current Assets	1,034,300	989,600	1,289,100	861,400	880,600	807,000	777,400	751,400
Total Assets	3,224,500	3,149,800	2,879,800	2,368,100	2,192,100	2,018,200	1,987,600	1,904,000
Current Liabilities	609,400	744,900	693,000	508,900	484,400	469,500	410,300	782,700
Long-Term Obligations	1,292,400	1,102,100	897,600	689,400	524,100	524,500	524,400	124,300
Total Liabilities	2,186,600	2,146,000	1,834,300	1,440,300	1,230,400	1,202,200	1,137,100	1,106,700
Stockholders' Equity	1,037,900	1,003,800	1,045,500	927,800	961,700	816,000	850,500	797,300
Shares Outstanding	116,500	116,500	118,300	118,200	119,500	119,000	124,800	123,700
Statistical Record								
Return on Assets %	11.12	10.84	11.69	12.59	12.49	10.59	6.33	9.17
Return on Equity %	32.84	31.89	31.08	30.39	29.59	25.45	14.96	21.14
EBITDA Margin %	12.35	15.98	19.69	19.68	18.59	16.14	11.76	14.47
Net Margin %	5.40	7.89	10.61	10.66	10.28	8.73	5.37	7.83
Asset Turnover	1.35	1.37	1.10	1.18	1.22	1.21	1.18	1.17
Current Ratio	1.70	1.33	1.86	1.69	1.82	1.72	1.89	0.96
Debt to Equity	1.25	1.10	0.86	0.74	0.54	0.64	0.62	0.16
Price Range	81.56-60.56	77.65-60.56	65.36-49.64	55.53-39.11	42.13-26.93	27.97-20.41	24.85-19.18	24.07-18.96
P/E Ratio	28.62-21.25	28.76-22.43	25.83-19.62	23.94-16.86	19.87-12.70	16.55-12.08	25.62-19.77	18.23-14.36
Average Yield %	1.92	1.93	2.12	2.29	2.36	3.04	2.88	2.72

Address: 5 Dakota Drive, Lake Success, NY 11042 **Telephone:** 516-472-5400	**Web Site:** www.broadridge.com **Officers:** Leslie A. Brun - Chairman Timothy C. Gokey - President, Chief Operating Officer, Senior Vice President, Chief Development Officer	**Auditors:** Deloitte & Touche LLP **Investor Contact:** 516-472-5400 **Transfer Agents:** Broadridge Corporate Issuer Solutions, Inc.

BROOKDALE SENIOR LIVING INC

Exchange	Symbol	Price	52Wk Range	Yield	P/E
NYS	BKD	$9.70 (12/29/2017)	16.27-8.81	N/A	N/A

*7 Year Price Score 43.14 *NYSE Composite Index=100 *12 Month Price Score 74.99

Interim Earnings (Per Share)

Qtr.	Mar	Jun	Sep	Dec
2014	(0.02)	(0.03)	(0.23)	(0.70)
2015	(0.71)	(0.46)	(0.37)	(0.94)
2016	(0.26)	(0.19)	(0.28)	(1.45)
2017	(0.68)	(0.25)	(2.22)	...

Interim Dividends (Per Share)

No Dividends Paid

Valuation Analysis | **Institutional Holding**

Forecast EPS	$-3.38	No of Institutions
	(01/16/2018)	356
Market Cap	$1.9 Billion	Shares
Book Value	$1.5 Billion	211,922,512
Price/Book	1.23	% Held
Price/Sales	0.39	106.11

TRADING VOLUME (thousand shares)

Business Summary: Hospitals & Health Care Facilities (MIC: 4.2.1 SIC: 8052 NAIC: 623311)

Brookdale Senior Living is a holding company. Through its subsidiaries, Co. operates independent living, assisted living and dementia-care communities and continuing care retirement centers (CCRCs). Through its ancillary services programs, Co. also provide a range of outpatient therapy, home health and hospice services to residents of many of its communities and to seniors living outside of its communities. As of Dec 31 2016, Co. operated 129 retirement center communities (24,339 units), 851 assisted living communities (58,477 units) and 75 CCRCs (20,558 units).

Recent Developments: For the quarter ended Sep 30 2017, net loss amounted to US$413.9 million versus a net loss of US$51.7 million in the year-earlier quarter. Revenues were US$1.18 billion, down 5.5% from US$1.25 billion the year before. Operating loss was US$351.0 million versus an income of US$47.6 million in the prior-year quarter. Direct operating expenses declined 7.6% to US$650.7 million from US$704.2 million in the comparable period the year before. Indirect operating expenses increased 77.7% to US$878.3 million from US$494.3 million in the equivalent prior-year period.

Prospects: Our evaluation of Brookdale Senior Living Inc. as of Jan. 21, 2018 is the result of our systematic analysis on three basic characteristics: earnings strength, relative valuation, and recent stock price movement. The company has produced a positive trend in earnings per share over the past 5 quarters. Because the company lacks sufficient analyst estimate data, we place greater weight on the historical EPS trend as the measure of earnings strength. Based on operating earnings yield, the company is overvalued when compared to all of the companies in our coverage universe. Share price changes over the past year indicates that BKD will perform poorly over the near term.

Financial Data

(US$ in Thousands)	9 Mos	6 Mos	3 Mos	12/31/2016	12/31/2015	12/31/2014	12/31/2013	12/31/2012
Earnings Per Share	(4.60)	(2.66)	(2.60)	(2.18)	(2.48)	(1.01)	(0.03)	(0.54)
Cash Flow Per Share	1.99	2.08	1.95	1.96	1.59	1.64	2.96	2.38
Tang Book Value Per Share	4.90	5.88	6.06	6.79	8.52	10.64	5.89	5.79
Income Statement								
Total Revenue	3,581,226	2,403,238	1,216,766	4,976,980	4,960,608	3,831,706	2,891,966	2,770,085
EBITDA	84,608	326,341	175,214	495,966	558,601	445,043	396,848	331,158
Depn & Amortn	364,025	246,047	126,090	514,200	721,000	529,100	264,100	248,500
Income Before Taxes	(526,241)	(87,816)	(43,314)	(400,918)	(549,560)	(330,902)	(3,312)	(60,113)
Income Taxes	50,075	81,293	84,028	5,378	(92,209)	(181,305)	1,756	2,044
Net Income	(586,476)	(172,591)	(126,304)	(404,397)	(457,477)	(148,990)	(3,584)	(65,645)
Average Shares	186,298	186,212	185,689	185,653	184,333	148,185	123,671	121,991
Balance Sheet								
Current Assets	935,852	560,924	473,717	619,504	497,943	614,789	294,862	309,038
Total Assets	8,092,166	8,192,792	8,238,088	9,217,687	10,048,564	10,521,363	4,737,757	4,665,978
Current Liabilities	1,128,396	1,077,548	706,328	731,142	840,148	877,762	870,844	1,121,503
Long-Term Obligations	4,868,863	4,573,668	4,933,655	5,829,912	6,196,809	5,993,691	2,434,624	2,169,826
Total Liabilities	6,582,079	6,276,533	6,283,149	7,139,705	7,589,676	7,639,639	3,716,820	3,663,261
Stockholders' Equity	1,510,087	1,916,259	1,954,939	2,077,982	2,458,888	2,881,724	1,020,937	1,002,717
Shares Outstanding	191,538	191,626	191,798	190,045	188,338	187,037	127,726	126,689
Statistical Record								
EBITDA Margin %	2.36	13.58	14.40	9.97	11.26	11.61	13.72	11.95
Asset Turnover	0.54	0.54	0.54	0.52	0.48	0.50	0.62	0.61
Current Ratio	0.83	0.52	0.67	0.85	0.59	0.70	0.34	0.28
Debt to Equity	3.22	2.39	2.52	2.81	2.52	2.08	2.38	2.16
Price Range	17.59-10.60	18.47-11.27	19.12-11.27	19.30-11.27	38.74-17.69	36.86-26.37	29.97-24.96	25.72-15.19

Address: 111 Westwood Place, Suite 400, Brentwood, TN 37027
Telephone: 615-221-2250

Web Site: www.brookdale.com
Officers: Daniel A. Decker - Executive Chairman
William B. Doniger - Vice-Chairman

Auditors: Ernst & Young LLP
Investor Contact: 615-564-8104
Transfer Agents: American Stock Transfer & Trust Company, New York, NY

BROWN & BROWN, INC.

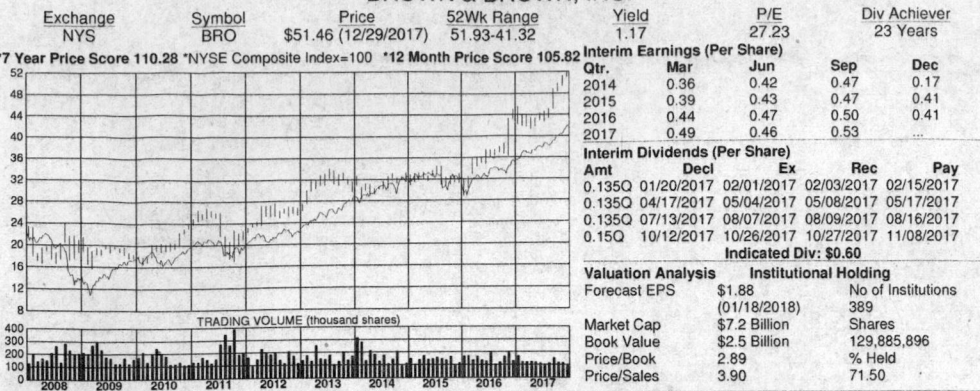

Exchange	Symbol	Price	52Wk Range	Yield	P/E	Div Achiever
NYS	BRO	$51.46 (12/29/2017)	51.93-41.32	1.17	27.23	23 Years

*7 Year Price Score 110.28 *NYSE Composite Index=100 *12 Month Price Score 105.82

Interim Earnings (Per Share)

Qtr.	Mar	Jun	Sep	Dec
2014	0.36	0.42	0.47	0.17
2015	0.39	0.43	0.47	0.41
2016	0.44	0.47	0.50	0.41
2017	0.49	0.46	0.53	...

Interim Dividends (Per Share)

Amt	Decl	Ex	Rec	Pay
0.135Q	01/20/2017	02/01/2017	02/03/2017	02/15/2017
0.135Q	04/17/2017	05/04/2017	05/08/2017	05/17/2017
0.135Q	07/13/2017	08/07/2017	08/09/2017	08/16/2017
0.15Q	10/12/2017	10/26/2017	10/27/2017	11/08/2017

Indicated Div: $0.60

Valuation Analysis		Institutional Holding	
Forecast EPS	$1.88	No of Institutions	
	(01/18/2018)	389	
Market Cap	$7.2 Billion	Shares	
Book Value	$2.5 Billion	129,885,896	
Price/Book	2.89	% Held	
Price/Sales	3.90	71.50	

Business Summary: Brokers & Intermediaries (MIC: 5.2.3 SIC: 6411 NAIC: 524210)

Brown & Brown is an insurance agency, wholesale brokerage, insurance programs and service organization. Co. markets and sells insurance products and services, primarily in the property, casualty and employee benefits areas. Co. has four segments: Retail, which provides a range of insurance products and services; National Programs, which provides programs, that can be grouped into five categories; Professional Programs, Arrowhead Insurance Programs, Commercial Programs, Public Entity-Related Programs, and the National Flood Program; Wholesale Brokerage, which markets and sells excess and surplus commercial and personal lines insurance; and Services, which provides insurance-related services.

Recent Developments: For the quarter ended Sep 30 2017, net income increased 6.1% to US$75.9 million from US$71.5 million in the year-earlier quarter. Revenues were US$475.6 million, up 2.9% from US$462.3 million the year before.

Prospects: Our evaluation of Brown & Brown Inc. as of Jan. 14, 2018 is the result of our systematic analysis on three basic characteristics: earnings strength, relative valuation, and recent stock price movement. The company has produced a positive trend in earnings per share over the past 5 quarters and while recent estimates for the company have been mixed, BRO has posted better than expected results. Based on operating earnings yield, the company is about fairly valued when compared to all of the companies in our coverage universe. Share price changes over the past year indicates that BRO will perform well over the near term.

Financial Data (US$ in Thousands)	9 Mos	6 Mos	3 Mos	12/31/2016	12/31/2015	12/31/2014	12/31/2013	12/31/2012
Earnings Per Share	1.89	1.86	1.87	1.82	1.70	1.41	1.48	1.26
Cash Flow Per Share	3.07	3.32	3.17	2.75	2.99	2.73	2.76	1.58
Dividends Per Share	0.540	0.527	0.515	0.502	0.453	0.410	0.370	0.345
Dividend Payout %	28.57	28.36	27.54	27.61	26.62	29.08	25.00	27.38
Income Statement								
Total Revenue	1,407,031	931,385	465,080	1,766,629	1,660,509	1,575,796	1,363,279	1,200,032
EBITDA	455,429	294,280	148,797	483,980	462,707	389,052	391,534	336,281
Depn & Amortn	83,092	55,755	28,148	21,000	20,900	20,895	17,485	15,373
Income Before Taxes	343,388	218,969	110,967	423,499	402,559	339,749	357,609	304,811
Income Taxes	131,263	82,757	40,857	166,008	159,241	132,853	140,497	120,766
Net Income	212,125	136,212	70,110	257,491	243,318	206,896	217,112	184,045
Average Shares	138,893	139,101	139,026	137,804	140,112	142,891	142,624	142,010
Balance Sheet								
Current Assets	3,916,383	1,778,932	1,696,965	1,760,737	1,537,389	1,570,108	928,036	759,512
Total Assets	7,414,277	5,279,009	5,197,444	5,287,343	5,012,739	4,956,458	3,649,508	3,128,058
Current Liabilities	3,631,514	1,419,537	1,337,908	1,445,157	1,328,547	1,269,153	906,877	567,781
Long-Term Obligations	860,741	965,391	1,005,044	1,018,372	1,079,878	1,152,846	380,000	450,000
Total Liabilities	4,930,630	2,820,776	2,781,648	2,927,132	2,862,963	2,842,713	1,642,367	1,320,725
Stockholders' Equity	2,483,647	2,458,233	2,415,796	2,360,211	2,149,776	2,113,745	2,007,141	1,807,333
Shares Outstanding	139,518	139,999	140,274	140,104	138,985	143,486	145,419	143,878
Statistical Record								
Return on Assets %	4.17	5.06	5.21	4.99	4.88	4.81	6.41	6.40
Return on Equity %	11.22	11.27	11.51	11.39	11.41	10.04	11.38	10.64
EBITDA Margin %	32.37	31.60	31.99	27.40	27.87	24.69	28.72	28.02
Net Margin %	15.08	14.62	15.07	14.58	14.65	13.13	15.93	15.34
Asset Turnover	0.28	0.35	0.35	0.34	0.33	0.37	0.40	0.42
Current Ratio	1.08	1.25	1.27	1.22	1.16	1.24	1.02	1.34
Debt to Equity	0.35	0.39	0.42	0.43	0.50	0.55	0.19	0.25
Price Range	48.87-36.21	45.56-35.90	45.56-34.30	45.11-28.87	34.47-30.74	33.26-28.28	34.12-25.46	27.64-22.29
P/E Ratio	25.86-19.16	24.49-19.30	24.36-18.34	24.79-15.86	20.28-18.08	23.59-20.06	23.05-17.20	21.94-17.69
Average Yield %	1.26	1.29	1.32	1.38	1.39	1.32	1.18	1.36

Address: 220 South Ridgewood Avenue, Daytona Beach, FL 32114 Telephone: 386-252-9601	Web Site: www.bbinsurance.com Officers: J. Hyatt Brown - Chairman J. Powell Brown - President, Chief Executive Officer	Auditors: Deloitte & Touche LLP Investor Contact: 386-252-9601 Transfer Agents: American Stock Transfer & Trust Co., Brooklyn, NY

BROWN-FORMAN CORP

Exchange	Symbol	Price	52Wk Range	Yield	P/E	Div Achiever
NYS	BF B	$68.67 (12/29/2017)	68.78-43.96	1.15	35.77	32 Years

*7 Year Price Score 100.38 *NYSE Composite Index=100 *12 Month Price Score 111.52

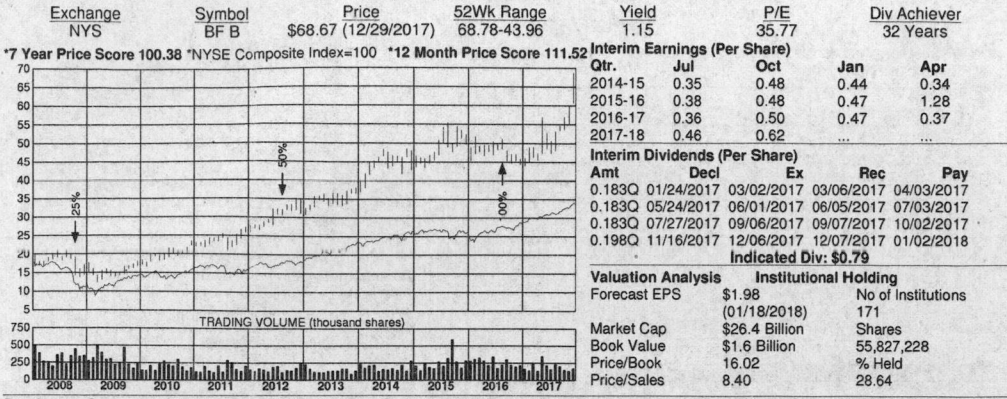

Interim Earnings (Per Share)

Qtr.	Jul	Oct	Jan	Apr
2014-15	0.35	0.48	0.44	0.34
2015-16	0.38	0.48	0.47	1.28
2016-17	0.36	0.50	0.47	0.37
2017-18	0.46	0.62	...	...

Interim Dividends (Per Share)

Amt	Decl	Ex	Rec	Pay
0.183Q	01/24/2017	03/02/2017	03/06/2017	04/03/2017
0.183Q	05/24/2017	06/01/2017	06/05/2017	07/03/2017
0.183Q	07/27/2017	09/06/2017	09/07/2017	10/02/2017
0.198Q	11/16/2017	12/06/2017	12/07/2017	01/02/2018

Indicated Div: $0.79

Valuation Analysis

Forecast EPS	$1.98
	(01/18/2018)
Market Cap	$26.4 Billion
Book Value	$1.6 Billion
Price/Book	16.02
Price/Sales	8.40

Institutional Holding

No of Institutions	171
Shares	55,827,228
% Held	28.64

TRADING VOLUME (thousand shares)

Business Summary: Beverages (MIC: 1.2.2 SIC: 2084 NAIC: 312130)

Brown-Forman primarily manufactures, bottles, imports, exports, markets, and sells a range of alcoholic beverage brands. Co.'s principal brands include, among other, Jack Daniel's Tennessee Whiskey; Jack Daniel's Tennessee Honey; Jack Daniel's RTDs; Gentleman Jack Rare Tennessee Whiskey; Jack Daniel's Tennessee Fire; Jack Daniel's Single Barrel Collection; Jack Daniel's Winter Jack; Jack Daniel's Sinatra Select; Jack Daniel's No. 27 Gold Tennessee Whiskey; Jack Daniel's Tennessee Rye; Korbel California Champagnes; Korbel California Brandy; Woodford Reserve Kentucky Bourbon; Woodford Reserve Double Oaked; Woodford Reserve Kentucky Rye Whiskey; Finlandia Vodkas; and Slane Irish Whiskey.

Recent Developments: For the quarter ended Oct 31 2017, net income increased 21.3% to US$239.0 million from US$197.0 million in the year-earlier quarter. Revenues were US$914.0 million, up 10.1% from US$830.0 million the year before. Operating income was US$346.0 million versus US$291.0 million in the prior-year quarter, an increase of 18.9%. Direct operating expenses rose 9.4% to US$304.0 million from US$278.0 million in the comparable period the year before. Indirect operating expenses increased 1.1% to US$264.0 million from US$261.0 million in the equivalent prior-year period.

Prospects: Our evaluation of Brown-Forman Corp. as of Jan. 14, 2018 is the result of our systematic analysis on three basic characteristics: earnings strength, relative valuation, and recent stock price movement. The company has produced a positive trend in earnings per share over the past 5 quarters and while recent estimates for the company have been raised by analysts, BF.B has posted better than expected results. Based on operating earnings yield, the company is about fairly valued when compared to all of the companies in our coverage universe. Share price changes over the past year indicates that BF.B will perform very well over the near term.

Financial Data

(US$ in Thousands)	6 Mos	3 Mos	04/30/2017	04/30/2016	04/30/2015	04/30/2014	04/30/2013	04/30/2012
Earnings Per Share	1.92	1.80	1.71	2.61	1.61	1.53	1.38	1.19
Cash Flow Per Share	1.78	1.60	1.65	1.29	1.44	1.52	1.26	1.20
Tang Book Value Per Share	0.60	0.01	N.M.	0.95	1.65	1.72	0.80	1.84
Dividends Per Share	0.730	0.718	0.705	0.655	0.605	0.545	2.488	0.447
Dividend Payout %	38.02	39.86	41.23	25.10	37.69	35.62	180.97	37.64
Income Statement								
Total Revenue	1,637,000	723,000	2,994,000	3,089,000	3,134,000	2,991,000	2,849,000	2,723,000
EBITDA	621,000	259,000	1,047,000	1,589,000	1,078,000	1,021,000	949,000	837,000
Depn & Amortn	31,000	15,000	58,000	56,000	51,000	50,000	51,000	49,000
Income Before Taxes	560,000	229,000	933,000	1,489,000	1,002,000	947,000	865,000	760,000
Income Taxes	143,000	51,000	264,000	422,000	318,000	288,000	274,000	247,000
Net Income	417,000	178,000	669,000	1,067,000	684,000	659,000	591,000	513,000
Average Shares	386,627	386,387	390,461	408,560	426,166	430,164	429,972	432,300
Balance Sheet								
Current Assets	2,661,000	2,503,000	2,351,000	2,233,000	2,254,000	2,177,000	1,821,000	1,749,000
Total Assets	4,978,000	4,802,000	4,625,000	4,183,000	4,193,000	4,103,000	3,626,000	3,477,000
Current Liabilities	1,052,000	1,089,000	970,000	791,000	958,000	561,000	473,000	404,000
Long-Term Obligations	1,719,000	1,720,000	1,689,000	1,230,000	748,000	997,000	997,000	503,000
Total Liabilities	3,331,000	3,382,000	3,255,000	2,621,000	2,288,000	2,071,000	1,998,000	1,408,000
Stockholders' Equity	1,647,000	1,420,000	1,370,000	1,562,000	1,905,000	2,032,000	1,628,000	2,069,000
Shares Outstanding	384,316	384,271	384,086	395,484	417,400	426,910	427,414	426,222
Statistical Record								
Return on Assets %	15.34	14.69	15.19	25.41	16.49	17.05	16.64	14.23
Return on Equity %	50.78	51.05	45.63	61.38	34.75	36.01	31.97	24.78
EBITDA Margin %	37.94	35.82	34.97	51.44	34.40	34.14	33.31	30.74
Net Margin %	25.47	24.62	22.34	34.54	21.83	22.03	20.74	18.84
Asset Turnover	0.65	0.64	0.68	0.74	0.76	0.77	0.80	0.76
Current Ratio	2.53	2.30	2.42	2.82	2.35	3.88	3.85	4.33
Debt to Equity	1.04	1.21	1.23	0.79	0.39	0.49	0.61	0.24
Price Range	57.02-43.96	56.92-43.96	51.06-43.96	55.41-45.12	48.52-41.81	45.24-33.25	35.93-28.00	28.86-20.75
P/E Ratio	29.70-22.90	31.62-24.42	29.86-25.71	21.23-17.29	30.14-25.97	29.57-21.73	26.04-20.29	24.25-17.43
Average Yield %	1.50	1.51	1.50	1.31	1.33	1.45	7.73	1.76

Address: 850 Dixie Highway, Louisville, KY 40210
Telephone: 502-585-1100
Fax: 502-774-7876

Web Site: www.brown-forman.com
Officers: Paul C. Varga - Chairman, Chief Executive Officer Geo. Garvin Brown - Chairman, Executive Vice President

Auditors: PricewaterhouseCoopers LLP
Transfer Agents: Computershare, Providence, RI

BRUNSWICK CORP.

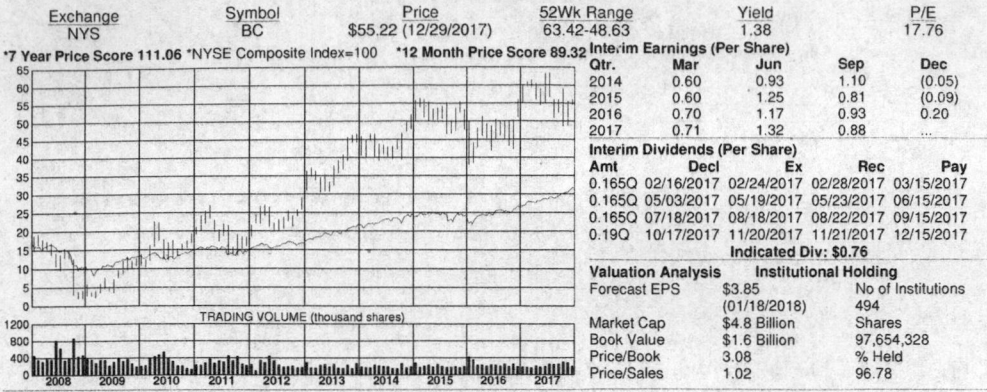

Exchange	Symbol	Price	52Wk Range	Yield	P/E
NYS	BC	$55.22 (12/29/2017)	63.42-48.63	1.38	17.76

*7 Year Price Score 111.06 *NYSE Composite Index=100 *12 Month Price Score 89.32

Interim Earnings (Per Share)

Qtr.	Mar	Jun	Sep	Dec
2014	0.60	0.93	1.10	(0.05)
2015	0.60	1.25	0.81	(0.09)
2016	0.70	1.17	0.93	0.20
2017	0.71	1.32	0.88	...

Interim Dividends (Per Share)

Amt	Decl	Ex	Rec	Pay
0.165Q	02/16/2017	02/24/2017	02/28/2017	03/15/2017
0.165Q	05/03/2017	05/19/2017	05/23/2017	06/15/2017
0.165Q	07/18/2017	08/18/2017	08/22/2017	09/15/2017
0.19Q	10/17/2017	11/20/2017	11/21/2017	12/15/2017

Indicated Div: $0.76

Valuation Analysis

		Institutional Holding	
Forecast EPS	$3.85 (01/18/2018)	No of Institutions	494
Market Cap	$4.8 Billion	Shares	97,654,328
Book Value	$1.6 Billion	% Held	96.78
Price/Book	3.08		
Price/Sales	1.02		

Business Summary: Leisure Equipment (MIC: 1.6.1 SIC: 3511 NAIC: 333611)

Brunswick is a designer, manufacturer and marketer of recreation products. Co. operates in three reportable segments: marine engine, which manufactures and markets a range of outboard, sterndrive and inboard engine and propulsion systems; boat, which designs, manufactures and markets fiberglass pleasure boats, yachts and sport yachts, sport cruisers and sport boats, fishing boats, pontoon boats, utility boats, deck boats, inflatable boats, and aluminum boats; and fitness, which designs, manufactures and markets a line of cardiovascular fitness equipment and strength-training equipment under the Life Fitness, Hammer Strength, Cybex, Indoor Cycling Group and SCIFIT brands.

Recent Developments: For the quarter ended Sep 30 2017, income from continuing operations decreased 7.4% to US$79.0 million from US$85.3 million in the year-earlier quarter. Net income decreased 7.5% to US$79.0 million from US$85.4 million in the year-earlier quarter. Revenues were US$1.14 billion, up 4.4% from US$1.09 billion the year before. Operating income was US$111.7 million versus US$122.5 million in the prior-year quarter, a decrease of 8.8%. Direct operating expenses rose 5.7% to US$828.2 million from US$783.3 million in the comparable period the year before. Indirect operating expenses increased 7.7% to US$201.6 million from US$187.2 million in the equivalent prior-year period.

Prospects: Our evaluation of Brunswick Corp. as of Jan. 14, 2018 is the result of our systematic analysis on three basic characteristics: earnings strength, relative valuation, and recent stock price movement. The company has managed to produce a neutral trend in earnings per share over the past 5 quarters and while recent estimates for the company have remained steady, BC has posted results that fell short of analysts expectations. Based on operating earnings yield, the company is undervalued when compared to all of the companies in our coverage universe. Share price changes over the past year indicates that BC will perform in line with the market over the near term.

Financial Data

(US$ in Thousands)	9 Mos	6 Mos	3 Mos	12/31/2016	12/31/2015	12/31/2014	12/31/2013	12/31/2012
Earnings Per Share	3.11	3.16	3.01	3.00	2.56	2.58	8.20	0.54
Cash Flow Per Share	4.47	4.27	4.76	4.61	3.48	2.53	1.87	1.78
Tang Book Value Per Share	11.16	10.91	10.01	9.65	10.21	8.94	7.70	N.M.
Dividends Per Share	0.660	0.645	0.630	0.615	0.525	0.450	0.100	0.050
Dividend Payout %	21.22	20.41	20.93	20.50	20.51	17.44	1.22	9.26
Income Statement								
Total Revenue	3,653,800	2,512,300	1,160,300	4,488,500	4,105,700	3,838,700	3,887,500	3,717,600
EBITDA	458,500	317,300	117,900	508,200	423,000	393,000	358,700	335,900
Depn & Amortn	83,200	55,200	27,200	97,100	85,900	78,300	84,800	85,900
Income Before Taxes	357,200	249,700	84,600	385,400	311,500	286,100	231,500	184,800
Income Taxes	99,100	69,100	22,000	115,300	87,800	93,000	(545,600)	33,600
Net Income	263,300	184,300	64,900	276,000	241,400	245,700	769,200	50,000
Average Shares	89,800	90,600	90,100	92,000	94,300	95,100	93,800	92,400
Balance Sheet								
Current Assets	1,776,700	1,777,800	1,671,000	1,688,500	1,984,900	1,967,800	1,508,600	1,360,100
Total Assets	3,399,200	3,383,700	3,273,900	3,284,700	3,152,500	3,134,400	2,915,800	2,424,200
Current Liabilities	980,100	985,800	956,500	964,900	908,100	900,100	883,100	937,200
Long-Term Obligations	437,600	438,200	435,400	436,500	442,500	450,200	453,400	563,600
Total Liabilities	1,829,100	1,835,900	1,800,300	1,844,600	1,871,200	1,962,900	1,877,400	2,346,500
Stockholders' Equity	1,570,100	1,547,800	1,473,600	1,440,100	1,281,300	1,171,500	1,038,400	77,700
Shares Outstanding	87,687	88,776	89,365	89,317	90,813	92,694	92,409	89,631
Statistical Record								
Return on Assets %	8.46	8.67	8.63	8.55	7.68	8.12	28.81	2.03
Return on Equity %	18.70	19.58	19.87	20.23	19.68	22.24	137.84	91.83
EBITDA Margin %	12.55	12.63	10.16	11.32	10.30	10.24	9.23	9.04
Net Margin %	7.21	7.34	5.59	6.15	5.88	6.40	19.79	1.34
Asset Turnover	1.43	1.41	1.43	1.39	1.31	1.27	1.46	1.51
Current Ratio	1.81	1.80	1.75	1.75	2.19	2.19	1.71	1.45
Debt to Equity	0.28	0.28	0.30	0.30	0.35	0.38	0.44	7.25
Price Range	63.42-42.19	63.34-42.19	61.46-41.82	56.03-37.98	56.39-46.50	51.94-38.95	46.48-29.09	29.09-18.49
P/E Ratio	20.39-13.57	20.04-13.35	20.42-13.89	18.68-12.66	22.03-18.16	20.13-15.10	5.67-3.55	53.87-34.24
Average Yield %	1.18	1.20	1.24	1.31	1.01	1.04	0.27	0.21

Address: 26125 N. Riverwoods Blvd., Suite 500, Mettawa, IL 60045-3420 **Telephone:** 847-735-4700	**Web Site:** www.brunswick.com **Officers:** Mark D. Schwabero - Chairman, President, Chief Executive Officer, Chief Operating Officer, Vice President, Division Officer Christopher E. Clawson - Vice President, Division Officer	**Auditors:** Deloitte & Touche LLP **Investor Contact:** 847-735-4612 **Transfer Agents:** ComputerShare Investor Services, Providence, RI

BUCKEYE PARTNERS LP

Exchange	Symbol	Price	52Wk Range	Yield	P/E	Div Achiever
NYS	BPL	$49.55 (12/29/2017)	72.62-44.59	10.19	15.29	21 Years

*7 Year Price Score 73.20 *NYSE Composite Index=100 *12 Month Price Score 74.51

Interim Earnings (Per Share)

Qtr.	Mar	Jun	Sep	Dec
2014	0.78	0.20	0.86	0.43
2015	0.87	0.71	0.78	1.04
2016	1.01	1.07	1.19	0.75
2017	0.88	0.80	0.81	...

Interim Dividends (Per Share)

Amt	Decl	Ex	Rec	Pay
1.238Q	02/10/2017	02/16/2017	02/21/2017	02/28/2017
1.25Q	05/05/2017	05/11/2017	05/15/2017	05/22/2017
1.263Q	08/04/2017	08/10/2017	08/14/2017	08/21/2017
1.263Q	11/03/2017	11/10/2017	11/13/2017	11/20/2017

Indicated Div: $5.05

Valuation Analysis

		Institutional Holding	
Forecast EPS	$3.41 (01/18/2018)	No of Institutions	527
Market Cap	$7.3 Billion	Shares	113,476,720
Book Value	N/A	% Held	73.86
Price/Book	N/A		
Price/Sales	2.00		

Business Summary: Equipment & Services (MIC: 9.1.3 SIC: 4613 NAIC: 486910)

Buckeye Partners is a holding company. Through its subsidiaries, Co. owns and operates integrated assets providing midstream logistic solutions, including transportation, storage, processing and marketing of liquid petroleum products. Co. has three segments: Domestic Pipelines & Terminals, which provide pipeline transportation services; Global Marine Terminals, which provide marine accessible bulk storage and blending services, rail and truck rack loading/unloading, along with petroleum processing services in the East Coast and Gulf Coast regions of the U.S. and in the Caribbean; and Merchant Services, which distribute refined petroleum products in the continental U.S. and in the Caribbean.

Recent Developments: For the quarter ended Sep 30 2017, net income decreased 25.0% to US$120.2 million from US$160.3 million in the year-earlier quarter. Revenues were US$922.6 million, up 20.4% from US$766.6 million the year before. Operating income was US$168.0 million versus US$206.2 million in the prior-year quarter, a decrease of 18.6%. Direct operating expenses rose 39.5% to US$664.6 million from US$476.6 million in the comparable period the year before. Indirect operating expenses increased 7.5% to US$90.1 million from US$83.8 million in the equivalent prior-year period.

Prospects: Our evaluation of Buckeye Partners, L.P. as of Jan. 14, 2018 is the result of our systematic analysis on three basic characteristics: earnings strength, relative valuation, and recent stock price movement. The company has managed to produce a neutral trend in earnings per share over the past 5 quarters. However, while recent estimates for the company have been lowered by analysts, BPL has posted results that fell short of analysts expectations. Based on operating earnings yield, the company is undervalued when compared to all of the companies in our coverage universe. Share price changes over the past year indicates that BPL will perform very poorly over the near term.

Financial Data

(US$ in Thousands)	9 Mos	6 Mos	3 Mos	12/31/2016	12/31/2015	12/31/2014	12/31/2013	12/31/2012
Earnings Per Share	3.24	3.62	3.89	4.03	3.40	2.28	1.49	2.32
Cash Flow Per Share	6.02	5.56	5.02	5.41	5.54	5.03	3.60	4.53
Dividends Per Share	4.975	4.925	4.875	4.825	4.625	4.425	4.225	4.150
Dividend Payout %	153.55	136.05	125.32	119.73	136.03	194.08	283.56	178.88
Income Statement								
Total Revenue	2,702,093	1,779,474	969,273	3,248,376	3,453,434	6,620,247	5,054,101	4,357,242
EBITDA	523,834	351,502	176,419	920,121	762,914	643,319	601,036	458,956
Depn & Amortn	13,053	8,722	4,361	186,600	158,700	148,400	122,700	120,200
Income Before Taxes	341,911	230,471	116,173	538,599	432,884	323,684	347,416	223,776
Income Taxes	1,709	1,261	222	1,460	874	451	1,060	(675)
Net Income	352,485	236,298	123,576	535,608	437,223	272,954	160,273	226,417
Average Shares	142,818	141,505	140,998	132,927	128,617	119,899	107,677	97,635
Balance Sheet								
Current Assets	558,330	575,498	605,390	1,318,897	551,550	632,299	901,086	634,322
Total Assets	10,112,500	9,880,703	9,866,845	9,421,103	8,369,281	8,086,088	7,005,563	5,981,009
Current Liabilities	509,274	538,422	547,786	399,548	504,309	621,955	685,043	594,366
Long-Term Obligations	4,593,635	4,579,943	4,561,032	4,217,695	3,732,824	3,388,986	3,092,711	2,735,244
Total Liabilities	5,481,968	5,500,522	5,494,318	5,009,380	4,633,892	4,383,460	3,939,898	3,608,696
Shares Outstanding	146,641	141,221	140,526	140,263	129,523	127,043	115,063	98,345
Statistical Record								
Return on Assets %	4.91	5.45	5.79	6.00	5.31	3.62	2.47	3.91
EBITDA Margin %	19.39	19.75	18.20	28.33	22.09	9.72	11.89	10.53
Net Margin %	13.04	13.28	12.75	16.49	12.66	4.12	3.17	5.20
Asset Turnover	0.39	0.38	0.38	0.36	0.42	0.88	0.78	0.75
Current Ratio	1.10	1.07	1.11	3.30	1.09	1.02	1.32	1.07
Price Range	72.62-54.55	74.40-60.11	74.40-62.51	74.40-50.35	82.04-54.00	83.91-66.87	73.13-45.41	64.17-44.65
P/E Ratio	22.41-16.84	20.55-16.60	19.13-16.07	18.46-12.49	24.13-15.88	36.80-29.33	49.08-30.48	27.66-19.25
Average Yield %	7.67	7.27	7.08	7.18	6.42	5.76	6.59	7.84

Address: One Greenway Plaza, Suite 600, Houston, TX 77046 **Telephone:** 832-615-8600	**Web Site:** www.buckeye.com **Officers:** Gary L. Bohnsack - Associate/Affiliate Company Officer Clark C. Smith - President, Chief Executive Officer, Chief Operating Officer, Associate/Affiliate Company Officer	**Auditors:** Deloitte & Touche LLP **Investor Contact:** 800-422-2825 **Transfer Agents:** First Chicago Trust Company a Division of Equiserv, Jersey City, NJ

BUNGE LTD.

Exchange	Symbol	Price	52Wk Range	Yield	P/E
NYS	BG	$67.08 (12/29/2017)	83.22-65.15	2.74	21.03

*7 Year Price Score 80.10 ***NYSE Composite Index=100** ***12 Month Price Score 86.18**

Interim Earnings (Per Share)

Qtr.	Mar	Jun	Sep	Dec
2014	(0.18)	1.81	1.90	(0.41)
2015	1.67	0.50	1.56	1.30
2016	1.54	0.78	0.83	1.82
2017	0.27	0.51	0.59	...

Interim Dividends (Per Share)

Amt	Decl	Ex	Rec	Pay
0.42Q	03/08/2017	05/17/2017	05/19/2017	06/02/2017
0.46Q	05/24/2017	08/18/2017	08/22/2017	09/05/2017
0.46Q	08/08/2017	11/17/2017	11/20/2017	12/04/2017
0.46Q	12/07/2017	02/15/2018	02/16/2018	03/02/2018

Indicated Div: $1.84

Valuation Analysis		Institutional Holding	
Forecast EPS	N/A	No of Institutions	608
Market Cap	$9.4 Billion	Shares	
Book Value	$7.5 Billion		132,897,472
Price/Book	1.25	% Held	
Price/Sales	0.21		73.88

Business Summary: Food (MIC: 1.2.1 SIC: 2079 NAIC: 311225)

Bunge is a holding company. Through its subsidiaries, Co. is an agribusiness and food company operating in the farm field to consumer foods. Co.'s segments include: Agribusiness, which purchases, stores, transports, processes and sells agricultural commodities and commodity products; Food and Ingredients, which include edible oil and milling products; Sugar and Bioenergy, in which Co. is a producer of sugar and ethanol in Brazil, and a trader and merchandiser of sugar; and Fertilizer, in which Co. produces, blends and distributes a range of nitrogen, phosphate and potassium fertilizers, including phosphate-based liquid and solid nitrogen fertilizers, through its operations in Argentina.

Recent Developments: For the quarter ended Sep 30 2017, income from continuing operations decreased 26.4% to US$92.0 million from US$125.0 million in the year-earlier quarter. Net income decreased 29.2% to US$92.0 million from US$130.0 million in the year-earlier quarter. Revenues were US$11.42 billion, unchanged from the year before. Direct operating expenses rose 0.6% to US$10.93 billion from US$10.87 billion in the comparable period the year before. Indirect operating expenses increased 4.9% to US$340.0 million from US$324.0 million in the equivalent prior-year period.

Prospects: Our evaluation of Bunge Ltd. as of July 19, 2015 is the result of our systematic analysis on three basic characteristics: earnings strength, relative valuation, and recent stock price movement. The company has produced a positive trend in earnings per share over the past 5 quarters. However, while recent estimates for the company have been lowered by analysts, BG has posted better than expected results. Based on operating earnings yield, the company is undervalued when compared to all of the companies in our coverage universe. Share price changes over the past year indicates that BG will perform well over the near term.

Financial Data

(US$ in Millions)	9 Mos	6 Mos	3 Mos	12/31/2016	12/31/2015	12/31/2014	12/31/2013	12/31/2012
Earnings Per Share	3.19	3.43	3.70	5.01	5.07	3.17	1.55	0.19
Cash Flow Per Share	6.88	15.03	12.74	13.58	4.25	9.57	15.12	(3.12)
Tang Book Value Per Share	42.69	40.34	46.09	41.18	35.14	49.08	57.17	65.09
Income Statement								
Total Revenue	34,189	22,766	11,121	42,679	43,455	57,161	61,347	60,991
EBITDA	839	497	265	1,696	1,784	1,570	1,825	1,117
Depn & Amortn	448	282	130	517	518	576	524	504
Income Before Taxes	229	108	82	996	1,051	734	1,014	372
Income Taxes	2	(27)	28	220	296	249	904	(6)
Net Income	220	128	47	745	791	515	306	64
Average Shares	141	141	140	148	152	147	148	147
Balance Sheet								
Current Assets	11,985	11,914	12,008	11,092	10,916	13,081	17,772	17,264
Total Assets	20,552	20,433	20,620	19,188	17,922	21,432	26,781	27,280
Current Liabilities	7,468	7,933	8,616	7,684	7,340	8,704	12,535	11,561
Long-Term Obligations	4,246	3,918	3,266	3,069	2,934	2,855	3,179	3,532
Total Liabilities	13,006	13,206	13,192	12,044	11,481	12,986	16,924	16,418
Stockholders' Equity	7,546	7,227	7,428	7,144	6,441	8,446	9,857	10,862
Shares Outstanding	140	140	127	139	142	145	147	146
Statistical Record								
Return on Assets %	2.42	2.43	2.82	4.00	4.02	2.14	1.13	0.25
Return on Equity %	6.71	7.20	7.85	10.94	10.63	5.63	2.95	0.57
EBITDA Margin %	2.45	2.18	2.38	3.97	4.11	2.75	2.97	1.83
Net Margin %	0.64	0.56	0.42	1.75	1.82	0.90	0.50	0.10
Asset Turnover	2.27	2.16	2.27	2.29	2.21	2.37	2.27	2.41
Current Ratio	1.60	1.50	1.39	1.44	1.49	1.50	1.42	1.49
Debt to Equity	0.56	0.54	0.44	0.43	0.46	0.34	0.32	0.33
Price Range	83.22-58.64	83.22-57.76	82.07-55.62	73.61-47.79	92.85-61.81	92.91-73.51	83.11-66.40	73.82-57.22
P/E Ratio	26.09-18.38	24.26-16.84	22.18-15.03	14.69-9.54	18.31-12.19	29.31-23.19	53.62-42.84	388.53-301.16

Address: 50 Main Street, White Plains, NY 10606
Telephone: 914-684-2800

Web Site: www.bunge.com
Officers: Soren Schroder - Chief Executive Officer, Region Officer D. Benedict Pearcy - Chief Development Officer, Division Officer

Auditors: Deloitte & Touche LLP
Transfer Agents: Computershare Investor Services LLC

BURLINGTON STORES INC

Exchange	Symbol	Price	52Wk Range	Yield	P/E
NYS	BURL	$123.03 (12/29/2017)	123.03-80.27	N/A	32.38

*7 Year Price Score N/A   *NYSE Composite Index=100   *12 Month Price Score 109.21

TRADING VOLUME (thousand shares)

Interim Earnings (Per Share)

Qtr.	Apr	Jul	Oct	Jan
2014-15	0.16	(0.09)	(0.46)	1.26
2015-16	0.34	0.14	0.20	1.30
2016-17	0.52	0.28	0.45	1.76
2017-18	0.73	0.66	0.65	...

Interim Dividends (Per Share)

No Dividends Paid

Valuation Analysis

Forecast EPS	$4.27
	(01/18/2018)
Market Cap	$8.4 Billion
Book Value	N/A
Price/Book	N/A
Price/Sales	1.43

Institutional Holding

No of Institutions	383
Shares	78,701,456
% Held	97.33

Business Summary: Retail - Apparel and Accessories (MIC: 2.1.5 SIC: 5311 NAIC: 452111)

Burlington Stores is a holding company. Through its indirect subsidiary, Burlington Coat Factory Warehouse Corporation, operated 592 retail stores, inclusive of an internet store, selling apparel, footwear and accessories for men, women and children. A majority of those stores provide a home furnishing and linens department and a juvenile furniture department. As of Jan 28 2017, Co. operated stores under the names Burlington Stores, Cohoes Fashions, Super Baby Depot, MJM Designer Shoes, Burlington Shoes and one online store. Co.'s trademarks include Burlington Stores, BCF, Burlington, Burlington Coat Factory, Cohoes, Luxury Linens, MJM Designer Shoes, and Baby Depot.

Recent Developments: For the quarter ended Oct 28 2017, net income increased 38.5% to US$44.9 million from US$32.4 million in the year-earlier quarter. Revenues were US$1.44 billion, up 7.1% from US$1.35 billion the year before. Direct operating expenses rose 5.3% to US$831.7 million from US$789.9 million in the comparable period the year before. Indirect operating expenses increased 7.0% to US$545.0 million from US$509.3 million in the equivalent prior-year period.

Prospects: Our evaluation of Burlington Stores Inc as of Jan. 14, 2018 is the result of our systematic analysis on three basic characteristics: earnings strength, relative valuation, and recent stock price movement. The company has managed to produce a neutral trend in earnings per share over the past 5 quarters and while recent estimates for the company have been mixed, BURL has posted better than expected results. Based on operating earnings yield, the company is about fairly valued when compared to all of the companies in our coverage universe. Share price changes over the past year indicates that BURL will perform poorly over the near term.

Financial Data
(US$ in Thousands)

	9 Mos	6 Mos	3 Mos	01/28/2017	01/30/2016	01/31/2015	02/01/2014	02/02/2013
Earnings Per Share	3.80	3.60	3.22	3.01	1.99	0.87	(0.39)	(2.92)
Cash Flow Per Share	7.94	8.31	8.66	8.57	4.43	4.09	0.79	9.68
Income Statement								
Total Revenue	4,165,771	2,721,199	1,352,219	5,590,950	5,129,843	4,849,634	4,461,987	4,165,504
EBITDA	251,453	167,669	89,428	551,073	448,175	336,981	307,697	290,892
Depn & Amortn	1,897	1,263	630	161,700	150,300	148,200	147,600	147,800
Income Before Taxes	206,147	138,348	75,284	333,212	238,876	105,036	32,358	29,165
Income Taxes	61,998	39,078	22,916	117,339	88,394	39,081	16,208	3,864
Net Income	144,149	99,270	52,368	215,873	150,482	65,955	16,150	25,301
Average Shares	69,541	70,801	71,505	71,721	75,443	75,865	370,040	45,982
Balance Sheet								
Current Assets	1,150,455	948,463	914,724	928,324	932,982	987,483	1,016,520	879,654
Total Assets	2,843,363	2,611,768	2,558,858	2,574,483	2,580,147	2,624,569	2,621,092	2,478,082
Current Liabilities	1,127,675	923,296	947,320	996,834	886,588	933,117	903,816	740,055
Long-Term Obligations	1,294,300	1,276,443	1,152,186	1,128,843	1,303,497	1,249,276	1,369,159	1,335,532
Total Liabilities	2,953,896	2,707,668	2,599,766	2,624,295	2,679,169	2,690,520	2,771,560	2,558,351
Stockholders' Equity	(110,533)	(95,900)	(40,908)	(49,812)	(99,022)	(65,951)	(150,468)	(80,269)
Shares Outstanding	68,247	68,972	69,821	70,180	72,071	75,254	73,686	51,835
Statistical Record								
Return on Assets %	9.75	9.94	8.93	8.40	5.80	2.52	0.64	1.00
EBITDA Margin %	6.04	6.16	6.61	9.86	8.74	6.95	6.90	6.98
Net Margin %	3.46	3.65	3.87	3.86	2.93	1.36	0.36	0.61
Asset Turnover	2.12	2.23	2.19	2.18	1.98	1.85	1.75	1.65
Current Ratio	1.02	1.03	0.97	0.93	1.05	1.06	1.12	1.19
Price Range	103.96-69.24	103.96-69.24	98.92-51.69	89.68-49.71	61.02-40.70	51.60-24.26	32.50-24.86	...
P/E Ratio	27.36-18.22	28.88-19.23	30.72-16.05	29.79-16.51	30.66-20.45	59.31-27.89	...	...

Address: 2006 Route 130 North, Burlington, NJ 08016	Web Site: www.burlingtonstores.com	Auditors: Deloitte & Touche LLP
Telephone: 609-387-7800	Officers: Thomas A. Kingsbury - Chairman, President, Chief Executive Officer Janet L. Dhillon - Executive Vice President, General Counsel, Corporate Secretary	Transfer Agents: American Stock Transfer & Trust Company, LLC, Brooklyn, NY

BWX TECHNOLOGIES INC

Exchange	Symbol	Price	52Wk Range	Yield	P/E
		$60.49 (12/29/2017)	62.45-39.22	0.73	30.55

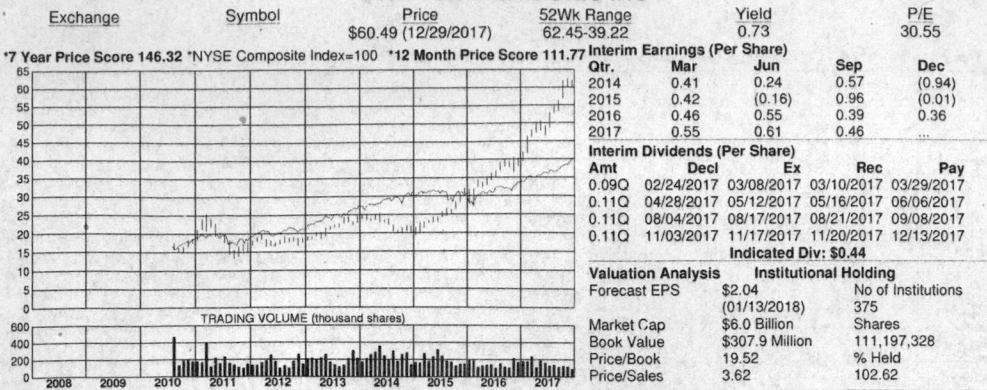

*7 Year Price Score 146.32 *NYSE Composite Index=100 *12 Month Price Score 111.77

Interim Earnings (Per Share)

Qtr.	Mar	Jun	Sep	Dec
2014	0.41	0.24	0.57	(0.94)
2015	0.42	(0.16)	0.96	(0.01)
2016	0.46	0.55	0.39	0.36
2017	0.55	0.61	0.46	...

Interim Dividends (Per Share)

Amt	Decl	Ex	Rec	Pay
0.09Q	02/24/2017	03/08/2017	03/10/2017	03/29/2017
0.11Q	04/28/2017	05/12/2017	05/16/2017	06/06/2017
0.11Q	08/04/2017	08/17/2017	08/21/2017	09/08/2017
0.11Q	11/03/2017	11/17/2017	11/20/2017	12/13/2017

Indicated Div: $0.44

Valuation Analysis | **Institutional Holding**

Forecast EPS	$2.04	No of Institutions
	(01/13/2018)	375
Market Cap	$6.0 Billion	Shares
Book Value	$307.9 Million	111,197,328
Price/Book	19.52	% Held
Price/Sales	3.62	102.62

Business Summary: Industrial Machinery & Equipment (MIC: 7.2.1 SIC: 3511 NAIC: 333611)

BWX Technologies is a manufacturer of nuclear components and a service provider. Co. operates in three reportable segments: Nuclear Operations, which designs and manufactures naval nuclear reactors for the U.S. Department of Energy/National Nuclear Security Administration's Naval Nuclear Propulsion Program; Technical Services, which provides various services to the U.S. Government, including uranium processing, environmental site restoration services and management and operating services for various U.S. Government-owned facilities; and Nuclear Energy, which supplies commercial nuclear steam generators and components to nuclear utility customers.

Recent Developments: For the quarter ended Sep 30 2017, net income increased 13.3% to US$46.7 million from US$41.2 million in the year-earlier quarter. Revenues were US$419.4 million, up 10.5% from US$379.5 million the year before. Operating income was US$73.7 million versus US$62.4 million in the prior-year quarter, an increase of 18.1%. Direct operating expenses rose 8.9% to US$295.3 million from US$271.2 million in the comparable period the year before. Indirect operating expenses increased 9.6% to US$50.4 million from US$46.0 million in the equivalent prior-year period.

Prospects: Our evaluation of BWX Technologies Inc. as of Jan. 14, 2018 is the result of our systematic analysis on three basic characteristics: earnings strength, relative valuation, and recent stock price movement. The company has generated a negative trend in earnings per share over the past 5 quarters. However, while recent estimates for the company have been mixed, BWXT has posted results that fell short of analysts expectations. Based on operating earnings yield, the company is about fairly valued when compared to all of the companies in our coverage universe. Share price changes over the past year indicates that BWXT will perform very well over the near term.

Financial Data
(US$ in Thousands)

	9 Mos	6 Mos	3 Mos	12/31/2016	12/31/2015	12/31/2014	12/31/2013	12/31/2012
Earnings Per Share	1.98	1.91	1.85	1.76	1.22	0.27	3.07	1.91
Cash Flow Per Share	3.05	2.43	2.04	2.33	3.09	0.69	1.23	1.56
Tang Book Value Per Share	N.M.	N.M.	N.M.	N.M.	0.37	4.77	7.26	6.12
Dividends Per Share	0.400	0.380	0.360	0.360	0.320	0.400	0.340	0.080
Dividend Payout %	20.20	19.90	19.46	20.45	26.23	148.15	11.07	4.19
Income Statement								
Total Revenue	1,257,600	838,240	428,229	1,550,573	1,415,529	2,923,019	3,269,208	3,291,359
EBITDA	281,267	196,932	93,859	297,341	242,819	63,161	512,987	314,353
Depn & Amortn	42,135	28,199	13,976	48,400	55,300	92,900	62,200	59,400
Income Before Taxes	228,622	161,658	76,503	241,199	207,669	(36,290)	449,115	252,709
Income Taxes	75,556	51,654	24,592	73,656	80,416	(15,991)	184,583	101,861
Net Income	163,534	116,982	55,719	183,057	131,465	29,388	346,078	227,695
Average Shares	100,260	100,150	100,690	103,840	107,583	108,761	112,685	119,021
Balance Sheet								
Current Assets	830,876	745,544	743,509	693,571	647,294	1,473,802	1,437,424	1,521,086
Total Assets	1,723,512	1,624,738	1,617,926	1,579,815	1,382,139	2,856,936	2,609,153	2,840,355
Current Liabilities	459,867	392,774	382,437	439,876	353,780	819,636	927,228	1,079,288
Long-Term Obligations	489,128	489,322	542,997	497,724	285,000	285,000	225	430
Total Liabilities	1,415,612	1,360,787	1,412,020	1,429,797	1,116,423	1,858,232	1,444,466	1,853,920
Stockholders' Equity	307,900	263,951	205,906	150,018	265,716	998,704	1,164,687	986,435
Shares Outstanding	99,356	99,282	99,019	99,290	105,297	106,688	110,468	115,235
Statistical Record								
Return on Assets %	12.94	12.81	12.74	12.33	6.20	1.08	12.70	8.07
Return on Equity %	93.77	69.69	80.25	87.82	20.79	2.72	32.18	25.06
EBITDA Margin %	22.37	23.49	21.92	19.18	17.15	2.16	15.69	9.55
Net Margin %	13.00	13.96	13.01	11.81	9.29	1.01	10.59	6.92
Asset Turnover	1.08	1.07	1.08	1.04	0.67	1.07	1.20	1.17
Current Ratio	1.81	1.90	1.94	1.58	1.83	1.80	1.55	1.41
Debt to Equity	1.59	1.85	2.64	3.32	1.07	0.29	N.M.	N.M.
Price Range	56.37-36.37	50.71-34.82	48.10-32.36	40.52-27.09	32.23-19.33	25.39-19.81	24.70-18.11	19.84-16.47
P/E Ratio	28.47-18.37	26.55-18.23	26.00-17.49	23.02-15.39	26.42-15.84	94.05-73.38	8.05-5.90	10.38-8.62
Average Yield %	0.87	0.90	0.93	1.02	1.28	1.77	1.59	0.44

Address: 800 Main Street, 4th Floor, Lynchburg, VA 24504
Telephone: 980-365-4300

Web Site: www.bwxt.com
Officers: John A. Fees - Chairman Rex D. Geveden - Chief Operating Officer, President, Chief Executive Officer

Auditors: Deloitte & Touche LLP
Investor Contact: 704-625-4944
Transfer Agents: Computershare Trust Company, N.A., Canton, MA

CABLE ONE INC

Exchange	Symbol	Price	52Wk Range	Yield	P/E
NYS	CABO	$703.35 (12/29/2017)	762.27-570.00	1.00	34.34

*7 Year Price Score N/A   *NYSE Composite Index=100   *12 Month Price Score 94.55

TRADING VOLUME (thousand shares)
2008 2009 2010 2011 2012 2013 2014 2015 2016 2017

Interim Earnings (Per Share)

Qtr.	Mar	Jun	Sep	Dec
2014	4.17	4.60	11.84	4.60
2015	3.78	3.67	3.30	4.44
2016	4.65	4.62	3.63	4.23
2017	5.80	4.97	5.48	...

Interim Dividends (Per Share)

Amt	Decl	Ex	Rec	Pay
1.50Q	02/07/2017	02/16/2017	02/21/2017	03/10/2017
1.50Q	05/02/2017	05/12/2017	05/16/2017	06/02/2017
1.75Q	08/02/2017	08/11/2017	08/15/2017	09/01/2017
1.75Q	11/07/2017	11/20/2017	11/21/2017	12/08/2017

Indicated Div: $7.00

Valuation Analysis / Institutional Holding

Valuation Analysis		Institutional Holding	
Forecast EPS	$22.04	No of Institutions	
	(01/11/2018)	283	
Market Cap	$4.0 Billion	Shares	
Book Value	$525.6 Million	4,709,475	
Price/Book	7.67	% Held	
Price/Sales	4.43	N/A	

Business Summary: Radio & Television (MIC: 2.3.1 SIC: 4841 NAIC: 515210)

Cable One is a provider of data, video and voice services in 19 Western, Midwestern and Southern states. Co. provides these broadband services to residential and business customers in more than 35 cable systems covering over 400 cities and towns. Co.'s product lines include residential data services, residential video services, residential voice services, business services, and advertising. As of Dec 31 2016, Co. provided service to 657,222 residential and business customers. Of these customers, 513,908 subscribed to data services, 320,246 to video services and 115,811 to voice services.

Recent Developments: For the quarter ended Sep 30 2017, net income increased 51.0% to US$31.5 million from US$20.9 million in the year-earlier quarter. Revenues were US$253.8 million, up 23.5% from US$205.5 million the year before. Operating income was US$61.9 million versus US$43.8 million in the prior-year quarter, an increase of 41.3%. Direct operating expenses rose 21.5% to US$91.9 million from US$75.6 million in the comparable period the year before. Indirect operating expenses increased 16.2% to US$100.1 million from US$86.1 million in the equivalent prior-year period.

Prospects: Our evaluation of Cable ONE Inc. as of Jan. 14, 2018 is the result of our systematic analysis on three basic characteristics: earnings strength, relative valuation, and recent stock price movement. The company has produced a positive trend in earnings per share over the past 5 quarters. However, while recent estimates for the company have been mixed, CABO has posted better than expected results. Based on operating earnings yield, the company is fairly valued when compared to all of the companies in our coverage universe. Share price changes over the past year indicates that CABO will perform well over the near term.

Financial Data
(US$ in Thousands)

	9 Mos	6 Mos	3 Mos	12/31/2016	12/31/2015	12/31/2014	12/31/2013	12/31/2012
Earnings Per Share	20.48	18.63	18.28	17.14	15.19	147,309.00	104,511.00	93,911.00
Cash Flow Per Share	48.95	45.28	44.53	43.73	42.10	...	...	...
Dividends Per Share	6.250	6.000	6.000	6.000	1.500	...	...	...
Dividend Payout %	30.52	32.21	32.82	35.01	9.87	...	...	...
Income Statement								
Total Revenue	702,315	448,469	207,427	819,625	807,266	814,812	825,707	804,992
EBITDA	308,925	203,357	99,440	335,528	302,110	372,009	289,811	276,711
Depn & Amortn	127,783	84,391	38,800	142,200	140,600	134,000	125,500	126,500
Income Before Taxes	147,734	99,577	53,034	163,107	145,420	238,009	164,311	150,211
Income Taxes	54,430	37,787	19,819	64,168	56,387	90,700	59,800	56,300
Net Income	93,304	61,790	33,215	98,939	89,033	147,309	104,511	93,911
Average Shares	5,753	5,745	5,730	5,770	5,860	...	...	...
Balance Sheet								
Current Assets	202,966	165,400	218,666	185,937	166,353	50,121	46,768	...
Total Assets	2,165,233	2,124,494	1,423,494	1,397,271	1,408,595	1,262,040	1,248,344	...
Current Liabilities	151,281	134,646	112,545	111,143	126,832	95,623	105,142	...
Long-Term Obligations	1,164,070	1,167,458	529,407	530,886	545,301	...	...	...
Total Liabilities	1,639,609	1,621,346	942,648	942,760	973,249	408,752	413,085	...
Stockholders' Equity	525,624	503,148	480,846	454,511	435,346	853,288	835,259	...
Shares Outstanding	5,728	5,725	5,723	5,708	5,833	...	...	...
Statistical Record								
Return on Assets %	6.63	6.12	7.50	7.03	...	11.74	...	...
Return on Equity %	24.44	22.90	23.28	22.18	...	17.45	...	...
EBITDA Margin %	43.99	45.34	47.94	40.94	37.42	45.66	35.10	34.37
Net Margin %	13.29	13.78	16.01	12.07	11.03	18.08	12.66	11.67
Asset Turnover	0.51	0.49	0.59	0.58	...	0.65	...	...
Current Ratio	1.34	1.23	1.94	1.67	1.31	0.52	0.44	...
Debt to Equity	2.21	2.32	1.10	1.17	1.25	...	...	...
Price Range	762.27-569.77	731.45-511.41	645.45-434.84	623.87-396.52	490.48-376.91	...	...	...
P/E Ratio	37.22-27.82	39.26-27.45	35.31-23.79	36.40-23.13	32.29-24.81	...	...	...
Average Yield %	0.95	0.98	1.07	1.18	0.35	...	...	...

Address: 210 E. Earll Drive, Phoenix, AZ 85012 **Telephone:** 602-364-6000	**Web Site:** www.cableone.net **Officers:** Julia M. Laulis - Chairman, President, Chief Executive Officer, Chief Operating Officer Kevin P. Coyle - Senior Vice President, Chief Financial Officer	**Auditors:** PricewaterhouseCoopers LLP **Transfer Agents:** Computershare Trust Company, N.A.

CABOT CORP.

Exchange	Symbol	Price	52Wk Range	Yield	P/E
NYS	CBT	$61.59 (12/29/2017)	64.26-50.75	2.05	16.21

*7 Year Price Score 99.07   *NYSE Composite Index=100   *12 Month Price Score 100.93

Interim Earnings (Per Share)

Qtr.	Dec	Mar	Jun	Sep
2012-13	0.31	0.42	0.90	0.73
2013-14	1.23	0.54	0.78	0.48
2014-15	0.69	0.41	(7.04)	0.61
2015-16	(0.11)	0.76	0.88	0.83
2016-17	0.85	1.18	0.71	1.06

Interim Dividends (Per Share)

Amt	Decl	Ex	Rec	Pay
0.315Q	05/10/2017	05/24/2017	05/26/2017	06/09/2017
0.315Q	07/14/2017	08/23/2017	08/25/2017	09/08/2017
0.315Q	11/10/2017	11/22/2017	11/24/2017	12/08/2017
0.315Q	01/12/2018	02/22/2018	02/23/2018	03/09/2018

Indicated Div: $1.26

Valuation Analysis

Forecast EPS	$3.80	
	(01/17/2018)	
Market Cap	$3.8 Billion	
Book Value	$1.5 Billion	
Price/Book	2.58	
Price/Sales	1.40	

Institutional Holding

No of Institutions	402
Shares	66,258,368
% Held	86.79

Business Summary: Specialty Chemicals (MIC: 8.3.2 SIC: 2895 NAIC: 325182)

Cabot is a chemicals and performance materials. Co.'s business segments are: Reinforcement Materials, which include rubber blacks products are used in tires and industrial products; Performance Chemicals, which designs, manufactures and sells materials that deliver performance in a customer applications across the automotive, construction and infrastructure; Purification Solutions, which include activated carbon products are used for the purification of water, air, food and beverages, pharmaceuticals and other liquids and gases; and Specialty Fluids, which produces and markets cesium formate as a drilling and completion fluid for use primarily in high pressure oil and gas well construction.

Recent Developments: For the year ended Sep 30 2017, income from continuing operations increased 63.2% to US$266.0 million from US$163.0 million a year earlier. Net income increased 62.2% to US$266.0 million from US$164.0 million in the prior year. Revenues were US$2.72 billion, up 12.7% from US$2.41 billion the year before. Operating income was US$336.0 million versus US$250.0 million in the prior year, an increase of 34.4%. Direct operating expenses rose 12.7% to US$2.07 billion from US$1.83 billion in the comparable period the year before. Indirect operating expenses decreased 3.7% to US$316.0 million from US$328.0 million in the equivalent prior-year period.

Prospects: Our evaluation of Cabot Corp. as of Jan. 14, 2018 is the result of our systematic analysis on three basic characteristics: earnings strength, relative valuation, and recent stock price movement. The company has managed to produce a neutral trend in earnings per share over the past 5 quarters and while recent estimates for the company have been raised by analysts, CBT has posted results that fell short of analysts expectations. Based on operating earnings yield, the company is undervalued when compared to all of the companies in our coverage universe. Share price changes over the past year indicates that CBT will perform poorly over the near term.

Financial Data

(US$ in Thousands)	09/30/2017	09/30/2016	09/30/2015	09/30/2014	09/30/2013	09/30/2012	09/30/2011	09/30/2010
Earnings Per Share	3.80	2.36	(5.27)	3.03	2.36	5.99	3.57	2.35
Cash Flow Per Share	5.46	6.26	7.87	4.89	6.57	6.53	3.02	3.89
Tang Book Value Per Share	19.21	15.79	14.84	16.45	17.77	15.83	22.66	19.26
Dividends Per Share	1.230	1.040	0.880	0.840	0.800	0.760	0.720	0.720
Dividend Payout %	32.37	44.07	...	27.72	33.90	12.69	20.17	30.64
Income Statement								
Total Revenue	2,717,000	2,411,000	2,871,000	3,647,000	3,463,000	3,300,000	3,102,000	2,893,000
EBITDA	479,000	397,000	(159,000)	544,000	438,000	440,000	378,000	388,000
Depn & Amortn	147,000	154,000	169,000	184,000	176,000	153,000	138,000	142,000
Income Before Taxes	288,000	194,000	(377,000)	308,000	205,000	245,000	203,000	208,000
Income Taxes	29,000	34,000	(45,000)	92,000	58,000	55,000	6,000	46,000
Net Income	241,000	149,000	(334,000)	199,000	153,000	388,000	236,000	154,000
Average Shares	62,700	62,900	63,400	65,100	64,500	64,200	65,400	64,000
Balance Sheet								
Current Assets	1,262,000	1,089,000	1,048,000	1,364,000	1,495,000	1,443,000	1,555,000	1,438,000
Total Assets	3,314,000	3,044,000	3,075,000	4,084,000	4,233,000	4,399,000	3,141,000	2,886,000
Current Liabilities	742,000	398,000	441,000	630,000	844,000	919,000	656,000	539,000
Long-Term Obligations	661,000	918,000	970,000	1,004,000	1,020,000	1,172,000	556,000	600,000
Total Liabilities	1,834,000	1,770,000	1,841,000	2,142,000	2,282,000	2,586,000	1,654,000	1,584,000
Stockholders' Equity	1,480,000	1,274,000	1,234,000	1,942,000	1,951,000	1,813,000	1,487,000	1,302,000
Shares Outstanding	61,884	62,210	62,458	64,382	63,970	63,347	63,860	65,370
Statistical Record								
Return on Assets %	7.58	4.86	N.M.	4.79	3.54	10.26	7.83	5.54
Return on Equity %	17.50	11.85	N.M.	10.22	8.13	23.45	16.92	12.64
EBITDA Margin %	17.63	16.47	N.M.	14.92	12.65	13.33	12.19	13.41
Net Margin %	8.87	6.18	N.M.	5.46	4.42	11.76	7.61	5.32
Asset Turnover	0.85	0.79	0.80	0.88	0.80	0.87	1.03	1.04
Current Ratio	1.70	2.74	2.38	2.17	1.77	1.57	2.37	2.67
Debt to Equity	0.45	0.72	0.79	0.52	0.52	0.65	0.37	0.46
Price Range	60.90-48.21	53.41-31.56	50.77-30.90	60.30-42.48	43.93-32.41	44.66-23.27	47.83-24.78	33.65-21.04
P/E Ratio	16.03-12.69	22.63-13.37	...	19.90-14.02	18.61-13.73	7.46-3.88	13.40-6.94	14.32-8.95
Average Yield %	2.27	2.33	2.11	1.58	2.09	2.07	1.86	2.59

Address: Two Seaport Lane, Suite 1300, Boston, MA 02210-2019	**Web Site:** www.cabotcorp.com	**Auditors:** DELOITTE & TOUCHE LLP
Telephone: 617-345-0100	**Officers:** Sean D. Keohane - President, Chief Executive Officer, Executive Vice President, Division Officer Eduardo E. Cordeiro - Executive Vice President, Chief Financial Officer, Region Officer	**Investor Contact:** 617-342-6090
		Transfer Agents: Computershare Trust Company, N.A., Providence, RI

CABOT OIL & GAS CORP.

Exchange	Symbol	Price	52Wk Range	Yield	P/E
NYS	COG	$28.60 (12/29/2017)	29.44-20.77	0.84	N/A

*7 Year Price Score 76.16   *NYSE Composite Index=100   *12 Month Price Score 107.04

Interim Earnings (Per Share)

Qtr.	Mar	Jun	Sep	Dec
2014	0.26	0.28	0.24	(0.53)
2015	0.10	(0.07)	(0.04)	(0.27)
2016	(0.12)	(0.14)	(0.02)	(0.64)
2017	0.23	0.05	0.04	...

Interim Dividends (Per Share)

Amt	Decl	Ex	Rec	Pay
0.05Q	05/03/2017	05/15/2017	05/17/2017	05/31/2017
0.05Q	07/27/2017	08/08/2017	08/10/2017	08/24/2017
0.05Q	10/25/2017	11/07/2017	11/08/2017	11/17/2017
0.06Q	01/03/2018	01/23/2018	01/24/2018	02/07/2018

Indicated Div: $0.24

Valuation Analysis

		Institutional Holding	
Forecast EPS	$0.51	No of Institutions	
	(01/18/2018)	732	
Market Cap	$13.2 Billion	Shares	
Book Value	$2.6 Billion	506,646,752	
Price/Book	5.00	% Held	
Price/Sales	7.87	90.57	

Business Summary: Production & Extraction (MIC: 9.1.1 SIC: 1311 NAIC: 211111)

Cabot Oil & Gas is an independent oil and gas company engaged in the development, exploitation and exploration of oil and gas properties. Co. also transports, stores, gathers and purchases natural gas for resale. Co.'s exploration, development and production operations are primarily concentrated in two unconventional plays: the Marcellus Shale in northeast Pennsylvania and the Eagle Ford Shale in south Texas. Co. also has operations in various other conventional and unconventional plays throughout the continental U.S. As of Dec 31 2016, Co. had proved natural gas reserves of 8.28 trillion cubic feet and proved crude oil and natural gas liquids reserves of 49.2 million barrels.

Recent Developments: For the quarter ended Sep 30 2017, net income amounted to US$17.6 million versus a net loss of US$10.3 million in the year-earlier quarter. Revenues were US$385.4 million, up 24.2% from US$310.4 million the year before. Operating income was US$40.0 million versus US$3.6 million in the prior-year quarter, an increase of. Direct operating expenses rose 10.3% to US$147.0 million from US$133.2 million in the comparable period the year before. Indirect operating expenses increased 14.3% to US$198.5 million from US$173.6 million in the equivalent prior-year period.

Prospects: Our evaluation of Cabot Oil & Gas Corp. as of Jan. 14, 2018 is the result of our systematic analysis on three basic characteristics: earnings strength, relative valuation, and recent stock price movement. The company has suffered a very negative trend in earnings per share over the past 5 quarters. However, while recent estimates for the company have been mixed, COG has posted results that fell short of analysts expectations. Based on operating earnings yield, the company is overvalued when compared to all of the companies in our coverage universe. Share price changes over the past year indicates that COG will perform in line with the market over the near term.

Financial Data

(US$ in Thousands)	9 Mos	6 Mos	3 Mos	12/31/2016	12/31/2015	12/31/2014	12/31/2013	12/31/2012
Earnings Per Share	(0.32)	(0.38)	(0.57)	(0.91)	(0.28)	0.25	0.66	0.31
Cash Flow Per Share	1.86	1.67	1.29	0.86	1.79	2.97	2.44	1.55
Tang Book Value Per Share	5.72	5.71	5.82	5.52	4.85	5.19	5.29	5.07
Dividends Per Share	0.140	0.110	0.080	0.080	0.080	0.080	0.060	0.040
Dividend Payout %	...	...	...	...	...	32.00	9.09	12.90
Income Statement								
Total Revenue	1,363,716	978,302	517,843	1,155,677	1,357,150	2,173,011	1,746,278	1,204,546
EBITDA	296,098	249,835	190,885	26,425	529,888	740,620	1,205,225	762,803
Depn & Amortn	3,579	2,384	1,189	595,211	626,665	637,514	654,745	456,670
Income Before Taxes	230,799	206,061	168,925	(657,122)	(193,688)	29,321	485,538	237,840
Income Taxes	85,965	78,814	63,205	(242,475)	(73,382)	(72,067)	205,765	106,110
Net Income	144,834	127,247	105,720	(417,124)	(113,891)	104,468	279,773	131,730
Average Shares	464,780	466,745	466,888	456,847	413,696	417,601	422,375	421,986
Balance Sheet								
Current Assets	718,029	735,824	748,313	715,881	144,786	413,447	378,899	270,310
Total Assets	5,128,766	5,219,459	5,244,388	5,122,569	5,261,899	5,437,716	4,981,080	4,616,313
Current Liabilities	438,234	234,422	224,395	257,812	235,552	499,018	407,905	444,139
Long-Term Obligations	1,284,551	1,521,211	1,520,870	1,520,530	2,005,000	1,752,000	1,147,000	1,012,000
Total Liabilities	2,484,172	2,577,428	2,537,209	2,554,902	3,252,711	3,294,983	2,776,478	2,484,866
Stockholders' Equity	2,644,594	2,642,031	2,707,179	2,567,667	2,009,188	2,142,733	2,204,602	2,131,447
Shares Outstanding	462,507	462,492	465,521	465,150	413,875	413,022	416,396	420,050
Statistical Record								
Return on Assets %	N.M.	N.M.	N.M.	N.M.	N.M.	2.01	5.83	2.94
Return on Equity %	N.M.	N.M.	N.M.	N.M.	N.M.	4.81	12.90	6.20
EBITDA Margin %	21.71	25.54	36.86	2.29	39.04	34.08	69.02	63.33
Net Margin %	10.62	13.01	20.42	N.M.	N.M.	4.81	16.02	10.94
Asset Turnover	0.32	0.30	0.25	0.22	0.25	0.42	0.36	0.27
Current Ratio	1.64	3.14	3.33	2.78	0.61	0.83	0.93	0.61
Debt to Equity	0.49	0.58	0.56	0.59	1.00	0.82	0.52	0.47
Price Range	26.96-20.05	26.50-20.05	26.50-20.05	26.50-15.48	35.40-15.03	41.61-28.48	39.93-23.77	25.54-14.77
P/E Ratio	...	...	...	...	...	166.44-113.92	60.50-36.01	82.37-47.65
Average Yield %	0.59	0.47	0.34	0.35	0.30	0.23	0.18	0.20

Address: Three Memorial City Plaza, 840 Gessner Road, Suite 1400, Houston, TX 77024 **Telephone:** 281-589-4600 **Fax:** 281-589-4653	**Web Site:** www.cabotog.com **Officers:** Dan O. Dinges - Chairman, President, Chief Executive Officer Steven W. Lindeman - Senior Vice President	**Auditors:** PricewaterhouseCoopers LLP **Investor Contact:** 281-589-4993 **Transfer Agents:** Wells Fargo Bank N.A., Mendota Heights, MN

CALATLANTIC GROUP INC

Exchange	Symbol	Price	52Wk Range	Yield	P/E
NYS	CAA	$56.39 (12/29/2017)	57.10-33.10	0.28	16.68

*7 Year Price Score 89.37 *NYSE Composite Index=100 *12 Month Price Score 128.80

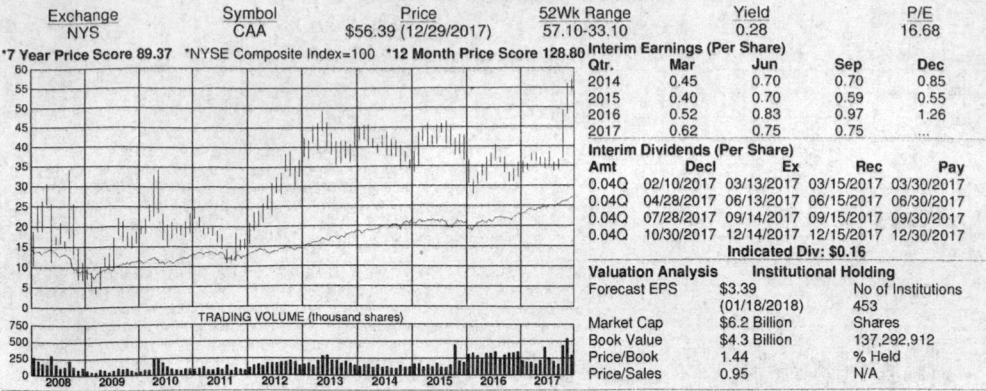

Interim Earnings (Per Share)

Qtr.	Mar	Jun	Sep	Dec
2014	0.45	0.70	0.70	0.85
2015	0.40	0.70	0.59	0.55
2016	0.52	0.83	0.97	1.26
2017	0.62	0.75	0.75	

Interim Dividends (Per Share)

Amt	Decl	Ex	Rec	Pay
0.04Q	02/10/2017	03/13/2017	03/15/2017	03/30/2017
0.04Q	04/28/2017	06/13/2017	06/15/2017	06/30/2017
0.04Q	07/28/2017	09/14/2017	09/15/2017	09/30/2017
0.04Q	10/30/2017	12/14/2017	12/15/2017	12/30/2017

Indicated Div: $0.16

Valuation Analysis

		Institutional Holding	
Forecast EPS	$3.39	No of Institutions	
	(01/18/2018)	453	
Market Cap	$6.2 Billion	Shares	
Book Value	$4.3 Billion	137,292,912	
Price/Book	1.44	% Held	
Price/Sales	0.95	N/A	

Business Summary: Builders (MIC: 2.2.5 SIC: 1531 NAIC: 236117)

CalAtlantic Group is a builder of single-family attached and detached homes, in over 40 metropolitan statistical areas spanning 17 states. Co. also provides mortgage, title and escrow services. Co. operates two principal businesses: homebuilding, which acquires and develops land and constructs and sells single-family attached and detached homes, and is divided into four reportable segments: North, Southeast, Southwest and West; and financial services, which consists of its mortgage financing, title, escrow and insurance services operations. Mortgage financing operation provides mortgage financing to Co.'s homebuyers in substantially all of the markets in which Co. operates.

Recent Developments: For the quarter ended Sep 30 2017, net income decreased 29.5% to US$93.4 million from US$132.3 million in the year-earlier quarter. Revenues were US$1.54 billion, down 9.2% from US$1.69 billion the year before. Direct operating expenses declined 6.3% to US$1.23 billion from US$1.31 billion in the comparable period the year before. Indirect operating expenses decreased 1.4% to US$168.4 million from US$170.8 million in the equivalent prior-year period.

Prospects: Our evaluation of CalAtlantic Group Inc. as of Jan. 14, 2018 is the result of our systematic analysis on three basic characteristics: earnings strength, relative valuation, and recent stock price movement. The company has generated a negative trend in earnings per share over the past 5 quarters. However, while recent estimates for the company have been mixed, CAA has posted results that fell short of analysts expectations. Based on operating earnings yield, the company is undervalued when compared to all of the companies in our coverage universe. Share price changes over the past year indicates that CAA will perform poorly over the near term.

Financial Data

(US$ in Thousands)	9 Mos	6 Mos	3 Mos	12/31/2016	12/31/2015	12/31/2014	12/31/2013	12/31/2012
Earnings Per Share	3.38	3.60	3.68	3.60	2.26	2.70	2.35	7.20
Cash Flow Per Share	0.28	2.28	3.86	2.72	(3.78)	(6.50)	(3.05)	(6.99)
Tang Book Value Per Share	30.34	29.50	28.95	28.29	24.14	30.47	26.46	29.45
Dividends Per Share	0.160	0.160	0.160	0.160	0.040	...	...	...
Dividend Payout %	4.73	4.44	4.35	4.44	1.77	...	...	...
Income Statement								
Total Revenue	4,535,050	2,999,046	1,357,655	6,476,735	3,540,113	2,435,297	1,939,519	1,258,258
EBITDA	436,810	290,998	130,274	828,557	397,298	364,029	269,340	96,304
Depn & Amortn	14,282	9,216	4,294	79,498	56,775	13,397	12,591	9,631
Income Before Taxes	422,528	281,782	125,980	749,059	340,523	350,632	256,749	80,277
Income Taxes	157,322	104,502	47,248	268,386	128,980	134,099	68,983	(453,234)
Net Income	274,966	181,614	82,620	484,730	213,509	215,865	188,715	531,421
Average Shares	124,449	131,636	132,505	135,984	81,512	63,257	58,234	44,103
Balance Sheet								
Current Assets	7,219,202	7,011,044	6,852,588	6,763,217	6,398,703	3,611,272	3,034,920	2,429,312
Total Assets	9,079,034	8,866,796	8,693,770	8,709,044	8,345,505	4,174,420	3,662,105	3,113,074
Current Liabilities	1,056,607	708,325	826,286	811,685	670,474	268,868	250,037	220,590
Long-Term Obligations	3,679,324	3,912,101	3,572,368	3,667,214	3,791,121	2,225,495	1,940,462	1,634,177
Total Liabilities	4,749,823	4,631,090	4,406,397	4,501,458	4,484,069	2,497,732	2,193,145	1,857,258
Stockholders' Equity	4,329,211	4,235,706	4,287,373	4,207,586	3,861,436	1,676,688	1,468,960	1,255,816
Shares Outstanding	110,217	110,204	114,587	114,429	121,286	55,028	55,523	42,649
Statistical Record								
Return on Assets %	4.99	5.49	5.78	5.67	3.41	5.51	5.57	19.95
Return on Equity %	10.44	11.62	12.02	11.98	7.71	13.72	13.85	56.39
EBITDA Margin %	9.63	9.70	9.60	12.79	11.22	14.95	13.89	7.65
Net Margin %	6.06	6.06	6.09	7.48	6.03	8.86	9.73	42.23
Asset Turnover	0.74	0.76	0.77	0.76	0.57	0.62	0.57	0.47
Current Ratio	6.83	9.90	8.29	8.33	9.54	13.43	12.14	11.01
Debt to Equity	0.85	0.92	0.83	0.87	0.98	1.33	1.32	1.30
Price Range	38.56-30.88	40.44-30.88	40.44-30.88	40.44-27.88	46.50-33.45	45.75-34.40	49.05-35.45	38.95-15.65
P/E Ratio	11.41-9.14	11.23-8.58	10.99-8.39	11.23-7.74	20.58-14.80	16.94-12.74	20.87-15.09	5.41-2.17
Average Yield %	0.46	0.45	0.46	0.47	0.10	...	...	...

Address: 1100 Wilson Boulevard, #2100, Arlington, VA 22209 Telephone: 240-532-3806	Web Site: www.calatlantichomes.com Officers: Scott D. Stowell - Executive Chairman, President, Chief Executive Officer, Chief Operating Officer Larry T. Nicholson - President, Chief Executive Officer	Auditors: Ernst & Young LLP Transfer Agents: Computershare Shareowner Services LLC, Pittsburgh, PA

CALIFORNIA WATER SERVICE GROUP (DE)

Exchange	Symbol	Price	52Wk Range	Yield	P/E	Div Achiever
NYS	CWT	$45.35 (12/29/2017)	45.60-32.50	1.59	31.94	49 Years

*7 Year Price Score 121.06 *NYSE Composite Index=100 *12 Month Price Score 109.03

Interim Earnings (Per Share)

Qtr.	Mar	Jun	Sep	Dec
2014	(0.11)	0.36	0.70	0.24
2015	0.03	0.21	0.52	0.18
2016	(0.02)	0.24	0.48	0.31
2017	0.02	0.39	0.70	...

Interim Dividends (Per Share)

Amt	Decl	Ex	Rec	Pay
0.18Q	01/25/2017	02/02/2017	02/06/2017	02/17/2017
0.18Q	04/26/2017	05/04/2017	05/08/2017	05/19/2017
0.18Q	07/26/2017	08/03/2017	08/07/2017	08/18/2017
0.18Q	10/25/2017	11/03/2017	11/06/2017	11/17/2017

Indicated Div: $0.72 (Div. Reinv. Plan)

Valuation Analysis / **Institutional Holding**

Forecast EPS	$1.31 (01/18/2018)	No of Institutions	277
Market Cap	$2.2 Billion	Shares	40,921,568
Book Value	$687.7 Million	% Held	63.99
Price/Book	3.17		
Price/Sales	3.32		

Business Summary: Water Utilities (MIC: 3.2.1 SIC: 4941 NAIC: 221310)

California Water Service Group is a holding company. Through its subsidiaries, Co. produces, purchases, stores, treats, tests, distributes and sells water for domestic, industrial, public and irrigation uses, and for fire protection. Co. also provides non-regulated water-related services under agreements with municipalities and other private companies. The non-regulated services include water system operation, billing and meter reading, the lease of communication antenna sites, lab services, and promotion of other non- regulated services. As of Dec 31 2016, Co. provided service to approximately 482,400 customers in approximately 100 California communities through 25 separate districts.

Recent Developments: For the quarter ended Sep 30 2017, net income increased 48.0% to US$33.8 million from US$22.9 million in the year-earlier quarter. Revenues were US$211.7 million, up 14.9% from US$184.3 million the year before. Operating income was US$41.2 million versus US$30.1 million in the prior-year quarter, an increase of 37.1%. Direct operating expenses rose 7.6% to US$102.5 million from US$95.3 million in the comparable period the year before. Indirect operating expenses increased 15.4% to US$68.0 million from US$58.9 million in the equivalent prior-year period.

Prospects: Our evaluation of California Water Service Group as of Jan. 14, 2018 is the result of our systematic analysis on three basic characteristics: earnings strength, relative valuation, and recent stock price movement. The company has generated a negative trend in earnings per share over the past 5 quarters and while recent estimates for the company have remained steady, CWT has posted better than expected results. Based on operating earnings yield, the company is about fairly valued when compared to all of the companies in our coverage universe. Share price changes over the past year indicates that CWT will perform very well over the near term.

Financial Data

(US$ in Thousands)	9 Mos	6 Mos	3 Mos	12/31/2016	12/31/2015	12/31/2014	12/31/2013	12/31/2012
Earnings Per Share	1.42	1.20	1.05	1.01	0.94	1.19	1.02	1.17
Cash Flow Per Share	3.05	2.84	2.98	3.32	3.02	2.68	2.68	3.14
Tang Book Value Per Share	14.27	13.73	13.51	13.69	13.36	13.05	12.49	11.24
Dividends Per Share	0.713	0.705	0.698	0.690	0.670	0.650	0.640	0.630
Dividend Payout %	50.18	58.75	66.43	68.32	71.28	54.62	62.75	53.85
Income Statement								
Total Revenue	504,899	293,168	122,036	609,370	588,368	597,499	584,103	559,966
EBITDA	163,935	84,473	28,122	170,036	160,783	174,346	156,421	154,252
Depn & Amortn	59,016	39,328	19,658	66,074	64,007	64,119	61,331	57,973
Income Before Taxes	79,611	28,414	248	73,479	69,545	83,465	66,301	68,184
Income Taxes	26,099	8,751	(884)	24,804	24,528	26,727	19,047	19,356
Net Income	53,512	19,663	1,132	48,675	45,017	56,738	47,254	48,828
Average Shares	48,017	48,020	47,984	47,956	47,880	47,829	46,417	41,892
Balance Sheet								
Current Assets	180,485	170,580	128,205	142,069	127,578	154,124	139,490	146,564
Total Assets	2,603,104	2,533,026	2,440,298	2,411,745	2,246,095	2,187,351	1,959,855	1,995,924
Current Liabilities	380,361	361,027	293,373	250,230	148,455	217,706	166,584	243,067
Long-Term Obligations	519,700	519,875	521,715	531,745	512,287	419,233	426,142	434,467
Total Liabilities	1,915,381	1,871,192	1,788,965	1,752,274	1,603,940	1,560,725	1,361,099	1,522,212
Stockholders' Equity	687,723	661,834	651,333	659,471	642,155	626,626	598,756	473,712
Shares Outstanding	48,015	48,018	48,022	47,964	47,875	47,806	47,740	41,908
Statistical Record								
Return on Assets %	2.75	2.36	2.14	2.08	2.03	2.74	2.39	2.53
Return on Equity %	10.24	8.88	7.88	7.46	7.10	9.26	8.81	10.55
EBITDA Margin %	32.47	28.81	23.04	27.90	27.33	29.18	26.78	27.55
Net Margin %	10.60	6.71	0.93	7.99	7.65	9.50	8.09	8.72
Asset Turnover	0.26	0.26	0.26	0.26	0.27	0.29	0.30	0.29
Current Ratio	0.47	0.47	0.44	0.57	0.86	0.71	0.84	0.60
Debt to Equity	0.76	0.79	0.80	0.81	0.80	0.67	0.71	0.92
Price Range	39.50-30.28	38.30-30.05	37.60-26.59	36.80-22.96	25.96-19.68	26.09-20.44	23.23-18.35	19.21-17.22
P/E Ratio	27.82-21.32	31.92-25.04	35.81-25.32	36.44-22.73	27.62-20.94	21.92-17.18	22.77-17.99	16.42-14.72
Average Yield %	2.02	2.08	2.16	2.31	2.87	2.78	3.12	3.46

Address: 1720 North First Street, San Jose, CA 95112 **Telephone:** 408-367-8200	**Web Site:** www.calwatergroup.com **Officers:** Peter C. Nelson - Chairman, President, Chief Executive Officer Martin A. Kropelnicki - President, Chief Executive Officer, Vice President, Chief Financial Officer, Chief Operating Officer	**Auditors:** Deloitte & Touche LLP **Investor Contact:** 408-367-8200 **Transfer Agents:** American Stock Transfer & Trust Company, Brooklyn, NY

CALLON PETROLEUM CO. (DE)

Exchange	Symbol	Price	52Wk Range	Yield	P/E
NYS	CPE	$12.15 (12/29/2017)	16.07-9.54	N/A	22.92

*7 Year Price Score 115.79 *NYSE Composite Index=100 *12 Month Price Score 89.27

Interim Earnings (Per Share)

Qtr.	Mar	Jun	Sep	Dec
2014	0.00	0.07	0.23	0.34
2015	(0.21)	(0.11)	(1.72)	(1.67)
2016	(0.51)	(0.61)	0.14	0.07
2017	0.22	0.16	0.08	...

Interim Dividends (Per Share)

No Dividends Paid

Valuation Analysis		Institutional Holding	
Forecast EPS	$0.40	No of Institutions	
	(01/18/2018)	367	
Market Cap	$2.5 Billion	Shares	
Book Value	$1.8 Billion	273,094,272	
Price/Book	1.34	% Held	
Price/Sales	7.73	71.26	

Business Summary: Production & Extraction (MIC: 9.1.1 SIC: 1311 NAIC: 211111)

Callon Petroleum is engaged in the exploration, development, acquisition and production of oil and natural gas properties in the Permian Basin in West Texas. As of Dec 31 2016, Co.'s estimated net proved reserves totaled 91.6 million barrels of oil equivalents and included 71.1 million barrels of oil and 122.6 billion cubic feet of natural gas.

Recent Developments: For the quarter ended Sep 30 2017, net income decreased 19.2% to US$17.1 million from US$21.1 million in the year-earlier quarter. Revenues were US$84.6 million, up 51.3% from US$55.9 million the year before. Operating income was US$31.4 million versus US$16.7 million in the prior-year quarter, an increase of 88.7%. Direct operating expenses rose 27.0% to US$17.1 million from US$13.4 million in the comparable period the year before. Indirect operating expenses increased 39.8% to US$36.1 million from US$25.8 million in the equivalent prior-year period.

Prospects: Our evaluation of Callon Petroleum Co. as of Jan. 14, 2018 is the result of our systematic analysis on three basic characteristics: earnings strength, relative valuation, and recent stock price movement. The company has generated a negative trend in earnings per share over the past 5 quarters and while recent estimates for the company have been mixed, CPE has posted results that fell short of analysts expectations. Based on operating earnings yield, the company is about fairly valued when compared to all of the companies in our coverage universe. Share price changes over the past year indicates that CPE will perform very poorly over the near term.

Financial Data

(US$ in Thousands)	9 Mos	6 Mos	3 Mos	12/31/2016	12/31/2015	12/31/2014	12/31/2013	12/31/2012
Earnings Per Share	0.53	0.59	(0.18)	(0.78)	(3.77)	0.65	(0.01)	0.07
Cash Flow Per Share	1.08	0.88	0.77	0.94	1.32	2.10	1.35	1.29
Tang Book Value Per Share	9.08	9.00	8.85	8.62	4.53	7.85	6.92	5.18
Income Statement								
Total Revenue	248,261	163,647	81,363	200,851	137,512	151,862	102,569	110,733
EBITDA	102,019	83,816	48,925	(79,163)	(179,689)	71,508	14,235	14,612
Depn & Amortn	1,695	1,254	665	793	865	836	750	760
Income Before Taxes	98,626	81,308	47,595	(91,827)	(201,665)	60,900	7,391	4,744
Income Taxes	1,026	789	466	(14)	38,474	23,134	3,104	2,223
Net Income	97,600	80,519	47,129	(91,813)	(240,139)	37,766	4,304	2,747
Average Shares	202,337	201,905	201,740	126,258	65,708	45,961	40,133	40,337
Balance Sheet								
Current Assets	149,498	228,570	115,996	725,126	62,252	60,457	29,564	19,923
Total Assets	2,614,083	2,581,664	2,335,579	2,267,587	788,594	876,770	423,953	378,173
Current Liabilities	178,092	161,874	155,409	131,550	87,877	98,812	62,793	38,477
Long-Term Obligations	595,115	595,138	390,536	390,219	328,565	335,000	75,748	120,668
Total Liabilities	781,218	765,767	555,546	534,185	425,836	443,035	144,859	172,202
Stockholders' Equity	1,832,865	1,815,897	1,780,033	1,733,402	362,758	433,735	279,094	205,971
Shares Outstanding	201,827	201,806	201,054	201,041	80,087	55,225	40,345	39,800
Statistical Record								
Return on Assets %	4.63	5.43	N.M.	N.M.	N.M.	5.81	1.07	0.73
Return on Equity %	6.53	8.08	N.M.	N.M.	N.M.	10.60	1.77	1.35
EBITDA Margin %	41.09	51.22	60.13	N.M.	N.M.	47.09	13.88	13.20
Net Margin %	39.31	49.20	57.92	N.M.	N.M.	24.87	4.20	2.48
Asset Turnover	0.15	0.16	0.16	0.13	0.17	0.23	0.26	0.30
Current Ratio	0.84	1.41	0.75	5.51	0.71	0.61	0.47	0.52
Debt to Equity	0.32	0.33	0.22	0.23	0.91	0.77	0.27	0.59
Price Range	17.64-9.54	17.64-9.69	17.64-8.50	17.64-5.23	10.01-4.78	11.94-4.14	7.59-3.27	7.65-3.88
P/E Ratio	33.28-18.00	29.90-16.42	...	...	...	18.37-6.37	...	109.29-55.43

Address: 200 North Canal Street, Natchez, MS 39120
Telephone: 601-442-1601

Web Site: www.callon.com
Officers: Joseph C. Gatto - President, Chief Executive Officer, Chief Financial Officer, Senior Vice President, Treasurer Bobby F. Weatherly - Executive Vice President, Chief Financial Officer, Chief Administrative Officer, Corporate Secretary

Auditors: Grant Thornton LLP
Investor Contact: 601-442-1601
Transfer Agents: American Stock Transfer & Trust Company, New York, NY

CALPINE CORP

Exchange	Symbol	Price	52Wk Range	Yield	P/E
NYS	CPN	$15.13 (12/29/2017)	15.14-9.59	N/A	N/A

*7 Year Price Score 60.43 *NYSE Composite Index=100 *12 Month Price Score 107.93

TRADING VOLUME (thousand shares)

Interim Earnings (Per Share)

Qtr.	Mar	Jun	Sep	Dec
2014	(0.04)	0.33	1.52	0.54
2015	(0.03)	0.05	0.76	(0.13)
2016	(0.56)	(0.08)	0.83	0.07
2017	(0.16)	(0.61)	0.63	...

Interim Dividends (Per Share)

No Dividends Paid

Valuation Analysis / Institutional Holding

Valuation Analysis		Institutional Holding	
Forecast EPS	$0.32	No of Institutions	
	(01/18/2018)	441	
Market Cap	$5.5 Billion	Shares	
Book Value	$3.2 Billion	341,312,256	
Price/Book	1.68	% Held	
Price/Sales	0.64	N/A	

Business Summary: Electric Utilities (MIC: 3.1.1 SIC: 4911 NAIC: 221122)

Calpine is a power generation company that owns and operates natural gas-fired and geothermal power plants in North America and has a presence in wholesale power markets in California, Texas and the Northeast and Mid-Atlantic regions. Co. sells wholesale power, steam, capacity, renewable energy credits and ancillary services to its customers, which include utilities, independent electric system operators, industrial and agricultural companies, retail power providers, municipalities, power marketers as well as retail commercial, industrial, governmental and residential customers. As of Dec 31 2016, Co. served customers in 25 states in the U.S. and in Canada and Mexico.

Recent Developments: For the quarter ended Sep 30 2017, net income decreased 23.3% to US$231.0 million from US$301.0 million in the year-earlier quarter. Revenues were US$2.59 billion, up 9.8% from US$2.36 billion the year before. Operating income was US$393.0 million versus US$462.0 million in the prior-year quarter, a decrease of 14.9%. Direct operating expenses rose 15.5% to US$1.95 billion from US$1.69 billion in the comparable period the year before. Indirect operating expenses increased 18.4% to US$244.0 million from US$206.0 million in the equivalent prior-year period.

Prospects: Our evaluation of Calpine Corp. as of Jan. 14, 2018 is the result of our systematic analysis on three basic characteristics: earnings strength, relative valuation, and recent stock price movement. The company has produced a positive trend in earnings per share over the past 5 quarters and while recent estimates for the company have remained steady, CPN has posted results that fell short of analysts expectations. Based on operating earnings yield, the company is overvalued when compared to all of the companies in our coverage universe. Share price changes over the past year indicates that CPN will perform well over the near term.

Financial Data

(US$ in Thousands)	9 Mos	6 Mos	3 Mos	12/31/2016	12/31/2015	12/31/2014	12/31/2013	12/31/2012
Earnings Per Share	(0.07)	0.13	0.66	0.26	0.64	2.31	0.03	0.42
Cash Flow Per Share	3.29	3.25	3.10	2.90	2.38	2.11	1.25	1.39
Tang Book Value Per Share	6.79	6.03	6.50	9.10	8.72	8.84	8.19	8.74
Income Statement								
Total Revenue	6,951,000	4,365,000	2,281,000	6,716,000	6,472,000	8,030,000	6,301,000	5,478,000
EBITDA	1,127,000	561,000	311,000	1,394,000	1,368,000	2,188,000	1,334,000	1,472,000
Depn & Amortn	691,000	510,000	265,000	628,000	595,000	591,000	654,000	557,000
Income Before Taxes	(33,000)	(262,000)	(113,000)	135,000	149,000	958,000	(10,000)	190,000
Income Taxes	...	2,000	(61,000)	48,000	(76,000)	22,000	2,000	19,000
Net Income	(47,000)	(272,000)	(56,000)	92,000	235,000	946,000	14,000	199,000
Average Shares	358,844	355,358	354,682	356,110	364,886	409,360	444,773	471,743
Balance Sheet								
Current Assets	2,388,000	3,187,000	3,521,000	4,432,000	4,095,000	4,220,000	2,856,000	2,832,000
Total Assets	16,792,000	17,975,000	18,576,000	19,317,000	18,833,000	18,378,000	16,559,000	16,549,000
Current Liabilities	1,794,000	2,873,000	3,120,000	3,702,000	3,048,000	3,199,000	1,531,000	1,318,000
Long-Term Obligations	11,281,000	11,307,000	11,344,000	11,431,000	11,868,000	11,083,000	10,908,000	10,635,000
Total Liabilities	13,548,000	14,979,000	15,364,000	16,049,000	15,724,000	15,000,000	13,045,000	12,555,000
Stockholders' Equity	3,244,000	2,996,000	3,212,000	3,268,000	3,109,000	3,378,000	3,514,000	3,994,000
Shares Outstanding	360,613	360,670	360,797	359,061	356,662	381,921	429,038	457,048
Statistical Record								
Return on Assets %	N.M.	0.26	1.26	0.48	1.26	5.42	0.08	1.17
Return on Equity %	N.M.	1.60	7.64	2.88	7.25	27.45	0.37	4.78
EBITDA Margin %	16.21	12.85	13.63	20.76	21.14	27.25	21.17	26.87
Net Margin %	N.M.	N.M.	N.M.	1.37	3.63	11.78	0.22	3.63
Asset Turnover	0.49	0.46	0.40	0.35	0.35	0.46	0.38	0.32
Current Ratio	1.33	1.11	1.13	1.20	1.34	1.32	1.87	2.15
Debt to Equity	3.48	3.77	3.53	3.50	3.82	3.28	3.10	2.66
Price Range	14.92-9.59	15.02-9.59	16.00-10.41	16.00-10.41	23.26-11.80	24.29-18.53	22.01-18.05	18.90-14.51
P/E Ratio	...	115.54-73.77	24.24-15.77	61.54-40.04	36.34-18.44	10.52-8.02	733.67-601.67	45.00-34.55

Address: 717 Texas Avenue, Suite 1000, Houston, TX 77002 **Telephone:** 713-830-2000	**Web Site:** www.calpine.com **Officers:** Frank Cassidy - Chairman John B. (Thad) Hill - President, Chief Executive Officer, Executive Vice President, Chief Operating Officer, Chief Commercial Officer	**Auditors:** PricewaterhouseCoopers LLP **Investor Contact:** 713-830-8775 **Transfer Agents:** Computershare, Inc., Providence, RI

CAMDEN PROPERTY TRUST

Exchange	Symbol	Price	52Wk Range	Yield	P/E
NYS	CPT	$92.06 (12/29/2017)	95.70-79.06	3.26	55.79

*7 Year Price Score 93.88 *NYSE Composite Index=100 *12 Month Price Score 100.01

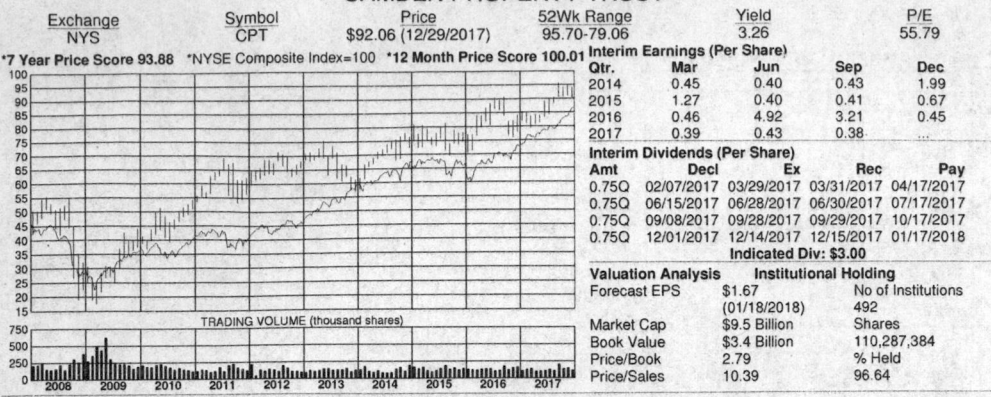

Interim Earnings (Per Share)

Qtr.	Mar	Jun	Sep	Dec
2014	0.45	0.40	0.43	1.99
2015	1.27	0.40	0.41	0.67
2016	0.46	4.92	3.21	0.45
2017	0.39	0.43	0.38	...

Interim Dividends (Per Share)

Amt	Decl	Ex	Rec	Pay
0.75Q	02/07/2017	03/29/2017	03/31/2017	04/17/2017
0.75Q	06/15/2017	06/28/2017	06/30/2017	07/17/2017
0.75Q	09/08/2017	09/28/2017	09/29/2017	10/17/2017
0.75Q	12/01/2017	12/14/2017	12/15/2017	01/17/2018

Indicated Div: $3.00

Valuation Analysis		Institutional Holding	
Forecast EPS	$1.67	No of Institutions	
	(01/18/2018)	492	
Market Cap	$9.5 Billion	Shares	
Book Value	$3.4 Billion	110,287,384	
Price/Book	2.79	% Held	
Price/Sales	10.39	96.64	

TRADING VOLUME (thousand shares)

Business Summary: REITs (MIC: 5.3.1 SIC: 6798 NAIC: 525930)

Camden Property Trust is a real estate investment trust. Co. is primarily engaged in the ownership, management, development, redevelopment, acquisition, and construction of multifamily apartment communities. Co.'s properties typically consist of mid-rise buildings or two and three story buildings in a landscaped setting and provide residents with a variety of amenities common to multifamily rental properties. As of Dec 31 2016, Co. owned interests in, operated, or was developing 159 multifamily properties comprised of 55,366 apartment homes across the U.S. Co. also own land holdings which it may develop into multifamily communities.

Recent Developments: For the quarter ended Sep 30 2017, income from continuing operations decreased 88.3% to US$35.5 million from US$303.4 million in the year-earlier quarter. Net income decreased 88.3% to US$35.5 million from US$303.4 million in the year-earlier quarter. Revenues were US$233.9 million, up 3.8% from US$225.4 million the year before. Revenues from property income rose 3.6% to US$228.2 million from US$220.2 million in the corresponding quarter a year earlier.

Prospects: Our evaluation of Camden Property Trust as of Jan. 14, 2018 is the result of our systematic analysis on three basic characteristics: earnings strength, relative valuation, and recent stock price movement. The company has produced a positive trend in earnings per share over the past 5 quarters. Because the company lacks sufficient analyst estimate data, we place greater weight on the historical EPS trend as the measure of earnings strength. Based on operating earnings yield, the company is overvalued when compared to all of the companies in our coverage universe. Share price changes over the past year indicates that CPT will perform very well over the near term.

Financial Data

(US$ in Thousands)	9 Mos	6 Mos	3 Mos	12/31/2016	12/31/2015	12/31/2014	12/31/2013	12/31/2012
Earnings Per Share	1.65	4.48	8.97	9.05	2.76	3.27	3.78	3.30
Cash Flow Per Share	4.61	4.71	4.67	4.93	4.75	4.75	4.64	3.86
Tang Book Value Per Share	32.96	30.29	30.60	30.82	28.87	28.85	27.85	26.64
Dividends Per Share	3.000	7.250	7.250	7.250	2.800	2.640	2.520	2.240
Dividend Payout %	181.82	161.83	80.82	80.11	101.45	80.73	66.67	67.88
Income Statement								
Total Revenue	688,581	454,639	225,886	891,024	900,260	858,589	810,048	744,315
EBITDA	368,263	245,692	120,699*	793,167	608,360	628,446	453,904	468,132
Depn & Amortn	195,781	128,767	63,734	250,146	257,082	238,989	223,198	213,480
Income Before Taxes	107,929	73,197	34,643	449,876	253,966	296,194	132,577	150,370
Income Taxes	1,008	496	471	1,617	1,872	1,903	1,826	1,208
Net Income	108,433	74,049	34,861	819,823	249,315	292,089	336,364	285,465
Average Shares	92,033	91,041	90,949	89,903	89,490	88,468	88,494	85,556
Balance Sheet								
Current Assets	383,072	48,222	277,338	369,854	41,688	185,793	52,117	66,285
Total Assets	6,168,895	5,798,600	5,935,346	6,028,152	6,037,612	6,056,907	5,632,141	5,385,172
Current Liabilities	270,546	234,660	214,094	256,015	242,851	256,767	205,742	180,317
Long-Term Obligations	2,204,251	2,303,892	2,450,295	2,480,588	2,724,687	2,743,539	2,530,766	2,510,468
Total Liabilities	2,781,988	2,837,452	2,944,025	3,013,279	3,221,055	3,241,305	2,940,605	2,822,073
Stockholders' Equity	3,386,907	2,961,148	2,991,321	3,014,873	2,816,557	2,815,602	2,691,536	2,563,099
Shares Outstanding	102,767	97,761	97,763	97,818	97,571	97,604	96,660	96,201
Statistical Record								
Return on Assets %	2.44	6.77	13.58	13.55	4.12	5.00	6.11	5.69
Return on Equity %	4.65	13.19	28.13	28.04	8.85	10.61	12.80	12.88
EBITDA Margin %	53.48	54.04	53.43	89.02	67.58	73.20	56.03	62.89
Net Margin %	15.75	16.29	15.43	92.01	27.69	34.02	41.52	38.35
Asset Turnover	0.15	0.15	0.15	0.15	0.15	0.15	0.15	0.15
Current Ratio	1.42	0.21	1.30	1.44	0.17	0.72	0.25	0.37
Debt to Equity	0.65	0.78	0.82	0.82	0.97	0.97	0.94	0.98
Price Range	95.70-76.00	90.67-76.00	90.67-76.00	90.67-70.55	81.28-69.45	77.87-56.88	75.46-56.79	71.59-59.61
P/E Ratio	58.00-46.06	20.24-16.96	10.11-8.47	10.02-7.80	29.45-25.16	23.81-17.39	19.96-15.02	21.69-18.06
Average Yield %	3.58	8.70	8.71	8.87	3.68	3.77	3.76	3.39

Address: 11 Greenway Plaza, Suite 2400, Houston, TX 77046 **Telephone:** 713-354-2500	**Web Site:** www.camdenliving.com **Officers:** Richard J. Campo - Chairman, Chief Executive Officer D. Keith Oden - President	**Auditors:** Deloitte & Touche LLP **Investor Contact:** 713-354-2549 **Transfer Agents:** American Stock Transfer and Trust Company, New York, NY

CAMPBELL SOUP CO.

Exchange	Symbol	Price	52Wk Range	Yield	P/E
NYS	CPB	$48.11 (12/29/2017)	63.84-45.13	2.91	16.82

*7 Year Price Score 93.14 ***NYSE Composite Index=100** ***12 Month Price Score 85.22**

TRADING VOLUME (thousand shares)

Interim Earnings (Per Share)

Qtr.	Oct	Jan	Apr	Jul
2014-15	0.74	0.66	0.58	0.23
2015-16	0.62	0.85	0.59	(0.26)
2016-17	0.94	0.33	0.58	1.04
2017-18	0.91	...	...	...

Interim Dividends (Per Share)

Amt	Decl	Ex	Rec	Pay
0.35Q	03/22/2017	04/10/2017	04/12/2017	05/01/2017
0.35Q	06/27/2017	07/11/2017	07/13/2017	07/31/2017
0.35Q	09/27/2017	10/12/2017	10/13/2017	10/30/2017
0.35Q	11/16/2017	01/09/2018	01/10/2018	01/29/2018

Indicated Div: $1.40 (Div. Reinv. Plan)

Valuation Analysis

Forecast EPS	$2.96 (01/18/2018)
Market Cap	$15.5 Billion
Book Value	$1.7 Billion
Price/Book	9.24
Price/Sales	1.98

Institutional Holding

No of Institutions	842
Shares	189,454,816
% Held	41.37

Business Summary: Food (MIC: 1.2.1 SIC: 2032 NAIC: 311422)

Campbell Soup is a manufacturer and marketer of food and beverage products. Co. manages its businesses in three segments: Americas Simple Meals and Beverages, which includes the retail and food service businesses in the U.S., Canada and Latin America; Global Biscuits and Snacks, which includes Pepperidge Farm cookies, crackers, bakery and frozen products in U.S. retail, Arnott's biscuits in Australia and Asia Pacific, and Kelsen cookies globally; and Campbell Fresh, which includes Bolthouse Farms fresh carrots, carrot ingredients, refrigerated beverages and refrigerated salad dressings, Garden Fresh Gourmet salsa, hummus, dips and tortilla chips, and the U.S. refrigerated soup business.

Recent Developments: For the quarter ended Oct 29 2017, net income decreased 5.8% to US$275.0 million from US$292.0 million in the year-earlier quarter. Revenues were US$2.16 billion, down 1.9% from US$2.20 billion the year before. Operating income was US$412.0 million versus US$457.0 million in the prior-year quarter, a decrease of 9.8%. Direct operating expenses rose 2.0% to US$1.38 billion from US$1.35 billion in the comparable period the year before. Indirect operating expenses decreased 5.8% to US$371.0 million from US$394.0 million in the equivalent prior-year period.

Prospects: Our evaluation of Campbell Soup Co. as of Jan. 14, 2018 is the result of our systematic analysis on three basic characteristics: earnings strength, relative valuation, and recent stock price movement. The company has generated a negative trend in earnings per share over the past 5 quarters. However, while recent estimates for the company have been lowered by analysts, CPB has posted results that fell short of analysts expectations. Based on operating earnings yield, the company is undervalued when compared to all of the companies in our coverage universe. Share price changes over the past year indicates that CPB will perform in line with the market over the near term.

Financial Data
(US$ in Thousands)

	3 Mos	07/31/2017	07/31/2016	08/02/2015	08/03/2014	07/28/2013	07/29/2012	07/31/2011
Earnings Per Share	2.86	2.89	1.81	2.21	2.59	1.44	2.41	2.42
Cash Flow Per Share	4.18	4.23	4.75	3.80	2.82	3.25	3.54	3.51
Dividends Per Share	1.400	1.400	1.248	1.248	1.248	1.160	1.160	1.145
Dividend Payout %	48.95	48.44	68.95	56.47	48.19	80.56	48.13	47.31
Income Statement								
Total Revenue	2,161,000	7,890,000	7,961,000	8,082,000	8,268,000	8,052,000	7,707,000	7,719,000
EBITDA	494,000	1,699,000	1,248,000	1,381,000	1,479,000	1,473,000	1,470,000	1,544,000
Depn & Amortn	82,000	299,000	288,000	286,000	287,000	393,000	258,000	265,000
Income Before Taxes	382,000	1,293,000	849,000	990,000	1,073,000	955,000	1,106,000	1,168,000
Income Taxes	107,000	406,000	286,000	299,000	347,000	275,000	342,000	366,000
Net Income	275,000	887,000	563,000	691,000	818,000	458,000	774,000	805,000
Average Shares	302,000	307,000	311,000	313,000	316,000	317,000	319,000	329,000
Balance Sheet								
Current Assets	1,996,000	1,900,000	1,908,000	2,092,000	2,100,000	2,221,000	1,771,000	1,963,000
Total Assets	7,746,000	7,726,000	7,837,000	8,089,000	8,113,000	8,323,000	6,530,000	6,862,000
Current Liabilities	2,583,000	2,395,000	2,555,000	2,806,000	2,989,000	3,282,000	2,070,000	1,989,000
Long-Term Obligations	2,269,000	2,499,000	2,314,000	2,552,000	2,244,000	2,544,000	2,004,000	2,427,000
Total Liabilities	6,065,000	6,089,000	6,312,000	6,709,000	6,498,000	7,106,000	5,632,000	5,774,000
Stockholders' Equity	1,681,000	1,637,000	1,525,000	1,380,000	1,615,000	1,217,000	898,000	1,088,000
Shares Outstanding	323,000	301,000	308,000	310,000	313,000	312,000	312,000	320,000
Statistical Record								
Return on Assets %	11.02	11.40	7.09	8.55	9.79	6.18	11.59	12.29
Return on Equity %	53.21	56.10	38.87	46.27	56.83	43.43	78.16	80.16
EBITDA Margin %	22.86	21.53	15.68	17.09	17.89	18.29	19.07	20.00
Net Margin %	12.73	11.24	7.07	8.55	9.89	5.69	10.04	10.43
Asset Turnover	0.99	1.01	1.00	1.00	0.99	1.09	1.15	1.18
Current Ratio	0.77	0.79	0.75	0.75	0.70	0.68	0.86	0.99
Debt to Equity	1.35	1.53	1.52	1.85	1.39	2.09	2.23	2.23
Price Range	63.84-45.13	63.84-50.96	67.55-46.15	49.31-41.60	47.89-38.60	48.14-32.47	34.44-29.77	37.47-32.77
P/E Ratio	22.32-15.78	22.09-17.63	37.32-25.50	22.31-18.82	18.49-14.90	33.43-22.55	14.29-12.35	15.48-13.54
Average Yield %	2.53	2.44	2.20	2.75	2.87	2.93	3.56	3.30

Address: 1 Campbell Place, Camden, NJ 08103-1799	Web Site: www.campbellsoupcompany.com	Auditors: PricewaterhouseCoopers LLP
Telephone: 856-342-4800	Officers: Les C. Vinney - Chairman Denise M. Morrison - President, Chief Executive Officer	Investor Contact: 180-084-02865
Fax: 856-342-3878		Transfer Agents: Computershare Trust Company, N.A., Providence, RI

CAPITAL ONE FINANCIAL CORP

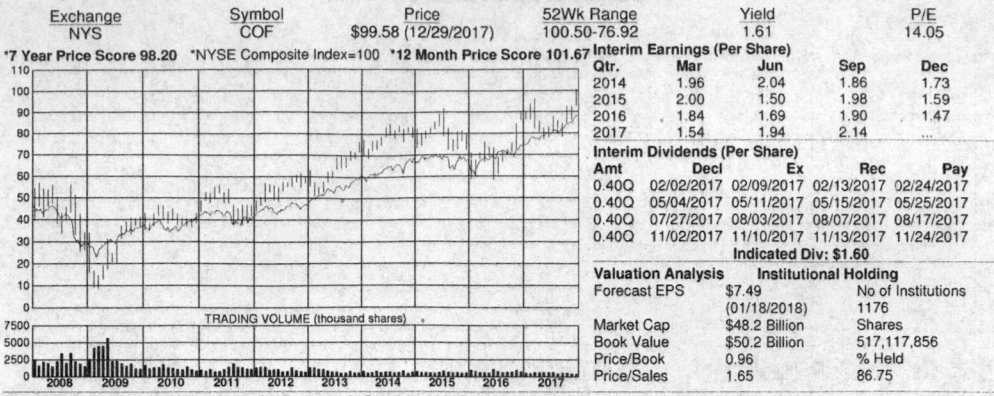

Exchange	Symbol	Price	52Wk Range	Yield	P/E
NYS	COF	$99.58 (12/29/2017)	100.50-76.92	1.61	14.05

*7 Year Price Score 98.20   ***NYSE Composite Index=100**   ***12 Month Price Score 101.67**

Interim Earnings (Per Share)

Qtr.	Mar	Jun	Sep	Dec
2014	1.96	2.04	1.86	1.73
2015	2.00	1.50	1.98	1.59
2016	1.84	1.69	1.90	1.47
2017	1.54	1.94	2.14	...

Interim Dividends (Per Share)

Amt	Decl	Ex	Rec	Pay
0.40Q	02/02/2017	02/09/2017	02/13/2017	02/24/2017
0.40Q	05/04/2017	05/11/2017	05/15/2017	05/25/2017
0.40Q	07/27/2017	08/03/2017	08/07/2017	08/17/2017
0.40Q	11/02/2017	11/10/2017	11/13/2017	11/24/2017

Indicated Div: $1.60

Valuation Analysis		Institutional Holding	
Forecast EPS	$7.49	No of Institutions	
	(01/18/2018)	1176	
Market Cap	$48.2 Billion	Shares	
Book Value	$50.2 Billion	517,117,856	
Price/Book	0.96	% Held	
Price/Sales	1.65	86.75	

Business Summary: Banking (MIC: 5.1.1 SIC: 6021 NAIC: 522110)

Capital One Financial is a financial services holding company with banking and non-banking subsidiaries. As of Dec 31 2016, Co.'s subsidiaries included: Capital One Bank (USA), NA, which provides credit and debit card products, other lending products and deposit products; and Capital One, NA, which provides banking products and financial services to consumers, small businesses and commercial clients. Co.'s principal operations are organized into three segments based on the products and services provided or the type of customer served: Credit Card, Consumer Banking and Commercial Banking. As of Dec 31 2016, Co. had total assets of $357.03 billion and total deposits of $236.77 billion.

Recent Developments: For the quarter ended Sep 30 2017, income from continuing operations increased 11.9% to US$1.14 billion from US$1.02 billion in the year-earlier quarter. Net income increased 10.1% to US$1.11 billion from US$1.01 billion in the year-earlier quarter. Net interest income increased 8.0% to US$5.70 billion from US$5.28 billion in the year-earlier quarter. Provision for loan losses was US$1.83 billion versus US$1.59 billion in the prior-year quarter, an increase of 15.4%. Non-interest income rose 8.5% to US$1.29 billion from US$1.18 billion, while non-interest expense advanced 6.1% to US$3.57 billion.

Prospects: Our evaluation of Capital One Financial Corp. as of Jan. 14, 2018 is the result of our systematic analysis on three basic characteristics: earnings strength, relative valuation, and recent stock price movement. The company has enjoyed a very positive trend in earnings per share over the past 5 quarters and while recent estimates for the company have been mixed, COF has posted results that fell short of analysts expectations. Based on operating earnings yield, the company is undervalued when compared to all of the companies in our coverage universe. Share price changes over the past year indicates that COF will perform poorly over the near term.

Financial Data

(US$ in Thousands)	9 Mos	6 Mos	3 Mos	12/31/2016	12/31/2015	12/31/2014	12/31/2013	12/31/2012
Earnings Per Share	7.09	6.85	6.60	6.89	7.07	7.59	6.96	6.16
Cash Flow Per Share	24.92	25.44	22.64	23.42	18.69	16.52	17.22	16.11
Tang Book Value Per Share	73.54	71.56	69.43	68.71	62.22	56.15	48.48	45.68
Dividends Per Share	1.600	1.600	1.600	1.600	1.500	1.200	0.950	0.200
Dividend Payout %	22.57	23.36	24.24	23.22	21.22	15.81	13.65	3.25
Income Statement								
Interest Income	18,618,000	12,198,000	6,070,000	22,891,000	20,459,000	19,397,000	19,898,000	18,964,000
Interest Expense	1,971,000	1,251,000	596,000	2,018,000	1,625,000	1,579,000	1,792,000	2,375,000
Net Interest Income	16,647,000	10,947,000	5,474,000	20,873,000	18,834,000	17,818,000	18,106,000	16,589,000
Provision for Losses	5,625,000	3,792,000	1,992,000	6,459,000	4,536,000	3,541,000	3,453,000	4,415,000
Non-Interest Income	3,577,000	2,292,000	1,061,000	4,628,000	4,579,000	4,472,000	4,278,000	4,807,000
Non-Interest Expense	10,415,000	6,848,000	3,434,000	13,558,000	12,996,000	12,180,000	12,514,000	11,946,000
Income Before Taxes	4,184,000	2,599,000	1,109,000	5,484,000	5,881,000	6,569,000	6,417,000	5,035,000
Income Taxes	1,205,000	757,000	314,000	1,714,000	1,869,000	2,146,000	2,025,000	1,301,000
Net Income	2,953,000	1,846,000	810,000	3,751,000	4,050,000	4,428,000	4,159,000	3,517,000
Average Shares	489,000	488,100	487,900	509,800	548,000	571,900	587,600	566,000
Balance Sheet								
Net Loans & Leases	246,570,000	237,909,000	234,339,000	240,126,000	225,625,000	204,559,000	193,102,000	200,934,000
Total Assets	361,402,000	350,593,000	348,549,000	357,033,000	334,048,000	308,854,000	297,048,000	312,918,000
Total Deposits	239,062,000	239,763,000	241,182,000	236,768,000	217,721,000	205,548,000	204,523,000	212,485,000
Total Liabilities	311,248,000	301,456,000	300,509,000	309,519,000	286,764,000	263,801,000	255,304,000	272,419,000
Stockholders' Equity	50,154,000	49,137,000	48,040,000	47,514,000	47,284,000	45,053,000	41,744,000	40,499,000
Shares Outstanding	484,419	483,692	482,765	480,218	527,259	553,391	572,675	582,207
Statistical Record								
Return on Assets %	1.06	1.06	1.05	1.08	1.26	1.46	1.36	1.35
Return on Equity %	7.61	7.49	7.41	7.89	8.77	10.20	10.11	10.00
Net Interest Margin %	88.79	89.31	90.18	91.18	92.06	91.86	90.99	87.48
Efficiency Ratio %	46.29	46.39	48.16	49.27	51.91	51.03	51.76	50.25
Loans to Deposits	1.03	0.99	0.97	1.01	1.04	1.00	0.94	0.95
Price Range	96.12-71.07	96.12-60.86	96.12-58.15	90.62-58.15	91.71-71.55	84.95-68.66	76.61-50.80	61.40-43.75
P/E Ratio	13.56-10.02	14.03-8.88	14.56-8.81	13.15-8.44	12.97-10.12	11.19-9.05	11.01-7.30	9.97-7.10
Average Yield %	1.92	2.01	2.08	2.24	1.88	1.53	1.50	0.37

Address: 1680 Capital One Drive, McLean, VA 22102 Telephone: 703-720-1000	Web Site: www.capitalone.com Officers: Richard D. Fairbank - Chairman, President, Chief Executive Officer Matthew W. Cooper - General Counsel	Auditors: Ernst & Young LLP Investor Contact: 703-720-2455 Transfer Agents: ComputerShare Investor Services, Providence, RI

CARDINAL HEALTH, INC.

Exchange	Symbol	Price	52Wk Range	Yield	P/E	Div Achiever
NYS	CAH	$61.27 (12/29/2017)	83.80-55.00	3.02	17.81	20 Years

*7 Year Price Score 89.06 *NYSE Composite Index=100 *12 Month Price Score 78.36

Interim Earnings (Per Share)

Qtr.	Sep	Dec	Mar	Jun
2014-15	0.78	0.86	1.09	0.88
2015-16	1.15	0.98	1.17	1.02
2016-17	0.96	1.02	1.20	0.86
2017-18	0.36	...	...	...

Interim Dividends (Per Share)

Amt	Decl	Ex	Rec	Pay
0.449Q	02/02/2017	03/30/2017	04/03/2017	04/15/2017
0.462Q	05/03/2017	06/29/2017	07/03/2017	07/15/2017
0.462Q	08/09/2017	09/29/2017	10/02/2017	10/15/2017
0.462Q	11/00/2017	12/29/2017	01/02/2018	01/15/2018

Indicated Div: $1.85

Valuation Analysis

		Institutional Holding	
Forecast EPS	$4.99 (01/18/2018)	No of Institutions	1049
Market Cap	$19.3 Billion	Shares	340,608,064
Book Value	$6.7 Billion	% Held	82.57
Price/Book	2.89		
Price/Sales	0.15		

Business Summary: Pharmaceuticals (MIC: 4.1.1 SIC: 5122 NAIC: 424210)

Cardinal Health is a healthcare services and products company. Co.'s segments are: Pharmaceutical and Medical. The Pharmaceutical segment distributes branded and generic pharmaceutical, specialty pharmaceutical, over-the-counter healthcare and consumer products; operates nuclear pharmacies and radiopharmaceutical manufacturing facilities; provides pharmacy management services to hospitals as well as medication therapy management and patient outcomes services. The Medical segment manufactures, sources and distributes Cardinal Health branded medical, surgical and laboratory products, which are sold in the U.S., Canada, Europe, Asia and other markets.

Recent Developments: For the quarter ended Sep 30 2017, net income decreased 62.3% to US$117.0 million from US$310.0 million in the year-earlier quarter. Revenues were US$32.64 billion, up 1.9% from US$32.04 billion the year before. Operating income was US$262.0 million versus US$535.0 million in the prior-year quarter, a decrease of 51.0%. Direct operating expenses rose 1.7% to US$30.97 billion from US$30.45 billion in the comparable period the year before. Indirect operating expenses increased 33.6% to US$1.41 billion from US$1.06 billion in the equivalent prior-year period.

Prospects: Our evaluation of Cardinal Health Inc. as of Jan. 14, 2018 is the result of our systematic analysis on three basic characteristics: earnings strength, relative valuation, and recent stock price movement. The company has generated a negative trend in earnings per share over the past 5 quarters and while recent estimates for the company have been raised by analysts, CAH has posted better than expected results. Based on operating earnings yield, the company is undervalued when compared to all of the companies in our coverage universe. Share price changes over the past year indicates that CAH will perform very poorly over the near term.

Financial Data

(US$ in Thousands)	3 Mos	06/30/2017	06/30/2016	06/30/2015	06/30/2014	06/30/2013	06/30/2012	06/30/2011
Earnings Per Share	3.44	4.03	4.32	3.62	3.38	0.97	3.06	2.72
Cash Flow Per Share	7.16	3.74	9.06	7.65	7.40	5.06	3.40	4.00
Tang Book Value Per Share	N.M.	N.M.	N.M.	0.73	1.58	1.18	5.40	4.53
Dividends Per Share	1.823	1.809	1.610	1.415	1.250	1.090	0.882	0.800
Dividend Payout %	52.98	44.89	37.27	39.07	36.98	112.37	28.84	29.41
Income Statement								
Total Revenue	32,641,000	129,976,000	121,546,000	102,531,000	91,084,000	101,093,000	107,552,000	102,644,200
EBITDA	488,000	2,439,000	2,731,000	2,362,000	2,196,000	1,270,000	2,034,000	1,854,100
Depn & Amortn	229,000	314,000	277,000	254,000	265,000	259,000	241,000	243,000
Income Before Taxes	178,000	1,924,000	2,276,000	1,967,000	1,798,000	888,000	1,698,000	1,518,300
Income Taxes	61,000	630,000	845,000	755,000	635,000	553,000	628,000	552,100
Net Income	115,000	1,288,000	1,427,000	1,215,000	1,166,000	334,000	1,069,000	959,000
Average Shares	318,000	320,000	330,000	335,000	345,000	344,000	349,000	352,500
Balance Sheet								
Current Assets	23,725,000	28,345,000	21,956,000	21,752,000	17,939,000	17,770,000	17,510,000	16,315,900
Total Assets	41,940,000	40,112,000	34,122,000	30,142,000	26,033,000	25,819,000	24,260,000	22,845,900
Current Liabilities	22,407,000	21,221,000	19,701,000	17,243,000	15,115,000	14,590,000	14,174,000	13,369,500
Long-Term Obligations	9,068,000	9,068,000	4,952,000	5,211,000	3,171,000	3,686,000	2,418,000	2,175,300
Total Liabilities	35,262,000	33,304,000	27,568,000	23,886,000	19,632,000	19,844,000	18,016,000	16,997,300
Stockholders' Equity	6,678,000	6,808,000	6,554,000	6,256,000	6,401,000	5,975,000	6,244,000	5,848,600
Shares Outstanding	315,000	316,000	322,000	328,000	337,000	339,000	343,000	351,100
Statistical Record								
Return on Assets %	2.87	3.47	4.43	4.33	4.50	1.33	4.53	4.48
Return on Equity %	16.59	19.28	22.22	19.20	18.84	5.47	17.63	17.24
EBITDA Margin %	1.50	1.88	2.25	2.30	2.41	1.26	1.89	1.81
Net Margin %	0.35	0.99	1.17	1.19	1.28	0.33	0.99	0.93
Asset Turnover	3.42	3.50	3.77	3.65	3.51	4.04	4.55	4.79
Current Ratio	1.06	1.34	1.11	1.26	1.19	1.22	1.24	1.22
Debt to Equity	1.36	1.33	0.76	0.83	0.50	0.62	0.39	0.37
Price Range	83.80-64.36	84.92-65.17	90.85-73.69	91.50-68.56	73.54-47.02	48.76-37.75	46.83-37.99	45.54-29.96
P/E Ratio	24.36-18.71	21.07-16.17	21.03-17.06	25.28-18.94	21.76-13.91	50.27-38.92	15.30-12.42	16.74-11.01
Average Yield %	2.45	2.35	1.95	1.74	2.01	2.54	2.10	2.10

Address: 7000 Cardinal Place, Dublin, OH 43017 **Telephone:** 614-757-5000	**Web Site:** www.cardinalhealth.com **Officers:** George S. Barrett - Executive Chairman, Chairman, Chief Executive Officer Gregory B. Kenny - Chairman	**Auditors:** Ernst & Young LLP **Investor Contact:** 614-757-7115 **Transfer Agents:** Computershare Trust Company, N.A., Canton, MA

CARLISLE COMPANIES INC.

Exchange	Symbol	Price	52Wk Range	Yield	P/E	Div Achiever
NYS	CSL	$113.65 (12/29/2017)	115.91-92.40	1.30	22.50	40 Years

*7 Year Price Score 104.64 *NYSE Composite Index=100 *12 Month Price Score 101.81

TRADING VOLUME (thousand shares)

Interim Earnings (Per Share)

Qtr.	Mar	Jun	Sep	Dec
2014	0.55	1.14	1.32	0.81
2015	0.59	1.43	1.56	1.24
2016	1.05	1.75	(0.15)	1.16
2017	0.94	1.58	1.37	...

Interim Dividends (Per Share)

Amt	Decl	Ex	Rec	Pay
0.35Q	02/07/2017	02/15/2017	02/17/2017	03/01/2017
0.35Q	04/26/2017	05/10/2017	05/12/2017	06/01/2017
0.37Q	08/07/2017	08/16/2017	08/18/2017	09/01/2017
0.37Q	11/06/2017	11/16/2017	11/17/2017	12/01/2017

Indicated Div: $1.48 (Div. Reinv. Plan)

Valuation Analysis **Institutional Holding**

Forecast EPS	$4.88	No of Institutions
	(01/17/2018)	479
Market Cap	$7.0 Billion	Shares
Book Value	$2.4 Billion	64,055,140
Price/Book	2.88	% Held
Price/Sales	1.79	87.44

Business Summary: Rubber Products (MIC: 8.4.1 SIC: 3069 NAIC: 326299)

Carlisle Companies is a holding company. Through its subsidiaries, Co. is a manufacturing company that designs, manufactures, and markets a range of products that are marketed as a component to original equipment manufacturers, distributors, as well as directly to end-users. Co.'s products include: rubber, thermoplastic polyolefin, and polyvinyl chloride membrane roofing systems; wire, cable, connectors, contacts, and cable assemblies for the transfer of power and data; industrial liquid and powder finishing equipment and integrated system solutions; brakes and friction material; and commercial and institutional foodservice permanentware, table coverings, cookware, and catering equipment.

Recent Developments: For the quarter ended Sep 30 2017, income from continuing operations was US$86.4 million compared with a loss of US$9.5 million in the year-earlier quarter. Net income amounted to US$86.3 million versus a net loss of US$9.8 million in the year-earlier quarter. Revenues were US$1.09 billion, up 9.9% from US$991.0 million the year before. Direct operating expenses rose 16.5% to US$777.6 million from US$667.4 million in the comparable period the year before. Indirect operating expenses decreased 41.3% to US$168.6 million from US$287.2 million in the equivalent prior-year period.

Prospects: Our evaluation of Carlisle Companies Inc. as of Jan. 14, 2018 is the result of our systematic analysis on three basic characteristics: earnings strength, relative valuation, and recent stock price movement. The company has managed to produce a neutral trend in earnings per share over the past 5 quarters. However, while recent estimates for the company have been mixed, CSL has posted better than expected results. Based on operating earnings yield, the company is about fairly valued when compared to all of the companies in our coverage universe. Share price changes over the past year indicates that CSL will perform poorly over the near term.

Financial Data

(US$ in Thousands)	9 Mos	6 Mos	3 Mos	12/31/2016	12/31/2015	12/31/2014	12/31/2013	12/31/2012
Earnings Per Share	5.05	3.53	3.70	3.82	4.82	3.82	3.22	4.22
Cash Flow Per Share	7.62	7.62	7.06	8.25	8.16	4.61	6.53	7.75
Tang Book Value Per Share	3.32	4.56	5.01	7.99	5.08	9.72	8.60	3.36
Dividends Per Share	1.420	1.400	1.350	1.300	1.100	0.940	0.840	0.760
Dividend Payout %	28.12	39.66	36.49	34.03	22.82	24.61	26.09	18.01
Income Statement								
Total Revenue	3,018,100	1,929,000	857,300	3,675,400	3,543,200	3,204,000	2,943,000	3,629,400
EBITDA	519,100	334,600	135,500	516,200	575,400	473,000	442,200	498,900
Depn & Amortn	120,700	79,100	38,800	75,100	73,500	64,700	75,400	74,600
Income Before Taxes	377,000	241,800	90,100	410,500	467,900	376,100	333,000	398,800
Income Taxes	126,800	78,000	28,600	159,700	148,300	124,400	97,800	131,500
Net Income	250,400	164,100	61,800	250,100	319,700	251,300	209,700	270,200
Average Shares	62,797	64,140	64,848	64,883	65,804	65,304	64,806	63,610
Balance Sheet								
Current Assets	1,361,700	1,336,200	1,191,200	1,355,200	1,319,500	1,611,500	1,535,000	1,205,300
Total Assets	4,317,900	4,228,900	4,070,700	3,965,800	3,954,100	3,758,700	3,493,000	3,457,300
Current Liabilities	635,600	601,900	508,300	513,500	605,900	392,200	376,400	470,600
Long-Term Obligations	781,900	706,700	596,500	596,400	598,700	749,800	751,000	752,500
Total Liabilities	1,881,600	1,756,400	1,552,500	1,498,900	1,606,700	1,553,700	1,506,900	1,669,200
Stockholders' Equity	2,436,300	2,472,500	2,518,200	2,466,900	2,347,400	2,205,000	1,986,100	1,788,100
Shares Outstanding	61,763	62,968	64,368	64,257	64,051	64,691	63,658	63,127
Statistical Record								
Return on Assets %	7.89	5.49	6.01	6.30	8.29	6.93	6.03	8.17
Return on Equity %	13.38	9.29	9.92	10.36	14.05	11.99	11.11	16.39
EBITDA Margin %	17.20	17.35	15.81	14.04	16.24	14.76	15.03	13.75
Net Margin %	8.30	8.51	7.21	6.80	9.02	7.84	7.13	7.44
Asset Turnover	0.94	0.91	0.92	0.93	0.92	0.88	0.85	1.10
Current Ratio	2.14	2.22	2.34	2.64	2.18	4.11	4.08	2.56
Debt to Equity	0.32	0.29	0.24	0.24	0.26	0.34	0.38	0.42
Price Range	115.96-92.40	115.96-93.50	115.96-98.38	115.96-77.82	104.60-84.11	91.54-71.67	79.62-58.76	59.36-45.56
P/E Ratio	22.96-18.30	32.85-26.49	31.34-26.59	30.36-20.37	21.70-17.45	23.96-18.76	24.73-18.25	14.07-10.80
Average Yield %	1.37	1.33	1.28	1.29	1.16	1.14	1.24	1.45

Address: 16430 North Scottsdale Road, Suite 400, Scottsdale, AZ 85254	Web Site: www.carlisle.com	Auditors: Deloitte & Touche LLP
Telephone: 480-781-5000	Officers: D. Christian Koch - President, Chief Operating Officer, Region Officer, Chief Executive Officer Robert M. Roche - Chief Financial Officer, Vice President	Investor Contact: 800-897-9071 Transfer Agents: Computershare Investor Services, LLC, Chicago, IL

CARMAX INC.

Exchange	Symbol	Price	52Wk Range	Yield	P/E
NYS	KMX	$64.13 (12/29/2017)	76.81-55.37	N/A	17.19

*7 Year Price Score 106.34 *NYSE Composite Index=100   *12 Month Price Score 99.27

Interim Earnings (Per Share)

Qtr.	May	Aug	Nov	Feb
2014-15	0.76	0.70	0.60	0.67
2015-16	0.86	0.82	0.63	0.71
2016-17	0.90	0.84	0.72	0.81
2017-18	1.13	0.98	0.81	...

Interim Dividends (Per Share)

No Dividends Paid

Valuation Analysis

		Institutional Holding	
Forecast EPS	$3.82 (01/18/2018)	No of Institutions	679
Market Cap	$11.6 Billion	Shares	238,826,368
Book Value	$3.3 Billion		
Price/Book	3.53	% Held	95.29
Price/Sales	0.68		

Business Summary: Retail - Automotive (MIC: 2.1.4 SIC: 5521 NAIC: 441120)

CarMax is a holding company. Through its subsidiaries, Co. is engaged as a retailer of used vehicles. Co. operates in two segments: CarMax Sales Operations, which sells used vehicles, purchases used vehicles from customers and other sources, sells related products and services, and arranges financing options for customers; and CarMax Auto Finance, which consists of finance operation that provides vehicle financing to customer buying vehicles from Co. Co.'s products and services include retail merchandising, wholesale auctions, extended protection plans, reconditioning and service, and customer credit. As of Feb 28 2017, Co. operated 173 used car stores in 86 U.S. television markets.

Recent Developments: For the quarter ended Nov 30 2017, net income increased 8.9% to US$148.8 million from US$136.6 million in the year-earlier quarter. Revenues were US$4.11 billion, up 11.0% from US$3.70 billion the year before. Direct operating expenses rose 11.6% to US$3.57 billion from US$3.20 billion in the comparable period the year before. Indirect operating expenses increased 10.8% to US$314.0 million from US$283.5 million in the equivalent prior-year period.

Prospects: Our evaluation of Carmax Inc. as of Jan. 14, 2018 is the result of our systematic analysis on three basic characteristics: earnings strength, relative valuation, and recent stock price movement. The company has managed to produce a neutral trend in earnings per share over the past 5 quarters and while recent estimates for the company have been raised by analysts, KMX has posted better than expected results. Based on operating earnings yield, the company is undervalued when compared to all of the companies in our coverage universe. Share price changes over the past year indicates that KMX will perform poorly over the near term.

Financial Data

(US$ in Thousands)	9 Mos	6 Mos	3 Mos	02/28/2017	02/29/2016	02/28/2015	02/28/2014	02/28/2013
Earnings Per Share	3.73	3.64	3.50	3.26	3.03	2.73	2.16	1.87
Cash Flow Per Share	(1.75)	(1.90)	(1.95)	(2.46)	(0.73)	(4.49)	(2.74)	(3.41)
Tang Book Value Per Share	18.19	17.60	17.14	16.66	14.92	15.11	14.96	13.36
Income Statement								
Total Revenue	13,035,991	8,928,974	4,542,334	15,875,118	15,149,675	14,268,716	12,574,299	10,962,818
EBITDA	1,037,739	750,037	398,785	1,203,521	1,173,302	1,099,504	918,556	816,008
Depn & Amortn	133,175	88,078	43,894	140,700	127,000	105,700	90,400	82,300
Income Before Taxes	853,485	628,285	338,053	1,006,405	1,009,944	969,331	797,322	701,351
Income Taxes	311,519	235,159	126,351	379,435	386,516	371,973	304,736	267,067
Net Income	541,966	393,126	211,702	626,970	623,428	597,358	492,586	434,284
Average Shares	184,033	184,696	186,859	192,215	205,540	218,691	227,584	231,823
Balance Sheet								
Current Assets	3,004,923	2,803,335	2,734,544	2,873,630	2,471,781	2,599,038	2,643,224	2,310,131
Total Assets	17,303,414	16,875,733	16,475,689	16,279,356	14,481,576	13,198,201	11,707,157	9,888,602
Current Liabilities	1,111,678	1,201,557	1,166,670	1,105,787	1,005,193	997,173	875,497	684,173
Long-Term Obligations	12,651,337	12,234,004	11,925,870	11,826,438	10,342,323	8,818,750	7,340,431	6,009,627
Total Liabilities	14,002,687	13,674,747	13,323,561	13,170,776	11,576,790	10,041,416	8,390,160	6,869,435
Stockholders' Equity	3,300,727	3,200,986	3,152,128	3,108,580	2,904,786	3,156,785	3,316,997	3,019,167
Shares Outstanding	181,489	181,903	183,872	186,548	194,712	208,869	221,685	225,906
Statistical Record								
Return on Assets %	4.20	4.21	4.24	4.08	4.49	4.80	4.56	4.77
Return on Equity %	21.99	21.79	21.66	20.85	20.51	18.45	15.55	15.26
EBITDA Margin %	7.96	8.40	8.78	7.58	7.74	7.71	7.31	7.44
Net Margin %	4.16	4.40	4.66	3.95	4.12	4.19	3.92	3.96
Asset Turnover	1.03	1.03	1.04	1.03	1.09	1.15	1.16	1.20
Current Ratio	2.70	2.33	2.34	2.60	2.46	2.61	3.02	3.38
Debt to Equity	3.83	3.82	3.78	3.80	3.56	2.79	2.21	1.99
Price Range	76.81-55.37	68.60-48.65	68.60-45.70	68.60-45.70	74.73-42.15	68.30-42.88	53.05-38.38	40.10-25.22
P/E Ratio	20.59-14.84	18.85-13.37	19.60-13.06	21.04-14.02	24.66-13.91	25.02-15.71	24.56-17.77	21.44-13.49

Address: 12800 Tuckahoe Creek Parkway, Richmond, VA 23238
Telephone: 804-747-0422

Web Site: www.carmax.com
Officers: William D. (Bill) Nash - President, Executive Vice President, Senior Vice President, Vice President, Chief Executive Officer William C. (Cliff) Wood - Chief Operating Officer, Executive Vice President, Executive Vice President (frmr), Senior Vice President

Auditors: KPMG LLP
Investor Contact: 804-935-4591
Transfer Agents: American Stock Transfer & Trust Company, LLC, Brooklyn, NY

141

CARNIVAL CORP

Exchange	Symbol	Price	52Wk Range	Yield	P/E
NYS	CCL	$66.37 (12/29/2017)	69.48-52.14	2.71	18.08

*7 Year Price Score 112.53 *NYSE Composite Index=100   *12 Month Price Score 99.36

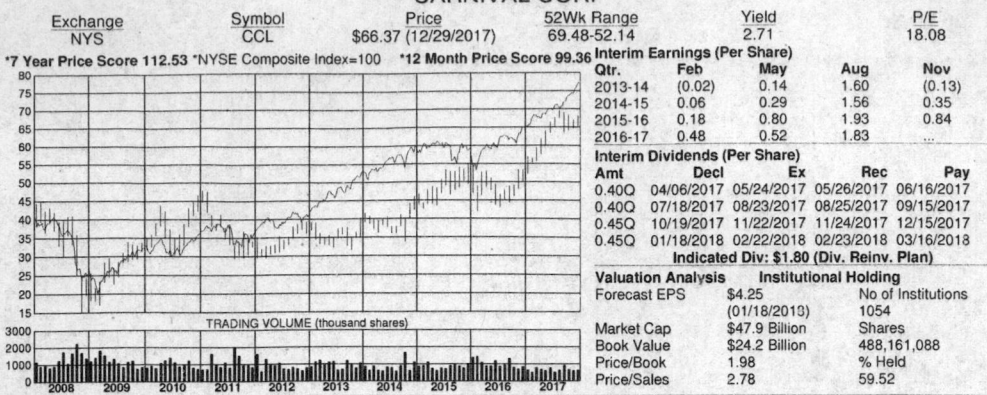

Interim Earnings (Per Share)

Qtr.	Feb	May	Aug	Nov
2013-14	(0.02)	0.14	1.60	(0.13)
2014-15	0.06	0.29	1.56	0.35
2015-16	0.18	0.80	1.93	0.84
2016-17	0.48	0.52	1.83	...

Interim Dividends (Per Share)

Amt	Decl	Ex	Rec	Pay
0.40Q	04/06/2017	05/24/2017	05/26/2017	06/16/2017
0.40Q	07/18/2017	08/23/2017	08/25/2017	09/15/2017
0.45Q	10/19/2017	11/22/2017	11/24/2017	12/15/2017
0.45Q	01/18/2018	02/22/2018	02/23/2018	03/16/2018

Indicated Div: $1.80 (Div. Reinv. Plan)

Valuation Analysis

		Institutional Holding	
Forecast EPS	$4.25	No of Institutions	
	(01/18/2018)	1054	
Market Cap	$47.9 Billion	Shares	
Book Value	$24.2 Billion	488,161,088	
Price/Book	1.98	% Held	
Price/Sales	2.78	59.52	

TRADING VOLUME (thousand shares)

Business Summary: Hotels, Restaurants & Travel (MIC: 2.2.1 SIC: 4489 NAIC: 483212)

Carnival is a leisure travel company. Co. operates ships within global, regional and national cruise brands that sell tailored cruise products and services. Co.'s North America segment includes Carnival Cruise Lines, Princess Cruises, Holland America Line, and Seabourn. Co.'s Europe, Australia & Asia segment includes Costa Cruises, AIDA Cruises, P&O Cruises (U.K.), P&O Cruises (Australia), and Cunard. Co. also has a Cruise Support segment that represents its port destinations and private islands. In additon, Co. has a Tour and Other segment, which includes Holland America Princess Alaska Tours, a tour company in Alaska and the Canadian Yukon.

Recent Developments: For the quarter ended Aug 31 2017, net income decreased 6.7% to US$1.33 billion from US$1.42 billion in the year-earlier quarter. Revenues were US$5.52 billion, up 8.2% from US$5.10 billion the year before. Operating income was US$1.39 billion versus US$1.56 billion in the prior-year quarter, a decrease of 10.8%. Direct operating expenses rose 17.6% to US$3.01 billion from US$2.56 billion in the comparable period the year before. Indirect operating expenses increased 14.1% to US$1.11 billion from US$972.0 million in the equivalent prior-year period.

Prospects: Our evaluation of Carnival Corp. as of Jan. 14, 2018 is the result of our systematic analysis on three basic characteristics: earnings strength, relative valuation, and recent stock price movement. The company has managed to produce a neutral trend in earnings per share over the past 5 quarters. However, while recent estimates for the company have been lowered by analysts, CCL has posted better than expected results. Based on operating earnings yield, the company is undervalued when compared to all of the companies in our coverage universe. Share price changes over the past year indicates that CCL will perform well over the near term.

Financial Data

(US$ in Thousands)	9 Mos	6 Mos	3 Mos	11/30/2016	11/30/2015	11/30/2014	11/30/2013	11/30/2012
Earnings Per Share	3.67	3.77	4.05	3.72	2.26	1.59	1.39	1.67
Cash Flow Per Share	7.36	7.32	7.27	6.87	5.85	4.42	3.66	3.84
Tang Book Value Per Share	27.69	N.M.	25.44	25.36	25.29	25.60	25.84	25.05
Dividends Per Share	1.500	1.450	1.400	1.350	1.100	1.000	1.500	1.000
Dividend Payout %	40.87	38.46	34.57	36.29	48.67	62.89	107.91	59.88
Income Statement								
Total Revenue	13,251,000	7,736,000	3,791,000	16,389,000	15,714,000	15,884,000	15,456,000	15,382,000
EBITDA	3,617,000	1,730,000	842,000	4,783,000	3,634,000	3,160,000	2,968,000	3,155,000
Depn & Amortn	1,368,000	896,000	439,000	1,738,000	1,626,000	1,635,000	1,588,000	1,527,000
Income Before Taxes	2,106,000	737,000	354,000	2,828,000	1,799,000	1,245,000	1,072,000	1,302,000
Income Taxes	46,000	7,000	2,000	49,000	42,000	9,000	(6,000)	4,000
Net Income	2,060,000	730,000	352,000	2,779,000	1,757,000	1,236,000	1,078,000	1,298,000
Average Shares	726,000	727,000	728,000	747,000	779,000	778,000	777,000	779,000
Balance Sheet								
Current Assets	1,661,000	1,774,000	1,597,000	1,689,000	2,451,000	1,503,000	1,937,000	1,821,000
Total Assets	40,643,000	40,451,000	38,703,000	38,936,000	39,237,000	39,532,000	40,104,000	39,161,000
Current Liabilities	7,969,000	9,058,000	7,465,000	7,072,000	6,956,000	6,921,000	6,720,000	7,340,000
Long-Term Obligations	7,723,000	7,635,000	7,796,000	8,357,000	7,413,000	7,363,000	8,092,000	7,168,000
Total Liabilities	16,471,000	17,487,000	16,043,000	16,339,000	15,466,000	15,244,000	15,548,000	15,232,000
Stockholders' Equity	24,172,000	22,964,000	22,660,000	22,597,000	23,771,000	24,288,000	24,556,000	23,929,000
Shares Outstanding	721,000	724,000	726,000	726,000	772,000	777,000	776,000	776,000
Statistical Record								
Return on Assets %	6.67	6.88	7.75	7.09	4.46	3.10	2.72	3.33
Return on Equity %	11.34	12.08	13.20	11.95	7.31	5.06	4.45	5.42
EBITDA Margin %	27.30	22.36	22.21	29.18	23.13	19.89	19.20	20.51
Net Margin %	15.55	9.44	9.29	16.96	11.18	7.78	6.97	8.44
Asset Turnover	0.43	0.42	0.43	0.42	0.40	0.40	0.39	0.39
Current Ratio	0.21	0.20	0.21	0.24	0.35	0.22	0.29	0.25
Debt to Equity	0.32	0.33	0.34	0.37	0.31	0.30	0.33	0.30
Price Range	69.48-44.37	64.07-43.18	56.93-43.18	55.14-41.92	54.08-42.39	44.16-33.88	39.32-31.60	39.16-29.48
P/E Ratio	18.93-12.09	16.99-11.45	14.06-10.66	14.82-11.27	23.93-18.76	27.77-21.31	28.29-22.73	23.45-17.65
Average Yield %	2.62	2.79	2.83	2.79	2.29	2.59	4.22	2.96

Address: 3655 N.W. 87th Avenue, Miami, FL 33178-2428	**Web Site:** www.carnivalcorporation.com	**Auditors:** PricewaterhouseCoopers LLP
Telephone: 305-599-2600	**Officers:** Micky Meir Arison - Chairman, Chief Executive Officer Arnold W. Donald - President, Chief Executive Officer, Associate/Affiliate Company Officer	**Investor Contact:** 305-406-5539 **Transfer Agents:** ComputerShare Investor Services, Providence, RI

CARPENTER TECHNOLOGY CORP.

Exchange	Symbol	Price	52Wk Range	Yield	P/E
NYS	CRS	$50.99 (12/29/2017)	52.84-34.66	1.41	31.48

*7 Year Price Score 70.98   *NYSE Composite Index=100   *12 Month Price Score 110.82

Interim Earnings (Per Share)

Qtr.	Sep	Dec	Mar	Jun
2014-15	0.25	0.45	(0.03)	0.43
2015-16	0.18	0.23	(0.51)	0.31
2016-17	(0.13)	0.15	0.44	0.54
2017-18	0.49	...	...	...

Interim Dividends (Per Share)

Amt	Decl	Ex	Rec	Pay
0.18Q	01/25/2017	02/03/2017	02/07/2017	03/02/2017
0.18Q	04/20/2017	04/28/2017	05/02/2017	06/01/2017
0.18Q	08/09/2017	08/18/2017	08/22/2017	09/07/2017
0.18Q	10/10/2017	10/23/2017	10/24/2017	12/07/2017

Indicated Div: $0.72

Valuation Analysis / Institutional Holding

Valuation Analysis		Institutional Holding	
Forecast EPS	$2.31 (01/17/2018)	No of Institutions	320
Market Cap	$2.4 Billion	Shares	52,881,028
Book Value	$1.2 Billion	% Held	89.43
Price/Book	1.94		
Price/Sales	1.26		

Business Summary: Non-Precious Metals (MIC: 8.2.2 SIC: 3312 NAIC: 331111)

Carpenter Technology is engaged in the manufacturing, fabrication and distribution of metals. Co. produces and distributes premium specialty alloys, including titanium alloys, powder metals, stainless steels, alloy steels, and tool steels as well as drilling tools. Co.'s superalloy and titanium powder technologies support a range of products and manufacturing techniques. Co.'s segments are Specialty Alloys Operations, which consists of alloy and stainless steel manufacturing operations; and Performance Engineered Products, which includes the Dynamet titanium business, the Carpenter Powder Products business, the Amega West business and the Latrobe and Mexico distribution businesses.

Recent Developments: For the quarter ended Sep 30 2017, net income amounted to US$23.4 million versus a net loss of US$6.2 million in the year-earlier quarter. Revenues were US$479.8 million, up 23.3% from US$389.0 million the year before. Operating income was US$41.7 million versus US$1.4 million in the prior-year quarter, an increase of. Direct operating expenses rose 14.9% to US$394.2 million from US$343.0 million in the comparable period the year before. Indirect operating expenses decreased 1.6% to US$43.9 million from US$44.6 million in the equivalent prior-year period.

Prospects: Our evaluation of Carpenter Technology Corp. as of Jan. 14, 2018 is the result of our systematic analysis on three basic characteristics: earnings strength, relative valuation, and recent stock price movement. The company has produced a positive trend in earnings per share over the past 5 quarters. However, while recent estimates for the company have been mixed, CRS has posted better than expected results. Based on operating earnings yield, the company is about fairly valued when compared to all of the companies in our coverage universe. Share price changes over the past year indicates that CRS will perform well over the near term.

Financial Data
(US$ in Thousands)

	3 Mos	06/30/2017	06/30/2016	06/30/2015	06/30/2014	06/30/2013	06/30/2012	06/30/2011
Earnings Per Share	1.62	0.99	0.23	1.11	2.47	2.73	2.53	1.59
Cash Flow Per Share	2.51	2.75	5.33	5.37	4.50	4.07	3.39	1.46
Tang Book Value Per Share	19.32	18.61	17.10	19.81	21.94	18.01	13.99	15.66
Dividends Per Share	0.720	0.720	0.720	0.720	0.720	0.720	0.720	0.720
Dividend Payout %	44.44	72.73	313.04	64.86	29.15	26.37	28.46	45.28
Income Statement								
Total Revenue	479,800	1,797,600	1,813,400	2,226,700	2,173,000	2,271,700	2,028,700	1,675,100
EBITDA	71,100	205,500	155,200	223,800	305,900	321,300	282,400	160,400
Depn & Amortn	28,700	105,800	106,500	107,200	93,300	85,100	71,500	59,200
Income Before Taxes	35,200	70,200	20,900	89,000	195,800	215,500	188,000	85,200
Income Taxes	11,800	23,200	10,200	30,400	63,600	70,300	67,000	16,100
Net Income	23,400	47,000	11,300	58,700	132,800	146,100	121,200	71,000
Average Shares	47,300	47,100	48,200	52,700	53,600	53,400	47,800	44,700
Balance Sheet								
Current Assets	1,111,700	1,093,600	1,010,700	1,070,400	1,194,500	1,281,500	1,249,700	1,157,600
Total Assets	2,892,500	2,878,100	2,794,300	2,905,900	3,057,500	2,882,900	2,627,800	1,991,900
Current Liabilities	381,600	396,000	298,800	322,100	430,600	421,200	554,200	395,400
Long-Term Obligations	549,200	550,000	611,300	607,100	604,300	604,200	305,900	407,800
Total Liabilities	1,661,500	1,679,500	1,689,400	1,580,000	1,553,200	1,579,800	1,524,000	1,226,200
Stockholders' Equity	1,231,000	1,198,600	1,104,900	1,325,900	1,504,300	1,303,100	1,103,800	765,700
Shares Outstanding	46,803	46,753	46,600	50,318	53,137	52,773	52,412	44,107
Statistical Record								
Return on Assets %	2.68	1.66	0.40	1.97	4.47	5.30	5.23	3.97
Return on Equity %	6.51	4.08	0.93	4.15	9.46	12.14	12.93	10.60
EBITDA Margin %	14.82	11.43	8.56	10.05	14.08	14.14	13.92	9.58
Net Margin %	4.88	2.61	0.62	2.64	6.11	6.43	5.97	4.24
Asset Turnover	0.66	0.63	0.63	0.75	0.73	0.82	0.88	0.94
Current Ratio	2.91	2.76	3.38	3.32	2.77	3.04	2.25	2.93
Debt to Equity	0.45	0.46	0.55	0.46	0.40	0.46	0.28	0.53
Price Range	48.03-31.25	43.63-31.25	40.56-25.16	64.32-35.69	66.64-45.59	55.70-43.77	59.53-41.32	57.68-30.58
P/E Ratio	29.65-19.29	44.07-31.57	176.35-109.39	57.95-32.15	26.98-18.46	20.40-16.03	23.53-16.33	36.28-19.23
Average Yield %	1.88	1.91	2.17	1.55	1.21	1.47	1.41	1.78

Address: 1735 Market Street, 15th Floor, Philadelphia, PA 19103 **Telephone:** 610-208-2000	**Web Site:** www.cartech.com **Officers:** Gregory A. Pratt - Interim Executive Chairman, Chairman, Interim President, Interim Chief Executive Officer Tony R. Thene - President, Chief Executive Officer, Senior Vice President, Chief Financial Officer	**Auditors:** PricewaterhouseCoopers LLP **Investor Contact:** 610-208-3476 **Transfer Agents:** American Stock Transfer & Trust Company

CARS.COM INC

Exchange	Symbol	Price	52Wk Range	Yield	P/E
NYS	CARS	$28.84 (12/29/2017)	29.98-22.00	N/A	47.28

*7 Year Price Score N/A   *NYSE Composite Index=100   *12 Month Price Score N/A

Interim Earnings (Per Share)

Qtr.	Mar	Jun	Sep	Dec
2016	0.47	0.59	0.72	(0.41)
2017	0.38	0.35	0.29	...

Interim Dividends (Per Share)

No Dividends Paid

Valuation Analysis   **Institutional Holding**

Forecast EPS	$1.30	No of Institutions
	(01/06/2018)	331
Market Cap	$2.1 Billion	Shares
Book Value	$1.5 Billion	85,002,056
Price/Book	1.37	% Held
Price/Sales	N/A	N/A

TRADING VOLUME (thousand shares)

2008 2009 2010 2011 2012 2013 2014 2015 2016 2017

Business Summary: IT Services (MIC: 6.3.1 SIC: 7374 NAIC: 518210)

Cars.com operates as an online research destination for car shoppers. Co. sells online subscription advertising products to car dealerships by its own direct sales force, as well as through its affiliate sales channel. Co. also sells display advertising to national advertisers. In addition, Co. offers online automotive marketplace service that connects buyers and sellers in Cars.com, Auto.com, DealerRater.com, NewCars.com, and PickupTrucks.com Websites. Co.'s Website hosts approximately 4.7 million vehicle listings at any given time and serves approximately 20,000 franchise and independent car dealers in 50 states.

Recent Developments: For the quarter ended Sep 30 2017, net income decreased 59.5% to US$21.0 million from US$51.8 million in the year-earlier quarter. Revenues were US$159.9 million, down 1.5% from US$162.3 million the year before. Operating income was US$39.4 million versus US$52.2 million in the prior-year quarter, a decrease of 24.5%. Indirect operating expenses increased 9.4% to US$120.5 million from US$110.1 million in the equivalent prior-year period.

Prospects: Our evaluation of Cars.com Inc. as of Jan. 14, 2018 is the result of our systematic analysis on three basic characteristics: earnings strength, relative valuation, and recent stock price movement. The company has suffered a very negative trend in earnings per share over the past 5 quarters and while recent estimates for the company have been mixed, CARS has posted results that fell short of analysts expectations. Based on operating earnings yield, the company is undervalued when compared to all of the companies in our coverage universe. Share price changes over the past year indicates that CARS will perform very poorly over the near term.

Financial Data

(US$ in Thousands)	9 Mos	6 Mos	3 Mos	12/31/2016	12/31/2015	12/31/2014
Earnings Per Share	0.61	1.04	1.28	1.37	...	...
Cash Flow Per Share	...	...	...	2.77	...	...
Tang Book Value Per Share	N.M.	N.M.	0.32	...	...	...
Income Statement						
Total Revenue	469,697	309,798	153,174	633,106	596,510	145,939
EBITDA	77,190	43,701	21,006	251,787	230,496	34,382
Depn & Amortn	(18,437)	(12,488)	(6,300)	74,829	72,658	18,164
Income Before Taxes	88,467	54,460	27,306	176,958	157,838	16,218
Income Taxes	15,782	2,763	418	588	...	...
Net Income	72,685	51,697	26,888	176,370	157,838	16,218
Average Shares	71,767	71,780	...	71,598	...	...
Balance Sheet						
Current Assets	138,803	151,644	105,500	119,541	98,517	...
Total Assets	2,527,924	2,559,885	2,515,497	2,547,266	2,473,667	...
Current Liabilities	97,086	100,592	65,887	71,984	88,370	...
Long-Term Obligations	597,468	647,752	...	...	...	...
Total Liabilities	1,021,452	1,076,352	116,376	129,981	169,148	...
Stockholders' Equity	1,506,472	1,483,533	2,399,121	2,417,285	2,304,519	...
Shares Outstanding	71,625	71,588	71,589	...	...	...
Statistical Record						
Return on Assets %	...	...	...	7.01	...	...
Return on Equity %	...	...	...	7.45	...	...
EBITDA Margin %	16.43	14.11	13.71	39.77	38.64	23.56
Net Margin %	15.47	16.69	17.55	27.86	26.46	11.11
Asset Turnover	...	...	...	0.25	...	...
Current Ratio	1.43	1.51	1.60	1.66	1.11	...
Debt to Equity	0.40	0.44	...	...	...	...
Price Range	29.14-23.12	29.14-25.34	...	...	...	...
P/E Ratio	47.77-37.90	28.02-24.37	...	...	...	...

Address: 300 S. Riverside Plaza, Suite 1000, Chicago, IL 60606 **Telephone:** 312-601-5000	**Web Site:** www.cars.com **Officers:** Scott E. Forbes - Chairman Thomas Alex Vetter - President, Chief Executive Officer	**Auditors:** Ernst & Young LLP **Transfer Agents:** Wells Fargo Shareowner Services, Mendota Heights, MN

CARTER'S INC

Exchange	Symbol	Price	52Wk Range	Yield	P/E
NYS	CRI	$117.49 (12/29/2017)	117.59-78.32	1.26	N/A

*7 Year Price Score 98.90   *NYSE Composite Index=100   *12 Month Price Score 111.00

Interim Earnings (Per Share)

Qtr.	Mar	Jun	Sep	Dec
2014	0.63	0.48	1.23	1.28
2015	0.94	0.68	1.51	1.38
2016	1.04	0.71	1.60	1.74
2017	0.95	0.78	1.71	...

Interim Dividends (Per Share)

Amt	Decl	Ex	Rec	Pay
0.37Q	02/15/2017	03/08/2017	03/10/2017	03/24/2017
0.37Q	05/17/2017	05/25/2017	05/30/2017	06/16/2017
0.37Q	08/17/2017	08/25/2017	08/29/2017	09/08/2017
0.37Q	11/08/2017	11/17/2017	11/20/2017	12/01/2017

Indicated Div: $1.48

Valuation Analysis / **Institutional Holding**

Valuation Analysis		Institutional Holding	
Forecast EPS	$5.63	No of Institutions	484
	(01/26/2018)		
Market Cap	$5.6 Billion	Shares	61,171,500
Book Value	$772.0 Million	% Held	87.62
Price/Book	7.22		
Price/Sales	N/A		

TRADING VOLUME (thousand shares)

Business Summary: Apparel, Footwear & Accessories (MIC: 1.4.2 SIC: 5641 NAIC: 315291)

Carter's is a marketer of apparel for babies and young children. Under its Carter's brand, Co. designs, sources, and markets a range of products, mainly for sizes newborn to eight. Under its OshKosh B'gosh (OshKosh) brand, Co. designs, sources, and markets a range of young children's apparel, mainly for children in sizes newborn to 12. Co. provides several product categories, including baby, sleepwear, playclothes, and related accessories. As of Dec 31 2016, Co. operated 495 Carter's and 138 OshKosh stores in the U.S., and its products are sold through 164 Co.-operated stores in Canada in addition to its international wholesale, licensing, and online channels.

Recent Developments: For the quarter ended Sep 30 2017, net income increased 2.1% to US$82.5 million from US$80.8 million in the year-earlier quarter. Revenues were US$948.2 million, up 5.2% from US$901.4 million the year before. Operating income was US$130.7 million versus US$130.9 million in the prior-year quarter, a decrease of 0.1%. Direct operating expenses rose 3.5% to US$544.4 million from US$525.9 million in the comparable period the year before. Indirect operating expenses increased 11.6% to US$273.1 million from US$244.7 million in the equivalent prior-year period.

Prospects: Our evaluation of Carter Holdings Inc. as of Jan. 21, 2018 is the result of our systematic analysis on three basic characteristics: earnings strength, relative valuation, and recent stock price movement. The company has enjoyed a very positive trend in earnings per share over the past 5 quarters and while recent estimates for the company have been mixed, CRI has posted better than expected results. Based on operating earnings yield, the company is undervalued when compared to all of the companies in our coverage universe. Share price changes over the past year indicates that CRI will perform in line with the market over the near term.

Financial Data

(US$ in Thousands)	9 Mos	6 Mos	3 Mos	12/31/2016	01/02/2016	01/03/2015	12/28/2013	12/29/2012
Earnings Per Share	...	5.07	5.00	5.08	4.50	3.62	2.75	2.69
Cash Flow Per Share	...	8.17	6.73	7.42	5.96	5.28	3.69	4.80
Tang Book Value Per Share	2.65	2.34	2.84	6.19	7.52	5.45	3.38	8.28
Dividends Per Share	1.440	1.400	1.360	1.320	0.880	0.760	0.480	...
Dividend Payout %	...	27.61	27.20	25.98	19.56	20.99	17.45	...
Income Statement								
Total Revenue	2,373,104	1,424,872	732,755	3,199,184	3,013,879	2,893,868	2,638,711	2,381,734
EBITDA	278,215	145,893	79,410	495,970	463,136	405,093	330,521	301,631
Depn & Amortn	2,830	2,041	623	73,419	68,417	74,937	68,288	39,500
Income Before Taxes	253,285	129,772	71,822	396,070	368,188	302,906	249,465	255,391
Income Taxes	86,210	45,183	25,158	137,964	130,366	108,236	89,058	94,241
Net Income	167,075	84,589	46,664	258,106	237,822	194,670	160,407	161,150
Average Shares	47,844	48,414	48,877	50,375	52,334	53,093	57,522	59,069
Balance Sheet								
Current Assets	1,049,100	993,697	841,850	1,057,086	1,131,465	1,041,458	970,381	957,703
Total Assets	2,104,063	2,031,859	1,885,463	1,946,597	2,009,113	1,893,096	1,812,484	1,630,109
Current Liabilities	327,909	311,984	225,047	277,609	262,718	247,971	269,139	244,235
Long-Term Obligations	687,074	661,846	581,621	580,376	584,431	586,000	586,000	186,000
Total Liabilities	1,332,100	1,281,948	1,113,500	1,158,473	1,134,062	1,106,412	1,111,753	644,630
Stockholders' Equity	771,963	749,911	771,963	788,124	875,051	786,684	700,731	985,479
Shares Outstanding	47,419	50,194	48,517	48,948	51,764	52,712	54,541	59,126
Statistical Record								
Return on Assets %	...	12.80	13.21	13.09	12.22	10.34	9.34	10.66
Return on Equity %	...	33.30	30.95	31.12	28.70	25.75	19.08	18.04
EBITDA Margin %	11.72	10.24	10.84	15.50	15.37	14.00	12.53	12.66
Net Margin %	7.04	5.94	6.37	8.07	7.89	6.73	6.08	6.77
Asset Turnover	...	1.65	1.69	1.62	1.55	1.54	1.54	1.57
Current Ratio	3.20	3.19	3.74	3.81	4.31	4.20	3.61	3.92
Debt to Equity	0.89	0.88	0.75	0.74	0.67	0.74	0.84	0.19
Price Range	98.75-78.32	111.47-78.32	111.47-78.32	111.47-84.16	108.98-80.98	87.31-64.84	77.33-55.55	57.44-39.49
P/E Ratio	...	21.99-15.45	22.29-15.66	21.94-16.57	24.22-18.00	24.12-17.91	28.12-20.20	21.35-14.68
Average Yield %	1.63	1.54	1.43	1.36	0.94	1.00	0.71	...

Address: Phipps Tower, 3438 Peachtree Road N.E., Suite 1800, Atlanta, GA 30326
Telephone: 678-791-1000

Web Site: www.carters.com
Officers: Michael Dennis Casey - Chairman, President, Chief Executive Officer Brian J. Lynch - President, Executive Vice President

Auditors: PricewaterhouseCoopers LLP
Investor Contact: 404-745-2889
Transfer Agents: American Stock Transfer & Trust Company, LLC, Brooklyn, NY

CATALENT INC

Exchange	Symbol	Price	52Wk Range	Yield	P/E
NYS	CTLT	$41.08 (12/29/2017)	43.02-25.88	N/A	47.22

*7 Year Price Score N/A *NYSE Composite Index=100 *12 Month Price Score 108.43

TRADING VOLUME (thousand shares)

Interim Earnings (Per Share)

Qtr.	Sep	Dec	Mar	Jun
2014-15	(0.18)	0.37	0.25	1.26
2015-16	0.07	0.24	0.08	0.50
2016-17	0.04	0.14	0.21	0.49
2017-18	0.03	...	...	...

Interim Dividends (Per Share)

No Dividends Paid

Valuation Analysis

		Institutional Holding
Forecast EPS	$1.63	No of Institutions
	(01/18/2018)	321
Market Cap	$5.5 Billion	Shares
Book Value	$1.0 Billion	154,730,480
Price/Book	5.25	% Held
Price/Sales	2.51	N/A

Business Summary: Pharmaceuticals (MIC: 4.1.1 SIC: 2834 NAIC: 325412)

Catalent is a holding company. Co. is a provider of delivery technologies and development solutions for drugs, biologics and consumer and animal health products. Co.'s segments include: Softgel Technologies, which provides formulation, development and manufacturing services for soft capsules; Drug Delivery Solutions, which provides various formulation delivery technologies, and related solutions including: development and manufacturing of a range of oral dose forms including fast-dissolve tablets and controlled release products; and Clinical Supply Services, which provides manufacturing, packaging, storage and inventory management for drugs and biologics in clinical trials.

Recent Developments: For the quarter ended Sep 30 2017, net income decreased 17.4% to US$3.8 million from US$4.6 million in the year-earlier quarter. Revenues were US$543.9 million, up 23.0% from US$442.2 million the year before. Operating income was US$31.9 million versus US$24.8 million in the prior-year quarter, an increase of 28.6%. Direct operating expenses rose 26.9% to US$403.8 million from US$318.1 million in the comparable period the year before. Indirect operating expenses increased 9.0% to US$108.2 million from US$99.3 million in the equivalent prior-year period.

Prospects: Our evaluation of Catalent Inc as of Jan. 14, 2018 is the result of our systematic analysis on three basic characteristics: earnings strength, relative valuation, and recent stock price movement. The company has managed to produce a neutral trend in earnings per share over the past 5 quarters and while recent estimates for the company have been raised by analysts, CTLT has posted better than expected results. Based on operating earnings yield, the company is about fairly valued when compared to all of the companies in our coverage universe. Share price changes over the past year indicates that CTLT will perform very well over the near term.

Financial Data

(US$ in Thousands)	3 Mos	06/30/2017	06/30/2016	06/30/2015	06/30/2014	06/30/2013	06/30/2012	06/30/2011
Earnings Per Share	0.87	0.87	0.89	1.75	0.21	(0.62)	(0.54)	(0.72)
Cash Flow Per Share	2.66	2.40	1.24	1.44	2.38	1.84	1.17	1.33
Income Statement								
Total Revenue	543,900	2,075,400	1,848,100	1,830,800	1,827,700	1,800,300	1,694,800	1,531,800
EBITDA	27,500	327,900	327,600	311,800	331,000	350,500	346,200	285,600
Depn & Amortn	1,300	102,200	94,200	94,300	100,500	171,200	144,400	125,500
Income Before Taxes	1,900	135,600	144,900	112,500	67,400	(23,900)	18,600	(5,400)
Income Taxes	(1,900)	25,800	33,700	(97,700)	49,500	24,100	16,500	23,700
Net Income	3,800	109,800	111,500	212,200	16,200	(46,700)	(40,400)	(54,000)
Average Shares	127,784	126,737	125,870	121,348	76,123	74,970	75,384	74,693
Balance Sheet								
Current Assets	1,330,100	1,059,800	790,200	737,500	687,500	677,900	704,700	205,100
Total Assets	3,784,800	3,454,300	3,091,100	3,145,400	3,090,200	3,056,800	3,139,000	2,729,100
Current Liabilities	457,100	469,000	391,200	399,000	453,000	410,300	439,300	...
Long-Term Obligations	2,082,900	2,055,100	1,832,800	1,864,100	2,685,400	2,656,600	2,640,300	...
Total Liabilities	2,746,000	2,730,800	2,455,200	2,511,400	3,461,400	3,467,500	3,489,700	...
Stockholders' Equity	1,038,800	723,500	635,900	634,000	(371,200)	(410,700)	(350,700)	...
Shares Outstanding	132,841	125,049	124,712	124,319	74,821	74,796	74,756	74,729
Statistical Record								
Return on Assets %	3.15	3.36	3.57	6.81	0.53	N.M.	N.M.	...
Return on Equity %	13.19	16.15	17.51	161.49	...	...	...	...
EBITDA Margin %	5.06	15.80	17.73	17.03	18.11	19.47	20.43	18.64
Net Margin %	0.70	5.29	6.03	11.59	0.89	N.M.	N.M.	N.M.
Asset Turnover	0.63	0.63	0.59	0.59	0.59	0.58	0.58	...
Current Ratio	2.91	2.26	2.02	1.85	1.52	1.65	1.60	...
Debt to Equity	2.01	2.84	2.88	2.94	...	...	...	...
Price Range	41.67-21.85	38.02-21.85	34.21-20.86	31.96-19.85	...	...	...	...
P/E Ratio	47.90-25.11	43.70-25.11	38.44-23.44	18.26-11.34	...	...	...	...

Address: 14 Schoolhouse Road, Somerset, NJ 08873 **Telephone:** 732-537-6200	**Web Site:** www.catalent.com **Officers:** John R. Chiminski - Chairman, President, Chief Executive Officer Matthew M. Walsh - Executive Vice President, Chief Financial Officer	**Auditors:** Ernst & Young LLP **Transfer Agents:** Computershare Trust Company, N.A.

CATERPILLAR INC.

Exchange	Symbol	Price	52Wk Range	Yield	P/E	Div Achiever
NYS	CAT	$157.58 (12/29/2017)	158.42-91.39	1.98	108.68	23 Years

*7 Year Price Score 95.47 *NYSE Composite Index=100 *12 Month Price Score 119.49

Interim Earnings (Per Share)

Qtr.	Mar	Jun	Sep	Dec
2014	1.44	1.57	1.63	1.24
2015	1.81	1.16	0.62	(0.12)
2016	0.46	0.93	0.48	(1.99)
2017	0.32	1.35	1.77	...

Interim Dividends (Per Share)

Amt	Decl	Ex	Rec	Pay
0.77Q	04/12/2017	04/20/2017	04/24/2017	05/20/2017
0.78Q	06/14/2017	07/18/2017	07/20/2017	08/19/2017
0.78Q	10/11/2017	10/20/2017	10/23/2017	11/20/2017
0.78Q	12/13/2017	01/19/2018	01/22/2018	02/20/2018

Indicated Div: $3.12 (Div. Reinv. Plan)

Valuation Analysis

		Institutional Holding
Forecast EPS	$6.47	No of Institutions
	(01/17/2018)	1780
Market Cap	$93.7 Billion	Shares
Book Value	$15.6 Billion	513,345,824
Price/Book	6.00	% Held
Price/Sales	2.22	62.10

Business Summary: Construction Services (MIC: 7.5.4 SIC: 3531 NAIC: 333120)

Caterpillar manufactures construction and mining equipment, diesel and natural gas engines, industrial gas turbines and diesel-electric locomotives. Co. has five segments: Construction Industries, which provides machinery for infrastructure, forestry and building construction applications; Resource Industries, which provides machinery for mining, quarry, waste, and material handling applications; Energy and Transportation, which provides reciprocating engines, turbines, diesel-electric locomotives and related parts; Financial Products Segment, which provides financing for Co.'s products; and All Other operating segments, which provides business strategy and product management.

Recent Developments: For the quarter ended Sep 30 2017, net income increased 274.9% to US$1.06 billion from US$283.0 million in the year-earlier quarter. Revenues were US$11.41 billion, up 24.6% from US$9.16 billion the year before. Operating income was US$1.58 billion versus US$481.0 million in the prior-year quarter, an increase of 227.9%. Direct operating expenses rose 16.9% to US$7.63 billion from US$6.53 billion in the comparable period the year before. Indirect operating expenses increased 2.4% to US$2.20 billion from US$2.15 billion in the equivalent prior-year period.

Prospects: Our evaluation of Caterpillar Inc. as of Jan. 14, 2018 is the result of our systematic analysis on three basic characteristics: earnings strength, relative valuation, and recent stock price movement. The company has enjoyed a very positive trend in earnings per share over the past 5 quarters and while recent estimates for the company have been raised by analysts, CAT has posted better than expected results. Based on operating earnings yield, the company is about fairly valued when compared to all of the companies in our coverage universe. Share price changes over the past year indicates that CAT will perform in line with the market over the near term.

Financial Data

(US$ in Thousands)	9 Mos	6 Mos	3 Mos	12/31/2016	12/31/2015	12/31/2014	12/31/2013	12/31/2012
Earnings Per Share	1.45	0.16	(0.26)	(0.11)	3.50	5.88	5.75	8.48
Cash Flow Per Share	11.48	11.40	11.34	9.57	11.23	13.05	15.80	8.01
Tang Book Value Per Share	12.20	9.54	8.91	8.13	9.23	11.51	16.08	10.04
Dividends Per Share	3.090	3.080	3.080	3.080	2.940	2.600	1.720	2.480
Dividend Payout %	213.10	1,925.00	...	...	84.00	44.22	29.91	29.25
Income Statement								
Total Revenue	32,566,000	21,153,000	9,822,000	38,537,000	47,011,000	55,184,000	55,656,000	65,875,000
EBITDA	5,970,000	3,443,000	1,281,000	3,947,000	6,654,000	8,986,000	9,030,000	11,921,000
Depn & Amortn	2,153,000	1,430,000	710,000	2,707,000	2,705,000	2,795,000	2,710,000	2,421,000
Income Before Taxes	2,971,000	1,448,000	289,000	139,000	2,855,000	5,083,000	5,128,000	8,236,000
Income Taxes	921,000	451,000	90,000	192,000	742,000	1,380,000	1,319,000	2,528,000
Net Income	2,053,000	994,000	192,000	(67,000)	2,102,000	3,695,000	3,789,000	5,681,000
Average Shares	600,100	595,400	593,200	584,300	601,300	628,900	658,600	669,600
Balance Sheet								
Current Assets	37,185,000	36,991,000	35,548,000	31,967,000	34,418,000	38,867,000	38,335,000	42,524,000
Total Assets	78,560,000	78,510,000	77,549,000	74,704,000	78,497,000	84,681,000	84,896,000	89,356,000
Current Liabilities	25,903,000	28,133,000	27,635,000	26,132,000	26,303,000	27,877,000	27,297,000	29,755,000
Long-Term Obligations	24,835,000	23,815,000	23,725,000	22,818,000	25,247,000	27,784,000	26,719,000	27,752,000
Total Liabilities	62,933,000	64,501,000	63,961,000	61,567,000	63,688,000	67,935,000	64,085,000	71,824,000
Stockholders' Equity	15,627,000	14,009,000	13,588,000	13,137,000	14,809,000	16,746,000	20,811,000	17,532,000
Shares Outstanding	594,933	590,972	589,090	586,486	582,321	606,166	637,822	655,048
Statistical Record								
Return on Assets %	1.14	0.14	N.M.	N.M.	2.58	4.36	4.35	6.63
Return on Equity %	5.64	0.73	N.M.	N.M.	13.32	19.68	19.76	37.25
EBITDA Margin %	18.33	16.28	13.04	10.24	14.15	16.28	16.22	18.10
Net Margin %	6.30	4.70	1.95	N.M.	4.47	6.70	6.81	8.62
Asset Turnover	0.54	0.51	0.50	0.50	0.58	0.65	0.64	0.77
Current Ratio	1.44	1.31	1.29	1.22	1.31	1.39	1.40	1.43
Debt to Equity	1.59	1.70	1.75	1.74	1.71	1.66	1.28	1.58
Price Range	125.23-81.11	107.60-74.38	99.02-69.43	97.33-57.91	91.88-63.79	111.40-86.17	99.49-80.43	116.20-79.64
P/E Ratio	86.37-55.94	672.50-464.88	...	...	26.25-18.23	18.95-14.65	17.30-13.99	13.70-9.39
Average Yield %	3.08	3.35	3.61	3.92	3.73	2.58	1.98	2.64

Address: 100 N.E. Adams Street, Peoria, IL 61629 Telephone: 309-675-1000 Fax: 309-675-4332	Web Site: www.caterpillar.com Officers: Donald James (Jim) Umpleby - Group President, Chief Executive Officer Bradley M. Halverson - Group President, Vice President, Chief Financial Officer, Controller	Auditors: PricewaterhouseCoopers LLP Investor Contact: 309-675-4549 Transfer Agents: ComputerShare, College Station, TX

CBRE GROUP INC

Exchange	Symbol	Price	52Wk Range	Yield	P/E
NYS	CBG	$43.31 (12/29/2017)	44.20-30.04	N/A	18.67

*7 Year Price Score 103.40 *NYSE Composite Index=100 *12 Month Price Score 109.23

Interim Earnings (Per Share)

Qtr.	Mar	Jun	Sep	Dec
2014	0.20	0.32	0.32	0.61
2015	0.28	0.37	0.44	0.54
2016	0.24	0.36	0.31	0.78
2017	0.38	0.58	0.58	...

Interim Dividends (Per Share)

No Dividends Paid

Valuation Analysis

Forecast EPS	$2.66
	(01/11/2018)
Market Cap	$14.7 Billion
Book Value	$3.8 Billion
Price/Book	3.87
Price/Sales	1.07

Institutional Holding

No of Institutions	696
Shares	399,112,832
% Held	N/A

TRADING VOLUME (thousand shares)

Business Summary: Property, Real Estate & Development (MIC: 5.3.2 SIC: 6531 NAIC: 531210)

CBRE Group is a holding company. Through its subsidiaries, Co. is a commercial real estate services and investment firm. Co. has five segments: The Americas, which consists of operations located in the U.S., Canada and Latin America; Europe, Middle East and Africa, which mainly consists of operations in Europe; Asia Pacific, which includes operations in Asia, Australia and New Zealand; Global Investment Management business, which consists of investment management operations in North America, Europe and Asia Pacific; and Development Services business, which consists of real estate development and investment activities primarily in the U.S.

Recent Developments: For the quarter ended Sep 30 2017, net income increased 78.0% to US$197.4 million from US$110.9 million in the year-earlier quarter. Revenues were US$3.55 billion, up 11.2% from US$3.19 billion the year before.

Prospects: Our evaluation of CBRE Group Inc. as of Jan. 14, 2018 is the result of our systematic analysis on three basic characteristics: earnings strength, relative valuation, and recent stock price movement. The company has generated a negative trend in earnings per share over the past 5 quarters and while recent estimates for the company have been mixed, CBG has posted better than expected results. Based on operating earnings yield, the company is undervalued when compared to all of the companies in our coverage universe. Share price changes over the past year indicates that CBG will perform well over the near term.

Financial Data
(US$ in Thousands)

	9 Mos	6 Mos	3 Mos	12/31/2016	12/31/2015	12/31/2014	12/31/2013	12/31/2012
Earnings Per Share	2.32	2.05	1.83	1.69	1.63	1.45	0.95	0.97
Cash Flow Per Share	2.22	1.39	1.30	1.34	1.96	2.00	2.27	0.90
Income Statement								
Total Revenue	9,873,396	6,323,419	2,981,204	13,071,589	10,855,810	9,049,918	7,184,794	6,514,099
EBITDA	669,164	429,646	201,796	971,375	966,650	904,150	671,456	672,374
Depn & Amortn	7,371	4,912	2,439	151,200	137,200	122,800	98,100	76,200
Income Before Taxes	564,837	359,132	167,758	683,375	716,881	675,548	444,563	428,749
Income Taxes	195,813	119,635	51,273	296,662	320,853	263,759	187,187	185,322
Net Income	523,079	326,762	129,597	571,973	547,132	484,503	316,538	315,555
Average Shares	341,186	340,882	339,690	338,424	336,414	334,171	331,762	327,044
Balance Sheet								
Current Assets	5,804,734	4,824,336	4,245,460	5,122,450	5,305,223	3,524,504	2,879,812	4,084,550
Total Assets	11,652,014	10,606,218	9,927,112	10,779,587	11,017,943	7,647,105	6,998,414	7,809,542
Current Liabilities	4,551,377	3,797,550	3,473,180	4,525,429	4,994,157	2,875,634	2,605,740	2,972,293
Long-Term Obligations	2,551,568	2,550,404	2,549,258	2,548,126	2,645,111	1,852,416	1,866,890	2,543,707
Total Liabilities	7,856,544	7,066,525	6,715,167	7,765,100	8,305,291	5,387,275	5,102,629	6,270,331
Stockholders' Equity	3,795,470	3,539,693	3,211,945	3,014,487	2,712,652	2,259,830	1,895,785	1,539,211
Shares Outstanding	339,459	337,929	337,874	337,279	334,230	332,991	331,927	330,082
Statistical Record								
Return on Assets %	7.02	6.77	6.27	5.23	5.86	6.62	4.28	4.19
Return on Equity %	23.39	21.73	20.55	19.92	22.01	23.32	18.43	23.39
EBITDA Margin %	6.78	6.79	6.77	7.43	8.90	9.99	9.35	10.32
Net Margin %	5.30	5.17	4.35	4.38	5.04	5.35	4.41	4.84
Asset Turnover	1.22	1.30	1.34	1.20	1.16	1.24	0.97	0.86
Current Ratio	1.28	1.27	1.22	1.13	1.06	1.23	1.11	1.37
Debt to Equity	0.67	0.72	0.79	0.85	0.98	0.82	0.98	1.65
Price Range	38.42-25.67	37.13-24.54	36.43-24.54	34.58-23.32	38.92-30.93	35.06-25.47	26.31-19.90	20.86-15.10
P/E Ratio	16.56-11.06	18.11-11.97	19.91-13.41	20.46-13.80	23.88-18.98	24.18-17.57	27.69-20.95	21.51-15.57

Address: 400 South Hope Street, 25th Floor, Los Angeles, CA 90071 **Telephone:** 213-613-3333	**Web Site:** www.cbre.com **Officers:** Robert E. Sulentic - President, Chief Executive Officer Michael J. Lafitte - Chief Operating Officer, Region Officer	**Auditors:** KPMG LLP **Investor Contact:** 213-613-3732 **Transfer Agents:** Broadridge Corporate Issuer Solutions, Inc., Edgewood, NY

CBS CORP

Exchange	Symbol	Price	52Wk Range	Yield	P/E
NYS	CBS	$59.00 (12/29/2017)	69.51-54.46	1.22	75.64

*7 Year Price Score 102.34 *NYSE Composite Index=100 *12 Month Price Score 86.27

Interim Earnings (Per Share)

Qtr.	Mar	Jun	Sep	Dec
2014	0.78	0.76	3.03	0.83
2015	0.78	0.67	0.88	0.56
2016	1.02	0.93	1.07	(0.21)
2017	(0.61)	0.14	1.46	...

Interim Dividends (Per Share)

Amt	Decl	Ex	Rec	Pay
0.18Q	01/26/2017	03/08/2017	03/10/2017	04/01/2017
0.18Q	05/19/2017	06/07/2017	06/09/2017	07/01/2017
0.18Q	07/20/2017	09/07/2017	09/00/2017	10/01/2017
0.18Q	11/21/2017	12/08/2017	12/11/2017	01/01/2018

Indicated Div: $0.72

Valuation Analysis / **Institutional Holding**

Forecast EPS	$4.36	No of Institutions
	(01/27/2018)	1067
Market Cap	$23.6 Billion	Shares
Book Value	$3.0 Billion	385,480,192
Price/Book	7.88	% Held
Price/Sales	1.90	N/A

TRADING VOLUME (thousand shares)

Business Summary: Radio & Television (MIC: 2.3.1 SIC: 4833 NAIC: 515120)

CBS is a mass media company. Co.'s segments include: Entertainment, which is composed of the CBS® Television Network, CBS Television Studios®, CBS Studios International™, CBS Television Distribution™, CBS Interactive™, CBS Films®, CBS All Access®, and CBSN®; Cable Networks, which is composed of Showtime Networks, CBS Sports Network®, and Smithsonian Networks™, which operates Smithsonian Channel™; Publishing, which is composed of Simon & Schuster, which publishes and distributes books under imprints such as Simon & Schuster®, Pocket Books®, Scribner®, Gallery Books®, Touchstone® and Atria Books®; and Local Media, which is composed of CBS Television Stations and CBS Local Digital Media™.

Recent Developments: For the quarter ended Sep 30 2017, income from continuing operations decreased 10.3% to US$418.0 million from US$466.0 million in the year-earlier quarter. Net income increased 23.8% to US$592.0 million from US$478.0 million in the year-earlier quarter. Revenues were US$3.17 billion, up 2.8% from US$3.08 billion the year before. Operating income was US$707.0 million versus US$721.0 million in the prior-year quarter, a decrease of 1.9%. Direct operating expenses rose 4.1% to US$1.86 billion from US$1.79 billion in the comparable period the year before. Indirect operating expenses increased 4.7% to US$602.0 million from US$575.0 million in the equivalent prior-year period.

Prospects: Our evaluation of CBS Corp. as of Jan. 21, 2018 is the result of our systematic analysis on three basic characteristics: earnings strength, relative valuation, and recent stock price movement. The company has managed to produce a neutral trend in earnings per share over the past 5 quarters. However, while recent estimates for the company have been mixed, CBS has posted better than expected results. Based on operating earnings yield, the company is undervalued when compared to all of the companies in our coverage universe. Share price changes over the past year indicates that CBS will perform in line with the market over the near term.

Financial Data

(US$ in Thousands)	9 Mos	6 Mos	3 Mos	12/31/2016	12/31/2015	12/31/2014	12/31/2013	12/31/2012
Earnings Per Share	0.78	0.39	1.18	2.81	2.89	5.27	3.01	2.39
Cash Flow Per Share	3.41	3.39	3.36	3.78	2.88	2.32	3.08	2.82
Dividends Per Share	0.720	0.720	0.690	0.660	0.600	0.540	0.480	0.440
Dividend Payout %	92.31	184.62	58.47	23.49	20.76	10.25	15.95	18.41
Income Statement								
Total Revenue	9,771,000	6,600,000	3,343,000	13,166,000	13,886,000	13,806,000	15,284,000	14,089,000
EBITDA	2,250,000	1,490,000	760,000	2,814,000	2,631,000	2,763,000	3,622,000	3,326,000
Depn & Amortn	166,000	111,000	55,000	205,000	240,000	249,000	357,000	369,000
Income Before Taxes	1,793,000	1,187,000	609,000	2,230,000	2,023,000	2,164,000	2,897,000	2,561,000
Income Taxes	479,000	307,000	138,000	628,000	587,000	762,000	978,000	892,000
Net Income	398,000	(194,000)	(252,000)	1,261,000	1,413,000	2,959,000	1,879,000	1,574,000
Average Shares	406,000	410,000	416,000	448,000	489,000	561,000	624,000	659,000
Balance Sheet								
Current Assets	6,294,000	5,686,000	5,620,000	6,063,000	5,747,000	5,589,000	5,370,000	5,720,000
Total Assets	23,894,000	22,653,000	23,022,000	24,238,000	23,765,000	24,072,000	26,387,000	26,466,000
Current Liabilities	4,052,000	3,230,000	3,424,000	3,708,000	3,560,000	4,033,000	4,207,000	3,941,000
Long-Term Obligations	9,080,000	8,898,000	8,900,000	8,902,000	8,226,000	6,510,000	5,940,000	5,904,000
Total Liabilities	20,900,000	20,026,000	20,137,000	20,549,000	18,202,000	17,102,000	16,421,000	16,253,000
Stockholders' Equity	2,994,000	2,627,000	2,885,000	3,689,000	5,563,000	6,970,000	9,966,000	10,213,000
Shares Outstanding	400,000	403,000	407,000	412,000	463,000	507,000	596,000	630,000
Statistical Record								
Return on Assets %	1.19	0.75	2.30	5.24	5.91	11.73	7.11	5.96
Return on Equity %	6.83	4.27	12.81	27.18	22.55	34.94	18.62	15.60
EBITDA Margin %	23.03	22.58	22.73	21.37	18.95	20.01	23.70	23.61
Net Margin %	4.07	N.M.	N.M.	9.58	10.18	21.43	12.29	11.17
Asset Turnover	0.52	0.55	0.54	0.55	0.58	0.55	0.58	0.53
Current Ratio	1.55	1.76	1.64	1.64	1.61	1.39	1.28	1.45
Debt to Equity	3.03	3.39	3.08	2.41	1.48	0.93	0.60	0.58
Price Range	69.51-54.74	69.51-49.97	69.36-49.97	64.85-42.65	63.35-38.67	67.55-48.91	63.74-37.52	38.05-27.27
P/E Ratio	89.12-70.18	178.23-128.13	58.78-42.35	23.08-15.18	21.92-13.38	12.82-9.28	21.18-12.47	15.92-11.41
Average Yield %	1.14	1.19	1.19	1.23	1.12	0.92	0.95	1.33

Address: 51 W. 52nd Street, New York, NY 10019	Web Site: www.cbscorporation.com	Auditors: PricewaterhouseCoopers LLP
Telephone: 212-975-4321	Officers: Leslie Moonves - Chairman, President, Chief Executive Officer Sumner M. Redstone - Chairman Emeritus, Executive Chairman	Investor Contact: 187-722-70787 Transfer Agents: Wells Fargo Shareowner Services, St. Paul, MN

CELANESE CORP (DE)

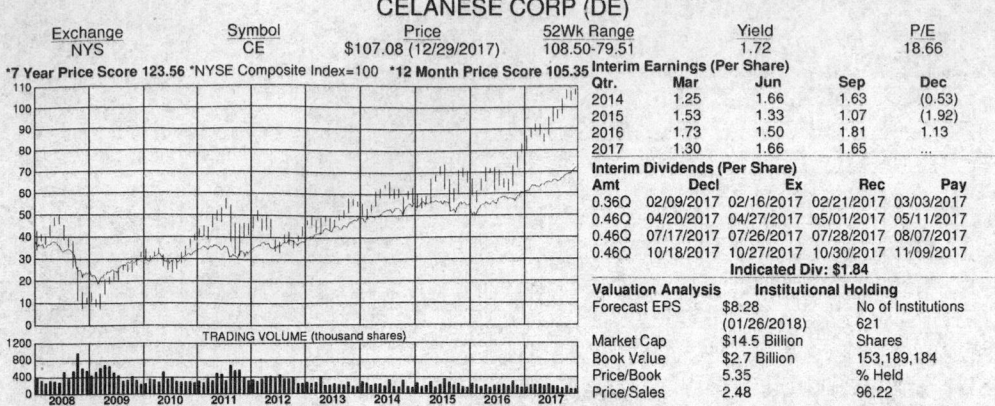

Exchange	Symbol	Price	52Wk Range	Yield	P/E
NYS	CE	$107.08 (12/29/2017)	108.50-79.51	1.72	18.66

*7 Year Price Score 123.56 *NYSE Composite Index=100 *12 Month Price Score 105.35

Interim Earnings (Per Share)

Qtr.	Mar	Jun	Sep	Dec
2014	1.25	1.66	1.63	(0.53)
2015	1.53	1.33	1.07	(1.92)
2016	1.73	1.50	1.81	1.13
2017	1.30	1.66	1.65	...

Interim Dividends (Per Share)

Amt	Decl	Ex	Rec	Pay
0.36Q	02/09/2017	02/16/2017	02/21/2017	03/03/2017
0.46Q	04/20/2017	04/27/2017	05/01/2017	05/11/2017
0.46Q	07/17/2017	07/26/2017	07/28/2017	08/07/2017
0.46Q	10/18/2017	10/27/2017	10/30/2017	11/09/2017

Indicated Div: $1.84

Valuation Analysis / Institutional Holding

Valuation Analysis		Institutional Holding	
Forecast EPS	$8.28	No of Institutions	
	(01/26/2018)	621	
Market Cap	$14.5 Billion	Shares	
Book Value	$2.7 Billion	153,189,184	
Price/Book	5.35	% Held	
Price/Sales	2.48	96.22	

Business Summary: Specialty Chemicals (MIC: 8.3.2 SIC: 5169 NAIC: 424690)

Celanese is a technology and specialty materials company. Co.'s segments include: Advanced Engineered Materials, which includes its engineered materials business that uses polymer technology to produce a portfolio of specialty polymers used automotive, medical and electronics products, as well as other consumer and industrial applications; Consumer Specialties, which includes Co.'s cellulose derivatives and food ingredients businesses; Industrial Specialties, which includes Co.'s emulsion polymers and ethylene vinyl acetate polymers businesses; and Acetyl Intermediates, which includes its intermediate chemistry business, which produces and supplies acetyl products.

Recent Developments: For the quarter ended Sep 30 2017, income from continuing operations decreased 12.8% to US$232.0 million from US$266.0 million in the year-earlier quarter. Net income decreased 13.3% to US$228.0 million from US$263.0 million in the year-earlier quarter. Revenues were US$1.57 billion, up 18.4% from US$1.32 billion the year before. Operating income was US$252.0 million versus US$246.0 million in the prior-year quarter, an increase of 2.4%. Direct operating expenses rose 22.0% to US$1.18 billion from US$968.0 million in the comparable period the year before. Indirect operating expenses increased 22.0% to US$133.0 million from US$109.0 million in the equivalent prior-year period.

Prospects: Our evaluation of Celanese Corp. as of Jan. 21, 2018 is the result of our systematic analysis on three basic characteristics: earnings strength, relative valuation, and recent stock price movement. The company has enjoyed a very positive trend in earnings per share over the past 5 quarters and while recent estimates for the company have been raised by analysts, CE has posted better than expected results. Based on operating earnings yield, the company is undervalued when compared to all of the companies in our coverage universe. Share price changes over the past year indicates that CE will perform well over the near term.

Financial Data

(US$ in Thousands)	9 Mos	6 Mos	3 Mos	12/31/2016	12/31/2015	12/31/2014	12/31/2013	12/31/2012
Earnings Per Share	5.74	5.90	5.74	6.18	2.00	4.00	6.91	3.79
Cash Flow Per Share	5.11	5.39	5.67	6.14	5.71	6.21	4.80	4.55
Tang Book Value Per Share	10.45	10.29	11.60	11.36	10.55	12.67	11.21	4.94
Dividends Per Share	1.640	1.540	1.440	1.380	1.150	0.930	0.525	0.270
Dividend Payout %	28.57	26.10	25.09	22.33	57.50	23.25	7.60	7.12
Income Statement								
Total Revenue	4,547,000	2,981,000	1,471,000	5,389,000	5,674,000	6,802,000	6,510,000	6,418,000
EBITDA	778,000	503,000	226,000	1,283,000	782,000	1,133,000	1,912,000	910,000
Depn & Amortn	14,000	9,000	4,000	290,000	357,000	292,000	312,000	312,000
Income Before Taxes	675,000	436,000	193,000	875,000	307,000	695,000	1,429,000	415,000
Income Taxes	153,000	96,000	56,000	122,000	201,000	314,000	508,000	48,000
Net Income	640,000	414,000	183,000	900,000	304,000	624,000	1,101,000	605,000
Average Shares	136,951	139,029	140,997	145,668	152,287	156,166	159,334	159,796
Balance Sheet								
Current Assets	2,613,000	2,583,000	2,389,000	2,472,000	2,787,000	2,698,000	3,182,000	2,839,000
Total Assets	9,062,000	8,883,000	8,288,000	8,357,000	8,586,000	8,818,000	9,018,000	9,000,000
Current Liabilities	1,550,000	1,424,000	1,015,000	1,077,000	1,550,000	1,338,000	1,545,000	1,355,000
Long-Term Obligations	2,954,000	2,931,000	2,851,000	2,890,000	2,468,000	2,608,000	2,887,000	2,930,000
Total Liabilities	6,347,000	6,189,000	5,677,000	5,769,000	6,208,000	6,000,000	6,319,000	7,270,000
Stockholders' Equity	2,715,000	2,694,000	2,611,000	2,588,000	2,378,000	2,818,000	2,699,000	1,730,000
Shares Outstanding	135,636	137,654	139,552	140,660	146,782	152,902	156,939	159,642
Statistical Record								
Return on Assets %	8.98	9.76	9.90	10.59	3.49	7.00	12.22	6.89
Return on Equity %	29.49	31.57	31.43	36.15	11.70	22.62	49.72	39.29
EBITDA Margin %	17.11	16.87	15.36	23.81	13.78	16.66	29.37	14.18
Net Margin %	14.08	13.89	12.44	16.70	5.36	9.17	16.91	9.43
Asset Turnover	0.66	0.66	0.65	0.63	0.62	0.76	0.72	0.73
Current Ratio	1.69	1.81	2.35	2.30	1.80	2.02	2.06	2.10
Debt to Equity	1.09	1.09	1.09	1.12	1.04	0.93	1.07	1.69
Price Range	104.34-63.37	95.63-60.97	92.46-60.97	83.30-55.81	73.72-53.41	66.05-48.83	58.25-41.97	52.22-33.28
P/E Ratio	18.18-11.04	16.21-10.33	16.11-10.62	13.48-9.03	36.86-26.70	16.51-12.21	8.43-6.07	13.78-8.78
Average Yield %	1.88	1.95	1.94	2.03	1.81	1.81	1.59	0.64

Address: 222 West Las Colinas Blvd., Suite 900N, Irving, TX 75039-5421
Telephone: 972-443-4000

Web Site: www.celanese.com
Officers: Mark C. Rohr - Chairman, Chief Executive Officer Peter G. Edwards - Executive Vice President, General Counsel

Auditors: KPMG LLP
Investor Contact: 972-443-4965
Transfer Agents: ComputerShare Investor Services, Providence, RI

CENTENE CORP

Exchange	Symbol	Price	52Wk Range	Yield	P/E
NYS	CNC	$100.88 (12/29/2017)	103.02-58.31	N/A	20.26

*7 Year Price Score 143.88 *NYSE Composite Index=100 *12 Month Price Score 113.73

Interim Earnings (Per Share)

Qtr.	Mar	Jun	Sep	Dec
2014	0.28	0.41	0.68	0.88
2015	0.51	0.72	0.76	0.89
2016	(0.14)	0.97	0.83	1.56
2017	0.79	1.47	1.16	...

Interim Dividends (Per Share)

No Dividends Paid

Valuation Analysis   **Institutional Holding**

Forecast EPS	$5.00	No of Institutions
	(01/18/2018)	773
Market Cap	$17.4 Billion	Shares
Book Value	$6.6 Billion	186,150,112
Price/Book	2.62	% Held
Price/Sales	0.37	100.11

Business Summary: Hospitals & Health Care Facilities (MIC: 4.2.1 SIC: 6324 NAIC: 524114)

Centene is a healthcare enterprise that provides a portfolio of services to government sponsored healthcare programs. Co. operates in two segments: Managed Care, which provides health plan coverage to individuals through government subsidized programs, including Medicaid, the State Children's Health Insurance Program, Long Term Care, Foster Care, dual-eligible individuals, the Supplemental Security Income Program, also known as the Aged, Blind or Disabled Program, Medicare, and Health Insurance Marketplace; and Specialty Services, which consists of Co.'s specialty companies providing a range of healthcare services and products.

Recent Developments: For the quarter ended Sep 30 2017, income from continuing operations increased 34.9% to US$201.0 million from US$149.0 million in the year-earlier quarter. Net income increased 35.8% to US$201.0 million from US$148.0 million in the year-earlier quarter. Revenues were US$11.90 billion, up 9.7% from US$10.85 billion the year before.

Prospects: Our evaluation of Centene Corp. as of Jan. 14, 2018 is the result of our systematic analysis on three basic characteristics: earnings strength, relative valuation, and recent stock price movement. The company has generated a negative trend in earnings per share over the past 5 quarters and while recent estimates for the company have been mixed, CNC has posted better than expected results. Based on operating earnings yield, the company is undervalued when compared to all of the companies in our coverage universe. Share price changes over the past year indicates that CNC will perform very well over the near term.

Financial Data

(US$ in Thousands)	9 Mos	6 Mos	3 Mos	12/31/2016	12/31/2015	12/31/2014	12/31/2013	12/31/2012
Earnings Per Share	4.98	4.65	4.15	3.43	2.88	2.25	1.47	0.01
Cash Flow Per Share	15.27	17.51	16.88	11.57	5.52	10.51	3.53	2.70
Tang Book Value Per Share	2.90	1.16	N.M.	N.M.	9.64	7.35	7.56	6.46
Income Statement								
Total Revenue	35,576,000	23,678,000	11,724,000	40,607,000	22,760,000	16,560,000	10,863,329	8,667,612
EBITDA	1,272,000	843,000	321,000	1,622,000	818,000	557,000	348,108	58,948
Depn & Amortn	117,000	79,000	40,000	248,000	78,000	65,000	52,234	50,112
Income Before Taxes	966,000	640,000	219,000	1,157,000	697,000	457,000	268,917	(11,624)
Income Taxes	381,000	256,000	87,000	599,000	339,000	196,000	107,080	(329)
Net Income	598,000	393,000	139,000	562,000	355,000	271,000	165,099	1,859
Average Shares	176,915	176,420	175,836	163,975	123,066	120,360	112,494	107,428
Balance Sheet								
Current Assets	9,660,000	9,648,000	9,408,000	8,365,000	3,605,000	3,034,000	1,800,173	1,373,602
Total Assets	22,000,000	21,840,000	21,362,000	20,197,000	7,339,000	5,838,000	3,529,300	2,741,682
Current Liabilities	9,709,000	8,966,000	9,202,000	8,623,000	3,629,000	2,900,000	1,559,121	1,197,090
Long-Term Obligations	4,717,000	4,716,000	4,643,000	4,651,000	1,216,000	888,000	665,697	535,481
Total Liabilities	15,360,000	15,462,000	15,292,000	14,302,000	5,182,000	4,094,000	2,295,259	1,788,626
Stockholders' Equity	6,640,000	6,378,000	6,070,000	5,895,000	2,157,000	1,744,000	1,234,041	953,056
Shares Outstanding	172,566	172,467	172,271	171,919	120,342	118,433	110,638	104,658
Statistical Record								
Return on Assets %	4.15	3.89	3.59	4.07	5.39	5.79	5.27	0.08
Return on Equity %	13.98	13.49	12.63	13.92	18.20	18.20	15.10	0.20
EBITDA Margin %	3.58	3.56	2.74	3.99	3.59	3.36	3.20	0.68
Net Margin %	1.68	1.66	1.19	1.38	1.56	1.64	1.52	0.02
Asset Turnover	2.28	2.25	2.27	2.94	3.45	3.54	3.46	3.51
Current Ratio	0.99	1.08	1.02	0.97	0.99	1.05	1.15	1.15
Debt to Equity	0.71	0.74	0.76	0.79	0.56	0.51	0.54	0.56
Price Range	98.16-50.68	84.15-50.68	75.39-50.68	75.39-50.68	81.48-51.92	53.58-27.83	33.19-20.45	25.40-13.42
P/E Ratio	19.71-10.18	18.10-10.90	18.17-12.21	21.98-14.78	28.29-18.03	23.81-12.37	22.58-13.91	N.M.

Address: 7700 Forsyth Boulevard, St. Louis, MO 63105 Telephone: 314-725-4477 Fax: 314-725-5180	Web Site: www.centene.com Officers: Michael F. Neidorff - Chairman, President, Chief Executive Officer Jeffrey A. Schwaneke - Executive Vice President, Senior Vice President, Vice President, Chief Financial Officer, Chief Accounting Officer, Corporate Controller, Treasurer	Auditors: KPMG LLP Transfer Agents: Broadridge Corporate Issuer Solutions, Inc., Philadelphia, PA

CENTERPOINT ENERGY, INC

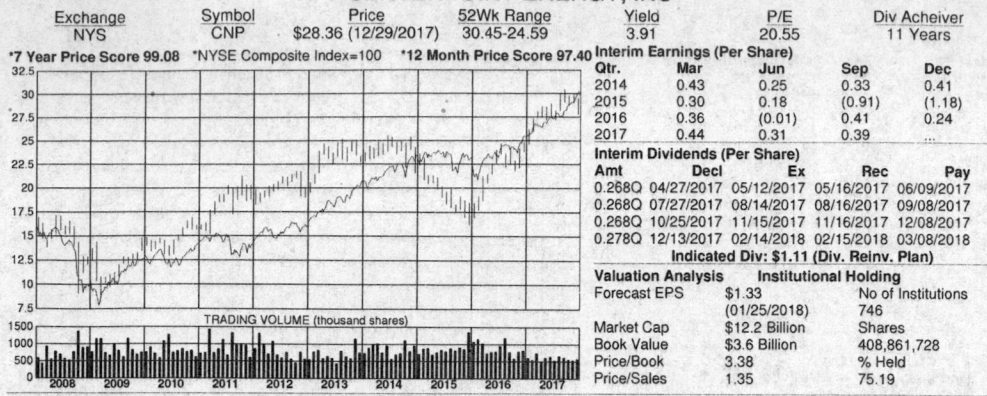

Exchange	Symbol	Price	52Wk Range	Yield	P/E	Div Acheiver
NYS	CNP	$28.36 (12/29/2017)	30.45-24.59	3.91	20.55	11 Years

*7 Year Price Score 99.08 *NYSE Composite Index=100 *12 Month Price Score 97.40

Interim Earnings (Per Share)

Qtr.	Mar	Jun	Sep	Dec
2014	0.43	0.25	0.33	0.41
2015	0.30	0.18	(0.91)	(1.18)
2016	0.36	(0.01)	0.41	0.24
2017	0.44	0.31	0.39	...

Interim Dividends (Per Share)

Amt	Decl	Ex	Rec	Pay
0.268Q	04/27/2017	05/12/2017	05/16/2017	06/09/2017
0.268Q	07/27/2017	08/14/2017	08/16/2017	09/08/2017
0.268Q	10/25/2017	11/15/2017	11/16/2017	12/08/2017
0.278Q	12/13/2017	02/14/2018	02/15/2018	03/08/2018

Indicated Div: $1.11 (Div. Reinv. Plan)

Valuation Analysis		Institutional Holding	
Forecast EPS	$1.33	No of Institutions	
	(01/25/2018)		746
Market Cap	$12.2 Billion	Shares	
Book Value	$3.6 Billion		408,861,728
Price/Book	3.38	% Held	
Price/Sales	1.35		75.19

Business Summary: Electric Utilities (MIC: 3.1.1 SIC: 4911 NAIC: 221111)

CenterPoint Energy is a public utility holding company whose subsidiaries include: CenterPoint Energy Houston Electric, LLC, which engages in the electric transmission and distribution business in the Texas Gulf Coast area; CenterPoint Energy Resources Corp. (CERC Corp.), which owns and operates natural gas distribution systems; and CenterPoint Energy Services, Inc., which obtains and provides variable and fixed-price physical natural gas supplies and services mainly to commercial and industrial customers and electric and natural gas utilities. CERC Corp. also owns interests in Enable Midstream Partners, LP, which owns, operates and develops natural gas and crude oil infrastructure assets.

Recent Developments: For the quarter ended Sep 30 2017, net income decreased 5.6% to US$169.0 million from US$179.0 million in the year-earlier quarter. Revenues were US$2.10 billion, up 11.1% from US$1.89 billion the year before. Operating income was US$279.0 million versus US$284.0 million in the prior-year quarter, a decrease of 1.8%. Direct operating expenses rose 22.6% to US$1.46 billion from US$1.19 billion in the comparable period the year before. Indirect operating expenses decreased 13.2% to US$362.0 million from US$417.0 million in the equivalent prior-year period.

Prospects: Our evaluation of Centerpoint Energy Inc. as of Jan. 21, 2018 is the result of our systematic analysis on three basic characteristics: earnings strength, relative valuation, and recent stock price movement. The company has generated a negative trend in earnings per share over the past 5 quarters and while recent estimates for the company have been mixed, CNP has posted results that fell short of analysts expectations. Based on operating earnings yield, the company is undervalued when compared to all of the companies in our coverage universe. Share price changes over the past year indicates that CNP will perform well over the near term.

Financial Data

(US$ in Thousands)	9 Mos	6 Mos	3 Mos	12/31/2016	12/31/2015	12/31/2014	12/31/2013	12/31/2012
Earnings Per Share	1.38	1.40	1.08	1.00	(1.61)	1.42	0.72	0.97
Cash Flow Per Share	3.50	3.60	3.74	4.46	4.34	3.25	3.76	4.34
Tang Book Value Per Share	6.38	6.25	6.20	6.03	6.10	8.62	8.13	6.62
Dividends Per Share	1.060	1.050	1.040	1.030	0.990	0.950	0.830	0.810
Dividend Payout %	76.81	75.00	96.30	103.00	...	66.90	115.28	83.51
Income Statement								
Total Revenue	6,976,000	4,878,000	2,735,000	7,528,000	7,386,000	9,226,000	8,106,000	7,452,000
EBITDA	889,000	586,000	331,000	2,033,000	1,930,000	2,061,000	1,608,000	1,857,000
Depn & Amortn	18,000	12,000	6,000	1,126,000	970,000	1,013,000	531,000	562,000
Income Before Taxes	578,000	379,000	227,000	478,000	503,000	577,000	593,000	726,000
Income Taxes	281,000	183,000	107,000	254,000	(438,000)	274,000	470,000	340,000
Net Income	496,000	327,000	192,000	432,000	(692,000)	611,000	311,000	417,000
Average Shares	434,000	434,000	433,348	431,000	430,000	432,000	430,930	429,794
Balance Sheet								
Current Assets	2,935,000	2,865,000	2,896,000	2,923,000	2,689,000	3,268,000	2,658,000	2,874,000
Total Assets	22,135,000	22,045,000	21,931,000	21,829,000	21,334,000	23,200,000	21,870,000	22,871,000
Current Liabilities	3,221,000	3,038,000	2,642,000	3,080,000	2,467,000	3,475,000	3,019,000	3,575,000
Long-Term Obligations	7,531,000	7,587,000	7,892,000	7,532,000	7,901,000	8,009,000	7,817,000	8,357,000
Total Liabilities	18,517,000	18,482,000	18,394,000	18,369,000	17,873,000	18,652,000	17,541,000	18,570,000
Stockholders' Equity	3,618,000	3,563,000	3,537,000	3,460,000	3,461,000	4,548,000	4,329,000	4,301,000
Shares Outstanding	431,030	431,021	430,958	430,682	430,000	430,000	429,000	428,000
Statistical Record								
Return on Assets %	2.75	2.82	2.19	2.00	N.M.	2.71	1.39	1.87
Return on Equity %	16.84	17.44	13.35	12.45	N.M.	13.77	7.21	9.76
EBITDA Margin %	12.74	12.01	12.10	27.01	26.13	22.34	19.84	24.92
Net Margin %	7.11	6.70	7.02	5.74	N.M.	6.62	3.84	5.60
Asset Turnover	0.42	0.41	0.39	0.35	0.33	0.41	0.36	0.33
Current Ratio	0.91	0.94	1.10	0.95	1.09	0.94	0.88	0.80
Debt to Equity	2.08	2.13	2.23	2.18	2.28	1.76	1.81	1.94
Price Range	30.45-21.84	28.93-21.84	28.09-20.51	24.84-16.90	23.63-16.14	25.54-21.54	25.16-19.25	21.75-18.23
P/E Ratio	22.07-15.83	20.66-15.60	26.01-18.99	24.84-16.90	...	17.99-15.17	34.94-26.74	22.42-18.79
Average Yield %	3.97	4.15	4.37	4.70	5.05	3.95	3.58	4.04

Address: 1111 Louisiana, Houston, TX 77002	**Web Site:** www.centerpointenergy.com	**Auditors:** Deloitte & Touche LLP
Telephone: 713-207-1111	**Officers:** Milton Carroll - Executive Chairman Scott M. Prochazka - President, Chief Executive Officer, Executive Vice President, Chief Operating Officer	**Investor Contact:** 713-207-6500
		Transfer Agents: CenterPoint Energy Investor Services

CENTURYLINK INC

Exchange	Symbol	Price	52Wk Range	Yield	P/E
NYS	CTL	$16.68 (12/29/2017)	27.31-13.62	12.95	28.76

*7 Year Price Score 52.01 *NYSE Composite Index=100 *12 Month Price Score 67.79

TRADING VOLUME (thousand shares)

Interim Earnings (Per Share)

Qtr.	Mar	Jun	Sep	Dec
2014	0.35	0.34	0.33	0.34
2015	0.34	0.26	0.37	0.61
2016	0.44	0.36	0.28	0.08
2017	0.30	0.03	0.17	...

Interim Dividends (Per Share)

Amt	Decl	Ex	Rec	Pay
0.54Q	02/21/2017	03/01/2017	03/03/2017	03/17/2017
0.54Q	05/24/2017	06/01/2017	06/05/2017	06/16/2017
0.54Q	08/22/2017	08/31/2017	09/05/2017	09/15/2017
0.54Q	11/14/2017	11/24/2017	11/27/2017	12/11/2017

Indicated Div: $2.16 (Div. Reinv. Plan)

Valuation Analysis / Institutional Holding

Forecast EPS	$1.63	No of Institutions
	(01/18/2018)	973
Market Cap	$9.2 Billion	Shares
Book Value	$13.0 Billion	524,205,696
Price/Book	0.71	% Held
Price/Sales	0.55	70.23

Business Summary: Services (MIC: 6.1.2 SIC: 4813 NAIC: 517110)

CenturyLink is a holding company. Through its subsidiaries, Co. is a communications company. Co.'s communications services include local and long-distance voice, broadband, Multi-Protocol Label Switching, private line (including special access), Ethernet, colocation, hosting (including cloud hosting and managed hosting), data integration, video, network, public access, Voice over Internet Protocol, information technology and other ancillary services. Co. has two segments: Business, which provides products and services to enterprise, wholesale and governmental customers, including other communication providers; and Consumer, which provides products and services to residential consumers.

Recent Developments: For the quarter ended Sep 30 2017, net income decreased 39.5% to US$92.0 million from US$152.0 million in the year-earlier quarter. Revenues were US$4.03 billion, down 7.9% from US$4.38 billion the year before. Operating income was US$487.0 million versus US$593.0 million in the prior-year quarter, a decrease of 17.9%. Direct operating expenses declined 3.5% to US$1.93 billion from US$2.00 billion in the comparable period the year before. Indirect operating expenses decreased 9.6% to US$1.62 billion from US$1.79 billion in the equivalent prior-year period.

Prospects: Our evaluation of CenturyLink, Inc. as of Jan. 14, 2018 is the result of our systematic analysis on three basic characteristics: earnings strength, relative valuation, and recent stock price movement. The company has managed to produce a neutral trend in earnings per share over the past 5 quarters. However, while recent estimates for the company have been mixed, CTL has posted results that fell short of analysts expectations. Based on operating earnings yield, the company is undervalued when compared to all of the companies in our coverage universe. Share price changes over the past year indicates that CTL will perform very poorly over the near term.

Financial Data

(US$ in Thousands)	9 Mos	6 Mos	3 Mos	12/31/2016	12/31/2015	12/31/2014	12/31/2013	12/31/2012
Earnings Per Share	0.58	0.69	1.02	1.16	1.58	1.36	(0.40)	1.25
Cash Flow Per Share	7.01	6.93	7.85	8.52	9.29	9.13	9.25	9.75
Dividends Per Share	2.160	2.160	2.160	2.160	2.160	2.160	2.160	2.900
Dividend Payout %	372.41	313.04	211.76	186.21	136.71	158.82	...	232.00
Income Statement								
Total Revenue	12,333,000	8,299,000	4,209,000	17,470,000	17,900,000	18,031,000	18,095,000	18,376,000
EBITDA	4,225,000	2,814,000	626,000	5,029,000	5,464,000	5,379,000	4,474,000	5,667,000
Depn & Amortn	2,739,000	1,829,000	1,000	2,691,000	2,836,000	2,958,000	2,952,000	3,098,000
Income Before Taxes	486,000	347,000	307,000	1,020,000	1,316,000	1,110,000	224,000	1,250,000
Income Taxes	214,000	167,000	144,000	394,000	438,000	338,000	463,000	473,000
Net Income	272,000	180,000	163,000	626,000	878,000	772,000	(239,000)	777,000
Average Shares	541,963	542,151	541,522	540,679	555,093	569,739	600,892	622,285
Balance Sheet								
Current Assets	2,694,000	2,908,000	4,968,000	5,162,000	2,650,000	3,576,000	3,907,000	3,613,000
Total Assets	50,536,000	50,925,000	46,602,000	47,017,000	47,604,000	50,147,000	51,787,000	54,020,000
Current Liabilities	3,266,000	3,243,000	5,096,000	5,349,000	4,604,000	3,918,000	4,409,000	4,595,000
Long-Term Obligations	24,854,000	24,881,000	18,180,000	18,185,000	18,722,000	20,121,000	20,181,000	19,400,000
Total Liabilities	37,576,000	37,839,000	33,296,000	33,618,000	33,544,000	35,124,000	34,596,000	34,731,000
Stockholders' Equity	12,960,000	13,086,000	13,306,000	13,399,000	14,060,000	15,023,000	17,191,000	19,289,000
Shares Outstanding	549,654	549,743	548,845	546,545	543,800	568,517	583,637	625,658
Statistical Record								
Return on Assets %	0.65	0.76	1.18	1.32	1.80	1.51	N.M.	1.41
Return on Equity %	2.34	2.76	4.05	4.55	6.04	4.79	N.M.	3.86
EBITDA Margin %	34.26	33.91	14.87	28.79	30.53	29.83	24.73	30.84
Net Margin %	2.21	2.17	3.87	3.58	4.91	4.28	N.M.	4.23
Asset Turnover	0.34	0.35	0.37	0.37	0.37	0.35	0.34	0.33
Current Ratio	0.82	0.90	0.97	0.97	0.58	0.91	0.89	0.79
Debt to Equity	1.92	1.90	1.37	1.36	1.33	1.34	1.17	1.01
Price Range	31.00-18.32	31.44-22.45	32.80-22.45	32.80-22.24	40.52-24.38	41.81-28.09	41.76-30.30	42.95-36.59
P/E Ratio	53.45-31.59	45.57-32.54	32.16-22.01	28.28-19.17	25.65-15.43	30.74-20.65	...	34.36-29.27
Average Yield %	9.00	8.29	7.98	7.73	6.87	5.92	6.18	7.37

Address: 100 CenturyLink Drive, Monroe, LA 71203	**Web Site:** www.centurylink.com	**Auditors:** KPMG LLP
Telephone: 318-388-9000	**Officers:** Glen F. Post - President, Chief Executive Officer David D. Cole - Executive Vice President, Senior Vice President, Controller, Assistant Secretary	**Investor Contact:** 800-833-1188
Fax: 318-789-8656		**Transfer Agents:** Computershare Trust Company, Providence, RI

CF INDUSTRIES HOLDINGS INC

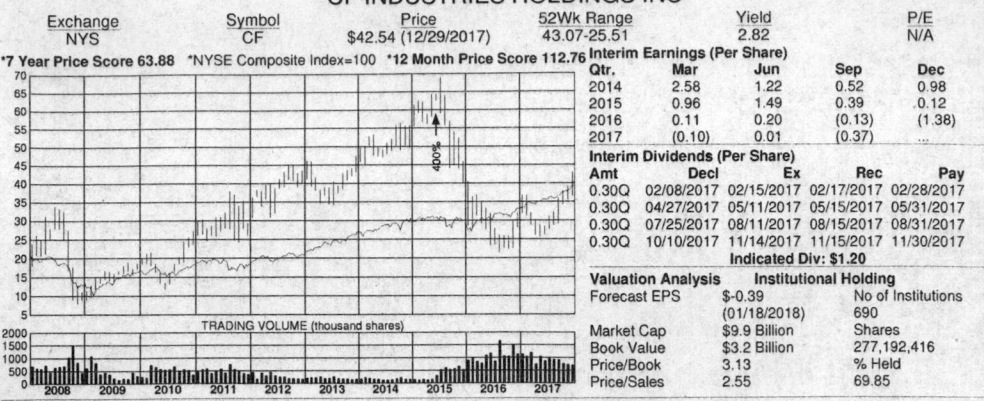

Exchange	Symbol	Price	52Wk Range	Yield	P/E
NYS	CF	$42.54 (12/29/2017)	43.07-25.51	2.82	N/A

*7 Year Price Score 63.88   *NYSE Composite Index=100   *12 Month Price Score 112.76

Interim Earnings (Per Share)

Qtr.	Mar	Jun	Sep	Dec
2014	2.58	1.22	0.52	0.98
2015	0.96	1.49	0.39	.0.12
2016	0.11	0.20	(0.13)	(1.38)
2017	(0.10)	0.01	(0.37)	...

Interim Dividends (Per Share)

Amt	Decl	Ex	Rec	Pay
0.30Q	02/08/2017	02/15/2017	02/17/2017	02/28/2017
0.30Q	04/27/2017	05/11/2017	05/15/2017	05/31/2017
0.30Q	07/25/2017	08/11/2017	08/15/2017	08/31/2017
0.30Q	10/10/2017	11/14/2017	11/15/2017	11/30/2017

Indicated Div: $1.20

Valuation Analysis	Institutional Holding
Forecast EPS $-0.39	No of Institutions
(01/18/2018)	690
Market Cap $9.9 Billion	Shares
Book Value $3.2 Billion	277,192,416
Price/Book 3.13	% Held
Price/Sales 2.55	69.85

Business Summary: Agricultural Chemicals (MIC: 8.3.3 SIC: 2879 NAIC: 325320)

CF Industries Holdings is a manufacturer and distributor of nitrogen fertilizer and other nitrogen products. Co.'s reportable segments include: ammonia, which produces anhydrous ammonia (ammonia), its nitrogen fertilizer product that contains 82.0% nitrogen; granular urea, which produces granular urea that contains 46.0% nitrogen; urea ammonium nitrate (UAN), which produces UAN, a liquid fertilizer product with a nitrogen content that ranges from 28.0% to 32.0%; ammonium nitrate (AN), which produces AN, a nitrogen-based product with a nitrogen content between 29.0% and 35.0%; and Other; which includes diesel exhaust fluid, urea liquor, nitric acid, as well as compound fertilizer products.

Recent Developments: For the quarter ended Sep 30 2017, net loss amounted to US$68.0 million versus net income of nil in the year-earlier quarter. Revenues were US$870.0 million, up 27.9% from US$680.0 million the year before. Operating loss was US$39.0 million versus a loss of US$101.0 million in the prior-year quarter. Direct operating expenses rose 27.0% to US$861.0 million from US$678.0 million in the comparable period the year before. Indirect operating expenses decreased 53.4% to US$48.0 million from US$103.0 million in the equivalent prior-year period.

Prospects: Our evaluation of CF Industries Holdings Inc. as of Jan. 14, 2018 is the result of our systematic analysis on three basic characteristics: earnings strength, relative valuation, and recent stock price movement. The company has managed to produce a neutral trend in earnings per share over the past 5 quarters. Because the company lacks sufficient analyst estimate data, we place greater weight on the historical EPS trend as the measure of earnings strength. Based on operating earnings yield, the company is overvalued when compared to all of the companies in our coverage universe. Share price changes over the past year indicates that CF will perform poorly over the near term.

Financial Data

(US$ in Thousands)	9 Mos	6 Mos	3 Mos	12/31/2016	12/31/2015	12/31/2014	12/31/2013	12/31/2012
Earnings Per Share	(1.84)	(1.60)	(1.41)	(1.19)	2.96	5.42	4.95	5.72
Cash Flow Per Share	6.12	5.82	2.69	2.64	5.12	5.50	4.98	7.42
Tang Book Value Per Share	3.42	3.90	3.98	4.30	7.06	8.76	10.51	12.04
Dividends Per Share	1.200	1.200	1.200	1.200	1.200	1.000	0.440	0.320
Dividend Payout %	...	...	...	...	40.54	18.46	8.89	5.60
Income Statement								
Total Revenue	3,031,000	2,161,000	1,037,000	3,685,000	4,308,300	4,743,200	5,474,700	6,104,000
EBITDA	781,000	589,000	259,000	190,000	1,289,600	2,375,400	2,726,100	3,333,300
Depn & Amortn	648,000	422,000	205,000	89,000	65,400	53,900	410,600	419,800
Income Before Taxes	(100,000)	10,000	(25,000)	(94,000)	1,092,600	2,144,200	2,168,000	2,782,500
Income Taxes	(55,000)	(8,000)	(13,000)	(81,000)	395,800	773,000	686,500	964,200
Net Income	(107,000)	(20,000)	(23,000)	(277,000)	699,900	1,390,300	1,464,600	1,848,700
Average Shares	233,200	233,700	233,100	233,100	236,100	256,500	296,000	323,500
Balance Sheet								
Current Assets	2,651,000	2,675,000	2,805,000	2,655,000	1,127,100	2,614,500	2,630,100	2,807,600
Total Assets	14,857,000	14,936,000	15,185,000	15,131,000	12,738,900	11,338,200	10,678,100	10,166,900
Current Liabilities	1,551,000	1,441,000	853,000	686,000	1,215,200	979,700	828,300	950,200
Long-Term Obligations	4,988,000	4,986,000	5,780,000	5,778,000	5,592,700	4,592,500	3,098,100	1,600,000
Total Liabilities	11,690,000	11,666,000	11,906,000	11,783,000	8,703,700	7,128,500	5,602,000	4,264,700
Stockholders' Equity	3,167,000	3,270,000	3,279,000	3,348,000	4,035,200	4,209,700	5,076,100	5,902,200
Shares Outstanding	233,257	233,232	233,184	233,114	233,081	241,673	279,240	314,753
Statistical Record								
Return on Assets %	N.M.	N.M.	N.M.	N.M.	5.81	12.63	14.05	19.26
Return on Equity %	N.M.	N.M.	N.M.	N.M.	16.98	29.94	26.68	35.29
EBITDA Margin %	25.77	27.26	24.98	5.16	29.93	50.08	49.79	54.61
Net Margin %	N.M.	N.M.	N.M.	N.M.	16.25	29.31	26.75	30.29
Asset Turnover	0.26	0.24	0.24	0.26	0.36	0.43	0.53	0.64
Current Ratio	1.71	1.86	3.29	3.87	0.93	2.67	3.18	2.95
Debt to Equity	1.57	1.52	1.76	1.73	1.39	1.09	0.61	0.27
Price Range	36.85-22.28	36.85-21.43	36.85-21.43	40.81-21.43	68.92-40.07	56.55-44.98	47.41-34.06	44.90-30.76
P/E Ratio	...	...	...	...	23.28-13.54	10.43-8.30	9.58-6.88	7.85-5.38
Average Yield %	4.07	4.31	4.23	4.22	2.13	1.99	1.09	0.83

Address: 4 Parkway North, Suite 400, Deerfield, IL 60015	**Web Site:** www.cfindustries.com	**Auditors:** KPMG LLP
Telephone: 847-405-2400	**Officers:** Stephen A. Furbacher - Chairman W. Anthony Will - President, Chief Executive Officer, Senior Vice President, Vice President	**Investor Contact:** 847-405-2550 **Transfer Agents:** Computershare, Providence, RI

CHARLES RIVER LABORATORIES INTERNATIONAL INC.

Exchange	Symbol	Price	52Wk Range	Yield	P/E
NYS	CRL	$109.45 (12/29/2017)	118.09-76.53	N/A	26.70

*7 Year Price Score 126.19 *NYSE Composite Index=100 *12 Month Price Score 104.06

TRADING VOLUME (thousand shares)

Interim Earnings (Per Share)

Qtr.	Mar	Jun	Sep	Dec
2014	0.67	0.74	0.68	0.57
2015	0.66	1.02	0.79	0.66
2016	0.78	0.73	0.79	0.93
2017	0.97	1.12	1.08	...

Interim Dividends (Per Share)

No Dividends Paid

Valuation Analysis **Institutional Holding**

Forecast EPS	$5.14	No of Institutions
	(01/16/2018)	468
Market Cap	$5.2 Billion	Shares
Book Value	$1.0 Billion	61,169,052
Price/Book	5.07	% Held
Price/Sales	2.81	96.80

Business Summary: Biotechnology (MIC: 4.1.2 SIC: 8731 NAIC: 541710)

Charles River Laboratories International is a contract research organization engaged in laboratory animal medicine and science to develop a portfolio of discovery and safety assessment services. Co. has three segments: Research Models and Services, which is engaged in supplying research models to the drug development industry; Discovery and Safety Assessment, which provides discovery and safety assessment services that include in vivo and in vitro studies, supporting laboratory services, and non-clinical consulting and program management to support product development; and Manufacturing Support, which includes its Microbial Solutions, Avian Vaccine Services and Biologics Testing Solutions.

Recent Developments: For the quarter ended Sep 30 2017, income from continuing operations increased 40.6% to US$53.0 million from US$37.7 million in the year-earlier quarter. Net income increased 39.2% to US$53.0 million from US$38.0 million in the year-earlier quarter. Revenues were US$464.2 million, up 9.0% from US$425.7 million the year before. Operating income was US$74.0 million versus US$58.8 million in the prior-year quarter, an increase of 25.8%. Direct operating expenses rose 6.5% to US$287.0 million from US$269.5 million in the comparable period the year before. Indirect operating expenses increased 5.9% to US$103.2 million from US$97.5 million in the equivalent prior-year period.

Prospects: Our evaluation of Charles River Laboratories International Inc. as of Jan. 14, 2018 is the result of our systematic analysis on three basic characteristics: earnings strength, relative valuation, and recent stock price movement. The company has generated a negative trend in earnings per share over the past 5 quarters and while recent estimates for the company have been mixed, CRL has posted better than expected results. Based on operating earnings yield, the company is undervalued when compared to all of the companies in our coverage universe. Share price changes over the past year indicates that CRL will perform very well over the near term.

Financial Data

(US$ in Thousands)	9 Mos	6 Mos	3 Mos	12/31/2016	12/26/2015	12/27/2014	12/28/2013	12/29/2012
Earnings Per Share	4.10	3.81	3.42	3.23	3.13	2.66	2.12	2.01
Cash Flow Per Share	6.49	6.69	6.22	6.29	6.22	5.42	4.39	4.35
Tang Book Value Per Share	N.M.	N.M.	N.M.	N.M.	0.29	3.64	6.85	6.37
Income Statement								
Total Revenue	1,379,124	914,892	445,763	1,681,432	1,363,302	1,297,662	1,165,528	1,129,530
EBITDA	280,371	189,542	95,565	376,015	304,386	284,848	255,202	243,774
Depn & Amortn	30,913	20,556	10,737	126,699	94,929	96,457	96,636	81,275
Income Before Taxes	227,902	154,963	78,047	222,921	195,428	177,595	138,327	129,746
Income Taxes	73,272	53,327	31,084	66,835	43,391	47,671	32,911	27,628
Net Income	153,204	100,730	46,778	154,765	149,313	126,698	102,828	97,295
Average Shares	48,390	48,342	48,421	47,958	47,634	47,558	48,489	48,406
Balance Sheet								
Current Assets	782,378	738,067	700,121	656,832	559,234	606,898	552,550	485,252
Total Assets	2,865,918	2,773,664	2,697,075	2,711,800	2,068,497	1,885,192	1,644,621	1,586,344
Current Liabilities	415,755	424,071	383,374	429,593	311,761	296,170	247,034	342,247
Long-Term Obligations	1,155,998	1,116,278	1,170,063	1,207,696	845,997	745,958	642,352	527,136
Total Liabilities	1,844,405	1,810,168	1,820,644	1,875,032	1,335,430	1,212,989	1,003,637	985,539
Stockholders' Equity	1,021,513	963,496	876,431	836,768	733,067	672,203	640,984	600,805
Shares Outstanding	47,324	47,586	47,635	47,363	46,698	47,327	47,553	48,220
Statistical Record								
Return on Assets %	7.12	6.62	6.85	6.37	7.57	7.20	6.38	6.20
Return on Equity %	20.95	20.41	19.85	19.40	21.31	19.35	16.61	17.32
EBITDA Margin %	20.33	20.72	21.44	22.36	22.33	21.95	21.90	21.58
Net Margin %	11.11	11.01	10.49	9.20	10.95	9.76	8.82	8.61
Asset Turnover	0.66	0.65	0.74	0.69	0.69	0.74	0.72	0.72
Current Ratio	1.88	1.74	1.83	1.53	1.79	2.05	2.24	1.42
Debt to Equity	1.13	1.16	1.34	1.44	1.15	1.11	1.00	0.88
Price Range	109.26-67.40	101.54-67.40	91.40-67.40	88.44-67.10	84.20-61.59	65.59-50.74	53.33-37.47	41.24-27.15
P/E Ratio	26.65-16.44	26.65-17.69	26.73-19.71	27.38-20.77	26.90-19.68	24.66-19.08	25.16-17.67	20.52-13.51

Address: 251 Ballardvale Street, Wilmington, MA 01887 **Telephone:** 781-222-6000	**Web Site:** www.criver.com **Officers:** James C. Foster - Chairman, President, Chief Executive Officer David R. Smith - Executive Vice President, Chief Financial Officer, Chief Accounting Officer	**Auditors:** PricewaterhouseCoopers LLP **Investor Contact:** 781-222-6000 **Transfer Agents:** ComputerShare Investor Services, Providence, RI

CHEMOURS CO (THE)

Exchange	Symbol	Price	52Wk Range	Yield	P/E
NYS	CC	$50.06 (12/29/2017)	57.23-21.22	0.52	34.52

*7 Year Price Score N/A   *NYSE Composite Index=100   *12 Month Price Score 114.39

Interim Earnings (Per Share)

Qtr.	Mar	Jun	Sep	Dec
2014	0.54	0.64	0.59	0.44
2015	0.24	(0.10)	(0.16)	(0.48)
2016	0.28	(0.10)	1.11	(1.26)
2017	0.79	0.84	1.08	...

Interim Dividends (Per Share)

Amt	Decl	Ex	Rec	Pay
0.03Q	04/27/2017	05/15/2017	05/17/2017	06/15/2017
0.03Q	08/02/2017	08/15/2017	08/17/2017	09/15/2017
0.03Q	11/07/2017	11/17/2017	11/20/2017	12/15/2017
0.17Q	11/30/2017	02/14/2018	02/15/2018	03/15/2018

Indicated Div: $0.26

Valuation Analysis

		Institutional Holding	
Forecast EPS	$3.71 (01/16/2018)	No of Institutions	570
Market Cap	$9.3 Billion	Shares	159,071,520
Book Value	$800.0 Million	% Held	N/A
Price/Book	11.58		
Price/Sales	1.56		

Business Summary: Specialty Chemicals (MIC: 8.3.2 SIC: 2899 NAIC: 325998)

Chemours is a provider of performance chemicals. Co. has three reportable segments: Titanium Technologies, Fluoroproducts and Chemical Solutions. Co.'s Titanium Technologies segment is a producer of titanium dioxide, a white pigment used to deliver whiteness, brightness, opacity and protection in a variety of applications. Co.'s Fluoroproducts segment is a provider of fluoroproducts, such as refrigerants and industrial fluoropolymer resins. Co.'s Chemical Solutions segment is a provider of industrial chemicals used in gold production, oil and gas, water treatment and other industries.

Recent Developments: For the quarter ended Sep 30 2017, net income increased 1.5% to US$207.0 million from US$204.0 million in the year-earlier quarter. Revenues were US$1.58 billion, up 13.3% from US$1.40 billion the year before. Direct operating expenses rose 5.8% to US$1.12 billion from US$1.06 billion in the comparable period the year before. Indirect operating expenses decreased 22.5% to US$176.0 million from US$227.0 million in the equivalent prior-year period.

Prospects: Our evaluation of The Chemours Company as of Jan. 14, 2018 is the result of our systematic analysis on three basic characteristics: earnings strength, relative valuation, and recent stock price movement. The company has produced a positive trend in earnings per share over the past 5 quarters and while recent estimates for the company have been mixed, CC has posted better than expected results. Based on operating earnings yield, the company is undervalued when compared to all of the companies in our coverage universe. Share price changes over the past year indicates that CC will perform very well over the near term.

Financial Data

(US$ in Millions)	9 Mos	6 Mos	3 Mos	12/31/2016	12/31/2015	12/31/2014	12/31/2013	12/31/2012
Earnings Per Share	1.45	1.48	0.54	0.04	(0.50)	2.21	2.34	...
Cash Flow Per Share	3.27	3.74	3.27	3.26	1.01	...	...	...
Tang Book Value Per Share	3.42	2.16	1.00	N.M.	N.M.	...	...	...
Dividends Per Share	0.120	0.120	0.120	0.120	0.580	...	...	...
Dividend Payout %	8.28	8.11	22.22	300.00	...	...	...	...
Income Statement								
Total Revenue	4,608	3,024	1,437	5,400	5,717	6,432	6,859	7,365
EBITDA	995	631	290	454	186	784	802	1,720
Depn & Amortn	211	143	73	281	264	254	255	260
Income Before Taxes	623	382	166	(40)	(210)	530	547	1,460
Income Taxes	130	87	22	(18)	(98)	149	152	427
Net Income	518	311	150	7	(90)	400	423	1,057
Average Shares	191	191	189	183	181	181	181	...
Balance Sheet								
Current Assets	3,433	3,440	2,711	2,553	2,301	1,962	1,980	...
Total Assets	7,120	7,052	6,282	6,060	6,298	5,978	5,621	...
Current Liabilities	1,570	1,750	1,735	1,771	1,466	1,407	1,471	...
Long-Term Obligations	4,081	4,056	3,538	3,529	3,915	...	...	...
Total Liabilities	6,320	6,485	5,929	5,960	6,172	2,309	2,407	...
Stockholders' Equity	800	567	353	100	126	3,669	3,214	...
Shares Outstanding	185	184	184	182	181	181	181	...
Statistical Record								
Return on Assets %	4.30	4.29	1.67	0.11	...	6.90	...	...
Return on Equity %	48.94	77.87	39.19	6.18	...	11.62	...	...
EBITDA Margin %	21.59	20.87	20.18	8.41	3.25	12.19	11.69	23.35
Net Margin %	11.24	10.28	10.44	0.13	N.M.	6.22	6.17	14.35
Asset Turnover	0.88	0.87	0.88	0.87	...	1.11	...	...
Current Ratio	2.19	1.97	1.56	1.44	1.57	1.39	1.35	...
Debt to Equity	5.10	7.15	10.02	35.29	31.07	...	...	...
Price Range	51.95-14.87	45.38-5.93	38.50-5.93	26.96-3.12	20.85-4.72	...	...	...
P/E Ratio	35.83-10.26	30.66-4.01	71.30-10.98	674.00-78.00	...	...	...	...
Average Yield %	0.35	0.48	0.68	1.04	6.49	...	...	...

Address: 1007 Market Street, Wilmington, DE 19899 **Telephone:** 302-773-1000	**Web Site:** www.chemours.com **Officers:** Richard H. Brown - Chairman Mark P. Vergnano - President, Chief Executive Officer, Holding/Parent Company Officer	**Auditors:** PricewaterhouseCoopers LLP **Transfer Agents:** Computershare Trust Company, N.A.

CHESAPEAKE ENERGY CORP.

Exchange	Symbol	Price	52Wk Range	Yield	P/E
NYS	CHK	$3.96 (12/29/2017)	7.18-3.51	N/A	N/A

*7 Year Price Score 23.52   *NYSE Composite Index=100   *12 Month Price Score 73.92

Interim Earnings (Per Share)

Qtr.	Mar	Jun	Sep	Dec
2014	0.54	0.22	0.26	0.83
2015	(5.72)	(6.27)	(7.08)	(3.36)
2016	(1.44)	(2.48)	(1.54)	(0.98)
2017	0.08	0.47	(0.05)	...

Interim Dividends (Per Share)

Dividend Payment Suspended

Valuation Analysis   Institutional Holding

Forecast EPS	$0.77	No of Institutions
	(01/18/2018)	777
Market Cap	$3.6 Billion	Shares
Book Value	N/A	683,341,952
Price/Book	N/A	% Held
Price/Sales	0.40	82.43

Business Summary: Production & Extraction (MIC: 9.1.1 SIC: 1311 NAIC: 211111)

Chesapeake Energy is an oil and natural gas exploration and production company engaged in the acquisition, exploration and development of properties for the production of oil, natural gas and natural gas liquids (NGL) from underground reservoirs. Co. also owns oil and natural gas marketing and natural gas gathering and compression businesses. Co.'s operations are located onshore in the U.S. Co. has two geographic operating divisions: Southern Division, and Northern Division. As of Dec 31 2016, Co. had estimated total proved reserves of 399.0 million barrels of oil, 6.50 trillion cubic feet of natural gas, and 226.0 million barrels of NGL.

Recent Developments: For the quarter ended Sep 30 2017, net loss amounted to US$17.0 million versus a net loss of US$1.21 billion in the year-earlier quarter. Revenues were US$1.94 billion, down 14.6% from US$2.28 billion the year before. Operating income was US$94.0 million versus a loss of US$1.23 billion in the prior-year quarter. Direct operating expenses declined 20.7% to US$1.52 billion from US$1.92 billion in the comparable period the year before. Indirect operating expenses decreased 79.3% to US$330.0 million from US$1.60 billion in the equivalent prior-year period.

Prospects: Our evaluation of Chesapeake Energy Corp. as of Jan. 14, 2018 is the result of our systematic analysis on three basic characteristics: earnings strength, relative valuation, and recent stock price movement. The company has suffered a very negative trend in earnings per share over the past 5 quarters and while recent estimates for the company have been raised by analysts, CHK has posted better than expected results. Based on operating earnings yield, the company is undervalued when compared to all of the companies in our coverage universe. Share price changes over the past year indicates that CHK will perform very poorly over the near term.

Financial Data
(US$ in Thousands)

	9 Mos	6 Mos	3 Mos	12/31/2016	12/31/2015	12/31/2014	12/31/2013	12/31/2012
Earnings Per Share	(0.48)	(1.97)	(4.92)	(6.45)	(22.43)	1.87	0.73	(1.46)
Cash Flow Per Share	0.02	0.07	0.35	(0.27)	1.86	7.03	7.07	4.40
Tang Book Value Per Share	...	...	...	...	...	20.87	19.47	18.83
Dividends Per Share	...	...	...	...	0.175	0.350	0.350	0.350
Dividend Payout %	...	...	...	...	...	18.72	47.95	...
Income Statement								
Total Revenue	6,977,000	5,034,000	2,753,000	7,872,000	12,764,000	20,951,000	17,506,000	12,316,000
EBITDA	1,612,000	1,267,000	455,000	(3,186,000)	(16,552,000)	6,204,000	4,572,000	1,914,000
Depn & Amortn	689,000	441,000	218,000	1,107,000	2,229,000	2,915,000	2,903,000	2,811,000
Income Before Taxes	621,000	638,000	142,000	(4,589,000)	(19,098,000)	3,200,000	1,442,000	(974,000)
Income Taxes	2,000	2,000	1,000	(190,000)	(4,463,000)	1,144,000	548,000	(380,000)
Net Income	616,000	634,000	140,000	(4,401,000)	(14,685,000)	1,917,000	724,000	(769,000)
Average Shares	909,000	1,114,000	907,000	764,000	662,000	772,000	653,000	643,000
Balance Sheet								
Current Assets	1,178,000	1,247,000	1,360,000	2,142,000	2,480,000	7,468,000	3,656,000	2,948,000
Total Assets	11,981,000	11,920,000	11,699,000	13,028,000	17,357,000	40,751,000	41,782,000	41,611,000
Current Liabilities	2,218,000	2,158,000	2,788,000	3,648,000	3,685,000	5,863,000	5,515,000	6,266,000
Long-Term Obligations	9,899,000	9,850,000	9,509,000	9,938,000	10,383,000	11,184,000	12,917,000	12,356,000
Total Liabilities	12,938,000	12,858,000	13,158,000	14,488,000	15,219,000	23,848,000	25,787,000	26,042,000
Stockholders' Equity	(957,000)	(938,000)	(1,459,000)	(1,460,000)	2,138,000	16,903,000	15,995,000	15,569,000
Shares Outstanding	906,338	905,640	905,674	895,058	663,357	663,329	664,190	664,319
Statistical Record								
Return on Assets %	0.33	N.M.	N.M.	N.M.	N.M.	4.65	1.74	N.M.
Return on Equity %	...	...	...	N.M.	N.M.	11.65	4.59	N.M.
EBITDA Margin %	23.10	25.17	16.53	N.M.	N.M.	29.61	26.12	15.54
Net Margin %	8.83	12.59	5.09	N.M.	N.M.	9.15	4.14	N.M.
Asset Turnover	0.73	0.73	0.64	0.52	0.44	0.51	0.42	0.29
Current Ratio	0.53	0.58	0.49	0.59	0.67	1.27	0.66	0.47
Debt to Equity	...	...	...	...	4.86	0.66	0.81	0.79
Price Range	7.72-3.61	8.05-4.18	8.05-3.61	8.05-1.59	21.26-3.72	29.50-16.71	27.13-15.62	24.07-12.75
P/E Ratio	...	...	...	...	...	15.78-8.94	37.17-21.39	...
Average Yield %	...	...	...	...	1.51	1.42	1.63	1.90

Address: 6100 North Western Avenue, Oklahoma City, OK 73118 **Telephone:** 405-848-8000	**Web Site:** www.chk.com **Officers:** R. Brad Martin - Chairman Archie W. Dunham - Chairman Emeritus	**Auditors:** PricewaterhouseCoopers LLP **Investor Contact:** 405-935-4763 **Transfer Agents:** Computershare Trust Company, N.A., Canton, MA

CHESAPEAKE UTILITIES CORP.

Exchange	Symbol	Price	52Wk Range	Yield	P/E	Div Achiever
NYS	CPK	$78.55 (12/29/2017)	85.55-63.40	1.65	29.31	13 Years

*7 Year Price Score 126.40 ***NYSE Composite Index=100** ***12 Month Price Score 102.39**

Interim Earnings (Per Share)

Qtr.	Mar	Jun	Sep	Dec
2014	1.21	0.35	0.22	0.69
2015	1.44	0.41	0.33	0.56
2016	1.33	0.52	0.29	0.72
2017	1.17	0.37	0.42	...

Interim Dividends (Per Share)

Amt	Decl	Ex	Rec	Pay
0.305Q	02/24/2017	03/13/2017	03/15/2017	04/05/2017
0.325Q	05/03/2017	06/13/2017	06/15/2017	07/05/2017
0.325Q	08/02/2017	09/14/2017	09/15/2017	10/05/2017
0.325Q	11/08/2017	12/14/2017	12/15/2017	01/05/2018

Indicated Div: $1.30 (Div. Reinv. Plan)

Valuation Analysis **Institutional Holding**

Forecast EPS	$2.87 (01/17/2018)	No of Institutions	201
Market Cap	$1.3 Billion	Shares	11,575,415
Book Value	$463.8 Million	% Held	54.31
Price/Book	2.77		
Price/Sales	2.22		

Business Summary: Gas Utilities (MIC: 3.3.1 SIC: 4923 NAIC: 221210)

Chesapeake Utilities is a energy company engaged, through its operating divisions and subsidiaries, in various energy and other businesses. Co. operates within two reportable segments: Regulated Energy and Unregulated Energy. Co.'s regulated energy businesses consist of: regulated natural gas distribution operations; regulated natural gas transmission operations; and regulated electric distribution operations. Co.'s unregulated energy segment provides propane distribution, propane and crude oil wholesale marketing operation, natural gas marketing operation, and Co.'s natural gas supply, gathering and processing operation.

Recent Developments: For the quarter ended Sep 30 2017, net income increased 54.7% to US$6.8 million from US$4.4 million in the year-earlier quarter. Revenues were US$126.9 million, up 17.2% from US$108.3 million the year before. Operating income was US$14.2 million versus US$10.2 million in the prior-year quarter, an increase of 40.2%. Direct operating expenses rose 14.8% to US$99.3 million from US$86.5 million in the comparable period the year before. Indirect operating expenses increased 14.8% to US$13.4 million from US$11.7 million in the equivalent prior-year period.

Prospects: Our evaluation of Chesapeake Utilities Corp. as of Jan. 14, 2018 is the result of our systematic analysis on three basic characteristics: earnings strength, relative valuation, and recent stock price movement. The company has enjoyed a very positive trend in earnings per share over the past 5 quarters and while recent estimates for the company have remained steady, CPK has posted better than expected results. Based on operating earnings yield, the company is about fairly valued when compared to all of the companies in our coverage universe. Share price changes over the past year indicates that CPK will perform very well over the near term.

Financial Data

(US$ in Thousands)	9 Mos	6 Mos	3 Mos	12/31/2016	12/31/2015	12/31/2014	12/31/2013	12/31/2012
Earnings Per Share	2.68	2.55	2.70	2.86	2.72	2.47	2.26	1.99
Cash Flow Per Share	7.31	7.69	7.41	6.62	6.97	5.45	5.05	4.57
Tang Book Value Per Share	26.75	27.22	27.19	26.32	22.35	20.08	18.78	17.35
Dividends Per Share	1.260	1.240	1.220	1.202	1.133	1.067	1.013	0.960
Dividend Payout %	47.01	48.63	45.19	42.05	41.64	43.18	44.84	48.16
Income Statement								
Total Revenue	437,180	310,244	185,160	498,860	459,244	498,834	444,306	392,502
EBITDA	67,926	51,396	36,338	90,989	85,029	76,096	69,229	62,453
Depn & Amortn	5,989	3,939	1,939	7,334	6,978	6,577	6,123	5,547
Income Before Taxes	52,804	41,646	31,660	73,016	68,045	60,037	54,872	48,159
Income Taxes	20,781	16,456	12,516	28,341	26,905	23,945	22,085	19,296
Net Income	32,023	25,190	19,144	44,675	41,140	36,092	32,787	28,863
Average Shares	16,389	16,382	16,363	15,613	15,143	14,604	14,543	14,507
Balance Sheet								
Current Assets	149,005	102,435	118,813	141,151	112,538	122,373	126,409	100,597
Total Assets	1,346,750	1,256,988	1,238,311	1,229,219	1,068,586	904,469	837,522	733,746
Current Liabilities	339,270	272,054	320,733	334,051	279,593	194,235	221,942	162,166
Long-Term Obligations	201,248	201,590	136,537	136,954	149,340	158,486	117,592	101,907
Total Liabilities	882,930	795,310	777,482	783,133	710,448	604,147	558,749	477,148
Stockholders' Equity	463,820	461,678	460,829	446,086	358,138	300,322	278,773	256,598
Shares Outstanding	16,344	16,344	16,331	16,303	15,270	14,588	14,457	14,396
Statistical Record								
Return on Assets %	3.53	3.52	3.75	3.88	4.17	4.14	4.17	3.99
Return on Equity %	9.73	9.86	10.41	11.08	12.50	12.46	12.25	11.57
EBITDA Margin %	15.54	16.57	19.63	18.24	18.51	15.25	15.58	15.91
Net Margin %	7.32	8.12	10.34	8.96	8.96	7.24	7.38	7.35
Asset Turnover	0.47	0.48	0.46	0.43	0.47	0.57	0.57	0.54
Current Ratio	0.44	0.38	0.37	0.42	0.40	0.63	0.57	0.62
Debt to Equity	0.43	0.44	0.30	0.31	0.42	0.53	0.42	0.40
Price Range	81.25-58.18	76.65-58.18	70.00-56.83	70.00-53.54	60.31-45.54	52.60-37.78	40.48-30.27	32.45-26.83
P/E Ratio	30.32-21.71	30.06-22.82	25.93-21.05	24.48-18.72	22.17-16.74	21.30-15.30	17.91-13.39	16.31-13.48
Average Yield %	1.79	1.85	1.92	1.93	2.21	2.44	2.88	3.25

Address: 909 Silver Lake Boulevard, Dover, DE 19904
Telephone: 302-734-6799

Web Site: www.chpk.com
Officers: John R. Schimkaitis - Vice-Chairman, Chief Executive Officer Michael P. McMasters - President, Executive Vice President, Chief Operating Officer

Auditors: Baker Tilly Virchow Krause, LLP
Investor Contact: 888-742-5275
Transfer Agents: Computershare Trust Company, N.A., Providence, RI

CHEVRON CORPORATION

Exchange	Symbol	Price	52Wk Range	Yield	P/E	Div Acheiver
NYS	CVX	$125.19 (12/29/2017)	125.98-103.04	3.45	36.50	29 Years

*7 Year Price Score 80.76   *NYSE Composite Index=100   *12 Month Price Score 101.21

Interim Earnings (Per Share)

Qtr.	Mar	Jun	Sep	Dec
2014	2.36	2.98	2.95	1.85
2015	1.37	0.30	1.09	(0.31)
2016	(0.39)	(0.78)	0.68	0.22
2017	1.41	0.77	1.03	...

Interim Dividends (Per Share)

Amt	Decl	Ex	Rec	Pay
1.08Q	01/25/2017	02/14/2017	02/16/2017	03/10/2017
1.08Q	04/26/2017	05/17/2017	05/19/2017	06/12/2017
1.08Q	07/26/2017	08/16/2017	08/18/2017	09/11/2017
1.08Q	10/25/2017	11/16/2017	11/17/2017	12/11/2017

Indicated Div: $4.32 (Div. Reinv. Plan)

Valuation Analysis / **Institutional Holding**

Forecast EPS	$4.21 (01/26/2018)	No of Institutions 2765
Market Cap	$237.8 Billion	Shares 1,556,319,744
Book Value	$146.7 Billion	% Held 59.08
Price/Book	1.62	
Price/Sales	1.75	

Business Summary: Refining & Marketing (MIC: 9.1.2 SIC: 2911 NAIC: 324110)

Chevron is engaged in energy and chemicals operations. Upstream operations consist of, among others, exploring for, developing and producing crude oil and natural gas; transporting, storage and marketing of natural gas; and a gas-to-liquids plant. Downstream operations consist of, among others, refining crude oil into petroleum products; marketing of crude oil and refined products; and manufacturing and marketing of commodity petrochemicals, plastics for industrial uses and fuel and lubricant additives. At Dec 31 2016, Co. had net proved reserves of 6.33 billion barrels of crude oil, condensate, natural gas liquids and synthetic oil, and 28.76 trillion cubic feet of natural gas.

Recent Developments: For the quarter ended Sep 30 2017, net income increased 52.7% to US$1.99 billion from US$1.30 billion in the year-earlier quarter. Revenues were US$36.21 billion, up 20.1% from US$30.14 billion the year before. Direct operating expenses rose 15.6% to US$23.71 billion from US$20.51 billion in the comparable period the year before. Indirect operating expenses increased 15.4% to US$9.83 billion from US$8.52 billion in the equivalent prior-year period.

Prospects: Our evaluation of Chevron Corporation as of Jan. 21, 2018 is the result of our systematic analysis on three basic characteristics: earnings strength, relative valuation, and recent stock price movement. The company has generated a negative trend in earnings per share over the past 5 quarters and while recent estimates for the company have been raised by analysts, CVX has posted results that fell short of analysts expectations. Based on operating earnings yield, the company is about fairly valued when compared to all of the companies in our coverage universe. Share price changes over the past year indicates that CVX will perform poorly over the near term.

Financial Data

(US$ in Millions)	9 Mos	6 Mos	3 Mos	12/31/2016	12/31/2015	12/31/2014	12/31/2013	12/31/2012
Earnings Per Share	3.43	3.08	1.53	(0.27)	2.45	10.14	11.09	13.32
Cash Flow Per Share	9.64	9.62	8.29	6.84	10.42	16.72	18.27	19.85
Tang Book Value Per Share	74.86	74.75	74.98	74.53	78.67	80.03	75.50	67.75
Dividends Per Share	4.320	4.310	4.300	4.290	4.280	4.210	3.900	3.510
Dividend Payout %	125.95	139.94	281.05	...	174.69	41.52	35.17	26.35
Income Statement								
Total Revenue	104,106	67,901	33,421	114,472	138,477	211,970	228,848	241,909
EBITDA	22,488	14,686	7,374	17,498	25,879	47,995	50,091	59,745
Depn & Amortn	14,614	9,505	4,194	19,457	21,037	16,793	14,186	13,413
Income Before Taxes	7,740	5,082	3,129	(2,160)	4,842	31,202	35,905	46,332
Income Taxes	1,589	917	430	(1,729)	132	11,892	14,308	19,996
Net Income	6,084	4,132	2,682	(497)	4,587	19,241	21,423	26,179
Average Shares	1,895	1,893	1,895	1,873	1,875	1,898	1,932	1,965
Balance Sheet								
Current Assets	29,398	26,626	29,568	29,619	35,347	42,232	50,250	55,720
Total Assets	255,160	254,599	259,111	260,078	266,103	266,026	253,753	232,982
Current Liabilities	28,223	27,956	28,426	31,785	26,464	31,926	33,018	34,212
Long-Term Obligations	34,075	34,082	36,959	35,286	33,664	24,028	20,057	12,065
Total Liabilities	108,447	108,396	112,519	114,522	113,387	110,998	104,640	96,458
Stockholders' Equity	146,713	146,203	146,592	145,556	152,716	155,028	149,113	136,524
Shares Outstanding	1,899	1,895	1,894	1,891	1,882	1,879	1,913	1,946
Statistical Record								
Return on Assets %	2.52	2.26	1.11	N.M.	1.72	7.40	8.80	11.80
Return on Equity %	4.43	3.97	1.96	N.M.	2.98	12.65	15.00	20.25
EBITDA Margin %	21.60	21.63	22.06	15.29	18.69	22.64	21.89	24.70
Net Margin %	5.84	6.09	8.02	N.M.	3.31	9.08	9.36	10.82
Asset Turnover	0.53	0.50	0.48	0.43	0.52	0.82	0.94	1.09
Current Ratio	1.04	0.95	1.04	0.93	1.34	1.32	1.52	1.63
Debt to Equity	0.23	0.23	0.25	0.24	0.22	0.15	0.13	0.09
Price Range	118.77-99.92	118.77-97.70	118.77-92.67	118.77-78.98	112.78-70.02	134.85-100.86	127.76-108.14	117.96-96.41
P/E Ratio	34.63-29.13	38.56-31.72	77.63-60.57	...	46.03-28.58	13.30-9.95	11.52-9.75	8.86-7.24
Average Yield %	3.96	4.02	4.06	4.30	4.44	3.49	3.25	3.26

Address: 6001 Bollinger Canyon Road, San Ramon, CA 94583-2324	Web Site: www.chevron.com	Auditors: PricewaterhouseCoopers LLP
Telephone: 925-842-1000	**Officers:** Christine L. Cavallo - Assistant Secretary, Managing Counsel Michael K. Wirth - Chairman, Vice-Chairman, Executive Vice President, Executive Vice President (frmr), Chief Executive Officer	**Investor Contact:** 925-842-5690
Fax: 925-894-6017		**Transfer Agents:** Computershare, Providence, RI

CHIMERA INVESTMENT CORP

Exchange	Symbol	Price	52Wk Range	Yield	P/E
NYS	CIM	$18.48 (12/29/2017)	20.83-17.09	10.82	5.69

*7 Year Price Score 93.76 ***NYSE Composite Index=100** ***12 Month Price Score 92.41**

Interim Earnings (Per Share)

Qtr.	Mar	Jun	Sep	Dec
2014	0.50	0.50	1.85	0.00
2015	0.33	0.57	(0.24)	0.60
2016	0.44	0.39	0.92	1.16
2017	0.84	0.56	0.69	...

Interim Dividends (Per Share)

Amt	Decl	Ex	Rec	Pay
0.50Q	02/14/2017	03/29/2017	03/31/2017	04/28/2017
0.50Q	05/01/2017	06/28/2017	06/30/2017	07/28/2017
0.50Q	08/01/2017	09/27/2017	09/28/2017	10/27/2017
0.50Q	11/01/2017	12/28/2017	12/29/2017	01/30/2018

Indicated Div: $2.00 (Div. Reinv. Plan)

Valuation Analysis   **Institutional Holding**

Forecast EPS	$2.33	No of Institutions
	(11/14/2017)	368
Market Cap	$3.5 Billion	Shares
Book Value	$3.6 Billion	201,454,000
Price/Book	0.95	% Held
Price/Sales	2.79	67.24

Business Summary: REITs (MIC: 5.3.1 SIC: 6798 NAIC: 525930)

Chimera Investment is a real estate investment trust engaged in investing in mortgage assets, Co.'s investment portfolio includes: Residential Mortgage-Backed Securities, which invests in mortgage pass-through certificates issued or guaranteed; Agency commercial mortgage-backed securities, which each Government National Mortgage Association Construction Loan Certificates is backed by a single multifamily property or health care facilities; residential mortgage loans, which invests in residential mortgage loans primarily through direct and secondary market purchases; and other Asset-Backed Securities, which invests in securities issued in various collaterized debt obligations offerings.

Recent Developments: For the quarter ended Sep 30 2017, net income decreased 19.4% to US$139.2 million from US$172.8 million in the year-earlier quarter. Revenues were US$305.8 million, up 5.9% from US$288.8 million the year before.

Prospects: Our evaluation of Chimera Investment Corp. as of Jan. 14, 2018 is the result of our systematic analysis on three basic characteristics: earnings strength, relative valuation, and recent stock price movement. The company has suffered a very negative trend in earnings per share over the past 5 quarters and while recent estimates for the company have remained steady, CIM has posted better than expected results. Based on operating earnings yield, the company is undervalued when compared to all of the companies in our coverage universe. Share price changes over the past year indicates that CIM will perform well over the near term.

Financial Data

(US$ in Thousands)	9 Mos	6 Mos	3 Mos	12/31/2016	12/31/2015	12/31/2014	12/31/2013	12/31/2012
Earnings Per Share	3.25	3.48	3.31	2.92	1.25	2.85	1.75	1.60
Cash Flow Per Share	3.19	3.31	2.70	2.94	1.99	0.89	1.48	1.63
Tang Book Value Per Share	19.42	19.05	18.70	16.64	15.70	17.55	16.21	17.24
Dividends Per Share	2.000	1.980	1.960	2.440	1.440	1.800	2.800	1.900
Dividend Payout %	61.54	56.90	59.21	83.56	115.20	63.16	160.00	118.75
Income Statement								
Total Revenue	888,944	583,193	305,591	992,902	603,111	768,360	498,786	513,493
EBITDA	412,080	282,400	157,523	557,001	271,308	528,190	299,773	276,037
Depn & Amortn	(5,152)	4,421	(5,300)	4,975	20,958	(61,017)	(62,915)	(51,731)
Income Before Taxes	417,232	277,979	162,823	552,026	250,350	589,207	362,688	327,768
Income Taxes	172	155	16	83	1,000.00	2	2	1,000.00
Net Income	417,060	277,824	162,807	551,943	250,349	589,205	362,686	327,767
Average Shares	188,192	188,142	188,195	188,024	199,650	205,508	205,514	205,499
Balance Sheet								
Current Assets	148,711	266,822	182,225	257,411	180,309	235,719	110,623	660,483
Total Assets	21,187,384	20,818,469	20,426,650	16,684,908	15,344,646	19,155,005	6,936,081	7,742,489
Current Liabilities	7,623,574	7,463,980	6,498,253	6,267,110	8,127,509	10,425,034	1,957,862	1,622,897
Long-Term Obligations	9,916,175	9,776,095	10,414,682	7,275,221	4,249,911	5,095,278	...	...
Total Liabilities	17,540,953	17,241,782	16,914,562	13,561,375	12,398,458	15,547,315	3,604,571	4,200,010
Stockholders' Equity	3,646,431	3,576,687	3,512,088	3,123,533	2,946,188	3,607,690	3,331,510	3,542,479
Shares Outstanding	187,781	187,779	187,779	187,739	187,711	205,546	205,525	205,519
Statistical Record								
Return on Assets %	3.33	3.50	3.54	3.44	1.45	4.52	4.94	4.22
Return on Equity %	19.12	20.57	19.66	18.14	7.64	16.98	10.55	9.92
EBITDA Margin %	46.36	48.42	51.55	56.10	44.98	68.74	60.10	53.76
Net Margin %	46.92	47.64	53.28	55.59	41.51	76.68	72.71	63.83
Asset Turnover	0.06	0.06	0.06	0.06	0.03	0.06	0.07	0.07
Current Ratio	0.02	0.04	0.03	0.04	0.02	0.02	0.06	0.41
Debt to Equity	2.72	2.73	2.97	2.33	1.44	1.41	...	...
Price Range	20.83-14.80	20.83-14.80	20.41-13.48	17.64-11.39	16.45-12.86	16.95-14.95	16.60-13.05	15.60-10.65
P/E Ratio	6.41-4.55	5.99-4.25	6.17-4.07	6.04-3.90	13.16-10.29	5.95-5.25	9.49-7.46	9.75-6.66
Average Yield %	10.95	11.24	11.91	16.17	9.79	11.36	18.40	14.05

Address: 520 Madison Avenue, 32nd Floor, New York, NY 10022
Telephone: 212-626-2300

Web Site: www.chimerareit.com
Officers: Matthew Lambiase - President, Chief Executive Officer Robert S. (Rob) Colligan - Chief Financial Officer

Auditors: Ernst & Young LLP
Investor Contact: 866-315-9930
Transfer Agents: Computershare Shareowner Services LLC, Jersey City, NJ

CHIPOTLE MEXICAN GRILL INC

Exchange	Symbol	Price	52Wk Range	Yield	P/E
NYS	CMG	$289.03 (12/29/2017)	496.14-268.70	N/A	56.12

*7 Year Price Score 66.77 *NYSE Composite Index=100 *12 Month Price Score 73.81

TRADING VOLUME (thousand shares)

Interim Earnings (Per Share)

Qtr.	Mar	Jun	Sep	Dec
2014	2.64	3.50	4.15	3.84
2015	3.88	4.45	4.59	2.18
2016	(0.88)	0.87	0.27	0.54
2017	1.60	2.32	0.69	...

Interim Dividends (Per Share)

No Dividends Paid

Valuation Analysis

		Institutional Holding	
Forecast EPS	$6.63	No of Institutions	
	(01/18/2018)	763	
Market Cap	$8.2 Billion	Shares	
Book Value	$1.4 Billion	29,571,282	
Price/Book	5.89	% Held	
Price/Sales	1.86	89.02	

Business Summary: Hotels, Restaurants & Travel (MIC: 2.2.1 SIC: 5812 NAIC: 722110)

Chipotle Mexican Grill together with its subsidiaries operates Chipotle Mexican Grill restaurants, which serve a focused menu of burritos, tacos, burrito bowls (a burrito without the tortilla) and salads. As of Dec 31 2016, Co. operated 2,198 Chipotle restaurants throughout the U.S., as well as 29 international Chipotle restaurants, and Co. also had 23 restaurants in operation in other non-Chipotle concepts. Co. also makes a variety of extras such as guacamole, salsas and tortilla chips seasoned with lime juice and salt. In addition to sodas, fruit and tea drinks and organic milk, most of Co.'s restaurants also provides a selection of beer and margaritas.

Recent Developments: For the quarter ended Sep 30 2017, net income increased 151.4% to US$19.6 million from US$7.8 million in the year-earlier quarter. Revenues were US$1.13 billion, up 8.8% from US$1.04 billion the year before. Direct operating expenses rose 6.4% to US$946.9 million from US$890.3 million in the comparable period the year before. Indirect operating expenses increased 9.7% to US$150.3 million from US$137.0 million in the equivalent prior-year period.

Prospects: Our evaluation of Chipotle Mexican Grill Inc. as of Jan. 14, 2018 is the result of our systematic analysis on three basic characteristics: earnings strength, relative valuation, and recent stock price movement. The company has suffered a very negative trend in earnings per share over the past 5 quarters. However, while recent estimates for the company have been mixed, CMG has posted results that fell short of analysts expectations. Based on operating earnings yield, the company is overvalued when compared to all of the companies in our coverage universe. Share price changes over the past year indicates that CMG will perform poorly over the near term.

Financial Data
(US$ in Thousands)

	9 Mos	6 Mos	3 Mos	12/31/2016	12/31/2015	12/31/2014	12/31/2013	12/31/2012
Earnings Per Share	5.15	4.73	3.28	0.77	15.10	14.13	10.47	8.75
Cash Flow Per Share	15.73	14.42	15.24	11.90	21.98	21.98	17.08	13.29
Tang Book Value Per Share	48.26	49.97	48.32	47.91	68.86	64.15	48.86	39.37
Income Statement								
Total Revenue	3,366,312	2,238,238	1,068,829	3,904,384	4,501,223	4,108,269	3,214,591	2,731,224
EBITDA	332,671	260,258	112,452	185,107	900,235	824,777	630,525	541,815
Depn & Amortn	121,906	80,360	39,279	146,368	130,368	110,474	96,054	84,130
Income Before Taxes	214,277	182,135	74,361	38,739	769,867	714,303	534,471	457,685
Income Taxes	81,817	69,285	28,241	15,801	294,265	268,929	207,033	179,685
Net Income	132,460	112,850	46,120	22,938	475,602	445,374	327,438	278,000
Average Shares	28,439	28,800	28,850	29,770	31,494	31,512	31,281	31,783
Balance Sheet								
Current Assets	655,936	663,965	663,964	522,374	814,647	878,479	666,307	546,607
Total Assets	2,064,377	2,068,551	2,062,262	2,026,103	2,725,066	2,546,285	2,009,280	1,668,667
Current Liabilities	323,402	267,785	306,323	281,793	279,942	245,710	199,228	186,852
Long-Term Obligations	...	...	...	...	...	...	...	3,386
Total Liabilities	677,251	618,355	654,540	623,610	597,092	533,916	470,992	422,741
Stockholders' Equity	1,387,126	1,450,196	1,407,722	1,402,493	2,127,974	2,012,369	1,538,288	1,245,926
Shares Outstanding	28,287	28,585	28,678	28,814	30,584	31,027	31,033	31,093
Statistical Record								
Return on Assets %	7.19	6.55	4.54	0.96	18.04	19.55	17.81	17.92
Return on Equity %	10.50	9.31	6.48	1.30	22.97	25.09	23.52	24.21
EBITDA Margin %	9.88	11.63	10.52	4.74	20.00	20.08	19.61	19.84
Net Margin %	3.93	5.04	4.32	0.59	10.57	10.84	10.19	10.18
Asset Turnover	2.13	2.07	1.97	1.64	1.71	1.80	1.75	1.76
Current Ratio	2.03	2.48	2.17	1.85	2.91	3.58	3.34	2.93
Price Range	496.14-297.09	496.14-359.92	470.97-359.92	533.69-359.92	757.77-479.85	692.69-476.28	546.97-280.94	440.40-236.24
P/E Ratio	96.34-57.69	104.89-76.09	143.59-109.73	693.10-467.43	50.18-31.78	49.02-33.71	52.24-26.83	50.33-27.00

Address: 1401 Wynkoop Street, Suite 500, Denver, CO 80202 **Telephone:** 303-595-4000	**Web Site:** www.chipotle.com **Officers:** M. Steven (Steve) Ells - Chairman, Chief Executive Officer, Co-Chief Executive Officer Scott Boatwright - Chief Restaurant Officer	**Auditors:** Ernst & Young LLP **Transfer Agents:** Wells Fargo Shareowner Services, Mendota Heights, MN

CHOICE HOTELS INTERNATIONAL, INC.

Exchange	Symbol	Price	52Wk Range	Yield	P/E
NYS	CHH	$77.60 (12/29/2017)	78.70-53.50	1.11	28.74

*7 Year Price Score 107.11 *NYSE Composite Index=100 *12 Month Price Score 110.29

Interim Earnings (Per Share)

Qtr.	Mar	Jun	Sep	Dec
2014	0.32	0.60	0.67	0.44
2015	0.37	0.62	0.72	0.51
2016	0.35	0.68	0.84	0.56
2017	0.51	0.79	0.84	....

Interim Dividends (Per Share)

Amt	Decl	Ex	Rec	Pay
0.215Q	02/28/2017	03/30/2017	04/03/2017	04/18/2017
0.215Q	04/24/2017	06/29/2017	07/03/2017	07/18/2017
0.215Q	09/18/2017	09/29/2017	10/02/2017	10/17/2017
0.215Q	12/18/2017	12/29/2017	01/02/2018	01/17/2018

Indicated Div: $0.86

Valuation Analysis

	Institutional Holding	
Forecast EPS	$2.88	No of Institutions
	(01/26/2018)	247
Market Cap	$4.4 Billion	Shares
Book Value	N/A	32,841,192
Price/Book	N/A	% Held
Price/Sales	4.49	N/A

Business Summary: Hotels, Restaurants & Travel (MIC: 2.2.1 SIC: 7011 NAIC: 721110)

Choice Hotels International is a hotel franchisor with 6,514 hotels (516,122 rooms) in 50 states, the District of Columbia and over 40 countries and territories outside the U.S. Co. franchises lodging properties under the following brand names: Comfort Inn®, Comfort Suites®, Quality®, Clarion®, Sleep Inn®, Econo Lodge®, Rodeway Inn®, MainStay Suites®, Suburban Extended Stay Hotel®, Cambria® hotels & suites, and Ascend Hotel Collection®. Co.'s brand names include Comfort Inn, Comfort Suites, Quality, Clarion, Ascend Hotel Collection, Sleep Inn, Econo Lodge, Rodeway Inn, MainStay Suites, Suburban Extended Stay Hotel and Cambria hotels & suites.

Recent Developments: For the quarter ended Sep 30 2017, net income was unchanged at US$47.6 million versus US$47.6 million the year-earlier quarter. Revenues were US$295.1 million, up 10.3% from US$267.6 million the year before. Operating income was US$77.8 million versus US$78.6 million in the prior-year quarter, a decrease of 1.0%. Direct operating expenses rose 10.4% to US$167.8 million from US$152.0 million in the comparable period the year before. Indirect operating expenses increased 34.0% to US$49.5 million from US$36.9 million in the equivalent prior-year period.

Prospects: Our evaluation of Choice Hotels International Inc. as of Jan. 21, 2018 is the result of our systematic analysis on three basic characteristics: earnings strength, relative valuation, and recent stock price movement. The company has generated a negative trend in earnings per share over the past 5 quarters and while recent estimates for the company have been mixed, CHH has posted better than expected results. Based on operating earnings yield, the company is about fairly valued when compared to all of the companies in our coverage universe. Share price changes over the past year indicates that CHH will perform well over the near term.

Financial Data
(US$ in Thousands)

	9 Mos	6 Mos	3 Mos	12/31/2016	12/31/2015	12/31/2014	12/31/2013	12/31/2012
Earnings Per Share	2.70	2.70	2.59	2.46	2.22	2.10	1.91	2.07
Cash Flow Per Share	4.07	3.36	3.56	2.71	2.81	3.19	2.62	2.79
Dividends Per Share	0.860	0.850	0.840	0.830	0.790	0.750	0.740	11.150
Dividend Payout %	31.85	31.48	32.43	33.74	35.59	35.71	38.74	538.65
Income Statement								
Total Revenue	769,785	474,697	197,898	924,641	859,878	757,970	724,307	691,509
EBITDA	219,313	137,606	56,474	245,999	230,439	217,241	199,374	197,005
Depn & Amortn	9,215	6,120	3,070	5,600	4,300	3,100	3,100	2,400
Income Before Taxes	180,491	111,703	43,463	199,488	184,886	174,416	156,284	168,956
Income Taxes	55,944	35,025	12,639	60,609	55,956	52,285	44,317	48,481
Net Income	121,334	73,739	28,744	139,371	128,029	123,160	112,601	120,687
Average Shares	56,506	56,428	56,286	56,155	57,273	58,256	58,335	57,653
Balance Sheet								
Current Assets	455,323	380,227	342,862	344,873	310,953	351,414	258,646	233,470
Total Assets	961,192	947,973	904,132	852,468	717,010	647,270	539,899	510,772
Current Liabilities	273,034	276,361	274,081	263,668	208,016	200,098	174,338	176,137
Long-Term Obligations	800,001	862,965	862,389	839,409	812,945	782,082	783,471	847,150
Total Liabilities	1,161,572	1,200,590	1,196,619	1,163,817	1,112,909	1,076,071	1,004,144	1,059,676
Stockholders' Equity	(200,380)	(252,617)	(292,487)	(311,349)	(395,899)	(428,801)	(464,245)	(548,904)
Shares Outstanding	56,593	56,496	56,448	56,299	56,336	57,337	58,638	58,171
Statistical Record								
Return on Assets %	16.95	17.10	17.38	17.71	18.77	20.75	21.43	25.11
EBITDA Margin %	28.49	28.99	28.54	26.60	26.80	28.66	27.53	28.49
Net Margin %	15.76	15.53	14.52	15.07	14.89	16.25	15.55	17.45
Asset Turnover	1.08	1.06	1.08	1.18	1.26	1.28	1.38	1.44
Current Ratio	1.67	1.38	1.25	1.31	1.49	1.76	1.48	1.33
Price Range	67.40-44.06	67.40-44.06	63.30-44.06	56.70-41.85	64.85-46.62	57.34-43.71	49.71-33.62	44.21-30.80
P/E Ratio	24.96-16.32	24.96-16.32	24.44-17.01	23.05-17.01	29.21-21.00	27.30-20.81	26.03-17.60	21.36-14.88
Average Yield %	1.46	1.54	1.64	1.71	1.43	1.52	1.79	31.06

Address: 1 Choice Hotels Circle, Suite 400, Rockville, MD 20850
Telephone: 301-592-5000

Web Site: www.choicehotels.com
Officers: Stewart Bainum - Chairman Patrick S. Pacious - President, Chief Operating Officer, Executive Vice President

Auditors: Ernst & Young LLP
Investor Contact: 301-592-5026
Transfer Agents: Computershare, Providence, RI

CHUBB LTD

Exchange	Symbol	Price	52Wk Range	Yield	P/E
NYS	CB	$146.13 (12/29/2017)	155.19-128.48	1.94	17.48

*7 Year Price Score 109.78 *NYSE Composite Index=100 *12 Month Price Score 99.03

TRADING VOLUME (thousand shares)

Interim Earnings (Per Share)

Qtr.	Mar	Jun	Sep	Dec
2014	2.14	2.28	2.32	1.67
2015	2.05	2.86	1.62	2.09
2016	0.97	1.54	2.88	3.43
2017	2.31	2.77	(0.15)	...

Interim Dividends (Per Share)

Amt	Decl	Ex	Rec	Pay
0.69Q	02/23/2017	03/29/2017	03/31/2017	04/21/2017
0.71Q	05/18/2017	06/28/2017	06/30/2017	07/21/2017
0.71Q	08/10/2017	09/28/2017	09/29/2017	10/20/2017
0.71Q	11/16/2017	12/28/2017	12/29/2017	01/19/2018

Indicated Div. $2.84 (Div. Reinv. Plan)

Valuation Analysis   **Institutional Holding**

Forecast EPS	N/A	No of Institutions 1303
Market Cap	$67.8 Billion	Shares
Book Value	$50.5 Billion	480,519,776
Price/Book	1.34	% Held
Price/Sales	2.09	N/A

Business Summary: General Insurance (MIC: 5.2.1 SIC: 6331 NAIC: 524130)

Chubb is a holding company. Through its subsidiaries, Co. is an insurance and reinsurance organization. Co. provides commercial insurance products and service offerings such as risk management programs. Co. provides insurance products ranging from Directors & Officers and professional liability to several specialty-casualty and umbrella and excess casualty lines. Co. also provides personal lines insurance coverage including homeowners, umbrella liability and recreational marine products. Co.'s segments are: North America Commercial P&C Insurance, North America Personal P&C Insurance, North America Agricultural Insurance, Overseas General Insurance, Global Reinsurance, and Life Insurance.

Recent Developments: For the quarter ended Sep 30 2017, net loss amounted to US$70.0 million versus net income of US$1.36 billion in the year-earlier quarter. Revenues were US$8.61 billion, up 1.0% from US$8.53 billion the year before. Net premiums earned were US$7.81 billion versus US$7.69 billion in the prior-year quarter, an increase of 1.5%. Net investment income rose 10.0% to US$813.0 million from US$739.0 million a year ago.

Prospects: Our evaluation of Chubb Ltd. as of Sep. 17, 2017 is the result of our systematic analysis on three basic characteristics: earnings strength, relative valuation, and recent stock price movement. The company has generated a negative trend in earnings per share over the past 5 quarters and while recent estimates for the company have been mixed, CB has posted better than expected results. Based on operating earnings yield, the company is undervalued when compared to all of the companies in our coverage universe. Share price changes over the past year indicates that CB will perform well over the near term.

Financial Data

(US$ in Thousands)	9 Mos	6 Mos	3 Mos	12/31/2016	12/31/2015	12/31/2014	12/31/2013	12/31/2012
Earnings Per Share	8.36	11.39	10.16	8.87	8.62	8.42	10.92	7.89
Cash Flow Per Share	10.43	10.21	11.27	11.41	11.87	13.40	11.80	11.72
Tang Book Value Per Share	60.77	60.89	58.14	56.18	72.26	72.61	68.93	66.28
Dividends Per Share	...	...	...	...	2.660	2.700	2.020	2.060
Dividend Payout %	...	...	...	...	30.86	32.07	18.50	26.11
Income Statement								
Premium Income	21,816,000	14,009,000	6,772,000	28,749,000	17,213,000	17,426,000	16,613,000	15,677,000
Total Revenue	24,228,000	15,618,000	7,510,000	31,469,000	18,987,000	19,171,000	19,261,000	17,936,000
Benefits & Claims	14,682,000	8,266,000	3,957,000	16,640,000	10,027,000	10,166,000	9,863,000	10,174,000
Income Before Taxes	2,269,000	2,527,000	1,168,000	4,686,000	3,183,000	3,256,000	4,119,000	2,896,000
Income Taxes	243,000	328,000	128,000	815,000	462,000	634,000	480,000	270,000
Net Income	2,328,000	2,398,000	1,093,000	4,135,000	2,834,000	2,853,000	3,758,000	2,706,000
Average Shares	466,370	471,853	472,731	465,949	328,835	338,986	344,147	342,746
Balance Sheet								
Total Assets	167,578,000	162,988,000	160,967,000	159,786,000	102,366,000	98,248,000	94,510,000	92,545,000
Total Liabilities	117,107,000	112,639,000	111,743,000	111,511,000	73,231,000	68,661,000	65,685,000	65,014,000
Stockholders' Equity	50,471,000	50,349,000	49,224,000	48,275,000	29,135,000	29,587,000	28,825,000	27,531,000
Shares Outstanding	464,158	465,375	467,223	465,968	324,563	328,659	339,793	340,321
Statistical Record								
Return on Assets %	2.39	3.32	3.02	3.15	2.83	2.96	4.02	3.00
Return on Equity %	7.97	11.00	10.07	10.65	9.65	9.77	13.34	10.37
Loss Ratio %	67.30	59.00	58.43	57.88	58.25	58.34	59.37	64.90
Net Margin %	9.61	15.35	14.55	13.14	14.93	14.88	19.51	15.09
Price Range	149.87-121.88	147.58-121.88	140.38-117.19	133.32-108.00	119.47-99.72	117.58-92.19	103.53-79.80	81.70-68.98
P/E Ratio	17.93-14.58	12.96-10.70	13.82-11.53	15.03-12.18	13.86-11.57	13.96-10.95	9.48-7.31	10.35-8.74
Average Yield %	...	...	...	...	2.43	2.60	2.21	2.76

Address: Baerengasse 32, Zurich, CH-8001 **Telephone:** 434-567-600	**Web Site:** www.acegroup.com **Officers:** Evan G. Greenberg - Chairman, Vice-Chairman, President, Chief Executive Officer, Chief Operating Officer John W. Keogh - Executive Vice Chairman, Vice-Chairman, Chief Operating Officer	**Auditors:** PricewaterhouseCoopers LLP

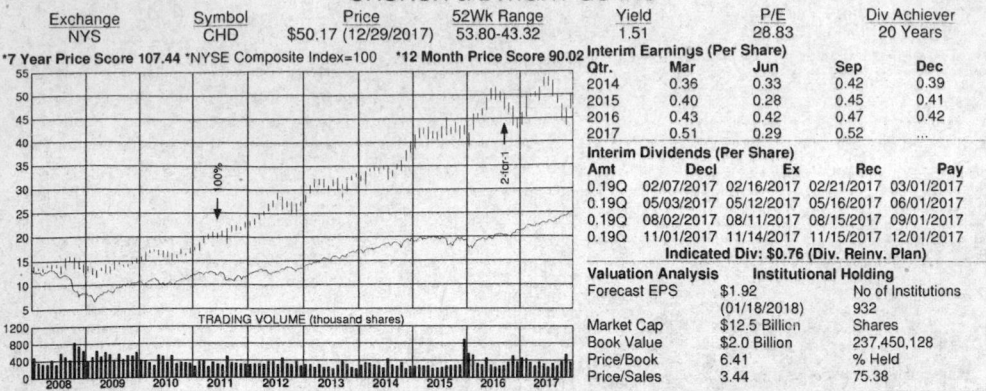

CHURCH & DWIGHT CO INC

Exchange	Symbol	Price	52Wk Range	Yield	P/E	Div Achiever
NYS	CHD	$50.17 (12/29/2017)	53.80-43.32	1.51	28.83	20 Years

*7 Year Price Score 107.44 *NYSE Composite Index=100 *12 Month Price Score 90.02

Interim Earnings (Per Share)

Qtr.	Mar	Jun	Sep	Dec
2014	0.36	0.33	0.42	0.39
2015	0.40	0.28	0.45	0.41
2016	0.43	0.42	0.47	0.42
2017	0.51	0.29	0.52	...

Interim Dividends (Per Share)

Amt	Decl	Ex	Rec	Pay
0.19Q	02/07/2017	02/16/2017	02/21/2017	03/01/2017
0.19Q	05/03/2017	05/12/2017	05/16/2017	06/01/2017
0.19Q	08/02/2017	08/11/2017	08/15/2017	09/01/2017
0.19Q	11/01/2017	11/14/2017	11/15/2017	12/01/2017

Indicated Div: $0.76 (Div. Reinv. Plan)

Valuation Analysis

		Institutional Holding	
Forecast EPS	$1.92	No of Institutions	
	(01/18/2018)	932	
Market Cap	$12.5 Billion	Shares	
Book Value	$2.0 Billion	237,450,128	
Price/Book	6.41	% Held	
Price/Sales	3.44	75.38	

Business Summary: Household & Personal Products (MIC: 1.7.1 SIC: 2841 NAIC: 325611)

Church & Dwight develops, manufactures and markets a range of household, personal care and specialty products. Co. sells its products under a variety of brands via a distribution platform that includes supermarkets, mass merchandisers, wholesale clubs, drugstores, convenience stores, home stores, dollar, pet and other specialty stores and websites. Co. has three segments: Consumer Domestic, which sells household and personal care products; Consumer International, which sells personal care products, some of which use the same brands as its domestic lines, in international markets; and Specialty Products Division, which has an animal productivity business with products for animal agriculture.

Recent Developments: For the quarter ended Sep 30 2017, net income increased 7.6% to US$133.4 million from US$124.0 million in the year-earlier quarter. Revenues were US$967.9 million, up 11.2% from US$870.7 million the year before. Operating income was US$198.7 million versus US$196.0 million in the prior-year quarter, an increase of 1.4%. Direct operating expenses rose 11.4% to US$529.4 million from US$475.1 million in the comparable period the year before. Indirect operating expenses increased 20.1% to US$239.8 million from US$199.6 million in the equivalent prior-year period.

Prospects: Our evaluation of Church & Dwight Co. Inc. as of Jan. 14, 2018 is the result of our systematic analysis on three basic characteristics: earnings strength, relative valuation, and recent stock price movement. The company has managed to produce a neutral trend in earnings per share over the past 5 quarters and while recent estimates for the company have been mixed, CHD has posted better than expected results. Based on operating earnings yield, the company is about fairly valued when compared to all of the companies in our coverage universe. Share price changes over the past year indicates that CHD will perform in line with the market over the near term.

Financial Data

(US$ in Thousands)	9 Mos	6 Mos	3 Mos	12/31/2016	12/31/2015	12/31/2014	12/31/2013	12/31/2012
Earnings Per Share	1.74	1.69	1.83	1.75	1.53	1.50	1.40	1.23
Cash Flow Per Share	2.34	2.43	2.40	2.54	2.31	2.00	1.80	1.86
Dividends Per Share	0.748	0.735	0.723	0.710	0.670	0.620	0.560	0.480
Dividend Payout %	42.96	43.49	39.59	40.57	43.65	41.20	40.14	39.18
Income Statement								
Total Revenue	2,743,100	1,775,200	877,200	3,493,100	3,394,800	3,297,600	3,194,300	2,921,900
EBITDA	611,600	378,500	225,600	784,100	730,000	697,800	682,400	603,600
Depn & Amortn	91,600	59,200	29,300	59,700	58,300	57,100	59,700	56,000
Income Before Taxes	486,100	301,800	188,100	696,700	641,200	613,300	595,000	533,600
Income Taxes	156,200	102,600	58,700	246,900	225,000	211,000	203,400	192,700
Net Income	337,800	204,400	131,500	459,000	410,400	413,900	394,400	349,800
Average Shares	255,300	255,600	259,700	262,100	267,200	275,000	282,400	285,400
Balance Sheet								
Current Assets	1,003,200	877,200	754,500	756,800	906,000	1,032,500	1,115,800	933,800
Total Assets	5,952,800	4,667,000	4,487,800	4,354,100	4,256,900	4,381,300	4,259,700	4,098,100
Current Liabilities	952,600	1,211,700	1,166,800	1,001,900	872,700	905,300	651,200	725,600
Long-Term Obligations	2,104,100	894,100	692,900	693,400	692,800	698,600	649,500	649,400
Total Liabilities	3,999,700	2,818,700	2,552,100	2,376,200	2,233,700	2,279,400	1,959,800	2,037,200
Stockholders' Equity	1,953,100	1,848,300	1,935,700	1,977,900	2,023,200	2,101,900	2,299,900	2,060,900
Shares Outstanding	249,715	249,283	251,895	253,962	259,908	266,703	277,929	277,562
Statistical Record								
Return on Assets %	8.76	9.78	10.88	10.63	9.50	9.58	9.44	9.67
Return on Equity %	22.01	22.73	24.77	22.88	19.90	18.81	18.09	17.01
EBITDA Margin %	22.30	21.32	25.72	22.45	21.50	21.16	21.36	20.66
Net Margin %	12.31	11.51	14.99	13.14	12.09	12.55	12.35	11.97
Asset Turnover	0.71	0.79	0.80	0.81	0.79	0.76	0.76	0.81
Current Ratio	1.05	0.72	0.65	0.76	1.04	1.14	1.71	1.29
Debt to Equity	1.08	0.48	0.36	0.35	0.34	0.33	0.28	0.32
Price Range	53.80-42.77	53.75-42.77	51.67-42.77	51.67-39.12	45.28-38.78	40.27-31.03	33.45-26.79	29.38-22.40
P/E Ratio	30.92-24.58	31.80-25.31	28.23-23.37	29.53-22.35	29.60-25.35	26.84-20.69	23.90-19.13	23.89-18.21
Average Yield %	1.53	1.52	1.51	1.52	1.58	1.79	1.81	1.85

Address: 500 Charles Ewing Boulevard, Ewing, NJ 08628 **Telephone:** 609-806-1200 **Fax:** 609-497-7269	**Web Site:** www.churchdwight.com **Officers:** James R. Craigie - Chairman, Chief Executive Officer Matthew Thomas Farrell - President, Chief Executive Officer, Executive Vice President, Chief Financial Officer, Chief Operating Officer	**Auditors:** Deloitte & Touche LLP **Investor Contact:** 609-497-7111 **Transfer Agents:** Computershare Inc., Canton, MA

CIENA CORP

Exchange	Symbol	Price	52Wk Range	Yield	P/E
NYS	CIEN	$20.93 (12/29/2017)	27.50-19.57	N/A	2.78

*7 Year Price Score 92.69   *NYSE Composite Index=100   *12 Month Price Score 84.26

Interim Earnings (Per Share)

Qtr.	Jan	Apr	Jul	Oct
2012-13	(0.47)	(0.27)	(0.01)	(0.09)
2013-14	(0.15)	(0.10)	0.15	(0.29)
2014-15	(0.17)	0.17	0.19	(0.12)
2015-16	(0.08)	0.10	0.23	0.25
2016-17	0.03	0.25	0.30	6.84

Interim Dividends (Per Share)

No Dividends Paid

Valuation Analysis		Institutional Holding	
Forecast EPS	$1.26	No of Institutions	480
	(01/16/2018)		
Market Cap	$3.0 Billion	Shares	182,799,792
Book Value	$2.1 Billion	% Held	
Price/Book	1.40		
Price/Sales	1.07	N/A	

Business Summary: IT Services (MIC: 6.3.1 SIC: 7373 NAIC: 541512)

Ciena provides equipment, software and services that support the transport, switching, aggregation, service delivery and management of voice, video and data traffic on communications networks. Co.'s Converged Packet Optical, Packet Networking, and Optical Transport products are used by communications service providers, cable and multiservice operators, Web-scale providers, submarine network operators, governments, enterprises, research and education institutions, and other network operators. To complement its solutions, Co. provides a range of transformation and automation services that help customers to design, optimize, integrate, deploy, manage and maintain their networks.

Recent Developments: For the year ended Oct 31 2017, net income increased to US$1.26 billion from US$72.6 million in the prior year. Revenues were US$2.80 billion, up 7.7% from US$2.60 billion the year before. Operating income was US$214.7 million versus US$156.2 million in the prior year, an increase of 37.5%. Direct operating expenses rose 8.1% to US$1.56 billion from US$1.44 billion in the comparable period the year before. Indirect operating expenses increased 2.6% to US$1.03 billion from US$1.01 billion in the equivalent prior-year period.

Prospects: Our evaluation of CIENA Corp. as of Jan. 14, 2018 is the result of our systematic analysis on three basic characteristics: earnings strength, relative valuation, and recent stock price movement. The company has generated a negative trend in earnings per share over the past 5 quarters. However, while recent estimates for the company have been lowered by analysts, CIEN has posted results that fell short of analysts expectations. Based on operating earnings yield, the company is undervalued when compared to all of the companies in our coverage universe. Share price changes over the past year indicates that CIEN will perform poorly over the near term.

Financial Data (US$ in Thousands)	10/31/2017	10/31/2016	10/31/2015	10/31/2014	10/31/2013	10/31/2012	10/31/2011	10/31/2010
Earnings Per Share	7.53	0.51	0.10	(0.38)	(0.83)	(1.45)	(2.04)	(3.58)
Cash Flow Per Share	1.65	2.09	2.21	0.85	0.44	1.08	(0.94)	(2.46)
Tang Book Value Per Share	12.36	2.52	1.19	...	...	...	N.M.	N.M.
Income Statement								
Total Revenue	2,801,687	2,600,573	2,445,669	2,288,289	2,082,546	1,833,923	1,741,970	1,236,636
EBITDA	322,061	269,682	202,050	125,295	89,203	45,951	(9,517)	(151,353)
Depn & Amortn	112,913	130,998	125,966	103,751	119,608	125,797	146,427	165,518
Income Before Taxes	156,126	86,718	23,764	(26,673)	(80,191)	(134,699)	(187,848)	(331,573)
Income Taxes	(1,105,827)	14,134	12,097	13,964	5,240	9,322	7,673	1,941
Net Income	1,261,953	72,584	11,667	(40,637)	(85,431)	(144,021)	(195,521)	(333,514)
Average Shares	169,919	150,704	120,101	105,783	102,350	99,341	95,854	93,103
Balance Sheet								
Current Assets	2,006,311	2,013,192	1,864,210	1,693,190	1,395,802	1,415,690	1,332,838	1,441,568
Total Assets	3,951,711	2,882,442	2,695,051	2,072,632	1,802,770	1,881,143	1,951,418	2,118,093
Current Liabilities	1,037,743	891,862	667,034	781,136	615,055	684,970	453,493	469,945
Long-Term Obligations	657,095	1,050,289	1,285,433	1,279,380	1,212,019	1,225,806	1,442,364	1,442,705
Total Liabilities	1,815,369	2,116,101	2,074,175	2,142,247	1,885,447	1,970,115	1,937,545	1,958,800
Stockholders' Equity	2,136,342	766,341	620,876	(69,615)	(82,677)	(88,972)	13,873	159,293
Shares Outstanding	143,043	139,767	135,612	106,979	103,705	100,601	97,440	94,060
Statistical Record								
Return on Assets %	36.93	2.60	0.49	N.M.	N.M.	N.M.	N.M.	N.M.
Return on Equity %	86.95	10.44	4.23	...	...	...	N.M.	N.M.
EBITDA Margin %	11.50	10.37	8.26	5.48	4.28	2.51	N.M.	N.M.
Net Margin %	45.04	2.79	0.48	N.M.	N.M.	N.M.	N.M.	N.M.
Asset Turnover	0.82	0.93	1.03	1.18	1.13	0.95	0.86	0.68
Current Ratio	1.93	2.26	2.79	2.17	2.27	2.07	2.94	3.07
Debt to Equity	0.31	1.37	2.07	...	...	...	103.97	9.06
Price Range	27.50-19.21	25.30-15.73	26.03-14.81	26.20-14.16	27.67-12.42	17.98-10.38	28.81-10.28	19.24-10.67
P/E Ratio	3.65-2.55	49.61-30.84	260.30-148.10	...	...	...	...	...

Address: 7035 Ridge Road, Hanover, MD 21076
Telephone: 410-694-5700
Fax: 410-694-5750

Web Site: www.ciena.com
Officers: Patrick H. Nettles - Executive Chairman
Gary B. Smith - President, Chief Executive Officer

Auditors: PricewaterhouseCoopers LLP
Transfer Agents: Computershare Trust Company, N.A., Providence, RI

CIGNA CORP

Exchange	Symbol	Price	52Wk Range	Yield	P/E
NYS	CI	$203.09 (12/29/2017)	211.73-135.72	0.02	22.24

*7 Year Price Score 135.80 *NYSE Composite Index=100 *12 Month Price Score 112.92

Interim Earnings (Per Share)
Qtr.	Mar	Jun	Sep	Dec
2014	1.92	2.12	2.01	1.78
2015	2.04	2.26	2.10	1.64
2016	2.00	1.97	1.76	1.47
2017	2.30	3.15	2.21	...

Interim Dividends (Per Share)
Amt	Decl	Ex	Rec	Pay
0.04A	02/26/2014	03/10/2014	03/12/2014	04/09/2014
0.04A	02/25/2015	03/10/2015	03/12/2015	04/10/2015
0.04A	02/24/2016	03/09/2016	03/11/2016	04/11/2016
0.04A	02/22/2017	03/08/2017	03/10/2017	04/10/2017

Indicated Div: $0.04 (Div. Reinv. Plan)

Valuation Analysis
Forecast EPS	$10.40
	(01/18/2018)
Market Cap	$50.1 Billion
Book Value	$14.1 Billion
Price/Book	3.54
Price/Sales	1.22

Institutional Holding
No of Institutions	1080
Shares	261,756,080
% Held	82.69

Business Summary: Life & Health (MIC: 5.2.2 SIC: 6324 NAIC: 524114)

Cigna is a holding company. Co. is a health services organization. Through its subsidiaries, Co. provides medical, dental, disability, life and accident insurance and related products and services, the majority of which are provide through employers and other groups such as governmental and non-governmental organizations, unions and associations. Co. also provides commercial health and dental insurance, Medicare and Medicaid products and health, life and accident insurance coverages to individuals in the U.S. and selected international markets. Co.'s segments include: Global Health Care; Global Supplemental Benefits; Group Disability and Life; and Other Operations.

Recent Developments: For the quarter ended Sep 30 2017, net income increased 24.3% to US$562.0 million from US$452.0 million in the year-earlier quarter. Revenues were US$10.38 billion, up 5.1% from US$9.88 billion the year before. Net premiums earned were US$8.03 billion versus US$7.61 billion in the prior-year quarter, an increase of 5.6%. Net investment income rose 5.7% to US$298.0 million from US$282.0 million a year ago.

Prospects: Our evaluation of Cigna Corp. as of Jan. 14, 2018 is the result of our systematic analysis on three basic characteristics: earnings strength, relative valuation, and recent stock price movement. The company has generated a negative trend in earnings per share over the past 5 quarters and while recent estimates for the company have been raised by analysts, CI has posted better than expected results. Based on operating earnings yield, the company is undervalued when compared to all of the companies in our coverage universe. Share price changes over the past year indicates that CI will perform very well over the near term.

Financial Data
(US$ in Millions)	9 Mos	6 Mos	3 Mos	12/31/2016	12/31/2015	12/31/2014	12/31/2013	12/31/2012
Earnings Per Share	9.13	8.68	7.50	7.19	8.04	7.83	5.18	5.61
Cash Flow Per Share	17.91	20.10	18.43	15.72	10.61	7.56	2.57	8.23
Tang Book Value Per Share	33.03	33.94	32.20	30.14	23.45	18.46	16.47	13.18
Dividends Per Share	0.040	0.040	0.040	0.040	0.040	0.040	0.040	0.040
Dividend Payout %	0.44	0.46	0.53	0.56	0.50	0.51	0.77	0.71
Income Statement								
Premium Income	24,143	16,113	8,103	30,626	29,642	27,214	28,976	26,187
Total Revenue	31,085	20,703	10,385	39,668	37,876	34,914	32,380	29,119
Benefits & Claims	4,044	12,611	1,367	24,486	23,290	21,334	20,865	17,859
Income Before Taxes	2,848	2,024	890	2,979	3,327	3,304	2,176	2,477
Income Taxes	883	621	297	1,136	1,250	1,210	698	853
Net Income	1,971	1,411	598	1,867	2,094	2,102	1,476	1,623
Average Shares	253	258	259	259	260	268	284	289
Balance Sheet								
Total Assets	61,936	61,738	61,147	59,360	57,088	55,896	54,336	53,734
Total Liabilities	47,791	47,192	46,921	45,637	45,053	45,122	43,769	43,965
Stockholders' Equity	14,145	14,546	14,226	13,723	12,035	10,774	10,567	9,769
Shares Outstanding	246	251	256	256	256	259	275	285
Statistical Record								
Return on Assets %	3.84	3.71	3.24	3.20	3.71	3.81	2.73	3.09
Return on Equity %	16.74	16.12	14.47	14.46	18.36	19.70	14.52	17.87
Loss Ratio %	16.75	78.27	16.87	79.95	78.57	78.39	72.01	68.20
Net Margin %	6.34	6.82	5.76	4.71	5.53	6.02	4.56	5.57
Price Range	187.62-116.03	170.68-116.03	154.00-116.03	146.55-116.03	169.77-101.06	105.20-75.64	88.18-53.46	54.49-39.66
P/E Ratio	20.55-12.71	19.66-13.37	20.53-15.47	20.38-16.14	21.12-12.57	13.44-9.66	17.02-10.32	9.71-7.07
Average Yield %	0.03	0.03	0.03	0.03	0.03	0.04	0.06	0.09

Address: 900 Cottage Grove Road, Bloomfield, CT 06002
Telephone: 860-226-6000
Fax: 860-226-6741

Web Site: www.cigna.com
Officers: Isaiah Harris - Chairman David M. Cordani - President, Chief Executive Officer

Auditors: PricewaterhouseCoopers LLP
Investor Contact: 215-761-1414
Transfer Agents: Computershare Shareowner Services, Providence, RI

CIMAREX ENERGY CO

Exchange	Symbol	Price	52Wk Range	Yield	P/E
NYS	XEC	$122.01 (12/29/2017)	142.47-91.33	0.26	32.28

*7 Year Price Score 91.12   *NYSE Composite Index=100   *12 Month Price Score 96.94

TRADING VOLUME (thousand shares)

Interim Earnings (Per Share)

Qtr.	Mar	Jun	Sep	Dec
2014	1.59	1.70	1.65	0.84
2015	(4.84)	(6.47)	(8.21)	(6.78)
2016	(2.00)	(2.91)	(0.14)	0.42
2017	1.38	1.02	0.96	...

Interim Dividends (Per Share)

Amt	Decl	Ex	Rec	Pay
0.08Q	02/24/2017	05/11/2017	05/15/2017	06/01/2017
0.08Q	05/12/2017	08/11/2017	08/15/2017	09/01/2017
0.08Q	09/01/2017	11/14/2017	11/15/2017	12/01/2017
0.08Q	12/08/2017	02/14/2018	02/15/2018	03/01/2018

Indicated Div: $0.32

Valuation Analysis / Institutional Holding

Forecast EPS	$4.56 (01/26/2018)	No of Institutions	678
Market Cap	$11.6 Billion	Shares	110,470,928
Book Value	$2.4 Billion	% Held	90.07
Price/Book	4.84		
Price/Sales	6.64		

Business Summary: Production & Extraction (MIC: 9.1.1 SIC: 1311 NAIC: 211111)

Cimarex Energy is an independent oil and gas exploration and production company. Co.'s operations are mainly located in Oklahoma, Texas and New Mexico. Co.'s operations are focused in two main areas: the Permian Basin and the Mid-Continent region. Co.'s Permian Basin region encompasses west Texas and southeast New Mexico. Co.'s Mid-Continent region consists of Oklahoma and the Texas Panhandle. As of Dec 31 2016, Co.'s proved oil and gas reserves totaled 2.89 trillion cubic feet of natural gas equivalent, consisted of 1.47 trillion cubic feet of gas, and 105.9 million barrels of oil and 130.6 million barrels of natural gas liquids.

Recent Developments: For the quarter ended Sep 30 2017, net income amounted to US$91.4 million versus a net loss of US$10.7 million in the year-earlier quarter. Revenues were US$463.7 million, up 38.1% from US$335.7 million the year before. Operating income was US$149.5 million versus a loss of US$4.1 million in the prior-year quarter. Direct operating expenses rose 21.0% to US$132.7 million from US$109.6 million in the comparable period the year before. Indirect operating expenses decreased 21.2% to US$181.5 million from US$230.2 million in the equivalent prior-year period.

Prospects: Our evaluation of Cimarex Energy Co as of Jan. 21, 2018 is the result of our systematic analysis on three basic characteristics: earnings strength, relative valuation, and recent stock price movement. The company has suffered a very negative trend in earnings per share over the past 5 quarters and while recent estimates for the company have been raised by analysts, XEC has posted better than expected results. Based on operating earnings yield, the company is about fairly valued when compared to all of the companies in our coverage universe. Share price changes over the past year indicates that XEC will perform very poorly over the near term.

Financial Data

(US$ in Thousands)	9 Mos	6 Mos	3 Mos	12/31/2016	12/31/2015	12/31/2014	12/31/2013	12/31/2012
Earnings Per Share	3.78	2.68	(1.25)	(4.62)	(25.92)	5.78	6.47	4.07
Cash Flow Per Share	9.90	9.53	8.18	6.40	7.44	18.90	15.53	14.03
Tang Book Value Per Share	18.70	17.74	16.72	18.29	22.96	44.30	39.03	32.96
Dividends Per Share	0.320	0.320	0.320	0.400	0.640	0.620	0.540	0.460
Dividend Payout %	8.47	11.94	...	...	...	10.73	8.35	11.30
Income Statement								
Total Revenue	1,367,309	903,628	447,176	1,257,345	1,452,619	2,424,176	1,998,051	1,623,938
EBITDA	863,420	597,921	319,505	(130,304)	(2,948,304)	1,648,862	1,533,030	1,088,609
Depn & Amortn	315,096	203,700	95,816	465,936	778,923	806,021	615,874	513,916
Income Before Taxes	507,795	365,157	209,278	(658,264)	(3,782,384)	805,901	893,700	560,550
Income Taxes	188,162	136,923	78,306	(227,215)	(1,373,436)	298,697	329,011	206,727
Net Income	319,633	228,234	130,972	(431,049)	(2,408,948)	507,204	564,689	353,823
Average Shares	93,531	93,435	93,428	93,379	92,992	85,810	85,409	85,034
Balance Sheet								
Current Assets	894,132	927,876	949,227	969,304	1,077,930	931,804	469,139	470,137
Total Assets	4,769,054	4,562,980	4,393,999	4,681,693	5,243,286	8,725,293	7,253,135	6,305,152
Current Liabilities	592,625	526,221	507,322	522,352	410,067	776,327	683,167	645,862
Long-Term Obligations	1,486,509	1,486,097	1,488,500	1,487,939	1,485,620	1,500,000	924,000	750,000
Total Liabilities	2,366,991	2,251,225	2,183,050	2,321,629	2,445,608	4,224,661	3,230,927	2,830,416
Stockholders' Equity	2,402,063	2,311,755	2,210,949	2,360,064	2,797,678	4,500,632	4,022,208	3,474,736
Shares Outstanding	95,260	95,341	95,116	95,123	94,820	87,592	87,152	86,595
Statistical Record								
Return on Assets %	7.69	5.58	N.M.	N.M.	N.M.	6.35	8.33	6.01
Return on Equity %	15.11	10.89	N.M.	N.M.	N.M.	11.90	15.06	10.68
EBITDA Margin %	63.15	66.17	71.45	N.M.	N.M.	68.02	76.73	67.04
Net Margin %	23.38	25.26	29.29	N.M.	N.M.	20.92	28.26	21.79
Asset Turnover	0.38	0.36	0.31	0.25	0.21	0.30	0.29	0.28
Current Ratio	1.51	1.76	1.87	1.86	2.63	1.20	0.69	0.73
Debt to Equity	0.62	0.64	0.67	0.63	0.53	0.33	0.23	0.22
Price Range	143.25-91.33	143.25-91.33	143.25-94.77	143.25-75.60	129.44-85.27	148.77-92.73	110.43-57.73	86.41-46.96
P/E Ratio	37.90-24.16	53.45-34.08	...	...	...	25.74-16.04	17.07-8.92	21.23-11.54
Average Yield %	0.27	0.26	0.26	0.35	0.58	0.51	0.67	0.74

Address: 1700 Lincoln Street, Suite 3700, Denver, CO 80203 Telephone: 303-295-3995	Web Site: www.cimarex.com Officers: Thomas E. Jorden - Chairman, Executive Vice President, President, Chief Executive Officer Krista L. Johnson - Division Officer	Auditors: KPMG LLP Investor Contact: 303-295-3995 Transfer Agents: Continental Stock Transfer & Trust Company, New York, NY

CINEMARK HOLDINGS INC

Exchange	Symbol	Price	52Wk Range	Yield	P/E
NYS	CNK	$34.82 (12/29/2017)	44.58-32.29	3.33	16.50

*7 Year Price Score 97.60   *NYSE Composite Index=100   *12 Month Price Score 85.16

Interim Earnings (Per Share)

Qtr.	Mar	Jun	Sep	Dec
2014	0.31	0.62	0.33	0.41
2015	0.37	0.61	0.40	0.50
2016	0.50	0.46	0.56	0.66
2017	0.68	0.44	0.33	...

Interim Dividends (Per Share)

Amt	Decl	Ex	Rec	Pay
0.29Q	02/23/2017	03/06/2017	03/08/2017	03/20/2017
0.29Q	05/25/2017	06/06/2017	06/08/2017	06/22/2017
0.29Q	08/10/2017	08/29/2017	08/31/2017	09/13/2017
0.29Q	11/17/2017	11/30/2017	12/01/2017	12/15/2017

Indicated Div: $1.16

Valuation Analysis

		Institutional Holding	
Forecast EPS	$1.95	No of Institutions	
	(01/18/2018)	414	
Market Cap	$4.1 Billion	Shares	
Book Value	$1.3 Billion	130,220,800	
Price/Book	3.03	% Held	
Price/Sales	1.38	86.88	

Business Summary: Entertainment (MIC: 2.3.2 SIC: 7832 NAIC: 512131)

Cinemark Holdings is a holding company. Through its subsidiaries, Co. is engaged in the motion picture exhibition industry, with theatres in the U. S., Brazil, Argentina, Chile, Colombia, Peru, Ecuador, Honduras, El Salvador, Nicaragua, Costa Rica, Panama, Guatemala, Bolivia, Curacao and Paraguay. At Dec 31 2016, Co. managed its business under two segments: U.S. markets and international markets. As of the same date, Co. operated 526 theatres and 5,903 screens in the U.S. and Latin America. Co. develops and expands new platforms and markets adaptive concepts for its theatre circuit, such as XD, Luxury Lounger recliner seats, Cinemark Reserve, motion seats, CineArts and other concepts.

Recent Developments: For the quarter ended Sep 30 2017, net income decreased 41.7% to US$38.5 million from US$66.1 million in the year-earlier quarter. Revenues were US$710.7 million, down 7.5% from US$768.6 million the year before. Operating income was US$74.2 million versus US$117.8 million in the prior-year quarter, a decrease of 37.0%. Direct operating expenses declined 8.7% to US$266.4 million from US$291.7 million in the comparable period the year before. Indirect operating expenses increased 3.1% to US$370.2 million from US$359.1 million in the equivalent prior-year period.

Prospects: Our evaluation of Cinemark Holdings Inc. as of Jan. 14, 2018 is the result of our systematic analysis on three basic characteristics: earnings strength, relative valuation, and recent stock price movement. The company has generated a negative trend in earnings per share over the past 5 quarters. However, while recent estimates for the company have been mixed, CNK has posted results that fell short of analysts expectations. Based on operating earnings yield, the company is undervalued when compared to all of the companies in our coverage universe. Share price changes over the past year indicates that CNK will perform in line with the market over the near term.

Financial Data
(US$ in Thousands)

	9 Mos	6 Mos	3 Mos	12/31/2016	12/31/2015	12/31/2014	12/31/2013	12/31/2012
Earnings Per Share	2.11	2.34	2.36	2.19	1.87	1.66	1.28	1.47
Cash Flow Per Share	4.19	4.20	4.62	3.90	3.96	3.97	2.72	3.48
Dividends Per Share	1.140	1.120	1.100	1.080	1.000	1.000	0.920	0.840
Dividend Payout %	54.03	47.86	46.61	49.32	53.48	60.24	71.88	57.14
Income Statement								
Total Revenue	2,241,553	1,530,805	779,610	2,918,765	2,852,609	2,626,990	2,682,894	2,473,531
EBITDA	485,732	352,784	195,126	637,692	610,472	548,557	522,345	544,395
Depn & Amortn	168,667	112,622	55,556	207,091	186,898	173,138	160,071	143,394
Income Before Taxes	242,252	189,984	114,534	328,684	319,541	267,320	241,182	283,709
Income Taxes	98,475	73,845	44,400	103,819	128,939	96,064	113,316	125,398
Net Income	169,106	130,967	79,728	255,091	216,869	192,610	148,470	168,949
Average Shares	116,104	116,072	115,915	115,783	115,399	114,966	114,396	113,824
Balance Sheet								
Current Assets	590,331	618,409	707,868	676,317	715,151	741,010	729,599	845,161
Total Assets	4,371,650	4,354,525	4,383,326	4,306,633	4,126,497	4,151,980	4,144,163	3,863,226
Current Liabilities	392,674	405,886	439,518	443,225	439,793	414,407	395,712	338,204
Long-Term Obligations	2,033,999	2,010,954	2,012,319	2,016,722	1,981,882	2,016,552	2,025,453	1,893,571
Total Liabilities	3,031,822	3,030,989	3,061,606	3,044,815	3,026,789	3,039,180	3,050,741	2,779,161
Stockholders' Equity	1,339,828	1,323,536	1,321,720	1,261,818	1,099,708	1,112,800	1,093,422	1,084,065
Shares Outstanding	116,467	116,468	116,422	116,210	115,924	115,700	115,382	114,949
Statistical Record								
Return on Assets %	5.76	6.39	6.49	6.03	5.24	4.64	3.71	4.56
Return on Equity %	19.22	21.79	22.45	21.54	19.60	17.46	13.64	16.07
EBITDA Margin %	21.67	23.05	25.03	21.85	21.40	20.88	19.47	22.01
Net Margin %	7.54	8.56	10.23	8.74	7.60	7.33	5.53	6.83
Asset Turnover	0.69	0.70	0.70	0.69	0.69	0.63	0.67	0.67
Current Ratio	1.50	1.52	1.61	1.53	1.63	1.79	1.84	2.50
Debt to Equity	1.52	1.52	1.52	1.60	1.80	1.81	1.85	1.75
Price Range	44.58-32.29	44.58-35.11	44.58-33.00	42.23-27.15	45.52-31.56	36.37-27.73	34.17-25.98	27.20-18.04
P/E Ratio	21.13-15.30	19.05-15.00	18.89-13.98	19.28-12.40	24.34-16.88	21.91-16.70	26.70-20.30	18.50-12.27
Average Yield %	2.86	2.78	2.85	2.99	2.62	3.07	3.06	3.66

Address: 3900 Dallas Parkway, Suite 500, Plano, TX 75093
Telephone: 972-665-1000

Web Site: www.cinemark.com
Officers: Lee Roy Mitchell - Chairman   Mark Zoradi - Chief Executive Officer

Auditors: Deloitte & Touche LLP
Investor Contact: 972-665-1500
Transfer Agents: Wells Fargo Shareholder Services

CITIGROUP INC

Exchange	Symbol	Price	52Wk Range	Yield	P/E
NYS	C	$74.41 (12/29/2017)	77.10-55.68	N/A	14.34

*7 Year Price Score 107.88 ***NYSE Composite Index=100** ***12 Month Price Score 106.98**

Interim Earnings (Per Share)

Qtr.	Mar	Jun	Sep	Dec
2014	1.23	0.03	0.88	0.06
2015	1.51	1.51	1.35	1.02
2016	1.10	1.24	1.24	1.14
2017	1.35	1.28	1.42	...

Interim Dividends (Per Share)

Amt	Decl	Ex	Rec	Pay
0.16Q	04/03/2017	04/27/2017	05/01/2017	05/26/2017
0.32Q	07/19/2017	08/03/2017	08/07/2017	08/25/2017
0.32Q	10/18/2017	11/03/2017	11/06/2017	11/22/2017
0.32Q	01/08/2018	02/02/2018	02/05/2018	02/23/2018

Indicated Div: $1.20

Valuation Analysis **Institutional Holding**

Forecast EPS	$6.40	No of Institutions	
(01/26/2018)		2163	
Market Cap	$196.7 Billion	Shares	2,790,900,736
Book Value	$227.6 Billion	% Held	
Price/Book	0.86		
Price/Sales	N/A	N/A	

Business Summary: Banking (MIC: 5.1.1 SIC: 6021 NAIC: 522110)

Citigroup is a financial services holding company, providing consumers, corporations, governments and institutions with a range of financial products and services. Co.'s activities are conducted through the: Global Consumer Banking, which provides traditional banking services to retail customers through retail banking, including commercial banking, and Citi-branded cards and Citi retail services; and Institutional Clients Group, which provides a range of wholesale banking products and services, including, among others, fixed income and equity sales and trading, and foreign exchange. As of Dec 31 2016, Co. had total assets of $1.82 trillion and total deposits of $950.00 billion.

Recent Developments: For the quarter ended Sep 30 2017, income from continuing operations increased 6.4% to US$4.14 billion from US$3.89 billion in the year-earlier quarter. Net income increased 7.1% to US$4.13 billion from US$3.86 billion in the year-earlier quarter. Net interest income decreased 0.3% to US$11.44 billion from US$11.48 billion in the year-earlier quarter. Provision for loan losses was US$1.97 billion versus US$1.70 billion in the prior-year quarter, an increase of 15.9%. Non-interest income rose 7.2% to US$6.73 billion from US$6.28 billion, while non-interest expense declined 2.3% to US$10.20 billion.

Prospects: Our evaluation of Citigroup Inc. as of Jan. 21, 2018 is the result of our systematic analysis on three basic characteristics: earnings strength, relative valuation, and recent stock price movement. The company has enjoyed a very positive trend in earnings per share over the past 5 quarters and while recent estimates for the company have been raised by analysts, C has posted better than expected results. Based on operating earnings yield, the company is undervalued when compared to all of the companies in our coverage universe. Share price changes over the past year indicates that C will perform well over the near term.

Financial Data

(US$ in Thousands)	9 Mos	6 Mos	3 Mos	12/31/2016	12/31/2015	12/31/2014	12/31/2013	12/31/2012
Earnings Per Share	5.19	5.01	4.97	4.72	5.40	2.20	4.35	2.44
Cash Flow Per Share	...	4.15	18.36	18.62	13.23	14.99	18.91	4.86
Tang Book Value Per Share	68.36	67.16	58.41	64.03	60.03	56.24	54.41	50.57
Dividends Per Share	0.800	0.640	0.530	0.420	0.160	0.040	0.040	0.040
Dividend Payout %	15.41	12.77	10.66	8.90	2.96	1.82	0.92	1.64
Income Statement								
Interest Income	45,445,000	29,624,000	14,423,000	57,615,000	58,551,000	61,683,000	62,970,000	68,138,000
Interest Expense	11,981,000	7,602,000	3,566,000	12,511,000	11,921,000	13,690,000	16,177,000	20,535,000
Net Interest Income	33,464,000	22,022,000	10,857,000	45,104,000	46,630,000	47,993,000	46,793,000	47,603,000
Provision for Losses	5,297,000	3,326,000	1,632,000	6,749,000	7,108,000	6,828,000	7,604,000	10,848,000
Non-Interest Income	20,730,000	13,999,000	7,263,000	24,771,000	29,724,000	28,889,000	29,573,000	22,570,000
Non-Interest Expense	31,235,000	21,036,000	10,507,000	41,649,000	44,420,000	55,690,000	49,265,000	51,389,000
Income Before Taxes	17,662,000	11,659,000	5,981,000	21,477,000	24,826,000	14,364,000	19,497,000	7,936,000
Income Taxes	5,524,000	3,658,000	1,863,000	6,444,000	7,440,000	6,864,000	5,867,000	27,000
Net Income	12,095,000	7,962,000	4,090,000	14,912,000	17,242,000	7,313,000	13,673,000	7,541,000
Average Shares	2,683,700	2,739,200	2,765,300	2,888,300	3,007,700	3,037,000	3,041,600	3,015,500
Balance Sheet								
Net Loans & Leases	640,817,000	632,670,000	616,565,000	612,309,000	604,991,000	628,641,000	645,824,000	630,009,000
Total Assets	1,889,133,000	1,864,063,000	1,821,635,000	1,792,077,000	1,731,210,000	1,842,530,000	1,880,382,000	1,864,660,000
Total Deposits	964,038,000	958,743,000	949,990,000	929,406,000	907,887,000	899,332,000	968,273,000	930,560,000
Total Liabilities	1,661,499,000	1,634,044,000	1,593,503,000	1,566,957,000	1,509,353,000	1,631,996,000	1,676,043,000	1,675,611,000
Stockholders' Equity	227,634,000	230,019,000	228,132,000	225,120,000	221,857,000	210,534,000	204,339,000	189,049,000
Shares Outstanding	2,644,002	2,724,556	3,099,523	2,772,392	2,953,279	3,023,918	3,029,243	3,028,884
Statistical Record								
Return on Assets %	...	0.83	0.86	0.84	0.96	0.39	0.73	0.40
Return on Equity %	...	6.66	6.80	6.65	7.98	3.53	6.95	4.10
Net Interest Margin %	72.32	73.45	75.28	78.29	79.64	77.81	74.31	69.86
Efficiency Ratio %	45.22	48.00	48.45	50.55	50.32	61.49	53.23	56.65
Loans to Deposits	0.66	0.66	0.65	0.66	0.67	0.70	0.67	0.68
Price Range	72.74-47.03	66.98-40.78	61.55-38.48	61.09-34.98	60.34-46.95	56.37-45.68	53.29-39.56	40.17-24.82
P/E Ratio	14.02-9.06	13.37-8.14	12.38-7.74	12.94-7.41	11.17-8.69	25.62-20.76	12.25-9.09	16.46-10.17
Average Yield %	1.32	1.17	1.05	0.91	0.30	0.08	0.08	0.12

Address: 388 Greenwich Street, New York, NY 10013 **Telephone:** 212-559-1000	**Web Site:** www.citigroup.com **Officers:** Michael E. O'Neill - Chairman Michael S. Helfer - Vice-Chairman, General Counsel, Corporate Secretary	**Auditors:** KPMG LLP **Investor Contact:** 212-559-2718 **Transfer Agents:** Computershare Trust Company, N.A., Providence, RI

169

CLEAN HARBORS INC

Exchange	Symbol	Price	52Wk Range	Yield	P/E
NYS	CLH	$54.20 (12/29/2017)	61.33-49.98	N/A	774.29

*7 Year Price Score 80.64 *NYSE Composite Index=100 *12 Month Price Score 89.92

Interim Earnings (Per Share)

Qtr.	Mar	Jun	Sep	Dec
2014	0.15	0.47	(1.55)	0.45
2015	(0.12)	0.18	0.69	0.02
2016	(0.36)	0.07	(0.18)	(0.22)
2017	(0.37)	0.45	0.21	...

Interim Dividends (Per Share)

No Dividends Paid

Valuation Analysis		Institutional Holding	
Forecast EPS	$0.32	No of Institutions	
	(01/18/2018)	354	
Market Cap	$3.1 Billion	Shares	
Book Value	$1.1 Billion	66,179,224	
Price/Book	2.73	% Held	
Price/Sales	1.07	95.00	

Business Summary: Sanitation Services (MIC: 7.5.3 SIC: 4953 NAIC: 562112)

Clean Harbors is a provider of environmental, energy and industrial services throughout North America. Co. has six operating segments: Technical Services, which provides a range of hazardous material management services; Industrial and Field Services, which provides industrial and specialty services; Safety-Kleen, which provides a range of environmental services such as parts cleaning, containerized waste services, used oil collection, and other complementary products and services; Oil, Gas and Lodging Services, which provides fluid handling, surface rentals, seismic support services, directional boring services, as well as lodges and remote workforce accommodation facilities.

Recent Developments: For the quarter ended Sep 30 2017, net income amounted to US$12.1 million versus a net loss of US$10.3 million in the year-earlier quarter. Revenues were US$755.8 million, up 3.6% from US$729.5 million the year before. Operating income was US$47.7 million versus US$16.8 million in the prior-year quarter, an increase of 183.7%. Direct operating expenses rose 5.6% to US$519.6 million from US$491.9 million in the comparable period the year before. Indirect operating expenses decreased 14.6% to US$188.6 million from US$220.8 million in the equivalent prior-year period.

Prospects: Our evaluation of Clean Harbors Inc. as of Jan. 14, 2018 is the result of our systematic analysis on three basic characteristics: earnings strength, relative valuation, and recent stock price movement. The company has enjoyed a very positive trend in earnings per share over the past 5 quarters and while recent estimates for the company have been mixed, CLH has posted results that fell short of analysts expectations. Based on operating earnings yield, the company is overvalued when compared to all of the companies in our coverage universe. Share price changes over the past year indicates that CLH will perform in line with the market over the near term.

Financial Data
(US$ in Thousands)

	9 Mos	6 Mos	3 Mos	12/31/2016	12/31/2015	12/31/2014	12/31/2013	12/31/2012
Earnings Per Share	0.07	(0.32)	(0.70)	(0.69)	0.76	(0.47)	1.57	2.40
Cash Flow Per Share	5.30	4.49	4.85	4.50	6.80	4.93	6.86	6.00
Tang Book Value Per Share	3.02	2.54	1.80	2.10	2.37	4.76	5.52	4.40
Income Statement								
Total Revenue	2,197,575	1,441,729	688,941	2,755,226	3,275,137	3,401,636	3,509,656	2,187,908
EBITDA	312,542	202,332	68,013	339,241	420,199	355,590	434,761	338,456
Depn & Amortn	191,762	126,860	64,129	247,000	234,000	239,400	212,500	163,439
Income Before Taxes	55,037	30,404	(18,692)	8,716	109,646	38,522	143,885	127,730
Income Taxes	38,492	25,917	2,701	48,589	65,544	66,850	48,319	(1,944)
Net Income	16,545	4,487	(21,393)	(39,873)	44,102	(28,328)	95,566	129,674
Average Shares	57,195	57,336	57,262	57,532	58,434	60,311	60,728	54,079
Balance Sheet								
Current Assets	1,160,258	1,234,734	1,061,771	1,092,871	921,196	1,126,433	1,171,179	1,086,793
Total Assets	3,748,353	3,806,282	3,645,653	3,681,920	3,431,428	3,704,278	3,953,678	3,825,806
Current Liabilities	529,540	619,300	488,581	504,668	517,120	572,471	639,545	569,052
Long-Term Obligations	1,625,971	1,626,505	1,633,968	1,633,272	1,382,543	1,395,000	1,401,435	1,402,879
Total Liabilities	2,620,006	2,705,345	2,582,023	2,597,679	2,335,146	2,441,407	2,478,039	2,393,734
Stockholders' Equity	1,128,347	1,100,937	1,063,630	1,084,241	1,096,282	1,262,871	1,475,639	1,432,072
Shares Outstanding	56,926	57,153	57,188	57,297	57,593	58,903	60,672	60,385
Statistical Record								
Return on Assets %	0.10	N.M.	N.M.	N.M.	1.24	N.M.	2.46	4.38
Return on Equity %	0.34	N.M.	N.M.	N.M.	3.74	N.M.	6.57	11.09
EBITDA Margin %	14.22	14.03	9.87	12.31	12.83	10.45	12.39	15.47
Net Margin %	0.75	0.31	N.M.	N.M.	1.35	N.M.	2.72	5.93
Asset Turnover	0.77	0.76	0.77	0.77	0.92	0.89	0.90	0.74
Current Ratio	2.19	1.99	2.17	2.17	1.78	1.97	1.83	1.91
Debt to Equity	1.44	1.48	1.54	1.51	1.26	1.10	0.95	0.98
Price Range	61.33-43.75	61.33-43.75	58.33-43.75	57.78-39.35	58.87-40.22	64.51-44.98	62.53-50.30	70.30-47.16
P/E Ratio	876.14-625.00	...	...	...	77.46-52.92	...	39.83-32.04	29.29-19.65

Address: 42 Longwater Drive, Norwell, MA 02061-9149 Telephone: 781-792-5000	Web Site: www.cleanharbors.com Officers: Alan S. McKim Chairman, President, Chief Executive Officer Eric W. Gerstenberg - Chief Operating Officer, Division Officer	Auditors: Deloitte & Touche LLP Investor Contact: 617-542-5300 Transfer Agents: American Stock Transfer & Trust Company, New York, NY

CLOROX CO (THE)

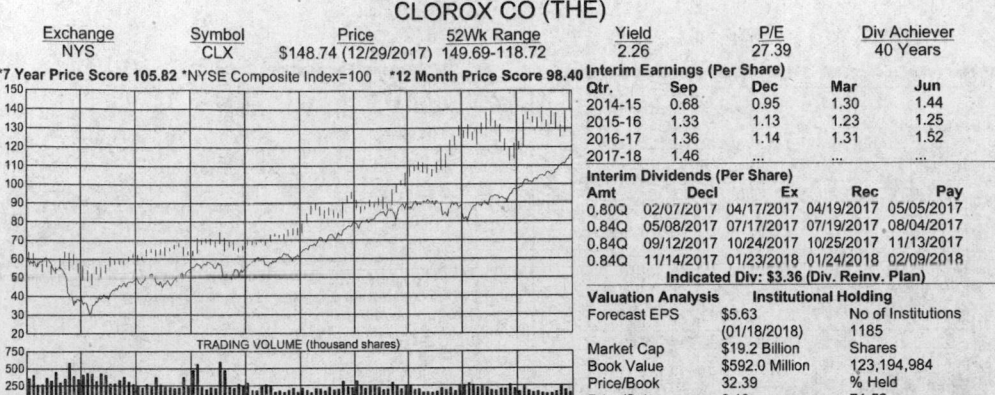

Exchange	Symbol	Price	52Wk Range	Yield	P/E	Div Achiever
NYS	CLX	$148.74 (12/29/2017)	149.69-118.72	2.26	27.39	40 Years

*7 Year Price Score 105.82 *NYSE Composite Index=100 *12 Month Price Score 98.40

Interim Earnings (Per Share)

Qtr.	Sep	Dec	Mar	Jun
2014-15	0.68	0.95	1.30	1.44
2015-16	1.33	1.13	1.23	1.25
2016-17	1.36	1.14	1.31	1.52
2017-18	1.46	...	...	...

Interim Dividends (Per Share)

Amt	Decl	Ex	Rec	Pay
0.80Q	02/07/2017	04/17/2017	04/19/2017	05/05/2017
0.84Q	05/08/2017	07/17/2017	07/19/2017	08/04/2017
0.84Q	09/12/2017	10/24/2017	10/25/2017	11/13/2017
0.84Q	11/14/2017	01/23/2018	01/24/2018	02/09/2018

Indicated Div: $3.36 (Div. Reinv. Plan)

Valuation Analysis — **Institutional Holding**

Forecast EPS	$5.63	No of Institutions
	(01/18/2018)	1185
Market Cap	$19.2 Billion	Shares
Book Value	$592.0 Million	123,194,984
Price/Book	32.39	% Held
Price/Sales	3.18	71.52

Business Summary: Household & Personal Products (MIC: 1.7.1 SIC: 2842 NAIC: 325612)

Clorox is a manufacturer and marketer of consumer products. Co. sells its products via mass retail and grocery outlets, warehouse, clubs, and e-commerce channels, among others. Co. markets consumer brand names, including its namesake bleach and cleaning products, Pine-Sol® cleaners, Liquid-Plumr® clog removers, Poett® home care products, Fresh Step® cat litter, Glad® bags, wraps and container products, Kingsford® and Match Light® charcoal, RenewLife® digestive health products, Hidden Valley® dressings and sauces, Brita® water-filtration products, and Burt's Bees® personal care products. Co. also markets to services channels, including infection control products for the healthcare industry.

Recent Developments: For the quarter ended Sep 30 2017, income from continuing operations increased 7.3% to US$192.0 million from US$179.0 million in the year-earlier quarter. Net income increased 7.3% to US$192.0 million from US$179.0 million in the year-earlier quarter. Revenues were US$1.50 billion, up 4.0% from US$1.44 billion the year before. Direct operating expenses rose 3.0% to US$827.0 million from US$803.0 million in the comparable period the year before. Indirect operating expenses increased 4.8% to US$394.0 million from US$376.0 million in the equivalent prior-year period.

Prospects: Our evaluation of Clorox Co. as of Jan. 14, 2018 is the result of our systematic analysis on three basic characteristics: earnings strength, relative valuation, and recent stock price movement. The company has generated a negative trend in earnings per share over the past 5 quarters and while recent estimates for the company have been raised by analysts, CLX has posted better than expected results. Based on operating earnings yield, the company is about fairly valued when compared to all of the companies in our coverage universe. Share price changes over the past year indicates that CLX will perform well over the near term.

Financial Data
(US$ in Thousands)

	3 Mos	06/30/2017	06/30/2016	06/30/2015	06/30/2014	06/30/2013	06/30/2012	06/30/2011
Earnings Per Share	5.43	5.33	4.92	4.37	4.23	4.30	4.09	4.02
Cash Flow Per Share	7.41	6.73	5.99	6.71	5.92	5.91	4.66	5.11
Dividends Per Share	3.240	3.200	3.080	2.960	2.840	2.560	2.400	2.200
Dividend Payout %	59.67	60.04	62.60	67.73	67.14	59.53	58.68	54.73
Income Statement								
Total Revenue	1,500,000	5,973,000	5,761,000	5,655,000	5,591,000	5,623,000	5,468,000	5,231,000
EBITDA	340,000	1,261,000	1,216,000	1,154,000	1,116,000	1,124,000	1,064,000	815,000
Depn & Amortn	40,000	163,000	165,000	165,000	169,000	171,000	167,000	162,000
Income Before Taxes	279,000	1,014,000	968,000	893,000	847,000	834,000	772,000	533,000
Income Taxes	87,000	330,000	335,000	315,000	299,000	279,000	248,000	276,000
Net Income	192,000	701,000	648,000	580,000	558,000	572,000	541,000	557,000
Average Shares	131,509	131,566	131,717	132,776	131,742	132,969	132,310	138,101
Balance Sheet								
Current Assets	1,520,000	1,514,000	1,485,000	1,429,000	1,395,000	1,420,000	1,376,000	1,279,000
Total Assets	4,600,000	4,573,000	4,518,000	4,164,000	4,258,000	4,311,000	4,355,000	4,163,000
Current Liabilities	1,376,000	1,809,000	1,558,000	1,405,000	1,638,000	1,134,000	2,061,000	1,365,000
Long-Term Obligations	1,787,000	1,391,000	1,797,000	1,796,000	1,595,000	2,170,000	1,571,000	2,125,000
Total Liabilities	4,008,000	4,031,000	4,221,000	4,046,000	4,104,000	4,165,000	4,490,000	4,249,000
Stockholders' Equity	592,000	542,000	297,000	118,000	154,000	146,000	(135,000)	(86,000)
Shares Outstanding	128,923	129,014	129,355	128,614	128,796	130,366	129,562	131,066
Statistical Record								
Return on Assets %	15.75	15.42	14.89	13.77	13.02	13.20	12.67	12.78
Return on Equity %	162.09	167.10	311.44	426.47	372.00	10,400.00	...	...
EBITDA Margin %	22.67	21.11	21.11	20.41	19.96	19.99	19.46	15.58
Net Margin %	12.80	11.74	11.25	10.26	9.98	10.17	9.89	10.65
Asset Turnover	1.33	1.31	1.32	1.34	1.30	1.30	1.28	1.20
Current Ratio	1.10	0.84	0.95	1.02	0.85	1.25	0.67	0.94
Debt to Equity	3.02	2.57	6.05	15.22	10.36	14.86	...	...
Price Range	141.15-112.25	141.15-112.25	138.39-100.63	111.93-86.39	95.83-81.49	89.53-70.10	74.55-63.71	71.26-61.57
P/E Ratio	25.99-20.67	26.48-21.06	28.13-21.14	25.61-19.77	22.65-19.26	20.82-16.30	18.23-15.58	17.73-15.32
Average Yield %	2.51	2.49	2.50	2.91	3.23	3.27	3.52	3.33

Address: 1221 Broadway, Oakland, CA 94612-1888
Telephone: 510-271-7000

Web Site: www.thecloroxcompany.com
Officers: Benno O. Dorer - Chairman, Chief Executive Officer, Executive Vice President, Senior Vice President, Division Officer Dawn C. Willoughby - Chief Operating Officer, Executive Vice President, Senior Vice President, Division Officer

Auditors: Ernst & Young LLP
Transfer Agents: Computershare, Providence, RI

CMS ENERGY CORP

Exchange	Symbol	Price	52Wk Range	Yield	P/E
NYS	CMS	$47.30 (12/29/2017)	50.55-41.51	2.81	24.51

*7 Year Price Score 113.80 *NYSE Composite Index=100 *12 Month Price Score 99.61

Interim Earnings (Per Share)

Qtr.	Mar	Jun	Sep	Dec
2014	0.75	0.30	0.34	0.35
2015	0.73	0.25	0.53	0.38
2016	0.59	0.45	0.67	0.28
2017	0.71	0.33	0.61	...

Interim Dividends (Per Share)

Amt	Decl	Ex	Rec	Pay
0.333Q	01/19/2017	02/01/2017	02/03/2017	02/28/2017
0.333Q	04/20/2017	05/03/2017	05/05/2017	05/31/2017
0.333Q	07/20/2017	08/02/2017	08/04/2017	08/31/2017
0.333Q	10/19/2017	11/02/2017	11/03/2017	11/30/2017

Indicated Div: $1.33

Valuation Analysis   **Institutional Holding**

Forecast EPS	$2.17	No of Institutions
	(01/18/2018)	685
Market Cap	$13.3 Billion	Shares
Book Value	$4.5 Billion	314,959,904
Price/Book	2.94	% Held
Price/Sales	2.07	91.20

Business Summary: Electric Utilities (MIC: 3.1.1 SIC: 4931 NAIC: 221119)

CMS Energy is a holding company. Co. has several subsidiaries, including Consumers Energy Company (Consumers), an electric and gas utility, and CMS Enterprises Company (CMS Enterprises), primarily a domestic independent power producer. Consumers serves individuals and businesses operating in the alternative energy, automotive, chemical, metal, and food products industries, as well as a group of other industries. CMS Enterprises, through its subsidiaries and equity investments, is engaged primarily in independent power production and owns power generation facilities fueled mostly by natural gas and renewable sources. Co. has three segments: electric utility, gas utility, and enterprises.

Recent Developments: For the quarter ended Sep 30 2017, net income decreased 7.5% to US$172.0 million from US$186.0 million in the year-earlier quarter. Revenues were US$1.53 billion, down 3.8% from US$1.59 billion the year before. Operating income was US$330.0 million versus US$375.0 million in the prior-year quarter, a decrease of 12.0%. Direct operating expenses declined 2.6% to US$942.0 million from US$967.0 million in the comparable period the year before. Indirect operating expenses increased 4.1% to US$255.0 million from US$245.0 million in the equivalent prior-year period.

Prospects: Our evaluation of CMS Energy Corp. as of Jan. 14, 2018 is the result of our systematic analysis on three basic characteristics: earnings strength, relative valuation, and recent stock price movement. The company has managed to produce a neutral trend in earnings per share over the past 5 quarters and while recent estimates for the company have remained steady, CMS has posted better than expected results. Based on operating earnings yield, the company is undervalued when compared to all of the companies in our coverage universe. Share price changes over the past year indicates that CMS will perform very well over the near term.

Financial Data

(US$ in Millions)	9 Mos	6 Mos	3 Mos	12/31/2016	12/31/2015	12/31/2014	12/31/2013	12/31/2012
Earnings Per Share	1.93	1.99	2.11	1.98	1.89	1.74	1.66	1.42
Cash Flow Per Share	5.65	5.89	5.89	5.85	5.95	5.35	5.37	4.75
Tang Book Value Per Share	16.10	15.80	15.61	15.23	14.21	13.34	12.98	12.09
Dividends Per Share	1.308	1.285	1.263	1.240	1.160	1.080	1.020	0.960
Dividend Payout %	67.75	64.57	59.83	62.63	61.38	62.07	61.45	67.61
Income Statement								
Total Revenue	4,805	3,278	1,829	6,399	6,456	7,179	6,566	6,253
EBITDA	1,626	1,099	656	2,053	1,916	1,801	1,766	1,587
Depn & Amortn	652	459	262	811	750	685	628	598
Income Before Taxes	654	428	291	813	782	714	743	605
Income Taxes	200	143	96	273	271	250	302	245
Net Income	463	291	199	551	523	477	452	382
Average Shares	281	280	279	278	276	274	271	268
Balance Sheet								
Current Assets	2,121	2,211	2,215	2,280	2,320	2,597	2,526	2,422
Total Assets	22,120	21,867	21,623	21,622	20,340	19,185	17,416	17,131
Current Liabilities	2,261	2,115	1,926	2,655	2,302	2,014	1,945	1,797
Long-Term Obligations	9,121	9,190	9,233	8,750	8,559	8,139	7,239	6,863
Total Liabilities	17,585	17,418	17,253	17,369	16,402	15,515	13,962	13,937
Stockholders' Equity	4,535	4,449	4,370	4,253	3,938	3,670	3,454	3,194
Shares Outstanding	281	281	280	279	277	275	266	264
Statistical Record								
Return on Assets %	2.51	2.62	2.81	2.62	2.65	2.61	2.62	2.27
Return on Equity %	12.28	12.88	13.82	13.42	13.75	13.39	13.60	12.25
EBITDA Margin %	33.84	33.53	35.87	32.08	29.68	25.09	26.90	25.38
Net Margin %	9.64	8.88	10.88	8.61	8.10	6.64	6.88	6.11
Asset Turnover	0.30	0.31	0.31	0.30	0.33	0.39	0.38	0.37
Current Ratio	0.94	1.05	1.15	0.86	1.01	1.29	1.30	1.35
Debt to Equity	2.01	2.07	2.11	2.06	2.17	2.22	2.10	2.15
Price Range	49.10-39.49	48.25-39.49	46.17-39.38	46.17-35.61	38.20-31.39	36.42-26.12	29.94-24.38	24.81-21.33
P/E Ratio	25.44-20.46	24.25-19.84	21.88-18.66	23.32-17.98	20.21-16.61	20.93-15.01	18.04-14.69	17.47-15.02
Average Yield %	2.94	2.95	2.97	2.99	3.35	3.60	3.77	4.16

Address: One Energy Plaza, Jackson, MI 49201	Web Site: www.cmsenergy.com	Auditors: PricewaterhouseCoopers LLP
Telephone: 517-788-0550	Officers: David W. Joos - Chairman Patricia K. Poppe - President, Chief Executive Officer, Division Officer	Investor Contact: 517-788-1868
		Transfer Agents: Investor Services Department, Jackson, MI

CNA FINANCIAL CORP

Exchange	Symbol	Price	52Wk Range	Yield	P/E
NYS	CNA	$53.05 (12/29/2017)	54.98-40.21	2.26	15.70

*7 Year Price Score 104.92 *NYSE Composite Index=100 *12 Month Price Score 105.78

TRADING VOLUME (thousand shares)

Interim Earnings (Per Share)

Qtr.	Mar	Jun	Sep	Dec
2014	0.05	0.98	0.79	0.73
2015	0.86	0.51	0.66	(0.26)
2016	0.25	0.77	1.26	0.89
2017	0.96	1.00	0.53	...

Interim Dividends (Per Share)

Amt	Decl	Ex	Rec	Pay
2.00Q	02/06/2017	02/15/2017	02/20/2017	03/08/2017
0.25Q	05/01/2017	05/11/2017	05/15/2017	05/31/2017
0.30Q	07/31/2017	08/10/2017	08/14/2017	08/30/2017
0.30Q	10/30/2017	11/10/2017	11/13/2017	11/29/2017

Indicated Div: $1.20

Valuation Analysis — **Institutional Holding**

Forecast EPS	$3.15 (01/18/2018)	No of Institutions 270
Market Cap	$14.4 Billion	Shares
Book Value	$12.2 Billion	275,799,616
Price/Book	1.18	% Held
Price/Sales	1.52	99.33

Business Summary: General Insurance (MIC: 5.2.1 SIC: 6331 NAIC: 524126)

CNA Financial is an insurance holding company. Co.'s insurance products include commercial property and casualty coverages, including surety. Co.'s services include risk management, information services, warranty and claims administration. Co.'s products and services are marketed through independent agents, brokers and managing general underwriters to a range of customers, including businesses, insurance companies, and other groups. Co.'s core business, commercial property and casualty insurance operations are reported in three segments: Specialty, Commercial and International. Co.'s non-core businesses are managed in two segments: Life & Group Non-Core and Corporate & Other Non-Core.

Recent Developments: For the quarter ended Sep 30 2017, net income decreased 58.0% to US$144.0 million from US$343.0 million in the year-earlier quarter. Revenues were US$2.40 billion, down 1.4% from US$2.43 billion the year before. Net premiums earned were US$1.81 billion versus US$1.77 billion in the prior-year quarter, an increase of 2.2%. Net investment income fell 2.9% to US$509.0 million from US$524.0 million a year ago.

Prospects: Our evaluation of CNA Financial Corp. as of Jan. 14, 2018 is the result of our systematic analysis on three basic characteristics: earnings strength, relative valuation, and recent stock price movement. The company has suffered a very negative trend in earnings per share over the past 5 quarters. However, while recent estimates for the company have been mixed, CNA has posted better than expected results. Based on operating earnings yield, the company is undervalued when compared to all of the companies in our coverage universe. Share price changes over the past year indicates that CNA will perform very well over the near term.

Financial Data

(US$ in Thousands)	9 Mos	6 Mos	3 Mos	12/31/2016	12/31/2015	12/31/2014	12/31/2013	12/31/2012
Earnings Per Share	3.38	4.11	3.88	3.17	1.77	2.55	3.47	2.33
Cash Flow Per Share	4.39	4.86	5.04	5.22	5.13	5.34	4.46	4.63
Tang Book Value Per Share	44.33	43.84	42.61	43.71	42.94	46.83	46.33	45.14
Dividends Per Share	3.050	3.000	3.000	3.000	3.000	2.000	0.800	0.600
Dividend Payout %	90.24	72.99	77.32	94.64	169.49	78.43	23.05	25.75
Income Statement								
Premium Income	5,185,000	3,379,000	1,645,000	6,924,000	6,921,000	7,212,000	7,271,000	6,882,000
Total Revenue	7,094,000	4,696,000	2,330,000	9,366,000	9,101,000	9,692,000	10,113,000	9,547,000
Benefits & Claims	...	...	...	5,283,000	5,384,000	5,591,000	5,947,000	5,896,000
Income Before Taxes	900,000	713,000	343,000	1,137,000	549,000	1,207,000	1,313,000	872,000
Income Taxes	224,000	181,000	83,000	278,000	70,000	319,000	376,000	244,000
Net Income	676,000	532,000	260,000	859,000	479,000	691,000	937,000	628,000
Average Shares	272,100	271,900	271,700	271,100	270,700	270,600	270,200	269,800
Balance Sheet								
Total Assets	56,582,000	56,205,000	55,201,000	55,233,000	55,047,000	55,566,000	57,194,000	58,522,000
Total Liabilities	44,413,000	44,177,000	43,508,000	43,264,000	43,291,000	42,772,000	44,543,000	46,208,000
Stockholders' Equity	12,169,000	12,028,000	11,693,000	11,969,000	11,756,000	12,794,000	12,651,000	12,314,000
Shares Outstanding	271,176	270,987	270,978	270,495	270,274	269,980	269,717	269,399
Statistical Record								
Return on Assets %	1.62	1.97	1.90	1.55	0.87	1.23	1.62	1.10
Return on Equity %	7.53	9.33	9.09	7.22	3.90	5.43	7.51	5.25
Loss Ratio %	...	...	...	76.30	77.79	77.52	81.79	85.67
Net Margin %	9.53	11.33	11.16	9.17	5.26	7.13	9.27	6.58
Price Range	53.28-34.04	48.75-30.37	44.57-29.42	42.07-28.21	43.40-34.24	43.08-36.29	42.89-28.01	30.67-25.91
P/E Ratio	15.76-10.07	11.86-7.39	11.49-7.58	13.27-8.90	24.52-19.34	16.89-14.23	12.36-8.07	13.16-11.12
Average Yield %	6.92	7.57	8.29	8.96	7.82	5.01	2.27	2.14

Address: 333 S. Wabash, Chicago, IL 60604
Telephone: 312-822-5000
Fax: 312-822-6419

Web Site: www.cna.com
Officers: Dino E. Robusto - Chairman, Chief Executive Officer D. Craig Mense - Executive Vice President, Chief Financial Officer

Auditors: Deloitte & Touche LLP
Investor Contact: 312-822-4278
Transfer Agents: Wells Fargo Bank, N.A., St. Paul, MN

CNX RESOURCES CORP

Exchange	Symbol	Price	52Wk Range	Yield	P/E
NYS	CNX	$14.63 (12/29/2017)	16.30-11.35	N/A	N/A

*7 Year Price Score 43.19   *NYSE Composite Index=100   *12 Month Price Score 98.16

Interim Earnings (Per Share)

Qtr.	Mar	Jun	Sep	Dec
2014	0.50	(0.11)	(0.01)	0.31
2015	0.34	(2.64)	0.52	0.13
2016	(0.43)	(2.05)	0.11	(1.34)
2017	(0.17)	0.73	(0.11)	...

Interim Dividends (Per Share)

Dividend Payment Suspended

Valuation Analysis	Institutional Holding	
Forecast EPS	$0.05	No of Institutions
	(01/25/2018)	462
Market Cap	$3.4 Billion	Shares
Book Value	$3.9 Billion	253,328,960
Price/Book	0.86	% Held
Price/Sales	1.25	98.17

Business Summary: Mining (MIC: 8.2.4 SIC: 1311 NAIC: 211111)

CNX Resources is an energy company operated through two primary divisions, Exploration and Production (E&P) and Pennsylvania (PA) Mining Operations. The E&P division is focused on Appalachian area natural gas and liquids activities, including production, gathering, processing and acquisition of natural gas properties in the Appalachian Basin. The PA Mining Operations division is focused on the extraction and preparation of coal, also in the Appalachian Basin. As of Dec 31 2016, Co. had total proved developed and undeveloped reserves of 6.25 trillion cubic feet equivalent.

Recent Developments: For the quarter ended Sep 30 2017, loss from continuing operations was US$25.7 million compared with income of US$62.6 million in the year-earlier quarter. Net loss amounted to US$25.7 million versus net income of US$27.6 million in the year-earlier quarter. Revenues were US$671.3 million, down 10.0% from US$745.6 million the year before. Direct operating expenses rose 9.2% to US$161.4 million from US$147.8 million in the comparable period the year before. Indirect operating expenses increased 5.5% to US$508.8 million from US$482.4 million in the equivalent prior-year period.

Prospects: Our evaluation of CNX Resources Corp. as of Jan. 21, 2018 is the result of our systematic analysis on three basic characteristics: earnings strength, relative valuation, and recent stock price movement. The company has generated a negative trend in earnings per share over the past 5 quarters. However, while recent estimates for the company have been mixed, CNX has posted results that fell short of analysts expectations. Based on operating earnings yield, the company is overvalued when compared to all of the companies in our coverage universe. Share price changes over the past year indicates that CNX will perform poorly over the near term.

Financial Data

(US$ in Thousands)	9 Mos	6 Mos	3 Mos	12/31/2016	12/31/2015	12/31/2014	12/31/2013	12/31/2012
Earnings Per Share	(0.89)	(0.67)	(3.45)	(3.70)	(1.64)	0.70	2.87	1.70
Cash Flow Per Share	2.41	2.34	2.38	2.04	2.21	4.07	2.88	3.19
Tang Book Value Per Share	17.09	17.15	16.36	16.55	20.53	23.14	21.85	17.33
Dividends Per Share	...	...	...	0.010	0.145	0.250	0.375	0.625
Dividend Payout %	...	...	...	...	...	35.71	13.07	36.76
Income Statement								
Total Revenue	2,235,942	1,564,660	698,709	2,026,375	3,114,401	3,726,804	3,299,685	5,430,307
EBITDA	698,608	507,229	105,895	264,024	349,970	977,879	726,395	1,344,772
Depn & Amortn	414,608	265,839	148,753	598,503	649,601	571,191	461,122	627,438
Income Before Taxes	154,633	153,525	(87,291)	(525,955)	(498,900)	183,124	46,075	497,274
Income Taxes	39,962	13,204	(53,789)	10,010	(134,425)	14,347	(33,189)	109,201
Net Income	104,104	130,544	(38,966)	(848,102)	(374,885)	163,090	660,442	388,470
Average Shares	230,080	232,198	229,817	229,387	229,186	231,580	230,077	229,141
Balance Sheet								
Current Assets	805,283	847,094	616,215	626,139	804,763	1,166,350	1,445,592	1,539,094
Total Assets	8,979,568	9,025,192	9,063,769	9,183,981	10,929,902	11,759,530	11,393,667	12,670,909
Current Liabilities	860,192	825,713	992,849	940,014	1,680,937	1,147,961	1,119,971	1,387,099
Long-Term Obligations	2,532,312	2,630,108	2,657,294	2,762,069	2,748,205	3,275,878	3,163,559	3,174,586
Total Liabilities	5,047,737	5,079,855	5,299,966	5,385,586	6,227,875	6,430,072	6,387,378	8,717,117
Stockholders' Equity	3,931,831	3,945,337	3,763,803	3,798,395	4,702,027	5,329,458	5,006,289	3,953,792
Shares Outstanding	230,090	230,067	230,034	229,443	229,054	230,265	229,145	228,094
Statistical Record								
Return on Assets %	N.M.	N.M.	N.M.	N.M.	N.M.	1.41	5.49	3.08
Return on Equity %	N.M.	N.M.	N.M.	N.M.	N.M.	3.16	14.74	10.24
EBITDA Margin %	31.24	32.42	15.16	13.03	11.24	26.24	22.01	24.76
Net Margin %	4.66	8.34	N.M.	N.M.	N.M.	4.38	20.02	7.15
Asset Turnover	0.29	0.29	0.22	0.20	0.27	0.32	0.27	0.43
Current Ratio	0.94	1.03	0.62	0.67	0.48	1.02	1.29	1.11
Debt to Equity	0.64	0.67	0.71	0.73	0.58	0.61	0.63	0.80
Price Range	18.39-11.35	18.39-11.35	18.39-9.00	18.39-4.16	28.64-5.42	39.58-26.80	32.05-22.11	32.84-22.35
P/E Ratio	...	...	...	...	...	56.54-38.28	11.17-7.70	19.32-13.15
Average Yield %	...	...	...	0.08	0.85	0.75	1.35	2.29

Address: 1000 Consol Energy Drive, Canonsburg, PA 15317-6506 **Telephone:** 724-485-4000	**Web Site:** www.consolenergy.com **Officers:** William N. Thorndike - Chairman Nicholas J. DeIuliis - President, Chief Executive Officer, Executive Vice President, Chief Operating Officer	**Auditors:** Ernst & Young LLP **Investor Contact:** 724-485-3157 **Transfer Agents:** ComputerShare, College Station, TX

COCA-COLA CO (THE)

Exchange	Symbol	Price	52Wk Range	Yield	P/E	Div Achiever
NYS	KO	$45.88 (12/29/2017)	47.43-40.44	3.23	44.12	54 Years

*7 Year Price Score 86.73   *NYSE Composite Index=100   *12 Month Price Score 98.07

Interim Earnings (Per Share)

Qtr.	Mar	Jun	Sep	Dec
2014	0.36	0.58	0.48	0.18
2015	0.35	0.71	0.33	0.28
2016	0.34	0.79	0.24	0.12
2017	0.27	0.32	0.33	...

Interim Dividends (Per Share)

Amt	Decl	Ex	Rec	Pay
0.37Q	02/16/2017	03/13/2017	03/15/2017	04/03/2017
0.37Q	04/27/2017	06/13/2017	06/15/2017	07/03/2017
0.37Q	07/20/2017	09/14/2017	09/15/2017	10/02/2017
0.37Q	10/10/2017	11/30/2017	12/01/2017	12/15/2017

Indicated Div: $1.48 (Div. Reinv. Plan)

Valuation Analysis		Institutional Holding	
Forecast EPS	$1.91	No of Institutions	2477
	(01/18/2018)		
Market Cap	$195.5 Billion	Shares	3,282,078,720
Book Value	$22.1 Billion	% Held	60.01
Price/Book	8.84		
Price/Sales	5.24		

Business Summary: Beverages (MIC: 1.2.2 SIC: 2086 NAIC: 312111)

Coca-Cola is a beverage company. Co. owns or licenses and markets nonalcoholic beverage brands including sparkling beverages and a variety of still beverages such as waters, flavored waters and enhanced waters, juices and juice drinks, ready-to-drink teas and coffees, sports drinks, dairy, and energy drinks. Co.'s nonalcoholic sparkling beverage brands include Coca-Cola and Sprite. Co. markets, manufactures and sells beverage concentrates and syrups, including fountain syrups; and finished sparkling and still beverages. Co.'s operating structure consists of the following operating segments: Europe, Middle East and Africa; Latin America; North America; Asia Pacific; and Bottling Investments.

Recent Developments: For the quarter ended Sep 29 2017, net income increased 37.5% to US$1.44 billion from US$1.05 billion in the year-earlier quarter. Revenues were US$9.08 billion, down 14.6% from US$10.63 billion the year before. Operating income was US$2.12 billion versus US$2.27 billion in the prior-year quarter, a decrease of 6.6%. Direct operating expenses declined 17.8% to US$3.40 billion from US$4.13 billion in the comparable period the year before. Indirect operating expenses decreased 15.8% to US$3.56 billion from US$4.23 billion in the equivalent prior-year period.

Prospects: Our evaluation of Coca-Cola Co as of Jan. 14, 2018 is the result of our systematic analysis on three basic characteristics: earnings strength, relative valuation, and recent stock price movement. The company has enjoyed a very positive trend in earnings per share over the past 5 quarters and while recent estimates for the company have been mixed, KO has posted better than expected results. Based on operating earnings yield, the company is about fairly valued when compared to all of the companies in our coverage universe. Share price changes over the past year indicates that KO will perform well over the near term.

Financial Data

(US$ in Thousands)	9 Mos	6 Mos	3 Mos	12/31/2016	12/31/2015	12/31/2014	12/31/2013	12/31/2012
Earnings Per Share	1.04	0.95	1.42	1.49	1.67	1.60	1.90	1.97
Cash Flow Per Share	1.87	1.96	2.09	2.03	2.42	2.42	2.38	2.36
Tang Book Value Per Share	1.30	1.13	0.96	0.45	0.33	0.90	1.26	1.22
Dividends Per Share	1.460	1.440	1.420	1.400	1.320	1.220	1.120	1.020
Dividend Payout %	140.38	151.58	100.00	93.96	79.04	76.25	58.95	51.78
Income Statement								
Total Revenue	27,898,000	18,820,000	9,118,000	41,863,000	44,294,000	45,998,000	46,854,000	48,017,000
EBITDA	5,984,000	4,338,000	1,756,000	8,989,000	11,112,000	10,181,000	12,547,000	12,639,000
Depn & Amortn	926,000	629,000	328,000	1,597,000	1,753,000	1,736,000	1,743,000	1,723,000
Income Before Taxes	4,922,000	3,606,000	1,391,000	7,301,000	9,116,000	8,556,000	10,875,000	10,990,000
Income Taxes	1,805,000	1,575,000	323,000	1,586,000	2,239,000	2,201,000	2,851,000	2,723,000
Net Income	4,000,000	2,553,000	1,182,000	6,527,000	7,351,000	7,098,000	8,584,000	9,019,000
Average Shares	4,319,999	4,326,999	4,333,999	4,366,999	4,404,999	4,449,999	4,508,999	4,583,999
Balance Sheet								
Current Assets	38,404,000	38,961,000	40,251,000	34,010,000	33,395,000	32,986,000	31,304,000	30,328,000
Total Assets	90,515,000	91,146,000	91,201,000	87,270,000	90,093,000	92,023,000	90,055,000	86,174,000
Current Liabilities	27,633,000	28,830,000	28,656,000	26,532,000	26,930,000	32,374,000	27,811,000	27,821,000
Long-Term Obligations	32,471,000	31,805,000	31,538,000	29,684,000	28,407,000	19,063,000	19,154,000	14,736,000
Total Liabilities	68,396,000	69,145,000	68,325,000	64,208,000	64,539,000	61,703,000	56,882,000	53,384,000
Stockholders' Equity	22,119,000	22,001,000	22,876,000	23,062,000	25,554,000	30,320,000	33,173,000	32,790,000
Shares Outstanding	4,262,000	4,268,000	4,273,000	4,288,000	4,323,999	4,365,999	4,401,999	4,468,999
Statistical Record								
Return on Assets %	4.93	4.48	6.82	7.34	8.07	7.80	9.74	10.83
Return on Equity %	18.88	17.06	26.06	26.78	26.31	22.36	26.03	27.92
EBITDA Margin %	21.45	23.05	19.26	21.47	25.09	22.13	26.78	26.32
Net Margin %	14.34	13.57	12.96	15.59	16.60	15.43	18.32	18.78
Asset Turnover	0.40	0.42	0.45	0.47	0.49	0.51	0.53	0.58
Current Ratio	1.39	1.35	1.40	1.28	1.24	1.02	1.13	1.09
Debt to Equity	1.47	1.45	1.38	1.29	1.11	0.63	0.58	0.45
Price Range	46.87-40.17	45.99-40.17	46.89-40.17	46.89-40.17	43.84-37.99	44.83-37.10	43.09-36.25	40.56-33.49
P/E Ratio	45.07-38.63	48.41-42.28	33.02-28.29	31.47-26.96	26.25-22.75	28.02-23.19	22.68-19.08	20.59-17.00
Average Yield %	3.38	3.36	3.29	3.22	3.20	2.99	2.82	2.75

Address: One Coca-Cola Plaza, Atlanta, GA 30313

Telephone: 404-676-2121

Fax: 404-676-6792

Web Site: www.coca-colacompany.com

Officers: Ahmet Muhtar Kent - Chairman, President, Chief Executive Officer James Quincey - President, Chief Executive Officer, Chief Operating Officer, Region Officer

Auditors: Ernst & Young LLP

Investor Contact: 404-676-7563

Transfer Agents: Computershare Trust Company, N.A., Providence, RI

COLGATE-PALMOLIVE CO.

Exchange	Symbol	Price	52Wk Range	Yield	P/E	Div Achiever
NYS	CL	$75.45 (12/29/2017)	77.23-64.53	2.12	29.13	54 Years

*7 Year Price Score 92.42   *NYSE Composite Index=100   *12 Month Price Score 95.18

Interim Earnings (Per Share)

Qtr.	Mar	Jun	Sep	Dec
2014	0.42	0.67	0.59	0.68
2015	0.59	0.63	0.80	(0.50)
2016	0.59	0.67	0.78	0.68
2017	0.64	0.59	0.68	...

Interim Dividends (Per Share)

Amt	Decl	Ex	Rec	Pay
0.40Q	03/09/2017	04/19/2017	04/21/2017	05/15/2017
0.40Q	06/08/2017	07/14/2017	07/18/2017	08/15/2017
0.40Q	09/26/2017	10/20/2017	10/23/2017	11/15/2017
0.40Q	01/11/2018	01/22/2018	01/23/2018	02/15/2018

Indicated Div: $1.60 (Div. Reinv. Plan)

Valuation Analysis   Institutional Holding

Forecast EPS	$2.87	No of Institutions
	(01/18/2018)	1904
Market Cap	$66.3 Billion	Shares
Book Value	N/A	756,209,728
Price/Book	N/A	% Held
Price/Sales	4.34	69.22

Business Summary: Household & Personal Products (MIC: 1.7.1 SIC: 2844 NAIC: 325611)

Colgate-Palmolive is engaged primarily in the manufacture and market a range of consumer products. Co. has two product segments. Oral, Personal and Home Care products include toothpaste, toothbrushes and mouthwash, bar and liquid hand soaps, shower gels, shampoos, conditioners, deodorants and antiperspirants, laundry and dishwashing detergents, fabric conditioners, household cleaners, bleaches and other similar items. These products are sold to retail trade customers and wholesale distributors. Pet Nutrition products include pet nutrition products manufactured and marketed by Hill's Pet Nutrition. The principal customers for Pet Nutrition products are pet supply retailers and veterinarians.

Recent Developments: For the quarter ended Sep 30 2017, net income decreased 12.9% to US$650.0 million from US$746.0 million in the year-earlier quarter. Revenues were US$3.97 billion, up 2.8% from US$3.87 billion the year before. Operating income was US$927.0 million versus US$1.07 billion in the prior-year quarter, a decrease of 13.4%. Direct operating expenses rose 3.1% to US$1.59 billion from US$1.54 billion in the comparable period the year before. Indirect operating expenses increased 16.2% to US$1.46 billion from US$1.25 billion in the equivalent prior-year period.

Prospects: Our evaluation of Colgate-Palmolive Co. as of Jan. 14, 2018 is the result of our systematic analysis on three basic characteristics: earnings strength, relative valuation, and recent stock price movement. The company has managed to produce a neutral trend in earnings per share over the past 5 quarters and while recent estimates for the company have been mixed, CL has posted results that fell short of analysts expectations. Based on operating earnings yield, the company is about fairly valued when compared to all of the companies in our coverage universe. Share price changes over the past year indicates that CL will perform in line with the market over the near term.

Financial Data

(US$ in Thousands)	9 Mos	6 Mos	3 Mos	12/31/2016	12/31/2015	12/31/2014	12/31/2013	12/31/2012
Earnings Per Share	2.59	2.69	2.77	2.72	1.52	2.36	2.38	2.58
Cash Flow Per Share	3.54	3.54	3.64	3.51	3.27	3.60	3.44	3.35
Dividends Per Share	1.580	1.570	1.560	1.550	1.500	1.420	1.330	1.220
Dividend Payout %	61.00	58.36	56.32	56.99	98.68	60.17	55.88	47.38
Income Statement								
Total Revenue	11,562,000	7,588,000	3,762,000	15,195,000	16,034,000	17,277,000	17,420,000	17,085,000
EBITDA	3,019,000	1,964,000	994,000	3,860,000	2,814,000	3,582,000	3,583,000	3,913,000
Depn & Amortn	354,000	226,000	109,000	33,000	33,000	32,000	32,000	31,000
Income Before Taxes	2,591,000	1,691,000	862,000	3,728,000	2,755,000	3,526,000	3,560,000	3,867,000
Income Taxes	770,000	520,000	251,000	1,152,000	1,215,000	1,194,000	1,155,000	1,243,000
Net Income	1,701,000	1,094,000	570,000	2,441,000	1,384,000	2,180,000	2,241,000	2,472,000
Average Shares	886,300	890,800	891,000	898,400	909,700	924,300	939,900	960,200
Balance Sheet								
Current Assets	4,736,000	4,555,000	4,596,000	4,338,000	4,384,000	4,863,000	4,822,000	4,556,000
Total Assets	12,775,000	12,580,000	12,448,000	12,123,000	11,958,000	13,459,000	13,876,000	13,394,000
Current Liabilities	3,854,000	3,780,000	3,809,000	3,305,000	3,534,000	3,946,000	4,470,000	3,736,000
Long-Term Obligations	6,520,000	6,506,000	6,466,000	6,520,000	6,269,000	5,644,000	4,749,000	4,926,000
Total Liabilities	12,883,000	12,822,000	12,761,000	12,366,000	12,257,000	12,314,000	11,571,000	11,205,000
Stockholders' Equity	(108,000)	(242,000)	(313,000)	(243,000)	(299,000)	1,145,000	2,305,000	2,189,000
Shares Outstanding	878,105	880,841	883,292	883,108	892,738	906,712	919,946	935,728
Statistical Record								
Return on Assets %	18.17	19.14	19.91	20.22	10.89	15.95	16.44	18.88
Return on Equity %	...	...	...	...	327.19	126.38	99.73	108.03
EBITDA Margin %	26.11	25.88	26.42	25.40	17.55	20.73	20.57	22.90
Net Margin %	14.71	14.42	15.15	16.06	8.63	12.62	12.86	14.47
Asset Turnover	1.20	1.21	1.22	1.26	1.26	1.26	1.28	1.30
Current Ratio	1.23	1.21	1.21	1.31	1.24	1.23	1.08	1.22
Debt to Equity	...	...	...	...	...	4.93	2.06	2.25
Price Range	77.23-64.53	77.23-64.53	75.27-64.53	75.27-62.45	71.46-60.37	71.00-60.17	66.26-52.27	55.31-44.13
P/E Ratio	29.82-24.92	28.71-23.99	27.17-23.30	27.67-22.96	47.01-39.72	30.08-25.50	27.84-21.96	21.44-17.10
Average Yield %	2.22	2.19	2.20	2.21	2.23	2.23	2.15	2.42

Address: 300 Park Avenue, New York, NY 10022	**Web Site:** www.colgatepalmolive.com	**Auditors:** PricewaterhouseCoopers LLP
Telephone: 212-310-2000	**Officers:** Ian M. Cook - Chairman, President, Chief Executive Officer Franck J. Moison - Vice-Chairman, Division Officer	**Investor Contact:** 212-310-2575
Fax: 212-310-3284		**Transfer Agents:** Computershare, Providence, RI

Exchange	Symbol	Price	52Wk Range	Yield	P/E
NYS	CFX	$39.62 (12/29/2017)	43.16-34.88	N/A	27.90

*7 Year Price Score 77.03 ***NYSE Composite Index=100** ***12 Month Price Score 91.42**

Interim Earnings (Per Share)

Qtr.	Mar	Jun	Sep	Dec
2014	0.22	1.53	0.59	0.64
2015	0.42	0.42	0.15	0.35
2016	0.18	0.32	0.23	0.31
2017	0.31	0.43	0.37	...

Interim Dividends (Per Share)

No Dividends Paid

Valuation Analysis — **Institutional Holding**

Forecast EPS	$1.78	No of Institutions
	(01/18/2018)	310
Market Cap	$4.9 Billion	Shares
Book Value	$3.3 Billion	98,025,424
Price/Book	1.48	% Held
Price/Sales	1.36	104.82

Business Summary: Industrial Machinery & Equipment (MIC: 7.2.1 SIC: 3561 NAIC: 333911)

Colfax provides gas- and fluid-handling and fabrication technology products and services to commercial and governmental customers. Co.'s gas- and fluid-handling segment is a supplier of a range of products, including centrifugal and axial fans, rotary heat exchangers, gas compressors, centrifugal and positive displacement pumps, which serves customers in the power generation, oil, gas and petrochemical, mining, marine (including defense) and general industrial and other end markets. Co.'s fabrication technology segment formulates, develops, manufactures and supplies consumable products and equipment for use in the cutting and joining of steels, aluminum and other metals and metal alloys.

Recent Developments: For the quarter ended Sep 30 2017, income from continuing operations increased 22.4% to US$49.6 million from US$40.5 million in the year-earlier quarter. Net income increased 60.6% to US$51.7 million from US$32.2 million in the year-earlier quarter. Revenues were US$844.5 million, up 10.2% from US$766.5 million the year before. Operating income was US$74.8 million versus US$58.7 million in the prior-year quarter, an increase of 27.3%. Direct operating expenses rose 9.9% to US$580.6 million from US$528.2 million in the comparable period the year before. Indirect operating expenses increased 5.3% to US$189.1 million from US$179.6 million in the equivalent prior-year period.

Prospects: Our evaluation of Colfax Corp. as of Jan. 14, 2018 is the result of our systematic analysis on three basic characteristics: earnings strength, relative valuation, and recent stock price movement. The company has generated a negative trend in earnings per share over the past 5 quarters and while recent estimates for the company have been raised by analysts, CFX has posted better than expected results. Based on operating earnings yield, the company is about fairly valued when compared to all of the companies in our coverage universe. Share price changes over the past year indicates that CFX will perform poorly over the near term.

Financial Data
(US$ in Thousands)

	9 Mos	6 Mos	3 Mos	12/31/2016	12/31/2015	12/31/2014	12/31/2013	12/31/2012
Earnings Per Share	1.42	1.28	1.17	1.04	1.34	3.02	1.56	(0.92)
Cash Flow Per Share	2.11	2.35	2.21	2.00	2.45	3.18	3.65	1.80
Income Statement								
Total Revenue	2,426,101	1,810,758	844,926	3,647,047	3,967,053	4,624,476	4,207,209	3,913,856
EBITDA	306,954	226,830	98,193	317,215	375,345	504,053	484,492	211,709
Depn & Amortn	101,843	68,606	31,972	79,200	90,700	94,500	78,100	71,700
Income Before Taxes	176,005	140,711	57,126	207,999	236,902	358,248	302,795	48,439
Income Taxes	46,128	40,749	15,639	62,808	49,724	(62,025)	93,652	90,703
Net Income	137,800	91,936	38,542	128,111	167,739	392,098	178,628	(64,402)
Average Shares	124,080	123,954	123,795	123,198	124,869	122,666	100,366	91,069
Balance Sheet								
Current Assets	2,314,869	1,958,417	1,780,577	1,785,597	1,759,765	2,099,463	2,138,346	2,130,782
Total Assets	6,838,316	6,730,279	6,429,745	6,385,459	6,732,919	7,245,098	6,582,853	6,129,727
Current Liabilities	1,288,630	1,146,755	1,081,854	1,106,674	1,116,344	1,285,535	1,375,090	1,175,458
Long-Term Obligations	1,334,627	1,322,442	1,244,902	1,286,738	1,411,755	1,529,389	1,457,642	1,693,512
Total Liabilities	3,538,692	3,567,166	3,419,358	3,488,588	3,662,944	4,098,272	4,068,964	4,217,375
Stockholders' Equity	3,299,624	3,163,113	3,010,387	2,896,871	3,069,975	3,146,826	2,513,889	1,912,352
Shares Outstanding	123,115	123,036	122,991	122,780	123,486	123,730	101,921	94,067
Statistical Record								
Return on Assets %	2.62	2.37	2.19	1.95	2.40	5.67	2.81	N.M.
Return on Equity %	5.60	5.15	4.76	4.28	5.40	13.85	8.07	N.M.
EBITDA Margin %	12.65	12.53	11.62	8.70	9.46	10.90	11.52	5.41
Net Margin %	5.68	5.08	4.56	3.51	4.23	8.48	4.25	N.M.
Asset Turnover	0.54	0.54	0.55	0.55	0.57	0.67	0.66	1.08
Current Ratio	1.80	1.71	1.65	1.61	1.58	1.63	1.56	1.81
Debt to Equity	0.40	0.42	0.41	0.44	0.46	0.49	0.58	0.89
Price Range	42.74-29.00	41.58-25.79	41.40-24.96	39.75-19.29	53.47-22.00	74.92-47.20	63.69-40.35	40.35-24.80
P/E Ratio	30.10-20.42	32.48-20.15	35.38-21.33	38.22-18.55	39.90-16.42	24.81-15.63	40.83-25.87	...

Address: 420 National Business Parkway, 5th Floor, Annapolis Junction, MD 20701 **Telephone:** 301-323-9000	**Web Site:** www.colfaxcorp.com **Officers:** Mitchell P. Rales - Chairman Shyam Kambeyanda - Senior Vice President, Division Officer	**Auditors:** Ernst & Young LLP **Investor Contact:** 301-323-9090 **Transfer Agents:** Registrar and Transfer Company, Cranford, NJ

COLONY NORTHSTAR INC

Exchange	Symbol	Price	52Wk Range	Yield	P/E
NYS	CLNS	$11.41 (12/29/2017)	14.70-11.41	9.47	N/A

*7 Year Price Score N/A   *NYSE Composite Index=100   ***12 Month Price Score 85.51**

Interim Earnings (Per Share)

Qtr.	Mar	Jun	Sep	Dec
2014	0.00	(0.12)	0.10	0.16
2015	0.11	0.19	0.21	0.09
2016	0.09	0.06	0.13	(0.07)
2017	(0.01)	0.07	0.00	...

Interim Dividends (Per Share)

Amt	Decl	Ex	Rec	Pay
0.24Q	02/28/2017	03/29/2017	03/31/2017	04/17/2017
0.27Q	05/04/2017	06/28/2017	06/30/2017	07/17/2017
0.27Q	08/03/2017	09/28/2017	09/30/2017	10/16/2017
0.27Q	11/02/2017	12/28/2017	12/29/2017	01/15/2018

Indicated Div: $1.08

Valuation Analysis

		Institutional Holding	
Forecast EPS	$0.10 (01/17/2018)	No of Institutions	429
Market Cap	$6.3 Billion	Shares	468,566,720
Book Value	$8.9 Billion	% Held	N/A
Price/Book	0.70		
Price/Sales	2.88		

TRADING VOLUME (thousand shares)

Business Summary: REITs (MIC: 5.3.1 SIC: 6531 NAIC: 531390)

NorthStar Asset Management Group is an asset management firm. Co.'s primary business lines are as follows: NorthStar Listed Companies, and Retail Companies, which provides asset management and other services on a fee basis by managing the day-to-day activities of the NorthStar Listed Companies, and Retail Companies;Broker-dealer, which raises capital in the retail market through NorthStar Securities and earned dealer manager fees for selling equity in the Retail Companies; Direct Investments, which invest in strategic partnerships and joint ventures with third-parties. As of Dec 31 2016, Co. had $56.00 billion of assets under management.

Recent Developments: For the quarter ended Sep 30 2017, net income increased 179.8% to US$72.6 million from US$25.9 million in the year-earlier quarter. Revenues were US$789.9 million, up 727.1% from US$95.5 million the year before.

Prospects: Our evaluation of Colony Northstar Inc. as of Jan. 14, 2018 is the result of our systematic analysis on three basic characteristics: earnings strength, relative valuation, and recent stock price movement. The company has generated a negative trend in earnings per share over the past 5 quarters and while recent estimates for the company have remained steady, CLNS has posted results that fell short of analysts expectations. Based on operating earnings yield, the company is overvalued when compared to all of the companies in our coverage universe. Share price changes over the past year indicates that CLNS will perform very well over the near term.

Financial Data

(US$ in Thousands)	9 Mos	6 Mos	3 Mos	12/31/2016	12/31/2015	12/31/2014	12/31/2013	12/31/2012
Earnings Per Share	(0.01)	0.12	0.11	0.21	0.60	0.10	...	...
Cash Flow Per Share	1.47	1.19	0.18	0.92	0.84	0.25	...	...
Tang Book Value Per Share	10.03	10.25	10.49	N.M.	0.92	1.03	...	...
Dividends Per Share	0.270	0.270	1.404	0.400	0.400	0.100	...	...
Dividend Payout %	...	225.00	1276.36	190.48	66.67	100.00	...	...
Income Statement								
Total Revenue	789,853	679,372	607,165	398,542	435,821	259,142	89,938	50,761
EBITDA	196,159	145,406	66,767	164,833	201,022	22,661	(1,921)	(17,257)
Depn & Amortn	153,111	162,694	137,420	75,121	59,253	900	74	65
Income Before Taxes	43,048	(17,288)	(70,653)	63,798	140,991	21,761	(1,995)	(17,322)
Income Taxes	(10,613)	(86)	3,709	11,022	21,869	1,622	...	...
Net Income	33,908	78,342	25,597	42,281	119,794	19,100	(1,995)	(17,322)
Average Shares	542,855	544,023	506,405	185,111	193,119	194,408	...	...
Balance Sheet								
Current Assets	1,557,190	1,125,923	1,132,784	241,011	220,077	198,950	30,724	19,851
Total Assets	25,990,764	25,288,332	24,909,731	850,627	374,821	266,987	31,709	20,257
Current Liabilities	1,303,123	1,011,582	1,046,369	91,165	197,148	65,239	3,283	2,343
Long-Term Obligations	10,791,975	10,418,978	10,249,548	468,425	...	...	...	...
Total Liabilities	17,054,592	16,198,167	15,729,857	666,515	199,756	65,239	3,341	2,382
Stockholders' Equity	8,936,172	9,090,165	9,179,874	184,112	175,065	201,748	28,368	17,875
Shares Outstanding	548,586	551,932	558,174	193,639	189,898	196,686	...	...
Statistical Record								
Return on Assets %	0.52	1.25	0.81	6.88	37.33	12.79	N.M.	...
Return on Equity %	1.49	3.44	2.22	23.48	63.58	16.60	N.M.	...
EBITDA Margin %	24.83	21.40	11.00	41.36	46.12	8.74	N.M.	N.M.
Net Margin %	4.29	11.53	4.22	10.61	27.49	7.37	N.M.	N.M.
Asset Turnover	0.12	0.11	0.19	0.65	1.36	1.74	3.46	...
Current Ratio	1.19	1.11	1.08	2.64	1.12	3.05	9.36	8.47
Debt to Equity	1.21	1.15	1.12	2.54	...	...	...	...
Price Range	14.70-12.55	14.68-12.65	14.68-12.87	...	...	...	...	...
P/E Ratio	N.M.	122.33-105.42	133.46-117.00	...	...	...	...	...
Average Yield %	1.97	1.97	10.13	...	...	...	...	...

Address: 515 South Flower Street, 44th Floor, Los Angeles, CA 90071
Telephone: 310-282-8820

Web Site: www.nsamgroup.com
Officers: David T. Hamamoto - Chairman, Chief Executive Officer, Holding/Parent Company Officer Albert Tylis - President, Holding/Parent Company Officer

Auditors: Ernst & Young LLP
Transfer Agents: American Stock Transfer & Trust Company, LLC, Brookly, NY

COLUMBIA PROPERTY TRUST INC

Exchange	Symbol	Price	52Wk Range	Yield	P/E
NYS	CXP	$22.95 (12/29/2017)	23.43-20.62	3.49	13.66

*7 Year Price Score N/A ***NYSE Composite Index=100** ***12 Month Price Score 96.31**

Interim Earnings (Per Share)

Qtr.	Mar	Jun	Sep	Dec
2014	0.03	0.06	0.20	0.45
2015	0.04	0.07	0.16	0.08
2016	0.05	0.11	0.30	0.22
2017	0.61	0.01	0.84	...

Interim Dividends (Per Share)

Amt	Decl	Ex	Rec	Pay
0.20Q	02/09/2017	02/27/2017	03/01/2017	03/15/2017
0.20Q	05/02/2017	05/30/2017	06/01/2017	06/15/2017
0.20Q	08/07/2017	08/30/2017	09/01/2017	09/15/2017
0.20Q	11/13/2017	11/30/2017	12/01/2017	01/04/2018

Indicated Div: $0.80

Valuation Analysis

		Institutional Holding	
Forecast EPS	$-0.01 (01/11/2018)	No of Institutions	271
Market Cap	$2.7 Billion	Shares	94,475,728
Book Value	$2.6 Billion	% Held	20.92
Price/Book	1.08		
Price/Sales	8.51		

Business Summary: REITs (MIC: 5.3.1 SIC: 6798 NAIC: 525930)

Columbia Property Trust is a real estate investment trust that owns and operates commercial real estate properties. Co. conducts its business primarily through Columbia Property Trust Operating Partnership, L.P., which acquires, develops, owns, leases, and operates real properties directly, through wholly owned subsidiaries, or through joint ventures. Co. typically invests in office properties. As of Dec 31 2016, Co. owned 21 office properties and one hotel located in nine states and the District of Columbia. All of the office properties are wholly owned except for one property, which is owned through an unconsolidated joint venture.

Recent Developments: For the quarter ended Sep 30 2017, loss from continuing operations was US$831,000 compared with income of nil in the year-earlier quarter. Net income increased 175.2% to US$101.5 million from US$36.9 million in the year-earlier quarter. Revenues were US$60.4 million, down 46.7% from US$113.3 million the year before.

Prospects: Our evaluation of Columbia Property Trust Inc as of Jan. 14, 2018 is the result of our systematic analysis on three basic characteristics: earnings strength, relative valuation, and recent stock price movement. The company has managed to produce a neutral trend in earnings per share over the past 5 quarters. Because the company lacks sufficient analyst estimate data, we place greater weight on the historical EPS trend as the measure of earnings strength. Based on operating earnings yield, the company is overvalued when compared to all of the companies in our coverage universe. Share price changes over the past year indicates that CXP will perform well over the near term.

Financial Data

(US$ in Thousands)	9 Mos	6 Mos	3 Mos	12/31/2016	12/31/2015	12/31/2014	12/31/2013	12/31/2012
Earnings Per Share	1.68	1.14	1.24	0.68	0.36	0.74	0.12	0.36
Cash Flow Per Share	0.75	1.15	1.28	1.56	1.79	1.90	1.63	1.84
Tang Book Value Per Share	21.08	20.26	20.44	20.04	20.40	21.03	21.14	22.33
Dividends Per Share	0.900	1.000	1.100	1.200	1.200	1.200	0.300	1.880
Dividend Payout %	53.57	87.72	88.71	176.47	333.33	162.16	250.00	522.22
Income Statement								
Total Revenue	217,375	157,013	82,156	473,543	566,065	540,797	526,578	576,691
EBITDA	123,626	89,590	46,305	188,826	231,811	206,241	214,067	227,930
Depn & Amortn	84,644	58,817	30,474	108,543	131,490	117,766	119,835	120,307
Income Before Taxes	2,342	6,023	3,066	19,962	22,279	20,039	26,320	41,103
Income Taxes	(378)	(381)	(388)	445	378	662	500	586
Net Income	177,389	75,855	74,722	84,281	44,619	92,635	15,720	48,039
Average Shares	120,529	121,909	122,329	123,228	124,847	124,918	134,085	136,672
Balance Sheet								
Current Assets	385,544	510,540	559,945	288,059	153,377	273,224	220,861	187,756
Total Assets	4,043,280	4,152,977	4,190,453	4,299,793	4,678,118	4,738,878	4,592,482	5,730,949
Current Liabilities	129,802	140,151	125,743	167,755	136,113	106,276	99,678	104,778
Long-Term Obligations	1,333,929	1,459,524	1,460,533	1,534,438	1,845,830	1,800,066	1,609,179	2,236,296
Total Liabilities	1,489,378	1,648,134	1,636,584	1,797,025	2,063,924	2,005,400	1,804,659	2,467,443
Stockholders' Equity	2,553,902	2,504,843	2,553,869	2,502,768	2,614,194	2,733,478	2,787,823	3,263,506
Shares Outstanding	119,803	121,235	122,450	122,184	124,363	124,973	124,830	136,900
Statistical Record								
Return on Assets %	4.90	3.25	3.45	1.87	0.95	1.99	0.30	0.83
Return on Equity %	8.05	5.57	5.96	3.29	1.67	3.36	0.52	1.43
EBITDA Margin %	56.87	57.06	56.36	39.88	40.95	38.14	40.65	39.52
Net Margin %	81.61	48.31	90.95	17.80	7.88	17.13	2.99	8.33
Asset Turnover	0.08	0.09	0.10	0.11	0.12	0.12	0.10	0.10
Current Ratio	2.97	3.64	4.45	1.72	1.13	2.57	2.22	1.79
Debt to Equity	0.52	0.58	0.57	0.61	0.71	0.66	0.58	0.69
Price Range	23.43-20.47	24.63-20.47	24.63-20.20	24.63-19.81	27.67-21.16	29.13-23.12	25.07-22.16	...
P/E Ratio	13.95-12.18	21.61-17.96	19.86-16.29	36.22-29.13	76.86-58.78	39.36-31.24	208.92-184.67	...
Average Yield %	4.12	4.49	4.97	5.46	4.81	4.67	1.29	...

Address: One Glenlake Parkway, Suite 1200, Atlanta, GA 30328 **Telephone:** 404-465-2200	**Web Site:** www.columbiapropertytrust.com **Officers:** John L. Dixon - Chairman E. Nelson Mills - President, Chief Executive Officer	**Auditors:** Deloitte & Touche LLP **Transfer Agents:** DST Systems Inc

COMERICA, INC.

Exchange	Symbol	Price	52Wk Range	Yield	P/E
NYS	CMA	$86.81 (12/29/2017)	87.74-64.46	1.38	19.64

*7 Year Price Score 127.09 *NYSE Composite Index=100 *12 Month Price Score 106.47

TRADING VOLUME (thousand shares)

Interim Earnings (Per Share)

Qtr.	Mar	Jun	Sep	Dec
2014	0.73	0.80	0.82	0.81
2015	0.73	0.73	0.74	0.64
2016	0.34	0.58	0.84	0.92
2017	1.11	1.13	1.26	...

Interim Dividends (Per Share)

Amt	Decl	Ex	Rec	Pay
0.23Q	01/24/2017	03/13/2017	03/15/2017	04/01/2017
0.26Q	04/25/2017	06/13/2017	06/15/2017	07/01/2017
0.30Q	07/25/2017	09/14/2017	09/15/2017	10/01/2017
0.30Q	11/07/2017	12/14/2017	12/15/2017	01/01/2018

Indicated Div: $1.20 (Div. Reinv. Plan)

Valuation Analysis **Institutional Holding**

Forecast EPS	$6.30	No of Institutions
	(01/18/2018)	736
Market Cap	$15.1 Billion	Shares
Book Value	$8.0 Billion	177,441,616
Price/Book	1.88	% Held
Price/Sales	4.76	79.00

Business Summary: Banking (MIC: 5.1.1 SIC: 6021 NAIC: 522110)

Comerica is a financial holding company. Co.'s principal activity is lending to and accepting deposits from businesses and individuals. Co.'s business segments are: Business Bank, which provides products and services to middle market businesses, multinational corporations and governmental entities; Retail Bank, which includes small business banking and personal financial services; and Wealth Management, which provides products and services consisting of fiduciary services, private banking, retirement services, investment management and advisory services, investment banking and brokerage services. As of Dec 31 2016, Co. had total assets of $72.98 billion and deposits of $58.99 billion.

Recent Developments: For the quarter ended Sep 30 2017, net income increased 51.7% to US$226.0 million from US$149.0 million in the year-earlier quarter. Net interest income increased 21.3% to US$546.0 million from US$450.0 million in the year-earlier quarter. Provision for loan losses was US$24.0 million versus US$16.0 million in the prior-year quarter, an increase of 50.0%. Non-interest income rose 1.1% to US$275.0 million from US$272.0 million, while non-interest expense declined 6.1% to US$463.0 million.

Prospects: Our evaluation of Comerica Inc. as of Jan. 14, 2018 is the result of our systematic analysis on three basic characteristics: earnings strength, relative valuation, and recent stock price movement. The company has generated a negative trend in earnings per share over the past 5 quarters and while recent estimates for the company have been raised by analysts, CMA has posted better than expected results. Based on operating earnings yield, the company is undervalued when compared to all of the companies in our coverage universe. Share price changes over the past year indicates that CMA will perform poorly over the near term.

Financial Data

(US$ in Thousands)	9 Mos	6 Mos	3 Mos	12/31/2016	12/31/2015	12/31/2014	12/31/2013	12/31/2012
Earnings Per Share	4.42	4.00	3.45	2.68	2.84	3.16	2.85	2.67
Cash Flow Per Share	5.48	5.20	3.74	2.86	4.90	3.57	4.57	3.94
Tang Book Value Per Share	46.09	45.39	44.69	44.47	43.03	41.35	39.24	36.87
Dividends Per Share	1.020	0.950	0.910	0.890	0.830	0.790	0.680	0.550
Dividend Payout %	23.08	23.75	26.38	33.21	29.23	25.00	23.86	20.60
Income Statement								
Interest Income	1,604,000	1,025,000	496,000	1,909,000	1,784,000	1,750,000	1,784,000	1,863,000
Interest Expense	88,000	55,000	26,000	112,000	95,000	95,000	112,000	135,000
Net Interest Income	1,516,000	970,000	470,000	1,797,000	1,689,000	1,655,000	1,672,000	1,728,000
Provision for Losses	57,000	33,000	16,000	248,000	147,000	27,000	46,000	79,000
Non-Interest Income	822,000	547,000	271,000	1,051,000	1,050,000	868,000	826,000	818,000
Non-Interest Expense	1,377,000	914,000	457,000	1,930,000	1,842,000	1,658,000	1,722,000	1,757,000
Income Before Taxes	904,000	570,000	268,000	670,000	750,000	870,000	730,000	710,000
Income Taxes	273,000	165,000	66,000	193,000	229,000	277,000	189,000	189,000
Net Income	631,000	405,000	202,000	477,000	521,000	593,000	541,000	521,000
Average Shares	177,000	179,000	180,000	177,000	181,000	185,000	187,000	192,000
Balance Sheet								
Net Loans & Leases	48,497,000	48,703,000	47,595,000	48,358,000	48,450,000	47,999,000	44,872,000	45,428,000
Total Assets	72,017,000	71,447,000	72,976,000	72,978,000	71,877,000	69,190,000	65,227,000	65,359,000
Total Deposits	57,819,000	56,781,000	58,863,000	58,985,000	59,853,000	57,486,000	53,292,000	52,202,000
Total Liabilities	63,983,000	63,462,000	65,046,000	65,182,000	64,317,000	61,788,000	58,074,000	58,417,000
Stockholders' Equity	8,034,000	7,985,000	7,930,000	7,796,000	7,560,000	7,402,000	7,153,000	6,942,000
Shares Outstanding	174,329	175,912	177,432	175,313	175,707	179,018	182,304	188,275
Statistical Record								
Return on Assets %	1.09	1.01	0.87	0.66	0.74	0.88	0.83	0.82
Return on Equity %	10.09	9.16	7.95	6.20	6.96	8.15	7.68	7.52
Net Interest Margin %	94.30	94.52	94.76	94.13	94.67	94.57	93.72	92.75
Efficiency Ratio %	54.22	56.77	59.58	65.20	65.00	63.33	65.98	65.54
Loans to Deposits	0.84	0.86	0.81	0.82	0.81	0.83	0.84	0.87
Price Range	76.26-47.32	74.62-39.15	74.58-36.55	70.03-31.02	52.65-40.41	52.37-43.06	47.63-30.34	33.57-26.72
P/E Ratio	17.25-10.71	18.66-9.79	21.62-10.59	26.13-11.57	18.54-14.23	16.57-13.63	16.71-10.65	12.57-10.01
Average Yield %	1.51	1.56	1.69	1.95	1.82	1.63	1.73	1.81

Address: Comerica Bank Tower, 1717 Main Street, MC 6404, Dallas, TX 75201 **Telephone:** 214-462-6831	**Web Site:** www.comerica.com **Officers:** Ralph W. Babb - Chairman, President, Chief Executive Officer Curtis C. Farmer - Vice-Chairman, President, Executive Vice President	**Auditors:** Ernst & Young LLP **Investor Contact:** 214-462-6831 **Transfer Agents:** Wells Fargo Shareowner Services, St. Paul, MN

COMMERCIAL METALS CO.

Exchange	Symbol	Price	52Wk Range	Yield	P/E
NYS	CMC	$21.32 (12/29/2017)	23.14-17.08	2.25	32.80

*7 Year Price Score 93.90 *NYSE Composite Index=100 *12 Month Price Score 95.16

Interim Earnings (Per Share)

Qtr.	Nov	Feb	May	Aug
2014-15	0.30	0.46	0.49	(0.05)
2015-16	0.21	0.09	0.17	0.00
2016-17	0.05	0.26	0.34	(0.26)
2017-18	0.31	...	...	...

Interim Dividends (Per Share)

Amt	Decl	Ex	Rec	Pay
0.12Q	03/22/2017	04/03/2017	04/05/2017	04/20/2017
0.12Q	06/21/2017	07/03/2017	07/06/2017	07/20/2017
0.12Q	10/24/2017	11/07/2017	11/08/2017	11/22/2017
0.12Q	01/02/2018	01/12/2018	01/16/2018	01/31/2018

Indicated Div: $0.48

Valuation Analysis

		Institutional Holding	
Forecast EPS	$1.48 (01/16/2018)	No of Institutions	332
Market Cap	$2.5 Billion	Shares	129,520,696
Book Value	$1.4 Billion	% Held	83.44
Price/Book	1.73		
Price/Sales	0.53		

Business Summary: Non-Precious Metals (MIC: 8.2.2 SIC: 3312 NAIC: 331111)

Commercial Metals manufactures, recycles and markets steel and metal products, related materials and services. Co. has five segments: Americas Recycling , which processes scrap metals; Americas Mills, which, via its mills, produces rebar, angles, flats, rounds, channels, fence post sections and other shapes; Americas Fabrication, which bends, welds, cuts and fabricates steel, and sells or rents products for the installation of concrete; International Mill, which comprises its mill, recycling and fabrication operations in Poland; and International Marketing and Distribution, which sells, distributes and processes steel products, ferrous and nonferrous metals and other industrial products.

Recent Developments: For the year ended Aug 31 2017, net income decreased 15.4% to US$46.3 million from US$54.8 million in the prior year. Revenues were US$4.57 billion, up 9.4% from US$4.18 billion the year before. Direct operating expenses rose 12.4% to US$4.02 billion from US$3.58 billion in the comparable period the year before. Indirect operating expenses decreased 5.1% to US$501.4 million from US$528.2 million in the equivalent prior-year period.

Prospects: Our evaluation of Commercial Metals Co. as of Jan. 14, 2018 is the result of our systematic analysis on three basic characteristics: earnings strength, relative valuation, and recent stock price movement. The company has produced a positive trend in earnings per share over the past 5 quarters and while recent estimates for the company have been raised by analysts, CMC has posted better than expected results. Based on operating earnings yield, the company is about fairly valued when compared to all of the companies in our coverage universe. Share price changes over the past year indicates that CMC will perform very poorly over the near term.

Financial Data

(US$ in Thousands)	3 Mos	08/31/2017	08/31/2016	08/31/2015	08/31/2014	08/31/2013	08/31/2012	08/31/2011
Earnings Per Share	0.65	0.39	0.47	1.20	0.97	0.66	1.78	(1.13)
Cash Flow Per Share	1.21	1.51	5.08	2.69	1.17	1.27	1.69	0.24
Tang Book Value Per Share	11.75	11.54	11.35	10.83	10.81	10.26	10.05	9.37
Dividends Per Share	0.480	0.480	0.480	0.480	0.480	0.480	0.480	0.480
Dividend Payout %	73.85	123.08	102.13	40.00	49.48	72.73	26.97	...
Income Statement								
Total Revenue	1,238,519	4,569,675	4,610,526	5,988,605	7,039,959	6,889,575	7,828,440	7,918,430
EBITDA	89,032	202,465	266,764	447,470	350,959	326,622	363,784	120,283
Depn & Amortn	32,193	113,414	119,343	125,182	128,407	124,078	131,495	159,576
Income Before Taxes	50,314	45,004	85,190	244,528	144,811	132,936	162,793	(110,099)
Income Taxes	11,778	12,454	12,647	83,206	42,724	57,979	(46,190)	19,328
Net Income	36,810	46,332	54,762	141,634	115,551	77,315	207,484	(129,617)
Average Shares	117,857	117,364	116,623	117,949	118,607	117,552	116,783	114,995
Balance Sheet								
Current Assets	1,600,497	1,713,900	2,048,125	2,307,101	2,553,791	2,366,195	2,239,831	2,326,253
Total Assets	2,898,576	2,975,131	3,130,869	3,372,302	3,688,520	3,494,801	3,441,246	3,683,131
Current Liabilities	500,123	608,438	821,118	617,348	891,153	781,109	901,134	1,198,854
Long-Term Obligations	803,785	805,580	757,948	1,277,882	1,281,042	1,278,814	1,157,073	1,167,497
Total Liabilities	1,463,776	1,574,374	1,763,597	2,053,101	2,340,040	2,224,802	2,194,878	2,522,706
Stockholders' Equity	1,434,800	1,400,757	1,367,272	1,319,201	1,348,480	1,269,999	1,246,368	1,160,425
Shares Outstanding	116,630	115,793	114,635	115,635	117,829	117,010	116,351	115,533
Statistical Record								
Return on Assets %	2.61	1.52	1.68	4.01	3.22	2.23	5.81	N.M.
Return on Equity %	5.56	3.35	4.07	10.62	8.83	6.14	17.19	N.M.
EBITDA Margin %	7.19	4.43	5.79	7.47	4.99	4.74	4.65	1.52
Net Margin %	2.97	1.01	1.19	2.37	1.64	1.12	2.65	N.M.
Asset Turnover	1.60	1.50	1.41	1.70	1.96	1.99	2.19	2.14
Current Ratio	3.20	2.82	2.49	3.74	2.87	3.03	2.49	1.94
Debt to Equity	0.56	0.58	0.55	0.97	0.95	1.01	0.93	1.01
Price Range	24.34-17.08	24.34-14.77	18.30-12.91	18.54-12.99	20.58-14.91	17.41-12.74	15.30-8.69	18.09-10.72
P/E Ratio	37.45-26.28	62.41-37.87	38.94-27.47	15.45-10.83	21.22-15.37	26.38-19.30	8.60-4.88	...
Average Yield %	2.45	2.51	3.07	3.02	2.61	3.21	3.70	3.17

Address: 6565 North MacArthur Blvd., Irving, TX 75039	**Web Site:** www.cmc.com	**Auditors:** DELOITTE & TOUCHE LLP
Telephone: 214-689-4300	**Officers:** Barbara R. Smith - Chairman, President,	**Investor Contact:** 214-689-4300
Fax: 214-689-5886	Chief Executive Officer, Chief Operating Officer, Chief Financial Officer, Senior Vice President Tracy L. Porter - Executive Vice President, Senior Vice President, Division Officer	**Transfer Agents:** StockTrans®, a Broadridge Company

COMMUNITY BANK SYSTEM INC

Exchange	Symbol	Price	52Wk Range	Yield	P/E	Div Achiever
NYS	CBU	$53.75 (12/29/2017)	62.32-49.11	2.53	24.66	25 Years

*7 Year Price Score 118.03 *NYSE Composite Index=100 *12 Month Price Score 91.92

Interim Earnings (Per Share)

Qtr.	Mar	Jun	Sep	Dec
2014	0.54	0.57	0.54	0.57
2015	0.54	0.58	0.60	0.47
2016	0.55	0.58	0.61	0.58
2017	0.57	0.35	0.68	...

Interim Dividends (Per Share)

Amt	Decl	Ex	Rec	Pay
0.32Q	02/21/2017	03/13/2017	03/15/2017	04/10/2017
0.32Q	05/18/2017	06/13/2017	06/15/2017	07/10/2017
0.34Q	08/16/2017	09/14/2017	09/15/2017	10/10/2017
0.34Q	11/16/2017	12/15/2017	12/15/2017	01/10/2018

Indicated Div: $1.36 (Div. Reinv. Plan)

Valuation Analysis **Institutional Holding**

Forecast EPS	$2.59	No of Institutions
	(01/18/2018)	250
Market Cap	$2.7 Billion	Shares
Book Value	$1.6 Billion	43,347,224
Price/Book	1.71	% Held
Price/Sales	5.44	71.89

Business Summary: Banking (MIC: 5.1.1 SIC: 6021 NAIC: 522110)

Community Bank System is a holding company. Through its Community Bank, N.A. subsidiary, Co. operates as a banking and financial services to retail, commercial, and municipal customers in northern, central, and western New York as well as northeast Pennsylvania. Through its Benefit Plans Administrative Services, Inc. subsidiary, Co. provides employee benefit services in the U.S. and Puerto Rico. Through other subsidiaries, Co. provides wealth management, retirement planning, higher educational planning, fiduciary, risk management, and personal financial planning services. At Dec 31 2016, Co. had total assets of $8.67 billion and total deposit of $7.08 billion.

Recent Developments: For the quarter ended Sep 30 2017, net income increased 29.8% to US$35.2 million from US$27.2 million in the year-earlier quarter. Net interest income increased 23.3% to US$84.4 million from US$68.5 million in the year-earlier quarter. Provision for loan losses was US$2.3 million versus US$1.8 million in the prior-year quarter, an increase of 29.3%. Non-interest income rose 32.5% to US$52.9 million from US$40.0 million, while non-interest expense advanced 26.5% to US$83.8 million.

Prospects: Our evaluation of Community Bank System Inc. as of Jan. 14, 2018 is the result of our systematic analysis on three basic characteristics: earnings strength, relative valuation, and recent stock price movement. The company has managed to produce a neutral trend in earnings per share over the past 5 quarters and while recent estimates for the company have been mixed, CBU has posted better than expected results. Based on operating earnings yield, the company is undervalued when compared to all of the companies in our coverage universe. Share price changes over the past year indicates that CBU will perform poorly over the near term.

Financial Data

(US$ in Thousands)	9 Mos	6 Mos	3 Mos	12/31/2016	12/31/2015	12/31/2014	12/31/2013	12/31/2012
Earnings Per Share	2.18	2.11	2.34	2.32	2.19	2.22	1.94	1.93
Cash Flow Per Share	3.35	3.21	3.28	2.97	2.84	3.04	2.58	2.76
Tang Book Value Per Share	15.20	14.68	14.73	16.14	15.00	14.75	12.00	13.01
Dividends Per Share	1.300	1.280	1.270	1.260	1.220	1.160	1.100	1.060
Dividend Payout %	59.63	60.66	54.27	54.31	55.71	52.25	56.70	54.92
Income Statement								
Interest Income	239,867	151,380	69,958	285,187	259,622	256,220	264,159	281,400
Interest Expense	10,169	6,077	2,684	11,291	11,202	11,792	26,065	50,976
Net Interest Income	229,698	145,303	67,274	273,896	248,420	244,428	238,094	230,424
Provision for Losses	5,603	3,289	1,828	8,076	6,447	7,178	7,992	9,108
Non-Interest Income	148,485	95,544	44,318	155,625	123,299	119,020	102,180	99,246
Non-Interest Expense	260,230	176,454	73,575	266,848	233,055	226,580	221,255	211,757
Income Before Taxes	112,350	61,104	36,189	154,597	132,217	129,690	111,027	108,805
Income Taxes	33,659	17,656	9,932	50,785	40,987	38,337	32,198	31,737
Net Income	78,691	43,448	26,257	103,812	91,230	91,353	78,829	77,068
Average Shares	51,288	49,151	45,987	44,485	41,401	41,029	40,504	39,671
Balance Sheet								
Net Loans & Leases	6,262,005	6,313,875	4,885,790	4,903,745	4,756,906	4,191,907	4,065,492	3,822,688
Total Assets	10,850,218	10,884,046	8,913,860	8,666,437	8,552,669	7,489,440	7,095,864	7,496,800
Total Deposits	8,605,990	8,625,605	7,336,877	7,075,954	6,873,474	5,935,264	5,896,044	5,628,039
Total Liabilities	9,256,973	9,311,146	7,617,830	7,468,337	7,412,022	6,501,536	6,220,052	6,594,022
Stockholders' Equity	1,593,245	1,572,900	1,296,030	1,198,100	1,140,647	987,904	875,812	902,778
Shares Outstanding	50,587	50,511	45,955	44,437	43,774	40,747	40,431	39,625
Statistical Record								
Return on Assets %	1.07	0.99	1.21	1.20	1.14	1.25	1.08	1.10
Return on Equity %	7.42	6.90	8.46	8.85	8.57	9.80	8.86	9.16
Net Interest Margin %	95.38	95.83	96.16	96.04	95.69	95.40	90.13	81.88
Efficiency Ratio %	59.24	77.56	64.38	60.54	60.86	60.38	60.40	55.63
Loans to Deposits	0.73	0.73	0.67	0.69	0.69	0.71	0.69	0.68
Price Range	62.32-46.07	62.32-39.96	62.32-36.78	62.24-34.47	43.13-33.60	39.91-32.84	40.27-27.36	29.38-25.55
P/E Ratio	28.59-21.13	29.54-18.94	26.63-15.72	26.83-14.86	19.69-15.34	17.98-14.79	20.76-14.10	15.22-13.24
Average Yield %	2.36	2.42	2.59	2.87	3.27	3.18	3.42	3.84

Address: 5790 Widewaters Parkway, DeWitt, NY 13214-1883 **Telephone:** 315-445-2282	**Web Site:** www.communitybankna.com **Officers:** Sally A. Steele - Chairman Mark E. Tryniski - President, Chief Executive Officer	**Auditors:** PricewaterhouseCoopers LLP **Investor Contact:** 315-445-3121 **Transfer Agents:** American Stock Transfer & Trust Company LLC, Brooklyn, NY

COMMUNITY HEALTH SYSTEMS, INC.

Exchange	Symbol	Price	52Wk Range	Yield	P/E
NYS	CYH	$4.26 (12/29/2017)	10.32-3.99	N/A	N/A

*7 Year Price Score 23.44 *NYSE Composite Index=100 *12 Month Price Score 56.48

Interim Earnings (Per Share)

Qtr.	Mar	Jun	Sep	Dec
2014	(1.04)	0.37	0.54	0.89
2015	0.68	0.95	0.44	(0.71)
2016	0.10	(12.91)	(0.71)	1.99
2017	(1.79)	(1.22)	(0.98)	...

Interim Dividends (Per Share)
Dividend Payment Suspended

Valuation Analysis

		Institutional Holding	
Forecast EPS	$-1.28	No of Institutions	
	(01/17/2018)	374	
Market Cap	$488.4 Million	Shares	
Book Value	$1.2 Billion	155,493,296	
Price/Book	0.40	% Held	
Price/Sales	0.03	96.07	

Business Summary: Hospitals & Health Care Facilities (MIC: 4.2.1 SIC: 8062 NAIC: 622110)

Community Health Systems is an operator of general acute care hospitals and outpatient facilities. Services provided via Co.'s hospitals and affiliated businesses include general acute care, emergency room, general and specialty surgery, critical care, internal medicine, obstetrics, diagnostic, psychiatric and rehabilitation services. Co. also provides additional outpatient services at urgent care centers, occupational medicine clinics, imaging centers, cancer centers, ambulatory surgery centers and home health and hospice agencies. At Dec 31 2016, Co. owned or leased 155 hospitals, comprised of 152 general acute care hospitals and three stand-alone rehabilitation or psychiatric hospitals.

Recent Developments: For the quarter ended Sep 30 2017, loss from continuing operations was US$88.0 million compared with a loss of US$54.0 million in the year-earlier quarter. Net loss amounted to US$90.0 million versus a net loss of US$56.0 million in the year-earlier quarter. Revenues were US$3.67 billion, down 16.3% from US$4.38 billion the year before. Operating income was US$90.0 million versus US$146.0 million in the prior-year quarter, a decrease of 38.4%. Indirect operating expenses decreased 15.5% to US$3.58 billion from US$4.23 billion in the equivalent prior-year period.

Prospects: Our evaluation of Community Health Systems Inc. as of Jan. 14, 2018 is the result of our systematic analysis on three basic characteristics: earnings strength, relative valuation, and recent stock price movement. The company has suffered a very negative trend in earnings per share over the past 5 quarters. Because the company lacks sufficient analyst estimate data, we place greater weight on the historical EPS trend as the measure of earnings strength. Based on operating earnings yield, the company is overvalued when compared to all of the companies in our coverage universe. Share price changes over the past year indicates that CYH will perform very poorly over the near term.

Financial Data
(US$ in Thousands)

	9 Mos	6 Mos	3 Mos	12/31/2016	12/31/2015	12/31/2014	12/31/2013	12/31/2012
Earnings Per Share	(5.98)	(5.71)	(17.40)	(15.54)	1.37	0.82	1.51	2.96
Cash Flow Per Share	8.43	9.01	9.75	10.24	8.05	14.47	11.75	14.31
Dividends Per Share	...	...	...	...	...	...	...	0.250
Dividend Payout %	...	...	...	...	...	...	...	8.45
Income Statement								
Total Revenue	12,295,000	8,629,000	4,486,000	18,438,000	19,437,000	18,639,000	12,997,693	13,028,985
EBITDA	904,000	610,000	286,000	304,000	2,495,000	1,341,000	1,661,043	1,810,229
Depn & Amortn	665,000	458,000	236,000	1,100,000	1,174,000	75,000	782,675	725,558
Income Before Taxes	(467,000)	(316,000)	(179,000)	(1,758,000)	348,000	294,000	263,221	461,738
Income Taxes	(74,000)	(15,000)	...	(104,000)	116,000	82,000	88,594	157,502
Net Income	(446,000)	(335,000)	(199,000)	(1,721,000)	158,000	92,000	141,203	265,640
Average Shares	111,935	111,909	111,252	110,730	115,272	112,549	93,815	89,806
Balance Sheet								
Current Assets	4,678,000	5,055,000	4,775,000	4,666,000	5,166,000	5,566,000	3,747,963	3,419,142
Total Assets	19,735,000	20,873,000	21,660,000	21,944,000	26,861,000	27,421,000	17,117,295	16,606,335
Current Liabilities	2,277,000	2,378,000	2,996,000	2,887,000	3,072,000	3,589,000	2,457,483	2,143,220
Long-Term Obligations	13,901,000	14,702,000	14,687,000	14,789,000	16,822,000	16,681,000	9,286,495	9,451,394
Total Liabilities	17,992,000	19,575,000	20,231,000	20,329,000	22,842,000	23,418,000	14,049,468	13,875,128
Stockholders' Equity	1,213,000	1,298,000	1,429,000	1,615,000	4,019,000	4,003,000	3,067,827	2,731,207
Shares Outstanding	114,658	114,758	114,690	113,876	112,757	116,725	95,011	91,950
Statistical Record								
Return on Assets %	N.M.	N.M.	N.M.	N.M.	0.58	0.41	0.84	1.67
Return on Equity %	N.M.	N.M.	N.M.	N.M.	3.94	2.60	4.87	10.33
EBITDA Margin %	7.35	7.07	6.38	1.65	12.84	7.19	12.78	13.89
Net Margin %	N.M.	N.M.	N.M.	N.M.	0.81	0.49	1.09	2.04
Asset Turnover	0.80	0.81	0.74	0.75	0.72	0.84	0.77	0.82
Current Ratio	2.05	2.13	1.59	1.62	1.68	1.55	1.53	1.60
Debt to Equity	11.46	11.33	10.28	9.16	4.19	4.17	3.03	3.46
Price Range	11.54-4.66	13.30-4.66	17.15-4.66	21.84-4.66	52.71-20.73	47.29-28.99	42.13-25.30	26.06-13.74
P/E Ratio	...	...	...	...	38.48-15.13	57.67-35.35	27.90-16.76	8.80-4.64
Average Yield %	...	...	...	...	...	...	...	1.21

Address: 4000 Meridian Boulevard, Franklin, TN 37067 **Telephone:** 615-465-7000	**Web Site:** www.chs.net **Officers:** Wayne T. Smith - Chairman, President, Chief Executive Officer Tim L. Hingtgen - President, Executive Vice President, Chief Operating Officer	**Auditors:** Deloitte & Touche LLP **Investor Contact:** 615-465-7000 **Transfer Agents:** Registrar and Transfer Company, Cranford, NJ

COMPASS MINERALS INTERNATIONAL INC

Exchange	Symbol	Price	52Wk Range	Yield	P/E	Div Achiever
NYS	CMP	$72.25 (12/29/2017)	83.60-60.10	3.99	17.00	12 Years

*7 Year Price Score 68.88 *NYSE Composite Index=100 *12 Month Price Score 93.20

Interim Earnings (Per Share)

Qtr.	Mar	Jun	Sep	Dec
2014	1.49	(0.02)	2.60	2.37
2015	1.79	0.39	0.80	1.72
2016	1.46	0.18	0.27	2.87
2017	0.63	(0.19)	0.94	...

Interim Dividends (Per Share)

Amt	Decl	Ex	Rec	Pay
0.72Q	02/02/2017	02/27/2017	03/01/2017	03/15/2017
0.72Q	05/04/2017	05/30/2017	06/01/2017	06/15/2017
0.72Q	08/04/2017	08/30/2017	09/01/2017	09/15/2017
0.72Q	11/09/2017	11/30/2017	12/01/2017	12/15/2017

Indicated Div: $2.88

Valuation Analysis | **Institutional Holding**

Forecast EPS $2.60 (01/18/2018)	No of Institutions 422
Market Cap $2.4 Billion	Shares 52,371,048
Book Value $748.0 Million	% Held
Price/Book 3.27	91.00
Price/Sales 1.81	

TRADING VOLUME (thousand shares)

Business Summary: Mining (MIC: 8.2.4 SIC: 1499 NAIC: 212399)

Compass Minerals International is a holding company. Through its wholly owned subsidiaries, Co. is a provider of minerals, including salt, plant nutrition minerals, and chemicals. Co. has three reportable segments: Salt, which products include rock salt, mechanically evaporated salt, solar evaporated salt, brine magnesium chloride and flake magnesium chloride; Plant Nutrition North America, which includes sulfate of potash specialty fertilizer and micronutrients; and Plant Nutrition South America, which manufactures, distributes and markets an array of specialty plant nutrients and supplements developed and formulated from primary and secondary nutrients, micronutrients and biostimulants.

Recent Developments: For the quarter ended Sep 30 2017, net income increased 251.6% to US$32.0 million from US$9.1 million in the year-earlier quarter. Revenues were US$290.7 million, up 61.9% from US$179.6 million the year before. Operating income was US$31.4 million versus US$19.5 million in the prior-year quarter, an increase of 61.0%. Direct operating expenses rose 59.7% to US$214.6 million from US$134.4 million in the comparable period the year before. Indirect operating expenses increased 73.9% to US$44.7 million from US$25.7 million in the equivalent prior-year period.

Prospects: Our evaluation of Compass Minerals International Inc. as of Jan. 14, 2018 is the result of our systematic analysis on three basic characteristics: earnings strength, relative valuation, and recent stock price movement. The company has enjoyed a very positive trend in earnings per share over the past 5 quarters and while recent estimates for the company have been raised by analysts, CMP has posted results that fell short of analysts expectations. Based on operating earnings yield, the company is about fairly valued when compared to all of the companies in our coverage universe. Share price changes over the past year indicates that CMP will perform very poorly over the near term.

Financial Data

(US$ in Thousands)	9 Mos	6 Mos	3 Mos	12/31/2016	12/31/2015	12/31/2014	12/31/2013	12/31/2012
Earnings Per Share	4.25	3.58	3.95	4.79	4.69	6.44	3.88	2.65
Cash Flow Per Share	5.53	4.75	5.86	4.94	4.09	7.24	7.13	4.57
Tang Book Value Per Share	5.19	4.16	4.66	4.36	14.73	14.25	14.39	12.89
Dividends Per Share	2.855	2.830	2.805	2.780	2.640	2.400	2.180	1.980
Dividend Payout %	67.18	79.05	71.01	58.04	56.29	37.27	56.19	74.72
Income Statement								
Total Revenue	906,500	615,800	387,800	1,138,000	1,098,700	1,282,500	1,129,600	941,900
EBITDA	80,000	46,800	42,100	325,100	315,500	391,100	266,200	195,300
Depn & Amortn	1,700	1,100	600	92,300	79,500	79,200	74,200	65,800
Income Before Taxes	38,800	19,700	27,800	198,700	214,500	291,800	174,100	111,300
Income Taxes	(7,700)	4,800	6,300	34,600	55,300	73,900	43,300	22,400
Net Income	47,100	15,100	21,500	162,700	159,200	217,900	130,800	88,900
Average Shares	33,825	33,823	33,803	33,780	33,692	33,581	33,420	33,135
Balance Sheet								
Current Assets	632,100	539,500	548,100	715,000	512,300	702,700	577,400	506,900
Total Assets	2,446,800	2,297,900	2,323,300	2,466,500	1,628,900	1,637,200	1,404,800	1,300,600
Current Liabilities	251,000	254,000	297,100	372,000	170,800	237,700	257,600	199,300
Long-Term Obligations	1,274,200	1,172,800	1,114,900	1,194,800	722,100	622,500	474,700	478,400
Total Liabilities	1,698,800	1,604,200	1,593,200	1,749,400	989,200	983,600	850,600	797,100
Stockholders' Equity	748,000	693,700	730,100	717,100	639,700	653,600	554,200	503,500
Shares Outstanding	33,826	33,823	33,822	33,789	33,701	33,609	33,476	33,272
Statistical Record								
Return on Assets %	6.36	6.16	6.77	7.92	9.75	14.33	9.67	7.08
Return on Equity %	20.45	17.68	18.78	23.92	24.62	36.08	24.73	18.66
EBITDA Margin %	8.83	7.60	10.86	28.57	28.72	30.50	23.57	20.73
Net Margin %	5.20	2.45	5.54	14.30	14.49	16.99	11.58	9.44
Asset Turnover	0.59	0.63	0.59	0.55	0.67	0.84	0.84	0.75
Current Ratio	2.52	2.12	1.84	1.92	3.00	2.96	2.24	2.54
Debt to Equity	1.70	1.69	1.53	1.67	1.13	0.95	0.86	0.95
Price Range	83.60-60.10	83.60-62.90	83.60-65.95	81.85-66.62	95.60-72.12	97.20-77.09	91.64-71.09	78.85-68.38
P/E Ratio	19.67-14.14	23.35-17.57	21.16-16.70	17.09-13.91	20.38-15.38	15.09-11.97	23.62-18.32	29.75-25.80
Average Yield %	4.00	3.89	3.74	3.76	3.08	2.76	2.78	2.68

Address: 9900 West 109th Street, Suite 100, Overland Park, KS 66210 **Telephone:** 913-344-9200	**Web Site:** www.compassminerals.com **Officers:** Francis Joseph Malecha - President, Chief Executive Officer James D. Standen - Interim Chief Financial Officer, Chief Financial Officer, Principal Financial Officer, Principal Accounting Officer, Treasurer, Vice President	**Auditors:** Ernst & Young LLP **Investor Contact:** 913-344-9200 **Transfer Agents:** Computershare Trust Company, N.A., Providence, RI

CONAGRA BRANDS INC

Exchange	Symbol	Price	52Wk Range	Yield	P/E
NYS	CAG	$37.67 (12/29/2017)	41.50-32.43	2.26	22.69

*7 Year Price Score 104.54 *NYSE Composite Index=100 *12 Month Price Score 92.78

TRADING VOLUME (thousand shares)

Interim Earnings (Per Share)

Qtr.	Aug	Nov	Feb	May
2014-15	1.12	0.02	(2.23)	0.49
2015-16	(2.65)	0.35	0.46	0.27
2016-17	0.42	0.28	0.41	0.35
2017-18	0.36	0.54	...	...

Interim Dividends (Per Share)

Amt	Decl	Ex	Rec	Pay
0.20Q	04/03/2017	04/26/2017	04/28/2017	05/30/2017
0.212Q	07/20/2017	07/27/2017	07/31/2017	08/31/2017
0.212Q	09/21/2017	10/30/2017	10/31/2017	11/30/2017
0.212Q	12/12/2017	01/29/2018	01/30/2018	03/01/2018

Indicated Div: $0.85 (Div. Reinv. Plan)

Valuation Analysis

Forecast EPS	$1.90
	(01/18/2018)
Market Cap	$15.1 Billion
Book Value	$3.7 Billion
Price/Book	4.08
Price/Sales	1.93

Institutional Holding

No of Institutions	997
Shares	409,552,800
% Held	65.82

Business Summary: Food (MIC: 1.2.1 SIC: 2038 NAIC: 311412)

Conagra Brands is a packaged goods food company. Co.'s segments are: Grocery & Snacks, which includes branded, shelf stable food products sold in various retail channels; Refrigerated & Frozen, which includes branded, temperature controlled food products sold in various retail channels; International, which includes branded food products sold in retail and foodservice channels outside of the U.S.; Foodservice, which includes branded and customized food products for sale to restaurants and other foodservice establishments; and Commercial Foods, which included commercially branded and private label food and ingredients, which were sold to commercial and industrial customers, among others.

Recent Developments: For the quarter ended Nov 26 2017, income from continuing operations increased 96.1% to US$224.1 million from US$114.3 million in the year-earlier quarter. Net income increased 78.3% to US$224.5 million from US$125.9 million in the year-earlier quarter. Revenues were US$2.17 billion, up 4.1% from US$2.09 billion the year before. Direct operating expenses rose 5.1% to US$1.52 billion from US$1.44 billion in the comparable period the year before. Indirect operating expenses decreased 26.8% to US$345.3 million from US$472.0 million in the equivalent prior-year period.

Prospects: Our evaluation of Conagra Brands Inc. as of Jan. 14, 2018 is the result of our systematic analysis on three basic characteristics: earnings strength, relative valuation, and recent stock price movement. The company has managed to produce a neutral trend in earnings per share over the past 5 quarters and while recent estimates for the company have been raised by analysts, CAG has posted better than expected results. Based on operating earnings yield, the company is undervalued when compared to all of the companies in our coverage universe. Share price changes over the past year indicates that CAG will perform in line with the market over the near term.

Financial Data (US$ in Thousands)	6 Mos	3 Mos	05/28/2017	05/29/2016	05/31/2015	05/25/2014	05/26/2013	05/27/2012
Earnings Per Share	1.66	1.40	1.46	(1.56)	(0.60)	0.70	1.85	1.12
Cash Flow Per Share	2.59	2.37	2.73	2.79	3.42	3.69	3.45	2.55
Dividends Per Share	0.825	0.863	0.900	1.000	1.000	1.000	0.990	0.950
Dividend Payout %	49.70	61.61	61.64	...	...	142.86	53.51	84.82
Income Statement								
Total Revenue	3,977,600	1,804,200	7,826,900	11,642,900	15,832,400	17,702,600	15,491,400	13,262,600
EBITDA	760,000	344,700	958,600	4,551,400	(55,100)	1,066,800	1,480,600	850,300
Depn & Amortn	129,000	64,700	33,600	3,670,000	108,500	111,400	56,200	21,100
Income Before Taxes	556,600	243,600	729,500	583,600	(495,500)	576,400	1,148,800	625,200
Income Taxes	229,500	120,000	254,700	225,400	234,000	298,200	400,200	195,800
Net Income	376,000	152,500	639,300	(677,000)	(252,600)	303,000	773,900	467,900
Average Shares	410,400	419,200	436,000	438,500	426,100	427,500	417,600	418,300
Balance Sheet								
Current Assets	2,056,300	2,125,000	2,013,200	3,576,700	3,667,700	4,230,800	4,379,800	3,218,800
Total Assets	10,400,100	10,225,600	10,096,300	13,390,600	17,542,200	19,366,400	20,405,300	11,441,900
Current Liabilities	1,850,300	2,053,600	1,720,500	2,532,400	3,310,200	2,642,400	3,401,300	2,225,200
Long-Term Obligations	3,261,800	2,767,000	2,769,200	4,917,800	6,888,900	8,767,600	8,886,900	2,858,600
Total Liabilities	6,702,400	6,431,800	6,105,500	9,677,000	13,016,200	14,107,900	15,140,900	7,002,400
Stockholders' Equity	3,697,700	3,793,800	3,990,800	3,713,600	4,526,000	5,258,500	5,264,400	4,439,500
Shares Outstanding	400,660	408,498	416,519	438,064	428,204	421,915	419,465	407,612
Statistical Record								
Return on Assets %	6.48	5.25	5.46	N.M.	N.M.	1.53	4.87	4.11
Return on Equity %	17.36	16.12	16.64	N.M.	N.M.	5.78	15.99	10.27
EBITDA Margin %	19.11	19.11	12.25	39.09	N.M.	6.03	9.56	6.41
Net Margin %	9.45	8.45	8.17	N.M.	N.M.	1.71	5.00	3.53
Asset Turnover	0.72	0.67	0.67	0.75	0.84	0.89	0.98	1.16
Current Ratio	1.11	1.03	1.17	1.41	1.11	1.60	1.29	1.45
Debt to Equity	0.88	0.73	0.69	1.32	1.52	1.67	1.69	0.64
Price Range	41.50-32.43	41.50-33.07	41.50-33.23	36.13-29.12	30.27-22.36	28.97-21.99	28.14-18.53	21.15-17.68
P/E Ratio	25.00-19.54	29.64-23.62	28.42-22.76	...	...	41.39-31.42	15.21-10.01	18.88-15.79
Average Yield %	2.22	2.30	2.38	3.04	3.74	3.96	4.29	4.79

Address: 222 Merchandise Mart Plaza, Suite 1300, Chicago, IL 60654 **Telephone:** 312-549-5000	**Web Site:** www.conagrafoods.com **Officers:** Sean M. Connolly - President, Chief Executive Officer David S. Marberger - Executive Vice President, Chief Financial Officer	**Auditors:** KPMG LLP **Investor Contact:** 402-240-4154 **Transfer Agents:** Wells Fargo Shareowner Services, St. Paul, MN

CUBESMART

Exchange	Symbol	Price	52Wk Range	Yield	P/E
NYS	CUBE	$28.92 (12/29/2017)	29.65-22.94	4.15	43.82

*7 Year Price Score 103.31 ***NYSE Composite Index=100** ***12 Month Price Score 103.91**

TRADING VOLUME (thousand shares)

Interim Earnings (Per Share)

Qtr.	Mar	Jun	Sep	Dec
2014	0.02	0.04	0.05	0.03
2015	0.04	0.07	0.10	0.21
2016	0.08	0.11	0.13	0.13
2017	0.14	0.18	0.21	...

Interim Dividends (Per Share)

Amt	Decl	Ex	Rec	Pay
0.27Q	02/14/2017	03/30/2017	04/03/2017	04/17/2017
0.27Q	05/31/2017	06/29/2017	07/03/2017	07/17/2017
0.27Q	07/25/2017	09/29/2017	10/02/2017	10/16/2017
0.30Q	12/14/2017	12/29/2017	01/02/2018	01/16/2018

Indicated Div: $1.20

Valuation Analysis

		Institutional Holding	
Forecast EPS	$0.72	No of Institutions	
	(01/16/2018)	347	
Market Cap	$5.2 Billion	Shares	
Book Value	$1.6 Billion	253,343,696	
Price/Book	3.24	% Held	
Price/Sales	9.55	N/A	

Business Summary: REITs (MIC: 5.3.1 SIC: 6798 NAIC: 525930)

CubeSmart is a real estate company focused primarily on the ownership, operation, management, acquisition, and development of self-storage properties. At Dec 31 2016, Co. owned 475 self-storage properties in 23 states and in the District of Columbia, and managed 316 stores for third parties in 26 states, bringing the total number of stores it owned and/or managed to 791. Co.'s customers rent storage cubes typically on a month-to-month basis. Additionally, some of Co.'s stores provide outside storage areas for vehicles and boats. Co.'s stores are designed to accommodate both residential and commercial customers, with features such as aisles and load-bearing capabilities for truck access.

Recent Developments: For the quarter ended Sep 30 2017, net income increased 50.3% to US$37.7 million from US$25.1 million in the year-earlier quarter. Revenues were US$143.9 million, up 8.9% from US$132.1 million the year before.

Prospects: Our evaluation of CubeSmart as of Jan. 14, 2018 is the result of our systematic analysis on three basic characteristics: earnings strength, relative valuation, and recent stock price movement. The company has produced a positive trend in earnings per share over the past 5 quarters and while recent estimates for the company have remained steady, CUBE has posted better than expected results. Based on operating earnings yield, the company is about fairly valued when compared to all of the companies in our coverage universe. Share price changes over the past year indicates that CUBE will perform well over the near term.

Financial Data

(US$ in Thousands)	9 Mos	6 Mos	3 Mos	12/31/2016	12/31/2015	12/31/2014	12/31/2013	12/31/2012
Earnings Per Share	0.66	0.58	0.51	0.45	0.42	0.14	0.26	(0.03)
Cash Flow Per Share	1.59	1.59	1.50	1.47	1.28	1.11	1.06	0.95
Tang Book Value Per Share	8.94	8.96	9.06	9.15	9.33	8.69	7.77	7.51
Dividends Per Share	1.080	1.020	0.960	0.900	0.690	0.550	0.460	0.430
Dividend Payout %	163.64	175.86	188.24	200.00	164.29	392.86	176.92	...
Income Statement								
Total Revenue	415,461	271,596	133,037	510,039	444,521	376,963	318,395	283,076
EBITDA	254,030	164,462	79,108	308,456	279,340	210,616	171,944	155,016
Depn & Amortn	112,885	76,337	38,825	164,442	154,113	129,003	117,488	118,573
Income Before Taxes	97,058	59,069	25,978	91,038	79,167	32,621	11,560	(7,551)
Net Income	94,741	57,444	24,986	87,905	77,712	26,379	41,448	1,817
Average Shares	181,286	181,189	181,265	179,533	170,191	150,863	137,742	124,548
Balance Sheet								
Current Assets	10,419	12,241	9,637	20,843	96,458	14,413	15,355	10,565
Total Assets	3,503,019	3,493,238	3,466,115	3,475,028	3,114,834	2,786,339	2,358,624	2,150,319
Current Liabilities	189,189	176,425	153,870	143,415	124,122	97,736	77,930	77,571
Long-Term Obligations	1,620,403	1,614,100	1,598,960	1,595,743	1,262,212	1,173,851	1,138,818	1,023,759
Total Liabilities	1,886,099	1,877,794	1,832,905	1,819,646	1,471,507	1,338,313	1,266,348	1,160,528
Stockholders' Equity	1,616,920	1,615,444	1,633,210	1,655,382	1,643,327	1,448,026	1,092,276	989,791
Shares Outstanding	180,880	180,197	180,173	180,083	174,667	163,956	139,328	131,794
Statistical Record								
Return on Assets %	3.46	3.18	2.91	2.66	2.63	1.03	1.84	0.09
Return on Equity %	7.23	6.58	5.86	5.32	5.03	2.08	3.98	0.19
EBITDA Margin %	61.14	60.55	59.46	60.48	62.84	55.87	54.00	54.76
Net Margin %	22.80	21.15	18.78	17.23	17.48	7.00	13.02	0.64
Asset Turnover	0.16	0.16	0.16	0.15	0.15	0.15	0.14	0.14
Current Ratio	0.06	0.07	0.06	0.15	0.78	0.15	0.20	0.14
Debt to Equity	1.00	1.00	0.98	0.96	0.77	0.81	1.04	1.03
Price Range	27.96-22.94	32.07-23.81	33.30-23.88	33.30-23.88	31.42-22.07	22.92-15.63	19.48-14.24	14.67-10.30
P/E Ratio	42.36-34.76	55.29-41.05	65.29-46.82	74.00-53.07	74.81-52.55	163.71-111.64	74.92-54.77	...
Average Yield %	4.24	3.85	3.43	3.10	2.71	2.96	2.80	3.50

Address: 5 Old Lancaster Road, Malvern, PA 19355
Telephone: 610-535-5000

Web Site: www.cubesmart.com
Officers: William M. Diefenderfer - Chairman
Christopher P. Marr - President, Chief Executive Officer, Chief Operating Officer, Chief Investment Officer, Treasurer

Auditors: KPMG LLP
Investor Contact: 610-293-5700
Transfer Agents: American Stock Transfer & Trust Co., LLC, Brooklyn, NY

CONCHO RESOURCES INC

Exchange	Symbol	Price	52Wk Range	Yield	P/E
NYS	CXO	$150.22 (12/29/2017)	153.92-108.05	N/A	38.03

*7 Year Price Score 94.22 *NYSE Composite Index=100 *12 Month Price Score 103.15

Interim Earnings (Per Share)

Qtr.	Mar	Jun	Sep	Dec
2014	0.87	0.11	2.69	1.15
2015	0.06	(1.02)	1.49	(0.02)
2016	(7.95)	(2.04)	(0.38)	(0.67)
2017	4.37	1.02	(0.77)	...

Interim Dividends (Per Share)

No Dividends Paid

Valuation Analysis		Institutional Holding	
Forecast EPS	$1.89	No of Institutions	
	(01/18/2018)	590	
Market Cap	$22.3 Billion	Shares	
Book Value	$8.6 Billion	161,191,680	
Price/Book	2.59	% Held	
Price/Sales	9.58	95.04	

Business Summary: Production & Extraction (MIC: 9.1.1 SIC: 1311 NAIC: 211111)

Concho Resources is an independent oil and natural gas company engaged in the acquisition, development, exploration and production of oil and natural gas properties. Co.'s four core operating areas include: Northern Delaware Basin, which comprised the Avalon Shale, Bone Spring and Wolfcamp; Southern Delaware Basin, where it mainly targets the Bone Spring and Wolfcamp formations; Midland Basin, where it mainly targets the Spraberry and Wolfcamp zones; and New Mexico Shelf, where it mainly targets the Yeso, San Andres and Grayburg formations. At Dec 31 2016, Co.'s total estimated proved reserves of 720.0 million barrels of oil equivalents consisted of about 59.5% oil and 40.5% natural gas.

Recent Developments: For the quarter ended Sep 30 2017, net loss amounted to US$113.0 million versus a net loss of US$51.0 million in the year-earlier quarter. Revenues were US$627.0 million, up 45.8% from US$430.0 million the year before. Operating loss was US$77.0 million versus an income of US$2.0 million in the prior-year quarter. Direct operating expenses rose 48.1% to US$154.0 million from US$104.0 million in the comparable period the year before. Indirect operating expenses increased 69.8% to US$550.0 million from US$324.0 million in the equivalent prior-year period.

Prospects: Our evaluation of Concho Resources Inc. as of Jan. 14, 2018 is the result of our systematic analysis on three basic characteristics: earnings strength, relative valuation, and recent stock price movement. The company has suffered a very negative trend in earnings per share over the past 5 quarters and while recent estimates for the company have been raised by analysts, CXO has posted better than expected results. Based on operating earnings yield, the company is overvalued when compared to all of the companies in our coverage universe. Share price changes over the past year indicates that CXO will perform very poorly over the near term.

Financial Data
(US$ in Thousands)

	9 Mos	6 Mos	3 Mos	12/31/2016	12/31/2015	12/31/2014	12/31/2013	12/31/2012
Earnings Per Share	3.95	4.34	1.28	(10.85)	0.54	4.88	2.39	4.15
Cash Flow Per Share	14.45	13.17	11.44	10.25	7.48	15.38	13.13	11.96
Tang Book Value Per Share	57.88	58.53	57.42	52.02	53.56	46.49	35.49	32.86
Income Statement								
Total Revenue	1,806,000	1,179,000	612,000	1,634,988	1,803,573	2,660,147	2,319,919	1,819,814
EBITDA	2,053,000	1,909,000	1,067,000	(2,114,418)	330,955	2,052,361	1,348,348	1,417,104
Depn & Amortn	848,000	564,000	6,000	20,600	18,300	979,740	772,608	575,128
Income Before Taxes	1,087,000	1,266,000	1,021,000	(2,338,536)	97,271	855,960	357,159	659,271
Income Taxes	398,000	464,000	371,000	(876,090)	31,371	317,785	118,237	251,041
Net Income	689,000	802,000	650,000	(1,462,446)	65,900	538,175	251,003	431,689
Average Shares	147,557	147,766	147,551	134,755	120,373	109,132	103,913	103,972
Balance Sheet								
Current Assets	535,000	1,304,000	1,353,000	546,494	1,314,550	1,188,396	520,875	458,882
Total Assets	13,482,000	13,591,000	13,319,000	12,119,326	12,641,876	11,799,963	9,591,164	8,589,437
Current Liabilities	810,000	766,000	780,000	753,186	596,420	1,427,193	756,868	740,086
Long-Term Obligations	2,738,000	2,741,000	2,741,000	2,740,580	3,332,188	3,517,320	3,630,421	3,101,103
Total Liabilities	4,851,000	4,862,000	4,787,000	4,496,633	5,699,325	6,519,175	5,833,215	5,123,241
Stockholders' Equity	8,631,000	8,729,000	8,532,000	7,622,693	6,942,551	5,280,788	3,757,949	3,466,196
Shares Outstanding	148,700	148,722	148,174	146,058	129,137	113,004	105,095	104,581
Statistical Record								
Return on Assets %	4.50	5.11	1.69	N.M.	0.54	5.03	2.76	5.58
Return on Equity %	7.13	8.55	2.83	N.M.	1.08	11.91	6.95	13.36
EBITDA Margin %	113.68	161.92	174.35	N.M.	18.35	77.15	58.12	77.87
Net Margin %	38.15	68.02	106.21	N.M.	3.65	20.23	10.82	23.72
Asset Turnover	0.19	0.17	0.16	0.13	0.15	0.25	0.26	0.24
Current Ratio	0.66	1.70	1.73	0.73	2.20	0.83	0.69	0.62
Debt to Equity	0.32	0.31	0.32	0.36	0.48	0.67	0.97	0.89
Price Range	144.46-108.05	144.46-113.88	144.46-97.48	143.25-72.52	128.31-86.67	148.00-83.01	120.72-80.14	113.43-77.80
P/E Ratio	36.57-27.35	33.29-26.24	112.86-76.16	...	237.61-160.50	30.33-17.01	50.51-33.53	27.33-18.75

Address: One Concho Center, 600 West Illinois Avenue, Midland, TX 79701
Telephone: 432-683-7443
Fax: 432-683-7441

Web Site: www.concho.com
Officers: Timothy A. Leach - Chairman, President, Chief Executive Officer Jack F. Harper - President, Chief Financial Officer, Executive Vice President, Treasurer, Senior Vice President, Chief of Staff

Auditors: Grant Thornton LLP
Investor Contact: 432-685-2533
Transfer Agents: American Stock Transfer & Trust Company, New York, NY

CONDUENT INC

Exchange	Symbol	Price	52Wk Range	Yield	P/E
NYS	CNDT	$16.16 (12/29/2017)	17.70-13.31	N/A	N/A

*7 Year Price Score N/A   *NYSE Composite Index=100   *12 Month Price Score 92.66

Interim Earnings (Per Share)

Qtr.	Mar	Jun	Sep	Dec
2016	(0.12)	(0.05)	0.00	(0.48)
2017	(0.04)	(0.03)	(0.09)	...

Interim Dividends (Per Share)

No Dividends Paid

Valuation Analysis   **Institutional Holding**

Forecast EPS	$0.79	No of Institutions
(11/20/2017)		338
Market Cap	$3.4 Billion	Shares
Book Value	$3.5 Billion	186,578,192
Price/Book	0.98	% Held
Price/Sales	0.56	N/A

TRADING VOLUME (thousand shares)

Business Summary: Business Services (MIC: 7.5.2 SIC: 7389 NAIC: 813910)

Conduent is a holding company. Through its subsidiaries, Co. is a provider of business process services in transaction-intensive processing, analytics and automation. Co.'s reportable segments are: Commercial Industries, which delivers end-to-end business-to-business and business-to-customer services including customer care, human resource management, finance and accounting, workforce learning services and legal business services; Healthcare, which provides services and solutions and subject matter personnel to providers, payers, pharmaceutical and life science companies and government agencies; and Public Sector, which provides government-centric business process services.

Recent Developments: For the quarter ended Sep 30 2017, loss from continuing operations was US$17.0 million compared with income of US$1.0 million in the year-earlier quarter. Net loss amounted to US$17.0 million versus net income of US$1.0 million in the year-earlier quarter. Revenues were US$1.48 billion, down 7.3% from US$1.60 billion the year before. Direct operating expenses declined 8.2% to US$1.22 billion from US$1.33 billion in the comparable period the year before. Indirect operating expenses decreased 6.8% to US$248.0 million from US$266.0 million in the equivalent prior-year period.

Prospects: Our evaluation of Conduent Inc. as of Jan. 14, 2018 is the result of our systematic analysis on three basic characteristics: earnings strength, relative valuation, and recent stock price movement. The company has suffered a very negative trend in earnings per share over the past 5 quarters and while recent estimates for the company have remained steady, CNDT has posted better than expected results. Based on operating earnings yield, the company is undervalued when compared to all of the companies in our coverage universe. Share price changes over the past year indicates that CNDT will perform poorly over the near term.

Financial Data
(US$ in Millions)

	9 Mos	6 Mos	3 Mos	12/31/2016	12/31/2015	12/31/2014	12/31/2013
Earnings Per Share	(4.84)	(4.75)	(4.77)	(4.85)	...	...	...
Cash Flow Per Share	1.03	1.21	0.59	0.53	...	...	...
Income Statement							
Total Revenue	4,529	3,049	1,553	6,408	6,662	6,938	6,879
EBITDA	92	41	16	(777)	(129)	523	709
Depn & Amortn	7	4	2	410	376	395	385
Income Before Taxes	(20)	(33)	(22)	(1,227)	(574)	10	207
Income Taxes	11	(19)	(12)	(244)	(238)	(24)	72
Net Income	(27)	(10)	(6)	(983)	(414)	(81)	182
Average Shares	204	203	203	202	...	...	...
Balance Sheet							
Current Assets	2,112	1,986	1,974	1,917	1,874	3,252	...
Total Assets	7,547	7,648	7,700	7,709	9,058	10,954	...
Current Liabilities	1,214	1,212	1,248	1,402	2,741	4,139	...
Long-Term Obligations	1,991	2,071	2,075	1,913	37	43	...
Total Liabilities	4,093	4,189	4,259	4,279	3,896	5,543	...
Stockholders' Equity	3,454	3,459	3,441	3,430	5,162	5,411	...
Shares Outstanding	210	209	203	202	...	...	...
Statistical Record							
EBITDA Margin %	2.03	1.34	1.03	N.M.	N.M.	7.54	10.31
Net Margin %	N.M.	N.M.	N.M.	N.M.	N.M.	N.M.	2.65
Asset Turnover	0.73	...	...	0.76	0.67	...	...
Current Ratio	1.74	1.64	1.58	1.37	0.68	0.79	...
Debt to Equity	0.58	0.60	0.60	0.56	0.01	0.01	...
Price Range	17.70-13.31	17.70-13.31	17.25-13.31	...	...	...	...

Address: 100 Campus Drive, Suite 200E, Florham Park, NJ 07932 **Telephone:** 844-663-2638	**Web Site:** www.conduent.com **Officers:** Ashok Vemuri - Chief Executive Officer Douglas H. Marshall - Secretary	**Auditors:** PricewaterhouseCoopers LLP **Transfer Agents:** Computershare Trust Company, N.A.

CONOCOPHILLIPS

Exchange	Symbol	Price	52Wk Range	Yield	P/E
NYS	COP	$54.89 (12/29/2017)	56.23-42.50	1.93	N/A

*7 Year Price Score 66.00 *NYSE Composite Index=100 *12 Month Price Score 102.97

Interim Earnings (Per Share)

Qtr.	Mar	Jun	Sep	Dec
2014	1.71	1.67	2.17	(0.03)
2015	0.22	(0.15)	(0.87)	(2.78)
2016	(1.18)	(0.86)	(0.84)	(0.03)
2017	0.47	(2.78)	0.34	

Interim Dividends (Per Share)

Amt	Decl	Ex	Rec	Pay
0.265Q	01/31/2017	02/10/2017	02/14/2017	03/01/2017
0.265Q	05/05/2017	05/11/2017	05/15/2017	06/01/2017
0.265Q	07/12/2017	07/20/2017	07/24/2017	09/01/2017
0.265Q	10/06/2017	10/13/2017	10/16/2017	12/01/2017

Indicated Div: $1.06 (Div. Reinv. Plan)

Valuation Analysis | **Institutional Holding**

Forecast EPS	$0.59	No of Institutions
	(01/18/2018)	1989
Market Cap	$65.5 Billion	Shares
Book Value	$30.5 Billion	1,071,484,224
Price/Book	2.15	% Held
Price/Sales	2.10	63.21

Business Summary: Production & Extraction (MIC: 9.1.1 SIC: 1311 NAIC: 211111)

ConocoPhillips explores for, produces, transports and markets crude oil, bitumen, natural gas, liquefied natural gas and natural gas liquids. Co. has six segments: Alaska, which operates in Alaska; Lower 48, which operates in the U.S. Lower 48 states and the Gulf of Mexico; Canada, which operates in western Canada and northeastern Alberta; Europe and North Africa, which has activities in Norway, the U.K. and Libya; Asia Pacific and Middle East, which has activities in China, Indonesia, Malaysia, Australia, Qatar, Timor-Leste and Brunei; and Other International, which has activities in Colombia and Chile. At Dec 31 2016, Co.'s proved reserves totaled 6.42 billion barrels of oil equivalent.

Recent Developments: For the quarter ended Sep 30 2017, net income amounted to US$436.0 million versus a net loss of US$1.03 billion in the year-earlier quarter. Revenues were US$7.20 billion, up 10.4% from US$6.52 billion the year before. Direct operating expenses declined 4.5% to US$4.15 billion from US$4.35 billion in the comparable period the year before. Indirect operating expenses decreased 37.5% to US$2.39 billion from US$3.83 billion in the equivalent prior-year period.

Prospects: Our evaluation of ConocoPhillips as of Jan. 14, 2018 is the result of our systematic analysis on three basic characteristics: earnings strength, relative valuation, and recent stock price movement. The company has generated a negative trend in earnings per share over the past 5 quarters and while recent estimates for the company have been raised by analysts, COP has posted better than expected results. Based on operating earnings yield, the company is overvalued when compared to all of the companies in our coverage universe. Share price changes over the past year indicates that COP will perform very poorly over the near term.

Financial Data

(US$ in Thousands)	9 Mos	6 Mos	3 Mos	12/31/2016	12/31/2015	12/31/2014	12/31/2013	12/31/2012
Earnings Per Share	(2.00)	(3.18)	(1.26)	(2.91)	(3.58)	5.51	7.38	6.72
Cash Flow Per Share	4.98	5.06	4.64	3.53	6.10	13.53	13.07	11.16
Tang Book Value Per Share	25.58	24.89	28.58	28.27	32.17	42.16	42.49	39.33
Dividends Per Share	1.045	1.030	1.015	1.000	2.940	2.840	2.700	2.640
Dividend Payout %	...	...	...	...	...	51.54	36.59	39.29
Income Statement								
Total Revenue	23,848,000	16,653,000	7,771,000	24,360,000	30,935,000	55,517,000	58,248,000	62,004,000
EBITDA	2,144,000	(368,000)	2,062,000	4,777,000	2,794,000	18,367,000	22,492,000	22,712,000
Depn & Amortn	5,212,000	3,604,000	1,979,000	9,062,000	9,113,000	8,329,000	7,434,000	6,580,000
Income Before Taxes	(3,940,000)	(4,593,000)	(232,000)	(5,530,000)	(7,239,000)	9,390,000	14,446,000	15,423,000
Income Taxes	(1,549,000)	(1,766,000)	(831,000)	(1,971,000)	(2,868,000)	3,583,000	6,409,000	7,942,000
Net Income	(2,434,000)	(2,854,000)	586,000	(3,615,000)	(4,428,000)	6,869,000	9,156,000	8,428,000
Average Shares	1,215,341	1,236,831	1,248,722	1,245,440	1,241,919	1,245,863	1,239,803	1,253,093
Balance Sheet								
Current Assets	16,954,000	19,879,000	10,728,000	8,609,000	8,789,000	15,068,000	19,023,000	23,989,000
Total Assets	74,861,000	78,004,000	87,973,000	89,772,000	97,484,000	116,539,000	118,057,000	117,144,000
Current Liabilities	7,131,000	9,926,000	7,526,000	6,909,000	9,256,000	11,537,000	15,129,000	17,443,000
Long-Term Obligations	19,673,000	19,670,000	25,340,000	26,186,000	23,453,000	22,383,000	21,073,000	20,770,000
Total Liabilities	44,361,000	47,718,000	52,620,000	54,798,000	57,722,000	64,628,000	65,967,000	69,157,000
Stockholders' Equity	30,500,000	30,286,000	35,353,000	34,974,000	39,762,000	51,911,000	52,090,000	47,987,000
Shares Outstanding	1,192,399	1,216,949	1,237,103	1,237,269	1,235,995	1,231,352	1,225,939	1,220,017
Statistical Record								
Return on Assets %	N.M.	N.M.	N.M.	N.M.	N.M.	5.86	7.79	6.22
Return on Equity %	N.M.	N.M.	N.M.	N.M.	N.M.	13.21	18.30	14.85
EBITDA Margin %	8.99	N.M.	26.53	19.61	9.03	33.08	38.61	36.63
Net Margin %	N.M.	N.M.	7.54	N.M.	N.M.	12.37	15.72	13.59
Asset Turnover	0.37	0.35	0.29	0.26	0.29	0.47	0.50	0.46
Current Ratio	2.38	2.00	1.43	1.25	0.95	1.31	1.26	1.38
Debt to Equity	0.65	0.65	0.72	0.75	0.59	0.43	0.40	0.43
Price Range	52.64-40.65	52.64-39.01	52.64-39.01	52.64-31.88	69.88-42.19	86.76-61.69	74.34-56.81	59.63-50.82
P/E Ratio	...	...	...	...	...	15.75-11.20	10.07-7.70	8.87-7.56
Average Yield %	2.25	2.26	2.26	2.35	5.05	3.83	4.24	4.71

Address: 600 North Dairy Ashford, Houston, TX 77079	Web Site: www.conocophillips.com	Auditors: Ernst & Young LLP
Telephone: 281-293-1000	Officers: Ryan M. Lance - Chairman, Chief Executive Officer, Division Officer Don E. Wallette - Executive Vice President, Chief Financial Officer, Executive Vice President (frmr)	Investor Contact: 212-207-1996
Fax: 281-661-7636		Transfer Agents: Computershare, Canton, MA

CONSOLIDATED EDISON INC

Exchange	Symbol	Price	52Wk Range	Yield	P/E	Div Achiever
NYS	ED	$84.95 (12/29/2017)	89.66-72.64	3.25	21.34	42 Years

*7 Year Price Score 99.27 *NYSE Composite Index=100 *12 Month Price Score 101.23

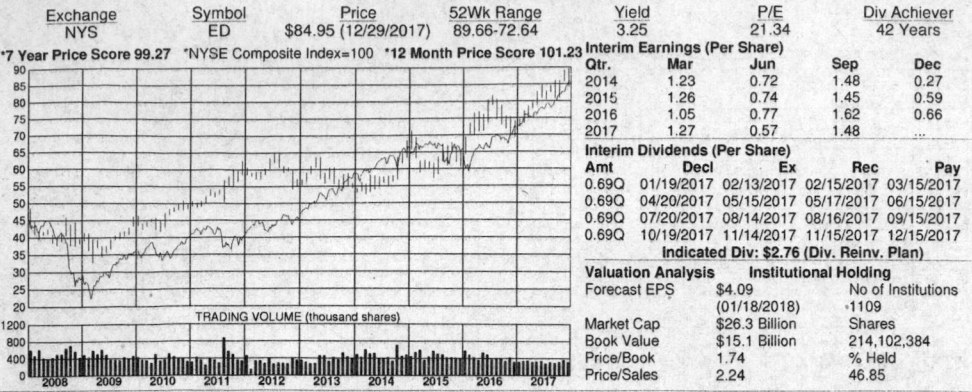

Interim Earnings (Per Share)

Qtr.	Mar	Jun	Sep	Dec
2014	1.23	0.72	1.48	0.27
2015	1.26	0.74	1.45	0.59
2016	1.05	0.77	1.62	0.66
2017	1.27	0.57	1.48	...

Interim Dividends (Per Share)

Amt	Decl	Ex	Rec	Pay
0.69Q	01/19/2017	02/13/2017	02/15/2017	03/15/2017
0.69Q	04/20/2017	05/15/2017	05/17/2017	06/15/2017
0.69Q	07/20/2017	08/14/2017	08/16/2017	09/15/2017
0.69Q	10/19/2017	11/14/2017	11/15/2017	12/15/2017

Indicated Div: $2.76 (Div. Reinv. Plan)

Valuation Analysis — **Institutional Holding**

Forecast EPS	$4.09
	(01/18/2018)
Market Cap	$26.3 Billion
Book Value	$15.1 Billion
Price/Book	1.74
Price/Sales	2.24

No of Institutions ·1109
Shares 214,102,384
% Held 46.85

TRADING VOLUME (thousand shares)

Business Summary: Electric Utilities (MIC: 3.1.1 SIC: 4931 NAIC: 221121)

Consolidated Edison is a holding company. Co. owns Consolidated Edison Company of New York, Inc., which at Dec 31 2016, provided electricity, gas and steam to about 3.4 million customers in New York City and Westchester County, 1.1 million customers in Manhattan, the Bronx, Queens and Westchester County, and 1,649 customers in Manhattan, respectively. Co. also owns Orange and Rockland Utilities, Inc., which delivers electricity and natural gas to customers in southeastern New York and northern New Jersey; The Clean Energy Businesses, which develop, own and operate renewable and energy infrastructure projects; and Consolidated Edison Transmission, LLC, which invests in transmission projects.

Recent Developments: For the quarter ended Sep 30 2017, net income decreased 8.0% to US$457.0 million from US$497.0 million in the year-earlier quarter. Revenues were US$3.21 billion, down 6.0% from US$3.42 billion the year before. Operating income was US$873.0 million versus US$940.0 million in the prior-year quarter, a decrease of 7.1%. Direct operating expenses declined 16.6% to US$1.46 billion from US$1.75 billion in the comparable period the year before. Indirect operating expenses increased 20.9% to US$881.0 million from US$729.0 million in the equivalent prior-year period.

Prospects: Our evaluation of Consolidated Edison Inc. as of Jan. 14, 2018 is the result of our systematic analysis on three basic characteristics: earnings strength, relative valuation, and recent stock price movement. The company has managed to produce a neutral trend in earnings per share over the past 5 quarters and while recent estimates for the company have remained steady, ED has posted results that fell short of analysts expectations. Based on operating earnings yield, the company is undervalued when compared to all of the companies in our coverage universe. Share price changes over the past year indicates that ED will perform very well over the near term.

Financial Data

(US$ in Thousands)	9 Mos	6 Mos	3 Mos	12/31/2016	12/31/2015	12/31/2014	12/31/2013	12/31/2012
Earnings Per Share	3.98	4.12	4.32	4.12	4.05	3.71	3.61	3.86
Cash Flow Per Share	10.88	11.14	11.09	11.48	11.18	9.67	8.71	8.85
Tang Book Value Per Share	46.97	45.58	45.73	45.07	43.08	41.46	40.33	39.05
Dividends Per Share	2.740	2.720	2.700	2.680	2.600	2.520	2.460	2.420
Dividend Payout %	68.84	66.02	62.50	65.05	64.20	67.92	68.14	62.69
Income Statement								
Total Revenue	9,072,000	5,861,000	3,228,000	12,075,000	12,554,000	12,919,000	12,354,000	12,188,000
EBITDA	2,071,000	1,191,000	765,000	3,645,000	3,529,000	3,424,000	3,291,000	3,342,000
Depn & Amortn	(93,000)	(62,000)	(31,000)	1,006,000	1,078,000	1,173,000	1,034,000	997,000
Income Before Taxes	1,619,000	893,000	615,000	1,943,000	1,798,000	1,660,000	1,538,000	1,741,000
Income Taxes	599,000	330,000	227,000	698,000	605,000	568,000	476,000	600,000
Net Income	1,020,000	563,000	388,000	1,245,000	1,193,000	1,092,000	1,062,000	1,141,000
Average Shares	309,300	306,800	306,300	301,900	294,400	294,000	294,400	294,500
Balance Sheet								
Current Assets	3,096,000	3,280,000	3,017,000	3,406,000	3,836,000	3,854,000	3,891,000	3,451,000
Total Assets	49,246,000	49,099,000	48,365,000	48,255,000	45,642,000	44,308,000	40,647,000	41,209,000
Current Liabilities	3,915,000	4,329,000	3,441,000	3,843,000	4,720,000	3,781,000	4,730,000	3,945,000
Long-Term Obligations	14,651,000	14,703,000	14,829,000	14,735,000	12,006,000	11,631,000	10,490,000	10,064,000
Total Liabilities	34,144,000	34,609,000	33,867,000	33,957,000	32,590,000	31,732,000	28,402,000	29,340,000
Stockholders' Equity	15,102,000	14,490,000	14,498,000	14,298,000	13,052,000	12,576,000	12,245,000	11,869,000
Shares Outstanding	310,000	306,000	305,000	305,000	293,000	292,876	292,872	292,871
Statistical Record								
Return on Assets %	2.54	2.63	2.82	2.64	2.65	2.57	2.59	2.83
Return on Equity %	8.35	8.90	9.56	9.08	9.31	8.80	8.81	9.68
EBITDA Margin %	22.83	20.32	23.70	30.19	28.11	26.50	26.64	27.42
Net Margin %	11.24	9.61	12.02	10.31	9.50	8.45	8.60	9.36
Asset Turnover	0.24	0.25	0.26	0.26	0.28	0.30	0.30	0.30
Current Ratio	0.79	0.76	0.88	0.89	0.81	1.02	0.82	0.87
Debt to Equity	0.97	1.01	1.02	1.03	0.92	0.92	0.86	0.85
Price Range	86.05-69.15	84.96-69.15	81.67-69.15	81.67-64.27	71.40-57.21	68.50-52.46	63.66-54.33	64.94-54.10
P/E Ratio	21.62-17.37	20.62-16.78	18.91-16.01	19.82-15.60	17.63-14.13	18.46-14.14	17.63-15.05	16.82-14.02
Average Yield %	3.52	3.55	3.60	3.62	4.11	4.39	4.25	4.07

Address: 4 Irving Place, New York, NY 10003	**Web Site:** www.conedison.com	**Auditors:** PricewaterhouseCoopers LLP
Telephone: 212-460-4600	**Officers:** John McAvoy - Chairman, President, Chief Executive Officer Elizabeth D. Moore - Senior Vice President, General Counsel	**Investor Contact:** 212-460-6611 **Transfer Agents:** Computershare, Pittsburgh, PA

CONSTELLATION BRANDS INC

Exchange	Symbol	Price	52Wk Range	Yield	P/E
NYS	STZ	$228.57 (12/29/2017)	228.57-146.75	0.91	24.93

*7 Year Price Score 156.93 *NYSE Composite Index=100 *12 Month Price Score 111.12

Interim Earnings (Per Share)

Qtr.	May	Aug	Nov	Feb
2014-15	1.03	0.98	1.10	1.06
2015-16	1.18	1.49	1.33	1.19
2016-17	1.55	1.75	1.98	2.25
2017-18	2.00	2.48	2.44	...

Interim Dividends (Per Share)

Amt	Decl	Ex	Rec	Pay
0.52Q	04/05/2017	05/08/2017	05/10/2017	05/24/2017
0.52Q	06/28/2017	08/07/2017	08/09/2017	08/23/2017
0.52Q	10/04/2017	11/06/2017	11/07/2017	11/21/2017
0.52Q	01/04/2018	02/08/2018	02/09/2018	02/23/2018

Indicated Div: $2.08

Valuation Analysis — **Institutional Holding**

Forecast EPS	$8.55
(01/18/2018)	No of Institutions 1056
Market Cap	$44.5 Billion
Book Value	$8.0 Billion
Shares	186,708,352
Price/Book	5.57
% Held	76.09
Price/Sales	5.98

Business Summary: Beverages (MIC: 1.2.2 SIC: 2084 NAIC: 312130)

Constellation Brands is an international beverage alcohol company. Co. produces and markets beer, wine and spirits with operations in the U.S., Mexico, New Zealand, Italy and Canada. Co. has two business divisions: Beer, which import, market and sells in the U.S. Mexican Beer brands in the import category and sells Ballast Point brand in the craft beer category; and Wine and Spirits, which sells a number of wine brands across all categories, such as table wine, sparkling wine and dessert wine, across popular, premium and luxury categories, complemented by certain premium spirits brands.

Recent Developments: For the quarter ended Nov 30 2017, net income increased 22.1% to US$494.7 million from US$405.0 million in the year-earlier quarter. Revenues were US$1.80 billion, down 0.6% from US$1.81 billion the year before. Operating income was US$486.8 million versus US$534.0 million in the prior-year quarter, a decrease of 8.8%. Direct operating expenses declined 3.0% to US$891.6 million from US$919.1 million in the comparable period the year before. Indirect operating expenses increased 17.7% to US$420.7 million from US$357.4 million in the equivalent prior-year period.

Prospects: Our evaluation of Constellation Brands Inc. as of Jan. 14, 2018 is the result of our systematic analysis on three basic characteristics: earnings strength, relative valuation, and recent stock price movement. The company has generated a negative trend in earnings per share over the past 5 quarters and while recent estimates for the company have been raised by analysts, STZ has posted better than expected results. Based on operating earnings yield, the company is about fairly valued when compared to all of the companies in our coverage universe. Share price changes over the past year indicates that STZ will perform very well over the near term.

Financial Data
(US$ in Thousands)

	9 Mos	6 Mos	3 Mos	02/28/2017	02/29/2016	02/28/2015	02/28/2014	02/28/2013
Earnings Per Share	9.17	8.71	7.98	7.52	5.18	4.17	9.83	2.04
Cash Flow Per Share	8.96	8.98	8.89	8.51	7.17	5.61	4.39	3.05
Dividends Per Share	1.960	1.840	1.720	1.600	1.240	...	...	...
Dividend Payout %	21.37	21.13	21.55	21.28	23.94	...	...	...
Income Statement								
Total Revenue	5,819,100	4,020,000	1,935,500	7,331,500	6,548,400	6,028,000	4,867,700	2,796,100
EBITDA	2,082,900	1,518,200	721,800	2,693,300	1,985,000	1,697,800	2,593,000	625,800
Depn & Amortn	333,200	245,000	160,400	293,900	221,000	202,000	155,300	115,400
Income Before Taxes	1,504,600	1,109,500	479,000	2,066,100	1,450,100	1,158,100	2,114,500	283,300
Income Taxes	352,300	202,800	74,100	554,200	440,600	343,400	259,200	128,600
Net Income	1,393,400	902,300	402,800	1,535,100	1,054,900	839,300	1,943,100	387,800
Average Shares	201,177	201,346	201,030	204,099	203,821	201,224	197,570	190,307
Balance Sheet								
Current Assets	3,545,600	3,373,400	3,360,500	3,230,000	2,977,600	2,910,800	2,747,200	2,471,200
Total Assets	20,107,100	19,418,400	18,959,400	18,602,400	16,965,000	15,144,500	14,302,100	7,638,100
Current Liabilities	2,535,900	2,090,000	2,182,400	2,697,600	2,272,300	1,130,700	2,025,700	677,900
Long-Term Obligations	8,114,200	8,036,900	8,077,200	7,720,700	6,816,200	7,137,500	6,373,300	3,277,800
Total Liabilities	12,113,200	11,490,300	11,569,700	11,711,200	10,405,400	9,373,800	9,320,800	4,777,800
Stockholders' Equity	7,993,900	7,928,100	7,389,700	6,891,200	6,559,600	5,770,700	4,981,300	2,860,300
Shares Outstanding	194,704	195,576	195,266	194,598	199,458	194,541	191,470	184,776
Statistical Record								
Return on Assets %	9.60	9.48	8.85	8.63	6.55	5.70	17.71	5.26
Return on Equity %	24.59	23.30	22.75	22.83	17.06	15.61	49.56	14.01
EBITDA Margin %	35.79	37.77	37.29	36.74	30.31	28.17	53.27	22.38
Net Margin %	23.95	22.45	20.81	20.94	16.11	13.92	39.92	13.87
Asset Turnover	0.39	0.40	0.40	0.41	0.41	0.41	0.44	0.38
Current Ratio	1.40	1.61	1.54	1.20	1.31	2.57	1.36	3.65
Debt to Equity	1.02	1.01	1.09	1.12	1.04	1.24	1.28	1.15
Price Range	221.88-145.34	200.10-145.34	184.14-145.34	171.24-138.71	154.36-110.91	115.78-77.97	82.07-43.25	44.71-18.69
P/E Ratio	24.20-15.85	22.97-16.69	23.08-18.21	22.77-18.45	29.80-21.41	27.76-18.70	8.35-4.40	21.92-9.16
Average Yield %	1.08	1.08	1.08	1.01	0.97	...	...	...

Address: 207 High Point Drive, Building 100, Victor, NY 14564	**Web Site:** www.cbrands.com	**Auditors:** KPMG LLP
Telephone: 585-678-7100	**Officers:** Richard Sands - Chairman Robert Sands - President, Chief Executive Officer	**Investor Contact:** 585-678-7483
		Transfer Agents: Computershare Shareowner Services, College Station, TX

CONTINENTAL RESOURCES INC.

Exchange NYS	Symbol CLR	Price $52.97 (12/29/2017)	52Wk Range 53.41-30.03	Yield N/A	P/E N/A

*7 Year Price Score 75.53   *NYSE Composite Index=100   *12 Month Price Score 107.75

Interim Earnings (Per Share)

Qtr.	Mar	Jun	Sep	Dec
2014	0.61	0.28	1.44	0.31
2015	(0.36)	0.00	(0.22)	(0.38)
2016	(0.54)	(0.32)	(0.30)	0.07
2017	0.00	(0.17)	0.03	...

Interim Dividends (Per Share)

No Dividends Paid

Valuation Analysis   Institutional Holding

Forecast EPS	$0.37	No of Institutions
	(01/18/2018)	505
Market Cap	$19.9 Billion	Shares
Book Value	$4.3 Billion	95,667,904
Price/Book	4.65	% Held
Price/Sales	7.58	24.79

Business Summary: Production & Extraction (MIC: 9.1.1 SIC: 1311 NAIC: 211111)

Continental Resources is an independent crude oil and natural gas company with properties in the North, South and East regions of the U.S. The North region consists of properties north of Kansas and west of the Mississippi River and includes North Dakota Bakken, Montana Bakken, and the Red River units. The South region includes all properties south of Nebraska and west of the Mississippi River including various plays in the South Central Oklahoma Oil Province, Sooner Trend Anadarko Canadian Kingfisher, and Arkoma Woodford areas of Oklahoma. As of Dec 31 2016, Co.'s estimated proved reserves were 1,275 million barrels of crude oil equivalent.

Recent Developments: For the quarter ended Sep 30 2017, net income amounted to US$10.6 million versus a net loss of US$109.6 million in the year-earlier quarter. Revenues were US$726.7 million, up 38.1% from US$526.2 million the year before. Operating income was US$91.8 million versus a loss of US$93.2 million in the prior-year quarter. Direct operating expenses rose 33.5% to US$139.1 million from US$104.2 million in the comparable period the year before. Indirect operating expenses decreased 3.7% to US$495.9 million from US$515.2 million in the equivalent prior-year period.

Prospects: Our evaluation of Continental Resources Inc. as of Jan. 14, 2018 is the result of our systematic analysis on three basic characteristics: earnings strength, relative valuation, and recent stock price movement. The company has generated a negative trend in earnings per share over the past 5 quarters and while recent estimates for the company have been raised by analysts, CLR has posted better than expected results. Based on operating earnings yield, the company is overvalued when compared to all of the companies in our coverage universe. Share price changes over the past year indicates that CLR will perform very poorly over the near term.

Financial Data

(US$ in Thousands)	9 Mos	6 Mos	3 Mos	12/31/2016	12/31/2015	12/31/2014	12/31/2013	12/31/2012
Earnings Per Share	(0.07)	(0.40)	(0.55)	(1.08)	(0.96)	2.64	2.06	2.04
Cash Flow Per Share	4.34	4.16	3.55	3.03	5.03	9.10	6.96	4.49
Tang Book Value Per Share	11.40	11.34	11.48	11.49	12.52	13.35	10.65	8.52
Income Statement								
Total Revenue	2,073,657	1,346,914	685,427	1,980,273	2,680,167	4,801,618	3,455,150	2,572,520
EBITDA	1,340,857	823,805	459,048	1,397,675	1,524,448	3,214,277	2,413,761	1,990,602
Depn & Amortn	1,199,715	774,810	381,385	1,709,567	1,746,454	1,368,311	965,437	694,698
Income Before Taxes	(77,530)	(94,921)	6,491	(632,454)	(535,085)	1,562,038	1,213,049	1,155,196
Income Taxes	(25,063)	(31,833)	6,022	(232,775)	(181,417)	584,697	448,830	415,811
Net Income	(52,467)	(63,088)	469	(399,679)	(353,668)	977,341	764,219	739,385
Average Shares	373,015	371,111	373,353	370,380	369,540	370,758	369,698	363,692
Balance Sheet								
Current Assets	1,060,975	934,042	929,506	913,233	822,339	1,389,601	1,147,266	946,783
Total Assets	13,995,087	13,871,257	13,826,060	13,811,776	14,919,808	15,145,070	11,941,182	9,140,009
Current Liabilities	1,129,459	1,094,978	1,005,321	932,393	923,028	1,952,013	1,473,156	1,125,865
Long-Term Obligations	6,612,281	6,553,740	6,508,209	6,577,697	7,115,644	5,995,837	4,713,821	3,537,771
Total Liabilities	9,718,308	9,616,922	9,516,706	9,509,780	10,250,908	10,177,226	7,988,064	5,976,310
Stockholders' Equity	4,276,779	4,254,335	4,309,354	4,301,996	4,668,900	4,967,844	3,953,118	3,163,699
Shares Outstanding	375,196	375,206	375,321	374,492	372,959	372,005	371,317	371,209
Statistical Record								
Return on Assets %	N.M.	N.M.	N.M.	N.M.	N.M.	7.22	7.25	9.97
Return on Equity %	N.M.	N.M.	N.M.	N.M.	N.M.	21.91	21.48	26.95
EBITDA Margin %	64.66	61.16	66.97	70.58	56.88	66.94	69.86	77.38
Net Margin %	N.M.	N.M.	0.07	N.M.	N.M.	20.35	22.12	28.74
Asset Turnover	0.19	0.17	0.16	0.14	0.18	0.35	0.33	0.35
Current Ratio	0.94	0.85	0.92	0.98	0.89	0.71	0.78	0.84
Debt to Equity	1.55	1.54	1.51	1.53	1.52	1.21	1.19	1.12
Price Range	58.01-30.03	58.01-30.39	58.01-29.18	58.01-16.04	52.63-20.00	80.64-30.95	60.50-36.53	47.47-31.29
P/E Ratio	...	...	...	...	...	30.55-11.72	29.37-17.74	23.27-15.34

Address: 20 N. Broadway, Oklahoma City, OK 73102 Telephone: 405-234-9000	Web Site: www.clr.com Officers: Harold G. Hamm - Chairman, Chief Executive Officer Jeffrey B. Hume - Vice-Chairman, President, Chief Operating Officer	Auditors: Grant Thornton LLP Investor Contact: 405-234-9127 Transfer Agents: American Stock Transfer & Trust Company, New York

CONVERGYS CORP

Exchange	Symbol	Price	52Wk Range	Yield	P/E
NYS	CVG	$23.50 (12/29/2017)	26.65-20.33	1.70	17.80

*7 Year Price Score 93.24 ***NYSE Composite Index=100** ***12 Month Price Score 95.76**

TRADING VOLUME (thousand shares)

Interim Earnings (Per Share)

Qtr.	Mar	Jun	Sep	Dec
2014	0.13	0.23	0.31	0.45
2015	0.37	0.28	0.56	0.40
2016	0.43	0.32	0.46	0.19
2017	0.38	0.40	0.35	...

Interim Dividends (Per Share)

Amt	Decl	Ex	Rec	Pay
0.09Q	02/21/2017	03/22/2017	03/24/2017	04/07/2017
0.10Q	05/08/2017	06/21/2017	06/23/2017	07/07/2017
0.10Q	08/08/2017	00/21/2017	09/22/2017	10/06/2017
0.10Q	11/07/2017	12/21/2017	12/22/2017	01/05/2018

Indicated Div: $0.40

Valuation Analysis

		Institutional Holding	
Forecast EPS	$1.86	No of Institutions	
	(11/20/2017)	384	
Market Cap	$2.2 Billion	Shares	
Book Value	$1.4 Billion	117,755,168	
Price/Book	1.57	% Held	
Price/Sales	0.76	84.39	

Business Summary: IT Services (MIC: 6.3.1 SIC: 7373 NAIC: 541512)

Convergys is a provider of integrated agent, analytics and technology solutions. Co.'s contact center technology solutions include: multichannel interaction solutions; cross-channel integration framework; real-time decisioning engine; robotic process automation; intelligent notifications; campaign management; personalized care; personalized selling; agent productivity; and retention. Co.'s team delivers data-driven insights to enhance customer experience through analytics and consulting, and software solutions, including integrated customer experience analytics and Voice of Customer SaaS software for measuring customer satisfaction. As of Dec 31 2016, Co. operated 149 contact centers.

Recent Developments: For the quarter ended Sep 30 2017, income from continuing operations decreased 7.7% to US$34.8 million from US$37.7 million in the year-earlier quarter. Net income decreased 27.0% to US$34.8 million from US$47.7 million in the year-earlier quarter. Revenues were US$688.3 million, down 7.1% from US$741.2 million the year before. Operating income was US$48.1 million versus US$50.6 million in the prior-year quarter, a decrease of 4.9%. Direct operating expenses declined 10.8% to US$428.1 million from US$479.8 million in the comparable period the year before. Indirect operating expenses increased 0.6% to US$212.1 million from US$210.8 million in the equivalent prior-year period.

Prospects: Our evaluation of Convergys Corp. as of Jan. 14, 2018 is the result of our systematic analysis on three basic characteristics: earnings strength, relative valuation, and recent stock price movement. The company has managed to produce a neutral trend in earnings per share over the past 5 quarters and while recent estimates for the company have remained steady, CVG has posted results that fell short of analysts expectations. Based on operating earnings yield, the company is undervalued when compared to all of the companies in our coverage universe. Share price changes over the past year indicates that CVG will perform well over the near term.

Financial Data

(US$ in Thousands)	9 Mos	6 Mos	3 Mos	12/31/2016	12/31/2015	12/31/2014	12/31/2013	12/31/2012
Earnings Per Share	1.32	1.43	1.35	1.40	1.61	1.13	0.56	0.86
Cash Flow Per Share	2.74	2.90	2.77	3.18	2.54	2.59	2.03	1.00
Tang Book Value Per Share	1.63	1.45	1.23	0.97	1.32	0.21	6.74	7.32
Dividends Per Share	0.380	0.370	0.360	0.350	0.310	0.270	0.240	0.150
Dividend Payout %	28.79	25.87	26.67	25.00	19.25	23.89	42.86	17.44
Income Statement								
Total Revenue	2,102,800	1,414,400	727,600	2,913,600	2,950,600	2,855,500	2,046,100	2,005,000
EBITDA	227,600	155,000	77,500	326,200	336,700	291,500	228,000	125,300
Depn & Amortn	80,600	54,500	27,400	122,200	141,500	142,900	85,500	82,400
Income Before Taxes	133,000	90,900	44,800	185,900	177,000	129,300	131,000	29,300
Income Taxes	20,500	13,200	6,900	52,900	8,600	12,800	72,500	1,100
Net Income	112,500	77,700	37,900	143,000	169,000	120,000	60,900	100,600
Average Shares	99,800	100,100	100,500	102,500	104,700	106,200	109,200	117,100
Balance Sheet								
Current Assets	819,000	820,200	824,100	784,800	823,400	890,900	1,060,400	1,100,600
Total Assets	2,387,400	2,405,200	2,401,100	2,371,800	2,358,100	2,516,500	1,956,700	2,037,900
Current Liabilities	315,000	330,100	307,200	347,600	338,400	368,500	292,600	286,500
Long-Term Obligations	279,200	288,800	343,300	297,000	337,400	368,400	60,200	59,900
Total Liabilities	1,007,500	1,041,600	1,065,500	1,055,900	1,081,900	1,289,300	667,100	666,000
Stockholders' Equity	1,379,900	1,363,600	1,335,600	1,315,900	1,276,200	1,227,200	1,289,600	1,371,900
Shares Outstanding	92,400	93,300	94,126	94,700	96,800	99,400	100,800	105,900
Statistical Record								
Return on Assets %	5.44	6.00	5.70	6.03	6.93	5.37	3.05	4.60
Return on Equity %	9.55	10.65	10.25	11.00	13.50	9.54	4.58	7.21
EBITDA Margin %	10.82	10.96	10.65	11.20	11.41	10.21	11.14	6.25
Net Margin %	5.35	5.49	5.21	4.91	5.73	4.20	2.98	5.02
Asset Turnover	1.20	1.22	1.22	1.23	1.21	1.28	1.02	0.92
Current Ratio	2.60	2.48	2.68	2.26	2.43	2.42	3.62	3.84
Debt to Equity	0.20	0.21	0.26	0.23	0.26	0.30	0.05	0.04
Price Range	30.42-20.33	30.78-20.33	30.78-20.33	30.78-22.83	26.47-19.16	22.60-17.45	21.22-15.88	16.83-12.19
P/E Ratio	23.05-15.40	21.52-14.22	22.80-15.06	21.99-16.31	16.44-11.90	20.00-15.44	37.89-28.36	19.57-14.17
Average Yield %	1.55	1.45	1.36	1.30	1.31	1.32	1.32	1.03

Address: 201 East Fourth Street, Cincinnati, OH 45202	**Web Site:** www.convergys.com	**Auditors:** Ernst & Young LLP
Telephone: 513-723-7000	**Officers:** Andrea J. Ayers - President, Chief Executive Officer, Division Officer Julia A. Houston - Senior Vice President, General Counsel, Corporate Secretary	**Investor Contact:** 513-723-7000 **Transfer Agents:** ComputerShare Investment Services, LLC, Canto

COOPER COMPANIES, INC. (THE)

Exchange	Symbol	Price	52Wk Range	Yield	P/E
NYS	COO	$217.88 (12/29/2017)	254.90-175.15	0.03	28.97

*7 Year Price Score 125.17 *NYSE Composite Index=100 *12 Month Price Score 99.00

Interim Earnings (Per Share)

Qtr.	Jan	Apr	Jul	Oct
2012-13	1.50	1.52	1.79	1.15
2013-14	1.47	1.62	1.80	0.62
2014-15	1.25	1.23	0.91	0.75
2015-16	1.05	1.52	1.79	1.23
2016-17	1.53	2.12	2.09	1.78

Interim Dividends (Per Share)

Amt	Decl	Ex	Rec	Pay
0.03S	07/07/2016	07/20/2016	07/22/2016	08/05/2016
0.03S	01/05/2017	01/19/2017	01/23/2017	02/09/2017
0.03S	07/06/2017	07/19/2017	07/21/2017	08/07/2017
0.03S	01/04/2018	01/22/2018	01/23/2018	02/09/2018

Indicated Div: $0.06

Valuation Analysis — **Institutional Holding**

Forecast EPS	$11.51	No of Institutions
(01/18/2018)		623
Market Cap	$10.6 Billion	Shares
Book Value	$3.2 Billion	60,521,832
Price/Book	3.35	% Held
Price/Sales	4.97	97.01

Business Summary: Medical Instruments & Equipment (MIC: 4.3.1 SIC: 3851 NAIC: 339115)

Cooper Companies is a medical device company. Co. operates through two business units, CooperVision, Inc. (CooperVision) and CooperSurgical, Inc. (CooperSurgical). CooperVision develops, manufactures and markets a range of soft contact lenses including single-use spherical, toric and multifocal lenses under Co.'s clariti 1day brand and a single-use silicone hydrogel spherical lens under MyDay®. CooperSurgical develops, manufactures and markets medical devices and procedure solutions to improve healthcare delivery to women with products in three categories: hospitals, obstetricians and gynecologists medical offices and fertility clinics.

Recent Developments: For the year ended Oct 31 2017, net income increased 35.6% to US$372.9 million from US$274.9 million in the prior year. Revenues were US$2.14 billion, up 8.8% from US$1.97 billion the year before. Operating income was US$429.1 million versus US$324.1 million in the prior year, an increase of 32.4%. Direct operating expenses declined 2.6% to US$773.2 million from US$793.7 million in the comparable period the year before. Indirect operating expenses increased 10.3% to US$936.7 million from US$849.0 million in the equivalent prior-year period.

Prospects: Our evaluation of Cooper Companies Inc. as of Jan. 14, 2018 is the result of our systematic analysis on three basic characteristics: earnings strength, relative valuation, and recent stock price movement. The company has managed to produce a neutral trend in earnings per share over the past 5 quarters and while recent estimates for the company have been raised by analysts, COO has posted better than expected results. Based on operating earnings yield, the company is about fairly valued when compared to all of the companies in our coverage universe. Share price changes over the past year indicates that COO will perform very well over the near term.

Financial Data

(US$ in Thousands)	10/31/2017	10/31/2016	10/31/2015	10/31/2014	10/31/2013	10/31/2012	10/31/2011	10/31/2010
Earnings Per Share	7.52	5.59	4.14	5.51	5.96	5.05	3.63	2.43
Cash Flow Per Share	12.14	10.47	8.07	9.46	8.56	6.56	7.17	5.88
Tang Book Value Per Share	6.48	1.93	1.23	N.M.	17.05	12.55	11.13	6.34
Dividends Per Share	0.060	0.060	0.060	0.060	0.060	0.060	0.060	0.060
Dividend Payout %	0.80	1.07	1.45	1.09	1.01	1.19	1.65	2.47
Income Statement								
Total Revenue	2,139,000	1,966,814	1,797,060	1,717,776	1,587,725	1,445,136	1,330,835	1,158,517
EBITDA	495,800	382,613	380,147	442,700	446,788	398,437	308,255	255,095
Depn & Amortn	68,400	60,790	146,559	138,201	125,349	111,214	98,149	94,001
Income Before Taxes	394,000	295,633	215,485	296,534	312,271	275,452	192,764	124,426
Income Taxes	21,100	20,699	10,341	24,705	15,365	26,808	17,334	11,623
Net Income	372,900	273,917	203,523	269,856	296,151	248,339	175,430	112,803
Average Shares	49,600	49,026	49,179	48,960	49,685	49,152	48,309	46,505
Balance Sheet								
Current Assets	953,200	934,458	841,818	791,617	747,241	657,860	540,347	491,340
Total Assets	4,858,700	4,475,918	4,460,610	4,458,340	3,137,261	2,941,384	2,624,518	2,525,018
Current Liabilities	396,100	536,455	569,172	442,182	321,253	262,552	267,206	199,520
Long-Term Obligations	1,149,300	1,107,448	1,105,764	1,280,833	301,670	348,422	327,453	591,977
Total Liabilities	1,683,000	1,776,051	1,793,101	1,888,462	732,726	748,633	687,030	858,242
Stockholders' Equity	3,175,700	2,699,867	2,667,509	2,569,878	2,404,535	2,192,751	1,937,488	1,666,776
Shares Outstanding	48,800	48,785	48,268	48,143	47,995	48,440	47,846	45,827
Statistical Record								
Return on Assets %	7.99	6.11	4.56	7.11	9.74	8.90	6.81	4.44
Return on Equity %	12.69	10.18	7.77	10.85	12.88	11.99	9.73	7.03
EBITDA Margin %	23.18	19.45	21.15	25.77	28.14	27.57	23.16	22.02
Net Margin %	17.43	13.93	11.33	15.71	18.65	17.18	13.18	9.74
Asset Turnover	0.46	0.44	0.40	0.45	0.52	0.52	0.52	0.46
Current Ratio	2.41	1.74	1.48	1.79	2.33	2.51	2.02	2.46
Debt to Equity	0.36	0.41	0.41	0.50	0.13	0.16	0.17	0.36
Price Range	254.90-159.50	189.90-121.01	189.09-137.62	164.29-117.30	134.97-89.40	100.67-56.64	83.00-48.98	50.82-28.45
P/E Ratio	33.90-21.21	33.97-21.65	45.67-33.24	29.82-21.29	22.65-15.00	19.93-11.22	22.87-13.49	20.91-11.71
Average Yield %	0.03	0.04	0.04	0.04	0.05	0.04	0.08	0.15

Address: 6140 Stoneridge Mall Road, Suite 590, Pleasanton, CA 94588	Web Site: www.coopercos.com	Auditors: KPMG LLP
Telephone: 925-460-3600	Officers: A. Thomas Bender - Chairman Agostino Ricupati - Chief Accounting Officer	Investor Contact: 925-460-3663
Fax: 925-460-3648		Transfer Agents: American Stock Transfer & Trust Company, New York, NY

COOPER TIRE & RUBBER CO.

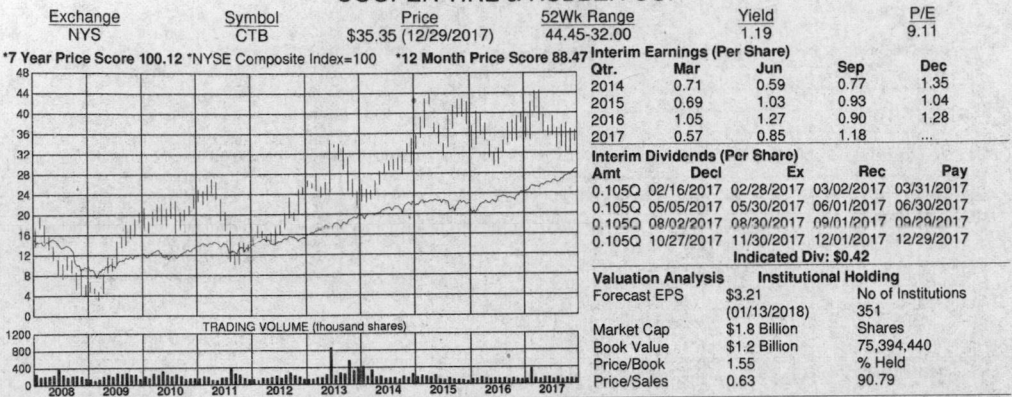

Exchange	Symbol	Price	52Wk Range	Yield	P/E
NYS	CTB	$35.35 (12/29/2017)	44.45-32.00	1.19	9.11

*7 Year Price Score 100.12 *NYSE Composite Index=100 *12 Month Price Score 88.47

Interim Earnings (Per Share)

Qtr.	Mar	Jun	Sep	Dec
2014	0.71	0.59	0.77	1.35
2015	0.69	1.03	0.93	1.04
2016	1.05	1.27	0.90	1.28
2017	0.57	0.85	1.18	...

Interim Dividends (Per Share)

Amt	Decl	Ex	Rec	Pay
0.105Q	02/16/2017	02/28/2017	03/02/2017	03/31/2017
0.105Q	05/05/2017	05/30/2017	06/01/2017	06/30/2017
0.105Q	08/02/2017	08/30/2017	09/01/2017	09/29/2017
0.105Q	10/27/2017	11/30/2017	12/01/2017	12/29/2017

Indicated Div: $0.42

Valuation Analysis   **Institutional Holding**

Forecast EPS	$3.21	No of Institutions
	(01/13/2018)	351
Market Cap	$1.8 Billion	Shares
Book Value	$1.2 Billion	75,394,440
Price/Book	1.55	% Held
Price/Sales	0.63	90.79

TRADING VOLUME (thousand shares)

Business Summary: Auto Parts (MIC: 1.8.2 SIC: 3011 NAIC: 326211)

Cooper Tire & Rubber is a manufacturer and marketer of replacement tires. In its Americas Tire Operations segment, Co. manufactures and markets passenger car and light truck tires, primarily for sale in the U.S. replacement market, and also supplies passenger car tires to the U.S., Mexican, Central American and South American markets. In its International Tire Operations segment, Co.'s U.K. entity manufactures and markets passenger car, light truck, motorcycle and racing tires and tire retread material for the domestic and global markets, and its Serbian entity manufactures light vehicle tires primarily for the European markets and for export.

Recent Developments: For the quarter ended Sep 30 2017, net income increased 24.1% to US$62.7 million from US$50.5 million in the year-earlier quarter. Revenues were US$733.8 million, down 2.3% from US$750.9 million the year before. Operating income was US$101.4 million versus US$78.2 million in the prior-year quarter, an increase of 29.6%. Direct operating expenses declined 4.8% to US$569.1 million from US$598.0 million in the comparable period the year before. Indirect operating expenses decreased 15.2% to US$63.4 million from US$74.7 million in the equivalent prior-year period.

Prospects: Our evaluation of Cooper Tire & Rubber Co. as of Jan. 14, 2018 is the result of our systematic analysis on three basic characteristics: earnings strength, relative valuation, and recent stock price movement. The company has managed to produce a neutral trend in earnings per share over the past 5 quarters and while recent estimates for the company have been mixed, CTB has posted better than expected results. Based on operating earnings yield, the company is undervalued when compared to all of the companies in our coverage universe. Share price changes over the past year indicates that CTB will perform very poorly over the near term.

Financial Data

(US$ in Thousands)	9 Mos	6 Mos	3 Mos	12/31/2016	12/31/2015	12/31/2014	12/31/2013	12/31/2012
Earnings Per Share	3.88	3.60	4.02	4.51	3.69	3.42	1.73	3.49
Cash Flow Per Share	2.28	3.32	4.81	5.67	5.27	5.20	4.30	7.24
Tang Book Value Per Share	19.05	18.01	17.14	16.65	14.81	11.82	12.81	9.32
Dividends Per Share	0.420	0.420	0.420	0.420	0.420	0.420	0.420	0.420
Dividend Payout %	10.82	11.67	10.45	9.31	11.38	12.28	24.28	12.03
Income Statement								
Total Revenue	2,097,621	1,363,778	643,025	2,924,869	2,972,901	3,424,809	3,439,233	4,200,836
EBITDA	254,874	143,950	58,885	562,634	523,215	550,230	427,101	570,191
Depn & Amortn	31,463	20,939	10,450	173,315	167,578	175,073	187,034	174,755
Income Before Taxes	205,115	110,531	42,410	367,093	334,028	348,519	212,971	368,450
Income Taxes	67,250	35,325	13,029	115,799	118,224	111,697	79,406	116,024
Net Income	137,558	75,872	30,561	248,381	212,766	213,578	111,013	220,371
Average Shares	52,435	53,191	53,422	55,090	57,623	62,401	64,282	63,224
Balance Sheet								
Current Assets	1,413,960	1,428,125	1,404,396	1,420,518	1,334,630	1,427,552	1,454,790	1,449,695
Total Assets	2,673,548	2,663,947	2,612,776	2,619,395	2,436,176	2,489,931	2,738,147	2,801,160
Current Liabilities	528,711	520,700	492,909	500,814	433,003	511,365	564,583	655,141
Long-Term Obligations	296,084	296,179	296,516	297,094	296,412	298,931	320,959	336,142
Total Liabilities	1,500,243	1,528,760	1,512,626	1,543,381	1,456,928	1,646,139	1,747,281	2,043,536
Stockholders' Equity	1,173,305	1,135,187	1,100,150	1,076,014	979,248	843,792	990,866	757,624
Shares Outstanding	51,503	52,390	52,930	52,999	55,832	58,151	63,386	63,158
Statistical Record								
Return on Assets %	7.93	7.53	8.66	9.80	8.64	8.17	4.01	8.29
Return on Equity %	18.52	17.81	20.78	24.10	23.34	23.28	12.70	32.91
EBITDA Margin %	12.15	10.56	9.16	19.24	17.60	16.07	12.42	13.57
Net Margin %	6.56	5.56	4.75	8.49	7.16	6.24	3.23	5.25
Asset Turnover	1.10	1.12	1.15	1.15	1.21	1.31	1.24	1.58
Current Ratio	2.67	2.74	2.85	2.84	3.08	2.79	2.58	2.21
Debt to Equity	0.25	0.26	0.27	0.28	0.30	0.35	0.32	0.44
Price Range	44.45-33.00	44.45-29.73	44.35-29.53	40.30-29.53	43.69-31.46	34.98-22.27	34.66-21.62	25.36-13.85
P/E Ratio	11.46-8.51	12.35-8.26	11.03-7.35	8.94-6.55	11.84-8.53	10.23-6.51	20.03-12.50	7.27-3.97
Average Yield %	1.11	1.13	1.17	1.19	1.10	1.49	1.53	2.29

Address: 701 Lima Avenue, Findlay, OH 45840	Web Site: www.coopertire.com	Auditors: Ernst & Young LLP
Telephone: 419-423-1321	Officers: Bradley E. Hughes - President, Chief Executive Officer, Chief Operating Officer, Senior Vice President, Chief Financial Officer, Vice President, Treasurer Ginger M. Jones - Chief Financial Officer, Vice President	Investor Contact: 419-424-4165
Fax: 419-424-4305		Transfer Agents: Computershare Inc., Canton, MA

CORECIVIC INC

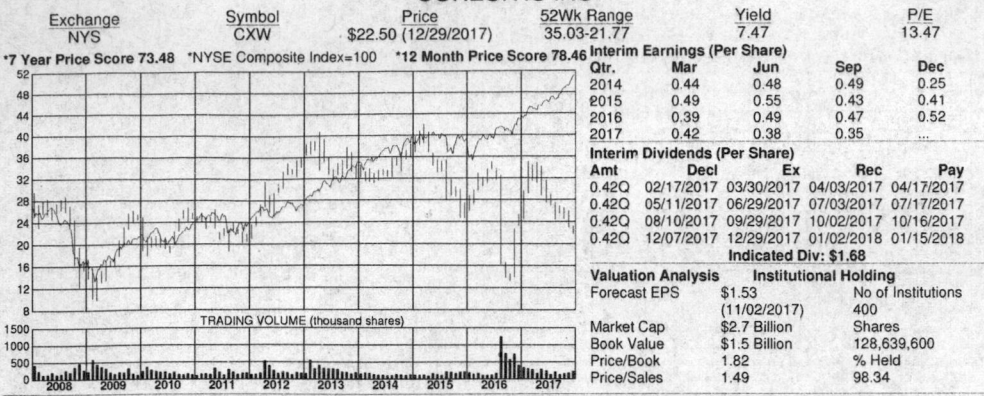

Exchange NYS	**Symbol** CXW	**Price** $22.50 (12/29/2017)	**52Wk Range** 35.03-21.77	**Yield** 7.47	**P/E** 13.47

*7 Year Price Score 73.48   ***NYSE Composite Index=100**   ***12 Month Price Score 78.46**

Interim Earnings (Per Share)

Qtr.	Mar	Jun	Sep	Dec
2014	0.44	0.48	0.49	0.25
2015	0.49	0.55	0.43	0.41
2016	0.39	0.49	0.47	0.52
2017	0.42	0.38	0.35	...

Interim Dividends (Per Share)

Amt	Decl	Ex	Rec	Pay
0.42Q	02/17/2017	03/30/2017	04/03/2017	04/17/2017
0.42Q	05/11/2017	06/29/2017	07/03/2017	07/17/2017
0.42Q	08/10/2017	09/29/2017	10/02/2017	10/16/2017
0.42Q	12/07/2017	12/29/2017	01/02/2018	01/15/2018

Indicated Div: $1.68

Valuation Analysis	Institutional Holding	
Forecast EPS	$1.53	No of Institutions
	(11/02/2017)	400
Market Cap	$2.7 Billion	Shares
Book Value	$1.5 Billion	128,639,600
Price/Book	1.82	% Held
Price/Sales	1.49	98.34

Business Summary: REITs (MIC: 5.3.1 SIC: 6798 NAIC: 525930)

CoreCivic is a real estate investment trust. Co. is the owner of partnership correctional, detention, and residential reentry facilities and prison operators. As of Dec 31 2016, Co. owned or controlled 49 correctional and detention facilities, owned or controlled 25 residential reentry facilities, and managed an additional 11 correctional and detention facilities owned by its government partners, in 20 states and the District of Columbia. In addition, Co.'s facilities provide a variety of rehabilitation and educational programs, such as basic education, and faith-based services. Co. also makes available to offenders' certain health care, food services, and work and recreational programs.

Recent Developments: For the quarter ended Sep 30 2017, net income decreased 25.6% to US$41.2 million from US$55.3 million in the year-earlier quarter. Revenues were US$442.8 million, down 6.8% from US$474.9 million the year before.

Prospects: Our evaluation of CoreCivic Inc. as of Jan. 14, 2018 is the result of our systematic analysis on three basic characteristics: earnings strength, relative valuation, and recent stock price movement. The company has generated a negative trend in earnings per share over the past 5 quarters and while recent estimates for the company have remained steady, CXW has posted better than expected results. Based on operating earnings yield, the company is undervalued when compared to all of the companies in our coverage universe. Share price changes over the past year indicates that CXW will perform in line with the market over the near term.

Financial Data

(US$ in Thousands)	9 Mos	6 Mos	3 Mos	12/31/2016	12/31/2015	12/31/2014	12/31/2013	12/31/2012
Earnings Per Share	1.67	1.79	1.90	1.87	1.88	1.66	2.70	1.56
Cash Flow Per Share	2.86	2.92	2.94	3.19	3.42	3.65	3.37	2.84
Tang Book Value Per Share	12.01	12.04	12.06	11.74	11.82	12.34	12.60	15.08
Dividends Per Share	1.680	1.800	1.920	2.040	2.160	2.040	8.600	0.600
Dividend Payout %	100.60	100.56	101.05	109.09	114.89	122.89	318.52	38.46
Income Statement								
Total Revenue	1,324,922	882,077	445,684	1,849,785	1,793,087	1,646,867	1,694,297	1,759,885
EBITDA	197,590	135,927	69,805	461,727	431,311	355,500	327,523	417,172
Depn & Amortn	2,349	1,566	783	165,800	151,400	114,000	112,800	114,100
Income Before Taxes	145,100	101,249	52,532	228,172	230,215	201,965	169,597	244,709
Income Taxes	8,400	5,727	2,485	8,253	8,361	6,943	(134,995)	87,586
Net Income	136,700	95,522	50,047	219,919	221,854	195,022	300,835	156,761
Average Shares	118,528	118,585	118,259	117,791	117,785	117,312	111,250	100,623
Balance Sheet								
Current Assets	304,056	279,052	281,582	298,824	342,058	365,985	352,734	350,742
Total Assets	3,242,766	3,224,316	3,240,618	3,271,604	3,356,018	3,127,191	3,007,425	2,974,742
Current Liabilities	277,573	254,828	253,187	272,193	324,595	318,988	254,406	166,458
Long-Term Obligations	1,411,210	1,407,196	1,421,182	1,435,169	1,447,077	1,200,000	1,205,000	1,111,545
Total Liabilities	1,784,085	1,760,972	1,777,457	1,812,641	1,893,270	1,645,691	1,504,918	1,453,122
Stockholders' Equity	1,458,681	1,463,344	1,463,161	1,458,963	1,462,748	1,481,500	1,502,507	1,521,620
Shares Outstanding	118,191	118,179	118,140	117,554	117,232	116,764	115,923	100,105
Statistical Record								
Return on Assets %	6.05	6.46	6.87	6.62	6.84	6.36	10.06	5.22
Return on Equity %	13.60	14.55	15.37	15.01	15.07	13.07	19.90	10.67
EBITDA Margin %	14.91	15.41	15.66	24.96	24.05	21.59	19.33	23.70
Net Margin %	10.32	10.83	11.23	11.89	12.37	11.84	17.76	8.91
Asset Turnover	0.55	0.56	0.57	0.56	0.55	0.54	0.57	0.59
Current Ratio	1.10	1.10	1.11	1.10	1.05	1.15	1.39	2.11
Debt to Equity	0.97	0.96	0.97	0.98	0.99	0.81	0.80	0.73
Price Range	35.03-13.18	35.03-13.18	35.03-13.18	35.02-13.18	42.10-24.62	38.33-31.13	40.78-31.60	35.87-20.96
P/E Ratio	20.98-7.89	19.57-7.36	18.44-6.94	18.73-7.05	22.39-13.10	23.09-18.75	15.10-11.70	22.99-13.44
Average Yield %	6.27	6.87	7.21	7.77	6.40	6.00	24.14	2.03

Address: 10 Burton Hills Blvd., Nashville, TN 37215	Web Site: www.cca.com	Auditors: Ernst & Young LLP
Telephone: 615-263-3000	Officers: John D. Ferguson - Chairman, Vice-Chairman, President, Chief Executive Officer Kim M. White - Executive Vice President	Investor Contact: 615-263-3005 Transfer Agents: American Stock Transfer and Trust Company LLC, New York, NY

CORELOGIC INC.

Exchange	Symbol	Price	52Wk Range	Yield	P/E
NYS	CLGX	$46.21 (12/29/2017)	49.10-35.01	N/A	43.59

*7 Year Price Score 111.20 *NYSE Composite Index=100 *12 Month Price Score 99.02

TRADING VOLUME (thousand shares)

Interim Earnings (Per Share)

Qtr.	Mar	Jun	Sep	Dec
2014	(0.03)	0.17	0.50	0.15
2015	0.32	0.36	0.31	0.41
2016	0.31	0.45	0.39	0.04
2017	0.18	0.48	0.36	...

Interim Dividends (Per Share)

No Dividends Paid

Valuation Analysis   **Institutional Holding**

Forecast EPS	$2.32	No of Institutions
	(01/17/2018)	311
Market Cap	$3.8 Billion	Shares
Book Value	$1.0 Billion	84,912,000
Price/Book	3.78	% Held
Price/Sales	2.03	N/A

Business Summary: Business Services (MIC: 7.5.2 SIC: 7374 NAIC: 519190)

CoreLogic is a property information, analytics and data-enabled services provider operating in North America, Western Europe and Asia Pacific. Co. has two segments: Property Intelligence, which owns or licenses real property, mortgage and consumer information, including loan information, property sales and characteristic information, and property risk and replacement cost; and Risk Management and Work Flow segment, which owns or licenses real property information, mortgage information and consumer information, including loan information, property sales and characteristic information, natural hazard data, parcel maps, employment verification, criminal records and eviction records.

Recent Developments: For the quarter ended Sep 30 2017, income from continuing operations decreased 14.4% to US$30.8 million from US$36.0 million in the year-earlier quarter. Net income decreased 12.3% to US$30.8 million from US$35.1 million in the year-earlier quarter. Revenues were US$483.1 million, down 7.8% from US$523.9 million the year before. Operating income was US$62.3 million versus US$85.7 million in the prior-year quarter, a decrease of 27.3%. Direct operating expenses declined 11.4% to US$244.2 million from US$275.5 million in the comparable period the year before. Indirect operating expenses increased 8.6% to US$176.6 million from US$162.7 million in the equivalent prior-year period.

Prospects: Our evaluation of CoreLogic Inc. as of Jan. 14, 2018 is the result of our systematic analysis on three basic characteristics: earnings strength, relative valuation, and recent stock price movement. The company has enjoyed a very positive trend in earnings per share over the past 5 quarters and while recent estimates for the company have been mixed, CLGX has posted better than expected results. Based on operating earnings yield, the company is about fairly valued when compared to all of the companies in our coverage universe. Share price changes over the past year indicates that CLGX will perform well over the near term.

Financial Data

(US$ in Thousands)	9 Mos	6 Mos	3 Mos	12/31/2016	12/31/2015	12/31/2014	12/31/2013	12/31/2012
Earnings Per Share	1.06	1.09	1.06	1.19	1.41	0.79	1.11	1.09
Cash Flow Per Share	4.43	4.50	5.00	4.71	3.69	3.54	3.72	3.52
Income Statement								
Total Revenue	1,396,960	913,829	439,851	1,952,557	1,528,110	1,405,040	1,330,630	1,567,633
EBITDA	171,005	151,110	55,538	303,957	308,216	241,940	246,708	297,044
Depn & Amortn	4,263	43,570	22,040	82,200	73,700	68,300	61,800	77,300
Income Before Taxes	122,713	79,804	19,705	163,974	173,226	106,658	137,259	167,276
Income Taxes	36,759	24,909	6,274	54,524	57,394	29,770	34,473	80,396
Net Income	87,453	56,698	15,438	106,550	127,844	73,200	107,728	112,293
Average Shares	85,090	86,097	86,341	89,122	90,564	92,429	97,109	104,050
Balance Sheet								
Current Assets	481,481	433,684	413,833	391,887	542,266	500,625	641,614	589,924
Total Assets	4,139,888	3,977,104	3,919,603	3,907,534	3,701,050	3,516,362	3,003,355	3,029,827
Current Liabilities	635,300	646,493	688,392	668,421	614,476	550,590	538,027	517,091
Long-Term Obligations	1,704,849	1,501,048	1,463,938	1,496,889	1,315,511	1,319,211	811,776	792,324
Total Liabilities	3,133,751	2,926,461	2,903,751	2,904,550	2,651,560	2,502,195	1,958,982	1,860,526
Stockholders' Equity	1,006,137	1,050,643	1,015,852	1,002,984	1,049,490	1,014,167	1,044,373	1,169,301
Shares Outstanding	82,374	84,303	84,630	84,368	88,228	89,343	91,254	97,698
Statistical Record								
Return on Assets %	2.23	2.38	2.51	2.79	3.54	2.25	3.57	3.65
Return on Equity %	8.73	8.82	8.95	10.35	12.39	7.11	9.73	9.29
EBITDA Margin %	12.24	16.54	12.63	15.57	20.17	17.22	18.54	18.95
Net Margin %	6.26	6.20	3.51	5.46	8.37	5.21	8.10	7.16
Asset Turnover	0.46	0.48	0.52	0.51	0.42	0.43	0.44	0.51
Current Ratio	0.76	0.67	0.60	0.59	0.88	0.91	1.19	1.14
Debt to Equity	1.69	1.43	1.44	1.49	1.25	1.30	0.78	0.68
Price Range	47.80-35.01	43.80-35.01	42.56-33.49	42.56-32.19	42.18-30.75	35.86-26.00	35.93-21.88	28.00-12.55
P/E Ratio	45.09-33.03	40.18-32.12	40.15-31.59	35.76-27.05	29.91-21.81	45.39-32.91	32.37-19.71	25.69-11.51

Address: 40 Pacifica, Irvine, CA 92618-7471 **Telephone:** 949-214-1000	**Web Site:** www.corelogic.com **Officers:** Paul F. Folino - Chairman Frank D. Martell - President, Interim President, Chief Executive Officer, Interim Chief Executive Officer, Chief Operating Officer, Chief Financial Officer, Principal Financial Officer	**Auditors:** PricewaterhouseCoopers LLP **Investor Contact:** 703-610-5410 **Transfer Agents:** Wells Fargo Shareowner Services, South Saint Paul, MN

CORNING INC

Exchange	Symbol	Price	52Wk Range	Yield	P/E
NYS	GLW	$31.99 (12/29/2017)	32.64-24.19	1.94	13.91

*7 Year Price Score 117.56 *NYSE Composite Index=100 *12 Month Price Score 103.51

TRADING VOLUME (thousand shares)

Interim Earnings (Per Share)

Qtr.	Mar	Jun	Sep	Dec
2014	0.20	0.11	0.72	0.70
2015	0.29	0.36	0.15	0.18
2016	(0.36)	1.87	0.26	1.42
2017	0.07	0.42	0.39	...

Interim Dividends (Per Share)

Amt	Decl	Ex	Rec	Pay
0.155Q	02/01/2017	02/24/2017	02/28/2017	03/31/2017
0.155Q	04/27/2017	05/26/2017	05/31/2017	06/30/2017
0.155Q	07/19/2017	08/29/2017	08/31/2017	09/29/2017
0.155Q	10/04/2017	11/15/2017	11/16/2017	12/15/2017

Indicated Div: $0.62

Valuation Analysis

Forecast EPS	$1.71
	(01/13/2018)
Market Cap	$27.8 Billion
Book Value	$17.3 Billion
Price/Book	1.61
Price/Sales	2.79

Institutional Holding

No of Institutions	1464
Shares	853,919,296
% Held	63.70

Business Summary: Electrical Equipment (MIC: 7.3.1 SIC: 3211 NAIC: 327211)

Corning is a provider of high-performance glass. Co. operates in five reportable segments: Display Technologies, which manufactures glass substrates for matrix liquid crystal displays; Optical Communications, which is engaged in delivering optical solutions; Environmental Technologies, which manufactures ceramic substrates and filter products for emissions control in mobile and stationary applications; Specialty Materials, which manufactures products that provide material formulations for glass, glass ceramics and fluoride crystals; and Life Sciences segment, which include consumables (plastic vessels, specialty surfaces and media), as well as general labware and equipment.

Recent Developments: For the quarter ended Sep 30 2017, net income increased 37.3% to US$390.0 million from US$284.0 million in the year-earlier quarter. Revenues were US$2.61 billion, up 4.0% from US$2.51 billion the year before. Operating income was US$453.0 million versus US$535.0 million in the prior-year quarter, a decrease of 15.3%. Direct operating expenses rose 5.8% to US$1.55 billion from US$1.47 billion in the comparable period the year before. Indirect operating expenses increased 19.2% to US$603.0 million from US$506.0 million in the equivalent prior-year period.

Prospects: Our evaluation of Corning Inc. as of Jan. 14, 2018 is the result of our systematic analysis on three basic characteristics: earnings strength, relative valuation, and recent stock price movement. The company has generated a negative trend in earnings per share over the past 5 quarters. However, while recent estimates for the company have been mixed, GLW has posted better than expected results. Based on operating earnings yield, the company is undervalued when compared to all of the companies in our coverage universe. Share price changes over the past year indicates that GLW will perform well over the near term.

Financial Data
(US$ in Thousands)

	9 Mos	6 Mos	3 Mos	12/31/2016	12/31/2015	12/31/2014	12/31/2013	12/31/2012
Earnings Per Share	2.30	2.17	3.62	3.23	1.00	1.73	1.34	1.15
Cash Flow Per Share	2.88	2.81	3.02	2.46	2.30	3.61	1.92	2.14
Tang Book Value Per Share	14.32	14.70	14.74	14.28	12.75	13.84	14.02	13.60
Dividends Per Share	0.600	0.580	0.560	0.540	0.480	0.400	0.390	0.315
Dividend Payout %	26.09	26.73	15.47	16.72	48.00	23.12	29.10	27.39
Income Statement								
Total Revenue	7,479,000	4,872,000	2,375,000	9,390,000	9,111,000	9,715,000	7,819,000	8,012,000
EBITDA	1,870,000	1,103,000	242,000	4,730,000	2,490,000	4,599,000	3,040,000	2,396,000
Depn & Amortn	848,000	556,000	277,000	1,195,000	1,184,000	1,200,000	1,002,000	997,000
Income Before Taxes	943,000	495,000	(60,000)	3,408,000	1,187,000	3,302,000	1,926,000	1,302,000
Income Taxes	176,000	87,000	(66,000)	(3,000)	147,000	1,096,000	512,000	389,000
Net Income	915,000	525,000	86,000	3,695,000	1,339,000	2,472,000	1,961,000	1,728,000
Average Shares	1,009,000	1,034,000	936,000	1,144,000	1,343,000	1,427,000	1,462,000	1,506,000
Balance Sheet								
Current Assets	8,254,000	8,431,000	8,718,000	9,048,000	8,269,000	10,238,000	8,891,000	9,695,000
Total Assets	28,094,000	27,830,000	28,305,000	27,899,000	28,547,000	30,063,000	28,478,000	29,375,000
Current Liabilities	3,065,000	2,808,000	2,421,000	2,751,000	2,814,000	2,324,000	1,746,000	1,956,000
Long-Term Obligations	3,994,000	3,302,000	3,669,000	3,646,000	3,910,000	3,227,000	3,272,000	3,382,000
Total Liabilities	10,777,000	9,818,000	9,997,000	10,006,000	9,759,000	8,484,000	7,316,000	7,889,000
Stockholders' Equity	17,317,000	18,012,000	18,308,000	17,893,000	18,788,000	21,579,000	21,162,000	21,486,000
Shares Outstanding	869,000	902,000	920,000	926,000	1,130,000	1,274,000	1,399,000	1,470,000
Statistical Record								
Return on Assets %	8.74	8.14	14.75	13.06	4.57	8.45	6.78	6.02
Return on Equity %	14.20	12.66	22.91	20.09	6.63	11.57	9.20	8.10
EBITDA Margin %	25.00	22.64	10.19	50.37	27.33	47.34	38.88	29.91
Net Margin %	12.23	10.78	3.62	39.35	14.70	25.45	25.08	21.57
Asset Turnover	0.35	0.34	0.35	0.33	0.31	0.33	0.27	0.28
Current Ratio	2.69	3.00	3.60	3.29	2.94	4.41	5.09	4.96
Debt to Equity	0.23	0.18	0.20	0.20	0.21	0.15	0.15	0.16
Price Range	32.13-22.33	30.50-19.93	28.20-18.32	24.94-16.69	25.00-15.97	23.32-17.05	17.82-11.79	14.62-10.88
P/E Ratio	13.97-9.71	14.06-9.18	7.79-5.06	7.72-5.17	25.00-15.97	13.48-9.86	13.30-8.80	12.71-9.46
Average Yield %	2.21	2.29	2.42	2.55	2.36	1.97	2.42	2.45

Address: One Riverfront Plaza, Corning, NY 14831	**Web Site:** www.corning.com	**Auditors:** PricewaterhouseCoopers LLP
Telephone: 607-974-9000	**Officers:** Wendell P. Weeks - Chairman, President, Chief Executive Officer Lawrence D. McRae - Vice-Chairman, Executive Vice President, Senior Vice President, Corporate Development Officer	**Investor Contact:** 888-267-6464
		Transfer Agents: ComputerShare Investor Services, Chicago, IL

CORPORATE OFFICE PROPERTIES TRUST

Exchange	Symbol	Price	52Wk Range	Yield	P/E
NYS	OFC	$29.20 (12/29/2017)	35.79-29.01	3.77	41.71

*7 Year Price Score 94.13 *NYSE Composite Index=100 *12 Month Price Score 88.17

Interim Earnings (Per Share)

Qtr.	Mar	Jun	Sep	Dec
2014	0.00	0.02	0.22	0.01
2015	0.10	0.13	0.91	0.59
2016	0.03	(0.54)	0.25	0.23
2017	0.18	0.08	0.21	...

Interim Dividends (Per Share)

Amt	Decl	Ex	Rec	Pay
0.275Q	02/07/2017	03/29/2017	03/31/2017	04/17/2017
0.275Q	05/11/2017	06/28/2017	06/30/2017	07/17/2017
0.275Q	08/11/2017	09/28/2017	09/30/2017	10/16/2017
0.275Q	11/09/2017	12/28/2017	12/29/2017	01/16/2018

Indicated Div: $1.10

Valuation Analysis · **Institutional Holding**

Forecast EPS	$0.73 (01/17/2018)	No of Institutions 353
Market Cap	$2.9 Billion	Shares 126,232,232
Book Value	$1.3 Billion	% Held 108.37
Price/Book	2.15	
Price/Sales	4.93	

Business Summary: REITs (MIC: 5.3.1 SIC: 6798 NAIC: 525930)

Corporate Office Properties Trust is a real estate investment trust. Through Corporate Office Properties, L.P. and subsidiaries, Co. is engaged in owning, managing, leasing, developing and acquiring office and data center properties. The majority of Co.'s portfolio is in locations that support U.S. Government agencies and their contractors, most of whom are engaged in national security, defense and information technology related activities. As of Dec 31 2016, Co.'s properties included the following: 164 operating office properties; 11 office properties under, or contractually committed for, construction or redevelopment; 1,227 acres of land that Co. controlled; and a wholesale data center.

Recent Developments: For the quarter ended Sep 30 2017, net income decreased 22.5% to US$22.7 million from US$29.3 million in the year-earlier quarter. Revenues were US$157.0 million, up 10.5% from US$142.1 million the year before. Revenues from property income fell 2.8% to US$127.2 million from US$131.0 million in the corresponding quarter a year earlier.

Prospects: Our evaluation of Corporate Office Properties Trust as of Jan. 14, 2018 is the result of our systematic analysis on three basic characteristics: earnings strength, relative valuation, and recent stock price movement. The company has produced a positive trend in earnings per share over the past 5 quarters. Because the company lacks sufficient analyst estimate data, we place greater weight on the historical EPS trend as the measure of earnings strength. Based on operating earnings yield, the company is about fairly valued when compared to all of the companies in our coverage universe. Share price changes over the past year indicates that OFC will perform very well over the near term.

Financial Data

(US$ in Thousands)	9 Mos	6 Mos	3 Mos	12/31/2016	12/31/2015	12/31/2014	12/31/2013	12/31/2012
Earnings Per Share	0.70	0.74	0.12	(0.03)	1.74	0.25	0.83	(0.03)
Cash Flow Per Share	2.35	2.28	2.50	2.45	2.17	2.20	1.87	2.60
Tang Book Value Per Share	12.89	12.86	12.92	12.92	13.19	12.96	12.78	11.81
Dividends Per Share	1.100	1.100	1.100	1.100	1.100	1.100	1.100	1.100
Dividend Payout %	157.14	148.65	916.67	...	63.22	440.00	132.53	...
Income Statement								
Total Revenue	448,253	291,236	139,801	574,328	625,466	586,473	523,360	528,007
EBITDA	215,954	141,099	70,351	184,019	345,394	258,146	228,094	208,502
Depn & Amortn	105,477	69,561	34,918	132,719	140,025	136,086	113,214	113,480
Income Before Taxes	57,522	36,690	18,165	(26,419)	120,812	34,590	36,704	7,570
Income Taxes	145	88	40	244	199	310	1,978	381
Net Income	60,133	39,217	21,355	11,439	178,300	40,255	93,707	20,977
Average Shares	99,258	99,196	98,566	94,502	97,667	88,263	85,224	73,454
Balance Sheet								
Current Assets	150,002	123,477	321,063	262,844	100,454	48,703	95,283	51,398
Total Assets	3,559,772	3,574,887	3,739,366	3,780,885	3,909,312	3,670,257	3,629,952	3,653,759
Current Liabilities	176,168	149,173	142,631	169,815	159,081	183,908	159,357	154,252
Long-Term Obligations	1,889,638	1,913,911	1,903,657	1,904,001	2,077,752	1,920,057	1,927,703	2,019,168
Total Liabilities	2,209,858	2,222,764	2,204,318	2,257,826	2,364,787	2,218,834	2,204,368	2,288,335
Stockholders' Equity	1,349,914	1,352,123	1,535,048	1,523,059	1,544,525	1,451,423	1,425,584	1,365,424
Shares Outstanding	99,608	99,471	99,390	98,498	94,531	93,255	87,394	80,952
Statistical Record								
Return on Assets %	2.36	2.46	0.68	0.30	4.70	1.10	2.57	0.56
Return on Equity %	6.10	6.55	1.70	0.74	11.90	2.80	6.71	1.67
EBITDA Margin %	48.18	48.45	50.32	32.04	55.22	44.02	43.58	39.49
Net Margin %	13.41	13.47	15.28	1.99	28.51	6.86	17.90	3.97
Asset Turnover	0.16	0.16	0.15	0.15	0.17	0.16	0.14	0.14
Current Ratio	0.85	0.83	2.25	1.55	0.63	0.26	0.60	0.33
Debt to Equity	1.40	1.42	1.24	1.25	1.35	1.32	1.35	1.48
Price Range	35.79-25.52	35.79-25.52	34.09-25.52	31.34-20.04	30.75-20.34	29.29-23.69	29.75-21.79	26.12-20.96
P/E Ratio	51.13-36.46	48.36-34.49	284.08-212.67	...	17.67-11.69	117.16-94.76	35.84-26.25	...
Average Yield %	3.43	3.55	3.77	4.10	4.36	4.06	4.31	4.69

Address: 6711 Columbia Gateway Drive, Suite 300, Columbia, MD 21046 **Telephone:** 443-285-5400	**Web Site:** www.copt.com **Officers:** Jay H. Shidler - Chairman Clay W. Hamlin - Vice-Chairman	**Auditors:** PricewaterhouseCoopers LLP **Investor Contact:** 443-285-5400 **Transfer Agents:** Wells Fargo Shareowner Services, St. Paul, MN

COTY, INC.

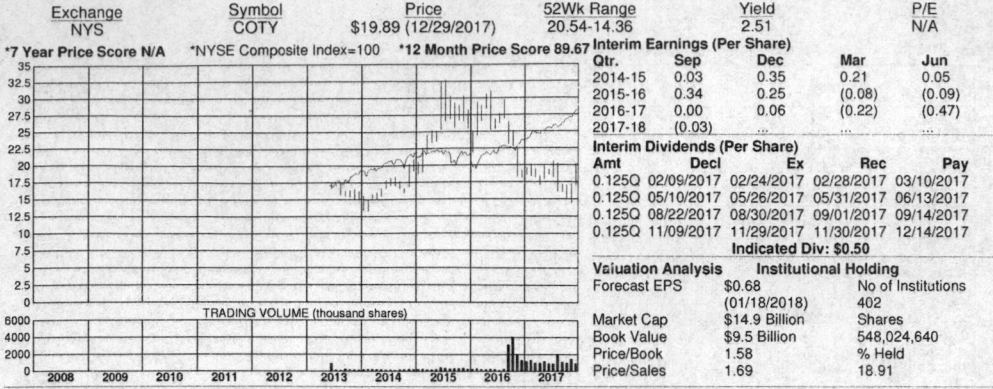

Exchange	Symbol	Price	52Wk Range	Yield	P/E
NYS	COTY	$19.89 (12/29/2017)	20.54-14.36	2.51	N/A

*7 Year Price Score N/A   *NYSE Composite Index=100   ***12 Month Price Score 89.67**

Interim Earnings (Per Share)

Qtr.	Sep	Dec	Mar	Jun
2014-15	0.03	0.35	0.21	0.05
2015-16	0.34	0.25	(0.08)	(0.09)
2016-17	0.00	0.06	(0.22)	(0.47)
2017-18	(0.03)	...		

Interim Dividends (Per Share)

Amt	Decl	Ex	Rec	Pay
0.125Q	02/09/2017	02/24/2017	02/28/2017	03/10/2017
0.125Q	05/10/2017	05/26/2017	05/31/2017	06/13/2017
0.125Q	08/22/2017	08/30/2017	09/01/2017	09/14/2017
0.125Q	11/09/2017	11/29/2017	11/30/2017	12/14/2017

Indicated Div: $0.50

Valuation Analysis   **Institutional Holding**

Forecast EPS	$0.68 (01/18/2018)	No of Institutions	402
Market Cap	$14.9 Billion	Shares	
Book Value	$9.5 Billion		548,024,640
Price/Book	1.58	% Held	
Price/Sales	1.69		18.91

Business Summary: Household & Personal Products (MIC: 1.7.1 SIC: 2844 NAIC: 325620)

Coty is a beauty company. Co. is organized into three divisions, which is also its operating and reportable segments: Consumer Beauty, which primarily focuses on color cosmetics, retail hair coloring and styling products, body care and mass fragrances primarily in the mass retail channel, e-commerce and social selling direct-to-consumer platform; Luxury, which primarily focuses on fragrances, skincare and cosmetics across various regions and channels, including travel retail; and Professional Beauty, which primarily focuses on servicing salon owners and salon personnel in both hair and nail care, covering salon segments and salon client needs.

Recent Developments: For the quarter ended Sep 30 2017, net loss amounted to US$16.1 million versus net income of US$9.8 million in the year-earlier quarter. Revenues were US$2.24 billion, up 107.2% from US$1.08 billion the year before. Operating income was US$28.7 million versus US$46.4 million in the prior-year quarter, a decrease of 38.1%. Direct operating expenses rose 96.6% to US$874.3 million from US$444.8 million in the comparable period the year before. Indirect operating expenses increased 126.7% to US$1.34 billion from US$589.0 million in the equivalent prior-year period.

Prospects: Our evaluation of Coty, Inc. as of Jan. 14, 2018 is the result of our systematic analysis on three basic characteristics: earnings strength, relative valuation, and recent stock price movement. The company has generated a negative trend in earnings per share over the past 5 quarters and while recent estimates for the company have been raised by analysts, COTY has posted better than expected results. Based on operating earnings yield, the company is overvalued when compared to all of the companies in our coverage universe. Share price changes over the past year indicates that COTY will perform very poorly over the near term.

Financial Data

(US$ in Thousands)	3 Mos	06/30/2017	06/30/2016	06/30/2015	06/30/2014	06/30/2013	06/30/2012	06/30/2011
Earnings Per Share	(0.66)	(0.66)	0.44	0.64	(0.26)	0.42	(0.87)	0.18
Cash Flow Per Share	1.02	1.18	1.45	1.49	1.41	1.22	1.58	1.27
Dividends Per Share	0.500	0.650	0.250	0.200	0.200	0.150	...	0.100
Dividend Payout %	...	...	56.82	31.25	...	35.71	...	55.56
Income Statement								
Total Revenue	2,238,300	7,650,300	4,349,100	4,395,200	4,551,600	4,649,100	4,611,300	4,086,100
EBITDA	192,700	(159,400)	373,100	462,500	189,400	564,600	(95,600)	410,300
Depn & Amortn	168,700	280,000	152,400	156,200	165,000	169,400	145,900	133,800
Income Before Taxes	(41,400)	(658,000)	138,800	233,300	(44,100)	318,700	(331,100)	185,000
Income Taxes	(25,300)	(259,500)	(40,400)	(26,100)	20,100	116,800	(37,800)	95,100
Net Income	(19,700)	(422,200)	156,900	232,500	(97,400)	168,000	(324,400)	61,700
Average Shares	748,600	642,800	354,200	362,900	381,700	396,400	373,000	339,100
Balance Sheet								
Current Assets	4,249,500	3,581,500	1,938,400	1,856,400	2,784,800	2,416,900	2,138,500	...
Total Assets	23,573,100	22,548,200	7,100,200	6,018,900	6,592,500	6,470,000	6,183,400	...
Current Liabilities	3,948,500	3,803,600	1,855,200	1,526,200	1,597,300	1,463,200	1,913,000	...
Long-Term Obligations	7,541,900	6,928,300	4,001,000	2,605,900	3,260,100	2,590,100	2,270,200	...
Total Liabilities	14,120,800	13,233,500	6,740,000	5,049,100	5,748,700	4,976,000	5,153,800	...
Stockholders' Equity	9,452,300	9,314,700	360,200	969,800	843,800	1,494,000	1,029,600	...
Shares Outstanding	749,400	747,900	337,100	360,800	353,900	383,800	381,900	370,000
Statistical Record								
Return on Assets %	N.M.	N.M.	2.39	3.69	N.M.	2.66	...	...
Return on Equity %	N.M.	N.M.	23.53	25.64	N.M.	13.31	...	...
EBITDA Margin %	8.61	N.M.	8.58	10.52	4.16	12.14	N.M.	10.04
Net Margin %	N.M.	N.M.	3.61	5.29	N.M.	3.61	N.M.	1.51
Asset Turnover	0.57	0.52	0.66	0.70	0.70	0.73	...	...
Current Ratio	1.08	0.94	1.04	1.22	1.74	1.65	1.12	...
Debt to Equity	0.80	0.74	11.11	2.69	3.86	1.73	2.20	...
Price Range	25.10-16.00	29.75-17.05	32.68-21.79	32.45-15.94	17.85-13.25	17.52-16.61	...	...
P/E Ratio	...	...	74.27-49.52	50.70-24.91	...	41.71-39.55	...	...
Average Yield %	2.62	3.07	0.91	0.96	1.26	0.38	...	...

Address: 350 Fifth Avenue, New York, NY 10118 **Telephone:** 212-389-7300	**Web Site:** www.coty.com **Officers:** Lambertus J.H. (Bart) Becht - Chairman, Interim Chief Executive Officer Camillo Pane - Chief Executive Officer, Executive Vice President	**Auditors:** Deloitte & Touche LLP **Investor Contact:** 212-389-7300

CRANE CO.

Exchange	Symbol	Price	52Wk Range	Yield	P/E
NYS	CR	$89.22 (12/29/2017)	90.46-71.55	1.48	40.01

*7 Year Price Score 105.13 *NYSE Composite Index=100 *12 Month Price Score 102.36

Interim Earnings (Per Share)

Qtr.	Mar	Jun	Sep	Dec
2014	0.82	1.00	0.47	0.95
2015	0.87	0.95	0.97	1.11
2016	0.93	1.15	1.07	(1.09)
2017	1.05	1.14	1.13	...

Interim Dividends (Per Share)

Amt	Decl	Ex	Rec	Pay
0.33Q	01/30/2017	02/24/2017	02/28/2017	03/09/2017
0.33Q	04/24/2017	05/26/2017	05/31/2017	06/09/2017
0.33Q	07/24/2017	08/29/2017	08/31/2017	09/08/2017
0.33Q	10/23/2017	11/29/2017	11/30/2017	12/08/2017

Indicated Div: $1.32

Valuation Analysis | **Institutional Holding**

Forecast EPS	$4.53	No of Institutions
	(01/17/2018)	440
Market Cap	$5.3 Billion	Shares
Book Value	$1.4 Billion	51,422,968
Price/Book	3.84	% Held
Price/Sales	1.92	70.02

Business Summary: Industrial Machinery & Equipment (MIC: 7.2.1 SIC: 3499 NAIC: 332999)

Crane is a manufacturer of industrial products. Co. has four segments: Fluid Handling, which provides fluid handling equipment; Payment and Merchandising Technologies, which provides technology payment acceptance products and vending equipment and related solutions; Aerospace and Electronics, which provides products such as custom designed, engineered products used in landing systems, sensing and utility systems, fluid management, seat actuation, power and microelectronic applications, and microwave systems; and Engineered Materials, which manufactures fiberglass-reinforced plastic panels and coils for use in the manufacturing of recreational vehicles, truck bodies, truck trailers.

Recent Developments: For the quarter ended Sep 30 2017, net income increased 7.5% to US$68.5 million from US$63.7 million in the year-earlier quarter. Revenues were US$695.9 million, up 0.2% from US$694.2 million the year before. Operating income was US$105.4 million versus US$103.8 million in the prior-year quarter, an increase of 1.5%. Direct operating expenses declined 1.7% to US$441.5 million from US$449.2 million in the comparable period the year before. Indirect operating expenses increased 5.5% to US$149.0 million from US$141.2 million in the equivalent prior-year period.

Prospects: Our evaluation of Crane Co. as of Jan. 14, 2018 is the result of our systematic analysis on three basic characteristics: earnings strength, relative valuation, and recent stock price movement. The company has managed to produce a neutral trend in earnings per share over the past 5 quarters and while recent estimates for the company have been mixed, CR has posted better than expected results. Based on operating earnings yield, the company is undervalued when compared to all of the companies in our coverage universe. Share price changes over the past year indicates that CR will perform poorly over the near term.

Financial Data

(US$ in Thousands)	9 Mos	6 Mos	3 Mos	12/31/2016	12/31/2015	12/31/2014	12/31/2013	12/31/2012
Earnings Per Share	2.23	2.17	2.18	2.07	3.89	3.23	3.73	3.72
Cash Flow Per Share	5.44	5.66	5.73	5.42	3.95	4.50	4.14	4.08
Dividends Per Share	1.320	1.320	1.320	1.320	1.320	1.260	1.160	1.080
Dividend Payout %	59.19	60.83	60.55	63.77	33.93	39.01	31.10	29.03
Income Statement								
Total Revenue	2,071,800	1,375,900	673,400	2,748,000	2,740,500	2,924,997	2,595,281	2,579,068
EBITDA	364,200	240,100	113,800	238,900	411,300	360,365	389,309	349,957
Depn & Amortn	54,000	35,500	17,400	40,200	39,100	41,700	38,700	40,400
Income Before Taxes	284,700	187,700	87,900	164,100	336,500	281,156	326,016	284,605
Income Taxes	83,600	55,100	24,600	40,300	106,500	87,587	105,065	88,416
Net Income	200,500	132,300	63,100	122,800	228,900	192,672	219,502	216,993
Average Shares	60,400	60,500	60,300	59,300	58,800	59,603	58,839	58,293
Balance Sheet								
Current Assets	1,422,800	1,352,300	1,318,500	1,315,700	1,203,500	1,195,184	1,149,092	1,180,521
Total Assets	3,607,100	3,533,800	3,451,000	3,428,000	3,341,600	3,450,785	3,559,607	2,889,878
Current Liabilities	535,200	487,200	484,100	520,800	572,800	640,025	668,902	511,888
Long-Term Obligations	745,900	745,700	745,500	745,300	749,300	749,213	749,170	399,092
Total Liabilities	2,228,000	2,215,300	2,231,000	2,294,200	2,202,200	2,391,033	2,355,288	1,971,495
Stockholders' Equity	1,379,100	1,318,500	1,220,000	1,133,800	1,139,400	1,059,752	1,204,319	918,383
Shares Outstanding	59,320	59,568	72,426	58,964	58,109	58,121	58,185	57,106
Statistical Record								
Return on Assets %	3.89	3.78	3.82	3.62	6.74	5.50	6.81	7.55
Return on Equity %	10.14	10.23	10.75	10.77	20.82	17.02	20.68	24.99
EBITDA Margin %	17.58	17.45	16.90	8.69	15.01	12.32	15.00	13.57
Net Margin %	9.68	9.62	9.37	4.47	8.35	6.59	8.46	8.41
Asset Turnover	0.78	0.79	0.81	0.81	0.81	0.83	0.80	0.90
Current Ratio	2.66	2.78	2.72	2.53	2.10	1.87	1.72	2.31
Debt to Equity	0.54	0.57	0.61	0.66	0.66	0.71	0.62	0.43
Price Range	84.22-60.43	80.45-55.65	77.36-52.31	77.36-43.14	69.78-45.27	76.33-53.63	67.25-46.28	51.07-35.53
P/E Ratio	37.77-27.10	37.07-25.65	35.49-24.00	37.37-20.84	17.94-11.64	23.63-16.60	18.03-12.41	13.73-9.55
Average Yield %	1.77	1.87	2.02	2.23	2.33	1.87	1.99	2.54

Address: 100 First Stamford Place, Stamford, CT 06902
Telephone: 203-363-7300

Web Site: www.craneco.com
Officers: R. S. Evans - Chairman Max H. Mitchell - President, Chief Executive Officer, Executive Vice President, Chief Operating Officer

Auditors: Deloitte & Touche LLP
Investor Contact: 203-363-7352
Transfer Agents: First Chicago Trust Company of New York, Jersey City, NJ

CROWN CASTLE INTERNATIONAL CORP

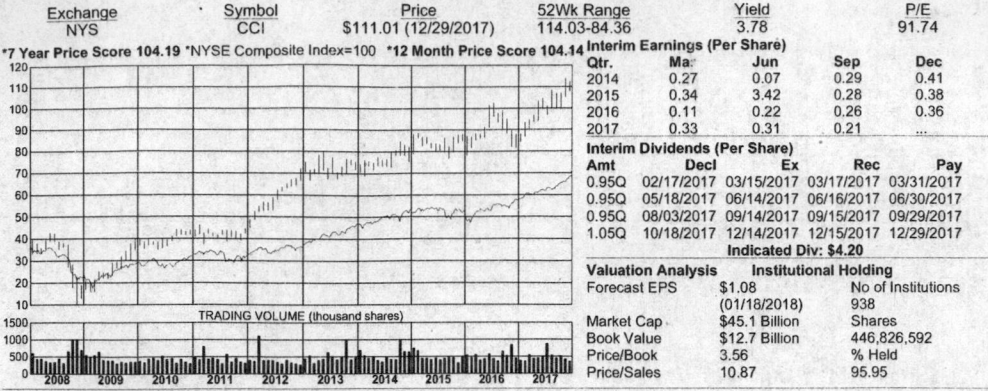

Exchange	Symbol	Price	52Wk Range	Yield	P/E
NYS	CCI	$111.01 (12/29/2017)	114.03-84.36	3.78	91.74

*7 Year Price Score 104.19 *NYSE Composite Index=100 *12 Month Price Score 104.14

Interim Earnings (Per Share)

Qtr.	Mar	Jun	Sep	Dec
2014	0.27	0.07	0.29	0.41
2015	0.34	3.42	0.28	0.38
2016	0.11	0.22	0.26	0.36
2017	0.33	0.31	0.21	...

Interim Dividends (Per Share)

Amt	Decl	Ex	Rec	Pay
0.95Q	02/17/2017	03/15/2017	03/17/2017	03/31/2017
0.95Q	05/18/2017	06/14/2017	06/16/2017	06/30/2017
0.95Q	08/03/2017	09/14/2017	09/15/2017	09/29/2017
1.05Q	10/18/2017	12/14/2017	12/15/2017	12/29/2017

Indicated Div: $4.20

Valuation Analysis

Forecast EPS	$1.08
	(01/18/2018)
Market Cap	$45.1 Billion
Book Value	$12.7 Billion
Price/Book	3.56
Price/Sales	10.87

Institutional Holding

No of Institutions	938
Shares	446,826,592
% Held	95.95

Business Summary: REITs (MIC: 5.3.1 SIC: 6798 NAIC: 525930)

Crown Castle International owns, operates and leases shared wireless infrastructure, including: towers and other structures, such as rooftops and fiber supporting small cell networks. Co.'s core business is providing access, including space or capacity, to its shared wireless infrastructure via long-term contracts in various forms, including license, sublease and lease agreements. As part of its effort to provide wireless infrastructure solutions, Co. also provides certain network services relating to its wireless infrastructure, consisting of site development services relating to existing or new tenant equipment installations on its wireless infrastructure and installation services.

Recent Developments: For the quarter ended Sep 30 2017, net income increased 17.1% to US$115.2 million from US$98.4 million in the year-earlier quarter. Revenues were US$1.06 billion, up 7.2% from US$992.0 million the year before. Revenues from property income rose 9.9% to US$892.8 million from US$812.0 million in the corresponding quarter a year earlier.

Prospects: Our evaluation of Crown Castle International Corp. as of Jan. 14, 2018 is the result of our systematic analysis on three basic characteristics: earnings strength, relative valuation, and recent stock price movement. The company has managed to produce a neutral trend in earnings per share over the past 5 quarters. However, while recent estimates for the company have been mixed, CCI has posted results that fell short of analysts expectations. Based on operating earnings yield, the company is overvalued when compared to all of the companies in our coverage universe. Share price changes over the past year indicates that CCI will perform very well over the near term.

Financial Data
(US$ in Thousands)

	9 Mos	6 Mos	3 Mos	12/31/2016	12/31/2015	12/31/2014	12/31/2013	12/31/2012
Earnings Per Share	1.21	1.26	1.17	0.95	4.42	1.04	0.26	0.64
Cash Flow Per Share	4.79	4.93	4.96	5.22	5.39	5.01	4.15	2.66
Tang Book Value Per Share	4.63	N.M.	N.M.	N.M.	N.M.	N.M.	N.M.	N.M.
Dividends Per Share	3.800	3.735	3.670	3.605	3.345	0.820	...	...
Dividend Payout %	314.05	296.43	313.68	379.47	75.68	78.85	...	...
Income Statement								
Total Revenue	3,117,515	2,054,277	1,015,942	3,921,225	3,663,851	3,689,884	3,022,384	2,432,680
EBITDA	783,190	520,274	260,460	1,720,790	1,773,951	1,718,209	1,442,904	1,136,215
Depn & Amortn	7,637	5,256	2,836	832,700	774,900	757,400	562,100	438,900
Income Before Taxes	357,736	240,159	123,507	373,854	473,829	388,134	292,529	100,827
Income Taxes	11,290	8,907	4,369	16,881	(51,457)	(10,640)	198,628	(100,061)
Net Income	346,446	231,252	119,138	356,973	1,520,992	390,513	90,111	188,584
Average Shares	397,035	365,832	361,727	340,879	334,062	333.265	299,293	291,270
Balance Sheet								
Current Assets	7,474,555	951,335	916,449	1,324,761	981,245	931,502	892,683	1,581,324
Total Assets	31,011,756	24,483,624	23,776,842	22,675,092	22,036,245	21,143,276	20,594,908	16,088,709
Current Liabilities	1,048,871	997,912	902,195	961,355	855,369	898,935	756,387	1,237,858
Long-Term Obligations	15,090,217	13,726,333	13,380,091	12,069,393	12,143,019	11,807,526	11,490,914	10,923,186
Total Liabilities	18,339,424	16,893,315	16,413,362	15,117,977	14,947,024	14,427,051	13,668,191	13,149,963
Stockholders' Equity	12,672,332	7,590,309	7,363,480	7,557,115	7,089,221	6,716,225	6,926,717	2,938,746
Shares Outstanding	406,274	366,115	361,355	360,536	333,771	333,856	334,070	293,164
Statistical Record								
Return on Assets %	1.77	1.95	1.88	1.59	7.04	1.87	0.49	1.41
Return on Equity %	4.85	6.25	5.90	4.86	22.03	5.72	1.83	6.68
EBITDA Margin %	25.12	25.33	25.64	43.88	48.42	46.57	47.74	46.71
Net Margin %	11.11	11.26	11.73	9.10	41.51	10.58	2.98	7.75
Asset Turnover	0.16	0.17	0.18	0.17	0.17	0.18	0.16	0.18
Current Ratio	7.13	0.95	1.02	1.38	1.15	1.04	1.18	1.28
Debt to Equity	1.19	1.81	1.82	1.60	1.71	1.76	1.66	3.72
Price Range	108.44-81.53	104.59-81.53	102.56-81.53	102.56-78.22	88.71-76.58	84.75-68.96	79.77-66.66	72.16-44.92
P/E Ratio	89.62-67.38	83.01-64.71	87.66-69.68	107.96-82.34	20.07-17.33	81.49-66.31	306.81-256.38	112.75-70.19
Average Yield %	4.03	4.02	4.03	4.01	4.00	1.07	...	...

Address: 1220 Augusta Drive, Suite 600, Houston, TX 77057-2261 **Telephone:** 713-570-3000	**Web Site:** www.crowncastle.com **Officers:** J. Landis Martin - Chairman W. Benjamin Moreland - Executive Vice-Chairman, President, Chief Executive Officer	**Auditors:** PricewaterhouseCoopers LLP **Investor Contact:** 713-570-3050 **Transfer Agents:** Mellon Investor Services LLC, Jersey City, NJ

CROWN HOLDINGS INC

Exchange	Symbol	Price	52Wk Range	Yield	P/E
NYS	CCK	$56.25 (12/29/2017)	61.17-52.48	N/A	16.07

*7 Year Price Score 97.44 *NYSE Composite Index=100 *12 Month Price Score 96.94

Interim Earnings (Per Share)

Qtr.	Mar	Jun	Sep	Dec
2014	0.17	0.76	1.76	0.09
2015	0.32	1.02	1.01	0.47
2016	0.57	1.21	1.31	0.47
2017	0.77	0.94	1.32	...

Interim Dividends (Per Share)

No Dividends Paid

Valuation Analysis | **Institutional Holding**

Forecast EPS	$4.03	No of Institutions
	(01/18/2018)	517
Market Cap	$7.6 Billion	Shares
Book Value	$798.0 Million	151,710,096
Price/Book	9.46	% Held
Price/Sales	0.89	82.09

TRADING VOLUME (thousand shares)

Business Summary: Metal Products (MIC: 8.2.3 SIC: 3411 NAIC: 332431)

Crown Holdings is engaged in the design, manufacture and sale of packaging products for consumer goods. Co.'s primary products include steel and aluminum cans for food, beverage, household and other consumer products, glass bottles for beverage products and metal vacuum closures and caps. These products are sold through Co.'s sales organization to the soft drink, food, citrus, brewing, household products, personal care and various other industries. Co.'s business is organized geographically within three divisions: Americas, which include Americas Beverage segment and North America Food segment; European, which includes European Beverage segment and European Food segment; and Asia-Pacific.

Recent Developments: For the quarter ended Sep 30 2017, net income increased 1.0% to US$208.0 million from US$206.0 million in the year-earlier quarter. Revenues were US$2.47 billion, up 6.1% from US$2.33 billion the year before. Operating income was US$347.0 million versus US$315.0 million in the prior-year quarter, an increase of 10.2%. Direct operating expenses rose 6.2% to US$2.02 billion from US$1.90 billion in the comparable period the year before. Indirect operating expenses decreased 7.3% to US$102.0 million from US$110.0 million in the equivalent prior-year period.

Prospects: Our evaluation of Crown Holdings Inc. as of Jan. 14, 2018 is the result of our systematic analysis on three basic characteristics: earnings strength, relative valuation, and recent stock price movement. The company has produced a positive trend in earnings per share over the past 5 quarters. However, while recent estimates for the company have been mixed, CCK has posted results that fell short of analysts' expectations. Based on operating earnings yield, the company is undervalued when compared to all of the companies in our coverage universe. Share price changes over the past year indicates that CCK will perform well over the near term.

Financial Data

(US$ in Thousands)	9 Mos	6 Mos	3 Mos	12/31/2016	12/31/2015	12/31/2014	12/31/2013	12/31/2012
Earnings Per Share	3.50	3.49	3.76	3.56	2.82	2.79	2.30	3.75
Cash Flow Per Share	7.78	6.64	7.35	6.70	6.93	6.65	6.34	4.22
Income Statement								
Total Revenue	6,530,000	4,062,000	1,901,000	8,284,000	8,762,000	9,097,000	8,656,000	8,470,000
EBITDA	1,027,000	617,000	297,000	1,247,000	1,135,000	952,000	941,000	1,035,000
Depn & Amortn	183,000	120,000	59,000	247,000	237,000	190,000	134,000	180,000
Income Before Taxes	667,000	380,000	179,000	769,000	639,000	516,000	576,000	636,000
Income Taxes	178,000	99,000	46,000	186,000	178,000	41,000	148,000	(17,000)
Net Income	412,000	235,000	107,000	496,000	393,000	387,000	324,000	557,000
Average Shares	134,400	135,700	139,000	139,310	139,140	138,500	140,700	148,400
Balance Sheet								
Current Assets	3,153,000	3,020,000	2,888,000	2,841,000	3,049,000	3,624,000	3,180,000	2,750,000
Total Assets	10,496,000	10,266,000	9,870,000	9,599,000	10,020,000	9,708,000	8,030,000	7,490,000
Current Liabilities	3,037,000	2,794,000	2,496,000	2,896,000	2,908,000	2,926,000	2,920,000	2,518,000
Long-Term Obligations	5,114,000	5,262,000	5,206,000	4,717,000	5,255,000	5,007,000	3,469,000	3,289,000
Total Liabilities	9,698,000	9,644,000	9,327,000	9,233,000	9,876,000	9,589,000	8,026,000	7,652,000
Stockholders' Equity	798,000	622,000	543,000	366,000	144,000	119,000	4,000	(162,000)
Shares Outstanding	134,272	135,006	136,086	139,840	139,441	139,000	138,207	143,136
Statistical Record								
Return on Assets %	4.66	4.82	5.29	5.04	3.98	4.36	4.18	7.74
Return on Equity %	75.30	102.77	132.32	193.98	298.86	629.27	...	...
EBITDA Margin %	15.73	15.19	15.62	15.05	12.95	10.46	10.87	12.22
Net Margin %	6.31	5.79	5.63	5.99	4.49	4.25	3.74	6.58
Asset Turnover	0.83	0.83	0.84	0.84	0.89	1.03	1.12	1.18
Current Ratio	1.04	1.08	1.16	0.98	1.05	1.24	1.09	1.09
Debt to Equity	6.41	8.46	9.59	12.89	36.49	42.08	867.25	...
Price Range	61.17-51.72	59.66-49.75	57.09-48.28	57.09-44.21	56.63-44.31	52.31-40.12	45.22-36.81	38.79-32.69
P/E Ratio	17.48-14.78	17.09-14.26	15.18-12.84	16.04-12.42	20.08-15.71	18.75-14.38	19.66-16.00	10.34-8.72

Address: One Crown Way, Philadelphia, PA 19154-4599 **Telephone:** 215-698-5100	**Web Site:** www.crowncork.com **Officers:** John W. Conway - Chairman, President, Chief Executive Officer, Chief Operating Officer Timothy J. Donahue - President, Chief Executive Officer, Executive Vice President, Chief Financial Officer, Chief Operating Officer	**Auditors:** PricewaterhouseCoopers LLP **Investor Contact:** 215-698-5341 **Transfer Agents:** Wells Fargo Shareowner Services, St. Paul, MN

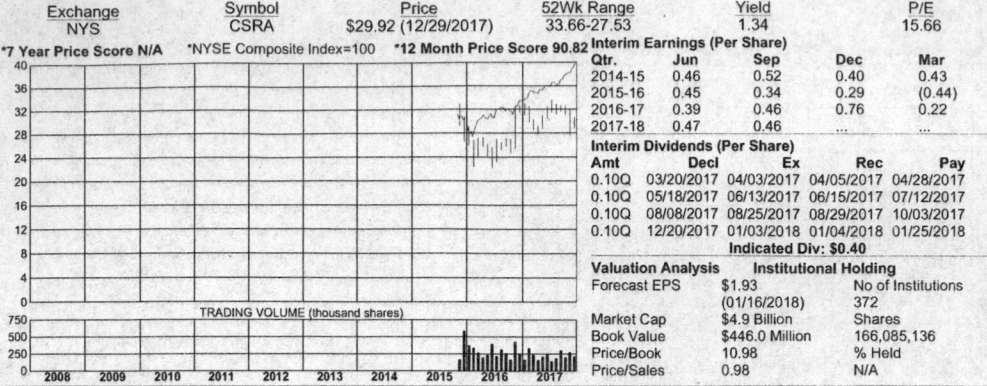

CSRA INC

Exchange	Symbol	Price	52Wk Range	Yield	P/E
NYS	CSRA	$29.92 (12/29/2017)	33.66-27.53	1.34	15.66

*7 Year Price Score N/A *NYSE Composite Index=100 *12 Month Price Score 90.82

Interim Earnings (Per Share)

Qtr.	Jun	Sep	Dec	Mar
2014-15	0.46	0.52	0.40	0.43
2015-16	0.45	0.34	0.29	(0.44)
2016-17	0.39	0.46	0.76	0.22
2017-18	0.47	0.46	...	...

Interim Dividends (Per Share)

Amt	Decl	Ex	Rec	Pay
0.10Q	03/20/2017	04/03/2017	04/05/2017	04/28/2017
0.10Q	05/18/2017	06/13/2017	06/15/2017	07/12/2017
0.10Q	08/08/2017	08/25/2017	08/29/2017	10/03/2017
0.10Q	12/20/2017	01/03/2018	01/04/2018	01/25/2018

Indicated Div: $0.40

Valuation Analysis

		Institutional Holding	
Forecast EPS	$1.93 (01/16/2018)	No of Institutions	372
Market Cap	$4.9 Billion	Shares	166,085,136
Book Value	$446.0 Million	% Held	N/A
Price/Book	10.98		
Price/Sales	0.98		

TRADING VOLUME (thousand shares)

Business Summary: Computer Hardware & Equipment (MIC: 6.2.1 SIC: 7373 NAIC: 541512)

CSRA is a pure-play provider of information technology services to the U.S. government. Co. provides a range of IT solutions and professional services to help its customers modernize their legacy systems, protect their networks and assets, and improve the mission-critical functions for its war fighters and its citizens. Co. operates through two segments: the Defense and Intelligence segment, where Co. provides services to the Department of Defense (DoD), National Security Agency, branches of the Armed Forces and other DoD and Intelligence agencies; and Civil segment, where Co. provides services to federal civil agencies including the Department of Homeland Security and Department of State.

Recent Developments: For the quarter ended Sep 29 2017, net income decreased 2.5% to US$78.0 million from US$80.0 million in the year-earlier quarter. Revenues were US$1.27 billion, up 0.7% from US$1.26 billion the year before. Operating income was US$134.0 million versus US$130.0 million in the prior-year quarter, an increase of 3.1%. Direct operating expenses rose 1.5% to US$1.02 billion from US$1.01 billion in the comparable period the year before. Indirect operating expenses decreased 7.9% to US$116.0 million from US$126.0 million in the equivalent prior-year period.

Prospects: Our evaluation of CSRA Inc. as of Jan. 14, 2018 is the result of our systematic analysis on three basic characteristics: earnings strength, relative valuation, and recent stock price movement. The company has managed to produce a neutral trend in earnings per share over the past 5 quarters and while recent estimates for the company have been raised by analysts, CSRA has posted results that fell short of analysts expectations. Based on operating earnings yield, the company is undervalued when compared to all of the companies in our coverage universe. Share price changes over the past year indicates that CSRA will perform poorly over the near term.

Financial Data
(US$ in Thousands)

	6 Mos	3 Mos	03/31/2017	04/01/2016	04/03/2015	03/28/2014	03/29/2013
Earnings Per Share	1.91	1.91	1.84	0.53	1.81	2.13	...
Cash Flow Per Share	2.67	2.56	3.00	3.42	...	...	...
Dividends Per Share	0.400	0.400	0.400	0.200	...	...	...
Dividend Payout %	20.94	20.94	21.74	37.74	...	...	...
Income Statement							
Total Revenue	2,501,000	1,229,000	4,993,000	4,250,447	4,069,746	4,102,636	4,675,701
EBITDA	422,000	191,100	859,900	384,806	597,336	576,094	618,928
Depn & Amortn	116,000	37,100	240,900	182,242	146,764	155,522	169,529
Income Before Taxes	249,000	126,000	495,000	149,089	428,708	400,276	431,223
Income Taxes	91,000	46,000	179,000	46,167	160,996	146,558	161,832
Net Income	153,000	77,000	304,000	87,145	251,757	296,382	280,701
Average Shares	165,251	164,980	164,836	163,584	139,128	139,128	...
Balance Sheet							
Current Assets	1,042,000	1,110,000	1,000,000	1,004,522	794,371	796,804	...
Total Assets	5,005,000	4,987,000	4,888,000	4,846,300	2,161,282	2,216,367	...
Current Liabilities	989,000	1,012,000	992,000	1,085,739	791,655	718,787	...
Long-Term Obligations	2,733,000	2,737,000	2,683,000	2,764,854	129,933	139,348	...
Total Liabilities	4,559,000	4,608,000	4,558,000	4,781,754	1,094,195	1,088,358	...
Stockholders' Equity	446,000	379,000	330,000	64,546	1,067,087	1,128,009	...
Shares Outstanding	163,718	163,367	163,216	162,925	139,128	139,128	...
Statistical Record							
Return on Assets %	6.47	6.47	6.26	2.49	11.32	...	...
Return on Equity %	101.61	126.40	154.52	15.44	22.57	...	...
EBITDA Margin %	16.87	15.55	17.22	9.05	14.68	14.04	13.24
Net Margin %	6.12	6.27	6.09	2.05	6.19	7.22	6.00
Asset Turnover	1.02	1.02	1.03	1.22	1.83	...	...
Current Ratio	1.05	1.10	1.01	0.93	1.00	1.11	...
Debt to Equity	6.13	7.22	8.13	42.84	0.12	0.12	...
Price Range	33.66-24.61	33.05-23.18	33.05-22.15	33.02-22.34	...	...	...
P/E Ratio	17.62-12.88	17.30-12.14	17.96-12.04	62.30-42.15	...	...	...
Average Yield %	1.31	1.39	1.44	0.73	...	...	...

Address: 3170 Fairview Park Drive, Falls Church, VA 22042 **Telephone:** 703-641-2000	**Web Site:** www.csra.com **Officers:** Nancy Killefer - Chairwoman Lawrence B. Prior - President, Chief Executive Officer	**Auditors:** Deloitte & Touche LLP **Transfer Agents:** Computershare Trust Company, N.A.

CULLEN/FROST BANKERS, INC.

Exchange	Symbol	Price	52Wk Range	Yield	P/E	Div Achiever
NYS	CFR	$94.65 (12/29/2017)	101.40-81.59	2.41	17.99	23 Years

*7 Year Price Score 105.30 *NYSE Composite Index=100   *12 Month Price Score 98.15

Interim Earnings (Per Share)
Qtr.	Mar	Jun	Sep	Dec
2014	0.96	1.02	1.19	1.11
2015	1.10	1.11	1.17	0.89
2016	1.07	1.11	1.24	1.28
2017	1.28	1.29	1.41	...

Interim Dividends (Per Share)
Amt	Decl	Ex	Rec	Pay
0.54Q	01/26/2017	02/24/2017	02/28/2017	03/15/2017
0.57Q	04/27/2017	05/26/2017	05/31/2017	06/15/2017
0.57Q	07/27/2017	08/29/2017	08/31/2017	09/15/2017
0.57Q	10/26/2017	11/29/2017	11/30/2017	12/15/2017

Indicated Div: $2.28

Valuation Analysis / Institutional Holding
Valuation Analysis		Institutional Holding	
Forecast EPS	$5.37 (01/17/2018)	No of Institutions	467
Market Cap	$6.0 Billion	Shares	66,183,596
Book Value	$3.2 Billion	% Held	76.26
Price/Book	1.87		
Price/Sales	4.96		

Business Summary: Banking (MIC: 5.1.1 SIC: 6021 NAIC: 522110)

Cullen/Frost Bankers is a financial holding company and a bank holding company. Through its subsidiaries, Co. provides commercial and consumer banking services, and trust and investment management, insurance, brokerage, mutual funds, leasing, treasury management, capital markets advisory and item processing services throughout various Texas markets. Co. has two segments: Banking, which includes commercial and consumer banking services, and its Frost Insurance Agency; and Frost Wealth Advisors, which includes fee-based services within private trust, retirement services, and financial management services. At Dec 31 2016, Co. had total assets of $30.20 billion and deposits of $25.81 billion.

Recent Developments: For the quarter ended Sep 30 2017, net income increased 16.1% to US$93.1 million from US$80.2 million in the year-earlier quarter. Net interest income increased 12.7% to US$219.2 million from US$194.5 million in the year-earlier quarter. Provision for loan losses was US$11.0 million versus US$5.0 million in the prior-year quarter, an increase of 117.6%. Non-interest income fell 0.6% to US$81.6 million from US$82.1 million, while non-interest expense advanced 3.5% to US$186.8 million.

Prospects: Our evaluation of Cullen/Frost Bankers Inc. as of Jan. 14, 2018 is the result of our systematic analysis on three basic characteristics: earnings strength, relative valuation, and recent stock price movement. The company has managed to produce a neutral trend in earnings per share over the past 5 quarters and while recent estimates for the company have been raised by analysts, CFR has posted better than expected results. Based on operating earnings yield, the company is undervalued when compared to all of the companies in our coverage universe. Share price changes over the past year indicates that CFR will perform in line with the market over the near term.

Financial Data
(US$ in Thousands)	9 Mos	6 Mos	3 Mos	12/31/2016	12/31/2015	12/31/2014	12/31/2013	12/31/2012
Earnings Per Share	5.26	5.09	4.91	4.70	4.28	4.29	3.80	3.86
Cash Flow Per Share	7.20	6.97	6.86	7.00	6.27	4.62	2.88	4.88
Tang Book Value Per Share	37.78	37.66	35.85	34.60	33.60	32.32	30.16	30.48
Dividends Per Share	2.220	2.190	2.160	2.150	2.100	2.030	1.980	1.900
Dividend Payout %	42.21	43.03	43.99	45.74	49.07	47.32	52.11	49.22
Income Statement								
Interest Income	658,652	431,066	211,792	788,412	749,496	701,471	642,500	631,612
Interest Expense	16,144	7,769	3,283	12,076	12,864	14,537	21,945	26,751
Net Interest Income	642,508	423,297	208,509	776,336	736,632	686,934	620,555	604,861
Provision for Losses	27,358	16,378	7,952	51,673	51,845	16,314	20,582	10,080
Non-Interest Income	246,395	164,780	83,700	349,708	328,730	320,144	302,818	288,787
Non-Interest Expense	562,789	375,966	187,915	732,960	693,718	654,740	611,910	575,093
Income Before Taxes	298,756	195,733	96,342	341,411	319,799	336,024	290,881	308,475
Income Taxes	35,131	25,239	11,401	37,150	40,471	58,047	53,015	70,523
Net Income	263,625	170,494	84,941	304,261	279,328	277,977	237,866	237,952
Average Shares	64,565	65,035	64,737	62,968	63,473	62,973	61,116	61,643
Balance Sheet								
Net Loans & Leases	12,552,001	12,362,780	12,032,589	11,822,347	11,350,672	10,887,993	9,423,262	9,119,395
Total Assets	30,989,972	30,206,314	30,524,705	30,196,319	28,567,118	28,277,775	24,312,939	23,124,069
Total Deposits	26,403,269	25,613,573	26,142,164	25,811,575	24,343,595	24,135,930	20,688,786	19,497,366
Total Liabilities	27,800,929	26,982,385	27,427,327	27,193,791	25,676,775	25,426,372	21,798,778	20,706,587
Stockholders' Equity	3,189,043	3,223,929	3,097,378	3,002,528	2,890,343	2,851,403	2,514,161	2,417,482
Shares Outstanding	63,113	64,225	63,915	63,474	61,982	63,149	60,566	61,479
Statistical Record								
Return on Assets %	1.15	1.13	1.09	1.03	0.98	1.06	1.00	1.09
Return on Equity %	10.94	10.52	10.52	10.30	9.73	10.36	9.65	10.10
Net Interest Margin %	96.32	97.95	98.45	98.47	98.28	97.93	96.58	95.76
Efficiency Ratio %	60.42	62.61	63.59	64.40	64.34	64.09	64.73	62.48
Loans to Deposits	0.48	0.48	0.46	0.46	0.47	0.45	0.46	0.47
Price Range	98.59-71.04	98.59-60.59	96.10-51.93	88.77-42.55	80.10-59.40	81.67-68.06	75.58-54.27	60.67-53.66
P/E Ratio	18.74-13.51	19.37-11.90	19.57-10.58	18.89-9.05	18.71-13.88	19.04-15.86	19.89-14.28	15.72-13.90
Average Yield %	2.52	2.65	2.88	3.27	3.05	2.66	2.98	3.36

Address: 100 W. Houston Street, San Antonio, TX 78205	**Web Site:** www.frostbank.com	**Auditors:** Ernst & Young LLP
Telephone: 210-220-4011	**Officers:** Phillip D. Green - Chairman, President, Chief Executive Officer, Group Executive Vice President, Chief Financial Officer Paul H. Bracher - President	**Investor Contact:** 210-220-5632
Fax: 210-220-5578		**Transfer Agents:** American Stock Transfer & Trust Company, LLC, Brooklyn, NY

CUMMINS, INC.

Exchange	Symbol	Price	52Wk Range	Yield	P/E	Div Achiever
NYS	CMI	$176.64 (12/29/2017)	180.35-137.42	2.45	17.95	11 Years

*7 Year Price Score 100.22 *NYSE Composite Index=100 *12 Month Price Score 100.15

TRADING VOLUME (thousand shares)

Interim Earnings (Per Share)

Qtr.	Mar	Jun	Sep	Dec
2014	1.83	2.43	2.32	2.44
2015	2.14	2.62	2.14	0.94
2016	1.87	2.40	1.72	2.24
2017	2.36	2.53	2.71	...

Interim Dividends (Per Share)

Amt	Decl	Ex	Rec	Pay
1.025Q	02/14/2017	02/22/2017	02/24/2017	03/06/2017
1.025Q	05/09/2017	05/17/2017	05/19/2017	06/01/2017
1.08Q	07/11/2017	08/16/2017	08/18/2017	09/01/2017
1.08Q	10/10/2017	11/16/2017	11/17/2017	12/01/2017

Indicated Div: $4.32 (Div. Reinv. Plan)

Valuation Analysis

		Institutional Holding	
Forecast EPS	$10.25	No of Institutions	
	(01/17/2018)	1257	
Market Cap	$29.4 Billion	Shares	
Book Value	$7.6 Billion	166,921,680	
Price/Book	3.86	% Held	
Price/Sales	1.51	73.27	

Business Summary: Auto Parts (MIC: 1.8.2 SIC: 3519 NAIC: 333618)

Cummins is a diesel engine manufacturer. Co.'s reportable operating segments consist of: Engine, which manufactures and markets diesel and natural gas powered engines; Distribution, which engages in wholesaling engines, generator sets and service parts, as well as performing service and repair activities on its products; Components, which sells filtration products, aftertreatment systems, turbochargers and fuel systems; and Power Systems, which designs, manufactures and sells engines for industrial applications (including mining, oil and gas and marine), standby and prime power generator sets, alternators and other power components.

Recent Developments: For the quarter ended Oct 1 2017, net income increased 52.3% to US$457.0 million from US$300.0 million in the year-earlier quarter. Revenues were US$5.29 billion, up 26.2% from US$4.19 billion the year before. Operating income was US$629.0 million versus US$384.0 million in the prior-year quarter, an increase of 63.8%. Direct operating expenses rose 27.0% to US$3.95 billion from US$3.11 billion in the comparable period the year before. Indirect operating expenses increased 2.2% to US$710.0 million from US$695.0 million in the equivalent prior-year period.

Prospects: Our evaluation of Cummins Inc. as of Jan. 14, 2018 is the result of our systematic analysis on three basic characteristics: earnings strength, relative valuation, and recent stock price movement. The company has managed to produce a neutral trend in earnings per share over the past 5 quarters and while recent estimates for the company have been raised by analysts, CMI has posted better than expected results. Based on operating earnings yield, the company is undervalued when compared to all of the companies in our coverage universe. Share price changes over the past year indicates that CMI will perform in line with the market over the near term.

Financial Data

(US$ in Thousands)	9 Mos	6 Mos	3 Mos	12/31/2016	12/31/2015	12/31/2014	12/31/2013	12/31/2012
Earnings Per Share	9.84	8.85	8.72	8.23	7.84	9.02	7.91	8.67
Cash Flow Per Share	12.60	12.12	12.24	11.42	11.56	12.41	11.17	8.07
Tang Book Value Per Share	33.79	39.77	37.75	36.05	37.65	38.02	35.84	30.50
Dividends Per Share	4.155	4.100	4.050	4.000	3.510	2.810	2.250	1.800
Dividend Payout %	42.23	46.33	46.44	48.60	44.77	31.15	28.45	20.76
Income Statement								
Total Revenue	14,952,000	9,667,000	4,589,000	17,509,000	19,110,000	19,221,000	17,301,000	17,334,000
EBITDA	1,822,000	1,182,000	566,000	2,410,000	2,485,000	2,826,000	2,451,000	2,565,000
Depn & Amortn	7,000	3,000	2,000	434,000	419,000	351,000	318,000	287,000
Income Before Taxes	1,769,000	1,147,000	548,000	1,930,000	2,025,000	2,434,000	2,119,000	2,271,000
Income Taxes	466,000	301,000	143,000	474,000	555,000	698,000	531,000	533,000
Net Income	1,273,000	820,000	396,000	1,394,000	1,399,000	1,651,000	1,483,000	1,645,000
Average Shares	167,000	167,800	168,000	169,336	178,406	183,079	187,417	189,668
Balance Sheet								
Current Assets	9,056,000	8,602,000	8,159,000	7,707,000	7,947,000	9,055,000	8,639,000	7,167,000
Total Assets	17,992,000	16,260,000	15,634,000	15,011,000	15,134,000	15,776,000	14,728,000	12,548,000
Current Liabilities	5,758,000	4,894,000	4,662,000	4,325,000	3,803,000	4,021,000	3,368,000	3,136,000
Long-Term Obligations	1,615,000	1,564,000	1,576,000	1,568,000	1,576,000	1,589,000	1,672,000	698,000
Total Liabilities	10,363,000	8,767,000	8,469,000	8,136,000	7,728,000	8,027,000	7,218,000	5,945,000
Stockholders' Equity	7,629,000	7,493,000	7,165,000	6,875,000	7,406,000	7,749,000	7,510,000	6,603,000
Shares Outstanding	166,600	167,600	167,900	168,200	175,200	182,200	186,700	189,800
Statistical Record								
Return on Assets %	9.97	9.51	9.65	9.22	9.05	10.82	10.87	13.55
Return on Equity %	22.67	20.72	20.86	19.47	18.46	21.64	21.02	27.13
EBITDA Margin %	12.19	12.23	12.33	13.76	13.00	14.70	14.17	14.80
Net Margin %	8.51	8.48	8.63	7.96	7.32	8.59	8.57	9.49
Asset Turnover	1.17	1.17	1.17	1.16	1.24	1.26	1.27	1.43
Current Ratio	1.57	1.76	1.75	1.78	2.09	2.25	2.57	2.29
Debt to Equity	0.21	0.21	0.22	0.23	0.21	0.21	0.22	0.11
Price Range	168.35-121.72	164.10-110.18	154.51-105.09	146.46-83.52	147.85-85.21	160.55-123.70	140.97-103.66	128.00-83.53
P/E Ratio	17.11-12.37	18.54-12.45	17.72-12.05	17.80-10.15	18.86-10.87	17.80-13.71	17.82-13.10	14.76-9.63
Average Yield %	2.78	2.94	3.14	3.44	2.80	1.95	1.85	1.76

Address: 500 Jackson Street, P.O. Box 3005, Columbus, IN 47202-3005 Telephone: 812-377-5000 Fax: 812-377-4937	Web Site: www.cummins.com Officers: Norman Thomas Linebarger - Chairman, President, Chief Executive Officer, Executive Vice President, Vice President, Chief Financial Officer, Chief Operating Officer, Division Officer Richard Joseph (Rich) Freeland - President, Vice President, Chief Operating Officer, Division Officer	Auditors: PricewaterhouseCoopers LLP Investor Contact: 812-377-3121 Transfer Agents: Wells Fargo Shareowner Services

CURTISS-WRIGHT CORP.

Exchange	Symbol	Price	52Wk Range	Yield	P/E
NYS	CW	$121.85 (12/29/2017)	124.20-83.41	0.49	25.33

*7 Year Price Score 129.06 ***NYSE Composite Index=100** ***12 Month Price Score 113.58**

Interim Earnings (Per Share)

Qtr.	Mar	Jun	Sep	Dec
2014	0.72	0.74	0.51	0.34
2015	0.33	0.53	0.71	1.48
2016	0.73	0.88	1.02	1.52
2017	0.73	1.13	1.43	...

Interim Dividends (Per Share)

Amt	Decl	Ex	Rec	Pay
0.13Q	02/07/2017	03/28/2017	03/30/2017	04/13/2017
0.13Q	05/17/2017	06/20/2017	06/22/2017	07/06/2017
0.15Q	09/13/2017	10/05/2017	10/06/2017	10/20/2017
0.15Q	11/10/2017	11/28/2017	11/29/2017	12/08/2017

Indicated Div: $0.60

Valuation Analysis **Institutional Holding**

Forecast EPS	$4.75 (01/17/2018)	No of Institutions	341
Market Cap	$5.4 Billion	Shares	45,600,936
Book Value	$1.5 Billion	% Held	82.00
Price/Book	3.65		
Price/Sales	2.42		

Business Summary: Industrial Machinery & Equipment (MIC: 7.2.1 SIC: 3599 NAIC: 333999)

Curtiss-Wright is a multinational manufacturing and service company that designs, manufactures, and overhauls precision components and provides engineered products and services to the aerospace, defense, power generation, and general industrial markets. Co. operates through three segments: Commercial/Industrial, which provide industrial vehicle products such as electronic throttle control devices and transmission shifters; Defense, which provide Commercial Off-the-Shelf embedded computing board level modules, integrated subsystems, flight test equipment, instrumentation and control systems; and Power, which provide a range of hardware, pumps, valves, and fastening systems.

Recent Developments: For the quarter ended Sep 30 2017, net income increased 39.2% to US$63.9 million from US$45.9 million in the year-earlier quarter. Revenues were US$567.9 million, up 12.0% from US$507.1 million the year before. Operating income was US$96.6 million versus US$76.6 million in the prior-year quarter, an increase of 26.1%. Direct operating expenses rose 10.7% to US$357.1 million from US$322.6 million in the comparable period the year before. Indirect operating expenses increased 5.9% to US$114.2 million from US$107.9 million in the equivalent prior-year period.

Prospects: Our evaluation of Curtiss-Wright Corp. as of Jan. 14, 2018 is the result of our systematic analysis on three basic characteristics: earnings strength, relative valuation, and recent stock price movement. The company has managed to produce a neutral trend in earnings per share over the past 5 quarters and while recent estimates for the company have been mixed, CW has posted better than expected results. Based on operating earnings yield, the company is about fairly valued when compared to all of the companies in our coverage universe. Share price changes over the past year indicates that CW will perform in line with the market over the near term.

Financial Data
(US$ in Thousands)

	9 Mos	6 Mos	3 Mos	12/31/2016	12/31/2015	12/31/2014	12/31/2013	12/31/2012
Earnings Per Share	4.81	4.40	4.15	4.15	3.05	2.31	2.88	2.40
Cash Flow Per Share	7.21	7.41	7.41	9.51	3.48	6.91	5.06	3.25
Tang Book Value Per Share	1.04	N.M.	N.M.	1.55	N.M.	2.73	N.M.	N.M.
Dividends Per Share	0.520	0.520	0.520	0.520	0.520	0.520	0.390	0.350
Dividend Payout %	10.81	11.82	12.53	12.53	17.05	22.51	13.54	14.58
Income Statement								
Total Revenue	1,659,145	1,091,244	523,591	2,108,931	2,205,683	2,243,126	2,510,771	2,097,716
EBITDA	306,686	184,961	76,465	371,809	375,932	349,338	306,573	224,491
Depn & Amortn	74,815	49,961	24,926	62,600	64,700	66,600	71,600	62,800
Income Before Taxes	200,287	113,873	41,162	267,961	275,194	246,944	197,953	135,362
Income Taxes	53,146	30,676	8,615	78,579	82,946	76,995	59,972	43,073
Net Income	147,141	83,197	32,547	187,329	145,461	113,338	137,981	113,844
Average Shares	44,686	44,807	44,860	45,045	47,616	49,075	47,912	47,412
Balance Sheet								
Current Assets	1,389,279	1,287,104	1,190,109	1,414,811	1,316,620	1,571,075	1,337,283	1,175,761
Total Assets	3,221,224	3,121,274	3,017,873	3,037,781	3,029,378	3,399,511	3,458,274	3,114,588
Current Liabilities	669,238	653,791	624,817	675,262	525,187	571,993	534,593	639,748
Long-Term Obligations	814,400	814,810	815,220	815,630	953,083	953,279	958,604	751,990
Total Liabilities	1,746,748	1,728,109	1,693,518	1,746,590	1,773,955	1,921,078	1,905,569	1,801,996
Stockholders' Equity	1,474,476	1,393,165	1,324,355	1,291,191	1,255,423	1,478,433	1,552,705	1,312,592
Shares Outstanding	44,129	44,137	44,284	44,181	44,621	47,904	47,638	46,449
Statistical Record								
Return on Assets %	6.92	6.48	6.25	6.16	4.53	3.31	4.20	3.94
Return on Equity %	15.63	14.83	14.33	14.67	10.64	7.48	9.63	8.93
EBITDA Margin %	18.48	16.95	14.60	17.63	17.04	15.57	12.21	10.70
Net Margin %	8.87	7.62	6.22	8.88	6.59	5.05	5.50	5.43
Asset Turnover	0.71	0.71	0.71	0.69	0.69	0.65	0.76	0.73
Current Ratio	2.08	1.97	1.90	2.10	2.51	2.75	2.50	1.84
Debt to Equity	0.55	0.58	0.62	0.63	0.76	0.64	0.62	0.57
Price Range	107.06-83.41	107.06-82.31	107.06-74.65	107.06-63.70	77.08-61.97	73.16-58.77	62.23-31.05	40.82-28.90
P/E Ratio	22.26-17.34	24.33-18.71	25.80-17.99	25.80-15.35	25.27-20.32	31.67-25.44	21.61-10.78	17.01-12.04
Average Yield %	0.55	0.56	0.58	0.62	0.75	0.78	0.94	1.06

Address: 13925 Ballantyne Corporate Place, Suite 400, Charlotte, NC 28277
Telephone: 704-869-4600

Web Site: www.curtisswright.com
Officers: David C. Adams - Chairman, Chief Executive Officer, President, Vice President, Co-Chief Operating Officer, Chief Operating Officer Thomas P. Quinly - Vice President, Chief Operating Officer

Auditors: Deloitte & Touche LLP
Investor Contact: 973-541-3700
Transfer Agents: Broadridge Corporate Issuer Solutions, Inc., Brentwood, NY

CVS HEALTH CORPORATION

Exchange	Symbol	Price	52Wk Range	Yield	P/E	Div Achiever
NYS	CVS	$72.50 (12/29/2017)	83.92-66.80	2.76	15.01	13 Years

*7 Year Price Score 86.80   *NYSE Composite Index=100   ***12 Month Price Score 87.68**

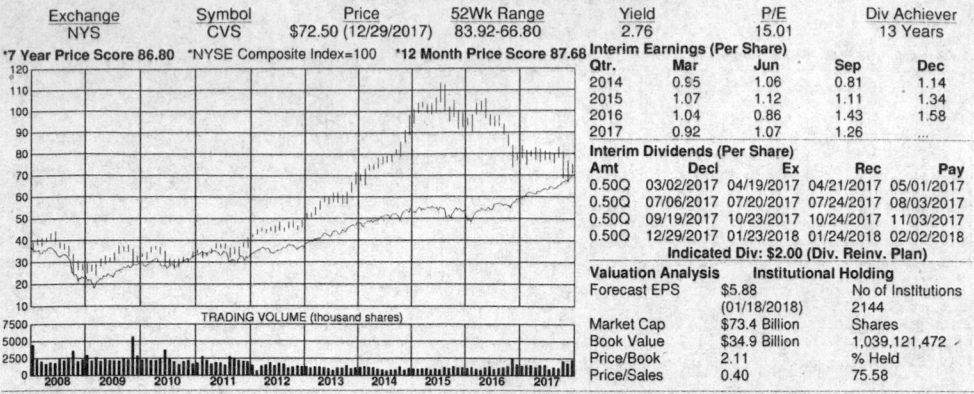

Interim Earnings (Per Share)

Qtr.	Mar	Jun	Sep	Dec
2014	0.95	1.06	0.81	1.14
2015	1.07	1.12	1.11	1.34
2016	1.04	0.86	1.43	1.58
2017	0.92	1.07	1.26	...

Interim Dividends (Per Share)

Amt	Decl	Ex	Rec	Pay
0.50Q	03/02/2017	04/19/2017	04/21/2017	05/01/2017
0.50Q	07/06/2017	07/20/2017	07/24/2017	08/03/2017
0.50Q	09/19/2017	10/23/2017	10/24/2017	11/03/2017
0.50Q	12/29/2017	01/23/2018	01/24/2018	02/02/2018

Indicated Div: $2.00 (Div. Reinv. Plan)

Valuation Analysis / Institutional Holding

Forecast EPS	$5.88 (01/18/2018)
Market Cap	$73.4 Billion
Book Value	$34.9 Billion
Price/Book	2.11
Price/Sales	0.40

No of Institutions	2144
Shares	1,039,121,472
% Held	75.58

TRADING VOLUME (thousand shares)

Business Summary: Retail - Food & Beverage, Drug & Tobacco (MIC: 2.1.2 SIC: 5912 NAIC: 446110)

CVS Health is a pharmacy health care provider. Co. has three reportable segments: Pharmacy Services, which provides pharmacy benefit management services, and through its SilverScript Insurance Company subsidiary, is a provider of drug benefits to eligible beneficiaries under the federal government's Medicare Part D program; Retail/LTC, which sells prescription drugs and a range of over-the-counter and personal care products, beauty and cosmetic products, and general merchandise (front store products); and Corporate, which provides management and administrative services to support the overall operations of Co.

Recent Developments: For the quarter ended Sep 30 2017, income from continuing operations decreased 16.7% to US$1.29 billion from US$1.54 billion in the year-earlier quarter. Net income decreased 16.6% to US$1.29 billion from US$1.54 billion in the year-earlier quarter. Revenues were US$46.18 billion, up 3.5% from US$44.62 billion the year before. Operating income was US$2.50 billion versus US$2.82 billion in the prior-year quarter, a decrease of 11.5%. Direct operating expenses rose 5.2% to US$39.06 billion from US$37.12 billion in the comparable period the year before. Indirect operating expenses decreased 0.9% to US$4.63 billion from US$4.67 billion in the equivalent prior-year period.

Prospects: Our evaluation of CVS Health Corp. as of Jan. 14, 2018 is the result of our systematic analysis on three basic characteristics: earnings strength, relative valuation, and recent stock price movement. The company has produced a positive trend in earnings per share over the past 5 quarters. However, while recent estimates for the company have been mixed, CVS has posted better than expected results. Based on operating earnings yield, the company is undervalued when compared to all of the companies in our coverage universe. Share price changes over the past year indicates that CVS will perform poorly over the near term.

Financial Data

(US$ in Thousands)	9 Mos	6 Mos	3 Mos	12/31/2016	12/31/2015	12/31/2014	12/31/2013	12/31/2012
Earnings Per Share	4.83	5.00	4.79	4.90	4.63	3.96	3.74	3.03
Cash Flow Per Share	10.10	11.36	10.86	9.36	7.52	7.01	4.75	5.23
Tang Book Value Per Share	N.M.	N.M.	N.M.	N.M.	N.M.	0.04	1.58	1.26
Dividends Per Share	1.925	1.850	1.775	1.700	1.400	1.100	0.900	0.650
Dividend Payout %	39.86	37.00	37.06	34.69	30.24	27.78	24.06	21.45
Income Statement								
Total Revenue	136,380,000	90,199,000	44,514,000	177,526,000	153,290,000	139,367,000	126,761,000	123,133,000
EBITDA	8,060,000	5,138,000	2,405,000	11,395,000	10,954,000	9,678,000	9,437,000	8,180,000
Depn & Amortn	1,857,000	1,242,000	619,000	1,700,000	1,500,000	1,400,000	1,400,000	1,300,000
Income Before Taxes	5,459,000	3,397,000	1,534,000	8,637,000	8,616,000	7,678,000	7,528,000	6,323,000
Income Taxes	2,115,000	1,338,000	572,000	3,317,000	3,386,000	3,033,000	2,928,000	2,441,000
Net Income	3,335,000	2,050,000	952,000	5,317,000	5,237,000	4,644,000	4,592,000	3,877,000
Average Shares	1,020,000	1,024,000	1,035,000	1,079,000	1,126,000	1,169,000	1,226,000	1,280,000
Balance Sheet								
Current Assets	29,923,000	29,404,000	29,457,000	31,042,000	30,378,000	25,983,000	25,325,000	19,852,000
Total Assets	92,853,000	92,525,000	92,670,000	94,462,000	93,657,000	74,252,000	71,526,000	65,912,000
Current Liabilities	28,513,000	26,857,000	27,288,000	26,250,000	23,169,000	19,027,000	15,425,000	13,790,000
Long-Term Obligations	23,386,000	25,622,000	25,622,000	25,615,000	26,267,000	11,695,000	12,841,000	9,133,000
Total Liabilities	57,990,000	58,383,000	58,833,000	57,632,000	56,461,000	36,294,000	33,588,000	28,208,000
Stockholders' Equity	34,863,000	34,142,000	33,837,000	36,830,000	37,196,000	37,958,000	37,938,000	37,704,000
Shares Outstanding	1,013,000	1,015,000	1,027,000	1,061,000	1,101,000	1,140,000	1,180,000	1,231,000
Statistical Record								
Return on Assets %	5.39	5.72	5.53	5.64	6.24	6.37	6.68	5.93
Return on Equity %	14.24	15.38	14.67	14.33	13.94	12.24	12.14	10.21
EBITDA Margin %	5.91	5.70	5.40	6.42	7.15	6.94	7.44	6.64
Net Margin %	2.45	2.27	2.14	3.00	3.42	3.33	3.62	3.15
Asset Turnover	1.95	1.95	1.93	1.88	1.83	1.91	1.84	1.88
Current Ratio	1.05	1.09	1.08	1.18	1.31	1.37	1.64	1.44
Debt to Equity	0.67	0.75	0.76	0.70	0.71	0.31	0.34	0.24
Price Range	88.99-73.53	98.06-73.53	106.10-73.53	106.10-73.53	113.45-91.56	98.25-65.44	71.58-48.35	49.24-41.46
P/E Ratio	18.42-15.22	19.61-14.71	22.15-15.35	21.65-15.01	24.50-19.78	24.81-16.53	19.14-12.93	16.25-13.68
Average Yield %	2.41	2.21	2.00	1.83	1.38	1.40	1.54	1.43

Address: One CVS Drive, Woonsocket, RI 02895
Telephone: 401-765-1500
Fax: 401-762-2137

Web Site: www.cvshealth.com
Officers: David W. Dorman - Chairman Larry J. Merlo - President, Chief Executive Officer

Auditors: Ernst & Young LLP
Investor Contact: 800-201-0938
Transfer Agents: Computershare, Providence, RI

DAVITA INC

Exchange	Symbol	Price	52Wk Range	Yield	P/E
NYS	DVA	$72.25 (12/29/2017)	72.36-53.89	N/A	27.68

*7 Year Price Score 81.82   *NYSE Composite Index=100   *12 Month Price Score 91.93

Interim Earnings (Per Share)

Qtr.	Mar	Jun	Sep	Dec
2014	0.85	0.68	0.85	0.95
2015	(0.52)	0.78	1.00	(0.02)
2016	0.47	0.26	2.76	0.81
2017	2.29	0.65	(1.14)	...

Interim Dividends (Per Share)

No Dividends Paid

Valuation Analysis   **Institutional Holding**

Forecast EPS	$3.43	No of Institutions
	(01/24/2018)	679
Market Cap	$13.7 Billion	Shares
Book Value	$4.8 Billion	183,834,752
Price/Book	2.86	% Held
Price/Sales	0.90	81.15

TRADING VOLUME (thousand shares)

Business Summary: Diagnostic & Health Related Services (MIC: 4.2.2 SIC: 8092 NAIC: 621492)

DaVita operates two divisions, DaVita Kidney Care (Kidney Care) and DaVita Medical Group (DMG). Kidney Care is comprised of Co.'s U.S. dialysis and related lab services, its ancillary services and strategic initiatives, for patients suffering from chronic kidney failure. Co.'s DMG division is a patient- and physician-focused integrated healthcare delivery and management company. As of Dec 31 2016, Co. provided dialysis and administrative services in the U.S. through a network of 2,350 outpatient dialysis centers in 46 states and the District of Columbia. Co. also provides acute inpatient dialysis services in approximately 900 hospitals and related laboratory services throughout the U.S.

Recent Developments: For the quarter ended Sep 30 2017, net loss amounted to US$172.0 million versus net income of US$612.2 million in the year-earlier quarter. Revenues were US$3.92 billion, up 5.2% from US$3.73 billion the year before. Operating loss was US$192.5 million versus an income of US$819.2 million in the prior-year quarter. Direct operating expenses rose 8.5% to US$2.93 billion from US$2.70 billion in the comparable period the year before. Indirect operating expenses increased 456.3% to US$1.19 billion from US$213.8 million in the equivalent prior-year period.

Prospects: Our evaluation of Davita Inc. as of Jan. 21, 2018 is the result of our systematic analysis on three basic characteristics: earnings strength, relative valuation, and recent stock price movement. The company has managed to produce a neutral trend in earnings per share over the past 5 quarters and while recent estimates for the company have been mixed, DVA has posted results that fell short of analysts expectations. Based on operating earnings yield, the company is undervalued when compared to all of the companies in our coverage universe. Share price changes over the past year indicates that DVA will perform very poorly over the near term.

Financial Data
(US$ in Thousands)

	9 Mos	6 Mos	3 Mos	12/31/2016	12/31/2015	12/31/2014	12/31/2013	12/31/2012
Earnings Per Share	2.61	6.51	6.12	4.29	1.25	3.33	2.95	2.73
Cash Flow Per Share	10.84	10.62	12.47	9.71	7.35	6.87	8.45	5.72
Income Statement								
Total Revenue	11,497,591	7,574,760	3,697,283	14,745,105	13,781,837	12,795,106	11,764,050	8,186,280
EBITDA	1,678,725	1,658,743	1,078,750	2,435,967	1,588,675	2,125,042	1,893,470	1,573,291
Depn & Amortn	593,527	390,244	190,206	545,734	475,484	428,309	373,107	299,810
Income Before Taxes	763,184	1,056,108	784,115	1,475,851	704,811	1,286,439	1,090,420	984,927
Income Taxes	276,005	401,747	287,765	455,813	295,726	446,343	381,013	359,845
Net Income	360,222	574,698	447,697	879,874	269,732	723,114	633,446	536,017
Average Shares	188,883	193,987	195,281	204,904	216,251	216,927	214,763	195,942
Balance Sheet								
Current Assets	4,033,549	4,023,768	4,603,900	3,980,228	4,503,280	3,876,797	3,472,278	2,878,794
Total Assets	19,013,339	19,341,784	19,388,264	18,741,257	18,514,875	17,942,715	17,098,877	16,018,596
Current Liabilities	2,874,793	2,773,325	2,813,577	2,696,445	2,399,138	2,088,652	2,462,049	2,018,174
Long-Term Obligations	8,908,703	8,910,814	8,918,878	8,947,327	9,001,308	8,383,280	8,141,231	8,326,534
Total Liabilities	14,228,758	14,257,470	14,248,335	14,093,210	13,644,095	12,772,202	12,666,398	12,255,459
Stockholders' Equity	4,784,581	5,084,314	5,139,929	4,648,047	4,870,780	5,170,513	4,432,479	3,763,137
Shares Outstanding	189,231	191,200	194,596	194,554	209,754	215,640	213,163	210,997
Statistical Record								
Return on Assets %	2.73	6.86	6.49	4.71	1.48	4.13	3.83	4.29
Return on Equity %	10.68	26.53	24.99	18.44	5.37	15.06	15.46	18.11
EBITDA Margin %	14.60	21.90	29.18	16.52	11.53	16.61	16.10	19.22
Net Margin %	3.13	7.59	12.11	5.97	1.96	5.65	5.38	6.55
Asset Turnover	0.80	0.79	0.78	0.79	0.76	0.73	0.71	0.66
Current Ratio	1.40	1.45	1.64	1.48	1.88	1.86	1.41	1.43
Debt to Equity	1.86	1.75	1.74	1.92	1.85	1.62	1.84	2.21
Price Range	70.09-55.16	78.44-55.16	78.44-55.16	78.44-55.16	84.23-67.79	78.07-62.74	65.59-53.76	57.49-38.56
P/E Ratio	26.85-21.13	12.05-8.47	12.82-9.01	18.28-12.86	67.38-54.23	23.44-18.84	22.24-18.22	21.06-14.13

Address: 2000 16th Street, Denver, CO 80202
Telephone: 303-405-2100

Web Site: www.davita.com
Officers: Kent J. Thiry - Chairman, Co Chairman, Chief Executive Officer Robert J. Margolis - Co-Chairman

Auditors: KPMG LLP
Investor Contact: 310-536-2585
Transfer Agents: Computershare

DANAHER CORP

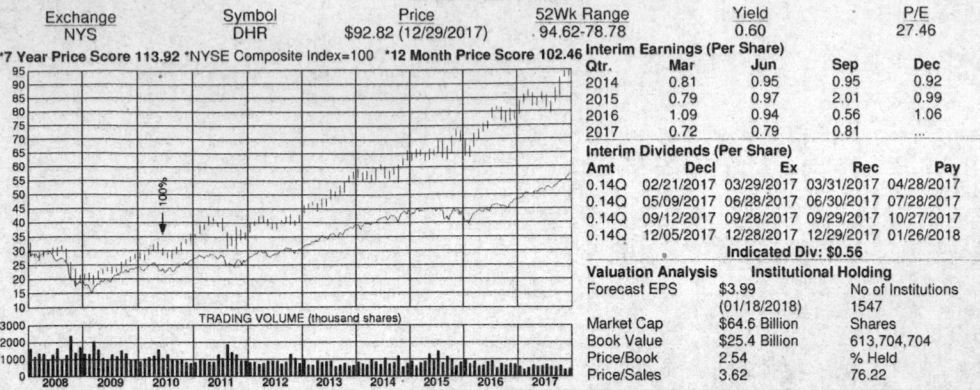

Exchange	Symbol	Price	52Wk Range	Yield	P/E
NYS	DHR	$92.82 (12/29/2017)	94.62-78.78	0.60	27.46

*7 Year Price Score 113.92 *NYSE Composite Index=100 *12 Month Price Score 102.46

Interim Earnings (Per Share)

Qtr.	Mar	Jun	Sep	Dec
2014	0.81	0.95	0.95	0.92
2015	0.79	0.97	2.01	0.99
2016	1.09	0.94	0.56	1.06
2017	0.72	0.79	0.81	...

Interim Dividends (Per Share)

Amt	Decl	Ex	Rec	Pay
0.14Q	02/21/2017	03/29/2017	03/31/2017	04/28/2017
0.14Q	05/09/2017	06/28/2017	06/30/2017	07/28/2017
0.14Q	09/12/2017	09/28/2017	09/29/2017	10/27/2017
0.14Q	12/05/2017	12/28/2017	12/29/2017	01/26/2018

Indicated Div: $0.56

Valuation Analysis / Institutional Holding

Valuation Analysis		Institutional Holding	
Forecast EPS	$3.99	No of Institutions	
	(01/18/2018)	1547	
Market Cap	$64.6 Billion	Shares	
Book Value	$25.4 Billion	613,704,704	
Price/Book	2.54	% Held	
Price/Sales	3.62	76.22	

Business Summary: Medical Instruments & Equipment (MIC: 4.3.1 SIC: 3823 NAIC: 334513)

Danaher designs, manufactures and markets professional, medical, industrial and commercial products and services, Co.'s business consists of four segments: Life Sciences, which provides research tools to study the basic building blocks of life; Diagnostics, which provides analytical instruments, reagents, consumables, software and services that hospitals, physicians' offices, and reference laboratories ; Dental, which provides products that are used to diagnose, treat and prevent disease and ailments of the teeth, gums and supporting bone; and Environmental & Applied Solutions, which its water quality business provides instrumentation, services and disinfection systems.

Recent Developments: For the quarter ended Sep 29 2017, income from continuing operations increased 42.1% to US$572.1 million from US$402.6 million in the year-earlier quarter. Net income increased 46.1% to US$572.1 million from US$391.6 million in the year-earlier quarter. Revenues were US$4.53 billion, up 9.6% from US$4.13 billion the year before. Operating income was US$767.5 million versus US$699.1 million in the prior-year quarter, an increase of 9.8%. Direct operating expenses rose 7.9% to US$1.99 billion from US$1.85 billion in the comparable period the year before. Indirect operating expenses increased 11.5% to US$1.77 billion from US$1.59 billion in the equivalent prior-year period.

Prospects: Our evaluation of Danaher Corp. as of Jan. 14, 2018 is the result of our systematic analysis on three basic characteristics: earnings strength, relative valuation, and recent stock price movement. The company has enjoyed a very positive trend in earnings per share over the past 5 quarters and while recent estimates for the company have remained steady, DHR has posted better than expected results. Based on operating earnings yield, the company is about fairly valued when compared to all of the companies in our coverage universe. Share price changes over the past year indicates that DHR will perform in line with the market over the near term.

Financial Data

(US$ in Thousands)	9 Mos	6 Mos	3 Mos	12/31/2016	12/31/2015	12/31/2014	12/31/2013	12/31/2012
Earnings Per Share	3.38	3.13	3.28	3.65	4.74	3.63	3.80	3.36
Cash Flow Per Share	4.73	4.37	4.77	5.08	5.45	5.35	5.15	4.91
Tang Book Value Per Share	N.M.	N.M.	N.M.	N.M.	N.M.	N.M.	0.14	N.M.
Dividends Per Share	0.545	0.530	0.550	0.570	0.540	0.400	0.100	0.100
Dividend Payout %	16.12	16.93	16.77	15.62	11.39	11.02	2.63	2.98
Income Statement								
Total Revenue	13,244,000	8,715,800	4,205,700	16,882,400	20,563,100	19,913,800	19,118,000	18,260,400
EBITDA	2,995,300	1,916,400	929,500	3,340,500	4,055,000	4,140,400	4,236,100	3,593,000
Depn & Amortn	920,200	608,800	305,600	545,000	573,500	552,600	529,900	497,800
Income Before Taxes	1,959,800	1,230,000	585,200	2,611,300	3,324,000	3,481,800	3,566,000	2,940,900
Income Taxes	346,600	188,900	101,400	457,900	725,300	883,400	871,000	711,500
Net Income	1,635,500	1,063,400	506,100	2,553,700	3,357,400	2,598,400	2,695,000	2,392,200
Average Shares	705,600	705,400	705,700	699,800	708,500	716,100	711,000	713,100
Balance Sheet								
Current Assets	6,260,200	6,256,600	6,318,900	6,665,100	7,836,700	9,431,300	9,113,700	7,587,800
Total Assets	45,851,300	45,646,800	45,245,100	45,295,300	48,222,200	36,991,700	34,672,200	32,941,000
Current Liabilities	4,387,500	4,202,600	6,003,100	6,874,000	6,170,400	5,396,400	4,527,400	4,206,100
Long-Term Obligations	10,726,800	11,422,500	9,729,300	9,674,200	12,025,200	3,401,500	3,436,700	5,287,600
Total Liabilities	20,475,900	21,056,800	21,459,300	22,292,500	24,531,900	13,613,600	12,286,900	13,924,500
Stockholders' Equity	25,375,400	24,590,000	23,785,800	23,002,800	23,690,300	23,378,100	22,385,300	19,016,500
Shares Outstanding	695,500	694,700	694,100	692,200	686,800	704,300	698,100	687,500
Statistical Record								
Return on Assets %	5.47	4.53	4.92	5.45	7.88	7.25	7.97	7.59
Return on Equity %	9.81	8.87	9.53	10.91	14.27	11.36	13.02	13.28
EBITDA Margin %	22.62	21.99	22.10	19.79	19.72	20.79	22.16	19.68
Net Margin %	12.35	12.20	12.03	15.13	16.33	13.05	14.10	13.10
Asset Turnover	0.41	0.36	0.40	0.36	0.48	0.56	0.57	0.58
Current Ratio	1.43	1.49	1.05	0.97	1.27	1.75	2.01	1.80
Debt to Equity	0.42	0.46	0.41	0.42	0.51	0.15	0.15	0.28
Price Range	88.45-75.86	87.76-75.86	87.76-70.24	81.84-63.35	73.78-62.06	65.98-54.34	58.51-42.37	43.07-36.63
P/E Ratio	26.17-22.44	28.04-24.24	26.76-21.42	22.42-17.36	15.57-13.09	18.18-14.97	15.40-11.15	12.82-10.90
Average Yield %	0.66	0.65	0.70	0.76	0.81	0.68	0.20	0.25

Address: 2200 Pennsylvania Avenue, N.W., Suite 800W, Washington, DC 20037-1701 Telephone: 202-828-0850 Fax: 202-828-0860	Web Site: www.danaher.com Officers: Steven M. Rales - Chairman Thomas Patrick (Tom) Joyce - President, Chief Executive Officer, Executive Vice President	Auditors: Ernst & Young LLP Investor Contact: 202-828-0850 Transfer Agents: Computershare, Providence, RI

DARDEN RESTAURANTS, INC.

Exchange	Symbol	Price	52Wk Range	Yield	P/E
NYS	DRI	$96.02 (12/29/2017)	97.50-71.55	2.62	24.62

*7 Year Price Score 117.93 *NYSE Composite Index=100 ***12 Month Price Score 98.78**

TRADING VOLUME (thousand shares)

2008 2009 2010 2011 2012 2013 2014 2015 2016 2017

Interim Earnings (Per Share)

Qtr.	Aug	Nov	Feb	May
2014-15	3.81	(0.26)	1.05	0.83
2015-16	0.67	0.33	0.82	1.08
2016-17	0.87	0.64	1.32	0.98
2017-18	0.93	0.67	...	...

Interim Dividends (Per Share)

Amt	Decl	Ex	Rec	Pay
0.56Q	03/22/2017	04/06/2017	04/10/2017	05/01/2017
0.63Q	06/26/2017	07/06/2017	07/10/2017	08/01/2017
0.63Q	09/21/2017	10/06/2017	10/10/2017	11/01/2017
0.63Q	12/14/2017	01/09/2018	01/10/2018	02/01/2018

Indicated Div: $2.52 (Div. Reinv. Plan)

Valuation Analysis | **Institutional Holding**

Forecast EPS	$4.76
	(01/18/2018)
Market Cap	$11.9 Billion
Book Value	$2.0 Billion
Price/Book	6.00
Price/Sales	1.55

No of Institutions	853
Shares	144,818,208
% Held	83.70

Business Summary: Hotels, Restaurants & Travel (MIC: 2.2.1 SIC: 5812 NAIC: 722110)

Darden Restaurants is a restaurant company. Co. has four reportable segments: Olive Garden; LongHorn Steakhouse; Fine Dining (which includes The Capital Grille and Eddie V's); and Other Business (which includes Cheddar's Scratch Kitchen, Yard House, Seasons 52, Bahama Breeze, consumer-packaged goods and franchise activities). As of May 28 2017, Co. owned and operated 1,695 restaurants through subsidiaries in the U.S. and Canada. As of May 28 2017, Co. also had 78 restaurants operated by independent third parties pursuant to area development and franchise agreements.

Recent Developments: For the quarter ended Nov 26 2017, income from continuing operations increased 11.2% to US$88.6 million from US$79.7 million in the year-earlier quarter. Net income increased 6.5% to US$84.7 million from US$79.5 million in the year-earlier quarter. Revenues were US$1.88 billion, up 14.6% from US$1.64 billion the year before. Operating income was US$128.9 million versus US$116.5 million in the prior-year quarter, an increase of 10.6%. Direct operating expenses rose 14.8% to US$1.52 billion from US$1.32 billion in the comparable period the year before. Indirect operating expenses increased 15.3% to US$235.8 million from US$204.5 million in the equivalent prior-year period.

Prospects: Our evaluation of Darden Restaurants Inc. as of Jan. 14, 2018 is the result of our systematic analysis on three basic characteristics: earnings strength, relative valuation, and recent stock price movement. The company has produced a positive trend in earnings per share over the past 5 quarters and while recent estimates for the company have been raised by analysts, DRI has posted better than expected results. Based on operating earnings yield, the company is undervalued when compared to all of the companies in our coverage universe. Share price changes over the past year indicates that DRI will perform poorly over the near term.

Financial Data

(US$ in Thousands)	6 Mos	3 Mos	05/28/2017	05/29/2016	05/31/2015	05/25/2014	05/26/2013	05/27/2012
Earnings Per Share	3.90	3.87	3.80	2.90	5.47	2.15	3.13	3.57
Cash Flow Per Share	7.59	7.38	7.41	6.46	6.74	4.25	7.38	5.87
Tang Book Value Per Share	N.M.	N.M.	N.M.	4.00	7.00	5.37	3.74	5.97
Dividends Per Share	2.380	2.310	2.240	2.100	2.200	2.200	2.000	1.720
Dividend Payout %	61.03	59.69	58.95	72.41	40.22	102.33	63.90	48.18
Income Statement								
Total Revenue	3,817,600	1,936,100	7,170,200	6,933,500	6,764,000	6,285,600	8,551,900	7,998,700
EBITDA	304,300	174,600	951,400	916,000	695,500	627,100	1,056,100	1,095,400
Depn & Amortn	900	100	273,900	293,800	327,900	318,200	407,800	355,800
Income Before Taxes	272,900	159,500	637,300	449,700	175,300	174,600	522,400	638,000
Income Taxes	63,000	38,200	154,800	90,000	(21,100)	(8,600)	109,800	161,500
Net Income	203,700	119,000	479,100	375,000	709,500	286,200	411,900	475,500
Average Shares	125,500	127,300	126,000	129,300	129,700	133,200	131,600	133,200
Balance Sheet								
Current Assets	485,200	483,000	799,800	820,300	1,056,400	1,976,400	764,900	757,600
Total Assets	5,317,600	5,223,500	5,504,200	4,582,600	5,994,700	7,100,700	6,936,900	5,944,200
Current Liabilities	1,418,000	1,258,300	1,289,200	1,187,100	1,196,700	1,618,500	1,416,400	1,774,100
Long-Term Obligations	935,600	936,600	936,600	440,000	1,452,300	2,533,400	2,548,700	1,508,100
Total Liabilities	3,341,500	3,164,800	3,402,500	2,630,600	3,661,200	4,943,800	4,877,400	4,102,200
Stockholders' Equity	1,976,100	2,058,700	2,101,700	1,952,000	2,333,500	2,156,900	2,059,500	1,842,000
Shares Outstanding	123,533	123,673	125,400	126,200	126,700	132,300	130,300	129,000
Statistical Record								
Return on Assets %	10.08	10.17	9.53	7.11	10.66	4.09	6.41	8.36
Return on Equity %	25.75	25.28	23.70	17.55	31.09	13.61	21.17	25.24
EBITDA Margin %	7.97	9.02	13.27	13.21	10.28	9.98	12.35	13.69
Net Margin %	5.34	6.15	6.68	5.41	10.49	4.55	4.82	5.94
Asset Turnover	1.56	1.54	1.43	1.31	1.02	0.90	1.33	1.41
Current Ratio	0.34	0.38	0.62	0.69	0.88	1.22	0.54	0.43
Debt to Equity	0.47	0.45	0.45	0.23	0.62	1.17	1.24	0.82
Price Range	92.69-71.55	92.69-60.63	88.40-59.68	67.78-53.93	62.44-39.18	48.94-40.99	51.23-39.79	48.02-37.19
P/E Ratio	23.77-18.35	23.95-15.67	23.26-15.71	23.37-18.60	11.41-7.16	22.76-19.07	16.37-12.71	13.45-10.42
Average Yield %	2.92	2.99	3.15	3.39	4.41	4.89	4.43	3.99

Address: 1000 Darden Center Drive, Orlando, FL 32837	**Web Site:** www.darden.com	**Auditors:** KPMG LLP
Telephone: 407-245-4000	**Officers:** Charles M. (Chuck) Sonsteby - Chairman Eugene I. (Gene) Lee - President, President (frmr), Chief Executive Officer, Interim Chief Executive Officer, Division Officer	**Investor Contact:** 800-832-7336 **Transfer Agents:** Wells Fargo Shareowner Services, Mendota Heights, MN

DANA INC

Exchange	Symbol	Price	52Wk Range	Yield	P/E
NYS	DAN	$32.01 (12/29/2017)	33.04-17.57	0.75	6.74

*7 Year Price Score 102.46 *NYSE Composite Index=100 *12 Month Price Score 126.35

Interim Earnings (Per Share)

Qtr.	Mar	Jun	Sep	Dec
2014	0.19	0.49	0.52	0.64
2015	0.38	0.36	0.75	(0.49)
2016	0.30	0.36	0.39	3.31
2017	0.51	0.47	0.46	...

Interim Dividends (Per Share)

Amt	Decl	Ex	Rec	Pay
0.06Q	02/16/2017	03/01/2017	03/03/2017	03/24/2017
0.06Q	04/27/2017	05/10/2017	05/12/2017	06/02/2017
0.06Q	07/26/2017	08/09/2017	08/11/2017	09/01/2017
0.06Q	10/25/2017	11/09/2017	11/10/2017	12/01/2017

Indicated Div: $0.24

Valuation Analysis — **Institutional Holding**

Forecast EPS	$2.44	No of Institutions
	(01/26/2018)	363
Market Cap	$4.6 Billion	Shares
Book Value	$1.2 Billion	169,137,776
Price/Book	3.90	% Held
Price/Sales	0.68	N/A

Business Summary: Auto Parts (MIC: 1.8.2 SIC: 3714 NAIC: 336399)

Dana is a holding company. Through its subsidiaries, Co is a provider of driveline, sealing and thermal-management products its customer base. Co. has four segments: Light Vehicle Driveline Technologies, which include front axles, rear axles, drive shafts, differentials, torque couplings and modular assemblies; Commercial Vehicle Driveline Technologies, which include steer axles, drive axles, drive shafts, and tire inflation systems; Off-Highway Driveline Technologies, which include front axles, rear axles, driveshafts, transmissions, torque converters, tire inflation systems, and electronic controls; and Power Technologies, which include gaskets, cover modules and heat shields.

Recent Developments: For the quarter ended Sep 30 2017, net income increased 19.7% to US$73.0 million from US$61.0 million in the year-earlier quarter. Revenues were US$1.83 billion, up 32.3% from US$1.38 billion the year before. Direct operating expenses rose 32.8% to US$1.56 billion from US$1.18 billion in the comparable period the year before. Indirect operating expenses increased 22.0% to US$144.0 million from US$118.0 million in the equivalent prior-year period.

Prospects: Our evaluation of Dana Inc. as of Jan. 21, 2018 is the result of our systematic analysis on three basic characteristics: earnings strength, relative valuation, and recent stock price movement. The company has generated a negative trend in earnings per share over the past 5 quarters and while recent estimates for the company have been mixed, DAN has posted better than expected results. Based on operating earnings yield, the company is undervalued when compared to all of the companies in our coverage universe. Share price changes over the past year indicates that DAN will perform very well over the near term.

Financial Data

(US$ in Thousands)	9 Mos	6 Mos	3 Mos	12/31/2016	12/31/2015	12/31/2014	12/31/2013	12/31/2012
Earnings Per Share	4.75	4.68	4.57	4.36	0.99	1.84	(0.09)	-1.40
Cash Flow Per Share	3.88	2.80	2.92	2.62	2.55	3.23	3.94	2.28
Tang Book Value Per Share	6.03	5.55	5.29	6.66	3.64	4.94	4.16	4.48
Dividends Per Share	0.240	0.240	0.240	0.240	0.230	0.200	0.200	0.200
Dividend Payout %	5.05	5.13	5.25	5.50	23.23	10.87	...	14.29
Income Statement								
Total Revenue	5,372,000	3,541,000	1,701,000	5,826,000	6,060,000	6,617,000	6,769,000	7,224,000
EBITDA	555,000	366,000	182,000	497,000	566,000	576,000	704,000	701,000
Depn & Amortn	176,000	113,000	53,000	182,000	174,000	213,000	262,000	277,000
Income Before Taxes	308,000	204,000	105,000	215,000	292,000	260,000	368,000	364,000
Income Taxes	94,000	61,000	30,000	(424,000)	82,000	(70,000)	119,000	51,000
Net Income	215,000	146,000	75,000	640,000	159,000	319,000	244,000	300,000
Average Shares	146,900	146,200	145,900	146,800	160,000	173,500	146,400	214,700
Balance Sheet								
Current Assets	2,843,000	2,775,000	2,504,000	2,284,000	2,474,000	2,954,000	3,165,000	2,953,000
Total Assets	5,710,000	5,597,000	5,290,000	4,860,000	4,326,000	4,930,000	5,129,000	5,144,000
Current Liabilities	1,653,000	1,587,000	1,616,000	1,253,000	1,091,000	1,261,000	1,268,000	1,310,000
Long-Term Obligations	1,765,000	1,841,000	1,623,000	1,595,000	1,553,000	1,613,000	1,567,000	803,000
Total Liabilities	4,522,000	4,478,000	4,212,000	3,703,000	3,598,000	3,850,000	3,820,000	3,301,000
Stockholders' Equity	1,188,000	1,119,000	1,078,000	1,157,000	728,000	1,080,000	1,309,000	1,843,000
Shares Outstanding	144,861	144,656	144,541	143,938	150,068	166,070	145,338	148,264
Statistical Record								
Return on Assets %	13.56	13.54	13.73	13.90	3.44	6.34	4.75	5.73
Return on Equity %	71.39	73.90	72.20	67.72	17.59	26.71	15.48	16.71
EBITDA Margin %	10.33	10.34	10.70	8.53	9.34	8.70	10.40	9.70
Net Margin %	4.00	4.12	4.41	10.99	2.62	4.82	3.60	4.15
Asset Turnover	1.32	1.25	1.25	1.26	1.31	1.32	1.32	1.38
Current Ratio	1.72	1.75	1.55	1.82	2.27	2.34	2.50	2.25
Debt to Equity	1.49	1.65	1.51	1.38	2.13	1.49	1.20	0.44
Price Range	28.08-14.29	22.34-10.09	20.34-10.09	19.74-10.09	23.20-13.11	24.60-17.21	23.32-15.52	16.55-11.31
P/E Ratio	5.91-3.01	4.77-2.16	4.45-2.21	4.53-2.31	23.43-13.24	13.37-9.35	...	11.82-8.08
Average Yield %	1.19	1.37	1.55	1.74	1.20	0.93	1.05	1.43

Address: 3939 Technology Drive, Maumee, OH 43537	**Web Site:** www.dana.com	**Auditors:** PricewaterhouseCoopers LLP
Telephone: 419-887-3000	**Officers:** James K. Kamsickas - President, Chief Executive Officer Jonathan M. Collins - Executive Vice President, Senior Vice President, Chief Financial Officer	**Investor Contact:** 800-537-8823
Fax: 419-887-5200		**Transfer Agents:** Wells Fargo Shareowner Services

DCT INDUSTRIAL TRUST INC

Exchange	Symbol	Price	52Wk Range	Yield	P/E
NYS	DCT	$58.78 (12/29/2017)	61.42-44.18	2.45	52.95

*7 Year Price Score 123.27 *NYSE Composite Index=100 ***12 Month Price Score 104.43**

Interim Earnings (Per Share)

Qtr.	Mar	Jun	Sep	Dec
2014	0.00	0.08	0.16	0.34
2015	0.32	0.20	0.09	0.43
2016	0.41	0.24	0.17	0.22
2017	0.16	0.45	0.28	...

Interim Dividends (Per Share)

Amt	Decl	Ex	Rec	Pay
0.31Q	02/02/2017	03/29/2017	03/31/2017	04/12/2017
0.31Q	05/03/2017	06/28/2017	06/30/2017	07/12/2017
0.31Q	08/03/2017	10/05/2017	10/00/2017	10/18/2017
0.36Q	11/02/2017	12/21/2017	12/22/2017	01/04/2018

Indicated Div: $1.44 (Div. Reinv. Plan)

Valuation Analysis

		Institutional Holding	
Forecast EPS	$1.05 (01/11/2018)	No of Institutions	354
Market Cap	$5.5 Billion	Shares	120,180,776
Book Value	$1.9 Billion	% Held	100.98
Price/Book	2.84		
Price/Sales	13.09		

Business Summary: REITs (MIC: 5.3.1 SIC: 6798 NAIC: 525930)

DCT Industrial Trust is an industrial real estate company engaged in the ownership, acquisition, development, leasing and management of bulk-distribution and light-industrial properties located in the U.S. As of Dec 31 2016, Co. owned interests in approximately 74.0 million square feet of properties leased to approximately 900 customers, including: 401 consolidated operating properties; 23 unconsolidated properties; three consolidated properties under redevelopment; and four consolidated properties which are shell-complete and in lease-up. In addition, Co. has 10 projects under construction and several projects in pre-development.

Recent Developments: For the quarter ended Sep 30 2017, net income increased 64.6% to US$27.0 million from US$16.4 million in the year-earlier quarter. Revenues were US$105.2 million, up 4.9% from US$100.3 million the year before. Revenues from property income rose 4.9% to US$104.9 million from US$99.9 million in the corresponding quarter a year earlier.

Prospects: Our evaluation of DCT Industrial Trust Inc. as of Jan. 14, 2018 is the result of our systematic analysis on three basic characteristics: earnings strength, relative valuation, and recent stock price movement. The company has managed to produce a neutral trend in earnings per share over the past 5 quarters and while recent estimates for the company have been mixed, DCT has posted better than expected results. Based on operating earnings yield, the company is overvalued when compared to all of the companies in our coverage universe. Share price changes over the past year indicates that DCT will perform very well over the near term.

Financial Data

(US$ in Thousands)	9 Mos	6 Mos	3 Mos	12/31/2016	12/31/2015	12/31/2014	12/31/2013	12/31/2012
Earnings Per Share	1.11	1.00	0.79	1.03	1.05	0.58	0.20	(0.24)
Cash Flow Per Share	2.66	2.86	2.49	2.46	2.27	2.04	2.05	1.87
Tang Book Value Per Share	20.67	20.70	20.27	20.35	19.84	19.88	19.28	18.97
Dividends Per Share	1.220	1.220	1.200	1.180	1.130	0.280	1.120	...
Dividend Payout %	109.91	122.00	151.90	114.56	107.62	48.28	560.00	...
Income Statement								
Total Revenue	315,597	210,417	105,896	392,776	354,697	336,526	289,005	260,779
EBITDA	256,247	171,855	72,772	319,327	306,533	250,734	188,584	171,674
Depn & Amortn	125,479	83,052	41,605	161,334	156,010	148,992	137,120	126,687
Income Before Taxes	81,173	55,231	14,407	94,509	96,428	40,069	(11,656)	(23,996)
Income Taxes	147	203	134	591	736	...	...	...
Net Income	82,374	56,593	14,959	93,060	94,048	49,164	15,870	(15,086)
Average Shares	93,078	92,429	91,884	89,982	88,514	83,572	74,692	63,707
Balance Sheet								
Current Assets	45,715	55,568	14,004	17,632	49,599	23,410	44,847	22,772
Total Assets	3,952,003	3,866,949	3,824,843	3,808,142	3,632,355	3,451,534	3,265,963	3,057,199
Current Liabilities	178,173	160,381	143,653	155,603	165,389	140,055	115,615	103,025
Long-Term Obligations	1,696,317	1,624,730	1,659,369	1,628,928	1,556,472	1,409,045	1,452,367	1,452,314
Total Liabilities	2,029,574	1,942,560	1,963,011	1,946,093	1,880,371	1,701,702	1,722,157	1,728,135
Stockholders' Equity	1,922,429	1,924,389	1,861,832	1,862,049	1,751,984	1,749,832	1,543,806	1,329,064
Shares Outstanding	93,018	92,956	91,844	91,516	88,313	88,012	80,066	70,077
Statistical Record								
Return on Assets %	2.66	2.43	1.91	2.49	2.66	1.46	0.50	N.M.
Return on Equity %	5.43	4.92	3.95	5.14	5.37	2.99	1.10	N.M.
EBITDA Margin %	81.19	81.67	68.72	81.30	86.42	74.51	65.25	65.83
Net Margin %	26.10	26.90	14.13	23.69	26.52	14.61	5.49	N.M.
Asset Turnover	0.11	0.11	0.11	0.11	0.10	0.10	0.09	0.09
Current Ratio	0.26	0.35	0.10	0.11	0.30	0.17	0.39	0.22
Debt to Equity	0.88	0.84	0.89	0.87	0.89	0.81	0.94	1.09
Price Range	59.82-43.47	55.20-43.47	50.43-39.46	50.43-33.99	38.60-31.31	36.47-27.64	33.32-25.96	27.44-20.28
P/E Ratio	53.89-39.16	55.20-43.47	63.84-49.95	48.96-33.00	36.76-29.82	62.88-47.66	166.60-129.80	...
Average Yield %	2.41	2.52	2.52	2.71	3.24	0.88	3.81	...

Address: 555 17th Street, Suite 3700, Denver, CO 80202 **Telephone:** 303-597-2400	**Web Site:** www.dctindustrial.com **Officers:** Thomas F. August - Chairman Philip L. Hawkins - President, Chief Executive Officer, President (frmr)	**Auditors:** Ernst & Young LLP **Investor Contact:** 303-597-1550 **Transfer Agents:** BNY Mellon Shareowner Services, Jersey City, NJ

DDR CORP

Exchange	Symbol	Price	52Wk Range	Yield	P/E
NYS	DDR	$8.96 (12/29/2017)	15.47-7.41	8.48	N/A

*7 Year Price Score 54.68   *NYSE Composite Index=100   *12 Month Price Score 71.37

Interim Earnings (Per Share)

Qtr.	Mar	Jun	Sep	Dec
2014	(0.07)	0.19	0.17	(0.05)
2015	(0.69)	0.03	0.15	0.24
2016	0.11	0.10	(0.18)	0.08
2017	(0.16)	0.06	(0.02)	...

Interim Dividends (Per Share)

Amt	Decl	Ex	Rec	Pay
0.19Q	02/10/2017	03/14/2017	03/16/2017	04/04/2017
0.19Q	05/10/2017	06/13/2017	06/15/2017	07/06/2017
0.19Q	09/13/2017	09/25/2017	09/26/2017	10/10/2017
0.19Q	11/10/2017	12/11/2017	12/12/2017	01/05/2018

Indicated Div: $0.76

Valuation Analysis		Institutional Holding	
Forecast EPS	$-0.08	No of Institutions	411
	(01/18/2018)		
Market Cap	$3.3 Billion	Shares	402,082,496
Book Value	$3.2 Billion	% Held	
Price/Book	1.03	N/A	
Price/Sales	3.48		

Business Summary: REITs (MIC: 5.3.1 SIC: 6798 NAIC: 525930)

DDR is a self-administered and self-managed real estate investment trust (REIT), engaged in the business of acquiring, owning, developing, redeveloping, expanding, leasing, financing and managing shopping centers. At Dec 31 2016, Co. owned and managed approximately 106.0 million total square feet of gross leasable area. Co.'s portfolio as of Feb 10 2017, consisted of 317 shopping centers (including 152 centers owned through joint ventures) and more than 650 acres of undeveloped land (of which approximately 100 acres are owned through unconsolidated joint ventures). The shopping centers are located in 35 states as well as Puerto Rico (14 assets).

Recent Developments: For the quarter ended Sep 30 2017, loss from continuing operations was US$43.1 million compared with a loss of US$81.4 million in the year-earlier quarter. Net income amounted to US$1.2 million versus a net loss of US$60.1 million in the year-earlier quarter. Revenues were US$227.4 million, down 10.4% from US$253.8 million the year before. Revenues from property income fell 13.6% to US$206.3 million from US$238.8 million in the corresponding quarter a year earlier.

Prospects: Our evaluation of DDR Corp. as of Jan. 14, 2018 is the result of our systematic analysis on three basic characteristics: earnings strength, relative valuation, and recent stock price movement. The company has suffered a very negative trend in earnings per share over the past 5 quarters. Because the company lacks sufficient analyst estimate data, we place greater weight on the historical EPS trend as the measure of earnings strength. Based on operating earnings yield, the company is overvalued when compared to all of the companies in our coverage universe. Share price changes over the past year indicates that DDR will perform very poorly over the near term.

Financial Data

(US$ in Thousands)	9 Mos	6 Mos	3 Mos	12/31/2016	12/31/2015	12/31/2014	12/31/2013	12/31/2012
Earnings Per Share	(0.04)	(0.20)	(0.16)	0.10	(0.27)	0.25	(0.14)	(0.21)
Cash Flow Per Share	1.13	1.20	1.29	1.26	1.20	1.17	1.15	1.04
Tang Book Value Per Share	6.69	6.84	6.92	7.24	7.67	8.43	8.62	8.93
Dividends Per Share	0.760	0.760	0.760	0.760	0.690	0.620	0.540	0.480
Dividend Payout %	...	...	...	760.00	...	248.00	...	...
Income Statement								
Total Revenue	704,032	476,608	240,421	1,005,805	1,028,071	985,675	888,788	800,375
EBITDA	(11,777)	(16,725)	(45,926)	546,096	380,784	664,370	541,388	421,954
Depn & Amortn	5,959	1,896	906	391,666	396,730	431,204	338,277	265,195
Income Before Taxes	(142,402)	(103,798)	(90,267)	(26,105)	(228,460)	11,973	(2,219)	(48,866)
Income Taxes	9,963	696	223	1,781	6,286	1,855	2,713	1,160
Net Income	(23,647)	(24,630)	(54,241)	60,012	(72,168)	117,282	(10,175)	(25,822)
Average Shares	367,686	367,030	366,430	365,561	360,946	358,122	326,426	291,726
Balance Sheet								
Current Assets	216,246	609,575	233,756	210,095	204,143	221,218	327,991	249,778
Total Assets	7,640,697	8,270,038	8,092,966	8,197,518	9,097,088	9,541,895	9,693,073	8,055,837
Current Liabilities	434,150	445,156	444,793	457,538	494,082	509,660	470,520	370,234
Long-Term Obligations	4,017,531	4,566,666	4,520,926	4,493,968	5,139,537	5,234,707	5,294,674	4,319,143
Total Liabilities	4,460,604	5,020,524	4,974,265	4,960,003	5,641,903	5,771,647	5,788,412	4,713,699
Stockholders' Equity	3,180,093	3,249,514	3,118,701	3,237,515	3,455,185	3,770,248	3,904,661	3,342,138
Shares Outstanding	367,146	366,482	365,965	365,350	364,347	359,754	358,348	314,261
Statistical Record								
Return on Assets %	0.12	N.M.	N.M.	0.69	N.M.	1.22	N.M.	N.M.
Return on Equity %	0.31	N.M.	N.M.	1.79	N.M.	3.06	N.M.	N.M.
EBITDA Margin %	N.M.	N.M.	N.M.	54.29	37.04	67.40	60.91	52.72
Net Margin %	N.M.	N.M.	N.M.	5.97	N.M.	11.90	N.M.	N.M.
Asset Turnover	0.12	0.11	0.12	0.12	0.11	0.10	0.10	0.10
Current Ratio	0.50	1.37	0.53	0.46	0.41	0.43	0.70	0.67
Debt to Equity	1.26	1.41	1.45	1.39	1.49	1.39	1.36	1.29
Price Range	17.43-8.38	19.91-8.38	19.91-12.47	19.91-14.76	20.36-14.75	18.70-15.06	19.41-14.95	15.86-12.28
P/E Ratio	...	...	...	199.10-147.60	...	74.80-60.24	...	...
Average Yield %	6.12	5.17	4.60	4.44	4.01	3.61	3.21	3.26

Address: 3300 Enterprise Parkway, Beachwood, OH 44122
Telephone: 216-755-5500
Fax: 216-755-1500

Web Site: www.ddr.com
Officers: Thomas F. August - President, Chief Executive Officer David R. Lukes - President, Chief Executive Officer

Auditors: PricewaterhouseCoopers LLP
Transfer Agents: Computershare, Providence, RI

DEAN FOODS CO.

Exchange	Symbol	Price	52Wk Range	Yield	P/E
NYS	DF	$11.56 (12/29/2017)	21.91-9.09	3.11	25.13

*7 Year Price Score 78.52 *NYSE Composite Index=100 *12 Month Price Score 65.70

Interim Earnings (Per Share)

Qtr.	Mar	Jun	Sep	Dec
2014	(0.09)	(0.01)	(0.17)	0.05
2015	(0.78)	0.28	0.22	0.20
2016	0.43	0.36	0.16	0.36
2017	(0.11)	0.19	0.02	...

Interim Dividends (Per Share)

Amt	Decl	Ex	Rec	Pay
0.09Q	03/08/2017	03/16/2017	03/20/2017	03/29/2017
0.09Q	05/10/2017	05/18/2017	05/22/2017	06/01/2017
0.09Q	00/09/2017	08/17/2017	08/21/2017	08/30/2017
0.09Q	11/08/2017	11/17/2017	11/20/2017	12/05/2017

Indicated Div: $0.36

Valuation Analysis

		Institutional Holding	
Forecast EPS	$0.80 (01/18/2018)	No of Institutions	407
Market Cap	$1.1 Billion	Shares	119,940,720
Book Value	$604.4 Million	% Held	N/A
Price/Book	1.74		
Price/Sales	0.13		

Business Summary: Food (MIC: 1.2.1 SIC: 2024 NAIC: 311520)

Dean Foods is a food and beverage company and a processor and direct-to-store distributor of fluid milk and other dairy and dairy case products. Co. manufactures, markets and distributes a branded and private label dairy and dairy case products, including fluid milk, ice cream, cultured dairy products, creamers, ice cream mix and other dairy products to retailers, educational institutions and governmental entities. Co.'s portfolio includes DairyPurewhite, TruMoo®, Alta Dena ®, Berkeley Farms ®, Country Fresh ®, Dean's ®, Friendly's ®, Garelick Farms ®, LAND O LAKES ®, Mayfield ® and more. Co. also makes and distributes ice cream, cultured products, juices, teas and bottled water.

Recent Developments: For the quarter ended Sep 30 2017, loss from continuing operations was US$10.0 million compared with income of US$14.5 million in the year-earlier quarter. Net income decreased 90.5% to US$1.4 million from US$14.5 million in the year-earlier quarter. Revenues were US$1.94 billion, down 1.4% from US$1.96 billion the year before. Operating income was US$2.2 million versus US$42.0 million in the prior-year quarter, a decrease of 94.7%. Direct operating expenses rose 1.4% to US$1.50 billion from US$1.48 billion in the comparable period the year before. Indirect operating expenses decreased 1.6% to US$439.5 million from US$446.8 million in the equivalent prior-year period.

Prospects: Our evaluation of Dean Foods Co. as of Jan. 14, 2018 is the result of our systematic analysis on three basic characteristics: earnings strength, relative valuation, and recent stock price movement. The company has enjoyed a very positive trend in earnings per share over the past 5 quarters and while recent estimates for the company have been mixed, DF has posted results that fell short of analysts expectations. Based on operating earnings yield, the company is undervalued when compared to all of the companies in our coverage universe. Share price changes over the past year indicates that DF will perform very poorly over the near term.

Financial Data

(US$ in Thousands)	9 Mos	6 Mos	3 Mos	12/31/2016	12/31/2015	12/31/2014	12/31/2013	12/31/2012
Earnings Per Share	0.46	0.60	0.77	1.31	(0.09)	(0.22)	8.58	1.70
Cash Flow Per Share	1.53	2.32	2.63	2.82	4.37	1.63	(3.38)	4.76
Tang Book Value Per Share	4.80	4.85	4.85	5.04	5.02	5.74	6.62	N.M.
Dividends Per Share	0.360	0.360	0.360	0.360	0.280	0.280	...	...
Dividend Payout %	78.26	60.00	46.75	27.48	...	...	...	...
Income Statement								
Total Revenue	5,860,028	3,922,408	1,995,686	7,710,226	8,121,661	9,503,196	9,016,321	11,462,277
EBITDA	68,296	60,187	9,063	442,098	224,856	168,125	649,061	675,077
Depn & Amortn	15,542	10,310	5,155	172,652	171,353	159,389	165,469	246,583
Income Before Taxes	2,344	15,994	(13,556)	202,651	(13,310)	(52,283)	283,034	263,922
Income Taxes	4,429	8,106	(3,797)	82,034	(5,229)	(32,096)	(42,325)	146,509
Net Income	9,270	7,888	(9,759)	119,929	(8,508)	(20,296)	813,178	158,622
Average Shares	90,939	91,369	90,709	91,510	93,298	93,916	94,796	93,065
Balance Sheet								
Current Assets	1,016,423	968,083	1,011,373	1,058,630	1,077,563	1,180,060	1,150,698	2,202,778
Total Assets	2,506,711	2,494,248	2,525,740	2,606,227	2,528,015	2,769,636	2,802,045	5,687,091
Current Liabilities	791,181	797,471	825,953	847,787	761,895	794,451	781,087	1,340,993
Long-Term Obligations	803,598	762,125	750,195	745,245	840,932	916,481	896,564	3,077,258
Total Liabilities	1,902,293	1,886,037	1,930,713	1,995,671	1,982,511	2,142,318	2,087,730	5,329,904
Stockholders' Equity	604,418	608,211	595,027	610,556	545,504	627,318	714,315	357,187
Shares Outstanding	91,004	90,913	90,872	90,586	91,428	94,080	94,831	92,781
Statistical Record								
Return on Assets %	1.66	2.20	2.85	4.66	N.M.	N.M.	19.16	2.77
Return on Equity %	7.05	9.29	12.10	20.69	N.M.	N.M.	151.78	124.66
EBITDA Margin %	1.17	1.53	0.45	5.73	2.77	1.77	7.20	5.89
Net Margin %	0.16	0.20	N.M.	1.56	N.M.	N.M.	9.02	1.38
Asset Turnover	3.11	3.14	3.14	3.00	3.07	3.41	2.12	2.00
Current Ratio	1.28	1.21	1.22	1.25	1.41	1.49	1.47	1.64
Debt to Equity	1.33	1.25	1.26	1.22	1.54	1.46	1.26	8.62
Price Range	22.00-10.40	22.00-15.88	22.00-15.88	22.00-15.88	19.56-15.41	19.40-12.70	22.70-14.35	17.48-9.82
P/E Ratio	47.83-22.61	36.67-26.47	28.57-20.62	16.79-12.12	...	...	2.65-1.67	10.28-5.78
Average Yield %	2.05	1.93	1.95	1.97	1.61	1.76	...	...

Address: 2711 North Haskell Avenue, Suite 3400, Dallas, TX 75204	Web Site: www.deanfoods.com	Auditors: Deloitte & Touche LLP
Telephone: 214-303-3400	Officers: Tom C. Davis - Chairman Ralph P. Scozzafava - Executive Vice President, Chief Operating Officer, Chief Commercial Officer, Chief Executive Officer	Investor Contact: 214-303-3400
Transfer Agents: Computershare Shareowner Services LLC, Providence, RI

DECKERS OUTDOOR CORP.

Exchange	Symbol	Price	52Wk Range	Yield	P/E
NYS	DECK	$80.25 (12/29/2017)	80.25-44.99	N/A	79.46

*7 Year Price Score 73.75   *NYSE Composite Index=100   *12 Month Price Score 108.30

TRADING VOLUME (thousand shares)

Interim Earnings (Per Share)

Qtr.	Jun	Sep	Dec	Mar
2014-15	(1.07)	1.17	4.50	0.07
2015-16	(1.43)	1.11	4.78	(0.70)
2016-17	(1.84)	1.21	1.27	(0.48)
2017-18	(1.32)	1.54	...	...

Interim Dividends (Per Share)

No Dividends Paid

Valuation Analysis   Institutional Holding

Forecast EPS	$4.30	No of Institutions
	(01/26/2018)	377
Market Cap	$2.6 Billion	Shares
Book Value	$968.8 Million	39,185,720
Price/Book	2.65	% Held
Price/Sales	1.41	95.56

Business Summary: Apparel, Footwear & Accessories (MIC: 1.4.2 SIC: 3021 NAIC: 316211)

Deckers Outdoor is engaged in designing, marketing and distributing footwear, apparel and accessories. Co. markets its products primarily under five brands. The UGG® brand is comprised of a line of footwear for women, men and children. Teva® is an outdoor active lifestyle brand, and the product line includes sandals, shoes, and boots. Sanuk® is a surf lifestyle footwear brand, and it includes Co.'s SIDEWALK SURFERS shoe, Yoga Mat and Beer Cozy sandal collections. Co.' other brands include: Hoka One One®, a line of running footwear; and Koolaburra® by UGG, a line of casual footwear using sheepskin and other plush materials. At Mar 31 2017, Co. had a total of 160 retail stores worldwide.

Recent Developments: For the quarter ended Sep 30 2017, net income increased 26.1% to US$49.6 million from US$39.3 million in the year-earlier quarter. Revenues were US$482.5 million, down 0.7% from US$485.9 million the year before. Operating income was US$67.4 million versus US$54.0 million in the prior-year quarter, an increase of 24.7%. Direct operating expenses declined 4.5% to US$257.3 million from US$269.5 million in the comparable period the year before. Indirect operating expenses decreased 2.9% to US$157.8 million from US$162.4 million in the equivalent prior-year period.

Prospects: Our evaluation of Deckers Outdoor Corp. as of Jan. 21, 2018 is the result of our systematic analysis on three basic characteristics: earnings strength, relative valuation, and recent stock price movement. The company has generated a negative trend in earnings per share over the past 5 quarters and while recent estimates for the company have been raised by analysts, DECK has posted better than expected results. Based on operating earnings yield, the company is undervalued when compared to all of the companies in our coverage universe. Share price changes over the past year indicates that DECK will perform poorly over the near term.

Financial Data
(US$ in Thousands)

	6 Mos	3 Mos	03/31/2017	03/31/2016	03/31/2015	03/31/2014	12/31/2013	12/31/2012
Earnings Per Share	1.01	0.68	0.18	3.70	4.66	(0.08)	4.18	3.45
Cash Flow Per Share	9.54	7.34	6.21	3.85	4.93	5.61	7.60	4.43
Tang Book Value Per Share	27.88	26.13	27.36	23.63	21.67	19.34	19.24	14.95
Income Statement								
Total Revenue	692,177	209,717	1,790,147	1,875,197	1,817,057	294,716	1,556,618	1,414,398
EBITDA	35,764	(43,764)	52,183	212,303	274,445	10,278	250,015	221,108
Depn & Amortn	24,453	12,268	52,628	50,024	49,293	10,569	41,439	33,367
Income Before Taxes	9,734	(56,587)	(6,986)	156,885	221,139	(742)	205,557	184,118
Income Taxes	2,296	(14,466)	(12,696)	34,620	59,359	1,943	59,868	55,104
Net Income	7,438	(42,121)	5,710	122,265	161,780	(2,685)	145,689	128,866
Average Shares	32,272	31,991	32,355	33,039	34,733	34,621	34,829	37,334
Balance Sheet								
Current Assets	1,152,911	903,380	820,821	785,765	686,593	623,862	829,304	691,586
Total Assets	1,520,288	1,272,858	1,191,780	1,278,068	1,169,933	1,064,204	1,259,729	1,068,064
Current Liabilities	474,047	285,875	159,051	238,498	167,542	122,215	320,518	267,017
Long-Term Obligations	31,803	31,943	32,082	32,631	33,154	...	...	...
Total Liabilities	551,462	359,184	237,525	310,597	232,921	175,355	371,610	329,263
Stockholders' Equity	968,826	913,674	954,255	967,471	937,012	888,849	888,119	738,801
Shares Outstanding	32,037	31,999	31,987	32,020	33,292	34,624	34,618	34,400
Statistical Record								
Return on Assets %	2.12	1.71	0.46	9.96	14.48	N.M.	12.52	11.61
Return on Equity %	3.40	2.46	0.59	12.80	17.72	N.M.	17.91	16.32
EBITDA Margin %	5.17	N.M.	2.92	11.32	15.10	3.49	16.06	15.63
Net Margin %	1.07	N.M.	0.32	6.52	8.90	N.M.	9.36	9.11
Asset Turnover	1.18	1.39	1.45	1.53	1.63	1.03	1.34	1.27
Current Ratio	2.43	3.16	5.16	3.29	4.10	5.10	2.59	2.59
Debt to Equity	0.03	0.03	0.03	0.03	0.04	...	...	...
Price Range	71.92-44.99	71.92-44.99	68.57-44.99	76.58-42.27	99.38-66.05	88.56-72.86	86.09-36.12	90.21-28.63
P/E Ratio	71.21-44.54	105.76-66.16	380.94-249.94	20.70-11.42	21.33-14.17	...	20.60-8.64	26.15-8.30

Address: 250 Coromar Drive, Goleta, CA 93117	**Web Site:** www.deckers.com	**Auditors:** KPMG LLP
Telephone: 805-967-7611	**Officers:** John M. Gibbons - Chairman David Powers - Chief Executive Officer, Division Officer	**Investor Contact:** 203-.68-2.8200
		Transfer Agents: Mellon Investor Services LLC, South Hackensack, NJ

DEERE & CO.

Exchange	Symbol	Price	52Wk Range	Yield	P/E
NYS	DE	$156.51 (12/29/2017)	158.75-104.05	1.53	23.43

*7 Year Price Score 106.47 *NYSE Composite Index=100 *12 Month Price Score 113.25

Interim Earnings (Per Share)

Qtr.	Jan	Apr	Jul	Oct
2012-13	1.65	2.76	2.56	2.12
2013-14	1.81	2.65	2.33	1.84
2014-15	1.12	2.03	1.53	1.10
2015-16	0.80	1.56	1.55	0.90
2016-17	0.61	2.49	1.97	1.57

Interim Dividends (Per Share)

Amt	Decl	Ex	Rec	Pay
0.60Q	02/22/2017	03/29/2017	03/31/2017	05/01/2017
0.60Q	05/31/2017	06/28/2017	06/30/2017	08/01/2017
0.60Q	08/30/2017	09/28/2017	09/29/2017	11/01/2017
0.60Q	12/06/2017	12/28/2017	12/29/2017	02/01/2018

Indicated Div: $2.40 (Div. Reinv. Plan)

Valuation Analysis **Institutional Holding**

Forecast EPS	$8.25 (01/18/2018)	No of Institutions 1482
Market Cap	$50.4 Billion	Shares
Book Value	$9.6 Billion	270,968,544
Price/Book	5.27	% Held
Price/Sales	1.69	54.77

TRADING VOLUME (thousand shares)

Business Summary: Industrial Machinery & Equipment (MIC: 7.2.1 SIC: 3523 NAIC: 332212)

Deere & Co. and its subsidiaries (collectively, John Deere) operates in three business segments: Agriculture and Turf, which manufactures and distributes agriculture and turf equipment and related service parts including tractors, loaders, harvesting equipment, scrapers, as well as tillage, seeding and application equipment; Construction and Forestry, which manufactures and distributes a range of machines and service parts used in construction, earthmoving, material handling and timber harvesting; and Financial Services, which primarily finances sales and leases by John Deere dealers of new and used agriculture and turf equipment and construction and forestry equipment.

Recent Developments: For the year ended Oct 29 2017, net income increased 41.9% to US$2.16 billion from US$1.52 billion in the prior year. Revenues were US$29.74 billion, up 11.6% from US$26.64 billion the year before. Direct operating expenses rose 9.4% to US$20.95 billion from US$19.15 billion in the comparable period the year before. Indirect operating expenses increased 5.0% to US$4.73 billion from US$4.50 billion in the equivalent prior-year period.

Prospects: Our evaluation of Deere & Co. as of Jan. 14, 2018 is the result of our systematic analysis on three basic characteristics: earnings strength, relative valuation, and recent stock price movement. The company has produced a positive trend in earnings per share over the past 5 quarters and while recent estimates for the company have been raised by analysts, DE has posted better than expected results. Based on operating earnings yield, the company is about fairly valued when compared to all of the companies in our coverage universe. Share price changes over the past year indicates that DE will perform in line with the market over the near term.

Financial Data
(US$ in Thousands)

	10/29/2017	10/31/2016	10/31/2015	10/31/2014	10/31/2013	10/31/2012	10/31/2011	10/31/2010
Earnings Per Share	6.68	4.81	5.77	8.63	9.09	7.63	6.63	4.35
Cash Flow Per Share	6.92	11.91	11.21	9.71	8.45	2.93	5.57	5.38
Tang Book Value Per Share	25.81	17.79	18.80	23.74	25.00	15.00	13.97	12.26
Dividends Per Share	2.400	2.400	2.400	2.220	1.990	1.790	1.520	1.160
Dividend Payout %	35.93	49.90	41.59	25.72	21.89	23.46	22.93	26.67
Income Statement								
Total Revenue	29,737,700	26,644,000	28,862,800	36,066,900	37,795,400	36,157,100	32,012,500	26,004,600
EBITDA	4,779,300	3,688,700	4,152,100	6,157,400	6,861,700	6,072,200	5,498,200	4,376,600
Depn & Amortn	726,000	701,000	692,000	696,000	637,000	555,000	516,000	540,000
Income Before Taxes	3,153,800	2,224,000	2,780,100	4,797,400	5,483,400	4,734,400	4,222,800	3,025,200
Income Taxes	971,100	700,100	840,100	1,626,500	1,945,900	1,659,400	1,423,600	1,161,600
Net Income	2,159,100	1,523,900	1,940,000	3,161,700	3,537,300	3,064,700	2,799,900	1,865,000
Average Shares	323,300	316,600	336,000	366,100	389,200	401,500	422,400	428,600
Balance Sheet								
Current Assets	18,851,400	12,176,600	12,492,000	14,019,600	15,316,900	16,942,400	13,478,600	11,510,500
Total Assets	65,786,300	57,981,400	57,947,600	61,336,400	59,521,300	56,265,800	48,207,400	43,266,800
Current Liabilities	22,692,600	19,236,100	20,408,600	21,232,500	21,979,000	19,092,000	17,552,100	14,220,500
Long-Term Obligations	25,891,000	23,760,000	23,833,000	24,381,000	21,578,000	22,453,000	16,960,000	16,815,000
Total Liabilities	56,229,000	51,461,400	51,204,200	52,273,800	49,255,500	49,423,700	41,407,100	36,976,500
Stockholders' Equity	9,557,300	6,520,000	6,743,400	9,062,600	10,265,800	6,842,100	6,800,300	6,290,300
Shares Outstanding	321,841	314,767	316,687	345,504	373,802	387,805	406,069	422,180
Statistical Record								
Return on Assets %	3.51	2.62	3.25	5.23	6.11	5.85	6.12	4.42
Return on Equity %	27.01	22.92	24.55	32.72	41.35	44.81	42.78	33.58
EBITDA Margin %	16.07	13.84	14.39	17.07	18.15	16.79	17.18	16.83
Net Margin %	7.26	5.72	6.72	8.77	9.36	8.48	8.75	7.17
Asset Turnover	0.48	0.46	0.48	0.60	0.65	0.69	0.70	0.62
Current Ratio	0.83	0.63	0.61	0.66	0.70	0.89	0.77	0.81
Debt to Equity	2.71	3.64	3.53	2.69	2.10	3.28	2.49	2.67
Price Range	133.25-88.06	88.30-71.78	97.33-72.89	94.53-80.01	95.05-80.90	88.40-70.59	99.24-61.72	77.25-46.30
P/E Ratio	19.95-13.18	18.36-14.92	16.87-12.63	10.95-9.27	10.46-8.90	11.59-9.25	14.97-9.31	17.76-10.64
Average Yield %	2.10	2.98	2.73	2.54	2.31	2.26	1.83	1.93

Address: One John Deere Place, Moline, IL 61265	**Web Site:** www.johndeere.com	**Auditors:** DELOITTE & TOUCHE LLP
Telephone: 309-765-8000	**Officers:** Samuel R. Allen - Chairman, President, Chief Executive Officer, Chief Operating Officer,	**Investor Contact:** 309-765-4491
Fax: 309-765-9929	Division Officer Rajesh Kalathur - Senior Vice President, Chief Financial Officer	**Transfer Agents:** ComputerShare, College Station, TX

DELEK US HOLDINGS INC

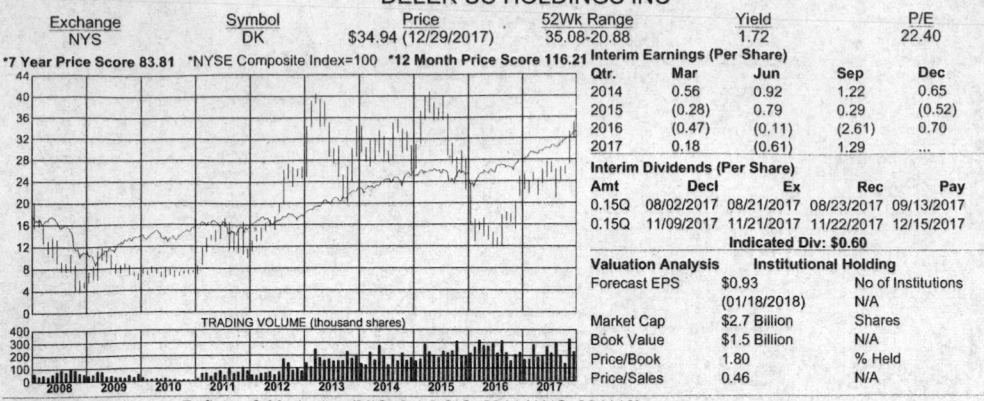

*7 Year Price Score 83.81   ***NYSE Composite Index=100**   ***12 Month Price Score 116.21**

Interim Earnings (Per Share)

Qtr.	Mar	Jun	Sep	Dec
2014	0.56	0.92	1.22	0.65
2015	(0.28)	0.79	0.29	(0.52)
2016	(0.47)	(0.11)	(2.61)	0.70
2017	0.18	(0.61)	1.29	

Interim Dividends (Per Share)

Amt	Decl	Ex	Rec	Pay
0.15Q	08/02/2017	08/21/2017	08/23/2017	09/13/2017
0.15Q	11/09/2017	11/21/2017	11/22/2017	12/15/2017

Indicated Div: $0.60

Valuation Analysis   **Institutional Holding**

Forecast EPS	$0.93	No of Institutions	
	(01/18/2018)	N/A	
Market Cap	$2.7 Billion	Shares	
Book Value	$1.5 Billion	N/A	
Price/Book	1.80	% Held	
Price/Sales	0.46	N/A	

TRADING VOLUME (thousand shares)

Business Summary: Refining & Marketing (MIC: 9.1.2 SIC: 2911 NAIC: 324110)

Delek US Holdings is an energy business focused on petroleum refining and the transportation, storage and wholesale distribution of crude oil, intermediate and refined products. Co. has two segments: refining, which operates independent refineries in Tyler, TX and El Dorado, AR; and logistics, which gathers, transports and stores crude oil and markets, distributes, transports and stores refined products in select regions of the southeastern U.S. and west Texas for both Co.'s refining segment and third parties. Co.'s refining segment also includes biodiesel facilities that are involved in the production of biodiesel fuels and related activities, located in Crossett, AR and Cleburne, TX.

Recent Developments: For the quarter ended Mar 31 2017, income from continuing operations was US$15.3 million compared with a loss of US$21.5 million in the year-earlier quarter. Net income amounted to US$15.3 million versus a net loss of US$23.9 million in the year-earlier quarter. Revenues were US$1.18 billion, up 33.4% from US$886.1 million the year before. Operating income was US$29.8 million versus a loss of US$13.6 million in the prior-year quarter. Direct operating expenses rose 27.0% to US$1.04 billion from US$815.8 million in the comparable period the year before. Indirect operating expenses increased 39.1% to US$116.7 million from US$83.9 million in the equivalent prior-year period.

Prospects: Our evaluation of Delek US Holdings Inc. as of Jan. 14, 2018 is the result of our systematic analysis on three basic characteristics: earnings strength, relative valuation, and recent stock price movement. The company has suffered a very negative trend in earnings per share over the past 5 quarters and while recent estimates for the company have been raised by analysts, DK has posted better than expected results. Based on operating earnings yield, the company is overvalued when compared to all of the companies in our coverage universe. Share price changes over the past year indicates that DK will perform poorly over the near term.

Financial Data

(US$ in Thousands)	9 Mos	6 Mos	3 Mos	12/31/2016	12/31/2015	12/31/2014	12/31/2013	12/31/2012
Earnings Per Share	1.56	(2.34)	(1.84)	(2.49)	0.32	3.35	1.96	4.57
Cash Flow Per Share	2.85	1.21	2.49	4.32	2.96	5.39	1.73	7.86
Tang Book Value Per Share	7.76	14.99	15.47	15.38	16.92	15.92	14.33	13.58
Dividends Per Share	0.150	0.600	0.600	0.600	0.600	1.000	0.950	0.600
Dividend Payout %	9.62	...	...	...	187.50	29.85	48.47	13.13
Income Statement								
Total Revenue	4,754,300	2,412,800	1,182,200	4,197,900	5,762,000	8,324,300	8,706,800	8,726,700
EBITDA	74,000	40,100	57,800	(179,800)	215,000	477,600	329,500	551,400
Depn & Amortn	900	57,000	28,000	115,100	132,700	110,200	85,500	78,300
Income Before Taxes	13,300	(43,500)	17,200	(347,800)	25,100	327,600	206,600	427,600
Income Taxes	111,500	(22,000)	5,000	(171,500)	(16,600)	101,600	70,900	151,600
Net Income	77,700	(26,700)	11,200	(153,700)	19,400	198,600	117,700	272,800
Average Shares	81,245	62,054	62,589	61,921	61,320	59,355	60,047	59,644
Balance Sheet								
Current Assets	2,270,600	1,311,700	1,367,300	1,402,200	988,800	1,247,400	1,410,500	1,359,700
Total Assets	5,569,100	2,876,500	2,958,000	2,985,100	3,324,900	2,891,400	2,834,400	2,623,700
Current Liabilities	2,084,200	875,800	918,900	940,500	759,700	857,200	1,080,800	999,100
Long-Term Obligations	1,076,800	731,100	740,500	748,500	880,500	533,300	376,600	310,000
Total Liabilities	4,088,700	1,905,400	1,960,100	1,993,200	2,171,600	1,889,700	1,899,400	1,724,400
Stockholders' Equity	1,480,400	971,100	997,900	991,900	1,153,300	1,001,700	935,000	899,300
Shares Outstanding	76,254	62,154	62,028	61,954	62,137	57,271	59,229	59,619
Statistical Record								
Return on Assets %	2.84	N.M.	N.M.	N.M.	0.62	6.94	4.31	11.21
Return on Equity %	10.04	N.M.	N.M.	N.M.	1.80	20.51	12.83	35.04
EBITDA Margin %	1.56	1.66	4.89	N.M.	3.73	5.74	3.78	6.32
Net Margin %	1.63	N.M.	0.95	N.M.	0.34	2.39	1.35	3.13
Asset Turnover	1.36	1.47	1.52	1.33	1.85	2.91	3.19	3.59
Current Ratio	1.09	1.50	1.49	1.49	1.30	1.46	1.31	1.36
Debt to Equity	0.73	0.75	0.74	0.75	0.76	0.53	0.40	0.34
Price Range	27.64-15.13	27.64-11.88	25.54-11.88	24.89-11.88	40.86-22.45	35.77-25.87	40.50-20.17	27.39-11.13
P/E Ratio	17.72-9.70	...	...	...	127.69-70.16	10.68-7.72	20.66-10.29	5.99-2.44
Average Yield %	0.65	2.89	3.30	3.67	1.84	3.25	3.08	3.07

Address: 7102 Commerce Way, Brentwood, TN 37027 Telephone: 615-771-6701	Web Site: www.Delekus.com Officers: Ezra Uzi Yemin - President, Chief Executive Officer Frederec C. Green - Chief Operating Officer, Executive Vice President	Auditors: Ernst & Young LLP Investor Contact: 615-435-1366 Transfer Agents: American Stock Transfer & Trust Company, Brooklyn, NY

DELL TECHNOLOGIES INC

Exchange	Symbol	Price	52Wk Range	Yield	P/E
NYS	DVMT	$81.28 (12/29/2017)	84.77-54.57	N/A	26.05

*7 Year Price Score N/A   ***NYSE Composite Index=100**   ***12 Month Price Score 108.75**

TRADING VOLUME (thousand shares)

Interim Earnings (Per Share)

Qtr.	Apr	Jul	Oct	Jan
2015-16	(1.24)	(0.65)	(0.44)	(0.38)
2016-17	0.14	1.41	0.78	0.65
2017-18	0.56	0.82	1.09	...

Interim Dividends (Per Share)

No Dividends Paid

Valuation Analysis   **Institutional Holding**

Forecast EPS	$5.05	No of Institutions
	(01/23/2018)	695
Market Cap	$62.5 Billion	Shares
Book Value	$9.9 Billion	191,848,032
Price/Book	6.33	% Held
Price/Sales	0.81	N/A

Business Summary: Computer Hardware & Equipment (MIC: 6.2.1 SIC: 3571 NAIC: 334111)

Dell Technologies is a holding company. Through its subsidiaries, Co. is engaged in providing information technology solutions. Co. is organized into three business units: Client Solutions Group, which has offerings that include hardware, such as desktop personal computers, notebooks and tablets, and peripherals, such as monitors, printers, and projectors, as well as third-party software, and peripherals; Infrastructure Solutions Group, which enables the digital transformation of Co.'s enterprise customers through Co.'s cloud and big data solutions, which are built upon a data center infrastructure; and VMware, which provides virtualization and cloud infrastructure solutions.

Recent Developments: For the quarter ended Nov 3 2017, loss from continuing operations was US$941.0 million compared with a loss of US$1.64 billion in the year-earlier quarter. Net loss amounted to US$941.0 million versus a net loss of US$2.08 billion in the year-earlier quarter. Revenues were US$19.61 billion, up 20.7% from US$16.25 billion the year before. Operating loss was US$533.0 million versus a loss of US$1.51 billion in the prior-year quarter. Direct operating expenses rose 17.0% to US$14.45 billion from US$12.35 billion in the comparable period the year before. Indirect operating expenses increased 5.3% to US$5.70 billion from US$5.41 billion in the equivalent prior-year period.

Prospects: Our evaluation of Dell Technologies Inc. as of Jan. 21, 2018 is the result of our systematic analysis on three basic characteristics: earnings strength, relative valuation, and recent stock price movement. The company has enjoyed a very positive trend in earnings per share over the past 5 quarters. Because the company lacks sufficient analyst estimate data, we place greater weight on the historical EPS trend as the measure of earnings strength. Based on operating earnings yield, the company is undervalued when compared to all of the companies in our coverage universe. Share price changes over the past year indicates that DVMT will perform well over the near term.

Financial Data
(US$ in Thousands)

	9 Mos	6 Mos	3 Mos	02/03/2017	01/29/2016	01/30/2015
Earnings Per Share	3.12	2.81	3.40	1.43	(2.72)	(3.02)
Cash Flow Per Share	5.66	3.20	3.27	3.18	5.35	6.31
Income Statement						
Total Revenue	56,725,000	37,115,000	17,816,000	61,642,000	50,911,000	54,142,000
EBITDA	(2,927,000)	(2,406,000)	(1,482,000)	(1,656,000)	714,000	885,000
Depn & Amortn	140,000	90,000	46,000	3,700,000	2,000,000	2,100,000
Income Before Taxes	(4,812,000)	(3,597,000)	(2,073,000)	(5,356,000)	(1,286,000)	(1,215,000)
Income Taxes	(1,510,000)	(1,236,000)	(690,000)	(1,619,000)	(118,000)	(107,000)
Net Income	(3,217,000)	(2,280,000)	(1,334,000)	(1,672,000)	(1,104,000)	(1,221,000)
Average Shares	202,000	203,000	207,000	217,000	405,000	404,000
Balance Sheet						
Current Assets	34,525,000	32,205,000	30,384,000	30,773,000	23,573,000	...
Total Assets	118,394,000	117,494,000	116,040,000	118,206,000	45,122,000	...
Current Liabilities	40,742,000	42,126,000	36,636,000	38,135,000	25,310,000	...
Long-Term Obligations	45,416,000	41,374,000	44,948,000	43,061,000	10,650,000	...
Total Liabilities	108,513,000	106,214,000	104,207,000	104,732,000	43,550,000	...
Stockholders' Equity	9,881,000	11,280,000	11,833,000	13,474,000	1,572,000	...
Shares Outstanding	769,000	773,000	405,000	778,000	405,000	...
Statistical Record						
EBITDA Margin %	N.M.	N.M.	N.M.	N.M.	1.40	1.63
Asset Turnover	0.63	0.79	0.84	0.74	...	...
Current Ratio	0.85	0.76	0.83	0.81	0.93	...
Debt to Equity	4.60	3.67	3.80	3.20	6.77	...
Price Range	83.88-48.62	69.39-42.75	67.57-42.75	64.35-42.75	...	...
P/E Ratio	26.89-15.58	24.69-15.21	19.87-12.57	45.00-29.90	...	...

Address: One Dell Way, Round Rock, TX 78682
Telephone: 800-289-3355

Web Site: www.delltechnologies.com
Officers: Michael S. Dell - Chairman, Chief Executive Officer Jeffrey W. Clarke - Vice-Chairman

Auditors: PricewaterhouseCoopers LLP
Investor Contact: 800-289-3355

DELTA AIR LINES INC (DE)

Exchange	Symbol	Price	52Wk Range	Yield	P/E
NYS	DAL	$56.00 (12/29/2017)	56.43-44.03	2.18	11.18

*7 Year Price Score 126.23 *NYSE Composite Index=100 *12 Month Price Score 99.75

Interim Earnings (Per Share)

Qtr.	Mar	Jun	Sep	Dec
2014	0.25	0.94	0.42	(0.83)
2015	0.90	1.83	1.65	1.26
2016	1.21	2.03	1.70	0.87
2017	0.82	1.68	1.64	...

Interim Dividends (Per Share)

Amt	Decl	Ex	Rec	Pay
0.203Q	02/10/2017	02/22/2017	02/24/2017	03/17/2017
0.203Q	05/05/2017	05/17/2017	05/19/2017	06/09/2017
0.305Q	08/09/2017	08/21/2017	08/23/2017	09/13/2017
0.305Q	11/03/2017	11/16/2017	11/17/2017	12/08/2017

Indicated Div: $1.22

Valuation Analysis

		Institutional Holding	
Forecast EPS	$6.35	No of Institutions	
	(01/24/2018)	1154	
Market Cap	$39.9 Billion	Shares	
Book Value	$14.0 Billion	754,060,288	
Price/Book	2.85	% Held	
Price/Sales	0.99	0.01	

Business Summary: Airlines/Air Freight (MIC: 7.4.4 SIC: 4512 NAIC: 481111)

Delta Air Lines provides scheduled air transportation for passengers and cargo in the U.S. and around the world. Co.'s route network is centered around a system of hub and international gateway airports that it operates in Amsterdam, Atlanta, Boston, Detroit, London-Heathrow, Los Angeles, Minneapolis-St. Paul, New York-LaGuardia, New York-JFK, Paris-Charles de Gaulle, Salt Lake City, Seattle and Tokyo-Narita. Each of these operations includes flights that gather and distribute traffic from markets in the geographic region surrounding the hub or gateway to domestic and international cities and to other hubs or gateways. Co.'s network is supported by a fleet of aircraft varied in size.

Recent Developments: For the quarter ended Sep 30 2017, net income decreased 6.4% to US$1.18 billion from US$1.26 billion in the year-earlier quarter. Revenues were US$11.06 billion, up 5.5% from US$10.48 billion the year before. Operating income was US$1.84 billion versus US$1.97 billion in the prior-year quarter, a decrease of 6.6%. Direct operating expenses rose 6.7% to US$4.54 billion from US$4.26 billion in the comparable period the year before. Indirect operating expenses increased 9.9% to US$4.68 billion from US$4.26 billion in the equivalent prior-year period.

Prospects: Our evaluation of Delta Air Lines Inc. as of Jan. 21, 2018 is the result of our systematic analysis on three basic characteristics: earnings strength, relative valuation, and recent stock price movement. The company has managed to produce a neutral trend in earnings per share over the past 5 quarters and while recent estimates for the company have been raised by analysts, DAL has posted better than expected results. Based on operating earnings yield, the company is undervalued when compared to all of the companies in our coverage universe. Share price changes over the past year indicates that DAL will perform poorly over the near term.

Financial Data

(US$ in Thousands)	9 Mos	6 Mos	3 Mos	12/31/2016	12/31/2015	12/31/2014	12/31/2013	12/31/2012
Earnings Per Share	5.01	5.07	5.42	5.79	5.63	0.78	12.29	1.19
Cash Flow Per Share	6.08	6.27	7.41	9.57	9.95	5.92	5.31	2.92
Dividends Per Share	0.912	0.810	0.743	0.675	0.450	0.300	0.120	...
Dividend Payout %	18.21	15.98	13.70	11.66	7.99	38.46	0.98	...
Income Statement								
Total Revenue	30,999,000	19,939,000	9,148,000	39,639,000	40,704,000	40,362,000	37,773,000	36,670,000
EBITDA	6,557,000	4,078,000	1,549,000	8,924,000	9,438,000	3,422,000	4,779,000	3,430,000
Depn & Amortn	1,649,000	1,075,000	540,000	1,900,000	1,800,000	1,700,000	1,400,000	1,400,000
Income Before Taxes	4,611,000	2,806,000	915,000	6,636,000	7,157,000	1,072,000	2,527,000	1,025,000
Income Taxes	1,606,000	979,000	312,000	2,263,000	2,631,000	413,000	(8,013,000)	16,000
Net Income	3,005,000	1,827,000	603,000	4,373,000	4,526,000	659,000	10,540,000	1,009,000
Average Shares	719,000	731,000	731,000	755,000	804,000	845,000	858,000	850,000
Balance Sheet								
Current Assets	7,083,000	7,177,000	6,880,000	7,451,000	9,056,000	12,465,000	9,651,000	8,272,000
Total Assets	51,928,000	51,815,000	51,459,000	51,261,000	53,134,000	54,121,000	52,252,000	44,550,000
Current Liabilities	16,496,000	16,631,000	15,953,000	15,239,000	17,526,000	16,879,000	14,152,000	13,270,000
Long-Term Obligations	7,584,000	7,916,000	8,187,000	6,201,000	6,766,000	8,561,000	9,795,000	11,082,000
Total Liabilities	37,927,000	38,336,000	38,514,000	38,974,000	42,284,000	45,308,000	40,609,000	46,681,000
Stockholders' Equity	14,001,000	13,479,000	12,945,000	12,287,000	10,850,000	8,813,000	11,643,000	(2,131,000)
Shares Outstanding	712,973	724,030	735,530	730,737	778.783	825,258	851,443	851,402
Statistical Record								
Return on Assets %	7.05	7.17	7.69	8.35	8.44	1.24	21.78	2.29
Return on Equity %	27.36	29.33	33.31	37.70	46.04	6.44	221.61	...
EBITDA Margin %	21.15	20.45	16.93	22.51	23.19	8.48	12.65	9.35
Net Margin %	9.69	9.16	6.59	11.03	11.12	1.63	27.90	2.75
Asset Turnover	0.79	0.77	0.75	0.76	0.76	0.76	0.78	0.83
Current Ratio	0.43	0.43	0.43	0.49	0.52	0.74	0.68	0.62
Debt to Equity	0.54	0.59	0.63	0.50	0.62	0.97	0.84	...
Price Range	55.48-38.94	53.87-35.58	51.78-33.36	51.78-33.36	52.26-40.00	49.23-27.47	29.34-11.87	12.10-8.01
P/E Ratio	11.07-7.77	10.63-7.02	9.55-6.15	8.94-5.76	9.28-7.10	63.12-35.22	2.39-0.97	10.17-6.73
Average Yield %	1.89	1.79	1.70	1.56	0.98	0.80	0.60	...

Address: Post Office Box 20706, Atlanta, GA 30320-6001
Telephone: 404-715-2600

Web Site: www.delta.com
Officers: Glen W. Hauenstein - President, Executive Vice President, Chief Revenue Officer, Executive Vice President (frmr) Edward H. Bastian - Chief Executive Officer, President, Executive Vice President, Chief Financial Officer, Senior Vice President, Vice President, Controller, Division Officer

Auditors: Ernst & Young LLP
Investor Contact: 404-715-2170
Transfer Agents: Wells Fargo Shareowner Services, St. Paul, MN

DELUXE CORP

Exchange	Symbol	Price	52Wk Range	Yield	P/E
NYS	DLX	$76.84 (12/29/2017)	76.84-67.03	1.56	18.88

*7 Year Price Score 113.59 *NYSE Composite Index=100 *12 Month Price Score 94.16

Interim Earnings (Per Share)

Qtr.	Mar	Jun	Sep	Dec
2014	0.93	0.99	0.88	1.16
2015	0.91	1.11	1.13	1.20
2016	1.18	1.18	1.19	1.10
2017	1.16	1.22	0.59	...

Interim Dividends (Per Share)

Amt	Decl	Ex	Rec	Pay
0.30Q	01/24/2017	02/16/2017	02/21/2017	03/06/2017
0.30Q	05/01/2017	05/18/2017	05/22/2017	06/05/2017
0.30Q	07/27/2017	08/17/2017	08/21/2017	09/05/2017
0.30Q	10/26/2017	11/17/2017	11/20/2017	12/04/2017

Indicated Div: $1.20

Valuation Analysis

		Institutional Holding	
Forecast EPS	$5.27	No of Institutions	
	(01/17/2018)	465	
Market Cap	$3.7 Billion	Shares	
Book Value	$950.5 Million	55,203,880	
Price/Book	3.89	% Held	
Price/Sales	1.90	83.33	

TRADING VOLUME (thousand shares)

Business Summary: Printing (MIC: 7.5.5 SIC: 2761 NAIC: 323116)

Deluxe is engaged in providing payment solutions. Co.'s product and service offerings are comprised of: Checks, which is a provider of checks in the U.S.; Marketing solutions and other services, which utilize digital printing and web-to-print solutions to provide promotional solutions such as postcards, brochures, retail packaging supplies, and apparel; Forms, which is a provider of printed forms to small businesses, including deposit tickets, billing forms, work orders, job proposals; and Accessories and other products, which provide small business owners with the customized documents necessary to manage their business.

Recent Developments: For the quarter ended June 30 2017, net income increased 2.0% to US$59.6 million from US$58.4 million in the year-earlier quarter. Revenues were US$485.2 million, up 7.7% from US$450.6 million the year before. Operating income was US$93.3 million versus US$90.9 million in the prior-year quarter, an increase of 2.6%. Direct operating expenses rose 12.1% to US$179.2 million from US$159.8 million in the comparable period the year before. Indirect operating expenses increased 6.4% to US$212.7 million from US$199.9 million in the equivalent prior-year period.

Prospects: Our evaluation of Deluxe Corp. as of Jan. 14, 2018 is the result of our systematic analysis on three basic characteristics: earnings strength, relative valuation, and recent stock price movement. The company has managed to produce a neutral trend in earnings per share over the past 5 quarters and while recent estimates for the company have remained steady, DLX has posted better than expected results. Based on operating earnings yield, the company is undervalued when compared to all of the companies in our coverage universe. Share price changes over the past year indicates that DLX will perform poorly over the near term.

Financial Data (US$ in Thousands)	9 Mos	6 Mos	3 Mos	12/31/2016	12/31/2015	12/31/2014	12/31/2013	12/31/2012
Earnings Per Share	4.07	4.67	4.63	4.65	4.36	3.96	3.65	3.32
Cash Flow Per Share	7.01	7.10	6.64	6.56	6.23	5.63	5.17	4.79
Dividends Per Share	1.200	1.200	1.200	1.200	1.200	1.150	1.000	1.000
Dividend Payout %	29.48	25.70	25.92	25.81	27.52	29.04	27.40	30.12
Income Statement								
Total Revenue	1,470,666	972,998	487,766	1,849,062	1,772,817	1,674,082	1,584,824	1,514,917
EBITDA	340,774	249,776	120,664	531,356	485,646	448,627	430,484	408,982
Depn & Amortn	105,982	69,639	34,604	168,668	137,400	114,917	111,124	111,382
Income Before Taxes	218,997	170,050	81,231	340,386	327,947	297,181	281,059	250,753
Income Taxes	73,551	53,405	24,165	111,004	109,318	97,387	94,407	80,261
Net Income	145,446	116,645	57,066	229,382	218,629	199,794	186,652	170,492
Average Shares	48,377	48,580	48,698	48,975	49,825	50,262	51,010	51,076
Balance Sheet								
Current Assets	372,519	354,279	391,523	398,230	325,988	318,890	319,313	219,743
Total Assets	2,179,980	2,168,755	2,162,289	2,184,338	1,844,402	1,688,391	1,569,529	1,412,440
Current Liabilities	401,085	409,216	410,269	415,684	751,043	467,248	490,071	220,110
Long-Term Obligations	714,432	680,652	701,651	722,806	196,222	393,401	385,115	652,581
Total Liabilities	1,229,435	1,219,766	1,249,129	1,303,368	1,099,333	1,040,894	1,019,072	979,505
Stockholders' Equity	950,545	948,989	913,160	880,970	745,069	647,497	550,457	432,935
Shares Outstanding	48,120	48,351	48,502	48,546	49,019	49,742	50,344	50,614
Statistical Record								
Return on Assets %	9.69	11.37	11.43	11.36	12.38	12.27	12.52	12.14
Return on Equity %	22.18	26.00	26.91	28.14	31.40	33.36	37.96	46.23
EBITDA Margin %	23.17	25.67	24.74	28.74	27.39	26.80	27.16	27.00
Net Margin %	9.89	11.99	11.70	12.41	12.33	11.93	11.78	11.25
Asset Turnover	0.95	0.95	0.94	0.92	1.00	1.03	1.06	1.08
Current Ratio	0.93	0.87	0.95	0.96	0.43	0.68	0.65	1.00
Debt to Equity	0.75	0.72	0.77	0.82	0.26	0.61	0.70	1.51
Price Range	75.79-59.67	75.79-59.67	75.79-59.67	73.04-51.00	69.57-53.36	63.54-45.52	52.19-32.24	32.24-21.51
P/E Ratio	18.62-14.66	16.23-12.78	16.37-12.89	15.71-10.97	15.96-12.24	16.05-11.49	14.30-8.83	9.71-6.48
Average Yield %	1.72	1.73	1.77	1.89	1.93	2.08	2.44	3.76

Address: 3680 Victoria St. N., Shoreview, MN 55126-2966
Telephone: 651-483-7111
Fax: 651-483-7337

Web Site: www.deluxe.com
Officers: Lee J. Schram - Chief Executive Officer
Pete J. Godich - Senior Vice President, Vice President

Auditors: PricewaterhouseCoopers LLP
Investor Contact: 651-787-1068
Transfer Agents: Wells Fargo Bank Minnesota, N.A., St. Paul, MN

DENBURY RESOURCES, INC. (DE)

Exchange	Symbol	Price	52Wk Range	Yield	P/E
NYS	DNR	$2.21 (12/29/2017)	3.88-0.96	N/A	N/A

*7 Year Price Score 13.59   ***NYSE Composite Index=100**   ***12 Month Price Score 82.95**

Interim Earnings (Per Share)

Qtr.	Mar	Jun	Sep	Dec
2014	0.17	(0.16)	0.77	1.04
2015	(0.31)	(3.28)	(6.41)	(2.56)
2016	(0.53)	(1.03)	(0.06)	(1.01)
2017	0.05	0.04	0.00	...

Interim Dividends (Per Share)

Dividend Payment Suspended

Valuation Analysis		Institutional Holding	
Forecast EPS	$0.09	No of Institutions	
	(01/17/2018)	356	
Market Cap	$889.0 Million	Shares	
Book Value	$517.4 Million	396,789,984	
Price/Book	1.72	% Held	
Price/Sales	0.83	88.75	

Business Summary: Production & Extraction (MIC: 9.1.1 SIC: 1311 NAIC: 211111)

Denbury Resources is an independent oil and natural gas company. Co.'s operations are focused in two key operating areas: the Gulf Coast and Rocky Mountain regions. Co.'s properties with proved and producing reserves in the Gulf Coast region are situated in Mississippi, Texas, Louisiana and Alabama, and in the Rocky Mountain region are situated in Montana, North Dakota and Wyoming. As of Dec 31 2016, Co.'s total estimated proved reserves were 254.5 million barrels of oil equivalent, which consisted of 247.1 million barrels of crude oil and 44.3 billion cubic feet of natural gas.

Recent Developments: For the quarter ended Sep 30 2017, net income amounted to US$442,000 versus a net loss of US$24.6 million in the year-earlier quarter. Revenues were US$266.6 million, up 5.0% from US$254.0 million the year before. Direct operating expenses rose 10.9% to US$119.1 million from US$107.4 million in the comparable period the year before. Indirect operating expenses decreased 13.2% to US$161.2 million from US$185.8 million in the equivalent prior-year period.

Prospects: Our evaluation of Denbury Resources Inc. as of Jan. 14, 2018 is the result of our systematic analysis on three basic characteristics: earnings strength, relative valuation, and recent stock price movement. The company has suffered a very negative trend in earnings per share over the past 5 quarters and while recent estimates for the company have been raised by analysts, DNR has posted better than expected results. Based on operating earnings yield, the company is about fairly valued when compared to all of the companies in our coverage universe. Share price changes over the past year indicates that DNR will perform very poorly over the near term.

Financial Data

(US$ in Thousands)	9 Mos	6 Mos	3 Mos	12/31/2016	12/31/2015	12/31/2014	12/31/2013	12/31/2012
Earnings Per Share	(0.92)	(0.98)	(2.05)	(2.61)	(12.57)	1.81	1.11	1.35
Cash Flow Per Share	0.52	0.60	0.62	0.58	2.48	3.50	3.71	3.65
Tang Book Value Per Share	1.29	1.29	1.24	1.18	3.55	12.51	11.08	10.20
Dividends Per Share	...	...	...	...	0.188	0.250	...	...
Dividend Payout %	...	...	...	...	13.81			
Income Statement								
Total Revenue	803,197	536,638	275,454	975,596	1,257,560	2,435,205	2,517,127	2,456,472
EBITDA	283,622	220,762	120,877	(549,159)	(5,625,933)	1,812,008	1,307,055	1,532,671
Depn & Amortn	154,448	102,347	51,195	846,043	560,781	606,448	523,966	522,233
Income Before Taxes	53,389	67,176	42,504	(1,520,347)	(6,325,982)	1,022,557	642,380	856,857
Income Taxes	17,018	31,247	20,974	(544,170)	(1,940,534)	387,066	232,783	331,497
Net Income	36,371	35,929	21,530	(976,177)	(4,385,448)	635,491	409,597	525,360
Average Shares	393,023	391,827	392,997	373,859	348,802	351,167	369,877	388,938
Balance Sheet								
Current Assets	187,592	186,229	188,269	181,126	344,708	812,680	414,559	1,542,754
Total Assets	4,440,929	4,425,341	4,308,659	4,274,578	5,919,824	12,727,802	11,788,737	11,139,342
Current Liabilities	354,548	329,341	356,279	433,496	373,015	640,125	675,199	616,421
Long-Term Obligations	3,057,439	3,060,048	2,956,385	2,909,732	3,277,866	3,535,900	3,260,625	3,104,462
Total Liabilities	3,923,482	3,911,142	3,814,900	3,806,130	4,670,912	7,023,946	6,487,331	6,024,453
Stockholders' Equity	517,447	514,199	493,759	468,448	1,248,912	5,703,856	5,301,406	5,114,889
Shares Outstanding	402,239	398,899	398,302	398,427	351,417	353,364	362,504	375,561
Statistical Record								
Return on Assets %	N.M.	N.M.	N.M.	N.M.	N.M.	5.18	3.57	4.91
Return on Equity %	N.M.	N.M.	N.M.	N.M.	N.M.	11.55	7.86	10.56
EBITDA Margin %	35.31	41.14	43.88	N.M.	N.M	74.41	51.93	62.39
Net Margin %	4.53	6.70	7.82	N.M.	N.M.	26.10	16.27	21.39
Asset Turnover	0.23	0.23	0.21	0.19	0.13	0.20	0.22	0.23
Current Ratio	0.53	0.57	0.53	0.42	0.92	1.27	0.61	2.50
Debt to Equity	5.91	5.95	5.99	6.21	2.62	0.62	0.62	0.61
Price Range	4.03-0.96	4.03-1.30	4.68-2.01	4.68-0.95	9.44-1.89	18.50-6.34	19.48-15.98	20.91-13.46
P/E Ratio	...	...	...	...	...	10.22-3.50	17.55-14.40	15.49-9.97
Average Yield %	...	...	...	...	3.35	1.65		

Address: 5320 Legacy Drive, Plano, TX 75024	**Web Site:** www.denbury.com	**Auditors:** PricewaterhouseCoopers LLP
Telephone: 972-673-2000	**Officers:** John P. Dielwart - Chairman Christian S. Kendall - President, Chief Executive Officer, Chief Operating Officer	**Investor Contact:** 972-673-2028
Fax: 972-673-2150		**Transfer Agents:** American Stock Transfer and Trust Company, New York, NY

DEVON ENERGY CORP.

Exchange	Symbol	Price	52Wk Range	Yield	P/E
NYS	DVN	$41.40 (12/29/2017)	49.01-29.54	0.58	13.80

*7 Year Price Score 53.31 *NYSE Composite Index=100 *12 Month Price Score 97.78

Interim Earnings (Per Share)

Qtr.	Mar	Jun	Sep	Dec
2014	0.79	1.64	2.47	(1.00)
2015	(8.88)	(6.94)	(8.64)	(11.10)
2016	(6.44)	(3.04)	1.89	0.70
2017	1.07	0.80	0.43	...

Interim Dividends (Per Share)

Amt	Decl	Ex	Rec	Pay
0.06Q	03/01/2017	06/13/2017	06/15/2017	06/30/2017
0.06Q	06/07/2017	09/14/2017	09/15/2017	09/29/2017
0.06Q	09/13/2017	12/14/2017	12/15/2017	12/29/2017
0.06Q	11/29/2017	03/14/2018	03/15/2018	03/29/2018

Indicated Div: $0.24

Valuation Analysis   **Institutional Holding**

Forecast EPS	$1.81	No of Institutions
	(01/18/2018)	1184
Market Cap	$21.7 Billion	Shares
Book Value	$7.1 Billion	510,294,784
Price/Book	3.05	% Held
Price/Sales	1.63	77.05

Business Summary: Production & Extraction (MIC: 9.1.1 SIC: 1311 NAIC: 211111)

Devon Energy is an independent energy company engaged primarily in the exploration, development and production of oil, natural gas and natural gas liquids. Co.'s operations are concentrated in various North American onshore areas in the U.S. and Canada. Co.'s operating areas consist of Barnett Shale, Delaware Basin, Eagle Ford, Heavy Oil, Rockies Oil, and the STACK development, located in Oklahoma's Canadian, Kingfisher and Blaine counties. Co. also owns natural gas pipelines, plants and treatment facilities through its ownership in EnLink Midstream Partners, LP. As of Dec 31 2016, Co. had 2.06 billion barrels of oil equivalent proved reserves.

Recent Developments: For the quarter ended Sep 30 2017, net income decreased 75.5% to US$247.0 million from US$1.01 billion in the year-earlier quarter. Revenues were US$3.16 billion, down 25.4% from US$4.23 billion the year before. Operating income was US$326.0 million versus US$1.47 billion in the prior-year quarter, a decrease of 77.7%. Direct operating expenses rose 20.1% to US$2.20 billion from US$1.84 billion in the comparable period the year before. Indirect operating expenses decreased 32.9% to US$626.0 million from US$933.0 million in the equivalent prior-year period.

Prospects: Our evaluation of Devon Energy Corp. as of Jan. 14, 2018 is the result of our systematic analysis on three basic characteristics: earnings strength, relative valuation, and recent stock price movement. The company has generated a negative trend in earnings per share over the past 5 quarters and while recent estimates for the company have been raised by analysts, DVN has posted better than expected results. Based on operating earnings yield, the company is about fairly valued when compared to all of the companies in our coverage universe. Share price changes over the past year indicates that DVN will perform very poorly over the near term.

Financial Data

(US$ in Thousands)	9 Mos	6 Mos	3 Mos	12/31/2016	12/31/2015	12/31/2014	12/31/2013	12/31/2012
Earnings Per Share	3.00	4.46	0.62	(6.52)	(35.55)	3.91	(0.06)	(0.52)
Cash Flow Per Share	5.68	5.59	4.68	3.43	13.23	14.77	13.52	12.36
Tang Book Value Per Share	6.03	5.58	4.76	3.75	4.83	37.25	36.06	37.44
Dividends Per Share	0.240	0.240	0.240	0.420	0.960	0.940	0.860	0.800
Dividend Payout %	8.00	5.38	38.71	...	...	24.04	...	...
Income Statement								
Total Revenue	9,976,000	6,820,000	3,547,000	12,197,000	13,145,000	19,566,000	10,397,000	9,502,000
EBITDA	2,860,000	2,061,000	771,000	(987,000)	(17,622,000)	7,904,000	3,346,000	2,864,000
Depn & Amortn	1,162,000	762,000	46,000	1,986,000	3,129,000	3,319,000	2,780,000	2,811,000
Income Before Taxes	1,328,000	1,056,000	598,000	(3,877,000)	(21,268,000)	4,059,000	149,000	(317,000)
Income Taxes	51,000	26,000	19,000	(173,000)	(6,065,000)	2,368,000	169,000	(132,000)
Net Income	1,218,000	990,000	565,000	(3,302,000)	(14,454,000)	1,607,000	(20,000)	(206,000)
Average Shares	523,000	523,000	522,000	507,000	407,000	407,000	402,000	400,000
Balance Sheet								
Current Assets	4,622,000	4,086,000	3,775,000	3,772,000	4,026,000	6,498,000	8,005,000	8,971,000
Total Assets	27,559,000	26,814,000	26,134,000	25,913,000	29,532,000	50,637,000	42,877,000	43,326,000
Current Liabilities	2,832,000	2,532,000	2,470,000	2,616,000	3,295,000	5,935,000	6,655,000	6,003,000
Long-Term Obligations	10,383,000	10,558,000	10,381,000	10,154,000	12,137,000	9,830,000	7,956,000	8,455,000
Total Liabilities	20,430,000	19,915,000	19,668,000	19,986,000	22,483,000	29,098,000	22,378,000	22,048,000
Stockholders' Equity	7,129,000	6,899,000	6,466,000	5,927,000	7,049,000	21,539,000	20,499,000	21,278,000
Shares Outstanding	525,000	526,000	526,000	523,000	418,000	409,000	406,000	406,000
Statistical Record								
Return on Assets %	5.70	8.56	1.16	N.M.	N.M.	3.44	N.M.	N.M.
Return on Equity %	23.89	39.40	4.95	N.M.	N.M.	7.65	N.M.	N.M.
EBITDA Margin %	28.67	30.22	21.74	N.M.	N.M.	40.40	32.18	30.14
Net Margin %	12.21	14.52	15.93	N.M.	N.M.	8.21	N.M.	N.M.
Asset Turnover	0.49	0.53	0.50	0.44	0.33	0.42	0.24	0.22
Current Ratio	1.63	1.61	1.53	1.44	1.22	1.09	1.20	1.49
Debt to Equity	1.46	1.53	1.61	1.71	1.72	0.46	0.39	0.40
Price Range	49.01-29.54	49.01-30.01	49.01-26.05	48.33-18.65	69.03-28.67	79.50-52.66	65.52-51.44	75.81-51.15
P/E Ratio	16.34-9.85	10.99-6.73	79.05-42.02	...	...	20.33-13.47	...	...
Average Yield %	0.61	0.58	0.59	1.17	1.81	1.39	1.49	1.30

Address: 333 West Sheridan Avenue, Oklahoma City, OK 73102-5015 **Telephone:** 405-235-3611	**Web Site:** www.devonenergy.com **Officers:** John Richels - Chairman, Vice-Chairman, President, Chief Executive Officer David A. Hager - President, Chief Executive Officer, Executive Vice President, Chief Operating Officer	**Auditors:** KPMG LLP **Investor Contact:** 405-552-4505 **Transfer Agents:** Computershare Trust Company, N.A., Providence, RI

DIAMOND OFFSHORE DRILLING, INC.

Exchange	Symbol	Price	52Wk Range	Yield	P/E
NYS	DO	$18.59 (12/29/2017)	19.49-10.22	N/A	15.36

*7 Year Price Score 26.41   *NYSE Composite Index=100   *12 Month Price Score 108.88

Interim Earnings (Per Share)

Qtr.	Mar	Jun	Sep	Dec
2014	1.05	0.65	0.38	0.72
2015	(1.86)	0.66	0.99	(1.79)
2016	0.64	(4.30)	0.10	0.84
2017	0.17	0.12	0.08	...

Interim Dividends (Per Share)

Dividend Payment Suspended

Valuation Analysis   **Institutional Holding**

Forecast EPS	$0.85	No of Institutions
	(01/18/2018)	449
Market Cap	$2.6 Billion	Shares
Book Value	$3.8 Billion	175,499,312
Price/Book	0.67	% Held
Price/Sales	1.67	99.71

Business Summary: Equipment & Services (MIC: 9.1.3 SIC: 1381 NAIC: 213111)

Diamond Offshore Drilling engaged in offshore drilling, providing contract drilling services to the energy industry around the globe with a fleet of 32 offshore drilling rigs, which includes four jack-up rigs that Co. markets for sale. As of Dec 31 2016, Co.'s fleet consists of 23 semisubmersibles, including the Ocean GreatWhite, which is under construction, five jack-ups and four dynamically positioned drillships, including the Ocean BlackLion. Co.'s fleet enables it to provide a range of services worldwide, primarily in the floater market (ultra-deepwater, deepwater and mid-water).

Recent Developments: For the quarter ended Sep 30 2017, net income decreased 22.5% to US$10.8 million from US$13.9 million in the year-earlier quarter. Revenues were US$366.0 million, up 4.8% from US$349.2 million the year before. Operating income was US$58.6 million versus US$54.1 million in the prior-year quarter, an increase of 8.3%. Direct operating expenses rose 6.0% to US$206.3 million from US$194.6 million in the comparable period the year before. Indirect operating expenses increased 0.7% to US$101.2 million from US$100.5 million in the equivalent prior-year period.

Prospects: Our evaluation of Diamond Offshore Drilling Inc. as of Jan. 14, 2018 is the result of our systematic analysis on three basic characteristics: earnings strength, relative valuation, and recent stock price movement. The company has suffered a very negative trend in earnings per share over the past 5 quarters. However, while recent estimates for the company have been lowered by analysts, DO has posted better than expected results. Based on operating earnings yield, the company is about fairly valued when compared to all of the companies in our coverage universe. Share price changes over the past year indicates that DO will perform very poorly over the near term.

Financial Data

(US$ in Thousands)	9 Mos	6 Mos	3 Mos	12/31/2016	12/31/2015	12/31/2014	12/31/2013	12/31/2012
Earnings Per Share	1.21	1.23	(3.19)	(2.72)	(2.00)	2.81	3.95	5.18
Cash Flow Per Share	3.80	3.77	3.67	4.70	5.37	7.22	7.67	9.41
Tang Book Value Per Share	27.73	27.63	27.51	27.34	29.99	32.46	33.35	32.92
Dividends Per Share	...	...	...	...	0.500	3.500	3.500	3.500
Dividend Payout %	...	...	...	...	...	124.56	88.61	67.57
Income Statement								
Total Revenue	1,139,538	773,515	374,226	1,600,342	2,419,393	2,814,671	2,920,421	2,986,508
EBITDA	358,195	250,929	145,112	2,627	202,426	1,032,926	1,186,474	1,352,300
Depn & Amortn	262,492	179,211	93,229	381,760	493,162	456,483	388,092	392,913
Income Before Taxes	13,641	17,442	24,462	(468,299)	(381,348)	515,191	774,240	918,081
Income Taxes	(36,646)	(22,046)	923	(95,796)	(107,063)	128,180	225,554	197,604
Net Income	50,287	39,488	23,539	(372,503)	(274,285)	387,011	548,686	720,477
Average Shares	137,241	137,227	137,250	137,168	137,157	137,523	139,064	139,048
Balance Sheet								
Current Assets	648,477	580,176	515,503	505,807	669,595	899,059	2,718,110	2,132,943
Total Assets	6,198,228	6,193,263	6,268,943	6,371,877	7,164,889	8,021,289	8,391,434	7,235,286
Current Liabilities	180,970	157,091	201,583	340,499	625,723	856,646	745,582	485,546
Long-Term Obligations	1,971,852	1,981,458	1,981,169	1,980,884	1,994,773	1,994,526	2,244,189	1,496,066
Total Liabilities	2,393,466	2,401,445	2,494,948	2,621,743	3,052,119	3,569,726	3,754,176	2,658,892
Stockholders' Equity	3,804,762	3,791,818	3,773,995	3,750,134	4,112,770	4,451,563	4,637,258	4,576,394
Shares Outstanding	137,227	137,224	137,180	137,169	137,158	137,147	139,035	139,031
Statistical Record								
Return on Assets %	2.64	2.67	N.M.	N.M.	N.M.	4.72	7.02	10.12
Return on Equity %	4.47	4.57	N.M.	N.M.	N.M.	8.52	11.91	16.13
EBITDA Margin %	31.43	32.44	38.78	0.16	8.37	36.70	40.63	45.28
Net Margin %	4.41	5.11	6.29	N.M.	N.M.	13.75	18.79	24.12
Asset Turnover	0.24	0.24	0.23	0.24	0.32	0.34	0.37	0.42
Current Ratio	3.58	3.69	2.56	1.49	1.07	1.05	3.65	4.39
Debt to Equity	0.52	0.52	0.52	0.53	0.49	0.45	0.48	0.33
Price Range	21.08-10.22	26.11-10.26	26.11-14.70	26.11-14.80	37.23-16.81	56.92-29.37	76.48-55.39	72.43-55.61
P/E Ratio	17.42-8.45	21.23-8.34	...	...	...	20.26-10.45	19.36-14.02	13.98-10.74
Average Yield %	...	...	...	...	1.91	7.82	5.24	5.37

Address: 15415 Katy Freeway, Houston, TX 77094 **Telephone:** 281-492-5300 **Fax:** 281-492-5316	**Web Site:** www.diamondoffshore.com **Officers:** James S. Tisch - Chairman Marc Gerard Rex Edwards - President, Chief Executive Officer	**Auditors:** Deloitte & Touche LLP **Investor Contact:** 281-492-5393 **Transfer Agents:** Computershare, Providence, R.I.

DICK'S SPORTING GOODS, INC

Exchange	Symbol	Price	52Wk Range	Yield	P/E
NYS	DKS	$28.74 (12/29/2017)	55.33-24.39	2.37	10.61

*7 Year Price Score 66.24   *NYSE Composite Index=100   *12 Month Price Score 68.40

Interim Earnings (Per Share)

Qtr.	Apr	Jul	Oct	Jan
2014-15	0.57	0.57	0.41	1.29
2015-16	0.53	0.77	0.41	1.12
2016-17	0.50	0.82	0.44	0.81
2017-18	0.52	1.03	0.35	...

Interim Dividends (Per Share)

Amt	Decl	Ex	Rec	Pay
0.17Q	02/14/2017	03/08/2017	03/10/2017	03/31/2017
0.17Q	05/11/2017	06/07/2017	06/09/2017	06/30/2017
0.17Q	08/10/2017	09/07/2017	09/08/2017	09/29/2017
0.17Q	11/09/2017	12/07/2017	12/08/2017	12/29/2017

Indicated Div: $0.68

Valuation Analysis

		Institutional Holding	
Forecast EPS	$2.98 (01/18/2018)	No of Institutions	589
Market Cap	$2.4 Billion	Shares	98,587,024
Book Value	$1.9 Billion	% Held	75.87
Price/Book	1.27		
Price/Sales	0.28		

Business Summary: Retail - Specialty (MIC: 2.1.3 SIC: 5941 NAIC: 451110)

Dick's Sporting Goods is an omni-channel sporting goods retailer offering sports equipment, apparel, footwear and accessories through a blend of dedicated associates, in-store services and specialty shop-in-shops. Co. also owns and operates Golf Galaxy, Field & Stream, and Dick's Team Sports HQ, an all-in-one youth sports digital platform offering free league management services, mobile apps for scheduling, communications and live scorekeeping, custom uniforms and FanWear. Co.'s Dick's Sporting Goods stores unites several sports specialty stores under one roof. Through eCommerce, Co. continues to develop its online content and capabilities to enhance the online experience.

Recent Developments: For the quarter ended Oct 28 2017, net income decreased 24.5% to US$36.9 million from US$48.9 million in the year-earlier quarter. Revenues were US$1.94 billion, up 7.4% from US$1.81 billion the year before. Operating income was US$50.0 million versus US$73.8 million in the prior-year quarter, a decrease of 32.2%. Direct operating expenses rose 12.1% to US$1.41 billion from US$1.26 billion in the comparable period the year before. Indirect operating expenses increased 1.1% to US$484.1 million from US$479.1 million in the equivalent prior-year period.

Prospects: Our evaluation of Dick's Sporting Goods Inc. as of Jan. 14, 2018 is the result of our systematic analysis on three basic characteristics: earnings strength, relative valuation, and recent stock price movement. The company has generated a negative trend in earnings per share over the past 5 quarters and while recent estimates for the company have been raised by analysts, DKS has posted better than expected results. Based on operating earnings yield, the company is undervalued when compared to all of the companies in our coverage universe. Share price changes over the past year indicates that DKS will perform very poorly over the near term.

Financial Data

(US$ in Thousands)	9 Mos	6 Mos	3 Mos	01/28/2017	01/30/2016	01/31/2015	02/01/2014	02/02/2013
Earnings Per Share	2.71	2.80	2,59	2.56	2.83	2.84	2.69	2.31
Cash Flow Per Share	6.64	7.22	7.20	6.85	5.60	5.10	3.30	3.55
Tang Book Value Per Share	17.93	14.35	14.41	13.99	13.24	12.88	11.52	10.47
Dividends Per Share	0.661	0.642	0.624	0.605	0.550	0.500	0.500	2.500
Dividend Payout %	24.40	22.95	24.08	23.63	19.43	17.61	18.59	108.23
Income Statement								
Total Revenue	5,926,350	3,982,164	1,825,252	7,921,981	7,270,965	6,814,479	6,213,173	5,836,119
EBITDA	493,898	375,692	145,991	670,878	715,387	720,829	702,836	621,159
Depn & Amortn	166,521	109,085	53,044	206,600	180,500	161,600	153,800	125,300
Income Before Taxes	321,058	263,127	91,683	458,422	530,875	556,014	546,107	489,825
Income Taxes	113,564	92,547	33,488	171,026	200,484	211,816	208,509	199,116
Net Income	207,494	170,580	58,195	287,396	330,391	344,198	337,598	290,709
Average Shares	105,814	108,679	111,406	112,216	116,794	121,238	125,628	125,995
Balance Sheet								
Current Assets	2,582,076	2,277,284	2,254,616	1,995,678	1,812,690	1,850,384	1,620,071	1,595,889
Total Assets	4,784,914	4,395,311	4,332,724	4,058,296	3,559,336	3,436,198	3,071,487	2,887,807
Current Liabilities	1,607,109	1,509,500	1,514,483	1,397,415	1,191,675	1,118,833	1,002,587	1,000,768
Long-Term Obligations	516,113	191,143	96,970	4,679	5,324	5,913	6,476	7,762
Total Liabilities	2,911,928	2,474,051	2,371,900	2,128,807	1,770,149	1,603,973	1,379,308	1,300,483
Stockholders' Equity	1,872,986	1,921,260	1,960,824	1,929,489	1,789,187	1,832,225	1,692,179	1,587,324
Shares Outstanding	82,693	107,200	109,369	110,330	111,751	118,106	120,966	123,005
Statistical Record								
Return on Assets %	6.49	7.39	7.03	7.57	9.47	10.61	11.36	9.72
Return on Equity %	15.91	16.51	15.34	15.50	18.30	19.59	20.64	17.76
EBITDA Margin %	8.33	9.43	8.00	8.47	9.84	10.58	11.31	10.64
Net Margin %	3.50	4.28	3.19	3.63	4.54	5.05	5.43	4.98
Asset Turnover	1.83	1.97	1.97	2.09	2.08	2.10	2.09	1.95
Current Ratio	1.61	1.51	1.49	1.43	1.52	1.65	1.62	1.59
Debt to Equity	0.28	0.10	0.05	N.M.	N.M.	N.M.	N.M.	N.M.
Price Range	62.25-24.67	62.25-35.12	62.25-38.10	62.25-36.57	58.98-34.24	57.26-41.90	58.58-45.11	53.93-41.37
P/E Ratio	22.97-9.10	22.23-12.54	24.03-14.71	24.32-14.29	20.84-12.10	20.16-14.75	21.78-16.77	23.35-17.91
Average Yield %	1.51	1.26	1.20	1.20	1.12	0.97	0.97	5.11

Address: 345 Court Street, Coraopolis, PA 15108
Telephone: 724-273-3400

Web Site: www.DICKS.com
Officers: Edward W. Stack - Chairman, Chief Executive Officer William J. Colombo - Vice-Chairman, Chief Marketing Officer

Auditors: Deloitte & Touche LLP
Transfer Agents: American Stock Transfer & Trust Company, New York, NY

DIEBOLD NIXDORF INC

Exchange	Symbol	Price	52Wk Range	Yield	P/E
NYS	DBD	$16.35 (12/29/2017)	31.60-16.15	2.45	N/A

*7 Year Price Score 61.31   *NYSE Composite Index=100   *12 Month Price Score 69.38

Interim Earnings (Per Share)

Qtr.	Mar	Jun	Sep	Dec
2014	0.15	0.64	0.51	0.46
2015	(0.04)	0.34	0.33	0.49
2016	2.56	(0.32)	(1.44)	(1.14)
2017	(0.78)	(0.41)	(0.47)	...

Interim Dividends (Per Share)

Amt	Decl	Ex	Rec	Pay
0.10Q	02/08/2017	02/23/2017	02/27/2017	03/17/2017
0.10Q	04/26/2017	05/17/2017	05/19/2017	06/09/2017
0.10Q	07/13/2017	08/23/2017	08/25/2017	09/15/2017
0.10Q	10/18/2017	11/16/2017	11/17/2017	12/08/2017

Indicated Div: $0.40 (Div. Reinv. Plan)

Valuation Analysis

		Institutional Holding	
Forecast EPS	$1.09 (01/18/2018)	No of Institutions	386
Market Cap	$1.2 Billion	Shares	114,951,960
Book Value	$572.2 Million	% Held	101.15
Price/Book	2.16		
Price/Sales	0.27		

Business Summary: Computer Hardware & Equipment (MIC: 6.2.1 SIC: 3578 NAIC: 333313)

Diebold Nixdorf provides connected commerce services, software and technology. Co.'s financial self-service products are primarily automated teller machines and other equipment primarily used in the banking industry which include both hardware and the software required for the equipment to operate as intended. Co. also provides provides global product sales, service, installation, project management for longer-term contracts and monitoring of original equipment manufacturer electronic security products to financial, government, retail and commercial customers. Co. also designs, manufactures and/or procures and installs physical security and facility products.

Recent Developments: For the quarter ended Sep 30 2017, loss from continuing operations was US$28.8 million compared with a loss of US$97.2 million in the year-earlier quarter. Net loss amounted to US$28.8 million versus a net loss of US$101.8 million in the year-earlier quarter. Revenues were US$1.12 billion, up 14.2% from US$983.3 million the year before. Operating loss was US$7.6 million versus a loss of US$86.7 million in the prior-year quarter. Direct operating expenses rose 12.2% to US$881.7 million from US$785.7 million in the comparable period the year before. Indirect operating expenses decreased 12.6% to US$248.6 million from US$284.3 million in the equivalent prior-year period.

Prospects: Our evaluation of Diebold Nixdorf Inc. as of Jan. 14, 2018 is the result of our systematic analysis on three basic characteristics: earnings strength, relative valuation, and recent stock price movement. The company has managed to produce a neutral trend in earnings per share over the past 5 quarters. However, while recent estimates for the company have been mixed, DBD has posted better than expected results. Based on operating earnings yield, the company is undervalued when compared to all of the companies in our coverage universe. Share price changes over the past year indicates that DBD will perform in line with the market over the near term.

Financial Data

(US$ in Thousands)	9 Mos	6 Mos	3 Mos	12/31/2016	12/31/2015	12/31/2014	12/31/2013	12/31/2012
Earnings Per Share	(2.80)	(3.77)	(3.68)	(0.48)	1.12	1.76	(2.85)	1.23
Cash Flow Per Share	(0.16)	0.65	1.03	0.41	0.57	2.90	1.95	2.14
Tang Book Value Per Share	N.M.	N.M.	N.M.	N.M.	3.86	5.56	6.51	8.49
Dividends Per Share	0.400	0.588	0.775	0.963	1.150	1.150	1.150	1.140
Dividend Payout %	...	...	...	...	102.68	65.34	...	92.68
Income Statement								
Total Revenue	3,359,400	2,236,700	1,102,800	3,316,300	2,419,300	3,051,053	2,857,491	2,991,693
EBITDA	96,300	33,400	8,200	(75,100)	119,000	250,211	(40,422)	199,203
Depn & Amortn	185,400	116,600	58,600	61,800	40,700	48,202	50,151	51,447
Income Before Taxes	(164,000)	(134,700)	(74,800)	(238,300)	45,800	170,589	(119,807)	117,426
Income Taxes	(59,400)	(58,900)	(22,600)	(67,600)	(13,700)	53,570	56,715	29,905
Net Income	(124,800)	(89,400)	(58,800)	(33,000)	73,700	114,417	(181,605)	78,454
Average Shares	75,500	75,500	75,300	69,100	65,600	65,154	63,659	63,914
Balance Sheet								
Current Assets	2,576,300	2,641,600	2,601,500	2,619,600	1,643,600	1,655,530	1,555,350	1,814,857
Total Assets	5,361,400	5,455,500	5,244,600	5,270,300	2,249,300	2,342,136	2,183,491	2,592,987
Current Liabilities	1,758,300	1,882,400	1,846,200	1,824,500	955,800	1,027,723	893,736	838,855
Long-Term Obligations	1,834,500	1,787,500	1,689,700	1,691,400	613,100	479,794	480,242	617,534
Total Liabilities	4,789,200	4,868,300	4,711,500	4,678,900	1,836,900	1,810,532	1,586,727	1,783,024
Stockholders' Equity	572,200	587,200	533,100	591,400	412,400	531,604	596,764	809,963
Shares Outstanding	75,527	75,504	75,461	75,144	65,001	64,632	64,068	63,240
Statistical Record								
Return on Assets %	N.M.	N.M.	N.M.	N.M.	3.21	5.06	N.M.	3.06
Return on Equity %	N.M.	N.M.	N.M.	N.M.	15.61	20.28	N.M.	9.56
EBITDA Margin %	2.87	1.49	0.74	N.M.	4.92	8.20	N.M.	6.66
Net Margin %	N.M.	N.M.	N.M.	N.M.	3.05	3.75	N.M.	2.62
Asset Turnover	0.83	0.94	1.04	0.88	1.05	1.35	1.20	1.17
Current Ratio	1.47	1.40	1.41	1.44	1.72	1.61	1.74	2.16
Debt to Equity	3.21	3.04	3.17	2.86	1.49	0.90	0.80	0.76
Price Range	31.60-18.15	31.60-21.20	31.60-21.20	30.09-21.20	37.83-29.36	40.61-32.35	35.10-27.61	40.68-28.26
P/E Ratio	...	...	...	...	33.78-26.21	23.07-18.38	...	33.07-22.98
Average Yield %	1.59	2.22	2.98	3.77	3.40	3.12	3.73	3.30

Address: 5995 Mayfair Road, P.O. Box 3077, North Canton, OH 44720-8077
Telephone: 330-490-4000

Web Site: www.diebold.com
Officers: Andreas W. Mattes - President, President (frmr), Chief Executive Officer Jurgen Wunram - Chief Operating Officer

Auditors: KPMG LLP
Investor Contact: 330-490-6319
Transfer Agents: Wells Fargo Shareowner Services

226

DIGITAL REALTY TRUST INC

Exchange	Symbol	Price	52Wk Range	Yield	P/E	Div Acheiver
NYS	DLR	$113.90 (12/29/2017)	126.04-99.36	3.27	92.60	12 Years

*7 Year Price Score 118.48 *NYSE Composite Index=100 *12 Month Price Score 97.56

Interim Earnings (Per Share)

Qtr.	Mar	Jun	Sep	Dec
2014	0.26	0.31	0.80	(0.40)
2015	0.75	0.86	0.28	(0.32)
2016	0.27	0.19	1.25	0.48
2017	0.41	0.36	(0.02)	...

Interim Dividends (Per Share)

Amt	Decl	Ex	Rec	Pay
0.93Q	03/01/2017	03/13/2017	03/15/2017	03/31/2017
0.93Q	05/08/2017	06/13/2017	06/15/2017	06/30/2017
0.93Q	08/07/2017	09/14/2017	09/15/2017	09/29/2017
0.93Q	11/03/2017	12/14/2017	12/15/2017	01/12/2010

Indicated Div: $3.72

Valuation Analysis   **Institutional Holding**

Forecast EPS	$1.16	No of Institutions
	(01/26/2018)	833
Market Cap	$23.4 Billion	Shares
Book Value	$10.5 Billion	242,373,184
Price/Book	2.24	% Held
Price/Sales	10.16	108.74

Business Summary: REITs (MIC: 5.3.1 SIC: 6798 NAIC: 525930)

Digital Realty Trust is engaged in the business of owning, acquiring, developing and managing data centers. Co. provides data center, colocation and interconnection solutions for domestic and international tenants ranging from financial services, cloud and information technology services, to manufacturing, energy, healthcare, and consumer products. As of Dec 31 2016, Co.'s portfolio consisted of 145 operating properties, including 14 properties held as investments in unconsolidated joint ventures and developable land and mainly located throughout North America, with 32 properties located in Europe, four properties in Asia and three properties in Australia.

Recent Developments: For the quarter ended Sep 30 2017, net income decreased 94.4% to US$12.5 million from US$222.4 million in the year-earlier quarter. Revenues were US$609.9 million, up 11.6% from US$546.3 million the year before. Revenues from property income rose 11.7% to US$549.9 million from US$492.4 million in the corresponding quarter a year earlier.

Prospects: Our evaluation of Digital Realty Trust Inc. as of Jan. 21, 2018 is the result of our systematic analysis on three basic characteristics: earnings strength, relative valuation, and recent stock price movement. The company has managed to produce a neutral trend in earnings per share over the past 5 quarters. However, while recent estimates for the company have been mixed, DLR has posted results that fell short of analysts expectations. Based on operating earnings yield, the company is overvalued when compared to all of the companies in our coverage universe. Share price changes over the past year indicates that DLR will perform very well over the near term.

Financial Data

(US$ in Thousands)	9 Mos	6 Mos	3 Mos	12/31/2016	12/31/2015	12/31/2014	12/31/2013	12/31/2012
Earnings Per Share	1.23	2.50	2.33	2.20	1.56	0.99	2.12	1.48
Cash Flow Per Share	5.65	6.44	5.98	6.07	5.78	4.92	5.13	4.68
Tang Book Value Per Share	27.54	20.73	20.31	20.94	19.67	20.87	22.70	23.14
Dividends Per Share	3.670	3.620	3.570	3.520	3.400	3.320	3.120	2.920
Dividend Payout %	298.37	144.80	153.22	160.00	217.95	335.35	147.17	197.30
Income Statement								
Total Revenue	1,726,483	1,116,558	550,569	2,142,213	1,763,336	1,616,438	1,482,259	1,279,067
EBITDA	512,321	371,318	186,876	1,387,107	1,074,431	941,142	988,010	759,770
Depn & Amortn	166,626	103,520	50,115	720,930	578,064	557,356	486,805	393,995
Income Before Taxes	164,373	155,284	81,462	425,133	292,551	195,364	311,945	210,559
Income Taxes	7,356	4,862	2,223	10,385	6,451	5,238	1,292	2,647
Net Income	174,624	162,189	83,538	426,187	296,689	200,183	314,488	210,334
Average Shares	170,194	161,781	160,421	150,679	138,865	133,637	128,127	116,006
Balance Sheet								
Current Assets	468,821	270,764	220,803	225,974	252,460	188,807	278,333	268,617
Total Assets	21,232,498	12,579,571	12,329,548	12,192,585	11,451,267	9,526,784	9,685,745	8,819,214
Current Liabilities	1,024,394	850,602	804,371	969,072	735,268	720,942	765,196	739,861
Long-Term Obligations	8,484,244	6,437,620	6,201,329	5,838,607	5,934,241	4,673,127	4,961,892	4,278,565
Total Liabilities	10,763,219	7,582,756	7,298,085	7,096,570	6,951,135	5,648,528	6,075,229	5,350,909
Stockholders' Equity	10,469,279	4,996,815	5,031,463	5,096,015	4,500,132	3,878,256	3,610,516	3,468,305
Shares Outstanding	205,433	162,183	159,539	159,019	146,384	135,626	128,455	125,140
Statistical Record								
Return on Assets %	1.61	3.99	3.77	3.60	2.83	2.08	3.40	2.81
Return on Equity %	3.45	10.26	9.50	8.86	7.08	5.35	8.89	7.00
EBITDA Margin %	29.67	33.26	33.94	64.75	60.93	58.22	66.66	59.40
Net Margin %	10.11	14.53	15.17	19.89	16.83	12.38	21.22	16.44
Asset Turnover	0.14	0.19	0.18	0.18	0.17	0.17	0.16	0.17
Current Ratio	0.46	0.32	0.27	0.23	0.34	0.26	0.36	0.36
Debt to Equity	0.81	1.29	1.23	1.15	1.32	1.20	1.37	1.23
Price Range	126.04-87.54	120.54-87.54	112.10-85.62	112.10-72.50	77.01-61.52	70.27-49.12	73.77-44.53	80.31-59.28
P/E Ratio	102.47-71.17	48.22-35.02	48.11-36.75	50.95-32.95	49.37-39.44	70.98-49.62	34.80-21.00	54.26-40.05
Average Yield %	3.43	3.49	3.62	3.80	5.01	5.56	5.21	4.12

Address: Four Embarcadero Center, Suite 3200, San Francisco, CA 94111 **Telephone:** 415-738-6500 **Fax:** 415-738-6501	**Web Site:** www.digitalrealty.com **Officers:** Dennis E. Singleton - Interim Chairman A. William Stein - Interim Chief Executive Officer, Chief Executive Officer, Chief Financial Officer, Chief Investment Officer	**Auditors:** KPMG LLP **Investor Contact:** 415-738-6500 **Transfer Agents:** American Stock Transfer & Trust Company, New York, NY

DILLARD'S INC.

Exchange	Symbol	Price	52Wk Range	Yield	P/E
NYS	DDS	$60.05 (12/29/2017)	78.87-46.93	0.67	16.10

*7 Year Price Score 58.38   *NYSE Composite Index=100   *12 Month Price Score 96.67

Interim Earnings (Per Share)

Qtr.	Apr	Jul	Oct	Jan
2014-15	2.56	0.80	1.30	3.12
2015-16	2.66	0.75	1.19	2.26
2016-17	2.17	0.35	0.67	1.69
2017-18	2.12	(0.58)	0.50	...

Interim Dividends (Per Share)

Amt	Decl	Ex	Rec	Pay
0.07Q	02/24/2017	03/29/2017	03/31/2017	05/01/2017
0.07Q	05/22/2017	06/28/2017	06/30/2017	07/31/2017
0.10Q	08/17/2017	09/28/2017	09/29/2017	10/30/2017
0.10Q	11/17/2017	12/28/2017	12/29/2017	02/05/2018

Indicated Div: $0.40

Valuation Analysis — **Institutional Holding**

Forecast EPS	$3.71 (01/18/2018)	No of Institutions	305
Market Cap	$1.7 Billion	Shares	35,875,952
Book Value	$1.6 Billion	% Held	70.48
Price/Book	1.08		
Price/Sales	0.27		

Business Summary: Retail - General Merchandise/Department Stores (MIC: 2.1.1 SIC: 5311 NAIC: 452111)

Dillard's is a fashion apparel, cosmetics and home furnishing retailer. As of Jan 28 2017, Co. operated 293 Dillard's stores, including 25 clearance centers, and an Internet store providing a selection of merchandise including fashion apparel for women, men and children, accessories, cosmetics, home furnishings and other consumer goods. Co. also operates a contracting construction company, CDI Contractors, LLC, a portion of whose business includes constructing and remodeling stores for Co. As of Jan 28 2017, Co. operated retail department stores in 29 states, primarily in the southwest, southeast and midwest regions of the U. S.

Recent Developments: For the quarter ended Oct 28 2017, net income decreased 36.2% to US$14.5 million from US$22.8 million in the year-earlier quarter. Revenues were US$1.40 billion, down 0.7% from US$1.41 billion the year before. Direct operating expenses rose 1.3% to US$890.1 million from US$878.9 million in the comparable period the year before. Indirect operating expenses decreased 1.6% to US$484.6 million from US$492.6 million in the equivalent prior-year period.

Prospects: Our evaluation of Dillard's Inc. as of Jan. 14, 2018 is the result of our systematic analysis on three basic characteristics: earnings strength, relative valuation, and recent stock price movement. The company has managed to produce a neutral trend in earnings per share over the past 5 quarters and while recent estimates for the company have been mixed, DDS has posted better than expected results. Based on operating earnings yield, the company is undervalued when compared to all of the companies in our coverage universe. Share price changes over the past year indicates that DDS will perform very poorly over the near term.

Financial Data

(US$ in Thousands)	9 Mos	6 Mos	3 Mos	01/28/2017	01/30/2016	01/31/2015	02/01/2014	02/02/2013
Earnings Per Share	3.73	3.90	4.83	4.93	6.91	7.79	7.10	6.87
Cash Flow Per Share	15.44	15.41	18.37	15.11	11.57	14.39	11.04	10.69
Tang Book Value Per Share	55.84	55.23	57.91	53.41	49.98	49.02	45.33	41.24
Dividends Per Share	0.310	0.280	0.280	0.280	0.260	0.240	0.220	5.200
Dividend Payout %	8.31	7.18	5.80	5.68	3.76	3.08	3.10	75.69
Income Statement								
Total Revenue	4,313,503	2,916,684	1,452,874	6,418,009	6,754,545	6,780,129	6,691,777	6,751,595
EBITDA	321,720	227,933	178,728	564,734	719,707	823,074	815,729	809,346
Depn & Amortn	178,528	121,033	60,585	244,000	250,000	251,000	255,000	260,000
Income Before Taxes	96,732	75,420	102,461	257,675	408,784	510,768	496,224	479,750
Income Taxes	33,005	26,220	36,170	88,500	140,770	179,480	173,400	145,060
Net Income	63,761	49,222	66,302	169,220	269,370	331,853	323,671	335,962
Average Shares	28,934	29,363	31,257	34,308	39,005	42,603	45,586	48,911
Balance Sheet								
Current Assets	2,170,770	1,759,873	2,092,742	1,837,921	1,668,883	1,888,442	1,660,156	1,491,980
Total Assets	4,135,334	3,749,335	4,114,905	3,888,136	3,865,625	4,170,071	4,050,739	4,048,744
Current Liabilities	1,526,837	1,122,682	1,235,696	976,517	751,216	885,323	778,311	767,116
Long-Term Obligations	568,561	568,806	729,888	730,094	822,054	820,704	821,544	822,309
Total Liabilities	2,544,687	2,146,614	2,424,493	2,170,719	2,070,320	2,150,801	2,058,542	2,078,569
Stockholders' Equity	1,590,647	1,602,721	1,690,412	1,717,417	1,795,305	2,019,270	1,992,197	1,970,175
Shares Outstanding	28,484	29,021	29,189	32,157	35,920	41,192	43,948	47,769
Statistical Record								
Return on Assets %	2.90	3.40	3.88	4.38	6.72	8.10	8.01	7.91
Return on Equity %	7.25	7.65	9.03	9.66	14.16	16.59	16.38	16.44
EBITDA Margin %	7.46	7.81	12.30	8.80	10.66	12.14	12.19	11.99
Net Margin %	1.48	1.69	4.56	2.64	3.99	4.89	4.84	4.98
Asset Turnover	1.51	1.66	1.56	1.66	1.69	1.65	1.66	1.59
Current Ratio	1.42	1.57	1.69	1.88	2.22	2.13	2.13	1.94
Debt to Equity	0.36	0.35	0.43	0.43	0.46	0.41	0.41	0.42
Price Range	78.87-46.93	78.87-46.93	74.92-46.94	87.74-54.65	142.22-61.24	125.81-83.60	97.21-75.77	89.05-45.22
P/E Ratio	21.14-12.58	20.22-12.03	15.51-9.72	17.80-11.09	20.58-8.86	16.15-10.73	13.69-10.67	12.96-6.58
Average Yield %	0.53	0.47	0.46	0.42	0.26	0.22	0.26	7.22

Address: 1600 Cantrell Road, Little Rock, AR 72201
Telephone: 501-376-5200

Web Site: www.dillards.com
Officers: William T. Dillard - Chairman, Chief Executive Officer Alex Dillard - President

Auditors: KPMG LLP
Investor Contact: 501-376-5965
Transfer Agents: Registrar and Transfer Company, Cranford, NJ

DISCOVER FINANCIAL SERVICES

Exchange	Symbol	Price	52Wk Range	Yield	P/E
NYS	DFS	$76.92 (12/29/2017)	77.50-57.66	1.82	13.19

*7 Year Price Score 104.59 *NYSE Composite Index=100 ***12 Month Price Score 101.79**

Interim Earnings (Per Share)

Qtr.	Mar	Jun	Sep	Dec
2014	1.31	1.35	1.37	0.88
2015	1.28	1.33	1.38	1.15
2016	1.35	1.47	1.56	1.41
2017	1.43	1.40	1.59	...

Interim Dividends (Per Share)

Amt	Decl	Ex	Rec	Pay
0.30Q	04/20/2017	05/09/2017	05/11/2017	05/25/2017
0.35Q	07/25/2017	08/22/2017	08/24/2017	09/07/2017
0.35Q	10/19/2017	11/21/2017	11/22/2017	12/07/2017
0.35Q	01/18/2018	02/21/2018	02/22/2018	03/08/2018

Indicated Div: $1.40

Valuation Analysis

		Institutional Holding	
Forecast EPS	$7.71	No of Institutions	
	(01/26/2018)	1075	
Market Cap	$28.2 Billion	Shares	
Book Value	$11.2 Billion	391,711,520	
Price/Book	2.52	% Held	
Price/Sales	2.51	71.16	

Business Summary: Credit & Lending (MIC: 5.4.1 SIC: 6141 NAIC: 522210)

Discover Financial Services is a bank holding and financial holding company. Co. operates two segments: Direct Banking, which includes Discover-branded credit cards issued to individuals on the Discover Network and other consumer products and services, including private student loans, personal loans, home equity loans, and other consumer lending and deposit products; and Payment Services, which includes PULSE electronic funds transfer network, Diners Club International global payments network, and its Network Partners business that provides payment transaction processing and settlement services. As of Dec 31 2016, Co. had total assets of $92.31 billion and total deposits of $51.99 billion.

Recent Developments: For the quarter ended Sep 30 2017, net income decreased 5.8% to US$602.0 million from US$639.0 million in the year-earlier quarter. Net interest income increased 12.3% to US$2.05 billion from US$1.83 billion in the year-earlier quarter. Provision for loan losses was US$674.0 million versus US$445.0 million in the prior-year quarter, an increase of 51.5%. Non-interest income fell 0.2% to US$475.0 million from US$476.0 million, while non-interest expense advanced 5.9% to US$948.0 million.

Prospects: Our evaluation of Discover Financial Services as of Jan. 21, 2018 is the result of our systematic analysis on three basic characteristics: earnings strength, relative valuation, and recent stock price movement. The company has produced a positive trend in earnings per share over the past 5 quarters and while recent estimates for the company have been mixed, DFS has posted better than expected results. Based on operating earnings yield, the company is undervalued when compared to all of the companies in our coverage universe. Share price changes over the past year indicates that DFS will perform poorly over the near term.

Financial Data (US$ in Thousands)	9 Mos	6 Mos	3 Mos	12/31/2016	12/31/2015	12/31/2014	12/31/2013	11/30/2012
Earnings Per Share	5.83	5.80	5.87	5.77	5.13	4.90	4.96	4.46
Cash Flow Per Share	13.14	12.25	11.09	10.90	8.82	8.28	7.24	5.84
Tang Book Value Per Share	27.89	27.40	26.90	26.60	24.41	22.58	20.71	17.56
Dividends Per Share	1.250	1.200	1.180	1.160	1.080	0.920	0.600	0.400
Dividend Payout %	21.44	20.69	20.10	20.10	21.05	18.78	12.10	8.97
Income Statement								
Total Revenue	8,495,000	5,544,000	2,725,000	10,497,000	10,002,000	9,611,000	9,370,000	8,984,000
Income Before Taxes	2,638,000	1,735,000	868,000	3,656,000	3,612,000	3,694,000	3,944,000	3,753,000
Income Taxes	926,000	625,000	304,000	1,263,000	1,315,000	1,371,000	1,474,000	1,408,000
Net Income	1,712,000	1,110,000	564,000	2,393,000	2,297,000	2,323,000	2,470,000	2,345,000
Average Shares	371,000	379,000	386,000	406,000	437,498	463,412	486,861	520,000
Balance Sheet								
Total Assets	97,608,000	93,757,000	94,795,000	92,308,000	86,936,000	83,126,000	79,340,000	75,283,000
Total Liabilities	86,421,000	82,498,000	83,530,000	80,985,000	75,661,000	71,992,000	68,531,000	65,505,000
Stockholders' Equity	11,187,000	11,259,000	11,265,000	11,323,000	11,275,000	11,134,000	10,809,000	9,778,000
Shares Outstanding	366,042	375,163	382,351	388,766	421,678	449,188	472,244	497,871
Statistical Record								
Return on Assets %	2.42	2.55	2.60	2.66	2.70	2.86	3.19	3.25
Return on Equity %	20.19	20.41	21.10	21.12	20.50	21.17	24.00	25.96
Net Margin %	20.15	20.02	20.70	22.80	22.97	24.17	26.36	26.10
Asset Turnover	0.12	0.12	0.12	0.12	0.12	0.12	0.12	0.12
Price Range	73.94-54.47	73.94-52.33	73.94-50.26	73.18-43.25	65.49-50.60	66.38-52.21	55.95-37.80	41.61-23.07
P/E Ratio	12.68-9.34	12.75-9.02	12.60-8.56	12.68-7.50	12.77-9.86	13.55-10.66	11.28-7.62	9.33-5.17
Average Yield %	1.95	1.90	1.93	2.07	1.89	1.52	1.28	1.19

Address: 2500 Lake Cook Road, Riverwoods, IL 60015 **Telephone:** 224-405-0900	**Web Site:** www.discover.com **Officers:** David W. Nelms - Chairman, Chief Executive Officer Roger C. Hochschild - President, Chief Operating Officer	**Auditors:** Deloitte & Touche LLP **Investor Contact:** 224-405-4555 **Transfer Agents:** Computershare, Jersey City, NJ

DISNEY (WALT) CO. (THE)

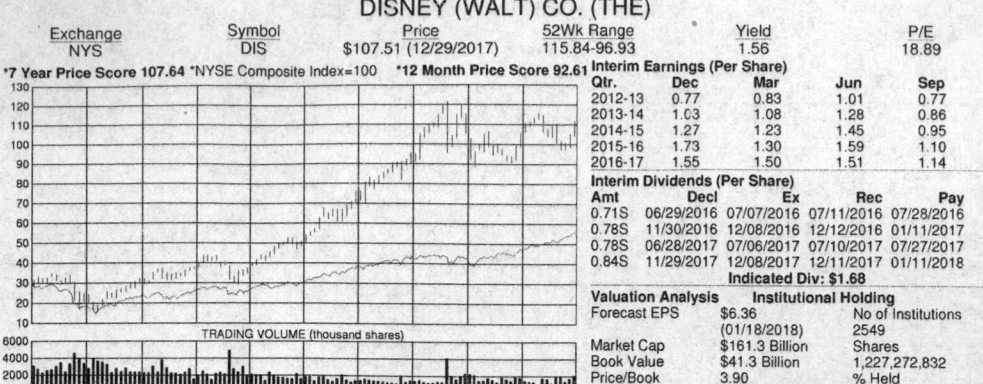

Exchange	Symbol	Price	52Wk Range	Yield	P/E
NYS	DIS	$107.51 (12/29/2017)	115.84-96.93	1.56	18.89

*7 Year Price Score 107.64 *NYSE Composite Index=100 *12 Month Price Score 92.61

Interim Earnings (Per Share)

Qtr.	Dec	Mar	Jun	Sep
2012-13	0.77	0.83	1.01	0.77
2013-14	1.03	1.08	1.28	0.86
2014-15	1.27	1.23	1.45	0.95
2015-16	1.73	1.30	1.59	1.10
2016-17	1.55	1.50	1.51	1.14

Interim Dividends (Per Share)

Amt	Decl	Ex	Rec	Pay
0.71S	06/29/2016	07/07/2016	07/11/2016	07/28/2016
0.78S	11/30/2016	12/08/2016	12/12/2016	01/11/2017
0.78S	06/28/2017	07/06/2017	07/10/2017	07/27/2017
0.84S	11/29/2017	12/08/2017	12/11/2017	01/11/2018

Indicated Div: $1.68

Valuation Analysis

Forecast EPS	$6.36
	(01/18/2018)
Market Cap	$161.3 Billion
Book Value	$41.3 Billion
Price/Book	3.90
Price/Sales	2.92

Institutional Holding

No of Institutions	2549
Shares	1,227,272,832
% Held	59.06

Business Summary: Entertainment (MIC: 2.3.2 SIC: 4841 NAIC: 515210)

Walt Disney is an entertainment company. Co.'s segments are: Media Networks, which includes cable and broadcast television networks, television production and distribution operations, domestic television stations and radio networks and stations; Parks and Resorts, which owns and operates the Disneyland Resort, and the Disney Cruise Line, among others; Studio Entertainment, which produces and acquires live-action and animated motion pictures, direct-to-video content, musical recordings and live stage plays; and Consumer Products and Interactive Media, which licenses Co.'s trade names, characters and visual and literary properties to manufacturers, game developers, publishers and retailers.

Recent Developments: For the year ended Sep 30 2017, net income decreased 4.3% to US$9.37 billion from US$9.79 billion in the prior year. Revenues were US$55.14 billion, down 0.9% from US$55.63 billion the year before. Direct operating expenses rose 1.0% to US$30.31 billion from US$29.99 billion in the comparable period the year before. Indirect operating expenses decreased 3.3% to US$11.06 billion from US$11.44 billion in the equivalent prior-year period.

Prospects: Our evaluation of Disney (Walt) Co. as of Jan. 14, 2018 is the result of our systematic analysis on three basic characteristics: earnings strength, relative valuation, and recent stock price movement. The company has managed to produce a neutral trend in earnings per share over the past 5 quarters and while recent estimates for the company have been raised by analysts, DIS has posted results that fell short of analysts expectations. Based on operating earnings yield, the company is undervalued when compared to all of the companies in our coverage universe. Share price changes over the past year indicates that DIS will perform poorly over the near term.

Financial Data

(US$ in Thousands)	09/30/2017	10/01/2016	10/03/2015	09/27/2014	09/28/2013	09/29/2012	10/01/2011	10/02/2010
Earnings Per Share	5.69	5.73	4.90	4.26	3.38	3.13	2.52	2.03
Cash Flow Per Share	7.89	8.13	6.34	5.64	5.29	4.45	3.73	3.44
Tang Book Value Per Share	1.93	5.32	5.95	5.65	5.96	5.41	4.61	4.40
Dividends Per Share	1.560	1.420	1.810	0.860	0.750	0.600	0.400	0.350
Dividend Payout %	27.42	24.78	36.94	20.19	22.19	19.17	15.87	17.24
Income Statement								
Total Revenue	55,137,000	55,632,000	52,465,000	48,813,000	45,041,000	42,278,000	40,893,000	38,063,000
EBITDA	16,635,000	16,729,000	15,525,000	13,657,000	11,140,000	10,989,000	9,642,000	8,198,000
Depn & Amortn	2,782,000	2,527,000	2,354,000	2,288,000	2,192,000	1,987,000	1,841,000	1,602,000
Income Before Taxes	13,468,000	13,942,000	13,054,000	11,392,000	8,713,000	8,633,000	7,458,000	6,187,000
Income Taxes	4,422,000	5,078,000	5,016,000	4,242,000	2,984,000	3,087,000	2,785,000	2,314,000
Net Income	8,980,000	9,391,000	8,382,000	7,501,000	6,136,000	5,682,000	4,807,000	3,963,000
Average Shares	1,578,000	1,639,000	1,709,000	1,759,000	1,813,000	1,818,000	1,909,000	1,948,000
Balance Sheet								
Current Assets	15,889,000	16,966,000	16,758,000	15,176,000	14,109,000	13,709,000	13,757,000	12,225,000
Total Assets	95,789,000	92,033,000	88,182,000	84,186,000	81,241,000	74,898,000	72,124,000	69,206,000
Current Liabilities	19,595,000	16,842,000	16,334,000	13,292,000	11,704,000	12,813,000	12,088,000	11,000,000
Long-Term Obligations	19,119,000	16,483,000	12,773,000	12,676,000	13,050,000	10,981,000	11,210,000	10,354,000
Total Liabilities	54,474,000	48,768,000	43,657,000	39,228,000	35,812,000	35,139,000	34,739,000	31,687,000
Stockholders' Equity	41,315,000	43,265,000	44,525,000	44,958,000	45,429,000	39,759,000	37,385,000	37,519,000
Shares Outstanding	1,500,000	1,600,000	1,600,000	1,707,000	1,800,000	1,780,000	1,762,200	1,896,900
Statistical Record								
Return on Assets %	9.59	10.45	9.57	9.09	7.88	7.75	6.82	6.01
Return on Equity %	21.29	21.45	18.43	16.64	14.45	14.77	12.87	11.15
EBITDA Margin %	30.17	30.07	29.59	27.98	24.73	25.99	23.58	21.54
Net Margin %	16.29	16.88	15.98	15.37	13.62	13.44	11.76	10.41
Asset Turnover	0.59	0.62	0.60	0.59	0.58	0.58	0.58	0.58
Current Ratio	0.81	1.01	1.03	1.14	1.21	1.07	1.14	1.11
Debt to Equity	0.46	0.38	0.29	0.28	0.29	0.28	0.30	0.28
Price Range	115.84-90.83	120.07-88.85	121.69-81.74	90.94-63.59	67.67-47.06	52.92-29.00	44.07-29.55	37.56-27.21
P/E Ratio	20.36-15.96	20.95-15.51	24.83-16.68	21.35-14.93	20.02-13.92	16.91-9.27	17.49-11.73	18.50-13.40
Average Yield %	1.49	1.41	1.77	1.09	1.29	1.41	1.04	1.08

Address: 500 South Buena Vista Street, Burbank, CA 91521
Telephone: 818-560-1000

Web Site: www.disney.com
Officers: Robert A. (Bob) Iger - Chairman, President, Chief Executive Officer Alan N. Braverman - Senior Executive Vice President, General Counsel, Secretary

Auditors: PricewaterhouseCoopers LLP
Investor Contact: 818-553-7200
Transfer Agents: Broadridge Corporate Issuer Solutions, Brentwood, NY

DOLBY LABORATORIES INC

Exchange	Symbol	Price	52Wk Range	Yield	P/E
NYS	DLB	$62.00 (12/29/2017)	63.25-46.06	1.03	31.79

*7 Year Price Score 100.44 *NYSE Composite Index=100 *12 Month Price Score 108.43

Interim Earnings (Per Share)

Qtr.	Dec	Mar	Jun	Sep
2012-13	0.50	0.60	0.29	0.45
2013-14	0.43	0.73	0.38	0.44
2014-15	0.40	0.56	0.34	0.46
2015-16	0.30	0.66	0.62	0.22
2016-17	0.51	0.49	0.73	0.22

Interim Dividends (Per Share)

Amt	Decl	Ex	Rec	Pay
0.14Q	01/25/2017	02/02/2017	02/06/2017	02/15/2017
0.14Q	04/26/2017	05/04/2017	05/08/2017	05/16/2017
0.14Q	07/24/2017	08/03/2017	08/07/2017	08/15/2017
0.16Q	10/25/2017	11/03/2017	11/06/2017	11/15/2017

Indicated Div: $0.64

Valuation Analysis

Forecast EPS	$2.21
	(01/17/2018)
Market Cap	$6.3 Billion
Book Value	$2.1 Billion
Price/Book	2.96
Price/Sales	5.86

Institutional Holding

No of Institutions	390
Shares	61,680,020
% Held	46.24

Business Summary: Manufacturing (MIC: 6.1.1 SIC: 3663 NAIC: 334220)

Dolby Laboratories designs and manufactures audio and imaging products for the cinema, television, broadcast, and entertainment industries. Co. has various licensing models: a two-tier model, an integrated licensing model, a patent licensing model, and collaboration arrangements. Co.'s Cinema Imaging Products include digital cinema server used on digital cinema projectors. Co.'s Dolby Cinema Audio Products include cinema processors, amplifiers, and loudspeakers. Co.'s Dolby Conference Phone is a hardware component of the Dolby Voice conferencing solution. Co.'s other products include broadcast hardware and software used to encode, transmit, and decode multiple channels of audio.

Recent Developments: For the year ended Sep 29 2017, net income increased 8.6% to US$202.4 million from US$186.4 million in the prior year. Revenues were US$1.08 billion, up 5.4% from US$1.03 billion the year before. Operating income was US$248.6 million versus US$231.8 million in the prior year, an increase of 7.3%. Direct operating expenses rose 8.6% to US$118.3 million from US$109.0 million in the comparable period the year before. Indirect operating expenses increased 4.3% to US$714.5 million from US$685.0 million in the equivalent prior-year period.

Prospects: Our evaluation of Dolby Laboratories Inc. as of Jan. 14, 2018 is the result of our systematic analysis on three basic characteristics: earnings strength, relative valuation, and recent stock price movement. The company has managed to produce a neutral trend in earnings per share over the past 5 quarters and while recent estimates for the company have remained steady, DLB has posted results that fell short of analysts expectations. Based on operating earnings yield, the company is about fairly valued when compared to all of the companies in our coverage universe. Share price changes over the past year indicates that DLB will perform in line with the market over the near term.

Financial Data

(US$ in Thousands)	09/29/2017	09/30/2016	09/25/2015	09/26/2014	09/27/2013	09/28/2012	09/30/2011	09/24/2010
Earnings Per Share	1.95	1.81	1.75	1.99	1.84	2.46	2.75	2.46
Cash Flow Per Share	3.66	3.49	3.03	3.55	2.70	3.66	3.56	2.89
Tang Book Value Per Share	16.01	14.25	13.58	13.38	11.40	13.41	12.33	10.19
Dividends Per Share	0.560	0.480	0.400	...	4.000	...	...	...
Dividend Payout %	28.72	26.52	22.86	...	217.39	...	...	...
Income Statement								
Total Revenue	1,081,454	1,025,738	970,638	960,176	909,674	926,264	955,505	922,713
EBITDA	300,594	282,345	289,621	310,672	284,773	393,376	454,740	448,217
Depn & Amortn	53,400	52,000	48,200	38,100	37,400	30,600	24,100	17,800
Income Before Taxes	256,644	235,904	245,782	276,099	250,646	368,991	440,643	437,012
Income Taxes	54,217	49,502	62,542	67,379	60,344	103,857	130,061	154,185
Net Income	201,802	185,860	181,390	206,103	189,271	264,302	309,267	283,447
Average Shares	103,286	102,424	103,862	103,632	102,788	107,541	112,554	115,388
Balance Sheet								
Current Assets	1,011,434	759,730	918,330	1,005,851	812,722	970,286	1,158,598	1,060,413
Total Assets	2,533,554	2,310,106	2,133,293	1,984,012	1,737,945	1,960,798	1,884,387	1,711,772
Current Liabilities	245,773	213,083	209,681	189,370	172,815	156,840	159,385	165,756
Total Liabilities	396,812	339,850	326,225	273,995	256,835	240,529	220,874	238,035
Stockholders' Equity	2,136,742	1,970,256	1,807,068	1,710,017	1,481,110	1,720,269	1,663,513	1,473,737
Shares Outstanding	102,155	101,422	101,034	102,268	101,739	103,095	109,420	112,084
Statistical Record								
Return on Assets %	8.36	8.23	8.84	11.11	10.26	13.78	16.92	17.26
Return on Equity %	9.85	9.68	10.34	12.95	11.86	15.66	19.40	20.19
EBITDA Margin %	27.80	27.53	29.84	32.36	31.30	42.47	47.59	48.58
Net Margin %	18.66	18.12	18.69	21.47	20.81	28.53	32.37	30.72
Asset Turnover	0.45	0.45	0.47	0.52	0.49	0.48	0.52	0.56
Current Ratio	4.12	3.57	4.38	5.31	4.70	6.19	7.27	6.40
Price Range	59.07-45.19	54.54-30.50	45.99-30.91	46.93-34.39	35.60-28.98	45.11-26.28	69.51-27.44	69.37-37.40
P/E Ratio	30.29-23.17	30.13-16.85	26.28-17.66	23.58-17.28	19.35-15.75	18.34-10.68	25.28-9.98	28.20-15.20
Average Yield %	1.11	1.15	1.02	...	12.23	...	...	...

Address: 1275 Market Street, San Francisco, CA 94103-1410 **Telephone:** 415-558-0200	**Web Site:** www.dolby.com **Officers:** Peter Gotcher - Chairman Kevin J. Yeaman - President, Chief Executive Officer	**Auditors:** KPMG LLP **Transfer Agents:** Computershare Trust Company, N.A., Providence, RI

DOLLAR GENERAL CORP

Exchange	Symbol	Price	52Wk Range	Yield	P/E
NYS	DG	$93.01 (12/29/2017)	93.38-68.35	1.12	20.62

*7 Year Price Score 99.06   *NYSE Composite Index=100   *12 Month Price Score 108.07

Interim Earnings (Per Share)

Qtr.	Apr	Jul	Oct	Jan
2014-15	0.72	0.83	0.78	1.17
2015-16	0.84	0.95	0.86	1.30
2016-17	1.03	1.08	0.84	1.48
2017-18	1.02	1.08	0.93	...

Interim Dividends (Per Share)

Amt	Decl	Ex	Rec	Pay
0.26Q	03/15/2017	04/07/2017	04/11/2017	04/25/2017
0.26Q	05/31/2017	07/07/2017	07/11/2017	07/25/2017
0.26Q	08/31/2017	10/06/2017	10/10/2017	10/24/2017
0.26Q	12/05/2017	01/08/2018	01/09/2018	01/23/2018

Indicated Div: $1.04

Valuation Analysis / **Institutional Holding**

Forecast EPS	$4.49
	(01/26/2018)
Market Cap	$25.3 Billion
Book Value	$5.7 Billion
Price/Book	4.40
Price/Sales	1.08

No of Institutions	823
Shares	292,289,760
% Held	N/A

Business Summary: Retail - General Merchandise/Department Stores (MIC: 2.1.1 SIC: 5331 NAIC: 452990)

Dollar General is a discount retailer providing a range of merchandise. At Mar 3 2017, Co. operated 13,429 stores located in 44 states, primarily in the southern, southwestern, midwestern and eastern U.S. Co.'s consumables category includes paper and cleaning products, packaged food, perishables, snacks, health and beauty; seasonal products include decorations, toys, batteries, small electronics, automotive and home office supplies; home products include kitchen supplies, cookware, frames, craft supplies and kitchen, and bed and bath soft goods; and apparel category includes casual everyday apparel, as well as socks, underwear, disposable diapers, shoes and accessories.

Recent Developments: For the quarter ended Nov 3 2017, net income increased 7.3% to US$252.5 million from US$235.3 million in the year-earlier quarter. Revenues were US$5.90 billion, up 11.0% from US$5.32 billion the year before. Operating income was US$417.4 million versus US$393.0 million in the prior-year quarter, an increase of 6.2%. Direct operating expenses rose 10.8% to US$4.14 billion from US$3.73 billion in the comparable period the year before. Indirect operating expenses increased 12.9% to US$1.35 billion from US$1.19 billion in the equivalent prior-year period.

Prospects: Our evaluation of Dollar General Inc. as of Jan. 21, 2018 is the result of our systematic analysis on three basic characteristics: earnings strength, relative valuation, and recent stock price movement. The company has managed to produce a neutral trend in earnings per share over the past 5 quarters and while recent estimates for the company have been raised by analysts, DG has posted results that fell short of analysts expectations. Based on operating earnings yield, the company is undervalued when compared to all of the companies in our coverage universe. Share price changes over the past year indicates that DG will perform poorly over the near term.

Financial Data

(US$ in Thousands)	9 Mos	6 Mos	3 Mos	02/03/2017	01/29/2016	01/30/2015	01/31/2014	02/01/2013
Earnings Per Share	4.51	4.42	4.42	4.43	3.95	3.49	3.17	2.85
Cash Flow Per Share	5.96	5.84	6.23	5.61	4.69	4.33	3.77	3.41
Tang Book Value Per Share	0.76	0.54	N.M.	N.M.	N.M.	0.56	N.M.	N.M.
Dividends Per Share	1.030	1.020	1.010	1.000	0.880	...	...	...
Dividend Payout %	22.84	23.08	22.85	22.57	22.28	...	...	...
Income Statement								
Total Revenue	17,341,536	11,437,930	5,609,625	21,986,598	20,368,562	18,909,588	17,504,167	16,022,128
EBITDA	1,679,441	1,161,055	568,879	2,441,749	2,290,568	2,104,993	2,032,614	1,902,520
Depn & Amortn	298,571	197,616	98,586	378,300	350,600	335,900	315,300	277,200
Income Before Taxes	1,308,123	914,687	445,289	1,965,628	1,853,024	1,680,861	1,628,330	1,497,394
Income Taxes	481,318	340,415	165,800	714,495	687,944	615,516	603,214	544,732
Net Income	826,805	574,272	279,489	1,251,133	1,165,080	1,065,345	1,025,116	952,662
Average Shares	272,881	274,132	275,215	282,261	295,211	305,681	323,854	334,469
Balance Sheet								
Current Assets	4,153,334	3,979,991	3,748,949	3,677,771	3,432,410	3,532,609	3,205,607	2,677,113
Total Assets	12,374,756	12,120,824	11,796,355	11,672,298	11,257,885	11,224,104	10,867,524	10,367,682
Current Liabilities	2,937,806	2,806,755	2,692,041	2,622,805	1,995,596	1,987,740	1,811,971	1,738,547
Long-Term Obligations	2,719,568	2,683,105	2,632,090	2,710,576	2,969,175	2,639,427	2,742,788	2,771,336
Total Liabilities	6,630,601	6,433,729	6,267,474	6,266,004	5,880,009	5,514,066	5,465,331	5,382,352
Stockholders' Equity	5,744,155	5,687,095	5,528,881	5,406,294	5,377,876	5,710,038	5,402,193	4,985,330
Shares Outstanding	271,563	273,259	274,225	275,212	286,694	303,447	317,058	327,069
Statistical Record								
Return on Assets %	10.22	10.31	10.69	10.74	10.39	9.67	9.68	9.53
Return on Equity %	22.35	22.05	22.63	22.83	21.07	19.23	19.79	19.78
EBITDA Margin %	9.68	10.15	10.14	11.11	11.25	11.13	11.61	11.87
Net Margin %	4.77	5.02	4.98	5.69	5.72	5.63	5.86	5.95
Asset Turnover	1.92	1.92	1.93	1.89	1.82	1.72	1.65	1.60
Current Ratio	1.41	1.42	1.39	1.40	1.72	1.78	1.77	1.54
Debt to Equity	0.47	0.47	0.48	0.50	0.55	0.46	0.51	0.56
Price Range	84.37-68.35	94.37-66.97	96.71-66.97	96.71-66.97	81.18-60.02	71.29-53.50	62.87-43.80	55.06-41.64
P/E Ratio	18.71-15.16	21.35-15.15	21.88-15.15	21.83-15.12	20.55-15.19	20.43-15.33	19.83-13.82	19.32-14.61
Average Yield %	1.38	1.38	1.29	1.25	1.21	...	...	...

Address: 100 Mission Ridge, Goodlettsville, TN 37072	**Web Site:** www.dollargeneral.com
Telephone: 615-855-4000	**Officers:** Michael M. Calbert - Chairman, Chairman (frmr) Todd J. Vasos - Chief Executive Officer,
Fax: 615-855-5527	Executive Vice President, Chief Merchandising Officer, Chief Operating Officer, Division Officer

Auditors: Ernst & Young LLP	
Investor Contact: 615-855-4000	
Transfer Agents: Wells Fargo Bank, N.A., St. Paul, MN	

DOMINION ENERGY INC

Exchange	Symbol	Price	52Wk Range	Yield	P/E	Div Achiever
NYS	D	$81.06 (12/29/2017)	84.91-71.68	3.80	23.91	13 Years

*7 Year Price Score 94.89 *NYSE Composite Index=100 *12 Month Price Score 99.21

Interim Earnings (Per Share)

Qtr.	Mar	Jun	Sep	Dec
2014	0.65	0.27	0.90	0.41
2015	0.91	0.70	1.00	0.60
2016	0.88	0.73	1.10	0.73
2017	1.01	0.62	1.03	...

Interim Dividends (Per Share)

Amt	Decl	Ex	Rec	Pay
0.755Q	01/24/2017	03/01/2017	03/03/2017	03/20/2017
0.755Q	05/10/2017	05/31/2017	06/02/2017	06/20/2017
0.755Q	08/01/2017	08/30/2017	09/01/2017	09/20/2017
0.77Q	10/12/2017	11/30/2017	12/01/2017	12/20/2017

Indicated Div: $3.08 (Div. Reinv. Plan)

Valuation Analysis		Institutional Holding	
Forecast EPS	$3.60	No of Institutions	
	(01/18/2018)	1439	
Market Cap	$52.2 Billion	Shares	
Book Value	$16.3 Billion	512,132,480	
Price/Book	3.21	% Held	
Price/Sales	4.19	59.19	

Business Summary: Electric Utilities (MIC: 3.1.1 SIC: 4911 NAIC: 221121)

Dominion Energy is a producer and transporter of energy. Co.'s subsidiary, Dominion Gas Holdings, LLC conducts business activities through a regulated interstate natural gas transmission pipeline and underground storage system in the Northeast, mid-Atlantic and Midwest states, regulated gas transportation and distribution operations in Ohio, and gas gathering and processing activities primarily in West Virginia, Ohio and Pennsylvania. Co.'s nonregulated operations include merchant generation, energy marketing and price risk management activities, and retail energy marketing operations. As of Dec 31 2016, Co. served over 6.0 million utility and retail energy customers in 14 states.

Recent Developments: For the quarter ended Sep 30 2017, net income decreased 4.4% to US$696.0 million from US$728.0 million in the year-earlier quarter. Revenues were US$3.18 billion, up 1.5% from US$3.13 billion the year before. Operating income was US$1.20 billion versus US$1.15 billion in the prior-year quarter, an increase of 4.8%. Direct operating expenses declined 7.6% to US$1.33 billion from US$1.44 billion in the comparable period the year before. Indirect operating expenses increased 18.7% to US$647.0 million from US$545.0 million in the equivalent prior-year period.

Prospects: Our evaluation of Dominion Energy Inc. as of Jan. 14, 2018 is the result of our systematic analysis on three basic characteristics: earnings strength, relative valuation, and recent stock price movement. The company has managed to produce a neutral trend in earnings per share over the past 5 quarters and while recent estimates for the company have been mixed, D has posted better than expected results. Based on operating earnings yield, the company is undervalued when compared to all of the companies in our coverage universe. Share price changes over the past year indicates that D will perform very well over the near term.

Financial Data (US$ in Thousands)	9 Mos	6 Mos	3 Mos	12/31/2016	12/31/2015	12/31/2014	12/31/2013	12/31/2012
Earnings Per Share	3.39	3.46	3.57	3.44	3.20	2.24	2.93	0.53
Cash Flow Per Share	6.86	7.09	6.84	6.68	7.55	5.90	5.93	7.20
Tang Book Value Per Share	15.33	13.61	13.54	12.08	14.77	13.57	14.20	12.43
Dividends Per Share	2.965	2.910	2.855	2.800	2.590	2.400	2.250	2.110
Dividend Payout %	87.46	84.10	79.97	81.40	80.94	107.14	76.79	398.11
Income Statement								
Total Revenue	9,376,000	6,197,000	3,384,000	11,737,000	11,683,000	12,436,000	13,120,000	13,093,000
EBITDA	5,024,000	3,190,000	1,789,000	5,726,000	5,401,000	4,531,000	4,971,000	2,822,000
Depn & Amortn	1,649,000	1,088,000	548,000	1,849,000	1,669,000	1,560,000	1,390,000	1,443,000
Income Before Taxes	2,470,000	1,502,000	949,000	2,867,000	2,828,000	1,778,000	2,704,000	497,000
Income Taxes	683,000	411,000	275,000	655,000	905,000	452,000	892,000	146,000
Net Income	1,687,000	1,022,000	632,000	2,123,000	1,899,000	1,310,000	1,697,000	302,000
Average Shares	642,500	629,200	628,100	617,100	593,700	584,500	579,500	573,900
Balance Sheet								
Current Assets	3,994,000	3,911,000	4,285,000	4,248,000	4,191,000	5,615,000	5,940,000	5,140,000
Total Assets	75,391,000	73,902,000	72,852,000	71,610,000	58,797,000	54,327,000	50,096,000	46,838,000
Current Liabilities	8,559,000	9,502,000	7,842,000	8,115,000	8,120,000	7,198,000	6,994,000	7,763,000
Long-Term Obligations	30,886,000	30,155,000	31,096,000	30,231,000	23,616,000	21,805,000	19,330,000	16,851,000
Total Liabilities	59,111,000	58,929,000	57,935,000	57,005,000	46,133,000	42,772,000	38,197,000	36,013,000
Stockholders' Equity	16,280,000	14,973,000	14,917,000	14,605,000	12,664,000	11,555,000	11,899,000	10,825,000
Shares Outstanding	644,000	630,000	629,000	628,000	596,000	585,000	581,000	576,000
Statistical Record								
Return on Assets %	2.96	3.21	3.37	3.25	3.36	2.51	3.50	0.65
Return on Equity %	13.73	14.84	16.05	15.53	15.68	11.17	14.94	2.67
EBITDA Margin %	53.58	51.48	52.87	48.79	46.23	36.43	37.89	21.55
Net Margin %	17.99	16.49	18.68	18.09	16.25	10.53	12.93	2.31
Asset Turnover	0.17	0.18	0.18	0.18	0.21	0.24	0.27	0.28
Current Ratio	0.47	0.41	0.55	0.52	0.52	0.78	0.85	0.66
Debt to Equity	1.90	2.01	2.08	2.07	1.86	1.89	1.62	1.56
Price Range	81.41-69.99	81.41-69.99	78.92-69.51	78.92-67.47	79.27-64.89	80.23-63.51	67.80-51.80	54.97-49.19
P/E Ratio	24.01-20.65	23.53-20.23	22.11-19.47	22.94-19.61	24.77-20.28	35.82-28.35	23.14-17.68	103.72-92.81
Average Yield %	3.88	3.88	3.83	3.82	3.65	3.43	3.79	4.05

Address: 120 Tredegar Street, Richmond, VA 23219	Web Site: www.dom.com	Auditors: Deloitte & Touche LLP
Telephone: 804-819-2000	Officers: Thomas F. Farrell - Chairman, President, Chief Executive Officer Mark F. McGettrick - Executive Vice President, Chief Financial Officer	Investor Contact: 804-819-2205
Fax: 804-775-5819		Transfer Agents: Dominion Resources Services, Inc. Richmond, VA

DOMINOS PIZZA INC.

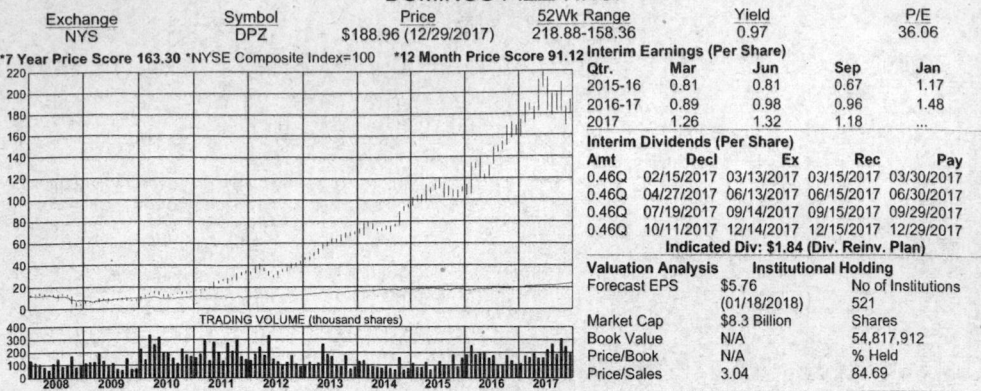

Exchange	Symbol	Price	52Wk Range	Yield	P/E
NYS	DPZ	$188.96 (12/29/2017)	218.88-158.36	0.97	36.06

*7 Year Price Score 163.30 *NYSE Composite Index=100 ***12 Month Price Score 91.12**

Interim Earnings (Per Share)

Qtr.	Mar	Jun	Sep	Jan
2015-16	0.81	0.81	0.67	1.17
2016-17	0.89	0.98	0.96	1.48
2017	1.26	1.32	1.18	...

Interim Dividends (Per Share)

Amt	Decl	Ex	Rec	Pay
0.46Q	02/15/2017	03/13/2017	03/15/2017	03/30/2017
0.46Q	04/27/2017	06/13/2017	06/15/2017	06/30/2017
0.46Q	07/19/2017	09/14/2017	09/15/2017	09/29/2017
0.46Q	10/11/2017	12/14/2017	12/15/2017	12/29/2017

Indicated Div: $1.84 (Div. Reinv. Plan)

Valuation Analysis | **Institutional Holding**

Forecast EPS	$5.76	No of Institutions
	(01/18/2018)	521
Market Cap	$8.3 Billion	Shares
Book Value	N/A	54,817,912
Price/Book	N/A	% Held
Price/Sales	3.04	84.69

Business Summary: Hotels, Restaurants & Travel (MIC: 2.2.1 SIC: 5812 NAIC: 722211)

Domino's Pizza is involved in the: retail sales of food through Co.-owned Domino's Pizza stores; sales of food, equipment and supplies to Co.-owned and franchised Domino's Pizza stores; and receipt of royalties and fees from domestic and international Domino's Pizza franchisees. Co.'s menu features pizza products with varying sizes and crust types. Co.'s typical store also provides oven-baked sandwiches, pasta, boneless chicken and wings, bread side items, desserts and Coca-Cola® soft drink products. International markets vary toppings by country and culture, such as squid topping in Japan, and feature regional specialty items, such as a banana and cinnamon dessert pizza in Brazil.

Recent Developments: For the quarter ended Sep 10 2017, net income increased 19.3% to US$56.4 million from US$47.2 million in the year-earlier quarter. Revenues were US$643.6 million, up 13.6% from US$566.7 million the year before. Operating income was US$117.1 million versus US$100.9 million in the prior-year quarter, an increase of 16.0%. Direct operating expenses rose 13.3% to US$445.2 million from US$392.8 million in the comparable period the year before. Indirect operating expenses increased 11.5% to US$81.4 million from US$73.0 million in the equivalent prior-year period.

Prospects: Our evaluation of Dominos Pizza Inc. as of Jan. 14, 2018 is the result of our systematic analysis on three basic characteristics: earnings strength, relative valuation, and recent stock price movement. The company has produced a positive trend in earnings per share over the past 5 quarters and while recent estimates for the company have been mixed, DPZ has posted better than expected results. Based on operating earnings yield, the company is about fairly valued when compared to all of the companies in our coverage universe. Share price changes over the past year indicates that DPZ will perform poorly over the near term.

Financial Data

(US$ in Thousands)	9 Mos	6 Mos	3 Mos	01/01/2017	01/03/2016	12/28/2014	12/29/2013	12/30/2012
Earnings Per Share	5.24	5.02	4.68	4.30	3.47	2.86	2.48	1.91
Cash Flow Per Share	7.53	6.94	7.44	5 92	5.33	3.51	3.51	3.13
Dividends Per Share	1.680	1.680	1.600	1.520	1.240	1.000	0.800	3.000
Dividend Payout %	32.06	33.47	34.19	35.35	35.73	34.97	32.26	157.07
Income Statement								
Total Revenue	1,896,470	1,252,828	624,217	2,472,628	2,216,528	1,993,833	1,802,223	1,678,439
EBITDA	355,405	231,615	117,434	498,600	450,266	386,895	345,688	320,098
Depn & Amortn	9,424	2,714	1,400	44,558	44,827	41,534	31,877	37,767
Income Before Taxes	263,597	179,046	90,514	344,658	306,215	258,623	225,099	181,187
Income Taxes	79,019	50,836	28,045	129,980	113,426	96,036	82,114	68,795
Net Income	184,578	128,210	62,469	214,678	192,789	162,587	142,985	112,392
Average Shares	47,715	49,776	49,706	49,923	55,532	56,931	57,720	58,997
Balance Sheet								
Current Assets	592,586	560,903	528,636	495,873	602,637	428,361	351,540	306,267
Total Assets	816,235	781,797	742,462	716,295	799,845	619,280	525,255	478,197
Current Liabilities	398,530	351,512	369,440	403,698	375,983	265,608	254,611	229,498
Long-Term Obligations	3,128,048	2,180,518	2,179,258	2,148,990	2,181,460	1,523,546	1,512,299	1,536,443
Total Liabilities	3,581,579	2,584,868	2,596,153	2,599,438	2,600,096	1,838,745	1,815,457	1,813,720
Stockholders' Equity	(2,765,344)	(1,803,071)	(1,853,691)	(1,883,143)	(1,800,251)	(1,219,465)	(1,290,202)	(1,335,523)
Shares Outstanding	43,734	48,247	48,089	48,100	49,838	55,553	55,768	56,313
Statistical Record								
Return on Assets %	34.47	34.61	29.64	28.40	26.73	28.49	28.58	23.51
EBITDA Margin %	18.74	18.49	18.81	20.16	20.31	19.40	19.18	19.07
Net Margin %	9.73	10.23	10.01	8.68	8.70	8.15	7.93	6.70
Asset Turnover	3.64	3.68	3.27	3.27	3.07	3.49	3.60	3.51
Current Ratio	1.49	1.60	1.43	1.23	1.60	1.61	1.38	1.33
Price Range	218.88-149.66	218.15-122.08	189.81-118.56	172.26-104.16	119.43-94.17	95.93-67.17	70.68-43.55	43.46-28.75
P/E Ratio	41.77-28.56	43.46-24.32	40.56-25.33	40.06-24.22	34.42-27.14	33.54-23.49	28.50-17.56	22.75-15.05
Average Yield %	0.93	1.00	1.05	1.09	1.16	1.29	1.36	8.44

Address: 30 Frank Lloyd Wright Drive, Ann Arbor, MI 48105
Telephone: 734-930-3030

Web Site: www.dominos.com
Officers: David A. Brandon - Chairman, Chief Executive Officer J. Patrick Doyle - President, Chief Executive Officer

Auditors: PricewaterhouseCoopers LLP
Investor Contact: 734-930-3008
Transfer Agents: ComputerShare Investor Services, Providence, RI

DOMTAR CORP

Exchange	Symbol	Price	52Wk Range	Yield	P/E	Div Acheiver
NYS	UFS	$62.23 (12/29/2017)	63.91-47.33	2.67	22.30	6 Years

*7 Year Price Score 89.42 *NYSE Composite Index=100 *12 Month Price Score 107.86

Interim Earnings (Per Share)

Qtr.	Mar	Jun	Sep	Dec
2014	0.60	0.61	4.33	1.10
2015	0.56	0.60	0.17	0.90
2016	0.06	0.29	0.94	0.75
2017	0.32	0.61	1.11	...

Interim Dividends (Per Share)

Amt	Decl	Ex	Rec	Pay
0.415Q	02/22/2017	03/30/2017	04/03/2017	04/17/2017
0.415Q	05/16/2017	06/29/2017	07/03/2017	07/17/2017
0.415Q	08/02/2017	09/29/2017	10/02/2017	10/16/2017
0.415Q	11/01/2017	12/29/2017	01/02/2018	01/15/2018

Indicated Div: $1.66

Valuation Analysis | **Institutional Holding**

Forecast EPS	$2.77	No of Institutions	
	(01/26/2018)	N/A	
Market Cap	$3.9 Billion	Shares	
Book Value	$2.9 Billion	N/A	
Price/Book	1.35	% Held	
Price/Sales	0.77	N/A	

Business Summary: Paper & Forest Products (MIC: 8.1.2 SIC: 2621 NAIC: 322121)

Domtar is engaged in designing, manufacturing, marketing and distributing a range of fiber-based products including communication papers, specialty and packaging papers and absorbent hygiene products. Co. is also a marketer and producer of a broad line of incontinence care products as well as infant diapers. Co. operates the following business segments: Pulp and Paper, which consists of the design, manufacturing, marketing and distribution of communication, specialty and packaging papers, as well as softwood, fluff and hardwood market pulp; and Personal Care, which consists of the design, manufacturing, marketing and distribution of absorbent hygiene products.

Recent Developments: For the quarter ended Sep 30 2017, net income increased 18.6% to US$70.0 million from US$59.0 million in the year-earlier quarter. Revenues were US$1.29 billion, up 1.7% from US$1.27 billion the year before. Operating income was US$89.0 million versus US$92.0 million in the prior-year quarter, a decrease of 3.3%. Direct operating expenses rose 4.4% to US$1.01 billion from US$969.0 million in the comparable period the year before. Indirect operating expenses decreased 8.6% to US$191.0 million from US$209.0 million in the equivalent prior-year period.

Prospects: Our evaluation of Domtar Corp. as of Jan. 21, 2018 is the result of our systematic analysis on three basic characteristics: earnings strength, relative valuation, and recent stock price movement. The company has managed to produce a neutral trend in earnings per share over the past 5 quarters and while recent estimates for the company have been raised by analysts, UFS has posted better than expected results. Based on operating earnings yield, the company is undervalued when compared to all of the companies in our coverage universe. Share price changes over the past year indicates that UFS will perform in line with the market over the near term.

Financial Data

(US$ in Thousands)	9 Mos	6 Mos	3 Mos	12/31/2016	12/31/2015	12/31/2014	12/31/2013	12/31/2012
Earnings Per Share	2.79	2.62	2.30	2.04	2.24	6.64	1.36	2.38
Cash Flow Per Share	7.64	7.38	7.33	7.41	7.16	9.78	6.17	7.63
Tang Book Value Per Share	26.73	25.15	24.35	24.25	24.06	25.96	30.94	33.07
Dividends Per Share	1.660	1.660	1.660	1.645	1.600	1.400	1.050	0.850
Dividend Payout %	59.50	63.36	72.17	80.64	71.43	21.08	77.21	35.71
Income Statement								
Total Revenue	3,820,000	2,528,000	1,304,000	5,098,000	5,264,000	5,563,000	5,391,000	5,482,000
EBITDA	434,000	265,000	122,000	552,000	628,000	727,000	527,000	752,000
Depn & Amortn	239,000	159,000	80,000	329,000	340,000	363,000	366,000	385,000
Income Before Taxes	145,000	72,000	25,000	157,000	156,000	261,000	72,000	236,000
Income Taxes	17,000	14,000	5,000	29,000	14,000	(170,000)	(20,000)	58,000
Net Income	128,000	58,000	20,000	128,000	142,000	431,000	91,000	172,000
Average Shares	62,900	62,700	62,800	62,700	63,400	64,900	66,800	72,200
Balance Sheet								
Current Assets	1,649,000	1,555,000	1,544,000	1,568,000	1,554,000	1,670,000	2,077,000	2,015,000
Total Assets	5,784,000	5,667,000	5,625,000	5,680,000	5,663,000	6,185,000	6,278,000	6,123,000
Current Liabilities	720,000	656,000	724,000	753,000	788,000	926,000	709,000	758,000
Long-Term Obligations	1,164,000	1,203,000	1,188,000	1,218,000	1,219,000	1,181,000	1,510,000	1,128,000
Total Liabilities	2,898,000	2,897,000	2,940,000	3,004,000	3,011,000	3,295,000	3,496,000	3,246,000
Stockholders' Equity	2,886,000	2,770,000	2,685,000	2,676,000	2,652,000	2,890,000	2,782,000	2,877,000
Shares Outstanding	62,692	62,654	62,632	62,588	62,849	64,010	64,837	69,692
Statistical Record								
Return on Assets %	3.01	2.87	2.53	2.25	2.40	6.92	1.47	2.86
Return on Equity %	6.21	5.98	5.31	4.79	5.12	15.20	3.22	5.87
EBITDA Margin %	11.36	10.48	9.36	10.83	11.93	13.07	9.78	13.72
Net Margin %	3.35	2.29	1.53	2.51	2.70	7.75	1.69	3.14
Asset Turnover	0.88	0.89	0.90	0.90	0.89	0.89	0.87	0.91
Current Ratio	2.29	2.37	2.13	2.08	1.97	1.80	2.93	2.66
Debt to Equity	0.40	0.43	0.44	0.46	0.46	0.41	0.54	0.39
Price Range	57.11-45.64	57.11-43.32	57.06-43.32	54.86-42.41	59.49-44.24	63.73-37.66	51.34-34.01	49.87-35.13
P/E Ratio	20.47-16.36	21.80-16.53	24.81-18.83	26.89-20.79	26.56-19.75	9.60-5.67	37.75-25.00	20.95-14.76
Average Yield %	3.26	3.28	3.29	3.31	3.37	3.04	2.88	2.64	2.07

Address: 234 Kingsley Park Drive, Fort Mill, SC 29715 **Telephone:** 803-802-7500	**Web Site:** www.domtar.com **Officers:** Harold H. MacKay - Chairman John D. Williams - President, Chief Executive Officer	**Auditors:** PricewaterhouseCoopers LLP **Investor Contact:** 514-848-5555 **Transfer Agents:** ComputerShare Investor Services, Providence, RI

DR PEPPER SNAPPLE GROUP INC

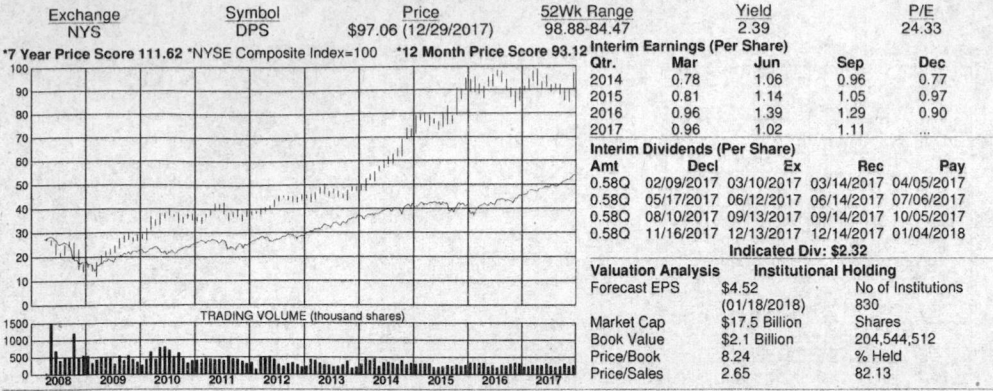

Exchange	Symbol	Price	52Wk Range	Yield	P/E
NYS	DPS	$97.06 (12/29/2017)	98.88-84.47	2.39	24.33

*7 Year Price Score 111.62 *NYSE Composite Index=100 *12 Month Price Score 93.12

Interim Earnings (Per Share)

Qtr.	Mar	Jun	Sep	Dec
2014	0.78	1.06	0.96	0.77
2015	0.81	1.14	1.05	0.97
2016	0.96	1.39	1.29	0.90
2017	0.96	1.02	1.11	...

Interim Dividends (Per Share)

Amt	Decl	Ex	Rec	Pay
0.58Q	02/09/2017	03/10/2017	03/14/2017	04/05/2017
0.58Q	05/17/2017	06/12/2017	06/14/2017	07/06/2017
0.58Q	08/10/2017	09/13/2017	09/14/2017	10/05/2017
0.58Q	11/16/2017	12/13/2017	12/14/2017	01/04/2018

Indicated Div: $2.32

Valuation Analysis

Forecast EPS	$4.52
	(01/18/2018)
Market Cap	$17.5 Billion
Book Value	$2.1 Billion
Price/Book	8.24
Price/Sales	2.65

Institutional Holding

No of Institutions	830
Shares	204,544,512
% Held	82.13

Business Summary: Beverages (MIC: 1.2.2 SIC: 2086 NAIC: 312111)

Dr Pepper Snapple Group is a brand owner, manufacturer and distributor of non-alcoholic beverages in the U.S., Canada and Mexico with a portfolio of flavored (non-cola) carbonated soft drinks (CSDs) and non-carbonated beverages (NCBs), including ready-to-drink teas, juices, juice drinks, water and mixers. In the CSD market, Co.'s primary brands are Dr Pepper, Canada Dry, 7UP, Crush, A&W, Sunkist soda, Schweppes and Squirt. In the NCB market segment in the U.S., Co. participates primarily in the ready-to-drink tea, juice, juice drinks and mixer categories. Co.'s segments are: Beverage Concentrates, Packaged Beverages and Latin America Beverages.

Recent Developments: For the quarter ended Sep 30 2017, net income decreased 15.4% to US$203.0 million from US$240.0 million in the year-earlier quarter. Revenues were US$1.74 billion, up 3.6% from US$1.68 billion the year before. Operating income was US$367.0 million versus US$373.0 million in the prior-year quarter, a decrease of 1.6%. Direct operating expenses rose 3.5% to US$707.0 million from US$683.0 million in the comparable period the year before. Indirect operating expenses increased 6.7% to US$666.0 million from US$624.0 million in the equivalent prior-year period.

Prospects: Our evaluation of Dr Pepper Snapple Group Inc. as of Jan. 14, 2018 is the result of our systematic analysis on three basic characteristics: earnings strength, relative valuation, and recent stock price movement. The company has managed to produce a neutral trend in earnings per share over the past 5 quarters. However, while recent estimates for the company have been mixed, DPS has posted results that fell short of analysts expectations. Based on operating earnings yield, the company is undervalued when compared to all of the companies in our coverage universe. Share price changes over the past year indicates that DPS will perform in line with the market over the near term.

Financial Data

(US$ in Thousands)	9 Mos	6 Mos	3 Mos	12/31/2016	12/31/2015	12/31/2014	12/31/2013	12/31/2012
Earnings Per Share	3.99	4.17	4.54	4.54	3.97	3.56	3.05	2.96
Cash Flow Per Share	5.45	5.14	4.68	5.05	5.19	5.22	4.27	2.17
Dividends Per Share	2.270	2.220	2.170	2.120	1.920	1.640	1.520	1.360
Dividend Payout %	56.89	53.24	47.80	46.70	48.36	46.07	49.84	45.95
Income Statement								
Total Revenue	5,047,000	3,307,000	1,510,000	6,440,000	6,282,000	6,121,000	5,997,000	5,995,000
EBITDA	1,093,000	696,000	331,000	1,618,000	1,491,000	1,379,000	859,000	1,304,000
Depn & Amortn	124,000	83,000	44,000	191,000	192,000	199,000	196,000	203,000
Income Before Taxes	848,000	531,000	248,000	1,283,000	1,184,000	1,073,000	542,000	978,000
Income Taxes	279,000	165,000	71,000	434,000	420,000	371,000	(81,000)	349,000
Net Income	568,000	365,000	177,000	847,000	764,000	703,000	624,000	629,000
Average Shares	182,100	183,700	184,600	186,600	192,400	197,400	204,500	212,300
Balance Sheet								
Current Assets	1,266,000	1,555,000	1,247,000	2,736,000	1,817,000	1,211,000	1,119,000	1,335,000
Total Assets	10,039,000	10,319,000	10,008,000	9,791,000	8,869,000	8,273,000	8,201,000	8,928,000
Current Liabilities	1,359,000	1,580,000	1,147,000	1,051,000	1,583,000	1,038,000	1,030,000	1,232,000
Long-Term Obligations	4,399,000	4,391,000	4,467,000	4,468,000	2,875,000	2,588,000	2,508,000	2,554,000
Total Liabilities	7,910,000	8,164,000	7,815,000	7,657,000	6,686,000	5,979,000	5,924,000	6,648,000
Stockholders' Equity	2,129,000	2,155,000	2,193,000	2,134,000	2,183,000	2,294,000	2,277,000	2,280,000
Shares Outstanding	180,640	182,216	183,795	183,119	187,841	192,957	197,979	205,292
Statistical Record								
Return on Assets %	7.83	8.22	9.17	9.05	8.91	8.53	7.29	6.89
Return on Equity %	34.43	35.84	39.21	39.13	34.13	30.76	27.39	27.62
EBITDA Margin %	21.66	21.05	21.92	25.12	23.73	22.53	14.32	21.75
Net Margin %	11.25	11.04	11.72	13.15	12.16	11.49	10.41	10.49
Asset Turnover	0.71	0.70	0.70	0.69	0.73	0.74	0.70	0.66
Current Ratio	0.93	0.98	1.09	2.60	1.15	1.17	1.09	1.08
Debt to Equity	2.07	2.04	2.04	2.09	1.32	1.13	1.10	1.12
Price Range	98.88-82.38	98.88-82.38	98.51-82.38	98.51-82.38	94.99-71.38	74.00-47.22	50.36-42.47	45.91-37.33
P/E Ratio	24.78-20.65	23.71-19.76	21.70-18.15	21.70-18.15	23.93-17.98	20.79-13.26	16.51-13.92	15.51-12.61
Average Yield %	2.49	2.40	2.36	2.32	2.39	2.77	3.28	3.22

Address: 5301 Legacy Drive, Plano, TX 75024
Telephone: 972-673-7000

Web Site: www.drpeppersnapplegroup.com
Officers: Wayne R. Sanders - Chairman Larry D. Young - President, Chief Executive Officer

Auditors: Deloitte & Touche LLP
Investor Contact: 972-673-7935
Transfer Agents: Computershare Investor Services, Canton, MA

DONALDSON CO. INC.

Exchange	Symbol	Price	52Wk Range	Yield	P/E	Div Achiever
NYS	DCI	$48.95 (12/29/2017)	49.90-41.29	1.47	27.66	21 Years

*7 Year Price Score 97.66 *NYSE Composite Index=100 *12 Month Price Score 99.31

Interim Earnings (Per Share)

Qtr.	Oct	Jan	Apr	Jul
2014-15	0.40	0.35	0.33	0.41
2015-16	0.29	0.28	0.41	0.45
2016-17	0.43	0.35	0.45	0.51
2017-18	0.46	...	...	...

Interim Dividends (Per Share)

Amt	Decl	Ex	Rec	Pay
0.175Q	01/27/2017	02/10/2017	02/14/2017	03/03/2017
0.175Q	05/24/2017	06/08/2017	06/12/2017	06/28/2017
0.18Q	07/28/2017	08/11/2017	08/15/2017	08/31/2017
0.18Q	11/17/2017	12/05/2017	12/06/2017	12/21/2017

indicated Div: $0.72 (Div. Reinv. Plan)

Valuation Analysis — **Institutional Holding**

Forecast EPS	$2.00	No of Institutions
	(01/17/2018)	477
Market Cap	$6.4 Billion	Shares
Book Value	$876.3 Million	128,950,000
Price/Book	7.25	% Held
Price/Sales	2.58	71.90

Business Summary: Industrial Machinery & Equipment (MIC: 7.2.1 SIC: 3564 NAIC: 333411)

Donaldson Company is a manufacturer of filtration systems and replacement parts. Co. has two reporting segments: Engine Products, with products including replacement filters for both air and liquid filtration applications, air filtration systems, liquid filtration systems for fuel, lube and hydraulic applications, and exhaust and emissions systems; and Industrial Products, with products including dust, fume and mist collectors, compressed air purification systems, air filtration systems for gas turbines, polytetrafluoroethylene membrane-based products and air and gas filtration systems for applications including hard disk drives and semi-conductor manufacturing.

Recent Developments: For the quarter ended Oct 31 2017, net income increased 5.0% to US$60.9 million from US$58.0 million in the year-earlier quarter. Revenues were US$644.8 million, up 16.6% from US$553.0 million the year before. Operating income was US$90.7 million versus US$76.4 million in the prior-year quarter, an increase of 18.7%. Direct operating expenses rose 17.2% to US$420.5 million from US$358.8 million in the comparable period the year before. Indirect operating expenses increased 13.4% to US$133.6 million from US$117.8 million in the equivalent prior-year period.

Prospects: Our evaluation of Donaldson Co. Inc. as of Jan. 14, 2018 is the result of our systematic analysis on three basic characteristics: earnings strength, relative valuation, and recent stock price movement. The company has enjoyed a very positive trend in earnings per share over the past 5 quarters. However, while recent estimates for the company have been mixed, DCI has posted better than expected results. Based on operating earnings yield, the company is about fairly valued when compared to all of the companies in our coverage universe. Share price changes over the past year indicates that DCI will perform in line with the market over the near term.

Financial Data (US$ in Thousands)	3 Mos	07/31/2017	07/31/2016	07/31/2015	07/31/2014	07/31/2013	07/31/2012	07/31/2011
Earnings Per Share	1.77	1.74	1.42	1.49	1.76	1.64	1.73	1.44
Cash Flow Per Share	2.10	2.34	2.13	1.55	2.18	2.13	1.72	1.59
Tang Book Value Per Share	4.61	4.37	3.76	3.81	5.70	6.01	4.75	4.70
Dividends Per Share	0.705	0.700	0.685	0.665	0.575	0.410	0.320	0.268
Dividend Payout %	39.83	40.23	48.24	44.63	32.67	25.00	18.50	18.64
Income Statement								
Total Revenue	644,800	2,371,900	2,220,300	2,371,213	2,473,466	2,436,948	2,493,248	2,294,029
EBITDA	91,300	410,300	346,900	370,660	432,903	417,891	437,569	379,288
Depn & Amortn	1,400	68,800	68,800	66,900	62,000	58,800	55,300	54,500
Income Before Taxes	84,700	322,000	257,400	288,603	360,703	348,181	370,780	312,263
Income Taxes	23,800	89,200	66,600	80,492	100,479	100,804	106,479	86,972
Net Income	60,900	232,800	190,800	208,111	260,224	247,377	264,301	225,291
Average Shares	132,700	134,100	134,800	139,381	147,641	150,455	152,940	157,196
Balance Sheet								
Current Assets	1,204,300	1,151,000	1,009,700	1,030,716	1,225,277	1,055,662	1,085,662	1,066,582
Total Assets	2,032,400	1,979,700	1,788,600	1,809,534	1,942,411	1,743,556	1,730,082	1,726,093
Current Liabilities	415,100	484,100	543,800	560,647	609,580	476,435	498,523	496,244
Long-Term Obligations	631,700	537,300	351,800	389,218	243,726	102,774	203,483	205,748
Total Liabilities	1,156,100	1,129,600	1,021,200	1,034,765	939,928	658,369	820,068	791,382
Stockholders' Equity	876,300	850,100	767,400	774,769	1,002,483	1,085,187	910,014	934,711
Shares Outstanding	129,849	130,605	132,892	134,598	140,405	146,152	147,662	150,794
Statistical Record								
Return on Assets %	12.32	12.36	10.58	11.09	14.12	14.24	15.25	13.97
Return on Equity %	28.45	28.79	24.68	23.42	24.93	24.80	28.58	26.80
EBITDA Margin %	14.16	17.30	15.62	15.63	17.50	17.15	17.55	16.53
Net Margin %	9.44	9.81	8.59	8.78	10.52	10.15	10.60	9.82
Asset Turnover	1.29	1.26	1.23	1.26	1.34	1.40	1.44	1.42
Current Ratio	2.90	2.38	1.86	1.84	2.01	2.22	2.18	2.15
Debt to Equity	0.72	0.63	0.46	0.50	0.24	0.09	0.22	0.22
Price Range	48.17-36.02	47.96-35.64	36.88-26.17	42.91-31.93	43.58-35.15	39.26-32.02	38.20-23.31	31.29-20.95
P/E Ratio	27.21-20.35	27.56-20.48	25.97-18.43	28.80-21.43	24.76-19.97	23.94-19.52	22.08-13.47	21.73-14.55
Average Yield %	1.58	1.66	2.20	1.75	1.41	1.15	0.97	0.98

Address: 1400 West 94th Street, Minneapolis, MN 55431 **Telephone:** 952-887-3131	**Web Site:** www.donaldson.com **Officers:** Tod E. Carpenter - President, Chief Executive Officer, Chief Operating Officer, Division Officer Scott J. Robinson - Chief Financial Officer, Vice President	**Auditors:** PricewaterhouseCoopers LLP **Investor Contact:** 952-887-3753 **Transfer Agents:** Wells Fargo Shareowner Services, St. Paul, MN

DOUGLAS EMMETT INC

Exchange	Symbol	Price	52Wk Range	Yield	P/E
NYS	DEI	$41.06 (12/29/2017)	41.39-36.46	2.44	77.47

*7 Year Price Score 109.26 *NYSE Composite Index=100   *12 Month Price Score 98.02

Interim Earnings (Per Share)

Qtr.	Mar	Jun	Sep	Dec
2014	0.09	0.09	0.05	0.07
2015	0.12	0.09	0.08	0.09
2016	0.10	0.12	0.21	0.13
2017	0.12	0.13	0.15	...

Interim Dividends (Per Share)

Amt	Decl	Ex	Rec	Pay
0.23Q	03/02/2017	03/29/2017	03/31/2017	04/14/2017
0.23Q	06/01/2017	06/28/2017	06/30/2017	07/14/2017
0.23Q	09/07/2017	09/28/2017	09/29/2017	10/13/2017
0.25Q	12/07/2017	12/28/2017	12/29/2017	01/15/2018

Indicated Div: $1.00

Valuation Analysis

		Institutional Holding	
Forecast EPS	$0.58 (01/18/2018)	No of Institutions	342
Market Cap	$7.0 Billion	Shares	212,022,608
Book Value	$2.4 Billion	% Held	99.45
Price/Book	2.86		
Price/Sales	8.73		

Business Summary: REITs (MIC: 5.3.1 SIC: 6798 NAIC: 525930)

Douglas Emmett is a real estate investment trust. Through its interest in Douglas Emmett Properties, LP and its subsidiaries, its consolidated joint ventures (JVs), and its investments in its unconsolidated institutional real estate funds, Co. owns or partially owns, acquires, develops and manages real estate, consisting primarily of office and multifamily properties. At Dec 31 2016, Co. owned a portfolio of 59 office properties (including ancillary retail space), which included seven office properties owned by its consolidated JVs, 10 multifamily properties containing 3,320 apartment units, and the fee interests in two parcels of land subject to ground leases.

Recent Developments: For the quarter ended Sep 30 2017, net income decreased 20.4% to US$28.5 million from US$35.8 million in the year-earlier quarter. Revenues were US$208.7 million, up 8.7% from US$192.1 million the year before.

Prospects: Our evaluation of Douglas Emmett Inc. as of Jan. 14, 2018 is the result of our systematic analysis on three basic characteristics: earnings strength, relative valuation, and recent stock price movement. The company has enjoyed a very positive trend in earnings per share over the past 5 quarters. However, while recent estimates for the company have been mixed, DEI has posted results that were in line with analysts expectations. Based on operating earnings yield, the company is overvalued when compared to all of the companies in our coverage universe. Share price changes over the past year indicates that DEI will perform well over the near term.

Financial Data

(US$ in Thousands)	9 Mos	6 Mos	3 Mos	12/31/2016	12/31/2015	12/31/2014	12/31/2013	12/31/2012
Earnings Per Share	0.53	0.58	0.57	0.55	0.39	0.30	0.31	0.16
Cash Flow Per Share	2.31	2.38	2.34	2.27	1.86	1.71	1.71	1.50
Tang Book Value Per Share	14.33	13.19	12.13	12.63	13.07	13.38	13.78	13.97
Dividends Per Share	0.920	0.910	0.900	0.890	0.850	0.810	0.740	0.630
Dividend Payout %	172.93	155.82	156.52	160.65	220.21	270.00	238.71	393.75
Income Statement								
Total Revenue	602,862	394,113	194,481	742,551	635,774	599,539	591,536	578,999
EBITDA	193,197	125,430	61,363	461,201	394,153	376,447	368,540	363,307
Depn & Amortn	10,348	6,543	2,629	241,102	197,639	198,799	188,253	186,559
Income Before Taxes	72,441	43,933	21,780	73,951	61,061	49,141	49,739	30,055
Net Income	64,907	39,293	19,049	85,397	58,384	44,621	45,311	22,942
Average Shares	165,520	155,952	153,655	153,190	150,604	176,221	174,802	173,120
Balance Sheet								
Current Assets	284,378	277,637	193,099	215,036	190,262	102,071	121,375	441,788
Total Assets	8,113,172	7,955,393	7,586,699	7,613,705	6,066,161	5,954,596	5,847,789	6,103,807
Current Liabilities	206,151	177,722	178,697	223,267	157,027	168,196	176,297	171,914
Long-Term Obligations	4,048,828	4,314,137	4,391,410	4,369,537	3,611,276	3,435,290	3,241,140	3,441,140
Total Liabilities	5,677,250	5,828,323	5,722,209	5,692,562	4,139,950	4,011,138	3,877,392	4,124,151
Stockholders' Equity	2,435,922	2,127,070	1,864,490	1,921,143	1,926,211	1,943,458	1,970,397	1,979,656
Shares Outstanding	169,487	160,743	153,144	151,530	146,919	144,869	142,605	141,245
Statistical Record								
Return on Assets %	1.07	1.19	1.20	1.25	0.97	0.76	0.76	0.37
Return on Equity %	3.91	4.60	4.74	4.43	3.02	2.28	2.29	1.19
EBITDA Margin %	32.05	31.83	31.55	62.11	62.00	62.79	62.30	62.75
Net Margin %	10.77	9.97	9.79	11.50	9.18	7.44	7.66	3.96
Asset Turnover	0.10	0.10	0.10	0.11	0.11	0.10	0.10	0.09
Current Ratio	1.38	1.56	1.08	0.96	1.21	0.61	0.69	2.57
Debt to Equity	1.66	2.03	2.36	2.27	1.87	1.77	1.64	1.74
Price Range	40.79-33.98	40.79-33.98	40.79-30.11	38.70-24.95	31.79-26.85	29.38-23.29	28.18-22.27	24.48-18.46
P/E Ratio	76.96-64.11	70.33-58.59	71.56-52.82	70.36-45.36	81.51-68.85	97.93-77.63	90.90-71.84	153.00-115.38
Average Yield %	2.43	2.43	2.50	2.65	2.89	2.96	3.02	2.78

Address: 808 Wilshire Boulevard, Suite 200, Santa Monica, CA 90401
Telephone: 310-255-7700

Web Site: www.douglasemmett.com
Officers: Dan A. Emmett - Chairman Jordan L. Kaplan - President, Chief Executive Officer

Auditors: Ernst & Young LLP
Investor Contact: 310-255-7751
Transfer Agents: Computershare Investor Services

DOVER CORP

Exchange	Symbol	Price	52Wk Range	Yield	P/E	Div Achiever
NYS	DOV	$100.99 (12/29/2017)	101.44-76.34	1.86	23.49	61 Years

*7 Year Price Score 99.70 *NYSE Composite Index=100 *12 Month Price Score 107.22

Interim Earnings (Per Share)

Qtr.	Mar	Jun	Sep	Dec
2014	0.93	1.27	1.38	1.02
2015	1.28	2.07	1.19	0.91
2016	0.64	0.76	0.83	1.03
2017	1.09	1.04	1.14	...

Interim Dividends (Per Share)

Amt	Decl	Ex	Rec	Pay
0.44Q	02/10/2017	02/24/2017	02/28/2017	03/15/2017
0.44Q	05/05/2017	05/26/2017	05/31/2017	06/15/2017
0.47Q	08/04/2017	08/29/2017	08/31/2017	09/15/2017
0.47Q	11/03/2017	11/29/2017	11/30/2017	12/15/2017

Indicated Div: $1.88 (Div. Reinv. Plan)

Valuation Analysis — **Institutional Holding**

Forecast EPS	$4.30	No of Institutions	911
	(01/18/2018)		
Market Cap	$15.7 Billion	Shares	166,232,032
Book Value	$4.3 Billion	% Held	77.70
Price/Book	3.68		
Price/Sales	2.07		

Business Summary: Industrial Machinery & Equipment (MIC: 7.2.1 SIC: 3559 NAIC: 333220)

Dover is a global manufacturer delivering equipment and components, specialty systems, consumable supplies, software and digital solutions and support services through four operating segments: Energy, which provides solutions and services for production and processing of fuels worldwide; Engineered Systems, which designs, manufactures and services critical equipment and components; Fluids, which is focused on the handling of critical fluids across the retail fueling, chemical, hygienic, oil and gas and industrial end markets; and Refrigeration & Food Equipment, which provides equipment and systems serving the commercial refrigeration and food service industries.

Recent Developments: For the quarter ended Sep 30 2017, net income increased 37.5% to US$178.9 million from US$130.1 million in the year-earlier quarter. Revenues were US$2.01 billion, up 17.5% from US$1.71 billion the year before. Operating income was US$273.8 million versus US$210.7 million in the prior-year quarter, an increase of 29.9%. Direct operating expenses rose 17.3% to US$1.26 billion from US$1.08 billion in the comparable period the year before. Indirect operating expenses increased 11.8% to US$470.5 million from US$421.0 million in the equivalent prior-year period.

Prospects: Our evaluation of Dover Corp. as of Jan. 14, 2018 is the result of our systematic analysis on three basic characteristics: earnings strength, relative valuation, and recent stock price movement. The company has enjoyed a very positive trend in earnings per share over the past 5 quarters and while recent estimates for the company have been mixed, DOV has posted better than expected results. Based on operating earnings yield, the company is about fairly valued when compared to all of the companies in our coverage universe. Share price changes over the past year indicates that DOV will perform in line with the market over the near term.

Financial Data

(US$ in Thousands)	9 Mos	6 Mos	3 Mos	12/31/2016	12/31/2015	12/31/2014	12/31/2013	12/31/2012
Earnings Per Share	4.30	3.99	3.71	3.25	5.46	4.59	5.78	4.41
Cash Flow Per Share	5.08	4.85	5.19	5.54	6.02	5.70	6.88	6.93
Dividends Per Share	1.790	1.760	1.740	1.720	1.640	1.550	1.450	1.330
Dividend Payout %	41.63	44.11	46.90	52.92	30.04	33.77	25.09	30.16
Income Statement								
Total Revenue	5,812,998	3,806,723	1,813,372	6,794,342	6,956,311	7,752,728	8,729,813	8,104,339
EBITDA	943,335	622,229	310,519	994,469	1,095,383	1,373,465	1,593,512	1,460,528
Depn & Amortn	141,029	91,043	44,718	175,495	167,516	152,079	235,358	201,816
Income Before Taxes	700,191	462,763	231,972	689,332	800,610	1,094,207	1,237,412	1,137,571
Income Taxes	184,974	126,458	59,725	180,440	204,729	316,067	271,607	304,452
Net Income	515,217	336,305	172,247	508,892	869,829	775,235	1,003,129	811,070
Average Shares	157,555	157,513	157,399	156,636	159,172	168,842	173,547	183,993
Balance Sheet								
Current Assets	2,868,771	2,759,584	2,761,919	2,589,191	2,420,779	2,896,822	3,240,162	3,027,844
Total Assets	10,493,390	10,292,423	10,238,308	10,115,991	8,619,763	9,090,385	10,838,172	10,443,943
Current Liabilities	2,167,256	2,215,346	2,319,203	1,940,318	1,367,182	2,039,354	1,615,580	1,986,628
Long-Term Obligations	2,985,048	2,925,472	2,887,962	3,206,637	2,617,342	2,253,041	2,599,201	2,189,350
Total Liabilities	6,217,700	6,219,989	6,284,893	6,316,245	4,975,188	5,389,660	5,460,776	5,524,713
Stockholders' Equity	4,275,690	4,072,434	3,953,415	3,799,746	3,644,575	3,700,725	5,377,396	4,919,230
Shares Outstanding	155,791	155,734	155,669	155,428	155,003	163,011	169,906	174,717
Statistical Record								
Return on Assets %	6.83	6.51	6.05	5.42	9.82	7.78	9.43	8.11
Return on Equity %	16.77	16.12	15.21	13.63	23.68	17.08	19.48	16.42
EBITDA Margin %	16.23	16.35	17.12	14.64	15.75	17.72	18.25	18.02
Net Margin %	8.86	8.83	9.50	7.49	12.50	10.00	11.49	10.01
Asset Turnover	0.77	0.76	0.73	0.72	0.79	0.78	0.82	0.81
Current Ratio	1.32	1.25	1.19	1.33	1.77	1.42	2.01	1.52
Debt to Equity	0.70	0.72	0.73	0.84	0.72	0.61	0.48	0.45
Price Range	92.43-65.53	83.71-65.53	81.82-62.31	77.13-52.65	77.77-55.99	91.07-67.76	80.08-54.51	55.26-42.26
P/E Ratio	21.50-15.24	20.98-16.42	22.05-16.80	23.73-16.20	14.24-10.25	19.84-14.76	13.86-9.43	12.53-9.58
Average Yield %	2.26	2.33	2.41	2.55	2.43	1.86	1.89	2.69

Address: 3005 Highland Parkway, Downers Grove, IL 60515	Web Site: www.dovercorporation.com	Auditors: PricewaterhouseCoopers LLC
Telephone: 630-541-1540	Officers: Michael F. Johnston - Chairman Robert A. Livingston - President, Chief Executive Officer	Investor Contact: 212-922-1640
		Transfer Agents: ComputerShare Investor Services, Providence, RI

DRIL-QUIP INC

Exchange	Symbol	Price	52Wk Range	Yield	P/E
NYS	DRQ	$47.70 (12/29/2017)	67.10-36.20	N/A	N/A

*7 Year Price Score 54.08 ***NYSE Composite Index=100** ***12 Month Price Score 86.52**

Interim Earnings (Per Share)

Qtr.	Mar	Jun	Sep	Dec
2014	1.04	1.27	1.40	1.49
2015	1.38	1.01	1.32	1.28
2016	0.97	0.96	0.51	0.03
2017	0.00	0.00	(0.78)	...

Interim Dividends (Per Share)

No Dividends Paid

Valuation Analysis

		Institutional Holding	
Forecast EPS	$0.20	No of Institutions	
	(01/17/2018)	357	
Market Cap	$1.8 Billion	Shares	
Book Value	$1.4 Billion	52,088,016	
Price/Book	1.32	% Held	
Price/Sales	3.98	99.79	

Business Summary: Equipment & Services (MIC: 9.1.3 SIC: 3533 NAIC: 333132)

Dril-Quip designs, manufactures, sells and services offshore drilling and production equipment. Co.'s primary products consist of subsea and surface wellheads, subsea and surface production trees, subsea control systems and manifolds, mudline hanger systems, specialty connectors and associated pipe, drilling and production riser systems, liner hangers, wellhead connectors and diverters. Co. also provides technical advisory assistance on an as-requested basis during installation of its products, as well as rework and reconditioning services for customer-owned Co.'s products. Co.'s customers may rent or purchase running tools from Co. for use in the installation and retrieval of its products.

Recent Developments: For the quarter ended Sep 30 2017, net loss amounted to US$29.3 million versus net income of US$19.0 million in the year-earlier quarter. Revenues were US$100.3 million, down 18.8% from US$123.6 million the year before. Operating loss was US$62.0 million versus an income of US$22.9 million in the prior-year quarter. Direct operating expenses declined 18.8% to US$63.1 million from US$77.6 million in the comparable period the year before. Indirect operating expenses increased 330.5% to US$99.3 million from US$23.1 million in the equivalent prior-year period.

Prospects: Our evaluation of Dril-Quip Inc. as of Jan. 14, 2018 is the result of our systematic analysis on three basic characteristics: earnings strength, relative valuation, and recent stock price movement. The company has enjoyed a very positive trend in earnings per share over the past 5 quarters. However, while recent estimates for the company have been mixed, DRQ has posted better than expected results. Based on operating earnings yield, the company is overvalued when compared to all of the companies in our coverage universe. Share price changes over the past year indicates that DRQ will perform very poorly over the near term.

Financial Data

(US$ in Thousands)	9 Mos	6 Mos	3 Mos	12/31/2016	12/31/2015	12/31/2014	12/31/2013	12/31/2012
Earnings Per Share	(0.75)	0.54	1.50	2.47	4.98	5.19	4.16	2.94
Cash Flow Per Share	2.66	3.26	5.48	6.55	4.96	3.74	3.99	(0.20)
Tang Book Value Per Share	33.77	34.12	33.88	34.19	34.90	31.98	30.54	26.35
Income Statement								
Total Revenue	347,498	247,150	119,228	538,731	844,310	930,957	872,372	733,031
EBITDA	(31,796)	20,729	8,962	144,459	279,335	309,948	252,845	187,916
Depn & Amortn	32,231	22,713	9,832	31,600	30,500	31,200	29,300	26,224
Income Before Taxes	(61,108)	(10)	52	115,868	249,771	279,380	224,097	162,122
Income Taxes	(31,959)	(120)	(42)	22,647	57,763	70,668	54,270	42,913
Net Income	(29,149)	110	94	93,221	192,008	208,712	169,827	119,209
Average Shares	37,528	37,718	37,693	37,667	38,531	40,190	40,865	40,523
Balance Sheet								
Current Assets	992,489	1,024,895	1,007,229	1,056,711	1,124,298	1,127,140	1,078,813	924,388
Total Assets	1,437,464	1,466,913	1,453,487	1,461,404	1,428,250	1,449,251	1,394,612	1,231,447
Current Liabilities	69,283	86,250	83,193	101,480	100,815	198,642	142,790	155,089
Total Liabilities	71,471	88,595	85,491	104,980	103,792	204,059	152,594	165,015
Stockholders' Equity	1,365,993	1,378,318	1,367,996	1,356,424	1,324,458	1,245,192	1,242,018	1,066,432
Shares Outstanding	37,857	37,835	37,831	37,797	37,951	38,932	40,673	40,475
Statistical Record								
Return on Assets %	N.M.	1.40	3.87	6.43	13.35	14.68	12.93	10.26
Return on Equity %	N.M.	1.49	4.14	6.94	14.94	16.78	14.71	11.94
EBITDA Margin %	N.M.	8.39	7.52	26.81	33.08	33.29	28.98	25.64
Net Margin %	N.M.	0.04	0.08	17.30	22.74	22.42	19.47	16.26
Asset Turnover	0.31	0.33	0.34	0.37	0.59	0.65	0.66	0.63
Current Ratio	14.33	11.88	12.11	10.41	11.15	5.67	7.56	5.96
Price Range	67.10-36.20	67.10-47.50	67.10-47.50	65.65-47.50	80.20-55.11	115.81-70.00	119.38-73.05	76.61-58.72
P/E Ratio	...	124.26-87.96	44.73-31.67	26.58-19.23	16.10-11.07	22.31-13.49	28.70-17.56	26.06-19.97

Address: 6401 N. Eldridge Parkway, Houston, TX 77041 **Telephone:** 713-939-7711 **Fax:** 713-939-8063	**Web Site:** www.dril-quip.com **Officers:** John V. Lovoi - Chairman Blake T. DeBerry - President, Chief Executive Officer, Senior Vice President	**Auditors:** PricewaterhouseCoopers LLP **Investor Contact:** 713-939-7711 **Transfer Agents:** Computershare, Jersey City, NJ

DST SYSTEMS INC (DE)

Exchange	Symbol	Price	52Wk Range	Yield	P/E
NYS	DST	$62.07 (12/29/2017)	62.63-50.58	1.16	9.48

*7 Year Price Score 104.90 *NYSE Composite Index=100 *12 Month Price Score 98.54

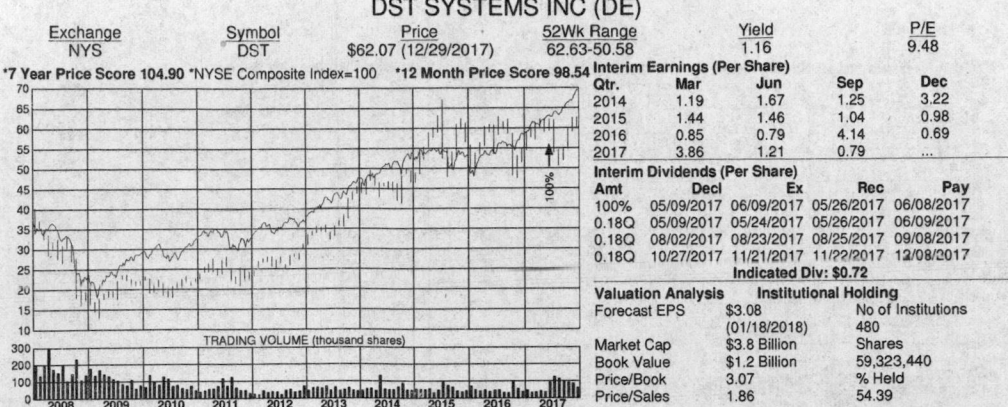

Interim Earnings (Per Share)

Qtr.	Mar	Jun	Sep	Dec
2014	1.19	1.67	1.25	3.22
2015	1.44	1.46	1.04	0.98
2016	0.85	0.79	4.14	0.69
2017	3.86	1.21	0.79	...

Interim Dividends (Per Share)

Amt	Decl	Ex	Rec	Pay
100%	05/09/2017	06/09/2017	05/26/2017	06/08/2017
0.18Q	05/09/2017	05/24/2017	05/26/2017	06/09/2017
0.18Q	08/02/2017	08/23/2017	08/25/2017	09/08/2017
0.18Q	10/27/2017	11/21/2017	11/22/2017	12/08/2017

Indicated Div: $0.72

Valuation Analysis

		Institutional Holding	
Forecast EPS	$3.08 (01/18/2018)	No of Institutions	480
Market Cap	$3.8 Billion	Shares	59,323,440
Book Value	$1.2 Billion	% Held	54.39
Price/Book	3.07		
Price/Sales	1.86		

Business Summary: IT Services (MIC: 6.3.1 SIC: 7374 NAIC: 518210)

DST Systems is a provider of technology-based information processing and servicing solutions. Co.'s segments are: Financial Services, which provides investor, investment, advisor/intermediary and asset distribution services to companies within the financial services industry; and Healthcare Services, which provides healthcare organizations with pharmacy, healthcare administration, and health outcomes optimization solutions, such as claims adjudication, benefit management, care management, business intelligence and other ancillary services. Co.'s Investments and Other Segment includes its investments in equity securities, private equity investments, real estate and other financial interests.

Recent Developments: For the quarter ended Sep 30 2017, net income decreased 82.3% to US$48.5 million from US$273.8 million in the year-earlier quarter. Revenues were US$562.6 million, up 45.5% from US$386.7 million the year before. Operating income was US$55.8 million versus US$74.3 million in the prior-year quarter, a decrease of 24.9%. Direct operating expenses rose 63.0% to US$472.1 million from US$289.6 million in the comparable period the year before. Indirect operating expenses increased 52.2% to US$34.7 million from US$22.8 million in the equivalent prior-year period.

Prospects: Our evaluation of DST Systems Inc. as of Jan. 14, 2018 is the result of our systematic analysis on three basic characteristics: earnings strength, relative valuation, and recent stock price movement. The company has generated a negative trend in earnings per share over the past 5 quarters. However, while recent estimates for the company have been mixed, DST has posted better than expected results. Based on operating earnings yield, the company is about fairly valued when compared to all of the companies in our coverage universe. Share price changes over the past year indicates that DST will perform very poorly over the near term.

Financial Data

(US$ in Thousands)	9 Mos	6 Mos	3 Mos	12/31/2016	12/31/2015	12/31/2014	12/31/2013	12/31/2012
Earnings Per Share	6.55	9.90	9.48	6.41	4.92	7.33	4.00	3.54
Cash Flow Per Share	1.87	1.70	2.90	2.86	3.06	3.91	4.57	2.40
Tang Book Value Per Share	2.27	2.29	2.26	7.13	5.93	9.30	7.45	5.70
Dividends Per Share	0.700	0.685	0.670	0.660	0.600	0.600	0.600	0.400
Dividend Payout %	10.69	6.92	7.07	10.30	12.21	8.19	15.00	11.30
Income Statement								
Total Revenue	1,624,300	1,061,700	405,500	1,556,700	2,825,100	2,749,300	2,658,600	2,576,600
EBITDA	456,300	373,800	255,100	353,700	615,600	897,800	683,700	669,900
Depn & Amortn	31,200	13,200	6,200	78,200	105,500	114,900	127,300	139,100
Income Before Taxes	405,400	347,800	243,000	252,000	486,000	756,300	521,900	487,300
Income Taxes	66,300	53,300	18,100	101,100	173,700	198,400	192,300	195,500
Net Income	370,300	321,800	246,400	427,300	358,200	593,300	352,600	324,000
Average Shares	61,600	62,500	64,000	66,600	72,800	81,000	88,200	91,600
Balance Sheet								
Current Assets	1,163,600	1,146,500	1,225,500	1,118,200	1,055,500	971,900	842,400	954,300
Total Assets	3,002,200	2,964,900	3,031,700	2,771,800	2,813,200	2,942,900	3,090,500	3,392,500
Current Liabilities	1,071,600	1,081,300	1,049,800	1,091,400	948,700	1,021,900	1,072,800	1,378,500
Long-Term Obligations	511,200	453,700	513,000	299,700	556,500	385,600	399,400	492,200
Total Liabilities	1,778,100	1,738,400	1,803,700	1,656,600	1,767,200	1,706,500	1,906,700	2,312,800
Stockholders' Equity	1,224,100	1,226,500	1,228,000	1,115,200	1,046,000	1,236,400	1,183,800	1,079,700
Shares Outstanding	60,500	61,700	63,000	64,000	68,600	75,200	83,600	88,600
Statistical Record								
Return on Assets %	14.84	22.92	21.84	15.26	12.45	19.67	10.88	9.47
Return on Equity %	34.70	58.70	55.31	39.43	31.39	49.03	31.16	34.02
EBITDA Margin %	28.09	35.21	62.91	22.72	21.79	32.66	25.72	26.00
Net Margin %	22.80	30.31	60.76	27.45	12.68	21.58	13.26	12.57
Asset Turnover	0.73	0.66	0.56	0.56	0.98	0.91	0.82	0.75
Current Ratio	1.09	1.06	1.17	1.02	1.11	0.95	0.79	0.69
Debt to Equity	0.42	0.37	0.42	0.27	0.53	0.31	0.34	0.46
Price Range	62.33-47.47	62.91-47.47	62.91-47.47	62.91-47.47	67.08-46.48	49.84-41.26	45.52-30.30	31.16-23.16
P/E Ratio	9.52-7.25	6.35-4.79	6.64-5.01	9.81-7.40	13.64-9.45	6.80-5.63	11.38-7.58	8.80-6.54
Average Yield %	1.24	1.18	1.17	1.17	1.07	1.30	1.64	1.48

Address: 333 West 11th Street, Kansas City, MO 64105 Telephone: 816-435-1000	Web Site: www.dstsystems.com Officers: Stephen C. Hooley - Chairman, President, Chief Executive Officer, Chief Operating Officer Jonathan J. Boehm - Executive Vice President	Auditors: PricewaterhouseCoopers LLP Transfer Agents: Computershare Trust Company, N.A., Providence, RI

DTE ENERGY CO

Exchange	Symbol	Price	52Wk Range	Yield	P/E
NYS	DTE	$109.46 (12/29/2017)	115.99-97.10	3.22	20.05

*7 Year Price Score 110.04 *NYSE Composite Index=100 *12 Month Price Score 99.57

Interim Earnings (Per Share)

Qtr.	Mar	Jun	Sep	Dec
2014	1.84	0.70	0.88	1.68
2015	1.53	0.61	1.47	0.44
2016	1.37	0.84	1.88	0.73
2017	2.23	0.99	1.51	...

Interim Dividends (Per Share)

Amt	Decl	Ex	Rec	Pay
0.825Q	02/03/2017	03/16/2017	03/20/2017	04/15/2017
0.825Q	05/08/2017	06/15/2017	06/19/2017	07/15/2017
0.825Q	06/22/2017	09/15/2017	09/18/2017	10/16/2017
0.882Q	11/03/2017	12/15/2017	12/18/2017	01/15/2018

Indicated Div: $3.53

Valuation Analysis

Forecast EPS	$5.52
	(01/18/2018)
Market Cap	$19.6 Billion
Book Value	$9.4 Billion
Price/Book	2.09
Price/Sales	1.61

Institutional Holding

No of Institutions	811
Shares	152,614,400
% Held	63.93

Business Summary: Electric Utilities (MIC: 3.1.1 SIC: 4911 NAIC: 221111)

DTE Energy is a holding company. Co. is engaged in the generation, purchase, distribution and sale of electricity in southeastern Michigan through its DTE Electric Company subsidiary, as well as in the purchase, storage, transportation, distribution and sale of natural gas throughout Michigan and the sale of storage and transportation capacity through its DTE Gas Company subsidiary. Co.'s non-utility operations are: natural gas pipelines, gathering and storage businesses; power and industrial projects; and energy marketing and trading operations. As of Dec 31 2016, DTE Electric and DTE Gas Company served approximately 2.2 million and 1.3 million, respectively, customers throughout Michigan.

Recent Developments: For the quarter ended Sep 30 2017, net income decreased 19.1% to US$263.0 million from US$325.0 million in the year-earlier quarter. Revenues were US$3.25 billion, up 10.8% from US$2.93 billion the year before. Operating income was US$418.0 million versus US$507.0 million in the prior-year quarter, a decrease of 17.6%. Direct operating expenses rose 17.8% to US$2.47 billion from US$2.10 billion in the comparable period the year before. Indirect operating expenses increased 10.2% to US$355.0 million from US$322.0 million in the equivalent prior-year period.

Prospects: Our evaluation of DTE Energy Co. as of Jan. 14, 2018 is the result of our systematic analysis on three basic characteristics: earnings strength, relative valuation, and recent stock price movement. The company has generated a negative trend in earnings per share over the past 5 quarters and while recent estimates for the company have been mixed, DTE has posted results that fell short of analysts expectations. Based on operating earnings yield, the company is undervalued when compared to all of the companies in our coverage universe. Share price changes over the past year indicates that DTE will perform very well over the near term.

Financial Data

(US$ in Thousands)	9 Mos	6 Mos	3 Mos	12/31/2016	12/31/2015	12/31/2014	12/31/2013	12/31/2012
Earnings Per Share	5.46	5.83	5.68	4.83	4.05	5.10	3.76	3.55
Cash Flow Per Share	10.43	11.15	11.90	11.61	10.68	10.39	12.31	12.88
Tang Book Value Per Share	34.54	32.93	33.81	32.79	37.14	35.07	32.64	30.29
Dividends Per Share	3.300	3.245	3.150	3.055	2.840	2.690	2.585	2.415
Dividend Payout %	60.44	55.66	55.46	63.25	70.12	52.75	68.75	68.03
Income Statement								
Total Revenue	9,336,000	6,091,000	3,236,000	10,630,000	10,337,000	12,301,000	9,661,000	8,791,000
EBITDA	1,507,000	1,013,000	638,000	1,641,000	1,478,000	1,771,000	1,420,000	1,465,000
Depn & Amortn	39,000	24,000	12,000	89,000	98,000	77,000	71,000	75,000
Income Before Taxes	1,073,000	736,000	504,000	1,100,000	943,000	1,275,000	922,000	960,000
Income Taxes	241,000	167,000	110,000	266,000	223,000	364,000	-254,000	286,000
Net Income	847,000	577,000	400,000	868,000	727,000	905,000	661,000	610,000
Average Shares	179,000	179,000	179,000	179,000	179,000	177,000	175,000	172,000
Balance Sheet								
Current Assets	2,815,000	2,631,000	2,567,000	2,762,000	2,575,000	3,087,000	2,806,000	2,915,000
Total Assets	33,071,000	32,582,000	32,149,000	32,041,000	28,737,000	27,974,000	25,935,000	26,339,000
Current Liabilities	2,598,000	2,747,000	1,834,000	2,437,000	2,528,000	2,577,000	3,189,000	2,768,000
Long-Term Obligations	11,795,000	11,358,000	11,758,000	11,269,000	8,835,000	8,343,000	7,214,000	7,014,000
Total Liabilities	23,698,000	23,494,000	22,955,000	23,030,000	19,965,000	19,647,000	18,014,000	18,966,000
Stockholders' Equity	9,373,000	9,088,000	9,194,000	9,011,000	8,772,000	8,327,000	7,921,000	7,373,000
Shares Outstanding	179,390	179,393	179,387	179,432	179,470	176,991	177,087	172,351
Statistical Record								
Return on Assets %	3.13	3.41	3.36	2.85	2.56	3.36	2.53	2.32
Return on Equity %	10.57	11.71	11.29	9.74	8.50	11.14	8.64	8.46
EBITDA Margin %	16.14	16.63	19.72	15.44	14.30	14.40	14.70	16.66
Net Margin %	9.07	9.47	12.36	8.17	7.03	7.36	6.84	6.94
Asset Turnover	0.39	0.39	0.37	0.35	0.36	0.46	0.37	0.33
Current Ratio	1.08	0.96	1.40	1.13	1.02	1.20	0.88	1.05
Debt to Equity	1.26	1.25	1.28	1.25	1.01	1.00	0.91	0.95
Price Range	113.51-90.97	111.19-90.97	102.56-85.07	100.10-78.38	91.54-73.78	90.18-65.10	72.90-60.05	62.10-52.96
P/E Ratio	20.79-16.66	19.07-15.60	18.06-14.98	20.72-16.23	22.60-18.22	17.68-12.76	19.39-15.97	17.49-14.92
Average Yield %	3.23	3.28	3.31	3.34	3.52	3.52	3.55	3.84	4.18

Address: One Energy Plaza, Detroit, MI 48226-1279	**Web Site:** www.dteenergy.com	**Auditors:** PricewaterhouseCoopers LLP
Telephone: 313-235-4000	**Officers:** Gerard M. Anderson - Chairman, President, Chief Executive Officer Jeffrey A. Jewell - Vice President, Controller, Chief Accounting Officer	**Transfer Agents:** Wells Fargo Bank, N.A.

DUKE ENERGY CORP

Exchange	Symbol	Price	52Wk Range	Yield	P/E	Div Achiever
NYS	DUK	$84.11 (12/29/2017)	91.09-76.50	4.23	27.76	12 Years

*7 Year Price Score 91.43   *NYSE Composite Index=100   *12 Month Price Score 98.50

TRADING VOLUME (thousand shares)

Interim Earnings (Per Share)

Qtr.	Mar	Jun	Sep	Dec
2014	(0.14)	0.86	1.80	0.14
2015	1.22	0.78	1.35	0.69
2016	1.01	0.74	1.70	(0.33)
2017	1.02	0.98	1.36	...

Interim Dividends (Per Share)

Amt	Decl	Ex	Rec	Pay
0.855Q	05/04/2017	05/17/2017	05/19/2017	06/16/2017
0.89Q	07/07/2017	08/16/2017	08/18/2017	09/18/2017
0.89Q	10/26/2017	11/16/2017	11/17/2017	12/18/2017
0.89Q	01/05/2018	02/15/2018	02/16/2018	03/16/2018

Indicated Div: $3.56 (Div. Reinv. Plan)

Valuation Analysis / Institutional Holding

Forecast EPS	$4.55	No of Institutions
	(01/18/2018)	1656
Market Cap	$58.9 Billion	Shares
Book Value	$41.6 Billion	534,536,832
Price/Book	1.41	% Held
Price/Sales	2.61	N/A

Business Summary: Electric Utilities (MIC: 3.1.1 SIC: 4931 NAIC: 221122)

Duke Energy is an energy company. Through its subsidiaries, Co. conducts its operations in three reportable operating segments: Electric Utilities and Infrastructure, which provides retail electric service through the generation, transmission, distribution and sale of electricity; Gas Utilities and Infrastructure, which conducts natural gas operations primarily through the regulated public utilities of Piedmont and Duke Energy Ohio; and Commercial Renewables, which primarily acquires, builds, develops and operates wind and solar renewable generation throughout the continental U.S. The portfolio includes nonregulated renewable energy and energy storage businesses.

Recent Developments: For the quarter ended Sep 30 2017, income from continuing operations decreased 4.4% to US$957.0 million from US$1.00 billion in the year-earlier quarter. Net income decreased 19.1% to US$955.0 million from US$1.18 billion in the year-earlier quarter. Revenues were US$6.48 billion, down 1.4% from US$6.58 billion the year before. Operating income was US$1.70 billion versus US$1.95 billion in the prior-year quarter, a decrease of 13.3%. Direct operating expenses declined 3.5% to US$3.37 billion from US$3.50 billion in the comparable period the year before. Indirect operating expenses increased 25.7% to US$1.41 billion from US$1.13 billion in the equivalent prior-year period.

Prospects: Our evaluation of Duke Energy Corp. Holding Co as of Jan. 14, 2018 is the result of our systematic analysis on three basic characteristics: earnings strength, relative valuation, and recent stock price movement. The company has managed to produce a neutral trend in earnings per share over the past 5 quarters. However, while recent estimates for the company have been mixed, DUK has posted better than expected results. Based on operating earnings yield, the company is undervalued when compared to all of the companies in our coverage universe. Share price changes over the past year indicates that DUK will perform very well over the near term.

Financial Data

(US$ in Thousands)	9 Mos	6 Mos	3 Mos	12/31/2016	12/31/2015	12/31/2014	12/31/2013	12/31/2012
Earnings Per Share	3.03	3.37	3.13	3.11	4.05	2.66	3.76	3.07
Cash Flow Per Share	8.88	9.07	9.18	9.81	9.62	9.32	9.04	9.11
Tang Book Value Per Share	31.73	31.23	31.57	30.87	33.99	34.73	35.40	34.40
Dividends Per Share	3.455	3.420	3.390	3.360	3.240	3.150	3.090	1.530
Dividend Payout %	114.03	101.48	108.31	108.04	80.00	118.42	82.18	49.84
Income Statement								
Total Revenue	17,766,000	11,284,000	5,729,000	22,743,000	23,459,000	23,925,000	24,598,000	19,624,000
EBITDA	7,764,000	4,944,000	2,514,000	9,524,000	9,256,000	9,076,000	8,547,000	6,147,000
Depn & Amortn	2,990,000	1,953,000	991,000	3,880,000	3,613,000	3,507,000	3,229,000	2,652,000
Income Before Taxes	3,299,000	2,014,000	1,032,000	3,749,000	4,068,000	4,004,000	3,798,000	2,303,000
Income Taxes	1,035,000	671,000	344,000	1,156,000	1,326,000	1,669,000	1,261,000	705,000
Net Income	2,356,000	1,402,000	716,000	2,152,000	2,816,000	1,883,000	2,665,000	1,768,000
Average Shares	700,000	700,000	700,000	691,000	694,000	707,000	706,000	575,000
Balance Sheet								
Current Assets	7,706,000	7,673,000	8,005,000	8,039,000	8,322,000	11,575,000	10,516,000	10,122,000
Total Assets	136,325,000	135,004,000	134,108,000	132,761,000	121,156,000	120,709,000	114,779,000	113,856,000
Current Liabilities	10,820,000	12,466,000	10,941,000	11,551,000	11,400,000	11,233,000	8,644,000	10,029,000
Long-Term Obligations	48,929,000	46,043,000	47,021,000	45,576,000	37,495,000	37,213,000	38,152,000	36,351,000
Total Liabilities	94,694,000	93,720,000	92,929,000	91,728,000	81,429,000	79,834,000	73,449,000	72,900,000
Stockholders' Equity	41,631,000	41,284,000	41,179,000	41,033,000	39,727,000	40,875,000	41,330,000	40,956,000
Shares Outstanding	700,000	700,000	689,000	700,000	688,000	707,000	706,000	704,000
Statistical Record								
Return on Assets %	1.60	1.82	1.70	1.69	2.33	1.60	2.33	2.00
Return on Equity %	5.19	5.79	5.36	5.31	6.99	4.58	6.48	5.53
EBITDA Margin %	43.70	43.81	43.88	41.88	39.46	37.94	34.75	31.32
Net Margin %	13.26	12.42	12.50	9.46	12.00	7.87	10.83	9.01
Asset Turnover	0.17	0.18	0.18	0.18	0.19	0.20	0.22	0.22
Current Ratio	0.71	0.62	0.73	0.70	0.73	1.03	1.22	1.01
Debt to Equity	1.18	1.12	1.14	1.11	0.94	0.91	0.92	0.89
Price Range	88.34-72.75	87.23-72.75	87.23-72.75	87.23-71.04	89.36-65.83	86.83-67.13	75.20-63.80	69.84-59.87
P/E Ratio	29.16-24.01	25.88-21.59	27.87-23.24	28.05-22.84	22.06-16.25	32.64-25.24	20.00-16.97	22.75-19.50
Average Yield %	4.24	4.23	4.25	4.27	4.33	4.27	4.46	2.36

Address: 550 South Tryon Street, Charlotte, NC 28202-1803	Web Site: www.duke-energy.com	Auditors: Deloitte & Touche LLP
Telephone: 704-382-3853	Officers: Lynn J. Good - Chairman, Vice-Chairman, President, Chief Executive Officer, Group Executive, Chief Financial Officer Dhiaa M. Jamil - Chief Operating Officer, Executive Vice President, Chief Officer	Investor Contact: 704-382-4070 Transfer Agents: Duke Energy, Charlotte, NC

DUKE REALTY CORP

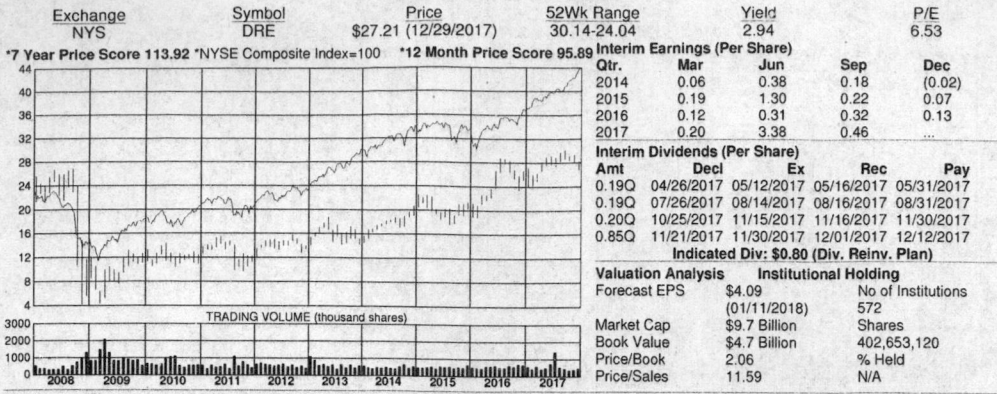

Exchange	Symbol	Price	52Wk Range	Yield	P/E
NYS	DRE	$27.21 (12/29/2017)	30.14-24.04	2.94	6.53

*7 Year Price Score 113.92 *NYSE Composite Index=100 *12 Month Price Score 95.89

Interim Earnings (Per Share)

Qtr.	Mar	Jun	Sep	Dec
2014	0.06	0.38	0.18	(0.02)
2015	0.19	1.30	0.22	0.07
2016	0.12	0.31	0.32	0.13
2017	0.20	3.38	0.46	...

Interim Dividends (Per Share)

Amt	Decl	Ex	Rec	Pay
0.19Q	04/26/2017	05/12/2017	05/16/2017	05/31/2017
0.19Q	07/26/2017	08/14/2017	08/16/2017	08/31/2017
0.20Q	10/25/2017	11/15/2017	11/16/2017	11/30/2017
0.85Q	11/21/2017	11/30/2017	12/01/2017	12/12/2017

Indicated Div: $0.80 (Div. Reinv. Plan)

Valuation Analysis

		Institutional Holding	
Forecast EPS	$4.09	No of Institutions	
	(01/11/2018)	572	
Market Cap	$9.7 Billion	Shares	
Book Value	$4.7 Billion	402,653,120	
Price/Book	2.06	% Held	
Price/Sales	11.59	N/A	

TRADING VOLUME (thousand shares)

Business Summary: REITs (MIC: 5.3.1 SIC: 6798 NAIC: 525930)

Duke Realty is a self-administered and self-managed real estate investment trust and is the sole general partner of Duke Realty Limited Partnership. As of Dec 31 2016, Co. owned or jointly controlled 561 industrial, medical office and other properties; and owned, including through ownership interests in unconsolidated joint ventures 2,190 acres of land and controlled an additional 1,600 acres through purchase options. Co. had three operating segments at Dec 31 2016, the first two of which consist of the ownership and rental of industrial and medical office real estate investments. The third segment consists of various real estate services such as property management.

Recent Developments: For the quarter ended Sep 30 2017, income from continuing operations decreased 61.3% to US$42.0 million from US$108.6 million in the year-earlier quarter. Net income increased 46.4% to US$165.6 million from US$113.2 million in the year-earlier quarter. Revenues were US$194.8 million, up 7.2% from US$181.7 million the year before. Revenues from property income rose 4.5% to US$169.6 million from US$162.3 million in the corresponding quarter a year earlier.

Prospects: Our evaluation of Duke Realty Corp. as of Jan. 14, 2018 is the result of our systematic analysis on three basic characteristics: earnings strength, relative valuation, and recent stock price movement. The company has generated a negative trend in earnings per share over the past 5 quarters. Because the company lacks sufficient analyst estimate data, we place greater weight on the historical EPS trend as the measure of earnings strength. Based on operating earnings yield, the company is overvalued when compared to all of the companies in our coverage universe. Share price changes over the past year indicates that DRE will perform very well over the near term.

Financial Data

(US$ in Thousands)	9 Mos	6 Mos	3 Mos	12/31/2016	12/31/2015	12/31/2014	12/31/2013	12/31/2012
Earnings Per Share	4.17	4.03	0.96	0.88	1.77	0.60	0.47	(0.48)
Cash Flow Per Share	1.30	1.38	1.39	1.28	1.10	1.32	1.35	1.11
Tang Book Value Per Share	13.23	12.97	9.75	9.77	9.22	8.31	7.86	7.04
Dividends Per Share	0.760	0.750	0.740	0.730	0.890	0.680	0.680	0.680
Dividend Payout %	18.23	18.61	77.08	82.95	50.28	113.33	144.68	...
Income Statement								
Total Revenue	565,315	370,487	227,314	902,244	949,432	1,164,704	1,081,790	1,109,440
EBITDA	460,456	336,091	181,009	658,239	611,171	639,454	517,941	414,918
Depn & Amortn	226,963	157,557	82,873	255,419	253,683	290,279	288,583	262,825
Income Before Taxes	177,289	136,760	68,164	265,279	188,581	130,808	2,350	(92,563)
Income Taxes	7,918	7,557	2,132	(589)	(3,928)	(844)	(5,080)	(103)
Net Income	1,446,012	1,280,743	70,200	312,143	615,310	243,588	190,592	(73,977)
Average Shares	362,102	361,981	360,700	357,076	352,197	340,446	326,712	267,900
Balance Sheet								
Current Assets	149,308	196,004	153,562	159,375	174,619	211,786	182,908	216,229
Total Assets	7,297,471	7,317,569	6,958,510	6,772,002	6,917,113	7,754,839	7,752,614	7,560,101
Current Liabilities	217,069	200,528	211,785	254,002	263,318	323,687	308,945	319,071
Long-Term Obligations	2,131,880	2,280,128	3,080,262	2,908,477	3,341,739	4,453,403	4,254,376	4,446,170
Total Liabilities	2,587,087	2,703,420	3,491,309	3,306,184	3,735,181	4,894,514	4,739,371	4,968,687
Stockholders' Equity	4,710,384	4,614,149	3,467,201	3,465,818	3,181,932	2,860,325	3,013,243	2,591,414
Shares Outstanding	356,130	355,713	355,587	354,756	345,285	344,112	326,399	279,423
Statistical Record								
Return on Assets %	21.10	20.31	4.89	4.55	8.39	3.14	2.49	N.M.
Return on Equity %	36.47	36.34	10.22	9.37	20.37	8.29	6.80	N.M.
EBITDA Margin %	81.45	90.72	79.63	72.96	64.37	54.90	47.88	37.40
Net Margin %	255.79	345.69	30.88	34.60	64.81	20.91	17.62	N.M.
Asset Turnover	0.12	0.12	0.13	0.13	0.13	0.15	0.14	0.15
Current Ratio	0.69	0.98	0.73	0.63	0.66	0.65	0.59	0.68
Debt to Equity	0.45	0.49	0.89	0.84	1.05	1.56	1.41	1.72
Price Range	30.14-23.38	29.18-23.38	28.79-21.70	28.79-18.76	22.58-17.61	20.63-14.53	18.71-13.87	15.77-12.02
P/E Ratio	7.23-5.61	7.24-5.80	29.99-22.60	32.72-21.32	12.76-9.95	34.38-24.22	39.81-29.51	...
Average Yield %	2.81	2.80	2.89	3.00	4.40	3.86	4.24	4.82

Address: 600 East 96th Street, Suite 100, Indianapolis, IN 46240
Telephone: 317-808-6000

Web Site: www.dukerealty.com
Officers: Dennis D. Oklak - Executive Chairman, Chairman, President, Chief Executive Officer, Associate/Affiliate Company Officer James B. Connor - Senior Executive Vice President, Chief Operating Officer, Region Officer, President, Chief Executive Officer

Auditors: KPMG LLP
Investor Contact: 317-808-6060
Transfer Agents: American Stock Transfer & Trust Company, New York, NY

DUN & BRADSTREET CORP (DE)

Exchange	Symbol	Price	52Wk Range	Yield	P/E
NYS	DNB	$118.41 (12/29/2017)	125.41-100.75	1.70	22.73

*7 Year Price Score 86.78 *NYSE Composite Index=100 *12 Month Price Score 99.69

Interim Earnings (Per Share)

Qtr.	Mar	Jun	Sep	Dec
2014	2.26	1.35	1.85	2.52
2015	1.13	(0.22)	1.62	2.11
2016	0.82	0.51	(0.80)	2.12
2017	0.42	1.22	1.45	...

Interim Dividends (Per Share)

Amt	Decl	Ex	Rec	Pay
0.502Q	02/08/2017	02/21/2017	02/23/2017	03/10/2017
0.502Q	05/10/2017	05/22/2017	05/24/2017	06/09/2017
0.502Q	08/02/2017	08/21/2017	08/23/2017	09/08/2017
0.502Q	10/19/2017	11/21/2017	11/22/2017	12/08/2017

Indicated Div: $2.01

Valuation Analysis — **Institutional Holding**

Forecast EPS	$7.17	No of Institutions	
	(11/15/2017)	501	
Market Cap	$4.4 Billion	Shares	
Book Value	N/A		44,515,976
Price/Book	N/A	% Held	
Price/Sales	2.51		70.85

TRADING VOLUME (thousand shares)

Business Summary: Business Services (MIC: 7.5.2 SIC: 7323 NAIC: 561450)

Dun & Bradstreet is a provider of commercial data, analytics and insight on businesses. Customers use Co.'s Risk Management Solutions™ to mitigate credit, compliance and supplier risk, increase cash flow and drive profitability, and Co.'s Sales & Marketing Solutions™ to use data to grow sales and improve marketing effectiveness and also for data management capabilities. Co. manages and reports its business through two segments: Americas, which consists of its operations in the U.S., Canada, and its Latin America Worldwide Network; and Non-Americas, which consists of its operations in the U.K., Greater China, India, and its European and Asia Pacific Worldwide Networks.

Recent Developments: For the quarter ended Sep 30 2017, income from continuing operations was US$54.1 million compared with a loss of US$28.5 million in the year-earlier quarter. Net income amounted to US$54.1 million versus a net loss of US$29.4 million in the year-earlier quarter. Revenues were US$428.3 million, up 3.8% from US$412.8 million the year before. Operating income was US$95.2 million versus US$96.8 million in the prior-year quarter, a decrease of 1.7%. Direct operating expenses rose 9.1% to US$142.6 million from US$130.7 million in the comparable period the year before. Indirect operating expenses increased 2.8% to US$190.5 million from US$185.3 million in the equivalent prior-year period.

Prospects: Our evaluation of Dun & Bradstreet Corp. as of Jan. 14, 2018 is the result of our systematic analysis on three basic characteristics: earnings strength, relative valuation, and recent stock price movement. The company has enjoyed a very positive trend in earnings per share over the past 5 quarters and while recent estimates for the company have remained steady, DNB has posted better than expected results. Based on operating earnings yield, the company is undervalued when compared to all of the companies in our coverage universe. Share price changes over the past year indicates that DNB will perform in line with the market over the near term.

Financial Data

(US$ in Thousands)	9 Mos	6 Mos	3 Mos	12/31/2016	12/31/2015	12/31/2014	12/31/2013	12/31/2012
Earnings Per Share	5.21	2.96	2.25	2.65	4.64	7.99	6.54	6.43
Cash Flow Per Share	7.97	8.63	8.59	8.82	9.51	8.64	8.52	7.83
Dividends Per Share	1.990	1.970	1.950	1.930	1.850	1.760	1.600	1.520
Dividend Payout %	38.20	66.55	86.67	72.83	39.87	22.03	24.46	23.64
Income Statement								
Total Revenue	1,215,500	787,200	381,500	1,703,700	1,637,100	1,681,800	1,655,200	1,663,000
EBITDA	240,000	136,200	48,600	264,200	335,600	398,500	443,500	428,200
Depn & Amortn	28,400	18,900	9,500	9,300	6,200	8,300	8,100	11,200
Income Before Taxes	167,900	88,400	24,900	203,600	280,000	348,600	396,000	378,300
Income Taxes	51,100	26,900	8,200	99,900	74,200	52,600	135,500	83,100
Net Income	114,700	60,600	15,500	97,400	168,800	294,400	258,500	295,500
Average Shares	37,200	37,100	37,100	36,800	36,400	36,900	39,500	46,000
Balance Sheet								
Current Assets	882,800	837,600	860,900	944,400	959,600	935,900	822,400	747,400
Total Assets	2,301,000	2,253,700	2,279,300	2,209,200	2,273,600	1,986,200	1,890,300	1,991,800
Current Liabilities	954,500	934,000	1,000,500	1,010,000	959,200	1,158,900	852,300	876,700
Long-Term Obligations	1,651,600	1,673,400	1,682,200	1,594,500	1,804,100	1,352,200	1,516,000	1,290,700
Total Liabilities	3,175,000	3,184,200	3,274,100	3,211,200	3,390,400	3,189,500	2,938,700	3,009,200
Stockholders' Equity	(874,000)	(930,500)	(994,800)	(1,002,000)	(1,116,800)	(1,203,300)	(1,048,400)	(1,017,400)
Shares Outstanding	36,800	36,957	36,900	36,800	36,100	35,900	37,800	41,300
Statistical Record								
Return on Assets %	8.93	4.94	3.72	4.33	7.93	15.19	13.32	14.85
EBITDA Margin %	19.74	17.30	12.74	15.51	20.50	23.69	26.79	25.75
Net Margin %	9.44	7.70	4.06	5.72	10.31	17.51	15.62	17.77
Asset Turnover	0.80	0.78	0.77	0.76	0.77	0.87	0.85	0.84
Current Ratio	0.92	0.90	0.86	0.94	1.00	0.81	0.96	0.85
Price Range	136.62-100.75	140.73-100.75	140.73-100.75	140.73-87.91	135.92-100.97	127.37-94.87	123.42-78.17	86.50-63.34
P/E Ratio	26.22-19.34	47.54-34.04	62.55-44.78	53.11-33.17	29.29-21.76	15.94-11.87	18.87-11.95	13.45-9.85
Average Yield %	1.75	1.65	1.60	1.64	1.55	1.58	1.64	1.95

Address: 103 JFK Parkway, Short Hills, NJ 07078	Web Site: www.dnb.com	Auditors: PricewaterhouseCoopers LLP
Telephone: 973-921-5500	Officers: Christopher J. Coughlin - Chairman Robert P. Carrigan - Chairman, President, Chief Executive Officer	Investor Contact: 973-921-5914
		Transfer Agents: Computershare Shareowner Services LLC, Providence, RI

DYCOM INDUSTRIES, INC.

Exchange	Symbol	Price	52Wk Range	Yield	P/E
NYS	DY	$111.43 (12/29/2017)	114.42-76.05	N/A	26.28

*7 Year Price Score 156.05 *NYSE Composite Index=100 *12 Month Price Score 107.93

Interim Earnings (Per Share)

Qtr.	Oct	Jan	Apr	Jul
2014-15	0.59	0.27	0.58	0.97
2015-16	0.91	0.46	1.00	1.52
2016-17	1.59	0.74	1.22	1.38
2017-18	0.90	...	...	...

Interim Dividends (Per Share)

No Dividends Paid

Valuation Analysis / **Institutional Holding**

Forecast EPS	$4.11	No of Institutions
	(01/17/2018)	443
Market Cap	$3.4 Billion	Shares
Book Value	$689.6 Million	43,864,480
Price/Book	5.00	% Held
Price/Sales	1.14	81.55

TRADING VOLUME (thousand shares)

Business Summary: Construction Services (MIC: 7.5.4 SIC: 1623 NAIC: 237130)

Dycom Industries is a provider of specialty contracting services throughout the U.S. and in Canada. Co. provides program management, engineering, construction, maintenance, and installation services for telecommunications providers, underground facility locating services for various utilities, including telecommunications providers, and other construction and maintenance services for electric and gas utilities. Co. provides the labor, tools and equipment to design, engineer, locate, maintain, expand, install and upgrade the telecommunications infrastructure. Also, Co. provides underground facility locating services to a variety of utility companies, including telecommunication providers.

Recent Developments: For the quarter ended Oct 28 2017, net income decreased 43.6% to US$28.8 million from US$51.1 million in the year-earlier quarter. Revenues were US$756.2 million, down 5.4% from US$799.2 million the year before. Direct operating expenses declined 2.3% to US$600.8 million from US$615.0 million in the comparable period the year before. Indirect operating expenses increased 13.2% to US$107.2 million from US$94.8 million in the equivalent prior-year period.

Prospects: Our evaluation of Dycom Industries Inc. as of Jan. 14, 2018 is the result of our systematic analysis on three basic characteristics: earnings strength, relative valuation, and recent stock price movement. The company has generated a negative trend in earnings per share over the past 5 quarters and while recent estimates for the company have been mixed, DY has posted better than expected results. Based on operating earnings yield, the company is about fairly valued when compared to all of the companies in our coverage universe. Share price changes over the past year indicates that DY will perform poorly over the near term.

Financial Data

(US$ in Thousands)	3 Mos	07/29/2017	07/30/2016	07/25/2015	07/26/2014	07/27/2013	07/28/2012	07/30/2011
Earnings Per Share	4.24	4.92	3.89	2.41	1.15	1.04	1.14	0.45
Cash Flow Per Share	11.42	8.20	7.96	4.18	2.50	3.24	1.94	1.25
Tang Book Value Per Share	6.16	5.35	1.57	3.43	2.93	1.06	5.01	3.61
Income Statement								
Total Revenue	756,215	3,066,880	2,672,542	2,022,312	1,811,593	1,608,612	1,201,119	1,035,868
EBITDA	95,892	410,914	346,561	241,940	167,663	146,289	137,465	100,122
Depn & Amortn	41,806	123,125	105,514	79,331	74,517	64,756	56,187	55,727
Income Before Taxes	44,379	250,425	206,327	135,584	66,319	58,199	64,561	28,484
Income Taxes	15,603	93,208	77,587	51,260	26,341	23,011	25,183	12,377
Net Income	28,776	157,217	128,740	84,324	39,978	35,188	39,378	16,107
Average Shares	31,891	31,984	33,115	35,026	34,816	33,782	34,481	35,754
Balance Sheet								
Current Assets	893,370	938,518	851,234	696,632	605,736	541,134	376,947	330,311
Total Assets	1,852,522	1,899,307	1,719,716	1,358,864	1,212,354	1,154,208	772,193	724,755
Current Liabilities	283,121	318,538	322,627	226,710	196,532	199,815	114,563	118,513
Long-Term Obligations	736,008	738,265	706,202	521,841	446,863	444,169	187,500	187,574
Total Liabilities	1,162,884	1,227,724	1,162,429	851,664	727,420	725,847	379,262	372,904
Stockholders' Equity	689,638	671,583	557,287	507,200	484,934	428,361	392,931	351,851
Shares Outstanding	30,938	31,087	31,420	33,381	33,990	33,264	33,587	33,487
Statistical Record								
Return on Assets %	7.31	8.71	8.23	6.58	3.39	3.66	5.28	2.30
Return on Equity %	20.71	25.66	23.80	17.05	8.78	8.59	10.60	4.33
EBITDA Margin %	12.68	13.40	12.97	11.96	9.26	9.09	11.44	9.67
Net Margin %	3.81	5.13	4.82	4.17	2.21	2.19	3.28	1.55
Asset Turnover	1.64	1.70	1.71	1.58	1.54	1.67	1.61	1.48
Current Ratio	3.16	2.95	2.64	3.07	3.08	2.71	3.29	2.79
Debt to Equity	1.07	1.10	1.27	1.03	0.92	1.04	0.48	0.53
Price Range	108.99-71.34	108.99-71.34	95.94-48.61	69.62-25.67	33.52-24.77	26.77-13.09	23.79-12.59	18.56-7.45
P/E Ratio	25.71-16.83	22.15-14.50	24.66-12.50	28.89-10.65	29.15-21.54	25.74-12.59	20.87-11.04	41.24-16.56

Address: 11780 US Highway 1, Suite 600, Palm Beach Gardens, FL 33408	Web Site: www.dycomind.com	Auditors: PricewaterhouseCoopers LLP
Telephone: 561-627-7171	Officers: Steven E. Nielsen - Chairman, President, Chief Executive Officer Timothy R. Estes - Executive Vice President, Chief Operating Officer	Investor Contact: 561-627-7171
Fax: 561-627-7709		Transfer Agents: American Stock Transfer & Trust Company, New York, NY

EAGLE MATERIALS INC

Exchange	Symbol	Price	52Wk Range	Yield	P/E
NYS	EXP	$113.30 (12/29/2017)	116.15-87.24	0.35	25.99

*7 Year Price Score 116.32 ***NYSE Composite Index=100** ***12 Month Price Score 102.51**

Interim Earnings (Per Share)

Qtr.	Jun	Sep	Dec	Mar
2014-15	0.75	1.00	1.03	0.93
2015-16	0.75	0.59	0.92	0.79
2016-17	0.93	1.25	1.17	0.75
2017-18	1.13	1.31	...	...

Interim Dividends (Per Share)

Amt	Decl	Ex	Rec	Pay
0.10Q	01/31/2017	04/11/2017	04/13/2017	05/12/2017
0.10Q	05/22/2017	06/19/2017	06/21/2017	07/21/2017
0.10Q	08/07/2017	10/05/2017	10/06/2017	11/07/2017
0.10Q	11/01/2017	12/21/2017	12/22/2017	01/26/2018

Indicated Div: $0.40

Valuation Analysis

		Institutional Holding	
Forecast EPS	$5.00	No of Institutions	
	(01/17/2018)	456	
Market Cap	$5.5 Billion	Shares	
Book Value	$1.3 Billion	54,612,760	
Price/Book	4.20	% Held	
Price/Sales	4.16	96.61	

TRADING VOLUME (thousand shares)

Business Summary: Construction Materials (MIC: 8.5.1 SIC: 3241 NAIC: 327310)

Eagle Materials is a holding company. Co. operates in five business segments: Cement, Gypsum Wallboard, Recycled Paperboard, Oil and Gas Proppants and Concrete and Aggregates. These operations are conducted in the U.S. and include the mining of limestone and the manufacture, production, distribution and sale of portland cement and slag, the grinding of slag, the mining of gypsum and the manufacture and sale of gypsum wallboard, the manufacture and sale of recycled paperboard to the gypsum wallboard industry and other paperboard converters, the sale of readymix concrete and the mining and sale of aggregates and sand used in hydraulic fracturing.

Recent Developments: For the quarter ended Sep 30 2017, net income increased 5.2% to US$63.4 million from US$60.2 million in the year-earlier quarter. Revenues were US$376.3 million, up 13.1% from US$332.7 million the year before. Direct operating expenses rose 15.8% to US$279.6 million from US$241.4 million in the comparable period the year before. Indirect operating income amounted to US$3.0 million compared with an income of US$3.8 million in the equivalent prior-year period.

Prospects: Our evaluation of Eagle Materials Inc. as of Jan. 14, 2018 is the result of our systematic analysis on three basic characteristics: earnings strength, relative valuation, and recent stock price movement. The company has produced a positive trend in earnings per share over the past 5 quarters and while recent estimates for the company have been raised by analysts, EXP has posted results that fell short of analysts expectations. Based on operating earnings yield, the company is about fairly valued when compared to all of the companies in our coverage universe. Share price changes over the past year indicates that EXP will perform in line with the market over the near term.

Financial Data

(US$ in Thousands)	6 Mos	3 Mos	03/31/2017	03/31/2016	03/31/2015	03/31/2014	03/31/2013	03/31/2012
Earnings Per Share	4.36	4.30	4.10	3.05	3.71	2.49	1.22	0.42
Cash Flow Per Share	6.75	6.88	6.92	5.36	4.72	3.48	2.67	1.37
Tang Book Value Per Share	22.04	21.02	19.98	18.03	15.91	13.40	10.78	7.10
Dividends Per Share	0.400	0.400	0.400	0.400	0.400	0.400	0.400	0.300
Dividend Payout %	9.17	9.30	9.76	13.11	10.78	16.06	32.79	71.43
Income Statement								
Total Revenue	742,436	366,121	1,211,220	1,143,492	1,066,368	898,396	642,562	495,023
EBITDA	223,594	105,774	360,764	280,952	289,403	229,575	122,512	58,905
Depn & Amortn	59,253	28,947	86,000	84,200	69,700	67,300	55,100	48,900
Income Before Taxes	150,018	69,654	252,133	180,169	207,960	143,993	51,589	(6,616)
Income Taxes	53,605	24,648	96,300	66,660	66,074	57,561	26,352	3,180
Net Income	118,244	54,882	198,219	152,592	186,853	124,243	57,744	18,732
Average Shares	48,504	48,655	48,361	50,070	50,372	49,939	47,340	44,515
Balance Sheet								
Current Assets	446,810	440,302	400,624	380,003	366,635	306,960	261,271	191,841
Total Assets	2,321,041	2,279,590	2,247,124	1,883,635	1,882,591	1,511,529	1,476,233	985,145
Current Liabilities	221,407	239,727	229,519	120,589	184,576	108,820	100,229	77,043
Long-Term Obligations	575,588	580,421	605,253	499,714	455,714	371,759	489,259	262,259
Total Liabilities	1,008,368	1,024,503	1,043,674	843,104	871,998	680,030	780,063	512,634
Stockholders' Equity	1,312,673	1,255,087	1,203,450	1,040,531	1,010,593	831,499	696,170	472,511
Shares Outstanding	48,624	48,547	48,453	48,526	50,245	50,053	49,503	45,269
Statistical Record								
Return on Assets %	9.97	9.97	9.60	8.08	11.01	8.32	4.69	1.90
Return on Equity %	17.49	17.98	17.67	14.84	20.29	16.27	9.88	4.01
EBITDA Margin %	30.12	28.89	29.79	24.57	27.14	25.55	19.07	11.90
Net Margin %	15.93	14.99	16.37	13.34	17.52	13.83	8.99	3.78
Asset Turnover	0.63	0.61	0.59	0.61	0.63	0.60	0.52	0.50
Current Ratio	2.02	1.84	1.75	3.15	1.99	2.82	2.61	2.49
Debt to Equity	0.44	0.46	0.50	0.48	0.45	0.45	0.70	0.56
Price Range	108.70-75.61	108.70-73.33	108.70-68.78	87.68-46.85	104.73-69.80	90.88-61.72	71.57-29.84	35.81-15.68
P/E Ratio	24.93-17.34	25.28-17.05	26.51-16.78	28.75-15.36	28.23-18.81	36.50-24.79	58.66-24.46	85.26-37.33
Average Yield %	0.42	0.44	0.46	0.46	0.56	0.54	0.83	1.18

Address: 3811 Turtle Creek Blvd., Suite 1100, Dallas, TX 75219
Telephone: 214-432-2000
Fax: 214-432-2100

Web Site: www.eaglematerials.com
Officers: Richard R. Stewart - Chairman David B. Powers - President, Chief Executive Officer, Executive Vice President, Division Officer

Auditors: Ernst & Young LLP
Investor Contact: 214-432-2000
Transfer Agents: Computershare, Inc., Providence , RI

EASTMAN CHEMICAL CO

Exchange	Symbol	Price	52Wk Range	Yield	P/E
NYS	EMN	$92.64 (12/29/2017)	93.42-75.92	2.42	13.43

*7 Year Price Score 95.54   ***NYSE Composite Index=100**   ***12 Month Price Score 102.57**

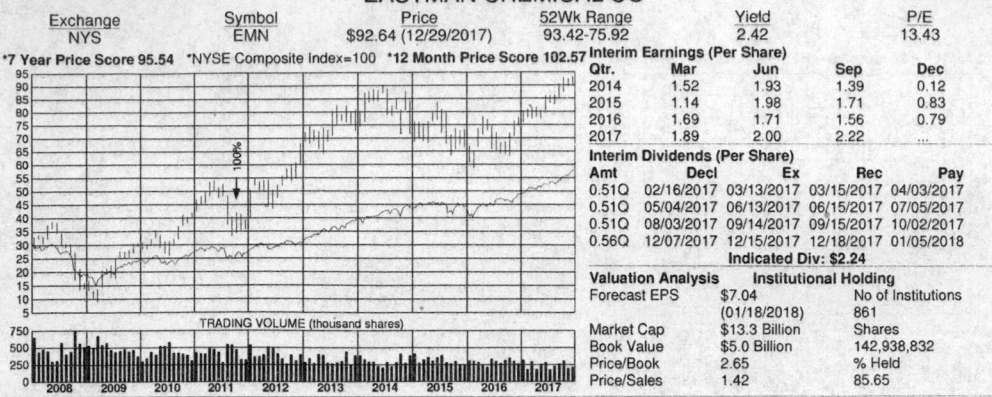

Interim Earnings (Per Share)

Qtr.	Mar	Jun	Sep	Dec
2014	1.52	1.93	1.39	0.12
2015	1.14	1.98	1.71	0.83
2016	1.69	1.71	1.56	0.79
2017	1.89	2.00	2.22	...

Interim Dividends (Per Share)

Amt	Decl	Ex	Rec	Pay
0.51Q	02/16/2017	03/13/2017	03/15/2017	04/03/2017
0.51Q	05/04/2017	06/13/2017	06/15/2017	07/05/2017
0.51Q	08/03/2017	09/14/2017	09/15/2017	10/02/2017
0.56Q	12/07/2017	12/15/2017	12/18/2017	01/05/2018

Indicated Div: $2.24

Valuation Analysis		Institutional Holding	
Forecast EPS	$7.04	No of Institutions	
	(01/18/2018)	861	
Market Cap	$13.3 Billion	Shares	
Book Value	$5.0 Billion	142,938,832	
Price/Book	2.65	% Held	
Price/Sales	1.42	85.65	

Business Summary: Plastics (MIC: 8.4.2 SIC: 2821 NAIC: 325211)

Eastman Chemical is a chemical company that produces a range of materials, specialty additives, chemicals, and fibers. Co.'s segments are: Additives & Functional Products, which manufactures chemicals for products in the coatings and tires industries; Adhesives & Plasticizers, which manufactures coatings and inks additives, adhesives resins, tire additives and others; Advanced Materials, which manufactures specialty plastics, interlayers, and performance films; Chemical Intermediates, which manufactures intermediates, plasticizers, and functional amines; and Fibers, which manufactures acetate tow, acetate yarn, and acetyl chemical products.

Recent Developments: For the quarter ended Sep 30 2017, net income increased 39.1% to US$324.0 million from US$233.0 million in the year-earlier quarter. Revenues were US$2.47 billion, up 7.8% from US$2.29 billion the year before. Operating income was US$460.0 million versus US$356.0 million in the prior-year quarter, an increase of 29.2%. Direct operating expenses rose 6.5% to US$1.77 billion from US$1.67 billion in the comparable period the year before. Indirect operating expenses decreased 12.8% to US$231.0 million from US$265.0 million in the equivalent prior-year period.

Prospects: Our evaluation of Eastman Chemical Co. as of Jan. 14, 2018 is the result of our systematic analysis on three basic characteristics: earnings strength, relative valuation, and recent stock price movement. The company has generated a negative trend in earnings per share over the past 5 quarters and while recent estimates for the company have been raised by analysts, EMN has posted better than expected results. Based on operating earnings yield, the company is undervalued when compared to all of the companies in our coverage universe. Share price changes over the past year indicates that EMN will perform in line with the market over the near term.

Financial Data

(US$ in Thousands)	9 Mos	6 Mos	3 Mos	12/31/2016	12/31/2015	12/31/2014	12/31/2013	12/31/2012
Earnings Per Share	6.90	6.24	5.95	5.75	5.66	4.97	7.44	2.93
Cash Flow Per Share	9.74	9.13	9.51	9.38	10.85	9.42	8.42	7.73
Dividends Per Share	2.040	1.990	1.940	1.890	1.660	1.450	1.250	1.080
Dividend Payout %	29.57	31.89	32.61	32.87	29.33	29.18	16.80	36.86
Income Statement								
Total Revenue	7,187,000	4,722,000	2,303,000	9,008,000	9,648,000	9,527,000	9,350,000	8,102,000
EBITDA	1,725,000	1,113,000	546,000	1,716,000	1,794,000	1,532,000	2,204,000	1,101,000
Depn & Amortn	440,000	292,000	145,000	412,000	402,000	355,000	345,000	309,000
Income Before Taxes	1,103,000	700,000	341,000	1,049,000	1,129,000	990,000	1,679,000	649,000
Income Taxes	206,000	127,000	62,000	190,000	275,000	235,000	507,000	206,000
Net Income	893,000	570,000	278,000	854,000	848,000	751,000	1,165,000	437,000
Average Shares	145,500	146,400	147,200	148,400	149,800	151,100	156,500	149,100
Balance Sheet								
Current Assets	3,245,000	3,262,000	3,165,000	2,866,000	2,878,000	3,173,000	2,840,000	2,594,000
Total Assets	16,024,000	15,964,000	15,755,000	15,457,000	15,611,000	16,072,000	11,845,000	11,619,000
Current Liabilities	1,771,000	1,596,000	1,637,000	1,795,000	2,056,000	2,022,000	1,470,000	1,364,000
Long-Term Obligations	6,325,000	6,669,000	6,578,000	6,311,000	6,608,000	7,248,000	4,254,000	4,779,000
Total Liabilities	11,001,000	11,152,000	11,104,000	10,925,000	11,670,000	12,562,000	8,049,000	8,676,000
Stockholders' Equity	5,023,000	4,812,000	4,651,000	4,532,000	3,941,000	3,510,000	3,796,000	2,943,000
Shares Outstanding	143,682	144,828	145,776	146,438	147,761	148,596	152,416	153,894
Statistical Record								
Return on Assets %	6.40	5.82	5.62	5.48	5.35	5.38	9.93	4.90
Return on Equity %	21.32	19.98	19.90	20.10	22.76	20.56	34.57	18.11
EBITDA Margin %	24.00	23.57	23.71	19.05	18.59	16.08	23.57	13.59
Net Margin %	12.43	12.07	12.07	9.48	8.79	7.88	12.46	5.39
Asset Turnover	0.59	0.58	0.58	0.58	0.61	0.68	0.80	0.91
Current Ratio	1.83	2.04	1.93	1.60	1.40	1.57	1.93	1.90
Debt to Equity	1.26	1.39	1.41	1.39	1.68	2.06	1.12	1.62
Price Range	90.49-63.17	86.00-63.17	81.47-63.17	78.21-58.43	83.75-63.30	90.20-71.49	82.60-64.06	68.05-40.09
P/E Ratio	13.11-9.16	13.78-10.12	13.69-10.62	13.60-10.16	14.80-11.18	18.15-14.38	11.10-8.61	23.23-13.68
Average Yield %	2.58	2.67	2.66	2.72	2.27	1.75	1.69	2.03

Address: 200 South Wilcox Drive, Kingsport, TN 37662 **Telephone:** 423-229-2000	**Web Site:** www.eastman.com **Officers:** Mark J. Costa - Chairman, Chief Executive Officer, President, Executive Vice President, Chief Marketing Officer Mark J. Costa - Chairman, Chief Executive Officer, President, Executive Vice President, Chief Marketing Officer	**Auditors:** PricewaterhouseCoopers LLP **Investor Contact:** 212-835-1620 **Transfer Agents:** American Stock Transfer & Trust Company, New York, NY

EATON CORP PLC

Exchange	Symbol	Price	52Wk Range	Yield	P/E
NYS	ETN	$79.01 (12/29/2017)	81.51-66.88	3.04	12.40

*7 Year Price Score 95.75   *NYSE Composite Index=100   *12 Month Price Score 97.47

Interim Earnings (Per Share)

Qtr.	Mar	Jun	Sep	Dec
2014	0.92	0.36	1.26	1.23
2015	0.99	1.14	0.96	1.14
2016	0.88	1.07	1.15	1.12
2017	0.96	1.15	3.14	...

Interim Dividends (Per Share)

Amt	Decl	Ex	Rec	Pay
0.60Q	02/22/2017	03/02/2017	03/06/2017	03/17/2017
0.60Q	04/25/2017	05/03/2017	05/05/2017	05/19/2017
0.60Q	07/25/2017	08/02/2017	08/04/2017	08/18/2017
0.60Q	10/24/2017	11/02/2017	11/03/2017	11/17/2017

Indicated Div: $2.40

Valuation Analysis

Forecast EPS	N/A
Market Cap	$34.8 Billion
Book Value	$16.6 Billion
Price/Book	2.10
Price/Sales	1.74

Institutional Holding

No of Institutions	1082
Shares	375,613,728
% Held	69.40

TRADING VOLUME (thousand shares)

Business Summary: Electrical Equipment (MIC: 7.3.1 SIC: 3599 NAIC: 336399)

Eaton is a power management company providing energy-efficient solutions. Co.'s segments are: Electrical Products, which includes electrical components, industrial components, residential products, and single phase power quality; Electrical Systems and Services, which includes power distribution and assemblies, three phase power quality, and hazardous duty electrical equipment; Hydraulics, which provides power products, fluid conveyance products, filtration systems solutions, industrial drum and disc brakes, and golf grips; Aerospace, which supplies aerospace fuel, hydraulics and pneumatic systems; and Vehicle, which provides drivetrain and powertrain systems and critical components.

Recent Developments: For the quarter ended Sep 30 2017, net income increased 168.0% to US$1.40 billion from US$522.0 million in the year-earlier quarter. Revenues were US$5.21 billion, up 4.5% from US$4.99 billion the year before. Direct operating expenses rose 2.9% to US$3.47 billion from US$3.37 billion in the comparable period the year before. Indirect operating expenses increased 6.4% to US$1.06 billion from US$999.0 million in the equivalent prior-year period.

Prospects: Our evaluation of Eaton Corp PLC as of Sep. 17, 2017 is the result of our systematic analysis on three basic characteristics: earnings strength, relative valuation, and recent stock price movement. The company has enjoyed a very positive trend in earnings per share over the past 5 quarters and while recent estimates for the company have remained steady, ETN has posted results that fell short of analysts expectations. Based on operating earnings yield, the company is undervalued when compared to all of the companies in our coverage universe. Share price changes over the past year indicates that ETN will perform in line with the market over the near term.

Financial Data

(US$ in Millions)	9 Mos	6 Mos	3 Mos	12/31/2016	12/31/2015	12/31/2014	12/31/2013	12/31/2012
Earnings Per Share	6.37	4.38	4.30	4.21	4.23	3.76	3.90	3.46
Cash Flow Per Share	5.48	5.54	5.89	5.59	5.09	3.96	4.83	4.77
Dividends Per Share	2.370	2.340	2.310	2.280	2.200	1.960	1.680	1.520
Dividend Payout %	37.21	53.42	53.72	54.16	52.01	52.13	43.08	43.93
Income Statement								
Total Revenue	15,191	9,980	4,848	19,747	20,855	22,552	22,046	16,311
EBITDA	3,591	1,608	750	2,846	2,856	2,502	2,671	2,057
Depn & Amortn	685	453	225	486	479	514	516	598
Income Before Taxes	2,725	1,034	464	2,127	2,145	1,761	1,884	1,251
Income Taxes	378	86	32	202	164	(42)	11	31
Net Income	2,346	947	432	1,922	1,979	1,793	1,861	1,217
Average Shares	445	448	451	456	467	476	476	350
Balance Sheet								
Current Assets	8,449	7,487	6,975	6,941	6,616	8,100	8,731	7,844
Total Assets	32,725	31,355	30,611	30,419	31,031	33,529	35,491	35,848
Current Liabilities	5,900	6,309	5,557	5,485	4,625	5,355	4,914	5,431
Long-Term Obligations	7,273	6,264	6,677	6,677	7,781	8,024	8,969	9,762
Total Liabilities	16,132	15,803	15,454	15,522	15,845	17,743	18,700	20,762
Stockholders' Equity	16,593	15,552	15,157	14,897	15,186	15,786	16,791	15,086
Shares Outstanding	440	444	447	449	458	467	475	470
Statistical Record								
Return on Assets %	8.91	6.32	6.27	6.24	6.13	5.20	5.22	4.52
Return on Equity %	17.81	12.79	12.71	12.74	12.78	11.01	11.68	10.76
EBITDA Margin %	23.64	16.11	15.47	14.41	13.69	11.09	12.12	12.61
Net Margin %	15.44	9.49	8.91	9.73	9.49	7.95	8.44	7.46
Asset Turnover	0.63	0.63	0.64	0.64	0.65	0.65	0.62	0.61
Current Ratio	1.43	1.19	1.26	1.27	1.43	1.51	1.78	1.44
Debt to Equity	0.44	0.40	0.44	0.45	0.51	0.51	0.53	0.65
Price Range	80.61-59.72	78.08-58.72	74.20-55.57	69.86-47.27	73.50-49.74	79.44-58.27	76.75-54.18	54.66-37.04
P/E Ratio	12.65-9.38	17.83-13.41	17.26-12.92	16.59-11.23	17.38-11.76	21.13-15.50	19.68-13.89	15.80-10.71
Average Yield %	3.29	3.38	3.38	3.69	3.50	2.75	2.57	3.25

Address: Eaton House, 30 Pembroke Road, Dublin 4, 44114-2584 Telephone: 353-163-72900	Web Site: www.eaton.com Officers: Craig Arnold - Chairman, Chief Executive Officer Richard H. Fearon - Vice-Chairman, Chief Financial Officer, Chief Planning Officer	Auditors: Ernst & Young LLP Investor Contact: 216-523-4205 Transfer Agents: Computershare Shareowner Services, Jersey City, NJ

EATON VANCE CORP

Exchange	Symbol	Price	52Wk Range	Yield	P/E	Div Achiever
NYS	EV	$56.39 (12/29/2017)	57.08-41.80	2.20	23.30	35 Years

*7 Year Price Score 102.55 *NYSE Composite Index=100 *12 Month Price Score 107.72

Interim Earnings (Per Share)

Qtr.	Jan	Apr	Jul	Oct
2012-13	0.38	0.50	0.18	0.46
2013-14	0.56	0.59	0.63	0.66
2014-15	0.21	0.58	0.57	0.53
2015-16	0.50	0.48	0.55	0.57
2016-17	0.53	0.62	0.58	0.69

Interim Dividends (Per Share)

Amt	Decl	Ex	Rec	Pay
0.28Q	04/12/2017	04/26/2017	04/28/2017	05/15/2017
0.28Q	07/12/2017	07/27/2017	07/31/2017	08/15/2017
0.31Q	10/12/2017	10/30/2017	10/31/2017	11/15/2017
0.31Q	01/10/2018	01/30/2018	01/31/2018	02/15/2018

Indicated Div: $1.24

Valuation Analysis

		Institutional Holding	
Forecast EPS	$3.39 (01/13/2018)	No of Institutions	515
Market Cap	$6.7 Billion	Shares	108,423,704
Book Value	$1.0 Billion	% Held	79.78
Price/Book	6.61		
Price/Sales	4.37		

Business Summary: Wealth Management (MIC: 5.5.2 SIC: 6282 NAIC: 523930)

Eaton Vance, through its subsidiaries, manages active equity, income and alternative strategies across a range of investment styles and asset classes, including U.S. and global equities, floating-rate bank loans, municipal bonds, global income, high-yield and investment grade bonds. Through its subsidiary, Parametric Portfolio Associates LLC, Co. provides portfolio implementation and overlay services, including tax-managed and non-tax-managed custom core equity strategies, centralized portfolio management of multi-manager portfolios and customized exposure management services. As of Oct 31 2016, Co. had $336.38 billion in assets under management.

Recent Developments: For the year ended Oct 31 2017, net income increased 15.7% to US$306.4 million from US$264.8 million in the prior year. Revenues were US$1.53 billion, up 13.9% from US$1.34 billion the year before. Operating income was US$482.8 million versus US$414.3 million in the prior year, an increase of 16.5%. Direct operating expenses rose 12.6% to US$132.9 million from US$118.0 million in the comparable period the year before. Indirect operating expenses increased 12.7% to US$913.4 million from US$810.6 million in the equivalent prior-year period.

Prospects: Our evaluation of Eaton Vance Corp. as of Jan. 14, 2018 is the result of our systematic analysis on three basic characteristics: earnings strength, relative valuation, and recent stock price movement. The company has produced a positive trend in earnings per share over the past 5 quarters and while recent estimates for the company have been raised by analysts, EV has posted results that fell short of analysts expectations. Based on operating earnings yield, the company is about fairly valued when compared to all of the companies in our coverage universe. Share price changes over the past year indicates that EV will perform in line with the market over the near term.

Financial Data
(US$ in Thousands)

	10/31/2017	10/31/2016	10/31/2015	10/31/2014	10/31/2013	10/31/2012	10/31/2011	10/31/2010
Earnings Per Share	2.42	2.12	1.92	2.44	1.53	1.72	1.75	1.40
Cash Flow Per Share	0.59	3.09	1.94	0.85	1.00	1.59	1.49	0.82
Tang Book Value Per Share	5.58	3.59	2.82	3.05	3.01	3.42	2.17	1.70
Dividends Per Share	1.150	1.075	1.015	0.910	1.820	0.770	0.730	0.660
Dividend Payout %	47.52	50.71	52.86	37.30	118.95	44.77	41.71	47.14
Income Statement								
Total Revenue	1,529,010	1,342,860	1,403,563	1,450,294	1,357,503	1,209,036	1,260,031	1,121,661
EBITDA	483,264	432,158	416,908	546,788	425,313	473,015	420,380	373,163
Depn & Amortn	9,100	10,900	11,400	10,900	13,000	16,900	15,800	15,400
Income Before Taxes	469,169	408,052	369,384	491,149	359,453	403,738	381,376	326,961
Income Taxes	173,666	153,630	143,214	186,710	143,896	142,385	156,844	126,263
Net Income	282,131	241,307	230,299	304,316	193,841	203,465	214,902	174,298
Average Shares	116,418	113,982	118,155	121,595	122,444	115,126	119,975	122,632
Balance Sheet								
Current Assets	811,008	610,346	816,015	580,522	668,767	632,423	657,959	499,274
Total Assets	2,330,901	1,732,576	2,116,471	1,860,086	2,407,249	1,979,491	1,831,300	1,280,607
Current Liabilities	320,079	269,937	277,047	275,719	255,222	227,985	210,723	258,001
Long-Term Obligations	631,441	573,967	970,850	725,637	1,100,415	946,605	977,699	500,000
Total Liabilities	1,319,505	1,028,787	1,496,240	1,204,910	1,737,465	1,367,419	1,370,885	870,322
Stockholders' Equity	1,011,396	703,789	620,231	655,176	669,784	612,072	460,415	410,285
Shares Outstanding	118,520	113,987	115,885	118,261	121,631	116,291	115,623	118,326
Statistical Record								
Return on Assets %	13.89	12.50	11.58	14.26	8.84	10.65	13.81	14.80
Return on Equity %	32.90	36.35	36.11	45.94	30.24	37.84	49.36	46.03
EBITDA Margin %	31.61	32.18	29.70	37.70	31.33	39.12	33.36	33.27
Net Margin %	18.45	17.97	16.41	20.98	14.28	16.83	17.06	15.54
Asset Turnover	0.75	0.70	0.71	0.68	0.62	0.63	0.81	0.95
Current Ratio	2.53	2.26	2.95	2.11	2.62	2.77	3.12	1.94
Debt to Equity	0.62	0.82	1.57	1.11	1.64	1.55	2.12	1.22
Price Range	51.90-34.60	40.18-27.18	44.00-33.06	43.63-34.29	44.18-28.14	29.70-21.78	33.92-20.84	35.72-25.90
P/E Ratio	21.45-14.30	18.95-12.82	22.92-17.22	17.88-14.05	28.88-18.39	17.27-12.66	19.38-11.91	25.51-18.50
Average Yield %	2.54	3.09	2.56	2.38	4.80	2.92	2.51	2.17

Address: Two International Place, Boston, MA 02110 **Telephone:** 617-482-8260 **Fax:** 617-482-2396	**Web Site:** www.eatonvance.com **Officers:** Thomas E. Faust - Chairman, President, Chief Executive Officer Jeffrey P. Beale - Vice President, Chief Administrative Officer	**Auditors:** DELOITTE & TOUCHE LLP **Investor Contact:** 617-482-8260 **Transfer Agents:** ComputerShare Investor Services, Providence, RI

ECOLAB INC

Exchange	Symbol	Price	52Wk Range	Yield	P/E	Div Achiever
NYS	ECL	$134.18 (12/29/2017)	137.42-117.86	1.22	30.22	24 Years

*7 Year Price Score 105.33 ***NYSE Composite Index=100** ***12 Month Price Score 97.85**

Stock price chart 2008–2017 with TRADING VOLUME (thousand shares)

Interim Earnings (Per Share)

Qtr.	Mar	Jun	Sep	Dec
2014	0.62	1.02	1.19	1.10
2015	0.77	1.00	0.86	0.69
2016	0.77	0.87	1.27	1.23
2017	0.86	1.01	1.34	...

Interim Dividends (Per Share)

Amt	Decl	Ex	Rec	Pay
0.37Q	02/23/2017	03/17/2017	03/21/2017	04/17/2017
0.37Q	05/04/2017	06/16/2017	06/20/2017	07/17/2017
0.37Q	08/03/2017	09/18/2017	09/19/2017	10/16/2017
0.41Q	12/07/2017	12/18/2017	12/19/2017	01/16/2018

Indicated Div: $1.64 (Div. Reinv. Plan)

Valuation Analysis / Institutional Holding

Forecast EPS	$4.70 (01/18/2018)	No of Institutions	1197
Market Cap	$38.8 Billion	Shares	272,534,016
Book Value	$7.2 Billion	% Held	94.94
Price/Book	5.37		
Price/Sales	2.86		

Business Summary: Specialty Chemicals (MIC: 8.3.2 SIC: 2842 NAIC: 325612)

Ecolab is a provider of water, hygiene and energy technologies and services that protect people and resources. Co.'s products and technologies are used in water treatment, pollution control, energy conservation, oil production and refining, steelmaking, and other industrial processes. Co. has four segments: Global Industrial, which consists of the Water, Food and Beverage, Paper and Textile Care operating segments; Global Institutional, which consists of the consists of the Institutional, Specialty and Healthcare operating segments; Global Energy, which consists of the Energy operating segment; as well as Other, which consists of the Pest Elimination and Equipment Care operating segments.

Recent Developments: For the quarter ended Sep 30 2017, net income increased 4.3% to US$395.8 million from US$379.5 million in the year-earlier quarter. Revenues were US$3.56 billion, up 5.2% from US$3.39 billion the year before. Operating income was US$579.8 million versus US$574.1 million in the prior-year quarter, an increase of 1.0%. Direct operating expenses rose 8.9% to US$1.89 billion from US$1.74 billion in the comparable period the year before. Indirect operating expenses increased 1.6% to US$1.09 billion from US$1.07 billion in the equivalent prior-year period.

Prospects: Our evaluation of Ecolab Inc. as of Jan. 14, 2018 is the result of our systematic analysis on three basic characteristics: earnings strength, relative valuation, and recent stock price movement. The company has enjoyed a very positive trend in earnings per share over the past 5 quarters. However, while recent estimates for the company have been mixed, ECL has posted better than expected results. Based on operating earnings yield, the company is about fairly valued when compared to all of the companies in our coverage universe. Share price changes over the past year indicates that ECL will perform well over the near term.

Financial Data
(US$ in Thousands)

	9 Mos	6 Mos	3 Mos	12/31/2016	12/31/2015	12/31/2014	12/31/2013	12/31/2012
Earnings Per Share	4.44	4.37	4.23	4.14	3.32	3.93	3.16	2.35
Cash Flow Per Share	6.55	6.64	6.51	6.61	6.75	6.05	5.20	4.10
Dividends Per Share	1.480	1.460	1.440	1.420	1.340	1.155	0.965	0.830
Dividend Payout %	33.33	33.41	34.04	34.30	40.36	29.39	30.54	35.32
Income Statement								
Total Revenue	10,187,600	6,624,300	3,161,600	13,152,800	13,545,100	14,280,500	13,253,400	11,838,700
EBITDA	2,057,600	1,249,500	589,300	2,476,000	2,121,300	2,513,000	2,074,600	1,757,300
Depn & Amortn	665,500	437,200	216,000	561,000	560,000	558,000	514,000	468,000
Income Before Taxes	1,214,900	690,200	310,800	1,650,400	1,317,700	1,698,400	1,298,300	1,012,600
Income Taxes	264,200	135,300	54,000	403,300	300,500	476,200	324,700	311,300
Net Income	942,500	550,100	253,500	1,229,600	1,002,100	1,202,800	967,800	703,600
Average Shares	293,400	294,100	295,000	296,700	301,400	305,900	305,900	298,900
Balance Sheet								
Current Assets	4,614,500	4,532,100	4,307,300	4,279,400	4,447,500	4,871,100	4,698,400	4,892,000
Total Assets	19,856,700	19,523,400	19,223,000	18,330,200	18,641,700	19,466,700	19,636,500	17,572,300
Current Liabilities	3,756,600	4,318,400	4,205,300	3,019,400	4,764,400	4,386,600	3,488,700	3,052,700
Long-Term Obligations	6,484,500	5,909,300	5,841,600	6,145,700	4,260,200	4,864,000	6,043,500	5,736,100
Total Liabilities	12,634,400	12,603,700	12,413,600	11,429,100	11,731,800	12,150,800	12,292,200	11,495,300
Stockholders' Equity	7,222,300	6,919,700	6,809,400	6,901,100	6,909,900	7,315,900	7,344,300	6,077,000
Shares Outstanding	288,914	289,400	290,000	291,825	295,967	299,852	301,135	294,722
Statistical Record								
Return on Assets %	6.85	6.84	6.67	6.63	5.26	6.15	5.20	3.92
Return on Equity %	18.58	19.09	18.70	17.76	14.09	16.41	14.42	11.95
EBITDA Margin %	20.20	18.86	18.64	18.82	15.66	17.60	15.65	14.84
Net Margin %	9.25	8.30	8.02	9.35	7.40	8.42	7.30	5.94
Asset Turnover	0.71	0.71	0.70	0.71	0.71	0.73	0.71	0.66
Current Ratio	1.23	1.05	1.02	1.42	0.93	1.11	1.35	1.60
Debt to Equity	0.90	0.85	0.86	0.89	0.62	0.66	0.82	0.94
Price Range	134.61-110.67	134.61-110.67	125.87-110.67	124.05-100.14	122.10-98.93	118.07-98.03	107.99-71.90	72.72-58.02
P/E Ratio	30.32-24.93	30.80-25.32	29.76-26.16	29.96-24.19	36.78-29.80	30.04-24.94	34.17-22.75	30.94-24.69
Average Yield %	1.18	1.19	1.21	1.23	1.18	1.06	1.08	1.27

Address: 1 Ecolab Place, St. Paul, MN 55102	**Web Site:** www.ecolab.com	**Auditors:** PricewaterhouseCoopers LLP
Telephone: 800-232-6522	**Officers:** Douglas M. Baker - Chairman, President, Chief Executive Officer, Chief Operating Officer Thomas W. Handley - President, Chief Operating Officer, Senior Executive Vice President, Division Officer	**Investor Contact:** 651-293-2545 **Transfer Agents:** Elavon Financial Services DAC

251

EDGEWELL PERSONAL CARE CO

Exchange	Symbol	Price	52Wk Range	Yield	P/E
NYS	EPC	$59.39 (12/29/2017)	81.71-56.64	N/A	593.90

*7 Year Price Score 77.06 *NYSE Composite Index=100 *12 Month Price Score 79.22

Interim Earnings (Per Share)

Qtr.	Dec	Mar	Jun	Sep
2012-13	2.07	1.35	1.38	1.67
2013-14	1.71	1.57	1.03	1.36
2014-15	1.69	(1.41)	(1.17)	(3.54)
2015-16	0.39	1.10	0.61	0.88
2016-17	0.58	1.14	0.95	(2.57)

Interim Dividends (Per Share)

No Dividends Paid

Valuation Analysis		Institutional Holding	
Forecast EPS	$3.89	No of Institutions	
	(01/18/2018)	510	
Market Cap	$3.3 Billion	Shares	
Book Value	$1.7 Billion	67,371,256	
Price/Book	1.91	% Held	
Price/Sales	1.45	79.04	

Business Summary: Household & Personal Products (MIC: 1.7.1 SIC: 2844 NAIC: 325620)

Edgewell Personal Care is a manufacturer and marketer of personal care products in the wet shave, sun and skin care, feminine care and infant care categories. Co. manages its business in four segments: Wet Shave, which manufactures and distributes Schick and Wilkinson Sword razor systems, composed of razor handles and refillable blades, and disposable shave products for men and women; Sun and Skin Care, in which Co. sells its products under the Banana Boat, Hawaiian Tropic, Bulldog® and Wet Ones brand names; Feminine Care, in which Co. markets products under the Playtex, Stayfree, Carefree and o.b. brands; and All Other, which includes infant care, pet care and miscellaneous other products.

Recent Developments: For the year ended Sep 30 2017, income from continuing operations decreased 96.8% to US$5.7 million from US$178.7 million a year earlier. Net income decreased 96.8% to US$5.7 million from US$178.7 million in the prior year. Revenues were US$2.30 billion, down 2.7% from US$2.36 billion the year before. Direct operating expenses declined 2.9% to US$1.17 billion from US$1.20 billion in the comparable period the year before. Indirect operating expenses increased 25.9% to US$1.18 billion from US$940.0 million in the equivalent prior-year period.

Prospects: Our evaluation of Edgewell Personal Care Co. as of Jan. 14, 2018 is the result of our systematic analysis on three basic characteristics: earnings strength, relative valuation, and recent stock price movement. The company has generated a negative trend in earnings per share over the past 5 quarters. However, while recent estimates for the company have been mixed, EPC has posted results that fell short of analysts expectations. Based on operating earnings yield, the company is undervalued when compared to all of the companies in our coverage universe. Share price changes over the past year indicates that EPC will perform in line with the market over the near term.

Financial Data

(US$ in Thousands)	09/30/2017	09/30/2016	09/30/2015	09/30/2014	09/30/2013	09/30/2012	09/30/2011	09/30/2010
Earnings Per Share	0.10	2.99	(4.44)	5.69	6.47	6.22	3.72	5.72
Cash Flow Per Share	5.17	2.97	2.40	9.23	12.08	9.71	5.93	9.32
Income Statement								
Total Revenue	2,298,400	2,362,000	2,421,200	4,447,700	4,466,000	4,567,200	4,645,700	4,248,300
EBITDA	90,400	365,300	(285,200)	716,400	863,100	829,400	681,900	788,100
Depn & Amortn	74,100	73,600	73,700	120,300	164,700	136,700	154,500	119,300
Income Before Taxes	(52,900)	219,900	(458,700)	473,500	567,900	565,400	406,000	543,400
Income Taxes	(58,600)	41,200	(162,600)	117,400	160,900	156,500	144,800	140,400
Net Income	5,700	178,700	(275,300)	356,100	407,000	408,900	261,200	403,000
Average Shares	57,500	59,700	62,000	62,600	62,900	65,700	70,300	70,500
Balance Sheet								
Current Assets	1,186,200	1,452,000	1,636,600	2,729,600	2,568,400	2,522,600	2,392,600	2,429,500
Total Assets	4,188,800	4,771,500	4,991,700	6,928,700	6,717,400	6,731,200	6,663,400	6,387,900
Current Liabilities	524,400	868,200	666,800	1,573,700	1,153,400	1,307,500	1,159,300	1,253,500
Long-Term Obligations	1,525,600	1,544,200	1,704,000	1,768,900	1,998,800	2,138,600	2,206,500	2,022,500
Total Liabilities	2,447,100	2,942,500	3,127,600	4,406,400	4,263,800	4,661,700	4,562,100	4,288,300
Stockholders' Equity	1,741,700	1,829,000	1,864,100	2,522,300	2,453,600	2,069,500	2,101,300	2,099,600
Shares Outstanding	56,017	57,914	60,176	61,824	62,324	61,522	67,075	70,355
Statistical Record								
Return on Assets %	0.13	3.65	N.M.	5.22	6.05	6.09	4.00	6.43
Return on Equity %	0.32	9.65	N.M.	14.31	18.00	19.55	12.44	20.87
EBITDA Margin %	3.93	15.47	N.M.	16.11	19.33	18.16	14.68	18.55
Net Margin %	0.25	7.57	N.M.	8.01	9.11	8.95	5.62	9.49
Asset Turnover	0.51	0.48	0.41	0.65	0.66	0.68	0.71	0.68
Current Ratio	2.26	1.67	2.45	1.73	2.23	1.93	2.06	1.94
Debt to Equity	0.88	0.84	0.91	0.70	0.81	1.03	1.05	0.96
Price Range	81.75-69.72	87.48-69.84	107.28-78.40	92.73-67.59	80.20-52.29	59.13-47.72	60.55-48.19	52.84-36.90
P/E Ratio	817.50-697.20	29.26-23.36	...	16.30-11.88	12.40-8.08	9.51-7.67	16.28-12.95	9.24-6.45

Address: 1350 Timberlake Manor Parkway, Chesterfield, MO 63017 **Telephone:** 314-594-1900	**Web Site:** www.edgewell.com **Officers:** David P. Hatfield - Chairman, President, Chief Executive Officer Colin Hutchison - Chief Operating Officer	**Auditors:** PricewaterhouseCoopers LLP **Investor Contact:** 314-982-2013 **Transfer Agents:** Continental Stock Transfer & Trust Company, New York, NY

EDISON INTERNATIONAL

Exchange	Symbol	Price	52Wk Range	Yield	P/E	Div Achiever
NYS	EIX	$63.24 (12/29/2017)	82.64-63.24	3.83	14.34	12 Years

*7 Year Price Score 107.50 *NYSE Composite Index=100 *12 Month Price Score 92.37

Interim Earnings (Per Share)

Qtr.	Mar	Jun	Sep	Dec
2014	0.54	1.63	1.46	1.27
2015	0.91	1.15	1.28	(0.24)
2016	0.82	0.84	1.27	1.03
2017	1.10	0.85	1.43	...

Interim Dividends (Per Share)

Amt	Decl	Ex	Rec	Pay
0.542Q	02/23/2017	03/29/2017	03/31/2017	04/30/2017
0.542Q	04/27/2017	06/28/2017	06/30/2017	07/31/2017
0.542Q	08/24/2017	09/28/2017	09/29/2017	10/31/2017
0.605Q	12/07/2017	12/28/2017	12/29/2017	01/31/2018

Indicated Div: $2.42 (Div. Reinv. Plan)

Valuation Analysis **Institutional Holding**

Forecast EPS	$4.30	No of Institutions
	(01/18/2018)	854
Market Cap	$20.6 Billion	Shares
Book Value	$12.4 Billion	310,354,304
Price/Book	1.66	% Held
Price/Sales	1.72	78.25

TRADING VOLUME (thousand shares)

Business Summary: Electric Utilities (MIC: 3.1.1 SIC: 4911 NAIC: 221111)

Edison International is a holding company. Through its principal subsidiary, Southern California Edison Company (SCE), Co. is primarily engaged in the business of supplying and delivering electricity. Co. is also the parent company of Edison Energy Group, a company that engaged in businesses focused on providing energy services and distributing solar to commercial and industrial customers. SCE supplies electricity to its customers through transmission and distribution networks. Its transmission facilities include sub-transmission facilities and are located primarily in California as well as in Nevada and Arizona.

Recent Developments: For the quarter ended Sep 30 2017, income from continuing operations increased 11.1% to US$501.0 million from US$451.0 million in the year-earlier quarter. Net income increased 11.1% to US$501.0 million from US$451.0 million in the year-earlier quarter. Revenues were US$3.67 billion, down 2.5% from US$3.77 billion the year before. Operating income was US$561.0 million versus US$695.0 million in the prior-year quarter, a decrease of 19.3%. Direct operating expenses rose 1.5% to US$2.50 billion from US$2.46 billion in the comparable period the year before. Indirect operating expenses increased 0.3% to US$615.0 million from US$613.0 million in the equivalent prior-year period.

Prospects: Our evaluation of Edison International as of Jan. 14, 2018 is the result of our systematic analysis on three basic characteristics: earnings strength, relative valuation, and recent stock price movement. The company has generated a negative trend in earnings per share over the past 5 quarters. However, while recent estimates for the company have been lowered by analysts, EIX has posted better than expected results. Based on operating earnings yield, the company is undervalued when compared to all of the companies in our coverage universe. Share price changes over the past year indicates that EIX will perform very well over the near term.

Financial Data

(US$ in Thousands)	9 Mos	6 Mos	3 Mos	12/31/2016	12/31/2015	12/31/2014	12/31/2013	12/31/2012
Earnings Per Share	4.41	4.25	4.24	3.97	3.10	4.89	2.78	(0.56)
Cash Flow Per Share	10.57	10.00	10.07	9.96	13.83	9.96	9.83	10.20
Tang Book Value Per Share	38.11	37.28	36.99	36.82	34.89	33.64	30.50	28.95
Dividends Per Share	2.170	2.107	2.045	1.982	1.732	1.482	1.367	1.313
Dividend Payout %	49.21	49.59	48.23	49.94	55.89	30.32	49.19	...
Income Statement								
Total Revenue	9,100,000	5,428,000	2,463,000	11,869,000	11,524,000	13,413,000	12,581,000	11,862,000
EBITDA	3,171,000	2,040,000	1,022,000	3,688,000	3,539,000	4,349,000	3,377,000	4,005,000
Depn & Amortn	1,591,000	1,048,000	520,000	1,520,000	1,420,000	1,815,000	1,622,000	1,634,000
Income Before Taxes	1,119,000	687,000	352,000	1,590,000	1,568,000	1,979,000	1,221,000	1,860,000
Income Taxes	(83,000)	(14,000)	(40,000)	177,000	486,000	443,000	242,000	267,000
Net Income	1,110,000	640,000	362,000	1,311,000	1,020,000	1,612,000	915,000	(183,000)
Average Shares	328,000	329,000	329,000	330,000	329,000	329,000	329,000	330,000
Balance Sheet								
Current Assets	2,758,000	2,546,000	2,046,000	2,123,000	2,654,000	4,019,000	3,312,000	2,672,000
Total Assets	53,592,000	52,753,000	51,740,000	51,319,000	50,310,000	50,186,000	46,646,000	44,394,000
Current Liabilities	5,409,000	4,602,000	4,416,000	5,912,000	4,927,000	5,479,000	4,881,000	3,744,000
Long-Term Obligations	11,638,000	11,662,000	11,662,000	10,175,000	10,964,000	10,234,000	9,825,000	9,231,000
Total Liabilities	41,176,000	40,607,000	39,689,000	39,323,000	38,942,000	39,226,000	36,708,000	34,962,000
Stockholders' Equity	12,416,000	12,146,000	12,051,000	11,996,000	11,368,000	10,960,000	9,938,000	9,432,000
Shares Outstanding	325,811	325,811	325,811	325,811	325,811	325,811	325,811	325,811
Statistical Record								
Return on Assets %	2.77	2.70	2.75	2.57	2.03	3.33	2.01	N.M.
Return on Equity %	12.02	11.86	11.95	11.19	9.14	15.43	9.45	N.M.
EBITDA Margin %	34.85	37.58	41.49	31.07	30.71	32.42	26.84	33.76
Net Margin %	12.20	11.79	14.70	11.05	8.85	12.02	7.27	N.M.
Asset Turnover	0.23	0.23	0.23	0.23	0.23	0.28	0.28	0.26
Current Ratio	0.51	0.55	0.46	0.36	0.54	0.73	0.68	0.71
Debt to Equity	0.94	0.96	0.97	0.85	0.96	0.93	0.99	0.98
Price Range	82.18-68.34	82.18-68.34	80.90-68.00	78.55-58.28	69.05-55.58	68.27-45.07	53.98-44.36	47.96-39.98
P/E Ratio	18.63-15.50	19.34-16.08	19.08-16.04	19.79-14.68	22.27-17.93	13.96-9.22	19.42-15.96	...
Average Yield %	2.84	2.80	2.79	2.81	2.82	2.82	2.63	2.85	2.96

Address: 2244 Walnut Grove Avenue, P.O. Box 976, Rosemead, CA 91770 Telephone: 626-302-2222	**Web Site:** www.edisoninvestor.com **Officers:** William P. Sullivan - Chairman Pedro J. Pizarro - President, Chief Executive Officer	**Auditors:** PricewaterhouseCoopers LLP **Transfer Agents:** Wells Fargo Shareowner Services, St. Paul, MN

EDUCATION REALTY TRUST INC

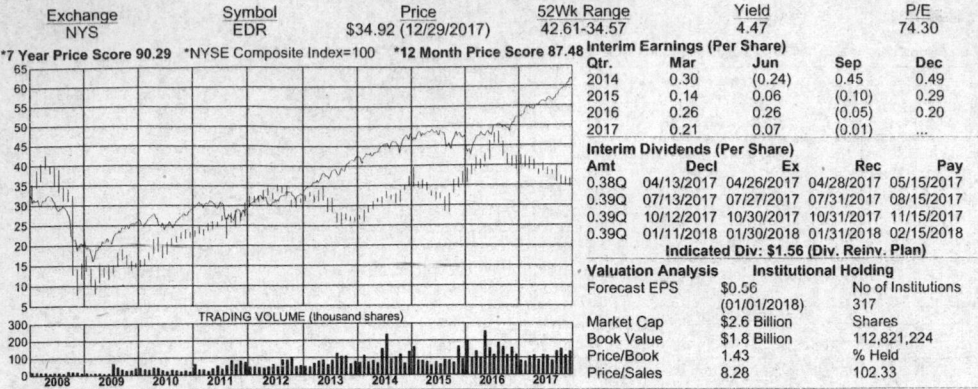

Exchange	Symbol	Price	52Wk Range	Yield	P/E
NYS	EDR	$34.92 (12/29/2017)	42.61-34.57	4.47	74.30

*7 Year Price Score 90.29   *NYSE Composite Index=100   *12 Month Price Score 87.48

Interim Earnings (Per Share)

Qtr.	Mar	Jun	Sep	Dec
2014	0.30	(0.24)	0.45	0.49
2015	0.14	0.06	(0.10)	0.29
2016	0.26	0.26	(0.05)	0.20
2017	0.21	0.07	(0.01)	...

Interim Dividends (Per Share)

Amt	Decl	Ex	Rec	Pay
0.38Q	04/13/2017	04/26/2017	04/28/2017	05/15/2017
0.39Q	07/13/2017	07/27/2017	07/31/2017	08/15/2017
0.39Q	10/12/2017	10/30/2017	10/31/2017	11/15/2017
0.39Q	01/11/2018	01/30/2018	01/31/2018	02/15/2018

Indicated Div: $1.56 (Div. Reinv. Plan)

Valuation Analysis — **Institutional Holding**

Forecast EPS	$0.56	No of Institutions
	(01/01/2018)	317
Market Cap	$2.6 Billion	Shares
Book Value	$1.8 Billion	112,821,224
Price/Book	1.43	% Held
Price/Sales	8.28	102.33

Business Summary: REITs (MIC: 5.3.1 SIC: 6798 NAIC: 525930)

Education Realty Trust is a real estate investment trust. Co. is engaged in developing, acquiring, owning and managing collegiate housing communities located near university campuses. Co. selectively develops collegiate housing communities for its own account and also provides third-party management services as well as third-party development consulting services on collegiate housing development projects for universities and other third parties. As of Dec 31 2016, Co. owned 64 collegiate housing communities located in 22 states containing 32,729 beds in 12,294 apartment units on or near 38 university campuses.

Recent Developments: For the quarter ended Sep 30 2017, net loss amounted to US$631,000 versus a net loss of US$3.9 million in the year-earlier quarter. Revenues were US$75.4 million, up 13.8% from US$66.2 million the year before. Revenues from property income rose 14.9% to US$71.1 million from US$61.9 million in the corresponding quarter a year earlier.

Prospects: Our evaluation of Education Realty Trust Inc. as of Jan. 14, 2018 is the result of our systematic analysis on three basic characteristics: earnings strength, relative valuation, and recent stock price movement. The company has produced a positive trend in earnings per share over the past 5 quarters. However, while recent estimates for the company have been mixed, EDR has posted better than expected results. Based on operating earnings yield, the company is overvalued when compared to all of the companies in our coverage universe. Share price changes over the past year indicates that EDR will perform well over the near term.

Financial Data

(US$ in Thousands)	9 Mos	6 Mos	3 Mos	12/31/2016	12/31/2015	12/31/2014	12/31/2013	12/31/2012
Earnings Per Share	0.47	0.43	0.62	0.65	0.40	1.09	0.12	0.24
Cash Flow Per Share	2.09	1.92	1.91	1.91	2.01	2.08	2.03	1.13
Tang Book Value Per Share	24.39	24.13	24.43	24.54	21.68	20.53	18.87	19.99
Dividends Per Share	1.530	1.520	1.510	1.500	1.460	1.380	1.260	1.020
Dividend Payout %	325.53	353.49	243.55	230.77	365.00	126.61	1,050.00	425.00
Income Statement								
Total Revenue	235,200	159,840	85,798	288,968	255,162	225,793	184,376	144,951
EBITDA	32,098	27,823	18,840	38,424	44,063	36,760	23,172	17,380
Depn & Amortn	1,185	779	421	1,700	1,500	900	600	2,438
Income Before Taxes	19,420	20,224	15,002	21,760	18,327	15,394	5,493	835
Income Taxes	(948)	(532)	(885)	684	347	261	203	(884)
Net Income	22,062	22,217	16,157	44,924	19,911	47,655	4,323	8,421
Average Shares	73,687	73,841	73,775	69,600	49,991	43,277	38,489	34,105
Balance Sheet								
Current Assets	53,482	41,569	42,636	46,679	48,787	32,993	40,355	30,621
Total Assets	2,926,079	2,802,943	2,719,848	2,506,185	2,001,831	1,811,637	1,610,565	1,324,687
Current Liabilities	214,155	954,833	855,041	148,599	104,694	94,170	91,144	75,087
Long-Term Obligations	808,081	29,751	29,776	517,196	638,707	711,137	779,581	477,846
Total Liabilities	1,078,694	1,037,111	931,847	706,166	765,132	822,848	884,841	566,965
Stockholders' Equity	1,847,385	1,765,832	1,788,001	1,800,019	1,236,699	988,789	725,724	757,722
Shares Outstanding	75,751	73,194	73,180	73,075	56,879	47,999	38,246	37,687
Statistical Record								
Return on Assets %	1.34	1.25	1.81	1.99	1.04	2.75	0.29	0.73
Return on Equity %	1.98	1.85	2.69	2.95	1.79	5.49	0.58	1.27
EBITDA Margin %	13.65	17.41	21.96	13.30	17.27	16.28	12.57	11.99
Net Margin %	9.38	13.90	18.83	15.55	7.80	20.84	2.34	5.81
Asset Turnover	0.12	0.12	0.12	0.13	0.13	0.13	0.13	0.13
Current Ratio	0.25	0.04	0.05	0.31	0.47	0.35	0.44	0.41
Debt to Equity	0.44	0.02	0.02	0.29	0.52	0.72	1.07	0.63
Price Range	43.14-35.86	48.47-37.45	48.47-38.87	48.47-35.63	39.59-28.08	37.38-25.95	35.13-25.20	35.37-29.49
P/E Ratio	91.79-76.30	112.72-87.09	78.18-62.69	74.57-54.82	98.98-70.20	34.29-23.81	292.75-210.00	147.38-122.88
Average Yield %	3.84	3.44	3.56	3.57	4.29	4.40	4.22	3.15

Address: 999 South Shady Grove Road, Suite 600, Memphis, TN 38120 Telephone: 901-259-2500	Web Site: www.edrtrust.com Officers: Randall L. Churchey - Chairman, President, Chief Executive Officer Thomas Trubiana - President, Executive Vice President, Senior Vice President, Chief Investment Officer	Auditors: Deloitte & Touche LLP Investor Contact: 901-259-2500 Transfer Agents: American Stock Transfer & Trust Co. LLC, New York, NY

EDWARDS LIFESCIENCES CORP

Exchange	Symbol	Price	52Wk Range	Yield	P/E
NYS	EW	$112.71 (12/29/2017)	120.15-89.49	N/A	32.86

*7 Year Price Score 132.93 *NYSE Composite Index=100 *12 Month Price Score 98.41

TRADING VOLUME (thousand shares)

Interim Earnings (Per Share)

Qtr.	Mar	Jun	Sep	Dec
2014	0.28	2.54	0.44	0.50
2015	0.56	0.51	0.54	0.64
2016	0.66	0.58	0.65	0.72
2017	1.06	0.86	0.79	...

Interim Dividends (Per Share)

Amt	Decl	Ex	Rec	Pay
100%	11/19/2015	12/14/2015	11/30/2015	12/11/2015

Valuation Analysis **Institutional Holding**

Forecast EPS	$3.76	No of Institutions
	(01/17/2018)	978
Market Cap	$23.8 Billion	Shares
Book Value	$3.2 Billion	198,870,848
Price/Book	7.54	% Held
Price/Sales	7.20	83.07

Business Summary: Medical Instruments & Equipment (MIC: 4.3.1 SIC: 3842 NAIC: 339113)

Edwards Lifesciences is engaged in patient-focused technology for structural heart disease and critical care monitoring. Co.'s products and technologies are categorized into three areas: Transcatheter Heart Valve Therapy, which provides transcatheter heart valve replacement technologies designed for the nonsurgical replacement of heart valves; Surgical Heart Valve Therapy, which provides surgical tissue heart valve products, surgical heart valve repair therapies and cardiac cannula devices; and Critical Care, which provides hemodynamic monitoring systems used to measure a patient's heart function and fluid status in surgical and intensive care settings.

Recent Developments: For the quarter ended Sep 30 2017, net income increased 20.3% to US$170.1 million from US$141.4 million in the year-earlier quarter. Revenues were US$821.5 million, up 11.1% from US$739.4 million the year before. Direct operating expenses rose 5.9% to US$213.3 million from US$201.4 million in the comparable period the year before. Indirect operating expenses increased 13.0% to US$394.7 million from US$349.2 million in the equivalent prior-year period.

Prospects: Our evaluation of Edwards Lifesciences Corp. as of Jan. 14, 2018 is the result of our systematic analysis on three basic characteristics: earnings strength, relative valuation, and recent stock price movement. The company has generated a negative trend in earnings per share over the past 5 quarters and while recent estimates for the company have been raised by analysts, EW has posted results that fell short of analysts expectations. Based on operating earnings yield, the company is about fairly valued when compared to all of the companies in our coverage universe. Share price changes over the past year indicates that EW will perform in line with the market over the near term.

Financial Data

(US$ in Thousands)	9 Mos	6 Mos	3 Mos	12/31/2016	12/31/2015	12/31/2014	12/31/2013	12/31/2012
Earnings Per Share	3.43	3.29	3.01	2.61	2.25	3.74	1.72	1.24
Cash Flow Per Share	3.97	3.48	3.44	3.30	2.55	4.80	2.12	1.62
Tang Book Value Per Share	8.35	7.42	6.63	8.45	7.75	8.31	5.11	4.50
Income Statement								
Total Revenue	2,546,800	1,725,300	883,500	2,963,700	2,493,700	2,322,900	2,045,500	1,899,600
EBITDA	775,600	543,000	317,100	809,900	690,400	1,212,300	574,000	435,400
Depn & Amortn	60,700	40,000	21,100	63,600	58,700	57,500	53,100	44,000
Income Before Taxes	711,000	499,200	293,600	737,900	622,400	1,144,000	515,700	391,800
Income Taxes	124,600	82,900	63,400	168,400	127,500	332,900	123,600	97,900
Net Income	586,400	416,300	230,200	569,500	494,900	811,100	391,700	293,200
Average Shares	216,200	215,700	216,400	217,800	220,300	217,000	227,600	236,600
Balance Sheet								
Current Assets	2,566,400	2,283,400	2,018,400	2,240,000	2,047,900	2,294,600	1,725,800	1,291,900
Total Assets	5,488,400	5,138,500	4,780,400	4,510,000	4,059,300	3,524,300	2,724,700	2,221,500
Current Liabilities	735,200	562,500	584,800	532,500	476,200	434,400	345,600	347,400
Long-Term Obligations	1,034,000	1,016,800	847,900	822,300	599,900	598,100	593,100	189,300
Total Liabilities	2,325,900	2,198,900	2,037,700	1,891,000	1,556,200	1,332,900	1,165,500	742,200
Stockholders' Equity	3,162,500	2,939,600	2,742,700	2,619,000	2,503,100	2,191,400	1,559,200	1,479,300
Shares Outstanding	211,590	211,100	210,400	211,600	215,400	215,600	218,600	228,600
Statistical Record								
Return on Assets %	15.16	15.59	15.21	13.26	13.05	25.96	15.84	13.92
Return on Equity %	25.45	26.47	26.05	22.18	21.08	43.25	25.78	20.76
EBITDA Margin %	30.45	31.47	35.89	27.33	27.69	52.19	28.06	22.92
Net Margin %	23.02	24.13	26.06	19.22	19.85	34.92	19.15	15.43
Asset Turnover	0.67	0.70	0.73	0.69	0.66	0.74	0.83	0.90
Current Ratio	3.49	4.06	3.45	4.21	4.30	5.28	4.99	3.72
Debt to Equity	0.33	0.35	0.31	0.31	0.24	0.27	0.38	0.13
Price Range	121.36-81.47	121.36-81.47	121.36-81.47	121.36-74.52	82.56-61.93	66.74-32.09	47.28-30.72	54.88-34.22
P/E Ratio	35.38-23.75	36.89-24.76	40.32-27.07	46.50-28.55	36.69-27.52	17.84-8.58	27.49-17.86	44.25-27.59

Address: One Edwards Way, Irvine, CA 92614 **Telephone:** 949-250-2500	**Web Site:** www.edwards.com **Officers:** Michael A. Mussallem - Chairman, Chief Executive Officer Scott B. Ullem - Corporate Vice-President, Chief Financial Officer	**Auditors:** PricewaterhouseCoopers LLP **Transfer Agents:** ComputerShare Investor Services, Providence, RI

EMCOR GROUP, INC.

Exchange	Symbol	Price	52Wk Range	Yield	P/E
NYS	EME	$81.75 (12/29/2017)	83.64-60.39	0.39	22.84

*7 Year Price Score 122.40 *NYSE Composite Index=100 *12 Month Price Score 110.07

Interim Earnings (Per Share)

Qtr.	Mar	Jun	Sep	Dec
2014	0.61	0.59	0.67	0.66
2015	0.52	0.74	0.66	0.81
2016	0.56	0.90	0.84	0.67
2017	0.87	0.95	1.09	...

Interim Dividends (Per Share)

Amt	Decl	Ex	Rec	Pay
0.08Q	04/05/2017	04/12/2017	04/17/2017	04/28/2017
0.08Q	07/06/2017	07/13/2017	07/17/2017	07/28/2017
0.08Q	10/03/2017	10/16/2017	10/17/2017	10/30/2017
0.08Q	01/05/2018	01/12/2018	01/16/2018	01/30/2018

Indicated Div: $0.32

TRADING VOLUME (thousand shares)

Valuation Analysis — **Institutional Holding**

Forecast EPS	$3.79	No of Institutions
(11/22/2017)		433
Market Cap	$4.8 Billion	Shares
Book Value	$1.6 Billion	74,977,072
Price/Book	2.97	% Held
Price/Sales	0.63	96.84

Business Summary: Construction Services (MIC: 7.5.4 SIC: 1731 NAIC: 238210)

EMCOR Group is an electrical and mechanical construction and facilities services firm. In addition, Co. provides a number of building services and industrial services. Co.'s services are provided through its operating subsidiaries and joint venture entities. Co. focuses on providing construction services relating to electrical and mechanical systems and in providing various services relating to the operation, maintenance and management of facilities, including refineries and petrochemical plants. Co. also provides its construction services indirectly by acting as a subcontractor to contractors, systems suppliers, property managers and other subcontractors.

Recent Developments: For the quarter ended Sep 30 2017, income from continuing operations increased 24.7% to US$64.8 million from US$52.0 million in the year-earlier quarter. Net income increased 25.3% to US$64.6 million from US$51.6 million in the year-earlier quarter. Revenues were US$1.89 billion, down 1.9% from US$1.92 billion the year before. Operating income was US$106.5 million versus US$86.1 million in the prior-year quarter, an increase of 23.7%. Direct operating expenses declined 3.8% to US$1.59 billion from US$1.66 billion in the comparable period the year before. Indirect operating expenses increased 3.6% to US$188.6 million from US$182.0 million in the equivalent prior-year period.

Prospects: Our evaluation of EMCOR Group Inc. as of Jan. 14, 2018 is the result of our systematic analysis on three basic characteristics: earnings strength, relative valuation, and recent stock price movement. The company has generated a negative trend in earnings per share over the past 5 quarters and while recent estimates for the company have been mixed, EME has posted better than expected results. Based on operating earnings yield, the company is undervalued when compared to all of the companies in our coverage universe. Share price changes over the past year indicates that EME will perform in line with the market over the near term.

Financial Data

(US$ in Thousands)	9 Mos	6 Mos	3 Mos	12/31/2016	12/31/2015	12/31/2014	12/31/2013	12/31/2012
Earnings Per Share	3.58	3.33	3.28	2.97	2.72	2.52	1.82	2.16
Cash Flow Per Share	6.33	5.39	4.96	4.34	4.25	3.72	2.24	2.76
Tang Book Value Per Share	1.86	0.99	0.03	1.17	2.63	1.27	1.34	6.51
Dividends Per Share	0.320	0.320	0.320	0.320	0.320	0.320	0.180	0.510
Dividend Payout %	8.94	9.61	9.76	10.77	11.76	12.70	9.89	23.61
Income Statement								
Total Revenue	5,674,360	3,787,669	1,891,732	7,551,524	6,718,726	6,424,965	6,417,158	6,346,679
EBITDA	318,374	199,852	94,955	388,266	361,277	364,344	277,620	310,929
Depn & Amortn	36,320	24,257	12,181	79,808	74,195	74,466	67,328	60,962
Income Before Taxes	273,197	169,785	79,960	296,494	278,823	281,645	202,651	244,248
Income Taxes	98,473	59,865	26,846	111,199	106,256	103,528	75,297	95,362
Net Income	173,995	109,398	52,640	181,935	172,286	168,664	123,792	146,584
Average Shares	59,419	59,639	60,111	61,206	63,307	67,062	68,076	67,738
Balance Sheet								
Current Assets	2,231,972	2,099,836	2,041,792	2,210,847	2,067,419	1,886,603	1,930,105	2,044,453
Total Assets	3,966,321	3,847,574	3,805,162	3,894,170	3,546,470	3,388,967	3,465,915	3,107,070
Current Liabilities	1,552,279	1,468,857	1,472,860	1,511,774	1,413,728	1,283,417	1,298,743	1,294,519
Long-Term Obligations	398,506	401,866	405,405	408,296	300,065	316,399	335,331	154,112
Total Liabilities	2,349,309	2,269,498	2,271,844	2,357,081	2,069,759	1,972,954	1,999,650	1,760,990
Stockholders' Equity	1,617,012	1,578,076	1,533,318	1,537,089	1,476,711	1,416,013	1,466,265	1,346,080
Shares Outstanding	58,806	59,171	59,255	59,946	61,067	62,981	66,896	66,964
Statistical Record								
Return on Assets %	5.46	5.27	5.52	4.88	4.97	4.92	3.77	4.78
Return on Equity %	13.42	12.95	13.28	12.04	11.91	11.70	8.80	11.33
EBITDA Margin %	5.61	5.28	5.02	5.14	5.38	5.67	4.33	4.90
Net Margin %	3.07	2.89	2.78	2.41	2.56	2.63	1.93	2.31
Asset Turnover	1.94	2.00	2.12	2.02	1.94	1.87	1.95	2.07
Current Ratio	1.44	1.43	1.39	1.46	1.46	1.47	1.49	1.58
Debt to Equity	0.25	0.25	0.26	0.27	0.20	0.22	0.23	0.11
Price Range	73.04-56.04	73.04-48.45	73.04-44.97	73.04-42.47	51.68-39.96	47.79-39.07	43.78-34.61	34.70-25.76
P/E Ratio	20.40-15.65	21.93-14.55	22.27-13.71	24.59-14.30	19.00-14.69	18.96-15.50	24.05-19.02	16.06-11.93
Average Yield %	0.49	0.51	0.55	0.60	0.69	0.73	0.46	1.76

Address: 301 Merritt Seven, Norwalk, CT 06851-1092	**Web Site:** www.emcorgroup.com	**Auditors:** Ernst & Young LLP
Telephone: 203-849-7800	**Officers:** Stephen W. Bershad - Chairman Anthony J. Guzzi - President, Chief Executive Officer	**Investor Contact:** 203-849-7938
		Transfer Agents: Computershare Shareowner Services, Pittsburgh, PA

EMERSON ELECTRIC CO.

Exchange	Symbol	Price	52Wk Range	Yield	P/E	Div Achiever
NYS	EMR	$69.69 (12/29/2017)	69.98-56.14	2.78	29.66	60 Years

*7 Year Price Score 84.91 *NYSE Composite Index=100 *12 Month Price Score 99.81

Interim Earnings (Per Share)

Qtr.	Dec	Mar	Jun	Sep
2012-13	0.62	0.77	0.27	1.10
2013-14	0.65	0.77	1.03	0.58
2014-15	0.75	1.42	0.84	0.98
2015-16	0.53	0.57	0.74	0.68
2016-17	0.48	0.45	0.64	0.78

Interim Dividends (Per Share)

Amt	Decl	Ex	Rec	Pay
0.48Q	02/07/2017	02/15/2017	02/17/2017	03/10/2017
0.48Q	05/02/2017	05/10/2017	05/12/2017	06/09/2017
0.48Q	08/01/2017	08/09/2017	08/11/2017	09/11/2017
0.485Q	11/07/2017	11/16/2017	11/17/2017	12/11/2017

Indicated Div: $1.94 (Div. Reinv. Plan)

Valuation Analysis | **Institutional Holding**

Forecast EPS	$2.90 (01/18/2018)	No of Institutions	1829
Market Cap	$44.7 Billion	Shares	573,642,304
Book Value	$8.7 Billion	% Held	65.60
Price/Book	5.13		
Price/Sales	2.93		

Business Summary: Electrical Equipment (MIC: 7.3.1 SIC: 3679 NAIC: 334419)

Emerson Electric is organized into five business segments: process management, which provides measurement, control and diagnostic capabilities for automated industrial processes producing items such as fuels, chemicals, foods, medicines and power; industrial automation, which brings integrated manufacturing solutions to various industries; climate technologies, which provides heating, air conditioning and refrigeration technology; commercial and residential solutions, which provides tools for professionals and homeowners, residential storage systems and appliance solutions.

Recent Developments: For the year ended Sep 30 2017, income from continuing operations increased 3.5% to US$1.68 billion from US$1.62 billion a year earlier. Net income decreased 6.9% to US$1.55 billion from US$1.66 billion in the prior year. Revenues were US$15.26 billion, up 5.1% from US$14.52 billion the year before. Direct operating expenses rose 7.3% to US$8.86 billion from US$8.26 billion in the comparable period the year before. Indirect operating expenses increased 3.9% to US$3.90 billion from US$3.76 billion in the equivalent prior-year period.

Prospects: Our evaluation of Emerson Electric Co. as of Jan. 14, 2018 is the result of our systematic analysis on three basic characteristics: earnings strength, relative valuation, and recent stock price movement. The company has managed to produce a neutral trend in earnings per share over the past 5 quarters and while recent estimates for the company have been raised by analysts, EMR has posted better than expected results. Based on operating earnings yield, the company is about fairly valued when compared to all of the companies in our coverage universe. Share price changes over the past year indicates that EMR will perform poorly over the near term.

Financial Data

(US$ in Thousands)	09/30/2017	09/30/2016	09/30/2015	09/30/2014	09/30/2013	09/30/2012	09/30/2011	09/30/2010
Earnings Per Share	2.35	2.52	3.99	3.03	2.76	2.67	3.27	2.84
Cash Flow Per Share	2.98	4.46	3.76	5.27	5.08	4.17	4.32	4.39
Tang Book Value Per Share	2.36	4.29	N.M.	1.79	1.99	0.60	N.M.	N.M.
Dividends Per Share	1.920	1.900	1.880	1.720	1.640	1.600	1.380	1.340
Dividend Payout %	81.70	75.40	47.12	56.77	59.42	59.93	42.20	47.18
Income Statement								
Total Revenue	15,264,000	14,522,000	22,304,000	24,537,000	24,669,000	24,412,000	24,222,000	21,039,000
EBITDA	3,050,000	2,979,000	5,053,000	4,285,000	4,155,000	4,085,000	4,637,000	3,878,000
Depn & Amortn	550,000	475,000	721,000	743,000	741,000	746,000	783,000	738,000
Income Before Taxes	2,335,000	2,316,000	4,161,000	3,348,000	3,196,000	3,115,000	3,631,000	2,879,000
Income Taxes	660,000	697,000	1,428,000	1,164,000	1,130,000	1,091,000	1,127,000	848,000
Net Income	1,518,000	1,635,000	2,710,000	2,147,000	2,004,000	1,968,000	2,480,000	2,164,000
Average Shares	643,400	646,800	676,500	704,100	722,900	734,600	753,500	757,000
Balance Sheet								
Current Assets	8,252,000	9,960,000	10,049,000	10,867,000	10,999,000	10,126,000	9,345,000	8,363,000
Total Assets	19,589,000	21,743,000	22,088,000	24,177,000	24,711,000	23,818,000	23,861,000	22,843,000
Current Liabilities	5,045,000	8,008,000	7,800,000	8,454,000	7,625,000	7,133,000	6,465,000	5,849,000
Long-Term Obligations	3,794,000	4,062,000	4,289,000	3,559,000	4,055,000	3,787,000	4,324,000	4,586,000
Total Liabilities	10,871,000	14,175,000	14,007,000	14,058,000	14,126,000	13,523,000	13,462,000	13,051,000
Stockholders' Equity	8,718,000	7,568,000	8,081,000	10,119,000	10,585,000	10,295,000	10,399,000	9,792,000
Shares Outstanding	641,691	642,796	654,608	696,605	706,660	724,113	738,877	752,690
Statistical Record								
Return on Assets %	7.35	7.44	11.72	8.78	8.26	8.23	10.62	10.16
Return on Equity %	18.64	20.84	29.78	20.74	19.20	18.97	24.57	23.59
EBITDA Margin %	19.98	20.51	22.66	17.46	16.84	16.73	19.14	18.43
Net Margin %	9.94	11.26	12.15	8.75	8.12	8.06	10.24	10.29
Asset Turnover	0.74	0.66	0.96	1.00	1.02	1.02	1.04	0.99
Current Ratio	1.64	1.24	1.29	1.29	1.44	1.42	1.45	1.43
Debt to Equity	0.44	0.54	0.53	0.35	0.38	0.37	0.42	0.47
Price Range	64.15-49.41	56.34-42.29	65.77-43.04	70.26-61.79	66.50-47.32	53.37-40.69	61.85-41.31	53.62-37.75
P/E Ratio	27.30-21.03	22.36-16.78	16.48-10.79	23.19-20.39	24.09-17.14	19.99-15.24	18.91-12.63	18.88-13.29
Average Yield %	3.30	3.75	3.25	2.60	2.93	3.27	2.84	2.91

Address: 8000 W. Florissant Avenue, P.O. Box 4100, St. Louis, MO 63136 **Telephone:** 314-553-2000	**Web Site:** www.emerson.com **Officers:** David N. Farr - Chairman, President, Chief Executive Officer Edward L. Monser - President, Chief Operating Officer	**Auditors:** KPMG LLP **Investor Contact:** 314-553-2197 **Transfer Agents:** Computershare, Inc., Providence, RI

EMPIRE STATE REALTY TRUST INC

Exchange	Symbol	Price	52Wk Range	Yield	P/E
NYS	ESRT	$20.53 (12/29/2017)	21.92-19.76	2.05	52.64

*7 Year Price Score N/A   *NYSE Composite Index=100   *12 Month Price Score 93.08

Interim Earnings (Per Share)

Qtr.	Mar	Jun	Sep	Dec
2014	0.05	0.10	0.09	0.03
2015	0.03	0.10	0.10	0.07
2016	0.06	0.09	0.12	0.11
2017	0.06	0.10	0.12	...

Interim Dividends (Per Share)

Amt	Decl	Ex	Rec	Pay
0.105Q	02/17/2017	03/13/2017	03/15/2017	03/31/2017
0.105Q	05/12/2017	06/13/2017	06/15/2017	06/30/2017
0.105Q	08/09/2017	09/14/2017	09/15/2017	09/29/2017
0.105Q	11/24/2017	12/14/2017	12/15/2017	12/29/2017

Indicated Div: $0.42

Valuation Analysis		Institutional Holding	
Forecast EPS	$0.38 (01/11/2018)	No of Institutions	228
Market Cap	$3.3 Billion	Shares	158,069,584
Book Value	$1.2 Billion	% Held	87.61
Price/Book	2.84		
Price/Sales	4.62		

TRADING VOLUME (thousand shares)

Business Summary: REITs (MIC: 5.3.1 SIC: 6798 NAIC: 525930)

Empire State Realty Trust is a real estate investment trust that owns, manages, operates, acquires and repositions office and retail properties in Manhattan and the greater New York metropolitan area. As of Dec 31 2016, Co. owned 14 office properties encompassing approximately 9.4 million rentable square feet of office space. Empire State Realty OP, L.P. conducts substantially all of Co.'s business. Co. has two segments: real estate, which includes all activities related to the ownership, management, operation, acquisition, repositioning and disposition of its real estate assets; and observatory, which operates the 86th and 102nd floor observatories at the Empire State Building.

Recent Developments: For the quarter ended Sep 30 2017, net income increased 7.9% to US$35.5 million from US$32.9 million in the year-earlier quarter. Revenues were US$187.3 million, up 6.5% from US$175.8 million the year before. Revenues from property income rose 5.9% to US$142.7 million from US$134.8 million in the corresponding quarter a year earlier.

Prospects: Our evaluation of Empire State Realty Trust Inc as of Jan. 14, 2018 is the result of our systematic analysis on three basic characteristics: earnings strength, relative valuation, and recent stock price movement. The company has produced a positive trend in earnings per share over the past 5 quarters and while recent estimates for the company have remained steady, ESRT has posted results that fell short of analysts expectations. Based on operating earnings yield, the company is overvalued when compared to all of the companies in our coverage universe. Share price changes over the past year indicates that ESRT will perform very well over the near term.

Financial Data

(US$ in Thousands)	9 Mos	6 Mos	3 Mos	12/31/2016	12/31/2015	12/31/2014	12/31/2013	10/06/2013
Earnings Per Share	0.12	0.10	0.06	0.38	0.29	0.27	0.79	...
Cash Flow Per Share	2.17	0.70	1.56	1.63	1.78	1.41	(5.86)	...
Tang Book Value Per Share	1.83	1.81	1.84	4.25	0.28	N.M.	N.M.	...
Dividends Per Share	0.105	0.105	0.105	0.400	0.340	0.340	0.080	...
Dividend Payout %	87.50	105.00	175.00	105.26	117.24	125.93	10.06	
Income Statement								
Total Revenue	187,320	177,124	164,954	678,000	657,634	635,326	127,583	206,072
EBITDA	54,975	52,230	36,949	290,886	259,688	230,826	256,525	49,028
Depn & Amortn	351	838	530	106,343	108,319	89,505	49,947	50,475
Income Before Taxes	37,734	33,915	18,677	113,396	83,877	74,865	193,431	(52,107)
Income Taxes	2,245	2,556	(468)	6,146	3,949	4,655	...	...
Net Income	19,040	16,818	10,219	52,392	34,666	27,143	75,245	(37,232)
Average Shares	297,871	298,398	297,962	277,568	266,621	254,506	95,611	...
Balance Sheet								
Current Assets	496,125	508,969	594,906	615,885	112,565	106,005	116,364	...
Total Assets	3,848,934	3,831,201	3,866,176	3,890,953	3,300,650	3,296,495	2,476,061	...
Current Liabilities	190,085	186,286	173,108	181,247	159,989	137,011	113,314	...
Long-Term Obligations	1,577,290	1,579,499	1,608,799	1,612,331	1,632,416	1,611,652	1,208,112	...
Total Liabilities	2,687,299	2,673,061	2,701,899	2,728,813	2,767,917	2,819,853	2,090,903	...
Stockholders' Equity	1,153,631	1,150,136	1,156,273	1,154,136	524,729	468,638	385,158	...
Shares Outstanding	159,427	158,573	157,784	155,840	120,023	107,191	95,606	...
Statistical Record								
Return on Assets %	1.97	1.75	1.07	1.45	1.05	0.94	...	...
Return on Equity %	6.56	5.85	3.59	6.22	6.98	6.36	...	...
EBITDA Margin %	29.35	29.49	22.40	42.90	39.49	36.33	201.07	23.79
Net Margin %	10.16	9.50	6.20	7.73	5.27	4.27	58.98	N.M.
Asset Turnover	0.19	0.18	0.17	0.19	0.20	0.22	...	...
Current Ratio	2.61	2.73	3.44	3.40	0.70	0.77	1.03	...
Debt to Equity	1.37	1.37	1.39	1.40	3.11	3.44	3.14	...
Price Range	21.92-18.81	22.17-18.79	22.17-17.53	22.17-14.67	18.96-15.94	17.88-14.19	15.55-13.27	13.20-13.10
P/E Ratio	182.67-156.75	221.70-187.90	369.50-292.17	58.34-38.61	65.38-54.97	66.22-52.56	19.68-16.80	...
Average Yield %	0.51	0.51	0.53	2.11	1.91	2.14	0.56	...

Address: 111 West 33rd Street, 12th Floor, New York, NY 10120 Telephone: 212-687-8700	Web Site: www.empirestaterealtytrust.com Officers: Anthony E. Malkin - Chairman, President, Chief Executive Officer John B. Kessler - President, Chief Operating Officer	Auditors: Ernst & Young LLP Transfer Agents: American Stock Transfer & Trust Company, LLC

ENCOMPASS HEALTH CORP

Exchange	Symbol	Price	52Wk Range	Yield	P/E
NYS	EHC	$49.41 (12/29/2017)	50.10-38.61	2.02	17.90

*7 Year Price Score 104.52 *NYSE Composite Index=100 *12 Month Price Score 101.93

Interim Earnings (Per Share)

Qtr.	Mar	Jun	Sep	Dec
2014	0.48	0.85	0.52	0.44
2015	0.44	0.45	0.52	0.50
2016	0.61	0.65	0.64	0.69
2017	0.70	0.70	0.67	...

Interim Dividends (Per Share)

Amt	Decl	Ex	Rec	Pay
0.24Q	02/17/2017	03/30/2017	04/03/2017	04/17/2017
0.24Q	05/04/2017	06/29/2017	07/03/2017	07/17/2017
0.25Q	07/20/2017	09/29/2017	10/02/2017	10/16/2017
0.25Q	10/20/2017	12/29/2017	01/02/2018	01/16/2018

Indicated Div: $1.00

Valuation Analysis | Institutional Holding

Forecast EPS	$2.72	No of Institutions 455
	(01/26/2018)	
Market Cap	$4.9 Billion	Shares 122,139,768
Book Value	$1.1 Billion	% Held N/A
Price/Book	4.27	
Price/Sales	1.26	

TRADING VOLUME (thousand shares)

Business Summary: Hospitals & Health Care Facilities (MIC: 4.2.1 SIC: 8093 NAIC: 623110)

Encompass Health is a provider of post-acute healthcare services, providing both facility-based and home-based post-acute services in 35 states and Puerto Rico through its network of inpatient rehabilitation hospitals, home health agencies, and hospice agencies. Co. manages its operations using two operating segments: inpatient rehabilitation and home health and hospice. As of Dec 31 2016, Co. operated hospitals in 30 states and Puerto Rico. Co. also managed five inpatient rehabilitation units. As of Dec 31 2016, Co.'s Encompass Home Health and Hospice business operated home health and hospice agencies in 25 states, with concentrations in the Southeast, Oklahoma, and Texas.

Recent Developments: For the quarter ended Sep 30 2017, income from continuing operations increased 9.0% to US$85.2 million from US$78.2 million in the year-earlier quarter. Net income increased 9.0% to US$85.1 million from US$78.1 million in the year-earlier quarter. Revenues were US$983.0 million, up 7.8% from US$912.0 million the year before. Direct operating expenses rose 8.9% to US$137.6 million from US$126.3 million in the comparable period the year before. Indirect operating expenses increased 9.5% to US$683.1 million from US$623.6 million in the equivalent prior-year period.

Prospects: Our evaluation of Encompass Health Corp. as of Jan. 21, 2018 is the result of our systematic analysis on three basic characteristics: earnings strength, relative valuation, and recent stock price movement. The company has managed to produce a neutral trend in earnings per share over the past 5 quarters and while recent estimates for the company have been raised by analysts, EHC has posted better than expected results. Based on operating earnings yield, the company is undervalued when compared to all of the companies in our coverage universe. Share price changes over the past year indicates that EHC will perform in line with the market over the near term.

Financial Data

(US$ in Thousands)	9 Mos	6 Mos	3 Mos	12/31/2016	12/31/2015	12/31/2014	12/31/2013	12/31/2012
Earnings Per Share	2.76	2.73	2.68	2.59	1.91	2.29	2.58	1.69
Cash Flow Per Share	6.36	6.93	7.06	6.78	5.42	5.13	5.34	4.34
Tang Book Value Per Share	N.M.	N.M.	N.M.	N.M.	N.M.	N.M.	N.M.	1.29
Dividends Per Share	0.970	0.960	0.950	0.940	0.880	0.780	0.360	...
Dividend Payout %	35.14	35.16	35.45	36.29	46.07	34.06	13.95	...
Income Statement								
Total Revenue	2,909,000	1,926,000	958,400	3,646,000	3,115,700	2,374,300	2,247,200	2,134,900
EBITDA	610,000	400,800	208,800	746,600	620,800	565,300	552,300	480,400
Depn & Amortn	137,200	91,000	45,200	102,300	91,000	79,900	67,900	59,000
Income Before Taxes	354,300	228,100	122,300	472,200	386,900	376,200	384,000	327,300
Income Taxes	111,400	68,300	39,700	163,900	141,900	110,700	12,700	108,600
Net Income	195,700	129,800	66,800	247,600	183,100	222,000	323,600	185,000
Average Shares	99,000	98,900	99,000	99,500	101,000	100,700	102,100	108,100
Balance Sheet								
Current Assets	687,400	693,500	682,300	654,500	598,700	686,600	580,400	636,800
Total Assets	4,883,400	4,840,000	4,703,800	4,681,900	4,606,100	3,408,800	2,534,400	2,423,800
Current Liabilities	511,200	493,300	487,300	475,600	426,400	364,300	311,600	300,900
Long-Term Obligations	2,591,300	2,625,100	2,915,500	2,979,300	3,134,700	2,110,800	1,505,200	1,239,900
Total Liabilities	3,747,000	3,736,300	3,924,100	3,946,000	3,994,700	2,842,400	2,096,600	1,790,000
Stockholders' Equity	1,136,400	1,103,700	779,700	735,900	611,400	566,400	437,800	633,800
Shares Outstanding	98,300	98,700	89,500	88,929	90,130	87,788	87,993	95,685
Statistical Record								
Return on Assets %	5.49	5.42	5.51	5.32	4.57	7.47	13.05	7.86
Return on Equity %	28.02	28.91	35.88	36.65	31.09	44.21	60.40	32.42
EBITDA Margin %	20.97	20.81	21.79	20.48	19.92	23.81	24.58	22.50
Net Margin %	6.73	6.74	6.97	6.79	5.88	9.35	14.40	8.67
Asset Turnover	0.81	0.80	0.80	0.78	0.78	0.80	0.91	0.91
Current Ratio	1.34	1.41	1.40	1.38	1.40	1.88	1.86	2.12
Debt to Equity	2.28	2.38	3.74	4.05	5.13	3.73	3.44	1.96
Price Range	49.06-38.34	49.06-38.25	43.05-35.04	43.05-30.91	47.93-33.04	41.74-30.05	36.48-21.11	24.63-16.82
P/E Ratio	17.78-13.89	17.97-14.01	16.06-13.07	16.62-11.93	25.09-17.30	18.23-13.12	14.14-8.18	14.57-9.95
Average Yield %	2.24	2.28	2.35	2.42	2.11	2.11	1.20	...

Address: 3660 Grandview Parkway, Suite 200, Birmingham, AL 35243 Telephone: 205-967-7116	Web Site: www.healthsouth.com Officers: Leo I. (Lee) Higdon - Chairman Jon F. Hanson - Chairman	Auditors: PricewaterhouseCoopers LLP Investor Contact: 205-968-6400 Transfer Agents: Computershare Investor Services, Canton, MA

ENERGEN CORP.

Exchange	Symbol	Price	52Wk Range	Yield	P/E
NYS	EGN	$57.57 (12/29/2017)	59.37-46.77	N/A	N/A

*7 Year Price Score 73.23   *NYSE Composite Index=100   *12 Month Price Score 97.77

Interim Earnings (Per Share)

Qtr.	Mar	Jun	Sep	Dec
2014	0.73	(0.11)	6.22	0.89
2015	(0.21)	(1.52)	(2.89)	(7.71)
2016	(2.34)	0.38	0.55	(0.56)
2017	0.34	0.30	(0.19)	...

Interim Dividends (Per Share)

Dividend Payment Suspended

Valuation Analysis   **Institutional Holding**

Forecast EPS	$0.53	No of Institutions
	(01/26/2018)	454
Market Cap	$5.6 Billion	Shares
Book Value	$3.2 Billion	112,683,272
Price/Book	1.76	% Held
Price/Sales	6.96	82.79

Business Summary: Production & Extraction (MIC: 9.1.1 SIC: 1311 NAIC: 211111)

Energen is an oil and natural gas exploration and production company engaged in the exploration, development and production of oil, natural gas liquids and natural gas. Co.'s operations are primarily located within the Midland Basin, the Delaware Basin and the Central Basin Platform areas of the Permian Basin in west Texas and New Mexico. In addition, Co. explores for and develops new reservoirs, primarily in areas in which it has an operating presence. As of Dec 31 2016, Co. had 316.3 million barrels of oil equivalents proved reserves, which consisted of 352.25 billion cubic feet of natural gas, 58.0 million barrels of natural gas liquids, and 199.6 million barrels of oil.

Recent Developments: For the quarter ended Sep 30 2017, net loss amounted to US$18.5 million versus net income of US$53.3 million in the year-earlier quarter. Revenues were US$191.5 million, up 3.9% from US$184.4 million the year before. Operating loss was US$17.8 million versus an income of US$90.3 million in the prior-year quarter. Direct operating expenses rose 12.4% to US$59.9 million from US$53.3 million in the comparable period the year before. Indirect operating expenses increased 266.2% to US$149.5 million from US$40.8 million in the equivalent prior-year period.

Prospects: Our evaluation of Energen Corp. as of Jan. 21, 2018 is the result of our systematic analysis on three basic characteristics: earnings strength, relative valuation, and recent stock price movement. The company has generated a negative trend in earnings per share over the past 5 quarters and while recent estimates for the company have been raised by analysts, EGN has posted better than expected results. Based on operating earnings yield, the company is overvalued when compared to all of the companies in our coverage universe. Share price changes over the past year indicates that EGN will perform poorly over the near term.

Financial Data

(US$ in Thousands)	9 Mos	6 Mos	3 Mos	12/31/2016	12/31/2015	12/31/2014	12/31/2013	12/31/2012
Earnings Per Share	(0.11)	0.63	0.71	(1.77)	(12.43)	7.75	2.82	3.51
Cash Flow Per Share	4.87	3.80	3.37	3.09	9.39	9.68	12.82	10.17
Tang Book Value Per Share	32.67	32.82	31.45	32.17	36.78	46.84	39.36	37.14
Dividends Per Share	...	...	...	...	0.080	0.470	0.580	0.560
Dividend Payout %	...	...	...	...	...	6.06	20.57	15.95
Income Statement								
Total Revenue	689,249	497,745	240,921	532,889	878,554	1,679,213	1,738,650	1,617,169
EBITDA	451,762	337,770	161,462	237,709	(843,389)	726,706	895,474	882,535
Depn & Amortn	352,957	221,201	99,652	447,961	593,789	548,564	527,845	419,598
Income Before Taxes	70,766	98,458	52,844	(247,151)	(1,480,736)	140,371	298,429	397,381
Income Taxes	26,368	35,574	19,441	(79,638)	(535,005)	40,728	105,282	143,819
Net Income	44,398	62,884	33,403	(167,513)	(945,731)	568,032	204,554	253,562
Average Shares	97,198	97,693	97,607	94,475	76,078	73,274	72,470	72,316
Balance Sheet								
Current Assets	163,340	166,894	232,987	505,911	246,340	919,360	427,231	425,120
Total Assets	4,853,576	4,746,732	4,598,715	4,579,823	4,613,693	6,138,258	6,622,212	6,175,890
Current Liabilities	282,768	273,313	308,675	338,204	287,521	560,323	1,109,893	1,159,782
Long-Term Obligations	765,759	659,158	527,557	527,443	776,087	1,038,563	1,343,464	1,103,528
Total Liabilities	1,680,296	1,558,990	1,444,164	1,459,221	1,717,833	2,723,654	3,764,193	3,499,200
Stockholders' Equity	3,173,280	3,187,742	3,154,551	3,120,602	2,895,860	3,414,604	2,858,019	2,676,690
Shares Outstanding	97,130	97,119	100,309	97,013	78,743	72,895	72,606	72,069
Statistical Record								
Return on Assets %	N.M.	1.33	1.53	N.M.	N.M.	8.90	3.20	4.43
Return on Equity %	N.M.	1.96	2.21	N.M.	N.M.	18.11	7.39	9.90
EBITDA Margin %	65.54	67.86	67.02	44.61	N.M.	43.28	51.50	54.57
Net Margin %	6.44	12.63	13.86	N.M.	N.M.	33.83	11.77	15.68
Asset Turnover	0.17	0.17	0.14	0.12	0.16	0.26	0.27	0.28
Current Ratio	0.58	0.61	0.75	1.50	0.86	1.64	0.38	0.37
Debt to Equity	0.24	0.21	0.17	0.17	0.27	0.30	0.47	0.41
Price Range	62.07-46.77	62.07-44.24	62.07-35.35	62.07-22.90	75.46-40.45	90.10-55.49	85.31-44.87	55.50-40.85
P/E Ratio	...	98.52-70.22	87.42-49.79	...	...	11.63-7.16	30.25-15.91	15.81-11.64
Average Yield %	...	...	...	...	0.13	0.62	0.97	1.15

Address: 605 Richard Arrington Jr. Boulevard North, Birmingham, AL 35203-2707 **Telephone:** 205-326-2700	**Web Site:** www.energen.com **Officers:** James T. McManus - Chairman, President, Chief Executive Officer, Chief Operating Officer Charles W. Porter - Vice President, Chief Financial Officer, Treasurer	**Auditors:** PricewaterhouseCoopers LLP **Investor Contact:** 205-326-8421 **Transfer Agents:** Computershare Shareowner Services LLC, Providence, RI

ENERGIZER HOLDINGS INC

Exchange	Symbol	Price	52Wk Range	Yield	P/E
NYS	ENR	$47.98 (12/29/2017)	59.82-41.14	2.42	14.90

*7 Year Price Score N/A   *NYSE Composite Index=100   *12 Month Price Score 86.86

TRADING VOLUME (thousand shares)

Interim Earnings (Per Share)

Qtr.	Dec	Mar	Jun	Sep
2014-15	0.99	(1.11)	(0.32)	0.38
2015-16	1.05	0.26	0.39	0.34
2016-17	1.52	0.75	0.40	0.55

Interim Dividends (Per Share)

Amt	Decl	Ex	Rec	Pay
0.275Q	01/30/2017	02/16/2017	02/21/2017	03/14/2017
0.275Q	05/01/2017	05/18/2017	05/22/2017	06/14/2017
0.275Q	07/31/2017	08/17/2017	08/21/2017	09/12/2017
0.29Q	11/13/2017	11/29/2017	11/30/2017	12/14/2017

Indicated Div: $1.16

Valuation Analysis

		Institutional Holding	
Forecast EPS	$3.05	No of Institutions	
	(01/18/2018)	381	
Market Cap	$2.9 Billion	Shares	
Book Value	$85.1 Million	65,541,776	
Price/Book	34.23	% Held	
Price/Sales	1.66	N/A	

Business Summary: Household & Personal Products (MIC: 1.7.1 SIC: 3692 NAIC: 335912)

Energizer Holdings is a manufacturer, marketer and distributor of household batteries, specialty batteries and lighting products under the Energizer® and Eveready® brand names, and a designer and marketer of automotive fragrance and appearance products marketed under the Refresh Your Car!®, California Scents®, Driven®, Bahama & Co.®, LEXOL®, and Eagle One® brands. Co. provides batteries using lithium, alkaline, carbon zinc, nickel metal hydride, zinc air and silver oxide. Co. also distributes, markets, and licenses lighting products including headlights, lanterns, children's lights and area lights. Co. markets its flashlights under the Hard Case®, Dolphin®, and WeatherReady® sub-brands.

Recent Developments: For the year ended Sep 30 2017, net income increased 57.8% to US$201.5 million from US$127.7 million in the prior year. Revenues were US$1.76 billion, up 7.4% from US$1.63 billion the year before. Direct operating expenses rose 2.5% to US$944.4 million from US$921.8 million in the comparable period the year before. Indirect operating expenses decreased 2.9% to US$478.2 million from US$492.7 million in the equivalent prior-year period.

Prospects: Our evaluation of Energizer Holdings Co. as of Jan. 14, 2018 is the result of our systematic analysis on three basic characteristics: earnings strength, relative valuation, and recent stock price movement. The company has generated a negative trend in earnings per share over the past 5 quarters and while recent estimates for the company have been raised by analysts, ENR has posted better than expected results. Based on operating earnings yield, the company is undervalued when compared to all of the companies in our coverage universe. Share price changes over the past year indicates that ENR will perform poorly over the near term.

Financial Data

(US$ in Thousands)	09/30/2017	09/30/2016	09/30/2015	09/30/2014	09/30/2013	09/30/2012
Earnings Per Share	3.22	2.04	(0.06)	...	...	...
Cash Flow Per Share	3.20	3.12	2.60	...	...	...
Dividends Per Share	1.100	1.000	0.250	...	...	...
Dividend Payout %	34.16	49.02	...	...	...	...
Income Statement						
Total Revenue	1,755,700	1,634,200	1,631,600	1,840,400	2,012,200	2,087,700
EBITDA	371,300	250,700	114,300	308,200	284,900	381,800
Depn & Amortn	44,900	30,700	37,100	40,300	54,800	55,300
Income Before Taxes	273,300	165,700	(700)	215,200	162,000	257,600
Income Taxes	71,800	38,000	3,300	57,900	47,100	70,600
Net Income	201,500	127,700	(4,000)	157,300	114,900	187,000
Average Shares	62,600	62,500	62,200	...	...	...
Balance Sheet						
Current Assets	1,020,200	889,500	1,126,500	747,100	753,000	...
Total Assets	1,823,600	1,731,500	1,629,600	1,194,700	1,238,800	...
Current Liabilities	582,000	533,100	467,800	380,400	395,100	...
Long-Term Obligations	978,500	981,700	995,000	...	...	...
Total Liabilities	1,738,500	1,761,500	1,689,700	470,200	501,100	...
Stockholders' Equity	85,100	(30,000)	(60,100)	724,500	737,700	...
Shares Outstanding	60,708	61,672	62,195	...	...	...
Statistical Record						
Return on Assets %	11.34	7.58	N.M.	...	...	...
Return on Equity %	731.40	...	N.M.	...	...	...
EBITDA Margin %	21.15	15.34	7.01	16.75	14.16	18.29
Net Margin %	11.48	7.81	N.M.	8.55	5.71	8.96
Asset Turnover	0.99	0.97	1.16	...	...	...
Current Ratio	1.75	1.67	2.41	1.96	1.91	...
Debt to Equity	11.50	...	...	...	...	...
Price Range	59.82-41.14	52.35-30.23	42.31-33.00	...	...	...
P/E Ratio	18.58-12.78	25.66-14.82	...	...	...	...
Average Yield %	2.23	2.35	0.64	...	...	...

Address: 533 Maryville University Drive, St. Louis, MO 63141 **Telephone:** 314-985-2000	**Web Site:** www.energizerholdings.com **Officers:** J. Patrick Mulcahy - Chairman Benjamin J. Angelette - Deputy General Counsel, Corporate Secretary	**Auditors:** PricewaterhouseCoopers LLP **Transfer Agents:** Continental Stock Transfer and Trust Company

ENERGY TRANSFER EQUITY LP

Exchange	Symbol	Price	52Wk Range	Yield	P/E	Div Achiever
NYS	ETE	$17.26 (12/29/2017)	19.86-15.15	6.84	21.05	10 Years

*7 Year Price Score 80.72   *NYSE Composite Index=100   *12 Month Price Score 89.77

Interim Earnings (Per Share)

Qtr.	Mar	Jun	Sep	Dec
2014	0.15	0.15	0.17	0.11
2015	0.26	0.28	0.28	0.30
2016	0.30	0.23	0.19	0.21
2017	0.21	0.18	0.22	...

Interim Dividends (Per Share)

Amt	Decl	Ex	Rec	Pay
0.285Q	01/26/2017	02/03/2017	02/07/2017	02/20/2017
0.285Q	04/28/2017	05/08/2017	05/10/2017	05/19/2017
0.285Q	07/27/2017	08/03/2017	08/07/2017	08/21/2017
0.295Q	10/26/2017	11/06/2017	11/07/2017	11/20/2017

Indicated Div: $1.18 (Div. Reinv. Plan)

Valuation Analysis

	Institutional Holding	
Forecast EPS	$1.13	No of Institutions
(01/18/2018)		489
Market Cap	$18.6 Billion	Shares
Book Value	N/A	585,071,104
Price/Book	N/A	% Held
Price/Sales	0.46	46.58

Business Summary: Equipment & Services (MIC: 9.1.3 SIC: 4922 NAIC: 486210)

Energy Transfer Equity is a holding company. Co.'s segments are: Investment in Energy Transfer Partners, L.P., which includes intrastate transportation and storage operations, interstate transportation and storage operations, midstream operations, liquids transportation and services operations, investment in Sunoco Logistics Partners L.P., and retail marketing operations; Investment in Sunoco LP, which includes wholesale and retail operations; and Investment in Lake Charles liquefied natural gas (LNG), which provides terminal services for shippers by receiving LNG at the facility for storage and delivering such LNG to shippers, either in liquid state or gaseous state after regasification.

Recent Developments: For the quarter ended Sep 30 2017, income from continuing operations increased to US$798.0 million from US$29.0 million in the year-earlier quarter. Net income increased to US$804.0 million from US$41.0 million in the year-earlier quarter. Revenues were US$9.47 billion, up 23.0% from US$7.71 billion the year before. Operating income was US$986.0 million versus US$646.0 million in the prior-year quarter, an increase of 52.6%. Direct operating expenses rose 22.5% to US$7.08 billion from US$5.78 billion in the comparable period the year before. Indirect operating expenses increased 9.9% to US$1.41 billion from US$1.28 billion in the equivalent prior-year period.

Prospects: Our evaluation of Energy Transfer Equity L.P. as of Jan. 14, 2018 is the result of our systematic analysis on three basic characteristics: earnings strength, relative valuation, and recent stock price movement. The company has managed to produce a neutral trend in earnings per share over the past 5 quarters. However, while recent estimates for the company have been mixed, ETE has posted results that fell short of analysts expectations. Based on operating earnings yield, the company is undervalued when compared to all of the companies in our coverage universe. Share price changes over the past year indicates that ETE will perform poorly over the near term.

Financial Data

(US$ in Thousands)	9 Mos	6 Mos	3 Mos	12/31/2016	12/31/2015	12/31/2014	12/31/2013	12/31/2012
Earnings Per Share	0.82	0.79	0.84	0.92	1.11	0.57	0.17	0.28
Cash Flow Per Share	4.01	3.10	3.09	3.26	2.89	2.92	2.16	1.01
Dividends Per Share	1.140	1.140	1.140	1.140	1.020	0.750	0.652	0.625
Dividend Payout %	139.02	144.30	135.71	123.91	91.89	130.43	372.50	221.24
Income Statement								
Total Revenue	27,637,000	18,163,000	11,247,000	37,504,000	42,126,000	55,691,000	48,335,000	16,964,000
EBITDA	4,461,000	2,775,000	729,000	3,475,000	4,136,000	3,677,000	2,488,000	3,044,000
Depn & Amortn	1,840,000	1,208,000	5,000	2,089,000	1,776,000	1,223,000	1,128,000	801,000
Income Before Taxes	1,150,000	601,000	238,000	(446,000)	717,000	1,085,000	139,000	1,225,000
Income Taxes	(97,000)	60,000	35,000	(217,000)	(100,000)	357,000	93,000	54,000
Net Income	703,000	451,000	239,000	995,000	1,189,000	633,000	196,000	304,000
Average Shares	1,148,300	1,141,300	1,139,000	1,078,600	1,064,400	1,090,800	1,121,800	1,066,888
Balance Sheet								
Current Assets	10,689,000	10,326,000	6,514,000	6,985,000	5,410,000	6,153,000	6,536,000	5,597,000
Total Assets	85,380,000	82,609,000	80,997,000	79,011,000	71,189,000	64,469,000	50,330,000	48,904,000
Current Liabilities	7,847,000	7,765,000	6,218,000	7,277,000	4,910,000	6,782,000	6,500,000	5,845,000
Long-Term Obligations	44,627,000	43,084,000	42,583,000	42,858,000	36,837,000	29,653,000	22,562,000	21,440,000
Total Liabilities	86,572,000	83,794,000	82,144,000	80,672,000	72,088,000	63,772,000	49,220,000	46,718,000
Stockholders' Equity	...	...	...	33,000	33,000	33,000	32,000	73,000
Shares Outstanding	1,079,185	1,079,100	1,079,100	1,046,947	1,046,923	1,080,613	1,122,926	1,119,822
Statistical Record								
Return on Assets %	1.15	1.14	1.20	1.32	1.75	1.10	0.40	0.87
Return on Equity %	...	...	...	3,006.91	3,603.03	1,947.69	373.33	420.65
EBITDA Margin %	16.14	15.28	6.48	9.27	9.82	6.60	5.15	17.94
Net Margin %	2.54	2.48	2.13	2.65	2.82	1.14	0.41	1.79
Asset Turnover	0.50	0.52	0.53	0.50	0.62	0.97	0.97	0.48
Current Ratio	1.36	1.33	1.05	0.96	1.10	0.91	1.01	0.96
Debt to Equity	...	...	...	1,298.73	1,116.27	898.58	705.06	293.70
Price Range	19.86-13.80	19.86-13.80	19.86-6.45	19.59-4.05	35.24-11.09	32.24-19.62	20.62-11.37	11.95-8.60
P/E Ratio	24.22-16.83	25.14-17.47	23.64-7.68	21.29-4.40	31.75-9.99	56.56-34.43	121.31-66.88	42.67-30.71
Average Yield %	6.44	6.50	7.11	8.51	3.71	2.85	4.23	5.89

Address: 8111 Westchester Drive, Suite 600, Dallas, TX 75225
Telephone: 214-981-0700

Web Site: www.energytransfer.com
Officers: Kelcy L. Warren - Chairman John W. McReynolds - President, Chief Financial Officer

Auditors: Grant Thornton LLP
Investor Contact: 214-981-0700
Transfer Agents: American Stock Transfer & Trust, Brooklyn, NY

ENERSYS

Exchange	Symbol	Price	52Wk Range	Yield	P/E
NYS	ENS	$69.63 (12/29/2017)	83.96-61.45	1.01	18.97

*7 Year Price Score 105.97 *NYSE Composite Index=100 ***12 Month Price Score 88.00**

TRADING VOLUME (thousand shares)

Interim Earnings (Per Share)

Qtr.	Jun.	Sep	Dec	Mar
2014-15	0.99	1.16	1.04	0.58
2015-16	1.03	0.87	0.86	0.23
2016-17	1.02	1.04	0.82	0.76
2017-18	1.09	1.00		

Interim Dividends (Per Share)

Amt	Decl	Ex	Rec	Pay
0.175Q	02/08/2017	03/15/2017	03/17/2017	03/31/2017
0.175Q	05/04/2017	06/14/2017	06/16/2017	06/30/2017
0.175Q	08/09/2017	09/14/2017	09/15/2017	09/29/2017
0.175Q	11/08/2017	12/14/2017	12/15/2017	12/29/2017

Indicated Div: $0.70

Valuation Analysis

		Institutional Holding	
Forecast EPS	$4.57 (01/18/2018)	No of Institutions	378
Market Cap	$2.9 Billion	Shares	51,325,032
Book Value	$1.1 Billion	% Held	
Price/Book	2.58		101.81
Price/Sales	1.21		

Business Summary: Electrical Equipment (MIC: 7.3.1 SIC: 5063 NAIC: 423610)

EnerSys is a manufacturer, marketer and distributor of industrial batteries. Co. also manufactures, markets and distributes products such as battery chargers, power equipment, battery accessories, and outdoor cabinet enclosures. Additionally, Co. provides related aftermarket and customer-support services for its products. Co. has two primary product lines: reserve power, which are used for backup power for the ongoing operation of applications in telecommunications systems, uninterruptible power systems, applications for computer and computer-controlled systems, and other power applications; and motive power products, which are used to provide power for electric industrial forklifts.

Recent Developments: For the quarter ended Oct 1 2017, net income increased 0.8% to US$43.2 million from US$42.8 million in the year-earlier quarter. Revenues were US$617.3 million, up 7.2% from US$576.0 million the year before. Operating income was US$64.0 million versus US$62.9 million in the prior-year quarter, an increase of 1.7%. Direct operating expenses rose 10.3% to US$457.4 million from US$414.8 million in the comparable period the year before. Indirect operating expenses decreased 2.5% to US$95.9 million from US$98.4 million in the equivalent prior-year period.

Prospects: Our evaluation of Enersys as of Jan. 14, 2018 is the result of our systematic analysis on three basic characteristics: earnings strength, relative valuation, and recent stock price movement. The company has generated a negative trend in earnings per share over the past 5 quarters and while recent estimates for the company have remained steady, ENS has posted better than expected results. Based on operating earnings yield, the company is undervalued when compared to all of the companies in our coverage universe. Share price changes over the past year indicates that ENS will perform poorly over the near term.

Financial Data

(US$ in Thousands)	6 Mos	3 Mos	03/31/2017	03/31/2016	03/31/2015	03/31/2014	03/31/2013	03/31/2012
Earnings Per Share	3.67	3.71	3.64	2.99	3.77	3.02	3.42	2.93
Cash Flow Per Share	4.14	4.61	5.67	6.93	4.26	4.08	5.09	4.18
Tang Book Value Per Share	15.13	15.41	14.29	11.58	11.63	14.01	15.05	12.09
Dividends Per Share	0.700	0.700	0.700	0.700	0.700	0.500	...	...
Dividend Payout %	19.07	18.87	19.23	23.41	18.57	16.56	...	...
Income Statement								
Total Revenue	1,239,914	622,625	2,367,149	2,316,249	2,505,512	2,474,433	2,277,559	2,283,369
EBITDA	154,932	79,899	280,280	251,966	318,244	230,545	296,828	256,275
Depn & Amortn	26,624	13,199	45,388	47,686	49,261	49,693	47,876	48,532
Income Before Taxes	116,065	60,966	212,695	181,937	249,339	163,747	230,233	191,259
Income Taxes	24,592	12,644	54,472	50,113	67,814	16,980	65,275	47,292
Net Income	91,423	48,201	160,214	136,150	181,188	150,328	166,508	144,003
Average Shares	43,327	44,163	44,012	45,474	48,052	49,788	48,635	49,216
Balance Sheet								
Current Assets	1,547,738	1,506,405	1,418,915	1,296,239	1,233,418	1,300,700	1,152,962	1,071,673
Total Assets	2,457,806	2,402,854	2,293,029	2,214,488	2,163,047	2,321,858	1,987,867	1,919,279
Current Liabilities	451,800	467,064	467,431	451,171	433,371	581,403	467,559	460,301
Long-Term Obligations	728,607	634,206	587,705	606,398	495,973	288,132	155,476	237,110
Total Liabilities	1,322,759	1,240,060	1,189,573	1,201,357	1,122,817	1,065,843	818,466	887,084
Stockholders' Equity	1,135,047	1,162,794	1,103,456	1,013,131	1,040,230	1,256,015	1,169,401	1,032,195
Shares Outstanding	42,124	43,401	43,447	43,189	44,068	46,942	47,840	47,800
Statistical Record								
Return on Assets %	6.84	7.11	7.11	6.20	8.08	6.98	8.52	7.66
Return on Equity %	14.64	14.98	15.14	13.22	15.78	12.40	15.13	14.31
EBITDA Margin %	12.50	12.83	11.84	10.88	12.70	9.32	13.03	11.22
Net Margin %	7.37	7.74	6.77	5.88	7.23	6.08	7.31	6.31
Asset Turnover	1.03	1.04	1.05	1.06	1.12	1.15	1.17	1.22
Current Ratio	3.43	3.23	3.04	2.87	2.85	2.24	2.47	2.33
Debt to Equity	0.64	0.55	0.53	0.60	0.48	0.23	0.13	0.23
Price Range	83.96-61.45	83.96-59.51	82.71-52.44	72.75-43.39	71.81-51.83	73.87-42.78	45.58-30.16	40.01-17.91
P/E Ratio	22.88-16.74	22.63-16.04	22.72-14.41	24.33-14.51	19.05-13.75	24.46-14.17	13.33-8.82	13.66-6.11
Average Yield %	0.94	0.94	1.01	1.17	1.11	0.84	...	...

Address: 2366 Bernville Road, Reading, PA 19605 Telephone: 610-208-1991	Web Site: www.enersys.com Officers: David M. Shaffer - President, Chief Executive Officer Todd M. Sechrist - Executive Vice President, Chief Operating Officer, Region Officer	Auditors: Ernst & Young LLP Investor Contact: 610-236-4040 Transfer Agents: Computershare

ENSCO PLC

Exchange	Symbol	Price	52Wk Range	Yield	P/E
NYS	ESV	$5.91 (12/29/2017)	11.81-4.16	0.68	N/A

*7 Year Price Score 15.44 *NYSE Composite Index=100 *12 Month Price Score 75.58

Interim Earnings (Per Share)

Qtr.	Mar	Jun	Sep	Dec
2014	1.25	(5.07)	1.83	(14.91)
2015	1.38	1.11	1.34	(10.61)
2016	0.74	2.04	0.28	0.06
2017	(0.09)	(0.15)	(0.08)	...

Interim Dividends (Per Share)

Amt	Decl	Ex	Rec	Pay
0.01Q	02/21/2017	03/02/2017	03/06/2017	03/17/2017
0.01Q	05/22/2017	06/01/2017	06/05/2017	06/16/2017
0.01Q	08/29/2017	09/08/2017	09/11/2017	09/22/2017
0.01Q	11/07/2017	12/01/2017	12/04/2017	12/15/2017

Indicated Div: $0.04

Valuation Analysis | **Institutional Holding**

Forecast EPS	N/A	No of Institutions	568
Market Cap	$1.8 Billion	Shares	
Book Value	$8.2 Billion		394,421,248
Price/Book	0.22	% Held	
Price/Sales	0.95	N/A	

TRADING VOLUME (thousand shares)

Business Summary: Equipment & Services (MIC: 9.1.3 SIC: 1381 NAIC: 213111)

Ensco is an offshore contract drilling company engaged in providing offshore contract drilling services to the international oil and gas industry. As of Dec 31 2016, Co. owned and operated an offshore drilling rig fleet of 57 rigs. Co.'s rig fleet includes eight drillships, 10 semisubmersible rigs, three moored semisubmersible rigs and 38 jackup rigs, including rigs under construction. Co.'s business consists of three operating segments: floaters, which includes its drillships and semisubmersible rigs; jackups; and other, which consists of management services on rigs owned by third-parties. Co.'s two reportable segments, floaters and jackups, provide one service, contract drilling.

Recent Developments: For the quarter ended Sep 30 2017, loss from continuing operations was US$28.0 million compared with income of US$88.0 million in the year-earlier quarter. Net loss amounted to US$28.2 million versus net income of US$87.3 million in the year-earlier quarter. Revenues were US$460.2 million, down 16.1% from US$548.2 million the year before. Operating income was US$35.8 million versus US$115.4 million in the prior-year quarter, a decrease of 69.0%. Direct operating expenses declined 4.1% to US$285.8 million from US$298.1 million in the comparable period the year before. Indirect operating expenses increased 2.9% to US$138.6 million from US$134.7 million in the equivalent prior-year period.

Prospects: Our evaluation of Ensco PLC as of July 26, 2015 is the result of our systematic analysis on three basic characteristics: earnings strength, relative valuation, and recent stock price movement. The company has suffered a very negative trend in earnings per share over the past 5 quarters. However, while recent estimates for the company have been mixed, ESV has posted better than expected results. Based on operating earnings yield, the company is undervalued when compared to all of the companies in our coverage universe. Share price changes over the past year indicates that ESV will perform well over the near term.

Financial Data

(US$ in Thousands)	9 Mos	6 Mos	3 Mos	12/31/2016	12/31/2015	12/31/2014	12/31/2013	12/31/2012
Earnings Per Share	(0.26)	0.10	2.29	3.13	(6.88)	(16.88)	6.07	5.04
Cash Flow Per Share	1.00	1.35	3.16	3.85	7.31	8.89	8.58	9.56
Tang Book Value Per Share	26.86	26.93	27.08	27.23	27.65	33.68	40.39	36.26
Dividends Per Share	0.040	0.040	0.040	0.040	0.600	3.000	2.250	1.500
Dividend Payout %	...	40.00	1.75	1.28	..	...	37.07	29.76
Income Statement								
Total Revenue	1,388,800	928,600	471,100	2,776,400	4,063,400	4,564,500	4,919,800	4,300,700
EBITDA	431,400	289,400	157,300	1,657,800	(692,300)	(1,862,500)	2,412,600	2,126,000
Depn & Amortn	316,600	210,600	105,800	445,300	572,500	537,900	611,900	558,600
Income Before Taxes	(29,900)	(25,300)	100	997,500	(1,471,200)	(2,548,800)	1,658,500	1,466,600
Income Taxes	66,800	43,400	24,100	108,500	(13,900)	140,500	225,600	244,400
Net Income	(96,600)	(71,200)	(25,700)	890,200	(1,594,800)	(3,902,600)	1,418,200	1,169,700
Average Shares	301,200	300,900	300,600	279,100	232,200	231,600	231,100	229,700
Balance Sheet								
Current Assets	2,461,500	2,531,800	2,713,600	3,279,300	2,285,100	2,934,800	1,535,200	1,723,900
Total Assets	13,682,900	13,723,900	13,972,300	14,374,500	13,637,000	16,059,900	19,472,900	18,565,300
Current Liabilities	488,700	503,000	546,100	854,400	775,500	1,104,600	1,047,300	989,700
Long-Term Obligations	4,747,700	4,744,700	4,905,900	4,942,600	5,895,100	5,885,600	4,718,900	4,798,400
Total Liabilities	5,517,700	5,539,300	5,751,100	6,123,900	7,124,100	7,844,900	6,681,300	6,718,900
Stockholders' Equity	8,165,200	8,184,600	8,221,200	8,250,600	6,512,900	8,215,000	12,791,600	11,846,400
Shares Outstanding	303,950	303,950	303,550	303,050	235,350	234,250	233,550	232,450
Statistical Record								
Return on Assets %	N.M.	0.39	5.00	6.34	N.M.	N.M.	7.46	6.40
Return on Equity %	N.M.	0.66	9.24	12.03	N.M.	N.M.	11.51	10.27
EBITDA Margin %	31.06	31.17	33.39	59.71	N.M.	N.M.	49.04	49.43
Net Margin %	N.M.	N.M.	N.M.	32.06	N.M.	N.M.	28.83	27.20
Asset Turnover	0.14	0.14	0.18	0.20	0.27	0.26	0.26	0.24
Current Ratio	5.04	5.03	4.97	3.84	2.95	2.66	1.47	1.74
Debt to Equity	0.58	0.58	0.60	0.60	0.91	0.72	0.37	0.41
Price Range	11.81-4.16	11.81-5.07	11.96-6.64	15.89-6.64	31.93-13.53	57.33-26.41	65.45-51.73	60.33-42.21
P/E Ratio	...	118.10-50.70	5.22-2.90	5.08-2.12	...	...	10.78-8.52	11.97-8.38
Average Yield %	0.51	0.46	0.42	0.42	2.86	...	6.34	3.83	2.80

Address: 6 Chesterfield Gardens, London, W1J5BQ Telephone: 207-659-4660	Web Site: www.enscoplc.com Officers: Robert W. Edwards - Division Officer Carl G. Trowell - President, Chief Executive Officer	Auditors: KPMG LLP Investor Contact: 713-430-4607 Transfer Agents: Computershare Trust Company, N.A.

ENTERGY CORP

Exchange	Symbol	Price	52Wk Range	Yield	P/E
NYS	ETR	$81.39 (12/29/2017)	87.42-70.44	4.37	N/A

*7 Year Price Score 84.83   ***NYSE Composite Index=100**   ***12 Month Price Score 102.21**

Interim Earnings (Per Share)

Qtr.	Mar	Jun	Sep	Dec
2014	2.24	1.05	1.27	0.66
2015	1.65	0.83	(4.04)	0.55
2016	1.28	3.16	2.16	(9.86)
2017	0.46	2.27	2.21	...

Interim Dividends (Per Share)

Amt	Decl	Ex	Rec	Pay
0.87Q	01/27/2017	02/07/2017	02/09/2017	03/01/2017
0.87Q	04/05/2017	05/09/2017	05/11/2017	06/01/2017
0.87Q	07/28/2017	08/08/2017	08/10/2017	09/01/2017
0.89Q	10/27/2017	11/08/2017	11/09/2017	12/01/2017

Indicated Div: $3.56

Valuation Analysis   **Institutional Holding**

Forecast EPS	$6.90 (01/18/2018)	No of Institutions	827
Market Cap	$14.6 Billion	Shares	179,099,808
Book Value	$8.9 Billion	% Held	84.14
Price/Book	1.64		
Price/Sales	1.32		

TRADING VOLUME (thousand shares)

Business Summary: Electric Utilities (MIC: 3.1.1 SIC: 4911 NAIC: 221122)

Entergy is engaged in electric power production and retail electric distribution operations. Co. operates through two business segments: Utility, which generates, transmits, distributes and sells electric power to retail and wholesale customers in Arkansas, Louisiana, Mississippi, and Texas, as well as provides natural gas utility services to customers in and around Baton Rouge, LA, and New Orleans, LA; and Entergy Wholesale Commodities, which includes theownership, operation, and decommissioning of nuclear power plants located in the northern U.S. and the sale of the electric power produced by its operating plants.

Recent Developments: For the quarter ended Sep 30 2017, net income increased 2.1% to US$401.6 million from US$393.2 million in the year-earlier quarter. Revenues were US$3.24 billion, up 3.8% from US$3.12 billion the year before. Operating income was US$729.5 million versus US$772.1 million in the prior-year quarter, a decrease of 5.5%. Direct operating expenses rose 8.3% to US$1.87 billion from US$1.73 billion in the comparable period the year before. Indirect operating expenses increased 3.0% to US$645.3 million from US$626.7 million in the equivalent prior-year period.

Prospects: Our evaluation of Entergy Corp. as of Jan. 14, 2018 is the result of our systematic analysis on three basic characteristics: earnings strength, relative valuation, and recent stock price movement. The company has enjoyed a very positive trend in earnings per share over the past 5 quarters and while recent estimates for the company have been mixed, ETR has posted better than expected results. Based on operating earnings yield, the company is undervalued when compared to all of the companies in our coverage universe. Share price changes over the past year indicates that ETR will perform very well over the near term.

Financial Data

(US$ in Thousands)	9 Mos	6 Mos	3 Mos	12/31/2016	12/31/2015	12/31/2014	12/31/2013	12/31/2012
Earnings Per Share	(4.92)	(4.97)	(4.08)	(3.26)	(0.99)	5.22	3.99	4.76
Cash Flow Per Share	13.69	14.30	16.70	16.72	18.37	21.67	17.90	16.54
Tang Book Value Per Share	47.41	45.66	43.93	44.15	51.56	54.91	53.07	50.65
Dividends Per Share	3.480	3.460	3.440	3.420	3.340	3.320	3.320	3.320
Dividend Payout %	...	...	...	...	...	63.60	83.21	69.75
Income Statement								
Total Revenue	8,450,636	5,207,008	2,588,458	10,845,645	11,513,251	12,494,921	11,390,947	10,302,079
EBITDA	2,671,896	1,400,996	730,685	1,262,772	1,773,982	4,157,567	3,373,366	3,112,375
Depn & Amortn	1,561,565	1,042,671	531,373	2,123,291	2,117,236	2,127,892	2,012,076	1,771,649
Income Before Taxes	813,509	170,070	93,814	(1,381,762)	(799,661)	1,549,854	956,553	899,218
Income Taxes	(87,555)	(329,350)	7,763	(817,259)	(642,927)	589,597	225,981	30,855
Net Income	901,064	492,528	82,605	(564,503)	(156,734)	960,257	730,572	868,363
Average Shares	180,464	180,234	179,842	178,885	179,176	180,296	178,570	177,737
Balance Sheet								
Current Assets	3,471,231	3,599,344	3,397,491	3,684,268	4,067,412	4,389,633	3,929,691	3,683,126
Total Assets	46,398,442	46,007,037	45,318,206	45,904,434	44,647,681	46,527,854	43,406,446	43,202,502
Current Liabilities	4,460,871	4,240,530	3,879,043	3,200,096	3,089,958	3,848,891	4,060,572	4,106,321
Long-Term Obligations	14,000,305	14,330,938	13,950,777	14,492,237	13,138,557	12,529,819	12,171,367	11,954,859
Total Liabilities	37,505,020	37,432,996	37,057,832	37,619,440	35,072,705	36,215,369	33,469,220	33,724,902
Stockholders' Equity	8,893,422	8,574,041	8,260,374	8,284,994	9,574,976	10,312,485	9,937,226	9,477,600
Shares Outstanding	179,625	179,519	179,433	179,129	178,389	179,240	178,370	177,807
Statistical Record								
Return on Assets %	N.M.	N.M.	N.M.	N.M.	N.M.	2.14	1.69	2.06
Return on Equity %	N.M.	N.M.	N.M.	N.M.	N.M.	9.48	7.53	9.25
EBITDA Margin %	31.62	26.91	28.23	11.64	15.41	33.27	29.61	30.21
Net Margin %	10.66	9.46	3.19	N.M.	N.M.	7.69	6.41	8.43
Asset Turnover	0.24	0.24	0.24	0.24	0.25	0.28	0.26	0.24
Current Ratio	0.78	0.85	0.88	1.15	1.32	1.14	0.97	0.90
Debt to Equity	1.57	1.67	1.69	1.75	1.37	1.22	1.22	1.26
Price Range	80.45-67.41	82.03-67.41	82.03-67.41	82.03-66.56	89.90-61.53	91.16-60.52	72.35-60.85	73.06-62.04
P/E Ratio	...	...	...	...	...	17.46-11.59	18.13-15.25	15.35-13.03
Average Yield %	4.64	4.58	4.56	4.55	4.58	4.47	5.06	4.91

Address: 639 Loyola Avenue, New Orleans, LA 70113
Telephone: 504-576-4000

Web Site: www.entergy.com
Officers: Leo P. Denault - Chairman, Chief Executive Officer, Executive Vice President, Chief Financial Officer Paul D. Hinnenkamp - Senior Vice President, Chief Operating Officer

Auditors: Deloitte & Touche LLP
Investor Contact: 504-576-4879
Transfer Agents: Wells Fargo Shareowner Services, St. Paul, MN

ENTERPRISE PRODUCTS PARTNERS L.P.

Exchange	Symbol	Price	52Wk Range	Yield	P/E	Div Achiever
NYS	EPD	$26.51 (12/29/2017)	29.86-23.89	6.41	21.21	18 Years

*7 Year Price Score 74.55   *NYSE Composite Index=100   *12 Month Price Score 88.16

TRADING VOLUME (thousand shares)

Interim Earnings (Per Share)

Qtr.	Mar	Jun	Sep	Dec
2014	0.42	0.34	0.37	0.34
2015	0.32	0.28	0.32	0.34
2016	0.32	0.27	0.30	0.31
2017	0.36	0.30	0.28	...

Interim Dividends (Per Share)

Amt	Decl	Ex	Rec	Pay
0.415Q	04/05/2017	04/26/2017	04/28/2017	05/08/2017
0.42Q	07/05/2017	07/27/2017	07/31/2017	08/07/2017
0.422Q	10/12/2017	10/30/2017	10/31/2017	11/07/2017
0.425Q	01/12/2018	01/30/2018	01/31/2018	02/07/2018

Indicated Div: $1.70 (Div. Reinv. Plan)

Valuation Analysis / Institutional Holding

Valuation Analysis		Institutional Holding	
Forecast EPS	$1.29	No of Institutions	
	(01/18/2018)	1196	
Market Cap	$57.1 Billion	Shares	
Book Value	N/A	893,246,656	
Price/Book	N/A	% Held	
Price/Sales	2.09	32.35	

Business Summary: Equipment & Services (MIC: 9.1.3 SIC: 4922 NAIC: 486210)

Enterprise Products Partners provides midstream energy services to producers and consumers of natural gas, natural gas liquids (NGLs), crude oil, petrochemicals and refined products. Co.'s midstream energy operations include: natural gas gathering, treating, processing, transportation and storage; NGL transportation, fractionation, storage, and export and import terminals (including liquefied petroleum gases, and ethane); crude oil gathering, transportation, storage and terminals; petrochemical and refined products transportation, storage and terminals, and related services; and a marine transportation business that operates on the U.S. inland and Intracoastal Waterway systems.

Recent Developments: For the quarter ended Sep 30 2017, net income decreased 3.4% to US$621.3 million from US$643.1 million in the year-earlier quarter. Revenues were US$6.89 billion, up 16.3% from US$5.92 billion the year before. Operating income was US$879.2 million versus US$905.0 million in the prior-year quarter, a decrease of 2.9%. Direct operating expenses rose 20.0% to US$6.08 billion from US$5.07 billion in the comparable period the year before. Indirect operating income amounted to US$72.1 million compared with an income of US$50.3 million in the equivalent prior-year period.

Prospects: Our evaluation of Enterprise Products Partners L.P. as of Jan. 14, 2018 is the result of our systematic analysis on three basic characteristics: earnings strength, relative valuation, and recent stock price movement. The company has managed to produce a neutral trend in earnings per share over the past 5 quarters and while recent estimates for the company have been mixed, EPD has posted results that fell short of analysts expectations. Based on operating earnings yield, the company is undervalued when compared to all of the companies in our coverage universe. Share price changes over the past year indicates that EPD will perform very poorly over the near term.

Financial Data
(US$ in Thousands)

	9 Mos	6 Mos	3 Mos	12/31/2016	12/31/2015	12/31/2014	12/31/2013	12/31/2012
Earnings Per Share	1.25	1.27	1.24	1.20	1.26	1.47	1.41	1.36
Cash Flow Per Share	1.97	2.12	1.90	1.95	2.04	2.25	2.16	1.67
Dividends Per Share	1.650	1.630	1.610	1.590	1.510	1.430	1.350	1.266
Dividend Payout %	132.00	128.35	129.84	132.50	119.84	97.28	95.74	93.45
Income Statement								
Total Revenue	20,814,900	13,928,000	7,320,400	23,022,300	27,027,900	47,951,200	47,727,000	42,583,100
EBITDA	3,468,300	2,383,600	1,249,000	4,412,700	4,305,700	4,630,900	4,311,300	4,018,000
Depn & Amortn	966,100	638,600	317,500	1,215,700	1,161,600	1,114,100	1,012,400	900,500
Income Before Taxes	1,763,200	1,249,900	682,200	2,214,400	2,182,300	2,597,100	2,497,300	2,346,500
Income Taxes	20,100	14,700	6,000	23,400	(2,500)	23,100	57,500	(17,200)
Net Income	2,025,300	1,414,400	760,700	2,513,100	2,521,200	2,787,400	2,596,900	2,419,900
Average Shares	2,160,600	2,154,300	2,134,900	2,089,100	1,998,600	1,895,200	1,842,600	1,786,400
Balance Sheet								
Current Assets	6,031,100	4,784,500	5,641,500	6,528,200	4,313,000	5,490,700	7,023,400	5,843,100
Total Assets	53,300,600	51,313,300	51,529,500	52,194,000	48,952,000	47,100,700	40,138,700	35,934,400
Current Liabilities	8,438,700	7,818,600	7,048,000	8,250,500	7,166,600	7,873,700	8,238,700	7,755,700
Long-Term Obligations	21,710,900	20,026,500	21,123,000	21,120,900	20,826,700	19,157,400	16,226,500	14,655,200
Total Liabilities	30,970,000	28,653,200	28,950,200	30,147,000	28,656,900	29,037,500	24,923,900	22,746,700
Shares Outstanding	2,152,703	2,148,036	2,136,371	2,117,588	2,012,553	1,937,324	1,871,370	1,806,667
Statistical Record								
Return on Assets %	5.13	5.27	5.16	4.96	5.25	6.39	6.83	6.89
EBITDA Margin %	16.66	17.11	17.06	19.17	15.93	9.66	9.03	9.44
Net Margin %	9.73	10.16	10.39	10.92	9.33	5.81	5.44	5.68
Asset Turnover	0.52	0.51	0.50	0.45	0.56	1.10	1.25	1.21
Current Ratio	0.71	0.61	0.80	0.79	0.60	0.70	0.85	0.75
Price Range	29.86-24.53	29.93-24.53	29.93-23.86	29.93-19.79	36.83-21.86	41.11-31.84	33.15-25.04	27.44-23.11
P/E Ratio	23.89-19.62	23.57-19.31	24.14-19.24	24.94-16.49	29.23-17.35	27.97-21.66	23.51-17.76	20.18-17.00
Average Yield %	6.14	6.00	5.94	6.12	5.04	3.91	4.50	4.94

Address: 1100 Louisiana Street, 10th Floor, Houston, TX 77002	**Web Site:** www.enterpriseproducts.com
Telephone: 713-381-6500	**Officers:** Randa Duncan Williams - Chairman Richard H. Bachmann - Vice-Chairman

Auditors: Deloitte & Touche LLP
Investor Contact: 866-230-0745
Transfer Agents: Wells Fargo Shareowner Services, South St. Paul, MN

ENVISION HEALTHCARE CORP

Exchange	Symbol	Price	52Wk Range	Yield	P/E
NYS	EVHC	$34.56 (12/29/2017)	72.48-24.79	N/A	N/A

*7 Year Price Score N/A   *NYSE Composite Index=100   *12 Month Price Score 54.05

TRADING VOLUME (thousand shares)

Interim Earnings (Per Share)

Qtr.	Mar	Jun	Sep	Dec
2016	0.53	0.80	0.69	(2.50)
2017	(3.84)	0.45	0.23	...

Interim Dividends (Per Share)

No Dividends Paid

Valuation Analysis   **Institutional Holding**

Forecast EPS	$2.73	No of Institutions	
	(01/17/2018)	N/A	
Market Cap	$4.2 Billion	Shares	
Book Value	$6.4 Billion	N/A	
Price/Book	0.65	% Held	
Price/Sales	0.58	N/A	

Business Summary: Hospitals & Health Care Facilities (MIC: 4.2.1 SIC: 8011 NAIC: 621399)

Envision Healthcare is a provider of healthcare services. Co. has three reportable segments: physician services, which include Co.'s hospital-based and non-hospital-based physician services businesses; medical transportation, which include Co.'s community-based medical transportation services, including emergency (911), non-emergency, managed transportation, air ambulance and disaster response services; and ambulatory services, which include Co.'s ambulatory surgery business, which acquires, develops, owns and operates ambulatory surgery centers and surgical hospitals in partnership with physicians and health systems.

Recent Developments: For the quarter ended Sep 30 2017, income from continuing operations decreased 4.4% to US$91.4 million from US$95.6 million in the year-earlier quarter. Net income decreased 17.4% to US$79.0 million from US$95.6 million in the year-earlier quarter. Revenues were US$1.99 billion, up 142.1% from US$822.2 million the year before. Operating income was US$178.9 million versus US$158.1 million in the prior-year quarter, an increase of 13.2%. Indirect operating expenses increased 172.8% to US$1.81 billion from US$664.1 million in the equivalent prior-year period.

Prospects: Our evaluation of Envision Healthcare Corp. as of Jan. 14, 2018 is the result of our systematic analysis on three basic characteristics: earnings strength, relative valuation, and recent stock price movement. The company has generated a negative trend in earnings per share over the past 5 quarters. However, while recent estimates for the company have been mixed, EVHC has posted results that fell short of analysts expectations. Based on operating earnings yield, the company is undervalued when compared to all of the companies in our coverage universe. Share price changes over the past year indicates that EVHC will perform very poorly over the near term.

Financial Data (US$ in Thousands)	9 Mos	6 Mos	3 Mos	12/31/2016	12/31/2015	12/31/2014	12/31/2013
Earnings Per Share	0.23	0.45	(3.84)	(0.47)	3.16	0.66	0.04
Cash Flow Per Share	6.03	9.63	3.41	7.10	11.19	1.51	0.36
Income Statement							
Total Revenue	1,990,700	1,947,000	1,878,600	3,696,000	2,566,900	4,397,644	3,728,312
EBITDA	291,900	300,500	261,800	371,100	626,700	474,109	354,675
Depn & Amortn	117,000	110,500	109,700	47,800	25,400	155,629	158,588
Income Before Taxes	113,500	133,900	99,700	180,900	479,800	209,110	10,178
Income Taxes	27,100	35,600	17,500	(900)	113,800	89,498	(994)
Net Income	28,300	56,300	(445,200)	(18,600)	163,000	125,508	5,995
Average Shares	122,700	119,581	119,475	59,002	51,612	189,921	156,962
Balance Sheet							
Current Assets	5,222,900	5,070,400	4,825,200	2,411,300	537,700	1,363,239	...
Total Assets	17,591,900	17,588,400	16,691,400	16,708,900	6,499,300	4,703,753	...
Current Liabilities	1,733,300	1,791,500	1,546,500	1,154,300	385,900	576,868	...
Long-Term Obligations	6,270,700	6,276,400	5,785,900	5,791,600	2,358,000	2,025,877	...
Total Liabilities	11,200,700	11,235,000	10,400,400	9,977,800	4,205,900	2,943,176	...
Stockholders' Equity	6,391,200	6,353,400	6,291,000	6,731,100	2,293,400	1,760,577	...
Shares Outstanding	120,889	118,560	117,520	117,478	54,294	183,679	...
Statistical Record							
Return on Assets %	0.64	1.32	N.M.	N.M.	2.91	...	...
Return on Equity %	1.76	3.57	N.M.	N.M.	8.04	...	...
EBITDA Margin %	14.66	15.43	13.94	10.04	24.41	10.78	9.51
Net Margin %	1.42	2.89	N.M.	N.M.	6.35	2.85	0.16
Asset Turnover	0.45	0.46	0.46	0.32	0.46	...	...
Current Ratio	3.01	2.83	3.12	2.09	1.39	2.36	...
Debt to Equity	0.98	0.99	0.92	0.86	1.03	1.15	...
Price Range	72.48-42.80	72.48-54.54	72.48-61.32	71.75-63.29	...	...	...
P/E Ratio	315.13-186.09	161.07-121.20	...	...	...	...	...

Address: 1A Burton Hills Boulevard, Nashville, TN 37215 Telephone: 615-665-1283	Web Site: www.evhc.net Officers: William A. Sanger - Executive Chairman Christopher A. Holden - President, Chief Executive Officer	Auditors: Deloitte & Touche LLP Transfer Agents: American Stock Transfer & Trust, Brooklyn, NY

EOG RESOURCES, INC.

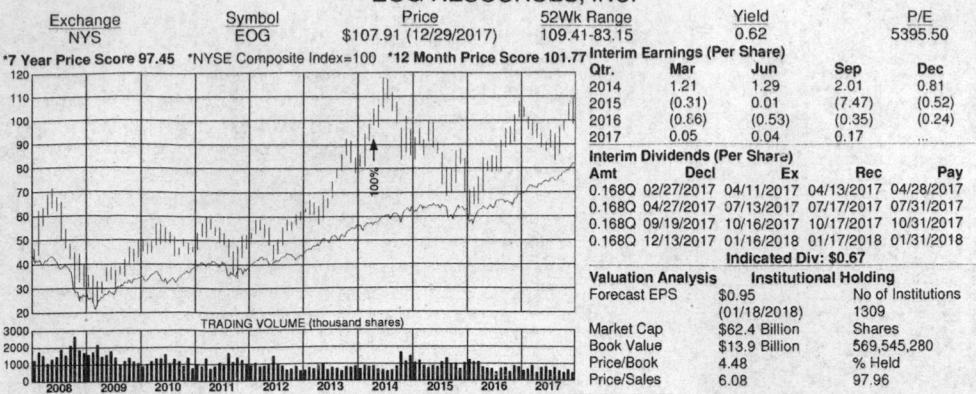

Exchange	Symbol	Price	52Wk Range
NYS	EOG	$107.91 (12/29/2017)	109.41-83.15

Yield	P/E
0.62	5395.50

*7 Year Price Score 97.45 *NYSE Composite Index=100 *12 Month Price Score 101.77

Interim Earnings (Per Share)

Qtr.	Mar	Jun	Sep	Dec
2014	1.21	1.29	2.01	0.81
2015	(0.31)	0.01	(7.47)	(0.52)
2016	(0.66)	(0.53)	(0.35)	(0.24)
2017	0.05	0.04	0.17	

Interim Dividends (Per Share)

Amt	Decl	Ex	Rec	Pay
0.168Q	02/27/2017	04/11/2017	04/13/2017	04/28/2017
0.168Q	04/27/2017	07/13/2017	07/17/2017	07/31/2017
0.168Q	09/19/2017	10/16/2017	10/17/2017	10/31/2017
0.168Q	12/13/2017	01/16/2018	01/17/2018	01/31/2018

Indicated Div: $0.67

Valuation Analysis

		Institutional Holding	
Forecast EPS	$0.95	No of Institutions	
	(01/18/2018)	1309	
Market Cap	$62.4 Billion	Shares	
Book Value	$13.9 Billion	569,545,280	
Price/Book	4.48	% Held	
Price/Sales	6.08	97.96	

Business Summary: Production & Extraction (MIC: 9.1.1 SIC: 1311 NAIC: 211111)

EOG Resources, together with its subsidiaries, explores for, develops, produces and markets crude oil and natural gas primarily in producing basins in the U.S., The Republic of Trinidad and Tobago, the U.K., The People's Republic of China, Canada and, from time to time, select other international areas. As of Dec 31 2016, Co.'s total estimated net proved reserves were 2.15 billion barrels of oil equivalent, of which 1,178.0 million barrels (MMBbl) were crude oil and condensate reserves, 416.0 MMBbl were natural gas liquids reserves and 3,318.00 billion cubic feet, or 553.0 million barrels of oil equivalent were natural gas reserves.

Recent Developments: For the quarter ended Sep 30 2017, net income amounted to US$100.5 million versus a net loss of US$190.0 million in the year-earlier quarter. Revenues were US$2.64 billion, up 24.8% from US$2.12 billion the year before. Operating income was US$214.8 million versus a loss of US$193.5 million in the prior-year quarter. Direct operating expenses declined 0.4% to US$468.1 million from US$470.2 million in the comparable period the year before. Indirect operating expenses increased 6.5% to US$1.96 billion from US$1.84 billion in the equivalent prior-year period.

Prospects: Our evaluation of EOG Resources Inc. as of Jan. 14, 2018 is the result of our systematic analysis on three basic characteristics: earnings strength, relative valuation, and recent stock price movement. The company has generated a negative trend in earnings per share over the past 5 quarters and while recent estimates for the company have been raised by analysts, EOG has posted better than expected results. Based on operating earnings yield, the company is overvalued when compared to all of the companies in our coverage universe. Share price changes over the past year indicates that EOG will perform very poorly over the near term.

Financial Data

(US$ in Thousands)	9 Mos	6 Mos	3 Mos	12/31/2016	12/31/2015	12/31/2014	12/31/2013	12/31/2012
Earnings Per Share	0.02	(0.50)	(1.07)	(1.98)	(8.29)	5.32	4.02	1.05
Cash Flow Per Share	6.51	6.16	5.17	4.25	6.59	15.92	13.56	9.76
Tang Book Value Per Share	24.06	24.08	24.13	24.24	23.54	32.30	28.23	24.45
Dividends Per Share	0.670	0.670	0.670	0.670	0.670	0.511	0.366	0.335
Dividend Payout %	3,350.00	...	...	...	...	9.61	9.11	31.75
Income Statement								
Total Revenue	7,867,881	5,223,037	2,610,565	7,650,632	8,757,428	18,035,340	14,487,118	11,682,636
EBITDA	2,986,481	1,925,197	926,933	2,277,593	(3,370,519)	9,193,814	7,273,322	4,663,995
Depn & Amortn	2,527,642	1,681,420	816,036	3,553,417	3,313,644	3,997,041	3,600,976	3,169,703
Income Before Taxes	247,829	101,849	39,382	(1,557,505)	(6,921,556)	4,995,315	3,436,886	1,280,740
Income Taxes	95,718	50,279	10,865	(460,819)	(2,397,041)	2,079,828	1,239,777	710,461
Net Income	152,111	51,570	28,517	(1,096,686)	(4,524,515)	2,915,487	2,197,109	570,279
Average Shares	578,736	578,483	578,593	553,384	545,697	548,539	546,228	541,524
Balance Sheet								
Current Assets	2,763,963	3,383,373	3,394,076	3,554,603	2,592,244	5,416,021	4,072,015	3,589,884
Total Assets	28,805,305	29,263,617	29,211,974	29,459,433	26,975,244	34,762,687	30,574,238	27,336,578
Current Liabilities	2,180,024	2,722,254	2,032,007	2,027,291	1,819,287	3,384,308	2,861,716	2,924,058
Long-Term Obligations	6,380,427	6,380,350	6,980,008	6,979,779	6,653,685	5,903,354	5,906,642	5,905,602
Total Liabilities	14,883,041	15,361,902	15,283,743	15,477,852	14,032,209	17,050,105	15,155,779	14,051,814
Stockholders' Equity	13,922,264	13,901,715	13,928,231	13,981,581	12,943,035	17,712,582	15,418,459	13,284,764
Shares Outstanding	578,570	577,395	577,258	576,700	549,858	548,294	546,171	543,264
Statistical Record								
Return on Assets %	0.04	N.M.	N.M.	N.M.	N.M.	8.92	7.59	2.18
Return on Equity %	0.08	N.M.	N.M.	N.M.	N.M.	17.60	15.31	4.39
EBITDA Margin %	37.96	36.86	35.51	29.77	N.M.	50.98	50.21	39.92
Net Margin %	1.93	0.99	1.09	N.M.	N.M.	16.17	15.17	4.88
Asset Turnover	0.38	0.35	0.32	0.27	0.28	0.55	0.50	0.45
Current Ratio	1.27	1.24	1.67	1.75	1.42	1.60	1.42	1.23
Debt to Equity	0.46	0.46	0.50	0.50	0.51	0.33	0.38	0.44
Price Range	108.01-83.15	108.01-78.70	108.01-70.31	108.01-60.24	99.74-68.36	117.98-80.87	92.58-56.72	62.19-41.98
P/E Ratio	N.M.	...	...	...	...	22.18-15.20	23.03-14.11	59.22-39.98
Average Yield %	0.71	0.71	0.74	0.80	0.79	0.52	0.50	0.62

Address: 1111 Bagby, Sky Lobby 2, Houston, TX 77002	**Web Site:** www.eogresources.com	**Auditors:** Deloitte & Touche LLP	
Telephone: 713-651-7000	**Officers:** William R. Thomas - Chairman, President, Chief Executive Officer, Senior Executive Vice President Gary L. Thomas - President, Senior Executive Vice President, Chief Operating Officer	**Investor Contact:** 713-651-7000 **Transfer Agents:** Computershare Trust Company, N.A., Providence, RI	

EPR PROPERTIES

Exchange	Symbol	Price	52Wk Range	Yield	P/E
NYS	EPR	$65.46 (12/29/2017)	77.56-63.11	6.23	19.48

*7 Year Price Score 99.40   *NYSE Composite Index=100   *12 Month Price Score 88.82

Interim Earnings (Per Share)

Qtr.	Mar	Jun	Sep	Dec
2014	0.71	0.65	0.68	0.82
2015	0.64	0.75	0.76	0.78
2016	0.77	0.77	0.81	0.82
2017	0.75	1.02	0.77	...

Interim Dividends (Per Share)

Amt	Decl	Ex	Rec	Pay
0.34M	09/18/2017	09/28/2017	09/29/2017	10/16/2017
0.34M	10/16/2017	10/30/2017	10/31/2017	11/15/2017
0.34M	11/17/2017	11/29/2017	11/30/2017	12/15/2017
0.34M	12/18/2017	12/28/2017	12/29/2017	01/15/2018

Indicated Div: $4.08 (Div. Reinv. Plan)

Valuation Analysis — **Institutional Holding**

Forecast EPS	$3.50 (01/16/2018)	No of Institutions 473
Market Cap	$4.8 Billion	Shares 86,817,032
Book Value	$2.9 Billion	% Held
Price/Book	1.67	N/A
Price/Sales	8.62	

Business Summary: REITs (MIC: 5.3.1 SIC: 6798 NAIC: 525930)

EPR Properties is a real estate investment trust. Co.'s operating segments are: Entertainment, which consists of investments in megaplex theatres, entertainment retail centers, family entertainment centers and other retail parcels; Education, which consists of investments in public charter schools, early education centers and K-12 private schools; Recreation, which consists of investments in ski areas, waterparks, golf entertainment complexes and other recreation; and Other, which consists of land under ground lease, property under development and land held for development related to the Adelaar casino and resort project in Sullivan County, NY.

Recent Developments: For the quarter ended Sep 30 2017, net income increased 9.4% to US$63.0 million from US$57.5 million in the year-earlier quarter. Revenues were US$151.4 million, up 20.5% from US$125.6 million the year before. Revenues from property income rose 19.3% to US$126.6 million from US$106.1 million in the corresponding quarter a year earlier.

Prospects: Our evaluation of EPR Properties as of Jan. 14, 2018 is the result of our systematic analysis on three basic characteristics: earnings strength, relative valuation, and recent stock price movement. The company has generated a negative trend in earnings per share over the past 5 quarters. Because the company lacks sufficient analyst estimate data, we place greater weight on the historical EPS trend as the measure of earnings strength. Based on operating earnings yield, the company is undervalued when compared to all of the companies in our coverage universe. Share price changes over the past year indicates that EPR will perform very well over the near term.

Financial Data
(US$ in Thousands)

	9 Mos	6 Mos	3 Mos	12/31/2016	12/31/2015	12/31/2014	12/31/2013	12/31/2012
Earnings Per Share	3.36	3.40	3.15	3.17	2.93	2.86	3.24	1.98
Cash Flow Per Share	5.30	4.56	4.87	4.82	4.79	4.61	4.87	4.42
Tang Book Value Per Share	39.21	39.39	34.57	34.11	33.95	33.57	32.54	31.13
Dividends Per Share	4.020	3.960	3.900	3.840	3.630	3.420	3.160	3.000
Dividend Payout %	119.64	116.47	123.81	121.14	123.89	119.58	97.52	151.52
Income Statement								
Total Revenue	428,291	276,894	129,112	493,242	421,017	385,051	343,064	321,786
EBITDA	394,926	261,783	114,371	425,960	359,661	322,977	291,819	256,797
Depn & Amortn	97,738	62,295	28,801	103,900	85,900	63,000	50,700	47,300
Income Before Taxes	199,335	135,829	54,878	224,916	193,846	178,707	160,063	132,841
Income Taxes	2,016	1,429	954	553	482	4,228	(14,176)	...
Net Income	197,405	134,451	53,916	224,982	194,532	179,633	180,226	121,556
Average Shares	73,724	73,225	64,102	63,474	58,328	54,444	48,214	47,049
Balance Sheet								
Current Assets	134,948	201,607	139,236	128,018	73,962	63,690	60,210	73,393
Total Assets	6,133,010	5,938,886	5,046,782	4,865,022	4,217,270	3,702,048	3,272,276	2,946,730
Current Liabilities	256,777	244,620	190,991	193,496	161,482	130,036	108,926	118,000
Long-Term Obligations	2,987,925	2,792,920	2,616,382	2,485,625	1,981,920	1,645,523	1,475,336	1,368,832
Total Liabilities	3,244,702	3,037,540	2,807,373	2,679,121	2,143,402	1,775,936	1,584,639	1,487,209
Stockholders' Equity	2,888,308	2,901,346	2,239,409	2,185,901	2,073,868	1,926,112	1,687,637	1,459,521
Shares Outstanding	73,664	73,660	64,771	63,647	60,823	57,125	51,655	46,887
Statistical Record								
Return on Assets %	4.75	4.81	4.79	4.94	4.91	5.15	5.80	4.27
Return on Equity %	10.07	9.82	10.15	10.53	9.73	9.94	11.45	8.28
EBITDA Margin %	92.21	94.54	88.58	86.36	85.43	83.88	85.06	79.80
Net Margin %	46.09	48.56	41.76	45.61	46.21	46.65	52.53	37.78
Asset Turnover	0.10	0.10	0.11	0.11	0.11	0.11	0.11	0.11
Current Ratio	0.53	0.82	0.73	0.66	0.46	0.49	0.55	0.62
Debt to Equity	1.03	0.96	1.17	1.14	0.96	0.85	0.87	0.94
Price Range	78.74-66.63	84.46-66.63	84.46-64.28	84.46-54.09	65.58-49.57	60.80-48.60	60.70-45.93	48.11-40.40
P/E Ratio	23.43-19.83	24.84-19.60	26.81-20.41	26.64-17.06	22.38-16.92	21.26-16.99	18.73-14.18	24.30-20.40
Average Yield %	5.57	5.31	5.28	5.43	6.33	6.32	6.23	6.72

Address: 909 Walnut Street, Suite 200, Kansas City, MO 64106
Telephone: 816-472-1700
Fax: 816-472-5794

Web Site: www.eprkc.com
Officers: Robert J. Druten - Chairman Gregory K. Silvers - President, Chief Executive Officer, Executive Vice President, Vice President, Chief Operating Officer, Chief Development Officer, Secretary, General Counsel

Auditors: KPMG LLP
Transfer Agents: Computershare Trust Company, N. A., Providence, RI

EQT CORP

Exchange	Symbol	Price	52Wk Range	Yield	P/E
NYS	EQT	$56.92 (12/29/2017)	67.02-50.83	0.21	299.58

*7 Year Price Score 68.32   *NYSE Composite Index=100   *12 Month Price Score 92.11

Interim Earnings (Per Share)

Qtr.	Mar	Jun	Sep	Dec
2014	1.26	0.73	0.65	(0.09)
2015	1.14	0.04	0.27	(0.88)
2016	0.04	(1.55)	(0.05)	(1.13)
2017	0.95	0.24	0.13	...

Interim Dividends (Per Share)

Amt	Decl	Ex	Rec	Pay
0.03Q	04/19/2017	05/10/2017	05/12/2017	06/01/2017
0.03Q	07/12/2017	08/09/2017	08/11/2017	09/01/2017
0.03Q	10/11/2017	11/09/2017	11/10/2017	12/01/2017
0.03Q	01/17/2018	02/13/2018	02/14/2018	03/01/2018

Indicated Div: $0.12

TRADING VOLUME (thousand shares)

Valuation Analysis — **Institutional Holding**

Forecast EPS	$0.79	No of Institutions
	(01/18/2018)	734
Market Cap	$9.9 Billion	Shares
Book Value	$6.1 Billion	212,429,008
Price/Book	1.62	% Held
Price/Sales	3.75	N/A

Business Summary: Production & Extraction (MIC: 9.1.1 SIC: 1311 NAIC: 211111)

EQT conducts its business through three business segments: EQT Production, which includes Co.'s exploration for, and development and production of, natural gas, natural gas liquids and a limited amount of crude oil, primarily in the Appalachian Basin; EQT Gathering, which includes the natural gas gathering activities of Co., consisting of assets that are owned and operated by its subsidiary, EQT Midstream Partners, LP (EQM); and EQT Transmission, which includes the natural gas transmission and storage activities of Co., consisting of assets that are owned and operated by EQM. As of Dec 31 2016, Co. had total proved reserves of 13.51 trillion cubic feet of natural gas.

Recent Developments: For the quarter ended Sep 30 2017, net income increased 50.4% to US$105.5 million from US$70.1 million in the year-earlier quarter. Revenues were US$660.3 million, up 18.6% from US$556.7 million the year before. Operating income was US$137.7 million versus US$108.5 million in the prior-year quarter, an increase of 27.0%. Direct operating expenses rose 33.5% to US$196.5 million from US$147.1 million in the comparable period the year before. Indirect operating expenses increased 8.3% to US$326.2 million from US$301.1 million in the equivalent prior-year period.

Prospects: Our evaluation of EQT Corp. as of Jan. 14, 2018 is the result of our systematic analysis on three basic characteristics: earnings strength, relative valuation, and recent stock price movement. The company has suffered a very negative trend in earnings per share over the past 5 quarters. However, while recent estimates for the company have been lowered by analysts, EQT has posted better than expected results. Based on operating earnings yield, the company is overvalued when compared to all of the companies in our coverage universe. Share price changes over the past year indicates that EQT will perform poorly over the near term.

Financial Data

(US$ in Thousands)	9 Mos	6 Mos	3 Mos	12/31/2016	12/31/2015	12/31/2014	12/31/2013	12/31/2012
Earnings Per Share	0.19	0.01	(1.78)	(2.71)	0.56	2.54	2.57	1.22
Cash Flow Per Share	8.69	7.96	7.47	6.36	7.99	9.33	7.97	5.47
Tang Book Value Per Share	35.12	34.98	34.73	33.91	33.29	30.23	26.74	24.01
Dividends Per Share	0.120	0.120	0.120	0.120	0.120	0.120	0.120	0.880
Dividend Payout %	63.16	1,200.00	...	...	21.43	4.72	4.67	72.13
Income Statement								
Total Revenue	2,248,729	1,588,416	897,523	1,608,348	2,339,762	2,469,710	1,862,011	1,641,608
EBITDA	1,454,305	1,063,192	625,943	681,313	1,392,308	1,539,546	1,340,416	985,611
Depn & Amortn	719,295	472,735	231,918	927,920	819,216	679,298	676,570	499,118
Income Before Taxes	597,900	503,724	351,370	(394,527)	426,561	723,711	521,158	301,707
Income Taxes	119,093	130,374	100,665	(263,464)	104,675	214,092	175,186	105,296
Net Income	228,458	205,118	163,992	(452,983)	85,171	386,965	390,572	183,395
Average Shares	173,675	173,582	173,511	166,978	152,939	152,513	151,787	150,506
Balance Sheet								
Current Assets	858,458	996,853	1,251,953	1,828,219	2,251,019	1,904,323	1,255,425	852,845
Total Assets	15,984,648	15,724,011	15,646,614	15,472,922	13,976,172	12,064,900	9,792,053	8,849,862
Current Liabilities	1,435,259	1,355,726	894,743	804,640	795,819	833,479	523,410	570,465
Long-Term Obligations	2,691,041	2,584,957	3,082,938	3,289,459	2,793,343	2,822,889	2,490,354	2,502,969
Total Liabilities	9,896,978	9,661,835	9,627,271	9,612,641	8,898,381	7,482,085	5,757,265	5,246,042
Stockholders' Equity	6,087,670	6,062,176	6,019,343	5,860,281	5,077,791	4,582,815	4,034,788	3,603,820
Shares Outstanding	173,343	173,327	173,316	172,827	152,554	151,596	150,884	150,109
Statistical Record								
Return on Assets %	0.24	0.03	N.M.	N.M.	0.65	3.54	4.19	2.08
Return on Equity %	0.60	0.08	N.M.	N.M.	1.76	8.98	10.23	5.08
EBITDA Margin %	64.67	66.93	69.74	42.36	59.51	62.34	71.99	60.04
Net Margin %	10.16	12.91	18.27	N.M.	3.64	15.67	20.98	11.17
Asset Turnover	0.17	0.17	0.13	0.11	0.18	0.23	0.20	0.19
Current Ratio	0.60	0.74	1.40	2.27	2.83	2.28	2.40	1.50
Debt to Equity	0.44	0.43	0.51	0.56	0.55	0.62	0.62	0.69
Price Range	74.70-50.83	79.33-50.83	79.33-56.76	79.33-49.53	91.95-47.75	109.84-75.38	92.56-57.19	62.74-44.00
P/E Ratio	393.16-267.53	N.M.	...	...	164.20-85.27	43.24-29.68	36.02-22.25	51.43-36.07
Average Yield %	0.19	0.18	0.18	0.18	0.16	0.12	0.15	1.64

Address: 625 Liberty Avenue, Suite 1700, Pittsburgh, PA 15222 **Telephone:** 412-553-5700	**Web Site:** www.eqt.com **Officers:** David L. Porges - Chairman, President, Chief Executive Officer, Associate/Affiliate Company Officer Steven T. Schlotterbeck - President, Executive Vice President, Senior Vice President, Vice President, Chief Executive Officer, Division Officer	**Auditors:** Ernst & Young LLP **Investor Contact:** 412-553-7833 **Transfer Agents:** Computershare, College Station, TX

EQUIFAX INC

Exchange	Symbol	Price	52Wk Range	Yield	P/E
NYS	EFX	$117.92 (12/29/2017)	146.26-92.98	1.32	26.62

*7 Year Price Score 124.29 *NYSE Composite Index=100 *12 Month Price Score 83.92

TRADING VOLUME (thousand shares)

Interim Earnings (Per Share)

Qtr.	Mar	Jun	Sep	Dec
2014	0.69	0.75	0.75	0.80
2015	0.73	0.92	0.98	0.93
2016	0.85	1.08	1.09	1.02
2017	1.26	1.36	0.79	...

Interim Dividends (Per Share)

Amt	Decl	Ex	Rec	Pay
0.39Q	02/08/2017	03/01/2017	03/03/2017	03/15/2017
0.39Q	05/04/2017	05/23/2017	05/25/2017	06/15/2017
0.39Q	08/04/2017	08/23/2017	08/25/2017	09/15/2017
0.39Q	11/09/2017	11/22/2017	11/24/2017	12/15/2017

Indicated Div: $1.56

Valuation Analysis — **Institutional Holding**

Forecast EPS	$5.92	No of Institutions	
	(01/13/2018)	839	
Market Cap	$14.2 Billion	Shares	
Book Value	$3.1 Billion		160,846,816
Price/Book	4.56	% Held	
Price/Sales	4.26		87.07

Business Summary: Business Services (MIC: 7.5.2 SIC: 7323 NAIC: 561450)

Equifax Inc. is a provider of information solutions and human resources business process outsourcing services for businesses, governments and consumers. Co.'s products and services are based on databases of consumer and business information. Co. uses statistical techniques and software tools to analyze all available data, creating insights, decision-making solutions and processing services for its clients. Co. also provides information, technology and services to support debt collections and recovery management. Additionally, Co. provides payroll-related and human resource management business process outsourcing services in the U.S.

Recent Developments: For the quarter ended Sep 30 2017, net income decreased 25.5% to US$100.5 million from US$134.9 million in the year-earlier quarter. Revenues were US$834.8 million, up 3.8% from US$804.1 million the year before. Operating income was US$152.9 million versus US$212.1 million in the prior-year quarter, a decrease of 27.9%. Direct operating expenses rose 3.2% to US$297.3 million from US$288.0 million in the comparable period the year before. Indirect operating expenses increased 26.5% to US$384.6 million from US$304.0 million in the equivalent prior-year period.

Prospects: Our evaluation of Equifax Inc. as of Jan. 14, 2018 is the result of our systematic analysis on three basic characteristics: earnings strength, relative valuation, and recent stock price movement. The company has managed to produce a neutral trend in earnings per share over the past 5 quarters and while recent estimates for the company have been mixed, EFX has posted better than expected results. Based on operating earnings yield, the company is undervalued when compared to all of the companies in our coverage universe. Share price changes over the past year indicates that EFX will perform poorly over the near term.

Financial Data

(US$ in Thousands)	9 Mos	6 Mos	3 Mos	12/31/2016	12/31/2015	12/31/2014	12/31/2013	12/31/2012
Earnings Per Share	4.43	4.73	4.45	4.04	3.55	2.97	2.84	2.22
Cash Flow Per Share	7.33	7.03	6.74	6.65	6.25	5.08	4.67	4.13
Dividends Per Share	1.500	1.440	1.380	1.320	1.160	1.000	0.880	0.720
Dividend Payout %	33.86	30.44	31.01	32.67	32.68	33.67	30.99	32.43
Income Statement								
Total Revenue	2,523,800	1,689,000	832,200	3,144,900	2,663,600	2,436,400	2,303,900	2,160,500
EBITDA	861,100	630,600	292,000	1,089,000	900,400	847,000	790,900	659,000
Depn & Amortn	216,700	143,500	72,100	268,700	200,000	204,200	190,300	163,400
Income Before Taxes	574,300	438,300	195,700	728,200	636,600	574,200	530,400	440,200
Income Taxes	150,800	115,300	40,300	233,100	201,800	200,200	188,900	159,400
Net Income	415,000	318,700	153,300	488,800	429,100	367,400	351,800	272,100
Average Shares	121,400	121,900	121,900	121,100	120,900	123,500	123,700	122,500
Balance Sheet								
Current Assets	899,300	1,000,700	705,200	672,900	561,600	605,100	648,400	529,700
Total Assets	7,115,700	7,058,300	6,789,000	6,664,000	4,509,000	4,674,200	4,539,900	4,511,100
Current Liabilities	1,336,300	1,343,400	1,201,300	1,259,600	603,800	823,100	662,500	646,500
Long-Term Obligations	2,038,700	2,038,100	2,037,400	2,086,800	1,145,900	1,145,700	1,145,500	1,447,400
Total Liabilities	4,015,300	4,037,300	3,900,900	4,001,300	2,198,100	2,474,100	2,239,200	2,577,900
Stockholders' Equity	3,100,400	3,021,000	2,888,100	2,662,700	2,310,900	2,200,100	2,300,700	1,933,200
Shares Outstanding	120,000	120,400	120,200	119,900	118,700	119,400	121,900	120,400
Statistical Record								
Return on Assets %	7.73	8.39	7.99	8.73	9.35	7.97	7.77	6.77
Return on Equity %	18.40	20.66	20.09	19.60	19.02	16.33	16.62	14.93
EBITDA Margin %	34.12	37.34	35.09	34.63	33.80	34.76	34.33	30.50
Net Margin %	16.44	18.87	18.42	15.54	16.11	15.08	15.27	12.59
Asset Turnover	0.48	0.48	0.48	0.56	0.58	0.53	0.51	0.54
Current Ratio	0.67	0.74	0.59	0.53	0.93	0.74	0.98	0.82
Debt to Equity	0.66	0.67	0.71	0.78	0.50	0.52	0.50	0.75
Price Range	146.26-92.98	142.58-111.54	136.98-111.54	136.43-93.22	113.61-80.00	82.15-65.04	69.35-53.13	54.93-38.42
P/E Ratio	33.02-20.99	30.14-23.58	30.78-25.07	33.77-23.07	32.00-22.54	27.66-21.90	24.42-18.71	24.74-17.31
Average Yield %	1.16	1.11	1.10	1.10	1.18	1.36	1.45	1.56

Address: 1550 Peachtree Street, N.W., Atlanta, GA 30309 Telephone: 404-885-8000	Web Site: www.equifax.com Officers: Paulino do Rego Barros - Interim Chief Executive Officer, Region Officer John W. Gamble - Chief Financial Officer, Corporate Vice-President	Auditors: Ernst & Young LLP Investor Contact: 404-885-8804 Transfer Agents: American Stock Transfer & Trust Company, Brookly, NY

EQUITY COMMONWEALTH

Exchange	Symbol	Price	52Wk Range	Yield	P/E
NYS	EQC	$30.51 (12/29/2017)	32.51-29.80	N/A	69.34

*7 Year Price Score 97.01 ***NYSE Composite Index=100** ***12 Month Price Score 92.24**

Interim Earnings (Per Share)

Qtr.	Mar	Jun	Sep	Dec
2014	0.08	(0.14)	1.16	(1.33)
2015	0.05	0.04	0.18	0.29
2016	0.31	0.56	0.67	0.08
2017	0.17	(0.06)	0.25	...

Interim Dividends (Per Share)

Dividend Payment Suspended

Valuation Analysis / Institutional Holding

Forecast EPS	$0.21	No of Institutions
	(01/13/2018)	359
Market Cap	$3.8 Billion	Shares
Book Value	$3.3 Billion	153,979,632
Price/Book	1.14	% Held
Price/Sales	10.16	N/A

Business Summary: REITs (MIC: 5.3.1 SIC: 6798 NAIC: 525930)

Equity Commonwealth is an internally managed and self-advised real estate investment trust engaged in the ownership and operation primarily of office buildings. At Dec 31 2016, Co.'s portfolio included 33 properties (64 buildings).

Recent Developments: For the quarter ended Sep 30 2017, net income decreased 61.5% to US$33.2 million from US$86.4 million in the year-earlier quarter. Revenues were US$77.8 million, down 32.1% from US$114.6 million the year before. Revenues from property income fell 34.1% to US$61.1 million from US$92.7 million in the corresponding quarter a year earlier.

Prospects: Our evaluation of Equity Commonwealth as of Jan. 14, 2018 is the result of our systematic analysis on three basic characteristics: earnings strength, relative valuation, and recent stock price movement. The company has managed to produce a neutral trend in earnings per share over the past 5 quarters. Because the company lacks sufficient analyst estimate data, we place greater weight on the historical EPS trend as the measure of earnings strength. Based on operating earnings yield, the company is overvalued when compared to all of the companies in our coverage universe. Share price changes over the past year indicates that EQC will perform well over the near term.

Financial Data
(US$ in Thousands)

	9 Mos	6 Mos	3 Mos	12/31/2016	12/31/2015	12/31/2014	12/31/2013	12/31/2012
Earnings Per Share	0.44	0.86	1.48	1.62	0.56	(0.19)	(1.97)	(1.81)
Cash Flow Per Share	0.89	0.93	1.11	1.30	1.41	1.60	2.09	3 30
Tang Book Value Per Share	25.82	25.51	25.52	25.33	23.62	22.64	23.06	29.49
Dividends Per Share	...	...	...	...	...	0.250	1.000	1.750
Income Statement								
Total Revenue	268,948	191,150	99,551	500,680	714,891	861,857	885,536	1,013,092
EBITDA	150,757	91,078	62,840	410,332	349,436	119,101	336,587	476,565
Depn & Amortn	75,567	53,361	28,201	102,695	145,888	166,076	178,353	188,123
Income Before Taxes	51,790	18,231	23,997	233,639	102,221	(188,644)	(13,548)	85,626
Income Taxes	555	220	175	745	2,364	3,191	2,634	3,207
Net Income	51,217	18,005	23,814	232,894	99,857	24,012	(177,060)	(95,421)
Average Shares	125,175	124,067	125,150	126,768	129,437	125,163	112,378	83,750
Balance Sheet								
Current Assets	2,628,192	2,367,586	2,322,370	2,253,237	2,009,650	644,874	468,319	372,239
Total Assets	4,260,289	4,491,116	4,518,756	4,526,075	5,244,372	5,761,639	6,646,434	8,189,634
Current Liabilities	83,799	100,852	87,960	103,555	133,925	176,248	187,216	231,002
Long-Term Obligations	850,576	1,100,355	1,141,628	1,141,667	1,710,324	2,207,665	3,005,410	4,349,821
Total Liabilities	936,729	1,205,781	1,233,273	1,265,628	1,875,885	2,442,056	3,282,848	5,084,206
Stockholders' Equity	3,323,560	3,285,335	3,285,483	3,260,447	3,368,487	3,319,583	3,363,586	3,105,428
Shares Outstanding	124,089	124,089	124,064	123,994	126,349	129,607	118,386	83,804
Statistical Record								
Return on Assets %	1.38	2.48	4.37	4.75	1.81	0.39	N.M.	N.M.
Return on Equity %	1.92	3.60	6.30	7.01	2.99	0.72	N.M.	N.M.
EBITDA Margin %	56.05	47.65	63.12	81.95	48.88	13.82	38.01	47.04
Net Margin %	19.04	9.42	23.92	46.52	13.97	2.79	N.M.	N.M.
Asset Turnover	0.08	0.09	0.10	0.10	0.13	0.14	0.12	0.13
Current Ratio	31.36	23.48	26.40	21.76	15.01	3.66	2.50	1.61
Debt to Equity	0.26	0.33	0.35	0.35	0.51	0.67	0.89	1.40
Price Range	32.51-28.62	32.51-28.62	31.97-26.99	31.77-25.41	29.67-25.21	28.06-22.40	26.26-15.71	20.61-13.58
P/E Ratio	73.89-65.05	37.80-33.28	21.60-18.24	19.61-15.69	52.98-45.02	...	...	...
Average Yield %	...	...	...	...	...	0.96	4.53	10.25

Address: Two North Riverside Plaza, Suite 2100, Chicago, IL 60606 Telephone: 312-646-2800 Fax: 617-332-2261	Web Site: www.eqcre.com Officers: Samuel Zell - Chairman David A. Helfand - President, Chief Executive Officer, Interim Chief Financial Officer	Auditors: Ernst & Young LLP Investor Contact: 617-796-8222 Transfer Agents: Wells Fargo Bank, National Association, Mendota Heights, MN

EQUITY LIFESTYLE PROPERTIES INC

Exchange	Symbol	Price	52Wk Range	Yield	P/E	Div Achiever
NYS	ELS	$89.02 (12/29/2017)	91.71-71.35	2.19	42.59	12 Years

*7 Year Price Score 127.28 *NYSE Composite Index=100 *12 Month Price Score 101.19

Interim Earnings (Per Share)

Qtr.	Mar	Jun	Sep	Dec
2014	0.46	0.30	0.31	0.35
2015	0.32	0.38	0.43	0.41
2016	0.60	0.42	0.48	0.43
2017	0.65	0.45	0.56	...

Interim Dividends (Per Share)

Amt	Decl	Ex	Rec	Pay
0.487Q	02/21/2017	03/29/2017	03/31/2017	04/14/2017
0.487Q	05/02/2017	06/28/2017	06/30/2017	07/14/2017
0.487Q	07/25/2017	09/28/2017	09/29/2017	10/13/2017
0.487Q	11/02/2017	12/28/2017	12/29/2017	01/12/2018

Indicated Div: $1.95

Valuation Analysis   **Institutional Holding**

Forecast EPS	$2.13	No of Institutions
	(01/17/2018)	330
Market Cap	$7.8 Billion	Shares
Book Value	$951.8 Million	96,756,432
Price/Book	8.18	% Held
Price/Sales	8.57	88.28

Business Summary: REITs (MIC: 5.3.1 SIC: 6798 NAIC: 525930)

Equity Lifestyle Properties is an owner and operator of lifestyle-oriented properties (Properties) consisting of manufactured home communities and recreational vehicle (RV) resorts and campgrounds. Co. owns the land and provides its customers the opportunity to place factory built homes, cottages, cabins or RVs either permanently or on a long-term or short-term basis. Co.'s customers may lease individual developed areas (Sites) or enter right-to-use contracts which provide them access to specific Properties for limited stays. Co. was a real estate networks with a portfolio, as of Dec 31 2016, of 391 Properties consisting of 146,610 residential Sites located throughout the U.S. and Canada.

Recent Developments: For the quarter ended Sep 30 2017, net income increased 17.3% to US$54.9 million from US$46.8 million in the year-earlier quarter. Revenues were US$241.6 million, up 6.8% from US$226.2 million the year before. Revenues from property income rose 6.7% to US$235.6 million from US$220.9 million in the corresponding quarter a year earlier.

Prospects: Our evaluation of Equity Lifestyle Properties Inc. as of Jan. 14, 2018 is the result of our systematic analysis on three basic characteristics: earnings strength, relative valuation, and recent stock price movement. The company has enjoyed a very positive trend in earnings per share over the past 5 quarters. Because the company lacks sufficient analyst estimate data, we place greater weight on the historical EPS trend as the measure of earnings strength. Based on operating earnings yield, the company is about fairly valued when compared to all of the companies in our coverage universe. Share price changes over the past year indicates that ELS will perform very well over the near term.

Financial Data

(US$ in Thousands)	9 Mos	6 Mos	3 Mos	12/31/2016	12/31/2015	12/31/2014	12/31/2013	12/31/2012
Earnings Per Share	2.09	2.01	1.98	1.92	1.54	1.41	1.28	0.66
Cash Flow Per Share	4.42	4.39	4.25	4.16	4.20	3.43	3.08	2.86
Tang Book Value Per Share	10.88	10.37	10.38	10.20	9.36	9.25	9.09	8.69
Dividends Per Share	1.888	1.825	1.763	1.700	1.500	1.300	1.000	0.875
Dividend Payout %	90.31	90.80	89.02	88.54	97.40	92.20	78.13	132.58
Income Statement								
Total Revenue	695,326	453,701	232,389	870,435	821,654	776,809	728,375	709,877
EBITDA	329,176	218,620	118,477	405,078	366,852	358,057	304,235	302,661
Depn & Amortn	94,921	63,572	31,673	118,521	114,698	111,872	110,505	105,578
Income Before Taxes	159,527	105,347	61,925	184,527	146,423	133,890	75,208	72,559
Net Income	152,578	100,998	59,185	173,263	139,371	128,005	116,199	69,391
Average Shares	93,324	93,063	93,011	92,569	91,907	91,511	91,196	90,862
Balance Sheet								
Current Assets	126,679	115,993	107,487	122,235	146,586	139,440	126,668	115,929
Total Assets	3,525,847	3,485,358	3,471,041	3,478,987	3,420,061	3,446,339	3,391,639	3,398,226
Current Liabilities	329,534	331,436	311,974	305,861	281,657	255,066	236,066	204,058
Long-Term Obligations	2,181,138	2,054,511	2,059,321	2,091,279	2,145,713	2,212,246	2,192,368	2,269,866
Total Liabilities	2,574,088	2,446,650	2,433,128	2,470,444	2,494,993	2,534,346	2,498,306	2,538,978
Stockholders' Equity	951,759	1,038,708	1,037,913	1,008,543	925,068	911,993	893,333	859,248
Shares Outstanding	87,499	87,004	86,841	85,529	84,253	83,879	83,313	83,193
Statistical Record								
Return on Assets %	5.48	5.27	5.22	5.01	4.06	3.74	3.42	2.01
Return on Equity %	19.65	18.07	18.10	17.87	15.17	14.18	13.26	7.75
EBITDA Margin %	47.34	48.19	50.98	46.54	44.65	46.09	41.77	42.64
Net Margin %	21.94	22.26	25.47	19.91	16.96	16.48	15.95	9.78
Asset Turnover	0.26	0.26	0.26	0.25	0.24	0.23	0.21	0.21
Current Ratio	0.38	0.35	0.34	0.40	0.52	0.55	0.54	0.57
Debt to Equity	2.29	1.98	1.98	2.07	2.32	2.43	2.45	2.64
Price Range	90.41-67.05	87.18-67.05	83.16-67.05	83.16-63.80	66.81-51.55	52.42-36.13	42.77-33.48	36.49-31.91
P/E Ratio	43.26-32.08	43.37-33.36	42.00-33.86	43.31-33.23	43.38-33.47	37.18-25.62	33.41-26.16	55.30-48.35
Average Yield %	2.38	2.36	2.36	2.33	2.64	2.98	2.67	2.57

Address: Two North Riverside Plaza, Suite 800, Chicago, IL 60606 Telephone: 312-279-1400	Web Site: www.equitylifestyleproperties.com Officers: Samuel Zell - Chairman Howard Walker - Co-Vice Chairman, Vice-Chairman	Auditors: Ernst & Young LLP Investor Contact: 180-024-75279 Transfer Agents: American Stock Transfer and Trust Company, LLC, New York, NY

EQUITY RESIDENTIAL

Exchange	Symbol	Price	52Wk Range	Yield	P/E
NYS	EQR	$63.77 (12/29/2017)	70.37-59.90	3.16	31.11

*7 Year Price Score 80.58 *NYSE Composite Index=100 ***12 Month Price Score 96.39**

Interim Earnings (Per Share)

Qtr.	Mar	Jun	Sep	Dec
2014	0.22	0.31	0.61	0.60
2015	0.49	0.78	0.53	0.56
2016	9.76	0.59	0.56	0.76
2017	0.39	0.53	0.37	...

Interim Dividends (Per Share)

Amt	Decl	Ex	Rec	Pay
0.504Q	03/16/2017	03/23/2017	03/27/2017	04/17/2017
0.504Q	06/15/2017	06/22/2017	06/26/2017	07/14/2017
0.504Q	09/15/2017	09/22/2017	09/25/2017	10/13/2017
0.504Q	12/19/2017	12/29/2017	01/02/2018	01/12/2018

Indicated Div: $2.02

Valuation Analysis		Institutional Holding	
Forecast EPS	$1.62	No of Institutions	
	(01/18/2018)	751	
Market Cap	$23.4 Billion	Shares	
Book Value	$10.3 Billion	450,237,856	
Price/Book	2.28	% Held	
Price/Sales	9.58	97.83	

Business Summary: REITs (MIC: 5.3.1 SIC: 6798 NAIC: 525930)

Equity Residential is a real estate investment trust focused on the acquisition, development and management of apartment properties. Co. is the general partner of, and as of Dec. 31, 2016 owned an approximate 96.2% ownership interest in ERP Operating Limited Partnership (ERPOP). All of Co.'s property ownership, development and related business operations are conducted through ERPOP and those entities/subsidiaries owned or controlled by ERPOP. As of Dec 31 2016, Co., directly or indirectly through investments in title holding entities, owned all or a portion of 302 properties located in 10 states and the District of Columbia.

Recent Developments: For the quarter ended Sep 30 2017, income from continuing operations decreased 33.6% to US$144.2 million from US$217.2 million in the year-earlier quarter. Net income decreased 33.7% to US$144.2 million from US$217.5 million in the year-earlier quarter. Revenues were US$624.1 million, up 3.0% from US$606.1 million the year before.

Prospects: Our evaluation of Equity Residential Properties Trust as of Jan. 14, 2018 is the result of our systematic analysis on three basic characteristics: earnings strength, relative valuation, and recent stock price movement. The company has produced a positive trend in earnings per share over the past 5 quarters and while recent estimates for the company have been mixed, EQR has posted better than expected results. Based on operating earnings yield, the company is overvalued when compared to all of the companies in our coverage universe. Share price changes over the past year indicates that EQR will perform very well over the near term.

Financial Data

(US$ in Thousands)	9 Mos	6 Mos	3 Mos	12/31/2016	12/31/2015	12/31/2014	12/31/2013	12/31/2012
Earnings Per Share	2.05	2.24	2.30	11.68	2.36	1.73	5.16	2.70
Cash Flow Per Share	3.42	3.23	3.28	3.04	3.73	3.67	2.45	3.45
Tang Book Value Per Share	27.82	27.92	27.90	27.86	28.60	28.44	29.01	22.27
Dividends Per Share	2.015	5.015	5.015	13.015	2.210	2.000	1.850	1.780
Dividend Payout %	98.29	223.88	218.04	111.43	93.64	115.61	35.85	65.93
Income Statement								
Total Revenue	1,840,702	1,216,580	604,100	2,425,800	2,744,965	2,614,748	2,387,702	2,123,715
EBITDA	1,200,636	790,358	391,618	1,617,140	1,779,145	1,675,625	1,501,328	1,476,136
Depn & Amortn	571,089	377,569	188,337	705,649	765,895	758,861	1,013,353	684,992
Income Before Taxes	340,229	212,735	95,376	416,612	558,380	448,485	(121,076)	312,108
Income Taxes	710	482	262	1,613	917	1,394	1,169	539
Net Income	478,012	339,783	143,742	4,292,163	870,120	631,308	1,830,613	841,719
Average Shares	382,945	382,692	382,280	381,992	380,620	377,735	354,305	319,766
Balance Sheet								
Current Assets	94,176	313,113	186,223	219,088	155,115	160,468	199,737	872,161
Total Assets	20,697,833	20,636,575	20,608,338	20,704,148	23,157,328	22,950,614	22,834,545	17,201,000
Current Liabilities	728,438	1,206,469	809,474	463,348	559,305	507,329	512,203	441,759
Long-Term Obligations	8,762,428	8,199,728	8,615,239	8,987,258	10,968,498	10,844,861	10,766,254	8,529,244
Total Liabilities	10,438,564	10,346,070	10,328,062	10,475,070	12,686,960	12,582,158	12,327,344	9,911,187
Stockholders' Equity	10,259,269	10,290,505	10,280,276	10,229,078	10,470,368	10,368,456	10,507,201	7,289,813
Shares Outstanding	367,462	367,298	367,137	365,870	364,755	362,855	360,479	325,054
Statistical Record								
Return on Assets %	3.60	3.94	4.05	19.52	3.77	2.76	9.14	4.96
Return on Equity %	7.41	7.70	7.95	41.36	8.35	6.05	20.57	12.96
EBITDA Margin %	65.23	64.97	64.83	66.66	64.81	64.08	62.88	69.51
Net Margin %	25.97	27.93	23.79	176.94	31.70	24.14	76.67	39.63
Asset Turnover	0.12	0.12	0.12	0.11	0.12	0.11	0.12	0.13
Current Ratio	0.13	0.26	0.23	0.47	0.28	0.32	0.39	1.97
Debt to Equity	0.85	0.80	0.84	0.88	1.05	1.05	1.02	1.17
Price Range	68.61-58.81	71.02-58.81	75.17-58.81	81.59-58.81	81.97-68.95	74.55-51.87	60.75-50.45	65.47-54.06
P/E Ratio	33.47-28.69	31.71-26.25	32.68-25.57	6.99-5.04	34.73-29.22	43.09-29.98	11.77-9.78	24.25-20.02
Average Yield %	3.14	7.83	7.72	19.16	2.90	3.19	3.34	3.00

Address: Two North Riverside Plaza, Chicago, IL 60606 **Telephone:** 312-474-1300	**Web Site:** www.equityresidential.com **Officers:** Samuel Zell - Chairman David J. Neithercut - President, Chief Executive Officer	**Auditors:** Ernst & Young LLP **Investor Contact:** 888-879-6356 **Transfer Agents:** Computershare Trust Company, N.A, Providence, RI

ESSEX PROPERTY TRUST INC

Exchange	Symbol	Price	52Wk Range	Yield	P/E	Div Acheiver
NYS	ESS	$241.37 (12/29/2017)	269.39-221.72	2.90	30.21	22 Years

*7 Year Price Score 103.79 *NYSE Composite Index=100   *12 Month Price Score 94.65

Interim Earnings (Per Share)

Qtr.	Mar	Jun	Sep	Dec
2014	0.58	0.08	0.85	0.66
2015	0.92	0.70	0.65	1.22
2016	1.19	1.10	1.00	2.98
2017	2.72	1.08	1.21	...

Interim Dividends (Per Share)

Amt	Decl	Ex	Rec	Pay
1.75Q	02/22/2017	03/29/2017	03/31/2017	04/17/2017
1.75Q	05/18/2017	06/28/2017	06/30/2017	07/14/2017
1.75Q	09/19/2017	09/28/2017	09/29/2017	10/16/2017
1.75Q	12/13/2017	12/28/2017	12/29/2017	01/16/2018

Indicated Div: $7.00 (Div. Reinv. Plan)

Valuation Analysis		Institutional Holding	
Forecast EPS	$6.12	No of Institutions	581
	(01/26/2018)		
Market Cap	$15.9 Billion	Shares	78,603,376
Book Value	$6.3 Billion	% Held	67.64
Price/Book	2.54		
Price/Sales	11.82		

TRADING VOLUME (thousand shares)

Business Summary: REITs (MIC: 5.3.1 SIC: 6798 NAIC: 525930)

Essex Property Trust is a self-administered and self-managed real estate investment trust. Co. owns all of its interest in its real estate and other investments directly or indirectly through Essex Portfolio, L.P. Co. is engaged primarily in the ownership, operation, management, acquisition, development and redevelopment of primarily apartment communities. As of Dec 31 2016, Co. owned or had ownership interests in 245 apartment communities (aggregating 59,645 apartment homes), two operating commercial buildings, and six active development projects. The communities are located in Southern California, Northern California and the Seattle metropolitan areas.

Recent Developments: For the quarter ended Sep 30 2017, net income increased 21.2% to US$85.0 million from US$70.2 million in the year-earlier quarter. Revenues were US$344.4 million, up 4.6% from US$329.2 million the year before. Revenues from property income rose 4.6% to US$342.0 million from US$327.1 million in the corresponding quarter a year earlier.

Prospects: Our evaluation of Essex Property Trust Inc. as of Jan. 21, 2018 is the result of our systematic analysis on three basic characteristics: earnings strength, relative valuation, and recent stock price movement. The company has enjoyed a very positive trend in earnings per share over the past 5 quarters. Because the company lacks sufficient analyst estimate data, we place greater weight on the historical EPS trend as the measure of earnings strength. Based on operating earnings yield, the company is overvalued when compared to all of the companies in our coverage universe. Share price changes over the past year indicates that ESS will perform very well over the near term.

Financial Data
(US$ in Thousands)

	9 Mos	6 Mos	3 Mos	12/31/2016	12/31/2015	12/31/2014	12/31/2013	12/31/2012
Earnings Per Share	7.99	7.78	7.80	6.27	3.49	2.06	4.04	3.41
Cash Flow Per Share	11.42	11.18	11.22	10.85	9.52	8.72	8.19	7.61
Tang Book Value Per Share	94.93	95.72	95.53	94.50	94.28	93.42	48.51	46.52
Dividends Per Share	6.850	6.700	6.550	6.400	5.760	5.110	4.840	4.400
Dividend Payout %	85.73	86.12	83.97	102.07	165.04	248.06	119.80	129.03
Income Statement								
Total Revenue	1,018,835	674,466	335,404	1,294,001	1,194,407	969,305	613,703	543,425
EBITDA	432,951	324,706	215,005	998,708	833,735	583,880	383,426	356,549
Depn & Amortn	(16,260)	(11,587)	(6,882)	412,237	421,673	336,595	193,518	170,686
Income Before Taxes	307,447	242,139	176,652	394,122	226,378	94,545	96,941	99,452
Income Taxes	...	...	...	4,410	...	...	...	...
Net Income	329,446	249,723	178,964	414,979	232,120	122,150	156,283	125,284
Average Shares	66,078	65,819	65,859	65,587	65,061	56,696	37,335	35,124
Balance Sheet								
Current Assets	369,404	406,531	290,084	350,461	279,825	237,583	212,105	201,002
Total Assets	12,512,523	12,524,951	12,447,427	12,217,408	12,005,091	11,562,874	5,186,839	4,847,223
Current Liabilities	403,385	308,435	340,941	284,305	272,634	261,248	125,857	115,302
Long-Term Obligations	5,615,222	5,663,395	5,602,507	5,563,260	5,315,464	5,109,817	3,033,524	2,818,683
Total Liabilities	6,247,015	6,208,178	6,183,406	6,025,230	5,767,358	5,540,202	3,297,871	3,078,070
Stockholders' Equity	6,265,508	6,316,773	6,264,021	6,192,178	6,237,733	6,022,672	1,888,968	1,769,153
Shares Outstanding	66,002	65,988	65,569	65,527	65,379	63,682	37,421	36,442
Statistical Record								
Return on Assets %	4.25	4.13	4.18	3.42	1.97	1.46	3.12	2.81
Return on Equity %	8.50	8.22	8.26	6.66	3.79	3.09	8.54	7.78
EBITDA Margin %	42.49	48.14	64.10	77.18	69.80	60.24	62.48	65.61
Net Margin %	32.34	37.03	53.36	32.07	19.43	12.60	25.47	23.05
Asset Turnover	0.11	0.11	0.11	0.11	0.10	0.12	0.12	0.12
Current Ratio	0.92	1.32	0.85	1.23	1.03	0.91	1.69	1.74
Debt to Equity	0.90	0.90	0.89	0.90	0.85	0.85	1.61	1.59
Price Range	269.39-204.62	268.39-204.62	236.77-204.62	240.04-192.26	244.29-206.60	212.86-143.51	170.47-141.49	160.33-136.94
P/E Ratio	33.72-25.61	34.50-26.30	30.36-26.23	38.28-30.66	70.00-59.20	103.33-69.67	42.20-35.02	47.02-40.16
Average Yield %	2.86	2.90	2.89	2.89	2.57	2.57	3.13	2.96

Address: 1100 Park Place Suite 200, San Mateo, CA 94403 Telephone: 650-655-7800	Web Site: www.essex.com Officers: George M. Marcus - Chairman Michael J. Schall - President, Chief Executive Officer, Senior Executive Vice President, Chief Operating Officer	Auditors: KPMG LLP Investor Contact: 650-494-3700 Transfer Agents: Computershare, LLC

ESTERLINE TECHNOLOGIES CORP

Exchange	Symbol	Price	52Wk Range	Yield	P/E
NYS	ESL	$74.70 (12/29/2017)	101.60-69.35	N/A	N/A

*7 Year Price Score 84.97   *NYSE Composite Index=100   *12 Month Price Score 82.30

TRADING VOLUME (thousand shares)

Interim Earnings (Per Share)

Qtr.	Jan	May	Aug	Oct
2013-14	0.93	1.14	1.19	(0.10)
Qtr.	Jan	May	Jul	Sep
2014-15	(0.26)	0.63	0.92	0.62
2015-16	0.17	0.50	0.99	1.76
Qtr.	Dec	Mar	Jun	Sep
2016-17	0.54	1.17	1.01	1.19

Interim Dividends (Per Share)

No Dividends Paid

Valuation Analysis		Institutional Holding	
Forecast EPS	$3.85 (01/16/2018)	No of Institutions	321
Market Cap	$2.2 Billion	Shares	
Book Value	N/A		35,421,904
Price/Book	N/A	% Held	
Price/Sales	N/A		97.30

Business Summary: Electronic Instruments & Related Products (MIC: 6.2.3 SIC: 3823 NAIC: 334513)

Esterline Technologies is a manufacturing company principally serving aerospace and defense customers. Co. designs, manufactures and markets engineered products and systems for application within the industries it serves. Co. focuses in three key technology segments: Avionics and Controls, which includes avionics systems, control and communication systems, and interface technologies capabilities; Sensors and Systems, which includes power systems, connection technologies and advanced sensors capabilities; and Advanced Materials, which includes engineered materials and defense technologies capabilities.

Recent Developments: For the year ended Sep 29 2017, income from continuing operations increased 6.6% to US$124.7 million from US$117.0 million a year earlier. Net income increased 15.4% to US$117.4 million from US$101.7 million in the prior year. Revenues were US$2.00 billion, up 0.5% from US$1.99 billion the year before. Direct operating expenses rose 0.4% to US$1.34 billion from US$1.33 billion in the comparable period the year before. Indirect operating expenses decreased 4.2% to US$470.6 million from US$491.1 million in the equivalent prior-year period.

Prospects: Our evaluation of Esterline Technologies Corp. as of Jan. 14, 2018 is the result of our systematic analysis on three basic characteristics: earnings strength, relative valuation, and recent stock price movement. The company has generated a negative trend in earnings per share over the past 5 quarters and while recent estimates for the company have been raised by analysts, ESL has posted results that fell short of analysts expectations. Based on operating earnings yield, the company is undervalued when compared to all of the companies in our coverage universe. Share price changes over the past year indicates that ESL will perform poorly over the near term.

Financial Data

(US$ in Thousands)	09/29/2017	09/30/2016	10/02/2015	10/31/2014	10/25/2013	10/26/2012	10/28/2011	10/29/2010
Earnings Per Share	3.91	3.42	1.91	3.16	5.19	3.60	4.27	4.66
Cash Flow Per Share	6.52	5.68	5.10	6.69	8.07	6.33	6.32	6.02
Tang Book Value Per Share	14.14	6.21	1.47	10.82	5.21	N.M.	N.M.	9.38
Income Statement								
Total Revenue	2,002,195	1,992,631	1,774,449	2,051,169	1,969,754	1,992,318	1,717,985	1,526,601
EBITDA	253,011	219,659	190,534	299,489	292,377	241,706	239,583	226,470
Depn & Amortn	58,200	49,500	45,000	56,200	55,400	52,400	42,500	39,500
Income Before Taxes	165,130	140,435	116,022	210,834	197,849	143,533	158,482	154,749
Income Taxes	38,928	22,535	18,956	44,274	30,085	29,958	24,938	24,504
Net Income	117,387	101,685	59,612	102,418	164,734	112,535	133,040	141,920
Average Shares	30,003	29,764	31,215	32,448	31,738	31,282	31,154	30,477
Balance Sheet								
Current Assets	1,280,457	1,175,788	1,128,814	1,169,504	1,091,715	1,035,693	1,039,313	1,076,585
Total Assets	3,130,323	3,032,031	3,007,030	3,193,467	3,262,112	3,227,117	3,378,586	2,587,738
Current Liabilities	393,430	398,498	410,809	408,129	408,092	396,346	418,361	324,377
Long-Term Obligations	759,424	853,796	867,786	609,720	667,859	838,060	1,020,028	598,972
Total Liabilities	1,293,716	1,431,474	1,469,563	1,305,650	1,388,507	1,616,636	1,815,751	1,174,942
Stockholders' Equity	1,836,607	1,600,557	1,537,467	1,887,817	1,873,605	1,610,481	1,562,835	1,412,796
Shares Outstanding	29,981	29,428	29,546	31,854	31,441	30,869	30,613	30,279
Statistical Record								
EBITDA Margin %	12.64	11.02	10.74	14.60	14.84	12.13	13.95	14.83
Net Margin %	5.86	5.10	3.36	4.99	8.36	5.65	7.74	9.30
Current Ratio	3.25	2.95	2.75	2.87	2.68	2.61	2.48	3.32
Debt to Equity	0.41	0.53	0.56	0.32	0.36	0.52	0.65	0.42
Price Range	101.60-69.90	95.78-51.76	120.06-71.14	121.48-78.27	84.80-55.42	75.20-48.71	81.96-48.54	60.44-37.71
P/E Ratio	25.98-17.88	28.01-15.13	62.86-37.25	38.44-24.77	16.34-10.68	20.89-13.53	19.19-11.37	12.97-8.09

Address: 500 108th Avenue N.E., Bellevue, WA 98004 **Telephone:** 425-453-9400	**Web Site:** www.esterline.com **Officers:** Curtis C. Reusser - Chairman, President, Chief Executive Officer Robert D. George - Executive Vice President, Vice President, Chief Financial Officer, Treasurer, Secretary	**Auditors:** Ernst & Young LLP **Investor Contact:** 425-453-9400 **Transfer Agents:** Mellon Investor Services LLC, Ridgefield , NJ

EVEREST RE GROUP LTD

Exchange	Symbol	Price	52Wk Range	Yield	P/E
NYS	RE	$221.26 (12/29/2017)	271.12-210.36	2.35	35.29

*7 Year Price Score 119.95 *NYSE Composite Index=100 *12 Month Price Score 87.60

Interim Earnings (Per Share)

Qtr.	Mar	Jun	Sep	Dec
2014	6.21	6.26	6.00	7.44
2015	7.19	4.68	2.00	8.18
2016	4.00	3.67	7.06	8.98
2017	7.07	5.95	(15.73)	...

Interim Dividends (Per Share)

Amt	Decl	Ex	Rec	Pay
1.25Q	02/22/2017	03/06/2017	03/08/2017	03/22/2017
1.25Q	05/17/2017	05/26/2017	05/31/2017	06/14/2017
1.25Q	08/23/2017	09/01/2017	09/06/2017	09/20/2017
1.30Q	11/09/2017	11/28/2017	11/29/2017	12/13/2017

Indicated Div: $5.20

Valuation Analysis

		Institutional Holding	
Forecast EPS	N/A	No of Institutions	626
Market Cap	$9.1 Billion	Shares	48,062,840
Book Value	$8.0 Billion	% Held	79.97
Price/Book	1.14		
Price/Sales	1.43		

Business Summary: General Insurance (MIC: 5.2.1 SIC: 6331 NAIC: 524126)

Everest Re Group is a holding company. Through its subsidiaries, Co.'s principal business is underwriting of reinsurance and insurance in the U.S., Bermuda and international markets. Co. operates following segments: U.S. Reinsurance, which writes property and casualty reinsurance and specialty lines of business, including Marine, Aviation, Surety and Accident and Health business; International, which writes foreign property and casualty reinsurance; Bermuda, which provides reinsurance and insurance to worldwide property and casualty markets and and reinsurance to the U.K and European markets; and Insurance, which writes property and casualty insurance within the U.S. and Canada.

Recent Developments: For the quarter ended Sep 30 2017, net loss amounted to US$639.4 million versus net income of US$295.4 million in the year-earlier quarter. Revenues were US$1.73 billion, up 14.2% from US$1.51 billion the year before. Net premiums earned were US$1.60 billion versus US$1.37 billion in the prior-year quarter, an increase of 16.6%. Net investment income rose 11.7% to US$137.0 million from US$122.7 million a year ago.

Prospects: Our evaluation of Everest Re Group Ltd. as of Sep. 17, 2017 is the result of our systematic analysis on three basic characteristics: earnings strength, relative valuation, and recent stock price movement. The company has suffered a very negative trend in earnings per share over the past 5 quarters. However, while recent estimates for the company have been mixed, RE has posted better than expected results. Based on operating earnings yield, the company is undervalued when compared to all of the companies in our coverage universe. Share price changes over the past year indicates that RE will perform very well over the near term.

Financial Data
(US$ in Thousands)

	9 Mos	6 Mos	3 Mos	12/31/2016	12/31/2015	12/31/2014	12/31/2013	12/31/2012
Earnings Per Share	6.27	29.06	26.78	23.68	22.10	25.91	25.44	15.79
Cash Flow Per Share	36.09	32.81	34.24	33.13	30.14	28.95	22.59	12.76
Tang Book Value Per Share	194.05	209.05	203.32	197.45	178.21	166.75	146.57	130.96
Dividends Per Share	5.000	4.900	4.800	4.700	4.000	3.200	2.190	1.920
Dividend Payout %	79.74	16.86	17.92	19.85	18.10	12.35	8.61	12.16
Income Statement								
Premium Income	4,280,653	2,681,778	1,312,097	5,320,466	5,481,459	5,169,135	4,753,543	4,164,628
Total Revenue	4,740,860	3,015,389	1,484,778	5,794,346	5,837,889	5,790,589	5,640,836	4,922,810
Benefits & Claims	3,842,145	1,632,063	770,788	3,139,629	3,101,915	2,906,534	2,800,251	2,745,265
Income Before Taxes	(290,121)	613,946	338,413	1,099,844	1,208,509	1,446,115	1,554,966	939,526
Income Taxes	(188,064)	76,629	46,770	103,500	134,021	187,652	289,706	110,572
Net Income	(102,057)	537,317	291,643	996,344	977,869	1,199,156	1,259,382	828,954
Average Shares	40,883	40,874	40,796	41,628	43,877	45,802	49,056	52,067
Balance Sheet								
Total Assets	23,936,269	22,521,891	22,192,953	21,321,504	21,426,175	20,817,824	19,808,036	19,777,907
Total Liabilities	15,966,938	13,937,093	13,845,077	13,246,108	13,817,590	13,366,704	12,839,760	13,044,440
Stockholders' Equity	7,969,331	8,584,798	8,347,876	8,075,396	7,608,585	7,451,120	6,968,276	6,733,467
Shares Outstanding	41,068	41,065	41,057	40,898	42,694	44,685	47,543	51,417
Statistical Record								
Return on Assets %	1.19	5.51	5.19	4.65	4.63	5.90	6.36	4.28
Return on Equity %	3.39	14.56	13.79	12.67	12.99	16.63	18.38	12.91
Loss Ratio %	89.76	60.86	58.74	59.01	56.59	56.23	58.91	65.92
Net Margin %	(2.15)	17.82	19.64	17.20	16.75	20.71	22.33	16.84
Price Range	271.12-184.24	258.12-177.74	239.15-169.21	218.38-169.21	191.54-166.99	176.27-137.48	159.13-109.95	114.60-83.35
P/E Ratio	43.24-29.38	8.88-6.12	8.93-6.32	9.22-7.15	8.67-7.56	6.80-5.31	6.26-4.32	7.26-5.28
Average Yield %	2.14	2.26	2.38	2.47	2.22	2.01	1.63	1.90

Address: Seon Place - 4th Floor, 141 Front Street, P.O. Box HM 845, Hamilton, HM 19
Telephone: 441-295-0006
Fax: 441-295-4828

Web Site: www.everestregroup.com
Officers: Joseph V. Taranto - Chairman, Chief Executive Officer Dominic James Addesso - President, Chief Executive Officer, Executive Vice President, Chief Financial Officer

Auditors: PricewaterhouseCoopers LLP
Investor Contact: 908-604-3169
Transfer Agents: Computershare Trust Company, N.A., Providence, RI

EVERSOURCE ENERGY

Exchange	Symbol	Price	52Wk Range	Yield	P/E	Div Achiever
NYS	ES	$63.18 (12/29/2017)	65.81-54.25	3.01	20.51	17 Years

*7 Year Price Score 101.73 *NYSE Composite Index=100   *12 Month Price Score 99.62

Interim Earnings (Per Share)

Qtr.	Mar	Jun	Sep	Dec
2014	0.74	0.40	0.74	0.69
2015	0.80	0.65	0.74	0.57
2016	0.77	0.64	0.83	0.72
2017	0.82	0.72	0.82	...

Interim Dividends (Per Share)

Amt	Decl	Ex	Rec	Pay
0.475Q	02/02/2017	02/28/2017	03/02/2017	03/31/2017
0.475Q	05/03/2017	05/26/2017	05/31/2017	06/30/2017
0.475Q	09/06/2017	09/18/2017	09/19/2017	09/29/2017
0.475Q	12/05/2017	12/15/2017	12/18/2017	12/29/2017

Indicated Div: $1.90 (Div. Reinv. Plan)

Valuation Analysis   Institutional Holding

Forecast EPS	$3.14	No of Institutions
(01/18/2018)		129
Market Cap	$20.0 Billion	Shares
Book Value	$11.0 Billion	24,691,984
Price/Book	1.82	% Held
Price/Sales	2.62	65.19

Business Summary: Electric Utilities (MIC: 3.1.1 SIC: 4911 NAIC: 221122)

Eversource Energy is a public utility holding company, which engaged primarily in the energy delivery business through its utility subsidiaries. As of Dec 31 2016, Connecticut Light and Power Company furnished retail franchise electric service to 1.2 million customers in Connecticut; NSTAR Electric Company served 1.2 million customers in Boston and 80 surrounding cities and towns in Massachusetts; Western Massachusetts Electric Company served 210,000 customers in 59 cities and towns in the western region of Massachusetts; and Public Service Company of New Hampshire served 511,000 retail customers in New Hampshire.

Recent Developments: For the quarter ended Sep 30 2017, net income decreased 1.9% to US$262.3 million from US$267.2 million in the year-earlier quarter. Revenues were US$1.99 billion, down 2.5% from US$2.04 billion the year before. Operating income was US$502.6 million versus US$509.9 million in the prior-year quarter, a decrease of 1.4%. Direct operating expenses declined 3.9% to US$952.2 million from US$990.5 million in the comparable period the year before. Indirect operating expenses decreased 1.0% to US$533.7 million from US$539.3 million in the equivalent prior-year period.

Prospects: Our evaluation of Eversource Energy as of Jan. 14, 2018 is the result of our systematic analysis on three basic characteristics: earnings strength, relative valuation, and recent stock price movement. The company has managed to produce a neutral trend in earnings per share over the past 5 quarters and while recent estimates for the company have remained steady, ES has posted results that fell short of analysts expectations. Based on operating earnings yield, the company is undervalued when compared to all of the companies in our coverage universe. Share price changes over the past year indicates that ES will perform well over the near term.

Financial Data

(US$ in Thousands)	9 Mos	6 Mos	3 Mos	12/31/2016	12/31/2015	12/31/2014	12/31/2013	12/31/2012
Earnings Per Share	3.08	3.09	3.01	2.96	2.76	2.58	2.49	1.89
Cash Flow Per Share	6.35	6.63	6.65	6.83	4.49	5.17	5.28	4.18
Tang Book Value Per Share	23.60	23.25	22.99	22.70	21.54	20.37	19.32	18.21
Dividends Per Share	1.870	1.840	1.810	1.780	1.670	1.570	1.470	1.323
Dividend Payout %	60.71	59.55	60.13	60.14	60.51	60.85	59.04	69.99
Income Statement								
Total Revenue	5,856,458	3,867,946	2,105,135	7,639,129	7,954,827	7,741,856	7,301,204	6,273,787
EBITDA	2,152,824	1,392,723	733,418	2,621,245	2,464,247	2,272,125	2,170,106	1,656,958
Depn & Amortn	629,210	392,896	210,822	715,466	665,856	614,657	610,777	519,010
Income Before Taxes	1,204,137	789,069	419,167	1,504,818	1,425,971	1,295,362	1,220,630	808,003
Income Taxes	447,921	295,103	157,829	554,997	539,967	468,297	426,941	274,926
Net Income	750,577	490,074	259,458	942,302	878,485	819,546	786,007	525,945
Average Shares	317,949	317,947	318,124	318,454	318,432	317,417	316,211	277,993
Balance Sheet								
Current Assets	2,403,470	2,330,814	2,511,399	2,477,672	2,618,786	2,692,465	2,087,049	2,227,295
Total Assets	33,163,620	32,658,840	32,355,176	32,053,173	30,580,309	29,777,975	27,795,537	28,302,824
Current Liabilities	2,620,431	3,785,709	3,333,765	3,638,605	2,989,790	3,134,381	3,275,651	3,643,690
Long-Term Obligations	10,468,193	8,899,021	9,267,891	8,829,354	8,805,574	8,606,017	7,776,833	7,200,156
Total Liabilities	22,165,583	21,773,317	21,550,980	21,341,439	20,228,094	19,801,160	18,184,009	19,065,774
Stockholders' Equity	10,998,037	10,885,523	10,804,196	10,711,734	10,352,215	9,976,815	9,611,528	9,237,050
Shares Outstanding	316,885	316,885	316,885	316,885	317,191	316,983	315,273	314,053
Statistical Record								
Return on Assets %	3.05	3.10	3.04	3.00	2.91	2.85	2.80	2.39
Return on Equity %	9.06	9.21	9.02	8.92	8.64	8.37	8.34	7.92
EBITDA Margin %	36.76	36.01	34.84	34.31	30.98	29.35	29.72	26.41
Net Margin %	12.82	12.67	12.33	12.34	11.04	10.59	10.77	8.38
Asset Turnover	0.24	0.24	0.24	0.24	0.26	0.27	0.26	0.28
Current Ratio	0.92	0.62	0.75	0.68	0.88	0.86	0.64	0.61
Debt to Equity	0.95	0.82	0.86	0.82	0.85	0.86	0.81	0.78
Price Range	64.11-51.10	63.24-51.10	60.25-51.10	60.25-50.58	56.40-45.41	56.15-41.52	45.33-38.67	40.57-33.53
P/E Ratio	20.81-16.59	20.47-16.54	20.02-16.98	20.35-17.09	20.43-16.45	21.76-16.09	18.20-15.53	21.47-17.74
Average Yield %	3.21	3.24	3.24	3.22	3.34	3.41	3.49	3.53

Address: 300 Cadwell Drive, Springfield, MA 01104	**Web Site:** www.eversource.com	**Auditors:** Deloitte & Touche LLP
Telephone: 800-286-5000	**Officers:** James J. Judge - President, Chief Executive Officer, Executive Vice President, Chief Financial Officer Philip J. Lembo - Executive Vice President, Senior Vice President, Chief Financial Officer, Treasurer	**Investor Contact:** 860-728-4650 **Transfer Agents:** ComputerShare Investor Services, Providence, RI

EXELON CORP

Exchange	Symbol	Price	52Wk Range	Yield	P/E
NYS	EXC	$39.41 (12/29/2017)	42.39-33.50	3.32	17.67

*7 Year Price Score 82.69 *NYSE Composite Index=100 *12 Month Price Score 103.13

Interim Earnings (Per Share)

Qtr.	Mar	Jun	Sep	Dec
2014	0.10	0.60	1.15	0.02
2015	0.80	0.74	0.69	0.32
2016	0.19	0.29	0.53	0.22
2017	1.07	0.09	0.85	...

Interim Dividends (Per Share)

Amt	Decl	Ex	Rec	Pay
0.328Q	01/31/2017	02/13/2017	02/15/2017	03/10/2017
0.328Q	04/25/2017	05/11/2017	05/15/2017	06/09/2017
0.328Q	07/25/2017	08/11/2017	08/15/2017	09/08/2017
0.328Q	09/25/2017	11/14/2017	11/15/2017	12/08/2017

Indicated Div: $1.31

Valuation Analysis

		Institutional Holding	
Forecast EPS	$2.65 (01/18/2018)	No of Institutions	1210
Market Cap	$37.9 Billion	Shares	878,229,696
Book Value	$28.1 Billion	% Held	72.43
Price/Book	1.35		
Price/Sales	1.15		

Business Summary: Electric Utilities (MIC: 3.1.1 SIC: 4931 NAIC: 221122)

Exelon is a utility services holding company engaged through its principal subsidiaries in the energy generation and energy distribution and transmission businesses. Co. has 12 reportable segments consisting of Exelon Generation Company, LLC's six reportable segments (Mid-Atlantic, Midwest, New England, New York, Electric Reliability Council of Texas and Other Power Regions in Generation), Commonwealth Edison Company; PECO Energy Company; and Baltimore Gas and Electric Company and Pepco Holdings, Inc.'s three utility reportable segments (Potomac Electric Power Company, Delmarva Power & Light Company and Atlantic City Electric Company).

Recent Developments: For the quarter ended Sep 30 2017, net income increased 64.8% to US$867.0 million from US$526.0 million in the year-earlier quarter. Revenues were US$8.77 billion, down 2.6% from US$9.00 billion the year before. Operating income was US$1.48 billion versus US$1.27 billion in the prior-year quarter, an increase of 16.4%. Direct operating expenses declined 4.1% to US$5.84 billion from US$6.09 billion in the comparable period the year before. Indirect operating expenses decreased 11.6% to US$1.45 billion from US$1.64 billion in the equivalent prior-year period.

Prospects: Our evaluation of Exelon Corp. as of Jan. 14, 2018 is the result of our systematic analysis on three basic characteristics: earnings strength, relative valuation, and recent stock price movement. The company has produced a positive trend in earnings per share over the past 5 quarters and while recent estimates for the company have been mixed, EXC has posted results that fell short of analysts expectations. Based on operating earnings yield, the company is undervalued when compared to all of the companies in our coverage universe. Share price changes over the past year indicates that EXC will perform very well over the near term.

Financial Data

(US$ in Thousands)	9 Mos	6 Mos	3 Mos	12/31/2016	12/31/2015	12/31/2014	12/31/2013	12/31/2012
Earnings Per Share	2.23	1.91	2.11	1.22	2.54	1.88	2.00	1.42
Cash Flow Per Share	7.03	7.27	8.81	9.11	8.56	5.18	7.41	7.49
Tang Book Value Per Share	22.30	21.74	21.44	20.74	25.34	23.41	23.68	22.33
Dividends Per Share	1.301	1.291	1.282	1.264	1.240	1.240	1.455	2.100
Dividend Payout %	58.32	67.59	60.73	103.61	48.82	65.96	72.75	147.89
Income Statement								
Total Revenue	25,149,000	16,381,000	8,757,000	31,360,000	29,447,000	27,429,000	24,888,000	23,489,000
EBITDA	4,208,000	2,159,000	1,760,000	9,861,000	9,222,000	8,007,000	8,055,000	7,556,000
Depn & Amortn	483,000	143,000	181,000	6,349,000	4,860,000	4,476,000	3,960,000	4,754,000
Income Before Taxes	2,531,000	1,207,000	1,206,000	1,989,000	3,330,000	2,506,000	2,763,000	1,889,000
Income Taxes	595,000	143,000	215,000	761,00	1,073,000	666,000	1,044,000	627,000
Net Income	1,899,000	1,076,000	995,000	1,134,000	2,269,000	1,623,000	1,719,000	1,160,000
Average Shares	965,000	936,000	930,000	927,000	893,000	864,000	860,000	819,000
Balance Sheet								
Current Assets	12,724,000	12,232,000	12,194,000	12,412,000	15,334,000	12,097,000	10,137,000	10,133,000
Total Assets	118,473,000	117,104,000	117,068,000	114,904,000	95,384,000	86,814,000	79,924,000	78,554,000
Current Liabilities	12,395,000	13,965,000	14,437,000	13,457,000	9,118,000	8,762,000	7,728,000	7,784,000
Long-Term Obligations	32,090,000	30,956,000	31,685,000	32,216,000	24,286,000	20,010,000	18,271,000	18,854,000
Total Liabilities	90,373,000	89,558,000	90,538,000	89,067,000	69,398,000	64,013,000	56,999,000	56,843,000
Stockholders' Equity	28,100,000	27,546,000	26,530,000	25,837,000	25,986,000	22,801,000	22,925,000	21,711,000
Shares Outstanding	960,852	960,087	926,000	924,035	919,924	859,833	857,290	854,781
Statistical Record								
Return on Assets %	1.81	1.54	1.71	1.08	2.49	1.95	2.17	1.73
Return on Equity %	7.77	6.61	7.46	4.36	9.30	7.10	7.70	6.39
EBITDA Margin %	16.73	13.18	20.10	31.44	31.32	29.19	32.36	32.17
Net Margin %	7.55	6.57	11.36	3.62	7.71	5.92	6.91	4.94
Asset Turnover	0.28	0.29	0.28	0.30	0.32	0.33	0.31	0.35
Current Ratio	1.03	0.88	0.84	0.92	1.68	1.38	1.31	1.30
Debt to Equity	1.14	1.12	1.19	1.25	0.93	0.88	0.80	0.87
Price Range	38.55-30.00	37.50-30.00	37.50-30.00	37.50-26.78	37.99-25.46	38.63-26.62	37.78-26.90	42.07-28.57
P/E Ratio	17.29-13.45	19.63-15.71	17.77-14.22	30.74-21.95	14.96-10.02	20.55-14.16	18.89-13.45	29.63-20.12
Average Yield %	3.66	3.69	3.69	3.76	3.87	3.70	4.69	5.72

Address: 10 South Dearborn Street, P.O. Box 805379, Chicago, IL 60680-5379 **Telephone:** 800-483-3220	**Web Site:** www.exeloncorp.com **Officers:** Mayo A. Shattuck - Chairman, Executive Chairman Christopher M. (Chris) Crane - President, Chief Executive Officer, Chief Operating Officer	**Auditors:** PricewaterhouseCoopers LLP **Investor Contact:** 312-394-2345 **Transfer Agents:** Wells Fargo

EXTENDED STAY AMERICA INC

Exchange	Symbol	Price	52Wk Range	Yield	P/E
NYS	STAY	$19.00 (12/29/2017)	20.87-15.50	4.42	46.34

*7 Year Price Score N/A   *NYSE Composite Index=100   *12 Month Price Score 93.78

Interim Earnings (Per Share)

Qtr.	Mar	Jun	Sep	Dec
2014	0.05	0.21	0.21	(0.29)
2015	0.11	0.28	0.18	(0.02)
2016	0.08	0.30	0.23	(0.26)
2017	0.12	0.27	0.28	...

Interim Dividends (Per Share)

Amt	Decl	Ex	Rec	Pay
0.19Q	02/28/2017	03/10/2017	03/14/2017	03/28/2017
0.21Q	04/27/2017	05/09/2017	05/11/2017	05/25/2017
0.21Q	08/01/2017	08/11/2017	08/15/2017	08/29/2017
0.21Q	11/07/2017	11/20/2017	11/21/2017	12/05/2017

Indicated Div: $0.84

Valuation Analysis   **Institutional Holding**

Forecast EPS	$0.97	No of Institutions
	(01/18/2018)	286
Market Cap	$3.7 Billion	Shares
Book Value	$854.3 Million	206,411,392
Price/Book	4.28	% Held
Price/Sales	2.86	97.10

TRADING VOLUME (thousand shares)

Business Summary: Hotels, Restaurants & Travel (MIC: 2.2.1 SIC: 7011 NAIC: 721110)

Extended Stay America is an owner/operator of company-branded hotels in North America. Co.'s business operates in the extended stay segment of the lodging industry. As of Dec 31 2016, Co. owned and operated 629 hotels comprising about 69,400 rooms located in 44 states across the U.S. and in Canada. Co. owns and operates the substantial majority of its hotels under its primary brand, Extended Stay America, which serves the mid-price extended stay segment. In addition, Co. owns and operates three Extended Stay Canada hotels. Extended Stay America-branded hotels feature: in-room kitchens; free WiFi; free grab-and-go breakfast; flat screen TVs with cable channels; and on-site guest laundry.

Recent Developments: For the quarter ended Sep 30 2017, net income increased 16.1% to US$66.3 million from US$57.1 million in the year-earlier quarter. Revenues were US$350.9 million, down 1.0% from US$354.5 million the year before. Operating income was US$117.9 million versus US$121.3 million in the prior-year quarter, a decrease of 2.8%. Direct operating expenses rose 1.5% to US$152.2 million from US$149.9 million in the comparable period the year before. Indirect operating expenses decreased 3.0% to US$80.8 million from US$83.3 million in the equivalent prior-year period.

Prospects: Our evaluation of Extended Stay America Inc as of Jan. 14, 2018 is the result of our systematic analysis on three basic characteristics: earnings strength, relative valuation, and recent stock price movement. The company has generated a negative trend in earnings per share over the past 5 quarters and while recent estimates for the company have been mixed, STAY has posted results that fell short of analysts expectations. Based on operating earnings yield, the company is undervalued when compared to all of the companies in our coverage universe. Share price changes over the past year indicates that STAY will perform poorly over the near term.

Financial Data
(US$ in Thousands)

	9 Mos	6 Mos	3 Mos	12/31/2016	12/31/2015	12/31/2014	12/31/2013	12/31/2012
Earnings Per Share	0.41	0.36	0.39	0.35	0.55	0.19	0.49	...
Cash Flow Per Share	2.35	2.32	2.28	2.08	2.10	1.82	1.78	...
Tang Book Value Per Share	4.05	3.84	3.69	3.65	3.89	3.43	3.20	...
Dividends Per Share	0.800	0.780	0.760	0.740	0.910	0.530	...	...
Dividend Payout %	195.12	216.67	194.87	211.43	165.45	278.95	...	...
Income Statement								
Total Revenue	980,220	629,354	290,991	1,270,593	1,284,753	1,213,475	1,132,818	1,011,462
EBITDA	448,476	270,978	113,814	583,549	701,237	532,182	480,178	414,210
Depn & Amortn	178,759	119,457	59,662	221,309	203,897	187,207	168,053	129,938
Income Before Taxes	172,759	86,214	20,546	197,703	359,558	195,611	77,666	26,923
Income Taxes	40,721	20,426	4,483	34,351	76,536	45,057	(4,990)	4,642
Net Income	128,752	74,874	23,101	69,932	113,040	39,596	86,231	20,732
Average Shares	193,331	193,944	195,386	200,736	204,567	204,508	176,268	...
Balance Sheet								
Current Assets	165,448	102,266	106,477	126,609	475,819	221,258	129,362	183,744
Total Assets	4,111,154	4,071,151	4,126,730	4,180,304	4,528,900	4,481,120	4,449,687	4,491,734
Current Liabilities	219,481	201,479	196,087	193,303	243,969	172,440	175,122	124,362
Long-Term Obligations	2,536,125	2,537,510	2,573,892	2,585,274	2,762,388	2,891,369	2,926,045	3,605,708
Total Liabilities	3,256,899	3,255,254	3,333,689	3,385,472	3,649,227	3,691,602	3,705,111	3,742,076
Stockholders' Equity	854,255	815,897	793,041	794,832	879,673	789,518	744,576	...
Shares Outstanding	192,293	192,505	194,282	195,406	204,593	204,517	204,788	...
Statistical Record								
Return on Assets %	1.78	1.58	1.78	1.60	2.51	0.89	1.93	0.47
Return on Equity %	8.34	7.79	9.11	8.33	13.54	5.16	...	...
EBITDA Margin %	45.75	43.06	39.11	45.93	54.58	43.86	42.39	40.95
Net Margin %	13.14	11.90	7.94	5.50	8.80	3.26	7.61	2.05
Asset Turnover	0.30	0.30	0.30	0.29	0.29	0.27	0.25	0.23
Current Ratio	0.75	0.51	0.54	0.65	1.95	1.28	0.74	1.48
Debt to Equity	2.97	3.11	3.25	3.25	3.14	3.66	3.93	...
Price Range	20.20-13.26	19.80-13.26	17.79-13.26	16 93-10.95	21.30-15.75	26.57-17.63	26.26-23.41	...
P/E Ratio	49.27-32.34	55.00-36.83	45.62-34.00	48.37-31.29	38.73-28.64	139.84-92.79	53.59-47.78	...
Average Yield %	4.64	4.88	4.97	5.06	4.82	2.33	...	...

Address: 11525 N. Community House Road, Suite 100, Charlotte, NC 28277
Telephone: 980-345-1600

Web Site: www.esa.com
Officers: Douglas G. Geoga - Chairman Gerardo I. Lopez - President, Chief Executive Officer

Auditors: Deloitte & Touche LLP
Transfer Agents: American Stock Transfer & Trust Company, LLC

EXTRA SPACE STORAGE INC

Exchange	Symbol	Price	52Wk Range	Yield	P/E
NYS	EXR	$87.45 (12/29/2017)	87.86-71.64	3.57	31.92

*7 Year Price Score 113.24 *NYSE Composite Index=100 *12 Month Price Score 102.50

Interim Earnings (Per Share)

Qtr.	Mar	Jun	Sep	Dec
2014	0.32	0.36	0.47	0.38
2015	0.46	0.47	0.58	0.05
2016	0.66	0.66	0.93	0.67
2017	0.64	0.69	0.74	...

Interim Dividends (Per Share)

Amt	Decl	Ex	Rec	Pay
0.78Q	02/16/2017	03/13/2017	03/15/2017	03/31/2017
0.78Q	05/22/2017	06/13/2017	06/15/2017	06/30/2017
0.78Q	08/25/2017	09/14/2017	09/15/2017	09/29/2017
0.78Q	11/10/2017	12/14/2017	12/15/2017	12/29/2017

Indicated Div: $3.12

Valuation Analysis | **Institutional Holding**

Forecast EPS	$2.81	No of Institutions	
	(01/13/2018)	513	
Market Cap	$11.0 Billion	Shares	
Book Value	$2.2 Billion	170,685,232	
Price/Book	4.97	% Held	
Price/Sales	10.16	95.74	

TRADING VOLUME (thousand shares)

Business Summary: REITs (MIC: 5.3.1 SIC: 6798 NAIC: 525930)

Extra Space Storage is a real estate investment trust. Substantially all of Co.'s business is conducted through Extra Space Storage LP. Co. operate in three segments: rental operations, which include rental operations of stores in which Co. has an ownership interest; tenant reinsurance, which include the reinsurance of risks relating to the loss of goods stored by tenants in Co.'s stores; and property management, acquisition and development, which include managing, acquiring, developing and selling stores. At Dec 31 2016, Co. had direct and indirect equity interests in 1,016 storage facilities, and Co. managed 411 stores for third parties.

Recent Developments: For the quarter ended Sep 30 2017, net income decreased 20.6% to US$101.1 million from US$127.2 million in the year-earlier quarter. Revenues were US$284.2 million, up 10.5% from US$257.2 million the year before. Revenues from property income rose 10.8% to US$248.6 million from US$224.5 million in the corresponding quarter a year earlier.

Prospects: Our evaluation of Extra Space Storage Inc. as of Jan. 14, 2018 is the result of our systematic analysis on three basic characteristics: earnings strength, relative valuation, and recent stock price movement. The company has managed to produce a neutral trend in earnings per share over the past 5 quarters. However, while recent estimates for the company have been mixed, EXR has posted better than expected results. Based on operating earnings yield, the company is about fairly valued when compared to all of the companies in our coverage universe. Share price changes over the past year indicates that EXR will perform very well over the near term.

Financial Data
(US$ in Thousands)

	9 Mos	6 Mos	3 Mos	12/31/2016	12/31/2015	12/31/2014	12/31/2013	12/31/2012
Earnings Per Share	2.74	2.93	2.90	2.91	1.56	1.53	1.53	1.14
Cash Flow Per Share	4.79	4.68	4.43	4.30	3.07	2.92	2.44	2.10
Tang Book Value Per Share	17.58	17.64	17.76	17.83	16.81	14.87	15.14	13.44
Dividends Per Share	3.120	3.120	3.120	2.930	2.240	1.810	1.450	0.850
Dividend Payout %	113.87	106.48	107.59	100.69	143.59	118.30	94.77	74.56
Income Statement								
Total Revenue	823,167	539,011	263,008	991,875	782,270	647,155	520,613	409,396
EBITDA	551,684	359,297	178,007	633,209	419,908	375,990	310,253	236,757
Depn & Amortn	157,212	104,706	53,804	174,906	123,751	109,531	104,963	79,516
Income Before Taxes	282,654	182,406	89,279	330,842	205,476	188,903	137,855	91,613
Income Taxes	9,154	5,991	3,124	15,847	11,148	7,570	9,984	5,413
Net Income	263,052	169,288	82,282	366,127	189,474	178,355	172,076	117,309
Average Shares	133,044	132,783	132,618	125,948	126,918	121,435	113,105	106,523
Balance Sheet								
Current Assets	81,009	48,412	41,542	74,353	244,197	126,293	187,741	78,720
Total Assets	7,086,955	7,037,463	7,034,357	7,091,446	6,071,407	4,402,107	3,977,140	3,223,477
Current Liabilities	231,661	210,061	194,458	468,083	120,916	204,193	61,272	137,299
Long-Term Obligations	4,195,598	4,171,326	4,174,103	3,941,223	3,499,621	2,232,597	1,948,723	1,496,425
Total Liabilities	4,871,689	4,815,672	4,798,241	4,846,554	3,982,330	2,664,682	2,218,670	1,731,670
Stockholders' Equity	2,215,266	2,221,791	2,236,116	2,244,892	2,089,077	1,737,425	1,758,470	1,491,807
Shares Outstanding	126,007	125,977	125,912	125,881	124,119	116,360	115,755	110,737
Statistical Record								
Return on Assets %	5.00	5.48	5.49	5.55	3.62	4.26	4.78	4.08
Return on Equity %	15.65	17.05	16.71	16.85	9.90	10.20	10.59	9.32
EBITDA Margin %	67.02	66.66	67.68	63.84	53.68	58.10	59.59	57.83
Net Margin %	31.96	31.41	31.28	36.91	24.22	27.56	33.05	28.65
Asset Turnover	0.16	0.16	0.15	0.15	0.15	0.15	0.14	0.14
Current Ratio	0.35	0.23	0.21	0.16	2.02	0.62	3.06	0.57
Debt to Equity	1.89	1.88	1.87	1.76	1.68	1.29	1.11	1.00
Price Range	82.25-68.78	94.38-68.78	94.38-68.78	94.38-68.78	90.22-58.64	60.12-41.79	48.65-36.39	36.39-24.00
P/E Ratio	30.02-25.10	32.21-23.47	32.54-23.72	32.43-23.64	57.83-37.59	39.29-27.31	31.80-23.78	31.92-21.05
Average Yield %	4.11	4.02	3.85	3.50	3.10	3.48	3.44	2.76

Address: 2795 East Cottonwood Parkway, Suite 300; Salt Lake City, UT 84121 **Telephone:** 801-365-4600	**Web Site:** www.extraspace.com **Officers:** Kenneth M. Woolley - Executive Chairman, Chairman, Chief Executive Officer Spencer F. Kirk - Chairman, President, Chief Executive Officer	**Auditors:** Ernst & Young LLP **Investor Contact:** 801-365-4600 **Transfer Agents:** American Stock Transfer & Trust Company

EXXON MOBIL CORP

Exchange	Symbol	Price	52Wk Range	Yield	P/E	Div Achiever
NYS	XOM	$83.64 (12/29/2017)	90.89-76.10	3.68	27.24	34 Years

*7 Year Price Score 74.23 ***NYSE Composite Index=100** ***12 Month Price Score 95.06**

Interim Earnings (Per Share)

Qtr.	Mar	Jun	Sep	Dec
2014	2.10	2.05	1.89	1.56
2015	1.17	1.00	1.01	0.67
2016	0.43	0.41	0.63	0.41
2017	0.95	0.78	0.93	...

Interim Dividends (Per Share)

Amt	Decl	Ex	Rec	Pay
0.75Q	01/25/2017	02/08/2017	02/10/2017	03/10/2017
0.77Q	04/26/2017	05/10/2017	05/12/2017	06/09/2017
0.77Q	07/26/2017	08/10/2017	08/14/2017	09/11/2017
0.77Q	10/25/2017	11/10/2017	11/13/2017	12/11/2017

Indicated Div: $3.08 (Div. Reinv. Plan)

Valuation Analysis

		Institutional Holding	
Forecast EPS	$3.65	No of Institutions	
	(01/18/2018)	3047	
Market Cap	$354.4 Billion	Shares	
Book Value	$182.3 Billion	2,883,930,624	
Price/Book	1.94	% Held	
Price/Sales	1.40	45.00	

TRADING VOLUME (thousand shares)

Business Summary: Production & Extraction (MIC: 9.1.1 SIC: 1311 NAIC: 211111)

Exxon Mobil is engaged in the exploration for, and production of, crude oil and natural gas, manufacture of petroleum products and transportation and sale of crude oil, natural gas and petroleum products. Co. is a manufacturer and marketer of commodity petrochemicals, including olefins, aromatics, polyethylene and polypropylene plastics and a variety of specialty products. As of Dec 31 2016, Co. had total proved reserves of 19.97 billion barrels of oil-equivalent, which consisted of 7.75 billion barrels of crude oil, 1.54 billion barrels of natural gas liquids, 701.0 million barrels of bitumen, 564.0 million barrels of synthetic oil, and 56.50 trillion cubic ft. of natural gas.

Recent Developments: For the quarter ended Sep 30 2017, net income increased 41.4% to US$4.09 billion from US$2.89 billion in the year-earlier quarter. Revenues were US$66.17 billion, up 12.8% from US$58.68 billion the year before. Direct operating expenses rose 10.8% to US$45.63 billion from US$41.18 billion in the comparable period the year before. Indirect operating expenses increased 4.8% to US$14.95 billion from US$14.27 billion in the equivalent prior-year period.

Prospects: Our evaluation of Exxon Mobil Corp. as of Jan. 14, 2018 is the result of our systematic analysis on three basic characteristics: earnings strength, relative valuation, and recent stock price movement. The company has managed to produce a neutral trend in earnings per share over the past 5 quarters and while recent estimates for the company have been raised by analysts, XOM has posted better than expected results. Based on operating earnings yield, the company is about fairly valued when compared to all of the companies in our coverage universe. Share price changes over the past year indicates that XOM will perform poorly over the near term.

Financial Data

(US$ in Thousands)	9 Mos	6 Mos	3 Mos	12/31/2016	12/31/2015	12/31/2014	12/31/2013	12/31/2012
Earnings Per Share	3.07	2.77	2.40	1.88	3.85	7.60	7.37	9.70
Cash Flow Per Share	7.04	6.53	6.02	5.27	7.23	10.54	10.16	12.10
Tang Book Value Per Share	43.02	42.29	41.81	40.34	41.10	41.51	40.14	36.84
Dividends Per Share	3.040	3.020	3.000	2.980	2.880	2.700	2.460	2.180
Dividend Payout %	99.02	109.03	125.00	158.51	74.81	35.53	33.38	22.47
Income Statement								
Total Revenue	192,328,000	126,163,000	63,287,000	226,094,000	268,882,000	411,939,000	438,255,000	482,295,000
EBITDA	30,123,000	19,549,000	10,583,000	30,730,000	40,325,000	69,213,000	74,902,000	94,941,000
Depn & Amortn	14,051,000	9,171,000	4,519,000	22,308,000	18,048,000	17,297,000	17,182,000	15,888,000
Income Before Taxes	15,657,000	10,074,000	5,918,000	7,969,000	21,966,000	51,630,000	57,711,000	78,726,000
Income Taxes	4,218,000	2,720,000	1,828,000	(406,000)	5,415,000	18,015,000	24,263,000	31,045,000
Net Income	11,330,000	7,360,000	4,010,000	7,840,000	16,150,000	32,520,000	32,580,000	44,880,000
Average Shares	4,271,000	4,271,000	4,223,000	4,177,000	4,196,000	4,282,000	4,418,999	4,627,999
Balance Sheet								
Current Assets	45,752,000	42,180,000	43,131,000	41,416,000	42,623,000	52,910,000	59,308,000	64,460,000
Total Assets	349,427,000	343,012,000	344,209,000	330,314,000	336,758,000	349,493,000	346,808,000	333,795,000
Current Liabilities	53,777,000	50,949,000	53,374,000	47,638,000	53,976,000	64,633,000	71,724,000	64,139,000
Long-Term Obligations	24,869,000	24,750,000	25,124,000	28,932,000	19,925,000	11,653,000	6,891,000	7,928,000
Total Liabilities	167,151,000	163,834,000	167,058,000	162,989,000	165,947,000	175,094,000	172,805,000	167,932,000
Stockholders' Equity	182,276,000	179,178,000	177,151,000	167,325,000	170,811,000	174,399,000	174,003,000	165,863,000
Shares Outstanding	4,237,000	4,237,000	4,237,000	4,148,000	4,156,000	4,201,000	4,334,999	4,501,999
Statistical Record								
Return on Assets %	3.78	3.41	2.92	2.34	4.71	9.34	9.57	13.46
Return on Equity %	7.37	6.68	5.75	4.62	9.36	18.67	19.17	27.95
EBITDA Margin %	15.66	15.50	16.72	13.59	15.00	16.80	17.09	19.69
Net Margin %	5.89	5.83	6.34	3.47	6.01	7.89	7.43	9.31
Asset Turnover	0.74	0.72	0.70	0.68	0.78	1.18	1.29	1.45
Current Ratio	0.85	0.83	0.81	0.87	0.79	0.82	0.83	1.01
Debt to Equity	0.14	0.14	0.14	0.17	0.12	0.07	0.04	0.05
Price Range	92.58-76.10	95.12-79.50	95.12-80.93	95.12-73.18	93.37-68.71	104.38-86.41	101.51-85.16	93.48-77.60
P/E Ratio	30.16-24.79	34.34-28.70	39.63-33.72	50.60-38.93	24.25-17.85	13.73-11.37	13.77-11.55	9.64-8.00
Average Yield %	3.66	3.54	3.45	3.46	3.48	2.78	2.72	2.52

Address: 5959 Las Colinas Boulevard, Irving, TX 75039-2298	Web Site: www.exxonmobil.com	Auditors: PricewaterhouseCoopers LLP
Telephone: 972-444-1000	Officers: Rex W. Tillerson - Chairman, President, Chief Executive Officer Darren W. Woods - President, Chairman, Senior Vice President, President, Vice President, Chief Executive Officer, Division Officer, Senior Vice President, Vice President, Division Officer	Investor Contact: 180-025-21800
Fax: 972-444-1505		Transfer Agents: ComputerShare, College Station, TX

FNB CORP

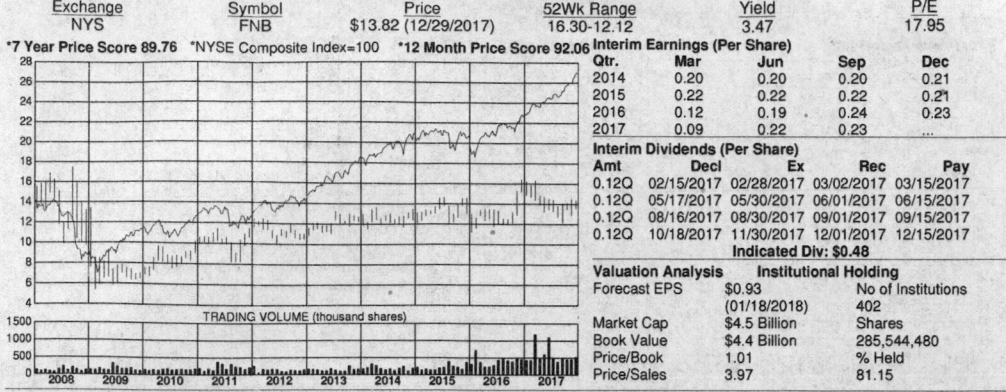

Exchange	Symbol	Price	52Wk Range	Yield	P/E
NYS	FNB	$13.82 (12/29/2017)	16.30-12.12	3.47	17.95

*7 Year Price Score 89.76   *NYSE Composite Index=100   *12 Month Price Score 92.06

Interim Earnings (Per Share)

Qtr.	Mar	Jun	Sep	Dec
2014	0.20	0.20	0.20	0.21
2015	0.22	0.22	0.22	0.21
2016	0.12	0.19	0.24	0.23
2017	0.09	0.22	0.23	...

Interim Dividends (Per Share)

Amt	Decl	Ex	Rec	Pay
0.12Q	02/15/2017	02/28/2017	03/02/2017	03/15/2017
0.12Q	05/17/2017	05/30/2017	06/01/2017	06/15/2017
0.12Q	08/16/2017	08/30/2017	09/01/2017	09/15/2017
0.12Q	10/18/2017	11/30/2017	12/01/2017	12/15/2017
			Indicated Div: $0.48	

Valuation Analysis

		Institutional Holding	
Forecast EPS	$0.93 (01/18/2018)	No of Institutions	402
Market Cap	$4.5 Billion	Shares	285,544,480
Book Value	$4.4 Billion		
Price/Book	1.01	% Held	81.15
Price/Sales	3.97		

Business Summary: Banking (MIC: 5.1.1 SIC: 6021 NAIC: 522110)

F.N.B. is a financial holding company. Through its subsidiaries, Co. provides commercial banking, consumer banking, insurance and wealth management solutions. Co.'s commercial banking solutions include corporate banking, small business banking, investment real estate financing, international banking, business credit, capital markets and lease financing. Co.'s consumer banking products and services include deposit products, mortgage lending, consumer lending, mobile and online banking services. Co.'s wealth management services include asset management, private banking and insurance. As of Dec 31 2016, Co. had total assets of $21.84 billion and total deposits of $16.07 billion.

Recent Developments: For the quarter ended Sep 30 2017, net income increased 48.9% to US$77.7 million from US$52.2 million in the year-earlier quarter. Net interest income increased 43.0% to US$225.2 million from US$157.5 million in the year-earlier quarter. Provision for loan losses was US$16.8 million versus US$14.6 million in the prior-year quarter, an increase of 14.5%. Non-interest income rose 24.3% to US$66.2 million from US$53.2 million, while non-interest expense advanced 35.3% to US$163.7 million.

Prospects: Our evaluation of F.N.B. Corp. as of Jan. 14, 2018 is the result of our systematic analysis on three basic characteristics: earnings strength, relative valuation, and recent stock price movement. The company has managed to produce a neutral trend in earnings per share over the past 5 quarters and while recent estimates for the company have been mixed, FNB has posted results that fell short of analysts expectations. Based on operating earnings yield, the company is undervalued when compared to all of the companies in our coverage universe. Share price changes over the past year indicates that FNB will perform poorly over the near term.

Financial Data

(US$ in Thousands)	9 Mos	6 Mos	3 Mos	12/31/2016	12/31/2015	12/31/2014	12/31/2013	12/31/2012
Earnings Per Share	0.77	0.78	0.75	0.78	0.86	0.80	0.80	0.79
Cash Flow Per Share	0.71	0.33	0.92	1.42	1.28	2.67	2.64	3.90
Tang Book Value Per Share	6.02	5.91	5.77	6.47	6.33	5.95	5.38	4.92
Dividends Per Share	0.480	0.480	0.480	0.480	0.480	0.480	0.480	0.480
Dividend Payout %	62.34	61.54	64.00	61.54	55.81	60.00	60.00	60.76
Income Statement								
Interest Income	709,241	445,727	194,693	678,963	546,795	508,983	440,386	431,906
Interest Expense	92,843	54,560	21,941	67,451	48,573	42,686	44,344	59,055
Net Interest Income	616,398	391,167	172,752	611,512	498,222	466,297	396,042	372,851
Provision for Losses	44,374	27,606	10,850	55,752	40,441	38,648	31,090	31,302
Non-Interest Income	187,345	121,194	55,116	201,761	162,410	158,274	135,778	131,463
Non-Interest Expense	515,012	351,269	187,555	511,133	390,549	379,253	338,170	318,829
Income Before Taxes	244,357	133,486	29,463	246,388	229,642	206,670	162,560	154,183
Income Taxes	69,279	36,101	6,484	75,497	69,993	62,620	44,756	43,773
Net Income	175,078	97,385	22,979	170,891	159,649	144,050	117,804	110,410
Average Shares	324,904	324,867	239,254	207,768	176,338	169,078	147,809	140,640
Balance Sheet								
Net Loans & Leases	20,761,198	20,536,326	20,092,138	14,738,884	12,048,428	11,121,112	9,395,310	8,033,345
Total Assets	31,123,295	30,753,726	30,190,695	21,844,817	17,557,662	16,127,090	13,563,405	12,023,976
Total Deposits	21,929,171	21,051,707	21,326,272	16,065,647	12,623,463	11,382,208	10,198,232	9,082,174
Total Liabilities	26,687,374	26,361,288	25,834,900	19,273,200	15,461,480	14,105,634	11,789,022	10,621,907
Stockholders' Equity	4,435,921	4,392,438	4,355,795	2,571,617	2,096,182	2,021,456	1,774,383	1,402,069
Shares Outstanding	323,301	323,226	322,906	211,059	175,441	173,992	158,967	139,929
Statistical Record								
Return on Assets %	0.86	0.77	0.66	0.87	0.95	0.97	0.92	1.01
Return on Equity %	6.46	5.79	4.88	7.30	7.75	7.59	7.42	8.43
Net Interest Margin %	85.47	87.01	88.73	90.07	91.12	91.61	89.93	86.33
Efficiency Ratio %	49.67	51.63	75.08	58.04	55.07	56.84	58.69	56.59
Loans to Deposits	0.95	0.98	0.94	0.92	0.95	0.98	0.92	0.88
Price Range	16.40-12.09	16.40-11.92	16.40-11.76	16.40-11.18	14.64-11.89	13.65-11.49	13.29-10.62	12.44-9.95
P/E Ratio	21.30-15.70	21.03-15.28	21.87-15.68	21.03-14.33	17.02-13.83	17.06-14.36	16.61-13.27	15.75-12.59
Average Yield %	3.37	3.43	3.50	3.69	3.60	3.84	3.99	4.28

Address: One North Shore Center, 12 Federal Street, Pittsburgh, PA 15212	Web Site: www.fnbcorporation.com	Auditors: Ernst & Young LLP
Telephone: 800-555-5455	Officers: Stephen J. Gurgovits - Chairman Vincent J. Delie - President, Chief Executive Officer, Division Officer	Investor Contact: 724-983-3429 Transfer Agents: ComputerShare, College Station, TX

FACTSET RESEARCH SYSTEMS INC.

Exchange	Symbol	Price	52Wk Range	Yield	P/E	Div Acheiver
NYS	FDS	$192.76 (12/29/2017)	204.87-155.53	1.16	29.12	17 Years

*7 Year Price Score 104.74 *NYSE Composite Index=100 *12 Month Price Score 105.90

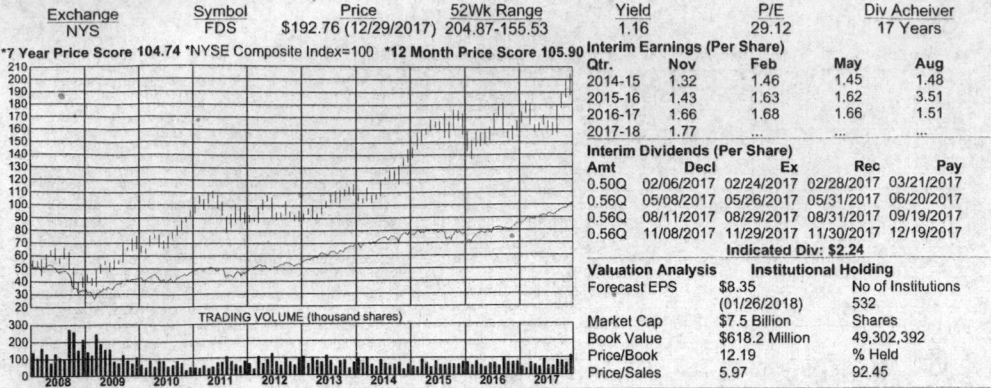

Interim Earnings (Per Share)

Qtr.	Nov	Feb	May	Aug
2014-15	1.32	1.46	1.45	1.48
2015-16	1.43	1.63	1.62	3.51
2016-17	1.66	1.68	1.66	1.51
2017-18	1.77	...	...	...

Interim Dividends (Per Share)

Amt	Decl	Ex	Rec	Pay
0.50Q	02/06/2017	02/24/2017	02/28/2017	03/21/2017
0.56Q	05/08/2017	05/26/2017	05/31/2017	06/20/2017
0.56Q	08/11/2017	08/29/2017	08/31/2017	09/19/2017
0.56Q	11/08/2017	11/29/2017	11/30/2017	12/19/2017

Indicated Div: $2.24

Valuation Analysis / **Institutional Holding**

Forecast EPS	$8.35	No of Institutions
	(01/26/2018)	532
Market Cap	$7.5 Billion	Shares
Book Value	$618.2 Million	49,302,392
Price/Book	12.19	% Held
Price/Sales	5.97	92.45

Business Summary: Business Services (MIC: 7.5.2 SIC: 7371 NAIC: 541511)

FactSet Research Systems provides financial information and analytical applications for the global investment community. Co. provides information to financial investment personnel through its analytics, service, content, and technology. Co. supports the workflow of both buy-side and sell-side clients. From streaming real-time data to historical information, including quotes, estimates, news and commentary, Co. provides content through desktop, wireless and off-platform solutions. Co.'s application provides tools and resources including company and industry analyses, screening tools, portfolio analysis, risk profiles, alpha-testing, portfolio optimization and research management solutions.

Recent Developments: For the quarter ended Nov 30 2017, net income increased 5.7% to US$70.4 million from US$66.6 million in the year-earlier quarter. Revenues were US$329.1 million, up 14.3% from US$288.1 million the year before. Operating income was US$89.1 million versus US$90.3 million in the prior-year quarter, a decrease of 1.4%. Direct operating expenses rose 26.9% to US$161.5 million from US$127.3 million in the comparable period the year before. Indirect operating expenses increased 11.4% to US$78.5 million from US$70.5 million in the equivalent prior-year period.

Prospects: Our evaluation of FactSet Research Systems Inc. as of Jan. 21, 2018 is the result of our systematic analysis on three basic characteristics: earnings strength, relative valuation, and recent stock price movement. The company has enjoyed a very positive trend in earnings per share over the past 5 quarters and while recent estimates for the company have been raised by analysts, FDS has posted better than expected results. Based on operating earnings yield, the company is about fairly valued when compared to all of the companies in our coverage universe. Share price changes over the past year indicates that FDS will perform poorly over the near term.

Financial Data

(US$ in Thousands)	3 Mos	08/31/2017	08/31/2016	08/31/2015	08/31/2014	08/31/2013	08/31/2012	08/31/2011
Earnings Per Share	6.62	6.51	8.19	5.71	4.92	4.45	4.12	3.61
Cash Flow Per Share	8.46	8.13	8.08	7.37	6.25	6.15	5.17	4.51
Tang Book Value Per Share	N.M.	N.M.	N.M.	4.44	4.39	0.02	5.94	5.34
Dividends Per Share	2.180	2.120	1.880	1.660	1.480	1.320	1.160	1.000
Dividend Payout %	32.93	32.57	22.95	29.07	30.08	29.66	28.16	27.70
Income Statement								
Total Revenue	329,141	1,221,179	1,127,092	1,006,768	920,335	858,112	805,793	726,510
EBITDA	100,465	378,912	485,429	356,854	329,364	299,310	300,805	266,858
Depn & Amortn	14,286	28,000	23,300	23,100	25,900	28,400	26,100	27,900
Income Before Taxes	86,179	344,312	460,993	333,754	303,464	270,910	274,705	238,958
Income Taxes	15,800	86,053	122,178	92,703	91,921	72,273	85,896	67,912
Net Income	70,379	258,259	338,815	241,051	211,543	198,637	188,809	171,046
Average Shares	39,680	39,642	41,365	42,235	42,970	44,624	45,810	47,355
Balance Sheet								
Current Assets	427,012	409,376	369,276	304,174	249,775	318,034	299,125	273,170
Total Assets	1,430,602	1,413,315	1,019,161	736,671	663,212	690,197	694,143	657,440
Current Liabilities	161,600	201,139	158,210	139,780	127,291	118,253	113,176	109,423
Long-Term Obligations	574,666	575,000	300,000	35,000	...	...	...	...
Total Liabilities	812,385	853,624	501,780	205,087	152,130	148,418	141,879	142,252
Stockholders' Equity	618,217	559,691	517,381	531,584	511,082	541,779	552,264	515,188
Shares Outstanding	39,110	39,023	40,038	41,316	41,792	43,324	44,279	45,055
Statistical Record								
Return on Assets %	21.16	21.23	38.49	34.44	31.26	28.70	27.86	26.27
Return on Equity %	47.01	47.96	64.42	46.24	40.18	36.31	35.28	33.62
EBITDA Margin %	30.52	31.03	43.07	35.45	35.79	34.88	37.33	36.73
Net Margin %	21.38	21.15	30.06	23.94	22.99	23.15	23.43	23.54
Asset Turnover	1.02	1.00	1.28	1.44	1.36	1.24	1.19	1.12
Current Ratio	2.64	2.04	2.33	2.18	1.96	2.69	2.64	2.50
Debt to Equity	0.93	1.03	0.58	0.07	...	...	...	...
Price Range	199.88-155.53	183.17-151.67	178.81-136.40	173.20-116.34	127.86-101.94	111.60-87.45	108.52-82.24	111.76-73.55
P/E Ratio	30.19-23.49	28.14-23.30	21.83-16.65	30.33-20.37	25.99-20.72	25.08-19.65	26.34-19.96	30.96-20.37
Average Yield %	1.28	1.28	1.18	1.11	1.33	1.36	1.23	1.05

Address: 601 Merritt 7, Norwalk, CT 06851	Web Site: www.factset.com	Auditors: Ernst & Young LLP
Telephone: 203-810-1000	Officers: Philip A. Hadley - Chairman, Chief Executive Officer F. Philip Snow - President, Chief Executive Officer	Transfer Agents: Computershare
Fax: 203-810-1001		

FAIR ISAAC CORP

Exchange	Symbol	Price	52Wk Range	Yield	P/E
NYS	FICO	$153.20 (12/29/2017)	158.13-120.17	N/A	38.49

*7 Year Price Score 145.87 *NYSE Composite Index=100 *12 Month Price Score 104.89

Interim Earnings (Per Share)

Qtr.	Dec	Mar	Jun	Sep
2012-13	0.65	0.51	0.54	0.79
2013-14	0.47	0.59	0.58	1.07
2014-15	0.43	0.58	0.62	1.02
2015-16	0.59	0.72	1.08	1.00
2016-17	1.16	0.78	0.78	1.25

Interim Dividends (Per Share)

Amt	Decl	Ex	Rec	Pay
0.02Q	05/12/2016	05/23/2016	05/25/2016	06/08/2016
0.02Q	08/24/2016	09/12/2016	09/14/2016	09/28/2016
0.02Q	10/26/2016	11/30/2016	12/02/2016	12/16/2016
0.02Q	02/15/2017	03/01/2017	03/03/2017	03/17/2017

Valuation Analysis   **Institutional Holding**

Forecast EPS	$5.45 (01/17/2018)	No of Institutions 365
Market Cap	$4.6 Billion	Shares
Book Value	$426.5 Million	38,225,668
Price/Book	10.86	% Held
Price/Sales	4.97	89.00

Business Summary: Internet & Software (MIC: 6.3.2 SIC: 7372 NAIC: 511210)

Fair Isaac provides a range of analytical solutions, credit scoring and credit account management products and services to banks, and credit reporting agencies. Co.'s segments are: Applications, which includes pre-configured decision management applications designed for a specific type of business problem or process; Scores, which includes Co.'s business-to-business scoring solutions and services, Co.'s myFICO® solutions for consumers, and associated services; and Decision Management Software, which is composed of analytic and decision management software tools that clients can use to create their own custom decision management applications, and its FICO® Decision Management Suite.

Recent Developments: For the year ended Sep 30 2017, net income increased 17.2% to US$128.3 million from US$109.4 million in the prior year. Revenues were US$932.2 million, up 5.8% from US$881.4 million the year before. Operating income was US$177.2 million versus US$169.6 million in the prior year, an increase of 4.5%. Direct operating expenses rose 8.3% to US$287.1 million from US$265.2 million in the comparable period the year before. Indirect operating expenses increased 4.8% to US$467.8 million from US$446.6 million in the equivalent prior-year period.

Prospects: Our evaluation of Fair, Isaac & Co. Inc. as of Jan. 14, 2018 is the result of our systematic analysis on three basic characteristics: earnings strength, relative valuation, and recent stock price movement. The company has enjoyed a very positive trend in earnings per share over the past 5 quarters and while recent estimates for the company have remained steady, FICO has posted results that fell short of analysts expectations. Based on operating earnings yield, the company is overvalued when compared to all of the companies in our coverage universe. Share price changes over the past year indicates that FICO will perform well over the near term.

Financial Data

(US$ in Thousands)	09/30/2017	09/30/2016	09/30/2015	09/30/2014	09/30/2013	09/30/2012	09/30/2011	09/30/2010
Earnings Per Share	3.98	3.39	2.65	2.72	2.48	2.64	1.79	1.42
Cash Flow Per Share	7.31	5.93	4.23	5.17	3.85	3.71	3.46	2.36
Dividends Per Share	0.040	0.080	0.080	0.080	0.080	0.080	0.080	0.080
Dividend Payout %	1.01	2.36	3.02	2.94	3.23	3.03	4.47	5.63
Income Statement								
Total Revenue	932,169	881,356	838,781	788,985	743,444	676,423	619,683	605,643
EBITDA	189,823	185,184	152,061	173,598	175,746	189,204	151,868	145,641
Depn & Amortn	12,709	13,982	13,673	11,917	13,535	21,544	24,241	30,901
Income Before Taxes	151,324	144,569	109,238	133,131	131,984	136,243	97,455	92,304
Income Taxes	23,068	35,121	22,736	38,252	41,889	44,239	25,893	27,847
Net Income	128,256	109,448	86,502	94,879	90,095	92,004	71,562	64,457
Average Shares	32,245	32,308	32,609	34,864	36,292	36,063	39,988	45,308
Balance Sheet								
Current Assets	310,931	267,638	286,602	288,527	249,188	259,325	364,481	347,175
Total Assets	1,255,620	1,221,052	1,230,163	1,192,298	1,161,547	1,158,611	1,129,468	1,123,716
Current Liabilities	326,655	246,077	243,875	341,404	165,880	209,605	146,498	122,147
Long-Term Obligations	462,801	494,000	516,000	376,000	447,000	455,000	504,000	512,000
Total Liabilities	829,083	774,224	793,165	737,684	630,870	684,205	663,974	648,802
Stockholders' Equity	426,537	446,828	436,998	454,614	530,677	474,406	465,494	474,914
Shares Outstanding	30,243	30,935	31,290	32,047	34,786	34,839	37,084	39,882
Statistical Record								
Return on Assets %	10.36	8.91	7.14	8.06	7.77	8.02	6.35	5.31
Return on Equity %	29.37	24.70	19.40	19.26	17.93	19.52	15.22	11.99
EBITDA Margin %	20.36	21.01	18.13	22.00	23.64	27.97	24.51	24.05
Net Margin %	13.76	12.42	10.31	12.03	12.12	13.60	11.55	10.64
Asset Turnover	0.75	0.72	0.69	0.67	0.64	0.59	0.55	0.50
Current Ratio	0.95	1.09	1.18	0.85	1.50	1.24	2.49	2.84
Debt to Equity	1.09	1.11	1.18	0.83	0.84	0.96	1.08	1.08
Price Range	145.54-111.42	132.87-81.01	97.25-53.89	64.88-51.00	55.29-40.62	45.95-20.26	31.61-21.19	26.57-18.07
P/E Ratio	36.57-27.99	39.19-23.90	36.70-20.34	23.85-18.75	22.29-16.38	17.41-7.67	17.66-11.84	18.71-12.73
Average Yield %	0.03	0.08	0.10	0.14	0.17	0.20	0.30	0.35

Address: 181 Metro Drive, Suite 700, San Jose, CA 95110-1346
Telephone: 408-535-1500

Web Site: www.fico.com
Officers: A. George Battle - Chairman William J. Lansing - Chief Executive Officer

Auditors: DELOITTE & TOUCHE LLP
Investor Contact: 800-213-5542
Transfer Agents: Computershare, College Station, TX

FEDERAL REALTY INVESTMENT TRUST (MD)

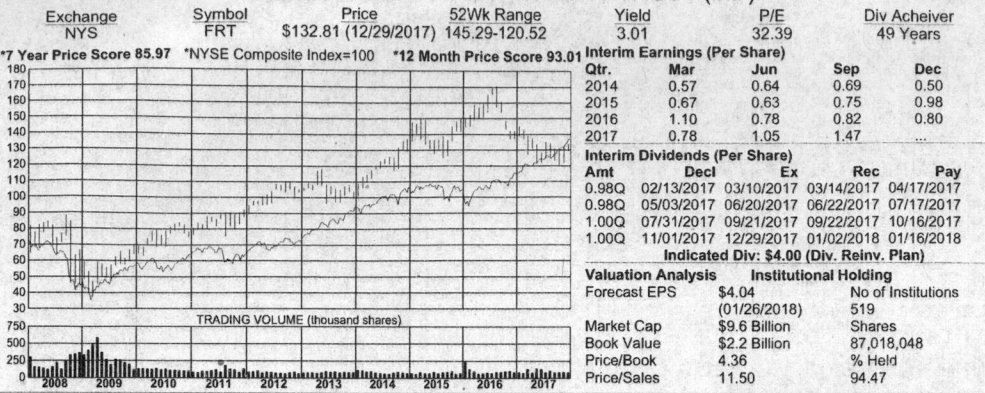

Exchange	Symbol	Price	52Wk Range	Yield	P/E	Div Acheiver
NYS	FRT	$132.81 (12/29/2017)	145.29-120.52	3.01	32.39	49 Years

*7 Year Price Score 85.97 *NYSE Composite Index=100 *12 Month Price Score 93.01

Interim Earnings (Per Share)

Qtr.	Mar	Jun	Sep	Dec
2014	0.57	0.64	0.69	0.50
2015	0.67	0.63	0.75	0.98
2016	1.10	0.78	0.82	0.80
2017	0.78	1.05	1.47	...

Interim Dividends (Per Share)

Amt	Decl	Ex	Rec	Pay
0.98Q	02/13/2017	03/10/2017	03/14/2017	04/17/2017
0.98Q	05/03/2017	06/20/2017	06/22/2017	07/17/2017
1.00Q	07/31/2017	09/21/2017	09/22/2017	10/16/2017
1.00Q	11/01/2017	12/29/2017	01/02/2018	01/16/2018

Indicated Div: $4.00 (Div. Reinv. Plan)

Valuation Analysis — **Institutional Holding**

Forecast EPS	$4.04
(01/26/2018)	No of Institutions 519
Market Cap	$9.6 Billion Shares
Book Value	$2.2 Billion 87,018,048
Price/Book	4.36 % Held
Price/Sales	11.50 94.47

TRADING VOLUME (thousand shares)

Business Summary: REITs (MIC: 5.3.1 SIC: 6798 NAIC: 525930)

Federal Realty Investment Trust is an equity real estate investment trust that focuses on the ownership, management, and redevelopment of retail and mixed-use properties. Co.'s properties are located primarily in communities in selected metropolitan markets in the Northeast and Mid-Atlantic regions of the U.S., as well as in California and South Florida. As of Dec 31 2016, Co. owned or had a majority interest in community and neighborhood shopping centers and mixed-use properties which were operated as 96 predominantly retail real estate projects.

Recent Developments: For the quarter ended Sep 30 2017, income from continuing operations increased 3.3% to US$58.1 million from US$56.3 million in the year-earlier quarter. Net income increased 77.9% to US$108.9 million from US$61.2 million in the year-earlier quarter. Revenues were US$218.0 million, up 8.3% from US$201.2 million the year before. Revenues from property income rose 7.4% to US$212.0 million from US$197.5 million in the corresponding quarter a year earlier.

Prospects: Our evaluation of Federal Realty Investment Trust as of Jan. 14, 2018 is the result of our systematic analysis on three basic characteristics: earnings strength, relative valuation, and recent stock price movement. The company has managed to produce a neutral trend in earnings per share over the past 5 quarters. Because the company lacks sufficient analyst estimate data, we place greater weight on the historical EPS trend as the measure of earnings strength. Based on operating earnings yield, the company is overvalued when compared to all of the companies in our coverage universe. Share price changes over the past year indicates that FRT will perform well over the near term.

Financial Data
(US$ in Thousands)

	9 Mos	6 Mos	3 Mos	12/31/2016	12/31/2015	12/31/2014	12/31/2013	12/31/2012
Earnings Per Share	4.10	3.45	3.18	3.50	3.03	2.41	2.46	2.35
Cash Flow Per Share	6.52	6.41	6.12	5.90	5.23	5.14	4.81	4.63
Tang Book Value Per Share	28.24	27.44	27.29	27.32	23.80	23.24	21.56	19.70
Dividends Per Share	3.940	3.920	3.880	3.840	3.620	3.300	3.020	2.840
Dividend Payout %	96.10	113.62	122.01	109.71	119.47	136.93	122.76	120.85
Income Statement								
Total Revenue	633,391	415,438	207,389	801,591	744,012	686,090	637,413	608,018
EBITDA	408,787	268,679	132,923	514,580	455,878	431,306	401,956	397,301
Depn & Amortn	159,656	104,045	51,379	193,585	174,796	170,814	161,099	142,039
Income Before Taxes	175,432	117,143	57,892	226,375	188,678	166,645	136,313	142,615
Net Income	239,258	132,481	56,190	249,910	210,219	164,535	162,681	151,925
Average Shares	72,206	72,124	72,005	71,049	68,981	67,492	65,483	64,056
Balance Sheet								
Current Assets	223,728	265,322	135,887	170,021	173,066	192,230	228,920	166,497
Total Assets	6,221,137	5,803,503	5,656,200	5,423,279	4,911,709	4,546,870	4,219,294	3,898,565
Current Liabilities	296,605	278,791	280,047	289,481	228,309	220,420	221,427	181,571
Long-Term Obligations	3,263,462	3,142,988	3,013,369	2,798,452	2,642,366	2,409,677	2,321,862	2,208,602
Total Liabilities	4,012,183	3,811,136	3,674,508	3,446,546	3,247,960	2,942,469	2,771,134	2,611,753
Stockholders' Equity	2,208,954	1,992,367	1,981,692	1,976,733	1,663,749	1,604,401	1,448,160	1,286,812
Shares Outstanding	72,542	72,251	72,236	71,995	69,493	68,605	66,701	64,815
Statistical Record								
Return on Assets %	5.12	4.54	4.25	4.82	4.45	3.75	4.01	4.01
Return on Equity %	14.22	12.74	11.95	13.69	12.86	10.78	11.90	12.11
EBITDA Margin %	64.54	64.67	64.09	64.19	61.27	62.86	63.06	65.34
Net Margin %	37.77	31.89	27.09	31.18	28.25	23.98	25.52	24.99
Asset Turnover	0.14	0.15	0.15	0.15	0.16	0.16	0.16	0.16
Current Ratio	0.75	0.95	0.49	0.59	0.76	0.87	1.03	0.92
Debt to Equity	1.48	1.58	1.52	1.42	1.59	1.50	1.60	1.72
Price Range	153.93-121.73	170.35-121.73	170.35-126.98	170.35-136.98	150.27-124.96	137.18-100.90	117.96-96.21	110.03-89.23
P/E Ratio	37.54-29.69	49.38-35.28	53.57-39.93	48.67-39.14	49.59-41.24	56.92-41.87	47.95-39.11	46.82-37.97
Average Yield %	2.93	2.74	2.60	2.52	2.60	2.75	2.85	2.80

Address: 1626 East Jefferson Street, Rockville, MD 20852
Telephone: 301-998-8100

Web Site: www.federalrealty.com
Officers: Donald C. Wood - President, Chief Executive Officer, Principal Financial Officer Dawn M. Becker - Executive Vice President, Chief Operating Officer, Secretary, General Counsel

Auditors: Grant Thornton LLP
Investor Contact: 800-658-8980
Transfer Agents: American Stock Transfer & Trust Company, New York, NY

FEDERATED INVESTORS INC (PA)

Exchange	Symbol	Price	52Wk Range	Yield	P/E
NYS	FII	$36.08 (12/29/2017)	36.53-25.26	2.77	16.94

*7 Year Price Score 83.07 *NYSE Composite Index=100 *12 Month Price Score 110.69

Interim Earnings (Per Share)

Qtr.	Mar	Jun	Sep	Dec
2014	0.34	0.35	0.36	0.37
2015	0.35	0.40	0.42	0.45
2016	0.44	0.51	0.54	0.55
2017	0.49	0.53	0.56	...

Interim Dividends (Per Share)

Amt	Decl	Ex	Rec	Pay
0.25Q	01/26/2017	02/06/2017	02/08/2017	02/15/2017
0.25Q	04/27/2017	05/04/2017	05/08/2017	05/15/2017
0.25Q	07/27/2017	08/04/2017	08/08/2017	08/15/2017
0.25Q	10/26/2017	11/07/2017	11/08/2017	11/15/2017

Indicated Div: $1.00

Valuation Analysis / **Institutional Holding**

Forecast EPS	$2.14 (01/17/2018)	No of Institutions	439
Market Cap	$3.6 Billion	Shares	118,247,464
Book Value	$653.8 Million	% Held	83.85
Price/Book	5.57		
Price/Sales	3.27		

Business Summary: Wealth Management (MIC: 5.5.2 SIC: 6282 NAIC: 523930)

Federated Investors, together with its subsidiaries, is a provider of investment management products and related financial services. Co. sponsors, markets and provides investment-related services to various investment products, including mutual funds and Separate Accounts (which include separately managed accounts, institutional accounts, sub-advised funds and other managed products) in both domestic and international markets. Co. markets these funds to banks, broker/dealers and other financial intermediaries who use them to meet the needs of their customers, including retail investors, corporations and retirement plans. As of Dec 31 2016, Co. had $365.91 billion in assets under management.

Recent Developments: For the quarter ended Sep 30 2017, net income decreased 2.8% to US$57.2 million from US$58.9 million in the year-earlier quarter. Revenues were US$278.3 million, down 5.5% from US$294.6 million the year before. Operating income was US$88.7 million versus US$88.6 million in the prior-year quarter, an increase of 0.1%. Indirect operating expenses decreased 7.9% to US$189.6 million from US$206.0 million in the equivalent prior-year period.

Prospects: Our evaluation of Federated Investors Inc. as of Jan. 14, 2018 is the result of our systematic analysis on three basic characteristics: earnings strength, relative valuation, and recent stock price movement. The company has managed to produce a neutral trend in earnings per share over the past 5 quarters and while recent estimates for the company have been mixed, FII has posted better than expected results. Based on operating earnings yield, the company is undervalued when compared to all of the companies in our coverage universe. Share price changes over the past year indicates that FII will perform well over the near term.

Financial Data

(US$ in Thousands)	9 Mos	6 Mos	3 Mos	12/31/2016	12/31/2015	12/31/2014	12/31/2013	12/31/2012
Earnings Per Share	2.13	2.11	2.09	2.03	1.62	1.42	1.55	1.79
Cash Flow Per Share	2.76	2.69	2.66	2.54	2.32	1.91	2.59	3.14
Dividends Per Share	2.000	2.000	2.000	2.000	1.000	1.000	0.980	2.470
Dividend Payout %	93.90	94.79	95.69	98.52	61.73	70.42	63.23	137.99
Income Statement								
Total Revenue	824,612	546,297	273,501	1,143,371	926,609	859,250	878,365	945,706
EBITDA	268,929	174,980	84,595	354,807	288,405	258,963	280,579	331,052
Depn & Amortn	6,580	4,879	2,608	9,700	9,200	10,000	9,100	8,100
Income Before Taxes	258,815	167,818	80,885	340,934	274,906	239,352	259,015	308,511
Income Taxes	95,888	62,132	29,858	119,420	102,920	89,530	92,660	110,883
Net Income	159,531	103,092	49,641	208,919	169,807	149,236	162,177	188,088
Average Shares	97,129	97,582	97,864	99,117	100,477	100,723	100,669	100,313
Balance Sheet								
Current Assets	385,689	344,383	335,474	359,760	395,828	342,055	339,318	300,062
Total Assets	1,181,508	1,140,791	1,133,216	1,155,107	1,187,203	1,140,519	1,135,797	1,090,061
Current Liabilities	115,814	94,679	127,573	162,538	159,208	149,321	214,205	181,134
Long-Term Obligations	175,000	178,500	159,375	165,750	191,250	216,750	198,333	276,250
Total Liabilities	527,711	509,162	520,526	560,281	539,387	531,025	569,678	594,629
Stockholders' Equity	653,797	631,629	612,690	594,826	647,816	609,494	566,119	495,432
Shares Outstanding	100,903	101,454	101,999	101,998	104,103	104,927	104,798	104,450
Statistical Record								
Return on Assets %	17.86	18.27	18.34	17.79	14.59	13.11	14.57	16.74
Return on Equity %	32.30	32.92	33.45	33.53	27.01	25.39	30.55	36.16
EBITDA Margin %	32.61	32.03	30.93	31.03	31.12	30.14	31.94	35.01
Net Margin %	19.35	18.87	18.15	18.27	18.33	17.37	18.46	19.89
Asset Turnover	0.92	0.97	0.99	0.97	0.80	0.75	0.79	0.84
Current Ratio	3.33	3.64	2.63	2.21	2.49	2.29	1.58	1.66
Debt to Equity	0.27	0.28	0.26	0.28	0.30	0.36	0.35	0.56
Price Range	29.96-24.90	32.93-24.90	32.93-24.90	32.93-23.29	35.34-28.29	33.86-25.73	30.52-20.23	23.45-15.83
P/E Ratio	14.07-11.69	15.61-11.80	15.76-11.91	16.22-11.47	21.81-17.46	23.85-18.12	19.69-13.05	13.10-8.84
Average Yield %	7.32	7.11	6.87	6.89	3.08	3.39	3.74	12.01

Address: Federated Investors Tower, Pittsburgh, PA 15222-3779
Telephone: 412-288-1900

Web Site: www.federatedinvestors.com
Officers: John F. Donahue - Chairman Paul A. Uhlman - Vice President

Auditors: Ernst & Young LLP
Transfer Agents: ComputerShare Investor Services, Providence, RI

FEDEX CORP

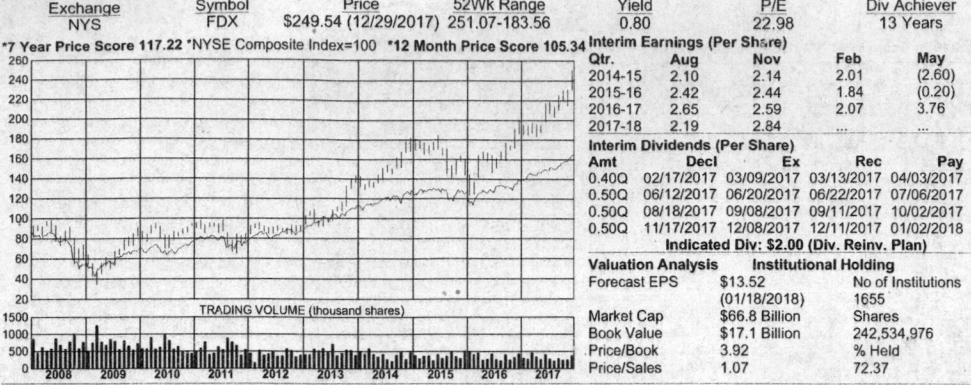

Exchange	Symbol	Price	52Wk Range	Yield	P/E	Div Achiever
NYS	FDX	$249.54 (12/29/2017)	251.07-183.56	0.80	22.98	13 Years

*7 Year Price Score 117.22 *NYSE Composite Index=100 *12 Month Price Score 105.34

Interim Earnings (Per Share)

Qtr.	Aug	Nov	Feb	May
2014-15	2.10	2.14	2.01	(2.60)
2015-16	2.42	2.44	1.84	(0.20)
2016-17	2.65	2.59	2.07	3.76
2017-18	2.19	2.84	...	...

Interim Dividends (Per Share)

Amt	Decl	Ex	Rec	Pay
0.40Q	02/17/2017	03/09/2017	03/13/2017	04/03/2017
0.50Q	06/12/2017	06/20/2017	06/22/2017	07/06/2017
0.50Q	08/18/2017	09/08/2017	09/11/2017	10/02/2017
0.50Q	11/17/2017	12/08/2017	12/11/2017	01/02/2018

Indicated Div: $2.00 (Div. Reinv. Plan)

Valuation Analysis

		Institutional Holding	
Forecast EPS	$13.52	No of Institutions	
	(01/18/2018)	1655	
Market Cap	$66.8 Billion	Shares	
Book Value	$17.1 Billion	242,534,976	
Price/Book	3.92	% Held	
Price/Sales	1.07	72.37	

Business Summary: Airlines/Air Freight (MIC: 7.4.4 SIC: 4513 NAIC: 492110)

FedEx provides transportation, e-commerce and business services through companies under the FedEx brand. These companies are included in the following segments: Federal Express Corporation, an express transportation company; TNT Express B.V., an international express transportation, small-package ground delivery and freight transportation company; FedEx Ground Package System, Inc., a provider of small-package ground delivery services; FedEx Freight, Inc., a provider of less-than-truckload freight services; and FedEx Corporate Services, Inc., which provides sales, marketing, information technology, communications, customer services, technical support, billing and collections services.

Recent Developments: For the quarter ended Nov 30 2017, net income increased 10.7% to US$775.0 million from US$700.0 million in the year-earlier quarter. Revenues were US$16.31 billion, up 9.3% from US$14.93 billion the year before. Operating income was US$1.26 billion versus US$1.17 billion in the prior-year quarter, an increase of 8.1%. Direct operating expenses rose 11.3% to US$6.91 billion from US$6.21 billion in the comparable period the year before. Indirect operating expenses increased 7.7% to US$8.14 billion from US$7.55 billion in the equivalent prior-year period.

Prospects: Our evaluation of FedEx Corp. as of Jan. 14, 2018 is the result of our systematic analysis on three basic characteristics: earnings strength, relative valuation, and recent stock price movement. The company has managed to produce a neutral trend in earnings per share over the past 5 quarters and while recent estimates for the company have been raised by analysts, FDX has posted better than expected results. Based on operating earnings yield, the company is undervalued when compared to all of the companies in our coverage universe. Share price changes over the past year indicates that FDX will perform poorly over the near term.

Financial Data

(US$ in Thousands)	6 Mos	3 Mos	05/31/2017	05/31/2016	05/31/2015	05/31/2014	05/31/2013	05/31/2012
Earnings Per Share	10.86	10.61	11.07	6.51	3.65	6.75	4.91	6.41
Cash Flow Per Share	14.15	16.97	18.53	20.62	18.96	13.89	14.88	15.31
Tang Book Value Per Share	36.32	34.44	33.25	26.50	39.60	39.27	46.05	38.93
Dividends Per Share	1.800	1.700	1.600	1.000	0.800	0.600	0.560	0.520
Dividend Payout %	16.57	16.02	14.45	15.36	21.92	8.89	11.41	8.11
Income Statement								
Total Revenue	31,610,000	15,297,000	60,319,000	50,365,000	47,453,000	45,567,000	44,287,000	42,680,000
EBITDA	3,866,000	1,847,000	7,958,000	5,655,000	4,448,000	6,031,000	4,816,000	5,280,000
Depn & Amortn	1,507,000	751,000	2,900,000	2,600,000	2,600,000	2,600,000	2,300,000	2,100,000
Income Before Taxes	2,121,000	982,000	4,579,000	2,740,000	1,627,000	3,289,000	2,455,000	3,141,000
Income Taxes	750,000	386,000	1,582,000	920,000	577,000	1,192,000	894,000	1,109,000
Net Income	1,371,000	596,000	2,997,000	1,820,000	1,050,000	2,097,000	1,561,000	2,032,000
Average Shares	272,000	272,000	270,000	279,000	287,000	310,000	317,000	317,000
Balance Sheet								
Current Assets	12,881,000	12,722,000	12,628,000	11,989,000	10,941,000	9,683,000	11,274,000	9,056,000
Total Assets	50,281,000	49,350,000	48,552,000	46,064,000	37,069,000	33,070,000	33,567,000	29,903,000
Current Liabilities	8,227,000	7,790,000	7,918,000	8,008,000	5,957,000	5,312,000	5,750,000	5,374,000
Long-Term Obligations	15,180,000	15,137,000	14,909,000	13,838,000	7,249,000	4,736,000	2,739,000	1,250,000
Total Liabilities	33,226,000	32,732,000	32,479,000	32,280,000	22,076,000	17,793,000	16,169,000	15,176,000
Stockholders' Equity	17,055,000	16,618,000	16,073,000	13,784,000	14,993,000	15,277,000	17,398,000	14,727,000
Shares Outstanding	267,889	268,147	268,257	265,524	282,430	318,000	318,000	317,000
Statistical Record								
Return on Assets %	6.11	6.06	6.34	4.37	2.99	6.29	4.92	7.07
Return on Equity %	18.70	18.71	20.08	12.61	6.94	12.84	9.72	13.53
EBITDA Margin %	12.23	12.07	13.19	11.23	9.37	13.24	10.87	12.37
Net Margin %	4.34	3.90	4.97	3.61	2.21	4.60	3.52	4.76
Asset Turnover	1.29	1.28	1.28	1.21	1.35	1.37	1.40	1.49
Current Ratio	1.57	1.63	1.59	1.50	1.84	1.82	1.96	1.69
Debt to Equity	0.89	0.91	0.93	1.00	0.48	0.31	0.16	0.08
Price Range	231.46-183.56	219.06-158.89	201.02-146.13	184.98-123.18	182.03-139.21	144.53-95.71	109.07-84.34	98.50-65.15
P/E Ratio	21.31-16.90	20.65-14.98	18.16-13.20	28.41-18.92	49.87-38.14	21.41-14.18	22.21-17.18	15.37-10.16
Average Yield %	0.88	0.89	0.89	0.64	0.49	0.48	0.60	0.61

Address: 942 South Shady Grove Road, Memphis, TN 38120	**Web Site:** www.fedex.com	**Auditors:** Ernst & Young LLP
Telephone: 901-818-7500	**Officers:** Frederick W. Smith - Chairman, President, Chief Executive Officer David J. Bronczek - President, Chief Executive Officer	**Investor Contact:** 901-818-7200
		Transfer Agents: ComputerShare Investor Services, Providence, RI

FIDELITY NATIONAL FINANCIAL INC

Exchange	Symbol	Price	52Wk Range	Yield	P/E
NYS	FNF	$39.24 (12/29/2017)	40.63-24.17	2.75	16.84

*7 Year Price Score N/A ***NYSE Composite Index=100** ***12 Month Price Score 115.85**

Interim Earnings (Per Share)

Qtr.	Mar	Jun	Sep	Dec
2014	(0.08)	0.41	0.40	0.35
2015	0.30	0.56	0.53	0.51
2016	0.26	0.67	0.58	0.83
2017	0.25	0.63	0.62	...

Interim Dividends (Per Share)

Amt	Decl	Ex	Rec	Pay
0.25Q	05/03/2017	06/14/2017	06/16/2017	06/30/2017
0.25Q	07/19/2017	09/14/2017	09/15/2017	09/29/2017
0.00Q	09/07/2017	10/02/2017	09/20/2017	09/29/2017
0.27Q	10/25/2017	12/14/2017	12/15/2017	12/29/2017
		Indicated Div: $1.08		

Valuation Analysis **Institutional Holding**

Forecast EPS	$2.46 (01/12/2018)	No of Institutions	588
Market Cap	$13.3 Billion	Shares	278,845,696
Book Value	$5.3 Billion	% Held	
Price/Book	2.52		101.20
Price/Sales	1.34		

Business Summary: General Insurance (MIC: 5.2.1 SIC: 6361 NAIC: 524127)

Fidelity National Financial is a title insurance holding company. Co. has organized its business into two groups, FNF Group and FNF Ventures (FNFV). Through its FNF Group, Co. provides title insurance, escrow and other title related services, including trust activities, trustee's sales guarantees, recordings and reconveyances and home warranty products and technology and transaction services to the real estate and mortgage industries. Through its FNFV group, Co. owns majority and minority equity investment stakes in a number of entities, including American Blue Ribbon Holdings, LLC, Ceridian HCM, Inc. and and Digital Insurance, Inc.

Recent Developments: For the quarter ended Sep 30 2017, income from continuing operations decreased 5.3% to US$144.0 million from US$152.0 million in the year-earlier quarter. Net income increased 3.6% to US$175.0 million from US$169.0 million in the year-earlier quarter. Revenues were US$2.27 billion, unchanged from the year before. Net premiums earned were US$1.28 billion versus US$1.27 billion in the prior-year quarter, an increase of 0.6%.

Prospects: Our evaluation of Fidelity National Financial Inc. as of Jan. 14, 2018 is the result of our systematic analysis on three basic characteristics: earnings strength, relative valuation, and recent stock price movement. The company has managed to produce a neutral trend in earnings per share over the past 5 quarters and while recent estimates for the company have been raised by analysts, FNF has posted better than expected results. Based on operating earnings yield, the company is about fairly valued when compared to all of the companies in our coverage universe. Share price changes over the past year indicates that FNF will perform very well over the near term.

Financial Data
(US$ in Thousands)

	9 Mos	6 Mos	3 Mos	12/31/2016	12/31/2015	12/31/2014	12/31/2013	12/31/2012
Earnings Per Share	2.33	2.29	2.33	2.34	1.89	0.75	1.71	2.68
Cash Flow Per Share	3.61	3.98	3.96	4.26	3.31	4.11	2.10	2.80
Tang Book Value Per Share	5.23	N.M.	N.M.	N.M.	N.M.	N.M.	10.18	7.48
Dividends Per Share	1.000	0.960	0.920	0.880	0.800	0.370	0.660	0.580
Dividend Payout %	42.92	41.92	39.48	37.61	42.33	49.33	38.60	21.64
Income Statement								
Premium Income	3,626,000	2,349,000	1,048,000	4,723,000	4,286,000	3,671,000	4,152,000	3,836,500
Total Revenue	6,901,000	5,104,000	2,217,000	9,554,000	9,132,000	8,024,000	8,565,000	7,201,700
Benefits & Claims	181,000	117,000	52,000	157,000	246,000	228,000	291,000	279,300
Income Before Taxes	861,000	691,000	161,000	1,072,000	867,000	392,000	651,000	843,400
Income Taxes	355,000	304,000	78,000	372,000	290,000	312,000	205,000	246,700
Net Income	533,000	368,000	72,000	650,000	527,000	583,000	402,000	606,500
Average Shares	276,000	277,000	279,000	280,000	286,000	142,000	235,000	226,000
Balance Sheet								
Total Assets	10,501,000	14,202,000	14,178,000	14,463,000	13,931,000	13,868,000	10,524,000	9,902,600
Total Liabilities	5,231,000	8,161,000	8,199,000	8,467,000	8,177,000	7,874,000	5,456,000	5,634,600
Stockholders' Equity	5,270,000	6,041,000	5,979,000	5,996,000	5,754,000	5,994,000	5,068,000	4,268,000
Shares Outstanding	338,019	337,954	338,665	338,622	347,999	371,777	250,340	228,545
Statistical Record								
Return on Assets %	6.08	5.22	4.61	4.57	3.79	4.78	3.94	6.81
Return on Equity %	13.57	12.61	11.07	11.03	8.97	10.54	8.61	15.31
Loss Ratio %	4.99	4.98	4.96	3.32	5.74	6.21	7.01	7.28
Net Margin %	7.72	7.21	3.25	6.80	5.77	7.27	4.69	8.42
Price Range	35.10-22.84	32.20-22.84	28.12-22.80	27.60-21.25	28.73-23.34	25.87-18.83	...	...
P/E Ratio	15.06-9.80	14.06-9.97	12.07-9.79	11.80-9.08	15.20-12.35	34.50-25.10	...	...
Average Yield %	3.48	3.57	3.60	3.55	3.04	1.76	...	...

Address: 601 Riverside Avenue, Jacksonville, FL 32204 **Telephone:** 904-854-8100	**Web Site:** www.fnf.com **Officers:** Michael J. Nolan - President, Co-Chief Operating Officer Raymond R. (Randy) Quirk - President, Chief Executive Officer	**Auditors:** Ernst & Young LLP **Investor Contact:** 904-854-8120 **Transfer Agents:** Continental Stock Transfer & Trust Company, New York, NY

FIDELITY NATIONAL INFORMATION SERVICES INC

Exchange	Symbol	Price	52Wk Range	Yield	P/E
NYS	FIS	$94.09 (12/29/2017)	96.62-76.98	1.23	58.44

*7 Year Price Score 124.09 *NYSE Composite Index=100 *12 Month Price Score 101.20

Interim Earnings (Per Share)

Qtr.	Mar	Jun	Sep	Dec
2014	0.53	0.62	0.52	0.68
2015	0.39	0.84	0.62	0.34
2016	0.17	0.37	0.56	0.62
2017	0.41	0.40	0.18	...

Interim Dividends (Per Share)

Amt	Decl	Ex	Rec	Pay
0.29Q	01/25/2017	03/15/2017	03/17/2017	03/31/2017
0.29Q	04/27/2017	06/14/2017	06/16/2017	06/30/2017
0.29Q	07/20/2017	09/14/2017	09/15/2017	09/29/2017
0.29Q	10/26/2017	12/14/2017	12/15/2017	12/29/2017

Indicated Div: $1.16

Valuation Analysis | **Institutional Holding**

Forecast EPS	$4.41	No of Institutions
	(01/17/2018)	881
Market Cap	$31.3 Billion	Shares
Book Value	$10.0 Billion	350,429,984
Price/Book	3.14	% Held
Price/Sales	3.39	N/A

Business Summary: Business Services (MIC: 7.5.2 SIC: 7389 NAIC: 561499)

Fidelity National Information Services is a provider of financial services technology. Co.'s segments are: Integrated Financial Solutions, which serves the regional and community bank and savings institution market for transaction and account processing, payment solutions, channel solutions, lending and wealth management solutions, digital channels, risk and compliance solutions, and services; Global Financial Solutions, which provides an array of capital markets and asset management and insurance solutions, as well as banking and payments solutions and consulting and transformation services; and Corporate and Other, which includes global commercial services and retail check processing.

Recent Developments: For the quarter ended Sep 30 2017, income from continuing operations decreased 62.8% to US$71.0 million from US$191.0 million in the year-earlier quarter. Net income decreased 62.8% to US$71.0 million from US$191.0 million in the year-earlier quarter. Revenues were US$2.20 billion, down 4.8% from US$2.31 billion the year before. Operating income was US$388.0 million versus US$398.0 million in the prior-year quarter, a decrease of 2.5%. Direct operating expenses declined 2.9% to US$1.48 billion from US$1.53 billion in the comparable period the year before. Indirect operating expenses decreased 14.8% to US$327.0 million from US$384.0 million in the equivalent prior-year period.

Prospects: Our evaluation of Fidelity National Information Services Inc. as of Jan. 14, 2018 is the result of our systematic analysis on three basic characteristics: earnings strength, relative valuation, and recent stock price movement. The company has enjoyed a very positive trend in earnings per share over the past 5 quarters and while recent estimates for the company have been mixed, FIS has posted better than expected results. Based on operating earnings yield, the company is undervalued when compared to all of the companies in our coverage universe. Share price changes over the past year indicates that FIS will perform well over the near term.

Financial Data

(US$ in Thousands)	9 Mos	6 Mos	3 Mos	12/31/2016	12/31/2015	12/31/2014	12/31/2013	12/31/2012
Earnings Per Share	1.61	1.99	1.96	1.72	2.19	2.35	1.68	1.55
Cash Flow Per Share	5.02	4.95	6.08	5.89	3.99	4.09	3.66	3.58
Dividends Per Share	1.130	1.100	1.070	1.040	1.040	0.960	0.880	0.800
Dividend Payout %	70.19	55.28	54.59	60.47	47.49	40.85	52.38	51.61
Income Statement								
Total Revenue	6,794,000	4,596,000	2,255,000	9,241,000	6,595,200	6,413,800	6,070,700	5,807,600
EBITDA	899,000	695,000	490,000	1,474,000	1,359,400	1,341,000	1,132,200	1,171,700
Depn & Amortn	15,000	17,000	174,000	185,000	139,100	130,100	119,000	117,800
Income Before Taxes	617,000	495,000	223,000	906,000	1,036,900	1,053,400	825,000	831,200
Income Taxes	262,000	211,000	79,000	317,000	378,800	335,100	309,200	270,900
Net Income	331,000	270,000	138,000	568,000	631,500	679,100	493,100	461,200
Average Shares	336,000	334,000	333,000	330,000	288,700	288,700	294,200	297,500
Balance Sheet								
Current Assets	3,324,000	4,062,000	3,409,000	4,282,000	3,511,400	2,473,100	2,351,900	1,844,200
Total Assets	24,294,000	24,970,000	25,086,000	26,031,000	26,268,800	14,520,500	13,960,100	13,549,700
Current Liabilities	2,658,000	2,729,000	3,138,000	3,151,000	2,363,900	1,598,900	1,672,700	1,256,800
Long-Term Obligations	8,813,000	9,415,000	9,154,000	10,146,000	11,497,800	5,054,600	4,339,800	4,231,600
Total Liabilities	14,309,000	15,079,000	15,208,000	16,290,000	16,947,800	7,963,800	7,379,600	6,908,800
Stockholders' Equity	9,985,000	9,891,000	9,878,000	9,741,000	9,321,000	6,556,700	6,580,500	6,640,900
Shares Outstanding	333,000	332,000	329,000	328,000	324,500	284,900	290,600	294,100
Statistical Record								
Return on Assets %	2.13	2.58	2.53	2.17	3.10	4.77	3.58	3.36
Return on Equity %	5.48	6.83	6.76	5.94	7.95	10.34	7.46	7.00
EBITDA Margin %	13.23	15.12	21.73	15.95	20.61	20.91	18.65	20.18
Net Margin %	4.87	5.87	6.12	6.15	9.58	10.59	8.12	7.94
Asset Turnover	0.37	0.36	0.36	0.35	0.32	0.45	0.44	0.42
Current Ratio	1.25	1.49	1.09	1.36	1.49	1.55	1.41	1.47
Debt to Equity	0.88	0.95	0.93	1.04	1.23	0.77	0.66	0.64
Price Range	93.54-73.92	86.77-73.68	83.84-63.31	80.84-56.04	73.50-58.52	64.04-48.87	53.68-34.81	36.97-26.43
P/E Ratio	58.10-45.91	43.60-37.03	42.78-32.30	47.00-32.58	33.56-26.72	27.25-20.80	31.95-20.72	23.85-17.05
Average Yield %	1.36	1.38	1.40	1.46	1.59	1.73	2.01	2.47

Address: 601 Riverside Avenue, Jacksonville, FL 32204 **Telephone:** 904-438-6000	**Web Site:** www.fisglobal.com **Officers:** Gary A. Norcross - President, Corporate Executive Vice President, Chief Operating Officer, Chief Executive Officer Marc M. Mayo - Executive Vice President, Chief Legal Officer	**Auditors:** KPMG LLP **Transfer Agents:** Computershare Investor Services, LLC, Chicago, IL

FIRST AMERICAN FINANCIAL CORP

Exchange	Symbol	Price	52Wk Range	Yield	P/E
NYS	FAF	$56.04 (12/29/2017)	57.02-36.83	2.71	22.15

'7 Year Price Score 120.99 **'NYSE Composite Index=100** **'12 Month Price Score 114.40**

Interim Earnings (Per Share)

Qtr.	Mar	Jun	Sep	Dec
2014	0.20	0.47	0.74	0.74
2015	0.34	0.85	0.69	0.74
2016	0.47	0.92	0.96	0.73
2017	0.52	1.09	0.19	...

Interim Dividends (Per Share)

Amt	Decl	Ex	Rec	Pay
0.34Q	01/19/2017	03/06/2017	03/08/2017	03/15/2017
0.34Q	05/09/2017	06/06/2017	06/08/2017	06/15/2017
0.38Q	08/16/2017	09/07/2017	09/08/2017	09/15/2017
0.38Q	11/08/2017	12/07/2017	12/08/2017	12/15/2017

Indicated Div: $1.52

Valuation Analysis / **Institutional Holding**

Forecast EPS	$3.49 (01/12/2018)	No of Institutions 402
Market Cap	$6.2 Billion	Shares
Book Value	$3.3 Billion	105,489,296
Price/Book	1.89	% Held
Price/Sales	1.07	93.40

Business Summary: General Insurance (MIC: 5.2.1 SIC: 6361 NAIC: 524127)

First American Financial is a holding company. Through its subsidiaries, Co. is engaged in the business of providing financial services through its two segments. The title insurance and services segment provides title insurance, closing and/or escrow services and similar or related services domestically and internationally in connection with residential and commercial real estate transactions. It maintains, manages and provides access to title plant records and images and, in addition, provides banking, trust, document custodial and investment advisory services. The specialty insurance segment issues property and casualty insurance policies and sells home warranty products.

Recent Developments: For the quarter ended Sep 30 2017, net income decreased 80.3% to US$21.2 million from US$107.4 million in the year-earlier quarter. Revenues were US$1.52 billion, up 0.7% from US$1.51 billion the year before. Net premiums earned were unchanged at US$1.28 billion versus the prior-year quarter. Net investment income fell 14.7% to US$37.5 million from US$43.9 million a year ago.

Prospects: Our evaluation of First American Financial Corp. as of Jan. 14, 2018 is the result of our systematic analysis on three basic characteristics: earnings strength, relative valuation, and recent stock price movement. The company has produced a positive trend in earnings per share over the past 5 quarters and while recent estimates for the company have been mixed, FAF has posted better than expected results. Based on operating earnings yield, the company is undervalued when compared to all of the companies in our coverage universe. Share price changes over the past year indicates that FAF will perform well over the near term.

Financial Data
(US$ in Thousands)

	9 Mos	6 Mos	3 Mos	12/31/2016	12/31/2015	12/31/2014	12/31/2013	12/31/2012
Earnings Per Share	2.53	3.30	3.13	3.09	2.62	2.15	1.71	2.77
Cash Flow Per Share	6.20	5.18	4.96	4.42	5.08	3.37	3.54	4.03
Tang Book Value Per Share	18.71	18.82	17.88	17.39	16.00	14.48	14.74	13.48
Dividends Per Share	1.400	1.360	1.280	1.200	1.000	0.840	0.480	0.360
Dividend Payout %	55.34	41.21	40.89	38.83	38.17	39.07	28.07	13.00
Income Statement								
Total Revenue	4,291,040	2,771,472	1,317,043	5,575,846	5,175,456	4,677,949	4,956,077	4,541,821
Income Before Taxes	285,996	268,034	83,880	477,581	432,765	350,560	310,708	467,406
Income Taxes	84,846	88,070	25,811	134,105	143,895	116,345	123,644	165,678
Net Income	201,922	180,539	58,282	342,993	288,086	233,534	186,367	301,041
Average Shares	112,575	112,199	111,822	111,156	109,826	108,688	109,102	108,542
Balance Sheet								
Total Assets	9,347,047	9,314,286	8,874,436	8,831,777	8,254,351	7,666,100	6,520,600	6,050,847
Total Liabilities	6,053,153	6,120,863	5,801,974	5,823,598	5,495,849	5,093,183	4,067,551	3,702,782
Stockholders' Equity	3,293,894	3,193,423	3,072,462	3,008,179	2,758,502	2,572,917	2,453,049	2,348,065
Shares Outstanding	110,817	110,721	110,528	109,944	109,098	107,541	105,900	107,239
Statistical Record								
Return on Assets %	3.04	4.06	4.07	4.00	3.62	3.29	2.96	5.26
Return on Equity %	8.96	12.03	11.79	11.86	10.81	9.29	7.76	13.72
Net Margin %	4.71	6.51	4.43	6.15	5.57	4.99	3.76	6.63
Asset Turnover	0.62	0.64	0.66	0.65	0.65	0.66	0.79	0.79
Price Range	49.97-35.81	45.43-35.81	43.35-35.37	43.35-32.44	42.36-32.65	34.30-24.92	28.26-20.53	24.69-12.75
P/E Ratio	19.75-14.15	13.77-10.85	13.85-11.30	14.03-10.50	16.17-12.46	15.95-11.59	16.53-12.01	8.91-4.60
Average Yield %	3.36	3.39	3.30	3.14	2.70	2.99	1.97	1.94

Address: 1 First American Way, Santa Ana, CA 92707-5913 **Telephone:** 714-250-3000 **Fax:** 714-250-3151	**Web Site:** www.firstam.com **Officers:** Parker S. Kennedy - Executive Chairman George L. Argyros - Chairman, Chief Executive Officer	**Auditors:** PricewaterhouseCoopers LLP **Investor Contact:** 714-250-5214 **Transfer Agents:** Wells Fargo Shareowner Services

FIRST DATA CORP

Exchange	Symbol	Price	52Wk Range	Yield	P/E
NYS	FDC	$16.71 (12/29/2017)	19.08-14.81	N/A	21.99

*7 Year Price Score N/A   *NYSE Composite Index=100   *12 Month Price Score 92.27

TRADING VOLUME (thousand shares)

Interim Earnings (Per Share)

Qtr.	Mar	Jun	Sep	Dec
2016	(0.06)	0.17	0.14	0.21
2017	0.04	0.20	0.31	...

Interim Dividends (Per Share)

No Dividends Paid

Valuation Analysis   Institutional Holding

Forecast EPS	$1.52	No of Institutions
	(01/25/2018)	477
Market Cap	$15.4 Billion	Shares
Book Value	$2.1 Billion	515,055,072
Price/Book	7.35	% Held
Price/Sales	1.30	N/A

Business Summary: IT Services (MIC: 6.3.1 SIC: 7389 NAIC: 561499)

First Data engages in commerce-enabling technology and solutions, for merchants, financial institutions, and card issuers. Co. segments are: Global Business Solutions, which provides retail point-of-sale (POS) merchant acquiring and eCommerce services as well as next-generation offerings, and cloud-based Clover POS operating system; Global Financial Solutions, which provides credit and retail private-label card processing, as well as licensed financial software systems, and lending solutions; and Network & Security Solutions, which provides electronic funds transfer network solutions, debit card processing solutions, stored value network solutions, and security and fraud solutions.

Recent Developments: For the quarter ended Sep 30 2017, net income increased 70.0% to US$340.0 million from US$200.0 million in the year-earlier quarter. Revenues were US$3.08 billion, up 4.8% from US$2.94 billion the year before. Operating income was US$418.0 million versus US$454.0 million in the prior-year quarter, a decrease of 7.9%. Direct operating expenses declined 0.5% to US$794.0 million from US$798.0 million in the comparable period the year before. Indirect operating expenses increased 10.7% to US$1.86 billion from US$1.68 billion in the equivalent prior-year period.

Prospects: Our evaluation of First Data Corp as of Jan. 21, 2018 is the result of our systematic analysis on three basic characteristics: earnings strength, relative valuation, and recent stock price movement. The company has enjoyed a very positive trend in earnings per share over the past 5 quarters. However, while recent estimates for the company have been mixed, FDC has posted results that fell short of analysts expectations. Based on operating earnings yield, the company is undervalued when compared to all of the companies in our coverage universe. Share price changes over the past year indicates that FDC will perform poorly over the near term.

Financial Data
(US$ in Thousands)

	9 Mos	6 Mos	3 Mos	12/31/2016	12/31/2015	12/31/2014	12/31/2013	12/31/2012
Earnings Per Share	0.76	0.59	0.56	0.46	(7.70)	...	...	...
Cash Flow Per Share	2.21	2.41	2.36	2.33	4.13	...	...	...
Income Statement								
Total Revenue	8,902,000	5,826,000	2,801,000	11,584,000	11,451,000	11,151,800	10,808,900	10,680,300
EBITDA	1,941,000	1,248,000	528,000	1,849,000	421,000	2,503,700	2,287,600	2,310,400
Depn & Amortn	806,000	526,000	258,000	300,000	290,000	1,163,300	1,211,900	1,330,900
Income Before Taxes	429,000	250,000	36,000	481,000	(1,406,000)	(402,000)	(793,900)	(909,500)
Income Taxes	(66,000)	40,000	12,000	81,000	101,000	82,100	86,500	(224,000)
Net Income	517,000	221,000	36,000	420,000	(1,481,000)	(457,800)	(869,100)	(700,900)
Average Shares	944,000	938,000	931,000	921,001	192,263	...	...	...
Balance Sheet								
Current Assets	17,886,000	12,577,000	12,055,000	17,417,000	10,786,000	9,954,400	10,076,100	11,883,400
Total Assets	41,645,000	35,605,000	35,017,000	40,292,000	34,362,000	34,269,300	35,239,800	37,899,000
Current Liabilities	17,545,000	11,754,000	11,339,000	16,717,000	10,645,000	9,530,600	9,618,000	11,344,900
Long-Term Obligations	17,795,000	18,033,000	18,123,000	18,131,000	18,737,000	20,711,400	22,556,800	22,528,900
Total Liabilities	39,547,000	33,970,000	33,654,000	39,072,000	33,694,000	34,721,200	36,729,400	38,497,500
Stockholders' Equity	2,098,000	1,635,000	1,363,000	1,220,000	668,000	(451,900)	(1,489,600)	(598,500)
Shares Outstanding	923,000	922,000	918,000	911,959	899,203	1,000.00	1,000.00	1,000.00
Statistical Record								
Return on Assets %	1.86	1.56	1.49	1.12	N.M.	N.M.	N.M.	N.M.
Return on Equity %	45.22	44.82	51.51	44.37	N.M.	...	...	...
EBITDA Margin %	21.80	21.42	18.85	15.96	3.68	22.45	21.16	21 63
Net Margin %	5.81	3.79	1.29	3.63	N.M.	N.M.	N.M.	N.M.
Asset Turnover	0.31	0.34	0.34	0.31	0.33	0.32	0.30	0.27
Current Ratio	1.02	1.07	1.06	1.04	1.01	1.04	1.05	1.05
Debt to Equity	8.48	11.03	13.30	14.86	28.05	...	...	...
Price Range	19.04-13.03	18.71-10.66	16.63-10.13	16.02-8.67	17.80-15.36	...	...	...
P/E Ratio	25.05-17.14	31.71-18.07	29.70-18.09	34.83-18.85	...	...	...	...

Address: 225 Liberty Street, 29th Floor, New York, NY 10281
Telephone: 800-735-3362

Web Site: www.firstdata.com
Officers: Frank J. Bisignano - Chairman, Chief Executive Officer Joseph J. Plumeri - Vice-Chairman

Auditors: Ernst & Young LLP
Investor Contact: 800-735-3362
Transfer Agents: Wells Fargo Bank Minnesota, South St. Paul, MN

FIRST HORIZON NATIONAL CORP

Exchange	Symbol	Price	52Wk Range	Yield	P/E
NYS	FHN	$19.99 (12/29/2017)	20.76-16.05	1.80	17.85

*7 Year Price Score 114.16 *NYSE Composite Index=100 *12 Month Price Score 98.78

Interim Earnings (Per Share)

Qtr.	Mar	Jun	Sep	Dec
2014	0.19	0.32	0.19	0.21
2015	(0.33)	0.22	0.25	0.20
2016	0.20	0.24	0.27	0.23
2017	0.23	0.38	0.28	...

Interim Dividends (Per Share)

Amt	Decl	Ex	Rec	Pay
0.09Q	01/24/2017	03/08/2017	03/10/2017	04/03/2017
0.09Q	04/25/2017	06/07/2017	06/09/2017	07/03/2017
0.09Q	07/25/2017	09/07/2017	09/08/2017	10/02/2017
0.09Q	10/24/2017	11/02/2017	11/03/2017	01/02/2018

Indicated Div: $0.36

Valuation Analysis

		Institutional Holding	
Forecast EPS	$1.11	No of Institutions	
	(01/16/2018)	409	
Market Cap	$4.7 Billion	Shares	
Book Value	$2.6 Billion	253,218,432	
Price/Book	1.81	% Held	
Price/Sales	3.34	74.42	

Business Summary: Banking (MIC: 5.1.1 SIC: 6021 NAIC: 522110)

First Horizon National is a bank holding company. Co. provides financial services primarily through its subsidiary, First Tennessee Bank National Association. Co. business segments are: regional banking, which provides financial products and services; fixed income, which consists of fixed income securities sales, trading, and strategies for institutional clients; corporate, which consists of unallocated corporate expenses, expense on subordinated debt issuances, and unallocated interest income; and non-strategic, which consists of the wind-down national consumer lending activities. As of Dec 31 2016, Co. had total assets of $28.56 billion and total deposits of $22.67 billion.

Recent Developments: For the quarter ended Sep 30 2017, net income increased 6.1% to US$71.8 million from US$67.6 million in the year-earlier quarter. Net interest income increased 13.3% to US$209.8 million from US$185.2 million in the year-earlier quarter. Provision for loan losses was nil versus US$4.0 million in the prior-year quarter, a decrease of 100.0%. Non-interest income fell 24.3% to US$112.4 million from US$148.5 million, while non-interest expense advanced 1.4% to US$236.9 million.

Prospects: Our evaluation of First Horizon National Corp. as of Jan. 14, 2018 is the result of our systematic analysis on three basic characteristics: earnings strength, relative valuation, and recent stock price movement. The company has managed to produce a neutral trend in earnings per share over the past 5 quarters. However, while recent estimates for the company have been mixed, FHN has posted better than expected results. Based on operating earnings yield, the company is undervalued when compared to all of the companies in our coverage universe. Share price changes over the past year indicates that FHN will perform poorly over the near term.

Financial Data

(US$ in Thousands)	9 Mos	6 Mos	3 Mos	12/31/2016	12/31/2015	12/31/2014	12/31/2013	12/31/2012
Earnings Per Share	1.12	1.11	0.97	0.94	0.34	0.91	0.10	(0.11)
Cash Flow Per Share	0.58	(1.02)	0.95	0.78	1.57	3.00	1.81	1.49
Tang Book Value Per Share	9.45	9.20	9.14	9.00	8.51	8.63	7.92	7.98
Dividends Per Share	0.340	0.320	0.300	0.280	0.240	0.200	0.200	0.040
Dividend Payout %	30.36	28.83	30.93	29.79	70.59	21.98	200.00	...
Income Statement								
Interest Income	702,297	454,152	218,811	817,909	736,405	709,249	732,053	798,953
Interest Expense	102,071	63,743	29,103	88,825	82,685	81,531	94,679	110,286
Net Interest Income	600,226	390,409	189,708	729,084	653,720	627,718	637,374	688,667
Provision for Losses	(3,000)	(3,000)	(1,000)	11,000	9,000	27,000	55,000	78,000
Non-Interest Income	357,029	244,612	116,939	552,441	517,325	550,044	584,577	671,329
Non-Interest Expense	676,991	440,122	222,205	925,204	1,053,791	841,211	1,158,601	1,383,701
Income Before Taxes	283,264	197,899	85,442	345,321	108,254	309,551	8,350	(101,705)
Income Taxes	57,903	44,307	27,054	106,810	10,941	78,501	(32,169)	(85,262)
Net Income	216,806	147,920	55,568	227,046	85,879	219,523	29,602	(27,759)
Average Shares	236,340	236,263	236,855	235,292	236,266	236,735	239,794	248,349
Balance Sheet								
Net Loans & Leases	20,311,004	20,224,833	18,993,562	19,498,700	17,602,602	16,139,003	15,505,417	16,833,556
Total Assets	29,622,636	29,369,956	29,618,600	28,555,231	26,195,136	25,672,887	23,789,833	25,520,140
Total Deposits	22,099,254	22,333,349	23,479,841	22,672,363	19,967,478	18,068,939	16,734,956	16,629,709
Total Liabilities	27,034,516	26,838,499	27,173,571	26,145,578	23,850,981	23,377,350	21,584,513	23,306,099
Stockholders' Equity	2,588,120	2,531,457	2,445,029	2,409,653	2,344,155	2,295,537	2,205,320	2,214,041
Shares Outstanding	234,230	234,135	233,883	233,623	238,586	234,219	236,369	243,597
Statistical Record								
Return on Assets %	0.94	0.94	0.82	0.83	0.33	0.89	0.12	N.M.
Return on Equity %	10.79	10.86	9.73	9.53	3.70	9.75	1.34	N.M.
Net Interest Margin %	84.55	85.28	86.70	89.14	88.77	88.50	87.07	86.20
Efficiency Ratio %	65.69	60.03	66.18	67.52	84.05	66.80	88.00	94.11
Loans to Deposits	0.92	0.91	0.81	0.86	0.88	0.89	0.93	1.01
Price Range	20.76-14.71	20.76-13.13	20.76-12.54	20.61-11.62	16.20-12.31	13.91-11.18	12.55-9.72	10.89-7.55
P/E Ratio	18.54-13.13	18.70-11.83	21.40-12.93	21.93-12.36	47.65-36.21	15.29-12.29	125.50-97.20	...
Average Yield %	1.88	1.84	1.84	1.83	1.90	1.65	1.66	1.80	0.44

Address: 165 Madison Avenue, Memphis, TN 38103	**Web Site:** www.firsthorizon.com	**Auditors:** KPMG LLP
Telephone: 901-523-4444	**Officers:** D. Bryan Jordan - Chairman, President, Chief Executive Officer Michael E. Kisber - President	**Investor Contact:** 800-410-4577 **Transfer Agents:** Wells Fargo

FIRST INDUSTRIAL REALTY TRUST INC

Exchange	Symbol	Price	52Wk Range	Yield	P/E
NYS	FR	$31.47 (12/29/2017)	32.82-25.35	2.67	29.41

*7 Year Price Score 119.82 *NYSE Composite Index=100 *12 Month Price Score 102.99

Interim Earnings (Per Share)

Qtr.	Mar	Jun	Sep	Dec
2014	0.02	0.04	0.19	0.17
2015	0.02	0.13	0.13	0.40
2016	0.14	0.43	0.27	0.20
2017	0.19	0.32	0.36	...

Interim Dividends (Per Share)

Amt	Decl	Ex	Rec	Pay
0.21Q	02/22/2017	03/29/2017	03/31/2017	04/17/2017
0.21Q	05/11/2017	06/28/2017	06/30/2017	07/17/2017
0.21Q	08/02/2017	09/28/2017	09/29/2017	10/16/2017
0.21Q	11/07/2017	12/28/2017	12/29/2017	01/16/2018

Indicated Div: $0.84

Valuation Analysis — **Institutional Holding**

Forecast EPS	$1.04	No of Institutions	
	(01/16/2018)	348	
Market Cap	$3.8 Billion	Shares	
Book Value	$1.3 Billion		153,296,240
Price/Book	2.80	% Held	
Price/Sales	9.62		101.48

Business Summary: REITs (MIC: 5.3.1 SIC: 6798 NAIC: 525930)

First Industrial Realty Trust is a real estate investment trust that owns, manages, acquires, sells, develops, and redevelops industrial real estate. As of Dec 31 2016, Co.'s in-service portfolio consisted of 215 light industrial properties, 53 R&D/flex properties, 167 bulk warehouse properties and 100 regional warehouse properties located in 23 states. Co.'s in-service portfolio includes properties that have reached stabilized occupancy, developed and redeveloped properties and acquired properties that are occupied at acquisition or one year from the acquisition date. Co.'s operations are conducted via First Industrial, L.P. and itss subsidiaries, of which Co. is the sole general partner.

Recent Developments: For the quarter ended Sep 30 2017, net income increased 36.7% to US$44.7 million from US$32.7 million in the year-earlier quarter. Revenues were US$99.3 million, up 6.1% from US$93.6 million the year before. Revenues from property income rose 6.1% to US$76.5 million from US$72.1 million in the corresponding quarter a year earlier.

Prospects: Our evaluation of First Industrial Realty Trust Inc. as of Jan. 14, 2018 is the result of our systematic analysis on three basic characteristics: earnings strength, relative valuation, and recent stock price movement. The company has produced a positive trend in earnings per share over the past 5 quarters. Because the company lacks sufficient analyst estimate data, we place greater weight on the historical EPS trend as the measure of earnings strength. Based on operating earnings yield, the company is about fairly valued when compared to all of the companies in our coverage universe. Share price changes over the past year indicates that FR will perform very well over the near term.

Financial Data

(US$ in Thousands)	9 Mos	6 Mos	3 Mos	12/31/2016	12/31/2015	12/31/2014	12/31/2013	12/31/2012
Earnings Per Share	1.07	0.98	1.09	1.05	0.67	0.42	0.24	(0.24)
Cash Flow Per Share	1.61	1.63	1.58	1.50	1.47	1.25	1.18	1.49
Tang Book Value Per Share	10.99	10.83	10.36	10.35	9.37	9.18	9.98	10.84
Dividends Per Share	0.820	0.800	0.780	0.760	0.510	0.410	0.340	...
Dividend Payout %	76.64	81.63	71.56	72.38	76.12	97.62	141.67	...
Income Statement								
Total Revenue	294,272	194,962	97,383	378,020	365,762	344,599	328,226	327,273
EBITDA	249,324	157,691	70,816	284,936	240,244	186,627	173,292	167,149
Depn & Amortn	95,092	63,248	32,090	95,514	92,955	93,457	94,271	100,074
Income Before Taxes	108,236	63,601	23,579	126,773	76,767	20,004	4,592	(17,017)
Income Taxes	1,236	1,257	88	1,089	117	238	(213)	5,522
Net Income	103,469	60,271	22,709	121,232	73,802	49,110	40,307	(1,318)
Average Shares	119,990	117,779	117,261	115,370	110,781	110,325	106,995	91,468
Balance Sheet								
Current Assets	88,754	90,659	99,624	26,218	32,604	18,685	13,282	9,534
Total Assets	2,927,826	2,863,963	2,805,058	2,793,263	2,718,051	2,581,995	2,597,510	2,608,842
Current Liabilities	154,527	139,262	138,174	151,146	148,664	128,596	115,859	111,901
Long-Term Obligations	1,368,291	1,340,541	1,371,297	1,347,092	1,442,411	1,349,846	1,296,806	1,335,766
Total Liabilities	1,579,308	1,535,802	1,562,684	1,551,822	1,644,951	1,533,045	1,470,660	1,505,463
Stockholders' Equity	1,348,518	1,328,161	1,242,374	1,241,441	1,073,100	1,048,950	1,126,850	1,103,379
Shares Outstanding	119,848	119,848	117,272	117,107	111,027	110,600	109,980	98,767
Statistical Record								
Return on Assets %	4.47	4.13	4.63	4.39	2.78	1.90	1.55	N.M.
Return on Equity %	9.92	9.13	11.16	10.45	6.96	4.51	3.61	N.M.
EBITDA Margin %	84.73	80.88	72.72	75.38	65.68	54.16	52.80	51.07
Net Margin %	35.16	30.91	23.32	32.07	20.18	14.25	12.28	N.M.
Asset Turnover	0.14	0.14	0.14	0.14	0.14	0.13	0.13	0.12
Current Ratio	0.57	0.65	0.72	0.17	0.22	0.15	0.11	0.09
Debt to Equity	1.01	1.01	1.10	1.09	1.34	1.29	1.15	1.21
Price Range	31.74-25.35	30.04-25.35	29.61-22.36	29.61-19.32	23.08-18.69	21.16-16.42	18.81-14.08	14.10-10.30
P/E Ratio	29.66-23.69	30.65-25.87	27.17-20.51	28.20-18.40	34.45-27.90	50.38-39.10	78.38-58.67	...
Average Yield %	2.92	2.90	2.93	3.01	2.44	2.21	2.05	...

Address: 311 S. Wacker Drive, Suite 3900, Chicago, IL 60606 **Telephone:** 312-344-4300 **Fax:** 312-922-6320	**Web Site:** www.firstindustrial.com **Officers:** Bruce W. Duncan - Chairman, President, Chief Executive Officer Peter E. Baccile - President, Chief Executive Officer	**Auditors:** PricewaterhouseCoopers LLP **Investor Contact:** 312-344-4320 **Transfer Agents:** Barack Ferrazzano Kirschbaum & Nagelberg LLP

FIRST REPUBLIC BANK (SAN FRANCISCO, CA)

Exchange	Symbol	Price	52Wk Range	Yield	P/E
NYS	FRC	$86.64 (12/29/2017)	105.17-86.62	0.78	20.43

*7 Year Price Score 136.74 *NYSE Composite Index=100 *12 Month Price Score 91.08

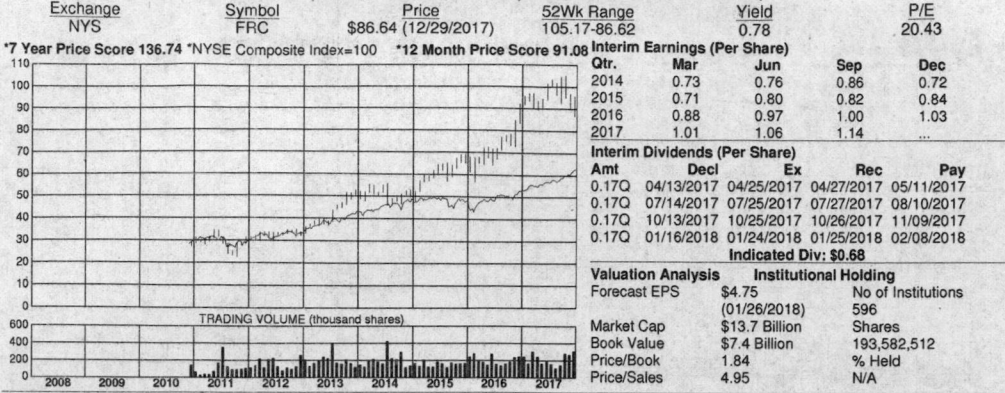

Interim Earnings (Per Share)

Qtr.	Mar	Jun	Sep	Dec
2014	0.73	0.76	0.86	0.72
2015	0.71	0.80	0.82	0.84
2016	0.88	0.97	1.00	1.03
2017	1.01	1.06	1.14	...

Interim Dividends (Per Share)

Amt	Decl	Ex	Rec	Pay
0.17Q	04/13/2017	04/25/2017	04/27/2017	05/11/2017
0.17Q	07/14/2017	07/25/2017	07/27/2017	08/10/2017
0.17Q	10/13/2017	10/25/2017	10/26/2017	11/09/2017
0.17Q	01/16/2018	01/24/2018	01/25/2018	02/08/2018

Indicated Div: $0.68

Valuation Analysis

		Institutional Holding	
Forecast EPS	$4.75	No of Institutions	
	(01/26/2018)	596	
Market Cap	$13.7 Billion	Shares	
Book Value	$7.4 Billion	193,582,512	
Price/Book	1.84	% Held	
Price/Sales	4.95	N/A	

Business Summary: Banking (MIC: 5.1.1 SIC: 6029 NAIC: 522110)

First Republic Bank is a commercial bank and trust company. Co. focuses on providing personalized, relationship-based services, including private banking, private business banking, real estate lending and wealth management services, including trust and custody services. Co. conducts its business through two reportable business segments: Commercial Banking and Wealth Management. Co. provides its services in the following areas: San Francisco, Palo Alto, Los Angeles, Santa Barbara, Newport Beach, San Diego, Portland, OR; Boston, New York City, Greenwich and Palm Beach, FL. As of Dec 31 2016, Co. had total assets of $73.28 billion and total deposits of $58.60 billion.

Recent Developments: For the quarter ended Sep 30 2017, net income increased 16.4% to US$200.0 million from US$171.8 million in the year-earlier quarter. Net interest income increased 19.6% to US$551.0 million from US$460.6 million in the year-earlier quarter. Provision for loan losses was US$10.1 million versus US$18.0 million in the prior-year quarter, a decrease of 43.8%. Non-interest income rose 22.7% to US$119.3 million from US$97.3 million, while non-interest expense advanced 23.9% to US$418.4 million.

Prospects: Our evaluation of First Republic Bank as of Jan. 21, 2018 is the result of our systematic analysis on three basic characteristics: earnings strength, relative valuation, and recent stock price movement. The company has managed to produce a neutral trend in earnings per share over the past 5 quarters. However, while recent estimates for the company have been lowered by analysts, FRC has posted better than expected results. Based on operating earnings yield, the company is undervalued when compared to all of the companies in our coverage universe. Share price changes over the past year indicates that FRC will perform in line with the market over the near term.

Financial Data
(US$ in Thousands)

	9 Mos	6 Mos	3 Mos	12/31/2016	12/31/2015	12/31/2014	12/31/2013	12/31/2012
Earnings Per Share	4.24	4.10	4.01	3.93	3.18	3.07	3.10	2.76
Cash Flow Per Share	...	...	...	5.72	...	3.64	4.28	3.37
Tang Book Value Per Share	38.50	37.44	36.77	34.94	29.80	26.21	22.61	19.93
Dividends Per Share	0.660	0.650	0.640	0.630	0.590	0.540	0.360	0.300
Dividend Payout %	15.57	15.85	15.96	16.03	18.55	17.59	11.61	10.87
Income Statement								
Total Revenue	2,118,981	1,362,481	653,954	2,375,685	1,989,145	1,801,364	1,600,368	1,455,940
Income Before Taxes	675,629	433,815	213,517	827,596	690,668	669,883	663,559	601,347
Income Taxes	112,246	70,441	36,743	154,168	168,523	182,877	201,489	197,337
Net Income	563,383	363,374	176,774	673,428	522,145	487,006	462,070	402,472
Average Shares	162,377	162,335	160,433	154,095	145,510	140,497	135,949	134,189
Balance Sheet								
Total Assets	84,320,096	80,978,231	76,504,351	73,277,772	58,981,285	48,353,330	42,112,763	34,387,677
Total Liabilities	76,892,150	73,718,148	69,415,606	66,369,120	53,275,602	43,574,863	37,952,716	30,989,133
Stockholders' Equity	7,427,946	7,260,083	7,088,745	6,908,652	5,705,683	4,778,467	4,160,047	3,398,544
Shares Outstanding	157,930	157,686	157,122	154,292	146,109	138,268	132,768	131,273
Statistical Record								
Return on Assets %	0.97	0.98	1.00	1.02	0.97	1.08	1.21	1.29
Return on Equity %	10.70	10.53	10.60	10.65	9.96	10.90	12.23	13.57
Net Margin %	26.59	26.67	27.03	28.35	26.25	27.04	28.87	27.64
Asset Turnover	0.04	0.04	0.04	0.04	0.04	0.04	0.04	0.05
Price Range	104.46-72.81	101.45-66.93	96.96-64.25	92.14-56.59	69.28-47.62	55.62-45.77	52.72-32.78	34.95-29.53
P/E Ratio	24.64-17.17	24.74-16.32	24.18-16.02	23.45-14.40	21.79-14.97	18.12-14.91	17.01-10.57	12.66-10.70
Average Yield %	0.71	0.76	0.81	0.87	0.97	1.06	0.85	0.92

Address: 111 Pine Street, 2nd Floor, San Francisco, CA 94111 **Telephone:** 415-392-1400	**Web Site:** www.firstrepublic.com **Officers:** James H. Herbert - Chairman, Chief Executive Officer Katherine August-deWilde - Vice-Chairman, President, Chief Operating Officer	**Auditors:** KPMG LLP **Investor Contact:** 415-392-1400 **Transfer Agents:** Common and Preferred Stock – Computershare Shareowner Services, LLC

FIRSTENERGY CORP

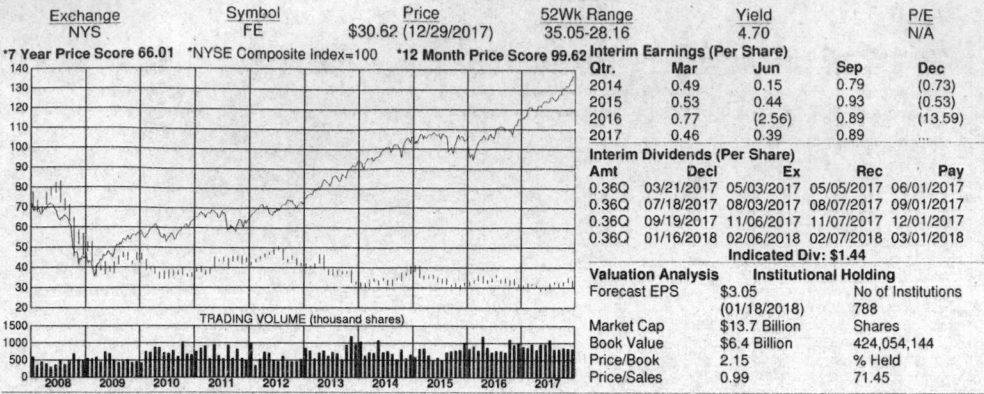

Exchange	Symbol	Price	52Wk Range	Yield	P/E
NYS	FE	$30.62 (12/29/2017)	35.05-28.16	4.70	N/A

*7 Year Price Score 66.01   *NYSE Composite index=100   *12 Month Price Score 99.62

Interim Earnings (Per Share)

Qtr.	Mar	Jun	Sep	Dec
2014	0.49	0.15	0.79	(0.73)
2015	0.53	0.44	0.93	(0.53)
2016	0.77	(2.56)	0.89	(13.59)
2017	0.46	0.39	0.89	...

Interim Dividends (Per Share)

Amt	Decl	Ex	Rec	Pay
0.36Q	03/21/2017	05/03/2017	05/05/2017	06/01/2017
0.36Q	07/18/2017	08/03/2017	08/07/2017	09/01/2017
0.36Q	09/19/2017	11/06/2017	11/07/2017	12/01/2017
0.36Q	01/16/2018	02/06/2018	02/07/2018	03/01/2018

Indicated Div: $1.44

Valuation Analysis

		Institutional Holding	
Forecast EPS	$3.05	No of Institutions	
	(01/18/2018)	788	
Market Cap	$13.7 Billion	Shares	
Book Value	$6.4 Billion	424,054,144	
Price/Book	2.15	% Held	
Price/Sales	0.99	71.45	

Business Summary: Electric Utilities (MIC: 3.1.1 SIC: 4911 NAIC: 221121)

FirstEnergy is a public utility holding company. Through its utility operating subsidiaries, Ohio Edison Company, The Cleveland Electric Illuminating Company, The Toledo Edison Company, Pennsylvania Power Company, Jersey Central Power & Light Company, Metropolitan Edison Company, Pennsylvania Electric Company, Monongahela Power Company, The Potomac Edison Company, West Penn Power Company, American Transmission Systems, Inc. and also Trans-Allegheny Interstate Line Company (the Utilities), Co. is engaged in providing electric service. The Utilities' combined service areas encompass approximately 65,000 square miles in Ohio, Pennsylvania, West Virginia, Maryland, New Jersey and New York.

Recent Developments: For the quarter ended Sep 30 2017, net income increased 4.2% to US$396.0 million from US$380.0 million in the year-earlier quarter. Revenues were US$3.71 billion, down 5.2% from US$3.92 billion the year before. Operating income was US$884.0 million versus US$861.0 million in the prior-year quarter, an increase of 2.7%. Direct operating expenses declined 9.1% to US$2.17 billion from US$2.38 billion in the comparable period the year before. Indirect operating expenses decreased 1.5% to US$664.0 million from US$674.0 million in the equivalent prior-year period.

Prospects: Our evaluation of FirstEnergy Corp. as of Jan. 14, 2018 is the result of our systematic analysis on three basic characteristics: earnings strength, relative valuation, and recent stock price movement. The company has enjoyed a very positive trend in earnings per share over the past 5 quarters and while recent estimates for the company have remained steady, FE has posted better than expected results. Based on operating earnings yield, the company is undervalued when compared to all of the companies in our coverage universe. Share price changes over the past year indicates that FE will perform very well over the near term.

Financial Data

(US$ in Thousands)	9 Mos	6 Mos	3 Mos	12/31/2016	12/31/2015	12/31/2014	12/31/2013	12/31/2012
Earnings Per Share	(11.85)	(11.85)	(14.80)	(14.49)	1.37	0.71	0.94	1.84
Cash Flow Per Share	8.00	7.64	7.94	7.89	8.17	6.46	6.37	5.54
Tang Book Value Per Share	1.76	1.58	1.17	1.41	14.17	14.25	14.99	15.87
Dividends Per Share	1.440	1.440	1.440	1.440	1.440	1.440	2.200	2.200
Dividend Payout %	...	...	...	...	105.11	202.82	234.04	119.57
Income Statement								
Total Revenue	10,575,000	6,861,000	3,552,000	14,562,000	15,026,000	15,049,000	14,917,000	15,303,000
EBITDA	3,328,000	1,951,000	990,000	(6,865,000)	3,190,000	2,346,000	2,713,000	3,377,000
Depn & Amortn	1,248,000	792,000	392,000	1,313,000	1,282,000	1,220,000	1,202,000	1,124,000
Income Before Taxes	1,257,000	622,000	331,000	(9,232,000)	893,000	171,000	570,000	1,324,000
Income Taxes	482,000	243,000	126,000	(3,055,000)	315,000	(42,000)	195,000	553,000
Net Income	775,000	379,000	205,000	(6,177,000)	578,000	299,000	392,000	770,000
Average Shares	446,000	445,000	444,000	426,000	424,000	421,000	419,000	419,000
Balance Sheet								
Current Assets	2,931,000	2,755,000	2,760,000	2,950,000	3,040,000	3,876,000	3,887,000	3,768,000
Total Assets	43,649,000	43,327,000	43,212,000	43,148,000	52,187,000	52,166,000	50,424,000	50,406,000
Current Liabilities	4,255,000	4,647,000	7,657,000	7,126,000	5,602,000	5,561,000	7,637,000	7,605,000
Long-Term Obligations	21,089,000	20,582,000	17,762,000	18,192,000	19,192,000	19,176,000	15,831,000	15,179,000
Total Liabilities	37,243,000	37,007,000	37,073,000	36,907,000	39,766,000	39,746,000	37,732,000	37,322,000
Stockholders' Equity	6,406,000	6,320,000	6,139,000	6,241,000	12,421,000	12,420,000	12,692,000	13,084,000
Shares Outstanding	448,858	444,304	443,740	442,344	423,560	421,102	418,628	418,216
Statistical Record								
Return on Assets %	N.M.	N.M.	N.M.	N.M.	1.11	0.58	0.78	1.57
Return on Equity %	N.M.	N.M.	N.M.	N.M.	4.65	2.38	3.04	5.83
EBITDA Margin %	31.47	28.44	27.87	N.M.	21.23	15.59	18.19	22.07
Net Margin %	7.33	5.52	5.77	N.M.	3.85	1.99	2.63	5.03
Asset Turnover	0.29	0.30	0.30	0.30	0.29	0.29	0.30	0.31
Current Ratio	0.69	0.59	0.36	0.41	0.54	0.70	0.51	0.50
Debt to Equity	3.29	3.26	2.89	2.91	1.55	1.54	1.25	1.16
Price Range	34.50-28.16	36.60-28.16	36.60-29.58	36.60-30.06	41.37-29.12	40.77-30.22	46.60-31.60	50.87-40.72
P/E Ratio	...	...	...	...	30.20-21.26	57.42-42.56	49.57-33.62	27.65-22.13
Average Yield %	4.64	4.55	4.40	4.32	4.22	4.26	5.67	4.88

Address: 76 South Main Street, Akron, OH 44308	**Web Site:** www.firstenergycorp.com	**Auditors:** PricewaterhouseCoopers LLP
Telephone: 800-736-3402	**Officers:** George M. Smart - Chairman Charles E. Jones - President, Chief Executive Officer, Division Officer	**Investor Contact:** 330-384-3859
		Transfer Agents: American Stock Transfer & Trust Company, LLC, New York, NY

FLEETCOR TECHNOLOGIES INC

Exchange	Symbol	Price	52Wk Range	Yield	P/E
NYS	FLT	$192.43 (12/29/2017)	193.38-131.26	N/A	32.73

*7 Year Price Score 113.68 *NYSE Composite Index=100 *12 Month Price Score 109.73

Interim Earnings (Per Share)

Qtr.	Mar	Jun	Sep	Dec
2014	0.88	1.03	1.11	1.22
2015	1.00	1.05	1.24	0.56
2016	1.17	1.21	1.36	1.00
2017	1.31	1.39	2.18	...

Interim Dividends (Per Share)

No Dividends Paid

Valuation Analysis		Institutional Holding	
Forecast EPS	$8.43	No of Institutions	460
	(01/17/2018)		
Market Cap	$17.2 Billion	Shares	
Book Value	$3.4 Billion		95,005,528
Price/Book	5.02	% Held	
Price/Sales	8.00		86.96

Business Summary: Business Services (MIC: 7.5.2 SIC: 7389 NAIC: 561499)

FleetCor Technologies is engaged in workforce payment products. Co. primarily go to market with its fuel card payments product solutions, corporate payments products, toll products, lodging cards and gift cards. Co.'s primary products are primarily sold to businesses, retailers, major oil companies and marketers and government entities. Co.'s payment programs enable its customers to manage and control their commercial payments, card programs, and employee spending and provide card-accepting merchants. Co. also provides a suite of fleet related and workforce payment solution products, including mobile telematics services, fleet maintenance management and employee benefit.

Recent Developments: For the quarter ended Sep 30 2017, net income increased 56.5% to US$202.8 million from US$129.6 million in the year-earlier quarter. Revenues were US$577.9 million, up 19.3% from US$484.4 million the year before. Operating income was US$232.6 million versus US$191.1 million in the prior-year quarter, an increase of 21.8%. Indirect operating expenses increased 17.7% to US$345.2 million from US$293.4 million in the equivalent prior-year period.

Prospects: Our evaluation of FleetCor Technologies Inc. as of Jan. 14, 2018 is the result of our systematic analysis on three basic characteristics: earnings strength, relative valuation, and recent stock price movement. The company has enjoyed a very positive trend in earnings per share over the past 5 quarters and while recent estimates for the company have been raised by analysts, FLT has posted better than expected results. Based on operating earnings yield, the company is about fairly valued when compared to all of the companies in our coverage universe. Share price changes over the past year indicates that FLT will perform poorly over the near term.

Financial Data
(US$ in Thousands)

	9 Mos	6 Mos	3 Mos	12/31/2016	12/31/2015	12/31/2014	12/31/2013	12/31/2012
Earnings Per Share	5.88	5.06	4.88	4.75	3.85	4.24	3.36	2.52
Cash Flow Per Share	7.95	7.35	6.93	7.60	8.20	7.21	4.59	1.62
Income Statement								
Total Revenue	1,639,547	1,061,670	520,433	1,831,546	1,702,865	1,199,390	895,171	707,534
EBITDA	965,723	542,841	259,651	949,306	855,251	657,634	486,243	370,283
Depn & Amortn	204,142	133,375	66,779	198,135	190,240	107,249	66,213	46,476
Income Before Taxes	685,259	362,488	169,745	679,275	593,672	521,529	403,569	310,790
Income Taxes	227,756	103,077	43,675	190,534	173,573	144,236	119,068	94,591
Net Income	457,503	254,680	123,693	452,385	362,431	368,707	284,501	216,199
Average Shares	93,001	94,223	94,560	95,213	94,139	86,982	84,655	85,736
Balance Sheet								
Current Assets	3,521,501	3,045,358	2,882,091	2,527,693	1,945,172	2,137,350	1,353,512	1,195,354
Total Assets	11,330,294	10,101,711	10,009,954	9,626,732	7,891,868	8,674,506	3,932,235	2,721,870
Current Liabilities	4,172,898	3,619,026	3,500,665	3,296,318	2,248,021	2,896,618	1,908,898	1,142,222
Long-Term Obligations	2,933,976	2,394,621	2,460,629	2,521,727	2,061,415	2,168,953	474,939	485,217
Total Liabilities	7,899,876	6,696,211	6,668,142	6,542,694	5,061,821	5,921,369	2,688,342	1,808,048
Stockholders' Equity	3,430,418	3,405,500	3,341,812	3,084,038	2,830,047	2,753,137	1,243,893	913,822
Shares Outstanding	89,558	91,878	92,257	91,836	92,376	91,662	82,471	81,037
Statistical Record								
Return on Assets %	5.20	5.22	5.14	5.15	4.38	5.85	8.55	8.55
Return on Equity %	16.73	14.79	14.63	15.26	12.98	18.45	26.37	24.99
EBITDA Margin %	58.90	51.13	49.89	51.83	50.22	54.83	54.32	52.33
Net Margin %	27.90	23.99	23.77	24.70	21.28	30.74	31.78	30.56
Asset Turnover	0.20	0.22	0.22	0.21	0.21	0.19	0.27	0.28
Current Ratio	0.84	0.84	0.82	0.77	0.87	0.74	0.71	1.05
Debt to Equity	0.86	0.70	0.74	0.82	0.73	0.79	0.38	0.53
Price Range	175.53-131.26	175.53-131.26	175.53-134.67	175.53-113.39	163.86-137.02	156.05-101.69	122.70-53.65	53.65-30.55
P/E Ratio	29.85-22.32	34.69-25.94	35.97-27.60	36.95-23.87	42.56-35.59	36.80-23.98	36.52-15.97	21.29-12.12

Address: 5445 Triangle Parkway, Peachtree Corners, GA 30092 **Telephone:** 770-449-0479	**Web Site:** www.fleetcor.com **Officers:** Ronald F. Clarke - Chairman, Chief Executive Officer Charles Freund - Executive Vice President	**Auditors:** Ernst & Young LLP **Investor Contact:** 770-449-0479 **Transfer Agents:** American Stock Transfer & Trust Company, LLC, Brooklyn, NY

FLOOR & DECOR HOLDINGS INC

Exchange	Symbol	Price	52Wk Range	Yield	P/E
NYS	FND	$48.68 (12/29/2017)	49.59-32.05	N/A	65.78

*7 Year Price Score N/A   *NYSE Composite Index=100   *12 Month Price Score N/A

Interim Earnings (Per Share)

Qtr.	Mar	Jun	Sep	Dec
2016	0.08	0.06	0.16	0.19
2017	0.13	0.20	0.22	

Interim Dividends (Per Share)

No Dividends Paid

Valuation Analysis   **Institutional Holding**

Forecast EPS	$0.67	No of Institutions
	(01/18/2018)	140
Market Cap	$4.6 Billion	Shares
Book Value	$388.2 Million	88,882,088
Price/Book	11.87	% Held
Price/Sales	3.62	N/A

Business Summary: Construction Materials (MIC: 8.5.1 SIC: 5211 NAIC: 423310)

Floor & Decor is a holding company. Through its subsidiaries, Co. is a highly differentiated, rapidly growing specialty retailer of hard surface flooring and related accessories. Co. offers a broad in-stock assortment of tile, wood, laminate, and natural stone flooring along with decorative and installation accessories at everyday low prices. Co.'s stores appeal to a variety of customers, including professional installers and commercial businesses, Do it Yourself customers and customers who buy the products for professional installation. Co. also sells products through its Website, FloorandDecor.com. As of Apr. 17, 2017, Co. operates 72 warehouse-format stores across 17 states.

Recent Developments: For the quarter ended Sep 28 2017, net income increased 63.5% to US$23.3 million from US$14.2 million in the year-earlier quarter. Revenues were US$343.9 million, up 26.8% from US$271.3 million the year before. Operating income was US$28.6 million versus US$24.6 million in the prior-year quarter, an increase of 16.4%. Direct operating expenses rose 25.6% to US$201.4 million from US$160.3 million in the comparable period the year before. Indirect operating expenses increased 31.8% to US$113.9 million from US$86.4 million in the equivalent prior-year period.

Prospects: Our evaluation of Floor & Decor Holdings Inc. as of Jan. 14, 2018 is the result of our systematic analysis on three basic characteristics: earnings strength, relative valuation, and recent stock price movement. The company has suffered a very negative trend in earnings per share over the past 5 quarters and while recent estimates for the company have been raised by analysts, FND has posted better than expected results. Based on operating earnings yield, the company is overvalued when compared to all of the companies in our coverage universe. Share price changes over the past year indicates that FND will perform very poorly over the near term.

Financial Data
(US$ in Thousands)

	9 Mos	6 Mos	3 Mos	12/29/2016	12/31/2015	12/25/2014
Earnings Per Share	0.74	0.68	0.54	0.49	0.31	0.18
Cash Flow Per Share	1.07	1.24	1.51	1.08	0.24	0.52
Tang Book Value Per Share	0.54	0.26	N.M.	N.M.	N.M.	...
Income Statement						
Total Revenue	995,266	651,343	307,296	1,050,759	784,012	584,588
EBITDA	77,562	49,785	21,917	79,828	70,923	58,440
Depn & Amortn	(2,366)	(1,547)	(755)	12,512	18,531	24,759
Income Before Taxes	68,551	42,565	17,258	54,513	43,006	24,732
Income Taxes	13,739	11,008	6,130	11,474	16,199	9,634
Net Income	54,812	31,557	11,128	43,039	26,807	15,098
Average Shares	103,899	99,918	88,645	88,430	86,280	85,651
Balance Sheet						
Current Assets	456,307	416,088	359,885	336,215	305,190	...
Total Assets	1,000,931	944,220	868,354	831,166	748,888	...
Current Liabilities	344,224	322,431	293,215	243,714	196,574	...
Long-Term Obligations	183,919	178,325	351,210	387,243	176,323	...
Total Liabilities	612,760	583,076	722,245	696,883	436,523	...
Stockholders' Equity	388,171	361,144	146,109	134,283	312,365	...
Shares Outstanding	94,685	94,084	83,575	83,518	83,373	83,333
Statistical Record						
Return on Assets %	...	...	...	5.46	...	...
Return on Equity %	...	...	...	19.32	...	...
EBITDA Margin %	7.79	7.64	7.13	7.60	9.05	10.00
Net Margin %	5.51	4.84	3.62	4.10	3.42	2.58
Asset Turnover	...	...	...	1.33	...	...
Current Ratio	1.33	1.29	1.23	1.38	1.55	...
Debt to Equity	0.47	0.49	2.40	2.88	0.56	...
Price Range	46.31-32.05	46.31-32.05	...	...	...	...
P/E Ratio	62.58-43.31	68.10-47.13	...	...	...	...

Address: 2233 Lake Park Drive, Smyrna, GA 30080 Telephone: 404-471-1634	Web Site: www.FloorandDecor.com Officers: Norman H. Axelrod - Chairman George Vincent West - Vice-Chairman	Auditors: Ernst & Young LLP Transfer Agents: American Stock Transfer & Trust Company, LLC

FLOWERS FOODS, INC.

Exchange	Symbol	Price	52Wk Range	Yield	P/E	Div Achiever
NYS	FLO	$19.31 (12/29/2017)	20.84-17.00	3.52	48.27	13 Years

*7 Year Price Score 81.07 ***NYSE Composite Index=100** ***12 Month Price Score 96.96**

Interim Earnings (Per Share)

Qtr.	Apr	Jul	Oct	Jan
2015-16	0.29	0.24	0.21	0.15
Qtr.	Apr	Jul	Oct	Dec
2016	0.28	0.24	0.19	0.06
2017	0.29	0.21	(0.16)	...

Interim Dividends (Per Share)

Amt	Decl	Ex	Rec	Pay
0.16Q	02/17/2017	03/01/2017	03/03/2017	03/17/2017
0.17Q	05/25/2017	06/07/2017	06/09/2017	06/23/2017
0.17Q	08/18/2017	08/30/2017	09/01/2017	09/15/2017
0.17Q	11/17/2017	11/30/2017	12/01/2017	12/15/2017

Indicated Div: $0.68 (Div. Reinv. Plan)

Valuation Analysis   **Institutional Holding**

Forecast EPS	$0.87	No of Institutions
	(01/17/2018)	404
Market Cap	$4.0 Billion	Shares
Book Value	$1.2 Billion	170,480,080
Price/Book	3.40	% Held
Price/Sales	1.03	94.84

Business Summary: Food (MIC: 1.2.1 SIC: 2053 NAIC: 311813)

Flowers Foods is a producer and marketer of bakery products. Co. operates two business segments: a direct-store-delivery (DSD) and a warehouse delivery (warehouse). The DSD segment produces breads, buns, rolls, tortillas and snack cakes to retail and foodservice customers. The Warehouse segment produces snack cakes and frozen breads and rolls. Co.'s fresh and frozen products are delivered to customers' warehouse nationwide through contract carriers. Co.'s Warehouse Segment markets a line of breads and rolls under the Alpine Valley bread brand primarily for retail and foodservice customers. This segment's snack cakes are sold under the Mrs. Freshley's, Broad Street Bakery, and store brands.

Recent Developments: For the quarter ended Oct 7 2017, net loss amounted to US$33.6 million versus net income of US$40.2 million in the year-earlier quarter. Revenues were US$932.8 million, up 1.5% from US$918.8 million the year before. Operating loss was US$53.8 million versus an income of US$66.1 million in the prior-year quarter. Direct operating expenses declined 0.1% to US$476.2 million from US$476.8 million in the comparable period the year before. Indirect operating expenses increased 35.8% to US$510.4 million from US$375.9 million in the equivalent prior-year period.

Prospects: Our evaluation of Flowers Foods Inc. as of Jan. 14, 2018 is the result of our systematic analysis on three basic characteristics: earnings strength, relative valuation, and recent stock price movement. The company has enjoyed a very positive trend in earnings per share over the past 5 quarters. However, while recent estimates for the company have been mixed, FLO has posted better than expected results. Based on operating earnings yield, the company is about fairly valued when compared to all of the companies in our coverage universe. Share price changes over the past year indicates that FLO will perform well over the near term.

Financial Data

(US$ in Thousands)	9 Mos	6 Mos	3 Mos	12/31/2016	01/02/2016	01/03/2015	12/28/2013	12/29/2012
Earnings Per Share	0.40	0.75	0.78	0.78	0.89	0.82	1.09	0.65
Cash Flow Per Share	1.30	1.49	1.44	1.66	1.54	1.47	1.30	1.06
Tang Book Value Per Share	N.M.	N.M.	N.M.	N.M.	N.M.	0.93	0.66	0.97
Dividends Per Share	0.660	0.650	0.640	0.625	0.568	0.485	0.444	0.420
Dividend Payout %	165.00	86.67	82.05	80.13	63.76	59.15	40.75	64.29
Income Statement								
Total Revenue	3,047,110	2,114,288	1,187,649	3,926,885	3,778,505	3,748,973	3,751,005	3,046,491
EBITDA	230,813	251,607	147,313	380,257	414,679	392,595	441,933	311,911
Depn & Amortn	114,288	81,316	47,188	116,367	116,800	117,200	106,700	93,400
Income Before Taxes	105,469	161,965	95,077	249,537	293,031	268,054	322,373	208,772
Income Taxes	33,882	56,807	34,659	85,761	103,840	92,315	91,479	72,651
Net Income	71,587	105,158	60,418	163,776	189,191	175,739	230,894	136,121
Average Shares	209,606	210,269	210,275	210,354	213,356	213,092	211,927	207,673
Balance Sheet								
Current Assets	524,021	489,276	487,517	476,842	537,515	460,563	487,405	464,451
Total Assets	2,682,679	2,721,708	2,736,725	2,761,068	2,885,168	2,408,974	2,504,014	1,995,849
Current Liabilities	408,532	358,001	352,931	340,624	403,738	315,553	327,782	354,958
Long-Term Obligations	843,639	834,865	881,787	946,667	933,932	728,940	892,478	535,016
Total Liabilities	1,490,705	1,457,121	1,491,940	1,550,988	1,642,086	1,285,930	1,427,825	1,137,229
Stockholders' Equity	1,191,974	1,264,587	1,244,785	1,210,080	1,243,082	1,123,044	1,076,189	858,620
Shares Outstanding	209,604	209,339	209,231	208,422	212,266	209,347	208,562	207,409
Statistical Record								
Return on Assets %	3.08	5.72	5.94	5.82	7.17	7.04	10.29	7.69
Return on Equity %	7.14	13.11	13.73	13.39	16.04	15.72	23.93	16.88
EBITDA Margin %	7.57	11.90	12.40	9.68	10.97	10.47	11.78	10.24
Net Margin %	2.35	4.97	5.09	4.17	5.01	4.69	6.16	4.47
Asset Turnover	1.43	1.41	1.41	1.39	1.43	1.50	1.67	1.72
Current Ratio	1.28	1.37	1.38	1.40	1.33	1.46	1.49	1.31
Debt to Equity	0.71	0.66	0.71	0.78	0.75	0.65	0.83	0.62
Price Range	20.84-14.71	20.84-14.60	20.84-14.60	21.85-14.60	27.09-18.85	22.19-17.67	25.39-15.51	16.09-12.30
P/E Ratio	52.10-36.78	27.79-19.47	26.72-18.72	28.01-18.72	30.44-21.18	27.06-21.55	23.29-14.23	24.75-18.92
Average Yield %	3.62	3.65	3.58	3.54	2.51	2.43	2.08	3.02

Address: 1919 Flowers Circle, Thomasville, GA 31757 Telephone: 229-226-9110	Web Site: www.flowersfoods.com Officers: Allen L. Shiver - President, Chief Executive Officer R. Steve Kinsey - Chief Financial Officer, Executive Vice President	Auditors: PricewaterhouseCoopers LLP Investor Contact: 229-227-2348 Transfer Agents: Computershare, Providence, RI

FLOWSERVE CORP

Exchange	Symbol	Price	52Wk Range	Yield	P/E
NYS	FLS	$42.13 (12/29/2017)	51.85-37.58	1.80	32.66

*7 Year Price Score 70.96   *NYSE Composite Index=100   *12 Month Price Score 86.34

Interim Earnings (Per Share)

Qtr.	Mar	Jun	Sep	Dec
2014	0.78	0.90	0.93	1.16
2015	0.20	0.56	0.70	0.54
2016	0.29	0.48	(0.16)	0.50
2017	0.11	0.32	0.36	...

Interim Dividends (Per Share)

Amt	Decl	Ex	Rec	Pay
0.19Q	02/16/2017	03/22/2017	03/24/2017	04/07/2017
0.19Q	05/18/2017	06/21/2017	06/23/2017	07/07/2017
0.19Q	09/05/2017	09/21/2017	09/22/2017	10/06/2017
0.19Q	12/21/2017	01/04/2018	01/05/2018	01/19/2018

Indicated Div: $0.76

Valuation Analysis

Forecast EPS	$1.37
	(01/18/2018)
Market Cap	$5.5 Billion
Book Value	$1.7 Billion
Price/Book	3.14
Price/Sales	1.48

Institutional Holding

No of Institutions	625
Shares	155,820,160
% Held	85.00

TRADING VOLUME (thousand shares)

Business Summary: Industrial Machinery & Equipment (MIC: 7.2.1 SIC: 3561 NAIC: 333911)

Flowserve manufactures and provides aftermarket service flow control systems. Co. develops and manufactures flow control equipment integral to the movement, control and protection of the flow of materials in its customers' processes. Co.'s segments include: Engineered Product Division for long lead time, custom and other engineered pumps and pump systems, mechanical seals, auxiliary systems and replacement parts and related services; Industrial Product Division for engineered and pre-configured industrial pumps and pump systems and related products and services; and Flow Control Division for engineered and industrial valves, control valves, actuators and controls and related services.

Recent Developments: For the quarter ended Sep 30 2017, net income amounted to US$48.7 million versus a net loss of US$15.0 million in the year-earlier quarter. Revenues were US$883.4 million, down 6.6% from US$945.9 million the year before. Operating income was US$74.0 million versus US$112,000 in the prior-year quarter, an increase of. Direct operating expenses declined 7.8% to US$615.8 million from US$668.0 million in the comparable period the year before. Indirect operating expenses decreased 30.4% to US$193.5 million from US$277.9 million in the equivalent prior-year period.

Prospects: Our evaluation of Flowserve Corp. as of Jan. 14, 2018 is the result of our systematic analysis on three basic characteristics: earnings strength, relative valuation, and recent stock price movement. The company has produced a positive trend in earnings per share over the past 5 quarters and while recent estimates for the company have remained steady, FLS has posted better than expected results. Based on operating earnings yield, the company is about fairly valued when compared to all of the companies in our coverage universe. Share price changes over the past year indicates that FLS will perform poorly over the near term.

Financial Data

(US$ in Thousands)	9 Mos	6 Mos	3 Mos	12/31/2016	12/31/2015	12/31/2014	12/31/2013	12/31/2012
Earnings Per Share	1.29	0.77	0.93	1.11	2.00	3.76	3.41	2.84
Cash Flow Per Share	1.85	2.07	1.83	1.74	3.13	4.17	3.44	3.29
Tang Book Value Per Share	2.49	2.20	1.94	1.76	1.66	5.34	4.39	4.75
Dividends Per Share	0.760	0.760	0.760	0.760	0.720	0.640	0.560	0.480
Dividend Payout %	58.91	98.70	81.72	68.47	36.00	17.02	16.42	16.92
Income Statement								
Total Revenue	2,626,762	1,743,381	863,626	3,991,462	4,561,030	4,877,885	4,954,619	4,751,339
EBITDA	317,285	207,349	59,349	369,430	575,041	873,024	797,681	725,751
Depn & Amortn	87,944	57,395	28,625	99,897	99,501	93,307	90,695	88,572
Income Before Taxes	187,025	121,573	16,652	212,200	412,335	721,075	654,004	594,613
Income Taxes	85,836	66,208	6,755	75,286	148,922	208,305	204,701	160,766
Net Income	108,534	60,929	14,823	145,060	267,669	518,824	485,530	448,339
Average Shares	131,396	131,341	131,275	130,975	133,811	137,843	142,429	157,968
Balance Sheet								
Current Assets	2,439,010	2,415,555	2,282,133	2,331,361	2,631,792	2,794,163	2,847,382	2,740,216
Total Assets	4,834,140	4,795,115	4,696,831	4,742,762	5,103,850	4,968,020	5,036,733	4,810,958
Current Liabilities	1,148,317	1,146,323	1,099,223	1,178,141	1,359,962	1,471,875	1,558,099	1,590,625
Long-Term Obligations	1,506,057	1,500,988	1,477,549	1,485,258	1,570,836	1,101,791	1,127,619	869,116
Total Liabilities	3,085,452	3,091,123	3,016,457	3,094,528	3,437,373	3,036,458	3,166,354	2,920,739
Stockholders' Equity	1,748,688	1,703,992	1,680,374	1,648,234	1,666,477	1,931,562	1,870,379	1,890,219
Shares Outstanding	130,290	130,291	130,218	129,813	129,090	134,349	137,163	144,405
Statistical Record								
Return on Assets %	3.50	2.07	2.52	2.94	5.32	10.37	9.86	9.48
Return on Equity %	9.84	5.85	7.17	8.73	14.88	27.29	25.82	21.50
EBITDA Margin %	12.08	11.89	6.87	9.26	12.61	17.90	16.10	15.27
Net Margin %	4.13	3.49	1.72	3.63	5.87	10.64	9.80	9.44
Asset Turnover	0.76	0.77	0.81	0.81	0.91	0.98	1.01	1.00
Current Ratio	2.12	2.11	2.08	1.98	1.94	1.90	1.83	1.72
Debt to Equity	0.86	0.88	0.88	0.90	0.94	0.57	0.60	0.46
Price Range	51.85-37.58	51.85-41.35	52.32-41.35	52.32-35.40	62.86-39.85	81.55-54.80	78.83-48.93	48.93-33.39
P/E Ratio	40.19-29.13	67.34-53.70	56.26-44.46	47.14-31.89	31.43-19.93	21.69-14.57	23.12-14.35	17.23-11.76
Average Yield %	1.64	1.60	1.61	1.67	1.42	0.88	0.96	1.19

Address: 5215 N. O'Connor Blvd., Suite 2300, Irving, TX 75039	**Web Site:** www.flowserve.com	**Auditors:** PricewaterhouseCoopers LLP
Telephone: 972-443-6500	**Officers:** Robert Scott Rowe - President, Chief Executive Officer Thomas L. Pajonas - Executive Vice	**Investor Contact:** 972-443-6500
Fax: 972-443-6800	President, Senior Vice President, Chief Operating Officer, Division Officer	**Transfer Agents:** Wells Fargo Bank, N.A., Mendota Heights, MN

FLUOR CORP.

Exchange	Symbol	Price	52Wk Range	Yield	P/E
NYS	FLR	$51.65 (12/29/2017)	58.17-37.23	1.63	36.12

*7 Year Price Score 64.56 *NYSE Composite Index=100 *12 Month Price Score 94.87

Interim Earnings (Per Share)

Qtr.	Mar	Jun	Sep	Dec
2014	0.92	0.48	0.44	1.36
2015	0.96	1.00	1.17	(0.32)
2016	0.74	0.72	0.03	0.50
2017	0.43	(0.17)	0.67	...

Interim Dividends (Per Share)

Amt	Decl	Ex	Rec	Pay
0.21Q	02/01/2017	02/28/2017	03/02/2017	04/04/2017
0.21Q	05/03/2017	05/31/2017	06/02/2017	07/05/2017
0.21Q	08/02/2017	08/31/2017	09/05/2017	10/03/2017
0.21Q	11/01/2017	12/04/2017	12/05/2017	01/03/2018

Indicated Div: $0.84

Valuation Analysis

		Institutional Holding	
Forecast EPS	$1.55 (01/18/2018)	No of Institutions	767
Market Cap	$7.2 Billion	Shares	138,187,136
Book Value	$3.3 Billion	% Held	
Price/Book	2.20		77.17
Price/Sales	0.37		

TRADING VOLUME (thousand shares)

Business Summary: Construction Services (MIC: 7.5.4 SIC: 1629 NAIC: 237990)

Fluor is a holding company. Through its subsidiaries, Co. provides engineering, procurement, construction, fabrication and modularization, commissioning and maintenance as well as project management services. Co. serves a set of industries including oil and gas, chemicals and petrochemicals, mining and metals, transportation, power, life sciences and manufacturing. Co. is also a service provider to the U.S. federal government and governments abroad; and it performs operations, maintenance and asset integrity activities for industrial clients. Co. has four segments: Energy, Chemicals & Mining; Industrial, Infrastructure & Power; Maintenance, Modification & Asset Integrity; and Government.

Recent Developments: For the quarter ended Sep 30 2017, net income increased 548.6% to US$112.9 million from US$17.4 million in the year-earlier quarter. Revenues were US$4.94 billion, up 3.7% from US$4.77 billion the year before. Direct operating expenses declined 0.2% to US$4.72 billion from US$4.73 billion in the comparable period the year before. Indirect operating expenses increased 40.9% to US$56.2 million from US$39.9 million in the equivalent prior-year period.

Prospects: Our evaluation of Fluor Corp. as of Jan. 14, 2018 is the result of our systematic analysis on three basic characteristics: earnings strength, relative valuation, and recent stock price movement. The company has produced a positive trend in earnings per share over the past 5 quarters and while recent estimates for the company have been mixed, FLR has posted better than expected results. Based on operating earnings yield, the company is about fairly valued when compared to all of the companies in our coverage universe. Share price changes over the past year indicates that FLR will perform very poorly over the near term.

Financial Data
(US$ in Thousands)

	9 Mos	6 Mos	3 Mos	12/31/2016	12/31/2015	12/31/2014	12/31/2013	12/31/2012
Earnings Per Share	1.43	0.79	1.68	2.00	2.81	3.20	4.06	2.71
Cash Flow Per Share	5.75	7.46	6.18	5.06	5.86	4.08	4.85	3.75
Tang Book Value Per Share	19.44	18.79	19.14	18.62	20.76	20.17	22.59	19.96
Dividends Per Share	0.840	0.840	0.840	0.840	0.840	0.840	0.640	0.640
Dividend Payout %	58.74	106.33	50.00	42.00	29.89	26.25	15.76	23.62
Income Statement								
Total Revenue	14,493,631	9,551,997	4,835,905	19,036,525	18,114,048	21,531,577	27,351,573	27,577,135
EBITDA	464,235	223,285	176,396	825,156	944,371	1,408,916	1,397,141	946,368
Depn & Amortn	199,031	133,671	71,443	225,913	189,738	192,594	207,098	212,381
Income Before Taxes	234,860	69,476	93,425	546,600	726,552	1,204,909	1,177,599	733,505
Income Taxes	51,249	(1,246)	16,071	219,151	245,888	352,815	354,573	162,438
Net Income	131,049	36,586	60,611	281,401	412,512	510,909	667,711	456,330
Average Shares	140,830	139,818	140,958	140,912	146,722	159,616	164,354	168,491
Balance Sheet								
Current Assets	5,514,894	5,613,818	5,560,338	5,610,270	5,278,287	5,758,047	6,003,683	6,094,137
Total Assets	9,193,527	9,221,808	9,160,335	9,216,417	7,631,506	8,194,429	8,323,850	8,276,043
Current Liabilities	3,543,574	3,733,271	3,676,369	3,816,029	2,935,352	3,330,853	3,407,160	3,887,114
Long-Term Obligations	1,580,974	1,560,471	1,526,023	1,517,949	992,664	991,685	496,604	520,205
Total Liabilities	5,910,219	6,044,122	5,939,500	6,091,226	4,634,159	5,083,558	4,566,863	4,934,748
Stockholders' Equity	3,283,308	3,177,686	3,220,835	3,125,191	2,997,347	3,110,871	3,756,987	3,341,295
Shares Outstanding	139,902	139,876	139,781	139,258	139,018	148,633	161,287	162,359
Statistical Record								
Return on Assets %	2.18	1.21	2.62	3.33	5.21	6.19	8.04	5.50
Return on Equity %	6.31	3.54	7.53	9.17	13.51	14.88	18.81	13.51
EBITDA Margin %	3.20	2.34	3.65	4.33	5.21	6.54	5.11	3.43
Net Margin %	0.90	0.38	1.25	1.48	2.28	2.37	2.44	1.65
Asset Turnover	2.11	2.09	2.14	2.25	2.29	2.61	3.30	3.32
Current Ratio	1.56	1.50	1.51	1.47	1.80	1.73	1.76	1.57
Debt to Equity	0.48	0.49	0.47	0.49	0.33	0.32	0.13	0.16
Price Range	58.17-37.23	58.17-43.77	58.17-44.58	57.14-41.11	61.20-40.94	83.65-56.29	80.29-54.16	63.99-45.12
P/E Ratio	40.68-26.03	73.63-55.41	34.63-26.54	28.57-20.56	21.78-14.57	26.14-17.59	19.78-13.34	23.61-16.65
Average Yield %	1.72	1.63	1.60	1.66	1.61	1.11	0.96	1.17

Address: 6700 Las Colinas Boulevard, Irving, TX 75039	Web Site: www.fluor.com	Auditors: Ernst & Young LLP
Telephone: 469-398-7000	Officers: David T. Seaton - Chairman, Chief Executive Officer, Chief Operating Officer Glenn Gilkey - Senior Vice President	Investor Contact: 469-398-7189
		Transfer Agents: Computershare, Pittsburgh, PA

FMC CORP.

Exchange	Symbol	Price	52Wk Range	Yield	P/E
NYS	FMC	$94.66 (12/29/2017)	95.54-57.03	0.70	591.63

*7 Year Price Score 106.07 *NYSE Composite Index=100 *12 Month Price Score 112.56

Interim Earnings (Per Share)

Qtr.	Mar	Jun	Sep	Dec
2014	0.49	0.81	0.42	0.57
2015	(0.35)	5.52	(0.02)	(1.52)
2016	0.36	0.49	0.59	0.12
2017	(0.93)	0.56	0.41	...

Interim Dividends (Per Share)

Amt	Decl	Ex	Rec	Pay
0.165Q	02/28/2017	03/29/2017	03/31/2017	04/20/2017
0.165Q	04/25/2017	06/28/2017	06/30/2017	07/20/2017
0.165Q	07/21/2017	09/28/2017	09/29/2017	10/19/2017
0.165Q	12/12/2017	12/28/2017	12/29/2017	01/18/2018

Indicated Div: $0.66

Valuation Analysis / Institutional Holding

Forecast EPS	$2.67	No of Institutions
	(01/18/2018)	715
Market Cap	$12.7 Billion	Shares
Book Value	$2.1 Billion	139,161,088
Price/Book	5.99	% Held
Price/Sales	4.60	87.63

Business Summary: Agricultural Chemicals (MIC: 8.3.3 SIC: 2812 NAIC: 325181)

FMC is chemical company serving agricultural, consumer and industrial markets globally. Co. operates in three business segments: FMC Agricultural Solutions, FMC Health and Nutrition and FMC Lithium. Co.'s FMC Agricultural Solutions segment develops, markets and sells three classes of crop protection chemicals, including insecticides, herbicides and fungicides. The FMC Health and Nutrition segment focuses on nutritional ingredients, health excipients, and functional health ingredients. Co.'s FMC Lithium segment manufactures lithium for use in a range of lithium products, which are used primarily in energy storage, specialty polymers and chemical synthesis application.

Recent Developments: For the quarter ended Sep 30 2017, income from continuing operations increased 46.2% to US$70.9 million from US$48.5 million in the year-earlier quarter. Net income decreased 29.9% to US$55.8 million from US$79.6 million in the year-earlier quarter. Revenues were US$646.2 million, up 2.8% from US$628.8 million the year before. Direct operating expenses declined 8.2% to US$380.3 million from US$414.2 million in the comparable period the year before. Indirect operating expenses increased 30.2% to US$188.2 million from US$144.6 million in the equivalent prior-year period.

Prospects: Our evaluation of FMC Corp as of Jan. 14, 2018 is the result of our systematic analysis on three basic characteristics: earnings strength, relative valuation, and recent stock price movement. The company has enjoyed a very positive trend in earnings per share over the past 5 quarters and while recent estimates for the company have been mixed, FMC has posted better than expected results. Based on operating earnings yield, the company is about fairly valued when compared to all of the companies in our coverage universe. Share price changes over the past year indicates that FMC will perform very well over the near term.

Financial Data

(US$ in Thousands)	9 Mos	6 Mos	3 Mos	12/31/2016	12/31/2015	12/31/2014	12/31/2013	12/31/2012
Earnings Per Share	0.16	0.34	0.27	1.56	3.66	2.29	2.16	3.00
Cash Flow Per Share	3.20	3.97	2.71	3.71	(2.68)	2.80	2.43	2.61
Tang Book Value Per Share	6.28	5.57	4.79	2.63	1.62	6.73	6.21	7.05
Dividends Per Share	0.660	0.660	0.660	0.660	0.660	0.600	0.540	0.405
Dividend Payout %	412.50	194.12	244.44	42.31	18.03	26.20	25.00	13.50
Income Statement								
Total Revenue	1,899,000	1,252,800	596,000	3,282,400	3,276,500	4,037,700	3,874,800	3,748,300
EBITDA	288,000	185,200	93,600	507,900	23,900	649,300	753,600	757,300
Depn & Amortn	71,200	46,100	23,600	86,400	74,100	103,900	94,600	99,100
Income Before Taxes	165,500	106,200	54,300	338,800	(130,300)	485,900	616,800	612,900
Income Taxes	1,100	12,700	9,400	93,900	47,400	73,500	148,600	146,700
Net Income	5,700	(49,500)	(124,200)	209,100	489,000	307,500	293,900	416,200
Average Shares	135,947	135,603	135,082	134,538	133,696	134,282	136,137	138,813
Balance Sheet								
Current Assets	3,574,200	3,485,800	3,554,200	2,849,200	2,971,900	2,934,400	2,945,000	2,181,800
Total Assets	6,056,800	5,984,300	6,036,300	6,139,300	6,325,900	5,340,500	5,235,200	4,373,900
Current Liabilities	1,630,600	1,541,900	1,488,800	1,438,200	1,453,300	1,910,400	1,986,700	1,135,400
Long-Term Obligations	1,492,900	1,592,300	1,790,400	1,798,800	2,036,300	1,153,400	1,154,100	908,800
Total Liabilities	3,936,500	3,972,400	4,159,000	4,181,600	4,460,200	3,810,000	3,715,400	2,893,600
Stockholders' Equity	2,120,300	2,011,900	1,877,300	1,957,700	1,865,700	1,530,500	1,519,800	1,480,300
Shares Outstanding	134,261	134,128	134,001	133,690	133,655	133,317	132,885	137,670
Statistical Record								
Return on Assets %	0.35	0.75	0.59	3.35	8.38	5.82	6.12	10.23
Return on Equity %	1.03	2.30	1.91	10.91	28.80	20.16	19.59	30.51
EBITDA Margin %	15.17	14.78	15.70	15.47	0.73	16.08	19.45	20.20
Net Margin %	0.30	N.M.	N.M.	6.37	14.92	7.62	7.58	11.10
Asset Turnover	0.45	0.48	0.50	0.53	0.56	0.76	0.81	0.92
Current Ratio	2.19	2.26	2.39	1.98	2.04	1.54	1.48	1.92
Debt to Equity	0.70	0.79	0.95	0.92	1.09	0.75	0.76	0.61
Price Range	92.14-46.09	76.77-44.16	69.59-36.90	59.00-33.53	64.59-32.93	83.10-51.60	75.46-55.45	58.59-43.48
P/E Ratio	575.88-288.06	225.79-129.88	257.74-136.67	37.82-21.49	17.65-9.00	36.29-22.53	34.94-25.67	19.53-14.49
Average Yield %	0.98	1.13	1.29	1.44	1.31	0.88	0.83	0.77

Address: 2929 Walnut Street, Philadelphia, PA 19104 **Telephone:** 215-299-6000 **Fax:** 215-299-5998	**Web Site:** www.fmc.com **Officers:** Pierre R. Brondeau - Chairman, President, Chief Executive Officer Paul W. Graves - Executive Vice President, Chief Financial Officer	**Auditors:** KPMG LLP **Investor Contact:** 215-299-6119 **Transfer Agents:** Wells Fargo Bank, N.A., Mendota Heights, MN

FOOT LOCKER, INC.

Exchange	Symbol	Price	52Wk Range	Yield	P/E
NYS	FL	$46.88 (12/29/2017)	77.35-29.24	2.65	11.81

*7 Year Price Score 93.06   *NYSE Composite Index=100   *12 Month Price Score 70.97

Interim Earnings (Per Share)

Qtr.	Apr	Jul	Oct	Jan
2014-15	1.10	0.63	0.82	1.01
2015-16	1.29	0.84	0.57	1.13
2016-17	1.39	0.94	1.17	1.41
2017-18	1.36	0.39	0.81	...

Interim Dividends (Per Share)

Amt	Decl	Ex	Rec	Pay
0.31Q	02/15/2017	04/11/2017	04/13/2017	04/28/2017
0.31Q	05/16/2017	07/12/2017	07/14/2017	07/28/2017
0.31Q	08/16/2017	10/12/2017	10/13/2017	10/27/2017
0.31Q	11/15/2017	01/18/2018	01/19/2018	02/02/2018

Indicated Div: $1.24

Valuation Analysis / **Institutional Holding**

Forecast EPS	$4.08 (01/26/2018)	No of Institutions 732
Market Cap	$6.3 Billion	Shares
Book Value	$2.7 Billion	143,216,016
Price/Book	2.35	% Held
Price/Sales	0.81	82.13

Business Summary: Retail - Apparel and Accessories (MIC: 2.1.5 SIC: 5661 NAIC: 448210)

Foot Locker is a retailer of athletically inspired shoes and apparel. Co. operates in two reportable segments: Athletic Stores and Direct-to-Customers. The Athletic Stores segment is an athletic footwear and apparel retailers, with formats that include Foot Locker, Kids Foot Locker, Lady Foot Locker, Champs Sports, Footaction, and Runners Point. The Direct-to-Customers segment includes Footlocker.com, Inc. and other affiliates, including Eastbay, Inc., and Co.'s international ecommerce businesses, which sell to customers through their Internet and mobile sites and catalogs. As of Jan 28 2017, Co. operated 3,363 mall-based stores in the U. S., Canada, Europe, Australia, and New Zealand.

Recent Developments: For the quarter ended Oct 28 2017, net income decreased 35.0% to US$102.0 million from US$157.0 million in the year-earlier quarter. Revenues were US$1.87 billion, down 0.8% from US$1.89 billion the year before. Operating income was US$155.0 million versus US$228.0 million in the prior-year quarter, a decrease of 32.0%. Direct operating expenses rose 3.5% to US$1.29 billion from US$1.25 billion in the comparable period the year before. Indirect operating expenses increased 3.2% to US$425.0 million from US$412.0 million in the equivalent prior-year period.

Prospects: Our evaluation of Foot Locker Inc. as of Jan. 21, 2018 is the result of our systematic analysis on three basic characteristics: earnings strength, relative valuation, and recent stock price movement. The company has managed to produce a neutral trend in earnings per share over the past 5 quarters and while recent estimates for the company have been raised by analysts, FL has posted better than expected results. Based on operating earnings yield, the company is undervalued when compared to all of the companies in our coverage universe. Share price changes over the past year indicates that FL will perform very poorly over the near term.

Financial Data

(US$ in Thousands)	9 Mos	6 Mos	3 Mos	01/28/2017	01/30/2016	01/31/2015	02/01/2014	02/02/2013
Earnings Per Share	3.97	4.33	4.88	4.91	3.84	3.56	2.85	2.58
Cash Flow Per Share	6.81	5.32	-5.81	6.11	5.37	4.96	3.58	2.71
Tang Book Value Per Share	18.40	20.53	19.98	19.11	17.17	16.26	15.58	14.61
Dividends Per Share	1.205	1.170	1.135	1.100	1.000	0.880	0.800	0.720
Dividend Payout %	30.35	27.02	23.26	22.40	26.04	24.72	28.07	27.91
Income Statement								
Total Revenue	5,572,000	3,702,000	2,001,000	7,766,000	7,412,000	7,151,000	6,505,000	6,182,000
EBITDA	624,000	424,000	310,000	1,164,000	989,000	953,000	801,000	730,000
Depn & Amortn	127,000	83,000	41,000	158,000	148,000	139,000	133,000	118,000
Income Before Taxes	498,000	342,000	269,000	1,004,000	837,000	809,000	663,000	607,000
Income Taxes	165,000	111,000	89,000	340,000	296,000	289,000	234,000	210,000
Net Income	333,000	231,000	180,000	664,000	541,000	520,000	429,000	397,000
Average Shares	126,400	132,000	132,600	135,100	140,800	146,000	150,500	154,000
Balance Sheet								
Current Assets	2,498,000	2,644,000	2,622,000	2,633,000	2,606,000	2,456,000	2,350,000	2,363,000
Total Assets	3,813,000	3,946,000	3,877,000	3,840,000	3,775,000	3,577,000	3,487,000	3,367,000
Current Liabilities	567,000	470,000	535,000	612,000	700,000	696,000	626,000	636,000
Long-Term Obligations	126,000	126,000	127,000	127,000	129,000	132,000	136,000	133,000
Total Liabilities	1,156,000	1,052,000	1,055,000	1,130,000	1,222,000	1,081,000	991,000	990,000
Stockholders' Equity	2,657,000	2,894,000	2,822,000	2,710,000	2,553,000	2,496,000	2,496,000	2,377,000
Shares Outstanding	133,336	131,100	131,296	131,496	136,977	140,864	145,427	150,070
Statistical Record								
Return on Assets %	13.91	14.97	17.11	17.49	14.76	14.76	12.55	12.17
Return on Equity %	19.74	21.09	23.76	25.30	21.49	20.89	17.66	17.41
EBITDA Margin %	11.20	11.45	15.49	14.99	13.34	13.33	12.31	11.81
Net Margin %	.5.98	6.24	9.00	8.55	7.30	7.27	6.59	6.42
Asset Turnover	2.05	2.00	2.04	2.05	2.02	2.03	1.90	1.90
Current Ratio	4.41	5.63	4.90	4.30	3.72	3.53	3.75	3.72
Debt to Equity	0.05	0.04	0.05	0.05	0.05	0.05	0.05	0.06
Price Range	79.20-30.95	79.20-45.05	79.20-51.79	79.20-51.79	75.76-52.43	57.98-36.73	41.44-31.79	37.27-26.53
P/E Ratio	19.95-7.80	18.29-10.40	16.23-10.61	16.13-10.55	19.73-13.65	16.29-10.32	14.54-11.15	14.45-10.28
Average Yield %	2.02	1.75	1.70	1.71	1.54	1.74	2.26	2.21

Address: 330 West 34th Street, New York, NY 10001 **Telephone:** 212-720-3700	**Web Site:** www.footlocker-inc.com **Officers:** Richard A. Johnson - President, Chief Executive Officer, Executive Vice President, Chief Operating Officer, Division Officer Lauren B. Peters - Chief Financial Officer, Executive Vice President	**Auditors:** KPMG LLP **Investor Contact:** 212-720-3700 **Transfer Agents:** Computershare, Providence, R.I.

303

FORD MOTOR CO. (DE)

Exchange	Symbol	Price	52Wk Range	Yield	P/E
NYS	F	$12.49 (12/29/2017)	13.17-10.56	4.80	11.35

*7 Year Price Score 68.38   *NYSE Composite Index=100   *12 Month Price Score 98.97

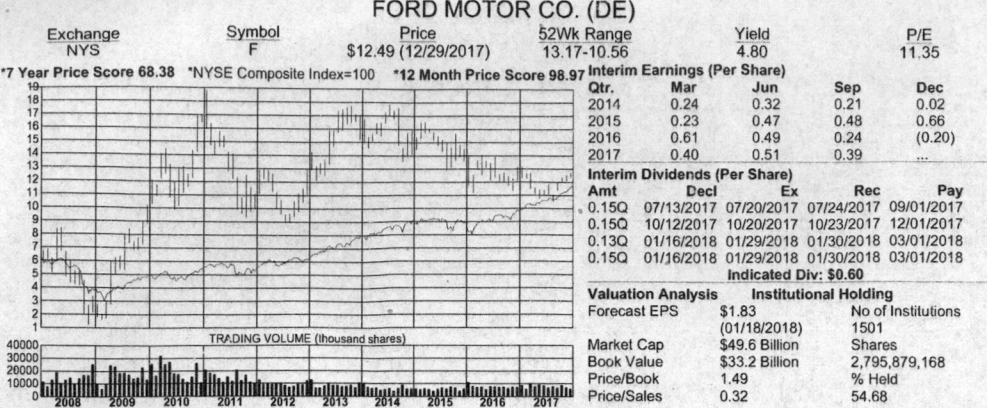

Interim Earnings (Per Share)

Qtr.	Mar	Jun	Sep	Dec
2014	0.24	0.32	0.21	0.02
2015	0.23	0.47	0.48	0.66
2016	0.61	0.49	0.24	(0.20)
2017	0.40	0.51	0.39	...

Interim Dividends (Per Share)

Amt	Decl	Ex	Rec	Pay
0.15Q	07/13/2017	07/20/2017	07/24/2017	09/01/2017
0.15Q	10/12/2017	10/20/2017	10/23/2017	12/01/2017
0.13Q	01/16/2018	01/29/2018	01/30/2018	03/01/2018
0.15Q	01/16/2018	01/29/2018	01/30/2018	03/01/2018

Indicated Div: $0.60

Valuation Analysis / Institutional Holding

Valuation Analysis		Institutional Holding	
Forecast EPS	$1.83	No of Institutions	
	(01/18/2018)	1501	
Market Cap	$49.6 Billion	Shares	
Book Value	$33.2 Billion	2,795,879,168	
Price/Book	1.49	% Held	
Price/Sales	0.32	54.68	

Business Summary: Autos- Manufacturing (MIC: 1.8.1 SIC: 3711 NAIC: 336111)

Ford Motor's business includes designing, manufacturing, marketing, and servicing Ford cars, trucks, and SUVs, as well as Lincoln luxury vehicles. Co. has four operating segments: Automotive, which includes the sale of Ford and Lincoln brand vehicles, service parts, and accessories; Financial Services, which includes its vehicle-related financing and leasing activities at its subsidiary, Ford Motor Credit Company LLC; Ford Smart Mobility LLC, a subsidiary formed to design, build, grow, and invest in emerging mobility services; and Central Treasury Operations, which engages in decision making for investments, risk management activities, and providing financing for the Automotive segment.

Recent Developments: For the quarter ended Sep 30 2017, net income increased 63.5% to US$1.57 billion from US$961.0 million in the year-earlier quarter. Revenues were US$36.45 billion, up 1.4% from US$35.94 billion the year before. Direct operating expenses declined 1.2% to US$30.29 billion from US$30.67 billion in the comparable period the year before. Indirect operating expenses increased 6.9% to US$5.19 billion from US$4.86 billion in the equivalent prior-year period.

Prospects: Our evaluation of Ford Motor Co. as of Jan. 14, 2018 is the result of our systematic analysis on three basic characteristics: earnings strength, relative valuation, and recent stock price movement. The company has enjoyed a very positive trend in earnings per share over the past 5 quarters and while recent estimates for the company have been mixed, F has posted better than expected results. Based on operating earnings yield, the company is undervalued when compared to all of the companies in our coverage universe. Share price changes over the past year indicates that F will perform poorly over the near term.

Financial Data

(US$ in Millions)	9 Mos	6 Mos	3 Mos	12/31/2016	12/31/2015	12/31/2014	12/31/2013	12/31/2012
Earnings Per Share	1.10	0.95	0.93	1.15	1.84	0.80	1.76	1.42
Cash Flow Per Share	4.47	4.50	5.04	4.97	4.07	3.71	2.65	2.36
Tang Book Value Per Share	8.37	7.95	7.69	7.34	7.22	6.27	6.69	4.04
Dividends Per Share	0.650	0.650	0.650	0.850	0.600	0.500	0.400	0.200
Dividend Payout %	59.09	68.42	69.89	73.91	32.61	62.50	22.73	14.08
Income Statement								
Total Revenue	115,450	78,999	39,146	151,800	149,558	144,077	146,917	134,252
EBITDA	5,840	4,237	2,083	10,283	15,681	10,475	13,522	14,343
Depn & Amortn	...	...	...	4,667	4,332	4,252	4,064	3,655
Income Before Taxes	5,324	3,883	1,897	5,016	8,434	3,067	5,932	7,132
Income Taxes	1,044	858	649	2,189	2,881	1,156	(147)	2,056
Net Income	5,193	3,629	1,587	4,596	7,373	3,187	7,155	5,665
Average Shares	3,997	3,997	4,000	4,000	4,003	4,046	4,088	4,016
Balance Sheet								
Current Assets	112,732	113,539	113,228	108,461	43,495	39,016	44,276	43,305
Total Assets	251,273	247,469	244,094	237,951	224,925	208,527	202,026	190,554
Current Liabilities	94,352	94,299	91,304	90,281	78,336	73,963	74,131	73,428
Long-Term Obligations	97,938	95,236	96,720	93,301	89,856	79,999	76,625	66,296
Total Liabilities	218,035	215,225	213,475	208,781	196,283	183,722	175,643	174,607
Stockholders' Equity	33,238	32,244	30,619	29,170	28,642	24,805	26,383	15,947
Shares Outstanding	3,973	4,058	3,983	3,975	3,970	3,956	3,944	3,923
Statistical Record								
Return on Assets %	1.81	1.56	1.55	1.98	3.40	1.55	3.65	3.06
Return on Equity %	13.63	12.00	12.39	15.86	27.59	12.45	33.81	36.48
EBITDA Margin %	5.06	5.36	5.32	6.77	10.48	7.27	9.20	10.68
Net Margin %	4.50	4.59	4.05	3.03	4.93	2.21	4.87	4.22
Asset Turnover	0.63	0.65	0.64	0.65	0.69	0.70	0.75	0.73
Current Ratio	1.19	1.20	1.24	1.20	0.56	0.53	0.60	0.59
Debt to Equity	2.95	2.95	3.16	3.20	3.14	3.23	2.90	4.16
Price Range	13.17-10.56	13.92-10.76	14.09-11.34	14.09-11.17	16.57-12.90	17.84-13.54	17.76-12.13	12.96-8.92
P/E Ratio	11.97-9.60	14.65-11.33	15.15-12.19	12.25-9.71	9.01-7.01	22.30-16.92	10.09-6.89	9.13-6.28
Average Yield %	5.53	5.38	5.16	6.73	4.00	3.15	2.61	1.83

Address: One American Road, Dearborn, MI 48126
Telephone: 313-322-3000

Web Site: www.corporate.ford.com
Officers: William Clay Ford - Executive Chairman, Chairman James Patrick Hackett - President, Chief Executive Officer

Auditors: PricewaterhouseCoopers LLP
Investor Contact: 313-845-8540
Transfer Agents: Computershare Trust Company, N.A., Providence, RI

FORTIVE CORP

Exchange	Symbol	Price	52Wk Range	Yield	P/E
NYS	FTV	$72.35 (12/29/2017)	74.65-53.66	0.39	27.30

*7 Year Price Score N/A   *NYSE Composite Index=100   *12 Month Price Score 106.87

TRADING VOLUME (thousand shares)

2008 2009 2010 2011 2012 2013 2014 2015 2016 2017

Interim Earnings (Per Share)

Qtr.	Mar	Jun	Sep	Dec
2016	0.53	0.69	0.65	0.64
2017	0.57	0.68	0.76	...

Interim Dividends (Per Share)

Amt	Decl	Ex	Rec	Pay
0.07Q	01/24/2017	02/22/2017	02/24/2017	03/31/2017
0.07Q	04/13/2017	05/24/2017	05/26/2017	06/30/2017
0.07Q	08/03/2017	08/23/2017	08/25/2017	09/29/2017
0.07Q	11/02/2017	11/22/2017	11/24/2017	12/29/2017

Indicated Div: $0.28

Valuation Analysis / Institutional Holding

Valuation Analysis		Institutional Holding	
Forecast EPS	$2.86 (01/18/2018)	No of Institutions	841
Market Cap	$25.1 Billion	Shares	291,310,816
Book Value	$3.5 Billion	% Held	N/A
Price/Book	7.24		
Price/Sales	3.88		

Business Summary: Industrial Machinery & Equipment (MIC: 7.2.1 SIC: 3823 NAIC: 334513)

Fortive is a diversified industrial growth company comprising businesses in recognized markets globally. Co. designs, develops, services, manufactures and markets engineered products, software and services. Co. operates through two segments: Professional Instrumentation, which provides essential products, software and services used to create actionable intelligence by measuring and monitoring a range of physical parameters in industrial applications, including electrical current, radio frequency signals, distance, pressure and temperature; and Industrial Technologies, which provides technical equipment, components, software and services for manufacturing, repair and transportation markets.

Recent Developments: For the quarter ended Sep 29 2017, net income increased 18.0% to US$267.8 million from US$226.9 million in the year-earlier quarter. Revenues were US$1.69 billion, up 7.5% from US$1.57 billion the year before. Operating income was US$355.9 million versus US$323.2 million in the prior-year quarter, an increase of 10.1%. Direct operating expenses rose 6.5% to US$845.9 million from US$794.5 million in the comparable period the year before. Indirect operating expenses increased 7.5% to US$483.5 million from US$449.7 million in the equivalent prior-year period.

Prospects: Our evaluation of Fortive Corp. as of Jan. 14, 2018 is the result of our systematic analysis on three basic characteristics: earnings strength, relative valuation, and recent stock price movement. The company has managed to produce a neutral trend in earnings per share over the past 5 quarters and while recent estimates for the company have been mixed, FTV has posted better than expected results. Based on operating earnings yield, the company is about fairly valued when compared to all of the companies in our coverage universe. Share price changes over the past year indicates that FTV will perform very well over the near term.

Financial Data

(US$ in Thousands)	9 Mos	6 Mos	3 Mos	12/31/2016	12/31/2015	12/31/2014	12/31/2013
Earnings Per Share	2.65	2.54	2.55	2.51	...	...	...
Cash Flow Per Share	2.96	3.00	3.19	3.28	...	...	...
Dividends Per Share	0.280	0.280	0.210	0.140	...	...	...
Dividend Payout %	10.57	11.02	8.24	5.58	...	...	...
Income Statement							
Total Revenue	4,849,300	3,164,000	1,535,200	6,224,300	6,178,800	6,337,200	5,961,900
EBITDA	1,128,100	717,000	331,600	1,337,000	1,357,700	1,357,200	1,221,200
Depn & Amortn	113,700	73,800	36,700	91,000	88,000	78,000	78,000
Income Before Taxes	946,200	597,900	272,300	1,197,000	1,269,700	1,279,200	1,143,200
Income Taxes	238,600	158,100	72,600	324,700	405,900	395,800	312,300
Net Income	707,600	439,800	199,700	872,300	863,800	883,400	830,900
Average Shares	352,900	352,200	351,500	347,300	...	...	...
Balance Sheet							
Current Assets	2,695,300	2,701,700	2,517,400	2,488,700	1,594,100	1,683,400	...
Total Assets	9,327,000	8,467,100	8,234,300	8,189,800	7,210,600	7,355,600	...
Current Liabilities	1,379,300	1,370,800	1,401,000	1,466,500	1,323,500	1,285,000	...
Long-Term Obligations	3,671,900	3,208,100	3,262,700	3,358,000	...	...	...
Total Liabilities	5,852,800	5,297,600	5,345,900	5,501,900	2,031,100	2,126,300	...
Stockholders' Equity	3,474,200	3,169,500	2,888,400	2,687,900	5,179,500	5,229,300	...
Shares Outstanding	347,500	347,000	346,600	345,900	...	...	...
Statistical Record							
Return on Assets %	10.68	10.97	...	11.30	11.86	...	...
Return on Equity %	30.91	32.18	...	22.11	16.60	...	...
EBITDA Margin %	23.26	22.66	21.60	21.48	21.97	21.42	20.48
Net Margin %	14.59	13.90	13.01	14.01	13.98	13.94	13.94
Asset Turnover	0.74	0.78	...	0.81	0.85	...	...
Current Ratio	1.95	1.97	1.80	1.70	1.20	1.31	...
Debt to Equity	1.06	1.01	1.13	1.25	...	...	...
Price Range	70.79-47.49	64.79-47.49	60.22-47.49	55.97-47.49	...	...	...
P/E Ratio	26.71-17.92	25.51-18.70	23.62-18.62	22.30-18.92	...	...	...
Average Yield %	0.47	0.50	0.39	0.27	...	...	...

Address: 6920 Seaway Blvd., Everett, WA 98203 Telephone: 425-446-5000	Web Site: www.fortive.com Officers: Alan G. Spoon - Chairman James A. Lico - President, Chief Executive Officer	Auditors: Ernst & Young LLP Transfer Agents: Computershare Trust Company, N.A.

FORTUNE BRANDS HOME & SECURITY, INC.

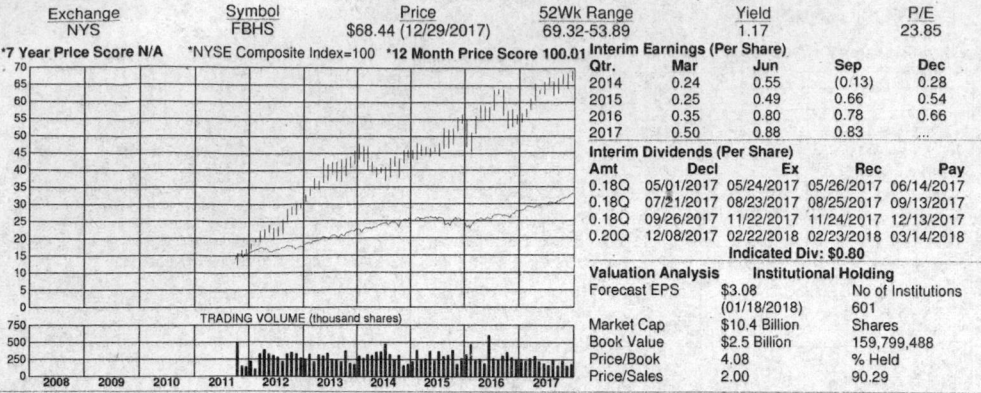

Exchange	Symbol	Price	52Wk Range	Yield	P/E
NYS	FBHS	$68.44 (12/29/2017)	69.32-53.89	1.17	23.85

*7 Year Price Score N/A   *NYSE Composite Index=100   *12 Month Price Score 100.01

Interim Earnings (Per Share)

Qtr.	Mar	Jun	Sep	Dec
2014	0.24	0.55	(0.13)	0.28
2015	0.25	0.49	0.66	0.54
2016	0.35	0.80	0.78	0.66
2017	0.50	0.88	0.83	...

Interim Dividends (Per Share)

Amt	Decl	Ex	Rec	Pay
0.18Q	05/01/2017	05/24/2017	05/26/2017	06/14/2017
0.18Q	07/21/2017	08/23/2017	08/25/2017	09/13/2017
0.18Q	09/26/2017	11/22/2017	11/24/2017	12/13/2017
0.20Q	12/08/2017	02/22/2018	02/23/2018	03/14/2018

Indicated Div: $0.80

Valuation Analysis   **Institutional Holding**

Forecast EPS	$3.08
	(01/18/2018)
Market Cap	$10.4 Billion
Book Value	$2.5 Billion
Price/Book	4.08
Price/Sales	2.00

No of Institutions 601
Shares 159,799,488
% Held 90.29

TRADING VOLUME (thousand shares)

Business Summary: Household Appliances, Electronics & Goods (MIC: 1.5.1 SIC: 1522 NAIC: 236115)

Fortune Brands Home & Security is a holding company, which provides home and security products. Co. has four business segments: Cabinets, which manufactures custom, semi-custom and stock cabinetry, and vanities; Plumbing, which manufactures or assembles and sells faucets, accessories, kitchen sinks and waste disposals; Doors, which manufactures and sells fiberglass and steel entry door systems and urethane millwork product lines; and Security, which manufactures and sells key-controlled and combination padlocks, bicycle and cable locks, built-in locker locks, door hardware, automotive, trailer and towing locks, electronic access control solutions, and other safety and security devices.

Recent Developments: For the quarter ended Sep 30 2017, income from continuing operations increased 6.3% to US$129.6 million from US$121.9 million in the year-earlier quarter. Net income increased 5.0% to US$129.6 million from US$123.4 million in the year-earlier quarter. Revenues were US$1.35 billion, up 5.4% from US$1.28 billion the year before. Operating income was US$201.8 million versus US$183.1 million in the prior-year quarter, an increase of 10.2%. Direct operating expenses rose 5.1% to US$841.6 million from US$801.0 million in the comparable period the year before. Indirect operating expenses increased 3.5% to US$305.2 million from US$294.9 million in the equivalent prior-year period.

Prospects: Our evaluation of Fortune Brands Home & Security Inc. as of Jan. 14, 2018 is the result of our systematic analysis on three basic characteristics: earnings strength, relative valuation, and recent stock price movement. The company has managed to produce a neutral trend in earnings per share over the past 5 quarters and while recent estimates for the company have been mixed, FBHS has posted better than expected results. Based on operating earnings yield, the company is undervalued when compared to all of the companies in our coverage universe. Share price changes over the past year indicates that FBHS will perform well over the near term.

Financial Data

(US$ in Thousands)	9 Mos	6 Mos	3 Mos	12/31/2016	12/31/2015	12/31/2014	12/31/2013	12/31/2012
Earnings Per Share	2.87	2.82	2.74	2.62	1.93	0.95	1.34	0.71
Cash Flow Per Share	4.06	4.26	4.26	4.20	2.58	1.57	1.80	1.76
Tang Book Value Per Share	N.M.	N.M.	N.M.	N.M.	N.M.	0.85	2.26	1.93
Dividends Per Share	0.700	0.680	0.660	0.640	0.560	0.480	0.300	...
Dividend Payout %	24.39	24.11	24.09	24.43	29.02	50.53	22.39	...
Income Statement								
Total Revenue	3,900,800	2,552,200	1,186,800	4,984,900	4,579,400	4,013,600	4,157,400	3,591,100
EBITDA	626,700	392,200	148,000	753,900	606,900	498,300	442,500	264,000
Depn & Amortn	97,800	65,000	32,300	122,700	115,100	96,000	90,440	101,300
Income Before Taxes	492,400	303,000	103,800	582,100	459,900	391,900	344,900	154,000
Income Taxes	145,100	85,300	26,400	169,700	153,400	118,300	114,000	34,300
Net Income	344,600	215,100	77,400	413,200	315,000	158,100	229,700	118,700
Average Shares	155,900	156,600	156,200	157,800	163,000	166,300	171,300	166,100
Balance Sheet								
Current Assets	1,598,300	1,553,100	1,456,100	1,445,200	1,418,700	1,299,100	1,327,400	1,228,000
Total Assets	5,349,300	5,253,400	5,134,100	5,128,500	4,878,600	4,052,900	4,178,100	3,873,700
Current Liabilities	852,500	791,100	707,800	842,800	757,900	699,600	738,700	632,600
Long-Term Obligations	1,462,200	1,391,900	1,491,500	1,431,100	1,171,600	643,700	350,000	297,500
Total Liabilities	2,805,000	2,686,200	2,704,900	2,767,000	2,427,700	1,793,400	1,528,700	1,492,600
Stockholders' Equity	2,544,300	2,567,200	2,429,200	2,361,500	2,450,900	2,259,500	2,649,400	2,381,100
Shares Outstanding	151,800	154,010	153,844	153,412	159,906	158,140	166,667	163,855
Statistical Record								
Return on Assets %	8.49	8.54	8.53	8.24	7.05	3.84	5.71	3.15
Return on Equity %	18.28	18.24	18.69	17.13	13.37	6.44	9.13	5.26
EBITDA Margin %	16.07	15.37	12.47	15.12	13.25	12.42	10.64	7.35
Net Margin %	8.83	8.43	6.52	8.29	6.88	3.94	5.53	3.31
Asset Turnover	0.99	0.99	1.01	0.99	1.03	0.98	1.03	0.95
Current Ratio	1.87	1.96	2.06	1.71	1.87	1.86	1.80	1.94
Debt to Equity	0.57	0.54	0.61	0.61	0.48	0.28	0.13	0.12
Price Range	67.30-52.31	66.05-52.31	64.04-52.31	64.04-45.27	56.47-43.04	47.83-36.77	45.70-29.22	30.33-16.82
P/E Ratio	23.45-18.23	23.42-18.55	23.37-19.09	24.44-17.28	29.26-22.30	50.35-38.71	34.10-21.81	42.72-23.69
Average Yield %	1.16	1.15	1.14	1.14	1.16	1.14	0.77	...

Address: 520 Lake Cook Road, Deerfield, IL 60015-5611 **Telephone:** 847-484-4400	**Web Site:** www.fbhs.com **Officers:** Christopher J. Klein - President, Chief Executive Officer E. Lee Wyatt - Senior Vice President, Chief Financial Officer	**Auditors:** PricewaterhouseCoopers LLP **Transfer Agents:** Wells Fargo Shareowner Services, Mendota Heights, MN

FRANKLIN RESOURCES, INC.

Exchange	Symbol	Price	52Wk Range	Yield	P/E	Div Achiever
NYS	BEN	$43.33 (12/29/2017)	47.28-39.74	2.12	14.40	27 Years

*7 Year Price Score 76.03   *NYSE Composite Index=100   *12 Month Price Score 94.34

TRADING VOLUME (thousand shares)

Interim Earnings (Per Share)

Qtr.	Dec	Mar	Jun	Sep
2012-13	0.81	0.90	0.86	0.80
2013-14	0.96	0.89	0.92	1.02
2014-15	0.91	0.98	0.82	0.59
2015-16	0.74	0.61	0.77	0.82
2016-17	0.77	0.74	0.73	0.76

Interim Dividends (Per Share)

Amt	Decl	Ex	Rec	Pay
0.20Q	02/15/2017	03/29/2017	03/31/2017	04/13/2017
0.20Q	06/14/2017	06/28/2017	06/30/2017	07/14/2017
0.20Q	08/23/2017	09/28/2017	09/29/2017	10/13/2017
0.23Q	12/12/2017	12/22/2017	12/26/2017	01/10/2018

Indicated Div: $0.92 (Div. Reinv. Plan)

Valuation Analysis   Institutional Holding

Forecast EPS	$3.10	No of Institutions
	(01/18/2018)	844
Market Cap	$24.0 Billion	Shares
Book Value	$12.6 Billion	295,912,096
Price/Book	1.91	% Held
Price/Sales	3.76	49.77

Business Summary: Wealth Management (MIC: 5.5.2 SIC: 6282 NAIC: 523930)

Franklin Resources is a holding company that, operates as Franklin Templeton Investments®. Co. is a global investment management organization that provides investment management and related services. Co. provides its investment products and services under its Franklin®, Templeton®, Franklin Mutual Series®, Franklin Bissett®, Fiduciary Trustâ,¢, Darby®, Balanced Equity Management®, K2® and LibertyShares® brand names. Co.'s products include investment funds and institutional and separately-managed accounts. Co.'s investment funds include U.S.-registered funds, non-U.S.-registered funds, and unregistered funds. At Sep 30 2017, Co.'s total assets under management were $753.20 billion.

Recent Developments: For the year ended Sep 30 2017, net income increased 1.8% to US$1.79 billion from US$1.76 billion in the prior year. Revenues were US$6.39 billion, down 3.4% from US$6.62 billion the year before. Operating income was US$2.26 billion versus US$2.37 billion in the prior year, a decrease of 4.3%. Direct operating expenses declined 3.6% to US$2.13 billion from US$2.21 billion in the comparable period the year before. Indirect operating expenses decreased 2.2% to US$2.00 billion from US$2.04 billion in the equivalent prior-year period.

Prospects: Our evaluation of Franklin Resources Inc. as of Jan. 14, 2018 is the result of our systematic analysis on three basic characteristics: earnings strength, relative valuation, and recent stock price movement. The company has generated a negative trend in earnings per share over the past 5 quarters and while recent estimates for the company have been raised by analysts, BEN has posted better than expected results. Based on operating earnings yield, the company is undervalued when compared to all of the companies in our coverage universe. Share price changes over the past year indicates that BEN will perform well over the near term.

Financial Data

(US$ in Thousands)	09/30/2017	09/30/2016	09/30/2015	09/30/2014	09/30/2013	09/30/2012	09/30/2011	09/30/2010
Earnings Per Share	3.01	2.94	3.29	3.79	3.37	2.98	2.87	2.11
Cash Flow Per Share	2.03	2.95	3.66	3.42	3.22	1.66	2.45	2.43
Tang Book Value Per Share	18.73	17.05	15.88	14.86	12.23	11.09	9.76	8.51
Dividends Per Share	0.800	0.720	1.100	0.480	1.390	1.027	0.333	1.363
Dividend Payout %	26.58	24.49	33.43	12.66	41.25	34.41	11.60	64.61
Income Statement								
Total Revenue	6,392,200	6,618,000	7,948,700	8,491,400	7,985,000	7,101,000	7,140,039	5,852,999
EBITDA	2,499,300	2,537,500	3,202,000	3,462,400	3,068,900	2,701,700	2,723,200	2,121,149
Depn & Amortn	81,500	81,000	81,600	82,600	76,900	67,900	71,500	67,700
Income Before Taxes	2,441,200	2,443,100	3,091,600	3,341,500	2,952,600	2,609,600	2,625,277	2,049,860
Income Taxes	759,400	742,100	923,700	997,900	855,900	762,700	803,424	618,312
Net Income	1,696,700	1,726,700	2,035,300	2,384,300	2,150,200	1,931,400	1,923,580	1,445,689
Average Shares	559,100	583,800	614,900	625,200	634,100	643,200	666,252	682,059
Balance Sheet								
Current Assets	9,751,600	9,277,600	9,306,800	8,644,100	7,474,400	6,996,500	8,372,635	6,932,798
Total Assets	17,534,000	16,098,800	16,335,700	16,357,100	15,390,300	14,751,500	13,775,843	10,708,085
Current Liabilities	1,114,700	997,300	1,117,800	1,220,200	1,731,800	1,709,100	2,202,253	1,662,390
Long-Term. Obligations	1,097,600	2,083,400	2,155,300	2,149,000	2,306,000	2,839,100	2,083,926	949,903
Total Liabilities	4,914,000	4,163,000	4,494,700	4,773,000	5,317,200	5,550,200	5,251,112	2,981,094
Stockholders' Equity	12,620,000	11,935,800	11,841,000	11,584,100	10,073,100	9,201,300	8,524,731	7,726,994
Shares Outstanding	554,865	570,345	603,517	622,893	630,917	636,626	653,080	672,023
Statistical Record								
Return on Assets %	10.09	10.62	12.45	15.02	14.27	13.50	15.71	14.33
Return on Equity %	13.82	14.48	17.38	22.02	22.31	21.73	23.67	18.83
EBITDA Margin %	39.10	38.34	40.28	40.78	38.43	38.05	38.14	36.24
Net Margin %	26.54	26.09	25.61	28.08	26.93	27.20	26.94	24.70
Asset Turnover	0.38	0.41	0.49	0.53	0.53	0.50	0.58	0.58
Current Ratio	8.75	9.30	8.33	7.08	4.32	4.09	3.80	4.17
Debt to Equity	0.09	0.17	0.18	0.19	0.23	0.31	0.24	0.12
Price Range	47.28-33.18	41.92-30.67	58.84-36.36	58.51-49.52	56.11-41.55	42.67-30.13	45.75-31.88	40.44-28.32
P/E Ratio	15.71-11.02	14.26-10.43	17.88-11.05	15.44-13.07	16.65-12.33	14.32-10.11	15.94-11.11	19.16-13.42
Average Yield %	1.93	1.97	2.17	0.88	2.94	2.78	0.83	3.92

Address: One Franklin Parkway, San Mateo, CA 94403	Web Site: www.franklinresources.com	Auditors: PricewaterhouseCoopers LLP
Telephone: 650-312-2000	Officers: Gregory E. Johnson - Chairman, President, Chief Executive Officer Rupert H. Johnson - Vice-Chairman	Investor Contact: 650-312-4091
Fax: 650-312-3655		Transfer Agents: Computershare, Pittsburgh, PA

FREEPORT-MCMORAN INC

Exchange	Symbol	Price	52Wk Range	Yield	P/E
NYS	FCX	$18.96 (12/29/2017)	19.27-11.21	N/A	23.12

*7 Year Price Score 40.24   *NYSE Composite Index=100   *12 Month Price Score 103.81

Interim Earnings (Per Share)

Qtr.	Mar	Jun	Sep	Dec
2014	0.49	0.46	0.53	(2.73)
2015	(2.38)	(1.78)	(3.58)	(3.54)
2016	(3.35)	(0.38)	0.16	0.29
2017	0.16	0.18	0.19	...

Interim Dividends (Per Share)

Dividend Payment Suspended

Valuation Analysis

Institutional Holding		
Forecast EPS	$1.14	No of Institutions
(01/18/2018)		1187
Market Cap	$27.5 Billion	Shares
Book Value	$7.0 Billion	1,160,030,080
Price/Book	3.94	% Held
Price/Sales	1.74	76.92

TRADING VOLUME (thousand shares)

Business Summary: Non-Precious Metals (MIC: 8.2.2 SIC: 1021 NAIC: 212234)

Freeport-McMoRan is a mining company. Co. operates assets with proven and probable reserves of copper, gold and molybdenum, and Co. is the publicly traded copper producer. Co.'s portfolio of assets includes the Grasberg minerals district in Indonesia (copper and gold deposits), and mining operations in the Americas, including the Morenci minerals district in North America and the Cerro Verde operation in South America. At Dec 31 2016, Co.'s estimated proved developed oil and natural gas reserves (all of which are located in the U.S.) totaled 18.0 million barrels of oil equivalents, comprised of 4.0 million barrels of oil and natural gas liquids and 87.00 billion cubic feet of natural gas.

Recent Developments: For the quarter ended Sep 30 2017, income from continuing operations decreased 17.1% to US$242.0 million from US$292.0 million in the year-earlier quarter. Net income decreased 14.3% to US$245.0 million from US$286.0 million in the year-earlier quarter. Revenues were US$4.31 billion, up 11.2% from US$3.88 billion the year before. Operating income was US$917.0 million versus US$359.0 million in the prior-year quarter, an increase of 155.4%. Direct operating expenses declined 5.6% to US$3.22 billion from US$3.41 billion in the comparable period the year before. Indirect operating expenses increased 61.7% to US$173.0 million from US$107.0 million in the equivalent prior-year period.

Prospects: Our evaluation of Freeport-McMoRan Inc. as of Jan. 14, 2018 is the result of our systematic analysis on three basic characteristics: earnings strength, relative valuation, and recent stock price movement. The company has suffered a very negative trend in earnings per share over the past 5 quarters and while recent estimates for the company have been raised by analysts, FCX has posted better than expected results. Based on operating earnings yield, the company is undervalued when compared to all of the companies in our coverage universe. Share price changes over the past year indicates that FCX will perform very poorly over the near term.

Financial Data

(US$ in Thousands)	9 Mos	6 Mos	3 Mos	12/31/2016	12/31/2015	12/31/2014	12/31/2013	12/31/2012
Earnings Per Share	0.82	0.79	0.23	(3.16)	(11.31)	(1.26)	2.64	3.19
Cash Flow Per Share	2.87	2.73	2.61	2.82	2.98	5.42	6.13	3.97
Tang Book Value Per Share	4.82	4.23	4.37	3.98	6.03	17.28	17.96	18.13
Dividends Per Share	...	...	...	...	0.573	1.250	2.250	1.188
Dividend Payout %	...	...	...	...	...	...	85.23	37.23
Income Statement								
Total Revenue	11,362,000	7,052,000	3,341,000	14,830,000	15,877,000	21,438,000	20,921,000	18,010,000
EBITDA	3,467,000	2,119,000	994,000	(107,000)	(9,879,000)	4,069,000	8,228,000	6,852,000
Depn & Amortn	1,257,000	839,000	389,000	2,610,000	3,497,000	3,863,000	2,797,000	1,179,000
Income Before Taxes	1,577,000	951,000	438,000	(3,472,000)	(14,021,000)	(424,000)	4,913,000	5,487,000
Income Taxes	747,000	360,000	174,000	371,000	(1,935,000)	324,000	1,475,000	1,510,000
Net Income	776,000	496,000	228,000	(4,315,000)	(12,195,000)	(1,268,000)	2,680,000	3,041,000
Average Shares	1,454,000	1,453,000	1,454,000	1,318,000	1,082,000	1,039,000	1,006,000	954,000
Balance Sheet								
Current Assets	11,150,000	10,417,000	9,767,000	10,435,000	7,462,000	9,045,000	9,972,000	10,297,000
Total Assets	37,327,000	37,043,000	36,576,000	37,317,000	46,577,000	58,795,000	63,473,000	35,440,000
Current Liabilities	5,517,000	4,944,000	4,842,000	4,265,000	4,307,000	5,172,000	4,773,000	3,343,000
Long-Term Obligations	12,567,000	13,138,000	13,135,000	14,795,000	19,779,000	18,492,000	20,394,000	3,525,000
Total Liabilities	30,354,000	30,370,000	30,258,000	31,266,000	38,749,000	40,508,000	42,539,000	17,897,000
Stockholders' Equity	6,973,000	6,673,000	6,318,000	6,051,000	7,828,000	18,287,000	20,934,000	17,543,000
Shares Outstanding	1,448,000	1,577,000	1,447,000	1,445,000	1,246,000	1,039,000	1,038,000	949,000
Statistical Record								
Return on Assets %	2.23	2.10	0.22	N.M.	N.M.	N.M.	5.42	8.98
Return on Equity %	14.97	15.42	1.72	N.M.	N.M.	N.M.	13.93	18.28
EBITDA Margin %	30.51	30.05	29.75	N.M.	N.M.	18.98	39.33	38.05
Net Margin %	6.83	7.03	6.82	N.M.	N.M.	N.M.	12.81	16.89
Asset Turnover	0.40	0.39	0.38	0.35	0.30	0.35	0.42	0.53
Current Ratio	2.02	2.11	2.02	2.45	1.73	1.75	2.09	3.08
Debt to Equity	1.80	1.97	2.08	2.45	2.53	1.01	0.97	0.20
Price Range	17.02-9.52	17.02-9.52	17.02-8.85	16.21-3.74	23.66-6.12	39.04-21.03	37.74-26.82	46.50-30.81
P/E Ratio	20.76-11.61	21.54-12.05	74.00-38.48	...	...	...	14.30-10.16	14.58-9.66
Average Yield %	...	...	...	...	3.70	3.80		3.19

Address: 333 North Central Avenue, Phoenix, AZ 85004-2189	Web Site: www.fcx.com	Auditors: Ernst & Young LLP
Telephone: 602-366-8100	Officers: James R. Moffett - Chairman Emeritus, Executive Chairman, Chief Executive Officer Richard C. Adkerson - Vice-Chairman, President, Chief Executive Officer, President (frmr) Chief Executive Officer (frmr), Chief Financial Officer	Investor Contact: 602-366-8400 Transfer Agents: Computershare, Canton, MA

FULLER (HB) COMPANY

Exchange	Symbol	Price	52Wk Range	Yield	P/E	Div Achiever
NYS	FUL	$53.87 (12/29/2017)	58.64-47.48	1.11	26.41	49 Years

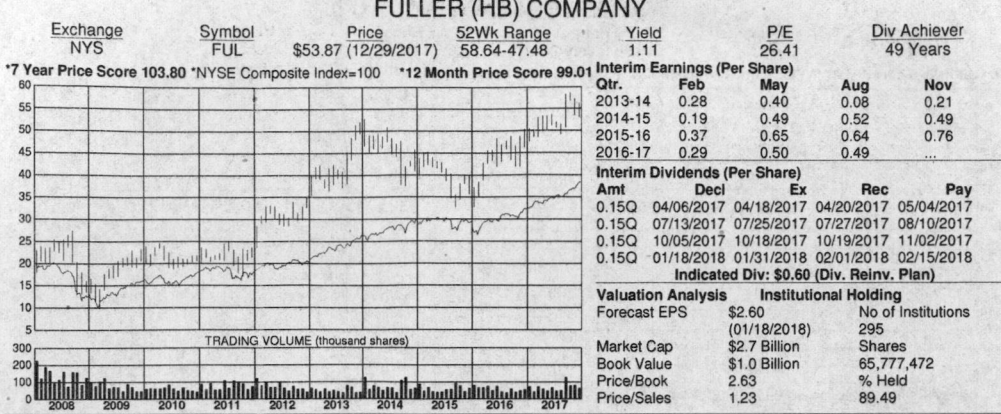

*7 Year Price Score 103.80 *NYSE Composite Index=100 *12 Month Price Score 99.01

Interim Earnings (Per Share)

Qtr.	Feb	May	Aug	Nov
2013-14	0.28	0.40	0.08	0.21
2014-15	0.19	0.49	0.52	0.49
2015-16	0.37	0.65	0.64	0.76
2016-17	0.29	0.50	0.49	...

Interim Dividends (Per Share)

Amt	Decl	Ex	Rec	Pay
0.15Q	04/06/2017	04/18/2017	04/20/2017	05/04/2017
0.15Q	07/13/2017	07/25/2017	07/27/2017	08/10/2017
0.15Q	10/05/2017	10/18/2017	10/19/2017	11/02/2017
0.15Q	01/18/2018	01/31/2018	02/01/2018	02/15/2018

Indicated Div: $0.60 (Div. Reinv. Plan)

Valuation Analysis		Institutional Holding	
Forecast EPS	$2.60	No of Institutions	
	(01/18/2018)	295	
Market Cap	$2.7 Billion	Shares	
Book Value	$1.0 Billion	65,777,472	
Price/Book	2.63	% Held	
Price/Sales	1.23	89.49	

Business Summary: Specialty Chemicals (MIC: 8.3.2 SIC: 2891 NAIC: 325520)

H.B. Fuller formulates, manufactures and markets adhesives, sealants and other chemical products. Co.'s Americas Adhesives, Europe, India, Middle East and Africa, and Asia Pacific segments manufacture and supply adhesives products in the assembly, packaging, converting, nonwoven and hygiene, performance wood, flooring, textile, flexible packaging, graphic arts, and envelope markets. Co.'s Construction Products segment provides floor preparation, grouts and mortars for tile setting as well as sealants and related products for heating, ventilation and air conditioning installations. Co.'s Engineering Adhesives segment provides adhesives to markets such as transportation and electronics.

Recent Developments: For the quarter ended Sep 2 2017, net income decreased 23.4% to US$25.1 million from US$32.8 million in the year-earlier quarter. Revenues were US$562.9 million, up 9.8% from US$512.9 million the year before. Direct operating expenses rose 12.5% to US$412.5 million from US$366.7 million in the comparable period the year before. Indirect operating expenses increased 16.2% to US$110.2 million from US$94.9 million in the equivalent prior-year period.

Prospects: Our evaluation of Fuller (H.B.) Company as of Jan. 14, 2018 is the result of our systematic analysis on three basic characteristics: earnings strength, relative valuation, and recent stock price movement. The company has managed to produce a neutral trend in earnings per share over the past 5 quarters. However, while recent estimates for the company have been mixed, FUL has posted results that fell short of analysts expectations. Based on operating earnings yield, the company is undervalued when compared to all of the companies in our coverage universe. Share price changes over the past year indicates that FUL will perform well over the near term.

Financial Data

(US$ in Thousands)	9 Mos	6 Mos	3 Mos	12/03/2016	11/28/2015	11/29/2014	11/30/2013	12/01/2012
Earnings Per Share	2.04	2.19	2.34	2.42	1.69	0.97	1.89	2.48
Cash Flow Per Share	2.39	2.89	3.38	3.84	4.20	0.60	2.67	2.20
Tang Book Value Per Share	6.94	6.29	5.59	7.30	6.11	8.71	8.91	5.82
Dividends Per Share	0.580	0.570	0.560	0.550	0.510	0.460	0.385	0.330
Dividend Payout %	28.43	26.03	23.93	22.73	30.18	47.42	20.37	13.31
Income Statement								
Total Revenue	1,627,843	1,064,974	503,323	2,094,605	2,083,660	2,104,454	2,046,968	1,886,239
EBITDA	169,694	109,060	46,002	270,424	237,746	164,236	204,722	162,100
Depn & Amortn	59,503	39,200	19,300	77,685	74,890	65,524	58,795	54,490
Income Before Taxes	85,563	53,332	18,322	167,425	138,345	79,312	127,544	89,548
Income Taxes	26,178	16,916	5,765	50,436	55,855	34,348	39,949	30,479
Net Income	65,800	40,662	14,795	124,128	86,680	49,773	96,761	125,622
Average Shares	51,605	51,686	51,460	51,270	51,393	51,255	51,136	50,618
Balance Sheet								
Current Assets	916,911	850,440	831,972	811,253	801,051	765,136	794,694	799,344
Total Assets	2,288,323	2,200,236	2,169,328	2,058,254	2,042,252	1,869,006	1,873,028	1,786,320
Current Liabilities	348,965	325,381	325,066	391,844	349,525	317,199	360,778	350,119
Long-Term Obligations	760,581	747,738	757,661	588,145	669,606	547,735	472,315	475,112
Total Liabilities	1,256,164	1,208,873	1,219,948	1,120,378	1,169,332	978,959	942,963	1,008,047
Stockholders' Equity	1,032,159	991,363	949,380	937,876	872,920	890,047	930,065	778,273
Shares Outstanding	50,297	50,517	50,490	50,141	50,074	50,310	50,228	49,903
Statistical Record								
Return on Assets %	4.80	5.27	5.72	5.96	4.44	2.67	5.30	8.36
Return on Equity %	10.53	11.72	13.05	13.49	9.86	5.48	11.36	16.98
EBITDA Margin %	10.42	10.24	9.14	12.91	11.41	7.80	10.00	8.59
Net Margin %	4.04	3.82	2.94	5.93	4.16	2.37	4.73	6.66
Asset Turnover	1.01	1.01	1.01	1.01	1.07	1.13	1.12	1.26
Current Ratio	2.63	2.61	2.56	2.07	2.29	2.41	2.20	2.28
Debt to Equity	0.74	0.75	0.80	0.63	0.77	0.62	0.51	0.61
Price Range	53.67-41.81	53.40-41.81	50.43-39.28	48.82-32.71	45.74-32.73	52.74-37.46	51.32-32.55	34.00-21.34
P/E Ratio	26.31-20.50	24.38-19.09	21.55-16.79	20.17-13.52	27.07-19.37	54.37-38.62	27.15-17.22	13.71-8.60
Average Yield %	1.17	1.19	1.22	1.28	1.25	0.99	0.95	1.11

Address: 1200 Willow Lake Boulevard, St. Paul, MN 55110-5101
Telephone: 651-236-5900
Fax: 651-236-5161

Web Site: www.hbfuller.com
Officers: Lee R. Mitau - Chairman R. William Van Sant - Vice-Chairman

Auditors: KPMG LLP
Investor Contact: 651-236-5062
Transfer Agents: Wells Fargo Shareholder Services, St. Paul, MN

GALLAGHER (ARTHUR J.) & CO.

Exchange	Symbol	Price	52Wk Range	Yield	P/E
NYS	AJG	$63.28 (12/29/2017)	66.96-52.24	2.47	25.31

*7 Year Price Score 105.41 *NYSE Composite Index=100 *12 Month Price Score 104.34

Interim Earnings (Per Share)
Qtr.	Mar	Jun	Sep	Dec
2014	0.36	0.70	0.58	0.30
2015	0.13	0.81	0.75	0.35
2016	0.26	0.84	0.69	0.53
2017	0.31	0.95	0.71	...

Interim Dividends (Per Share)
Amt	Decl	Ex	Rec	Pay
0.39Q	01/25/2017	03/01/2017	03/03/2017	03/17/2017
0.39Q	04/26/2017	05/31/2017	06/02/2017	06/16/2017
0.39Q	07/26/2017	08/30/2017	09/01/2017	09/15/2017
0.39Q	10/25/2017	11/30/2017	12/01/2017	12/15/2017

Indicated Div: $1.56 (Div. Reinv. Plan)

Valuation Analysis
		Institutional Holding	
Forecast EPS	$2.99	No of Institutions	
	(01/18/2018)	713	
Market Cap	$11.4 Billion	Shares	
Book Value	$4.1 Billion	184,769,824	
Price/Book	2.78	% Held	
Price/Sales	1.92	90.81	

Business Summary: Brokers & Intermediaries (MIC: 5.2.3 SIC: 6411 NAIC: 524210)

Arthur J. Gallagher & Co. is a holding company. Through its subsidiaries, Co. provides insurance brokerage and consulting services and third-party claims settlement and administration services. Co.'s segments are brokerage, which comprised of retail and wholesale insurance brokerage operations; and risk management, which provides contract claim settlement and administration services for enterprises that choose to self-insure some or all of their property/casualty coverages and for insurance companies that choose to outsource some or all of their property/casualty claims departments. Co. also provides integrated disability management programs, and information services, among others.

Recent Developments: For the quarter ended Sep 30 2017, net income increased 5.7% to US$137.8 million from US$130.4 million in the year-earlier quarter. Revenues were US$1.58 billion, up 6.9% from US$1.48 billion the year before.

Prospects: Our evaluation of Gallagher (Arthur J.) & Co. as of Jan. 14, 2018 is the result of our systematic analysis on three basic characteristics: earnings strength, relative valuation, and recent stock price movement. The company has managed to produce a neutral trend in earnings per share over the past 5 quarters and while recent estimates for the company have been raised by analysts, AJG has posted better than expected results. Based on operating earnings yield, the company is undervalued when compared to all of the companies in our coverage universe. Share price changes over the past year indicates that AJG will perform well over the near term.

Financial Data
(US$ in Thousands)	9 Mos	6 Mos	3 Mos	12/31/2016	12/31/2015	12/31/2014	12/31/2013	12/31/2012
Earnings Per Share	2.50	2.48	2.37	2.32	2.06	1.97	2.06	1.59
Cash Flow Per Share	3.84	3.79	3.81	3.49	3.79	2.63	2.71	2.83
Dividends Per Share	1.550	1.540	1.530	1.520	1.480	1.440	1.400	1.360
Dividend Payout %	62.00	62.10	64.56	65.52	71.84	73.10	67.96	85.53
Income Statement								
Total Revenue	4,560,600	2,976,100	1,412,700	5,594,800	5,392,400	4,626,500	3,179,600	2,520,300
EBITDA	411,600	275,900	88,000	460,500	387,400	336,800	327,900	286,700
Depn & Amortn	115,600	76,600	35,700	103,600	93,900	69,400	53,400	41,400
Income Before Taxes	296,000	199,300	52,300	356,900	293,500	267,400	274,500	245,300
Income Taxes	(90,000)	(48,900)	(15,500)	(88,100)	(95,600)	(36,000)	5,900	50,300
Net Income	358,000	227,600	55,700	414,400	356,800	303,400	268,600	195,000
Average Shares	182,500	181,600	180,600	178,400	173,200	154,300	130,500	122,500
Balance Sheet								
Current Assets	5,087,400	5,107,200	4,483,200	4,416,100	4,335,800	3,811,200	2,875,600	2,429,500
Total Assets	12,810,400	12,569,600	11,780,600	11,489,600	10,913,800	10,010,000	6,860,500	5,352,300
Current Liabilities	4,705,200	4,858,000	4,784,700	4,611,700	4,191,700	3,642,700	3,284,800	2,362,900
Long-Term Obligations	2,741,700	2,644,800	2,144,700	2,144,600	2,075,000	2,125,000	825,000	725,000
Total Liabilities	8,700,400	8,724,900	8,118,100	7,893,000	7,275,500	6,780,600	4,775,000	3,693,700
Stockholders' Equity	4,110,000	3,844,700	3,662,500	3,596,600	3,638,300	3,229,400	2,085,500	1,658,600
Shares Outstanding	180,800	180,200	179,500	178,300	176,900	164,600	133,600	125,600
Statistical Record								
Return on Assets %	3.77	3.72	3.77	3.69	3.41	3.60	4.40	3.95
Return on Equity %	11.62	11.97	11.67	11.42	10.39	11.42	14.35	13.40
EBITDA Margin %	9.03	9.27	6.23	8.23	7.18	7.28	10.31	11.38
Net Margin %	7.85	7.65	3.94	7.41	6.62	6.56	8.45	7.74
Asset Turnover	0.50	0.49	0.51	0.50	0.52	0.55	0.52	0.51
Current Ratio	1.08	1.05	0.94	0.96	1.03	1.05	0.88	1.03
Debt to Equity	0.67	0.69	0.59	0.60	0.57	0.66	0.40	0.44
Price Range	61.63-47.35	59.01-47.35	57.76-43.43	52.12-36.24	49.50-40.08	49.39-43.59	48.11-34.65	37.73-32.76
P/E Ratio	24.65-18.94	23.79-19.09	24.37-18.32	22.47-15.62	24.03-19.46	25.07-22.13	23.35-16.82	23.73-20.60
Average Yield %	2.81	2.92	3.05	3.27	3.23	3.11	3.26	3.84

Address: 2850 W. Golf Road, Rolling Meadows, IL 60008-4050 **Telephone:** 630-773-3800	**Web Site:** www.ajg.com **Officers:** J. Patrick Gallagher - Chairman, President, Chief Executive Officer Douglas K. Howell - Corporate Vice-President, Chief Financial Officer	**Auditors:** Ernst & Young LLP **Investor Contact:** 630-285-3501 **Transfer Agents:** Computershare Investor Services, Canton, MA

GAMESTOP CORP

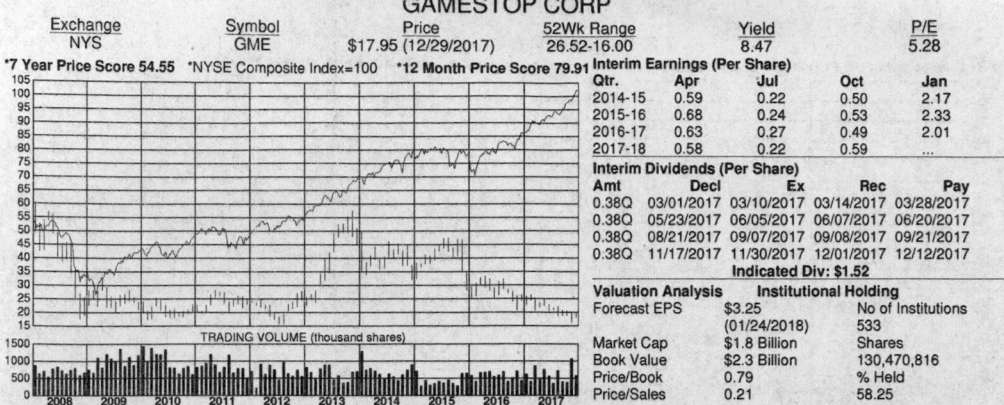

Exchange	Symbol	Price	52Wk Range	Yield	P/E
NYS	GME	$17.95 (12/29/2017)	26.52-16.00	8.47	5.28

*7 Year Price Score 54.55 *NYSE Composite Index=100 *12 Month Price Score 79.91

Interim Earnings (Per Share)

Qtr.	Apr	Jul	Oct	Jan
2014-15	0.59	0.22	0.50	2.17
2015-16	0.68	0.24	0.53	2.33
2016-17	0.63	0.27	0.49	2.01
2017-18	0.58	0.22	0.59	

Interim Dividends (Per Share)

Amt	Decl	Ex	Rec	Pay
0.38Q	03/01/2017	03/10/2017	03/14/2017	03/28/2017
0.38Q	05/23/2017	06/05/2017	06/07/2017	06/20/2017
0.38Q	08/21/2017	09/07/2017	09/08/2017	09/21/2017
0.38Q	11/17/2017	11/30/2017	12/01/2017	12/12/2017

Indicated Div: $1.52

Valuation Analysis

		Institutional Holding	
Forecast EPS	$3.25	No of Institutions	
	(01/24/2018)	533	
Market Cap	$1.8 Billion	Shares	
Book Value	$2.3 Billion	130,470,816	
Price/Book	0.79	% Held	
Price/Sales	0.21	58.25	

Business Summary: Retail - Appliances and Electronics (MIC: 2.1.7 SIC: 5734 NAIC: 443120)

GameStop is a family of specialty retail brands. Through its video game brand stores and e-commerce sites, Co. is the omnichannel retailer of video game products. Co. also provide mobile and consumer technology products through its AT&T® authorized retailer stores, Cricket Wireless™ reseller pre-paid wireless stores and Simply Mac stores. In addition, Co. is a retailer of collectible pop-culture themed products. Co. has five reportable segments, which are comprised of four geographic Video Game Brands segments: U.S., Canada, Australia and Europe, and a Technology Brands segment. Co.'s Technology Brands segment includes its Spring Mobile and Simply Mac businesses.

Recent Developments: For the quarter ended Oct 28 2017, net income increased 16.9% to US$59.4 million from US$50.8 million in the year-earlier quarter. Revenues were US$1.99 billion, up 1.5% from US$1.96 billion the year before. Operating income was US$87.6 million versus US$98.8 million in the prior-year quarter, a decrease of 11.3%. Direct operating expenses rose 3.9% to US$1.30 billion from US$1.25 billion in the comparable period the year before. Indirect operating expenses decreased 1.2% to US$601.8 million from US$609.4 million in the equivalent prior-year period.

Prospects: Our evaluation of GameStop Corp. as of Jan. 21, 2018 is the result of our systematic analysis on three basic characteristics: earnings strength, relative valuation, and recent stock price movement. The company has generated a negative trend in earnings per share over the past 5 quarters. However, while recent estimates for the company have been mixed, GME has posted better than expected results. Based on operating earnings yield, the company is undervalued when compared to all of the companies in our coverage universe. Share price changes over the past year indicates that GME will perform poorly over the near term.

Financial Data

(US$ in Thousands)	9 Mos	6 Mos	3 Mos	01/28/2017	01/30/2016	01/31/2015	02/01/2014	02/02/2013
Earnings Per Share	3.40	3.30	3.35	3.40	3.78	3.47	2.99	(2.13)
Cash Flow Per Share	3.83	6.52	6.48	5.21	6.21	4.29	6.53	4.92
Tang Book Value Per Share	1.11	1.00	0.31	0.21	2.65	4.08	5.57	6.34
Dividends Per Share	1.510	1.500	1.490	1.480	1.440	1.320	1.100	0.800
Dividend Payout %	44.41	45.45	44.48	43.53	38.10	38.04	36.79	...
Income Statement								
Total Revenue	5,722,100	3,733,500	2,045,900	8,607,900	9,363,800	9,296,000	9,039,500	8,886,700
EBITDA	345,500	220,900	139,400	709,400	793,100	762,800	726,400	138,500
Depn & Amortn	113,200	76,200	38,300	151,700	144,900	144,500	152,900	180,100
Income Before Taxes	190,100	116,400	87,200	504,700	625,200	608,300	568,800	(44,900)
Income Taxes	49,500	35,200	28,200	151,500	222,400	215,200	214,600	224,900
Net Income	140,600	81,200	59,000	353,200	402,800	393,100	354,200	(269,700)
Average Shares	101,500	101,500	101,400	103,800	106,700	113,200	118,400	126,400
Balance Sheet								
Current Assets	2,671,000	1,790,600	1,847,000	2,140,700	1,938,800	2,062,500	1,949,600	2,010,900
Total Assets	5,474,000	4,609,800	4,683,400	4,975,900	4,334,900	4,246,300	4,091,400	4,133,600
Current Liabilities	2,217,500	1,337,700	1,465,600	1,761,500	1,794,400	1,639,700	1,726,000	1,715,300
Long-Term Obligations	817,200	816,400	815,700	815,000	350,000	350,600	1,600	...
Total Liabilities	3,160,300	2,298,100	2,414,500	2,721,800	2,253,900	2,178,600	1,840,000	1,847,300
Stockholders' Equity	2,313,700	2,311,700	2,268,900	2,254,100	2,081,000	2,067,700	2,251,400	2,286,300
Shares Outstanding	101,300	101,300	101,300	101,000	103,300	107,700	115,300	118,200
Statistical Record								
Return on Assets %	6.53	7.79	7.59	7.61	9.41	9.46	8.64	N.M.
Return on Equity %	15.74	15.27	15.66	16.34	19.47	18.25	15.65	N.M.
EBITDA Margin %	6.04	5.92	6.81	8.24	8.47	8.21	8.04	1.56
Net Margin %	2.46	2.17	2.88	4.10	4.30	4.23	3.92	N.M.
Asset Turnover	1.64	2.00	1.90	1.85	2.19	2.24	2.20	1.95
Current Ratio	1.20	1.34	1.26	1.22	1.08	1.26	1.13	1.17
Debt to Equity	0.35	0.35	0.36	0.36	0.17	0.17	N.M.	...
Price Range	26.52-18.50	32.16-20.46	32.80-20.70	33.38-20.73	47.44-25.06	46.10-31.92	57.59-23.54	27.83-15.73
P/E Ratio	7.80-5.44	9.75-6.20	9.79-6.18	9.82-6.10	12.55-6.63	13.29-9.20	19.26-7.87	...
Average Yield %	6.67	6.09	5.68	5.33	3.62	3.36	2.65	3.69

Address: 625 Westport Parkway, Grapevine, TX 76051
Telephone: 817-424-2000

Web Site: www.gamestop.com
Officers: Daniel A. DeMatteo - Executive Chairman, Interim Chief Executive Officer Tony D. Bartel - President, Chief Operating Officer

Auditors: Deloitte & Touche LLP
Transfer Agents: Computershare, Providence, RI

GARTNER INC

Exchange	Symbol	Price	52Wk Range	Yield	P/E
NYS	IT	$123.15 (12/29/2017)	129.53-90.56	N/A	N/A

*7 Year Price Score 125.47 ***NYSE Composite Index=100** ***12 Month Price Score 98.59**

TRADING VOLUME (thousand shares)

Interim Earnings (Per Share)

Qtr.	Mar	Jun	Sep	Dec
2014	0.40	0.58	0.38	0.66
2015	0.32	0.61	0.36	0.77
2016	0.48	0.57	0.36	0.79
2017	0.43	(1.03)	(0.53)	...

Interim Dividends (Per Share)

No Dividends Paid

Valuation Analysis

		Institutional Holding	
Forecast EPS	$3.45	No of Institutions	
	(01/25/2018)	545	
Market Cap	$11.2 Billion	Shares	
Book Value	$863.4 Million	151,730,256	
Price/Book	12.93	% Held	
Price/Sales	3.72	88.45	

Business Summary: IT Services (MIC: 6.3.1 SIC: 8741 NAIC: 561110)

Gartner is an information technology research and advisory company. Co. works with clients to research, analyze and interpret the business of IT within the context of their individual roles. Co. manages its business through three reportable segments: Research, Consulting and Events. The Research segment consists primarily of subscription-based research products, access to research inquiry, peer networking services, and membership programs. The Consulting segment consists primarily of consulting, measurement engagements, and advisory services. The Events segment consists of various symposia, conferences and exhibitions.

Recent Developments: For the quarter ended Sep 30 2017, net loss amounted to US$48.2 million versus net income of US$30.5 million in the year-earlier quarter. Revenues were US$828.1 million, up 44.3% from US$574.1 million the year before. Operating loss was US$24.3 million versus an income of US$48.7 million in the prior-year quarter. Direct operating expenses rose 48.9% to US$332.2 million from US$223.1 million in the comparable period the year before. Indirect operating expenses increased 72.1% to US$520.2 million from US$302.2 million in the equivalent prior-year period.

Prospects: Our evaluation of Gartner Inc. as of Jan. 21, 2018 is the result of our systematic analysis on three basic characteristics: earnings strength, relative valuation, and recent stock price movement. The company has enjoyed a very positive trend in earnings per share over the past 5 quarters and while recent estimates for the company have remained steady, IT has posted better than expected results. Based on operating earnings yield, the company is overvalued when compared to all of the companies in our coverage universe. Share price changes over the past year indicates that IT will perform in line with the market over the near term.

Financial Data

(US$ in Thousands)	9 Mos	6 Mos	3 Mos	12/31/2016	12/31/2015	12/31/2014	12/31/2013	12/31/2012
Earnings Per Share	(0.34)	0.55	2.15	2.31	2.06	2.03	1.93	1.73
Cash Flow Per Share	3.48	3.30	3.95	4.42	4.12	3.88	3.39	2.99
Income Statement								
Total Revenue	2,296,985	1,468,900	625,169	2,444,540	2,163,056	2,021,441	1,784,213	1,615,808
EBITDA	(8,697)	(6,620)	65,111	375,544	340,135	324,996	309,722	274,257
Depn & Amortn	58,873	37,772	10,708	61,997	47,142	39,426	34,446	29,802
Income Before Taxes	(156,194)	(94,254)	48,497	288,431	272,211	274,683	266,439	235,596
Income Taxes	(52,166)	(38,406)	12,064	94,849	96,576	90,917	83,638	69,693
Net Income	(104,028)	(55,848)	36,433	193,582	175,635	183,766	182,801	165,903
Average Shares	90,624	89,297	84,095	83,820	85,056	90,719	94,830	95,842
Balance Sheet								
Current Assets	1,812,283	1,759,974	2,175,695	1,343,196	1,140,997	1,096,658	1,084,882	927,466
Total Assets	7,011,492	6,994,887	3,365,300	2,367,335	2,174,686	1,904,351	1,783,582	1,621,277
Current Liabilities	2,482,035	2,243,907	1,470,356	1,460,249	1,323,492	1,215,218	1,159,923	1,070,000
Long-Term Obligations	2,922,229	3,140,307	1,599,331	664,391	790,000	385,000	136,250	115,000
Total Liabilities	6,148,082	6,141,212	3,262,483	2,306,457	2,307,086	1,743,180	1,422,266	1,314,604
Stockholders' Equity	863,410	853,675	102,817	60,878	(132,400)	161,171	361,316	306,673
Shares Outstanding	90,645	90,614	83,018	82,651	82,338	87,520	91,965	93,361
Statistical Record								
Return on Assets %	N.M.	0.88	6.50	8.50	8.61	9.97	10.74	11.03
Return on Equity %	N.M.	10.27	...	...	1,220.92	70.34	54.73	67.74
EBITDA Margin %	N.M.	N.M.	10.41	15.36	15.72	16.08	17.36	16.97
Net Margin %	N.M.	N.M.	5.83	7.92	8.12	9.09	10.25	10.27
Asset Turnover	0.65	0.59	0.90	1.07	1.06	1.10	1.05	1.07
Current Ratio	0.73	0.78	1.48	0.92	0.86	0.90	0.94	0.87
Debt to Equity	3.38	3.68	15.56	10.91	...	2.39	0.38	0.37
Price Range	129.53-85.17	124.61-85.17	111.93-85.17	104.93 79.86	93.87-77.92	87.40-62.51	71.22-46.02	51.01-34.67
P/E Ratio	...	226.56-154.85	52.06-39.61	45.42-34.57	45.57-37.83	43.05-30.79	36.90-23.84	29.49-20.04

Address: P.O. Box 10212, 56 Top Gallant Road, Stamford, CT 06902-7700 **Telephone:** 203-316-1111	**Web Site:** www.gartner.com **Officers:** James C. Smith - Chairman Eugene A. Hall - Chief Executive Officer	**Auditors:** KPMG LLP **Investor Contact:** 203-316-6537 **Transfer Agents:** American Stock Transfer & Trust Company, LLC, New York, NY

GATX CORP

Exchange	Symbol	Price	52Wk Range	Yield	P/E
NYS	GATX	$62.16 (12/29/2017)	65.54-56.54	2.70	12.84

*7 Year Price Score 95.21 ***NYSE Composite Index=100** ***12 Month Price Score 93.96**

Interim Earnings (Per Share)

Qtr.	Mar	Jun	Sep	Dec
2014	0.90	1.15	1.14	1.30
2015	1.39	1.03	0.91	1.36
2016	1.66	1.49	2.36	0.80
2017	1.44	1.35	1.25	...

Interim Dividends (Per Share)

Amt	Decl	Ex	Rec	Pay
0.42Q	01/27/2017	03/08/2017	03/10/2017	03/31/2017
0.42Q	05/05/2017	06/13/2017	06/15/2017	06/30/2017
0.42Q	07/28/2017	09/14/2017	09/15/2017	09/30/2017
0.42Q	10/27/2017	12/14/2017	12/15/2017	12/31/2017

Indicated Div: $1.68 (Div. Reinv. Plan)

Valuation Analysis

		Institutional Holding	
Forecast EPS	$4.64	No of Institutions	
	(01/23/2018)	340	
Market Cap	$2.4 Billion	Shares	
Book Value	$1.5 Billion	58,321,988	
Price/Book	1.62	% Held	
Price/Sales	1.72	91.92	

Business Summary: Miscellaneous Transportation Services (MIC: 7.4.5 SIC: 4741 NAIC: 488210)

GATX is a railcar lessor, owning fleets in North America, Europe, and Asia. In addition, Co. operates a fleet of U.S.-flagged vessels on the Great Lakes and jointly with Rolls-Royce plc, Co. owns aircraft spare engine lease portfolios. Co. leases tank cars, freight cars, and locomotives in North America, tank cars and freight cars in Europe and freight cars in India and Russia. As of Dec 31 2016, Co. had a wholly owned fleet of approximately 146,300 railcars. As of the same date, Co. also had an ownership interest in an affiliate investment that owned approximately 2,200 railcars, and Co. managed approximately 400 railcars for other third-party owners.

Recent Developments: For the quarter ended Sep 30 2017, net income decreased 48.8% to US$49.0 million from US$95.7 million in the year-earlier quarter. Revenues were US$359.6 million, down 0.9% from US$362.9 million the year before. Direct operating expenses rose 2.0% to US$218.2 million from US$213.9 million in the comparable period the year before. Indirect operating expenses decreased 11.9% to US$51.3 million from US$58.2 million in the equivalent prior-year period.

Prospects: Our evaluation of GATX Corp. as of Jan. 21, 2018 is the result of our systematic analysis on three basic characteristics: earnings strength, relative valuation, and recent stock price movement. The company has generated a negative trend in earnings per share over the past 5 quarters and while recent estimates for the company have been raised by analysts, GATX has posted results that fell short of analysts expectations. Based on operating earnings yield, the company is undervalued when compared to all of the companies in our coverage universe. Share price changes over the past year indicates that GATX will perform very poorly over the near term.

Financial Data

(US$ in Thousands)	9 Mos	6 Mos	3 Mos	12/31/2016	12/31/2015	12/31/2014	12/31/2013	12/31/2012
Earnings Per Share	4.84	5.95	6.09	6.29	4.69	4.48	3.59	2.88
Cash Flow Per Share	13.23	15.68	15.24	15.42	12.40	9.98	8.64	7.89
Tang Book Value Per Share	36.17	35.13	33.42	32.18	28.60	27.78	28.39	24.57
Dividends Per Share	1.660	1.640	1.620	1.600	1.520	1.320	1.240	1.200
Dividend Payout %	34.30	27.56	26.60	25.44	32.41	29.46	34.54	41.67
Income Statement								
Total Revenue	1,024,100	664,500	316,100	1,418,300	1,449,900	1,451,000	1,321,000	1,243,200
EBITDA	547,500	367,400	183,800	763,700	728,700	676,600	593,400	559,800
Depn & Amortn	238,500	155,800	75,200	310,200	303,300	287,000	267,800	249,400
Income Before Taxes	189,600	132,400	69,400	305,400	270,300	231,200	159,000	143,800
Income Taxes	60,300	39,900	20,600	95,700	110,900	75,700	65,500	26,100
Net Income	159,900	110,900	57,500	257,100	205,300	205,000	169,300	137,300
Average Shares	39,200	39,500	39,900	40,900	43,800	45,800	47,100	47,600
Balance Sheet								
Current Assets	418,700	500,300	364,800	538,600	455,200	576,700	804,900	620,600
Total Assets	7,261,900	7,272,100	7,096,900	7,105,400	6,894,200	6,937,500	6,549,600	6,055,400
Current Liabilities	149,500	212,200	146,300	178,600	178,300	238,000	183,200	451,000
Long-Term Obligations	4,279,500	4,274,300	4,264,400	4,268,100	4,196,800	4,202,100	3,847,400	3,294,300
Total Liabilities	5,791,700	5,829,100	5,711,700	5,758,200	5,614,000	5,623,500	5,152,600	4,811,200
Stockholders' Equity	1,470,200	1,443,000	1,385,200	1,347,200	1,280,200	1,314,000	1,397,000	1,244,200
Shares Outstanding	38,311	38,720	39,093	39,442	41,970	44,198	45,868	46,898
Statistical Record								
Return on Assets %	2.66	3.31	3.46	3.66	2.97	3.04	2.69	2.30
Return on Equity %	13.43	17.26	18.23	19.52	15.83	15.12	12.82	11.55
EBITDA Margin %	53.46	55.29	58.15	53.85	50.26	46.63	44.92	45.03
Net Margin %	15.61	16.69	18.19	18.13	14.16	14.13	12.82	11.04
Asset Turnover	0.19	0.19	0.20	0.20	0.21	0.22	0.21	0.21
Current Ratio	2.80	2.36	2.49	3.02	2.55	2.42	4.39	1.38
Debt to Equity	2.91	2.96	3.08	3.17	3.28	3.20	2.75	2.65
Price Range	65.54-42.65	65.54-40.83	64.17-40.83	64.17-35.12	62.95-39.87	69.10-51.00	53.85-43.30	44.90-35.93
P/E Ratio	13.54-8.81	11.02-6.86	10.54-6.70	10.20-5.58	13.42-8.50	15.42-11.38	15.00-12.06	15.59-12.48
Average Yield %	2.85	3.04	3.23	3.47	2.90	2.12	2.54	2.88

Address: 222 West Adams Street,	Web Site: www.gatx.com	Auditors: Ernst & Young LLP
Chicago, IL 60606-5314	Officers: Brian A. Kenney - Chairman, President,	Investor Contact: 312-621-6262
Telephone: 312-621-6200	Chief Executive Officer N. Gokce Tezel - Vice	Transfer Agents: Computershare,
	President, Senior Vice President, Division Officer	Canton, MA

GENERAL DYNAMICS CORP.

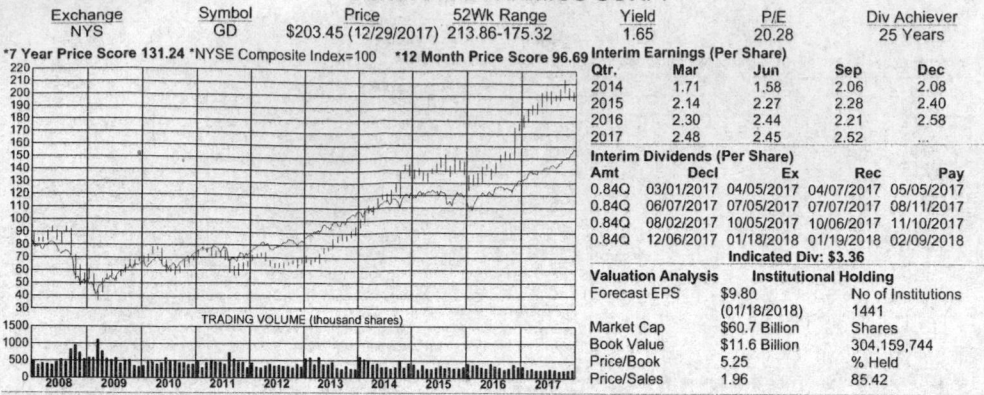

Exchange	Symbol	Price	52Wk Range	Yield	P/E	Div Achiever
NYS	GD	$203.45 (12/29/2017)	213.86-175.32	1.65	20.28	25 Years

*7 Year Price Score 131.24 *NYSE Composite Index=100 ***12 Month Price Score 96.69**

Interim Earnings (Per Share)

Qtr.	Mar	Jun	Sep	Dec
2014	1.71	1.58	2.06	2.08
2015	2.14	2.27	2.28	2.40
2016	2.30	2.44	2.21	2.58
2017	2.48	2.45	2.52	...

Interim Dividends (Per Share)

Amt	Decl	Ex	Rec	Pay
0.84Q	03/01/2017	04/05/2017	04/07/2017	05/05/2017
0.84Q	06/07/2017	07/05/2017	07/07/2017	08/11/2017
0.84Q	08/02/2017	10/05/2017	10/06/2017	11/10/2017
0.84Q	12/06/2017	01/18/2018	01/19/2018	02/09/2018

Indicated Div: $3.36

Valuation Analysis — **Institutional Holding**

Forecast EPS	$9.80 (01/18/2018)	No of Institutions 1441
Market Cap	$60.7 Billion	Shares
Book Value	$11.6 Billion	304,159,744
Price/Book	5.25	% Held
Price/Sales	1.96	85.42

TRADING VOLUME (thousand shares)

Business Summary: Aerospace (MIC: 7.1.1 SIC: 3721 NAIC: 336411)

General Dynamics is an aerospace and defense company. Co. has four business groups: Aerospace, which produces Gulfstream aircraft, provides aircraft services and performs aircraft completions for other original equipment manufacturers; Combat Systems, which provides combat vehicles, weapons systems and munitions; Information Systems and Technology, which provides command, control, communication, computers, intelligence, surveillance and reconnaissance solutions and information technology services; and Marine Systems, which designs, constructs and repairs surface ships and submarines. Co. also does business with non-U.S. governments and corporate and individual buyers of business aircraft.

Recent Developments: For the quarter ended Oct 1 2017, income from continuing operations increased 4.5% to US$764.0 million from US$731.0 million in the year-earlier quarter. Net income increased 18.1% to US$764.0 million from US$647.0 million in the year-earlier quarter. Revenues were US$7.58 billion, down 1.0% from US$7.66 billion the year before. Operating income was US$1.05 billion versus US$1.02 billion in the prior-year quarter, an increase of 3.6%. Direct operating expenses declined 2.5% to US$6.02 billion from US$6.17 billion in the comparable period the year before. Indirect operating expenses increased 8.3% to US$510.0 million from US$471.0 million in the equivalent prior-year period.

Prospects: Our evaluation of General Dynamics Corp. as of Jan. 14, 2018 is the result of our systematic analysis on three basic characteristics: earnings strength, relative valuation, and recent stock price movement. The company has managed to produce a neutral trend in earnings per share over the past 5 quarters. However, while recent estimates for the company have been mixed, GD has posted better than expected results. Based on operating earnings yield, the company is undervalued when compared to all of the companies in our coverage universe. Share price changes over the past year indicates that GD will perform in line with the market over the near term.

Financial Data

(US$ in Millions)	9 Mos	6 Mos	3 Mos	12/31/2016	12/31/2015	12/31/2014	12/31/2013	12/31/2012
Earnings Per Share	10.03	9.77	9.71	9.52	9.08	7.42	6.67	(0.94)
Cash Flow Per Share	9.08	7.79	7.60	7.19	7.78	11.12	8.86	7.58
Tang Book Value Per Share	N.M.	N.M.	N.M.	N.M.	N.M.	N.M.	3.70	N.M.
Dividends Per Share	3.200	3.120	3.040	2.970	2.690	2.420	2.190	2.040
Dividend Payout %	31.90	32.10	31.31	31.20	29.63	32.61	32.83	...
Income Statement								
Total Revenue	22,696	15,116	7,441	31,353	31,469	30,852	31,218	31,513
EBITDA	3,471	2,311	1,146	4,776	4,667	4,384	4,249	1,317
Depn & Amortn	326	220	111	454	482	496	556	620
Income Before Taxes	3,069	2,042	1,010	4,231	4,102	3,802	3,607	541
Income Taxes	793	530	247	1,169	1,137	1,129	1,121	873
Net Income	2,276	1,512	763	2,955	2,965	2,533	2,357	(332)
Average Shares	303	303	307	310	326	341	353	353
Balance Sheet								
Current Assets	18,080	17,126	16,614	15,447	14,571	17,407	17,886	15,744
Total Assets	34,914	33,793	33,211	32,872	31,997	35,355	35,448	34,309
Current Liabilities	13,209	13,503	13,165	12,846	12,445	13,751	12,194	11,620
Long-Term Obligations	3,979	2,989	2,988	2,988	2,898	3,410	3,908	3,908
Total Liabilities	23,350	22,841	22,628	21,896	21,259	23,526	20,947	22,919
Stockholders' Equity	11,564	10,952	10,583	10,976	10,738	11,829	14,501	11,390
Shares Outstanding	298	299	301	302	312	332	353	353
Statistical Record								
Return on Assets %	9.09	9.13	9.25	9.09	8.80	7.16	6.76	N.M.
Return on Equity %	26.86	27.27	28.36	27.14	26.28	19.24	18.21	N.M.
EBITDA Margin %	15.29	15.29	15.40	15.23	14.83	14.21	13.61	4.18
Net Margin %	10.03	10.00	10.25	9.42	9.42	8.21	7.55	N.M.
Asset Turnover	0.92	0.95	0.96	0.96	0.93	0.87	0.90	0.91
Current Ratio	1.37	1.27	1.26	1.20	1.17	1.27	1.47	1.35
Debt to Equity	0.34	0.27	0.28	0.27	0.27	0.29	0.27	0.34
Price Range	206.80-149.60	204.52-138.41	193.27-130.84	178.67-124.18	153.28-131.27	145.36-94.46	95.55-64.57	74.09-61.96
P/E Ratio	20.62-14.92	21.04-14.24	19.90-13.47	18.77-13.04	16.88-14.46	19.59-12.73	14.33-9.68	...
Average Yield %	1.72	1.36	1.91	2.03	1.91	2.04	2.11	3.73

Address: 2941 Fairview Park Drive, Suite 100, Falls Church, VA 22042-4513 **Telephone:** 703-876-3000	**Web Site:** www.generaldynamics.com **Officers:** Phebe N. Novakovic - Chairman, President, Chief Executive Officer, Senior Vice President, Chief Operating Officer Mark C. Roualet - Executive Vice President, Vice President, Division Officer

Auditors: KPMG LLP
Investor Contact: 703-876-3583
Transfer Agents: Computershare, Providence, RI

GENERAL ELECTRIC CO

Exchange	Symbol	Price	52Wk Range	Yield	P/E
NYS	GE	$17.45 (12/29/2017)	31.70-17.36	2.75	22.09

*7 Year Price Score 82.92 *NYSE Composite Index=100 *12 Month Price Score 66.83

Interim Earnings (Per Share)

Qtr.	Mar	Jun	Sep	Dec
2014	0.30	0.35	0.35	0.50
2015	(1.35)	(0.13)	0.25	0.62
2016	(0.01)	0.30	0.22	0.38
2017	0.07	0.13	0.21	...

Interim Dividends (Per Share)

Amt	Decl	Ex	Rec	Pay
0.24Q	02/10/2017	02/23/2017	02/27/2017	04/25/2017
0.24Q	06/09/2017	06/15/2017	06/19/2017	07/25/2017
0.24Q	09/07/2017	09/15/2017	09/18/2017	10/25/2017
0.12Q	12/08/2017	12/26/2017	12/27/2017	01/25/2018

Indicated Div: $0.48 (Div. Reinv. Plan)

Valuation Analysis		Institutional Holding	
Forecast EPS	$1.05	No of Institutions	
	(01/18/2018)	2950	
Market Cap	$151.3 Billion	Shares	
Book Value	$79.5 Billion	6,197,349,888	
Price/Book	1.90	% Held	
Price/Sales	1.22	49.22	

TRADING VOLUME (thousand shares)

Business Summary: Electrical Equipment (MIC: 7.3.1 SIC: 3699 NAIC: 335999)

General Electric is a digital industrial company. Co.'s segments include: Power, which serves power generation, industrial, government and other customers worldwide with products and services related to energy production and water reuse; GE Renewable Energy, which makes renewable power sources; Oil & Gas, which serves all segments of the oil and gas industry, from drilling, completion, production and oil field operations, to transportation via liquefied natural gas and pipelines; Aviation, which designs and produces commercial and military aircraft engines, integrated digital components, electric power and mechanical aircraft systems; and Healthcare, which provides healthcare technologies.

Recent Developments: For the quarter ended Sep 30 2017, income from continuing operations decreased 12.5% to US$1.80 billion from US$2.06 billion in the year-earlier quarter. Net income decreased 13.2% to US$1.69 billion from US$1.95 billion in the year-earlier quarter. Revenues were US$33.47 billion, up 14.4% from US$29.27 billion the year before. Direct operating expenses rose 18.4% to US$25.92 billion from US$21.89 billion in the comparable period the year before. Indirect operating expenses increased 14.8% to US$6.09 billion from US$5.30 billion in the equivalent prior-year period.

Prospects: Our evaluation of General Electric Co as of Jan. 14, 2018 is the result of our systematic analysis on three basic characteristics: earnings strength, relative valuation, and recent stock price movement. The company has generated a negative trend in earnings per share over the past 5 quarters and while recent estimates for the company have remained steady, GE has posted results that fell short of analysts expectations. Based on operating earnings yield, the company is undervalued when compared to all of the companies in our coverage universe. Share price changes over the past year indicates that GE will perform poorly over the near term.

Financial Data

(US$ in Millions)	9 Mos	6 Mos	3 Mos	12/31/2016	12/31/2015	12/31/2014	12/31/2013	12/31/2012
Earnings Per Share	0.79	0.80	0.97	0.89	(0.61)	1.50	1.27	1.29
Cash Flow Per Share	0.59	0.60	(0.06)	(0.03)	2.00	2.76	2.80	2.97
Tang Book Value Per Share	N.M.	N.M.	N.M.	N.M.	1.71	3.72	3.84	3.61
Dividends Per Share	0.960	0.950	0.940	0.930	0.920	0.890	0.790	0.700
Dividend Payout %	121.52	118.75	96.91	104.49	...	59.33	62.20	54.26
Income Statement								
Total Revenue	90,691	57,219	27,660	123,693	117,386	148,589	146,045	147,359
EBITDA	11,072	6,977	3,164	20,887	13,302	28,500	27,978	31,529
Depn & Amortn	3,715	2,318	1,193	6,832	1,653	1,789	1,711	1,615
Income Before Taxes	3,812	2,346	832	9,030	8,186	17,229	16,151	17,406
Income Taxes	(303)	31	16	(464)	6,485	1,772	676	2,504
Net Income	3,856	2,020	653	8,831	(6,126)	15,233	13,057	13,641
Average Shares	8,732	8,760	8,811	9,130	10,016	10,123	10,289	10,564
Balance Sheet								
Current Assets	129,424	128,307	127,889	138,872	151,993	179,041	171,249	162,740
Total Assets	378,038	355,473	351,643	365,183	492,692	648,349	656,560	685,328
Current Liabilities	79,517	79,334	77,811	81,998	108,197	208,440	206,572	221,403
Long-Term Obligations	108,265	104,358	100,342	105,080	145,301	200,414	221,665	236,084
Total Liabilities	298,491	278,132	274,055	289,356	394,418	520,190	525,994	562,302
Stockholders' Equity	79,546	77,341	77,588	75,828	98,274	128,159	130,566	123,026
Shares Outstanding	8,672	8,658	8,684	8,742	9,379	10,057	10,060	10,405
Statistical Record								
Return on Assets %	1.96	2.04	2.27	2.05	N.M.	2.33	1.95	1.94
Return on Equity %	9.15	9.33	10.76	10.12	N.M.	11.78	10.30	11.36
EBITDA Margin %	12.21	12.19	11.44	16.89	11.33	19.18	19.16	21.40
Net Margin %	4.25	3.53	2.36	7.14	N.M.	10.25	8.94	9.26
Asset Turnover	0.32	0.32	0.30	0.29	0.21	0.23	0.22	0.21
Current Ratio	1.63	1.62	1.64	1.69	1.40	0.86	0.83	0.74
Debt to Equity	1.36	1.35	1.29	1.39	1.48	1.56	1.70	1.92
Price Range	32.25-23.72	32.93-27.01	32.93-28.28	32.93-27.45	31.28-23.27	28.03-23.95	28.03-20.90	23.12-18.15
P/E Ratio	40.82-30.03	41.16-33.76	33.95-29.15	37.00-30.84	...	18.69-15.97	22.07-16.46	17.92-14.07
Average Yield %	3.36	3.16	3.08	3.06	3.43	3.42	3.29	3.46

Address: 41 Farnsworth Street, Boston, MA 02210	Web Site: www.ge.com	Auditors: KPMG LLP
Telephone: 617-443-3000	**Officers:** John Leonard Flannery - Chairman, Chief Executive Officer, Division Officer Jeffrey S. Bornstein - Vice-Chairman, Senior Vice President, Chief Financial Officer	**Investor Contact:** 203-373-2460 **Transfer Agents:** Computershare, Pittsburgh, PA

GENERAL MILLS, INC.

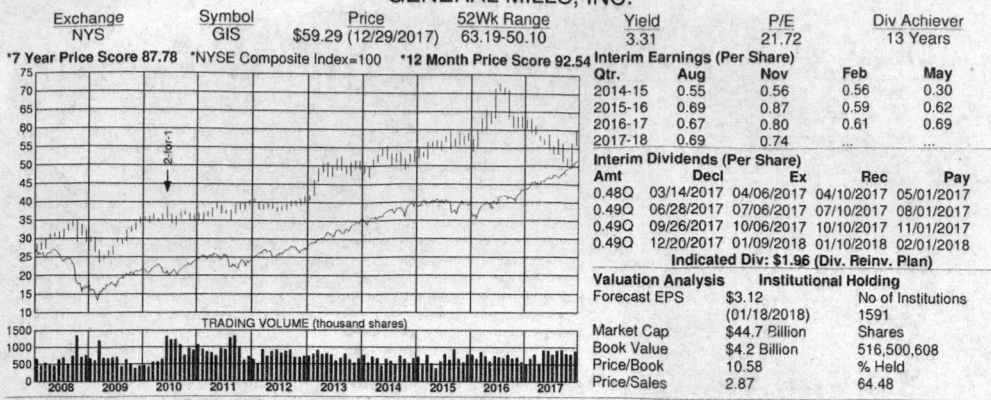

Exchange NYS	Symbol GIS	Price $59.29 (12/29/2017)	52Wk Range 63.19-50.10	Yield 3.31	P/E 21.72	Div Achiever 13 Years

*7 Year Price Score 87.78   *NYSE Composite Index=100   *12 Month Price Score 92.54

Interim Earnings (Per Share)

Qtr.	Aug	Nov	Feb	May
2014-15	0.55	0.56	0.56	0.30
2015-16	0.69	0.87	0.59	0.62
2016-17	0.67	0.80	0.61	0.69
2017-18	0.69	0.74	...	...

Interim Dividends (Per Share)

Amt	Decl	Ex	Rec	Pay
0.48Q	03/14/2017	04/06/2017	04/10/2017	05/01/2017
0.49Q	06/28/2017	07/06/2017	07/10/2017	08/01/2017
0.49Q	09/26/2017	10/06/2017	10/10/2017	11/01/2017
0.49Q	12/20/2017	01/09/2018	01/10/2018	02/01/2018

Indicated Div: $1.96 (Div. Reinv. Plan)

Valuation Analysis		Institutional Holding	
Forecast EPS	$3.12	No of Institutions	
	(01/18/2018)	1591	
Market Cap	$44.7 Billion	Shares	
Book Value	$4.2 Billion	516,500,608	
Price/Book	10.58	% Held	
Price/Sales	2.87	64.48	

TRADING VOLUME (thousand shares)

Business Summary: Food (MIC: 1.2.1 SIC: 2043 NAIC: 311230)

General Mills manufactures and markets branded consumer foods sold through retail stores. Co. has four segments: North America Retail, which provides cereals, refrigerated yogurt, soup, meal kits, refrigerated and frozen dough products, dessert and baking mixes, frozen pizza and pizza snacks, grain, fruit and savory snacks, and organic products; Convenience Stores & Foodservice, which provides cereals, snacks, yogurt, frozen meals, frozen dough products, and baking mixes; Europe & Australia, which includes retail and foodservice businesses in the Europe and Australia region; and Asia & Latin America, which includes retail and foodservice businesses in the Asia and South America regions.

Recent Developments: For the quarter ended Nov 26 2017, net income decreased 10.5% to US$443.8 million from US$495.8 million in the year-earlier quarter. Revenues were US$4.20 billion, up 2.1% from US$4.11 billion the year before. Operating income was US$729.8 million versus US$768.9 million in the prior-year quarter, a decrease of 5.1%. Direct operating expenses rose 6.3% to US$2.76 billion from US$2.59 billion in the comparable period the year before. Indirect operating expenses decreased 5.0% to US$713.2 million from US$750.6 million in the equivalent prior-year period.

Prospects: Our evaluation of General Mills Inc. as of Jan. 14, 2018 is the result of our systematic analysis on three basic characteristics: earnings strength, relative valuation, and recent stock price movement. The company has managed to produce a neutral trend in earnings per share over the past 5 quarters and while recent estimates for the company have been raised by analysts, GIS has posted better than expected results. Based on operating earnings yield, the company is undervalued when compared to all of the companies in our coverage universe. Share price changes over the past year indicates that GIS will perform poorly over the near term.

Financial Data

(US$ in Thousands)	6 Mos	3 Mos	05/28/2017	05/29/2016	05/31/2015	05/25/2014	05/26/2013	05/27/2012
Earnings Per Share	2.73	2.79	2.77	2.77	1.97	2.83	2.79	2.35
Cash Flow Per Share	5.06	4.54	3.95	4.40	4.15	4.05	4.52	3.72
Dividends Per Share	1.940	1.930	1.920	1.780	1.670	1.550	1.320	1.220
Dividend Payout %	71.06	69.18	69.31	64.26	84.77	54.77	47.31	51.91
Income Statement								
Total Revenue	7,967,900	3,769,200	15,619,800	16,563,100	17,630,300	17,909,600	17,774,100	16,657,900
EBITDA	1,646,400	770,900	3,170,000	3,315,500	2,665,600	3,542,800	3,439,800	3,103,900
Depn & Amortn	290,800	145,100	603,600	608,100	588,300	585,400	588,000	541,500
Income Before Taxes	1,208,300	553,400	2,271,300	2,403,600	1,761,900	2,655,000	2,534,900	2,210,500
Income Taxes	403,400	168,500	655,200	755,200	586,800	883,300	741,200	709,600
Net Income	835,200	404,700	1,657,500	1,697,400	1,221,300	1,824,400	1,855,200	1,567,300
Average Shares	580,300	586,900	598,000	611,900	618,800	645,700	665,600	666,700
Balance Sheet								
Current Assets	4,334,100	4,338,500	4,061,400	3,937,200	3,785,700	4,393,500	4,298,900	3,691,400
Total Assets	22,191,500	22,209,600	21,812,600	21,712,300	21,964,500	23,145,700	22,658,000	21,096,800
Current Liabilities	5,349,500	5,889,900	5,330,800	5,014,700	4,890,100	5,423,500	5,293,900	3,843,200
Long-Term Obligations	8,228,300	7,822,700	7,642,900	7,057,700	7,607,700	6,423,500	5,926,100	6,161,900
Total Liabilities	17,960,800	18,305,800	17,484,700	16,782,100	16,967,800	16,610,900	15,985,800	14,675,100
Stockholders' Equity	4,230,700	3,903,800	4,327,900	4,930,200	4,996,700	6,534,800	6,672,200	6,421,700
Shares Outstanding	754,600	568,200	576,900	596,800	598,700	612,300	640,800	648,500
Statistical Record								
Return on Assets %	7.32	7.49	7.64	7.79	5.33	7.99	8.50	7.90
Return on Equity %	38.09	37.52	35.90	34.29	20.84	27.70	28.41	24.58
EBITDA Margin %	20.66	20.45	20.29	20.02	15.12	19.78	19.35	18.63
Net Margin %	10.48	10.74	10.61	10.25	6.93	10.19	10.44	9.41
Asset Turnover	0.71	0.70	0.72	0.76	0.77	0.78	0.81	0.84
Current Ratio	0.81	0.74	0.76	0.79	0.77	0.81	0.81	0.96
Debt to Equity	1.94	2.00	1.77	1.43	1.52	0.98	0.89	0.96
Price Range	63.87-50.10	71.42-53.28	72.64-55.91	65.36-54.12	57.14-48.86	54.40-46.86	50.93-37.55	41.05-34.95
P/E Ratio	23.40-18.35	25.60-19.10	26.22-20.18	23.60-19.54	29.01-24.80	19.22-16.56	18.25-13.46	17.47-14.87
Average Yield %	3.39	3.22	3.03	3.05	3.14	3.09	3.13	3.16

Address: Number One General Mills Boulevard, Minneapolis, MN 55426 Telephone: 763-764-7600 Fax: 763-764-8330	Web Site: www.generalmills.com Officers: Jeffrey L. (Jeff) Harmening - Chairman, President, Chief Executive Officer, Chief Operating Officer, Executive Vice President, Region Officer Donal L. Mulligan - Chief Financial Officer, Executive Vice President	Auditors: KPMG LLP Investor Contact: 180-024-55703 Transfer Agents: Wells Fargo Bank, N.A., St. Paul, MN

GENERAL MOTORS CO

Exchange	Symbol	Price	52Wk Range	Yield	P/E
NYS	GM	$40.99 (12/29/2017)	46.48-32.42	3.71	21.02

*7 Year Price Score 92.37   *NYSE Composite Index=100   *12 Month Price Score 106.97

TRADING VOLUME (thousand shares)

Interim Earnings (Per Share)

Qtr.	Mar	Jun	Sep	Dec
2014	0.06	0.11	0.81	0.66
2015	0.56	0.67	0.84	3.84
2016	1.24	1.81	1.76	1.19
2017	1.70	1.09	(2.03)	...

Interim Dividends (Per Share)

Amt	Decl	Ex	Rec	Pay
0.38Q	02/06/2017	03/08/2017	03/10/2017	03/24/2017
0.38Q	04/27/2017	06/07/2017	06/09/2017	06/23/2017
0.38Q	07/24/2017	09/07/2017	09/08/2017	09/22/2017
0.38Q	10/23/2017	12/07/2017	12/08/2017	12/21/2017

Indicated Div: $1.52

Valuation Analysis		Institutional Holding	
Forecast EPS	$6.35	No of Institutions	
	(01/26/2018)	1230	
Market Cap	$57.4 Billion	Shares	
Book Value	$42.2 Billion	1,174,297,216	
Price/Book	1.36	% Held	
Price/Sales	0.37	73.63	

Business Summary: Autos- Manufacturing (MIC: 1.8.1 SIC: 3711 NAIC: 336111)

General Motors designs, builds and sells cars, trucks, crossovers and automobile parts. Co. also provides automotive financing services through its subsidiary, General Motors Financial Company, Inc. Co.'s automotive operations serves customers through its automotive segments: GM North America, GM Europe, GM International Operations and GM South America. In addition to the products sold to its dealers for consumer retail sales, Co. also sells vehicles directly or through its dealer network to fleet customers, including daily rental car companies, commercial fleet customers, leasing companies and governments. Co. also provides aftersale vehicle services and products via its dealer network.

Recent Developments: For the quarter ended Sep 30 2017, income from continuing operations decreased 95.8% to US$114.0 million from US$2.71 billion in the year-earlier quarter. Net loss amounted to US$2.98 billion versus net income of US$2.71 billion in the year-earlier quarter. Revenues were US$33.62 billion, down 13.5% from US$38.89 billion the year before. Operating income was US$1.92 billion versus US$3.15 billion in the prior-year quarter, a decrease of 39.1%. Direct operating expenses declined 11.8% to US$29.40 billion from US$33.34 billion in the comparable period the year before. Indirect operating expenses decreased 4.0% to US$2.30 billion from US$2.40 billion in the equivalent prior-year period.

Prospects: Our evaluation of General Motors Co. as of Jan. 21, 2018 is the result of our systematic analysis on three basic characteristics: earnings strength, relative valuation, and recent stock price movement. The company has generated a negative trend in earnings per share over the past 5 quarters and while recent estimates for the company have been raised by analysts, GM has posted better than expected results. Based on operating earnings yield, the company is undervalued when compared to all of the companies in our coverage universe. Share price changes over the past year indicates that GM will perform well over the near term.

Financial Data

(US$ in Millions)	9 Mos	6 Mos	3 Mos	12/31/2016	12/31/2015	12/31/2014	12/31/2013	12/31/2012
Earnings Per Share	1.95	5.74	6.46	6.00	5.91	1.65	2.38	2.92
Cash Flow Per Share	10.00	12.12	12.46	10.71	7.55	6.27	9.07	6.75
Tang Book Value Per Share	25.99	27.13	26.36	25.09	21.96	18.04	20.30	12.49
Dividends Per Share	1.520	1.520	1.520	1.520	1.380	1.200	...	....
Dividend Payout %	77.95	26.48	23.53	25.33	23.35	72.73	...	....
Income Statement								
Total Revenue	107,873	74,250	41,200	166,380	152,356	155,929	155,427	152,256
EBITDA	16,522	5,630	5,628	14,312	10,566	7,135	9,997	(22,705)
Depn & Amortn	9,084	108	2,883	4,767	5,220	5,403	5,078	7,908
Income Before Taxes	7,285	5,355	2,762	9,402	5,524	2,152	5,648	(30,257)
Income Taxes	3,637	1,321	700	2,416	(1,897)	228	2,127	(34,831)
Net Income	1,287	4,268	2,608	9,427	9,687	3,949	5,346	6,188
Average Shares	1,472	1,519	1,532	1,570	1,640	1,687	1,676	1,675
Balance Sheet								
Current Assets	76,618	85,081	79,598	76,203	78,007	83,670	81,501	69,996
Total Assets	229,502	240,300	230,793	221,690	194,520	177,677	166,344	149,422
Current Liabilities	81,849	94,306	90,904	85,181	71,466	65,701	62,412	53,992
Long-Term Obligations	67,066	59,081	57,200	55,600	43,549	31,853	22,025	10,532
Total Liabilities	187,259	194,779	184,821	177,854	154,649	142,220	123,737	113,178
Stockholders' Equity	42,243	45,521	45,972	43,836	39,871	35,457	42,607	36,244
Shares Outstanding	1,400	1,457	1,509	1,497	1,544	1,611	1,589	1,366
Statistical Record								
Return on Assets %	1.40	3.94	4.64	4.52	5.21	2.30	3.39	4.20
Return on Equity %	7.18	19.91	23.20	22.46	25.72	10.12	13.56	16.60
EBITDA Margin %	15.32	7.58	13.66	8.60	6.94	4.58	6.43	N.M.
Net Margin %	1.19	5.75	6.33	5.67	6.36	2.53	3.44	4.06
Asset Turnover	0.70	0.73	0.78	0.80	0.82	0.91	0.98	1.03
Current Ratio	0.94	0.90	0.88	0.89	1.09	1.27	1.31	1.30
Debt to Equity	1.59	1.30	1.24	1.27	1.09	0.90	0.52	0.29
Price Range	40.58-30.96	38.28-28.17	38.28-27.51	37.66-26.90	38.87-27.28	40.95-29.69	41.53-26.33	28.83-18.80
P/E Ratio	20.81-15.88	6.67-4.91	5.93-4.26	6.28-4.48	6.58-4.62	24.82-17.99	17.45-11.06	9.87-6.44
Average Yield %	4.32	4.50	4.62	4.85	4.02	3.47	...	....

Address: 300 Renaissance Center, Detroit, MI 48265-3000 Telephone: 313-667-1500	Web Site: www.gm.com Officers: Mary T. Barra - Chairman, Chief Executive Officer, Senior Vice President Daniel (Dan) Ammann - President, Senior Vice President, Chief Financial Officer	Auditors: Deloitte & Touche LLP Transfer Agents: Computershare Trust Company, N.A., Providence, RI

GENESEE & WYOMING INC.

Exchange	Symbol	Price	52Wk Range	Yield	P/E
NYS	GWR	$78.73 (12/29/2017)	79.48-62.60	N/A	37.49

*7 Year Price Score 74.98 *NYSE Composite Index=100 *12 Month Price Score 102.24

Interim Earnings (Per Share)

Qtr.	Mar	Jun	Sep	Dec
2014	0.70	1.07	1.27	1.53
2015	0.42	0.92	1.10	1.47
2016	0.47	0.83	0.98	0.14
2017	0.42	0.74	0.80	...

Interim Dividends (Per Share)

No Dividends Paid

Valuation Analysis

		Institutional Holding	
Forecast EPS	$2.89	No of Institutions	
	(01/18/2018)	391	
Market Cap	$4.9 Billion	Shares	
Book Value	$3.1 Billion	69,785,256	
Price/Book	1.58	% Held	
Price/Sales	2.28	90.43	

Business Summary: Rail (MIC: 7.4.3 SIC: 4011 NAIC: 482111)

Genesee & Wyoming owns and operates freight railroads worldwide that are organized in 10 operating regions. Co. has three segments: North American Operations, which includes eight regions that serve 41 U.S. states and four Canadian provinces and includes 115 short line and regional freight railroads with more than 13,000 track-miles; Australian Operations, which provides rail freight services in New South Wales, including in the Hunter Valley coal supply chain, the Northern Territory and South Australia; and U.K./European Operations, which is led by Freightliner Group Limited, a rail maritime intermodal operator and a rail freight company.

Recent Developments: For the quarter ended Sep 30 2017, net income decreased 6.0% to US$53.4 million from US$56.8 million in the year-earlier quarter. Revenues were US$576.9 million, up 15.2% from US$501.0 million the year before. Operating income was US$111.5 million versus US$91.9 million in the prior-year quarter, an increase of 21.4%. Direct operating expenses rose 16.4% to US$190.4 million from US$163.6 million in the comparable period the year before. Indirect operating expenses increased 12.0% to US$275.0 million from US$245.6 million in the equivalent prior-year period.

Prospects: Our evaluation of Genesee & Wyoming Inc. as of Jan. 14, 2018 is the result of our systematic analysis on three basic characteristics: earnings strength, relative valuation, and recent stock price movement. The company has generated a negative trend in earnings per share over the past 5 quarters and while recent estimates for the company have been mixed, GWR has posted results that fell short of analysts expectations. Based on operating earnings yield, the company is about fairly valued when compared to all of the companies in our coverage universe. Share price changes over the past year indicates that GWR will perform poorly over the near term.

Financial Data
(US$ in Thousands)

	9 Mos	6 Mos	3 Mos	12/31/2016	12/31/2015	12/31/2014	12/31/2013	12/31/2012
Earnings Per Share	2.10	2.28	2.37	2.42	3.89	4.58	4.79	1.02
Cash Flow Per Share	7.36	7.63	6.74	7.08	8.37	8.89	7.69	3.99
Tang Book Value Per Share	5.67	4.64	4.87	4.77	9.77	21.13	16.87	12.51
Income Statement								
Total Revenue	1,636,468	1,059,541	519,108	2,001,527	2,000,401	1,639,012	1,569,011	874,916
EBITDA	476,503	300,571	136,129	462,325	526,623	557,830	501,510	209,116
Depn & Amortn	186,509	122,287	60,774	172,300	159,100	135,000	119,200	66,600
Income Before Taxes	210,834	126,942	49,217	215,491	300,931	368,113	318,387	83,396
Income Taxes	82,032	51,525	21,928	74,395	75,894	107,107	46,296	46,402
Net Income	122,485	72,245	26,238	141,137	225,037	260,755	271,296	52,433
Average Shares	62,477	62,415	62,353	58,256	57,848	56,972	56,679	51,316
Balance Sheet								
Current Assets	590,911	561,251	488,266	485,338	576,560	548,426	548,330	465,252
Total Assets	8,029,168	7,935,930	7,710,611	7,634,958	6,795,604	5,595,753	5,319,821	5,226,115
Current Liabilities	453,862	445,405	449,220	479,110	533,814	464,238	456,508	416,744
Long-Term Obligations	2,353,524	2,398,070	2,305,753	2,306,915	2,223,306	1,548,051	1,540,346	1,770,566
Total Liabilities	4,912,685	4,906,035	4,762,359	4,740,376	4,276,143	3,238,894	3,172,026	3,331,654
Stockholders' Equity	3,116,483	3,029,895	2,948,252	2,894,582	2,519,461	2,356,859	2,147,795	1,894,461
Shares Outstanding	62,381	62,334	62,263	62,120	57,738	53,958	53,543	47,088
Statistical Record								
Return on Assets %	1.79	1.90	1.95	1.95	3.63	4.78	5.15	1.39
Return on Equity %	4.55	4.91	5.08	5.20	9.23	11.58	13.42	3.66
EBITDA Margin %	29.12	28.37	26.22	23.10	26.33	34.03	31.96	23.90
Net Margin %	7.48	6.82	5.05	7.05	11.25	15.91	17.29	5.99
Asset Turnover	0.29	0.29	0.28	0.28	0.32	0.30	0.30	0.23
Current Ratio	1.30	1.26	1.09	1.01	1.08	1.18	1.20	1.12
Debt to Equity	0.76	0.79	0.78	0.80	0.88	0.66	0.72	0.93
Price Range	80.01-62.60	80.01-58.58	80.01-52.86	80.01-44.55	105.15-50.28	105.51-83.33	101.77-76.08	76.28-48.08
P/E Ratio	38.10-29.81	35.09-25.69	33.76-22.30	33.06-18.41	27.03-12.93	23.04-18.19	21.25-15.88	74.78-47.14

Address: 20 West Avenue, Darien, CT 06820 **Telephone:** 203-202-8900	**Web Site:** www.gwrr.com **Officers:** John C. Hellmann - Chairman, President, Chief Executive Officer Mark W. Hastings - Executive Vice President	**Auditors:** PricewaterhouseCoopers LLP **Transfer Agents:** Computershare, Providence, RI

GENESIS ENERGY L.P.

Exchange	Symbol	Price	52Wk Range	Yield	P/E	Div Achiever
NYS	GEL	$22.35 (12/29/2017)	37.86-20.50	9.13	31.48	13 Years

*7 Year Price Score 60.86   *NYSE Composite Index=100   *12 Month Price Score 71.83

Interim Earnings (Per Share)

Qtr.	Mar	Jun	Sep	Dec
2014	0.34	0.24	0.33	0.28
2015	0.21	0.12	3.38	0.16
2016	0.32	0.22	0.28	0.19
2017	0.23	0.28	0.01	...

Interim Dividends (Per Share)

Amt	Decl	Ex	Rec	Pay
0.72Q	04/11/2017	04/26/2017	04/28/2017	05/15/2017
0.723Q	07/12/2017	07/27/2017	07/31/2017	08/14/2017
0.50Q	10/12/2017	10/30/2017	10/31/2017	11/14/2017
0.51Q	01/10/2018	01/30/2018	01/31/2018	02/14/2018

Indicated Div: $2.04

Valuation Analysis   **Institutional Holding**

Forecast EPS	$0.88 (01/18/2018)	No of Institutions 238
Market Cap	$2.7 Billion	Shares
Book Value	$691.7 Million	101,648,600
Price/Book	3.96	% Held
Price/Sales	1.58	79.75

Business Summary: Equipment & Services (MIC: 9.1.3 SIC: 5171 NAIC: 424710)

Genesis Energy is a limited partnership focused on the midstream segment of the crude oil and natural gas industry. Co. business segments are: offshore pipeline transportation, which develop reservoir, crude oil and natural gas properties in the Gulf of Mexico; refinery services, which operate storage and transportation assets in relation to those services; marine transportation, which is a provider of transportation services by tank barge primarily for refined petroleum products; and supply and logistics, which owns and/or leases its integrated suite of onshore crude oil and refined products infrastructure, including pipelines, trucks, terminals, railcars, and rail loading.

Recent Developments: For the quarter ended Sep 30 2017, net income decreased 80.7% to US$6.2 million from US$32.0 million in the year-earlier quarter. Revenues were US$486.1 million, up 5.7% from US$460.1 million the year before. Operating income was US$43.1 million versus US$55.2 million in the prior-year quarter, a decrease of 21.9%. Direct operating expenses rose 6.0% to US$359.9 million from US$339.4 million in the comparable period the year before. Indirect operating expenses increased 27.0% to US$83.1 million from US$65.5 million in the equivalent prior-year period.

Prospects: Our evaluation of Genesis Energy L.P. as of Jan. 14, 2018 is the result of our systematic analysis on three basic characteristics: earnings strength, relative valuation, and recent stock price movement. The company has produced a positive trend in earnings per share over the past 5 quarters and while recent estimates for the company have remained steady, GEL has posted results that fell short of analysts expectations. Based on operating earnings yield, the company is about fairly valued when compared to all of the companies in our coverage universe. Share price changes over the past year indicates that GEL will perform very poorly over the near term.

Financial Data

(US$ in Thousands)	9 Mos	6 Mos	3 Mos	12/31/2016	12/31/2015	12/31/2014	12/31/2013	12/31/2012
Earnings Per Share	0.71	0.98	0.92	1.00	4.09	1.18	1.03	1.23
Cash Flow Per Share	2.35	3.09	2.72	2.62	2.81	3.23	1.65	2.41
Tang Book Value Per Share	1.46	...	...	...	...	...	...	...
Dividends Per Share	2.853	2.820	2.773	2.717	2.470	2.230	2.015	1.823
Dividend Payout %	401.76	287.76	301.36	271.75	60.39	188.98	195.63	148.17
Income Statement								
Total Revenue	1,308,328	822,214	415,491	1,712,493	2,246,529	3,846,164	4,134,830	4,070,057
EBITDA	310,086	212,667	101,603	400,427	595,918	205,751	157,057	151,090
Depn & Amortn	155,218	98,623	49,006	194,000	124,200	73,200	46,300	37,400
Income Before Taxes	32,751	39,315	15,858	66,480	371,122	65,912	62,174	72,769
Income Taxes	878	558	255	3,342	3,987	2,845	845	(9,205)
Net Income	67,135	60,823	27,090	113,249	422,528	106,202	86,109	96,319
Average Shares	122,579	122,579	118,388	113,433	103,004	90,060	83,957	78,363
Balance Sheet								
Current Assets	590,824	327,710	352,568	359,569	306,316	355,366	535,223	404,034
Total Assets	7,137,634	5,640,376	5,686,191	5,702,592	5,459,599	3,230,374	2,862,202	2,109,664
Current Liabilities	364,011	237,196	231,454	260,803	302,136	363,145	446,553	312,651
Long-Term Obligations	3,730,549	3,027,259	3,024,712	3,091,369	2,922,054	1,601,039	1,283,572	850,895
Total Liabilities	4,368,533	3,480,678	3,471,998	3,572,261	3,430,498	2,001,171	1,764,465	1,193,169
Stockholders' Equity	691,708	...	...	...	...	...	...	...
Shares Outstanding	122,579	122,579	122,579	117,979	109,979	95,029	88,690	81,202
Statistical Record								
Return on Assets %	1.40	2.04	1.86	2.02	9.72	3.49	3.46	5.00
EBITDA Margin %	23.70	25.87	24.45	23.38	26.53	5.35	3.80	3.71
Net Margin %	5.13	7.40	6.52	6.61	18.81	2.76	2.08	2.37
Asset Turnover	0.27	0.30	0.31	0.31	0.52	1.26	1.66	2.11
Current Ratio	1.62	1.38	1.52	1.38	1.01	0.98	1.20	1.29
Debt to Equity	5.39	...	...	...	...	...	...	...
Price Range	37.97-25.76	40.90-28.19	40.90-29.44	40.90-20.43	49.93-32.02	57.30-36.23	55.54-35.72	35.87-27.33
P/E Ratio	53.48-36.28	41.73-28.77	44.46-32.00	40.90-20.43	12.21-7.83	48.56-30.70	53.92-34.68	29.16-22.22
Average Yield %	8.83	8.20	7.85	8.07	5.70	4.26	4.17	5.81

Address: 919 Milam, Suite 2100, Houston, TX 77002 **Telephone:** 713-860-2500	**Web Site:** www.genesisenergy.com **Officers:** Grant E. Sims - Chairman, Chief Executive Officer Robert V. Deere - Chief Financial Officer	**Auditors:** Ernst & Young LLP **Transfer Agents:** American Stock Transfer & Trust Company, New York, NY

GENESIS HEALTHCARE INC

Exchange	Symbol	Price	52Wk Range	Yield	P/E
NYS	GEN	$0.76 (12/29/2017)	4.69-0.69	N/A	N/A

*7 Year Price Score 28.62   *NYSE Composite Index=100   *12 Month Price Score 37.74

Interim Earnings (Per Share)

Qtr.	Mar	Jun	Sep	Dec
2014	0.03	(0.07)	0.02	0.00
2015	(1.50)	(0.22)	(0.32)	(3.07)
2016	(0.48)	(0.26)	(0.23)	0.14
2017	(0.55)	(0.70)	(3.94)	...

Interim Dividends (Per Share)

No Dividends Paid

Valuation Analysis   **Institutional Holding**

Forecast EPS	$-5.50	No of Institutions
	(01/23/2018)	28
Market Cap	$119.3 Million	Shares
Book Value	N/A	1,463,447
Price/Book	N/A	% Held
Price/Sales	0.02	36.90

Business Summary: Hospitals & Health Care Facilities (MIC: 4.2.1 SIC: 8051 NAIC: 623110)

Genesis Healthcare is a holding company. As of Dec 31 2016, Co. provided inpatient services through its network of 499 nursing and assisted/senior living facilities across 34 states, consisting of 473 skilled nursing facilities and 26 stand-alone assisted/senior living facilities. Co. has three operating segments: inpatient services, which includes the operation of nursing facilities and assisted/senior living facilities; rehabilitation therapy services, which includes Co.'s integrated and third-party rehabilitation and respiratory therapy services; and all other services, which provides a range of other specialty medical services, including physician services.

Recent Developments: For the quarter ended Sep 30 2017, loss from continuing operations was US$615.0 million compared with a loss of US$52.4 million in the year-earlier quarter. Net loss amounted to US$615.0 million versus a net loss of US$52.4 million in the year-earlier quarter. Revenues were US$1.32 billion, down 7.3% from US$1.42 billion the year before. Indirect operating expenses increased 33.1% to US$1.80 billion from US$1.35 billion in the equivalent prior-year period.

Prospects: Our evaluation of Genesis Healthcare Inc. as of Jan. 21, 2018 is the result of our systematic analysis on three basic characteristics: earnings strength, relative valuation, and recent stock price movement. The company has produced a positive trend in earnings per share over the past 5 quarters. Because the company lacks sufficient analyst estimate data, we place greater weight on the historical EPS trend as the measure of earnings strength. Based on operating earnings yield, the company is overvalued when compared to all of the companies in our coverage universe. Share price changes over the past year indicates that GEN will perform very poorly over the near term.

Financial Data

(US$ in Thousands)	9 Mos	6 Mos	3 Mos	12/31/2016	12/31/2015	12/31/2014	12/31/2013	12/31/2012
Earnings Per Share	(5.05)	(1.34)	(0.90)	(0.82)	(4.97)	(0.02)	(0.28)	0.57
Cash Flow Per Share	1.06	1.22	0.96	0.76	0.10	0.69	1.28	1.14
Tang Book Value Per Share	...	...	...	...	...	0.20	0.11	N.M.
Income Statement								
Total Revenue	4,045,860	2,730,408	1,389,132	5,732,430	5,619,224	833,256	842,272	872,623
EBITDA	(241,266)	188,408	106,681	624,445	371,445	51,958	46,485	93,535
Depn & Amortn	183,986	124,596	64,369	234,700	218,800	24,300	23,600	24,200
Income Before Taxes	(798,725)	(185,230)	(82,442)	(138,799)	(355,164)	(3,582)	(11,038)	32,087
Income Taxes	5,683	4,087	1,284	(17,435)	172,524	(1,248)	(2,905)	12,438
Net Income	(489,741)	(115,917)	(50,761)	(64,013)	(426,195)	(907)	(10,484)	21,597
Average Shares	94,940	93,273	91,880	152,532	85,755	38,125	37,533	37,589
Balance Sheet								
Current Assets	998,792	986,330	1,030,549	1,058,987	1,011,493	161,383	142,417	138,825
Total Assets	4,926,928	5,514,788	5,688,509	5,779,201	6,091,470	650,956	643,416	682,636
Current Liabilities	5,502,595	784,566	824,043	857,560	798,665	115,292	97,788	104,303
Long-Term Obligations	338,699	5,019,113	4,985,319	5,011,424	5,335,573	398,389	411,495	435,629
Total Liabilities	5,915,884	6,131,279	6,237,327	6,269,524	6,527,777	555,697	551,184	582,805
Stockholders' Equity	(988,956)	(616,491)	(548,818)	(490,323)	(436,307)	95,259	92,232	99,831
Shares Outstanding	156,321	156,321	154,532	154,531	153,554	39,994	39,793	38,543
Statistical Record								
Return on Assets %	N.M.	N.M.	N.M.	N.M.	N.M.	N.M.	N.M.	3.13
Return on Equity %	...	...	...	...	...	N.M.	N.M.	24.33
EBITDA Margin %	N.M.	6.90	7.68	10.89	6.61	6.24	5.52	10.72
Net Margin %	N.M.	N.M.	N.M.	N.M.	N.M.	N.M.	N.M.	2.47
Asset Turnover	1.01	0.97	0.97	0.96	1.67	1.29	1.27	1.26
Current Ratio	0.18	1.26	1.25	1.23	1.27	1.40	1.46	1.33
Debt to Equity	...	...	...	...	...	4.18	4.46	4.36
Price Range	4.69-0.97	4.69-1.59	4.69-1.38	4.36-1.38	9.22-3.42	8.91-4.28	7.36-4.20	8.02-5.18
P/E Ratio	...	...	...	...	...	...	...	14.07-9.09

Address: 101 East State Street, Kennett Square, PA 19348
Telephone: 610-444-6350

Web Site: www.genesishcc.com
Officers: George V. Hager - Chief Executive Officer
Paul D. Bach - Chief Operating Officer

Auditors: KPMG LLP
Transfer Agents: Wells Fargo Shareowner Services, South St. Paul, MN

GENPACT LTD

Exchange	Symbol	Price	52Wk Range	Yield	P/E
NYS	G	$31.74 (12/29/2017)	32.66-23.37	0.76	23.17

*7 Year Price Score 104.85 *NYSE Composite Index=100 *12 Month Price Score 109.01

Interim Earnings (Per Share)

Qtr.	Mar	Jun	Sep	Dec
2014	0.21	0.22	0.21	0.20
2015	0.20	0.28	0.31	0.29
2016	0.27	0.31	0.33	0.37
2017	0.26	0.36	0.38	...

Interim Dividends (Per Share)

Amt	Decl	Ex	Rec	Pay
0.06Q	02/10/2017	03/08/2017	03/10/2017	03/28/2017
0.06Q	06/01/2017	06/08/2017	06/12/2017	06/28/2017
0.06Q	08/18/2017	09/07/2017	09/08/2017	09/21/2017
0.06Q	11/22/2017	12/07/2017	12/08/2017	12/20/2017

Indicated Div: $0.24

Valuation Analysis / **Institutional Holding**

Forecast EPS	N/A	No of Institutions	298
Market Cap	$6.1 Billion	Shares	189,093,056
Book Value	$1.3 Billion	% Held	88.09
Price/Book	4.66		
Price/Sales	2.28		

Business Summary: Business Services (MIC: 7.5.2 SIC: 8742 NAIC: 541618)

Genpact is engaged in business process management and services. Co.'s business focuses on industry verticals in banking and financial services, capital markets, consumer product goods, healthcare, high tech, infrastructure, manufacturing and services, insurance, and life sciences. In addition, Co.'s process knowledge spans a number of service areas, including analytics and research, collections and customer services, consulting and transformation services, core industry operations services, enterprise application services, finance and accounting services, IT infrastructure management services, and supply chain and procurement services.

Recent Developments: For the quarter ended Sep 30 2017, net income increased 7.3% to US$73.2 million from US$68.2 million in the year-earlier quarter. Revenues were US$708.8 million, up 9.3% from US$648.8 million the year before. Operating income was US$97.5 million versus US$87.1 million in the prior-year quarter, an increase of 11.9%. Direct operating expenses rose 9.4% to US$429.2 million from US$392.4 million in the comparable period the year before. Indirect operating expenses increased 7.7% to US$182.2 million from US$169.2 million in the equivalent prior-year period.

Prospects: Our evaluation of Genpact Ltd. as of Sep. 17, 2017 is the result of our systematic analysis on three basic characteristics: earnings strength, relative valuation, and recent stock price movement. The company has managed to produce a neutral trend in earnings per share over the past 5 quarters and while recent estimates for the company have remained steady, G has posted better than expected results. Based on operating earnings yield, the company is undervalued when compared to all of the companies in our coverage universe. Share price changes over the past year indicates that G will perform well over the near term.

Financial Data

(US$ in Thousands)	9 Mos	6 Mos	3 Mos	12/31/2016	12/31/2015	12/31/2014	12/31/2013	12/31/2012
Earnings Per Share	1.37	1.32	1.27	1.28	1.09	0.85	0.97	0.78
Cash Flow Per Share	2.01	1.99	1.95	1.67	1.51	1.23	1.36	1.38
Tang Book Value Per Share	N.M.	N.M.	0.08	0.73	0.79	0.52	1.17	0.44
Dividends Per Share	...	...	...	...	...	...	...	2.240
Dividend Payout %	...	...	...	...	...	...	...	287.18
Income Statement								
Total Revenue	2,002,516	1,293,692	622,995	2,570,756	2,461,044	2,279,438	2,131,997	1,901,971
EBITDA	327,488	206,886	93,583	426,536	409,892	356,352	399,175	348,457
Depn & Amortn	59,854	37,718	18,847	73,009	76,186	72,572	70,053	69,351
Income Before Taxes	243,567	153,825	69,243	337,343	312,554	254,385	305,982	262,992
Income Taxes	44,297	27,716	12,245	62,098	61,937	57,419	71,100	78,419
Net Income	196,029	122,284	53,338	269,684	239,817	192,002	229,717	178,216
Average Shares	194,947	193,732	202,655	210,126	219,145	225,168	235,754	229,532
Balance Sheet								
Current Assets	1,354,614	1,324,954	1,218,692	1,227,037	1,195,069	1,188,508	1,276,144	1,128,767
Total Assets	3,349,891	3,239,434	2,911,730	2,885,880	2,793,489	2,742,537	2,689,367	2,605,927
Current Liabilities	823,153	766,120	523,322	731,355	594,480	622,114	461,693	517,818
Long-Term Obligations	1,019,354	1,029,508	1,038,867	700,652	739,536	651,974	656,258	659,412
Total Liabilities	2,035,538	1,981,014	1,730,086	1,599,232	1,489,133	1,457,401	1,366,628	1,437,516
Stockholders' Equity	1,314,353	1,258,420	1,181,644	1,286,648	1,304,356	1,285,136	1,322,739	1,168,411
Shares Outstanding	193,033	192,868	192,727	198,794	211,472	218,684	231,262	225,480
Statistical Record								
Return on Assets %	8.75	8.83	9.19	9.47	8.66	7.07	8.68	7.10
Return on Equity %	20.83	20.55	20.90	20.76	18.52	14.72	18.44	13.66
EBITDA Margin %	16.35	15.99	15.02	16.59	16.66	15.63	18.72	18.32
Net Margin %	9.79	9.45	8.56	10.49	9.74	8.42	10.77	9.37
Asset Turnover	0.86	0.86	0.90	0.90	0.89	0.84	0.81	0.76
Current Ratio	1.65	1.73	2.33	1.68	2.01	1.91	2.76	2.18
Debt to Equity	0.78	0.82	0.88	0.54	0.57	0.51	0.50	0.56
Price Range	29.99-22.76	28.16-22.70	28.39-22.70	28.39-22.70	25.85-18.87	19.30-14.28	21.19-15.46	18.66-14.45
P/E Ratio	21.89-16.61	21.33-17.20	22.35-17.87	22.18-17.73	23.72-17.31	22.71-16.80	21.85-15.94	23.92-18.53
Average Yield %	...	...	...	...	...	...	...	13.73

Address: Canon's Court, 22 Victoria Street, Hamilton, HM12
Telephone: 441-295-2244

Web Site: www.genpact.com
Officers: N. V. Tyagarajan - President, Chief Executive Officer Edward J. Fitzpatrick - Senior Vice President, Chief Financial Officer

Auditors: KPMG
Transfer Agents: Computershare, Providence, RI

GENUINE PARTS CO.

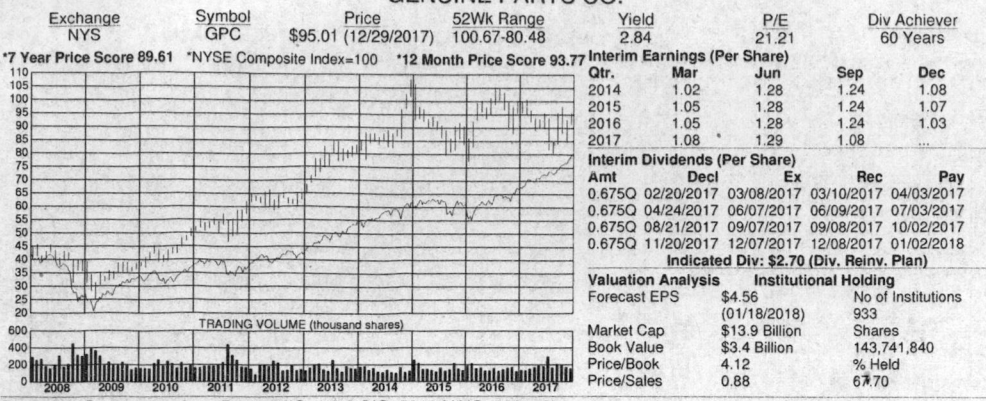

Exchange	Symbol	Price	52Wk Range	Yield	P/E	Div Achiever
NYS	GPC	$95.01 (12/29/2017)	100.67-80.48	2.84	21.21	60 Years

*7 Year Price Score 89.61   *NYSE Composite Index=100   *12 Month Price Score 93.77

Interim Earnings (Per Share)

Qtr.	Mar	Jun	Sep	Dec
2014	1.02	1.28	1.24	1.08
2015	1.05	1.28	1.24	1.07
2016	1.05	1.28	1.24	1.03
2017	1.08	1.29	1.08	...

Interim Dividends (Per Share)

Amt	Decl	Ex	Rec	Pay
0.675Q	02/20/2017	03/08/2017	03/10/2017	04/03/2017
0.675Q	04/24/2017	06/07/2017	06/09/2017	07/03/2017
0.675Q	08/21/2017	09/07/2017	09/08/2017	10/02/2017
0.675Q	11/20/2017	12/07/2017	12/08/2017	01/02/2018

Indicated Div: $2.70 (Div. Reinv. Plan)

Valuation Analysis

		Institutional Holding	
Forecast EPS	$4.56 (01/18/2018)	No of Institutions	933
Market Cap	$13.9 Billion	Shares	143,741,840
Book Value	$3.4 Billion	% Held	67.70
Price/Book	4.12		
Price/Sales	0.88		

Business Summary: Auto Parts (MIC: 1.8.2 SIC: 5013 NAIC: 423120)

Genuine Parts is a service organization engaged in the distribution of automotive replacement parts, industrial replacement parts, office products and electrical/electronic materials. Co.'s Automotive Parts Group distributes automotive parts and accessory items. Co.'s Industrial Parts Group distributes industrial replacement parts and related supplies such as bearings and material handling products. Co.'s Office Products Group engages in the wholesale distribution a line of office and other business related products. Co.'s Electrical/Electronic Materials Group distributes materials to electrical and electronic manufacturers, and industrial assembly and specialty wire and cable markets.

Recent Developments: For the quarter ended Sep 30 2017, net income decreased 14.5% to US$158.4 million from US$185.3 million in the year-earlier quarter. Revenues were US$4.10 billion, up 3.9% from US$3.94 billion the year before. Direct operating expenses rose 4.6% to US$2.87 billion from US$2.74 billion in the comparable period the year before. Indirect operating expenses increased 8.1% to US$980.5 million from US$907.2 million in the equivalent prior-year period.

Prospects: Our evaluation of Genuine Parts Co. as of Jan. 14, 2018 is the result of our systematic analysis on three basic characteristics: earnings strength, relative valuation, and recent stock price movement. The company has managed to produce a neutral trend in earnings per share over the past 5 quarters. However, while recent estimates for the company have been mixed, GPC has posted results that fell short of analysts expectations. Based on operating earnings yield, the company is about fairly valued when compared to all of the companies in our coverage universe. Share price changes over the past year indicates that GPC will perform poorly over the near term.

Financial Data

(US$ in Thousands)	9 Mos	6 Mos	3 Mos	12/31/2016	12/31/2015	12/31/2014	12/31/2013	12/31/2012
Earnings Per Share	4.48	4.64	4.63	4.59	4.63	4.61	4.40	4.14
Cash Flow Per Share	5.09	5.17	6.16	6.33	7.64	5.15	6.83	5.82
Tang Book Value Per Share	11.35	10.97	10.93	10.91	11.89	12.50	13.39	16.15
Dividends Per Share	2.683	2.665	2.648	2.630	2.460	2.300	2.150	1.980
Dividend Payout %	59.88	57.44	57.18	57.30	53.13	49.89	48.86	47.83
Income Statement								
Total Revenue	12,101,725	8,005,819	3,905,641	15,339,713	15,280,044	15,341,647	14,077,843	13,013,868
EBITDA	904,907	618,276	281,907	1,242,911	1,287,018	1,291,140	1,205,232	1,137,797
Depn & Amortn	117,640	77,364	38,132	147,487	141,675	148,313	133,957	98,383
Income Before Taxes	787,267	540,912	243,775	1,074,340	1,123,681	1,117,739	1,044,304	1,018,932
Income Taxes	278,693	190,780	83,615	387,100	418,009	406,453	359,345	370,891
Net Income	508,574	350,132	160,160	687,240	705,672	711,286	684,959	648,041
Average Shares	147,222	147,650	148,788	149,804	152,496	154,375	155,714	156,420
Balance Sheet								
Current Assets	6,316,608	6,301,416	6,194,062	5,948,431	5,555,316	5,592,525	5,221,491	4,820,131
Total Assets	9,494,234	9,412,144	9,166,826	8,859,400	8,144,771	8,246,238	7,680,297	6,807,061
Current Liabilities	4,802,667	4,801,167	4,579,833	4,244,150	3,940,654	3,584,115	3,183,044	2,487,638
Long-Term Obligations	550,000	550,000	550,000	589,221	287,642	540,040	527,815	283,748
Total Liabilities	6,115,999	6,124,020	5,947,853	5,665,672	4,998,204	4,944,990	4,331,223	3,809,174
Stockholders' Equity	3,378,235	3,288,124	3,218,973	3,193,728	3,146,567	3,301,248	3,349,074	2,997,887
Shares Outstanding	146,613	146,830	147,394	148,410	150,081	153,113	153,773	154,841
Statistical Record								
Return on Assets %	7.25	7.62	7.83	8.06	8.61	8.93	9.46	10.19
Return on Equity %	19.73	21.09	21.37	21.62	21.89	21.39	21.58	22.36
EBITDA Margin %	7.48	7.72	7.22	8.10	8.42	8.42	8.56	8.74
Net Margin %	4.20	4.37	4.10	4.48	4.62	4.64	4.87	4.98
Asset Turnover	1.74	1.74	1.76	1.80	1.86	1.93	1.94	2.05
Current Ratio	1.32	1.31	1.35	1.40	1.41	1.56	1.64	1.94
Debt to Equity	0.16	0.17	0.17	0.18	0.09	0.16	0.16	0.09
Price Range	100.67-80.48	105.24-87.67	105.24-87.67	105.24-77.40	106.57-79.53	108.31-77.75	85.03-63.58	66.38-58.53
P/E Ratio	22.47-17.96	22.68-18.89	22.73-18.94	22.93-16.86	23.02-17.18	23.49-16.87	19.32-14.45	16.03-14.14
Average Yield %	2.91	2.77	2.72	2.75	2.72	2.59	2.77	3.16

Address: 2999 Wildwood Parkway, Atlanta, GA 30339 Telephone: 678-934-5000	Web Site: www.genpt.com Officers: Paul D. Donahue - President, Chief Executive Officer, Executive Vice President, Division Officer Carol B. Yancey - Executive Vice President, Chief Financial Officer, Corporate Secretary, Vice President	Auditors: Ernst & Young LLP Investor Contact: 770-953-1700 Transfer Agents: Computershare, Providence, RI

GENWORTH FINANCIAL, INC. (HOLDING CO)

Exchange	Symbol	Price	52Wk Range	Yield	P/E
NYS	GNW	$3.11 (12/29/2017)	4.16-3.11	N/A	4.64

*7 Year Price Score 35.72 ***NYSE Composite Index=100** ***12 Month Price Score 85.42**

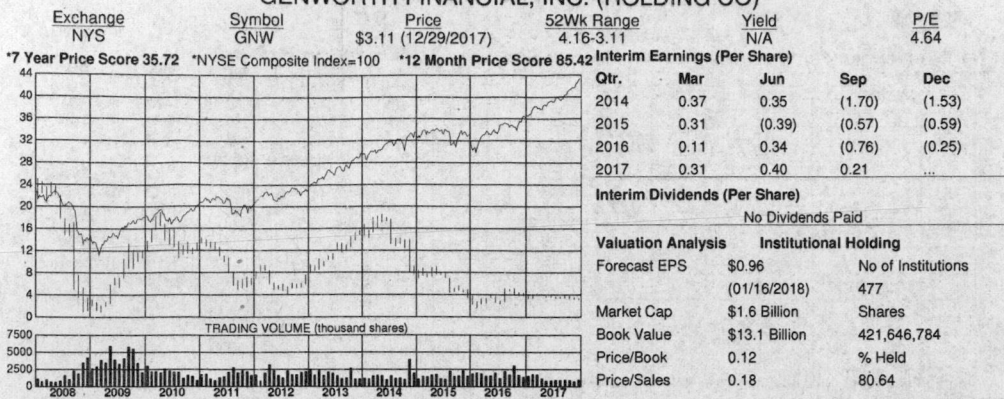

Interim Earnings (Per Share)

Qtr.	Mar	Jun	Sep	Dec
2014	0.37	0.35	(1.70)	(1.53)
2015	0.31	(0.39)	(0.57)	(0.59)
2016	0.11	0.34	(0.76)	(0.25)
2017	0.31	0.40	0.21	...

Interim Dividends (Per Share)

No Dividends Paid

Valuation Analysis		Institutional Holding	
Forecast EPS	$0.96	No of Institutions	
	(01/16/2018)	477	
Market Cap	$1.6 Billion	Shares	
Book Value	$13.1 Billion	421,646,784	
Price/Book	0.12	% Held	
Price/Sales	0.18	80.64	

Business Summary: Life & Health (MIC: 5.2.2 SIC: 6311 NAIC: 524113)

Genworth Financial is a holding company. Co. operates its business through five operating segments: U.S. Mortgage Insurance, which provides mortgage insurance products predominantly insuring prime-based, individually underwritten residential mortgage loans; Canada Mortgage Insurance, which provides flow mortgage insurance and also provide bulk mortgage insurance in Canada; Australia Mortgage Insurance, which provides flow mortgage insurance and also provide bulk mortgage insurance in Australia; U.S. Life Insurance, which provides long-term care insurance products, and service life insurance; and Runoff, which includes the results of non-strategic products which are no longer actively sold.

Recent Developments: For the quarter ended Sep 30 2017, income from continuing operations was US$184.0 million compared with a loss of US$347.0 million in the year-earlier quarter. Net income amounted to US$175.0 million versus a net loss of US$332.0 million in the year-earlier quarter. Revenues were US$2.22 billion, up 3.0% from US$2.15 billion the year before. Net premiums earned were US$1.14 billion versus US$1.11 billion in the prior-year quarter, an increase of 2.4%. Net investment income fell 1.0% to US$797.0 million from US$805.0 million a year ago.

Prospects: Our evaluation of Genworth Financial Inc. as of Jan. 14, 2018 is the result of our systematic analysis on three basic characteristics: earnings strength, relative valuation, and recent stock price movement. The company has managed to produce a neutral trend in earnings per share over the past 5 quarters and while recent estimates for the company have been raised by analysts, GNW has posted results that fell short of analysts expectations. Based on operating earnings yield, the company is undervalued when compared to all of the companies in our coverage universe. Share price changes over the past year indicates that GNW will perform well over the near term.

Financial Data
(US$ in Millions)

	9 Mos	6 Mos	3 Mos	12/31/2016	12/31/2015	12/31/2014	12/31/2013	12/31/2012
Earnings Per Share	0.67	(0.30)	(0.36)	(0.56)	(1.24)	(2.51)	1.12	0.65
Cash Flow Per Share	3.98	4.20	4.51	3.71	3.20	4.91	2.83	1.95
Tang Book Value Per Share	25.56	25.42	24.91	24.69	25.03	29.45	26.52	30.34
Income Statement								
Premium Income	3,382	2,247	1,136	4,160	4,579	5,431	5,148	5,038
Total Revenue	6,609	4,394	2,171	8,369	8,548	9,565	9,403	10,023
Income Before Taxes	1,019	733	332	320	(15)	(1,276)	1,050	712
Income Taxes	348	246	116	358	(9)	(228)	324	189
Net Income	464	357	155	(277)	(615)	(1,244)	560	323
Average Shares	501	501	501	498	497	496	498	494
Balance Sheet								
Total Assets	104,629	105,016	104,686	104,658	106,431	111,358	108,045	113,312
Total Liabilities	91,560	91,998	91,874	92,014	93,607	96,435	93,652	96,775
Stockholders' Equity	13,069	13,018	12,812	12,644	12,824	14,923	14,393	16,537
Shares Outstanding	499	499	499	498	498	497	495	492
Statistical Record								
Return on Assets %	0.32	N.M.	N.M.	N.M.	N.M.	N.M.	0.51	0.28
Return on Equity %	2.45	N.M.	N.M.	N.M.	N.M.	N.M.	3.62	1.95
Net Margin %	7.02	8.12	7.14	(3.31)	(7.19)	(13.01)	5.96	3.22
Price Range	5.22-3.30	5.22-2.35	5.22-2.35	5.22-1.61	9.15-3.47	18.60-7.64	15.63-7.51	9.34-4.12
P/E Ratio	7.79-4.93	...	...	...	...	...	13.96-6.71	14.37-6.34

Address: 6620 West Broad Street, Richmond, VA 23230 Telephone: 804-281-6000	Web Site: www.genworth.com Officers: Thomas J. McInerney - President, Chief Executive Officer Kelly L. Groh - Executive Vice President, Chief Financial Officer, Controller, Division Officer	Auditors: KPMG LLP Transfer Agents: Computershare Shareowner Services LLC, College Station, TX

GGP INC

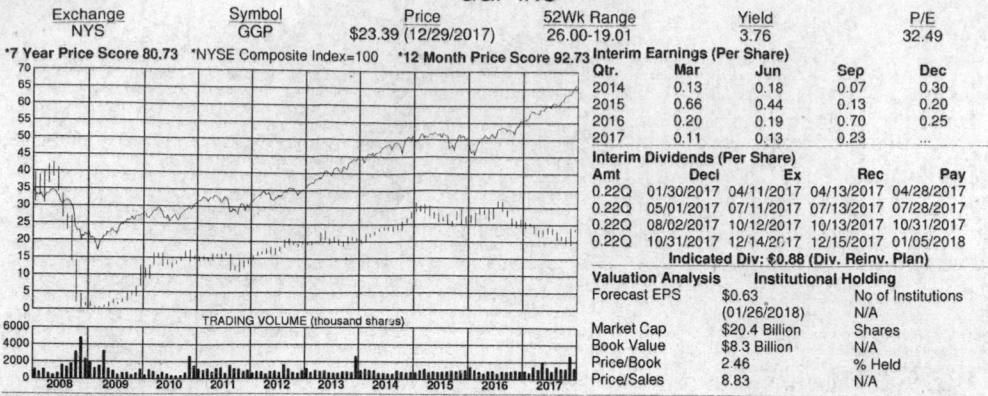

Exchange	Symbol	Price	52Wk Range	Yield	P/E
NYS	GGP	$23.39 (12/29/2017)	26.00-19.01	3.76	32.49

*7 Year Price Score 80.73   *NYSE Composite Index=100   *12 Month Price Score 92.73

Interim Earnings (Per Share)

Qtr.	Mar	Jun	Sep	Dec
2014	0.13	0.18	0.07	0.30
2015	0.66	0.44	0.13	0.20
2016	0.20	0.19	0.70	0.25
2017	0.11	0.13	0.23	...

Interim Dividends (Per Share)

Amt	Decl	Ex	Rec	Pay
0.22Q	01/30/2017	04/11/2017	04/13/2017	04/28/2017
0.22Q	05/01/2017	07/11/2017	07/13/2017	07/28/2017
0.22Q	08/02/2017	10/12/2017	10/13/2017	10/31/2017
0.22Q	10/31/2017	12/14/2017	12/15/2017	01/05/2018

Indicated Div: $0.88 (Div. Reinv. Plan)

Valuation Analysis

		Institutional Holding	
Forecast EPS	$0.63	No of Institutions	
	(01/26/2018)	N/A	
Market Cap	$20.4 Billion	Shares	
Book Value	$8.3 Billion	N/A	
Price/Book	2.46	% Held	
Price/Sales	8.83	N/A	

Business Summary: REITs (MIC: 5.3.1 SIC: 6798 NAIC: 525930)

GGP is a self-administered and self-managed real estate investment trust. Co., through its subsidiaries and affiliates, is an owner and operator of retail properties with a property portfolio primarily comprised of Class A retail real estate. As of Dec 31 2016, Co. owned, either entirely or with joint venture partners, 127 retail properties located throughout the U.S. Co. provides management and other services to substantially all of its properties, including properties which Co. owns through joint venture arrangements. Substantially all of Co.'s business is conducted through GGP Operating Partnership, LP, GGP Nimbus, LP, and GGP Limited Partnership.

Recent Developments: For the quarter ended Sep 30 2017, net income decreased 66.8% to US$226.3 million from US$681.7 million in the year-earlier quarter. Revenues were US$578.4 million, up 4.3% from US$554.5 million the year before. Revenues from property income rose 2.5% to US$529.2 million from US$516.2 million in the corresponding quarter a year earlier.

Prospects: Our evaluation of GGP Inc. as of Jan. 21, 2018 is the result of our systematic analysis on three basic characteristics: earnings strength, relative valuation, and recent stock price movement. The company has enjoyed a very positive trend in earnings per share over the past 5 quarters. Because the company lacks sufficient analyst estimate data, we place greater weight on the historical EPS trend as the measure of earnings strength. Based on operating earnings yield, the company is about fairly valued when compared to all of the companies in our coverage universe. Share price changes over the past year indicates that GGP will perform poorly over the near term.

Financial Data

(US$ in Thousands)	9 Mos	6 Mos	3 Mos	12/31/2016	12/31/2015	12/31/2014	12/31/2013	12/31/2012
Earnings Per Share	0.72	1.19	1.25	1.34	1.43	0.69	0.31	(0.52)
Cash Flow Per Share	1.42	1.23	1.28	1.28	1.20	1.07	0.96	0.86
Tang Book Value Per Share	8.90	8.95	9.02	9.13	8.63	7.68	7.77	6.99
Dividends Per Share	1.120	1.090	1.060	1.060	0.710	0.630	0.510	0.420
Dividend Payout %	155.56	91.60	84.80	79.10	49.65	91.30	164.52	...
Income Statement								
Total Revenue	1,700,487	1,122,129	566,332	2,346,446	2,403,906	2,535,559	2,527,387	2,511,850
EBITDA	758,968	436,394	210,247	1,578,398	1,575,382	1,091,273	1,051,835	350,236
Depn & Amortn	27,369	22,155	14,195	41,154	62,106	76,615	84,229	105,871
Income Before Taxes	380,423	183,095	81,665	1,026,004	954,855	343,986	238,745	(563,805)
Income Taxes	15,347	8,354	4,510	901	(38,334)	7,253	345	9,091
Net Income	455,803	233,022	107,160	1,288,367	1,374,561	665,850	302,528	(481,233)
Average Shares	940,184	945,325	949,516	952,333	951,062	944,721	934,068	938,049
Balance Sheet								
Current Assets	1,103,749	1,175,848	1,297,724	1,475,449	1,306,451	1,036,239	1,056,170	885,675
Total Assets	23,326,016	22,277,446	22,467,454	22,732,746	24,073,555	25,335,734	25,762,303	27,282,405
Current Liabilities	972,542	786,875	807,740	972,706	797,170	929,250	963,183	1,170,509
Long-Term Obligations	13,705,458	12,707,705	12,779,245	12,642,004	14,433,745	16,216,555	15,891,340	16,186,358
Total Liabilities	15,036,454	13,851,361	13,953,565	14,096,982	15,803,512	17,729,815	17,659,182	19,660,707
Stockholders' Equity	8,289,562	8,426,085	8,513,889	8,635,764	8,270,043	7,605,919	8,103,121	7,621,698
Shares Outstanding	872,760	882,008	882,605	884,097	882,397	884,912	911,194	939,049
Statistical Record								
Return on Assets %	3.01	4.99	5.23	5.49	5.56	2.61	1.14	N.M.
Return on Equity %	8.08	13.67	14.36	15.20	17.32	8.48	3.85	N.M.
EBITDA Margin %	44.63	38.89	37.12	67.27	65.53	43.04	41.62	13.94
Net Margin %	26.80	20.77	18.92	54.91	57.18	26.26	11.97	N.M.
Asset Turnover	0.10	0.10	0.10	0.10	0.10	0.10	0.10	0.09
Current Ratio	1.13	1.49	1.61	1.52	1.64	1.12	1.10	0.76
Debt to Equity	1.65	1.51	1.50	1.46	1.75	2.13	1.96	2.12
Price Range	27.60-20.50	31.97-21.61	31.97-22.66	31.97-24.25	31.46-24.37	28.66-19.54	23.33-18.69	20.99-14.36
P/E Ratio	38.33-28.47	26.87-18.16	25.58-18.13	23.86-18.10	22.00-17.04	41.54-28.32	75.26-60.29	...
Average Yield %	4.72	4.23	3.92	3.81	2.56	2.67	2.52	2.34

Address: 110 N. Wacker Dr., Chicago, IL 60606	Web Site: www.ggp.com	Auditors: Deloitte & Touche LLP
Telephone: 312-960-5000	Officers: John Bucksbaum - Chairman Shobi Khan - President, Chief Operating Officer	Investor Contact: 312-960-5529
		Transfer Agents: American Stock Transfer & Trust Company, LLC, Brooklyn, NY

GLOBAL PARTNERS LP

Exchange	Symbol	Price	52Wk Range	Yield	P/E
NYS	GLP	$16.70 (12/29/2017)	21.55-16.05	11.08	N/A

*7 Year Price Score 53.21 *NYSE Composite Index=100 *12 Month Price Score 88.61

Interim Earnings (Per Share)

Qtr.	Mar	Jun	Sep	Dec
2014	2.03	(0.50)	1.50	0.92
2015	0.92	0.15	0.16	(0.09)
2016	(0.21)	(0.22)	(3.54)	(1.94)
2017	0.68	0.07	0.44	...

Interim Dividends (Per Share)

Amt	Decl	Ex	Rec	Pay
0.463Q	01/30/2017	02/07/2017	02/09/2017	02/14/2017
0.463Q	04/28/2017	05/08/2017	05/10/2017	05/15/2017
0.463Q	07/28/2017	08/07/2017	08/09/2017	08/14/2017
0.463Q	10/27/2017	11/08/2017	11/09/2017	11/14/2017

Indicated Div: $1.85

Valuation Analysis

		Institutional Holding	
Forecast EPS	$1.32	No of Institutions	
	(01/18/2018)	85	
Market Cap	$565.7 Million	Shares	
Book Value	N/A	16,275,167	
Price/Book	N/A	% Held	
Price/Sales	0.06	41.85	

Business Summary: Equipment & Services (MIC: 9.1.3 SIC: 5171 NAIC: 424710)

Global Partners is a midstream logistics and marketing company that engages in the purchasing, selling, storing and logistics of transporting petroleum and related products. Co.'s segments are: Wholesale, which sells, gathers, stores and transports refined petroleum products, renewable fuels, crude oil and propane; Gasoline Distribution and Station Operations, which sells branded and unbranded gasoline to gasoline station operators and sub-jobbers; and Commercial, which includes sales and deliveries to end user customers in the public sector and to commercial and industrial end users of unbranded gasoline, home heating oil, diesel, kerosene, residual oil, bunker fuel and natural gas.

Recent Developments: For the quarter ended Sep 30 2017, net income amounted to US$14.5 million versus a net loss of US$156.6 million in the year-earlier quarter. Revenues were US$2.16 billion, up 6.4% from US$2.03 billion the year before. Operating income was US$34.4 million versus a loss of US$132.2 million in the prior-year quarter. Direct operating expenses rose 5.9% to US$2.01 billion from US$1.90 billion in the comparable period the year before. Indirect operating expenses decreased 56.3% to US$115.7 million from US$264.9 million in the equivalent prior-year period.

Prospects: For the Quarter ended Mar. 31, 2017, Co. posted a solid first quarter and continued to position the Partnership for growth. Net income attributable to the Partnership in the first quarter of 2017 was $22.9 million, or $0.68 per diluted limited partner unit, compared with a net loss attributable to the Partnership of $7.0 million, or $0.21 per limited partner unit, in the first quarter of 2016. EBITDA in the first quarter of 2017 was $71.9 million compared with EBITDA of $42.6 million in the comparable period of 2016. Adjusted EBITDA was $60.1 million in the first quarter of 2017 compared with Adjusted EBITDA of $48.7 million in the same period of 2016.

Financial Data

(US$ in Thousands)	9 Mos	6 Mos	3 Mos	12/31/2016	12/31/2015	12/31/2014	12/31/2013	12/31/2012
Earnings Per Share	(0.75)	(4.73)	(5.02)	(5.91)	1.11	3.95	1.42	1.71
Cash Flow Per Share	6.79	4.47	1.53	(3.57)	1.94	12.58	9.34	8.78
Dividends Per Share	1.850	1.850	1.850	1.850	2.735	2.527	2.340	2.058
Dividend Payout %	...	...	...	...	246.40	63.99	164.79	120.32
Income Statement								
Total Revenue	6,520,060	4,360,314	2,270,784	8,239,639	10,314,852	17,269,954	19,589,608	17,625,997
EBITDA	110,800	74,700	47,829	(49,651)	217,023	233,207	143,309	123,088
Depn & Amortn	5,936	4,199	2,201	102,600	102,300	67,500	57,900	38,500
Income Before Taxes	39,028	25,291	22,341	(238,570)	41,391	117,943	41,872	48,320
Income Taxes	72	795	(164)	53	(1,873)	963	819	1,577
Net Income	40,198	25,320	22,946	(199,412)	43,563	114,709	42,615	46,743
Average Shares	33,945	33,652	33,610	33,525	32,323	27,502	27,560	26,567
Balance Sheet								
Current Assets	722,930	730,780	856,065	1,075,466	867,035	961,223	1,374,311	1,506,933
Total Assets	2,148,178	2,197,580	2,328,329	2,564,020	2,663,675	2,039,977	2,427,922	2,329,752
Current Liabilities	476,602	460,964	577,476	799,225	594,734	707,491	972,572	1,045,195
Long-Term Obligations	1,103,572	1,163,642	1,162,971	1,025,850	1,075,564	601,936	909,968	762,754
Total Liabilities	1,760,168	1,809,091	1,927,766	2,171,365	2,015,886	1,453,035	2,012,685	1,893,291
Shares Outstanding	33,874	33,784	33,784	33,773	33,737	30,835	27,491	27,540
Statistical Record								
Return on Assets %	N.M.	N.M.	N.M.	N.M.	1.85	5.13	1.79	2.22
EBITDA Margin %	1.70	1.71	2.11	N.M.	2.10	1.35	0.73	0.70
Net Margin %	0.62	0.58	1.01	N.M.	0.42	0.66	0.22	0.27
Asset Turnover	3.90	3.55	3.52	3.14	4.39	7.73	8.23	8.37
Current Ratio	1.52	1.59	1.48	1.35	1.46	1.36	1.41	1.44
Price Range	21.55-15.15	21.55-13.06	21.55-12.31	19.50-12.31	41.82-15.26	45.32-31.68	40.65-25.35	27.81-20.19
P/E Ratio	...	...	...	...	37.68-13.75	11.47-8.02	28.63-17.85	16.26-11.81
Average Yield %	10.27	10.68	11.60	12.54	8.21	6.37	6.74	8.67

Address: P.O. Box 9161, 800 South Street, Waltham, MA 02454-9161
Telephone: 781-894-8800

Web Site: www.globalp.com
Officers: Richard Slifka - Chairman Eric S. Slifka - President, Chief Executive Officer, Associate/Affiliate Company Officer

Auditors: Ernst & Young LLP
Investor Contact: 781-894-8800
Transfer Agents: American Stock Transfer and Trust Company, New Yor, NY

GLOBAL PAYMENTS INC

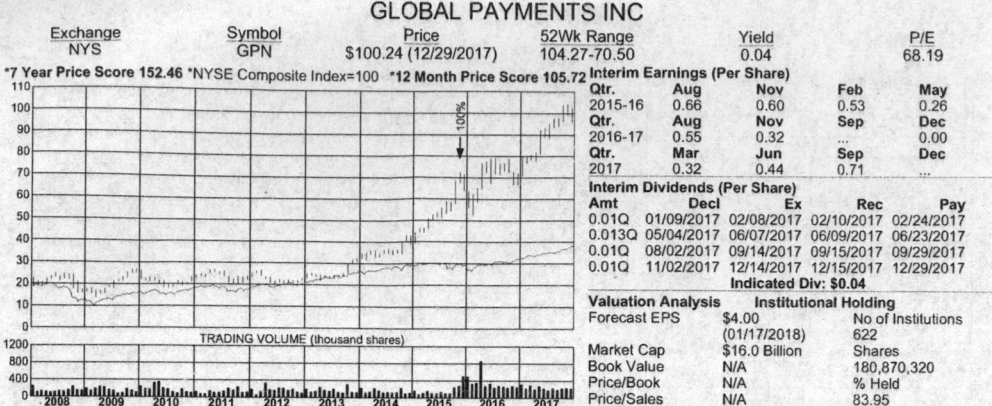

Exchange	Symbol	Price	52Wk Range	Yield	P/E
NYS	GPN	$100.24 (12/29/2017)	104.27-70.50	0.04	68.19

*7 Year Price Score 152.46 *NYSE Composite Index=100 *12 Month Price Score 105.72

Interim Earnings (Per Share)

Qtr.	Aug	Nov	Feb	May
2015-16	0.66	0.60	0.53	0.26
Qtr.	Aug	Nov	Sep	Dec
2016-17	0.55	0.32	...	0.00
Qtr.	Mar	Jun	Sep	Dec
2017	0.32	0.44	0.71	...

Interim Dividends (Per Share)

Amt	Decl	Ex	Rec	Pay
0.01Q	01/09/2017	02/08/2017	02/10/2017	02/24/2017
0.013Q	05/04/2017	06/07/2017	06/09/2017	06/23/2017
0.01Q	08/02/2017	09/14/2017	09/15/2017	09/29/2017
0.01Q	11/02/2017	12/14/2017	12/15/2017	12/29/2017

Indicated Div: $0.04

Valuation Analysis

		Institutional Holding	
Forecast EPS	$4.00	No of Institutions	
	(01/17/2018)	622	
Market Cap	$16.0 Billion	Shares	
Book Value	N/A		180,870,320
Price/Book	N/A	% Held	
Price/Sales	N/A		83.95

Business Summary: Business Services (MIC: 7.5.2 SIC: 7389 NAIC: 561499)

Global Payments provides payment technology services. Co.'s payment solutions enable its merchant customers to accept card, electronic, check and digital-based payments at the point of sale. Co.'s products include terminal sales and deployment, authorization processing, settlement and funding processing, customer support and help-desk functions, chargeback resolution, industry compliance, Payment Card Industry security, consolidated billing and statements and on-line reporting. Through its wholesale channel, Co. provides payment services to merchants via independent sales organizations. Co.'s credit and debit card transaction processing includes the processing of international card brands.

Recent Developments: For the quarter ended Nov 30 2016, net income decreased 36.7% to US$52.6 million from US$83.1 million in the year-earlier quarter. Revenues were US$941.8 million, up 30.4% from US$722.4 million the year before. Operating income was US$105.3 million versus US$123.2 million in the prior-year quarter, a decrease of 14.5%. Direct operating expenses rose 73.1% to US$468.4 million from US$270.6 million in the comparable period the year before. Indirect operating expenses increased 12.0% to US$368.2 million from US$328.6 million in the equivalent prior-year period.

Prospects: Our evaluation of Global Payments Inc. as of Jan 14, 2018 is the result of our systematic analysis on three basic characteristics: earnings strength, relative valuation, and recent stock price movement. The company has managed to produce a neutral trend in earnings per share over the past 5 quarters and while recent estimates for the company have remained steady, GPN has posted better than expected results. Based on operating earnings yield, the company is about fairly valued when compared to all of the companies in our coverage universe. Share price changes over the past year indicates that GPN will perform well over the near term.

Financial Data

(US$ in Thousands)	9 Mos	6 Mos	3 Mos	12/31/2016	05/31/2016	05/31/2015	05/31/2014	05/31/2013
Earnings Per Share	1.47	0.76	0.64	0.81	2.04	2.06	1.69	1.38
Cash Flow Per Share	0.80	...	7.83	5.59	4.41	3.17	1.35	1.55
Dividends Per Share	0.033	0.013	0.010	0.020	0.040	0.040	0.040	0.040
Dividend Payout %	2.25	1.71	1.56	2.47	1.96	1.94	2.37	2.90
Income Statement								
Total Revenue	1,038,907	962,240	919,762	2,202,896	2,898,150	2,773,718	2,554,236	2,375,923
EBITDA	256,449	131,852	189,019	432,280	538,633	594,084	527,544	468,978
Depn & Amortn	83,978	...	84,049	194,329	113,689	137,487	122,045	111,765
Income Before Taxes	134,054	85,323	65,280	173,344	360,912	417,110	377,350	334,284
Income Taxes	15,692	...	12,321	35,661	70,695	107,995	107,398	95,571
Net Income	110,740	66,909	48,813	124,931	271,666	278,040	245,286	216,125
Average Shares	155,402	153,555	153,255	154,231	133,167	134,922	145,376	156,454
Balance Sheet								
Current Assets	3,550,297	2,516,071	2,399,180	3,116,006	2,851,313	3,302,295	1,643,444	1,214,492
Total Assets	12,281,549	10,036,781	9,959,716	10,664,350	10,509,952	5,793,548	4,018,650	3,125,056
Current Liabilities	3,123,911	2,098,464	2,092,862	2,851,956	2,430,707	3,015,904	1,211,618	704,114
Long-Term Obligations	4,677,910	4,175,411	4,221,258	4,260,827	4,379,744	1,680,000	1,376,002	891,134
Total Liabilities	8,750,200	7,185,799	7,228,837	8,033,559	7,763,476	5,035,572	3,021,423	1,978,971
Stockholders' Equity	3,531,349	2,850,982	2,730,879	2,630,791	2,746,476	757,976	997,227	1,146,085
Shares Outstanding	158,762	152,556	152,502	152,185	154,421	130,557	137,691	150,852
Statistical Record								
EBITDA Margin %	24.68	13.70	20.55	19.62	18.59	21.42	20.65	19.74
Net Margin %	10.66	6.95	5.31	5.67	9.37	10.02	9.60	9.10
Current Ratio	1.14	1.20	1.15	1.09	1.17	1.09	1.36	1.72
Debt to Equity	1.32	1.46	1.55	1.62	1.59	2.22	1.38	0.78
Price Range	98.08-66.42	93.31-66.42	80.89-64.77	79.23-66.42	77.69-51.09	52.70-33.98	36.50-22.91	25.50-19.94
P/E Ratio	66.72-45.18	122.78-87.40	126.39-101.20	97.81-82.00	38.08-25.04	25.58-16.50	21.60-13.55	18.48-14.45
Average Yield %	0.04	0.02	0.01	0.03	0.06	0.10	0.13	0.18

Address: 3550 Lenox Road, Atlanta, GA 30326 **Telephone:** 770-829-8000	**Web Site:** www.globalpaymentsinc.com **Officers:** William I. Jacobs - Chairman David E. Mangum - President, Senior Executive Vice President, Chief Financial Officer, Chief Operating Officer	**Auditors:** Deloitte & Touche LLP **Investor Contact:** 770-829-8234 **Transfer Agents:** Computershare Trust Company, N.A, Canton, MA

GLOBUS MEDICAL INC

Exchange	Symbol	Price	52Wk Range	Yield	P/E
NYS	GMED	$41.10 (12/29/2017)	41.64-24.79	N/A	37.36

*7 Year Price Score N/A   *NYSE Composite Index=100   *12 Month Price Score 113.13

TRADING VOLUME (thousand shares)

Interim Earnings (Per Share)

Qtr.	Mar	Jun	Sep	Dec
2014	0.22	0.22	0.24	0.29
2015	0.26	0.25	0.28	0.39
2016	0.29	0.27	0.27	0.25
2017	0.30	0.29	0.26	...

Interim Dividends (Per Share)

No Dividends Paid

Valuation Analysis   Institutional Holding

Forecast EPS	$1.27	No of Institutions
	(01/18/2018)	N/A
Market Cap	$4.0 Billion	Shares
Book Value	$935.3 Million	N/A
Price/Book	4.23	% Held
Price/Sales	6.48	N/A

Business Summary: Medical Instruments & Equipment (MIC: 4.3.1 SIC: 3841 NAIC: 339112)

Globus Medical is a medical device company focused on the design, development and commercialization of musculoskeletal implants. Co. provides a portfolio of products addressing a range of spinal pathologies, anatomies and surgical approaches. All of Co.'s products fall into one of two categories: Innovative Fusion or Disruptive Technologies. Co.'s Innovative Fusion products are used to treat degenerative, deformity, tumor, and trauma conditions. Co.'s pipeline of Disruptive Technology products includes products that allow for minimally invasive surgical techniques, regenerative biologics technologies; and interventional pain management solutions.

Recent Developments: For the quarter ended Sep 30 2017, net income decreased 2.4% to US$25.6 million from US$26.2 million in the year-earlier quarter. Revenues were US$151.7 million, up 11.9% from US$135.7 million the year before. Operating income was US$35.8 million versus US$37.7 million in the prior-year quarter, a decrease of 4.9%. Direct operating expenses rose 17.0% to US$36.8 million from US$31.5 million in the comparable period the year before. Indirect operating expenses increased 18.9% to US$79.2 million from US$66.5 million in the equivalent prior-year period.

Prospects: Our evaluation of Globus Medical Inc as of Jan. 14, 2018 is the result of our systematic analysis on three basic characteristics: earnings strength, relative valuation, and recent stock price movement. The company has managed to produce a neutral trend in earnings per share over the past 5 quarters and while recent estimates for the company have been mixed, GMED has posted better than expected results. Based on operating earnings yield, the company is about fairly valued when compared to all of the companies in our coverage universe. Share price changes over the past year indicates that GMED will perform poorly over the near term.

Financial Data
(US$ in Thousands)

	9 Mos	6 Mos	3 Mos	12/31/2016	12/31/2015	12/31/2014	12/31/2013	12/31/2012
Earnings Per Share	1.10	1.11	1.09	1.08	1.17	0.97	0.73	0.80
Cash Flow Per Share	1.73	1.80	1.77	1.79	1.28	0.84	1.01	0.85
Tang Book Value Per Share	7.56	7.30	7.30	6.93	6.19	5.26	4.54	3.96
Income Statement								
Total Revenue	459,943	308,199	155,809	563,994	544,753	474,371	434,459	385,994
EBITDA	116,840	80,818	42,004	196,050	195,327	159,686	120,870	132,293
Depn & Amortn	2,258	1,855	1,008	38,771	22,522	21,044	18,869	17,640
Income Before Taxes	119,328	81,971	42,414	157,279	172,805	138,642	102,001	114,653
Income Taxes	36,356	24,590	13,700	52,938	60,021	46,157	33,389	40,822
Net Income	82,972	57,381	28,714	104,341	112,784	92,485	68,612	73,831
Average Shares	97,849	97,818	97,148	96,432	96,073	95,457	94,192	92,208
Balance Sheet								
Current Assets	563,562	535,129	540,899	513,766	544,799	470,025	416,808	360,110
Total Assets	1,037,160	995,014	960,421	927,637	834,100	703,547	566,304	447,133
Current Liabilities	74,927	69,061	75,369	79,892	82,691	89,412	67,942	39,508
Total Liabilities	101,896	89,714	91,536	95,559	118,776	118,093	93,944	60,631
Stockholders' Equity	935,264	905,300	868,885	832,078	715,324	585,454	472,360	386,502
Shares Outstanding	96,367	96,288	96,077	95,929	95,319	94,705	93,442	91,270
Statistical Record								
Return on Assets %	11.07	11.57	11.67	11.81	14.67	14.57	13.54	18.96
Return on Equity %	12.29	12.81	12.99	13.45	17.34	17.49	15.98	22.01
EBITDA Margin %	25.40	26.22	26.96	34.76	35.86	33.66	27.82	34.27
Net Margin %	18.04	18.62	18.43	18.50	20.70	19.50	15.79	19.13
Asset Turnover	0.63	0.64	0.64	0.64	0.71	0.75	0.86	0.99
Current Ratio	7.52	7.75	7.18	6.43	6.59	5.26	6.13	9.11
Price Range	33.95-20.65	33.95-20.65	29.96-20.65	27.82-20.65	28.24-20.66	26.95-18.14	20.18-10.49	18.75-10.37
P/E Ratio	30.86-18.77	30.59-18.60	27.49-18.94	25.76-19.12	24.14-17.66	27.78-18.70	27.64-14.37	23.44-12.96

Address: 2560 General Armistead Avenue, Audubon, PA 19403 Telephone: 610-930-1800 Fax: 302-636-5454	Web Site: www.globusmedical.com Officers: David C. Paul - Chairman, Chief Executive Officer Anthony L. Williams - President, Vice President, Corporate Counsel, Secretary	Auditors: Deloitte & Touche LLP Investor Contact: 610-930-1800 Transfer Agents: Broadridge Corporate Issuer Solutions, Inc., Philadelphia, PA

GODADDY INC

Exchange	Symbol	Price	52Wk Range	Yield	P/E
NYS	GDDY	$50.28 (12/29/2017)	51.06-34.41	N/A	193.38

*7 Year Price Score N/A *NYSE Composite Index=100 *12 Month Price Score 109.77

Interim Earnings (Per Share)

Qtr.	Mar	Jun	Sep	Dec
2015	(0.34)	(0.46)	(0.04)	0.01
2016	(0.15)	(0.11)	0.05	(0.02)
2017	0.01	0.10	0.17	...

Interim Dividends (Per Share)

No Dividends Paid

Valuation Analysis   **Institutional Holding**

Forecast EPS	$0.23	No of Institutions
	(01/18/2018)	245
Market Cap	$8.4 Billion	Shares
Book Value	$395.2 Million	144,299,808
Price/Book	21.15	% Held
Price/Sales	3.95	N/A

TRADING VOLUME (thousand shares)

Business Summary: Internet & Software (MIC: 6.3.2 SIC: 7373 NAIC: 541512)

GoDaddy is a holding company. Co. is a technology provider to small businesses, web design personnel and individuals, delivering cloud-based products and personalized Customer Care. Co. provides website building, hosting and security tools to help customers construct and protect their online presence. Co. provides applications and access to relevant third party products helping them connect to their customers, manage and grow their businesses and get found online. Co. has designed and developed a set of cloud-based technology products enabling its customers to establish a digital presence, connect with their customers and manage their ventures.

Recent Developments: For the quarter ended Sep 30 2017, income from continuing operations decreased 14.5% to US$7.1 million from US$8.3 million in the year-earlier quarter. Net income increased 261.4% to US$30.0 million from US$8.3 million in the year-earlier quarter. Revenues were US$582.2 million, up 23.3% from US$472.1 million the year before. Operating income was US$32.1 million versus US$21.2 million in the prior-year quarter, an increase of 51.4%. Direct operating expenses rose 18.4% to US$200.3 million from US$169.2 million in the comparable period the year before. Indirect operating expenses increased 24.2% to US$349.8 million from US$281.7 million in the equivalent prior-year period.

Prospects: Our evaluation of GoDaddy Inc as of Jan. 14, 2018 is the result of our systematic analysis on three basic characteristics: earnings strength, relative valuation, and recent stock price movement. The company has suffered a very negative trend in earnings per share over the past 5 quarters and while recent estimates for the company have remained steady, GDDY has posted results that were in line with analysts expectations. Based on operating earnings yield, the company is overvalued when compared to all of the companies in our coverage universe. Share price changes over the past year indicates that GDDY will perform well over the near term.

Financial Data

(US$ in Thousands)	9 Mos	6 Mos	3 Mos	12/31/2016	12/31/2015	12/31/2014	12/31/2013	12/31/2012
Earnings Per Share	0.26	0.14	(0.07)	(0.21)	(0.81)	(1.11)	(1.58)	(2.21)
Cash Flow Per Share	4.01	4.21	4.55	4.83	4.42	1.40	1.21	0.84
Income Statement								
Total Revenue	1,629,700	1,047,500	489,700	1,847,900	1,607,300	1,387,262	1,130,845	910,903
EBITDA	227,100	138,600	42,300	104,700	9,900	(5,558)	(79,874)	(125,033)
Depn & Amortn	147,100	87,100	31,600	69,000	61,300	55,574	50,174	75,145
Income Before Taxes	20,800	16,700	(2,100)	(21,500)	(120,600)	(146,129)	(201,026)	(279,270)
Income Taxes	(6,600)	(3,600)	1,000	400	(200)	(2,824)	(1,142)	(218)
Net Income	43,800	21,400	600	(16,500)	(47,400)	(143,305)	(199,884)	(279,052)
Average Shares	175,219	176,716	100,242	79,835	58,676	128,567	126,663	126,098
Balance Sheet								
Current Assets	1,003,600	1,605,000	1,046,200	932,800	693,900	460,882	405,875	...
Total Assets	5,695,000	6,253,900	3,889,900	3,786,900	3,498,800	3,264,805	3,213,130	...
Current Liabilities	1,750,500	2,324,100	1,323,000	1,262,200	1,113,600	972,749	858,529	...
Long-Term Obligations	2,635,900	2,605,400	1,229,000	1,035,700	1,039,800	1,413,939	1,083,934	...
Total Liabilities	5,299,800	5,868,500	3,291,300	3,224,400	3,073,000	2,854,414	2,342,382	...
Stockholders' Equity	395,200	385,400	598,600	562,500	425,800	410,391	870,748	...
Shares Outstanding	166,211	164,745	169,043	167,112	157,481	129,003	127,559	126,200
Statistical Record								
Return on Assets %	0.89	0.49	N.M.	N.M.	N.M.	N.M.	...	...
Return on Equity %	9.32	5.88	N.M.	N.M.	N.M.	N.M.	...	...
EBITDA Margin %	13.94	13.23	8.64	5.67	0.62	N.M.	N.M.	N.M.
Net Margin %	2.69	2.04	0.12	N.M.	N.M.	N.M.	N.M.	N.M.
Asset Turnover	0.45	0.40	0.51	0.51	0.48	0.43	...	...
Current Ratio	0.57	0.69	0.79	0.74	0.62	0.47	0.47	...
Debt to Equity	6.67	6.76	2.05	1.84	2.44	3.45	1.24	...
Price Range	45.30-31.80	43.59-28.31	37.90-28.31	36.82-24.25	34.24-23.59	...	...	...
P/E Ratio	174.23-122.31	311.36-202.21	...	...	...	...	...	...

Address: 14455 N. Hayden Road, Scottsdale, AZ 85260
Telephone: 480-505-8800

Web Site: www.godaddy.com
Officers: Charles J. (Chuck) Robel - Chairman Scott W. Wagner - President, Chief Operating Officer, Chief Financial Officer, Chief Executive Officer

Auditors: Ernst & Young LLP
Transfer Agents: American Stock Transfer & Trust Company, LLC, Brooklyn, NY

GORMAN-RUPP COMPANY (THE)

Exchange	Symbol	Price	52Wk Range	Yield	P/E	Div Acheiver
NYS	GRC	$31.21 (12/29/2017)	33.47-24.07	1.60	34.68	44 Years

*7 Year Price Score 86.04   *NYSE Composite Index=100   *12 Month Price Score 99.46

TRADING VOLUME (thousand shares)

Interim Earnings (Per Share)

Qtr.	Mar	Jun	Sep	Dec
2014	0.38	0.34	0.36	0.30
2015	0.28	0.25	0.22	0.21
2016	0.24	0.25	0.27	0.19
2017	0.19	0.30	0.22	...

Interim Dividends (Per Share)

Amt	Decl	Ex	Rec	Pay
0.115Q	04/28/2017	05/11/2017	05/15/2017	06/09/2017
0.115Q	07/28/2017	08/11/2017	08/15/2017	09/08/2017
0.125Q	10/27/2017	11/14/2017	11/15/2017	12/08/2017
0.125Q	01/26/2018	02/14/2018	02/15/2018	03/09/2018

Indicated Div: $0.50

Valuation Analysis   **Institutional Holding**

Forecast EPS	$1.22 (01/03/2018)	No of Institutions	137
Market Cap	$814.8 Million	Shares	16,531,148
Book Value	$319.0 Million	% Held	54.10
Price/Book	2.55		
Price/Sales	2.15		

Business Summary: Industrial Machinery & Equipment (MIC: 7.2.1 SIC: 3561 NAIC: 333911)

Gorman-Rupp designs, manufactures and globally sells pumps and pump systems for use in water, wastewater, construction, dewatering, industrial, petroleum, original equipment, agriculture, fire protection, heating, ventilating and air conditioning, military and other liquid-handling applications. Co.'s product line consists of pump models ranging in size from 1/4 inch to nearly 15 feet. The types of pumps which Co. produces include self priming centrifugal, standard centrifugal, magnetic drive centrifugal, axial and mixed flow, vertical turbine line shaft, submersible, high pressure booster, rotary gear, diaphragm, bellows and oscillating.

Recent Developments: For the quarter ended Sep 30 2017, net income decreased 17.7% to US$5.7 million from US$6.9 million in the year-earlier quarter. Revenues were US$94.0 million, up 2.9% from US$91.3 million the year before. Operating income was US$7.9 million versus US$9.9 million in the prior-year quarter, a decrease of 20.2%. Direct operating expenses declined 1.3% to US$67.8 million from US$68.7 million in the comparable period the year before. Indirect operating expenses increased 43.1% to US$18.3 million from US$12.8 million in the equivalent prior-year period.

Prospects: Our evaluation of Gorman-Rupp Co. as of Jan. 21, 2018 is the result of our systematic analysis on three basic characteristics: earnings strength, relative valuation, and recent stock price movement. The company has managed to produce a neutral trend in earnings per share over the past 5 quarters and while recent estimates for the company have been raised by analysts, GRC has posted better than expected results. Based on operating earnings yield, the company is about fairly valued when compared to all of the companies in our coverage universe. Share price changes over the past year indicates that GRC will perform in line with the market over the near term.

Financial Data
(US$ in Thousands)

	9 Mos	6 Mos	3 Mos	12/31/2016	12/31/2015	12/31/2014	12/31/2013	12/31/2012
Earnings Per Share	0.90	0.95	0.90	0.95	0.96	1.38	1.15	1.07
Cash Flow Per Share	1.33	1.68	1.57	2.04	1.55	1.10	1.92	1.24
Tang Book Value Per Share	10.77	10.42	10.12	9.96	9.43	9.22	8.86	7.71
Dividends Per Share	0.460	0.450	0.440	0.430	0.405	0.370	0.330	0.312
Dividend Payout %	51.11	47.37	48.89	45.26	42.19	26.81	28.70	29.10
Income Statement								
Total Revenue	284,451	190,475	92,603	382,071	406,150	434,925	391,665	375,691
EBITDA	38,490	26,560	11,074	52,011	52,548	68,349	57,865	54,513
Depn & Amortn	11,406	7,433	3,754	15,529	15,282	14,615	13,588	12,066
Income Before Taxes	27,084	19,127	7,320	36,482	37,266	53,734	44,277	42,447
Income Taxes	8,469	6,214	2,255	11,599	12,157	17,593	14,173	14,244
Net Income	18,615	12,913	5,065	24,883	25,109	36,141	30,104	28,203
Average Shares	26,106	26,096	26,093	26,087	26,192	26,256	26,249	26,242
Balance Sheet								
Current Assets	225,123	215,481	209,359	203,900	189,391	200,709	189,289	175,675
Total Assets	396,664	393,466	386,288	382,818	364,201	380,904	355,638	335,183
Current Liabilities	47,280	47,951	48,763	49,352	43,460	64,346	60,760	64,821
Total Liabilities	77,655	79,076	79,513	79,930	77,180	98,937	91,498	100,464
Stockholders' Equity	319,009	314,390	306,775	302,888	287,021	281,967	264,140	234,719
Shares Outstanding	26,106	26,099	26,093	26,093	26,083	26,260	26,253	26,246
Statistical Record								
Return on Assets %	6.04	6.50	6.25	6.64	6.74	9.81	8.72	8.87
Return on Equity %	7.63	8.15	7.90	8.41	8.83	13.24	12.07	12.51
EBITDA Margin %	13.53	13.94	11.96	13.61	12.94	15.72	14.77	14.51
Net Margin %	6.54	6.78	5.47	6.51	6.18	8.31	7.69	7.51
Asset Turnover	0.97	0.98	0.99	1.02	1.09	1.18	1.13	1.18
Current Ratio	4.76	4.49	4.29	4.13	4.36	3.12	3.12	2.71
Price Range	33.94-22.34	33.94-22.34	33.94-22.34	33.94-21.26	32.12-22.19	39.18-28.87	34.13-21.44	27.51-20.89
P/E Ratio	37.71-24.82	35.73-23.52	37.71-24.82	35.73-22.38	33.46-23.11	28.39-20.92	29.68-18.64	25.71-19.52
Average Yield %	1.60	1.59	1.54	1.59	1.47	1.23	1.23	1.35

Address: 600 South Airport Road, Mansfield, OH 44903
Telephone: 419-755-1011
Fax: 419-755-1233

Web Site: www.gormanrupp.com
Officers: James C. Gorman - Chairman Jeffrey S. Gorman - President, Chief Executive Officer

Auditors: Ernst & Young LLP
Investor Contact: 419-755-1397
Transfer Agents: Broadridge Corporate Issuer Solutions, Inc., Brentwood, NY

GRACE (WR) & CO

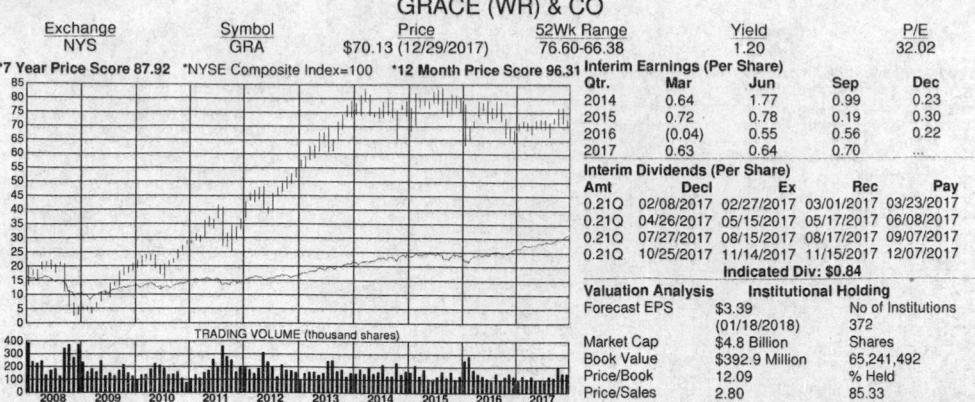

Exchange	Symbol	Price	52Wk Range	Yield	P/E
NYS	GRA	$70.13 (12/29/2017)	76.60-66.38	1.20	32.02

*7 Year Price Score 87.92   *NYSE Composite Index=100   *12 Month Price Score 96.31

Interim Earnings (Per Share)

Qtr.	Mar	Jun	Sep	Dec
2014	0.64	1.77	0.99	0.23
2015	0.72	0.78	0.19	0.30
2016	(0.04)	0.55	0.56	0.22
2017	0.63	0.64	0.70	...

Interim Dividends (Per Share)

Amt	Decl	Ex	Rec	Pay
0.21Q	02/08/2017	02/27/2017	03/01/2017	03/23/2017
0.21Q	04/26/2017	05/15/2017	05/17/2017	06/08/2017
0.21Q	07/27/2017	08/15/2017	08/17/2017	09/07/2017
0.21Q	10/25/2017	11/14/2017	11/15/2017	12/07/2017

Indicated Div: $0.84

Valuation Analysis

	Institutional Holding	
Forecast EPS	$3.39 (01/18/2018)	No of Institutions 372
Market Cap	$4.8 Billion	Shares
Book Value	$392.9 Million	65,241,492
Price/Book	12.09	% Held
Price/Sales	2.80	85.33

Business Summary: Specialty Chemicals (MIC: 8.3.2 SIC: 2819 NAIC: 331311)

Grace (W.R.) is engaged in the production and sale of specialty chemicals and specialty materials through two reportable business segments: Grace Catalysts Technologies; and Grace Materials Technologies. Grace Catalysts Technologies produces and sells catalysts and related products and technologies used in refining, petrochemical and other chemical manufacturing applications. Grace Materials Technologies produces and sells specialty materials, including silica-based and silica-alumina-based materials, used in coatings, consumer, industrial, and pharmaceutical applications, as follows: coatings and print media applications, consumer/pharma applications, and chemical Process applications.

Recent Developments: For the quarter ended Sep 30 2017, income from continuing operations increased 14.0% to US$47.1 million from US$41.3 million in the year-earlier quarter. Net income increased 18.6% to US$47.1 million from US$39.7 million in the year-earlier quarter. Revenues were US$429.5 million, up 6.2% from US$404.5 million the year before. Direct operating expenses rose 8.4% to US$256.2 million from US$236.3 million in the comparable period the year before. Indirect operating expenses increased 6.6% to US$114.6 million from US$107.5 million in the equivalent prior-year period.

Prospects: Our evaluation of Grace (W.R.) Co. as of Jan. 14, 2018 is the result of our systematic analysis on three basic characteristics: earnings strength, relative valuation, and recent stock price movement. The company has generated a negative trend in earnings per share over the past 5 quarters and while recent estimates for the company have been mixed, GRA has posted better than expected results. Based on operating earnings yield, the company is undervalued when compared to all of the companies in our coverage universe. Share price changes over the past year indicates that GRA will perform in line with the market over the near term.

Financial Data
(US$ in Thousands)

	9 Mos	6 Mos	3 Mos	12/31/2016	12/31/2015	12/31/2014	12/31/2013	12/31/2012
Earnings Per Share	2.19	2.05	1.96	1.33	1.99	3.63	3.30	1.23
Cash Flow Per Share	4.82	3.97	3.42	3.81	0.19	(19.55)	6.75	6.04
Tang Book Value Per Share	N.M.	N.M.	N.M.	N.M.	N.M.	N.M.	N.M.	0.38
Dividends Per Share	0.800	0.760	0.720	0.510	...	...	...	...
Dividend Payout %	36.53	37.07	36.73	38.35	...	...	...	...
Income Statement								
Total Revenue	1,257,000	827,500	398,000	1,598,600	3,051,500	3,243,000	3,060,700	3,155,500
EBITDA	307,100	203,900	100,300	302,400	499,400	552,900	490,100	194,000
Depn & Amortn	82,600	54,200	27,100	85,700	109,300	112,500	108,600	108,200
Income Before Taxes	164,800	110,900	53,900	136,200	289,200	314,600	337,700	39,300
Income Taxes	49,200	37,600	18,000	59,000	164,700	57,000	102,900	(37,300)
Net Income	134,200	86,800	42,900	94,100	144,200	276,300	256,100	94,100
Average Shares	68,000	68,400	68,500	70,500	72,600	76,200	77,700	76,300
Balance Sheet								
Current Assets	715,400	715,500	628,800	654,800	1,184,500	1,690,900	2,294,400	2,440,200
Total Assets	2,985,900	2,989,900	2,890,800	2,911,800	3,676,000	4,095,200	5,396,100	5,090,200
Current Liabilities	449,600	470,000	434,000	480,800	707,400	1,182,100	635,600	646,300
Long-Term Obligations	1,521,900	1,516,500	1,511,000	1,507,600	2,144,300	1,919,000	29,600	35,800
Total Liabilities	2,593,000	2,587,500	2,498,700	2,543,000	3,468,200	3,729,300	4,835,500	4,781,800
Stockholders' Equity	392,900	402,400	392,100	368,800	207,800	365,900	560,600	308,400
Shares Outstanding	67,758	68,226	68,342	68,309	70,533	72,922	77,046	75,565
Statistical Record								
Return on Assets %	5.00	4.76	4.73	2.85	3.71	5.82	4.88	1.96
Return on Equity %	33.88	31.97	34.92	32.55	50.27	59.64	58.94	40.12
EBITDA Margin %	24.43	24.64	25.20	18.92	16.37	17.05	16.01	6.15
Net Margin %	10.68	10.49	10.78	5.89	4.73	8.52	8.37	2.98
Asset Turnover	0.57	0.56	0.57	0.48	0.79	0.68	0.58	0.66
Current Ratio	1.59	1.52	1.45	1.36	1.67	1.43	3.61	3.78
Debt to Equity	3.87	3.77	3.85	4.09	10.32	5.24	0.05	0.12
Price Range	73.80-63.91	79.10-63.91	79.44-63.91	79.93-63.12	83.89-68.23	83.47-65.35	79.35-53.96	54.98-37.05
P/E Ratio	33.70-29.18	38.59-31.18	40.53-32.61	60.10-47.46	42.15-34.29	22.99-18.00	24.05-16.35	44.70-30.12
Average Yield %	1.15	1.07	0.99	0.70	...	...	...	...

Address: 7500 Grace Drive, Columbia, MD 21044-4098 Telephone: 410-531-4000	Web Site: www.grace.com Officers: Alfred E. Festa - Chairman, President, Chief Executive Officer Hudson La Force - President, Senior Vice President, Chief Operating Officer, Chief Financial Officer	Auditors: PricewaterhouseCoopers LLP Investor Contact: 410-531-4167 Transfer Agents: Computershare Shareowner Services LLC, Providence, RI

GRACO INC

Exchange	Symbol	Price	52Wk Range	Yield	P/E	Div Achiever
NYS	GGG	$45.22 (12/29/2017)	45.63-27.78	1.17	71.78	17 Years

*7 Year Price Score 122.86 *NYSE Composite Index=100 *12 Month Price Score 111.88

Interim Earnings (Per Share)

Qtr.	Mar	Jun	Sep	Dec
2014	0.27	0.36	0.32	0.27
2015	0.38	0.97	0.29	0.32
2016	0.23	0.30	0.32	(0.61)
2017	0.35	0.46	0.43	...

Interim Dividends (Per Share)

Amt	Decl	Ex	Rec	Pay
0.12Q	06/16/2017	07/13/2017	07/17/2017	08/02/2017
0.12Q	09/22/2017	10/13/2017	10/16/2017	11/01/2017
3-for-1	12/08/2017	12/28/2017	12/18/2017	12/27/2017
0.133Q	12/08/2017	01/19/2018	01/22/2018	02/07/2018

Indicated Div: $0.53

Valuation Analysis

		Institutional Holding	
Forecast EPS	$1.46 (01/11/2018)	No of Institutions	508
Market Cap	$7.6 Billion	Shares	63,445,816
Book Value	$720.0 Million	% Held	81.61
Price/Book	10.58		
Price/Sales	5.26		

TRADING VOLUME (thousand shares)

Business Summary: Industrial Machinery & Equipment (MIC: 7.2.1 SIC: 3561 NAIC: 333911)

Graco, together with its subsidiaries, design, manufacture and market equipment used to move, measure, control, dispense and spray fluid and powder materials. Co. has three segments: Industrial, which includes Co.'s Industrial Products and Applied Fluid Technologies divisions and markets equipment and pre-engineered packages for moving and applying paints, coatings, sealants, adhesives and other fluids; Process, which includes Co.'s Process, Oil and Natural Gas, and Lubrication divisions and markets pumps, valves, meters and accessories to move and dispense fluids; and Contractor, which markets sprayers for architectural coatings for painting, corrosion control, texture and line striping.

Recent Developments:
For the quarter ended Sep 29 2017, net income increased 38.7% to US$75.5 million from US$54.4 million in the year-earlier quarter. Revenues were US$379.8 million, up 16.1% from US$327.2 million the year before. Operating income was US$99.6 million versus US$81.5 million in the prior-year quarter, an increase of 22.3%. Direct operating expenses rose 17.1% to US$176.3 million from US$150.6 million in the comparable period the year before. Indirect operating expenses increased 9.1% to US$103.8 million from US$95.1 million in the equivalent prior-year period.

Prospects:
Our evaluation of Graco Inc. as of Jan. 14, 2018 is the result of our systematic analysis on three basic characteristics: earnings strength, relative valuation, and recent stock price movement. The company has generated a negative trend in earnings per share over the past 5 quarters and while recent estimates for the company have been mixed, GGG has posted better than expected results. Based on operating earnings yield, the company is about fairly valued when compared to all of the companies in our coverage universe. Share price changes over the past year indicates that GGG will perform well over the near term.

Financial Data

(US$ in Thousands)	9 Mos	6 Mos	3 Mos	12/30/2016	12/25/2015	12/26/2014	12/27/2013	12/28/2012
Earnings Per Share	0.63	0.51	0.35	0.24	1.95	1.22	1.12	0.81
Cash Flow Per Share	1.86	1.89	1.76	1.59	1.10	1.34	1.33	1.05
Tang Book Value Per Share	1.58	1.16	0.69	0.80	0.06	0.70	1.60	0.65
Dividends Per Share	1.410	1.380	1.350	1.320	1.200	1.100	1.000	0.900
Dividend Payout %	223.81	268.80	385.60	557.67	61.43	90.41	89.29	111.57
Income Statement								
Total Revenue	1,099,885	720,073	340,590	1,329,293	1,286,485	1,221,130	1,104,024	1,012,456
EBITDA	319,301	207,750	96,724	143,045	518,056	357,906	330,369	258,799
Depn & Amortn	33,620	22,362	11,094	28,800	25,700	24,100	23,400	22,200
Income Before Taxes	273,571	177,179	81,575	96,655	474,713	315,073	288,822	217,326
Income Taxes	57,551	36,619	20,843	55,981	129,000	89,500	78,000	68,200
Net Income	216,020	140,560	60,732	40,674	345,713	225,573	210,822	149,126
Average Shares	174,612	173,781	173,136	170,880	177,021	185,235	188,370	185,133
Balance Sheet								
Current Assets	642,399	579,705	556,648	503,362	509,017	859,507	792,593	776,996
Total Assets	1,404,223	1,341,777	1,313,850	1,243,109	1,391,352	1,544,778	1,327,228	1,321,734
Current Liabilities	288,271	264,089	253,707	177,985	194,616	174,480	168,853	151,671
Long-Term Obligations	225,000	236,015	302,655	305,685	392,695	615,000	408,370	556,480
Total Liabilities	684,234	690,215	746,839	669,289	755,801	948,746	692,863	867,620
Stockholders' Equity	719,989	651,562	567,011	573,820	635,551	596,032	634,365	454,114
Shares Outstanding	168,390	167,988	166,656	167,503	167,297	177,595	183,009	182,300
Statistical Record								
Return on Assets %	7.91	6.50	4.51	3.04	23.61	15.75	15.96	13.62
Return on Equity %	15.62	13.67	10.28	6.62	56.30	36.77	38.84	38.50
EBITDA Margin %	29.03	28.85	28.40	10.76	40.27	29.31	29.92	25.56
Net Margin %	19.64	19.52	17.83	3.06	26.87	18.47	19.10	14.73
Asset Turnover	1.03	1.00	0.99	0.99	0.88	0.85	0.84	0.92
Current Ratio	2.23	2.20	2.19	2.83	2.62	4.93	4.69	5.12
Debt to Equity	0.31	0.36	0.53	0.53	0.62	1.03	0.64	1.23
Price Range	41.23-23.37	37.90-23.37	31.58-23.37	28.67-21.19	27.14-21.60	27.14-22.00	26.29-16.95	18.67-13.32
P/E Ratio	65.44-37.09	74.32-45.82	90.24-66.76	119.47-88.28	13.92-11.08	22.25-18.04	23.47-15.13	23.05-16.44
Average Yield %	4.35	4.73	4.99	5.12	4.98	4.37	4.54	5.52

Address: 88 - 11th Avenue Northeast, Minneapolis, MN 55413
Telephone: 612-623-6000
Fax: 612-623-6777

Web Site: www.graco.com
Officers: Lee R. Mitau - Chairman Patrick J. McHale - President, Chief Executive Officer

Auditors: Deloitte & Touche LLP
Transfer Agents: Wells Fargo Bank, N.A., St. Paul, MN

GRAHAM HOLDINGS CO.

Exchange	Symbol	Price	52Wk Range	Yield	P/E
NYS	GHC	$558.35 (12/29/2017)	610.10-514.95	0.95	25.13

*7 Year Price Score 109.35 *NYSE Composite Index=100   ***12 Month Price Score 93.09**

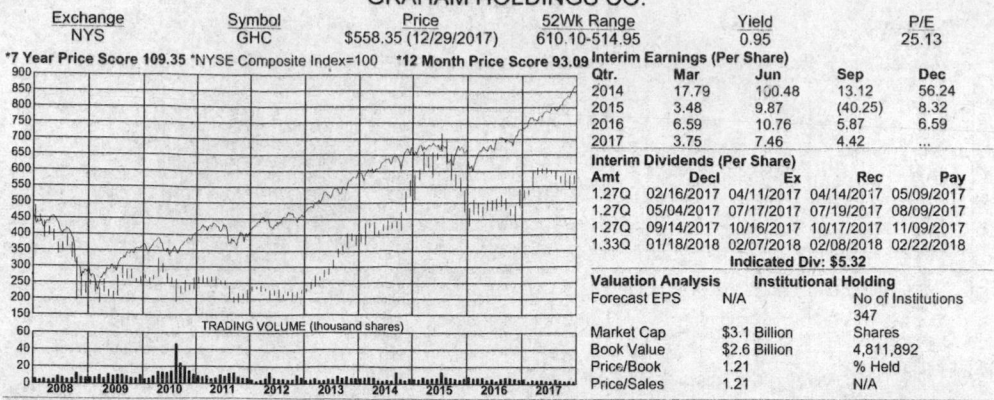

Interim Earnings (Per Share)

Qtr.	Mar	Jun	Sep	Dec
2014	17.79	100.48	13.12	56.24
2015	3.48	9.87	(40.25)	8.32
2016	6.59	10.76	5.87	6.59
2017	3.75	7.46	4.42	...

Interim Dividends (Per Share)

Amt	Decl	Ex	Rec	Pay
1.27Q	02/16/2017	04/11/2017	04/14/2017	05/09/2017
1.27Q	05/04/2017	07/17/2017	07/19/2017	08/09/2017
1.27Q	09/14/2017	10/16/2017	10/17/2017	11/09/2017
1.33Q	01/18/2018	02/07/2018	02/08/2018	02/22/2018

Indicated Div: $5.32

Valuation Analysis   **Institutional Holding**

Forecast EPS	N/A	No of Institutions 347
Market Cap	$3.1 Billion	Shares
Book Value	$2.6 Billion	4,811,892
Price/Book	1.21	% Held
Price/Sales	1.21	N/A

Business Summary: Educational Services (MIC: 2.2.2 SIC: 8299 NAIC: 611699)

Graham Holdings is an education and media company. Co.'s Kaplan, Inc. subsidiary provides a variety of educational services, both domestically and outside the U.S. Co.'s education business includes Kaplan University, which focuses on online education; its test preparation businesses; and businesses in Europe and the Asia Pacific region. Co.'s media operations comprise the ownership and operation of television broadcasting, plus Slate and Foreign Policy magazines. As of Dec 31 2016, Co. owned and operated seven television broadcast stations. Also, as of Dec 31 2016, Co. owned home health and hospice providers, three industrial companies and Social Code LLC, a marketing solutions provider.

Recent Developments: For the quarter ended Sep 30 2017, net income decreased 25.0% to US$24.8 million from US$33.1 million in the year-earlier quarter. Revenues were US$657.2 million, up 5.7% from US$621.6 million the year before. Operating income was US$44.6 million versus US$68.0 million in the prior-year quarter, a decrease of 34.5%. Direct operating expenses rose 20.3% to US$352.6 million from US$293.2 million in the comparable period the year before. Indirect operating expenses decreased 0.2% to US$260.0 million from US$260.4 million in the equivalent prior-year period.

Prospects: Our evaluation of Graham Holdings Co. as of Jan. 14, 2018 is the result of our systematic analysis on three basic characteristics: earnings strength, relative valuation, and recent stock price movement. The company has generated a negative trend in earnings per share over the past 5 quarters. Because the company lacks sufficient analyst estimate data, we place greater weight on the historical EPS trend as the measure of earnings strength. Based on operating earnings yield, the company is undervalued when compared to all of the companies in our coverage universe. Share price changes over the past year indicates that GHC will perform in line with the market over the near term.

Financial Data

(US$ in Thousands)	9 Mos	6 Mos	3 Mos	12/31/2016	12/31/2015	12/31/2014	12/31/2013	12/31/2012
Earnings Per Share	22.22	23.67	26.97	29.80	(17.87)	195.03	32.05	17.39
Cash Flow Per Share	61.24	46.46	55.31	46.87	13.06	57.55	45.30	64.66
Tang Book Value Per Share	164.94	160.59	188.53	207.30	231.59	204.94	195.10	93.42
Dividends Per Share	5.020	4.960	4.900	4.840	9.100	10.200	...	19.600
Dividend Payout %	22.59	20.95	18.17	16.24	...	5.23	...	112.71
Income Statement								
Total Revenue	1,916,029	1,258,804	582,717	2,481,890	2,586,114	3,535,166	3,487,864	4,017,653
EBITDA	223,682	150,223	51,391	382,163	7,530	1,483,888	568,612	429,119
Depn & Amortn	74,815	47,890	21,488	91,271	96,978	222,697	246,798	290,044
Income Before Taxes	126,481	87,705	23,137	258,595	(120,193)	1,226,741	288,011	106,524
Income Taxes	40,000	26,600	2,700	81,200	20,500	406,100	110,000	71,600
Net Income	87,866	63,082	21,086	168,590	(100,655)	1,293,843	236,865	132,113
Average Shares	5,554	5,577	5,569	5,589	5,727	6,559	7,333	7,404
Balance Sheet								
Current Assets	1,617,859	1,597,425	1,759,891	1,871,346	1,860,722	1,690,703	1,702,387	1,453,762
Total Assets	4,619,915	4,508,439	4,416,105	4,432,670	4,352,951	5,752,319	5,811,046	5,105,069
Current Liabilities	813,181	755,224	778,993	818,961	725,149	1,050,792	934,109	1,126,286
Long-Term Obligations	486,242	489,717	487,186	485,719	399,926	399,545	447,608	453,384
Total Liabilities	2,059,238	1,972,067	1,935,527	1,979,729	1,862,253	2,601,510	2,500,314	2,507,945
Stockholders' Equity	2,560,677	2,536,372	2,480,578	2,452,941	2,490,698	3,150,809	3,310,732	2,597,124
Shares Outstanding	5,531	5,592	5,590	5,576	5,803	5,798	7,387	7,427
Statistical Record								
Return on Assets %	2.76	3.01	3.48	3.83	N.M.	22.38	4.34	2.60
Return on Equity %	4.92	5.32	6.17	6.80	N.M.	40.05	8.02	5.06
EBITDA Margin %	11.67	11.93	8.82	15.40	0.29	41.98	16.30	10.68
Net Margin %	4.59	5.01	3.62	6.79	N.M.	36.60	6.79	3.29
Asset Turnover	0.56	0.57	0.56	0.56	0.51	0.61	0.64	0.79
Current Ratio	1.99	2.12	2.26	2.29	2.57	1.61	1.82	1.29
Debt to Equity	0.19	0.19	0.20	0.20	0.16	0.13	0.14	0.17
Price Range	610.10-443.05	610.10-443.05	599.55-443.05	541.95-428.09	718.70-471.59	571.19-370.98	406.93-220.66	241.68-198.03
P/E Ratio	27.46-19.94	25.78-18.72	22.23-16.43	18.19-14.37	...	2.93-1.90	12.70-6.88	13.90-11.39
Average Yield %	0.91	0.93	0.97	0.99	1.50	2.33	...	8.91

Address: 1300 North 17th Street, Arlington, VA 22209 Telephone: 703-345-6300	Web Site: www.ghco.com Officers: Donald E. Graham - Chairman, Chief Executive Officer Timothy J. O'Shaughnessy - President, Chief Executive Officer	Auditors: PricewaterhouseCoopers LLP Investor Contact: 703-345-6300 Transfer Agents: ComputerShare Investor Services, Providence, RI

GRAINGER (W.W.) INC.

Exchange	Symbol	Price	52Wk Range	Yield	P/E	Div Achiever
NYS	GWW	$236.25 (12/29/2017)	258.16-156.25	2.17	27.99	45 Years

*7 Year Price Score 74.23   *NYSE Composite Index=100   *12 Month Price Score 101.07

TRADING VOLUME (thousand shares)

Interim Earnings (Per Share)

Qtr.	Mar	Jun	Sep	Dec
2014	3.07	2.94	3.30	2.15
2015	3.07	3.25	2.92	2.34
2016	2.98	2.79	3.05	1.05
2017	2.93	1.67	2.79	...

Interim Dividends (Per Share)

Amt	Decl	Ex	Rec	Pay
1.22Q	01/25/2017	02/09/2017	02/13/2017	03/01/2017
1.28Q	04/26/2017	05/04/2017	05/08/2017	06/01/2017
1.28Q	07/26/2017	08/10/2017	08/14/2017	09/01/2017
1.28Q	10/25/2017	11/10/2017	11/13/2017	12/01/2017

Indicated Div: $5.12

Valuation Analysis / Institutional Holding

Forecast EPS	$10.72 (01/17/2018)	No of Institutions	844
Market Cap	$13.5 Billion	Shares	59,381,104
Book Value	$1.8 Billion	% Held	69.42
Price/Book	7.62		
Price/Sales	1.31		

Business Summary: Electrical Equipment (MIC: 7.3.1 SIC: 5099 NAIC: 423990)

W.W. Grainger is a distributor of maintenance, repair and operating (MRO) supplies and other related products and services used by businesses and institutions mainly in the U.S. and Canada, and also in Europe, Asia and Latin America. Co.'s U.S. segment provides MRO supplies and other related products and services through sales representatives, catalogs, eCommerce and local branches. Co.'s Canadian segment, through its Acklands – Grainger Inc. subsidiary, distributes tools, fasteners, safety supplies, welding and shop equipment and other items. Co.'s Other businesses include Zoro Tools, Inc. in the U.S. and MonotaRO Co., Ltd. in Japan and other operations in Europe, Asia and Latin America.

Recent Developments: For the quarter ended Sep 30 2017, net income decreased 11.7% to US$170.8 million from US$193.4 million in the year-earlier quarter. Revenues were US$2.64 billion, up 1.5% from US$2.60 billion the year before. Operating income was US$281.2 million versus US$322.6 million in the prior-year quarter, a decrease of 12.8%. Direct operating expenses rose 4.0% to US$1.62 billion from US$1.56 billion in the comparable period the year before. Indirect operating expenses increased 2.6% to US$736.0 million from US$717.2 million in the equivalent prior-year period.

Prospects: Our evaluation of Grainger (W.W.) Inc. as of Jan. 14, 2018 is the result of our systematic analysis on three basic characteristics: earnings strength, relative valuation, and recent stock price movement. The company has managed to produce a neutral trend in earnings per share over the past 5 quarters and while recent estimates for the company have been raised by analysts, GWW has posted better than expected results. Based on operating earnings yield, the company is undervalued when compared to all of the companies in our coverage universe. Share price changes over the past year indicates that GWW will perform very poorly over the near term.

Financial Data

(US$ in Thousands)	9 Mos	6 Mos	3 Mos	12/31/2016	12/31/2015	12/31/2014	12/31/2013	12/31/2012
Earnings Per Share	8.44	8.70	9.82	9.87	11.58	11.45	11.13	9.52
Cash Flow Per Share	18.38	18.08	17.54	16.55	15.19	14.05	14.20	11.66
Tang Book Value Per Share	11.27	10.30	11.55	11.64	19.68	40.08	39.58	35.70
Dividends Per Share	5.000	4.940	4.880	4.830	4.590	4.170	3.590	3.060
Dividend Payout %	59.24	56.78	49.69	48.94	39.64	36.42	32.26	32.14
Income Statement								
Total Revenue	7,792,397	5,156,398	2,541,129	10,137,204	9,973,384	9,964,953	9,437,758	8,950,045
EBITDA	1,004,619	656,785	358,082	1,281,866	1,456,850	1,550,737	1,478,203	1,290,256
Depn & Amortn	194,338	128,195	62,249	166,000	162,000	208,326	180,613	159,049
Income Before Taxes	752,997	492,364	279,047	1,050,251	1,262,445	1,334,386	1,287,599	1,117,789
Income Taxes	267,239	188,057	87,820	386,220	465,531	522,090	479,850	418,940
Net Income	434,671	272,665	174,744	605,928	768,996	801,729	797,036	689,881
Average Shares	57,521	58,287	59,202	60,839	65,765	69,205	70,576	71,181
Balance Sheet								
Current Assets	3,175,060	3,186,347	3,096,183	3,020,229	3,048,642	2,967,549	3,044,285	2,900,640
Total Assets	5,825,060	5,861,881	5,782,549	5,694,307	5,857,755	5,284,252	5,266,328	5,014,598
Current Liabilities	1,392,523	1,410,578	1,688,430	1,628,937	1,788,534	1,261,716	1,195,790	1,080,003
Long-Term Obligations	2,270,001	2,267,872	1,847,717	1,840,946	1,388,414	404,536	445,513	467,048
Total Liabilities	4,057,563	4,138,553	3,987,747	3,896,372	3,591,121	2,074,380	2,015,890	1,990,686
Stockholders' Equity	1,767,497	1,723,328	1,794,802	1,797,935	2,266,634	3,209,872	3,250,438	3,023,912
Shares Outstanding	56,983	57,690	58,405	58,804	62,028	67,432	68,853	69,478
Statistical Record								
Return on Assets %	8.46	8.78	10.11	10.46	13.80	15.20	15.51	14.14
Return on Equity %	26.00	26.92	29.24	29.73	28.08	24.82	25.41	24.34
EBITDA Margin %	12.89	12.74	14.09	12.65	14.61	15.56	15.66	14.42
Net Margin %	5.58	5.29	6.88	5.98	7.71	8.05	8.45	7.71
Asset Turnover	1.75	1.73	1.73	1.75	1.79	1.89	1.84	1.83
Current Ratio	2.28	2.26	1.83	1.85	1.70	2.35	2.55	2.69
Debt to Equity	1.28	1.32	1.03	1.02	0.61	0.13	0.14	0.15
Price Range	258.16-156.25	258.16-169.51	258.16-203.08	239.62-182.78	255.22-190.83	269.22-229.29	274.01-202.37	219.90-177.10
P/E Ratio	30.59-18.51	29.67-19.48	26.29-20.68	24.28-18.52	22.04-16.48	23.51-20.03	24.62-18.18	23.10-18.60
Average Yield %	2.42	2.24	2.12	2.18	2.02	1.67	1.45	1.52

Address: 100 Grainger Parkway, Lake Forest, IL 60045-5201
Telephone: 847-535-1000
Fax: 847-535-0878

Web Site: www.grainger.com
Officers: Donald G. Macpherson - Chairman, Chief Executive Officer, Chief Operating Officer John L. Howard - Senior Vice President, General Counsel

Auditors: Ernst & Young LLP
Investor Contact: 847-535-0409
Transfer Agents: Computershare Trust Company, N.A., Providence, RI

GRANITE CONSTRUCTION INC.

Exchange	Symbol	Price	52Wk Range	Yield	P/E
NYS	GVA	$63.43 (12/29/2017)	66.66-45.71	0.82	48.42

*7 Year Price Score 117.18 *NYSE Composite Index=100 *12 Month Price Score 109.96

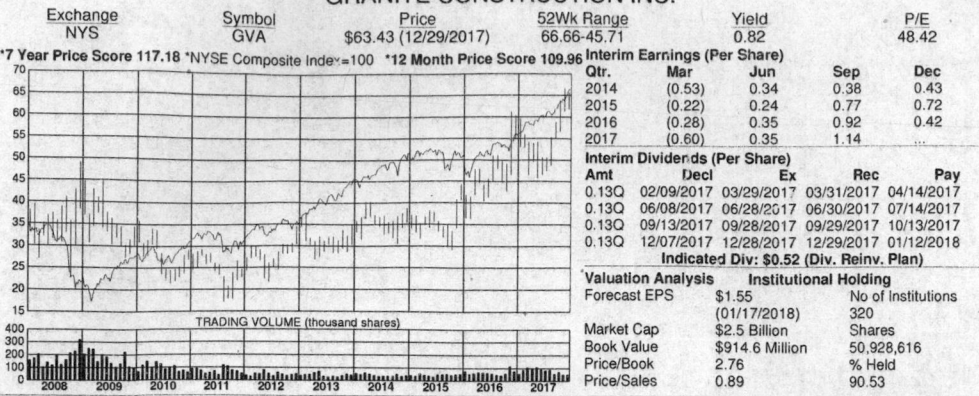

Interim Earnings (Per Share)

Qtr.	Mar	Jun	Sep	Dec
2014	(0.53)	0.34	0.38	0.43
2015	(0.22)	0.24	0.77	0.72
2016	(0.28)	0.35	0.92	0.42
2017	(0.60)	0.35	1.14	...

Interim Dividends (Per Share)

Amt	Decl	Ex	Rec	Pay
0.13Q	02/09/2017	03/29/2017	03/31/2017	04/14/2017
0.13Q	06/08/2017	06/28/2017	06/30/2017	07/14/2017
0.13Q	09/13/2017	09/28/2017	09/29/2017	10/13/2017
0.13Q	12/07/2017	12/28/2017	12/29/2017	01/12/2018

Indicated Div: $0.52 (Div. Reinv. Plan)

Valuation Analysis

Forecast EPS	$1.55
	(01/17/2018)
Market Cap	$2.5 Billion
Book Value	$914.6 Million
Price/Book	2.76
Price/Sales	0.89

Institutional Holding

No of Institutions	320
Shares	50,928,616
% Held	90.53

TRADING VOLUME (thousand shares)

Business Summary: Construction Services (MIC: 7.5.4 SIC: 1629 NAIC: 237990)

Granite Construction is a holding company. Through its subsidiaries, Co. is a heavy civil contractor and a construction materials producer. Co.'s segments are: Construction, which performs construction management and civil construction projects focused on new construction and improvement of streets, roads, highways, bridges, site work and other infrastructure projects; Large Project Construction, which focuses on infrastructure projects such as highways, mass transit facilities, bridges, tunnels, waterway locks and dams, pipelines and airport infrastructure; and Construction Materials, which mines and processes aggregates and operates plants that produce construction materials.

Recent Developments: For the quarter ended Sep 30 2017, net income increased 25.9% to US$48.1 million from US$38.2 million in the year-earlier quarter. Revenues were US$957.1 million, up 19.1% from US$803.9 million the year before. Operating income was US$66.8 million versus US$53.9 million in the prior-year quarter, an increase of 24.0%. Direct operating expenses rose 21.0% to US$842.6 million from US$696.2 million in the comparable period the year before. Indirect operating expenses decreased 11.2% to US$47.7 million from US$53.8 million in the equivalent prior-year period.

Prospects: Our evaluation of Granite Construction Inc. as of Jan. 14, 2018 is the result of our systematic analysis on three basic characteristics: earnings strength, relative valuation, and recent stock price movement. The company has enjoyed a very positive trend in earnings per share over the past 5 quarters. However, while recent estimates for the company have been mixed, GVA has posted better than expected results. Based on operating earnings yield, the company is overvalued when compared to all of the companies in our coverage universe. Share price changes over the past year indicates that GVA will perform in line with the market over the near term.

Financial Data

(US$ in Thousands)	9 Mos	6 Mos	3 Mos	12/31/2016	12/31/2015	12/31/2014	12/31/2013	12/31/2012
Earnings Per Share	1.31	1.09	1.09	1.42	1.52	0.64	(0.94)	1.15
Cash Flow Per Share	3.97	3.76	2.44	1.84	1.70	1.10	0.14	2.38
Tang Book Value Per Share	21.60	20.52	20.24	21.00	19.93	18.90	18.71	20.00
Dividends Per Share	0.520	0.520	0.520	0.520	0.520	0.520	0.520	0.520
Dividend Payout %	39.69	47.71	47.71	36.62	34.21	81.25	...	45.22
Income Statement								
Total Revenue	2,188,439	1,231,313	468,400	2,514,617	2,371,029	2,275,270	2,266,901	2,083,037
EBITDA	105,673	20,208	(20,922)	159,326	173,339	131,883	9,968	138,818
Depn & Amortn	48,522	31,148	14,649	61,000	61,000	64,900	62,700	51,800
Income Before Taxes	52,410	(14,162)	(37,263)	89,185	100,217	54,696	(65,333)	79,041
Income Taxes	16,841	(4,408)	(12,496)	30,162	35,179	19,721	(19,263)	21,109
Net Income	36,325	(9,657)	(23,790)	57,122	60,485	25,346	(36,423)	45,283
Average Shares	40,387	40,393	39,649	40,225	39,868	39,795	38,803	39,076
Balance Sheet								
Current Assets	1,285,967	1,149,557	1,027,534	1,088,992	985,222	970,178	950,203	1,022,057
Total Assets	1,947,288	1,803,145	1,678,219	1,733,453	1,627,860	1,620,494	1,617,155	1,729,487
Current Liabilities	717,191	612,551	501,179	529,934	466,045	462,826	497,570	531,272
Long-Term Obligations	225,922	227,114	228,306	229,498	245,081	275,621	276,868	271,070
Total Liabilities	1,032,732	931,749	818,702	847,465	788,623	826,109	835,215	899,534
Stockholders' Equity	914,556	871,396	859,517	885,988	839,237	794,385	781,940	829,953
Shares Outstanding	39,850	39,837	39,815	39,621	39,412	39,186	38,917	38,730
Statistical Record								
Return on Assets %	2.86	2.55	2.71	3.39	3.72	1.57	N.M.	2.76
Return on Equity %	5.98	5.21	5.28	6.60	7.41	3.22	N.M.	5.54
EBITDA Margin %	4.83	1.64	N.M.	6.34	7.31	5.80	0.44	6.66
Net Margin %	1.66	N.M.	N.M.	2.27	2.55	1.11	N.M.	2.17
Asset Turnover	1.53	1.55	1.55	1.49	1.46	1.41	1.35	1.27
Current Ratio	1.79	1.88	2.05	2.05	2.11	2.10	1.91	1.92
Debt to Equity	0.25	0.26	0.27	0.26	0.29	0.35	0.35	0.33
Price Range	61.30-42.71	61.30-42.71	61.30-40.33	61.30-36.25	44.25-29.12	40.29-30.52	37.54-26.83	34.43-21.66
P/E Ratio	46.79-32.60	56.24-39.18	56.24-37.00	43.17-25.53	29.11-19.16	62.95-47.69	...	29.94-18.83
Average Yield %	1.00	1.02	1.05	1.11	1.46	1.46	1.66	1.89

Address: 585 West Beach Street, Watsonville, CA 95076 **Telephone:** 831-724-1011	**Web Site:** www.graniteconstruction.com **Officers:** David H. Watts - Chairman James H. Roberts - President, Chief Executive Officer, Executive Vice President, Chief Operating Officer (frmr), Interim Chief Operating Officer, Division Officer	**Auditors:** PricewaterhouseCoopers LLP **Investor Contact:** 831-724-1011 **Transfer Agents:** Computershare, Canton, MA

GRAPHIC PACKAGING HOLDING CO

Exchange	Symbol	Price	52Wk Range	Yield	P/E
NYS	GPK	$15.45 (12/29/2017)	15.83-12.26	1.94	29.71

*7 Year Price Score 106.87 *NYSE Composite Index=100 *12 Month Price Score 105.20

Interim Earnings (Per Share)
Qtr.	Mar	Jun	Sep	Dec
2014	0.11	(0.12)	0.16	0.12
2015	0.17	0.17	0.18	0.18
2016	0.18	0.24	0.18	0.11
2017	0.12	0.14	0.15	...

Interim Dividends (Per Share)
Amt	Decl	Ex	Rec	Pay
0.075Q	03/13/2017	03/27/2017	03/29/2017	04/05/2017
0.075Q	05/24/2017	06/13/2017	06/15/2017	07/05/2017
0.075Q	07/28/2017	09/14/2017	09/15/2017	10/05/2017
0.075Q	11/16/2017	12/14/2017	12/15/2017	01/05/2018

Indicated Div: $0.30

Valuation Analysis / Institutional Holding
Forecast EPS	$0.65	No of Institutions	348
	(01/17/2018)		
Market Cap	$4.8 Billion	Shares	
Book Value	$1.1 Billion		466,931,808
Price/Book	4.22	% Held	
Price/Sales	1.10		74.27

Business Summary: Containers & Packaging (MIC: 8.1.3 SIC: 2657 NAIC: 322212)

Graphic Packaging Holding is a provider of paper-based packaging solutions for a range of products to food, beverage and other consumer products companies. Co. is a producer of folding cartons. Co. operates in three geographic areas: Americas, Europe and Asia Pacific. Co. has three segments: Paperboard Mills, which produces primarily coated unbleached kraft and coated recycled board; Americas Paperboard Packaging, which includes paperboard packaging folding cartons sold primarily to Consumer Packaged Goods (CPG) companies in the Americas; and Europe Paperboard Packaging, which includes paperboard packaging folding cartons sold primarily to CPG companies in Europe.

Recent Developments: For the quarter ended June 30 2017, net income decreased 46.0% to US$42.0 million from US$77.8 million in the year-earlier quarter. Revenues were US$1.09 billion, down 0.8% from US$1.10 billion the year before. Operating income was US$87.6 million versus US$105.6 million in the prior-year quarter, a decrease of 17.0%. Direct operating expenses rose 2.2% to US$917.8 million from US$898.4 million in the comparable period the year before. Indirect operating expenses decreased 10.0% to US$89.3 million from US$99.2 million in the equivalent prior-year period.

Prospects: Our evaluation of Graphic Packaging Holding Co. as of Jan. 14, 2018 is the result of our systematic analysis on three basic characteristics: earnings strength, relative valuation, and recent stock price movement. The company has enjoyed a very positive trend in earnings per share over the past 5 quarters. However, while recent estimates for the company have been mixed, GPK has posted results that fell short of analysts expectations. Based on operating earnings yield, the company is about fairly valued when compared to all of the companies in our coverage universe. Share price changes over the past year indicates that GPK will perform poorly over the near term.

Financial Data
(US$ in Thousands)	9 Mos	6 Mos	3 Mos	12/31/2016	12/31/2015	12/31/2014	12/31/2013	12/31/2012
Earnings Per Share	0.52	0.55	0.65	0.71	0.70	0.27	0.42	0.31
Cash Flow Per Share	1.78	1.80	1.95	1.99	1.79	1.60	1.32	1.19
Dividends Per Share	0.300	0.275	0.250	0.225	0.200	...	...	...
Dividend Payout %	57.69	50.00	38.46	31.69	28.57	...	...	...
Income Statement								
Total Revenue	3,293,800	2,156,200	1,061,500	4,298,100	4,160,200	4,240,500	4,478,100	4,337,100
EBITDA	495,700	313,300	150,500	636,000	654,700	435,000	547,000	534,100
Depn & Amortn	237,200	150,200	75,000	240,000	227,600	221,600	232,500	222,700
Income Before Taxes	192,100	119,300	54,200	319,400	359,300	132,700	212,600	200,300
Income Taxes	67,100	41,200	17,600	93,200	130,400	45,400	67,400	82,500
Net Income	126,300	79,000	37,000	228,000	230,100	89,700	146,600	122,600
Average Shares	310,900	311,100	314,100	321,500	330,700	330,500	349,700	396,200
Balance Sheet								
Current Assets	1,222,600	1,152,000	1,145,300	1,114,900	1,066,800	1,220,900	1,232,200	1,203,100
Total Assets	4,839,800	4,691,400	4,661,800	4,603,400	4,256,100	4,331,300	4,559,300	4,620,800
Current Liabilities	817,400	769,300	757,400	779,800	732,200	676,700	711,200	752,900
Long-Term Obligations	2,225,200	2,165,700	2,183,800	2,088,500	1,838,900	1,942,100	2,176,200	2,253,500
Total Liabilities	3,706,100	3,594,700	3,581,000	3,546,900	3,154,400	3,319,000	3,497,000	3,646,800
Stockholders' Equity	1,133,700	1,096,700	1,080,800	1,056,500	1,101,700	1,012,300	1,062,300	974,000
Shares Outstanding	309,713	310,108	311,283	313,533	324,688	327,044	324,746	344,534
Statistical Record								
Return on Assets %	3.37	3.65	4.44	5.13	5.36	2.02	3.19	2.64
Return on Equity %	14.38	15.73	19.03	21.07	21.77	8.65	14.40	11.42
EBITDA Margin %	15.05	14.53	14.18	14.80	15.74	10.26	12.22	12.31
Net Margin %	3.83	3.66	3.49	5.30	5.53	2.12	3.27	2.83
Asset Turnover	0.91	0.92	0.92	0.97	0.97	0.95	0.98	0.93
Current Ratio	1.50	1.50	1.51	1.43	1.46	1.80	1.73	1.60
Debt to Equity	1.96	1.97	2.02	1.98	1.67	1.92	2.05	2.31
Price Range	14.15-12.26	14.60-12.26	14.60-12.06	14.60-10.74	15.75-12.24	14.05-9.17	9.60-6.46	6.50-4.49
P/E Ratio	27.21-23.58	26.55-22.29	22.46-18.55	20.56-15.13	22.50-17.49	52.04-33.96	22.86-15.38	20.97-14.48
Average Yield %	2.27	2.07	1.90	1.73	1.41	...	...	...

Address: 1500 Riveredge Parkway, Suite 100, Atlanta, GA 30328
Telephone: 770-240-7200

Web Site: www.graphicpkg.com
Officers: Philip R. Martens - Chairman Stephen M. Humphrey - Vice-Chairman

Auditors: Ernst & Young LLP
Transfer Agents: Broadridge Corporate Issuer Solutions, Inc., Ardmore, PA

GREAT PLAINS ENERGY INC

Exchange NYS	Symbol GXP	Price $32.24 (12/29/2017)	52Wk Range 34.70-26.87	Yield 3.41	P/E 169.68

*7 Year Price Score 93.99 *NYSE Composite Index=100 *12 Month Price Score 104.37

Interim Earnings (Per Share)

Qtr.	Mar	Jun	Sep	Dec
2014	0.15	0.34	0.95	0.13
2015	0.12	0.28	0.82	0.15
2016	0.17	0.20	0.86	0.38
2017	(0.11)	(0.10)	0.02	...

Interim Dividends (Per Share)

Amt	Decl	Ex	Rec	Pay
0.275Q	02/14/2017	02/23/2017	02/27/2017	03/20/2017
0.275Q	05/02/2017	05/25/2017	05/30/2017	06/20/2017
0.275Q	08/08/2017	08/25/2017	08/29/2017	09/20/2017
0.275Q	10/31/2017	11/28/2017	11/29/2017	12/20/2017

Indicated Div: $1.10 (Div. Reinv. Plan)

Valuation Analysis

Forecast EPS	$1.72 (01/17/2018)
Market Cap	$7.0 Billion
Book Value	$5.1 Billion
Price/Book	1.36
Price/Sales	2.59

Institutional Holding

No of Institutions	527
Shares	224,198,944
% Held	84.43

Business Summary: Electric Utilities (MIC: 3.1.1 SIC: 4911 NAIC: 221122)

Great Plains Energy is a public utility holding company. Co.'s wholly owned direct subsidiaries with operations are as follows: Kansas City Power & Light Co., a regulated electric utility that provides electricity to customers primarily in Missouri and Kansas; and KCP&L Greater Missouri Operations Co., a regulated electric utility that provides electricity to customers in Missouri and regulated steam service to certain customers in St. Joseph, MO. Co. also wholly owns GPE Transmission Holding Company, LLC (GPETHC), which owns 13.5% of Transource Energy, LLC, and focuses on developing electric transmission projects.

Recent Developments: For the quarter ended Sep 30 2017, net income decreased 92.1% to US$10.5 million from US$133.6 million in the year-earlier quarter. Revenues were US$857.2 million, up 0.0% from US$856.8 million the year before. Operating income was US$305.9 million versus US$281.9 million in the prior-year quarter, an increase of 8.5%. Direct operating expenses declined 5.1% to US$394.6 million from US$415.6 million in the comparable period the year before. Indirect operating expenses decreased 1.6% to US$156.7 million from US$159.3 million in the equivalent prior-year period.

Prospects: Our evaluation of Great Plains Energy Inc. as of Jan. 14, 2018 is the result of our systematic analysis on three basic characteristics: earnings strength, relative valuation, and recent stock price movement. The company has suffered a very negative trend in earnings per share over the past 5 quarters. However, while recent estimates for the company have been mixed, GXP has posted better than expected results. Based on operating earnings yield, the company is overvalued when compared to all of the companies in our coverage universe. Share price changes over the past year indicates that GXP will perform very well over the near term.

Financial Data

(US$ in Thousands)	9 Mos	6 Mos	3 Mos	12/31/2016	12/31/2015	12/31/2014	12/31/2013	12/31/2012
Earnings Per Share	0.19	1.03	1.33	1.61	1.37	1.57	1.62	1.35
Cash Flow Per Share	3.47	3.57	3.46	4.62	4.88	4.54	5.06	4.55
Tang Book Value Per Share	22.97	23.21	23.58	23.95	22.59	22.17	21.48	20.65
Dividends Per Share	1.100	1.087	1.075	1.063	0.998	0.935	0.882	0.855
Dividend Payout %	578.95	105.58	80.83	65.99	72.81	59.55	54.48	63.33
Income Statement								
Total Revenue	2,110,500	1,253,300	570,700	2,676,000	2,502,200	2,568,200	2,446,300	2,309,900
EBITDA	400,100	239,300	82,800	930,500	833,200	923,800	946,300	856,300
Depn & Amortn	78,200	60,600	32,500	308,800	299,400	376,800	368,300	330,600
Income Before Taxes	79,100	(33,200)	(16,300)	460,200	334,500	358,500	379,600	304,900
Income Taxes	87,200	(15,100)	(5,800)	172,200	122,700	115,700	129,200	104,600
Net Income	(6,100)	(16,600)	(9,600)	290,000	213,000	242,800	250,200	199,900
Average Shares	215,700	215,500	215,300	169,800	154,800	154,100	153,700	147,200
Balance Sheet								
Current Assets	1,860,900	7,249,700	7,258,600	3,059,500	664,200	718,900	767,000	723,700
Total Assets	12,428,900	17,806,400	17,797,500	13,570,000	10,738,600	10,475,700	9,795,400	9,647,300
Current Liabilities	1,292,300	1,613,500	1,816,200	1,384,800	915,700	1,070,800	769,800	1,449,500
Long-Term Obligations	3,312,000	7,571,700	7,275,900	3,365,200	3,745,100	3,488,000	3,515,700	2,756,800
Total Liabilities	7,306,400	11,795,500	11,709,500	7,408,000	7,043,100	6,850,600	6,282,000	6,268,300
Stockholders' Equity	5,122,500	6,010,900	6,088,000	6,162,000	3,695,500	3,625,100	3,513,400	3,379,000
Shares Outstanding	215,661	215,647	215,599	215,351	154,403	154,162	153,866	153,529
Statistical Record								
Return on Assets %	0.78	1.49	1.78	2.38	2.01	2.40	2.57	2.12
Return on Equity %	2.07	4.45	5.22	5.87	5.82	6.80	7.26	6.25
EBITDA Margin %	18.96	19.09	14.51	34.77	33.30	35.97	38.68	37.07
Net Margin %	N.M.	N.M.	N.M.	10.84	8.51	9.45	10.23	8.65
Asset Turnover	0.23	0.19	0.19	0.22	0.24	0.25	0.25	0.25
Current Ratio	1.44	4.49	4.00	2.21	0.73	0.67	1.00	0.50
Debt to Equity	0.65	1.26	1.20	0.55	1.01	0.96	1.00	0.82
Price Range	31.58-26.20	31.22-26.20	32.68-26.20	32.68-26.20	30.06-24.16	29.38-23.85	24.76-20.31	22.81-19.54
P/E Ratio	166.21-137.89	30.31-25.44	24.57-19.70	20.30-16.27	21.94-17.64	18.71-15.19	15.28-12.54	16.90-14.47
Average Yield %	3.82	3.84	3.75	3.67	3.76	3.62	3.85	4.08

Address: 1200 Main Street, Kansas City, MO 64105 **Telephone:** 816-556-2200	**Web Site:** www.greatplainsenergy.com **Officers:** Terry Bassham - Chairman, President, Chief Executive Officer, Executive Vice President Kevin E. Bryant - Senior Vice President, Chief Financial Officer	**Auditors:** Deloitte & Touche LLP **Investor Contact:** 816-654-1763 **Transfer Agents:** Computershare Trust Company, N. A., Providence, RI

GREIF INC

Exchange	Symbol	Price	52Wk Range	Yield	P/E
NYS	GEF	$60.58 (12/29/2017)	64.87-51.20	2.77	29.99

*7 Year Price Score 92.38 *NYSE Composite Index=100 *12 Month Price Score 93.59

Interim Earnings (Per Share)

Qtr.	Jan	Apr	Jul	Oct
2012-13	0.43	0.70	0.80	0.63
2013-14	0.51	0.61	0.21	0.24
2014-15	0.52	0.35	0.15	0.21
2015-16	(0.19)	0.53	0.78	0.15
2016-17	0.10	0.61	0.74	0.57

Interim Dividends (Per Share)

Amt	Decl	Ex	Rec	Pay
0.42Q	02/28/2017	03/15/2017	03/17/2017	04/01/2017
0.42Q	06/06/2017	06/15/2017	06/19/2017	07/01/2017
0.42Q	08/29/2017	09/15/2017	09/18/2017	10/01/2017
0.42Q	12/05/2017	12/15/2017	12/18/2017	01/01/2018

Indicated Div: $1.68

Valuation Analysis

		Institutional Holding	
Forecast EPS	$3.40 (01/17/2018)	No of Institutions	300
Market Cap	$2.9 Billion	Shares	29,230,532
Book Value	$1.0 Billion	% Held	47.66
Price/Book	2.78		
Price/Sales	0.80		

Business Summary: Containers & Packaging (MIC: 8.1.3 SIC: 2655 NAIC: 322214)

Greif is a producer of industrial packaging products and services. Co. has four segments: Rigid Industrial Packaging and Services, which provides steel, fibre and plastic drums, rigid intermediate bulk containers, closure systems for industrial packaging products, transit protection products, water bottles and reconditioned containers, and services; Paper Packaging and Services, which sells containerboard, corrugated sheets, corrugated containers and other corrugated products; Flexible Products and Services, which produces flexible intermediate bulk containers and related services; and Land Management, which focuses on the harvesting and regeneration of its U.S. timber properties.

Recent Developments: For the year ended Oct 31 2017, net income increased 78.9% to US$135.1 million from US$75.5 million in the prior year. Revenues were US$3.64 billion, up 9.5% from US$3.32 billion the year before. Operating income was US$272.4 million versus US$225.6 million in the prior year, an increase of 20.7%. Direct operating expenses rose 10.8% to US$2.92 billion from US$2.64 billion in the comparable period the year before. Indirect operating expenses decreased 3.7% to US$442.3 million from US$459.3 million in the equivalent prior-year period.

Prospects: Our evaluation of Greif Bros. Corp. as of Jan. 14, 2018 is the result of our systematic analysis on three basic characteristics: earnings strength, relative valuation, and recent stock price movement. The company has produced a positive trend in earnings per share over the past 5 quarters. However, while recent estimates for the company have been mixed, GEF has posted better than expected results. Based on operating earnings yield, the company is undervalued when compared to all of the companies in our coverage universe. Share price changes over the past year indicates that GEF will perform well over the near term.

Financial Data

(US$ in Thousands)	10/31/2017	10/31/2016	10/31/2015	10/31/2014	10/31/2013	10/31/2012	10/31/2011	10/31/2010
Earnings Per Share	2.02	1.28	1.23	1.56	2.52	2.17	3.01	3.58
Cash Flow Per Share	6.38	6.28	4.32	5.49	5.27	9.98	3.65	3.78
Tang Book Value Per Share	3.32	1.72	1.59	2.00	2.08	0.55	0.01	8.39
Dividends Per Share	1.680	1.680	1.680	1.680	1.680	1.680	1.680	1.600
Dividend Payout %	83.17	131.25	136.59	107.69	66.67	77.42	55.81	44.69
Income Statement								
Total Revenue	3,638,200	3,323,600	3,616,700	4,239,100	4,353,400	4,269,500	4,247,954	3,461,537
EBITDA	367,200	324,000	303,000	369,600	459,400	408,400	445,665	416,776
Depn & Amortn	106,800	107,400	113,400	129,800	131,900	131,400	122,700	98,500
Income Before Taxes	200,300	141,200	114,800	158,000	243,700	187,100	243,413	252,489
Income Taxes	67,200	66,500	48,400	115,000	97,600	56,800	71,077	40,571
Net Income	118,600	74,900	71,900	91,500	147,300	126,100	176,040	209,985
Average Shares	25,822	25,756	25,674	25,552	25,400	25,200	25,044	24,959
Balance Sheet								
Current Assets	994,500	920,300	1,008,500	1,154,700	1,094,000	1,064,000	1,305,337	1,165,889
Total Assets	3,232,300	3,153,000	3,315,700	3,667,400	3,882,200	3,856,900	4,207,282	3,498,445
Current Liabilities	687,900	659,200	647,000	851,700	801,700	862,000	929,768	761,811
Long-Term Obligations	937,800	974,600	1,116,200	1,087,400	1,207,200	1,175,300	1,345,138	953,066
Total Liabilities	2,189,900	2,173,800	2,300,100	2,525,300	2,599,000	2,656,100	2,971,931	2,219,724
Stockholders' Equity	1,042,400	979,200	1,015,600	1,142,100	1,283,200	1,200,800	1,235,351	1,278,721
Shares Outstanding	47,843	47,791	47,813	47,723	47,576	47,403	47,092	47,169
Statistical Record								
Return on Assets %	3.71	2.31	2.06	2.42	3.81	3.12	4.57	6.65
Return on Equity %	11.73	7.49	6.66	7.55	11.86	10.32	14.00	17.71
EBITDA Margin %	10.09	9.75	8.38	8.72	10.55	9.57	10.49	12.04
Net Margin %	3.26	2.25	1.99	2.16	3.38	2.95	4.14	6.07
Asset Turnover	1.14	1.02	1.04	1.12	1.13	1.06	1.10	1.10
Current Ratio	1.45	1.40	1.56	1.36	1.36	1.23	1.40	1.53
Debt to Equity	0.90	1.00	1.10	0.95	0.94	0.98	1.09	0.75
Price Range	61.23-45.59	49.59-24.00	48.17-27.84	55.74-42.68	57.43-40.00	56.50-38.90	67.04-41.65	60.83-46.52
P/E Ratio	30.31-22.57	38.74-18.75	39.16-22.63	35.73-27.36	22.79-15.87	26.04-17.93	22.27-13.84	16.99-12.99
Average Yield %	3.01	4.66	4.35	3.28	3.36	3.63	2.82	2.86

Address: 425 Winter Road, Delaware, OH 43015
Telephone: 740-549-6000

Web Site: www.greif.com
Officers: Michael J. Gasser - Chairman Peter G. Watson - President, Chief Executive Officer, Chief Operating Officer, Division Officer

Auditors: DELOITTE & TOUCHE LLP
Investor Contact: 740-549-6000
Transfer Agents: The Bank of NEw York Mellon (Luxembourg) S.A., Luxembourg

GROUP 1 AUTOMOTIVE, INC.

Exchange	Symbol	Price	52Wk Range	Yield	P/E
NYS	GPI	$70.97 (12/29/2017)	83.40-53.21	1.41	11.27

*7 Year Price Score 84.56 *NYSE Composite Index=100 *12 Month Price Score 104.87

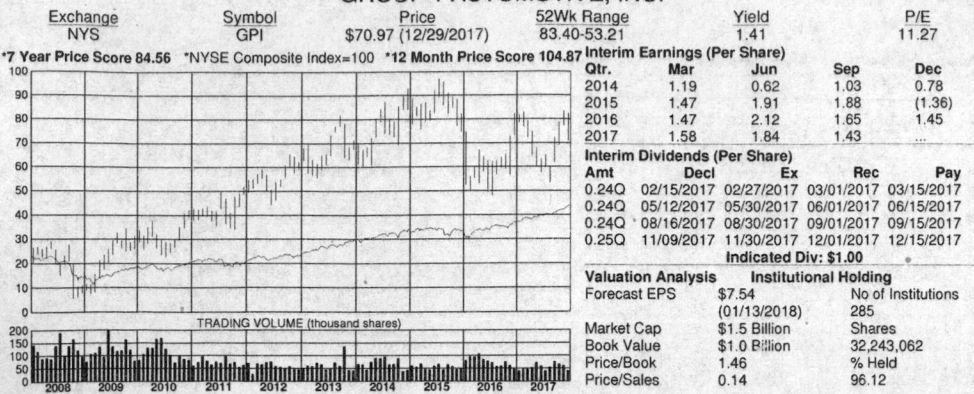

Interim Earnings (Per Share)

Qtr.	Mar	Jun	Sep	Dec
2014	1.19	0.62	1.03	0.78
2015	1.47	1.91	1.88	(1.36)
2016	1.47	2.12	1.65	1.45
2017	1.58	1.84	1.43	...

Interim Dividends (Per Share)

Amt	Decl	Ex	Rec	Pay
0.24Q	02/15/2017	02/27/2017	03/01/2017	03/15/2017
0.24Q	05/12/2017	05/30/2017	06/01/2017	06/15/2017
0.24Q	08/16/2017	08/30/2017	09/01/2017	09/15/2017
0.25Q	11/09/2017	11/30/2017	12/01/2017	12/15/2017

Indicated Div: $1.00

Valuation Analysis   **Institutional Holding**

Forecast EPS	$7.54	No of Institutions
	(01/13/2018)	285
Market Cap	$1.5 Billion	Shares
Book Value	$1.0 Billion	32,243,062
Price/Book	1.46	% Held
Price/Sales	0.14	96.12

Business Summary: Retail - Automotive (MIC: 2.1.4 SIC: 5511 NAIC: 441110)

Group 1 Automotive is an operator in the automotive retail industry. At Dec 31 2016, Co. owned and operated 210 franchises, representing 31 brands of automobiles, at 159 dealership locations and 38 collision centers. Co. owns 146 franchises at 111 dealership locations and 29 collision service centers in the U.S., 41 franchises at 30 dealership locations and eight collision centers in the U.K. and 23 franchises at 18 dealership locations and one collision center in Brazil. Via its dealerships, Co. sells new and used cars and light trucks, arranges related vehicle financing; sells service and insurance contracts; provides automotive maintenance and repair services; and sells vehicle parts.

Recent Developments: For the quarter ended Sep 30 2017, net income decreased 15.5% to US$29.9 million from US$35.4 million in the year-earlier quarter. Revenues were US$3.01 billion, up 6.7% from US$2.82 billion the year before. Operating income was US$78.5 million versus US$83.9 million in the prior-year quarter, a decrease of 6.4%. Direct operating expenses rose 6.8% to US$2.58 billion from US$2.42 billion in the comparable period the year before. Indirect operating expenses increased 9.3% to US$352.9 million from US$322.8 million in the equivalent prior-year period.

Prospects: Our evaluation of Group 1 Automotive Inc. as of Jan. 14, 2018 is the result of our systematic analysis on three basic characteristics: earnings strength, relative valuation, and recent stock price movement. The company has produced a positive trend in earnings per share over the past 5 quarters and while recent estimates for the company have been raised by analysts, GPI has posted better than expected results. Based on operating earnings yield, the company is undervalued when compared to all of the companies in our coverage universe. Share price changes over the past year indicates that GPI will perform poorly over the near term.

Financial Data

(US$ in Thousands)	9 Mos	6 Mos	3 Mos	12/31/2016	12/31/2015	12/31/2014	12/31/2013	12/31/2012
Earnings Per Share	6.30	6.52	6.80	6.67	3.90	3.60	4.32	4.19
Cash Flow Per Share	15.24	13.00	16.45	18.14	6.09	8.48	2.27	(3.47)
Tang Book Value Per Share	N.M.	N.M.	N.M.	N.M.	N.M.	N.M.	1.05	5.03
Dividends Per Share	0.950	0.940	0.930	0.910	0.830	0.700	0.650	0.590
Dividend Payout %	15.08	14.42	13.68	13.64	21.28	19.44	15.05	14.08
Income Statement								
Total Revenue	8,203,316	5,191,024	2,518,829	10,887,612	10,632,505	9,937,889	8,918,581	7,476,100
EBITDA	253,728	174,217	81,049	391,434	325,538	298,007	308,333	261,496
Depn & Amortn	2,852	1,849	912	51,200	47,200	42,300	35,800	31,500
Income Before Taxes	160,029	112,886	51,196	227,371	182,171	164,400	191,895	160,735
Income Taxes	57,076	39,814	17,257	80,306	88,172	71,396	77,903	60,526
Net Income	102,953	73,072	33,939	147,065	93,999	93,004	113,992	100,209
Average Shares	20,225	20,522	20,698	21,170	23,152	24,885	25,314	22,688
Balance Sheet								
Current Assets	2,232,655	2,293,872	2,153,077	2,150,587	2,202,955	2,035,219	1,967,938	1,566,181
Total Assets	4,730,994	4,644,585	4,489,363	4,461,903	4,414,929	4,141,492	3,819,478	3,023,015
Current Liabilities	2,136,283	2,126,854	2,021,275	2,053,117	2,039,470	1,922,199	1,865,176	1,395,578
Long-Term Obligations	1,292,689	1,263,845	1,224,718	1,212,809	1,203,436	1,008,837	663,689	555,016
Total Liabilities	3,719,847	3,672,937	3,520,403	3,531,703	3,496,677	3,163,482	2,755,209	2,130,226
Stockholders' Equity	1,011,147	971,648	968,960	930,200	918,252	978,010	1,064,269	892,789
Shares Outstanding	20,862	20,863	21,472	21,405	23,415	24,339	24,314	22,726
Statistical Record								
Return on Assets %	2.92	3.05	3.25	3.30	2.20	2.34	3.33	3.63
Return on Equity %	14.10	15.14	15.59	15.87	9.91	9.11	11.65	11.76
EBITDA Margin %	3.09	3.36	3.22	3.60	3.06	3.00	3.46	3.50
Net Margin %	1.26	1.41	1.35	1.35	0.88	0.94	1.28	1.34
Asset Turnover	2.38	2.34	2.39	2.45	2.49	2.50	2.61	2.71
Current Ratio	1.05	1.08	1.07	1.05	1.08	1.06	1.06	1.12
Debt to Equity	1.28	1.30	1.26	1.30	1.31	1.03	0.62	0.62
Price Range	83.05-53.21	83.05-48.20	83.05-48.20	82.35-48.20	96.97-74.61	92.94-60.32	81.74-55.45	65.51-44.29
P/E Ratio	13.18-8.45	12.74-7.39	12.21-7.09	12.35-7.23	24.86-19.13	25.82-16.76	18.92-12.84	15.63-10.57
Average Yield %	1.40	1.40	1.41	1.49	0.97	0.93	0.97	1.06

Address: 800 Gessner, Suite 500, Houston, TX 77024 **Telephone:** 713-647-5700 **Fax:** 713-647-5858	**Web Site:** www.group1auto.com **Officers:** Earl J. Hesterberg - President, Chief Executive Officer John C. Rickel - Senior Vice President, Chief Financial Officer	**Auditors:** Ernst & Young LLP **Transfer Agents:** American Stock Transfer & Trust Company LLC, Brooklyn, NY

GUIDEWIRE SOFTWARE INC

Exchange	Symbol	Price	52Wk Range	Yield	P/E
NYS	GWRE	$74.26 (12/29/2017)	82.77-50.93	N/A	275.04

*7 Year Price Score N/A   *NYSE Composite Index=100   *12 Month Price Score 106.39

TRADING VOLUME (thousand shares)

Interim Earnings (Per Share)

Qtr.	Oct	Jan	Apr	Jul
2014-15	(0.04)	0.06	(0.04)	0.17
2015-16	(0.02)	0.01	(0.01)	0.22
2016-17	(0.11)	0.05	(0.02)	0.36
2017-18	(0.12)	...	...	...

Interim Dividends (Per Share)

No Dividends Paid

Valuation Analysis   Institutional Holding

Forecast EPS	$0.88	No of Institutions
	(01/11/2018)	289
Market Cap	$5.6 Billion	Shares
Book Value	$988.4 Million	88,053,456
Price/Book	5.66	% Held
Price/Sales	10.59	97.47

Business Summary: Internet & Software (MIC: 6.3.2 SIC: 7372 NAIC: 511210)

Guidewire Software is a provider of software products and subscription services for the property and casualty industry. Guidewire InsurancePlatform™ consists of applications to support core operations, data management and analytics, and digital engagement. Guidewire InsuranceSuite™ and Guidewire InsuranceNow™ provide transactional systems of record that support the insurance lifecycle. Guidewire InsuranceSuite is a system comprised of three primary applications (ClaimCenter, PolicyCenter and BillingCenter) that can be deployed on-premise or in the cloud. Guidewire InsuranceNow is a cloud-based system that provides policy, billing and claims management functionality to insurers.

Recent Developments: For the quarter ended Oct 31 2017, net loss amounted to US$8.9 million versus a net loss of US$7.9 million in the year-earlier quarter. Revenues were US$108.2 million, up 14.9% from US$94.1 million the year before. Operating loss was US$32.7 million versus a loss of US$18.3 million in the prior-year quarter. Direct operating expenses rose 49.7% to US$62.9 million from US$42.0 million in the comparable period the year before. Indirect operating expenses increased 10.8% to US$78.0 million from US$70.4 million in the equivalent prior-year period.

Prospects: Our evaluation of Guidewire Software Inc as of Jan. 14, 2018 is the result of our systematic analysis on three basic characteristics: earnings strength, relative valuation, and recent stock price movement. The company has managed to produce a neutral trend in earnings per share over the past 5 quarters and while recent estimates for the company have remained steady, GWRE has posted better than expected results. Based on operating earnings yield, the company is overvalued when compared to all of the companies in our coverage universe. Share price changes over the past year indicates that GWRE will perform very well over the near term.

Financial Data (US$ in Thousands)	3 Mos	07/31/2017	07/31/2016	07/31/2015	07/31/2014	07/31/2013	07/31/2012	07/31/2011
Earnings Per Share	0.27	0.28	0.20	0.14	0.21	0.25	0.25	0.76
Cash Flow Per Share	1.58	1.85	1.38	0.91	1.15	0.58	0.49	1.97
Tang Book Value Per Share	10.35	9.07	10.13	9.52	9.21	3.67	3.41	...
Income Statement								
Total Revenue	108,171	514,284	424,446	380,537	350,246	300,649	232,061	172,472
EBITDA	(30,867)	34,023	22,432	20,495	23,896	21,214	25,471	9,640
Depn & Amortn	2,110	6,600	6,500	6,000	5,300	4,500	2,600	1,500
Income Before Taxes	(31,069)	33,277	20,782	16,740	19,946	17,212	23,179	8,296
Income Taxes	(22,155)	12,053	5,806	6,855	5,225	1,829	7,979	(27,262)
Net Income	(8,914)	21,224	14,976	9,885	14,721	15,383	15,200	35,558
Average Shares	75,187	75,328	73,765	72,314	69,112	61,943	41,509	17,763
Balance Sheet								
Current Assets	667,634	679,240	707,672	661,644	516,430	210,093	262,465	94,842
Total Assets	1,150,148	1,078,901	916,178	799,947	757,227	312,270	284,247	126,540
Current Liabilities	135,432	163,616	119,083	104,409	95,386	74,784	93,187	82,301
Total Liabilities	161,747	185,620	132,243	110,559	106,541	83,841	100,285	108,388
Stockholders' Equity	988,401	893,281	783,935	689,388	650,686	228,429	183,962	18,152
Shares Outstanding	75,362	75,007	73,039	71,005	69,082	57,909	53,956	14,422
Statistical Record								
Return on Assets %	1.96	2.13	1.74	1.27	2.75	5.16	7.38	38.11
Return on Equity %	2.26	2.53	2.03	1.48	3.35	7.46	15.00	...
EBITDA Margin %	N.M.	6.62	5.29	5.39	6.82	7.06	10.98	5.59
Net Margin %	N.M.	4.13	3.53	2.60	4.20	5.12	6.55	20.62
Asset Turnover	0.51	0.52	0.49	0.49	0.65	1.01	1.13	1.85
Current Ratio	4.93	4.15	5.94	6.34	5.41	2.81	2.82	1.15
Price Range	80.06-49.33	72.81-49.33	63.79-43.05	60.08-39.76	57.38-34.85	45.47-24.64	35.37-17.12	...
P/E Ratio	296.52-182.70	260.04-176.18	318.95-215.25	429.14-284.00	273.24-165.95	181.88-98.56	141.48-68.48	...

Address: 1001 E. Hillsdale Blvd., Suite 800, Foster City, CA 94404 **Telephone:** 650-357-9100 **Fax:** 650-357-9101	**Web Site:** www.guidewire.com **Officers:** Peter P. Gassner - Chairman Marcus S. Ryu - President, Chief Executive Officer	**Auditors:** KPMG LLP **Investor Contact:** 650-357-5282 **Transfer Agents:** Computershare Shareowner Services LLC, Canton, MA

HALLIBURTON COMPANY

Exchange	Symbol	Price	52Wk Range	Yield	P/E
NYS	HAL	$48.87 (12/29/2017)	58.21-38.66	1.47	195.48

*7 Year Price Score 82.32   *NYSE Composite Index=100   *12 Month Price Score 90.06

Interim Earnings (Per Share)

Qtr.	Mar	Jun	Sep	Dec
2014	0.73	0.91	1.41	1.06
2015	(0.76)	0.06	(0.06)	(0.03)
2016	(2.81)	(3.73)	0.01	(0.16)
2017	(0.04)	0.03	0.42	...

Interim Dividends (Per Share)

Amt	Decl	Ex	Rec	Pay
0.18Q	02/08/2017	02/27/2017	03/01/2017	03/22/2017
0.18Q	05/18/2017	06/05/2017	06/07/2017	06/28/2017
0.18Q	07/14/2017	09/01/2017	09/06/2017	09/27/2017
0.18Q	11/03/2017	12/06/2017	12/07/2017	12/28/2017

Indicated Div: $0.72

Valuation Analysis

		Institutional Holding	
Forecast EPS	$1.15	No of Institutions	
	(01/18/2018)	1426	
Market Cap	$42.6 Billion	Shares	857,211,520
Book Value	$9.2 Billion	% Held	
Price/Book	4.62		70.89
Price/Sales	2.28		

Business Summary: Equipment & Services (MIC: 9.1.3 SIC: 1389 NAIC: 213112)

Halliburton provides services and products to the oil and natural gas industry throughout the lifecycle of the reservoir, from locating hydrocarbons and managing geological data, to drilling and formation evaluation, well construction and completion, and optimizing production. Co. has two segments: Completion and Production, which delivers cementing, stimulation, intervention, pressure control, specialty chemicals, artificial lift and completion services; and Drilling and Evaluation, which provides field and reservoir modeling, drilling, evaluation and precise wellbore placement solutions that enable customers to model, measure, drill and optimize their well construction activities.

Recent Developments: For the quarter ended Sep 30 2017, income from continuing operations increased to US$361.0 million from US$7.0 million in the year-earlier quarter. Net income increased to US$361.0 million from US$7.0 million in the year-earlier quarter. Revenues were US$5.44 billion, up 42.0% from US$3.83 billion the year before. Operating income was US$634.0 million versus US$128.0 million in the prior-year quarter, an increase of 395.3%. Direct operating expenses rose 29.8% to US$4.76 billion from US$3.66 billion in the comparable period the year before. Indirect operating expenses increased 27.9% to US$55.0 million from US$43.0 million in the equivalent prior-year period.

Prospects: Our evaluation of Halliburton Co. as of Jan. 14, 2018 is the result of our systematic analysis on three basic characteristics: earnings strength, relative valuation, and recent stock price movement. The company has enjoyed a very positive trend in earnings per share over the past 5 quarters and while recent estimates for the company have been mixed, HAL has posted better than expected results. Based on operating earnings yield, the company is overvalued when compared to all of the companies in our coverage universe. Share price changes over the past year indicates that HAL will perform very poorly over the near term.

Financial Data

(US$ in Thousands)	9 Mos	6 Mos	3 Mos	12/31/2016	12/31/2015	12/31/2014	12/31/2013	12/31/2012
Earnings Per Share	0.25	(0.16)	(3.92)	(6.69)	(0.79)	4.11	2.36	2.84
Cash Flow Per Share	2.89	2.82	(1.76)	(1.97)	3.41	4.79	4.95	3.94
Tang Book Value Per Share	7.49	7.48	7.53	8.08	15.60	16.44	13.44	14.67
Dividends Per Share	0.720	0.720	0.720	0.720	0.720	0.630	0.525	0.360
Dividend Payout %	288.00	...	...	...	...	15.33	22.25	12.68
Income Statement								
Total Revenue	14,680,000	9,236,000	4,279,000	15,887,000	23,633,000	32,870,000	29,402,000	28,503,000
EBITDA	2,079,000	1,074,000	568,000	(5,483,000)	1,346,000	7,221,000	4,995,000	5,748,000
Depn & Amortn	1,163,000	769,000	383,000	1,503,000	1,835,000	2,126,000	1,900,000	1,628,000
Income Before Taxes	438,000	(58,000)	(57,000)	(7,625,000)	(936,000)	4,712,000	2,764,000	3,822,000
Income Taxes	81,000	(54,000)	(25,000)	(1,858,000)	(274,000)	1,275,000	648,000	1,235,000
Net Income	361,000	(4,000)	(32,000)	(5,763,000)	(671,000)	3,500,000	2,125,000	2,635,000
Average Shares	873,000	871,000	867,000	861,000	853,000	852,000	902,000	928,000
Balance Sheet								
Current Assets	10,144,000	10,260,000	9,828,000	11,677,000	21,609,000	15,068,000	13,704,000	13,086,000
Total Assets	25,790,000	25,325,000	24,885,000	27,000,000	36,942,000	32,240,000	29,223,000	27,410,000
Current Liabilities	4,601,000	4,068,000	3,842,000	4,023,000	5,359,000	5,883,000	5,026,000	4,752,000
Long-Term Obligations	10,423,000	10,816,000	10,812,000	12,214,000	14,687,000	7,840,000	7,816,000	4,820,000
Total Liabilities	16,573,000	16,408,000	15,934,000	17,591,000	21,480,000	15,973,000	15,642,000	11,645,000
Stockholders' Equity	9,217,000	8,917,000	8,951,000	9,409,000	15,462,000	16,267,000	13,581,000	15,765,000
Shares Outstanding	872,000	870,000	867,000	866,000	856,000	848,000	849,000	929,000
Statistical Record								
Return on Assets %	0.81	N.M.	N.M.	N.M.	N.M.	11.39	7.50	10.29
Return on Equity %	2.24	N.M.	N.M.	N.M.	N.M.	23.45	14.48	18.15
EBITDA Margin %	14.16	11.63	13.27	N.M.	5.70	21.97	16.99	20.17
Net Margin %	2.46	N.M.	N.M.	N.M.	N.M.	10.65	7.23	9.24
Asset Turnover	0.71	0.64	0.54	0.50	0.68	1.07	1.04	1.11
Current Ratio	2.20	2.52	2.56	2.90	4.03	2.56	2.73	2.75
Debt to Equity	1.13	1.21	1.21	1.30	0.95	0.48	0.58	0.31
Price Range	58.21-38.66	58.21-40.95	58.21-34.00	55.07-28.48	49.21-33.40	74.02-37.82	56.26-34.69	38.51-26.70
P/E Ratio	232.84-154.64	...	...	...	...	18.01-9.20	23.84-14.70	13.56-9.40
Average Yield %	1.51	1.49	1.53	1.72	1.75	1.07	1.16	1.09

Address: 3000 North Sam Houston Parkway East, Houston, TX 77032 **Telephone:** 281-871-2699	**Web Site:** www.halliburton.com **Officers:** David J. Lesar - Executive Chairman, Chairman, President, Chief Executive Officer Jeffrey Allen Miller - President, Chief Operating Officer, Executive Vice President, Chief Executive Officer	**Auditors:** KPMG LLP **Investor Contact:** 888-669-3920 **Transfer Agents:** Computershare Shareowner Services, Jersey City, NJ

Exchange	Symbol	Price	52Wk Range	Yield	P/E
NYS	HYH	$46.18 (12/29/2017)	48.63-35.52	N/A	38.48

*7 Year Price Score N/A   *NYSE Composite Index=100   *12 Month Price Score 106.90

Interim Earnings (Per Share)

Qtr.	Mar	Jun	Sep	Dec
2014	0.89	(0.10)	(0.16)	(0.05)
2015	0.46	0.17	(10.10)	0.31
2016	0.30	0.14	0.19	0.22
2017	0.27	0.36	0.35	...

Interim Dividends (Per Share)

No Dividends Paid

Valuation Analysis   **Institutional Holding**

Forecast EPS	$2.08	No of Institutions
	(01/13/2018)	386
Market Cap	$2.2 Billion	Shares
Book Value	$1.2 Billion	48,412,144
Price/Book	1.83	% Held
Price/Sales	1.35	N/A

TRADING VOLUME (thousand shares)

Business Summary: Medical Instruments & Equipment (MIC: 4.3.1 SIC: 3842 NAIC: 339113)

Halyard Health is a medical technology company focused on eliminating pain, speeding recovery and preventing infection for healthcare providers and patients. Co. is organized into two operating segments based on product groupings: Medical Devices, which focused on pain management, respiratory and digestive health to improve patient outcomes and reduce the cost of care that include post-operative pain management solutions, and minimally invasive interventional (or chronic) pain therapies; and Surgical and Infection Prevention, which provides healthcare supplies and solutions that target the prevention of healthcare-associated infections.

Recent Developments: For the quarter ended Sep 30 2017, net income increased 82.4% to US$16.6 million from US$9.1 million in the year-earlier quarter. Revenues were US$401.4 million, up 1.0% from US$397.5 million the year before. Operating income was US$28.8 million versus US$20.9 million in the prior-year quarter, an increase of 37.8%. Direct operating expenses declined 0.5% to US$258.1 million from US$259.5 million in the comparable period the year before. Indirect operating expenses decreased 2.2% to US$114.5 million from US$117.1 million in the equivalent prior-year period.

Prospects: Our evaluation of Halyard Health Inc. as of Jan. 14, 2018 is the result of our systematic analysis on three basic characteristics: earnings strength, relative valuation, and recent stock price movement. The company has managed to produce a neutral trend in earnings per share over the past 5 quarters and while recent estimates for the company have remained steady, HYH has posted better than expected results. Based on operating earnings yield, the company is about fairly valued when compared to all of the companies in our coverage universe. Share price changes over the past year indicates that HYH will perform in line with the market over the near term.

Financial Data

(US$ in Thousands)	9 Mos	6 Mos	3 Mos	12/31/2016	12/31/2015	12/31/2014	12/31/2013	12/31/2012
Earnings Per Share	1.20	1.04	0.82	0.85	(9.15)	0.58	...	...
Cash Flow Per Share	2.67	3.24	3.93	4.04	2.09	3.18	...	...
Tang Book Value Per Share	N.M.	N.M.	N.M.	N.M.	0.59	N.M.	...	...
Income Statement								
Total Revenue	1,196,200	794,800	395,600	1,592,300	1,574,400	1,672,100	1,677,500	1,684,000
EBITDA	117,300	77,500	37,300	130,400	(337,700)	147,300	265,200	266,300
Depn & Amortn	33,000	22,000	11,000	43,000	40,000	53,000	39,900	38,300
Income Before Taxes	62,400	41,000	19,100	55,300	(410,500)	91,200	227,800	229,800
Income Taxes	15,900	11,100	6,300	15,500	15,800	64,100	73,200	77,200
Net Income	46,500	29,900	12,800	39,800	(426,300)	27,100	154,600	152,600
Average Shares	47,600	47,300	47,400	47,000	46,600	46,538	...	...
Balance Sheet								
Current Assets	681,000	654,800	614,400	593,500	676,000	684,900	585,100	593,700
Total Assets	2,148,900	2,124,900	2,086,400	2,071,800	2,000,200	2,527,600	2,484,000	2,534,200
Current Liabilities	319,400	321,800	310,000	324,400	315,200	356,000	310,400	359,100
Long-Term Obligations	580,400	579,900	579,400	579,000	578,100	632,300	...	...
Total Liabilities	968,200	968,100	955,500	969,300	944,900	1,036,400	404,900	478,500
Stockholders' Equity	1,180,700	1,156,800	1,130,900	1,102,500	1,055,300	1,491,200	2,079,100	2,055,700
Shares Outstanding	46,835	46,791	46,695	46,681	46,614	46,535	...	...
Statistical Record								
Return on Assets %	2.66	2.31	1.87	1.95	N.M.	...	6.16	...
Return on Equity %	4.95	4.36	3.47	3.68	N.M.	...	7.48	...
EBITDA Margin %	9.81	9.75	9.43	8.19	N.M.	8.81	15.81	15.81
Net Margin %	3.89	3.76	3.24	2.50	N.M.	1.62	9.22	9.06
Asset Turnover	0.76	0.76	0.78	0.78	0.70	...	0.67	...
Current Ratio	2.13	2.03	1.98	1.83	2.14	1.92	1.88	1.65
Debt to Equity	0.49	0.50	0.51	0.53	0.55	0.42	...	...
Price Range	46.51-31.99	41.54-31.99	41.54-26.71	39.06-23.29	50.41-27.00	45.47-35.82	...	...
P/E Ratio	38.76-26.66	39.94-30.76	50.66-32.57	45.95-27.40	...	78.40-61.76	...	...

Address: 5405 Windward Parkway, Suite 100 South, Alpharetta, GA 30004
Telephone: 678-425-9273

Web Site: www.halyardhealth.com
Officers: Ronald W. Dollens - Chairman Joseph Fralin Woody - Chief Executive Officer

Auditors: Deloitte & Touche LLP
Transfer Agents: Computershare

HANESBRANDS INC

Exchange	Symbol	Price	52Wk Range	Yield	P/E
NYS	HBI	$20.91 (12/29/2017)	25.67-18.98	2.87	12.99

*7 Year Price Score 93.16 *NYSE Composite Index=100 ***12 Month Price Score 87.85**

TRADING VOLUME (thousand shares)

Interim Earnings (Per Share)

Qtr.	Mar	Jun	Sep	Dec
2014	0.10	0.38	0.29	0.55
2015	0.13	0.23	0.40	0.30
2016	0.21	0.34	0.45	0.41
2017	0.18	0.47	0.55	...

Interim Dividends (Per Share)

Amt	Decl	Ex	Rec	Pay
0.15Q	01/24/2017	02/10/2017	02/14/2017	03/07/2017
0.15Q	04/25/2017	05/12/2017	05/16/2017	06/06/2017
0.15Q	07/25/2017	08/11/2017	08/15/2017	09/06/2017
0.15Q	10/24/2017	11/13/2017	11/14/2017	12/05/2017

Indicated Div: $0.60

Valuation Analysis   Institutional Holding

Forecast EPS	$1.94	No of Institutions
	(01/26/2018)	845
Market Cap	$7.6 Billion	Shares
Book Value	$1.2 Billion	397,344,128
Price/Book	6.19	% Held
Price/Sales	1.19	89.59

Business Summary: Apparel, Footwear & Accessories (MIC: 1.4.2 SIC: 2389 NAIC: 313312)

Hanesbrands is a marketer of basic innerwear and activewear apparel in the U.S., Europe, Australia and Asia/Pacific under several apparel brands. Co. has four segments: Innerwear, which focuses on main apparel products, such as intimate apparel, men's underwear, women's panties, children's underwear, socks and hosiery; Activewear, which sells products such as T-shirts and fleece to both retailers and wholesalers as well as provides uniforms for athletic programs; Direct to Consumer, which includes Co.'s domestic Co.-operated outlet stores and website operations; and International, which includes products in Innerwear and Activewear segments.

Recent Developments: For the quarter ended Sep 30 2017, income from continuing operations increased 17.7% to US$203.4 million from US$172.8 million in the year-earlier quarter. Net income increased 17.0% to US$203.4 million from US$173.9 million in the year-earlier quarter. Revenues were US$1.80 billion, up 2.2% from US$1.76 billion the year before. Operating income was US$253.3 million versus US$228.4 million in the prior-year quarter, an increase of 10.9%. Direct operating expenses rose 0.8% to US$1.12 billion from US$1.11 billion in the comparable period the year before. Indirect operating expenses increased 1.0% to US$425.2 million from US$421.0 million in the equivalent prior-year period.

Prospects: Our evaluation of Hanesbrands Inc. as of Jan. 21, 2018 is the result of our systematic analysis on three basic characteristics: earnings strength, relative valuation, and recent stock price movement. The company has managed to produce a neutral trend in earnings per share over the past 5 quarters. However, while recent estimates for the company have been mixed, HBI has posted results that were in line with analysts expectations. Based on operating earnings yield, the company is undervalued when compared to all of the companies in our coverage universe. Share price changes over the past year indicates that HBI will perform poorly over the near term.

Financial Data
(US$ in Thousands)

	9 Mos	6 Mos	3 Mos	12/31/2016	01/02/2016	01/03/2015	12/28/2013	12/29/2012
Earnings Per Share	1.61	1.51	1.38	1.40	1.06	1.32	1.08	0.55
Cash Flow Per Share	1.99	2.10	2.32	1.59	0.57	1.66	1.98	1.86
Tang Book Value Per Share	N.M.	N.M.	N.M.	N.M.	N.M.	N.M.	0.76	1.13
Dividends Per Share	0.560	0.520	0.480	0.440	0.400	0.300	0.150	...
Dividend Payout %	34.78	34.44	34.78	31.43	37.74	22.67	13.85	...
Income Statement								
Total Revenue	4,826,235	3,026,965	1,380,355	6,028,199	5,731,549	5,324,746	4,627,802	4,525,721
EBITDA	711,947	418,578	155,834	827,066	695,811	659,557	588,575	492,836
Depn & Amortn	113,357	71,411	35,950	103,175	103,903	98,202	90,890	93,036
Income Before Taxes	468,406	260,900	77,747	571,199	473,873	464,968	395,801	262,945
Income Taxes	19,804	15,654	4,665	34,272	45,018	60,449	65,307	30,502
Net Income	446,505	243,149	70,617	539,382	428,855	404,519	330,494	164,681
Average Shares	368,160	367,992	375,251	384,566	403,659	306,033	305,469	300,807
Balance Sheet								
Current Assets	3,560,026	3,578,002	3,458,807	3,298,420	2,917,867	2,765,232	2,243,666	2,027,525
Total Assets	7,280,723	7,236,971	7,055,928	6,907,734	5,619,040	5,221,781	4,090,048	3,631,700
Current Liabilities	1,896,629	1,778,588	1,762,494	1,602,922	1,503,909	1,486,620	999,278	875,668
Long-Term Obligations	3,566,547	3,797,245	3,763,119	3,507,685	2,254,162	1,613,997	1,467,000	1,317,500
Total Liabilities	6,049,556	6,158,645	6,097,868	5,683,820	4,343,149	3,835,009	2,859,425	2,744,834
Stockholders' Equity	1,231,167	1,078,326	958,060	1,223,914	1,275,891	1,386,772	1,230,623	886,866
Shares Outstanding	364,571	364,435	364,146	378,687	391,670	300,591	298,366	294,809
Statistical Record								
Return on Assets %	8.28	8.29	8.23	8.64	7.93	8.55	8.58	4.31
Return on Equity %	49.93	53.96	55.47	43.27	32.30	30.41	31.30	21.06
EBITDA Margin %	14.75	13.83	11.29	13.72	12.14	12.39	12.72	10.89
Net Margin %	9.25	8.03	5.12	8.95	7.48	7.60	7.14	3.64
Asset Turnover	0.88	0.92	0.96	0.97	1.06	1.13	1.20	1.18
Current Ratio	1.88	2.01	1.96	2.06	1.94	1.86	2.25	2.32
Debt to Equity	2.90	3.52	3.93	2.87	1.77	1.16	1.19	1.49
Price Range	25.91-18.98	27.90-18.98	29.53-18.98	31.18-21.53	34.58-26.54	28.93-16.04	17.74-8.90	9.13-5.46
P/E Ratio	16.09-11.79	18.48-12.57	21.40-13.75	22.27-15.38	32.62-25.03	21.92-12.15	16.42-8.24	16.59-9.94
Average Yield %	2.47	2.23	1.94	1.66	1.29	1.31	1.12	...

Address: 1000 East Hanes Mill Road, Winston-Salem, NC 27105 Telephone: 336-519-8080	Web Site: www.Hanes.com Officers: Richard A. Noll - Executive Chairman, Chairman, Chief Executive Officer Michael E. Faircloth - President, Chief Information Officer, Chief Global Supply Chain	Auditors: PricewaterhouseCoopers LLP Investor Contact: 336-519-8080 Transfer Agents: ComputerShare Investor Services, Providence, RI

HANOVER INSURANCE GROUP INC

Exchange	Symbol	Price	52Wk Range	Yield	P/E	Div Achiever
NYS	THG	$108.08 (12/29/2017)	108.85-80.59	2.00	38.06	11 Years

*7 Year Price Score 114.76 *NYSE Composite Index=100 *12 Month Price Score 106.31

Interim Earnings (Per Share)

Qtr.	Mar	Jun	Sep	Dec
2014	1.22	1.84	1.22	2.00
2015	1.22	2.68	1.74	1.76
2016	1.80	0.05	2.06	(0.30)
2017	1.05	1.83	0.26	...

Interim Dividends (Per Share)

Amt	Decl	Ex	Rec	Pay
0.50Q	02/21/2017	03/08/2017	03/10/2017	03/31/2017
0.50Q	05/16/2017	06/07/2017	06/09/2017	06/30/2017
0.50Q	08/15/2017	09/14/2017	09/15/2017	09/29/2017
0.54Q	12/05/2017	12/14/2017	12/15/2017	12/29/2017

Indicated Div: $2.16

Valuation Analysis | **Institutional Holding**

Forecast EPS	$4.60
	(01/17/2018)
Market Cap	$4.6 Billion
Book Value	$3.0 Billion
Price/Book	1.54
Price/Sales	0.90

No of Institutions 397
Shares 50,109,824
% Held N/A

Business Summary: General Insurance (MIC: 5.2.1 SIC: 6331 NAIC: 524126)

The Hanover Insurance Group is a holding company. Through its subsidiaries, Co. provides property and casualty insurance products and services. Co. has four segments: Commercial Lines, which include commercial multiple peril, commercial automobile, workers' compensation, and other commercial coverages; Personal Lines, which include personal automobile, homeowners, and other personal coverages; Chaucer Holdings Limited, which includes marine and aviation, property, energy, casualty and other coverages; and Other, which provides investment advisory services to affiliates and also manages assets for unaffiliated institutions such as insurance companies, retirement plans and foundations.

Recent Developments: For the quarter ended Sep 30 2017, income from continuing operations decreased 86.1% to US$12.3 million from US$88.3 million in the year-earlier quarter. Net income decreased 87.4% to US$11.1 million from US$88.4 million in the year-earlier quarter. Revenues were US$1.33 billion, up 6.8% from US$1.24 billion the year before. Net premiums earned were US$1.23 billion versus US$1.16 billion in the prior-year quarter, an increase of 5.7%. Net investment income rose 13.0% to US$76.6 million from US$67.8 million a year ago.

Prospects: Our evaluation of Hanover Insurance Group Inc. as of Jan. 14, 2018 is the result of our systematic analysis on three basic characteristics: earnings strength, relative valuation, and recent stock price movement. The company has suffered a very negative trend in earnings per share over the past 5 quarters. However, while recent estimates for the company have been mixed, THG has posted better than expected results. Based on operating earnings yield, the company is overvalued when compared to all of the companies in our coverage universe. Share price changes over the past year indicates that THG will perform in line with the market over the near term.

Financial Data
(US$ in Thousands)

	9 Mos	6 Mos	3 Mos	12/31/2016	12/31/2015	12/31/2014	12/31/2013	12/31/2012
Earnings Per Share	2.84	4.64	2.86	3.59	7.40	6.28	5.59	1.23
Cash Flow Per Share	16.79	17.78	16.82	17.19	9.99	12.83	8.71	9.11
Tang Book Value Per Share	65.72	65.74	64.05	63.04	61.82	60.58	55.14	54.41
Dividends Per Share	2.000	1.960	1.920	1.880	1.690	1.520	1.360	1.230
Dividend Payout %	70.42	42.24	67.13	52.37	22.84	24.20	24.33	100.00
Income Statement								
Premium Income	3,589,400	2,362,500	1,181,300	4,628,100	4,704,800	4,710,300	4,450,500	4,239,100
Total Revenue	3,852,200	2,527,000	1,260,900	4,945,800	5,034,000	5,067,600	4,793,700	4,590,700
Benefits & Claims	2,369,500	1,491,500	766,500	2,964,700	2,884,100	2,927,500	2,761,100	2,974,400
Income Before Taxes	178,900	170,000	59,000	192,300	439,400	378,000	329,100	28,700
Income Taxes	43,000	46,400	13,800	36,200	108,600	95,700	83,400	(17,400)
Net Income	134,700	123,600	45,200	155,100	331,500	282,000	251,000	55,900
Average Shares	42,900	42,800	42,900	43,200	44,800	44,900	44,900	45,300
Balance Sheet								
Total Assets	15,389,300	14,792,700	14,490,800	14,220,400	13,790,900	13,759,700	13,378,700	13,484,900
Total Liabilities	12,417,300	11,820,200	11,577,300	11,362,900	10,946,500	10,915,700	10,784,200	10,889,500
Stockholders' Equity	2,972,000	2,972,500	2,913,500	2,857,500	2,844,400	2,844,000	2,594,500	2,595,400
Shares Outstanding	42,400	42,400	42,600	42,400	43,000	43,900	43,700	44,300
Statistical Record								
Return on Assets %	0.81	1.37	0.86	1.10	2.41	2.08	1.87	0.43
Return on Equity %	4.03	6.64	4.16	5.43	11.66	10.37	9.67	2.18
Loss Ratio %	66.01	63.13	64.89	64.06	61.30	62.15	62.04	70.17
Net Margin %	3.50	4.89	3.58	3.14	6.59	5.56	5.24	1.22
Price Range	99.63-74.88	91.66-74.10	91.66-74.10	91.66-74.10	86.58-68.18	73.30-53.14	60.99-38.74	41.39-33.99
P/E Ratio	35.08-26.37	19.75-15.97	32.05-25.91	25.53-20.64	11.70-9.21	11.67-8.46	10.91-6.93	33.65-27.63
Average Yield %	2.27	2.33	2.28	2.27	2.22	2.44	2.67	3.25

Address: 440 Lincoln Street, Worcester, MA 01653	**Web Site:** www.hanover.com	**Auditors:** PricewaterhouseCoopers LLP
Telephone: 508-855-1000	**Officers:** Micheal P. Angelini - Chairman Mark Leo Berthiaume - Executive Vice President, Chief Administrative Officer	**Investor Contact:** 508-855-2063
Fax: 508-855-6332		**Transfer Agents:** ComputerShare Investor Services, Providence, RI

HARLEY-DAVIDSON INC

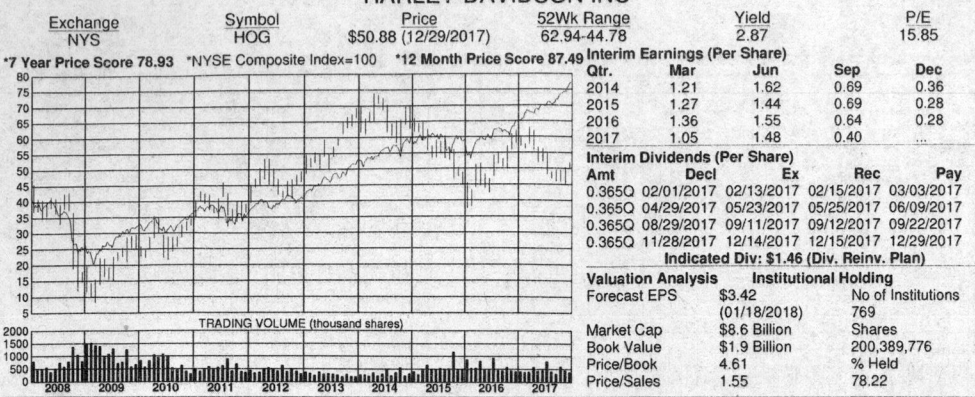

Exchange	Symbol	Price	52Wk Range	Yield	P/E
NYS	HOG	$50.88 (12/29/2017)	62.94-44.78	2.87	15.85

*7 Year Price Score 78.93 *NYSE Composite Index=100 *12 Month Price Score 87.49

Interim Earnings (Per Share)

Qtr.	Mar	Jun	Sep	Dec
2014	1.21	1.62	0.69	0.36
2015	1.27	1.44	0.69	0.28
2016	1.36	1.55	0.64	0.28
2017	1.05	1.48	0.40	...

Interim Dividends (Per Share)

Amt	Decl	Ex	Rec	Pay
0.365Q	02/01/2017	02/13/2017	02/15/2017	03/03/2017
0.365Q	04/29/2017	05/23/2017	05/25/2017	06/09/2017
0.365Q	08/29/2017	09/11/2017	09/12/2017	09/22/2017
0.365Q	11/28/2017	12/14/2017	12/15/2017	12/29/2017

Indicated Div: $1.46 (Div. Reinv. Plan)

Valuation Analysis

		Institutional Holding	
Forecast EPS	$3.42 (01/18/2018)	No of Institutions	769
Market Cap	$8.6 Billion	Shares	200,389,776
Book Value	$1.9 Billion	% Held	78.22
Price/Book	4.61		
Price/Sales	1.55		

Business Summary: Autos- Manufacturing (MIC: 1.8.1 SIC: 3751 NAIC: 336991)

Harley-Davidson is the parent company for the groups of companies doing business as Harley-Davidson Motor Company and Harley-Davidson Financial Services (HDFS). Co. operates in two reportable segments: Motorcycles & Related Products (Motorcycles) and Financial Services. The primary business of the Motorcycles segment is to design, manufacture and sell at wholesale on-road Harley-Davidson motorcycles as well as a line of motorcycle parts, accessories, general merchandise and related services. HDFS is engaged in the business of financing and servicing wholesale inventory receivables and retail consumer loans, primarily for the purchase of Harley-Davidson motorcycles.

Recent Developments: For the quarter ended Sep 24 2017, net income decreased 40.2% to US$68.2 million from US$114.1 million in the year-earlier quarter. Revenues were US$1.15 billion, down 9.7% from US$1.27 billion the year before. Operating income was US$96.7 million versus US$178.4 million in the prior-year quarter, a decrease of 45.8%. Direct operating expenses declined 5.4% to US$760.6 million from US$803.7 million in the comparable period the year before. Indirect operating expenses increased 0.4% to US$293.9 million from US$292.7 million in the equivalent prior-year period.

Prospects: Our evaluation of Harley-Davidson Inc. as of Jan. 14, 2018 is the result of our systematic analysis on three basic characteristics: earnings strength, relative valuation, and recent stock price movement. The company has enjoyed a very positive trend in earnings per share over the past 5 quarters. However, while recent estimates for the company have been mixed, HOG has posted better than expected results. Based on operating earnings yield, the company is undervalued when compared to all of the companies in our coverage universe. Share price changes over the past year indicates that HOG will perform very poorly over the near term.

Financial Data

(US$ in Thousands)	9 Mos	6 Mos	3 Mos	12/31/2016	12/31/2015	12/31/2014	12/31/2013	12/31/2012
Earnings Per Share	3.21	3.45	3.52	3.83	3.69	3.88	3.28	2.72
Cash Flow Per Share	7.04	7.71	7.35	6.52	5.43	5.30	4.39	3.52
Tang Book Value Per Share	10.70	11.67	11.08	10.61	9.67	13.60	13.54	11.18
Dividends Per Share	1.445	1.430	1.415	1.400	1.240	1.100	0.840	0.620
Dividend Payout %	45.02	41.45	40.20	36.55	33.60	28.35	25.61	22.79
Income Statement								
Total Revenue	4,418,296	3,267,101	1,501,932	5,996,458	5,995,402	6,228,508	5,899,872	5,580,506
EBITDA	860,471	739,366	314,511	1,359,069	1,463,875	1,466,782	1,326,633	1,176,523
Depn & Amortn	68,164	44,850	22,154	305,488	301,595	179,300	167,072	168,978
Income Before Taxes	769,012	679,117	284,684	1,023,911	1,150,163	1,283,320	1,114,305	961,512
Income Taxes	255,567	233,881	98,315	331,747	397,956	438,709	380,312	337,587
Net Income	513,445	445,236	186,369	692,164	752,207	844,611	733,993	623,925
Average Shares	170,688	175,324	177,070	180,535	203,686	217,706	224,071	229,229
Balance Sheet								
Current Assets	3,788,142	4,244,602	4,237,920	3,853,852	3,983,154	3,948,095	3,988,803	4,050,936
Total Assets	10,088,359	10,487,771	10,281,855	9,890,240	9,991,167	9,528,097	9,405,040	9,170,773
Current Liabilities	3,216,351	3,354,761	2,556,739	2,862,562	2,752,578	2,389,286	2,509,586	1,503,082
Long-Term Obligations	4,607,791	4,678,350	5,320,797	4,666,975	4,845,388	3,761,528	3,416,713	4,370,544
Total Liabilities	8,231,539	8,441,604	8,288,446	7,970,082	8,151,513	6,618,811	6,395,554	6,613,149
Stockholders' Equity	1,856,820	2,046,167	1,993,409	1,920,158	1,839,654	2,909,286	3,009,486	2,557,624
Shares Outstanding	168,295	170,594	175,038	175,947	184,733	211,876	219,959	226,100
Statistical Record								
Return on Assets %	5.52	5.82	6.05	6.94	7.71	8.92	7.90	6.60
Return on Equity %	29.13	29.82	32.32	36.72	31.68	28.54	26.37	25.00
EBITDA Margin %	19.48	22.63	20.94	22.66	24.42	23.55	22.49	21.08
Net Margin %	11.62	13.63	12.41	11.54	12.55	13.56	12.44	11.18
Asset Turnover	0.54	0.54	0.55	0.60	0.61	0.66	0.64	0.59
Current Ratio	1.18	1.27	1.66	1.35	1.45	1.65	1.59	2.70
Debt to Equity	2.48	2.29	2.67	2.43	2.63	1.29	1.14	1.71
Price Range	62.94-45.93	62.94-42.39	62.94-42.39	62.07-37.49	66.13-45.12	73.94-55.48	69.36-48.69	53.49-39.33
P/E Ratio	19.61-14.31	18.24-12.29	17.88-12.04	16.21-9.79	17.92-12.23	19.06-14.30	21.15-14.84	19.67-14.46
Average Yield %	2.62	2.57	2.66	2.82	2.20	1.66	1.45	1.35

Address: 3700 West Juneau Avenue, Milwaukee, WI 53208	**Web Site:** www.harley-davidson.com	**Auditors:** Ernst & Young LLP
Telephone: 414-342-4680	**Officers:** Michael J. Cave - Chairman Matthew S. Levatich - President, Chief Executive Officer	**Investor Contact:** 187-743-78625
		Transfer Agents: Computershare, Inc., Providence, RI

HARRIS CORP.

Exchange	Symbol	Price	52Wk Range	Yield	P/E	Div Achiever
NYS	HRS	$141.65 (12/29/2017)	144.50-99.99	1.61	31.62	15 Years

*7 Year Price Score 131.62 *NYSE Composite Index=100 *12 Month Price Score 112.09

Interim Earnings (Per Share)

Qtr.	Sep	Dec	Mar	Jun
2014-15	1.18	1.32	1.20	(0.58)
2015-16	1.18	(1.23)	1.34	1.28
2016-17	1.27	1.40	0.69	1.07
2017-18	1.32	...	...	...

Interim Dividends (Per Share)

Amt	Decl	Ex	Rec	Pay
0.53Q	03/03/2017	03/10/2017	03/14/2017	03/24/2017
0.53Q	04/28/2017	05/31/2017	06/02/2017	06/16/2017
0.57Q	08/25/2017	09/07/2017	09/08/2017	09/22/2017
0.57Q	10/26/2017	11/16/2017	11/17/2017	12/01/2017

Indicated Div: $2.28 (Div. Reinv. Plan)

Valuation Analysis — **Institutional Holding**

Forecast EPS	$6.05	No of Institutions	883
(01/18/2018)			
Market Cap	$16.9 Billion	Shares	146,922,320
Book Value	$3.0 Billion		
Price/Book	5.65	% Held	77.71
Price/Sales	2.74		

TRADING VOLUME (thousand shares)

Business Summary: Defense (MIC: 7.1.2 SIC: 3812 NAIC: 334511)

Harris, together with its subsidiaries, provides technology-based solutions. Co. has three segments: Communication Systems, which serves markets in tactical communications and defense products and in public safety networks; Electronic Systems, which provides electronic warfare, avionics, and command, control, communications, computers, intelligence, surveillance and reconnaissance solutions and air traffic management solutions; and Space and Intelligence Systems, which provides intelligence, space protection, geospatial, Earth observation, universe exploration, positioning, navigation and timing, and environmental solutions for national security, defense, civil and commercial customers.

Recent Developments: For the quarter ended Sep 29 2017, income from continuing operations increased 15.2% to US$167.0 million from US$145.0 million in the year-earlier quarter. Net income increased 0.6% to US$161.0 million from US$160.0 million in the year-earlier quarter. Revenues were US$1.41 billion, down 0.5% from US$1.42 billion the year before. Operating income was US$272.0 million versus US$246.0 million in the prior-year quarter, an increase of 10.6%. Direct operating expenses rose 0.1% to US$898.0 million from US$897.0 million in the comparable period the year before. Indirect operating expenses decreased 12.3% to US$243.0 million from US$277.0 million in the equivalent prior-year period.

Prospects: Our evaluation of Harris Corp. as of Jan. 14, 2018 is the result of our systematic analysis on three basic characteristics: earnings strength, relative valuation, and recent stock price movement. The company has managed to produce a neutral trend in earnings per share over the past 5 quarters. However, while recent estimates for the company have been mixed, HRS has posted better than expected results. Based on operating earnings yield, the company is about fairly valued when compared to all of the companies in our coverage universe. Share price changes over the past year indicates that HRS will perform well over the near term.

Financial Data
(US$ in Thousands)	3 Mos	06/30/2017	07/01/2016	07/03/2015	06/27/2014	06/28/2013	06/29/2012	07/01/2011
Earnings Per Share	4.48	4.44	2.59	3.11	4.95	1.01	0.26	4.60
Cash Flow Per Share	5.21	4.65	7.48	7.95	8.03	7.56	7.49	6.67
Dividends Per Share	2.160	2.120	2.000	1.880	1.680	1.480	1.220	1.000
Dividend Payout %	48.21	47.75	77.22	60.45	33.94	146.53	469.23	21.74
Income Statement								
Total Revenue	1,413,000	5,900,000	7,467,000	5,083,000	5,012,000	5,111,700	5,451,300	5,924,600
EBITDA	334,000	1,222,000	992,000	760,000	1,028,300	917,800	1,095,200	1,103,700
Depn & Amortn	62,000	147,000	200,000	155,000	142,100	146,400	143,000	135,400
Income Before Taxes	231,000	905,000	611,000	477,000	795,400	664,500	841,500	880,700
Income Taxes	64,000	267,000	266,000	143,000	256,200	202,700	286,000	293,600
Net Income	161,000	553,000	324,000	334,000	534,800	113,000	30,600	588,000
Average Shares	121,200	124,300	125,000	106,800	107,300	111,200	114,800	126,300
Balance Sheet								
Current Assets	2,127,000	2,073,000	2,608,000	3,524,000	1,991,300	1,948,100	2,600,400	2,216,800
Total Assets	10,099,000	10,090,000	11,996,000	13,129,000	4,931,200	4,858,400	5,592,800	6,172,800
Current Liabilities	1,918,000	1,926,000	1,964,000	2,281,000	1,114,600	1,297,400	1,414,400	1,430,500
Long-Term Obligations	3,395,000	3,396,000	4,120,000	5,053,000	1,575,800	1,577,100	1,883,000	1,887,200
Total Liabilities	7,112,000	7,162,000	8,940,000	9,732,000	3,105,200	3,297,100	3,653,900	3,670,800
Stockholders' Equity	2,987,000	2,928,000	3,056,000	3,397,000	1,826,000	1,561,300	1,938,900	2,502,000
Shares Outstanding	119,045	119,628	124,643	123,675	105,509	106,933	112,147	123,118
Statistical Record								
Return on Assets %	5.06	5.02	2.59	3.64	10.96	2.17	0.52	10.81
Return on Equity %	18.34	18.53	10.07	12.58	31.66	6.47	1.38	25.13
EBITDA Margin %	23.64	20.71	13.29	14.95	20.52	17.95	20.09	18.63
Net Margin %	11.39	9.37	4.34	6.57	10.67	2.21	0.56	9.92
Asset Turnover	0.56	0.54	0.60	0.55	1.03	0.98	0.93	1.09
Current Ratio	1.11	1.08	1.33	1.54	1.79	1.50	1.84	1.55
Debt to Equity	1.14	1.16	1.35	1.49	0.86	1.01	0.97	0.75
Price Range	131.80-88.98	113.82-81.54	89.48-70.28	82.46-61.52	77.55-49.08	51.97-39.95	45.70-33.23	53.13-41.09
P/E Ratio	29.42-19.86	25.64-18.36	34.55-27.14	26.51-19.78	15.67-9.92	51.46-39.55	175.77-127.81	11.55-8.93
Average Yield %	1.98	2.10	2.52	2.57	2.54	3.14	3.08	2.16

Address: 1025 West NASA Boulevard, Melbourne, FL 32919	Web Site: www.harris.com	Auditors: Ernst & Young LLP
Telephone: 321-727-9100	Officers: William M. Brown - Chairman, President, Chief Executive Officer Rahul Ghai - Chief Financial Officer, Senior Vice President	Investor Contact: 321-727-9383 Transfer Agents: Computershare, Canton, MA

HARTFORD FINANCIAL SERVICES GROUP INC.

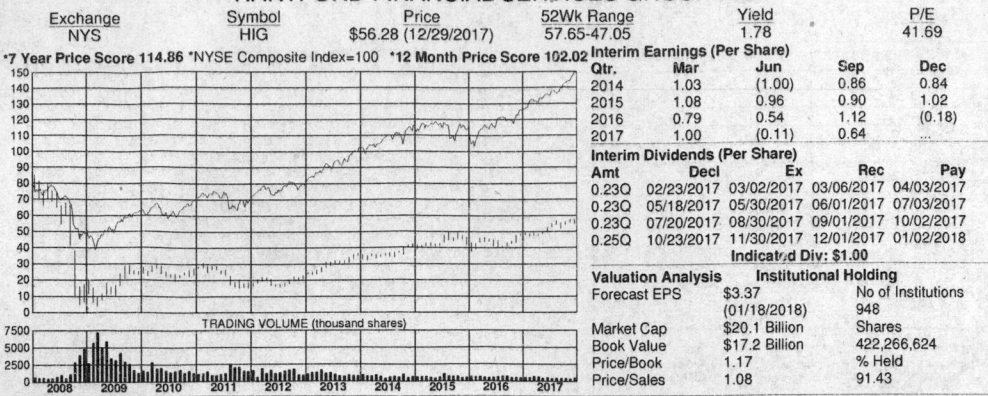

Exchange	Symbol	Price	52Wk Range	Yield	P/E
NYS	HIG	$56.28 (12/29/2017)	57.65-47.05	1.78	41.69

*7 Year Price Score 114.86 *NYSE Composite Index=100 *12 Month Price Score 102.02

Interim Earnings (Per Share)

Qtr.	Mar	Jun	Sep	Dec
2014	1.03	(1.00)	0.86	0.84
2015	1.08	0.96	0.90	1.02
2016	0.79	0.54	1.12	(0.18)
2017	1.00	(0.11)	0.64	...

Interim Dividends (Per Share)

Amt	Decl	Ex	Rec	Pay
0.23Q	02/23/2017	03/02/2017	03/06/2017	04/03/2017
0.23Q	05/18/2017	05/30/2017	06/01/2017	07/03/2017
0.23Q	07/20/2017	08/30/2017	09/01/2017	10/02/2017
0.25Q	10/23/2017	11/30/2017	12/01/2017	01/02/2018

Indicated Div: $1.00

Valuation Analysis / **Institutional Holding**

Forecast EPS	$3.37	No of Institutions
	(01/18/2018)	948
Market Cap	$20.1 Billion	Shares
Book Value	$17.2 Billion	422,266,624
Price/Book	1.17	% Held
Price/Sales	1.08	91.43

Business Summary: General Insurance (MIC: 5.2.1 SIC: 6331 NAIC: 524126)

Hartford Financial Services Group is a holding company. Through its subsidiaries, Co. provides property and casualty insurance, group life and disability products, mutual funds and exchange-traded products. Co. has six segments: Commercial Lines, which provides workers' compensation, property, automobile, marine, livestock, liability and umbrella coverages; Personal Lines, which provides automobile, homeowners and personal umbrella coverages; Property & Casualty Other Operations, which includes property and casualty operations; Group Benefits, which provides group life, accident and disability coverage, voluntary benefits and group retiree health; Mutual Funds; and Talcott Resolution.

Recent Developments: For the quarter ended Sep 30 2017, net income decreased 46.6% to US$234.0 million from US$438.0 million in the year-earlier quarter. Revenues were US$4.68 billion, down 0.7% from US$4.72 billion the year before. Net premiums earned were US$3.47 billion versus US$3.48 billion in the prior-year quarter, a decrease of 0.3%. Net investment income fell 5.6% to US$729.0 million from US$772.0 million a year ago.

Prospects: Our evaluation of Hartford Financial Services Group Inc. as of Jan. 14, 2018 is the result of our systematic analysis on three basic characteristics: earnings strength, relative valuation, and recent stock price movement. The company has suffered a very negative trend in earnings per share over the past 5 quarters. However, while recent estimates for the company have been mixed, HIG has posted better than expected results. Based on operating earnings yield, the company is undervalued when compared to all of the companies in our coverage universe. Share price changes over the past year indicates that HIG will perform well over the near term.

Financial Data

(US$ in Thousands)	9 Mos	6 Mos	3 Mos	12/31/2016	12/31/2015	12/31/2014	12/31/2013	12/31/2012
Earnings Per Share	1.35	1.83	2.48	2.27	3.96	1.73	0.34	(0.18)
Cash Flow Per Share	6.07	5.86	5.10	5.31	6.63	4.27	2.76	6.11
Tang Book Value Per Share	46.61	46.09	44.53	43.69	42.67	42.93	40.61	48.67
Dividends Per Share	0.920	0.900	0.880	0.860	0.780	0.660	0.500	0.400
Dividend Payout %	68.15	49.18	35.48	37.89	19.70	38.15	147.06	...
Income Statement								
Premium Income	10,437,000	6,963,000	3,473,000	13,811,000	13,577,000	13,336,000	13,226,000	13,631,000
Total Revenue	14,108,000	9,424,000	4,655,000	18,300,000	18,377,000	18,614,000	26,236,000	26,412,000
Income Before Taxes	604,000	348,000	487,000	804,000	1,978,000	1,699,000	63,000	(527,000)
Income Taxes	32,000	10,000	109,000	(92,000)	305,000	350,000	(247,000)	(494,000)
Net Income	572,000	338,000	378,000	896,000	1,682,000	798,000	176,000	(38,000)
Average Shares	367,000	366,000	378,600	394,800	425,200	460,200	484,400	437,700
Balance Sheet								
Total Assets	224,211,000	225,863,000	225,388,000	223,432,000	228,348,000	245,013,000	277,884,000	298,513,000
Total Liabilities	206,978,000	208,575,000	208,379,000	206,529,000	210,706,000	226,293,000	258,979,000	276,066,000
Stockholders' Equity	17,233,000	17,288,000	17,009,000	16,903,000	17,642,000	18,720,000	18,905,000	22,447,000
Shares Outstanding	357,540	362,819	369,196	373,949	401,821	424,415	453,290	436,305
Statistical Record								
Return on Assets %	0.22	0.31	0.42	0.40	0.71	0.31	0.06	N.M.
Return on Equity %	2.74	3.88	5.42	5.17	9.25	4.24	0.85	N.M.
Net Margin %	4.05	3.59	8.12	4.90	9.15	4.29	0.67	(0.14)
Price Range	56.81-42.50	52.75-39.85	49.87-39.85	48.58-37.63	49.53-38.90	42.27-32.18	36.62-22.44	22.88-15.93
P/E Ratio	42.08-31.48	28.83-21.78	20.11-16.07	21.40-16.58	12.51-9.82	24.43-18.60	107.71-66.00	...
Average Yield %	1.86	1.94	1.95	1.97	1.78	1.81	1.68	2.07

Address: One Hartford Plaza, Hartford, CT 06155	Web Site: www.thehartford.com	Auditors: Deloitte & Touche LLP
Telephone: 860-547-5000	Officers: Christopher J. Swift - Chairman, Chief Executive Officer, Executive Vice President, Chief Financial Officer, Principal Accounting Officer Douglas G. Elliot - President, Executive Vice President, Division Officer	Investor Contact: 860-547-8691 Transfer Agents: BNY Mellon Shareowner Services, Jersey City, NY

HAWAIIAN ELECTRIC INDUSTRIES INC

Exchange	Symbol	Price	52Wk Range	Yield	P/E
NYS	HE	$36.15 (12/29/2017)	38.35-31.83	3.43	22.18

*7 Year Price Score 93.62   *NYSE Composite Index=100   *12 Month Price Score 103.08

Interim Earnings (Per Share)

Qtr.	Mar	Jun	Sep	Dec
2014	0.45	0.41	0.46	0.32
2015	0.31	0.33	0.47	0.39
2016	0.30	0.41	1.17	0.41
2017	0.31	0.36	0.55	...

Interim Dividends (Per Share)

Amt	Decl	Ex	Rec	Pay
0.31Q	02/13/2017	02/22/2017	02/24/2017	03/10/2017
0.31Q	05/04/2017	05/22/2017	05/24/2017	06/12/2017
0.31Q	08/01/2017	08/21/2017	08/23/2017	09/12/2017
0.31Q	10/31/2017	11/21/2017	11/22/2017	12/12/2017

Indicated Div: $1.24

Valuation Analysis

		Institutional Holding	
Forecast EPS	$1.64	No of Institutions	360
	(01/06/2018)		
Market Cap	$3.9 Billion	Shares	66,143,780
Book Value	$2.1 Billion	% Held	46.77
Price/Book	1.84		
Price/Sales	1.56		

Business Summary: Electric Utilities (MIC: 3.1.1 SIC: 4911 NAIC: 221122)

Hawaiian Electric Industries is a holding company. Through its subsidiaries, Co. is engaged in electric utility and banking businesses. Co.'s subsidiary, Hawaiian Electric Company, Inc., and its subsidiaries, Hawaii Electric Light Company, Inc. and Maui Electric Company, Limited, are regulated electric public utilities engaged in the production, purchase, transmission, distribution and sale of electricity. In addition, Co.'s subsidiary, American Savings Bank, F.S.B. is engaged in the origination, purchase and sale of loans, residential mortgage lending, construction and development lending, multifamily residential and commercial real estate lending, consumer lending and commercial lending.

Recent Developments: For the quarter ended Sep 30 2017, net income decreased 52.6% to US$60.5 million from US$127.6 million in the year-earlier quarter. Revenues were US$673.2 million, up 4.2% from US$646.1 million the year before. Operating income was US$109.5 million versus US$105.4 million in the prior-year quarter, an increase of 3.9%. Direct operating expenses rose 4.3% to US$563.6 million from US$540.6 million in the comparable period the year before.

Prospects: Our evaluation of Hawaiian Electric Industries Inc. as of Jan. 14, 2018 is the result of our systematic analysis on three basic characteristics: earnings strength, relative valuation, and recent stock price movement. The company has managed to produce a neutral trend in earnings per share over the past 5 quarters and while recent estimates for the company have been mixed, HE has posted results that fell short of analysts expectations. Based on operating earnings yield, the company is undervalued when compared to all of the companies in our coverage universe. Share price changes over the past year indicates that HE will perform very well over the near term.

Financial Data

(US$ in Thousands)	9 Mos	6 Mos	3 Mos	12/31/2016	12/31/2015	12/31/2014	12/31/2013	12/31/2012
Earnings Per Share	1.63	2.25	2.30	2.29	1.50	1.64	1.62	1.42
Cash Flow Per Share	3.47	4.19	3.85	4.57	3.34	2.96	3.31	2.41
Tang Book Value Per Share	18.89	18.63	18.55	18.59	17.49	17.00	16.58	15.79
Dividends Per Share	1.240	1.240	1.240	1.240	1.240	1.240	1.240	1.240
Dividend Payout %	76.07	55.11	53.91	54.15	82.67	75.61	76.54	87.32
Income Statement								
Total Revenue	1,897,028	1,223,843	591,562	2,380,654	2,602,982	3,239,542	3,238,470	3,374,995
EBITDA	427,696	255,347	122,684	640,773	513,447	508,457	481,041	441,592
Depn & Amortn	165,485	106,163	52,423	194,273	183,966	172,762	160,061	150,389
Income Before Taxes	206,347	111,208	51,582	373,841	254,788	261,922	247,747	217,407
Income Taxes	72,003	37,408	16,916	123,695	93,021	91,712	84,341	76,859
Net Income	134,344	73,800	34,666	250,146	161,767	170,210	163,406	140,548
Average Shares	108,865	108,797	108,858	108,309	106,721	102,937	99,623	97,338
Balance Sheet								
Current Assets	476,305	471,626	498,352	527,620	553,922	558,540	659,367	678,507
Total Assets	12,742,850	12,693,805	12,543,275	12,425,506	11,790,196	11,184,161	10,340,044	10,149,132
Current Liabilities	5,964,205	5,991,054	5,865,616	5,717,433	5,292,882	4,954,148	4,717,006	4,552,246
Long-Term Obligations	1,771,998	1,806,777	1,818,805	1,811,637	1,915,128	1,797,202	1,737,459	1,618,798
Total Liabilities	10,605,535	10,584,483	10,443,394	10,324,460	9,828,263	9,358,440	8,578,681	8,520,974
Stockholders' Equity	2,137,315	2,109,322	2,099,881	2,101,046	1,961,933	1,825,721	1,761,363	1,628,158
Shares Outstanding	108,785	108,785	108,745	108,583	107,460	102,565	101,259	97,928
Statistical Record								
Return on Assets %	1.44	2.00	2.06	2.06	1.41	1.58	1.60	1.42
Return on Equity %	8.46	12.00	12.36	12.28	8.54	9.49	9.64	8.78
EBITDA Margin %	22.55	20.86	20.74	26.92	19.73	15.70	14.85	13.08
Net Margin %	7.08	6.03	5.86	10.51	6.21	5.25	5.05	4.16
Asset Turnover	0.20	0.20	0.20	0.20	0.23	0.30	0.32	0.34
Current Ratio	0.08	0.08	0.08	0.09	0.10	0.11	0.14	0.15
Debt to Equity	0.83	0.86	0.87	0.86	0.98	0.98	0.99	0.99
Price Range	34.42-28.40	33.96-28.40	34.48-28.40	34.48-27.74	34.83-27.23	34.62-23.22	28.30-23.97	29.24-24.00
P/E Ratio	21.12-17.42	15.09-12.62	14.99-12.35	15.06-12.11	23.22-18.15	21.11-14.16	17.47-14.80	20.59-16.90
Average Yield %	3.82	3.89	3.90	4.00	4.05	4.77	4.72	4.69

Address: 1001 Bishop Streetm Suite 2900, Honolulu, HI 96813 **Telephone:** 808-543-5662 **Fax:** 808-543-7966	**Web Site:** www.hei.com **Officers:** Jeffrey N. Watanabe - Chairman Constance H. Lau - President, Chief Executive Officer	**Auditors:** Deloitte & Touche LLP **Investor Contact:** 808-543-7384 **Transfer Agents:** Continental Stock Transfer & Trust Company, New York, NY

347

HCA HEALTHCARE INC

Exchange	Symbol	Price	52Wk Range	Yield	P/E
NYS	HCA	$87.84 (12/29/2017)	90.49-74.22	N/A	12.53

*7 Year Price Score N/A   *NYSE Composite Index=100   *12 Month Price Score 95.20

TRADING VOLUME (thousand shares)

Interim Earnings (Per Share)

Qtr.	Mar	Jun	Sep	Dec
2014	0.76	1.07	1.16	1.18
2015	1.36	1.18	1.05	1.39
2016	1.69	1.65	1.59	2.37
2017	1.74	1.75	1.15	...

Interim Dividends (Per Share)

Dividend Payment Suspended

Valuation Analysis   Institutional Holding

Forecast EPS	$6.56	No of Institutions
	(01/18/2018)	745
Market Cap	$31.4 Billion	Shares
Book Value	N/A	309,684,224
Price/Book	N/A	% Held
Price/Sales	0.73	N/A

Business Summary: Hospitals & Health Care Facilities (MIC: 4.2.1 SIC: 8062 NAIC: 622110)

HCA Healthcare is a holding company. Through its subsidiaries, partnerships and joint ventures (collectively, its affiliates), Co. owns and operates hospitals and related health care entities. At Dec 31 2016, these affiliates operated 170 hospitals, comprised of 166 general, acute care hospitals, three psychiatric hospitals, and one rehabilitation hospital; as well as operated 118 surgery centers. Co. also operates outpatient health care facilities, such as ambulatory surgery centers, emergency care facilities, urgent care facilities, walk-in clinics, diagnostic and imaging centers, rehabilitation and physical therapy centers, radiation and oncology therapy centers, and physician practices.

Recent Developments: For the quarter ended Sep 30 2017, net income decreased 28.9% to US$530.0 million from US$745.0 million in the year-earlier quarter. Revenues were US$10.70 billion, up 4.1% from US$10.27 billion the year before. Indirect operating expenses increased 7.2% to US$9.92 billion from US$9.25 billion in the equivalent prior-year period.

Prospects: Our evaluation of HCA Healthcare Inc. as of Jan. 14, 2018 is the result of our systematic analysis on three basic characteristics: earnings strength, relative valuation, and recent stock price movement. The company has generated a negative trend in earnings per share over the past 5 quarters. However, while recent estimates for the company have been mixed, HCA has posted results that fell short of analysts expectations. Based on operating earnings yield, the company is undervalued when compared to all of the companies in our coverage universe. Share price changes over the past year indicates that HCA will perform poorly over the near term.

Financial Data

(US$ in Millions)	9 Mos	6 Mos	3 Mos	12/31/2016	12/31/2015	12/31/2014	12/31/2013	12/31/2012
Earnings Per Share	7.01	7.45	7.35	7.30	4.99	4.16	3.37	3.49
Cash Flow Per Share	14.97	15.28	14.95	14.70	11.43	10.21	8.27	9.46
Dividends Per Share	...	...	...	...	...	...	...	6.500
Dividend Payout %	...	...	...	...	...	...	...	186.25
Income Statement								
Total Revenue	32,052	21,356	10,623	41,490	39,678	36,918	34,182	33,013
EBITDA	4,248	3,049	1,483	8,409	7,456	6,979	6,498	6,329
Depn & Amortn	23	16	8	1,946	1,880	1,798	1,733	1,673
Income Before Taxes	2,968	2,203	1,056	4,756	3,911	3,438	2,917	2,858
Income Taxes	902	654	289	1,378	1,261	1,108	950	888
Net Income	1,742	1,316	659	2,890	2,129	1,875	1,556	1,605
Average Shares	369	375	379	395	426	450	461	459
Balance Sheet								
Current Assets	9,448	9,337	9,037	9,086	9,232	8,930	8,037	7,763
Total Assets	35,731	34,566	33,795	33,758	32,744	31,199	28,831	28,075
Current Liabilities	5,611	5,771	5,463	5,834	5,516	5,480	5,695	6,172
Long-Term Obligations	32,751	31,448	31,302	31,160	30,255	29,307	27,590	27,495
Total Liabilities	42,511	41,358	40,812	41,060	40,343	39,093	37,101	37,735
Stockholders' Equity	(6,780)	(6,792)	(7,017)	(7,302)	(7,599)	(7,894)	(8,270)	(9,660)
Shares Outstanding	356	362	368	370	398	420	439	443
Statistical Record								
Return on Assets %	7.73	8.42	8.58	8.67	6.66	6.25	5.47	5.82
EBITDA Margin %	13.25	14.28	13.96	20.27	18.79	18.90	19.01	19.17
Net Margin %	5.43	6.16	6.20	6.97	5.37	5.08	4.55	4.86
Asset Turnover	1.24	1.25	1.26	1.24	1.24	1.23	1.20	1.20
Current Ratio	1.68	1.62	1.65	1.56	1.67	1.63	1.41	1.26
Price Range	90.49-69.58	90.49-69.58	90.49-69.58	82.02-62.83	94.81-64.47	75.00-47.65	48.54-30.17	33.87-20.80
P/E Ratio	12.91-9.93	12.15-9.34	12.31-9.47	11.24-8.61	19.00-12.92	18.03-11.45	14.40-8.95	9.70-5.96
Average Yield %	...	...	...	...	...	...	...	23.25

Address: One Park Plaza, Nashville, TN 37203
Telephone: 615-344-9551

Web Site: www.hcahealthcare.com
Officers: R. Milton Johnson - Chairman, President, Chief Executive Officer, Chief Financial Officer
Samuel N. Hazen - President, Chief Operating Officer, President

Auditors: Ernst & Young LLP
Investor Contact: 615-344-2688
Transfer Agents: Wells Fargo Shareowner Services, St. Paul, MN

HCP INC

Exchange	Symbol	Price	52Wk Range	Yield	P/E
NYS	HCP	$26.08 (12/29/2017)	33.39-25.21	5.67	23.50

*7 Year Price Score 65.45   *NYSE Composite Index=100   *12 Month Price Score 83.96

Interim Earnings (Per Share)

Qtr.	Mar	Jun	Sep	Dec
2014	0.56	0.48	0.54	0.42
2015	(0.52)	0.36	0.25	(1.29)
2016	0.25	0.64	0.32	0.12
2017	0.97	0.04	(0.02)	...

Interim Dividends (Per Share)

Amt	Decl	Ex	Rec	Pay
0.37Q	02/02/2017	02/13/2017	02/15/2017	03/02/2017
0.37Q	04/27/2017	05/04/2017	05/08/2017	05/23/2017
0.37Q	07/27/2017	08/03/2017	08/07/2017	08/22/2017
0.37Q	10/26/2017	11/03/2017	11/06/2017	11/21/2017

Indicated Div: $1.48 (Div. Reinv. Plan)

Valuation Analysis

		Institutional Holding	
Forecast EPS	$1.17	No of Institutions	
	(01/17/2018)	887	
Market Cap	$12.2 Billion	Shares	
Book Value	$5.5 Billion	528,402,944	
Price/Book	2.21	% Held	
Price/Sales	7.76	N/A	

Business Summary: REITs (MIC: 5.3.1 SIC: 6798 NAIC: 525930)

HCP is a real estate investment trust, which, together with its consolidated entities, invests primarily in real estate serving the healthcare industry in the U.S. Co. acquires, develops, leases, manages and disposes of healthcare real estate and provides financing to healthcare providers. Co.'s portfolio is comprised of investments in the following healthcare segments: senior housing triple-net (SH NNN), senior housing operating portfolio (SHOP), life science, and medical office. At Dec 31 2016, Co. had interests in and managed 15 hospitals, 61 care homes in the U.K., five post-acute/skilled nursing facilities (SNFs), four of which were owned by Co.'s unconsolidated joint ventures.

Recent Developments: For the quarter ended Sep 30 2017, loss from continuing operations was US$5.7 million compared with income of US$45.8 million in the year-earlier quarter. Net loss amounted to US$5.7 million versus net income of US$154.0 million in the year-earlier quarter. Revenues were US$454.0 million, down 14.4% from US$530.6 million the year before. Revenues from property income fell 13.5% to US$429.0 million from US$495.8 million in the corresponding quarter a year earlier.

Prospects: Our evaluation of HCP Inc. as of Jan. 14, 2018 is the result of our systematic analysis on three basic characteristics: earnings strength, relative valuation, and recent stock price movement. The company has produced a positive trend in earnings per share over the past 5 quarters. Because the company lacks sufficient analyst estimate data, we place greater weight on the historical EPS trend as the measure of earnings strength. Based on operating earnings yield, the company is about fairly valued when compared to all of the companies in our coverage universe. Share price changes over the past year indicates that HCP will perform very well over the near term.

Financial Data

(US$ in Thousands)	9 Mos	6 Mos	3 Mos	12/31/2016	12/31/2015	12/31/2014	12/31/2013	12/31/2012
Earnings Per Share	1.11	1.45	2.05	1.34	(1.21)	2.00	2.13	1.90
Cash Flow Per Share	1.82	2.09	2.43	2.59	2.64	2.72	2.53	2.42
Tang Book Value Per Share	10.84	11.18	11.45	10.74	18.65	22.19	22.28	21.95
Dividends Per Share	1.480	1.685	1.890	2.095	2.260	2.180	2.100	2.000
Dividend Payout %	133.33	116.21	92.20	156.34	...	109.00	98.59	105.26
Income Statement								
Total Revenue	1,405,119	951,096	492,168	2,129,294	2,544,312	2,266,279	2,099,878	1,900,722
EBITDA	719,197	652,920	549,087	830,490	(88,546)	1,332,231	1,280,621	1,171,691
Depn & Amortn	22,006	14,794	7,623	(1,197)	(1,295)	(949)	(6,646)	(2,232)
Income Before Taxes	461,357	473,620	454,746	367,284	(566,847)	893,438	852,015	756,793
Income Taxes	(14,630)	(9,149)	(6,162)	4,473	(9,011)	250	5,815	(1,636)
Net Income	472,871	480,528	461,145	627,747	(559,235)	922,233	970,837	832,540
Average Shares	468,975	468,839	475,173	467,403	462,795	458,796	455,702	428,316
Balance Sheet								
Current Assets	195,593	490,415	856,420	182,106	456,045	269,125	365,279	319,671
Total Assets	13,904,081	14,102,575	14,855,868	15,759,265	21,449,849	21,369,940	20,075,870	19,915,555
Current Liabilities	381,189	389,690	344,908	475,505	511,512	517,657	417,237	399,903
Long-Term Obligations	7,466,203	7,485,326	8,141,452	9,189,495	11,069,003	9,759,773	8,661,627	8,693,820
Total Liabilities	8,372,648	8,400,528	9,014,520	10,211,670	12,106,206	10,634,643	9,352,570	9,364,318
Stockholders' Equity	5,531,433	5,702,047	5,841,348	5,547,595	9,343,643	10,735,297	10,723,300	10,551,237
Shares Outstanding	469,034	468,879	468,446	468,081	465,488	459,746	456,960	453,191
Statistical Record								
Return on Assets %	3.03	3.92	5.40	3.36	N.M.	4.45	4.86	4.45
Return on Equity %	7.22	9.22	12.91	8.41	N.M.	8.60	9.13	8.48
EBITDA Margin %	51.18	68.65	111.56	39.00	N.M.	58.78	60.99	61.64
Net Margin %	33.65	50.52	93.70	29.48	N.M.	40.69	46.23	43.80
Asset Turnover	0.09	0.10	0.11	0.11	0.12	0.11	0.11	0.10
Current Ratio	0.51	1.26	2.48	0.38	0.89	0.52	0.88	0.80
Debt to Equity	1.35	1.31	1.39	1.66	1.18	0.91	0.81	0.82
Price Range	34.55-27.66	36.72-27.94	36.72-27.94	36.72-23.79	43.89-29.81	41.49-32.94	50.32-32.46	42.98-34.48
P/E Ratio	31.12-24.92	25.32-19.27	17.91-13.63	27.40-17.75	...	20.75-16.47	23.63-15.24	22.62-18.15
Average Yield %	4.81	5.27	5.94	6.62	6.26	5.82	5.14	5.10

Address: 1920 Main Street, Suite 1200, Irvine, CA 92614
Telephone: 949-407-0700
Fax: 562-733-5200

Web Site: www.hcpi.com
Officers: Michael D. McKee - Executive Chairman, Acting President, Acting Chief Executive Officer
Thomas M. Herzog - Chief Executive Officer, Chief Financial Officer, Chief Financial Officer (frmr), Executive Vice President

Auditors: Deloitte & Touche LLP
Investor Contact: 562-733-5309
Transfer Agents: Wells Fargo Shareowner Services, Saint Paul, MN

HEALTHCARE REALTY TRUST, INC.

Exchange	Symbol	Price	52Wk Range	Yield	P/E
NYS	HR	$32.12 (12/29/2017)	36.17-29.80	3.74	32.44

*7 Year Price Score 97.46 *NYSE Composite Index=100 ***12 Month Price Score 94.57**

Interim Earnings (Per Share)

Qtr.	Mar	Jun	Sep	Dec
2014	0.04	0.06	0.04	0.19
2015	0.05	0.18	0.27	0.19
2016	0.09	0.12	0.10	0.47
2017	0.28	0.22	0.02	...

Interim Dividends (Per Share)

Amt	Decl	Ex	Rec	Pay
0.30Q	01/31/2017	02/10/2017	02/14/2017	02/28/2017
0.30Q	05/02/2017	05/12/2017	05/16/2017	05/31/2017
0.30Q	08/01/2017	08/09/2017	08/11/2017	08/31/2017
0.30Q	10/31/2017	11/15/2017	11/16/2017	11/30/2017

Indicated Div: $1.20 (Div. Reinv. Plan)

Valuation Analysis — **Institutional Holding**

Forecast EPS	$0.57	No of Institutions
	(01/17/2018)	318
Market Cap	$4.0 Billion	Shares
Book Value	$1.9 Billion	146,704,400
Price/Book	2.15	% Held
Price/Sales	9.50	97.30

Business Summary: REITs (MIC: 5.3.1 SIC: 6798 NAIC: 525930)

Healthcare Realty Trust is a self-managed and self-administered real estate investment trust that owns, leases, manages, acquires, finances, develops and redevelops income-producing real estate properties associated primarily with the delivery of outpatient healthcare services. Co. had gross investments in 202 real estate properties, construction in progress, land held for development and corporate property at Dec 31 2016. Co. also provided property management services for 146 healthcare-related properties nationwide, as of Dec 31 2016.

Recent Developments: For the quarter ended Sep 30 2017, income from continuing operations decreased 73.3% to US$3.2 million from US$11.9 million in the year-earlier quarter. Net income decreased 73.2% to US$3.2 million from US$11.8 million in the year-earlier quarter. Revenues were US$107.0 million, up 3.2% from US$103.7 million the year before. Revenues from property income rose 3.9% to US$106.6 million from US$102.5 million in the corresponding quarter a year earlier.

Prospects: Our evaluation of Healthcare Realty Trust Inc. as of Jan. 14, 2018 is the result of our systematic analysis on three basic characteristics: earnings strength, relative valuation, and recent stock price movement. The company has managed to produce a neutral trend in earnings per share over the past 5 quarters. Because the company lacks sufficient analyst estimate data, we place greater weight on the historical EPS trend as the measure of earnings strength. Based on operating earnings yield, the company is overvalued when compared to all of the companies in our coverage universe. Share price changes over the past year indicates that HR will perform very well over the near term.

Financial Data

(US$ in Thousands)	9 Mos	6 Mos	3 Mos	12/31/2016	12/31/2015	12/31/2014	12/31/2013	12/31/2012
Earnings Per Share	0.99	1.07	0.97	0.78	0.70	0.33	0.08	0.07
Cash Flow Per Share	1.50	1.53	1.37	1.39	1.62	1.32	1.33	1.47
Tang Book Value Per Share	14.93	14.13	14.19	13.99	12.02	12.13	12.76	12.60
Dividends Per Share	1.200	1.200	1.200	1.200	1.200	1.200	1.200	1.200
Dividend Payout %	121.21	112.15	123.71	153.85	171.43	363.64	1,500.00	1,714.29
Income Statement								
Total Revenue	316,768	209,814	104,569	411,630	388,471	370,855	336,926	316,350
EBITDA	101,006	151,536	75,834	259,590	230,900	205,776	149,623	167,987
Depn & Amortn	(1,319)	66,056	29,817	116,483	106,530	99,384	88,380	85,122
Income Before Taxes	60,247	57,082	31,858	85,756	58,836	33,979	(12,268)	7,812
Net Income	60,243	57,070	31,845	85,571	69,436	31,887	6,946	5,465
Average Shares	119,181	115,674	115,507	109,387	99,880	96,759	90,940	80,127
Balance Sheet								
Current Assets	205,753	19,951	121,493	127,307	76,302	75,019	196,018	225,067
Total Assets	3,145,704	2,958,498	3,039,236	3,040,647	2,816,726	2,757,510	2,729,662	2,539,972
Current Liabilities	69,918	62,121	62,746	78,880	75,522	70,612	74,853	65,809
Long-Term Obligations	1,166,060	1,203,146	1,278,662	1,264,370	1,431,494	1,403,692	1,348,459	1,293,044
Total Liabilities	1,281,442	1,312,221	1,385,945	1,387,233	1,573,979	1,536,456	1,486,185	1,419,028
Stockholders' Equity	1,864,262	1,646,277	1,653,291	1,653,414	1,242,747	1,221,054	1,243,477	1,120,944
Shares Outstanding	124,890	116,545	116,511	116,417	101,517	98,828	95,924	87,514
Statistical Record								
Return on Assets %	3.67	4.16	3.68	2.91	2.49	1.16	0.26	0.22
Return on Equity %	6.44	8.10	7.35	5.89	5.64	2.59	0.59	0.51
EBITDA Margin %	31.89	72.22	72.52	63.06	59.44	55.49	44.41	53.10
Net Margin %	19.02	27.20	30.45	20.79	17.87	8.60	2.06	1.73
Asset Turnover	0.14	0.14	0.14	0.14	0.14	0.14	0.13	0.12
Current Ratio	2.94	0.32	1.94	1.61	1.01	1.06	2.62	3.42
Debt to Equity	0.63	0.73	0.77	0.76	1.15	1.15	1.08	1.15
Price Range	36.17-27.74	36.50-27.74	36.50-27.74	36.50-27.74	30.94-22.11	27.81-21.22	30.52-20.98	24.93-18.56
P/E Ratio	36.54-28.02	34.11-25.93	37.63-28.60	46.79-35.56	44.20-31.59	84.27-64.30	381.50-262.25	356.14-265.14
Average Yield %	3.74	3.68	3.74	3.80	4.62	4.86	4.76	5.30

Address: 3310 West End Avenue, Suite 700, Nashville, TN 37203 Telephone: 615-269-8175	Web Site: www.healthcarerealty.com Officers: David R. Emery - Chairman, Chief Executive Officer Robert E. Hull - Executive Vice President	Auditors: BDO USA, LLP Transfer Agents: Wells Fargo Shareowner Services, Mendota Heights, MN

HEALTHCARE TRUST OF AMERICA INC

Exchange	Symbol	Price	52Wk Range	Yield	P/E
NYS	HTA	$30.04 (12/29/2017)	32.92-28.69	4.06	120.16

*7 Year Price Score N/A   *NYSE Composite Index=100   *12 Month Price Score 93.94

Interim Earnings (Per Share)

Qtr.	Mar	Jun	Sep	Dec
2014	0.04	0.02	0.14	0.17
2015	0.05	0.07	0.05	0.08
2016	0.08	0.09	0.04	0.12
2017	0.09	(0.03)	0.07	...

Interim Dividends (Per Share)

Amt	Decl	Ex	Rec	Pay
0.30Q	02/15/2017	04/06/2017	04/10/2017	04/13/2017
0.30Q	04/26/2017	06/30/2017	07/05/2017	07/11/2017
0.305Q	07/31/2017	09/29/2017	10/02/2017	10/06/2017
0.305Q	10/24/2017	12/29/2017	01/02/2018	01/09/2018

Indicated Div: $1.22

Valuation Analysis		Institutional Holding	
Forecast EPS	$0.21 (01/18/2018)	No of Institutions	347
Market Cap	$6.0 Billion	Shares	241,276,608
Book Value	$3.2 Billion	% Held	68.40
Price/Book	1.90		
Price/Sales	10.72		

TRADING VOLUME (thousand shares)

Business Summary: REITs (MIC: 5.3.1 SIC: 6798 NAIC: 525930)

Healthcare Trust of America is a real estate investment trust and an owners and operators of medical office buildings (MOBs) in the U.S. Co. focuses on owning and operating MOBs that serve healthcare delivery and are located on health system campuses, near university medical centers, or in community core outpatient locations. Co.'s properties include health systems such as Highmark-Allegheny Health Network, Greenville Health System, Tufts Medical Center, Hospital Corporation of America, Providence St. Joseph Health and Steward Health Care System. As of Dec 31 2016, Co.'s portfolio consisted of approximately 17.7 million square feet of gross leasable area.

Recent Developments: For the quarter ended Sep 30 2017, net income increased 110.2% to US$14.0 million from US$6.6 million in the year-earlier quarter. Revenues were US$176.0 million, up 48.7% from US$118.3 million the year before. Revenues from property income rose 48.4% to US$175.4 million from US$118.3 million in the corresponding quarter a year earlier.

Prospects: Our evaluation of Healthcare Trust Of America as of Jan. 14, 2018 is the result of our systematic analysis on three basic characteristics: earnings strength, relative valuation, and recent stock price movement. The company has produced a positive trend in earnings per share over the past 5 quarters and while recent estimates for the company have remained steady, HTA has posted results that fell short of analysts expectations. Based on operating earnings yield, the company is overvalued when compared to all of the companies in our coverage universe. Share price changes over the past year indicates that HTA will perform very well over the near term.

Financial Data

(US$ in Thousands)	9 Mos	6 Mos	3 Mos	12/31/2016	12/31/2015	12/31/2014	12/31/2013	12/31/2012
Earnings Per Share	0.25	0.22	0.34	0.33	0.26	0.37	0.20	(0.22)
Cash Flow Per Share	1.42	1.40	1.48	1.49	1.52	1.41	1.30	1.05
Tang Book Value Per Share	15.29	15.51	11.36	11.58	10.53	11.22	11.29	9.05
Dividends Per Share	1.205	1.200	0.895	1.190	1.170	0.290	...	...
Dividend Payout %	482.00	545.45	263.24	360.61	450.00	78.38	...	...
Income Statement								
Total Revenue	440,220	264,226	124,347	460,928	403,822	371,505	319,899	299,644
EBITDA	203,739	114,112	76,595	283,432	244,047	246,753	820,036	100,625
Depn & Amortn	121,500	71,700	46,213	175,285	151,614	140,400	755,000	72,000
Income Before Taxes	21,724	8,085	14,000	47,345	33,557	45,994	23,577	(24,368)
Net Income	21,390	7,627	13,545	45,912	32,931	45,371	24,261	(24,424)
Average Shares	204,795	176,464	146,117	140,259	128,004	121,168	114,969	111,356
Balance Sheet								
Current Assets	26,879	124,620	24,077	198,506	170,665	175,318	145,532	46,896
Total Assets	6,413,522	6,366,758	3,753,017	3,747,844	3,172,300	3,041,650	2,752,334	2,414,090
Current Liabilities	159,070	135,214	98,222	105,034	94,933	101,042	82,893	63,443
Long-Term Obligations	2,856,522	2,784,162	1,811,208	1,768,905	1,590,696	1,412,461	1,214,241	1,037,539
Total Liabilities	3,237,957	3,145,692	2,096,016	2,060,570	1,792,876	1,594,511	1,365,128	1,159,824
Stockholders' Equity	3,175,565	3,221,066	1,657,001	1,687,274	1,379,424	1,447,139	1,387,206	1,254,266
Shares Outstanding	200,686	200,646	141,825	141,719	127,026	125,087	118,440	107,326
Statistical Record								
Return on Assets %	0.75	0.62	1.40	1.32	1.06	1.57	0.94	N.M.
Return on Equity %	1.55	1.26	3.20	2.99	2.33	3.20	1.84	N.M.
EBITDA Margin %	46.28	43.19	61.60	61.49	60.43	66.42	256.34	33.58
Net Margin %	4.86	2.89	10.89	9.96	8.15	12.21	7.58	N.M.
Asset Turnover	0.11	0.10	0.14	0.13	0.13	0.13	0.12	0.13
Current Ratio	0.17	0.92	0.25	1.89	1.80	1.74	1.76	0.74
Debt to Equity	0.90	0.86	1.09	1.05	1.15	0.98	0.88	0.83
Price Range	32.92-27.23	34.64-27.23	34.64-27.23	34.64-26.30	29.94-22.69	27.40-19.66	26.56-19.46	21.78-18.28
P/E Ratio	131.68-108.92	157.45-123.77	101.88-80.09	104.97-79.70	115.15-87.27	74.05-53.14	132.80-97.30	...
Average Yield %	3.96	3.86	2.91	3.95	4.50	1.22	...	...

Address: 16435 N. Scottsdale Road, Suite 320, Scottsdale, AZ 85254 Telephone: 480-998-3478 Fax: 480-991-0755	Web Site: www.htareit.com Officers: Scott D. Peters - Chairman, President, Chief Executive Officer Robert A. Milligan - Executive Vice President, Chief Financial Officer, Secretary, Treasurer	Auditors: Deloitte & Touche LLP Investor Contact: 480-998-3478 Transfer Agents: DST Systems, Inc., Kansas City, MO

HEICO CORP

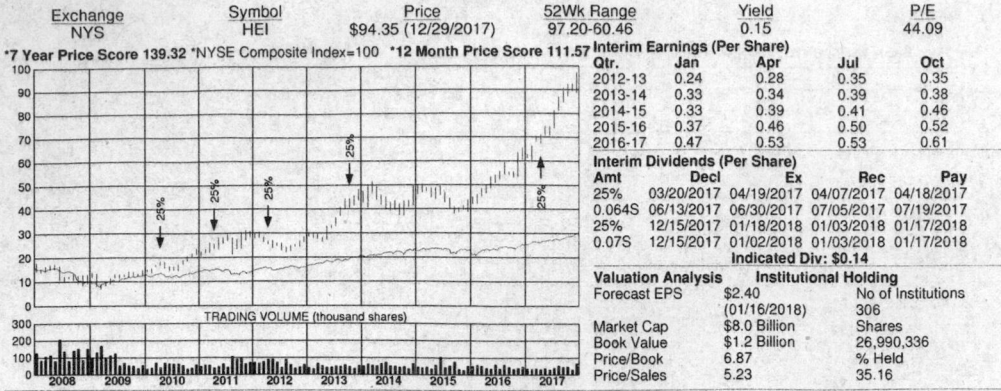

Exchange	Symbol	Price	52Wk Range	Yield	P/E
NYS	HEI	$94.35 (12/29/2017)	97.20-60.46	0.15	44.09

*7 Year Price Score 139.32 *NYSE Composite Index=100 *12 Month Price Score 111.57

Interim Earnings (Per Share)

Qtr.	Jan	Apr	Jul	Oct
2012-13	0.24	0.28	0.35	0.35
2013-14	0.33	0.34	0.39	0.38
2014-15	0.33	0.39	0.41	0.46
2015-16	0.37	0.46	0.50	0.52
2016-17	0.47	0.53	0.53	0.61

Interim Dividends (Per Share)

Amt	Decl	Ex	Rec	Pay
25%	03/20/2017	04/19/2017	04/07/2017	04/18/2017
0.064S	06/13/2017	06/30/2017	07/05/2017	07/19/2017
25%	12/15/2017	01/18/2018	01/03/2018	01/17/2018
0.07S	12/15/2017	01/02/2018	01/03/2018	01/17/2018

Indicated Div: $0.14

Valuation Analysis

Forecast EPS	$2.40
	(01/16/2018)
Market Cap	$8.0 Billion
Book Value	$1.2 Billion
Price/Book	6.87
Price/Sales	5.23

Institutional Holding

No of Institutions	306
Shares	26,990,336
% Held	35.16

Business Summary: Aerospace (MIC: 7.1.1 SIC: 3724 NAIC: 336412)

HEICO is a holding company engaged as a manufacturer of Federal Aviation Administration-approved jet engine and aircraft component replacement parts, other than the original equipment manufacturers and their subcontractors. Co. also manufactures a range of electronic equipment for the aviation, defense, space, medical, telecommunications and electronics industries. Co. has two operating segments: Flight Support Group, which uses proprietary technology to design and manufacture jet engine and aircraft component replacement parts for sale; and Electronic Technologies Group, which designs, manufactures and sells various types of electronic, microwave and electro-optical products.

Recent Developments: For the year ended Oct 31 2017, net income increased 17.9% to US$207.7 million from US$176.2 million in the prior year. Revenues were US$1.52 billion, up 10.8% from US$1.38 billion the year before. Operating income was US$306.7 million versus US$265.3 million in the prior year, an increase of 15.6%. Direct operating expenses rose 10.4% to US$950.1 million from US$860.8 million in the comparable period the year before. Indirect operating expenses increased 7.2% to US$268.1 million from US$250.1 million in the equivalent prior-year period.

Prospects: Our evaluation of Heico Corp. as of Jan. 14, 2018 is the result of our systematic analysis on three basic characteristics: earnings strength, relative valuation, and recent stock price movement. The company has managed to produce a neutral trend in earnings per share over the past 5 quarters and while recent estimates for the company have been raised by analysts, HEI has posted better than expected results. Based on operating earnings yield, the company is overvalued when compared to all of the companies in our coverage universe. Share price changes over the past year indicates that HEI will perform very well over the near term.

Financial Data

(US$ in Thousands)	10/31/2017	10/31/2016	10/31/2015	10/31/2014	10/31/2013	10/31/2012	10/31/2011	10/31/2010
Earnings Per Share	2.14	1.83	1.58	1.44	1.22	1.02	0.88	0.66
Cash Flow Per Share	3.26	2.97	2.07	2.30	1.59	1.68	1.54	1.27
Tang Book Value Per Share	N.M.	N.M.	N.M.	N.M.	N.M.	N.M.	0.09	0.43
Dividends Per Share	0.152	0.128	0.112	0.376	1.453	0.069	0.055	0.044
Dividend Payout %	7.10	6.99	7.11	26.11	118.69	6.75	6.32	6.67
Income Statement								
Total Revenue	1,524,813	1,376,258	1,188,648	1,132,311	1,008,757	897,347	764,891	617,020
EBITDA	329,650	285,722	247,390	221,113	197,878	175,207	147,135	118,231
Depn & Amortn	21,900	20,400	17,800	17,100	13,400	11,600	8,640	8,668
Income Before Taxes	297,960	257,050	224,964	198,572	180,761	161,175	138,353	109,055
Income Taxes	90,300	80,900	71,400	59,800	56,200	54,500	42,900	36,700
Net Income	185,985	156,192	133,364	121,293	102,396	85,147	72,820	54,938
Average Shares	86,776	85,212	84,763	84,316	83,727	83,279	83,010	82,448
Balance Sheet								
Current Assets	631,892	584,221	503,612	431,293	441,472	367,911	316,638	259,249
Total Assets	2,512,431	2,039,475	1,736,387	1,489,214	1,533,015	1,192,846	941,069	781,643
Current Liabilities	249,437	214,421	168,387	152,220	161,286	131,514	123,390	81,832
Long-Term Obligations	673,528	457,814	367,241	328,691	376,818	131,194	39,823	14,073
Total Liabilities	1,351,351	1,076,096	926,524	789,730	926,669	576,173	411,998	312,531
Stockholders' Equity	1,161,080	963,379	809,863	699,484	606,346	616,673	529,071	469,112
Shares Outstanding	84,482	84,111	83,591	83,182	82,970	82,598	82,181	80,540
Statistical Record								
Return on Assets %	8.17	8.25	8.27	8.03	7.51	7.96	8.45	7.25
Return on Equity %	17.51	17.57	17.67	18.58	16.74	14.82	14.59	11.85
EBITDA Margin %	21.62	20.76	20.81	19.53	19.62	19.52	19.24	19.16
Net Margin %	12.20	11.35	11.22	10.71	10.15	9.49	9.52	8.90
Asset Turnover	0.67	0.73	0.74	0.75	0.74	0.84	0.89	0.81
Current Ratio	2.53	2.72	2.99	2.83	2.74	2.80	2.57	3.17
Debt to Equity	0.58	0.48	0.45	0.47	0.62	0.21	0.08	0.03
Price Range	92.29-53.14	59.39-38.69	50.28-38.00	51.62-37.19	44.36-24.29	31.17-21.89	30.35-19.83	20.58-12.24
P/E Ratio	43.13-24.83	32.45-21.14	31.82-24.05	35.84-25.83	36.36-19.91	30.56-21.47	34.49-22.54	31.19-18.54
Average Yield %	0.21	0.26	0.25	0.87	4.49	0.26	0.22	

Address: 3000 Taft Street, Hollywood, FL 33021	Web Site: www.heico.com	Auditors: DELOITTE & TOUCHE LLP
Telephone: 954-987-4000	Officers: Laurans A. Mendelson - Chairman, Chief Executive Officer Eric A. Mendelson - Co-President, Division Officer	Investor Contact: 954-987-4000 Transfer Agents: Computershare Shareowner Services LLC, Providence, RI

HELMERICH & PAYNE, INC.

Exchange	Symbol	Price	52Wk Range	Yield	P/E	Div Achiever
NYS	HP	$64.64 (12/29/2017)	81.11-42.34	4.33	N/A	40 Years

*7 Year Price Score 70.23   *NYSE Composite Index=100   *12 Month Price Score 94.49

Interim Earnings (Per Share)

Qtr.	Dec	Mar	Jun	Sep
2012-13	1.48	1.39	2.46	1.46
2013-14	1.59	1.59	1.75	1.54
2014-15	1.85	1.37	0.83	(0.19)
2015-16	0.15	0.19	(0.20)	(0.67)
2016-17	(0.33)	(0.45)	(0.21)	(0.21)

Interim Dividends (Per Share)

Amt	Decl	Ex	Rec	Pay
0.70Q	03/01/2017	05/17/2017	05/19/2017	06/01/2017
0.70Q	06/07/2017	08/16/2017	08/18/2017	09/01/2017
0.70Q	09/06/2017	11/10/2017	11/13/2017	12/01/2017
0.70Q	12/05/2017	02/09/2018	02/12/2018	03/01/2018

Indicated Div: $2.80

Valuation Analysis

		Institutional Holding	
Forecast EPS	$-0.34 (01/18/2018)	No of Institutions	735
Market Cap	$7.0 Billion	Shares	148,720,160
Book Value	$4.2 Billion		
Price/Book	1.69	% Held	92.01
Price/Sales	3.89		

Business Summary: Equipment & Services (MIC: 9.1.3 SIC: 1381 NAIC: 213111)

Helmerich & Payne is primarily engaged in contract drilling of oil and gas wells for others. Co.'s contract drilling business is composed of three segments: U.S. Land, which drills primarily in Oklahoma, California, Texas, Wyoming, Colorado, Louisiana, Mississippi, Pennsylvania, Ohio, New Mexico and North Dakota; Offshore, which is conducted in the Gulf of Mexico and Equatorial Guinea; and International Land, which conducts drilling operations in five international locations: Ecuador, Colombia, Argentina, Bahrain and United Arab Emirates. Co. is also engaged in the ownership, development and operation of commercial real estate and the research and development of rotary steerable technology.

Recent Developments: For the year ended Sep 30 2017, loss from continuing operations was US$127.9 million compared with a loss of US$53.0 million a year earlier. Net loss amounted to US$128.2 million versus a net loss of US$56.8 million in the prior year. Revenues were US$1.80 billion, up 11.1% from US$1.62 billion the year before. Operating loss was US$172.5 million versus a loss of US$26.0 million in the prior year. Direct operating expenses rose 39.0% to US$1.25 billion from US$898.8 million in the comparable period the year before. Indirect operating expenses decreased 3.1% to US$728.0 million from US$751.4 million in the equivalent prior-year period.

Prospects: Our evaluation of Helmerich & Payne Inc. as of Jan. 14, 2018 is the result of our systematic analysis on three basic characteristics: earnings strength, relative valuation, and recent stock price movement. The company has produced a positive trend in earnings per share over the past 5 quarters. Because the company lacks sufficient analyst estimate data, we place greater weight on the historical EPS trend as the measure of earnings strength. Based on operating earnings yield, the company is overvalued when compared to all of the companies in our coverage universe. Share price changes over the past year indicates that HP will perform very poorly over the near term.

Financial Data

(US$ in Thousands)	09/30/2017	09/30/2016	09/30/2015	09/30/2014	09/30/2013	09/30/2012	09/30/2011	09/30/2010
Earnings Per Share	(1.20)	(0.54)	3.87	6.46	6.79	5.34	3.99	1.45
Cash Flow Per Share	3.29	6.96	13.17	10.38	9.38	9.34	9.17	4.37
Tang Book Value Per Share	37.40	42.20	45.44	45.19	41.64	36.28	30.54	26.53
Dividends Per Share	2.800	2.763	2.750	2.438	0.870	0.280	0.250	0.210
Dividend Payout %	...	...	71.06	37.73	12.81	5.24	6.27	14.48
Income Statement								
Total Revenue	1,804,741	1,624,232	3,165,441	3,719,707	3,387,614	3,151,802	2,543,894	1,875,162
EBITDA	414,777	545,667	1,281,841	1,622,934	1,574,396	1,297,402	1,017,939	716,241
Depn & Amortn	585,543	598,587	606,992	523,549	455,623	387,549	315,468	262,658
Income Before Taxes	(184,598)	(72,667)	665,647	1,096,314	1,114,297	902,580	687,067	438,236
Income Taxes	(56,735)	(19,677)	243,375	387,548	392,844	328,971	252,399	152,155
Net Income	(128,212)	(56,828)	422,225	708,719	736,639	581,045	434,186	156,312
Average Shares	108,500	107,996	108,570	109,141	107,879	108,377	108,632	107,404
Balance Sheet								
Current Assets	1,235,267	1,572,686	1,439,007	1,277,366	1,258,211	895,228	956,313	652,804
Total Assets	6,439,988	6,832,019	7,152,012	6,721,861	6,264,827	5,721,085	5,003,891	4,265,370
Current Liabilities	344,385	330,120	351,228	507,526	452,273	381,164	416,729	232,638
Long-Term Obligations	492,902	491,847	492,443	40,000	80,000	195,000	235,000	360,000
Total Liabilities	2,275,397	2,271,094	2,254,560	1,830,884	1,821,100	1,886,087	1,733,844	1,457,905
Stockholders' Equity	4,164,591	4,560,925	4,897,452	4,890,977	4,443,727	3,834,998	3,270,047	2,807,465
Shares Outstanding	108,604	108,077	107,767	108,232	106,716	105,697	107,086	105,819
Statistical Record								
Return on Assets %	N.M.	N.M.	6.09	10.91	12.29	10.81	9.37	3.71
Return on Equity %	N.M.	N.M.	8.63	15.18	17.80	16.31	14.29	5.69
EBITDA Margin %	22.98	33.60	40.49	43.63	46.48	41.16	40.01	38.20
Net Margin %	N.M.	N.M.	13.34	19.05	21.75	18.44	17.07	8.34
Asset Turnover	0.27	0.23	0.46	0.57	0.57	0.59	0.55	0.45
Current Ratio	3.59	4.76	4.10	2.52	2.78	2.35	2.29	2.81
Debt to Equity	0.12	0.11	0.10	0.01	0.02	0.05	0.07	0.13
Price Range	83.46-42.34	69.77-42.85	97.87-46.50	118.29-68.95	70.82-45.22	65.13-37.39	72.60-40.26	48.58-33.42
P/E Ratio	...	...	25.29-12.02	18.31-10.67	10.43-6.66	12.20-7.00	18.20-10.09	33.50-23.05
Average Yield %	4.48	4.75	4.01	2.52	1.44	0.54	0.44	0.52

Address: 1437 South Boulder Avenue, Tulsa, OK 74119	**Web Site:** www.hpinc.com	**Auditors:** Ernst & Young LLP
Telephone: 918-742-5531	**Officers:** Hans Helmerich - Chairman, President, Chief Executive Officer John W. Lindsay - President,	**Investor Contact:** 918-588-5207
Fax: 918-742-0237	Chief Executive Officer, Executive Vice President, Chief Operating Officer	**Transfer Agents:** Computershare Investor Services LLC, Providence, RI

HERBALIFE LTD

Exchange	Symbol	Price	52Wk Range	Yield	P/E
NYS	HLF	$67.72 (12/29/2017)	78.76-49.19	N/A	15.39

*7 Year Price Score 93.03   *NYSE Composite Index=100   *12 Month Price Score 99.04

TRADING VOLUME (thousand shares)

Interim Earnings (Per Share)

Qtr.	Mar	Jun	Sep	Dec
2014	0.74	1.31	0.13	1.18
2015	0.92	0.97	1.09	0.98
2016	1.13	(0.28)	1.01	1.15
2017	0.98	1.61	0.66	...

Interim Dividends (Per Share)

Dividend Payment Suspended

Valuation Analysis / **Institutional Holding**

Forecast EPS	N/A	No of Institutions
		328
Market Cap	$6.0 Billion	Shares
Book Value	$219.0 Million	107,306,608
Price/Book	27.61	% Held
Price/Sales	1.38	79.98

Business Summary: Household & Personal Products (MIC: 1.7.1 SIC: 5122 NAIC: 424210)

Herbalife is a holding company. Through its subsidiaries, Co. is a nutrition company that sells its products to and through a network of independent members. Co. has five product groups: weight management, which provides for meal replacement, protein shakes, drink mixes, weight loss solutions and healthy snacks; targeted nutrition, which provides dietary and nutritional supplements; energy, sports and fitness, which provide products that support a healthy active lifestyle; outer nutrition, which provides for facial skin care, body care, and hair care; and literature, promotional and other, which provide start-up kits, sales tools, and educational materials.

Recent Developments: For the quarter ended Sep 30 2017, net income decreased 37.9% to US$54.5 million from US$87.7 million in the year-earlier quarter. Revenues were US$1.09 billion, down 3.3% from US$1.12 billion the year before. Operating income was US$119.3 million versus US$151.5 million in the prior-year quarter, a decrease of 21.3%. Direct operating expenses rose 3.0% to US$215.4 million from US$209.1 million in the comparable period the year before. Indirect operating expenses decreased 1.4% to US$750.7 million from US$761.4 million in the equivalent prior-year period.

Prospects: Our evaluation of Herbalife Ltd. as of Aug. 2, 2015 is the result of our systematic analysis on three basic characteristics: earnings strength, relative valuation, and recent stock price movement. The company has managed to produce a neutral trend in earnings per share over the past 5 quarters. However, while recent estimates for the company have been mixed, HLF has posted better than expected results. Based on operating earnings yield, the company is undervalued when compared to all of the companies in our coverage universe. Share price changes over the past year indicates that HLF will perform poorly over the near term.

Financial Data
(US$ in Thousands)

	9 Mos	6 Mos	3 Mos	12/31/2016	12/31/2015	12/31/2014	12/31/2013	12/31/2012
Earnings Per Share	4.40	4.75	2.86	3.02	3.97	3.40	4.91	4.05
Cash Flow Per Share	6.56	3.40	4.83	4.41	7.61	5.93	7.53	5.04
Tang Book Value Per Share	N.M.	N.M.	N.M.	N.M.	...	...	1.34	0.04
Dividends Per Share	...	...	...	...	...	0.300	1.200	1.200
Dividend Payout %	...	...	...	...	...	8.82	24.44	29.63
Income Statement								
Total Revenue	3,334,400	2,249,000	1,102,100	4,488,400	4,469,000	4,958,600	4,825,308	4,072,330
EBITDA	541,800	397,300	168,300	538,800	663,800	582,000	816,377	732,347
Depn & Amortn	73,800	48,600	24,500	80,700	82,500	81,500	81,100	70,900
Income Before Taxes	361,500	280,600	113,600	364,700	486,400	421,300	716,717	650,906
Income Taxes	84,200	57,800	28,400	104,700	147,300	112,600	189,192	173,716
Net Income	277,300	222,800	85,200	260,000	339,100	308,700	527,525	477,190
Average Shares	83,000	85,300	86,700	86,100	85,300	90,800	107,445	117,856
Balance Sheet								
Current Assets	2,274,100	2,269,400	2,409,500	1,462,500	1,566,300	1,393,400	1,643,120	963,848
Total Assets	3,422,500	3,410,000	3,560,300	2,565,400	2,477,900	2,374,900	2,473,701	1,703,944
Current Liabilities	858,800	862,800	940,600	791,500	1,024,400	874,800	922,178	716,891
Long-Term Obligations	2,176,600	2,188,100	2,199,200	1,438,400	1,392,500	1,711,700	850,019	431,305
Total Liabilities	3,203,500	3,210,000	3,292,900	2,369,100	2,531,400	2,709,300	1,922,255	1,283,189
Stockholders' Equity	219,000	200,000	267,400	196,300	(53,500)	(334,400)	551,446	420,755
Shares Outstanding	89,300	90,200	91,100	93,100	92,700	92,200	101,100	106,900
Statistical Record								
Return on Assets %	12.65	13.61	8.39	10.28	13.98	12.73	25.25	30.21
Return on Equity %	219.84	348.11	150.11	363.15	...	284.46	108.52	97.03
EBITDA Margin %	16.25	17.67	15.27	12.00	14.85	11.74	16.92	17.98
Net Margin %	8.32	9.91	7.73	5.79	7.59	6.23	10.93	11.72
Asset Turnover	1.47	1.47	1.50	1.78	1.84	2.05	2.31	2.58
Current Ratio	2.65	2.63	2.56	1.85	1.53	1.59	1.78	1.34
Debt to Equity	9.94	10.94	8.22	7.33	...	...	1.54	1.03
Price Range	74.11-47.99	74.11-47.99	68.01-47.99	68.01-43.42	60.77-29.70	81.81-37.16	80.81-32.20	72.69-26.06
P/E Ratio	16.84-10.91	15.60-10.10	23.78-16.78	22.52-14.38	15.31-7.48	24.06-10.93	16.46-6.56	17.95-6.43
Average Yield %	...	...	...	...	...	0.54	2.25	2.26

Address: P.O. Box 309GT, Ugland House, South Church Street, George Town, KY1-1104 Telephone: 213-745-0500	Web Site: www.herbalife.com Officers: Michael O. Johnson - Chairman, Chief Executive Officer David Pezzullo - Chief Operating Officer, Chief	Auditors: PricewaterhouseCoopers LLP Transfer Agents: Mellon Investor Services LLC, South Hackensack, NJ

HERSHEY COMPANY (THE)

Exchange	Symbol	Price	52Wk Range	Yield	P/E
NYS	HSY	$113.51 (12/29/2017)	115.96-102.87	2.31	33.88

*7 Year Price Score 97.04   *NYSE Composite Index=100   *12 Month Price Score 96.20

Interim Earnings (Per Share)

Qtr.	Mar	Jun	Sep	Dec
2014	1.11	0.75	1.00	0.91
2015	1.10	(0.47)	0.70	0.97
2016	1.06	0.68	1.06	0.54
2017	0.58	0.95	1.28	...

Interim Dividends (Per Share)

Amt	Decl	Ex	Rec	Pay
0.618Q	02/03/2017	02/22/2017	02/24/2017	03/15/2017
0.618Q	05/02/2017	05/23/2017	05/25/2017	06/15/2017
0.656Q	07/25/2017	08/23/2017	08/25/2017	09/15/2017
0.656Q	10/05/2017	11/21/2017	11/22/2017	12/15/2017

Indicated Div: $2.62 (Div. Reinv. Plan)

Valuation Analysis		Institutional Holding	
Forecast EPS	$4.81 (01/18/2018)	No of Institutions	1044
Market Cap	$23.9 Billion	Shares	137,158,752
Book Value	$823.3 Million	% Held	
Price/Book	29.05		52.81
Price/Sales	3.17		

Business Summary: Food (MIC: 1.2.1 SIC: 2064 NAIC: 311320)

Hershey is engaged in the production of chocolate and non-chocolate confectionery. Co. has two reportable segments: North America, which is responsible for Co.'s chocolate and sugar confectionery market position, as well as Co.'s grocery and growing snacks market positions, in the U.S. and Canada; and International and Other, which includes all other countries where Co. manufactures, imports, markets, sells or distributes chocolate and non-chocolate confectionery and other products. Co.'s principal product offerings include chocolate and non-chocolate confectionery products; gum and mint refreshment products; pantry items; and snack items such as spreads, meat snacks, bars and snack bites.

Recent Developments: For the quarter ended Oct 1 2017, net income increased 20.5% to US$274.0 million from US$227.4 million in the year-earlier quarter. Revenues were US$2.03 billion, up 1.5% from US$2.00 billion the year before. Operating income was US$439.0 million versus US$374.0 million in the prior-year quarter, an increase of 17.4%. Direct operating expenses declined 5.2% to US$1.09 billion from US$1.15 billion in the comparable period the year before. Indirect operating expenses increased 5.1% to US$501.2 million from US$476.8 million in the equivalent prior-year period.

Prospects: Our evaluation of Hershey Foods Corp. as of Jan. 14, 2018 is the result of our systematic analysis on three basic characteristics: earnings strength, relative valuation, and recent stock price movement. The company has generated a negative trend in earnings per share over the past 5 quarters and while recent estimates for the company have been mixed, HSY has posted better than expected results. Based on operating earnings yield, the company is about fairly valued when compared to all of the companies in our coverage universe. Share price changes over the past year indicates that HSY will perform well over the near term.

Financial Data

(US$ in Thousands)	9 Mos	6 Mos	3 Mos	12/31/2016	12/31/2015	12/31/2014	12/31/2013	12/31/2012
Earnings Per Share	3.35	3.13	2.86	3.34	2.32	3.77	3.61	2.89
Cash Flow Per Share	5.60	4.56	4.51	4.58	5.54	3.77	5.30	4.85
Tang Book Value Per Share	N.M.	N.M.	N.M.	N.M.	N.M.	1.66	3.72	1.05
Dividends Per Share	2.510	2.472	2.437	2.402	2.236	2.040	1.810	1.560
Dividend Payout %	74.93	78.98	85.21	71.92	96.38	54.11	50.14	53.98
Income Statement								
Total Revenue	5,575,790	3,542,669	1,879,678	7,440,181	7,386,626	7,421,768	7,146,079	6,644,252
EBITDA	1,117,048	629,424	257,054	1,421,359	1,252,548	1,601,107	1,540,708	1,321,185
Depn & Amortn	194,313	132,079	64,952	231,735	244,928	211,532	201,033	210,037
Income Before Taxes	850,279	449,478	168,361	1,099,481	901,847	1,306,043	1,251,319	1,015,579
Income Taxes	275,291	148,503	70,113	379,437	388,896	459,131	430,849	354,648
Net Income	601,848	328,545	125,044	720,044	512,951	846,912	820,470	660,931
Average Shares	213,392	275,260	275,142	215,304	220,651	224,837	227,203	228,337
Balance Sheet								
Current Assets	2,214,454	1,911,529	1,873,861	1,816,778	1,848,598	2,247,047	2,487,334	2,113,485
Total Assets	5,655,477	5,380,228	5,342,385	5,524,333	5,344,371	5,629,516	5,357,488	4,754,839
Current Liabilities	2,337,670	1,742,205	1,710,917	1,909,443	2,217,912	1,935,647	1,408,022	1,471,110
Long-Term Obligations	2,054,132	2,349,756	2,350,941	2,347,455	1,557,091	1,548,963	1,795,142	1,530,967
Total Liabilities	4,832,207	4,524,923	4,512,307	4,738,477	4,346,374	4,174,454	3,752,654	3,718,090
Stockholders' Equity	823,270	855,305	830,078	785,856	997,997	1,455,062	1,604,834	1,036,749
Shares Outstanding	210,668	212,414	212,750	212,259	216,777	221,044	223,894	223,786
Statistical Record								
Return on Assets %	12.50	12.29	11.56	13.21	9.35	15.42	16.23	14.38
Return on Equity %	83.63	84.99	74.06	80.51	41.82	55.36	62.12	69.91
EBITDA Margin %	20.03	17.77	13.68	19.10	16.96	21.57	21.56	19.88
Net Margin %	10.79	9.27	6.65	9.68	6.94	11.41	11.48	9.95
Asset Turnover	1.31	1.37	1.41	1.37	1.35	1.35	1.41	1.45
Current Ratio	0.95	1.10	1.10	0.95	0.83	1.16	1.77	1.44
Debt to Equity	2.50	2.75	2.83	2.99	1.56	1.06	1.12	1.48
Price Range	115.96-94.63	115.96-94.63	113.89-89.60	113.89-83.32	110.78-83.58	108.07-88.15	100.90-72.22	74.64-59.49
P/E Ratio	34.61-28.25	37.05-30.23	39.82-31.33	34.10-24.95	47.75-36.03	28.67-23.38	27.95-20.01	25.83-20.58
Average Yield %	2.37	2.34	2.41	2.48	2.36	2.09	2.02	2.29

Address: 100 Crystal A Drive, Hershey, PA 17033	**Web Site:** www.hersheys.com	**Auditors:** KPMG LLP
Telephone: 717-534-4200	**Officers:** John P. Bilbrey - Chairman, President, Chief Executive Officer Michele G. Buck - President, Chief	**Investor Contact:** 800-539-0261
Fax: 717-531-6161	Operating Officer, Executive Vice President, Chief Executive Officer, Senior Vice President, Executive Vice President, Global Chief Marketing Officer, Chief Operating Officer, Region Officer, Senior Vice President, Global Chief Marketing Officer, Region Officer	**Transfer Agents:** Computershare, Providence, RI

HESS CORP

Exchange	Symbol	Price	52Wk Range	Yield	P/E
NYS	HES	$47.47 (12/29/2017)	62.82-38.09	2.11	N/A

*7 Year Price Score 57.66   ***NYSE Composite Index=100**   ***12 Month Price Score 91.63**

Interim Earnings (Per Share)

Qtr.	Mar	Jun	Sep	Dec
2014	1.20	2.96	3.31	0.09
2015	(1.37)	(1.99)	(0.98)	(6.43)
2016	(1.72)	(1.29)	(1.12)	(15.81)
2017	(1.07)	(1.46)	(2.02)	...

Interim Dividends (Per Share)

Amt	Decl	Ex	Rec	Pay
0.25Q	03/01/2017	03/13/2017	03/15/2017	03/31/2017
0.25Q	06/06/2017	06/14/2017	06/16/2017	06/30/2017
0.25Q	09/06/2017	09/15/2017	09/18/2017	09/29/2017
0.25Q	12/06/2017	12/15/2017	12/18/2017	12/29/2017

Indicated Div: $1.00

Valuation Analysis		Institutional Holding	
Forecast EPS	$-4.47	No of Institutions	
	(01/18/2018)	786	
Market Cap	$15.1 Billion	Shares	
Book Value	$13.1 Billion	341,073,184	
Price/Book	1.15	% Held	
Price/Sales	2.72	N/A	

Business Summary: Production & Extraction (MIC: 9.1.1 SIC: 1311 NAIC: 211111)

Hess is an exploration and production company engaged in exploration, development, production, transportation, purchase and sale of crude oil, natural gas liquids, and natural gas with production operations located primarily in the U.S., Denmark, Equatorial Guinea, the Malaysia/Thailand Joint Development Area, Malaysia, and Norway. The Bakken Midstream operating segment provides services, including storing and terminaling propane. As of Dec 31 2016, Co. had total proved developed and undeveloped reserves of 1.11 billion barrels of oil equivalent, consisted of 826.0 million barrels of crude oil and condensate and natural gas liquids, as well as 1.70 billion cubic feet of natural gas.

Recent Developments: For the quarter ended Sep 30 2017, net loss amounted to US$593.0 million versus a net loss of US$317.0 million in the year-earlier quarter. Revenues were US$1.67 billion, up 39.3% from US$1.20 billion the year before. Direct operating expenses rose 10.3% to US$739.0 million from US$670.0 million in the comparable period the year before. Indirect operating expenses increased 201.5% to US$3.49 billion from US$1.16 billion in the equivalent prior-year period.

Prospects: Our evaluation of Hess Corp. as of Jan. 14, 2018 is the result of our systematic analysis on three basic characteristics: earnings strength, relative valuation, and recent stock price movement. The company has generated a negative trend in earnings per share over the past 5 quarters. Because the company lacks sufficient analyst estimate data, we place greater weight on the historical EPS trend as the measure of earnings strength. Based on earnings yield, the company is overvalued when compared to all of the companies in our coverage universe. Share price changes over the past year indicates that HES will perform very poorly over the near term.

Financial Data

(US$ in Thousands)	9 Mos	6 Mos	3 Mos	12/31/2016	12/31/2015	12/31/2014	12/31/2013	12/31/2012
Earnings Per Share	(20.36)	(19.46)	(19.29)	(19.92)	(10.78)	7.53	14.82	5.95
Cash Flow Per Share	2.95	3.73	3.84	2.56	6.99	14.70	14.47	16.68
Tang Book Value Per Share	40.19	42.25	43.32	44.73	66.46	71.18	70.24	55.29
Dividends Per Share	1.000	1.000	1.000	1.000	1.000	1.000	0.700	0.400
Dividend Payout %	...	...	...	...	...	13.28	4.72	6.72
Income Statement								
Total Revenue	4,169,000	2,503,000	1,275,000	4,844,000	6,561,000	11,439,000	24,421,000	38,373,000
EBITDA	(819,000)	910,000	512,000	(272,000)	38,000	5,983,000	7,669,000	7,106,000
Depn & Amortn	2,237,000	1,478,000	737,000	3,244,000	3,955,000	3,224,000	2,770,000	2,949,000
Income Before Taxes	(3,301,000)	(734,000)	(309,000)	(3,854,000)	(4,258,000)	2,436,000	4,493,000	3,738,000
Income Taxes	(1,995,000)	(21,000)	(13,000)	2,222,000	(1,299,000)	744,000	525,000	1,675,000
Net Income	(1,397,000)	(773,000)	(324,000)	(6,132,000)	(3,056,000)	2,317,000	5,052,000	2,025,000
Average Shares	314,500	314,400	313,900	309,900	283,600	307,700	340,900	340,300
Balance Sheet								
Current Assets	4,083,000	4,270,000	4,171,000	4,276,000	4,404,000	6,687,000	8,599,000	8,387,000
Total Assets	26,600,000	27,798,000	28,100,000	28,621,000	34,195,000	38,578,000	42,754,000	43,441,000
Current Liabilities	2,214,000	2,118,000	2,126,000	2,251,000	2,628,000	4,851,000	6,558,000	8,382,000
Long-Term Obligations	6,592,000	6,612,000	6,669,000	6,694,000	6,544,000	5,919,000	5,420,000	7,324,000
Total Liabilities	13,468,000	14,018,000	13,952,000	14,087,000	14,809,000	16,373,000	18,034,000	22,351,000
Stockholders' Equity	13,132,000	13,780,000	14,148,000	14,534,000	19,386,000	22,205,000	24,720,000	21,090,000
Shares Outstanding	317,754	317,843	317,916	316,523	286,045	285,834	325,314	341,527
Statistical Record								
Return on Assets %	N.M.	N.M.	N.M.	N.M.	N.M.	5.70	11.72	4.89
Return on Equity %	N.M.	N.M.	N.M.	N.M.	N.M.	9.88	22.06	10.20
EBITDA Margin %	N.M.	36.36	40.16	N.M.	0.58	52.30	31.40	18.52
Net Margin %	N.M.	N.M.	N.M.	N.M.	N.M.	20.26	20.69	5.28
Asset Turnover	0.18	0.16	0.16	0.15	0.18	0.28	0.57	0.93
Current Ratio	1.84	2.02	1.96	1.90	1.68	1.38	1.31	1.00
Debt to Equity	0.50	0.48	0.47	0.46	0.34	0.27	0.22	0.35
Price Range	65.14-38.09	65.14-40.31	65.14-45.67	65.14-34.38	78.09-47.44	101.10-65.45	84.06-52.96	67.00-39.95
P/E Ratio	...	...	...	...	...	13.43-8.69	5.67-3.57	11.26-6.71
Average Yield %	2.03	1.92	1.83	1.90	1.56	1.15	0.97	0.77

Address: 1185 Avenue of the Americas, New York, NY 10036	**Web Site:** www.hess.com	**Auditors:** Ernst & Young LLP
Telephone: 212-997-8500	**Officers:** James H. Quigley - Chairman John B. Hess - Chairman, Chief Executive Officer	**Investor Contact:** 212-536-8940
		Transfer Agents: Computershare, Providence, RI

HEWLETT PACKARD ENTERPRISE CO

Exchange	Symbol	Price	52Wk Range	Yield	P/E
NYS	HPE	$14.36 (12/29/2017)	15.14-13.06	2.09	68.38

*7 Year Price Score N/A   *NYSE Composite Index=100   *12 Month Price Score 94.59

Interim Earnings (Per Share)

Qtr.	Jan	Apr	Jul	Oct
2014-15	0.30	0.16	0.13	0.75
2015-16	0.15	0.18	1.32	0.18
2016-17	0.16	(0.37)	0.10	0.32

Interim Dividends (Per Share)

Amt	Decl	Ex	Rec	Pay
0.065Q	07/20/2017	09/12/2017	09/13/2017	10/04/2017
0.00Q	08/04/2017	09/01/2017	08/21/2017	09/01/2017
0.075Q	11/09/2017	12/12/2017	12/13/2017	01/03/2018
0.075Q	01/18/2018	03/13/2018	03/14/2018	04/04/2018

Indicated Div: $0.30 (Div. Reinv. Plan)

Valuation Analysis

		Institutional Holding	
Forecast EPS	$1.18	No of Institutions	
	(01/18/2018)	821	
Market Cap	$22.9 Billion	Shares	
Book Value	$23.5 Billion	1,440,601,600	
Price/Book	0.98	% Held	
Price/Sales	0.79	N/A	

TRADING VOLUME (thousand shares)

Business Summary: IT Services (MIC: 6.3.1 SIC: 7379 NAIC: 541519)

Hewlett Packard Enterprise is a technology company. Co. organizes its business into the following five segments: Enterprise Group, which provides customers with technology infrastructure they need to optimize IT; Software, which allows customers to automate IT operations to accelerate and secure business processes; Enterprise Services, which brings Co.'s solutions together through its consulting and support personnel; Financial Services, which enables IT consumption models, financial architectures and customized investment solutions for customers; and Corporate Investments, which includes Hewlett Packard Labs and certain cloud-related business incubation projects, among others.

Recent Developments: For the year ended Oct 31 2017, income from continuing operations decreased 86.5% to US$436.0 million from US$3.24 billion a year earlier. Net income decreased 89.1% to US$344.0 million from US$3.16 billion in the prior year. Revenues were US$28.87 billion, down 4.7% from US$30.28 billion the year before. Operating income was US$625.0 million versus US$3.90 billion in the prior year, a decrease of 84.0%. Direct operating expenses declined 1.7% to US$19.91 billion from US$20.26 billion in the comparable period the year before. Indirect operating expenses increased 36.2% to US$8.33 billion from US$6.12 billion in the equivalent prior-year period.

Prospects: Our evaluation of Hewlett Packard Enterprise Co. as of Jan. 14, 2018 is the result of our systematic analysis on three basic characteristics: earnings strength, relative valuation, and recent stock price movement. The company has generated a negative trend in earnings per share over the past 5 quarters and while recent estimates for the company have remained steady, HPE has posted better than expected results. Based on operating earnings yield, the company is undervalued when compared to all of the companies in our coverage universe. Share price changes over the past year indicates that HPE will perform poorly over the near term.

Financial Data

(US$ in Millions)	10/31/2017	10/31/2016	10/31/2015	10/31/2014	10/31/2013	10/31/2012
Earnings Per Share	0.21	1.82	1.34	...	...	...
Cash Flow Per Share	0.54	2.88	2.03	...	...	...
Tang Book Value Per Share	3.08	3.71	2.49	...	...	...
Dividends Per Share	0.260	0.220	...	...	...	...
Dividend Payout %	123.81	12.09	...	...	...	...
Income Statement						
Total Revenue	28,871	50,123	52,107	55,123	57,371	61,042
EBITDA	3,408	8,471	5,715	6,718	7,692	(8,981)
Depn & Amortn	2,521	3,755	3,952	4,106	4,428	4,841
Income Before Taxes	295	4,155	1,470	2,244	2,871	(14,314)
Income Taxes	(164)	918	(991)	596	820	447
Net Income	344	3,161	2,461	1,648	2,051	(14,761)
Average Shares	1,674	1,739	1,834	...	...	...
Balance Sheet						
Current Assets	21,444	28,917	31,173	22,031	24,379	...
Total Assets	61,406	79,679	81,270	65,071	68,775	...
Current Liabilities	18,924	22,531	22,151	19,760	20,912	...
Long-Term Obligations	10,182	12,608	15,103	485	617	...
Total Liabilities	37,940	48,231	47,735	28,295	30,787	...
Stockholders' Equity	23,466	31,448	33,535	36,776	37,988	...
Shares Outstanding	1,595	1,666	1,742	...	...	...
Statistical Record						
Return on Assets %	0.49	3.92	...	2.46	...	...
Return on Equity %	1.25	9.70	...	4.41	...	...
EBITDA Margin %	11.80	16.90	10.97	12.19	13.41	N.M.
Net Margin %	1.19	6.31	4.72	2.99	3.57	N.M.
Asset Turnover	0.41	0.62	...	0.82	...	...
Current Ratio	1.13	1.28	1.41	1.11	1.17	...
Debt to Equity	0.43	0.40	0.45	0.01	0.02	...
Price Range	15.14-12.95	13.81-7.17	10.10-8.75	...	...	...
P/E Ratio	72.10-61.68	7.59-3.94	7.54-6.53	...	...	...
Average Yield %	1.86	2.11	...	...	...	...

Address: 3000 Hanover Street, Palo Alto, CA 94304 **Telephone:** 650-687-5817	**Web Site:** www.hpe.com **Officers:** Patricia F. Russo - Chairman Antonio F. Neri - President, Executive Vice President, Division Officer	**Auditors:** Ernst & Young LLP **Transfer Agents:** Wells Fargo Shareowner Services

HEXCEL CORP.

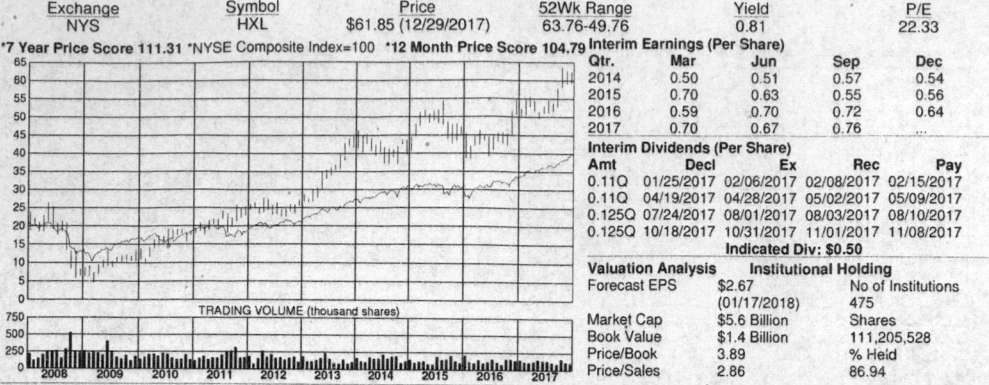

Exchange	Symbol	Price	52Wk Range	Yield	P/E
NYS	HXL	$61.85 (12/29/2017)	63.76-49.76	0.81	22.33

*7 Year Price Score 111.31 *NYSE Composite Index=100 *12 Month Price Score 104.79

Interim Earnings (Per Share)

Qtr.	Mar	Jun	Sep	Dec
2014	0.50	0.51	0.57	0.54
2015	0.70	0.63	0.55	0.56
2016	0.59	0.70	0.72	0.64
2017	0.70	0.67	0.76	...

Interim Dividends (Per Share)

Amt	Decl	Ex	Rec	Pay
0.11Q	01/25/2017	02/06/2017	02/08/2017	02/15/2017
0.11Q	04/19/2017	04/28/2017	05/02/2017	05/09/2017
0.125Q	07/24/2017	08/01/2017	08/03/2017	08/10/2017
0.125Q	10/18/2017	10/31/2017	11/01/2017	11/08/2017

Indicated Div: $0.50

Valuation Analysis — **Institutional Holding**

Forecast EPS	$2.67
	(01/17/2018)
Market Cap	$5.6 Billion
Book Value	$1.4 Billion
Price/Book	3.89
Price/Sales	2.86

No of Institutions	475
Shares	111,205,528
% Held	86.94

TRADING VOLUME (thousand shares)

Business Summary: Plastics (MIC: 8.4.2 SIC: 2821 NAIC: 325211)

Hexcel is a composites company with two reportable segments. The Composite Materials segment manufactures and markets carbon fibers, fabrics and specialty reinforcements, prepregs and other fiber-reinforced matrix materials, structural adhesives, honeycomb, molding compounds, tooling materials, polyurethane systems and laminates that are incorporated into several applications, including military and commercial aircraft, wind turbine blades, recreational products, transport (cars, boats, trains) and other industrial applications. The Engineered Products segment manufactures and markets composite structures and precision machined honeycomb parts primarily for use in the aerospace industry.

Recent Developments: For the quarter ended Sep 30 2017, net income increased 2.2% to US$69.7 million from US$68.2 million in the year-earlier quarter. Revenues were US$491.5 million, down 1.8% from US$500.5 million the year before. Operating income was unchanged at US$89.1 million versus the prior-year quarter. Direct operating expenses declined 2.4% to US$355.9 million from US$364.8 million in the comparable period the year before. Indirect operating expenses decreased 0.2% to US$46.5 million from US$46.6 million in the equivalent prior-year period.

Prospects: Our evaluation of Hexcel Corp. as of Jan. 14, 2018 is the result of our systematic analysis on three basic characteristics: earnings strength, relative valuation, and recent stock price movement. The company has enjoyed a very positive trend in earnings per share over the past 5 quarters. However, while recent estimates for the company have been mixed, HXL has posted better than expected results. Based on operating earnings yield, the company is about fairly valued when compared to all of the companies in our coverage universe. Share price changes over the past year indicates that HXL will perform in line with the market over the near term.

Financial Data

(US$ in Thousands)	9 Mos	6 Mos	3 Mos	12/31/2016	12/31/2015	12/31/2014	12/31/2013	12/31/2012
Earnings Per Share	2.77	2.73	2.76	2.65	2.44	2.12	1.84	1.61
Cash Flow Per Share	4.70	4.95	4.87	4.31	3.14	3.29	2.73	2.31
Tang Book Value Per Share	15.06	14.00	13.12	12.83	11.99	11.41	11.12	9.37
Dividends Per Share	0.455	0.440	0.440	0.430	0.400	...	...	...
Dividend Payout %	16.43	16.12	15.94	16.23	16.39	...	...	...
Income Statement								
Total Revenue	1,461,600	970,100	478,800	2,004,300	1,861,200	1,855,500	1,678,200	1,578,200
EBITDA	258,000	168,700	79,000	453,000	408,800	376,500	329,200	304,900
Depn & Amortn	600	400	400	93,300	76,400	71,200	59,300	57,200
Income Before Taxes	237,400	155,300	72,400	337,600	318,200	297,300	262,600	237,700
Income Taxes	44,300	30,700	8,600	90,300	83,000	89,300	76,000	74,100
Net Income	195,900	126,200	64,600	249,800	237,200	209,400	187,900	164,300
Average Shares	91,400	92,000	92,900	94,200	97,200	98,700	102,100	102,000
Balance Sheet								
Current Assets	707,500	648,400	686,800	607,000	633,800	681,700	656,400	575,700
Total Assets	2,737,200	2,627,300	2,575,500	2,400,600	2,187,400	2,036,400	1,836,100	1,603,100
Current Liabilities	257,800	270,800	274,800	271,900	292,600	310,600	268,700	235,300
Long-Term Obligations	829,600	817,300	837,000	684,400	576,500	415,000	292,000	240,000
Total Liabilities	1,310,500	1,297,000	1,312,800	1,155,700	1,007,800	886,500	675,700	609,000
Stockholders' Equity	1,426,700	1,330,300	1,262,700	1,244,900	1,179,600	1,149,900	1,160,400	994,100
Shares Outstanding	89,800	89,800	90,700	91,400	93,500	95,500	98,900	99,900
Statistical Record								
Return on Assets %	9.96	10.16	10.55	10.86	11.23	10.81	10.93	11.00
Return on Equity %	19.02	19.87	20.84	20.55	20.36	18.13	17.44	18.24
EBITDA Margin %	17.65	17.39	16.50	22.60	21.96	20.29	19.62	19.32
Net Margin %	13.40	13.01	13.49	12.46	12.74	11.29	11.20	10.41
Asset Turnover	0.76	0.78	0.81	0.87	0.88	0.96	0.98	1.06
Current Ratio	2.74	2.39	2.50	2.23	2.17	2.19	2.44	2.45
Debt to Equity	0.58	0.61	0.66	0.55	0.49	0.36	0.25	0.24
Price Range	57.92-42.04	55.63-40.82	55.63-39.15	54.97-38.38	54.48-40.38	46.40-36.92	44.69-26.50	27.80-22.53
P/E Ratio	20.91-15.18	20.38-14.95	20.16-14.18	20.74-14.48	22.33-16.55	21.89-17.42	24.29-14.40	17.27-13.99
Average Yield %	0.88	0.90	0.94	0.97	0.83	...	...	...

Address: Two Stamford Plaza, 281 Tresser Boulevard, Stamford, CT 06901-3238 **Telephone:** 203-969-0666	**Web Site:** www.hexcel.com **Officers:** Patrick Winterlich - Executive Vice President, Chief Financial Officer Nick L. Stanage - Chairman, President, Chief Executive Officer, Chief Operating Officer	**Auditors:** Ernst & Young LLP **Investor Contact:** 203-969-0666 **Transfer Agents:** American Stock Transfer & Trust Company, New York, NY

HIGHWOODS PROPERTIES, INC.

Exchange	Symbol	Price	52Wk Range	Yield	P/E
NYS	HIW	$50.91 (12/29/2017)	53.19-48.87	3.46	35.11

*7 Year Price Score 98.44 *NYSE Composite Index=100 *12 Month Price Score 94.36

Interim Earnings (Per Share)

Qtr.	Mar	Jun	Sep	Dec
2014	0.13	0.25	0.57	0.23
2015	0.21	0.27	0.31	0.21
2016	4.49	0.32	0.32	0.22
2017	0.31	0.37	0.55	...

Interim Dividends (Per Share)

Amt	Decl	Ex	Rec	Pay
0.44Q	02/07/2017	02/16/2017	02/21/2017	03/07/2017
0.44Q	04/20/2017	05/15/2017	05/17/2017	06/06/2017
0.44Q	08/02/2017	08/10/2017	08/14/2017	09/06/2017
0.44Q	10/19/2017	11/13/2017	11/14/2017	12/05/2017

Indicated Div: $1.76

Valuation Analysis | **Institutional Holding**

Forecast EPS	$1.24	No of Institutions
	(01/13/2018)	375
Market Cap	$5.3 Billion	Shares
Book Value	$2.2 Billion	120,405,952
Price/Book	2.39	% Held
Price/Sales	7.57	104.85

Business Summary: REITs (MIC: 5.3.1 SIC: 6798 NAIC: 525930)

Highwoods Properties is an integrated office real estate investment trust that that owns, develops, acquires, leases and manages properties primarily in the business districts of Atlanta, Greensboro, Memphis, Nashville, Orlando, Pittsburgh, Raleigh, Richmond and Tampa. Co.'s primary business is the operation, acquisition and development of office properties. Co. provides a line of real estate services to its customers. Co. provides its customers with services such as build-to-suit construction and space modification, including tenant improvements and expansions. Co. conducts its activities through Highwoods Realty Limited Partnership.

Recent Developments: For the quarter ended June 30 2017, income from continuing operations increased 18.0% to US$39.6 million from US$33.5 million in the year-earlier quarter. Net income increased 18.0% to US$39.6 million from US$33.5 million in the year-earlier quarter. Revenues were US$177.3 million, up 6.2% from US$166.9 million the year before.

Prospects: Our evaluation of Highwoods Properties Inc. as of Jan. 14, 2018 is the result of our systematic analysis on three basic characteristics: earnings strength, relative valuation, and recent stock price movement. The company has enjoyed a very positive trend in earnings per share over the past 5 quarters. Because the company lacks sufficient analyst estimate data, we place greater weight on the historical EPS trend as the measure of earnings strength. Based on operating earnings yield, the company is about fairly valued when compared to all of the companies in our coverage universe. Share price changes over the past year indicates that HIW will perform well over the near term.

Financial Data

(US$ in Thousands)	9 Mos	6 Mos	3 Mos	12/31/2016	12/31/2015	12/31/2014	12/31/2013	12/31/2012
Earnings Per Share	1.45	1.22	1.17	5.30	1.00	1.19	1.44	1.02
Cash Flow Per Share	3.33	3.32	3.21	3.10	3.06	2.94	3.01	2.54
Tang Book Value Per Share	21.04	20.95	20.71	20.73	16.36	16.09	16.11	14.08
Dividends Per Share	2.545	2.530	2.515	2.500	1.700	1.700	1.700	1.700
Dividend Payout %	175.52	207.38	214.96	47.17	170.00	142.86	118.06	166.67
Income Statement								
Total Revenue	526,876	346,691	169,408	665,634	604,671	608,468	556,810	516,102
EBITDA	178,426	106,322	50,993	415,770	387,910	397,498	336,792	299,864
Depn & Amortn	3,193	2,224	1,284	224,707	223,384	203,324	190,227	165,420
Income Before Taxes	125,831	71,329	32,530	116,753	80,443	113,761	60,459	45,683
Net Income	128,172	70,509	32,297	524,290	97,078	110,964	125,457	79,595
Average Shares	106,145	105,386	104,661	101,398	97,406	93,800	88,836	79,678
Balance Sheet								
Current Assets	272,080	242,041	236,632	268,832	201,274	214,021	176,797	173,550
Total Assets	4,560,466	4,560,499	4,548,816	4,561,050	4,493,432	4,004,909	3,807,101	3,350,428
Current Liabilities	227,575	200,981	207,144	313,885	248,107	237,633	218,962	172,146
Long-Term Obligations	1,966,398	2,005,038	2,042,486	1,948,047	2,499,614	2,094,908	1,982,963	1,888,520
Total Liabilities	2,359,068	2,368,489	2,406,792	2,424,695	2,892,125	2,480,698	2,329,801	2,190,288
Stockholders' Equity	2,201,398	2,192,010	2,142,024	2,136,355	1,601,307	1,524,211	1,477,300	1,160,140
Shares Outstanding	103,248	103,236	102,018	101,665	96,091	92,907	89,920	80,311
Statistical Record								
Return on Assets %	3.41	2.83	2.72	11.55	2.28	2.84	3.51	2.43
Return on Equity %	7.09	6.06	5.88	27.98	6.21	7.39	9.51	7.41
EBITDA Margin %	33.86	30.67	30.10	62.46	64.15	65.33	60.49	58.10
Net Margin %	24.33	20.34	19.06	78.77	16.05	18.24	22.53	15.42
Asset Turnover	0.15	0.15	0.15	0.15	0.14	0.16	0.16	0.16
Current Ratio	1.20	1.20	1.14	0.86	0.81	0.90	0.81	1.01
Debt to Equity	0.89	0.91	0.95	0.91	1.56	1.37	1.34	1.63
Price Range	53.19-45.86	55.74-45.86	55.74-45.32	55.74-39.01	48.14-36.82	45.13-35.82	41.07-33.00	35.48-29.71
P/E Ratio	36.68-31.63	45.69-37.59	47.64-38.74	10.52-7.36	48.14-36.82	37.92-30.10	28.52-22.92	34.78-29.13
Average Yield %	5.04	4.96	5.00	5.15	3.96	4.21	4.64	5.17

Address: 3100 Smoketree Court, Suite 600, Raleigh, NC 27604	Web Site: www.highwoods.com	Auditors: Deloitte & Touch LLP
Telephone: 919-872-4924	Officers: O. Temple Sloan - Chairman Edward J. Fritsch - President, Chief Executive Officer	Investor Contact: 919-431-1529
Fax: 919-431-1439		Transfer Agents: Wells Fargo Shareholder Services, Mendota Heights, MN

HILL-ROM HOLDINGS, INC.

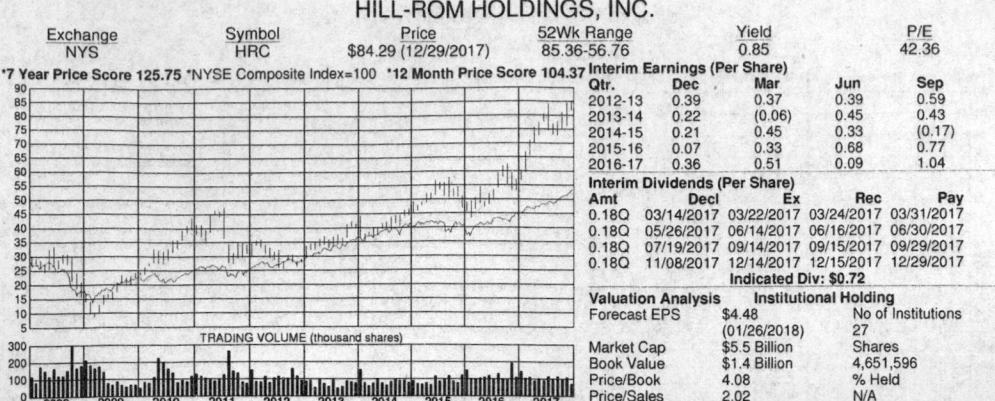

Exchange	Symbol	Price	52Wk Range	Yield	P/E
NYS	HRC	$84.29 (12/29/2017)	85.36-56.76	0.85	42.36

*7 Year Price Score 125.75 *NYSE Composite Index=100 *12 Month Price Score 104.37

Interim Earnings (Per Share)

Qtr.	Dec	Mar	Jun	Sep
2012-13	0.39	0.37	0.39	0.59
2013-14	0.22	(0.06)	0.45	0.43
2014-15	0.21	0.45	0.33	(0.17)
2015-16	0.07	0.33	0.68	0.77
2016-17	0.36	0.51	0.09	1.04

Interim Dividends (Per Share)

Amt	Decl	Ex	Rec	Pay
0.18Q	03/14/2017	03/22/2017	03/24/2017	03/31/2017
0.18Q	05/26/2017	06/14/2017	06/16/2017	06/30/2017
0.18Q	07/19/2017	09/14/2017	09/15/2017	09/29/2017
0.18Q	11/08/2017	12/14/2017	12/15/2017	12/29/2017
		Indicated Div: $0.72		

Valuation Analysis

		Institutional Holding	
Forecast EPS	$4.48	No of Institutions	
	(01/26/2018)	27	
Market Cap	$5.5 Billion	Shares	
Book Value	$1.4 Billion	4,651,596	
Price/Book	4.08	% Held	
Price/Sales	2.02	N/A	

TRADING VOLUME (thousand shares)

Business Summary: Medical Instruments & Equipment (MIC: 4.3.1 SIC: 3841 NAIC: 339112)

Hill-Rom Holdings is a medical technology company. Co.'s products and services include: Patient Support Systems, which include a variety of specialty frames and surfaces, such as Medical Surgical beds, Intensive Care Unit beds, and Bariatric patient beds, patient mobility solutions, non-invasive therapeutic products and surfaces, and Co.'s communications technologies and software solutions; Front Line Care, which include its patient monitoring and diagnostics products from its Welch Allyn Holdings, Inc. and Mortara Instruments, Inc. and its respiratory health products; and Surgical Solutions, which include surgical tables, lights, and pendants utilized within the operating room setting.

Recent Developments: For the year ended Sep 30 2017, net income increased 7.7% to US$132.3 million from US$122.8 million in the prior year. Revenues were US$2.74 billion, up 3.3% from US$2.66 billion the year before. Operating income was US$273.4 million versus US$230.3 million in the prior year, an increase of 18.7%. Direct operating expenses rose 1.8% to US$1.42 billion from US$1.40 billion in the comparable period the year before. Indirect operating expenses increased 2.0% to US$1.05 billion from US$1.03 billion in the equivalent prior-year period.

Prospects: Our evaluation of Hil-Rom Holdings, Inc. as of Jan. 21, 2018 is the result of our systematic analysis on three basic characteristics: earnings strength, relative valuation, and recent stock price movement. The company has generated a negative trend in earnings per share over the past 5 quarters and while recent estimates for the company have been raised by analysts, HRC has posted better than expected results. Based on operating earnings yield, the company is about fairly valued when compared to all of the companies in our coverage universe. Share price changes over the past year indicates that HRC will perform well over the near term.

Financial Data
(US$ in Thousands)

	09/30/2017	09/30/2016	09/30/2015	09/30/2014	09/30/2013	09/30/2012	09/30/2011	09/30/2010
Earnings Per Share	1.99	1.86	0.82	1.04	1.74	1.94	2.09	1.97
Cash Flow Per Share	4.74	4.29	3.73	3.65	4.39	4.20	3.52	2.22
Tang Book Value Per Share	N.M.	N.M.	N.M.	2.53	4.50	3.07	8.57	7.80
Dividends Per Share	0.710	0.670	0.632	0.595	0.525	0.487	0.430	0.410
Dividend Payout %	35.68	36.02	77.13	57.21	30.17	25.13	20.57	20.81
Income Statement								
Total Revenue	2,743,700	2,655,200	1,988,200	1,686,100	1,716,200	1,634,300	1,591,700	1,469,600
EBITDA	482,700	437,700	201,700	231,400	224,700	243,900	242,500	264,400
Depn & Amortn	210,800	209,000	118,200	106,400	71,200	73,900	74,300	72,800
Income Before Taxes	183,000	138,300	65,100	115,200	144,000	163,500	159,700	182,900
Income Taxes	50,700	15,500	18,300	54,600	39,000	42,700	26,200	56,900
Net Income	133,600	124,100	47,700	60,600	105,000	120,800	133,300	125,300
Average Shares	67,225	66,596	58,536	58,523	60,250	62,120	63,899	63,739
Balance Sheet								
Current Assets	1,166,200	1,082,100	1,141,000	779,300	688,000	681,800	791,700	739,200
Total Assets	4,528,700	4,262,400	4,457,600	1,752,100	1,586,800	1,627,600	1,299,100	1,245,600
Current Liabilities	658,700	662,300	578,800	442,300	345,400	378,100	334,000	288,700
Long-Term Obligations	2,120,400	1,938,400	2,175,200	364,900	225,800	237,500	50,800	98,500
Total Liabilities	3,170,500	3,035,200	3,310,700	945,600	728,100	815,000	557,400	538,100
Stockholders' Equity	1,358,200	1,227,200	1,146,900	806,500	858,700	812,600	741,700	707,500
Shares Outstanding	65,813	65,705	65,165	57,439	58,523	60,796	61,686	62,786
Statistical Record								
Return on Assets %	3.04	2.84	1.54	3.63	6.53	8.23	10.48	10.11
Return on Equity %	10.33	10.43	4.88	7.28	12.57	15.50	18.40	19.03
EBITDA Margin %	17.59	16.48	10.14	13.72	13.09	14.92	15.24	17.99
Net Margin %	4.87	4.67	2.40	3.59	6.12	7.39	8.37	8.53
Asset Turnover	0.62	0.61	0.64	1.01	1.07	1.11	1.25	1.19
Current Ratio	1.77	1.63	1.97	1.76	1.99	1.80	2.37	2.56
Debt to Equity	1.56	1.58	1.90	0.45	0.26	0.29	0.07	0.14
Price Range	84.17-52.92	61.98-43.29	57.79-40.58	44.39-35.13	37.62-26.40	35.96-25.30	47.48-27.37	35.89-19.59
P/E Ratio	42.30-26.59	33.32-23.27	70.48-49.49	42.68-33.78	21.62-15.17	18.54-13.04	22.72-13.10	18.22-9.94
Average Yield %	1.04	1.31	1.28	1.49	1.59	1.55	1.10	1.48

Address: 130 East Randolph Street, Suite 1000, Chicago, IL 60601 **Telephone:** 312-819-7200 **Fax:** 812-934-8189	**Web Site:** www.Hill-Rom.com **Officers:** John J. Greisch - President, Chief Executive Officer Carlos Alonso - Senior Vice President	**Auditors:** PricewaterhouseCoopers LLP **Investor Contact:** 812-931-2199 **Transfer Agents:** Computershare Trust Company, N.A., Providence, RI

HILTON GRAND VACATIONS INC

Exchange	Symbol	Price	52Wk Range	Yield	P/E
NYS	HGV	$41.95 (12/29/2017)	42.71-24.99	N/A	22.80

7 Year Price Score N/A   **NYSE Composite Index=100**   **12 Month Price Score 110.12**

Interim Earnings (Per Share)

Qtr.	Mar	Jun	Sep	Dec
2016	0.48	0.48	0.35	0.39
2017	0.51	0.51	0.43	...

Interim Dividends (Per Share)

No Dividends Paid

Valuation Analysis   Institutional Holding

Forecast EPS	$1.95	No of Institutions
	(01/01/2018)	242
Market Cap	$4.2 Billion	Shares
Book Value	$333.0 Million	98,424,200
Price/Book	12.48	% Held
Price/Sales	2.48	N/A

Business Summary: Hotels, Restaurants & Travel (MIC: 2.2.1 SIC: 7011 NAIC: 721110)

Hilton Grand Vacations is a timeshare company engaged in developing, marketing, selling and managing timeshare resorts primarily under the Hilton Grand Vacations brand. Co.'s operations primarily consist of: selling vacation ownership intervals for Co. and third parties; operating its resorts; financing and servicing loans provided to consumers for their timeshare purchases; and managing its points-based Hilton Grand Vacations Club exchange program. As of Dec 31 2016, Co. had 47 timeshare properties, comprised of 7,657 units, located in the U.S. and Europe and feature condominium-style accommodations.

Recent Developments: For the quarter ended Sep 30 2017, net income increased 22.9% to US$43.0 million from US$35.0 million in the year-earlier quarter. Revenues were US$426.0 million, up 4.7% from US$407.0 million the year before. Direct operating expenses declined 9.1% to US$40.0 million from US$44.0 million in the comparable period the year before. Indirect operating expenses increased 7.3% to US$310.0 million from US$289.0 million in the equivalent prior-year period.

Prospects: Our evaluation of Hilton Grand Vacations Inc. as of Jan. 14, 2018 is the result of our systematic analysis on three basic characteristics: earnings strength, relative valuation, and recent stock price movement. The company has managed to produce a neutral trend in earnings per share over the past 5 quarters. However, while recent estimates for the company have been mixed, HGV has posted results that fell short of analysts expectations. Based on operating earnings yield, the company is undervalued when compared to all of the companies in our coverage universe. Share price changes over the past year indicates that HGV will perform very well over the near term.

Financial Data
(US$ in Millions)

	9 Mos	6 Mos	3 Mos	12/31/2016	12/31/2015	12/31/2014	12/31/2013
Earnings Per Share	1.84	1.76	1.73	1.70	...	...	...
Cash Flow Per Share	3.27	2.52	2.60	1.59	...	...	...
Tang Book Value Per Share	2.63	2.14	1.59	0.98	...	...	...
Income Statement							
Total Revenue	1,264	838	399	1,583	1,475	1,317	1,224
EBITDA	255	177	84	334	331	324	274
Depn & Amortn	4	3	1	12	10	8	8
Income Before Taxes	230	160	76	293	292	280	218
Income Taxes	87	59	26	125	118	113	90
Net Income	144	101	50	168	174	167	128
Average Shares	100	99	99	99	...	...	...
Balance Sheet							
Current Assets	1,918	1,902	1,913	1,812	1,556	1,445	...
Total Assets	2,348	2,287	2,307	2,180	1,724	1,621	...
Current Liabilities	426	365	371	334	304	278	...
Long-Term Obligations	1,096	1,131	1,183	1,184	1,136	1,344	...
Total Liabilities	2,015	2,004	2,081	2,013	1,830	1,994	...
Stockholders' Equity	333	283	226	167	(106)	(373)	...
Shares Outstanding	99	99	99	98	...	...	...
Statistical Record							
Return on Assets %	...	...	...	8.58	10.40	...	...
Return on Equity %	...	...	...	549.31	...	...	...
EBITDA Margin %	20.17	21.12	21.05	21.10	22.44	24.60	22.39
Net Margin %	11.39	12.05	12.53	10.61	11.80	12.68	10.46
Asset Turnover	...	...	...	0.81	0.88	...	...
Current Ratio	4.50	5.21	5.16	5.43	5.12	5.20	...
Debt to Equity	3.29	4.00	5.23	7.09	...	...	...
Price Range	39.26-24.99	37.40-24.99	30.91-24.99	...	...	...	...
P/E Ratio	21.34-13.58	21.25-14.20	17.87-14.45	...	...	...	...

Address: 6355 MetroWest Boulevard, Suite 180, Orlando, FL 32835 **Telephone:** 407-613-3100	**Web Site:** www.hiltongrandvacations.com **Officers:** Leonard A. Potter - Chairman Mark D. Wang - President, Chief Executive Officer	**Auditors:** Ernst & Young LLP **Transfer Agents:** Wells Fargo Bank

HNI CORP

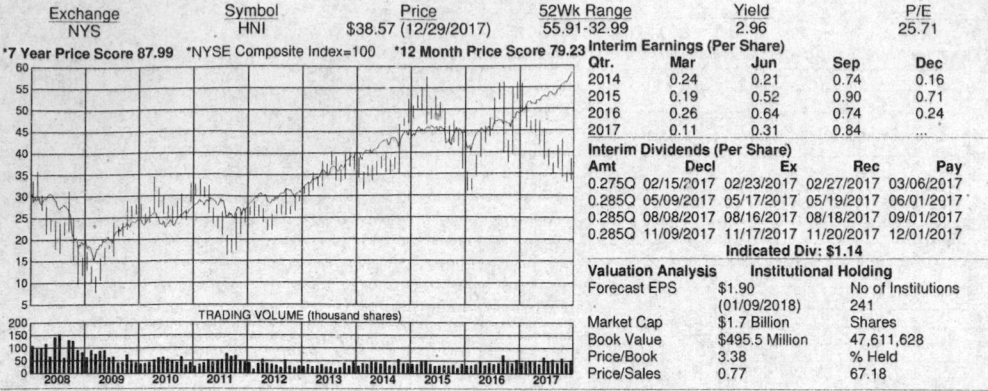

Exchange	Symbol	Price	52Wk Range	Yield	P/E
NYS	HNI	$38.57 (12/29/2017)	55.91-32.99	2.96	25.71

*7 Year Price Score 87.99   *NYSE Composite Index=100   *12 Month Price Score 79.23

Interim Earnings (Per Share)

Qtr.	Mar	Jun	Sep	Dec
2014	0.24	0.21	0.74	0.16
2015	0.19	0.52	0.90	0.71
2016	0.26	0.64	0.74	0.24
2017	0.11	0.31	0.84	...

Interim Dividends (Per Share)

Amt	Decl	Ex	Rec	Pay
0.275Q	02/15/2017	02/23/2017	02/27/2017	03/06/2017
0.285Q	05/09/2017	05/17/2017	05/19/2017	06/01/2017
0.285Q	08/08/2017	08/16/2017	08/18/2017	09/01/2017
0.285Q	11/09/2017	11/17/2017	11/20/2017	12/01/2017

Indicated Div: $1.14

Valuation Analysis

		Institutional Holding	
Forecast EPS	$1.90	No of Institutions	
	(01/09/2018)	241	
Market Cap	$1.7 Billion	Shares	
Book Value	$495.5 Million	47,611,628	
Price/Book	3.38	% Held	
Price/Sales	0.77	67.18	

Business Summary: Office Equipment & Furniture (MIC: 7.5.1 SIC: 2522 NAIC: 337214)

HNI is a provider of office furniture and hearth products. Co. designs, manufactures and markets a range of office furniture systems and seating across a range of price points. Co.'s office furniture portfolio includes panel-based and freestanding furniture systems and complementary products such as seating, storage, tables and relocatable architectural walls. In addition, Co. manufactures and markets prefabricated fireplaces, hearth stoves and related products. Co.'s line of hearth products includes a range of gas, wood and pellet burning fireplaces, inserts, stoves, facings and accessories. Co.'s products are marketed predominantly in the U.S. and Canada.

Recent Developments: For the quarter ended Sep 30 2017, net income increased 10.4% to US$37.3 million from US$33.8 million in the year-earlier quarter. Revenues were US$599.5 million, up 2.5% from US$584.6 million the year before. Operating income was US$57.7 million versus US$51.7 million in the prior-year quarter, an increase of 11.7%. Direct operating expenses rose 4.2% to US$378.2 million from US$363.1 million in the comparable period the year before. Indirect operating expenses decreased 3.7% to US$163.5 million from US$169.9 million in the equivalent prior-year period.

Prospects: Our evaluation of HNI Corp. as of Jan. 14, 2018 is the result of our systematic analysis on three basic characteristics: earnings strength, relative valuation, and recent stock price movement. The company has generated a negative trend in earnings per share over the past 5 quarters and while recent estimates for the company have been mixed, HNI has posted better than expected results. Based on operating earnings yield, the company is undervalued when compared to all of the companies in our coverage universe. Share price changes over the past year indicates that HNI will perform very poorly over the near term.

Financial Data

(US$ in Thousands)	9 Mos	6 Mos	3 Mos	12/31/2016	01/02/2016	01/03/2015	12/28/2013	12/29/2012
Earnings Per Share	1.50	1.40	1.73	1.88	2.32	1.35	1.39	1.07
Cash Flow Per Share	3.82	3.72	4.80	5.04	3.93	3.69	3.66	3.21
Tang Book Value Per Share	N.M.	4.62	4.76	4.76	4.51	3.06	3.33	2.94
Dividends Per Share	1.120	1.110	1.100	1.090	1.045	0.990	0.960	0.950
Dividend Payout %	74.67	79.29	63.58	57.98	45.04	73.33	69.06	88.79
Income Statement								
Total Revenue	1,591,607	992,152	477,667	2,203,489	2,304,419	2,222,695	2,059,964	2,004,003
EBITDA	141,826	66,047	26,773	190,892	210,176	158,949	142,287	130,987
Depn & Amortn	54,524	36,464	18,839	57,200	46,500	46,100	36,300	43,360
Income Before Taxes	83,541	27,586	6,959	128,911	157,170	104,931	96,707	77,604
Income Taxes	27,573	8,949	2,178	43,273	51,764	43,776	33,338	29,278
Net Income	55,956	18,685	4,837	85,577	105,436	61,471	63,683	48,967
Average Shares	44,479	45,305	45,452	45,502	45,440	45,578	45,956	45,819
Balance Sheet								
Current Assets	488,143	467,242	418,018	433,041	438,370	455,559	433,228	404,940
Total Assets	1,425,416	1,401,159	1,326,283	1,330,234	1,263,925	1,239,334	1,134,705	1,079,631
Current Liabilities	450,905	484,363	465,991	463,473	435,900	457,333	411,584	395,885
Long-Term Obligations	295,000	240,000	175,000	180,000	185,000	197,736	150,197	150,372
Total Liabilities	929,953	907,168	825,173	829,631	786,971	824,747	698,377	659,272
Stockholders' Equity	495,463	493,991	501,110	500,603	476,954	414,587	436,328	420,359
Shares Outstanding	43,427	44,056	44,239	44,078	44,158	44,165	44,981	44,950
Statistical Record								
Return on Assets %	4.80	4.60	5.96	6.62	8.45	5.09	5.77	4.60
Return on Equity %	13.11	12.68	15.88	17.56	23.72	14.21	14.91	11.70
EBITDA Margin %	8.91	6.66	5.60	8.66	9.12	7.15	6.91	6.54
Net Margin %	3.52	1.88	1.01	3.88	4.58	2.77	3.09	2.44
Asset Turnover	1.56	1.57	1.65	1.70	1.85	1.84	1.87	1.88
Current Ratio	1.08	0.96	0.90	0.93	1.01	1.00	1.05	1.02
Debt to Equity	0.60	0.49	0.35	0.36	0.39	0.48	0.34	0.36
Price Range	56.20-34.82	56.26-37.54	56.26-37.54	56.26-30.91	57.58-36.06	52.53-31.50	40.34-30.02	31.68-21.95
P/E Ratio	37.47-23.21	40.19-26.81	32.52-21.70	29.93-16.44	24.82-15.54	38.91-23.33	29.02-21.60	29.61-20.51
Average Yield %	2.54	2.34	2.32	2.47	2.17	2.55	2.70	3.59

Address: 600 East Second Street, Muscatine, IA 52761-0071	**Web Site:** www.hnicorp.com	**Auditors:** KPMG LLP	
Telephone: 563-272-7400	**Officers:** Stanley A. Askren - Chairman, President, Chief Executive Officer Marshall H. Bridges - Vice President, Chief Financial Officer	**Investor Contact:** 563-272-7400	
Fax: 563-272-7114		**Transfer Agents:** Wells Fargo Shareowner Services, St. Paul, MN	

HOLLYFRONTIER CORP

Exchange	Symbol	Price	52Wk Range	Yield	P/E
NYS	HFC	$51.22 (12/29/2017)	51.63-23.90	2.58	26.96

*7 Year Price Score 66.68 *NYSE Composite Index=100 *12 Month Price Score 132.57

TRADING VOLUME (thousand shares)

Interim Earnings (Per Share)

Qtr.	Mar	Jun	Sep	Dec
2014	0.76	0.89	0.88	(1.11)
2015	1.16	1.88	1.04	(0.19)
2016	0.12	(2.33)	0.42	0.30
2017	(0.26)	0.33	1.53	...

Interim Dividends (Per Share)

Amt	Decl	Ex	Rec	Pay
0.33Q	02/15/2017	02/24/2017	02/28/2017	03/14/2017
0.33Q	05/10/2017	05/19/2017	05/23/2017	06/14/2017
0.33Q	07/31/2017	08/21/2017	08/23/2017	09/20/2017
0.33Q	11/08/2017	11/20/2017	11/21/2017	12/13/2017

Indicated Div: $1.32

Valuation Analysis

		Institutional Holding	
Forecast EPS	$2.42 (01/26/2018)	No of Institutions	583
Market Cap	$9.1 Billion	Shares	187,330,272
Book Value	$4.8 Billion	% Held	N/A
Price/Book	1.87		
Price/Sales	0.69		

Business Summary: Refining & Marketing (MIC: 9.1.2 SIC: 2911 NAIC: 324110)

HollyFrontier is a petroleum refiner that produces products such as gasoline, diesel fuel, jet fuel, specialty lubricant products, and asphalt. Co. has two reportable segments, Refining and its subsidiary, Holly Energy Partners, L.P. (HEP). Refining segment activities involve the purchase and refining of crude oil and wholesale of refined products, such as gasoline, diesel fuel and jet fuel. The HEP segment includes all of the operations of HEP, which owns and operates logistics and refinery assets consisting of petroleum product and crude oil pipelines, terminals, tankage, loading rack facilities and processing units in the Mid-Continent, Southwest and Rocky Mountain regions of the U.S.

Recent Developments: For the quarter ended Sep 30 2017, net income increased 228.2% to US$287.7 million from US$87.7 million in the year-earlier quarter. Revenues were US$3.72 billion, up 30.6% from US$2.85 billion the year before. Operating income was US$449.3 million versus US$124.8 million in the prior-year quarter, an increase of 260.1%. Direct operating expenses rose 18.6% to US$2.78 billion from US$2.34 billion in the comparable period the year before. Indirect operating expenses increased 29.5% to US$492.6 million from US$380.4 million in the equivalent prior-year period.

Prospects: Our evaluation of HollyFrontier Corp. as of Jan. 21, 2018 is the result of our systematic analysis on three basic characteristics: earnings strength, relative valuation, and recent stock price movement. The company has enjoyed a very positive trend in earnings per share over the past 5 quarters and while recent estimates for the company have been raised by analysts, HFC has posted better than expected results. Based on operating earnings yield, the company is undervalued when compared to all of the companies in our coverage universe. Share price changes over the past year indicates that HFC will perform well over the near term.

Financial Data

(US$ in Thousands)	9 Mos	6 Mos	3 Mos	12/31/2016	12/31/2015	12/31/2014	12/31/2013	12/31/2012
Earnings Per Share	1.90	0.79	(1.87)	(1.48)	3.90	1.42	3.64	8.38
Cash Flow Per Share	5.36	4.34	3.16	3.41	5.19	3.85	4.34	8.08
Tang Book Value Per Share	14.86	13.59	13.50	14.99	16.21	16.28	18.45	18.25
Dividends Per Share	1.320	1.320	1.320	1.320	1.310	3.260	3.200	3.100
Dividend Payout %	69.47	167.09	...	...	33.59	229.58	87.91	36.99
Income Statement								
Total Revenue	10,258,594	6,539,347	3,080,483	10,535,700	13,237,920	19,764,327	20,160,560	20,090,724
EBITDA	858,984	398,540	77,791	131,854	1,485,685	770,523	1,437,565	3,067,372
Depn & Amortn	288,883	297,127	107,863	247,900	233,300	261,800	213,600	182,900
Income Before Taxes	486,636	45,605	(56,411)	(185,747)	1,212,306	469,507	1,161,471	2,785,072
Income Taxes	173,593	15,207	(16,789)	19,411	406,060	141,172	391,576	1,027,962
Net Income	284,313	12,299	(45,468)	(260,453)	740,101	281,292	735,842	1,727,172
Average Shares	176,530	176,302	176,210	176,101	188,940	197,428	201,234	206,184
Balance Sheet								
Current Assets	2,797,061	2,293,763	2,168,839	2,851,009	1,448,065	2,782,998	3,896,444	4,470,265
Total Assets	10,148,355	9,643,035	9,542,352	9,435,661	8,388,299	9,230,640	10,056,739	10,328,997
Current Liabilities	1,401,015	1,220,448	1,141,656	1,083,229	860,615	1,251,403	1,674,490	1,654,444
Long-Term Obligations	2,236,514	2,227,951	2,231,542	2,235,137	1,040,040	1,054,890	997,519	1,336,238
Total Liabilities	5,299,491	5,029,132	4,948,881	4,754,267	3,134,884	3,707,056	4,057,119	4,276,043
Stockholders' Equity	4,848,864	4,613,903	4,593,471	4,681,394	5,253,415	5,523,584	5,999,620	6,052,954
Shares Outstanding	177,276	177,279	177,359	177,345	180,234	196,086	198,830	203,551
Statistical Record								
Return on Assets %	3.60	1.53	N.M.	N.M.	8.40	2.92	7.22	16.69
Return on Equity %	7.10	3.03	N.M.	N.M.	13.73	4.88	12.21	30.60
EBITDA Margin %	8.37	6.09	2.53	1.25	11.22	3.90	7.13	15.27
Net Margin %	2.77	0.19	N.M.	N.M.	5.59	1.42	3.65	8.60
Asset Turnover	1.41	1.35	1.28	1.18	1.50	2.05	1.98	1.94
Current Ratio	2.00	1.88	1.90	2.63	1.68	2.22	2.33	2.70
Debt to Equity	0.46	0.48	0.49	0.48	0.20	0.19	0.17	0.22
Price Range	35.99-22.70	34.30-22.31	37.38-22.31	41.11-22.31	53.80-30.19	52.63-36.11	58.43-39.73	47.38-25.24
P/E Ratio	18.94-11.95	43.42-28.24	...	...	13.79-7.74	37.06-25.43	16.05-10.91	5.65-3.01
Average Yield %	4.65	4.86	4.72	4.51	3.01	7.06	6.81	8.65

Address: 2828 N. Harwood, Suite 1300, Dallas, TX 75201 **Telephone:** 214-871-3555	**Web Site:** www.hollyfrontier.com **Officers:** George J. Damiris - President, Chief Executive Officer, Executive Vice President, Chief Operating Officer, Senior Vice President Richard L. Voliva - Executive Vice President, Senior Vice President, Chief Financial Officer	**Auditors:** Ernst & Young LLP **Investor Contact:** 214-871-3555 **Transfer Agents:** Wells Fargo Shareowner Services, Mendota Heights, MN

HOME DEPOT INC

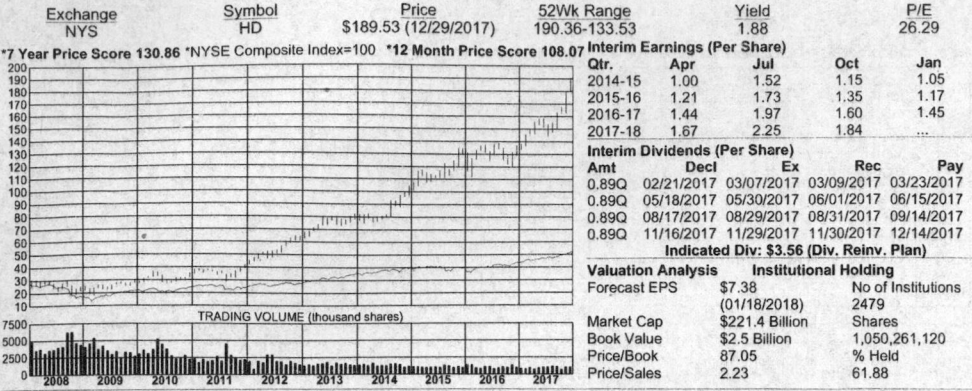

Exchange	Symbol	Price	52Wk Range	Yield	P/E
NYS	HD	$189.53 (12/29/2017)	190.36-133.53	1.88	26.29

*7 Year Price Score 130.86 *NYSE Composite Index=100 *12 Month Price Score 108.07

Interim Earnings (Per Share)

Qtr.	Apr	Jul	Oct	Jan
2014-15	1.00	1.52	1.15	1.05
2015-16	1.21	1.73	1.35	1.17
2016-17	1.44	1.97	1.60	1.45
2017-18	1.67	2.25	1.84	...

Interim Dividends (Per Share)

Amt	Decl	Ex	Rec	Pay
0.89Q	02/21/2017	03/07/2017	03/09/2017	03/23/2017
0.89Q	05/18/2017	05/30/2017	06/01/2017	06/15/2017
0.89Q	08/17/2017	08/29/2017	08/31/2017	09/14/2017
0.89Q	11/16/2017	11/29/2017	11/30/2017	12/14/2017

Indicated Div: $3.56 (Div. Reinv. Plan)

Valuation Analysis

Institutional Holding	
Forecast EPS	$7.38
	(01/18/2018)
Market Cap	$221.4 Billion
Book Value	$2.5 Billion
Price/Book	87.05
Price/Sales	2.23

No of Institutions 2479
Shares 1,050,261,120
% Held 61.88

TRADING VOLUME (thousand shares)

Business Summary: Retail - Hardware & Home Improvement (MIC: 2.1.8 SIC: 5211 NAIC: 444110)

The Home Depot is a home improvement retailer that sells a range of building materials, home improvement products and lawn and garden products and provides a number of services. As of Jan 29 2017, Co. had 2,278 The Home Depot stores located throughout the U.S., including the Commonwealth of Puerto Rico and the territories of the U.S. Virgin Islands and Guam, Canada and Mexico. Co. serves three primary customer groups: Do-It-Yourself customers, Do-It-For-Me customers, and professional customers. Co.'s products include Thomasville® Studio 1904 kitchen cabinets; DEWALT FLEXVOLT® system for power tools; Makita® subcompact drills; and Milwaukee M18 FUEL® with ONE KEYâ„¢ power tools.

Recent Developments: For the quarter ended Oct 29 2017, net income increased 10.0% to US$2.17 billion from US$1.97 billion in the year-earlier quarter. Revenues were US$25.03 billion, up 8.1% from US$23.15 billion the year before. Operating income was US$3.68 billion versus US$3.32 billion in the prior-year quarter, an increase of 10.8%. Direct operating expenses rose 8.4% to US$16.38 billion from US$15.11 billion in the comparable period the year before. Indirect operating expenses increased 5.2% to US$4.97 billion from US$4.72 billion in the equivalent prior-year period.

Prospects: Our evaluation of Home Depot Inc. as of Jan. 14, 2018 is the result of our systematic analysis on three basic characteristics: earnings strength, relative valuation, and recent stock price movement. The company has managed to produce a neutral trend in earnings per share over the past 5 quarters and while recent estimates for the company have been raised by analysts, HD has posted better than expected results. Based on operating earnings yield, the company is about fairly valued when compared to all of the companies in our coverage universe. Share price changes over the past year indicates that HD will perform in line with the market over the near term.

Financial Data

(US$ in Thousands)	9 Mos	6 Mos	3 Mos	01/29/2017	01/31/2016	02/01/2015	02/02/2014	02/03/2013
Earnings Per Share	7.21	6.97	6.69	6.45	5.46	4.71	3.76	3.00
Cash Flow Per Share	9.94	9.10	8.94	7.98	7.36	6.18	5.37	4.58
Tang Book Value Per Share	0.28	1.12	1.56	1.86	3.37	6.10	8.14	11.19
Dividends Per Share	3.360	3.160	2.960	2.760	2.360	1.880	1.560	1.160
Dividend Payout %	46.60	45.34	44.25	42.79	43.22	39.92	41.49	38.67
Income Statement								
Total Revenue	77,021,000	51,995,000	23,887,000	94,595,000	88,519,000	83,176,000	78,812,000	74,754,000
EBITDA	13,025,000	8,827,000	3,854,000	15,400,000	13,637,000	12,255,000	10,923,000	9,450,000
Depn & Amortn	1,533,000	1,015,000	505,000	1,973,000	1,863,000	1,786,000	1,757,000	1,684,000
Income Before Taxes	10,755,000	7,322,000	3,108,000	12,491,000	11,021,000	9,976,000	8,467,000	7,221,000
Income Taxes	3,904,000	2,636,000	1,094,000	4,534,000	4,012,000	3,631,000	3,082,000	2,686,000
Net Income	6,851,000	4,686,000	2,014,000	7,957,000	7,009,000	6,345,000	5,385,000	4,535,000
Average Shares	1,174,000	1,189,000	1,204,000	1,234,000	1,283,000	1,346,000	1,434,000	1,511,000
Balance Sheet								
Current Assets	19,682,000	20,511,000	19,896,000	17,724,000	16,993,000	15,302,000	15,279,000	15,372,000
Total Assets	45,023,000	45,959,000	44,944,000	42,966,000	42,549,000	39,946,000	40,518,000	41,084,000
Current Liabilities	16,002,000	15,823,000	16,438,000	14,133,000	12,526,000	11,269,000	10,749,000	11,462,000
Long-Term Obligations	24,266,000	24,422,000	22,393,000	22,349,000	20,888,000	16,869,000	14,691,000	9,475,000
Total Liabilities	42,480,000	42,405,000	40,982,000	38,633,000	36,233,000	30,624,000	27,996,000	23,307,000
Stockholders' Equity	2,543,000	3,554,000	3,962,000	4,333,000	6,316,000	9,322,000	12,522,000	17,777,000
Shares Outstanding	1,168,000	1,181,000	1,197,000	1,203,000	1,252,000	1,307,000	1,380,000	1,484,000
Statistical Record								
Return on Assets %	19.20	18.62	18.25	18.66	17.04	15.81	13.23	10.94
Return on Equity %	210.53	164.51	158.65	149.85	89.89	58.25	35.64	25.01
EBITDA Margin %	16.91	16.98	16.13	16.28	15.41	14.73	13.86	12.64
Net Margin %	8.89	9.01	8.43	8.41	7.92	7.63	6.83	6.07
Asset Turnover	2.22	2.16	2.14	2.22	2.15	2.07	1.94	1.80
Current Ratio	1.23	1.30	1.21	1.25	1.36	1.36	1.42	1.34
Debt to Equity	9.54	6.87	5.65	5.16	3.31	1.81	1.17	0.53
Price Range	167.65-119.89	158.81-119.89	156.12-119.89	138.77-111.85	134.74-104.43	107.62-74.97	82.34-63.92	67.82-45.17
P/E Ratio	23.25-16.63	22.78-17.20	23.34-17.92	21.51-17.34	24.68-19.13	22.85-15.92	21.90-17.00	22.61-15.06
Average Yield %	2.28	2.25	2.24	2.11	2.00	2.15	2.06	2.08

Address: 2455 Paces Ferry Road, Atlanta, GA 30339	Web Site: www.homedepot.com	Auditors: KPMG LLP
Telephone: 770-433-8211	Officers: Craig A. Menear - Chairman, President, Chief Executive Officer, Executive Vice President, Region Officer Carol B. Tome - Executive Vice President, Chief Financial Officer	Investor Contact: 770-384-4388
Fax: 770-431-2707		Transfer Agents: Computershare Trust Company, N.A., Providence, RI

HONEYWELL INTERNATIONAL INC

Exchange	Symbol	Price	52Wk Range	Yield	P/E
NYS	HON	$153.36 (12/29/2017)	155.96-116.18	1.94	23.24

*7 Year Price Score 116.99 *NYSE Composite Index=100 *12 Month Price Score 106.48

Interim Earnings (Per Share)

Qtr.	Mar	Jun	Sep	Dec
2014	1.28	1.38	1.47	1.20
2015	1.41	1.51	1.60	1.53
2016	1.53	1.66	1.60	1.34
2017	1.71	1.80	1.75	...

Interim Dividends (Per Share)

Amt	Decl	Ex	Rec	Pay
0.665Q	02/09/2017	02/22/2017	02/24/2017	03/10/2017
0.665Q	04/24/2017	05/17/2017	05/19/2017	06/09/2017
0.665Q	07/28/2017	08/16/2017	08/18/2017	09/08/2017
0.745Q	09/29/2017	11/16/2017	11/17/2017	12/08/2017

Indicated Div: $2.98 (Div. Reinv. Plan)

Valuation Analysis

		Institutional Holding	
Forecast EPS	$7.10	No of Institutions	
	(01/18/2018)	2017	
Market Cap	$116.8 Billion	Shares	709,749,568
Book Value	$21.1 Billion	% Held	
Price/Book	5.54	80.82	
Price/Sales	2.94		

TRADING VOLUME (thousand shares)

Business Summary: Auto Parts (MIC: 1.8.2 SIC: 3714 NAIC: 336312)

Honeywell International is a technology and manufacturing company. Co. has four segments: Aerospace, which supplies products, software and services for aircraft and vehicles; Home and Building Technologies, which provides products, software, solutions and technologies that assist owners of homes stay connected and in control of their comfort, security and energy use; Performance Materials and Technologies, which provides advanced materials, process technologies and automation solutions; and Safety and Productivity Solutions, which provides safety products such as personal protection equipment and footwear, and productivity solutions products and services such as gas detection technology.

Recent Developments: For the quarter ended Sep 30 2017, net income increased 9.4% to US$1.37 billion from US$1.25 billion in the year-earlier quarter. Revenues were US$10.12 billion, up 3.2% from US$9.80 billion the year before. Direct operating expenses declined 0.4% to US$6.87 billion from US$6.90 billion in the comparable period the year before. Indirect operating expenses increased 5.9% to US$1.45 billion from US$1.37 billion in the equivalent prior-year period.

Prospects: Our evaluation of Honeywell International Inc. as of Jan. 14, 2018 is the result of our systematic analysis on three basic characteristics: earnings strength, relative valuation, and recent stock price movement. The company has managed to produce a neutral trend in earnings per share over the past 5 quarters and while recent estimates for the company have been mixed, HON has posted better than expected results. Based on operating earnings yield, the company is undervalued when compared to all of the companies in our coverage universe. Share price changes over the past year indicates that HON will perform well over the near term.

Financial Data

(US$ in Thousands)	9 Mos	6 Mos	3 Mos	12/31/2016	12/31/2015	12/31/2014	12/31/2013	12/31/2012
Earnings Per Share	6.60	6.45	6.31	6.20	6.04	5.33	4.92	3.69
Cash Flow Per Share	7.66	7.96	8.10	7.17	6.99	6.40	5.51	4.48
Tang Book Value Per Share	N.M.	N.M.	N.M.	N.M.	N.M.	3.68	2.65	N.M.
Dividends Per Share	2.660	2.590	2.520	2.450	2.148	1.867	1.680	1.528
Dividend Payout %	40.30	40.16	39.94	39.52	35.55	35.04	34.15	41.40
Income Statement								
Total Revenue	29,691,000	19,570,000	9,492,000	39,302,000	38,581,000	40,306,000	39,055,000	37,665,000
EBITDA	6,352,000	4,203,000	2,070,000	7,374,000	7,434,000	6,665,000	6,304,000	4,783,000
Depn & Amortn	832,000	547,000	271,000	726,000	672,000	667,000	670,000	660,000
Income Before Taxes	5,285,000	3,502,000	1,724,000	6,416,000	6,556,000	5,782,000	5,376,000	3,830,000
Income Taxes	1,188,000	770,000	392,000	1,601,000	1,739,000	1,489,000	1,450,000	944,000
Net Income	4,066,000	2,718,000	1,326,000	4,809,000	4,768,000	4,239,000	3,924,000	2,926,000
Average Shares	771,400	774,000	773,900	775,300	789,300	795,200	797,300	791,900
Balance Sheet								
Current Assets	24,644,000	24,064,000	23,580,000	23,058,000	20,053,000	22,191,000	21,164,000	17,598,000
Total Assets	56,768,000	55,668,000	54,779,000	54,146,000	49,316,000	45,451,000	45,435,000	41,853,000
Current Liabilities	18,225,000	17,981,000	17,281,000	16,331,000	18,371,000	14,773,000	14,181,000	13,045,000
Long-Term Obligations	11,453,000	11,329,000	11,181,000	12,182,000	5,554,000	6,046,000	6,801,000	6,395,000
Total Liabilities	35,691,000	35,240,000	34,453,000	34,774,000	30,743,000	27,575,000	27,801,000	28,728,000
Stockholders' Equity	21,077,000	20,428,000	20,326,000	19,372,000	18,573,000	17,876,000	17,634,000	13,125,000
Shares Outstanding	761,822	760,569	762,338	760,800	770,400	782,200	783,800	782,800
Statistical Record								
Return on Assets %	9.25	9.34	9.29	9.27	10.06	9.33	8.99	7.15
Return on Equity %	25.33	25.47	25.34	25.28	26.16	23.87	25.51	24.39
EBITDA Margin %	21.39	21.48	21.81	18.76	19.27	16.54	16.14	12.70
Net Margin %	13.69	13.89	13.97	12.24	12.36	10.52	10.05	7.77
Asset Turnover	0.72	0.74	0.75	0.76	0.81	0.89	0.89	0.92
Current Ratio	1.35	1.34	1.36	1.41	1.09	1.50	1.49	1.35
Debt to Equity	0.54	0.55	0.55	0.63	0.30	0.34	0.39	0.49
Price Range	141.75-105.78	135.84-105.78	127.25-105.78	119.20-95.69	106.69-91.07	101.40-84.63	90.85-63.11	63.92-52.62
P/E Ratio	21.48-16.03	21.06-16.40	20.17-16.76	19.23-15.43	17.66-15.08	19.02-15.88	18.47-12.83	17.32-14.26
Average Yield %	2.12	2.15	2.17	2.20	2.11	2.00	2.13	2.60

Address: 115 Tabor Road, Morris Plains, NJ 07950	**Web Site:** www.honeywell.com	**Auditors:** Deloitte & Touche LLP
Telephone: 973-455-2000	**Officers:** David M. Cote - Chairman, President, Chief Executive Officer Darius Adamczyk - President, Chief Executive Officer, Chief Operating Officer, Division Officer	**Investor Contact:** 973-455-2222
Fax: 973-455-4807		**Transfer Agents:** American Stock Transfer & Trust Company, LLC, Brookly, NY

HORMEL FOODS CORP.

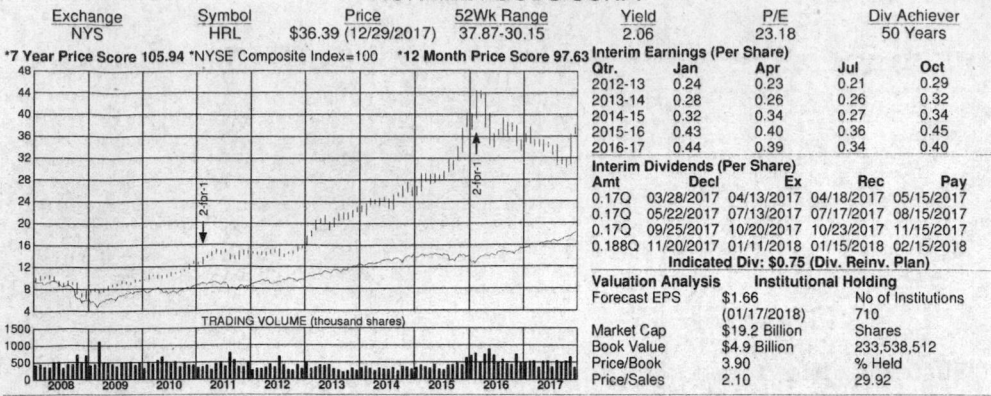

Exchange	Symbol	Price	52Wk Range	Yield	P/E	Div Achiever
NYS	HRL	$36.39 (12/29/2017)	37.87-30.15	2.06	23.18	50 Years

*7 Year Price Score 105.94 *NYSE Composite Index=100 *12 Month Price Score 97.63

Interim Earnings (Per Share)

Qtr.	Jan	Apr	Jul	Oct
2012-13	0.24	0.23	0.21	0.29
2013-14	0.28	0.26	0.26	0.32
2014-15	0.32	0.34	0.27	0.34
2015-16	0.43	0.40	0.36	0.45
2016-17	0.44	0.39	0.34	0.40

Interim Dividends (Per Share)

Amt	Decl	Ex	Rec	Pay
0.17Q	03/28/2017	04/13/2017	04/18/2017	05/15/2017
0.17Q	05/22/2017	07/13/2017	07/17/2017	08/15/2017
0.17Q	09/25/2017	10/20/2017	10/23/2017	11/15/2017
0.188Q	11/20/2017	01/11/2018	01/15/2018	02/15/2018

Indicated Div: $0.75 (Div. Reinv. Plan)

Valuation Analysis		Institutional Holding	
Forecast EPS	$1.66	No of Institutions	
	(01/17/2018)	710	
Market Cap	$19.2 Billion	Shares	
Book Value	$4.9 Billion	233,538,512	
Price/Book	3.90	% Held	
Price/Sales	2.10	29.92	

Business Summary: Food (MIC: 1.2.1 SIC: 2011 NAIC: 311611)

Hormel Foods is engaged in the production of a variety of meat and food products and the marketing of those products throughout the U.S. and internationally. Co.'s business is reported in five segments: Grocery Products, which processes, markets, and sells shelf-stable food products; Refrigerated Foods, which processes, markets, and sells pork, beef, chicken, and turkey products; Jennie-O Turkey Store, which processes, markets, and sells turkey products; Specialty Foods, which processes, markets, and sells nutritional and private label shelf-stable products; and International and Other, which manufactures, markets, and sells Co.'s products internationally.

Recent Developments: For the year ended Oct 29 2017, net income decreased 4.9% to US$847.1 million from US$890.5 million in the prior year. Revenues were US$9.17 billion, down 3.7% from US$9.52 billion the year before. Operating income was US$1.28 billion versus US$1.32 billion in the prior year, a decrease of 3.3%. Direct operating expenses declined 2.7% to US$7.16 billion from US$7.37 billion in the comparable period the year before. Indirect operating expenses decreased 13.4% to US$722.7 million from US$834.3 million in the equivalent prior-year period.

Prospects: Our evaluation of Hormel Foods Corp. as of Jan. 14, 2018 is the result of our systematic analysis on three basic characteristics: earnings strength, relative valuation, and recent stock price movement. The company has managed to produce a neutral trend in earnings per share over the past 5 quarters and while recent estimates for the company have been raised by analysts, HRL has posted better than expected results. Based on operating earnings yield, the company is undervalued when compared to all of the companies in our coverage universe. Share price changes over the past year indicates that HRL will perform well over the near term.

Financial Data

(US$ in Thousands)	10/29/2017	10/30/2016	10/25/2015	10/26/2014	10/27/2013	10/28/2012	10/30/2011	10/31/2010
Earnings Per Share	1.57	1.64	1.27	1.12	0.97	0.93	0.87	0.73
Cash Flow Per Share	1.92	1.85	1.88	1.42	1.21	0.99	0.92	0.90
Tang Book Value Per Share	3.39	3.24	2.78	3.46	3.79	3.93	3.59	3.06
Dividends Per Share	0.680	0.580	0.500	0.400	0.340	0.300	0.255	0.210
Dividend Payout %	43.31	35.37	39.37	35.87	34.87	32.26	29.31	28.77
Income Statement								
Total Revenue	9,167,519	9,523,224	9,263,863	9,316,256	8,751,654	8,230,670	7,895,089	7,220,719
EBITDA	1,380,239	1,425,565	1,185,009	1,053,431	919,805	854,452	849,168	769,572
Depn & Amortn	139,360	140,355	141,576	139,396	134,329	128,469	133,641	136,123
Income Before Taxes	1,239,055	1,278,530	1,033,256	904,567	777,994	719,644	692,079	611,425
Income Taxes	431,542	426,698	369,879	316,126	268,431	253,374	239,640	224,775
Net Income	846,735	890,052	686,088	602,677	526,211	500,050	474,195	395,587
Average Shares	539,116	542,473	541,002	540,432	540,448	537,782	543,830	541,396
Balance Sheet								
Current Assets	2,026,523	2,029,912	2,063,032	2,132,771	2,047,413	2,320,684	1,998,231	1,858,166
Total Assets	6,975,908	6,370,067	6,139,831	5,455,619	4,915,880	4,563,966	4,244,391	4,053,918
Current Liabilities	1,058,212	1,053,196	1,214,025	954,692	784,009	786,300	778,186	1,101,213
Long-Term Obligations	250,000	250,000	250,000	250,000	250,000	250,000	250,000	...
Total Liabilities	2,040,001	1,922,061	2,141,633	1,849,941	1,604,840	1,744,511	1,587,809	1,653,261
Stockholders' Equity	4,935,907	4,448,006	3,998,198	3,605,678	3,311,040	2,819,455	2,656,582	2,400,657
Shares Outstanding	528,424	528,483	528,411	527,226	527,316	526,088	527,926	531,926
Statistical Record								
Return on Assets %	12.72	14.00	11.87	11.65	11.13	11.39	11.46	10.05
Return on Equity %	18.10	20.73	18.10	17.47	17.21	18.31	18.80	17.21
EBITDA Margin %	15.06	14.97	12.79	11.31	10.51	10.38	10.76	10.66
Net Margin %	9.24	9.35	7.41	6.47	6.01	6.08	6.01	5.48
Asset Turnover	1.38	1.50	1.60	1.80	1.85	1.87	1.91	1.83
Current Ratio	1.92	1.93	1.70	2.23	2.61	2.95	2.57	1.69
Debt to Equity	0.05	0.06	0.06	0.07	0.08	0.09	0.09	...
Price Range	38.50-30.27	44.47-33.09	34.24-25.07	26.27-21.11	22.06-14.77	15.34-13.74	15.19-11.40	11.48-9.21
P/E Ratio	24.52-19.28	27.12-20.17	26.96-19.74	23.46-18.85	22.74-15.22	16.49-14.77	17.45-13.10	15.73-12.62
Average Yield %	1.99	1.52	1.75	1.69	1.77	2.07	1.87	2.03

Address: 1 Hormel Place, Austin, MN 55912-3680	**Web Site:** www.hormel.com	**Auditors:** Ernst & Young LLP
Telephone: 507-437-5611	**Officers:** James P. Snee - Chairman, President, Chief Executive Officer, Chief Operating Officer, Vice President, Group Vice President, Division Officer Steven G. Binder - Executive Vice President, Division Officer	**Investor Contact:** 507-437-5248
Fax: 507-437-5489		**Transfer Agents:** Wells Fargo Shareowner Services, Mendota Heights, MN

HORTON (DR) INC

Exchange	Symbol	Price	52Wk Range	Yield	P/E
NYS	DHI	$51.07 (12/29/2017)	51.45-27.56	0.98	18.64

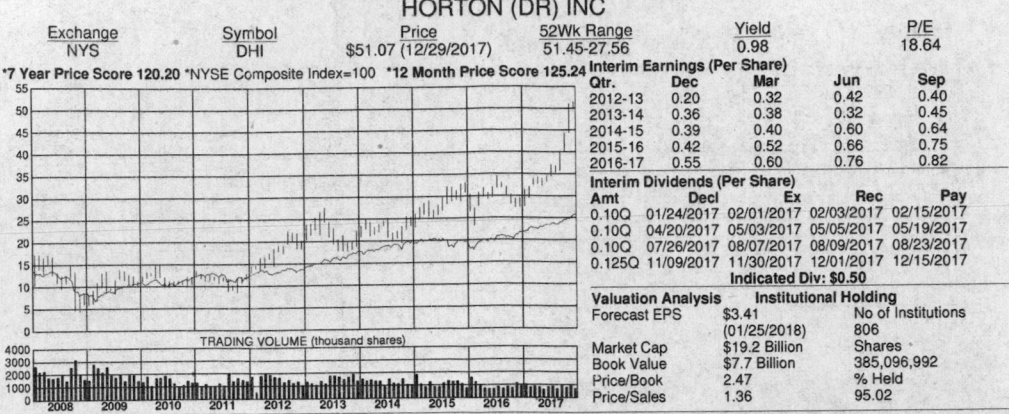

*7 Year Price Score 120.20 *NYSE Composite Index=100 *12 Month Price Score 125.24

Interim Earnings (Per Share)

Qtr.	Dec	Mar	Jun	Sep
2012-13	0.20	0.32	0.42	0.40
2013-14	0.36	0.38	0.32	0.45
2014-15	0.39	0.40	0.60	0.64
2015-16	0.42	0.52	0.66	0.75
2016-17	0.55	0.60	0.76	0.82

Interim Dividends (Per Share)

Amt	Decl	Ex	Rec	Pay
0.10Q	01/24/2017	02/01/2017	02/03/2017	02/15/2017
0.10Q	04/20/2017	05/03/2017	05/05/2017	05/19/2017
0.10Q	07/26/2017	08/07/2017	08/09/2017	08/23/2017
0.125Q	11/09/2017	11/30/2017	12/01/2017	12/15/2017

Indicated Div: $0.50

Valuation Analysis / Institutional Holding

Forecast EPS	$3.41 (01/25/2018)	No of Institutions	806
Market Cap	$19.2 Billion	Shares	385,096,992
Book Value	$7.7 Billion		
Price/Book	2.47	% Held	95.02
Price/Sales	1.36		

Business Summary: Builders (MIC: 2.2.5 SIC: 1531 NAIC: 236117)

D.R. Horton a homebuilding company. Co. constructs and sells homes under the D.R. Horton, America's Builder, Emerald Homes, Express Homes, Freedom Homes and Pacific Ridge Homes names. Co.'s business operations consist of homebuilding, financial services and other activities. Co. sells single-family detached homes, as well as attached homes, such as townhomes, duplexes, triplexes and condominiums. Co.'s financial services operations provide mortgage financing and title agency services to homebuyers in its homebuilding markets. In addition, Co. has subsidiaries that engage in conducting insurance-related operations, constructing and owning income-producing rental properties, among others.

Recent Developments: For the year ended Sep 30 2017, net income increased 17.2% to US$1.04 billion from US$886.3 million in the prior year. Revenues were US$14.09 billion, up 15.9% from US$12.16 billion the year before. Direct operating expenses rose 16.2% to US$11.04 billion from US$9.50 billion in the comparable period the year before. Indirect operating expenses increased 11.1% to US$1.45 billion from US$1.30 billion in the equivalent prior-year period.

Prospects: Our evaluation of Horton (D.R.) Inc. as of Jan. 21, 2018 is the result of our systematic analysis on three basic characteristics: earnings strength, relative valuation, and recent stock price movement. The company has managed to produce a neutral trend in earnings per share over the past 5 quarters and while recent estimates for the company have been raised by analysts, DHI has posted better than expected results. Based on operating earnings yield, the company is undervalued when compared to all of the companies in our coverage universe. Share price changes over the past year indicates that DHI will perform very well over the near term.

Financial Data
(US$ in Thousands)

	09/30/2017	09/30/2016	09/30/2015	09/30/2014	09/30/2013	09/30/2012	09/30/2011	09/30/2010
Earnings Per Share	2.74	2.36	2.03	1.50	1.33	2.77	0.23	0.77
Cash Flow Per Share	1.16	1.66	1.91	(1.94)	(3.82)	(0.93)	0.05	2.23
Tang Book Value Per Share	20.45	18.00	15.75	13.77	12.45	11.07	8.24	8.15
Dividends Per Share	0.400	0.320	0.250	0.138	0.188	0.150	0.150	0.150
Dividend Payout %	14.60	13.56	12.32	9.17	14.10	5.42	65.22	19.48
Income Statement								
Total Revenue	14,091,000	12,157,400	10,824,000	8,024,900	6,259,300	4,354,000	3,636,800	4,400,200
EBITDA	1,637,000	1,390,800	1,161,200	840,600	676,700	278,400	74,300	194,900
Depn & Amortn	49,400	50,800	50,300	36,600	22,300	18,800	19,900	17,200
Income Before Taxes	1,602,100	1,353,500	1,123,400	814,200	657,800	242,900	12,100	99,500
Income Taxes	563,700	467,200	372,700	280,700	195,100	(713,400)	(59,700)	(145,600)
Net Income	1,038,400	886,300	750,700	533,500	462,700	956,300	71,800	245,100
Average Shares	378,900	375,100	369,800	366,600	364,900	359,000	318,500	318,600
Balance Sheet								
Current Assets	10,366,900	9,778,200	9,376,200	8,549,300	7,397,900	5,821,500	4,778,800	5,125,700
Total Assets	12,184,600	11,558,900	11,151,000	10,202,500	8,856,400	7,248,200	5,358,400	5,938,600
Current Liabilities	911,400	849,200	784,600	747,300	636,400	377,600	294,500	186,700
Long-Term Obligations	2,871,600	3,271,300	3,811,500	3,682,800	3,509,000	2,493,100	1,704,600	2,171,800
Total Liabilities	4,437,500	4,766,400	5,256,700	5,086,700	4,797,900	3,656,100	2,737,800	3,325,400
Stockholders' Equity	7,747,100	6,792,500	5,894,300	5,115,800	4,058,500	3,592,100	2,620,600	2,613,200
Shares Outstanding	374,986	372,923	368,647	364,586	322,943	320,891	316,043	318,823
Statistical Record								
Return on Assets %	8.75	7.78	7.03	5.60	5.75	15.13	1.27	3.86
Return on Equity %	14.28	13.93	13.64	11.63	12.10	30.70	2.74	10.06
EBITDA Margin %	11.62	11.44	10.73	10.47	10.81	6.39	2.04	4.43
Net Margin %	7.37	7.29	6.94	6.65	7.39	21.96	1.97	5.57
Asset Turnover	1.19	1.07	1.01	0.84	0.78	0.69	0.64	0.69
Current Ratio	11.37	11.51	11.95	11.44	11.62	15.42	16.23	27.45
Debt to Equity	0.37	0.48	0.65	0.72	0.86	0.69	0.65	0.83
Price Range	39.93-27.28	34.41-23.23	32.21-19.49	25.10-17.69	27.60-17.77	22.37-8.45	13.50-8.94	14.97-9.71
P/E Ratio	14.57-9.96	14.58-9.84	15.87-9.60	16.73-11.79	20.75-13.36	8.08-3.05	58.70-38.87	19.44-12.61
Average Yield %	1.24	1.05	0.95	0.63	0.86	0.98	1.33	1.29

Address: 1341 Horton Circle, Arlington, TX 76102 Telephone: 817-390-8200	Web Site: www.drhorton.com Officers: Donald R. Horton - Chairman David V. Auld - President, Chief Executive Officer, Executive Vice President, Chief Operating Officer, Division Officer	Auditors: PricewaterhouseCoopers LLP Investor Contact: 817-390-8200 Transfer Agents: American Stock Transfer & Trust Co., New York, NY

HP INC

Exchange	Symbol	Price	52Wk Range	Yield	P/E
NYS	HPQ	$21.01 (12/29/2017)	22.46-14.58	2.65	14.20

*7 Year Price Score 105.86 *NYSE Composite Index=100 *12 Month Price Score 108.05

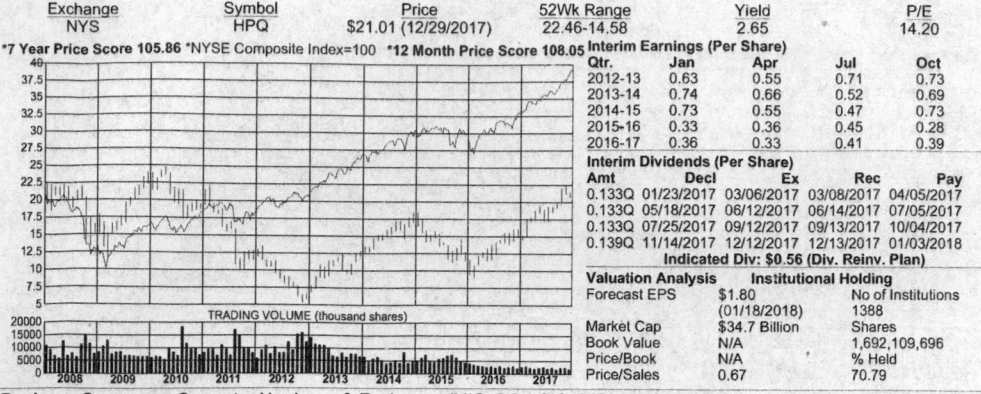

Interim Earnings (Per Share)

Qtr.	Jan	Apr	Jul	Oct
2012-13	0.63	0.55	0.71	0.73
2013-14	0.74	0.66	0.52	0.69
2014-15	0.73	0.55	0.47	0.73
2015-16	0.33	0.36	0.45	0.28
2016-17	0.36	0.33	0.41	0.39

Interim Dividends (Per Share)

Amt	Decl	Ex	Rec	Pay
0.133Q	01/23/2017	03/06/2017	03/08/2017	04/05/2017
0.133Q	05/18/2017	06/12/2017	06/14/2017	07/05/2017
0.133Q	07/25/2017	09/12/2017	09/13/2017	10/04/2017
0.139Q	11/14/2017	12/12/2017	12/13/2017	01/03/2018

Indicated Div: $0.56 (Div. Reinv. Plan)

Valuation Analysis / Institutional Holding

Forecast EPS	$1.80	No of Institutions
	(01/18/2018)	1388
Market Cap	$34.7 Billion	Shares
Book Value	N/A	1,692,109,696
Price/Book	N/A	% Held
Price/Sales	0.67	70.79

Business Summary: Computer Hardware & Equipment (MIC: 6.2.1 SIC: 3571 NAIC: 334111)

HP is a provider of personal computing and other access devices, imaging and printing products, and related technologies, solutions and services. Co. has three business segments: Personal Systems, which provides commercial personal computers (PCs), consumer PCs, workstations, thin clients, commercial tablets and mobility devices, retail point-of-sale systems, displays and other related accessories, software, support, and services for the commercial and consumer markets; Printing, which provides consumer and commercial printer hardware, supplies, media, solutions and services, and scanning devices; and Corporate Investments, which includes HP Labs and certain business incubation projects.

Recent Developments: For the year ended Oct 31 2017, income from continuing operations decreased 5.3% to US$2.53 billion from US$2.67 billion a year earlier. Net income increased 1.2% to US$2.53 billion from US$2.50 billion in the prior year. Revenues were US$52.06 billion, up 7.9% from US$48.24 billion the year before. Operating income was US$3.52 billion versus US$3.55 billion in the prior year, a decrease of 0.8%. Direct operating expenses rose 8.3% to US$42.48 billion from US$39.24 billion in the comparable period the year before. Indirect operating expenses increased 11.2% to US$6.06 billion from US$5.45 billion in the equivalent prior-year period.

Prospects: Our evaluation of HP Inc as of Jan. 14, 2018 is the result of our systematic analysis on three basic characteristics: earnings strength, relative valuation, and recent stock price movement. The company has enjoyed a very positive trend in earnings per share over the past 5 quarters and while recent estimates for the company have remained steady, HPQ posted results that fell short of analysts expectations. Based on operating earnings yield, the company is undervalued when compared to all of the companies in our coverage universe. Share price changes over the past year indicates that HPQ will perform well over the near term.

Financial Data
(US$ in Millions)

	10/31/2017	10/31/2016	10/31/2015	10/31/2014	10/31/2013	10/31/2012	10/31/2011	10/31/2010
Earnings Per Share	1.48	1.43	2.48	2.62	2.62	(6.41)	3.32	3.69
Cash Flow Per Share	2.18	1.86	3.58	6.55	6.00	5.34	6.04	5.14
Dividends Per Share	0.531	0.496	0.672	0.610	0.554	0.504	0.400	0.320
Dividend Payout %	35.86	34.69	27.10	23.30	21.16	...	12.05	8.67
Income Statement								
Total Revenue	52,056	48,238	103,355	111,454	112,298	120,357	127,245	126,033
EBITDA	3,939	3,881	9,090	11,485	11,704	(5,973)	14,684	15,758
Depn & Amortn	354	332	4,031	4,300	4,573	5,084	5,007	4,784
Income Before Taxes	3,276	3,761	4,732	6,557	6,510	(11,933)	8,982	10,974
Income Taxes	750	1,095	178	1,544	1,397	717	1,908	2,213
Net Income	2,526	2,496	4,554	5,013	5,113	(12,650)	7,074	8,761
Average Shares	1,702	1,743	1,836	1,912	1,950	1,974	2,128	2,373
Balance Sheet								
Current Assets	22,318	18,468	51,787	50,145	50,364	50,637	51,021	54,184
Total Assets	32,913	29,010	106,882	103,206	105,676	108,768	129,517	124,503
Current Liabilities	22,412	18,800	42,191	43,735	45,521	46,666	50,442	49,403
Long-Term Obligations	6,747	6,758	21,780	16,039	16,608	21,789	22,551	15,258
Total Liabilities	36,321	32,899	79,114	76,475	78,407	86,332	90,892	84,054
Stockholders' Equity	(3,408)	(3,889)	27,768	26,731	27,269	22,436	38,625	40,449
Shares Outstanding	1,650	1,712	1,803	1,839	1,907	1,962	1,990	2,204
Statistical Record								
Return on Assets %	8.16	3.66	4.34	4.80	4.77	N.M.	5.57	7.32
Return on Equity %	...	20.85	16.71	18.57	20.57	N.M.	17.89	21.64
EBITDA Margin %	7.57	8.05	8.79	10.30	10.42	N.M.	11.54	12.50
Net Margin %	4.85	5.17	4.41	4.50	4.55	N.M.	5.56	6.95
Asset Turnover	1.68	0.71	0.98	1.07	1.05	1.01	1.00	1.05
Current Ratio	1.00	0.98	1.23	1.15	1.11	1.09	1.01	1.10
Debt to Equity	...	...	0.78	0.60	0.61	0.97	0.58	0.38
Price Range	22.12-14.35	15.65-9.02	18.49-11.15	17.32-11.06	12.39-5.32	13.57-6.29	22.24-10.08	24.75-17.25
P/E Ratio	14.95-9.70	10.94-6.31	7.45-4.50	6.61-4.22	4.73-2.03	...	6.70-3.04	6.71-4.68
Average Yield %	2.99	3.90	4.48	4.20	5.93	4.91	2.37	1.48

Address: 1501 Page Mill Road, Palo Alto, CA 94304
Telephone: 650-857-1501

Web Site: www.hp.com
Officers: Charles V. (Chip) Bergh - Chairman Dion J. Weisler - President, Chief Executive Officer, Division Officer

Auditors: Ernst & Young LLP
Investor Contact: 800-286-5977
Transfer Agents: Wells Fargo Shareowner Services, St. Paul, MN

HOST HOTELS & RESORTS INC

Exchange	Symbol	Price	52Wk Range	Yield	P/E
NYS	HST	$19.85 (12/29/2017)	20.58-17.38	4.03	24.81

*7 Year Price Score 82.02 *NYSE Composite Index=100 *12 Month Price Score 100.83

Interim Earnings (Per Share)

Qtr.	Mar	Jun	Sep	Dec
2014	0.24	0.21	0.19	0.33
2015	0.13	0.28	0.11	0.21
2016	0.24	0.47	0.14	0.17
2017	0.21	0.28	0.14	...

Interim Dividends (Per Share)

Amt	Decl	Ex	Rec	Pay
0.20Q	06/15/2017	06/28/2017	06/30/2017	07/17/2017
0.20Q	09/18/2017	09/28/2017	09/29/2017	10/16/2017
0.05Q	12/14/2017	12/28/2017	12/29/2017	01/16/2018
0.20Q	12/14/2017	12/28/2017	12/29/2017	01/16/2018

Indicated Div: $0.80

Valuation Analysis   **Institutional Holding**

Forecast EPS	$0.79	No of Institutions
	(01/26/2018)	715
Market Cap	$14.7 Billion	Shares
Book Value	$7.1 Billion	972,459,520
Price/Book	2.07	% Held
Price/Sales	2.73	102.31

Business Summary: REITs (MIC: 5.3.1 SIC: 6798 NAIC: 525930)

Host Hotels & Resorts is a real estate investment trust, which owns properties and conducts operations through Host Hotels & Resorts, L.P. Co.'s lodging portfolio consisted 96 hotels located in the U.S., and with seven of the properties located outside of the U.S. in Australia, Brazil, Canada and Mexico. In addition, Co. owns non-controlling interests in two international joint ventures: approximately a 33% interest in a joint venture in Europe; and a 9% indirect interest, through joint ventures, in five operating hotels and two hotels in the final stages of completion in India. Co. also hold non-controlling investments in three domestic hotels and a timeshare joint venture in Hawaii.

Recent Developments: For the quarter ended Sep 30 2017, net income decreased 2.8% to US$105.0 million from US$108.0 million in the year-earlier quarter. Revenues were US$1.25 billion, down 3.2% from US$1.30 billion the year before.

Prospects: Our evaluation of Host Marriott Corp. as of Jan. 21, 2018 is the result of our systematic analysis on three basic characteristics: earnings strength, relative valuation, and recent stock price movement. The company has generated a negative trend in earnings per share over the past 5 quarters. However, while recent estimates for the company have been mixed, HST has posted results that were in line with analysts' expectations. Based on operating earnings yield, the company is about fairly valued when compared to all of the companies in our coverage universe. Share price changes over the past year indicates that HST will perform in line with the market over the near term.

Financial Data
(US$ in Millions)

	9 Mos	6 Mos	3 Mos	12/31/2016	12/31/2015	12/31/2014	12/31/2013	12/31/2012
Earnings Per Share	0.80	0.80	0.99	1.02	0.74	0.96	0.42	0.08
Cash Flow Per Share	1.69	1.76	1.75	1.75	1.56	1.52	1.37	1.09
Tang Book Value Per Share	9.58	9.61	9.51	9.48	9.41	9.71	9.58	9.42
Dividends Per Share	0.850	0.850	0.850	0.850	0.800	0.750	0.460	0.300
Dividend Payout %	106.25	106.25	85.86	83.33	108.11	78.13	109.52	375.00
Income Statement								
Total Revenue	4,043	2,789	1,348	5,430	5,387	5,354	5,166	5,286
EBITDA	648	462	187	1,672	1,477	1,670	558	395
Depn & Amortn	5	3	1	731	737	725	10	3
Income Before Taxes	522	379	148	790	510	735	248	42
Income Taxes	63	21	(6)	40	9	14	21	31
Net Income	472	368	158	762	558	732	317	61
Average Shares	739	738	738	743	752	786	747	719
Balance Sheet								
Current Assets	905	766	546	374	254	684	893	453
Total Assets	11,771	11,854	11,776	11,408	11,784	12,207	12,814	12,994
Current Liabilities	250	221	218	278	243	298	214	194
Long-Term Obligations	3,961	3,992	3,988	3,649	4,017	3,992	4,759	5,411
Total Liabilities	4,692	4,753	4,750	4,414	4,720	4,871	5,586	6,169
Stockholders' Equity	7,079	7,101	7,026	6,994	7,064	7,336	7,228	6,825
Shares Outstanding	738	738	738	737	750	755	754	724
Statistical Record								
Return on Assets %	5.13	5.13	6.29	6.55	4.65	5.85	2.46	0.47
Return on Equity %	8.44	8.42	10.51	10.81	7.75	10.05	4.51	0.90
EBITDA Margin %	16.03	16.57	13.87	30.79	27.42	31.19	10.80	7.47
Net Margin %	11.67	13.19	11.72	14.03	10.36	13.67	6.14	1.15
Asset Turnover	0.46	0.46	0.46	0.47	0.45	0.43	0.40	0.40
Current Ratio	3.62	3.47	2.50	1.35	1.05	2.30	4.17	2.34
Debt to Equity	0.56	0.56	0.57	0.52	0.57	0.54	0.66	0.79
Price Range	19.34-14.83	19.34-14.83	19.34-14.58	19.18-12.82	24.14-15.20	24.33-18.00	19.44-15.67	17.25-13.78
P/E Ratio	24.18-18.54	24.18-18.54	19.54-14.73	18.80-12.57	32.62-20.54	25.34-18.75	46.29-37.31	215.63-172.25
Average Yield %	4.74	4.82	5.00	5.24	4.12	3.49	2.60	1.92

Address: 6903 Rockledge Drive, Suite 1500, Bethesda, MD 20817 **Telephone:** 240-744-1000	**Web Site:** www.hosthotels.com **Officers:** Richard E. Marriott - Chairman James F. Risoleo - President, Chief Executive Officer, Executive Vice President, Chief Investment Officer, Region Officer
	Auditors: KPMG LLP **Transfer Agents:** Computershare Trust Company, N.A., Providence, RI

HOWARD HUGHES CORP

Exchange	Symbol	Price	52Wk Range	Yield	P/E
NYS	HHC	$131.27 (12/29/2017)	131.79-105.33	N/A	90.53

*7 Year Price Score 90.76 *NYSE Composite Index=100 *12 Month Price Score 98.89

Interim Earnings (Per Share)

Qtr.	Mar	Jun	Sep	Dec
2014	(2.19)	(0.37)	0.48	0.81
2015	(2.68)	0.18	0.76	0.59
2016	2.69	0.16	0.19	1.01
2017	0.13	0.07	0.24	...

Interim Dividends (Per Share)

No Dividends Paid

TRADING VOLUME (thousand shares)

Valuation Analysis

		Institutional Holding	
Forecast EPS	$0.72	No of Institutions	
	(01/18/2018)	313	
Market Cap	$5.7 Billion	Shares	
Book Value	$3.0 Billion	43,566,160	
Price/Book	1.87	% Held	
Price/Sales	5.24	81.57	

Business Summary: Property, Real Estate & Development (MIC: 5.3.2 SIC: 6552 NAIC: 531312)

Howard Hughes is engaged in the development of master planned communities, in the ownership, management and redevelopment of revenue-generating real estate assets, and in the development of other real estate assets in the form of entitled and unentitled land and residential condominium developments. Co.'s segments are: Master Planned Communities, which includes the development and sale of residential and commercial land, primarily in large-scale long-term projects; Operating Assets, which contains properties, investments and other assets that generate revenue; and Strategic Developments, which focuses on development projects, in which it creates or executes strategic plans for these assets.

Recent Developments: For the quarter ended Sep 30 2017, net income increased 31.5% to US$10.5 million from US$8.0 million in the year-earlier quarter. Revenues were US$258.7 million, up 6.8% from US$242.3 million the year before.

Prospects: Our evaluation of Howard Hughes Corp as of Jan. 14, 2018 is the result of our systematic analysis on three basic characteristics: earnings strength, relative valuation, and recent stock price movement. The company has suffered a very negative trend in earnings per share over the past 5 quarters and while recent estimates for the company have been mixed, HHC has posted results that fell short of analysts expectations. Based on operating earnings yield, the company is overvalued when compared to all of the companies in our coverage universe. Share price changes over the past year indicates that HHC will perform well over the near term.

Financial Data

(US$ in Thousands)	9 Mos	6 Mos	3 Mos	12/31/2016	12/31/2015	12/31/2014	12/31/2013	12/31/2012
Earnings Per Share	1.45	1.40	1.49	4.73	1.60	(0.60)	(1.87)	(3.36)
Cash Flow Per Share	3.49	2.43	1.09	1.49	0.61	(1.48)	3.28	4.00
Tang Book Value Per Share	67.66	66.20	62.20	64.53	59.43	56.10	56.56	58.36
Income Statement								
Total Revenue	799,137	540,401	231,762	1,035,005	797,088	634,565	474,610	376,886
EBITDA	169,453	110,621	51,366	410,201	286,603	53,409	(68,211)	(113,357)
Depn & Amortn	97,757	63,297	27,294	81,878	82,275	50,683	29,637	19,455
Income Before Taxes	25,320	16,425	6,836	263,958	146,999	16,104	(78,553)	(124,339)
Income Taxes	31,846	26,000	9,697	118,450	24,001	62,960	9,570	6,887
Net Income	19,283	8,779	5,659	202,303	126,719	(23,531)	(73,790)	(128,288)
Average Shares	43,267	43,051	42,757	42,729	42,754	39,464	39,449	38,127
Balance Sheet								
Current Assets	1,107,617	1,260,497	1,085,215	825,933	619,114	721,665	1,383,235	680,397
Total Assets	6,723,696	6,667,449	6,408,142	6,367,382	5,721,582	5,119,931	4,567,868	3,503,042
Current Liabilities	650,226	625,416	957,149	1,105,125	913,731	898,955	808,099	503,733
Long-Term Obligations	2,993,448	3,002,846	2,750,254	2,690,747	2,443,962	1,993,470	1,514,623	688,312
Total Liabilities	3,697,086	3,703,728	3,794,608	3,799,644	3,361,465	2,896,168	2,329,284	1,197,804
Stockholders' Equity	3,026,610	2,963,721	2,613,534	2,567,738	2,360,117	2,223,763	2,238,584	2,305,238
Shares Outstanding	43,206	43,185	40,311	39,790	39,714	39,638	39,576	39,498
Statistical Record								
Return on Assets %	0.95	0.94	1.03	3.34	2.34	N.M.	N.M.	N.M.
Return on Equity %	2.27	2.21	2.51	8.19	5.53	N.M.	N.M.	N.M.
EBITDA Margin %	21.20	20.47	22.16	39.63	35.96	8.42	N.M.	N.M.
Net Margin %	2.41	1.62	2.44	19.55	15.90	N.M.	N.M.	N.M.
Asset Turnover	0.16	0.17	0.17	0.17	0.15	0.13	0.12	0.11
Current Ratio	1.70	2.02	1.13	0.75	0.68	0.80	1.71	1.35
Debt to Equity	0.99	1.01	1.05	1.05	1.04	0.90	0.68	0.30
Price Range	130.00-103.30	130.00-103.30	121.71-98.43	121.71-81.34	159.12-108.49	160.00-118.04	121.13-71.25	75.12-44.27
P/E Ratio	89.66-71.24	92.86-73.79	81.68-66.06	25.73-17.20	99.45-67.81	...	...	...

Address: 13355 Noel Road, 22nd Floor, Dallas, TX 75240	**Web Site:** www.howardhughes.com	**Auditors:** Ernst & Young LLP
Telephone: 214-741-7744	**Officers:** William A. Ackman - Chairman Saul Scherl - Executive Vice President	**Transfer Agents:** Computershare, Jersey City, NJ
Fax: 214-741-3021		

HRG GROUP INC

Exchange	Symbol	Price	52Wk Range	Yield	P/E
NYS	HRG	$16.95 (12/29/2017)	20.07-14.26	N/A	31.98

*7 Year Price Score 120.90 *NYSE Composite Index=100 *12 Month Price Score 89.64

TRADING VOLUME (thousand shares)

Interim Earnings (Per Share)

Qtr.	Dec	Mar	Jun	Sep
2012-13	0.03	(0.33)	0.25	(0.97)
2013-14	(0.28)	(0.63)	0.00	0.00
2014-15	(0.56)	(1.16)	(0.38)	(0.72)
2015-16	(0.17)	(0.18)	(0.66)	(0.04)
2016-17	1.06	(0.41)	0.01	(0.13)

Interim Dividends (Per Share)
No Dividends Paid

Valuation Analysis

Valuation Analysis		Institutional Holding	
Forecast EPS	N/A	No of Institutions	215
Market Cap	$3.4 Billion	Shares	
Book Value	$758.0 Million	219,061,056	
Price/Book	4.49	% Held	
Price/Sales	0.68	N/A	

Business Summary: Household & Personal Products (MIC: 1.7.1 SIC: 3691 NAIC: 335911)

HRG Group is a holding company. Co.'s principal operating subsidiaries include the following: Spectrum Brands Holdings, Inc., its subsidiary that provides global branded consumer products; Fidelity & Guaranty Life, its subsidiary that provides life insurance and annuity products; and Front Street Re (Delaware) Ltd., its subsidiary engaged in the business of providing long-term reinsurance, including reinsurance to the specialty insurance sector of fixed, deferred and payout annuities.

Recent Developments: For the year ended Sep 30 2017, income from continuing operations decreased 28.6% to US$102.9 million from US$144.2 million a year earlier. Net income amounted to US$273.2 million versus a net loss of US$33.9 million in the prior year. Revenues were US$5.01 billion, down 0.8% from US$5.05 billion the year before. Operating income was US$516.3 million versus US$573.5 million in the prior year, a decrease of 10.0%. Direct operating expenses rose 0.4% to US$3.13 billion from US$3.12 billion in the comparable period the year before. Indirect operating expenses were unchanged at US$1.36 billion versus the equivalent prior-year period.

Prospects: Our evaluation of HRG Group Inc. as of Jan. 21, 2018 is the result of our systematic analysis on three basic characteristics: earnings strength, relative valuation, and recent stock price movement. The company has enjoyed a very positive trend in earnings per share over the past 5 quarters. Because the company lacks sufficient analyst estimate data, we place greater weight on the historical EPS trend as the measure of earnings strength. Based on operating earnings yield, the company is overvalued when compared to all of the companies in our coverage universe. Share price changes over the past year indicates that HRG will perform very poorly over the near term.

Financial Data
(US$ in Thousands)

	09/30/2017	09/30/2016	09/30/2015	09/30/2014	09/30/2013	09/30/2012	09/30/2011	12/31/2010
Earnings Per Share	0.53	(0.99)	(2.81)	(0.51)	(0.67)	0.15	0.04	(1.16)
Cash Flow Per Share	4.20	4.59	1.43	3.73	3.73	4.43	1.10	(0.72)
Tang Book Value Per Share	N.M.	N.M.	N.M.	N.M.	N.M.	N.M.	N.M.	6.44
Income Statement								
Total Revenue	5,008,500	5,215,400	5,815,900	5,963,000	5,543,400	4,480,716	3,477,782	...
EBITDA	606,500	812,700	210,800	740,200	806,600	384,068	404,781	(17,965)
Depn & Amortn	95,200	183,700	221,900	205,100	176,400	107,650	104,851	358
Income Before Taxes	151,200	231,900	(440,800)	213,200	118,300	25,386	50,670	(23,066)
Income Taxes	48,300	41,500	71,600	111,500	187,300	(85,282)	50,555	(758)
Net Income	106,000	(198,800)	(556,800)	(10,300)	(45,800)	89,556	34,795	(22,305)
Average Shares	199,990	201,600	198,142	162,941	139,856	139,818	158,384	19,286
Balance Sheet								
Current Assets	1,615,400	3,444,600	2,802,700	2,724,400	3,381,000	2,797,438	2,673,412	111,798
Total Assets	35,849,700	35,792,800	32,334,100	30,100,200	27,908,800	25,200,491	23,579,554	483,934
Current Liabilities	1,115,600	989,800	1,137,700	1,033,000	1,012,700	679,265	662,354	10,142
Long-Term Obligations	5,774,100	5,430,900	6,382,700	5,157,800	4,896,100	2,150,625	2,127,690	345,146
Total Liabilities	35,091,700	35,154,700	31,747,400	28,658,600	26,854,700	23,703,669	22,398,940	359,635
Stockholders' Equity	758,000	638,100	586,700	1,441,600	1,054,100	1,496,822	1,180,614	124,299
Shares Outstanding	200,624	200,789	201,383	202,295	142,381	140,184	139,346	19,292
Statistical Record								
Return on Assets %	0.30	N.M.	N.M.	N.M.	N.M.	0.37	0.29	N.M.
Return on Equity %	15.19	N.M.	N.M.	N.M.	N.M.	6.67	5.33	N.M.
EBITDA Margin %	12.11	15.58	3.62	12.41	14.55	8.57	11.64	...
Net Margin %	2.12	N.M.	N.M.	N.M.	N.M.	2.00	1.00	...
Asset Turnover	0.14	0.15	0.19	0.21	0.21	0.18	0.29	...
Current Ratio	1.45	3.48	2.46	2.64	3.34	4.12	4.04	11.02
Debt to Equity	7.62	8.51	10.88	3.58	4.64	1.44	1.80	2.78
Price Range	20.07-14.32	16.28-10.34	14.53-11.45	13.24-9.90	10.60-7.40	10.34-4.01	6.46-4.01	7.43-4.33
P/E Ratio	37.87-27.02	...	...	...	...	68.93-26.73	161.50-100.25	...

Address: 450 Park Avenue, 29th Floor, New York, NY 10022	Web Site: www.harbingergroupinc.com	Auditors: KPMG LLP
Telephone: 212-906-8555	Officers: Joseph S. Steinberg - Chief Executive Officer David M. Maura - Executive Vice President, Managing Director	Investor Contact: 212-905-8560 Transfer Agents: American Stock Transfer & Trust, New York, NY

HUBBELL INC.

Exchange	Symbol	Price	52Wk Range	Yield	P/E
NYS	HUBB	$135.34 (12/29/2017)	137.50-109.89	2.28	26.08

*7 Year Price Score 95.17 ***NYSE Composite Index=100** ***12 Month Price Score 100.60**

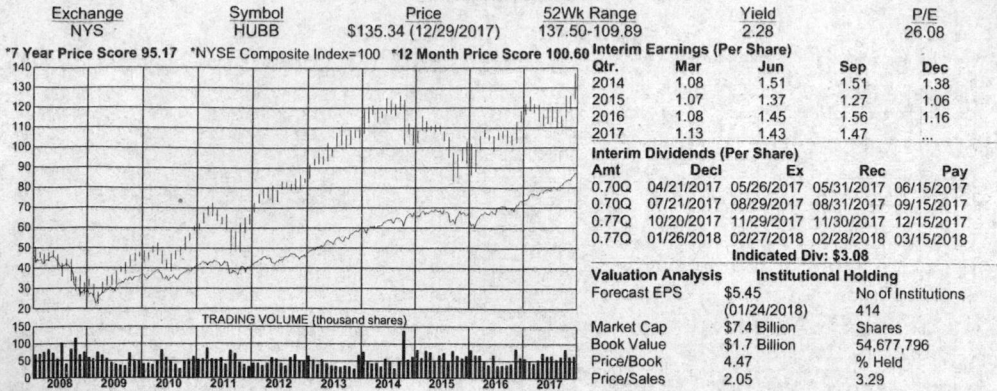

Interim Earnings (Per Share)

Qtr.	Mar	Jun	Sep	Dec
2014	1.08	1.51	1.51	1.38
2015	1.07	1.37	1.27	1.06
2016	1.08	1.45	1.56	1.16
2017	1.13	1.43	1.47	...

Interim Dividends (Per Share)

Amt	Decl	Ex	Rec	Pay
0.70Q	04/21/2017	05/26/2017	05/31/2017	06/15/2017
0.70Q	07/21/2017	08/29/2017	08/31/2017	09/15/2017
0.77Q	10/20/2017	11/29/2017	11/30/2017	12/15/2017
0.77Q	01/26/2018	02/27/2018	02/28/2018	03/15/2018

Indicated Div: $3.08

Valuation Analysis

Forecast EPS	$5.45
	(01/24/2018)
Market Cap	$7.4 Billion
Book Value	$1.7 Billion
Price/Book	4.47
Price/Sales	2.05

Institutional Holding

No of Institutions	414
Shares	54,677,796
% Held	3.29

Business Summary: Electrical Equipment (MIC: 7.3.1 SIC: 3613 NAIC: 334417)

Hubbell is primarily engaged in the design, manufacture and sale of electrical and electronic products a range of non-residential and residential construction, industrial and utility applications. Co. has two segments: electrical, which comprised of businesses that sell stock and custom products including standard and application wiring device products, rough-in electrical products, connector and grounding products, lighting fixtures and controls, as well as other electrical equipment; and power, which consists of operations that design and manufacture various distribution, transmission, substation and telecommunications products primarily used by the electrical utility industry.

Recent Developments: For the quarter ended Sep 30 2017, net income decreased 6.0% to US$82.8 million from US$88.1 million in the year-earlier quarter. Revenues were US$950.5 million, up 4.7% from US$907.4 million the year before. Operating income was US$146.4 million versus US$136.0 million in the prior-year quarter, an increase of 7.6%. Direct operating expenses rose 4.0% to US$643.6 million from US$618.7 million in the comparable period the year before. Indirect operating expenses increased 5.1% to US$160.5 million from US$152.7 million in the equivalent prior-year period.

Prospects: Hubbell Inc. acquired Jiangsu Xin Yuan Electric Equipment Co., Ltd. in 2016. With this acquisition, there will be some improvements in earnings forcast. Recentlly the company has generated a negative trend in earnings per share over the past quarters. However, with this acquisition, there were some improvements in the annual and quarted earnings.

Financial Data
(US$ in Thousands)

	9 Mos	6 Mos	3 Mos	12/31/2016	12/31/2015	12/31/2014	12/31/2013	12/31/2012
Earnings Per Share	5.19	5.28	5.30	5.24	4.77	5.48	5.47	5.00
Cash Flow Per Share	6.71	7.45	7.30	7.16	5.74	6.66	6.46	5.89
Tang Book Value Per Share	2.84	1.59	2.74	3.07	7.61	12.47	13.85	10.43
Dividends Per Share	2.800	2.730	2.660	2.590	...	...	1.850	1.680
Dividend Payout %	53.95	51.70	50.19	49.43	...	...	33.82	33.60
Income Statement								
Total Revenue	2,751,100	1,800,600	852,300	3,505,200	3,390,400	3,359,400	3,183,900	3,044,400
EBITDA	441,500	280,700	126,200	527,200	500,800	566,600	549,900	516,700
Depn & Amortn	76,000	50,400	24,200	53,400	51,200	49,900	45,300	44,100
Income Before Taxes	331,200	207,600	90,900	430,400	418,600	485,500	473,800	441,800
Income Taxes	103,700	62,900	27,000	132,600	136,500	158,300	144,000	139,700
Net Income	222,700	141,900	62,800	293,000	277,300	325,300	326,500	299,700
Average Shares	54,900	55,100	55,600	55,700	58,000	59,200	59,600	59,800
Balance Sheet								
Current Assets	1,685,000	1,609,600	1,517,600	1,551,300	1,387,800	1,629,400	1,632,400	1,456,200
Total Assets	3,743,200	3,666,700	3,494,600	3,525,000	3,208,700	3,322,800	3,187,200	2,947,000
Current Liabilities	740,600	1,025,300	576,000	589,600	603,100	499,200	467,000	447,400
Long-Term Obligations	986,700	691,800	990,900	990,500	595,900	597,600	597,200	596,700
Total Liabilities	2,087,200	2,074,400	1,915,900	1,932,200	1,468,100	1,395,700	1,280,800	1,285,800
Stockholders' Equity	1,656,000	1,592,300	1,578,700	1,592,800	1,740,600	1,927,100	1,906,400	1,661,200
Shares Outstanding	54,706	54,700	55,041	55,532	57,836	58,496	59,172	59,236
Statistical Record								
Return on Assets %	7.94	8.27	8.55	8.68	8.49	9.99	10.65	10.32
Return on Equity %	17.50	18.53	18.75	17.53	15.12	16.97	18.30	19.10
EBITDA Margin %	16.05	15.59	14.81	15.04	14.77	16.87	17.27	16.97
Net Margin %	8.09	7.88	7.37	8.36	8.18	9.68	10.25	9.84
Asset Turnover	1.00	1.01	1.02	1.04	1.04	1.03	1.04	1.05
Current Ratio	2.28	1.57	2.63	2.63	2.30	3.26	3.50	3.25
Debt to Equity	0.60	0.43	0.63	0.62	0.34	0.31	0.31	0.36
Price Range	125.74-101.55	125.74-101.55	125.74-98.17	118.54-86.29	116.29-82.96	126.41-101.44	110.90-84.63	86.48-67.80
P/E Ratio	24.23-19.57	23.81-19.23	23.72-18.52	22.62-16.47	24.38-17.39	23.07-18.51	20.27-15.47	17.30-13.56
Average Yield %	2.43	2.42	2.41	2.48	...	...	1.84	2.12

Address: 40 Waterview Drive, Shelton, CT 06484
Telephone: 475-882-4000

Web Site: www.hubbell.com
Officers: David G. Nord - Chairman, President, Chief Executive Officer, Senior Vice President, Chief Operating Officer, Chief Financial Officer William R. Sperry - Senior Vice President, Chief Financial Officer

Auditors: PricewaterhouseCoopers LLP
Transfer Agents: Computershare Inc.

HUDSON PACIFIC PROPERTIES INC

Exchange	Symbol	Price	52Wk Range	Yield	P/E
NYS	HPP	$34.25 (12/29/2017)	36.65-31.73	2.92	79.65

*7 Year Price Score 108.62 *NYSE Composite Index=100 *12 Month Price Score 95.36

Interim Earnings (Per Share)

Qtr.	Mar	Jun	Sep	Dec
2014	0.02	0.05	0.11	(0.04)
2015	0.25	(0.28)	(0.04)	(0.07)
2016	0.03	0.01	0.02	0.20
2017	0.14	0.02	0.07	...

Interim Dividends (Per Share)

Amt	Decl	Ex	Rec	Pay
0.25Q	03/09/2017	03/16/2017	03/20/2017	03/30/2017
0.25Q	06/09/2017	06/16/2017	06/20/2017	06/30/2017
0.25Q	09/08/2017	09/18/2017	09/19/2017	09/29/2017
0.25Q	12/08/2017	12/15/2017	12/18/2017	12/28/2017

Indicated Div: $1.00

Valuation Analysis | **Institutional Holding**

Forecast EPS	$0.31 (01/18/2018)	No of Institutions	260
Market Cap	$5.3 Billion	Shares	176,779,488
Book Value	$3.7 Billion	% Held	101.81
Price/Book	1.45		
Price/Sales	7.53		

Business Summary: REITs (MIC: 5.3.1 SIC: 6531 NAIC: 531312)

Hudson Pacific Properties is a holding company operating through Hudson Pacific Properties, L.P. Co. is focused on acquiring, repositioning, developing and operating office and media and entertainment properties throughout Northern and Southern California and the Pacific Northwest. Co. has two segments: office properties and media and entertainment properties. As of Dec 31 2016, the office properties segment included 54 properties totaling approximately 14.1 million square feet, while the media and entertainment segment included two properties, the Sunset Gower Studios property and the Sunset Bronson Studios property, totaling approximately 0.9 million square feet located in Hollywood, CA.

Recent Developments: For the quarter ended Sep 30 2017, net income increased 178.1% to US$14.5 million from US$5.2 million in the year-earlier quarter. Revenues were US$190.0 million, up 15.5% from US$164.6 million the year before.

Prospects: Our evaluation of Hudson Pacific Properties Inc as of Jan. 14, 2018 is the result of our systematic analysis on three basic characteristics: earnings strength, relative valuation, and recent stock price movement. The company has enjoyed a very positive trend in earnings per share over the past 5 quarters and while recent estimates for the company have remained steady, HPP has posted better than expected results. Based on operating earnings yield, the company is overvalued when compared to all of the companies in our coverage universe. Share price changes over the past year indicates that HPP will perform well over the near term.

Financial Data

(US$ in Thousands)	9 Mos	6 Mos	3 Mos	12/31/2016	12/31/2015	12/31/2014	12/31/2013	12/31/2012
Earnings Per Share	0.43	0.38	0.37	0.25	(0.19)	0.15	(0.27)	(0.41)
Cash Flow Per Share	1.69	1.63	1.71	2.06	2.03	0.96	0.75	1.03
Tang Book Value Per Share	23.55	23.65	23.87	22.75	18.70	15.50	15.02	14.71
Dividends Per Share	0.950	0.900	0.850	0.800	0.575	0.500	0.500	0.500
Dividend Payout %	220.93	236.84	229.73	320.00	...	333.33	...	...
Income Statement								
Total Revenue	538,806	348,785	168,285	639,639	520,850	253,415	205,558	166,156
EBITDA	115,310	76,670	46,425	390,843	272,841	125,194	98,660	72,895
Depn & Amortn	3,697	1,984	372	271,301	238,380	75,606	72,047	59,136
Income Before Taxes	45,617	31,107	24,153	43,758	(16,082)	23,686	1,415	(5,006)
Net Income	36,615	25,096	21,116	27,984	(16,397)	9,955	(14,833)	(17,190)
Average Shares	156,093	156,095	149,950	110,369	85,927	66,509	55,182	41,640
Balance Sheet								
Current Assets	215,705	187,707	220,549	202,325	181,040	109,518	77,389	63,833
Total Assets	6,907,090	6,864,034	6,701,761	6,678,998	6,254,035	2,340,885	2,131,274	1,559,690
Current Liabilities	162,938	134,237	135,198	278,061	254,105	137,634	86,625	67,908
Long-Term Obligations	2,424,358	2,598,780	2,388,388	2,688,010	2,260,716	918,059	931,308	582,085
Total Liabilities	3,250,044	3,182,743	2,985,718	3,565,538	4,578,024	1,151,534	1,117,353	707,002
Stockholders' Equity	3,657,046	3,681,291	3,716,043	3,113,460	1,676,011	1,189,351	1,013,921	852,688
Shares Outstanding	155,302	155,301	155,279	136,492	89,153	66,797	57,230	47,496
Statistical Record								
Return on Assets %	0.85	0.72	0.71	0.43	N.M.	0.45	N.M.	N.M.
Return on Equity %	1.81	1.68	1.68	1.17	N.M.	0.90	N.M.	N.M.
EBITDA Margin %	21.40	21.98	27.59	61.10	52.38	49.40	48.00	43.87
Net Margin %	6.80	7.20	12.55	4.37	N.M.	3.93	N.M.	N.M.
Asset Turnover	0.11	0.10	0.10	0.10	0.12	0.11	0.11	0.12
Current Ratio	1.32	1.40	1.63	0.73	0.71	0.80	0.89	0.94
Debt to Equity	0.66	0.71	0.64	0.86	1.35	0.77	0.92	0.68
Price Range	36.65-31.73	36.65-29.03	36.65-27.16	35.27-22.97	33.95-27.17	30.34-21.42	23.99-19.03	21.06-13.62
P/E Ratio	85.23-73.79	96.45-76.39	99.05-73.41	141.08-91.88	... 202.27-142.80		...	...
Average Yield %	2.81	2.66	2.62	2.65	1.90	2.00	2.34	2.93

Address: 11601 Wilshire Blvd., Ninth Floor, Los Angeles, CA 90025	Web Site: www.hudsonpacificproperties.com	Auditors: Ernst & Young LLP
Telephone: 310-445-5700	Officers: Victor J. Coleman - Chairman, Chief Executive Officer Mark T. Lammas - Chief Financial Officer, Chief Operating Officer, Treasurer	Investor Contact: 310-829-5400
Fax: 310-445-5710		Transfer Agents: Computershare, Canton, MA

HUMANA INC.

Exchange	Symbol	Price	52Wk Range	Yield	P/E
NYS	HUM	$248.07 (12/29/2017)	260.86-195.24	0.64	19.49

*7 Year Price Score 133.78 *NYSE Composite Index=100 *12 Month Price Score 101.74

TRADING VOLUME (thousand shares)

Interim Earnings (Per Share)

Qtr.	Mar	Jun	Sep	Dec
2014	2.35	2.19	1.85	0.97
2015	2.82	2.85	2.09	0.67
2016	1.56	2.06	2.98	(2.66)
2017	7.49	4.46	3.44	...

Interim Dividends (Per Share)

Amt	Decl	Ex	Rec	Pay
0.40Q	02/14/2017	03/29/2017	03/31/2017	04/28/2017
0.40Q	04/20/2017	06/28/2017	06/30/2017	07/31/2017
0.40Q	08/17/2017	09/28/2017	09/29/2017	10/27/2017
0.40Q	11/02/2017	12/28/2017	12/29/2017	01/26/2018

Indicated Div: $1.60

Valuation Analysis

		Institutional Holding	
Forecast EPS	$11.64 (01/18/2018)	No of Institutions	920
Market Cap	$35.4 Billion	Shares	165,735,568
Book Value	$11.2 Billion	% Held	88.13
Price/Book	3.16		
Price/Sales	0.66		

Business Summary: Life & Health (MIC: 5.2.2 SIC: 6324 NAIC: 524114)

Humana is a holding company. Through its subsidiaries, Co. is a health and well-being company. Co. manages its business with three segments: Retail, which consists of Medicare and commercial insured medical and specialty health insurance benefits, including dental, vision, and other supplemental health and financial protection products; Group, which consists of employer group commercial fully-insured medical and specialty health insurance benefits, including dental, vision, and other supplemental health and voluntary benefit products; and Healthcare Services, which includes pharmacy solutions, provider services, home based services, clinical programs, and predictive modeling, among others.

Recent Developments: For the quarter ended Sep 30 2017, net income increased 10.9% to US$499.0 million from US$450.0 million in the year-earlier quarter. Revenues were US$13.28 billion, down 3.0% from US$13.69 billion the year before. Net premiums earned were US$12.96 billion versus US$13.37 billion in the prior-year quarter, a decrease of 3.1%.

Prospects: Our evaluation of Humana Inc. as of Jan. 14, 2018 is the result of our systematic analysis on three basic characteristics: earnings strength, relative valuation, and recent stock price movement. The company has generated a negative trend in earnings per share over the past 5 quarters and while recent estimates for the company have been raised by analysts, HUM has posted better than expected results. Based on operating earnings yield, the company is undervalued when compared to all of the companies in our coverage universe. Share price changes over the past year indicates that HUM will perform in line with the market over the near term.

Financial Data

(US$ in Thousands)	9 Mos	6 Mos	3 Mos	12/31/2016	12/31/2015	12/31/2014	12/31/2013	12/31/2012
Earnings Per Share	12.73	12.27	9.87	4.07	8.44	7.36	7.73	7.47
Cash Flow Per Share	29.05	40.31	38.28	12.93	5.81	10.49	10.90	11.88
Tang Book Value Per Share	55.51	53.09	48.19	49.65	47.75	39.67	36.25	32.89
Dividends Per Share	1.780	1.380	1.270	0.870	1.150	1.110	1.070	1.030
Dividend Payout %	13.98	11.25	12.87	21.38	13.63	15.08	13.84	13.79
Income Statement								
Premium Income	39,556,000	26,601,000	13,398,000	53,021,000	52,409,000	45,959,000	38,829,000	37,009,000
Total Revenue	40,578,000	27,296,000	13,762,000	54,379,000	54,289,000	48,500,000	41,313,000	39,126,000
Benefits & Claims	32,857,000	22,215,000	11,326,000	45,007,000	44,269,000	38,166,000	32,564,000	30,985,000
Income Before Taxes	3,530,000	2,731,000	1,689,000	1,552,000	2,431,000	2,170,000	1,921,000	1,911,000
Income Taxes	1,266,000	966,000	574,000	938,000	1,155,000	1,023,000	690,000	689,000
Net Income	2,264,000	1,765,000	1,115,000	614,000	1,276,000	1,147,000	1,231,000	1,222,000
Average Shares	145,360	145,634	148,872	150,917	151,142	155,874	159,151	163,457
Balance Sheet								
Total Assets	32,956,000	32,253,000	31,712,000	25,396,000	24,705,000	23,466,000	20,735,000	19,979,000
Total Liabilities	21,745,000	21,300,000	21,478,000	14,711,000	14,359,000	13,820,000	11,419,000	11,132,000
Stockholders' Equity	11,211,000	10,953,000	10,234,000	10,685,000	10,346,000	9,646,000	9,316,000	8,847,000
Shares Outstanding	142,860	144,517	144,314	149,305	148,288	149,604	154,030	158,331
Statistical Record								
Return on Assets %	5.97	6.10	5.03	2.44	5.30	5.19	6.05	6.47
Return on Equity %	16.56	16.62	14.21	5.82	12.77	12.10	13.56	14.41
Loss Ratio %	83.06	83.51	84.54	84.89	84.47	83.04	83.87	83.72
Net Margin %	5.58	6.47	8.10	1.13	2.35	2.36	2.98	3.12
Price Range	258.75-165.31	240.62-153.38	219.25-153.38	216.76-153.38	214.92-139.09	149.07-95.59	105.25-66.01	95.50-61.60
P/E Ratio	20.33-12.99	19.61-12.50	22.21-15.54	53.26-37.69	25.46-16.48	20.25-12.99	13.62-8.54	12.78-8.25
Average Yield %	0.82	0.69	0.68	0.49	0.65	0.91	1.26	1.32

Address: 500 West Main Street, Louisville, KY 40202 Telephone: 502-580-1000	Web Site: www.humana.com Officers: Kurt J. Hilzinger - Chairman Bruce D. Broussard - President, Chief Executive Officer	Auditors: PricewaterhouseCoopers LLP Investor Contact: 502-580-3644 Transfer Agents: American Stock Transfer & Trust Company, LLC, Brooklyn, NY

HUNTINGTON INGALLS INDUSTRIES, INC.

Exchange	Symbol	Price	52Wk Range	Yield	P/E
NYS	HII	$235.70 (12/29/2017)	251.96-185.22	1.22	17.79

*7 Year Price Score N/A   *NYSE Composite Index=100   ***12 Month Price Score 106.85**

TRADING VOLUME (thousand shares)

Interim Earnings (Per Share)

Qtr.	Mar	Jun	Sep	Dec
2014	1.81	2.04	1.96	1.06
2015	1.79	3.20	2.29	1.08
2016	2.87	2.80	2.27	4.21
2017	2.56	3.21	3.27	...

Interim Dividends (Per Share)

Amt	Decl	Ex	Rec	Pay
0.60Q	02/17/2017	03/01/2017	03/03/2017	03/10/2017
0.60Q	05/03/2017	05/24/2017	05/26/2017	06/09/2017
0.60Q	07/25/2017	08/23/2017	08/25/2017	09/08/2017
0.72Q	11/07/2017	11/22/2017	11/24/2017	12/08/2017

Indicated Div: $2.88

Valuation Analysis   **Institutional Holding**

Forecast EPS	$12.00 (01/18/2018)	No of Institutions	543
Market Cap	$10.7 Billion	Shares	44,535,892
Book Value	$1.7 Billion	% Held	86.12
Price/Book	6.24		
Price/Sales	1.45		

Business Summary: Defense (MIC: 7.1.2 SIC: 3731 NAIC: 336611)

Huntington Ingalls Industries is a military shipbuilding company and a provider of professional services to partners in government and industry. Co. has three segments: Ingalls Shipbuilding, which designs and constructs non-nuclear ships for the U.S. Navy and U.S. Coast Guard, including amphibious assault ships, and surface combatants; Newport News Shipbuilding, which is designing and constructing nuclear-powered ships, such as aircraft carriers and submarines, and the refueling and overhaul and the inactivation of such ships; and Technical Solutions, which includes businesses that are focused on life-cycle sustainment services to the U.S. Navy fleet and other maritime customers.

Recent Developments: For the quarter ended Sep 30 2017, net income increased 39.3% to US$149.0 million from US$107.0 million in the year-earlier quarter. Revenues were US$1.86 billion, up 10.7% from US$1.68 billion the year before. Operating income was US$237.0 million versus US$175.0 million in the prior-year quarter, an increase of 35.4%. Direct operating expenses rose 9.6% to US$1.50 billion from US$1.37 billion in the comparable period the year before. Indirect operating expenses decreased 9.2% to US$128.0 million from US$141.0 million in the equivalent prior-year period.

Prospects: Our evaluation of Huntington Ingalls Industries Inc. as of Jan. 14, 2018 is the result of our systematic analysis on three basic characteristics: earnings strength, relative valuation, and recent stock price movement. The company has generated a negative trend in earnings per share over the past 5 quarters and while recent estimates for the company have been raised by analysts, HII has posted better than expected results. Based on operating earnings yield, the company is undervalued when compared to all of the companies in our coverage universe. Share price changes over the past year indicates that HII will perform in line with the market over the near term.

Financial Data

(US$ in Thousands)	9 Mos	6 Mos	3 Mos	12/31/2016	12/31/2015	12/31/2014	12/31/2013	12/31/2012
Earnings Per Share	13.25	12.25	11.84	12.14	8.36	6.86	5.18	2.91
Cash Flow Per Share	15.97	19.32	18.70	17.52	17.29	14.67	4.75	6.70
Tang Book Value Per Share	N.M.	N.M.	N.M.	N.M.	0.83	N.M.	2.30	N.M.
Dividends Per Share	2.400	2.300	2.200	2.100	1.700	1.000	0.500	0.100
Dividend Payout %	18.11	18.78	18.58	17.30	20.33	14.58	9.65	3.44
Income Statement								
Total Revenue	5,445,000	3,582,000	1,724,000	7,068,000	7,020,000	6,957,000	6,820,000	6,708,000
EBITDA	795,000	505,000	219,000	1,044,000	949,000	850,000	738,000	542,000
Depn & Amortn	157,000	105,000	-54,000	186,000	180,000	194,000	226,000	184,000
Income Before Taxes	585,000	365,000	147,000	784,000	632,000	507,000	394,000	241,000
Income Taxes	170,000	99,000	28,000	211,000	228,000	169,000	133,000	95,000
Net Income	415,000	266,000	119,000	573,000	404,000	338,000	261,000	146,000
Average Shares	45,500	45,800	46,400	47,200	48,300	49,300	50,400	50,100
Balance Sheet								
Current Assets	1,939,000	2,033,000	2,063,000	2,142,000	2,284,000	2,546,000	2,676,000	2,484,000
Total Assets	6,172,000	6,190,000	6,234,000	6,352,000	6,024,000	6,269,000	6,225,000	6,392,000
Current Liabilities	1,275,000	1,247,000	1,273,000	1,343,000	1,274,000	1,312,000	1,392,000	1,384,000
Long-Term Obligations	1,282,000	1,281,000	1,280,000	1,278,000	1,273,000	1,592,000	1,700,000	1,779,000
Total Liabilities	4,460,000	4,540,000	4,596,000	4,699,000	4,534,000	4,904,000	4,704,000	5,725,000
Stockholders' Equity	1,712,000	1,650,000	1,638,000	1,653,000	1,490,000	1,365,000	1,521,000	667,000
Shares Outstanding	45,300	45,500	46,200	46,200	46,900	48,300	48,700	49,600
Statistical Record								
Return on Assets %	10.05	9.46	9.17	9.23	6.57	5.41	4.14	2.35
Return on Equity %	36.39	34.95	35.20	36.36	28.30	23.42	23.86	18.92
EBITDA Margin %	14.60	14.10	12.70	14.77	13.52	12.22	10.82	8.08
Net Margin %	7.62	7.43	6.90	8.11	5.75	4.86	3.83	2.18
Asset Turnover	1.21	1.19	1.16	1.14	1.14	1.11	1.08	1.08
Current Ratio	1.52	1.63	1.62	1.59	1.79	1.94	1.92	1.79
Debt to Equity	0.75	0.78	0.78	0.77	0.85	1.17	1.12	2.67
Price Range	226.44-146.75	219.47-146.75	219.47-136.94	187.96-121.41	143.55-103.98	115.48-87.91	90.01-43.17	44.96-31.80
P/E Ratio	17.09-11.08	17.92-11.98	18.54-11.57	15.48-10.00	17.17-12.44	16.83-12.81	17.38-8.33	15.45-10.93
Average Yield %	1.24	1.25	1.28	1.36	1.38	1.00	0.82	0.26

Address: 4101 Washington Avenue, Newport News, VA 23607 **Telephone:** 757-380-2000	**Web Site:** www.huntingtoningalls.com **Officers:** Thomas B. Fargo - Chairman C. Michael Petters - President, Chief Executive Officer	**Auditors:** Deloitte & Touche LLP **Investor Contact:** 757-688-5572 **Transfer Agents:** Computershare Trust Company, N.A., Providence, RI

HUNTSMAN CORP

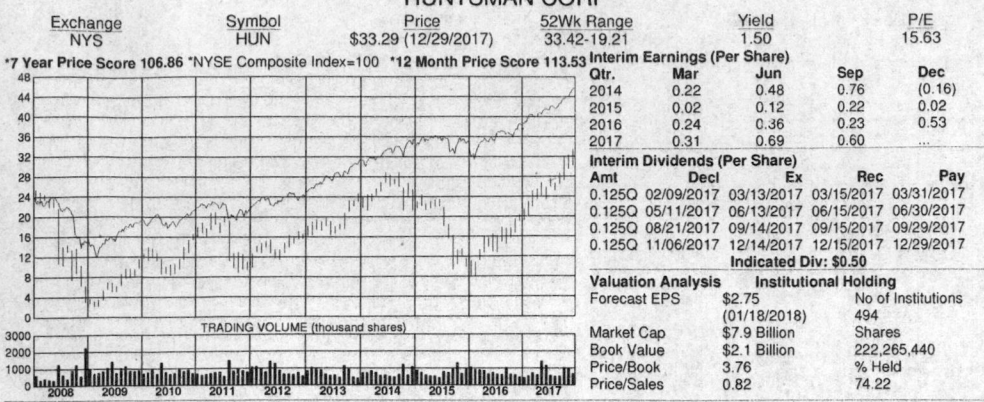

Exchange	Symbol	Price	52Wk Range	Yield	P/E
NYS	HUN	$33.29 (12/29/2017)	33.42-19.21	1.50	15.63

*7 Year Price Score 106.86 *NYSE Composite Index=100 *12 Month Price Score 113.53

Interim Earnings (Per Share)

Qtr.	Mar	Jun	Sep	Dec
2014	0.22	0.48	0.76	(0.16)
2015	0.02	0.12	0.22	0.02
2016	0.24	0.36	0.23	0.53
2017	0.31	0.69	0.60	...

Interim Dividends (Per Share)

Amt	Decl	Ex	Rec	Pay
0.125Q	02/09/2017	03/13/2017	03/15/2017	03/31/2017
0.125Q	05/11/2017	06/13/2017	06/15/2017	06/30/2017
0.125Q	08/21/2017	09/14/2017	09/15/2017	09/29/2017
0.125Q	11/06/2017	12/14/2017	12/15/2017	12/29/2017

Indicated Div: $0.50

Valuation Analysis

		Institutional Holding	
Forecast EPS	$2.75 (01/18/2018)	No of Institutions	494
Market Cap	$7.9 Billion	Shares	222,265,440
Book Value	$2.1 Billion	% Held	74.22
Price/Book	3.76		
Price/Sales	0.82		

Business Summary: Specialty Chemicals (MIC: 8.3.2 SIC: 2899 NAIC: 325199)

Huntsman is a manufacturer of organic chemical products and of inorganic chemical products. Co. operates in five segments: Polyurethanes, which provides polyurethane chemicals, including methyl diphenyl diisocyanate products, propylene oxide, polyols, propylene glycol and thermoplastic polyurethane; Performance Products, which provides amines, surfactants and maleic anhydride; Advanced Materials, which provides epoxy, acrylic and polyurethane-based polymer products; Textile Effects, which provides textile chemicals, dyes and digital inks; and Pigments and Additives, which provides titanium dioxide, functional additives, color pigments, timber treatment and water treatment chemicals.

Recent Developments: For the quarter ended Sep 30 2017, income from continuing operations increased 190.0% to US$116.0 million from US$40.0 million in the year-earlier quarter. Net income increased 179.7% to US$179.0 million from US$64.0 million in the year-earlier quarter. Revenues were US$2.17 billion, up 18.5% from US$1.83 billion the year before. Operating income was US$223.0 million versus US$101.0 million in the prior-year quarter, an increase of 120.8%. Direct operating expenses rose 14.9% to US$1.70 billion from US$1.48 billion in the comparable period the year before. Indirect operating expenses decreased 1.6% to US$251.0 million from US$255.0 million in the equivalent prior-year period.

Prospects: Our evaluation of Huntsman Corp. as of Jan. 14, 2018 is the result of our systematic analysis on three basic characteristics: earnings strength, relative valuation, and recent stock price movement. The company has enjoyed a very positive trend in earnings per share over the past 5 quarters and while recent estimates for the company have been raised by analysts, HUN has posted better than expected results. Based on operating earnings yield, the company is undervalued when compared to all of the companies in our coverage universe. Share price changes over the past year indicates that HUN will perform well over the near term.

Financial Data

(US$ in Thousands)	9 Mos	6 Mos	3 Mos	12/31/2016	12/31/2015	12/31/2014	12/31/2013	12/31/2012
Earnings Per Share	2.13	1.76	1.43	1.36	0.38	1.31	0.53	1.51
Cash Flow Per Share	4.12	4.36	4.60	4.59	2.37	3.14	2.95	3.25
Tang Book Value Per Share	8.03	6.09	5.24	4.65	5.23	6.41	7.33	6.66
Dividends Per Share	0.500	0.500	0.500	0.500	0.500	0.500	0.500	0.400
Dividend Payout %	23.47	28.41	34.97	36.76	131.58	38.17	94.34	26.49
Income Statement								
Total Revenue	6,155,000	5,085,000	2,469,000	9,657,000	10,299,000	11,578,000	11,079,000	11,187,000
EBITDA	796,000	651,000	270,000	1,045,000	752,000	1,016,000	876,000	1,165,000
Depn & Amortn	235,000	214,000	106,000	400,000	377,000	413,000	415,000	399,000
Income Before Taxes	427,000	342,000	116,000	443,000	170,000	398,000	271,000	540,000
Income Taxes	78,000	68,000	23,000	87,000	46,000	51,000	125,000	169,000
Net Income	390,000	243,000	76,000	326,000	93,000	323,000	128,000	363,000
Average Shares	244,000	243,700	242,500	239,600	245,400	246,000	242,400	240,600
Balance Sheet								
Current Assets	5,767,000	3,980,000	3,835,000	3,555,000	3,834,000	5,039,000	4,159,000	4,119,000
Total Assets	9,983,000	9,688,000	9,488,000	9,189,000	9,820,000	11,002,000	9,188,000	8,884,000
Current Liabilities	3,090,000	1,883,000	1,855,000	1,778,000	1,917,000	2,332,000	2,159,000	2,181,000
Long-Term Obligations	2,845,000	4,072,000	4,161,000	4,136,000	4,626,000	4,939,000	3,639,000	3,418,000
Total Liabilities	7,872,000	8,021,000	8,036,000	7,902,000	8,378,000	9,224,000	7,208,000	7,111,000
Stockholders' Equity	2,111,000	1,667,000	1,452,000	1,287,000	1,442,000	1,778,000	1,980,000	1,773,000
Shares Outstanding	238,609	238,427	238,152	236,370	237,080	243,416	240,401	238,273
Statistical Record								
Return on Assets %	5.26	4.39	3.58	3.42	0.89	3.20	1.42	4.13
Return on Equity %	28.01	26.66	23.45	23.83	5.78	17.19	6.82	21.08
EBITDA Margin %	12.93	12.80	10.94	10.82	7.30	8.78	7.91	10.41
Net Margin %	6.34	4.78	3.08	3.38	0.90	2.79	1.16	3.24
Asset Turnover	0.98	1.01	1.01	1.01	0.99	1.15	1.23	1.27
Current Ratio	1.87	2.11	2.07	2.00	2.00	2.16	1.93	1.89
Debt to Equity	1.35	2.44	2.87	3.21	3.21	2.78	1.84	1.93
Price Range	28.64-15.66	26.71-12.79	25.07-12.70	20.33-7.91	24.40-9.33	28.88-21.22	24.60-15.90	17.07-9.82
P/E Ratio	13.45-7.35	15.18-7.27	17.53-8.88	14.95-5.82	64.21-24.55	22.05-16.20	46.42-30.00	11.30-6.50
Average Yield %	2.20	2.50	2.50	2.86	3.38	2.71	1.98	2.84

Address: 10003 Woodloch Forest Drive, The Woodlands, TX 77380
Telephone: 281-719-6000

Web Site: www.huntsman.com
Officers: Jon M. Huntsman - Chairman Peter R Huntsman - President, Chief Executive Officer

Auditors: Deloitte & Touche LLP
Investor Contact: 801-584-5959
Transfer Agents: Computershare, Providence, RI

HYATT HOTELS CORP

Exchange	Symbol	Price	52Wk Range	Yield	P/E
NYS	H	$73.54 (12/29/2017)	73.88-50.64	N/A	44.04

*7 Year Price Score 94.28   *NYSE Composite Index=100   *12 Month Price Score 111.89

Interim Earnings (Per Share)

Qtr.	Mar	Jun	Sep	Dec
2014	0.36	0.49	0.21	1.18
2015	0.15	0.27	0.18	0.26
2016	0.25	0.49	0.47	0.31
2017	0.54	0.68	0.14	...

Interim Dividends (Per Share)

No Dividends Paid

Valuation Analysis		Institutional Holding	
Forecast EPS	$1.75	No of Institutions	
	(01/18/2018)	251	
Market Cap	$8.9 Billion	Shares	
Book Value	$3.7 Billion	48,275,896	
Price/Book	2.45	% Held	
Price/Sales	1.95	24.57	

TRADING VOLUME (thousand shares)

Business Summary: Hotels, Restaurants & Travel (MIC: 2.2.1 SIC: 7011 NAIC: 721110)

Hyatt Hotels is a hospitality company engaged in the development, ownership, operation, management, franchising, licensing or provision of services to a portfolio of properties, consisting of service hotels, select service hotels, resorts and other properties, including timeshare, fractional and other forms of residential and vacation properties. Co.'s hotels and resorts operate under seven brands: Park Hyatt, Grand Hyatt, Hyatt Regency, Hyatt, Andaz, Hyatt Centric and The Unbound Collection by Hyatt. Co.'s two select service brands are Hyatt Place and Hyatt House, an extended stay brand. As of Dec 31 2016, Co.'s worldwide hotel portfolio consisted of 657 hotels (171,133 rooms).

Recent Developments: For the quarter ended Sep 30 2017, net income decreased 72.6% to US$17.0 million from US$62.0 million in the year-earlier quarter. Revenues were US$1.12 billion, up 2.8% from US$1.09 billion the year before. Direct operating expenses rose 2.7% to US$881.0 million from US$858.0 million in the comparable period the year before. Indirect operating expenses increased 12.4% to US$181.0 million from US$161.0 million in the equivalent prior-year period.

Prospects: Our evaluation of Hyatt Hotels Corp. as of Jan. 14, 2018 is the result of our systematic analysis on three basic characteristics: earnings strength, relative valuation, and recent stock price movement. The company has suffered a very negative trend in earnings per share over the past 5 quarters. However, while recent estimates for the company have been mixed, H has posted better than expected results. Based on operating earnings yield, the company is overvalued when compared to all of the companies in our coverage universe. Share price changes over the past year indicates that H will perform poorly over the near term.

Financial Data

(US$ in Thousands)	9 Mos	6 Mos	3 Mos	12/31/2016	12/31/2015	12/31/2014	12/31/2013	12/31/2012
Earnings Per Share	1.67	2.00	1.81	1.52	0.86	2.23	1.30	0.53
Cash Flow Per Share	4.74	4.53	4.53	3.67	3.77	3.09	2.88	3.02
Tang Book Value Per Share	23.18	24.07	23.19	24.30	24.33	26.44	25.82	26.53
Income Statement								
Total Revenue	3,501,000	2,382,000	1,187,000	4,429,000	4,328,000	4,415,000	4,184,000	3,949,000
EBITDA	181,000	152,000	19,000	574,000	603,000	869,000	673,000	470,000
Depn & Amortn	(19,000)	(12,000)	(6,000)	315,000	289,000	324,000	320,000	327,000
Income Before Taxes	275,000	245,000	114,000	221,000	258,000	500,000	322,000	117,000
Income Taxes	100,000	86,000	41,000	85,000	70,000	179,000	116,000	8,000
Net Income	173,000	157,000	70,000	204,000	124,000	344,000	207,000	88,000
Average Shares	125,407	126,804	130,997	133,939	143,999	154,350	159,189	165,377
Balance Sheet								
Current Assets	1,268,000	1,363,000	1,048,000	1,139,000	1,124,000	1,709,000	1,163,000	1,758,000
Total Assets	7,861,000	7,901,000	7,763,000	7,749,000	7,596,000	8,143,000	8,177,000	7,640,000
Current Liabilities	1,200,000	1,073,000	1,109,000	924,000	1,107,000	730,000	871,000	618,000
Long-Term Obligations	1,444,000	1,446,000	1,445,000	1,445,000	1,047,000	1,381,000	1,289,000	1,229,000
Total Liabilities	4,210,000	4,064,000	4,049,000	3,846,000	3,605,000	3,516,000	3,408,000	2,819,000
Stockholders' Equity	3,651,000	3,837,000	3,714,000	3,903,000	3,991,000	4,627,000	4,769,000	4,821,000
Shares Outstanding	121,550	125,513	125,461	130,815	136,233	149,081	156,111	162,066
Statistical Record								
Return on Assets %	2.76	3.33	3.06	2.65	1.58	4.22	2.62	1.16
Return on Equity %	5.66	6.63	6.23	5.15	2.88	7.32	4.32	1.82
EBITDA Margin %	5.17	6.38	1.60	12.96	13.93	19.68	16.09	11.90
Net Margin %	4.94	6.59	5.90	4.61	2.87	7.79	4.95	2.23
Asset Turnover	0.59	0.58	0.58	0.58	0.55	0.54	0.53	0.52
Current Ratio	1.06	1.27	0.94	1.23	1.02	2.34	1.34	2.84
Debt to Equity	0.40	0.38	0.39	0.37	0.26	0.30	0.27	0.25
Price Range	61.83-48.67	58.52-48.52	57.69-45.34	57.69-35.77	61.76-45.86	63.74-45.88	49.85-38.57	44.10-33.74
P/E Ratio	37.02-29.14	29.26-24.26	31.87-25.05	37.95-23.53	71.81-53.33	28.58-20.57	38.35-29.67	83.21-63.66

Address: 150 North Riverside Plaza, Chicago, IL 60606
Telephone: 312-750-1234

Web Site: www.hyatt.com
Officers: Thomas J. Pritzker - Executive Chairman
Mark S. Hoplamazian - President, Chief Executive Officer

Auditors: Deloitte & Touche LLP
Investor Contact: 312-750-1234
Transfer Agents: Wells Fargo Shareowner Services, South St. Paul, MN

IDACORP INC

Exchange	Symbol	Price	52Wk Range	Yield	P/E
NYS	IDA	$91.36 (12/29/2017)	98.81-77.98	2.58	22.23

*7 Year Price Score 115.59 *NYSE Composite Index=100 ***12 Month Price Score 102.63**

TRADING VOLUME (thousand shares)

Interim Earnings (Per Share)

Qtr.	Mar	Jun	Sep	Dec
2014	0.55	0.89	1.73	0.69
2015	0.47	1.31	1.46	0.63
2016	0.51	1.12	1.65	0.66
2017	0.66	0.99	1.80	...

Interim Dividends (Per Share)

Amt	Decl	Ex	Rec	Pay
0.55Q	01/19/2017	02/02/2017	02/06/2017	02/28/2017
0.55Q	04/20/2017	05/03/2017	05/05/2017	05/30/2017
0.55Q	07/20/2017	08/04/2017	08/08/2017	08/30/2017
0.59Q	10/19/2017	11/03/2017	11/06/2017	11/30/2017

Indicated Div: $2.36 (Div. Reinv. Plan)

Valuation Analysis — **Institutional Holding**

Forecast EPS	$4.10 (01/01/2018)	No of Institutions 351
Market Cap	$4.6 Billion	Shares
Book Value	$2.2 Billion	54,366,304
Price/Book	2.05	% Held
Price/Sales	3.44	75.01

Business Summary: Electric Utilities (MIC: 3.1.1 SIC: 4911 NAIC: 221122)

Idacorp is a holding company. Co.'s principal operating subsidiary, Idaho Power Co. (Idaho Power), is an electric utility engaged in the generation, transmission, distribution, sale, and purchase of electric energy and capacity and is regulated by the state regulatory commissions of Idaho and Oregon and by the Federal Energy Regulatory Commission. Idaho Power's joint venture, Idaho Energy Resources Co., mines and supplies coal to the Jim Bridger generating plant owned in part by Idaho Power. As of Dec 31 2016, Idaho Power provided electric utility service to about 535,000 general business customers in southern Idaho and eastern Oregon, of which over 444,000 were residential customers.

Recent Developments: For the quarter ended Sep 30 2017, net income increased 9.7% to US$91.1 million from US$83.0 million in the year-earlier quarter. Revenues were US$408.3 million, up 9.8% from US$372.0 million the year before. Operating income was US$120.9 million versus US$97.9 million in the prior-year quarter, an increase of 23.5%. Direct operating expenses rose 4.0% to US$235.2 million from US$226.2 million in the comparable period the year before. Indirect operating expenses increased 8.9% to US$52.2 million from US$47.9 million in the equivalent prior-year period.

Prospects: Our evaluation of Idacorp Inc. as of Jan. 14, 2018 is the result of our systematic analysis on three basic characteristics: earnings strength, relative valuation, and recent stock price movement. The company has managed to produce a neutral trend in earnings per share over the past 5 quarters. However, while recent estimates for the company have been mixed, IDA has posted better than expected results. Based on operating earnings yield, the company is undervalued when compared to all of the companies in our coverage universe. Share price changes over the past year indicates that IDA will perform very well over the near term.

Financial Data

(US$ in Thousands)	9 Mos	6 Mos	3 Mos	12/31/2016	12/31/2015	12/31/2014	12/31/2013	12/31/2012
Earnings Per Share	4.11	3.96	4.09	3.94	3.87	3.85	3.64	3.37
Cash Flow Per Share	8.36	7.97	7.85	6.89	7.03	7.27	6.10	4.98
Tang Book Value Per Share	44.45	43.16	42.69	42.55	40.65	38.58	36.53	34.71
Dividends Per Share	2.200	2.160	2.120	2.080	1.920	1.760	1.570	1.370
Dividend Payout %	53.53	54.55	51.83	52.79	49.61	45.71	43.13	40.65
Income Statement								
Total Revenue	1,043,874	635,550	302,544	1,262,020	1,270,289	1,282,524	1,246,214	1,080,662
EBITDA	396,679	227,538	95,207	447,342	449,151	410,942	453,348	393,185
Depn & Amortn	122,262	82,002	36,763	143,661	138,110	132,987	129,735	123,941
Income Before Taxes	212,328	104,188	37,744	221,646	229,107	198,154	242,581	195,375
Income Taxes	45,420	23,124	6,183	36,429	45,760	16,772	72,226	26,113
Net Income	173,567	82,933	33,102	198,288	194,679	193,480	182,417	168,761
Average Shares	50,421	50,407	50,397	50,373	50,292	50,199	50,126	50,010
Balance Sheet								
Current Assets	457,928	420,078	409,057	440,312	462,036	442,101	476,611	367,253
Total Assets	6,367,183	6,277,399	6,229,948	6,289,897	6,023,314	5,716,853	5,364,563	5,319,516
Current Liabilities	225,792	190,670	180,784	249,715	242,306	241,781	250,372	351,303
Long-Term Obligations	1,745,746	1,745,368	1,744,991	1,744,614	1,725,410	1,614,438	1,615,258	1,466,632
Total Liabilities	4,119,591	4,094,556	4,070,799	4,135,991	3,965,430	3,763,652	3,513,913	3,560,763
Stockholders' Equity	2,247,592	2,182,843	2,159,149	2,153,906	2,057,884	1,953,201	1,850,650	1,758,753
Shares Outstanding	50,393	50,393	50,390	50,396	50,340	50,269	50,232	50,156
Statistical Record								
Return on Assets %	3.31	3.22	3.33	3.21	3.32	3.49	3.41	3.27
Return on Equity %	9.41	9.33	9.75	9.39	9.71	10.17	10.11	9.85
EBITDA Margin %	38.00	35.80	31.47	35.45	35.36	32.04	36.38	36.38
Net Margin %	16.63	13.05	10.94	15.71	15.33	15.09	14.64	15.62
Asset Turnover	0.21	0.21	0.21	0.20	0.22	0.23	0.23	0.21
Current Ratio	2.03	2.20	2.26	1.76	1.91	1.83	1.90	1.05
Debt to Equity	0.78	0.80	0.81	0.81	0.84	0.83	0.87	0.83
Price Range	91.88-73.37	89.97-73.37	83.51-70.17	81.87-65.73	70.34-55.77	69.99-50.77	53.88-43.31	44.80-38.28
P/E Ratio	22.36-17.85	22.72-18.53	20.42-17.16	20.78-16.68	18.18-14.41	18.18-13.19	14.80-11.90	13.29-11.36
Average Yield %	2.66	2.68	2.73	2.77	3.05	3.13	3.22	3.28

Address: 1221 W. Idaho Street, Boise, ID 83702-5627 **Telephone:** 208-388-2200	**Web Site:** www.idacorpinc.com **Officers:** Robert A. Tinstman - Chairman Darrel T. Anderson - President, Chief Executive Officer, Executive Vice President, Chief Financial Officer	**Auditors:** Deloitte & Touche LLP **Investor Contact:** 208-388-2664 **Transfer Agents:** Wells Fargo Shareowner Services, Mendota Heights, MN

IDEX CORPORATION

Exchange	Symbol	Price	52Wk Range	Yield	P/E
NYS	IEX	$131.97 (12/29/2017)	135.57-89.34	1.12	33.84

*7 Year Price Score 125.27 *NYSE Composite Index=100 *12 Month Price Score 111.55

Interim Earnings (Per Share)

Qtr.	Mar	Jun	Sep	Dec
2014	0.91	0.88	0.88	0.77
2015	0.84	0.89	1.02	0.87
2016	0.89	0.99	0.91	0.75
2017	0.99	1.08	1.08	...

Interim Dividends (Per Share)

Amt	Decl	Ex	Rec	Pay
0.37Q	04/26/2017	05/11/2017	05/15/2017	05/31/2017
0.37Q	06/20/2017	07/12/2017	07/14/2017	07/31/2017
0.37Q	09/14/2017	10/13/2017	10/16/2017	10/31/2017
0.37Q	12/04/2017	01/11/2018	01/15/2018	01/30/2018

Indicated Div: $1.48 (Div. Reinv. Plan)

Valuation Analysis

		Institutional Holding	
Forecast EPS	$4.27 (01/18/2018)	No of Institutions	470
Market Cap	$10.1 Billion	Shares	88,003,360
Book Value	$1.8 Billion	% Held	93.57
Price/Book	5.59		
Price/Sales	4.53		

Business Summary: Industrial Machinery & Equipment (MIC: 7.2.1 SIC: 3561 NAIC: 333911)

IDEX is an applied solutions business that sells of pumps, valves, flow meters and other fluidics systems and components and engineered products. Co. has three segments: Fluid and Metering Technologies, which designs, produces and distributes displacement pumps, valves, flow meters, injectors, and other fluid-handling pump modules and systems; Health and Science Technologies, which distribute fluidics, rotary lobe pumps, roll compaction and drying systems used in beverage, food processing, pharmaceutical and cosmetics; and Fire and Safety/Diversified Products, which produces firefighting pumps and controls, rescue tools, lifting bags and other components for the fire and rescue industry.

Recent Developments: For the quarter ended Sep 30 2017, net income increased 19.9% to US$83.8 million from US$69.9 million in the year-earlier quarter. Revenues were US$574.5 million, up 8.3% from US$530.4 million the year before. Operating income was US$126.5 million versus US$109.7 million in the prior-year quarter, an increase of 15.3%. Direct operating expenses rose 5.7% to US$316.6 million from US$299.5 million in the comparable period the year before. Indirect operating expenses increased 8.5% to US$131.4 million from US$121.2 million in the equivalent prior-year period.

Prospects: Our evaluation of IDEX Corp. as of Jan. 14, 2018 is the result of our systematic analysis on three basic characteristics: earnings strength, relative valuation, and recent stock price movement. The company has managed to produce a neutral trend in earnings per share over the past 5 quarters and while recent estimates for the company have been mixed, IEX has posted better than expected results. Based on operating earnings yield, the company is about fairly valued when compared to all of the companies in our coverage universe. Share price changes over the past year indicates that IEX will perform very well over the near term.

Financial Data

(US$ in Thousands)	9 Mos	6 Mos	3 Mos	12/31/2016	12/31/2015	12/31/2014	12/31/2013	12/31/2012
Earnings Per Share	3.90	3.73	3.64	3.53	3.62	3.45	3.09	0.45
Cash Flow Per Share	5.40	5.43	5.45	5.26	4.67	4.62	4.93	3.93
Dividends Per Share	1.420	1.390	1.360	1.340	1.240	1.070	0.890	0.770
Dividend Payout %	36.41	37.27	37.36	37.96	34.25	31.01	28.80	171.11
Income Statement								
Total Revenue	1,701,408	1,126,918	553,552	2,113,043	2,020,668	2,147,767	2,024,130	1,954,258
EBITDA	401,961	265,292	128,097	463,166	476,407	477,522	439,662	169,939
Depn & Amortn	36,370	24,552	12,118	49,038	42,426	43,187	44,327	41,485
Income Before Taxes	331,671	217,884	104,427	368,512	392,345	392,440	353,129	86,204
Income Taxes	88,160	58,141	28,528	97,403	-109,538	113,054	97,914	48,574
Net Income	243,511	159,743	75,899	271,109	282,807	279,386	255,215	37,630
Average Shares	77,523	77,320	76,894	76,758	77,972	80,728	82,489	83,641
Balance Sheet								
Current Assets	955,478	861,418	823,680	822,721	862,684	1,075,791	990,953	881,865
Total Assets	3,317,761	3,224,165	3,163,785	3,154,944	2,805,443	2,908,070	2,887,577	2,785,390
Current Liabilities	336,851	313,905	278,455	309,158	309,597	411,968	304,609	291,427
Long-Term Obligations	874,853	888,495	950,283	1,014,235	839,707	765,006	772,005	779,241
Total Liabilities	1,507,449	1,497,154	1,522,480	1,611,050	1,362,152	1,421,619	1,314,588	1,320,392
Stockholders' Equity	1,810,312	1,727,011	1,641,305	1,543,894	1,443,291	1,486,451	1,572,989	1,464,998
Shares Outstanding	76,659	76,645	76,554	76,440	76,534	78,765	81,195	82,726
Statistical Record								
Return on Assets %	9.14	9.06	8.84	9.07	9.90	9.64	9.00	1.34
Return on Equity %	17.88	17.80	17.80	18.10	19.31	18.26	16.80	2.52
EBITDA Margin %	23.63	23.54	23.14	21.92	23.58	22.23	21.72	8.70
Net Margin %	14.31	14.18	13.71	12.83	14.00	13.01	12.61	1.93
Asset Turnover	0.68	0.69	0.69	0.71	0.71	0.74	0.71	0.69
Current Ratio	2.84	2.74	2.96	2.66	2.79	2.61	3.25	3.03
Debt to Equity	0.48	0.51	0.58	0.66	0.58	0.51	0.49	0.53
Price Range	123.58-84.97	114.82-80.70	96.14-79.29	95.64-68.33	80.00-68.86	81.58-66.43	73.85-46.53	46.53-36.00
P/E Ratio	31.69-21.79	30.78-21.64	26.41-21.78	27.09-19.36	22.10-19.02	23.65-19.26	23.90-15.06	103.40-80.00
Average Yield %	1.41	1.43	1.53	1.58	1.64	1.43	1.43	1.87

Address: 1925 West Field Court, Lake Forest, IL 60045 **Telephone:** 847-498-7070	**Web Site:** www.idexcorp.com **Officers:** Andrew K. Silvernail - Chairman, President, Chief Executive Officer William K. Grogan - Senior Vice President, Chief Financial Officer	**Auditors:** Deloitte & Touche LLP **Investor Contact:** 847-498-7070 **Transfer Agents:** Computershare, Providence, RI

ILLINOIS TOOL WORKS, INC.

Exchange	Symbol	Price	52Wk Range	Yield	P/E	Div Achiever
NYS	ITW	$166.85 (12/29/2017)	169.25-121.61	1.87	25.55	54 Years

*7 Year Price Score 128.82 ***NYSE Composite Index=100** ***12 Month Price Score 108.14**

TRADING VOLUME (thousand shares)

Interim Earnings (Per Share)

Qtr.	Mar	Jun	Sep	Dec
2014	1.11	3.66	1.34	1.19
2015	1.21	1.30	1.39	1.23
2016	1.29	1.46	1.50	1.45
2017	1.54	1.69	1.85	...

Interim Dividends (Per Share)

Amt	Decl	Ex	Rec	Pay
0.65Q	02/10/2017	03/29/2017	03/31/2017	04/11/2017
0.65Q	05/05/2017	06/28/2017	06/30/2017	07/12/2017
0.78Q	08/04/2017	09/28/2017	09/29/2017	10/10/2017
0.78Q	10/27/2017	12/28/2017	12/29/2017	01/10/2018

Indicated Div: $3.12 (Div. Reinv. Plan)

Valuation Analysis

Forecast EPS	$6.69
	(01/18/2018)
Market Cap	$57.2 Billion
Book Value	$5.0 Billion
Price/Book	11.38
Price/Sales	4.06

Institutional Holding

No of Institutions	1503
Shares	354,589,856
% Held	64.67

Business Summary: Industrial Machinery & Equipment (MIC: 7.2.1 SIC: 3569 NAIC: 333999)

Illinois Tool Works manufactures industrial products and equipment. Co. has seven segments: Automotive original equipment manufacturers, which produces components and fasteners; Food Equipment, which produces commercial food equipment; Test & Measurement and Electronics, which produces equipment, consumables, and related software; Welding, which produces arc welding equipment, consumables and accessories; Polymers & Fluids, which produces adhesives, sealants, lubrication and cutting fluids; Construction Products, which produce engineered fastening systems and solutions; and Specialty Products, which produces beverage packaging equipment and consumables, product coding and marking equipment.

Recent Developments: For the quarter ended Sep 30 2017, net income increased 19.6% to US$640.0 million from US$535.0 million in the year-earlier quarter. Revenues were US$3.62 billion, up 3.4% from US$3.50 billion the year before. Operating income was US$961.0 million versus US$808.0 million in the prior-year quarter, an increase of 18.9%. Direct operating expenses rose 3.3% to US$2.09 billion from US$2.03 billion in the comparable period the year before. Indirect operating expenses decreased 15.2% to US$560.0 million from US$660.0 million in the equivalent prior-year period.

Prospects: Our evaluation of Illinois Tool Works Inc. as of Jan. 14, 2018 is the result of our systematic analysis on three basic characteristics: earnings strength, relative valuation, and recent stock price movement. The company has managed to produce a neutral trend in earnings per share over the past 5 quarters and while recent estimates for the company have been mixed, ITW has posted better than expected results. Based on operating earnings yield, the company is about fairly valued when compared to all of the companies in our coverage universe. Share price changes over the past year indicates that ITW will perform well over the near term.

Financial Data

(US$ in Thousands)	9 Mos	6 Mos	3 Mos	12/31/2016	12/31/2015	12/31/2014	12/31/2013	12/31/2012
Earnings Per Share	6.53	6.18	5.95	5.70	5.13	7.28	3.74	6.06
Cash Flow Per Share	6.90	6.43	6.60	6.47	6.25	4.02	5.67	4.40
Tang Book Value Per Share	N.M.	N.M.	N.M.	N.M.	N.M.	0.92	6.55	6.09
Dividends Per Share	2.730	2.600	2.500	2.400	2.070	1.810	1.600	1.480
Dividend Payout %	41.81	42.07	42.02	42.11	40.35	24.86	42.78	24.42
Income Statement								
Total Revenue	10,685,000	7,070,000	3,471,000	13,599,000	13,405,000	14,484,000	14,135,000	17,924,000
EBITDA	3,012,000	1,925,000	927,000	3,516,000	3,372,000	265,135,000	3,099,000	3,485,000
Depn & Amortn	344,000	228,000	114,000	470,000	475,000	262,242,000	549,000	611,000
Income Before Taxes	2,474,000	1,568,000	749,000	2,847,000	2,723,000	2,708,000	2,361,000	3,633,000
Income Taxes	711,000	445,000	213,000	873,000	820,000	809,000	717,000	1,108,000
Net Income	1,763,000	1,123,000	536,000	2,035,000	1,899,000	2,946,000	1,679,000	2,870,000
Average Shares	346,000	347,500	349,000	357,100	370,100	404,600	449,300	473,200
Balance Sheet								
Current Assets	6,912,000	6,570,000	6,430,000	6,123,000	6,720,000	8,076,000	9,816,000	7,960,000
Total Assets	16,314,000	15,922,000	15,529,000	15,201,000	15,729,000	17,678,000	19,966,000	19,309,000
Current Liabilities	2,867,000	2,826,000	2,875,000	2,760,000	2,368,000	3,533,000	6,034,000	2,651,000
Long-Term Obligations	7,439,000	7,360,000	7,205,000	7,177,000	6,896,000	5,981,000	2,793,000	4,589,000
Total Liabilities	11,291,000	11,151,000	11,036,000	10,947,000	10,505,000	10,859,000	10,263,000	8,748,000
Stockholders' Equity	5,023,000	4,771,000	4,493,000	4,254,000	5,224,000	6,819,000	9,703,000	10,561,000
Shares Outstanding	342,600	344,100	345,500	346,900	363,710	382,900	430,200	455,100
Statistical Record								
Return on Assets %	14.18	13.90	13.58	13.12	11.37	15.65	8.55	15.35
Return on Equity %	46.27	44.56	43.31	42.82	31.54	35.66	16.57	27.82
EBITDA Margin %	28.19	27.23	26.71	25.85	25.15	1,830.54	21.92	19.44
Net Margin %	16.50	15.88	15.44	14.96	14.17	20.34	11.88	16.01
Asset Turnover	0.88	0.90	0.89	0.88	0.80	0.77	0.72	0.96
Current Ratio	2.41	2.32	2.24	2.22	2.84	2.29	1.63	3.00
Debt to Equity	1.48	1.54	1.60	1.69	1.32	0.88	0.29	0.43
Price Range	150.18-111.84	150.18-103.91	135.50-98.70	127.93-81.05	99.81-80.09	97.21-76.78	84.08-59.77	62.95-47.79
P/E Ratio	23.00-17.13	24.30-16.81	22.77-16.59	22.44-14.22	19.46-15.61	13.35-10.55	22.48-15.98	10.39-7.89
Average Yield %	2.05	2.04	2.13	2.21	2.24	2.10	2.27	2.61

Address: 155 Harlem Avenue, Glenview, IL 60025	**Web Site:** www.itw.com	**Auditors:** Deloitte & Touche LLP
Telephone: 847-724-7500	**Officers:** E. Scott Santi - Chairman, Chief Executive Officer, Vice-Chairman, President, Chief Operating Officer Christopher A. O'Herlihy - Vice-Chairman, Executive Vice President	**Investor Contact:** 847-657-4104 **Transfer Agents:** Computershare Trust Company, N.A., Providence, RI

INTERCONTINENTAL EXCHANGE INC

Exchange	Symbol	Price	52Wk Range	Yield	P/E
NYS	ICE	$70.56 (12/29/2017)	72.07-56.22	1.13	25.75

*7 Year Price Score 120.77 *NYSE Composite Index=100 *12 Month Price Score 103.22

Interim Earnings (Per Share)

Qtr.	Mar	Jun	Sep	Dec
2014	0.45	0.39	0.36	0.51
2015	0.56	0.51	0.55	0.66
2016	0.62	0.60	0.57	0.58
2017	0.84	0.70	0.62	...

Interim Dividends (Per Share)

Amt	Decl	Ex	Rec	Pay
0.20Q	02/07/2017	09/14/2017	09/15/2017	09/29/2017
0.20Q	02/07/2017	06/14/2017	06/16/2017	06/30/2017
0.20Q	02/07/2017	12/13/2017	12/14/2017	12/29/2017
0.20Q	02/07/2017	03/14/2017	03/16/2017	03/31/2017

Indicated Div: $0.80

Valuation Analysis | **Institutional Holding**

Forecast EPS	$2.94 (01/18/2018)	No of Institutions	850
Market Cap	$41.3 Billion	Shares	575,729,280
Book Value	$16.0 Billion	% Held	86.82
Price/Book	2.59		
Price/Sales	7.03		

Business Summary: Finance Intermediaries & Services (MIC: 5.5.1 SIC: 6231 NAIC: 523210)

IntercontinentalExchange is an operator of regulated exchanges, clearing houses and listings venues, and a provider of data services for commodity and financial markets. Co. operates regulated marketplaces for listing, trading and clearing a range of derivatives and securities contracts across main asset classes, including energy and agricultural commodities, interest rates, equities, equity derivatives, exchange traded funds, credit derivatives, bonds and currencies. Co. provides end-to-end market data services to support the trading, investment, risk management and connectivity needs of customers. Co.'s business is conducted as two segments: Trading and Clearing and Data and Listings.

Recent Developments: For the quarter ended Sep 30 2017, net income increased 7.1% to US$375.0 million from US$350.0 million in the year-earlier quarter. Revenues were US$1.43 billion, up 1.1% from US$1.42 billion the year before. Operating income was US$596.0 million versus US$474.0 million in the prior-year quarter, an increase of 25.7%. Direct operating expenses declined 14.5% to US$289.0 million from US$338.0 million in the comparable period the year before. Indirect operating expenses decreased 9.4% to US$547.0 million from US$604.0 million in the equivalent prior-year period.

Prospects: Our evaluation of IntercontinentalExchange Inc. as of Jan. 14, 2018 is the result of our systematic analysis on three basic characteristics: earnings strength, relative valuation, and recent stock price movement. The company has managed to produce a neutral trend in earnings per share over the past 5 quarters and while recent estimates for the company have been mixed, ICE has posted better than expected results. Based on operating earnings yield, the company is about fairly valued when compared to all of the companies in our coverage universe. Share price changes over the past year indicates that ICE will perform well over the near term.

Financial Data

(US$ in Thousands)	9 Mos	6 Mos	3 Mos	12/31/2016	12/31/2015	12/31/2014	12/31/2013	12/31/2012
Earnings Per Share	2.74	2.69	2.59	2.37	2.28	1.71	0.64	1.50
Cash Flow Per Share	3.49	3.63	3.64	3.60	2.36	2.57	1.88	2.01
Tang Book Value Per Share	N.M.	N.M.	N.M.	N.M.	N.M.	N.M.	N.M.	2.50
Dividends Per Share	0.770	0.740	0.710	0.680	0.580	0.520	0.130	...
Dividend Payout %	28.10	27.51	27.46	28.69	25.46	30.41	20.25	...
Income Statement								
Total Revenue	4,395,000	2,963,000	1,469,000	5,958,000	4,682,000	4,221,000	1,795,000	1,362,965
EBITDA	2,389,000	1,654,000	902,000	2,462,000	1,963,000	1,685,000	638,000	888,368
Depn & Amortn	404,000	276,000	134,000	255,000	213,000	182,000	85,000	61,400
Income Before Taxes	1,848,000	1,288,000	723,000	2,029,000	1,653,000	1,407,000	500,000	789,692
Income Taxes	537,000	352,000	213,000	580,000	358,000	402,000	230,000	227,955
Net Income	1,289,000	920,000	502,000	1,422,000	1,274,000	981,000	254,000	551,576
Average Shares	592,000	595,000	599,000	599,000	560,000	575,000	395,000	366,830
Balance Sheet								
Current Assets	55,239,000	56,448,000	55,073,000	57,133,000	53,313,000	50,245,000	44,259,000	33,750,087
Total Assets	79,118,000	80,324,000	79,463,000	82,003,000	77,987,000	68,279,000	64,818,000	37,214,842
Current Liabilities	54,600,000	56,819,000	56,006,000	58,617,000	54,743,000	50,539,000	44,342,000	32,245,697
Long-Term Obligations	4,865,000	3,874,000	3,872,000	3,871,000	4,717,000	2,247,000	3,923,000	969,500
Total Liabilities	63,126,000	64,426,000	63,708,000	66,286,000	63,179,000	55,919,000	52,235,000	33,571,465
Stockholders' Equity	15,992,000	15,898,000	15,755,000	15,717,000	14,808,000	12,360,000	12,583,000	3,643,377
Shares Outstanding	586,000	589,000	599,000	595,000	595,000	565,000	575,000	362,370
Statistical Record								
Return on Assets %	2.11	2.08	1.96	1.77	1.74	1.47	0.50	1.50
Return on Equity %	10.42	10.36	10.10	9.29	9.38	7.87	3.13	16.26
EBITDA Margin %	54.36	55.82	61.40	41.32	41.93	39.92	35.54	65.18
Net Margin %	29.33	31.05	34.17	23.87	27.21	23.24	14.15	40.47
Asset Turnover	0.08	0.08	0.07	0.07	0.06	0.06	0.04	0.04
Current Ratio	1.01	0.99	0.98	0.97	0.97	0.99	1.00	1.05
Debt to Equity	0.30	0.24	0.25	0.25	0.32	0.18	0.31	0.27
Price Range	68.70-52.61	66.14-50.55	61.55-46.50	59.66-45.99	52.83-40.97	45.56-36.69	45.21-24.76	28.47-22.43
P/E Ratio	25.07-19.20	24.59-18.79	23.76-17.95	25.17-19.41	23.17-17.97	26.65-21.46	70.64-38.69	18.98-14.95
Average Yield %	1.28	1.29	1.30	1.30	1.23	1.28	0.37	...

Address: 5660 New Northside Drive, Atlanta, GA 30328	Web Site: www.theice.com	Auditors: Ernst & Young LLP
Telephone: 770-857-4700	Officers: Jeffrey C. Sprecher - Chairman, Chief Executive Officer Benjamin Jackson - President, Chief Commercial Officer	Investor Contact: 770-857-4726
Fax: 770-937-0020		Transfer Agents: Computershare Trust Company, N.A., Providence, RI

INGERSOLL-RAND PLC

Exchange	Symbol	Price	52Wk Range	Yield	P/E
NYS	IR	$89.19 (12/29/2017)	95.61-74.90	2.02	22.19

*7 Year Price Score 113.70 ***NYSE Composite Index=100** ***12 Month Price Score 94.93**

TRADING VOLUME (thousand shares)

Interim Earnings (Per Share)

Qtr.	Mar	Jun	Sep	Dec
2014	0.28	1.12	1.07	0.95
2015	0.19	0.29	1.12	0.88
2016	0.58	2.86	1.44	0.76
2017	0.45	1.38	1.43	...

Interim Dividends (Per Share)

Amt	Decl	Ex	Rec	Pay
0.40Q	02/08/2017	03/08/2017	03/10/2017	03/31/2017
0.40Q	04/05/2017	06/07/2017	06/09/2017	06/30/2017
0.45Q	08/04/2017	09/07/2017	09/08/2017	09/29/2017
0.45Q	10/03/2017	12/07/2017	12/08/2017	12/29/2017

Indicated Div: $1.80

Valuation Analysis

		Institutional Holding	
Forecast EPS	N/A	No of Institutions	N/A
Market Cap	$22.3 Billion	Shares	N/A
Book Value	$6.8 Billion	% Held	N/A
Price/Book	3.30		N/A
Price/Sales	1.60		

Business Summary: Industrial Machinery & Equipment (MIC: 7.2.1 SIC: 3585 NAIC: 333415)

Ingersoll-Rand provides products, services and solutions to enhance air in homes and buildings, transport and protect food. Co.'s segments are: Climate. which includes Trane® and American Standard® Heating & Air Conditioning, providing heating, ventilation and air conditioning systems, and commercial and residential building services, parts, support and controls, energy services and building automation as well as transport temperature control solutions; and Industrial, which includes compressed air and gas systems and services, power tools, material handling systems, ARO® fluid management equipment, as well as Club Car ® golf, utility and rough terrain vehicles.

Recent Developments: For the quarter ended Sep 30 2017, income from continuing operations increased 0.1% to US$368.2 million from US$367.7 million in the year-earlier quarter. Net income decreased 2.6% to US$371.9 million from US$381.9 million in the year-earlier quarter. Revenues were US$3.67 billion, up 2.9% from US$3.57 billion the year before. Operating income was US$506.1 million versus US$511.7 million in the prior-year quarter, a decrease of 1.1%. Direct operating expenses rose 3.2% to US$2.49 billion from US$2.41 billion in the comparable period the year before. Indirect operating expenses increased 4.9% to US$674.5 million from US$643.2 million in the equivalent prior-year period.

Prospects: Our evaluation of Ingersoll-Rand Plc. as of Sep. 17, 2017 is the result of our systematic analysis on three basic characteristics: earnings strength, relative valuation, and recent stock price movement. The company has produced a positive trend in earnings per share over the past 5 quarters and while recent estimates for the company have remained steady, IR has posted better than expected results. Based on operating earnings yield, the company is undervalued when compared to all of the companies in our coverage universe. Share price changes over the past year indicates that IR will perform well over the near term.

Financial Data

(US$ in Thousands)	9 Mos	6 Mos	3 Mos	12/31/2016	12/31/2015	12/31/2014	12/31/2013	12/31/2012
Earnings Per Share	4.02	4.03	5.51	5.65	2.48	3.40	2.07	3.28
Cash Flow Per Share	5.02	5.80	5.66	5.77	3.21	3.60	3.98	3.88
Dividends Per Share	1.650	1.520	1.440	1.360	1.160	1.000	0.630	0.690
Dividend Payout %	41.04	37.72	26.13	24.07	46.77	29.41	30.43	21.04
Income Statement								
Total Revenue	10,579,500	6,909,000	3,000,600	13,508,900	13,300,700	12,891,400	12,350,500	14,034,900
EBITDA	1,510,100	926,100	293,900	1,774,500	1,657,200	1,613,600	1,297,700	1,758,600
Depn & Amortn	261,900	174,100	86,700	216,700	209,500	199,900	199,500	238,800
Income Before Taxes	1,092,900	648,300	156,300	1,344,300	1,205,300	1,201,600	832,200	1,282,600
Income Taxes	243,200	166,800	28,700	281,500	540,800	293,700	189,000	227,000
Net Income	842,500	475,700	117,100	1,476,200	664,600	931,700	618,800	1,018,600
Average Shares	256,700	259,700	262,600	261,700	267,800	274,300	298,300	310,600
Balance Sheet								
Current Assets	5,813,900	5,855,000	5,414,000	5,579,300	4,609,400	5,707,900	5,716,700	4,942,700
Total Assets	17,722,800	17,773,500	17,259,500	17,397,400	16,738,800	17,298,500	17,658,100	18,492,900
Current Liabilities	4,688,600	3,903,500	3,534,100	3,590,300	3,648,400	3,666,100	3,408,600	4,161,300
Long-Term Obligations	2,955,900	3,704,500	3,711,100	3,709,400	3,734,800	3,741,700	3,153,500	2,269,300
Total Liabilities	10,946,600	11,051,900	10,675,700	10,753,600	10,922,100	11,311,100	10,589,200	11,345,100
Stockholders' Equity	6,776,200	6,721,600	6,583,800	6,643,800	5,816,700	5,987,400	7,068,900	7,147,800
Shares Outstanding	250,500	253,667	257,400	259,006	261,251	262,899	282,700	295,605
Statistical Record								
Return on Assets %	5.88	5.98	8.42	8.63	3.91	5.33	3.42	5.45
Return on Equity %	15.38	16.02	23.28	23.63	11.26	14.27	8.71	14.43
EBITDA Margin %	14.27	13.40	9.79	13.14	12.46	12.52	10.51	12.53
Net Margin %	7.97	6.89	3.90	10.93	5.00	7.23	5.01	7.26
Asset Turnover	0.79	0.79	0.80	0.79	0.78	0.74	0.68	0.75
Current Ratio	1.24	1.50	1.53	1.55	1.26	1.56	1.68	1.19
Debt to Equity	0.44	0.55	0.56	0.56	0.64	0.62	0.45	0.32
Price Range	93.73-64.60	92.59-63.08	81.98-59.18	78.75-48.80	70.91-50.61	64.59-53.57	71.42-47.96	48.87-31.86
P/E Ratio	23.32-16.07	22.98-15.65	14.88-10.74	13.94-8.64	28.59-20.41	19.00-15.76	34.50-23.17	14.90-9.71
Average Yield %	2.02	1.99	2.04	2.11	1.85	1.66	1.08	1.62

Address: 170/175 Lakeview Dr., Airside Business Park, Swords **Telephone:** 018-707-400	**Web Site:** www.ingersollrand.com **Officers:** Michael W. Lamach - Chairman, President, Chief Executive Officer, Chief Operating Officer Susan K. Carter - Senior Vice President, Chief Financial Officer	**Auditors:** PricewaterhouseCoopers LLP **Transfer Agents:** The Bank of New York Mellon, New York, NY

INGREDION INC

*7 Year Price Score 117.93 ***NYSE Composite Index=100** ***12 Month Price Score 103.99**

TRADING VOLUME (thousand shares)

Interim Earnings (Per Share)

Qtr.	Mar	Jun	Sep	Dec
2014	0.96	1.35	1.60	0.85
2015	1.15	1.47	1.48	1.42
2016	1.73	1.58	1.93	1.26
2017	1.68	1.78	2.26	...

Interim Dividends (Per Share)

Amt	Decl	Ex	Rec	Pay
0.50Q	03/15/2017	03/29/2017	03/31/2017	04/25/2017
0.50Q	05/17/2017	06/28/2017	06/30/2017	07/25/2017
0.60Q	09/15/2017	09/29/2017	10/02/2017	10/25/2017
0.60Q	12/15/2017	12/29/2017	01/02/2018	01/25/2018

Indicated Div: $2.40

Valuation Analysis

	Institutional Holding	
Forecast EPS	$7.71	No of Institutions
	(01/18/2018)	649
Market Cap	$10.0 Billion	Shares
Book Value	$2.8 Billion	84,120,800
Price/Book	3.55	% Held
Price/Sales	1.73	N/A

Business Summary: Food (MIC: 1.2.1 SIC: 2046 NAIC: 311221)

Ingredion is an ingredients solutions provider. Co. supplies a range of customers in various industries, including the food, beverage, paper and corrugating, brewing, pharmaceutical, textile and personal care industries. Co.'s product line includes starches and sweeteners, animal feed products and edible corn oil. Co.'s starch-based products include both food-grade and industrial starches, and biomaterials. Co.'s sweetener products include glucose syrups, high maltose syrups, high fructose corn syrup, caramel color, dextrose, polyols, maltodextrins and glucose and syrup solids. Co. operates four segments: North America, South America, Asia Pacific and Europe, Middle East and Africa.

Recent Developments: For the quarter ended Sep 30 2017, net income increased 15.8% to US$169.0 million from US$146.0 million in the year-earlier quarter. Revenues were US$1.49 billion, unchanged from the year before. Operating income was US$233.0 million versus US$221.0 million in the prior-year quarter, an increase of 5.4%. Direct operating expenses declined 2.1% to US$1.10 billion from US$1.12 billion in the comparable period the year before. Indirect operating expenses increased 4.7% to US$155.0 million from US$148.0 million in the equivalent prior-year period.

Prospects: Our evaluation of Ingredion Inc as of Jan. 14, 2018 is the result of our systematic analysis on three basic characteristics: earnings strength, relative valuation, and recent stock price movement. The company has managed to produce a neutral trend in earnings per share over the past 5 quarters and while recent estimates for the company have remained steady, INGR has posted better than expected results. Based on operating earnings yield, the company is undervalued when compared to all of the companies in our coverage universe. Share price changes over the past year indicates that INGR will perform in line with the market over the near term.

Financial Data

(US$ in Thousands)	9 Mos	6 Mos	3 Mos	12/31/2016	12/31/2015	12/31/2014	12/31/2013	12/31/2012
Earnings Per Share	6.98	6.65	6.45	6.55	5.51	4.74	5.05	5.47
Cash Flow Per Share	10.47	11.24	11.16	10.63	9.58	9.93	8.04	9.54
Tang Book Value Per Share	21.28	19.18	17.94	17.66	15.82	19.76	20.97	20.13
Dividends Per Share	2.100	2.000	1.950	1.900	1.740	1.680	1.560	0.920
Dividend Payout %	30.09	30.08	30.23	29.01	31.58	35.44	30.89	16.82
Income Statement								
Total Revenue	4,395,000	2,910,000	1,453,000	5,704,000	5,621,000	5,668,000	6,328,000	6,532,000
EBITDA	738,000	468,000	225,000	1,001,000	848,000	775,000	804,000	874,000
Depn & Amortn	156,000	103,000	51,000	196,000	194,000	195,000	194,000	211,000
Income Before Taxes	582,000	365,000	174,000	742,000	599,000	520,000	547,000	596,000
Income Taxes	153,000	105,000	47,000	246,000	187,000	157,000	144,000	167,000
Net Income	420,000	254,000	124,000	485,000	402,000	355,000	396,000	428,000
Average Shares	73,300	73,200	73,700	74,100	73,000	74,900	78,300	78,200
Balance Sheet								
Current Assets	2,266,000	2,208,000	2,227,000	2,252,000	1,950,000	2,144,000	2,214,000	2,360,000
Total Assets	5,893,000	5,789,000	5,799,000	5,782,000	5,074,000	5,091,000	5,360,000	5,592,000
Current Liabilities	940,000	874,000	933,000	978,000	742,000	721,000	820,000	933,000
Long-Term Obligations	1,731,000	1,838,000	1,895,000	1,850,000	1,819,000	1,804,000	1,717,000	1,724,000
Total Liabilities	3,062,000	3,111,000	3,215,000	3,217,000	2,930,000	2,914,000	2,956,000	3,155,000
Stockholders' Equity	2,831,000	2,678,000	2,584,000	2,565,000	2,144,000	2,177,000	2,404,000	2,437,000
Shares Outstanding	71,846	71,685	71,608	72,414	71,616	71,322	74,311	77,031
Statistical Record								
Return on Assets %	8.97	8.85	8.67	8.91	7.91	6.79	7.23	7.83
Return on Equity %	19.10	19.21	19.61	20.54	18.61	15.50	16.36	18.80
EBITDA Margin %	16.79	16.08	15.49	17.55	15.09	13.67	12.71	13.38
Net Margin %	9.56	8.73	8.53	8.50	7.15	6.26	6.26	6.55
Asset Turnover	1.01	1.04	1.05	1.05	1.11	1.08	1.16	1.19
Current Ratio	2.41	2.53	2.39	2.30	2.63	2.97	2.70	2.53
Debt to Equity	0.61	0.69	0.73	0.72	0.85	0.83	0.71	0.71
Price Range	134.80-114.09	139.64-114.09	139.64-104.75	139.64-86.60	99.34-76.49	86.85-58.88	74.01-61.70	66.59-45.59
P/E Ratio	19.31-16.35	21.00-17.16	21.65-16.24	21.32-13.22	18.03-13.88	18.32-12.42	14.66-12.22	12.17-8.33
Average Yield %	1.72	1.60	1.57	1.60	2.03	2.27	2.24	1.65

Address: 5 Westbrook Corporate Center, Westchester, IL 60154	**Web Site:** www.ingredion.com	**Auditors:** KPMG LLP
Telephone: 708-551-2600	**Officers:** Ilene S. Gordon - Chairman, President, Chief Executive Officer James D. Gray - Chief Financial Officer, Executive Vice President	**Investor Contact:** 708-551-2592
Fax: 708-551-2700		**Transfer Agents:** Computershare, Providence, RI

INTERNATIONAL BUSINESS MACHINES CORP

Exchange	Symbol	Price	52Wk Range	Yield	P/E	Div Achiever
NYS	IBM	$153.42 (12/29/2017)	181.95-139.70	3.91	12.83	21 Years

*7 Year Price Score 71.74   *NYSE Composite Index=100   *12 Month Price Score 90.76

Interim Earnings (Per Share)

Qtr.	Mar	Jun	Sep	Dec
2014	2.29	4.12	0.02	5.46
2015	2.35	3.51	3.01	4.57
2016	2.09	2.61	2.98	4.71
2017	1.85	2.48	2.92	...

Interim Dividends (Per Share)

Amt	Decl	Ex	Rec	Pay
1.40Q	01/31/2017	02/08/2017	02/10/2017	03/10/2017
1.50Q	04/25/2017	05/08/2017	05/10/2017	06/10/2017
1.50Q	07/25/2017	08/08/2017	08/10/2017	09/09/2017
1.50Q	10/31/2017	11/09/2017	11/10/2017	12/09/2017

Indicated Div: $6.00 (Div. Reinv. Plan)

Valuation Analysis

Valuation Analysis		Institutional Holding	
Forecast EPS	$13.80 (01/18/2018)	No of Institutions	2556
Market Cap	$142.0 Billion	Shares	714,231,872
Book Value	$19.6 Billion	% Held	49.71
Price/Book	7.24		
Price/Sales	1.81		

Business Summary: IT Services (MIC: 6.3.1 SIC: 7379 NAIC: 541519)

International Business Machines consist of five segments: Cognitive Solutions, comprises a portfolio that help clients to identify insights and inform decision-making; Global Business Services, provides clients with consulting, application management services and global process services; Technology Services & Cloud Platforms, provides IT infrastructure services creating business value for clients; Systems, provides clients with infrastructure technologies to help meet the new requirements; and Global Financing, facilitates clients' acquisition of information technology systems, software and services.

Recent Developments: For the quarter ended Sep 30 2017, income from continuing operations decreased 4.5% to US$2.73 billion from US$2.85 billion in the year-earlier quarter. Net income decreased 4.5% to US$2.73 billion from US$2.85 billion in the year-earlier quarter. Revenues were US$19.15 billion, down 0.4% from US$19.23 billion the year before. Direct operating expenses rose 1.4% to US$10.35 billion from US$10.21 billion in the comparable period the year before. Indirect operating expenses increased 1.4% to US$5.68 billion from US$5.60 billion in the equivalent prior-year period.

Prospects: Our evaluation of International Business Machines Corp. as of Jan. 14, 2018 is the result of our systematic analysis on three basic characteristics: earnings strength, relative valuation, and recent stock price movement. The company has produced a positive trend in earnings per share over the past 5 quarters. However, while recent estimates for the company have been mixed, IBM has posted better than expected results. Based on operating earnings yield, the company is undervalued when compared to all of the companies in our coverage universe. Share price changes over the past year indicates that IBM will perform poorly over the near term.

Financial Data

(US$ in Thousands)	9 Mos	6 Mos	3 Mos	12/31/2016	12/31/2015	12/31/2014	12/31/2013	12/31/2012
Earnings Per Share	11.96	12.02	12.15	12.38	13.42	11.90	14.94	14.37
Cash Flow Per Share	15.76	16.36	16.20	17.70	17.38	16.80	15.85	17.10
Dividends Per Share	5.800	5.700	5.600	5.500	5.000	4.250	3.700	3.300
Dividend Payout %	48.49	47.42	46.09	44.43	37.26	35.71	24.77	22.96
Income Statement								
Total Revenue	56,597,000	37,443,000	18,155,000	79,919,000	81,741,000	92,793,000	99,751,000	104,507,000
EBITDA	10,672,000	6,302,000	2,628,000	17,233,000	20,196,000	24,872,000	24,530,000	26,928,000
Depn & Amortn	3,392,000	2,216,000	1,099,000	4,381,000	3,855,000	4,492,000	4,678,000	4,676,000
Income Before Taxes	6,931,000	3,867,000	1,424,000	12,330,000	15,945,000	19,986,000	19,524,000	21,902,000
Income Taxes	120,000	(218,000)	(329,000)	449,000	2,581,000	4,234,000	3,041,000	5,298,000
Net Income	6,807,000	4,082,000	1,750,000	11,872,000	13,190,000	12,022,000	16,483,000	16,604,000
Average Shares	933,200	939,600	947,800	958,714	982,700	1,010,000	1,094,486	1,155,449
Balance Sheet								
Current Assets	44,742,000	45,013,000	42,889,000	43,888,000	42,504,000	49,422,000	51,350,000	49,433,000
Total Assets	121,636,000	120,495,000	117,495,000	117,470,000	110,495,000	117,532,000	126,223,000	119,213,000
Current Liabilities	31,697,000	35,966,000	36,481,000	36,275,000	34,269,000	39,600,000	40,154,000	43,625,000
Long-Term Obligations	41,327,000	37,612,000	34,441,000	34,655,000	33,428,000	35,073,000	32,856,000	24,088,000
Total Liabilities	102,009,000	102,076,000	99,168,000	99,224,000	96,233,000	105,664,000	103,431,000	100,353,000
Stockholders' Equity	19,627,000	18,419,000	18,327,000	18,246,000	14,262,000	11,868,000	22,792,000	18,860,000
Shares Outstanding	925,791	931,940	939,496	945,867	965,728	990,523	1,054,390	1,117,367
Statistical Record								
Return on Assets %	9.53	9.59	9.82	10.39	11.57	9.86	13.43	14.05
Return on Equity %	61.73	66.97	69.82	72.84	100.96	69.37	79.15	84.92
EBITDA Margin %	18.86	16.83	14.48	21.56	24.71	26.80	24.59	25.77
Net Margin %	12.03	10.90	9.64	14.86	16.14	12.96	16.52	15.89
Asset Turnover	0.66	0.66	0.67	0.70	0.72	0.76	0.81	0.88
Current Ratio	1.41	1.25	1.18	1.21	1.24	1.25	1.28	1.13
Debt to Equity	2.11	2.04	1.88	1.90	2.34	2.96	1.44	1.28
Price Range	181.95-139.70	181.95-149.63	181.95-143.50	168.51-117.85	174.40-131.75	197.77-151.41	215.80-172.80	211.00-179.16
P/E Ratio	15.21-11.68	15.14-12.45	14.98-11.81	13.61-9.52	13.00-9.82	16.62-12.72	14.44-11.57	14.68-12.47
Average Yield %	3.64	3.50	3.49	3.66	3.22	2.33	1.91	1.68

Address: One New Orchard Road, Armonk, NY 10504	Web Site: www.ibm.com	Auditors: PricewaterhouseCoopers LLP
Telephone: 914-499-1900	Officers: Virginia M. (Ginni) Rometty - Chairman, President, Chief Executive Officer, Senior Vice President Martin J. Schroeter - Senior Vice President, Chief Financial Officer, General Manager	Investor Contact: 914-499-7777
Fax: 914-765-4190		Transfer Agents: Computershare Trust Company, N.A., Providence, RI

INTERNATIONAL FLAVORS & FRAGRANCES INC.

Exchange	Symbol	Price	52Wk Range	Yield	P/E	Div Achiever
NYS	IFF	$152.61 (12/29/2017)	155.44-115.26	1.81	29.24	14 Years

*7 Year Price Score 111.84 *NYSE Composite Index=100 *12 Month Price Score 105.04

Interim Earnings (Per Share)

Qtr.	Mar	Jun	Sep	Dec
2014	1.30	1.35	1.31	1.11
2015	1.57	1.29	1.31	0.98
2016	1.47	1.46	1.12	1.00
2017	1.45	1.38	1.39	...

Interim Dividends (Per Share)

Amt	Decl	Ex	Rec	Pay
0.64Q	03/07/2017	03/23/2017	03/27/2017	04/07/2017
0.64Q	05/03/2017	06/22/2017	06/27/2017	07/07/2017
0.69Q	08/02/2017	09/22/2017	09/25/2017	10/06/2017
0.69Q	12/13/2017	12/28/2017	12/29/2017	01/08/2018

Indicated Div: $2.76 (Div. Reinv. Plan)

Valuation Analysis — **Institutional Holding**

Forecast EPS	$5.80 (01/18/2018)	No of Institutions 669
Market Cap	$12.1 Billion	Shares 89,229,808
Book Value	$1.8 Billion	% Held 76.37
Price/Book	6.86	
Price/Sales	3.64	

Business Summary: Specialty Chemicals (MIC: 8.3.2 SIC: 2869 NAIC: 325199)

International Flavors & Fragrances and its subsidiaries is a manufacturer of flavors and fragrances (including cosmetic active ingredients) used to impart flavor or fragrance in a variety of consumer products. Co.'s products are sold principally to manufacturers of perfumes and cosmetics, hair and other personal care products, soaps and detergents, cleaning products, dairy, meat and other processed foods, beverages, snacks and savory foods, sweet and baked goods, and pharmaceutical and oral care products. Co. operates in two business segments, Flavors, which develops different flavors and taste for Co.'s customers; and Fragrances, which has two sources, Fragrance Compounds and Ingredients.

Recent Developments: For the quarter ended Sep 30 2017, net income increased 22.8% to US$110.3 million from US$89.8 million in the year-earlier quarter. Revenues were US$872.9 million, up 12.3% from US$777.0 million the year before. Operating income was US$157.7 million versus US$124.4 million in the prior-year quarter, an increase of 26.7%. Direct operating expenses rose 14.0% to US$490.9 million from US$430.7 million in the comparable period the year before. Indirect operating expenses increased 1.1% to US$224.4 million from US$221.8 million in the equivalent prior-year period.

Prospects: Our evaluation of International Flavors & Fragrances Inc. as of Jan. 14, 2018 is the result of our systematic analysis on three basic characteristics: earnings strength, relative valuation, and recent stock price movement. The company has managed to produce a neutral trend in earnings per share over the past 5 quarters and while recent estimates for the company have been mixed, IFF has posted better than expected results. Based on operating earnings yield, the company is about fairly valued when compared to all of the companies in our coverage universe. Share price changes over the past year indicates that IFF will perform very well over the near term.

Financial Data

(US$ in Thousands)	9 Mos	6 Mos	3 Mos	12/31/2016	12/31/2015	12/31/2014	12/31/2013	12/31/2012
Earnings Per Share	5.22	4.95	5.03	5.05	5.16	5.06	4.29	3.09
Cash Flow Per Share	5.13	5.55	6.64	6.70	5.39	6.40	5.01	3.98
Tang Book Value Per Share	2.27	1.31	1.46	3.29	4.29	9.49	9.42	6.70
Dividends Per Share	2.610	2.560	2.480	2.400	2.060	1.720	1.460	1.300
Dividend Payout %	50.00	51.72	49.30	47.52	39.92	33.99	34.03	42.07
Income Statement								
Total Revenue	2,544,094	1,671,154	828,293	3,116,350	3,023,189	3,088,533	2,952,896	2,821,446
EBITDA	495,764	326,451	158,360	679,069	659,963	684,482	615,204	561,835
Depn & Amortn	24,327	15,561	7,066	102,363	74,800	89,354	83,227	76,667
Income Before Taxes	421,853	280,527	138,487	523,717	539,101	549,061	485,210	443,415
Income Taxes	86,033	54,968	22,723	118,686	119,854	134,518	131,666	189,281
Net Income	335,820	225,559	115,764	405,031	419,247	414,543	353,544	254,134
Average Shares	79,362	79,305	79,409	79,981	80,891	81,494	81,930	81,833
Balance Sheet								
Current Assets	1,849,747	1,993,926	1,711,433	1,609,014	1,455,884	1,710,027	1,652,903	1,572,559
Total Assets	4,520,438	4,618,875	4,252,259	4,016,984	3,721,454	3,494,621	3,331,731	3,249,600
Current Liabilities	696,121	861,223	985,824	898,297	742,128	518,808	560,366	622,732
Long-Term Obligations	1,625,502	1,636,338	1,186,417	1,066,855	937,844	934,232	932,665	881,104
Total Liabilities	2,763,125	2,944,517	2,626,182	2,390,740	2,131,136	1,976,060	1,868,659	2,000,792
Stockholders' Equity	1,757,313	1,674,358	1,626,077	1,626,244	1,590,318	1,518,561	1,463,072	1,248,808
Shares Outstanding	78,977	78,975	78,948	79,213	80,022	80,777	81,384	81,626
Statistical Record								
Return on Assets %	9.65	9.01	9.56	10.44	11.62	12.15	10.74	8.16
Return on Equity %	24.09	23.61	24.70	25.12	26.97	27.81	26.07	21.54
EBITDA Margin %	19.49	19.53	19.12	21.79	21.83	22.16	20.83	19.91
Net Margin %	13.20	13.50	13.98	13.00	13.87	13.42	11.97	9.01
Asset Turnover	0.77	0.73	0.75	0.80	0.84	0.90	0.90	0.91
Current Ratio	2.66	2.32	1.74	1.79	1.96	3.30	2.95	2.53
Debt to Equity	0.92	0.98	0.73	0.66	0.59	0.62	0.64	0.71
Price Range	145.01-115.26	142.97-115.26	142.97-113.77	142.97-100.49	122.77-98.15	105.43-83.84	89.89-66.54	67.41-52.88
P/E Ratio	27.78-22.08	28.88-23.28	28.42-22.62	28.31-19.90	23.79-19.02	20.84-16.57	20.95-15.51	21.82-17.11
Average Yield %	2.00	1.97	1.96	1.93	1.81	1.77	1.85	2.21

Address: 521 West 57th Street, New York, NY 10019-2960 **Telephone:** 212-765-5500	**Web Site:** www.iff.com **Officers:** Andreas Fibig - Chairman, Chief Executive Officer Richard A. O'Leary - Executive Vice President, Senior Vice President, Vice President, Chief Financial Officer, Interim Chief Financial Officer, Chief Accounting Officer, Controller	**Auditors:** PricewaterhouseCoopers LLP **Investor Contact:** 212-765-5500 **Transfer Agents:** American Stock Transfer & Trust Company, New York, NY

INTERNATIONAL PAPER CO

Exchange	Symbol	Price	52Wk Range	Yield	P/E
NYS	IP	$57.94 (12/29/2017)	58.67-49.64	3.28	26.70

*7 Year Price Score 99.96   *NYSE Composite Index=100   *12 Month Price Score 96.60

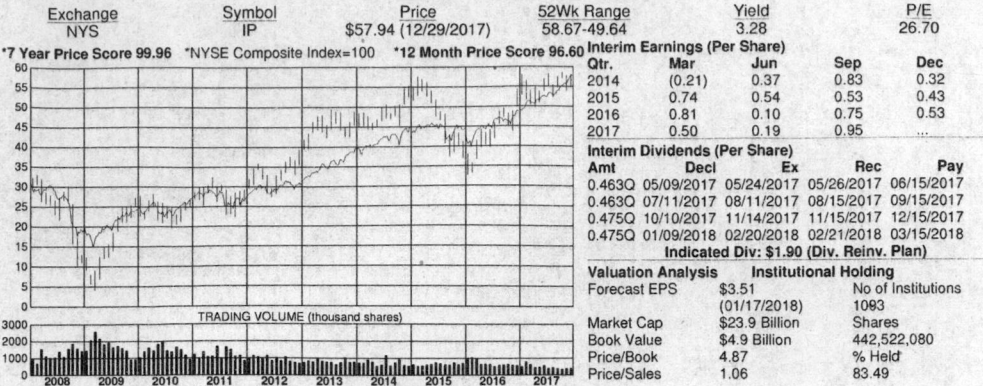

Interim Earnings (Per Share)

Qtr.	Mar	Jun	Sep	Dec
2014	(0.21)	0.37	0.83	0.32
2015	0.74	0.54	0.53	0.43
2016	0.81	0.10	0.75	0.53
2017	0.50	0.19	0.95	

Interim Dividends (Per Share)

Amt	Decl	Ex	Rec	Pay
0.463Q	05/09/2017	05/24/2017	05/26/2017	06/15/2017
0.463Q	07/11/2017	08/11/2017	08/15/2017	09/15/2017
0.475Q	10/10/2017	11/14/2017	11/15/2017	12/15/2017
0.475Q	01/09/2018	02/20/2018	02/21/2018	03/15/2018

Indicated Div: $1.90 (Div. Reinv. Plan)

Valuation Analysis

		Institutional Holding	
Forecast EPS	$3.51	No of Institutions	
	(01/17/2018)	1093	
Market Cap	$23.9 Billion	Shares	
Book Value	$4.9 Billion	442,522,080	
Price/Book	4.87	% Held	
Price/Sales	1.06	83.49	

Business Summary: Containers & Packaging (MIC: 8.1.3 SIC: 2621 NAIC: 322121)

International Paper is a paper and packaging company with markets and manufacturing operations in North America, Europe, Latin America, Russia, Asia, Africa and the Middle East. Co.'s businesses are separated into three segments: Industrial Packaging, which manufactures containerboard in the U.S. and its products include linerboard, medium, whitetop, recycled linerboard, recycled medium and saturating kraft; Printing Papers, produces printing and writing papers and its products include uncoated papers and pulp; and Consumer Packaging, produces solid bleached sulfate board and its brands include Everest®, Fortress®, and Starcote®.£

Recent Developments: For the quarter ended Sep 30 2017, income from continuing operations increased 27.8% to US$395.0 million from US$309.0 million in the year-earlier quarter. Net income increased 27.8% to US$395.0 million from US$309.0 million in the year-earlier quarter. Revenues were US$5.91 billion, up 12.3% from US$5.27 billion the year before. Direct operating expenses rose 11.1% to US$4.02 billion from US$3.62 billion in the comparable period the year before. Indirect operating expenses increased 8.3% to US$1.23 billion from US$1.14 billion in the equivalent prior-year period.

Prospects: Our evaluation of International Paper Co. as of Jan. 14, 2018 is the result of our systematic analysis on three basic characteristics: earnings strength, relative valuation, and recent stock price movement. The company has enjoyed a very positive trend in earnings per share over the past 5 quarters and while recent estimates for the company have been mixed, IP has posted better than expected results. Based on operating earnings yield, the company is undervalued when compared to all of the companies in our coverage universe. Share price changes over the past year indicates that IP will perform poorly over the near term.

Financial Data

(US$ in Millions)	9 Mos	6 Mos	3 Mos	12/31/2016	12/31/2015	12/31/2014	12/31/2013	12/31/2012
Earnings Per Share	2.17	1.97	1.88	2.18	2.23	1.29	3.11	1.80
Cash Flow Per Share	3.55	6.13	6.04	6.01	6.18	7.19	6.83	6.80
Tang Book Value Per Share	3.62	2.75	2.84	2.38	1.31	3.19	9.44	4.52
Dividends Per Share	1.850	1.827	1.805	1.783	1.640	1.450	1.250	1.087
Dividend Payout %	85.25	92.77	96.01	81.77	73.54	112.40	40.19	60.42
Income Statement								
Total Revenue	17,196	11,283	5,511	21,079	22,365	23,617	29,080	27,833
EBITDA	2,146	1,150	710	2,676	3,034	2,787	2,884	3,095
Depn & Amortn	997	656	324	1,200	1,213	1,308	1,423	1,399
Income Before Taxes	718	215	244	956	1,266	872	849	1,024
Income Taxes	147	(6)	83	247	466	123	(523)	331
Net Income	684	289	209	904	938	555	1,395	794
Average Shares	417	416	416	415	420	432	448	440
Balance Sheet								
Current Assets	7,211	7,237	6,721	6,969	6,477	7,959	9,025	8,905
Total Assets	33,813	33,877	33,301	33,345	30,587	28,684	31,528	32,153
Current Liabilities	4,869	5,002	4,267	4,072	3,924	4,909	5,127	4,998
Long-Term Obligations	11,373	10,392	10,823	11,075	8,900	8,631	8,827	9,696
Total Liabilities	28,899	29,332	28,726	29,004	26,703	23,569	23,423	25,849
Stockholders' Equity	4,914	4,545	4,575	4,341	3,884	5,115	8,105	6,304
Shares Outstanding	412	412	412	411	420	420	436	439
Statistical Record								
Return on Assets %	2.72	2.51	2.42	2.82	3.17	1.84	4.38	2.68
Return on Equity %	19.77	19.12	17.69	21.92	20.85	8.40	19.36	12.25
EBITDA Margin %	12.48	10.19	12.88	12.70	13.57	11.80	9.92	11.12
Net Margin %	3.98	2.56	3.79	4.29	4.19	2.35	4.80	2.85
Asset Turnover	0.68	0.67	0.67	0.66	0.75	0.78	0.91	0.94
Current Ratio	1.48	1.45	1.58	1.71	1.65	1.62	1.76	1.78
Debt to Equity	2.31	2.29	2.37	2.55	2.29	1.69	1.09	1.54
Price Range	58.17-43.60	57.99-41.76	57.99-39.60	54.28-32.58	57.59-36.80	55.25-44.25	49.48-39.28	39.28-27.42
P/E Ratio	26.81-20.09	29.44-21.20	30.85-21.06	24.90-14.94	25.83-16.50	42.83-34.30	15.91-12.63	21.82-15.23
Average Yield %	3.51	3.63	3.80	4.09	3.41	3.00	2.77	3.29

Address: 6400 Poplar Avenue, Memphis, TN 38197	**Web Site:** www.internationalpaper.com	**Auditors:** Deloitte & Touche LLP
Telephone: 901-419-7000	**Officers:** Mark S. Sutton - Chairman, President, Chief Executive Officer, Chief Operating Officer Tommy S. Joseph - Senior Vice President	**Investor Contact:** 901-419-1731
		Transfer Agents: Computershare Trust Company, N.A., Canton, MA

INTERPUBLIC GROUP OF COMPANIES INC.

Exchange	Symbol	Price	52Wk Range	Yield	P/E
NYS	IPG	$20.16 (12/29/2017)	25.57-18.45	3.57	14.00

*7 Year Price Score 101.56 *NYSE Composite Index=100 ***12 Month Price Score 83.18**

Interim Earnings (Per Share)

Qtr.	Mar	Jun	Sep	Dec
2014	(0.05)	0.23	0.21	0.73
2015	0.00	0.29	0.18	0.62
2016	0.01	0.38	0.32	0.78
2017	0.05	0.24	0.37	...

Interim Dividends (Per Share)

Amt	Decl	Ex	Rec	Pay
0.18Q	02/10/2017	02/27/2017	03/01/2017	03/15/2017
0.18Q	05/25/2017	06/01/2017	06/05/2017	06/19/2017
0.18Q	07/26/2017	08/30/2017	09/01/2017	09/15/2017
0.18Q	10/25/2017	11/30/2017	12/01/2017	12/15/2017

Indicated Div: $0.72

Valuation Analysis

Valuation Analysis		Institutional Holding	
Forecast EPS	$1.40	No of Institutions	
	(01/12/2018)	713	
Market Cap	$8.1 Billion	Shares	
Book Value	$2.0 Billion	491,871,904	
Price/Book	4.00	% Held	
Price/Sales	1.03	88.43	

Business Summary: Advertising (MIC: 2.3.4 SIC: 7311 NAIC: 541810)

Interpublic Group of Companies is engaged in providing advertising and marketing services. Co. has two reportale segments: Integrated Agency Networks (IAN) and Constituency Management Group (CMG). Within IAN, Co.'s agencies provide a range of communications and marketing services. Co.'s digital agencies provide digital capabilities and service their own client rosters while also serving as digital partners. In addition, Co.'s domestic integrated agencies provide advertising, marketing communications services and/or marketing services. CMG provides clients with a range of services such as public relations, meeting and event production, and sports and entertainment marketing, among others.

Recent Developments: For the quarter ended Sep 30 2017, net income increased 12.1% to US$148.8 million from US$132.7 million in the year-earlier quarter. Revenues were US$1.90 billion, down 1.0% from US$1.92 billion the year before. Operating income was US$219.1 million versus US$208.0 million in the prior-year quarter, an increase of 5.3%. Indirect operating expenses decreased 1.8% to US$1.68 billion from US$1.71 billion in the equivalent prior-year period.

Prospects: Our evaluation of Interpublic Group of Cos. Inc. as of Jan. 14, 2018 is the result of our systematic analysis on three basic characteristics: earnings strength, relative valuation, and recent stock price movement. The company has managed to produce a neutral trend in earnings per share over the past 5 quarters. However, while recent estimates for the company have been mixed, IPG has posted results that fell short of analysts expectations. Based on operating earnings yield, the company is undervalued when compared to all of the companies in our coverage universe. Share price changes over the past year indicates that IPG will perform poorly over the near term.

Financial Data
(US$ in Thousands)	9 Mos	6 Mos	3 Mos	12/31/2016	12/31/2015	12/31/2014	12/31/2013	12/31/2012
Earnings Per Share	1.44	1.39	1.53	1.49	1.09	1.12	0.61	0.94
Cash Flow Per Share	1.05	2.33	2.02	1.29	1.65	1.60	1.41	0.82
Dividends Per Share	0.690	0.660	0.630	0.600	0.480	0.380	0.300	0.240
Dividend Payout %	47.92	47.48	41.18	40.27	44.04	33.93	49.18	25.53
Income Statement								
Total Revenue	5,541,400	3,638,800	1,753,900	7,846,600	7,613,800	7,537,100	7,122,300	6,956,200
EBITDA	494,800	270,400	61,600	1,039,000	956,100	910,500	696,600	903,100
Depn & Amortn	64,000	48,800	31,100	138,300	130,900	132,300	130,600	124,300
Income Before Taxes	377,200	184,900	14,800	830,200	762,200	720,700	468,000	674,800
Income Taxes	115,800	73,300	(2,100)	198,000	282,800	216,500	181,200	213,300
Net Income	262,400	116,200	21,500	608,500	454,600	477,100	267,900	446,700
Average Shares	397,200	400,300	399,300	408,000	415,700	425,400	429,600	481,400
Balance Sheet								
Current Assets	6,463,800	6,486,500	6,589,500	7,438,000	7,693,100	7,810,200	8,084,000	8,738,300
Total Assets	11,716,100	11,678,200	11,697,900	12,485,200	12,585,100	12,747,200	12,905,000	13,493,900
Current Liabilities	6,946,300	6,946,200	6,990,700	7,706,000	7,584,300	7,463,300	8,165,300	7,701,700
Long-Term Obligations	1,285,000	1,283,100	1,281,900	1,280,700	1,610,300	1,623,500	1,129,800	2,060,800
Total Liabilities	9,702,700	9,695,700	9,734,900	10,468,100	10,619,600	10,630,900	10,689,800	11,073,300
Stockholders' Equity	2,013,400	1,982,500	1,963,000	2,017,100	1,965,500	2,116,300	2,215,200	2,420,600
Shares Outstanding	399,400	399,300	395,110	391,600	403,200	413,800	424,500	417,500
Statistical Record								
Return on Assets %	4.92	4.82	5.38	4.84	3.59	3.72	2.03	3.38
Return on Equity %	29.33	28.27	31.99	30.47	22.27	22.03	11.56	18.25
EBITDA Margin %	8.93	7.43	3.51	13.24	12.56	12.08	9.78	12.98
Net Margin %	4.74	3.19	1.23	7.75	5.97	6.33	3.76	6.42
Asset Turnover	0.66	0.67	0.68	0.62	0.60	0.59	0.54	0.53
Current Ratio	0.93	0.93	0.94	0.97	1.01	1.05	0.99	1.13
Debt to Equity	0.64	0.65	0.65	0.63	0.82	0.77	0.51	0.85
Price Range	25.57-19.58	25.21-21.83	24.74-21.83	24.60-20.30	23.65-18.27	20.83-16.05	17.70-11.02	11.97-9.45
P/E Ratio	17.76-13.60	18.14-15.71	16.17-14.27	16.51-13.62	21.70-16.76	18.60-14.33	29.02-18.07	12.73-10.05
Average Yield %	2.96	2.79	2.69	2.63	2.27	2.06	2.01	2.20

Address: 909 Third Avenue, New York, NY 10022 **Telephone:** 212-704-1200	**Web Site:** www.interpublic.com **Officers:** Michael I. Roth - Chairman, Chief Executive Officer Philippe Krakowsky - Executive Vice President, Chief Strategy Officer, Chief Talent Officer	**Auditors:** PricewaterhouseCoopers LLP **Transfer Agents:** Computershare Shareowner Services LLC, Jersey City, NJ

INTREXON CORP

Exchange NYS	Symbol XON	Price $11.52 (12/29/2017)	52Wk Range 26.25-11.33	Yield N/A	P/E N/A

*7 Year Price Score N/A   *NYSE Composite Index=100   *12 Month Price Score 62.50

Interim Earnings (Per Share)

Qtr.	Mar	Jun	Sep	Dec
2014	0.04	(0.53)	(0.53)	0.19
2015	0.25	(0.37)	(0.34)	(0.29)
2016	(0.55)	(0.42)	(0.24)	(0.37)
2017	(0.26)	(0.16)	(0.33)	...

Interim Dividends (Per Share)

No Dividends Paid

Valuation Analysis   Institutional Holding

Forecast EPS	$-1.08	No of Institutions
	(01/16/2018)	N/A
Market Cap	$1.4 Billion	Shares
Book Value	$533.6 Million	N/A
Price/Book	2.60	% Held
Price/Sales	6.94	N/A

Business Summary: Biotechnology (MIC: 4.1.2 SIC: 8731 NAIC: 541710)

Intrexon is engaged in the business of synthetic biology. Co. designs, builds and regulates gene programs, which are DNA sequences that consist of primary genetic components. Co.'s synthetic biology capabilities include the ability to control the amount, location and modification of biological molecules to control the function and output of living cells. Co.'s technologies include: its UltraVector gene design and fabrication platform and its library of modular DNA components; Cell Systems Informatics; RheoSwitch inducible gene switch; AttSite Recombinases; Protein Engineering; Laser-Enabled Analysis and Processing; and ActoBiotics platform.

Recent Developments: For the quarter ended Sep 30 2017, net loss amounted to US$40.8 million versus a net loss of US$30.0 million in the year-earlier quarter. Revenues were US$46.0 million, down 6.1% from US$49.0 million the year before. Operating loss was US$44.7 million versus a loss of US$28.8 million in the prior-year quarter. Direct operating expenses was unchanged at US$15.0 million versus the comparable period the year before. Indirect operating expenses increased 20.5% to US$75.7 million from US$62.8 million in the equivalent prior-year period.

Prospects: Our evaluation of Intrexon Corp as of Jan. 14, 2018 is the result of our systematic analysis on three basic characteristics: earnings strength, relative valuation, and recent stock price movement. The company has suffered a very negative trend in earnings per share over the past 5 quarters. Because the company lacks sufficient analyst estimate data, we place greater weight on the historical EPS trend as the measure of earnings strength. Based on operating earnings yield, the company is overvalued when compared to all of the companies in our coverage universe. Share price changes over the past year indicates that XON will perform very poorly over the near term.

Financial Data

(US$ in Thousands)	9 Mos	6 Mos	3 Mos	12/31/2016	12/31/2015	12/31/2014	12/31/2013	12/31/2012
Earnings Per Share	(1.12)	(1.03)	(1.29)	(1.58)	(0.76)	(0.83)	(1.40)	(18.77)
Cash Flow Per Share	(0.78)	(0.74)	(0.65)	(0.47)	0.32	(0.20)	(1.31)	(11.09)
Tang Book Value Per Share	1.04	1.21	1.23	1.50	2.41	2.17	3.20	9.82
Income Statement								
Total Revenue	153,953	107,937	53,747	190,926	173,605	71,930	23,760	13,925
EBITDA	(88,671)	(48,148)	(29,428)	(172,973)	(70,802)	(74,421)	(35,836)	(76,591)
Depn & Amortn	9,034	5,964	2,980	9,387	7,872	6,178	4,325	4,957
Income Before Taxes	(83,766)	(45,105)	(27,963)	(173,031)	(78,034)	(80,459)	(40,302)	(81,600)
Income Taxes	(2,164)	(1,346)	(533)	(3,877)	1,016	(103)	...	...
Net Income	(89,752)	(50,063)	(31,399)	(186,612)	(84,493)	(81,822)	(38,980)	(81,874)
Average Shares	120,518	119,731	118,956	117,983	111,066	99,170	40,951	5,533
Balance Sheet								
Current Assets	179,740	234,117	281,670	315,181	323,801	174,773	187,556	13,533
Total Assets	898,261	933,986	915,928	949,068	982,046	576,272	469,472	151,646
Current Liabilities	87,796	95,686	90,650	94,605	75,904	47,482	19,829	16,717
Long-Term Obligations	7,673	7,684	7,608	7,562	7,598	8,694	1,663	42
Total Liabilities	364,648	383,116	387,390	388,831	287,968	191,511	102,750	66,540
Stockholders' Equity	533,613	550,870	528,538	560,237	694,078	384,761	366,722	85,106
Shares Outstanding	120,624	120,404	119,552	118,688	116,658	100,557	97,053	5,661
Statistical Record								
Asset Turnover	0.21	0.21	0.21	0.20	0.22	0.14	0.08	0.10
Current Ratio	2.05	2.45	3.11	3.33	4.27	3.68	9.46	0.81
Debt to Equity	0.01	0.01	0.01	0.01	0.01	0.02	N.M.	N.M.
Price Range	32.35-17.30	32.35-18.92	37.64-18.93	38.53-21.17	68.05-24.90	35.16-14.61	28.36-16.85	...

Address: 20374 Seneca Meadows Parkway, Germantown, MD 20876 Telephone: 301-556-9900	Web Site: www.dna.com Officers: Randal J. Kirk - Chairman, Chief Executive Officer Andrew J. Last - Chief Operating Officer	Auditors: PricewaterhouseCoopers LLP Transfer Agents: American Stock Transfer & Trust Company, LLC

INVESCO LTD

Exchange	Symbol	Price	52Wk Range	Yield	P/E
NYS	IVZ	$36.54 (12/29/2017)	37.67-28.92	3.15	15.89

*7 Year Price Score 85.49   *NYSE Composite Index=100   *12 Month Price Score 101.74

Interim Earnings (Per Share)

Qtr.	Mar	Jun	Sep	Dec
2014	0.43	0.63	0.59	0.62
2015	0.60	0.60	0.58	0.48
2016	0.38	0.54	0.58	0.55
2017	0.52	0.58	0.65	...

Interim Dividends (Per Share)

Amt	Decl	Ex	Rec	Pay
0.28Q	01/26/2017	02/14/2017	02/16/2017	03/03/2017
0.29Q	04/26/2017	05/10/2017	05/12/2017	06/02/2017
0.29Q	07/27/2017	08/15/2017	08/17/2017	09/01/2017
0.29Q	10/25/2017	11/13/2017	11/14/2017	12/04/2017

Indicated Div: $1.15

Valuation Analysis / **Institutional Holding**

Forecast EPS	N/A	No of Institutions
		773
Market Cap	$14.9 Billion	Shares
Book Value	$8.3 Billion	410,742,304
Price/Book	1.79	% Held
Price/Sales	2.99	N/A

Business Summary: Wealth Management (MIC: 5.5.2 SIC: 6282 NAIC: 523930)

Invesco is an investment manager. Co. provides a range of investment capabilities and outcomes, delivered through a set of investment vehicles. Co. sole business is investment management. Co. operates in the retail and institutional markets in North America, Europe, Middle East and Africa, and Asia Pacific. Co.'s asset classes include money market, balanced, equity, fixed income, and alternatives. Co.'s distribution channels consist of: Retail, which is a provider of retail investment solutions to clients in primary markets; and Institutional, which provides investment solutions to institutional investors. As of Dec 31 2016, Co.'s assets under management was US$812.90 billion.

Recent Developments: For the quarter ended Sep 30 2017, net income increased 7.3% to US$274.6 million from US$255.9 million in the year-earlier quarter. Revenues were US$1.34 billion, up 11.3% from US$1.20 billion the year before. Operating income was US$355.3 million versus US$306.3 million in the prior-year quarter, an increase of 16.0%. Indirect operating expenses increased 9.7% to US$982.4 million from US$895.3 million in the equivalent prior-year period.

Prospects: Our evaluation of Invesco Ltd as of Sep. 17, 2017 is the result of our systematic analysis on three basic characteristics: earnings strength, relative valuation, and recent stock price movement. The company has managed to produce a neutral trend in earnings per share over the past 5 quarters and while recent estimates for the company have remained steady, IVZ has posted better than expected results. Based on operating earnings yield, the company is undervalued when compared to all of the companies in our coverage universe. Share price changes over the past year indicates that IVZ will perform well over the near term.

Financial Data

(US$ in Thousands)	9 Mos	6 Mos	3 Mos	12/31/2016	12/31/2015	12/31/2014	12/31/2013	12/31/2012
Earnings Per Share	2.30	2.23	2.19	2.06	2.26	2.27	2.10	1.49
Cash Flow Per Share	1.46	1.80	1.26	0.31	2.46	2.76	1.74	1.81
Tang Book Value Per Share	0.44	0.75	0.23	N.M.	0.85	1.16	0.60	N.M.
Dividends Per Share	1.140	1.130	1.120	1.110	1.060	0.975	0.848	0.640
Dividend Payout %	49.57	50.67	51.14	53.88	46.90	42.95	40.36	42.95
Income Statement								
Total Revenue	3,784,700	2,447,000	1,192,600	4,734,400	5,122,900	5,147,100	4,644,600	4,177,000
EBITDA	1,135,100	699,500	319,600	1,365,800	1,414,600	1,426,500	1,258,900	847,500
Depn & Amortn	82,200	52,500	26,300	87,300	83,000	76,800	71,300	65,400
Income Before Taxes	988,700	603,900	272,200	1,197,300	1,327,000	1,362,300	1,219,700	829,800
Income Taxes	291,400	168,300	75,700	338,300	398,000	390,600	336,900	272,200
Net Income	719,100	451,600	212,000	854,200	968,100	988,100	940,300	677,100
Average Shares	410,500	410,300	408,000	415,000	429,300	435,600	448,500	453,800
Balance Sheet								
Current Assets	21,690,800	20,024,100	18,474,300	17,529,100	16,888,400	12,009,700	10,505,200	3,907,600
Total Assets	30,372,500	28,248,500	26,598,900	25,734,300	25,073,200	20,462,500	19,270,500	17,492,400
Current Liabilities	14,423,800	12,982,200	11,130,300	1,466,700	1,524,400	3,852,600	3,737,500	2,713,000
Long-Term Obligations	6,398,900	6,004,300	6,366,500	6,505,500	7,509,800	6,738,900	5,770,300	5,085,400
Total Liabilities	22,058,500	20,276,000	18,935,600	18,230,500	17,187,900	12,136,500	10,877,900	9,175,600
Stockholders' Equity	8,314,000	7,972,500	7,663,300	7,503,800	7,885,300	8,326,000	8,392,600	8,316,800
Shares Outstanding	407,100	406,891	406,856	403,800	417,500	429,900	433,100	441,400
Statistical Record								
Return on Assets %	3.47	3.55	3.68	3.35	4.25	4.97	5.12	3.67
Return on Equity %	11.78	11.76	11.63	11.07	11.94	11.82	11.25	8.22
EBITDA Margin %	29.99	28.59	26.80	28.85	27.61	27.71	27.10	20.29
Net Margin %	19.00	18.46	17.78	18.04	18.90	19.20	20.25	16.21
Asset Turnover	0.18	0.19	0.19	0.19	0.23	0.26	0.25	0.23
Current Ratio	1.50	1.54	1.63	11.95	11.08	3.12	2.81	1.44
Debt to Equity	0.77	0.75	0.83	0.87	0.95	0.81	0.69	0.61
Price Range	36.53-27.67	35.40-24.77	33.35-23.16	33.48-23.16	41.85-30.39	41.28-31.77	36.55-25.64	26.84-20.35
P/E Ratio	15.88-12.03	15.87-11.11	15.23-10.58	16.25-11.24	18.52-13.45	18.19-14.00	17.40-12.21	18.01-13.66
Average Yield %	3.54	3.65	3.70	3.74	2.88	2.61	2.70	2.69

Address: 1555 Peachtree Street N.E., Suite 1800, Atlanta, GA 30309
Telephone: 404-892-0896

Web Site: www.invesco.com
Officers: Ben F. Johnson - Chairman Martin L. Flanagan - President, Chief Executive Officer

Auditors: PricewaterhouseCoopers LLP
Investor Contact: 404-439-4605
Transfer Agents: BNY Mellon Shareowner Services, Pittsburg, PA

INVITATION HOMES INC

Exchange	Symbol	Price	52Wk Range	Yield	P/E
NYS	INVH	$23.57 (12/29/2017)	24.10-20.00	1.36	N/A

*7 Year Price Score N/A   *NYSE Composite Index=100   *12 Month Price Score N/A

TRADING VOLUME (thousand shares)

Interim Earnings (Per Share)

Qtr.	Mar	Jun	Sep	Dec
2017	(0.08)	0.02	(0.07)	...

Interim Dividends (Per Share)

Amt	Decl	Ex	Rec	Pay
0.06Q	05/05/2017	05/11/2017	05/15/2017	05/31/2017
0.08Q	08/04/2017	08/11/2017	08/15/2017	08/31/2017
0.08Q	10/13/2017	10/23/2017	10/24/2017	11/07/2017

Indicated Div: $0.32

Valuation Analysis	Institutional Holding
Forecast EPS	$-0.24	No of Institutions
	(01/11/2018)	199
Market Cap	$7.3 Billion	Shares
Book Value	$3.6 Billion	329,236,864
Price/Book	2.04	% Held
Price/Sales	7.65	N/A

Business Summary: Property, Real Estate & Development (MIC: 5.3.2 SIC: 6519 NAIC: 531190)

Invitation Homes is a owner and operator of single-family homes for lease, providing residents homes in neighborhoods across America. Co. operates one reportable segment related to acquiring, renovating, leasing, and operating single-family homes as rental properties, including single-family homes in planned unit developments. As of Dec 31 2016, Co. owned 48,298 single-family rental homes and had 36,469 homes in its Same Store portfolio.

Recent Developments: For the quarter ended Sep 30 2017, loss from continuing operations was US$26.3 million compared with a loss of US$24.9 million in the year-earlier quarter. Net loss amounted to US$22.5 million versus a net loss of US$21.9 million in the year-earlier quarter. Revenues were US$243.5 million, up 4.5% from US$233.0 million the year before.

Prospects: Our evaluation of Invitation Homes Inc as of Jan. 14, 2018 is the result of our systematic analysis on three basic characteristics: earnings strength, relative valuation, and recent stock price movement. The company has managed to produce a neutral trend in earnings per share over the past 5 quarters. Because the company lacks sufficient analyst estimate data, we place greater weight on the historical EPS trend as the measure of earnings strength. Based on operating earnings yield, the company is overvalued when compared to all of the companies in our coverage universe. Share price changes over the past year indicates that INVH will perform very poorly over the near term.

Financial Data
(US$ in Thousands)

	9 Mos	6 Mos	3 Mos	12/31/2016	12/31/2015	12/31/2014
Earnings Per Share	(0.13)	(0.06)	(0.08)	...	...	...
Cash Flow Per Share	0.87	0.84	0.78	0.48	...	...
Tang Book Value Per Share	11.57	11.74	11.79	...	...	...
Dividends Per Share	0.140	0.060	...	...	...	...
Income Statement						
Total Revenue	724,502	480,966	238,750	922,587	836,049	658,722
EBITDA	326,674	222,372	26,381	452,312	356,321	173,475
Depn & Amortn	231,559	157,787	14,521	263,093	245,965	207,289
Income Before Taxes	(87,611)	(61,345)	(56,712)	(96,829)	(162,480)	(269,626)
Net Income	(59,372)	(36,862)	(42,391)	(78,239)	(160,208)	(269,861)
Average Shares	311,599	312,271	311,651	519,372		...
Balance Sheet						
Current Assets	288,222	297,198	336,619	420,211	493,992	561,715
Total Assets	9,524,524	9,519,326	9,588,161	9,732,351	9,796,978	9,199,653
Current Liabilities	249,650	199,700	189,139	174,565	163,986	163,142
Long-Term Obligations	5,644,275	5,645,195	5,714,391	7,570,279	7,725,957	6,564,643
Total Liabilities	5,922,511	5,875,355	5,930,119	7,774,928	7,909,947	6,743,052
Stockholders' Equity	3,602,013	3,643,971	3,658,042	1,957,423	1,887,031	2,456,601
Shares Outstanding	311,354	310,376	310,376	...	...	...
Statistical Record						
EBITDA Margin %	45.09	46.23	11.05	49.03	42.62	26.34
Asset Turnover	...	...	...	0.09	0.09	...
Current Ratio	1.15	1.49	1.78	2.41	3.01	3.44
Debt to Equity	1.57	1.55	1.56	3.87	4.09	2.67
Price Range	23.53-20.00	21.93-20.00	21.92-20.00	...	...	...
Average Yield %	0.64	0.28	...	...	...	...

Address: 1717 Main Street, Suite 2000, Dallas, TX 75201 Telephone: 972-421-3600	Web Site: www.invitationhomes.com Officers: Bryce Blair - Executive Chairman Nicholas C. Gould - Vice-Chairman	Auditors: Deloitte & Touche LLP Investor Contact: 972-421-3600 Transfer Agents: Computershare Trust Company, N.A.

IQVIA HOLDINGS INC

Exchange	Symbol	Price	52Wk Range	Yield	P/E
NYS	IQV	$97.90 (12/29/2017)	108.56-75.35	N/A	N/A

*7 Year Price Score N/A   ***NYSE Composite Index=100**   ***12 Month Price Score 107.97**

Interim Earnings (Per Share)

Qtr.	Mar	Jun	Sep	Dec
2014	0.68	0.64	0.71	0.69
2015	0.68	0.67	0.89	0.84
2016	0.88	0.71	0.82	(1.65)
2017	0.31	0.34	0.38	...

Interim Dividends (Per Share)

No Dividends Paid

Valuation Analysis

		Institutional Holding	
Forecast EPS	$4.62	No of Institutions	
	(01/16/2018)	549	
Market Cap	$23.1 Billion	Shares	
Book Value	$7.3 Billion	216,495,824	
Price/Book	3.18	% Held	
Price/Sales	2.44	6.20	

Business Summary: Biotechnology (MIC: 4.1.2 SIC: 8731 NAIC: 541710)

IQVIA Holdings is an integrated information and technology-enabled healthcare service provider. Co. has three operating segments: Commercial Solutions, Research & Development Solutions and Integrated Engagement Services. Co.'s principal Commercial Solutions offerings include: national information offerings and sub-national information offerings. Co.'s principal Research & Development Solutions offerings include: project management and clinical monitoring, clinical trial support services, and Q2 Solutions. Co.'s principal Integrated Engagement Services offerings include: health care provider engagement services, patient engagement services, and medical affairs services.

Recent Developments: For the quarter ended Sep 30 2017, net income decreased 14.4% to US$89.0 million from US$104.0 million in the year-earlier quarter. Revenues were US$2.47 billion, up 64.7% from US$1.50 billion the year before. Operating income was US$197.0 million versus US$168.0 million in the prior-year quarter, an increase of 17.3%. Direct operating expenses rose 52.6% to US$1.61 billion from US$1.06 billion in the comparable period the year before. Indirect operating expenses increased 140.7% to US$657.0 million from US$273.0 million in the equivalent prior-year period.

Prospects: Our evaluation of IQVIA Holdings Inc. as of Jan. 14, 2018 is the result of our systematic analysis on three basic characteristics: earnings strength, relative valuation, and recent stock price movement. The company has produced a positive trend in earnings per share over the past 5 quarters and while recent estimates for the company have been mixed, IQV has posted better than expected results. Based on operating earnings yield, the company is about fairly valued when compared to all of the companies in our coverage universe. Share price changes over the past year indicates that IQV will perform very well over the near term.

Financial Data
(US$ in Thousands)

	9 Mos	6 Mos	3 Mos	12/31/2016	12/31/2015	12/31/2014	12/31/2013	12/31/2012
Earnings Per Share	(0.62)	(0.18)	0.19	0.76	3.08	2.72	1.77	1.51
Cash Flow Per Share	5.53	4.63	3.49	5.75	3.87	3.37	3.20	2.89
Income Statement								
Total Revenue	7,162,000	4,697,000	2,322,000	6,878,000	5,737,619	5,459,998	5,099,545	4,865,513
EBITDA	495,000	317,000	167,000	941,000	781,263	727,069	572,016	506,257
Depn & Amortn	9,000	7,000	5,000	322,000	144,793	127,701	129,329	107,525
Income Before Taxes	242,000	157,000	89,000	479,000	538,995	502,189	323,116	267,428
Income Taxes	5,000	5,000	12,000	345,000	158,989	150,056	95,965	93,364
Net Income	233,000	149,000	74,000	115,000	387,205	356,383	226,591	177,546
Average Shares	219,000	222,300	234,900	152,000	125,630	131,083	127,862	117,796
Balance Sheet								
Current Assets	3,492,000	3,259,000	3,117,000	3,337,000	2,411,985	2,146,083	1,945,688	1,509,994
Total Assets	22,445,000	21,782,000	21,183,000	21,208,000	3,926,316	3,305,832	3,066,797	2,499,153
Current Liabilities	2,853,000	2,660,000	2,596,000	2,705,000	1,594,176	1,471,900	1,482,247	1,317,964
Long-Term Obligations	9,651,000	8,858,000	8,254,000	7,108,000	2,419,293	2,292,491	2,035,586	2,366,268
Total Liabilities	15,181,000	14,243,000	13,612,000	12,575,000	4,490,533	4,009,893	3,734,210	3,858,676
Stockholders' Equity	7,264,000	7,539,000	7,571,000	8,633,000	(564,217)	(704,061)	(667,413)	(1,359,523)
Shares Outstanding	236,300	216,400	249,500	235,400	119,377	124,129	129,652	115,764
Statistical Record								
Return on Assets %	0.42	0.55	0.65	0.91	10.71	11.18	8.14	7.34
Return on Equity %	1.59	1.99	2.31	2.84	...	...	...	...
EBITDA Margin %	6.91	6.75	7.19	13.68	13.62	13.32	11.22	10.41
Net Margin %	3.25	3.17	3.19	1.67	6.75	6.53	4.44	3.65
Asset Turnover	0.71	0.66	0.61	0.55	1.59	1.71	1.83	2.01
Current Ratio	1.22	1.23	1.20	1.23	1.51	1.46	1.31	1.15
Debt to Equity	1.33	1.17	1.09	0.82	...	...	...	...
Price Range	98.82-71.66	91.08-65.32	82.30-61.32	81.06-55.91	79.10-57.07	60.66-45.80	46.48-41.58	...
P/E Ratio	...	...	433.16-322.74	106.66-73.57	25.68-18.53	22.30-16.84	26.26-23.49	...

Address: 4820 Emperor Blvd., Durham, NC 27703 Telephone: 919-998-2000	Web Site: www.quintiles.com Officers: Ari Bousbib - Chairman, President, Chief Executive Officer Michael R. McDonnell - Executive Vice President, Chief Financial Officer, Chief Financial Officer	Auditors: PricewaterhouseCoopers LLP Transfer Agents: American Stock Transfer & Trust Company, LLC, Brooklyn, NY

IRON MOUNTAIN INC

Exchange	Symbol	Price	52Wk Range	Yield	P/E
NYS	IRM	$37.73 (12/29/2017)	41.44-33.10	6.23	47.16

*7 Year Price Score 87.81 *NYSE Composite Index=100 *12 Month Price Score 101.60

TRADING VOLUME (thousand shares)

Interim Earnings (Per Share)

Qtr.	Mar	Jun	Sep	Dec
2014	0.22	1.40	0.00	0.04
2015	0.19	0.25	0.11	0.03
2016	0.30	(0.06)	0.03	0.19
2017	0.22	0.30	0.09	...

Interim Dividends (Per Share)

Amt	Decl	Ex	Rec	Pay
0.55Q	02/15/2017	03/13/2017	03/15/2017	04/03/2017
0.55Q	05/24/2017	06/13/2017	06/15/2017	07/03/2017
0.55Q	07/27/2017	09/14/2017	09/15/2017	10/02/2017
0.588Q	10/24/2017	12/14/2017	12/15/2017	01/02/2018

Indicated Div: $2.35

Valuation Analysis	Institutional Holding	
Forecast EPS	$1.15	No of Institutions
	(01/18/2018)	563
Market Cap	$10.1 Billion	Shares
Book Value	$1.9 Billion	266,606,352
Price/Book	5.39	% Held
Price/Sales	2.66	91.13

Business Summary: REITs (MIC: 5.3.1 SIC: 4225 NAIC: 493110)

Iron Mountain stores records, primarily physical records and data backup media, and provides information management services that help organizations protect their information, comply with regulations, and enable corporate disaster recovery. Co. provides storage and information management services to commercial, legal, financial, healthcare, insurance, life sciences, energy, businesses services, entertainment and government organizations. Co. operates in the following business segments: North American Records and Information Management Business, North American Data Management Business, Western European Business, Other International Business, and Corporate and Other Business.

Recent Developments: For the quarter ended Sep 30 2017, income from continuing operations increased 340.7% to US$25.4 million from US$5.8 million in the year-earlier quarter. Net income increased 211.8% to US$24.3 million from US$7.8 million in the year-earlier quarter. Revenues were US$965.7 million, up 2.4% from US$942.8 million the year before. Operating income was US$176.8 million versus US$135.5 million in the prior-year quarter, an increase of 30.5%. Direct operating expenses declined 2.7% to US$418.3 million from US$429.8 million in the comparable period the year before. Indirect operating expenses decreased 1.8% to US$370.6 million from US$377.6 million in the equivalent prior-year period.

Prospects: Our evaluation of Iron Mountain Inc. as of Jan. 14, 2018 is the result of our systematic analysis on three basic characteristics: earnings strength, relative valuation, and recent stock price movement. The company has produced a positive trend in earnings per share over the past 5 quarters and while recent estimates for the company have remained steady, IRM has posted better than expected results. Based on operating earnings yield, the company is about fairly valued when compared to all of the companies in our coverage universe. Share price changes over the past year indicates that IRM will perform very well over the near term.

Financial Data

(US$ in Thousands)	9 Mos	6 Mos	3 Mos	12/31/2016	12/31/2015	12/31/2014	12/31/2013	12/31/2012
Earnings Per Share	0.80	0.74	0.38	0.42	0.58	1.66	0.51	0.98
Cash Flow Per Share	2.41	2.49	2.22	2.20	2.57	2.42	2.66	2.49
Dividends Per Share	2.200	2.135	2.070	2.005	1.910	5.371	1.080	5.120
Dividend Payout %	275.00	288.51	544.74	477.38	329.31	323.57	211.76	522.45
Income Statement								
Total Revenue	2,854,343	1,888,682	938,876	3,511,453	3,007,976	3,117,693	3,025,923	3,005,255
EBITDA	862,806	610,266	285,891	822,832	727,156	788,647	700,048	821,563
Depn & Amortn	401,850	266,587	131,772	365,526	301,219	304,557	282,856	280,598
Income Before Taxes	195,946	167,658	68,064	146,644	162,066	223,373	163,018	298,366
Income Taxes	29,497	27,229	9,220	44,944	37,713	(97,275)	63,057	114,873
Net Income	161,100	136,755	58,125	104,824	123,241	326,119	97,262	171,708
Average Shares	266,139	264,930	264,809	247,267	212,118	196,749	192,412	174,867
Balance Sheet								
Current Assets	1,328,224	1,205,876	1,198,637	1,112,107	857,912	917,719	933,607	1,024,092
Total Assets	10,260,006	9,814,693	9,672,134	9,486,800	6,350,587	6,570,342	6,653,005	6,358,339
Current Liabilities	1,232,369	1,474,606	1,418,469	1,046,557	841,831	856,736	959,101	904,953
Long-Term Obligations	6,700,094	6,028,985	5,922,748	6,078,206	4,757,610	4,611,436	4,119,139	3,732,116
Total Liabilities	8,393,018	7,958,905	7,769,409	7,550,253	5,841,746	5,713,987	5,605,667	5,208,368
Stockholders' Equity	1,866,988	1,855,788	1,902,725	1,936,547	508,841	856,355	1,047,338	1,149,971
Shares Outstanding	266,882	264,379	264,110	263,682	211,340	209,818	191,426	190,005
Statistical Record								
Return on Assets %	2.08	1.97	1.24	1.32	1.91	4.93	1.50	2.76
Return on Equity %	10.52	9.46	8.35	8.55	18.05	34.26	8.85	14.30
EBITDA Margin %	30.23	32.31	30.45	23.43	24.17	25.30	23.14	27.34
Net Margin %	5.64	7.24	6.19	2.99	4.10	10.46	3.21	5.71
Asset Turnover	0.38	0.39	0.46	0.44	0.47	0.47	0.47	0.48
Current Ratio	1.08	0.82	0.85	1.06	1.02	1.07	0.97	1.13
Debt to Equity	3.59	3.25	3.11	3.14	9.35	5.38	3.93	3.25
Price Range	40.38-31.46	41.25-31.46	41.25-31.46	41.25-24.56	41.09-26.13	40.27-25.90	39.54-25.30	37.69-27.41
P/E Ratio	50.48-39.33	55.74-42.51	108.55-82.79	98.21-58.48	70.84-45.05	24.26-15.60	77.53-49.61	38.46-27.97
Average Yield %	6.24	6.00	5.76	5.85	5.76	16.71	3.47	16.15

Address: One Federal Street, Boston, MA 02110
Telephone: 617-535-4766

Web Site: www.ironmountain.com
Officers: William L. Meaney - Chief Executive Officer Stuart B. Brown - Executive Vice President, Chief Financial Officer

Auditors: Deloitte & Touche LLP
Investor Contact: 617-535-4766
Transfer Agents: Computershare, Providence, RI

ITT INC

Exchange	Symbol	Price	52Wk Range	Yield	P/E	Div Achiever
NYS	ITT	$53.37 (12/29/2017)	54.31-38.01	0.96	22.91	14 Years

7 Year Price Score 96.07   **NYSE Composite Index=100**   **12 Month Price Score 113.40**

Interim Earnings (Per Share)

Qtr.	Mar	Jun	Sep	Dec
2014	0.35	0.41	0.86	0.37
2015	0.46	1.58	1.45	0.41
2016	0.41	0.36	1.00	0.29
2017	0.52	0.54	0.98	...

Interim Dividends (Per Share)

Amt	Decl	Ex	Rec	Pay
0.128Q	02/14/2017	03/09/2017	03/13/2017	04/03/2017
0.128Q	05/10/2017	06/08/2017	06/12/2017	07/03/2017
0.128Q	08/09/2017	09/08/2017	09/11/2017	10/02/2017
0.128Q	10/11/2017	12/07/2017	12/08/2017	12/29/2017

Indicated Div: $0.51

Valuation Analysis   **Institutional Holding**

Forecast EPS	$2.53 (01/17/2018)	No of Institutions	542
Market Cap	$4.7 Billion	Shares	113,612,768
Book Value	$1.7 Billion	% Held	N/A
Price/Book	2.84		
Price/Sales	1.89		

Business Summary: Industrial Machinery & Equipment (MIC: 7.2.1 SIC: 3561 NAIC: 333911)

ITT is a manufacturer of components and customized technology solutions for the energy, transportation and industrial markets. Co.'s segments are: Industrial Process, which manufactures engineered fluid process equipment and provides plant and aftermarket services and parts; Motion Technologies, which manufactures brake components and specialized sealing solutions, shock absorbers and damping technologies; Interconnect Solutions, which manufactures and designs a range of engineered harsh environment connector solutions; and Control Technologies, which manufactures equipment, including fuel management, actuation, noise and energy absorption, and environmental control system components.

Recent Developments: For the quarter ended Sep 30 2017, income from continuing operations decreased 1.6% to US$87.0 million from US$88.4 million in the year-earlier quarter. Net income decreased 3.7% to US$86.9 million from US$90.2 million in the year-earlier quarter. Revenues were US$645.0 million, up 10.9% from US$581.7 million the year before. Operating income was US$127.8 million versus US$134.8 million in the prior-year quarter, a decrease of 5.2%. Direct operating expenses rose 11.1% to US$441.9 million from US$397.8 million in the comparable period the year before. Indirect operating expenses increased 53.4% to US$75.3 million from US$49.1 million in the equivalent prior-year period.

Prospects: Our evaluation of ITT Inc as of Jan. 14, 2018 is the result of our systematic analysis on three basic characteristics: earnings strength, relative valuation, and recent stock price movement. The company has managed to produce a neutral trend in earnings per share over the past 5 quarters. However, while recent estimates for the company have been mixed, ITT has posted better than expected results. Based on operating earnings yield, the company is undervalued when compared to all of the companies in our coverage universe. Share price changes over the past year indicates that ITT will perform in line with the market over the near term.

Financial Data

(US$ in Thousands)	9 Mos	6 Mos	3 Mos	12/31/2016	12/31/2015	12/31/2014	12/31/2013	12/31/2012
Earnings Per Share	2.33	2.35	2.17	2.07	3.88	1.99	5.29	1.33
Cash Flow Per Share	3.10	2.96	2.96	2.69	2.56	2.67	2.49	2.65
Tang Book Value Per Share	6.43	5.25	4.80	5.13	4.12	5.11	4.61	N.M.
Dividends Per Share	0.508	0.504	0.500	0.372	0.473	0.440	0.400	0.364
Dividend Payout %	21.80	21.45	23.04	17.97	12.20	22.11	7.56	27.37
Income Statement								
Total Revenue	1,901,700	1,256,700	625,800	2,405,400	2,485,600	2,654,600	2,496,900	2,227,800
EBITDA	298,200	150,900	73,100	331,700	450,500	336,400	245,200	201,000
Depn & Amortn	57,200	37,500	18,300	74,100	70,700	72,900	63,400	54,600
Income Before Taxes	241,000	113,400	54,800	258,400	382,300	262,000	180,500	149,100
Income Taxes	60,300	19,700	9,100	76,000	70,100	71,300	(309,600)	39,600
Net Income	180,700	93,800	46,000	186,100	351,800	184,500	488,500	125,400
Average Shares	88,700	89,000	89,200	89,900	90,700	92,800	92,300	94,100
Balance Sheet								
Current Assets	1,465,200	1,404,200	1,378,900	1,401,800	1,497,700	1,636,200	1,665,500	1,540,400
Total Assets	3,800,100	3,730,600	3,670,400	3,601,700	3,723,600	3,631,500	3,740,200	3,386,100
Current Liabilities	925,400	892,900	885,800	866,200	953,100	775,400	832,600	805,300
Total Liabilities	2,148,500	2,186,200	2,180,000	2,175,300	2,361,500	2,416,600	2,539,200	2,682,900
Stockholders' Equity	1,651,600	1,544,400	1,490,400	1,426,400	1,362,100	1,214,900	1,201,000	703,200
Shares Outstanding	88,000	88,000	88,700	88,400	89,500	91,000	91,000	92,100
Statistical Record								
Return on Assets %	5.49	5.61	5.21	5.07	9.57	5.01	13.71	3.54
Return on Equity %	13.29	14.17	13.37	13.31	27.30	15.27	51.31	17.90
EBITDA Margin %	15.68	12.01	11.68	13.79	18.12	12.67	9.82	9.02
Net Margin %	9.50	7.46	7.35	7.74	14.15	6.95	19.56	5.63
Asset Turnover	0.66	0.65	0.65	0.65	0.68	0.72	0.70	0.63
Current Ratio	1.58	1.57	1.56	1.62	1.57	2.11	2.00	1.91
Price Range	44.51-33.26	43.36-30.71	43.36-30.53	42.73-29.89	43.40-33.05	49.24-37.55	43.50-23.46	24.95-17.14
P/E Ratio	19.10-14.27	18.45-13.07	19.98-14.07	20.64-14.44	11.19-8.52	24.74-18.87	8.22-4.43	18.76-12.89
Average Yield %	1.27	1.32	1.35	1.05	1.22	1.00	1.25	1.72

Address: 1133 Westchester Avenue, White Plains, NY 10604
Telephone: 914-641-2000

Web Site: www.itt.com
Officers: Denise L. Ramos - President, Chief Executive Officer, Senior Vice President, Chief Financial Officer Luca Savi - Executive Vice President, Senior Vice President, Chief Operating Officer, Division Officer

Auditors: Deloitte & Touche LLP
Investor Contact: 914-641-2030
Transfer Agents: Wells Fargo Shareowner Services

JABIL INC

Exchange	Symbol	Price	52Wk Range	Yield	P/E
NYS	JBL	$26.25 (12/29/2017)	31.46-22.99	1.22	46.87

*7 Year Price Score 102.32 *NYSE Composite Index=100 *12 Month Price Score 93.81

Interim Earnings (Per Share)

Qtr.	Nov	Feb	May	Aug
2014-15	0.37	0.27	0.37	0.45
2015-16	0.68	0.41	0.03	0.20
2016-17	0.47	0.11	(0.14)	0.24
2017-18	0.35	...	...	...

Interim Dividends (Per Share)

Amt	Decl	Ex	Rec	Pay
0.08Q	01/26/2017	02/13/2017	02/15/2017	03/01/2017
0.08Q	04/20/2017	05/11/2017	05/15/2017	06/01/2017
0.08Q	07/20/2017	08/11/2017	08/15/2017	09/01/2017
0.08Q	10/19/2017	11/14/2017	11/15/2017	12/01/2017

Indicated Div: $0.32

Valuation Analysis | **Institutional Holding**

Forecast EPS	$2.60	No of Institutions	
	(01/13/2018)	503	
Market Cap	$4.6 Billion	Shares	
Book Value	$2.3 Billion	211,395,600	
Price/Book	1.99	% Held	
Price/Sales	0.24	76.01	

Business Summary: Electrical Equipment (MIC: 7.3.1 SIC: 3672 NAIC: 334412)

Jabil provides electronics design, production and product management services to companies in the automotive and transportation, capital equipment, consumer lifestyles and wearable technologies, computing and storage, defense and aerospace, digital home, healthcare, industrial and energy, mobility, networking and telecommunications, packaging, point of sale and printing industries. Co. has two segments: Electronics Manufacturing Services, which is focused around Information Technology, supply chain design and engineering, technologies centered on core electronics; and Diversified Manufacturing Services, which provides engineering solutions and a focus on material sciences and technologies.

Recent Developments: For the year ended Aug 31 2017, income from continuing operations decreased 50.1% to US$127.2 million from US$254.9 million a year earlier. Net income decreased 50.1% to US$127.2 million from US$254.9 million in the prior year. Revenues were US$19.06 billion, up 3.9% from US$18.35 billion the year before. Operating income was US$410.2 million versus US$522.8 million in the prior year, a decrease of 21.5%. Direct operating expenses rose 4.1% to US$17.52 billion from US$16.83 billion in the comparable period the year before. Indirect operating expenses increased 13.0% to US$1.14 billion from US$1.00 billion in the equivalent prior-year period.

Prospects: Our evaluation of Jabil Circuit Inc. as of Jan. 14, 2018 is the result of our systematic analysis on three basic characteristics: earnings strength, relative valuation, and recent stock price movement. The company has suffered a very negative trend in earnings per share over the past 5 quarters. However, while recent estimates for the company have been lowered by analysts, JBL has posted results that fell short of analysts expectations. Based on operating earnings yield, the company is undervalued when compared to all of the companies in our coverage universe. Share price changes over the past year indicates that JBL will perform very well over the near term.

Financial Data

(US$ in Thousands)	3 Mos	08/31/2017	08/31/2016	08/31/2015	08/31/2014	08/31/2013	08/31/2012	08/31/2011
Earnings Per Share	0.56	0.69	1.32	1.45	1.19	1.79	1.87	1.73
Cash Flow Per Share	5.94	6.91	4.80	6.40	2.46	5.98	3.07	3.86
Tang Book Value Per Share	7.93	8.22	8.27	8.17	8.32	7.85	9.18	8.56
Dividends Per Share	0.320	0.320	0.320	0.320	0.320	0.320	0.320	0.280
Dividend Payout %	57.14	46.38	24.24	22.07	26.89	17.88	17.11	16.18
Income Statement								
Total Revenue	5,585,532	19,063,121	18,353,086	17,899,196	15,762,146	18,336,894	17,151,941	16,518,827
EBITDA	149,851	1,142,162	1,199,374	1,069,333	681,594	923,379	966,513	894,899
Depn & Amortn	9,979	760,380	696,621	529,149	485,157	418,154	353,525	319,151
Income Before Taxes	107,439	256,233	375,345	422,046	72,123	386,064	508,900	481,187
Income Taxes	43,520	129,066	120,449	127,861	73,711	15,973	112,811	98,229
Net Income	63,795	129,000	254,095	284,019	241,313	371,482	394,687	381,063
Average Shares	180,203	185,838	192,750	196,005	202,497	207,815	211,181	220,719
Balance Sheet								
Current Assets	6,922,128	6,626,683	5,848,381	5,866,309	5,359,017	5,820,245	5,639,328	5,135,360
Total Assets	11,519,565	11,095,995	10,322,677	9,603,207	8,479,746	9,153,781	7,803,141	7,057,940
Current Liabilities	7,249,724	6,870,593	5,568,056	5,675,141	4,321,097	4,864,434	3,858,996	3,889,888
Long-Term Obligations	1,693,433	1,632,592	2,074,012	1,346,558	1,669,585	1,690,426	1,658,326	1,112,594
Total Liabilities	9,189,826	8,742,481	7,884,506	7,288,351	6,237,918	6,818,494	5,698,084	5,190,820
Stockholders' Equity	2,329,739	2,353,514	2,438,171	2,314,856	2,241,828	2,335,287	2,105,057	1,867,120
Shares Outstanding	176,305	177,727	186,998	192,068	194,113	203,164	206,028	203,416
Statistical Record								
Return on Assets %	0.95	1.21	2.54	3.14	2.74	4.38	5.30	5.68
Return on Equity %	4.46	5.39	10.66	12.47	10.54	16.73	19.82	22.12
EBITDA Margin %	2.68	5.99	6.53	5.97	4.32	5.04	5.64	5.42
Net Margin %	1.14	0.68	1.38	1.59	1.53	2.03	2.30	2.31
Asset Turnover	1.77	1.78	1.84	1.98	1.79	2.16	2.30	2.46
Current Ratio	0.95	0.96	1.05	1.03	1.24	1.20	1.46	1.32
Debt to Equity	0.73	0.69	0.85	0.58	0.74	0.72	0.79	0.60
Price Range	31.46-20.50	31.46-20.41	25.93-16.88	24.83-17.66	24.04-15.67	23.90-16.57	27.13-15.76	22.98-10.25
P/E Ratio	56.18-36.61	45.59-29.58	19.64-12.79	17.12-12.18	20.20-13.17	13.35-9.26	14.51-8.43	13.28-5.92
Average Yield %	1.14	1.23	1.55	1.49	1.63	1.63	1.51	1.54

Address: 10560 Dr. Martin Luther King, Jr. Street North, St. Petersburg, FL 33716
Telephone: 727-577-9749

Web Site: www.jabil.com
Officers: Timothy L. Main - Chairman, President, Chief Executive Officer Thomas A. Sansone - Vice-Chairman

Auditors: Ernst & Young LLP
Investor Contact: 727-803-3349
Transfer Agents: Computershare, Providence, RI

JACOBS ENGINEERING GROUP, INC.

Exchange	Symbol	Price	52Wk Range	Yield	P/E
NYS	JEC	$65.96 (12/29/2017)	68.51-49.58	0.91	27.26

*7 Year Price Score 91.18 *NYSE Composite Index=100 *12 Month Price Score 106.40

Interim Earnings (Per Share)

Qtr.	Dec	Mar	Jun	Sep
2012-13	0.76	0.80	0.83	0.84
2013-14	0.71	0.63	0.49	0.65
2014-15	0.77	0.64	0.73	0.25
2015-16	0.38	0.54	0.57	0.24
2016-17	0.50	0.41	0.74	0.78

Interim Dividends (Per Share)

Amt	Decl	Ex	Rec	Pay
0.15Q	05/04/2017	05/17/2017	05/19/2017	06/16/2017
0.15Q	07/18/2017	08/02/2017	08/04/2017	09/01/2017
0.15Q	09/27/2017	10/12/2017	10/13/2017	11/10/2017
0.15Q	01/18/2018	02/15/2018	02/16/2018	03/16/2018

Indicated Div: $0.60

Valuation Analysis

		Institutional Holding	
Forecast EPS	$3.73 (01/17/2018)	No of Institutions	736
Market Cap	$7.9 Billion	Shares	
Book Value	$4.4 Billion		131,299,608
Price/Book	1.79	% Held	
Price/Sales	0.79		89.03

Business Summary: Construction Services (MIC: 7.5.4 SIC: 1629 NAIC: 236210)

Jacobs Engineering Group provides four categories of services: Project Services, which designs and engineers process plants, buildings, infrastructure projects, technology and manufacturing facilities, consumer products manufacturing facilities, power plants and stations, pulp and paper plants, and other facilities; Process, Scientific, and Systems Consulting Services, which provides a range of consulting services; Construction Services, which provides field construction services to private and public sector clients; and Operations and Maintenance Services, which provides management and support services over all aspects of the operations of a facility.

Recent Developments: For the year ended Sep 29 2017, net income increased 34.0% to US$287.4 million from US$214.5 million in the prior year. Revenues were US$10.02 billion, down 8.6% from US$10.96 billion the year before. Operating income was US$392.3 million versus US$338.6 million in the prior year, an increase of 15.9%. Direct operating expenses declined 10.3% to US$8.25 billion from US$9.20 billion in the comparable period the year before. Indirect operating expenses decreased 3.4% to US$1.38 billion from US$1.43 billion in the equivalent prior-year period.

Prospects: Our evaluation of Jacobs Engineering Group Inc. as of Jan. 14, 2018 is the result of our systematic analysis on three basic characteristics: earnings strength, relative valuation, and recent stock price movement. The company has managed to produce a neutral trend in earnings per share over the past 5 quarters and while recent estimates for the company have been raised by analysts, JEC has posted better than expected results. Based on operating earnings yield, the company is undervalued when compared to all of the companies in our coverage universe. Share price changes over the past year indicates that JEC will perform in line with the market over the near term.

Financial Data
(US$ in Thousands)

	09/29/2017	09/30/2016	10/02/2015	09/26/2014	09/27/2013	09/28/2012	09/30/2011	10/01/2010
Earnings Per Share	2.42	1.73	2.40	2.48	3.23	2.94	2.60	1.96
Cash Flow Per Share	4.83	5.68	3.81	5.55	3.48	2.36	1.89	1.59
Tang Book Value Per Share	9.02	7.02	7.22	7.61	14.98	11.30	10.24	13.03
Dividends Per Share	0.450	...	...	...	...	...	...	...
Dividend Payout %	18.60	...	...	...	...	...	...	...
Income Statement								
Total Revenue	10,022,788	10,964,157	12,114,832	12,695,157	11,818,376	10,893,778	10,381,664	9,915,517
EBITDA	519,017	424,106	591,670	689,322	767,933	699,797	615,913	485,512
Depn & Amortn	122,513	129,971	149,292	145,412	98,874	100,824	95,370	88,495
Income Before Taxes	393,217	286,723	430,137	542,166	661,548	593,336	516,661	391,934
Income Taxes	105,842	72,208	101,255	190,054	221,366	202,382	181,440	145,647
Net Income	293,727	210,463	302,971	328,108	423,093	378,954	331,029	245,974
Average Shares	120,147	121,483	126,110	132,371	130,945	128,692	127,235	125,790
Balance Sheet								
Current Assets	2,996,180	2,864,470	3,282,976	3,892,071	4,039,558	3,612,077	3,157,353	2,767,042
Total Assets	7,380,859	7,360,022	7,785,926	8,453,659	7,274,144	6,839,433	6,049,428	4,683,917
Current Liabilities	1,926,227	1,782,686	1,981,166	2,349,846	1,887,619	1,747,052	2,058,045	1,239,453
Long-Term Obligations	235,000	385,330	584,434	764,075	415,086	528,260	2,042	509
Total Liabilities	2,952,507	3,094,746	3,494,181	3,984,404	3,061,047	3,116,960	2,736,440	1,824,869
Stockholders' Equity	4,428,352	4,265,276	4,291,745	4,469,255	4,213,097	3,722,473	3,312,988	2,859,048
Shares Outstanding	120,385	120,950	123,152	131,752	131,639	129,935	127,784	125,909
Statistical Record								
Return on Assets %	4.00	2.79	3.67	4.18	6.01	5.90	6.19	5.41
Return on Equity %	6.78	4.93	6.80	7.58	10.69	10.80	10.76	8.99
EBITDA Margin %	5.18	3.87	4.88	5.43	6.50	6.42	5.93	4.90
Net Margin %	2.93	1.92	2.50	2.58	3.58	3.48	3.19	2.48
Asset Turnover	1.36	1.45	1.47	1.62	1.68	1.70	1.94	2.18
Current Ratio	1.56	1.61	1.66	1.66	2.14	2.07	1.53	2.23
Debt to Equity	0.05	0.09	0.14	0.17	0.10	0.14	N.M.	N.M.
Price Range	62.17-49.25	55.57-35.06	49.68-36.65	66.81-49.52	62.33-38.43	47.61-31.55	53.01-31.88	49.97-34.02
P/E Ratio	25.69-20.35	32.12-20.27	20.70-15.27	26.94-19.97	19.30-11.90	16.19-10.73	20.39-12.26	25.49-17.36
Average Yield %	0.82	...	...	...	...	...	...	...

Address: 1999 Bryan Street, Suite 1200, Dallas, TX 75201	**Web Site:** www.jacobs.com	**Auditors:** Ernst & Young, LLP
Telephone: 214-583-8500	**Officers:** Steven J. Demetriou - Chairman, President, Chief Executive Officer Kevin C. Berryman - Executive Vice President, Chief Financial Officer	**Transfer Agents:** Wells Fargo Shareowner Services, South St. Paul, MN

JBG SMITH PROPERTIES

Exchange	Symbol	Price	52Wk Range	Yield	P/E
NYS	JBGS	$34.73 (12/29/2017)	37.24-31.10	N/A	N/A

*7 Year Price Score N/A   *NYSE Composite Index=100   *12 Month Price Score N/A

Interim Earnings (Per Share)

No earnings information available

Interim Dividends (Per Share)

No Dividends Paid

Valuation Analysis		Institutional Holding	
Forecast EPS	N/A	No of Institutions	
		255	
Market Cap	$4.1 Billion	Shares	
Book Value	$3.1 Billion	88,417,304	
Price/Book	1.33	% Held	
Price/Sales	N/A	N/A	

TRADING VOLUME (thousand shares)

2008 2009 2010 2011 2012 2013 2014 2015 2016 2017

Business Summary: REITs (MIC: 5.3.1 SIC: 6798 NAIC: 525930)

JBG SMITH Properties operates as a real estate investment trust. Co. owns, operates, and develops mixed use real estate properties. Co. manages residential, office, retail, and mixed-use properties.

Recent Developments: For the quarter ended Sep 30 2017, net loss amounted to US$78.0 million versus net income of US$21.0 million in the year-earlier quarter. Revenues were US$152.4 million, up 23.5% from US$123.4 million the year before. Revenues from property income rose 24.1% to US$151.2 million from US$121.8 million in the corresponding quarter a year earlier.

Prospects: Our evaluation of JBG SMITH Properties as of Jan. 14, 2018 is the result of our systematic analysis on three basic characteristics: earnings strength, relative valuation, and recent stock price movement. The company has produced a positive trend in earnings per share over the past 5 quarters. Because the company lacks sufficient analyst estimate data, we place greater weight on the historical EPS trend as the measure of earnings strength. Based on operating earnings yield, the company is overvalued when compared to all of the companies in our coverage universe. Share price changes over the past year indicates that JBGS will perform very poorly over the near term.

Financial Data (US$ in Thousands)	9 Mos	6 Mos	12/31/2016	12/31/2015	12/31/2014
Earnings Per Share	...	...	(107.00)	...	...
Cash Flow Per Share	...	...	1.35	...	...
Tang Book Value Per Share	23.96	17.39	...	...	...
Income Statement					
Total Revenue	386,642	234,292	478,519	470,607	472,923
EBITDA	(11,555)	111,698	249,799	249,493	251,345
Depn & Amortn	6,647	66,563	133,719	144,188	111,388
Income Before Taxes	(60,649)	18,376	64,299	54,482	82,820
Income Taxes	(317)	717	1,083	420	242
Net Income	(57,851)	17,659	61,974	49,628	81,299
Average Shares	114,744	...	118,049	...	...
Balance Sheet					
Current Assets	435,891	312,580	65,643	110,883	...
Total Assets	6,015,027	3,909,945	3,660,640	3,575,878	...
Current Liabilities	131,627	321,683	324,155	137,004	...
Long-Term Obligations	2,139,814	1,376,077	1,165,014	1,302,956	...
Total Liabilities	2,943,618	1,748,100	1,538,951	1,516,902	...
Stockholders' Equity	3,071,409	2,161,845	2,121,689	2,058,976	...
Shares Outstanding	117,957	118,200	...	...	...
Statistical Record					
Return on Assets %	...	...	1.71	...	...
Return on Equity %	...	...	2.96	...	...
EBITDA Margin %	N.M.	47.67	52.20	53.02	53.15
Net Margin %	N.M.	7.54	12.95	10.55	17.19
Asset Turnover	...	...	0.13	...	...
Current Ratio	3.31	0.97	0.20	0.81	...
Debt to Equity	0.70	0.64	0.55	0.63	...
Price Range	37.24-32.22	...	...	...	...

Address: 4445 Willard Avenue, Suite 400, Chevy Chase, MD 20815
Telephone: 240-333-3600

Web Site: www.jbgsmith.com
Officers: Steven Roth - Chairman Robert A. Stewart - Executive Vice-Chairman

Auditors: Deloitte & Touche LLP
Transfer Agents: American Stock Transfer & Trust Company, LLC, Brookly, NY

JOHNSON & JOHNSON

Exchange	Symbol	Price	52Wk Range	Yield	P/E	Div Achiever
NYS	JNJ	$139.72 (12/29/2017)	143.62-111.76	2.40	24.26	52 Years

*7 Year Price Score 107.62 *NYSE Composite Index=100 ***12 Month Price Score 101.83**

TRADING VOLUME (thousand shares)

Interim Earnings (Per Share)

Qtr.	Mar	Jun	Sep	Dec
2014	1.64	1.51	1.66	0.89
2015	1.53	1.61	1.20	1.15
2016	1.54	1.43	1.53	1.38
2017	1.61	1.40	1.37	...

Interim Dividends (Per Share)

Amt	Decl	Ex	Rec	Pay
0.84Q	04/27/2017	05/25/2017	05/30/2017	06/13/2017
0.84Q	07/17/2017	08/25/2017	08/29/2017	09/12/2017
0.84Q	10/19/2017	11/27/2017	11/28/2017	12/12/2017
0.84Q	01/02/2018	02/26/2018	02/27/2018	03/13/2018

Indicated Div: $3.36 (Div. Reinv. Plan)

Valuation Analysis		Institutional Holding	
Forecast EPS	$7.28	No of Institutions	
	(01/18/2018)	3193	
Market Cap	$375.1 Billion	Shares	
Book Value	$74.0 Billion	2,283,337,216	
Price/Book	5.07	% Held	
Price/Sales	5.04	66.52	

Business Summary: Pharmaceuticals (MIC: 4.1.1 SIC: 2834 NAIC: 325412)

Johnson & Johnson, is engaged in the research and development, manufacture and sale of a range of products in the health care field. Co. is organized into three business segments: Consumer, which includes a range of products used in the baby care, oral care, beauty, over-the-counter pharmaceutical, women's health and wound care markets. Pharmaceutical, which is focused on five therapeutic areas: immunology, infectious diseases and vaccines, neuroscience, oncology, and cardiovascular and metabolic diseases. Medical Devices, which includes products used in the orthopaedic, surgery, cardiovascular, diabetes care and vision care fields.

Recent Developments: For the quarter ended Oct 1 2017, net income decreased 11.9% to US$3.76 billion from US$4.27 billion in the year-earlier quarter. Revenues were US$19.65 billion, up 10.3% from US$17.82 billion the year before. Direct operating expenses rose 25.8% to US$6.90 billion from US$5.49 billion in the comparable period the year before. Indirect operating expenses increased 12.8% to US$7.96 billion from US$7.05 billion in the equivalent prior-year period.

Prospects: Our evaluation of Johnson & Johnson as of Jan. 14, 2018 is the result of our systematic analysis on three basic characteristics: earnings strength, relative valuation, and recent stock price movement. The company has produced a positive trend in earnings per share over the past 5 quarters. However, while recent estimates for the company have been mixed, JNJ has posted better than expected results. Based on operating earnings yield, the company is undervalued when compared to all of the companies in our coverage universe. Share price changes over the past year indicates that JNJ will perform well over the near term.

Financial Data

(US$ in Millions)	9 Mos	6 Mos	3 Mos	01/01/2017	01/03/2016	12/28/2014	12/29/2013	12/30/2012
Earnings Per Share	5.76	5.92	5.95	5.93	5.48	5.70	4.81	3.86
Cash Flow Per Share	8.05	7.69	7.36	6.87	6.84	6.58	6.22	5.61
Tang Book Value Per Share	N.M.	N.M.	5.95	7.66	8.62	7.44	8.26	4.91
Dividends Per Share	3.280	3.240	3.200	3.150	2.950	2.760	2.590	2.400
Dividend Payout %	56.94	54.73	53.78	53.12	53.83	48.42	53.85	62.18
Income Statement								
Total Revenue	56,255	36,605	17,766	71,890	70,074	74,331	71,312	67,224
EBITDA	19,246	12,590	6,570	23,861	23,320	24,927	19,942	17,889
Depn & Amortn	3,773	2,062	912	3,700	3,700	3,898	4,063	3,646
Income Before Taxes	15,113	10,323	5,575	19,803	19,196	20,563	15,471	13,775
Income Taxes	3,100	2,074	1,153	3,263	3,787	4,240	1,640	3,261
Net Income	12,013	8,249	4,422	16,540	15,409	16,323	13,831	10,853
Average Shares	2,738	2,742	2,755	2,789	2,813	2,864	2,878	2,813
Balance Sheet								
Current Assets	41,829	38,789	63,347	65,032	60,210	59,311	56,407	46,116
Total Assets	155,658	152,807	144,918	141,208	133,411	131,119	132,683	121,347
Current Liabilities	31,806	28,872	25,119	26,287	27,747	25,085	25,675	24,262
Long-Term Obligations	26,675	27,363	27,015	22,442	12,857	15,122	13,328	11,489
Total Liabilities	81,679	80,885	74,577	70,790	62,261	61,367	58,630	56,521
Stockholders' Equity	73,979	71,922	70,341	70,418	71,150	69,752	74,053	64,826
Shares Outstanding	2,686	2,686	2,695	2,707	2,756	2,784	2,821	2,779
Statistical Record								
Return on Assets %	10.69	11.16	11.74	12.08	11.46	12.41	10.92	9.26
Return on Equity %	21.57	22.63	23.09	23.43	21.52	22.76	19.97	17.85
EBITDA Margin %	34.21	34.39	36.98	33.19	33.28	33.54	27.96	26.61
Net Margin %	21.35	22.54	24.89	23.01	21.99	21.96	19.40	16.14
Asset Turnover	0.50	0.50	0.51	0.53	0.52	0.57	0.56	0.57
Current Ratio	1.32	1.34	2.52	2.47	2.17	2.36	2.20	1.90
Debt to Equity	0.36	0.38	0.38	0.32	0.18	0.22	0.18	0.18
Price Range	136.57-110.99	136.43-110.99	128.96-108.59	125.40-95.75	106.39-90.73	109.07-86.62	95.63-70.10	72.52-61.78
P/E Ratio	23.71-19.27	23.05-18.75	21.67-18.25	21.15-16.15	19.41-16.56	19.14-15.20	19.88-14.57	18.79-16.01
Average Yield %	2.65	2.68	2.72	2.77	2.96	2.74	3.02	3.58

Address: One Johnson & Johnson Plaza, New Brunswick, NJ 08933	Web Site: www.jnj.com	Auditors: PricewaterhouseCoopers LLP
Telephone: 732-524-0400	Officers: Alex Gorsky - Chairman, Chief Executive Officer, Division Officer Dominic J. Caruso - Executive Vice President, Vice President, Chief Financial Officer	Investor Contact: 800-950-5089
Fax: 732-214-0332		Transfer Agents: Computershare Trust Company, N.A., Canton, MA

JONES LANG LASALLE INC

Exchange	Symbol	Price	52Wk Range	Yield	P/E
NYS	JLL	$148.93 (12/29/2017)	153.03-99.21	0.50	19.94

*7 Year Price Score 86.27 *NYSE Composite Index=100 *12 Month Price Score 112.15

Interim Earnings (Per Share)

Qtr.	Mar	Jun	Sep	Dec
2014	0.35	1.58	2.30	4.28
2015	0.92	1.98	2.43	4.31
2016	0.56	1.73	1.05	3.63
2017	0.24	1.71	1.89	...

Interim Dividends (Per Share)

Amt	Decl	Ex	Rec	Pay
0.31S	04/27/2016	05/11/2016	05/13/2016	06/15/2016
0.33S	11/02/2016	11/10/2016	11/15/2016	12/15/2016
0.35S	05/05/2017	05/11/2017	05/15/2017	06/15/2017
0.37S	11/06/2017	11/15/2017	11/16/2017	12/15/2017

Indicated Div: $0.74

Valuation Analysis / Institutional Holding

Forecast EPS	$8.35	No of Institutions
	(01/09/2018)	490
Market Cap	$6.8 Billion	Shares
Book Value	$3.1 Billion	50,769,544
Price/Book	2.15	% Held
Price/Sales	0.89	94.50

TRADING VOLUME (thousand shares)

Business Summary: Property, Real Estate & Development (MIC: 5.3.2 SIC: 6531 NAIC: 531210)

Jones Lang LaSalle is a financial services company that provides real estate services on a local, regional and global basis to owner, occupier, investor and developer clients. Services provided include: agency leasing; capital markets; corporate finance; energy and sustainability services; facility management outsourcing (occupiers); investment management; logistics and supply-chain management; mortgage origination and servicing; project and development management/construction; property management (investors); real estate investment banking/merchant banking; research; consulting and advisory services; tenant representation; valuations; and value recovery and receivership services.

Recent Developments: For the quarter ended Sep 30 2017, net income increased 81.5% to US$87.5 million from US$48.2 million in the year-earlier quarter. Revenues were US$1.95 billion, up 14.2% from US$1.71 billion the year before.

Prospects: Our evaluation of Jones Lang LaSalle Inc. as of Jan. 14, 2018 is the result of our systematic analysis on three basic characteristics: earnings strength, relative valuation, and recent stock price movement. The company has produced a positive trend in earnings per share over the past 5 quarters and while recent estimates for the company have been raised by analysts, JLL has posted better than expected results. Based on operating earnings yield, the company is undervalued when compared to all of the companies in our coverage universe. Share price changes over the past year indicates that JLL will perform well over the near term.

Financial Data

(US$ in Thousands)	9 Mos	6 Mos	3 Mos	12/31/2016	12/31/2015	12/31/2014	12/31/2013	12/31/2012
Earnings Per Share	7.47	6.63	6.65	6.98	9.65	8.52	5.98	4.63
Cash Flow Per Share	14.60	10.65	7.48	4.74	8.36	11.16	6.62	7.45
Tang Book Value Per Share	2.98	0.76	N.M.	N.M.	7.11	9.82	5.26	1.17
Dividends Per Share	0.680	0.680	0.640	0.640	0.560	0.480	0.440	0.400
Dividend Payout %	9.10	10.26	9.62	9.17	5.80	5.63	7.36	8.64
Income Statement								
Total Revenue	5,396,900	3,449,900	1,615,200	6,803,800	5,965,671	5,429,603	4,461,591	3,932,830
EBITDA	367,000	207,100	61,600	633,600	664,756	583,869	439,819	355,603
Depn & Amortn	122,300	80,500	39,300	179,700	134,958	118,205	71,000	66,200
Income Before Taxes	202,100	99,000	9,300	408,600	501,671	437,343	334,101	254,230
Income Taxes	57,300	29,100	3,600	108,000	132,805	97,588	92,092	69,244
Net Income	175,800	89,200	10,800	318,200	438,672	386,063	269,865	208,050
Average Shares	45,814	45,782	45,689	45,528	45,414	45,260	45,072	44,799
Balance Sheet								
Current Assets	2,986,300	3,399,300	2,796,200	3,299,700	2,650,807	2,118,176	1,724,228	1,515,529
Total Assets	7,554,300	7,897,900	7,236,000	7,629,400	6,205,159	5,075,336	4,597,353	4,351,499
Current Liabilities	2,582,400	2,851,800	2,230,900	2,966,300	2,505,193	2,047,011	1,658,424	1,661,971
Long-Term Obligations	1,117,800	1,327,100	1,429,300	1,178,100	529,999	275,000	430,000	444,000
Total Liabilities	4,410,600	4,892,800	4,369,700	4,839,700	3,516,396	2,688,539	2,417,684	2,400,316
Stockholders' Equity	3,143,700	3,005,100	2,866,300	2,789,700	2,688,763	2,386,797	2,179,669	1,951,183
Shares Outstanding	45,361	45,290	45,286	45,213	45,049	44,828	44,447	44,054
Statistical Record								
Return on Assets %	4.65	4.25	4.47	4.59	7.78	7.98	6.03	5.01
Return on Equity %	11.49	10.50	10.83	11.58	17.29	16.91	13.07	11.39
EBITDA Margin %	6.80	6.00	3.81	9.31	11.14	10.75	9.86	9.04
Net Margin %	3.26	2.59	0.67	4.68	7.35	7.11	6.05	5.29
Asset Turnover	1.03	1.03	1.04	0.98	1.06	1.12	1.00	0.95
Current Ratio	1.16	1.19	1.25	1.11	1.06	1.03	1.04	0.91
Debt to Equity	0.36	0.44	0.50	0.42	0.20	0.12	0.20	0.23
Price Range	132.87-88.65	125.21-88.65	124.34-88.65	160.19-88.65	179.35-142.69	153.43-101.95	102.80-82.15	87.08-63.21
P/E Ratio	17.79-11.87	18.89-13.37	18.70-13.33	22.95-12.70	18.59-14.79	18.01-11.97	17.19-13.74	18.81-13.65
Average Yield %	0.61	0.62	0.59	0.57	0.35	0.38	0.47	0.53

Address: 200 East Randolph Drive, Chicago, IL 60601	**Web Site:** www.jll.com	**Auditors:** KPMG LLP
Telephone: 312-782-5800	**Officers:** Sheila A. Penrose - Chairman Christian Ulbrich - President, Chief Executive Officer, Region Officer	**Investor Contact:** 312-782-5800
Fax: 312-782-4339		**Transfer Agents:** Computershare, Pittsburgh, PA

JPMORGAN CHASE & CO

Exchange	Symbol	Price	52Wk Range	Yield	P/E
NYS	JPM	$106.94 (12/29/2017)	107.83-82.15	2.09	15.41

*7 Year Price Score 123.03 *NYSE Composite Index=100 ***12 Month Price Score 106.09**

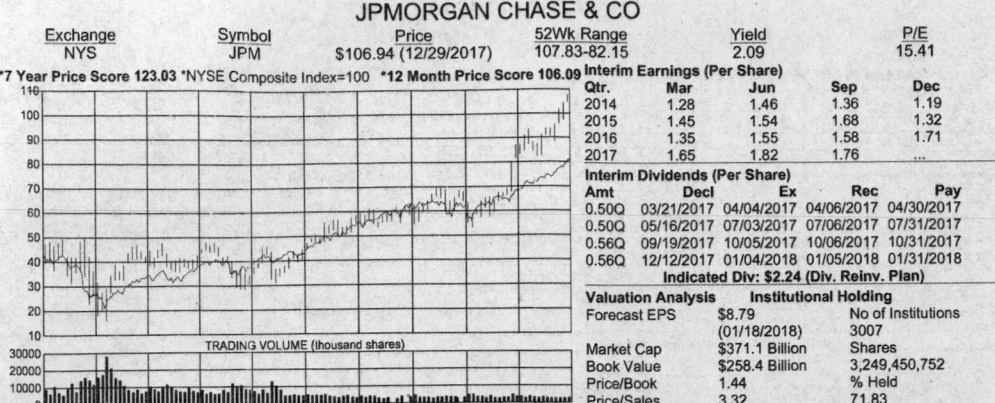

TRADING VOLUME (thousand shares)

Interim Earnings (Per Share)

Qtr.	Mar	Jun	Sep	Dec
2014	1.28	1.46	1.36	1.19
2015	1.45	1.54	1.68	1.32
2016	1.35	1.55	1.58	1.71
2017	1.65	1.82	1.76	...

Interim Dividends (Per Share)

Amt	Decl	Ex	Rec	Pay
0.50Q	03/21/2017	04/04/2017	04/06/2017	04/30/2017
0.50Q	05/16/2017	07/03/2017	07/06/2017	07/31/2017
0.56Q	09/19/2017	10/05/2017	10/06/2017	10/31/2017
0.56Q	12/12/2017	01/04/2018	01/05/2018	01/31/2018

Indicated Div: $2.24 (Div. Reinv. Plan)

Valuation Analysis

		Institutional Holding	
Forecast EPS	$8.79	No of Institutions	
	(01/18/2018)	3007	
Market Cap	$371.1 Billion	Shares	
Book Value	$258.4 Billion	3,249,450,752	
Price/Book	1.44	% Held	
Price/Sales	3.32	71.83	

Business Summary: Banking (MIC: 5.1.1 SIC: 6021 NAIC: 522110)

JPMorgan Chase is a financial holding company. Through its subsidiaries, Co. acts as a financial services firm and banking institution providing investment banking, financial services for consumers and businesses, commercial banking, financial transaction processing and asset management. Co.'s consumer business is the Consumer and Community Banking segment. Co.'s wholesale business segments are Corporate and Investment Bank, Commercial Banking, and Asset and Wealth Management. Under the J.P. Morgan and Chase brands, Co. serves customers in the corporate, institutional and government clients. As of Dec 31 2016, Co. had total assets of $2.49 trillion and total deposits of $1.38 trillion.

Recent Developments: For the quarter ended Sep 30 2017, net income increased 7.1% to US$6.73 billion from US$6.29 billion in the year-earlier quarter. Net interest income increased 10.3% to US$12.80 billion from US$11.60 billion in the year-earlier quarter. Provision for loan losses was US$1.45 billion versus US$1.27 billion in the prior-year quarter, an increase of 14.2%. Non-interest income fell 4.1% to US$12.53 billion from US$13.07 billion, while non-interest expense declined 1.0% to US$14.32 billion.

Prospects: Our evaluation of J.P. Morgan Chase & Co. as of Jan. 14, 2018 is the result of our systematic analysis on three basic characteristics: earnings strength, relative valuation, and recent stock price movement. The company has generated a negative trend in earnings per share over the past 5 quarters. Because the company lacks sufficient analyst estimate data, we place greater weight on the historical EPS trend as the measure of earnings strength. Based on operating earnings yield, the company is undervalued when compared to all of the companies in our coverage universe. Share price changes over the past year indicates that JPM will perform in line with the market over the near term.

Financial Data
(US$ in Millions)

	9 Mos	6 Mos	3 Mos	12/31/2016	12/31/2015	12/31/2014	12/31/2013	12/31/2012
Earnings Per Share	6.94	6.76	6.49	6.19	6.00	5.29	4.35	5.20
Cash Flow Per Share	6.47	8.42	5.98	5.57	19.85	9.72	28.54	6.57
Tang Book Value Per Share	51.43	50.74	49.42	48.83	45.46	41.92	37.46	36.01
Dividends Per Share	1.960	1.940	1.880	1.840	1.680	1.560	1.360	1.150
Dividend Payout %	28.24	28.70	28.97	29.73	28.00	29.49	31.26	22.12
Income Statement								
Interest Income	47,379	30,692	15,042	55,901	50,973	51,531	52,996	56,063
Interest Expense	10,309	6,420	2,978	9,818	7,463	7,897	9,677	11,153
Net Interest Income	37,070	24,272	12,064	46,083	43,510	43,634	43,319	44,910
Provision for Losses	3,982	2,530	1,315	5,361	3,827	3,139	225	3,385
Non-Interest Income	38,401	25,873	12,611	49,585	50,033	50,571	53,287	52,121
Non-Interest Expense	43,843	29,525	15,019	55,771	59,014	61,274	70,467	64,729
Income Before Taxes	27,646	18,090	8,341	34,536	30,702	29,792	25,914	28,917
Income Taxes	7,437	4,613	1,893	9,803	6,260	8,030	7,991	7,633
Net Income	20,209	13,477	6,448	24,733	24,442	21,762	17,923	21,284
Average Shares	3,560	3,600	3,631	3,650	3,733	3,798	3,815	3,823
Balance Sheet								
Net Loans & Leases	900,222	895,404	882,561	880,989	823,744	743,151	722,154	711,860
Total Assets	2,563,074	2,563,174	2,546,290	2,490,972	2,351,698	2,573,126	2,415,689	2,359,141
Total Deposits	1,439,027	1,439,473	1,422,999	1,375,179	1,279,715	1,363,427	1,287,765	1,193,593
Total Liabilities	2,304,692	2,304,691	2,290,427	2,236,782	2,104,125	2,341,061	2,204,511	2,155,072
Stockholders' Equity	258,382	258,483	255,863	254,190	247,573	232,065	211,178	204,069
Shares Outstanding	3,470	3,519	3,553	3,562	3,664	3,715	3,757	3,804
Statistical Record								
Return on Assets %	1.06	1.05	1.03	1.02	0.99	0.87	0.75	0.92
Return on Equity %	10.51	10.37	10.14	9.83	10.19	9.82	8.63	10.95
Net Interest Margin %	76.69	78.01	80.20	82.44	85.36	84.68	81.74	80.11
Efficiency Ratio %	49.01	50.17	54.31	52.87	58.43	60.01	66.30	59.83
Loans to Deposits	0.63	0.62	0.62	0.64	0.64	0.55	0.56	0.60
Price Range	95.51-66.51	93.60-59.55	93.60-57.32	87.13-53.07	70.08-54.38	63.15-53.31	58.48-43.97	46.27-31.00
P/E Ratio	13.76-9.58	13.85-8.81	14.42-8.83	14.08-8.57	11.68-9.06	11.94-10.08	13.44-10.11	8.90-5.96
Average Yield %	2.29	2.46	2.58	2.80	2.63	2.68	2.62	2.93

Address: 270 Park Avenue, New York, NY 10017
Telephone: 212-270-6000

Web Site: www.jpmorganchase.com
Officers: James Dimon - Chairman, President, Chief Executive Officer Marianne Lake - Chief Financial Officer, Division Officer

Auditors: PricewaterhouseCoopers LLP
Investor Contact: 212-270-7325
Transfer Agents: Computershare Shareowner Services LLC, Jersey City, NY

JUNIPER NETWORKS INC

Exchange	Symbol	Price	52Wk Range	Yield	P/E
NYS	JNPR	$28.50 (12/29/2017)	30.89-24.40	1.40	17.07

*7 Year Price Score 89.58   *NYSE Composite Index=100   *12 Month Price Score 92.82

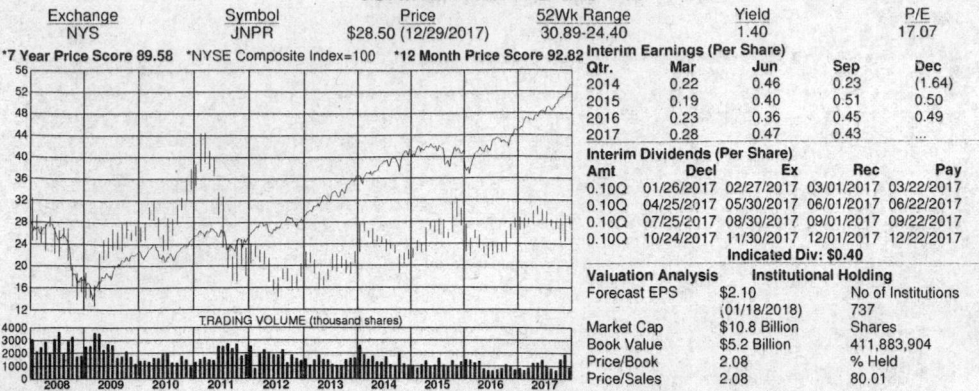

Interim Earnings (Per Share)

Qtr.	Mar	Jun	Sep	Dec
2014	0.22	0.46	0.23	(1.64)
2015	0.19	0.40	0.51	0.50
2016	0.23	0.36	0.45	0.49
2017	0.28	0.47	0.43	...

Interim Dividends (Per Share)

Amt	Decl	Ex	Rec	Pay
0.10Q	01/26/2017	02/27/2017	03/01/2017	03/22/2017
0.10Q	04/25/2017	05/30/2017	06/01/2017	06/22/2017
0.10Q	07/25/2017	08/30/2017	09/01/2017	09/22/2017
0.10Q	10/24/2017	11/30/2017	12/01/2017	12/22/2017

Indicated Div: $0.40

Valuation Analysis

Forecast EPS	$2.10
	(01/18/2018)
Market Cap	$10.8 Billion
Book Value	$5.2 Billion
Price/Book	2.08
Price/Sales	2.08

Institutional Holding

No of Institutions	737
Shares	411,883,904
% Held	80.01

Business Summary: Peripherals (MIC: 6.2.2 SIC: 3661 NAIC: 334210)

Juniper Networks designs, develops, and sells products and services for networks. Co. sells its products in three geographic regions: Americas; Europe, Middle East, and Africa; and Asia Pacific. Co. sells its network products and service offerings across routing, switching, and security. Co.'s products address network requirements for service providers, cloud providers, national governments, research and public sector organizations and other enterprises. Co.'s portfolio addresses various domains in the network: core; edge; access and aggregation; data centers; and campus and branch. Co.'s product families and service offerings are routing products, switching products, and security products.

Recent Developments: For the quarter ended Sep 30 2017, net income decreased 3.9% to US$165.7 million from US$172.4 million in the year-earlier quarter. Revenues were US$1.26 billion, down 2.1% from US$1.29 billion the year before. Operating income was US$230.9 million versus US$250.0 million in the prior-year quarter, a decrease of 7.6%. Direct operating expenses declined 0.1% to US$485.4 million from US$485.8 million in the comparable period the year before. Indirect operating expenses decreased 1.5% to US$541.5 million from US$549.5 million in the equivalent prior-year period.

Prospects: Our evaluation of Juniper Networks Inc. as of Jan. 14, 2018 is the result of our systematic analysis on three basic characteristics: earnings strength, relative valuation, and recent stock price movement. The company has generated a negative trend in earnings per share over the past 5 quarters. However, while recent estimates for the company have been mixed, JNPR has posted better than expected results. Based on operating earnings yield, the company is undervalued when compared to all of the companies in our coverage universe. Share price changes over the past year indicates that JNPR will perform in line with the market over the near term.

Financial Data

(US$ in Thousands)	9 Mos	6 Mos	3 Mos	12/31/2016	12/31/2015	12/31/2014	12/31/2013	12/31/2012
Earnings Per Share	1.67	1.69	1.58	1.53	1.59	(0.73)	0.86	0.35
Cash Flow Per Share	3.65	3.74	3.88	2.89	2.28	1.67	1.68	1.23
Tang Book Value Per Share	5.11	4.95	4.74	4.59	4.04	4.48	6.34	5.53
Dividends Per Share	0.400	0.400	0.400	0.400	0.400	0.200	...	...
Dividend Payout %	23.95	23.67	25.32	26.14	25.16	...	...	...
Income Statement								
Total Revenue	3,787,700	2,529,900	1,221,000	4,990,100	4,857,800	4,627,100	4,669,100	4,365,400
EBITDA	819,800	525,800	211,300	1,074,200	1,055,200	112,500	723,400	492,800
Depn & Amortn	169,700	112,100	55,800	184,500	141,500	141,900	148,200	159,400
Income Before Taxes	611,600	385,800	140,600	827,400	852,200	(86,300)	525,500	291,500
Income Taxes	157,300	97,200	31,800	234,700	218,500	248,000	85,700	105,000
Net Income	454,300	288,600	108,800	592,700	633,700	(334,300)	439,800	186,500
Average Shares	382,700	385,600	388,000	387,800	399,400	457,400	510,300	526,200
Balance Sheet								
Current Assets	4,283,300	4,145,100	3,993,800	3,971,900	2,912,400	2,971,900	3,703,900	3,600,700
Total Assets	9,744,300	9,752,900	9,638,000	9,656,500	8,619,200	8,403,100	10,326,000	9,832,100
Current Liabilities	1,585,300	1,672,800	1,582,600	1,735,900	1,801,900	1,527,700	1,441,400	1,422,000
Long-Term Obligations	2,135,700	2,135,000	2,134,400	2,133,700	1,648,800	1,349,000	999,300	999,200
Total Liabilities	4,586,200	4,666,700	4,619,600	4,694,000	4,044,800	3,484,000	3,023,800	2,833,100
Stockholders' Equity	5,158,100	5,086,200	5,018,400	4,962,500	4,574,400	4,919,100	7,302,200	6,999,000
Shares Outstanding	377,200	380,500	382,500	381,100	384,000	416,200	495,200	508,400
Statistical Record								
Return on Assets %	6.81	6.91	6.58	6.47	7.45	N.M.	4.36	1.88
Return on Equity %	12.95	13.31	12.64	12.40	13.35	N.M.	6.15	2.64
EBITDA Margin %	21.64	20.78	17.31	21.53	21.72	2.43	15.49	11.29
Net Margin %	11.99	11.41	8.91	11.88	13.05	N.M.	9.42	4.27
Asset Turnover	0.55	0.55	0.55	0.54	0.57	0.49	0.46	0.44
Current Ratio	2.70	2.48	2.52	2.29	1.62	1.95	2.57	2.53
Debt to Equity	0.41	0.42	0.43	0.43	0.36	0.27	0.14	0.14
Price Range	30.89-22.43	30.89-21.92	28.90-21.24	28.68-21.24	32.23-21.39	27.95-18.57	22.57-15.69	23.88-14.27
P/E Ratio	18.50-13.43	18.28-12.97	18.29-13.44	18.75-13.88	20.27-13.45	...	26.24-18.24	68.23-40.77
Average Yield %	1.44	1.51	1.60	1.64	1.52	0.84	...	...

Address: 1133 Innovation Way, Sunnyvale, CA 94089
Telephone: 408-745-2000
Fax: 408-745-2100

Web Site: www.juniper.net
Officers: Scott G. Kriens - Chairman, Chief Executive Officer Pradeep S. Sindhu - Chairman, Vice-Chairman, Executive Vice President, Chief Scientific Officer, Chief Technology Officer

Auditors: Ernst & Young LLP
Investor Contact: 408-936-5396
Transfer Agents: Wells Fargo Shareowner Services, Mendota Heights, MN

KANSAS CITY SOUTHERN

Exchange	Symbol	Price	52Wk Range	Yield	P/E
NYS	KSU	$105.22 (12/29/2017)	113.44-80.82	1.37	20.71

*7 Year Price Score 84.68 *NYSE Composite Index=100 *12 Month Price Score 104.31

Interim Earnings (Per Share)

Qtr.	Mar	Jun	Sep	Dec
2014	0.85	1.18	1.25	1.28
2015	0.91	1.01	1.20	1.28
2016	0.99	1.11	1.12	1.20
2017	1.38	1.27	1.23	...

Interim Dividends (Per Share)

Amt	Decl	Ex	Rec	Pay
0.33Q	01/26/2017	03/09/2017	03/13/2017	04/05/2017
0.33Q	05/05/2017	06/08/2017	06/12/2017	07/05/2017
0.36Q	08/15/2017	09/08/2017	09/11/2017	10/04/2017
0.36Q	11/10/2017	12/28/2017	12/29/2017	01/17/2018

Indicated Div: $1.44

Valuation Analysis

		Institutional Holding	
Forecast EPS	$5.21	No of Institutions	
	(01/17/2018)	738	
Market Cap	$10.9 Billion	Shares	
Book Value	$4.1 Billion	115,906,192	
Price/Book	2.67	% Held	
Price/Sales	4.33	89.72	

Business Summary: Rail (MIC: 7.4.3 SIC: 4011 NAIC: 482111)

Kansas City Southern is a holding company that has railroad investments in the U.S., Mexico and Panama. Co. is engaged primarily in the freight rail transportation business operating through a single coordinated rail network. As of Dec 31 2016, Co.'s coordinated rail network comprised approximately 6,600 route miles extending from the midwest and southeast portions of the U.S. south into Mexico and connected with all other Class I railroads, providing shippers with an alternative to other railroad routes and giving direct access to Mexico and the southeast and southwest U.S. through alternate interchange hubs.

Recent Developments: For the quarter ended Sep 30 2017, net income increased 7.4% to US$129.9 million from US$121.0 million in the year-earlier quarter. Revenues were US$656.6 million, up 8.6% from US$604.5 million the year before. Operating income was US$233.8 million versus US$199.8 million in the prior-year quarter, an increase of 17.0%. Direct operating expenses rose 18.5% to US$80.1 million from US$67.6 million in the comparable period the year before. Indirect operating expenses increased 1.7% to US$342.7 million from US$337.1 million in the equivalent prior-year period.

Prospects: Our evaluation of Kansas City Southern Industries Inc. as of Jan. 14, 2018 is the result of our systematic analysis on three basic characteristics: earnings strength, relative valuation, and recent stock price movement. The company has generated a negative trend in earnings per share over the past 5 quarters. However, while recent estimates for the company have been mixed, KSU has posted better than expected results. Based on operating earnings yield, the company is undervalued when compared to all of the companies in our coverage universe. Share price changes over the past year indicates that KSU will perform very well over the near term.

Financial Data

(US$ in Thousands)	9 Mos	6 Mos	3 Mos	12/31/2016	12/31/2015	12/31/2014	12/31/2013	12/31/2012
Earnings Per Share	5.08	4.97	4.81	4.43	4.40	4.55	3.18	3.43
Cash Flow Per Share	9.23	8.64	8.32	8.47	8.29	8.22	7.26	6.12
Tang Book Value Per Share	39.39	39.73	39.10	38.31	36.03	33.96	30.52	28.06
Dividends Per Share	1.350	1.320	1.320	1.320	1.320	1.120	0.860	0.780
Dividend Payout %	26.57	26.56	27.44	29.80	30.00	24.62	27.04	22.74
Income Statement								
Total Revenue	1,922,500	1,265,900	609,500	2,334,200	2,418,800	2,577,100	2,369,300	2,238,600
EBITDA	987,900	671,700	337,900	1,050,800	1,020,800	1,022,900	836,700	896,300
Depn & Amortn	241,600	159,700	79,300	305,000	284,600	258,100	223,300	198,800
Income Before Taxes	671,400	462,300	233,900	648,100	654,300	692,000	532,800	597,100
Income Taxes	269,600	187,600	91,000	182,800	187,300	208,800	198,300	237,000
Net Income	410,300	281,000	146,600	478,100	483,500	502,600	351,400	377,300
Average Shares	104,678	105,758	106,326	107,761	109,915	110,433	110,340	110,080
Balance Sheet								
Current Assets	640,500	711,400	633,000	648,000	537,000	818,300	942,400	522,300
Total Assets	9,100,300	9,067,600	8,878,200	8,817,500	8,341,000	8,091,000	7,435,400	6,395,900
Current Liabilities	924,800	821,300	708,200	744,400	757,600	898,800	730,600	424,800
Long-Term Obligations	2,238,400	2,243,600	2,263,600	2,271,500	2,045,000	1,841,000	1,856,900	1,547,600
Total Liabilities	5,009,700	4,875,000	4,724,200	4,727,600	4,426,700	4,335,500	4,064,800	3,299,300
Stockholders' Equity	4,090,600	4,192,600	4,154,000	4,089,900	3,914,300	3,755,500	3,370,600	3,096,600
Shares Outstanding	103,694	105,382	106,080	106,606	108,461	110,392	110,229	110,131
Statistical Record								
Return on Assets %	6.02	5.99	6.01	5.56	5.88	6.47	5.08	5.99
Return on Equity %	13.23	12.94	12.77	11.91	12.61	14.11	10.87	12.84
EBITDA Margin %	51.39	53.06	55.44	45.02	42.20	39.69	35.31	40.04
Net Margin %	21.34	22.20	24.05	20.48	19.99	19.50	14.83	16.85
Asset Turnover	0.28	0.28	0.28	0.27	0.29	0.33	0.34	0.36
Current Ratio	0.69	0.87	0.89	0.87	0.71	0.91	1.29	1.23
Debt to Equity	0.55	0.54	0.54	0.56	0.52	0.49	0.55	0.50
Price Range	108.68-80.82	104.65-80.82	99.47-80.82	99.47-64.35	122.03-70.01	125.88-91.12	125.20-83.48	83.82-62.54
P/E Ratio	21.39-15.91	21.06-16.26	20.68-16.80	22.45-14.53	27.73-15.91	27.67-20.03	39.37-26.25	24.44-18.23
Average Yield %	1.45	1.46	1.47	1.50	1.35	1.02	0.79	1.06

Address: 427 West 12th Street, Kansas City, MO 64105	Web Site: www.kcsouthern.com	Auditors: PricewaterhouseCoopers LLP
Telephone: 816-983-1303	Officers: Robert J. Druten - Chairman Patrick J. Ottensmeyer - President, Chief Executive Officer, Executive Vice President	Investor Contact: 816-983-1551
Fax: 816-556-0297		Transfer Agents: Computershare Trust Company, N.A., Providence, RI

KAR AUCTION SERVICES INC.

Exchange	Symbol	Price	52Wk Range	Yield	P/E
NYS	KAR	$50.51 (12/29/2017)	51.43-40.31	2.77	29.71

*7 Year Price Score 117.93 *NYSE Composite Index=100 *12 Month Price Score 104.07

Interim Earnings (Per Share)

Qtr.	Mar	Jun	Sep	Dec
2014	0.15	0.36	0.33	0.35
2015	0.38	0.41	0.37	0.35
2016	0.44	0.44	0.39	0.33
2017	0.50	0.41	0.46	...

Interim Dividends (Per Share)

Amt	Decl	Ex	Rec	Pay
0.32Q	02/21/2017	03/20/2017	03/22/2017	04/04/2017
0.32Q	05/09/2017	06/19/2017	06/21/2017	07/06/2017
0.32Q	08/08/2017	09/19/2017	09/20/2017	10/03/2017
0.35Q	10/31/2017	12/19/2017	12/20/2017	01/05/2018

Indicated Div: $1.40

Valuation Analysis		Institutional Holding	
Forecast EPS	$2.36	No of Institutions	
	(01/17/2018)	N/A	
Market Cap	$6.8 Billion	Shares	
Book Value	$1.4 Billion	N/A	
Price/Book	4.87	% Held	
Price/Sales	1.99	N/A	

Business Summary: Retail - Automotive (MIC: 2.1.4 SIC: 5521 NAIC: 441120)

KAR Auction Services is a provider of used car auction services and salvage auction services in North America and the U.K. Co. operates three business segments: ADESA Inc. Auctions, which encompasses all physical and online wholesale auctions throughout North America (U.S., Canada and Mexico); Insurance Auto Auctions, Inc., which encompasses all salvage auctions throughout North America (U.S. and Canada); and Automotive Finance Corporation, which engaged in the business of providing short-term, inventory-secured financing to independent, used vehicle dealers. As of Dec 31 2016, Co. had a North American network of 77 whole car auction locations and 172 salvage vehicle auction sites.

Recent Developments: For the quarter ended Sep 30 2017, net income increased 15.4% to US$62.8 million from US$54.4 million in the year-earlier quarter. Revenues were US$843.0 million, up 8.9% from US$773.8 million the year before. Operating income was US$141.9 million versus US$123.3 million in the prior-year quarter, an increase of 15.1%. Direct operating expenses rose 8.0% to US$479.2 million from US$443.7 million in the comparable period the year before. Indirect operating expenses increased 7.3% to US$221.9 million from US$206.8 million in the equivalent prior-year period.

Prospects: Our evaluation of KAR Aucton Services Inc. as of Jan. 14, 2018 is the result of our systematic analysis on three basic characteristics: earnings strength, relative valuation, and recent stock price movement. The company has managed to produce a neutral trend in earnings per share over the past 5 quarters. However, while recent estimates for the company have been mixed, KAR has posted better than expected results. Based on operating earnings yield, the company is undervalued when compared to all of the companies in our coverage universe. Share price changes over the past year indicates that KAR will perform in line with the market over the near term.

Financial Data
(US$ in Thousands)

	9 Mos	6 Mos	3 Mos	12/31/2016	12/31/2015	12/31/2014	12/31/2013	12/31/2012
Earnings Per Share	1.70	1.63	1.66	1.60	1.51	1.19	0.48	0.66
Cash Flow Per Share	4.14	4.20	3.17	2.61	3.39	3.08	3.15	2.12
Dividends Per Share	1.280	1.250	1.220	1.190	1.080	1.020	0.820	0.190
Dividend Payout %	75.29	76.69	73.49	74.38	71.52	85.71	170.83	28.79
Income Statement								
Total Revenue	2,567,600	1,724,600	866,600	3,150,100	2,639,600	2,364,500	2,173,300	1,963,400
EBITDA	424,600	279,900	146,100	583,700	506,700	419,000	318,200	343,400
Depn & Amortn	7,800	5,100	2,500	89,600	74,800	67,800	64,300	72,400
Income Before Taxes	294,900	194,400	103,300	355,300	340,500	265,000	149,200	151,600
Income Taxes	105,700	68,000	34,100	132,900	125,900	95,700	81,500	59,600
Net Income	189,200	126,400	69,200	222,400	214,600	169,300	67,700	92,000
Average Shares	137,700	138,400	138,300	139,100	142,300	141,800	140,800	139,000
Balance Sheet								
Current Assets	3,174,100	3,136,100	2,887,600	2,841,200	2,446,100	2,074,900	1,791,500	1,581,400
Total Assets	6,905,600	6,856,700	6,580,200	6,557,600	5,791,800	5,351,500	5,127,200	4,922,300
Current Liabilities	2,347,600	2,262,900	2,333,600	2,335,000	2,226,100	1,590,600	1,434,600	1,286,900
Long-Term Obligations	2,671,000	2,675,200	2,360,500	2,365,100	1,719,300	1,736,600	1,734,700	1,774,600
Total Liabilities	5,502,900	5,394,900	5,149,800	5,160,300	4,405,700	3,804,400	3,645,400	3,478,600
Stockholders' Equity	1,402,700	1,461,800	1,430,400	1,397,300	1,386,100	1,547,100	1,481,800	1,443,700
Shares Outstanding	135,261	137,322	137,129	136,639	137,795	141,316	139,027	136,657
Statistical Record								
Return on Assets %	3.48	3.37	3.53	3.59	3.85	3.23	1.35	1.89
Return on Equity %	16.30	15.49	16.18	15.94	14.63	11.18	4.63	6.58
EBITDA Margin %	16.54	16.23	16.86	18.53	19.20	17.72	14.64	17.49
Net Margin %	7.37	7.33	7.99	7.06	8.13	7.16	3.12	4.69
Asset Turnover	0.51	0.50	0.50	0.51	0.47	0.45	0.43	0.40
Current Ratio	1.35	1.39	1.24	1.22	1.10	1.30	1.25	1.23
Debt to Equity	1.90	1.83	1.65	1.69	1.24	1.12	1.17	1.23
Price Range	47.74-38.66	46.70-38.66	46.70-36.41	43.88-31.98	39.52-33.77	35.18-26.44	30.15-19.30	20.63-13.49
P/E Ratio	28.08-22.74	28.65-23.72	28.13-21.93	27.43-19.99	26.17-22.36	29.56-22.22	62.81-40.21	31.26-20.44
Average Yield %	2.95	2.90	2.89	2.99	2.91	3.33	3.33	1.11

Address: 13085 Hamilton Crossing Boulevard, Carmel, IN 46032 Telephone: 800-923-3725	Web Site: www.karauctionservices.com Officers: James P. Hallett - Chief Executive Officer Eric M. Loughmiller - Executive Vice President, Chief Financial Officer	Auditors: KPMG LLP Investor Contact: 317-249-4390

KB HOME

Exchange	Symbol	Price	52Wk Range	Yield	P/E
NYS	KBH	$31.95 (12/29/2017)	32.25-16.11	0.31	22.99

*7 Year Price Score 113.86 *NYSE Composite Index=100 *12 Month Price Score 125.73

Interim Earnings (Per Share)

Qtr.	Feb	May	Aug	Nov
2013-14	0.12	0.27	0.28	8.57
2014-15	0.08	0.10	0.23	0.43
2015-16	0.14	0.17	0.42	0.40
2016-17	0.15	0.33	0.51	...

Interim Dividends (Per Share)

Amt	Decl	Ex	Rec	Pay
0.025Q	01/26/2017	02/07/2017	02/09/2017	02/23/2017
0.025Q	04/13/2017	05/02/2017	05/04/2017	05/18/2017
0.025Q	07/13/2017	08/01/2017	08/03/2017	08/17/2017
0.025Q	10/05/2017	11/01/2017	11/02/2017	11/16/2017

Indicated Div: $0.10

Valuation Analysis   **Institutional Holding**

Forecast EPS	$1.47 (01/18/2018)	No of Institutions 390
Market Cap	$2.8 Billion	Shares 101,227,968
Book Value	$1.8 Billion	% Held 94.29
Price/Book	1.50	
Price/Sales	0.66	

Business Summary: Builders (MIC: 2.2.5 SIC: 1531 NAIC: 236115)

KB Home is a builder of attached and detached single-family residential homes, townhomes and condominiums. Co. has five segments, comprised of four homebuilding segments and one financial services segment. Co. organizes its homebuilding operations into four segments: West Coast, Southwest, Central and Southeast. Co.'s financial services segment provides property and casualty insurance and, in certain instances, earthquake, flood and personal property insurance to its homebuyers in the same markets as its homebuilding segments, and provides title services in the majority of its markets located within its Central and Southeast homebuilding segments.

Recent Developments: For the quarter ended Aug 31 2017, net income increased 27.6% to US$50.2 million from US$39.4 million in the year-earlier quarter. Revenues were US$1.14 billion, up 25.3% from US$913.3 million the year before. Direct operating expenses rose 25.5% to US$955.9 million from US$761.4 million in the comparable period the year before. Indirect operating expenses increased 11.2% to US$109.1 million from US$98.1 million in the equivalent prior-year period.

Prospects: Our evaluation of KB HOME as of Jan. 14, 2018 is the result of our systematic analysis on three basic characteristics: earnings strength, relative valuation, and recent stock price movement. The company has managed to produce a neutral trend in earnings per share over the past 5 quarters and while recent estimates for the company have been raised by analysts, KBH has posted better than expected results. Based on operating earnings yield, the company is undervalued when compared to all of the companies in our coverage universe. Share price changes over the past year indicates that KBH will perform very well over the near term.

Financial Data

(US$ in Thousands)	9 Mos	6 Mos	3 Mos	11/30/2016	11/30/2015	11/30/2014	11/30/2013	11/30/2012
Earnings Per Share	1.39	1.30	1.14	1.12	0.85	9.25	0.46	(0.76)
Cash Flow Per Share	4.59	3.41	2.99	2.20	1.97	(7.07)	(5.37)	0.45
Tang Book Value Per Share	21.28	20.72	20.36	18.23	16.51	15.60	5.69	4.29
Dividends Per Share	0.100	0.100	0.100	0.100	0.100	0.100	0.100	0.138
Dividend Payout %	7.19	7.69	8.77	8.93	11.76	1.08	21.74	...
Income Statement								
Total Revenue	2,965,391	1,821,390	818,596	3,594,646	3,032,030	2,400,949	2,097,130	1,560,115
EBITDA	162,294	81,587	28,473	163,887	149,353	126,229	103,094	(9,964)
Depn & Amortn	5,006	3,314	1,665	3,600	3,400	2,400	1,900	1,600
Income Before Taxes	151,728	72,366	20,699	154,916	124,555	93,522	39,296	(80,850)
Income Taxes	56,400	27,400	7,200	43,700	42,400	(823,400)	(1,600)	(20,100)
Net Income	96,249	46,041	14,259	105,615	84,643	918,349	39,963	(58,953)
Average Shares	98,912	97,732	96,273	96,278	102,857	99,314	91,559	77,106
Balance Sheet								
Current Assets	4,244,784	4,080,987	4,015,224	4,229,657	4,038,359	3,731,616	2,946,327	2,338,519
Total Assets	5,099,559	4,958,795	4,922,580	5,131,624	5,015,371	4,757,550	3,193,635	2,561,698
Current Liabilities	497,311	454,319	438,982	302,920	262,795	238,508	193,844	165,936
Long-Term Obligations	2,502,379	2,510,121	2,504,449	2,640,149	2,625,536	2,576,525	2,150,498	1,722,815
Total Liabilities	3,258,617	3,186,407	3,186,120	3,408,479	3,324,537	3,161,640	2,657,549	2,184,892
Stockholders' Equity	1,840,942	1,772,388	1,736,460	1,723,145	1,690,834	1,595,910	536,086	376,806
Shares Outstanding	86,500	85,548	85,273	94,504	102,411	102,289	94,246	87,837
Statistical Record								
Return on Assets %	2.64	2.49	2.17	2.08	1.73	23.10	1.39	N.M.
Return on Equity %	7.59	7.22	6.37	6.17	5.15	86.15	8.76	N.M.
EBITDA Margin %	5.47	4.48	3.48	4.56	4.93	5.26	4.92	N.M.
Net Margin %	3.25	2.53	1.74	2.94	2.79	38.25	1.91	N.M.
Asset Turnover	0.82	0.80	0.76	0.71	0.62	0.60	0.73	0.61
Current Ratio	8.54	8.98	9.15	13.96	15.37	15.65	15.20	14.09
Debt to Equity	1.36	1.42	1.44	1.53	1.55	1.61	4.01	4.57
Price Range	24.18-14.16	21.52-13.81	17.80-12.20	16.62-9.58	17.32-11.87	20.67-13.78	24.82-14.04	16.90-6.34
P/E Ratio	17.40-10.19	16.55-10.62	15.61-10.70	14.84-8.55	20.38-13.96	2.23-1.49	53.96-30.52	...
Average Yield %	0.53	0.59	0.66	0.71	0.68	0.62	0.54	1.32

Address: 10990 Wilshire Boulevard, Los Angeles, CA 90024
Telephone: 310-231-4000
Fax: 310-231-4222

Web Site: www.kbhome.com
Officers: Jeffrey T. Mezger - Chairman, President, Chief Executive Officer Jeff J. Kaminski - Chief Financial Officer, Executive Vice President

Auditors: Ernst & Young LLP
Investor Contact: 310-231-4000
Transfer Agents: ComputerShare Investor Services, Providence, RI

KBR INC

Exchange	Symbol	Price	52Wk Range	Yield	P/E
NYS	KBR	$19.83 (12/29/2017)	21.09-13.63	1.61	38.88

*7 Year Price Score 54.28   *NYSE Composite Index=100   *12 Month Price Score 110.61

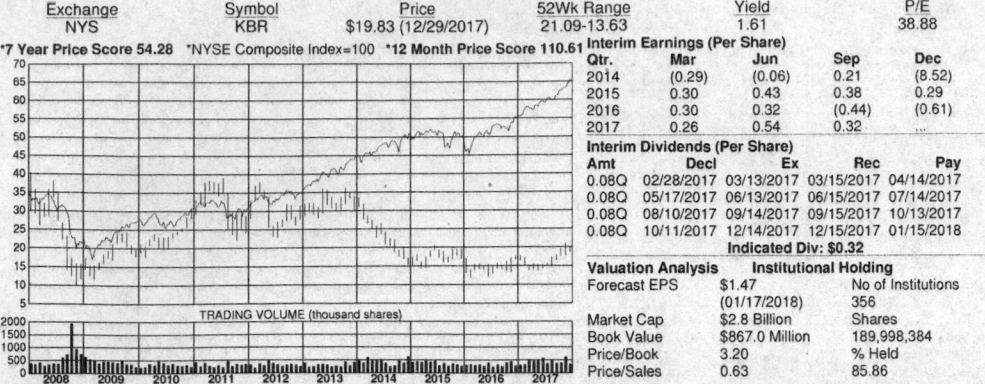

Interim Earnings (Per Share)

Qtr.	Mar	Jun	Sep	Dec
2014	(0.29)	(0.06)	0.21	(8.52)
2015	0.30	0.43	0.38	0.29
2016	0.30	0.32	(0.44)	(0.61)
2017	0.26	0.54	0.32	...

Interim Dividends (Per Share)

Amt	Decl	Ex	Rec	Pay
0.08Q	02/28/2017	03/13/2017	03/15/2017	04/14/2017
0.08Q	05/17/2017	06/13/2017	06/15/2017	07/14/2017
0.08Q	08/10/2017	09/14/2017	09/15/2017	10/13/2017
0.08Q	10/11/2017	12/14/2017	12/15/2017	01/15/2018

Indicated Div: $0.32

Valuation Analysis | **Institutional Holding**

Forecast EPS	$1.47	No of Institutions
	(01/17/2018)	356
Market Cap	$2.8 Billion	Shares
Book Value	$867.0 Million	189,998,384
Price/Book	3.20	% Held
Price/Sales	0.63	85.86

Business Summary: Construction Services (MIC: 7.5.4 SIC: 1629 NAIC: 237990)

KBR is a provider of differentiated, professional services and technologies across the asset and program life-cycle within the government services and hydrocarbons industries. Co.'s segments include: Government Services, which provides life-cycle support solutions to defense, space, aviation and other programs and missions for government agencies; Technology & Consulting, which provides licensed technologies and consulting services to the hydrocarbons value chain, from wellhead to crude refining and through refining and petrochemicals to specialty chemicals production; and Engineering & Construction, which provides project and program delivery capability globally.

Recent Developments: For the quarter ended Sep 30 2017, net income amounted to US$47.0 million versus a net loss of US$57.0 million in the year-earlier quarter. Revenues were US$1.03 billion, down 3.6% from US$1.07 billion the year before. Operating income was US$73.0 million versus a loss of US$67.0 million in the prior-year quarter. Direct operating expenses declined 14.6% to US$947.0 million from US$1.11 billion in the comparable period the year before. Indirect operating expenses decreased 54.8% to US$14.0 million from US$31.0 million in the equivalent prior-year period.

Prospects: Our evaluation of KBR Inc. as of Jan. 14, 2018 is the result of our systematic analysis on three basic characteristics: earnings strength, relative valuation, and recent stock price movement. The company has enjoyed a very positive trend in earnings per share over the past 5 quarters. However, while recent estimates for the company have been lowered by analysts, KBR has posted better than expected results. Based on operating earnings yield, the company is undervalued when compared to all of the companies in our coverage universe. Share price changes over the past year indicates that KBR will perform poorly over the near term.

Financial Data

(US$ in Thousands)	9 Mos	6 Mos	3 Mos	12/31/2016	12/31/2015	12/31/2014	12/31/2013	12/31/2012
Earnings Per Share	0.51	(0.25)	(0.47)	(0.43)	1.40	(8.66)	1.54	0.97
Cash Flow Per Share	2.08	2.01	(0.23)	0.43	0.33	1.16	1.96	0.96
Tang Book Value Per Share	N.M.	N.M.	N.M.	N.M.	4.97	3.98	11.88	11.27
Dividends Per Share	0.320	0.320	0.320	0.320	0.320	0.320	0.320	0.200
Dividend Payout %	62.75	...	...	...	22.86	...	20.78	20.62
Income Statement								
Total Revenue	3,234,000	2,200,000	1,106,000	4,268,000	5,096,000	6,366,000	7,283,000	7,921,000
EBITDA	204,000	147,000	55,000	(27,000)	198,000	(879,000)	385,000	360,000
Depn & Amortn	38,000	27,000	13,000	31,000	35,000	61,000	54,000	65,000
Income Before Taxes	150,000	110,000	42,000	(58,000)	163,000	(940,000)	326,000	288,000
Income Taxes	50,000	34,000	13,000	84,000	86,000	421,000	136,000	86,000
Net Income	159,000	114,000	37,000	(61,000)	203,000	(1,262,000)	229,000	144,000
Average Shares	140,000	141,000	143,000	142,000	144,000	146,000	149,000	149,000
Balance Sheet								
Current Assets	1,518,000	1,495,000	1,881,000	2,047,000	1,844,000	2,544,000	3,010,000	3,668,000
Total Assets	3,601,000	3,581,000	3,962,000	4,144,000	3,412,000	4,199,000	5,516,000	5,767,000
Current Liabilities	1,172,000	1,199,000	1,343,000	1,559,000	1,412,000	2,024,000	1,828,000	2,277,000
Long-Term Obligations	502,000	501,000	685,000	684,000	51,000	63,000	...	84,000
Total Liabilities	2,734,000	2,758,000	3,159,000	3,387,000	2,347,000	3,257,000	2,899,000	3,225,000
Stockholders' Equity	867,000	823,000	803,000	757,000	1,065,000	942,000	2,617,000	2,542,000
Shares Outstanding	140,079	139,877	143,146	142,803	142,058	144,837	148,195	147,584
Statistical Record								
Return on Assets %	1.84	N.M.	N.M.	N.M.	5.33	N.M.	4.06	2.51
Return on Equity %	7.28	N.M.	N.M.	N.M.	20.23	N.M.	8.88	5.70
EBITDA Margin %	6.31	6.68	4.97	N.M.	3.89	N.M.	5.29	4.54
Net Margin %	4.92	5.18	3.35	N.M.	3.98	N.M.	3.14	1.82
Asset Turnover	1.13	1.27	1.19	1.13	1.34	1.31	1.29	1.38
Current Ratio	1.30	1.25	1.40	1.31	1.31	1.26	1.65	1.61
Debt to Equity	0.58	0.61	0.85	0.90	0.05	0.07	...	0.03
Price Range	18.04-13.24	17.67-12.93	17.67-12.19	17.60-11.76	20.60-14.26	33.62-15.23	36.29-28.01	37.93-22.91
P/E Ratio	35.37-25.96	...	...	...	14.71-10.19	...	23.56-18.19	39.10-23.62
Average Yield %	2.04	2.09	2.10	2.16	1.82	1.35	1.00	0.68

Address: 601 Jefferson Street, Suite 3400, Houston, TX 77002
Telephone: 713-753-3011

Web Site: www.kbr.com
Officers: William P. Utt - Chairman, President, Chief Executive Officer Stuart J.B. Bradie - President, Chief Executive Officer

Auditors: KPMG LLP
Investor Contact: 713-753-5082
Transfer Agents: American Stock Transfer & Trust Company, Brooklyn, NY

KELLOGG CO

Exchange	Symbol	Price	52Wk Range	Yield	P/E	Div Achiever
NYS	K	$67.98 (12/29/2017)	76.44-58.87	3.18	30.35	12 Years

*7 Year Price Score 85.13 *NYSE Composite Index=100 *12 Month Price Score 89.16

Interim Earnings (Per Share)

Qtr.	Mar	Jun	Sep	Dec
2014	1.12	0.82	0.62	(0.81)
2015	0.64	0.63	0.58	(0.12)
2016	0.49	0.79	0.82	(0.15)
2017	0.74	0.80	0.85	...

Interim Dividends (Per Share)

Amt	Decl	Ex	Rec	Pay
0.52Q	02/17/2017	02/27/2017	03/01/2017	03/15/2017
0.52Q	04/28/2017	05/30/2017	06/01/2017	06/15/2017
0.54Q	07/28/2017	08/30/2017	09/01/2017	09/15/2017
0.54Q	10/20/2017	11/30/2017	12/01/2017	12/15/2017

Indicated Div: $2.16 (Div. Reinv. Plan)

Valuation Analysis

		Institutional Holding	
Forecast EPS	$4.04 (01/18/2018)	No of Institutions	998
Market Cap	$23.5 Billion	Shares	
Book Value	$1.9 Billion		458,277,248
Price/Book	12.17	% Held	
Price/Sales	1.83		69.81

Business Summary: Food (MIC: 1.2.1 SIC: 2043 NAIC: 311230)

Kellogg manufactures and markets cereal and convenience foods. Co.'s products are cereals and foods such as cookies, crackers, savory snacks, toaster pastries, cereal bars, fruit-flavored snacks, frozen waffles and veggie foods. Co.'s cereal products are marketed under the Kellogg's name and sold to the grocery trade. Co. also markets cookies, crackers, crisps, and other convenience foods, under brands such as Kellogg's, Keebler, Cheez-It, Murray, Austin and Famous Amos. Co. operates the following segments: U.S. Morning Foods; U.S. Snacks; U.S. Specialty; North America Other; Europe; Latin America; and Asia Pacific.

Recent Developments: For the quarter ended Sep 30 2017, net income increased 1.7% to US$297.0 million from US$292.0 million in the year-earlier quarter. Revenues were US$3.27 billion, up 0.6% from US$3.25 billion the year before. Operating income was US$464.0 million versus US$410.0 million in the prior-year quarter, an increase of 13.2%. Direct operating expenses rose 2.6% to US$2.04 billion from US$1.99 billion in the comparable period the year before. Indirect operating expenses decreased 10.1% to US$768.0 million from US$854.0 million in the equivalent prior-year period.

Prospects: Our evaluation of Kellogg Co as of Jan. 14, 2018 is the result of our systematic analysis on three basic characteristics: earnings strength, relative valuation, and recent stock price movement. The company has managed to produce a neutral trend in earnings per share over the past 5 quarters and while recent estimates for the company have been mixed, K has posted better than expected results. Based on operating earnings yield, the company is undervalued when compared to all of the companies in our coverage universe. Share price changes over the past year indicates that K will perform in line with the market over the near term.

Financial Data

(US$ in Thousands)	9 Mos	6 Mos	3 Mos	12/31/2016	01/02/2016	01/03/2015	12/28/2013	12/29/2012
Earnings Per Share	2.24	2.21	2.20	1.96	1.72	1.75	4.94	2.67
Cash Flow Per Share	5.01	4.68	5.23	4.66	4.79	4.93	4.99	4.92
Dividends Per Share	2.100	2.080	2.060	2.040	1.980	1.900	1.800	1.740
Dividend Payout %	93.75	94.12	93.64	104.08	115.12	108.57	36.44	65.17
Income Statement								
Total Revenue	9,714,000	6,441,000	3,254,000	13,014,000	13,525,000	14,580,000	14,792,000	14,197,000
EBITDA	1,638,000	1,050,000	484,000	1,850,000	1,534,000	1,537,000	3,373,000	2,034,000
Depn & Amortn	366,000	240,000	121,000	517,000	534,000	503,000	532,000	448,000
Income Before Taxes	1,084,000	686,000	302,000	927,000	773,000	825,000	2,606,000	1,325,000
Income Taxes	248,000	144,000	42,000	233,000	159,000	186,000	792,000	363,000
Net Income	841,000	544,000	262,000	694,000	614,000	632,000	1,807,000	961,000
Average Shares	348,000	352,000	354,000	354,000	356,000	360,000	365,000	360,000
Balance Sheet								
Current Assets	3,172,000	3,167,000	3,146,000	2,940,000	3,236,000	3,340,000	3,267,000	3,380,000
Total Assets	15,641,000	15,535,000	15,427,000	15,111,000	15,265,000	15,153,000	15,474,000	15,184,000
Current Liabilities	4,647,000	4,688,000	4,732,000	4,474,000	5,739,000	4,364,000	3,835,000	4,523,000
Long-Term Obligations	7,216,000	7,123,000	6,715,000	6,698,000	5,289,000	5,935,000	6,330,000	6,082,000
Total Liabilities	13,714,000	13,701,000	13,421,000	13,201,000	13,137,000	12,364,000	11,929,000	12,765,000
Stockholders' Equity	1,927,000	1,834,000	2,006,000	1,910,000	2,128,000	2,789,000	3,545,000	2,419,000
Shares Outstanding	345,000	346,000	350,000	351,069	350,024	356,002	362,801	361,266
Statistical Record								
Return on Assets %	5.09	5.06	5.08	4.58	4.05	4.06	11.82	7.12
Return on Equity %	38.33	40.95	38.69	34.47	25.04	19.63	60.76	46.12
EBITDA Margin %	16.86	16.30	14.87	14.22	11.34	10.54	22.80	14.33
Net Margin %	8.66	8.45	8.05	5.33	4.54	4.33	12.22	6.77
Asset Turnover	0.83	0.83	0.84	0.86	0.89	0.94	0.97	1.05
Current Ratio	0.68	0.68	0.66	0.66	0.56	0.77	0.85	0.75
Debt to Equity	3.74	3.88	3.35	3.51	2.49	2.13	1.79	2.51
Price Range	77.47-62.37	86.98-68.69	86.98-70.96	86.98-69.96	73.51-61.31	69.39-56.90	67.46-55.85	56.86-46.51
P/E Ratio	34.58-27.84	39.36-31.08	39.54-32.25	44.38-35.69	42.74-35.65	39.65-32.51	13.66-11.31	21.30-17.42
Average Yield %	2.93	2.77	2.70	2.67	2.99	2.98	2.89	3.38

Address: One Kellogg Square, P.O. Box 3599, Battle Creek, MI 49016-3599 **Telephone:** 269-961-2000	**Web Site:** www.kelloggcompany.com **Officers:** John A. Bryant - Executive Chairman, Chairman, President, Chief Executive Officer Gary H. Pilnick - Vice-Chairman, Corporate Development Officer, Chief Legal Officer, Senior Vice President, General Counsel, Secretary	**Auditors:** PricewaterhouseCoopers LLP **Investor Contact:** 269-961-2800 **Transfer Agents:** Wells Fargo Bank, N.A., St. Paul, MN

KEMPER CORP. (DE)

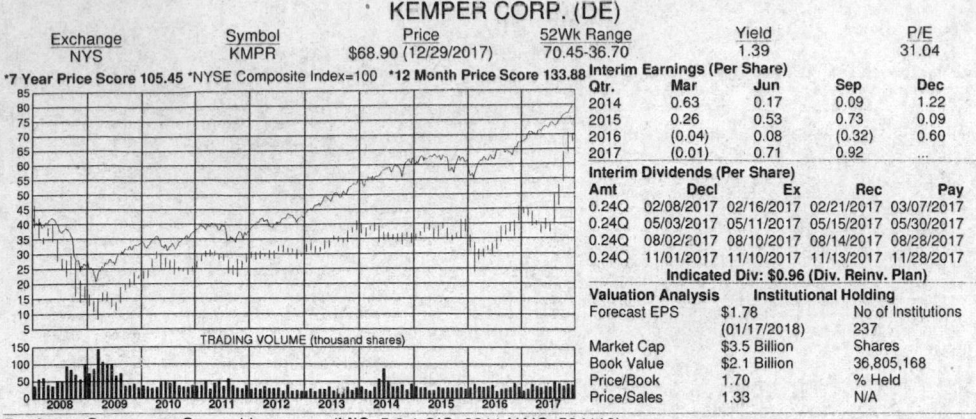

Exchange	Symbol	Price	52Wk Range	Yield	P/E
NYS	KMPR	$68.90 (12/29/2017)	70.45-36.70	1.39	31.04

*7 Year Price Score 105.45 *NYSE Composite Index=100 *12 Month Price Score 133.88

Interim Earnings (Per Share)

Qtr.	Mar	Jun	Sep	Dec
2014	0.63	0.17	0.09	1.22
2015	0.26	0.53	0.73	0.09
2016	(0.04)	0.08	(0.32)	0.60
2017	(0.01)	0.71	0.92	...

Interim Dividends (Per Share)

Amt	Decl	Ex	Rec	Pay
0.24Q	02/08/2017	02/16/2017	02/21/2017	03/07/2017
0.24Q	05/03/2017	05/11/2017	05/15/2017	05/30/2017
0.24Q	08/02/2017	08/10/2017	08/14/2017	08/28/2017
0.24Q	11/01/2017	11/10/2017	11/13/2017	11/28/2017

Indicated Div: $0.96 (Div. Reinv. Plan)

Valuation Analysis

Forecast EPS	$1.78
	(01/17/2018)
Market Cap	$3.5 Billion
Book Value	$2.1 Billion
Price/Book	1.70
Price/Sales	1.33

Institutional Holding

No of Institutions	237
Shares	36,805,168
% Held	N/A

Business Summary: General Insurance (MIC: 5.2.1 SIC: 6311 NAIC: 524113)

Kemper is an insurance holding company, with subsidiaries that provide automobile, homeowners, life, health, and other insurance products to individuals and businesses. Co. conducts its operations through two operating segments: Property and Casualty Insurance and Life and Health Insurance. The Property and Casualty Insurance segment's principal products are personal automobile insurance, both preferred and nonstandard, homeowners insurance, other personal insurance and commercial automobile insurance. The Life and Health Insurance segment's principal products are individual life, accident, health and property insurance. Co. conducts its operations solely in the U.S.

Recent Developments: For the quarter ended Sep 30 2017, income from continuing operations was US$47.8 million compared with a loss of US$18.3 million in the year-earlier quarter. Net income amounted to US$47.7 million versus a net loss of US$16.3 million in the year-earlier quarter. Revenues were US$690.3 million, up 7.7% from US$640.7 million the year before. Net premiums earned were US$598.2 million versus US$558.9 million in the prior-year quarter, an increase of 7.0%. Net investment income rose 10.6% to US$85.9 million from US$77.7 million a year ago.

Prospects: Our evaluation of Kemper Corp. as of Jan. 14, 2018 is the result of our systematic analysis on three basic characteristics: earnings strength, relative valuation, and recent stock price movement. The company has produced a positive trend in earnings per share over the past 5 quarters and while recent estimates for the company have been mixed, KMPR has posted better than expected results. Based on operating earnings yield, the company is overvalued when compared to all of the companies in our coverage universe. Share price changes over the past year indicates that KMPR will perform very well over the near term.

Financial Data

(US$ in Thousands)	9 Mos	6 Mos	3 Mos	12/31/2016	12/31/2015	12/31/2014	12/31/2013	12/31/2012
Earnings Per Share	0.92	0.71	(0.01)	0.33	1.65	2.12	3.80	1.74
Cash Flow Per Share	4.67	4.36	3.82	4.69	4.17	2.49	2.15	1.11
Tang Book Value Per Share	34.20	33.35	32.37	32.22	32.52	33.94	31.26	31.65
Dividends Per Share	0.240	0.240	0.240	0.960	0.960	0.960	0.960	0.960
Dividend Payout %	26.09	33.80	...	290.91	58.18	45.28	25.26	55.17
Income Statement								
Premium Income	598,200	582,500	563,400	2,220,000	2,009,600	1,862,200	2,025,800	2,107,100
Total Revenue	690,300	684,400	651,400	2,521,900	2,340,800	2,196,600	2,426,500	2,462,300
Income Before Taxes	68,300	52,100	(3,500)	3,500	100,300	160,200	314,400	122,400
Income Taxes	20,500	15,500	(3,100)	(9,200)	20,100	47,600	99,900	30,600
Net Income	47,700	36,600	(300)	16,800	85,700	114,500	217,700	103,400
Average Shares	51,566	51,411	51,273	51,214	51,683	53,867	56,983	58,999
Balance Sheet								
Total Assets	8,301,000	8,211,400	8,306,800	8,210,500	8,036,100	7,833,400	7,656,400	8,009,100
Total Liabilities	6,218,600	6,178,000	6,323,200	6,235,300	6,043,700	5,742,700	5,604,900	5,847,400
Stockholders' Equity	2,082,400	2,033,400	1,983,600	1,975,200	1,992,400	2,090,700	2,051,500	2,161,700
Shares Outstanding	51,448	51,293	51,295	51,270	51,326	52,418	55,653	58,454
Statistical Record								
Return on Assets %	2.29	1.78	N.M.	0.21	1.08	1.48	2.78	1.28
Return on Equity %	9.20	7.31	N.M.	0.84	4.20	5.53	10.33	4.71
Net Margin %	6.91	5.35	(0.05)	0.67	3.66	5.21	8.97	4.20
Price Range	53.00-35.60	45.65-30.98	45.65-28.76	45.65-23.80	41.44-34.25	40.88-32.97	41.13-29.50	32.93-27.98
P/E Ratio	57.61-38.70	64.30-43.63	...	138.33-72.12	25.12-20.76	19.28-15.55	10.82-7.76	18.93-16.08
Average Yield %	0.57	0.61	0.64	2.79	2.56	2.62	2.79	3.18

Address: One East Wacker Drive, Chicago, IL 60601 **Telephone:** 312-661-4600	**Web Site:** www.kemper.com **Officers:** Robert Joseph Joyce - Chairman Joseph P. Lacher - President, Chief Executive Officer	**Auditors:** Deloitte & Touche LLP **Investor Contact:** 312-661-4930 **Transfer Agents:** Computershare Trust Company, N.A., Providence, RI

KENNAMETAL INC.

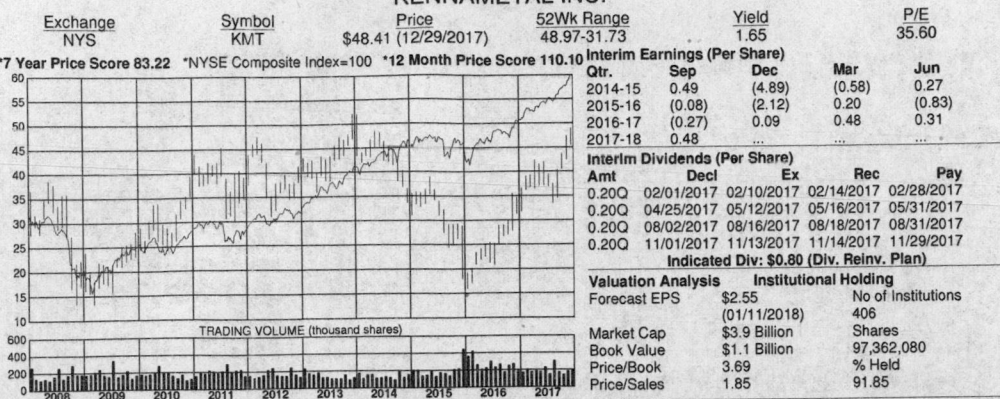

Exchange	Symbol	Price	52Wk Range	Yield	P/E
NYS	KMT	$48.41 (12/29/2017)	48.97-31.73	1.65	35.60

*7 Year Price Score 83.22 *NYSE Composite Index=100 *12 Month Price Score 110.10

Interim Earnings (Per Share)

Qtr.	Sep	Dec	Mar	Jun
2014-15	0.49	(4.89)	(0.58)	0.27
2015-16	(0.08)	(2.12)	0.20	(0.83)
2016-17	(0.27)	0.09	0.48	0.31
2017-18	0.48	...	...	...

Interim Dividends (Per Share)

Amt	Decl	Ex	Rec	Pay
0.20Q	02/01/2017	02/10/2017	02/14/2017	02/28/2017
0.20Q	04/25/2017	05/12/2017	05/16/2017	05/31/2017
0.20Q	08/02/2017	08/16/2017	08/18/2017	08/31/2017
0.20Q	11/01/2017	11/13/2017	11/14/2017	11/29/2017

Indicated Div: $0.80 (Div. Reinv. Plan)

Valuation Analysis | **Institutional Holding**

Forecast EPS	$2.55	No of Institutions
	(01/11/2018)	406
Market Cap	$3.9 Billion	Shares
Book Value	$1.1 Billion	97,362,080
Price/Book	3.69	% Held
Price/Sales	1.85	91.85

Business Summary: Industrial Machinery & Equipment (MIC: 7.2.1 SIC: 3541 NAIC: 333512)

Kennametal engages in the development and application of tungsten carbides, ceramics, materials and solutions used in metal cutting and mission-critical wear applications. Co.'s product offering includes a selection of standard and customized technologies for metalworking applications, such as turning, milling, hole making, tooling systems and services. End users of Co.'s metalworking products include manufacturers engaged in a range of industries including: the manufacturers of transportation vehicles and components, machine tools and light and heavy machinery; airframe and aerospace components; and energy-related components for the oil and gas industry, as well as power generation.

Recent Developments: For the quarter ended Sep 30 2017, net income amounted to US$39.6 million versus a net loss of US$21.2 million in the year-earlier quarter. Revenues were US$542.5 million, up 13.7% from US$477.1 million the year before. Operating income was US$56.5 million versus a loss of US$9.2 million in the prior-year quarter. Direct operating expenses rose 7.1% to US$357.5 million from US$333.6 million in the comparable period the year before. Indirect operating expenses decreased 15.9% to US$128.5 million from US$152.7 million in the equivalent prior-year period.

Prospects: Our evaluation of Kennametal Inc. as of Jan. 14, 2018 is the result of our systematic analysis on three basic characteristics: earnings strength, relative valuation, and recent stock price movement. The company has produced a positive trend in earnings per share over the past 5 quarters and while recent estimates for the company have been raised by analysts, KMT has posted better than expected results. Based on operating earnings yield, the company is undervalued when compared to all of the companies in our coverage universe. Share price changes over the past year indicates that KMT will perform in line with the market over the near term.

Financial Data

(US$ in Thousands)	3 Mos	06/30/2017	06/30/2016	06/30/2015	06/30/2014	06/30/2013	06/30/2012	06/30/2011
Earnings Per Share	1.36	0.61	(2.83)	(4.71)	1.99	2.52	3.77	2.76
Cash Flow Per Share	1.86	2.39	2.74	4.43	3.46	3.58	3.60	2.81
Tang Book Value Per Share	7.03	6.51	5.75	8.09	7.76	10.76	8.50	12.01
Dividends Per Share	0.800	0.800	0.800	0.720	0.720	0.640	0.540	0.480
Dividend Payout %	58.82	131.15	...	...	36.18	25.40	14.32	17.39
Income Statement								
Total Revenue	542,454	2,058,368	2,098,436	2,647,195	2,837,190	2,589,373	2,736,246	2,403,493
EBITDA	82,827	218,373	(53,353)	(224,485)	391,482	407,185	521,257	412,364
Depn & Amortn	26,438	107,656	117,466	131,664	130,222	113,104	104,073	93,471
Income Before Taxes	49,240	81,875	(198,571)	(387,615)	228,809	266,609	389,969	296,133
Income Taxes	9,602	29,895	25,313	(16,654)	66,611	59,693	79,136	63,856
Net Income	39,183	49,138	(225,968)	(373,896)	158,366	203,265	307,230	229,727
Average Shares	82,123	81,169	79,835	79,342	79,667	80,612	81,439	83,173
Balance Sheet								
Current Assets	1,075,915	1,113,901	1,075,341	1,258,546	1,525,196	1,499,473	1,282,962	1,287,585
Total Assets	2,399,700	2,415,496	2,368,793	2,849,529	3,868,086	3,301,039	3,034,188	2,754,469
Current Liabilities	396,967	461,478	427,275	482,744	562,756	467,593	578,622	841,521
Long-Term Obligations	695,357	694,991	699,558	735,885	981,666	703,626	490,608	1,919
Total Liabilities	1,337,720	1,398,202	1,404,470	1,503,722	1,938,830	1,519,213	1,390,338	1,116,397
Stockholders' Equity	1,061,980	1,017,294	964,323	1,345,807	1,929,256	1,781,826	1,643,850	1,638,072
Shares Outstanding	80,967	80,665	79,694	79,375	78,672	77,842	80,085	81,129
Statistical Record								
Return on Assets %	4.67	2.05	N.M.	N.M.	4.42	6.42	10.59	9.15
Return on Equity %	11.00	4.96	N.M.	N.M.	8.53	11.87	18.67	15.56
EBITDA Margin %	15.27	10.61	N.M.	N.M.	13.80	15.73	19.05	17.16
Net Margin %	7.22	2.39	N.M.	N.M.	5.58	7.85	11.23	9.56
Asset Turnover	0.90	0.86	0.80	0.79	0.79	0.82	0.94	0.96
Current Ratio	2.71	2.41	2.52	2.61	2.71	3.21	2.22	1.53
Debt to Equity	0.65	0.68	0.73	0.55	0.51	0.39	0.30	N.M.
Price Range	42.40-26.96	42.40-20.67	34.12-15.91	46.35-30.99	52.07-38.16	43.34-32.19	47.51-29.93	44.01-24.34
P/E Ratio	31.18-19.82	69.51-33.89	...	...	26.17-19.18	17.20-12.77	12.60-7.94	15.95-8.82
Average Yield %	2.22	2.40	3.23	1.89	1.58	1.65	1.39	1.35

Address: 600 Grant Street, Suite 5100, Pittsburgh, PA 15219-2706	**Web Site:** www.kennametal.com	**Auditors:** PricewaterhouseCoopers LLP
Telephone: 412-248-8000	**Officers:** Patrick S. Watson - Vice President, Corporate Controller Ronald M. (Ron) DeFeo - President, Chief Executive Officer, Executive Chairman	**Investor Contact:** 724-539-6559 **Transfer Agents:** Computershare, Jersey City, NJ

KEYCORP

Exchange	Symbol	Price	52Wk Range	Yield	P/E
NYS	KEY	$20.17 (12/29/2017)	20.44-16.47	2.08	17.69

*7 Year Price Score 117.18 *NYSE Composite Index=100 *12 Month Price Score 98.17

Interim Earnings (Per Share)

Qtr.	Mar	Jun	Sep	Dec
2014	0.26	0.24	0.21	0.28
2015	0.26	0.27	0.25	0.26
2016	0.22	0.23	0.17	0.19
2017	0.27	0.36	0.32	...

Interim Dividends (Per Share)

Amt	Decl	Ex	Rec	Pay
0.095Q	05/17/2017	05/25/2017	05/30/2017	06/15/2017
0.095Q	07/12/2017	08/25/2017	08/29/2017	09/15/2017
0.105Q	11/16/2017	11/27/2017	11/28/2017	12/15/2017
0.105Q	01/11/2018	02/26/2018	02/27/2018	03/15/2018

Indicated Div: $0.42 (Div. Reinv. Plan)

Valuation Analysis / **Institutional Holding**

Forecast EPS	$1.31
(01/18/2018)	No of Institutions 973
Market Cap	$21.8 Billion
Book Value	$15.2 Billion — Shares 1,037,040,512
Price/Book	1.43 — % Held 70.65
Price/Sales	3.21

Business Summary: Banking (MIC: 5.1.1 SIC: 6021 NAIC: 522110)

KeyCorp is a bank holding company. Through its subsidiaries, Co. provides a range of retail and commercial banking, commercial leasing, investment management, consumer finance, commercial mortgage servicing and other servicing, and investment banking products and services to individual, corporate and institutional clients through two main segments: Key Community Bank and Key Corporate Bank. Co.'s bank and trust company subsidiary also provide personal and institutional trust custody services, securities lending, personal financial and planning services, and access to mutual funds, among others. At Dec 31 2016, Co. had total assets of $136.45 billion and total deposits of $104.09 billion.

Recent Developments: For the quarter ended Sep 30 2017, income from continuing operations increased 111.0% to US$363.0 million from US$172.0 million in the year-earlier quarter. Net income increased 110.4% to US$364.0 million from US$173.0 million in the year-earlier quarter. Net interest income increased 21.5% to US$948.0 million from US$780.0 million in the year-earlier quarter. Provision for loan losses was US$51.0 million versus US$59.0 million in the prior-year quarter, a decrease of 13.6%. Non-interest income rose 7.8% to US$592.0 million from US$549.0 million, while non-interest expense declined 8.3% to US$992.0 million.

Prospects: Our evaluation of KeyCorp as of Jan. 14, 2018 is the result of our systematic analysis on three basic characteristics: earnings strength, relative valuation, and recent stock price movement. The company has generated a negative trend in earnings per share over the past 5 quarters and while recent estimates for the company have been mixed, KEY has posted results that fell short of analysts expectations. Based on operating earnings yield, the company is undervalued when compared to all of the companies in our coverage universe. Share price changes over the past year indicates that KEY will perform poorly over the near term.

Financial Data

(US$ in Thousands)	9 Mos	6 Mos	3 Mos	12/31/2016	12/31/2015	12/31/2014	12/31/2013	12/31/2012
Earnings Per Share	1.14	0.99	0.86	0.80	1.05	0.99	0.97	0.89
Cash Flow Per Share	1.78	0.35	0.85	1.82	1.35	1.51	1.74	1.44
Tang Book Value Per Share	10.50	10.37	10.17	9.96	11.16	10.57	10.00	9.54
Dividends Per Share	0.360	0.350	0.340	0.330	0.290	0.250	0.215	0.180
Dividend Payout %	31.58	35.35	39.53	41.25	27.62	25.25	22.16	20.22
Income Statement								
Interest Income	3,276,000	2,167,000	1,050,000	3,319,000	2,622,000	2,554,000	2,620,000	2,705,000
Interest Expense	437,000	276,000	132,000	400,000	274,000	261,000	295,000	441,000
Net Interest Income	2,839,000	1,891,000	918,000	2,919,000	2,348,000	2,293,000	2,325,000	2,264,000
Provision for Losses	180,000	129,000	63,000	266,000	166,000	59,000	130,000	229,000
Non-Interest Income	1,822,000	1,230,000	577,000	2,071,000	1,880,000	1,797,000	1,766,000	1,967,000
Non-Interest Expense	3,000,000	2,008,000	1,013,000	3,756,000	2,840,000	2,759,000	2,820,000	2,907,000
Income Before Taxes	1,481,000	984,000	419,000	968,000	1,222,000	1,272,000	1,141,000	1,095,000
Income Taxes	386,000	252,000	94,000	179,000	303,000	326,000	271,000	239,000
Net Income	1,100,000	736,000	324,000	791,000	916,000	900,000	910,000	858,000
Average Shares	1,088,841	1,093,039	1,086,540	938,536	844,489	878,199	912,571	943,259
Balance Sheet								
Net Loans & Leases	86,953,000	87,376,000	86,639,000	86,284,000	59,719,000	57,321,000	54,220,000	52,533,000
Total Assets	136,733,000	135,824,000	134,476,000	136,453,000	95,133,000	93,821,000	92,934,000	89,236,000
Total Deposits	103,446,000	102,821,000	103,982,000	104,087,000	71,046,000	71,998,000	69,262,000	65,993,000
Total Liabilities	121,484,000	120,571,000	119,500,000	121,213,000	84,387,000	83,291,000	82,631,000	78,965,000
Stockholders' Equity	15,249,000	15,253,000	14,976,000	15,240,000	10,746,000	10,530,000	10,303,000	10,271,000
Shares Outstanding	1,079,038	1,092,738	1,097,478	1,079,313	835,751	859,403	890,724	925,768
Statistical Record								
Return on Assets %	0.98	0.96	0.80	0.68	0.97	0.96	1.00	0.96
Return on Equity %	8.79	8.56	7.12	6.07	8.61	8.64	8.85	8.48
Net Interest Margin %	85.48	87.11	87.43	87.95	89.55	89.78	88.74	83.70
Efficiency Ratio %	58.32	56.21	62.26	69.68	63.08	63.41	64.30	62.22
Loans to Deposits	0.84	0.85	0.83	0.83	0.84	0.80	0.78	0.80
Price Range	19.37-12.15	19.36-10.68	19.36-10.29	18.54-10.00	15.65-12.16	14.51-12.14	13.46-8.42	9.04-6.89
P/E Ratio	16.99-10.66	19.56-10.79	22.51-11.97	23.17-12.50	14.90-11.58	14.66-12.26	13.88-8.68	10.16-7.74
Average Yield %	2.05	2.19	2.35	2.60	2.08	1.85	1.94	2.22

Address: 127 Public Square, Cleveland, OH 44114-1306	Web Site: www.key.com	Auditors: Ernst & Young LLP
Telephone: 216-689-3000	Officers: Beth E. Mooney - Chairman, Vice-Chairman, President, Chief Executive Officer, Chief Operating Officer Christopher M. Gorman - Co-Vice Chairman, Division Officer	Investor Contact: 216-689-3000 Transfer Agents: Computershare Investor Services LLC, Providence, RI

KEYSIGHT TECHNOLOGIES INC

Exchange	Symbol	Price	52Wk Range	Yield	P/E
NYS	KEYS	$41.60 (12/29/2017)	45.41-35.30	N/A	74.29

*7 Year Price Score N/A   *NYSE Composite Index=100   *12 Month Price Score 102.82

Interim Earnings (Per Share)

Qtr.	Jan	Apr	Jul	Oct
2013-14	0.44	0.66	0.64	0.61
2014-15	0.41	0.56	0.41	1.62
2015-16	0.37	0.51	0.53	0.54
2016-17	0.63	0.27	(0.10)	(0.22)

Interim Dividends (Per Share)

No Dividends Paid

Valuation Analysis   **Institutional Holding**

Valuation Analysis		Institutional Holding	
Forecast EPS	$2.79	No of Institutions	
	(01/12/2018)	409	
Market Cap	$7.7 Billion	Shares	
Book Value	$2.3 Billion	179,623,296	
Price/Book	3.35	% Held	
Price/Sales	2.43	N/A	

TRADING VOLUME (thousand shares)

Business Summary: Industrial Machinery & Equipment (MIC: 7.2.1 SIC: 3823 NAIC: 334513)

Keysight Technologies is a measurement company providing electronic design and test solutions to communications and electronics industries. Co. provides electronic design and test instruments and systems and related software, software design tools, and related services that are used in the design, development, manufacture, installation, deployment and operation of electronics equipment. Related services include start-up assistance, instrument productivity, application services and instrument calibration and repair. Co. also provides customization, consulting and optimization services throughout the customer's product lifecycle.

Recent Developments: For the year ended Oct 31 2017, net income decreased 69.6% to US$102.0 million from US$335.0 million in the prior year. Revenues were US$3.19 billion, up 9.3% from US$2.92 billion the year before. Operating income was US$239.0 million versus US$406.0 million in the prior year, a decrease of 41.1%. Direct operating expenses rose 14.9% to US$1.49 billion from US$1.29 billion in the comparable period the year before. Indirect operating expenses increased 20.1% to US$1.46 billion from US$1.22 billion in the equivalent prior-year period.

Prospects: Our evaluation of Keysight Technologies Inc. as of Jan. 14, 2018 is the result of our systematic analysis on three basic characteristics: earnings strength, relative valuation, and recent stock price movement. The company has enjoyed a very positive trend in earnings per share over the past 5 quarters and while recent estimates for the company have been raised by analysts, KEYS has posted better than expected results. Based on operating earnings yield, the company is undervalued when compared to all of the companies in our coverage universe. Share price changes over the past year indicates that KEYS will perform in line with the market over the near term.

Financial Data
(US$ in Millions)

	10/31/2017	10/31/2016	10/31/2015	10/31/2014	10/31/2013	10/31/2012	10/31/2011
Earnings Per Share	0.56	1.95	3.00	2.35	...	...	...
Cash Flow Per Share	1.74	2.44	2.22	3.37	...	...	...
Tang Book Value Per Share	N.M.	3.35	2.10	2.14	...	...	...
Income Statement							
Total Revenue	3,189	2,918	2,856	2,933	2,888	3,315	3,316
EBITDA	344	495	514	552	566	801	793
Depn & Amortn	92	85	81	74	65	55	44
Income Before Taxes	179	366	388	475	501	746	749
Income Taxes	77	31	(125)	83	44	(95)	(38)
Net Income	102	335	513	392	457	841	787
Average Shares	182	172	171	167	...	...	...
Balance Sheet							
Current Assets	2,177	1,854	1,579	1,850	972	993	...
Total Assets	5,933	3,803	3,508	3,050	2,028	2,133	...
Current Liabilities	819	644	686	769	560	595	...
Long-Term Obligations	2,038	1,100	1,099	1,099	...	...	...
Total Liabilities	3,623	2,290	2,206	2,281	783	828	...
Stockholders' Equity	2,310	1,513	1,302	769	1,245	1,305	...
Shares Outstanding	186	169	169	167	...	...	...
Statistical Record							
Return on Assets %	2.10	9.14	15.65	...	21.97	...	...
Return on Equity %	5.34	23.74	49.54	...	35.84	...	...
EBITDA Margin %	10.79	16.96	18.00	18.82	19.60	24.16	23.91
Net Margin %	3.20	11.48	17.96	13.37	15.82	25.37	23.73
Asset Turnover	0.66	0.80	0.87	...	1.39	...	...
Current Ratio	2.66	2.88	2.30	2.41	1.74	1.67	...
Debt to Equity	0.88	0.73	0.84	1.43	...	...	...
Price Range	44.67-31.82	33.37-21.18	38.89-29.54	31.50-28.25	...	...	...
P/E Ratio	79.77-56.82	17.11-10.86	12.96-9.85	13.40-12.02	...	...	...

Address: 1400 Fountaingrove Parkway, Santa Rosa, CA 95403
Telephone: 800-829-4444

Web Site: www.keysight.com
Officers: Paul N. Clark - Chairman Ronald S. Nersesian - President, Chief Executive Officer

Auditors: PricewaterhouseCoopers LLP
Transfer Agents: Computershare Trust Company, N.A.

KILROY REALTY CORP

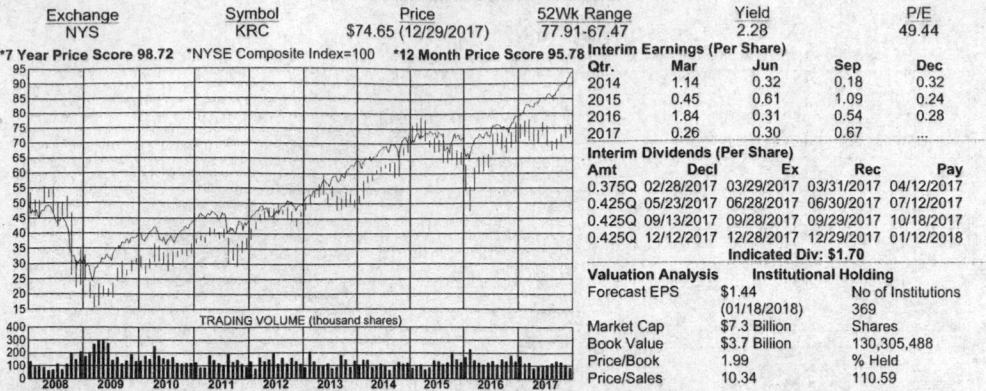

Exchange	Symbol	Price	52Wk Range	Yield	P/E
NYS	KRC	$74.65 (12/29/2017)	77.91-67.47	2.28	49.44

*7 Year Price Score 98.72   *NYSE Composite Index=100   *12 Month Price Score 95.78

Interim Earnings (Per Share)

Qtr.	Mar	Jun	Sep	Dec
2014	1.14	0.32	0.18	0.32
2015	0.45	0.61	1.09	0.24
2016	1.84	0.31	0.54	0.28
2017	0.26	0.30	0.67	...

Interim Dividends (Per Share)

Amt	Decl	Ex	Rec	Pay
0.375Q	02/28/2017	03/29/2017	03/31/2017	04/12/2017
0.425Q	05/23/2017	06/28/2017	06/30/2017	07/12/2017
0.425Q	09/13/2017	09/28/2017	09/29/2017	10/18/2017
0.425Q	12/12/2017	12/28/2017	12/29/2017	01/12/2018

Indicated Div: $1.70

Valuation Analysis		Institutional Holding	
Forecast EPS	$1.44	No of Institutions	
	(01/18/2018)	369	
Market Cap	$7.3 Billion	Shares	
Book Value	$3.7 Billion	130,305,488	
Price/Book	1.99	% Held	
Price/Sales	10.34	110.59	

Business Summary: REITs (MIC: 5.3.1 SIC: 6798 NAIC: 525930)

Kilroy Realty is a real estate investment trust, which owns, develops, acquires and manages real estate assets, consisting primarily of Class A properties in the coastal regions of Los Angeles, Orange County, San Diego County, the San Francisco Bay Area and greater Seattle. Co. owns its interests in all of its properties through Kilroy Realty, L.P. (the Operating Partnership) and Kilroy Realty Finance Partnership, L.P. and generally conducts substantially all of its operations through the Operating Partnership. As of Dec 31 2016, Co. had a stabilized portfolio of 108 office properties and one residential property.

Recent Developments: For the quarter ended Sep 30 2017, net income increased 33.9% to US$75.5 million from US$56.4 million in the year-earlier quarter. Revenues were US$181.5 million, up 7.8% from US$168.3 million the year before.

Prospects: Our evaluation of Kilroy Realty Corp. as of Jan. 14, 2018 is the result of our systematic analysis on three basic characteristics: earnings strength, relative valuation, and recent stock price movement. The company has enjoyed a very positive trend in earnings per share over the past 5 quarters. Because the company lacks sufficient analyst estimate data, we place greater weight on the historical EPS trend as the measure of earnings strength. Based on operating earnings yield, the company is overvalued when compared to all of the companies in our coverage universe. Share price changes over the past year indicates that KRC will perform well over the near term.

Financial Data

(US$ in Thousands)	9 Mos	6 Mos	3 Mos	12/31/2016	12/31/2015	12/31/2014	12/31/2013	12/31/2012
Earnings Per Share	1.51	1.38	1.39	2.97	2.42	1.95	0.36	2.56
Cash Flow Per Share	3.75	3.93	3.73	3.73	3.03	2.95	3.11	2.59
Tang Book Value Per Share	37.51	37.22	37.27	35.94	32.28	28.68	27.62	26.66
Dividends Per Share	3.500	3.450	3.400	3.375	1.400	1.400	1.400	1.400
Dividend Payout %	231.79	250.00	244.60	113.64	57.85	71.79	388.89	54.69
Income Statement								
Total Revenue	541,440	359,906	179,308	642,572	581,275	521,725	465,098	404,912
EBITDA	197,379	106,834	53,518	529,837	455,543	280,123	235,372	209,613
Depn & Amortn	1,457	1,025	(50)	172,000	159,500	153,800	145,300	125,900
Income Before Taxes	148,075	72,587	37,281	303,798	238,604	59,313	15,837	5,447
Net Income	136,083	64,973	33,525	293,758	234,081	180,219	43,880	270,914
Average Shares	98,911	98,827	98,018	93,023	90,395	84,967	79,108	69,639
Balance Sheet								
Current Assets	520,666	659,005	740,353	497,339	270,943	274,582	233,031	396,317
Total Assets	6,838,299	6,995,367	6,993,665	6,706,633	5,939,469	5,633,736	5,111,028	4,616,084
Current Liabilities	507,210	468,055	461,498	424,697	281,315	258,729	229,957	183,658
Long-Term Obligations	2,435,209	2,564,841	2,566,026	2,320,123	2,238,508	2,469,413	2,204,938	2,040,935
Total Liabilities	3,148,436	3,238,898	3,234,342	3,163,638	2,768,503	2,967,526	2,649,716	2,426,454
Stockholders' Equity	3,689,863	3,756,469	3,759,323	3,542,995	3,170,966	2,666,210	2,461,312	2,189,630
Shares Outstanding	98,382	98,351	98,275	93,219	92,258	86,259	82,153	74,926
Statistical Record								
Return on Assets %	2.56	2.28	2.32	4.63	4.05	3.35	0.90	6.70
Return on Equity %	4.72	4.28	4.32	8.73	8.02	7.03	1.89	15.19
EBITDA Margin %	36.45	29.68	29.85	82.46	78.37	53.69	50.61	51.77
Net Margin %	25.13	18.05	18.70	45.72	40.27	34.54	9.43	66.91
Asset Turnover	0.11	0.10	0.10	0.10	0.10	0.10	0.10	0.10
Current Ratio	1.03	1.41	1.60	1.17	0.96	1.06	1.01	2.16
Debt to Equity	0.66	0.68	0.68	0.65	0.71	0.93	0.90	0.93
Price Range	77.91-66.73	77.91-66.06	77.91-59.89	76.88-47.38	78.86-62.83	71.10-50.18	59.58-47.37	49.88-37.92
P/E Ratio	51.60-44.19	56.46-47.87	56.05-43.09	25.89-15.95	32.59-25.96	36.46-25.73	165.50-131.58	19.48-14.81
Average Yield %	4.84	4.77	4.88	5.16	2.00	2.29	2.69	3.05

Address: 12200 W. Olympic Boulevard, Suite 200, Los Angeles, CA 90064	Web Site: www.kilroyrealty.com	Auditors: Deloitte & Touche LLP
Telephone: 310-481-8400	**Officers:** John B. Kilroy - Chairman, President, Chief Executive Officer Justin William Smart - Executive Vice President	**Investor Contact:** 310-481-8400
		Transfer Agents: Computershare Trust Company, N.A., Canton, MA

KIMBERLY-CLARK CORP.

Exchange	Symbol	Price	52Wk Range	Yield	P/E	Div Achiever
NYS	KMB	$120.66 (12/29/2017)	135.00-109.87	3.22	19.88	42 Years

*7 Year Price Score 96.24 *NYSE Composite Index=100 *12 Month Price Score 89.23

Interim Earnings (Per Share)

Qtr.	Mar	Jun	Sep	Dec
2014	1.41	1.35	1.50	(0.21)
2015	1.27	(0.83)	1.41	0.92
2016	1.50	1.56	1.52	1.41
2017	1.57	1.49	1.60	...

Interim Dividends (Per Share)

Amt	Decl	Ex	Rec	Pay
0.97Q	01/24/2017	03/08/2017	03/10/2017	04/04/2017
0.97Q	04/20/2017	06/07/2017	06/09/2017	07/05/2017
0.97Q	08/01/2017	09/07/2017	09/08/2017	10/03/2017
0.97Q	11/16/2017	12/07/2017	12/08/2017	01/03/2018

Indicated Div: $3.88 (Div. Reinv. Plan)

Valuation Analysis | **Institutional Holding**

Forecast EPS	$6.20	No of Institutions
	(01/18/2018)	1796
Market Cap	$42.4 Billion	Shares
Book Value	$259.0 Million	333,184,320
Price/Book	163.87	% Held
Price/Sales	2.33	64.22

TRADING VOLUME (thousand shares)

Business Summary: Household & Personal Products (MIC: 1.7.1 SIC: 2679 NAIC: 322299)

Kimberly-Clark is engaged in the manufacturing and marketing of a range of products made from natural or synthetic fibers using technologies in fibers, nonwovens and absorbency. Co. is organized into three operating segments: personal care brands, which provides disposable diapers, training and youth pants, swimpants, baby wipes, feminine and incontinence care products, and other related products; consumer tissue, which provides facial and bathroom tissue, paper towels, napkins and related products; and K-C professional, which provides wipers, tissue, towels, apparel, soaps and sanitizers.

Recent Developments: For the quarter ended Sep 30 2017, net income increased 2.8% to US$579.0 million from US$563.0 million in the year-earlier quarter. Revenues were US$4.64 billion, up 1.0% from US$4.59 billion the year before. Operating income was US$854.0 million versus US$836.0 million in the prior-year quarter, an increase of 2.2%. Direct operating expenses rose 1.9% to US$2.98 billion from US$2.92 billion in the comparable period the year before. Indirect operating expenses decreased 3.5% to US$805.0 million from US$834.0 million in the equivalent prior-year period.

Prospects: Our evaluation of Kimberly-Clark Corp. as of Jan. 14, 2018 is the result of our systematic analysis on three basic characteristics: earnings strength, relative valuation, and recent stock price movement. The company has produced a positive trend in earnings per share over the past 5 quarters and while recent estimates for the company have been mixed, KMB has posted better than expected results. Based on operating earnings yield, the company is undervalued when compared to all of the companies in our coverage universe. Share price changes over the past year indicates that KMB will perform well over the near term.

Financial Data

(US$ in Thousands)	9 Mos	6 Mos	3 Mos	12/31/2016	12/31/2015	12/31/2014	12/31/2013	12/31/2012
Earnings Per Share	6.07	5.99	6.06	5.99	2.77	4.04	5.53	4.42
Cash Flow Per Share	8.33	8.69	8.75	8.97	6.34	7.60	7.92	8.34
Tang Book Value Per Share	N.M.	N.M.	N.M.	...	...	N.M.	3.95	5.01
Dividends Per Share	3.830	3.780	3.730	3.680	3.520	3.360	3.240	2.960
Dividend Payout %	63.10	63.11	61.55	61.44	127.08	83.17	58.59	66.97
Income Statement								
Total Revenue	13,677,000	9,037,000	4,483,000	18,202,000	18,591,000	19,724,000	21,152,000	21,063,000
EBITDA	3,027,000	1,991,000	1,012,000	4,022,000	2,359,000	3,383,000	3,247,000	2,715,000
Depn & Amortn	540,000	358,000	178,000	705,000	746,000	862,000	39,000	29,000
Income Before Taxes	2,248,000	1,469,000	753,000	3,009,000	1,335,000	2,255,000	2,945,000	2,420,000
Income Taxes	633,000	409,000	207,000	922,000	418,000	856,000	929,000	768,000
Net Income	1,661,000	1,094,000	563,000	2,166,000	1,013,000	1,526,000	2,142,000	1,750,000
Average Shares	354,800	356,700	358,600	361,700	366,300	377,400	387,300	396,100
Balance Sheet								
Current Assets	5,226,000	5,390,000	5,112,000	5,115,000	5,426,000	5,559,000	6,550,000	6,589,000
Total Assets	15,049,000	15,070,000	14,758,000	14,602,000	14,842,000	15,526,000	18,919,000	19,873,000
Current Liabilities	5,412,000	5,889,000	5,864,000	5,846,000	6,349,000	6,226,000	5,848,000	6,091,000
Long-Term Obligations	7,057,000	6,777,000	6,425,000	6,439,000	6,106,000	5,630,000	5,386,000	5,070,000
Total Liabilities	14,790,000	14,968,000	14,622,000	14,646,000	14,952,000	14,725,000	13,991,000	14,339,000
Stockholders' Equity	259,000	102,000	136,000	(44,000)	(110,000)	801,000	4,928,000	5,534,000
Shares Outstanding	351,757	353,302	354,928	356,568	360,860	365,336	380,799	389,275
Statistical Record								
Return on Assets %	14.47	14.40	14.77	14.67	6.67	8.86	11.04	8.89
Return on Equity %	776.34	1,442.28	1,782.86	...	293.20	53.27	40.95	30.81
EBITDA Margin %	22.13	22.03	22.57	22.10	12.69	17.15	15.35	12.89
Net Margin %	12.14	12.11	12.56	11.90	5.45	7.74	10.13	8.31
Asset Turnover	1.22	1.22	1.23	1.23	1.22	1.15	1.09	1.07
Current Ratio	0.97	0.92	0.87	0.87	0.85	0.89	1.12	1.08
Debt to Equity	27.25	66.44	47.24	...	...	7.03	1.09	0.92
Price Range	135.00-112.15	137.94-112.15	138.13-112.15	138.13-112.15	129.54-103.35	118.28-98.99	105.15-80.54	84.28-68.18
P/E Ratio	22.24-18.48	23.03-18.72	22.79-18.51	23.06-18.72	46.77-37.31	29.28-24.50	19.02-14.56	19.07-15.42
Average Yield %	3.10	3.01	2.97	2.91	3.13	3.16	3.45	3.85

Address: P.O. Box 619100, Dallas, TX 75261-9100	Web Site: www.kimberly-clark.com	Auditors: Deloitte & Touche LLP
Telephone: 972-281-1200	Officers: Thomas J. Falk - Chairman, President, Chief Executive Officer Michael D. Hsu - President, Chief Operating Officer, Division Officer	Investor Contact: 972-281-1440 Transfer Agents: ComputerShare Investor Services, Providence, RI

KIMCO REALTY CORP

Exchange	Symbol	Price	52Wk Range	Yield	P/E
NYS	KIM	$18.15 (12/29/2017)	26.07 17.30	6.17	21.10

*7 Year Price Score 72.63   *NYSE Composite Index=100   *12 Month Price Score 85.38

Interim Earnings (Per Share)

Qtr.	Mar	Jun	Sep	Dec
2014	0.18	0.18	0.44	0.10
2015	0.71	0.27	0.15	0.86
2016	0.31	0.46	(0.13)	0.16
2017	0.15	0.31	0.24	...

Interim Dividends (Per Share)

Amt	Decl	Ex	Rec	Pay
0.27Q	02/02/2017	04/03/2017	04/05/2017	04/17/2017
0.27Q	04/26/2017	07/03/2017	07/06/2017	07/17/2017
0.27Q	07/26/2017	10/03/2017	10/04/2017	10/16/2017
0.28Q	10/25/2017	12/29/2017	01/02/2018	01/16/2018

Indicated Div: $1.12 (Div. Reinv. Plan)

Valuation Analysis   Institutional Holding

Forecast EPS	$0.86	No of Institutions	
	(01/13/2018)	628	
Market Cap	$7.7 Billion	Shares	
Book Value	$5.2 Billion	472,102,688	
Price/Book	1.48	% Held	
Price/Sales	6.53	93.66	

TRADING VOLUME (thousand shares)

Business Summary: REITs (MIC: 5.3.1 SIC: 6798 NAIC: 525930)

Kimco Realty is a real estate investment trust engages in the ownership, management, development and operation of open-air shopping centers. As of Dec 31 2016, Co. had interests in 525 shopping center properties located in 34 states, Puerto Rico and Canada. In addition, as of Dec 31 2016, Co. had 384 other property interests, through Co.'s preferred equity investments and other real estate investments. Co.'s ownership interests in real estate consist of its consolidated portfolio and portfolios where it owns an economic interest, such as properties in Co.'s investment real estate management programs, where Co. partners with institutional investors and also retains management.

Recent Developments: For the quarter ended Sep 30 2017, income from continuing operations was US$81.7 million compared with a loss of US$51.3 million in the year-earlier quarter. Net income amounted to US$122.2 million versus a net loss of US$41.5 million in the year-earlier quarter. Revenues were US$294.8 million, up 3.4% from US$285.1 million the year before. Revenues from property income rose 4.2% to US$290.9 million from US$279.3 million in the corresponding quarter a year earlier.

Prospects: Our evaluation of Kimco Realty Corp. as of Jan. 14, 2018 is the result of our systematic analysis on three basic characteristics: earnings strength, relative valuation, and recent stock price movement. The company has enjoyed a very positive trend in earnings per share over the past 5 quarters. Because the company lacks sufficient analyst estimate data, we place greater weight on the historical EPS trend as the measure of earnings strength. Based on operating earnings yield, the company is undervalued when compared to all of the companies in our coverage universe. Share price changes over the past year indicates that KIM will perform in line with the market over the near term.

Financial Data (US$ in Thousands)	9 Mos	6 Mos	3 Mos	12/31/2016	12/31/2015	12/31/2014	12/31/2013	12/31/2012
Earnings Per Share	0.86	0.49	0.64	0.79	2.00	0.89	0.43	0.42
Cash Flow Per Share	1.51	1.60	1.45	1.41	1.20	1.54	1.40	1.18
Tang Book Value Per Share	12.25	12.29	12.24	12.37	12.21	11.59	11.31	11.69
Dividends Per Share	1.065	1.050	1.035	1.035	0.975	0.915	0.855	0.780
Dividend Payout %	123.84	214.29	161.72	131.01	48.75	102.81	198.84	185.71
Income Statement								
Total Revenue	885,609	590,764	293,588	1,170,792	1,166,769	993,897	946,673	922,304
EBITDA	536,240	348,604	185,984	614,416	693,273	577,993	489,434	522,236
Depn & Amortn	275,787	187,344	92,074	355,320	344,527	273,093	257,855	262,742
Income Before Taxes	120,623	68,688	47,428	68,025	168,916	102,107	34,667	34,069
Income Taxes	(2,224)	(1,527)	(493)	72,545	60,230	22,438	34,520	3,939
Net Income	341,179	220,149	76,733	378,850	894,115	424,001	236,281	266,073
Average Shares	424,311	424,944	424,146	419,709	412,851	411,038	408,614	406,689
Balance Sheet								
Current Assets	352,644	334,493	351,210	332,410	372,351	449,943	375,860	339,529
Total Assets	11,702,241	11,558,320	11,248,419	11,230,600	11,344,171	10,285,728	9,663,630	9,740,807
Current Liabilities	123,270	124,679	124,680	4,197,519	4,026,569	3,432,819	3,414,833	3,400,526
Long-Term Obligations	5,551,271	5,390,186	5,124,883	1,139,117	1,614,982	1,428,131	1,035,354	1,003,190
Total Liabilities	6,488,909	6,326,997	6,037,084	5,974,461	6,297,871	5,510,943	5,031,213	4,975,647
Stockholders' Equity	5,213,332	5,231,323	5,211,335	5,256,139	5,046,300	4,774,785	4,632,417	4,765,160
Shares Outstanding	425,633	425,637	425,639	425,034	413,430	411,819	409,731	407,782
Statistical Record								
Return on Assets %	3.66	2.22	2.80	3.35	8.27	4.25	2.44	2.74
Return on Equity %	7.98	4.83	6.06	7.33	18.21	9.01	5.03	5.61
EBITDA Margin %	60.55	59.01	63.35	52.48	59.42	58.15	51.70	56.62
Net Margin %	38.52	37.27	26.14	32.36	76.63	42.66	24.96	28.85
Asset Turnover	0.10	0.10	0.10	0.10	0.11	0.10	0.10	0.10
Current Ratio	2.86	2.68	2.82	0.08	0.09	0.13	0.11	0.10
Debt to Equity	1.06	1.03	0.98	0.22	0.32	0.30	0.22	0.21
Price Range	28.95-17.30	32.17-17.30	32.17-21.59	32.17-24.71	28.33-22.26	25.91-19.75	25.00-19.25	21.03-16.27
P/E Ratio	33.66-20.12	65.65-35.31	50.27-33.73	40.72-31.28	14.16-11.13	29.11-22.19	58.14-44.77	50.07-38.74
Average Yield %	4.75	4.17	3.77	3.67	3.85	4.00	3.93	4.08

Address: 3333 New Hyde Park Road, New Hyde Park, NY 11042 **Telephone:** 516-869-9000	**Web Site:** www.kimcorealty.com **Officers:** Milton Cooper - Executive Chairman Ross Cooper - President, Chief Investment Officer	**Auditors:** PricewaterhouseCoopers LLP **Investor Contact:** 866-831-4297 **Transfer Agents:** Wells Fargo Shareholder Services, St. Paul, MN

KINDRED HEALTHCARE INC

Exchange	Symbol	Price	52Wk Range	Yield	P/E
NYS	KND	$9.70 (12/29/2017)	11.70-5.60	N/A	N/A

*7 Year Price Score 45.32   *NYSE Composite Index=100   *12 Month Price Score 87.03

Interim Earnings (Per Share)

Qtr.	Mar	Jun	Sep	Dec
2014	0.15	(0.67)	(0.07)	0.00
2015	(1.84)	0.25	(0.17)	0.00
2016	0.15	0.26	(7.89)	0.00
2017	(0.07)	(4.68)	(1.09)	...

Interim Dividends (Per Share)

Amt	Decl	Ex	Rec	Pay
0.12Q	05/04/2016	05/16/2016	05/18/2016	06/10/2016
0.12Q	08/04/2016	08/16/2016	08/18/2016	09/02/2016
0.12Q	11/07/2016	11/17/2016	11/21/2016	12/09/2016
0.12Q	02/27/2017	03/09/2017	03/13/2017	03/31/2017

Valuation Analysis   **Institutional Holding**

Forecast EPS	$0.31	No of Institutions	273
	(01/09/2018)		
Market Cap	$843.2 Million	Shares	95,400,320
Book Value	N/A	% Held	93.85
Price/Book	N/A		
Price/Sales	N/A		

Business Summary: Hospitals & Health Care Facilities (MIC: 4.2.1 SIC: 8059 NAIC: 623110)

Kindred Healthcare is a healthcare services company, which operates a home health, hospice and community care business, transitional care hospitals, inpatient rehabilitation hospitals (IRFs), a contract rehabilitation services business, nursing centers, and assisted living facilities. Co. has four divisions: the Kindred at Home, which provides home health, hospice, and community care services; the hospital, which provides long-term acute care services; the Kindred Rehabilitation Services, which operates IRFs, manages hospital-based acute rehabilitation units and provides rehabilitation services; and the nursing center, which operates nursing centers and assisted living facilities.

Recent Developments: For the quarter ended Sep 30 2017, loss from continuing operations was US$18.4 million compared with a loss of US$649.2 million in the year-earlier quarter. Net loss amounted to US$81.7 million versus a net loss of US$671.3 million in the year-earlier quarter. Revenues were US$1.48 billion, down 5.5% from US$1.56 billion the year before. Indirect operating expenses decreased 22.4% to US$1.50 billion from US$1.93 billion in the equivalent prior-year period.

Prospects: Our evaluation of Kindred Healthcare Inc. as of Jan. 14, 2018 is the result of our systematic analysis on three basic characteristics: earnings strength, relative valuation, and recent stock price movement. The company has managed to produce a neutral trend in earnings per share over the past 5 quarters. However, while recent estimates for the company have been mixed, KND has posted better than expected results. Based on operating earnings yield, the company is overvalued when compared to all of the companies in our coverage universe. Share price changes over the past year indicates that KND will perform very poorly over the near term.

Financial Data
(US$ in Thousands)

	9 Mos	6 Mos	3 Mos	12/31/2016	12/31/2015	12/31/2014	12/31/2013	12/31/2012
Earnings Per Share	(1.09)	(4.68)	(0.07)	(7.65)	(1.11)	(1.36)	(3.23)	(0.78)
Cash Flow Per Share	0.38	4.25	(4.31)	2.13	1.93	1.80	3.82	5.07
Tang Book Value Per Share	N.M.	N.M.	N.M.	N.M.	N.M.	0.62	N.M.	N.M.
Dividends Per Share	...	...	0.120	0.480	0.480	0.480	0.240	...
Income Statement								
Total Revenue	1,477,141	1,532,022	1,768,396	7,219,519	7,054,907	5,027,599	4,900,510	6,181,291
EBITDA	67,117	(33,154)	105,425	90,815	265,135	308,021	185,233	293,737
Depn & Amortn	25,585	30,365	34,960	159,373	127,400	133,900	135,200	179,100
Income Before Taxes	(19,614)	(124,320)	11,131	(303,205)	(94,660)	5,358	(58,016)	6,741
Income Taxes	(1,225)	...	2,302	314,330	(42,797)	462	(13,204)	39,112
Net Income	(95,786)	(409,118)	(5,748)	(664,230)	(93,384)	(79,837)	(168,492)	(40,367)
Average Shares	87,597	87,506	87,085	86,800	84,558	58,634	52,249	51,659
Balance Sheet								
Current Assets	1,618,631	1,823,565	1,574,016	1,516,538	1,500,899	1,390,062	1,196,728	1,273,766
Total Assets	5,871,751	5,977,969	6,144,609	6,112,724	6,518,936	5,652,964	3,945,869	4,237,946
Current Liabilities	1,043,342	1,207,542	924,725	1,005,728	1,111,212	857,263	792,421	835,331
Long-Term Obligations	3,302,936	3,303,539	3,344,511	3,215,062	3,137,025	2,852,531	1,579,391	1,648,706
Total Liabilities	5,567,793	5,584,559	5,345,286	5,300,173	5,019,082	4,211,097	2,863,212	2,981,787
Stockholders' Equity	303,958	393,410	799,323	812,551	1,499,854	1,441,867	1,082,657	1,256,159
Shares Outstanding	86,980	87,025	85,691	85,166	83,792	69,977	54,165	53,280
Statistical Record								
EBITDA Margin %	4.54	N.M.	5.96	1.26	3.76	6.13	3.78	4.75
Current Ratio	1.55	1.51	1.70	1.51	1.35	1.62	1.51	1.52
Debt to Equity	10.87	8.40	4.18	3.96	2.09	1.98	1.46	1.31
Price Range	11.70-5.60	12.42-6.15	14.90-6.15	14.90-6.15	24.42-11.44	26.66-17.84	19.87-9.76	13.41-7.79
Average Yield %	...	...	1.21	4.54	2.52	2.21	1.79	...

Address: 680 South Fourth Street, Louisville, KY 40202-2412 **Telephone:** 502-596-7300	**Web Site:** www.kindredhealthcare.com **Officers:** Edward L. Kuntz - Chairman Paul J. Diaz - Executive Vice-Chairman, President, Chief Executive Officer	**Auditors:** PricewaterhouseCoopers LLP **Investor Contact:** 502-596-7734 **Transfer Agents:** Computershare

KINDER MORGAN INC.

Exchange	Symbol	Price	52Wk Range	Yield	P/E
NYS	KMI	$18.07 (12/29/2017)	22.94-16.76	2.77	32.27

*7 Year Price Score N/A   *NYSE Composite Index=100   *12 Month Price Score 83.79

Interim Earnings (Per Share)

Qtr.	Mar	Jun	Sep	Dec
2014	0.28	0.27	0.32	0.02
2015	0.20	0.15	0.08	(0.33)
2016	0.12	0.15	(0.10)	0.08
2017	0.18	0.15	0.15	...

Interim Dividends (Per Share)

Amt	Decl	Ex	Rec	Pay
0.125Q	04/19/2017	04/27/2017	05/01/2017	05/15/2017
0.125Q	07/19/2017	07/27/2017	07/31/2017	08/15/2017
0.125Q	10/18/2017	10/30/2017	10/31/2017	11/15/2017
0.125Q	01/17/2018	01/30/2018	01/31/2018	02/15/2018

Indicated Div: $0.50 (Div. Reinv. Plan)

Valuation Analysis

		Institutional Holding	
Forecast EPS	$0.75	No of Institutions	
	(01/26/2018)	1241	
Market Cap	$40.3 Billion	Shares	
Book Value	$35.2 Billion	1,646,998,656	
Price/Book	1.14	% Held	
Price/Sales	2.99	48.99	

Business Summary: Equipment & Services (MIC: 9.1.3 SIC: 4923 NAIC: 221210)

Kinder Morgan is an energy infrastructure company in North America. Co.'s segments are: Natural Gas Pipelines, which include natural gas sales, transportation, storage, gathering, processing and treating, and the terminaling of liquified natural gas; carbon dioxide (CO_2), which produces, transports, and markets CO_2 to oil fields; Terminals, which includes the ownership and/or operation of liquids and bulk terminal facilities and Jones Act tankers; Products Pipelines, which includes the operation of refined petroleum products, natural gas liquids and crude oil and condensate pipelines; and Kinder Morgan Canada, which includes the ownership and operation of the Trans Mountain pipeline system.

Recent Developments: For the quarter ended Sep 30 2017, net income amounted to US$387.0 million versus a net loss of US$183.0 million in the year-earlier quarter. Revenues were US$3.28 billion, down 1.5% from US$3.33 billion the year before. Operating income was US$830.0 million versus US$882.0 million in the prior-year quarter, a decrease of 5.9%. Direct operating expenses rose 4.5% to US$1.62 billion from US$1.55 billion in the comparable period the year before. Indirect operating expenses decreased 7.3% to US$835.0 million from US$901.0 million in the equivalent prior-year period.

Prospects: Our evaluation of Kinder Morgan, Inc. as of Jan. 21, 2018 is the result of our systematic analysis on three basic characteristics: earnings strength, relative valuation, and recent stock price movement. The company has produced a positive trend in earnings per share over the past 5 quarters and while recent estimates for the company have been raised by analysts, KMI has posted better than expected results. Based on operating earnings yield, the company is about fairly valued when compared to all of the companies in our coverage universe. Share price changes over the past year indicates that KMI will perform very poorly over the near term.

Financial Data

(US$ in Thousands)	9 Mos	6 Mos	3 Mos	12/31/2016	12/31/2015	12/31/2014	12/31/2013	12/31/2012
Earnings Per Share	0.56	0.31	0.31	0.25	0.10	0.89	1.15	0.35
Cash Flow Per Share	2.06	2.07	2.07	2.14	2.42	3.93	3.92	3.07
Tang Book Value Per Share	4.44	4.39	4.14	4.02	3.49	3.35	N.M.	N.M.
Dividends Per Share	0.500	0.500	0.500	0.500	1.930	1.700	1.560	1.340
Dividend Payout %	89.29	161.29	161.29	200.00	1,930.00	191.01	135.65	382.86
Income Statement								
Total Revenue	10,073,000	6,792,000	3,424,000	13,058,000	14,403,000	16,226,000	14,070,000	9,973,000
EBITDA	2,792,000	1,938,000	996,000	4,917,000	4,468,000	6,345,000	5,891,000	3,913,000
Depn & Amortn	45,000	30,000	15,000	1,970,000	2,059,000	1,862,000	1,663,000	1,324,000
Income Before Taxes	1,360,000	980,000	516,000	1,141,000	358,000	2,685,000	2,553,000	1,190,000
Income Taxes	622,000	462,000	246,000	917,000	564,000	648,000	742,000	139,000
Net Income	1,189,000	816,000	440,000	708,000	253,000	1,026,000	1,193,000	315,000
Average Shares	2,231,000	2,230,000	2,230,000	2,230,000	2,193,000	1,137,000	1,036,000	908,000
Balance Sheet								
Current Assets	2,613,000	2,726,000	2,675,000	3,229,000	2,824,000	3,752,000	3,868,000	3,674,000
Total Assets	80,351,000	80,203,000	79,793,000	80,305,000	84,104,000	83,198,000	75,185,000	68,185,000
Current Liabilities	6,174,000	6,363,000	6,689,000	5,924,000	4,065,000	6,362,000	6,075,000	5,209,000
Long-Term Obligations	35,116,000	35,100,000	35,464,000	37,354,000	42,406,000	40,246,000	33,887,000	32,000,000
Total Liabilities	45,126,000	45,054,000	45,148,000	45,874,000	48,985,000	49,122,000	62,092,000	54,320,000
Stockholders' Equity	35,225,000	35,149,000	34,645,000	34,431,000	35,119,000	34,076,000	13,093,000	13,865,000
Shares Outstanding	2,231,148	2,230,167	2,230,150	2,230,103	2,229,224	2,125,147	1,030,677	1,035,668
Statistical Record								
Return on Assets %	1.73	1.02	1.02	0.86	0.30	1.30	1.66	0.64
Return on Equity %	4.00	2.38	2.39	2.03	0.73	4.35	8.85	3.66
EBITDA Margin %	27.72	28.53	29.09	37.66	31.02	39.10	41.87	39.24
Net Margin %	11.80	12.01	12.85	5.42	1.76	6.32	8.48	3.16
Asset Turnover	0.17	0.16	0.16	0.16	0.17	0.20	0.20	0.20
Current Ratio	0.42	0.43	0.40	0.55	0.69	0.39	0.64	0.71
Debt to Equity	1.00	1.00	1.02	1.08	1.21	1.18	2.59	2.31
Price Range	23.13-18.40	23.13-18.29	23.13-16.85	23.13-12.01	44.57-14.54	43.01-30.96	41.09-32.58	39.85-30.76
P/E Ratio	41.30-32.86	74.61-59.00	74.61-54.35	92.52-48.04	445.70-145.40	48.33-34.79	35.73-28.33	113.86-87.89
Average Yield %	2.43	2.38	2.44	2.61	5.52	4.70	4.20	3.87

Address: 1001 Louisiana Street, Suite 1000, Houston, TX 77002	Web Site: www.kindermorgan.com	Auditors: PricewaterhouseCoopers LLP
Telephone: 713-369-9000	Officers: Richard D. Kinder - Executive Chairman, Chairman, Chief Executive Officer Steven J. Kean - President, Chief Executive Officer, Chief Operating Officer, Executive Vice President	Investor Contact: 713-369-9449 Transfer Agents: Computershare Investor Services, LLC

KIRBY CORP.

Exchange	Symbol	Price	52Wk Range	Yield	P/E
NYS	KEX	$66.80 (12/29/2017)	73.10-60.05	N/A	31.66

*7 Year Price Score 72.78   *NYSE Composite Index=100   *12 Month Price Score 93.88

TRADING VOLUME (thousand shares)

Interim Earnings (Per Share)

Qtr.	Mar	Jun	Sep	Dec
2014	1.09	1.31	1.34	1.19
2015	1.09	1.04	1.04	0.94
2016	0.71	0.72	0.59	0.60
2017	0.51	0.48	0.52	...

Interim Dividends (Per Share)

No Dividends Paid

Valuation Analysis		Institutional Holding	
Forecast EPS	$2.03	No of Institutions	
	(01/18/2018)	370	
Market Cap	$4.0 Billion	Shares	
Book Value	$2.9 Billion	74,817,224	
Price/Book	1.39	% Held	
Price/Sales	2.05	94.09	

Business Summary: Shipping (MIC: 7.4.2 SIC: 4449 NAIC: 483211)

Kirby is a tank barge operator. Co. has two segments: marine transportation, which provides marine transportation services, operating tank barges and towing vessels transporting bulk liquid products throughout the Mississippi River System, coastwise along all three U.S. coasts, and in Alaska and Hawaii; and diesel engine services, which provides services for diesel engines, reduction gears and ancillary products for marine and power generation applications, distributes and services diesel engines, transmissions and pumps, and manufactures oilfield service equipment for land-based oilfield service and oil and gas operator and producer markets.

Recent Developments: For the quarter ended Sep 30 2017, net income decreased 11.0% to US$28.8 million from US$32.4 million in the year-earlier quarter. Revenues were US$541.3 million, up 24.5% from US$434.7 million the year before. Operating income was US$53.4 million versus US$56.2 million in the prior-year quarter, a decrease of 5.0%. Direct operating expenses rose 34.1% to US$378.3 million from US$282.2 million in the comparable period the year before. Indirect operating expenses increased 13.7% to US$109.6 million from US$96.4 million in the equivalent prior-year period.

Prospects: Our evaluation of Kirby Corp. as of Jan. 14, 2018 is the result of our systematic analysis on three basic characteristics: earnings strength, relative valuation, and recent stock price movement. The company has enjoyed a very positive trend in earnings per share over the past 5 quarters and while recent estimates for the company have been mixed, KEX has posted better than expected results. Based on operating earnings yield, the company is about fairly valued when compared to all of the companies in our coverage universe. Share price changes over the past year indicates that KEX will perform very poorly over the near term.

Financial Data
(US$ in Thousands)

	9 Mos	6 Mos	3 Mos	12/31/2016	12/31/2015	12/31/2014	12/31/2013	12/31/2012
Earnings Per Share	2.11	2.18	2.42	2.62	4.11	4.93	4.44	3.73
Cash Flow Per Share	6.15	7.43	7.24	7.72	9.53	7.74	10.67	5.86
Tang Book Value Per Share	32.73	34.73	33.95	33.63	31.31	29.24	24.97	19.42
Income Statement								
Total Revenue	1,506,307	965,033	491,705	1,770,673	2,147,532	2,566,318	2,242,195	2,112,658
EBITDA	171,193	109,385	53,382	478,166	605,469	672,779	612,260	519,578
Depn & Amortn	25,009	16,450	7,927	233,262	225,470	197,312	176,058	154,943
Income Before Taxes	131,874	84,013	40,998	227,214	361,261	454,006	408,330	340,250
Income Taxes	49,468	30,396	13,353	84,942	133,742	169,782	152,379	127,907
Net Income	81,868	53,261	27,483	141,406	226,684	282,006	253,061	209,438
Average Shares	54,803	53,645	53,609	53,512	54,826	56,867	56,552	55,674
Balance Sheet								
Current Assets	890,764	603,645	609,588	646,555	640,776	803,154	544,006	596,256
Total Assets	5,200,415	4,225,356	4,257,292	4,303,499	4,156,266	4,141,909	3,682,517	3,653,128
Current Liabilities	462,190	341,994	333,536	358,338	361,917	594,027	345,989	355,020
Long-Term Obligations	1,031,028	591,535	674,552	722,802	778,834	600,000	749,150	1,070,110
Total Liabilities	2,327,737	1,751,462	1,827,122	1,894,181	1,887,455	1,887,873	1,671,831	1,958,160
Stockholders' Equity	2,872,678	2,473,894	2,430,170	2,409,318	2,268,811	2,254,036	2,010,686	1,694,968
Shares Outstanding	59,688	54,006	53,968	53,855	53,720	56,870	56,846	56,585
Statistical Record								
Return on Assets %	2.42	2.77	3.13	3.33	5.46	7.21	6.90	6.32
Return on Equity %	4.35	4.88	5.52	6.03	10.02	13.23	13.66	13.31
EBITDA Margin %	11.37	11.33	10.86	27.00	28.19	26.22	27.31	24.59
Net Margin %	5.44	5.52	5.59	7.99	10.56	10.99	11.29	9.91
Asset Turnover	0.41	0.43	0.43	0.42	0.52	0.66	0.61	0.64
Current Ratio	1.93	1.77	1.83	1.80	1.77	1.35	1.57	1.68
Debt to Equity	0.36	0.24	0.28	0.30	0.34	0.27	0.37	0.63
Price Range	73.10-55.65	73.10-51.90	73.00-51.90	72.71-45.77	83.90-50.86	123.25-80.32	99.25-61.89	70.00-45.39
P/E Ratio	34.64-26.37	33.53-23.81	30.17-21.45	27.75-17.47	20.41-12.37	25.00-16.29	22.35-13.94	18.77-12.17

Address: 55 Waugh Drive, Suite 1000, Houston, TX 77007
Telephone: 713-435-1000
Fax: 713-435-1010

Web Site: www.kirbycorp.com
Officers: Joseph H. Pyne - Chairman, President, Chief Executive Officer David W. Grzebinski - President, Chief Executive Officer, Interim Chief Financial Officer, Chief Operating Officer, Chief Financial Officer, Executive Vice President

Auditors: KPMG LLP
Transfer Agents: Computershare Trust Company, N.A., Providence, RI

KNOWLES CORP

Exchange	Symbol	Price	52Wk Range	Yield	P/E
NYS	KN	$14.66 (12/29/2017)	19.59-14.15	N/A	733.00

*7 Year Price Score N/A   *NYSE Composite Index=100   *12 Month Price Score 87.34

Interim Earnings (Per Share)

Qtr.	Mar	Jun	Sep	Dec
2014	0.09	(0.93)	(0.17)	(0.01)
2015	(0.19)	(0.19)	(0.17)	2.15)
2016	(0.33)	(0.28)	(0.08)	0.22
2017	(0.04)	(0.33)	0.17	...

Interim Dividends (Per Share)

No Dividends Paid

Valuation Analysis   **Institutional Holding**

Forecast EPS	$0.87	No of Institutions
	(01/17/2018)	315
Market Cap	$1.3 Billion	Shares
Book Value	$1.0 Billion	123,327,928
Price/Book	1.26	% Held
Price/Sales	1.55	83.99

TRADING VOLUME (thousand shares)

Business Summary: Electronic Instruments & Related Products (MIC: 6.2.3 SIC: 3651 NAIC: 334310)

Knowles is supplier of micro-acoustic, audio processing and specialty component solutions, serving the mobile consumer electronics, communications, medical, military, aerospace and industrial markets. Co.'s Mobile Consumer Electronics segment designs and manufactures acoustic products, including microphones and audio processing technologies used in mobile handsets, tablets and other consumer electronic devices. Co.'s Specialty Components segment specializes in the design and manufacture of specialized electronic components used in medical and life science applications, as well as solutions and components used in communications infrastructure and other markets.

Recent Developments: For the quarter ended Sep 30 2017, income from continuing operations decreased 26.3% to US$15.4 million from US$20.9 million in the year-earlier quarter. Net income amounted to US$15.7 million versus a net loss of US$7.6 million in the year-earlier quarter. Revenues were US$221.7 million, down 8.8% from US$243.1 million the year before. Operating income was US$20.9 million versus US$26.5 million in the prior-year quarter, a decrease of 21.1%. Direct operating expenses declined 6.1% to US$139.2 million from US$148.2 million in the comparable period the year before. Indirect operating expenses decreased 9.9% to US$61.6 million from US$68.4 million in the equivalent prior-year period.

Prospects: Our evaluation of Knowles Corp. as of Jan. 14, 2018 is the result of our systematic analysis on three basic characteristics: earnings strength, relative valuation, and recent stock price movement. The company has generated a negative trend in earnings per share over the past 5 quarters. However, while recent estimates for the company have been lowered by analysts, KN has posted better than expected results. Based on operating earnings yield, the company is about fairly valued when compared to all of the companies in our coverage universe. Share price changes over the past year indicates that KN will perform poorly over the near term.

Financial Data

(US$ in Thousands)	9 Mos	6 Mos	3 Mos	12/31/2016	12/31/2015	12/31/2014	12/31/2013	12/31/2012
Earnings Per Share	0.02	(0.23)	(0.18)	(0.47)	(2.69)	(1.02)	1.24	0.93
Cash Flow Per Share	1.13	1.33	1.19	1.21	0.90	1.36	2.05	2.05
Tang Book Value Per Share	0.80	0.48	0.49	0.41	N.M.	0.60	7.14	...
Income Statement								
Total Revenue	605,600	383,900	193,700	859,300	1,084,600	1,141,300	1,214,803	1,117,992
EBITDA	8,800	(13,900)	2,000	104,200	(100,500)	102,100	274,446	250,264
Depn & Amortn	5,500	3,700	1,700	53,000	135,700	151,600	130,912	114,878
Income Before Taxes	(12,100)	(27,900)	(4,900)	30,800	(248,900)	(55,100)	101,510	78,916
Income Taxes	7,500	7,100	(200)	11,700	(15,100)	31,900	(4,304)	(181)
Net Income	(17,200)	(32,900)	(3,200)	(42,300)	(233,800)	(87,000)	105,814	79,097
Average Shares	90,373	89,361	88,973	89,182	86,802	85,046	85,019	85,019
Balance Sheet								
Current Assets	371,100	334,800	324,300	330,100	419,300	474,000	501,823	377,280
Total Assets	1,553,900	1,516,500	1,530,300	1,515,100	1,697,700	1,998,500	2,170,116	2,051,092
Current Liabilities	155,400	156,800	147,600	149,000	226,900	288,600	209,975	233,422
Long-Term Obligations	297,900	284,800	286,600	301,700	400,000	385,000	...	528,812
Total Liabilities	517,000	506,600	502,900	506,600	690,900	762,300	282,989	862,985
Stockholders' Equity	1,036,900	1,009,900	1,027,400	1,008,500	1,006,800	1,236,200	1,887,127	1,188,107
Shares Outstanding	89,467	89,409	89,233	88,737	88,451	85,061	85,027	...
Statistical Record								
Return on Assets %	0.13	N.M.	N.M.	N.M.	N.M.	N.M.	5.01	...
Return on Equity %	0.20	N.M.	N.M.	N.M.	N.M.	N.M.	6.88	...
EBITDA Margin %	1.45	N.M.	1.03	12.13	N.M.	9.03	22.59	22.39
Net Margin %	N.M.	N.M.	N.M.	N.M.	N.M.	N.M.	8.71	7.07
Asset Turnover	0.54	0.55	0.55	0.53	0.59	0.55	0.58	...
Current Ratio	2.39	2.14	2.20	2.22	1.85	1.64	2.39	1.62
Debt to Equity	0.29	0.28	0.28	0.30	0.40	0.31	...	0.45
Price Range	19.59-13.91	19.59-12.87	19.49-12.27	17.36-9.98	24.67-12.88	33.54-18.13	...	...
P/E Ratio	979.50-695.50	...	...	...	...	...	...	...

Address: 1151 Maplewood Drive, Itasca, IL 60143
Telephone: 630-250-5100
Fax: 630-250-0575

Web Site: www.knowles.com
Officers: Jean-Pierre M. Ergas - Chairman Jeffrey S. Niew - President, Chief Executive Officer

Auditors: PricewaterhouseCoopers LLP

KOHL'S CORP.

Exchange	Symbol	Price	52Wk Range	Yield	P/E
NYS	KSS	$54.23 (12/29/2017)	56.87-35.32	4.06	14.42

*7 Year Price Score 65.01 *NYSE Composite Index=100 *12 Month Price Score 108.70

Interim Earnings (Per Share)

Qtr.	Apr	Jul	Oct	Jan
2014-15	0.60	1.13	0.70	1.81
2015-16	0.63	0.66	0.63	1.54
2016-17	0.09	0.77	0.83	1.43
2017-18	0.39	1.24	0.70	...

Interim Dividends (Per Share)

Amt	Decl	Ex	Rec	Pay
0.55Q	02/22/2017	03/06/2017	03/08/2017	03/22/2017
0.55Q	05/10/2017	06/05/2017	06/07/2017	06/21/2017
0.55Q	08/08/2017	09/01/2017	09/06/2017	09/20/2017
0.55Q	11/08/2017	12/05/2017	12/06/2017	12/20/2017

Indicated Div: $2.20

Valuation Analysis

Forecast EPS	$4.08
	(01/18/2018)
Market Cap	$9.1 Billion
Book Value	$5.0 Billion
Price/Book	1.81
Price/Sales	0.49

Institutional Holding

No of Institutions	872
Shares	227,516,080
% Held	81.31

Business Summary: Retail - General Merchandise/Department Stores (MIC: 2.1.1 SIC: 5311 NAIC: 452111)

Kohl's sells private label, exclusive and national brand apparel, footwear, accessories, beauty and home products. As of Jan 28 2017, Co. operated 1,154 department stores, a website (www.Kohls.com), 12 FILA outlets, and three Off-Aisle clearance centers. Co.'s website includes merchandise that is available in its stores, as well as merchandise that is available only on-line. Co.'s private brands include Apt. 9, Croft & Barrow, Jumping Beans, SO and Sonoma Goods for Life. Co.'s exclusive brands include Food Network, Jennifer Lopez, Marc Anthony, Rock & Republic and Simply Vera Vera Wang.

Recent Developments: For the quarter ended Oct 28 2017, net income decreased 19.9% to US$117.0 million from US$146.0 million in the year-earlier quarter. Revenues were US$4.33 billion, unchanged from the year before. Operating income was US$257.0 million versus US$301.0 million in the prior-year quarter, a decrease of 14.6%. Direct operating expenses rose 0.6% to US$2.74 billion from US$2.72 billion in the comparable period the year before. Indirect operating expenses increased 2.5% to US$1.34 billion from US$1.31 billion in the equivalent prior-year period.

Prospects: Our evaluation of Kohl's Corp. as of Jan. 14, 2018 is the result of our systematic analysis on three basic characteristics: earnings strength, relative valuation, and recent stock price movement. The company has managed to produce a neutral trend in earnings per share over the past 5 quarters and while recent estimates for the company have been raised by analysts, KSS has posted results that fell short of analysts expectations. Based on operating earnings yield, the company is undervalued when compared to all of the companies in our coverage universe. Share price changes over the past year indicates that KSS will perform very poorly over the near term.

Financial Data

(US$ in Thousands)	9 Mos	6 Mos	3 Mos	01/28/2017	01/30/2016	01/31/2015	02/01/2014	02/02/2013
Earnings Per Share	3.76	3.89	3.42	3.11	3.46	4.24	4.05	4.17
Cash Flow Per Share	10.46	9.99	12.08	12.10	7.66	10.00	8.67	5.30
Tang Book Value Per Share	29.93	29.83	29.20	29.75	29.52	29.81	28.33	27.24
Dividends Per Share	2.150	2.100	2.050	2.000	1.800	1.560	1.400	1.280
Dividend Payout %	57.18	53.98	59.94	64.31	52.02	36.79	34.57	30.70
Income Statement								
Total Revenue	12,319,000	7,987,000	3,843,000	18,686,000	19,204,000	19,023,000	19,031,000	19,279,000
EBITDA	1,573,000	1,073,000	423,000	2,121,000	2,318,000	2,575,000	2,631,000	2,723,000
Depn & Amortn	724,000	482,000	238,000	938,000	934,000	886,000	889,000	833,000
Income Before Taxes	624,000	441,000	109,000	875,000	1,057,000	1,349,000	1,404,000	1,561,000
Income Taxes	233,000	167,000	43,000	319,000	384,000	482,000	515,000	575,000
Net Income	391,000	274,000	66,000	556,000	673,000	867,000	889,000	986,000
Average Shares	166,000	168,000	171,000	179,000	195,000	204,000	220,000	237,000
Balance Sheet								
Current Assets	5,700,000	4,740,000	4,944,000	5,247,000	5,076,000	5,698,000	5,292,000	4,719,000
Total Assets	13,900,000	13,038,000	13,244,000	13,574,000	13,606,000	14,431,000	14,378,000	13,905,000
Current Liabilities	3,505,000	2,615,000	2,839,000	2,974,000	2,714,000	2,859,000	2,736,000	2,535,000
Long-Term Obligations	4,418,000	4,433,000	4,452,000	4,480,000	4,581,000	4,651,000	4,722,000	4,448,000
Total Liabilities	8,871,000	8,010,000	8,250,000	8,397,000	8,115,000	8,440,000	8,400,000	7,857,000
Stockholders' Equity	5,029,000	5,028,000	4,994,000	5,177,000	5,491,000	5,991,000	5,978,000	6,048,000
Shares Outstanding	168,000	168,579	171,000	174,000	186,000	201,000	211,000	222,000
Statistical Record								
Return on Assets %	4.60	5.10	4.56	4.10	4.81	6.04	6.30	6.93
Return on Equity %	12.71	13.14	11.76	10.45	11.75	14.53	14.83	15.45
EBITDA Margin %	12.77	13.43	11.01	11.35	12.07	13.54	13.82	14.12
Net Margin %	3.17	3.43	1.72	2.98	3.50	4.56	4.67	5.11
Asset Turnover	1.32	1.40	1.40	1.38	1.37	1.32	1.35	1.35
Current Ratio	1.63	1.81	1.74	1.76	1.87	1.99	1.93	1.86
Debt to Equity	0.88	0.88	0.89	0.87	0.83	0.78	0.79	0.74
Price Range	59.43-35.32	59.43-35.32	59.43-34.49	59.43-34.49	79.07-42.85	62.50-49.09	58.47-45.21	55.11-41.81
P/E Ratio	15.81-9.39	15.28-9.08	17.38-10.08	19.11-11.09	22.85-12.38	14.74-11.58	14.44-11.16	13.22-10.03
Average Yield %	5.08	4.92	4.81	4.55	3.05	2.78	2.72	2.63

Address: N56 W17000 Ridgewood Drive, Menomonee Falls, WI 53051 Telephone: 262-703-7000 Fax: 262-703-6373	Web Site: www.kohls.com Officers: Sona Chawla - President-elect, Chief Operating Officer Michelle D. Gass - Chief Executive Officer-elect, Chief Customer Officer, Chief Merchandising Officer	Auditors: Ernst & Young LLP Investor Contact: 262-703-1440 Transfer Agents: Wells Fargo Shareowner Services, St. Paul, MN

KOSMOS ENERGY LTD

Exchange	Symbol	Price	52Wk Range	Yield	P/E
NYS	KOS	$6.85 (12/29/2017)	8.53-5.59	N/A	N/A

*7 Year Price Score N/A   *NYSE Composite Index=100   *12 Month Price Score 106.41

TRADING VOLUME (thousand shares)

Interim Earnings (Per Share)

Qtr.	Mar	Jun	Sep	Dec
2014	0.19	0.15	0.05	0.33
2015	(0.21)	(0.20)	0.15	0.07
2016	(0.15)	(0.28)	(0.15)	(0.15)
2017	(0.07)	(0.02)	(0.16)	...

Interim Dividends (Per Share)

No Dividends Paid

Valuation Analysis | **Institutional Holding**

Forecast EPS	N/A	No of Institutions
		161
Market Cap	$2.7 Billion	Shares
Book Value	$1.0 Billion	537,058,752
Price/Book	2.64	% Held
Price/Sales	4.04	84.23

Business Summary: Production & Extraction (MIC: 9.1.1 SIC: 1311 NAIC: 211111)

Kosmos is a holding company. Through its subsidiaries, Co. operates as an independent oil and gas exploration and production company focused on areas along the Atlantic Margins. Co.'s assets include existing production and development projects offshore Ghana, discoveries and exploration potential offshore Mauritania and Senegal, as well as exploration licenses with hydrocarbon potential offshore Sao Tome and Principe, Suriname, Morocco and Western Sahara. As of Dec 31 2016, Co. had total net proved developed and undeveloped reserves of 74 million barrels of oil, condensate and natural gas liquids; and 15 billion cubit feet of natural gas.

Recent Developments: For the quarter ended Sep 30 2017, net loss amounted to US$63.4 million versus a net loss of US$59.8 million in the year-earlier quarter. Revenues were US$151.2 million, up 127.0% from US$66.6 million the year before. Direct operating expenses rose 188.7% to US$39.2 million from US$13.6 million in the comparable period the year before. Indirect operating expenses increased 68.0% to US$177.0 million from US$105.3 million in the equivalent prior-year period.

Prospects: Our evaluation of Kosmos Energy Ltd as of Sep. 17, 2017 is the result of our systematic analysis on three basic characteristics: earnings strength, relative valuation, and recent stock price movement. The company has produced a positive trend in earnings per share over the past 5 quarters. Because the company lacks sufficient analyst estimate data, we place greater weight on the historical EPS trend as the measure of earnings strength. Based on operating earnings yield, the company is overvalued when compared to all of the companies in our coverage universe. Share price changes over the past year indicates that KOS will perform poorly over the near term.

Financial Data

(US$ in Thousands)	9 Mos	6 Mos	3 Mos	12/31/2016	12/31/2015	12/31/2014	12/31/2013	12/31/2012
Earnings Per Share	(0.40)	(0.39)	(0.65)	(0.74)	(0.18)	0.72	(0.24)	(0.18)
Cash Flow Per Share	0.55	0.15	0.02	0.13	1.15	1.17	1.39	1.00
Tang Book Value Per Share	2.59	2.73	2.74	2.80	3.44	3.46	2.56	2.65
Income Statement								
Total Revenue	449,732	298,490	151,966	385,355	471,556	882,738	852,428	672,209
EBITDA	171,717	147,259	42,622	(118,917)	269,245	812,116	326,465	264,963
Depn & Amortn	173,300	102,400	32,500	131,500	146,600	188,300	213,700	178,600
Income Before Taxes	(56,312)	8,608	(6,664)	(294,564)	85,436	578,268	75,954	34,156
Income Taxes	44,401	45,916	22,177	(10,784)	155,272	298,898	166,998	101,184
Net Income	(100,713)	(37,308)	(28,841)	(283,780)	(69,836)	279,370	(91,044)	(67,028)
Average Shares	389,058	387,952	387,312	385,402	382,610	386,119	376,819	371,847
Balance Sheet								
Current Assets	469,149	513,475	545,791	475,187	734,148	1,010,476	734,961	750,118
Total Assets	2,970,448	3,076,359	3,183,049	3,341,465	3,203,050	2,972,766	2,345,826	2,366,123
Current Liabilities	283,122	282,340	344,752	370,025	456,741	448,771	219,324	190,253
Long-Term Obligations	1,080,352	1,127,503	1,174,677	1,321,874	860,878	794,269	900,000	1,000,000
Total Liabilities	1,961,205	2,013,506	2,121,737	2,260,266	1,877,537	1,633,807	1,353,491	1,337,217
Stockholders' Equity	1,009,243	1,062,853	1,061,312	1,081,199	1,325,513	1,338,959	992,335	1,028,906
Shares Outstanding	389,356	389,160	387,641	386,757	385,090	386,887	387,574	388,691
Statistical Record								
Return on Assets %	N.M.	N.M.	N.M.	N.M.	N.M.	10.51	N.M.	N.M.
Return on Equity %	N.M.	N.M.	N.M.	N.M.	N.M.	23.97	N.M.	N.M.
EBITDA Margin %	38.18	49.33	28.05	N.M.	57.10	92.00	38.30	39.42
Net Margin %	N.M.	N.M.	N.M.	N.M.	N.M.	31.65	N.M.	N.M.
Asset Turnover	0.21	0.18	0.15	0.12	0.15	0.33	0.36	0.27
Current Ratio	1.66	1.82	1.58	1.28	1.61	2.25	3.35	3.94
Debt to Equity	1.07	1.06	1.11	1.22	0.65	0.59	0.91	0.97
Price Range	8.13-4.62	7.84-4.62	7.25-4.62	7.05-3.50	9.78-4.73	11.23-7.09	13.00-9.75	14.73-9.29
P/E Ratio	...	...	...	...	...	15.60-9.85	...	...

Address: Clarendon House, 2 Church Street, Hamilton, HM 11 **Telephone:** 441-295-5950	**Web Site:** www.kosmosenergy.com **Officers:** Andrew G. Inglis - Chairman, Chief Executive Officer Thomas P. Chambers - Senior Vice President, Chief Financial Officer	**Auditors:** Ernst & Young LLP **Investor Contact:** 214-445-9669 **Transfer Agents:** Computershare Trust Company, N.A., United States

KROGER CO (THE)

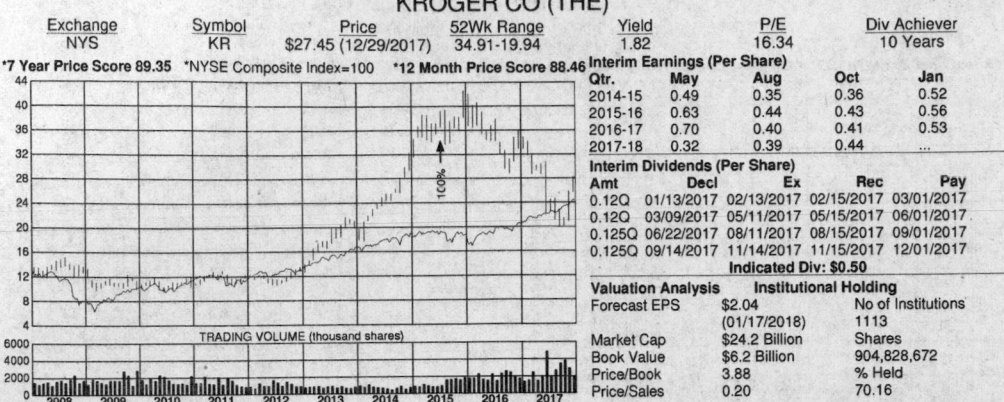

Exchange	Symbol	Price	52Wk Range	Yield	P/E	Div Achiever
NYS	KR	$27.45 (12/29/2017)	34.91-19.94	1.82	16.34	10 Years

*7 Year Price Score 89.35 *NYSE Composite Index=100 *12 Month Price Score 88.46

Interim Earnings (Per Share)

Qtr.	May	Aug	Oct	Jan
2014-15	0.49	0.35	0.36	0.52
2015-16	0.63	0.44	0.43	0.56
2016-17	0.70	0.40	0.41	0.53
2017-18	0.32	0.39	0.44	...

Interim Dividends (Per Share)

Amt	Decl	Ex	Rec	Pay
0.12Q	01/13/2017	02/13/2017	02/15/2017	03/01/2017
0.12Q	03/09/2017	05/11/2017	05/15/2017	06/01/2017
0.125Q	06/22/2017	08/11/2017	08/15/2017	09/01/2017
0.125Q	09/14/2017	11/14/2017	11/15/2017	12/01/2017

Indicated Div: $0.50

Valuation Analysis / Institutional Holding

Forecast EPS	$2.04	No of Institutions	
	(01/17/2018)	1113	
Market Cap	$24.2 Billion	Shares	
Book Value	$6.2 Billion	904,828,672	
Price/Book	3.88	% Held	
Price/Sales	0.20	70.16	

Business Summary: Retail - Food & Beverage, Drug & Tobacco (MIC: 2.1.2 SIC: 5411 NAIC: 445110)

Kroger operates supermarkets, multi-department stores, jewelry stores, and convenience stores. Co. also manufactures and processes some of the food for sale in its supermarkets. As of Jan 28 2017, Co. operated 2,796 supermarkets under a variety of local banner names in 35 states and the District of Columbia of which 2,255 have pharmacies and 1,445 have fuel centers. In addition to the supermarkets, Co. operated 784 convenience stores, 319 jewelry stores and an online retailer. The convenience stores provide a limited assortment of staple food items and general merchandise and, in most cases, sell fuel.

Recent Developments: For the quarter ended Nov 4 2017, net income increased 1.6% to US$389.0 million from US$383.0 million in the year-earlier quarter. Revenues were US$27.75 billion, up 4.5% from US$26.56 billion the year before. Operating income was US$740.0 million versus US$713.0 million in the prior-year quarter, an increase of 3.8%. Direct operating expenses rose 4.3% to US$21.53 billion from US$20.65 billion in the comparable period the year before. Indirect operating expenses increased 5.5% to US$5.48 billion from US$5.19 billion in the equivalent prior-year period.

Prospects: Our evaluation of Kroger Co. as of Jan. 14, 2018 is the result of our systematic analysis on three basic characteristics: earnings strength, relative valuation, and recent stock price movement. The company has enjoyed a very positive trend in earnings per share over the past 5 quarters and while recent estimates for the company have been raised by analysts, KR has posted better than expected results. Based on operating earnings yield, the company is undervalued when compared to all of the companies in our coverage universe. Share price changes over the past year indicates that KR will perform very poorly over the near term.

Financial Data

(US$ in Thousands)	9 Mos	6 Mos	3 Mos	01/28/2017	01/30/2016	01/31/2015	02/01/2014	02/02/2013
Earnings Per Share	1.68	1.65	1.66	2.05	2.06	1.72	1.45	1.39
Cash Flow Per Share	4.36	5.09	4.96	4.55	5.02	4.26	3.30	2.61
Tang Book Value Per Share	2.37	2.21	2.19	2.72	3.15	2.41	2.51	2.89
Dividends Per Share	0.485	0.485	0.480	0.450	0.395	0.340	0.308	0.248
Dividend Payout %	28.87	29.39	28.92	21.95	19.17	19.77	21.21	17.87
Income Statement								
Total Revenue	91,631,000	63,882,000	36,285,000	115,337,000	109,830,000	108,465,000	98,375,000	96,751,000
EBITDA	3,912,000	2,599,000	1,358,000	5,776,000	5,665,000	5,085,000	4,428,000	4,416,000
Depn & Amortn	1,871,000	1,299,000	736,000	2,340,000	2,089,000	1,948,000	1,703,000	1,652,000
Income Before Taxes	1,588,000	985,000	445,000	2,914,000	3,094,000	2,649,000	2,282,000	2,302,000
Income Taxes	552,000	337,000	148,000	957,000	1,045,000	902,000	751,000	794,000
Net Income	1,053,000	656,000	303,000	1,975,000	2,039,000	1,728,000	1,519,000	1,497,000
Average Shares	893,000	905,000	925,000	958,000	980,000	994,000	1,040,000	1,074,000
Balance Sheet								
Current Assets	10,925,000	10,147,000	9,538,000	10,340,000	9,892,000	8,911,000	8,830,000	7,959,000
Total Assets	37,028,000	36,600,000	35,799,000	36,505,000	33,897,000	30,556,000	29,281,000	24,652,000
Current Liabilities	12,890,000	11,618,000	12,515,000	12,860,000	12,971,000	11,403,000	10,705,000	11,057,000
Long-Term Obligations	13,118,000	13,100,000	11,590,000	11,825,000	9,709,000	9,771,000	9,653,000	6,145,000
Total Liabilities	30,793,000	30,441,000	29,654,000	29,807,000	27,077,000	25,144,000	23,897,000	20,445,000
Stockholders' Equity	6,235,000	6,159,000	6,145,000	6,698,000	6,820,000	5,412,000	5,384,000	4,207,000
Shares Outstanding	881,000	893,000	901,000	924,000	967,000	974,000	1,016,000	1,028,000
Statistical Record								
Return on Assets %	4.24	4.36	4.55	5.63	6.34	5.79	5.65	6.12
Return on Equity %	24.27	24.39	25.23	29.30	33.43	32.10	31.76	35.97
EBITDA Margin %	4.27	4.07	3.74	5.01	5.16	4.69	4.50	4.56
Net Margin %	1.15	1.03	0.84	1.71	1.86	1.59	1.54	1.55
Asset Turnover	3.24	3.31	3.36	3.29	3.42	3.64	3.66	3.96
Current Ratio	0.85	0.87	0.76	0.80	0.76	0.78	0.82	0.72
Debt to Equity	2.10	2.13	1.89	1.77	1.42	1.81	1.79	1.46
Price Range	35.96-19.94	35.96-22.29	37.86-28.60	40.65-28.84	42.64-33.66	34.67-17.69	21.71-13.84	13.95-10.56
P/E Ratio	21.40-11.87	21.79-13.51	22.81-17.23	19.83-14.07	20.70-16.34	20.16-10.28	14.97-9.54	10.03-7.59
Average Yield %	1.74	1.61	1.47	1.30	1.05	1.33	1.68	2.07

Address: 1014 Vine Street, Cincinnati, OH 45202
Telephone: 513-762-4000
Fax: 513-762-1400

Web Site: www.thekrogerco.com
Officers: W. Rodney McMullen - Chairman, Vice-Chairman, President, Chief Executive Officer, Chief Operating Officer Michael J. Donnelly - Chief Operating Officer, Executive Vice President, Executive Vice President (frmr), Senior Vice President

Auditors: PricewaterhouseCoopers LLP
Investor Contact: 513-762-4366
Transfer Agents: Wells Fargo Shareowner Services, Saint Paul, MN

LABORATORY CORPORATION OF AMERICA HOLDINGS

Exchange	Symbol	Price	52Wk Range	Yield	P/E
NYS	LH	$159.51 (12/29/2017)	163.95-129.07	N/A	22.25

*7 Year Price Score 105.33 *NYSE Composite Index=100 *12 Month Price Score 100.03

Interim Earnings (Per Share)

Qtr.	Mar	Jun	Sep	Dec
2014	1.31	1.64	1.59	1.38
2015	0.01	1.64	1.49	1.10
2016	1.55	1.91	1.71	1.77
2017	1.84	1.82	1.74	...

Interim Dividends (Per Share)

No Dividends Paid

Valuation Analysis

		Institutional Holding	
Forecast EPS	$9.53	No of Institutions	
	(01/18/2018)	984	
Market Cap	$16.3 Billion	Shares	
Book Value	$6.1 Billion	119,831,808	
Price/Book	2.66	% Held	
Price/Sales	1.62	85.89	

TRADING VOLUME (thousand shares)

Business Summary: Diagnostic & Health Related Services (MIC: 4.2.2 SIC: 8071 NAIC: 621511)

Laboratory Corporation of America Holdings is a life sciences company, providing clinical laboratory and end-to-end drug development services. Co. reports its business in two segments: LabCorp Diagnostics (LCD) and Covance Drug Development (CDD). LCD is an independent clinical laboratory business providing testing through an integrated network of primary and specialty laboratories supported by information technology system, logistics, local labs providing response testing and approximately 1,750 patient service centers located throughout the U.S. CDD provides a range of drug research and development and market access services to biopharmaceutical companies and medical device companies.

Recent Developments: For the quarter ended Sep 30 2017, net income increased 2.0% to US$183.4 million from US$179.8 million in the year-earlier quarter. Revenues were US$2.66 billion, up 10.0% from US$2.41 billion the year before. Operating income was US$341.3 million versus US$324.0 million in the prior-year quarter, an increase of 5.3%. Direct operating expenses rose 9.0% to US$1.77 billion from US$1.63 billion in the comparable period the year before. Indirect operating expenses increased 16.6% to US$541.5 million from US$464.4 million in the equivalent prior-year period.

Prospects: Our evaluation of Laboratory Corp. of America Holdings as of Jan. 14, 2018 is the result of our systematic analysis on three basic characteristics: earnings strength, relative valuation, and recent stock price movement. The company has enjoyed a very positive trend in earnings per share over the past 5 quarters and while recent estimates for the company have been mixed, LH has posted better than expected results. Based on operating earnings yield, the company is undervalued when compared to all of the companies in our coverage universe. Share price changes over the past year indicates that LH will perform poorly over the near term.

Financial Data
(US$ in Thousands)

	9 Mos	6 Mos	3 Mos	12/31/2016	12/31/2015	12/31/2014	12/31/2013	12/31/2012
Earnings Per Share	7.17	7.14	7.23	7.02	4.34	5.91	6.25	5.99
Cash Flow Per Share	13.15	12.24	12.55	11.44	9.94	8.71	9.08	8.77
Income Statement								
Total Revenue	7,645,100	4,989,900	2,447,000	9,641,800	8,680,100	6,011,600	5,808,300	5,671,400
EBITDA	1,391,400	920,500	457,900	1,627,800	1,266,900	1,079,500	1,139,900	1,158,400
Depn & Amortn	388,200	255,100	128,100	311,100	269,900	157,600	144,700	141,100
Income Before Taxes	835,900	558,000	277,400	1,097,600	722,100	812,400	898,700	922,800
Income Taxes	281,100	183,400	87,200	372,300	294,100	314,100	340,200	359,400
Net Income	561,400	380,800	192,200	732,100	436,900	511,200	573,800	583,100
Average Shares	103,700	103,700	104,300	104,300	100,600	86,400	91,800	97,400
Balance Sheet								
Current Assets	2,900,600	2,515,700	2,486,000	2,478,700	2,663,000	1,692,700	1,432,100	1,391,800
Total Assets	16,691,800	14,902,500	14,428,000	14,247,000	14,221,700	7,301,800	6,965,900	6,795,000
Current Liabilities	1,537,200	1,805,500	1,753,200	1,827,600	1,701,500	976,300	735,700	1,028,500
Long-Term Obligations	7,200,300	5,608,300	5,401,900	5,300,000	5,992,100	2,682,700	2,889,100	2,175,000
Total Liabilities	10,565,900	9,024,400	8,777,300	8,741,200	9,277,300	4,481,300	4,474,600	4,077,600
Stockholders' Equity	6,125,900	5,878,100	5,650,700	5,505,800	4,944,400	2,820,500	2,491,300	2,717,400
Shares Outstanding	102,100	102,000	102,600	102,700	101,300	84,600	85,700	93,500
Statistical Record								
Return on Assets %	4.78	5.12	5.23	5.13	4.06	7.17	8.34	8.99
Return on Equity %	12.80	13.31	13.95	13.97	11.25	19.25	22.03	22.28
EBITDA Margin %	18.20	18.45	18.71	16.88	14.60	17.96	19.63	20.43
Net Margin %	7.34	7.63	7.85	7.59	5.03	8.50	9.88	10.28
Asset Turnover	0.65	0.68	0.67	0.68	0.81	0.84	0.84	0.87
Current Ratio	1.89	1.39	1.42	1.36	1.57	1.73	1.95	1.35
Debt to Equity	1.18	0.95	0.96	0.96	1.21	0.95	1.16	0.80
Price Range	161.17-121.63	154.14-121.63	144.27-117.13	140.98-100.94	128.18-106.86	109.58-87.86	107.39-86.41	95.25-82.37
P/E Ratio	22.48-16.96	21.59-17.04	19.95-16.20	20.08-14.38	29.53-24.62	18.54-14.87	17.18-13.83	15.90-13.75

Address: 358 South Main Street, Burlington, NC 27215	**Web Site:** www.labcorp.com	**Auditors:** PricewaterhouseCoopers LLP
Telephone: 336-229-1127	**Officers:** David P. King - Chairman, President, Chief Executive Officer Glenn A. Eisenberg - Executive Vice President, Chief Financial Officer, Principal Accounting Officer, Treasurer	**Investor Contact:** 336-436-5076 **Transfer Agents:** American Stock Transfer & Trust Company, Brooklyn, NY

420

L BRANDS, INC

Exchange	Symbol	Price	52Wk Range	Yield	P/E
NYS	LB	$60.22 (12/29/2017)	67.34-36.06	3.99	18.36

*7 Year Price Score 65.82 *NYSE Composite Index=100 *12 Month Price Score 102.45

Interim Earnings (Per Share)

Qtr.	Apr	Jul	Oct	Jan
2014-15	0.53	0.63	0.44	1.90
2015-16	0.84	0.68	0.55	2.14
2016-17	0.52	0.87	0.42	2.17
2017-18	0.33	0.48	0.30	...

Interim Dividends (Per Share)

Amt	Decl	Ex	Rec	Pay
0.60Q	02/02/2017	02/15/2017	02/17/2017	03/03/2017
0.60Q	05/19/2017	05/31/2017	06/02/2017	06/16/2017
0.60Q	08/04/2017	08/17/2017	08/21/2017	09/01/2017
0.60Q	11/10/2017	11/22/2017	11/24/2017	12/08/2017

Indicated Div: $2.40 (Div. Reinv. Plan)

Valuation Analysis | **Institutional Holding**

Forecast EPS	$3.10	No of Institutions
(01/18/2018)		704
Market Cap	$17.0 Billion	Shares
Book Value	N/A	265,595,488
Price/Book	N/A	% Held
Price/Sales	1.38	N/A

TRADING VOLUME (thousand shares)

Business Summary: Retail - Apparel and Accessories (MIC: 2.1.5 SIC: 5621 NAIC: 448120)

L Brands is a retailer of women's apparel, personal care, beauty and home fragrance categories. Co. sells its merchandise through company-owned retail stores in the U.S., Canada, the U.K. and Greater China, and through its websites and other channels. Co.'s other international operations are primarily through franchise, license and wholesale partners. Co. operates the following retail brands: Victoria's Secret, PINK, Bath & Body Works, La Senza, and Henri Bendel. Co. has three segments: Victoria's Secret, Bath & Body Works and Victoria's Secret and Bath & Body Works International. As of Jan 28 2017, Co. had a total of 3,074 company-owned retail stores in operation.

Recent Developments: For the quarter ended Oct 28 2017, net income decreased 29.5% to US$86.0 million from US$122.0 million in the year-earlier quarter. Revenues were US$2.62 billion, up 1.4% from US$2.58 billion the year before. Operating income was US$232.0 million versus US$284.0 million in the prior-year quarter, a decrease of 18.3%. Direct operating expenses rose 4.7% to US$1.63 billion from US$1.56 billion in the comparable period the year before. Indirect operating expenses increased 2.2% to US$757.0 million from US$741.0 million in the equivalent prior-year period.

Prospects: Our evaluation of L Brands, Inc. as of Jan. 14, 2018 is the result of our systematic analysis on three basic characteristics: earnings strength, relative valuation, and recent stock price movement. The company has enjoyed a very positive trend in earnings per share over the past 5 quarters. However, while recent estimates for the company have been mixed, LB has posted better than expected results. Based on operating earnings yield, the company is undervalued when compared to all of the companies in our coverage universe. Share price changes over the past year indicates that LB will perform in line with the market over the near term.

Financial Data

(US$ in Thousands)	9 Mos	6 Mos	3 Mos	01/28/2017	01/30/2016	01/31/2015	02/01/2014	02/02/2013
Earnings Per Share	3.28	3.40	3.79	3.98	4.22	3.50	3.05	2.54
Cash Flow Per Share	6.03	5.89	7.03	6.60	6.44	6.13	4.32	4.58
Dividends Per Share	2.400	2.400	2.400	4.400	4.000	2.360	1.200	5.000
Dividend Payout %	73.17	70.59	63.32	110.55	94.79	67.43	39.34	196.85
Income Statement								
Total Revenue	7,809,000	5,192,000	2,437,000	12,574,000	12,154,000	11,454,000	10,773,000	10,459,000
EBITDA	1,161,000	795,000	349,000	2,608,000	2,725,000	2,398,000	2,166,000	1,983,000
Depn & Amortn	391,000	258,000	130,000	518,000	457,000	438,000	406,000	386,000
Income Before Taxes	470,000	336,000	118,000	1,696,000	1,934,000	1,636,000	1,446,000	1,281,000
Income Taxes	151,000	103,000	24,000	538,000	681,000	594,000	543,000	528,000
Net Income	319,000	233,000	94,000	1,158,000	1,253,000	1,042,000	903,000	753,000
Average Shares	285,000	289,000	289,000	291,000	297,000	298,000	296,000	297,000
Balance Sheet								
Current Assets	2,930,000	2,957,000	3,152,000	3,465,000	4,156,000	3,232,000	3,150,000	2,205,000
Total Assets	7,816,000	7,763,000	7,882,000	8,170,000	8,493,000	7,544,000	7,198,000	6,019,000
Current Liabilities	2,019,000	1,758,000	1,831,000	2,014,000	1,875,000	1,679,000	1,826,000	1,538,000
Long-Term Obligations	5,705,000	5,704,000	5,702,000	5,700,000	5,715,000	4,765,000	4,761,000	4,477,000
Total Liabilities	8,937,000	8,677,000	8,718,000	8,899,000	8,752,000	7,526,000	7,568,000	7,034,000
Stockholders' Equity	(1,121,000)	(914,000)	(836,000)	(729,000)	(259,000)	18,000	(370,000)	(1,015,000)
Shares Outstanding	282,000	286,000	286,000	286,000	290,000	292,000	291,000	289,000
Statistical Record								
Return on Assets %	12.29	12.90	14.37	13.94	15.67	14.18	13.70	12.22
EBITDA Margin %	14.87	15.31	14.32	20.74	22.42	20.94	20.11	18.96
Net Margin %	4.09	4.49	3.86	9.21	10.31	9.10	8.38	7.20
Asset Turnover	1.59	1.60	1.62	1.51	1.52	1.56	1.63	1.70
Current Ratio	1.45	1.68	1.72	1.72	2.22	1.92	1.73	1.43
Debt to Equity	...	...	...	...	...	264.72	...	...
Price Range	75.12-36.06	78.02-43.10	80.18-43.10	96.56-59.01	100.22-77.87	87.05-50.87	65.60-42.85	52.15-40.83
P/E Ratio	22.90-10.99	22.95-12.68	21.16-11.37	24.26-14.83	23.75-18.45	24.87-14.53	21.51-14.05	20.53-16.07
Average Yield %	4.59	3.96	3.67	5.98	4.41	3.62	2.21	10.56

Address: Three Limited Parkway, Columbus, OH 43230
Telephone: 614-415-7000

Web Site: www.lb.com
Officers: Leslie H. Wexner - Chairman, Chief Executive Officer Stuart B. Burgdoerfer - Executive Vice President, Chief Financial Officer

Auditors: Ernst & Young LLP
Investor Contact: 614-415-6400
Transfer Agents: American Stock Transfer & Trust Company, Brookly, NY

LAREDO PETROLEUM, INC

Exchange	Symbol	Price	52Wk Range	Yield	P/E
NYS	LPI	$10.61 (12/29/2017)	15.21-9.49	N/A	20.80

*7 Year Price Score N/A   *NYSE Composite Index=100   *12 Month Price Score 80.52

Interim Earnings (Per Share)

Qtr.	Mar	Jun	Sep	Dec
2014	0.00	(0.13)	0.58	1.40
2015	0.00	(1.88)	(4.01)	(4.72)
2016	(0.85)	(0.33)	0.04	(0.07)
2017	0.28	0.25	0.05	...

Interim Dividends (Per Share)

No Dividends Paid

Valuation Analysis — **Institutional Holding**

Valuation Analysis		Institutional Holding	
Forecast EPS	$0.52	No of Institutions	
	(01/18/2018)	217	
Market Cap	$2.6 Billion	Shares	
Book Value	$346.2 Million	351,201,184	
Price/Book	7.43	% Held	
Price/Sales	3.36	N/A	

Business Summary: Production & Extraction (MIC: 9.1.1 SIC: 1311 NAIC: 211111)

Laredo Petroleum is an independent energy company focused on the acquisition, exploration and development of oil and natural gas properties, and the transportation of oil and natural gas from such properties. Co. operates through two segments: exploration and production of oil and natural gas properties, which is conducted by Co. through the exploration and development of its acreage in the Permian Basin; and midstream and marketing, which buys, sells, gathers and transports oil, natural gas and water through Co.'s subsidiary, Laredo Midstream Services, LLC. As of Dec 31 2016, Co.'s total estimated proved reserves were 167.1 million barrels of oil equivalent, of which 84.0% were developed.

Recent Developments: For the quarter ended Sep 30 2017, net income increased 16.3% to US$11.0 million from US$9.5 million in the year-earlier quarter. Revenues were US$205.8 million, up 28.9% from US$159.7 million the year before. Operating income was US$60.5 million versus US$25.5 million in the prior-year quarter, an increase of 137.1%. Direct operating expenses rose 8.5% to US$79.2 million from US$73.0 million in the comparable period the year before. Indirect operating expenses increased 8.1% to US$66.2 million from US$61.3 million in the equivalent prior-year period.

Prospects: Our evaluation of Laredo Petroleum, Inc. as of Jan. 14, 2018 is the result of our systematic analysis on three basic characteristics: earnings strength, relative valuation, and recent stock price movement. The company has suffered a very negative trend in earnings per share over the past 5 quarters and while recent estimates for the company have been mixed, LPI has posted results that fell short of analysts expectations. Based on operating earnings yield, the company is undervalued when compared to all of the companies in our coverage universe. Share price changes over the past year indicates that LPI will perform poorly over the near term.

Financial Data

(US$ in Thousands)	9 Mos	6 Mos	3 Mos	12/31/2016	12/31/2015	12/31/2014	12/31/2013	12/31/2012
Earnings Per Share	0.51	0.50	(0.08)	(1.16)	(11.10)	1.85	0.88	0.48
Cash Flow Per Share	1.60	1.57	1.52	1.58	1.59	3.53	2.75	2.96
Tang Book Value Per Share	1.43	1.34	1.04	0.75	0.61	10.88	8.92	6.48
Income Statement								
Total Revenue	581,825	376,007	189,006	597,378	606,640	793,885	665,257	588,080
EBITDA	204,698	171,640	88,836	(171,119)	(2,284,387)	556,030	295,619	183,416
Depn & Amortn	3,132	2,094	1,053	5,900	6,500	5,100	4,400	3,300
Income Before Taxes	132,503	123,847	65,208	(270,142)	(2,393,680)	430,051	191,055	94,603
Income Taxes	...	...	...	...	(176,945)	164,286	74,507	32,949
Net Income	140,413	129,386	68,276	(260,739)	(2,209,936)	265,573	118,000	61,654
Average Shares	244,887	244,417	244,379	225,512	199,158	143,554	134,378	128,171
Balance Sheet								
Current Assets	142,465	167,664	152,629	154,777	332,232	365,253	307,609	137,437
Total Assets	2,066,326	1,941,254	1,818,596	1,782,346	1,813,287	3,932,549	2,623,760	2,338,304
Current Liabilities	223,260	172,083	162,335	187,945	216,815	425,025	253,969	262,068
Long-Term Obligations	1,440,968	1,390,277	1,349,591	1,353,909	1,416,226	1,801,295	1,051,538	1,216,760
Total Liabilities	1,720,101	1,616,851	1,565,686	1,601,773	1,681,840	2,369,348	1,351,504	1,506,581
Stockholders' Equity	346,225	324,403	252,910	180,573	131,447	1,563,201	1,272,256	831,723
Shares Outstanding	242,526	242,534	242,573	241,929	213,808	143,686	142,671	128,298
Statistical Record								
Return on Assets %	6.38	6.78	N.M.	N.M.	N.M.	8.10	4.76	3.10
Return on Equity %	45.75	72.22	N.M.	N.M.	N.M.	18.73	11.22	7.73
EBITDA Margin %	35.18	45.65	47.00	N.M.	N.M.	70.04	44.44	31.19
Net Margin %	24.13	34.41	36.12	N.M.	N.M.	33.45	17.74	10.48
Asset Turnover	0.40	0.41	0.39	0.33	0.21	0.24	0.27	0.30
Current Ratio	0.64	0.97	0.94	0.82	1.53	0.86	1.21	0.52
Debt to Equity	4.16	4.29	5.34	7.50	10.77	1.15	0.83	1.46
Price Range	15.99-9.69	15.99-9.42	15.99-7.47	15.99-4.10	15.80-7.05	30.98-7.39	33.52-15.95	26.80-17.41
P/E Ratio	31.35-19.00	31.98-18.84	...	...	...	16.75-3.99	38.09-18.13	55.83-36.27

Address: 15 W. Sixth Street, Suite 900, Tulsa, OK 74119	Web Site: www.laredopetro.com	Auditors: Grant Thornton LLP
Telephone: 918-513-4570	Officers: Randy A. Foutch - Chairman, Chief Executive Officer Richard C. Buterbaugh - Executive Vice President, Chief Financial Officer	Investor Contact: 918-858-5504 Transfer Agents: American Stock Transfer and Trust Company, Brooklyn, NY

LAS VEGAS SANDS CORP

Exchange	Symbol	Price	52Wk Range	Yield	P/E
NYS	LVS	$69.49 (12/29/2017)	71.97-51.69	4.20	26.22

*7 Year Price Score 86.51 *NYSE Composite Index=100 *12 Month Price Score 106.49

Interim Earnings (Per Share)

Qtr.	Mar	Jun	Sep	Dec
2014	0.95	0.83	0.83	0.90
2015	0.64	0.59	0.65	0.59
2016	0.40	0.41	0.65	0.64
2017	0.60	0.69	0.72	...

Interim Dividends (Per Share)

Amt	Decl	Ex	Rec	Pay
0.73Q	01/24/2017	03/21/2017	03/23/2017	03/31/2017
0.73Q	04/26/2017	06/20/2017	06/22/2017	06/30/2017
0.73Q	07/26/2017	09/20/2017	09/21/2017	09/29/2017
0.73Q	10/24/2017	12/20/2017	12/21/2017	12/29/2017

Indicated Div: $2.92

Valuation Analysis | **Institutional Holding**

Forecast EPS	$2.92
	(01/18/2018)
Market Cap	$54.9 Billion
Book Value	$5.9 Billion
Price/Book	9.31
Price/Sales	4.38

No of Institutions 793
Shares 347,001,952
% Held 41.93

Business Summary: Hotels, Restaurants & Travel (MIC: 2.2.1 SIC: 7011 NAIC: 721120)

Las Vegas Sands is a developer of destination properties (integrated resorts) that feature accommodations, gaming, entertainment and retail, convention and exhibition facilities, restaurants and other amenities. Through its 70.1% ownership of Sands China Ltd., Co. owns and operates resort properties, including The Venetian Macao Resort Hotel, Sands Cotai Central, the Four Seasons Hotel Macao, Cotai Strip and the Plaza Casino, and the Sands Macao. In Singapore, Co. owns and operates the Marina Bay Sands, while its properties in the U.S. include The Venetian Resort Hotel Casino and The Palazzo Resort Hotel Casino, the Sands Expo and Convention Center and the Sands Casino Resort Bethlehem.

Recent Developments: For the quarter ended Sep 30 2017, net income increased 13.1% to US$685.0 million from US$605.5 million in the year-earlier quarter. Revenues were US$3.20 billion, up 7.8% from US$2.97 billion the year before. Operating income was US$856.0 million versus US$719.6 million in the prior-year quarter, an increase of 19.0%. Direct operating expenses rose 11.4% to US$1.61 billion from US$1.45 billion in the comparable period the year before. Indirect operating expenses decreased 8.8% to US$731.0 million from US$801.6 million in the equivalent prior-year period.

Prospects: Our evaluation of Las Vegas Sands Corp. as of Jan. 14, 2018 is the result of our systematic analysis on three basic characteristics: earnings strength, relative valuation, and recent stock price movement. The company has generated a negative trend in earnings per share over the past 5 quarters and while recent estimates for the company have been raised by analysts, LVS has posted better than expected results. Based on operating earnings yield, the company is about fairly valued when compared to all of the companies in our coverage universe. Share price changes over the past year indicates that LVS will perform well over the near term.

Financial Data

(US$ in Thousands)	9 Mos	6 Mos	3 Mos	12/31/2016	12/31/2015	12/31/2014	12/31/2013	12/31/2012
Earnings Per Share	2.65	2.58	2.30	2.10	2.47	3.52	2.79	1.85
Cash Flow Per Share	5.61	5.51	5.30	5.07	4.33	6.00	5.40	3.78
Tang Book Value Per Share	7.35	7.37	7.45	7.64	8.49	8.93	9.24	8.48
Dividends Per Share	2.910	2.900	2.890	2.880	2.600	2.000	1.400	3.750
Dividend Payout %	109.81	112.40	125.65	137.14	105.26	56.82	50.18	202.70
Income Statement								
Total Revenue	9,446,000	6,247,000	3,106,000	11,410,000	11,688,461	14,583,849	13,769,885	11,131,132
EBITDA	2,406,000	1,551,000	742,000	3,708,000	3,949,486	5,200,486	4,498,054	3,275,631
Depn & Amortn	56,000	38,000	20,000	1,189,000	1,077,469	1,119,237	1,099,668	977,743
Income Before Taxes	2,121,000	1,363,000	647,000	2,255,000	2,621,882	3,832,711	3,143,512	2,062,576
Income Taxes	220,000	147,000	69,000	239,000	236,185	244,640	188,836	180,763
Net Income	1,595,000	1,025,000	480,000	1,670,000	1,966,236	2,840,629	2,305,997	1,524,093
Average Shares	792,000	792,000	795,000	795,000	797,596	808,019	826,316	824,556
Balance Sheet								
Current Assets	2,836,000	3,100,000	2,820,000	3,098,000	3,609,250	5,190,499	5,515,539	4,477,514
Total Assets	19,808,000	20,142,000	20,042,000	20,469,000	20,987,421	22,361,691	22,724,264	22,163,052
Current Liabilities	2,661,000	2,559,000	2,512,000	2,806,000	2,464,135	2,712,494	3,129,665	2,622,823
Long-Term Obligations	9,483,000	10,014,000	9,671,000	9,428,000	9,372,645	9,892,913	9,382,752	10,132,265
Total Liabilities	13,912,000	14,219,000	14,045,000	14,292,000	14,170,680	15,148,105	15,058,770	15,101,810
Stockholders' Equity	5,896,000	5,923,000	5,997,000	6,177,000	6,816,741	7,213,586	7,665,494	7,061,842
Shares Outstanding	790,000	791,000	792,000	794,960	794,645	798,258	818,702	824,297
Statistical Record								
Return on Assets %	10.39	9.95	9.05	8.03	9.07	12.60	10.27	6.85
Return on Equity %	34.37	33.15	28.97	25.63	28.03	38.18	31.32	20.38
EBITDA Margin %	25.47	24.83	23.89	32.50	33.79	35.66	32.67	29.43
Net Margin %	16.89	16.41	15.45	14.64	16.82	19.48	16.75	13.69
Asset Turnover	0.62	0.60	0.58	0.55	0.54	0.65	0.61	0.50
Current Ratio	1.07	1.21	1.12	1.10	1.46	1.91	1.76	1.71
Debt to Equity	1.61	1.69	1.61	1.53	1.37	1.37	1.22	1.43
Price Range	66.12-51.69	66.12-42.80	62.84-41.82	62.84-36.97	60.56-36.98	87.81-52.31	78.87-46.16	61.05-36.41
P/E Ratio	24.95-19.51	25.63-16.59	27.32-18.18	29.92-17.60	24.52-14.97	24.95-14.86	28.27-16.54	33.00-19.68
Average Yield %	4.96	5.18	5.48	5.69	5.08	2.81	2.35	7.91

Address: 3355 Las Vegas Boulevard South, Las Vegas, NV 89109 Telephone: 702-414-1000	Web Site: www.sands.com Officers: Sheldon Gary Adelson - Chairman, Chief Executive Officer, Treasurer George Tanasijevich - Managing Director	Auditors: Deloitte & Touche LLP Transfer Agents: American Stock Transfer & Trust Company, New York, NY

LASALLE HOTEL PROPERTIES

Exchange	Symbol	Price	52Wk Range	Yield	P/E
NYS	LHO	$28.07 (12/29/2017)	31.65-27.60	6.41	17.33

*7 Year Price Score 79.19 *NYSE Composite Index=100 *12 Month Price Score 91.85

TRADING VOLUME (thousand shares)

Interim Earnings (Per Share)

Qtr.	Mar	Jun	Sep	Dec
2014	(0.09)	0.82	0.94	0.21
2015	0.00	0.49	0.39	0.21
2016	0.05	0.49	1.34	0.19
2017	0.67	0.49	0.27	

Interim Dividends (Per Share)

Amt	Decl	Ex	Rec	Pay
0.45Q	03/15/2017	03/29/2017	03/31/2017	04/17/2017
0.45Q	06/15/2017	06/28/2017	06/30/2017	07/17/2017
0.45Q	09/15/2017	09/28/2017	09/29/2017	10/16/2017
0.45Q	12/15/2017	12/28/2017	12/29/2017	01/16/2018

Indicated Div: $1.80

Valuation Analysis	Institutional Holding
Forecast EPS $1.58 (01/27/2018)	No of Institutions 355
Market Cap $3.2 Billion	Shares
Book Value $2.5 Billion	148,992,992
Price/Book 1.27	% Held
Price/Sales 2.80	105.52

Business Summary: REITs (MIC: 5.3.1 SIC: 6798 NAIC: 525930)

LaSalle Hotel Properties is a self-administered and self-managed real estate investment trust. Co. primarily buys, owns, redevelops and leases full-service hotels located in convention, resort and urban business markets. As of Dec 31 2016, Co. owned interests in 46 hotels located in nine states and the District of Columbia. Substantially all of Co.'s assets are held directly or indirectly by, and all of its operations are conducted through, the LaSalle Hotel Operating Partnership, L.P. (Operating Partnership). Co. owned, through a combination of direct and indirect interests, 99.9% of the common units of the Operating Partnership at Dec 31 2016.

Recent Developments: For the quarter ended Sep 30 2017, income from continuing operations decreased 33.7% to US$35.2 million from US$53.1 million in the year-earlier quarter. Net income decreased 77.6% to US$35.3 million from US$157.7 million in the year-earlier quarter. Revenues were US$285.9 million, down 12.6% from US$326.9 million the year before.

Prospects: Our evaluation of LaSalle Hotel Properties as of Jan. 21, 2018 is the result of our systematic analysis on three basic characteristics: earnings strength, relative valuation, and recent stock price movement. The company has managed to produce a neutral trend in earnings per share over the past 5 quarters. Because the company lacks sufficient analyst estimate data, we place greater weight on the historical EPS trend as the measure of earnings strength. Based on operating earnings yield, the company is about fairly valued when compared to all of the companies in our coverage universe. Share price changes over the past year indicates that LHO will perform poorly over the near term.

Financial Data

(US$ in Thousands)	9 Mos	6 Mos	3 Mos	12/31/2016	12/31/2015	12/31/2014	12/31/2013	12/31/2012
Earnings Per Share	1.62	2.69	2.69	2.07	1.09	1.88	0.73	0.52
Cash Flow Per Share	2.68	2.95	3.10	3.18	3.00	2.72	2.53	2.52
Tang Book Value Per Share	22.12	22.30	22.84	22.62	21.02	21.64	20.23	19.41
Dividends Per Share	1.800	1.800	1.800	1.800	1.725	1.495	0.960	0.710
Dividend Payout %	111.11	66.91	66.91	86.96	158.26	74.73	131.51	136.54
Income Statement								
Total Revenue	847,305	561,449	254,405	1,227,619	1,216,584	1,109,778	977,293	867,075
EBITDA	265,339	173,628	61,756	386,454	377,099	340,212	287,844	254,179
Depn & Amortn	141,536	96,119	49,603	191,791	191,167	162,798	149,282	125,127
Income Before Taxes	95,935	58,716	2,468	154,441	134,537	122,598	90,725	80,639
Income Taxes	2,208	230	(4,773)	5,784	(1,292)	2,306	470	9,062
Net Income	179,022	143,799	81,489	252,781	135,552	212,845	89,935	71,296
Average Shares	113,383	113,342	113,306	113,164	113,096	104,545	97,228	85,897
Balance Sheet								
Current Assets	502,434	517,869	443,471	185,090	71,181	166,039	63,773	80,989
Total Assets	3,870,553	3,894,129	3,969,450	3,944,079	4,074,817	3,699,949	3,581,038	3,256,570
Current Liabilities	242,658	246,723	234,159	263,766	267,540	230,473	216,513	145,420
Long-Term Obligations	1,119,733	1,119,429	1,119,054	1,118,707	1,429,794	1,021,090	1,255,062	1,252,220
Total Liabilities	1,365,734	1,369,509	1,383,650	1,386,014	1,700,550	1,258,240	1,477,647	1,403,444
Stockholders' Equity	2,504,819	2,524,620	2,585,800	2,558,065	2,374,267	2,441,709	2,103,391	1,853,126
Shares Outstanding	113,231	113,193	113,219	113,088	112,959	112,824	103,963	95,445
Statistical Record								
Return on Assets %	5.24	8.23	8.10	6.29	3.49	5.85	2.63	2.34
Return on Equity %	8.11	13.15	13.26	10.22	5.63	9.37	4.55	3.93
EBITDA Margin %	31.32	30.92	24.27	31.48	31.00	30.66	29.45	29.31
Net Margin %	21.13	25.61	32.03	20.59	11.14	19.18	9.20	8.22
Asset Turnover	0.29	0.30	0.30	0.31	0.31	0.30	0.29	0.28
Current Ratio	2.07	2.10	1.89	0.70	0.27	0.72	0.29	0.56
Debt to Equity	0.45	0.44	0.43	0.44	0.60	0.42	0.60	0.68
Price Range	31.65-23.23	31.65-23.23	31.65-22.01	30.91-20.15	43.47-25.10	41.64-28.89	32.13-23.36	30.12-22.57
P/E Ratio	19.54-14.34	11.77-8.64	11.77-8.18	14.93-9.73	39.88-23.03	22.15-15.37	44.01-32.00	57.92-43.40
Average Yield %	6.27	6.42	6.77	7.16	4.99	4.25	4.05	2.65

Address: 7550 Wisconsin Avenue, 10th Floor, Bethesda, MD 20814 **Telephone:** 301-941-1500 **Fax:** 301-941-1553	**Web Site:** www.lasallehotels.com **Officers:** Stuart L. Scott - Acting Chairman Michael D. Barnello - President, Chief Executive Officer	**Auditors:** KPMG LLP **Investor Contact:** 301-941-1516 **Transfer Agents:** Wells Fargo Bank, N.A., Saint Paul, MN

LAUDER (ESTEE) COS., INC. (THE)

Exchange	Symbol	Price	52Wk Range	Yield	P/E
NYS	EL	$127.24 (12/29/2017)	129.62-77.33	1.19	34.39

*7 Year Price Score 104.38 *NYSE Composite Index=100 *12 Month Price Score 119.24

TRADING VOLUME (thousand shares)

Interim Earnings (Per Share)

Qtr.	Sep	Dec	Mar	Jun
2014-15	0.59	1.13	0.71	0.40
2015-16	0.82	1.19	0.71	0.25
2016-17	0.79	1.15	0.80	0.61
2017-18	1.14	...	...	...

Interim Dividends (Per Share)

Amt	Decl	Ex	Rec	Pay
0.34Q	02/02/2017	02/24/2017	02/28/2017	03/15/2017
0.34Q	05/03/2017	05/26/2017	05/31/2017	06/15/2017
0.34Q	08/18/2017	08/29/2017	08/31/2017	09/15/2017
0.38Q	11/01/2017	11/29/2017	11/30/2017	12/15/2017

Indicated Div: $1.52 (Div. Reinv. Plan)

Valuation Analysis / Institutional Holding

Valuation Analysis		Institutional Holding	
Forecast EPS	$4.16 (01/18/2018)	No of Institutions	947
Market Cap	$46.9 Billion	Shares	237,680,944
Book Value	$4.7 Billion	% Held	84.11
Price/Book	9.91		
Price/Sales	3.83		

Business Summary: Household & Personal Products (MIC: 1.7.1 SIC: 2844 NAIC: 325620)

Estee Lauder Companies is a manufacturer and marketer of skin care, makeup, fragrance and hair care products. Co.'s products are sold under a number of brand names including: Estee Lauder, Clinique, Origins, M.A.C, Bobbi Brown, La Mer, Jo Malone London, Aveda and Too Faced. Co. is also the licensee for fragrances and/or cosmetics sold under various designer brand names, including Tommy Hilfiger, Donna Karan New York, DKNY, Michael Kors and Tom Ford. Additionally, Co. manufactures and sells products under the Prescriptives, RODIN olio lusso and FLIRT! brands. Co. also develops and sells products under a license from Kiton.

Recent Developments: For the quarter ended Sep 30 2017, net income increased 45.3% to US$430.0 million from US$296.0 million in the year-earlier quarter. Revenues were US$3.27 billion, up 14.3% from US$2.87 billion the year before. Operating income was US$568.0 million versus US$418.0 million in the prior-year quarter, an increase of 35.9%. Direct operating expenses rose 19.3% to US$711.0 million from US$596.0 million in the comparable period the year before. Indirect operating expenses increased 7.8% to US$2.00 billion from US$1.85 billion in the equivalent prior-year period.

Prospects: Our evaluation of Lauder (Estee) Cos. Inc. as of Jan. 14, 2018 is the result of our systematic analysis on three basic characteristics: earnings strength, relative valuation, and recent stock price movement. The company has produced a positive trend in earnings per share over the past 5 quarters and while recent estimates for the company have been raised by analysts, EL has posted better than expected results. Based on operating earnings yield, the company is about fairly valued when compared to all of the companies in our coverage universe. Share price changes over the past year indicates that EL will perform very well over the near term.

Financial Data

(US$ in Thousands)	3 Mos	06/30/2017	06/30/2016	06/30/2015	06/30/2014	06/30/2013	06/30/2012	06/30/2011
Earnings Per Share	3.70	3.35	2.96	2.82	3.06	2.58	2.16	1.74
Cash Flow Per Share	5.55	4.90	4.82	5.12	3.98	3.16	2.89	2.61
Tang Book Value Per Share	4.05	3.10	5.44	5.79	7.32	5.76	4.27	3.86
Dividends Per Share	1.360	1.320	1.140	0.920	0.780	1.080	0.525	0.375
Dividend Payout %	36.76	39.40	38.51	32.62	25.49	41.86	24.31	21.55
Income Statement								
Total Revenue	3,274,000	11,824,000	11,262,300	10,780,400	10,968,800	10,181,700	9,713,600	8,810,000
EBITDA	680,000	2,120,000	2,011,500	2,006,300	2,205,700	1,878,900	1,609,100	1,372,900
Depn & Amortn	112,000	428,000	401,200	400,000	378,100	329,800	286,900	283,500
Income Before Taxes	549,000	1,617,000	1,555,200	1,560,600	1,776,800	1,475,200	1,261,100	1,025,500
Income Taxes	119,000	361,000	434,400	467,200	567,700	451,400	400,600	321,700
Net Income	427,000	1,249,000	1,114,600	1,088,900	1,204,100	1,019,800	856,900	700,800
Average Shares	375,400	373,000	376,600	385,700	393,100	394,900	397,000	402,400
Balance Sheet								
Current Assets	5,507,000	4,964,000	4,225,100	4,468,500	4,825,200	4,297,200	3,855,100	3,686,500
Total Assets	12,202,000	11,568,000	9,223,300	8,239,200	7,868,800	7,145,200	6,593,000	6,273,900
Current Liabilities	3,142,000	2,823,000	2,680,500	2,135,600	2,056,700	1,934,600	2,125,800	1,943,300
Long-Term Obligations	3,383,000	3,383,000	1,910,000	1,607,500	1,324,700	1,326,000	1,069,100	1,080,100
Total Liabilities	7,471,000	7,184,000	5,651,400	4,596,000	4,013,900	3,858,300	3,859,800	3,644,500
Stockholders' Equity	4,731,000	4,384,000	3,571,900	3,643,200	3,854,900	3,286,900	2,733,200	2,629,400
Shares Outstanding	368,522	368,103	367,759	374,882	382,884	387,994	388,897	394,562
Statistical Record								
Return on Assets %	12.83	12.01	12.73	13.52	16.04	14.85	13.28	12.07
Return on Equity %	32.95	31.40	30.81	29.04	33.72	33.88	31.87	30.62
EBITDA Margin %	20.77	17.93	17.86	18.61	20.11	18.45	16.57	15.58
Net Margin %	13.04	10.56	9.90	10.10	10.98	10.02	8.82	7.95
Asset Turnover	1.14	1.14	1.29	1.34	1.46	1.48	1.51	1.52
Current Ratio	1.75	1.76	1.58	2.09	2.35	2.22	1.81	1.90
Debt to Equity	0.72	0.77	0.53	0.44	0.34	0.40	0.39	0.41
Price Range	110.35-75.84	98.19-75.84	97.13-75.73	90.22-70.40	76.77-64.71	71.80-50.56	65.35-42.10	52.59-27.86
P/E Ratio	29.82-20.50	29.31-22.64	32.81-25.58	31.99-24.96	25.09-21.15	27.83-19.60	30.25-19.49	30.23-16.01
Average Yield %	1.52	1.52	1.30	1.17	1.10	1.74	1.22	0.94

Address: 767 Fifth Avenue, New York, NY 10153	Web Site: www.elcompanies.com	Auditors: KPMG LLP
Telephone: 212-572-4200	Officers: William P. Lauder - Executive Chairman Leonard A. Lauder - Chairman Emeritus, Chairman	Investor Contact: 800-308-2334 Transfer Agents: Computershare, Providence, RI

LAZARD LTD

Exchange	Symbol	Price	52Wk Range	Yield	P/E
NYS	LAZ	$52.50 (12/29/2017)	52.50-40.61	3.12	15.00

*7 Year Price Score 88.77 ***NYSE Composite Index=100** ***12 Month Price Score 102.66**

Interim Earnings (Per Share)

Qtr.	Mar	Jun	Sep	Dec
2014	0.61	0.64	0.67	1.29
2015	0.42	2.82	2.99	1.18
2016	0.50	0.61	0.85	0.96
2017	0.81	0.91	0.82	...

Interim Dividends (Per Share)

Amt	Decl	Ex	Rec	Pay
0.38Q	02/01/2017	02/09/2017	02/13/2017	02/24/2017
0.41Q	04/26/2017	05/04/2017	05/08/2017	05/19/2017
0.41Q	07/26/2017	08/03/2017	08/07/2017	08/18/2017
0.41Q	10/25/2017	11/03/2017	11/06/2017	11/17/2017

Indicated Div: $1.64

Valuation Analysis | **Institutional Holding**

Forecast EPS	N/A	No of Institutions 421
Market Cap	$6.3 Billion	Shares
Book Value	$1.3 Billion	108,928,072
Price/Book	4.82	% Held
Price/Sales	2.33	87.66

Business Summary: Finance Intermediaries & Services (MIC: 5.5.1 SIC: 6282 NAIC: 523930)

Lazard is a financial advisory and asset management firm. Co. focuses primarily on two business segments: Financial Advisory, which provides a range of financial advisory services regarding mergers and acquisitions and other strategic matters, restructurings, capital structure, capital raising and various other financial matters; and Asset Management, which provides a range of global investment solutions and investment management services in equity and fixed income strategies, alternative investments and private equity funds to corporations, public funds, sovereign entities, endowments and foundations, labor funds, financial intermediaries and private clients.

Recent Developments: For the quarter ended Sep 30 2017, net income decreased 1.0% to US$111.5 million from US$112.6 million in the year-earlier quarter. Revenues were US$638.1 million, up 2.7% from US$621.1 million the year before. Operating income was US$144.2 million versus US$149.0 million in the prior-year quarter, a decrease of 3.2%. Direct operating expenses rose 8.8% to US$13.3 million from US$12.2 million in the comparable period the year before. Indirect operating expenses increased 4.5% to US$480.6 million from US$459.9 million in the equivalent prior-year period.

Prospects: Our evaluation of Lazard Ltd. as of Sep. 17, 2017 is the result of our systematic analysis on three basic characteristics: earnings strength, relative valuation, and recent stock price movement. The company has managed to produce a neutral trend in earnings per share over the past 5 quarters. However, while recent estimates for the company have been lowered by analysts, LAZ has posted better than expected results. Based on operating earnings yield, the company is undervalued when compared to all of the companies in our coverage universe. Share price change over the past year indicates that LAZ will perform very well over the near term.

Financial Data

(US$ in Thousands)	9 Mos	6 Mos	3 Mos	12/31/2016	12/31/2015	12/31/2014	12/31/2013	12/31/2012
Earnings Per Share	3.50	3.53	3.23	2.92	7.40	3.20	1.21	0.65
Cash Flow Per Share	8.08	7.04	6.48	4.81	7.08	6.02	4.36	4.11
Tang Book Value Per Share	7.62	7.02	6.23	6.99	7.86	2.94	1.63	1.53
Dividends Per Share	2.780	2.750	2.720	2.690	2.350	1.200	1.000	1.160
Dividend Payout %	79.43	77.90	84.21	92.12	31.76	37.50	82.64	178.46
Income Statement								
Total Revenue	2,005,497	1,367,366	637,420	2,383,663	2,404,767	2,363,017	2,064,733	1,994,013
EBITDA	757,075	536,656	246,537	585,972	21,986	560,316	261,671	163,099
Depn & Amortn	290,165	213,958	96,340	68,511	38,606	40,851	44,864	39,214
Income Before Taxes	466,910	322,698	150,197	517,461	(16,620)	519,465	216,807	123,885
Income Taxes	124,109	91,367	39,767	123,769	(1,009,552)	85,402	51,693	31,100
Net Income	337,141	227,931	107,553	387,698	986,373	427,277	160,212	84,309
Average Shares	132,393	132,139	132,689	132,633	133,244	133,813	133,737	129,325
Balance Sheet								
Current Assets	2,493,751	2,401,365	2,025,252	2,245,765	2,054,105	1,875,226	1,661,082	1,685,959
Total Assets	4,836,388	4,769,762	4,385,258	4,556,508	4,486,766	3,332,236	3,011,137	2,986,893
Current Liabilities	1,192,858	1,208,272	914,784	1,113,149	1,186,512	942,468	803,528	740,989
Long-Term Obligations	1,189,936	1,189,489	1,195,956	1,195,805	1,007,378	1,060,365	1,064,184	1,094,713
Total Liabilities	3,528,546	3,526,736	3,232,181	3,320,521	3,173,311	2,625,492	2,450,928	2,417,237
Stockholders' Equity	1,307,842	1,243,026	1,153,077	1,235,987	1,313,455	706,744	560,209	569,656
Shares Outstanding	120,118	121,605	122,886	122,137	125,512	122,315	120,739	115,413
Statistical Record								
Return on Assets %	10.18	10.43	10.20	8.55	25.23	13.47	5.34	2.77
Return on Equity %	36.47	39.21	36.96	30.33	97.65	67.45	28.36	12.98
EBITDA Margin %	37.75	39.25	38.68	24.58	0.91	23.71	12.67	8.18
Net Margin %	16.81	16.67	16.87	16.26	41.02	18.08	7.76	4.23
Asset Turnover	0.59	0.60	0.60	0.53	0.62	0.75	0.69	0.66
Current Ratio	2.09	1.99	2.21	2.02	1.73	1.99	2.07	2.28
Debt to Equity	0.91	0.96	1.04	0.97	0.77	1.50	1.90	1.92
Price Range	48.01-34.18	46.81-29.39	45.99-27.00	45.01-27.00	58.78-41.47	54.96-41.37	45.32-29.84	31.49-22.33
P/E Ratio	13.72-9.77	13.26-8.33	14.24-8.36	15.41-9.25	7.94-5.60	17.18-12.93	37.45-24.66	48.45-34.35
Average Yield %	6.50	6.81	7.19	7.45	4.65	2.44	2.77	4.18

Address: Clarendon House, 2 Church Street, Hamilton, HM 11 **Telephone:** 441-295-1422	**Web Site:** www.lazard.com **Officers:** Kenneth M. Jacobs - Chairman, Chief Executive Officer Evan Russo - Chief Financial Officer, Associate/Affiliate Company Officer	**Auditors:** Deloitte & Touche LLP **Investor Contact:** 212-632-6637 **Transfer Agents:** Computershare, Pittsburgh, PA

LEAR CORP.

Exchange	Symbol	Price	52Wk Range	Yield	P/E
NYS	LEA	$176.66 (12/29/2017)	180.89-132.08	1.13	11.02

*7 Year Price Score 134.79 *NYSE Composite Index=100 *12 Month Price Score 109.12

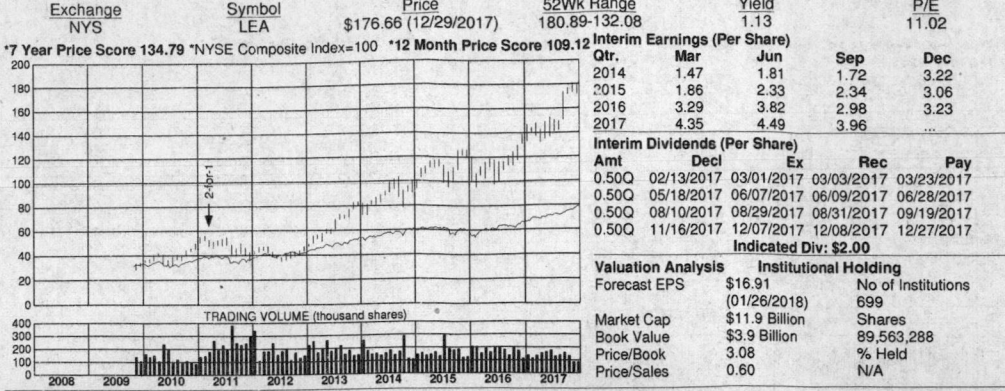

Interim Earnings (Per Share)

Qtr.	Mar	Jun	Sep	Dec
2014	1.47	1.81	1.72	3.22
2015	1.86	2.33	2.34	3.06
2016	3.29	3.82	2.98	3.23
2017	4.35	4.49	3.96	...

Interim Dividends (Per Share)

Amt	Decl	Ex	Rec	Pay
0.50Q	02/13/2017	03/01/2017	03/03/2017	03/23/2017
0.50Q	05/18/2017	06/07/2017	06/09/2017	06/28/2017
0.50Q	08/10/2017	08/29/2017	08/31/2017	09/19/2017
0.50Q	11/16/2017	12/07/2017	12/08/2017	12/27/2017

Indicated Div: $2.00

Valuation Analysis   **Institutional Holding**

Forecast EPS	$16.91	No of Institutions	
	(01/26/2018)	699	
Market Cap	$11.9 Billion	Shares	
Book Value	$3.9 Billion	89,563,288	
Price/Book	3.08	% Held	
Price/Sales	0.60	N/A	

TRADING VOLUME (thousand shares)

Business Summary: Auto Parts (MIC: 1.8.2 SIC: 3714 NAIC: 336360)

Lear is a designer and manufacturer of automotive seating and electrical distribution systems and related components. Co. has two segments: seating, which consists of the design, development, engineering, assembly and delivery of seat systems, and the design, development, engineering and manufacture of seat components, including seat covers and surface materials such as leather and fabric, and seating-related electrical and electronics (including software products); and e-systems, which consists of the design, development, engineering, manufacture, assembly and supply of electrical distribution systems, electronic modules and related components and software for light vehicles globally.

Recent Developments: For the quarter ended Sep 30 2017, net income increased 34.0% to US$315.0 million from US$235.0 million in the year-earlier quarter. Revenues were US$4.98 billion, up 10.1% from US$4.53 billion the year before. Direct operating expenses rose 10.3% to US$4.43 billion from US$4.01 billion in the comparable period the year before. Indirect operating expenses increased 1.1% to US$170.7 million from US$168.8 million in the equivalent prior-year period.

Prospects: Our evaluation of Lear Corp. as of Jan. 21, 2018 is the result of our systematic analysis on three basic characteristics: earnings strength, relative valuation, and recent stock price movement. The company has managed to produce a neutral trend in earnings per share over the past 5 quarters and while recent estimates for the company have been raised by analysts, LEA has posted better than expected results. Based on operating earnings yield, the company is undervalued when compared to all of the companies in our coverage universe. Share price changes over the past year indicates that LEA will perform in line with the market over the near term.

Financial Data

(US$ in Thousands)	9 Mos	6 Mos	3 Mos	12/31/2016	12/31/2015	12/31/2014	12/31/2013	12/31/2012
Earnings Per Share	16.03	15.05	14.38	13.33	9.59	8.23	4.99	12.85
Cash Flow Per Share	25.12	23.90	23.11	22.32	16.56	11.57	9.64	7.40
Tang Book Value Per Share	36.77	34.52	31.93	27.88	25.16	28.62	28.34	28.57
Dividends Per Share	1.800	1.600	1.400	1.200	1.000	0.800	0.680	0.560
Dividend Payout %	11.23	10.63	9.74	9.00	10.43	9.72	13.63	4.36
Income Statement								
Total Revenue	15,103,200	10,121,700	4,998,500	18,557,600	18,211,400	17,727,300	16,234,000	14,567,000
EBITDA	1,536,500	1,017,800	509,900	1,799,000	1,466,000	1,165,800	964,000	938,400
Depn & Amortn	313,200	201,500	96,900	378,200	347,800	310,900	285,500	239,600
Income Before Taxes	1,159,400	774,100	392,200	1,338,300	1,031,500	787,400	610,100	648,900
Income Taxes	240,200	162,400	89,100	370,200	285,500	121,400	192,700	(638,000)
Net Income	912,900	617,700	305,800	975,100	745,500	672,400	431,400	1,282,800
Average Shares	68,834	69,448	70,327	73,124	77,767	81,728	86,415	99,825
Balance Sheet								
Current Assets	6,563,000	6,341,900	6,228,900	5,649,300	5,286,600	5,379,600	4,922,500	4,873,500
Total Assets	11,712,000	11,237,200	10,600,500	9,900,600	9,405,800	9,150,200	8,330,900	8,194,100
Current Liabilities	4,893,000	4,942,300	4,630,700	4,182,300	3,839,600	3,957,800	3,579,100	3,216,900
Long-Term Obligations	1,953,000	1,877,100	1,889,000	1,898,000	1,931,700	1,475,000	1,057,100	626,300
Total Liabilities	7,840,900	7,615,300	7,269,500	6,843,400	6,478,400	6,191,400	5,285,000	4,707,000
Stockholders' Equity	3,871,100	3,621,900	3,331,000	3,057,200	2,927,400	2,958,800	3,045,900	3,487,100
Shares Outstanding	67,560	68,063	68,947	69,431	74,464	78,021	80,751	95,942
Statistical Record								
Return on Assets %	10.39	9.94	10.04	10.07	8.04	7.69	5.22	16.83
Return on Equity %	32.89	32.01	32.42	32.50	25.33	22.40	13.21	43.19
EBITDA Margin %	10.17	10.06	10.20	9.69	8.05	6.58	5.94	6.44
Net Margin %	6.04	6.10	6.12	5.25	4.09	3.79	2.66	8.81
Asset Turnover	1.80	1.80	1.84	1.92	1.96	2.03	1.96	1.91
Current Ratio	1.34	1.28	1.35	1.35	1.38	1.36	1.38	1.51
Debt to Equity	0.50	0.52	0.57	0.62	0.66	0.50	0.35	0.18
Price Range	173.89-112.84	152.87-99.45	148.20-97.71	138.80-94.98	126.34-93.40	103.28-71.97	83.11-46.84	47.01-34.81
P/E Ratio	10.85-7.04	10.16-6.61	10.31-6.79	10.41-7.13	13.17-9.74	12.55-8.74	16.66-9.39	3.66-2.71
Average Yield %	1.29	1.22	1.14	1.05	0.90	0.90	1.06	1.35

Address: 21557 Telegraph Road, Southfield, MI 48033
Telephone: 248-447-1500
Fax: 248-447-5250

Web Site: www.lear.com
Officers: Matthew J. Simoncini - President, Chief Executive Officer, Senior Vice President, Chief Financial Officer, Chief Accounting Officer Terrence B. Larkin - Executive Vice President, Senior Vice President, General Counsel, Corporate Secretary

Auditors: Ernst & Young LLP
Investor Contact: 248-447-1500
Transfer Agents: Computershare Trust Company, Canton, MA

LEGG MASON, INC.

Exchange	Symbol	Price	52Wk Range	Yield	P/E
NYS	LM	$41.98 (12/29/2017)	42.15-30.70	2.67	16.46

*7 Year Price Score 79.80 ***NYSE Composite Index=100** ***12 Month Price Score 99.94**

TRADING VOLUME (thousand shares)

Interim Earnings (Per Share)

Qtr.	Jun	Sep	Dec	Mar
2014-15	0.61	0.04	0.67	0.72
2015-16	0.84	0.58	(1.31)	(0.42)
2016-17	0.31	0.63	0.50	0.75
2017-18	0.52	0.78	...	

Interim Dividends (Per Share)

Amt	Decl	Ex	Rec	Pay
0.22Q	02/01/2017	03/14/2017	03/16/2017	04/17/2017
0.28Q	04/26/2017	06/09/2017	06/13/2017	07/10/2017
0.28Q	07/26/2017	10/04/2017	10/05/2017	10/23/2017
0.28Q	10/31/2017	12/19/2017	12/20/2018	01/15/2018

Indicated Div: $1.12

Valuation Analysis / Institutional Holding

Valuation Analysis		Institutional Holding	
Forecast EPS	$2.91	No of Institutions	
	(01/18/2018)	529	
Market Cap	$3.9 Billion	Shares	
Book Value	$4.0 Billion	109,597,224	
Price/Book	0.97	% Held	
Price/Sales	1.29	71.80	

Business Summary: Wealth Management (MIC: 5.5.2 SIC: 6282 NAIC: 523930)

Legg Mason is a holding company. Through its subsidiaries, Co. is an asset management company that provides investment management and related services to institutional and individual clients, company-sponsored mutual funds and other pooled investment vehicles. Co.'s investment advisory services include discretionary and non-discretionary management of separate investment accounts in numerous investment styles for institutional and individual investors. Co.'s investment products include proprietary mutual funds ranging from money market and other liquidity products. Co. also provides other domestic and offshore funds. As of Mar 31 2017, Co. had assets under management of $728.41 billion.

Recent Developments: For the quarter ended Sep 30 2017, net income increased 1.3% to US$87.6 million from US$86.5 million in the year-earlier quarter. Revenues were US$768.3 million, up 2.7% from US$748.4 million the year before. Operating income was US$144.4 million versus US$127.6 million in the prior-year quarter, an increase of 13.2%. Indirect operating expenses increased 0.5% to US$523.9 million from US$620.7 million in the equivalent prior-year period.

Prospects: Our evaluation of Legg Mason Inc. as of Jan. 14, 2018 is the result of our systematic analysis on three basic characteristics: earnings strength, relative valuation, and recent stock price movement. The company has generated a negative trend in earnings per share over the past 5 quarters and while recent estimates for the company have been raised by analysts, LM has posted better than expected results. Based on operating earnings yield, the company is undervalued when compared to all of the companies in our coverage universe. Share price changes over the past year indicates that LM will perform in line with the market over the near term.

Financial Data

(US$ in Thousands)	6 Mos	3 Mos	03/31/2017	03/31/2016	03/31/2015	03/31/2014	03/31/2013	03/31/2012
Earnings Per Share	2.55	2.40	2.18	(0.25)	2.04	2.33	(2.65)	1.54
Cash Flow Per Share	6.21	6.24	5.37	4.22	5.07	3.59	2.28	3.46
Tang Book Value Per Share	N.M.	N.M.	N.M.	N.M.	N.M.	2.67	2.96	3.90
Dividends Per Share	0.940	0.940	0.880	0.800	0.640	0.520	0.440	0.320
Dividend Payout %	36.86	39.17	40.37	...	31.37	22.32	...	20.78
Income Statement								
Total Revenue	1,562,180	793,842	2,886,902	2,660,844	2,819,106	2,741,757	2,612,650	2,662,574
EBITDA	299,275	132,660	557,449	77,908	473,913	529,030	(367,430)	472,981
Depn & Amortn	25,883	13,070	80,213	60,297	55,086	62,845	87,848	93,795
Income Before Taxes	218,089	91,792	370,878	(25,218)	367,993	419,641	(510,607)	303,083
Income Taxes	66,928	28,255	84,175	7,692	125,284	137,805	(150,859)	72,052
Net Income	126,584	50,920	227,256	(25,032)	237,080	284,784	(353,327)	220,817
Average Shares	93,496	95,297	100,799	107,406	113,246	122,383	133,226	143,349
Balance Sheet								
Current Assets	1,751,556	1,605,601	1,801,747	2,385,128	1,922,035	2,128,383	1,942,862	2,457,794
Total Assets	8,195,665	8,054,429	8,290,415	7,520,446	7,073,977	7,111,349	7,269,660	8,555,747
Current Liabilities	699,018	586,384	809,387	841,553	815,046	821,245	702,466	975,782
Long-Term Obligations	2,221,839	2,221,853	2,221,867	1,740,985	1,058,089	1,038,826	1,302,351	1,407,321
Total Liabilities	4,229,494	4,087,897	4,307,041	3,306,883	2,589,076	2,386,625	2,451,309	2,878,456
Stockholders' Equity	3,966,171	3,966,532	3,983,374	4,213,563	4,484,901	4,724,724	4,818,351	5,677,291
Shares Outstanding	91,892	94,119	95,726	107,011	111,469	117,173	125,341	139,874
Statistical Record								
Return on Assets %	3.09	2.99	2.87	N.M.	3.34	3.96	N.M.	2.55
Return on Equity %	6.33	6.07	5.54	N.M.	5.15	5.97	N.M.	3.85
EBITDA Margin %	19.16	16.71	19.31	2.93	16.81	19.30	N.M.	17.76
Net Margin %	8.10	6.41	7.87	N.M.	8.41	10.39	N.M.	8.29
Asset Turnover	0.36	0.36	0.37	0.36	0.40	0.38	0.33	0.31
Current Ratio	2.51	2.74	2.23	2.83	2.36	2.59	2.77	2.52
Debt to Equity	0.56	0.56	0.56	0.41	0.24	0.22	0.27	0.25
Price Range	41.41-28.35	40.55-28.35	37.72-27.77	55.58-35.20	58.92-43.36	49.04-29.76	32.15-22.38	37.53-22.95
P/E Ratio	16.24-11.12	16.90-11.81	17.30-12.74	...	28.88-21.25	21.05-12.77	...	24.37-14.90
Average Yield %	2.64	2.74	2.67	1.83	1.24	1.39	1.68	1.10

Address: 100 International Drive, Baltimore, MD 21202 **Telephone:** 410-539-0000	**Web Site:** www.leggmason.com **Officers:** Joseph A. Sullivan - Chairman, President, Chief Executive Officer, Acting Chief Executive Officer, Senior Executive Vice President, Chief Administrative Officer Peter H. Nachtwey - Chief Financial Officer, Senior Executive Vice President	**Auditors:** PricewaterhouseCoopers LLP **Investor Contact:** 410-454-5246 **Transfer Agents:** American Stock Transfer & Trust Company, New York, NY

LEGGETT & PLATT, INC.

Exchange	Symbol	Price	52Wk Range	Yield	P/E	Div Achiever
NYS	LEG	$47.73 (12/29/2017)	54.04-43.50	3.02	19.48	45 Years

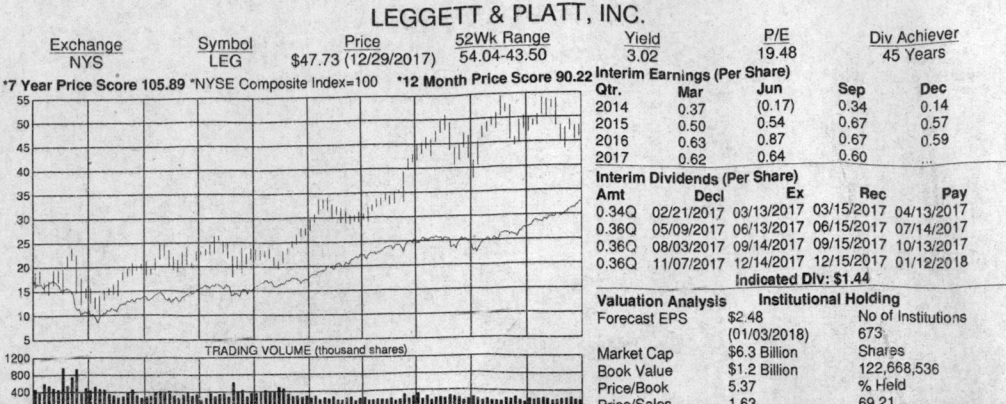

*7 Year Price Score 105.89 *NYSE Composite Index=100 *12 Month Price Score 90.22

Interim Earnings (Per Share)

Qtr.	Mar	Jun	Sep	Dec
2014	0.37	(0.17)	0.34	0.14
2015	0.50	0.54	0.67	0.57
2016	0.63	0.87	0.67	0.59
2017	0.62	0.64	0.60	...

Interim Dividends (Per Share)

Amt	Decl	Ex	Rec	Pay
0.34Q	02/21/2017	03/13/2017	03/15/2017	04/13/2017
0.36Q	05/09/2017	06/13/2017	06/15/2017	07/14/2017
0.36Q	08/03/2017	09/14/2017	09/15/2017	10/13/2017
0.36Q	11/07/2017	12/14/2017	12/15/2017	01/12/2018

Indicated Div: $1.44

Valuation Analysis / **Institutional Holding**

Forecast EPS	$2.48	No of Institutions
	(01/03/2018)	673
Market Cap	$6.3 Billion	Shares
Book Value	$1.2 Billion	122,668,536
Price/Book	5.37	% Held
Price/Sales	1.63	69.21

Business Summary: Furniture (MIC: 1.6.2 SIC: 2519 NAIC: 337121)

Leggett & Platt designs and produces engineered components and products. Co. has four segments: Residential Furnishings, which supplies a variety of components used by bedding and upholstered furniture manufacturers in the assembly of their finished products; Commercial Products, which designs, manufactures, and distributes a range of components and products primarily for the office seating market; Industrial Materials, which supplies steel wire; and Specialized Products, which designs, manufactures and sells products including automotive seating components, tubing for the aerospace industry, machinery and equipment, and service van interiors.

Recent Developments: For the quarter ended Sep 30 2017, income from continuing operations decreased 10.8% to US$83.5 million from US$93.6 million in the year-earlier quarter. Net income decreased 11.8% to US$82.6 million from US$93.6 million in the year-earlier quarter. Revenues were US$1.01 billion, up 6.4% from US$948.9 million the year before. Operating income was US$109.2 million versus US$130.2 million in the prior-year quarter, a decrease of 16.1%. Direct operating expenses rose 10.0% to US$793.9 million from US$721.5 million in the comparable period the year before. Indirect operating expenses increased 9.7% to US$106.6 million from US$97.2 million in the equivalent prior-year period.

Prospects: Our evaluation of Leggett & Platt Inc. as of Jan. 14, 2018 is the result of our systematic analysis on three basic characteristics: earnings strength, relative valuation, and recent stock price movement. The company has produced a positive trend in earnings per share over the past 5 quarters and while recent estimates for the company have been mixed, LEG has posted better than expected results. Based on operating earnings yield, the company is undervalued when compared to all of the companies in our coverage universe. Share price changes over the past year indicates that LEG will perform poorly over the near term.

Financial Data

(US$ in Thousands)	9 Mos	6 Mos	3 Mos	12/31/2016	12/31/2015	12/31/2014	12/31/2013	12/31/2012
Earnings Per Share	2.45	2.52	2.75	2.76	2.28	0.68	1.34	1.70
Cash Flow Per Share	3.16	3.28	3.65	4.00	2.55	2.70	2.87	3.11
Tang Book Value Per Share	1.36	1.06	0.58	1.01	0.64	0.89	1.87	1.67
Dividends Per Share	1.400	1.380	1.360	1.340	1.260	1.220	1.180	1.140
Dividend Payout %	57.14	54.76	49.45	48.55	55.26	179.41	88.06	67.06
Income Statement								
Total Revenue	2,959,300	1,949,600	960,300	3,749,900	3,917,200	3,782,300	3,746,000	3,720,800
EBITDA	441,800	300,400	146,200	628,700	590,800	441,100	400,900	457,400
Depn & Amortn	94,400	62,200	30,300	106,700	104,300	109,600	116,100	116,100
Income Before Taxes	321,400	220,700	107,300	487,100	449,800	295,500	247,800	304,400
Income Taxes	64,200	47,000	21,200	120,000	121,800	70,300	55,000	56,300
Net Income	256,300	173,700	86,100	385,800	325,100	98,000	197,300	248,200
Average Shares	136,900	137,400	138,100	140,000	142,900	143,200	147,300	145,963
Balance Sheet								
Current Assets	1,549,700	1,540,200	1,413,100	1,324,900	1,311,200	1,429,600	1,281,700	1,339,100
Total Assets	3,323,700	3,281,500	3,119,500	2,984,100	2,967,600	3,140,600	3,108,100	3,254,900
Current Liabilities	891,500	741,700	716,600	706,600	701,200	992,200	829,500	731,000
Long-Term Obligations	1,044,400	1,183,500	1,119,900	956,200	945,400	766,700	688,400	853,900
Total Liabilities	2,151,500	2,148,400	2,055,500	1,892,500	1,882,000	1,994,100	1,716,800	1,820,400
Stockholders' Equity	1,172,200	1,133,100	1,064,000	1,091,600	1,085,600	1,146,500	1,391,300	1,434,500
Shares Outstanding	131,817	132,285	132,307	133,500	135,600	137,800	139,400	142,100
Statistical Record								
Return on Assets %	10.57	11.05	12.45	12.93	10.64	3.14	6.20	8.02
Return on Equity %	29.73	31.76	35.69	35.34	29.13	7.72	13.96	18.12
EBITDA Margin %	14.93	15.41	15.22	16.77	15.08	11.66	10.70	12.29
Net Margin %	8.66	8.91	8.97	10.29	8.30	2.59	5.27	6.67
Asset Turnover	1.21	1.20	1.23	1.26	1.28	1.21	1.18	1.20
Current Ratio	1.74	2.08	1.97	1.88	1.87	1.44	1.55	1.83
Debt to Equity	0.89	1.04	1.05	0.88	0.87	0.67	0.49	0.60
Price Range	54.04-43.50	54.53-44.39	54.53-44.39	54.53-37.79	51.00-40.68	42.95-29.06	34.19-27.22	27.85-19.49
P/E Ratio	22.06-17.76	21.64-17.62	19.83-16.14	19.76-13.69	22.37-17.84	63.16-42.74	25.51-20.31	16.38-11.46
Average Yield %	2.84	2.76	2.76	2.80	2.76	3.53	3.83	4.88

Address: No. 1 Leggett Road, Carthage, MO 64836	Web Site: www.leggett.com	Auditors: PricewaterhouseCoopers LLP
Telephone: 417-358-8131	Officers: Robert Ted Enloe - Chairman Karl G. Glassman - President, Chief Executive Officer, Executive Vice President, Chief Operating Officer	Investor Contact: 417-358-8131 Transfer Agents: Wells Fargo Shareowner Services, St. Paul, MN

LEIDOS HOLDINGS INC

Exchange	Symbol	Price	52Wk Range	Yield	P/E
NYS	LDOS	$64.57 (12/29/2017)	65.22-48.31	1.98	34.72

*7 Year Price Score 100.76 *NYSE Composite Index=100 *12 Month Price Score 107.09

Interim Earnings (Per Share)

Qtr.	Mar	Jun	Sep	Dec
2015	0.55	0.50	0.67	1.55
2016	0.66	0.55	0.80	0.22
2017	0.47	0.64	0.53	...

Interim Dividends (Per Share)

Amt	Decl	Ex	Rec	Pay
0.32Q	02/17/2017	03/13/2017	03/15/2017	03/30/2017
0.32Q	05/12/2017	06/13/2017	06/15/2017	06/30/2017
0.32Q	09/08/2017	09/15/2017	09/18/2017	09/29/2017
0.32Q	12/08/2017	12/15/2017	12/18/2017	12/29/2017

Indicated Div: $1.28 (Div. Reinv. Plan)

Valuation Analysis / **Institutional Holding**

Forecast EPS	$3.70	No of Institutions
	(01/25/2018)	531
Market Cap	$9.8 Billion	Shares
Book Value	$3.3 Billion	154,051,808
Price/Book	2.96	% Held
Price/Sales	0.95	N/A

Business Summary: IT Services (MIC: 6.3.1 SIC: 7373 NAIC: 541330)

Leidos Holdings is a holding company. Through its subsidiaries, Co. provides technology and engineering services and solutions in the defense, intelligence, civil and health markets. Co. operates these segments: National Security Solutions, which deploys solutions in the areas of intelligence surveillance and reconnaissance, integrated systems and cybersecurity and global services; Information Systems & Global Solutions, which focuses on being a provider of information technology, management and engineering services; and Health and Infrastructure, which provides services and solutions focused on information technology and behavioral health and life sciences offerings.

Recent Developments: For the quarter ended Sep 29 2017, net income decreased 14.1% to US$79.0 million in the year-earlier quarter. Revenues were US$2.50 billion, up 34.0% from US$1.87 billion the year before. Operating income was US$151.0 million versus US$101.0 million in the prior-year quarter, an increase of 49.5%. Direct operating expenses rose 34.3% to US$2.19 billion from US$1.63 billion in the comparable period the year before. Indirect operating expenses increased 19.0% to US$163.0 million from US$137.0 million in the equivalent prior-year period.

Prospects: Our evaluation of Leidos Holdings Inc. as of Jan. 21, 2018 is the result of our systematic analysis on three basic characteristics: earnings strength, relative valuation, and recent stock price movement. The company has generated a negative trend in earnings per share over the past 5 quarters and while recent estimates for the company have been mixed, LDOS has posted better than expected results. Based on operating earnings yield, the company is undervalued when compared to all of the companies in our coverage universe. Share price changes over the past year indicates that LDOS will perform well over the near term.

Financial Data
(US$ in Millions)

	9 Mos	6 Mos	3 Mos	12/30/2016	01/01/2016	01/30/2015	01/31/2014	01/31/2013
Earnings Per Share	1.86	2.13	2.04	2.35	3.27	(4.36)	1.94	6.16
Cash Flow Per Share	3.45	3.16	2.51	4.38	5.96	5.37	2.35	4.13
Tang Book Value Per Share	N.M.	N.M.	N.M.	N.M.	N.M.	N.M.	N.M.	2.73
Dividends Per Share	1.280	14.920	14.920	14.920	1.280	1.280	0.640	1.920
Dividend Payout %	68.82	700.47	731.37	634.89	39.14	...	32.99	31.17
Income Statement								
Total Revenue	7,654	5,151	2,580	7,043	4,712	5,063	5,772	11,173
EBITDA	501	339	150	432	437	(162)	237	855
Depn & Amortn	42	26	13	38	33	47	81	113
Income Before Taxes	354	243	101	308	355	(283)	88	658
Income Taxes	108	71	34	72	112	47	4	135
Net Income	252	170	72	244	242	(323)	164	525
Average Shares	154	153	153	104	74	74	83	83
Balance Sheet								
Current Assets	2,571	2,434	2,395	2,381	1,793	1,618	1,794	3,079
Total Assets	8,923	8,882	9,140	9,132	3,377	3,281	4,162	5,875
Current Liabilities	2,021	1,910	1,983	2,016	1,040	951	1,009	1,793
Long-Term Obligations	3,043	3,147	3,188	3,225	1,086	1,164	1,331	1,296
Total Liabilities	5,629	5,658	5,963	5,997	2,309	2,283	2,567	3,257
Stockholders' Equity	3,294	3,224	3,177	3,135	1,068	998	1,595	2,618
Shares Outstanding	151	151	151	150	72	74	80	85
Statistical Record								
Return on Assets %	3.36	5.21	4.20	3.91	6.99	N.M.	3.27	8.35
Return on Equity %	9.70	14.72	12.29	11.64	19.80	N.M.	7.79	21.82
EBITDA Margin %	6.55	6.58	5.81	6.13	9.27	N.M.	4.11	7.65
Net Margin %	3.29	3.30	2.79	3.46	5.14	N.M.	2.84	4.70
Asset Turnover	1.11	1.56	1.33	1.13	1.36	1.36	1.15	1.78
Current Ratio	1.27	1.27	1.21	1.18	1.72	1.70	1.78	1.72
Debt to Equity	0.92	0.98	1.00	1.03	1.02	1.17	0.83	0.50
Price Range	59.43-41.18	56.37-38.50	54.87-38.50	56.19-38.50	59.05-38.05	46.07-33.21	49.02-31.06	37.34-28.48
P/E Ratio	31.95-22.14	26.46-18.08	26.90-18.87	23.91-16.38	18.06-11.64	...	25.27-16.01	6.06-4.62
Average Yield %	2.47	30.33	30.91	31.53	2.83	3.26	1.35	5.91

Address: 11951 Freedom Drive, Reston, VA 20190
Telephone: 571-526-6000

Web Site: www.leidos.com
Officers: John P. Jumper - Chairman, President, Chief Executive Officer Roger A. Krone - Chief Executive Officer

Auditors: Deloitte & Touche LLP
Investor Contact: 703-676-2283
Transfer Agents: BNY Mellon Shareowner Services

430

LENNAR CORP

Exchange	Symbol	Price	52Wk Range	Yield	P/E
NYS	LEN	$63.24 (12/29/2017)	64.00-42.19	0.25	18.22

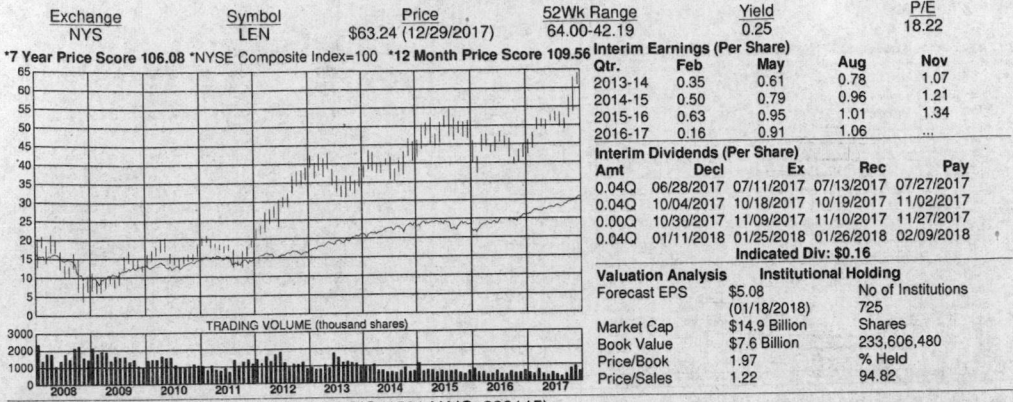

*7 Year Price Score 106.08 *NYSE Composite Index=100 *12 Month Price Score 109.56

Interim Earnings (Per Share)

Qtr.	Feb	May	Aug	Nov
2013-14	0.35	0.61	0.78	1.07
2014-15	0.50	0.79	0.96	1.21
2015-16	0.63	0.95	1.01	1.34
2016-17	0.16	0.91	1.06	...

Interim Dividends (Per Share)

Amt	Decl	Ex	Rec	Pay
0.04Q	06/28/2017	07/11/2017	07/13/2017	07/27/2017
0.04Q	10/04/2017	10/18/2017	10/19/2017	11/02/2017
0.00Q	10/30/2017	11/09/2017	11/10/2017	11/27/2017
0.04Q	01/11/2018	01/25/2018	01/26/2018	02/09/2018

Indicated Div: $0.16

Valuation Analysis / Institutional Holding

Valuation Analysis		Institutional Holding	
Forecast EPS	$5.08	No of Institutions	725
	(01/18/2018)		
Market Cap	$14.9 Billion	Shares	233,606,480
Book Value	$7.6 Billion	% Held	94.82
Price/Book	1.97		
Price/Sales	1.22		

Business Summary: Builders (MIC: 2.2.5 SIC: 1521 NAIC: 236115)

Lennar is a homebuilder, a provider of real estate related financial services, a commercial real estate, investment management and finance company and a developer of multifamily rental properties. Co.'s homebuilding operations include the construction and sale of single-family attached and detached homes as well as the purchase, development and sale of residential land. Co.'s Lennar Financial Services Operations provides mortgage financing and title insurance and closing services; while its Rialto Operations primarily manages third-party capital and originates commercial mortgage loans. Co.'s Lennar Multifamily Operations develops, constructs and manages multifamily rental properties.

Recent Developments: For the quarter ended Aug 31 2017, net income increased 4.5% to US$243.6 million from US$233.1 million in the year-earlier quarter. Revenues were US$3.26 billion, up 15.1% from US$2.83 billion the year before. Direct operating expenses rose 14.9% to US$2.81 billion from US$2.45 billion in the comparable period the year before. Indirect operating expenses increased 19.1% to US$72.9 million from US$61.2 million in the equivalent prior-year period.

Prospects: Our evaluation of Lennar Corp. as of Jan. 14, 2018 is the result of our systematic analysis on three basic characteristics: earnings strength, relative valuation, and recent stock price movement. The company has enjoyed a very positive trend in earnings per share over the past 5 quarters and while recent estimates for the company have been raised by analysts, LEN has posted results that fell short of analysts expectations. Based on operating earnings yield, the company is undervalued when compared to all of the companies in our coverage universe. Share price changes over the past year indicates that LEN will perform in line with the market over the near term.

Financial Data
(US$ in Thousands)

	9 Mos	6 Mos	3 Mos	11/30/2016	11/30/2015	11/30/2014	11/30/2013	11/30/2012
Earnings Per Share	3.47	3.42	3.46	3.93	3.46	2.80	2.15	3.11
Cash Flow Per Share	3.60	2.25	3.46	2.32	(2.05)	(3.90)	(4.24)	(2.27)
Tang Book Value Per Share	31.26	30.39	29.44	29.80	26.57	23.54	20.39	17.83
Dividends Per Share	0.160	0.160	0.160	0.160	0.160	0.160	0.160	0.160
Dividend Payout %	4.61	4.68	4.62	4.07	4.62	5.71	7.44	5.14
Income Statement								
Total Revenue	8,860,796	5,599,320	2,337,428	10,949,999	9,474,008	7,779,812	5,935,095	4,104,706
EBITDA	721,869	358,316	40,440	1,344,728	1,180,426	992,888	783,815	351,191
Depn & Amortn	7,079	5,059	3,132	64,838	63,540	59,929	53,846	49,531
Income Before Taxes	714,790	353,257	37,308	1,275,264	1,104,432	896,408	636,056	207,307
Income Taxes	253,656	128,861	19,969	417,378	390,416	341,091	177,015	(435,218)
Net Income	500,890	251,725	38,080	911,844	802,894	638,916	479,674	679,124
Average Shares	232,674	232,219	232,196	230,712	230,812	228,240	225,920	218,695
Balance Sheet								
Current Assets	11,884,905	11,507,616	11,490,984	10,911,843	10,171,054	9,230,259	7,700,479	6,609,544
Total Assets	16,939,373	16,754,505	16,230,113	15,361,781	14,419,509	12,958,267	11,273,247	10,362,206
Current Liabilities	524,852	492,734	473,802	478,546	475,909	412,558	271,365	220,690
Long-Term Obligations	6,860,644	7,342,157	6,964,623	4,575,977	5,025,130	4,690,213	4,194,432	4,005,051
Total Liabilities	9,385,113	9,431,934	9,124,060	8,335,739	8,770,565	8,131,247	7,104,346	6,947,442
Stockholders' Equity	7,554,260	7,322,571	7,106,053	7,026,042	5,648,944	4,827,020	4,168,901	3,414,764
Shares Outstanding	235,263	234,495	234,464	234,475	211,145	205,039	204,411	191,547
Statistical Record								
Return on Assets %	5.10	5.07	5.30	6.11	5.87	5.27	4.43	6.94
Return on Equity %	11.55	11.92	12.47	14.35	15.33	14.20	12.65	22.16
EBITDA Margin %	8.15	6.40	1.73	12.28	12.46	12.76	13.21	8.56
Net Margin %	5.65	4.50	1.63	8.33	8.47	8.21	8.08	16.55
Asset Turnover	0.77	0.75	0.74	0.73	0.69	0.64	0.55	0.42
Current Ratio	22.64	23.35	24.25	22.80	21.37	22.37	28.38	29.95
Debt to Equity	0.91	1.00	0.98	0.65	0.89	0.97	1.01	1.17
Price Range	53.67-39.65	52.07-39.65	48.32-39.65	51.42-37.16	54.64-40.62	46.70-33.64	43.13-30.99	38.38-17.92
P/E Ratio	15.47-11.43	15.22-11.59	13.97-11.46	13.08-9.45	15.79-11.74	16.68-12.01	20.06-14.42	12.34-5.76
Average Yield %	0.34	0.35	0.36	0.36	0.33	0.41	0.48	0.57

Address: 700 Northwest 107th Avenue, Miami, FL 33172	**Web Site:** www.lennar.com	**Auditors:** Deloitte & Touche LLP
Telephone: 305-559-4000	**Officers:** Stuart A. Miller - President, Chief Executive Officer Richard (Rick) Beckwitt - President	**Investor Contact:** 305-559-4000
		Transfer Agents: ComputerShare Investor Services, Providence, RI

LENNOX INTERNATIONAL INC

Exchange	Symbol	Price	52Wk Range	Yield	P/E
NYS	LII	$208.26 (12/29/2017)	210.66-148.51	0.98	29.46

*7 Year Price Score 143.27 *NYSE Composite Index=100 ***12 Month Price Score 108.58**

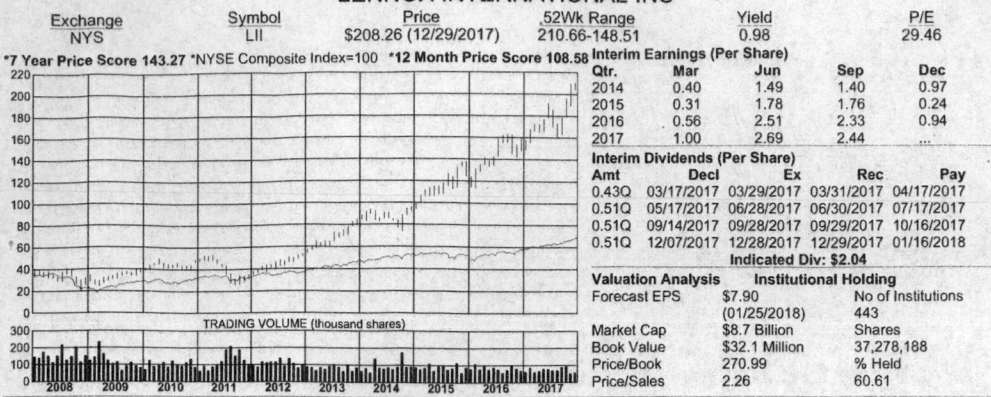

Interim Earnings (Per Share)

Qtr.	Mar	Jun	Sep	Dec
2014	0.40	1.49	1.40	0.97
2015	0.31	1.78	1.76	0.24
2016	0.56	2.51	2.33	0.94
2017	1.00	2.69	2.44	...

Interim Dividends (Per Share)

Amt	Decl	Ex	Rec	Pay
0.43Q	03/17/2017	03/29/2017	03/31/2017	04/17/2017
0.51Q	05/17/2017	06/28/2017	06/30/2017	07/17/2017
0.51Q	09/14/2017	09/28/2017	09/29/2017	10/16/2017
0.51Q	12/07/2017	12/28/2017	12/29/2017	01/16/2018

Indicated Div: $2.04

Valuation Analysis	Institutional Holding	
Forecast EPS	$7.90	No of Institutions
	(01/25/2018)	443
Market Cap	$8.7 Billion	Shares
Book Value	$32.1 Million	37,278,188
Price/Book	270.99	% Held
Price/Sales	2.26	60.61

Business Summary: Industrial Machinery & Equipment (MIC: 7.2.1 SIC: 3585 NAIC: 333415)

Lennox International is a provider of climate control solutions and designs, manufactures and markets products for the heating, ventilation, air conditioning and refrigeration markets. Co. has three segments: Residential Heating and Cooling, which provides furnaces, air conditioners, heat pumps, packaged heating and cooling systems, and comfort control products, among others, for the residential replacement and new construction markets; Commercial Heating and Cooling, which manufactures and sells unitary heating and cooling equipment for light commercial applications; and Refrigeration, which provides condensing units, unit coolers, fluid coolers, and air-cooled condensers, among others.

Recent Developments: For the quarter ended Sep 30 2017, income from continuing operations increased 2.3% to US$104.0 million from US$101.7 million in the year-earlier quarter. Net income increased 1.8% to US$103.5 million from US$101.7 million in the year-earlier quarter. Revenues were US$1.05 billion, up 4.2% from US$1.01 billion the year before. Operating income was US$154.6 million versus US$156.9 million in the prior-year quarter, a decrease of 1.5%. Direct operating expenses rose 5.6% to US$738.6 million from US$699.7 million in the comparable period the year before. Indirect operating expenses increased 3.7% to US$159.1 million from US$153.4 million in the equivalent prior-year period.

Prospects: Our evaluation of Lennox International Inc. as of Jan. 21, 2018 is the result of our systematic analysis on three basic characteristics: earnings strength, relative valuation, and recent stock price movement. The company has managed to produce a neutral trend in earnings per share over the past 5 quarters and while recent estimates for the company have been mixed, LII has posted better than expected results. Based on operating earnings yield, the company is about fairly valued when compared to all of the companies in our coverage universe. Share price changes over the past year indicates that LII will perform in line with the market over the near term.

Financial Data

(US$ in Thousands)	9 Mos	6 Mos	3 Mos	12/31/2016	12/31/2015	12/31/2014	12/31/2013	12/31/2012
Earnings Per Share	7.07	6.96	6.78	6.32	4.09	4.23	3.39	1.75
Cash Flow Per Share	8.99	8.21	8.42	8.15	7.38	3.86	4.22	4.35
Tang Book Value Per Share	N.M.	N.M.	...	N.M.	N.M.	N.M.	5.46	5.43
Dividends Per Share	1.880	1.800	1.720	1.650	1.380	1.140	0.920	0.760
Dividend Payout %	26.59	25.86	25.37	26.11	33.74	26.95	27.14	43.43
Income Statement								
Total Revenue	2,947,900	1,895,600	793,400	3,641,600	3,467,400	3,367,400	3,199,100	2,949,400
EBITDA	423,600	257,400	71,000	469,400	355,600	381,800	335,500	263,700
Depn & Amortn	48,100	32,000	15,700	58,100	62,800	60,800	58,900	55,400
Income Before Taxes	352,200	209,700	47,900	384,300	269,200	303,800	262,100	191,200
Income Taxes	103,800	60,700	9,900	124,100	95,400	109,500	94,400	66,700
Net Income	262,500	159,000	43,500	277,800	186,600	205,800	171,800	90,000
Average Shares	42,400	42,900	43,500	44,000	45,600	48,600	50,600	51,400
Balance Sheet								
Current Assets	1,270,600	1,366,700	1,186,400	1,005,900	938,200	1,014,000	902,400	987,100
Total Assets	2,055,700	2,145,800	1,950,600	1,760,300	1,680,200	1,764,300	1,626,700	1,691,900
Current Liabilities	1,023,700	989,500	1,037,500	888,600	824,000	827,300	714,000	639,600
Long-Term Obligations	775,700	922,600	693,900	615,700	508,600	675,000	233,200	351,200
Total Liabilities	2,023,600	2,135,600	1,952,000	1,722,700	1,579,000	1,755,900	1,141,800	1,195,100
Stockholders' Equity	32,100	10,200	(1,400)	37,600	101,200	8,400	484,900	496,800
Shares Outstanding	41,768	42,177	42,733	42,974	44,678	44,635	49,103	50,232
Statistical Record								
Return on Assets %	15.22	14.45	15.55	16.10	10.83	12.14	10.35	5.28
Return on Equity %	1,084.08	1,462.14	...	399.19	340.51	83.44	35.00	18.61
EBITDA Margin %	14.37	13.58	8.95	12.89	10.26	11.34	10.49	8.94
Net Margin %	8.90	8.39	5.48	7.63	5.38	6.11	5.37	3.05
Asset Turnover	1.93	1.82	1.95	2.11	2.01	1.99	1.93	1.73
Current Ratio	1.24	1.38	1.14	1.13	1.14	1.23	1.26	1.54
Debt to Equity	24.17	90.45	...	16.38	5.03	80.36	0.48	0.71
Price Range	191.87-141.53	191.87-141.53	172.11-133.08	163.16-113.97	137.79-93.85	96.04-73.66	85.12-52.52	53.84-34.74
P/E Ratio	27.14-20.02	27.57-20.33	25.38-19.63	25.82-18.03	33.69-22.95	22.70-17.41	25.11-15.49	30.77-19.85
Average Yield %	1.14	1.12	1.13	1.16	1.20	1.31	1.35	1.71

Address: 2140 Lake Park Blvd., Richardson, TX 75080	Web Site: www.lennoxinternational.com	Auditors: KPMG LLP
Telephone: 972-497-5000	Officers: Todd M. Bluedorn - Chairman, Chief Executive Officer Joseph William Reitmeier - Executive Vice President, Chief Financial Officer, Division Officer	Investor Contact: 972-497-6670 Transfer Agents: Computershare, Providence, RI

LEUCADIA NATIONAL CORP.

Exchange	Symbol	Price	52Wk Range	Yield	P/E
NYS	LUK	$26.49 (12/29/2017)	27.20-22.27	1.51	17.09

*7 Year Price Score 80.40   *NYSE Composite Index=100   *12 Month Price Score 96.52

Interim Earnings (Per Share)

Qtr.	Mar	Jun	Sep	Dec
2014	0.25	0.17	0.14	(0.02)
2015	0.99	0.04	(0.47)	0.15
2016	(0.60)	0.15	0.41	0.37
2017	0.75	0.16	0.27	...

Interim Dividends (Per Share)

Amt	Decl	Ex	Rec	Pay
0.063Q	02/27/2017	03/16/2017	03/20/2017	03/31/2017
0.063Q	05/25/2017	06/15/2017	06/19/2017	06/30/2017
0.10Q	07/27/2017	09/15/2017	09/18/2017	09/29/2017
0.10Q	10/26/2017	12/12/2017	12/13/2017	12/27/2017

Indicated Div: $0.40

Valuation Analysis   **Institutional Holding**

Forecast EPS	$1.59	No of Institutions
	(11/26/2017)	651
Market Cap	$9.4 Billion	Shares
Book Value	$10.6 Billion	305,860,704
Price/Book	0.89	% Held
Price/Sales	0.84	91.50

Business Summary: Agricultural Livestock (MIC: 1.1.2 SIC: 5147 NAIC: 311612)

Leucadia National is a holding company. Co.'s financial services businesses include Jefferies (investment banking and capital markets), Leucadia Asset Management (asset management), Berkadia (commercial mortgage banking, investment sales and servicing), FXCM Group, LLC (provider of online foreign exchange trading services), HomeFed (a real estate company) and Foursight Capital (vehicle finance). Co. also owns and has investments in an array of other businesses, including beef processing, insurance and consumer products, oil and gas exploration and development, automobile dealerships, fixed wireless broadband services in Italy, manufacturing, and a gold and silver mining project.

Recent Developments: For the quarter ended Sep 30 2017, net income decreased 22.4% to US$136.8 million from US$176.2 million in the year-earlier quarter. Revenues were US$2.90 billion, up 8.2% from US$2.68 billion the year before. Direct operating expenses rose 11.8% to US$1.89 billion from US$1.69 billion in the comparable period the year before. Indirect operating expenses increased 8.3% to US$838.5 million from US$773.9 million in the equivalent prior-year period.

Prospects: Our evaluation of Leucadia National Corp. as of Jan. 14, 2018 is the result of our systematic analysis on three basic characteristics: earnings strength, relative valuation, and recent stock price movement. The company has suffered a very negative trend in earnings per share over the past 5 quarters. Because the company lacks sufficient analyst estimate data, we place greater weight on the historical EPS trend as the measure of earnings strength. Based on operating earnings yield, the company is undervalued when compared to all of the companies in our coverage universe. Share price changes over the past year indicates that LUK will perform poorly over the near term.

Financial Data

(US$ in Thousands)	9 Mos	6 Mos	3 Mos	12/31/2016	12/31/2015	12/31/2014	12/31/2013	12/31/2012
Earnings Per Share	1.55	1.69	1.68	0.34	0.74	0.54	1.06	3.44
Cash Flow Per Share	3.51	2.83	3.63	1.64	(2.05)	(2.65)	2.07	0.90
Tang Book Value Per Share	22.75	22.66	22.30	21.53	21.72	20.97	20.46	24.18
Dividends Per Share	0.287	0.250	0.250	0.250	0.250	0.250	0.250	0.250
Dividend Payout %	18.55	14.79	14.88	73.53	33.78	46.30	23.58	7.27
Income Statement								
Total Revenue	8,496,884	5,600,362	2,867,982	10,062,617	10,886,458	11,486,485	10,429,491	9,193,689
EBITDA	903,180	700,453	557,596	437,324	529,740	499,613	576,930	1,229,214
Depn & Amortn	13,418	7,986	3,541	166,789	172,073	139,744	138,964	170,113
Income Before Taxes	807,219	637,249	526,671	161,832	246,255	242,695	353,002	966,520
Income Taxes	218,054	154,794	104,174	122,109	109,947	165,971	110,741	376,494
Net Income	442,155	341,632	282,424	130,001	283,650	208,368	372,637	854,466
Average Shares	370,198	371,552	375,721	371,518	372,431	373,333	347,734	248,914
Balance Sheet								
Current Assets	29,401,279	30,131,039	28,890,027	12,952,561	12,075,445	15,583,132	14,499,058	2,521,266
Total Assets	47,666,944	48,376,102	45,979,997	45,071,307	46,339,812	52,623,908	47,866,781	9,349,118
Current Liabilities	8,890,541	9,060,567	7,738,383	8,343,947	11,187,884	11,389,283	19,336,501	1,280,479
Long-Term Obligations	8,985,334	8,847,929	9,035,623	7,380,443	7,407,594	8,527,929	8,180,865	918,126
Total Liabilities	37,090,034	37,759,795	35,456,839	34,818,207	35,813,601	42,196,750	37,639,319	2,581,850
Stockholders' Equity	10,576,910	10,616,307	10,523,158	10,253,100	10,526,211	10,427,158	10,227,462	6,767,268
Shares Outstanding	356,189	358,644	359,815	359,425	362,617	367,498	364,541	244,582
Statistical Record								
Return on Assets %	1.24	1.36	1.42	0.28	0.57	0.41	1.30	9.16
Return on Equity %	5.59	6.10	6.12	1.25	2.71	2.02	4.39	13.17
EBITDA Margin %	10.63	12.51	19.44	4.35	4.87	4.35	5.53	13.37
Net Margin %	5.20	6.10	9.85	1.29	2.61	1.81	3.57	9.29
Asset Turnover	0.24	0.24	0.24	0.22	0.22	0.23	0.36	0.99
Current Ratio	3.31	3.33	3.73	1.55	1.08	1.37	0.75	1.97
Debt to Equity	0.85	0.83	0.86	0.72	0.70	0.82	0.80	0.14
Price Range	27.20-17.91	27.20-16.88	27.20-15.42	24.00-14.45	25.20-16.08	28.65-21.04	32.20-23.79	29.72-19.84
P/E Ratio	17.55-11.55	16.09-9.99	16.19-9.18	70.59-42.50	34.05-21.73	53.06-38.96	30.38-22.44	8.64-5.77
Average Yield %	1.20	1.12	1.23	1.38	1.14	0.98	0.91	1.06

Address: 520 Madison Avenue, New York, NY 10022	Web Site: www.leucadia.com	Auditors: Deloitte & Touche LLP
Telephone: 212-460-1900	Officers: Joseph S. Steinberg - Chairman, President	Investor Contact: 212-460-1900
Fax: 212-598-4869	Brian P. Friedman - President	Transfer Agents: American Stock Transfer & Trust Company, LLC, Brooklyn, NY

LIBERTY PROPERTY TRUST

Exchange	Symbol	Price	52Wk Range	Yield	P/E
NYS	LPT	$43.01 (12/29/2017)	45.29-37.56	3.72	18.15

*7 Year Price Score 88.72   *NYSE Composite Index=100   *12 Month Price Score 101.00

Interim Earnings (Per Share)

Qtr.	Mar	Jun	Sep	Dec
2014	0.49	0.20	0.23	0.55
2015	0.21	0.24	0.61	0.54
2016	0.39	0.34	0.37	1.33
2017	0.29	0.35	0.40	...

Interim Dividends (Per Share)

Amt	Decl	Ex	Rec	Pay
0.40Q	02/17/2017	03/29/2017	03/31/2017	04/15/2017
0.40Q	05/24/2017	06/29/2017	07/03/2017	07/15/2017
0.40Q	09/07/2017	09/29/2017	10/02/2017	10/15/2017
0.40Q	12/08/2017	12/29/2017	01/02/2018	01/15/2018

Indicated Div: $1.60 (Div. Reinv. Plan)

Valuation Analysis

		Institutional Holding	
Forecast EPS	$1.20 (01/18/2018)	No of Institutions	502
Market Cap	$6.3 Billion	Shares	180,533,488
Book Value	$3.0 Billion	% Held	101.16
Price/Book	2.10		
Price/Sales	8.67		

Business Summary: REITs (MIC: 5.3.1 SIC: 6798 NAIC: 525930)

Liberty Property Trust is a self-administered and self-managed real estate investment trust. Substantially all of Co.'s operations are conducted directly or indirectly, by its subsidiary, Liberty Property Limited Partnership. Co. provides leasing, property management, development and other tenant-related services for a portfolio of industrial and office properties. As of Dec 31 2016, Co. owned and operated 450 industrial and 55 office properties. At Dec 31 2016, Co. owned 25 properties under development, and 1,643 acres of developable land. Co. also had an ownership interest, through unconsolidated joint ventures, in 49 industrial and 14 office properties; and 360 acres of developable land.

Recent Developments: For the quarter ended Sep 30 2017, net income increased 9.7% to US$61.2 million from US$55.7 million in the year-earlier quarter. Revenues were US$193.7 million, up 1.5% from US$190.9 million the year before.

Prospects: Our evaluation of Liberty Property Trust as of Jan. 14, 2018 is the result of our systematic analysis on three basic characteristics: earnings strength, relative valuation, and recent stock price movement. The company has managed to produce a neutral trend in earnings per share over the past 5 quarters. Because the company lacks sufficient analyst estimate data, we place greater weight on the historical EPS trend as the measure of earnings strength. Based on operating earnings yield, the company is overvalued when compared to all of the companies in our coverage universe. Share price changes over the past year indicates that LPT will perform very well over the near term.

Financial Data

(US$ in Thousands)	9 Mos	6 Mos	3 Mos	12/31/2016	12/31/2015	12/31/2014	12/31/2013	12/31/2012
Earnings Per Share	2.37	2.34	2.33	2.43	1.60	1.47	1.60	1.17
Cash Flow Per Share	2.10	2.28	2.20	2.27	2.60	2.29	2.43	2.71
Tang Book Value Per Share	20.44	20.38	20.35	20.77	20.35	20.79	20.73	17.65
Dividends Per Share	1.675	1.750	1.825	1.900	1.900	1.900	1.900	1.900
Dividend Payout %	70.68	74.79	78.33	78.19	118.75	129.25	118.75	162.39
Income Statement								
Total Revenue	552,149	358,496	175,366	746,708	808,773	792,631	645,930	685,552
EBITDA	210,294	130,642	60,539	614,073	538,446	481,553	374,223	386,428
Depn & Amortn	2,811	1,874	937	166,800	181,000	179,100	162,500	140,600
Income Before Taxes	145,723	88,287	39,135	346,146	244,530	168,235	94,487	135,487
Income Taxes	1,528	946	622	1,971	3,233	2,967	2,799	976
Net Income	153,982	94,443	43,032	356,817	238,039	217,910	209,738	137,436
Average Shares	147,596	147,508	147,221	146,889	148,843	147,886	130,909	117,694
Balance Sheet								
Current Assets	77,748	47,372	62,213	179,264	177,501	213,061	328,726	189,119
Total Assets	6,309,674	6,159,635	6,083,901	5,992,813	6,557,629	6,625,536	6,775,560	5,177,971
Current Liabilities	173,222	138,240	151,500	159,293	149,323	148,809	167,506	109,260
Long-Term Obligations	2,847,208	2,730,501	2,670,230	2,556,936	3,147,016	3,163,395	3,253,519	2,657,398
Total Liabilities	3,296,860	3,158,046	3,088,060	2,989,422	3,604,701	3,597,864	3,739,716	3,086,959
Stockholders' Equity	3,012,814	3,001,589	2,995,841	3,003,391	2,952,928	3,027,672	3,035,844	2,091,012
Shares Outstanding	147,399	147,304	147,203	146,993	147,577	148,557	146,596	118,470
Statistical Record								
Return on Assets %	5.36	5.40	5.43	5.67	3.61	3.25	3.51	2.70
Return on Equity %	11.88	11.71	11.60	11.95	7.96	7.19	8.18	*6.54
EBITDA Margin %	38.09	36.44	34.52	82.24	66.58	60.75	57.94	56.37
Net Margin %	27.89	26.34	24.54	47.79	29.43	27.49	32.47	20.05
Asset Turnover	0.11	0.11	0.12	0.12	0.12	0.12	0.11	0.13
Current Ratio	0.45	0.34	0.41	1.13	1.19	1.43	1.96	1.73
Debt to Equity	0.95	0.91	0.89	0.85	1.07	1.04	1.07	1.27
Price Range	43.35-36.37	42.48-36.37	42.25-33.12	42.25-27.30	41.42-29.91	40.08-32.77	44.70-32.12	38.57-30.91
P/E Ratio	18.29-15.35	18.15-15.54	18.13-14.21	17.39-11.23	25.89-18.69	27.27-22.29	27.94-20.07	32.97-26.42
Average Yield %	4.16	4.38	4.71	5.20	5.49	5.24	5.03	5.36

Address: 500 Chesterfield Parkway, Malvern, PA 19355 Telephone: 610-648-1700	Web Site: www.libertyproperty.com Officers: William P. (Bill) Hankowsky - Chairman, President, Chief Executive Officer Robert E. Fenza - Executive Vice President, Chief Operating Officer	Auditors: Ernst & Young LLP Investor Contact: 610-648-1704 Transfer Agents: Wells Fargo Shareholder Services, St. Paul, MN

LIFE STORAGE INC

Exchange	Symbol	Price	52Wk Range	Yield	P/E
NYS	LSI	$89.07 (12/29/2017)	91.12-70.59	4.49	44.53

*7 Year Price Score 86.24   *NYSE Composite Index=100   *12 Month Price Score 102.31

Interim Earnings (Per Share)

Qtr.	Mar	Jun	Sep	Dec
2014	0.51	0.62	0.77	0.76
2015	0.65	0.80	0.88	0.83
2016	0.73	1.03	(0.10)	0.38
2017	0.44	0.42	0.76	...

Interim Dividends (Per Share)

Amt	Decl	Ex	Rec	Pay
1.00Q	04/05/2017	04/13/2017	04/18/2017	04/26/2017
1.00Q	07/05/2017	07/13/2017	07/17/2017	07/26/2017
1.00Q	10/03/2017	10/12/2017	10/13/2017	10/26/2017
1.00Q	01/03/2018	01/12/2018	01/16/2018	01/26/2018

Indicated Div: $4.00

Valuation Analysis

		Institutional Holding	
Forecast EPS	$2.36 (01/17/2018)	No of Institutions	371
Market Cap	$4.1 Billion	Shares	60,626,432
Book Value	$2.0 Billion	% Held	94.59
Price/Book	2.03		
Price/Sales	7.89		

Business Summary: REITs (MIC: 5.3.1 SIC: 6798 NAIC: 525930)

Life Storage is a self-administered and self-managed real estate investment trust that acquires, owns and manages self-storage properties. Co. owns its assets and conducts its operations via Life Storage LP (the Operating Partnership) and subsidiaries of the Operating Partnership. At Dec 31 2016, Co. had an ownership interest in and/or managed 659 self-storage properties in 29 states under the names Life Storage® and Uncle Bob's Self Storage®. Co.'s self-storage facilities provides storage space to residential and commercial users on a month-to-month basis. Individual storage spaces are secured by a lock furnished by the customer to provide the customer with control of access to the space.

Recent Developments: For the quarter ended Sep 30 2017, net income amounted to US$35.7 million versus a net loss of US$5.0 million in the year-earlier quarter. Revenues were US$135.6 million, up 6.1% from US$127.8 million the year before. Revenues from property income rose 4.8% to US$124.0 million from US$118.3 million in the corresponding quarter a year earlier.

Prospects: Our evaluation of Life Storage Inc. as of Jan. 14, 2018 is the result of our systematic analysis on three basic characteristics: earnings strength, relative valuation, and recent stock price movement. The company has enjoyed a very positive trend in earnings per share over the past 5 quarters. Because the company lacks sufficient analyst estimate data, we place greater weight on the historical EPS trend as the measure of earnings strength. Based on operating earnings yield, the company is about fairly valued when compared to all of the companies in our coverage universe. Share price changes over the past year indicates that LSI will perform well over the near term.

Financial Data

(US$ in Thousands)	9 Mos	6 Mos	3 Mos	12/31/2016	12/31/2015	12/31/2014	12/31/2013	12/31/2012
Earnings Per Share	2.00	1.14	1.75	1.96	3.16	2.67	2.36	1.87
Cash Flow Per Share	5.53	5.20	4.66	5.21	5.26	4.42	3.85	3.36
Tang Book Value Per Share	43.53	43.76	44.22	44.96	32.75	28.61	26.76	23.93
Dividends Per Share	3.900	3.850	3.800	3.700	3.200	2.720	2.020	1.800
Dividend Payout %	195.00	337.72	217.14	188.78	101.27	101.87	85.59	96.26
Income Statement								
Total Revenue	396,673	261,105	128,320	462,608	366,602	326,080	273,507	236,007
EBITDA	123,072	94,073	35,843	262,497	206,481	174,200	147,864	123,689
Depn & Amortn	2,496	24,700	832	126,769	59,690	52,691	46,380	42,515
Income Before Taxes	73,364	38,451	19,804	81,291	109,672	86,971	69,524	48,012
Net Income	75,280	39,785	20,429	85,225	112,524	88,531	74,126	55,128
Average Shares	46,520	46,477	46,418	43,407	35,601	33,191	31,453	29,489
Balance Sheet								
Current Assets	23,172	23,903	22,287	37,026	20,747	21,417	22,298	16,508
Total Assets	3,884,335	3,890,671	3,857,633	3,857,984	2,122,172	1,854,800	1,561,875	1,484,441
Current Liabilities	412,093	407,154	354,535	84,832	55,350	50,841	44,449	43,082
Long-Term Obligations	1,401,572	1,401,232	1,400,891	1,653,552	830,993	801,127	626,254	684,251
Total Liabilities	1,842,226	1,836,371	1,785,131	1,769,490	919,857	878,931	691,166	755,711
Stockholders' Equity	2,042,109	2,054,300	2,072,502	2,088,494	1,202,315	975,869	870,709	728,730
Shares Outstanding	46,536	46,565	46,496	46,454	36,710	34,105	32,532	30,446
Statistical Record								
Return on Assets %	2.42	1.45	2.45	2.84	5.66	5.18	4.87	3.89
Return on Equity %	4.51	2.54	4.37	5.17	10.33	9.59	9.27	7.94
EBITDA Margin %	31.03	36.03	27.93	56.74	56.32	53.42	54.06	52.41
Net Margin %	18.98	15.24	15.92	18.42	30.69	27.15	27.10	23.36
Asset Turnover	0.14	0.14	0.16	0.15	0.18	0.19	0.18	0.17
Current Ratio	0.06	0.06	0.06	0.44	0.37	0.42	0.50	0.38
Debt to Equity	0.69	0.68	0.68	0.79	0.69	0.82	0.72	0.94
Price Range	88.94-70.59	107.23-73.13	117.95-79.15	117.95-79.15	110.00-86.13	88.94-63.30	78.83-60.67	62.78-43.10
P/E Ratio	44.47-35.30	94.06-64.15	67.40-45.23	60.18-40.38	34.81-27.26	33.31-23.71	33.40-25.71	33.57-23.05
Average Yield %	4.87	4.51	4.08	3.73	3.40	3.55	2.98	3.37

Address: 6467 Main Street, Williamsville, NY 14221
Telephone: 716-633-1850
Fax: 716-633-1860

Web Site: www.unclebobs.com
Officers: Robert J. Attea - Chairman, Chief Executive Officer Kenneth F. Myszka - President, Chief Operating Officer

Auditors: Ernst & Young LLP
Investor Contact: 716-633-1850
Transfer Agents: American Stock Transfer & Trust Company, Brooklyn, NY

LILLY (ELI) & CO

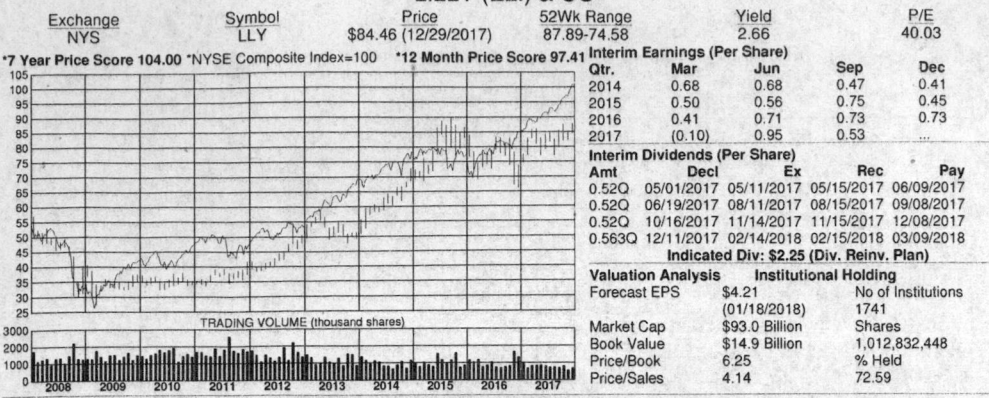

Exchange	Symbol	Price	52Wk Range	Yield	P/E
NYS	LLY	$84.46 (12/29/2017)	87.89-74.58	2.66	40.03

*7 Year Price Score 104.00 *NYSE Composite Index=100 *12 Month Price Score 97.41

Interim Earnings (Per Share)

Qtr.	Mar	Jun	Sep	Dec
2014	0.68	0.68	0.47	0.41
2015	0.50	0.56	0.75	0.45
2016	0.41	0.71	0.73	0.73
2017	(0.10)	0.95	0.53	...

Interim Dividends (Per Share)

Amt	Decl	Ex	Rec	Pay
0.52Q	05/01/2017	05/11/2017	05/15/2017	06/09/2017
0.52Q	06/19/2017	08/11/2017	08/15/2017	09/08/2017
0.52Q	10/16/2017	11/14/2017	11/15/2017	12/08/2017
0.563Q	12/11/2017	02/14/2018	02/15/2018	03/09/2018

Indicated Div: $2.25 (Div. Reinv. Plan)

Valuation Analysis | **Institutional Holding**

Forecast EPS	$4.21	No of Institutions
	(01/18/2018)	1741
Market Cap	$93.0 Billion	Shares
Book Value	$14.9 Billion	1,012,832,448
Price/Book	6.25	% Held
Price/Sales	4.14	72.59

TRADING VOLUME (thousand shares)

Business Summary: Pharmaceuticals (MIC: 4.1.1 SIC: 2834 NAIC: 325412)

Eli Lilly & Company is engaged in discovering, developing, manufacturing, and marketing products in two business segments: human pharmaceutical products and animal health products. Co.'s human pharmaceutical products include: endocrinology products, neurosciences products, oncology products, and cardiovascular products. Co.'s animal health products are comprised of products for animals, which include Rumensin, a cattle feed additive, and Tylan, an antibiotic used to control certain diseases in cattle, swine, and poultry; as well as products for companion animals, which include Trifexis and Comfortis, a chewable tablet that kills fleas and prevents flea infestations on dogs.

Recent Developments: For the quarter ended Sep 30 2017, net income decreased 28.6% to US$555.6 million from US$778.0 million in the year-earlier quarter. Revenues were US$5.66 billion, up 9.0% from US$5.19 billion the year before. Direct operating expenses rose 11.8% to US$1.57 billion from US$1.40 billion in the comparable period the year before. Indirect operating expenses increased 22.4% to US$3.49 billion from US$2.85 billion in the equivalent prior-year period.

Prospects: Our evaluation of Lilly (Eli) & Co. as of Jan. 14, 2018 is the result of our systematic analysis on three basic characteristics: earnings strength, relative valuation, and recent stock price movement. The company has managed to produce a neutral trend in earnings per share over the past 5 quarters and while recent estimates for the company have been mixed, LLY has posted better than expected results. Based on operating earnings yield, the company is undervalued when compared to all of the companies in our coverage universe. Share price changes over the past year indicates that LLY will perform well over the near term.

Financial Data

(US$ in Thousands)	9 Mos	6 Mos	3 Mos	12/31/2016	12/31/2015	12/31/2014	12/31/2013	12/31/2012
Earnings Per Share	2.11	2.31	2.07	2.58	2.26	2.23	4.32	3.66
Cash Flow Per Share	5.69	5.47	5.22	4.57	2.61	4.08	5.31	4.75
Tang Book Value Per Share	5.68	4.78	4.65	5.16	4.97	9.66	11.91	8.75
Dividends Per Share	2.070	2.060	2.050	2.040	2.000	1.960	1.960	1.960
Dividend Payout %	98.10	89.18	99.03	79.07	88.50	87.89	45.37	53.55
Income Statement								
Total Revenue	16,710,600	11,052,600	5,228,300	21,222,100	19,958,700	19,615,600	23,113,100	22,603,400
EBITDA	3,116,200	2,134,900	462,100	4,166,700	3,581,800	3,787,200	6,704,500	6,235,000
Depn & Amortn	1,155,400	782,500	386,900	716,200	717,600	759,100	774,800	754,000
Income Before Taxes	1,913,300	1,321,700	61,200	3,374,000	2,790,000	3,000,300	5,889,300	5,408,200
Income Taxes	460,500	424,500	172,000	636,400	381,600	609,800	1,204,500	1,319,600
Net Income	1,452,800	897,200	(110,800)	2,737,600	2,408,400	2,390,500	4,684,800	4,088,600
Average Shares	1,056,000	1,057,100	1,056,300	1,061,825	1,065,720	1,074,286	1,084,766	1,117,294
Balance Sheet								
Current Assets	17,428,400	15,746,500	12,976,200	15,101,400	12,573,600	12,179,800	13,104,700	13,038,700
Total Assets	43,010,400	40,946,500	37,624,300	38,805,900	35,568,900	37,178,200	35,248,700	34,398,900
Current Liabilities	12,666,500	11,294,500	10,448,000	10,986,600	8,229,600	11,207,500	8,916,600	8,389,500
Long-Term Obligations	9,926,600	9,867,900	7,637,500	8,367,800	7,972,400	5,367,700	4,200,300	5,519,400
Total Liabilities	28,120,100	26,845,700	23,593,300	24,798,200	20,997,600	21,805,000	17,617,300	19,633,700
Stockholders' Equity	14,890,300	14,100,800	14,031,000	14,007,700	14,571,300	15,373,200	17,631,400	14,765,200
Shares Outstanding	1,101,094	1,100,988	1,103,388	1,100,875	1,105,267	1,110,627	1,116,795	1,143,643
Statistical Record								
Return on Assets %	5.52	6.32	6.05	7.34	6.62	6.60	13.45	11.98
Return on Equity %	14.60	17.03	15.06	19.11	16.09	14.49	28.92	28.81
EBITDA Margin %	18.65	19.32	8.84	19.63	17.95	19.31	29.01	27.58
Net Margin %	8.69	8.12	N.M.	12.90	12.07	12.19	20.27	18.09
Asset Turnover	0.56	0.57	0.60	0.57	0.55	0.54	0.66	0.66
Current Ratio	1.38	1.39	1.24	1.37	1.53	1.09	1.47	1.55
Debt to Equity	0.67	0.70	0.54	0.60	0.55	0.35	0.24	0.37
Price Range	86.25-65.97	86.25-65.97	85.88-65.97	84.26-65.97	89.98-68.41	72.83-50.73	58.33-47.65	53.81-38.49
P/E Ratio	40.88-31.27	37.34-28.56	41.49-31.87	32.66-25.57	39.81-30.27	32.66-22.75	13.50-11.03	14.70-10.52
Average Yield %	2.60	2.82	2.65	2.67	2.54	3.18	3.72	4.50

Address: Lilly Corporate Center,	Web Site: www.lilly.com	Auditors: Ernst & Young LLP
Indianapolis, IN 46285	Officers: David A. Ricks - Chairman, President, Chief	Investor Contact: 317-276-2000
Telephone: 317-276-2000	Executive Officer, Senior Vice President, Division	Transfer Agents: Wells Fargo
	Officer Jan M. Lundberg - Executive Vice President,	Shareowner Services, St. Paul, MN
	Division Officer	

LINCOLN NATIONAL CORP.

Exchange	Symbol	Price	52Wk Range	Yield	P/E
NYS	LNC	$76.87 (12/29/2017)	78.54-63.23	1.72	11.94

*7 Year Price Score 124.14 *NYSE Composite Index=100 *12 Month Price Score 102.02

TRADING VOLUME (thousand shares)

Interim Earnings (Per Share)

Qtr.	Mar	Jun	Sep	Dec
2014	1.21	1.48	1.65	1.33
2015	1.15	1.35	0.87	1.14
2016	0.82	1.35	2.00	0.87
2017	1.89	1.81	1.87	...

Interim Dividends (Per Share)

Amt	Decl	Ex	Rec	Pay
0.29Q	02/23/2017	04/06/2017	04/10/2017	05/01/2017
0.29Q	05/26/2017	07/06/2017	07/10/2017	08/01/2017
0.29Q	08/10/2017	10/06/2017	10/10/2017	11/01/2017
0.33Q	11/01/2017	01/09/2018	01/10/2018	02/01/2018

Indicated Div: $1.32 (Div. Reinv. Plan)

Valuation Analysis

		Institutional Holding	
Forecast EPS	$7.72	No of Institutions	
	(01/18/2018)	940	
Market Cap	$16.9 Billion	Shares	
Book Value	$16.3 Billion	226,562,176	
Price/Book	1.03	% Held	
Price/Sales	1.22	77.34	

Business Summary: Life & Health (MIC: 5.2.2 SIC: 6311 NAIC: 524113)

Lincoln National is a holding company. Co. operates multiple insurance and retirement businesses through its subsidiary companies. Co. sells a range of wealth protection, accumulation and retirement income products and solutions. These products include fixed and indexed annuities, variable annuities, universal life insurance (UL), variable universal life insurance, linked-benefit UL, indexed universal life insurance, term life insurance, employer-sponsored retirement plans and services, and group life, disability and dental. Co. provides products and services through its Annuities, Retirement Plan Services, Life Insurance and Group Protection segments.

Recent Developments: For the quarter ended Sep 30 2017, net income decreased 10.5% to US$418.0 million from US$467.0 million in the year-earlier quarter. Revenues were US$3.51 billion, down 0.4% from US$3.53 billion the year before. Net premiums earned were US$774.0 million versus US$708.0 million in the prior-year quarter, an increase of 9.3%. Net investment income fell 1.6% to US$1.24 billion from US$1.26 billion a year ago.

Prospects: Our evaluation of Lincoln National Corp. (ID) as of Jan. 14, 2018 is the result of our systematic analysis on three basic characteristics: earnings strength, relative valuation, and recent stock price movement. The company has generated a negative trend in earnings per share over the past 5 quarters and while recent estimates for the company have been raised by analysts, LNC has posted better than expected results. Based on operating earnings yield, the company is undervalued when compared to all of the companies in our coverage universe. Share price changes over the past year indicates that LNC will perform poorly over the near term.

Financial Data

(US$ in Thousands)	9 Mos	6 Mos	3 Mos	12/31/2016	12/31/2015	12/31/2014	12/31/2013	12/31/2012
Earnings Per Share	6.44	6.57	6.11	5.03	4.51	5.67	4.52	4.56
Cash Flow Per Share	5.45	4.21	4.81	5.42	8.95	9.68	3.01	4.51
Tang Book Value Per Share	63.96	61.75	56.47	53.92	46.52	52.49	42.52	46.79
Dividends Per Share	1.120	1.080	1.040	1.000	0.800	0.640	0.480	0.320
Dividend Payout %	17.39	16.44	17.02	19.88	17.74	11.29	10.62	7.02
Income Statement								
Premium Income	2,382,000	1,608,000	807,000	2,987,000	3,246,000	2,988,000	2,687,000	2,462,000
Total Revenue	10,588,000	7,077,000	3,500,000	13,330,000	13,572,000	13,554,000	11,969,000	11,532,000
Benefits & Claims	3,839,000	2,578,000	1,290,000	4,692,000	5,044,000	4,679,000	3,862,000	3,538,000
Income Before Taxes	1,518,000	1,008,000	475,000	1,458,000	1,430,000	1,997,000	1,631,000	1,568,000
Income Taxes	254,000	162,000	40,000	266,000	276,000	483,000	387,000	282,000
Net Income	1,264,000	846,000	435,000	1,192,000	1,154,000	1,515,000	1,244,000	1,313,000
Average Shares	223,872	227,313	230,103	236,830	254,938	267,963	275,148	287,590
Balance Sheet								
Total Assets	276,785,000	271,651,000	267,468,000	261,627,000	251,937,000	253,377,000	236,945,000	218,869,000
Total Liabilities	260,471,000	255,655,000	252,495,000	247,149,000	238,320,000	237,637,000	223,493,000	203,896,000
Stockholders' Equity	16,314,000	15,996,000	14,973,000	14,478,000	13,617,000	15,740,000	13,452,000	14,973,000
Shares Outstanding	219,544	222,237	224,888	226,335	243,835	256,551	262,896	271,402
Statistical Record								
Return on Assets %	0.54	0.56	0.54	0.46	0.46	0.62	0.55	0.62
Return on Equity %	8.93	9.44	9.58	8.46	7.86	10.38	8.75	8.99
Loss Ratio %	161.17	160.32	159.85	157.08	155.39	156.59	143.73	143.70
Net Margin %	11.94	11.95	12.43	8.94	8.50	11.18	10.39	11.39
Price Range	74.34-46.98	73.08-37.10	73.08-35.50	68.48-30.78	61.65-46.07	58.80-45.67	51.95-25.90	27.29-19.29
P/E Ratio	11.54-7.30	11.12-5.65	11.96-5.81	13.61-6.12	13.67-10.22	10.37-8.05	11.49-5.73	5.98-4.23
Average Yield %	1.70	1.82	1.95	2.17	1.45	1.22	1.24	1.37

Address: 150 N. Radnor Chester Road, Suite A305, Radnor, PA 19087 **Telephone:** 484-583-1400	**Web Site:** www.lfg.com **Officers:** Dennis R. Glass - President, Chief Executive Officer Lisa M. Buckingham - Executive Vice President, Senior Vice President, Chief Human Resources Officer	**Auditors:** Ernst & Young LLP **Transfer Agents:** Computershare, Providence, RI

LINDSAY CORP

Exchange	Symbol	Price	52Wk Range	Yield	P/E	Div Achiever
NYS	LNN	$88.20 (12/29/2017)	95.05-74.03	1.36	37.06	14 Years

*7 Year Price Score 88.54 *NYSE Composite Index=100 *12 Month Price Score 98.91

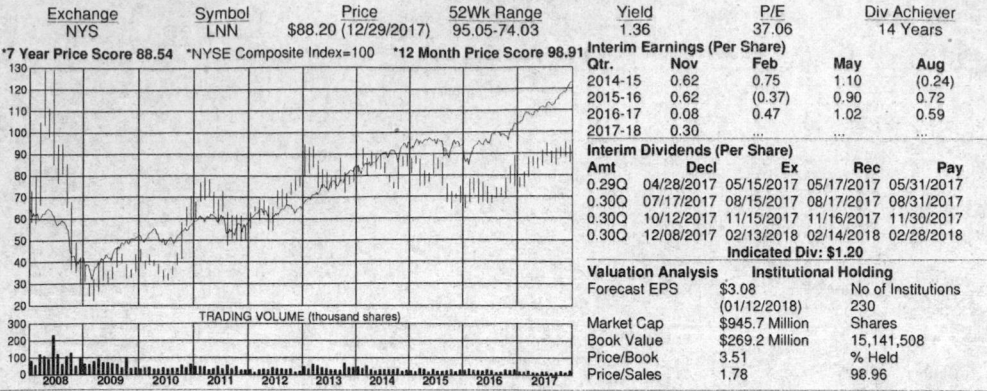

Interim Earnings (Per Share)

Qtr.	Nov	Feb	May	Aug
2014-15	0.62	0.75	1.10	(0.24)
2015-16	0.62	(0.37)	0.90	0.72
2016-17	0.08	0.47	1.02	0.59
2017-18	0.30	...	...	...

Interim Dividends (Per Share)

Amt	Decl	Ex	Rec	Pay
0.29Q	04/28/2017	05/15/2017	05/17/2017	05/31/2017
0.30Q	07/17/2017	08/15/2017	08/17/2017	08/31/2017
0.30Q	10/12/2017	11/15/2017	11/16/2017	11/30/2017
0.30Q	12/08/2017	02/13/2018	02/14/2018	02/28/2018

Indicated Div: $1.20

Valuation Analysis

		Institutional Holding	
Forecast EPS	$3.08	No of Institutions	
	(01/12/2018)	230	
Market Cap	$945.7 Million	Shares	
Book Value	$269.2 Million	15,141,508	
Price/Book	3.51	% Held	
Price/Sales	1.78	98.96	

Business Summary: Industrial Machinery & Equipment (MIC: 7.2.1 SIC: 3523 NAIC: 333111)

Lindsay is a provider of water management and road infrastructure products and services. Co.'s irrigation segment includes the manufacture and marketing of center pivot, lateral move, hose reel irrigation systems, and repair and replacement parts, and the design and manufacture of water pumping stations and controls for the agriculture, golf, landscape and municipal markets. Co.'s infrastructure segment includes the manufacture and marketing of moveable barriers, specialty barriers, crash cushions and end terminals, road marking and road safety equipment, large diameter steel tubing, and railroad signals and structures, and the provision of outsourced manufacturing and production services.

Recent Developments: For the quarter ended Nov 30 2017, net income increased 264.8% to US$3.2 million from US$873,000 in the year-earlier quarter. Revenues were US$124.5 million, up 12.8% from US$110.4 million the year before. Operating income was US$6.2 million versus US$2.7 million in the prior-year quarter, an increase of 126.7%. Direct operating expenses rose 12.3% to US$92.1 million from US$82.0 million in the comparable period the year before. Indirect operating expenses increased 2.2% to US$26.2 million from US$25.6 million in the equivalent prior-year period.

Prospects: Our evaluation of Lindsay Corp. as of Jan. 14, 2018 is the result of our systematic analysis on three basic characteristics: earnings strength, relative valuation, and recent stock price movement. The company has produced a positive trend in earnings per share over the past 5 quarters and while recent estimates for the company have been raised by analysts, LNN has posted results that fell short of analysts expectations. Based on operating earnings yield, the company is about fairly valued when compared to all of the companies in our coverage universe. Share price changes over the past year indicates that LNN will perform in line with the market over the near term.

Financial Data

(US$ in Thousands)	3 Mos	08/31/2017	08/31/2016	08/31/2015	08/31/2014	08/31/2013	08/31/2012	08/31/2011
Earnings Per Share	2.38	2.17	1.85	2.22	4.00	5.47	3.38	2.90
Cash Flow Per Share	2.46	3.70	3.02	4.12	7.15	4.48	4.12	3.43
Tang Book Value Per Share	14.03	14.03	12.00	14.16	25.21	23.87	20.11	17.05
Dividends Per Share	1.180	1.170	1.130	1.090	0.920	0.475	0.385	0.345
Dividend Payout %	49.58	53.92	61.08	49.10	23.00	8.68	11.39	11.90
Income Statement								
Total Revenue	124,526	517,985	516,411	560,181	617,933	690,848	551,255	478,890
EBITDA	9,988	51,494	45,594	60,446	88,913	116,915	74,696	65,961
Depn & Amortn	4,335	12,200	12,200	11,700	10,800	9,800	9,600	9,000
Income Before Taxes	4,792	35,715	29,288	46,751	78,655	107,307	65,108	56,514
Income Taxes	1,607	12,536	9,021	20,442	27,143	36,737	21,831	19,712
Net Income	3,185	23,179	20,267	26,309	51,512	70,570	43,277	36,802
Average Shares	10,740	10,694	10,930	11,855	12,882	12,901	12,810	12,692
Balance Sheet								
Current Assets	296,234	292,934	292,124	322,167	374,058	368,791	298,865	257,693
Total Assets	503,407	506,032	499,565	536,468	526,551	512,296	415,531	381,144
Current Liabilities	90,123	92,037	87,870	95,112	116,367	102,092	80,438	79,319
Long-Term Obligations	116,724	116,775	116,976	117,173	...	...	...	4,285
Total Liabilities	234,175	235,977	247,998	247,908	143,904	131,658	104,693	105,479
Stockholders' Equity	269,232	270,055	251,567	288,560	382,647	380,638	310,838	275,665
Shares Outstanding	10,722	10,697	10,630	11,290	12,440	12,873	12,723	12,676
Statistical Record								
Return on Assets %	5.18	4.61	3.90	4.95	9.92	15.21	10.83	10.42
Return on Equity %	9.85	8.89	7.48	7.84	13.50	20.41	14.72	14.57
EBITDA Margin %	8.02	9.94	8.83	10.79	14.39	16.92	13.55	13.77
Net Margin %	2.56	4.47	3.92	4.70	8.34	10.21	7.85	7.68
Asset Turnover	1.08	1.03	0.99	1.05	1.19	1.49	1.38	1.36
Current Ratio	3.29	3.18	3.32	3.39	3.21	3.61	3.72	3.25
Debt to Equity	0.43	0.43	0.46	0.41	...	...	...	0.02
Price Range	95.05-74.03	94.74-69.30	78.57-64.06	89.70-73.48	92.93-72.00	94.57-65.36	73.84-49.53	79.19-36.87
P/E Ratio	39.94-31.11	43.66-31.94	42.47-34.63	40.41-33.10	23.23-18.00	17.29-11.95	21.85-14.65	27.31-12.71
Average Yield %	1.38	1.43	1.60	1.33	1.12	0.60	0.63	0.55

Address: 2222 North 111th Street, Omaha, NE 68164	**Web Site:** www.lindsay.com	**Auditors:** KPMG LLP
Telephone: 402-829-6800	**Officers:** Michael C. Nahl - Chairman Timothy Hassinger - President, Chief Executive Officer	**Investor Contact:** 402-827-6579
Fax: 402-829-6834		**Transfer Agents:** Wells Fargo Shareowner Services, St. Paul, MN

LITHIA MOTORS INC

Exchange	Symbol	Price	52Wk Range	Yield	P/E
NYS	LAD	$113.59 (12/29/2017)	122.28-81.12	0.95	13.80

*7 Year Price Score 118.78 *NYSE Composite Index=100 *12 Month Price Score 107.14

TRADING VOLUME (thousand shares)

Interim Earnings (Per Share)

Qtr.	Mar	Jun	Sep	Dec
2014	0.94	1.45	1.31	1.55
2015	1.53	1.93	1.64	1.81
2016	1.55	2.01	2.14	2.03
2017	2.01	2.12	2.07	...

Interim Dividends (Per Share)

Amt	Decl	Ex	Rec	Pay
0.25Q	02/15/2017	03/08/2017	03/10/2017	03/24/2017
0.27Q	04/19/2017	05/10/2017	05/12/2017	05/26/2017
0.27Q	07/28/2017	08/09/2017	08/11/2017	08/25/2017
0.27Q	10/23/2017	11/09/2017	11/10/2017	11/24/2017

Indicated Div: $1.08

Valuation Analysis — **Institutional Holding**

Forecast EPS	$8.35 (01/16/2018)	No of Institutions 318
Market Cap	$2.8 Billion	Shares 31,916,712
Book Value	$1.0 Billion	% Held 84.77
Price/Book	2.75	
Price/Sales	0.29	

Business Summary: Retail - Automotive (MIC: 2.1.4 SIC: 5511 NAIC: 441110)

Lithia Motors is an operator of automotive franchises and a retailer of new and used vehicles and related services. As of Feb 28 2017, Co provided 30 brands of new vehicles and all brands of used vehicles in 154 stores and online at Lithia.com, DCHauto.com and CarboneCars.com. Co. sells new and used cars and replacement parts; provide vehicle maintenance, warranty, paint and repair services; arrange related financing; and sell vehicle service contracts, vehicle protection products and credit insurance. Co.'s business segments are Domestic, Import and Luxury. The franchises in each segment also sell used vehicles, parts and automotive services, and automotive finance and insurance products.

Recent Developments: For the quarter ended Sep 30 2017, net income decreased 4.0% to US$51.9 million from US$54.0 million in the year-earlier quarter. Revenues were US$2.68 billion, up 18.1% from US$2.27 billion the year before. Operating income was US$106.0 million versus US$93.4 million in the prior-year quarter, an increase of 13.4%. Direct operating expenses rose 17.8% to US$2.28 billion from US$1.93 billion in the comparable period the year before. Indirect operating expenses increased 21.8% to US$297.1 million from US$243.8 million in the equivalent prior-year period.

Prospects: Our evaluation of Lithia Motors Inc. as of Jan. 14, 2018 is the result of our systematic analysis on three basic characteristics: earnings strength, relative valuation, and recent stock price movement. The company has managed to produce a neutral trend in earnings per share over the past 5 quarters and while recent estimates for the company have been mixed, LAD has posted results that fell short of analysts' expectations. Based on operating earnings yield, the company is undervalued when compared to all of the companies in our coverage universe. Share price changes over the past year indicates that LAD will perform in line with the market over the near term.

Financial Data

(US$ in Thousands)	9 Mos	6 Mos	3 Mos	12/31/2016	12/31/2015	12/31/2014	12/31/2013	12/31/2012
Earnings Per Share	8.23	8.30	8.19	7.72	6.91	5.26	4.05	3.07
Cash Flow Per Share	6.29	7.93	7.09	3.40	2.82	1.16	1.24	(8.25)
Tang Book Value Per Share	31.01	29.11	27.46	18.58	17.44	12.31	15.99	12.99
Dividends Per Share	1.040	1.020	1.000	0.950	0.760	0.610	0.390	0.470
Dividend Payout %	12.64	12.29	12.21	12.31	11.00	11.60	9.63	15.31
Income Statement								
Total Revenue	7,383,479	4,703,137	2,236,101	8,678,157	7,864,252	5,390,326	4,005,749	3,316,487
EBITDA	348,998	227,093	108,725	381,630	343,329	261,461	206,546	168,208
Depn & Amortn	41,598	26,770	12,739	49,369	41,600	26,363	20,035	17,314
Income Before Taxes	255,642	169,099	81,263	283,523	262,704	210,495	165,788	128,457
Income Taxes	99,829	65,172	30,536	86,465	79,705	74,955	60,574	49,062
Net Income	155,813	103,927	50,727	197,058	182,999	138,720	106,000	80,362
Average Shares	25,076	25,106	25,250	25,521	26,490	26,382	26,191	26,170
Balance Sheet								
Current Assets	2,511,268	2,323,768	2,233,496	2,287,194	1,878,865	1,615,509	1,081,549	933,209
Total Assets	4,371,593	3,976,495	3,801,964	3,844,150	3,227,299	2,880,932	1,725,121	1,492,702
Current Liabilities	2,074,762	1,957,652	1,939,866	1,921,994	1,590,825	1,442,600	872,511	721,304
Long-Term Obligations	991,333	777,814	666,135	769,916	606,463	609,066	245,471	286,876
Total Liabilities	3,340,217	2,988,668	2,851,798	2,933,374	2,399,135	2,207,827	1,190,399	1,064,601
Stockholders' Equity	1,031,376	987,827	950,166	910,776	828,164	673,105	534,722	428,101
Shares Outstanding	24,966	25,019	25,153	25,144	26,218	26,233	25,891	25,678
Statistical Record								
Return on Assets %	5.22	5.74	5.87	5.56	5.99	6.02	6.59	6.07
Return on Equity %	21.83	23.19	23.52	22.60	24.38	22.97	22.02	20.16
EBITDA Margin %	4.73	4.83	4.86	4.40	4.37	4.85	5.16	5.07
Net Margin %	2.11	2.21	2.27	2.27	2.33	2.57	2.65	2.42
Asset Turnover	2.44	2.54	2.53	2.45	2.57	2.34	2.49	2.51
Current Ratio	1.21	1.19	1.15	1.19	1.18	1.12	1.24	1.29
Debt to Equity	0.96	0.79	0.70	0.85	0.73	0.90	0.46	0.67
Price Range	120.31-77.71	104.52-70.41	104.52-69.23	106.67-69.23	126.06-80.98	96.37-54.17	73.67-37.42	37.42-21.17
P/E Ratio	14.62-9.44	12.59-8.48	12.76-8.45	13.82-8.97	18.24-11.72	18.32-10.30	18.19-9.24	12.19-6.90
Average Yield %	1.08	1.13	1.13	1.11	0.72	0.80	0.80	1.66

Address: 150 N. Bartlett Street, Medford, OR 97501 **Telephone:** 541-776-6401	**Web Site:** www.lithia.com **Officers:** Sidney B. DeBoer - Executive Chairman, Chairman, Chief Executive Officer, Secretary M. L. Dick Heimann - Vice-Chairman	**Auditors:** KPMG LLP **Investor Contact:** 877-331-3084 **Transfer Agents:** Broadridge Financial Solutions, Inc., Philadelphia, PA

LIVE NATION ENTERTAINMENT INC

Exchange	Symbol	Price	52Wk Range	Yield	P/E
NYS	LYV	$42.57 (12/29/2017)	46.41-27.29	N/A	1419.00

*7 Year Price Score 136.97 *NYSE Composite Index=100 *12 Month Price Score 113.80

Interim Earnings (Per Share)

Qtr.	Mar	Jun	Sep	Dec
2014	(0.16)	0.11	0.49	(0.94)
2015	(0.31)	0.06	0.38	(0.47)
2016	(0.29)	0.13	0.49	(0.57)
2017	(0.22)	0.29	0.53	...

Interim Dividends (Per Share)

No Dividends Paid

Valuation Analysis   **Institutional Holding**

Forecast EPS	$0.07	No of Institutions
	(01/18/2018)	449
Market Cap	$8.8 Billion	Shares
Book Value	$1.4 Billion	160,462,400
Price/Book	6.38	% Held
Price/Sales	0.92	73.67

Business Summary: Entertainment (MIC: 2.3.2 SIC: 7929 NAIC: 711410)

Live Nation Entertainment is a live entertainment company. Co.'s reportable segments are: Concerts, which promotes live music events globally, produces music festivals, operates and manages music venues and creates associated content; Sponsorship and Advertising, which manages the development of strategic sponsorship programs, and sells international, national and local sponsorships and placement of advertising across Co.'s distribution network; Ticketing, which manages Co.'s global ticketing operations and is responsible for Co.'s primary websites, www.livenation.com and www.ticketmaster.com; and Artist Nation, which provides management services to music artists and other clients.

Recent Developments: For the quarter ended Sep 30 2017, net income increased 12.1% to US$148.8 million from US$132.8 million in the year-earlier quarter. Revenues were US$3.56 billion, up 12.3% from US$3.17 billion the year before. Operating income was US$201.3 million versus US$191.3 million in the prior-year quarter, an increase of 5.3%. Direct operating expenses rose 12.6% to US$2.73 billion from US$2.43 billion in the comparable period the year before. Indirect operating expenses increased 13.4% to US$625.1 million from US$551.1 million in the equivalent prior-year period.

Prospects: Our evaluation of Live Nation Entertainment, Inc. as of Jan. 14, 2018 is the result of our systematic analysis on three basic characteristics: earnings strength, relative valuation, and recent stock price movement. The company has suffered a very negative trend in earnings per share over the past 5 quarters and while recent estimates for the company have remained steady, LYV has posted results that fell short of analysts expectations. Based on operating earnings yield, the company is overvalued when compared to all of the companies in our coverage universe. Share price changes over the past year indicates that LYV will perform very well over the near term.

Financial Data

(US$ in Thousands)	9 Mos	6 Mos	3 Mos	12/31/2016	12/31/2015	12/31/2014	12/31/2013	12/31/2012
Earnings Per Share	0.03	(0.01)	(0.17)	(0.23)	(0.33)	(0.49)	(0.22)	(0.87)
Cash Flow Per Share	4.36	4.35	4.13	2.95	1.49	1.35	2.15	1.96
Income Statement								
Total Revenue	7,791,292	4,231,874	1,413,181	8,354,934	7,245,731	6,866,964	6,478,547	5,819,047
EBITDA	614,455	301,172	85,192	309,349	238,352	125,888	222,759	102,081
Depn & Amortn	315,653	202,797	103,716	139,288	134,148	127,168	122,164	124,593
Income Before Taxes	221,685	46,414	(43,589)	66,128	4,851	(103,986)	(5,993)	(142,082)
Income Taxes	42,190	16,505	6,521	28,029	22,122	4,630	30,878	29,736
Net Income	184,878	48,485	(32,993)	2,942	(32,508)	(90,807)	(43,378)	(163,227)
Average Shares	223,132	213,879	203,730	202,076	200,973	198,874	193,885	186,955
Balance Sheet								
Current Assets	3,563,629	3,984,278	3,601,449	2,673,551	2,288,315	2,267,691	2,160,104	1,812,812
Total Assets	7,810,524	8,251,426	7,823,517	6,764,266	6,156,241	5,988,361	5,683,521	5,290,806
Current Liabilities	3,212,877	3,836,657	3,539,331	2,460,344	2,101,206	2,010,781	2,255,518	1,768,172
Long-Term Obligations	2,240,461	2,249,157	2,258,820	2,259,736	2,002,662	2,015,915	1,530,484	1,677,955
Total Liabilities	6,431,550	7,024,787	6,706,774	5,638,250	4,919,288	4,691,407	4,274,293	3,935,388
Stockholders' Equity	1,378,974	1,226,639	1,116,743	1,126,016	1,236,953	1,296,954	1,409,228	1,355,418
Shares Outstanding	206,799	206,137	205,610	204,067	202,483	201,193	199,566	190,853
Statistical Record								
Return on Assets %	1.17	0.76	0.20	0.05	N.M.	N.M.	N.M.	N.M.
Return on Equity %	6.28	4.82	1.26	0.25	N.M.	N.M.	N.M.	N.M.
EBITDA Margin %	7.89	7.12	6.03	3.70	3.29	1.83	3.44	1.75
Net Margin %	2.37	1.15	N.M.	0.04	N.M.	N.M.	N.M.	N.M.
Asset Turnover	1.35	1.20	1.16	1.29	1.19	1.18	1.18	1.12
Current Ratio	1.11	1.04	1.02	1.09	1.09	1.13	0.96	1.03
Debt to Equity	1.62	1.83	2.02	2.01	1.62	1.55	1.09	1.24
Price Range	43.58-26.60	36.42-23.19	30.72-21.08	28.78-19.36	29.21-23.58	27.36-19.76	19.82-9.31	10.88-8.21

Address: 9348 Civic Center Drive, Beverly Hills, CA 90210
Telephone: 310-867-7000

Web Site: www.livenation.com; www.ticketmaster.com
Officers: Irving L. Azoff - Executive Chairman
Michael Rapino - President, Chief Executive Officer

Auditors: Ernst & Young LLP
Investor Contact: 310-867-7000
Transfer Agents: Computershare, Providence, RI

LOCKHEED MARTIN CORP

Exchange	Symbol	Price	52Wk Range	Yield	P/E	Div Achiever
NYS	LMT	$321.05 (12/29/2017)	322.82-250.90	2.49	25.75	14 Years

*7 Year Price Score 133.76 *NYSE Composite Index=100 *12 Month Price Score 103.42

Interim Earnings (Per Share)

Qtr.	Mar	Jun	Sep	Dec
2014	2.87	2.76	2.76	2.82
2015	2.74	2.94	2.77	3.01
2016	2.58	3.32	7.93	3.39
2017	2.61	3.23	3.24	...

Interim Dividends (Per Share)

Amt	Decl	Ex	Rec	Pay
1.82Q	01/26/2017	02/27/2017	03/01/2017	03/24/2017
1.82Q	04/26/2017	05/30/2017	06/01/2017	06/23/2017
1.82Q	06/22/2017	08/30/2017	09/01/2017	09/22/2017
2.00Q	09/28/2017	11/30/2017	12/01/2017	12/29/2017

Indicated Div: $8.00 (Div. Reinv. Plan)

Valuation Analysis

Forecast EPS	$13.11 (01/18/2018)
Market Cap	$92.1 Billion
Book Value	$2.1 Billion
Price/Book	43.88
Price/Sales	1.85

Institutional Holding

No of Institutions	1704
Shares	285,151,584
% Held	83.15

TRADING VOLUME (thousand shares)

Business Summary: Defense (MIC: 7.1.2 SIC: 3761 NAIC: 336414)

Lockheed Martin is a security and aerospace company. Co. has four segments: Aeronautics, designs, develops, manufactures, integrates, sustains, supports, and upgrades military aircraft; Missiles and Fire Control, provides air and missile defense systems, tactical missiles and air-to-ground precision strike weapon systems; Rotary and Mission Systems, designs, manufactures, services and supports military and civil helicopters, ship and submarine mission and combat systems; and Space Systems, engages in the research and development, design, engineering and production of satellites, strategic and defensive missile systems and space transportation systems.

Recent Developments: For the quarter ended Sep 24 2017, income from continuing operations decreased 13.8% to US$939.0 million from US$1.09 billion in the year-earlier quarter. Net income decreased 60.8% to US$939.0 million from US$2.40 billion in the year-earlier quarter. Revenues were US$12.17 billion, up 5.4% from US$11.55 billion the year before. Operating income was US$1.43 billion versus US$1.59 billion in the prior-year quarter, a decrease of 10.1%. Direct operating expenses rose 6.4% to US$10.82 billion from US$10.17 billion in the comparable period the year before. Indirect operating income amounted to US$77.0 million compared with an income of US$204.0 million in the equivalent prior-year period.

Prospects: Our evaluation of Lockheed Martin Corp. as of Jan. 14, 2018 is the result of our systematic analysis on three basic characteristics: earnings strength, relative valuation, and recent stock price movement. The company has produced a positive trend in earnings per share over the past 5 quarters and while recent estimates for the company have been raised by analysts, LMT has posted results that fell short of analysts expectations. Based on operating earnings yield, the company is about fairly valued when compared to all of the companies in our coverage universe. Share price changes over the past year indicates that LMT will perform well over the near term.

Financial Data

(US$ in Millions)	9 Mos	6 Mos	3 Mos	12/31/2016	12/31/2015	12/31/2014	12/31/2013	12/31/2012
Earnings Per Share	12.47	17.16	17.25	17.49	11.46	11.21	9.13	8.36
Cash Flow Per Share	19.83	18.23	18.25	17.29	16.44	12.20	14.17	4.81
Dividends Per Share	7.280	7.110	6.940	6.770	6.150	5.490	4.780	4.150
Dividend Payout %	58.38	41.43	40.23	38.71	53.66	48.97	52.35	49.64
Income Statement								
Total Revenue	35,911	23,742	11,057	47,248	46,132	45,600	45,358	47,182
EBITDA	4,934	3,214	1,435	6,764	6,492	6,592	5,495	5,443
Depn & Amortn	880	581	285	1,215	1,026	994	990	988
Income Before Taxes	3,577	2,318	995	4,886	5,023	5,258	4,155	4,072
Income Taxes	933	613	232	1,133	1,418	1,644	1,205	1,327
Net Income	2,644	1,705	763	5,302	3,605	3,614	2,981	2,745
Average Shares	290	291	292	303	314	322	326	328
Balance Sheet								
Current Assets	17,208	16,566	16,586	15,108	16,198	12,329	13,329	13,855
Total Assets	48,946	48,711	48,836	47,806	49,128	37,073	36,188	38,657
Current Liabilities	13,084	13,641	13,597	12,542	14,057	11,112	11,120	12,155
Long-Term Obligations	14,268	14,283	14,276	14,282	14,305	6,169	6,152	6,158
Total Liabilities	46,848	47,446	47,353	46,295	46,031	33,673	31,270	38,618
Stockholders' Equity	2,098	1,265	1,483	1,511	3,097	3,400	4,918	39
Shares Outstanding	286	287	289	289	303	314	319	321
Statistical Record								
Return on Assets %	7.44	10.27	10.44	10.91	8.36	9.87	7.97	7.15
Return on Equity %	164.31	238.76	221.76	229.49	110.97	86.90	120.27	526.44
EBITDA Margin %	13.74	13.54	12.98	14.32	14.07	14.46	12.11	11.54
Net Margin %	7.36	7.18	6.90	11.22	7.81	7.93	6.57	5.82
Asset Turnover	1.02	0.99	1.00	0.97	1.07	1.24	1.21	1.23
Current Ratio	1.32	1.21	1.22	1.20	1.15	1.11	1.20	1.14
Debt to Equity	6.80	11.29	9.63	9.45	4.62	1.81	1.25	157.90
Price Range	308.54-230.52	283.65-230.52	272.03-219.06	267.62-206.08	226.43-185.52	196.84-146.07	148.84-86.70	94.87-79.98
P/E Ratio	24.74-18.49	16.53-13.43	15.77-12.70	15.30-11.78	19.76-16.19	17.56-13.03	16.30-9.50	11.35-9.57
Average Yield %	2.70	2.75	2.79	2.85	3.03	3.25	4.24	4.68

Address: 6801 Rockledge Drive, Bethesda, MD 20817 **Telephone:** 301-897-6000	**Web Site:** www.lockheedmartin.com **Officers:** Marillyn A. Hewson - Chairman, President, President (frmr), President (frmr-frmr), Chief Executive Officer, Chief Executive Officer (frmr), Executive Vice President, Chief Operating Officer Bruce L. Tanner - Executive Vice President, Chief Financial Officer	**Auditors:** Ernst & Young LLP **Investor Contact:** 301-897-6584 **Transfer Agents:** Computershare Trust Company, N.A., Providence, RI

LOEWS CORP.

Exchange	Symbol	Price	52Wk Range	Yield	P/E
NYS	L	$50.03 (12/29/2017)	50.65-45.12	0.50	17.43

*7 Year Price Score 88.16 *NYSE Composite Index=100 *12 Month Price Score 98.86

Interim Earnings (Per Share)

Qtr.	Mar	Jun	Sep	Dec
2014	0.15	0.30	0.55	0.55
2015	0.29	0.46	0.50	(0.53)
2016	0.30	(0.19)	0.97	0.85
2017	0.87	0.69	0.46	...

Interim Dividends (Per Share)

Amt	Decl	Ex	Rec	Pay
0.063Q	02/14/2017	02/27/2017	03/01/2017	03/14/2017
0.063Q	05/09/2017	05/26/2017	05/31/2017	06/13/2017
0.063Q	08/08/2017	08/28/2017	08/30/2017	09/12/2017
0.063Q	11/14/2017	11/28/2017	11/29/2017	12/12/2017

Indicated Div: $0.25

Valuation Analysis

Forecast EPS	$2.80
	(01/17/2018)
Market Cap	$16.8 Billion
Book Value	$19.0 Billion
Price/Book	0.89
Price/Sales	1.25

Institutional Holding

No of Institutions	677
Shares	269,322,912
% Held	56.19

Business Summary: General Insurance (MIC: 5.2.1 SIC: 6331 NAIC: 524126)

Loews is a holding company. Co. is engaged in: commercial property and casualty insurance, including surety through its 90.0% owned subsidiary, CNA Financial Corporation; operation of offshore oil and gas drilling rigs through its 53.0% owned subsidiary, Diamond Offshore Drilling, Inc.; transportation and storage of natural gas and natural gas liquids and gathering and processing of natural gas through its 53% owned subsidiary, Boardwalk Pipeline Partners, LP; and operation a chain of hotels in the U.S. and Canada through its Loews Hotels Holding Corporation subsidiary.

Recent Developments:
For the quarter ended Sep 30 2017, net income decreased 46.1% to US$212.0 million from US$393.0 million in the year-earlier quarter. Revenues were US$3.52 billion, up 7.1% from US$3.29 billion the year before. Net premiums earned were US$1.81 billion versus US$1.77 billion in the prior-year quarter, an increase of 2.2%. Net investment income fell 0.7% to US$557.0 million from US$561.0 million a year ago.

Prospects:
Our evaluation of Loews Corp. as of Jan. 14, 2018 is the result of our systematic analysis on three basic characteristics: earnings strength, relative valuation, and recent stock price movement. The company has generated a negative trend in earnings per share over the past 5 quarters and while recent estimates for the company have been raised by analysts, L has posted better than expected results. Based on operating earnings yield, the company is undervalued when compared to all of the companies in our coverage universe. Share price changes over the past year indicates that L will perform in line with the market over the near term.

Financial Data
(US$ in Thousands)	9 Mos	6 Mos	3 Mos	12/31/2016	12/31/2015	12/31/2014	12/31/2013	12/31/2012
Earnings Per Share	2.87	3.38	2.50	1.93	0.72	1.55	1.53	1.43
Cash Flow Per Share	6.97	8.05	6.24	6.65	9.79	7.83	5.40	7.20
Tang Book Value Per Share	54.56	53.98	53.88	52.93	50.63	50.70	49.36	47.12
Dividends Per Share	0.250	0.250	0.250	0.250	0.250	0.250	0.250	0.250
Dividend Payout %	8.71	7.40	10.00	12.95	34.72	16.13	16.34	17.48
Income Statement								
Premium Income	5,185,000	3,379,000	1,645,000	6,924,000	6,921,000	7,212,000	7,271,000	6,882,000
Total Revenue	10,180,000	6,659,000	3,300,000	13,105,000	13,415,000	14,325,000	15,053,000	14,552,000
Benefits & Claims	4,053,000	2,573,000	1,293,000	5,283,000	5,384,000	5,591,000	5,947,000	5,896,000
Income Before Taxes	1,121,000	857,000	510,000	936,000	244,000	1,810,000	1,429,000	1,399,000
Income Taxes	240,000	188,000	119,000	220,000	(43,000)	457,000	360,000	289,000
Net Income	683,000	526,000	295,000	654,000	260,000	591,000	595,000	568,000
Average Shares	337,790	337,720	337,680	338,310	362,690	382,550	389,510	395,870
Balance Sheet								
Total Assets	79,527,000	79,101,000	77,114,000	76,594,000	76,029,000	78,367,000	79,939,000	80,021,000
Total Liabilities	60,506,000	60,285,000	58,626,000	58,431,000	58,468,000	59,087,000	60,481,000	60,562,000
Stockholders' Equity	19,021,000	18,816,000	18,488,000	18,163,000	17,561,000	19,280,000	19,458,000	19,459,000
Shares Outstanding	336,753	336,601	336,699	336,621	339,897	372,934	386,960	391,805
Statistical Record								
Return on Assets %	1.23	1.44	1.10	0.85	0.34	0.75	0.74	0.73
Return on Equity %	5.22	6.22	4.66	3.65	1.41	3.05	3.06	2.96
Loss Ratio %	78.17	76.15	78.60	76.30	77.79	77.52	81.79	85.67
Net Margin %	6.71	7.90	8.94	4.99	1.94	4.13	3.95	3.90
Price Range	49.19-40.80	48.14-39.90	47.90-37.52	47.90-34.21	42.53-35.36	48.24-39.07	49.20-40.75	43.17-37.31
P/E Ratio	17.14-14.22	14.24-11.80	19.16-15.01	24.82-17.73	59.07-49.11	31.12-25.21	32.16-26.63	30.19-26.09
Average Yield %	0.54	0.56	0.58	0.62	0.64	0.58	0.55	0.62

Address: 667 Madison Avenue, New York, NY 10065-8087 **Telephone:** 212-521-2000	**Web Site:** www.loews.com **Officers:** Andrew H. Tisch - Co-Chairman Jonathan M. Tisch - Co-Chairman	**Auditors:** Deloitte & Touche LLP **Transfer Agents:** Computershare Shareowner Services, Jersey City, NJ

LOUISIANA-PACIFIC CORP

Exchange	Symbol	Price	52Wk Range	Yield	P/E
NYS	LPX	$26.26 (12/29/2017)	29.14-18.83	N/A	12.69

*7 Year Price Score 120.18 *NYSE Composite Index=100 *12 Month Price Score 102.06

Interim Earnings (Per Share)

Qtr.	Mar	Jun	Sep	Dec
2014	(0.10)	0.01	(0.14)	(0.30)
2015	(0.24)	(0.14)	(0.19)	(0.05)
2016	0.07	0.22	0.45	0.29
2017	0.38	0.65	0.75	...

Interim Dividends (Per Share)

No Dividends Paid

Valuation Analysis / Institutional Holding

Valuation Analysis		Institutional Holding	
Forecast EPS	$2.19	No of Institutions	439
	(01/17/2018)		
Market Cap	$3.8 Billion	Shares	
Book Value	$1.5 Billion	166,027,696	
Price/Book	2.60	% Held	
Price/Sales	1.48	97.24	

TRADING VOLUME (thousand shares)

Business Summary: Paper & Forest Products (MIC: 8.1.2 SIC: 2493 NAIC: 321219)

Louisiana-Pacific is a manufacturer of building products. Co.'s products are used primarily in new home construction, repair and remodeling and outdoor structures. Co. operates in four segments: North America oriented strand board (OSB), which manufactures and distributes OSB structural panel products; siding, which includes SmartSide siding products and related accessories, and CanExel siding and accessories; engineered wood products, which manufactures and distributes laminated veneer lumber, I-Joists, laminated strand lumber and other related products; and South America, which manufactures and distributes OSB and siding products in South America and certain export markets.

Recent Developments: For the quarter ended Sep 30 2017, income from continuing operations increased 69.1% to US$110.9 million from US$65.6 million in the year-earlier quarter. Net income increased 67.4% to US$109.8 million from US$65.6 million in the year-earlier quarter. Revenues were US$718.3 million, up 20.4% from US$596.4 million the year before. Operating income was US$158.9 million versus US$76.9 million in the prior-year quarter, an increase of 106.6%. Direct operating expenses rose 8.3% to US$479.3 million from US$442.6 million in the comparable period the year before. Indirect operating expenses increased 4.2% to US$80.1 million from US$76.9 million in the equivalent prior-year period.

Prospects: Our evaluation of Louisiana-Pacific Corp. as of Jan. 14, 2018 is the result of our systematic analysis on three basic characteristics: earnings strength, relative valuation, and recent stock price movement. The company has generated a negative trend in earnings per share over the past 5 quarters. However, while recent estimates for the company have been mixed, LPX has posted results that fell short of analysts expectations. Based on operating earnings yield, the company is undervalued when compared to all of the companies in our coverage universe. Share price changes over the past year indicates that LPX will perform well over the near term.

Financial Data
(US$ in Thousands)

	9 Mos	6 Mos	3 Mos	12/31/2016	12/31/2015	12/31/2014	12/31/2013	12/31/2012
Earnings Per Share	2.07	1.77	1.34	1.03	(0.62)	(0.53)	1.23	0.20
Cash Flow Per Share	2.82	2.77	2.55	2.38	0.21	(0.37)	1.74	0.81
Tang Book Value Per Share	10.05	9.25	8.60	8.22	7.04	7.78	8.62	7.46
Income Statement								
Total Revenue	2,023,300	1,305,000	610,900	2,233,400	1,892,500	1,934,800	2,085,200	1,715,800
EBITDA	460,500	264,000	105,000	309,800	37,700	25,500	333,900	161,200
Depn & Amortn	91,300	60,200	30,600	112,800	101,900	100,700	91,300	73,900
Income Before Taxes	354,400	198,200	69,400	164,900	(95,400)	(105,000)	206,600	38,000
Income Taxes	97,900	51,500	15,500	19,800	(2,700)	(27,200)	41,100	7,600
Net Income	259,200	149,500	55,000	149,800	(88,100)	(75,400)	177,100	28,800
Average Shares	146,500	146,200	145,900	145,300	142,400	141,100	144,300	142,600
Balance Sheet								
Current Assets	1,290,800	1,155,700	1,074,000	1,016,500	769,100	950,300	1,034,200	995,600
Total Assets	2,308,000	2,162,800	2,080,200	2,031,200	2,176,300	2,353,500	2,493,300	2,331,000
Current Liabilities	245,800	230,600	215,500	228,800	143,000	172,700	166,200	239,300
Long-Term Obligations	353,000	352,600	374,600	374,400	751,800	759,500	762,700	782,700
Total Liabilities	842,700	814,400	826,100	835,500	1,159,300	1,237,700	1,267,000	1,297,200
Stockholders' Equity	1,465,300	1,348,400	1,254,100	1,195,700	1,017,000	1,115,800	1,226,300	1,033,800
Shares Outstanding	144,855	144,797	144,663	144,316	142,984	142,226	141,124	138,534
Statistical Record								
Return on Assets %	12.72	11.60	9.06	7.10	N.M.	N.M.	7.34	1.28
Return on Equity %	23.03	21.15	16.87	13.50	N.M.	N.M.	15.67	2.82
EBITDA Margin %	22.76	20.23	17.19	13.87	1.99	1.32	16.01	9.40
Net Margin %	12.81	11.46	9.00	6.71	N.M.	N.M.	8.49	1.68
Asset Turnover	1.09	1.11	1.09	1.06	0.84	0.80	0.86	0.77
Current Ratio	5.25	5.01	4.98	4.44	5.38	5.50	6.22	4.16
Debt to Equity	0.24	0.26	0.30	0.31	0.74	0.68	0.62	0.76
Price Range	29.14-17.50	26.73-17.35	24.82-15.92	20.86-13.78	18.70-14.19	18.79-12.61	22.18-14.75	19.32-7.68
P/E Ratio	14.08-8.45	15.10-9.80	18.52-11.88	20.25-13.38	...	...	18.03-11.99	96.60-38.40

Address: 414 Union Street, Nashville, TN 37219
Telephone: 615-986-5600
Fax: 615-986-5666

Web Site: www.lpcorp.com
Officers: E. Gary Cook - Chairman Mark A. Fuchs - Vice President, Secretary

Auditors: Deloitte & Touche LLP
Transfer Agents: Computershare Trust Company, N.A., Providence, RI

LOWE'S COMPANIES INC

Exchange	Symbol	Price	52Wk Range	Yield	P/E	Div Achiever
NYS	LOW	$92.94 (12/29/2017)	92.94-70.95	1.76	22.29	55 Years

*7 Year Price Score 116.36 *NYSE Composite Index=100 *12 Month Price Score 99.86

TRADING VOLUME (thousand shares)

Interim Earnings (Per Share)

Qtr.	Apr	Jul	Oct	Jan
2014-15	0.61	1.04	0.59	0.47
2015-16	0.70	1.20	0.80	0.03
2016-17	0.98	1.31	0.43	0.74
2017-18	0.70	1.68	1.05	...

Interim Dividends (Per Share)

Amt	Decl	Ex	Rec	Pay
0.35Q	03/24/2017	04/24/2017	04/26/2017	05/10/2017
0.41Q	06/02/2017	07/24/2017	07/26/2017	08/09/2017
0.41Q	08/18/2017	10/24/2017	10/25/2017	11/08/2017
0.41Q	11/10/2017	01/23/2018	01/24/2018	02/07/2018

Indicated Div: $1.64 (Div. Reinv. Plan)

Valuation Analysis

		Institutional Holding	
Forecast EPS	$4.52	No of Institutions	
	(01/18/2018)	1803	
Market Cap	$77.2 Billion	Shares	
Book Value	$5.7 Billion	794,999,680	
Price/Book	13.45	% Held	
Price/Sales	1.12	62.94	

Business Summary: Retail - Hardware & Home Improvement (MIC: 2.1.8 SIC: 5211 NAIC: 444110)

Lowe's Companies is a home improvement retailer. As of Feb. 3 2017, Co. operated 2,129 home improvement and hardware stores in the U.S., Canada and Mexico. Co. operated 87 Orchard Supply Hardware stores. Co. sells products in the following categories: Lumber and Building Materials; Tools and Hardware; Appliances; Fashion Fixtures; Rough Plumbing and Electrical; Seasonal Living; Lawn and Garden; Paint; Millwork; Flooring; Kitchens; Outdoor Power Equipment; and Home Fashions. Co.'s services includes installation services through independent contractors, and extended protection plans and repair services.

Recent Developments: For the quarter ended Nov 3 2017, net income increased 130.1% to US$872.0 million from US$379.0 million in the year-earlier quarter. Revenues were US$16.77 billion, up 6.6% from US$15.74 billion the year before. Operating income was US$1.55 billion versus US$939.0 million in the prior-year quarter, an increase of 64.7%. Direct operating expenses rose 7.0% to US$11.06 billion from US$10.33 billion in the comparable period the year before. Indirect operating expenses decreased 6.8% to US$4.17 billion from US$4.47 billion in the equivalent prior-year period.

Prospects: Our evaluation of Lowe's Companies Inc. as of Jan. 14, 2018 is the result of our systematic analysis on three basic characteristics: earnings strength, relative valuation, and recent stock price movement. The company has generated a negative trend in earnings per share over the past 5 quarters and while recent estimates for the company have been raised by analysts, LOW has posted better than expected results. Based on operating earnings yield, the company is undervalued when compared to all of the companies in our coverage universe. Share price changes over the past year indicates that LOW will perform very poorly over the near term.

Financial Data

(US$ in Thousands)	9 Mos	6 Mos	3 Mos	02/03/2017	01/29/2016	01/30/2015	01/31/2014	02/01/2013
Earnings Per Share	4.17	3.55	3.18	3.47	2.73	2.71	2.14	1.69
Cash Flow Per Share	6.88	7.21	6.64	6.28	5.17	5.00	3.89	3.28
Tang Book Value Per Share	5.31	5.11	5.22	6.18	8.41	10.38	11.51	12.48
Dividends Per Share	1.520	1.460	1.400	1.330	1.070	0.870	0.700	0.620
Dividend Payout %	36.45	41.13	44.03	38.33	39.19	32.10	32.71	36.69
Income Statement								
Total Revenue	53,125,000	36,355,000	16,860,000	65,017,000	59,074,000	56,223,000	53,417,000	50,521,000
EBITDA	6,172,000	4,245,000	1,484,000	7,346,000	6,455,000	6,277,000	5,611,000	5,083,000
Depn & Amortn	1,148,000	768,000	389,000	1,500,000	1,484,000	1,485,000	1,462,000	1,523,000
Income Before Taxes	4,545,000	3,158,000	934,000	5,201,000	4,419,000	4,276,000	3,673,000	3,137,000
Income Taxes	1,652,000	1,137,000	332,000	2,108,000	1,873,000	1,578,000	1,387,000	1,178,000
Net Income	2,893,000	2,021,000	602,000	3,093,000	2,546,000	2,698,000	2,286,000	1,959,000
Average Shares	832,000	842,000	858,000	881,000	929,000	990,000	1,061,000	1,152,000
Balance Sheet								
Current Assets	14,009,000	14,033,000	15,276,000	12,000,000	10,561,000	10,080,000	10,296,000	9,784,000
Total Assets	36,783,000	36,668,000	37,613,000	34,408,000	31,266,000	31,827,000	32,732,000	32,666,000
Current Liabilities	13,738,000	13,625,000	14,686,000	11,974,000	10,492,000	9,348,000	8,876,000	7,708,000
Long-Term Obligations	15,570,000	15,788,000	15,770,000	14,394,000	11,545,000	10,815,000	10,086,000	9,030,000
Total Liabilities	31,041,000	31,132,000	32,082,000	27,974,000	23,612,000	21,859,000	20,879,000	18,809,000
Stockholders' Equity	5,742,000	5,536,000	5,531,000	6,434,000	7,654,000	9,968,000	11,853,000	13,857,000
Shares Outstanding	831,000	837,000	853,000	866,000	910,000	960,000	1,030,000	1,110,000
Statistical Record								
Return on Assets %	9.86	8.38	7.52	9.27	8.09	8.38	7.01	5.93
Return on Equity %	57.63	49.21	44.12	43.20	28.98	24.80	17.83	12.93
EBITDA Margin %	11.62	11.68	8.80	11.30	10.93	11.16	10.50	10.06
Net Margin %	5.45	5.56	3.57	4.76	4.31	4.80	4.28	3.88
Asset Turnover	1.91	1.86	1.78	1.95	1.88	1.75	1.64	1.53
Current Ratio	1.02	1.03	1.04	1.00	1.01	1.08	1.16	1.27
Debt to Equity	2.71	2.85	2.85	2.24	1.51	1.08	0.85	0.65
Price Range	86.06-66.25	86.06-65.63	86.00-65.63	82.94-63.40	77.61-66.25	70.44-44.63	51.95-35.86	38.58-24.85
P/E Ratio	20.64-15.89	24.24-18.49	27.04-20.64	23.90-18.27	28.43-24.27	25.99-16.47	24.28-16.76	22.83-14.70
Average Yield %	1.96	1.91	1.83	1.79	1.49	1.64	1.59	2.03

Address: 1000 Lowe's Blvd., Mooresville, NC 28117 **Telephone:** 704-758-1000	**Web Site:** www.lowes.com **Officers:** Robert A. Niblock - Chairman, President, Chief Executive Officer Matthew V. Hollifield - Senior Vice President, Chief Accounting Officer	**Auditors:** Deloitte & Touche LLP **Investor Contact:** 704-758-2033 **Transfer Agents:** Computershare Trust Company N.A., Providence, RI

L3 TECHNOLOGIES INC

Exchange	Symbol	Price	52Wk Range	Yield	P/E	Div Achiever
NYS	LLL	$197.85 (12/29/2017)	199.05-145.71	1.52	27.21	12 Years

*7 Year Price Score 122.34 *NYSE Composite Index=100 *12 Month Price Score 104.31

Interim Earnings (Per Share)

Qtr.	Mar	Jun	Sep	Dec
2014	2.01	1.53	1.78	2.35
2015	1.25	1.44	(3.74)	(2.02)
2016	2.87	1.88	1.88	2.38
2017	2.07	2.54	0.28	...

Interim Dividends (Per Share)

Amt	Decl	Ex	Rec	Pay
0.75Q	02/13/2017	02/27/2017	03/01/2017	03/15/2017
0.75Q	05/09/2017	05/17/2017	05/19/2017	06/15/2017
0.75Q	07/19/2017	08/15/2017	08/17/2017	09/15/2017
0.75Q	10/17/2017	11/16/2017	11/17/2017	12/15/2017

Indicated Div: $3.00 (Div. Reinv. Plan)

Valuation Analysis		Institutional Holding	
Forecast EPS	$8.57	No of Institutions	
	(01/18/2018)	841	
Market Cap	$15.4 Billion	Shares	
Book Value	$5.0 Billion	85,197,024	
Price/Book	3.09	% Held	
Price/Sales	1.40	76.40	

Business Summary: Aerospace (MIC: 7.1.1 SIC: 3812 NAIC: 334511)

L3 Technologies together with its subsidiaries, is a contractor in Intelligence, Surveillance and Reconnaissance systems, aircraft sustainment (including modifications, logistics and maintenance), simulation and training, night vision and image intensification equipment, and security and detection systems. Co. is also a provider of a range of communication and electronic systems and products used on military and commercial platforms. Co.'s customers include the U.S. Department of Defense and its contractors. Co. has three reportable segments: Electronic Systems, Aerospace Systems, and Communication Systems.

Recent Developments: For the quarter ended Sep 29 2017, income from continuing operations decreased 82.8% to US$26.0 million from US$151.0 million in the year-earlier quarter. Net income decreased 83.4% to US$25.0 million from US$151.0 million in the year-earlier quarter. Revenues were US$2.65 billion, up 5.6% from US$2.51 billion the year before. Operating income was US$63.0 million versus US$215.0 million in the prior-year quarter, a decrease of 70.7%. Direct operating expenses rose 4.6% to US$2.40 billion from US$2.29 billion in the comparable period the year before.

Prospects: Our evaluation of L3 Technologies Inc. as of Jan. 14, 2018 is the result of our systematic analysis on three basic characteristics: earnings strength, relative valuation, and recent stock price movement. The company has generated a negative trend in earnings per share over the past 5 quarters and while recent estimates for the company have been raised by analysts, LLL has posted better than expected results. Based on operating earnings yield, the company is about fairly valued when compared to all of the companies in our coverage universe. Share price changes over the past year indicates that LLL will perform well over the near term.

Financial Data

(US$ in Thousands)	9 Mos	6 Mos	3 Mos	12/31/2016	12/31/2015	12/31/2014	12/31/2013	12/31/2012
Earnings Per Share	7.27	8.87	8.21	9.01	(2.93)	7.56	8.54	8.30
Cash Flow Per Share	15.15	13.83	13.77	14.13	12.91	13.17	14.13	12.75
Dividends Per Share	2.250	1.500	0.750	2.800	2.600	2.400	2.200	2.000
Dividend Payout %	30.95	16.91	9.14	31.08	...	31.75	25.76	24.10
Income Statement								
Total Revenue	8,047,000	5,401,000	2,669,000	10,511,000	10,466,000	12,124,000	12,629,000	13,146,000
EBITDA	840,000	707,000	323,000	1,163,000	640,000	1,257,000	1,424,000	1,508,000
Depn & Amortn	212,000	142,000	70,000	162,000	166,000	172,000	166,000	170,000
Income Before Taxes	515,000	489,000	216,000	850,000	322,000	925,000	1,096,000	1,162,000
Income Taxes	114,000	114,000	48,000	189,000	25,000	248,000	309,000	374,000
Net Income	388,000	366,000	164,000	710,000	(240,000)	664,000	778,000	810,000
Average Shares	79,800	79,500	79,300	78,800	81,900	87,800	91,100	97,600
Balance Sheet								
Current Assets	4,099,000	4,021,000	3,872,000	3,697,000	4,232,000	4,737,000	4,649,000	4,571,000
Total Assets	12,468,000	12,432,000	12,164,000	11,865,000	12,085,000	13,836,000	14,009,000	13,826,000
Current Liabilities	2,283,000	2,195,000	2,229,000	2,135,000	2,879,000	2,525,000	2,523,000	2,597,000
Long-Term Obligations	3,345,000	3,342,000	3,340,000	3,338,000	3,153,000	3,940,000	3,645,000	3,653,000
Total Liabilities	7,469,000	7,456,000	7,433,000	7,312,000	7,730,000	8,551,000	7,986,000	8,363,000
Stockholders' Equity	4,999,000	4,976,000	4,731,000	4,553,000	4,355,000	5,285,000	6,023,000	5,463,000
Shares Outstanding	78,075	78,003	77,895	77,232	78,133	82,040	85,828	90,433
Statistical Record								
Return on Assets %	4.74	5.82	5.37	5.91	N.M.	4.77	5.59	5.51
Return on Equity %	12.04	14.84	14.21	15.90	N.M.	11.74	13.55	13.35
EBITDA Margin %	10.44	13.09	12.10	11.06	6.12	10.37	11.28	11.47
Net Margin %	4.82	6.78	6.14	6.75	N.M.	5.48	6.16	6.16
Asset Turnover	0.91	0.90	0.90	0.88	0.81	0.87	0.91	0.89
Current Ratio	1.80	1.83	1.74	1.73	1.47	1.88	1.84	1.76
Debt to Equity	0.67	0.67	0.71	0.73	0.72	0.75	0.61	0.67
Price Range	190.32-134.05	173.94-134.05	170.81-118.50	161.56-108.05	132.87-101.90	128.34-101.39	107.13-74.86	77.91-66.91
P/E Ratio	26.18-18.44	19.61-15.11	20.81-14.43	17.93-11.99	...	16.98-13.41	12.54-8.77	9.39-8.06
Average Yield %	1.37	0.96	0.50	2.03	2.18	2.07	2.48	2.80

Address: 600 Third Avenue, New York, NY 10016
Telephone: 212-697-1111

Web Site: www.l-3com.com
Officers: Michael T. Strianese - Executive Chairman, Chairman, President, Chief Executive Officer
Christopher E. Kubasik - President, Incoming Chief Executive Officer, Chief Operating Officer, Associate/Affiliate Company Officer

Auditors: PricewaterhouseCoopers LLP
Investor Contact: 212-697-1111
Transfer Agents: Computershare Trust Company, N.A, Providence, RI

M & T BANK CORP

Exchange	Symbol	Price	52Wk Range	Yield	P/E
NYS	MTB	$170.99 (12/29/2017)	173.90-142.47	1.75	19.74

*7 Year Price Score 109.85 ***NYSE Composite Index=100** ***12 Month Price Score 98.12**

TRADING VOLUME (thousand shares)

Interim Earnings (Per Share)

Qtr.	Mar	Jun	Sep	Dec
2014	1.61	1.98	1.91	1.92
2015	1.65	1.98	1.93	1.62
2016	1.73	1.98	2.10	1.98
2017	2.12	2.35	2.21	...

Interim Dividends (Per Share)

Amt	Decl	Ex	Rec	Pay
0.75Q	02/22/2017	03/02/2017	03/06/2017	03/31/2017
0.75Q	05/16/2017	05/30/2017	06/01/2017	06/30/2017
0.75Q	08/15/2017	08/30/2017	09/01/2017	09/29/2017
0.75Q	11/21/2017	11/30/2017	12/01/2017	12/29/2017

Indicated Div: $3.00 (Div. Reinv. Plan)

Valuation Analysis / Institutional Holding

Valuation Analysis		Institutional Holding	
Forecast EPS	$12.07 (01/26/2018)	No of Institutions	822
Market Cap	$26.1 Billion	Shares	141,890,944
Book Value	$16.3 Billion	% Held	87.42
Price/Book	1.60		
Price/Sales	4.41		

Business Summary: Banking (MIC: 5.1.1 SIC: 6022 NAIC: 522110)

M&T Bank is a bank holding company. Through subsidiaries, Co. provides individuals, corporations and other businesses, and institutions with commercial and retail banking services, including loans and deposits, trust, mortgage banking, asset management, insurance and other financial services. Banking activities are primarily focused on consumers residing in New York State, Maryland, New Jersey, Pennsylvania, Delaware, Connecticut, Virginia, West Virginia and the District of Columbia and on small and medium-size businesses in those areas. Certain subsidiaries also conduct activities in other areas. At Dec 31 2016, Co. had total assets of $123.45 billion and deposits of $95.49 billion.

Recent Developments: For the quarter ended Sep 30 2017, net income increased 1.7% to US$355.9 million from US$350.0 million in the year-earlier quarter. Net interest income increased 11.5% to US$957.1 million from US$858.3 million in the year-earlier quarter. Provision for loan losses was US$30.0 million versus US$47.0 million in the prior-year quarter, a decrease of 36.2%. Non-interest income fell 6.5% to US$459.4 million from US$491.4 million, while non-interest expense advanced 7.1% to US$806.0 million.

Prospects: Our evaluation of M & T Bank Corp. as of Jan. 21, 2018 is the result of our systematic analysis on three basic characteristics: earnings strength, relative valuation, and recent stock price movement. The company has produced a positive trend in earnings per share over the past 5 quarters and while recent estimates for the company have been raised by analysts, MTB has posted better than expected results. Based on operating earnings yield, the company is undervalued when compared to all of the companies in our coverage universe. Share price changes over the past year indicates that MTB will perform poorly over the near term.

Financial Data

(US$ in Thousands)	9 Mos	6 Mos	3 Mos	12/31/2016	12/31/2015	12/31/2014	12/31/2013	12/31/2012
Earnings Per Share	8.66	8.55	8.18	7.78	7.18	7.42	8.20	7.54
Cash Flow Per Share	14.39	14.11	13.09	7.53	12.74	8.39	7.25	3.96
Tang Book Value Per Share	68.28	68.00	66.94	67.64	63.98	57.02	52.33	44.39
Dividends Per Share	2.950	2.900	2.850	2.800	2.800	2.800	2.800	2.800
Dividend Payout %	34.06	33.92	34.84	35.99	39.00	37.74	34.15	37.14
Income Statement								
Interest Income	3,093,656	2,036,446	1,006,033	3,895,871	3,170,844	2,956,877	2,957,334	2,941,685
Interest Expense	284,062	183,986	91,773	425,984	328,257	280,431	284,105	343,169
Net Interest Income	2,809,594	1,852,460	914,260	3,469,887	2,842,587	2,676,446	2,673,229	2,598,516
Provision for Losses	137,000	107,000	55,000	190,000	170,000	124,000	185,000	204,000
Non-Interest Income	1,367,090	907,661	446,845	1,825,996	1,839,304	1,795,945	1,881,331	1,688,781
Non-Interest Expense	2,344,512	1,538,487	787,852	3,047,485	2,822,932	2,742,857	2,635,885	2,509,260
Income Before Taxes	1,695,172	1,114,634	518,253	2,058,398	1,688,959	1,605,534	1,733,675	1,574,037
Income Taxes	609,269	384,654	169,326	743,284	595,025	522,616	579,069	523,028
Net Income	1,085,903	729,980	348,927	1,315,114	1,079,667	1,066,246	1,138,480	1,029,498
Average Shares	151,691	153,276	154,949	157,304	137,533	131,844	129,603	126,405
Balance Sheet								
Net Loans & Leases	86,911,808	88,072,330	88,311,572	89,864,419	86,533,507	65,749,394	63,156,483	65,645,097
Total Assets	120,401,804	120,896,567	123,223,251	123,449,206	122,787,884	96,685,535	85,162,391	83,008,803
Total Deposits	93,513,393	93,540,938	97,042,521	95,493,876	91,957,841	73,582,053	67,118,612	65,611,253
Total Liabilities	104,083,752	104,613,030	107,010,147	106,962,584	106,614,595	84,349,639	73,856,859	72,806,210
Stockholders' Equity	16,318,052	16,283,537	16,213,104	16,486,622	16,173,289	12,335,896	11,305,532	10,202,593
Shares Outstanding	152,539	152,539	153,781	156,180	159,563	132,312	130,516	128,176
Statistical Record								
Return on Assets %	1.15	1.15	1.10	1.07	0.98	1.17	1.35	1.28
Return on Equity %	8.67	8.61	8.39	8.03	7.57	9.02	10.59	10.54
Net Interest Margin %	90.53	91.05	90.88	89.07	89.65	90.52	90.39	88.33
Efficiency Ratio %	53.15	50.34	54.23	53.26	56.34	57.71	54.48	54.19
Loans to Deposits	0.93	0.94	0.91	0.94	0.94	0.89	0.94	1.00
Price Range	172.21-113.17	172.21-112.00	172.21-107.81	158.10-100.78	133.20-112.28	128.03-109.30	119.30-96.55	104.88-76.98
P/E Ratio	19.89-13.07	20.14-13.10	21.05-13.18	20.32-12.95	18.55-15.64	17.25-14.73	14.55-11.77	13.91-10.21
Average Yield %	1.93	2.03	2.16	2.35	2.28	2.32	2.57	3.18

Address: One M & T Plaza, Buffalo, NY 14203	Web Site: www.mtb.com	Auditors: PricewaterhouseCoopers LLP
Telephone: 716-635-4000	Officers: Robert G. Wilmers - Chairman, Chief Executive Officer Marie King - Group Vice President, Corporate Secretary	Investor Contact: 716-842-5138 Transfer Agents: Registrar and Transfer Company, Cranford, NJ

MACERICH CO (THE)

Exchange	Symbol	Price	52Wk Range	Yield	P/E
NYS	MAC	$65.68 (12/29/2017)	72.69-52.72	4.51	61.96

*7 Year Price Score 74.01 *NYSE Composite Index=100 *12 Month Price Score 95.47

Interim Earnings (Per Share)

Qtr.	Mar	Jun	Sep	Dec
2014	0.13	0.11	0.25	9.96
2015	0.15	0.09	0.21	2.63
2016	2.76	0.31	0.09	0.27
2017	0.48	0.19	0.12	...

Interim Dividends (Per Share)

Amt	Decl	Ex	Rec	Pay
0.71Q	02/09/2017	02/16/2017	02/21/2017	03/03/2017
0.71Q	04/20/2017	05/03/2017	05/05/2017	06/02/2017
0.71Q	08/04/2017	08/16/2017	08/18/2017	09/07/2017
0.74Q	10/24/2017	11/09/2017	11/10/2017	12/01/2017

Indicated Div: $2.96 (Div. Reinv. Plan)

Valuation Analysis

		Institutional Holding	
Forecast EPS	$1.06 (01/11/2018)	No of Institutions	488
Market Cap	$9.3 Billion	Shares	180,745,216
Book Value	$3.7 Billion	% Held	98.50
Price/Book	2.47		
Price/Sales	9.17		

Business Summary: REITs (MIC: 5.3.1 SIC: 6798 NAIC: 525930)

Macerich is a self-administered and self-managed real estate investment trust. Co. is involved in the acquisition, ownership, development, redevelopment, management and leasing of regional and community/power shopping centers. Co. is the sole general partner of, and owns a majority of the ownership interests in The Macerich Partnership, L.P. (the Operating Partnership). As of Dec 31 2016, the Operating Partnership owned or had an ownership interest in 50 regional shopping centers and seven community/power shopping centers. Co. conducts all of its operations through the Operating Partnership and its management companies.

Recent Developments: For the quarter ended Sep 30 2017, net income increased 45.7% to US$19.2 million from US$13.2 million in the year-earlier quarter. Revenues were US$242.5 million, down 4.3% from US$253.4 million the year before. Revenues from property income fell 4.4% to US$230.8 million from US$241.3 million in the corresponding quarter a year earlier.

Prospects: Our evaluation of Macerich Co. as of Jan. 14, 2018 is the result of our systematic analysis on three basic characteristics: earnings strength, relative valuation, and recent stock price movement. The company has managed to produce a neutral trend in earnings per share over the past 5 quarters. Because the company lacks sufficient analyst estimate data, we place greater weight on the historical EPS trend as the measure of earnings strength. Based on operating earnings yield, the company is overvalued when compared to all of the companies in our coverage universe. Share price changes over the past year indicates that MAC will perform in line with the market over the near term.

Financial Data

(US$ in Thousands)	9 Mos	6 Mos	3 Mos	12/31/2016	12/31/2015	12/31/2014	12/31/2013	12/31/2012
Earnings Per Share	1.06	1.03	1.15	3.52	3.08	10.45	3.00	2.51
Cash Flow Per Share	2.82	2.82	2.87	2.84	3.42	2.80	3.02	2.61
Tang Book Value Per Share	26.21	26.76	27.26	27.93	29.59	33.53	22.94	21.46
Dividends Per Share	2.840	2.810	2.780	2.750	6.630	2.510	2.360	2.230
Dividend Payout %	267.92	272.82	241.74	78.13	215.26	24.02	78.67	88.84
Income Statement								
Total Revenue	736,919	494,468	247,045	1,041,271	1,288,149	1,105,247	1,029,475	881,323
EBITDA	422,641	306,687	178,811	939,565	1,041,445	2,021,903	456,788	661,387
Depn & Amortn	229,615	155,030	82,028	277,270	354,977	289,178	269,790	271,025
Income Before Taxes	66,139	68,035	55,482	498,620	474,525	1,542,036	(10,249)	213,584
Income Taxes	(178)	(3,047)	(3,484)	722	(3,223)	(4,269)	(1,692)	(4,159)
Net Income	113,379	95,881	69,243	516,995	487,562	1,499,042	420,090	337,426
Average Shares	141,310	141,728	143,655	146,711	158,060	143,291	139,680	134,148
Balance Sheet								
Current Assets	314,161	335,071	335,025	280,995	257,901	230,463	186,055	271,862
Total Assets	9,606,911	9,682,206	9,712,064	9,958,148	11,258,576	13,121,778	9,075,250	9,311,209
Current Liabilities	371,699	379,239	380,610	427,481	815,382	684,122	440,099	388,425
Long-Term Obligations	5,050,431	4,987,514	4,902,408	4,965,900	5,283,742	6,292,400	4,582,727	5,261,370
Total Liabilities	5,860,590	5,822,650	5,754,611	5,852,261	6,543,162	7,481,658	5,716,501	6,233,680
Stockholders' Equity	3,746,321	3,859,556	3,957,453	4,105,887	4,715,414	5,640,120	3,358,749	3,077,529
Shares Outstanding	140,918	141,556	141,912	143,985	154,404	158,201	140,733	137,507
Statistical Record								
Return on Assets %	1.54	1.49	1.66	4.86	4.00	13.51	4.57	3.90
Return on Equity %	3.81	3.63	3.83	11.69	9.42	33.32	13.05	11.42
EBITDA Margin %	57.35	62.02	72.38	90.23	80.85	182.94	44.37	75.04
Net Margin %	15.39	19.39	28.03	49.65	37.85	135.63	40.81	38.29
Asset Turnover	0.10	0.10	0.10	0.10	0.11	0.10	0.11	0.10
Current Ratio	0.85	0.88	0.88	0.66	0.32	0.34	0.42	0.70
Debt to Equity	1.35	1.29	1.24	1.21	1.12	1.12	1.36	1.71
Price Range	80.87-52.72	89.76-56.80	89.76-62.84	89.76-67.09	94.89-72.53	84.87-55.58	70.84-55.25	62.29-50.30
P/E Ratio	76.29-49.74	87.15-55.15	78.05-54.64	25.50-19.06	30.81-23.55	8.12-5.32	23.61-18.42	24.82-20.04
Average Yield %	4.44	3.95	3.68	3.52	8.13	3.80	3.86	3.89

Address: 401 Wilshire Boulevard, Suite 700, Santa Monica, CA 90401
Telephone: 310-394-6000

Web Site: www.macerich.com
Officers: Arthur M. Coppola - Chairman, President, Chief Executive Officer Edward C. Coppola President, Senior Executive Vice President, Chief Investment Officer

Auditors: KPMG LLP
Transfer Agents: Computershare Trust Company, N.A., Providence, RI

MACK CALI REALTY CORP

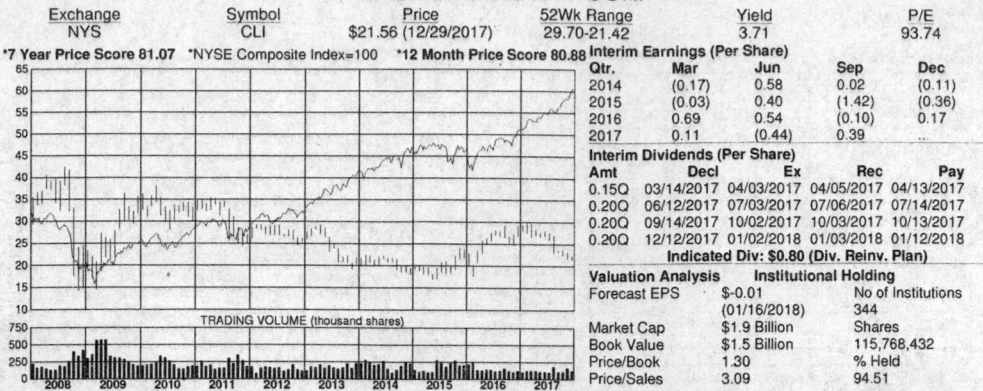

Exchange	Symbol	Price	52Wk Range	Yield	P/E
NYS	CLI	$21.56 (12/29/2017)	29.70-21.42	3.71	93.74

*7 Year Price Score 81.07   *NYSE Composite Index=100   *12 Month Price Score 80.88

Interim Earnings (Per Share)

Qtr.	Mar	Jun	Sep	Dec
2014	(0.17)	0.58	0.02	(0.11)
2015	(0.03)	0.40	(1.42)	(0.36)
2016	0.69	0.54	(0.10)	0.17
2017	0.11	(0.44)	0.39	...

Interim Dividends (Per Share)

Amt	Decl	Ex	Rec	Pay
0.15Q	03/14/2017	04/03/2017	04/05/2017	04/13/2017
0.20Q	06/12/2017	07/03/2017	07/06/2017	07/14/2017
0.20Q	09/14/2017	10/02/2017	10/03/2017	10/13/2017
0.20Q	12/12/2017	01/02/2018	01/03/2018	01/12/2018

Indicated Div: $0.80 (Div. Reinv. Plan)

Valuation Analysis

Valuation Analysis	Institutional Holding	
Forecast EPS	$-0.01	No of Institutions
	(01/16/2018)	344
Market Cap	$1.9 Billion	Shares
Book Value	$1.5 Billion	115,768,432
Price/Book	1.30	% Held
Price/Sales	3.09	94.51

Business Summary: REITs (MIC: 5.3.1 SIC: 6798 NAIC: 525930)

Mack-Cali Realty is a self-administered and self-managed real estate investment trust that owns and operates a real estate portfolio comprised primarily of Class A office and office/flex properties located primarily in the Northeast. Co. operates in three business segments: commercial and other real estate, multi-family real estate, and multi-family services. Co. provides leasing, property management, acquisition, development, construction and tenant-related services for its commercial and other real estate and multi-family real estate portfolio. As of Dec 31 2016, Co. owned or had interests in 248 properties, consisting of 119 office and 110 flex properties.

Recent Developments: For the quarter ended Sep 30 2017, net income amounted to US$44.7 million versus a net loss of US$9.6 million in the year-earlier quarter. Revenues were US$160.0 million, up 1.6% from US$157.5 million the year before. Revenues from property income fell 1.0% to US$150.8 million from US$152.4 million in the corresponding quarter a year earlier.

Prospects: Our evaluation of Mack Cali Realty Corp. as of Jan. 14, 2018 is the result of our systematic analysis on three basic characteristics: earnings strength, relative valuation, and recent stock price movement. The company has managed to produce a neutral trend in earnings per share over the past 5 quarters. Because the company lacks sufficient analyst estimate data, we place greater weight on the historical EPS trend as the measure of earnings strength. Based on operating earnings yield, the company is overvalued when compared to all of the companies in our coverage universe. Share price changes over the past year indicates that CLI will perform in line with the market over the near term.

Financial Data

(US$ in Thousands)	9 Mos	6 Mos	3 Mos	12/31/2016	12/31/2015	12/31/2014	12/31/2013	12/31/2012
Earnings Per Share	0.23	(0.26)	0.72	1.30	(1.41)	0.32	(0.17)	0.47
Cash Flow Per Share	1.75	1.54	1.40	1.11	1.90	1.79	2.26	2.78
Tang Book Value Per Share	16.52	16.30	16.98	16.99	16.22	18.21	18.58	20.15
Dividends Per Share	0.650	0.600	0.600	0.600	0.600	0.900	1.500	1.800
Dividend Payout %	282.61	...	83.33	46.15	...	281.25	...	382.98
Income Statement								
Total Revenue	472,671	312,653	149,887	613,398	594,883	636,799	667,031	704,743
EBITDA	111,731	37,312	45,139	403,616	145,276	331,703	231,048	363,491
Depn & Amortn	9,002	5,691	2,512	198,835	181,899	188,626	197,609	198,966
Income Before Taxes	33,189	(13,047)	22,780	111,506	(138,880)	33,814	(87,359)	42,192
Net Income	20,603	(17,451)	19,879	117,224	(125,752)	28,567	(14,909)	40,922
Average Shares	100,727	100,370	100,637	100,498	100,222	100,041	99,785	99,996
Balance Sheet								
Current Assets	239,121	191,139	338,373	196,232	203,420	196,255	386,735	226,747
Total Assets	4,995,519	5,076,494	4,914,227	4,296,766	4,063,490	4,192,247	4,515,328	4,526,045
Current Liabilities	266,989	261,623	255,447	230,070	224,862	221,582	234,107	253,149
Long-Term Obligations	2,839,186	2,950,219	2,731,204	2,340,009	2,154,920	2,088,654	2,362,766	2,204,389
Total Liabilities	3,507,053	3,607,825	3,385,937	2,769,595	2,607,814	2,567,466	2,872,969	2,759,071
Stockholders' Equity	1,488,466	1,468,669	1,528,290	1,527,171	1,455,676	1,624,781	1,642,359	1,766,974
Shares Outstanding	89,913	89,913	89,844	89,696	89,583	89,076	88,247	87,536
Statistical Record								
Return on Assets %	0.76	N.M.	1.64	2.80	N.M.	0.66	N.M.	0.93
Return on Equity %	2.38	N.M.	4.95	7.84	N.M.	1.75	N.M.	2.23
EBITDA Margin %	23.64	11.93	30.12	65.80	24.42	52.09	34.64	51.58
Net Margin %	4.36	N.M.	13.26	19.11	N.M.	4.49	N.M.	5.81
Asset Turnover	0.13	0.13	0.13	0.15	0.14	0.15	0.15	0.16
Current Ratio	0.90	0.73	1.32	0.85	0.90	0.89	1.65	0.90
Debt to Equity	1.91	2.01	1.79	1.53	1.48	1.29	1.44	1.25
Price Range	29.70-22.89	29.70-24.73	29.70-22.88	29.22-17.65	24.12-16.90	22.57-18.02	29.27-19.14	29.33-24.59
P/E Ratio	129.13-99.52	...	41.25-31.78	22.48-13.58	...	70.53-56.31	...	62.40-52.32
Average Yield %	2.43	2.18	2.22	2.38	3.02	4.38	6.12	6.58

Address: Harborside 3, 210 Hudson St., Ste. 400, Jersey City, NJ 07311 Telephone: 732-590-1010	Web Site: www.mack-cali.com Officers: William L. Mack - Chairman Michael J. DeMarco - President, Chief Operating Officer, Chief Executive Officer	Auditors: PricewaterhouseCoopers LLP Transfer Agents: Computershare Trust Company, N.A., Providence, RI

MACQUARIE INFRASTRUCTURE CORP

Exchange	Symbol	Price	52Wk Range	Yield	P/E
NYS	MIC	$64.20 (12/29/2017)	82.84-63.85	8.85	31.17

'7 Year Price Score 101.51 **'NYSE Composite Index=100** **'12 Month Price Score 83.38**

Interim Earnings (Per Share)

Qtr.	Mar	Jun	Sep	Dec
2014	0.36	0.17	13.87	(0.51)
2015	(1.22)	(0.80)	0.13	0.44
2016	0.28	0.24	0.51	0.82
2017	0.44	0.32	0.48	...

Interim Dividends (Per Share)

Amt	Decl	Ex	Rec	Pay
1.31Q	02/21/2017	03/01/2017	03/03/2017	03/08/2017
1.32Q	05/02/2017	05/11/2017	05/15/2017	05/18/2017
1.38Q	08/02/2017	08/10/2017	08/14/2017	08/17/2017
1.42Q	11/01/2017	11/10/2017	11/13/2017	11/16/2017

Indicated Div: $5.68

Valuation Analysis

		Institutional Holding	
Forecast EPS	$1.80	No of Institutions	
	(01/18/2018)	516	
Market Cap	$5.4 Billion	Shares	
Book Value	$2.9 Billion	74,980,856	
Price/Book	1.86	% Held	
Price/Sales	3.05	81.60	

Business Summary: Business Services (MIC: 7.5.2 SIC: 4581 NAIC: 488119)

Macquarie Infrastructure is a holding company. Co. owns and operates a portfolio of businesses that provide services to other businesses, government agencies and individuals. The businesses that Co. owns and operates are: International-Matex Tank Terminals, which provides bulk liquid storage, handling and other services; Atlantic Aviation, which provides fuel, terminal, aircraft hangaring and other services to owners and operators of general aviation jet aircraft; Contracted Power, which comprises a gas-fired facility and controlling interests in wind and solar facilities; and MIC Hawaii, which includes an energy company that processes and distributes gas and provides related services.

Recent Developments: For the quarter ended Sep 30 2017, net income decreased 14.8% to US$36.2 million from US$42.5 million in the year-earlier quarter. Revenues were US$453.1 million, up 7.7% from US$420.5 million the year before. Operating income was US$86.0 million versus US$75.7 million in the prior-year quarter, an increase of 13.6%. Direct operating expenses rose 8.3% to US$188.9 million from US$174.4 million in the comparable period the year before. Indirect operating expenses increased 4.5% to US$178.2 million from US$170.5 million in the equivalent prior-year period.

Prospects: Our evaluation of Macquarie Infrastructure Corp. as of Jan. 14, 2018 is the result of our systematic analysis on three basic characteristics: earnings strength, relative valuation, and recent stock price movement. The company has generated a negative trend in earnings per share over the past 5 quarters and while recent estimates for the company have been mixed, MIC has posted results that fell short of analysts expectations. Based on operating earnings yield, the company is about fairly valued when compared to all of the companies in our coverage universe. Share price changes over the past year indicates that MIC will perform in line with the market over the near term.

Financial Data
(US$ in Thousands)

	9 Mos	6 Mos	3 Mos	12/31/2016	12/31/2015	12/31/2014	12/31/2013	12/31/2012
Earnings Per Share	2.06	2.09	2.01	1.85	(1.39)	16.10	0.61	0.29
Cash Flow Per Share	6.23	6.45	6.58	6.91	4.89	3.99	3.02	4.66
Tang Book Value Per Share	N.M.	N.M.	0.07	0.48	0.98	N.M.	N.M.	N.M.
Dividends Per Share	5.300	5.170	5.050	4.890	2.240	3.888	3.350	2.200
Dividend Payout %	257.28	247.37	251.24	264.32	...	24.15	549.18	758.62
Income Statement								
Income Before Taxes	160,120	98,400	54,711	226,126	(178,968)	988,518	7,008	(15,791)
Income Taxes	65,284	39,737	22,073	71,257	(65,161)	(24,374)	18,043	2,285
Net Income	102,130	62,035	36,015	156,381	(108,537)	1,042,028	31,254	13,321
Average Shares	87,916	82,439	82,147	82,218	77,997	64,925	51,396	46,655
Balance Sheet								
Total Assets	7,955,363	7,634,911	7,538,562	7,559,253	7,378,828	6,625,188	2,500,865	2,223,694
Total Liabilities	5,044,589	4,792,665	4,636,994	4,606,359	4,348,638	3,838,025	1,458,637	1,568,666
Stockholders' Equity	2,910,774	2,842,246	2,901,568	2,952,894	3,030,190	2,787,163	1,042,228	655,028
Shares Outstanding	84,481	82,589	82,306	82,047	80,006	71,089	56,295	47,453
Statistical Record								
Return on Assets %	2.29	2.37	2.29	2.09	N.M.	22.84	1.32	0.60
Return on Equity %	5.97	6.14	5.78	5.21	N.M.	54.42	3.68	1.96
Price Range	83.82-71.84	84.13-73.50	84.13-66.30	84.13-52.89	87.24-65.32	73.04-51.59	59.55-45.56	45.85-27.57
P/E Ratio	40.69-34.87	40.25-35.17	41.86-32.99	45.48-28.59	...	4.54-3.20	97.62-74.69	158.10-95.07
Average Yield %	6.74	6.48	6.50	6.62	2.84	6.18	6.27	6.03

Address: 125 West 55th Street, New York, NY 10019
Telephone: 212-231-1000

Web Site: www.macquarie.com/mic
Officers: Martin Stanley - Chairman, Alternate Chairman Christopher Frost - President, Chief Operating Officer, Chief Executive Officer

Auditors: KPMG LLP
Investor Contact: 212-231-1825
Transfer Agents: Computershare Shareowner Services LLC, Pittsburgh, PA

MACY'S INC

Exchange	Symbol	Price	52Wk Range	Yield	P/E
NYS	M	$25.19 (12/29/2017)	35.84-17.53	5.99	11.15

*7 Year Price Score 47.74   *NYSE Composite Index=100   *12 Month Price Score 85.74

Interim Earnings (Per Share)

Qtr.	Apr	Jul	Oct	Jan
2014-15	0.60	0.80	0.61	2.21
2015-16	0.56	0.64	0.36	1.66
2016-17	0.37	0.03	0.05	1.53
2017-18	0.23	0.38	0.12	...

Interim Dividends (Per Share)

Amt	Decl	Ex	Rec	Pay
0.378Q	02/24/2017	03/13/2017	03/15/2017	04/03/2017
0.378Q	05/11/2017	06/13/2017	06/15/2017	07/03/2017
0.378Q	08/25/2017	09/14/2017	09/15/2017	10/02/2017
0.378Q	10/27/2017	12/14/2017	12/15/2017	01/02/2018

Indicated Div: $1.51 (Div. Reinv. Plan)

Valuation Analysis   **Institutional Holding**

Forecast EPS	$3.65	No of Institutions
(01/18/2018)		883
Market Cap	$7.7 Billion	Shares
Book Value	$4.2 Billion	322,040,832
Price/Book	1.81	% Held
Price/Sales	0.31	N/A

Business Summary: Retail - General Merchandise/Department Stores (MIC: 2.1.1 SIC: 5311 NAIC: 452111)

Macy's is an omnichannel retail organization operating stores, websites and mobile applications under three brands (Macy's, Bloomingdale's and Bluemercury) that sell a range of merchandise, including apparel and accessories (men's, women's and children's), cosmetics, home furnishings and other consumer goods. As of Jan 28 2017, Co. operated 829 stores in 45 states, the District of Columbia, Guam and Puerto Rico. As of Jan 28 2017, Co.'s operations were conducted through Macy's, Bloomingdale's, Bloomingdale's The Outlet, Macy's Backstage, Bluemercury and Macy's China Limited.

Recent Developments: For the quarter ended Oct 28 2017, net income increased 126.7% to US$34.0 million from US$15.0 million in the year-earlier quarter. Revenues were US$5.28 billion, down 6.1% from US$5.63 billion the year before. Operating income was US$121.0 million versus US$107.0 million in the prior-year quarter, an increase of 13.1%. Direct operating expenses declined 6.2% to US$3.18 billion from US$3.39 billion in the comparable period the year before. Indirect operating expenses decreased 6.9% to US$1.99 billion from US$2.13 billion in the equivalent prior-year period.

Prospects: Our evaluation of Macy's Inc. as of Jan. 14, 2018 is the result of our systematic analysis on three basic characteristics: earnings strength, relative valuation, and recent stock price movement. The company has enjoyed a very positive trend in earnings per share over the past 5 quarters and while recent estimates for the company have been raised by analysts, M has posted better than expected results. Based on operating earnings yield, the company is undervalued when compared to all of the companies in our coverage universe. Share price changes over the past year indicates that M will perform very poorly over the near term.

Financial Data

(US$ in Thousands)	9 Mos	6 Mos	3 Mos	01/28/2017	01/30/2016	01/31/2015	02/01/2014	02/02/2013
Earnings Per Share	2.26	2.19	1.84	1.99	3.22	4.22	3.86	3.24
Cash Flow Per Share	6.16	5.82	6.65	5.85	6.06	7.65	6.76	5.49
Tang Book Value Per Share	N.M.	N.M.	N.M.	N.M.	N.M.	3.34	5.42	4.51
Dividends Per Share	1.510	1.510	1.510	1.492	1.393	1.188	0.950	0.800
Dividend Payout %	66.81	68.95	82.07	75.00	43.25	28.14	24.61	24.69
Income Statement								
Total Revenue	16,171,000	10,890,000	5,338,000	25,778,000	27,079,000	28,105,000	27,931,000	27,686,000
EBITDA	583,000	463,000	460,000	2,359,000	3,086,000	3,814,000	3,690,000	3,557,000
Depn & Amortn	(10,000)	(10,000)	243,000	1,044,000	1,047,000	1,031,000	1,012,000	1,033,000
Income Before Taxes	356,000	310,000	133,000	952,000	1,678,000	2,390,000	2,290,000	2,102,000
Income Taxes	140,000	127,000	63,000	341,000	608,000	864,000	804,000	767,000
Net Income	222,000	187,000	71,000	619,000	1,072,000	1,526,000	1,486,000	1,335,000
Average Shares	306,500	306,500	306,900	310,800	333,000	361,700	384,800	412,200
Balance Sheet								
Current Assets	8,250,000	6,557,000	7,569,000	7,626,000	7,652,000	8,679,000	8,688,000	7,876,000
Total Assets	20,215,000	18,579,000	19,641,000	19,851,000	20,576,000	21,461,000	21,634,000	20,991,000
Current Liabilities	6,391,000	4,610,000	5,601,000	5,647,000	5,728,000	5,536,000	5,726,000	5,075,000
Long-Term Obligations	6,297,000	6,301,000	6,412,000	6,562,000	6,995,000	7,265,000	6,728,000	6,806,000
Total Liabilities	15,984,000	14,191,000	15,339,000	15,528,000	16,326,000	16,083,000	15,385,000	14,940,000
Stockholders' Equity	4,231,000	4,388,000	4,302,000	4,323,000	4,250,000	5,378,000	6,249,000	6,051,000
Shares Outstanding	304,566	304,558	304,506	304,062	310,256	340,573	364,935	387,701
Statistical Record								
Return on Assets %	3.36	3.55	2.88	3.07	5.11	7.10	6.99	6.10
Return on Equity %	17.41	16.10	13.59	14.48	22.33	26.32	24.23	21.92
EBITDA Margin %	3.61	4.25	8.62	9.15	11.40	13.57	13.21	12.85
Net Margin %	1.37	1.72	1.33	2.40	3.96	5.43	5.32	4.82
Asset Turnover	1.19	1.31	1.27	1.28	1.29	1.31	1.31	1.26
Current Ratio	1.29	1.42	1.35	1.35	1.34	1.57	1.52	1.55
Debt to Equity	1.49	1.44	1.49	1.52	1.65	1.35	1.08	1.12
Price Range	44.91-19.49	44.91-21.08	44.91-27.93	44.91-29.11	72.80-34.50	67.81-50.91	56.23-38.52	41.73-32.83
P/E Ratio	19.87-8.62	20.51-9.63	24.41-15.18	22.57-14.63	22.61-10.71	16.07-12.06	14.57-9.98	12.88-10.13
Average Yield %	5.37	4.72	4.37	3.99	2.43	2.00	2.03	2.09

Address: 151 West 34th Street, New York, NY 10001 **Telephone:** 212-494-1602 **Fax:** 212-494-1838	**Web Site:** www.macys.com **Officers:** Terry J. Lundgren - Chairman, President, Chief Executive Officer Harry A. (Hal) Lawton - President	**Auditors:** KPMG LLP **Investor Contact:** 513-579-7028 **Transfer Agents:** Computershare Shareowner Services, Pittsburgh, PA

MAGELLAN MIDSTREAM PARTNERS LP

Exchange	Symbol	Price	52Wk Range	Yield	P/E	Div Achiever
NYS	MMP	$70.94 (12/29/2017)	81.46-64.06	5.10	19.17	15 Years

*7 Year Price Score 95.22   *NYSE Composite Index=100   *12 Month Price Score 88.64

Interim Earnings (Per Share)

Qtr.	Mar	Jun	Sep	Dec
2014	1.07	0.64	0.87	1.11
2015	0.81	0.78	1.10	0.90
2016	0.91	0.82	0.85	0.93
2017	0.98	0.92	0.87	...

Interim Dividends (Per Share)

Amt	Decl	Ex	Rec	Pay
0.855Q	01/24/2017	02/01/2017	02/03/2017	02/14/2017
0.873Q	04/20/2017	04/27/2017	05/01/2017	05/15/2017
0.89Q	07/20/2017	07/27/2017	07/31/2017	08/14/2017
0.905Q	10/19/2017	11/01/2017	11/02/2017	11/14/2017

Indicated Div: $3.62

Valuation Analysis / Institutional Holding

Forecast EPS	$3.91 (01/18/2018)	No of Institutions 771
Market Cap	$16.2 Billion	Shares 160,014,048
Book Value	N/A	% Held
Price/Book	N/A	58.21
Price/Sales	6.60	

Business Summary: Equipment & Services (MIC: 9.1.3 SIC: 4613 NAIC: 486910)

Magellan Midstream Partners transports, stores and distributes refined petroleum products and crude oil. Co.'s segments are: refined products, which consists of its common carrier refined products pipeline system, independent terminals and its ammonia pipeline system; crude oil, which comprises crude oil pipelines and storage facilities and ships crude oil as a common carrier for customers including crude oil producers, end users such as refiners, and marketing and trading companies; and marine storage, which consists of marine terminals that provide distribution, storage, blending, inventory management and additive injection services for refiners, marketers, traders and other end users.

Recent Developments: For the quarter ended Sep 30 2017, net income increased 2.0% to US$198.5 million from US$194.6 million in the year-earlier quarter. Revenues were US$572.8 million, up 3.8% from US$551.8 million the year before. Operating income was US$229.7 million versus US$234.5 million in the prior-year quarter, a decrease of 2.1%. Direct operating expenses rose 13.4% to US$287.2 million from US$253.2 million in the comparable period the year before. Indirect operating expenses decreased 12.7% to US$56.0 million from US$64.1 million in the equivalent prior-year period.

Prospects: Our evaluation of Magellan Midstream Partners L.P. as of Jan. 14, 2018 is the result of our systematic analysis on three basic characteristics: earnings strength, relative valuation, and recent stock price movement. The company has generated a negative trend in earnings per share over the past 5 quarters. However, while recent estimates for the company have been mixed, MMP has posted results that fell short of analysts expectations. Based on operating earnings yield, the company is undervalued when compared to all of the companies in our coverage universe. Share price changes over the past year indicates that MMP will perform poorly over the near term.

Financial Data
(US$ in Thousands)

	9 Mos	6 Mos	3 Mos	12/31/2016	12/31/2015	12/31/2014	12/31/2013	12/31/2012
Earnings Per Share	3.70	3.68	3.58	3.52	3.59	3.69	2.56	1.92
Cash Flow Per Share	4.91	4.95	4.47	4.22	4.70	4.87	3.41	2.84
Dividends Per Share	3.455	3.385	3.315	3.245	2.915	2.505	2.098	1.784
Dividend Payout %	93.38	91.98	92.60	92.19	81.20	67.89	81.93	92.90
Income Statement								
Total Revenue	1,834,362	1,261,514	642,074	2,205,410	2,188,453	2,303,723	1,897,606	1,772,074
EBITDA	705,860	487,542	251,405	1,069,403	1,062,252	1,102,931	832,757	673,710
Depn & Amortn	6,658	4,846	2,548	176,700	164,100	159,000	136,400	126,700
Income Before Taxes	556,141	387,866	202,134	727,293	754,975	824,745	580,575	435,331
Income Taxes	2,678	1,752	844	3,218	2,336	4,620	4,613	2,622
Net Income	631,636	433,136	222,736	802,771	819,122	839,519	582,237	435,670
Average Shares	228,260	228,245	228,159	228,057	227,888	227,626	227,094	226,608
Balance Sheet								
Current Assets	407,428	325,656	302,428	370,394	338,854	402,667	396,733	700,278
Total Assets	7,103,447	6,930,722	6,829,879	6,772,073	6,041,567	5,517,285	4,820,812	4,420,067
Current Liabilities	809,714	456,575	397,599	481,656	713,072	536,155	638,276	392,620
Long-Term Obligations	4,051,411	4,231,912	4,203,080	4,087,192	3,189,287	2,982,895	2,435,316	2,393,408
Total Liabilities	4,968,152	4,796,453	4,713,672	4,679,968	4,019,831	3,649,052	3,173,370	2,904,365
Shares Outstanding	228,025	228,025	228,025	227,784	227,427	227,068	226,679	226,200
Statistical Record								
Return on Assets %	12.05	12.57	12.38	12.50	14.17	16.24	12.60	10.27
EBITDA Margin %	38.48	38.65	39.16	48.49	48.54	47.88	43.88	38.02
Net Margin %	34.43	34.33	34.69	36.40	37.43	36.44	30.68	24.59
Asset Turnover	0.35	0.36	0.35	0.34	0.38	0.45	0.41	0.42
Current Ratio	0.50	0.71	0.76	0.77	0.48	0.75	0.62	1.78
Price Range	81.46-64.06	81.46-65.17	81.46-64.05	77.40-56.97	85.01-55.08	89.12-60.52	63.27-43.19	45.34-32.51
P/E Ratio	22.02-17.31	22.14-17.71	22.75-17.89	21.99-16.18	23.68-15.34	24.15-16.40	24.71-16.87	23.61-16.93
Average Yield %	4.77	4.63	4.58	4.67	3.98	3.23	3.23	4.66

Address: One Williams Center, P.O. Box 22186, Tulsa, OK 74121-2186 **Telephone:** 918-574-7000	**Web Site:** www.magellanlp.com **Officers:** Michael N. Mears - Chairman, President, Chief Executive Officer Michael J. Aaronson - Senior Vice President

Auditors: Ernst & Young LLP
Investor Contact: 918-574-7650
Transfer Agents: Computershare Trust Company, N.A., Providence, RI

MANPOWERGROUP

Exchange	Symbol	Price	52Wk Range	Yield	P/E
NYS	MAN	$126.11 (12/29/2017)	130.38-89.81	1.47	18.82

*7 Year Price Score 119.47 *NYSE Composite Index=100 *12 Month Price Score 108.79

Interim Earnings (Per Share)

Qtr.	Mar	Jun	Sep	Dec
2014	0.86	1.35	1.61	1.48
2015	0.83	1.33	1.61	1.65
2016	0.98	1.60	1.87	1.85
2017	1.09	1.72	2.04	...

Interim Dividends (Per Share)

Amt	Decl	Ex	Rec	Pay
0.86S	05/03/2016	05/27/2016	06/01/2016	06/15/2016
0.86S	11/02/2016	11/29/2016	12/01/2016	12/15/2016
0.93S	05/02/2017	05/30/2017	06/01/2017	06/15/2017
0.93S	11/01/2017	11/30/2017	12/01/2017	12/15/2017

Indicated Div: $1.86 (Div. Reinv. Plan)

Valuation Analysis

		Institutional Holding	
Forecast EPS	$6.91	No of Institutions	
	(01/17/2018)	583	
Market Cap	$8.4 Billion	Shares	
Book Value	$2.6 Billion	86,136,088	
Price/Book	3.17	% Held	
Price/Sales	0.41	86.99	

Business Summary: Business Services (MIC: 7.5.2 SIC: 7363 NAIC: 561330)

ManpowerGroup provides a range of workforce solutions and services, which include recruitment and assessment, training and development, career management, outsourcing, and workforce consulting. Its brands and offerings include Manpower, Experis, Right Management and ManpowerGroup Solutions. Co.'s portfolio of recruitment services include permanent, temporary and contract recruitment of professionals, as well as administrative and industrial positions, which are provided under its Manpower and Experis brands. Experis focuses on the areas of information technology, engineering, and finance, while Right Management is focused on talent and career management workforce solutions.

Recent Developments: For the quarter ended Sep 30 2017, net income increased 6.6% to US$137.7 million from US$129.2 million in the year-earlier quarter. Revenues were US$5.46 billion, up 7.4% from US$5.09 billion the year before. Operating income was US$227.9 million versus US$211.1 million in the prior-year quarter, an increase of 8.0%. Direct operating expenses rose 7.9% to US$4.56 billion from US$4.23 billion in the comparable period the year before. Indirect operating expenses increased 3.9% to US$672.7 million from US$647.2 million in the equivalent prior-year period.

Prospects: Our evaluation of ManpowerGroup as of Jan. 14, 2018 is the result of our systematic analysis on three basic characteristics: earnings strength, relative valuation, and recent stock price movement. The company has managed to produce a neutral trend in earnings per share over the past 5 quarters and while recent estimates for the company have been mixed, MAN has posted better than expected results. Based on operating earnings yield, the company is undervalued when compared to all of the companies in our coverage universe. Share price changes over the past year indicates that MAN will perform well over the near term.

Financial Data

(US$ in Thousands)	9 Mos	6 Mos	3 Mos	12/31/2016	12/31/2015	12/31/2014	12/31/2013	12/31/2012
Earnings Per Share	6.70	6.53	6.41	6.27	5.40	5.30	3.62	2.47
Cash Flow Per Share	7.26	7.21	9.25	8.54	6.66	3.85	5.09	4.16
Tang Book Value Per Share	15.43	13.94	13.41	12.36	14.25	20.24	19.08	14.73
Dividends Per Share	1.790	1.790	1.720	1.720	1.600	0.980	0.920	0.860
Dividend Payout %	26.72	27.41	26.83	27.43	29.63	18.49	25.41	34.82
Income Statement								
Total Revenue	15,396,800	9,932,000	4,757,200	19,654,100	19,329,900	20,762,800	20,250,500	20,678,000
EBITDA	600,300	353,200	140,700	820,900	771,900	796,900	603,200	504,100
Depn & Amortn	62,300	40,700	20,300	85,300	77,700	83,800	94,300	100,500
Income Before Taxes	513,300	296,300	112,100	701,300	660,700	681,600	475,500	368,400
Income Taxes	184,200	104,900	37,700	257,600	241,500	254,000	187,500	170,800
Net Income	329,100	191,400	74,400	443,700	419,200	427,600	288,000	197,600
Average Shares	67,600	68,000	68,400	70,800	77,700	80,700	79,600	80,100
Balance Sheet								
Current Assets	5,973,600	5,621,100	5,300,800	5,132,900	5,092,500	5,033,700	5,243,000	5,060,600
Total Assets	8,581,700	8,139,500	7,678,900	7,574,200	7,517,500	7,182,500	7,288,300	7,012,600
Current Liabilities	4,626,200	4,356,700	3,647,200	3,658,800	3,451,000	3,374,400	3,509,600	3,677,200
Long-Term Obligations	470,600	454,800	796,000	785,600	810,900	423,900	481,900	462,100
Total Liabilities	5,949,000	5,627,500	5,233,500	5,212,300	4,892,800	4,239,500	4,374,100	4,511,800
Stockholders' Equity	2,632,700	2,512,000	2,445,400	2,361,900	2,624,700	2,943,000	2,914,200	2,500,800
Shares Outstanding	66,252	66,701	67,226	66,969	73,038	78,114	79,355	76,647
Statistical Record								
Return on Assets %	5.60	5.73	5.86	5.86	5.70	5.91	4.03	2.83
Return on Equity %	18.17	18.08	17.68	17.75	15.06	14.60	10.64	7.91
EBITDA Margin %	3.90	3.56	2.96	4.18	3.99	3.84	2.98	2.44
Net Margin %	2.14	1.93	1.56	2.26	2.17	2.06	1.42	0.96
Asset Turnover	2.50	2.55	2.60	2.60	2.63	2.87	2.83	2.96
Current Ratio	1.29	1.29	1.45	1.40	1.48	1.49	1.49	1.38
Debt to Equity	0.18	0.18	0.33	0.33	0.31	0.14	0.17	0.18
Price Range	119.93-71.50	111.65-60.67	103.61-59.90	92.83-59.90	96.56-63.79	86.73-59.00	86.66-42.44	47.90-32.41
P/E Ratio	17.90-10.67	17.10-9.29	16.16-9.34	14.81-9.55	17.88-11.81	16.36-11.13	23.94-11.72	19.39-13.12
Average Yield %	1.82	2.04	2.11	2.25	1.89	1.21	1.45	2.18

Address: 100 Manpower Place, Milwaukee, WI 53212	Web Site: www.manpower.com	Auditors: Deloitte & Touche LLP
Telephone: 414-961-1000	Officers: Jonas Prising - Chairman, President, Chief Executive Officer, Executive Vice President Darryl Green - President, Chief Operating Officer, Executive Vice President, Region Officer	Investor Contact: 414-906-6807
Fax: 414-332-0796		Transfer Agents: ComputerShare, College Station, TX

MARATHON OIL CORP.

Exchange	Symbol	Price	52Wk Range	Yield	P/E
NYS	MRO	$16.93 (12/29/2017)	18.18-10.77	1.18	N/A

*7 Year Price Score 44.04   *NYSE Composite Index=100   *12 Month Price Score 102.44

Interim Earnings (Per Share)

Qtr.	Mar	Jun	Sep	Dec
2014	1.65	0.80	0.64	1.36
2015	(0.41)	(0.57)	(1.11)	(1.17)
2016	(0.56)	(0.20)	(0.23)	(1.66)
2017	(5.84)	(0.16)	(0.70)	...

Interim Dividends (Per Share)

Amt	Decl	Ex	Rec	Pay
0.05Q	01/25/2017	02/13/2017	02/15/2017	03/10/2017
0.05Q	04/26/2017	05/15/2017	05/17/2017	06/12/2017
0.05Q	07/26/2017	08/14/2017	08/16/2017	09/11/2017
0.05Q	10/25/2017	11/14/2017	11/15/2017	12/11/2017

Indicated Div: $0.20 (Div. Reinv. Plan)

Valuation Analysis | **Institutional Holding**

Forecast EPS	$-0.34	No of Institutions
	(01/18/2018)	967
Market Cap	$14.4 Billion	Shares
Book Value	$11.8 Billion	870,581,504
Price/Book	1.22	% Held
Price/Sales	3.02	76.21

TRADING VOLUME (thousand shares)

Business Summary: Production & Extraction (MIC: 9.1.1 SIC: 1311 NAIC: 211111)

Marathon Oil is an exploration and production company. Co. has three segments: North America Exploration and Production (E&P), which explores for, produces and markets crude oil and condensate, natural gas liquids (NGLs) and natural gas in North America; International E&P, which explores for, produces and markets crude oil and condensate, NGLs and natural gas outside of North America; and Oil Sands Mining, which mines, extracts and transports bitumen from oil sands deposits in Alberta, Canada, and upgrades the bitumen to produce and market synthetic crude oil and vacuum gas oil. As of Dec 31 2016, Co. had total proved reserves of 2.10 billion barrels of oil equivalent.

Recent Developments: For the quarter ended Sep 30 2017, loss from continuing operations was US$599.0 million compared with a loss of US$206.0 million in the year-earlier quarter. Net loss amounted to US$599.0 million versus a net loss of US$192.0 million in the year-earlier quarter. Revenues were US$1.25 billion, up 26.5% from US$990.0 million the year before. Operating loss was US$377.0 million versus a loss of US$224.0 million in the prior-year quarter. Direct operating expenses declined 16.8% to US$352.0 million from US$423.0 million in the comparable period the year before. Indirect operating expenses increased 61.4% to US$1.28 billion from US$791.0 million in the equivalent prior-year period.

Prospects: Our evaluation of Marathon Oil Corp. as of Jan. 14, 2018 is the result of our systematic analysis on three basic characteristics: earnings strength, relative valuation, and recent stock price movement. The company has generated a negative trend in earnings per share over the past 5 quarters. Because the company lacks sufficient analyst estimate data, we place greater weight on the historical EPS trend as the measure of earnings strength. Based on operating earnings yield, the company is overvalued when compared to all of the companies in our coverage universe. Share price changes over the past year indicates that MRO will perform very poorly over the near term.

Financial Data

(US$ in Thousands)	9 Mos	6 Mos	3 Mos	12/31/2016	12/31/2015	12/31/2014	12/31/2013	12/31/2012
Earnings Per Share	(8.36)	(7.89)	(7.93)	(2.61)	(3.26)	4.46	2.47	2.23
Cash Flow Per Share	2.28	2.05	1.77	1.31	2.31	8.07	7.48	5.67
Tang Book Value Per Share	13.72	14.46	14.67	20.57	27.23	30.46	27.04	25.12
Dividends Per Share	0.200	0.200	0.200	0.200	0.680	0.800	0.720	0.680
Dividend Payout %	...	...	...	...	...	17.94	29.15	30.49
Income Statement								
Total Revenue	3,383,000	2,131,000	1,072,000	4,650,000	5,861,000	11,258,000	14,959,000	16,221,000
EBITDA	1,402,000	1,184,000	618,000	1,510,000	300,000	4,493,000	8,015,000	8,821,000
Depn & Amortn	1,789,000	1,148,000	556,000	2,395,000	2,957,000	2,861,000	2,790,000	2,478,000
Income Before Taxes	(586,000)	(128,000)	(16,000)	(1,235,000)	(2,958,000)	1,361,000	4,930,000	6,113,000
Income Taxes	216,000	75,000	34,000	905,000	(754,000)	392,000	3,337,000	4,531,000
Net Income	(5,695,000)	(5,096,000)	(4,957,000)	(2,140,000)	(2,204,000)	3,046,000	1,753,000	1,582,000
Average Shares	850,000	850,000	849,000	819,000	677,000	683,000	709,000	710,000
Balance Sheet								
Current Assets	3,690,000	4,424,000	3,743,000	3,665,000	2,590,000	4,593,000	2,975,000	3,762,000
Total Assets	22,947,000	24,241,000	24,537,000	31,094,000	32,311,000	36,011,000	35,620,000	35,306,000
Current Liabilities	1,762,000	2,082,000	3,099,000	2,240,000	1,729,000	4,379,000	4,333,000	5,081,000
Long-Term Obligations	6,488,000	6,715,000	5,723,000	6,589,000	7,276,000	5,323,000	6,394,000	6,512,000
Total Liabilities	11,172,000	11,836,000	11,953,000	13,553,000	13,758,000	14,991,000	16,276,000	17,023,000
Stockholders' Equity	11,775,000	12,405,000	12,584,000	17,541,000	18,553,000	21,020,000	19,344,000	18,283,000
Shares Outstanding	850,000	850,000	850,000	847,000	677,000	675,000	697,000	707,000
Statistical Record								
Return on Assets %	N.M.	N.M.	N.M.	N.M.	N.M.	8.50	4.94	4.73
Return on Equity %	N.M.	N.M.	N.M.	N.M.	N.M.	15.09	9.32	8.90
EBITDA Margin %	41.44	55.56	57.65	32.47	5.12	39.91	53.58	54.38
Net Margin %	N.M.	N.M.	N.M.	N.M.	N.M.	27.06	11.72	9.75
Asset Turnover	0.17	0.17	0.17	0.15	0.17	0.31	0.42	0.49
Current Ratio	2.09	2.12	1.21	1.64	1.50	1.05	0.69	0.74
Debt to Equity	0.55	0.54	0.45	0.38	0.39	0.25	0.33	0.36
Price Range	18.80-10.77	18.80-11.35	18.80-10.53	18.80-6.73	31.19-12.38	41.69-24.80	37.93-29.85	35.06-23.32
P/E Ratio	...	...	...	...	...	9.35-5.56	15.36-12.09	15.72-10.46
Average Yield %	1.37	1.31	1.32	1.49	2.99	2.23	2.08	2.32

Address: 5555 San Felipe Street, Houston, TX 77056-2723	Web Site: www.marathonoil.com	Auditors: PriceWaterHouseCoopers LLP
Telephone: 713-629-6600	Officers: Lee M. Tillman - President, Chief Executive Officer Patrick J. Wagner - Vice President, Interim Chief Financial Officer	Investor Contact: 713-296-4114 Transfer Agents: Computershare, Providence, RI

MARATHON PETROLEUM CORP.

Exchange	Symbol	Price	52Wk Range	Yield	P/E
NYS	MPC	$65.98 (12/29/2017)	66.84-47.71	2.42	20.68

*7 Year Price Score N/A   *NYSE Composite Index=100   *12 Month Price Score 110.42

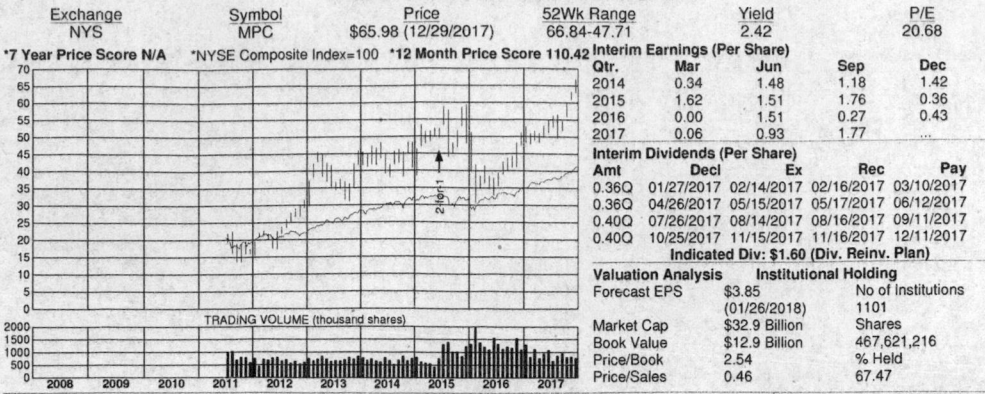

Interim Earnings (Per Share)

Qtr.	Mar	Jun	Sep	Dec
2014	0.34	1.48	1.18	1.42
2015	1.62	1.51	1.76	0.36
2016	0.00	1.51	0.27	0.43
2017	0.06	0.93	1.77	...

Interim Dividends (Per Share)

Amt	Decl	Ex	Rec	Pay
0.36Q	01/27/2017	02/14/2017	02/16/2017	03/10/2017
0.36Q	04/26/2017	05/15/2017	05/17/2017	06/12/2017
0.40Q	07/26/2017	08/14/2017	08/16/2017	09/11/2017
0.40Q	10/25/2017	11/15/2017	11/16/2017	12/11/2017

Indicated Div: $1.60 (Div. Reinv. Plan)

Valuation Analysis

		Institutional Holding	
Forecast EPS	$3.85	No of Institutions	
	(01/26/2018)	1101	
Market Cap	$32.9 Billion	Shares	
Book Value	$12.9 Billion	467,621,216	
Price/Book	2.54	% Held	
Price/Sales	0.46	67.47	

Business Summary: Refining & Marketing (MIC: 9.1.2 SIC: 1311 NAIC: 211111)

Marathon Petroleum is an independent petroleum refining, marketing, retail and transportation company. Co. has three segments: Refining and Marketing, which refines crude oil and other feedstocks at its refineries in the Gulf Coast and Midwest regions of the U.S., purchases refined products and ethanol for resale and distributes refined products; Speedway, which sells transportation fuels and convenience products in the retail market in the Midwest, East Coast and Southeast regions of the U.S.; and Midstream, which gathers, processes and transports natural gas; gathers, transports, fractionates, stores and markets natural gas liquids and transports and stores crude oil and refined products.

Recent Developments: For the quarter ended Sep 30 2017, net income increased 358.4% to US$1.00 billion from US$219.0 million in the year-earlier quarter. Revenues were US$19.39 billion, up 17.8% from US$16.46 billion the year before. Operating income was US$1.58 billion versus US$435.0 million in the prior-year quarter, an increase of 262.3%. Direct operating expenses rose 11.9% to US$16.77 billion from US$14.99 billion in the comparable period the year before. Indirect operating expenses increased 0.6% to US$1.05 billion from US$1.04 billion in the equivalent prior-year period.

Prospects: Our evaluation of Marathon Petroleum Corp. as of Jan. 21, 2018 is the result of our systematic analysis on three basic characteristics: earnings strength, relative valuation, and recent stock price movement. The company has enjoyed a very positive trend in earnings per share over the past 5 quarters and while recent estimates for the company have been mixed, MPC has posted better than expected results. Based on operating earnings yield, the company is undervalued when compared to all of the companies in our coverage universe. Share price changes over the past year indicates that MPC will perform poorly over the near term.

Financial Data

(US$ in Millions)	9 Mos	6 Mos	3 Mos	12/31/2016	12/31/2015	12/31/2014	12/31/2013	12/31/2012
Earnings Per Share	3.19	1.69	2.27	2.21	5.26	4.39	3.32	4.95
Cash Flow Per Share	9.63	6.55	9.09	7.53	7.55	5.46	5.40	6.59
Tang Book Value Per Share	18.76	17.89	18.27	18.88	17.36	16.76	16.80	16.16
Dividends Per Share	1.480	1.440	1.400	1.360	1.140	0.920	0.770	0.600
Dividend Payout %	46.39	85.21	61.67	61.54	21.67	20.96	23.19	12.13
Income Statement								
Total Revenue	54,133	34,747	16,393	63,364	72,258	98,102	100,254	82,492
EBITDA	2,876	1,290	300	4,416	6,302	5,356	4,624	6,317
Depn & Amortn	46	30	15	2,062	1,646	1,326	1,220	995
Income Before Taxes	2,385	966	142	1,822	4,374	3,835	3,246	5,238
Income Taxes	706	291	41	609	1,506	1,280	1,113	1,845
Net Income	1,416	513	30	1,174	2,852	2,524	2,112	3,389
Average Shares	508	517	530	530	542	574	634	684
Balance Sheet								
Current Assets	11,631	10,443	11,042	10,401	9,471	11,339	12,737	13,029
Total Assets	46,806	45,447	45,821	44,413	43,115	30,460	28,385	27,223
Current Liabilities	7,647	6,758	6,866	7,146	6,345	8,579	9,824	8,203
Long-Term Obligations	12,753	12,577	12,570	10,544	11,896	6,610	3,373	3,342
Total Liabilities	33,876	32,811	32,751	30,856	29,878	19,709	17,465	15,529
Stockholders' Equity	12,930	12,636	13,070	13,557	13,237	10,751	10,920	11,694
Shares Outstanding	498	506	519	528	531	548	594	666
Statistical Record								
Return on Assets %	3.65	1.98	2.75	2.68	7.75	8.58	7.60	12.76
Return on Equity %	12.48	6.77	9.26	8.74	23.78	23.29	18.68	31.89
EBITDA Margin %	5.31	3.71	1.83	6.97	8.72	5.46	4.61	7.66
Net Margin %	2.62	1.48	0.18	1.85	3.95	2.57	2.11	4.11
Asset Turnover	1.59	1.53	1.53	1.44	1.96	3.33	3.61	3.11
Current Ratio	1.52	1.55	1.61	1.46	1.49	1.32	1.30	1.59
Debt to Equity	0.99	1.00	0.96	0.78	0.90	0.61	0.31	0.29
Price Range	56.53-40.59	55.03-35.48	52.93-32.81	51.84-30.73	59.34-38.42	48.46-37.90	45.87-30.13	31.50-15.48
P/E Ratio	17.72-12.72	32.56-20.99	23.32-14.45	23.46-13.90	11.28-7.31	11.04-8.63	13.81-9.07	6.36-3.13
Average Yield %	2.96	3.08	3.25	3.38	2.25	2.11	2.02	2.57

Address: 539 South Main Street, Findlay, OH 45840-3229	Web Site: www.marathonpetroleum.com	Auditors: PricewaterhouseCoopers LLP
Telephone: 419-422-2121	Officers: Gary R. Heminger - Chairman, President, Chief Executive Officer Donald C. Templin - President, Senior Vice President, Chief Financial Officer, Division Officer	Investor Contact: 419-429-5640 Transfer Agents: Computershare, Canton, MA

MARKEL CORP (HOLDING CO)

Exchange	Symbol	Price	52Wk Range	Yield	P/E
NYS	MKL	$1139 (12/29/2017)	1147.10-891.25	N/A	253.14

*7 Year Price Score 117.78 ***NYSE Composite Index=100** ***12 Month Price Score 102.82**

TRADING VOLUME (thousand shares)

Interim Earnings (Per Share)

Qtr.	Mar	Jun	Sep	Dec
2014	6.25	2.66	5.30	8.06
2015	13.49	6.72	7.39	14.14
2016	11.15	5.41	5.60	9.11
2017	3.90	10.31	(18.82)	...

Interim Dividends (Per Share)
No Dividends Paid

Valuation Analysis		Institutional Holding	
Forecast EPS	$2.30	No of Institutions	
	(01/12/2018)	573	
Market Cap	$15.8 Billion	Shares	
Book Value	$8.9 Billion	13,429,601	
Price/Book	1.78	% Held	
Price/Sales	2.72	75.91	

Business Summary: General Insurance (MIC: 5.2.1 SIC: 6331 NAIC: 524126)

Markel is a financial holding company. Co.'s principal business markets and underwrites specialty insurance products. Co. also owns interests in various industrial and service businesses that operate outside of the specialty insurance marketplace. Co. has three segments: U.S. Insurance, which includes all direct business and facultative placements written by Co.'s insurance subsidiaries domiciled in the U.S.; International Insurance, which includes all direct business and facultative placements written by Co.'s insurance subsidiaries domiciled outside of the U.S.; and Reinsurance, which includes property and casualty treaty reinsurance products provided through the broker market.

Recent Developments: For the quarter ended Sep 30 2017, net loss amounted to US$261.0 million versus net income of US$83.4 million in the year-earlier quarter. Revenues were US$1.51 billion, up 5.2% from US$1.43 billion the year before. Net premiums earned were US$1.10 billion versus US$974.2 million in the prior-year quarter, an increase of 12.9%. Net investment income rose 12.2% to US$104.5 million from US$93.1 million a year ago.

Prospects: Our evaluation of Markel Corp. as of Jan. 14, 2018 is the result of our systematic analysis on three basic characteristics: earnings strength, relative valuation, and recent stock price movement. The company has suffered a very negative trend in earnings per share over the past 5 quarters. However, while recent estimates for the company have been mixed, MKL has posted results that fell short of analysts expectations. Based on operating earnings yield, the company is overvalued when compared to all of the companies in our coverage universe. Share price changes over the past year indicates that MKL will perform well over the near term.

Financial Data
(US$ in Thousands)

	9 Mos	6 Mos	3 Mos	12/31/2016	12/31/2015	12/31/2014	12/31/2013	12/31/2012
Earnings Per Share	4.50	28.92	24.02	31.27	41.74	22.27	22.48	25.89
Cash Flow Per Share	58.00	50.25	46.52	38.05	46.58	51.26	59.46	40.61
Tang Book Value Per Share	467.33	498.02	487.36	472.67	420.80	418.50	367.58	294.88
Income Statement								
Premium Income	3,116,038	2,016,176	982,602	3,865,870	3,823,532	3,840,912	3,231,616	2,147,128
Total Revenue	4,399,392	2,893,244	1,411,751	5,612,026	5,369,983	5,133,667	4,323,083	3,000,112
Benefits & Claims	2,210,129	1,134,697	611,719	2,050,744	1,938,745	2,202,467	1,816,273	1,154,068
Income Before Taxes	(56,359)	303,589	94,044	629,920	742,105	440,378	361,743	312,050
Income Taxes	(17,791)	81,122	23,004	169,477	152,963	116,690	77,898	53,802
Net Income	(39,612)	219,529	69,869	455,689	582,772	321,182	281,021	253,385
Average Shares	13,990	14,019	14,046	14,078	14,061	14,057	12,586	9,666
Balance Sheet								
Total Assets	28,519,411	27,203,341	26,400,679	25,875,299	24,941,271	25,200,357	23,955,511	12,556,588
Total Liabilities	19,610,526	18,248,932	17,747,479	17,414,372	17,107,121	17,605,539	17,281,934	8,667,931
Stockholders' Equity	8,908,885	8,954,409	8,653,200	8,460,927	7,834,150	7,594,818	6,673,577	3,888,657
Shares Outstanding	13,894	13,918	13,950	13,954	13,959	13,961	13,985	9,629
Statistical Record								
Return on Assets %	0.34	1.63	1.40	1.79	2.32	1.31	1.54	2.10
Return on Equity %	1.07	5.01	4.32	5.58	7.55	4.50	5.32	6.95
Loss Ratio %	70.93	56.28	62.26	53.05	50.71	57.34	56.20	53.75
Net Margin %	(0.90)	7.59	4.95	8.12	10.85	6.26	6.50	8.45
Price Range	1086.44-825.07	992.04-825.07	986.73-825.07	982.84-810.26	934.76-662.59	703.95-529.00	580.35-433.42	500.68-399.12
P/E Ratio	241.43-183.35	34.30-28.53	41.08-34.35	31.43-25.91	22.39-15.87	31.61-23.75	25.82-19.28	19.34-15.42

Address: 4521 Highwoods Parkway, Glen Allen, VA 23060-6148 Telephone: 804-747-0136	Web Site: www.markelcorp.com Officers: Alan I. Kirshner - Chairman, Chief Executive Officer Steven A. Markel - Vice-Chairman	Auditors: KPMG LLP Investor Contact: 800-446-6671 Transfer Agents: American Stock Transfer & Trust Co., LLC, Brooklyn, NY

MARSH & MCLENNAN COMPANIES INC.

Exchange	Symbol	Price	52Wk Range	Yield	P/E
NYS	MMC	$81.39 (12/29/2017)	85.97-67.41	1.84	22.30

*7 Year Price Score 120.31 ***NYSE Composite Index=100** ***12 Month Price Score 101.63**

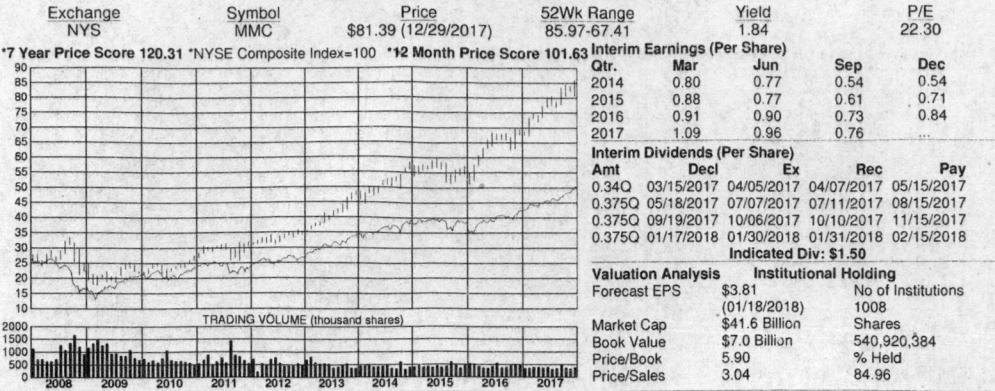

Interim Earnings (Per Share)

Qtr.	Mar	Jun	Sep	Dec
2014	0.80	0.77	0.54	0.54
2015	0.88	0.77	0.61	0.71
2016	0.91	0.90	0.73	0.84
2017	1.09	0.96	0.76	...

Interim Dividends (Per Share)

Amt	Decl	Ex	Rec	Pay
0.34Q	03/15/2017	04/05/2017	04/07/2017	05/15/2017
0.375Q	05/18/2017	07/07/2017	07/11/2017	08/15/2017
0.375Q	09/19/2017	10/06/2017	10/10/2017	11/15/2017
0.375Q	01/17/2018	01/30/2018	01/31/2018	02/15/2018

Indicated Div: $1.50

Valuation Analysis **Institutional Holding**

Forecast EPS	$3.81	No of Institutions
(01/18/2018)		1008
Market Cap	$41.6 Billion	Shares
Book Value	$7.0 Billion	540,920,384
Price/Book	5.90	% Held
Price/Sales	3.04	84.96

Business Summary: Brokers & Intermediaries (MIC: 5.2.3 SIC: 6411 NAIC: 524210)

Marsh & McLennan Companies is a holding company, engaged in providing clients advice and solutions in risk, strategy and people. Co.'s segments include: Risk and Insurance Services, which conducts its business through Marsh that provides, among others risk management, insurance program management services, risk consulting, and analytical modeling, and Guy Carpenter that creates and executes reinsurance and risk management solutions; and Consulting, which conducts its business through Mercer that operates in health, retirement, investments, and talent areas and Oliver Wyman Group that provides advisory services to clients through Oliver Wyman, Lippincott and NERA Economic Consulting.

Recent Developments: For the quarter ended Sep 30 2017, net income increased 3.4% to US$397.0 million from US$384.0 million in the year-earlier quarter. Revenues were US$3.34 billion, up 6.6% from US$3.14 billion the year before.

Prospects: Our evaluation of Marsh & McLennan Cos. Inc. as of Jan. 14, 2018 is the result of our systematic analysis on three basic characteristics: earnings strength, relative valuation, and recent stock price movement. The company has managed to produce a neutral trend in earnings per share over the past 5 quarters and while recent estimates for the company have been mixed, MMC has posted better than expected results. Based on operating earnings yield, the company is undervalued when compared to all of the companies in our coverage universe. Share price changes over the past year indicates that MMC will perform very well over the near term.

Financial Data

(US$ in Thousands)	9 Mos	6 Mos	3 Mos	12/31/2016	12/31/2015	12/31/2014	12/31/2013	12/31/2012
Earnings Per Share	3.65	3.62	3.56	3.38	2.98	2.65	2.43	2.13
Cash Flow Per Share	3.97	4.13	4.25	3.86	3.56	3.88	2.44	2.42
Tang Book Value Per Share	N.M.	N.M.	N.M.	N.M.	N.M.	N.M.	0.99	N.M.
Dividends Per Share	1.395	1.360	1.330	1.300	1.180	1.060	0.960	0.900
Dividend Payout %	38.22	37.57	37.36	38.46	39.60	40.00	39.51	42.25
Income Statement								
Total Revenue	10,339,000	6,998,000	3,503,000	13,211,000	12,893,000	12,951,000	12,261,000	11,924,000
EBITDA	2,295,000	1,658,000	849,000	2,794,000	2,566,000	2,287,000	2,194,000	1,925,000
Depn & Amortn	122,000	80,000	40,000	130,000	109,000	86,000	72,000	72,000
Income Before Taxes	2,001,000	1,464,000	753,000	2,480,000	2,307,000	2,057,000	1,973,000	1,696,000
Income Taxes	519,000	379,000	175,000	685,000	671,000	586,000	594,000	492,000
Net Income	1,463,000	1,070,000	569,000	1,768,000	1,599,000	1,465,000	1,357,000	1,176,000
Average Shares	519,000	520,000	522,000	524,000	536,000	553,000	558,000	552,000
Balance Sheet								
Current Assets	5,215,000	5,182,000	4,981,000	4,884,000	5,044,000	6,055,000	6,300,000	5,963,000
Total Assets	19,690,000	19,442,000	18,969,000	18,190,000	18,216,000	17,840,000	16,980,000	16,288,000
Current Liabilities	3,814,000	3,649,000	3,588,000	4,082,000	3,708,000	3,705,000	3,809,000	3,564,000
Long-Term Obligations	5,475,000	5,479,000	5,479,000	4,495,000	4,402,000	3,376,000	2,621,000	2,658,000
Total Liabilities	12,644,000	12,449,000	12,437,000	11,998,000	11,703,000	10,786,000	9,075,000	9,746,000
Stockholders' Equity	7,046,000	6,993,000	6,532,000	6,192,000	6,513,000	7,054,000	7,905,000	6,542,000
Shares Outstanding	511,156	512,803	515,024	514,491	521,897	540,142	546,759	545,507
Statistical Record								
Return on Assets %	9.98	10.05	10.01	9.69	8.87	8.41	8.16	7.39
Return on Equity %	27.69	27.69	28.10	27.76	23.57	19.59	18.79	18.88
EBITDA Margin %	22.20	23.69	24.24	21.15	19.90	17.66	17.89	16.14
Net Margin %	14.15	15.29	16.24	13.38	12.40	11.31	11.07	9.86
Asset Turnover	0.72	0.72	0.72	0.72	0.72	0.74	0.74	0.75
Current Ratio	1.37	1.42	1.39	1.20	1.36	1.63	1.65	1.67
Debt to Equity	0.78	0.78	0.84	0.73	0.68	0.48	0.33	0.41
Price Range	84.22-62.70	80.27-62.70	75.14-60.17	69.77-51.29	59.84-51.54	58.56-44.40	48.36-34.47	35.78-30.72
P/E Ratio	23.07-17.18	22.17-17.32	21.11-16.90	20.64-15.17	20.08-17.30	22.10-16.75	19.90-14.19	16.80-14.42
Average Yield %	1.90	1.94	1.97	2.04	2.10	2.07	2.34	2.72

Address: 1166 Avenue of the Americas, New York, NY 10036-2774	Web Site: www.mmc.com	Auditors: Deloitte & Touche LLP
Telephone: 212-345-5000	Officers: H. Edward Hanway - Chairman Daniel S.	Investor Contact: 212-345-5462
Fax: 212-345-4809	(Dan) Glaser - President, Chief Executive Officer, Chief Operating Officer, Division Officer	Transfer Agents: Wells Fargo Shareowner Services, St. Paul, MN

MARTIN MARIETTA MATERIALS, INC.

Exchange	Symbol	Price	52Wk Range	Yield	P/E
NYS	MLM	$221.04 (12/29/2017)	242.00-195.54	0.80	32.22

*7 Year Price Score 128.86 *NYSE Composite Index=100 *12 Month Price Score 91.29

Interim Earnings (Per Share)

Qtr.	Mar	Jun	Sep	Dec
2014	(0.47)	1.27	0.79	1.01
2015	0.07	1.22	1.74	1.26
2016	0.69	1.90	2.49	1.55
2017	0.67	2.25	2.39	...

Interim Dividends (Per Share)

Amt	Decl	Ex	Rec	Pay
0.42Q	02/24/2017	03/02/2017	03/06/2017	03/31/2017
0.42Q	05/19/2017	05/30/2017	06/01/2017	06/30/2017
0.44Q	08/24/2017	08/31/2017	09/05/2017	09/29/2017
0.44Q	11/16/2017	11/30/2017	12/01/2017	12/29/2017

Indicated Div: $1.76

Valuation Analysis

		Institutional Holding	
Forecast EPS	$6.81	No of Institutions	
	(01/18/2018)	704	
Market Cap	$13.9 Billion	Shares	
Book Value	$4.3 Billion		70,443,784
Price/Book	3.21	% Held	
Price/Sales	3.52		101.75

TRADING VOLUME (thousand shares)

Business Summary: Construction Materials (MIC: 8.5.1 SIC: 1411 NAIC: 212311)

Martin Marietta Materials is a supplier of aggregates products (crushed stone, sand, and gravel) used for the construction of infrastructure, nonresidential, and residential projects. Co.'s Aggregates business consists primarily of mining, processing, and selling granite, limestone, sand and gravel, as well as includes aggregates-related downstream product lines, its heavy building materials; Co.'s Cement business produces Portland and specialty cements; Co.'s Magnesia Specialties business manufactures and markets magnesia-based chemical products used in industrial, agricultural, and environmental applications, and dolomitic lime sold primarily to customers in the steel industry.

Recent Developments: For the quarter ended Sep 30 2017, net income decreased 5.0% to US$151.5 million from US$159.5 million in the year-earlier quarter. Revenues were US$1.09 billion, down 1.5% from US$1.10 billion the year before. Operating income was US$227.0 million versus US$242.7 million in the prior-year quarter, a decrease of 6.5%. Direct operating expenses declined 1.8% to US$796.1 million from US$810.6 million in the comparable period the year before. Indirect operating expenses increased 27.8% to US$64.7 million from US$50.6 million in the equivalent prior-year period.

Prospects: Our evaluation of Martin Marietta Materials Inc. as of Jan. 14, 2018 is the result of our systematic analysis on three basic characteristics: earnings strength, relative valuation, and recent stock price movement. The company has generated a negative trend in earnings per share over the past 5 quarters. However, while recent estimates for the company have been mixed, MLM has posted results that fell short of analysts expectations. Based on operating earnings yield, the company is about fairly valued when compared to all of the companies in our coverage universe. Share price changes over the past year indicates that MLM will perform very poorly over the near term.

Financial Data

(US$ in Thousands)	9 Mos	6 Mos	3 Mos	12/31/2016	12/31/2015	12/31/2014	12/31/2013	12/31/2012
Earnings Per Share	6.86	6.96	6.61	6.63	4.29	2.71	2.61	1.83
Cash Flow Per Share	10.86	11.21	10.88	10.64	8.58	6.71	6.69	4.85
Tang Book Value Per Share	33.53	31.38	29.42	23.26	22.93	25.07	18.86	16.17
Dividends Per Share	1.700	1.680	1.660	1.640	1.600	1.600	1.600	1.600
Dividend Payout %	24.78	24.14	25.11	24.74	37.30	59.04	61.30	87.43
Income Statement								
Total Revenue	2,995,116	1,907,383	843,859	3,818,749	3,539,570	2,957,951	2,155,551	2,037,667
EBITDA	744,819	442,060	148,062	957,640	736,962	526,477	386,026	328,192
Depn & Amortn	221,418	146,102	70,376	268,935	246,874	211,242	168,333	171,940
Income Before Taxes	455,364	251,062	56,835	607,028	413,801	249,178	164,226	102,913
Income Taxes	119,277	66,514	14,528	181,584	124,863	94,847	44,045	16,950
Net Income	336,159	184,613	42,334	425,386	288,792	155,601	121,337	84,474
Average Shares	63,158	63,141	63,319	63,861	67,020	57,088	46,285	45,970
Balance Sheet								
Current Assets	1,277,989	1,244,297	1,123,242	1,086,385	1,082,168	1,288,816	755,366	700,401
Total Assets	7,566,785	7,515,860	7,393,791	7,300,905	6,961,732	7,464,392	3,259,826	3,160,926
Current Liabilities	468,503	534,325	631,558	546,588	367,191	396,648	210,549	173,335
Long-Term Obligations	1,642,502	1,641,944	1,556,246	1,506,153	1,553,649	1,571,059	1,018,518	1,042,183
Total Liabilities	3,235,564	3,318,089	3,320,423	3,160,927	2,904,448	3,113,226	1,721,949	1,750,381
Stockholders' Equity	4,331,221	4,197,771	4,073,368	4,139,978	4,057,284	4,351,166	1,537,877	1,410,545
Shares Outstanding	62,859	62,840	62,778	63,176	64,479	67,293	46,261	46,002
Statistical Record								
Return on Assets %	5.82	6.01	5.85	5.95	4.00	2.90	3.78	2.67
Return on Equity %	10.25	10.79	10.55	10.35	6.87	5.28	8.23	5.97
EBITDA Margin %	24.87	23.18	17.55	25.08	20.82	17.80	17.91	16.11
Net Margin %	11.22	9.68	5.02	11.14	8.16	5.26	5.63	4.15
Asset Turnover	0.53	0.54	0.54	0.53	0.49	0.55	0.67	0.64
Current Ratio	2.73	2.33	1.78	1.99	2.95	3.25	3.59	4.04
Debt to Equity	0.38	0.39	0.38	0.36	0.38	0.36	0.66	0.74
Price Range	242.00-169.19	242.00-169.19	242.00-159.36	233.52-117.00	176.51-104.58	134.91-98.70	112.09-93.56	95.59-64.56
P/E Ratio	35.28-24.66	34.77-24.31	36.61-24.11	35.22-17.65	41.14-24.38	49.78-36.42	42.95-35.85	52.23-35.28
Average Yield %	0.79	0.80	0.84	0.92	1.09	1.31	1.60	1.96

Address: 2710 Wycliff Road, Raleigh, NC 27607-3033	**Web Site:** www.martinmarietta.com	**Auditors:** PricewaterhouseCoopers LLP
Telephone: 919-781-4550	**Officers:** C. Howard Nye - Chairman, President, Chief Executive Officer James A.J. Nickolas - Chief Financial Officer, Senior Vice President	**Transfer Agents:** American Stock Transfer & Trust Company, LLC, Brooklyn, NY

MASCO CORP.

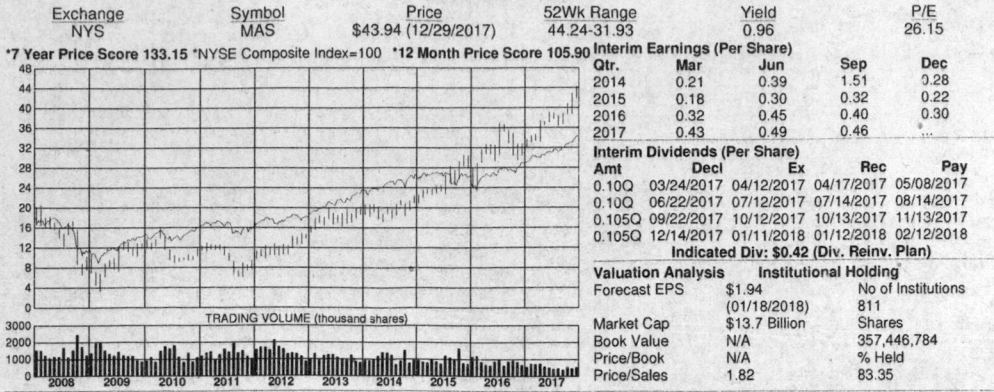

Exchange	Symbol	Price	52Wk Range	Yield	P/E
NYS	MAS	$43.94 (12/29/2017)	44.24-31.93	0.96	26.15

*7 Year Price Score 133.15 *NYSE Composite Index=100 *12 Month Price Score 105.90

Interim Earnings (Per Share)

Qtr.	Mar	Jun	Sep	Dec
2014	0.21	0.39	1.51	0.28
2015	0.18	0.30	0.32	0.22
2016	0.32	0.45	0.40	0.30
2017	0.43	0.49	0.46	...

Interim Dividends (Per Share)

Amt	Decl	Ex	Rec	Pay
0.10Q	03/24/2017	04/12/2017	04/17/2017	05/08/2017
0.10Q	06/22/2017	07/12/2017	07/14/2017	08/14/2017
0.105Q	09/22/2017	10/12/2017	10/13/2017	11/13/2017
0.105Q	12/14/2017	01/11/2018	01/12/2018	02/12/2018

Indicated Div: $0.42 (Div. Reinv. Plan)

Valuation Analysis | **Institutional Holding**

Forecast EPS	$1.94	No of Institutions
(01/18/2018)		811
Market Cap	$13.7 Billion	Shares
Book Value	N/A	357,446,784
Price/Book	N/A	% Held
Price/Sales	1.82	83.35

TRADING VOLUME (thousand shares)

Business Summary: Construction Materials (MIC: 8.5.1 SIC: 2434 NAIC: 337110)

Masco designs, manufactures and distributes home improvement and building products. Co. has four segments: Plumbing Products, which includes faucets, valves, showerheads, bathtubs, toilets, and spas; Architectural Products, which includes cabinet, door and window; Cabinetry Products, kitchen and bath cabinets; home office; entertainment centers; and storage products; and Windows and Other Specialty Products, which includes windows, window frame components, patio doors, staples, and other fastening tools.

Recent Developments: For the quarter ended Sep 30 2017, net income increased 9.6% to US$160.0 million from US$146.0 million in the year-earlier quarter. Revenues were US$1.94 billion, up 3.1% from US$1.88 billion the year before. Operating income was US$295.0 million versus US$269.0 million in the prior-year quarter, an increase of 9.7%. Direct operating expenses rose 1.8% to US$1.29 billion from US$1.26 billion in the comparable period the year before. Indirect operating expenses increased 2.9% to US$355.0 million from US$345.0 million in the equivalent prior-year period.

Prospects: Our evaluation of Masco Corp. as of Jan. 14, 2018 is the result of our systematic analysis on three basic characteristics: earnings strength, relative valuation, and recent stock price movement. The company has generated a negative trend in earnings per share over the past 5 quarters and while recent estimates for the company have been mixed, MAS has posted results that fell short of analysts expectations. Based on operating earnings yield, the company is about fairly valued when compared to all of the companies in our coverage universe. Share price changes over the past year indicates that MAS will perform in line with the market over the near term.

Financial Data

(US$ in Thousands)	9 Mos	6 Mos	3 Mos	12/31/2016	12/31/2015	12/31/2014	12/31/2013	12/31/2012
Earnings Per Share	1.68	1.62	1.58	1.47	1.02	2.38	0.76	(0.33)
Cash Flow Per Share	2.59	2.43	2.14	2.22	2.07	1.72	1.84	0.80
Dividends Per Share	0.400	0.395	0.390	0.385	0.365	0.330	0.300	0.300
Dividend Payout %	23.81	24.38	24.68	26.19	35.78	13.87	39.47	...
Income Statement								
Total Revenue	5,770,000	3,834,000	1,777,000	7,357,000	7,142,000	8,521,000	8,173,000	7,745,000
EBITDA	963,000	664,000	256,000	1,183,000	1,030,000	956,000	842,000	497,000
Depn & Amortn	...	...	...	124,000	116,000	157,000	175,000	202,000
Income Before Taxes	724,000	468,000	213,000	830,000	689,000	575,000	434,000	42,000
Income Taxes	243,000	147,000	63,000	296,000	293,000	(333,000)	111,000	83,000
Net Income	446,000	298,000	140,000	491,000	355,000	856,000	272,000	(114,000)
Average Shares	316,000	319,000	321,000	330,000	341,000	352,000	352,000	349,000
Balance Sheet								
Current Assets	3,308,000	3,306,000	2,958,000	2,934,000	3,328,000	3,863,000	3,468,000	3,217,000
Total Assets	5,483,000	5,489,000	5,139,000	5,137,000	5,680,000	7,167,000	6,933,000	6,875,000
Current Liabilities	1,708,000	1,692,000	1,424,000	1,460,000	2,506,000	2,211,000	1,782,000	1,862,000
Long-Term Obligations	2,969,000	2,967,000	2,996,000	2,995,000	2,418,000	2,919,000	3,421,000	3,422,000
Total Liabilities	5,642,000	5,620,000	5,407,000	5,435,000	5,815,000	6,243,000	6,398,000	6,553,000
Stockholders' Equity	(159,000)	(131,000)	(268,000)	(298,000)	(135,000)	924,000	535,000	322,000
Shares Outstanding	311,500	315,400	316,100	318,000	330,500	345,000	349,500	349,000
Statistical Record								
Return on Assets %	10.02	9.80	8.93	9.05	5.53	12.14	3.94	N.M.
Return on Equity %	...	...	...	...	89.99	117.34	63.48	N.M.
EBITDA Margin %	16.69	17.32	14.41	16.08	14.42	11.22	10.30	6.42
Net Margin %	7.73	7.77	7.88	6.67	4.97	10.05	3.33	N.M.
Asset Turnover	1.39	1.38	1.27	1.36	1.11	1.21	1.18	1.09
Current Ratio	1.94	1.95	2.08	2.01	1.33	1.75	1.95	1.73
Debt to Equity	...	...	...	...	...	3.16	6.39	10.63
Price Range	39.14-29.43	39.14-29.43	36.87-29.28	36.87-23.46	30.50-20.84	22.33-17.18	20.05-14.65	15.02-9.65
P/E Ratio	23.30-17.52	24.16-18.17	23.34-18.53	25.08-15.96	29.90-20.43	9.38-7.22	26.38-19.27	...
Average Yield %	1.14	1.16	1.19	1.22	1.45	1.67	1.69	2.48

Address: 17450 College Parkway, Livonia, MI 48152
Telephone: 313-274-7400

Web Site: www.masco.com
Officers: J. Michael Losh - Chairman Richard A. Manoogian - Chairman Emeritus, Executive Chairman, Chairman, President, Chief Executive Officer, Vice President

Auditors: PricewaterhouseCoopers LLP
Investor Contact: 313-792-5500
Transfer Agents: Computershare, Providence, RI

MASTERCARD INC

Exchange	Symbol	Price	52Wk Range	Yield	P/E
NYS	MA	$151.36 (12/29/2017)	154.19-105.00	0.66	35.20

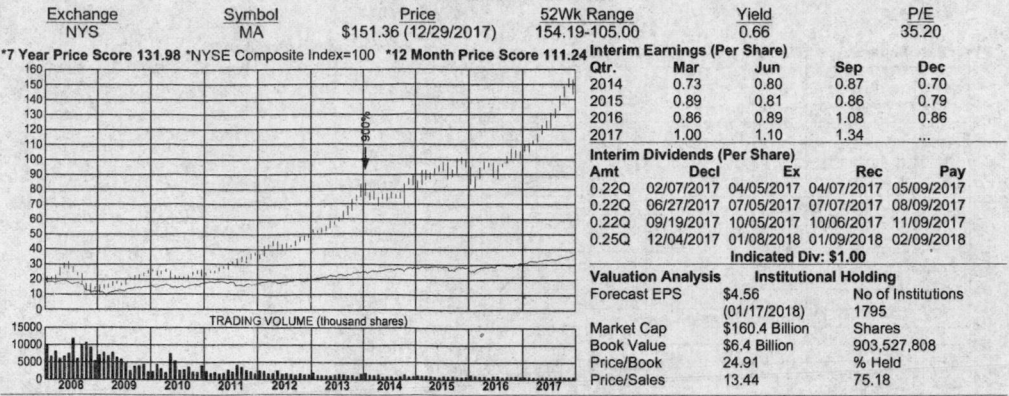

*7 Year Price Score 131.98 *NYSE Composite Index=100 *12 Month Price Score 111.24

Interim Earnings (Per Share)

Qtr.	Mar	Jun	Sep	Dec
2014	0.73	0.80	0.87	0.70
2015	0.89	0.81	0.86	0.79
2016	0.86	0.89	1.08	0.86
2017	1.00	1.10	1.34	...

Interim Dividends (Per Share)

Amt	Decl	Ex	Rec	Pay
0.22Q	02/07/2017	04/05/2017	04/07/2017	05/09/2017
0.22Q	06/27/2017	07/05/2017	07/07/2017	08/09/2017
0.22Q	09/19/2017	10/05/2017	10/06/2017	11/09/2017
0.25Q	12/04/2017	01/08/2018	01/09/2018	02/09/2018

Indicated Div: $1.00

Valuation Analysis / **Institutional Holding**

Forecast EPS	$4.56 (01/17/2018)	No of Institutions	1795
Market Cap	$160.4 Billion	Shares	903,527,808
Book Value	$6.4 Billion	% Held	75.18
Price/Book	24.91		
Price/Sales	13.44		

Business Summary: Business Services (MIC: 7.5.2 SIC: 7389 NAIC: 561499)

MasterCard is a technology company in the global payments industry that connects consumers, financial institutions, merchants, governments and businesses worldwide, enabling them to use electronic forms of payment instead of cash and checks. Co. facilitates the switching (authorization, clearing and settlement) of payment transactions and delivers related products and services. Co. creates a range of payment solutions and services using its family of brands, including MasterCard®, Maestro® and Cirrus®. Co. also provides offerings such as safety and security products, information services and consulting, issuer and acquirer processing and loyalty and reward programs.

Recent Developments: For the quarter ended Sep 30 2017, net income increased 20.8% to US$1.43 billion from US$1.18 billion in the year-earlier quarter. Revenues were US$3.40 billion, up 18.0% from US$2.88 billion the year before. Operating income was US$1.94 billion versus US$1.67 billion in the prior-year quarter, an increase of 16.2%. Indirect operating expenses increased 20.4% to US$1.46 billion from US$1.21 billion in the equivalent prior-year period.

Prospects: Our evaluation of MasterCard Inc. as of Jan. 14, 2018 is the result of our systematic analysis on three basic characteristics: earnings strength, relative valuation, and recent stock price movement. The company has enjoyed a very positive trend in earnings per share over the past 5 quarters and while recent estimates for the company have been mixed, MA has posted better than expected results. Based on operating earnings yield, the company is about fairly valued when compared to all of the companies in our coverage universe. Share price changes over the past year indicates that MA will perform well over the near term.

Financial Data

(US$ in Thousands)	9 Mos	6 Mos	3 Mos	12/31/2016	12/31/2015	12/31/2014	12/31/2013	12/31/2012
Earnings Per Share	4.30	4.04	3.83	3.69	3.35	3.10	2.56	2.19
Cash Flow Per Share	4.50	4.16	3.92	4.07	3.57	2.92	3.41	2.35
Tang Book Value Per Share	2.15	1.84	2.25	2.94	2.99	3.95	4.76	4.18
Dividends Per Share	0.850	0.820	0.790	0.760	0.640	0.440	0.210	0.105
Dividend Payout %	19.77	20.30	20.63	20.60	19.10	14.19	8.20	4.79
Income Statement								
Total Revenue	9,185,000	5,787,000	2,734,000	10,776,000	9,667,000	9,473,000	8,346,000	7,391,000
EBITDA	5,912,000	3,680,000	1,783,000	5,893,000	5,150,000	5,208,000	4,573,000	4,000,000
Depn & Amortn	761,000	496,000	266,000	152,000	131,000	107,000	92,000	84,000
Income Before Taxes	5,038,000	3,106,000	1,478,000	5,646,000	4,958,000	5,079,000	4,500,000	3,932,000
Income Taxes	1,350,000	848,000	397,000	1,587,000	1,150,000	1,462,000	1,384,000	1,174,000
Net Income	3,688,000	2,258,000	1,081,000	4,059,000	3,808,000	3,617,000	3,116,000	2,759,000
Average Shares	1,068,000	1,075,000	1,082,000	1,101,000	1,137,000	1,169,000	1,215,000	1,260,000
Balance Sheet								
Current Assets	13,231,000	12,542,000	12,885,000	13,228,000	10,985,000	10,997,000	10,950,000	9,357,000
Total Assets	20,914,000	19,839,000	18,570,000	18,675,000	16,269,000	15,329,000	14,242,000	12,462,000
Current Liabilities	7,984,000	7,583,000	7,095,000	7,206,000	6,269,000	6,222,000	6,032,000	4,906,000
Long-Term Obligations	5,393,000	5,326,000	5,216,000	5,180,000	3,287,000	1,494,000	...	...
Total Liabilities	14,472,000	13,987,000	12,959,000	13,019,000	10,241,000	8,539,000	6,758,000	5,545,000
Stockholders' Equity	6,442,000	5,852,000	5,611,000	5,656,000	6,028,000	6,790,000	7,484,000	6,917,000
Shares Outstanding	1,060,000	1,067,000	1,395,000	1,081,000	1,116,000	1,152,561	1,194,188	1,232,439
Statistical Record								
Return on Assets %	24.17	24.22	24.26	23.17	24.10	24.46	23.34	23.77
Return on Equity %	73.00	74.86	75.40	69.29	59.42	50.68	43.27	43.04
EBITDA Margin %	64.37	63.59	65.22	54.69	53.27	54.98	54.79	54.12
Net Margin %	40.15	39.02	39.54	37.67	39.39	38.18	37.34	37.33
Asset Turnover	0.62	0.63	0.64	0.62	0.61	0.64	0.63	0.64
Current Ratio	1.66	1.65	1.82	1.84	1.75	1.77	1.82	1.91
Debt to Equity	0.84	0.91	0.93	0.92	0.55	0.22	...	...
Price Range	142.49-100.18	125.90-86.83	112.83-86.83	107.02-80.65	101.50-80.74	89.08-68.68	83.55-49.13	49.85-33.91
P/E Ratio	33.14-23.30	31.16-21.49	29.46-22.67	29.00-21.86	30.30-24.10	28.74-22.15	32.64-19.19	22.76-15.48
Average Yield %	0.73	0.77	0.78	0.79	0.69	0.57	0.34	0.24

Address: 2000 Purchase Street, Purchase, NY 10577	Web Site: www.mastercard.com	Auditors: PricewaterhouseCoopers LLP
Telephone: 914-249-2000	Officers: Richard Haythornthwaite - Chairman Walter M. Macnee - Vice-Chairman	Investor Contact: 914-249-4565
		Transfer Agents: Computershare, Jersey City, NJ

MATADOR RESOURCES CO

Exchange	Symbol	Price	52Wk Range	Yield	P/E
NYS	MTDR	$31.13 (12/29/2017)	31.35-20.30	N/A	15.26

*7 Year Price Score N/A   *NYSE Composite Index=100   *12 Month Price Score 108.08

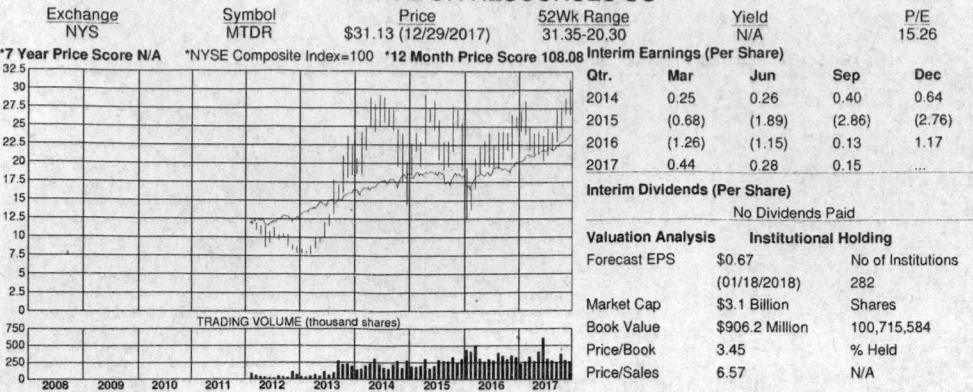

Interim Earnings (Per Share)

Qtr.	Mar	Jun	Sep	Dec
2014	0.25	0.26	0.40	0.64
2015	(0.68)	(1.89)	(2.86)	(2.76)
2016	(1.26)	(1.15)	0.13	1.17
2017	0.44	0.28	0.15	...

Interim Dividends (Per Share)

No Dividends Paid

Valuation Analysis   Institutional Holding

Forecast EPS	$0.67	No of Institutions
	(01/18/2018)	282
Market Cap	$3.1 Billion	Shares
Book Value	$906.2 Million	100,715,584
Price/Book	3.45	% Held
Price/Sales	6.57	N/A

TRADING VOLUME (thousand shares)

Business Summary: Production & Extraction (MIC: 9.1.1 SIC: 1311 NAIC: 211111)

Matador Resources is an independent energy company engaged in the exploration, development, production and acquisition of oil and natural gas resources. Additionally, Co. conducts midstream operations primarily, as of Feb 17 2017, through its midstream joint venture, San Mateo Midstream, LLC, in support of its exploration, development and production operations and provides natural gas processing, natural gas, oil and salt water gathering services and salt water disposal services to third parties. As of Dec 31 2016, Co.'s estimated proved developed and undeveloped reserves were 56,977 thousand barrels of oil and 292.6 billion cubic feet of natural gas.

Recent Developments: For the quarter ended Sep 30 2017, net income increased 49.2% to US$18.0 million from US$12.0 million in the year-earlier quarter. Revenues were US$126.3 million, up 42.3% from US$88.7 million the year before. Operating income was US$26.5 million versus US$16.9 million in the prior-year quarter, an increase of 57.5%. Direct operating expenses rose 24.6% to US$35.5 million from US$28.4 million in the comparable period the year before. Indirect operating expenses increased 48.0% to US$64.3 million from US$43.4 million in the equivalent prior-year period.

Prospects: Our evaluation of Matador Resources Co as of Jan. 14, 2018 is the result of our systematic analysis on three basic characteristics: earnings strength, relative valuation, and recent stock price movement. The company has suffered a very negative trend in earnings per share over the past 5 quarters and while recent estimates for the company have been raised by analysts, MTDR has posted better than expected results. Based on operating earnings yield, the company is overvalued when compared to all of the companies in our coverage universe. Share price changes over the past year indicates that MTDR will perform very poorly over the near term.

Financial Data

(US$ in Thousands)	9 Mos	6 Mos	3 Mos	12/31/2016	12/31/2015	12/31/2014	12/31/2013	12/31/2012
Earnings Per Share	2.04	2.02	0.59	(1.07)	(8.34)	1.56	0.77	(0.62)
Cash Flow Per Share	2.59	2.05	1.77	1.47	2.56	3.58	3.05	2.30
Tang Book Value Per Share	9.02	8.87	8.51	6.94	5.70	11.81	8.67	6.82
Income Statement								
Total Revenue	390,703	264,425	134,814	264,422	316,169	431,036	260,889	165,156
EBITDA	121,898	95,330	54,399	53,302	(627,804)	313,855	158,648	46,541
Depn & Amortn	103	64	44	123,196	179,699	134,737	98,395	80,454
Income Before Taxes	95,566	77,587	45,900	(98,093)	(826,892)	175,129	54,791	(34,691)
Income Taxes	...	...	...	(1,036)	(147,368)	64,375	9,697	(1,430)
Net Income	87,532	72,493	43,984	(97,421)	(679,785)	110,771	45,094	(33,261)
Average Shares	100,504	100,227	100,298	91,273	81,537	70,906	58,929	53,852
Balance Sheet								
Current Assets	150,345	246,787	309,976	279,182	127,007	113,323	42,172	38,197
Total Assets	1,848,537	1,777,076	1,686,393	1,464,665	1,140,861	1,436,291	890,330	632,029
Current Liabilities	252,095	212,184	167,305	169,505	136,830	161,787	100,327	96,492
Long-Term Obligations	574,027	573,988	573,968	573,924	391,254	340,000	200,000	150,000
Total Liabilities	942,334	887,334	834,128	774,540	652,858	569,883	321,406	252,925
Stockholders' Equity	906,203	889,742	852,265	690,125	488,003	866,408	568,924	379,104
Shares Outstanding	100,439	100,324	100,135	99,511	85,564	73,342	65,652	55,577
Statistical Record								
Return on Assets %	12.67	13.17	3.80	N.M.	N.M.	9.52	5.92	N.M.
Return on Equity %	28.55	28.76	7.88	N.M.	N.M.	15.43	9.51	N.M.
EBITDA Margin %	31.20	36.05	40.35	20.16	N.M.	72.81	60.81	28.18
Net Margin %	22.40	27.42	32.63	N.M.	N.M.	25.70	17.28	N.M.
Asset Turnover	0.31	0.31	0.25	0.20	0.25	0.37	0.34	0.31
Current Ratio	0.60	1.16	1.85	1.65	0.93	0.70	0.42	0.40
Debt to Equity	0.63	0.65	0.67	0.83	0.80	0.39	0.35	0.40
Price Range	28.46-20.30	28.46-19.31	28.46-18.65	26.64-12.58	29.35-18.30	29.28-14.44	23.72-7.72	12.07-7.88
P/E Ratio	13.95-9.95	14.09-9.56	48.24-31.61	...	...	18.77-9.26	30.81-10.03	...

Address: 5400 LBJ Freeway, Suite 1500, Dallas, TX 75240 **Telephone:** 972-371-5200	**Web Site:** www.matadorresources.com **Officers:** Joseph Wm. Foran - Chairman, President, Chief Executive Officer, Secretary Matthew V. Hairford - President, Executive Vice President	**Auditors:** KPMG LLP **Transfer Agents:** Registrar & Transfer Company, Cranford, NJ

MAXIMUS INC.

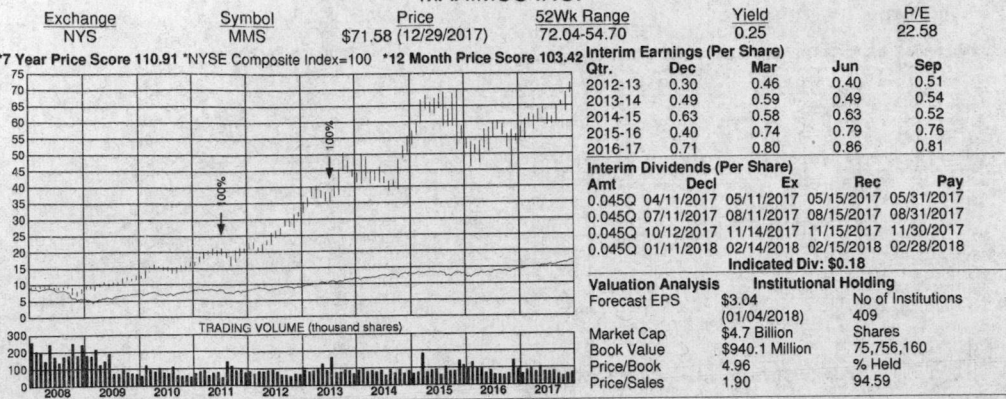

Exchange	Symbol	Price	52Wk Range	Yield	P/E
NYS	MMS	$71.58 (12/29/2017)	72.04-54.70	0.25	22.58

*7 Year Price Score 110.91 *NYSE Composite Index=100 *12 Month Price Score 103.42

Interim Earnings (Per Share)

Qtr.	Dec	Mar	Jun	Sep
2012-13	0.30	0.46	0.40	0.51
2013-14	0.49	0.59	0.49	0.54
2014-15	0.63	0.58	0.63	0.52
2015-16	0.40	0.74	0.79	0.76
2016-17	0.71	0.80	0.86	0.81

Interim Dividends (Per Share)

Amt	Decl	Ex	Rec	Pay
0.045Q	04/11/2017	05/11/2017	05/15/2017	05/31/2017
0.045Q	07/11/2017	08/11/2017	08/15/2017	08/31/2017
0.045Q	10/12/2017	11/14/2017	11/15/2017	11/30/2017
0.045Q	01/11/2018	02/14/2018	02/15/2018	02/28/2018

Indicated Div: $0.18

Valuation Analysis / **Institutional Holding**

Forecast EPS	$3.04 (01/04/2018)	No of Institutions	409
Market Cap	$4.7 Billion	Shares	75,756,160
Book Value	$940.1 Million	% Held	94.59
Price/Book	4.96		
Price/Sales	1.90		

Business Summary: Business Services (MIC: 7.5.2 SIC: 7389 NAIC: 561499)

MAXIMUS is an operator of government health and human services programs. Co.'s segments are: Health Services, which provides business process services, assessments and appeals, and related consulting services, primarily for state, provincial and national government programs; U.S. Federal Services, which provides business process services for federal government programs, assessment and appeals services for both federal and similar state-based programs, and technology solutions for federal civilian programs; and Human Services, which provides national, state and local human services agencies with a variety of business process services and related consulting services for government programs.

Recent Developments: For the year ended Sep 30 2017, net income increased 17.8% to US$212.2 million from US$180.2 million in the prior year. Revenues were US$2.45 billion, up 2.0% from US$2.40 billion the year before. Operating income was US$313.5 million versus US$286.6 million in the prior year, an increase of 9.4%. Direct operating expenses was unchanged at US$1.84 billion versus the comparable period the year before. Indirect operating expenses increased 8.3% to US$298.4 million from US$275.6 million in the equivalent prior-year period.

Prospects: Our evaluation of Maximus Inc. as of Jan. 14, 2018 is the result of our systematic analysis on three basic characteristics: earnings strength, relative valuation, and recent stock price movement. The company has generated a negative trend in earnings per share over the past 5 quarters and while recent estimates for the company have remained steady, MMS has posted better than expected results. Based on operating earnings yield, the company is undervalued when compared to all of the companies in our coverage universe. Share price changes over the past year indicates that MMS will perform well over the near term.

Financial Data

(US$ in Thousands)	09/30/2017	09/30/2016	09/30/2015	09/30/2014	09/30/2013	09/30/2012	09/30/2011	09/30/2010
Earnings Per Share	3.17	2.69	2.35	2.11	1.67	1.10	1.14	0.98
Cash Flow Per Share	5.14	2.73	3.09	3.16	1.77	1.70	1.41	1.99
Tang Book Value Per Share	6.32	3.26	1.55	4.60	4.02	4.21	4.01	3.42
Dividends Per Share	0.180	0.180	0.180	0.180	0.180	0.180	0.150	0.120
Dividend Payout %	5.68	6.69	7.66	8.53	10.78	16.44	13.16	12.24
Income Statement								
Total Revenue	2,450,961	2,403,360	2,099,821	1,700,912	1,331,279	1,050,145	929,633	831,749
EBITDA	373,805	352,679	307,565	264,098	212,508	146,375	137,501	120,306
Depn & Amortn	57,408	62,577	46,348	38,790	26,300	18,800	15,100	12,900
Income Before Taxes	314,235	285,968	259,819	227,369	189,059	131,751	125,896	108,322
Income Taxes	102,053	105,808	99,770	81,973	71,934	55,652	43,754	38,925
Net Income	209,426	178,362	157,772	145,440	116,731	76,133	81,168	70,409
Average Shares	65,632	66,229	67,275	69,087	69,893	69,612	71,062	71,860
Balance Sheet								
Current Assets	657,242	620,980	580,899	532,460	489,599	448,684	391,276	356,149
Total Assets	1,350,662	1,348,819	1,280,171	900,996	857,978	695,293	565,279	527,741
Current Liabilities	316,266	340,756	356,380	265,321	262,307	199,136	163,893	164,688
Long-Term Obligations	527	165,338	210,618	...	1,319	1,558	1,654	1,411
Total Liabilities	410,577	599,738	667,793	345,034	328,470	244,187	190,822	188,952
Stockholders' Equity	940,085	749,081	612,378	555,962	529,508	451,106	374,457	338,789
Shares Outstanding	65,137	65,223	65,437	66,613	68,525	67,970	67,586	68,696
Statistical Record								
Return on Assets %	15.52	13.53	14.47	16.54	15.03	12.05	14.85	14.65
Return on Equity %	24.80	26.13	27.01	26.80	23.81	18.39	22.76	22.14
EBITDA Margin %	15.25	14.67	14.65	15.53	15.96	13.94	14.79	14.46
Net Margin %	8.54	7.42	7.51	8.55	8.77	7.25	8.73	8.47
Asset Turnover	1.82	1.82	1.93	1.93	1.71	1.66	1.70	1.73
Current Ratio	2.08	1.82	1.63	2.01	1.87	2.25	2.39	2.16
Debt to Equity	N.M.	0.22	0.34	...	N.M.	N.M.	N.M.	N.M.
Price Range	65.06-45.25	69.80-45.94	69.22-39.00	50.41-38.57	45.29-27.31	29.86-16.95	21.23-14.73	16.20-11.12
P/E Ratio	20.52-14.27	25.95-17.08	29.46-16.60	23.89-18.28	27.12-16.35	27.15-15.41	18.62-12.92	16.53-11.34
Average Yield %	0.30	0.32	0.30	0.41	0.50	0.72	0.83	0.86

Address: 1891 Metro Center Drive, Reston, VA 20190 **Telephone:** 703-251-8500	**Web Site:** www.maximus.com **Officers:** Peter B. Pond - Chairman Bruce L. Caswell - President, Division Officer	**Auditors:** Ernst & Young LLP **Investor Contact:** 703-251-8637 **Transfer Agents:** American Stock Transfer & Trust Company, New York, NY

461

MCCORMICK & CO INC

Exchange	Symbol	Price	52Wk Range	Yield	P/E	Div Achiever
NYS	MKC	$101.91 (12/29/2017)	105.92-89.79	2.04	28.23	30 Years

*7 Year Price Score 103.87 *NYSE Composite Index=100 *12 Month Price Score 96.09

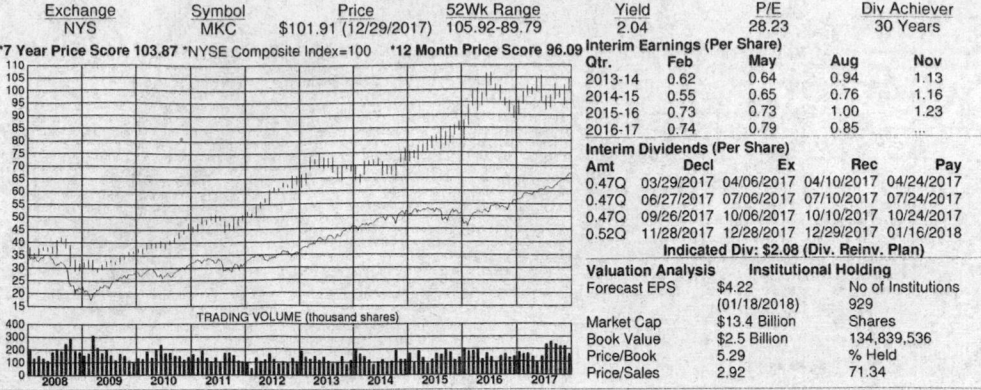

Interim Earnings (Per Share)

Qtr.	Feb	May	Aug	Nov
2013-14	0.62	0.64	0.94	1.13
2014-15	0.55	0.65	0.76	1.16
2015-16	0.73	0.73	1.00	1.23
2016-17	0.74	0.79	0.85	...

Interim Dividends (Per Share)

Amt	Decl	Ex	Rec	Pay
0.47Q	03/29/2017	04/06/2017	04/10/2017	04/24/2017
0.47Q	06/27/2017	07/06/2017	07/10/2017	07/24/2017
0.47Q	09/26/2017	10/06/2017	10/10/2017	10/24/2017
0.52Q	11/28/2017	12/28/2017	12/29/2017	01/16/2018

Indicated Div: $2.08 (Div. Reinv. Plan)

Valuation Analysis | **Institutional Holding**

Forecast EPS	$4.22	No of Institutions
	(01/18/2018)	929
Market Cap	$13.4 Billion	Shares
Book Value	$2.5 Billion	134,839,536
Price/Book	5.29	% Held
Price/Sales	2.92	71.34

Business Summary: Food (MIC: 1.2.1 SIC: 2099 NAIC: 311942)

McCormick & Co. manufactures, markets and distributes spices, seasoning mixes, condiments and other flavorful products to the food industry-retailers, food manufacturers and foodservice businesses. The consumer segment sells to retailers, that include grocery, mass merchandise, warehouse clubs, discount and drug stores, and e-commerce retailers served directly and indirectly through distributors or wholesalers. In addition to marketing its branded products to these customers, Co. is also a supplier of private label items, also known as store brands.

Recent Developments: For the quarter ended Aug 31 2017, net income decreased 15.3% to US$108.2 million from US$127.7 million in the year-earlier quarter. Revenues were US$1.19 billion, up 8.6% from US$1.09 billion the year before. Operating income was US$168.7 million versus US$167.8 million in the prior-year quarter, an increase of 0.5%. Direct operating expenses rose 10.0% to US$700.8 million from US$637.1 million in the comparable period the year before. Indirect operating expenses increased 10.3% to US$315.7 million from US$286.1 million in the equivalent prior-year period.

Prospects: Our evaluation of McCormick & Co. Inc. as of Jan. 14, 2018 is the result of our systematic analysis on three basic characteristics: earnings strength, relative valuation, and recent stock price movement. The company has enjoyed a very positive trend in earnings per share over the past 5 quarters and while recent estimates for the company have been mixed, MKC has posted better than expected results. Based on operating earnings yield, the company is about fairly valued when compared to all of the companies in our coverage universe. Share price changes over the past year indicates that MKC will perform well over the near term.

Financial Data

(US$ in Thousands)	9 Mos	6 Mos	3 Mos	11/30/2016	11/30/2015	11/30/2014	11/30/2013	11/30/2012
Earnings Per Share	3.61	3.76	3.70	3.69	3.11	3.34	2.91	3.04
Cash Flow Per Share	5.06	4.99	4.99	5.18	4.61	3.88	3.52	3.42
Dividends Per Share	1.840	1.800	1.760	1.720	1.600	1.480	1.360	1.240
Dividend Payout %	50.97	47.87	47.57	46.61	51.45	44.31	46.74	40.79
Income Statement								
Total Revenue	3,343,200	2,158,000	1,043,700	4,411,500	4,296,300	4,243,200	4,123,400	4,014,200
EBITDA	512,200	326,200	162,600	753,900	655,400	706,800	658,700	683,500
Depn & Amortn	89,600	58,100	28,300	108,700	105,900	102,700	106,000	102,800
Income Before Taxes	371,100	238,700	119,800	589,200	496,200	554,400	499,400	526,100
Income Taxes	93,600	60,600	33,300	153,000	131,300	145,900	133,600	139,800
Net Income	301,700	193,500	93,500	472,300	401,600	437,900	389,000	407,800
Average Shares	127,800	126,400	126,900	128,000	129,200	131,000	133,600	134,300
Balance Sheet								
Current Assets	1,642,600	1,425,900	1,385,100	1,421,800	1,406,500	1,416,200	1,370,200	1,285,400
Total Assets	10,381,700	4,872,100	4,751,100	4,635,900	4,507,800	4,414,300	4,449,700	4,165,400
Current Liabilities	1,734,200	1,801,400	1,738,400	1,422,700	1,240,200	1,122,000	1,063,100	1,187,600
Long-Term Obligations	4,702,300	804,300	803,500	1,054,000	1,052,700	1,014,100	1,019,000	779,200
Total Liabilities	7,860,100	3,074,000	3,031,900	3,009,300	2,837,600	2,622,100	2,517,200	2,482,500
Stockholders' Equity	2,521,600	1,798,100	1,719,200	1,626,600	1,670,200	1,792,200	1,932,500	1,682,900
Shares Outstanding	130,998	124,597	124,678	125,300	127,300	128,400	131,100	132,500
Statistical Record								
Return on Assets %	6.08	10.06	10.32	10.30	9.00	9.88	9.03	9.86
Return on Equity %	21.46	26.93	27.55	28.57	23.20	23.51	21.52	24.76
EBITDA Margin %	15.32	15.12	15.58	17.09	15.25	16.66	15.97	17.03
Net Margin %	9.02	8.97	8.96	10.71	9.35	10.32	9.43	10.16
Asset Turnover	0.61	0.94	0.97	0.96	0.96	0.96	0.96	0.97
Current Ratio	0.95	0.79	0.80	1.00	1.13	1.26	1.29	1.08
Debt to Equity	1.86	0.45	0.47	0.65	0.63	0.57	0.53	0.46
Price Range	105.92-88.78	107.07-88.78	107.07-88.78	107.07-79.78	86.03-71.39	74.33-63.03	74.76-61.23	66.37-48.54
P/E Ratio	29.34-24.59	28.48-23.61	28.94-23.99	29.02-21.62	27.66-22.95	22.25-18.87	25.69-21.04	21.83-15.97
Average Yield %	1.90	1.84	1.82	1.81	2.04	2.14	1.97	2.17

Address: 18 Loveton Circle, P. O. Box 6000, Sparks, MD 21152-6000
Telephone: 410-771-7301
Fax: 410-771-7462

Web Site: www.mccormickcorporation.com
Officers: Lawrence E. Kurzius - Chairman, President, Chief Executive Officer, Region Officer Michael R. Smith - Executive Vice President, Senior Vice President, Chief Financial Officer, Region Officer

Auditors: Ernst & Young LLP
Investor Contact: 410-771-7244
Transfer Agents: Wells Fargo Bank, N.A. Shareowner Services, Mendota Heights, MN

MCDONALD'S CORP

Exchange	Symbol	Price	52Wk Range	Yield	P/E	Div Achiever
NYS	MCD	$172.12 (12/29/2017)	174.20-119.48	2.35	24.87	40 Years

*7 Year Price Score 109.95 *NYSE Composite Index=100 *12 Month Price Score 108.35

TRADING VOLUME (thousand shares)

Interim Earnings (Per Share)

Qtr.	Mar	Jun	Sep	Dec
2014	1.21	1.40	1.09	1.13
2015	0.84	1.26	1.40	1.31
2016	1.23	1.25	1.50	1.43
2017	1.47	1.70	2.32	...

Interim Dividends (Per Share)

Amt	Decl	Ex	Rec	Pay
0.94Q	01/26/2017	02/27/2017	03/01/2017	03/15/2017
0.94Q	05/24/2017	06/01/2017	06/05/2017	06/19/2017
0.94Q	07/27/2017	08/30/2017	09/01/2017	09/18/2017
1.01Q	09/21/2017	11/30/2017	12/01/2017	12/15/2017

Indicated Div: $4.04 (Div. Reinv. Plan)

Valuation Analysis | **Institutional Holding**

Forecast EPS	$6.52	No of Institutions
	(01/18/2018)	2375
Market Cap	$137.2 Billion	Shares
Book Value	N/A	709,419,776
Price/Book	N/A	% Held
Price/Sales	5.84	60.51

Business Summary: Hotels, Restaurants & Travel (MIC: 2.2.1 SIC: 5812 NAIC: 722211)

McDonald's operates and franchises McDonald's restaurants. Co.'s menu includes hamburgers and cheeseburgers, Big Mac, Quarter Pounder with Cheese, Filet-O-Fish, several chicken sandwiches, Chicken McNuggets, wraps, french fries, salads, oatmeal, shakes, McFlurry desserts, sundaes, soft serve cones, pies, soft drinks, coffee, McCafé beverages and other beverages. Co.'s restaurants also provides breakfast menu that include Egg McMuffin, Sausage McMuffin with Egg, McGriddles, biscuit and bagel sandwiches and hotcakes. At Dec 31 2016, Co. had a total of 36,899 restaurants.

Recent Developments: For the quarter ended Sep 30 2017, net income increased 47.7% to US$1.88 billion from US$1.28 billion in the year-earlier quarter. Revenues were US$5.75 billion, down 10.4% from US$6.42 billion the year before. Operating income was US$3.08 billion versus US$2.14 billion in the prior-year quarter, an increase of 44.1%. Direct operating expenses declined 23.5% to US$2.48 billion from US$3.24 billion in the comparable period the year before. Indirect operating expenses decreased 81.3% to US$195.4 million from US$1.05 billion in the equivalent prior-year period.

Prospects: Our evaluation of McDonald's Corp. as of Jan. 14, 2018 is the result of our systematic analysis on three basic characteristics: earnings strength, relative valuation, and recent stock price movement. The company has managed to produce a neutral trend in earnings per share over the past 5 quarters and while recent estimates for the company have been mixed, MCD has posted results that fell short of analysts expectations. Based on operating earnings yield, the company is about fairly valued when compared to all of the companies in our coverage universe. Share price changes over the past year indicates that MCD will perform very well over the near term.

Financial Data
(US$ in Thousands)

	9 Mos	6 Mos	3 Mos	12/31/2016	12/31/2015	12/31/2014	12/31/2013	12/31/2012
Earnings Per Share	6.92	6.10	5.65	5.44	4.80	4.82	5.55	5.36
Cash Flow Per Share	6.53	7.18	7.15	7.07	6.96	6.86	7.13	6.88
Tang Book Value Per Share	...	...	...	...	5.04	10.51	13.26	12.46
Dividends Per Share	3.760	3.710	3.660	3.610	3.440	3.280	3.120	2.870
Dividend Payout %	54.34	60.82	64.78	66.36	71.67	68.05	56.22	53.54
Income Statement								
Total Revenue	17,480,200	11,725,600	5,675,900	24,621,900	25,413,000	27,441,300	28,105,700	27,567,000
EBITDA	8,287,700	4,913,100	2,312,300	9,086,700	8,778,800	9,490,700	10,147,000	9,854,300
Depn & Amortn	1,020,600	664,800	325,300	1,390,700	1,438,000	1,539,300	1,498,800	1,402,200
Income Before Taxes	6,587,300	3,798,700	1,766,600	6,811,200	6,702,500	7,380,900	8,126,300	7,935,500
Income Taxes	2,194,800	1,259,000	592,700	2,179,500	2,026,400	2,614,200	2,618,600	2,614,200
Net Income	4,493,600	2,609,900	1,214,800	4,686,500	4,529,300	4,757,800	5,585,900	5,464,800
Average Shares	813,500	819,200	825,200	861,200	944,600	986,300	1,006,000	1,020,200
Balance Sheet								
Current Assets	4,790,300	5,892,500	5,907,200	4,848,600	9,643,000	4,185,500	5,050,100	4,922,100
Total Assets	32,559,600	32,785,200	32,120,300	31,023,900	37,938,700	34,281,400	36,626,300	35,386,500
Current Liabilities	3,740,200	2,743,300	3,220,700	3,468,300	2,950,400	2,747,900	3,170,000	3,403,100
Long-Term Obligations	28,402,600	28,150,900	26,984,200	25,878,500	24,122,100	14,989,700	14,129,800	13,632,500
Total Liabilities	36,037,200	34,785,800	34,151,100	33,228,200	30,850,800	21,428,000	20,616,600	20,092,900
Stockholders' Equity	(3,477,600)	(2,000,600)	(2,030,800)	(2,204,300)	7,087,900	12,853,400	16,009,700	15,293,600
Shares Outstanding	797,200	810,000	815,070	819,300	906,800	962,900	990,400	1,002,700
Statistical Record								
Return on Assets %	17.49	15.41	14.49	13.55	12.54	13.42	15.51	15.94
Return on Equity %	...	...	521.40	191.40	45.43	32.97	35.69	36.72
EBITDA Margin %	47.41	41.90	40.74	36.90	34.54	34.59	36.10	35.75
Net Margin %	25.71	22.26	21.40	19.03	17.82	17.34	19.87	19.82
Asset Turnover	0.72	0.73	0.74	0.71	0.70	0.77	0.78	0.80
Current Ratio	1.28	2.15	1.83	1.40	3.27	1.52	1.59	1.45
Debt to Equity	...	...	...	...	3.40	1.17	0.88	0.89
Price Range	161.53-110.57	154.80-110.57	131.60-110.57	131.60-110.57	120.07-88.78	103.53-88.46	103.59-88.21	101.74-84.05
P/E Ratio	23.34-15.98	25.38-18.13	23.29-19.57	24.19-20.33	25.01-18.50	21.48-18.35	18.66-15.89	18.98-15.68
Average Yield %	2.77	2.94	3.01	3.00	3.43	3.41	3.21	3.10

Address: One McDonald's Plaza, Oak Brook, IL 60523	**Web Site:** www.mcdonalds.com	**Auditors:** Ernst & Young LLP
Telephone: 630-623-3000	**Officers:** Andrew J. McKenna - Chairman Emeritus Enrique Hernandez - Chairman	**Investor Contact:** 800-228-9623
		Transfer Agents: Computershare, Providence, RI

MCKESSON CORP

Exchange	Symbol	Price	52Wk Range	Yield	P/E
NYS	MCK	$155.95 (12/29/2017)	168.12-135.00	0.87	7.61

*7 Year Price Score 81.81 *NYSE Composite Index=100 *12 Month Price Score 92.74

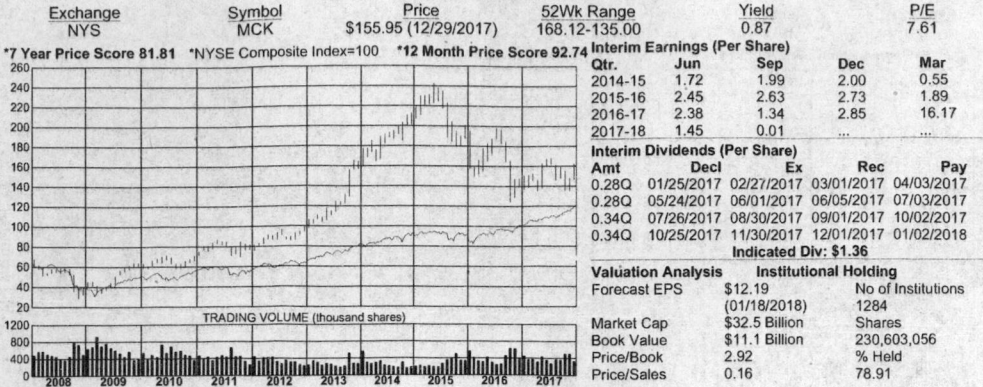

Interim Earnings (Per Share)

Qtr.	Jun	Sep	Dec	Mar
2014-15	1.72	1.99	2.00	0.55
2015-16	2.45	2.63	2.73	1.89
2016-17	2.38	1.34	2.85	16.17
2017-18	1.45	0.01	...	...

Interim Dividends (Per Share)

Amt	Decl	Ex	Rec	Pay
0.28Q	01/25/2017	02/27/2017	03/01/2017	04/03/2017
0.28Q	05/24/2017	06/01/2017	06/05/2017	07/03/2017
0.34Q	07/26/2017	08/30/2017	09/01/2017	10/02/2017
0.34Q	10/25/2017	11/30/2017	12/01/2017	01/02/2018

Indicated Div: $1.36

Valuation Analysis		Institutional Holding	
Forecast EPS	$12.19	No of Institutions	
	(01/18/2018)	1284	
Market Cap	$32.5 Billion	Shares	
Book Value	$11.1 Billion	230,603,056	
Price/Book	2.92	% Held	
Price/Sales	0.16	78.91	

Business Summary: Pharmaceuticals (MIC: 4.1.1 SIC: 5122 NAIC: 325412)

McKesson provides pharmaceuticals and medical supplies and services to its customers. Co. operates its business through two segments: McKesson Distribution Solutions and McKesson Technology Solutions. Co.'s Distribution Solutions segment distributes pharmaceutical drugs and other healthcare-related products internationally and provides practice management, technology, clinical support and business solutions to community-based oncology and other practices. Co.'s Technology Solutions segment provides clinical, financial and supply chain management solutions to healthcare organizations and includes its equity method investment in Change Healthcare, LLC.

Recent Developments: For the quarter ended Sep 30 2017, income from continuing operations decreased 82.8% to US$56.0 million from US$325.0 million in the year-earlier quarter. Net income decreased 82.7% to US$56.0 million from US$324.0 million in the year-earlier quarter. Revenues were US$52.06 billion, up 4.2% from US$49.96 billion the year before. Operating income was US$239.0 million versus US$580.0 million in the prior-year quarter, a decrease of 58.8%. Direct operating expenses rose 4.3% to US$49.23 billion from US$47.20 billion in the comparable period the year before. Indirect operating expenses increased 19.3% to US$2.60 billion from US$2.18 billion in the equivalent prior-year period.

Prospects: Our evaluation of McKesson Corp. as of Jan. 14, 2018 is the result of our systematic analysis on three basic characteristics: earnings strength, relative valuation, and recent stock price movement. The company has generated a negative trend in earnings per share over the past 5 quarters and while recent estimates for the company have been raised by analysts, MCK has posted better than expected results. Based on operating earnings yield, the company is undervalued when compared to all of the companies in our coverage universe. Share price changes over the past year indicates that MCK will perform poorly over the near term.

Financial Data

(US$ in Thousands)	6 Mos	3 Mos	03/31/2017	03/31/2016	03/31/2015	03/31/2014	03/31/2013	03/31/2012
Earnings Per Share	20.48	21.81	22.73	9.70	6.27	5.41	5.59	5.59
Cash Flow Per Share	15.10	17.18	21.47	15.92	13.41	13.69	10.57	11.96
Tang Book Value Per Share	N.M.	N.M.	N.M.	N.M.	N.M.	N.M.	N.M.	0.21
Dividends Per Share	1.180	1.120	1.120	1.080	0.960	0.920	0.800	0.800
Dividend Payout %	5.76	5.14	4.93	11.13	15.31	17.01	14.31	14.31
Income Statement								
Total Revenue	103,112,000	51,051,000	198,533,000	190,884,000	179,045,000	137,609,000	122,455,000	122,734,000
EBITDA	1,236,000	753,000	7,464,000	3,851,000	3,305,000	2,565,000	2,280,000	2,282,000
Depn & Amortn	463,000	227,000	324,000	281,000	306,000	186,000	146,000	140,000
Income Before Taxes	636,000	458,000	6,861,000	3,235,000	2,645,000	2,099,000	1,916,000	1,910,000
Income Taxes	217,000	95,000	1,614,000	908,000	815,000	742,000	581,000	516,000
Net Income	310,000	309,000	5,070,000	2,258,000	1,476,000	1,263,000	1,338,000	1,403,000
Average Shares	210,000	213,000	223,000	233,000	235,000	233,000	239,000	251,000
Balance Sheet								
Current Assets	39,794,000	37,697,000	36,948,000	38,437,000	36,670,000	32,573,000	23,170,000	23,603,000
Total Assets	63,846,000	61,816,000	60,969,000	56,563,000	53,870,000	51,759,000	34,786,000	33,093,000
Current Liabilities	37,765,000	35,799,000	35,612,000	35,071,000	33,497,000	29,501,000	21,357,000	21,686,000
Long-Term Obligations	7,490,000	7,424,000	7,305,000	6,535,000	8,180,000	8,949,000	4,521,000	3,072,000
Total Liabilities	52,703,000	50,513,000	49,874,000	47,639,000	45,869,000	43,237,000	27,716,000	26,262,000
Stockholders' Equity	11,143,000	11,303,000	11,095,000	8,924,000	8,001,000	8,522,000	7,070,000	6,831,000
Shares Outstanding	208,474	210,000	211,000	225,000	232,000	231,000	227,000	235,000
Statistical Record								
Return on Assets %	7.42	8.08	8.63	4.08	2.79	2.92	3.94	4.37
Return on Equity %	44.01	47.07	50.65	26.61	17.87	16.20	19.25	19.92
EBITDA Margin %	1.20	1.47	3.76	2.02	1.85	1.86	1.86	1.86
Net Margin %	0.30	0.61	2.55	1.18	0.82	0.92	1.09	1.14
Asset Turnover	3.31	3.34	3.38	3.45	3.39	3.18	3.61	3.83
Current Ratio	1.05	1.05	1.04	1.10	1.09	1.10	1.08	1.09
Debt to Equity	0.67	0.66	0.66	0.73	1.02	1.05	0.64	0.45
Price Range	168.12-124.11	198.44-124.11	198.44-124.11	242.75-150.03	230.26-164.68	185.35-104.18	111.23-85.48	88.59-69.35
P/E Ratio	8.21-6.06	9.10-5.69	8.73-5.46	25.03-15.47	36.72-26.26	34.26-19.26	19.90-15.29	15.85-12.41
Average Yield %	0.78	0.71	0.68	0.54	0.48	0.46	0.85	1.00

Address: One Post Street, San Francisco, CA 94104	Web Site: www.mckesson.com	Auditors: DELOITTE & TOUCHE LLP
Telephone: 415-983-8300	Officers: John H. Hammergren - Chairman, President, Chief Executive Officer James A. Beer - Executive Vice President, Chief Financial Officer, Principal Financial Officer	Investor Contact: 415-983-8391
		Transfer Agents: Wells Fargo Shareowner Services, Mendota Heights, MN

MDU RESOURCES GROUP INC

Exchange	Symbol	Price	52Wk Range	Yield	P/E	Div Achiever
NYS	MDU	$26.88 (12/29/2017)	29.43-25.45	2.94	22.59	26 Years

*7 Year Price Score 86.60   *NYSE Composite Index=100   *12 Month Price Score 94.78

Interim Earnings (Per Share)

Qtr.	Mar	Jun	Sep	Dec
2014	0.30	0.28	0.53	0.44
2015	(1.57)	(1.18)	(0.72)	0.27
2016	0.13	(0.56)	0.42	0.34
2017	0.19	0.21	0.45	...

Interim Dividends (Per Share)

Amt	Decl	Ex	Rec	Pay
0.193Q	02/16/2017	03/07/2017	03/09/2017	04/01/2017
0.193Q	05/10/2017	06/06/2017	06/08/2017	07/01/2017
0.193Q	08/17/2017	09/13/2017	09/14/2017	10/01/2017
0.198Q	11/16/2017	12/13/2017	12/14/2017	01/01/2018

Indicated Div: $0.79 (Div. Reinv. Plan)

Valuation Analysis / **Institutional Holding**

Forecast EPS	$1.18	No of Institutions
	(11/20/2017)	495
Market Cap	$5.2 Billion	Shares
Book Value	$2.4 Billion	154,296,304
Price/Book	2.23	% Held
Price/Sales	1.22	56.70

Business Summary: Electric Utilities (MIC: 3.1.1 SIC: 4911 NAIC: 221122)

MDU Resources Group is a regulated energy delivery and construction materials and services business. As of Dec 31 2016, Co.'s electric segment served 142,948 residential, commercial, industrial and municipal customers in 178 communities and adjacent rural areas, while its natural gas distribution operations served 922,408 residential, commercial and industrial customers in 335 communities and adjacent rural areas across eight states. Co.'s other businesses include pipeline and midstream, construction materials and contracting, construction services, as well as other, which includes the activities of Centennial Holdings Capital LLC, which insures various types of risks as a captive insurer.

Recent Developments: For the quarter ended Sep 30 2017, income from continuing operations increased 1.3% to US$89.5 million from US$88.4 million in the year-earlier quarter. Net income increased 5.3% to US$87.4 million from US$83.0 million in the year-earlier quarter. Revenues were US$1.27 billion, up 5.3% from US$1.21 billion the year before. Operating income was US$156.4 million versus US$146.7 million in the prior-year quarter, an increase of 6.6%. Direct operating expenses rose 5.5% to US$1.03 billion from US$971.7 million in the comparable period the year before. Indirect operating expenses increased 0.9% to US$91.0 million from US$90.2 million in the equivalent prior-year period.

Prospects: Our evaluation of MDU Resources Group Inc. as of Jan. 14, 2018 is the result of our systematic analysis on three basic characteristics: earnings strength, relative valuation, and recent stock price movement. The company has generated a negative trend in earnings per share over the past 5 quarters and while recent estimates for the company have remained steady, MDU has posted results that fell short of analysts expectations. Based on operating earnings yield, the company is undervalued when compared to all of the companies in our coverage universe. Share price changes over the past year indicates that MDU will perform well over the near term.

Financial Data

(US$ in Thousands)	9 Mos	6 Mos	3 Mos	12/31/2016	12/31/2015	12/31/2014	12/31/2013	12/31/2012
Earnings Per Share	1.19	1.16	0.39	0.33	(3.20)	1.55	1.47	(0.01)
Cash Flow Per Share	2.34	2.56	2.58	2.36	3.29	3.20	3.93	3.09
Tang Book Value Per Share	8.80	8.53	8.51	8.52	8.91	12.74	11.40	10.49
Dividends Per Share	0.770	0.765	0.760	0.755	0.735	0.715	0.695	0.675
Dividend Payout %	64.71	65.95	194.87	228.79	...	46.13	47.28	...
Income Statement								
Total Revenue	3,278,112	2,005,565	937,925	4,128,828	4,191,549	4,670,558	4,462,404	4,075,431
EBITDA	461,115	251,572	119,454	630,394	501,095	899,555	886,523	385,054
Depn & Amortn	155,138	102,983	51,325	216,318	227,730	401,368	386,856	359,205
Income Before Taxes	243,999	107,521	47,826	326,228	180,297	411,171	415,750	(50,850)
Income Taxes	74,406	27,478	12,188	93,132	65,603	119,969	136,736	(31,146)
Net Income	165,891	78,539	37,325	64,433	(622,435)	298,233	278,933	(754)
Average Shares	195,783	195,304	196,023	195,618	194,986	192,587	189,693	188,826
Balance Sheet								
Current Assets	1,099,242	1,015,970	942,073	977,475	1,021,042	1,194,973	1,116,688	1,128,081
Total Assets	6,344,445	6,230,498	6,148,458	6,284,467	6,627,608	7,809,978	7,061,332	6,682,491
Current Liabilities	856,568	693,805	618,034	669,659	947,639	968,694	784,900	850,115
Long-Term Obligations	1,592,053	1,677,977	1,659,507	1,746,561	1,627,443	1,825,278	1,842,286	1,610,867
Total Liabilities	3,990,528	3,927,546	3,834,553	3,968,223	4,231,103	4,675,937	4,238,168	4,034,243
Stockholders' Equity	2,353,917	2,302,952	2,313,905	2,316,244	2,396,505	3,134,041	2,823,164	2,648,248
Shares Outstanding	195,304	195,304	195,304	195,304	195,265	194,215	189,329	188,830
Statistical Record								
Return on Assets %	3.65	3.60	1.20	1.00	N.M.	4.01	4.06	N.M.
Return on Equity %	9.99	10.01	3.27	2.73	N.M.	10.01	10.20	N.M.
EBITDA Margin %	14.07	12.54	12.74	15.27	11.95	19.26	19.87	9.45
Net Margin %	5.06	3.92	3.98	1.56	N.M.	6.39	6.25	N.M.
Asset Turnover	0.68	0.67	0.66	0.64	0.58	0.63	0.65	0.61
Current Ratio	1.28	1.46	1.52	1.46	1.08	1.23	1.42	1.33
Debt to Equity	0.68	0.73	0.72	0.75	0.68	0.58	0.65	0.61
Price Range	29.62-24.63	29.62-23.03	29.62-18.91	29.62-16.03	24.36-16.36	35.93-21.44	30.87-21.24	23.06-19.76
P/E Ratio	24.89-20.70	25.53-19.85	75.95-48.49	89.76-48.58	...	23.18-13.83	21.00-14.45	...
Average Yield %	2.86	2.90	3.04	3.34	3.70	2.31	2.62	3.09

Address: 1200 West Century Avenue, P.O. Box 5650, Bismarck, ND 58506-5650	Web Site: www.mdu.com	Auditors: Deloitte & Touche LLP
	Officers: Harry Jonathan Pearce - Chairman David L. Goodin - President, Chief Executive Officer, Division Officer	Investor Contact: 866-866-8919
Telephone: 701-530-1000		Transfer Agents: Wells Fargo Bank, N.A., St. Paul, MN

MEDICAL PROPERTIES TRUST INC

Exchange	Symbol	Price	52Wk Range	Yield	P/E
NYS	MPW	$13.78 (12/29/2017)	14.16-12.15	6.97	18.62

*7 Year Price Score 81.80   *NYSE Composite Index=100   *12 Month Price Score 98.26

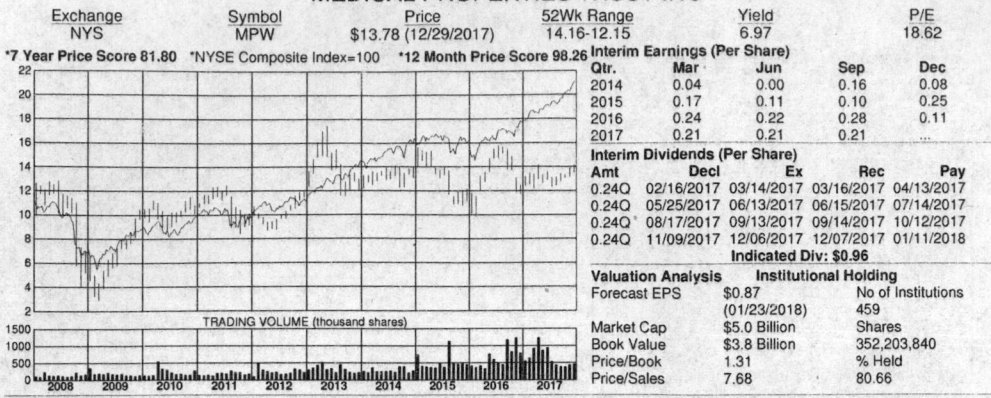

Interim Earnings (Per Share)

Qtr.	Mar	Jun	Sep	Dec
2014	0.04	0.00	0.16	0.08
2015	0.17	0.11	0.10	0.25
2016	0.24	0.22	0.28	0.11
2017	0.21	0.21	0.21	...

Interim Dividends (Per Share)

Amt	Decl	Ex	Rec	Pay
0.24Q	02/16/2017	03/14/2017	03/16/2017	04/13/2017
0.24Q	05/25/2017	06/13/2017	06/15/2017	07/14/2017
0.24Q	08/17/2017	09/13/2017	09/14/2017	10/12/2017
0.24Q	11/09/2017	12/06/2017	12/07/2017	01/11/2018

Indicated Div: $0.96

Valuation Analysis

		Institutional Holding	
Forecast EPS	$0.87	No of Institutions	
	(01/23/2018)	459	
Market Cap	$5.0 Billion	Shares	
Book Value	$3.8 Billion	352,203,840	
Price/Book	1.31	% Held	
Price/Sales	7.68	80.66	

TRADING VOLUME (thousand shares)

Business Summary: REITs (MIC: 5.3.1 SIC: 6798 NAIC: 525930)

Medical Properties Trust is a self-advised real estate investment trust (REIT) focused on investing in and owning net-leased healthcare facilities across the U.S. and selectively in foreign jurisdictions. Co. acquires and develops healthcare facilities and leases the facilities to healthcare operating companies. Co. also makes mortgage loans to healthcare operators collateralized by their real estate assets. In addition, Co. selectively makes loans to certain of its operators through its REIT subsidiaries. At Feb 24 2017, Co.'s portfolio consisted of 232 properties, including 136 general acute care hospitals, 79 inpatient rehabilitation hospitals, and 17 long-term acute care hospitals.

Recent Developments: For the quarter ended Sep 30 2017, income from continuing operations increased 9.0% to US$76.9 million from US$70.5 million in the year-earlier quarter. Net income increased 9.0% to US$76.9 million from US$70.5 million in the year-earlier quarter. Revenues were US$176.6 million, up 39.5% from US$126.6 million the year before. Revenues from property income rose 38.1% to US$147.6 million from US$106.8 million in the corresponding quarter a year earlier.

Prospects: Our evaluation of Medical Properties Trust Inc. as of Jan. 21, 2018 is the result of our systematic analysis on three basic characteristics: earnings strength, relative valuation, and recent stock price movement. The company has produced a positive trend in earnings per share over the past 5 quarters. However, while recent estimates for the company have been mixed, MPW has posted results that fell short of analysts expectations. Based on operating earnings yield, the company is undervalued when compared to all of the companies in our coverage universe. Share price changes over the past year indicates that MPW will perform well over the near term.

Financial Data

(US$ in Thousands)	9 Mos	6 Mos	3 Mos	12/31/2016	12/31/2015	12/31/2014	12/31/2013	12/31/2012
Earnings Per Share	0.74	0.81	0.82	0.86	0.63	0.29	0.63	0.67
Cash Flow Per Share	0.87	0.81	0.81	1.01	0.95	0.88	0.93	0.79
Tang Book Value Per Share	10.51	10.49	10.12	10.13	8.88	8.00	8.33	7.70
Dividends Per Share	0.950	0.940	0.930	0.910	0.880	0.840	0.810	0.800
Dividend Payout %	128.38	116.05	113.41	105.81	139.68	289.66	128.57	119.40
Income Statement								
Total Revenue	499,784	323,204	156,397	541,137	441,878	312,532	242,523	201,397
EBITDA	336,210	218,345	106,117	485,035	336,782	201,521	195,915	171,405
Depn & Amortn	4,748	3,139	1,617	105,214	77,912	60,267	42,377	39,050
Income Before Taxes	210,964	137,467	66,471	220,224	138,581	48,579	86,473	72,450
Income Taxes	...	...	...	(6,830)	1,503	340	726	...
Net Income	217,849	141,385	67,970	225,048	139,598	50,522	96,991	89,900
Average Shares	365,046	350,319	321,423	261,072	218,304	170,540	152,598	132,333
Balance Sheet								
Current Assets	354,366	384,119	576,827	257,799	324,635	244,806	150,307	118,460
Total Assets	8,927,040	7,327,837	6,780,730	6,418,536	5,609,351	3,747,336	2,904,570	2,178,886
Current Liabilities	199,537	239,635	213,722	227,644	166,714	139,830	118,098	86,570
Long-Term Obligations	4,832,264	3,221,054	3,277,986	2,909,341	3,322,541	2,201,654	1,421,681	1,025,160
Total Liabilities	5,100,596	3,510,527	3,533,949	3,170,158	3,507,083	2,365,289	1,560,362	1,129,072
Stockholders' Equity	3,826,444	3,817,310	3,246,781	3,248,378	2,102,268	1,382,047	1,344,208	1,049,814
Shares Outstanding	364,084	364,020	320,801	320,514	236,744	172,743	161,310	136,335
Statistical Record								
Return on Assets %	3.47	4.09	3.76	3.73	2.98	1.52	3.82	4.72
Return on Equity %	7.47	8.52	8.74	8.39	8.01	3.71	8.10	9.54
EBITDA Margin %	67.27	67.56	67.85	89.63	76.22	64.48	80.78	85.11
Net Margin %	43.59	43.74	43.46	41.59	31.59	16.17	39.99	44.64
Asset Turnover	0.09	0.10	0.09	0.09	0.09	0.09	0.10	0.11
Current Ratio	1.78	1.60	2.70	1.13	1.95	1.75	1.27	1.37
Debt to Equity	1.26	0.84	1.01	0.90	1.58	1.59	1.06	0.98
Price Range	14.86-11.75	15.80-11.75	15.80-11.75	15.80-9.86	15.62-10.73	14.09-12.20	17.46-11.51	11.96-8.69
P/E Ratio	20.08-15.88	19.51-14.51	19.27-14.33	18.37-11.47	24.79-17.03	48.59-42.07	27.71-18.27	17.85-12.97
Average Yield %	7.31	6.93	6.76	6.78	6.70	6.36	5.80	7.91

Address: 1000 Urban Center Drive, Suite 501, Birmingham, AL 35242	Web Site: www.medicalpropertiestrust.com	Auditors: PricewaterhouseCoopers LLP
Telephone: 205-969-3755	Officers: Edward K. Aldag - Chairman, President, Chief Executive Officer William G. McKenzie - Vice-Chairman	Investor Contact: 205-397-8897
Fax: 205-969-3756		Transfer Agents: American Stock Transfer & Trust Company, New York, NY

MEDNAX, INC.

Exchange	Symbol	Price	52Wk Range	Yield	P/E
NYS	MD	$53.44 (12/29/2017)	72.03-41.19	N/A	18.88

*7 Year Price Score 81.92 *NYSE Composite Index=100 *12 Month Price Score 83.34

Interim Earnings (Per Share)

Qtr.	Mar	Jun	Sep	Dec
2014	0.63	0.79	0.86	0.90
2015	0.72	0.90	0.97	0.99
2016	0.73	0.89	1.04	0.84
2017	0.59	0.69	0.71	...

Interim Dividends (Per Share)

No Dividends Paid

Valuation Analysis — **Institutional Holding**

Forecast EPS	$3.30	No of Institutions
	(01/01/2018)	489
Market Cap	$5.0 Billion	Shares
Book Value	$2.9 Billion	111,137,880
Price/Book	1.71	% Held
Price/Sales	1.48	N/A

Business Summary: Diagnostic & Health Related Services (MIC: 4.2.2 SIC: 8069 NAIC: 622310)

MEDNAX is a provider of physician services including newborn, anesthesia, maternal-fetal, teleradiology, pediatric cardiology and other pediatric subspecialty care. Co.'s network comprised of physicians who provide: neonatal clinical care to babies born prematurely or with medical complications; anesthesia care to patients in connection with surgical and other procedures, as well as pain management; maternal-fetal and obstetrical medical care to expectant mothers experiencing complicated pregnancies; pediatric intensive care; pediatric cardiology care; hospital-based pediatric care; pediatric surgical care; and pediatric ear, nose and throat and pediatric ophthalmology services.

Recent Developments: For the quarter ended Sep 30 2017, net income decreased 31.7% to US$65.9 million from US$96.4 million in the year-earlier quarter. Revenues were US$869.0 million, up 4.9% from US$828.0 million the year before. Operating income was US$126.4 million versus US$156.9 million in the prior-year quarter, a decrease of 19.4%. Indirect operating expenses increased 10.6% to US$742.5 million from US$671.1 million in the equivalent prior-year period.

Prospects: Our evaluation of Mednax, Inc. as of Jan. 14, 2018 is the result of our systematic analysis on three basic characteristics: earnings strength, relative valuation, and recent stock price movement. The company has managed to produce a neutral trend in earnings per share over the past 5 quarters and while recent estimates for the company have been mixed, MD has posted better than expected results. Based on operating earnings yield, the company is undervalued when compared to all of the companies in our coverage universe. Share price changes over the past year indicates that MD will perform very poorly over the near term.

Financial Data
(US$ in Thousands)

	9 Mos	6 Mos	3 Mos	12/31/2016	12/31/2015	12/31/2014	12/31/2013	12/31/2012
Earnings Per Share	2.83	3.16	3.36	3.49	3.58	3.18	2.78	2.42
Cash Flow Per Share	4.82	4.80	4.93	4.79	3.96	4.29	4.09	3.34
Income Statement								
Total Revenue	2,547,492	1,678,541	835,597	3,183,159	2,779,996	2,438,913	2,154,012	1,816,612
EBITDA	359,627	231,622	107,996	602,706	581,912	531,627	469,327	407,216
Depn & Amortn	4,078	2,740	1,383	29,000	22,200	15,900	15,500	15,800
Income Before Taxes	300,834	192,595	88,861	510,614	536,602	506,836	448,412	388,171
Income Taxes	117,811	75,692	34,967	189,203	204,038	191,413	167,895	147,264
Net Income	184,269	118,389	54,691	324,914	336,320	317,281	280,517	240,907
Average Shares	92,881	92,812	93,143	93,109	93,960	99,887	100,969	99,382
Balance Sheet								
Current Assets	653,323	557,570	562,438	587,128	527,769	467,052	408,839	359,044
Total Assets	5,680,523	5,407,396	5,424,885	5,339,400	4,547,214	3,608,795	3,049,430	2,750,337
Current Liabilities	475,994	350,148	328,613	448,949	428,771	416,273	326,792	268,338
Long-Term Obligations	1,797,150	1,746,131	1,877,996	1,683,628	1,262,820	558,855	27,143	144,233
Total Liabilities	2,763,949	2,569,148	2,662,415	2,578,633	2,109,686	1,344,176	706,442	714,969
Stockholders' Equity	2,916,574	2,838,248	2,762,470	2,760,767	2,437,528	2,264,619	2,342,988	2,035,368
Shares Outstanding	93,556	93,480	92,904	93,718	93,739	96,030	101,207	100,038
Statistical Record								
Return on Assets %	4.76	5.76	6.20	6.55	8.25	9.53	9.67	9.57
Return on Equity %	9.40	10.86	11.94	12.47	14.30	13.77	12.81	12.76
EBITDA Margin %	14.12	13.80	12.92	18.93	20.93	21.80	21.79	22.42
Net Margin %	7.23	7.05	6.55	10.21	12.10	13.01	13.02	13.26
Asset Turnover	0.61	0.66	0.65	0.64	0.68	0.73	0.74	0.72
Current Ratio	1.37	1.59	1.71	1.31	1.23	1.12	1.25	1.34
Debt to Equity	0.62	0.62	0.68	0.61	0.52	0.25	0.01	0.07
Price Range	72.03-41.19	76.29-53.95	76.29-60.38	76.29-60.38	85.47-64.53	67.20-51.25	56.31-39.76	40.67-30.00
P/E Ratio	25.45-14.55	24.14-17.07	22.71-17.97	21.86-17.30	23.87-18.03	21.13-16.12	20.25-14.30	16.81-12.40

Address: 1301 Concord Terrace, Sunrise, FL 33323 **Telephone:** 954-384-0175	**Web Site:** www.mednax.com **Officers:** Cesar L. Alvarez - Chairman Joseph M. Calabro - President, Chief Operating Officer	**Auditors:** PricewaterhouseCoopers LLP **Transfer Agents:** ComputerShare Investor Services, Providence, RI

MEDTRONIC PLC

Exchange	Symbol	Price	52Wk Range	Yield	P/E
NYS	MDT	$80.75 (12/29/2017)	89.30-70.61	2.24	22.12

*7 Year Price Score 104.03 *NYSE Composite Index=100 *12 Month Price Score 93.96

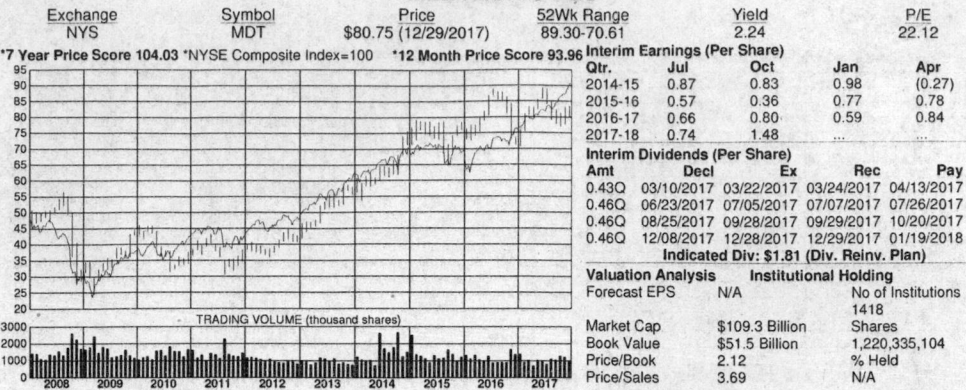

Interim Earnings (Per Share)

Qtr.	Jul	Oct	Jan	Apr
2014-15	0.87	0.83	0.98	(0.27)
2015-16	0.57	0.36	0.77	0.78
2016-17	0.66	0.80	0.59	0.84
2017-18	0.74	1.48	...	...

Interim Dividends (Per Share)

Amt	Decl	Ex	Rec	Pay
0.43Q	03/10/2017	03/22/2017	03/24/2017	04/13/2017
0.46Q	06/23/2017	07/05/2017	07/07/2017	07/26/2017
0.46Q	08/25/2017	09/28/2017	09/29/2017	10/20/2017
0.46Q	12/08/2017	12/28/2017	12/29/2017	01/19/2018

Indicated Div: $1.81 (Div. Reinv. Plan)

Valuation Analysis | **Institutional Holding**

Forecast EPS	N/A	No of Institutions	1418
Market Cap	$109.3 Billion	Shares	
Book Value	$51.5 Billion	1,220,335,104	
Price/Book	2.12	% Held	
Price/Sales	3.69	N/A	

Business Summary: Medical Instruments & Equipment (MIC: 4.3.1 SIC: 3845 NAIC: 334510)

Medtronic is a medical technology, services and solutions company. Co.'s operating segments are: Cardiac and Vascular, which include products for cardiac rhythm disorders and cardiovascular disease, as well as services to diagnose, treat, and manage heart and vascular-related disorders and diseases; Minimally Invasive Therapies, which provides products for surgical care and patient monitoring, patient care, renal care, and airway and ventilation; Restorative Therapies, which provides products focusing on the spine, bone graft substitutes, biologic products, trauma, implantable neurostimulation therapies and drug delivery systems; and Diabetes, which include products for diabetes management.

Recent Developments: For the quarter ended Oct 27 2017, net income increased 81.2% to US$2.01 billion from US$1.11 billion in the year-earlier quarter. Revenues were US$7.05 billion, down 4.0% from US$7.35 billion the year before. Operating income was US$1.90 billion versus US$1.39 billion in the prior-year quarter, an increase of 37.3%. Direct operating expenses declined 8.9% to US$2.12 billion from US$2.33 billion in the comparable period the year before. Indirect operating expenses decreased 16.6% to US$3.03 billion from US$3.63 billion in the equivalent prior-year period.

Prospects: Our evaluation of Medtronic PLC as of Sep. 17, 2017 is the result of our systematic analysis on three basic characteristics: earnings strength, relative valuation, and recent stock price movement. The company has managed to produce a neutral trend in earnings per share over the past 5 quarters. However, while recent estimates for the company have been lowered by analysts, MDT has posted better than expected results. Based on operating earnings yield, the company is undervalued when compared to all of the companies in our coverage universe. Share price changes over the past year indicates that MDT will perform in line with the market over the near term.

Financial Data

(US$ in Thousands)	6 Mos	3 Mos	04/28/2017	04/29/2016	04/24/2015	04/25/2014	04/26/2013	04/27/2012
Earnings Per Share	3.65	2.97	2.89	2.48	2.41	3.02	3.37	3.41
Cash Flow Per Share	4.06	4.45	5.00	3.64	4.49	4.96	4.80	4.25
Tang Book Value Per Share	N.M.	N.M.	N.M.	N.M.	N.M.	6.57	5.58	4.37
Dividends Per Share	1.780	1.750	1.720	1.520	1.220	1.120	1.040	0.970
Dividend Payout %	48.77	58.92	59.52	61.29	50.62	37.09	30.86	28.45
Income Statement								
Total Revenue	14,440,000	7,390,000	29,710,000	28,833,000	20,261,000	17,005,000	16,590,000	16,184,000
EBITDA	3,270,000	1,379,000	8,247,000	8,111,000	5,072,000	4,663,000	5,221,000	5,127,000
Depn & Amortn	(20,000)	(10,000)	2,917,000	2,820,000	1,306,000	850,000	819,000	833,000
Income Before Taxes	2,923,000	1,195,000	4,602,000	4,336,000	3,486,000	3,705,000	4,251,000	4,145,000
Income Taxes	(99,000)	186,000	578,000	798,000	811,000	640,000	784,000	730,000
Net Income	3,033,000	1,016,000	4,028,000	3,538,000	2,675,000	3,065,000	3,467,000	3,617,000
Average Shares	1,365,800	1,375,600	1,391,400	1,425,900	1,109,000	1,013,600	1,027,500	1,059,900
Balance Sheet								
Current Assets	25,162,000	24,779,000	24,873,000	23,600,000	30,844,000	21,210,000	17,793,000	9,515,000
Total Assets	94,458,000	100,250,000	99,816,000	99,782,000	106,685,000	37,943,000	34,841,000	33,083,000
Current Liabilities	10,496,000	15,148,000	14,220,000	7,165,000	9,173,000	5,559,000	3,891,000	5,857,000
Long-Term Obligations	25,941,000	25,953,000	25,921,000	30,247,000	33,752,000	10,315,000	9,741,000	7,359,000
Total Liabilities	42,989,000	49,578,000	49,522,000	47,719,000	53,455,000	18,500,000	16,170,000	15,970,000
Stockholders' Equity	51,469,000	50,672,000	50,294,000	52,063,000	53,230,000	19,443,000	18,671,000	17,113,000
Shares Outstanding	1,353,591	1,354,591	1,369,424	1,399,018	1,421,648	998,999	1,016,014	1,037,194
Statistical Record								
Return on Assets %	5.20	4.14	4.05	3.37	3.71	8.45	10.24	11.42
Return on Equity %	9.87	8.11	7.89	6.61	7.38	16.13	19.43	21.93
EBITDA Margin %	22.65	18.66	27.76	28.13	25.03	27.42	31.47	31.68
Net Margin %	21.00	13.75	13.56	12.27	13.20	18.02	20.90	22.35
Asset Turnover	0.31	0.30	0.30	0.27	0.28	0.47	0.49	0.51
Current Ratio	2.40	1.64	1.75	3.29	3.36	3.82	4.57	1.62
Debt to Equity	0.50	0.51	0.52	0.58	0.63	0.53	0.52	0.43
Price Range	89.30-70.61	89.30-70.61	88.92-70.61	79.78-64.52	79.25-58.21	62.31-46.36	47.72-35.89	43.20-30.41
P/E Ratio	24.47-19.35	30.07-23.77	30.77-24.43	32.17-26.02	32.88-24.15	20.63-15.35	14.16-10.65	12.67-8.92
Average Yield %	2.21	2.13	2.11	2.02	1.78	2.02	2.47	2.62

Address: 20 On Hatch, Lower Hatch Street, Dublin, 2	Web Site: www.medtronic.com	Auditors: PricewaterhouseCoopers LLP
Telephone: 143-817-00	Officers: Chris Lee - Senior Vice President, Division Officer Omar Ishrak - Chairman, Chief Executive Officer	Transfer Agents: Wells Fargo Shareowner Services, Mendota Heights, MN

MERCK & CO INC

Exchange	Symbol	Price	52Wk Range	Yield	P/E
NYS	MRK	$56.27 (12/29/2017)	66.58-54.10	3.41	54.11

*7 Year Price Score 95.46 *NYSE Composite Index=100 *12 Month Price Score 84.59

TRADING VOLUME (thousand shares)

Interim Earnings (Per Share)

Qtr.	Mar	Jun	Sep	Dec
2014	0.57	0.68	0.31	2.50
2015	0.33	0.24	0.64	0.34
2016	0.40	0.43	0.78	(0.21)
2017	0.56	0.71	(0.02)	...

Interim Dividends (Per Share)

Amt	Decl	Ex	Rec	Pay
0.47Q	02/28/2017	03/13/2017	03/15/2017	04/07/2017
0.47Q	05/23/2017	06/13/2017	06/15/2017	07/10/2017
0.47Q	07/25/2017	09/14/2017	09/15/2017	10/06/2017
0.48Q	11/28/2017	12/14/2017	12/15/2017	01/08/2018

Indicated Div: $1.92 (Div. Reinv. Plan)

Valuation Analysis

Forecast EPS	$3.95
	(01/18/2018)
Market Cap	$153.4 Billion
Book Value	$38.2 Billion
Price/Book	4.01
Price/Sales	3.85

Institutional Holding

No of Institutions	2565
Shares	2,389,780,736
% Held	N/A

Business Summary: Pharmaceuticals (MIC: 4.1.1 SIC: 2834 NAIC: 325412)

Merck & Co. is a health care company that provides health solutions through its prescription medicines, vaccines, biologic therapies and animal health products. Co.'s operations are comprised of three operating segments: pharmaceutical, which includes human health pharmaceutical and vaccine products marketed either directly by Co. or through joint ventures; animal health, which discovers, develops, manufactures and markets animal health products, including vaccines, which Co. sells to veterinarians, distributors and animal producers; and healthcare services.

Recent Developments: For the quarter ended Sep 30 2017, net loss amounted to US$51.0 million versus net income of US$2.19 billion in the year-earlier quarter. Revenues were US$10.33 billion, down 2.0% from US$10.54 billion the year before. Direct operating expenses declined 4.0% to US$3.27 billion from US$3.41 billion in the comparable period the year before. Indirect operating expenses increased 64.5% to US$6.94 billion from US$4.22 billion in the equivalent prior-year period.

Prospects: Our evaluation of Merck & Co. Inc. as of Jan. 14, 2018 is the result of our systematic analysis on three basic characteristics: earnings strength, relative valuation, and recent stock price movement. The company has generated a negative trend in earnings per share over the past 5 quarters and while recent estimates for the company have remained steady, MRK has posted better than expected results. Based on operating earnings yield, the company is undervalued when compared to all of the companies in our coverage universe. Share price changes over the past year indicates that MRK will perform in line with the market over the near term.

Financial Data

(US$ in Thousands)	9 Mos	6 Mos	3 Mos	12/31/2016	12/31/2015	12/31/2014	12/31/2013	12/31/2012
Earnings Per Share	1.04	1.84	1.56	1.41	1.56	4.07	1.47	2.00
Cash Flow Per Share	2.22	3.73	3.10	3.74	4.41	2.72	3.93	3.29
Tang Book Value Per Share	1.75	1.83	1.68	1.68	1.56	5.38	4.67	3.90
Dividends Per Share	1.880	1.870	1.860	1.850	1.810	1.770	1.730	1.690
Dividend Payout %	180.77	101.63	119.23	131.21	116.03	43.49	117.69	84.50
Income Statement								
Total Revenue	29,689,000	19,365,000	9,434,000	39,807,000	39,498,000	42,237,000	44,033,000	47,267,000
EBITDA	8,420,000	6,986,000	3,294,000	6,538,000	7,179,000	19,992,000	12,666,000	15,557,000
Depn & Amortn	3,509,000	2,355,000	1,193,000	1,600,000	1,600,000	2,500,000	6,988,000	6,978,000
Income Before Taxes	4,631,000	4,450,000	2,016,000	4,573,000	5,196,000	17,026,000	5,141,000	8,097,000
Income Taxes	1,186,000	935,000	447,000	718,000	942,000	5,349,000	1,028,000	2,440,000
Net Income	3,440,000	3,496,000	1,551,000	3,920,000	4,442,000	11,920,000	4,404,000	6,168,000
Average Shares	2,727,000	2,752,000	2,766,000	2,787,000	2,841,000	2,928,000	2,996,000	3,076,000
Balance Sheet								
Current Assets	27,919,000	28,167,000	31,530,000	30,614,000	29,764,000	33,173,000	35,685,000	34,857,000
Total Assets	91,676,000	92,804,000	96,561,000	95,377,000	101,779,000	98,335,000	105,645,000	106,132,000
Current Liabilities	19,467,000	18,758,000	19,823,000	17,204,000	19,203,000	18,766,000	17,868,000	18,348,000
Long-Term Obligations	21,838,000	21,706,000	23,437,000	24,274,000	23,929,000	18,699,000	20,539,000	16,254,000
Total Liabilities	53,428,000	53,341,000	56,724,000	55,289,000	57,103,000	49,688,000	55,880,000	53,112,000
Stockholders' Equity	38,248,000	39,463,000	39,837,000	40,088,000	44,676,000	48,647,000	49,765,000	53,020,000
Shares Outstanding	2,726,405	2,727,129	2,740,436	2,748,732	2,781,128	2,838,140	2,927,527	3,026,636
Statistical Record								
Return on Assets %	3.00	5.37	4.45	3.97	4.44	11.69	4.16	5.82
Return on Equity %	6.94	12.28	10.39	9.22	9.52	24.22	8.57	11.44
EBITDA Margin %	28.36	36.08	34.92	16.42	18.18	47.33	28.76	32.91
Net Margin %	11.59	18.05	16.44	9.85	11.25	28.22	10.00	13.05
Asset Turnover	0.42	0.42	0.41	0.40	0.39	0.41	0.42	0.45
Current Ratio	1.43	1.50	1.59	1.78	1.55	1.77	2.00	1.90
Debt to Equity	0.57	0.55	0.59	0.61	0.54	0.38	0.41	0.31
Price Range	66.58-58.43	66.58-57.61	66.58-52.91	64.96-48.59	63.03-48.42	61.88-49.49	50.18-40.85	47.96-37.18
P/E Ratio	64.02-56.18	36.18-31.31	42.68-33.92	46.07-34.46	40.40-31.04	15.20-12.16	34.14-27.79	23.98-18.59
Average Yield %	2.98	2.99	3.08	3.22	3.20	3.10	3.73	4.09

Address: 2000 Galloping Hill Road, Keniworth, NJ 07033	**Web Site:** www.merck.com	**Auditors:** PricewaterhouseCoopers LLP
Telephone: 908-740-4000	**Officers:** Kenneth C. Frazier - Chairman, President, Chief Executive Officer Robert M. Davis - Executive Vice President, Chief Financial Officer, Division Officer	**Investor Contact:** 908-423-5881
Fax: 908-735-1500		**Transfer Agents:** Wells Fargo Shareowner Services, South St. Paul, MN

MERCURY GENERAL CORP.

Exchange	Symbol	Price	52Wk Range	Yield	P/E	Div Achiever
NYS	MCY	$53.44 (12/29/2017)	64.15-51.87	4.68	29.85	30 Years

*7 Year Price Score 92.59   *NYSE Composite Index=100   *12 Month Price Score 89.01

TRADING VOLUME (thousand shares)

Interim Earnings (Per Share)

Qtr.	Mar	Jun	Sep	Dec
2014	1.32	1.73	0.57	(0.39)
2015	0.47	0.17	0.28	0.42
2016	0.42	0.88	0.49	(0.47)
2017	0.49	0.93	0.84	...

Interim Dividends (Per Share)

Amt	Decl	Ex	Rec	Pay
0.623Q	02/06/2017	03/14/2017	03/16/2017	03/30/2017
0.623Q	05/01/2017	06/13/2017	06/15/2017	06/29/2017
0.623Q	07/31/2017	09/13/2017	09/14/2017	09/28/2017
0.625Q	10/30/2017	12/13/2017	12/14/2017	12/28/2017

Indicated Div: $2.50

Valuation Analysis | **Institutional Holding**

Forecast EPS	$1.85	No of Institutions
(01/01/2018)		285
Market Cap	$3.0 Billion	Shares
Book Value	$1.8 Billion	35,284,820
Price/Book	1.66	% Held
Price/Sales	0.90	38.14

Business Summary: General Insurance (MIC: 5.2.1 SIC: 6331 NAIC: 524126)

Mercury General is an insurance holding company. Through its subsidiaries, Co. is primarily engaged in writing personal automobile insurance in 11 states, principally California. Co. also writes homeowners, commercial automobile, commercial property, mechanical breakdown, and umbrella insurance. Co. provides the following types of automobile coverage: collision, property damage, bodily injury, comprehensive, personal injury protection, underinsured and uninsured motorist, and other hazards. Co. provides the following types of homeowner's coverage: dwelling, liability, personal property, fire, and other hazards. Co. sells its policies through independent agents.

Recent Developments: For the quarter ended Sep 30 2017, net income increased 72.6% to US$46.5 million from US$26.9 million in the year-earlier quarter. Revenues were US$858.4 million, up 6.2% from US$808.2 million the year before. Net premiums earned were US$801.2 million versus US$790.9 million in the prior-year quarter, an increase of 1.3%. Net investment income rose 2.0% to US$31.0 million from US$30.4 million a year ago.

Prospects: Our evaluation of Mercury General Corp. as of Jan. 14, 2018 is the result of our systematic analysis on three basic characteristics: earnings strength, relative valuation, and recent stock price movement. The company has suffered a very negative trend in earnings per share over the past 5 quarters and while recent estimates for the company have been raised by analysts, MCY has posted better than expected results. Based on operating earnings yield, the company is about fairly valued when compared to all of the companies in our coverage universe. Share price changes over the past year indicates that MCY will perform in line with the market over the near term.

Financial Data (US$ in Thousands)	9 Mos	6 Mos	3 Mos	12/31/2016	12/31/2015	12/31/2014	12/31/2013	12/31/2012
Earnings Per Share	1.79	1.44	1.39	1.32	1.35	3.23	2.04	2.13
Cash Flow Per Share	6.41	6.52	5.71	5.19	3.45	4.48	3.82	2.69
Tang Book Value Per Share	30.94	30.69	30.35	30.46	31.66	32.60	31.62	31.90
Dividends Per Share	2.490	2.487	2.485	2.482	2.473	2.462	2.453	2.442
Dividend Payout %	139.11	172.74	178.78	188.07	183.15	76.24	120.22	114.67
Income Statement								
Premium Income	2,388,641	1,587,436	789,770	3,131,773	2,957,897	2,796,195	2,698,187	2,574,920
Total Revenue	2,558,708	1,700,351	847,504	3,227,683	3,009,300	3,011,773	2,821,041	2,783,370
Benefits & Claims	1,790,550	1,195,260	606,665	2,355,138	2,145,495	1,986,122	1,962,690	1,961,448
Income Before Taxes	157,598	99,351	30,599	70,724	70,567	247,425	132,096	135,310
Income Taxes	32,500	20,738	3,619	(2,320)	(3,912)	69,476	19,953	18,399
Net Income	125,098	78,613	26,980	73,044	74,479	177,949	112,143	116,911
Average Shares	55,334	55,323	55,312	55,304	55,209	55,020	54,964	54,922
Balance Sheet								
Total Assets	5,025,599	4,938,983	4,863,989	4,788,718	4,628,645	4,600,289	4,315,181	4,189,686
Total Liabilities	3,249,408	3,175,791	3,118,020	3,036,316	2,807,760	2,724,843	2,492,695	2,347,189
Stockholders' Equity	1,776,191	1,763,192	1,745,969	1,752,402	1,820,885	1,875,446	1,822,486	1,842,497
Shares Outstanding	55,332	55,311	55,311	55,289	55,164	55,121	54,975	54,922
Statistical Record								
Return on Assets %	2.02	1.64	1.61	1.55	1.61	3.99	2.64	2.82
Return on Equity %	5.51	4.43	4.32	4.08	4.03	9.62	6.12	6.30
Loss Ratio %	74.96	75.30	76.82	75.20	72.53	71.03	72.74	76.18
Net Margin %	4.89	4.62	3.18	2.26	2.47	5.91	3.98	4.20
Price Range	64.15-50.45	64.15-50.45	64.15-49.93	60.87-43.06	60.20-45.64	58.86-42.97	50.74-36.22	45.63-36.14
P/E Ratio	35.84-28.18	44.55-35.03	46.15-35.92	46.11-32.62	44.59-33.81	18.22-13.30	24.87-17.75	21.42-16.97
Average Yield %	4.33	4.38	4.46	4.66	4.56	5.03	5.60	5.85

Address: 4484 Wilshire Boulevard, Los Angeles, CA 90010 Telephone: 323-937-1060 Fax: 323-857-7116	Web Site: www.mercuryinsurance.com. Officers: George Joseph - Chairman Gabriel Tirador - President, Chief Executive Officer	Auditors: KPMG LLP Transfer Agents: Computershare Trust Company, N.A., Canton, MA

MEREDITH CORP

Exchange	Symbol	Price	52Wk Range	Yield	P/E	Div Achiever
NYS	MDP	$66.05 (12/29/2017)	71.80-51.15	3.15	15.95	23 Years

*7 Year Price Score 103.99 *NYSE Composite Index=100 *12 Month Price Score 102.18

Interim Earnings (Per Share)

Qtr.	Sep	Dec	Mar	Jun
2014-15	0.65	0.87	0.56	0.94
2015-16	0.24	0.72	1.79	(1.99)
2016-17	0.75	1.58	0.87	0.96
2017-18	0.73	...	...	...

Interim Dividends (Per Share)

Amt	Decl	Ex	Rec	Pay
0.52Q	01/30/2017	02/24/2017	02/28/2017	03/15/2017
0.52Q	05/10/2017	05/26/2017	05/31/2017	06/15/2017
0.52Q	08/09/2017	08/29/2017	08/31/2017	09/15/2017
0.52Q	11/08/2017	11/29/2017	11/30/2017	12/15/2017

Indicated Div: $2.08 (Div. Reinv. Plan)

Valuation Analysis | **Institutional Holding**

Forecast EPS	$3.37	No of Institutions	
	(01/03/2018)	358	
Market Cap	$3.0 Billion	Shares	
Book Value	$1.0 Billion	60,702,304	
Price/Book	2.93	% Held	
Price/Sales	1.73	69.79	

Business Summary: Advertising (MIC: 2.3.4 SIC: 2721 NAIC: 511120)

Meredith is a media company engaged in providing consumers with content and delivering the messages of Co.'s advertising and marketing partners. Co. operates two business segments: local media and national media. As of June 30 2017, Co.'s local media segment consisted of 17 television stations located across the U.S. in markets with related digital and mobile media assets. The national media segment includes national consumer media brands delivered via multiple media platforms including print magazines and digital and mobile media, brand licensing activities, database-related activities, and business-to-business marketing products and services.

Recent Developments: For the quarter ended Sep 30 2017, net income decreased 1.6% to US$33.4 million from US$34.0 million in the year-earlier quarter. Revenues were US$392.8 million, down 1.8% from US$399.9 million the year before. Operating income was US$56.8 million versus US$60.8 million in the prior-year quarter, a decrease of 6.5%. Direct operating expenses rose 3.7% to US$155.8 million from US$150.2 million in the comparable period the year before. Indirect operating expenses decreased 4.6% to US$180.2 million from US$188.9 million in the equivalent prior-year period.

Prospects: Our evaluation of Meredith Corp. as of Jan. 14, 2018 is the result of our systematic analysis on three basic characteristics: earnings strength, relative valuation, and recent stock price movement. The company has generated a negative trend in earnings per share over the past 5 quarters and while recent estimates for the company have remained steady, MDP has posted better than expected results. Based on operating earnings yield, the company is undervalued when compared to all of the companies in our coverage universe. Share price changes over the past year indicates that MDP will perform well over the near term.

Financial Data

(US$ in Thousands)	3 Mos	06/30/2017	06/30/2016	06/30/2015	06/30/2014	06/30/2013	06/30/2012	06/30/2011
Earnings Per Share	4.14	4.16	0.75	3.02	2.50	2.74	2.31	2.78
Cash Flow Per Share	5.26	4.92	5.07	4.32	3.99	4.25	4.05	4.72
Dividends Per Share	2.055	2.030	1.905	1.780	1.680	1.580	1.403	0.970
Dividend Payout %	49.64	48.80	254.00	58.94	67.20	57.66	60.71	34.89
Income Statement								
Total Revenue	392,771	1,713,361	1,649,628	1,594,176	1,468,708	1,471,340	1,376,687	1,400,480
EBITDA	74,219	361,473	186,774	297,606	230,927	254,101	229,629	272,073
Depn & Amortn	17,421	52,350	56,165	55,494	44,412	43,267	43,858	46,782
Income Before Taxes	51,720	290,334	110,207	222,760	174,339	197,404	172,875	212,353
Income Taxes	18,279	101,406	76,270	85,969	60,798	73,754	68,503	80,743
Net Income	33,441	188,928	33,937	136,791	113,541	123,650	104,372	127,432
Average Shares	45,620	45,447	45,357	45,323	45,410	45,085	45,100	45,832
Balance Sheet								
Current Assets	535,723	505,253	481,156	482,531	470,012	407,692	359,436	333,738
Total Assets	2,769,363	2,729,623	2,628,285	2,843,282	2,543,800	2,140,059	2,016,299	1,712,829
Current Liabilities	494,764	459,670	477,892	531,001	483,103	456,671	482,586	408,992
Long-Term Obligations	642,759	635,737	620,000	732,500	627,500	300,000	275,000	145,000
Total Liabilities	1,761,602	1,733,651	1,739,242	1,891,432	1,652,148	1,285,763	1,218,854	937,844
Stockholders' Equity	1,007,761	995,972	889,043	951,850	891,652	854,296	797,445	774,985
Shares Outstanding	44,676	44,552	44,556	44,620	44,476	44,566	44,507	45,058
Statistical Record								
Return on Assets %	6.97	7.05	1.24	5.08	4.85	5.95	5.58	7.41
Return on Equity %	19.70	20.05	3.68	14.84	13.01	14.97	13.24	17.42
EBITDA Margin %	18.90	21.10	11.32	18.67	15.72	17.27	16.68	19.43
Net Margin %	8.51	11.03	2.06	8.58	7.73	8.40	7.58	9.10
Asset Turnover	0.63	0.64	0.60	0.59	0.63	0.71	0.74	0.81
Current Ratio	1.08	1.10	1.01	0.91	0.97	0.89	0.74	0.82
Debt to Equity	0.64	0.64	0.70	0.77	0.70	0.35	0.34	0.19
Price Range	65.70-44.15	65.70-44.15	52.76-36.46	56.96-42.33	53.34-42.96	48.04-29.68	34.76-21.48	36.81-29.26
P/E Ratio	15.87-10.66	15.79-10.61	70.35-48.61	18.86-14.02	21.34-17.18	17.53-10.83	15.05-9.30	13.24-10.53
Average Yield %	3.59	3.60	4.12	3.51	3.56	4.35	4.84	2.92

Address: 1716 Locust Street, Des Moines, IA 50309-3023	Web Site: www.meredith.com	Auditors: KPMG LLP
Telephone: 515-284-3000	Officers: Stephen M. Lacy - Chairman, President, Chief Executive Officer, Principal Accounting Officer, Principal Financial Officer, Acting Vice President D. Mell Meredith Frazier - Vice-Chairman	Investor Contact: 515-284-3622
		Transfer Agents: Wells Fargo Bank, N.A., St. Paul, MN

METLIFE INC

Exchange	Symbol	Price	52Wk Range	Yield	P/E
NYS	MET	$50.56 (12/29/2017)	55.73-44.39	3.16	N/A

*7 Year Price Score 93.78 *NYSE Composite Index=100 *12 Month Price Score 101.63

Interim Earnings (Per Share)
Qtr.	Mar	Jun	Sep	Dec
2014	1.14	1.17	1.81	1.30
2015	1.87	0.92	1.06	0.71
2016	1.98	0.06	0.51	(1.92)
2017	0.75	0.77	(0.08)	...

Interim Dividends (Per Share)
Amt	Decl	Ex	Rec	Pay
0.00Q	06/29/2017	08/07/2017	07/19/2017	08/04/2017
0.40Q	07/07/2017	08/03/2017	08/07/2017	09/13/2017
0.40Q	10/24/2017	11/03/2017	11/06/2017	12/13/2017
0.40Q	01/05/2018	02/02/2018	02/05/2018	03/13/2018

Indicated Div: $1.60

Valuation Analysis		Institutional Holding	
Forecast EPS	$4.42	No of Institutions	
	(01/18/2018)	1455	
Market Cap	$53.3 Billion	Shares	
Book Value	$56.7 Billion	970,999,232	
Price/Book	0.94	% Held	
Price/Sales	0.86	77.61	

Business Summary: Life & Health (MIC: 5.2.2 SIC: 6311 NAIC: 524113)

MetLife is a holding company. Through its subsidiaries and affiliates, Co. is a provider of life insurance, annuities, employee benefits and asset management. In the U.S., Co. provides a range of insurance and financial services products, including life, dental, disability, property and casualty, guaranteed interest, stable value and annuities to both individuals and groups. Outside the U.S., Co. provides life, medical, dental, credit and other accident and health insurance, annuities, endowment and retirement and savings products to both individuals and groups. Co. has six segments: U.S.; Asia; Latin America; Europe, the Middle East and Africa; MetLife Holdings; and Brighthouse Financial.

Recent Developments: For the quarter ended Sep 30 2017, income from continuing operations decreased 12.8% to US$893.0 million from US$1.02 billion in the year-earlier quarter. Net loss amounted to US$75.0 million versus net income of US$573.0 million in the year-earlier quarter. Revenues were US$16.10 billion, up 1.7% from US$15.83 billion the year before. Net premiums earned were US$12.30 billion versus US$11.18 billion in the prior-year quarter, an increase of 10.1%. Net investment income fell 6.8% to US$4.30 billion from US$4.61 billion a year ago.

Prospects: Our evaluation of MetLife Inc. as of Jan. 14, 2018 is the result of our systematic analysis on three basic characteristics: earnings strength, relative valuation, and recent stock price movement. The company has generated a negative trend in earnings per share over the past 5 quarters. However, while recent estimates for the company have been mixed, MET has posted better than expected results. Based on operating earnings yield, the company is undervalued when compared to all of the companies in our coverage universe. Share price changes over the past year indicates that MET will perform well over the near term.

Financial Data
(US$ in Millions)	9 Mos	6 Mos	3 Mos	12/31/2016	12/31/2015	12/31/2014	12/31/2013	12/31/2012
Earnings Per Share	(0.48)	0.11	(0.60)	0.63	4.57	5.42	2.91	1.12
Cash Flow Per Share	14.95	13.10	13.72	13.44	12.64	14.51	14.59	15.98
Tang Book Value Per Share	44.73	56.49	54.17	53.02	53.32	55.02	46.25	50.03
Dividends Per Share	1.600	1.600	1.600	1.575	1.475	1.325	1.010	0.740
Dividend Payout %	...	1,454.55	...	250.00	32.28	24.45	34.71	66.07
Income Statement								
Premium Income	33,573	23,854	11,617	48,359	48,052	49,013	47,125	46,531
Total Revenue	46,315	33,514	16,269	63,476	69,951	73,316	68,199	68,150
Benefits & Claims	28,923	20,161	9,859	40,804	38,714	39,102	38,107	37,987
Income Before Taxes	2,482	1,819	817	(195)	7,470	8,804	4,052	1,442
Income Taxes	(148)	103	(12)	(999)	2,148	2,465	661	128
Net Income	1,629	1,710	826	800	5,310	6,309	3,368	1,324
Average Shares	1,071	1,082	1,098	1,108	1,128	1,142	1,116	1,076
Balance Sheet								
Total Assets	720,515	925,199	914,687	898,764	877,933	902,337	885,296	836,781
Total Liabilities	663,801	855,744	846,758	831,455	809,907	830,185	822,856	772,207
Stockholders' Equity	56,714	69,455	67,929	67,309	68,026	72,152	62,440	64,574
Shares Outstanding	1,054	1,063	1,081	1,095	1,098	1,131	1,122	1,091
Statistical Record								
Return on Assets %	N.M.	0.02	N.M.	0.09	0.60	0.71	0.39	0.16
Return on Equity %	N.M.	0.27	N.M.	1.18	7.58	9.38	5.30	2.12
Loss Ratio %	86.15	84.52	84.87	84.38	80.57	79.78	80.86	81.64
Net Margin %	3.52	5.10	5.08	1.26	7.59	8.61	4.94	1.94
Price Range	51.95-39.54	51.14-33.73	51.14-32.55	51.14-31.38	51.42-41.05	50.99-41.94	48.14-29.35	35.16-24.79
P/E Ratio	...	464.92-306.62	...	81.18-49.80	11.25-8.98	9.41-7.74	16.54-10.09	31.40-22.13
Average Yield %	3.40	3.61	3.77	3.94	3.22	2.81	2.56	2.44

Address: 200 Park Avenue, New York, NY 10166-0188 **Telephone:** 212-578-9500	**Web Site:** www.metlife.com **Officers:** Steven A. Kandarian - Chairman, President, Chief Executive Officer Esther S. Lee - Executive Vice President, Chief Marketing Officer	**Auditors:** Deloitte & Touche LLP **Transfer Agents:** ComputerShare Investor Services, Providence, RI	

METTLER-TOLEDO INTERNATIONAL, INC.

Exchange	Symbol	Price	52Wk Range	Yield	P/E
NYS	MTD	$619.52 (12/29/2017)	689.11-414.52	N/A	37.66

*7 Year Price Score 148.86 *NYSE Composite Index=100 *12 Month Price Score 107.64

Interim Earnings (Per Share)

Qtr.	Mar	Jun	Sep	Dec
2014	1.93	2.49	2.89	4.14
2015	2.19	2.73	3.16	4.41
2016	2.40	2.93	3.77	5.14
2017	3.48	3.84	3.99	...

Interim Dividends (Per Share)

No Dividends Paid

Valuation Analysis — **Institutional Holding**

Forecast EPS	$17.52
	(01/13/2018)
Market Cap	$15.8 Billion
Book Value	$513.0 Million
Price/Book	30.89
Price/Sales	5.96

No of Institutions	657
Shares	31,167,148
% Held	84.02

Business Summary: Industrial Machinery & Equipment (MIC: 7.2.1 SIC: 3826 NAIC: 334516)

Mettler-Toledo International is a supplier of precision instruments and services. Co. provides weighing instruments for use in laboratory, industrial and food retailing applications. Co. also provides analytical instruments for use in life science, reaction engineering and real-time analytic systems used in drug and chemical compound development, and process analytics instruments used for in-line measurement in production processes. In addition, Co. supplies end-of-line inspection systems used in production and packaging for food, pharmaceutical and other industries. Co. has five segments: U.S. Operations, Swiss Operations, Western European Operations, Chinese Operations, and Other.

Recent Developments: For the quarter ended Sep 30 2017, net income increased 3.6% to US$105.0 million from US$101.3 million in the year-earlier quarter. Revenues were US$698.8 million, up 7.4% from US$650.6 million the year before. Direct operating expenses rose 6.2% to US$298.5 million from US$281.1 million in the comparable period the year before. Indirect operating expenses increased 10.1% to US$251.5 million from US$228.4 million in the equivalent prior-year period.

Prospects: Our evaluation of Mettler-Toledo International Inc. as of Jan. 14, 2018 is the result of our systematic analysis on three basic characteristics: earnings strength, relative valuation, and recent stock price movement. The company has managed to produce a neutral trend in earnings per share over the past 5 quarters and while recent estimates for the company have been raised by analysts, MTD has posted better than expected results. Based on operating earnings yield, the company is about fairly valued when compared to all of the companies in our coverage universe. Share price changes over the past year indicates that MTD will perform very well over the near term.

Financial Data
(US$ in Thousands)

	9 Mos	6 Mos	3 Mos	12/31/2016	12/31/2015	12/31/2014	12/31/2013	12/31/2012
Earnings Per Share	16.45	16.23	15.32	14.22	12.48	11.44	9.96	9.14
Cash Flow Per Share	19.68	19.31	18.32	16.66	15.42	14.50	11.55	10.53
Tang Book Value Per Share	N.M.	N.M.	N.M.	N.M.	0.70	5.76	12.37	8.46
Income Statement								
Total Revenue	1,947,022	1,248,223	594,567	2,508,257	2,395,447	2,485,983	2,378,972	2,341,528
EBITDA	459,913	292,820	139,600	564,962	523,962	503,158	460,185	438,786
Depn & Amortn	55,431	36,213	18,011	32,743	33,087	33,617	34,765	33,421
Income Before Taxes	380,322	240,695	113,848	504,193	463,424	445,004	402,709	382,601
Income Taxes	81,326	46,649	21,382	119,823	110,604	106,763	96,615	91,754
Net Income	298,996	194,046	92,466	384,370	352,820	338,241	306,094	290,847
Average Shares	26,303	26,439	26,586	27,023	28,269	29,571	30,728	31,824
Balance Sheet								
Current Assets	986,564	913,753	912,865	896,784	862,815	849,430	913,987	864,920
Total Assets	2,497,199	2,247,950	2,203,764	2,166,777	2,018,485	2,009,110	2,152,819	2,117,400
Current Liabilities	652,358	588,809	561,162	587,515	595,127	678,890	564,188	562,677
Long-Term Obligations	1,050,681	947,781	944,211	875,056	576,984	335,790	395,960	347,131
Total Liabilities	1,984,220	1,786,031	1,763,912	1,731,834	1,438,028	1,289,515	1,217,767	1,290,181
Stockholders' Equity	512,979	461,919	439,852	434,943	580,457	719,595	935,052	827,219
Shares Outstanding	25,579	25,668	25,821	26,020	27,090	28,243	29,487	30,410
Statistical Record								
Return on Assets %	18.51	20.10	19.40	18.32	17.52	16.25	14.34	13.43
Return on Equity %	86.19	90.82	83.64	75.50	54.28	40.88	34.74	36.07
EBITDA Margin %	23.62	23.46	23.48	22.52	21.87	20.24	19.34	18.74
Net Margin %	15.36	15.55	15.55	15.32	14.73	13.61	12.87	12.42
Asset Turnover	1.13	1.21	1.21	1.20	1.19	1.19	1.11	1.08
Current Ratio	1.51	1.55	1.63	1.53	1.45	1.25	1.62	1.54
Debt to Equity	2.05	2.05	2.15	2.01	0.99	0.47	0.42	0.42
Price Range		635.17-397.73	601.16-363.19	486.90-344.76	429.91-298.14	346.92-277.62	305.89-223.80	253.27-193.30	195.00-148.68
P/E Ratio		38.61-24.18	37.04-22.38	31.78-22.50	30.23-20.97	27.80-22.25	26.74-19.56	25.47-19.41	21.33-16.27

Address: 1900 Polaris Parkway, Columbus, OH 43240 **Telephone:** 614-438-4511 **Fax:** 614-438-4646	**Web Site:** www.mt.com **Officers:** Robert F. Spoerry - Chairman Olivier A. Filliol - President, Chief Executive Officer	**Auditors:** PricewaterhouseCoopers LLP **Investor Contact:** 614-438-4748 **Transfer Agents:** Computershare Shareowner Services LLC, Jersey City, NJ

MFA FINANCIAL, INC.

Exchange	Symbol	Price	52Wk Range	Yield	P/E
NYS	MFA	$7.92 (12/29/2017)	8.87-7.76	10.10	10.70

*7 Year Price Score 83.10   ***NYSE Composite Index=100**   ***12 Month Price Score 91.71**

TRADING VOLUME (thousand shares)

Interim Earnings (Per Share)

Qtr.	Mar	Jun	Sep	Dec
2014	0.20	0.20	0.20	0.21
2015	0.21	0.20	0.20	0.19
2016	0.20	0.20	0.21	0.19
2017	0.20	0.20	0.15	...

Interim Dividends (Per Share)

Amt	Decl	Ex	Rec	Pay
0.20Q	03/08/2017	03/27/2017	03/29/2017	04/28/2017
0.20Q	06/12/2017	06/27/2017	06/29/2017	07/28/2017
0.20Q	09/14/2017	09/27/2017	09/28/2017	10/31/2017
0.20Q	12/13/2017	12/27/2017	12/28/2017	01/31/2018

Indicated Div: $0.80

Valuation Analysis		Institutional Holding	
Forecast EPS	$0.74	No of Institutions	
	(01/18/2018)	384	
Market Cap	$3.1 Billion	Shares	
Book Value	$3.3 Billion	377,810,048	
Price/Book	0.97	% Held	
Price/Sales	6.92	84.33	

Business Summary: REITs (MIC: 5.3.1 SIC: 6798 NAIC: 525930)

MFA Financial is a real estate investment trust holding company. Co. is primarily engaged in the real estate finance business. Co. engages in its business through subsidiaries that invest in residential mortgage assets, including Non-Agency mortgage-backed securities (MBS), which include Legacy Non-Agency MBS, and 3 Year Step-up securities; Agency MBS; residential whole loans, which are comprised of pools of fixed and adjustable rate residential mortgage loans acquired through consolidated trusts in secondary market transactions at discounted purchase prices; and CRT securities, which refer to credit risk transfer securities which are general obligations of Fannie Mae and Freddie Mac.

Recent Developments: For the quarter ended Sep 30 2017, net income decreased 23.1% to US$63.8 million from US$83.0 million in the year-earlier quarter. Revenues were US$134.2 million, down 8.1% from US$146.1 million the year before.

Prospects: Our evaluation of MFA Financial, Inc. as of Jan. 14, 2018 is the result of our systematic analysis on three basic characteristics: earnings strength, relative valuation, and recent stock price movement. The company has generated a negative trend in earnings per share over the past 5 quarters. However, while recent estimates for the company have been mixed, MFA has posted results that fell short of analysts expectations. Based on operating earnings yield, the company is undervalued when compared to all of the companies in our coverage universe. Share price changes over the past year indicates that MFA will perform well over the near term.

Financial Data
(US$ in Thousands)

	9 Mos	6 Mos	3 Mos	12/31/2016	12/31/2015	12/31/2014	12/31/2013	12/31/2012
Earnings Per Share	0.74	0.80	0.80	0.80	0.80	0.81	0.78	0.83
Cash Flow Per Share	0.27	0.38	0.24	0.23	0.76	0.69	0.82	0.87
Tang Book Value Per Share	8.19	8.24	8.18	8.14	7.99	8.64	8.59	9.24
Dividends Per Share	0.800	0.800	0.800	0.800	0.800	0.800	1.640	0.880
Dividend Payout %	108.11	100.00	100.00	100.00	100.00	98.77	210.26	106.02
Income Statement								
Interest Income	332,546	227,414	117,257	457,169	492,143	463,817	482,940	499,157
Interest Expense	148,646	99,371	50,349	193,355	176,948	159,808	164,013	171,670
Net Interest Income	183,900	128,043	66,908	263,814	315,195	304,009	318,927	327,487
Non-Interest Income	93,002	63,905	27,579	(485)	(705)	...	...	(1,200)
Non-Interest Expense	55,103	33,953	16,427	59,984	52,429	44,128	35,720	33,569
Net Income	221,799	157,995	78,060	312,668	313,226	313,504	302,709	306,839
Average Shares	396,698	386,303	372,579	371,122	372,114	369,048	362,399	356,762
Balance Sheet								
Net Loans & Leases	1,742,734	1,744,790	1,441,869	1,405,222	895,121	351,395	...	...
Total Assets	11,103,459	11,536,816	11,900,106	12,484,022	13,167,323	12,354,744	12,471,908	13,517,550
Total Liabilities	7,845,808	8,262,172	8,844,159	9,450,120	10,200,062	9,151,472	9,329,657	10,206,544
Stockholders' Equity	3,257,651	3,274,644	3,055,947	3,033,902	2,967,261	3,203,272	3,142,251	3,311,006
Shares Outstanding	396,939	396,311	372,819	371,854	370,584	370,084	365,125	357,546
Statistical Record								
Return on Assets %	2.47	2.57	2.53	2.43	2.45	2.53	2.33	2.42
Return on Equity %	9.36	10.08	10.57	10.39	10.15	9.88	9.38	10.54
Net Interest Margin %	53.13	55.50	57.06	57.71	64.05	65.55	66.04	65.61
Efficiency Ratio %	15.76	11.96	11.34	13.13	10.67	...	...	6.74
Price Range	8.87-7.07	8.63-7.07	8.15-6.71	8.01-5.78	8.19-6.48	8.46-7.06	9.59-7.00	8.70-6.68
P/E Ratio	11.99-9.55	10.79-8.84	10.19-8.39	10.01-7.23	10.24-8.10	10.44-8.72	12.29-8.97	10.48-8.05
Average Yield %	9.87	10.22	10.64	11.15	10.67	9.97	19.93	11.28

Address: 350 Park Avenue, 20th Floor, New York, NY 10022
Telephone: 212-207-6400
Fax: 212-207-6420

Web Site: www.mfafinancial.com
Officers: George H. Krauss - Chairman Bryan Wulfsohn - Senior Vice President

Auditors: KPMG LLP
Transfer Agents: Computershare Shareowner Services LLC, Providence, RI

MGM RESORTS INTERNATIONAL

Exchange	Symbol	Price	52Wk Range	Yield	P/E
NYS	MGM	$33.39 (12/29/2017)	34.27-25.43	N/A	32.74

*7 Year Price Score 120.66 *NYSE Composite Index=100 *12 Month Price Score 100.76

TRADING VOLUME (thousand shares)

Interim Earnings (Per Share)

Qtr.	Mar	Jun	Sep	Dec
2014	0.21	0.21	(0.04)	(0.70)
2015	0.33	0.17	0.12	(1.43)
2016	0.12	0.83	0.93	0.04
2017	0.36	0.36	0.26	...

Interim Dividends (Per Share)

No Dividends Paid

Valuation Analysis		Institutional Holding	
Forecast EPS	$1.11	No of Institutions	
	(01/18/2018)	689	
Market Cap	$18.9 Billion	Shares	
Book Value	$6.3 Billion	554,330,368	
Price/Book	2.99	% Held	
Price/Sales	1.78	65.66	

Business Summary: Hotels, Restaurants & Travel (MIC: 2.2.1 SIC: 7011 NAIC: 721120)

MGM Resorts International is a holding company. Through its subsidiaries, Co. owns and operates casino resorts, which provides gaming, hotel, convention, dining, entertainment, retail and other resort amenities. At Dec 31 2016, Co.'s domestic resorts consisted of the following casino resorts: Bellagio, MGM Grand Las Vegas, Mandalay Bay, The Mirage, Luxor, New York-New York, Excalibur, Monte Carlo and Circus Circus Las Vegas in Las Vegas, NV; MGM Grand Detroit in Detroit, MI; Beau Rivage in Biloxi, MS; Gold Strike Tunica in Tunica, MS; Borgata in Atlantic City, NJ; and MGM National Harbor in Prince George's County, MD.

Recent Developments: For the quarter ended Sep 30 2017, net income decreased 68.6% to US$176.5 million from US$561.3 million in the year-earlier quarter. Revenues were US$2.83 billion, up 12.4% from US$2.52 billion the year before. Direct operating expenses rose 11.8% to US$1.59 billion from US$1.43 billion in the comparable period the year before. Indirect operating expenses increased 96.3% to US$739.6 million from US$376.8 million in the equivalent prior-year period.

Prospects: Our evaluation of MGM Resorts International as of Jan. 14, 2018 is the result of our systematic analysis on three basic characteristics: earnings strength, relative valuation, and recent stock price movement. The company has suffered a very negative trend in earnings per share over the past 5 quarters. However, while recent estimates for the company have been mixed, MGM has posted results that fell short of analysts expectations. Based on operating earnings yield, the company is about fairly valued when compared to all of the companies in our coverage universe. Share price changes over the past year indicates that MGM will perform poorly over the near term.

Financial Data

(US$ in Thousands)	9 Mos	6 Mos	3 Mos	12/31/2016	12/31/2015	12/31/2014	12/31/2013	12/31/2012
Earnings Per Share	1.02	1.69	2.16	1.92	(0.82)	(0.31)	(0.32)	(3.62)
Cash Flow Per Share	3.48	3.23	2.99	2.69	1.85	2.30	2.68	1.85
Tang Book Value Per Share	1.02	1.27	0.92	0.55	N.M.	N.M.	N.M.	N.M.
Dividends Per Share	0.330	0.220	0.110	...	...	...	...	...
Dividend Payout %	32.35	13.02	5.09	...	...	...	...	...
Income Statement								
Total Revenue	8,176,656	5,349,916	2,708,179	9,455,123	9,190,068	10,081,984	9,809,663	9,160,844
EBITDA	1,368,326	934,090	465,505	2,369,493	436,078	2,105,320	1,943,896	519,633
Depn & Amortn	25,931	17,717	8,844	890,020	866,163	853,415	884,506	1,001,086
Income Before Taxes	830,991	568,256	282,602	784,700	(1,227,664)	434,844	202,043	(1,597,811)
Income Taxes	251,551	136,436	62,375	22,299	(6,594)	283,708	31,263	(117,301)
Net Income	566,573	417,458	206,847	1,101,440	(447,720)	(149,873)	(156,606)	(1,767,691)
Average Shares	580,676	582,056	580,165	573,317	542,873	490,875	489,661	488,988
Balance Sheet								
Current Assets	2,794,536	2,485,131	2,172,718	2,229,587	2,408,749	3,027,160	2,719,439	2,507,092
Total Assets	29,101,890	28,542,931	28,303,092	28,173,301	25,215,178	26,702,511	26,110,185	26,284,738
Current Liabilities	2,735,760	2,679,568	2,124,764	2,293,421	2,237,951	3,407,925	2,215,328	1,925,611
Long-Term Obligations	13,026,927	12,725,268	13,099,190	12,979,220	12,368,311	12,913,882	13,447,230	13,589,283
Total Liabilities	22,793,347	22,031,523	21,926,597	21,953,121	20,095,251	22,611,594	21,879,006	21,919,190
Stockholders' Equity	6,308,543	6,511,408	6,376,495	6,220,180	5,119,927	4,090,917	4,231,179	4,365,548
Shares Outstanding	565,493	575,008	574,466	574,123	564,838	491,292	490,360	489,234
Statistical Record								
Return on Assets %	2.08	3.55	4.62	4.11	N.M.	N.M.	N.M.	N.M.
Return on Equity %	9.46	16.24	21.45	19.37	N.M.	N.M.	N.M.	N.M.
EBITDA Margin %	16.73	17.46	17.19	25.06	4.75	20.88	19.82	5.67
Net Margin %	6.93	7.80	7.64	11.65	N.M.	N.M.	N.M.	N.M.
Asset Turnover	0.37	0.37	0.37	0.35	0.35	0.38	0.37	0.34
Current Ratio	1.02	0.93	1.02	0.97	1.08	0.89	1.23	1.30
Debt to Equity	2.06	1.95	2.05	2.09	2.42	3.16	3.18	3.11
Price Range	34.27-25.43	34.16-22.55	29.95-21.27	29.95-16.56	24.14-17.57	28.39-18.01	23.52-11.64	14.74-9.00
P/E Ratio	33.60-24.93	20.21-13.34	13.87-9.85	15.60-8.63	...	...	...	...
Average Yield %	1.11	0.80	0.43	...	...	...	...	...

Address: 3600 Las Vegas Boulevard South, Las Vegas, NV 89109 Telephone: 702-693-7120	Web Site: www.mgmresorts.com Officers: James J. Murren - Chairman, Chief Executive Officer William J. Hornbuckle - President, Chief Marketing Officer, Division Officer	Auditors: Deloitte & Touche LLP Transfer Agents: ComputerShare Investor Services, Providence, RI

MICHAEL KORS HOLDINGS LTD

Exchange NYS	Symbol KORS	Price $62.95 (12/29/2017)	52Wk Range 64.03-33.05	Yield N/A	P/E 17.25

*7 Year Price Score N/A   ***NYSE Composite Index=100**   ***12 Month Price Score 126.48**

Interim Earnings (Per Share)

Qtr.	Jun	Sep	Dec	Mar
2014-15	0.91	1.00	1.48	0.90
2015-16	0.87	1.01	1.59	0.99
2016-17	0.83	0.95	1.64	(0.11)
2017-18	0.80	1.32	...	...

Interim Dividends (Per Share)

No Dividends Paid

Valuation Analysis   Institutional Holding

Forecast EPS	N/A	No of Institutions 499
Market Cap	$9.6 Billion	Shares
Book Value	$1.8 Billion	151,302,480
Price/Book	5.30	% Held
Price/Sales	2.12	83.12

Business Summary: Retail - Apparel and Accessories (MIC: 2.1.5 SIC: 3199 NAIC: 316999)

Michael Kors Holdings designs, markets, distributes and a retailer of branded women's apparel and accessories and men's apparel. Co. operates its business through three operating segments: Retail, which include women's apparel, accessories (handbags and small leather goods), men's apparel, footwear and licensed products, such as watches, jewelry, fragrances and beauty, and eyewear; Wholesale, which include accessories (handbags and small leather goods), footwear and women's and men's apparel; and Licensing, which includes royalties earned on licensed products and use of Co.'s trademarks, and rights granted to third parties for the right to operate retail stores and/or sell Co.'s products.

Recent Developments: For the quarter ended Sep 30 2017, net income increased 26.1% to US$202.7 million from US$160.7 million in the year-earlier quarter. Revenues were US$1.15 billion, up 5.4% from US$1.09 billion the year before. Operating income was US$199.1 million versus US$203.7 million in the prior-year quarter, a decrease of 2.3%. Direct operating expenses rose 2.8% to US$455.8 million from US$443.5 million in the comparable period the year before. Indirect operating expenses increased 11.5% to US$491.7 million from US$441.0 million in the equivalent prior-year period.

Prospects: Our evaluation of Michael Kors Holdings Ltd. as of Sep. 17, 2017 is the result of our systematic analysis on three basic characteristics: earnings strength, relative valuation, and recent stock price movement. The company has generated a negative trend in earnings per share over the past 5 quarters. However, while recent estimates for the company have been lowered by analysts, KORS has posted better than expected results. Based on operating earnings yield, the company is undervalued when compared to all of the companies in our coverage universe. Share price changes over the past year indicates that KORS will perform very poorly over the near term.

Financial Data
(US$ in Thousands)

	6 Mos	3 Mos	04/01/2017	04/02/2016	03/28/2015	03/29/2014	03/30/2013	03/31/2012
Earnings Per Share	3.65	3.28	3.29	4.44	4.28	3.22	1.97	0.78
Cash Flow Per Share	6.67	5.82	6.21	6.49	4.24	3.13	1.82	0.73
Tang Book Value Per Share	8.41	6.91	6.77	10.80	10.85	8.54	5.02	2.22
Income Statement								
Total Revenue	2,099,000	952,400	4,493,700	4,712,100	4,371,469	3,310,843	2,181,732	1,302,254
EBITDA	477,500	193,400	890,400	1,346,200	1,387,438	1,084,640	681,351	286,311
Depn & Amortn	86,400	42,200	197,700	172,200	131,400	76,600	52,700	36,000
Income Before Taxes	389,200	150,100	688,600	1,172,300	1,255,823	1,007,647	627,127	248,816
Income Taxes	61,000	24,600	137,100	334,600	374,800	346,162	229,525	101,452
Net Income	328,400	125,500	552,500	839,100	881,023	661,485	397,602	147,364
Average Shares	154,168	156,871	168,123	189,054	205,865	205,638	201,540	189,299
Balance Sheet								
Current Assets	1,330,700	1,185,000	1,164,700	1,669,800	2,017,431	1,777,169	989,189	464,063
Total Assets	2,531,700	2,413,000	2,409,600	2,566,800	2,691,893	2,216,973	1,289,565	674,425
Current Liabilities	474,700	581,000	565,800	435,500	330,081	308,370	164,248	165,006
Long-Term Obligations	...	...	...	2,300	...	...	...	...
Total Liabilities	726,700	832,100	817,000	571,100	450,928	410,842	242,319	218,188
Stockholders' Equity	1,805,000	1,580,900	1,592,600	1,995,700	2,240,965	1,806,131	1,047,246	456,237
Shares Outstanding	152,066	151,593	155,833	176,441	199,656	204,261	201,454	192,731
Statistical Record								
Return on Assets %	21.67	20.80	22.27	31.40	35.99	37.83	40.60	27.52
Return on Equity %	32.87	31.83	30.88	38.97	43.66	46.49	53.04	50.24
EBITDA Margin %	22.75	20.31	19.81	28.57	31.74	32.76	31.23	21.99
Net Margin %	15.65	13.18	12.29	17.81	20.15	19.98	18.22	11.32
Asset Turnover	1.71	1.75	1.81	1.76	1.79	1.89	2.23	2.43
Current Ratio	2.80	2.04	2.06	3.83	6.11	5.76	6.02	2.81
Price Range	51.76-33.05	52.90-33.05	56.35-36.02	66.26-35.57	97.01-64.33	99.84-52.36	64.84-36.04	49.59-24.10
P/E Ratio	14.18-9.05	16.13-10.08	17.13-10.95	14.92-8.01	22.67-15.03	31.01-16.26	32.91-18.29	63.58-30.90

Address: 33 Kingsway, London, WC2B 6UF Telephone: 207-632-8600	Web Site: www.michaelkors.com Officers: John D. Idol - Chairman, Chief Executive Officer Michael David Kors - Honorary Chairman, Chief Creative Officer	Auditors: Ernst & Young LLP Investor Contact: 203-682-8200 Transfer Agents: American Stock Transfer & Trust Company, LLC, Brooklyn, NY

MID-AMERICA APARTMENT COMMUNITIES INC

Exchange	Symbol	Price	52Wk Range	Yield	P/E
NYS	MAA	$100.56 (12/29/2017)	110.32-93.78	3.67	46.13

*7 Year Price Score 103.03 *NYSE Composite Index=100 *12 Month Price Score 94.70

Interim Earnings (Per Share)

Qtr.	Mar	Jun	Sep	Dec
2014	0.20	0.42	0.89	0.46
2015	0.81	1.81	1.22	0.57
2016	0.58	0.60	1.12	0.40
2017	0.36	0.42	1.00	...

Interim Dividends (Per Share)

Amt	Decl	Ex	Rec	Pay
0.87Q	03/23/2017	04/11/2017	04/13/2017	04/28/2017
0.87Q	05/23/2017	07/12/2017	07/14/2017	07/31/2017
0.87Q	09/26/2017	10/12/2017	10/13/2017	10/31/2017
0.922Q	12/05/2017	01/11/2018	01/12/2018	01/31/2018

Indicated Div: $3.69 (Div. Reinv. Plan)

Valuation Analysis — **Institutional Holding**

Forecast EPS	$2.28 (01/18/2018)	No of Institutions 545
Market Cap	$11.4 Billion	Shares 123,165,288
Book Value	$6.3 Billion	% Held 94.47
Price/Book	1.81	
Price/Sales	7.86	

Business Summary: REITs (MIC: 5.3.1 SIC: 6798 NAIC: 525930)

Mid-America Apartment Communities is a self-administered and self-managed real estate investment trust. Co. owns, operates, acquires and develops apartment communities mainly located in the Southeast and Southwest regions of the U.S. As of Dec 31 2016, Co.'s activities included ownership and operation of 302 multi-family properties and four commercial properties located in Alabama, Arizona, Arkansas, Florida, Georgia, Kansas, Kentucky, Maryland, Mississippi, Missouri, Nevada, North Carolina, South Carolina, Tennessee, Texas, Virginia and Washington, D.C. Co.'s business is conducted principally through Mid-America Apartments, L.P., in which Co. is the sole general partner.

Recent Developments: For the quarter ended Sep 30 2017, net income increased 33.8% to US$119.0 million from US$88.9 million in the year-earlier quarter. Revenues were US$384.6 million, up 38.9% from US$276.9 million the year before.

Prospects: Our evaluation of Mid-America Apartment Communities Inc. as of Jan. 14, 2018 is the result of our systematic analysis on three basic characteristics: earnings strength, relative valuation, and recent stock price movement. The company has generated a negative trend in earnings per share over the past 5 quarters. Because the company lacks sufficient analyst estimate data, we place greater weight on the historical EPS trend as the measure of earnings strength. Based on operating earnings yield, the company is overvalued when compared to all of the companies in our coverage universe. Share price changes over the past year indicates that MAA will perform very well over the near term.

Financial Data

(US$ in Thousands)	9 Mos	6 Mos	3 Mos	12/31/2016	12/31/2015	12/31/2014	12/31/2013	12/31/2012
Earnings Per Share	2.18	2.30	2.48	2.69	4.41	1.97	2.25	2.56
Cash Flow Per Share	5.71	5.01	4.57	6.15	6.17	5.12	5.22	5.13
Tang Book Value Per Share	55.68	55.52	55.99	56.49	39.77	38.45	39.39	21.61
Dividends Per Share	3.430	3.380	3.330	3.280	3.080	2.920	2.780	2.640
Dividend Payout %	157.34	146.96	134.27	121.93	69.84	148.22	123.56	103.13
Income Statement								
Total Revenue	1,146,249	761,699	378,908	1,125,348	1,042,779	989,296	634,734	497,165
EBITDA	312,756	159,867	74,468	669,270	754,146	545,035	297,550	261,519
Depn & Amortn	(8,035)	(6,023)	(3,147)	313,463	279,382	280,462	183,803	131,428
Income Before Taxes	213,418	94,154	43,710	225,860	352,420	145,109	37,832	71,340
Income Taxes	1,910	1,269	651	1,699	1,673	2,050	893	...
Net Income	204,929	90,220	41,905	212,222	332,287	147,980	115,281	105,223
Average Shares	113,653	113,614	117,864	78,800	75,176	74,982	53,116	42,937
Balance Sheet								
Current Assets	128,104	67,518	58,499	121,800	63,641	53,582	133,694	9,883
Total Assets	11,532,801	11,534,129	11,559,699	11,604,491	6,847,781	6,831,028	6,841,925	2,751,068
Current Liabilities	38,875	37,195	37,766	30,799	17,545	18,921	24,337	11,255
Long-Term Obligations	4,492,834	4,573,052	4,557,184	4,499,712	3,427,568	3,524,515	3,472,718	1,673,848
Total Liabilities	5,205,070	5,225,380	5,199,505	5,190,599	3,847,434	3,934,593	3,890,064	1,832,303
Stockholders' Equity	6,327,731	6,308,749	6,360,194	6,413,892	3,000,347	2,896,435	2,951,861	918,765
Shares Outstanding	113,627	113,607	113,574	113,518	75,408	75,267	74,830	42,316
Statistical Record								
Return on Assets %	2.65	2.32	2.29	2.29	4.86	2.16	2.40	3.97
Return on Equity %	5.24	4.61	4.51	4.50	11.27	5.06	5.96	12.79
EBITDA Margin %	27.29	20.99	19.65	59.47	72.32	55.09	46.88	52.60
Net Margin %	17.88	11.84	11.06	18.86	31.87	14.96	18.16	21.16
Asset Turnover	0.16	0.15	0.13	0.12	0.15	0.14	0.13	0.19
Current Ratio	3.30	1.82	1.55	3.95	3.63	2.83	5.49	0.88
Debt to Equity	0.71	0.72	0.72	0.70	1.14	1.22	1.18	1.82
Price Range	110.32-85.94	110.32-85.94	109.67-85.94	109.67-84.64	92.40-71.15	76.24-60.74	74.41-59.70	70.20-58.49
P/E Ratio	50.61-39.42	47.97-37.37	44.22-34.65	40.77-31.46	20.95-16.13	38.70-30.83	33.07-26.53	27.42-22.85
Average Yield %	3.44	3.43	3.41	3.41	3.87	4.19	4.22	4.02

Address: 6584 Poplar Avenue, Memphis, TN 38138	Web Site: www.maac.com	Auditors: Ernst & Young LLP
Telephone: 901-682-6600	Officers: H. Eric Bolton - Chairman, President, Chief Executive Officer Thomas L. Grimes - Executive Vice President, Chief Operating Officer	Investor Contact: 901-682-6600
Fax: 901-682-6667		Transfer Agents: American Stock Transfer & Trust Company

MINERALS TECHNOLOGIES, INC.

Exchange	Symbol	Price	52Wk Range	Yield	P/E
NYS	MTX	$68.85 (12/29/2017)	83.70-62.95	0.29	15.68

*7 Year Price Score 108.47 *NYSE Composite Index=100   *12 Month Price Score 90.03

Interim Earnings (Per Share)

Qtr.	Mar	Jun	Sep	Dec
2014	0.45	0.53	1.06	0.60
2015	1.01	0.76	0.83	0.48
2016	0.97	0.60	1.18	1.04
2017	0.97	1.21	1.17	...

Interim Dividends (Per Share)

Amt	Decl	Ex	Rec	Pay
0.05Q	01/18/2017	02/15/2017	02/17/2017	03/09/2017
0.05Q	05/16/2017	05/26/2017	05/31/2017	06/09/2017
0.05Q	07/19/2017	08/23/2017	08/25/2017	09/07/2017
0.05Q	11/15/2017	11/24/2017	11/27/2017	12/08/2017

Indicated Div: $0.20

Valuation Analysis

		Institutional Holding	
Forecast EPS	$4.56	No of Institutions	
	(11/02/2017)	311	
Market Cap	$2.4 Billion	Shares	
Book Value	$1.2 Billion	41,556,984	
Price/Book	2.07	% Held	
Price/Sales	1.48	93.01	

Business Summary: Specialty Chemicals (MIC: 8.3.2 SIC: 2819 NAIC: 325188)

Minerals Technologies is a resource- and technology-based company. Co.'s segments are: Specialty Minerals, which provides synthetic mineral product precipitated calcium carbonate and processed mineral product quicklime, and mines mineral ores and processes and sells mineral products; Refractories, which provides monolithic and shaped refractory materials and specialty products, and calcium metal and metallurgical wire products; Performance Materials, which supplies bentonite and bentonite-related products; Construction Technologies, which provides products for non-residential construction, environmental and infrastructure projects; and Energy Services, which serves the oil and gas industry.

Recent Developments: For the quarter ended Oct 1 2017, net income increased 0.9% to US$42.9 million from US$42.5 million in the year-earlier quarter. Revenues were US$424.4 million, up 6.2% from US$399.5 million the year before. Operating income was US$66.8 million versus US$67.3 million in the prior-year quarter, a decrease of 0.7%. Direct operating expenses rose 7.4% to US$305.2 million from US$284.3 million in the comparable period the year before. Indirect operating expenses increased 9.4% to US$52.4 million from US$47.9 million in the equivalent prior-year period.

Prospects: Our evaluation of Minerals Technologies Inc. as of Jan. 14, 2018 is the result of our systematic analysis on three basic characteristics: earnings strength, relative valuation, and recent stock price movement. The company has managed to produce a neutral trend in earnings per share over the past 5 quarters and while recent estimates for the company have remained steady, MTX has posted better than expected results. Based on operating earnings yield, the company is undervalued when compared to all of the companies in our coverage universe. Share price changes over the past year indicates that MTX will perform very poorly over the near term.

Financial Data

(US$ in Thousands)	9 Mos	6 Mos	3 Mos	12/31/2016	12/31/2015	12/31/2014	12/31/2013	12/31/2012
Earnings Per Share	4.39	4.40	3.79	3.79	3.08	2.65	2.30	2.09
Cash Flow Per Share	5.99	5.72	5.69	6.43	7.78	9.61	3.89	3.95
Tang Book Value Per Share	5.61	3.81	2.13	0.67	N.M.	N.M.	22.80	20.73
Dividends Per Share	0.200	0.200	0.200	0.200	0.200	0.200	0.200	0.125
Dividend Payout %	4.56	4.55	5.28	5.28	6.49	7.55	8.70	5.98
Income Statement								
Total Revenue	1,243,500	819,100	405,000	1,638,000	1,797,600	1,725,000	1,018,181	1,005,619
EBITDA	256,700	167,800	79,000	300,100	283,400	246,200	168,657	155,799
Depn & Amortn	67,000	43,200	21,700	75,400	89,900	81,400	44,700	48,700
Income Before Taxes	157,200	102,600	45,500	170,300	132,600	123,000	123,710	107,046
Income Taxes	35,600	23,500	10,100	35,300	22,800	30,800	34,515	30,777
Net Income	119,300	77,600	34,600	133,400	107,900	92,400	80,330	74,147
Average Shares	35,600	35,600	35,600	35,200	35,000	34,800	34,976	35,529
Balance Sheet								
Current Assets	860,800	804,000	786,100	751,100	803,600	924,600	815,117	764,485
Total Assets	2,983,400	2,917,000	2,896,700	2,863,400	2,980,000	3,226,700	1,217,547	1,211,189
Current Liabilities	323,700	298,300	297,400	295,500	318,600	352,900	180,894	250,098
Long-Term Obligations	990,200	1,019,300	1,050,700	1,069,900	1,255,300	1,455,500	75,000	8,478
Total Liabilities	1,807,100	1,803,400	1,840,700	1,856,900	2,069,500	2,363,700	370,009	420,778
Stockholders' Equity	1,176,300	1,113,600	1,056,000	1,006,500	910,500	863,000	847,538	790,411
Shares Outstanding	35,366	35,093	35,086	34,969	34,784	34,649	34,350	34,949
Statistical Record								
Return on Assets %	5.27	5.32	4.56	4.55	3.48	4.16	6.61	6.22
Return on Equity %	14.25	15.00	13.36	13.88	12.17	10.80	9.81	9.65
EBITDA Margin %	20.64	20.49	19.51	18.32	15.77	14.27	16.56	15.49
Net Margin %	9.59	9.47	8.54	8.14	6.00	5.36	7.89	7.37
Asset Turnover	0.56	0.55	0.56	0.56	0.58	0.78	0.84	0.84
Current Ratio	2.66	2.70	2.64	2.54	2.52	2.62	4.51	3.06
Debt to Equity	0.84	0.92	0.99	1.06	1.38	1.69	0.09	0.01
Price Range	83.70-62.95	83.70-56.00	83.70-52.53	82.90-37.03	74.74-45.35	77.40-48.81	60.40-38.43	39.92-28.79
P/E Ratio	19.07-14.34	19.02-12.73	22.08-13.86	21.87-9.77	24.27-14.72	29.21-18.42	26.26-16.71	19.10-13.77
Average Yield %	0.27	0.27	0.29	0.33	0.32	0.32	0.42	0.37

Address: 622 Third Avenue, New York, NY 10017-6707	Web Site: www.mineralstech.com	Auditors: KPMG LLP
Telephone: 212-878-1800	Officers: Duane R. Dunham - Chairman Douglas T. Dietrich - Chief Executive Officer, Interim Co-Chief Executive Officer, Chief Financial Officer, Senior Vice President, Vice President	Investor Contact: 212-878-1831 Transfer Agents: Computershare Trust Company, N. A., Providence, RI

MOHAWK INDUSTRIES, INC.

Exchange	Symbol	Price	52Wk Range	Yield	P/E
NYS	MHK	$275.90 (12/29/2017)	284.82-201.74	N/A	21.37

*7 Year Price Score 132.22 *NYSE Composite Index=100 *12 Month Price Score 106.35

Interim Earnings (Per Share)

Qtr.	Mar	Jun	Sep	Dec
2014	1.11	2.08	2.06	2.00
2015	0.30	2.53	2.89	2.58
2016	2.30	3.42	3.62	3.14
2017	2.68	3.48	3.61	...

Interim Dividends (Per Share)

No Dividends Paid

Valuation Analysis | Institutional Holding

Forecast EPS	$13.52	No of Institutions
	(01/18/2018)	741
Market Cap	$20.5 Billion	Shares
Book Value	$6.8 Billion	72,657,376
Price/Book	3.02	% Held
Price/Sales	2.20	82.98

TRADING VOLUME (thousand shares)

Business Summary: Construction Materials (MIC: 8.5.1 SIC: 2273 NAIC: 314110)

Mohawk Industries is a flooring manufacturer for residential and commercial spaces. Co. has three segments: Global Ceramic, which designs, manufactures, sources and markets a line of ceramic tile, porcelain tile, natural stone and other products; Flooring North America, which designs, manufactures, sources and markets its floor covering product lines, including carpets, rugs, carpet pad, hardwood, laminate and vinyl products, including vinyl tile; and Flooring Rest of the World, which designs, manufactures, sources, licenses and markets laminate, hardwood flooring, roofing elements, insulation boards, medium-density fiberboard, chipboards, other wood products and vinyl products.

Recent Developments:
For the quarter ended Sep 30 2017, net income increased 0.1% to US$271.0 million from US$270.8 million in the year-earlier quarter. Revenues were US$2.45 billion, up 6.7% from US$2.29 billion the year before. Operating income was US$380.1 million versus US$378.3 million in the prior-year quarter, an increase of 0.5%. Direct operating expenses rose 6.2% to US$1.67 billion from US$1.57 billion in the comparable period the year before. Indirect operating expenses increased 15.8% to US$403.2 million from US$348.3 million in the equivalent prior-year period.

Prospects:
Our evaluation of Mohawk Industries Inc. as of Jan. 14, 2018 is the result of our systematic analysis on three basic characteristics: earnings strength, relative valuation, and recent stock price movement. The company has managed to produce a neutral trend in earnings per share over the past 5 quarters and while recent estimates for the company have been mixed, MHK has posted better than expected results. Based on operating earnings yield, the company is undervalued when compared to all of the companies in our coverage universe. Share price changes over the past year indicates that MHK will perform very well over the near term.

Financial Data

(US$ in Thousands)	9 Mos	6 Mos	3 Mos	12/31/2016	12/31/2015	12/31/2014	12/31/2013	12/31/2012
Earnings Per Share	12.91	12.92	12.86	12.48	8.31	7.25	4.82	3.61
Cash Flow Per Share	16.37	16.04	18.27	17.87	12.40	9.09	7.32	8.49
Tang Book Value Per Share	46.33	42.39	39.41	35.96	21.97	28.96	26.32	25.74
Income Statement								
Total Revenue	7,122,193	4,673,683	2,220,645	8,959,087	8,071,563	7,803,446	7,348,754	5,787,980
EBITDA	1,337,552	845,224	382,640	1,647,905	1,148,433	1,077,938	814,249	596,598
Depn & Amortn	328,300	214,785	105,024	366,233	328,486	315,840	276,432	217,393
Income Before Taxes	985,398	613,844	269,414	1,241,125	748,861	663,891	445,571	304,492
Income Taxes	251,572	151,040	68,358	307,559	131,875	131,637	78,385	53,599
Net Income	731,260	461,235	200,554	930,362	615,302	531,965	348,786	250,258
Average Shares	74,841	74,801	74,754	74,568	74,043	73,363	72,301	69,306
Balance Sheet								
Current Assets	3,997,110	4,010,723	3,734,982	3,471,512	3,249,972	3,132,270	3,085,718	2,550,046
Total Assets	11,822,813	11,589,491	10,727,517	10,230,596	9,942,364	8,285,544	8,494,177	6,303,684
Current Liabilities	2,697,018	3,220,735	2,828,327	2,718,320	3,259,028	1,955,814	1,320,811	828,649
Long-Term Obligations	1,544,665	1,174,440	1,132,268	1,128,747	1,196,928	1,402,135	2,132,790	1,327,729
Total Liabilities	5,033,761	5,143,013	4,670,105	4,454,145	5,088,191	3,867,538	4,033,120	2,584,067
Stockholders' Equity	6,789,052	6,446,478	6,057,412	5,776,451	4,854,173	4,418,006	4,461,057	3,719,617
Shares Outstanding	74,338	74,338	74,302	74,168	73,929	72,913	72,686	69,153
Statistical Record								
Return on Assets %	8.68	8.81	9.13	9.20	6.75	6.34	4.71	3.99
Return on Equity %	15.50	16.32	17.12	17.46	13.27	11.98	8.53	7.00
EBITDA Margin %	18.78	18.08	17.23	18.39	14.23	13.81	11.08	10.31
Net Margin %	10.27	9.87	9.03	10.38	7.62	6.82	4.75	4.32
Asset Turnover	0.84	0.84	0.86	0.89	0.89	0.93	0.99	0.92
Current Ratio	1.48	1.25	1.32	1.28	1.00	1.60	2.34	3.08
Debt to Equity	0.23	0.18	0.19	0.20	0.25	0.32	0.48	0.36
Price Range	259.69-176.98	246.65-176.98	231.90-176.98	216.22-151.78	211.33-152.74	157.60-124.77	148.90-90.47	91.29-59.39
P/E Ratio	20.12-13.71	19.09-13.70	18.03-13.76	17.33-12.16	25.43-18.38	21.74-17.21	30.89-18.77	25.29-16.45

Address: 160 S. Industrial Blvd., Calhoun, GA 30701 Telephone: 706-629-7721	Web Site: www.mohawkind.com Officers: Jeffrey S. Lorberbaum - Chairman, Chief Executive Officer W. Christopher Wellborn - President, Chief Operating Officer	Auditors: KPMG LLP Investor Contact: 706-624-2695 Transfer Agents: American Stock Transfer and Trust Company, Addison, TX

MOLINA HEALTHCARE INC

Exchange	Symbol	Price	52Wk Range	Yield	P/E
NYS	MOH	$76.68 (12/29/2017)	79.18-42.70	N/A	N/A

*7 Year Price Score 110.04 *NYSE Composite Index=100 *12 Month Price Score 113.91

TRADING VOLUME (thousand shares)

Interim Earnings (Per Share)

Qtr.	Mar	Jun	Sep	Dec
2014	0.09	0.16	0.33	0.70
2015	0.56	0.72	0.77	0.51
2016	0.43	0.58	0.76	(0.85)
2017	1.37	(4.10)	(1.70)	...

Interim Dividends (Per Share)

No Dividends Paid

Valuation Analysis		Institutional Holding	
Forecast EPS	$-3.51	No of Institutions	
	(01/18/2018)	354	
Market Cap	$4.4 Billion	Shares	
Book Value	$1.4 Billion	69,360,544	
Price/Book	3.06	% Held	
Price/Sales	0.22	74.21	

Business Summary: Hospitals & Health Care Facilities (MIC: 4.2.1 SIC: 6324 NAIC: 524114)

Molina Healthcare provides Medicaid-related solutions for low-income families and individuals, and to assist government agencies in their administration of the Medicaid program. Co. has three reportable segments: Health Plans, which consists of health plans in 12 states and the Commonwealth of Puerto Rico, and includes Co.'s direct delivery business; Molina Medicaid Solutions, which provides support to state government agencies in the administration of their Medicaid programs including business processing, information technology development, and administrative services; and Others, which includes primarily Co.'s Pathways behavioral health and social services provider.

Recent Developments: For the quarter ended Sep 30 2017, net loss amounted to US$97.0 million versus net income of US$42.0 million in the year-earlier quarter. Revenues were US$5.03 billion, up 10.7% from US$4.55 billion the year before. Net premiums earned were US$4.88 billion versus US$4.32 billion in the prior-year quarter, an increase of 13.1%.

Prospects: Our evaluation of Molina Healthcare Inc. as of Jan. 14, 2018 is the result of our systematic analysis on three basic characteristics: earnings strength, relative valuation, and recent stock price movement. The company has produced a positive trend in earnings per share over the past 5 quarters. Because the company lacks sufficient analyst estimate data, we place greater weight on the historical EPS trend as the measure of earnings strength. Based on operating earnings yield, the company is overvalued when compared to all of the companies in our coverage universe. Share price changes over the past year indicates that MOH will perform poorly over the near term.

Financial Data
(US$ in Thousands)

	9 Mos	6 Mos	3 Mos	12/31/2016	12/31/2015	12/31/2014	12/31/2013	12/31/2012
Earnings Per Share	(5.28)	(2.82)	1.86	0.92	2.58	1.29	1.13	0.21
Cash Flow Per Share	17.49	19.05	22.38	12.20	21.63	22.59	4.16	7.48
Tang Book Value Per Share	15.75	14.91	17.12	15.60	16.36	13.06	12.28	11.84
Income Statement								
Total Revenue	14,934,000	9,903,000	4,904,000	17,782,000	14,178,000	9,666,601	6,588,934	6,028,763
EBITDA	(187,000)	(114,000)	165,000	351,000	437,000	226,715	159,817	56,334
Depn & Amortn	24,000	16,000	8,000	45,000	49,000	34,600	26,600	20,500
Income Before Taxes	(296,000)	(183,000)	131,000	205,000	322,000	135,304	81,146	19,065
Income Taxes	(46,000)	(30,000)	54,000	153,000	179,000	72,726	36,316	9,275
Net Income	(250,000)	(153,000)	77,000	52,000	143,000	62,223	52,929	9,790
Average Shares	57,000	56,000	56,000	56,000	56,000	48,340	46,862	46,999
Balance Sheet								
Current Assets	7,708,000	7,169,000	6,402,000	5,988,000	5,306,000	3,245,397	2,039,664	1,349,126
Total Assets	8,954,000	8,583,000	8,038,000	7,449,000	6,576,000	4,477,215	3,002,937	1,934,822
Current Liabilities	5,962,000	5,793,000	4,422,000	4,570,000	3,822,000	2,174,773	1,293,976	828,037
Long-Term Obligations	1,515,000	1,215,000	1,653,000	1,173,000	1,160,000	905,048	602,854	261,784
Total Liabilities	7,525,000	7,062,000	6,311,000	5,800,000	5,019,000	3,466,773	2,110,000	1,152,508
Stockholders' Equity	1,429,000	1,521,000	1,727,000	1,649,000	1,557,000	1,010,442	892,937	782,314
Shares Outstanding	57,000	57,000	57,000	57,000	56,000	49,727	45,871	46,762
Statistical Record								
Return on Assets %	N.M.	N.M.	1.38	0.74	2.59	1.66	2.14	0.54
Return on Equity %	N.M.	N.M.	6.33	3.24	11.14	6.54	6.32	1.27
EBITDA Margin %	N.M.	N.M.	3.36	1.97	3.08	2.35	2.43	0.93
Net Margin %	N.M.	N.M.	1.57	0.29	1.01	0.64	0.80	0.16
Asset Turnover	2.36	2.41	2.41	2.53	2.57	2.58	2.67	3.35
Current Ratio	1.29	1.24	1.45	1.31	1.39	1.49	1.58	1.63
Debt to Equity	1.06	0.80	0.96	0.71	0.75	0.90	0.68	0.33
Price Range	72.05-42.70	71.33-42.70	67.72-42.70	67.72-45.34	81.50-49.87	54.09-32.73	40.69-25.73	36.78-17.77
P/E Ratio	...	...	36.41-22.96	73.61-49.28	31.59-19.33	41.93-25.37	36.01-22.77	175.14-84.62

Address: 200 Oceangate, Suite 100, Long Beach, CA 90802	**Web Site:** www.molinahealthcare.com	**Auditors:** Ernst & Young LLP
Telephone: 562-435-3666	**Officers:** Joseph M. Zubretsky - President, Chief Executive Officer Joseph W. White - Interim President, Interim Chief Executive Officer, Chief Financial Officer, Treasurer, Chief Accounting Officer, Vice President	**Transfer Agents:** American Stock Transfer & Trust Company, New York, NY
Fax: 562-437-1335		

MOLSON COORS BREWING CO.

Exchange	Symbol	Price	52Wk Range	Yield	P/E
NYS	TAP	$82.07 (12/29/2017)	101.59-76.52	2.00	7.86

*7 Year Price Score 104.93 *NYSE Composite Index=100 *12 Month Price Score 83.64

Interim Earnings (Per Share)

Qtr.	Mar	Jun	Sep	Dec
2014	0.88	1.56	(0.19)	0.50
2015	0.43	1.23	0.09	0.18
2016	0.78	0.80	0.94	6.73
2017	0.93	1.49	1.29	...

Interim Dividends (Per Share)

Amt	Decl	Ex	Rec	Pay
0.41Q	02/16/2017	02/24/2017	02/28/2017	03/15/2017
0.41Q	05/18/2017	05/26/2017	05/31/2017	06/15/2017
0.41Q	07/13/2017	08/29/2017	08/31/2017	09/15/2017
0.41Q	11/16/2017	11/29/2017	11/30/2017	12/15/2017

Indicated Div: $1.64

Valuation Analysis / Institutional Holding

Forecast EPS	$4.32	No of Institutions
	(01/18/2018)	752
Market Cap	$17.7 Billion	Shares
Book Value	$12.5 Billion	195,717,552
Price/Book	1.42	% Held
Price/Sales	1.65	70.86

TRADING VOLUME (thousand shares)

Business Summary: Beverages (MIC: 1.2.2 SIC: 2082 NAIC: 312120)

Molson Coors Brewing is a holding company. Co. is a brewer and has a portfolio of owned and partner brands, including primary brands Carling, Coors Light, Miller Lite, Molson Canadian and Staropramen, as well as craft and specialty beers such as the Blue Moon Brewing Company brands, Creemore Springs, Cobra and Doom Bar. Co.'s reporting segments include: MillerCoors LLC, operating in the U.S.; Molson Coors Canada, operating in Canada; Molson Coors Europe, operating in Bulgaria, Croatia, Czech Republic, Hungary, Montenegro, Republic of Ireland, Romania, Serbia, the U.K. and various other European countries; and Molson Coors International, operating in various other countries.

Recent Developments: For the quarter ended Sep 30 2017, income from continuing operations increased 40.5% to US$286.3 million from US$203.8 million in the year-earlier quarter. Net income increased 40.4% to US$286.1 million from US$203.8 million in the year-earlier quarter. Revenues were US$2.88 billion, up 204.3% from US$947.6 million the year before. Operating income was US$506.7 million versus US$289.2 million in the prior-year quarter, an increase of 75.2%. Direct operating expenses rose 193.7% to US$1.59 billion from US$541.3 million in the comparable period the year before. Indirect operating expenses increased 572.0% to US$786.9 million from US$117.1 million in the equivalent prior-year period.

Prospects: Our evaluation of Molson Coors Brewing Co. as of Jan. 14, 2018 is the result of our systematic analysis on three basic characteristics: earnings strength, relative valuation, and recent stock price movement. The company has managed to produce a neutral trend in earnings per share over the past 5 quarters and while recent estimates for the company have been raised by analysts, TAP has posted results that were in line with analysts expectations. Based on operating earnings yield, the company is undervalued when compared to all of the companies in our coverage universe. Share price changes over the past year indicates that TAP will perform poorly over the near term.

Financial Data

(US$ in Thousands)	9 Mos	6 Mos	3 Mos	12/31/2016	12/31/2015	12/31/2014	12/31/2013	12/29/2012
Earnings Per Share	10.44	10.09	9.40	9.26	1.93	2.76	3.08	2.44
Cash Flow Per Share	7.62	7.80	5.13	5.30	3.76	6.88	6.35	5.46
Tang Book Value Per Share	N.M.	N.M.	N.M.	N.M.	1.70	N.M.	N.M.	N.M.
Dividends Per Share	1.640	1.640	1.640	1.640	1.640	1.480	1.280	1.280
Dividend Payout %	15.71	16.25	17.45	17.71	84.97	53.62	41.56	52.46
Income Statement								
Total Revenue	8,423,200	5,540,000	2,448,700	4,885,000	3,567,500	4,146,300	4,206,100	3,916,500
EBITDA	1,430,400	919,800	376,100	3,085,100	290,900	426,600	558,100	496,500
Depn & Amortn	17,600	11,200	6,500	306,300	284,500	268,400	272,500	230,300
Income Before Taxes	1,154,400	722,800	273,000	2,534,400	(105,600)	24,500	115,500	81,200
Income Taxes	332,900	187,600	64,600	1,050,700	51,800	69,000	84,000	154,500
Net Income	804,600	524,600	201,300	1,975,900	359,500	514,000	567,300	443,000
Average Shares	216,500	216,400	216,500	213,400	186,400	186,100	184,200	181,800
Balance Sheet								
Current Assets	2,916,400	2,489,000	2,279,200	2,169,600	1,258,800	1,578,900	1,537,700	1,748,000
Total Assets	30,677,700	30,118,600	29,542,900	29,341,500	12,276,300	13,996,300	15,880,100	16,212,200
Current Liabilities	4,256,200	3,308,100	3,048,700	3,157,500	1,217,200	2,325,300	2,142,100	2,598,700
Long-Term Obligations	10,574,200	11,185,100	11,443,100	11,387,700	2,908,700	2,337,100	3,213,000	3,422,500
Total Liabilities	18,189,500	18,022,700	17,944,600	17,922,800	5,233,300	6,133,000	6,941,200	8,245,300
Stockholders' Equity	12,488,200	12,095,900	11,598,300	11,418,700	7,043,000	7,863,300	8,638,900	7,966,900
Shares Outstanding	215,400	215,300	215,300	214,900	184,500	185,500	184,200	181,500
Statistical Record								
Return on Assets %	8.48	9.53	9.00	9.47	2.74	3.48	3.55	3.10
Return on Equity %	20.02	19.73	18.74	21.35	4.82	6.23	6.80	5.69
EBITDA Margin %	16.98	16.60	15.36	63.15	8.15	10.29	13.27	12.68
Net Margin %	9.55	9.47	8.22	40.45	10.08	12.40	13.49	11.31
Asset Turnover	0.41	0.39	0.30	0.23	0.27	0.28	0.26	0.27
Current Ratio	0.69	0.75	0.75	0.69	1.03	0.68	0.72	0.67
Debt to Equity	0.85	0.92	0.99	1.00	0.41	0.30	0.37	0.43
Price Range	111.25-81.35	111.25-85.77	111.25-92.30	111.25-83.63	95.14-65.19	77.75-51.32	56.15-41.83	46.00-38.28
P/E Ratio	10.66-7.79	11.03-8.50	11.84-9.82	12.01-9.03	49.30-33.78	28.17-18.59	18.23-13.58	18.85-15.69
Average Yield %	1.72	1.66	1.64	1.68	2.10	2.21	2.56	3.01

Address: 1555 Notre Dame Street East, Montreal, H2L 2R5 Telephone: 514-521-1786	Web Site: www.molsoncoors.com Officers: Geoffrey E. Molson - Chairman Peter H. Coors - Chairman, Chairman (frmr), Vice-Chairman, Chief Customer Relations Officer, Vice-Chairman (frmr)	Auditors: PricewaterhouseCoopers LLP Investor Contact: 303-927-2448 Transfer Agents: CST Trust Company, Toronto, Ontario, Canada

MONSANTO CO

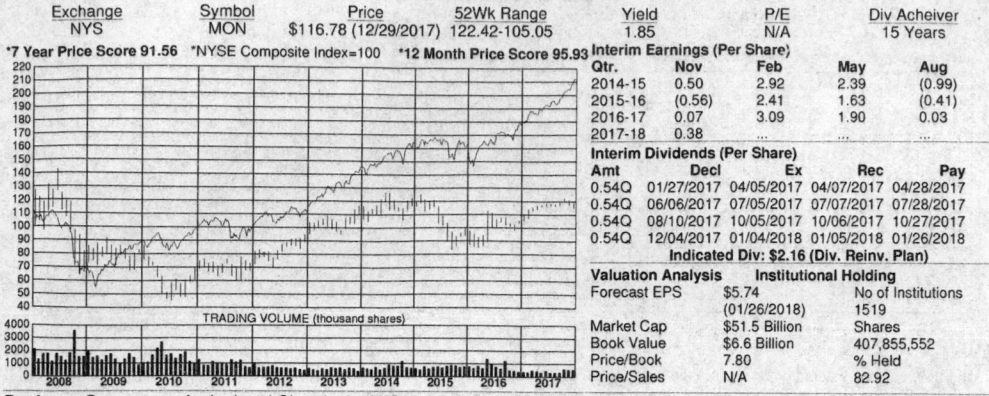

Exchange	Symbol	Price	52Wk Range	Yield	P/E	Div Acheiver
NYS	MON	$116.78 (12/29/2017)	122.42-105.05	1.85	N/A	15 Years

*7 Year Price Score 91.56 *NYSE Composite Index=100 *12 Month Price Score 95.93

Interim Earnings (Per Share)

Qtr.	Nov	Feb	May	Aug
2014-15	0.50	2.92	2.39	(0.99)
2015-16	(0.56)	2.41	1.63	(0.41)
2016-17	0.07	3.09	1.90	0.03
2017-18	0.38	...	...	...

Interim Dividends (Per Share)

Amt	Decl	Ex	Rec	Pay
0.54Q	01/27/2017	04/05/2017	04/07/2017	04/28/2017
0.54Q	06/06/2017	07/05/2017	07/07/2017	07/28/2017
0.54Q	08/10/2017	10/05/2017	10/06/2017	10/27/2017
0.54Q	12/04/2017	01/04/2018	01/05/2018	01/26/2018

Indicated Div: $2.16 (Div. Reinv. Plan)

Valuation Analysis

		Institutional Holding	
Forecast EPS	$5.74	No of Institutions	
	(01/26/2018)	1519	
Market Cap	$51.5 Billion	Shares	
Book Value	$6.6 Billion	407,855,552	
Price/Book	7.80	% Held	
Price/Sales	N/A	82.92	

Business Summary: Agricultural Chemicals (MIC: 8.3.3 SIC: 2879 NAIC: 325320)

Monsanto, along with its subsidiaries, is a provider of agricultural products for farmers. Co. has two business segments: Seeds and Genomics, and Agricultural Productivity. Through its Seeds and Genomics segment, Co. produces seed brands, including DEKALB, Asgrow, Deltapine, Seminis and De Ruiter, and Co. develops biotechnology traits that assist farmers in controlling insects and weeds. Co. also provides other seed companies with technology and genetic material for their seed brands. Through its Agricultural Productivity segment, Co. manufactures Roundup brand herbicides and other herbicides and provides lawn-and-garden herbicide products for the residential market.

Recent Developments: For the quarter ended Nov 30 2017, income from continuing operations increased 580.0% to US$170.0 million from US$25.0 million in the year-earlier quarter. Net income increased 388.6% to US$171.0 million from US$35.0 million in the year-earlier quarter. Revenues were US$2.66 billion, up 0.3% from US$2.65 billion the year before. Operating income was US$242.0 million versus US$247.0 million in the prior-year quarter, a decrease of 2.0%. Direct operating expenses declined 3.2% to US$1.35 billion from US$1.39 billion in the comparable period the year before. Indirect operating expenses increased 5.7% to US$1.07 billion from US$1.01 billion in the equivalent prior-year period.

Prospects: Our evaluation of Monsanto Co. as of Jan. 21, 2018 is the result of our systematic analysis on three basic characteristics: earnings strength, relative valuation, and recent stock price movement. The company has enjoyed a very positive trend in earnings per share over the past 5 quarters and while recent estimates for the company have been raised by analysts, MON has posted results that fell short of analysts expectations. Based on operating earnings yield, the company is undervalued when compared to all of the companies in our coverage universe. Share price changes over the past year indicates that MON will perform in line with the market over the near term.

Financial Data

(US$ in Millions)	3 Mos	08/31/2017	08/31/2016	08/31/2015	08/31/2014	08/31/2013	08/31/2012	08/31/2011
Earnings Per Share	...	5.09	2.99	4.81	5.22	4.60	3.79	2.96
Cash Flow Per Share	...	7.35	5.83	6.52	5.88	5.13	5.70	5.25
Tang Book Value Per Share	3.45	3.02	N.M.	3.41	4.13	14.77	13.40	12.84
Dividends Per Share	2.160	2.160	2.160	1.960	1.720	1.500	1.200	1.120
Dividend Payout %	...	42.44	72.24	40.75	32.95	32.61	31.66	37.84
Income Statement								
Total Revenue	2,658	14,640	13,502	15,001	15,855	14,861	13,504	11,822
EBITDA	527	4,010	3,080	4,205	4,664	4,124	3,724	3,075
Depn & Amortn	188	748	727	716	691	615	622	613
Income Before Taxes	230	2,886	1,991	3,161	3,827	3,429	2,988	2,374
Income Taxes	60	626	695	864	1,078	915	901	717
Net Income	169	2,260	1,336	2,314	2,740	2,482	2,045	1,607
Average Shares	445	443	447	481	524	539	540	542
Balance Sheet								
Current Assets	10,560	8,651	8,157	10,625	9,675	10,077	9,658	8,809
Total Assets	23,136	21,333	19,736	21,920	21,981	20,664	20,224	19,844
Current Liabilities	8,258	6,398	6,729	5,177	5,112	4,336	4,221	4,729
Long-Term Obligations	6,949	7,254	7,453	8,429	7,528	2,061	2,038	1,543
Total Liabilities	16,535	14,895	15,202	14,930	14,106	8,105	8,391	8,299
Stockholders' Equity	6,601	6,438	4,534	6,990	7,875	12,559	11,833	11,545
Shares Outstanding	440	439	437	467	485	529	534	535
Statistical Record								
Return on Assets %	...	11.01	6.40	10.54	12.85	12.14	10.18	8.52
Return on Equity %	...	41.20	23.12	31.13	26.82	20.35	17.45	14.85
EBITDA Margin %	19.83	27.39	22.81	28.03	29.42	27.75	27.58	26.01
Net Margin %	6.36	15.44	9.89	15.43	17.28	16.70	15.14	13.59
Asset Turnover	...	0.71	0.65	0.68	0.74	0.73	0.67	0.63
Current Ratio	1.28	1.35	1.21	2.05	1.89	2.32	2.29	1.86
Debt to Equity	1.05	1.13	1.64	1.21	0.96	0.16	0.17	0.13
Price Range	122.42-102.71	118.75-97.90	112.47-83.11	125.46-89.42	126.73-99.18	109.22-83.84	88.62-60.04	76.42-47.77
P/E Ratio	...	23.33-19.23	37.62-27.80	26.08-18.59	24.28-19.00	23.74-18.23	23.38-15.84	25.82-16.14
Average Yield %	1.88	1.95	2.25	1.71	1.52	1.53	1.57	1.69

Address: 800 North Lindbergh Blvd., St. Louis, MO 63167
Telephone: 314-694-1000
Fax: 314-694-1057

Web Site: www.monsanto.com
Officers: Hugh Grant - Chairman, President, Chief Executive Officer Pierre C. Courduroux - Senior Vice President, Chief Financial Officer

Auditors: DELOITTE & TOUCHE LLP
Transfer Agents: ComputerShare, College Station, TX

MOODY'S CORP.

Exchange	Symbol	Price	52Wk Range	Yield	P/E
NYS	MCO	$147.61 (12/29/2017)	152.57-94.67	1.03	52.16

*7 Year Price Score 124.72 ***NYSE Composite Index=100** ***12 Month Price Score 111.25**

TRADING VOLUME (thousand shares)

Interim Earnings (Per Share)

Qtr.	Mar	Jun	Sep	Dec
2014	1.00	1.48	1.00	1.13
2015	1.11	1.28	1.14	1.09
2016	0.93	1.30	1.31	(2.19)
2017	1.78	1.61	1.63	...

Interim Dividends (Per Share)

Amt	Decl	Ex	Rec	Pay
0.38Q	12/20/2016	02/15/2017	02/20/2017	03/10/2017
0.38Q	04/25/2017	05/18/2017	05/22/2017	06/12/2017
0.38Q	07/11/2017	08/18/2017	08/22/2017	09/12/2017
0.38Q	10/24/2017	11/20/2017	11/21/2017	12/12/2017

Indicated Div: $1.52

Valuation Analysis / Institutional Holding

Valuation Analysis		Institutional Holding	
Forecast EPS	$5.95 (01/17/2018)	No of Institutions	794
Market Cap	$28.2 Billion	Shares	210,365,376
Book Value	N/A	% Held	85.98
Price/Book	N/A		
Price/Sales	7.09		

Business Summary: Business Services (MIC: 7.5.2 SIC: 7323 NAIC: 561450)

Moody's provides credit ratings; credit, capital markets and economic related research, data and analytical tools; software solutions and related risk management services; quantitative credit risk measures, financial services training and certification services; and research and analytical services to financial institution customers. Co. operates two segments: Moody's Investors Service, which publishes credit ratings on debt obligations and the entities that issue such obligations; and Moody's Analytics, which develops a range of products and services that support financial analysis and risk management activities of institutional participants in global financial markets.

Recent Developments: For the quarter ended Sep 30 2017, net income increased 24.6% to US$319.7 million from US$256.6 million in the year-earlier quarter. Revenues were US$1.06 billion, up 15.9% from US$917.1 million the year before. Operating income was US$445.4 million versus US$397.5 million in the prior-year quarter, an increase of 12.1%. Direct operating expenses rose 25.3% to US$317.2 million from US$253.2 million in the comparable period the year before. Indirect operating expenses increased 12.7% to US$300.3 million from US$266.4 million in the equivalent prior-year period.

Prospects: Our evaluation of Moody's Corp. as of Jan. 14, 2018 is the result of our systematic analysis on three basic characteristics: earnings strength, relative valuation, and recent stock price movement. The company has generated a negative trend in earnings per share over the past 5 quarters and while recent estimates for the company have been raised by analysts, MCO has posted better than expected results. Based on operating earnings yield, the company is about fairly valued when compared to all of the companies in our coverage universe. Share price changes over the past year indicates that MCO will perform very well over the near term.

Financial Data
(US$ in Thousands)

	9 Mos	6 Mos	3 Mos	12/31/2016	12/31/2015	12/31/2014	12/31/2013	12/31/2012
Earnings Per Share	2.83	2.51	2.20	1.36	4.63	4.61	3.60	3.05
Cash Flow Per Share	3.73	3.40	2.49	6.35	5.77	4.83	4.22	3.68
Dividends Per Share	1.510	1.500	1.490	1.480	1.360	1.120	0.900	0.640
Dividend Payout %	53.36	59.76	67.73	108.82	29.37	24.30	25.00	20.98
Income Statement								
Total Revenue	3,038,600	1,975,700	975,200	3,604,200	3,484,500	3,334,300	2,972,500	2,730,300
EBITDA	1,444,500	960,200	465,500	811,100	1,596,400	1,663,800	1,345,700	1,176,500
Depn & Amortn	108,400	65,400	32,500	126,700	113,500	95,600	93,400	93,500
Income Before Taxes	1,200,600	807,400	390,600	546,600	1,367,800	1,451,400	1,160,500	1,019,200
Income Taxes	399,900	253,800	105,400	282,200	430,000	455,000	353,400	324,300
Net Income	975,100	657,800	345,600	266,600	941,300	988,700	804,500	690,000
Average Shares	194,100	193,800	194,300	195,400	203,400	214,700	223,500	226,600
Balance Sheet								
Current Assets	2,278,900	4,559,100	3,485,500	3,253,100	3,243,100	2,686,400	2,968,800	2,525,700
Total Assets	8,304,900	6,536,300	5,435,900	5,327,300	5,123,400	4,669,000	4,395,100	3,960,900
Current Liabilities	1,982,700	1,237,200	1,423,800	2,428,200	1,218,500	1,199,700	1,141,300	1,164,900
Long-Term Obligations	5,107,300	4,887,100	3,861,900	3,063,000	3,401,000	2,547,300	2,101,800	1,607,400
Total Liabilities	8,674,000	7,216,100	6,363,000	6,552,300	5,688,400	4,856,800	4,058,100	3,575,700
Stockholders' Equity	(369,100)	(679,800)	(927,100)	(1,225,000)	(565,000)	(187,800)	337,000	385,200
Shares Outstanding	191,080	191,036	191,307	190,694	196,075	204,363	213,960	223,252
Statistical Record								
Return on Assets %	8.20	8.37	8.11	5.09	19.23	21.82	19.26	20.13
Return on Equity %	...	...	...	...	...	1,325.34	222.79	636.55
EBITDA Margin %	47.54	48.60	47.73	22.50	45.81	49.90	45.27	43.09
Net Margin %	32.09	33.29	35.44	7.40	27.01	29.65	27.06	25.27
Asset Turnover	0.60	0.66	0.71	0.69	0.71	0.74	0.71	0.80
Current Ratio	1.15	3.69	2.45	1.34	2.66	2.24	2.60	2.17
Debt to Equity	...	...	...	...	...	...	6.24	4.17
Price Range	139.21-94.27	122.25-92.58	113.56-87.88	110.16-78.45	112.90-89.32	101.84-72.65	78.47-43.37	51.54-34.09
P/E Ratio	49.19-33.31	48.71-36.88	51.62-39.95	81.00-57.68	24.38-19.29	22.09-15.76	21.80-12.05	16.90-11.18
Average Yield %	1.32	1.40	1.45	1.51	1.32	1.28	1.44	1.56

Address: 7 World Trade Center, 250 Greenwich Street, New York, NY 10007 **Telephone:** 212-553-0300	**Web Site:** www.moodys.com **Officers:** Henry A. McKinnell - Chairman Raymond W. McDaniel - Chairman, President, Chief Executive Officer
Auditors: KPMG LLP **Investor Contact:** 212-553-4857 **Transfer Agents:** American Stock Transfer & Trust Company, LLC, Brooklyn, NY	

MORGAN STANLEY

Exchange	Symbol	Price	52Wk Range	Yield	P/E
NYS	MS	$52.47 (12/29/2017)	53.85-40.69	1.91	14.53

*7 Year Price Score 120.62 *NYSE Composite Index=100 *12 Month Price Score 105.21

Interim Earnings (Per Share)

Qtr.	Mar	Jun	Sep	Dec
2014	0.74	0.92	0.83	(0.89)
2015	1.18	0.85	0.48	0.39
2016	0.55	0.75	0.81	0.81
2017	1.00	0.87	0.93	...

Interim Dividends (Per Share)

Amt	Decl	Ex	Rec	Pay
0.20Q	04/19/2017	04/27/2017	05/01/2017	05/15/2017
0.25Q	07/19/2017	07/27/2017	07/31/2017	08/15/2017
0.25Q	10/17/2017	10/30/2017	10/31/2017	11/15/2017
0.25Q	01/18/2018	01/30/2018	01/31/2018	02/15/2018

Indicated Div: $1.00 (Div. Reinv. Plan)

Valuation Analysis — **Institutional Holding**

Forecast EPS	$4.50	No of Institutions
(01/26/2018)		1363
Market Cap	$95.1 Billion	Shares
Book Value	$79.0 Billion	1,864,482,048
Price/Book	1.20	% Held
Price/Sales	2.23	77.91

Business Summary: Finance Intermediaries & Services (MIC: 5.5.1 SIC: 6211 NAIC: 523110)

Morgan Stanley is a financial holding company. Through its subsidiaries and affiliates, Co. provides its products and services to corporations, governments, financial institutions and individuals. Co. has three segments: Institutional Securities, which provides capital raising and financial advisory services, sales and trading, lending, financing and market-making activities in equity, fixed income securities and related products; Wealth Management, which provides brokerage and investment advisory services; and Investment Management, which provides a range of investment strategies. As of Dec 31 2016, Co. had total assets of $814.95 billion and total deposits of $155.86 billion.

Recent Developments: For the quarter ended Sep 30 2017, income from continuing operations increased 9.4% to US$1.79 billion from US$1.63 billion in the year-earlier quarter. Net income increased 9.2% to US$1.79 billion from US$1.64 billion in the year-earlier quarter. Revenues were US$10.75 billion, up 11.6% from US$9.64 billion the year before. Direct operating expenses rose 113.0% to US$1.56 billion from US$731.0 million in the comparable period the year before. Indirect operating expenses increased 2.9% to US$6.72 billion from US$6.53 billion in the equivalent prior-year period.

Prospects: Our evaluation of Morgan Stanley Dean Witter & Co. as of Jan. 21, 2018 is the result of our systematic analysis on three basic characteristics: earnings strength, relative valuation, and recent stock price movement. The company has managed to produce a neutral trend in earnings per share over the past 5 quarters and while recent estimates for the company have been raised by analysts, MS has posted better than expected results. Based on operating earnings yield, the company is undervalued when compared to all of the companies in our coverage universe. Share price changes over the past year indicates that MS will perform in line with the market over the near term.

Financial Data

(US$ in Thousands)	9 Mos	6 Mos	3 Mos	12/31/2016	12/31/2015	12/31/2014	12/31/2013	12/31/2012
Earnings Per Share	3.61	3.49	3.37	2.92	2.90	1.60	1.36	(0.02)
Cash Flow Per Share	(6.46)	(13.00)	(1.83)	1.32	1.92	0.59	18.65	12.98
Tang Book Value Per Share	33.86	33.24	32.49	31.97	30.26	28.26	27.16	25.41
Dividends Per Share	0.850	0.800	0.750	0.700	0.550	0.350	0.200	0.200
Dividend Payout %	23.55	22.92	22.26	23.97	18.97	21.88	14.71	...
Income Statement								
Interest Income	6,411,000	4,071,000	1,965,000	7,016,000	5,835,000	5,413,000	5,209,000	5,725,000
Interest Expense	4,106,000	2,549,000	1,194,000	3,318,000	2,742,000	3,678,000	4,431,000	5,924,000
Net Interest Income	2,305,000	1,522,000	771,000	3,698,000	3,093,000	1,735,000	778,000	(199,000)
Non-Interest Income	26,140,000	17,726,000	8,974,000	30,933,000	32,062,000	32,540,000	31,639,000	26,311,000
Non-Interest Expense	20,513,000	13,798,000	6,937,000	25,783,000	26,660,000	30,684,000	27,935,000	25,597,000
Income Before Taxes	7,932,000	5,450,000	2,808,000	8,848,000	8,495,000	3,591,000	4,482,000	515,000
Income Taxes	2,358,000	1,661,000	815,000	2,726,000	2,200,000	(90,000)	826,000	(239,000)
Net Income	5,468,000	3,687,000	1,930,000	5,979,000	6,127,000	3,467,000	2,932,000	68,000
Average Shares	1,818,000	1,830,000	1,842,000	1,887,000	1,952,815	1,970,535	1,956,519	1,918,811
Balance Sheet								
Net Loans & Leases	104,431,000	97,639,000	95,953,000	94,248,000	85,759,000	66,577,000	42,874,000	29,046,000
Total Assets	853,693,000	841,016,000	832,391,000	814,949,000	787,465,000	801,510,000	832,702,000	780,960,000
Total Deposits	154,639,000	144,913,000	152,109,000	155,863,000	156,034,000	133,544,000	112,379,000	83,266,000
Total Liabilities	774,715,000	762,190,000	754,467,000	738,899,000	712,283,000	730,610,000	766,781,000	718,851,000
Stockholders' Equity	78,978,000	78,826,000	77,924,000	76,050,000	75,182,000	70,900,000	65,921,000	62,109,000
Shares Outstanding	1,812,472	1,839,578	1,851,942	1,852,481	1,920,024	1,950,980	1,944,868	1,974,042
Statistical Record								
Return on Assets %	0.86	0.83	0.83	0.74	0.77	0.42	0.36	0.01
Return on Equity %	9.14	8.91	8.80	7.89	8.39	5.07	4.58	0.11
Net Interest Margin %	33.46	35.66	39.24	52.71	53.01	32.05	14.94	N.M.
Efficiency Ratio %	62.44	63.19	63.42	67.94	70.35	80.85	75.81	79.90
Loans to Deposits	0.68	0.67	0.63	0.60	0.55	0.50	0.38	0.35
Price Range	48.31-31.73	46.83-25.00	46.83-23.61	43.73-21.69	40.54-31.01	39.00-28.47	31.62-19.12	21.17-12.36
P/E Ratio	13.38-8.79	13.42-7.16	13.90-7.01	14.98-7.43	13.98-10.69	24.38-17.79	23.25-14.06	...
Average Yield %	1.98	2.07	2.18	2.34	1.53	1.07	0.78	1.21

Address: 1585 Broadway, New York, NY 10036	**Web Site:** www.morganstanley.com	**Auditors:** Deloitte & Touche LLP
Telephone: 212-761-4000	**Officers:** James P. Gorman - Chairman, President, Chief Executive Officer Thomas Colm Kelleher - President, Executive Vice President	**Transfer Agents:** Computershare, Providence, RI

MOSAIC CO (THE)

Exchange	Symbol	Price	52Wk Range	Yield	P/E
NYS	MOS	$25.66 (12/29/2017)	34.02-19.39	0.39	N/A

*7 Year Price Score 43.89   *NYSE Composite Index=100   *12 Month Price Score 89.11

TRADING VOLUME (thousand shares)

Interim Earnings (Per Share)

Qtr.	Mar	Jun	Sep	Dec
2014	0.54	0.64	0.54	0.96
2015	0.80	1.08	0.45	0.45
2016	0.73	(0.03)	0.11	0.04
2017	0.00	0.28	0.65	...

Interim Dividends (Per Share)

Amt	Decl	Ex	Rec	Pay
0.15Q	05/18/2017	05/30/2017	06/01/2017	06/15/2017
0.15Q	08/17/2017	09/06/2017	09/07/2017	09/21/2017
0.025Q	10/31/2017	12/06/2017	12/07/2017	12/21/2017
0.025Q	12/14/2017	02/28/2018	03/01/2018	03/15/2018

Indicated Div: $0.10

Valuation Analysis   Institutional Holding

Forecast EPS	$1.02	No of Institutions
	(01/26/2018)	759
Market Cap	$9.0 Billion	Shares
Book Value	$10.1 Billion	324,920,320
Price/Book	0.89	% Held
Price/Sales	1.25	N/A

Business Summary: Agricultural Chemicals (MIC: 8.3.3 SIC: 2874 NAIC: 325312)

Mosaic is a producer and marketer of concentrated phosphate and potash crop nutrients. Co. mines phosphate rock in Florida and processes rock into finished phosphate products at facilities in Florida and Louisiana; and mines potash in Saskatchewan and New Mexico. Co. is organized into three reportable business segments: Phosphates, which sells phosphate-based crop nutrients and animal feed ingredients; Potash, which sells potash, primarily as fertilizer, but also for use in industrial applications and, to a lesser degree, as animal feed ingredients; and International Distribution, which serves as a distribution outlet for Co.'s Phosphates and Potash segments.

Recent Developments: For the quarter ended Sep 30 2017, net income increased 464.1% to US$229.6 million from US$40.7 million in the year-earlier quarter. Revenues were US$1.98 billion, up 1.7% from US$1.95 billion the year before. Operating income was US$213.9 million versus US$69.7 million in the prior-year quarter, an increase of 206.9%. Direct operating expenses was unchanged at US$1.74 billion versus the comparable period the year before. Indirect operating expenses decreased 81.3% to US$26.9 million from US$143.6 million in the equivalent prior-year period.

Prospects: Our evaluation of Mosaic Co as of Jan. 21, 2018 is the result of our systematic analysis on three basic characteristics: earnings strength, relative valuation, and recent stock price movement. The company has produced a positive trend in earnings per share over the past 5 quarters and while recent estimates for the company have been raised by analysts, MOS has posted better than expected results. Based on operating earnings yield, the company is undervalued when compared to all of the companies in our coverage universe. Share price changes over the past year indicates that MOS will perform very poorly over the near term.

Financial Data

(US$ in Thousands)	9 Mos	6 Mos	3 Mos	12/31/2016	12/31/2015	12/31/2014	12/31/2013	05/31/2013
Earnings Per Share	0.97	0.43	0.12	0.85	2.78	2.68	0.80	4.42
Cash Flow Per Share	2.41	2.30	3.27	3.60	5.04	6.13	3.60	4.43
Tang Book Value Per Share	23.96	23.06	22.74	22.71	22.51	24.21	22.32	27.20
Dividends Per Share	0.850	0.975	1.100	1.100	1.075	1.000	0.500	1.000
Dividend Payout %	87.63	226.74	916.67	129.41	38.67	37.31	62.50	22.62
Income Statement								
Total Revenue	5,317,500	3,332,700	1,578,100	7,162,800	8,895,300	9,055,800	4,765,900	9,974,100
EBITDA	906,700	464,300	193,300	1,058,600	1,933,300	2,075,800	883,700	2,800,500
Depn & Amortn	493,500	324,700	158,800	703,800	732,200	750,900	386,200	604,800
Income Before Taxes	314,800	77,400	8,700	242,400	1,103,300	1,217,300	484,200	2,214,500
Income Taxes	4,700	(12,900)	9,700	(74,200)	99,100	184,700	152,600	341,000
Net Income	323,900	96,400	(900)	297,800	1,000,400	1,028,600	340,000	1,888,700
Average Shares	352,200	352,000	350,500	351,700	360,300	375,600	422,000	426,900
Balance Sheet								
Current Assets	3,375,500	3,337,200	3,216,200	3,057,700	4,144,700	5,364,200	8,105,800	6,880,500
Total Assets	17,803,100	17,444,400	17,096,400	16,840,700	17,412,400	18,283,000	19,554,000	18,086,000
Current Liabilities	1,897,800	1,872,000	1,633,400	1,476,800	2,048,300	1,600,400	3,265,900	1,764,900
Long-Term Obligations	3,722,300	3,799,700	3,786,600	3,779,300	3,791,100	3,778,000	3,008,900	1,009,600
Total Liabilities	7,688,900	7,688,300	7,474,600	7,256,100	7,880,600	7,579,900	8,251,700	4,660,600
Stockholders' Equity	10,114,200	9,756,100	9,621,800	9,584,600	9,531,800	10,703,100	11,302,300	13,425,400
Shares Outstanding	351,049	351,049	351,017	350,238	352,515	367,540	426,005	425,817
Statistical Record								
Return on Assets %	1.92	0.84	0.23	1.73	5.61	5.44	3.20	10.86
Return on Equity %	3.37	1.50	0.41	3.11	9.89	9.35	4.98	14.87
EBITDA Margin %	17.05	13.93	12.25	14.78	21.73	22.92	18.54	28.08
Net Margin %	6.09	2.89	N.M.	4.16	11.25	11.36	7.13	18.94
Asset Turnover	0.41	0.41	0.41	0.42	0.50	0.48	0.45	0.57
Current Ratio	1.78	1.78	1.97	2.07	2.02	3.35	2.48	3.90
Debt to Equity	0.37	0.39	0.39	0.39	0.40	0.35	0.27	0.08
Price Range	34.02-19.39	34.02-21.87	34.02-22.83	31.42-22.10	53.56-27.24	50.79-40.76	61.80-40.68	64.30-45.62
P/E Ratio	35.07-19.99	79.12-50.86	283.50-190.25	36.96-26.00	19.27-9.80	18.95-15.21	77.25-50.85	14.55-10.32
Average Yield %	3.28	3.56	3.95	4.12	2.57	2.13	1.04	1.75

Address: 3033 Campus Drive, Suite E490, Plymouth, MN 55441	**Web Site:** www.mosaicco.com	**Auditors:** KPMG LLP
Telephone: 800-918-8270	**Officers:** James C. O'Rourke - President, Chief Executive Officer, Executive Vice President, Chief Operating Officer Richard L. Mack - Executive Vice President, Chief Financial Officer, General Counsel, Corporate Secretary, Principal Accounting Officer	**Investor Contact:** 763-577-8213
Fax: 763-577-2990		**Transfer Agents:** American Stock Transfer & Trust Company, New York, NY

MOTOROLA SOLUTIONS INC.

Exchange	Symbol	Price	52Wk Range	Yield	P/E
NYS	MSI	$90.34 (12/29/2017)	94.53-77.34	2.30	23.16

*7 Year Price Score 107.27 *NYSE Composite Index=100 *12 Month Price Score 100.80

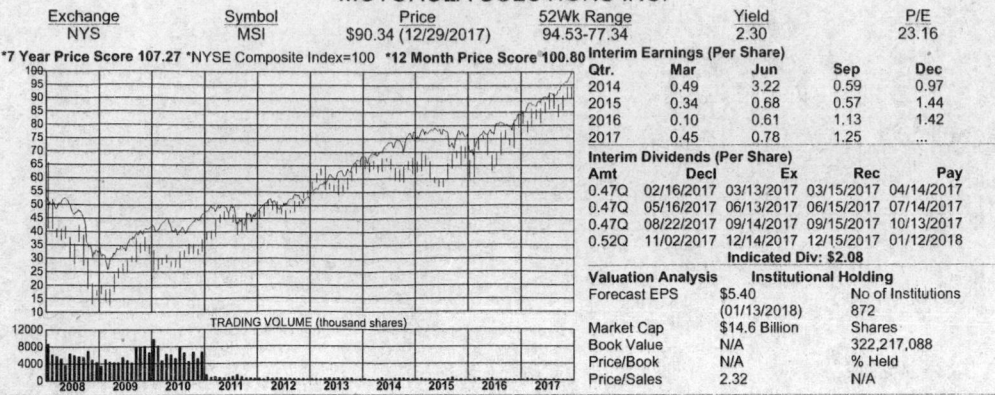

Interim Earnings (Per Share)

Qtr.	Mar	Jun	Sep	Dec
2014	0.49	3.22	0.59	0.97
2015	0.34	0.68	0.57	1.44
2016	0.10	0.61	1.13	1.42
2017	0.45	0.78	1.25	...

Interim Dividends (Per Share)

Amt	Decl	Ex	Rec	Pay
0.47Q	02/16/2017	03/13/2017	03/15/2017	04/14/2017
0.47Q	05/16/2017	06/13/2017	06/15/2017	07/14/2017
0.47Q	08/22/2017	09/14/2017	09/15/2017	10/13/2017
0.52Q	11/02/2017	12/14/2017	12/15/2017	01/12/2018

Indicated Div: $2.08

Valuation Analysis

		Institutional Holding	
Forecast EPS	$5.40	No of Institutions	
	(01/13/2018)	872	
Market Cap	$14.6 Billion	Shares	
Book Value	N/A	322,217,088	
Price/Book	N/A	% Held	
Price/Sales	2.32	N/A	

Business Summary: Manufacturing (MIC: 6.1.1 SIC: 3663 NAIC: 334220)

Motorola Solutions is a provider of communication infrastructure, devices, accessories, software and services. Co.'s Products segment provides a portfolio of infrastructure, devices, accessories, and software to government, public safety and first-responder agencies, municipalities, and commercial and industrial customers who operate private communications networks and manage a mobile workforce. Co.'s Services segment provides a set of service offerings for government, public safety, and commercial communication networks including: Integration services, Managed and Support services, and Integrated Digital Enhanced Network services.

Recent Developments: For the quarter ended Sep 30 2017, net income increased 10.4% to US$213.0 million from US$193.0 million in the year-earlier quarter. Revenues were US$1.65 billion, up 7.4% from US$1.53 billion the year before. Operating income was US$338.0 million versus US$341.0 million in the prior-year quarter, a decrease of 0.9%. Direct operating expenses rose 10.5% to US$851.0 million from US$770.0 million in the comparable period the year before. Indirect operating expenses increased 8.3% to US$456.0 million from US$421.0 million in the equivalent prior-year period.

Prospects: Our evaluation of Motorola Solutions Inc. as of Jan. 14, 2018 is the result of our systematic analysis on three basic characteristics: earnings strength, relative valuation, and recent stock price movement. The company has managed to produce a neutral trend in earnings per share over the past 5 quarters and while recent estimates for the company have been mixed, MSI has posted better than expected results. Based on operating earnings yield, the company is undervalued when compared to all of the companies in our coverage universe. Share price changes over the past year indicates that MSI will perform in line with the market over the near term.

Financial Data

(US$ in Millions)	9 Mos	6 Mos	3 Mos	12/31/2016	12/31/2015	12/31/2014	12/31/2013	12/31/2012
Earnings Per Share	3.90	3.78	3.61	3.24	3.02	5.29	4.06	2.96
Cash Flow Per Share	6.77	7.21	7.88	6.85	5.04	(2.79)	3.55	3.65
Tang Book Value Per Share	...	...	...	...	...	10.60	8.11	5.96
Dividends Per Share	1.880	1.820	1.760	1.700	1.430	1.300	1.140	0.960
Dividend Payout %	48.21	48.15	48.75	52.47	47.35	24.57	28.08	32.43
Income Statement								
Total Revenue	4,423	2,777	1,281	6,038	5,695	5,881	8,696	8,698
EBITDA	1,017	592	252	1,344	1,240	(862)	1,486	1,489
Depn & Amortn	254	166	80	295	150	173	228	208
Income Before Taxes	609	324	121	844	917	(1,161)	1,145	1,215
Income Taxes	188	114	42	282	274	(465)	40	337
Net Income	420	208	77	560	610	1,299	1,099	881
Average Shares	169	169	169	173	201	245	270	297
Balance Sheet								
Current Assets	3,336	3,211	3,073	3,468	4,582	6,879	7,020	7,401
Total Assets	8,618	8,295	8,140	8,463	8,387	10,423	11,851	12,679
Current Liabilities	2,563	2,410	2,385	2,668	2,193	2,250	3,220	3,335
Long-Term Obligations	4,423	4,421	4,414	4,392	4,386	3,396	2,457	1,859
Total Liabilities	9,448	9,283	9,190	9,427	8,493	7,688	8,192	9,414
Stockholders' Equity	(830)	(988)	(1,050)	(964)	(106)	2,735	3,659	3,265
Shares Outstanding	162	162	163	164	174	219	254	276
Statistical Record								
Return on Assets %	7.69	7.67	7.20	6.63	6.49	11.66	8.96	6.60
Return on Equity %	...	...	...	...	46.41	40.63	31.74	20.72
EBITDA Margin %	22.99	21.32	19.67	22.26	21.77	N.M.	17.09	17.12
Net Margin %	9.50	7.49	6.01	9.27	10.71	22.09	12.64	10.13
Asset Turnover	0.73	0.74	0.71	0.71	0.61	0.53	0.71	0.65
Current Ratio	1.30	1.33	1.29	1.30	2.09	3.06	2.18	2.22
Debt to Equity	...	...	...	...	...	1.24	0.67	0.57
Price Range	92.21-71.29	88.64-64.77	86.22-63.08	84.00-60.36	72.45-56.79	67.87-58.50	67.50-54.01	55.68-44.94
P/E Ratio	23.64-18.28	23.45-17.13	23.88-17.47	25.93-18.63	23.99-18.80	12.83-11.06	16.63-13.30	18.81-15.18
Average Yield %	2.26	2.29	2.31	2.34	2.21	2.02	1.90	1.93

Address: 500 West Monroe Street, Chicago, IL 60661 **Telephone:** 847-576-5000 **Fax:** 847-576-3477	**Web Site:** www.motorolasolutions.com **Officers:** Gregory Q. Brown - Chairman, President, Chief Executive Officer, Division Officer Gino A. Bonanotte - Executive Vice President, Corporate Vice-President, Acting Chief Financial Officer, Chief Financial Officer, Acting Chief Financial Officer, Chief Financial Officer	**Auditors:** KPMG LLP **Investor Contact:** 847-576-6899 **Transfer Agents:** Computershare, Jersey City, NJ

MSA SAFETY INC

Exchange	Symbol	Price	52Wk Range	Yield	P/E	Div Achiever
NYS	MSA	$77.52 (12/29/2017)	86.00-66.16	1.81	35.56	46 Years

*7 Year Price Score 119.51 *NYSE Composite Index=100 *12 Month Price Score 100.49

Interim Earnings (Per Share)

Qtr.	Mar	Jun	Sep	Dec
2014	0.37	0.59	0.51	0.86
2015	0.26	0.63	0.42	0.55
2016	0.31	0.82	0.63	0.66
2017	0.37	0.32	0.83	...

Interim Dividends (Per Share)

Amt	Decl	Ex	Rec	Pay
0.35Q	05/12/2017	05/19/2017	05/23/2017	06/10/2017
0.35Q	08/01/2017	08/14/2017	08/16/2017	09/10/2017
0.35Q	10/25/2017	11/13/2017	11/14/2017	12/10/2017
0.35Q	01/09/2018	02/13/2018	02/14/2018	03/10/2018

Indicated Div: $1.40

Valuation Analysis — **Institutional Holding**

Forecast EPS	$3.28	No of Institutions
	(10/25/2017)	317
Market Cap	$2.9 Billion	Shares
Book Value	$616.7 Million	31,853,788
Price/Book	4.78	% Held
Price/Sales	2.57	N/A

TRADING VOLUME (thousand shares)

Business Summary: Office Equipment & Furniture (MIC: 7.5.1 SIC: 3842 NAIC: 922160)

Mine Safety Appliances develops, manufactures and supplies safety products that protect people and facility infrastructures. Co. manufactures and sells safety products to protect the safety of workers and facility infrustructures in the oil and gas, fire service, construction, and mining industries. Co. also sells products designed for specific industrial and military applications. Co.'s products protect people against a variety of hazardous or life-threatening situations. Co.'s core products include fixed gas and flame detection systems, breathing apparatus, portable gas detection instruments, industrial head protection products, fire and rescue helmets, and fall protection devices.

Recent Developments: For the quarter ended Sep 30 2017, income from continuing operations increased 22.4% to US$32.2 million from US$26.3 million in the year-earlier quarter. Net income increased 28.8% to US$32.2 million from US$25.0 million in the year-earlier quarter. Revenues were US$296.1 million, up 6.4% from US$278.2 million the year before. Operating income was US$40.6 million versus US$40.0 million in the prior-year quarter, an increase of 1.5%. Direct operating expenses rose 9.5% to US$163.6 million from US$149.5 million in the comparable period the year before. Indirect operating expenses increased 3.5% to US$91.9 million from US$88.7 million in the equivalent prior-year period.

Prospects: Our evaluation of MSA Safety Inc. as of Jan. 14, 2018 is the result of our systematic analysis on three basic characteristics: earnings strength, relative valuation, and recent stock price movement. The company has produced a positive trend in earnings per share over the past 5 quarters and while recent estimates for the company have remained steady, MSA has posted better than expected results. Based on operating earnings yield, the company is about fairly valued when compared to all of the companies in our coverage universe. Share price changes over the past year indicates that MSA will perform well over the near term.

Financial Data

(US$ in Thousands)	9 Mos	6 Mos	3 Mos	12/31/2016	12/31/2015	12/31/2014	12/31/2013	12/31/2012
Earnings Per Share	2.18	1.98	2.48	2.42	1.87	2.33	2.34	2.42
Cash Flow Per Share	7.69	7.06	6.42	3.59	1.48	2.88	3.00	4.10
Tang Book Value Per Share	0.26	4.67	4.26	3.82	2.21	6.58	7.20	5.43
Dividends Per Share	1.360	1.340	1.320	1.310	1.270	1.230	1.180	1.380
Dividend Payout %	62.39	67.68	53.23	54.13	67.91	52.79	50.43	57.02
Income Statement								
Total Revenue	850,669	554,540	265,765	1,149,530	1,129,922	1,136,650	1,111,883	1,179,895
EBITDA	104,067	52,539	28,829	192,495	148,780	163,246	157,910	177,332
Depn & Amortn	27,665	17,736	8,752	27,000	26,900	26,200	27,100	31,681
Income Before Taxes	65,836	28,198	16,486	151,911	111,026	127,195	120,133	134,290
Income Taxes	6,306	894	1,796	57,804	44,407	41,044	35,145	42,529
Net Income	59,011	26,945	14,413	91,936	70,807	88,506	88,247	90,637
Average Shares	38,702	38,780	38,593	37,986	37,710	37,728	37,450	37,042
Balance Sheet								
Current Assets	576,539	532,140	494,801	472,806	505,027	497,869	500,966	463,548
Total Assets	1,595,217	1,362,036	1,258,154	1,353,920	1,424,818	1,264,792	1,234,270	1,111,746
Current Liabilities	273,088	263,342	202,015	221,410	251,905	234,057	191,564	188,800
Long-Term Obligations	445,717	242,679	268,568	363,836	459,959	245,000	260,667	272,333
Total Liabilities	978,478	762,407	681,813	795,755	908,322	730,983	667,818	648,791
Stockholders' Equity	616,739	599,629	576,341	558,165	516,496	533,809	566,452	462,955
Shares Outstanding	38,025	38,183	37,942	37,736	37,372	37,448	37,202	37,007
Statistical Record								
Return on Assets %	5.55	5.47	7.00	6.60	5.27	7.08	7.52	8.12
Return on Equity %	14.21	13.23	16.95	17.06	13.48	16.09	17.15	20.16
EBITDA Margin %	12.23	9.47	10.85	16.75	13.17	14.36	14.20	15.03
Net Margin %	6.94	4.86	5.42	8.00	6.27	7.79	7.94	7.68
Asset Turnover	0.76	0.81	0.84	0.83	0.84	0.91	0.95	1.06
Current Ratio	2.11	2.02	2.45	2.14	2.00	2.13	2.62	2.46
Debt to Equity	0.72	0.40	0.47	0.65	0.89	0.46	0.46	0.59
Price Range	83.37-55.16	83.37-51.69	74.51-46.55	70.97-38.31	53.09-38.69	61.02-47.29	54.73-42.71	43.40-32.88
P/E Ratio	38.24-25.30	42.11-26.11	30.04-18.77	29.33-15.83	28.39-20.69	26.19-20.30	23.39-18.25	17.93-13.59
Average Yield %	1.92	2.03	2.23	2.49	2.72	2.28	2.41	3.62

Address: 1000 Cranberry Woods Drive, Cranberry Township, PA 16066-5207 **Telephone:** 724-776-8600	**Web Site:** www.msasafety.com **Officers:** William M. Lambert - Chairman, President, Chief Executive Officer Bob Willem Leenen - Vice President, Division Officer	**Auditors:** Ernst & Young LLP **Investor Contact:** 724-741-8534 **Transfer Agents:** Wells Fargo Shareowner Services, South St.Paul, MN

MSC INDUSTRIAL DIRECT CO INC

Exchange	Symbol	Price	52Wk Range	Yield	P/E	Div Achiever
NYS	MSM	$96.66 (12/29/2017)	105.50-65.62	2.40	23.87	13 Years

*7 Year Price Score 89.20   *NYSE Composite Index=100   *12 Month Price Score 96.25

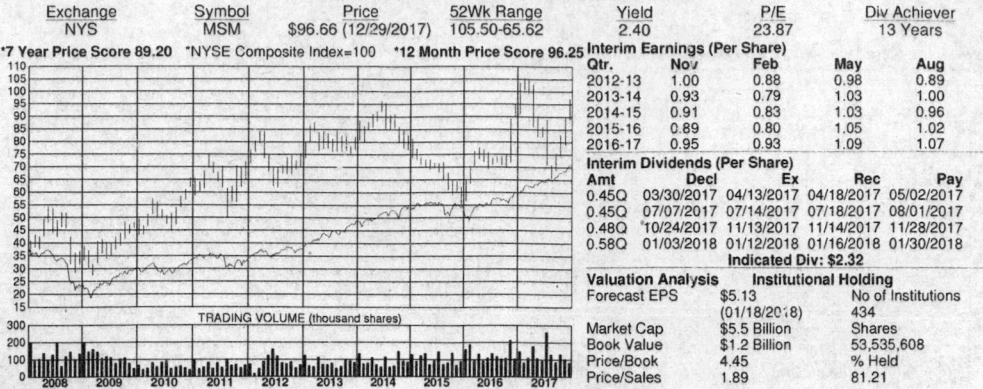

Interim Earnings (Per Share)
Qtr.	Nov	Feb	May	Aug
2012-13	1.00	0.88	0.98	0.89
2013-14	0.93	0.79	1.03	1.00
2014-15	0.91	0.83	1.03	0.96
2015-16	0.89	0.80	1.05	1.02
2016-17	0.95	0.93	1.09	1.07

Interim Dividends (Per Share)
Amt	Decl	Ex	Rec	Pay
0.45Q	03/30/2017	04/13/2017	04/18/2017	05/02/2017
0.45Q	07/07/2017	07/14/2017	07/18/2017	08/01/2017
0.48Q	10/24/2017	11/13/2017	11/14/2017	11/28/2017
0.58Q	01/03/2018	01/12/2018	01/16/2018	01/30/2018

Indicated Div: $2.32

Valuation Analysis   Institutional Holding
Forecast EPS	$5.13 (01/18/2018)	No of Institutions	434
Market Cap	$5.5 Billion	Shares	53,535,608
Book Value	$1.2 Billion	% Held	81.21
Price/Book	4.45		
Price/Sales	1.89		

Business Summary: Industrial Machinery & Equipment (MIC: 7.2.1 SIC: 5084 NAIC: 423830)

MSC Industrial Direct is a distributor of metalworking and maintenance, repair and operations (MRO) products and services. Co. serves a range of customers throughout the U.S., Canada and the U.K., from individual machine shops, to manufacturing companies, to government agencies such as the General Services Administration and the Department of Defense. Co.'s range of MRO products include cutting tools, measuring instruments, tooling components, metalworking products, fasteners, flat stock, raw materials, abrasives, machinery hand and power tools, safety and janitorial supplies, plumbing supplies, materials handling products, power transmission components, and electrical supplies.

Recent Developments: For the year ended Sep 2 2017, net income increased 0.1% to US$231.4 million from US$231.2 million in the prior year. Revenues were US$2.89 billion, up 0.8% from US$2.86 billion the year before. Operating income was US$379.0 million versus US$376.0 million in the prior year, an increase of 0.8%. Direct operating expenses rose 1.7% to US$1.60 billion from US$1.57 billion in the comparable period the year before. Indirect operating expenses decreased 0.6% to US$907.2 million from US$912.9 million in the equivalent prior-year period.

Prospects: Our evaluation of MSC Industrial Direct Co. Inc. as of Jan. 14, 2018 is the result of our systematic analysis on three basic characteristics: earnings strength, relative valuation, and recent stock price movement. The company has enjoyed a very positive trend in earnings per share over the past 5 quarters and while recent estimates for the company have been raised by analysts, MSM has posted results that fell short of analysts expectations. Based on operating earnings yield, the company is undervalued when compared to all of the companies in our coverage universe. Share price changes over the past year indicates that MSM will perform very poorly over the near term.

Financial Data
(US$ in Thousands)	09/02/2017	09/03/2016	08/29/2015	08/30/2014	08/31/2013	09/01/2012	08/27/2011	08/28/2010
Earnings Per Share	4.05	3.77	3.74	3.76	3.75	4.09	3.43	2.37
Cash Flow Per Share	4.37	6.48	4.09	4.40	5.21	3.69	3.35	2.41
Tang Book Value Per Share	8.53	6.52	9.56	10.24	9.53	13.48	10.63	9.23
Dividends Per Share	1.800	1.720	4.600	1.320	1.200	1.000	1.880	0.820
Dividend Payout %	44.44	45.62	122.99	35.11	32.00	24.45	54.81	34.60
Income Statement								
Total Revenue	2,887,744	2,863,505	2,910,379	2,787,122	2,457,649	2,355,918	2,021,792	1,692,041
EBITDA	434,060	433,936	431,509	430,714	421,645	436,863	371,000	260,512
Depn & Amortn	54,356	57,052	52,799	47,729	36,169	24,676	21,470	18,709
Income Before Taxes	367,992	371,731	373,141	379,525	383,429	412,142	349,330	240,828
Income Taxes	136,561	140,515	141,833	143,458	145,434	153,111	130,544	90,455
Net Income	231,431	231,216	231,308	236,067	237,995	259,031	218,786	150,373
Average Shares	56,971	61,076	61,487	62,339	63,011	62,803	63,324	62,930
Balance Sheet								
Current Assets	1,005,579	981,491	1,032,076	961,415	893,489	920,111	758,434	676,536
Total Assets	2,098,912	2,064,951	2,101,206	2,060,747	1,943,003	1,444,876	1,244,423	1,153,323
Current Liabilities	557,725	478,602	422,337	309,164	213,579	170,515	172,202	190,285
Long-Term Obligations	200,991	339,772	214,789	240,235	241,566	2,189	...	...
Total Liabilities	873,772	966,575	768,336	662,184	552,620	257,765	251,311	253,443
Stockholders' Equity	1,225,140	1,098,376	1,332,870	1,398,563	1,390,383	1,187,111	993,112	899,880
Shares Outstanding	56,391	56,581	61,658	61,618	63,434	62,800	62,800	62,777
Statistical Record								
Return on Assets %	11.15	10.92	11.15	11.82	14.09	18.95	18.30	13.05
Return on Equity %	19.98	18.71	16.98	16.98	18.52	23.38	23.18	17.68
EBITDA Margin %	15.03	15.15	14.83	15.45	17.16	18.54	18.35	15.40
Net Margin %	8.01	8.07	7.95	8.47	9.68	10.99	10.82	8.89
Asset Turnover	1.39	1.35	1.40	1.40	1.45	1.72	1.69	1.47
Current Ratio	1.80	2.05	2.44	3.11	4.18	5.40	4.40	3.56
Debt to Equity	0.16	0.31	0.16	0.17	0.17	N.M.	...	...
Price Range	105.50-65.62	77.76-55.01	91.09-65.04	96.13-75.55	87.79-67.18	84.27-56.13	75.04-44.57	57.47-38.92
P/E Ratio	26.05-16.20	20.63-14.59	24.36-17.39	25.57-20.09	23.41-17.91	20.60-13.72	21.88-12.99	24.25-16.42
Average Yield %	2.09	2.53	6.06	1.55	1.54	1.43	3.02	1.70

Address: 75 Maxess Road, Melville, NY 11747	**Web Site:** www.mscdirect.com	**Auditors:** Ernst & Young LLP
Telephone: 516-812-2000	**Officers:** Mitchell Jacobson - Chairman David K. Sandler - Executive Vice-Chairman, Vice-Chairman, President, Chief Executive Officer	**Investor Contact:** 516-812-1216
Fax: 516-349-7096		**Transfer Agents:** Computershare Trust Company, N.A., Providence, RI

MSCI INC

Exchange	Symbol	Price	52Wk Range	Yield	P/E
NYS	MSCI	$126.54 (12/29/2017)	129.35-78.71	1.20	37.89

*7 Year Price Score 146.94 *NYSE Composite Index=100 *12 Month Price Score 111.44

Interim Earnings (Per Share)

Qtr.	Mar	Jun	Sep	Dec
2014	0.68	0.91	0.44	0.40
2015	0.39	0.50	0.59	0.56
2016	0.60	0.69	0.68	0.72
2017	0.80	0.89	0.93	...

Interim Dividends (Per Share)

Amt	Decl	Ex	Rec	Pay
0.28Q	02/01/2017	02/15/2017	02/17/2017	03/15/2017
0.28Q	05/02/2017	05/17/2017	05/19/2017	05/31/2017
0.38Q	08/01/2017	08/16/2017	08/18/2017	08/31/2017
0.38Q	10/31/2017	11/16/2017	11/17/2017	11/30/2017

Indicated Div: $1.52

Valuation Analysis   **Institutional Holding**

Forecast EPS	$3.84 (01/27/2018)	No of Institutions 464
Market Cap	$11.4 Billion	Shares
Book Value	$360.3 Million	100,974,992
Price/Book	31.63	% Held
Price/Sales	9.25	94.51

Business Summary: Publishing (MIC: 2.3.3 SIC: 7389 NAIC: 523999)

MSCI provides products and services to support the needs of institutional investors throughout their investment processes. Co. operates in four segments: Index, which used in many areas of the investment process, including index-linked product creation and performance benchmarking; Analytics, which provides institutional investors an integrated view of risk and return; environmental, social and governance, which include screening service that is designed to enable institutional investors to manage ESG standards and restrictions; and Real Estate, which provide real estate performance analysis for funds, investors, managers and lenders.

Recent Developments: For the quarter ended Sep 30 2017, net income increased 30.4% to US$85.2 million from US$65.3 million in the year-earlier quarter. Revenues were US$322.1 million, up 11.7% from US$288.4 million the year before. Operating income was US$148.7 million versus US$123.3 million in the prior-year quarter, an increase of 20.6%. Direct operating expenses rose 8.7% to US$68.5 million from US$63.0 million in the comparable period the year before. Indirect operating expenses increased 2.7% to US$104.9 million from US$102.2 million in the equivalent prior-year period.

Prospects: Our evaluation of MSCI Inc. as of Jan. 21, 2018 is the result of our systematic analysis on three basic characteristics: earnings strength, relative valuation, and recent stock price movement. The company has managed to produce a neutral trend in earnings per share over the past 5 quarters and while recent estimates for the company have been mixed, MSCI has posted better than expected results. Based on operating earnings yield, the company is about fairly valued when compared to all of the companies in our coverage universe. Share price changes over the past year indicates that MSCI will perform very well over the near term.

Financial Data

(US$ in Thousands)	9 Mos	6 Mos	3 Mos	12/31/2016	12/31/2015	12/31/2014	12/31/2013	12/31/2012
Earnings Per Share	3.34	3.09	2.89	2.70	2.03	2.43	1.83	1.48
Cash Flow Per Share	4.42	4.91	4.84	4.52	2.80	2.64	2.67	2.84
Dividends Per Share	1.220	1.120	1.060	1.000	0.800	0.180	...	...
Dividend Payout %	36.53	36.25	36.68	37.04	39.41	7.41	...	...
Income Statement								
Total Revenue	939,393	617,296	301,207	1,150,669	1,075,013	996,680	1,035,667	950,141
EBITDA	485,767	317,016	150,617	566,016	488,585	413,624	451,358	426,881
Depn & Amortn	62,834	42,071	20,900	81,333	77,810	74,317	80,503	81,998
Income Before Taxes	339,939	219,136	101,625	385,938	349,554	308,338	345,621	289,409
Income Taxes	100,569	64,919	28,674	125,083	119,516	109,396	123,064	105,171
Net Income	239,370	154,217	72,951	260,855	223,648	284,113	222,557	184,238
Average Shares	91,868	91,708	91,624	96,540	109,926	116,706	121,074	123,204
Balance Sheet								
Current Assets	1,153,081	1,083,438	988,651	1,055,670	1,063,271	770,632	637,035	514,835
Total Assets	3,154,472	3,090,097	3,005,138	3,082,578	3,146,987	2,894,175	3,134,537	3,019,639
Current Liabilities	563,517	552,397	496,348	536,570	498,116	472,912	503,041	509,945
Long-Term Obligations	2,077,370	2,076,647	2,075,924	2,075,201	1,579,404	800,000	788,010	811,623
Total Liabilities	2,794,158	2,782,897	2,726,300	2,764,973	2,245,500	1,461,342	1,558,173	1,594,408
Stockholders' Equity	360,314	307,200	278,838	317,605	901,487	1,432,833	1,576,364	1,425,231
Shares Outstanding	90,067	90,129	90,450	91,279	101,013	112,072	118,083	120,114
Statistical Record								
Return on Assets %	9.52	9.79	9.37	8.35	7.40	9.43	7.23	6.01
Return on Equity %	67.47	68.32	61.14	42.68	19.16	18.88	14.83	13.46
EBITDA Margin %	51.71	51.36	50.00	49.19	45.45	41.50	43.58	44.93
Net Margin %	25.48	24.98	24.22	22.67	20.80	28.51	21.49	19.39
Asset Turnover	0.38	0.41	0.40	0.37	0.36	0.33	0.34	0.31
Current Ratio	2.05	1.96	1.99	1.97	2.13	1.63	1.27	1.01
Debt to Equity	5.77	6.76	7.44	6.53	1.75	0.56	0.50	0.57
Price Range	117.74-77.14	106.17-76.78	99.31-71.86	90.12-63.16	72.85-47.24	48.98-40.28	44.71-30.99	37.81-25.59
P/E Ratio	35.25-23.10	34.36-24.85	34.36-24.87	33.38-23.39	35.89-23.27	20.16-16.58	24.43-16.93	25.55-17.29
Average Yield %	1.28	1.28	1.28	1.29	1.29	0.40	...	...

Address: 7 World Trade Center, 250 Greenwich Street, 49th Floor, New York, NY 10007
Telephone: 212-804-3900

Web Site: www.msci.com
Officers: Henry A. Fernandez - Chairman, President, Chief Executive Officer C.D. Baer Pettit - President, Chief Operating Officer, Head

Auditors: PricewaterhouseCoopers LLP
Investor Contact: 212-804-3900
Transfer Agents: Broadridge Financial Solutions, Inc.

MURPHY OIL CORP

Exchange	Symbol	Price	52Wk Range	Yield	P/E
NYS	MUR	$31.05 (12/29/2017)	32.18-22.63	3.22	N/A

*7 Year Price Score 47.74 *NYSE Composite Index=100 *12 Month Price Score 101.83

Interim Earnings (Per Share)

Qtr.	Mar	Jun	Sep	Dec
2014	0.85	0.72	1.37	2.09
2015	(0.08)	(0.42)	(9.26)	(3.41)
2016	(1.16)	0.02	(0.09)	(0.36)
2017	0.34	(0.10)	(0.38)	...

Interim Dividends (Per Share)

Amt	Decl	Ex	Rec	Pay
0.25Q	02/01/2017	02/09/2017	02/13/2017	03/01/2017
0.25Q	04/05/2017	05/11/2017	05/15/2017	06/01/2017
0.25Q	08/02/2017	08/10/2017	08/14/2017	09/01/2017
0.25Q	10/04/2017	11/10/2017	11/13/2017	12/01/2017

Indicated Div: $1.00

Valuation Analysis / Institutional Holding

Forecast EPS	$-0.20 (01/18/2018)	No of Institutions	616
Market Cap	$5.4 Billion	Shares	
Book Value	$5.0 Billion	Shares	192,538,880
Price/Book	1.08	% Held	76.86
Price/Sales	2.50		

Business Summary: Production & Extraction (MIC: 9.1.1 SIC: 2911 NAIC: 324110)

Murphy Oil is a holding company, engaged in oil and gas exploration and production company. Co. explores for and produces crude oil, natural gas and natural gas liquids. Co.'s principal exploration and production activities are conducted in the U.S. by wholly owned Murphy Exploration & Production Company - USA, in Malaysia, Australia, Brunei, and Vietnam by wholly owned Murphy Exploration & Production Company - International (Murphy Expro International) and its subsidiaries, and in Western Canada and offshore Eastern Canada by wholly-owned Murphy Oil Company Ltd. At Dec 31 2016, Co. had proved reserves of 329.0 million barrels of oil, and 1,878.00 billion cubic feet of natural gas.

Recent Developments: For the quarter ended Sep 30 2017, loss from continuing operations was US$66.3 million compared with a loss of US$14.6 million in the year-earlier quarter. Net loss amounted to US$65.9 million versus a net loss of US$16.2 million in the year-earlier quarter. Revenues were US$498.3 million, up 2.6% from US$485.5 million the year before. Operating income was US$32.8 million versus US$7.5 million in the prior-year quarter, an increase of 339.5%. Direct operating expenses declined 4.4% to US$123.6 million from US$129.3 million in the comparable period the year before. Indirect operating expenses decreased 2.0% to US$341.9 million from US$348.8 million in the equivalent prior-year period.

Prospects: Our evaluation of Murphy Oil Corp. as of Jan. 14, 2018 is the result of our systematic analysis on three basic characteristics: earnings strength, relative valuation, and recent stock price movement. The company has suffered a very negative trend in earnings per share over the past 5 quarters. Because the company lacks sufficient analyst estimate data, we place greater weight on the historical EPS trend as the measure of earnings strength. Based on operating earnings yield, the company is overvalued when compared to all of the companies in our coverage universe. Share price changes over the past year indicates that MUR will perform very poorly over the near term.

Financial Data

(US$ in Thousands)	9 Mos	6 Mos	3 Mos	12/31/2016	12/31/2015	12/31/2014	12/31/2013	12/31/2012
Earnings Per Share	(0.50)	(0.21)	(0.09)	(1.60)	(13.03)	5.03	5.94	4.99
Cash Flow Per Share	6.61	6.25	5.01	3.48	6.79	17.05	19.36	15.72
Tang Book Value Per Share	28.86	28.84	25.42	28.55	30.85	48.30	46.65	46.68
Dividends Per Share	1.000	1.000	1.100	1.200	1.400	1.325	1.250	3.675
Dividend Payout %	...	...	...	...	...	26.34	21.04	73.65
Income Statement								
Total Revenue	1,683,238	1,139,116	664,619	1,874,129	3,033,080	5,476,084	5,390,089	28,626,046
EBITDA	248,707	243,031	209,436	756,347	(1,462,455)	3,357,119	3,173,336	3,166,059
Depn & Amortn	40,859	20,306	9,957	1,101,292	1,702,432	1,989,030	1,628,749	1,528,145
Income Before Taxes	69,425	132,983	154,882	(493,115)	(3,282,262)	1,252,270	1,472,687	1,622,982
Income Taxes	95,602	92,842	97,387	(219,172)	(1,026,490)	227,297	584,550	658,936
Net Income	(25,000)	40,893	58,464	(275,970)	(2,270,833)	905,611	1,123,473	970,876
Average Shares	172,573	172,557	173,088	172,173	174,351	180,070	189,271	194,668
Balance Sheet								
Current Assets	1,447,157	1,540,583	1,609,856	1,559,183	1,448,416	3,279,149	3,508,643	4,108,583
Total Assets	10,192,759	10,136,801	10,271,987	10,295,860	11,493,812	16,742,307	17,509,484	17,522,643
Current Liabilities	831,530	1,357,642	1,468,649	1,502,432	1,674,629	3,147,887	3,224,031	3,409,081
Long-Term Obligations	2,908,285	2,367,059	2,421,611	2,422,750	3,040,594	2,536,238	2,936,563	2,245,201
Total Liabilities	5,212,625	5,159,113	5,313,504	5,379,181	6,187,084	8,168,873	8,913,754	8,580,608
Stockholders' Equity	4,980,134	4,977,688	4,958,483	4,916,679	5,306,728	8,573,434	8,595,730	8,942,035
Shares Outstanding	172,572	172,572	195,055	172,202	172,034	177,499	183,406	190,641
Statistical Record								
Return on Assets %	N.M.	N.M.	N.M.	N.M.	N.M.	5.29	6.41	6.12
Return on Equity %	N.M.	N.M.	N.M.	N.M.	N.M.	10.55	12.81	10.93
EBITDA Margin %	14.78	21.34	31.51	40.36	N.M.	61.31	58.87	11.06
Net Margin %	N.M.	3.59	8.80	N.M.	N.M	16.54	20.84	3.39
Asset Turnover	0.21	0.21	0.19	0.17	0.21	0.32	0.31	1.80
Current Ratio	1.74	1.13	1.10	1.04	0.86	1.04	1.09	1.21
Debt to Equity	0.58	0.48	0.49	0.49	0.57	0.30	0.34	0.25
Price Range	34.30-22.63	34.30-24.06	36.24-23.49	36.24-15.76	51.77-21.71	67.75-44.39	65.55-51.20	55.89-37.67
P/E Ratio	...	...	...	...	...	13.47-8.83	11.04-8.62	11.20-7.55
Average Yield %	3.63	3.52	3.74	4.39	3.68	2.25	2.29	7.72

Address: 300 Peach Street, El Dorado, AR 71730-7000	**Web Site:** www.murphyoilcorp.com
Telephone: 870-862-6411	**Officers:** Claiborne P. Deming - Chairman, President, Chief Executive Officer Roger W. Jenkins - President,
Fax: 870-864-3673	Chief Executive Officer, Executive Vice President, Chief Operating Officer

Auditors: KPMG LLP
Investor Contact: 870-864-6501
Transfer Agents: Computershare Trust Company, N.A., Chicago, IL

MURPHY USA INC

Exchange	Symbol	Price	52Wk Range	Yield	P/E
NYS	MUSA	$80.36 (12/29/2017)	81.00-61.03	N/A	17.94

*7 Year Price Score N/A   *NYSE Composite Index=100   *12 Month Price Score 102.77

Price chart 2008-2017 with TRADING VOLUME (thousand shares)

Interim Earnings (Per Share)

Qtr.	Mar	Jun	Sep	Dec
2014	0.21	1.57	1.36	2.13
2015	0.50	0.59	1.41	1.55
2016	2.08	1.17	1.16	1.15
2017	(0.08)	1.51	1.90	...

Interim Dividends (Per Share)
No Dividends Paid

Valuation Analysis

		Institutional Holding
Forecast EPS	$4.52 (01/17/2018)	No of Institutions N/A
Market Cap	$2.8 Billion	Shares
Book Value	$665.1 Million	N/A
Price/Book	4.20	% Held
Price/Sales	0.22	N/A

Business Summary: Retail - General Merchandise/Department Stores (MIC: 2.1.1 SIC: 5541 NAIC: 447110)

Murphy USA's business consists primarily of the marketing of retail motor fuel products and convenience merchandise through a chain of 1,401 as of Dec 31 2016 retail stores operated by Co. located in 26 states, primarily in the Southwest, Southeast and Midwest U.S. As of Dec 31 2016, of these stores, 1,152 were branded Murphy USA® and 249 were standalone Murphy Express locations. Co.'s business also includes certain product supply and wholesale assets, including product distribution terminals and pipeline positions. In addition to the motor fuel sold at its stores, Co.'s stores carry a selection of snacks, beverages, tobacco products and non-food merchandise.

Recent Developments: For the quarter ended Sep 30 2017, net income increased 49.2% to US$67.9 million from US$45.5 million in the year-earlier quarter. Revenues were US$3.24 billion, up 6.4% from US$3.04 billion the year before. Operating income was US$117.9 million versus US$78.9 million in the prior-year quarter, an increase of 49.3%. Direct operating expenses rose 5.3% to US$2.93 billion from US$2.78 billion in the comparable period the year before. Indirect operating expenses increased 3.4% to US$191.4 million from US$185.0 million in the equivalent prior-year period.

Prospects: Our evaluation of Murphy USA Inc. as of Jan. 14, 2018 is the result of our systematic analysis on three basic characteristics: earnings strength, relative valuation, and recent stock price movement. The company has produced a positive trend in earnings per share over the past 5 quarters and while recent estimates for the company have been raised by analysts, MUSA has posted better than expected results. Based on operating earnings yield, the company is undervalued when compared to all of the companies in our coverage universe. Share price changes over the past year indicates that MUSA will perform poorly over the near term.

Financial Data
(US$ in Thousands)

	9 Mos	6 Mos	3 Mos	12/31/2016	12/31/2015	12/31/2014	12/31/2013	12/31/2012
Earnings Per Share	4.48	3.74	3.40	5.59	4.02	5.26	5.02	...
Cash Flow Per Share	8.30	5.73	5.82	8.57	4.97	6.63	7.63	...
Tang Book Value Per Share	19.11	18.88	18.29	18.87	19.01	18.79	14.04	...
Income Statement								
Total Revenue	9,447,029	6,210,678	2,999,618	11,594,553	12,699,411	17,209,919	18,083,335	19,655,436
EBITDA	305,364	155,439	26,626	489,767	336,211	485,059	345,217	222,695
Depn & Amortn	83,514	54,525	27,012	98,610	86,568	79,234	74,130	76,622
Income Before Taxes	188,813	80,137	(9,837)	352,031	218,289	369,423	257,677	145,740
Income Taxes	68,389	27,600	(6,811)	130,539	80,698	126,341	101,351	62,172
Net Income	120,424	52,537	(3,026)	221,492	176,340	243,863	235,033	83,568
Average Shares	35,745	36,861	36,880	39,646	43,794	46,417	46,858	...
Balance Sheet								
Current Assets	575,760	565,744	396,946	515,554	435,667	665,882	682,416	821,962
Total Assets	2,279,507	2,223,186	2,002,736	2,088,740	1,886,241	1,934,257	1,881,242	1,992,465
Current Liabilities	486,009	409,261	454,851	514,560	392,292	413,080	526,517	733,909
Long-Term Obligations	864,975	869,086	620,206	629,622	490,160	492,443	547,578	1,124
Total Liabilities	1,614,414	1,542,545	1,329,968	1,391,664	1,093,951	1,075,552	1,224,906	888,014
Stockholders' Equity	665,093	680,641	672,768	697,076	792,290	858,705	656,336	1,104,451
Shares Outstanding	34,796	36,051	36,775	36,935	41,678	45,710	46,743	...
Statistical Record								
Return on Assets %	7.58	6.59	6.59	11.11	9.23	12.78	...	4.41
Return on Equity %	23.06	19.72	18.96	29.66	21.36	32.19	...	7.50
EBITDA Margin %	3.23	2.50	0.89	4.22	2.65	2.82	1.91	1.13
Net Margin %	1.27	0.85	N.M.	1.91	1.39	1.42	1.30	0.43
Asset Turnover	5.77	5.72	6.02	5.82	6.65	9.02	...	10.38
Current Ratio	1.18	1.38	0.87	1.00	1.11	1.61	1.30	1.12
Debt to Equity	1.30	1.28	0.92	0.90	0.62	0.57	0.83	N.M.
Price Range	76.85-57.80	79.29-57.80	79.29-57.42	79.29-54.24	73.48-48.70	69.37-37.55	46.31-37.51	...
P/E Ratio	17.15-12.90	21.20-15.45	23.32-16.89	14.18-9.70	18.28-12.11	13.19-7.14	9.23-7.47	...

Address: 200 Peach Street, El Dorado, AR 71730-5836 **Telephone:** 870-875-7600	**Web Site:** www.murphyusa.com **Officers:** R. Madison Murphy - Chairman R. Andrew Clyde - President, Chief Executive Officer	**Auditors:** KPMG LLP **Transfer Agents:** Computershare Trust Company, N.A.

491

NABORS INDUSTRIES LTD

Exchange	Symbol	Price	52Wk Range	Yield	P/E
NYS	NBR	$6.83 (12/29/2017)	18.19-5.48	3.51	N/A

*7 Year Price Score 48.91   *NYSE Composite Index=100   *12 Month Price Score 58.70

Interim Earnings (Per Share)

Qtr.	Mar	Jun	Sep	Dec
2014	0.16	0.21	0.35	(3.01)
2015	0.42	(0.13)	(1.02)	(0.57)
2016	(1.41)	(0.65)	(0.39)	(1.18)
2017	(0.52)	(0.46)	(0.52)	...

Interim Dividends (Per Share)

Amt	Decl	Ex	Rec	Pay
0.06Q	02/17/2017	03/10/2017	03/14/2017	04/04/2017
0.06Q	04/21/2017	06/12/2017	06/14/2017	07/05/2017
0.06Q	07/28/2017	09/11/2017	09/12/2017	10/03/2017
0.06Q	10/28/2017	12/12/2017	12/13/2017	01/03/2018

Indicated Div: $0.24

Valuation Analysis   **Institutional Holding**

Forecast EPS	N/A	No of Institutions
		586
Market Cap	$2.0 Billion	Shares
Book Value	$2.9 Billion	341,421,312
Price/Book	0.67	% Held
Price/Sales	0.82	89.05

Business Summary: Production & Extraction (MIC: 9.1.1 SIC: 3533 NAIC: 333132)

Nabors Industries is a holding company. Co. owns and operates land-based drilling rig fleet and is a provider of offshore platform drilling rigs in the U.S. and multiple international markets. Co. also provides wellbore placement services, drilling software and performance tools, drilling equipment and technologies throughout the world's oil and gas markets. Co.'s Drilling & Rig Services business is comprised of its global land-based and offshore drilling rig operations and other rig services, consisting of equipment manufacturing and rig instrumentation. Co. also focuses on wellbore placement solutions and provides directional drilling and measurement while drilling systems and services.

Recent Developments: For the quarter ended Sep 30 2017, loss from continuing operations was US$119.3 million compared with a loss of US$97.8 million in the year-earlier quarter. Net loss amounted to US$146.4 million versus a net loss of US$110.0 million in the year-earlier quarter. Revenues were US$662.5 million, up 27.4% from US$520.0 million the year before. Direct operating expenses rose 44.0% to US$441.3 million from US$306.4 million in the comparable period the year before. Indirect operating expenses increased 3.7% to US$355.2 million from US$342.5 million in the equivalent prior-year period.

Prospects: Our evaluation of Nabors Industries Ltd. as of Sep. 17, 2017 is the result of our systematic analysis on three basic characteristics: earnings strength, relative valuation, and recent stock price movement. The company has produced a positive trend in earnings per share over the past 5 quarters. Because the company lacks sufficient analyst estimate data, we place greater weight on the historical EPS trend as the measure of earnings strength. Based on operating earnings yield, the company is overvalued when compared to all of the companies in our coverage universe. Share price changes over the past year indicates that NBR will perform very poorly over the near term.

Financial Data

(US$ in Thousands)	9 Mos	6 Mos	3 Mos	12/31/2016	12/31/2015	12/31/2014	12/31/2013	12/31/2012
Earnings Per Share	(2.68)	(2.55)	(2.74)	(3.64)	(1.29)	(2.28)	0.47	0.56
Cash Flow Per Share	0.33	0.67	1.12	1.92	3.03	6.13	4.82	5.37
Tang Book Value Per Share	9.54	10.08	10.53	10.85	14.64	16.36	18.71	19.08
Dividends Per Share	0.060	0.060	...	0.060	0.060	0.060	0.040	...
Dividend Payout %	...	...	...	...	...	...	8.51	...
Income Statement								
Total Revenue	1,856,222	1,193,742	563,273	2,007,108	3,791,664	6,809,727	6,248,631	6,751,390
EBITDA	(255,961)	(183,700)	(110,486)	(157,315)	734,970	729,004	1,457,981	1,592,526
Depn & Amortn	20,429	13,303	6,233	855,400	980,577	1,155,671	1,128,403	1,066,291
Income Before Taxes	(442,203)	(308,209)	(173,237)	(1,198,075)	(427,535)	(604,615)	106,160	274,683
Income Taxes	(59,814)	(45,105)	(25,609)	(186,831)	(98,038)	62,666	(55,181)	32,628
Net Income	(430,467)	(281,935)	(148,984)	(1,029,742)	(372,675)	(670,659)	139,982	164,034
Average Shares	279,313	278,916	277,781	276,475	282,982	290,694	296,592	292,323
Balance Sheet								
Current Assets	1,174,921	1,174,168	1,122,656	1,155,839	1,475,897	2,741,874	2,753,830	3,132,857
Total Assets	8,088,585	8,092,458	8,095,312	8,187,015	9,537,840	11,879,942	12,159,811	12,656,022
Current Liabilities	830,674	876,567	771,649	821,934	1,606,499	1,567,475	1,311,424	1,132,382
Long-Term Obligations	3,958,615	3,740,248	3,661,665	3,578,335	3,655,200	4,348,859	3,904,117	4,379,336
Total Liabilities	5,187,180	5,043,223	4,917,364	4,939,990	5,255,130	6,971,323	6,121,537	6,641,905
Stockholders' Equity	2,901,405	3,049,235	3,177,948	3,247,025	4,282,710	4,908,619	6,038,274	6,014,117
Shares Outstanding	285,877	285,826	285,894	283,925	281,184	289,408	295,297	290,399
Statistical Record								
Return on Assets %	N.M.	N.M.	N.M.	N.M.	N.M.	N.M.	1.13	1.28
Return on Equity %	N.M.	N.M.	N.M.	N.M.	N.M.	N.M.	2.32	2.80
EBITDA Margin %	N.M.	N.M.	N.M.	N.M.	19.38	10.71	23.33	23.59
Net Margin %	N.M.	N.M.	N.M.	N.M.	N.M.	N.M.	2.24	2.43
Asset Turnover	0.29	0.27	0.25	0.23	0.35	0.57	0.50	0.53
Current Ratio	1.41	1.34	1.45	1.41	1.47	1.75	2.10	2.77
Debt to Equity	1.36	1.23	1.15	1.10	0.85	0.89	0.65	0.73
Price Range	18.19-6.27	18.19-7.42	18.19-7.93	17.49-5.53	16.70-7.73	30.04-10.00	18.14-14.45	22.31-12.65
P/E Ratio	...	...	...	...	...	...	38.60-30.74	39.84-22.59
Average Yield %	0.51	0.49	...	0.59	0.50	0.27	0.25	...

Address: Crown House, Second Floor, 4 Par-la-Ville Road, Hamilton, HM08 **Telephone:** 441-292-1510	**Web Site:** www.nabors.com **Officers:** Anthony G. Petrello - Chairman, Deputy Chairman, President, Chief Executive Officer, Chief Operating Officer William J. Restrepo - Chief Financial Officer	**Auditors:** PricewaterhouseCoopers LLP **Investor Contact:** 441-292-1510 **Transfer Agents:** Computershare Trust Company, N.A., Providence, RI

NACCO INDUSTRIES INC

Exchange	Symbol	Price	52Wk Range	Yield	P/E	Div Achiever
NYS	NC	$37.65 (12/29/2017)	88.85-31.90	1.75	5.82	10 Years

*7 Year Price Score 97.01 ***NYSE Composite Index=100** ***12 Month Price Score 59.53**

Interim Earnings (Per Share)

Qtr.	Mar	Jun	Sep	Dec
2014	(0.19)	(0.47)	1.02	(5.35)
2015	0.14	(0.04)	0.45	2.58
2016	0.41	0.45	(0.07)	3.52
2017	0.73	0.99	1.23	...

Interim Dividends (Per Share)

Amt	Decl	Ex	Rec	Pay
0.265Q	02/14/2017	2/27//2017	3/01//2017	03/15/2017
0.273Q	05/10/2017	05/30/2017	06/01/2017	06/15/2017
0.273Q	08/21/2017	08/30/2017	09/01/2017	09/15/2017
0.165Q	11/07/2017	11/30/2017	12/01/2017	12/15/2017

Indicated Div: $0.66

Valuation Analysis　　**Institutional Holding**

Forecast EPS	N/A	No of Institutions 133
Market Cap	$257.8 Million	Shares
Book Value	$207.1 Million	4,211,599
Price/Book	1.24	% Held
Price/Sales	0.39	46.18

Business Summary: Household Appliances, Electronics & Goods (MIC: 1.5.1 SIC: 3639 NAIC: 443111)

NACCO Industries is a holding company with the following principal businesses: mining, small appliances, and specialty retail. Co.'s subsidiary, The North American Coal Corporation and its affiliated companies, mine coal primarily for use in power generation and provide services for natural resource companies. Co.'s subsidiary, Hamilton Beach Brands, Inc., is a designer, marketer and distributor of small electric household appliances and housewares appliances, as well as commercial products for restaurants, bars and hotels. Co.'s subsidiary, The Kitchen Collection, LLC (KC), is a retailer of kitchenware. KC operated 223 retail stores under the Kitchen Collection® store name at Dec 31 2016.

Recent Developments: For the quarter ended Sep 30 2017, income from continuing operations was US$3.3 million compared with a loss of US$2.1 million in the year-earlier quarter. Net income amounted to US$8.4 million versus a net loss of US$441,000 in the year-earlier quarter. Revenues were US$21.9 million, down 32.3% from US$32.4 million the year before. Operating income was US$7.0 million versus a loss of US$12.8 million in the prior-year quarter. Direct operating expenses declined 36.7% to US$19.5 million from US$30.8 million in the comparable period the year before. Indirect operating income amounted to US$4.5 million compared with an expense of US$14.4 million in the equivalent prior-year period.

Prospects: Our evaluation of NACCO Industries Inc. as of Jan. 14, 2018 is the result of our systematic analysis on three basic characteristics: earnings strength, relative valuation, and recent stock price movement. The company has generated a negative trend in earnings per share over the past 5 quarters. Because the company lacks sufficient analyst estimate data, we place greater weight on the historical EPS trend as the measure of earnings strength. Based on operating earnings yield, the company is undervalued when compared to all of the companies in our coverage universe. Share price changes over the past year indicates that NC will perform very well over the near term.

Financial Data

(US$ in Thousands)	9 Mos	6 Mos	3 Mos	12/31/2016	12/31/2015	12/31/2014	12/31/2013	12/31/2012
Earnings Per Share	6.47	5.17	4.63	4.32	3.13	(5.02)	5.47	20.82
Cash Flow Per Share	10.95	11.00	8.16	13.74	15.43	2.61	6.55	17.02
Tang Book Value Per Share	23.81	25.40	24.33	23.76	20.19	19.96	30.25	25.33
Dividends Per Share	1.080	1.075	1.070	1.065	1.045	1.023	1.000	5.378
Dividend Payout %	16.69	20.79	23.11	24.65	33.39	...	18.28	25.83
Income Statement								
Total Revenue	78,341	349,658	168,582	856,438	915,860	896,782	932,666	873,400
EBITDA	(19,019)	(9,892)	(7,120)	2,987	4,938	(89,464)	37,202	32,500
Depn & Amortn	387	296	148	19,284	23,687	28,100	24,568	15,200
Income Before Taxes	(22,212)	(12,925)	(8,615)	(21,989)	(25,673)	(125,130)	7,859	11,200
Income Taxes	4,564	4,358	1,670	4,863	2,815	(38,455)	11,270	15,800
Net Income	20,164	11,766	4,978	29,607	21,984	(38,118)	44,450	108,700
Average Shares	6,866	6,850	6,843	6,854	7,022	7,590	8,124	8,414
Balance Sheet								
Current Assets	164,248	343,959	330,895	381,732	361,434	465,713	461,290	486,800
Total Assets	384,949	621,260	620,291	668,021	655,408	770,520	809,956	776,300
Current Liabilities	43,223	186,049	167,204	221,828	191,746	254,681	238,119	227,200
Long-Term Obligations	57,573	99,918	125,313	120,295	160,113	191,431	152,431	135,400
Total Liabilities	177,886	390,300	395,765	447,728	454,270	559,046	512,176	494,900
Stockholders' Equity	207,063	230,960	224,526	220,293	201,138	211,474	297,780	281,400
Shares Outstanding	6,846	6,836	6,833	6,778	6,837	7,235	7,871	8,352
Statistical Record								
Return on Assets %	8.44	5.76	5.18	4.46	3.08	N.M.	5.60	8.41
Return on Equity %	21.96	16.49	14.90	14.01	10.66	N.M.	15.35	25.28
EBITDA Margin %	N.M.	N.M.	N.M.	0.35	0.54	N.M.	3.99	3.72
Net Margin %	25.74	3.37	2.95	3.46	2.40	N.M.	4.77	12.45
Asset Turnover	1.25	1.39	1.39	1.29	1.28	1.13	1.18	0.68
Current Ratio	3.80	1.85	1.98	1.72	1.88	1.83	1.94	2.14
Debt to Equity	0.28	0.43	0.56	0.55	0.80	0.91	0.51	0.48
Price Range	97.55-62.60	97.55-54.89	97.55-50.97	97.55-42.20	62.37-40.48	63.56-47.69	66.35-48.54	60.69-31.20
P/E Ratio	15.08-9.68	18.87-10.62	21.07-11.01	22.58-9.77	19.93-12.93	...	12.13-8.87	2.91-1.50
Average Yield %	1.43	1.47	1.56	1.70	1.99	1.87	1.72	13.03

Address: 5875 Landerbrook Drive, Suite 220, Cleveland, OH 44124-4069 Telephone: 440-229-5151	Web Site: www.nacco.com Officers: J. C. Butler - Senior Vice President, Vice President, Chief Administrative Officer, Treasurer, President, Chief Executive Officer Lauren E. Miller - Vice President	Auditors: Ernst & Young LLP Investor Contact: 440-229-5130 Transfer Agents: Computershare, Canton, MA

NATIONAL FUEL GAS CO. (NJ)

Exchange	Symbol	Price	52Wk Range	Yield	P/E	Div Achiever
NYS	NFG	$54.91 (12/29/2017)	60.91-53.32	3.02	16.64	45 Years

*7 Year Price Score 75.40   *NYSE Composite Index=100   *12 Month Price Score 93.97

Interim Earnings (Per Share)

Qtr.	Dec	Mar	Jun	Sep
2012-13	0.81	1.02	0.69	0.56
2013-14	0.97	1.12	0.76	0.67
2014-15	1.00	0.20	(3.44)	(2.25)
2015-16	(2.23)	(1.74)	0.10	0.44
2016-17	1.04	1.04	0.69	0.53

Interim Dividends (Per Share)

Amt	Decl	Ex	Rec	Pay
0.405Q	03/09/2017	03/29/2017	03/31/2017	04/14/2017
0.415Q	06/15/2017	06/28/2017	06/30/2017	07/14/2017
0.415Q	09/14/2017	09/28/2017	09/29/2017	10/13/2017
0.415Q	12/07/2017	12/28/2017	12/29/2017	01/12/2018

Indicated Div: $1.66 (Div. Reinv. Plan)

Valuation Analysis

		Institutional Holding	
Forecast EPS	$2.92 (01/18/2018)	No of Institutions	506
Market Cap	$4.7 Billion	Shares	74,854,768
Book Value	$1.7 Billion	% Held	63.54
Price/Book	2.76		
Price/Sales	2.97		

Business Summary: Gas Utilities (MIC: 3.3.1 SIC: 4924 NAIC: 221210)

National Fuel Gas is a holding company. Co. operates five segments: Exploration and Production, which is engaged in the exploration for, and the development and production of, natural gas and oil reserves; Pipeline and Storage, which provides interstate natural gas transportation and storage services; Gathering, which builds, owns and operates natural gas processing and pipeline gathering facilities; Utility, which sells natural gas or provides natural gas transportation services; and Energy Marketing, which markets natural gas. At Sept 30 2017, Co. had U.S. proved developed and undeveloped reserves of 30,207 thousand barrels of oil and 1,973,120 million cubic feet of natural gas.

Recent Developments: For the year ended Sep 30 2017, net income amounted to US$283.5 million versus a net loss of US$291.0 million in the prior year. Revenues were US$1.58 billion, up 8.8% from US$1.45 billion the year before. Operating income was US$552.8 million versus a loss of US$416.5 million in the prior year. Direct operating expenses rose 21.8% to US$717.8 million from US$589.5 million in the comparable period the year before. Indirect operating expenses decreased 75.8% to US$309.2 million from US$1.28 billion in the equivalent prior-year period.

Prospects: Our evaluation of National Fuel Gas Co. as of Jan. 14, 2018 is the result of our systematic analysis on three basic characteristics: earnings strength, relative valuation, and recent stock price movement. The company has generated a negative trend in earnings per share over the past 5 quarters and while recent estimates for the company have been raised by analysts, NFG has posted better than expected results. Based on operating earnings yield, the company is undervalued when compared to all of the companies in our coverage universe. Share price changes over the past year indicates that NFG will perform in line with the market over the near term.

Financial Data

(US$ in Thousands)	09/30/2017	09/30/2016	09/30/2015	09/30/2014	09/30/2013	09/30/2012	09/30/2011	09/30/2010
Earnings Per Share	3.30	(3.43)	(4.50)	3.52	3.08	2.63	3.09	2.73
Cash Flow Per Share	8.02	6.92	10.11	10.84	8.84	7.93	8.21	5.65
Tang Book Value Per Share	19.85	17.88	23.88	28.58	26.17	23.46	22.78	21.19
Dividends Per Share	1.640	1.600	1.560	1.520	1.480	1.440	1.400	1.360
Dividend Payout %	49.70	...	...	43.18	48.05	54.75	45.31	49.82
Income Statement								
Total Revenue	1,579,881	1,452,416	1,760,913	2,113,081	1,829,551	1,626,853	1,778,842	1,760,503
EBITDA	784,083	(157,281)	(266,856)	962,915	849,295	724,712	725,274	635,898
Depn & Amortn	224,195	249,417	336,158	383,781	326,760	271,530	226,527	191,809
Income Before Taxes	444,164	(523,507)	(698,563)	489,027	432,759	370,631	423,542	353,872
Income Taxes	160,682	(232,549)	(319,136)	189,614	172,758	150,554	164,381	137,227
Net Income	283,482	(290,958)	(379,427)	299,413	260,001	220,077	258,402	225,913
Average Shares	86,021	84,847	84,387	84,952	84,341	83,739	83,670	82,660
Balance Sheet								
Current Assets	818,280	413,031	513,001	377,332	448,677	355,576	385,312	775,377
Total Assets	6,103,320	5,636,387	6,702,139	6,739,597	6,218,347	5,935,142	5,284,742	5,105,625
Current Liabilities	646,039	303,737	446,140	490,576	302,171	734,479	528,618	524,324
Long-Term Obligations	2,083,681	2,086,252	2,084,009	1,649,000	1,649,000	1,149,000	899,000	1,049,000
Total Liabilities	4,399,585	4,109,383	4,676,699	4,328,914	4,023,618	3,975,047	3,392,857	3,359,654
Stockholders' Equity	1,703,735	1,527,004	2,025,440	2,410,683	2,194,729	1,960,095	1,891,885	1,745,971
Shares Outstanding	85,543	85,118	84,594	84,157	83,661	83,330	82,812	82,075
Statistical Record								
Return on Assets %	4.83	N.M.	N.M.	4.62	4.28	3.91	4.97	4.58
Return on Equity %	17.55	N.M.	N.M.	13.00	12.52	11.40	14.21	13.55
EBITDA Margin %	49.63	N.M.	N.M.	45.57	46.42	44.55	40.77	36.12
Net Margin %	17.94	N.M.	N.M.	14.17	14.21	13.53	14.53	12.83
Asset Turnover	0.27	0.23	0.26	0.33	0.30	0.29	0.34	0.36
Current Ratio	1.27	1.36	1.15	0.77	1.48	0.48	0.73	1.48
Debt to Equity	1.22	1.37	1.03	0.68	0.75	0.59	0.48	0.60
Price Range	60.91-50.68	59.45-37.90	71.90-48.82	78.30-65.45	68.76-48.69	63.58-42.17	75.40-48.68	54.32-42.98
P/E Ratio	18.46-15.36	...	...	22.24-18.59	22.32-15.81	24.17-16.03	24.40-15.75	19.90-15.74
Average Yield %	2.88	3.13	2.49	2.10	2.52	2.85	2.13	2.78

Address: 6363 Main Street, Williamsville, NY 14221	**Web Site:** www.nationalfuelgas.com	**Auditors:** PricewaterhouseCoopers LLP
Telephone: 716-857-7000	**Officers:** David F. Smith - Chairman, Chief Executive Officer Ronald J. Tanski - President, Chief Operating Officer, Chief Executive Officer	**Investor Contact:** 716-857-6987 **Transfer Agents:** Wells Fargo Shareowner Services, Saint Paul, MN

NATIONAL HEALTH INVESTORS, INC.

Exchange	Symbol	Price	52Wk Range	Yield	P/E	Div Acheiver
NYS	NHI	$75.38 (12/29/2017)	80.81-69.30	5.04	18.84	14 Years

*7 Year Price Score 96.57   ***NYSE Composite Index=100**   ***12 Month Price Score 96.32**

Interim Earnings (Per Share)

Qtr.	Mar	Jun	Sep	Dec
2014	0.71	0.77	0.76	0.80
2015	0.79	0.83	0.89	1.44
2016	0.85	1.16	0.83	1.03
2017	1.10	0.93	0.94	

Interim Dividends (Per Share)

Amt	Decl	Ex	Rec	Pay
0.95Q	02/17/2017	03/29/2017	03/31/2017	05/10/2017
0.95Q	05/11/2017	06/28/2017	06/30/2017	08/10/2017
0.95Q	08/09/2017	09/28/2017	09/29/2017	11/10/2017
0.95Q	11/08/2017	12/28/2017	12/29/2017	01/31/2018

Indicated Div: $3.80

Valuation Analysis

		Institutional Holding	
Forecast EPS	$3.90 (01/24/2018)	No of Institutions	286
Market Cap	$3.1 Billion	Shares	36,835,784
Book Value	$1.3 Billion	% Held	68.67
Price/Book	2.36		
Price/Sales	11.48		

TRADING VOLUME (thousand shares)

Business Summary: REITs (MIC: 5.3.1 SIC: 6798 NAIC: 525930)

National Health Investors is a real estate investment trust which focuses on sale-leaseback, joint-venture, mortgage and mezzanine financing of senior housing and medical investments. Co.'s portfolio consists of investments in independent living facilities, assisted living facilities, entrance-fee communities, senior living campuses, skilled nursing facilities, specialty hospitals and medical office buildings. At Dec 31 2016, Co. had investments in real estate, mortgage and other notes receivable involving 205 facilities located in 32 states. These investments involve senior housing properties, skilled nursing facilities, hospitals, medical office buildings and other notes receivable.

Recent Developments: For the quarter ended Sep 30 2017, net income increased 16.9% to US$39.1 million from US$33.4 million in the year-earlier quarter. Revenues were US$71.4 million, up 12.8% from US$63.3 million the year before. Revenues from property income rose 15.1% to US$68.2 million from US$59.3 million in the corresponding quarter a year earlier.

Prospects: Our evaluation of National Health Investors Inc. as of Jan. 21, 2018 is the result of our systematic analysis on three basic characteristics: earnings strength, relative valuation, and recent stock price movement. The company has enjoyed a very positive trend in earnings per share over the past 5 quarters. Because the company lacks sufficient analyst estimate data, we place greater weight on the historical EPS trend as the measure of earnings strength. Based on operating earnings yield, the company is undervalued when compared to all of the companies in our coverage universe. Share price changes over the past year indicates that NHI will perform very well over the near term.

Financial Data

(US$ in Thousands)	9 Mos	6 Mos	3 Mos	12/31/2016	12/31/2015	12/31/2014	12/31/2013	12/31/2012
Earnings Per Share	4.00	3.89	4.12	3.87	3.95	3.04	3.74	3.26
Cash Flow Per Share	4.72	4.61	4.62	4.53	4.37	3.78	3.67	3.09
Tang Book Value Per Share	31.97	31.39	31.41	30.36	29.52	27.74	23.19	16.41
Dividends Per Share	3.750	3.700	3.650	3.600	3.400	3.080	3.120	2.640
Dividend Payout %	93.75	95.12	88.59	93.02	86.08	101.32	83.42	80.98
Income Statement								
Total Revenue	207,576	136,225	66,388	248,500	228,988	177,509	117,828	96,953
EBITDA	175,402	117,588	61,617	214,244	204,537	141,201	99,832	91,599
Depn & Amortn	53,836	35,113	17,387	59,565	53,163	38,078	20,658	16,981
Income Before Taxes	121,566	82,475	44,230	154,679	151,374	103,123	79,174	74,618
Income Taxes	...	...	...	749	(707)	...	...	...
Net Income	121,566	82,475	44,230	151,540	148,862	101,609	106,183	90,731
Average Shares	41,448	41,245	40,108	39,155	37,644	33,416	28,397	27,838
Balance Sheet								
Current Assets	94,150	90,496	85,412	77,350	73,063	38,441	30,003	21,542
Total Assets	2,519,932	2,511,042	2,515,979	2,403,633	2,146,349	1,982,960	1,455,820	705,981
Current Liabilities	80,973	79,611	83,004	55,866	52,784	47,582	34,904	33,350
Long-Term Obligations	1,111,292	1,145,005	1,145,691	1,115,981	926,257	862,726	617,080	203,250
Total Liabilities	1,192,265	1,224,616	1,228,695	1,194,043	1,013,057	943,035	689,274	248,799
Stockholders' Equity	1,327,667	1,286,426	1,287,284	1,209,590	1,133,292	1,039,925	766,546	457,182
Shares Outstanding	41,531	40,984	40,978	39,847	38,396	37,485	33,051	27,857
Statistical Record								
Return on Assets %	6.63	6.47	6.97	6.64	7.21	5.91	9.82	14.08
Return on Equity %	12.84	12.76	13.49	12.90	13.70	11.25	17.35	20.09
EBITDA Margin %	84.50	86.32	92.81	86.21	89.32	79.55	84.73	94.48
Net Margin %	58.56	60.54	66.62	60.98	65.01	57.24	90.12	93.58
Asset Turnover	0.11	0.11	0.11	0.11	0.11	0.10	0.11	0.15
Current Ratio	1.16	1.14	1.03	1.38	1.38	0.81	0.86	0.65
Debt to Equity	0.84	0.89	0.89	0.92	0.82	0.83	0.81	0.44
Price Range	80.71-67.68	82.39-67.68	82.39-65.22	82.39-55.73	76.46-54.10	71.19-55.13	72.30-53.28	57.14-43.70
P/E Ratio	20.18-16.92	21.18-17.40	20.00-15.83	21.29-14.40	19.36-13.70	23.42-18.13	19.33-14.25	17.53-13.40
Average Yield %	4.99	4.91	4.96	5.08	5.25	4.94	5.04	5.18

Address: 222 Robert Rose Drive, Murfreesboro, TN 37129 **Telephone:** 615-890-9100	**Web Site:** www.nhireit.com **Officers:** W. Andrew Adams - Chairman, Chief Executive Officer, Acting Chief Financial Officer Eric Mendelsohn - Interim President, Interim Chief Executive Officer, President, Chief Executive Officer	**Auditors:** BDO USA, LLP **Investor Contact:** 615-890-9100 **Transfer Agents:** Computershare Trust Company, N.A. Providence, RI

NATIONAL OILWELL VARCO INC

Exchange	Symbol	Price	52Wk Range	Yield	P/E
NYS	NOV	$36.02 (12/29/2017)	41.74-29.94	0.56	N/A

*7 Year Price Score 49.96 *NYSE Composite Index=100 *12 Month Price Score 90.65

Interim Earnings (Per Share)

Qtr.	Mar	Jun	Sep	Dec
2014	1.37	1.44	1.62	1.39
2015	0.76	0.74	0.41	(3.91)
2016	(0.32)	(0.58)	(3.62)	(1.88)
2017	(0.32)	(0.20)	(0.07)	...

Interim Dividends (Per Share)

Amt	Decl	Ex	Rec	Pay
0.05Q	02/24/2017	03/15/2017	03/17/2017	03/31/2017
0.05Q	05/18/2017	06/14/2017	06/16/2017	06/30/2017
0.05Q	08/17/2017	09/14/2017	09/15/2017	09/29/2017
0.05Q	11/16/2017	12/07/2017	12/08/2017	12/22/2017

Indicated Div: $0.20 (Div. Reinv. Plan)

Valuation Analysis

		Institutional Holding	
Forecast EPS	$-0.42	No of Institutions	
	(01/18/2018)	963	
Market Cap	$13.7 Billion	Shares	
Book Value	$14.1 Billion	418,393,856	
Price/Book	0.97	% Held	
Price/Sales	1.95	86.41	

Business Summary: Equipment & Services (MIC: 9.1.3 SIC: 3533 NAIC: 333132)

National Oilwell Varco is an oilfield equipment manufacturer and technology provider. Co. operates in four segments: Rig Systems, which designs, manufactures and sells land rigs, offshore drilling equipment packages, and drilling rig components; Rig Aftermarket, which provides aftermarket products and services to support land and offshore rigs, and drilling rig components; Wellbore Technologies, which designs, manufactures, rents, and sells equipment used to perform drilling operations; and Completion and Production Solutions, which designs, manufactures, and sells equipment and technologies for hydraulic fracture stimulation, well intervention, onshore production and offshore production.

Recent Developments: For the quarter ended Sep 30 2017, net loss amounted to US$27.0 million versus a net loss of US$1.36 billion in the year-earlier quarter. Revenues were US$1.84 billion, up 11.5% from US$1.65 billion the year before. Operating loss was US$7.0 million versus a loss of US$1.19 billion in the prior-year quarter. Direct operating expenses declined 1.1% to US$1.55 billion from US$1.57 billion in the comparable period the year before. Indirect operating expenses decreased 76.9% to US$292.0 million from US$1.27 billion in the equivalent prior-year period.

Prospects: Our evaluation of National-Oilwell Inc. as of Jan. 14, 2018 is the result of our systematic analysis on three basic characteristics: earnings strength, relative valuation, and recent stock price movement. The company has produced a positive trend in earnings per share over the past 5 quarters. Because the company lacks sufficient analyst estimate data, we place greater weight on the historical EPS trend as the measure of earnings strength. Based on operating earnings yield, the company is overvalued when compared to all of the companies in our coverage universe. Share price changes over the past year indicates that NOV will perform very poorly over the near term.

Financial Data

(US$ in Thousands)	9 Mos	6 Mos	3 Mos	12/31/2016	12/31/2015	12/31/2014	12/31/2013	12/31/2012
Earnings Per Share	(2.47)	(6.02)	(6.40)	(6.41)	(1.99)	5.82	5.44	5.83
Cash Flow Per Share	1.76	1.30	1.20	2.55	3.44	6.11	7.97	1.45
Tang Book Value Per Share	11.95	11.54	11.55	11.47	14.78	18.40	18.97	19.50
Dividends Per Share	0.200	0.200	0.200	0.610	1.840	1.640	0.910	0.490
Dividend Payout %	...	...	...	...	...	28.18	16.73	8.40
Income Statement								
Total Revenue	5,335,000	3,500,000	1,741,000	7,251,000	14,757,000	21,440,000	22,869,000	20,041,000
EBITDA	338,000	177,000	67,000	(2,142,000)	(122,000)	3,936,000	3,774,000	3,809,000
Depn & Amortn	523,000	349,000	175,000	370,000	391,000	413,000	392,000	323,000
Income Before Taxes	(243,000)	(215,000)	(129,000)	(2,602,000)	(602,000)	3,436,000	3,283,000	3,447,000
Income Taxes	(26,000)	(23,000)	(9,000)	(207,000)	178,000	1,039,000	1,018,000	1,022,000
Net Income	(223,000)	(197,000)	(122,000)	(2,412,000)	(769,000)	2,502,000	2,327,000	2,491,000
Average Shares	377,000	377,000	376,000	376,000	387,000	430,000	428,000	427,000
Balance Sheet								
Current Assets	7,825,000	7,741,000	7,744,000	7,876,000	11,801,000	16,162,000	16,423,000	15,678,000
Total Assets	20,934,000	20,887,000	20,904,000	21,140,000	26,725,000	33,562,000	34,812,000	31,484,000
Current Liabilities	2,842,000	2,851,000	2,852,000	3,047,000	4,249,000	7,374,000	6,678,000	5,649,000
Long-Term Obligations	2,707,000	2,708,000	2,707,000	2,708,000	3,928,000	3,014,000	3,149,000	3,148,000
Total Liabilities	6,850,000	6,934,000	6,983,000	7,200,000	10,342,000	12,870,000	12,582,000	11,245,000
Stockholders' Equity	14,084,000	13,953,000	13,921,000	13,940,000	16,383,000	20,692,000	22,230,000	20,239,000
Shares Outstanding	380,053	380,052	380,060	378,637	375,764	418,977	428,433	426,928
Statistical Record								
Return on Assets %	N.M.	N.M.	N.M.	N.M.	N.M.	7.32	7.02	8.72
Return on Equity %	N.M.	N.M.	N.M.	N.M.	N.M.	11.66	10.96	13.12
EBITDA Margin %	6.34	5.06	3.85	N.M.	N.M.	18.36	16.50	19.01
Net Margin %	N.M.	N.M.	N.M.	N.M.	N.M.	11.67	10.18	12.43
Asset Turnover	0.33	0.31	0.30	0.30	0.49	0.63	0.69	0.70
Current Ratio	2.75	2.72	2.72	2.58	2.78	2.19	2.46	2.78
Debt to Equity	0.19	0.19	0.19	0.19	0.24	0.15	0.14	0.16
Price Range	41.74-29.94	41.74-31.27	41.74-27.32	40.32-26.34	65.53-33.27	86.43-61.55	75.97-57.80	78.57-54.07
P/E Ratio	...	...	...	...	...	14.85-10.58	13.97-10.63	13.48-9.27
Average Yield %	0.56	0.56	0.57	1.84	4.01	2.22	1.38	0.73

Address: 7909 Parkwood Circle Drive, Houston, TX 77036-6565 **Telephone:** 713-346-7500	**Web Site:** www.nov.com **Officers:** Clay C. Williams - Chairman, President, Chief Executive Officer, Chief Operating Officer, Chief Financial Officer, Executive Vice President, Senior Vice President Jose A. Bayardo - Chief Financial Officer, Senior Vice President	**Auditors:** Ernst & Young LLP **Investor Contact:** 713-346-7500 **Transfer Agents:** American Stock Transfer & Trust Company, New York, NY

NATIONAL RETAIL PROPERTIES INC

Exchange	Symbol	Price	52Wk Range	Yield	P/E	Div Achiever
NYS	NNN	$43.13 (12/29/2017)	46.13-36.72	4.41	31.03	27 Years

*7 Year Price Score 91.21   *NYSE Composite Index=100   *12 Month Price Score 94.65

Interim Earnings (Per Share)

Qtr.	Mar	Jun	Sep	Dec
2014	0.28	0.30	0.31	0.35
2015	0.34	0.28	0.34	0.24
2016	0.44	0.30	0.29	0.36
2017	0.35	0.33	0.35	...

Interim Dividends (Per Share)

Amt	Decl	Ex	Rec	Pay
0.455Q	04/13/2017	04/26/2017	04/28/2017	05/15/2017
0.475Q	07/14/2017	07/27/2017	07/31/2017	08/15/2017
0.475Q	10/16/2017	10/30/2017	10/31/2017	11/15/2017
0.475Q	01/16/2018	01/30/2018	01/31/2018	02/15/2018

Indicated Div: $1.90 (Div. Reinv. Plan)

Valuation Analysis

		Institutional Holding	
Forecast EPS	$1.35	No of Institutions	
	(01/09/2018)	463	
Market Cap	$6.5 Billion	Shares	
Book Value	$3.8 Billion	180,156,592	
Price/Book	1.74	% Held	
Price/Sales	11.36	N/A	

Business Summary: REITs (MIC: 5.3.1 SIC: 6798 NAIC: 525930)

National Retail Properties is a real estate investment trust. Co.'s assets primarily include: real estate assets, mortgages and notes receivable. Co. acquires, owns, invests in and develops properties that are leased primarily to retail tenants under long-term net leases and are primarily held for investment. Co. owned 2,535 properties located in 48 states as of Dec 31 2016.

Recent Developments: For the quarter ended Sep 30 2017, net income increased 20.4% to US$61.1 million from US$50.8 million in the year-earlier quarter. Revenues were US$147.7 million, up 9.8% from US$134.5 million the year before. Revenues from property income rose 10.0% to US$147.5 million from US$134.0 million in the corresponding quarter a year earlier.

Prospects: Our evaluation of National Retail Properties Inc. as of Jan. 14, 2018 is the result of our systematic analysis on three basic characteristics: earnings strength, relative valuation, and recent stock price movement. The company has produced a positive trend in earnings per share over the past 5 quarters. Because the company lacks sufficient analyst estimate data, we place greater weight on the historical EPS trend as the measure of earnings strength. Based on operating earnings yield, the company is about fairly valued when compared to all of the companies in our coverage universe. Share price changes over the past year indicates that NNN will perform well over the near term.

Financial Data

(US$ in Thousands)	9 Mos	6 Mos	3 Mos	12/31/2016	12/31/2015	12/31/2014	12/31/2013	12/31/2012
Earnings Per Share	1.39	1.33	1.30	1.38	1.20	1.24	1.10	1.11
Cash Flow Per Share	2.89	2.98	2.93	2.87	2.55	2.39	2.32	2.13
Tang Book Value Per Share	20.66	20.48	20.48	20.37	19.62	18.99	18.05	18.01
Dividends Per Share	1.840	1.820	1.800	1.780	1.710	1.650	1.600	1.560
Dividend Payout %	132.37	136.84	138.46	128.99	142.50	133.06	145.45	140.54
Income Statement								
Total Revenue	434,686	286,981	141,432	533,647	482,914	434,847	392,327	331,752
EBITDA	259,445	171,557	87,223	464,742	428,442	386,076	345,552	280,699
Depn & Amortn	5,270	3,466	1,722	156,236	140,714	121,221	106,304	83,096
Income Before Taxes	172,322	114,378	59,024	212,324	197,829	179,702	155,458	117,333
Income Taxes	...	...	...	...	10,318	(75)	618	(7,086)
Net Income	192,805	131,685	73,657	239,500	197,836	190,601	160,145	142,015
Average Shares	149,667	148,719	147,279	144,660	134,489	124,710	119,864	109,117
Balance Sheet								
Current Assets	283,644	32,346	63,078	323,059	43,133	39,276	30,389	30,646
Total Assets	6,626,220	6,337,128	6,114,772	6,334,151	5,460,044	4,926,714	4,454,523	3,988,026
Current Liabilities	37,055	235,421	36,379	19,665	20,113	17,396	63,542	191,727
Long-Term Obligations	2,708,861	2,313,301	2,312,489	2,311,689	1,975,944	1,741,054	1,523,659	1,412,764
Total Liabilities	2,860,967	2,648,943	2,439,961	2,417,352	2,117,910	1,844,199	1,677,478	1,691,741
Stockholders' Equity	3,765,253	3,688,185	3,674,811	3,916,799	3,342,134	3,082,515	2,777,045	2,296,285
Shares Outstanding	151,627	149,206	148,578	147,149	141,007	132,010	121,991	111,554
Statistical Record								
Return on Assets %	4.15	4.10	4.16	4.05	3.81	4.06	3.79	3.82
Return on Equity %	7.05	6.87	6.82	6.58	6.16	6.51	6.31	6.59
EBITDA Margin %	59.69	59.78	61.67	87.09	88.72	88.78	88.08	84.61
Net Margin %	44.36	45.89	52.08	44.88	40.97	43.83	40.82	42.81
Asset Turnover	0.09	0.09	0.09	0.09	0.09	0.09	0.09	0.09
Current Ratio	7.65	0.14	1.73	16.43	2.14	2.26	0.48	0.16
Debt to Equity	0.72	0.63	0.63	0.59	0.59	0.56	0.55	0.62
Price Range	50.85-36.72	53.46-36.72	53.46-40.89	53.46-39.00	44.24-33.99	40.34-30.33	41.89-30.09	32.25-26.10
P/E Ratio	36.58-26.42	40.20-27.61	41.12-31.45	38.74-28.26	36.87-28.33	32.53-24.46	38.08-27.35	29.05-23.51
Average Yield %	4.34	4.04	3.87	3.85	4.44	4.42	4.68	5.42

Address: 450 South Orange Avenue, Suite 900, Orlando, FL 32801
Telephone: 407-265-7348
Fax: 407-423-2894

Web Site: www.nnnreit.com
Officers: Craig Macnab - Chairman, Chief Executive Officer Julian E. Whitehurst - President, Chief Executive Officer, Chief Operating Officer

Auditors: Ernst & Young LLP
Investor Contact: 407-650-1228
Transfer Agents: American Stock Transfer & Trust Company, Brooklyn, NY

NAVISTAR INTERNATIONAL CORP.

Exchange	Symbol	Price	52Wk Range	Yield	P/E
NYS	NAV	$42.88 (12/29/2017)	45.30-22.89	N/A	134.00

*7 Year Price Score 80.47 *NYSE Composite Index=100 *12 Month Price Score 120.51

Interim Earnings (Per Share)

Qtr.	Jan	Apr	Jul	Oct
2012-13	(1.53)	(4.65)	(3.06)	(1.92)
2013-14	(3.05)	(3.65)	(0.02)	(0.87)
2014-15	(0.52)	(0.78)	(0.34)	(0.61)
2015-16	(0.40)	0.05	(0.42)	(0.42)
2016-17	(0.76)	(0.86)	0.38	1.47

Interim Dividends (Per Share)

No Dividends Paid

Valuation Analysis	Institutional Holding	
Forecast EPS	$2.00	No of Institutions
	(01/17/2018)	246
Market Cap	$4.2 Billion	Shares
Book Value	N/A	94,898,976
Price/Book	N/A	% Held
Price/Sales	0.49	100.88

Business Summary: Autos- Manufacturing (MIC: 1.8.1 SIC: 3711 NAIC: 336211)

Navistar International, manufactures International® brand commercial and military trucks, diesel engines, IC Bus™ brand school and commercial buses, and provides service parts as well as retail, wholesale, and lease financing services for its trucks and parts. Co. operates four segments: Truck, which provides Class 4 through 8 trucks and buses; Parts, and other standard truck, trailer, and engine service parts; Global Operations, consisting of engine and truck operations in Brazil; and Financial Services.

Recent Developments: For the year ended Oct 31 2017, income from continuing operations was US$54.0 million compared with a loss of US$65.0 million a year earlier. Net income amounted to US$55.0 million versus a net loss of US$65.0 million in the prior year. Revenues were US$8.57 billion, up 5.7% from US$8.11 billion the year before. Direct operating expenses rose 3.3% to US$7.04 billion from US$6.81 billion in the comparable period the year before. Indirect operating expenses increased 5.9% to US$1.50 billion from US$1.41 billion in the equivalent prior-year period.

Prospects: Our evaluation of Navistar International Corp. as of Jan. 14, 2018 is the result of our systematic analysis on three basic characteristics: earnings strength, relative valuation, and recent stock price movement. The company has produced a positive trend in earnings per share over the past 5 quarters and, while recent estimates for the company have been raised by analysts, NAV has posted better than expected results. Based on operating earnings yield, the company is overvalued when compared to all of the companies in our coverage universe. Share price changes over the past year indicates that NAV will perform well over the near term.

Financial Data

(US$ in Millions)	10/31/2017	10/31/2016	10/31/2015	10/31/2014	10/31/2013	10/31/2012	10/31/2011	10/31/2010
Earnings Per Share	0.32	(1.19)	(2.25)	(7.60)	(11.17)	(43.56)	22.64	3.05
Cash Flow Per Share	1.17	3.26	0.56	(4.13)	1.24	8.80	12.09	15.44
Income Statement								
Total Revenue	8,570	8,111	10,140	10,806	10,775	12,948	13,958	12,145
EBITDA	482	368	274	63	(269)	(596)	937	882
Depn & Amortn	73	79	76	314	395	298	299	289
Income Before Taxes	58	(38)	(109)	(565)	(985)	(1,153)	391	340
Income Taxes	10	33	51	26	(171)	1,780	(1,458)	23
Net Income	30	(97)	(184)	(619)	(898)	(3,010)	1,723	223
Average Shares	93	81	81	81	80	69	76	73
Balance Sheet								
Current Assets	4,160	3,759	4,622	5,013	5,459	5,837	7,235	5,835
Total Assets	6,135	5,653	6,692	7,443	8,315	9,102	12,291	9,730
Current Liabilities	3,645	3,203	3,788	4,231	4,261	4,353	4,798	3,589
Long-Term Obligations	3,889	3,997	4,188	3,929	3,922	3,566	3,477	4,238
Total Liabilities	10,713	10,951	11,859	12,095	11,960	12,407	12,313	10,703
Stockholders' Equity	(4,578)	(5,298)	(5,167)	(4,652)	(3,645)	(3,305)	(22)	(973)
Shares Outstanding	98	81	81	81	80	79	70	71
Statistical Record								
Return on Assets %	0.51	N.M.	N.M.	N.M.	N.M.	N.M.	15.65	2.26
EBITDA Margin %	5.62	4.54	2.70	0.58	N.M.	N.M.	6.71	7.26
Net Margin %	0.35	N.M.	N.M.	N.M.	N.M.	N.M.	12.34	1.84
Asset Turnover	1.45	1.31	1.43	1.37	1.24	1.21	1.27	1.23
Current Ratio	1.14	1.17	1.22	1.18	1.28	1.34	1.51	1.63
Price Range	44.68-22.30	23.69-6.23	37.76-11.36	40.90-29.49	39.71-18.75	47.42-18.51	70.17-30.68	56.89-32.18
P/E Ratio	139.63-69.69	...	...	...	...	...	3.10-1.36	18.65-10.55

Address: 2701 Navistar Drive, Lisle, IL 60532
Telephone: 331-332-5000

Web Site: www.navistar.com
Officers: Troy A. Clarke - President, Chief Executive Officer, Chief Operating Officer, Division Officer Persio V. Lisboa - Chief Operating Officer, Executive Vice President

Auditors: KPMG LLP
Investor Contact: 331-332-2143
Transfer Agents: Computershare Investor Services, Jersey City, NJ

NCR CORP

Exchange	Symbol	Price	52Wk Range	Yield	P/E
NYS	NCR	$33.99 (12/29/2017)	49.59-29.57	N/A	20.60

*7 Year Price Score 105.96 *NYSE Composite Index=100 *12 Month Price Score 76.25

TRADING VOLUME (thousand shares)

Interim Earnings (Per Share)

Qtr.	Mar	Jun	Sep	Dec
2014	0.31	0.53	0.09	0.20
2015	0.23	(2.03)	0.57	0.13
2016	0.16	0.49	0.68	0.35
2017	(0.14)	0.67	0.77	...

Interim Dividends (Per Share)

No Dividends Paid

Valuation Analysis   Institutional Holding

Forecast EPS	$3.16	No of Institutions
	(01/05/2018)	592
Market Cap	$4.1 Billion	Shares
Book Value	$1.6 Billion	142,290,256
Price/Book	2.63	% Held
Price/Sales	0.63	92.22

Business Summary: Computer Hardware & Equipment (MIC: 6.2.1 SIC: 3578 NAIC: 334119)

NCR is a provider of omni-channel technology solutions that help businesses connect, interact and transact with their customers. Co.'s offerings include automated teller machines, point of sale terminals and devices, self-service kiosks, omni-channel platform software and other software applications, and a complete suite of consulting, implementation, maintenance and managed services. Co. also resell third-party networking products and provide related service offerings in the telecommunications and technology sectors. Co. provides solutions for customers of varying sizes in a range of industries such as financial services, retail, hospitality, travel and telecommunications and technology.

Recent Developments: For the quarter ended Sep 30 2017, income from continuing operations increased 9.2% to US$119.0 million from US$109.0 million in the year-earlier quarter. Net income increased 11.2% to US$119.0 million from US$107.0 million in the year-earlier quarter. Revenues were US$1.66 billion, down 0.8% from US$1.68 billion the year before. Operating income was US$200.0 million versus US$189.0 million in the prior-year quarter, an increase of 5.8%. Direct operating expenses declined 0.8% to US$1.19 billion from US$1.20 billion in the comparable period the year before. Indirect operating expenses decreased 5.2% to US$273.0 million from US$288.0 million in the equivalent prior-year period.

Prospects: Our evaluation of NCR Corp. as of Jan. 14, 2018 is the result of our systematic analysis on three basic characteristics: earnings strength, relative valuation, and recent stock price movement. The company has generated a negative trend in earnings per share over the past 5 quarters. However, while recent estimates for the company have been lowered by analysts, NCR has posted better than expected results. Based on operating earnings yield, the company is undervalued when compared to all of the companies in our coverage universe. Share price changes over the past year indicates that NCR will perform very poorly over the near term.

Financial Data

(US$ in Thousands)	9 Mos	6 Mos	3 Mos	12/31/2016	12/31/2015	12/31/2014	12/31/2013	12/31/2012
Earnings Per Share	1.65	1.56	1.38	1.71	(1.09)	1.12	2.62	0.89
Cash Flow Per Share	6.55	7.31	7.44	7.10	4.06	3.12	1.70	(1.13)
Income Statement								
Total Revenue	4,734,000	3,071,000	1,478,000	6,543,000	6,373,000	6,591,000	6,123,000	5,730,000
EBITDA	736,000	453,000	195,000	635,000	164,000	395,000	719,000	282,000
Depn & Amortn	263,000	172,000	85,000	90,000	91,000	83,000	68,000	64,000
Income Before Taxes	351,000	201,000	71,000	379,000	(95,000)	137,000	554,000	182,000
Income Taxes	78,000	47,000	14,000	92,000	55,000	(48,000)	98,000	42,000
Net Income	277,000	159,000	57,000	270,000	(178,000)	191,000	443,000	146,000
Average Shares	153,100	152,700	122,800	157,400	167,600	171,200	169,300	163,800
Balance Sheet								
Current Assets	2,900,000	2,816,000	2,780,000	2,757,000	2,549,000	3,088,000	4,339,000	3,406,000
Total Assets	7,850,000	7,767,000	7,725,000	7,673,000	7,635,000	8,607,000	8,108,000	6,371,000
Current Liabilities	2,046,000	2,113,000	2,159,000	1,965,000	1,781,000	2,070,000	1,881,000	1,742,000
Long-Term Obligations	2,984,000	3,015,000	3,076,000	3,001,000	3,239,000	3,472,000	3,320,000	1,891,000
Total Liabilities	6,281,000	6,339,000	6,419,000	6,131,000	6,117,000	6,736,000	6,339,000	5,124,000
Stockholders' Equity	1,569,000	1,428,000	1,306,000	1,542,000	1,518,000	1,871,000	1,769,000	1,247,000
Shares Outstanding	121,500	121,400	121,200	124,600	133,000	168,600	166,600	162,800
Statistical Record								
Return on Assets %	4.29	4.14	3.81	3.52	N.M.	2.29	6.12	2.43
Return on Equity %	21.72	22.89	22.31	17.60	N.M.	10.49	29.38	14.23
EBITDA Margin %	15.55	14.75	13.19	9.71	2.57	5.99	11.74	4.92
Net Margin %	5.85	5.18	3.86	4.13	N.M.	2.90	7.24	2.55
Asset Turnover	0.84	0.84	0.85	0.85	0.78	0.79	0.85	0.96
Current Ratio	1.42	1.33	1.29	1.40	1.43	1.49	2.31	1.96
Debt to Equity	1.90	2.11	2.36	1.95	2.13	1.86	1.88	1.52
Price Range	49.59-29.85	49.59-27.55	49.59-25.36	41.75-19.08	34.73-22.39	37.50-23.54	41.56-25.48	25.64-16.48
P/E Ratio	30.05-18.09	31.79-17.66	35.93-18.38	24.42-11.16	...	33.48-21.02	15.86-9.73	28.81-18.52

Address: 3097 Satellite Boulevard, Duluth, GA 30096 **Telephone:** 937-445-5000	**Web Site:** www.ncr.com **Officers:** William R. Nuti - Chairman, President, Chief Executive Officer Mark D. Benjamin - President, Chief Operating Officer	**Auditors:** PricewaterhouseCoopers LLP **Investor Contact:** 212-589-8569 **Transfer Agents:** Wells Fargo Shareowner Services, St. Paul, MN

NEW JERSEY RESOURCES CORP

Exchange	Symbol	Price	52Wk Range	Yield	P/E	Div Achiever
NYS	NJR	$40.20 (12/29/2017)	45.00-34.25	2.71	26.45	21 Years

*7 Year Price Score 112.66 *NYSE Composite Index=100 *12 Month Price Score 98.24

Interim Earnings (Per Share)

Qtr.	Dec	Mar	Jun	Sep
2012-13	0.72	0.54	0.35	(0.23)
2013-14	0.09	2.04	(0.17)	(0.29)
2014-15	1.44	0.71	(0.09)	0.05
2015-16	0.56	0.84	(0.20)	0.29
2016-17	0.40	1.32	0.22	(0.42)

Interim Dividends (Per Share)

Amt	Decl	Ex	Rec	Pay
0.255Q	01/24/2017	03/13/2017	03/15/2017	04/03/2017
0.255Q	05/09/2017	06/13/2017	06/15/2017	07/03/2017
0.273Q	07/11/2017	09/21/2017	09/22/2017	10/02/2017
0.273Q	11/14/2017	12/14/2017	12/15/2017	01/02/2018

Indicated Div: $1.09 (Div. Reinv. Plan)

Valuation Analysis | **Institutional Holding**
Forecast EPS	$1.82	No of Institutions	351
	(01/13/2018)	
Market Cap	$3.5 Billion	Shares
Book Value	$1.2 Billion	72,787,872
Price/Book	2.81	% Held	56.42
Price/Sales	1.53	

Business Summary: Gas Utilities (MIC: 3.3.1 SIC: 4924 NAIC: 221210)

New Jersey Resources is an energy services holding company whose principal business is the distribution of natural gas through a regulated utility. Co.'s business segments are: Natural Gas Distribution, which consists of regulated natural gas services, off-system sales, capacity and storage management operations; Clean Energy Ventures, which consists of capital investments in clean energy projects; Energy Services, which consists of unregulated wholesale energy operations; and Midstream, which consists of investments in the midstream natural gas market, such as natural gas transportation and storage facilities.

Recent Developments: For the year ended Sep 30 2017, net income increased 0.3% to US$132.1 million from US$131.7 million in the prior year. Revenues were US$2.27 billion, up 20.6% from US$1.88 billion the year before. Operating income was US$167.0 million versus US$167.5 million in the prior year, a decrease of 0.3%. Direct operating expenses rose 23.1% to US$1.97 billion from US$1.60 billion in the comparable period the year before. Indirect operating expenses increased 16.2% to US$131.2 million from US$113.0 million in the equivalent prior-year period.

Prospects: Our evaluation of New Jersey Resources Corp. as of Jan. 14, 2018 is the result of our systematic analysis on three basic characteristics: earnings strength, relative valuation, and recent stock price movement. The company has suffered a very negative trend in earnings per share over the past 5 quarters and while recent estimates for the company have been mixed, NJR has posted results that fell short of analysts expectations. Based on operating earnings yield, the company is undervalued when compared to all of the companies in our coverage universe. Share price changes over the past year indicates that NJR will perform very well over the near term.

Financial Data

(US$ in Thousands)	09/30/2017	09/30/2016	09/30/2015	09/30/2014	09/30/2013	09/30/2012	09/30/2011	09/30/2010
Earnings Per Share	1.52	1.52	2.10	1.67	1.38	1.12	1.22	1.41
Cash Flow Per Share	2.87	1.66	4.55	4.24	1.37	0.61	3.02	1.69
Tang Book Value Per Share	13.81	13.55	12.94	11.45	10.57	9.78	9.37	8.81
Dividends Per Share	1.038	0.975	0.915	0.855	0.810	0.770	0.720	0.680
Dividend Payout %	68.26	64.14	43.57	51.20	58.91	69.06	59.02	48.23
Income Statement								
Total Revenue	2,268,617	1,880,905	2,733,987	3,738,145	3,198,068	2,248,923	3,009,209	2,639,304
EBITDA	263,281	249,431	316,395	261,483	211,324	152,461	181,948	226,575
Depn & Amortn	81,800	72,700	61,399	52,742	47,310	41,643	35,200	33,192
Income Before Taxes	136,595	145,687	227,275	183,278	140,035	89,974	127,125	172,132
Income Taxes	18,343	23,530	59,724	51,840	35,575	7,729	37,665	64,692
Net Income	132,065	131,672	180,960	141,970	114,809	92,879	101,299	117,457
Average Shares	87,144	86,731	86,265	84,922	83,628	83,264	83,136	83,260
Balance Sheet								
Current Assets	579,444	607,264	544,511	682,731	745,898	647,344	732,367	785,008
Total Assets	3,928,507	3,727,082	3,339,038	3,158,804	3,004,783	2,770,005	2,649,444	2,563,133
Current Liabilities	802,918	571,608	436,100	791,086	851,833	653,139	703,384	705,798
Long-Term Obligations	997,080	1,063,550	843,595	598,209	512,886	525,169	426,797	428,925
Total Liabilities	2,691,864	2,560,491	2,232,082	2,192,638	2,117,399	1,956,140	1,873,187	1,837,650
Stockholders' Equity	1,236,643	1,166,591	1,106,956	966,166	887,384	813,865	776,257	725,483
Shares Outstanding	86,555	86,086	85,531	84,356	83,923	83,239	82,843	82,347
Statistical Record								
Return on Assets %	3.45	3.72	5.57	4.61	3.98	3.42	3.89	4.81
Return on Equity %	10.99	11.55	17.46	15.32	13.50	11.65	13.49	16.60
EBITDA Margin %	11.61	13.26	11.57	6.99	6.61	6.78	6.05	8.58
Net Margin %	5.82	7.00	6.62	3.80	3.59	4.13	3.37	4.45
Asset Turnover	0.59	0.53	0.84	1.21	1.11	0.83	1.15	1.08
Current Ratio	0.72	1.06	1.25	0.86	0.88	0.99	1.04	1.11
Debt to Equity	0.81	0.91	0.76	0.62	0.58	0.65	0.55	0.59
Price Range	44.25-31.07	38.71-28.14	33.48-24.81	28.66-21.30	23.60-19.50	25.00-20.39	23.57-19.59	19.61-17.02
P/E Ratio	29.11-20.44	25.47-18.51	15.94-11.81	17.16-12.75	17.10-14.13	22.33-18.20	19.32-16.05	13.91-12.07
Average Yield %	2.68	2.85	3.10	3.50	3.72	3.38	3.34	3.70

Address: 1415 Wyckoff Road, Wall, NJ 07719	**Web Site:** www.njresources.com	**Auditors:** DELOITTE & TOUCHE LLP
Telephone: 732-938-1480	**Officers:** Laurence M. Downes - Chairman, President, Chief Executive Officer Patrick J. Migliaccio - Chief Financial Officer, Senior Vice President	**Investor Contact:** 732-378-4967
		Transfer Agents: Wells Fargo Shareowner Services, St. Paul, MN

NEW RESIDENTIAL INVESTMENT CORP

Exchange	Symbol	Price	52Wk Range	Yield	P/E
NYS	NRZ	$17.88 (12/29/2017)	18.30-15.15	11.19	5.73

*7 Year Price Score N/A *NYSE Composite Index=100 *12 Month Price Score 100.16

Interim Earnings (Per Share)

Qtr.	Mar	Jun	Sep	Dec
2014	0.38	0.88	0.88	0.37
2015	0.25	0.37	0.24	0.47
2016	0.48	0.30	0.41	0.93
2017	0.42	1.04	0.73	...

Interim Dividends (Per Share)

Amt	Decl	Ex	Rec	Pay
0.48Q	01/30/2017	03/23/2017	03/27/2017	04/28/2017
0.50Q	06/21/2017	06/29/2017	07/03/2017	07/28/2017
0.50Q	09/22/2017	09/29/2017	10/02/2017	10/27/2017
0.50Q	12/18/2017	12/28/2017	12/29/2017	01/30/2018

Indicated Div: $2.00

Valuation Analysis		Institutional Holding	
Forecast EPS	$2.75	No of Institutions	
	(01/26/2018)	364	
Market Cap	$5.5 Billion	Shares	
Book Value	$4.6 Billion	192,736,128	
Price/Book	1.20	% Held	
Price/Sales	2.84	61.45	

Business Summary: REITs (MIC: 5.3.1 SIC: 6798 NAIC: 525930)

New Residential Investment is a real estate investment trust primarily focused on investing in, and managing investments related to residential real estate. Co.'s portfolio is composed of: mortgage servicing related assets, which provides a mortgage servicer with the right to service a pool of residential mortgage loans; residential mortgage backed securities, which includes Government-Sponsored Enterprise and Government Guaranteed Loans, and Non-GSE or Government Guaranteed Loans; residential mortgage loans, which packaged into pools held in securitization entities; and other investments, which include investment in consumer loans.

Recent Developments: For the quarter ended Sep 30 2017, net income increased 82.9% to US$239.7 million from US$131.1 million in the year-earlier quarter. Revenues were US$340.3 million, up 59.8% from US$213.0 million the year before.

Prospects: Our evaluation of New Residential Investment Corp. as of Jan. 21, 2018 is the result of our systematic analysis on three basic characteristics: earnings strength, relative valuation, and recent stock price movement. The company has suffered a very negative trend in earnings per share over the past 5 quarters and while recent estimates for the company have been mixed, NRZ has posted better than expected results. Based on operating earnings yield, the company is undervalued when compared to all of the companies in our coverage universe. Share price changes over the past year indicates that NRZ will perform well over the near term.

Financial Data
(US$ in Thousands)

	9 Mos	6 Mos	3 Mos	12/31/2016	12/31/2015	12/31/2014	12/31/2013	12/31/2012
Earnings Per Share	3.12	2.80	2.06	2.12	1.32	2.53	2.06	...
Cash Flow Per Share	(1.89)	(0.41)	0.04	2.35	1.60	1.14	1.21	...
Tang Book Value Per Share	14.87	17.64	13.35	13.00	12.13	11.28	10.00	2.99
Dividends Per Share	1.940	2.360	1.860	1.840	1.750	0.380	0.990	...
Dividend Payout %	62.18	84.29	90.29	86.79	132.58	15.02	48.06	...
Income Statement								
Total Revenue	1,439,375	973,752	339,984	1,257,241	687,101	721,945	328,575	51,182
EBITDA	23,413	17,615	(49,670)	(126,305)	(254,417)	186,648	251,715	35,908
Depn & Amortn	(811,922)	(545,386)	(192,424)	(747,932)	(525,298)	(278,408)	(13,908)	(5,339)
Income Before Taxes	835,335	563,001	142,754	621,627	270,881	465,056	265,623	41,247
Income Taxes	121,053	88,440	5,596	38,911	(11,001)	22,957	...	...
Net Income	669,231	443,110	121,378	504,453	268,636	352,877	265,949	41,247
Average Shares	309,207	309,392	288,241	238,486	202,907	139,565	128,684	...
Balance Sheet								
Current Assets	439,890	728,006	394,930	1,978,390	1,788,417	212,985	271,994	...
Total Assets	21,404,833	23,000,015	20,029,987	18,365,035	15,192,722	8,093,690	5,958,658	534,876
Current Liabilities	16,572,839	18,250,538	15,452,129	6,805,056	4,937,019	3,301,202	1,956,965	156,520
Long-Term Obligations	...	...	...	7,990,605	7,249,568	2,913,209	2,488,618	...
Total Liabilities	16,833,221	18,575,211	15,927,875	15,104,935	12,396,789	6,497,601	4,692,808	156,520
Stockholders' Equity	4,571,612	4,424,804	4,102,112	3,260,100	2,795,933	1,596,089	1,265,850	378,356
Shares Outstanding	307,361	250,773	307,334	250,773	230,471	141,434	126,598	126,512
Statistical Record								
Return on Assets %	4.57	3.75	2.73	3.00	2.31	5.02	8.19	14.21
Return on Equity %	23.23	21.20	14.93	16.61	12.23	24.66	32.35	19.67
EBITDA Margin %	1.63	1.81	N.M.	N.M.	N.M.	25.85	76.61	70.16
Net Margin %	46.49	45.51	35.70	40.12	39.10	48.88	80.94	80.59
Asset Turnover	0.10	0.09	0.08	0.07	0.06	0.10	0.10	0.18
Current Ratio	0.03	0.04	0.03	0.29	0.36	0.06	0.14	...
Debt to Equity	...	...	...	2.45	2.59	1.83	1.97	...
Price Range	17.75-13.43	17.75-12.85	17.15-11.41	16.36-9.86	17.78-10.43	13.72-11.58	14.00-11.70	...
P/E Ratio	5.69-4.30	6.34-4.59	8.33-5.54	7.72-4.65	13.47-7.90	5.42-4.58	6.80-5.68	...
Average Yield %	12.12	15.33	12.87	13.97	12.18	3.00	7.58	...

Address: 1345 Avenue of the Americas, New York, NY 10105
Telephone: 212-798-3150
Web Site: www.newresi.com
Officers: Wesley R. Edens - Chairman Kenneth M. Riis - President, Chief Executive Officer
Auditors: Ernst & Young LLP
Transfer Agents: American Stock Transfer & Trust Company, LLC

NEW YORK COMMUNITY BANCORP INC.

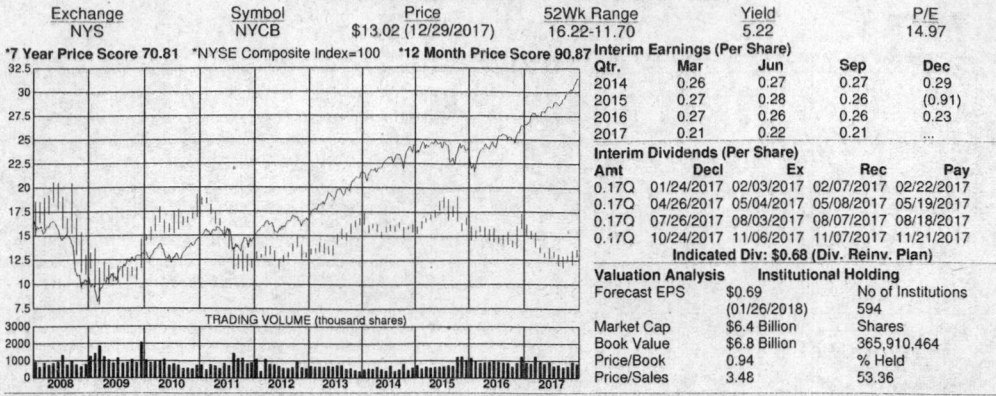

Exchange	Symbol	Price	52Wk Range	Yield	P/E
NYS	NYCB	$13.02 (12/29/2017)	16.22-11.70	5.22	14.97

*7 Year Price Score 70.81 ***NYSE Composite Index=100** ***12 Month Price Score 90.87**

Interim Earnings (Per Share)

Qtr.	Mar	Jun	Sep	Dec
2014	0.26	0.27	0.27	0.29
2015	0.27	0.28	0.26	(0.91)
2016	0.27	0.26	0.26	0.23
2017	0.21	0.22	0.21	...

Interim Dividends (Per Share)

Amt	Decl	Ex	Rec	Pay
0.17Q	01/24/2017	02/03/2017	02/07/2017	02/22/2017
0.17Q	04/26/2017	05/04/2017	05/08/2017	05/19/2017
0.17Q	07/26/2017	08/03/2017	08/07/2017	08/18/2017
0.17Q	10/24/2017	11/06/2017	11/07/2017	11/21/2017

Indicated Div: $0.68 (Div. Reinv. Plan)

Valuation Analysis   **Institutional Holding**

Forecast EPS	$0.69	No of Institutions
	(01/26/2018)	594
Market Cap	$6.4 Billion	Shares
Book Value	$6.8 Billion	365,910,464
Price/Book	0.94	% Held
Price/Sales	3.48	53.36

Business Summary: Banking (MIC: 5.1.1 SIC: 6036 NAIC: 522120)

New York Community Bancorp is a bank holding company. Co. has two subsidiaries: New York Community Bank (Community Bank), which provides multi-family loans, commercial real estate loans, and acquisition, development, and construction loans, among others; and New York Commercial Bank (Commercial Bank), which provides installment loans, revolving lines of credit, cash management services, and online banking, among others. As of Dec 31 2016, the Community Bank had 225 branches in Metro New York, New Jersey, Ohio, Florida, and Arizona, and the Commercial Bank had 30 branches in Metro New York. At Dec 31 2016, Co. had total assets of $48.93 billion and total deposits of $28.89 billion.

Recent Developments: For the quarter ended Sep 30 2017, net income decreased 11.8% to US$110.5 million from US$125.3 million in the year-earlier quarter. Net interest income decreased 13.2% to US$276.3 million from US$318.4 million in the year-earlier quarter. Provision for loan losses was US$44.6 million versus a credit for loan losses of US$55,000 in the prior-year quarter. Non-interest income rose 168.3% to US$108.9 million from US$40.6 million, while non-interest expense advanced 0.3% to US$162.2 million.

Prospects: Our evaluation of New York Community Bancorp Inc. as of Jan. 21, 2018 is the result of our systematic analysis on three basic characteristics: earnings strength, relative valuation, and recent stock price movement. The company has produced a positive trend in earnings per share over the past 5 quarters and while recent estimates for the company have been mixed, NYCB has posted results that fell short of analysts expectations. Based on operating earnings yield, the company is undervalued when compared to all of the companies in our coverage universe. Share price changes over the past year indicates that NYCB will perform very poorly over the near term.

Financial Data

(US$ in Thousands)	9 Mos	6 Mos	3 Mos	12/31/2016	12/31/2015	12/31/2014	12/31/2013	12/31/2012
Earnings Per Share	0.87	0.92	0.96	1.01	(0.11)	1.09	1.08	1.13
Cash Flow Per Share	3.44	2.06	1.67	1.55	(0.94)	1.64	3.13	1.31
Tang Book Value Per Share	7.81	7.76	7.10	7.09	6.70	7.03	6.90	6.93
Dividends Per Share	0.680	0.680	0.680	0.680	1.000	1.000	1.000	1.000
Dividend Payout %	78.16	73.91	70.83	67.33	...	91.74	92.59	88.50
Income Statement								
Interest Income	1,191,869	798,194	399,119	1,674,869	1,691,584	1,683,067	1,708,098	1,791,101
Interest Expense	332,840	215,508	104,202	387,487	1,283,509	542,714	541,482	631,080
Net Interest Income	859,029	582,686	294,917	1,287,382	408,075	1,140,353	1,166,616	1,160,021
Provision for Losses	34,316	(10,269)	(4,008)	4,180	(15,004)	(18,587)	30,758	62,988
Non-Interest Income	191,537	82,609	32,172	145,572	210,763	201,593	218,830	297,353
Non-Interest Expense	492,942	330,708	166,943	649,255	760,511	579,170	591,778	593,833
Income Before Taxes	523,308	344,856	164,154	777,128	(132,013)	773,066	747,126	780,909
Income Taxes	193,628	125,644	60,197	281,727	(84,857)	287,669	271,579	279,803
Net Income	329,680	219,212	103,957	495,401	(47,156)	485,397	475,547	501,106
Average Shares	487,274	487,282	486,511	485,150	448,982	440,988	439,251	437,712
Balance Sheet								
Net Loans & Leases	37,452,219	38,900,080	38,973,215	39,308,016	38,011,995	35,647,639	32,727,507	31,580,636
Total Assets	48,457,891	48,347,658	48,824,564	48,926,555	50,317,796	48,559,217	46,688,287	44,145,100
Total Deposits	28,893,197	28,893,565	28,726,546	28,887,903	28,426,758	28,328,734	25,660,992	24,877,521
Total Liabilities	41,698,237	41,612,880	42,177,213	42,802,564	44,383,100	42,777,402	40,952,625	38,488,836
Stockholders' Equity	6,759,654	6,734,778	6,647,351	6,123,991	5,934,696	5,781,815	5,735,662	5,656,264
Shares Outstanding	489,061	489,023	488,953	487,056	484,943	442,587	440,809	439,050
Statistical Record								
Return on Assets %	0.91	0.94	0.96	1.00	N.M.	1.02	1.05	1.16
Return on Equity %	6.90	7.17	7.43	8.19	N.M.	8.43	8.35	8.91
Net Interest Margin %	70.20	72.11	73.89	76.86	24.12	67.75	68.30	64.77
Efficiency Ratio %	32.28	36.43	38.71	35.66	39.98	30.73	30.71	28.43
Loans to Deposits	1.30	1.35	1.36	1.36	1.34	1.26	1.28	1.27
Price Range	17.30-11.70	17.30-12.67	17.30-13.78	17.30-13.78	19.16-15.25	17.34-14.82	16.85-12.96	14.95-11.57
P/E Ratio	19.89-13.45	18.80-13.77	18.02-14.35	17.13-13.64	...	15.91-13.60	15.60-12.00	13.23-10.24
Average Yield %	4.85	4.68	4.53	4.49	5.81	6.30	6.86	7.61

Address: 615 Merrick Avenue, Westbury, NY 11590	Web Site: www.mynycb.com	Auditors: KPMG LLP
Telephone: 516-683-4100	Officers: Joseph R. Ficalora - Chairman, President, Chief Executive Officer Thomas R. Cangemi - Senior Executive Vice President, Chief Financial Officer	Transfer Agents: Computershare, Providence, RI

NEW YORK TIMES CO.

Exchange	Symbol	Price	52Wk Range	Yield	P/E
NYS	NYT	$18.50 (12/29/2017)	20.00-13.05	0.86	30.83

*7 Year Price Score 110.02 *NYSE Composite Index=100 *12 Month Price Score 100.91

Interim Earnings (Per Share)

Qtr.	Mar	Jun	Sep	Dec
2014	0.01	0.06	(0.08)	0.21
2015	(0.09)	0.10	0.06	0.31
2016	(0.05)	0.00	0.00	0.23
2017	0.08	0.09	0.20	...

Interim Dividends (Per Share)

Amt	Decl	Ex	Rec	Pay
0.04Q	02/16/2017	04/03/2017	04/05/2017	04/20/2017
0.04Q	06/29/2017	07/10/2017	07/12/2017	07/27/2017
0.04Q	09/20/2017	10/03/2017	10/04/2017	10/19/2017
0.04Q	12/14/2017	01/09/2018	01/10/2018	01/25/2018

Indicated Div: $0.16 (Div. Reinv. Plan)

Valuation Analysis

		Institutional Holding	
Forecast EPS	$0.72 (01/16/2018)	No of Institutions	321
Market Cap	$3.0 Billion	Shares	153,003,904
Book Value	$918.7 Million	% Held	77.19
Price/Book	3.27		
Price/Sales	1.84		

TRADING VOLUME (thousand shares)

Business Summary: Publishing (MIC: 2.3.3 SIC: 2711 NAIC: 511110)

New York Times principal business consists of distributing content generated by its newsroom through its print, web and mobile platforms. In addition, Co. distributes selected content on third-party platforms. Co.'s businesses include: newspaper, The New York Times; websites, including NYTimes.com; mobile applications, including The Times's core news applications, as well as interest-specific applications such as NYT Cooking, Crossword and others; and related businesses, such as The Times news services division, product review and recommendation websites The Wirecutter and The Sweethome, digital archive distribution, NYT Live and other products and services under The Times brand.

Recent Developments: For the quarter ended Sep 24 2017, income from continuing operations increased to US$36.5 million from US$283,000 in the year-earlier quarter. Net income increased to US$36.0 million from US$283,000 in the year-earlier quarter. Revenues were US$385.6 million, up 6.1% from US$363.5 million the year before. Operating income was US$33.0 million versus US$9.0 million in the prior-year quarter, an increase of 267.9%. Direct operating expenses declined 4.3% to US$149.9 million from US$156.6 million in the comparable period the year before. Indirect operating expenses increased 2.4% to US$202.7 million from US$198.0 million in the equivalent prior-year period.

Prospects: Our evaluation of New York Times Co. as of Jan. 14, 2018 is the result of our systematic analysis on three basic characteristics: earnings strength, relative valuation, and recent stock price movement. The company has generated a negative trend in earnings per share over the past 5 quarters and while recent estimates for the company have remained steady, NYT has posted better than expected results. Based on operating earnings yield, the company is about fairly valued when compared to all of the companies in our coverage universe. Share price changes over the past year indicates that NYT will perform well over the near term.

Financial Data

(US$ in Thousands)	9 Mos	6 Mos	3 Mos	12/25/2016	12/27/2015	12/28/2014	12/29/2013	12/30/2012
Earnings Per Share	0.60	0.40	0.31	0.18	0.38	0.20	0.41	0.87
Cash Flow Per Share	1.02	1.00	0.90	0.59	1.07	0.54	0.23	0.53
Tang Book Value Per Share	4.78	4.62	4.48	4.43	4.45	4.06	4.78	3.43
Dividends Per Share	0.160	0.160	0.160	0.160	0.160	0.160	0.040	...
Dividend Payout %	26.67	40.00	51.61	88.89	42.11	80.00	9.76	...
Income Statement								
Total Revenue	1,191,513	805,878	398,804	1,555,342	1,579,215	1,588,528	1,577,230	1,990,080
EBITDA	136,652	87,962	45,162	163,327	198,182	171,403	241,564	426,890
Depn & Amortn	46,961	31,284	16,153	61,723	61,597	79,455	85,477	103,775
Income Before Taxes	74,573	46,220	23,684	66,799	97,535	38,218	98,014	260,300
Income Taxes	40,873	17,453	10,742	4,421	33,910	(3,541)	37,892	103,482
Net Income	61,109	28,780	13,181	29,068	63,246	33,307	65,105	133,173
Average Shares	164,405	163,808	162,592	162,817	166,423	161,323	157,774	152,693
Balance Sheet								
Current Assets	767,763	775,407	767,931	796,178	862,532	1,148,095	1,172,267	1,308,408
Total Assets	2,238,958	2,195,168	2,170,226	2,185,395	2,417,690	2,566,474	2,572,552	2,806,335
Current Liabilities	418,672	398,456	387,845	398,737	563,585	600,508	348,511	422,577
Long-Term Obligations	249,375	248,568	247,785	246,978	242,851	426,458	684,142	696,914
Total Liabilities	1,320,280	1,307,465	1,309,626	1,337,580	1,590,939	1,840,146	1,729,642	2,173,835
Stockholders' Equity	918,678	887,703	860,600	847,815	826,751	726,328	842,910	632,500
Shares Outstanding	162,160	161,975	161,522	161,152	161,389	150,337	149,927	148,605
Statistical Record								
Return on Assets %	4.28	2.93	2.25	1.27	2.54	1.30	2.43	4.61
Return on Equity %	11.45	7.85	6.10	3.48	8.17	4.26	8.85	23.01
EBITDA Margin %	11.47	10.92	11.32	10.50	12.55	10.79	15.32	21.45
Net Margin %	5.13	3.57	3.31	1.87	4.00	2.10	4.13	6.69
Asset Turnover	0.71	0.71	0.70	0.68	0.64	0.62	0.59	0.69
Current Ratio	1.83	1.95	1.98	2.00	1.53	1.91	3.36	3.10
Debt to Equity	0.27	0.28	0.29	0.29	0.29	0.59	0.81	1.10
Price Range	19.95-10.80	17.90-10.80	16.25-10.80	14.10-10.80	14.46-11.56	17.26-11.22	15.47-8.18	10.88-5.98
P/E Ratio	33.25-18.00	44.75-27.00	52.42-34.84	78.33-60.00	38.05-30.42	86.30-56.10	37.73-19.95	12.51-6.87
Average Yield %	1.05	1.16	1.24	1.28	1.20	1.13	0.36	...

Address: 620 Eighth Avenue, New York, NY 10018	Web Site: www.nytco.com	Auditors: Ernst & Young LLP
Telephone: 212-556-1234	Officers: Arthur Sulzberger - Chairman, Interim Chief Executive Officer Mark Thompson - President, Chief Executive Officer	Investor Contact: 212-556-4317 Transfer Agents: Computershare, Providence, RI

NEWELL BRANDS INC

Exchange	Symbol	Price	52Wk Range	Yield	P/E
NYS	NWL	$30.90 (12/29/2017)	54.85-27.97	2.98	11.93

*7 Year Price Score 109.98 *NYSE Composite Index=100 *12 Month Price Score 67.68

Interim Earnings (Per Share)

Qtr.	Mar	Jun	Sep	Dec
2014	0.19	0.54	0.44	0.19
2015	0.20	0.55	0.50	0.05
2016	0.15	0.30	0.38	0.34
2017	1.31	0.46	0.48	...

Interim Dividends (Per Share)

Amt	Decl	Ex	Rec	Pay
0.19Q	02/10/2017	02/24/2017	02/28/2017	03/15/2017
0.23Q	05/08/2017	05/26/2017	05/31/2017	06/15/2017
0.23Q	08/09/2017	08/29/2017	08/31/2017	09/15/2017
0.23Q	11/08/2017	11/29/2017	11/30/2017	12/15/2017

Indicated Div: $0.92

Valuation Analysis — **Institutional Holding**

Forecast EPS	$2.81	No of Institutions
(01/18/2018)		939
Market Cap	$15.1 Billion	Shares
Book Value	$12.7 Billion	537,393,216
Price/Book	1.19	% Held
Price/Sales	1.00	81.85

Business Summary: Plastics (MIC: 8.4.2 SIC: 3089 NAIC: 326299)

Newell Brands is a marketer of consumer and commercial products. Co.'s key brands in each of its segment include: Writing, which includes Sharpie®, Paper Mate®, Expo® and Prismacolor®; Home Solutions, which includes Rubbermaid® and Contigo®; Tools, which includes Irwin® and Lenox®; Commercial Products, which includes Rubbermaid Commercial Products®; Baby and Parenting, which includes Graco® and Baby Jogger®; Branded Consumables, which includes Yankee Candle® and Diamond®; Consumer Solutions, which includes Crock-Pot® and FoodSaver®; Outdoor Solutions, which includes Coleman® and Jostens®; and Process Solutions, which includes Jarden Plastic Solutions and Jarden Applied Materials.

Recent Developments: For the quarter ended Sep 30 2017, income from continuing operations increased 25.7% to US$234.4 million from US$186.5 million in the year-earlier quarter. Net income increased 25.7% to US$234.4 million from US$186.5 million in the year-earlier quarter. Revenues were US$3.68 billion, down 7.0% from US$3.95 billion the year before. Operating income was US$323.4 million versus US$323.9 million in the prior-year quarter, a decrease of 0.2%. Direct operating expenses declined 10.0% to US$2.41 billion from US$2.68 billion in the comparable period the year before. Indirect operating expenses decreased 0.7% to US$944.3 million from US$950.9 million in the equivalent prior-year period.

Prospects: Our evaluation of Newell Brands Inc. as of Jan. 14, 2018 is the result of our systematic analysis on three basic characteristics: earnings strength, relative valuation, and recent stock price movement. The company has managed to produce a neutral trend in earnings per share over the past 5 quarters and while recent estimates for the company have been mixed, NWL has posted results that fell short of analysts expectations. Based on operating earnings yield, the company is undervalued when compared to all of the companies in our coverage universe. Share price changes over the past year indicates that NWL will perform poorly over the near term.

Financial Data

(US$ in Thousands)	9 Mos	6 Mos	3 Mos	12/31/2016	12/31/2015	12/31/2014	12/31/2013	12/31/2012
Earnings Per Share	2.59	2.49	2.33	1.25	1.29	1.35	1.63	1.37
Cash Flow Per Share	1.90	2.61	3.74	4.33	2.10	2.30	2.10	2.12
Dividends Per Share	0.840	0.800	0.760	0.760	0.760	0.660	0.600	0.430
Dividend Payout %	32.43	32.13	32.62	60.80	58.91	48.89	36.81	31.39
Income Statement								
Total Revenue	10,999,100	7,320,900	3,266,300	13,264,000	5,915,700	5,727,000	5,692,500	5,902,700
EBITDA	1,789,300	1,436,500	980,900	1,433,100	503,800	615,700	700,200	750,100
Depn & Amortn	210,000	139,000	68,600	214,100	93,000	93,200	100,400	106,700
Income Before Taxes	1,226,300	1,060,700	790,100	814,500	330,900	462,100	539,500	567,300
Income Taxes	130,400	199,200	151,600	286,000	78,200	89,100	122,100	166,300
Net Income	1,095,900	861,500	638,500	527,800	350,000	377,800	474,600	401,300
Average Shares	491,500	485,900	485,800	423,100	271,500	278,900	291,800	293,600
Balance Sheet								
Current Assets	6,949,300	7,130,900	6,488,700	7,484,500	2,493,500	2,426,600	2,285,600	2,271,100
Total Assets	33,888,000	33,950,000	33,335,300	33,837,500	7,278,000	6,681,100	6,069,700	6,222,000
Current Liabilities	4,774,200	4,791,300	4,318,200	4,292,000	1,988,600	1,890,700	1,604,500	1,570,800
Long-Term Obligations	10,184,400	10,172,800	10,332,100	11,290,900	2,687,600	2,084,500	1,661,600	1,706,500
Total Liabilities	21,153,600	21,705,600	21,339,700	22,488,700	5,455,100	4,829,700	3,998,200	4,225,300
Stockholders' Equity	12,734,400	12,244,400	11,995,600	11,348,800	1,822,900	1,851,400	2,071,500	1,996,700
Shares Outstanding	490,100	483,400	483,100	482,500	267,200	269,200	278,600	286,900
Statistical Record								
Return on Assets %	3.69	3.57	4.63	2.56	5.01	5.93	7.72	6.46
Return on Equity %	10.44	10.30	16.35	7.99	19.05	19.26	23.33	20.81
EBITDA Margin %	16.27	19.62	30.03	10.80	8.52	10.75	12.30	12.71
Net Margin %	9.96	11.77	19.55	3.98	5.92	6.60	8.34	6.80
Asset Turnover	0.44	0.45	0.63	0.64	0.85	0.90	0.93	0.95
Current Ratio	1.46	1.49	1.50	1.74	1.25	1.28	1.42	1.45
Debt to Equity	0.80	0.83	0.86	0.99	1.47	1.13	0.80	0.85
Price Range	54.85-40.96	54.89-44.23	54.89-43.42	54.89-33.76	48.16-36.77	38.41-28.49	32.41-21.80	22.27-16.23
P/E Ratio	21.18-15.81	22.04-17.76	23.56-18.64	43.91-27.01	37.33-28.50	28.45-21.10	19.88-13.37	16.26-11.85
Average Yield %	1.72	1.61	1.56	1.63	1.85	2.04	2.25	2.30

Address: 221 River Street, Hoboken, NJ 07030 **Telephone:** 201-610-6600	**Web Site:** www.newellrubbermaid.com **Officers:** Michael T. Cowhig - Chairman Mark S. Tarchetti - President, Executive Vice President, Chief Development Officer	**Auditors:** PricewaterhouseCoopers LLP **Investor Contact:** 800-424-1941 **Transfer Agents:** ComputerShare Investor Services, Providence, RI

NEWFIELD EXPLORATION CO

Exchange	Symbol	Price	52Wk Range	Yield	P/E
NYS	NFX	$31.53 (12/29/2017)	43.67-24.51	N/A	17.52

*7 Year Price Score 69.25 ***NYSE Composite Index=100** ***12 Month Price Score 89.27**

Interim Earnings (Per Share)

Qtr.	Mar	Jun	Sep	Dec
2014	2.07	(0.16)	2.02	2.60
2015	(3.30)	(6.09)	(7.52)	(4.01)
2016	(3.52)	(3.36)	0.24	0.14
2017	0.73	0.49	0.44	...

Interim Dividends (Per Share)

No Dividends Paid

Valuation Analysis | Institutional Holding

Forecast EPS	$2.11	No of Institutions
	(01/18/2018)	631
Market Cap	$6.3 Billion	Shares
Book Value	$1.3 Billion	229,998,624
Price/Book	4.84	% Held
Price/Sales	3.76	92.95

TRADING VOLUME (thousand shares)

Business Summary: Production & Extraction (MIC: 9.1.1 SIC: 1311 NAIC: 211111)

Newfield Exploration is an independent energy company engaged in the exploration, development and production of crude oil, natural gas and natural gas liquids. Co.'s principal areas of operation are the Anadarko and Arkoma basins of Oklahoma, the Williston Basin of North Dakota and the Uinta Basin of Utah. In addition, Co. has oil producing assets offshore China. As of Dec 31 2016, Co. had proved reserves of 513.0 million barrels of oil equivalent, which consisted of 190.0 million barrels of oil and condensate, 1,366.00 billion cubic feet of natural gas, and 95.0 million barrels of natural gas liquids.

Recent Developments: For the quarter ended Sep 30 2017, net income increased 81.3% to US$87.0 million from US$48.0 million in the year-earlier quarter. Revenues were US$439.0 million, up 12.0% from US$392.0 million the year before. Operating income was US$112.0 million versus US$45.0 million in the prior-year quarter, an increase of 148.9%. Direct operating expenses rose 3.5% to US$149.0 million from US$144.0 million in the comparable period the year before. Indirect operating expenses decreased 12.3% to US$178.0 million from US$203.0 million in the equivalent prior-year period.

Prospects: Our evaluation of Newfield Exploration Co. as of Jan. 14, 2018 is the result of our systematic analysis on three basic characteristics: earnings strength, relative valuation, and recent stock price movement. The company has suffered a very negative trend in earnings per share over the past 5 quarters and while recent estimates for the company have been raised by analysts, NFX has posted better than expected results. Based on operating earnings yield, the company is undervalued when compared to all of the companies in our coverage universe. Share price changes over the past year indicates that NFX will perform very poorly over the near term.

Financial Data

(US$ in Thousands)	9 Mos	6 Mos	3 Mos	12/31/2016	12/31/2015	12/31/2014	12/31/2013	12/31/2012
Earnings Per Share	1.80	1.60	(2.25)	(6.36)	(21.18)	6.52	0.94	(8.80)
Cash Flow Per Share	4.42	4.60	4.63	4.27	7.60	10.12	10.70	8.47
Tang Book Value Per Share	6.52	6.06	5.53	4.71	8.43	28.35	21.70	20.54
Income Statement								
Total Revenue	1,258,000	819,000	417,000	1,472,000	1,557,000	2,288,000	1,789,000	2,567,000
EBITDA	735,000	521,000	282,000	(533,000)	(3,899,000)	2,082,000	1,252,000	104,000
Depn & Amortn	340,000	216,000	106,000	572,000	917,000	903,000	930,000	955,000
Income Before Taxes	329,000	261,000	154,000	(1,208,000)	(4,947,000)	1,032,000	170,000	(988,000)
Income Taxes	(3,000)	16,000	7,000	22,000	(1,585,000)	382,000	62,000	196,000
Net Income	332,000	245,000	147,000	(1,230,000)	(3,362,000)	900,000	147,000	(1,184,000)
Average Shares	200,000	200,000	200,000	193,000	159,000	138,000	136,000	135,000
Balance Sheet								
Current Assets	836,000	883,000	865,000	949,000	625,000	940,000	901,000	866,000
Total Assets	4,744,000	4,595,000	4,388,000	4,312,000	4,768,000	9,598,000	9,321,000	7,912,000
Current Liabilities	712,000	678,000	583,000	684,000	647,000	1,101,000	1,290,000	959,000
Long-Term Obligations	2,433,000	2,432,000	2,432,000	2,431,000	2,467,000	2,892,000	3,694,000	3,045,000
Total Liabilities	3,443,000	3,388,000	3,288,000	3,374,000	3,389,000	5,705,000	6,365,000	5,132,000
Stockholders' Equity	1,301,000	1,207,000	1,100,000	938,000	1,379,000	3,893,000	2,956,000	2,780,000
Shares Outstanding	199,609	199,331	198,966	198,954	163,490	137,328	136,221	135,314
Statistical Record								
Return on Assets %	7.70	6.89	N.M.	N.M.	N.M.	9.51	1.71	N.M.
Return on Equity %	31.12	29.44	N.M.	N.M.	N.M.	26.28	5.13	N.M.
EBITDA Margin %	58.43	63.61	67.63	N.M.	N.M.	91.00	69.98	4.05
Net Margin %	26.39	29.91	35.25	N.M.	N.M.	39.34	8.22	N.M.
Asset Turnover	0.37	0.37	0.35	0.32	0.22	0.24	0.21	0.30
Current Ratio	1.17	1.30	1.48	1.39	0.97	0.85	0.70	0.90
Debt to Equity	1.87	2.01	2.21	2.59	1.79	0.74	1.25	1.10
Price Range	47.88-24.51	47.88-27.40	47.88-31.61	47.88-22.31	41.05-22.73	44.98-23.56	31.68-19.84	42.25-23.88
P/E Ratio	26.60-13.62	29.93-17.13	...	...	...	6.90-3.61	33.70-21.11	...

Address: 4 Waterway Square Place, Suite 100, The Woodlands, TX 77380
Telephone: 281-210-5100
Fax: 281-210-5101

Web Site: www.newfield.com
Officers: Lee K. Boothby - Chairman, President, Chief Executive Officer Gary D. Packer - Executive Vice President, Chief Operating Officer

Auditors: PricewaterhouseCoopers LLP
Investor Contact: 281-210-5201
Transfer Agents: American Stock Transfer & Trust Company, New York, NY

NEWMARKET CORP

Exchange	Symbol	Price	52Wk Range	Yield	P/E	Div Achiever
NYS	NEU	$397.39 (12/29/2017)	476.18-381.23	1.76	19.93	10 Years

*7 Year Price Score 103.18 ***NYSE Composite Index=100** ***12 Month Price Score 85.34**

TRADING VOLUME (thousand shares)

Interim Earnings (Per Share)

Qtr.	Mar	Jun	Sep	Dec
2014	4.43	5.24	4.53	4.18
2015	5.14	4.72	5.08	4.51
2016	5.22	5.43	6.03	3.86
2017	5.39	5.29	5.40	...

Interim Dividends (Per Share)

Amt	Decl	Ex	Rec	Pay
1.75Q	02/23/2017	03/13/2017	03/15/2017	04/03/2017
1.75Q	04/27/2017	06/13/2017	06/15/2017	07/03/2017
1.75Q	08/03/2017	09/14/2017	09/15/2017	10/02/2017
1.75Q	10/26/2017	12/14/2017	12/15/2017	01/02/2018

Indicated Div: $7.00

Valuation Analysis **Institutional Holding**

Forecast EPS	$19.34 (11/05/2017)	No of Institutions	356
Market Cap	$4.7 Billion	Shares	9,248,870
Book Value	$628.4 Million	% Held	
Price/Book	7.50	N/A	
Price/Sales	2.20		

Business Summary: Specialty Chemicals (MIC: 8.3.2 SIC: 2869 NAIC: 325199)

NewMarket is a holding company and is the parent company of Afton Chemical Corporation (Afton), Ethyl Corporation (Ethyl), NewMarket Services Corporation (NewMarket Services), and NewMarket Development Corporation (NewMarket Development). Afton manufactures and sells petroleum additives, while Ethyl represents the sale of tetraethyl lead in North America and certain contracted manufacturing and services. NewMarket Development manages the property that Co. owns in Virginia. NewMarket Services provides various administrative services to Co., Afton, Ethyl, and NewMarket Development. Co.'s business is composed of one segment, petroleum additives.

Recent Developments: For the quarter ended Sep 30 2017, net income decreased 16.3% to US$59.8 million from US$71.4 million in the year-earlier quarter. Revenues were US$548.4 million, up 6.3% from US$516.1 million the year before. Operating income was US$82.4 million versus US$101.8 million in the prior-year quarter, a decrease of 19.1%. Direct operating expenses rose 14.6% to US$388.1 million from US$338.7 million in the comparable period the year before. Indirect operating expenses increased 3.1% to US$77.9 million from US$75.6 million in the equivalent prior-year period.

Prospects: Our evaluation of NewMarket Corp. as of Jan. 14, 2018 is the result of our systematic analysis on three basic characteristics: earnings strength, relative valuation, and recent stock price movement. The company has managed to produce a neutral trend in earnings per share over the past 5 quarters and while recent estimates for the company have remained steady, NEU has posted results that fell short of analysts expectations. Based on operating earnings yield, the company is undervalued when compared to all of the companies in our coverage universe. Share price changes over the past year indicates that NEU will perform in line with the market over the near term.

Financial Data
(US$ in Thousands)

	9 Mos	6 Mos	3 Mos	12/31/2016	12/31/2015	12/31/2014	12/31/2013	12/31/2012
Earnings Per Share	19.94	20.57	20.71	20.54	19.45	18.38	19.90	17.85
Cash Flow Per Share	22.97	21.82	26.49	29.80	21.90	18.54	20.92	20.30
Tang Book Value Per Share	40.61	48.39	43.93	39.91	31.52	32.47	41.92	27.70
Dividends Per Share	6.850	6.700	6.550	6.400	5.800	4.700	3.800	28.000
Dividend Payout %	34.35	32.57	31.63	31.16	29.82	25.57	19.10	156.86
Income Statement								
Total Revenue	1,638,422	1,090,006	542,818	2,049,451	2,140,830	2,335,405	2,280,355	2,223,309
EBITDA	306,192	209,078	106,111	401,993	388,623	389,666	394,107	386,206
Depn & Amortn	39,196	24,623	12,306	42,000	35,000	34,000	35,000	34,000
Income Before Taxes	250,500	173,523	88,233	343,208	338,971	339,099	341,311	341,391
Income Taxes	64,063	46,858	24,296	99,767	100,368	105,844	98,964	101,798
Net Income	186,437	126,665	63,937	243,441	238,603	233,255	264,742	239,593
Average Shares	11,829	11,829	11,829	11,828	12,241	12,671	13,286	13,405
Balance Sheet								
Current Assets	847,776	995,315	941,940	836,883	774,767	797,191	897,319	735,495
Total Assets	1,705,193	1,636,783	1,557,785	1,416,436	1,289,915	1,231,925	1,327,274	1,257,510
Current Liabilities	309,430	290,482	292,603	294,590	263,680	259,674	247,614	216,671
Long-Term Obligations	611,687	627,976	601,413	507,275	494,586	363,526	349,467	424,407
Total Liabilities	1,076,743	1,053,078	1,026,770	933,185	902,351	810,884	754,826	855,305
Stockholders' Equity	628,450	583,705	531,015	483,251	387,564	421,041	572,448	402,205
Shares Outstanding	11,853	11,852	11,852	11,845	11,948	12,446	13,099	13,417
Statistical Record								
Return on Assets %	14.93	16.28	17.07	17.94	18.92	18.23	20.48	19.51
Return on Equity %	41.99	47.99	53.23	55.76	59.02	46.96	54.33	50.21
EBITDA Margin %	18.69	19.18	19.55	19.61	18.15	16.69	17.28	17.37
Net Margin %	11.38	11.62	11.78	11.88	11.15	9.99	11.61	10.78
Asset Turnover	1.38	1.41	1.45	1.51	1.70	1.83	1.76	1.81
Current Ratio	2.74	3.43	3.22	2.84	2.94	3.07	3.62	3.39
Debt to Equity	0.97	1.08	1.13	1.05	1.28	0.86	0.61	1.06
Price Range	476.18-390.97	476.18-390.97	453.36-387.41	442.62-324.89	480.33-354.59	413.39-311.61	337.22-241.65	277.43-173.46
P/E Ratio	23.88-19.61	23.15-19.01	21.89-18.71	21.55-15.82	24.70-18.23	22.49-16.95	16.95-12.14	15.54-9.72
Average Yield %	1.57	1.54	1.56	1.59	1.36	1.23	1.35	12.43

Address: 330 South Fourth Street, Richmond, VA 23219-4350 Telephone: 804-788-5000	Web Site: www.newmarket.com Officers: Thomas E. Gottwald - Chairman, President, Chief Executive Officer Bruce R. Hazelgrove - Executive Vice President, Vice President, Chief Administrative Officer	Auditors: PricewaterhouseCoopers LLP Investor Contact: 804-788-5555 Transfer Agents: ComputerShare Investor Services, Providence, RI

NEWMONT MINING CORP (HOLDING CO)

Exchange	Symbol	Price	52Wk Range	Yield	P/E
NYS	NEM	$37.52 (12/29/2017)	39.60-31.89	0.67	250.13

*7 Year Price Score 75.57 *NYSE Composite Index=100 *12 Month Price Score 96.29

Interim Earnings (Per Share)

Qtr.	Mar	Jun	Sep	Dec
2014	0.20	0.36	0.43	0.03
2015	0.37	0.14	0.42	(0.50)
2016	0.10	0.04	(0.67)	(0.65)
2017	0.09	0.33	0.38	...

Interim Dividends (Per Share)

Amt	Decl	Ex	Rec	Pay
0.05Q	02/16/2017	03/07/2017	03/09/2017	03/23/2017
0.05Q	04/19/2017	06/06/2017	06/08/2017	06/22/2017
0.075Q	07/19/2017	09/13/2017	09/14/2017	09/28/2017
0.075Q	10/24/2017	12/07/2017	12/08/2017	12/28/2017

Indicated Div: $0.25

Valuation Analysis

		Institutional Holding	
Forecast EPS	$1.46 (01/18/2018)	No of Institutions	923
Market Cap	$20.0 Billion	Shares	560,869,440
Book Value	$11.1 Billion	% Held	71.32
Price/Book	1.80		
Price/Sales	2.78		

TRADING VOLUME (thousand shares)

Business Summary: Mining (MIC: 8.2.4 SIC: 1041 NAIC: 212221)

Newmont Mining is primarily a gold producer with operations and/or assets in the U.S., Australia, Peru, Ghana and Suriname. Co. is also engaged in the production of copper, principally through Boddington in Australia and Phoenix in the U.S. Co.'s regions include: North America, which consists primarily of Carlin, Phoenix, Twin Creeks and Long Canyon in the state of Nevada and Cripple Creek &Victor in the state of Colorado; South America, which consists primarily of Yanacocha in Peru and Merian in Suriname; Asia Pacific, which consists primarily of Boddington, Tanami and Kalgoorlie in Australia; and Africa, which consists primarily of Ahafo and Akyem in Ghana.

Recent Developments: For the quarter ended Sep 30 2017, income from continuing operations increased 51.9% to US$205.0 million from US$135.0 million in the year-earlier quarter. Net income amounted to US$198.0 million versus a net loss of US$313.0 million in the year-earlier quarter. Revenues were US$1.88 billion, up 4.9% from US$1.79 billion the year before. Direct operating expenses rose 7.1% to US$1.05 billion from US$983.0 million in the comparable period the year before. Indirect operating expenses decreased 2.5% to US$504.0 million from US$517.0 million in the equivalent prior-year period.

Prospects: Our evaluation of Newmont Mining Corp. as of Jan. 14, 2018 is the result of our systematic analysis on three basic characteristics: earnings strength, relative valuation, and recent stock price movement. The company has generated a negative trend in earnings per share over the past 5 quarters. However, while recent estimates for the company have been mixed, NEM has posted better than expected results. Based on operating earnings yield, the company is about fairly valued when compared to all of the companies in our coverage universe. Share price changes over the past year indicates that NEM will perform poorly over the near term.

Financial Data

(US$ in Thousands)	9 Mos	6 Mos	3 Mos	12/31/2016	12/31/2015	12/31/2014	12/31/2013	12/31/2012
Earnings Per Share	0.15	(0.90)	(1.19)	(1.18)	0.43	1.02	(4.94)	3.63
Cash Flow Per Share	4.16	4.48	4.96	5.24	4.16	2.88	3.10	4.77
Tang Book Value Per Share	20.88	20.49	20.17	20.21	21.14	20.17	19.91	27.08
Dividends Per Share	0.225	0.175	0.150	0.125	0.100	0.225	1.225	1.400
Dividend Payout %	150.00	...	...	...	23.26	22.06	...	38.57
Income Statement								
Total Revenue	5,413,000	3,534,000	1,659,000	6,711,000	7,729,000	7,292,000	8,322,000	9,868,000
EBITDA	1,901,000	1,261,000	553,000	1,279,000	2,530,000	2,092,000	(1,933,000)	4,383,000
Depn & Amortn	928,000	601,000	293,000	1,220,000	1,239,000	1,229,000	1,362,000	1,032,000
Income Before Taxes	805,000	529,000	193,000	(214,000)	966,000	506,000	(3,585,000)	3,114,000
Income Taxes	349,000	277,000	110,000	563,000	644,000	133,000	(813,000)	869,000
Net Income	429,000	223,000	46,000	(627,000)	220,000	508,000	(2,462,000)	1,809,000
Average Shares	536,000	535,000	533,000	532,000	516,000	499,000	498,000	499,000
Balance Sheet								
Current Assets	4,808,000	5,098,000	4,838,000	4,677,000	4,983,000	5,439,000	4,874,000	5,945,000
Total Assets	20,836,000	21,142,000	20,969,000	21,031,000	25,182,000	24,916,000	24,764,000	29,650,000
Current Liabilities	1,150,000	1,572,000	1,565,000	1,750,000	1,416,000	2,198,000	2,740,000	3,141,000
Long-Term Obligations	4,046,000	4,046,000	4,049,000	4,049,000	6,087,000	6,480,000	6,145,000	6,288,000
Total Liabilities	9,698,000	10,214,000	10,214,000	10,310,000	13,832,000	14,642,000	14,623,000	15,877,000
Stockholders' Equity	11,138,000	10,928,000	10,755,000	10,721,000	11,350,000	10,274,000	10,141,000	13,773,000
Shares Outstanding	533,336	533,271	533,233	530,465	529,650	498,670	497,678	496,723
Statistical Record								
Return on Assets %	0.38	N.M.	N.M.	N.M.	0.88	2.05	N.M.	6.32
Return on Equity %	0.76	N.M.	N.M.	N.M.	2.03	4.98	N.M.	13.53
EBITDA Margin %	35.12	35.68	33.33	19.06	32.73	28.69	N.M.	44.42
Net Margin %	7.93	6.31	2.77	N.M.	2.85	6.97	N.M.	18.33
Asset Turnover	0.32	0.31	0.32	0.29	0.31	0.29	0.31	0.34
Current Ratio	4.18	3.24	3.09	2.67	3.52	2.47	1.78	1.89
Debt to Equity	0.36	0.37	0.38	0.38	0.54	0.63	0.61	0.46
Price Range	39.60-30.91	45.86-30.91	45.86-26.30	45.86-16.31	27.69-15.55	27.09-17.78	46.90-22.49	64.04-43.39
P/E Ratio	264.00-206.07	...	...	...	64.40-36.16	26.56-17.43	...	17.64-11.95
Average Yield %	0.65	0.48	0.42	0.38	0.47	0.96	3.74	2.75

| **Address:** 6363 South Fiddler's Green Circle, Greenwood Village, CO 80111
Telephone: 303-863-7414
Fax: 303-837-5837 | **Web Site:** www.newmont.com
Officers: Noreen Doyle - Chair Gary J. Goldberg - President, Chief Executive Officer, Executive Vice President, Chief Operating Officer | **Auditors:** Ernst & Young LLP
Investor Contact: 303-837-5362
Transfer Agents: Computershare, Providence, RI |

NEXTERA ENERGY INC

Exchange	Symbol	Price	52Wk Range	Yield	P/E	Div Achiever
NYS	NEE	$156.19 (12/29/2017)	159.25-118.35	2.52	17.55	21 Years

*7 Year Price Score 116.63 *NYSE Composite Index=100* ***12 Month Price Score 103.94**

TRADING VOLUME (thousand shares)

Interim Earnings (Per Share)

Qtr.	Mar	Jun	Sep	Dec
2014	0.98	1.12	1.50	2.00
2015	1.45	1.59	1.93	1.09
2016	1.41	1.16	1.62	2.06
2017	3.37	1.68	1.79	...

Interim Dividends (Per Share)

Amt	Decl	Ex	Rec	Pay
0.983Q	02/17/2017	02/24/2017	02/28/2017	03/15/2017
0.983Q	05/18/2017	05/25/2017	05/30/2017	06/15/2017
0.983Q	07/27/2017	08/23/2017	08/25/2017	09/15/2017
0.983Q	10/13/2017	11/22/2017	11/24/2017	12/15/2017

Indicated Div: $3.93 (Div. Reinv. Plan)

Valuation Analysis / Institutional Holding

Forecast EPS	$6.75	No of Institutions
	(01/18/2018)	1681
Market Cap	$73.5 Billion	Shares
Book Value	$26.4 Billion	435,214,624
Price/Book	2.78	% Held
Price/Sales	4.35	N/A

Business Summary: Electric Utilities (MIC: 3.1.1 SIC: 4911 NAIC: 221121)

NextEra Energy is a holding company. Co. is an electric power company in North America and a generator of renewable energy from the wind and sun. Co. also owns and/or operates generation, transmission and distribution facilities to support its services to retail and wholesale customers, and has investments in gas infrastructure assets. Co. operates mainly through two subsidiaries, Florida Power & Light Company (FPL) and NextEra Energy Resources, LLC (NEER). FPL is engaged primarily in the generation, transmission, distribution and sale of electric energy in Florida. NEER focuses on the development, acquisition and operation of long-term contracted assets with a focus on renewable projects.

Recent Developments: For the quarter ended Sep 30 2017, net income increased 8.5% to US$856.0 million from US$789.0 million in the year-earlier quarter. Revenues were US$4.81 billion, unchanged from the year before. Operating income was US$1.40 billion versus US$1.28 billion in the prior-year quarter, an increase of 9.4%. Direct operating expenses declined 5.1% to US$1.95 billion from US$2.05 billion in the comparable period the year before. Indirect operating expenses decreased 0.8% to US$1.46 billion from US$1.48 billion in the equivalent prior-year period.

Prospects: Our evaluation of NextEra Energy Inc. as of Jan. 14, 2018 is the result of our systematic analysis on three basic characteristics: earnings strength, relative valuation, and recent stock price movement. The company has managed to produce a neutral trend in earnings per share over the past 5 quarters and while recent estimates for the company have been mixed, NEE has posted better than expected results. Based on operating earnings yield, the company is undervalued when compared to all of the companies in our coverage universe. Share price changes over the past year indicates that NEE will perform very well over the near term.

Financial Data

(US$ in Thousands)	9 Mos	6 Mos	3 Mos	12/31/2016	12/31/2015	12/31/2014	12/31/2013	12/31/2012
Earnings Per Share	8.90	8.73	8.21	6.25	6.06	5.60	4.47	4.56
Cash Flow Per Share	13.21	13.32	13.17	13.64	13.58	12.66	12.03	9.55
Tang Book Value Per Share	56.12	55.28	54.48	52.01	48.97	44.96	41.47	37.90
Dividends Per Share	3.817	3.705	3.592	3.480	3.080	2.900	2.640	2.400
Dividend Payout %	42.89	42.44	43.76	55.68	50.83	51.79	59.06	52.63
Income Statement								
Total Revenue	13,185,000	8,377,000	3,972,000	16,155,000	17,486,000	17,021,000	15,136,000	14,256,000
EBITDA	5,750,000	4,156,000	2,648,000	8,542,000	8,141,000	7,592,000	5,997,000	5,247,000
Depn & Amortn	210,000	143,000	72,000	3,377,000	3,203,000	2,896,000	2,521,000	1,772,000
Income Before Taxes	4,428,000	3,262,000	2,235,000	4,240,000	3,883,000	3,552,000	2,496,000	2,590,000
Income Taxes	1,329,000	964,000	675,000	1,383,000	1,228,000	1,176,000	801,000	692,000
Net Income	3,223,000	2,376,000	1,583,000	2,912,000	2,762,000	2,469,000	1,908,000	1,911,000
Average Shares	473,500	471,700	470,200	465,800	454,000	440,100	427,000	419,200
Balance Sheet								
Current Assets	7,027,000	5,947,000	5,827,000	7,409,000	6,795,000	6,944,000	5,842,000	5,237,000
Total Assets	96,781,000	92,890,000	91,205,000	89,993,000	82,479,000	74,929,000	69,306,000	64,439,000
Current Liabilities	11,604,000	8,950,000	9,761,000	10,919,000	10,107,000	9,663,000	9,189,000	8,879,000
Long-Term Obligations	30,345,000	30,392,000	28,539,000	27,818,000	26,681,000	24,367,000	23,969,000	23,177,000
Total Liabilities	70,383,000	66,964,000	65,708,000	65,652,000	59,905,000	55,013,000	51,266,000	48,371,000
Stockholders' Equity	26,398,000	25,926,000	25,497,000	24,341,000	22,574,000	19,916,000	18,040,000	16,068,000
Shares Outstanding	470,397	469,000	468,000	468,000	461,000	443,000	435,000	424,000
Statistical Record								
Return on Assets %	4.54	4.59	4.37	3.37	3.51	3.42	2.85	3.13
Return on Equity %	16.65	16.68	15.87	12.38	13.00	13.01	11.19	12.29
EBITDA Margin %	43.61	49.61	66.67	52.88	46.56	44.60	39.62	36.81
Net Margin %	24.44	28.36	39.85	18.03	15.80	14.51	12.61	13.40
Asset Turnover	0.18	0.19	0.19	0.19	0.22	0.24	0.23	0.23
Current Ratio	0.61	0.66	0.60	0.68	0.67	0.72	0.64	0.59
Debt to Equity	1.15	1.17	1.12	1.14	1.18	1.22	1.33	1.44
Price Range	151.40-112.95	144.23-112.95	132.80-112.91	130.89-103.57	111.66-94.62	110.50-84.25	89.06-69.19	72.05-58.79
P/E Ratio	17.01-12.69	16.52-12.94	16.18-13.75	20.94-16.57	18.43-15.61	19.73-15.04	19.92-15.48	15.80-12.89
Average Yield %	2.89	2.92	2.93	2.91	3.00	3.01	3.31	3.65

Address: 700 Universe Boulevard, Juno Beach, FL 33408	**Web Site:** www.nexteraenergy.com	**Auditors:** Deloitte & Touche LLP
Telephone: 561-694-4000	**Officers:** James L. Robo - Chairman, President, Chief Executive Officer, Chief Operating Officer Armando Pimentel - Executive Vice President, Chief Financial Officer	**Investor Contact:** 561-694-4697
Fax: 561-694-4620		**Transfer Agents:** Computershare Trust Company, N.A., Canton, MA

NGL ENERGY PARTNERS LP

Exchange	Symbol	Price	52Wk Range	Yield	P/E
NYS	NGL	$14.05 (12/29/2017)	25.75-8.70	11.10	N/A

*7 Year Price Score N/A   *NYSE Composite Index=100   *12 Month Price Score 76.29

Interim Earnings (Per Share)

Qtr.	Jun	Sep	Dec	Mar
2014-15	(0.61)	(0.34)	(0.26)	0.88
2015-16	(0.56)	(0.41)	0.03	(1.46)
2016-17	1.38	(0.71)	(0.07)	0.13
2017-18	(0.61)	(1.56)	...	

Interim Dividends (Per Share)

Amt	Decl	Ex	Rec	Pay
0.39Q	01/19/2017	02/01/2017	02/03/2017	02/14/2017
0.39Q	04/24/2017	05/04/2017	05/08/2017	05/15/2017
0.39Q	07/20/2017	08/02/2017	08/04/2017	08/14/2017
0.39Q	10/19/2017	11/03/2017	11/06/2017	11/14/2017

Indicated Div: $1.56

Valuation Analysis

Forecast EPS	$-1.28 (01/18/2018)
Market Cap	$1.7 Billion
Book Value	$71.0 Million
Price/Book	23.87
Price/Sales	0.11

Institutional Holding

No of Institutions	134
Shares	78,707,064
% Held	48.85

Business Summary: Refining & Marketing (MIC: 9.1.2 SIC: 5172 NAIC: 424720)

NGL Energy Partners is a limited partnership company. At Mar 31 2017, Co.'s operations include: crude oil logistics segment, which purchases crude oil from producers and transports it to refineries or for resale; water solutions segment, which provides services for the treatment and disposal of wastewater generated from crude oil and natural gas production; liquids segment, which supplies natural gas liquids to retailers, wholesalers, refiners, and petrochemical plants; retail propane segment, which sells propane, distillates, equipment and supplies to end users; and refined products and renewables segment, which conducts gasoline, diesel, ethanol, and biodiesel marketing operations.

Recent Developments: For the quarter ended Sep 30 2017, net loss amounted to US$173.6 million versus a net loss of US$66.7 million in the year-earlier quarter. Revenues were US$3.92 billion, up 28.8% from US$3.05 billion the year before. Operating loss was US$129.1 million versus a loss of US$35.8 million in the prior-year quarter. Direct operating expenses rose 28.7% to US$3.77 billion from US$2.93 billion in the comparable period the year before. Indirect operating expenses increased 84.6% to US$281.7 million from US$152.6 million in the equivalent prior-year period.

Prospects: On April 17, 2017, we entered into a purchase and sale agreement with the party owning the 50% noncontrolling interest in NGL Solids Solutions, LLC. Total consideration was $23.1 million, which consisted of cash of $20.0 million and the termination of a non-compete agreement that we valued at $3.1 million and in return we received the following, the remaining 50% interest in NGL Solids Solutions, LLC; and two parcels of land to develop saltwater disposal wells.

Financial Data
(US$ in Thousands)

	6 Mos	3 Mos	03/31/2017	03/31/2016	03/31/2015	03/31/2014	03/31/2013	03/31/2012
Earnings Per Share	(2.11)	(1.26)	0.95	(2.35)	(0.29)	0.51	0.96	0.32
Cash Flow Per Share	0.33	0.38	(0.25)	3.34	3.04	1.38	3.20	5.94
Dividends Per Share	1.560	1.560	1.560	2.538	2.366	2.014	1.688	0.854
Dividend Payout %	...	...	164.21	...	...	394.85	175.78	267.00
Income Statement								
Total Revenue	7,704,895	3,781,566	13,022,228	11,742,110	16,802,057	9,699,274	4,417,767	1,310,473
EBITDA	(74,969)	16,506	412,914	66,442	229,982	166,551	120,994	25,893
Depn & Amortn	66,132	32,344	119,707	136,938	105,700	59,900	39,196	10,573
Income Before Taxes	(240,560)	(65,064)	142,729	(203,585)	14,159	47,797	50,065	8,465
Income Taxes	570	459	1,939	(367)	(3,622)	937	1,875	601
Net Income	(236,733)	(63,362)	137,042	(198,929)	16,661	47,655	47,940	7,876
Average Shares	121,314	120,535	111,850	104,838	86,359	61,970	41,353	15,169
Balance Sheet								
Current Assets	1,546,220	1,333,734	1,484,207	1,028,480	1,645,344	1,309,299	762,119	198,624
Total Assets	6,209,658	6,118,715	6,320,379	5,560,155	6,547,501	4,167,223	2,291,347	749,137
Current Liabilities	989,881	816,645	938,598	706,017	1,112,996	995,792	659,288	144,419
Long-Term Obligations	2,993,461	2,834,325	2,963,483	2,912,837	2,745,299	1,629,834	740,436	199,177
Total Liabilities	4,169,537	3,838,074	4,116,433	3,903,797	4,421,707	2,640,644	1,407,669	344,236
Stockholders' Equity	71,009	67,048	63,890	...	...	...	...	...
Shares Outstanding	120,633	120,853	120,299	104,273	103,898	79,420	53,676	29,244
Statistical Record								
Return on Assets %	N.M.	N.M.	2.31	N.M.	0.31	1.48	3.15	1.72
EBITDA Margin %	N.M.	0.44	3.17	0.57	1.37	1.72	2.74	1.98
Net Margin %	N.M.	N.M.	1.05	N.M.	0.10	0.49	1.09	0.60
Asset Turnover	2.44	2.32	2.19	1.93	3.14	3.00	2.91	2.86
Current Ratio	1.56	1.63	1.58	1.46	1.48	1.31	1.16	1.38
Debt to Equity	42.16	42.27	46.38	...	...	...	...	...
Price Range	25.75-8.70	25.75-11.60	25.75-7.18	33.63-5.70	45.67-23.44	37.72-26.65	26.90-20.15	23.15-18.40
P/E Ratio	...	27.11-7.56	27.11-7.56	...	...	73.96-52.25	28.02-20.99	72.34-57.50
Average Yield %	9.08	8.21	8.47	12.60	6.56	7.14	4.08

Address: 6120 South Yale Avenue, Suite 805, Tulsa, OK 74136 **Telephone:** 918-481-1119	**Web Site:** www.nglenergypartners.com **Officers:** Shawn W. Coady - President, Division Officer H. Michael Krimbill - Chief Executive Officer, Chief Financial Officer	**Auditors:** GRANT THORNTON LLP **Investor Contact:** 918-481-1119 **Transfer Agents:** Wells Fargo Bank, N.A., St. Paul, MN

NIELSEN HOLDINGS PLC

Exchange	Symbol	Price	52Wk Range	Yield	P/E
NYS	NLSN	$36.40 (12/29/2017)	45.50-35.67	3.74	25.45

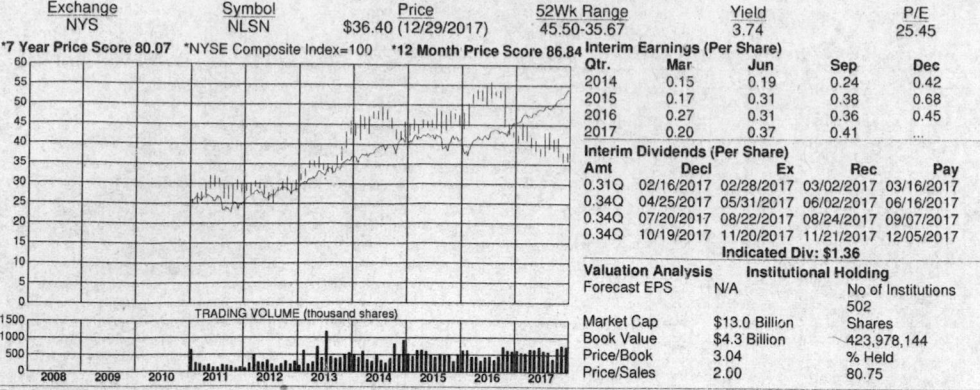

*7 Year Price Score 80.07   ***NYSE Composite Index=100**   ***12 Month Price Score 86.84**

Interim Earnings (Per Share)

Qtr.	Mar	Jun	Sep	Dec
2014	0.15	0.19	0.24	0.42
2015	0.17	0.31	0.38	0.68
2016	0.27	0.31	0.36	0.45
2017	0.20	0.37	0.41	...

Interim Dividends (Per Share)

Amt	Decl	Ex	Rec	Pay
0.31Q	02/16/2017	02/28/2017	03/02/2017	03/16/2017
0.34Q	04/25/2017	05/31/2017	06/02/2017	06/16/2017
0.34Q	07/20/2017	08/22/2017	08/24/2017	09/07/2017
0.34Q	10/19/2017	11/20/2017	11/21/2017	12/05/2017

Indicated Div: $1.36

Valuation Analysis   **Institutional Holding**

Forecast EPS	N/A	No of Institutions: 502
Market Cap	$13.0 Billion	Shares
Book Value	$4.3 Billion	423,978,144
Price/Book	3.04	% Held
Price/Sales	2.00	80.75

Business Summary: Business Services (MIC: 7.5.2 SIC: 7389 NAIC: 561499)

Nielsen Holdings is an information and measurement company that provides clients with consumer behavior. Co. delivers media and marketing information, analytics and manufacturer and retailer insight about what and where consumers buy and what consumers read, watch and listen to. Co. has two segments: Buy and Watch. Co.'s Buy segment provides retail transactional measurement data, consumer behavior information and analytics primarily to businesses in the consumer packaged goods industry. Co.'s Watch segment provides viewership and listening data and analytics primarily to the media and advertising industries across the television, radio, online and mobile viewing and listening platforms.

Recent Developments: For the quarter ended Sep 30 2017, net income increased 13.6% to US$150.0 million from US$132.0 million in the year-earlier quarter. Revenues were US$1.64 billion, up 4.5% from US$1.57 billion the year before. Operating income was US$337.0 million versus US$296.0 million in the prior-year quarter, an increase of 13.9%. Direct operating expenses rose 7.8% to US$692.0 million from US$642.0 million in the comparable period the year before. Indirect operating expenses decreased 3.2% to US$612.0 million from US$632.0 million in the equivalent prior-year period.

Prospects: Our evaluation of Nielsen Holdings PLC as of Sep. 17, 2017 is the result of our systematic analysis on three basic characteristics: earnings strength, relative valuation, and recent stock price movement. The company has produced a positive trend in earnings per share over the past 5 quarters and while recent estimates for the company have remained steady, NLSN has posted better than expected results. Based on operating earnings yield, the company is about fairly valued when compared to all of the companies in our coverage universe. Share price changes over the past year indicates that NLSN will perform poorly over the near term.

Financial Data

(US$ in Millions)	9 Mos	6 Mos	3 Mos	12/31/2016	12/31/2015	12/31/2014	12/31/2013	12/31/2012
Earnings Per Share	1.43	1.38	1.32	1.39	1.54	1.00	1.94	0.75
Cash Flow Per Share	3.78	3.55	3.49	3.60	3.21	2.88	2.40	2.16
Dividends Per Share	1.300	1.270	1.240	1.210	1.090	0.950	0.720	...
Dividend Payout %	90.91	92.03	93.94	87.05	70.78	95.00	37.11	...
Income Statement								
Total Revenue	4,811	3,170	1,526	6,309	6,172	6,288	5,703	5,612
EBITDA	1,333	837	360	1,310	1,428	1,080	996	1,000
Depn & Amortn	477	317	155	165	160	162	169	183
Income Before Taxes	582	340	116	816	961	621	520	408
Income Taxes	226	134	43	309	383	236	91	140
Net Income	348	202	71	502	570	384	740	273
Average Shares	357	358	359	362	370	384	380	366
Balance Sheet								
Current Assets	2,272	2,217	2,101	2,222	1,908	2,019	2,134	1,676
Total Assets	16,585	16,494	16,332	15,730	15,303	15,376	15,530	14,585
Current Liabilities	1,608	1,575	1,635	1,594	1,687	1,798	1,535	1,751
Long-Term Obligations	8,377	8,360	8,180	7,738	7,028	6,465	6,492	6,229
Total Liabilities	12,326	12,303	12,209	11,628	10,870	10,320	9,801	9,655
Stockholders' Equity	4,259	4,191	4,123	4,102	4,433	5,056	5,729	4,930
Shares Outstanding	356	356	357	357	362	372	378	362
Statistical Record								
Return on Assets %	3.14	3.05	2.96	3.23	3.72	2.48	4.91	1.87
Return on Equity %	11.92	11.60	10.95	11.73	12.01	7.12	13.88	5.69
EBITDA Margin %	27.71	26.40	23.59	20.76	23.14	17.18	17.46	17.82
Net Margin %	7.23	6.37	4.65	7.96	9.24	6.11	12.98	4.86
Asset Turnover	0.40	0.40	0.40	0.41	0.40	0.41	0.38	0.38
Current Ratio	1.41	1.41	1.29	1.39	1.13	1.12	1.39	0.96
Debt to Equity	1.97	1.99	1.98	1.89	1.59	1.28	1.13	1.26
Price Range	54.93-37.14	55.81-37.14	55.81-40.54	55.81-41.95	49.06-42.20	49.51-41.04	45.93-30.59	31.80-25.03
P/E Ratio	38.41-25.97	40.44-26.91	42.28-30.71	40.15-30.18	31.86-27.40	49.51-41.04	23.68-15.77	42.40-33.37
Average Yield %	3.08	2.79	2.54	2.42	2.39	2.10	2.01	...

Address: 85 Broad Street, New York, NY 10004	Web Site: www.nielsen.com	Auditors: Ernst & Young LLP
Telephone: 646-654-5000	Officers: Dwight M. (Mitch) Barns - Chief Executive Officer, Division Officer Jamere Jackson - Chief Financial Officer	Investor Contact: 646-654-4602
		Transfer Agents: Computershare

NIKE INC

Exchange	Symbol	Price	52Wk Range	Yield	P/E	Div Achiever
NYS	NKE	$62.55 (12/29/2017)	64.81-50.83	1.28	27.08	15 Years

*7 Year Price Score 106.51 *NYSE Composite Index=100 *12 Month Price Score 101.31

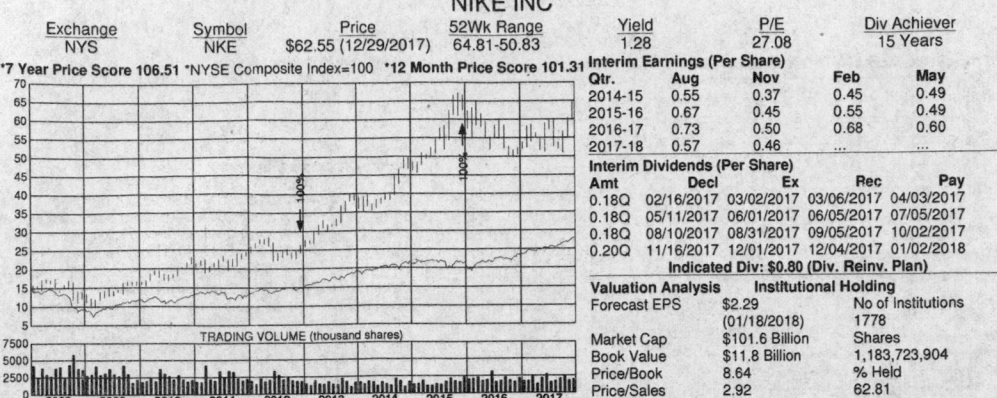

Interim Earnings (Per Share)

Qtr.	Aug	Nov	Feb	May
2014-15	0.55	0.37	0.45	0.49
2015-16	0.67	0.45	0.55	0.49
2016-17	0.73	0.50	0.68	0.60
2017-18	0.57	0.46	...	...

Interim Dividends (Per Share)

Amt	Decl	Ex	Rec	Pay
0.18Q	02/16/2017	03/02/2017	03/06/2017	04/03/2017
0.18Q	05/11/2017	06/01/2017	06/05/2017	07/05/2017
0.18Q	08/10/2017	08/31/2017	09/05/2017	10/02/2017
0.20Q	11/16/2017	12/01/2017	12/04/2017	01/02/2018

Indicated Div: $0.80 (Div. Reinv. Plan)

Valuation Analysis / **Institutional Holding**

Forecast EPS	$2.29 (01/18/2018)	No of Institutions	1778
Market Cap	$101.6 Billion	Shares	1,183,723,904
Book Value	$11.8 Billion	% Held	62.81
Price/Book	8.64		
Price/Sales	2.92		

Business Summary: Apparel, Footwear & Accessories (MIC: 1.4.2 SIC: 3021 NAIC: 316211)

NIKE is mainly engaged in the design, development, marketing and selling of athletic footwear, apparel, equipment, accessories and services. Co. sells its products to retail accounts, via Co.-owned retail stores, internet websites, and mobile applications (which Co. refers to as its Direct to Consumer operations), and via a mix of independent distributors and licensees throughout the world. Co. focuses its NIKE Brand offerings in nine key categories: Running, NIKE Basketball, the Jordan Brand, Football (Soccer), Men's Training, Women's Training, Action Sports, Sportswear (its sports lifestyle products) and Golf. Men's Training includes Co.'s baseball and American football product offerings.

Recent Developments: For the quarter ended Nov 30 2017, net income decreased 8.9% to US$767.0 million from US$842.0 million in the year-earlier quarter. Revenues were US$8.55 billion, up 4.6% from US$8.18 billion the year before. Direct operating expenses rose 6.8% to US$4.88 billion from US$4.56 billion in the comparable period the year before. Indirect operating expenses increased 11.9% to US$2.80 billion from US$2.50 billion in the equivalent prior-year period.

Prospects: Our evaluation of NIKE Inc. as of Jan. 14, 2018 is the result of our systematic analysis on three basic characteristics: earnings strength, relative valuation, and recent stock price movement. The company has generated a negative trend in earnings per share over the past 5 quarters. However, while recent estimates for the company have been mixed, NKE has posted better than expected results. Based on operating earnings yield, the company is about fairly valued when compared to all of the companies in our coverage universe. Share price changes over the past year indicates that NKE will perform poorly over the near term.

Financial Data

(US$ in Thousands)	6 Mos	3 Mos	05/31/2017	05/31/2016	05/31/2015	05/31/2014	05/31/2013	05/31/2012
Earnings Per Share	2.31	2.35	2.51	2.16	1.85	1.49	1.36	1.18
Cash Flow Per Share	2.37	2.13	2.20	1.82	2.72	1.70	1.69	1.03
Tang Book Value Per Share	6.98	7.07	7.29	7.04	7.17	5.98	5.95	5.26
Dividends Per Share	0.720	0.880	0.680	0.620	0.540	0.465	0.405	0.425
Dividend Payout %	31.17	37.45	27.09	28.70	29.19	31.31	29.89	35.94
Income Statement								
Total Revenue	17,624,000	9,070,000	34,350,000	32,376,000	30,601,000	27,799,000	25,313,000	24,128,000
EBITDA	2,356,000	1,273,000	5,651,000	5,291,000	4,839,000	4,095,000	3,707,000	3,359,000
Depn & Amortn	376,000	185,000	706,000	649,000	606,000	518,000	438,000	373,000
Income Before Taxes	1,951,000	1,072,000	4,886,000	4,623,000	4,205,000	3,544,000	3,272,000	2,983,000
Income Taxes	234,000	122,000	646,000	863,000	932,000	851,000	808,000	760,000
Net Income	1,717,000	950,000	4,240,000	3,760,000	3,273,000	2,693,000	2,485,000	2,223,000
Average Shares	1,660,900	1,676,900	1,692,000	1,742,500	1,768,800	1,811,600	1,832,800	1,879,200
Balance Sheet								
Current Assets	16,582,000	16,192,000	16,061,000	15,025,000	15,976,000	13,696,000	13,626,000	11,531,000
Total Assets	24,055,000	23,647,000	23,259,000	21,396,000	21,600,000	18,594,000	17,584,000	15,465,000
Current Liabilities	6,750,000	6,056,000	5,474,000	5,358,000	6,334,000	5,027,000	3,926,000	3,865,000
Long-Term Obligations	3,472,000	3,472,000	3,471,000	2,010,000	1,079,000	1,199,000	1,210,000	228,000
Total Liabilities	12,297,000	11,654,000	10,852,000	9,138,000	8,893,000	7,770,000	6,428,000	5,084,000
Stockholders' Equity	11,758,000	11,993,000	12,407,000	12,258,000	12,707,000	10,824,000	11,156,000	10,381,000
Shares Outstanding	1,624,000	1,637,000	1,643,000	1,682,000	1,714,000	1,740,000	1,788,000	1,832,000
Statistical Record								
Return on Assets %	16.55	17.59	18.99	17.44	16.29	14.89	15.04	14.55
Return on Equity %	32.11	32.63	34.38	30.04	27.82	24.50	23.08	21.92
EBITDA Margin %	13.37	14.04	16.45	16.34	15.81	14.73	14.64	13.92
Net Margin %	9.74	10.47	12.34	11.61	10.70	9.69	9.82	9.21
Asset Turnover	1.49	1.53	1.54	1.50	1.52	1.54	1.53	1.58
Current Ratio	2.46	2.67	2.93	2.80	2.52	2.72	3.47	2.98
Debt to Equity	0.30	0.29	0.28	0.16	0.08	0.11	0.11	0.02
Price Range	60.42-50.07	60.14-49.62	60.22-49.62	67.17-50.67	52.49-37.27	39.93-29.98	32.95-21.95	28.60-19.65
P/E Ratio	26.16-21.68	25.59-21.11	23.99-19.77	31.09-23.46	28.37-20.15	26.80-20.12	24.23-16.14	24.24-16.65
Average Yield %	1.31	1.42	1.25	1.04	1.20	1.30	1.55	1.76

Address: One Bowerman Drive, Beaverton, OR 97005-6453 **Telephone:** 503-671-6453	**Web Site:** www.nike.com **Officers:** Mark G. Parker - Chairman, President, Chief Executive Officer Eric D. Sprunk - Chief Operating Officer, Vice President
Auditors: PricewaterhouseCoopers LLP **Transfer Agents:** Computershare Trust Company, N.A., Providence, RI	

NISOURCE INC. (HOLDING CO.)

Exchange	Symbol	Price	52Wk Range	Yield	P/E
NYS	NI	$25.67 (12/29/2017)	27.58-21.84	2.73	31.30

*7 Year Price Score 124.79 *NYSE Composite Index=100 *12 Month Price Score 99.49

Interim Earnings (Per Share)

Qtr.	Mar	Jun	Sep	Dec
2014	0.85	0.25	0.10	0.48
2015	0.85	(0.11)	(0.02)	0.19
2016	0.56	0.09	0.08	0.27
2017	0.65	(0.14)	0.04	

Interim Dividends (Per Share)

Amt	Decl	Ex	Rec	Pay
0.175Q	01/27/2017	02/08/2017	02/10/2017	02/17/2017
0.175Q	03/21/2017	04/26/2017	04/28/2017	05/19/2017
0.175Q	05/09/2017	07/27/2017	07/31/2017	08/18/2017
0.175Q	08/08/2017	10/30/2017	10/31/2017	11/20/2017

Indicated Div: $0.70

Valuation Analysis

		Institutional Holding	
Forecast EPS	$1.19	No of Institutions	
	(01/12/2018)	666	
Market Cap	$8.6 Billion	Shares	
Book Value	$4.4 Billion	332,535,808	
Price/Book	1.98	% Held	
Price/Sales	1.80	86.63	

Business Summary: Equipment & Services (MIC: 9.1.3 SIC: 4923 NAIC: 221210)

NiSource is an energy holding company. Through its subsidiaries, Co. is a natural gas distribution company. Co.'s reportable segments are: Gas Distribution Operations and Electric Operations. At Dec 31 2016, Co.'s natural gas distribution operations served approximately 3.4 million customers in seven states and operated approximately 59,000 miles of pipeline. Through its electric operations, Co. generates, transmits and distributes electricity through its subsidiary, Northern Indiana Public Service Company, and engages in wholesale and transmission transactions. At Dec 31 2016, the electric operations served approximately 466,000 customers in 20 counties in the northern part of Indiana.

Recent Developments: For the quarter ended Sep 30 2017, income from continuing operations decreased 40.9% to US$14.0 million from US$23.7 million in the year-earlier quarter. Net income decreased 48.5% to US$14.0 million from US$27.2 million in the year-earlier quarter. Revenues were US$917.0 million, up 6.5% from US$861.3 million the year before. Operating income was US$99.6 million versus US$113.7 million in the prior-year quarter, a decrease of 12.4%. Direct operating expenses rose 7.1% to US$233.6 million from US$218.2 million in the comparable period the year before. Indirect operating expenses increased 10.3% to US$583.8 million from US$529.4 million in the equivalent prior-year period.

Prospects: Our evaluation of NiSource Inc. as of Jan. 14, 2018 is the result of our systematic analysis on three basic characteristics: earnings strength, relative valuation, and recent stock price movement. The company has generated a negative trend in earnings per share over the past 5 quarters and while recent estimates for the company have remained steady, NI has posted results that were in line with analysts expectations. Based on operating earnings yield, the company is undervalued when compared to all of the companies in our coverage universe. Share price changes over the past year indicates that NI will perform very well over the near term.

Financial Data

(US$ in Thousands)	9 Mos	6 Mos	3 Mos	12/31/2016	12/31/2015	12/31/2014	12/31/2013	12/31/2012
Earnings Per Share	0.82	0.86	1.09	1.02	0.90	1.67	1.70	1.39
Cash Flow Per Share	2.42	2.98	2.82	2.49	4.58	4.19	4.60	4.36
Tang Book Value Per Share	7.24	6.74	6.97	6.62	5.95	7.10	6.20	5.13
Dividends Per Share	0.690	0.680	0.660	0.640	0.830	1.020	0.980	0.940
Dividend Payout %	84.15	79.07	60.55	62.75	92.22	61.08	57.65	67.63
Income Statement								
Total Revenue	3,506,300	2,589,300	1,598,600	4,492,500	4,651,800	6,470,600	5,657,300	5,061,200
EBITDA	967,400	720,000	561,000	1,411,000	1,252,400	1,849,800	1,714,800	1,578,600
Depn & Amortn	428,500	285,500	143,300	554,700	533,100	615,500	586,700	571,600
Income Before Taxes	278,100	261,600	332,500	510,200	339,900	794,500	716,900	593,900
Income Taxes	97,100	94,600	121,200	182,100	141,300	310,400	261,900	215,500
Net Income	180,900	166,900	211,300	331,500	286,500	530,000	532,100	416,100
Average Shares	332,400	325,100	325,300	323,500	319,836	316,600	313,600	300,400
Balance Sheet								
Current Assets	1,332,400	1,280,800	1,471,200	1,762,100	1,577,200	2,466,500	2,159,200	2,352,400
Total Assets	19,269,500	18,822,700	18,635,900	18,691,900	17,492,500	24,866,300	22,653,900	21,844,700
Current Liabilities	2,566,800	2,778,300	3,664,100	3,452,200	2,657,500	3,954,900	3,178,400	3,301,600
Long-Term Obligations	7,518,600	6,777,400	5,590,700	6,058,200	5,948,500	8,155,900	7,593,200	6,819,100
Total Liabilities	14,906,500	14,699,900	14,444,800	14,620,700	13,649,000	18,691,000	16,767,300	16,290,400
Stockholders' Equity	4,363,000	4,122,800	4,191,100	4,071,200	3,843,500	6,175,300	5,886,600	5,554,300
Shares Outstanding	336,691	325,756	324,474	323,159	319,110	316,037	313,675	310,280
Statistical Record								
Return on Assets %	1.44	1.55	1.97	1.83	1.35	2.23	2.39	1.95
Return on Equity %	6.60	7.13	8.83	8.35	5.72	8.79	9.30	7.87
EBITDA Margin %	27.59	27.81	35.09	31.41	26.92	28.59	30.31	31.19
Net Margin %	5.16	6.45	13.22	7.38	6.16	8.19	9.41	8.22
Asset Turnover	0.26	0.26	0.26	0.25	0.22	0.27	0.25	0.24
Current Ratio	0.52	0.46	0.40	0.51	0.59	0.62	0.68	0.71
Debt to Equity	1.72	1.64	1.33	1.49	1.55	1.32	1.29	1.23
Price Range	27.23-21.41	26.77-21.41	26.77-21.41	26.77-19.46	19.83-16.10	17.41-12.69	12.92-9.78	10.15-8.83
P/E Ratio	33.21-26.11	31.13-24.90	24.56-19.64	26.25-19.08	22.03-17.88	10.43-7.60	7.60-5.75	7.30-6.35
Average Yield %	2.86	2.86	2.80	2.76	4.67	6.85	8.43	9.77

Address: 801 East 86th Avenue, Merrillville, IN 46410
Telephone: 877-647-5990

Web Site: www.nisource.com
Officers: Richard L. Thompson - Chairman Joseph Hamrock - President, Chief Executive Officer, Division Officer

Auditors: Deloitte & Touche LLP
Investor Contact: 219-647-5200
Transfer Agents: Computershare, Providence, R.I.

NOBLE ENERGY INC

Exchange	Symbol	Price	52Wk Range	Yield	P/E
NYS	NBL	$29.14 (12/29/2017)	40.30-23.02	1.37	N/A

*7 Year Price Score 51.68   *NYSE Composite Index=100   *12 Month Price Score 84.26

Interim Earnings (Per Share)

Qtr.	Mar	Jun	Sep	Dec
2014	0.55	0.52	1.12	1.06
2015	(0.06)	(0.28)	(0.67)	(5.02)
2016	(0.67)	(0.73)	(0.33)	(0.59)
2017	0.08	(3.20)	(0.28)	...

Interim Dividends (Per Share)

Amt	Decl	Ex	Rec	Pay
0.10Q	01/24/2017	02/02/2017	02/06/2017	02/21/2017
0.10Q	04/24/2017	05/04/2017	05/08/2017	05/22/2017
0.10Q	07/25/2017	08/03/2017	08/07/2017	08/21/2017
0.10Q	10/24/2017	11/03/2017	11/06/2017	11/20/2017

Indicated Div: $0.40

Valuation Analysis   **Institutional Holding**

Forecast EPS	$0.01	No of Institutions
(01/18/2018)		780
Market Cap	$14.3 Billion	Shares
Book Value	$9.5 Billion	510,949,184
Price/Book	1.51	% Held
Price/Sales	3.51	91.90

Business Summary: Production & Extraction (MIC: 9.1.1 SIC: 1311 NAIC: 211111)

Noble Energy is engaged in crude oil, natural gas and natural gas liquids exploration and production. Co.'s properties consist primarily of interests in developed and undeveloped crude oil and natural gas leases and concessions. Co. also owns natural gas processing plants, gathering systems and other pipeline systems. Co. has operations in these areas: the DJ Basin, the Marcellus Shale, Eagle Ford Shale, Permian Basin, the deepwater Gulf of Mexico, offshore West Africa and Eastern Mediterranean. As of Dec 31 2016, Co. had total proved reserves of 1.44 billion barrels of oil equivalent (BoE), of which 486.0 million BoE are proved undeveloped and 951.0 million BoE are proved developed.

Recent Developments: For the quarter ended Sep 30 2017, net loss amounted to US$115.0 million versus a net loss of US$143.0 million in the year-earlier quarter. Revenues were US$960.0 million, up 5.5% from US$910.0 million the year before. Operating income was US$2.0 million versus a loss of US$250.0 million in the prior-year quarter. Direct operating expenses declined 0.7% to US$280.0 million from US$282.0 million in the comparable period the year before. Indirect operating expenses decreased 22.8% to US$678.0 million from US$878.0 million in the equivalent prior-year period.

Prospects: Our evaluation of Noble Energy Inc. as of Jan. 14, 2018 is the result of our systematic analysis on three basic characteristics: earnings strength, relative valuation, and recent stock price movement. The company has generated a negative trend in earnings per share over the past 5 quarters. Because the company lacks sufficient analyst estimate data, we place greater weight on the historical EPS trend as the measure of earnings strength. Based on operating earnings yield, the company is overvalued when compared to all of the companies in our coverage universe. Share price changes over the past year indicates that NBL will perform very poorly over the near term.

Financial Data

(US$ in Thousands)	9 Mos	6 Mos	3 Mos	12/31/2016	12/31/2015	12/31/2014	12/31/2013	12/31/2012
Earnings Per Share	(3.99)	(4.04)	(1.57)	(2.32)	(6.07)	3.27	2.69	2.86
Cash Flow Per Share	3.52	3.79	3.80	3.13	5.13	9.71	8.18	8.22
Tang Book Value Per Share	16.68	17.03	21.36	21.43	24.02	26.61	23.78	21.29
Dividends Per Share	0.400	0.400	0.400	0.400	0.720	0.680	0.545	0.455
Dividend Payout %	...	...	...	...	...	20.80	20.26	15.94
Income Statement								
Total Revenue	3,055,000	2,095,000	1,036,000	3,491,000	3,133,000	5,101,000	5,015,000	4,223,000
EBITDA	(658,000)	(1,061,000)	674,000	1,065,000	288,000	3,679,000	3,072,000	2,883,000
Depn & Amortn	1,554,000	1,031,000	528,000	2,509,000	2,244,000	1,759,000	1,570,000	1,403,000
Income Before Taxes	(2,483,000)	(2,275,000)	59,000	(1,772,000)	(2,219,000)	1,710,000	1,344,000	1,356,000
Income Taxes	(917,000)	(824,000)	12,000	(787,000)	222,000	496,000	437,000	391,000
Net Income	(1,612,000)	(1,476,000)	36,000	(998,000)	(2,441,000)	1,214,000	978,000	1,027,000
Average Shares	487,000	472,000	431,000	430,000	402,000	367,000	363,000	360,000
Balance Sheet								
Current Assets	1,542,000	1,577,000	1,445,000	1,955,000	2,276,000	3,075,000	2,611,000	2,771,000
Total Assets	21,649,000	21,574,000	21,008,000	21,011,000	24,196,000	22,553,000	19,642,000	17,554,000
Current Liabilities	1,622,000	1,595,000	1,493,000	1,478,000	1,805,000	2,522,000	2,342,000	2,532,000
Long-Term Obligations	7,487,000	7,133,000	6,995,000	7,011,000	7,976,000	6,103,000	4,566,000	3,736,000
Total Liabilities	12,183,000	11,939,000	11,716,000	11,723,000	13,826,000	12,228,000	10,458,000	9,296,000
Stockholders' Equity	9,466,000	9,635,000	9,292,000	9,288,000	10,370,000	10,325,000	9,184,000	8,258,000
Shares Outstanding	490,000	490,000	435,000	433,399	431,792	364,693	359,905	358,000
Statistical Record								
Return on Assets %	N.M.	N.M.	N.M.	N.M.	N.M.	5.75	5.26	6.03
Return on Equity %	N.M.	N.M.	N.M.	N.M.	N.M.	12.45	11.21	13.20
EBITDA Margin %	N.M.	N.M.	65.06	30.51	9.19	72.12	61.26	68.27
Net Margin %	N.M.	N.M.	3.47	N.M.	N.M.	23.80	19.50	24.32
Asset Turnover	0.18	0.18	0.17	0.15	0.13	0.24	0.27	0.25
Current Ratio	0.95	0.99	0.97	1.32	1.26	1.22	1.11	1.09
Debt to Equity	0.79	0.74	0.75	0.75	0.77	0.59	0.50	0.45
Price Range	41.64-23.02	41.64-27.76	41.64-30.00	41.64-25.72	53.47-29.58	79.23-43.00	77.13-50.87	52.28-38.80
P/E Ratio	...	...	...	...	...	24.23-13.15	28.67-18.91	18.28-13.56
Average Yield %	1.22	1.14	1.11	1.16	1.77	1.03	0.88	0.97

Address: 1001 Noble Energy Way, Houston, TX 77070	**Web Site:** www.nobleenergyinc.com	**Auditors:** KPMG LLP
Telephone: 281-872-3100	**Officers:** David L. Stover - Chairman, President, Chief Executive Officer, Chief Operating Officer	**Investor Contact:** 281-.87-2.3125
Fax: 281-872-3111	Kenneth M. Fisher - Executive Vice President, Senior Vice President, Chief Financial Officer	**Transfer Agents:** Wells Fargo Bank, N.A., Mendota Heights, MN

NORDSTROM, INC.

Exchange	Symbol	Price	52Wk Range	Yield	P/E
NYS	JWN	$47.38 (12/29/2017)	50.01-38.30	3.12	16.68

*7 Year Price Score 63.11   *NYSE Composite Index=100   *12 Month Price Score 92.69

Interim Earnings (Per Share)

Qtr.	Apr	Jul	Oct	Jan
2014-15	0.72	0.95	0.73	1.32
2015-16	0.66	1.09	0.42	0.98
2016-17	0.26	0.67	(0.06)	1.15
2017-18	0.37	0.65	0.67	...

Interim Dividends (Per Share)

Amt	Decl	Ex	Rec	Pay
0.37Q	02/17/2017	02/27/2017	03/01/2017	03/15/2017
0.37Q	05/16/2017	05/24/2017	05/26/2017	06/12/2017
0.37Q	08/16/2017	08/24/2017	08/28/2017	09/12/2017
0.37Q	11/15/2017	11/24/2017	11/27/2017	12/12/2017

Indicated Div: $1.48

Valuation Analysis		Institutional Holding	
Forecast EPS	$2.95	No of Institutions	
	(01/18/2018)	828	
Market Cap	$7.9 Billion	Shares	
Book Value	$854.0 Million	127,519,064	
Price/Book	9.24	% Held	
Price/Sales	0.52	50.77	

Business Summary: Retail - General Merchandise/Department Stores (MIC: 2.1.1 SIC: 5651 NAIC: 448140)

Nordstrom is a retailer that provides brands focused on apparel, shoes, cosmetics and accessories for women, men, young adults and children. Co. has two segments: Retail, which included 117 Nordstrom-branded stores in the U.S. and Nordstrom.com, 216 off-price Nordstrom Rack stores, five Canada stores, Nordstromrack.com/HauteLook, seven Trunk Club clubhouses and TrunkClub.com, two Jeffrey boutiques and two clearance stores that operate as Last Chance, as of Mar 20 2017; and Credit, which customers can access payment products and services, including a Nordstrom-branded private label card, two Nordstrom-branded Visa credit cards and a debit card for Nordstrom purchases, as of Jan 28 2017.

Recent Developments: For the quarter ended Oct 28 2017, net income amounted to US$114.0 million versus a net loss of US$10.0 million in the year-earlier quarter. Revenues were US$3.63 billion, up 2.5% from US$3.54 billion the year before. Operating income was US$208.0 million versus US$55.0 million in the prior-year quarter, an increase of 278.2%. Direct operating expenses rose 2.4% to US$2.32 billion from US$2.26 billion in the comparable period the year before. Indirect operating expenses decreased 9.8% to US$1.11 billion from US$1.23 billion in the equivalent prior-year period.

Prospects: Our evaluation of Nordstrom Inc. as of Jan. 14, 2018 is the result of our systematic analysis on three basic characteristics: earnings strength, relative valuation, and recent stock price movement. The company has managed to produce a neutral trend in earnings per share over the past 5 quarters and while recent estimates for the company have been mixed, JWN has posted better than expected results. Based on operating earnings yield, the company is undervalued when compared to all of the companies in our coverage universe. Share price changes over the past year indicates that JWN will perform very poorly over the near term.

Financial Data

(US$ in Thousands)	9 Mos	6 Mos	3 Mos	01/28/2017	01/30/2016	01/31/2015	02/01/2014	02/02/2013
Earnings Per Share	2.84	2.11	2.13	2.02	3.15	3.72	3.71	3.56
Cash Flow Per Share	8.24	8.24	9.36	9.54	13.19	6.44	6.81	5.38
Tang Book Value Per Share	3.70	3.29	2.64	3.72	2.51	10.55	9.96	8.82
Dividends Per Share	1.480	1.480	1.480	1.480	6.330	1.320	1.200	1.080
Dividend Payout %	52.11	70.14	69.48	73.27	200.95	35.48	32.35	30.34
Income Statement								
Total Revenue	10,776,000	7,148,000	3,354,000	14,757,000	14,437,000	13,506,000	12,540,000	12,148,000
EBITDA	513,000	320,000	125,000	1,375,000	1,661,000	1,821,000	1,794,000	1,711,000
Depn & Amortn	(62,000)	(48,000)	(26,000)	570,000	560,000	498,000	444,000	366,000
Income Before Taxes	471,000	292,000	103,000	684,000	976,000	1,185,000	1,189,000	1,185,000
Income Taxes	185,000	119,000	40,000	330,000	376,000	465,000	455,000	450,000
Net Income	286,000	173,000	63,000	354,000	600,000	720,000	734,000	735,000
Average Shares	168,800	168,500	169,100	175,600	190,100	193,600	197,700	206,700
Balance Sheet								
Current Assets	3,479,000	3,473,000	3,169,000	3,242,000	3,014,000	5,224,000	5,228,000	5,081,000
Total Assets	8,186,000	8,161,000	7,771,000	7,858,000	7,698,000	9,245,000	8,574,000	8,089,000
Current Liabilities	3,471,000	3,451,000	3,145,000	3,029,000	2,911,000	2,800,000	2,541,000	2,226,000
Long-Term Obligations	2,681,000	2,729,000	2,731,000	2,763,000	2,795,000	3,123,000	3,106,000	3,124,000
Total Liabilities	7,332,000	7,376,000	7,094,000	6,988,000	6,827,000	6,805,000	6,494,000	6,176,000
Stockholders' Equity	854,000	785,000	677,000	870,000	871,000	2,440,000	2,080,000	1,913,000
Shares Outstanding	166,600	166,200	166,000	170,000	173,500	190,100	191,200	197,000
Statistical Record								
Return on Assets %	6.04	4.47	4.80	4.56	7.10	8.10	8.83	8.72
Return on Equity %	56.94	42.28	47.81	40.78	36.34	31.95	36.87	37.38
EBITDA Margin %	4.76	4.48	3.73	9.32	11.51	13.48	14.31	14.08
Net Margin %	2.65	2.42	1.88	2.40	4.16	5.33	5.85	6.05
Asset Turnover	1.87	1.84	1.92	1.90	1.71	1.52	1.51	1.44
Current Ratio	1.00	1.01	1.01	1.07	1.04	1.87	2.06	2.28
Debt to Equity	3.14	3.48	4.03	3.18	3.21	1.28	1.49	1.63
Price Range	61.49-40.14	61.49-40.14	61.49-36.20	61.49-36.20	82.32-45.45	79.78-55.38	63.43-52.45	58.20-46.80
P/E Ratio	21.65-14.13	29.14-19.02	28.87-17.00	30.44-17.92	26.13-14.43	21.45-14.89	17.10-14.14	16.35-13.15
Average Yield %	3.16	3.06	3.14	3.01	8.99	1.93	2.05	2.01

Address: 1617 Sixth Avenue, Seattle, WA 98101	Web Site: www.nordstrom.com	Auditors: Deloitte & Touche LLP
Telephone: 206-628-2111	**Officers:** Blake W. Nordstrom - Co-President, Interim Chief Financial Officer, President, Co-President (tmr), Executive Vice President Peter E. Nordstrom - Co-President, Executive Vice President, Division Officer	**Investor Contact:** 206-303-3200 **Transfer Agents:** Computershare, Providence, RI

NORFOLK SOUTHERN CORP.

Exchange	Symbol	Price	52Wk Range	Yield	P/E
NYS	NSC	$144.90 (12/29/2017)	145.91-106.99	1.68	22.82

*7 Year Price Score 108.44 *NYSE Composite Index=100 *12 Month Price Score 105.26

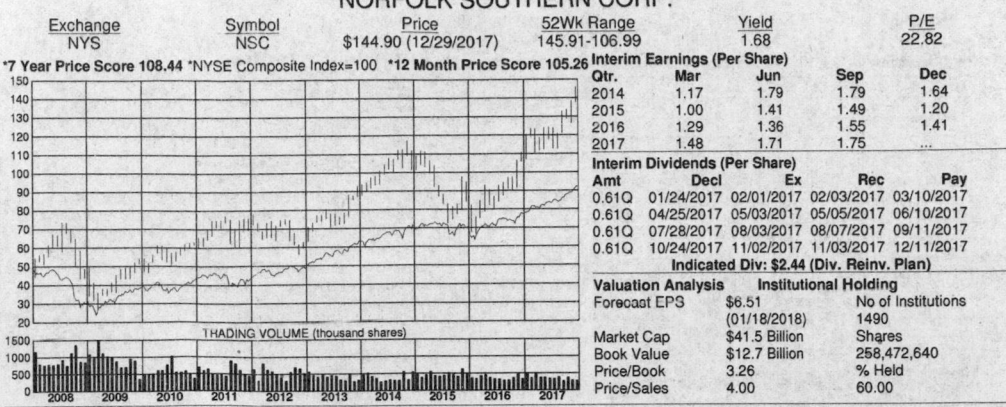

Interim Earnings (Per Share)

Qtr.	Mar	Jun	Sep	Dec
2014	1.17	1.79	1.79	1.64
2015	1.00	1.41	1.49	1.20
2016	1.29	1.36	1.55	1.41
2017	1.48	1.71	1.75	...

Interim Dividends (Per Share)

Amt	Decl	Ex	Rec	Pay
0.61Q	01/24/2017	02/01/2017	02/03/2017	03/10/2017
0.61Q	04/25/2017	05/03/2017	05/05/2017	06/10/2017
0.61Q	07/28/2017	08/03/2017	08/07/2017	09/11/2017
0.61Q	10/24/2017	11/02/2017	11/03/2017	12/11/2017

Indicated Div: $2.44 (Div. Reinv. Plan)

Valuation Analysis | **Institutional Holding**

Forecast EPS	$6.51	No of Institutions	
	(01/18/2018)	1490	
Market Cap	$41.5 Billion	Shares	
Book Value	$12.7 Billion	258,472,640	
Price/Book	3.26	% Held	
Price/Sales	4.00	60.00	

Business Summary: Rail (MIC: 7.4.3 SIC: 4011 NAIC: 482111)

Norfolk Southern is a holding company engaged principally in the rail transportation business, operating primarily in the East and Midwest. Co.'s Norfolk Southern Railway Company subsidiary and its railroad subsidiaries transport raw materials, intermediate products and finished goods classified in the following commodity groups: intermodal; chemicals; agriculture/consumer products/government; coal; metals/construction; automotive; and, paper/clay/forest products. At Dec 31 2016, Co.'s railroad operated approximately 19,500 miles of road in 22 states and the District of Columbia. Co. also transports overseas freight through several Atlantic and Gulf Coast ports.

Recent Developments: For the quarter ended Sep 30 2017, net income increased 10.0% to US$506.0 million from US$460.0 million in the year-earlier quarter. Revenues were US$2.67 billion, up 5.8% from US$2.52 billion the year before. Operating income was US$911.0 million versus US$820.0 million in the prior-year quarter, an increase of 11.1%. Direct operating expenses declined 2.1% to US$739.0 million from US$755.0 million in the comparable period the year before. Indirect operating expenses increased 7.5% to US$1.02 billion from US$949.0 million in the equivalent prior-year period.

Prospects: Our evaluation of Norfolk Southern Corp. as of Jan. 14, 2018 is the result of our systematic analysis on three basic characteristics: earnings strength, relative valuation, and recent stock price movement. The company has managed to produce a neutral trend in earnings per share over the past 5 quarters and while recent estimates for the company have been raised by analysts, NSC has posted better than expected results. Based on operating earnings yield, the company is about fairly valued when compared to all of the companies in our coverage universe. Share price changes over the past year indicates that NSC will perform in line with the market over the near term.

Financial Data

(US$ in Thousands)	9 Mos	6 Mos	3 Mos	12/31/2016	12/31/2015	12/31/2014	12/31/2013	12/31/2012
Earnings Per Share	6.35	6.15	5.80	5.62	5.10	6.39	6.04	5.37
Cash Flow Per Share	11.10	11.00	10.34	10.30	9.53	9.22	9.87	9.53
Tang Book Value Per Share	44.48	43.94	43.23	42.73	40.93	40.25	36.55	31.08
Dividends Per Share	2.420	2.400	2.380	2.360	2.360	2.220	2.040	1.940
Dividend Payout %	38.11	39.02	41.03	41.99	46.27	34.74	33.77	36.13
Income Statement								
Total Revenue	7,882,000	5,212,000	2,575,000	9,888,000	10,511,000	11,624,000	11,245,000	11,040,000
EBITDA	3,442,000	2,242,000	1,057,000	4,171,000	4,042,000	4,638,000	4,374,000	4,142,000
Depn & Amortn	791,000	525,000	260,000	1,030,000	1,059,000	956,000	922,000	922,000
Income Before Taxes	2,235,000	1,435,000	655,000	2,582,000	2,442,000	3,134,000	2,923,000	2,724,000
Income Taxes	799,000	505,000	222,000	914,000	886,000	1,134,000	1,055,000	1,009,000
Net Income	1,436,000	930,000	433,000	1,668,000	1,556,000	2,000,000	1,910,000	1,749,000
Average Shares	287,100	289,000	292,800	296,000	304,400	312,500	315,500	325,200
Balance Sheet								
Current Assets	1,999,000	1,936,000	2,327,000	2,291,000	2,633,000	2,778,000	3,075,000	2,242,000
Total Assets	35,153,000	34,922,000	35,145,000	34,892,000	34,260,000	33,241,000	32,483,000	30,342,000
Current Liabilities	2,413,000	2,343,000	2,443,000	2,339,000	2,231,000	1,780,000	2,305,000	2,081,000
Long-Term Obligations	9,280,000	9,273,000	9,569,000	9,562,000	9,393,000	8,924,000	8,903,000	8,432,000
Total Liabilities	22,426,000	22,260,000	22,618,000	22,483,000	22,072,000	20,833,000	21,194,000	20,582,000
Stockholders' Equity	12,727,000	12,662,000	12,527,000	12,409,000	12,188,000	12,408,000	11,289,000	9,760,000
Shares Outstanding	286,148	288,181	289,782	290,417	297,795	308,240	308,878	314,034
Statistical Record								
Return on Assets %	5.31	5.22	4.97	4.81	4.61	6.09	6.08	5.92
Return on Equity %	14.74	14.49	13.85	13.53	12.65	16.88	18.15	17.73
EBITDA Margin %	43.67	43.02	41.05	42.18	38.45	39.90	38.90	37.52
Net Margin %	18.22	17.84	16.82	16.87	14.80	17.21	16.99	15.84
Asset Turnover	0.30	0.30	0.29	0.29	0.31	0.35	0.36	0.37
Current Ratio	0.83	0.83	0.95	0.98	1.18	1.56	1.33	1.08
Debt to Equity	0.73	0.73	0.76	0.77	0.77	0.72	0.79	0.86
Price Range	132.79-90.03	124.50-83.90	123.53-78.72	110.69-66.60	111.73-72.44	117.20-87.76	92.87-61.84	78.24-56.34
P/E Ratio	20.91-14.18	20.24-13.64	21.30-13.57	19.70-11.85	21.91-14.20	18.34-13.73	15.38-10.24	14.57-10.49
Average Yield %	2.12	2.25	2.42	2.61	2.67	2.54	2.18	2.83

Address: Three Commercial Place, Norfolk, VA 23510-2191 **Telephone:** 757-629-2680	**Web Site:** www.norfolksouthern.com **Officers:** James A. Squires - Chairman, President, Chief Executive Officer, Executive Vice President, Chief Financial Officer, Executive Vice President Cynthia C. Earhart - Executive Vice President, Executive Vice President (frmr), Vice President, Chief Financial Officer, Chief Information Officer	**Auditors:** KPMG LLP **Investor Contact:** 757-629-2861 **Transfer Agents:** American Stock Transfer & Trust Company, LLC, Brooklyn, NY

NORTHROP GRUMMAN CORP

Exchange	Symbol	Price	52Wk Range	Yield	P/E	Div Achiever
NYS	NOC	$306.91 (12/29/2017)	310.47-226.96	1.30	22.87	13 Years

*7 Year Price Score 147.62 *NYSE Composite Index=100 *12 Month Price Score 107.91

Interim Earnings (Per Share)

Qtr.	Mar	Jun	Sep	Dec
2014	2.63	2.37	2.26	2.47
2015	2.41	2.74	2.75	2.50
2016	3.03	2.85	3.35	2.96
2017	3.63	3.15	3.68	...

Interim Dividends (Per Share)

Amt	Decl	Ex	Rec	Pay
0.90Q	02/16/2017	03/02/2017	03/06/2017	03/22/2017
1.00Q	05/16/2017	06/01/2017	06/05/2017	06/21/2017
1.00Q	08/16/2017	08/24/2017	08/28/2017	09/13/2017
1.00Q	11/15/2017	12/01/2017	12/04/2017	12/20/2017

Indicated Div: $4.00 (Div. Reinv. Plan)

Valuation Analysis | **Institutional Holding**

Forecast EPS	$13.14 (01/18/2018)	No of Institutions 1240
Market Cap	$53.4 Billion	Shares
Book Value	$6.5 Billion	200,722,704
Price/Book	8.23	% Held
Price/Sales	2.09	72.08

Business Summary: Defense (MIC: 7.1.2 SIC: 3812 NAIC: 334511)

Northrop Grumman is a global security company. Co. has three segments: Aerospace Systems, which designs, develops, integrates and produces manned aircraft, autonomous systems, spacecraft, high-energy laser systems, microelectronics and other systems/subsystems; Mission Systems, which provides in advanced mission solutions and multifunction systems for Department of Defense, intelligence community, international, federal civil and commercial customers; and Technology Services, which provides logistics solutions supporting the life cycle of platforms and systems for global defense and federal-civil customers.

Recent Developments: For the quarter ended Sep 30 2017, net income increased 7.1% to US$645.0 million from US$602.0 million in the year-earlier quarter. Revenues were US$6.53 billion, up 6.0% from US$6.16 billion the year before. Operating income was US$845.0 million versus US$826.0 million in the prior-year quarter, an increase of 2.3%. Direct operating expenses rose 7.5% to US$5.02 billion from US$4.67 billion in the comparable period the year before. Indirect operating expenses increased 0.6% to US$666.0 million from US$662.0 million in the equivalent prior-year period.

Prospects: Our evaluation of Northrop Grumman Corp. as of Jan. 14, 2018 is the result of our systematic analysis on three basic characteristics: earnings strength, relative valuation, and recent stock price movement. The company has generated a negative trend in earnings per share over the past 5 quarters and while recent estimates for the company have been raised by analysts, NOC has posted better than expected results. Based on operating earnings yield, the company is about fairly valued when compared to all of the companies in our coverage universe. Share price changes over the past year indicates that NOC will perform well over the near term.

Financial Data
(US$ in Thousands)

	9 Mos	6 Mos	3 Mos	12/31/2016	12/31/2015	12/31/2014	12/31/2013	12/31/2012
Earnings Per Share	13.42	13.09	12.79	12.19	10.39	9.75	8.35	7.81
Cash Flow Per Share	14.56	13.39	13.92	15.68	11.41	12.42	10.81	10.59
Dividends Per Share	3.800	3.700	3.600	3.500	3.100	2.710	2.380	2.150
Dividend Payout %	28.32	28.27	28.15	28.71	29.84	27.79	28.50	27.53
Income Statement								
Total Revenue	19,169,000	12,642,000	6,267,000	24,508,000	23,526,000	23,979,000	24,661,000	25,218,000
EBITDA	2,911,000	1,942,000	952,000	3,680,000	3,558,000	3,681,000	3,615,000	3,625,000
Depn & Amortn	322,000	211,000	104,000	456,000	467,000	462,000	495,000	448,000
Income Before Taxes	2,365,000	1,580,000	773,000	2,923,000	2,790,000	2,937,000	2,863,000	2,965,000
Income Taxes	528,000	388,000	133,000	723,000	800,000	868,000	911,000	987,000
Net Income	1,837,000	1,192,000	640,000	2,200,000	1,990,000	2,069,000	1,952,000	1,978,000
Average Shares	175,300	175,500	176,100	180,500	191,600	212,100	233,900	253,400
Balance Sheet								
Current Assets	7,599,000	6,864,000	6,568,000	6,856,000	6,334,000	8,184,000	9,488,000	8,392,000
Total Assets	26,513,000	25,813,000	25,413,000	25,614,000	24,454,000	26,572,000	26,381,000	26,543,000
Current Liabilities	6,300,000	6,186,000	5,168,000	5,630,000	5,457,000	5,892,000	5,815,000	6,056,000
Long-Term Obligations	6,227,000	6,219,000	7,060,000	7,058,000	6,416,000	5,925,000	5,928,000	3,930,000
Total Liabilities	20,020,000	19,894,000	19,855,000	20,355,000	18,932,000	19,337,000	15,761,000	17,029,000
Stockholders' Equity	6,493,000	5,919,000	5,558,000	5,259,000	5,522,000	7,235,000	10,620,000	9,514,000
Shares Outstanding	174,077	174,150	174,675	175,068	181,303	198,930	217,599	239,209
Statistical Record								
Return on Assets %	9.33	9.30	9.26	8.76	7.80	7.81	7.38	7.59
Return on Equity %	38.53	39.98	40.86	40.70	31.20	23.18	19.39	19.88
EBITDA Margin %	15.19	15.36	15.19	15.02	15.12	15.35	14.66	14.37
Net Margin %	9.58	9.43	10.21	8.98	8.46	8.63	7.92	7.84
Asset Turnover	1.01	1.01	1.01	0.98	0.92	0.91	0.93	0.97
Current Ratio	1.21	1.11	1.27	1.22	1.16	1.39	1.63	1.39
Debt to Equity	0.96	1.05	1.27	1.34	1.16	0.82	0.56	0.41
Price Range	287.72-212.48	261.27-208.36	251.80-197.90	251.80-178.19	191.48-143.37	152.24-110.80	115.32-64.38	71.13-57.11
P/E Ratio	21.44-15.83	19.96-15.92	19.69-15.47	20.66-14.62	18.43-13.80	15.61-11.36	13.81-7.71	9.11-7.31
Average Yield %	1.54	1.58	1.61	1.65	1.85	2.16	2.76	3.37

Address: 2980 Fairview Park Drive, Falls Church, VA 22042
Telephone: 703-280-2900

Web Site: www.northropgrumman.com
Officers: Wesley G. Bush - Chairman, President, Chief Executive Officer, Vice President, Chief Financial Officer, Chief Operating Officer Kathy J. Warden - President, Corporate Vice-President, Chief Operating Officer, Division Officer

Auditors: Deloitte & Touche LLP
Investor Contact: 703-280-2268
Transfer Agents: Computershare, Providence, RI

NORTHWEST NATURAL GAS CO.

Exchange	Symbol	Price	52Wk Range	Yield	P/E	Div Achiever
NYS	NWN	$59.65 (12/29/2017)	69.15-56.85	3.17	26.99	61 Years

*7 Year Price Score 98.57   *NYSE Composite Index=100   *12 Month Price Score 99.20

Interim Earnings (Per Share)

Qtr.	Mar	Jun	Sep	Dec
2014	1.40	0.04	(0.32)	1.05
2015	1.04	0.08	(0.24)	1.08
2016	1.33	0.07	(0.29)	1.01
2017	1.40	0.10	(0.30)	...

Interim Dividends (Per Share)

Amt	Decl	Ex	Rec	Pay
0.47Q	04/05/2017	04/26/2017	04/28/2017	05/15/2017
0.47Q	07/06/2017	07/27/2017	07/31/2017	08/15/2017
0.472Q	10/05/2017	10/30/2017	10/31/2017	11/15/2017
0.472Q	01/12/2018	01/30/2018	01/31/2018	02/15/2018

Indicated Div: $1.89 (Div. Reinv. Plan)

Valuation Analysis

		Institutional Holding	
Forecast EPS	$2.19 (01/17/2018)	No of Institutions	300
Market Cap	$1.7 Billion	Shares	24,831,188
Book Value	$846.7 Million	% Held	58.20
Price/Book	2.02		
Price/Sales	2.27		

TRADING VOLUME (thousand shares)

Business Summary: Gas Utilities (MIC: 3.3.1 SIC: 4924 NAIC: 221210)

Northwest Natural Gas is engaged in the distribution of natural gas. Co. operates in two segments: local gas distribution, which is a regulated utility principally engaged in the purchase, sale, and delivery of natural gas and related services to customers in Oregon and southwest Washington; and gas storage, which includes natural gas storage services provided to customers primarily from two underground natural gas storage facilities, Co.'s Gill Ranch gas storage facility, and the non-utility portion of Co.'s Mist gas storage facility. At Dec 31 2016, Co. had 725,146 utility customers with approximately 89.0% of its customers located in Oregon and 11.0% located in Washington.

Recent Developments: For the quarter ended Sep 30 2017, net loss amounted to US$8.5 million versus a net loss of US$8.0 million in the year-earlier quarter. Revenues were US$88.2 million, up 0.5% from US$87.7 million the year before. Operating loss was US$6.7 million versus a loss of US$4.4 million in the prior-year quarter. Direct operating expenses declined 3.6% to US$27.2 million from US$28.3 million in the comparable period the year before. Indirect operating expenses increased 5.8% to US$67.6 million from US$63.9 million in the equivalent prior-year period.

Prospects: Our evaluation of Northwest Natural Gas Co. as of Jan. 14, 2018 is the result of our systematic analysis on three basic characteristics: earnings strength, relative valuation, and recent stock price movement. The company has managed to produce a neutral trend in earnings per share over the past 5 quarters. However, while recent estimates for the company have been mixed, NWN has posted better than expected results. Based on operating earnings yield, the company is about fairly valued when compared to all of the companies in our coverage universe. Share price changes over the past year indicates that NWN will perform very well over the near term.

Financial Data

(US$ in Thousands)	9 Mos	6 Mos	3 Mos	12/31/2016	12/31/2015	12/31/2014	12/31/2013	12/31/2012
Earnings Per Share	2.21	2.22	2.19	2.12	1.96	2.16	2.24	2.22
Cash Flow Per Share	7.27	7.57	7.72	8.01	6.75	7.94	6.54	6.28
Tang Book Value Per Share	29.49	30.19	30.53	29.71	28.47	28.12	27.77	27.23
Dividends Per Share	1.880	1.877	1.875	1.873	1.863	1.845	1.825	1.790
Dividend Payout %	85.07	84.57	85.62	88.33	95.03	85.42	81.47	80.63
Income Statement								
Total Revenue	521,751	433,561	297,323	675,967	723,791	754,037	758,518	730,607
EBITDA	109,017	108,820	88,170	249,849	234,422	243,426	234,409	220,133
Depn & Amortn	22,956	17,596	11,061	111,112	102,427	98,528	86,994	73,017
Income Before Taxes	57,017	71,631	67,233	99,609	89,456	100,335	102,243	103,959
Income Taxes	22,473	28,592	26,923	40,714	35,753	41,643	41,705	44,104
Net Income	34,544	43,039	40,310	58,895	53,703	58,692	60,538	59,855
Average Shares	28,678	28,717	28,723	27,779	27,417	27,223	27,027	26,907
Balance Sheet								
Current Assets	199,546	192,004	265,893	288,053	332,063	362,560	330,448	283,699
Total Assets	3,105,607	3,065,154	3,070,656	3,079,801	3,076,692	3,064,945	2,970,911	2,818,753
Current Liabilities	202,951	235,082	235,019	274,517	477,714	469,410	432,791	368,436
Long-Term Obligations	757,429	658,118	657,716	679,334	576,700	621,700	681,700	691,700
Total Liabilities	2,258,925	2,199,725	2,196,041	2,229,304	2,295,720	2,297,624	2,219,039	2,085,720
Stockholders' Equity	846,682	865,429	874,615	850,497	780,972	767,321	751,872	733,033
Shares Outstanding	28,713	28,662	28,644	28,630	27,427	27,284	27,075	26,917
Statistical Record								
Return on Assets %	2.07	2.11	2.06	1.91	1.75	1.94	2.09	2.15
Return on Equity %	7.73	7.60	7.44	7.20	6.94	7.73	8.15	8.25
EBITDA Margin %	20.89	25.10	29.65	36.96	32.39	32.28	30.90	30.13
Net Margin %	6.62	9.93	13.56	8.71	7.42	7.78	7.98	8.19
Asset Turnover	0.25	0.25	0.24	0.22	0.24	0.25	0.26	0.26
Current Ratio	0.98	0.82	1.13	1.05	0.70	0.77	0.76	0.77
Debt to Equity	0.89	0.76	0.75	0.80	0.74	0.81	0.91	0.94
Price Range	68.40-54.85	65.60-54.85	65.60-49.55	65.60-49.44	51.98-42.18	52.46-40.36	46.40-40.07	50.47-41.72
P/E Ratio	30.95-24.82	29.55-24.71	29.95-22.63	30.94-23.32	26.52-21.52	24.29-18.69	20.71-17.89	22.73-18.79
Average Yield %	3.11	3.12	3.19	3.28	4.01	4.14	4.21	3.83

Address: 220 N.W. Second Avenue, Portland, OR 97209
Telephone: 503-226-4211

Web Site: www.nwnatural.com
Officers: Tod R. Hamachek - Chairman Frank Burkhartsmeyer - Senior Vice President, Chief Financial Officer

Auditors: PricewaterhouseCoopers LLP
Investor Contact: 503-226-4211ext.24
Transfer Agents: American Stock Transfer & Trust Company, Brooklyn, NY

NORTHWESTERN CORP.

Exchange	Symbol	Price	52Wk Range	Yield	P/E	Div Acheiver
NYS	NWE	$59.70 (12/29/2017)	64.26-56.09	3.52	18.04	11 Years

*7 Year Price Score 99.19 *NYSE Composite Index=100 *12 Month Price Score 97.17

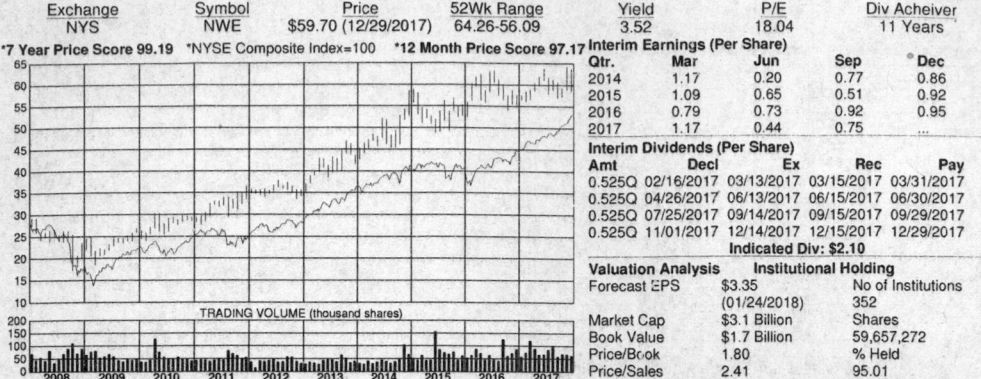

Interim Earnings (Per Share)

Qtr.	Mar	Jun	Sep	Dec
2014	1.17	0.20	0.77	0.86
2015	1.09	0.65	0.51	0.92
2016	0.79	0.73	0.92	0.95
2017	1.17	0.44	0.75	...

Interim Dividends (Per Share)

Amt	Decl	Ex	Rec	Pay
0.525Q	02/16/2017	03/13/2017	03/15/2017	03/31/2017
0.525Q	04/26/2017	06/13/2017	06/15/2017	06/30/2017
0.525Q	07/25/2017	09/14/2017	09/15/2017	09/29/2017
0.525Q	11/01/2017	12/14/2017	12/15/2017	12/29/2017

Indicated Div: $2.10

Valuation Analysis | **Institutional Holding**

Forecast EPS	$3.35	No of Institutions
	(01/24/2018)	352
Market Cap	$3.1 Billion	Shares
Book Value	$1.7 Billion	59,657,272
Price/Book	1.80	% Held
Price/Sales	2.41	95.01

TRADING VOLUME (thousand shares)

Business Summary: Electric Utilities (MIC: 3.1.1 SIC: 4931 NAIC: 221121)

Northwestern is engaged in providing electricity and natural gas to customers in Montana, South Dakota and Nebraska. Co. has two operating segments: Electric and Natural Gas. Co.'s regulated electric utility business in Montana includes generation, transmission and distribution, while its South Dakota electric utility business operates as a vertically integrated generation, transmission and distribution utility. Co.'s regulated natural gas utility business in Montana includes production, storage, transmission and distribution. As of Dec 31 2016, Co. provided electricity and natural gas to approximately 709, 600 customers in Montana, South Dakota and Nebraska.

Recent Developments: For the quarter ended Sep 30 2017, net income decreased 18.4% to US$36.4 million from US$44.6 million in the year-earlier quarter. Revenues were US$309.9 million, up 3.0% from US$301.0 million the year before. Operating income was US$61.5 million versus US$56.1 million in the prior-year quarter, an increase of 9.7%. Direct operating expenses rose 1.4% to US$97.5 million from US$96.2 million in the comparable period the year before. Indirect operating expenses increased 1.4% to US$150.9 million from US$148.7 million in the equivalent prior-year period.

Prospects: Our evaluation of Northwestern Corp. as of Jan. 21, 2018 is the result of our systematic analysis on three basic characteristics: earnings strength, relative valuation, and recent stock price movement. The company has generated a negative trend in earnings per share over the past 5 quarters. However, while recent estimates for the company have been mixed, NWE has posted better than expected results. Based on operating earnings yield, the company is undervalued when compared to all of the companies in our coverage universe. Share price changes over the past year indicates that NWE will perform very well over the near term.

Financial Data

(US$ in Thousands)	9 Mos	6 Mos	3 Mos	12/31/2016	12/31/2015	12/31/2014	12/31/2013	12/31/2012
Earnings Per Share	3.31	3.48	3.77	3.39	3.17	2.99	2.46	2.66
Cash Flow Per Share	6.84	6.72	6.28	5.97	7.18	6.23	5.08	6.80
Tang Book Value Per Share	26.23	25.94	25.95	27.28	25.79	23.93	17.44	15.55
Dividends Per Share	2.075	2.050	2.025	2.000	1.920	1.600	1.520	1.480
Dividend Payout %	62.69	58.91	53.71	59.00	60.57	53.51	61.79	55.64
Income Statement								
Total Revenue	961,104	651,171	367,312	1,257,247	1,214,299	1,204,863	1,154,519	1,070,342
EBITDA	198,383	134,854	87,845	410,831	418,101	311,992	291,601	287,601
Depn & Amortn	3,585	2,392	1,201	159,336	144,702	123,776	112,831	106,044
Income Before Taxes	124,841	85,654	63,244	156,525	181,246	110,414	108,284	116,495
Income Taxes	10,032	7,257	6,677	(7,647)	30,037	(10,272)	14,301	18,089
Net Income	114,809	78,397	56,567	164,172	151,209	120,686	93,983	98,406
Average Shares	48,551	48,581	48,386	48,475	47,642	40,431	38,227	37,040
Balance Sheet								
Current Assets	253,713	248,017	244,652	280,195	286,660	350,885	320,956	303,128
Total Assets	5,628,955	5,556,932	5,500,301	5,499,321	5,278,640	4,973,943	3,715,260	3,485,533
Current Liabilities	601,780	578,428	545,070	613,832	571,200	614,582	463,588	449,265
Long-Term Obligations	1,816,850	1,817,117	1,817,469	1,817,684	1,808,453	1,690,261	1,184,992	1,086,636
Total Liabilities	3,902,767	3,848,335	3,791,098	3,823,094	3,678,466	3,496,160	2,684,590	2,551,501
Stockholders' Equity	1,726,188	1,708,597	1,709,203	1,676,227	1,600,174	1,477,783	1,030,670	934,032
Shares Outstanding	52,175	52,091	52,085	48,331	48,172	46,914	38,745	37,221
Statistical Record								
Return on Assets %	2.92	3.11	3.40	3.04	2.95	2.78	2.61	2.93
Return on Equity %	9.53	10.13	10.99	9.99	9.83	9.62	9.57	10.95
EBITDA Margin %	20.64	20.71	23.92	32.68	34.43	25.89	25.26	26.87
Net Margin %	11.95	12.04	15.40	13.06	12.45	10.02	8.14	9.19
Asset Turnover	0.23	0.24	0.24	0.23	0.24	0.28	0.32	0.32
Current Ratio	0.42	0.43	0.45	0.46	0.50	0.57	0.69	0.67
Debt to Equity	1.05	1.06	1.06	1.08	1.13	1.14	1.15	1.16
Price Range	63.78-54.09	63.78-54.09	63.33-54.09	63.33-52.47	59.10-48.75	58.55-42.67	47.01-34.73	37.79-33.43
P/E Ratio	19.27-16.34	18.33-15.54	16.80-14.35	18.68-15.48	18.64-15.38	19.58-14.27	19.11-14.12	14.21-12.57
Average Yield %	3.54	3.50	3.48	3.44	3.60	3.31	3.67	4.17

Address: 3010 W. 69th Street, Sioux Falls, SD 57108
Telephone: 605-978-2900

Web Site: www.northwesternenergy.com
Officers: E. Linn Draper - Chairman Robert C. Rowe - President, Chief Executive Officer

Auditors: Deloitte & Touche LLP
Investor Contact: 605-978-2900

NOW INC

Exchange	Symbol	Price	52Wk Range	Yield	P/E
NYS	DNOW	$11.03 (12/29/2017)	22.67-9.88	N/A	N/A

*7 Year Price Score N/A   ***NYSE Composite Index=100**   ***12 Month Price Score 64.17**

Interim Earnings (Per Share)

Qtr.	Mar	Jun	Sep	Dec
2014	0.38	0.25	0.30	0.13
2015	(0.09)	(0.18)	(2.09)	(2.32)
2016	(0.59)	(0.40)	(0.53)	(0.66)
2017	(0.21)	(0.16)	(0.08)	...

Interim Dividends (Per Share)

No Dividends Paid

Valuation Analysis   **Institutional Holding**

Forecast EPS	$-0.33	No of Institutions
	(01/17/2018)	346
Market Cap	$1.2 Billion	Shares
Book Value	$1.2 Billion	124,146,224
Price/Book	1.00	% Held
Price/Sales	0.47	N/A

Business Summary: Equipment & Services (MIC: 9.1.3 SIC: 3533 NAIC: 333132)

NOW is a distributor to the oil and gas and industrial markets. Co. operates primarily under the DistributionNOW and Wilson Export brands. Co.'s product offering includes consumable maintenance, repair and operating supplies, pipe, valves, fittings, flanges, gaskets, fasteners, electrical, instrumentation, pumps, paint and coatings, mill tools, safety supplies and spare parts. Co. operates through three reportable segments: U.S., which serve the upstream, midstream and downstream energy and industrial markets; Canada, which serves the energy exploration, production, mining and drilling business; and International, which provides inventory and support to drilling and exploration activities.

Recent Developments: For the quarter ended Sep 30 2017, net loss amounted to US$9.0 million versus a net loss of US$56.0 million in the year-earlier quarter. Revenues were US$697.0 million, up 34.0% from US$520.0 million the year before. Operating loss was US$6.0 million versus a loss of US$53.0 million in the prior-year quarter. Direct operating expenses rose 29.8% to US$562.0 million from US$433.0 million in the comparable period the year before. Indirect operating expenses increased 0.7% to US$141.0 million from US$140.0 million in the equivalent prior-year period.

Prospects: Our evaluation of NOW Inc. as of Jan. 14, 2018 is the result of our systematic analysis on three basic characteristics: earnings strength, relative valuation, and recent stock price movement. The company has generated a negative trend in earnings per share over the past 5 quarters. Because the company lacks sufficient analyst estimate data, we place greater weight on the historical EPS trend as the measure of earnings strength. Based on operating earnings yield, the company is overvalued when compared to all of the companies in our coverage universe. Share price changes over the past year indicates that DNOW will perform very poorly over the near term.

Financial Data

(US$ in Millions)	9 Mos	6 Mos	3 Mos	12/31/2016	12/31/2015	12/31/2014	12/31/2013	12/31/2012
Earnings Per Share	(1.11)	(1.56)	(1.80)	(2.18)	(4.68)	1.06	...	...
Cash Flow Per Share	(0.54)	0.06	1.16	2.19	3.03	1.01	...	...
Tang Book Value Per Share	6.38	6.29	6.32	6.40	9.67	14.45	...	...
Income Statement								
Total Revenue	1,979	1,282	631	2,107	3,010	4,105	4,296	3,414
EBITDA	(11)	(14)	(10)	(198)	(493)	194	233	173
Depn & Amortn	38	26	13	32	25	16	11	8
Income Before Taxes	(49)	(40)	(23)	(230)	(518)	178	222	165
Income Taxes	...	...	...	4	(16)	62	75	57
Net Income	(49)	(40)	(23)	(234)	(502)	116	147	108
Average Shares	108	108	108	107	107	108	...	...
Balance Sheet								
Current Assets	1,149	1,065	1,025	959	1,292	2,047	1,662	1,882
Total Assets	1,780	1,698	1,663	1,603	1,832	2,596	2,183	2,373
Current Liabilities	422	386	399	347	307	620	363	391
Long-Term Obligations	163	128	82	65	108	...	...	...
Total Liabilities	593	522	488	420	429	630	381	402
Stockholders' Equity	1,187	1,176	1,175	1,183	1,403	1,966	...	...
Shares Outstanding	107	107	107	107	107	107	...	...
Statistical Record								
Return on Assets %	N.M.	N.M.	N.M.	N.M.	N.M.	4.85	6.45	...
EBITDA Margin %	N.M.	N.M.	N.M.	N.M.	N.M.	4.73	5.42	5.07
Net Margin %	N.M.	N.M.	N.M.	N.M.	N.M.	2.83	3.42	3.16
Asset Turnover	1.44	1.33	1.29	1.22	1.36	1.72	1.89	...
Current Ratio	2.72	2.76	2.57	2.76	4.21	3.30	4.58	4.81
Debt to Equity	0.14	0.11	0.07	0.05	0.08	...	...	...
Price Range	23.21-11.49	23.21-15.05	23.21-15.75	23.21-12.48	26.79-14.80	37.19-22.50	...	...
P/E Ratio	...	...	...	...	...	35.08-21.23	...	...

Address: 7402 North Eldridge Parkway, Houston, TX 77041
Telephone: 281-823-4700

Web Site: www.distributionnow.com
Officers: J. Wayne Richards - Chairman Robert R. Workman - President, Chief Executive Officer

Auditors: Ernst & Young LLP
Transfer Agents: American Stock Transfer & Trust Co., LLC , Brooklyn, NY

NRG ENERGY INC

Exchange	Symbol	Price	52Wk Range	Yield	P/E
NYS	NRG	$28.48 (12/29/2017)	29.49-12.30	0.42	N/A

*7 Year Price Score 74.97 *NYSE Composite Index=100 *12 Month Price Score 124.74

TRADING VOLUME (thousand shares)

Interim Earnings (Per Share)

Qtr.	Mar	Jun	Sep	Dec
2014	(0.18)	(0.30)	0.48	0.21
2015	(0.37)	(0.06)	0.18	(19.21)
2016	0.24	(0.61)	1.27	(3.13)
2017	(0.52)	(1.98)	0.53	...

Interim Dividends (Per Share)

Amt	Decl	Ex	Rec	Pay
0.03Q	01/18/2017	01/30/2017	02/01/2017	02/15/2017
0.03Q	04/07/2017	04/27/2017	05/01/2017	05/15/2017
0.03Q	07/20/2017	07/28/2017	08/01/2017	08/15/2017
0.03Q	10/18/2017	10/31/2017	11/01/2017	11/15/2017

Indicated Div: $0.12

Valuation Analysis

Valuation Analysis		Institutional Holding	
Forecast EPS	$0.73	No of Institutions	
	(01/18/2018)	591	
Market Cap	$9.0 Billion	Shares	
Book Value	$1.2 Billion	370,606,400	
Price/Book	7.62	% Held	
Price/Sales	0.82	101.23	

Business Summary: Electric Utilities (MIC: 3.1.1 SIC: 4911 NAIC: 221121)

NRG Energy is a power company, which produces, sells and delivers electricity and related products and services in power markets in the U.S. Co. owns and operates approx. 47,000 megawatt (MW) of generation; engages in the trading of wholesale energy, capacity and related products; transacts in and trades fuel and transportation services; and directly sells energy, services, and products and services to retail customers under the names NRG, Reliant and other retail brand names owned by Co.

Recent Developments: For the quarter ended Sep 30 2017, income from continuing operations increased 48.4% to US$190.0 million from US$128.0 million in the year-earlier quarter. Net income decreased 58.5% to US$163.0 million from US$393.0 million in the year-earlier quarter. Revenues were US$3.05 billion, down 10.9% from US$3.42 billion the year before. Operating income was US$376.0 million versus US$428.0 million in the prior-year quarter, a decrease of 12.1%. Direct operating expenses declined 11.6% to US$2.16 billion from US$2.44 billion in the comparable period the year before. Indirect operating expenses decreased 6.5% to US$517.0 million from US$553.0 million in the equivalent prior-year period.

Prospects: Our evaluation of NRG Energy Inc. as of Jan. 14, 2018 is the result of our systematic analysis on three basic characteristics: earnings strength, relative valuation, and recent stock price movement. The company has enjoyed a very positive trend in earnings per share over the past 5 quarters. However, while recent estimates for the company have been lowered by analysts, NRG has posted results that fell short of analysts expectations. Based on operating earnings yield, the company is about fairly valued when compared to all of the companies in our coverage universe. Share price changes over the past year indicates that NRG will perform very well over the near term.

Financial Data

(US$ in Thousands)	9 Mos	6 Mos	3 Mos	12/31/2016	12/31/2015	12/31/2014	12/31/2013	12/31/2012
Earnings Per Share	(5.10)	(4.36)	(2.99)	(2.22)	(19.46)	0.23	(1.22)	2.35
Cash Flow Per Share	3.61	4.03	4.59	6.54	3.98	4.52	3.93	4.94
Tang Book Value Per Share	N.M.	N.M.	N.M.	N.M.	N.M.	14.59	20.77	22.03
Dividends Per Share	0.120	0.120	0.120	0.235	0.580	0.540	0.450	0.180
Dividend Payout %	...	...	...	...	...	234.78	...	7.66
Income Statement								
Total Revenue	8,132,000	5,083,000	2,759,000	12,351,000	14,674,000	15,868,000	11,295,000	8,422,000
EBITDA	975,000	518,000	88,000	250,000	(3,921,000)	1,280,000	256,000	1,022,000
Depn & Amortn	187,000	120,000	31,000	91,000	81,000	64,000	49,000	146,000
Income Before Taxes	96,000	(73,000)	(212,000)	(902,000)	(5,130,000)	97,000	(641,000)	215,000
Income Taxes	5,000	(1,000)	(4,000)	16,000	1,342,000	3,000	(282,000)	(327,000)
Net Income	(619,000)	(790,000)	(163,000)	(774,000)	(6,382,000)	134,000	(386,000)	559,000
Average Shares	322,000	316,000	316,000	316,000	329,000	339,000	323,000	234,000
Balance Sheet								
Current Assets	4,760,000	4,469,000	5,440,000	6,395,000	7,391,000	8,582,000	7,596,000	7,956,000
Total Assets	25,470,000	25,205,000	29,420,000	30,355,000	32,882,000	40,665,000	33,902,000	35,128,000
Current Liabilities	3,705,000	3,520,000	4,197,000	4,382,000	4,375,000	4,859,000	4,204,000	4,677,000
Long-Term Obligations	15,658,000	15,842,000	17,672,000	18,006,000	18,983,000	19,900,000	15,767,000	15,733,000
Total Liabilities	24,287,000	24,184,000	27,795,000	28,314,000	29,873,000	30,612,000	24,051,000	24,864,000
Stockholders' Equity	1,183,000	1,021,000	1,625,000	2,041,000	3,009,000	10,053,000	9,851,000	10,264,000
Shares Outstanding	316,638	316,122	316,080	315,443	314,190	336,662	323,779	322,606
Statistical Record								
Return on Assets %	N.M.	N.M.	N.M.	N.M.	N.M.	0.36	N.M.	1.80
Return on Equity %	N.M.	N.M.	N.M.	N.M.	N.M.	1.35	N.M.	6.19
EBITDA Margin %	11.99	10.19	3.19	2.02	N.M.	8.07	2.27	12.13
Net Margin %	N.M.	N.M.	N.M.	N.M.	N.M.	0.84	N.M.	6.64
Asset Turnover	0.39	0.42	0.38	0.39	0.40	0.43	0.33	0.27
Current Ratio	1.28	1.27	1.30	1.46	1.69	1.77	1.81	1.70
Debt to Equity	13.24	15.52	10.88	8.82	6.31	1.98	1.60	1.53
Price Range	25.86-9.89	18.90-9.89	18.73-9.89	17.90-8.98	27.50-9.00	37.66-25.83	30.11-22.68	23.65-14.34
P/E Ratio	...	...	...	...	...	163.74-112.30	...	10.06-6.10
Average Yield %	0.70	0.83	0.86	1.85	2.81	1.74	1.69	0.96

Address: 804 Carnegie Center, Princeton, NJ 08540 **Telephone:** 609-524-4500	**Web Site:** www.nrgenergy.com **Officers:** Lawrence S. Coben - Chairman Mauricio Gutierrez - President, Chief Executive Officer, Executive Vice President, Chief Operating Officer	**Auditors:** KPMG LLP **Investor Contact:** 609-524-4526 **Transfer Agents:** Computershare Shareowner Services LLC, College Station, TX

NU SKIN ENTERPRISES, INC.

Exchange	Symbol	Price	52Wk Range	Yield	P/E	Div Acheiver
NYS	NUS	$68.23 (12/29/2017)	69.97-47.22	2.11	24.90	15 Years

*7 Year Price Score 84.87   *NYSE Composite Index=100   *12 Month Price Score 105.89

Interim Earnings (Per Share)

Qtr.	Mar	Jun	Sep	Dec
2014	1.05	0.32	1.12	0.77
2015	0.60	0.75	0.28	0.62
2016	0.06	0.79	0.98	0.70
2017	0.51	0.77	0.76	...

Interim Dividends (Per Share)

Amt	Decl	Ex	Rec	Pay
0.36Q	02/16/2017	02/23/2017	02/27/2017	03/15/2017
0.36Q	05/03/2017	05/24/2017	05/26/2017	06/14/2017
0.36Q	08/02/2017	08/23/2017	08/25/2017	09/13/2017
0.36Q	11/01/2017	11/16/2017	11/17/2017	12/06/2017

Indicated Div: $1.44

Valuation Analysis

		Institutional Holding	
Forecast EPS	$3.25	No of Institutions	
	(01/25/2018)	370	
Market Cap	$3.6 Billion	Shares	
Book Value	$717.5 Million	49,681,320	
Price/Book	5.02	% Held	
Price/Sales	1.68	65.95	

Business Summary: Household & Personal Products (MIC: 1.7.1 SIC: 5122 NAIC: 424210)

NU Skin Enterprises develops and distributes consumer products, as well as providing a line of beauty and wellness solutions. Co. has two primary product categories, each operating under its own brand: Nu Skin, which provides anti-aging personal care products including ageLOC Me customized skin care system, ageLOC Spa systems and ageLOC Transformation anti-aging skin care system; and Pharmanex, with a product line that includes ageLOC Youth nutritional supplement, ageLOC TR90 weight management and body shaping system and LifePak nutritional supplements. As of Dec 31 2016, Co. sold and distributed its products in approximately 50 markets worldwide.

Recent Developments: For the quarter ended Sep 30 2017, net income decreased 26.7% to US$41.7 million from US$56.9 million in the year-earlier quarter. Revenues were US$563.7 million, down 6.7% from US$604.2 million the year before. Operating income was US$64.4 million versus US$82.4 million in the prior-year quarter, a decrease of 21.9%. Direct operating expenses declined 4.0% to US$120.8 million from US$125.9 million in the comparable period the year before. Indirect operating expenses decreased 4.4% to US$378.5 million from US$395.9 million in the equivalent prior-year period.

Prospects: Our evaluation of NU Skin Enterprises Inc. as of Jan. 21, 2018 is the result of our systematic analysis on three basic characteristics: earnings strength, relative valuation, and recent stock price movement. The company has produced a positive trend in earnings per share over the past 5 quarters and while recent estimates for the company have been mixed, NUS has posted results that were in line with analysts expectations. Based on operating earnings yield, the company is undervalued when compared to all of the companies in our coverage universe. Share price changes over the past year indicates that NUS will perform well over the near term.

Financial Data
(US$ in Thousands)

	9 Mos	6 Mos	3 Mos	12/31/2016	12/31/2015	12/31/2014	12/31/2013	12/31/2012
Earnings Per Share	2.74	2.96	2.98	2.55	2.25	3.11	5.94	3.52
Cash Flow Per Share	4.65	4.22	5.68	4.95	5.55	(0.96)	9.05	5.12
Tang Book Value Per Share	10.11	9.90	9.66	9.23	11.54	12.80	11.24	6.60
Dividends Per Share	1.435	1.430	1.425	1.420	1.400	1.380	1.200	0.800
Dividend Payout %	52.37	48.31	47.82	55.69	62.22	44.37	20.20	22.73
Income Statement								
Total Revenue	1,612,898	1,049,200	499,099	2,207,797	2,247,047	2,569,495	3,176,718	2,169,664
EBITDA	219,418	138,783	59,320	273,639	273,559	345,007	584,040	370,742
Depn & Amortn	52,525	35,080	17,625	60,800	61,600	46,500	27,100	25,500
Income Before Taxes	166,893	103,703	41,695	212,839	211,959	298,507	556,940	345,242
Income Taxes	55,691	34,173	14,206	69,753	78,913	109,331	192,052	123,597
Net Income	111,202	69,530	27,489	143,086	133,046	189,176	364,888	221,645
Average Shares	54,834	54,839	54,057	56,097	59,057	60,887	61,448	63,025
Balance Sheet								
Current Assets	749,229	720,299	705,839	714,337	706,392	834,667	1,118,334	599,403
Total Assets	1,547,331	1,507,145	1,494,416	1,474,045	1,505,843	1,614,434	1,821,062	1,152,907
Current Liabilities	419,825	400,502	394,917	399,011	407,597	418,329	776,792	320,103
Long-Term Obligations	316,519	324,059	329,001	334,165	181,745	164,567	113,852	154,963
Total Liabilities	829,808	807,575	806,831	809,975	680,222	671,996	962,443	562,295
Stockholders' Equity	717,523	699,570	687,585	664,070	825,621	942,438	858,619	590,612
Shares Outstanding	52,800	53,000	52,900	52,600	56,000	59,000	59,000	58,400
Statistical Record								
Return on Assets %	9.06	10.01	11.13	9.58	8.53	11.01	24.54	20.62
Return on Equity %	19.01	21.52	22.47	19.16	15.05	21.01	50.36	37.95
EBITDA Margin %	13.60	13.23	11.89	12.39	12.17	13.43	18.39	17.09
Net Margin %	6.89	6.63	5.51	6.48	5.92	7.36	11.49	10.22
Asset Turnover	1.30	1.33	1.49	1.48	1.44	1.50	2.14	2.02
Current Ratio	1.78	1.80	1.79	1.79	1.73	2.00	1.44	1.87
Debt to Equity	0.44	0.46	0.48	0.50	0.22	0.17	0.13	0.26
Price Range	65.89-47.22	65.89-45.17	65.89-37.01	65.89-28.13	62.20-31.89	138.22-38.28	138.66-37.05	61.50-33.05
P/E Ratio	24.05-17.23	22.26-15.26	22.11-12.42	25.84-11.03	27.64-14.17	44.44-12.31	23.34-6.24	17.47-9.39
Average Yield %	2.54	2.59	2.80	3.05	3.04	2.09	1.59	1.71

Address: 75 West Center Street, Provo, UT 84601	**Web Site:** www.nuskinenterprises.com	**Auditors:** PricewaterhouseCoopers LLP
Telephone: 801-345-1000	**Officers:** Blake M. Roney - Chairman Steven J. Lund - Vice-Chairman	**Investor Contact:** 801-345-2657
		Transfer Agents: American Stock Transfer & Trust Co. LLC, Brooklyn, NY

NUCOR CORP.

Exchange	Symbol	Price	52Wk Range	Yield	P/E	Div Achiever
NYS	NUE	$63.58 (12/29/2017)	64.73-53.48	2.39	17.71	44 Years

*7 Year Price Score 96.69   *NYSE Composite Index=100   *12 Month Price Score 94.65

Interim Earnings (Per Share)

Qtr.	Mar	Jun	Sep	Dec
2014	0.35	0.46	0.76	0.65
2015	0.21	0.39	0.71	(0.19)
2016	0.22	0.73	0.84	0.69
2017	1.11	1.00	0.79	...

Interim Dividends (Per Share)

Amt	Decl	Ex	Rec	Pay
0.378Q	02/21/2017	03/29/2017	03/31/2017	05/11/2017
0.378Q	06/06/2017	06/28/2017	06/30/2017	08/11/2017
0.378Q	09/14/2017	09/28/2017	09/29/2017	11/09/2017
0.38Q	12/01/2017	12/28/2017	12/29/2017	02/09/2018

Indicated Div: $1.52 (Div. Reinv. Plan)

Valuation Analysis	Institutional Holding	
Forecast EPS	$3.48	No of Institutions
(01/18/2018)		1052
Market Cap	$20.2 Billion	Shares
Book Value	$8.5 Billion	318,896,544
Price/Book	2.38	% Held
Price/Sales	1.06	77.33

TRADING VOLUME (thousand shares)

Business Summary: Non-Precious Metals (MIC: 8.2.2 SIC: 3312 NAIC: 331111)

Nucor is engaged in the manufacturing of steel and steel products. Co. has three segments: steel mills, which produces and distributes sheet steel (hot-rolled, cold-rolled and galvanized), tubular products, plate steel, structural steel and bar steel; steel products, which produces steel joists and joist girders, steel deck, fabricated concrete reinforcing steel, cold finished steel, steel fasteners, metal building systems, steel grating, and wire and wire mesh; and raw materials, which produces direct reduced iron (DRI); brokers ferrous and nonferrous metals, pig iron, hot briquetted iron and DRI; supplies ferro-alloys; and processes ferrous and nonferrous scrap metal.

Recent Developments: For the quarter ended Sep 30 2017, net income decreased 19.7% to US$266.1 million from US$331.4 million in the year-earlier quarter. Revenues were US$5.17 billion, up 20.5% from US$4.29 billion the year before. Direct operating expenses rose 27.2% to US$4.59 billion from US$3.61 billion in the comparable period the year before. Indirect operating expenses increased 5.2% to US$208.4 million from US$198.1 million in the equivalent prior-year period.

Prospects: Our evaluation of Nucor Corp. as of Jan. 14, 2018 is the result of our systematic analysis on three basic characteristics: earnings strength, relative valuation, and recent stock price movement. The company has suffered a very negative trend in earnings per share over the past 5 quarters. However, while recent estimates for the company have been mixed, NUE has posted better than expected results. Based on operating earnings yield, the company is undervalued when compared to all of the companies in our coverage universe. Share price changes over the past year indicates that NUE will perform very poorly over the near term.

Financial Data

(US$ in Thousands)	9 Mos	6 Mos	3 Mos	12/31/2016	12/31/2015	12/31/2014	12/31/2013	12/31/2012
Earnings Per Share	3.59	3.64	3.37	2.48	1.11	2.22	1.52	1.58
Cash Flow Per Share	4.15	3.83	4.47	5.42	6.73	4.20	3.38	3.76
Tang Book Value Per Share	16.85	16.44	15.63	15.56	14.58	15.18	15.07	14.73
Dividends Per Share	1.510	1.508	1.505	1.502	1.492	1.482	1.472	1.462
Dividend Payout %	42.06	41.41	44.66	60.58	134.46	66.78	96.88	92.56
Income Statement								
Total Revenue	15,160,065	9,989,948	4,815,179	16,208,122	16,439,276	21,105,141	19,052,046	19,429,273
EBITDA	2,072,626	1,486,959	764,717	2,042,338	1,503,197	2,012,328	1,464,573	1,562,648
Depn & Amortn	543,216	363,721	180,893	613,192	625,757	652,000	535,852	534,010
Income Before Taxes	1,397,915	1,035,053	540,219	1,259,902	703,909	1,191,072	781,826	866,263
Income Taxes	442,239	337,739	171,327	398,243	213,154	388,787	205,594	259,814
Net Income	934,797	679,947	356,899	796,271	357,659	713,946	488,025	504,619
Average Shares	320,763	321,226	321,146	319,822	320,693	320,127	319,266	318,240
Balance Sheet								
Current Assets	7,500,647	7,182,692	6,878,193	6,506,393	5,754,380	6,441,888	6,410,046	5,661,364
Total Assets	16,503,834	16,112,725	15,875,460	15,223,518	14,250,399	15,615,927	15,203,283	14,152,059
Current Liabilities	3,555,466	3,325,306	2,837,796	2,389,966	1,385,173	2,097,776	1,960,216	2,029,568
Long-Term Obligations	3,241,488	3,240,694	3,739,908	3,739,141	4,360,600	4,360,600	4,376,900	3,380,200
Total Liabilities	7,998,449	7,735,660	7,741,437	7,343,653	6,833,521	7,843,457	7,557,514	6,510,488
Stockholders' Equity	8,505,385	8,377,065	8,134,023	7,879,865	7,416,878	7,772,470	7,645,769	7,641,571
Shares Outstanding	317,916	319,425	319,051	318,737	317,962	319,033	318,328	317,663
Statistical Record								
Return on Assets %	7.32	7.55	7.15	5.39	2.40	4.63	3.32	3.50
Return on Equity %	14.25	14.69	13.91	10.38	4.71	9.26	6.38	6.66
EBITDA Margin %	13.67	14.88	15.88	12.60	9.14	9.53	7.69	8.04
Net Margin %	6.17	6.81	7.41	4.91	2.18	3.38	2.56	2.60
Asset Turnover	1.21	1.18	1.14	1.10	1.10	1.37	1.30	1.35
Current Ratio	2.11	2.16	2.42	2.72	4.15	3.07	3.27	2.79
Debt to Equity	0.38	0.39	0.46	0.47	0.59	0.56	0.57	0.44
Price Range	66.75-46.54	66.75-45.35	66.75-45.35	66.75-34.86	49.77-37.00	58.09-46.62	54.62-42.23	45.41-34.39
P/E Ratio	18.59-12.96	18.34-12.46	19.81-13.46	26.92-14.06	44.84-33.33	26.17-21.00	35.93-27.78	28.74-21.77
Average Yield %	2.60	2.68	2.78	3.06	3.34	2.87	3.12	3.64

Address: 1915 Rexford Road, Charlotte, NC 28211	Web Site: www.nucor.com	Auditors: PricewaterhouseCoopers LLP
Telephone: 704-366-7000	Officers: John J. Ferriola - Chairman, President, Chief Executive Officer, Chief Operating Officer James D. Frias - Executive Vice President, Chief Financial Officer, Treasurer	Transfer Agents: American Stock Transfer & Trust Company, New York, NY
Fax: 704-362-4208		

NVR INC.

Exchange	Symbol	Price	52Wk Range	Yield	P/E
NYS	NVR	$3508 (12/29/2017)	3525.73-1649.99	N/A	25.85

*7 Year Price Score 149.50 ***NYSE Composite Index=100** ***12 Month Price Score 126.48**

TRADING VOLUME (thousand shares)

Interim Earnings (Per Share)

Qtr.	Mar	Jun	Sep	Dec
2014	5.16	15.17	20.70	22.91
2015	9.22	21.91	27.11	31.67
2016	15.79	22.01	28.46	37.37
2017	25.12	35.19	38.02	...

Interim Dividends (Per Share)

No Dividends Paid

Valuation Analysis / Institutional Holding

Valuation Analysis		Institutional Holding	
Forecast EPS	$146.40	No of Institutions	512
	(01/18/2018)		
Market Cap	$13.1 Billion	Shares	
Book Value	$1.7 Billion		3,888,561
Price/Book	7.94	% Held	
Price/Sales	2.09		74.40

Business Summary: Builders (MIC: 2.2.5 SIC: 1531 NAIC: 236117)

NVR is engaged in the construction and sale of single-family detached homes, townhomes and condominium buildings, all of which are primarily constructed on a pre-sold basis. Co.'s homebuilding operations construct and sell single-family detached homes, townhomes and condominium buildings under three trade names: NVHomes and Heartland Homes, which are marketed primarily to move-up and up-scale buyers, and Ryan Homes, which is marketed primarily to first-time and first-time move-up buyers. Co. also operates a mortgage banking and title services business. Co.'s mortgage banking operations are operated primarily through a wholly owned subsidiary, NVR Mortgage Finance, Inc.

Recent Developments: For the quarter ended Sep 30 2017, net income increased 38.1% to US$162.1 million from US$117.4 million in the year-earlier quarter. Revenues were US$1.67 billion, up 8.5% from US$1.54 billion the year before. Direct operating expenses rose 5.3% to US$1.31 billion from US$1.24 billion in the comparable period the year before. Indirect operating expenses increased 5.4% to US$113.9 million from US$108.1 million in the equivalent prior-year period.

Prospects: Our evaluation of NVR Inc. as of Jan. 14, 2018 is the result of our systematic analysis on three basic characteristics: earnings strength, relative valuation, and recent stock price movement. The company has produced a positive trend in earnings per share over the past 5 quarters and while recent estimates for the company have been mixed, NVR has posted better than expected results. Based on operating earnings yield, the company is about fairly valued when compared to all of the companies in our coverage universe. Share price changes over the past year indicates that NVR will perform very well over the near term.

Financial Data

(US$ in Thousands)	9 Mos	6 Mos	3 Mos	12/31/2016	12/31/2015	12/31/2014	12/31/2013	12/31/2012
Earnings Per Share	135.70	126.14	112.96	103.61	89.99	63.50	54.81	35.12
Cash Flow Per Share	169.14	149.49	146.05	99.67	50.57	43.14	57.04	52.62
Tang Book Value Per Share	428.33	396.24	363.28	339.27	304.87	264.25	271.93	289.44
Income Statement								
Total Revenue	4,500,334	2,828,163	1,280,164	5,834,585	5,169,562	4,453,139	4,220,908	3,193,204
EBITDA	620,550	364,373	143,696	705,673	648,305	494,300	454,472	290,706
Depn & Amortn	17,087	11,494	5,699	22,269	21,534	17,614	13,391	8,100
Income Before Taxes	585,593	341,129	132,161	661,697	603,212	453,546	418,696	275,077
Income Taxes	172,691	90,329	29,238	236,435	220,285	171,916	152,219	94,489
Net Income	412,902	250,800	102,923	425,262	382,927	281,630	266,477	180,588
Average Shares	4,263	4,202	4,097	4,104	4,255	4,435	4,861	5,141
Balance Sheet								
Current Assets	2,039,763	1,934,038	1,761,840	1,506,923	1,430,852	1,414,424	1,604,150	1,830,732
Total Assets	3,049,511	2,918,087	2,742,299	2,643,943	2,515,131	2,351,335	2,486,148	2,604,842
Current Liabilities	463,137	467,508	418,705	405,847	370,693	337,174	304,483	283,819
Long-Term Obligations	596,913	596,760	596,607	596,455	599,260	599,230	602,440	603,562
Total Liabilities	1,398,835	1,382,310	1,334,019	1,339,502	1,275,966	1,227,080	1,224,796	1,124,365
Stockholders' Equity	1,650,676	1,535,777	1,408,280	1,304,441	1,239,165	1,124,255	1,261,352	1,480,477
Shares Outstanding	3,735	3,747	3,735	3,693	3,890	4,049	4,433	4,914
Statistical Record								
Return on Assets %	19.74	18.48	17.52	16.44	15.74	11.64	10.47	8.22
Return on Equity %	38.23	35.88	34.74	33.35	32.40	23.61	19.44	12.61
EBITDA Margin %	13.79	12.88	11.22	12.09	12.54	11.10	10.77	9.10
Net Margin %	9.17	8.87	8.04	7.29	7.41	6.32	6.31	5.66
Asset Turnover	2.19	2.18	2.26	2.26	2.12	1.84	1.66	1.45
Current Ratio	4.40	4.14	4.21	3.71	3.86	4.19	5.27	6.45
Debt to Equity	0.36	0.39	0.42	0.46	0.48	0.53	0.48	0.41
Price Range	2873.37-1497.19	2488.59-1497.19	2106.88-1497.19	1830.00-1497.19	1720.00-1224.13	1276.68-997.49	1080.11-835.74	959.25-671.00
P/E Ratio	21.17-11.03	19.73-11.87	18.65-13.25	17.66-14.45	19.11-13.60	20.11-15.71	19.71-15.25	27.31-19.11

Address: 11700 Plaza America Drive, Suite 500, Reston, VA 20190 **Telephone:** 703-956-4000	**Web Site:** www.nvrinc.com **Officers:** Dwight C. Schar - Chairman Jeffrey D. Martchek - Division Officer	**Auditors:** KPMG LLP **Transfer Agents:** Computershare Trust Company, N.A., Providence, RI

OCCIDENTAL PETROLEUM CORP

Exchange	Symbol	Price	52Wk Range	Yield	P/E	Div Achiever
NYS	OXY	$73.66 (12/29/2017)	73.70-58.02	4.18	103.75	14 Years

*7 Year Price Score 62.47 *NYSE Composite Index=100 *12 Month Price Score 102.00

Interim Earnings (Per Share)

Qtr.	Mar	Jun	Sep	Dec
2014	1.75	1.82	1.55	(4.34)
2015	(0.28)	0.23	(3.42)	(6.77)
2016	0.10	(0.18)	(0.32)	(0.35)
2017	0.15	0.66	0.25	...

Interim Dividends (Per Share)

Amt	Decl	Ex	Rec	Pay
0.76Q	.02/16/2017	03/08/2017	03/10/2017	04/14/2017
0.76Q	05/11/2017	06/07/2017	06/09/2017	07/14/2017
0.77Q	07/13/2017	09/08/2017	09/11/2017	10/16/2017
0.77Q	10/05/2017	12/08/2017	12/11/2017	01/16/2018

Indicated Div: $3.08 (Div. Reinv. Plan)

Valuation Analysis — **Institutional Holding**

Forecast EPS	$0.87	No. of Institutions
	(01/18/2018)	1466
Market Cap	$56.4 Billion	Shares
Book Value	$20.7 Billion	767,431,552
Price/Book	2.73	% Held
Price/Sales	4.51	75.68

Business Summary: Production & Extraction (MIC: 9.1.1 SIC: 1311 NAIC: 211111)

Occidental Petroleum conducts its operations through various subsidiaries and affiliates. Co.'s principal businesses consist of three segments: oil and gas, which explores for, develops and produces oil and condensate, natural gas liquids (NGLs) and natural gas; chemical, which manufactures and markets basic chemicals and vinyls; and midstream and marketing, which gathers, processes, transports, stores, purchases and markets oil, condensate, NGLs, natural gas, carbon dioxide and power. At Dec 31 2016, Co. had 2.41 billion barrels of oil equivalent of proved reserves, which consisted of 1.36 billion barrels of oil, 420.0 million barrels of NGLs and 3.77 trillion cubic feet of natural gas.

Recent Developments: For the quarter ended Sep 30 2017, income from continuing operations was US$190.0 million compared with a loss of US$238.0 million in the year-earlier quarter. Net income amounted to US$190.0 million versus a net loss of US$241.0 million in the year-earlier quarter. Revenues were US$3.11 billion, up 13.6% from US$2.73 billion the year before. Direct operating expenses rose 1.4% to US$1.36 billion from US$1.34 billion in the comparable period the year before. Indirect operating expenses decreased 10.9% to US$1.53 billion from US$1.72 billion in the equivalent prior-year period.

Prospects: Our evaluation of Occidental Petroleum Corp. as of Jan. 14, 2018 is the result of our systematic analysis on three basic characteristics: earnings strength, relative valuation, and recent stock price movement. The company has generated a negative trend in earnings per share over the past 5 quarters and while recent estimates for the company have been raised by analysts, OXY has posted better than expected results. Based on operating earnings yield, the company is overvalued when compared to all of the companies in our coverage universe. Share price changes over the past year indicates that OXY will perform poorly over the near term.

Financial Data

(US$ in Thousands)	9 Mos	6 Mos	3 Mos	12/31/2016	12/31/2015	12/31/2014	12/31/2013	12/31/2012
Earnings Per Share	0.71	0.14	(0.70)	(0.75)	(10.23)	0.79	7.32	5.67
Cash Flow Per Share	5.87	5.32	4.38	4.42	4.38	14.17	16.08	13.94
Tang Book Value Per Share	27.01	27.51	27.57	28.13	31.89	39.26	48.46	49.68
Dividends Per Share	3.050	3.040	3.030	3.020	2.970	2.880	2.560	2.160
Dividend Payout %	429.58	2,171.43	...	...	...	364.56	34.97	38.10
Income Statement								
Total Revenue	9,686,000	6,581,000	2,978,000	10,398,000	12,699,000	21,947,000	25,736,000	24,253,000
EBITDA	4,169,000	2,868,000	1,188,000	2,715,000	(4,993,000)	5,562,000	14,747,000	12,031,000
Depn & Amortn	2,926,000	1,931,000	942,000	4,268,000	4,544,000	4,261,000	5,347,000	4,511,000
Income Before Taxes	985,000	770,000	165,000	(1,845,000)	(9,684,000)	1,224,000	9,282,000	7,390,000
Income Taxes	448,000	363,000	78,000	(662,000)	(1,330,000)	1,685,000	3,755,000	3,118,000
Net Income	814,000	624,000	117,000	(574,000)	(7,829,000)	616,000	5,903,000	4,598,000
Average Shares	766,400	765,900	765,200	763,800	765,600	781,100	804,600	810,000
Balance Sheet								
Current Assets	7,045,000	8,075,000	8,238,000	8,428,000	9,402,000	13,873,000	11,323,000	9,492,000
Total Assets	41,443,000	41,982,000	42,465,000	43,109,000	43,437,000	56,259,000	69,443,000	64,210,000
Current Liabilities	6,362,000	6,391,000	6,852,000	6,362,000	6,842,000	8,244,000	8,434,000	7,290,000
Long-Term Obligations	9,326,000	9,324,000	9,322,000	9,819,000	6,883,000	6,838,000	6,939,000	7,023,000
Total Liabilities	20,774,000	20,945,000	21,386,000	21,612,000	19,087,000	21,300,000	26,317,000	24,194,000
Stockholders' Equity	20,669,000	21,037,000	21,079,000	21,497,000	24,350,000	34,959,000	43,126,000	40,016,000
Shares Outstanding	765,245	764,573	764,581	764,237	763,678	890,557	889,919	805,514
Statistical Record								
Return on Assets %	1.30	0.26	N.M.	N.M.	N.M.	0.98	8.83	7.38
Return on Equity %	2.52	0.50	N.M.	N.M.	N.M.	1.58	14.20	11.81
EBITDA Margin %	43.04	43.58	39.89	26.11	N.M.	25.34	57.30	49.61
Net Margin %	8.40	9.48	3.93	N.M.	N.M.	2.81	22.94	18.96
Asset Turnover	0.30	0.29	0.26	0.24	0.25	0.35	0.39	0.39
Current Ratio	1.11	1.26	1.20	1.32	1.37	1.68	1.34	1.30
Debt to Equity	0.45	0.44	0.44	0.46	0.28	0.20	0.16	0.18
Price Range	75.03-58.02	78.00-58.02	78.31-62.06	78.31-59.60	83.08-63.61	100.90-73.13	95.32-73.49	101.16-70.58
P/E Ratio	105.68-81.72	557.14-414.43	...	...	...	127.73-92.57	13.02-10.04	17.84-12.45
Average Yield %	4.70	4.44	4.22	4.20	3.99	3.18	2.99	2.56

Address: 5 Greenway Plaza, Suite 110, Houston, TX 77046	Web Site: www.oxy.com	Auditors: KPMG LLP
Telephone: 713-215-7000	Officers: Eugene L. (Gene) Batchelder - Chairman Vicki A. Hollub - President, Chief Executive Officer, Chief Operating Officer, Senior Executive Vice President, Division Officer	Transfer Agents: American Stock Transfer and Trust Company, LLC, Brooklyn, NY

OCEANEERING INTERNATIONAL, INC.

Exchange	Symbol	Price	52Wk Range	Yield	P/E
NYS	OII	$21.14 (12/29/2017)	29.35-18.28	2.84	N/A

*7 Year Price Score 39.71   *NYSE Composite Index=100   *12 Month Price Score 76.98

Interim Earnings (Per Share)

Qtr.	Mar	Jun	Sep	Dec
2014	0.84	1.02	1.16	0.99
2015	0.70	0.66	0.70	0.28
2016	0.26	0.23	(0.12)	(0.11)
2017	(0.08)	0.02	(0.02)	...

Interim Dividends (Per Share)

Amt	Decl	Ex	Rec	Pay
0.15Q	10/27/2016	11/22/2016	11/25/2016	12/16/2016
0.15Q	02/08/2017	02/22/2017	02/24/2017	03/17/2017
0.15Q	04/26/2017	05/24/2017	05/26/2017	06/16/2017
0.15Q	07/26/2017	08/23/2017	08/25/2017	09/15/2017

Indicated Div: $0.60

Valuation Analysis / Institutional Holding

Forecast EPS	$-0.10 (01/18/2018)	No of Institutions 433
Market Cap	$2.1 Billion	Shares 123,776,400
Book Value	$1.5 Billion	% Held 89.47
Price/Book	1.39	
Price/Sales	1.08	

Business Summary: Equipment & Services (MIC: 9.1.3 SIC: 1389 NAIC: 213112)

Oceaneering International provides engineered services and products, primarily to the offshore oil and gas industry, with a focus on deepwater applications. Co. also serves the defense, aerospace and commercial theme park industries. Co.'s services and products include remotely operated vehicles, specialty subsea hardware, engineering and project management, subsea intervention services, including manned diving, survey and positioning services and asset integrity and nondestructive testing services. Co. operates two businesses: Oilfield business, which includes its Remotely Operated Vehicles, Subsea Products, Subsea Projects and Asset Integrity segments; and Advanced Technologies business.

Recent Developments: For the quarter ended Sep 30 2017, net loss amounted to US$1.8 million versus a net loss of US$11.8 million in the year-earlier quarter. Revenues were US$476.1 million, down 13.3% from US$549.3 million the year before. Operating income was US$10.5 million versus a loss of US$11.9 million in the prior-year quarter. Direct operating expenses declined 18.0% to US$421.2 million from US$513.8 million in the comparable period the year before. Indirect operating expenses decreased 6.2% to US$44.4 million from US$47.3 million in the equivalent prior-year period.

Prospects: Our evaluation of Oceaneering International Inc. as of Jan. 14, 2018 is the result of our systematic analysis on three basic characteristics: earnings strength, relative valuation, and recent stock price movement. The company has enjoyed a very positive trend in earnings per share over the past 5 quarters. Because the company lacks sufficient analyst estimate data, we place greater weight on the historical EPS trend as the measure of earnings strength. Based on operating earnings yield, the company is overvalued when compared to all of the companies in our coverage universe. Share price changes over the past year indicates that OII will perform very poorly over the near term.

Financial Data

(US$ in Thousands)	9 Mos	6 Mos	3 Mos	12/31/2016	12/31/2015	12/31/2014	12/31/2013	12/31/2012
Earnings Per Share	(0.19)	(0.29)	(0.08)	0.25	2.34	4.00	3.42	2.66
Cash Flow Per Share	2.26	3.03	3.52	3.46	5.69	6.77	4.89	4.05
Tang Book Value Per Share	10.48	10.59	10.62	10.05	10.81	12.70	15.07	13.46
Dividends Per Share	0.600	0.720	0.840	0.960	1.080	1.030	0.840	0.690
Dividend Payout %	...	...	...	384.00	46.15	25.75	24.56	25.94
Income Statement								
Total Revenue	1,437,332	961,212	446,176	2,271,603	3,062,754	3,659,624	3,287,019	2,782,604
EBITDA	176,350	113,593	50,957	314,767	599,709	857,722	746,071	599,015
Depn & Amortn	160,480	106,967	53,663	250,247	241,235	229,779	202,228	176,483
Income Before Taxes	(1,268)	(3,859)	(7,637)	43,102	334,031	623,528	542,203	420,249
Income Taxes	4,104	169	(1,083)	18,760	105,250	195,148	170,836	132,905
Net Income	(7,170)	(5,402)	(7,534)	24,586	231,011	428,329	371,500	289,017
Average Shares	98,270	98,751	98,138	98,424	98,808	107,091	108,731	108,617
Balance Sheet								
Current Assets	1,232,775	1,261,705	1,246,730	1,262,595	1,517,493	1,713,550	1,433,275	1,202,990
Total Assets	3,144,683	3,091,801	3,090,996	3,130,315	3,429,536	3,511,701	3,128,500	2,768,118
Current Liabilities	461,456	482,906	477,528	508,364	615,956	679,137	727,088	617,185
Long-Term Obligations	795,805	794,099	793,908	793,058	795,836	750,000	...	94,000
Total Liabilities	1,650,079	1,600,656	1,601,863	1,613,672	1,850,802	1,854,081	1,085,060	952,658
Stockholders' Equity	1,494,604	1,491,145	1,489,133	1,516,643	1,578,734	1,657,620	2,043,440	1,815,460
Shares Outstanding	98,276	98,266	98,258	98,065	97,849	99,613	108,197	107,907
Statistical Record								
Return on Assets %	N.M.	N.M.	N.M.	0.75	6.66	12.90	12.60	11.15
Return on Equity %	N.M.	N.M.	N.M.	1.58	14.28	23.15	19.25	17.09
EBITDA Margin %	12.27	11.82	11.42	13.86	19.58	23.44	22.70	21.53
Net Margin %	N.M.	N.M.	N.M.	1.08	7.54	11.70	11.30	10.39
Asset Turnover	0.60	0.62	0.65	0.69	0.88	1.10	1.11	1.07
Current Ratio	2.67	2.61	2.61	2.48	2.46	2.52	1.97	1.95
Debt to Equity	0.53	0.53	0.53	0.52	0.50	0.45	...	0.05
Price Range	31.53-21.03	31.53-21.03	36.65-22.75	38.78-22.75	59.12-37.06	78.88-57.49	86.68-53.79	57.42-43.76
P/E Ratio	...	...	...	155.12-91.00	25.26-15.84	19.72-14.37	25.35-15.73	21.59-16.45
Average Yield %	2.31	2.68	2.93	3.24	2.27	1.44	1.14	1.34

Address: 11911 FM 529, Houston, TX 77041	**Web Site:** www.oceaneering.com	**Auditors:** Ernst & Young LLP
Telephone: 713-329-4500	**Officers:** John R. Huff - Chairman Roderick A. Larson - President, Chief Executive Officer, Chief Operating Officer, Senior Vice President	**Investor Contact:** 713-329-4500
		Transfer Agents: Computershare Trust Company, N.A., Providence, RI

OGE ENERGY CORP.

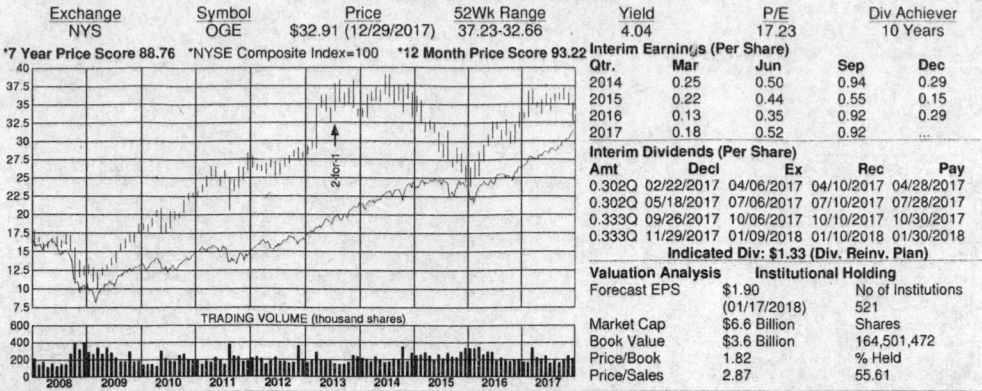

Exchange	Symbol	Price	52Wk Range	Yield	P/E	Div Achiever
NYS	OGE	$32.91 (12/29/2017)	37.23-32.66	4.04	17.23	10 Years

*7 Year Price Score 88.76   *NYSE Composite Index=100   *12 Month Price Score 93.22

Interim Earnings (Per Share)

Qtr.	Mar	Jun	Sep	Dec
2014	0.25	0.50	0.94	0.29
2015	0.22	0.44	0.55	0.15
2016	0.13	0.35	0.92	0.29
2017	0.18	0.52	0.92	...

Interim Dividends (Per Share)

Amt	Decl	Ex	Rec	Pay
0.302Q	02/22/2017	04/06/2017	04/10/2017	04/28/2017
0.302Q	05/18/2017	07/06/2017	07/10/2017	07/28/2017
0.333Q	09/26/2017	10/06/2017	10/10/2017	10/30/2017
0.333Q	11/29/2017	01/09/2018	01/10/2018	01/30/2018

Indicated Div: $1.33 (Div. Reinv. Plan)

Valuation Analysis

Forecast EPS: $1.90 (01/17/2018)
Market Cap: $6.6 Billion
Book Value: $3.6 Billion
Price/Book: 1.82
Price/Sales: 2.87

Institutional Holding

No of Institutions: 521
Shares: 164,501,472
% Held: 55.61

Business Summary: Electric Utilities (MIC: 3.1.1 SIC: 4911 NAIC: 221121)

OGE Energy is a holding company. Through its subsidiaries, Co. is an energy and energy services provider providing physical delivery and related services for both electricity and natural gas primarily in the south central U.S. Co. conducts these activities through two business segments: electric utility, which generates, transmits, distributes and sells electric energy in Oklahoma and western Arkansas; and natural gas midstream operations, which consist of Co.'s investment in Enable Midstream Partners, LP (Enable). Enable is engaged in the business of gathering, processing, transporting and storing natural gas. Enable also owns a crude oil gathering business in the Bakken shale formation.

Recent Developments: For the quarter ended Sep 30 2017, net income decreased 0.1% to US$183.4 million from US$183.6 million in the year-earlier quarter. Revenues were US$716.8 million, down 3.6% from US$743.9 million the year before. Operating income was US$243.3 million versus US$257.3 million in the prior-year quarter, a decrease of 5.4%. Direct operating expenses declined 58.2% to US$194.6 million from US$465.1 million in the comparable period the year before. Indirect operating expenses increased 7.9% to US$23.2 million from US$21.5 million in the equivalent prior-year period.

Prospects: Our evaluation of OGE Energy Corp. as of Jan. 14, 2018 is the result of our systematic analysis on three basic characteristics: earnings strength, relative valuation, and recent stock price movement. The company has generated a negative trend in earnings per share over the past 5 quarters. However, while recent estimates for the company have been lowered by analysts, OGE has posted results that fell short of analysts expectations. Based on operating earnings yield, the company is undervalued when compared to all of the companies in our coverage universe. Share price changes over the past year indicates that OGE will perform very well over the near term.

Financial Data

(US$ in Thousands)	9 Mos	6 Mos	3 Mos	12/31/2016	12/31/2015	12/31/2014	12/31/2013	12/31/2012
Earnings Per Share	1.91	1.91	1.74	1.69	1.36	1.98	1.94	1.79
Cash Flow Per Share	3.41	3.39	3.32	3.22	4.34	3.62	3.14	5.29
Tang Book Value Per Share	18.11	17.49	17.25	17.24	16.65	16.27	15.30	13.16
Dividends Per Share	1.210	1.183	1.155	1.127	1.025	0.925	0.835	0.785
Dividend Payout %	63.35	61.91	66.38	66.72	75.37	46.72	43.04	43.85
Income Statement								
Total Revenue	1,759,200	1,042,400	456,000	2,259,200	2,196,900	2,453,100	2,867,700	3,671,200
EBITDA	689,800	344,800	111,000	849,200	810,100	825,800	868,300	1,058,400
Depn & Amortn	207,200	130,300	55,600	322,600	307,900	281,400	298,600	374,800
Income Before Taxes	374,600	142,400	20,400	384,500	353,200	396,000	422,200	520,100
Income Taxes	149,000	66,600	20,000	148,100	97,400	172,800	130,300	135,100
Net Income	324,200	140,800	36,000	338,200	271,300	395,800	387,600	355,000
Average Shares	200,100	199,900	200,000	199,900	199,600	199,900	199,400	198,200
Balance Sheet								
Current Assets	599,800	632,500	538,100	549,500	570,200	705,800	694,600	794,200
Total Assets	10,463,700	10,420,500	10,134,900	9,939,600	9,597,400	9,527,800	9,134,700	9,922,200
Current Liabilities	953,500	926,200	915,000	1,027,200	752,800	573,300	1,093,800	1,276,400
Long-Term Obligations	2,749,500	2,863,000	2,703,200	2,405,800	2,645,600	2,755,300	2,300,100	2,848,600
Total Liabilities	6,846,900	6,928,500	6,690,500	6,495,800	6,271,400	6,283,400	6,097,600	7,155,000
Stockholders' Equity	3,616,800	3,492,000	3,444,400	3,443,800	3,326,000	3,244,400	3,037,100	2,767,200
Shares Outstanding	199,705	199,704	199,704	199,700	199,700	199,400	198,500	197,600
Statistical Record								
Return on Assets %	3.77	3.81	3.55	3.45	2.84	4.24	4.07	3.76
Return on Equity %	10.82	11.22	10.35	9.96	8.26	12.60	13.36	13.28
EBITDA Margin %	39.21	33.08	24.34	37.59	36.87	33.66	30.28	28.83
Net Margin %	18.43	13.51	7.89	14.97	12.35	16.13	13.52	9.67
Asset Turnover	0.23	0.23	0.23	0.23	0.23	0.26	0.30	0.39
Current Ratio	0.63	0.68	0.59	0.53	0.76	1.23	0.64	0.62
Debt to Equity	0.76	0.82	0.78	0.70	0.80	0.85	0.76	1.03
Price Range	37.02-29.62	37.02-29.62	37.02-27.30	33.89-23.86	36.20-24.37	39.08-33.18	38.36-28.16	29.09-25.20
P/E Ratio	19.38-15.51	19.38-15.51	21.28-15.69	20.05-14.12	26.62-17.92	19.74-16.76	19.77-14.51	16.25-14.08
Average Yield %	3.53	3.56	3.61	3.77	3.42	2.56	2.44	2.90

Address: 321 North Harvey, P.O. Box 321, Oklahoma City, OK 73101-0321
Telephone: 405-553-3000

Web Site: www.oge.com
Officers: Sean Trauschke - Chairman, President, Chief Executive Officer Stephen E. Merrill - Vice President, Chief Financial Officer

Auditors: Ernst & Young LLP
Investor Contact: 405-553-3966
Transfer Agents: Computershare, Providence, RI

OIL-DRI CORP. OF AMERICA

Exchange	Symbol	Price	52Wk Range	Yield	P/E	Div Achiever
NYS	ODC	$41.50 (12/29/2017)	50.33-32.82	2.22	25.78	14 Years

*7 Year Price Score 104.71 *NYSE Composite Index=100 *12 Month Price Score 102.87

Interim Earnings (Per Share)

Qtr.	Oct	Jan	Apr	Jul
2014-15	0.30	0.39	0.19	0.71
2015-16	0.75	0.53	(0.13)	0.72
2016-17	0.28	0.58	0.44	0.18
2017-18	0.41	...	...	...

Interim Dividends (Per Share)

Amt	Decl	Ex	Rec	Pay
0.22Q	03/16/2017	05/17/2017	05/19/2017	06/02/2017
0.23Q	06/14/2017	08/16/2017	08/18/2017	09/01/2017
0.23Q	10/18/2017	11/16/2017	11/17/2017	12/01/2017
0.23Q	12/13/2017	02/15/2018	02/16/2018	03/02/2018

Indicated Div: $0.92

Valuation Analysis   **Institutional Holding**

Forecast EPS	N/A	No of Institutions
		89
Market Cap	$303.7 Million	Shares
Book Value	$128.1 Million	4,234,622
Price/Book	2.37	% Held
Price/Sales	1.16	52.88

Business Summary: Household & Personal Products (MIC: 1.7.1 SIC: 3999 NAIC: 339999)

Oil-Dri Corp of America is engaged in developing, manufacturing and/or marketing sorbent products. Co.'s sorbent products are mainly produced from hydrated aluminosilicate minerals, primarily consisting of calcium bentonite, attapulgite and diatomaceous shale, which it refers to collectively as its clay or its minerals. Co.'s sorbent technologies include absorbent and adsorbent products, which draw liquids up into their pores. Co. also sells some nonclay-based products. Co.'s products include agricultural and horticultural products, animal health and nutrition products, bleaching clay and purification aid products, cat litter products, industrial and automotive products and sports products.

Recent Developments: For the quarter ended Oct 31 2017, net income increased 51.8% to US$3.1 million from US$2.0 million in the year-earlier quarter. Revenues were US$66.6 million, unchanged from the year before. Operating income was US$3.9 million versus US$3.0 million in the prior-year quarter, an increase of 28.6%. Direct operating expenses rose 3.9% to US$47.7 million from US$45.9 million in the comparable period the year before. Indirect operating expenses decreased 14.9% to US$15.1 million from US$17.7 million in the equivalent prior-year period.

Prospects: Our evaluation of Oil-Dri Corp. of America as of Jan. 14, 2018 is the result of our systematic analysis on three basic characteristics: earnings strength, relative valuation, and recent stock price movement. The company has suffered a very negative trend in earnings per share over the past 5 quarters. Because the company lacks sufficient analyst estimate data, we place greater weight on the historical EPS trend as the measure of earnings strength. Based on operating earnings yield, the company is about fairly valued when compared to all of the companies in our coverage universe. Share price changes over the past year indicates that ODC will perform very well over the near term.

Financial Data

(US$ in Thousands)	3 Mos	07/31/2017	07/31/2016	07/31/2015	07/31/2014	07/31/2013	07/31/2012	07/31/2011
Earnings Per Share	1.61	1.47	1.87	1.59	1.17	2.07	0.85	1.26
Cash Flow Per Share	3.96	3.80	3.57	3.87	2.33	3.40	3.33	1.87
Tang Book Value Per Share	15.69	15.43	13.95	13.44	12.36	13.79	11.40	12.39
Dividends Per Share	0.890	0.880	0.840	0.800	0.760	0.720	0.680	0.640
Dividend Payout %	55.28	59.86	44.92	50.31	64.96	34.78	80.00	50.79
Income Statement								
Total Revenue	66,646	262,307	262,313	261,402	266,313	250,583	240,681	226,755
EBITDA	3,961	26,882	26,145	25,835	22,172	28,177	19,677	22,636
Depn & Amortn	(25)	11,544	10,782	10,352	9,289	8,939	9,287	8,503
Income Before Taxes	3,839	14,545	14,357	14,169	11,337	17,499	8,361	12,141
Income Taxes	789	3,753	744	2,801	2,981	2,913	2,263	3,090
Net Income	3,050	10,792	13,613	11,368	8,356	14,586	6,098	9,051
Average Shares	7,211	7,158	7,094	7,037	7,004	6,927	7,062	7,103
Balance Sheet								
Current Assets	88,901	97,017	91,173	82,643	83,516	103,372	95,202	91,816
Total Assets	206,917	212,575	204,933	190,031	186,204	183,559	174,267	173,393
Current Liabilities	27,747	32,954	30,740	28,888	29,500	31,447	29,122	26,480
Long-Term Obligations	6,085	9,161	12,333	15,417	18,900	22,400	25,900	29,700
Total Liabilities	78,807	86,538	89,382	79,503	81,896	80,621	88,959	78,095
Stockholders' Equity	128,110	126,037	115,551	110,528	104,308	102,938	85,308	95,298
Shares Outstanding	7,318	7,296	7,260	7,068	7,071	7,021	6,924	7,156
Statistical Record								
Return on Assets %	5.81	5.17	6.87	6.04	4.52	8.15	3.50	5.53
Return on Equity %	9.66	8.93	12.01	10.58	8.06	15.50	6.73	9.74
EBITDA Margin %	5.94	10.25	9.97	9.88	8.33	11.24	8.18	9.98
Net Margin %	4.58	4.11	5.19	4.35	3.14	5.82	2.53	3.99
Asset Turnover	1.29	1.26	1.32	1.39	1.44	1.40	1.38	1.39
Current Ratio	3.20	2.94	2.97	2.86	2.83	3.29	3.27	3.47
Debt to Equity	0.05	0.07	0.11	0.14	0.18	0.22	0.30	0.31
Price Range	50.33-32.82	43.58-32.82	38.30-22.11	33.85-24.60	40.64-28.97	31.88-21.00	22.35-16.95	22.95-18.91
P/E Ratio	31.26-20.39	29.65-22.33	20.48-11.82	21.29-15.47	34.74-24.76	15.40-10.14	26.29-19.94	18.21-15.01
Average Yield %	2.28	2.62	2.62	2.65	2.26	2.79	3.39	3.06

Address: 410 North Michigan Avenue, Suite 400, Chicago, IL 60611-4213 **Telephone:** 312-321-1515 **Fax:** 312-321-9525	**Web Site:** www.oildri.com **Officers:** Richard M. Jaffee - Chairman Daniel S. Jaffee - President, Chief Executive Officer	**Auditors:** GRANT THORNTON LLP **Investor Contact:** 312-321-1515 **Transfer Agents:** ComputerShare Investor Services, Chicago, IL

527

OLD REPUBLIC INTERNATIONAL CORP.

Exchange	Symbol	Price	52Wk Range	Yield	P/E	Div Acheiver
NYS	ORI	$21.38 (12/29/2017)	21.46-18.11	3.55	15.72	35 Years

*7 Year Price Score 104.91 *NYSE Composite Index=100 *12 Month Price Score 97.84

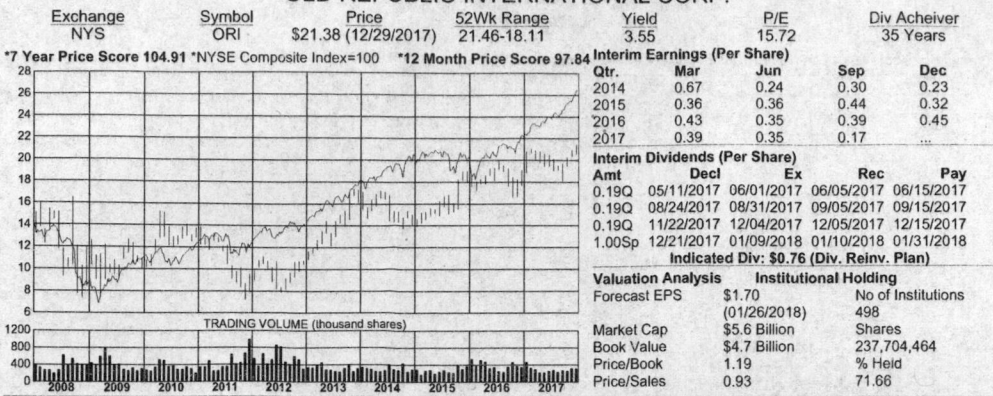

Interim Earnings (Per Share)

Qtr.	Mar	Jun	Sep	Dec
2014	0.67	0.24	0.30	0.23
2015	0.36	0.36	0.44	0.32
2016	0.43	0.35	0.39	0.45
2017	0.39	0.35	0.17	...

Interim Dividends (Per Share)

Amt	Decl	Ex	Rec	Pay
0.19Q	05/11/2017	06/01/2017	06/05/2017	06/15/2017
0.19Q	08/24/2017	08/31/2017	09/05/2017	09/15/2017
0.19Q	11/22/2017	12/04/2017	12/05/2017	12/15/2017
1.00Sp	12/21/2017	01/09/2018	01/10/2018	01/31/2018

Indicated Div: $0.76 (Div. Reinv. Plan)

Valuation Analysis		Institutional Holding	
Forecast EPS	$1.70	No of Institutions	
	(01/26/2018)	498	
Market Cap	$5.6 Billion	Shares	
Book Value	$4.7 Billion	237,704,464	
Price/Book	1.19	% Held	
Price/Sales	0.93	71.66	

Business Summary: General Insurance (MIC: 5.2.1 SIC: 6351 NAIC: 524113)

Old Republic International is a holding company engaged in the business of insurance underwriting and related services. Through its regulated insurance company subsidiaries, Co. conducts its operations in three main segments: General Insurance Group, which is a commercial lines insurance business focused on liability insurance coverages; Title Insurance Group, which consists mainly of the issuance of policies to real estate purchasers and investors based upon searches of the public records, which contain information concerning interests in real property; and the Republic Financial Indemnity Group Run-off Business, which consists of mortgage guaranty and consumer credit indemnity operations.

Recent Developments: For the quarter ended Sep 30 2017, net income decreased 58.4% to US$46.1 million from US$110.9 million in the year-earlier quarter. Revenues were US$1.59 billion, up 6.5% from US$1.50 billion the year before. Net premiums earned were US$1.31 billion versus US$1.24 billion in the prior-year quarter, an increase of 5.9%. Net investment income rose 7.8% to US$103.1 million from US$95.6 million a year ago.

Prospects: Our evaluation of Old Republic International Corp. as of Jan. 21, 2018 is the result of our systematic analysis on three basic characteristics: earnings strength, relative valuation, and recent stock price movement. The company has generated a negative trend in earnings per share over the past 5 quarters. However, while recent estimates for the company have been mixed, ORI has posted better than expected results. Based on operating earnings yield, the company is undervalued when compared to all of the companies in our coverage universe. Share price changes over the past year indicates that ORI will perform in line with the market over the near term.

Financial Data
(US$ in Thousands)

	9 Mos	6 Mos	3 Mos	12/31/2016	12/31/2015	12/31/2014	12/31/2013	12/31/2012
Earnings Per Share	1.36	1.58	1.58	1.62	1.48	1.44	1.74	(0.27)
Cash Flow Per Share	2.90	2.81	2.52	2.45	2.65	(0.70)	2.67	2.07
Tang Book Value Per Share	17.93	17.68	17.44	17.02	14.81	15.04	14.49	13.86
Dividends Per Share	0.757	0.755	0.752	0.750	0.740	0.730	0.720	0.710
Dividend Payout %	55.70	47.78	47.63	46.30	50.00	50.69	41.38	...
Income Statement								
Premium Income	3,752,600	2,440,600	1,201,300	4,868,900	4,758,800	4,446,300	4,456,600	4,043,800
Total Revenue	4,536,900	2,943,800	1,444,800	5,900,500	5,766,100	5,530,700	5,442,700	4,970,100
Benefits & Claims	...	...	...	2,329,800	2,441,300	2,500,000	2,223,000	2,747,400
Income Before Taxes	370,700	311,000	164,700	686,000	631,800	...	...	...
Income Taxes	109,700	96,200	51,600	219,000	209,600	199,700	225,000	(59,800)
Net Income	260,900	214,700	113,100	466,900	422,100	409,700	447,800	(68,600)
Average Shares	298,529	298,313	298,239	296,379	296,088	295,073	293,684	255,812
Balance Sheet								
Total Assets	19,747,400	19,357,100	18,905,400	18,591,600	17,110,500	16,988,100	16,534,400	16,226,800
Total Liabilities	15,017,300	14,695,300	14,308,800	14,119,900	13,229,600	13,064,000	12,759,400	12,630,600
Stockholders' Equity	4,730,000	4,661,800	4,596,600	4,471,600	3,880,800	3,924,000	3,775,000	3,596,200
Shares Outstanding	263,806	263,687	263,586	262,719	261,968	260,946	260,462	259,490
Statistical Record								
Return on Assets %	2.04	2.45	2.51	2.61	2.48	2.44	2.73	N.M.
Return on Equity %	8.56	10.12	10.46	11.15	10.82	10.64	12.15	N.M.
Loss Ratio %	...	...	...	47.85	51.30	56.23	49.88	67.94
Net Margin %	5.75	7.29	7.83	7.91	7.32	7.41	8.23	(1.38)
Price Range	21.08-16.58	21.08-16.58	21.08-16.58	19.98-16.58	19.02-13.87	17.27-13.74	17.36-10.65	11.19-7.83
P/E Ratio	15.50-12.19	13.34-10.49	13.34-10.49	12.33-10.23	12.85-9.37	11.99-9.54	9.98-6.12	...
Average Yield %	3.91	3.92	3.97	4.07	4.61	4.67	5.15	7.27

Address: 307 North Michigan Avenue, Chicago, IL 60601 **Telephone:** 312-346-8100	**Web Site:** www.oldrepublic.com **Officers:** Aldo C. Zucaro - Chairman, Chief Executive Officer R. Scott Rager - President, Senior Vice President, Chief Operating Officer, Division Officer	**Auditors:** KPMG LLP **Investor Contact:** 800-468-9716 **Transfer Agents:** Wells Fargo Shareholder Services, St. Paul, MN

OLIN CORP.

Exchange	Symbol	Price	52Wk Range	Yield	P/E
NYS	OLN	$35.58 (12/29/2017)	37.15-25.98	2.25	77.35

*7 Year Price Score 103.30 *NYSE Composite Index=100 *12 Month Price Score 104.93

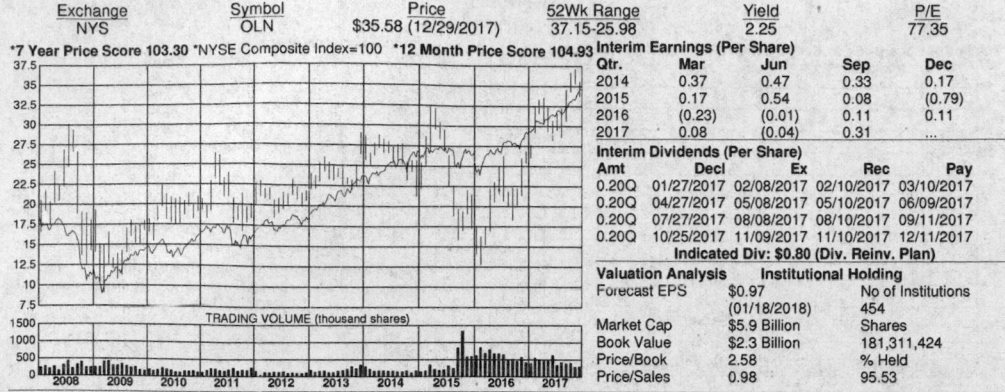

Interim Earnings (Per Share)

Qtr.	Mar	Jun	Sep	Dec
2014	0.37	0.47	0.33	0.17
2015	0.17	0.54	0.08	(0.79)
2016	(0.23)	(0.01)	0.11	0.11
2017	0.08	(0.04)	0.31	...

Interim Dividends (Per Share)

Amt	Decl	Ex	Rec	Pay
0.20Q	01/27/2017	02/08/2017	02/10/2017	03/10/2017
0.20Q	04/27/2017	05/08/2017	05/10/2017	06/09/2017
0.20Q	07/27/2017	08/08/2017	08/10/2017	09/11/2017
0.20Q	10/25/2017	11/09/2017	11/10/2017	12/11/2017

Indicated Div: $0.80 (Div. Reinv. Plan)

Valuation Analysis   **Institutional Holding**

Forecast EPS	$0.97 (01/18/2018)	No of Institutions 454
Market Cap	$5.9 Billion	Shares 181,311,424
Book Value	$2.3 Billion	% Held
Price/Book	2.58	95.53
Price/Sales	0.98	

Business Summary: Diversified Chemicals (MIC: 8.3.1 SIC: 2812 NAIC: 325181)

Olin is a manufacturer with three segments. The Chlor Alkali Products and Vinyls segment manufactures and sells chlorine and caustic soda, ethylene dichloride and vinyl chloride monomer, methyl chloride, methylene chloride, chloroform, carbon tetrachloride, perchloroethylene, trichloroethylene and vinylidene chloride, hydrochloric acid, hydrogen, bleach products and potassium hydroxide. The Epoxy segment produces and sells epoxy materials, including allyl chloride, epichlorohydrin, liquid epoxy resins and converted epoxy resins. The Winchester segment produces and sells sporting ammunition, reloading components, small caliber military ammunition and components, and industrial cartridges.

Recent Developments: For the quarter ended Sep 30 2017, net income increased 201.1% to US$52.7 million from US$17.5 million in the year-earlier quarter. Revenues were US$1.55 billion, up 7.0% from US$1.45 billion the year before. Operating income was US$112.6 million versus US$67.8 million in the prior-year quarter, an increase of 66.1%. Direct operating expenses rose 4.8% to US$1.35 billion from US$1.28 billion in the comparable period the year before. Indirect operating expenses decreased 3.8% to US$96.7 million from US$100.5 million in the equivalent prior-year period.

Prospects: Our evaluation of Olin Corp. as of Jan. 14, 2018 is the result of our systematic analysis on three basic characteristics: earnings strength, relative valuation, and recent stock price movement. The company has enjoyed a very positive trend in earnings per share over the past 5 quarters. However, while recent estimates for the company have been mixed, OLN has posted better than expected results. Based on operating earnings yield, the company is overvalued when compared to all of the companies in our coverage universe. Share price changes over the past year indicates that OLN will perform in line with the market over the near term.

Financial Data

(US$ in Thousands)	9 Mos	6 Mos	3 Mos	12/31/2016	12/31/2015	12/31/2014	12/31/2013	12/31/2012
Earnings Per Share	0.46	0.26	0.29	(0.02)	(0.01)	1.33	2.21	1.85
Cash Flow Per Share	3.92	3.88	3.96	3.64	2.10	2.03	3.97	3.48
Tang Book Value Per Share	N.M.	N.M.	N.M.	N.M.	N.M.	1.84	2.72	1.23
Dividends Per Share	0.800	0.800	0.800	0.800	0.800	0.800	0.800	0.800
Dividend Payout %	173.91	307.69	275.86	...	...	60.15	36.20	43.24
Income Statement								
Total Revenue	4,648,500	3,093,600	1,567,100	5,550,600	2,854,400	2,241,200	2,515,000	2,184,700
EBITDA	623,400	371,600	204,700	662,100	324,800	342,600	420,500	358,500
Depn & Amortn	411,400	272,200	135,100	509,500	223,900	139,100	135,300	110,900
Income Before Taxes	55,000	(4,900)	17,400	(35,900)	5,000	161,000	247,200	222,200
Income Taxes	(3,700)	(11,400)	4,500	(30,300)	8,100	57,700	71,400	75,600
Net Income	60,200	7,500	13,400	(3,900)	(1,400)	105,700	178,600	149,600
Average Shares	168,500	166,100	167,900	165,200	103,400	79,700	80,900	81,000
Balance Sheet								
Current Assets	1,717,900	1,691,000	1,669,700	1,546,200	1,933,400	816,100	839,900	749,100
Total Assets	9,366,500	8,794,300	8,813,200	8,762,600	9,321,800	2,698,100	2,802,800	2,777,700
Current Liabilities	999,300	1,006,400	985,400	922,600	1,147,700	377,700	407,500	434,000
Long-Term Obligations	3,663,500	3,518,900	3,530,800	3,537,100	3,675,200	658,700	678,400	690,100
Total Liabilities	7,068,000	6,535,700	6,541,600	6,489,600	6,903,000	1,684,800	1,701,700	1,779,300
Stockholders' Equity	2,298,500	2,258,600	2,271,600	2,273,000	2,418,800	1,013,300	1,101,100	998,400
Shares Outstanding	166,400	166,300	165,890	165,400	165,100	77,400	79,400	80,200
Statistical Record								
Return on Assets %	0.86	0.48	0.53	N.M.	N.M.	3.84	6.40	5.71
Return on Equity %	3.36	1.85	2.04	N.M.	N.M.	10.00	17.01	15.04
EBITDA Margin %	13.41	12.01	13.06	11.93	11.38	15.29	16.72	16.41
Net Margin %	1.30	0.24	0.86	N.M.	N.M.	4.72	7.10	6.85
Asset Turnover	0.66	0.67	0.64	0.61	0.47	0.81	0.90	0.83
Current Ratio	1.72	1.68	1.69	1.68	1.68	2.16	2.06	1.73
Debt to Equity	1.59	1.56	1.55	1.56	1.52	0.65	0.62	0.69
Price Range	34.53-20.08	33.54-18.27	33.34-16.87	26.83-12.78	32.41-15.82	28.85-21.22	29.03-21.59	23.19-18.51
P/E Ratio	75.07-43.65	129.00-70.27	114.97-58.17	...	...	21.69-15.95	13.14-9.77	12.54-10.01
Average Yield %	2.77	3.03	3.32	3.88	3.31	3.31	3.03	3.80

Address: 190 Carondelet Plaza, Suite 1530, Clayton, MO 63105
Telephone: 314-480-1400

Web Site: www.olin.com
Officers: John E. Fischer - Chairman, President, Chief Executive Officer, Chief Operating Officer, Senior Vice President, Vice President, Controller, Chief Financial Officer Todd A. Slater - Chief Financial Officer, Vice President, Vice President (frmr), Controller

Auditors: KPMG LLP
Investor Contact: 314-480-1452
Transfer Agents: Wells Fargo Shareowner Services, Mendota Heights, MN

OMEGA HEALTHCARE INVESTORS, INC.

Exchange	Symbol	Price	52Wk Range	Yield	P/E	Div Achiever
NYS	OHI	$27.54 (12/29/2017)	34.98-26.78	9.59	33.18	14 Years

*7 Year Price Score 81.95   *NYSE Composite Index=100   *12 Month Price Score 82.93

Interim Earnings (Per Share)

Qtr.	Mar	Jun	Sep	Dec
2014	0.45	0.37	0.48	0.44
2015	0.32	0.22	0.43	0.32
2016	0.29	0.57	0.40	0.64
2017	0.53	0.33	(0.67)	...

Interim Dividends (Per Share)

Amt	Decl	Ex	Rec	Pay
0.63Q	04/13/2017	04/27/2017	05/01/2017	05/15/2017
0.64Q	07/13/2017	07/28/2017	08/01/2017	08/15/2017
0.65Q	10/12/2017	10/30/2017	10/31/2017	11/15/2017
0.66Q	01/16/2018	01/30/2018	01/31/2018	02/15/2018

Indicated Div: $2.64 (Div. Reinv. Plan)

Valuation Analysis / Institutional Holding

Valuation Analysis		Institutional Holding	
Forecast EPS	$0.63	No of Institutions	
	(01/18/2018)	569	
Market Cap	$5.5 Billion	Shares	
Book Value	$3.6 Billion	185,761,936	
Price/Book	1.51	% Held	
Price/Sales	5.92	101.87	

Business Summary: REITs (MIC: 5.3.1 SIC: 6798 NAIC: 525930)

Omega Healthcare Investors is a real estate investment trust, investing in healthcare facilities, mainly long-term care facilities in the U.S. and the U.K. Co. provides lease or mortgage financing to operators of skilled nursing facilities (SNFs), assisted living facilities (ALFs), independent living facilities and rehabilitation and acute care facilities. As of Dec 31 2016, Co.'s portfolio of investments included 996 healthcare facilities located in 42 states and the U.K. operated by 79 third-party operators, comprising: 809 SNFs, 101 ALFs, 16 specialty facilities and one medical office building; fixed rate mortgages on 44 SNFs and two ALFs; and 23 facilities closed or held-for-sale.

Recent Developments: For the quarter ended Sep 30 2017, net loss amounted to US$137.5 million versus net income of US$82.1 million in the year-earlier quarter. Revenues were US$219.6 million, down 2.2% from US$224.6 million the year before. Revenues from property income rose 4.4% to US$194.1 million from US$185.8 million in the corresponding quarter a year earlier.

Prospects: Our evaluation of Omega Healthcare Investors Inc. as of Jan. 14, 2018 is the result of our systematic analysis on three basic characteristics: earnings strength, relative valuation, and recent stock price movement. The company has generated a negative trend in earnings per share over the past 5 quarters. Because the company lacks sufficient analyst estimate data, we place greater weight on the historical EPS trend as the measure of earnings strength. Based on operating earnings yield, the company is undervalued when compared to all of the companies in our coverage universe. Share price changes over the past year indicates that OHI will perform well over the near term.

Financial Data

(US$ in Thousands)	9 Mos	6 Mos	3 Mos	12/31/2016	12/31/2015	12/31/2014	12/31/2013	12/31/2012
Earnings Per Share	0.83	1.90	2.14	1.90	1.29	1.74	1.46	1.12
Cash Flow Per Share	3.03	3.06	3.11	3.25	2.69	2.67	2.39	1.93
Tang Book Value Per Share	14.96	16.14	16.36	16.39	16.50	10.98	10.52	9.00
Dividends Per Share	2.500	2.460	2.410	2.360	2.180	2.020	1.860	1.690
Dividend Payout %	301.20	129.47	112.62	124.21	168.99	116.09	127.40	150.89
Income Statement								
Total Revenue	687,179	467,541	231,744	900,827	743,617	504,787	418,714	350,460
EBITDA	218,568	306,693	156,525	838,040	661,266	482,537	385,700	350,947
Depn & Amortn	8,367	9,038	(594)	278,319	243,817	134,363	121,172	124,182
Income Before Taxes	40,716	177,777	109,580	384,333	234,526	221,349	172,521	120,698
Income Taxes	2,690	1,691	1,100	1,405	1,211	...	...	...
Net Income	38,019	169,697	104,440	366,415	224,524	221,349	172,521	120,698
Average Shares	206,662	206,672	206,174	201,635	180,508	127,294	118,100	108,011
Balance Sheet								
Current Assets	304,660	321,920	325,053	347,311	223,893	201,741	181,879	163,551
Total Assets	8,890,646	8,946,654	8,842,118	8,949,260	8,019,009	3,921,645	3,462,216	2,982,005
Current Liabilities	903,221	899,292	1,094,875	9,906	15,352	...	...	...
Long-Term Obligations	3,741,307	3,530,595	3,205,990	4,366,854	3,569,086	2,378,503	2,024,418	1,824,932
Total Liabilities	5,283,818	5,118,355	4,978,624	5,090,515	4,281,023	2,520,318	2,162,113	1,970,676
Stockholders' Equity	3,606,828	3,828,299	3,863,494	3,858,745	3,737,986	1,401,327	1,300,103	1,011,329
Shares Outstanding	198,065	197,224	196,761	196,142	187,399	127,606	123,530	112,393
Statistical Record								
Return on Assets %	1.82	4.24	4.76	4.31	3.76	6.00	5.35	4.35
Return on Equity %	4.37	9.84	10.99	9.62	8.74	16.39	14.93	12.74
EBITDA Margin %	31.81	65.60	67.54	93.03	88.93	95.59	92.12	100.14
Net Margin %	5.53	36.30	45.07	40.68	30.19	43.85	41.20	34.44
Asset Turnover	0.10	0.11	0.11	0.11	0.12	0.14	0.13	0.13
Current Ratio	0.34	0.36	0.30	35.06	14.58	...	...	...
Debt to Equity	1.04	0.92	0.83	1.13	0.95	1.70	1.56	1.80
Price Range	35.45-28.31	38.02-28.31	38.02-28.31	38.02-27.46	45.16-32.08	40.29-29.56	37.61-23.85	24.75-19.19
P/E Ratio	42.71-34.11	20.01-14.90	17.77-13.23	20.01-14.45	35.01-24.87	23.16-16.99	25.76-16.34	22.10-17.13
Average Yield %	7.80	7.47	7.30	7.12	5.91	5.68	6.10	7.59

Address: 303 International Circle, Suite 200, Hunt Valley, MD 21030
Telephone: 410-427-1700
Fax: 410-427-8800

Web Site: www.omegahealthcare.com
Officers: Bernard J. Korman - Chairman C. Taylor Pickett - President, Chief Executive Officer

Auditors: Ernst & Young LLP
Investor Contact: 410-427-1700
Transfer Agents: Registrar and Transfer Company, Cranford , NJ

OMNICOM GROUP, INC.

Exchange	Symbol	Price	52Wk Range	Yield	P/E
NYS	OMC	$72.83 (12/29/2017)	87.39-65.52	3.30	14.51

*7 Year Price Score 93.80   *NYSE Composite Index=100   *12 Month Price Score 85.11

Interim Earnings (Per Share)

Qtr.	Mar	Jun	Sep	Dec
2014	0.77	1.23	0.95	1.29
2015	0.83	1.26	0.97	1.35
2016	0.90	1.36	1.06	1.47
2017	1.02	1.40	1.13	...

Interim Dividends (Per Share)

Amt	Decl	Ex	Rec	Pay
0.55Q	02/02/2017	03/07/2017	03/09/2017	04/07/2017
0.55Q	05/25/2017	06/12/2017	06/14/2017	07/12/2017
0.55Q	07/13/2017	09/21/2017	09/22/2017	10/10/2017
0.60Q	12/04/2017	12/18/2017	12/19/2017	01/09/2018

Indicated Div: $2.40

Valuation Analysis — **Institutional Holding**

Forecast EPS	$5.10	No of Institutions
	(01/18/2018)	988
Market Cap	$16.8 Billion	Shares
Book Value	$2.5 Billion	304,628,800
Price/Book	6.66	% Held
Price/Sales	1.09	82.86

Business Summary: Advertising (MIC: 2.3.4 SIC: 7311 NAIC: 541810)

Omnicom Group is a holding company, engaged in providing advertising, marketing and corporate communications services. Co.'s networks and agencies provide a range of services in four fundamental disciplines: advertising, customer relationship management, public relations and specialty communications. Services in these disciplines include: advertising, brand consultancy, content marketing, corporate social responsibility consulting, crisis communications, custom publishing, data analytics, database management, direct marketing, entertainment marketing, environmental design, experiential marketing, field marketing, graphic arts/digital imaging, and instore design, among others.

Recent Developments: For the quarter ended Sep 30 2017, net income increased 3.1% to US$286.9 million from US$278.2 million in the year-earlier quarter. Revenues were US$3.72 billion, down 1.9% from US$3.79 billion the year before. Operating income was US$464.2 million versus US$453.1 million in the prior-year quarter, an increase of 2.4%. Direct operating expenses declined 2.3% to US$3.09 billion from US$3.16 billion in the comparable period the year before. Indirect operating expenses decreased 5.1% to US$168.1 million from US$177.2 million in the equivalent prior-year period.

Prospects: Our evaluation of Omnicom Group Inc. as of Jan. 14, 2018 is the result of our systematic analysis on three basic characteristics: earnings strength, relative valuation, and recent stock price movement. The company has managed to produce a neutral trend in earnings per share over the past 5 quarters and while recent estimates for the company have remained steady, OMC has posted better than expected results. Based on operating earnings yield, the company is undervalued when compared to all of the companies in our coverage universe. Share price changes over the past year indicates that OMC will perform poorly over the near term.

Financial Data

(US$ in Thousands)	9 Mos	6 Mos	3 Mos	12/31/2016	12/31/2015	12/31/2014	12/31/2013	12/31/2012
Earnings Per Share	5.02	4.95	4.91	4.78	4.41	4.24	3.71	3.61
Cash Flow Per Share	6.31	8.58	9.37	8.10	8.90	5.82	6.99	5.39
Dividends Per Share	2.200	2.200	2.200	2.150	2.000	1.900	1.600	1.200
Dividend Payout %	43.82	44.44	44.81	44.98	45.35	44.81	43.13	33.24
Income Statement								
Total Revenue	11,097,100	7,377,600	3,587,400	15,416,900	15,134,400	15,317,800	14,584,500	14,219,400
EBITDA	1,638,300	1,119,300	482,600	2,301,800	2,211,200	2,238,500	2,110,100	2,086,900
Depn & Amortn	198,700	143,800	72,700	292,900	291,100	294,400	284,800	282,700
Income Before Taxes	1,308,400	890,600	370,300	1,841,800	1,778,600	1,810,000	1,660,900	1,659,600
Income Taxes	406,700	274,700	108,000	600,500	583,600	593,100	565,200	527,100
Net Income	834,000	570,400	241,800	1,148,600	1,093,900	1,104,000	991,100	998,300
Average Shares	232,700	234,000	236,500	239,200	245,200	255,300	260,400	270,000
Balance Sheet								
Current Assets	11,417,400	11,505,100	11,728,800	12,722,000	11,980,500	11,190,500	11,652,300	11,661,400
Total Assets	22,207,500	22,163,400	22,237,300	23,165,400	22,110,700	21,559,700	22,098,700	22,151,900
Current Liabilities	12,621,200	12,863,700	13,070,100	14,010,900	14,219,600	12,061,100	12,277,700	11,875,800
Long-Term Obligations	4,927,400	4,930,400	4,914,500	4,920,500	3,564,200	4,562,600	4,033,400	4,448,500
Total Liabilities	19,685,000	19,907,300	20,102,700	21,003,400	19,658,300	18,709,700	18,516,300	18,691,100
Stockholders' Equity	2,522,500	2,256,100	2,134,600	2,162,000	2,452,400	2,850,000	3,582,400	3,460,800
Shares Outstanding	230,532	230,754	232,744	234,700	239,700	246,700	257,600	262,000
Statistical Record								
Return on Assets %	5.43	5.45	5.41	5.06	5.01	5.06	4.48	4.67
Return on Equity %	48.87	51.76	51.97	49.65	41.26	34.33	28.14	28.59
EBITDA Margin %	14.76	15.17	13.45	14.93	14.61	14.61	14.47	14.68
Net Margin %	7.52	7.73	6.74	7.45	7.23	7.21	6.80	7.02
Asset Turnover	0.70	0.72	0.72	0.68	0.69	0.70	0.66	0.66
Current Ratio	0.90	0.89	0.90	0.91	0.84	0.93	0.95	0.98
Debt to Equity	1.95	2.19	2.30	2.28	1.45	1.60	1.13	1.29
Price Range	88.47-71.73	88.47-79.00	88.47-77.57	88.47-67.94	80.52-64.79	78.41-64.93	74.37-49.96	54.23-44.04
P/E Ratio	17.62-14.29	17.87-15.96	18.02-15.80	18.51-14.21	18.26-14.69	18.49-15.31	20.05-13.47	15.02-12.20
Average Yield %	2.67	2.62	2.62	2.62	2.71	2.64	2.64	2.43

Address: 437 Madison Avenue, New York, NY 10022	**Web Site:** www.omnicomgroup.com	**Auditors:** KPMG LLP
Telephone: 212-415-3600	**Officers:** Bruce Crawford - Chairman John D. Wren - President, Chief Executive Officer	**Investor Contact:** 212-415-3393
Fax: 212-415-3393		**Transfer Agents:** Wells Fargo Bank, NA, South St. Paul, MN

ONE GAS, INC.

Exchange	Symbol	Price	52Wk Range	Yield	P/E
NYS	OGS	$73.26 (12/29/2017)	79.25-62.30	2.51	24.50

*7 Year Price Score N/A ***NYSE Composite Index=100** ***12 Month Price Score 101.68**

TRADING VOLUME (thousand shares)

Interim Earnings (Per Share)

Qtr.	Mar	Jun	Sep	Dec
2014	1.13	0.18	0.09	0.69
2015	1.13	0.23	0.14	0.74
2016	1.22	0.38	0.24	0.80
2017	1.44	0.39	0.36	...

Interim Dividends (Per Share)

Amt	Decl	Ex	Rec	Pay
0.42Q	05/01/2017	05/11/2017	05/15/2017	06/01/2017
0.42Q	07/24/2017	08/10/2017	08/14/2017	09/01/2017
0.42Q	10/30/2017	11/10/2017	11/13/2017	12/01/2017
0.46Q	01/16/2018	02/22/2018	02/23/2018	03/09/2018

Indicated Div: $1.84 (Div. Reinv. Plan)

Valuation Analysis

		Institutional Holding	
Forecast EPS	$3.07 (01/27/2018)	No of Institutions	330
Market Cap	$3.8 Billion	Shares	44,550,568
Book Value	$1.9 Billion	% Held	64.49
Price/Book	1.98		
Price/Sales	2.52		

Business Summary: Electric Utilities (MIC: 3.1.1 SIC: 4924 NAIC: 221210)

ONE Gas is a regulated natural gas distribution utility. Co. provide natural gas distribution services through its divisions in Oklahoma, Kansas and Texas through Oklahoma Natural Gas, Kansas Gas Service and Texas Gas Service, respectively. Co. serves residential, commercial, industrial and transportation customers in all three states. In addition, Co. also provides natural gas distribution services to wholesale and public authority customers. As of Dec 31 2016, Co. served a total of 2.0 million customers in Oklahoma, Kansas and Texas.

Recent Developments: For the quarter ended Sep 30 2017, net income increased 47.6% to US$18.8 million from US$12.7 million in the year-earlier quarter. Revenues were US$247.1 million, up 6.4% from US$232.2 million the year before. Operating income was US$40.8 million versus US$30.9 million in the prior-year quarter, an increase of 32.0%. Direct operating expenses rose 12.5% to US$58.8 million from US$52.3 million in the comparable period the year before. Indirect operating expenses decreased 1.0% to US$147.6 million from US$149.0 million in the equivalent prior-year period.

Prospects: Our evaluation of One Gas Inc. as of Jan. 21, 2018 is the result of our systematic analysis on three basic characteristics: earnings strength, relative valuation, and recent stock price movement. The company has generated a negative trend in earnings per share over the past 5 quarters. However, while recent estimates for the company have been lowered by analysts, OGS has posted better than expected results. Based on operating earnings yield, the company is about fairly valued when compared to all of the companies in our coverage universe. Share price changes over the past year indicates that OGS will perform very well over the near term.

Financial Data
(US$ in Thousands)

	9 Mos	6 Mos	3 Mos	12/31/2016	12/31/2015	12/31/2014	12/31/2013	12/31/2012
Earnings Per Share	2.99	2.87	2.86	2.65	2.24	2.07	...	...
Cash Flow Per Share	5.76	5.59	5.02	5.35	7.50	4.71	...	...
Tang Book Value Per Share	33.94	33.97	34.08	33.10	32.22	31.41	...	...
Dividends Per Share	1.610	1.540	1.470	1.400	1.200	0.840	...	...
Dividend Payout %	53.85	53.66	51.40	52.83	53.57	40.58	...	...
Income Statement								
Total Revenue	1,077,239	830,097	550,408	1,427,232	1,547,692	1,818,906	1,689,952	1,376,649
EBITDA	325,174	245,373	163,057	412,906	369,602	349,692	367,591	347,303
Depn & Amortn	113,293	74,870	37,019	143,829	133,023	125,722	144,758	130,150
Income Before Taxes	177,600	147,717	114,557	225,338	192,009	178,128	161,467	156,360
Income Taxes	61,724	50,638	38,101	85,243	72,979	68,338	62,272	59,851
Net Income	115,876	97,079	76,456	140,095	119,030	109,790	99,195	96,509
Average Shares	52,926	52,969	53,056	52,963	53,254	52,946	...	...
Balance Sheet								
Current Assets	445,553	411,579	481,132	568,923	482,845	667,501	602,184	457,094
Total Assets	4,971,063	4,873,130	4,889,874	4,942,791	4,644,410	4,649,210	3,846,475	3,491,332
Current Liabilities	392,228	292,685	307,943	443,933	304,221	392,433	769,077	578,702
Long-Term Obligations	1,193,052	1,192,848	1,192,647	1,192,446	1,201,305	1,201,311	1,028,949	1,028,954
Total Liabilities	3,039,071	2,939,834	2,945,296	3,054,511	2,802,855	2,855,173	2,607,452	2,336,535
Stockholders' Equity	1,931,992	1,933,296	1,944,578	1,888,280	1,841,555	1,794,037	1,239,023	1,154,797
Shares Outstanding	52,273	52,267	52,431	52,283	52,259	52,083	...	...
Statistical Record								
Return on Assets %	3.27	3.21	3.20	2.91	2.56	2.58	2.70	...
Return on Equity %	8.34	7.99	7.97	7.49	6.55	7.24	8.29	...
EBITDA Margin %	30.19	29.56	29.62	28.93	23.88	19.23	21.75	25.23
Net Margin %	10.76	11.69	13.89	9.82	7.69	6.04	5.87	7.01
Asset Turnover	0.31	0.32	0.31	0.30	0.33	0.43	0.46	...
Current Ratio	1.14	1.41	1.56	1.28	1.59	1.70	0.78	0.79
Debt to Equity	0.62	0.62	0.61	0.63	0.65	0.67	0.83	0.89
Price Range	75.73-56.75	72.40-56.75	68.59-56.75	66.59-48.40	51.34-39.38	44.19-32.25	...	...
P/E Ratio	25.33-18.98	25.23-19.77	23.98-19.84	25.13-18.26	22.92-17.58	21.35-15.58	...	...
Average Yield %	2.40	2.38	2.36	2.32	2.70	2.28	...	...

Address: 15 East Fifth Street, Tulsa, OK 74103
Telephone: 918-947-7000

Web Site: www.onegas.com
Officers: John W. Gibson - Chairman Mark A. Bender - Senior Vice President, Chief Information Officer

Auditors: PricewaterhouseCoopers LLP

ONEMAIN HOLDINGS INC

Exchange	Symbol	Price	52Wk Range	Yield	P/E
NYS	OMF	$25.99 (12/29/2017)	32.61-22.03	N/A	20.63

*7 Year Price Score N/A   *NYSE Composite Index=100   *12 Month Price Score 99.41

Interim Earnings (Per Share)

Qtr.	Mar	Jun	Sep	Dec
2014	0.45	0.63	3.70	(0.41)
2015	0.00	(0.09)	(0.08)	(1.71)
2016	1.13	0.19	0.19	0.20
2017	0.25	0.30	0.51	...

Interim Dividends (Per Share)

No Dividends Paid

Valuation Analysis		Institutional Holding	
Forecast EPS	$3.53	No of Institutions	
	(Q1/16/2018)	170	
Market Cap	$3.5 Billion	Shares	
Book Value	$3.2 Billion	133,549,936	
Price/Book	1.09	% Held	
Price/Sales	0.96	85.78	

TRADING VOLUME (thousand shares)

Business Summary: Credit & Lending (MIC: 5.4.1 SIC: 6141 NAIC: 522298)

OneMain Holdings is a financial services holding. Co.'s business segments are Consumer and Insurance, which originates and services personal loans through branch operations and centralized operations and provides credit insurance (life insurance, disability insurance, and involuntary unemployment insurance), non-credit insurance, and ancillary products; Acquisitions and Servicing, which consists of unsecured and secured loans by subordinate residential real estate mortgages and includes both closed-end accounts and open-end lines of credit; and Real Estate, which services and hold real estate loans secured by first or second mortgages on residential real estate.

Recent Developments: For the quarter ended Sep 30 2017, net income increased 176.0% to US$69.0 million from US$25.0 million in the year-earlier quarter. Net interest income increased 8.3% to US$601.0 million from US$555.0 million in the year-earlier quarter. Provision for loan losses was US$243.0 million versus US$263.0 million in the prior-year quarter, a decrease of 7.6%. Non-interest income fell 3.8% to US$152.0 million from US$158.0 million, while non-interest expense declined 6.7% to US$389.0 million.

Prospects: Our evaluation of Onemain Holdings, Inc. as of Jan. 14, 2018 is the result of our systematic analysis on three basic characteristics: earnings strength, relative valuation, and recent stock price movement. The company has enjoyed a very positive trend in earnings per share over the past 5 quarters and while recent estimates for the company have been mixed, OMF has posted results that fell short of analysts expectations. Based on operating earnings yield, the company is undervalued when compared to all of the companies in our coverage universe. Share price changes over the past year indicates that OMF will perform very poorly over the near term.

Financial Data
(US$ in Thousands)

	9 Mos	6 Mos	3 Mos	12/31/2016	12/31/2015	12/31/2014	12/31/2013	12/31/2012
Earnings Per Share	1.26	0.94	0.83	1.59	(1.89)	4.38	(0.19)	(2.19)
Cash Flow Per Share	10.55	10.41	10.04	9.82	5.71	3.49	6.56	2.15
Tang Book Value Per Share	10.02	9.37	8.91	8.54	5.59	17.45	13.20	11.71
Income Statement								
Total Revenue	2,753,000	1,793,000	900,000	3,883,000	2,192,000	2,814,104	2,307,138	1,800,495
Income Before Taxes	244,000	123,000	57,000	356,000	(269,000)	904,496	77,557	(306,856)
Income Taxes	100,000	48,000	24,000	113,000	(147,000)	297,046	(16,185)	(88,222)
Net Income	144,000	75,000	33,000	215,000	(242,000)	504,636	(19,301)	(218,634)
Average Shares	135,253	135,513	135,573	135,135	127,910	115,265	102,917	100,000
Balance Sheet								
Total Assets	19,050,000	18,698,000	17,973,000	18,123,000	21,056,000	11,057,864	15,402,686	14,673,515
Total Liabilities	15,820,000	15,544,000	14,868,000	15,057,000	18,305,000	9,032,595	13,862,666	13,473,388
Stockholders' Equity	3,230,000	3,154,000	3,105,000	3,066,000	2,751,000	2,025,269	1,540,020	1,200,127
Shares Outstanding	135,306	135,301	135,301	134,867	134,494	114,832	114,788	100,000
Statistical Record								
Return on Assets %	0.91	0.68	0.60	1.09	N.M.	3.81	N.M.	N.M.
Return on Equity %	5.45	4.11	3.68	7.37	N.M.	28.31	N.M.	N.M.
Net Margin %	5.23	4.18	3.67	5.54	N.M.	17.93	N.M.	N.M.
Asset Turnover	0.20	0.20	0.20	0.20	0.14	0.21	0.15	0.12
Price Range	31.47-16.90	31.47-16.90	32.26-16.90	41.54-16.90	53.83-31.60	39.86-22.35	25.28-19.26	...
P/E Ratio	24.98-13.41	33.48-17.98	38.87-20.36	26.13-10.63	...	9.10-5.10	...	...

Address: 601 N.W. Second Street, Evansville, IN 47708
Telephone: 812-424-8031

Web Site: www.springleaf.com
Officers: Wesley R. Edens - Chairman Jay N. Levine - President, Chief Executive Officer

Auditors: PricewaterhouseCoopers LLP
Transfer Agents: American Stock Transfer & Trust Company, LLC

ONEOK INC

Exchange	Symbol	Price	52Wk Range	Yield	P/E	Div Achiever
NYS	OKE	$53.45 (12/29/2017)	58.83-47.41	5.76	33.41	14 Years

*7 Year Price Score 90.65 *NYSE Composite Index=100 *12 Month Price Score 92.07

TRADING VOLUME (thousand shares)

Interim Earnings (Per Share)

Qtr.	Mar	Jun	Sep	Dec
2014	0.45	0.29	0.31	0.45
2015	0.29	0.36	0.39	0.12
2016	0.40	0.40	0.43	0.43
2017	0.41	0.33	0.43	...

Interim Dividends (Per Share)

Amt	Decl	Ex	Rec	Pay
0.615Q	04/20/2017	04/27/2017	05/01/2017	05/15/2017
0.745Q	07/26/2017	08/03/2017	08/07/2017	08/14/2017
0.745Q	10/25/2017	11/03/2017	11/06/2017	11/14/2017
0.77Q	01/17/2018	01/26/2018	01/29/2018	02/14/2018

Indicated Div: $3.08 (Div. Reinv. Plan)

Valuation Analysis

		Institutional Holding	
Forecast EPS	$1.73	No of Institutions	
	(01/18/2018)	981	
Market Cap	$20.4 Billion	Shares	
Book Value	$5.4 Billion	309,524,608	
Price/Book	3.80	% Held	
Price/Sales	1.85	70.03	

Business Summary: Equipment & Services (MIC: 9.1.3 SIC: 4923 NAIC: 221210)

Oneok's operations is comprised of the following business segments: Natural Gas Gathering and Processing, which provides midstream services to contracted producers in North Dakota, Montana, Wyoming, Kansas and Oklahoma; Natural Gas Liquids (NGLs), which owns and operates facilities that gather, fractionate, treat and distribute NGLs and store NGL products, primarily in Oklahoma, Kansas, Texas, New Mexico and the Rocky Mountain region where it provides midstream services to producers of NGLs and delivers those products to the two primary market centers; and Natural Gas Pipelines, which provides transportation and storage services to end users through ONEOK Partners' wholly owned assets.

Recent Developments: For the quarter ended Sep 30 2017, income from continuing operations decreased 14.5% to US$166.5 million from US$194.8 million in the year-earlier quarter. Net income decreased 14.3% to US$166.5 million from US$194.2 million in the year-earlier quarter. Revenues were US$2.91 billion, up 23.3% from US$2.36 billion the year before. Operating income was US$351.9 million versus US$329.4 million in the prior-year quarter, an increase of 6.8%. Direct operating expenses rose 24.7% to US$2.51 billion from US$2.02 billion in the comparable period the year before. Indirect operating expenses increased 216.5% to US$40.3 million from US$12.7 million in the equivalent prior-year period.

Prospects: Our evaluation of Oneok Inc. as of Jan. 14, 2018 is the result of our systematic analysis on three basic characteristics: earnings strength, relative valuation, and recent stock price movement. The company has produced a positive trend in earnings per share over the past 5 quarters. However, while recent estimates for the company have been mixed, OKE has posted results that fell short of analysts expectations. Based on operating earnings yield, the company is about fairly valued when compared to all of the companies in our coverage universe. Share price changes over the past year indicates that OKE will perform poorly over the near term.

Financial Data

(US$ in Thousands)	9 Mos	6 Mos	3 Mos	12/31/2016	12/31/2015	12/31/2014	12/31/2013	12/31/2012
Earnings Per Share	1.60	1.60	1.67	1.66	1.16	1.49	1.27	1.71
Cash Flow Per Share	3.59	6.91	6.57	6.38	4.79	6.14	6.28	4.79
Tang Book Value Per Share	11.44	11.60	N.M.	N.M.	N.M.	N.M.	5.59	5.53
Dividends Per Share	2.590	2.460	2.460	2.460	2.430	2.125	1.480	1.270
Dividend Payout %	161.88	153.75	147.31	148.19	209.48	142.62	116.54	74.27
Income Statement								
Total Revenue	8,381,749	5,475,383	2,749,611	8,920,934	7,763,206	12,195,091	14,602,717	12,632,559
EBITDA	1,269,669	817,237	417,443	1,679,502	1,167,983	1,441,071	1,348,409	1,459,579
Depn & Amortn	302,566	200,268	99,419	391,585	354,620	306,038	384,377	335,852
Income Before Taxes	605,635	382,034	201,562	818,266	396,576	778,870	629,826	821,422
Income Taxes	195,913	98,785	54,941	212,406	136,600	151,158	163,382	215,195
Net Income	324,796	159,054	87,361	352,039	244,977	314,101	266,533	360,619
Average Shares	383,419	214,012	213,602	212,383	210,541	210,427	209,695	210,710
Balance Sheet								
Current Assets	1,518,865	1,447,811	1,378,447	1,429,684	975,210	1,307,244	2,370,802	2,764,660
Total Assets	16,764,841	16,672,923	16,067,558	16,138,751	15,446,111	15,304,560	17,707,558	15,855,275
Current Liabilities	2,741,080	2,860,519	2,731,974	2,836,701	1,638,266	2,392,345	2,696,407	2,812,994
Long-Term Obligations	8,092,000	7,835,606	7,919,826	7,919,996	8,323,582	7,192,929	7,754,975	6,515,372
Total Liabilities	11,405,346	11,265,176	15,829,176	15,950,006	15,110,313	14,712,445	15,369,707	13,725,666
Stockholders' Equity	5,359,495	5,407,747	238,382	188,745	335,798	592,115	2,337,851	2,129,609
Shares Outstanding	381,285	380,004	210,906	210,681	209,731	208,322	206,618	204,935
Statistical Record								
Return on Assets %	2.54	2.10	2.26	2.22	1.59	1.90	1.59	2.43
Return on Equity %	14.90	12.11	135.53	133.86	52.80	21.44	11.93	16.47
EBITDA Margin %	15.15	14.93	15.18	18.83	15.05	11.82	9.23	11.55
Net Margin %	3.88	2.90	3.18	3.95	3.16	2.58	1.83	2.85
Asset Turnover	0.67	0.65	0.63	0.56	0.50	0.74	0.87	0.85
Current Ratio	0.55	0.51	0.50	0.50	0.60	0.55	0.88	0.98
Debt to Equity	1.51	1.45	33.22	41.96	24.79	12.15	3.32	3.06
Price Range	59.03-46.44	59.03-42.99	59.03-28.37	59.03-19.62	51.07-18.93	70.98-44.50	62.18-40.00	49.39-39.49
P/E Ratio	36.89-29.02	36.89-26.87	35.35-16.99	35.56-11.82	44.03-16.32	47.64-29.73	48.96-31.50	28.88-23.09
Average Yield %	4.86	4.45	5.07	5.99	6.22	3.44	2.96	2.92

Address: 100 West Fifth Street, Tulsa, OK 74103

Telephone: 918-588-7000

Fax: 918-588-7273

Web Site: www.oneok.com

Officers: Terry K. Spencer - President, Chief Executive Officer Derek S. Reiners - Chief Financial Officer, Senior Vice President, Chief Accounting Officer, Treasurer

Auditors: PricewaterhouseCoopers LLP

Investor Contact: 918 588-7163

Transfer Agents: Wells Fargo Shareowner Services, St Paul, MN

ORACLE CORP

Exchange	Symbol	Price	52Wk Range	Yield	P/E
NYS	ORCL	$47.28 (12/29/2017)	52.80-38.45	1.61	20.29

*7 Year Price Score 97.59 *NYSE Composite Index=100 *12 Month Price Score 99.51

Interim Earnings (Per Share)

Qtr.	Aug	Nov	Feb	May
2014-15	0.48	0.56	0.56	0.62
2015-16	0.40	0.52	0.50	0.66
2016-17	0.43	0.48	0.53	0.76
2017-18	0.52	0.52	...	...

Interim Dividends (Per Share)

Amt	Decl	Ex	Rec	Pay
0.19Q	03/15/2017	04/10/2017	04/12/2017	04/26/2017
0.19Q	06/21/2017	07/17/2017	07/19/2017	08/02/2017
0.19Q	09/12/2017	10/10/2017	10/11/2017	10/25/2017
0.19Q	12/13/2017	01/09/2018	01/10/2018	01/24/2018

Indicated Div: $0.76

Valuation Analysis / **Institutional Holding**

Forecast EPS	$2.94 (01/18/2018)	No of Institutions	2302
Market Cap	$195.9 Billion	Shares	2,990,932,736
Book Value	$55.9 Billion	% Held	53.04
Price/Book	3.51		
Price/Sales	5.03		

TRADING VOLUME (thousand shares)

Business Summary: Internet & Software (MIC: 6.3.2 SIC: 7372 NAIC: 511210)

Oracle provides products and services that address all aspects of corporate information technology environments: application, platform and infrastructure. Co. has three businesses that deliver its application, platform and infrastructure technologies. These businesses are: cloud and on-premise software, which is comprised of three operating segments: cloud software and on-premise software, cloud infrastructure as a service, and software license updates and product support; hardware systems, which is comprised of two operating segments: hardware products and hardware support; and services, which provides consulting services, support services and education services.

Recent Developments: For the quarter ended Nov 30 2017, net income increased 9.9% to US$2.23 billion from US$2.03 billion in the year-earlier quarter. Revenues were US$9.62 billion, up 6.5% from US$9.04 billion the year before. Operating income was US$3.07 billion versus US$3.04 billion in the prior-year quarter, an increase of 1.1%. Direct operating expenses rose 9.3% to US$1.97 billion from US$1.80 billion in the comparable period the year before. Indirect operating expenses increased 9.2% to US$4.59 billion from US$4.20 billion in the equivalent prior-year period.

Prospects: Our evaluation of Oracle Corp. as of Jan. 14, 2018 is the result of our systematic analysis on three basic characteristics: earnings strength, relative valuation, and recent stock price movement. The company has managed to produce a neutral trend in earnings per share over the past 5 quarters and while recent estimates for the company have been mixed, ORCL has posted better than expected results. Based on operating earnings yield, the company is undervalued when compared to all of the companies in our coverage universe. Share price changes over the past year indicates that ORCL will perform very well over the near term.

Financial Data
(US$ in Thousands)

	6 Mos	3 Mos	05/31/2017	05/31/2016	05/31/2015	05/31/2014	05/31/2013	05/31/2012
Earnings Per Share	2.33	2.29	2.21	2.07	2.21	2.38	2.26	1.96
Cash Flow Per Share	3.51	3.57	3.43	3.20	3.26	3.30	2.98	2.73
Tang Book Value Per Share	1.47	1.38	0.76	1.88	1.88	2.48	2.30	2.18
Dividends Per Share	0.720	0.680	0.640	0.600	0.510	0.480	0.300	0.240
Dividend Payout %	30.90	29.69	28.96	28.99	23.08	20.17	13.27	12.24
Income Statement								
Total Revenue	18,809,000	9,187,000	37,728,000	37,047,000	38,226,000	38,275,000	37,180,000	37,121,000
EBITDA	7,318,000	3,540,000	15,082,000	14,996,000	16,602,000	17,361,000	17,501,000	16,532,000
Depn & Amortn	1,384,000	696,000	2,451,000	2,509,000	2,861,000	2,908,000	2,931,000	2,916,000
Income Before Taxes	5,451,000	2,585,000	11,635,000	11,558,000	12,947,000	13,802,000	14,010,000	13,081,000
Income Taxes	1,009,000	375,000	2,182,000	2,541,000	2,896,000	2,749,000	2,973,000	2,981,000
Net Income	4,442,000	2,210,000	9,335,000	8,901,000	9,938,000	10,955,000	10,925,000	9,981,000
Average Shares	4,283,000	4,284,000	4,217,000	4,304,999	4,502,999	4,603,999	4,843,999	5,094,999
Balance Sheet								
Current Assets	78,545,000	73,335,000	74,515,000	64,313,000	63,183,000	48,138,000	41,692,000	40,023,000
Total Assets	138,762,000	133,597,000	134,991,000	112,180,000	110,903,000	90,344,000	81,812,000	78,327,000
Current Liabilities	15,494,000	20,226,000	24,178,000	17,208,000	15,291,000	14,389,000	12,872,000	15,388,000
Long-Term Obligations	58,170,000	48,293,000	48,112,000	40,105,000	39,959,000	22,667,000	18,494,000	13,524,000
Total Liabilities	82,894,000	77,638,000	81,131,000	64,891,000	62,240,000	43,466,000	37,164,000	34,639,000
Stockholders' Equity	55,868,000	55,959,000	53,860,000	47,289,000	48,663,000	46,878,000	44,648,000	43,688,000
Shares Outstanding	4,143,000	4,171,000	4,137,000	4,131,000	4,342,999	4,463,999	4,645,999	4,904,999
Statistical Record								
Return on Assets %	7.56	7.56	7.55	7.96	9.88	12.73	13.64	13.11
Return on Equity %	19.01	18.79	18.46	18.50	20.80	23.94	24.74	23.85
EBITDA Margin %	38.91	38.53	39.98	40.48	43.43	45.36	47.07	44.54
Net Margin %	23.62	24.06	24.74	24.03	26.00	28.62	29.38	26.89
Asset Turnover	0.30	0.30	0.31	0.33	0.38	0.44	0.46	0.49
Current Ratio	5.07	3.63	3.08	3.74	4.13	3.35	3.24	2.60
Debt to Equity	1.04	0.86	0.89	0.85	0.82	0.48	0.41	0.31
Price Range	52.80-38.45	51.17-37.93	45.73-37.93	44.91-33.94	46.23-37.56	42.20-29.96	36.34-26.00	34.22-24.78
P/E Ratio	22.66-16.50	22.34-16.56	20.69-17.16	21.70-16.40	20.92-17.00	17.73-12.59	16.08-11.50	17.46-12.64
Average Yield %	1.57	1.57	1.56	1.55	1.22	1.34	0.93	0.81

Address: 500 Oracle Parkway, Redwood City, CA 94065 **Telephone:** 650-506-7000	**Web Site:** www.oracle.com **Officers:** Lawrence J. Ellison - Executive Chairman, Chief Technology Officer, Chairman, Chief Executive Officer Jeffrey O. Henley - Vice-Chairman, Chairman	**Auditors:** Ernst & Young LLP **Investor Contact:** 650-506-4073 **Transfer Agents:** American Stock Transfer & Trust Company, LLC, Brooklyn, NY

ORBITAL ATK INC

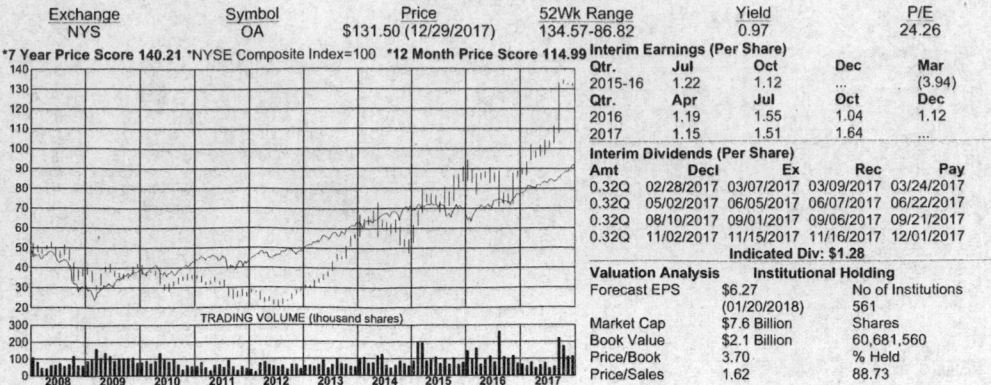

Exchange	Symbol	Price	52Wk Range	Yield	P/E
NYS	OA	$131.50 (12/29/2017)	134.57-86.82	0.97	24.26

*7 Year Price Score 140.21 *NYSE Composite Index=100 *12 Month Price Score 114.99

Interim Earnings (Per Share)

Qtr.	Jul	Oct	Dec	Mar
2015-16	1.22	1.12	...	(3.94)
Qtr.	**Apr**	**Jul**	**Oct**	**Dec**
2016	1.19	1.55	1.04	1.12
2017	1.15	1.51	1.64	...

Interim Dividends (Per Share)

Amt	Decl	Ex	Rec	Pay
0.32Q	02/28/2017	03/07/2017	03/09/2017	03/24/2017
0.32Q	05/02/2017	06/05/2017	06/07/2017	06/22/2017
0.32Q	08/10/2017	09/01/2017	09/06/2017	09/21/2017
0.32Q	11/02/2017	11/15/2017	11/16/2017	12/01/2017

Indicated Div: $1.28

Valuation Analysis		Institutional Holding	
Forecast EPS	$6.27	No of Institutions	
	(01/20/2018)	561	
Market Cap	$7.6 Billion	Shares	
Book Value	$2.1 Billion	60,681,560	
Price/Book	3.70	% Held	
Price/Sales	1.62	88.73	

Business Summary: Defense (MIC: 7.1.2 SIC: 3761 NAIC: 336415)

Orbital ATK is an aerospace and defense systems company and supplier of related products. Co.'s products include launch vehicles and related propulsion systems; satellites and associated components and services; composite aerospace structures; tactical missiles, subsystems and defense electronics; and precision weapons. Co. has three segments: Flight Systems Group, which develops rockets; Defense Systems Group, which develops and produces small-, medium- and large-caliber ammunition, precision weapons and munitions; and Space Systems Group, which develops and produces small- and medium-class satellites that are used to enable global and regional communications and broadcasting.

Recent Developments: For the quarter ended Oct 1 2017, net income increased 56.7% to US$94.0 million from US$60.0 million in the year-earlier quarter. Revenues were US$1.22 billion, up 16.6% from US$1.04 billion the year before. Operating income was US$142.0 million versus US$91.0 million in the prior-year quarter, an increase of 56.0%. Direct operating expenses rose 13.0% to US$941.0 million from US$833.0 million in the comparable period the year before. Indirect operating expenses increased 11.8% to US$133.0 million from US$119.0 million in the equivalent prior-year period.

Prospects: Our evaluation of Orbital ATK Inc. as of Jan. 21, 2018 is the result of our systematic analysis on three basic characteristics: earnings strength, relative valuation, and recent stock price movement. The company has enjoyed a very positive trend in earnings per share over the past 5 quarters and while recent estimates for the company have been raised by analysts, OA has posted better than expected results. Based on operating earnings yield, the company is undervalued when compared to all of the companies in our coverage universe. Share price changes over the past year indicates that OA will perform very well over the near term.

Financial Data
(US$ in Thousands)

	9 Mos	6 Mos	3 Mos	12/31/2016	12/31/2015	03/31/2015	03/31/2014	03/31/2013
Earnings Per Share	5.42	4.82	4.86	5.01	3.04	5.60	10.42	8.34
Cash Flow Per Share	9.99	7.19	9.81	8.92	6.78	8.78	12.25	8.43
Tang Book Value Per Share	2.60	0.73	N.M.	N.M.	N.M.	N.M.	N.M.	3.96
Dividends Per Share	1.260	1.240	1.220	1.200	0.780	1.280	1.100	0.920
Dividend Payout %	23.25	25.73	25.10	23.95	25.66	22.86	10.56	11.03
Income Statement								
Total Revenue	3,416,000	2,200,000	1,085,000	4,455,000	3,399,089	3,173,967	4,775,128	4,362,145
EBITDA	504,000	324,000	112,000	631,000	446,265	290,354	708,082	563,932
Depn & Amortn	115,000	77,000	1,000	159,000	123,878	85,027	117,776	106,062
Income Before Taxes	338,000	213,000	94,000	404,000	265,224	116,651	510,514	392,484
Income Taxes	90,000	59,000	28,000	111,000	83,659	39,117	169,428	120,243
Net Income	248,000	154,000	66,000	293,000	182,430	202,484	340,915	271,805
Average Shares	58,000	58,000	58,000	58,000	59,915	36,140	32,723	32,608
Balance Sheet								
Current Assets	2,415,000	2,310,000	2,405,000	2,235,000	2,240,442	2,388,906	2,461,598	2,218,732
Total Assets	5,537,000	5,479,000	5,570,000	5,418,000	5,353,556	5,504,402	5,771,146	4,383,010
Current Liabilities	1,293,000	1,223,000	1,374,000	1,342,000	966,979	1,096,784	1,130,150	906,855
Long-Term Obligations	1,370,000	1,454,000	1,464,000	1,398,000	1,450,000	1,528,504	1,843,750	1,023,877
Total Liabilities	3,485,000	3,526,000	3,698,000	3,612,000	3,416,416	3,727,404	3,859,571	2,880,841
Stockholders' Equity	2,052,000	1,953,000	1,872,000	1,806,000	1,937,140	1,776,998	1,911,575	1,502,169
Shares Outstanding	57,686	57,610	57,685	57,487	58,729	59,427	31,842	32,318
Statistical Record								
Return on Assets %	5.74	5.17	5.10	5.43	4.35	3.59	6.71	6.09
Return on Equity %	16.06	14.85	14.63	15.61	12.58	10.98	19.97	19.92
EBITDA Margin %	14.75	14.73	10.32	14.16	13.13	9.15	14.83	12.93
Net Margin %	7.26	7.00	6.08	6.58	5.37	6.38	7.14	6.23
Asset Turnover	0.86	0.84	0.81	0.82	0.81	0.56	0.94	0.98
Current Ratio	1.87	1.89	1.75	1.67	2.32	2.18	2.18	2.45
Debt to Equity	0.67	0.74	0.78	0.77	0.75	0.86	0.96	0.68
Price Range	133.16-72.19	104.32-70.79	102.11-70.79	94.55-70.79	90.98-68.04	79.78-47.42	66.96-32.49	33.75-20.50
P/E Ratio	24.57-13.32	21.64-14.69	21.01-14.57	18.87-14.13	29.93-22.38	14.25-8.47	6.43-3.12	4.05-2.46
Average Yield %	1.32	1.41	1.43	1.44	1.00		2.09	2.27	3.53

Address: 45101 Warp Drive, Dulles, VA 20166
Telephone: 703-406-5000

Web Site: www.orbitalatk.com
Officers: Ronald R. Fogleman - Chairman David W. Thompson - President, Chief Executive Officer

Auditors: Deloitte & Touche LLP
Investor Contact: 952-351-3056
Transfer Agents: Computershare, Providence, R.I.

OSHKOSH CORP

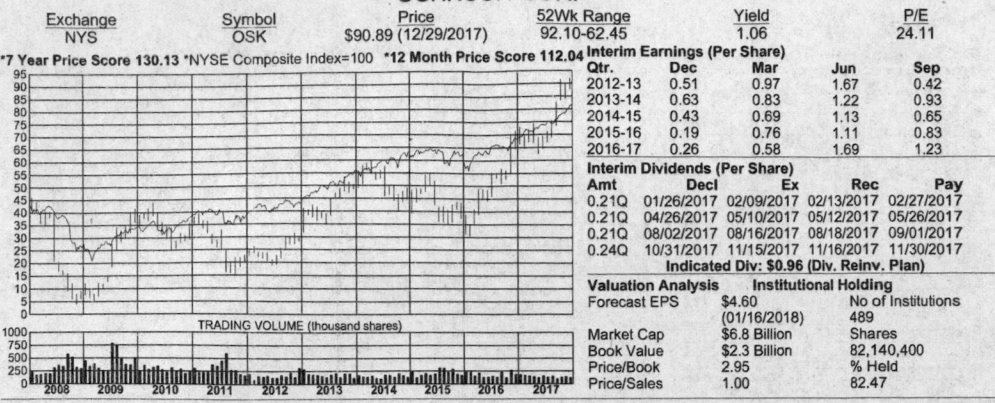

Exchange	Symbol	Price	52Wk Range	Yield	P/E
NYS	OSK	$90.89 (12/29/2017)	92.10-62.45	1.06	24.11

*7 Year Price Score 130.13 *NYSE Composite Index=100 *12 Month Price Score 112.04

Interim Earnings (Per Share)

Qtr.	Dec	Mar	Jun	Sep
2012-13	0.51	0.97	1.67	0.42
2013-14	0.63	0.83	1.22	0.93
2014-15	0.43	0.69	1.13	0.65
2015-16	0.19	0.76	1.11	0.83
2016-17	0.26	0.58	1.69	1.23

Interim Dividends (Per Share)

Amt	Decl	Ex	Rec	Pay
0.21Q	01/26/2017	02/09/2017	02/13/2017	02/27/2017
0.21Q	04/26/2017	05/10/2017	05/12/2017	05/26/2017
0.21Q	08/02/2017	08/16/2017	08/18/2017	09/01/2017
0.24Q	10/31/2017	11/15/2017	11/16/2017	11/30/2017

Indicated Div: $0.96 (Div. Reinv. Plan)

Valuation Analysis — **Institutional Holding**

Forecast EPS	$4.60 (01/16/2018)	No of Institutions 489
Market Cap	$6.8 Billion	Shares 82,140,400
Book Value	$2.3 Billion	% Held 82.47
Price/Book	2.95	
Price/Sales	1.00	

Business Summary: Autos- Manufacturing (MIC: 1.8.1 SIC: 3711 NAIC: 336120)

Oshkosh is a designer, manufacturer and marketer a range of specialty vehicles and vehicle bodies. Co. has four reportable segments: access equipment, used in a variety of construction, agricultural, industrial, institutional and general maintenance applications to position workers and materials at elevated heights, as well as carriers and wreckers; defense, which manufacture tactical trucks, trailers and supply parts and services; fire and emergency, which manufacture custom and commercial firefighting vehicles and equipment; and commercial, which manufacture concrete mixers, refuse collection vehicles, portable and stationary concrete batch plants.

Recent Developments: For the year ended Sep 30 2017, net income increased 32.0% to US$285.6 million from US$216.4 million in the prior year. Revenues were US$6.83 billion, up 8.8% from US$6.28 billion the year before. Operating income was US$463.0 million versus US$364.0 million in the prior year, an increase of 27.2%. Direct operating expenses rose 8.3% to US$5.66 billion from US$5.22 billion in the comparable period the year before. Indirect operating expenses increased 2.8% to US$711.4 million from US$691.8 million in the equivalent prior-year period.

Prospects: Our evaluation of Oshkosh Corp. as of Jan. 14, 2018 is the result of our systematic analysis on three basic characteristics: earnings strength, relative valuation, and recent stock price movement. The company has managed to produce a neutral trend in earnings per share over the past 5 quarters and while recent estimates for the company have been raised by analysts, OSK has posted better than expected results. Based on operating earnings yield, the company is undervalued when compared to all of the companies in our coverage universe. Share price changes over the past year indicates that OSK will perform well over the near term.

Financial Data (US$ in Thousands)	09/30/2017	09/30/2016	09/30/2015	09/30/2014	09/30/2013	09/30/2012	09/30/2011	09/30/2010
Earnings Per Share	3.77	2.91	2.90	3.61	3.55	2.51	2.99	8.69
Cash Flow Per Share	3.30	7.83	1.06	2.03	4.99	2.93	4.27	6.89
Tang Book Value Per Share	10.49	5.67	4.02	3.78	4.07	0.48	N.M.	N.M.
Dividends Per Share	0.840	0.740	0.680	0.150	...	...	...	...
Dividend Payout %	22.28	25.43	23.45	4.16	...	...	...	...
Income Statement								
Total Revenue	6,829,600	6,279,200	6,098,100	6,808,200	7,665,100	8,180,900	7,584,700	9,842,400
EBITDA	593,500	491,100	511,800	621,900	621,500	484,100	641,800	1,539,400
Depn & Amortn	127,300	125,800	118,100	120,600	121,900	123,300	139,300	144,300
Income Before Taxes	411,300	307,000	326,100	431,900	445,000	286,700	416,500	1,211,500
Income Taxes	127,200	92,400	99,200	125,000	131,700	57,400	143,600	414,300
Net Income	285,600	216,400	229,500	309,300	318,000	230,800	273,400	790,000
Average Shares	75,790	74,432	78,981	85,457	88,953	91,893	91,573	90,954
Balance Sheet								
Current Assets	3,039,800	2,417,500	2,429,300	2,384,300	2,553,400	2,694,500	2,454,600	2,215,900
Total Assets	5,098,900	4,513,800	4,613,000	4,586,700	4,765,700	4,947,800	4,826,900	4,708,600
Current Liabilities	1,683,100	1,367,600	1,458,100	1,311,600	1,380,700	1,704,500	1,691,800	1,812,000
Long-Term Obligations	807,900	826,200	855,000	875,000	890,000	955,000	1,020,000	1,086,400
Total Liabilities	2,791,500	2,537,300	2,701,900	2,601,700	2,657,900	3,094,300	3,230,400	3,382,000
Stockholders' Equity	2,307,400	1,976,500	1,911,100	1,985,000	2,107,800	1,853,500	1,596,500	1,326,600
Shares Outstanding	75,013	73,925	75,454	79,845	86,534	91,557	91,323	90,662
Statistical Record								
Return on Assets %	5.94	4.73	4.99	6.61	6.55	4.71	5.73	16.67
Return on Equity %	13.33	11.10	11.78	15.11	16.06	13.34	18.71	85.84
EBITDA Margin %	8.69	7.82	8.39	9.13	8.11	5.92	8.46	15.64
Net Margin %	4.18	3.45	3.76	4.54	4.15	2.82	3.60	8.03
Asset Turnover	1.42	1.37	1.33	1.46	1.58	1.67	1.59	2.08
Current Ratio	1.81	1.77	1.67	1.82	1.85	1.58	1.45	1.22
Debt to Equity	0.35	0.42	0.45	0.44	0.42	0.52	0.64	0.82
Price Range	82.68-52.58	56.90-30.33	54.90-35.23	60.03-44.15	49.12-26.85	29.76-14.51	39.27-15.74	43.84-24.88
P/E Ratio	21.93-13.95	19.55-10.42	18.93-12.15	16.63-12.23	13.84-7.56	11.86-5.78	13.13-5.26	5.04-2.86
Average Yield %	1.24	1.71	1.51	0.29	...	...	...	...

Address: P.O. Box 2566, Oshkosh, WI 54903-2566
Telephone: 920-235-9151

Web Site: www.oshkoshcorporation.com
Officers: Richard M. Donnelly - Chairman Craig P. Omtvedt - Incoming Chairman

Auditors: DELOITTE & TOUCHE LLP
Investor Contact: 920-966-5939
Transfer Agents: Computershare Investor Services, LLC, Providence, RI

OUTFRONT MEDIA INC

Exchange	Symbol	Price	52Wk Range	Yield	P/E
NYS	OUT	$23.20 (12/29/2017)	27.65-20.88	6.21	27.29

*7 Year Price Score N/A   *NYSE Composite Index=100   *12 Month Price Score 91.91

Interim Earnings (Per Share)

Qtr.	Mar	Jun	Sep	Dec
2014	0.09	0.19	2.06	0.20
2015	0.01	0.16	0.15	(0.53)
2016	(0.02)	0.21	0.28	0.20
2017	0.02	0.27	0.36	...

Interim Dividends (Per Share)

Amt	Decl	Ex	Rec	Pay
0.36Q	02/22/2017	03/08/2017	03/10/2017	03/31/2017
0.36Q	04/25/2017	06/07/2017	06/09/2017	06/30/2017
0.36Q	07/25/2017	09/07/2017	09/08/2017	09/29/2017
0.36Q	10/25/2017	12/07/2017	12/08/2017	12/29/2017

Indicated Div: $1.44

Valuation Analysis

	Institutional Holding	
Forecast EPS	$0.91 (01/11/2018)	No of Institutions 302
Market Cap	$3.2 Billion	Shares
Book Value	$1.2 Billion	156,306,416
Price/Book	2.69	% Held
Price/Sales	2.12	N/A

TRADING VOLUME (thousand shares)

Business Summary: REITs (MIC: 5.3.1 SIC: 6798 NAIC: 525930)

OUTFRONT Media is a real estate investment trust that provides advertising space on out-of-home advertising structures and sites in the U.S. and Canada. Co.'s inventory consists of billboard displays, which are primarily located on the heavily traveled highways and roadways, and transit advertising displays operated under multi-year contracts with municipalities in cities across the U.S. and Canada. As of Dec 31 2016, Co. had displays in over 150 markets in the U.S. and Canada. Co. manages its operations through three operating segments: U.S. Billboard and Transit, International, and Sports Marketing.

Recent Developments: For the quarter ended Sep 30 2017, net income increased 33.1% to US$50.7 million from US$38.1 million in the year-earlier quarter. Revenues were US$392.4 million, up 2.5% from US$382.8 million the year before.

Prospects: Our evaluation of OUTFRONT Media Inc. as of Jan. 14, 2018 is the result of our systematic analysis on three basic characteristics: earnings strength, relative valuation, and recent stock price movement. The company has managed to produce a neutral trend in earnings per share over the past 5 quarters. However, while recent estimates for the company have been mixed, OUT has posted better than expected results. Based on operating earnings yield, the company is about fairly valued when compared to all of the companies in our coverage universe. Share price changes over the past year indicates that OUT will perform well over the near term.

Financial Data

(US$ in Thousands)	9 Mos	6 Mos	3 Mos	12/31/2016	12/31/2015	12/31/2014	12/31/2013	12/31/2012
Earnings Per Share	0.85	0.77	0.71	0.66	(0.21)	2.67	1.48	1.17
Cash Flow Per Share	1.94	1.89	2.06	2.08	2.13	2.30	2.87	3.20
Tang Book Value Per Share	N.M.	N.M.	N.M.	N.M.	N.M.	N.M.	5.41	5.64
Dividends Per Share	1.420	1.400	1.380	1.360	1.420	5.670	...	...
Dividend Payout %	167.06	181.82	194.37	206.06	...	212.36	...	...
Income Statement								
Total Revenue	1,119,200	726,800	330,600	1,513,900	1,513,800	1,353,800	1,294,000	1,284,600
EBITDA	244,500	140,300	50,800	313,700	113,786,000	290,000	342,100	306,100
Depn & Amortn	72,900	49,200	24,800	108,900	113,700,000	107,200	104,500	105,900
Income Before Taxes	85,700	34,400	(2,100)	91,000	(28,800)	98,000	237,600	200,200
Income Taxes	(800)	(2,800)	(3,700)	5,400	5,400	(206,000)	96,600	89,000
Net Income	90,300	39,600	2,500	90,900	(29,400)	306,900	143,500	113,400
Average Shares	140,900	139,300	138,900	138,400	137,300	114,800	97,000	97,000
Balance Sheet								
Current Assets	360,800	350,200	311,500	378,200	416,600	355,300	317,200	315,000
Total Assets	3,813,900	3,800,700	3,656,500	3,738,500	3,845,200	4,023,600	3,355,500	3,464,900
Current Liabilities	293,800	297,400	210,700	251,500	265,600	255,200	212,200	205,600
Long-Term Obligations	2,144,700	2,143,600	2,142,500	2,136,800	2,251,700	2,198,300	...	...
Total Liabilities	2,618,900	2,618,800	2,471,300	2,505,600	2,632,600	2,578,100	601,100	621,000
Stockholders' Equity	1,195,000	1,181,900	1,185,200	1,232,900	1,212,600	1,445,500	2,754,400	2,843,900
Shares Outstanding	138,636	138,600	138,600	138,044	137,583	136,624	97,000	97,000
Statistical Record								
Return on Assets %	3.08	2.75	2.57	2.39	N.M.	8.32	4.21	...
Return on Equity %	9.56	8.56	8.13	7.41	N.M.	14.61	5.13	...
EBITDA Margin %	21.85	19.30	15.37	20.72	7,516.58	21.42	26.44	23.83
Net Margin %	8.07	5.45	0.76	6.00	N.M.	22.67	11.09	8.83
Asset Turnover	0.40	0.40	0.40	0.40	0.38	0.37	0.38	...
Current Ratio	1.23	1.18	1.48	1.50	1.57	1.39	1.49	1.53
Debt to Equity	1.79	1.81	1.81	1.73	1.86	1.52	...	...
Price Range	27.65-20.88	27.65-20.78	27.65-20.75	25.37-18.18	30.82-20.71	35.15-26.03	...	...
P/E Ratio	32.53-24.56	35.91-26.99	38.94-29.23	38.44-27.55	...	13.16-9.75	...	...
Average Yield %	5.90	5.79	5.82	6.10	5.50	18.34	...	...

Address: 405 Lexington Avenue, 17th Floor, New York, NY 10174 **Telephone:** 212-297-6400	**Web Site:** www.outfrontmedia.com **Officers:** Jeremy J. Male - Chairman, Chief Executive Officer Donald R. Shassian - Executive Vice President, Chief Financial Officer	**Auditors:** PricewaterhouseCoopers LLP **Transfer Agents:** Wells Fargo Bank, National Association

OWENS-ILLINOIS, INC.

Exchange	Symbol	Price	52Wk Range	Yield	P/E
NYS	OI	$22.17 (12/29/2017)	25.68-17.95	N/A	14.98

*7 Year Price Score 73.33   *NYSE Composite Index=100   *12 Month Price Score 98.56

Interim Earnings (Per Share)

Qtr.	Mar	Jun	Sep	Dec
2014	0.61	0.68	0.37	(1.21)
2015	0.44	0.25	0.10	(1.26)
2016	0.41	0.64	0.66	(0.43)
2017	0.30	0.85	0.76	...

Interim Dividends (Per Share)

No Dividends Paid

Valuation Analysis | **Institutional Holding**

Forecast EPS	$2.64	No of Institutions
	(01/18/2018)	507
Market Cap	$3.6 Billion	Shares
Book Value	$822.0 Million	188,693,376
Price/Book	4.40	% Held
Price/Sales	0.53	93.05

TRADING VOLUME (thousand shares)

Business Summary: Containers & Packaging (MIC: 8.1.3 SIC: 3221 NAIC: 327213)

Owens-Illinois is a manufacturer of glass containers. Co. produces glass containers for alcoholic beverages, including beer, flavored malt beverages, spirits and wine. Co. also produces glass packaging for a variety of food items, soft drinks, teas, juices and pharmaceuticals. Co. manufactures glass containers in a range of sizes, shapes and colors. Co. has four reportable segments based on its geographic locations: Europe, North America, South America and Asia Pacific.

Recent Developments: For the quarter ended Sep 30 2017, income from continuing operations increased 15.4% to US$135.0 million from US$117.0 million in the year-earlier quarter. Net income increased 16.7% to US$133.0 million in the year-earlier quarter. Revenues were US$1.79 billion, up 4.6% from US$1.71 billion the year before. Direct operating expenses rose 4.5% to US$1.44 billion from US$1.38 billion in the comparable period the year before. Indirect operating expenses decreased 6.4% to US$176.0 million from US$188.0 million in the equivalent prior-year period.

Prospects: Our evaluation of Owens-Illinois Inc. as of Jan. 14, 2018 is the result of our systematic analysis on three basic characteristics: earnings strength, relative valuation, and recent stock price movement. The company has managed to produce a neutral trend in earnings per share over the past 5 quarters and while recent estimates for the company have been mixed, OI has posted better than expected results. Based on operating earnings yield, the company is undervalued when compared to all of the companies in our coverage universe. Share price changes over the past year indicates that OI will perform very well over the near term.

Financial Data

(US$ in Thousands)	9 Mos	6 Mos	3 Mos	12/31/2016	12/31/2015	12/31/2014	12/31/2013	12/31/2012
Earnings Per Share	1.48	1.38	1.17	1.28	(0.47)	0.45	1.11	1.11
Cash Flow Per Share	3.49	4.33	4.41	4.63	3.77	4.10	4.15	3.49
Income Statement								
Total Revenue	5,157,000	3,366,000	1,615,000	6,702,000	6,156,000	6,784,000	6,967,000	7,000,000
EBITDA	514,000	312,000	263,000	956,000	573,000	719,000	847,000	881,000
Depn & Amortn	(31,000)	(20,000)	127,000	388,000	323,000	335,000	350,000	378,000
Income Before Taxes	341,000	191,000	58,000	296,000	(1,000)	154,000	268,000	264,000
Income Taxes	65,000	28,000	20,000	119,000	106,000	92,000	120,000	108,000
Net Income	314,000	188,000	49,000	209,000	(74,000)	75,000	184,000	184,000
Average Shares	164,993	164,482	163,840	162,825	161,169	166,047	165,828	165,768
Balance Sheet								
Current Assets	2,667,000	2,554,000	2,419,000	2,254,000	2,334,000	2,371,000	2,550,000	2,648,000
Total Assets	9,999,000	9,780,000	9,459,000	9,135,000	9,421,000	7,858,000	8,419,000	8,598,000
Current Liabilities	2,177,000	2,015,000	1,859,000	2,060,000	2,122,000	2,328,000	2,254,000	2,162,000
Long-Term Obligations	5,378,000	5,471,000	5,431,000	5,133,000	5,345,000	2,972,000	3,245,000	3,454,000
Total Liabilities	9,177,000	9,110,000	8,843,000	8,881,000	8,955,000	6,700,000	6,963,000	7,717,000
Stockholders' Equity	822,000	670,000	616,000	254,000	466,000	1,158,000	1,456,000	881,000
Shares Outstanding	162,991	162,875	162,698	162,337	160,961	164,197	164,714	163,963
Statistical Record								
Return on Assets %	2.50	2.32	2.00	2.25	N.M.	0.92	2.16	2.09
Return on Equity %	39.90	40.07	37.02	57.90	N.M.	5.74	15.75	21.34
EBITDA Margin %	9.97	9.27	16.28	14.26	9.31	10.60	12.16	12.59
Net Margin %	6.09	5.59	3.03	3.12	N.M.	1.11	2.64	2.63
Asset Turnover	0.70	0.69	0.70	0.72	0.71	0.83	0.82	0.80
Current Ratio	1.23	1.27	1.30	1.09	1.10	1.02	1.13	1.22
Debt to Equity	6.54	8.17	8.82	20.21	11.47	2.57	2.23	3.92
Price Range	25.22-17.00	23.92-16.81	20.46-15.46	20.18-12.06	26.99-16.94	35.78-23.53	35.78-21.27	24.83-17.07
P/E Ratio	17.04-11.49	17.33-12.18	17.49-13.21	15.77-9.42	...	79.51-52.29	32.23-19.16	22.37-15.38

Address: One Michael Owens Way, Perrysburg, OH 43551
Telephone: 567-336-5000

Web Site: www.o-i.com
Officers: Andres Alberto Lopez - President, Chief Executive Officer, Chief Operating Officer, Division Officer Jan A. Bertsch - Senior Vice President, Chief Financial Officer

Auditors: Ernst & Young LLP
Investor Contact: 567-336-2400
Transfer Agents: Computershare Trust Company, N.A., Providence, RI

OWENS CORNING

Exchange	Symbol	Price	52Wk Range	Yield	P/E
NYS	OC	$91.94 (12/29/2017)	92.75-51.66	0.91	27.44

*7 Year Price Score 124.23 *NYSE Composite Index=100 *12 Month Price Score 119.70

Interim Earnings (Per Share)

Qtr.	Mar	Jun	Sep	Dec
2014	1.01	0.18	0.44	0.28
2015	0.15	0.77	0.95	0.92
2016	0.49	1.19	0.97	0.76
2017	0.89	0.85	0.85	

Interim Dividends (Per Share)

Amt	Decl	Ex	Rec	Pay
0.20Q	02/03/2017	03/08/2017	03/10/2017	04/03/2017
0.20Q	06/15/2017	07/13/2017	07/17/2017	08/02/2017
0.20Q	09/21/2017	10/13/2017	10/16/2017	11/02/2017
0.21Q	12/07/2017	12/29/2017	01/02/2018	01/17/2018

Indicated Div: $0.84

Valuation Analysis	Institutional Holding
Forecast EPS $4.35	No of Institutions
(01/26/2018)	515
Market Cap $10.2 Billion	Shares
Book Value $4.1 Billion	131,256,776
Price/Book 2.51	% Held
Price/Sales 1.66	82.61

Business Summary: Construction Materials (MIC: 8.5.1 SIC: 3292 NAIC: 327910)

Owens Corning is a holding company. Through its subsidiaries, Co. produces glass fiber reinforcements and other materials for composites and of residential and commercial building materials. Co.'s products range from glass fiber used to reinforce composite materials for transportation, electronics, marine, infrastructure, wind-energy and other markets to insulation and roofing for residential, commercial and industrial applications. Co.'s segments are Composites, which includes Reinforcements and Downstream businesses; Insulation, which products include thermal and acoustical batts, and loosefill insulation; and Roofing, which main products are laminate and strip asphalt roofing shingles.

Recent Developments: For the quarter ended Sep 30 2017, net income decreased 15.0% to US$96.0 million from US$113.0 million in the year-earlier quarter. Revenues were US$1.70 billion, up 12.2% from US$1.52 billion the year before. Operating income was US$227.0 million versus US$207.0 million in the prior-year quarter, an increase of 9.7%. Direct operating expenses rose 11.8% to US$1.28 billion from US$1.14 billion in the comparable period the year before. Indirect operating expenses increased 18.0% to US$197.0 million from US$167.0 million in the equivalent prior-year period.

Prospects: Our evaluation of Owens Corning as of Jan. 21, 2018 is the result of our systematic analysis on three basic characteristics: earnings strength, relative valuation, and recent stock price movement. The company has managed to produce a neutral trend in earnings per share over the past 5 quarters and while recent estimates for the company have been raised by analysts, OC has posted results that fell short of analysts expectations. Based on operating earnings yield, the company is undervalued when compared to all of the companies in our coverage universe. Share price changes over the past year indicates that OC will perform very well over the near term.

Financial Data

(US$ in Millions)	9 Mos	6 Mos	3 Mos	12/31/2016	12/31/2015	12/31/2014	12/31/2013	12/31/2012
Earnings Per Share	3.35	3.47	3.81	3.41	2.79	1.91	1.71	(0.16)
Cash Flow Per Share	8.63	9.04	7.90	8.22	6.33	3.75	3.54	2.76
Tang Book Value Per Share	10.74	10.16	12.80	12.20	13.57	12.79	13.47	11.41
Dividends Per Share	0.780	0.760	0.760	0.740	0.680	0.640	...	...
Dividend Payout %	23.28	21.90	19.95	21.70	24.37	33.51	...	...
Income Statement								
Total Revenue	4,778	3,075	1,478	5,677	5,350	5,276	5,295	5,172
EBITDA	785	528	254	1,016	831	629	695	402
Depn & Amortn	269	168	84	318	278	283	310	328
Income Before Taxes	435	307	144	590	453	232	273	(40)
Income Taxes	142	110	43	188	120	5	68	(28)
Net Income	293	197	101	393	330	226	204	(19)
Average Shares	112	113	113	115	118	118	119	119
Balance Sheet								
Current Assets	1,963	1,988	1,833	1,586	1,538	1,807	1,848	1,612
Total Assets	8,656	8,690	7,966	7,741	7,380	7,555	7,647	7,568
Current Liabilities	1,185	1,116	975	963	1,117	983	992	906
Long-Term Obligations	2,539	2,686	2,256	2,099	1,702	1,991	2,024	2,076
Total Liabilities	4,582	4,714	4,061	3,892	3,641	3,863	3,854	4,030
Stockholders' Equity	4,074	3,976	3,905	3,849	3,739	3,692	3,793	3,538
Shares Outstanding	111	111	112	112	115	117	117	118
Statistical Record								
Return on Assets %	4.59	4.74	5.67	5.18	4.42	2.97	2.68	N.M.
Return on Equity %	9.51	10.08	11.36	10.33	8.88	6.04	5.57	N.M.
EBITDA Margin %	16.43	17.17	17.19	17.90	15.53	11.92	13.13	7.77
Net Margin %	6.13	6.41	6.83	6.92	6.17	4.28	3.85	N.M.
Asset Turnover	0.75	0.72	0.77	0.75	0.72	0.69	0.70	0.68
Current Ratio	1.66	1.78	1.88	1.65	1.38	1.84	1.86	1.78
Debt to Equity	0.62	0.68	0.58	0.55	0.46	0.54	0.53	0.59
Price Range	77.39-46.58	67.38-46.58	62.43-46.07	56.03-40.52	48.08-35.04	46.05-29.00	44.95-35.62	37.05-26.13
P/E Ratio	23.10-13.90	19.42-13.42	16.39-12.09	16.43-11.88	17.23-12.56	24.11-15.18	26.29-20.83	...
Average Yield %	1.29	1.35	1.43	1.48	1.59	1.69	...	...

Address: One Owens Corning Parkway, Toledo, OH 43659	Web Site: www.owenscorning.com	Auditors: PricewaterhouseCoopers LLP
Telephone: 419-248-8000	Officers: Michael H. Thaman - Chairman, President, Chief Executive Officer Ava Harter - Senior Vice President, General Counsel, Secretary	Investor Contact: 419-248-5748 Transfer Agents: Wells Fargo Shareowner Services, Mendota Heights, MN

OWENS & MINOR, INC.

Exchange	Symbol	Price	52Wk Range	Yield	P/E	Div Achiever
NYS	OMI	$18.88 (12/29/2017)	36.95-18.10	5.46	14.98	19 Years

*7 Year Price Score 72.19   *NYSE Composite Index=100   *12 Month Price Score 60.24

Interim Earnings (Per Share)

Qtr.	Mar	Jun	Sep	Dec
2014	0.41	0.32	0.11	0.22
2015	0.30	0.39	0.45	0.51
2016	0.39	0.45	0.48	0.44
2017	0.31	0.33	0.18	...

Interim Dividends (Per Share)

Amt	Decl	Ex	Rec	Pay
0.258Q	02/14/2017	03/13/2017	03/15/2017	03/31/2017
0.258Q	05/04/2017	06/13/2017	06/15/2017	06/30/2017
0.258Q	08/01/2017	09/14/2017	09/15/2017	09/29/2017
0.258Q	11/01/2017	12/14/2017	12/15/2017	12/29/2017

Indicated Div: $1.03 (Div. Reinv. Plan)

Valuation Analysis / **Institutional Holding**

Forecast EPS $1.78 (01/18/2018)
No of Institutions 401

Market Cap $1.2 Billion
Shares 76,036,896

Book Value $1.0 Billion
% Held 65.15

Price/Book 1.15

Price/Sales 0.12

Business Summary: Medical Instruments & Equipment (MIC: 4.3.1 SIC: 5047 NAIC: 423450)

Owens & Minor is a healthcare services company that connects medical products to the point of care. Co. provides supply chain assistance to the providers of healthcare services and the manufacturers of healthcare products, supplies and devices. Co. organizes its operations into three business units: Domestic, International and Clinical & Procedural Solutions (CPS). Co.'s Domestic unit is Co.'s U.S. distribution, logistics and services business, while the International unit is Co.'s European distribution, logistics and value-added services business. CPS provides product-related solutions, including surgical and procedural kitting and sourcing.

Recent Developments: For the quarter ended Sep 30 2017, net income decreased 63.6% to US$10.9 million from US$29.8 million in the year-earlier quarter. Revenues were US$2.33 billion, down 3.4% from US$2.42 billion the year before. Operating income was US$29.7 million versus US$53.6 million in the prior-year quarter, a decrease of 44.6%. Direct operating expenses declined 4.1% to US$2.03 billion from US$2.12 billion in the comparable period the year before. Indirect operating expenses increased 12.2% to US$272.3 million from US$242.7 million in the equivalent prior-year period.

Prospects: Our evaluation of Owens & Minor Inc. as of Jan. 14, 2018 is the result of our systematic analysis on three basic characteristics: earnings strength, relative valuation, and recent stock price movement. The company has produced a positive trend in earnings per share over the past 5 quarters and while recent estimates for the company have remained steady, OMI has posted results that fell short of analysts expectations. Based on operating earnings yield, the company is undervalued when compared to all of the companies in our coverage universe. Share price changes over the past year indicates that OMI will perform poorly over the near term.

Financial Data
(US$ in Thousands)

	9 Mos	6 Mos	3 Mos	12/31/2016	12/31/2015	12/31/2014	12/31/2013	12/31/2012
Earnings Per Share	1.26	1.56	1.68	1.76	1.65	1.06	1.76	1.72
Cash Flow Per Share	0.81	1.03	1.93	3.05	4.34	(0.06)	2.24	3.47
Tang Book Value Per Share	1.33	8.01	7.72	7.58	7.61	7.28	11.22	10.36
Dividends Per Share	1.028	1.025	1.023	1.020	1.010	1.000	0.960	0.880
Dividend Payout %	81.55	65.71	60.86	57.95	61.21	94.34	54.55	51.16
Income Statement								
Total Revenue	6,928,441	4,594,480	2,328,573	9,723,431	9,772,946	9,440,182	9,071,532	8,908,145
EBITDA	139,084	93,559	48,075	232,099	236,659	180,146	231,183	222,853
Depn & Amortn	41,060	25,206	12,558	32,500	36,300	35,500	33,100	26,100
Income Before Taxes	75,806	54,873	28,773	172,542	173,210	126,483	184,985	183,356
Income Taxes	26,010	15,947	9,988	63,755	69,801	59,980	74,103	74,353
Net Income	49,796	38,926	18,785	108,787	103,409	66,503	110,882	109,003
Average Shares	59,849	59,863	60,013	61,093	62,117	62,226	62,661	62,844
Balance Sheet								
Current Assets	2,131,921	2,022,853	1,942,994	1,962,039	1,974,700	1,870,706	1,725,932	1,628,894
Total Assets	3,334,156	2,795,137	2,700,549	2,717,752	2,777,840	2,735,406	2,324,042	2,207,701
Current Liabilities	1,204,291	1,063,364	1,007,695	1,034,638	1,063,589	1,004,555	989,179	924,287
Long-Term Obligations	917,256	579,117	564,145	564,583	572,559	608,551	213,815	215,383
Total Liabilities	2,330,372	1,801,566	1,730,592	1,757,714	1,785,250	1,744,568	1,300,129	1,235,175
Stockholders' Equity	1,003,784	993,571	969,957	960,038	992,590	990,838	1,023,913	972,526
Shares Outstanding	61,249	61,226	61,202	61,031	62,803	63,070	63,096	63,271
Statistical Record								
Return on Assets %	2.51	3.45	3.76	3.95	3.75	2.63	4.89	5.23
Return on Equity %	7.73	9.64	10.48	11.11	10.43	6.60	11.11	11.50
EBITDA Margin %	2.01	2.04	2.06	2.39	2.42	1.91	2.55	2.50
Net Margin %	0.72	0.85	0.81	1.12	1.06	0.70	1.22	1.22
Asset Turnover	3.03	3.38	3.49	3.53	3.55	3.73	4.00	4.28
Current Ratio	1.77	1.90	1.93	1.90	1.86	1.86	1.74	1.76
Debt to Equity	0.91	0.58	0.58	0.59	0.58	0.61	0.21	0.22
Price Range	36.95-27.07	38.01-31.49	41.20-31.94	41.20-31.94	39.02-31.94	37.49-31.72	38.23-28.51	31.28-27.01
P/E Ratio	29.33-21.48	24.37-20.19	24.52-19.01	23.41-18.15	23.65-19.36	35.37-29.92	21.72-16.20	18.19-15.70
Average Yield %	3.12	2.98	2.88	2.84	2.91	2.91	2.83	3.02

Address: 9120 Lockwood Boulevard, Mechanicsville, VA 23116
Telephone: 804-723-7000
Fax: 804-723-7100

Web Site: www.owens-minor.com
Officers: Paul Cody Phipps - Chairman, President, Chief Executive Officer Richard A. Meier - Executive Vice President, Chief Financial Officer, Division Officer

Auditors: KPMG LLP
Investor Contact: 804-723-7555
Transfer Agents: Computershare Shareowner Services LLC, Providence, RI

PACKAGING CORP OF AMERICA

Exchange	Symbol	Price	52Wk Range	Yield	P/E
NYS	PKG	$120.55 (12/29/2017)	120.92-85.00	2.09	22.32

*7 Year Price Score 136.40 *NYSE Composite Index=100 *12 Month Price Score 103.68

Interim Earnings (Per Share)

Qtr.	Mar	Jun	Sep	Dec
2014	0.92	1.01	1.06	1.00
2015	0.92	1.16	1.31	1.08
2016	1.09	1.23	1.26	1.17
2017	1.24	1.52	1.47	...

Interim Dividends (Per Share)

Amt	Decl	Ex	Rec	Pay
0.63Q	03/01/2017	03/13/2017	03/15/2017	04/14/2017
0.63Q	05/17/2017	06/13/2017	06/15/2017	07/14/2017
0.63Q	08/25/2017	09/14/2017	09/15/2017	10/13/2017
0.63Q	12/14/2017	12/22/2017	12/26/2017	01/12/2018

Indicated Div: $2.52

Valuation Analysis | **Institutional Holding**

Forecast EPS	$5.98	No of Institutions
	(01/17/2018)	674
Market Cap	$11.4 Billion	Shares
Book Value	$2.0 Billion	121,662,008
Price/Book	5.71	% Held
Price/Sales	1.82	84.54

Business Summary: Containers & Packaging (MIC: 8.1.3 SIC: 2652 NAIC: 322213)

Packaging Corporation of America is a producer of containerboard products and uncoated freesheet. Co. has three reportable segments: Packaging, which produces corrugated packaging products, including shipping containers used to protect and transport manufactured goods, multi-color boxes and displays, as well as produces packaging for meat, fresh fruit and vegetables, processed food, beverages, and other industrial and consumer products; Paper, which manufactures and sells white papers, including both commodity and specialty papers; and Corporate and Other, which includes corporate support staff services.

Recent Developments: For the quarter ended Sep 30 2017, net income increased 16.6% to US$139.1 million from US$119.3 million in the year-earlier quarter. Revenues were US$1.64 billion, up 10.5% from US$1.48 billion the year before. Operating income was US$242.3 million versus US$206.4 million in the prior-year quarter, an increase of 17.4%. Direct operating expenses rose 7.6% to US$1.24 billion from US$1.15 billion in the comparable period the year before. Indirect operating expenses increased 25.9% to US$155.0 million from US$123.1 million in the equivalent prior-year period.

Prospects: Our evaluation of Packaging Corp. of America as of Jan. 14, 2018 is the result of our systematic analysis on three basic characteristics: earnings strength, relative valuation, and recent stock price movement. The company has produced a positive trend in earnings per share over the past 5 quarters and while recent estimates for the company have been mixed, PKG has posted results that fell short of analysts expectations. Based on operating earnings yield, the company is undervalued when compared to all of the companies in our coverage universe. Share price changes over the past year indicates that PKG will perform well over the near term.

Financial Data

(US$ in Thousands)	9 Mos	6 Mos	3 Mos	12/31/2016	12/31/2015	12/31/2014	12/31/2013	12/31/2012
Earnings Per Share	5.40	5.19	4.90	4.75	4.47	3.99	4.47	1.68
Cash Flow Per Share	8.51	8.73	8.29	8.55	7.89	7.59	6.30	4.18
Tang Book Value Per Share	9.69	8.68	7.74	6.95	8.51	6.92	4.85	8.80
Dividends Per Share	2.520	2.520	2.440	2.360	2.200	1.600	1.513	1.000
Dividend Payout %	46.67	48.55	49.80	49.68	49.22	40.10	33.84	59.52
Income Statement								
Total Revenue	4,760,600	3,120,500	1,536,500	5,779,000	5,741,700	5,852,600	3,665,308	2,843,877
EBITDA	938,200	606,900	287,500	780,624	1,073,000	1,050,900	664,807	609,459
Depn & Amortn	259,000	170,000	84,400	324	323,000	348,200	191,200	166,000
Income Before Taxes	604,600	387,700	179,100	688,500	664,500	614,300	415,332	380,559
Income Taxes	204,900	127,100	61,700	238,900	227,700	221,700	(20,951)	216,739
Net Income	399,700	260,600	117,400	449,600	436,800	392,600	436,283	163,820
Average Shares	93,800	93,600	93,600	93,700	96,700	97,100	97,547	97,497
Balance Sheet								
Current Assets	2,001,800	1,863,400	1,779,100	1,696,300	1,554,500	1,578,600	1,487,204	937,033
Total Assets	6,027,200	5,903,200	5,843,400	5,777,000	5,284,600	5,348,500	5,199,974	2,453,768
Current Liabilities	824,300	760,200	776,000	625,400	561,900	611,000	660,539	259,846
Long-Term Obligations	2,475,600	2,477,000	2,478,400	2,640,300	2,324,300	2,371,700	2,532,719	803,534
Total Liabilities	4,033,000	3,996,600	4,018,700	4,017,200	3,651,300	3,827,100	3,886,959	1,484,307
Stockholders' Equity	1,994,200	1,906,600	1,824,700	1,759,800	1,633,300	1,521,400	1,313,015	969,461
Shares Outstanding	94,400	94,400	94,200	94,213	96,129	98,368	98,172	98,142
Statistical Record								
Return on Assets %	8.67	8.76	8.37	8.11	8.22	7.44	11.40	6.71
Return on Equity %	27.41	27.49	27.13	26.43	27.69	27.70	38.23	17.21
EBITDA Margin %	19.71	19.45	18.71	13.51	18.69	17.96	18.14	21.43
Net Margin %	8.40	8.35	7.64	7.78	7.61	6.71	11.90	5.76
Asset Turnover	1.06	1.09	1.07	1.04	1.08	1.11	0.96	1.17
Current Ratio	2.43	2.45	2.29	2.71	2.77	2.58	2.25	3.61
Debt to Equity	1.24	1.30	1.36	1.50	1.42	1.56	1.93	0.83
Price Range	119.28-78.67	112.77-65.44	96.62-58.89	87.51-45.15	84.24-59.34	79.69-58.61	64.27-38.43	38.47-25.00
P/E Ratio	22.09-14.57	21.73-12.61	19.72-12.02	18.42-9.51	18.85-13.28	19.97-14.69	14.38-8.60	22.90-14.88
Average Yield %	2.60	2.86	3.08	3.38	3.12	2.32	2.97	3.22

Address: 1955 West Field Court, Lake Forest, IL 60045 **Telephone:** 847-482-3000	**Web Site:** www.packagingcorp.com **Officers:** Mark W. Kowlzan - Chairman, Chief Executive Officer, Senior Vice President Robert P. Mundy - Senior Vice President, Chief Financial Officer	**Auditors:** KPMG LLP **Investor Contact:** 877-454-2509 **Transfer Agents:** Computershare Trust Company N.A., Providence, RI

PALO ALTO NETWORKS, INC

Exchange	Symbol	Price	52Wk Range	Yield	P/E
NYS	PANW	$144.94 (12/29/2017)	156.91-108.01	N/A	N/A

*7 Year Price Score N/A   *NYSE Composite Index=100   *12 Month Price Score 101.83

Interim Earnings (Per Share)

Qtr.	Oct	Jan	Apr	Jul
2014-15	(0.38)	(0.53)	(0.56)	(0.55)
2015-16	(0.45)	(0.72)	(0.80)	(0.61)
2016-17	(0.69)	(0.67)	(0.67)	(0.42)
2017-18	(0.70)	...	...	...

Interim Dividends (Per Share)

No Dividends Paid

Valuation Analysis | **Institutional Holding**

Forecast EPS	$3.39
	(01/18/2018)
Market Cap	$13.3 Billion
Book Value	$704.7 Million
Price/Book	18.90
Price/Sales	7.13

No of Institutions 698

Shares 91,405,536

% Held 82.37

Business Summary: IT Services (MIC: 6.3.1 SIC: 3577 NAIC: 423430)

Palo Alto Networks provides a platform that allows enterprises, service providers, and government entities to secure their organizations. Co.'s Next-Generation Security Platform consists of three elements: Next-Generation Firewall, which delivers application, user, and content visibility and control, and protection against cyber threats integrated within the firewall; Advanced Endpoint Protection, which prevents cyberattacks that aim to run malicious code or exploit software vulnerabilities; and Threat Intelligence Cloud, which provides central intelligence capabilities, security for software as a service applications, and automated delivery of preventative measures against cyberattacks.

Recent Developments: For the quarter ended Oct 31 2017, net loss amounted to US$64.0 million versus a net loss of US$56.9 million in the year-earlier quarter. Revenues were US$505.5 million, up 27.0% from US$398.1 million the year before. Operating loss was US$54.3 million versus a loss of US$49.0 million in the prior-year quarter. Direct operating expenses rose 39.7% to US$141.4 million from US$101.2 million in the comparable period the year before. Indirect operating expenses increased 21.0% to US$418.4 million from US$345.9 million in the equivalent prior-year period.

Prospects: Our evaluation of Palo Alto Networks, Inc as of Jan. 14, 2018 is the result of our systematic analysis on three basic characteristics: earnings strength, relative valuation, and recent stock price movement. The company has produced a positive trend in earnings per share over the past 5 quarters and while recent estimates for the company have been mixed, PANW has posted better than expected results. Based on operating earnings yield, the company is overvalued when compared to all of the companies in our coverage universe. Share price changes over the past year indicates that PANW will perform poorly over the near term.

Financial Data
(US$ in Thousands)

	3 Mos	07/31/2017	07/31/2016	07/31/2015	07/31/2014	07/31/2013	07/31/2012	07/31/2011
Earnings Per Share	(2.46)	(2.39)	(2.59)	(2.02)	(3.05)	(0.43)	...	(0.88)
Cash Flow Per Share	10.33	9.59	7.54	4.29	1.19	1.67	3.94	2.26
Tang Book Value Per Share	4.51	5.10	6.44	4.24	3.34	3.80	3.38	...
Income Statement								
Total Revenue	505,500	1,761,600	1,378,500	928,052	598,179	396,107	255,138	118,597
EBITDA	(42,700)	(125,900)	(139,200)	(105,052)	(203,346)	(9,229)	8,838	(9,888)
Depn & Amortn	6,800	58,400	42,500	28,200	16,931	9,911	6,057	2,167
Income Before Taxes	(55,800)	(194,100)	(205,100)	(155,577)	(222,160)	(18,656)	2,799	(12,052)
Income Taxes	8,200	22,500	20,800	9,405	4,292	10,590	2,062	476
Net Income	(64,000)	(216,600)	(225,900)	(164,982)	(226,452)	(29,246)	737	(12,528)
Average Shares	90,900	90,600	87,100	81,619	74,291	68,682	19,569	14,201
Balance Sheet								
Current Assets	2,039,500	1,976,300	1,719,100	1,074,030	958,326	529,699	381,657	76,840
Total Assets	3,486,500	3,438,300	2,761,200	1,965,178	1,478,466	585,606	407,804	91,172
Current Liabilities	1,743,000	1,201,300	846,800	1,032,227	348,171	206,102	122,006	67,101
Long-Term Obligations	...	524,700	508,200	...	466,875	...	...	...
Total Liabilities	2,781,800	2,678,700	1,971,300	1,389,363	1,009,883	313,186	178,733	98,135
Stockholders' Equity	704,700	759,600	789,900	575,815	468,583	272,420	229,071	(6,963)
Shares Outstanding	91,900	91,500	90,500	84,788	79,519	71,612	67,852	19,751
Statistical Record								
Return on Assets %	N.M.	N.M.	N.M.	N.M.	N.M.	N.M.	0.29	N.M.
Return on Equity %	N.M.	N.M.	N.M.	N.M.	N.M.	N.M.	0.66	...
EBITDA Margin %	N.M.	N.M.	N.M.	N.M.	N.M.	N.M.	3.46	N.M.
Net Margin %	N.M.	N.M.	N.M.	N.M.	N.M.	N.M.	0.29	N.M.
Asset Turnover	0.58	0.57	0.58	0.54	0.58	0.80	1.02	1.83
Current Ratio	1.17	1.65	2.03	1.04	2.75	2.57	3.13	1.15
Debt to Equity	...	0.69	0.64	...	1.00	...	...	...
Price Range	164.15-108.01	164.15-108.01	193.54-115.69	197.09-78.67	84.21-40.99	71.75-39.56	59.88-51.51	...

Address: 3000 Tannery Way, Santa Clara, CA 95054 Telephone: 408-753-4000	Web Site: www.paloaltonetworks.com Officers: Mark D. McLaughlin - Chairman, President, Chief Executive Officer Mark F. Anderson - President, Senior Vice President	Auditors: Ernst & Young LLP Investor Contact: 408-753-3872 Transfer Agents: Computershare, Canton, MA

PANDORA MEDIA INC

Exchange	Symbol	Price	52Wk Range	Yield	P/E
NYS	P	$4.82 (12/29/2017)	13.58-4.49	N/A	N/A

*7 Year Price Score N/A *NYSE Composite Index=100 *12 Month Price Score 55.29

Interim Earnings (Per Share)

Qtr.	Mar	Jun	Sep	Dec
2014	(0.14)	(0.06)	(0.01)	0.06
2015	(0.23)	(0.08)	(0.40)	(0.08)
2016	(0.51)	(0.33)	(0.27)	(0.39)
2017	(0.56)	(1.20)	(0.34)	...

Interim Dividends (Per Share)

No Dividends Paid

Valuation Analysis		Institutional Holding	
Forecast EPS	$-0.58	No of Institutions	
	(01/26/2018)	329	
Market Cap	$1.2 Billion	Shares	
Book Value	$652.9 Million	319,795,520	
Price/Book	1.84	% Held	
Price/Sales	0.82	98.02	

TRADING VOLUME (thousand shares)

Business Summary: Internet & Software (MIC: 6.3.2 SIC: 4832 NAIC: 515112)

Pandora Media is a music discovery platform providing music through earbuds, car speakers or live on stage. Co. provides local and national advertisers capabilities to deliver targeted messages to its listeners using a combination of audio, display and video advertisements. Co. has two models: Ad-Supported Service, which allows listeners to access Co.'s music and comedy catalogs and personalized playlist generating system; and Subscription Service, which subscription service, Pandora Plus and Pandora One are premium monthly or annual paid versions of the Pandora service, which include ad-free access, higher quality audio on supported devices and longer timeout-free listening.

Recent Developments: For the quarter ended Sep 30 2017, net loss amounted to US$66.2 million versus a net loss of US$61.5 million in the year-earlier quarter. Revenues were US$378.6 million, up 7.6% from US$351.9 million the year before. Operating loss was US$58.9 million versus a loss of US$55.2 million in the prior-year quarter. Direct operating expenses rose 12.6% to US$242.8 million from US$215.5 million in the comparable period the year before. Indirect operating expenses increased 1.7% to US$194.8 million from US$191.6 million in the equivalent prior-year period.

Prospects: Our evaluation of Pandora Media Inc as of Jan. 21, 2018 is the result of our systematic analysis on three basic characteristics: earnings strength, relative valuation, and recent stock price movement. The company has produced a positive trend in earnings per share over the past 5 quarters. Because the company lacks sufficient analyst estimate data, we place greater weight on the historical EPS trend as the measure of earnings strength. Based on operating earnings yield, the company is overvalued when compared to all of the companies in our coverage universe. Share price changes over the past year indicates that P will perform in line with the market over the near term.

Financial Data

(US$ in Thousands)	9 Mos	6 Mos	3 Mos	12/31/2016	12/31/2015	12/31/2014	12/31/2013	01/31/2013
Earnings Per Share	(2.49)	(2.42)	(1.55)	(1.49)	(0.79)	(0.15)	(0.15)	(0.23)
Cash Flow Per Share	(0.90)	(1.09)	(0.86)	(0.79)	(0.20)	0.10	(0.02)	(0.00)
Tang Book Value Per Share	2.25	1.21	0.30	0.67	1.46	2.76	2.56	0.57
Income Statement								
Total Revenue	1,071,477	692,838	316,004	1,384,826	1,164,043	920,802	600,233	427,145
EBITDA	(435,380)	(382,135)	(119,613)	(277,562)	(148,611)	(13,322)	(16,365)	(30,603)
Depn & Amortn	15,012	9,872	4,939	39,500	22,600	16,500	10,100	7,100
Income Before Taxes	(472,769)	(406,792)	(131,933)	(343,206)	(171,211)	(29,822)	(26,923)	(38,143)
Income Taxes	877	611	334	(228)	(1,550)	584	94	5
Net Income	(473,646)	(407,403)	(132,267)	(342,978)	(169,661)	(30,406)	(27,017)	(38,148)
Average Shares	245,810	241,320	237,515	230,693	213,790	205,273	180,968	168,294
Balance Sheet								
Current Assets	912,153	801,885	543,902	625,821	683,506	588,414	518,783	198,614
Total Assets	1,165,531	1,030,645	1,098,148	1,184,810	1,240,657	749,290	673,335	218,832
Current Liabilities	218,152	265,755	254,076	254,117	231,831	149,160	156,006	115,970
Long-Term Obligations	267,396	352,157	347,223	342,247	234,577	...	...	...
Total Liabilities	512,616	643,613	635,245	630,551	497,270	165,933	165,104	119,843
Stockholders' Equity	652,915	387,032	462,903	554,259	743,387	583,357	508,231	98,989
Shares Outstanding	248,681	242,412	240,334	235,162	224,970	209,071	195,395	172,506
Statistical Record								
Asset Turnover	1.22	1.31	1.23	1.14	1.17	1.29	1.54	2.15
Current Ratio	4.18	3.02	2.14	2.46	2.95	3.94	3.33	1.71
Debt to Equity	0.41	0.91	0.75	0.62	0.32	...	...	...
Price Range	14.77-6.91	14.77-6.91	14.77-8.17	14.77-7.88	21.98-11.51	39.43-16.90	31.56-11.36	14.66-7.18

Address: 2101 Webster Street, Suite 1650, Oakland, CA 94612 **Telephone:** 510-451-4100 **Fax:** 510-451-4286	**Web Site:** www.pandora.com/about **Officers:** Roger J. Lynch - President, Chief Executive Officer David Gerbitz - Executive Vice President	**Auditors:** Ernst & Young LLP **Investor Contact:** 510-451-4100 **Transfer Agents:** Computershare Trust Company, N.A.

PBF ENERGY INC

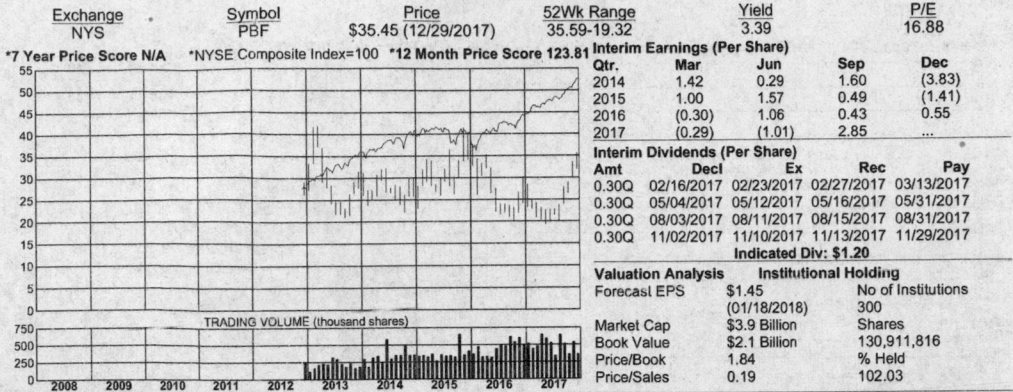

Exchange	Symbol	Price	52Wk Range	Yield	P/E
NYS	PBF	$35.45 (12/29/2017)	35.59-19.32	3.39	16.88

*7 Year Price Score N/A   *NYSE Composite Index=100   *12 Month Price Score 123.81

Interim Earnings (Per Share)

Qtr.	Mar	Jun	Sep	Dec
2014	1.42	0.29	1.60	(3.83)
2015	1.00	1.57	0.49	(1.41)
2016	(0.30)	1.06	0.43	0.55
2017	(0.29)	(1.01)	2.85	...

Interim Dividends (Per Share)

Amt	Decl	Ex	Rec	Pay
0.30Q	02/16/2017	02/23/2017	02/27/2017	03/13/2017
0.30Q	05/04/2017	05/12/2017	05/16/2017	05/31/2017
0.30Q	08/03/2017	08/11/2017	08/15/2017	08/31/2017
0.30Q	11/02/2017	11/10/2017	11/13/2017	11/29/2017

Indicated Div: $1.20

Valuation Analysis | **Institutional Holding**

Forecast EPS	$1.45 (01/18/2018)	No of Institutions 300
Market Cap	$3.9 Billion	Shares
Book Value	$2.1 Billion	130,911,816
Price/Book	1.84	% Held
Price/Sales	0.19	102.03

Business Summary: Refining & Marketing (MIC: 9.1.2 SIC: 2911 NAIC: 324110)

PBF Energy is a holding company. Through its subsidiaries, Co. is engaged as an independent petroleum refiner and supplier of unbranded transportation fuels, heating oil, petrochemical feedstocks, lubricants and other petroleum products in the U.S. Co. operates in two business segments: refining, which Co. produces a variety of products at each of its refineries such as gasoline, ultra-low-sulfur diesel, heating oil, jet fuel, lubricants, petrochemicals and asphalt; and logistics, which through its PBF Logistics LP subsidiary, Co. owns or leases, operates, develops and acquires crude oil and refined petroleum products terminals, pipelines, storage facilities and similar logistics assets.

Recent Developments: For the quarter ended Sep 30 2017, net income increased 515.2% to US$347.2 million from US$56.4 million in the year-earlier quarter. Revenues were US$5.48 billion, up 21.4% from US$4.51 billion the year before. Operating income was US$587,2 million versus US$129.7 million in the prior-year quarter, an increase of 352.7%. Direct operating expenses rose 11.6% to US$4.83 billion from US$4.33 billion in the comparable period the year before. Indirect operating expenses increased 13.7% to US$60.9 million from US$53.5 million in the equivalent prior-year period.

Prospects: Our evaluation of PBF Energy Inc as of Jan. 14, 2018 is the result of our systematic analysis on three basic characteristics: earnings strength, relative valuation, and recent stock price movement. The company has enjoyed a very positive trend in earnings per share over the past 5 quarters. However, while recent estimates for the company have been mixed, PBF has posted better than expected results. Based on operating earnings yield, the company is undervalued when compared to all of the companies in our coverage universe. Share price changes over the past year indicates that PBF will perform in line with the market over the near term.

Financial Data

(US$ in Thousands)	9 Mos	6 Mos	3 Mos	12/31/2016	12/31/2015	12/31/2014	12/31/2013	12/31/2012
Earnings Per Share	2.10	(0.32)	1.75	1.74	1.65	(0.51)	1.20	0.08
Cash Flow Per Share	5.34	3.69	4.66	6.61	6.36	6.13	8.97	34.47
Tang Book Value Per Share	19.25	16.65	17.93	18.54	16.84	14.86	16.47	17.76
Dividends Per Share	1.200	1.200	1.200	1.200	1.200	1.200	1.200	...
Dividend Payout %	57.14	...	68.57	68.97	72.73	...	100.00	...
Income Statement								
Total Revenue	15,250,649	9,771,698	4,754,473	15,920,424	13,123,929	19,828,155	19,151,455	20,138,687
EBITDA	665,857	(2,795)	61,633	629,842	483,226	269,542	403,963	978,888
Depn & Amortn	215,052	134,595	63,527	116,629	94,781	114,919	79,413	64,947
Income Before Taxes	335,934	(215,271)	(39,077)	363,168	282,258	55,859	230,766	805,312
Income Taxes	112,889	(91,090)	(19,047)	137,650	86,725	(22,412)	16,681	1,275
Net Income	173,625	(140,740)	(31,077)	170,811	146,401	(38,237)	39,540	1,956
Average Shares	113,882	108,779	108,760	103,606	94,138	74,464	33,061	97,230
Balance Sheet								
Current Assets	3,445,873	2,733,099	3,125,291	3,407,255	3,022,011	2,346,671	2,200,506	2,307,904
Total Assets	7,999,457	7,481,220	7,512,237	7,621,927	6,105,124	5,196,288	4,413,808	4,253,702
Current Liabilities	2,292,296	2,064,671	2,000,799	2,056,547	1,495,506	1,542,822	1,644,510	1,603,074
Long-Term Obligations	2,158,327	2,159,547	2,112,113	2,108,570	1,840,355	1,260,349	735,547	729,980
Total Liabilities	5,887,159	5,654,065	5,545,521	5,596,883	4,457,827	3,978,075	3,759,678	3,833,948
Stockholders' Equity	2,112,298	1,827,155	1,966,716	2,025,044	1,647,297	1,218,213	654,130	419,754
Shares Outstanding	109,747	109,722	109,667	109,204	97,781	81,981	39,665	23,571
Statistical Record								
Return on Assets %	2.95	N.M.	2.47	2.48	2.59	N.M.	0.91	...
Return on Equity %	11.85	N.M.	9.50	9.28	10.22	N.M.	7.36	...
EBITDA Margin %	4.37	N.M.	1.30	3.96	3.68	1.36	2.11	4.86
Net Margin %	1.14	N.M.	N.M.	1.07	1.12	N.M.	0.21	0.01
Asset Turnover	2.59	2.63	2.61	2.31	2.32	4.13	4.42	...
Current Ratio	1.50	1.32	1.56	1.66	2.02	1.52	1.34	1.44
Debt to Equity	1.02	1.18	1.07	1.04	1.12	1.03	1.12	1.74
Price Range	30.17-19.32	30.17-19.32	35.29-19.82	37.67-19.82	41.48-22.95	32.24-22.12	41.98-20.98	29.05-26.25
P/E Ratio	14.37-9.20	...	20.17-11.33	21.65-11.39	25.14-13.91	...	34.98-17.48	363.13-328.13
Average Yield %	5.19	5.23	4.84	4.46	3.91	4.42	4.18	...

Address: One Sylvan Way, Second Floor, Parsippany, NJ 07054 **Telephone:** 973-455-7500	**Web Site:** www.pbfenergy.com **Officers:** Thomas J. Nimbley - Chairman, Chief Executive Officer Matthew C. Lucey - President, Executive Vice President, Senior Vice President, Chief Financial Officer, Vice President	**Auditors:** Deloitte & Touche LLP **Investor Contact:** 973-455-7578 **Transfer Agents:** American Stock Transfer & Trust Company, Brooklyn, NY

PARAMOUNT GROUP INC

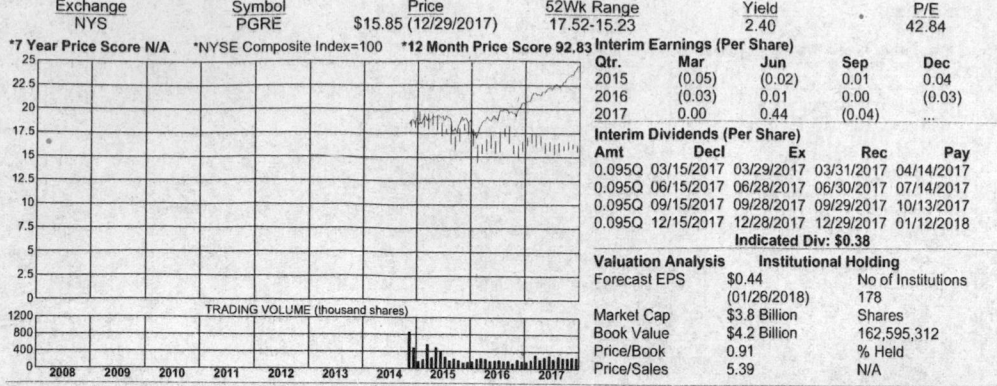

Exchange	Symbol	Price	52Wk Range	Yield	P/E
NYS	PGRE	$15.85 (12/29/2017)	17.52-15.23	2.40	42.84

*7 Year Price Score N/A   *NYSE Composite Index=100   *12 Month Price Score 92.83

Interim Earnings (Per Share)

Qtr.	Mar	Jun	Sep	Dec
2015	(0.05)	(0.02)	0.01	0.04
2016	(0.03)	0.01	0.00	(0.03)
2017	0.00	0.44	(0.04)	...

Interim Dividends (Per Share)

Amt	Decl	Ex	Rec	Pay
0.095Q	03/15/2017	03/29/2017	03/31/2017	04/14/2017
0.095Q	06/15/2017	06/28/2017	06/30/2017	07/14/2017
0.095Q	09/15/2017	09/28/2017	09/29/2017	10/13/2017
0.095Q	12/15/2017	12/28/2017	12/29/2017	01/12/2018

Indicated Div: $0.38

Valuation Analysis

		Institutional Holding	
Forecast EPS	$0.44	No of Institutions	
	(01/26/2018)	178	
Market Cap	$3.8 Billion	Shares	
Book Value	$4.2 Billion	162,595,312	
Price/Book	0.91	% Held	
Price/Sales	5.39	N/A	

Business Summary: REITs (MIC: 5.3.1 SIC: 6798 NAIC: 525930)

Paramount Group is a real estate investment trust focused on owning, operating, managing, acquiring and redeveloping Class A office properties in select central business district submarkets of New York City, Washington, D.C. and San Francisco. Co. conducts its business through, and substantially all its interests in properties and investments are held by, Paramount Group Operating Partnership LP, a Delaware limited partnership (the Operating Partnership). Co. is the sole general partner of, and owned approximately 87.0% of, the Operating Partnership as of Dec 31 2016. As of Dec 31 2016, Co.'s portfolio consisted of 13 Class A office properties.

Recent Developments: For the quarter ended Sep 30 2017, net loss amounted to US$25.4 million versus net income of US$4.5 million in the year-earlier quarter. Revenues were US$179.8 million, up 4.9% from US$171.3 million the year before.

Prospects: Our evaluation of Paramount Group Inc as of Jan. 21, 2018 is the result of our systematic analysis on three basic characteristics: earnings strength, relative valuation, and recent stock price movement. The company has produced a positive trend in earnings per share over the past 5 quarters. However, while recent estimates for the company have been mixed, PGRE has posted results that fell short of analysts expectations. Based on operating earnings yield, the company is overvalued when compared to all of the companies in our coverage universe. Share price changes over the past year indicates that PGRE will perform well over the near term.

Financial Data

(US$ in Thousands)	9 Mos	6 Mos	3 Mos	12/31/2016	12/31/2015	12/31/2014	11/23/2014	12/31/2013
Earnings Per Share	0.37	0.41	(0.02)	(0.05)	(0.02)	0.27	...	...
Cash Flow Per Share	0.75	0.41	0.35	0.66	(0.08)	(3.65)	...	...
Tang Book Value Per Share	15.88	16.04	15.58	15.55	15.32	15.28	...	...
Dividends Per Share	0.380	0.380	0.380	0.380	0.419	...	...	...
Dividend Payout %	102.70	92.68	...	...	...	...	...	...
Income Statement								
Total Revenue	538,710	358,940	181,236	683,341	662,408	66,135	227,389	419,890
EBITDA	280,500	254,359	59,205	249,601	319,807	134,409	164,557	345,606
Depn & Amortn	58,352	40,423	17,774	94,935	128,603	17,260	10,592	11,016
Income Before Taxes	118,650	145,063	5,911	3,854	23,709	73,227	127,859	313,868
Income Taxes	4,242	5,252	4,282	1,785	2,566	505	18,461	11,029
Net Income	93,174	103,388	372	(9,934)	(4,419)	57,308	21,510	16,514
Average Shares	239,445	235,010	230,958	218,053	212,106	212,107	...	...
Balance Sheet								
Current Assets	468,263	527,542	423,684	393,678	295,864	530,445	...	359,763
Total Assets	8,924,008	8,517,503	8,885,514	8,867,168	8,794,143	9,030,441	...	2,922,691
Current Liabilities	124,978	113,735	116,825	156,346	200,758	162,966	...	11,419
Long-Term Obligations	3,539,071	3,308,845	3,677,798	3,594,898	2,961,524	2,852,287	...	499,859
Total Liabilities	4,738,388	4,331,629	4,891,499	4,877,163	5,033,126	5,119,579	...	2,600,922
Stockholders' Equity	4,185,620	4,185,874	3,994,015	3,990,005	3,761,017	3,910,862	...	321,769
Shares Outstanding	240,073	238,283	231,379	230,015	212,112	212,106	...	...
Statistical Record								
Return on Assets %	1.00	1.14	N.M.	N.M.	N.M.	9.21	...	0.60
Return on Equity %	2.17	2.42	N.M.	N.M.	N.M.	26.01	...	4.45
EBITDA Margin %	52.07	70.86	32.67	36.53	48.28	203.23	72.37	82.31
Net Margin %	17.30	28.80	0.21	N.M.	N.M.	86.65	9.46	3.93
Asset Turnover	0.08	0.08	0.08	0.08	0.07	0.11	...	0.15
Current Ratio	3.75	4.64	3.63	2.52	1.47	3.25	...	31.51
Debt to Equity	0.85	0.79	0.92	0.90	0.79	0.73	...	1.55
Price Range	17.52-14.86	18.25-14.86	18.25-14.86	18.25-14.38	19.75-15.72	18.80-18.06	18.43-18.15	...
P/E Ratio	47.35-40.16	44.51-36.24	...	...	...	69.63-66.89	...	...
Average Yield %	2.35	2.31	2.31	2.33	2.31	...	...	...

Address: 1633 Broadway, Suite 1801, New York, NY 10019 **Telephone:** 212-237-3100	**Web Site:** www.paramount-group.com **Officers:** Albert P. Behler - Chairman, President, Chief Executive Officer Wilbur N. Paes - Chief Financial Officer, Executive Vice President, Treasurer, Senior Vice President, Chief Accounting Officer	**Auditors:** Deloitte & Touche LLP **Transfer Agents:** Computershare Trust Company, N.A.

PARKER HANNIFIN CORP

Exchange	Symbol	Price	52Wk Range	Yield	P/E
NYS	PH	$199.58 (12/29/2017)	199.69-140.78	1.32	25.62

*7 Year Price Score 115.42 *NYSE Composite Index=100 *12 Month Price Score 107.56

TRADING VOLUME (thousand shares)

Interim Earnings (Per Share)

Qtr.	Sep	Dec	Mar	Jun
2014-15	1.85	1.80	2.02	1.29
2015-16	1.41	1.33	1.37	1.77
2016-17	1.55	1.78	1.75	2.16
2017-18	2.10	...	...	...

Interim Dividends (Per Share)

Amt	Decl	Ex	Rec	Pay
0.66Q	04/20/2017	05/08/2017	05/10/2017	06/02/2017
0.66Q	08/17/2017	08/24/2017	08/28/2017	09/08/2017
0.66Q	10/25/2017	11/09/2017	11/10/2017	12/01/2017
0.66Q	01/25/2018	02/08/2018	02/09/2018	03/02/2018

Indicated Div: $2.64 (Div. Reinv. Plan)

Valuation Analysis / Institutional Holding

Forecast EPS	$9.64 (01/23/2018)	No of Institutions 930
Market Cap	$26.6 Billion	Shares 125,034,344
Book Value	$5.5 Billion	% Held 75.82
Price/Book	4.81	
Price/Sales	2.10	

Business Summary: Industrial Machinery & Equipment (MIC: 7.2.1 SIC: 3492 NAIC: 332912)

Parker Hannifin is a manufacturer of motion and control technologies and systems, providing engineered solutions for a variety of mobile, industrial and aerospace markets. Co. has two reporting segments: Diversified Industrial and Aerospace Systems. Co.'s Diversified Industrial segment consist of a range of motion-control and fluid systems and components, which are categorized into the following groups: Engineered Materials, Filtration, Fluid Connectors, Motion Systems, and Instrumentation. The principal products of Co.'s Aerospace Systems Segment are used on commercial and military airframe and engine programs and include control actuation systems and components.

Recent Developments: For the quarter ended Sep 30 2017, net income increased 35.8% to US$285.5 million from US$210.2 million in the year-earlier quarter. Revenues were US$3.36 billion, up 22.7% from US$2.74 billion the year before. Direct operating expenses rose 20.3% to US$2.53 billion from US$2.11 billion in the comparable period the year before. Indirect operating expenses increased 24.4% to US$401.7 million from US$323.0 million in the equivalent prior-year period.

Prospects: Our evaluation of Parker Hannifin Corp. as of Jan. 21, 2018 is the result of our systematic analysis on three basic characteristics: earnings strength, relative valuation, and recent stock price movement. The company has managed to produce a neutral trend in earnings per share over the past 5 quarters and while recent estimates for the company have been raised by analysts, PH has posted better than expected results. Based on operating earnings yield, the company is about fairly valued when compared to all of the companies in our coverage universe. Share price changes over the past year indicates that PH will perform well over the near term.

Financial Data
(US$ in Thousands)

	3 Mos	06/30/2017	06/30/2016	06/30/2015	06/30/2014	06/30/2013	06/30/2012	06/30/2011
Earnings Per Share	7.79	7.25	5.89	6.97	6.87	6.26	7.45	6.37
Cash Flow Per Share	10.72	9.77	8.62	9.11	9.31	7.98	10.09	7.24
Tang Book Value Per Share	N.M.	N.M.	5.59	8.29	15.44	8.20	5.85	7.72
Dividends Per Share	2.610	2.580	2.520	2.370	1.860	1.700	1.540	1.250
Dividend Payout %	33.50	35.59	42.78	34.00	27.07	27.16	20.67	19.62
Income Statement								
Total Revenue	3,364,651	12,029,312	11,360,753	12,711,744	13,215,971	13,015,704	13,145,942	12,345,870
EBITDA	543,964	1,693,945	1,441,553	1,753,422	1,854,251	1,616,275	1,879,996	1,742,663
Depn & Amortn	116,107	202,868	190,308	202,776	214,965	213,722	210,508	229,238
Income Before Taxes	374,302	1,328,641	1,114,728	1,432,240	1,556,720	1,311,001	1,576,698	1,413,721
Income Taxes	88,767	344,797	307,512	419,687	515,302	362,217	421,206	356,571
Net Income	285,397	983,412	806,840	1,012,140	1,041,048	948,427	1,151,823	1,049,130
Average Shares	135,794	135,559	136,911	145,112	151,444	151,588	154,664	164,798
Balance Sheet								
Current Assets	5,004,618	4,779,718	5,207,787	5,583,092	6,071,580	5,531,186	4,498,114	4,305,256
Total Assets	15,731,279	15,489,904	12,056,738	12,295,037	13,274,362	12,540,898	11,170,282	10,886,805
Current Liabilities	3,467,124	3,395,860	2,365,941	2,350,130	3,252,796	3,520,203	2,486,013	2,391,043
Long-Term Obligations	4,788,147	4,861,895	2,675,000	2,723,960	1,508,142	1,495,960	1,503,946	1,691,086
Total Liabilities	10,206,339	10,228,255	7,481,483	7,190,750	6,614,934	6,802,472	6,273,767	5,502,951
Stockholders' Equity	5,524,940	5,261,649	4,575,255	5,104,287	6,659,428	5,738,426	4,896,515	5,383,854
Shares Outstanding	133,226	133,191	134,012	138,558	148,902	149,288	149,630	155,090
Statistical Record								
Return on Assets %	7.64	7.14	6.61	7.92	8.07	8.00	10.42	10.09
Return on Equity %	20.82	19.99	16.63	17.21	16.79	17.84	22.35	21.52
EBITDA Margin %	16.17	14.08	12.69	13.79	14.03	12.42	14.30	14.12
Net Margin %	8.48	8.18	7.10	7.96	7.88	7.29	8.76	8.50
Asset Turnover	0.91	0.87	0.93	0.99	1.02	1.10	1.19	1.19
Current Ratio	1.44	1.41	2.20	2.38	1.87	1.57	1.81	1.80
Debt to Equity	0.87	0.92	0.58	0.53	0.23	0.26	0.31	0.31
Price Range	177.11-119.29	165.22-107.07	117.15-86.51	132.78-102.96	129.52-95.32	100.96-71.84	91.58-60.81	98.49-54.80
P/E Ratio	22.74-15.31	22.79-14.77	19.89-14.69	19.05-14.77	18.85-13.87	16.13-11.48	12.29-8.16	15.46-8.60
Average Yield %	1.72	1.84	2.38	1.96	1.61	1.95	1.93	1.56

Address: 6035 Parkland Boulevard, Cleveland, OH 44124-4141	**Web Site:** www.parker.com	**Auditors:** DELOITTE & TOUCHE LLP
Telephone: 216-896-3000	**Officers:** Thomas L. Williams - Chairman, Chief Executive Officer, Executive Vice President Lee C. Banks - President, Chief Operating Officer, Executive Vice President	**Investor Contact:** 216-896-2240 **Transfer Agents:** Wells Fargo Bank, N.A., St. Paul, MN

PARSLEY ENERGY INC

Exchange	Symbol	Price	52Wk Range	Yield	P/E
NYS	PE	$29.44 (12/29/2017)	36.88-23.86	N/A	420.57

*7 Year Price Score N/A   *NYSE Composite Index=100   *12 Month Price Score 88.27

TRADING VOLUME (thousand shares)

Interim Earnings (Per Share)

Qtr.	Mar	Jun	Sep	Dec
2014	0.00	(1.19)	0.18	0.89
2015	(0.17)	(0.18)	0.01	(0.12)
2016	(0.14)	(0.13)	(0.02)	(0.18)
2017	0.13	0.17	(0.05)	...

Interim Dividends (Per Share)

No Dividends Paid

Valuation Analysis / Institutional Holding

Forecast EPS	$0.50	No of Institutions
	(01/18/2018)	420
Market Cap	$9.3 Billion	Shares
Book Value	$4.6 Billion	264,088,368
Price/Book	2.01	% Held
Price/Sales	11.40	N/A

Business Summary: Production & Extraction (MIC: 9.1.1 SIC: 1311 NAIC: 211111)

Parsley Energy is a holding company. Co. is an independent oil and natural gas company focused on the acquisition and development of unconventional oil and natural gas reserves in the Permian Basin. The Permian Basin is located in West Texas and Southeastern New Mexico and is comprised of three primary sub-areas: the Midland Basin, the Central Basin Platform and the Delaware Basin. Co.'s properties are located in the Midland and Delaware Basins, where Co. focuses on horizontal development drilling. As of Dec 31 2016, Co.'s estimated proved reserves consisted of 136.5 million barrels (MMBbls) of oil, 223.61 billion cubic feet of natural gas, and 48.5 MMBbls of natural gas liquids.

Recent Developments: For the quarter ended Sep 30 2017, net loss amounted to US$15.2 million versus a net loss of US$1.6 million in the year-earlier quarter. Revenues were US$241.0 million, up 81.9% from US$132.5 million the year before. Operating income was US$63.1 million versus US$12.3 million in the prior-year quarter, an increase of 411.1%. Direct operating expenses rose 78.8% to US$44.3 million from US$24.8 million in the comparable period the year before. Indirect operating expenses increased 40.1% to US$133.6 million from US$95.4 million in the equivalent prior-year period.

Prospects: Our evaluation of Parsley Energy Inc as of Jan. 14, 2018 is the result of our systematic analysis on three basic characteristics: earnings strength, relative valuation, and recent stock price movement. The company has suffered a very negative trend in earnings per share over the past 5 quarters and while recent estimates for the company have been raised by analysts, PE has posted better than expected results. Based on operating earnings yield, the company is overvalued when compared to all of the companies in our coverage universe. Share price changes over the past year indicates that PE will perform very poorly over the near term.

Financial Data

(US$ in Thousands)	9 Mos	6 Mos	3 Mos	12/31/2016	12/31/2015	12/31/2014	12/31/2013	12/31/2012
Earnings Per Share	0.07	0.10	(0.20)	(0.46)	(0.45)	0.42	...	...
Cash Flow Per Share	2.21	2.05	1.13	1.41	1.55	3.36	...	...
Tang Book Value Per Share	14.65	14.61	14.93	10.07	7.49	5.61	...	...
Income Statement								
Total Revenue	655,556	414,535	200,858	457,773	266,057	301,757	121,018	37,679
EBITDA	166,317	163,798	141,011	176,092	122,395	132,949	44,046	19,571
Depn & Amortn	2,439	1,545	67,354	227,200	173,600	1,500	1,100	100
Income Before Taxes	104,461	124,702	56,692	(106,341)	(96,786)	92,842	29,232	13,186
Income Taxes	25,538	30,618	18,402	(17,424)	(23,755)	36,468	1,906	554
Net Income	56,855	70,188	29,442	(74,182)	(50,484)	23,429	27,510	12,899
Average Shares	246,518	246,792	221,697	161,793	111,271	55,239	...	...
Balance Sheet								
Current Assets	474,367	727,046	2,209,176	299,488	488,326	204,161	137,326	49,078
Total Assets	8,049,433	8,085,602	6,664,129	3,938,782	2,514,192	2,051,079	742,556	181,239
Current Liabilities	513,749	507,317	344,568	344,954	228,497	220,865	191,497	59,059
Long-Term Obligations	1,487,271	1,490,597	1,490,022	1,041,324	555,924	676,845	429,970	112,913
Total Liabilities	3,444,853	3,493,109	2,565,765	1,849,144	1,249,700	1,343,838	634,524	175,222
Stockholders' Equity	4,604,580	4,592,493	4,098,364	2,089,638	1,264,492	707,241	108,032	6,017
Shares Outstanding	314,395	314,380	274,495	207,599	168,768	126,046	...	...
Statistical Record								
Return on Assets %	0.44	0.65	N.M.	N.M.	N.M.	1.68	5.96	...
Return on Equity %	0.78	1.15	N.M.	N.M.	N.M.	5.75	48.24	...
EBITDA Margin %	25.37	39.51	70.20	38.47	46.00	44.06	36.40	51.94
Net Margin %	8.67	16.93	14.66	N.M.	N.M.	7.76	22.73	34.23
Asset Turnover	0.14	0.12	0.13	0.14	0.12	0.22	0.26	...
Current Ratio	0.92	1.43	6.41	0.87	2.14	0.92	0.72	0.83
Debt to Equity	0.32	0.32	0.36	0.50	0.44	0.96	3.98	18.77
Price Range	38.27-23.86	38.27-25.86	38.27-21.76	38.27-15.66	19.82-13.50	25.16-11.26	...	...
P/E Ratio	546.71-340.86	382.70-258.60	...	...	...	59.90-26.81	...	...

Address: 303 Colorado Street, Suite 3000, Austin, TX 78701 **Telephone:** 737-704-2300	**Web Site:** www.parsleyenergy.com **Officers:** Bryan Sheffield - Chairman, President, Chief Executive Officer Brad Smith - Division Officer	**Auditors:** KPMG LLP **Transfer Agents:** American Stock Transfer & Trust Company, LLC

PEABODY ENERGY CORP

Exchange	Symbol	Price	52Wk Range	Yield	P/E
NYS	BTU	$39.37 (12/29/2017)	39.54-23.01	N/A	N/A

*7 Year Price Score N/A   *NYSE Composite Index=100   *12 Month Price Score N/A

TRADING VOLUME (thousand shares)

Interim Earnings (Per Share)

Qtr.	Mar	Jun	Sep	Dec
2014	(2.70)	(4.05)	(8.40)	(28.80)
2015	(9.75)	(57.60)	(16.73)	(25.75)
2016	(9.03)	(12.71)	(7.41)	(11.14)
2017	6.57	(0.21)	1.47	...

Interim Dividends (Per Share)

Dividend Payment Suspended

Valuation Analysis   Institutional Holding

Forecast EPS	$4.43	No of Institutions
	(01/26/2018)	414
Market Cap	$4.0 Billion	Shares
Book Value	$3.3 Billion	138,070,688
Price/Book	1.21	% Held
Price/Sales	0.73	75.79

Business Summary: Mining (MIC: 8.2.4 SIC: 5052 NAIC: 213113)

Peabody Energy engages in the mining of thermal coal and metallurgical coal. Co.'s mining operations are located in the U.S. and Australia, including an equity-affiliate mining operation in Australia. Co. also markets and brokers coal from other coal producers, both as principal and agent, and trades coal and freight-related contracts. Co.'s other energy-related commercial activities include managing its coal reserve and real estate holdings and supporting the development of clean coal technologies. At Dec 31 2016, Co. had estimated 5.60 billion tons of proven and probable coal reserves.

Recent Developments:
For the quarter ended Sep 30 2017, income from continuing operations was US$233.7 million compared with a loss of US$97.7 million in the year-earlier quarter. Net income amounted to US$230.0 million versus a net loss of US$135.8 million in the year-earlier quarter. Revenues were US$1.48 billion, up 22.4% from US$1.21 billion the year before. Operating income was US$202.9 million versus a loss of US$21.6 million in the prior-year quarter. Direct operating expenses declined 1.9% to US$1.04 billion from US$1.06 billion in the comparable period the year before. Indirect operating expenses increased 40.0% to US$229.4 million from US$163.9 million in the equivalent prior-year period.

Prospects:
Our evaluation of Peabody Energy Corp. as of Jan. 8, 2017 is the result of our systematic analysis on three basic characteristics: earnings strength, relative valuation, and recent stock price movement. The company has produced a positive trend in earnings per share over the past 5 quarters. Because the company lacks sufficient analyst estimate data, we place greater weight on the historical EPS trend as the measure of earnings strength. Based on operating earnings yield, the company is overvalued when compared to all of the companies in our coverage universe. Share price changes over the past year indicates that BTUUQ will perform very poorly over the near term.

Financial Data

(US$ in Thousands)	9 Mos	6 Mos	3 Mos	12/31/2016	12/31/2015	12/31/2014	12/31/2013	12/31/2012
Earnings Per Share	(3.31)	(12.19)	(24.69)	(40.45)	(109.98)	(44.10)	(29.55)	(32.85)
Cash Flow Per Share	5.46	4.85	34.13	(2.88)	(0.80)	18.83	40.57	84.57
Tang Book Value Per Share	25.86	23.78	26.09	17.11	49.56	150.43	217.07	273.91
Dividends Per Share	...	...	...	...	0.075	5.100	5.100	5.100
Income Statement								
Total Revenue	2,735,500	1,258,300	1,326,200	4,715,300	5,609,200	6,792,200	7,013,700	8,077,500
EBITDA	652,600	278,600	261,600	(16,200)	(944,500)	628,200	455,700	897,100
Depn & Amortn	342,800	148,300	119,900	465,400	572,200	655,700	740,300	663,400
Income Before Taxes	229,500	90,400	111,500	(774,500)	(1,974,400)	(440,300)	(694,100)	(147,400)
Income Taxes	(79,400)	4,700	(4,500)	(84,000)	(176,400)	201,200	(448,300)	262,300
Net Income	319,800	94,900	122,100	(739,800)	(1,996,000)	(787,000)	(524,900)	(585,700)
Average Shares	103,100	96,800	18,400	18,300	18,100	17,873	17,806	17,866
Balance Sheet								
Current Assets	1,942,600	1,978,100	3,206,200	2,090,600	1,378,000	1,711,000	1,992,700	2,575,500
Total Assets	8,073,400	8,315,200	12,836,500	11,777,700	11,021,300	13,191,100	14,133,400	15,809,000
Current Liabilities	1,113,100	1,337,200	986,200	1,011,800	7,392,300	1,863,100	1,775,500	1,674,100
Long-Term Obligations	1,612,000	1,768,100	950,500	...	385,200	5,965,600	5,970,700	6,205,100
Total Liabilities	4,725,900	5,131,800	12,353,900	11,447,500	10,104,400	10,466,300	10,224,700	10,904,100
Stockholders' Equity	3,347,500	3,183,400	482,600	330,200	916,900	2,724,800	3,908,700	4,904,900
Shares Outstanding	102,700	100,200	18,500	19,300	18,500	18,113	18,006	17,906
Statistical Record								
Return on Assets %	2.35	N.M.	N.M.	N.M.	N.M.	N.M.	N.M.	N.M.
Return on Equity %	12.32	N.M.	N.M.	N.M.	N.M.	N.M.	N.M.	N.M.
EBITDA Margin %	23.86	22.14	19.73	N.M.	N.M.	9.25	6.50	11.11
Net Margin %	11.69	7.54	9.21	N.M.	N.M.	N.M.	N.M.	N.M.
Asset Turnover	0.54	0.51	0.41	0.41	0.46	0.50	0.47	0.50
Current Ratio	1.75	1.48	3.25	2.07	0.19	0.92	1.12	1.54
Debt to Equity	0.48	0.56	1.97	...	0.42	2.19	1.53	1.27
Price Range	31.00-23.01	31.00-23.01	...	...	...	...	...	...

Address: 701 Market Street, St. Louis, MO 63101-1826 **Telephone:** 314-342-3400	**Web Site:** www.peabodyenergy.com **Officers:** Glenn L. Kellow - President, Chief Operating Officer, Chief Executive Officer Amy B. Schwetz - Executive Vice President, Chief Financial Officer	**Auditors:** Ernst & Young LLP **Investor Contact:** 314-342-7900 **Transfer Agents:** American Stock Transfer & Trust Company

PENNEY (J.C.) CO.,INC. (HOLDING CO.)

Exchange	Symbol	Price	52Wk Range	Yield	P/E
NYS	JCP	$3.16 (12/29/2017)	8.47-2.37	N/A	N/A

*7 Year Price Score 25.17 ***NYSE Composite Index=100** ***12 Month Price Score 58.75**

Interim Earnings (Per Share)

Qtr.	Apr	Jul	Oct	Jan
2014-15	(1.15)	(0.56)	(0.62)	(0.20)
2015-16	(0.55)	(0.45)	(0.45)	(0.23)
2016-17	(0.22)	(0.18)	(0.22)	0.62
2017-18	(0.58)	(0.20)	(0.41)	...

Interim Dividends (Per Share)

Dividend Payment Suspended

Valuation Analysis **Institutional Holding**

Forecast EPS	$0.08	No of Institutions
	(01/18/2018)	502
Market Cap	$983.1 Million	Shares
Book Value	$1.1 Billion	293,681,984
Price/Book	0.91	% Held
Price/Sales	0.08	63.32

Business Summary: Retail - General Merchandise/Department Stores (MIC: 2.1.1 SIC: 5311 NAIC: 452111)

J.C. Penney Company is a holding company whose principal operating subsidiary is J. C. Penney Corporation, Inc. Co.'s business consists of selling merchandise and services to consumers through its department stores and its website at jcpenney.com. Co. sells family apparel and footwear, accessories, fine and fashion jewelry, beauty products through Sephora inside JCPenney and home furnishings. In addition, Co.'s department stores provide its customers with services such as styling salon, optical, portrait photography and custom decorating. As of Jan 28 2017, Co. operated 1,013 department stores in 49 states and Puerto Rico.

Recent Developments: For the quarter ended Oct 28 2017, net loss amounted to US$128.0 million versus a net loss of US$67.0 million in the year-earlier quarter. Revenues were US$2.81 billion, down 1.8% from US$2.86 billion the year before. Operating loss was US$79.0 million versus an income of US$23.0 million in the prior-year quarter. Direct operating expenses rose 3.2% to US$1.85 billion from US$1.80 billion in the comparable period the year before. Indirect operating expenses decreased 0.5% to US$1.03 billion from US$1.04 billion in the equivalent prior-year period.

Prospects: Our evaluation of Penney (J.C.) Co.,Inc. as of Jan. 14, 2018 is the result of our systematic analysis on three basic characteristics: earnings strength, relative valuation, and recent stock price movement. The company has suffered a very negative trend in earnings per share over the past 5 quarters and while recent estimates for the company have been raised by analysts, JCP has posted better than expected results. Based on operating earnings yield, the company is undervalued when compared to all of the companies in our coverage universe. Share price changes over the past year indicates that JCP will perform very poorly over the near term.

Financial Data

(US$ in Thousands)	9 Mos	6 Mos	3 Mos	01/28/2017	01/30/2016	01/31/2015	02/01/2014	02/02/2013
Earnings Per Share	(0.57)	(0.38)	(0.36)	...	(1.68)	(2.53)	(5.57)	(4.49)
Cash Flow Per Share	1.77	1.92	1.23	1.09	1.44	0.79	(7.30)	(0.04)
Tang Book Value Per Share	3.47	3.72	3.89	2.64	2.64	4.64	8.38	11.78
Dividends Per Share	...	...	...	...	...	...	...	0.200
Income Statement								
Total Revenue	8,475,000	5,668,000	2,706,000	12,547,000	12,625,000	12,257,000	11,859,000	12,985,000
EBITDA	254,000	202,000	40,000	974,000	517,000	289,000	(933,000)	(767,000)
Depn & Amortn	420,000	289,000	145,000	609,000	616,000	631,000	601,000	543,000
Income Before Taxes	(410,000)	(253,000)	(192,000)	2,000	(504,000)	(748,000)	(1,886,000)	(1,536,000)
Income Taxes	(40,000)	(11,000)	(12,000)	1,000	9,000	23,000	(498,000)	(551,000)
Net Income	(370,000)	(242,000)	(180,000)	1,000	(513,000)	(771,000)	(1,388,000)	(985,000)
Average Shares	311,600	310,800	309,600	313,000	305,900	305,200	249,300	219,200
Balance Sheet								
Current Assets	3,793,000	3,314,000	3,540,000	4,097,000	4,018,000	4,331,000	4,833,000	3,683,000
Total Assets	8,744,000	8,326,000	8,587,000	9,314,000	9,442,000	10,404,000	11,801,000	9,781,000
Current Liabilities	2,638,000	2,282,000	2,247,000	2,419,000	2,412,000	2,241,000	2,846,000	2,583,000
Long-Term Obligations	4,253,000	4,052,000	4,283,000	4,558,000	4,678,000	5,360,000	4,901,000	2,956,000
Total Liabilities	7,666,000	7,171,000	7,382,000	7,960,000	8,133,000	8,490,000	8,714,000	6,610,000
Stockholders' Equity	1,078,000	1,155,000	1,205,000	1,354,000	1,309,000	1,914,000	3,087,000	3,171,000
Shares Outstanding	311,100	310,300	309,800	308,300	306,100	304,900	304,600	219,300
Statistical Record								
Return on Assets %	N.M.	N.M.	N.M.	0.01	N.M.	N.M.	N.M.	N.M.
Return on Equity %	N.M.	N.M.	N.M.	0.08	N.M.	N.M.	N.M.	N.M.
EBITDA Margin %	3.00	3.56	1.48	7.76	4.10	2.36	N.M.	N.M.
Net Margin %	N.M.	N.M.	N.M.	0.01	N.M.	N.M.	N.M.	N.M.
Asset Turnover	1.36	1.43	1.40	1.34	1.28	1.11	1.10	1.20
Current Ratio	1.44	1.45	1.58	1.69	1.67	1.93	1.70	1.43
Debt to Equity	3.95	3.51	3.55	3.37	3.57	2.80	1.59	0.93
Price Range	10.56-3.12	11.29-4.33	11.29-5.38	11.86-6.45	9.98-6.31	11.20-5.08	22.47-5.77	43.13-16.28
Average Yield %	...	...	...	...	...	...	...	0.75

Address: 6501 Legacy Drive, Plano, TX 75024-3698
Telephone: 972-431-1000

Web Site: www.jcpenney.com
Officers: Joseph M. McFarland - Executive Vice President Marvin R. Ellison - Chairman, President, Chief Executive Officer - Designate

Auditors: KPMG LLP
Investor Contact: 972-431-5500
Transfer Agents: ComputerShare Investor Services, Providence, RI

PENTAIR PLC

Exchange	Symbol	Price	52Wk Range	Yield	P/E
NYS	PNR	$70.62 (12/29/2017)	71.17-56.57	1.98	21.40

*7 Year Price Score 90.28   *NYSE Composite Index=100   *12 Month Price Score 101.31

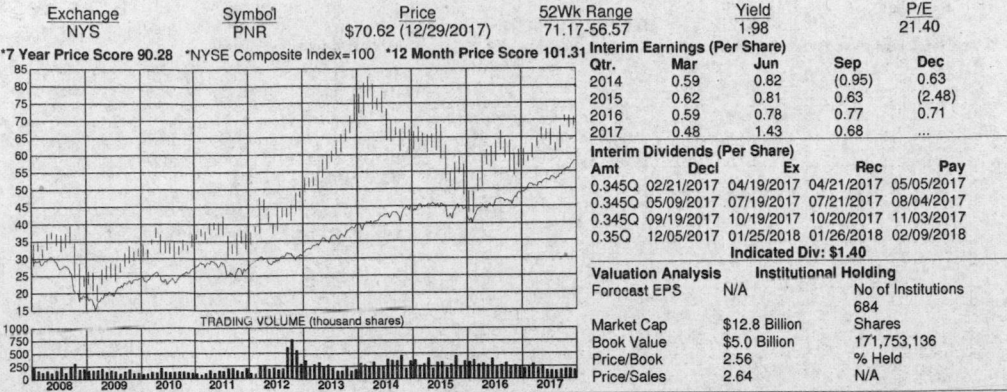

TRADING VOLUME (thousand shares)

Interim Earnings (Per Share)

Qtr.	Mar	Jun	Sep	Dec
2014	0.59	0.82	(0.95)	0.63
2015	0.62	0.81	0.63	(2.48)
2016	0.59	0.78	0.77	0.71
2017	0.48	1.43	0.68	...

Interim Dividends (Per Share)

Amt	Decl	Ex	Rec	Pay
0.345Q	02/21/2017	04/19/2017	04/21/2017	05/05/2017
0.345Q	05/09/2017	07/19/2017	07/21/2017	08/04/2017
0.345Q	09/19/2017	10/19/2017	10/20/2017	11/03/2017
0.35Q	12/05/2017	01/25/2018	01/26/2018	02/09/2018

Indicated Div: $1.40

Valuation Analysis   **Institutional Holding**

Forecast EPS	N/A	No of Institutions
		684
Market Cap	$12.8 Billion	Shares
Book Value	$5.0 Billion	171,753,136
Price/Book	2.56	% Held
Price/Sales	2.64	N/A

Business Summary: Industrial Machinery & Equipment (MIC: 7.2.1 SIC: 3559 NAIC: 333298)

Pentair is an industrial manufacturing company. Co. has three segments: Water Quality Systems, which designs, manufactures, markets and services water system products for filtration and fluid management in food and beverage, water, swimming pools and aquaculture applications; Flow & Filtration Solutions, which designs, manufactures, markets and services solutions for the filtration, separation, flow and fluid management in agriculture, food and beverage processing, water supply and disposal and industrial applications; and Technical Solutions, which designs, manufactures, markets and services products that guard and protect electrical and electronic equipment, and heat management solutions.

Recent Developments: For the quarter ended Sep 30 2017, income from continuing operations increased 8.2% to US$127.1 million from US$117.5 million in the year-earlier quarter. Net income decreased 11.1% to US$125.4 million from US$141.0 million in the year-earlier quarter. Revenues were US$1.23 billion, up 1.3% from US$1.21 billion the year before. Operating income was US$192.2 million versus US$182.8 million in the prior-year quarter, an increase of 5.1%. Direct operating expenses rose 0.2% to US$771.5 million from US$769.8 million in the comparable period the year before. Indirect operating expenses increased 1.9% to US$263.1 million from US$258.1 million in the equivalent prior-year period.

Prospects: Our evaluation of Pentair PLC as of Sep. 17, 2017 is the result of our systematic analysis on three basic characteristics: earnings strength, relative valuation, and recent stock price movement. The company has enjoyed a very positive trend in earnings per share over the past 5 quarters and while recent estimates for the company have remained steady, PNR has posted results that fell short of analysts expectations. Based on operating earnings yield, the company is undervalued when compared to all of the companies in our coverage universe. Share price changes over the past year indicates that PNR will perform in line with the market over the near term.

Financial Data

(US$ in Thousands)	9 Mos	6 Mos	3 Mos	12/31/2016	12/31/2015	12/31/2014	12/31/2013	12/31/2012
Earnings Per Share	3.30	3.39	2.74	2.85	(0.42)	1.11	2.62	(0.84)
Cash Flow Per Share	3.67	3.56	4.23	4.74	4.10	5.29	4.55	0.53
Dividends Per Share	1.375	1.370	1.355	1.340	...	...	...	0.880
Dividend Payout %	41.67	40.41	49.45	47.02	...	...	...	...
Income Statement								
Total Revenue	3,675,600	2,448,800	1,183,500	4,890,000	6,449,000	7,039,000	7,479,700	4,416,146
EBITDA	575,300	340,400	183,800	781,400	313,500	990,400	942,600	(30,651)
Depn & Amortn	137,100	90,600	45,400	84,600	139,500	138,700	148,900	87,835
Income Before Taxes	364,000	189,500	103,400	556,700	71,300	783,100	724,600	(186,121)
Income Taxes	88,800	41,100	22,900	109,400	139,100	177,300	183,800	(79,353)
Net Income	476,900	351,500	87,800	522,200	(76,400)	214,900	536,800	(107,186)
Average Shares	183,500	183,800	184,000	183,100	182,600	193,700	204,600	127,368
Balance Sheet								
Current Assets	1,705,800	1,754,800	2,841,100	2,672,000	2,780,600	2,894,100	3,232,100	3,260,368
Total Assets	8,628,800	8,669,100	11,818,000	11,534,800	11,857,000	10,655,200	11,743,300	11,795,311
Current Liabilities	1,072,600	1,048,400	1,397,600	1,471,200	1,486,500	1,639,500	1,610,200	1,537,921
Long-Term Obligations	1,503,400	1,698,900	4,528,900	4,278,400	4,709,300	2,997,400	2,552,600	2,454,278
Total Liabilities	3,620,200	3,765,600	7,443,200	7,280,400	7,848,200	5,991,400	5,648,000	5,428,451
Stockholders' Equity	5,008,600	4,903,500	4,374,800	4,254,400	4,008,800	4,663,800	6,095,300	6,366,860
Shares Outstanding	181,597	181,479	182,200	181,800	180,500	182,500	228,600	206,137
Statistical Record								
Return on Assets %	5.99	6.11	4.21	4.45	N.M.	1.92	4.56	N.M.
Return on Equity %	12.98	13.75	11.88	12.60	N.M.	3.99	8.61	N.M.
EBITDA Margin %	15.65	13.90	15.53	15.98	4.86	14.07	12.60	N.M.
Net Margin %	12.97	14.35	7.42	10.68	N.M.	3.05	7.18	N.M.
Asset Turnover	0.48	0.47	0.45	0.42	0.57	0.63	0.64	0.54
Current Ratio	1.59	1.67	2.03	1.82	1.87	1.77	2.01	2.12
Debt to Equity	0.30	0.35	1.04	1.01	1.17	0.64	0.42	0.39
Price Range	67.96-53.92	67.73-53.92	66.77-50.70	66.77-42.88	68.75-48.21	82.81-59.84	77.67-49.15	49.25-34.12
P/E Ratio	20.59-16.34	19.98-15.91	24.37-18.50	23.43-15.05	...	74.60-53.91	29.65-18.76	...
Average Yield %	2.23	2.23	2.28	2.36	...	...	...	2.09

Address: 43 London Wall, London, 55416-1259	Web Site: www.pentair.com	Auditors: Deloitte & Touche LLP
Telephone: 207-347-8925	Officers: Randall J. Hogan - Chairman, Division Officer, President (frmr), Chief Executive Officer, Executive Vice President (frmr), Chief Operating Officer (frmr) John L. Stauch - Incoming Chief Executive Officer, Chief Financial Officer, Executive Vice President	Investor Contact: 763-656-5575 Transfer Agents: Wells Fargo

PERFORMANCE FOOD GROUP CO

Exchange	Symbol	Price	52Wk Range	Yield	P/E
NYS	PFGC	$33.10 (12/29/2017)	33.20-21.90	N/A	32.14

*7 Year Price Score N/A   *NYSE Composite Index=100   *12 Month Price Score 105.49

Interim Earnings (Per Share)

Qtr.	Sep	Dec	Mar	Jun
2014-15	0.08	0.15	0.03	0.39
2015-16	0.14	0.17	0.09	0.30
2016-17	0.12	0.22	0.20	0.39
2017-18	0.22	...	...	...

Interim Dividends (Per Share)

No Dividends Paid

Valuation Analysis   **Institutional Holding**

Forecast EPS	$1.43	No of Institutions
	(01/17/2018)	182
Market Cap	$3.3 Billion	Shares
Book Value	$949.4 Million	90,405,568
Price/Book	3.52	% Held
Price/Sales	0.20	N/A

TRADING VOLUME (thousand shares)

Business Summary: Retail - Food & Beverage, Drug & Tobacco (MIC: 2.1.2 SIC: 5141 NAIC: 445110)

Performance Food Group, through its subsidiaries, markets and distributes approximately 150,000 food and food-related products from 76 distribution centers to over 150,000 customer locations across the U.S. Co.'s products include a line of frozen foods, such as meats, fully prepared appetizers and entrees, fruits, vegetables, and desserts; a line of canned and dry foods; fresh meats; dairy products; beverage products; and imported specialties. Co. also supplies a variety of non-food items including paper products such as pizza boxes, disposable napkins, plates and cups; tableware such as china and silverware; cookware such as pots, pans, and utensils; restaurant; and cleaning supplies.

Recent Developments: For the quarter ended Sep 30 2017, net income increased 85.2% to US$22.6 million from US$12.2 million in the year-earlier quarter. Revenues were US$4.36 billion, up 7.9% from US$4.05 billion the year before. Operating income was US$50.5 million versus US$31.6 million in the prior-year quarter, an increase of 59.8%. Direct operating expenses rose 7.8% to US$3.81 billion from US$3.53 billion in the comparable period the year before. Indirect operating expenses increased 5.1% to US$504.2 million from US$479.7 million in the equivalent prior-year period.

Prospects: Our evaluation of Performance Food Group Company as of Jan. 14, 2018 is the result of our systematic analysis on three basic characteristics: earnings strength, relative valuation, and recent stock price movement. The company has managed to produce a neutral trend in earnings per share over the past 5 quarters and while recent estimates for the company have been raised by analysts, PFGC has posted better than expected results. Based on operating earnings yield, the company is about fairly valued when compared to all of the companies in our coverage universe. Share price changes over the past year indicates that PFGC will perform well over the near term.

Financial Data

(US$ in Thousands)	3 Mos	07/01/2017	07/02/2016	06/27/2015	06/28/2014	06/29/2013
Earnings Per Share	1.03	0.93	0.70	0.64	0.18	0.10
Cash Flow Per Share	2.90	2.02	2.40	1.47	1.38	1.62
Tang Book Value Per Share	N.M.	0.06	N.M.	N.M.	N.M.	...
Dividends Per Share	...	...	...	...	...	2.530
Dividend Payout %	...	...	...	...	...	2,530.00
Income Statement						
Total Revenue	4,364,900	16,761,800	16,104,800	15,270,000	13,685,700	12,826,500
EBITDA	83,400	338,700	317,000	303,600	249,000	233,400
Depn & Amortn	32,600	126,100	118,600	121,300	132,700	120,000
Income Before Taxes	36,200	157,700	114,500	96,600	30,200	19,500
Income Taxes	13,600	61,400	46,200	40,100	14,700	11,100
Net Income	22,600	96,300	68,300	56,500	15,500	8,400
Average Shares	103,900	103,036	98,128	87,613	87,533	87,458
Balance Sheet						
Current Assets	2,132,800	2,084,900	1,938,900	1,900,300	1,727,300	...
Total Assets	3,883,300	3,804,100	3,455,400	3,390,900	3,239,800	...
Current Liabilities	1,375,200	1,383,300	1,316,700	1,277,000	1,170,400	...
Long-Term Obligations	1,351,800	1,285,900	1,143,100	1,429,600	1,449,000	...
Total Liabilities	2,933,900	2,878,600	2,652,600	2,897,900	2,805,700	...
Stockholders' Equity	949,400	925,500	802,800	493,000	434,100	...
Shares Outstanding	101,000	100,805	99,901	86,878	86,874	...
Statistical Record						
Return on Assets %	2.88	2.66	1.96	1.71	...	...
Return on Equity %	12.06	11.17	10.37	12.22	...	...
EBITDA Margin %	1.91	2.02	1.97	1.99	1.82	1.82
Net Margin %	0.52	0.57	0.42	0.37	0.11	0.07
Asset Turnover	4.61	4.63	4.63	4.62	...	...
Current Ratio	1.55	1.51	1.47	1.49	1.48	...
Debt to Equity	1.42	1.39	1.42	2.90	3.34	...
Price Range	29.40-20.45	28.85-20.45	27.43-19.20	...	...	...
P/E Ratio	28.54-19.85	31.02-21.99	39.19-27.43	...	...	...

Address: 12500 West Creek Parkway, Richmond, VA 23238
Telephone: 804-484-7700

Web Site: www.pfgc.com
Officers: Douglas M. Steenland - Chairman Thomas G. Ondrof - Executive Vice President, Chief Financial Officer

Auditors: DELOITTE & TOUCHE LLP
Transfer Agents: Computershare Trust Company, N.A.

PERKINELMER, INC.

Exchange	Symbol	Price	52Wk Range	Yield	P/E
NYS	PKI	$73.12 (12/29/2017)	73.84-51.57	0.38	20.37

*7 Year Price Score 117.88 *NYSE Composite Index=100 *12 Month Price Score 106.37

Interim Earnings (Per Share)

Qtr.	Mar	Jun	Sep	Dec
2014	0.30	0.44	0.37	0.27
2015	0.36	0.43	0.48	0.60
2016	0.43	0.58	0.53	0.58
2017	0.35	1.84	0.82	...

Interim Dividends (Per Share)

Amt	Decl	Ex	Rec	Pay
0.07Q	01/27/2017	04/11/2017	04/14/2017	05/10/2017
0.07Q	04/28/2017	07/19/2017	07/21/2017	08/10/2017
0.07Q	07/24/2017	10/19/2017	10/20/2017	11/10/2017
0.07Q	10/27/2017	01/18/2018	01/19/2018	02/09/2018

Indicated Div: $0.28

Valuation Analysis — **Institutional Holding**

Forecast EPS	$2.88	No of Institutions
(01/18/2018)		519
Market Cap	$8.1 Billion	Shares
Book Value	$2.5 Billion	140,572,752
Price/Book	3.18	% Held
Price/Sales	3.89	88.52

TRADING VOLUME (thousand shares)

Business Summary: Biotechnology (MIC: 4.1.2 SIC: 3826 NAIC: 334516)

PerkinElmer is a provider of products, services and solutions to the diagnostics, research, environmental, industrial, food and laboratory services markets. The principal products and services of Co.'s two operating segments are: Diagnostics, which develops diagnostics, tools and applications focused on clinically-oriented customers, particularly within the reproductive health, market diagnostics and applied genomics markets; and Discovery & Analytical Solutions, which provides products and services targeted towards the environmental, industrial, food, life sciences research and laboratory services markets.

Recent Developments: For the quarter ended Oct 1 2017, income from continuing operations increased 79.1% to US$96.5 million from US$53.9 million in the year-earlier quarter. Net income increased 56.7% to US$91.1 million from US$58.1 million in the year-earlier quarter. Revenues were US$554.3 million, up 7.7% from US$514.5 million the year before. Operating income was US$79.8 million versus US$75.8 million in the prior-year quarter, an increase of 5.3%. Direct operating expenses rose 7.3% to US$285.5 million from US$265.9 million in the comparable period the year before. Indirect operating expenses increased 9.4% to US$189.0 million from US$172.8 million in the equivalent prior-year period.

Prospects: Our evaluation of PerkinElmer Inc. as of Jan. 14, 2018 is the result of our systematic analysis on three basic characteristics: earnings strength, relative valuation, and recent stock price movement. The company has enjoyed a very positive trend in earnings per share over the past 5 quarters and while recent estimates for the company have remained steady, PKI has posted better than expected results. Based on operating earnings yield, the company is about fairly valued when compared to all of the companies in our coverage universe. Share price changes over the past year indicates that PKI will perform in line with the market over the near term.

Financial Data (US$ in Thousands)	9 Mos	6 Mos	3 Mos	01/01/2017	01/03/2016	12/28/2014	12/29/2013	12/30/2012
Earnings Per Share	3.59	3.30	2.04	2.12	1.87	1.39	1.47	0.61
Cash Flow Per Share	2.81	2.95	3.40	3.21	2.51	2.51	1.42	1.34
Dividends Per Share	0.280	0.280	0.280	0.280	0.280	0.280	0.280	0.280
Dividend Payout %	7.80	8.48	13.73	13.21	14.97	20.14	19.05	45.90
Income Statement								
Total Revenue	1,615,352	1,061,077	514,115	2,115,517	2,262,359	2,237,219	2,166,232	2,115,205
EBITDA	253,003	137,072	54,340	313,394	314,739	238,506	240,706	131,227
Depn & Amortn	6,176	5,471	2,761	28,500	33,400	33,300	38,100	35,600
Income Before Taxes	215,829	110,775	39,983	244,068	244,015	169,603	153,332	50,587
Income Taxes	20,495	11,987	3,921	28,362	31,327	8,437	(14,592)	(17,854)
Net Income	333,750	242,672	38,603	234,299	212,425	157,778	167,212	69,940
Average Shares	110,993	110,762	110,204	110,313	113,315	113,739	113,503	114,860
Balance Sheet								
Current Assets	1,545,660	1,433,826	1,116,579	1,189,931	1,033,161	1,068,551	1,044,838	971,754
Total Assets	4,738,955	4,605,104	4,340,501	4,276,683	4,166,295	4,134,075	3,946,712	3,901,762
Current Liabilities	597,512	589,388	600,608	603,355	561,485	597,310	602,796	581,100
Long-Term Obligations	1,109,269	1,089,395	1,052,677	1,045,254	1,011,762	1,051,892	932,104	938,824
Total Liabilities	2,202,926	2,166,468	2,131,514	2,123,113	2,055,854	2,091,973	1,952,225	1,961,950
Stockholders' Equity	2,536,029	2,438,636	2,208,987	2,153,570	2,110,441	2,042,102	1,994,487	1,939,812
Shares Outstanding	110,207	110,196	109,859	109,617	112,034	112,481	112,626	115,036
Statistical Record								
Return on Assets %	8.82	8.31	5.27	5.57	5.04	3.92	4.27	1.81
Return on Equity %	17.07	16.15	10.59	11.02	10.07	7.84	8.52	3.71
EBITDA Margin %	15.66	12.92	10.57	14.81	13.91	10.66	11.11	6.20
Net Margin %	20.66	22.87	7.51	11.08	9.39	7.05	7.72	3.31
Asset Turnover	0.46	0.47	0.49	0.50	0.54	0.56	0.55	0.55
Current Ratio	2.59	2.43	1.86	1.97	1.84	1.79	1.73	1.67
Debt to Equity	0.44	0.45	0.48	0.49	0.48	0.52	0.47	0.48
Price Range	69.94-49.95	68.45-49.95	58.06-48.58	56.92-41.45	54.36-42.66	48.25-39.83	41.18-30.35	32.29-20.00
P/E Ratio	19.48-13.91	20.74-15.14	28.46-23.81	26.85-19.55	29.07-22.81	34.71-28.65	28.01-20.65	52.93-32.79
Average Yield %	0.47	0.50	0.52	0.54	0.56	0.63	0.79	1.02

Address: 940 Winter Street, Waltham, MA 02451	**Web Site:** www.perkinelmer.com	**Auditors:** Deloitte & Touche LLP
Telephone: 781-663-6900	**Officers:** Robert F. Friel - Chairman, President, Chief Executive Officer James Corbett - Executive Vice President, Senior Vice President, Division Officer	**Investor Contact:** 781-663-6900
Fax: 781-663-6052		**Transfer Agents:** Computershare, Inc., Providence , RI

PENSKE AUTOMOTIVE GROUP INC

*7 Year Price Score 96.89 ***NYSE Composite Index=100** ***12 Month Price Score 96.37**

Interim Earnings (Per Share)

Qtr.	Mar	Jun	Sep	Dec
2014	0.75	0.81	0.83	0.79
2015	0.83	1.04	0.96	0.79
2016	0.90	1.10	1.03	0.97
2017	0.96	1.23	1.10	...

Interim Dividends (Per Share)

Amt	Decl	Ex	Rec	Pay
0.30Q	02/09/2017	02/15/2017	02/20/2017	03/01/2017
0.31Q	05/10/2017	05/18/2017	05/22/2017	06/01/2017
0.32Q	07/26/2017	08/08/2017	08/10/2017	09/01/2017
0.33Q	10/11/2017	11/09/2017	11/10/2017	12/01/2017

Indicated Div: $1.32

Valuation Analysis | **Institutional Holding**

Forecast EPS	$4.31	No of Institutions
	(01/16/2018)	337
Market Cap	$4.1 Billion	Shares
Book Value	$2.1 Billion	100,014,000
Price/Book	1.97	% Held
Price/Sales	0.20	N/A

Business Summary: Retail - Automotive (MIC: 2.1.4 SIC: 5511 NAIC: 441110)

Penske Automotive Group is a holding company. Through its subsidiaries, Co. operates in four segments: Retail Automotive, consisting of its retail automotive dealership operations; Retail Commercial Truck, consisting of its retail commercial truck dealership operations in the U.S. and Canada; Other, consisting of its commercial vehicle and power systems distribution operations and other non-automotive consolidated operations; and Non-Automotive Investments, consisting of its equity method investments in non-automotive operations. At Dec 31 2016, Co. operated 355 retail automotive franchises, of which 164 franchises were located in the U.S. and 191 franchises were located outside of the U.S.

Recent Developments: For the quarter ended Sep 30 2017, income from continuing operations increased 6.6% to US$94.2 million from US$88.4 million in the year-earlier quarter. Net income increased 6.6% to US$94.3 million from US$88.5 million in the year-earlier quarter. Revenues were US$5.52 billion, up 7.2% from US$5.15 billion the year before. Operating income was US$152.2 million versus US$141.5 million in the prior-year quarter, an increase of 7.6%. Direct operating expenses rose 6.7% to US$4.70 billion from US$4.41 billion in the comparable period the year before. Indirect operating expenses increased 11.2% to US$670.4 million from US$602.7 million in the equivalent prior year period.

Prospects: Our evaluation of Penske Automotive Group Inc. as of Jan. 14, 2018 is the result of our systematic analysis on three basic characteristics: earnings strength, relative valuation, and recent stock price movement. The company has managed to produce a neutral trend in earnings per share over the past 5 quarters and while recent estimates for the company have been mixed, PAG has posted better than expected results. Based on operating earnings yield, the company is undervalued when compared to all of the companies in our coverage universe. Share price changes over the past year indicates that PAG will perform very poorly over the near term.

Financial Data

(US$ in Thousands)	9 Mos	6 Mos	3 Mos	12/31/2016	12/31/2015	12/31/2014	12/31/2013	12/31/2012
Earnings Per Share	4.26	4.19	4.06	3.99	3.63	3.17	2.70	2.05
Cash Flow Per Share	4.37	4.90	5.63	4.24	4.36	4.06	3.49	3.62
Tang Book Value Per Share	N.M.	N.M.	N.M.	0.46	0.66	0.00	0.61	0.51
Dividends Per Share	1.220	1.180	1.140	1.100	0.940	0.780	0.620	0.460
Dividend Payout %	28.64	28.16	28.08	27.57	25.90	24.61	22.96	22.44
Income Statement								
Total Revenue	15,988,900	10,464,500	5,081,100	20,118,500	19,284,900	17,177,200	14,705,400	13,163,517
EBITDA	544,400	367,900	172,600	664,600	644,500	590,100	497,900	401,100
Depn & Amortn	70,000	45,700	22,400	89,700	78,000	70,000	61,700	53,995
Income Before Taxes	349,600	241,600	111,500	438,600	452,600	421,200	344,700	261,416
Income Taxes	136,000	91,300	41,100	160,700	158,000	153,200	124,300	94,330
Net Income	283,200	188,800	82,600	342,900	326,100	286,700	244,200	185,540
Average Shares	85,966	86,141	85,600	86,000	89,759	90,354	90,330	90,342
Balance Sheet								
Current Assets	4,842,800	4,664,500	4,589,500	4,421,500	4,408,100	3,867,700	3,346,600	2,773,083
Total Assets	10,282,300	9,711,900	9,395,400	8,861,100	8,022,700	7,228,200	6,415,500	5,378,990
Current Liabilities	4,676,600	4,559,700	4,420,200	4,229,600	4,286,900	3,630,300	3,331,800	2,693,556
Long-Term Obligations	2,170,500	1,955,800	1,989,000	1,828,800	1,255,100	1,316,000	1,033,200	918,024
Total Liabilities	8,203,300	7,727,600	7,527,700	7,110,200	6,232,500	5,575,400	4,911,100	4,074,775
Stockholders' Equity	2,079,000	1,984,300	1,867,700	1,750,900	1,790,200	1,652,800	1,504,400	1,304,215
Shares Outstanding	85,768	86,020	86,140	85,214	89,524	90,244	90,243	90,294
Statistical Record								
Return on Assets %	3.88	4.04	3.94	4.05	4.28	4.20	4.14	3.75
Return on Equity %	19.10	19.50	19.51	19.31	18.94	18.16	17.39	15.17
EBITDA Margin %	3.40	3.52	3.40	3.30	3.34	3.44	3.39	3.05
Net Margin %	1.77	1.80	1.63	1.70	1.69	1.67	1.66	1.41
Asset Turnover	2.22	2.31	2.32	2.38	2.53	2.52	2.49	2.66
Current Ratio	1.04	1.02	1.04	1.05	1.03	1.07	1.00	1.03
Debt to Equity	1.04	0.99	1.06	1.04	0.70	0.80	0.69	0.70
Price Range	55.98-39.04	55.98-29.96	55.98-29.96	55.98-29.96	54.21-41.79	51.16-37.51	47.42-28.40	32.11-18.58
P/E Ratio	13.14-9.16	13.36-7.15	13.79-7.38	14.03-7.51	14.93-11.51	16.14-11.83	17.56-10.52	15.66-9.06
Average Yield %	2.61	2.55	2.57	2.71	1.89	1.72	1.72	1.77

Address: 2555 Telegraph Road, Bloomfield Hills, MI 48302-0954	**Web Site:** www.penskeautomotive.com	**Auditors:** Deloitte & Touche LLP
Telephone: 248-648-2500	**Officers:** Roger S. Penske - Chairman, Chief Executive Officer Bud Denke - Executive Vice President	**Investor Contact:** 866-715-5289
Fax: 248-648-2525		**Transfer Agents:** ComputerShare Investor Services, Providence, RI

PFIZER INC

Exchange	Symbol	Price	52Wk Range	Yield	P/E
NYS	PFE	$36.22 (12/29/2017)	37.20-31.15	3.75	22.22

*7 Year Price Score 92.10   *NYSE Composite Index=100   *12 Month Price Score 99.72

TRADING VOLUME (thousand shares)

Interim Earnings (Per Share)

Qtr.	Mar	Jun	Sep	Dec
2014	0.36	0.45	0.42	0.19
2015	0.38	0.42	0.34	(0.03)
2016	0.49	0.33	0.21	0.14
2017	0.51	0.51	0.47	...

Interim Dividends (Per Share)

Amt	Decl	Ex	Rec	Pay
0.32Q	04/27/2017	05/10/2017	05/12/2017	06/01/2017
0.32Q	06/22/2017	08/02/2017	08/04/2017	09/01/2017
0.32Q	09/27/2017	11/09/2017	11/10/2017	12/01/2017
0.34Q	12/18/2017	02/01/2018	02/02/2018	03/01/2018

Indicated Div: $1.36

Valuation Analysis

		Institutional Holding	
Forecast EPS	$2.60	No of Institutions	
	(01/26/2018)	2847	
Market Cap	$215.9 Billion	Shares	
Book Value	$60.8 Billion	5,417,055,232	
Price/Book	3.55	% Held	
Price/Sales	4.11	58.06	

Business Summary: Pharmaceuticals (MIC: 4.1.1 SIC: 2834 NAIC: 325412)

Pfizer is a research-based biopharmaceutical company involved in the discovery, development and manufacture of healthcare products. Co. manages its commercial operations through two distinct business segments: Pfizer Innovative Health (IH) and Pfizer Essential Health (EH). IH focuses on developing and commercializing medicines and vaccines that improve patients' lives, as well as products for consumer healthcare with key therapeutic areas that include internal medicine, vaccines, oncology, inflammation & immunology, rare diseases and consumer healthcare. EH includes legacy brands, branded generics, generic sterile injectable products, biosimilars and its contract manufacturing business.

Recent Developments: For the quarter ended Oct 1 2017, income from continuing operations increased 110.9% to US$2.86 billion from US$1.36 billion in the year-earlier quarter. Net income increased 110.9% to US$2.86 billion from US$1.36 billion in the year-earlier quarter. Revenues were US$13.17 billion, up 0.9% from US$13.05 billion the year before. Direct operating expenses declined 7.7% to US$2.85 billion from US$3.09 billion in the comparable period the year before. Indirect operating expenses decreased 19.4% to US$6.74 billion from US$8.36 billion in the equivalent prior-year period.

Prospects: Our evaluation of Pfizer Inc. as of Jan. 21, 2018 is the result of our systematic analysis on three basic characteristics: earnings strength, relative valuation, and recent stock price movement. The company has produced a positive trend in earnings per share over the past 5 quarters. However, while recent estimates for the company have been mixed, PFE has posted better than expected results. Based on operating earnings yield, the company is undervalued when compared to all of the companies in our coverage universe. Share price changes over the past year indicates that PFE will perform well over the near term.

Financial Data

(US$ in Thousands)	9 Mos	6 Mos	3 Mos	12/31/2016	12/31/2015	12/31/2014	12/31/2013	12/31/2012
Earnings Per Share	1.63	1.37	1.19	1.17	1.11	1.42	3.19	1.94
Cash Flow Per Share	2.64	2.60	2.64	2.60	2.35	2.66	2.61	2.29
Dividends Per Share	1.260	1.240	1.220	1.200	1.120	1.040	0.960	0.880
Dividend Payout %	77.30	90.51	102.52	102.56	100.90	73.24	30.09	45.36
Income Statement								
Total Revenue	38,843,000	25,675,000	12,779,000	52,824,000	48,851,000	49,605,000	51,584,000	58,986,000
EBITDA	15,588,000	10,607,000	5,365,000	13,123,000	13,421,000	17,214,000	21,326,000	18,396,000
Depn & Amortn	3,571,000	2,394,000	1,186,000	4,056,000	3,728,000	4,039,000	4,599,000	5,175,000
Income Before Taxes	11,351,000	7,767,000	3,951,000	8,351,000	8,965,000	12,240,000	15,716,000	12,080,000
Income Taxes	2,287,000	1,560,000	821,000	1,123,000	1,990,000	3,120,000	4,306,000	2,562,000
Net Income	9,034,000	6,194,000	3,121,000	7,215,000	6,960,000	9,135,000	22,003,000	14,570,000
Average Shares	6,040,999	6,036,999	6,091,999	6,158,999	6,256,999	6,423,999	6,895,001	7,508,001
Balance Sheet								
Current Assets	40,291,000	36,385,000	35,878,000	38,949,000	43,804,000	57,702,000	56,244,000	61,415,000
Total Assets	172,151,000	168,558,000	168,784,000	171,615,000	167,460,000	169,274,000	172,101,000	185,798,000
Current Liabilities	28,217,000	27,182,000	24,864,000	31,115,000	29,399,000	21,631,000	23,366,000	28,619,000
Long-Term Obligations	34,503,000	34,191,000	36,330,000	31,398,000	28,818,000	31,541,000	30,462,000	31,036,000
Total Liabilities	111,381,000	110,189,000	110,349,000	112,072,000	102,741,000	97,973,000	95,794,000	104,538,000
Stockholders' Equity	60,770,000	58,368,000	58,435,000	59,544,000	64,720,000	71,301,000	76,307,000	81,260,000
Shares Outstanding	5,960,707	5,947,348	5,967,844	6,069,999	6,174,999	6,290,999	6,398,999	7,276,001
Statistical Record								
Return on Assets %	5.64	4.94	4.41	4.24	4.13	5.35	12.30	7.77
Return on Equity %	15.95	13.83	12.05	11.58	10.23	12.38	27.93	17.78
EBITDA Margin %	40.13	41.31	41.98	24.84	27.47	34.70	41.34	31.19
Net Margin %	23.26	24.12	24.42	13.66	14.25	18.42	42.65	24.70
Asset Turnover	0.30	0.31	0.32	0.31	0.29	0.29	0.29	0.31
Current Ratio	1.43	1.34	1.44	1.25	1.49	2.67	2.41	2.15
Debt to Equity	0.57	0.59	0.62	0.53	0.45	0.44	0.40	0.38
Price Range	35.99-29.89	37.31-29.89	37.31-29.89	37.31-28.56	36.15-30.82	32.75-27.70	32.20-25.08	26.04-20.95
P/E Ratio	22.08-18.34	27.23-21.82	31.35-25.12	31.89-24.41	32.57-27.77	23.06-19.51	10.09-7.86	13.42-10.80
Average Yield %	3.80	3.70	3.63	3.66	3.32	3.43	3.31	3.79

Address: 235 East 42nd Street, New York, NY 10017 **Telephone:** 212-733-2323	**Web Site:** www.pfizer.com **Officers:** Ian C. Read - Chairman, President, Chief Executive Officer Frank A. D'Amelio - Executive Vice President, Senior Vice President, Chief Financial Officer	**Auditors:** KPMG LLP **Transfer Agents:** Computershare Trust Company, N.A., Canton, MA

PG&E CORP (HOLDING CO)

Exchange	Symbol	Price	52Wk Range	Yield	P/E
NYS	PCG	$44.83 (12/29/2017)	71.56-44.45	N/A	10.26

*7 Year Price Score 99.14 *NYSE Composite Index=100 *12 Month Price Score 77.16

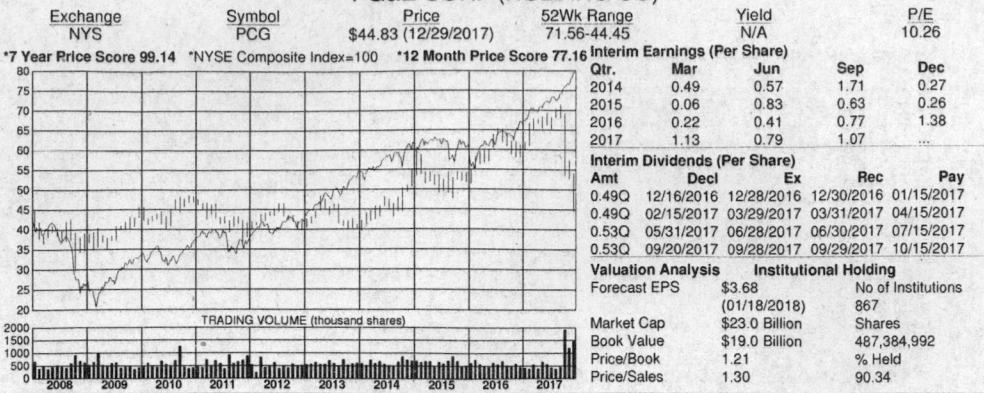

Interim Earnings (Per Share)

Qtr.	Mar	Jun	Sep	Dec
2014	0.49	0.57	1.71	0.27
2015	0.06	0.83	0.63	0.26
2016	0.22	0.41	0.77	1.38
2017	1.13	0.79	1.07	...

Interim Dividends (Per Share)

Amt	Decl	Ex	Rec	Pay
0.49Q	12/16/2016	12/28/2016	12/30/2016	01/15/2017
0.49Q	02/15/2017	03/29/2017	03/31/2017	04/15/2017
0.53Q	05/31/2017	06/28/2017	06/30/2017	07/15/2017
0.53Q	09/20/2017	09/28/2017	09/29/2017	10/15/2017

Valuation Analysis — **Institutional Holding**

Forecast EPS	$3.68	No of Institutions
	(01/18/2018)	867
Market Cap	$23.0 Billion	Shares
Book Value	$19.0 Billion	487,384,992
Price/Book	1.21	% Held
Price/Sales	1.30	90.34

TRADING VOLUME (thousand shares)

Business Summary: Electric Utilities (MIC: 3.1.1 SIC: 4931 NAIC: 221122)

PG&E is a holding company. Through its subsidiary, Pacific Gas and Electric Company (Utility), Co. is engaged in the sale and delivery of electricity and natural gas to customers. The Utility generates electricity and provides electricity transmission and distribution services throughout its service territory in northern and central California to residential, commercial, industrial, and agricultural customers. The Utility also provides natural gas transportation services to small commercial and residential customers and industrial, commercial, and natural gas-fired electric generation facilities that are connected to the Utility's gas system in its service territory.

Recent Developments: For the quarter ended Sep 30 2017, net income increased 41.4% to US$553.0 million from US$391.0 million in the year-earlier quarter. Revenues were US$4.52 billion, down 6.1% from US$4.81 billion the year before. Operating income was US$899.0 million versus US$640.0 million in the prior-year quarter, an increase of 40.5%. Direct operating expenses declined 16.3% to US$2.91 billion from US$3.48 billion in the comparable period the year before. Indirect operating expenses increased 2.3% to US$710.0 million from US$694.0 million in the equivalent prior-year period.

Prospects: Our evaluation of PG&E Corp. as of Jan. 14, 2018 is the result of our systematic analysis on three basic characteristics: earnings strength, relative valuation, and recent stock price movement. The company has generated a negative trend in earnings per share over the past 5 quarters and while recent estimates for the company have remained steady, PCG has posted better than expected results. Based on operating earnings yield, the company is undervalued when compared to all of the companies in our coverage universe. Share price changes over the past year indicates that PCG will perform very well over the near term.

Financial Data

(US$ in Thousands)	9 Mos	6 Mos	3 Mos	12/31/2016	12/31/2015	12/31/2014	12/31/2013	12/31/2012
Earnings Per Share	4.37	4.07	3.69	2.78	1.79	3.06	1.83	1.92
Cash Flow Per Share	11.50	10.54	9.70	8.81	7.75	7.86	7.72	11.48
Tang Book Value Per Share	37.05	36.39	35.94	35.39	33.69	33.09	31.41	30.35
Dividends Per Share	2.040	2.000	1.960	1.925	1.820	1.820	1.820	1.820
Dividend Payout %	46.68	49.14	53.12	69.24	101.68	59.48	99.45	94.79
Income Statement								
Total Revenue	13,035,000	8,518,000	4,268,000	17,666,000	16,833,000	17,090,000	15,598,000	15,040,000
EBITDA	4,720,000	3,086,000	1,613,000	5,023,000	4,237,000	4,953,000	3,879,000	4,035,000
Depn & Amortn	2,134,000	1,424,000	712,000	2,755,000	2,612,000	2,433,000	2,077,000	2,272,000
Income Before Taxes	1,945,000	1,232,000	688,000	1,462,000	861,000	1,795,000	1,096,000	1,067,000
Income Taxes	403,000	243,000	109,000	55,000	(27,000)	345,000	268,000	237,000
Net Income	1,542,000	989,000	579,000	1,407,000	888,000	1,450,000	828,000	830,000
Average Shares	516,000	513,000	511,000	501,000	487,000	470,000	445,000	425,000
Balance Sheet								
Current Assets	6,383,000	6,071,000	5,980,000	6,164,000	5,822,000	6,389,000	5,977,000	5,121,000
Total Assets	71,526,000	70,055,000	69,164,000	68,598,000	63,339,000	60,127,000	55,605,000	52,449,000
Current Liabilities	7,473,000	6,948,000	6,538,000	7,564,000	6,363,000	5,920,000	7,493,000	6,256,000
Long-Term Obligations	16,619,000	16,616,000	16,813,000	16,220,000	16,030,000	15,050,000	12,717,000	12,517,000
Total Liabilities	52,492,000	51,416,000	50,811,000	50,658,000	46,763,000	44,379,000	41,263,000	39,375,000
Stockholders' Equity	19,034,000	18,639,000	18,353,000	17,940,000	16,576,000	15,748,000	14,342,000	13,074,000
Shares Outstanding	513,773	512,220	510,610	506,891	492,025	475,913	456,670	430,718
Statistical Record								
Return on Assets %	3.24	3.05	2.80	2.13	1.44	2.51	1.53	1.62
Return on Equity %	12.30	11.73	10.73	8.13	5.49	9.64	6.04	6.58
EBITDA Margin %	36.21	36.23	37.79	28.43	25.17	28.98	24.87	26.83
Net Margin %	11.83	11.61	13.57	7.96	5.28	8.48	5.31	5.52
Asset Turnover	0.26	0.27	0.27	0.27	0.27	0.30	0.29	0.29
Current Ratio	0.85	0.87	0.91	0.81	0.91	1.08	0.80	0.82
Debt to Equity	0.87	0.89	0.92	0.90	0.97	0.96	0.89	0.96
Price Range	71.56-58.04	69.22-58.04	67.86-56.62	65.39-51.29	60.15-47.60	54.98-39.60	48.44-40.07	46.51-39.71
P/E Ratio	16.38-13.28	17.01-14.26	18.39-15.34	23.52-18.45	33.60-26.59	17.97-12.94	26.47-21.90	24.22-20.68
Average Yield %	3.14	3.21	3.17	3.22	3.44	3.97	4.21	4.23

Address: 77 Beale Street, P.O. Box 770000, San Francisco, CA 94177
Telephone: 415-973-1000
Fax: 415-267-7265

Web Site: www.pgecorp.com
Officers: Geisha J. Williams - President, Chief Economist John R. Simon - Executive Vice President, Senior Vice President

Auditors: Deloitte & Touche LLP
Investor Contact: 415-972-7080
Transfer Agents: American Stock Transfer and Trust Company, LLC, Brooklyn, NY

PHILIP MORRIS INTERNATIONAL INC

Exchange	Symbol	Price	52Wk Range	Yield	P/E
NYS	PM	$105.65 (12/29/2017)	122.90-90.40	4.05	23.32

*7 Year Price Score 98.03 *NYSE Composite Index=100 *12 Month Price Score 89.48

Interim Earnings (Per Share)

Qtr.	Mar	Jun	Sep	Dec
2014	1.18	1.17	1.38	1.03
2015	1.16	1.21	1.25	0.80
2016	0.98	1.15	1.25	1.10
2017	1.02	1.14	1.27	...

Interim Dividends (Per Share)

Amt	Decl	Ex	Rec	Pay
1.04Q	03/09/2017	03/21/2017	03/23/2017	04/11/2017
1.04Q	06/09/2017	06/21/2017	06/23/2017	07/11/2017
1.07Q	09/13/2017	09/26/2017	09/27/2017	10/12/2017
1.07Q	12/07/2017	12/20/2017	12/21/2017	01/11/2018

Indicated Div: $4.28

Valuation Analysis		Institutional Holding	
Forecast EPS	$4.75 (01/18/2018)	No of Institutions	2124
Market Cap	$164.1 Billion	Shares	1,333,330,304
Book Value	N/A	% Held	60.77
Price/Book	N/A		
Price/Sales	2.17		

Business Summary: Tobacco Products (MIC: 1.3.1 SIC: 2111 NAIC: 312221)

Philip Morris International is a holding company. Through its subsidiaries and affiliates and their licensees, Co. manufactures and sells cigarettes, other tobacco products and other nicotine-containing products in markets outside the U.S. Co. has a range of premium, mid-price and low-price brands. Co.'s portfolio of international and local brands includes Marlboro, L&M, Bond Street, and Champion. Co. also focuses on the development and commercialization of Reduced-Risk Products that produces lower quantities of harmful compounds than found in cigarette smoke. Co.'s other tobacco products include tobacco for roll-your-own and make-your-own cigarettes, pipe tobacco, cigars and cigarillos.

Recent Developments: For the quarter ended Sep 30 2017, net income increased 0.8% to US$2.05 billion from US$2.03 billion in the year-earlier quarter. Revenues were US$20.64 billion, up 3.5% from US$19.94 billion the year before. Operating income was US$3.07 billion versus US$2.98 billion in the prior-year quarter, an increase of 3.1%. Direct operating expenses rose 3.3% to US$15.90 billion from US$15.39 billion in the comparable period the year before. Indirect operating expenses increased 6.2% to US$1.67 billion from US$1.57 billion in the equivalent prior-year period.

Prospects: Our evaluation of Philip Morris International Inc. as of Jan. 14, 2018 is the result of our systematic analysis on three basic characteristics: earnings strength, relative valuation, and recent stock price movement. The company has produced a positive trend in earnings per share over the past 5 quarters and while recent estimates for the company have remained steady, PM has posted results that fell short of analysts expectations. Based on operating earnings yield, the company is undervalued when compared to all of the companies in our coverage universe. Share price changes over the past year indicates that PM will perform very well over the near term.

Financial Data
(US$ in Thousands)

	9 Mos	6 Mos	3 Mos	12/31/2016	12/31/2015	12/31/2014	12/31/2013	12/31/2012
Earnings Per Share	4.53	4.51	4.52	4.48	4.42	4.76	5.26	5.17
Cash Flow Per Share	5.24	6.00	5.45	5.19	5.08	4.94	6.25	5.55
Dividends Per Share	4.190	4.160	4.140	4.120	4.040	3.880	3.580	3.240
Dividend Payout %	92.49	92.24	91.59	91.96	91.40	81.51	68.06	62.67
Income Statement								
Total Revenue	56,513,000	35,875,000	16,556,000	74,953,000	73,908,000	80,106,000	80,029,000	77,393,000
EBITDA	8,250,000	5,161,000	2,418,000	11,558,000	11,377,000	12,591,000	14,397,000	14,744,000
Depn & Amortn	65,000	44,000	22,000	743,000	754,000	889,000	882,000	898,000
Income Before Taxes	7,530,000	4,685,000	2,177,000	9,924,000	9,615,000	10,650,000	12,542,000	12,987,000
Income Taxes	2,042,000	1,230,000	541,000	2,768,000	2,688,000	3,097,000	3,670,000	3,833,000
Net Income	5,341,000	3,371,000	1,590,000	6,967,000	6,873,000	7,493,000	8,576,000	8,800,000
Average Shares	1,553,000	1,553,000	1,553,000	1,551,000	1,549,000	1,566,000	1,622,000	1,692,000
Balance Sheet								
Current Assets	20,859,000	18,432,000	16,884,000	17,608,000	15,804,000	15,484,000	16,852,000	16,590,000
Total Assets	41,951,000	38,660,000	36,627,000	36,851,000	33,956,000	35,187,000	38,168,000	37,670,000
Current Liabilities	18,514,000	17,243,000	13,355,000	16,467,000	15,386,000	15,112,000	17,066,000	17,016,000
Long-Term Obligations	28,065,000	26,595,000	28,588,000	25,851,000	25,250,000	26,929,000	24,023,000	17,639,000
Total Liabilities	53,358,000	50,668,000	49,019,000	49,539,000	47,200,000	47,816,000	45,934,000	41,146,000
Stockholders' Equity	(11,407,000)	(12,008,000)	(12,392,000)	(12,688,000)	(13,244,000)	(12,629,000)	(7,766,000)	(3,476,000)
Shares Outstanding	1,553,195	1,553,187	1,553,140	1,551,385	1,549,344	1,546,899	1,589,002	1,653,612
Statistical Record								
Return on Assets %	18.19	19.11	19.73	19.63	19.88	20.43	22.62	23.99
EBITDA Margin %	14.60	14.39	14.60	15.42	15.39	15.72	17.99	19.05
Net Margin %	9.45	9.40	9.60	9.30	9.30	9.35	10.72	11.37
Asset Turnover	1.95	2.04	2.10	2.11	2.14	2.18	2.11	2.11
Current Ratio	1.13	1.07	1.26	1.07	1.03	1.02	0.99	0.97
Price Range	122.90-87.33	122.90-87.33	114.01-87.33	103.63-85.80	90.15-75.33	91.34-75.39	96.44-82.95	93.74-73.26
P/E Ratio	27.13-19.28	27.25-19.36	25.22-19.32	23.13-19.15	20.40-17.04	19.19-15.84	18.33-15.77	18.13-14.17
Average Yield %	3.92	4.04	4.19	4.29	4.86	4.60	4.01	3.74

Address: 120 Park Avenue, New York, NY 10017	Web Site: www.pmi.com	Auditors: PricewaterhouseCoopers SA
Telephone: 917-663-2000	Officers: Louis C. Camilleri - Chairman, Chief Executive Officer Andre Calantzopoulos - Chief	Investor Contact: 191-766-32233
Fax: 917-663-5372	Executive Officer, Chief Operating Officer	Transfer Agents: ComputerShare LLC, Providence, RI

PHILLIPS 66

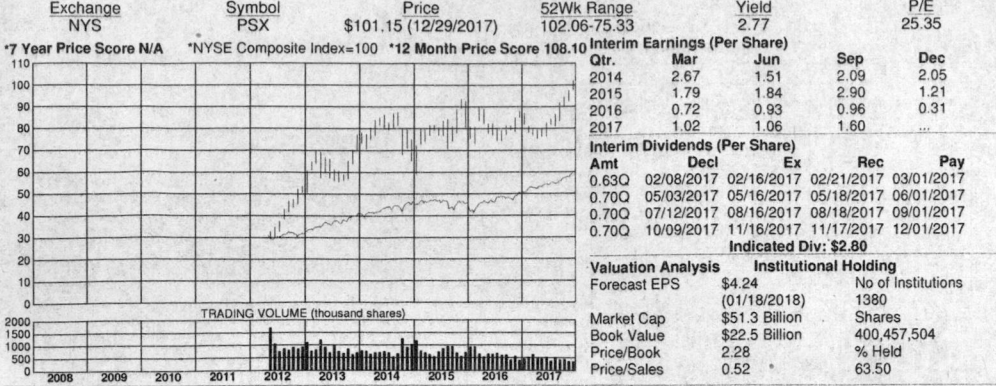

Exchange	Symbol	Price	52Wk Range	Yield	P/E
NYS	PSX	$101.15 (12/29/2017)	102.06-75.33	2.77	25.35

*7 Year Price Score N/A *NYSE Composite Index=100 ***12 Month Price Score 108.10**

Interim Earnings (Per Share)

Qtr.	Mar	Jun	Sep	Dec
2014	2.67	1.51	2.09	2.05
2015	1.79	1.84	2.90	1.21
2016	0.72	0.93	0.96	0.31
2017	1.02	1.06	1.60	...

Interim Dividends (Per Share)

Amt	Decl	Ex	Rec	Pay
0.63Q	02/08/2017	02/16/2017	02/21/2017	03/01/2017
0.70Q	05/03/2017	05/16/2017	05/18/2017	06/01/2017
0.70Q	07/12/2017	08/16/2017	08/18/2017	09/01/2017
0.70Q	10/09/2017	11/16/2017	11/17/2017	12/01/2017

Indicated Div: $2.80

Valuation Analysis

		Institutional Holding	
Forecast EPS	$4.24	No of Institutions	
	(01/18/2018)	1380	
Market Cap	$51.3 Billion	Shares	
Book Value	$22.5 Billion	400,457,504	
Price/Book	2.28	% Held	
Price/Sales	0.52	63.50	

Business Summary: Refining & Marketing (MIC: 9.1.2 SIC: 2911 NAIC: 324110)

Phillips 66 is an energy manufacturing and logistics company with midstream, chemicals, refining, and marketing and specialties businesses. Co. has four segments: Midstream, which gathers, processes, transports and markets natural gas as well as transports, stores, fractionates and markets natural gas liquids; Chemicals, which manufactures and markets petrochemicals and plastics on a worldwide basis; Refining, which buys, sells and refines crude oil and other feedstocks into petroleum products (such as gasoline, distillates and aviation fuels); and Marketing and Specialties, which purchases for resale and markets refined petroleum products, mainly in the U.S. and Europe.

Recent Developments: For the quarter ended Sep 30 2017, net income increased 58.4% to US$849.0 million from US$536.0 million in the year-earlier quarter. Revenues were US$26.21 billion, up 18.9% from US$22.04 billion the year before. Direct operating expenses rose 21.0% to US$20.60 billion from US$17.02 billion in the comparable period the year before. Indirect operating expenses increased 3.5% to US$4.35 billion from US$4.21 billion in the equivalent prior-year period.

Prospects: Our evaluation of Phillips 66 Inc. as of Jan. 14, 2018 is the result of our systematic analysis on three basic characteristics: earnings strength, relative valuation, and recent stock price movement. The company has enjoyed a very positive trend in earnings per share over the past 5 quarters. However, while recent estimates for the company have been mixed, PSX has posted better than expected results. Based on operating earnings yield, the company is about fairly valued when compared to all of the companies in our coverage universe. Share price changes over the past year indicates that PSX will perform in line with the market over the near term.

Financial Data

(US$ in Millions)	9 Mos	6 Mos	3 Mos	12/31/2016	12/31/2015	12/31/2014	12/31/2013	12/31/2012
Earnings Per Share	3.99	3.35	3.22	2.92	7.73	8.33	6.02	6.48
Cash Flow Per Share	4.65	5.54	4.13	5.60	10.53	6.24	9.83	6.81
Tang Book Value Per Share	36.25	35.60	35.26	35.14	35.74	31.88	30.76	26.79
Dividends Per Share	2.660	2.590	2.520	2.450	2.180	1.890	1.327	0.450
Dividend Payout %	66.67	77.31	78.26	83.90	28.20	22.69	22.05	6.94
Income Statement								
Total Revenue	74,499	48,293	23,712	85,777	100,949	164,093	174,809	182,922
EBITDA	4,197	2,492	1,217	3,697	7,432	7,007	6,748	7,790
Depn & Amortn	972	635	315	1,168	1,078	995	947	913
Income Before Taxes	2,901	1,645	797	2,191	6,044	5,745	5,526	6,631
Income Taxes	908	501	234	547	1,764	1,654	1,844	2,500
Net Income	1,908	1,085	535	1,555	4,227	4,762	3,726	4,124
Average Shares	515	520	524	530	546	571	618	636
Balance Sheet								
Current Assets	12,935	12,456	12,170	12,680	12,256	16,696	19,237	17,962
Total Assets	52,712	51,828	51,405	51,653	48,580	48,741	49,798	48,073
Current Liabilities	9,905	8,874	8,730	9,463	7,531	11,094	12,931	12,482
Long-Term Obligations	9,495	9,472	9,601	9,588	8,843	7,842	6,131	6,961
Total Liabilities	30,189	29,460	29,041	29,263	25,480	27,151	27,848	27,298
Stockholders' Equity	22,523	22,368	22,364	22,390	23,100	21,590	21,950	20,775
Shares Outstanding	506	511	516	518	529	546	590	623
Statistical Record								
Return on Assets %	4.02	3.44	3.42	3.09	8.69	9.67	7.61	9.01
Return on Equity %	9.12	7.78	7.55	6.82	18.92	21.87	17.44	18.68
EBITDA Margin %	5.63	5.16	5.13	4.31	7.36	4.27	3.86	4.26
Net Margin %	2.56	2.25	2.26	1.81	4.19	2.90	2.13	2.25
Asset Turnover	1.91	1.84	1.84	1.71	2.07	3.33	3.57	4.00
Current Ratio	1.31	1.40	1.39	1.34	1.63	1.50	1.49	1.44
Debt to Equity	0.42	0.42	0.43	0.43	0.38	0.36	0.28	0.34
Price Range	91.80-75.33	88.17-74.26	88.95-74.26	90.16-72.90	93.68-59.09	87.51-65.09	77.13-50.58	53.58-29.35
P/E Ratio	23.01-18.88	26.32-22.17	27.62-23.06	30.88-24.97	12.12-7.64	10.51-7.81	12.81-8.40	8.27-4.53
Average Yield %	3.25	3.24	3.12	3.03	2.74	2.40	2.14	1.09

Address: 2331 CityWest Blvd., Houston, TX 77042 **Telephone:** 281-293-6600	**Web Site:** www.Phillips66.com **Officers:** Greg C. Garland - Chairman, President, Chief Executive Officer Kevin J. Mitchell - Chief Financial Officer, Executive Vice President	**Auditors:** Ernst & Young LLP **Investor Contact:** 800-624-6440 **Transfer Agents:** Computershare, Canton, MA

PIEDMONT OFFICE REALTY TRUST INC

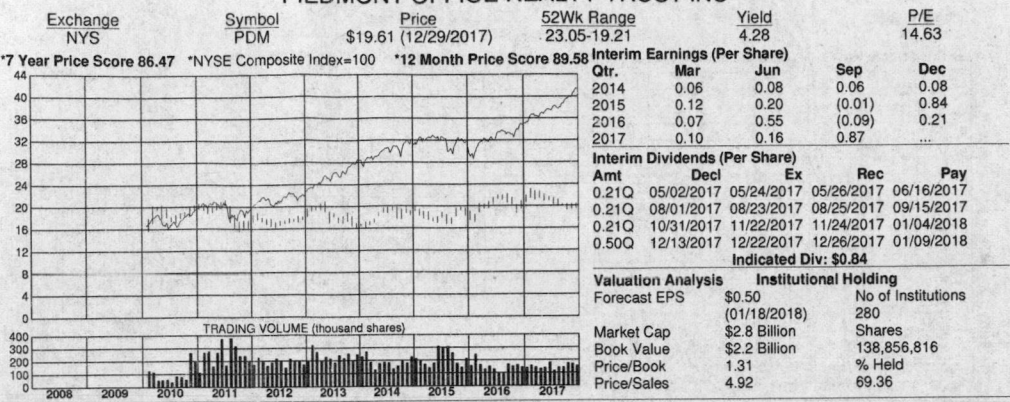

Exchange	Symbol	Price	52Wk Range	Yield	P/E
NYS	PDM	$19.61 (12/29/2017)	23.05-19.21	4.28	14.63

*7 Year Price Score 86.47   *NYSE Composite Index=100   *12 Month Price Score 89.58

Interim Earnings (Per Share)

Qtr.	Mar	Jun	Sep	Dec
2014	0.06	0.08	0.06	0.08
2015	0.12	0.20	(0.01)	0.84
2016	0.07	0.55	(0.09)	0.21
2017	0.10	0.16	0.87	

Interim Dividends (Per Share)

Amt	Decl	Ex	Rec	Pay
0.21Q	05/02/2017	05/24/2017	05/26/2017	06/16/2017
0.21Q	08/01/2017	08/23/2017	08/25/2017	09/15/2017
0.21Q	10/31/2017	11/22/2017	11/24/2017	01/04/2018
0.50Q	12/13/2017	12/22/2017	12/26/2017	01/09/2018

Indicated Div: $0.84

Valuation Analysis

Institutional Holding	
Forecast EPS	$0.50 (01/18/2018)
No of Institutions	280
Market Cap	$2.8 Billion
Shares	138,856,816
Book Value	$2.2 Billion
Price/Book	1.31
% Held	69.36
Price/Sales	4.92

Business Summary: REITs (MIC: 5.3.1 SIC: 6798 NAIC: 525930)

Piedmont Office Realty Trust is a self-managed real estate investment trust engaged in the acquisition, development, management, and ownership of commercial real estate properties. Co. conducts business primarily through Piedmont Operating Partnership, L.P., and performs the management of its buildings through two subsidiaries, Piedmont Government Services, LLC and Piedmont Office Management, LLC. As of Dec 31 2016, Co. owned and operated 65 office properties, one redevelopment asset, two development assets, and one building through an unconsolidated joint venture. Co.'s primary markets are Atlanta, Boston, Chicago, Dallas, Minneapolis, New York, Orlando, and Washington, D.C.

Recent Developments: For the quarter ended Sep 30 2017, income from continuing operations was US$16.6 million compared with a loss of US$13.1 million in the year-earlier quarter. Net income amounted to US$126.1 million versus a net loss of US$13.1 million in the year-earlier quarter. Revenues were US$137.6 million, down 0.6% from US$138.5 million the year before.

Prospects: Our evaluation of Piedmont Office Realty Trust Inc. as of Jan. 14, 2018 is the result of our systematic analysis on three basic characteristics: earnings strength, relative valuation, and recent stock price movement. The company has managed to produce a neutral trend in earnings per share over the past 5 quarters. Because the company lacks sufficient analyst estimate data, we place greater weight on the historical EPS trend as the measure of earnings strength. Based on operating earnings yield, the company is overvalued when compared to all of the companies in our coverage universe. Share price changes over the past year indicates that PDM will perform in line with the market over the near

Financial Data (US$ in Thousands)	9 Mos	6 Mos	3 Mos	12/31/2016	12/31/2015	12/31/2014	12/31/2013	12/31/2012
Earnings Per Share	1.34	0.38	0.77	0.74	1.15	0.28	0.60	0.55
Cash Flow Per Share	1.65	1.68	1.63	1.62	1.44	1.40	1.30	1.31
Tang Book Value Per Share	14.27	13.61	13.67	13.06	13.27	13.35	14.00	14.35
Dividends Per Share	0.840	0.840	0.840	0.840	0.840	0.810	0.800	0.800
Dividend Payout %	62.69	221.05	109.09	113.51	73.04	289.29	133.33	145.45
Income Statement								
Total Revenue	434,729	297,142	148,463	555,715	584,769	566,252	554,505	536,382
EBITDA	246,962	169,400	84,506	201,541	212,633	253,554	274,667	240,757
Depn & Amortn	149,187	100,671	51,306	127,733	134,503	138,679	123,566	113,649
Income Before Taxes	45,114	32,251	15,143	8,948	4,132	40,429	75,166	62,918
Net Income	164,947	38,814	15,104	107,887	172,990	43,348	98,728	93,204
Average Shares	145,719	145,813	145,833	145,634	150,880	154,585	165,137	170,441
Balance Sheet								
Current Assets	48,910	33,865	32,002	33,486	31,780	40,017	38,118	160,294
Total Assets	4,060,650	4,320,312	4,350,740	4,449,347	4,434,535	4,795,501	4,666,088	4,254,875
Current Liabilities	108,120	111,011	116,077	165,410	128,465	133,988	128,818	127,263
Long-Term Obligations	1,703,586	2,053,182	2,065,814	2,020,475	2,029,510	2,277,589	2,002,205	1,416,525
Total Liabilities	1,888,519	2,241,867	2,265,522	2,272,347	2,239,116	2,485,095	2,206,538	1,615,989
Stockholders' Equity	2,172,131	2,078,445	2,085,218	2,177,000	2,195,419	2,310,406	2,459,550	2,638,886
Shares Outstanding	145,294	145,489	145,319	145,235	145,511	154,324	157,460	167,556
Statistical Record								
Return on Assets %	4.62	1.31	2.59	2.42	3.75	0.92	2.21	2.14
Return on Equity %	8.99	2.63	5.31	4.92	7.68	1.82	3.87	3.44
EBITDA Margin %	56.81	57.01	56.92	36.27	36.36	44.78	49.53	44.89
Net Margin %	37.94	13.06	10.17	19.41	29.58	7.66	17.80	17.38
Asset Turnover	0.14	0.13	0.13	0.12	0.13	0.12	0.12	0.12
Current Ratio	0.45	0.31	0.28	0.20	0.25	0.30	0.30	1.26
Debt to Equity	0.78	0.99	0.99	0.93	0.92	0.99	0.81	0.54
Price Range	23.05-18.62	23.05-18.62	23.05-18.62	22.22-17.10	20.01-16.74	20.00-16.09	20.94-15.96	18.91-16.19
P/E Ratio	17.20-13.90	60.66-49.00	29.94-24.18	30.03-23.11	17.40-14.56	71.43-57.46	34.90-26.60	34.38-29.44
Average Yield %	4.01	3.96	4.02	4.17	4.56	4.43	4.33	4.59

Address: 11695 Johns Creek Parkway, Suite 350, Johns Creek, GA 30097 Telephone: 770-418-8800	Web Site: www.piedmontreit.com Officers: C. Brent Smith - Co-Chief Investment Officer, Chief Investment Officer Michael R. Buchanan - Chairman	Auditors: Ernst & Young LLP Transfer Agents: Computershare Inc.

PINNACLE FOODS INC.

Exchange	Symbol	Price	52Wk Range	Yield	P/E
NYS	PF	$59.47 (12/29/2017)	66.17-52.74	2.19	39.91

*7 Year Price Score N/A *NYSE Composite Index=100 *12 Month Price Score 92.38

Interim Earnings (Per Share)

Qtr.	Mar	Jun	Sep	Dec
2014	0.35	0.30	1.16	0.31
2015	0.35	0.37	0.41	0.67
2016	0.21	0.39	0.44	0.75
2017	0.19	0.16	0.39	...

Interim Dividends (Per Share)

Amt	Decl	Ex	Rec	Pay
0.285Q	02/08/2017	02/16/2017	02/21/2017	04/07/2017
0.285Q	05/24/2017	06/02/2017	06/06/2017	07/07/2017
0.325Q	08/16/2017	08/25/2017	08/29/2017	10/09/2017
0.325Q	12/06/2017	12/18/2017	12/19/2017	01/10/2018

Indicated Div: $1.30

Valuation Analysis

		Institutional Holding	
Forecast EPS	$2.55	No of Institutions	402
	(01/17/2018)		
Market Cap	$7.1 Billion	Shares	129,372,968
Book Value	$2.0 Billion	% Held	92.87
Price/Book	3.60		
Price/Sales	2.27		

Business Summary: Food (MIC: 1.2.1 SIC: 2099 NAIC: 311999)

Pinnacle Foods is a holding company. Co. is a manufacturer, marketer and distributor of convenience food products. Co.'s operations are managed and reported in four operating segments: the frozen segment, which is comprised of the retail businesses of Co.'s legacy frozen brands; the grocery segment, which is comprised of the retail businesses of Co.'s grocery brands; the boulder segment, which is comprised of the retail businesses of Co.'s health and wellness lifestyle brands; and the specialty segment, which includes Co.'s snack products (Tim's Cascade and Snyder of Berlin) and all of its U.S. foodservice and private label businesses.

Recent Developments: For the quarter ended Sep 24 2017, net income decreased 11.0% to US$46.6 million from US$52.4 million in the year-earlier quarter. Revenues were US$749.8 million, down 1.2% from US$758.8 million the year before. Operating income was US$94.1 million versus US$118.3 million in the prior-year quarter, a decrease of 20.5%. Direct operating expenses rose 0.1% to US$530.5 million from US$530.1 million in the comparable period the year before. Indirect operating expenses increased 13.4% to US$125.2 million from US$110.4 million in the equivalent prior-year period.

Prospects: Our evaluation of Pinnacle Foods Inc. as of Jan. 14, 2018 is the result of our systematic analysis on three basic characteristics: earnings strength, relative valuation, and recent stock price movement. The company has produced a positive trend in earnings per share over the past 5 quarters. However, while recent estimates for the company have been mixed, PF has posted better than expected results. Based on operating earnings yield, the company is about fairly valued when compared to all of the companies in our coverage universe. Share price changes over the past year indicates that PF will perform in line with the market over the near term.

Financial Data
(US$ in Thousands)

	9 Mos	6 Mos	3 Mos	12/25/2016	12/27/2015	12/28/2014	12/29/2013	12/30/2012
Earnings Per Share	1.49	1.54	1.77	1.79	1.81	2.13	0.82	0.61
Cash Flow Per Share	3.60	3.75	4.03	4.18	3.22	4.77	2.46	2.46
Dividends Per Share	1.180	1.140	1.110	1.080	0.980	0.890	0.570	...
Dividend Payout %	79.19	74.03	62.71	60.34	54.14	41.78	69.51	...
Income Statement								
Total Revenue	2,260,496	1,510,682	766,074	3,127,938	2,655,792	2,591,183	2,463,802	2,478,485
EBITDA	347,009	227,825	135,288	568,445	500,808	578,981	355,387	365,889
Depn & Amortn	97,727	72,597	24,080	88,800	76,106	66,710	62,350	82,295
Income Before Taxes	110,984	46,018	30,492	340,547	336,387	416,218	160,824	85,220
Income Taxes	22,636	4,251	7,343	129,430	123,879	167,800	71,475	32,701
Net Income	88,176	41,595	22,926	211,117	212,508	248,418	89,349	52,519
Average Shares	119,690	119,607	119,332	118,161	117,323	116,885	108,618	86,494
Balance Sheet								
Current Assets	991,307	909,533	912,270	1,150,515	857,634	715,709	792,309	705,277
Total Assets	6,477,195	6,430,006	6,496,258	6,739,645	5,340,083	5,200,945	5,081,191	4,399,988
Current Liabilities	550,894	528,870	563,064	571,696	405,647	383,436	331,304	333,724
Long-Term Obligations	2,936,375	2,940,800	2,944,179	3,140,496	2,272,932	2,285,984	2,476,167	2,576,386
Total Liabilities	4,510,759	4,486,128	4,534,265	4,791,637	3,534,554	3,486,956	3,483,150	3,511,262
Stockholders' Equity	1,966,436	1,943,878	1,961,993	1,948,008	1,805,529	1,713,989	1,598,041	888,726
Shares Outstanding	119,009	119,786	118,422	118,127	116,619	116,293	117,231	81,210
Statistical Record								
Return on Assets %	2.69	2.81	3.22	3.50	4.04	4.85	1.89	1.17
Return on Equity %	9.18	9.63	11.11	11.28	12.11	15.04	7.21	5.96
EBITDA Margin %	15.35	15.08	17.66	18.17	18.86	22.34	14.42	14.76
Net Margin %	3.90	2.75	2.99	6.75	8.00	9.59	3.63	2.12
Asset Turnover	0.48	0.48	0.48	0.52	0.51	0.51	0.52	0.55
Current Ratio	1.80	1.72	1.62	2.01	2.11	1.87	2.39	2.11
Debt to Equity	1.49	1.51	1.50	1.61	1.26	1.33	1.55	2.90
Price Range	66.17-46.62	66.17-43.34	58.96-41.82	53.25-39.89	47.41-34.77	35.60-26.51	28.56-22.21	...
P/E Ratio	44.41-31.29	42.97-28.14	33.31-23.63	29.75-22.28	26.19-19.21	16.71-12.45	34.83-27.09	...
Average Yield %	2.10	2.13	2.24	2.32	2.35	2.86	2.21	...

Address: 399 Jefferson Road, Parsippany, NJ 07054	Web Site: www.pinnaclefoods.com	Auditors: Deloitte & Touche LLP
Telephone: 973-541-6620	Officers: Mark A. Clouse - Chief Executive Officer D. Michael Wittman - Executive Vice President, Chief Supply Chain Officer	Transfer Agents: Computershare Trust Company, N.A.

PINNACLE WEST CAPITAL CORP

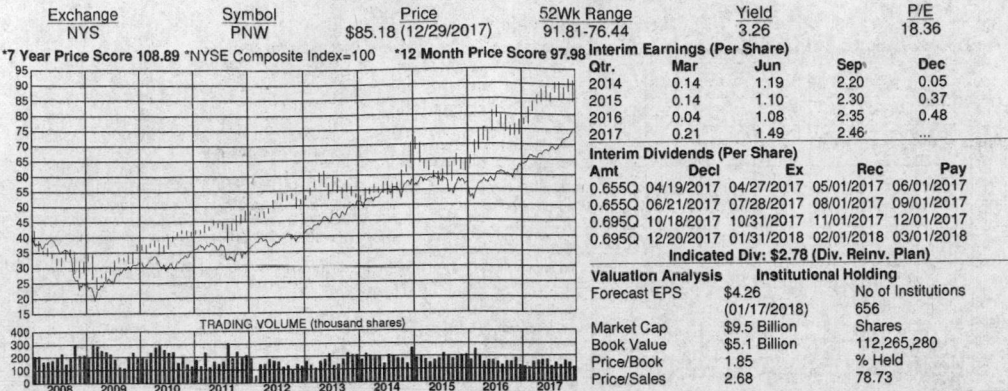

Exchange	Symbol	Price	52Wk Range	Yield	P/E
NYS	PNW	$85.18 (12/29/2017)	91.81-76.44	3.26	18.36

*7 Year Price Score 108.89 *NYSE Composite Index=100 *12 Month Price Score 97.98

Interim Earnings (Per Share)

Qtr.	Mar	Jun	Sep	Dec
2014	0.14	1.19	2.20	0.05
2015	0.14	1.10	2.30	0.37
2016	0.04	1.08	2.35	0.48
2017	0.21	1.49	2.46	...

Interim Dividends (Per Share)

Amt	Decl	Ex	Rec	Pay
0.655Q	04/19/2017	04/27/2017	05/01/2017	06/01/2017
0.655Q	06/21/2017	07/28/2017	08/01/2017	09/01/2017
0.695Q	10/18/2017	10/31/2017	11/01/2017	12/01/2017
0.695Q	12/20/2017	01/31/2018	02/01/2018	03/01/2018

Indicated Div: $2.78 (Div. Reinv. Plan)

Valuation Analysis

		Institutional Holding	
Forecast EPS	$4.26	No of Institutions	
	(01/17/2018)	656	
Market Cap	$9.5 Billion	Shares	
Book Value	$5.1 Billion	112,265,280	
Price/Book	1.85	% Held	
Price/Sales	2.68	78.73	

Business Summary: Electric Utilities (MIC: 3.1.1 SIC: 4911 NAIC: 221122)

Pinnacle West Capital is a holding company. Through its subsidiary, Arizona Public Service Company, Co. provides either retail or wholesale electric service to most of the State of Arizona, with the exceptions of about one-half of the Phoenix metropolitan area, Tucson metropolitan area and Mohave County in northwestern Arizona. Co.'s business segment is its regulated electricity segment, which consists of regulated retail and wholesale electricity businesses (primarily electric service to Native Load customers) and related activities and includes electricity generation, transmission and distribution. As of Dec 31 2016, APS provided electric service to approximately 1.2 million customers.

Recent Developments: For the quarter ended Sep 30 2017, net income increased 4.9% to US$280.9 million from US$267.9 million in the year-earlier quarter. Revenues were US$1.18 billion, up 1.4% from US$1.17 billion the year before. Operating income was US$466.1 million versus US$451.3 million in the prior-year quarter, an increase of 3.3%. Direct operating expenses declined 3.4% to US$534.8 million from US$553.7 million in the comparable period the year before. Indirect operating expenses increased 12.7% to US$182.5 million from US$162.0 million in the equivalent prior-year period.

Prospects: Our evaluation of Pinnacle West Capital Corp. as of Jan. 14, 2018 is the result of our systematic analysis on three basic characteristics: earnings strength, relative valuation, and recent stock price movement. The company has generated a negative trend in earnings per share over the past 5 quarters. However, while recent estimates for the company have been mixed, PNW has posted better than expected results. Based on operating earnings yield, the company is undervalued when compared to all of the companies in our coverage universe. Share price changes over the past year indicates that PNW will perform very well over the near term.

Financial Data
(US$ in Thousands)

	9 Mos	6 Mos	3 Mos	12/31/2016	12/31/2015	12/31/2014	12/31/2013	12/31/2012
Earnings Per Share	4.64	4.53	4.12	3.95	3.92	3.58	3.66	3.45
Cash Flow Per Share	9.21	7.97	9.12	9.16	9.86	9.94	10.49	10.66
Tang Book Value Per Share	46.05	43.53	43.28	43.14	41.30	39.50	38.07	36.20
Dividends Per Share	2.620	2.590	2.560	2.530	2.410	2.297	2.203	2.120
Dividend Payout %	56.47	57.17	62.14	64.05	61.48	64.18	60.18	61.45
Income Statement								
Total Revenue	2,805,637	1,622,315	677,728	3,498,682	3,495,443	3,491,632	3,454,628	3,301,804
EBITDA	846,108	376,608	75,139	1,330,632	1,309,409	1,335,338	1,353,886	1,196,826
Depn & Amortn	(18,153)	(13,663)	(4,172)	603,163	573,281	537,244	523,512	364,546
Income Before Taxes	718,944	293,680	32,396	584,743	593,131	644,401	670,557	656,310
Income Taxes	237,497	93,178	4,211	123,216	136,941	220,705	230,591	237,317
Net Income	466,827	190,755	23,312	442,034	437,257	397,595	406,074	381,542
Average Shares	112,401	112,345	112,195	112,046	111,552	111,178	110,806	110,527
Balance Sheet								
Current Assets	1,174,205	1,068,204	794,996	822,219	890,516	973,435	1,043,609	1,005,726
Total Assets	16,977,867	16,669,727	16,192,825	16,004,253	15,028,258	14,313,532	13,508,686	13,379,615
Current Liabilities	1,303,143	1,638,594	1,193,813	1,292,946	1,442,317	1,559,143	1,618,644	1,083,542
Long-Term Obligations	4,491,048	4,192,520	4,273,890	4,021,785	3,462,391	3,031,215	2,796,465	3,199,088
Total Liabilities	11,835,799	11,810,315	11,364,049	11,200,631	10,444,341	9,946,039	9,314,216	9,406,809
Stockholders' Equity	5,142,068	4,859,412	4,828,776	4,803,622	4,583,917	4,367,493	4,194,470	3,972,806
Shares Outstanding	111,657	111,623	111,557	111,336	110,980	110,571	110,181	109,742
Statistical Record								
Return on Assets %	3.17	3.15	2.94	2.84	2.98	2.86	3.02	2.87
Return on Equity %	10.41	10.74	9.78	9.39	9.77	9.29	9.94	9.76
EBITDA Margin %	30.16	23.21	11.09	38.03	37.46	38.24	39.19	36.25
Net Margin %	16.64	11.76	3.44	12.63	12.51	11.39	11.75	11.56
Asset Turnover	0.22	0.22	0.22	0.22	0.24	0.25	0.26	0.25
Current Ratio	0.90	0.65	0.67	0.64	0.62	0.62	0.64	0.93
Debt to Equity	0.87	0.86	0.89	0.84	0.76	0.69	0.67	0.81
Price Range	90.75-72.69	89.22-72.69	84.20-70.75	82.56-63.26	72.47-56.31	70.63-51.28	61.48-50.98	54.32-46.06
P/E Ratio	19.56-15.67	19.70-16.05	20.44-17.17	20.90-16.02	18.49-14.36	19.73-14.32	16.80-13.93	15.74-13.35
Average Yield %	3.19	3.25	3.33	3.42	3.83	4.05	3.94	4.21

Address: 400 North Fifth Street, P.O. Box 53999, Phoenix, AZ 85072-3999
Telephone: 602-250-1000
Fax: 602-379-2625

Web Site: www.pinnaclewest.com
Officers: Donald E. Brandt - Chairman, President, Chief Executive Officer James R. Hatfield - Executive Vice President, Senior Vice President, Chief Financial Officer, Treasurer

Auditors: Deloitte & Touche LLP
Investor Contact: 602-250-5668
Transfer Agents: Computershare, Providence, RI

PIONEER NATURAL RESOURCES CO

Exchange	Symbol	Price	52Wk Range	Yield	P/E
NYS	PXD	$172.85 (12/29/2017)	198.90-127.94	0.05	233.58

*7 Year Price Score 90.01   ***NYSE Composite Index=100**   ***12 Month Price Score 90.60**

Interim Earnings (Per Share)

Qtr.	Mar	Jun	Sep	Dec
2014	0.85	0.01	2.58	2.94
2015	(0.52)	(1.46)	4.27	(4.15)
2016	(1.65)	(1.63)	0.13	(0.24)
2017	(0.25)	1.36	(0.13)	...

Interim Dividends (Per Share)

Amt	Decl	Ex	Rec	Pay
0.04S	03/02/2016	03/29/2016	03/31/2016	04/12/2016
0.04S	08/25/2016	09/28/2016	09/30/2016	10/12/2016
0.04S	02/28/2017	03/29/2017	03/31/2017	04/12/2017
0.04S	08/24/2017	09/28/2017	09/29/2017	10/12/2017

Indicated Div: $0.08

Valuation Analysis | **Institutional Holding**

Forecast EPS	$1.74	No of Institutions
	(01/18/2018)	971
Market Cap	$29.4 Billion	Shares
Book Value	$10.6 Billion	178,729,200
Price/Book	2.78	% Held
Price/Sales	5.14	95.92

Business Summary: Production & Extraction (MIC: 9.1.1 SIC: 1311 NAIC: 211111)

Pioneer Natural Resources is a holding company. Through its subsidiaries, Co. is engaged as an oil and gas exploration and production company. Co. explores for, develops and produces oil, natural gas liquids and gas within the U.S. Co.'s operations are primarily located in the Permian Basin in West Texas, the Eagle Ford Shale play in South Texas, the Raton field in southeast Colorado and the West Panhandle field in the Texas Panhandle. As of Dec 31 2016, Co. had proved reserves of 725.9 million barrels of oil equivalent.

Recent Developments: For the quarter ended Sep 30 2017, net loss amounted to US$23.0 million versus net income of US$22.0 million in the year-earlier quarter. Revenues were US$1.46 billion, up 23.1% from US$1.19 billion the year before. Direct operating expenses rose 27.3% to US$1.30 billion from US$1.02 billion in the comparable period the year before. Indirect operating expenses decreased 11.6% to US$199.0 million from US$225.0 million in the equivalent prior-year period.

Prospects: Our evaluation of Pioneer Natural Resources Co as of Jan. 14, 2018 is the result of our systematic analysis on three basic characteristics: earnings strength, relative valuation, and recent stock price movement. The company has generated a negative trend in earnings per share over the past 5 quarters and while recent estimates for the company have been raised by analysts, PXD has posted better than expected results. Based on operating earnings yield, the company is overvalued when compared to all of the companies in our coverage universe. Share price changes over the past year indicates that PXD will perform very poorly over the near term.

Financial Data

(US$ in Thousands)	9 Mos	6 Mos	3 Mos	12/31/2016	12/31/2015	12/31/2014	12/31/2013	12/31/2012
Earnings Per Share	0.74	1.00	(1.99)	(3.34)	(1.83)	6.38	(6.16)	1.50
Cash Flow Per Share	10.80	10.71	10.30	9.00	8.38	16.43	15.76	14.90
Tang Book Value Per Share	60.65	60.71	59.20	59.70	54.20	55.77	44.36	43.70
Dividends Per Share	0.080	0.080	0.080	0.080	0.080	0.080	0.080	0.080
Dividend Payout %	10.81	8.00	...	...	...	1.25	...	5.33
Income Statement								
Total Revenue	4,557,000	3,099,000	1,468,000	3,824,000	4,825,000	5,055,000	3,719,510	3,228,308
EBITDA	1,459,000	1,083,000	332,000	817,000	1,241,000	2,912,000	600,107	1,314,968
Depn & Amortn	1,094,000	721,000	359,000	1,569,000	1,475,000	1,131,000	978,076	830,689
Income Before Taxes	·247,000	281,000	(73,000)	(959,000)	(421,000)	1,597,000	(561,719)	280,057
Income Taxes	79,000	90,000	(31,000)	(403,000)	(155,000)	556,000	(211,775)	92,384
Net Income	168,000	191,000	(42,000)	(556,000)	(273,000)	930,000	(838,414)	192,285
Average Shares	170,000	170,000	170,000	166,000	149,000	144,000	136,130	126,320
Balance Sheet								
Current Assets	2,901,000	3,064,000	2,940,000	3,298,000	3,194,000	2,359,000	1,728,434	1,050,355
Total Assets	16,465,000	16,271,000	15,749,000	16,459,000	15,154,000	14,926,000	12,292,788	13,069,030
Current Liabilities	1,715,000	1,558,000	952,000	1,566,000	1,462,000	1,580,000	1,250,106	1,034,790
Long-Term Obligations	2,282,000	2,281,000	2,729,000	2,728,000	3,207,000	2,665,000	2,653,059	3,721,193
Total Liabilities	5,874,000	5,674,000	5,408,000	6,055,000	6,786,000	6,345,000	5,691,204	7,379,676
Stockholders' Equity	10,591,000	10,597,000	10,341,000	10,404,000	8,368,000	8,581,000	6,601,584	5,689,354
Shares Outstanding	170,165	170,097	170,093	169,724	149,379	149,000	142,627	123,355
Statistical Record								
Return on Assets %	0.76	1.03	N.M.	N.M.	N.M.	6.83	N.M.	1.56
Return on Equity %	1.19	1.62	N.M.	N.M.	N.M.	12.25	N.M.	3.43
EBITDA Margin %	32.02	34.95	22.62	21.37	25.72	57.61	16.13	40.73
Net Margin %	3.69	6.16	N.M.	N.M.	N.M.	18.40	N.M.	5.96
Asset Turnover	0.35	0.33	0.29	0.24	0.32	0.37	0.29	0.26
Current Ratio	1.69	1.97	3.09	2.11	2.18	1.49	1.38	1.02
Debt to Equity	0.22	0.22	0.26	0.26	0.38	0.31	0.40	0.65
Price Range	198.90-127.94	198.90-148.83	198.90-138.44	193.24-107.75	180.23-107.24	233.07-130.60	224.95-106.59	116.24-78.78
P/E Ratio	268.78-172.89	198.90-148.83	...	...	...	36.53-20.47	...	77.49-52.52
Average Yield %	0.05	0.05	0.05	0.05	0.06	0.04	0.05	0.08

Address: 5205 N. O'Connor Blvd., Suite 200, Irving, TX 75039 **Telephone:** 972-444-9001 **Fax:** 972-969-3587	**Web Site:** www.pxd.com **Officers:** Scott D. Sheffield - Executive Chairman, Chairman, Chief Executive Officer Timothy L. Dove - President, Chief Executive Officer, Chief Operating Officer	**Auditors:** Ernst & Young LLP **Investor Contact:** 972-444-9001 **Transfer Agents:** Continental Stock Transfer & Trust Company, New York, NY

PITNEY BOWES INC

Exchange	Symbol	Price	52Wk Range	Yield	P/E
NYS	PBI	$11.18 (12/29/2017)	16.59-9.64	6.71	23.29

*7 Year Price Score 55.89   *NYSE Composite Index=100   *12 Month Price Score 74.15

Interim Earnings (Per Share)

Qtr.	Mar	Jun	Sep	Dec
2014	0.22	0.46	0.65	0.31
2015	0.40	0.75	0.44	0.44
2016	0.30	0.28	0.35	(0.44)
2017	0.35	0.26	0.31	...

Interim Dividends (Per Share)

Amt	Decl	Ex	Rec	Pay
0.188Q	02/06/2017	02/15/2017	02/17/2017	03/13/2017
0.188Q	05/08/2017	05/24/2017	05/26/2017	06/12/2017
0.188Q	08/04/2017	08/23/2017	08/25/2017	09/12/2017
0.188Q	11/10/2017	11/20/2017	11/21/2017	12/12/2017

Indicated Div: $0.75 (Div. Reinv. Plan)

Valuation Analysis

		Institutional Holding	
Forecast EPS	$1.38 (01/12/2018)	No of Institutions	573
Market Cap	$2.1 Billion	Shares	199,238,368
Book Value	$100.8 Million	% Held	84.94
Price/Book	20.69		
Price/Sales	0.62		

Business Summary: Office Equipment & Furniture (MIC: 7.5.1 SIC: 7372 NAIC: 511210)

Pitney Bowes is a technology company. Co.'s solutions include: Small and Medium Business Solutions, which provides a range of equipment, software, supplies and services that enable Co.'s clients to create physical and digital mail, evidence postage and print shipping labels for the sending of mail, flats and parcels; Enterprise Business Solutions, which includes equipment and services that enable large enterprises to process inbound and outbound mail; and Digital Commerce Solutions, which provide a range of solutions, including customer information management, location intelligence, customer engagement software and shipping management and cross border ecommerce solutions.

Recent Developments: For the quarter ended Sep 30 2017, income from continuing operations decreased 18.5% to US$57.4 million from US$70.4 million in the year-earlier quarter. Net income decreased 18.2% to US$57.4 million from US$70.1 million in the year-earlier quarter. Revenues were US$842.8 million, up 0.5% from US$839.0 million the year before. Direct operating expenses rose 6.8% to US$388.7 million from US$364.0 million in the comparable period the year before. Indirect operating expenses decreased 0.6% to US$379.2 million from US$381.4 million in the equivalent prior-year period.

Prospects: Our evaluation of Pitney Bowes Inc. as of Jan. 14, 2018 is the result of our systematic analysis on three basic characteristics: earnings strength, relative valuation, and recent stock price movement. The company has generated a negative trend in earnings per share over the past 5 quarters and while recent estimates for the company have remained steady, PBI has posted results that fell short of analysts expectations. Based on operating earnings yield, the company is undervalued when compared to all of the companies in our coverage universe. Share price changes over the past year indicates that PBI will perform very poorly over the near term.

Financial Data

(US$ in Thousands)	9 Mos	6 Mos	3 Mos	12/31/2016	12/31/2015	12/31/2014	12/31/2013	12/31/2012
Earnings Per Share	0.48	0.52	0.54	0.49	2.03	1.64	0.70	2.21
Cash Flow Per Share	2.84	2.80	3.15	2.60	2.58	3.25	3.10	3.29
Dividends Per Share	0.750	0.750	0.750	0.750	0.750	0.750	0.938	1.500
Dividend Payout %	156.25	144.23	138.89	153.06	36.95	45.73	133.93	67.87
Income Statement								
Total Revenue	2,500,831	1,658,011	836,640	3,406,575	3,578,060	3,821,504	3,869,401	4,904,015
EBITDA	477,679	317,655	179,494	528,581	906,199	765,646	751,541	1,003,999
Depn & Amortn	131,989	88,160	44,295	138,000	136,000	165,000	158,000	211,000
Income Before Taxes	225,367	150,402	96,549	246,370	610,825	431,196	403,177	604,613
Income Taxes	53,975	36,368	31,416	131,819	189,778	112,815	83,069	150,305
Net Income	171,392	114,034	65,133	92,805	407,943	333,755	142,835	445,163
Average Shares	187,757	187,377	186,875	188,975	200,945	203,961	202,957	201,366
Balance Sheet								
Current Assets	3,220,557	2,491,577	2,233,134	2,325,183	2,319,808	2,760,120	2,838,212	3,212,127
Total Assets	6,781,407	6,037,348	5,747,171	5,837,133	6,141,462	6,485,693	6,772,708	7,859,891
Current Liabilities	2,264,730	2,633,107	2,448,440	2,327,619	2,279,051	2,360,623	2,227,755	2,877,037
Long-Term Obligations	3,562,672	2,543,476	2,499,025	2,750,405	2,507,912	2,927,127	3,346,295	3,642,375
Total Liabilities	6,680,574	6,007,975	5,793,509	5,940,793	5,962,740	6,408,434	6,584,305	7,749,260
Stockholders' Equity	100,833	29,373	(46,338)	(103,660)	178,721	77,259	188,403	110,631
Shares Outstanding	186,560	186,370	186,307	185,668	195,521	201,027	202,082	200,884
Statistical Record								
Return on Assets %	1.34	1.59	1.70	1.55	6.46	5.03	1.95	5.55
Return on Equity %	75.27	176.00	259.70	246.60	318.73	251.26	95.53	1,239.30
EBITDA Margin %	19.10	19.16	21.45	15.52	25.33	20.04	19.42	20.47
Net Margin %	6.85	6.88	7.79	2.72	11.40	8.73	3.69	9.08
Asset Turnover	0.52	0.56	0.58	0.57	0.57	0.58	0.53	0.61
Current Ratio	1.42	0.95	0.91	1.00	1.02	1.17	1.27	1.12
Debt to Equity	35.33	86.59	...	...	14.03	37.89	17.76	32.92
Price Range	18.16-12.49	19.31-12.49	21.70-12.49	21.70-14.24	24.42-18.82	28.18-21.13	24.09-10.64	19.54-10.41
P/E Ratio	37.83-26.02	37.13-24.02	40.19-23.13	44.29-29.06	12.03-9.27	17.18-12.88	34.41-15.20	8.84-4.71
Average Yield %	5.13	4.75	4.42	4.13	3.45	2.93	5.67	10.01

Address: 3001 Summer Street, Stamford, CT 06926	**Web Site:** www.pb.com	**Auditors:** PricewaterhouseCoopers LLP
Telephone: 203-356-5000	**Officers:** Jason Dies - Executive Vice President, Division Officer Marc B. Lautenbach - President, Chief Executive Officer	**Investor Contact:** 203-351-6349
Fax: 203-351-7336		**Transfer Agents:** Computershare Trust Company, N.A., Providence, RI

PLANTRONICS, INC.

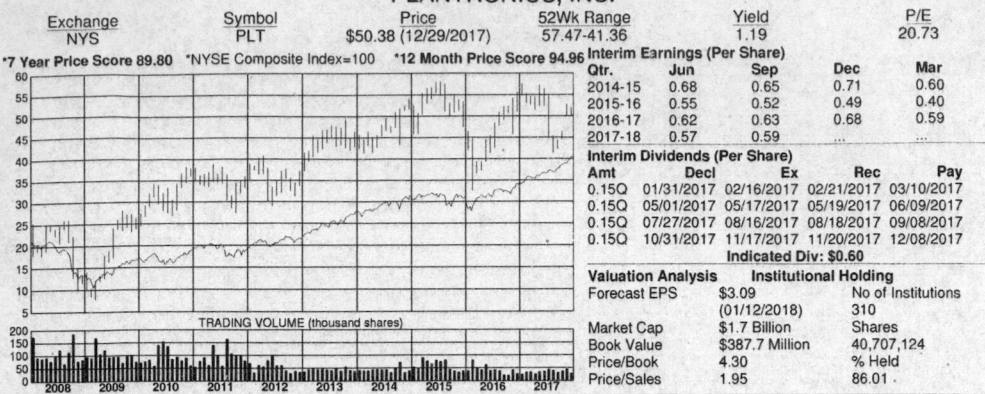

Exchange	Symbol	Price	52Wk Range	Yield	P/E
NYS	PLT	$50.38 (12/29/2017)	57.47-41.36	1.19	20.73

*7 Year Price Score 89.80 ***NYSE Composite Index=100** ***12 Month Price Score 94.96**

Interim Earnings (Per Share)

Qtr.	Jun	Sep	Dec	Mar
2014-15	0.68	0.65	0.71	0.60
2015-16	0.55	0.52	0.49	0.40
2016-17	0.62	0.63	0.68	0.59
2017-18	0.57	0.59	...	...

Interim Dividends (Per Share)

Amt	Decl	Ex	Rec	Pay
0.15Q	01/31/2017	02/16/2017	02/21/2017	03/10/2017
0.15Q	05/01/2017	05/17/2017	05/19/2017	06/09/2017
0.15Q	07/27/2017	08/16/2017	08/18/2017	09/08/2017
0.15Q	10/31/2017	11/17/2017	11/20/2017	12/08/2017

Indicated Div: $0.60

Valuation Analysis / Institutional Holding

Valuation Analysis		Institutional Holding	
Forecast EPS	$3.09	No of Institutions	
	(01/12/2018)	310	
Market Cap	$1.7 Billion	Shares	
Book Value	$387.7 Million	40,707,124	
Price/Book	4.30	% Held	
Price/Sales	1.95	86.01	

Business Summary: Manufacturing (MIC: 6.1.1 SIC: 3661 NAIC: 334210)

Plantronics designs, manufactures, and markets lightweight communications headsets, telephone headset systems, other communication endpoints, and accessories for the business and consumer markets. Co. also manufactures and markets specialty telephone products, such as telephones for the hearing impaired, and related products. Co.'s product categories are Enterprise, which includes headsets optimized for Unified Communications, other corded and cordless communication headsets, audio processors, and telephone systems; and Consumer, which includes Bluetooth and corded products for mobile device applications, personal computer, gaming headsets, and products for the hearing impaired.

Recent Developments: For the quarter ended Sep 30 2017, net income decreased 2.5% to US$20.0 million from US$20.5 million in the year-earlier quarter. Revenues were US$210.3 million, down 2.7% from US$216.2 million the year before. Operating income was US$30.2 million versus US$32.0 million in the prior-year quarter, a decrease of 5.6%. Direct operating expenses declined 2.9% to US$102.7 million from US$105.7 million in the comparable period the year before. Indirect operating expenses decreased 1.3% to US$77.5 million from US$78.5 million in the equivalent prior-year period.

Prospects: Our evaluation of Plantronics Inc. as of Jan. 14, 2018 is the result of our systematic analysis on three basic characteristics: earnings strength, relative valuation, and recent stock price movement. The company has generated a negative trend in earnings per share over the past 5 quarters and while recent estimates for the company have remained steady, PLT has posted better than expected results. Based on operating earnings yield, the company is undervalued when compared to all of the companies in our coverage universe. Share price changes over the past year indicates that PLT will perform very poorly over the near term.

Financial Data

(US$ in Thousands)	6 Mos	3 Mos	03/31/2017	03/31/2016	03/31/2015	03/31/2014	03/31/2013	03/31/2012
Earnings Per Share	2.43	2.47	2.51	1.96	2.63	2.59	2.49	2.41
Cash Flow Per Share	3.73	3.71	4.27	4.29	3.70	3.33	3.01	3.18
Tang Book Value Per Share	11.26	11.10	10.97	8.90	17.10	16.00	14.56	12.06
Dividends Per Share	0.600	0.600	0.600	0.600	0.600	0.400	0.400	0.200
Dividend Payout %	24.69	24.29	23.90	30.61	22.81	15.44	16.06	8.30
Income Statement								
Total Revenue	414,226	203,926	881,176	856,907	865,010	818,607	762,226	713,368
EBITDA	57,064	24,716	151,595	127,225	167,585	155,624	153,897	154,653
Depn & Amortn	725	362	20,700	19,900	18,500	15,500	15,800	13,300
Income Before Taxes	41,776	17,051	101,665	82,176	145,251	141,139	138,425	142,602
Income Taxes	2,995	(1,777)	19,066	13,784	32,950	28,722	32,023	33,566
Net Income	38,781	18,828	82,599	68,392	112,301	112,417	106,402	109,036
Average Shares	32,809	33,211	32,963	34,938	42,643	43,364	42,738	45,265
Balance Sheet								
Current Assets	734,386	715,366	698,977	596,995	602,654	556,287	566,490	524,174
Total Assets	1,022,382	1,009,994	1,017,159	933,437	876,042	811,815	764,605	672,470
Current Liabilities	114,053	102,635	117,170	109,167	94,822	97,607	103,486	86,193
Long-Term Obligations	491,784	491,421	491,059	489,609	34,500	...	...	37,000
Total Liabilities	634,715	621,573	635,003	621,038	148,645	113,151	118,158	145,226
Stockholders' Equity	387,667	388,421	382,156	312,399	727,397	698,664	646,447	527,244
Shares Outstanding	33,066	33,607	33,416	33,319	41,601	42,649	43,283	42,512
Statistical Record								
Return on Assets %	8.12	8.35	8.47	7.54	13.31	14.26	14.81	15.35
Return on Equity %	22.42	23.19	23.78	13.12	15.75	16.71	18.13	18.71
EBITDA Margin %	13.78	12.12	17.20	14.85	19.37	19.01	20.19	21.68
Net Margin %	9.36	9.23	9.37	7.98	12.98	13.73	13.96	15.28
Asset Turnover	0.86	0.89	0.90	0.94	1.02	1.04	1.06	1.00
Current Ratio	6.44	6.97	5.97	5.47	6.36	5.70	5.47	6.08
Debt to Equity	1.27	1.27	1.28	1.57	0.05	...	...	0.07
Price Range	57.47-41.36	57.47-42.47	57.47-37.28	58.09-32.55	55.45-41.57	49.56-41.41	45.61-28.95	40.26-27.45
P/E Ratio	23.65-17.02	23.27-17.19	22.90-14.85	29.64-16.61	21.03-15.81	19.14-15.99	18.32-11.63	16.71-11.39
Average Yield %	1.16	1.15	1.22	1.19	1.24	0.89	1.12	0.58

Address: 345 Encinal Street, Santa Cruz, CA 95060	**Web Site:** www.plantronics.com	**Auditors:** PricewaterhouseCoopers LLP
Telephone: 831-426-5858	**Officers:** Marvin Tseu - Chairman S. Kenneth Kannappan - Executive Vice Chairman, President,	**Investor Contact:** 831-426-5858
Fax: 831-426-6098	Chief Executive Officer	**Transfer Agents:** Computershare Trust Company, N.A., Providence, RI

PLATFORM SPECIALTY PRODUCTS CORP

Exchange	Symbol	Price	52Wk Range	Yield	P/E
NYS	PAH	$9.92 (12/29/2017)	14.58-9.45	N/A	N/A

*7 Year Price Score N/A   *NYSE Composite Index=100   *12 Month Price Score 77.91

Interim Earnings (Per Share)

Qtr.	Mar	Jun	Sep	Dec
2014	(0.07)	0.00	0.08	(1.97)
2015	(0.14)	(0.06)	(0.58)	(0.71)
2016	(0.59)	(0.04)	(0.15)	0.06
2017	(0.09)	(0.21)	(0.24)	...

Interim Dividends (Per Share)

No Dividends Paid

Valuation Analysis

Valuation Analysis		Institutional Holding	
Forecast EPS	$0.78	No of Institutions	258
	(01/17/2018)		
Market Cap	$2.8 Billion	Shares	
Book Value	$2.9 Billion	286,272,128	
Price/Book	0.99	% Held	
Price/Sales	0.78	N/A	

TRADING VOLUME (thousand shares)

Business Summary: Specialty Chemicals (MIC: 8.3.2 SIC: 5169 NAIC: 325998)

Platform Specialty Products is a producer of chemical products. Co.'s business involves the formulation of a range of chemicals, which are sold into various industries, including agricultural, animal health, electronics, and graphic arts. Co. manages its business in two reportable segments: Performance Solutions, which formulates and markets chemistry solutions that are used in electronics, automotive production, oil and gas production, drilling, commercial packaging and printing; and Agricultural Solutions, which provides to growers a range crop protection solutions from weeds (herbicides), insects (insecticides) and diseases (fungicides), in foliar and seed treatment applications.

Recent Developments: For the quarter ended Sep 30 2017, net loss amounted to US$66.3 million versus net income of US$65.9 million in the year-earlier quarter. Revenues were US$904.3 million, up 1.5% from US$890.5 million the year before. Operating income was US$83.5 million versus US$79.9 million in the prior-year quarter, an increase of 4.5%. Direct operating expenses rose 3.5% to US$533.2 million from US$515.4 million in the comparable period the year before. Indirect operating expenses decreased 2.6% to US$287.6 million from US$295.2 million in the equivalent prior-year period.

Prospects: Our evaluation of Platform Specialty Products as of Jan. 14, 2018 is the result of our systematic analysis on three basic characteristics: earnings strength, relative valuation, and recent stock price movement. The company has suffered a very negative trend in earnings per share over the past 5 quarters and while recent estimates for the company have been mixed, PAH has posted results that fell short of analysts expectations. Based on operating earnings yield, the company is undervalued when compared to all of the companies in our coverage universe. Share price changes over the past year indicates that PAH will perform very poorly over the near term.

Financial Data
(US$ in Thousands)

	9 Mos	6 Mos	3 Mos	12/31/2016	12/31/2015	12/31/2014	12/31/2013
Earnings Per Share	(0.48)	(0.39)	(0.22)	(0.65)	(1.52)	(1.94)	(2.10)
Cash Flow Per Share	1.02	1.00	0.97	0.76	1.58	0.73	0.08
Income Statement							
Total Revenue	2,707,200	1,802,900	861,800	3,585,900	2,542,300	843,200	118,239
EBITDA	235,800	157,700	101,800	402,600	33,500	26,300	(192,172)
Depn & Amortn	58,400	37,100	17,300	75,000	48,900	19,300	3,900
Income Before Taxes	(82,600)	(53,800)	(4,900)	(48,100)	(229,300)	(30,900)	(201,444)
Income Taxes	67,300	29,800	18,700	28,600	75,100	(6,700)	(5,819)
Net Income	(154,700)	(85,500)	(24,400)	(73,700)	(308,600)	(29,900)	(194,222)
Average Shares	286,700	286,100	284,500	272,300	203,200	135,300	92,563
Balance Sheet							
Current Assets	2,296,600	2,342,400	2,255,500	2,071,200	2,270,500	1,578,400	383,239
Total Assets	10,438,600	10,386,300	10,349,900	10,054,100	10,190,200	4,557,600	2,241,888
Current Liabilities	1,120,400	1,204,900	1,200,900	1,082,700	1,062,400	242,600	119,420
Long-Term Obligations	5,332,700	5,271,100	5,141,800	5,122,900	5,173,600	1,400,800	744,291
Total Liabilities	7,548,100	7,563,600	7,442,900	7,318,000	7,440,400	2,098,000	1,188,321
Stockholders' Equity	2,890,500	2,822,700	2,907,000	2,736,100	2,749,800	2,459,600	1,053,567
Shares Outstanding	287,100	286,291	285,700	284,221	229,464	182,066	103,571
Statistical Record							
Return on Assets %	N.M.	N.M.	0.35	N.M.	N.M.	N.M.	...
Return on Equity %	N.M.	N.M.	1.26	N.M.	N.M.	N.M.	...
EBITDA Margin %	8.71	8.75	11.81	11.23	1.32	3.12	N.M.
Asset Turnover	0.34	0.35	0.35	0.35	0.34	0.25	...
Current Ratio	2.05	1.94	1.88	1.91	2.14	6.51	3.21
Debt to Equity	1.84	1.87	1.77	1.87	1.88	0.57	0.71
Price Range	14.58-7.17	14.32-7.17	13.47-7.17	12.83-5.55	28.35-10.12	28.70-13.83	...

Address: 1450 Centrepark Boulevard, Suite 210, West Palm Beach, FL 33401
Telephone: 561-207-9600

Web Site: www.platformspecialtyproducts.com
Officers: Martin E. Franklin - Chairman Rakesh Sachdev - Chief Executive Officer

Auditors: PricewaterhouseCoopers LLP

PNC FINANCIAL SERVICES GROUP (THE)

Exchange	Symbol	Price	52Wk Range	Yield	P/E
NYS	PNC	$144.29 (12/29/2017)	146.26-113.93	2.08	17.62

*7 Year Price Score 119.50 *NYSE Composite Index=100 *12 Month Price Score 103.67

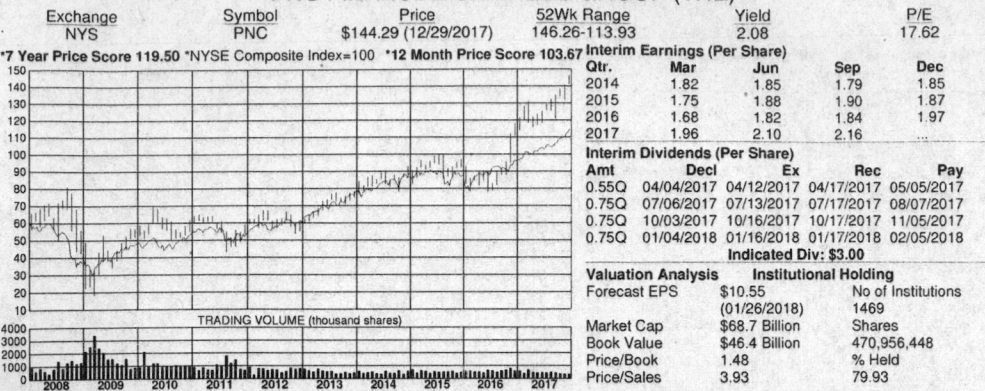

Interim Earnings (Per Share)

Qtr.	Mar	Jun	Sep	Dec
2014	1.82	1.85	1.79	1.85
2015	1.75	1.88	1.90	1.87
2016	1.68	1.82	1.84	1.97
2017	1.96	2.10	2.16	...

Interim Dividends (Per Share)

Amt	Decl	Ex	Rec	Pay
0.55Q	04/04/2017	04/12/2017	04/17/2017	05/05/2017
0.75Q	07/06/2017	07/13/2017	07/17/2017	08/07/2017
0.75Q	10/03/2017	10/16/2017	10/17/2017	11/05/2017
0.75Q	01/04/2018	01/16/2018	01/17/2018	02/05/2018

Indicated Div: $3.00

Valuation Analysis — **Institutional Holding**

Forecast EPS	$10.55	No of Institutions
	(01/26/2018)	1469
Market Cap	$68.7 Billion	Shares
Book Value	$46.4 Billion	470,956,448
Price/Book	1.48	% Held
Price/Sales	3.93	79.93

Business Summary: Banking (MIC: 5.1.1 SIC: 6021 NAIC: 522110)

PNC Financial Services Group is a bank holding company and a financial services company that provides its products and services nationally. Co.'s main markets are in Pennsylvania, Ohio, New Jersey, Michigan, Illinois, Maryland, Indiana, Florida, North Carolina, Kentucky, Washington, D.C., Delaware, Virginia, Georgia, Alabama, Missouri, Wisconsin and South Carolina. Co. also provides certain products and services internationally. Co. has six segments: retail banking, corporate and institutional banking, asset management group, residential mortgage banking, BlackRock, and non-strategic assets portfolio. At Dec 31 2016, Co. had total assets of $366.38 billion and deposits of $257.16 billion.

Recent Developments: For the quarter ended Sep 30 2017, net income increased 11.9% to US$1.13 billion from US$1.01 billion in the year-earlier quarter. Net interest income increased 11.9% to US$2.35 billion from US$2.10 billion in the year-earlier quarter. Provision for loan losses was US$130.0 million versus US$87.0 million in the prior-year quarter, an increase of 49.4%. Non-interest income rose 2.7% to US$1.78 billion from US$1.73 billion, while non-interest expense advanced 2.6% to US$2.46 billion.

Prospects: Our evaluation of PNC Financial Services Group as of Jan. 21, 2018 is the result of our systematic analysis on three basic characteristics: earnings strength, relative valuation, and recent stock price movement. The company has enjoyed a very positive trend in earnings per share over the past 5 quarters and while recent estimates for the company have been raised by analysts, PNC has posted better than expected results. Based on operating earnings yield, the company is undervalued when compared to all of the companies in our coverage universe. Share price changes over the past year indicates that PNC will perform in line with the market over the near term.

Financial Data

(US$ in Thousands)	9 Mos	6 Mos	3 Mos	12/31/2016	12/31/2015	12/31/2014	12/31/2013	12/31/2012
Earnings Per Share	8.19	7.87	7.59	7.30	7.39	7.30	7.39	5.30
Cash Flow Per Share	12.87	10.66	10.20	7.34	10.69	10.50	10.52	12.94
Tang Book Value Per Share	74.31	73.03	71.72	71.83	59.89	56.71	50.99	46.48
Dividends Per Share	2.400	2.200	2.160	2.120	2.010	1.880	1.720	1.550
Dividend Payout %	29.30	27.95	28.46	29.04	27.20	25.75	23.27	29.25
Income Statement								
Interest Income	7,989,000	5,194,000	2,520,000	9,652,000	9,323,000	9,431,000	10,007,000	10,734,000
Interest Expense	1,226,000	776,000	360,000	1,261,000	1,045,000	906,000	860,000	1,094,000
Net Interest Income	6,763,000	4,418,000	2,160,000	8,391,000	8,278,000	8,525,000	9,147,000	9,640,000
Provision for Losses	316,000	186,000	88,000	433,000	255,000	273,000	643,000	987,000
Non-Interest Income	5,306,000	3,526,000	1,724,000	6,771,000	6,947,000	6,850,000	6,865,000	5,872,000
Non-Interest Expense	7,337,000	4,881,000	2,402,000	9,476,000	9,463,000	9,488,000	9,801,000	10,582,000
Income Before Taxes	4,416,000	2,877,000	1,394,000	5,253,000	5,507,000	5,614,000	5,568,000	3,943,000
Income Taxes	1,119,000	706,000	320,000	1,268,000	1,364,000	1,407,000	1,341,000	942,000
Net Income	3,258,000	2,144,000	1,057,000	3,903,000	4,106,000	4,184,000	4,220,000	3,013,000
Average Shares	483,000	488,000	492,000	500,000	521,000	537,000	532,000	529,000
Balance Sheet								
Net Loans & Leases	220,268,000	217,503,000	211,679,000	210,748,000	205,509,000	203,748,000	194,259,000	185,513,000
Total Assets	375,191,000	372,190,000	370,944,000	366,380,000	358,493,000	345,072,000	320,296,000	305,107,000
Total Deposits	260,735,000	259,176,000	260,710,000	257,164,000	249,002,000	232,234,000	220,931,000	213,142,000
Total Liabilities	328,803,000	326,106,000	325,190,000	320,681,000	313,783,000	300,521,000	277,888,000	266,104,000
Stockholders' Equity	46,388,000	46,084,000	45,754,000	45,699,000	44,710,000	44,551,000	42,408,000	39,003,000
Shares Outstanding	476,000	480,000	485,000	485,000	504,000	523,000	533,000	528,000
Statistical Record								
Return on Assets %	1.15	1.13	1.10	1.07	1.17	1.26	1.35	1.04
Return on Equity %	9.30	9.07	8.88	8.61	9.20	9.62	10.37	8.23
Net Interest Margin %	83.90	84.44	85.71	86.94	88.79	90.39	91.41	89.81
Efficiency Ratio %	53.68	55.38	56.60	57.70	58.16	58.28	58.09	63.72
Loans to Deposits	0.84	0.84	0.81	0.82	0.83	0.88	0.88	0.87
Price Range	134.77-87.94	130.85-78.83	130.85-77.88	118.31-77.88	99.86-82.42	92.93-76.60	78.20-58.31	67.33-53.69
P/E Ratio	16.46-10.74	16.63-10.02	17.24-10.26	16.21-10.67	13.51-11.15	12.73-10.49	10.58-7.89	12.70-10.13
Average Yield %	2.02	2.04	2.18	2.35	2.16	2.22	2.44	2.55

Address: The Tower at PNC Plaza, 300 Fifth Avenue, Pittsburgh, PA 15222-2401	**Web Site:** www.pnc.com	**Auditors:** PricewaterhouseCoopers LLP
Telephone: 412-762-2000	**Officers:** William S. Demchak - Chairman, President, Chief Executive Officer Robert Q. Reilly - Executive Vice President, Chief Financial Officer	**Investor Contact:** 412-762-8257
Fax: 412-762-5798		**Transfer Agents:** Computershare Trust Company, N. A., Canton, MA

PNM RESOURCES INC

Exchange	Symbol	Price	52Wk Range	Yield	P/E
NYS	PNM	$40.45 (12/29/2017)	45.50-33.45	2.62	20.33

*7 Year Price Score 116.14 ***NYSE Composite Index=100** ***12 Month Price Score 104.38**

Interim Earnings (Per Share)

Qtr.	Mar	Jun	Sep	Dec
2014	0.16	0.36	0.69	0.24
2015	0.18	0.40	0.76	(1.14)
2016	0.13	0.34	0.68	0.31
2017	0.29	0.47	0.92	...

Interim Dividends (Per Share)

Amt	Decl	Ex	Rec	Pay
0.242Q	02/24/2017	04/27/2017	05/01/2017	05/15/2017
0.242Q	07/26/2017	08/03/2017	08/07/2017	08/14/2017
0.242Q	09/19/2017	10/27/2017	10/30/2017	11/14/2017
0.265Q	12/01/2017	01/17/2018	01/18/2018	02/01/2018

Indicated Div: $1.06

Valuation Analysis		Institutional Holding	
Forecast EPS	$1.88	No of Institutions	
	(01/18/2018)	338	
Market Cap	$3.2 Billion	Shares	
Book Value	$1.8 Billion	97,335,336	
Price/Book	1.81	% Held	
Price/Sales	2.22	79.10	

TRADING VOLUME (thousand shares)

Business Summary: Electric Utilities (MIC: 3.1.1 SIC: 4911 NAIC: 221121)

PNM Resources is a holding company with two regulated utilities providing electricity and electric services in New Mexico and Texas. Co.'s primary subsidiaries are Public Service Company of New Mexico (PNM) and Texas-New Mexico Power Company (TNMP). PNM is an electric utility that provides electric generation, transmission, and distribution service to its rate-regulated customers in New Mexico. TNMP is a regulated utility engaged in providing transmission and distribution services in Texas under the provisions of Texas Electric Choice Act and the Texas Public Utility Regulatory Act. As of Dec 31 2016, PNM had 520,449 customers, while TNMP had 246,620 customers.

Recent Developments: For the quarter ended Sep 30 2017, net income increased 33.8% to US$78.3 million from US$58.6 million in the year-earlier quarter. Revenues were US$419.9 million, up 4.9% from US$400.4 million the year before. Operating income was US$142.5 million versus US$108.1 million in the prior-year quarter, an increase of 31.8%. Direct operating expenses declined 11.7% to US$152.5 million from US$172.7 million in the comparable period the year before. Indirect operating expenses increased 4.5% to US$124.9 million from US$119.6 million in the equivalent prior-year period.

Prospects: Our evaluation of PNM Resources Inc. as of Jan. 14, 2018 is the result of our systematic analysis on three basic characteristics: earnings strength, relative valuation, and recent stock price movement. The company has generated a negative trend in earnings per share over the past 5 quarters. However, while recent estimates for the company have been mixed, PNM has posted better than expected results. Based on operating earnings yield, the company is undervalued when compared to all of the companies in our coverage universe. Share price changes over the past year indicates that PNM will perform very well over the near term.

Financial Data

(US$ in Thousands)	9 Mos	6 Mos	3 Mos	12/31/2016	12/31/2015	12/31/2014	12/31/2013	12/31/2012
Earnings Per Share	1.99	1.75	1.62	1.46	0.20	1.45	1.25	1.31
Cash Flow Per Share	6.40	6.20	5.72	5.19	4.85	5.20	4.85	3.52
Tang Book Value Per Share	18.82	18.34	17.83	17.69	17.43	18.26	17.66	16.84
Dividends Per Share	0.948	0.925	0.902	0.880	0.800	0.740	0.640	0.560
Dividend Payout %	47.61	52.86	55.71	60.27	400.00	51.03	51.20	42.75
Income Statement								
Total Revenue	1,112,398	692,498	330,178	1,362,951	1,439,082	1,435,853	1,387,923	1,342,403
EBITDA	505,233	287,214	129,928	543,547	377,376	521,658	453,355	489,307
Depn & Amortn	200,286	131,861	65,888	242,033	222,861	209,867	166,881	206,499
Income Before Taxes	221,158	100,088	37,221	195,174	46,153	200,647	175,069	175,035
Income Taxes	75,154	32,411	10,775	63,278	15,075	69,738	59,513	54,910
Net Income	134,552	60,681	22,994	117,377	16,168	116,782	101,035	106,075
Average Shares	80,154	80,131	80,112	80,132	80,139	80,279	79,845	80,417
Balance Sheet								
Current Assets	374,535	353,587	326,769	378,039	385,570	432,817	401,539	442,191
Total Assets	6,697,254	6,584,445	6,477,679	6,471,080	6,009,328	5,829,325	5,500,210	5,372,583
Current Liabilities	710,885	766,570	962,136	805,108	641,120	704,282	492,671	434,103
Long-Term Obligations	2,282,390	2,199,105	1,969,304	2,119,364	1,966,969	1,642,024	1,670,420	1,669,760
Total Liabilities	4,919,988	4,845,656	4,779,510	4,783,599	4,342,986	4,096,250	3,815,112	3,752,867
Stockholders' Equity	1,777,266	1,738,789	1,698,169	1,687,481	1,666,342	1,733,075	1,685,098	1,619,716
Shares Outstanding	79,653	79,653	79,653	79,653	79,653	79,653	79,653	79,653
Statistical Record								
Return on Assets %	2.43	2.17	2.03	1.88	0.27	2.06	1.86	2.00
Return on Equity %	9.17	8.20	7.74	6.98	0.95	6.83	6.11	6.60
EBITDA Margin %	45.42	41.48	39.35	39.88	26.22	36.33	32.66	36.45
Net Margin %	12.10	8.76	6.96	8.61	1.12	8.13	7.28	7.90
Asset Turnover	0.22	0.22	0.22	0.22	0.24	0.25	0.26	0.25
Current Ratio	0.53	0.46	0.34	0.47	0.60	0.61	0.82	1.02
Debt to Equity	1.28	1.26	1.16	1.26	1.18	0.95	0.99	1.03
Price Range	42.95-31.16	40.00-31.16	37.60-30.63	36.05-29.35	31.17-24.60	31.39-23.53	24.29-20.28	22.32-17.52
P/E Ratio	21.58-15.66	22.86-17.81	23.21-18.91	24.69-20.10	155.85-123.00	21.65-16.23	19.43-16.22	17.04-13.37
Average Yield %	2.59	2.66	2.68	2.69	2.89	2.74	2.82	2.85

Address: 414 Silver Ave. S.W., Albuquerque, NM 87102-3289 Telephone: 505-241-2700	Web Site: www.pnmresources.com Officers: Patricia K. Vincent-Collawn - Chairman, President, Chief Executive Officer Charles N. Eldred - Executive Vice President, Chief Financial Officer	Auditors: KPMG LLP Investor Contact: 505-241-2211 Transfer Agents: Computershare, Providence, RI

POLARIS INDUSTRIES INC.

Exchange	Symbol	Price	52Wk Range	Yield	P/E	Div Achiever
NYS	PII	$123.99 (12/29/2017)	133.70-78.82	1.87	39.11	21 Years

*7 Year Price Score 77.24 *NYSE Composite Index=100 *12 Month Price Score 121.41

Interim Earnings (Per Share)

Qtr.	Mar	Jun	Sep	Dec
2014	1.19	1.42	2.06	1.97
2015	1.30	1.49	2.30	1.66
2016	0.71	1.09	0.50	0.97
2017	(0.05)	0.97	1.28	...

Interim Dividends (Per Share)

Amt	Decl	Ex	Rec	Pay
0.58Q	01/26/2017	02/27/2017	03/01/2017	03/15/2017
0.58Q	04/27/2017	05/30/2017	06/01/2017	06/15/2017
0.58Q	07/26/2017	08/30/2017	09/01/2017	09/15/2017
0.58Q	10/26/2017	11/30/2017	12/01/2017	12/15/2017

Indicated Div: $2.32 (Div. Reinv. Plan)

Valuation Analysis **Institutional Holding**

Forecast EPS	$4.85 (01/18/2018)	No of Institutions 603
Market Cap	$7.8 Billion	Shares
Book Value	$907.3 Million	68,835,312
Price/Book	8.55	% Held
Price/Sales	1.49	73.89

Business Summary: Autos- Manufacturing (MIC: 1.8.1 SIC: 3799 NAIC: 336999)

Polaris Industries are engaged in the design, engineering, manufacturing and marketing of Off-Road Vehicles, which includes the RZR® sport side-by-side, the RANGER® utility side-by-side, the GENERALâ‚¢crossover side-by-side, the Sportsman® ATV and the Polaris ACE®; Snowmobiles, which include covers, traction products, reverse kits, electric starters, tracks, bags, windshields, oil and lubricants; Motorcycles, which include saddle bags, handlebars, backrests, exhaust, windshields, seats, oil and various chrome accessories; and Global Adjacent Markets vehicles, which provides a military version ATV and side-by-side vehicles with features designed for ultra-light tactical military applications.

Recent Developments: For the quarter ended Sep 30 2017, net income increased 153.4% to US$81.9 million from US$32.3 million in the year-earlier quarter. Revenues were US$1.48 billion, up 24.8% from US$1.19 billion the year before. Operating income was US$116.9 million versus US$57.4 million in the prior-year quarter, an increase of 103.7%. Direct operating expenses rose 20.6% to US$1.11 billion from US$924.3 million in the comparable period the year before. Indirect operating expenses increased 21.5% to US$247.1 million from US$203.4 million in the equivalent prior-year period.

Prospects: Our evaluation of Polaris Industries Inc. as of Jan. 14, 2018 is the result of our systematic analysis on three basic characteristics: earnings strength, relative valuation, and recent stock price movement. The company has produced a positive trend in earnings per share over the past 5 quarters and while recent estimates for the company have been mixed, PII has posted better than expected results. Based on operating earnings yield, the company is about fairly valued when compared to all of the companies in our coverage universe. Share price changes over the past year indicates that PII will perform well over the near term.

Financial Data

(US$ in Thousands)	9 Mos	6 Mos	3 Mos	12/31/2016	12/31/2015	12/31/2014	12/31/2013	12/31/2012
Earnings Per Share	3.17	2.39	2.51	3.27	6.75	6.65	5.35	4.40
Cash Flow Per Share	10.22	7.75	7.66	8.87	6.67	8.00	7.18	6.03
Tang Book Value Per Share	1.96	1.24	0.93	1.31	11.56	9.82	4.79	8.50
Dividends Per Share	2.290	2.260	2.230	2.200	2.120	1.920	1.680	1.480
Dividend Payout %	72.24	94.56	88.84	67.28	31.41	28.87	31.40	33.64
Income Statement								
Total Revenue	3,997,428	2,518,702	1,153,782	4,516,629	4,719,290	4,479,648	3,777,068	3,209,782
EBITDA	368,196	201,939	54,019	503,955	856,133	842,187	675,153	556,534
Depn & Amortn	138,105	91,124	44,538	167,512	152,138	127,507	92,100	70,580
Income Before Taxes	205,653	94,869	1,567	320,124	692,539	703,441	576,843	480,022
Income Taxes	59,796	32,503	2,578	100,303	230,376	245,288	193,360	167,533
Net Income	141,018	59,130	(2,911)	212,948	455,361	454,029	377,292	312,310
Average Shares	63,885	63,807	64,133	65,158	67,484	68,229	70,546	71,005
Balance Sheet								
Current Assets	1,248,650	1,216,879	1,250,477	1,190,989	1,154,725	1,096,555	865,698	1,017,841
Total Assets	3,133,066	3,114,972	3,135,999	3,099,597	2,387,462	2,074,935	1,685,488	1,486,492
Current Liabilities	1,195,038	1,048,106	986,385	959,751	826,783	850,810	748,070	631,029
Long-Term Obligations	892,149	1,064,966	1,174,853	1,138,063	458,220	223,620	284,342	104,292
Total Liabilities	2,225,771	2,250,470	2,290,904	2,223,829	1,396,340	1,200,140	1,141,462	795,962
Stockholders' Equity	907,295	864,502	845,095	875,768	991,122	874,795	544,026	690,530
Shares Outstanding	62,540	62,557	62,989	63,109	65,309	66,307	65,623	68,647
Statistical Record								
Return on Assets %	7.27	5.59	5.92	7.74	20.41	24.15	23.79	22.95
Return on Equity %	22.07	17.12	18.25	22.75	48.81	64.00	61.12	52.32
EBITDA Margin %	9.21	8.02	4.68	11.16	18.14	18.80	17.88	17.34
Net Margin %	3.53	2.35	N.M.	4.71	9.65	10.14	9.99	9.73
Asset Turnover	1.86	1.79	1.70	1.64	2.12	2.38	2.38	2.36
Current Ratio	1.04	1.16	1.27	1.24	1.40	1.29	1.16	1.61
Debt to Equity	0.98	1.23	1.39	1.30	0.46	0.26	0.52	0.15
Price Range	108.26-74.02	98.75-70.50	101.03-70.50	101.03-69.61	157.62-83.30	158.43-119.98	145.78-83.24	88.35-54.67
P/E Ratio	34.15-23.35	41.32-29.50	40.25-28.09	30.90-21.29	23.35-12.34	23.82-18.04	27.25-15.56	20.08-12.43
Average Yield %	2.63	2.64	2.60	2.56	1.59	1.37	1.58	1.96

Address: 2100 Highway 55, Medina, MN 55340 Telephone: 763-542-0500	Web Site: www.polaris.com Officers: Scott W. Wine - Chairman, Chief Executive Officer Michael T. Speetzen - Executive Vice President, Chief Financial Officer	Auditors: Ernst & Young LLP Investor Contact: 763-513-3477 Transfer Agents: Wells Fargo Shareowner Services, Mendota Heights, MN

POLYONE CORP.

Exchange	Symbol	Price	52Wk Range	Yield	P/E
NYS	POL	$43.50 (12/29/2017)	46.48-31.83	1.61	N/A

*7 Year Price Score 105.03 *NYSE Composite Index=100 *12 Month Price Score 110.82

Interim Earnings (Per Share)

Qtr.	Mar	Jun	Sep	Dec
2014	0.31	0.34	0.35	(0.14)
2015	0.34	0.74	0.50	0.05
2016	0.46	0.59	0.50	0.40
2017	0.57	(2.22)	0.47	...

Interim Dividends (Per Share)

Amt	Decl	Ex	Rec	Pay
0.135Q	02/15/2017	03/10/2017	03/14/2017	04/06/2017
0.135Q	05/11/2017	06/14/2017	06/16/2017	07/07/2017
0.135Q	07/13/2017	09/14/2017	09/15/2017	10/05/2017
0.175Q	10/12/2017	12/14/2017	12/15/2017	01/10/2018

Indicated Div: $0.70

Valuation Analysis | **Institutional Holding**

Forecast EPS	$2.51 (01/27/2018)	No of Institutions 353
Market Cap	$3.5 Billion	Shares
Book Value	$567.9 Million	95,827,096
Price/Book	6.19	% Held
Price/Sales	1.06	93.75

Business Summary: Plastics (MIC: 8.4.2 SIC: 2821 NAIC: 325211)

PolyOne is a provider of polymer materials, services and solutions. Co. has five segments: Color, Additives and Inks, which provide color and additive concentrates in solid and liquid form, dispersions, as well as specialty inks, plastisols, and vinyl slush molding solutions; Specialty Engineered Materials, which provide polymer formulations, services and solutions; Designed Structures and Solutions, which produce sheet, custom rollstock and film, laminate and acrylic solutions; Performance Products and Solutions, which comprised of the Geon performance Materials and producer services business units; and PolyOne Distribution, which distributes engineering and commodity grade resins.

Recent Developments: For the quarter ended Sep 30 2017, income from continuing operations decreased 6.1% to US$40.2 million from US$42.8 million in the year-earlier quarter. Net income decreased 8.3% to US$38.8 million from US$42.3 million in the year-earlier quarter. Revenues were US$818.5 million, up 9.6% from US$746.7 million the year before. Operating income was US$67.7 million versus US$72.0 million in the prior-year quarter, a decrease of 6.0%. Direct operating expenses rose 10.1% to US$639.0 million from US$580.6 million in the comparable period the year before. Indirect operating expenses increased 18.8% to US$111.8 million from US$94.1 million in the equivalent prior-year period.

Prospects: Our evaluation of PolyOne Corp. as of Jan. 21, 2018 is the result of our systematic analysis on three basic characteristics: earnings strength, relative valuation, and recent stock price movement. The company has produced a positive trend in earnings per share over the past 5 quarters and while recent estimates for the company have been mixed, POL has posted better than expected results. Based on operating earnings yield, the company is undervalued when compared to all of the companies in our coverage universe. Share price changes over the past year indicates that POL will perform well over the near term.

Financial Data (US$ in Thousands)	9 Mos	6 Mos	3 Mos	12/31/2016	12/31/2015	12/31/2014	12/31/2013	12/31/2012
Earnings Per Share	(0.78)	(0.75)	2.06	1.95	1.63	0.85	2.53	0.80
Cash Flow Per Share	2.53	2.64	2.76	2.63	2.59	2.26	1.14	1.20
Tang Book Value Per Share	N.M.	N.M.	N.M.	N.M.	N.M.	N.M.	0.55	N.M.
Dividends Per Share	0.540	0.525	0.510	0.495	0.420	0.340	0.260	0.200
Dividend Payout %	...	...	24.76	25.38	25.77	40.00	10.28	25.00
Income Statement								
Total Revenue	2,429,300	1,610,800	898,800	3,339,800	3,377,600	3,835,500	3,771,200	2,992,600
EBITDA	229,100	162,100	100,600	364,100	316,200	255,300	278,600	197,000
Depn & Amortn	900	900	20,300	82,000	84,400	104,700	91,000	56,600
Income Before Taxes	182,900	131,400	65,700	222,300	167,700	88,400	124,100	89,600
Income Taxes	44,800	33,500	18,800	57,300	23,000	11,200	58,100	41,200
Net Income	(95,700)	(134,500)	46,900	165,200	144,600	79,200	243,800	71,900
Average Shares	82,000	82,500	82,700	84,600	88,700	93,500	96,500	89,800
Balance Sheet								
Current Assets	1,044,000	1,135,300	985,000	949,500	960,800	1,042,700	1,253,600	866,900
Total Assets	2,649,500	2,712,600	2,776,700	2,723,300	2,595,100	2,711,200	2,944,100	2,128,000
Current Liabilities	533,900	546,200	517,600	509,600	498,100	601,200	608,900	459,800
Long-Term Obligations	1,319,500	1,382,500	1,279,200	1,239,800	1,128,000	962,000	976,200	703,100
Total Liabilities	2,081,600	2,155,300	2,043,100	1,998,600	1,890,900	1,934,900	1,967,300	1,498,900
Stockholders' Equity	567,900	557,300	733,600	724,700	704,200	776,300	976,800	629,100
Shares Outstanding	80,804	81,791	81,755	82,600	85,300	89,300	95,100	89,500
Statistical Record								
Return on Assets %	N.M.	N.M.	6.41	6.20	5.45	2.80	9.61	3.41
Return on Equity %	N.M.	N.M.	24.26	23.06	19.53	9.04	30.36	11.78
EBITDA Margin %	9.43	10.06	11.19	10.90	9.36	6.66	7.39	6.58
Net Margin %	N.M.	N.M.	5.22	4.95	4.28	2.06	6.46	2.40
Asset Turnover	1.23	1.25	1.26	1.25	1.27	1.36	1.49	1.42
Current Ratio	1.96	2.08	1.90	1.86	1.93	1.73	2.06	1.89
Debt to Equity	2.32	2.48	1.74	1.71	1.60	1.24	1.00	1.12
Price Range	40.56-29.06	39.40-29.06	38.21-29.06	38.21-24.30	40.89-29.27	43.14-32.19	35.44-20.42	20.74-11.77
P/E Ratio	...	...	18.55-14.11	19.59-12.46	25.09-17.96	50.75-37.87	14.01-8.07	25.92-14.71
Average Yield %	1.54	1.53	1.51	1.53	1.17	0.90	0.97	1.30

Address: 33587 Walker Road, Avon Lake, OH 44012 **Telephone:** 440-930-1000	**Web Site:** www.polyone.com **Officers:** Robert M. Patterson - Chairman, President, Chief Executive Officer, Senior Vice President, Chief Financial Officer, Chief Operating Officer Scott Horn - Senior Vice President, Division Officer	**Auditors:** Ernst & Young LLP **Investor Contact:** 440-930-1226 **Transfer Agents:** Wells Fargo Shareowner Services, Mendota Heights, MN

PORTLAND GENERAL ELECTRIC CO.

Exchange	Symbol	Price	52Wk Range	Yield	P/E	Div Achiever
NYS	POR	$45.58 (12/29/2017)	49.72-42.83	2.98	19.90	10 Years

*7 Year Price Score 106.03 *NYSE Composite Index=100 *12 Month Price Score 98.31

Interim Earnings (Per Share)

Qtr.	Mar	Jun	Sep	Dec
2014	0.73	0.43	0.47	0.55
2015	0.62	0.44	0.40	0.57
2016	0.68	0.42	0.38	0.67
2017	0.82	0.36	0.44	...

Interim Dividends (Per Share)

Amt	Decl	Ex	Rec	Pay
0.32Q	02/15/2017	03/23/2017	03/27/2017	04/17/2017
0.34Q	04/26/2017	06/22/2017	06/26/2017	07/17/2017
0.34Q	07/26/2017	09/22/2017	09/25/2017	10/16/2017
0.34Q	10/25/2017	12/22/2017	12/26/2017	01/16/2018

Indicated Div: $1.36

Valuation Analysis — Institutional Holding

Forecast EPS	$2.27	No of Institutions
	(01/16/2018)	380
Market Cap	$4.1 Billion	Shares
Book Value	$2.4 Billion	110,321,136
Price/Book	1.69	% Held
Price/Sales	2.01	105.94

Business Summary: Electric Utilities (MIC: 3.1.1 SIC: 4911 NAIC: 221122)

Portland General Electric is an electric utility engaged in the generation, wholesale purchase, transmission, distribution, and retail sale of electricity in the state of Oregon. Co. also participates in the wholesale market by purchasing and selling electricity and natural gas to its retail customers. Co.'s service area includes 51 incorporated cities in Oregon, principally in Portland and Salem, within a state-approved service area allocation of approximately 4,000 square miles. As of Dec 31 2016, Co. served a total of 863,000 retail customers.

Recent Developments: For the quarter ended Sep 30 2017, net income increased 17.6% to US$40.0 million from US$34.0 million in the year-earlier quarter. Revenues were US$515.0 million, up 6.4% from US$484.0 million the year before. Operating income was US$77.0 million versus US$64.0 million in the prior-year quarter, an increase of 20.3%. Direct operating expenses rose 3.2% to US$257.0 million from US$249.0 million in the comparable period the year before. Indirect operating expenses increased 5.8% to US$181.0 million from US$171.0 million in the equivalent prior-year period.

Prospects: Our evaluation of Portland General Electric Co. as of Jan. 14, 2018 is the result of our systematic analysis on three basic characteristics: earnings strength, relative valuation, and recent stock price movement. The company has generated a negative trend in earnings per share over the past 5 quarters and while recent estimates for the company have been mixed, POR has posted better than expected results. Based on operating earnings yield, the company is undervalued when compared to all of the companies in our coverage universe. Share price changes over the past year indicates that POR will perform very well over the near term.

Financial Data

(US$ in Millions)	9 Mos	6 Mos	3 Mos	12/31/2016	12/31/2015	12/31/2014	12/31/2013	12/31/2012
Earnings Per Share	2.29	2.23	2.29	2.16	2.04	2.18	1.35	1.87
Cash Flow Per Share	6.46	6.15	6.31	6.20	6.14	6.63	7.08	6.53
Tang Book Value Per Share	26.96	26.86	26.80	26.35	25.43	24.43	23.29	22.87
Dividends Per Share	1.320	1.300	1.280	1.260	1.180	1.115	1.095	1.075
Dividend Payout %	57.64	58.30	55.90	58.33	57.84	51.15	81.11	57.49
Income Statement								
Total Revenue	1,494	979	530	1,923	1,898	1,900	1,810	1,805
EBITDA	538	368	210	399	369	356	248	334
Depn & Amortn	257	170	84	44	38	25	22	22
Income Before Taxes	191	138	96	243	217	235	125	204
Income Taxes	46	33	23	50	45	61	21	64
Net Income	145	105	73	193	172	175	105	141
Average Shares	89	89	89	89	84	80	77	75
Balance Sheet								
Current Assets	466	412	485	463	557	699	591	622
Total Assets	7,759	7,653	7,612	7,527	7,221	7,042	6,101	5,670
Current Liabilities	491	512	548	577	626	873	393	521
Long-Term Obligations	2,277	2,200	2,200	2,200	2,071	2,126	1,916	1,536
Total Liabilities	5,357	5,261	5,225	5,183	4,963	5,131	4,282	3,942
Stockholders' Equity	2,402	2,392	2,387	2,344	2,258	1,911	1,819	1,728
Shares Outstanding	89	89	89	88	88	78	78	75
Statistical Record								
Return on Assets %	2.71	2.65	2.74	2.61	2.41	2.66	1.78	2.47
Return on Equity %	8.74	8.52	8.76	8.36	8.25	9.38	5.92	8.29
EBITDA Margin %	36.01	37.59	39.62	20.75	19.44	18.74	13.70	18.50
Net Margin %	9.71	10.73	13.77	10.04	9.06	9.21	5.80	7.81
Asset Turnover	0.27	0.26	0.26	0.26	0.27	0.29	0.31	0.32
Current Ratio	0.95	0.80	0.89	0.30	0.89	0.80	1.50	1.19
Debt to Equity	0.95	0.92	0.92	0.94	0.92	1.11	1.05	0.89
Price Range	48.19-40.32	48.02-40.32	45.75-37.91	45.04-35.80	40.79-33.16	40.09-29.07	32.72-27.36	27.99-24.33
P/E Ratio	21.04-17.61	21.53-18.08	19.98-16.55	20.85-16.57	20.00-16.25	18.39-13.33	24.24-20.27	14.97-13.01
Average Yield %	2.96	2.96	3.01	3.06	3.26	3.35	3.67	4.12

Address: 121 S.W. Salmon Street, Portland, OR 97204	**Web Site:** www.portlandgeneral.com	**Auditors:** Deloitte & Touche LLP
Telephone: 503-464-8000	**Officers:** Jack E. Davis - Chairman James F. Lobdell - Chief Financial Officer, Senior Vice President, Treasurer, Vice President	**Investor Contact:** 503-464-8586
Fax: 503-464-2676		**Transfer Agents:** American Stock Transfer & Trust Company, New York, NY

POST HOLDINGS INC

Exchange	Symbol	Price	52Wk Range	Yield	P/E
NYS	POST	$79.23 (12/29/2017)	88.41-76.24	N/A	158.46

*7 Year Price Score N/A   ***NYSE Composite Index=100**   ***12 Month Price Score 90.45**

TRADING VOLUME (thousand shares)

Interim Earnings (Per Share)

Qtr.	Dec	Mar	Jun	Sep
2012-13	0.23	0.13	0.03	(0.10)
2013-14	(0.15)	(0.67)	(0.92)	(7.19)
2014-15	(2.04)	0.45	0.33	(1.31)
2015-16	0.15	0.02	0.00	(0.58)
2016-17	1.22	(0.11)	(0.93)	0.16

Interim Dividends (Per Share)

No Dividends Paid

Valuation Analysis		Institutional Holding	
Forecast EPS	$3.85	No of Institutions	
	(01/18/2018)	360	
Market Cap	$5.2 Billion	Shares	
Book Value	$2.8 Billion	77,913,120	
Price/Book	1.88	% Held	
Price/Sales	1.00	N/A	

Business Summary: Food (MIC: 1.2.1 SIC: 2041 NAIC: 311211)

Post Holdings is a consumer packaged goods holding company. Co. operates in five segments:Post Consumer Brands segment includes the North American ready-to-eat (RTE) cereal and granola businesses, inclusive of the Weetabix North American RTE cereal business; Michael Foods Group segment includes foodservice and food ingredient egg, potato and pasta businesses and a retail cheese business; Active Nutrition segment includes protein shakes, bars and powders and nutritional supplements; Private Brands segment primarily consists of peanut and other nut butters and dried fruit and nuts; and the Weetabix segment includes the international (primarily the U.K.) RTE cereal and muesli business.

Recent Developments: For the year ended Sep 30 2017, net income amounted to US$48.3 million versus a net loss of US$3.3 million in the prior year. Revenues were US$5.23 billion, up 4.0% from US$5.03 billion the year before. Operating income was US$520.3 million versus US$545.7 million in the prior year, a decrease of 4.7%. Direct operating expenses rose 5.0% to US$3.65 billion from US$3.48 billion in the comparable period the year before. Indirect operating expenses increased 5.2% to US$1.05 billion from US$1.00 billion in the equivalent prior-year period.

Prospects: Our evaluation of Post Holdings Inc. as of Jan. 14, 2018 is the result of our systematic analysis on three basic characteristics: earnings strength, relative valuation, and recent stock price movement. The company has enjoyed a very positive trend in earnings per share over the past 5 quarters and while recent estimates for the company have been raised by analysts, POST has posted results that fell short of analysts expectations. Based on operating earnings yield, the company is about fairly valued when compared to all of the companies in our coverage universe. Share price changes over the past year indicates that POST will perform in line with the market over the near term.

Financial Data
(US$ in Thousands)

	09/30/2017	09/30/2016	09/30/2015	09/30/2014	09/30/2013	09/30/2012	09/30/2011	09/30/2010
Earnings Per Share	0.50	(0.41)	(2.33)	(9.03)	0.30	1.45	...	...
Cash Flow Per Share	5.70	7.28	7.96	4.61	3.65	4.20	...	...
Income Statement								
Total Revenue	5,225,800	5,026,800	4,648,200	2,411,100	1,034,100	958,900	968,200	996,700
EBITDA	712,300	579,200	393,000	(87,400)	184,600	203,900	(261,600)	246,200
Depn & Amortn	323,100	302,800	272,800	155,800	76,800	63,200	58,700	55,400
Income Before Taxes	74,400	(30,100)	(167,300)	(426,900)	22,300	80,400	(371,800)	139,300
Income Taxes	26,100	(26,800)	(52,000)	(83,700)	7,100	30,500	(6,300)	49,500
Net Income	48,300	(3,300)	(115,300)	(343,200)	15,200	49,900	(361,300)	92,000
Average Shares	69,900	68,800	56,700	39,700	33,000	34,500	...	...
Balance Sheet								
Current Assets	2,615,900	2,076,900	1,781,700	1,219,000	668,100	209,700	135,300	147,000
Total Assets	11,876,800	9,360,600	9,220,400	7,731,100	3,473,800	2,732,300	2,786,200	3,348,000
Current Liabilities	704,400	634,000	611,000	519,900	146,000	126,400	134,300	74,200
Long-Term Obligations	7,149,100	4,551,200	4,511,400	3,830,500	1,408,600	930,300	716,500	716,500
Total Liabilities	9,096,800	6,352,000	6,244,400	5,447,900	1,975,200	1,500,800	1,288,500	1,286,300
Stockholders' Equity	2,780,000	3,008,600	2,976,000	2,283,200	1,498,600	1,231,500	1,497,700	2,061,700
Shares Outstanding	66,100	64,900	60,300	43,000	30,900	32,650	...	...
Statistical Record								
Return on Assets %	0.45	N.M.	N.M.	N.M.	0.49	...	N.M.	...
Return on Equity %	1.67	N.M.	N.M.	N.M.	1.11	...	N.M.	...
EBITDA Margin %	13.63	11.52	8.45	N.M.	17.85	21.26	N.M.	24.70
Net Margin %	0.92	N.M.	N.M.	N.M.	1.47	5.20	N.M.	9.23
Asset Turnover	0.49	0.54	0.55	0.43	0.33	...	0.32	...
Current Ratio	3.71	3.28	2.92	2.34	4.58	1.66	1.01	1.98
Debt to Equity	2.57	1.51	1.52	1.68	0.94	0.76	0.48	0.35
Price Range	88.41-70.68	87.85-53.86	69.73-31.67	60.18-33.18	49.14-30.05	33.98-26.02	...	...
P/E Ratio	176.82-141.36			...	163.80-100.17	23.43-17.94	...	...

Address: 2503 S. Hanley Road, St. Louis, MO 63144	Web Site: www.postholdings.com	Auditors: PricewaterhouseCoopers LLP
Telephone: 314-644-7600	Officers: Robert V. Vitale - President, Chief Executive Officer, Chief Financial Officer Jeff A. Zadoks - Executive Vice President, Senior Vice President, Chief Financial Officer, Chief Accounting Officer, Principal Financial Officer, Principal Accounting Officer, Corporate Controller	Investor Contact: 314-644-7600 Transfer Agents: Computershare Trust Company, N.A., Providence, RI

PPG INDUSTRIES INC

Exchange	Symbol	Price	52Wk Range	Yield	P/E	Div Achiever
NYS	PPG	$116.82 (12/29/2017)	118.67-95.25	1.54	16.96	45 Years

*7 Year Price Score 99.92   *NYSE Composite Index=100   *12 Month Price Score 100.96

Interim Earnings (Per Share)

Qtr.	Mar	Jun	Sep	Dec
2014	4.49	1.38	1.33	0.31
2015	1.17	1.23	1.59	1.16
2016	1.29	1.37	(0.69)	1.30
2017	1.29	1.94	2.36	...

Interim Dividends (Per Share)

Amt	Decl	Ex	Rec	Pay
0.40Q	04/20/2017	05/08/2017	05/10/2017	06/12/2017
0.45Q	07/20/2017	08/08/2017	08/10/2017	09/12/2017
0.45Q	10/19/2017	11/09/2017	11/10/2017	12/12/2017
0.45Q	01/18/2018	02/15/2018	02/16/2018	03/12/2018

Indicated Div: $1.80 (Div. Reinv. Plan)

Valuation Analysis   **Institutional Holding**

Forecast EPS	$5.87	No of Institutions
	(01/18/2018)	1111
Market Cap	$29.7 Billion	Shares
Book Value	$5.9 Billion	228,841,472
Price/Book	5.04	% Held
Price/Sales	2.03	63.31

Business Summary: Specialty Chemicals (MIC: 8.3.2 SIC: 2851 NAIC: 325510)

PPG Industries manufactures and distributes a range of coatings and specialty materials. Co. has three segments: Performance Coatings, which primarily supplies a variety of protective and decorative coatings, sealants and finishes along with paint strippers, stains and related chemicals, as well as transparencies and transparent armor; Industrial Coatings, which primarily supplies a variety of protective and decorative coatings and finishes along with adhesives, sealants, metal pretreatment products, optical monomers and coatings, precipitated silicas and other specialty materials; and Glass, which primarily supplies continuous-strand fiber glass products.

Recent Developments: For the quarter ended Sep 30 2017, income from continuing operations was US$398.0 million compared with a loss of US$206.0 million in the year-earlier quarter. Net income amounted to US$615.0 million versus a net loss of US$179.0 million in the year-earlier quarter. Revenues were US$3.78 billion, up 3.2% from US$3.66 billion the year before. Direct operating expenses rose 6.2% to US$2.10 billion from US$1.98 billion in the comparable period the year before. Indirect operating expenses decreased 45.2% to US$1.16 billion from US$2.11 billion in the equivalent prior-year period.

Prospects: Our evaluation of PPG Industries Inc. as of Jan. 14, 2018 is the result of our systematic analysis on three basic characteristics: earnings strength, relative valuation, and recent stock price movement. The company has managed to produce a neutral trend in earnings per share over the past 5 quarters. However, while recent estimates for the company have been mixed, PPG has posted results that fell short of analysts expectations. Based on operating earnings yield, the company is undervalued when compared to all of the companies in our coverage universe. Share price changes over the past year indicates that PPG will perform well over the near term.

Financial Data

(US$ in Thousands)	9 Mos	6 Mos	3 Mos	12/31/2016	12/31/2015	12/31/2014	12/31/2013	12/31/2012
Earnings Per Share	6.89	3.84	3.27	3.28	5.14	7.51	11.14	3.03
Cash Flow Per Share	6.26	6.99	4.95	4.98	6.77	5.52	6.24	5.81
Tang Book Value Per Share	N.M.	N.M.	N.M.	N.M.	N.M.	N.M.	2.11	0.71
Dividends Per Share	1.650	1.600	1.600	1.560	1.415	1.310	1.210	1.170
Dividend Payout %	23.95	41.67	48.93	47.56	27.53	17.43	10.87	38.61
Income Statement								
Total Revenue	11,068,000	7,292,000	3,569,000	14,751,000	15,330,000	15,360,000	15,108,000	15,200,000
EBITDA	1,942,000	1,314,000	552,000	1,255,000	2,320,000	1,802,000	2,006,000	1,917,000
Depn & Amortn	245,000	160,000	83,000	341,000	363,000	350,000	356,000	355,000
Income Before Taxes	1,632,000	1,111,000	448,000	815,000	1,871,000	1,315,000	1,497,000	1,391,000
Income Taxes	392,000	269,000	109,000	241,000	456,000	259,000	333,000	338,000
Net Income	1,444,000	835,000	334,000	877,000	1,406,000	2,102,000	3,231,000	941,000
Average Shares	258,200	259,000	259,500	267,400	273,600	279,600	290,200	310,200
Balance Sheet								
Current Assets	7,638,000	7,145,000	6,646,000	6,452,000	6,554,000	6,850,000	7,214,000	7,715,000
Total Assets	17,615,000	16,977,000	16,154,000	15,769,000	17,076,000	17,583,000	15,863,000	15,878,000
Current Liabilities	4,618,000	4,441,000	4,273,000	4,240,000	4,656,000	4,876,000	4,135,000	4,461,000
Long-Term Obligations	4,089,000	3,998,000	3,817,000	3,787,000	4,042,000	3,544,000	3,372,000	3,368,000
Total Liabilities	11,713,000	11,347,000	10,962,000	10,943,000	12,093,000	12,403,000	10,931,000	11,815,000
Stockholders' Equity	5,902,000	5,630,000	5,192,000	4,826,000	4,983,000	5,180,000	4,932,000	4,063,000
Shares Outstanding	254,475	256,479	256,196	257,330	266,876	271,964	277,292	307,132
Statistical Record								
Return on Assets %	10.49	5.81	5.16	5.33	8.11	12.57	20.36	6.20
Return on Equity %	32.71	18.13	16.69	17.83	27.67	41.57	71.84	25.67
EBITDA Margin %	17.55	18.02	15.47	8.51	15.13	11.73	13.28	12.61
Net Margin %	13.05	11.45	9.36	5.95	9.17	13.68	21.39	6.19
Asset Turnover	0.86	0.86	0.89	0.90	0.88	0.92	0.95	1.00
Current Ratio	1.65	1.61	1.56	1.52	1.41	1.40	1.74	1.73
Debt to Equity	0.69	0.71	0.74	0.78	0.81	0.68	0.68	0.83
Price Range	113.60-91.22	111.57-91.22	116.55-91.22	116.55-89.27	118.85-84.51	116.23-88.30	94.83-65.04	67.67-42.16
P/E Ratio	16.49-13.24	29.05-23.76	35.64-27.90	35.53-27.22	23.12-16.44	15.48-11.76	8.51-5.84	22.33-13.92
Average Yield %	1.60	1.56	1.56	1.53	1.31	1.31	1.54	2.19

Address: One PPG Place, Pittsburgh, PA 15272
Telephone: 412-434-3131

Web Site: www.ppg.com
Officers: Michael H. McGarry - Chairman, President, Chief Executive Officer, Executive Vice President, Senior Vice President, Chief Operating Officer Vincent J. Morales - Senior Vice President, Chief Financial Officer

Auditors: PricewaterhouseCoopers LLP
Investor Contact: 412-434-3740
Transfer Agents: Computershare, Providence, R.I.

PPL CORP

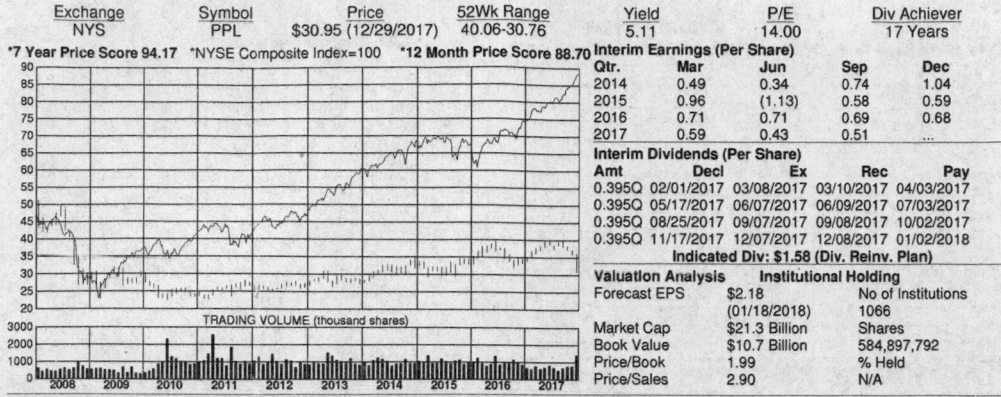

Exchange	Symbol	Price	52Wk Range	Yield	P/E	Div Achiever
NYS	PPL	$30.95 (12/29/2017)	40.06-30.76	5.11	14.00	17 Years

*7 Year Price Score 94.17 *NYSE Composite Index=100 *12 Month Price Score 88.70

Interim Earnings (Per Share)

Qtr.	Mar	Jun	Sep	Dec
2014	0.49	0.34	0.74	1.04
2015	0.96	(1.13)	0.58	0.59
2016	0.71	0.71	0.69	0.68
2017	0.59	0.43	0.51	...

Interim Dividends (Per Share)

Amt	Decl	Ex	Rec	Pay
0.395Q	02/01/2017	03/08/2017	03/10/2017	04/03/2017
0.395Q	05/17/2017	06/07/2017	06/09/2017	07/03/2017
0.395Q	08/25/2017	09/07/2017	09/08/2017	10/02/2017
0.395Q	11/17/2017	12/07/2017	12/08/2017	01/02/2018

Indicated Div: $1.58 (Div. Reinv. Plan)

Valuation Analysis

		Institutional Holding	
Forecast EPS	$2.18	No of Institutions	
	(01/18/2018)	1066	
Market Cap	$21.3 Billion	Shares	
Book Value	$10.7 Billion	584,897,792	
Price/Book	1.99	% Held	
Price/Sales	2.90	N/A	

Business Summary: Electric Utilities (MIC: 3.1.1 SIC: 4911 NAIC: 221122)

PPL is a utility holding company. Through its regulated utility subsidiaries, Co. delivers electricity to customers in the U.K., Pennsylvania, Kentucky, Virginia and Tennessee; delivers natural gas to customers in Kentucky; and generates electricity from power plants in Kentucky. Co. has three segments: U.K. Regulated, which has regulated electricity distribution operations in the U.K; Kentucky Regulated, which is engaged in the regulated generation, transmission, distribution and sale of electricity in Kentucky, Virginia and Tennessee, and the distribution and sale of natural gas in Kentucky; and Pennsylvania Regulated, which delivers electricity in eastern and central Pennsylvania.

Recent Developments: For the quarter ended Sep 30 2017, net income decreased 24.9% to US$355.0 million from US$473.0 million in the year-earlier quarter. Revenues were US$1.85 billion, down 2.3% from US$1.89 billion the year before. Operating income was US$777.0 million versus US$786.0 million in the prior-year quarter, a decrease of 1.1%. Direct operating expenses declined 6.7% to US$742.0 million from US$795.0 million in the comparable period the year before. Indirect operating expenses increased 5.8% to US$326.0 million from US$308.0 million in the equivalent prior-year period.

Prospects: Our evaluation of PPL Corp. as of Jan. 14, 2018 is the result of our systematic analysis on three basic characteristics: earnings strength, relative valuation, and recent stock price movement. The company has managed to produce a neutral trend in earnings per share over the past 5 quarters and while recent estimates for the company have been mixed, PPL has posted better than expected results. Based on operating earnings yield, the company is undervalued when compared to all of the companies in our coverage universe. Share price changes over the past year indicates that PPL will perform very well over the near term.

Financial Data (US$ in Thousands)	9 Mos	6 Mos	3 Mos	12/31/2016	12/31/2015	12/31/2014	12/31/2013	12/31/2012
Earnings Per Share	2.21	2.39	2.67	2.79	1.01	2.61	1.76	2.60
Cash Flow Per Share	3.52	3.67	3.62	4.25	3.90	5.21	4.69	4.75
Tang Book Value Per Share	10.02	9.77	9.40	9.03	8.44	13.06	11.57	9.27
Dividends Per Share	1.565	1.550	1.535	1.520	1.500	1.490	1.470	1.440
Dividend Payout %	70.81	64.85	57.49	54.48	148.51	57.09	83.52	55.38
Income Statement								
Total Revenue	5,521,000	3,676,000	1,951,000	7,517,000	7,669,000	11,499,000	11,860,000	12,286,000
EBITDA	2,857,000	1,872,000	1,014,000	4,361,000	3,822,000	4,620,000	3,473,000	4,146,000
Depn & Amortn	817,000	533,000	265,000	926,000	883,000	1,237,000	1,161,000	1,100,000
Income Before Taxes	1,371,000	900,000	532,000	2,550,000	2,072,000	2,364,000	1,309,000	2,090,000
Income Taxes	321,000	205,000	129,000	648,000	469,000	781,000	180,000	545,000
Net Income	1,050,000	695,000	403,000	1,902,000	682,000	1,737,000	1,130,000	1,526,000
Average Shares	688,746	686,351	683,084	680,446	672,586	665,973	663,073	581,626
Balance Sheet								
Current Assets	2,331,000	2,166,000	2,227,000	2,067,000	2,646,000	6,159,000	5,153,000	5,068,000
Total Assets	40,758,000	39,964,000	39,034,000	38,315,000	39,301,000	48,864,000	46,259,000	43,634,000
Current Liabilities	4,149,000	4,350,000	4,256,000	3,837,000	3,876,000	7,443,000	4,912,000	5,625,000
Long-Term Obligations	19,110,000	18,397,000	17,958,000	17,808,000	18,563,000	18,856,000	20,592,000	18,725,000
Total Liabilities	30,066,000	29,474,000	28,925,000	28,416,000	29,382,000	35,236,000	33,793,000	33,154,000
Stockholders' Equity	10,692,000	10,490,000	10,109,000	9,899,000	9,919,000	13,628,000	12,466,000	10,480,000
Shares Outstanding	688,133	685,473	682,427	679,731	673,857	665,849	630,321	581,944
Statistical Record								
Return on Assets %	3.85	4.11	4.69	4.89	1.55	3.65	2.51	3.53
Return on Equity %	14.66	15.69	18.36	19.14	5.79	13.31	9.85	14.28
EBITDA Margin %	51.75	50.92	51.97	58.02	49.84	40.18	29.28	33.75
Net Margin %	19.02	18.91	20.66	25.30	8.89	15.11	9.53	12.42
Asset Turnover	0.19	0.19	0.19	0.19	0.17	0.24	0.26	0.28
Current Ratio	0.56	0.50	0.52	0.54	0.68	0.83	1.05	0.90
Debt to Equity	1.79	1.75	1.78	1.80	1.87	1.38	1.65	1.79
Price Range	40.06-32.19	40.06-32.19	39.68-32.19	39.68-32.19	34.75-29.14	35.21-27.46	30.97-26.40	27.98-24.84
P/E Ratio	18.13-14.57	16.76-13.47	14.86-12.06	14.22-11.54	34.41-28.85	13.49-10.52	17.60-15.00	10.76-9.55
Average Yield %	4.27	4.31	4.28	4.25	4.68	4.80	5.19	5.47

Address: Two North Ninth Street, Allentown, PA 18101-1179 **Telephone:** 610-774-5151	**Web Site:** www.pplweb.com **Officers:** William H. Spence - Chairman, President, Chief Executive Officer, Chief Operating Officer Joanne H. Raphael - Senior Vice President, Secretary, General Counsel	**Auditors:** Ernst & Young LLP **Transfer Agents:** Wells Fargo Bank, N.A., Shareowner Services, Mendota Heights, MN

PRAXAIR INC

Exchange	Symbol	Price	52Wk Range	Yield	P/E	Div Achiever
NYS	PX	$154.68 (12/29/2017)	156.36-115.67	2.04	27.52	24 Years

*7 Year Price Score 88.48 *NYSE Composite Index=100 *12 Month Price Score 108.30

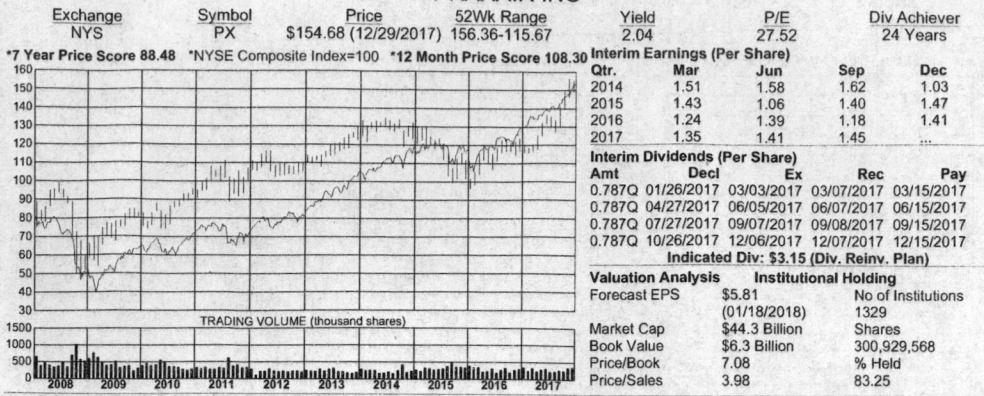

Interim Earnings (Per Share)

Qtr.	Mar	Jun	Sep	Dec
2014	1.51	1.58	1.62	1.03
2015	1.43	1.06	1.40	1.47
2016	1.24	1.39	1.18	1.41
2017	1.35	1.41	1.45	...

Interim Dividends (Per Share)

Amt	Decl	Ex	Rec	Pay
0.787Q	01/26/2017	03/03/2017	03/07/2017	03/15/2017
0.787Q	04/27/2017	06/05/2017	06/07/2017	06/15/2017
0.787Q	07/27/2017	09/07/2017	09/08/2017	09/15/2017
0.787Q	10/26/2017	12/06/2017	12/07/2017	12/15/2017

Indicated Div: $3.15 (Div. Reinv. Plan)

Valuation Analysis   **Institutional Holding**

Forecast EPS	$5.81	No of Institutions
	(01/18/2018)	1329
Market Cap	$44.3 Billion	Shares
Book Value	$6.3 Billion	300,929,568
Price/Book	7.08	% Held
Price/Sales	3.98	83.25

Business Summary: Specialty Chemicals (MIC: 8.3.2 SIC: 2819 NAIC: 325188)

Praxair is an industrial gas company in North and South America. Co.'s primary products in its industrial gases business are atmospheric gases (oxygen, nitrogen, argon, rare gases) and process gases (carbon dioxide, helium, hydrogen, electronic gases, specialty gases, acetylene). Co. also designs, engineers, and builds equipment that produces industrial gases primarily for internal use. Co.'s surface technologies segment supplies wear-resistant and high-temperature corrosion-resistant metallic and ceramic coatings and powders. Co.'s subsidiary, Praxair Surface Technologies, supplies wear-resistant and high-temperature corrosion-resistant metallic and ceramic coatings and powders.

Recent Developments: For the quarter ended Sep 30 2017, net income increased 26.5% to US$435.0 million from US$344.0 million in the year-earlier quarter. Revenues were US$2.92 billion, up 7.6% from US$2.72 billion the year before. Operating income was US$626.0 million versus US$497.0 million in the prior-year quarter, an increase of 26.0%. Direct operating expenses rose 7.8% to US$1.65 billion from US$1.53 billion in the comparable period the year before. Indirect operating expenses decreased 6.1% to US$644.0 million from US$686.0 million in the equivalent prior-year period.

Prospects: Our evaluation of Praxair Inc. as of Jan. 14, 2018 is the result of our systematic analysis on three basic characteristics: earnings strength, relative valuation, and recent stock price movement. The company has managed to produce a neutral trend in earnings per share over the past 5 quarters and while recent estimates for the company have been mixed, PX has posted better than expected results. Based on operating earnings yield, the company is about fairly valued when compared to all of the companies in our coverage universe. Share price changes over the past year indicates that PX will perform in line with the market over the near term.

Financial Data

(US$ in Thousands)	9 Mos	6 Mos	3 Mos	12/31/2016	12/31/2015	12/31/2014	12/31/2013	12/31/2012
Earnings Per Share	5.62	5.35	5.33	5.21	5.35	5.73	5.87	5.61
Cash Flow Per Share	10.23	10.22	10.28	9.68	9.34	9.81	9.87	9.20
Tang Book Value Per Share	8.59	7.19	6.36	4.64	2.93	6.56	9.58	11.42
Dividends Per Share	3.112	3.075	3.038	3.000	2.860	2.600	2.400	2.200
Dividend Payout %	55.38	57.48	56.99	57.58	53.46	45.38	40.89	39.22
Income Statement								
Total Revenue	8,484,000	5,562,000	2,728,000	10,534,000	10,776,000	12,273,000	11,925,000	11,224,000
EBITDA	2,689,000	1,765,000	869,000	3,360,000	3,427,000	3,778,000	3,734,000	3,438,000
Depn & Amortn	877,000	579,000	287,000	1,122,000	1,106,000	1,170,000	1,109,000	1,001,000
Income Before Taxes	1,692,000	1,107,000	541,000	2,048,000	2,160,000	2,395,000	2,447,000	2,296,000
Income Taxes	468,000	306,000	149,000	551,000	612,000	691,000	649,000	586,000
Net Income	1,214,000	795,000	389,000	1,500,000	1,547,000	1,694,000	1,755,000	1,692,000
Average Shares	289,216	288,535	287,384	287,757	289,055	295,608	298,965	301,845
Balance Sheet								
Current Assets	3,243,000	3,119,000	3,014,000	2,880,000	2,626,000	2,839,000	2,916,000	2,792,000
Total Assets	20,375,000	19,965,000	19,665,000	19,332,000	18,319,000	19,802,000	20,255,000	18,090,000
Current Liabilities	2,922,000	3,043,000	2,249,000	2,478,000	1,893,000	2,490,000	2,664,000	2,479,000
Long-Term Obligations	8,243,000	8,177,000	8,947,000	8,917,000	8,975,000	8,669,000	8,026,000	6,685,000
Total Liabilities	14,119,000	14,158,000	14,136,000	14,311,000	13,930,000	14,179,000	13,646,000	12,026,000
Stockholders' Equity	6,256,000	5,807,000	5,529,000	5,021,000	4,389,000	5,623,000	6,609,000	6,064,000
Shares Outstanding	286,305	286,024	285,353	284,900	284,879	289,261	294,133	296,229
Statistical Record								
Return on Assets %	8.05	7.74	7.92	7.95	8.12	8.46	9.15	9.80
Return on Equity %	28.17	28.14	29.43	31.79	30.90	27.70	27.70	29.21
EBITDA Margin %	31.69	31.73	31.85	31.90	31.80	30.78	31.31	30.63
Net Margin %	14.31	14.29	14.26	14.24	14.36	13.80	14.72	15.07
Asset Turnover	0.55	0.55	0.56	0.56	0.57	0.61	0.62	0.65
Current Ratio	1.11	1.02	1.34	1.16	1.39	1.14	1.09	1.13
Debt to Equity	1.32	1.41	1.62	1.78	2.04	1.54	1.21	1.10
Price Range	141.06-114.50	136.62-111.48	123.92-107.01	123.92-96.13	130.28-99.17	134.67-118.81	130.03-107.69	116.47-102.09
P/E Ratio	25.10-20.37	25.54-20.84	23.25-20.08	23.79-18.45	24.35-18.54	23.50-20.73	22.15-18.35	20.76-18.20
Average Yield %	2.50	2.55	2.60	2.64	2.45	2.01	2.04	2.03

Address: 10 Riverview Drive, Danbury, CT 06810-6268 **Telephone:** 203-837-2000	**Web Site:** www.praxair.com **Officers:** Stephen F. Angel - Chairman, Chief Executive Officer Matthew J. White - Senior Vice President, Vice President, Controller, Chief Financial Officer	**Auditors:** PricewaterhouseCoopers LLP **Investor Contact:** 203-837-2210 **Transfer Agents:** Registrar and Transfer Company, Cranford, NJ

PRESTIGE BRANDS HOLDINGS INC

Exchange	Symbol	Price	52Wk Range	Yield	P/E
NYS	PBH	$44.41 (12/29/2017)	57.92-40.63	N/A	22.20

*7 Year Price Score 119.57 ***NYSE Composite Index=100** ***12 Month Price Score 82.03**

TRADING VOLUME (thousand shares)

Interim Earnings (Per Share)

Qtr.	Jun	Sep	Dec	Mar
2014-15	0.32	0.31	0.40	0.45
2015-16	0.49	0.60	0.53	0.26
2016-17	(0.10)	0.60	0.59	0.21
2017-18	0.63	0.57	...	...

Interim Dividends (Per Share)

No Dividends Paid

Valuation Analysis   **Institutional Holding**

Forecast EPS	$2.62	No of Institutions
	(01/13/2018)	330
Market Cap	$2.4 Billion	Shares
Book Value	$896.0 Million	72,904,528
Price/Book	2.63	% Held
Price/Sales	2.42	101.66

Business Summary: Pharmaceuticals (MIC: 4.1.1 SIC: 2834 NAIC: 325412)

Prestige Brands Holdings is a holding company. Through its subsidiaries, Co. markets, sells and distributes over-the-counter (OTC) healthcare and household cleaning brands to mass merchandisers, drug, food, dollar, convenience, and club stores in North America (the U.S. and Canada) and in Australia and certain other international markets. Co.'s portfolio of OTC Healthcare products includes DenTek oral care products, Monistat women's health products, Nix lice treatment, Chloraseptic sore throat treatments, Clear Eyes eye care products, Efferdent denture care products and Luden's throat drops. Co.'s portfolio of Household Cleaning brands includes the Chore Boy, Comet and Spic and Span brands.

Recent Developments: For the quarter ended Sep 30 2017, net income decreased 4.6% to US$30.7 million from US$32.2 million in the year-earlier quarter. Revenues were US$258.0 million, up 20.0% from US$215.1 million the year before. Operating income was US$76.2 million versus US$71.1 million in the prior-year quarter, an increase of 7.2%. Direct operating expenses rose 25.1% to US$113.9 million from US$91.1 million in the comparable period the year before. Indirect operating expenses increased 28.4% to US$67.9 million from US$52.9 million in the equivalent prior-year period.

Prospects: Our evaluation of Prestige Brands Holdings Inc. as of Jan. 21, 2018 is the result of our systematic analysis on three basic characteristics: earnings strength, relative valuation, and recent stock price movement. The company has managed to produce a neutral trend in earnings per share over the past 5 quarters and while recent estimates for the company have been mixed, PBH has posted results that fell short of analysts expectations. Based on operating earnings yield, the company is undervalued when compared to all of the companies in our coverage universe. Share price changes over the past year indicates that PBH will perform poorly over the near term.

Financial Data
(US$ in Thousands)	6 Mos	3 Mos	03/31/2017	03/31/2016	03/31/2015	03/31/2014	03/31/2013	03/31/2012
Earnings Per Share	2.00	2.03	1.30	1.88	1.49	1.39	1.27	0.73
Cash Flow Per Share	2.94	2.85	2.79	3.30	3.00	2.16	2.72	1.34
Income Statement								
Total Revenue	514,599	256,573	882,060	806,247	714,623	601,881	623,597	441,085
EBITDA	158,680	80,775	210,193	247,545	212,492	173,530	192,041	103,177
Depn & Amortn	3,494	1,746	6,000	5,200	3,800	3,200	1,600	700
Income Before Taxes	102,009	52,688	110,850	157,185	127,458	101,748	106,034	61,157
Income Taxes	37,545	18,929	41,455	57,278	49,198	29,133	40,529	23,945
Net Income	64,464	33,759	69,395	99,907	78,260	72,615	65,505	37,212
Average Shares	53,539	53,509	53,362	53,143	52,670	52,349	51,440	50,748
Balance Sheet								
Current Assets	331,072	328,225	334,434	249,013	201,707	177,185	164,173	147,035
Total Assets	3,902,193	3,899,561	3,911,348	2,948,791	2,669,405	1,795,663	1,739,799	1,758,276
Current Liabilities	160,722	153,617	162,009	106,684	99,037	84,358	96,668	63,923
Long-Term Obligations	2,092,088	2,145,409	2,193,732	1,625,309	1,588,711	934,414	970,900	1,123,908
Total Liabilities	3,006,227	3,041,014	3,088,799	2,204,455	2,041,781	1,232,303	1,261,856	1,355,548
Stockholders' Equity	895,966	858,547	822,549	744,336	627,624	563,360	477,943	402,728
Shares Outstanding	53,039	52,955	52,955	52,760	52,296	51,815	51,130	50,285
Statistical Record								
Return on Assets %	3.18	3.21	2.02	3.55	3.51	4.11	3.75	2.64
Return on Equity %	12.83	13.62	8.86	14.52	13.14	13.95	14.88	9.71
EBITDA Margin %	30.84	31.48	23.83	30.70	29.73	28.83	30.80	23.39
Net Margin %	12.53	13.16	7.87	12.39	10.95	12.06	10.50	8.44
Asset Turnover	0.29	0.27	0.26	0.29	0.32	0.34	0.36	0.31
Current Ratio	2.06	2.14	2.06	2.33	2.04	2.10	1.70	2.30
Debt to Equity	2.34	2.50	2.67	2.18	2.53	1.66	2.03	2.79
Price Range	57.92-45.28	57.92-45.28	57.92-45.28	54.19-39.25	42.89-26.38	36.14-25.70	25.78-13.24	17.73-8.33
P/E Ratio	28.96-22.64	28.53-22.31	44.55-34.83	28.82-20.88	28.79-17.70	26.00-18.49	20.30-10.43	24.29-11.41

Address: 660 White Plains Road, Tarrytown, NY 10591 **Telephone:** 914-524-6800	**Web Site:** www.prestigebrands.com **Officers:** Ronald M. Lombardi - Chief Financial Officer, President, Chief Executive Officer, Interim Chief Financial Officer Christine Sacco - Chief Financial Officer	**Auditors:** PricewaterhouseCoopers LLP **Investor Contact:** 914-524-6819 **Transfer Agents:** Computershare Ltd., Canton, MA

PRIMERICA INC

Exchange	Symbol	Price	52Wk Range	Yield	P/E
NYS	PRI	$101.55 (12/29/2017)	105.30-69.95	0.79	19.72

*7 Year Price Score 142.03 *NYSE Composite index=100 *12 Month Price Score 114.36

Interim Earnings (Per Share)

Qtr.	Mar	Jun	Sep	Dec
2014	0.81	0.89	0.75	0.85
2015	0.82	0.94	0.98	0.97
2016	0.92	1.23	1.22	1.22
2017	1.11	1.36	1.46	...

Interim Dividends (Per Share)

Amt	Decl	Ex	Rec	Pay
0.19Q	02/07/2017	02/15/2017	02/20/2017	03/17/2017
0.19Q	05/08/2017	05/17/2017	05/19/2017	06/15/2017
0.20Q	08/07/2017	08/16/2017	08/18/2017	09/15/2017
0.20Q	11/06/2017	11/16/2017	11/17/2017	12/15/2017

Indicated Div: $0.80

Valuation Analysis		Institutional Holding	
Forecast EPS	$5.35	No of Institutions	
	(01/12/2018)	316	
Market Cap	$4.5 Billion	Shares	
Book Value	$1.3 Billion	50,783,576	
Price/Book	3.52	% Held	
Price/Sales	2.75	68.33	

Business Summary: Life & Health (MIC: 5.2.2 SIC: 6311 NAIC: 524113)

Primerica is a holding company. Through its subsidiaries, Co. distributes financial products to households in the U.S. and Canada. Co. has three operating segments: Term Life Insurance, which provides term life insurance to clients in the U.S., its territories, the District of Columbia and Canada; Investment and Savings Products, which includes mutual funds and annuities, segregated funds, and an individual annuity savings product that it underwrites in Canada; and Corporate and Other Distributed Products, which provides other products, including prepaid legal services, auto and homeowners' insurance referrals, credit information services, long-term care insurance and health insurance.

Recent Developments: For the quarter ended Sep 30 2017, net income increased 14.8% to US$66.6 million from US$58.0 million in the year-earlier quarter. Revenues were US$427.3 million, up 11.4% from US$383.6 million the year before. Net premiums earned were US$248.4 million versus US$216.9 million in the prior-year quarter, an increase of 14.5%. Net investment income rose 2.7% to US$19.9 million from US$19.4 million a year ago.

Prospects: Our evaluation of Primerica Inc as of Jan. 14, 2018 is the result of our systematic analysis on three basic characteristics: earnings strength, relative valuation, and recent stock price movement. The company has produced a positive trend in earnings per share over the past 5 quarters and while recent estimates for the company have been mixed, PRI has posted better than expected results. Based on operating earnings yield, the company is undervalued when compared to all of the companies in our coverage universe. Share price changes over the past year indicates that PRI will perform well over the near term.

Financial Data

(US$ in Thousands)	9 Mos	6 Mos	3 Mos	12/31/2016	12/31/2015	12/31/2014	12/31/2013	12/31/2012
Earnings Per Share	5.15	4.91	4.78	4.59	3.70	3.29	2.83	2.71
Cash Flow Per Share	7.44	6.70	6.69	6.15	5.09	4.36	3.37	1.96
Tang Book Value Per Share	27.67	27.00	26.18	25.51	22.52	22.68	21.03	21.39
Dividends Per Share	0.760	0.740	0.720	0.700	0.640	0.480	0.440	0.240
Dividend Payout %	14.76	15.07	15.06	15.25	17.30	14.59	15.55	8.86
Income Statement								
Total Revenue	1,246,161	818,860	405,164	1,519,084	1,405,314	1,340,030	1,267,448	1,190,715
Income Before Taxes	271,432	171,230	74,842	337,595	290,981	275,722	251,198	266,888
Income Taxes	89,619	56,054	22,772	118,181	101,110	95,888	88,473	93,082
Net Income	181,813	115,176	52,070	219,414	189,871	181,412	162,725	173,806
Average Shares	45,408	46,071	46,374	47,453	50,913	54,598	56,625	62,401
Balance Sheet								
Total Assets	12,206,839	11,945,298	11,669,997	11,438,943	10,612,119	10,738,114	10,329,950	10,337,877
Total Liabilities	10,926,309	10,676,045	10,423,499	10,217,569	9,466,347	9,492,988	9,107,923	9,062,461
Stockholders' Equity	1,280,530	1,269,253	1,246,498	1,221,374	1,145,772	1,245,126	1,222,027	1,275,416
Shares Outstanding	44,380	45,035	45,550	45,721	48,297	52,169	54,834	56,374
Statistical Record								
Return on Assets %	2.02	1.99	2.00	1.98	1.78	1.72	1.57	1.70
Return on Equity %	19.08	18.58	18.71	18.49	15.88	14.71	13.03	12.85
Net Margin %	14.59	14.07	12.85	14.44	13.51	13.54	12.84	14.60
Asset Turnover	0.14	0.14	0.14	0.14	0.13	0.13	0.12	0.12
Price Range	85.65-53.03	85.65-50.04	83.40-42.89	72.50-39.93	55.09-41.01	55.60-39.51	43.97-30.01	30.26-23.34
P/E Ratio	16.63-10.30	17.44-10.19	17.45-8.97	15.80-8.70	14.89-11.08	16.90-12.01	15.54-10.60	11.17-8.61
Average Yield %	1.02	1.08	1.16	1.31	1.34	1.01	1.18	0.89

Address: 1 Primerica Parkway, Duluth, GA 30099
Telephone: 770-381-1000

Web Site: www.primerica.com
Officers: Peter W. Schneider - President, Executive Vice President, Chief Administrative Officer, Corporate Secretary, General Counsel Glenn J. Williams - President, Chief Executive Officer

Auditors: KPMG LLP
Investor Contact: 866-694-0420
Transfer Agents: American Stock Transfer & Trust Company, Brooklyn, NY

PROASSURANCE CORP

Exchange	Symbol	Price	52Wk Range	Yield	P/E
NYS	PRA	$57.15 (12/29/2017)	63.00-51.30	2.17	21.25

*7 Year Price Score 96.62   *NYSE Composite Index=100   *12 Month Price Score 96.27

Interim Earnings (Per Share)

Qtr.	Mar	Jun	Sep	Dec
2014	0.76	0.84	0.59	1.11
2015	0.67	0.60	0.19	0.65
2016	0.36	0.81	0.63	1.02
2017	0.77	0.36	0.54	...

Interim Dividends (Per Share)

Amt	Decl	Ex	Rec	Pay
0.31Q	05/31/2017	06/23/2017	06/27/2017	07/12/2017
0.31Q	09/06/2017	09/28/2017	09/29/2017	10/10/2017
4.69Q	11/29/2017	12/20/2017	12/21/2017	01/10/2018
0.31Q	11/29/2017	12/20/2017	12/21/2017	01/10/2018

Indicated Div: $1.24

Valuation Analysis

		Institutional Holding	
Forecast EPS	$2.10 (01/16/2018)	No of Institutions	331
Market Cap	$3.1 Billion	Shares	51,317,692
Book Value	$1.9 Billion	% Held	74.89
Price/Book	1.65		
Price/Sales	3.41		

Business Summary: General Insurance (MIC: 5.2.1 SIC: 6331 NAIC: 524126)

ProAssurance is a holding company for property and casualty insurance companies. Co. has four segments: Specialty Property and Casualty, which includes its professional liability business and its medical technology and life sciences business; Workers' Compensation, which includes its workers' compensation business provided to employers, groups and associations in the Mid-Atlantic, Southeast, Midwest, and Gulf South regions of the continental U.S.; Lloyd's Syndicate, which provides property and casualty insurance and reinsurance lines through Lloyd's of London Syndicate 1729; and Corporate, which includes Co.'s investment operations, which are managed at the corporate level.

Recent Developments: For the quarter ended Sep 30 2017, net income decreased 14.4% to US$28.9 million from US$33.8 million in the year-earlier quarter. Revenues were US$228.5 million, up 1.8% from US$224.4 million the year before. Net premiums earned were US$192.3 million versus US$185.3 million in the prior-year quarter, an increase of 3.8%. Net investment income fell 6.1% to US$23.7 million from US$25.3 million a year ago.

Prospects: Our evaluation of ProAssurance Corp. as of Jan. 14, 2018 is the result of our systematic analysis on three basic characteristics: earnings strength, relative valuation, and recent stock price movement. The company has generated a negative trend in earnings per share over the past 5 quarters and while recent estimates for the company have been mixed, PRA has posted better than expected results. Based on operating earnings yield, the company is about fairly valued when compared to all of the companies in our coverage universe. Share price changes over the past year indicates that PRA will perform well over the near term.

Financial Data
(US$ in Thousands)

	9 Mos	6 Mos	3 Mos	12/31/2016	12/31/2015	12/31/2014	12/31/2013	12/31/2012
Earnings Per Share	2.69	2.78	3.23	2.83	2.11	3.30	4.80	4.46
Cash Flow Per Share	2.59	2.56	3.20	3.17	2.04	1.62	0.63	1.48
Tang Book Value Per Share	29.13	28.94	28.69	28.24	31.17	32.66	35.64	33.34
Dividends Per Share	5.930	5.930	5.930	5.930	2.240	3.860	1.050	3.125
Dividend Payout %	220.45	213.31	183.59	209.54	106.16	116.97	21.88	70.07
Income Statement								
Premium Income	555,559	363,256	182,903	733,281	694,149	699,731	527,919	550,664
Total Revenue	657,031	428,575	222,998	870,214	772,079	852,326	740,178	715,854
Benefits & Claims	364,058	234,701	119,151	515,242	456,862	379,232	243,015	161,726
Income Before Taxes	94,389	59,416	40,231	176,201	128,855	262,005	397,159	395,966
Income Taxes	4,467	(1,557)	(1,224)	25,120	12,658	65,440	99,636	120,496
Net Income	89,922	60,973	41,455	151,081	116,197	196,565	297,523	275,470
Average Shares	53,614	53,607	53,535	53,448	55,017	59,525	62,020	61,833
Balance Sheet								
Total Assets	4,925,154	4,861,716	4,872,641	5,065,181	4,908,163	5,169,160	5,150,891	4,876,578
Total Liabilities	3,074,264	3,023,620	3,046,955	3,266,479	2,949,809	3,011,216	2,756,477	2,605,998
Stockholders' Equity	1,850,890	1,838,096	1,825,686	1,798,702	1,958,354	2,157,944	2,394,414	2,270,580
Shares Outstanding	53,413	53,413	53,396	53,251	53,100	56,533	61,196	61,623
Statistical Record								
Return on Assets %	2.91	3.04	3.55	3.02	2.31	3.81	5.93	5.56
Return on Equity %	7.44	7.74	9.09	8.02	5.65	8.64	12.76	12.39
Loss Ratio %	65.53	64.61	65.14	70.27	65.82	54.20	46.03	29.37
Net Margin %	13.69	14.23	18.59	17.36	15.05	23.06	40.20	38.48
Price Range	62.85-50.75	62.85-50.75	62.85-47.73	62.85-46.22	53.42-43.73	48.48-42.90	55.28-42.19	46.48-39.35
P/E Ratio	23.36-18.87	22.61-18.26	19.46-14.78	22.21-16.33	25.32-20.73	14.69-13.00	11.52-8.79	10.42-8.82
Average Yield %	10.35	10.51	10.99	11.41	4.69	8.52	2.18	7.12

Address: 100 Brookwood Place, Birmingham, AL 35209
Telephone: 205-877-4400
Fax: 205-802-4799

Web Site: www.proassurance.com
Officers: W. Stancil Starnes - Chairman, Chief Executive Officer Victor T. Adamo - President

Auditors: Ernst & Young LLP
Investor Contact: 205-877-4461
Transfer Agents: Mellon Investor Services, LLC, Ridgefield Park, NJ

PROCTER & GAMBLE COMPANY (THE)

Exchange	Symbol	Price	52Wk Range	Yield	P/E	Div Achiever
NYS	PG	$91.88 (12/29/2017)	94.40-83.49	3.00	16.12	63 Years

*7 Year Price Score 90.11   *NYSE Composite Index=100   *12 Month Price Score 94.52

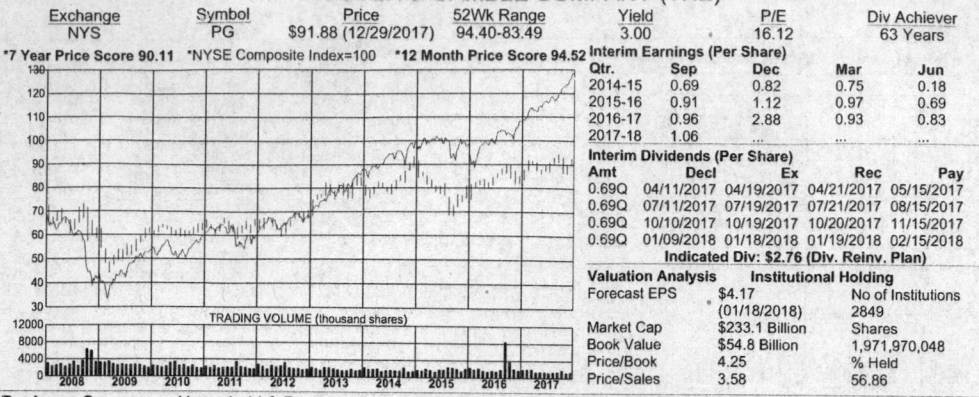

Interim Earnings (Per Share)

Qtr.	Sep	Dec	Mar	Jun
2014-15	0.69	0.82	0.75	0.18
2015-16	0.91	1.12	0.97	0.69
2016-17	0.96	2.88	0.93	0.83
2017-18	1.06	...	...	...

Interim Dividends (Per Share)

Amt	Decl	Ex	Rec	Pay
0.69Q	04/11/2017	04/19/2017	04/21/2017	05/15/2017
0.69Q	07/11/2017	07/19/2017	07/21/2017	08/15/2017
0.69Q	10/10/2017	10/19/2017	10/20/2017	11/15/2017
0.69Q	01/09/2018	01/18/2018	01/19/2018	02/15/2018

Indicated Div: $2.76 (Div. Reinv. Plan)

Valuation Analysis

Forecast EPS	$4.17
	(01/18/2018)
Market Cap	$233.1 Billion
Book Value	$54.8 Billion
Price/Book	4.25
Price/Sales	3.58

Institutional Holding

No of Institutions	2849
Shares	1,971,970,048
% Held	56.86

Business Summary: Household & Personal Products (MIC: 1.7.1 SIC: 2841 NAIC: 325611)

Procter & Gamble provides consumer packaged goods. Co.'s products are sold mainly through mass merchandisers, grocery stores, membership club stores, drug stores, department stores, distributors, wholesalers, baby stores, beauty stores, e-commerce, high-frequency stores and pharmacies. At June 30 2017, Co. had five reportable segments: Beauty, which includes hair care, and skin and personal care products; Grooming, which includes shave care products; Health Care, which includes oral care and personal health care products; Fabric and Home Care, which includes fabric and home care products; and Baby, Feminine and Family Care, which includes baby care, feminine care and family care products.

Recent Developments: For the quarter ended Sep 30 2017, income from continuing operations decreased 0.2% to US$2.87 billion from US$2.88 billion in the year-earlier quarter. Net income increased 4.1% to US$2.87 billion from US$2.76 billion in the year-earlier quarter. Revenues were US$16.65 billion, up 0.8% from US$16.52 billion the year before. Operating income was US$3.74 billion versus US$3.77 billion in the prior-year quarter, a decrease of 1.0%. Direct operating expenses rose 1.6% to US$8.23 billion from US$8.10 billion in the comparable period the year before. Indirect operating expenses increased 0.9% to US$4.69 billion from US$4.65 billion in the equivalent prior-year period.

Prospects: Our evaluation of Procter & Gamble Co. as of Jan. 14, 2018 is the result of our systematic analysis on three basic characteristics: earnings strength, relative valuation, and recent stock price movement. The company has managed to produce a neutral trend in earnings per share over the past 5 quarters and while recent estimates for the company have been raised by analysts, PG has posted better than expected results. Based on operating earnings yield, the company is undervalued when compared to all of the companies in our coverage universe. Share price changes over the past year indicates that PG will perform well over the near term.

Financial Data
(US$ in Millions)

	3 Mos	06/30/2017	06/30/2016	06/30/2015	06/30/2014	06/30/2013	06/30/2012	06/30/2011
Earnings Per Share	5.70	5.59	3.69	2.44	4.01	3.86	3.66	3.93
Cash Flow Per Share	5.24	4.91	5.70	5.39	5.13	5.42	4.82	4.72
Dividends Per Share	2.718	2.698	2.658	2.594	2.448	2.288	2.137	1.970
Dividend Payout %	47.69	48.27	72.04	106.30	61.05	59.26	58.39	50.14
Income Statement								
Total Revenue	16,653	65,058	65,299	76,279	83,062	84,167	83,680	82,559
EBITDA	4,509	16,371	16,844	15,455	18,635	18,405	16,758	18,858
Depn & Amortn	692	2,820	3,078	3,134	3,141	2,982	3,204	2,838
Income Before Taxes	3,751	13,257	13,369	11,846	14,885	14,843	12,785	15,189
Income Taxes	881	3,063	3,342	2,916	3,178	3,441	3,468	3,392
Net Income	2,853	15,326	10,508	7,036	11,643	11,312	10,756	11,797
Average Shares	2,691	2,741	2,845	2,884	2,905	2,931	2,942	3,002
Balance Sheet								
Current Assets	28,096	26,494	33,782	29,646	31,617	23,990	21,910	21,970
Total Assets	122,851	120,406	127,136	129,495	144,266	139,263	132,244	138,354
Current Liabilities	30,724	30,210	30,770	29,790	33,726	30,037	24,907	27,293
Long-Term Obligations	20,188	18,038	18,945	18,329	19,811	19,111	21,080	22,033
Total Liabilities	68,033	65,222	69,795	67,076	75,052	71,199	68,805	70,714
Stockholders' Equity	54,818	55,184	57,341	62,419	69,214	68,064	63,439	67,640
Shares Outstanding	2,537	2,554	2,669	2,715	2,711	2,743	2,749	2,766
Statistical Record								
Return on Assets %	12.28	12.38	8.17	5.14	8.21	8.33	7.93	8.85
Return on Equity %	27.35	27.24	17.50	10.69	16.96	17.20	16.37	18.32
EBITDA Margin %	27.08	25.16	25.80	20.26	22.44	21.87	20.03	22.84
Net Margin %	17.13	23.56	16.09	9.22	14.02	13.44	12.85	14.29
Asset Turnover	0.52	0.53	0.51	0.56	0.59	0.62	0.62	0.62
Current Ratio	0.91	0.88	1.10	1.00	0.94	0.80	0.88	0.80
Debt to Equity	0.37	0.33	0.33	0.29	0.29	0.28	0.33	0.33
Price Range	94.40-81.86	91.67-81.86	84.67-68.06	93.46-77.32	85.41-75.59	82.54-61.19	67.90-58.51	67.46-59.34
P/E Ratio	16.56-14.36	16.40-14.64	22.95-18.44	38.30-31.69	21.30-18.85	21.38-15.85	18.55-15.99	17.17-15.10
Average Yield %	3.08	3.09	3.39	3.09	3.06	3.18	3.13	3.13

Address: One Procter & Gamble Plaza, Cincinnati, OH 45202 **Telephone:** 513-983-1100	**Web Site:** www.pg.com **Officers:** David S. Taylor - Chairman, President, Chief Executive Officer, Division Officer Jon R. Moeller - Vice-Chairman, Chief Financial Officer
Auditors: DELOITTE & TOUCHE LLP **Investor Contact:** 800-742-6253 **Transfer Agents:** Computershare, Canton, MA	

PROGRESSIVE CORP. (OH)

Exchange	Symbol	Price	52Wk Range	Yield	P/E
NYS	PGR	$56.32 (12/29/2017)	56.51-35.53	1.21	23.56

*7 Year Price Score 123.14 *NYSE Composite Index=100 *12 Month Price Score 112.53

Interim Earnings (Per Share)

Qtr.	Mar	Jun	Sep	Dec
2014	0.54	0.49	0.50	0.62
2015	0.50	0.62	0.47	0.55
2016	0.44	0.33	0.34	0.65
2017	0.73	0.63	0.38	...

Interim Dividends (Per Share)

Amt	Decl	Ex	Rec	Pay
0.686A	12/19/2014	02/02/2015	02/04/2015	02/13/2015
0.888A	12/04/2015	02/01/2016	02/03/2016	02/12/2016
0.681A	12/02/2016	02/01/2017	02/03/2017	02/10/2017
0.00A	12/08/2017	02/01/2018	02/02/2018	02/09/2018

Indicated Div: $0.68

Valuation Analysis — **Institutional Holding**

Forecast EPS	$2.45 (01/18/2018)	No of Institutions 848
Market Cap	$32.8 Billion	Shares 556,782,464
Book Value	$9.3 Billion	% Held 69.20
Price/Book	3.53	
Price/Sales	1.27	

TRADING VOLUME (thousand shares)

Business Summary: General Insurance (MIC: 5.2.1 SIC: 6331 NAIC: 524126)

Progressive is an insurance holding company. Through its insurance subsidiaries and affiliates, Co. provides personal and commercial auto insurance, residential property insurance, and other specialty property-casualty insurance and related services. Co.'s Personal Lines segment writes insurance for personal autos and recreational and other vehicles, while its commercial lines business writes primary liability, physical damage, and other auto-related insurance for automobiles and trucks owned and/or operated mainly by businesses as a part of the commercial auto market. Co.'s service businesses primarily include: Commercial Auto Insurance Procedures/Plans and its commission-based businesses.

Recent Developments: For the quarter ended Sep 30 2017, net income increased 4.5% to US$214.8 million from US$205.5 million in the year-earlier quarter. Revenues were US$6.79 billion, up 14.4% from US$5.94 billion the year before. Net premiums earned were US$6.54 billion versus US$5.72 billion in the prior-year quarter, an increase of 14.3%. Net investment income rose 19.8% to US$142.9 million from US$119.3 million a year ago.

Prospects: Our evaluation of Progressive Corp. as of Jan. 14, 2018 is the result of our systematic analysis on three basic characteristics: earnings strength, relative valuation, and recent stock price movement. The company has generated a negative trend in earnings per share over the past 5 quarters and while recent estimates for the company have been raised by analysts, PGR has posted better than expected results. Based on operating earnings yield, the company is about fairly valued when compared to all of the companies in our coverage universe. Share price changes over the past year indicates that PGR will perform very well over the near term.

Financial Data

(US$ in Thousands)	9 Mos	6 Mos	3 Mos	12/31/2016	12/31/2015	12/31/2014	12/31/2013	12/31/2012
Earnings Per Share	2.39	2.35	2.05	1.76	2.15	2.15	1.93	1.48
Cash Flow Per Share	6.28	5.48	5.16	4.63	3.92	2.92	3.17	2.80
Tang Book Value Per Share	14.53	14.01	13.18	12.20	10.88	11.79	10.39	9.94
Dividends Per Share	0.681	0.681	0.681	0.888	0.686	1.493	0.284	1.407
Dividend Payout %	28.49	28.97	33.21	50.47	31.92	69.44	14.74	95.08
Income Statement								
Premium Income	18,884,000	12,340,000	6,026,700	22,474,000	19,899,100	18,398,500	17,103,400	16,018,000
Total Revenue	19,719,200	12,927,400	6,321,700	23,441,400	20,853,800	19,391,400	18,170,900	17,083,900
Benefits & Claims	13,928,800	8,878,300	4,263,400	16,879,600	14,342,000	13,306,200	12,472,400	11,948,000
Income Before Taxes	1,447,500	1,196,100	641,500	1,470,700	1,911,600	1,907,400	1,720,000	1,317,700
Income Taxes	429,700	393,100	211,200	413,500	611,100	626,400	554,600	415,400
Net Income	1,015,900	791,900	424,300	1,031,000	1,267,600	1,281,000	1,165,400	902,300
Average Shares	585,600	583,800	583,300	585,000	589,200	594,800	603,600	607,800
Balance Sheet								
Total Assets	38,932,600	36,689,800	34,810,500	33,427,500	29,819,300	25,787,600	24,408,200	22,694,700
Total Liabilities	29,643,200	27,698,300	26,287,600	25,470,400	22,529,900	18,859,000	18,218,700	16,687,700
Stockholders' Equity	9,289,400	8,991,500	8,522,900	7,957,100	7,289,400	6,928,600	6,189,500	6,007,000
Shares Outstanding	581,600	581,000	580,900	579,900	583,600	587,800	595,800	604,600
Statistical Record								
Return on Assets %	3.86	4.00	3.65	3.25	4.56	5.10	4.95	4.04
Return on Equity %	16.10	16.33	14.89	13.49	17.83	19.53	19.11	15.23
Loss Ratio %	73.76	71.95	70.74	75.11	72.07	72.32	72.92	74.59
Net Margin %	5.15	6.13	6.71	4.40	6.08	6.61	6.41	5.28
Price Range	48.89-30.88	44.83-30.77	40.31-30.77	35.74-29.49	33.64-25.85	27.35-22.59	28.14-21.10	23.30-19.24
P/E Ratio	20.46-12.92	19.08-13.09	19.66-15.01	20.31-16.76	15.65-12.02	12.72-10.51	14.58-10.93	15.74-13.00
Average Yield %	1.71	1.88	1.99	2.72	2.37	5.96	1.12	6.64

Address: 6300 Wilson Mills Road, Mayfield Village, OH 44143
Telephone: 440-461-5000
Fax: 440-446-7168

Web Site: www.progressive.com
Officers: Susan Patricia (Tricia) Griffith - President, Chief Executive Officer, Personal Lines Chief Operating Officer, Division Officer Steven A. Broz - Chief Financial Officer

Auditors: PricewaterhouseCoopers LLP
Investor Contact: 440-395-2222
Transfer Agents: American Stock Transfer & Trust Company, Brookly, NY

PROLOGIS INC

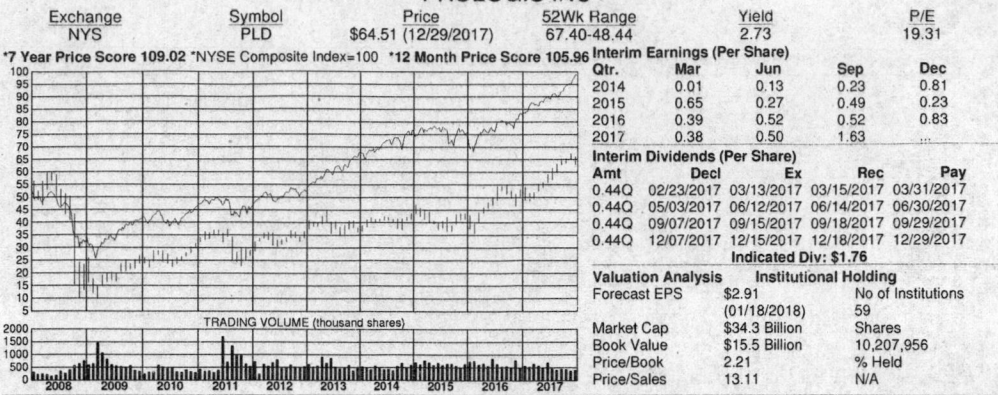

Exchange	Symbol	Price	52Wk Range	Yield	P/E
NYS	PLD	$64.51 (12/29/2017)	67.40-48.44	2.73	19.31

*7 Year Price Score 109.02 *NYSE Composite Index=100 ***12 Month Price Score 105.96**

Interim Earnings (Per Share)

Qtr.	Mar	Jun	Sep	Dec
2014	0.01	0.13	0.23	0.81
2015	0.65	0.27	0.49	0.23
2016	0.39	0.52	0.52	0.83
2017	0.38	0.50	1.63	...

Interim Dividends (Per Share)

Amt	Decl	Ex	Rec	Pay
0.44Q	02/23/2017	03/13/2017	03/15/2017	03/31/2017
0.44Q	05/03/2017	06/12/2017	06/14/2017	06/30/2017
0.44Q	09/07/2017	09/15/2017	09/18/2017	09/29/2017
0.44Q	12/07/2017	12/15/2017	12/18/2017	12/29/2017

Indicated Div: $1.76

Valuation Analysis — **Institutional Holding**

Forecast EPS	$2.91	No of Institutions
(01/18/2018)		59
Market Cap	$34.3 Billion	Shares
Book Value	$15.5 Billion	10,207,956
Price/Book	2.21	% Held
Price/Sales	13.11	N/A

TRADING VOLUME (thousand shares)

Business Summary: REITs (MIC: 5.3.1 SIC: 6798 NAIC: 525930)

Prologis is a real estate investment trust. Co. owns, manages and develops logistics facilities. The majority of Co.'s consolidated properties are in the U.S.; while outside the U.S., Co.'s properties are generally held in co-investment ventures. Co. is principally an owner-operator in the U.S. and a manager-developer outside the U.S. Co. has two operating segments: Real Estate Operations, which represents the ownership and development of operating properties, and includes development activities that lead to rental operations, including land held for development and properties under development; and Strategic Capital, which represents the management of unconsolidated co-investment ventures.

Recent Developments: For the quarter ended Sep 30 2017, net income increased 197.3% to US$913.4 million from US$307.2 million in the year-earlier quarter. Revenues were US$602.9 million, down 14.4% from US$704.6 million the year before. Revenues from property income fell 5.2% to US$531.2 million from US$560.3 million in the corresponding quarter a year earlier.

Prospects: Our evaluation of Prologis Inc. as of Jan. 14, 2018 is the result of our systematic analysis on three basic characteristics: earnings strength, relative valuation, and recent stock price movement. The company has generated a negative trend in earnings per share over the past 5 quarters. Because the company lacks sufficient analyst estimate data, we place greater weight on the historical EPS trend as the measure of earnings strength. Based on operating earnings yield, the company is overvalued when compared to all of the companies in our coverage universe. Share price changes over the past year indicates that PLD will perform very well over the near term.

Financial Data
(US$ in Thousands)

	9 Mos	6 Mos	3 Mos	12/31/2016	12/31/2015	12/31/2014	12/31/2013	12/31/2012
Earnings Per Share	3.34	2.23	2.25	2.27	1.64	1.24	0.64	(0.18)
Cash Flow Per Share	3.35	2.99	2.84	2.69	1.85	1.41	1.00	1.01
Tang Book Value Per Share	29.07	27.80	27.67	27.70	27.82	27.28	27.29	27.04
Dividends Per Share	1.740	1.720	1.700	1.680	1.520	1.320	1.120	1.120
Dividend Payout %	52.10	77.13	75.56	74.01	92.68	106.45	175.00	...
Income Statement								
Total Revenue	1,998,212	1,395,338	629,155	2,533,135	2,197,074	1,760,787	1,750,486	2,005,961
EBITDA	1,427,291	506,073	223,409	2,258,082	1,853,116	1,548,602	1,265,568	1,151,775
Depn & Amortn	(67,819)	(53,363)	(28,402)	822,240	787,894	686,145	674,147	788,467
Income Before Taxes	1,292,147	415,849	181,684	1,140,797	789,343	579,340	239,042	(121,298)
Income Taxes	42,328	24,381	9,600	54,564	23,090	(25,656)	106,733	3,580
Net Income	1,351,439	473,546	204,929	1,209,932	869,439	636,183	342,921	(39,720)
Average Shares	554,163	552,114	550,010	546,666	533,944	506,391	491,546	459,895
Balance Sheet								
Current Assets	568,726	271,354	395,829	1,026,999	454,456	548,355	758,629	448,820
Total Assets	29,654,150	30,150,395	29,814,958	30,249,932	31,394,767	25,818,223	24,572,307	27,310,145
Current Liabilities	707,049	554,775	549,836	847,034	994,282	895,883	1,074,229	611,770
Long-Term Obligations	9,721,065	11,081,922	10,966,932	10,608,294	11,626,831	9,380,199	9,011,216	11,790,794
Total Liabilities	14,110,399	15,303,099	15,068,091	15,258,851	16,726,832	11,842,714	10,861,149	14,241,128
Stockholders' Equity	15,543,751	14,847,296	14,746,867	14,991,081	14,667,935	13,975,509	13,711,158	13,069,017
Shares Outstanding	532,081	531,338	530,213	528,671	524,512	509,498	498,799	461,770
Statistical Record								
Return on Assets %	5.93	3.93	3.94	3.91	3.04	2.53	1.32	N.M.
Return on Equity %	11.82	8.10	8.20	8.14	6.07	4.60	2.56	N.M.
EBITDA Margin %	71.43	36.27	35.51	89.14	84.34	87.95	72.30	57.42
Net Margin %	67.63	33.94	32.57	47.76	39.57	36.13	19.59	N.M.
Asset Turnover	0.09	0.09	0.08	0.08	0.08	0.07	0.07	0.07
Current Ratio	0.80	0.49	0.72	1.21	0.46	0.61	0.71	0.73
Debt to Equity	0.63	0.75	0.74	0.71	0.79	0.67	0.66	0.90
Price Range	65.29-46.38	59.19-46.38	54.61-43.65	54.61-35.57	47.13-36.45	43.64-36.51	44.77-34.78	36.91-28.50
P/E Ratio	19.55-13.89	26.54-20.80	24.27-19.40	24.06-15.67	28.74-22.23	35.19-29.44	69.95-54.34	...
Average Yield %	3.18	3.27	3.38	3.52	3.67	3.26	2.87	3.33

Address: Pier 1, Bay 1, San Francisco, CA 94111	**Web Site:** www.prologis.com	**Auditors:** KPMG LLP
Telephone: 415-394-9000	**Officers:** Hamid R. Moghadam - Chairman, Chief Executive Officer, Co-Chief Executive Officer Thomas S. Olinger - Chief Financial Officer, Chief Integration Officer	**Investor Contact:** 415-733-9565
Fax: 415-394-9001		**Transfer Agents:** Computershare Investor Services, Canton, MA

PROSPERITY BANCSHARES INC.

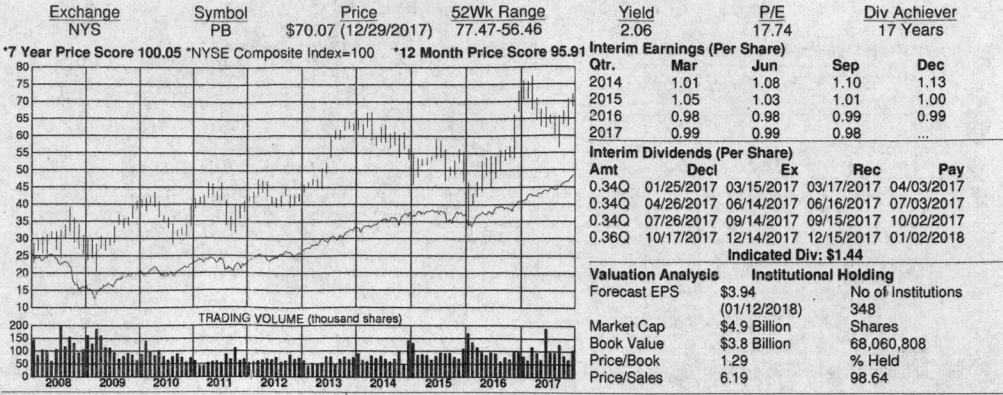

Exchange	Symbol	Price	52Wk Range	Yield	P/E	Div Achiever
NYS	PB	$70.07 (12/29/2017)	77.47-56.46	2.06	17.74	17 Years

*7 Year Price Score 100.05 *NYSE Composite Index=100 *12 Month Price Score 95.91

Interim Earnings (Per Share)

Qtr.	Mar	Jun	Sep	Dec
2014	1.01	1.08	1.10	1.13
2015	1.05	1.03	1.01	1.00
2016	0.98	0.98	0.99	0.99
2017	0.99	0.99	0.98	...

Interim Dividends (Per Share)

Amt	Decl	Ex	Rec	Pay
0.34Q	01/25/2017	03/15/2017	03/17/2017	04/03/2017
0.34Q	04/26/2017	06/14/2017	06/16/2017	07/03/2017
0.34Q	07/26/2017	09/14/2017	09/15/2017	10/02/2017
0.36Q	10/17/2017	12/14/2017	12/15/2017	01/02/2018

Indicated Div: $1.44

Valuation Analysis / Institutional Holding

Forecast EPS	$3.94	No of Institutions	348
	(01/12/2018)		
Market Cap	$4.9 Billion	Shares	68,060,808
Book Value	$3.8 Billion	% Held	98.64
Price/Book	1.29		
Price/Sales	6.19		

Business Summary: Banking (MIC: 5.1.1 SIC: 6022 NAIC: 522110)

Prosperity Bancshares is a financial holding company. Through its subsidiary, Prosperity Bank®, Co. provides financial products and services to small and medium-sized businesses and consumers. Co. is a real estate lender with commercial real estate and one-four family residential loans. Co. also provides commercial loans, loans for automobiles and other consumer durables, home equity loans, debit and credit cards, internet banking and other cash management services, mobile banking, trust and wealth management, retail brokerage services, mortgage banking services and automated telephone banking. As of Dec 31 2016, Co. had total assets of $22.33 billion and total deposits of $17.31 billion.

Recent Developments: For the quarter ended Sep 30 2017, net income decreased 1.1% to US$67.9 million from US$68.7 million in the year-earlier quarter. Net interest income increased 1.4% to US$156.1 million from US$154.1 million in the year-earlier quarter. Provision for loan losses was US$6.9 million versus US$2.0 million in the prior-year quarter, an increase of 245.0%. Non-interest income fell 2.9% to US$28.8 million from US$29.7 million, while non-interest expense declined 2.5% to US$77.5 million.

Prospects: Our evaluation of Prosperity Bancshares Inc. as of Jan. 14, 2018 is the result of our systematic analysis on three basic characteristics: earnings strength, relative valuation, and recent stock price movement. The company has managed to produce a neutral trend in earnings per share over the past 5 quarters and while recent estimates for the company have been raised by analysts, PB has posted better than expected results. Based on operating earnings yield, the company is undervalued when compared to all of the companies in our coverage universe. Share price changes over the past year indicates that PB will perform poorly over the near term.

Financial Data

(US$ in Thousands)	9 Mos	6 Mos	3 Mos	12/31/2016	12/31/2015	12/31/2014	12/31/2013	12/31/2012
Earnings Per Share	3.95	3.96	3.95	3.94	4.09	4.32	3.65	3.23
Cash Flow Per Share	4.73	4.54	4.57	4.79	4.44	5.06	5.09	4.04
Tang Book Value Per Share	26.48	25.81	25.11	24.40	22.06	18.80	16.25	14.99
Dividends Per Share	1.360	1.320	1.280	1.240	1.117	0.993	0.885	0.800
Dividend Payout %	34.43	33.33	32.41	31.47	27.32	22.97	24.25	24.77
Income Statement								
Interest Income	505,516	333,097	165,050	675,779	669,701	714,795	539,297	419,842
Interest Expense	44,703	28,431	12,615	43,159	39,191	43,641	40,471	39,136
Net Interest Income	460,813	304,666	152,435	632,620	630,510	671,154	498,826	380,706
Provision for Losses	12,325	5,425	2,675	24,000	7,560	18,275	17,240	6,100
Non-Interest Income	87,413	58,604	30,824	118,425	120,781	122,872	95,427	75,535
Non-Interest Expense	232,013	154,504	78,062	318,387	313,536	330,002	247,196	198,457
Income Before Taxes	303,888	203,341	102,522	408,658	430,195	445,749	329,817	251,684
Income Taxes	98,861	66,222	33,957	134,192	143,549	148,308	108,419	83,783
Net Income	205,027	137,119	68,565	274,466	286,646	297,441	221,398	167,901
Average Shares	69,485	69,487	69,482	69,680	70,049	68,911	60,578	51,941
Balance Sheet								
Net Loans & Leases	9,824,390	9,780,236	9,655,158	9,536,734	9,357,205	9,163,421	7,707,939	5,127,376
Total Assets	22,143,263	22,296,543	22,477,419	22,331,072	22,037,216	21,507,733	18,642,028	14,583,573
Total Deposits	16,907,476	17,070,530	17,035,572	17,307,302	17,681,119	17,693,158	15,291,271	11,641,844
Total Liabilities	18,361,905	18,560,355	18,788,337	18,688,761	18,574,306	18,262,907	15,855,210	12,494,184
Stockholders' Equity	3,781,358	3,736,188	3,689,082	3,642,311	3,462,910	3,244,826	2,786,818	2,089,389
Shares Outstanding	69,484	69,488	69,479	69,491	70,021	69,779	66,048	56,447
Statistical Record								
Return on Assets %	1.26	1.25	1.23	1.23	1.32	1.48	1.33	1.37
Return on Equity %	7.42	7.54	7.63	7.70	8.55	9.86	9.08	9.16
Net Interest Margin %	90.56	90.59	92.36	93.61	94.15	93.89	92.50	90.68
Efficiency Ratio %	38.52	39.04	39.85	40.09	39.66	39.40	38.95	40.06
Loans to Deposits	0.58	0.57	0.57	0.55	0.53	0.52	0.50	0.44
Price Range	77.47-53.38	77.47-47.69	77.47-43.90	73.20-33.73	59.23-45.79	67.00-53.21	65.07-42.00	47.31-39.10
P/E Ratio	19.61-13.51	19.56-12.04	19.61-11.11	18.58-8.56	14.48-11.20	15.51-12.32	17.83-11.51	14.65-12.11
Average Yield %	2.07	2.08	2.15	2.38	2.13	1.65	1.63	1.89

Address: Prosperity Bank Plaza, 4295 San Felipe, Houston, TX 77027	**Web Site:** www.prosperitybankusa.com	**Auditors:** Deloitte & Touche LLP
Telephone: 281-269-7199	**Officers:** David Zalman - Chairman, President, Chief Executive Officer H. E. Timanus - Vice-Chairman	**Investor Contact:** 713-693-9300
		Transfer Agents: Computershare Investor Services, Golden, Co

PRUDENTIAL FINANCIAL, INC.

Exchange	Symbol	Price	52Wk Range	Yield	P/E
NYS	PRU	$114.98 (12/29/2017)	117.15-98.65	2.61	11.51

*7 Year Price Score 110.05 *NYSE Composite Index=100 *12 Month Price Score 99.12

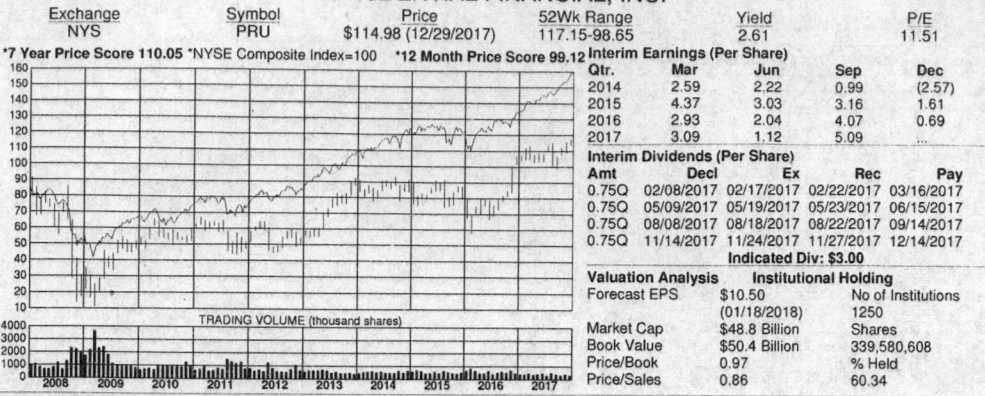

Interim Earnings (Per Share)

Qtr.	Mar	Jun	Sep	Dec
2014	2.59	2.22	0.99	(2.57)
2015	4.37	3.03	3.16	1.61
2016	2.93	2.04	4.07	0.69
2017	3.09	1.12	5.09	...

Interim Dividends (Per Share)

Amt	Decl	Ex	Rec	Pay
0.75Q	02/08/2017	02/17/2017	02/22/2017	03/16/2017
0.75Q	05/09/2017	05/19/2017	05/23/2017	06/15/2017
0.75Q	08/08/2017	08/18/2017	08/22/2017	09/14/2017
0.75Q	11/14/2017	11/24/2017	11/27/2017	12/14/2017

Indicated Div: $3.00

Valuation Analysis

		Institutional Holding	
Forecast EPS	$10.50	No of Institutions	
	(01/18/2018)	1250	
Market Cap	$48.8 Billion	Shares	
Book Value	$50.4 Billion	339,580,608	
Price/Book	0.97	% Held	
Price/Sales	0.86	60.34	

Business Summary: Life & Health (MIC: 5.2.2 SIC: 6311 NAIC: 524113)

Prudential Financial is a holding company. Through its subsidiaries and affiliates, Co. provides financial products and services, including life insurance, annuities, retirement-related services, mutual funds and investment management. The U.S. Retirement Solutions and Investment Management division consists of Co.'s Individual Annuities, Retirement and Asset Management segments. The U.S. Individual Life and Group Insurance division consists of Co.'s Individual Life and Group Insurance segments. The International Insurance division consists of Co.'s International Insurance segment. As of Dec 31 2016, Co. had operations in the U.S., Asia, Europe and Latin America.

Recent Developments: For the quarter ended Sep 30 2017, net income increased 22.3% to US$2.24 billion from US$1.83 billion in the year-earlier quarter. Revenues were US$16.31 billion, down 3.8% from US$16.96 billion the year before. Net premiums earned were US$7.80 billion versus US$9.64 billion in the prior-year quarter, a decrease of 19.1%. Net investment income rose 0.1% to US$4.08 billion from US$4.07 billion a year ago.

Prospects: Our evaluation of Prudential Financial Inc. as of Jan. 14, 2018 is the result of our systematic analysis on three basic characteristics: earnings strength, relative valuation, and recent stock price movement. The company has managed to produce a neutral trend in earnings per share over the past 5 quarters and while recent estimates for the company have been raised by analysts, PRU has posted better than expected results. Based on operating earnings yield, the company is undervalued when compared to all of the companies in our coverage universe. Share price changes over the past year indicates that PRU will perform poorly over the near term.

Financial Data
(US$ in Millions)

	9 Mos	6 Mos	3 Mos	12/31/2016	12/31/2015	12/31/2014	12/31/2013	12/31/2012
Earnings Per Share	9.99	8.97	9.89	9.71	12.17	3.23	(1.55)	0.94
Cash Flow Per Share	15.25	13.99	23.56	33.63	30.76	42.30	18.24	44.78
Tang Book Value Per Share	118.60	113.44	108.98	106.76	93.69	91.84	76.19	82.95
Dividends Per Share	2.950	2.900	2.850	2.800	2.440	2.170	1.730	1.600
Dividend Payout %	29.53	32.33	28.82	28.84	20.05	67.18	...	170.21
Income Statement								
Premium Income	22,602	14,807	6,481	30,964	28,521	29,293	26,237	65,354
Total Revenue	43,424	27,111	13,670	58,779	57,119	54,105	41,461	84,815
Benefits & Claims	23,546	15,353	7,025	33,632	30,627	31,587	26,733	65,131
Income Before Taxes	5,371	2,350	1,742	5,705	7,769	1,759	(1,684)	676
Income Taxes	1,320	520	395	1,335	2,072	349	(1,058)	204
Net Income	4,098	1,860	1,369	4,368	5,642	1,381	(667)	469
Average Shares	435	437	439	446	460	467	463	468
Balance Sheet								
Total Assets	821,131	812,590	797,365	783,962	757,388	766,655	731,781	709,298
Total Liabilities	770,758	764,146	750,581	738,099	715,498	724,885	696,503	670,723
Stockholders' Equity	50,373	48,444	46,784	45,863	41,890	41,770	35,278	38,575
Shares Outstanding	424	427	429	429	447	454	463	465
Statistical Record								
Return on Assets %	0.53	0.49	0.56	0.57	0.74	0.18	N.M.	0.07
Return on Equity %	8.21	7.67	9.17	9.93	13.49	3.58	N.M.	1.23
Loss Ratio %	104.18	103.69	108.39	108.62	107.38	107.83	101.89	99.66
Net Margin %	9.44	6.86	10.01	7.43	9.88	2.55	(1.61)	0.55
Price Range	115.23-81.43	113.82-68.74	113.82-66.93	107.10-58.00	91.68-74.22	93.16-77.61	92.43-53.33	64.65-44.74
P/E Ratio	11.53-8.15	12.69-7.66	11.51-6.77	11.03-5.97	7.53-6.10	28.84-24.03	...	68.78-47.60
Average Yield %	2.84	3.02	3.22	3.53	2.93	2.51	2.41	2.93

Address: 751 Broad Street, Newark, NJ 07102
Telephone: 973-802-6000

Web Site: www.investor.prudential.com
Officers: John R. Strangfeld - Chairman, President, Chief Executive Officer, Division Officer Mark B. Grier - Vice-Chairman, Division Officer

Auditors: PricewaterhouseCoopers LLP
Transfer Agents: Computershare Trust Company, N.A., Providence, RI

PUBLIC SERVICE ENTERPRISE GROUP INC

Exchange	Symbol	Price	52Wk Range	Yield	P/E
NYS	PEG	$51.50 (12/29/2017)	53.07-41.85	3.34	49.52

*7 Year Price Score 95.06   ***NYSE Composite Index=100**   ***12 Month Price Score 105.69**

Interim Earnings (Per Share)

Qtr.	Mar	Jun	Sep	Dec
2014	0.76	0.42	0.88	0.94
2015	1.15	0.68	0.87	0.60
2016	0.93	0.37	0.64	(0.19)
2017	0.23	0.22	0.78	...

Interim Dividends (Per Share)

Amt	Decl	Ex	Rec	Pay
0.43Q	02/21/2017	03/08/2017	03/10/2017	03/31/2017
0.43Q	04/18/2017	06/07/2017	06/09/2017	06/30/2017
0.43Q	07/18/2017	09/07/2017	09/08/2017	09/29/2017
0.43Q	11/21/2017	12/07/2017	12/08/2017	12/29/2017

Indicated Div: $1.72

Valuation Analysis

		Institutional Holding	
Forecast EPS	$2.90	No of Institutions	1015
	(01/27/2018)		
Market Cap	$26.0 Billion	Shares	411,738,912
Book Value	$13.1 Billion	% Held	63.36
Price/Book	1.98		
Price/Sales	2.86		

TRADING VOLUME (thousand shares)

Business Summary: Electric Utilities (MIC: 3.1.1 SIC: 4931 NAIC: 221119)

Public Service Enterprise Group is a holding company. Through its subsidiaries, Co. is engaged in the energy industry. Co. conducts its business through two subsidiaries, Public Service Electric and Gas Company (PSE&G) and PSEG Power LLC (Power). PSE&G is a public utility, which is engaged in the transmission of electricity and distribution of electricity and natural gas in certain areas of New Jersey, and Power is a multi-regional energy supply company that integrates the operations of its merchant nuclear and fossil generating assets with its power marketing businesses through energy sales in energy markets and fuel supply functions primarily in the Northeast and Mid-Atlantic U.S.

Recent Developments: For the quarter ended Sep 30 2017, net income increased 20.8% to US$395.0 million from US$327.0 million in the year-earlier quarter. Revenues were US$2.26 billion, down 7.6% from US$2.45 billion the year before. Operating income was US$693.0 million versus US$577.0 million in the prior-year quarter, an increase of 20.1%. Direct operating expenses declined 19.7% to US$1.32 billion from US$1.64 billion in the comparable period the year before. Indirect operating expenses increased 9.1% to US$252.0 million from US$231.0 million in the equivalent prior-year period.

Prospects: Our evaluation of Public Service Enterprise Group Inc. as of Jan. 21, 2018 is the result of our systematic analysis on three basic characteristics: earnings strength, relative valuation, and recent stock price movement. The company has generated a negative trend in earnings per share over the past 5 quarters and while recent estimates for the company have been mixed, PEG has posted results that fell short of analysts expectations. Based on operating earnings yield, the company is undervalued when compared to all of the companies in our coverage universe. Share price changes over the past year indicates that PEG will perform well over the near term.

Financial Data (US$ in Thousands)	9 Mos	6 Mos	3 Mos	12/31/2016	12/31/2015	12/31/2014	12/31/2013	12/31/2012
Earnings Per Share	1.04	0.90	1.05	1.75	3.30	2.99	2.45	2.51
Cash Flow Per Share	6.50	6.62	6.52	6.54	7.76	6.25	6.24	5.49
Tang Book Value Per Share	25.78	25.31	25.51	25.78	25.63	23.89	22.85	21.21
Dividends Per Share	1.700	1.680	1.660	1.640	1.560	1.480	1.440	1.420
Dividend Payout %	163.46	186.67	158.10	93.71	47.27	49.50	58.78	56.57
Income Statement								
Total Revenue	6,988,000	4,725,000	2,592,000	9,061,000	10,415,000	10,886,000	9,968,000	9,781,000
EBITDA	1,213,000	479,000	242,000	2,945,000	4,114,000	3,816,000	3,449,000	3,264,000
Depn & Amortn	152,000	101,000	54,000	1,476,000	1,214,000	1,227,000	1,178,000	1,054,000
Income Before Taxes	947,000	303,000	140,000	1,202,000	2,668,000	2,443,000	2,044,000	1,999,000
Income Taxes	340,000	88,000	29,000	326,000	1,001,000	938,000	812,000	736,000
Net Income	618,000	223,000	114,000	887,000	1,679,000	1,518,000	1,243,000	1,275,000
Average Shares	507,000	507,000	508,000	508,000	508,000	508,000	507,525	507,086
Balance Sheet								
Current Assets	3,081,000	3,188,000	2,716,000	3,254,000	3,494,000	4,119,000	3,614,000	3,869,000
Total Assets	41,157,000	40,524,000	39,664,000	40,070,000	37,535,000	35,333,000	32,522,000	31,725,000
Current Liabilities	3,831,000	3,164,000	3,111,000	3,276,000	3,575,000	3,478,000	3,063,000	3,777,000
Long-Term Obligations	11,274,000	11,621,000	10,898,000	10,895,000	8,834,000	8,261,000	7,862,000	6,687,000
Total Liabilities	28,033,000	27,606,000	26,659,000	26,940,000	24,469,000	23,148,000	20,914,000	20,945,000
Stockholders' Equity	13,124,000	12,918,000	13,005,000	13,130,000	13,066,000	12,185,000	11,608,000	10,780,000
Shares Outstanding	505,000	505,000	505,000	504,866	505,282	505,836	505,857	505,892
Statistical Record								
Return on Assets %	1.29	1.14	1.36	2.28	4.61	4.47	3.87	4.13
Return on Equity %	3.91	3.45	4.03	6.75	13.30	12.76	11.10	12.08
EBITDA Margin %	17.36	10.14	9.34	32.50	39.50	35.05	34.60	33.37
Net Margin %	8.84	4.72	4.40	9.79	16.12	13.94	12.47	13.04
Asset Turnover	0.23	0.23	0.23	0.23	0.29	0.32	0.31	0.32
Current Ratio	0.80	1.01	0.87	0.99	0.98	1.18	1.18	1.02
Debt to Equity	0.86	0.90	0.84	0.83	0.68	0.68	0.68	0.62
Price Range	47.30-39.57	46.75-39.57	47.32-39.57	47.32-38.42	44.30-37.02	43.53-31.33	36.61-29.78	34.00-29.09
P/E Ratio	45.48-38.05	51.94-43.97	45.07-37.69	27.04-21.95	13.42-11.22	14.56-10.48	14.94-12.16	13.55-11.59
Average Yield %	3.88		3.86	3.78	3.80	3.93	4.36	4.54

Address: 80 Park Plaza, Newark, NJ 07102	Web Site: www.pseg.com	Auditors: Deloitte & Touche LLP
Telephone: 973-430-7000	Officers: Ralph Izzo - Chairman, President, Chief Executive Officer Daniel J. Cregg - Executive Vice President, Chief Financial Officer	Investor Contact: 973-430-6565 Transfer Agents: Wells Fargo Bank, N.A., Mendota Heights, MN

PULTEGROUP INC

Exchange	Symbol	Price	52Wk Range	Yield	P/E
NYS	PHM	$33.25 (12/29/2017)	34.44-18.46	1.08	16.71

*7 Year Price Score 114.94 *NYSE Composite Index=100 *12 Month Price Score 122.05

TRADING VOLUME (thousand shares)

Interim Earnings (Per Share)

Qtr.	Mar	Jun	Sep	Dec
2014	0.19	0.11	0.37	0.59
2015	0.15	0.28	0.30	0.63
2016	0.24	0.34	0.37	0.81
2017	0.28	0.32	0.58	...

Interim Dividends (Per Share)

Amt	Decl	Ex	Rec	Pay
0.09Q	02/10/2017	03/08/2017	03/10/2017	04/04/2017
0.09Q	05/03/2017	06/06/2017	06/08/2017	07/05/2017
0.09Q	09/06/2017	09/18/2017	09/19/2017	10/03/2017
0.09Q	12/01/2017	12/11/2017	12/12/2017	01/03/2018

Indicated Div: $0.36

Valuation Analysis / Institutional Holding

Valuation Analysis		Institutional Holding	
Forecast EPS	$2.02	No of Institutions	
	(01/18/2018)	701	
Market Cap	$9.8 Billion	Shares	
Book Value	$4.3 Billion	305,982,016	
Price/Book	2.25	% Held	
Price/Sales	1.18	77.73	

Business Summary: Builders (MIC: 2.2.5 SIC: 1531 NAIC: 236117)

PulteGroup is engaged in the homebuilding business. Homebuilding, its main business, includes the acquisition and development of land primarily for residential purposes within the U.S. and the construction of housing on such land. Through its brands, which include Centex, Pulte Homes, Del Webb, DiVosta Homes, and John Wieland Homes and Neighborhoods, Co. provides home designs, including single-family detached, townhouses, condominiums, and duplexes. Co. Homebuilding operations has six segment: Northeast, Southeast, Florida, Midwest, Texas, and West. Co. also has a reportable segment for its financial services operations, which consist principally of mortgage banking and title operations.

Recent Developments: For the quarter ended Sep 30 2017, net income increased 38.2% to US$177.5 million from US$128.5 million in the year-earlier quarter. Revenues were US$2.13 billion, up 9.6% from US$1.94 billion the year before. Direct operating expenses rose 11.2% to US$1.62 billion from US$1.46 billion in the comparable period the year before. Indirect operating expenses decreased 5.3% to US$237.5 million from US$250.9 million in the equivalent prior-year period.

Prospects: Our evaluation of Pultegroup Inc. as of Jan. 14, 2018 is the result of our systematic analysis on three basic characteristics: earnings strength, relative valuation, and recent stock price movement. The company has enjoyed a very positive trend in earnings per share over the past 5 quarters and while recent estimates for the company have been mixed, PHM has posted results that fell short of analysts' expectations. Based on operating earnings yield, the company is undervalued when compared to all of the companies in our coverage universe. Share price changes over the past year indicates that PHM will perform very well over the near term.

Financial Data

(US$ in Thousands)	9 Mos	6 Mos	3 Mos	12/31/2016	12/31/2015	12/31/2014	12/31/2013	12/31/2012
Earnings Per Share	1.99	1.78	1.80	1.75	1.36	1.26	6.72	0.54
Cash Flow Per Share	2.12	1.82	0.54	0.20	(0.98)	0.83	2.30	1.99
Tang Book Value Per Share	14.29	14.15	14.27	14.12	13.32	12.67	11.84	5.28
Dividends Per Share	0.360	0.360	0.360	0.360	0.330	0.230	0.150	...
Dividend Payout %	18.09	20.22	20.00	20.57	24.26	18.25	2.23	
Income Statement								
Total Revenue	5,779,694	3,649,675	1,628,828	7,668,476	5,981,964	5,822,363	5,679,595	4,819,998
EBITDA	522,320	272,121	140,826	976,963	852,549	717,400	541,509	192,301
Depn & Amortn	(10,350)	6,900	3,450	54,000	46,200	39,833	18,500	16,900
Income Before Taxes	534,216	266,382	138,072	925,513	808,668	681,350	526,692	179,495
Income Taxes	160,255	69,545	47,747	331,147	321,933	215,420	(2,092,294)	(22,591)
Net Income	369,807	192,268	91,518	602,703	494,090	474,338	2,620,116	206,145
Average Shares	300,228	313,880	320,085	342,123	359,793	374,102	386,866	384,564
Balance Sheet								
Current Assets	7,567,249	7,330,019	7,452,198	7,534,903	6,332,065	5,854,026	5,752,801	5,844,850
Total Assets	9,971,269	9,812,878	9,920,814	10,178,200	8,967,160	8,569,410	8,734,143	6,734,409
Current Liabilities	748,122	698,581	649,866	745,133	652,636	547,715	629,884	571,133
Long-Term Obligations	3,438,808	3,263,697	3,250,385	3,460,919	2,387,982	1,981,057	2,163,832	2,648,408
Total Liabilities	5,626,184	5,368,876	5,260,669	5,518,837	4,207,835	3,764,456	4,085,191	4,544,793
Stockholders' Equity	4,345,085	4,444,002	4,660,145	4,659,363	4,759,325	4,804,954	4,648,952	2,189,616
Shares Outstanding	293,936	303,699	316,032	319,089	349,148	369,458	381,299	386,608
Statistical Record								
Return on Assets %	6.48	6.15	6.18	6.28	5.63	5.48	33.88	3.02
Return on Equity %	14.26	12.82	12.95	12.76	10.33	10.03	76.63	9.96
EBITDA Margin %	9.04	7.46	8.65	12.74	14.25	12.32	9.53	3.99
Net Margin %	6.40	5.27	5.62	7.86	8.26	8.15	46.13	4.28
Asset Turnover	0.83	0.84	0.80	0.80	0.68	0.67	0.73	0.71
Current Ratio	10.11	10.49	11.47	10.11	9.70	10.69	9.13	10.23
Debt to Equity	0.79	0.73	0.70	0.74	0.50	0.41	0.47	1.21
Price Range	27.33-18.01	24.53-18.01	23.83-17.21	22.11-15.36	23.24-17.18	21.72-16.66	24.25-15.11	18.61-6.52
P/E Ratio	13.73-9.05	13.78-10.12	13.24-9.56	12.63-8.78	17.09-12.63	17.24-13.22	3.61-2.25	34.46-12.07
Average Yield %	1.62	1.70	1.81	1.91	1.63		1.18	0.80	...

Address: 3350 Peachtree Road N.E., Suite 150, Atlanta, GA 30326 **Telephone:** 404-978-6400	**Web Site:** www.pultegroupinc.com **Officers:** Richard J. Dugas - Executive Chairman, Chairman, President, Chief Executive Officer Ryan R. Marshall - President, Region Officer, Chief Executive Officer	**Auditors:** Ernst & Young LLP **Investor Contact:** 248-433-4502 **Transfer Agents:** Computershare Trust Company N.A., Providence, RI

PVH CORP

Exchange	Symbol	Price	52Wk Range	Yield	P/E
NYS	PVH	$137.21 (12/29/2017)	137.56-85.48	0.11	20.39

*7 Year Price Score 86.52 *NYSE Composite Index=100 *12 Month Price Score 111.11

Interim Earnings (Per Share)

Qtr.	Apr	Jul	Oct	Jan
2014-15	0.42	1.52	2.71	0.61
2015-16	1.37	1.22	2.67	1.63
2016-17	2.83	1.11	1.56	1.27
2017-18	0.89	1.52	3.05	...

Interim Dividends (Per Share)

Amt	Decl	Ex	Rec	Pay
0.037Q	02/01/2017	02/22/2017	02/24/2017	03/24/2017
0.037Q	04/27/2017	05/16/2017	05/18/2017	06/20/2017
0.037Q	07/27/2017	08/22/2017	08/24/2017	09/22/2017
0.037Q	10/24/2017	11/21/2017	11/22/2017	12/20/2017

Indicated Div: $0.15

Valuation Analysis

		Institutional Holding	
Forecast EPS	$7.80 (01/18/2018)	No of Institutions	668
Market Cap	$10.6 Billion	Shares	83,239,672
Book Value	$5.2 Billion	% Held	
Price/Book	2.01		
Price/Sales	1.24	N/A	

Business Summary: Apparel, Footwear & Accessories (MIC: 1.4.2 SIC: 2321 NAIC: 315211)

PVH is an apparel company that designs and markets branded dress shirts, neckwear, sportswear, jeanswear, accessories, footwear and other related products and licenses its owned brands over a range of products. Co.'s brand portfolio includes CALVIN KLEIN and Tommy Hilfiger, as well as Van Heusen, IZOD, ARROW, Warner's, Olga and Eagle, which are owned brands, and Speedo, Geoffrey Beene, Kenneth Cole New York, Kenneth Cole Reaction, Sean John, MICHAEL Michael Kors, Michael Kors Collection and Chaps, which are licensed, as well as various other owned, licensed and private label brands. Co. aggregates its segments into three main businesses: Calvin Klein, Tommy Hilfiger and Heritage Brands.

Recent Developments: For the quarter ended Oct 29 2017, net income increased 89.3% to US$238.7 million from US$126.1 million in the year-earlier quarter. Revenues were US$2.36 billion, up 5.0% from US$2.24 billion the year before. Direct operating expenses rose 0.7% to US$1.06 billion from US$1.05 billion in the comparable period the year before. Indirect operating expenses increased 11.1% to US$1.02 billion from US$918.0 million in the equivalent prior-year period.

Prospects: Our evaluation of PVH Corp. as of Jan. 14, 2018 is the result of our systematic analysis on three basic characteristics: earnings strength, relative valuation, and recent stock price movement. The company has produced a positive trend in earnings per share over the past 5 quarters. However, while recent estimates for the company have been mixed, PVH has posted better than expected results. Based on operating earnings yield, the company is undervalued when compared to all of the companies in our coverage universe. Share price changes over the past year indicates that PVH will perform well over the near term.

Financial Data

(US$ in Thousands)	9 Mos	6 Mos	3 Mos	01/29/2017	01/31/2016	02/01/2015	02/02/2014	02/03/2013
Earnings Per Share	6.73	5.24	4.83	6.79	6.89	5.27	1.74	5.87
Cash Flow Per Share	8.04	9.63	10.24	11.94	10.95	9.60	5.09	7.96
Dividends Per Share	0.150	0.150	0.150	0.150	0.150	0.150	0.150	0.150
Dividend Payout %	2.23	2.86	3.11	2.21	2.18	2.85	8.62	2.56
Income Statement								
Total Revenue	6,415,900	4,058,900	1,989,000	8,203,100	8,020,300	8,241,200	8,186,351	6,042,999
EBITDA	807,600	449,400	190,000	1,017,500	954,700	713,800	695,081	777,339
Depn & Amortn	239,000	157,800	77,200	228,400	210,800	193,800	189,675	122,424
Income Before Taxes	479,300	233,200	84,100	674,100	630,900	381,500	320,710	537,665
Income Taxes	56,900	45,800	14,400	125,500	75,100	(47,500)	185,284	109,272
Net Income	429,300	190,100	70,400	549,000	572,400	439,000	143,537	433,840
Average Shares	78,500	78,700	79,000	80,900	83,100	83,300	82,618	73,876
Balance Sheet								
Current Assets	3,144,100	2,935,500	2,655,200	2,879,600	2,812,600	2,901,200	2,998,592	2,437,006
Total Assets	11,658,200	11,453,900	10,912,300	11,067,900	10,696,400	10,931,800	11,575,578	7,781,549
Current Liabilities	1,726,300	1,633,200	1,378,200	1,564,800	1,527,200	1,428,600	1,552,397	1,162,447
Long-Term Obligations	3,182,700	3,185,400	3,157,100	3,197,300	3,054,300	3,438,700	3,878,221	2,211,642
Total Liabilities	6,408,400	6,358,700	6,037,300	6,263,400	6,144,100	6,567,500	7,240,399	4,528,980
Stockholders' Equity	5,249,800	5,095,200	4,875,000	4,804,500	4,552,300	4,364,300	4,335,179	3,252,569
Shares Outstanding	77,080	77,574	78,018	78,551	81,487	82,512	82,166	72,910
Statistical Record								
Return on Assets %	4.66	3.68	3.56	5.06	5.31	3.91	1.49	5.87
Return on Equity %	10.55	8.43	7.97	11.77	12.87	10.12	3.79	14.30
EBITDA Margin %	12.59	11.07	9.55	12.40	11.90	8.66	8.49	12.86
Net Margin %	6.69	4.68	3.54	6.69	7.14	5.33	1.75	7.18
Asset Turnover	0.75	0.74	0.76	0.76	0.74	0.73	0.85	0.82
Current Ratio	1.82	1.80	1.93	1.84	1.84	2.03	1.93	2.10
Debt to Equity	0.61	0.63	0.65	0.67	0.67	0.79	0.89	0.68
Price Range	130.00-85.48	119.94-85.48	114.00-83.15	114.00-70.46	118.98-66.41	133.66-107.87	137.62-103.85	120.86-72.70
P/E Ratio	19.32-12.70	22.89-16.31	23.60-17.22	16.79-10.38	17.27-9.64	25.36-20.47	79.09-59.68	20.59-12.39
Average Yield %	0.14	0.15	0.15	0.15	0.15	0.12	0.12	0.16

Address: 200 Madison Avenue, New York, NY 10016
Telephone: 212-381-3500

Web Site: www.pvh.com
Officers: Emanuel (Manny) Chirico - Chairman, Chief Executive Officer Michael A. Shaffer - Executive Vice President, Chief Financial Officer, Chief Operating Officer

Auditors: Ernst & Young LLP
Transfer Agents: Wells Fargo Bank, N.A., St. Paul, MN

QEP RESOURCES INC

Exchange	Symbol	Price	52Wk Range	Yield	P/E
NYS	QEP	$9.57 (12/29/2017)	19.23-7.09	N/A	319.00

*7 Year Price Score 35.12   *NYSE Composite Index=100   *12 Month Price Score 80.80

TRADING VOLUME (thousand shares)

Interim Earnings (Per Share)

Qtr.	Mar	Jun	Sep	Dec
2014	0.22	(0.51)	0.94	3.70
2015	(0.32)	(0.43)	0.12	(0.22)
2016	(4.55)	(0.90)	(0.21)	(0.47)
2017	0.32	0.19	(0.01)	...

Interim Dividends (Per Share)

Dividend Payment Suspended

Valuation Analysis   Institutional Holding

Forecast EPS	$-0.45	No of Institutions
	(01/17/2018)	415
Market Cap	$2.3 Billion	Shares
Book Value	$3.6 Billion	251,764,032
Price/Book	0.63	% Held
Price/Sales	1.45	90.15

Business Summary: Production & Extraction (MIC: 9.1.1 SIC: 1311 NAIC: 211111)

QEP Resources is an independent crude oil and natural gas exploration and production company focused in two regions of the U.S.: the Northern Region (primarily in North Dakota, Wyoming and Utah) and the Southern Region (primarily in Texas and Louisiana). Co. sells gas volumes to wholesale marketers, industrial users, local distribution companies and utilities. Co. sells oil and natural gas liquids volumes to refiners, marketers and other companies. As of Dec 31 2016, Co. had estimated proved reserves of 731.4 million barrels of oil equivalent, consisting of 238.6 million barrels of oil, 2,553.80 billion cubic feet of gas, and 67.2 million barrels of natural gas liquids.

Recent Developments: For the quarter ended Sep 30 2017, net loss amounted to US$3.3 million versus a net loss of US$50.9 million in the year-earlier quarter. Revenues were US$390.1 million, up 2.0% from US$382.4 million the year before. Operating income was US$132.1 million versus a loss of US$93.1 million in the prior-year quarter. Direct operating expenses declined 9.3% to US$173.5 million from US$191.3 million in the comparable period the year before. Indirect operating expenses decreased 70.3% to US$84.5 million from US$284.2 million in the equivalent prior-year period.

Prospects: Our evaluation of QEP Resources Inc. as of Jan. 14, 2018 is the result of our systematic analysis on three basic characteristics: earnings strength, relative valuation, and recent stock price movement. The company has generated a negative trend in earnings per share over the past 5 quarters. Because the company lacks sufficient analyst estimate data, we place greater weight on the historical EPS trend as the measure of earnings strength. Based on operating earnings yield, the company is overvalued when compared to all of the companies in our coverage universe. Share price changes over the past year indicates that QEP will perform very poorly over the near term.

Financial Data

(US$ in Thousands)	9 Mos	6 Mos	3 Mos	12/31/2016	12/31/2015	12/31/2014	12/31/2013	12/31/2012
Earnings Per Share	0.03	(0.17)	(1.26)	(5.62)	(0.85)	4.36	0.89	0.72
Cash Flow Per Share	2.55	3.07	3.04	2.99	2.73	8.58	6.65	7.27
Tang Book Value Per Share	15.10	15.11	14.90	14.62	22.33	23.23	18.87	17.97
Dividends Per Share	...	...	...	...	0.080	0.080	0.080	0.080
Dividend Payout %	...	...	...	...	...	1.83	8.99	11.11
Income Statement								
Total Revenue	1,193,900	803,800	420,100	1,377,100	2,018,600	3,414,300	2,935,800	2,349,800
EBITDA	294,100	264,600	157,200	(958,100)	786,900	561,300	1,465,900	1,218,200
Depn & Amortn	4,800	3,100	1,500	877,500	887,300	1,047,300	1,022,400	910,200
Income Before Taxes	188,700	195,200	122,500	(1,953,200)	(243,000)	(642,300)	285,400	191,700
Income Taxes	69,700	72,900	45,600	(708,200)	(93,600)	(232,500)	119,800	66,500
Net Income	119,000	122,300	76,900	(1,245,000)	(149,400)	784,400	159,400	128,300
Average Shares	240,700	240,600	240,300	221,700	176,600	179,800	179,500	178,700
Balance Sheet								
Current Assets	941,000	424,300	512,600	640,100	931,800	2,001,500	519,000	649,700
Total Assets	7,347,400	7,265,500	7,235,000	7,245,400	8,425,500	9,286,800	9,376,800	9,108,500
Current Liabilities	606,200	519,100	414,200	514,800	641,600	1,344,800	641,500	761,900
Long-Term Obligations	1,890,600	1,889,000	2,022,400	2,020,900	2,042,000	2,218,100	2,997,500	3,206,900
Total Liabilities	3,709,900	3,630,500	3,652,000	3,742,700	4,477,600	5,211,500	6,000,200	5,842,500
Stockholders' Equity	3,637,500	3,635,000	3,583,000	3,502,700	3,947,900	4,075,300	3,376,600	3,266,000
Shares Outstanding	240,935	240,500	240,500	239,600	176,800	175,400	178,900	178,400
Statistical Record								
Return on Assets %	N.M.	N.M.	N.M.	N.M.	N.M.	8.41	1.72	1.55
Return on Equity %	N.M.	N.M.	N.M.	N.M.	N.M.	21.05	4.80	3.90
EBITDA Margin %	24.63	32.92	37.42	N.M.	38.98	16.44	49.93	51.84
Net Margin %	9.97	15.22	18.31	N.M.	N.M.	22.97	5.43	5.46
Asset Turnover	0.22	0.22	0.21	0.18	0.23	0.37	0.32	0.28
Current Ratio	1.55	0.82	1.24	1.24	1.45	1.49	0.81	0.85
Debt to Equity	0.52	0.52	0.56	0.58	0.52	0.54	0.89	0.98
Price Range	20.45-7.09	20.45-9.06	20.45-11.98	20.45-9.29	23.76-11.31	35.57-18.64	33.48-26.86	34.90-24.52
P/E Ratio	681.67-236.33	...	...	...	...	8.16-4.28	37.62-30.18	48.47-34.06
Average Yield %	...	...	...	...	0.46	0.27	0.27	0.27

Address: 1050 17th Street, Suite 800, Denver, CO 80265	**Web Site:** www.qepres.com	**Auditors:** PricewaterhouseCoopers LLP
Telephone: 303-672-6900	**Officers:** Charles B. Stanley - Chairman, President, Chief Executive Officer Richard J. Doleshek - Executive Vice President, Chief Financial Officer, Chief Accounting Officer, Treasurer	**Investor Contact:** 303-405-6665
		Transfer Agents: Wells Fargo Shareowner Services, Saint Paul, MN

QUANTA SERVICES, INC.

Exchange	Symbol	Price	52Wk Range	Yield	P/E
NYS	PWR	$39.11 (12/29/2017)	39.50-30.66	N/A	21.26

*7 Year Price Score 101.56 *NYSE Composite Index=100 ***12 Month Price Score 99.11**

Interim Earnings (Per Share)

Qtr.	Mar	Jun	Sep	Dec
2014	0.25	0.37	0.43	0.30
2015	0.25	0:22	1.15	0.06
2016	0.13	0.11	0.48	0.56
2017	0.31	0.41	0.56	...

Interim Dividends (Per Share)

No Dividends Paid

Valuation Analysis		Institutional Holding	
Forecast EPS	$1.95	No of Institutions	
	(01/17/2018)	649	
Market Cap	$5.9 Billion	Shares	
Book Value	$3.7 Billion	182,687,760	
Price/Book	1.59	% Held	
Price/Sales	0.65	87.23	

TRADING VOLUME (thousand shares)

Business Summary: Construction Services (MIC: 7.5.4 SIC: 1731 NAIC: 238210)

Quanta Services provides contracting services, including infrastructure solutions to the electric power and oil and gas industries in the U.S., Canada and Australia and other international markets. Co.'s services include the design, installation, upgrade, repair and maintenance of infrastructure within the industries that it serves, such as electric power transmission and distribution networks, substation facilities, renewable energy facilities, pipeline transmission and distribution systems and facilities, and infrastructure services for the offshore and inland water energy markets. Co. operates two segments: Electric Power Infrastructure Services and Oil and Gas Infrastructure Services.

Recent Developments: For the quarter ended Sep 30 2017, income from continuing operations increased 22.2% to US$89.8 million from US$73.5 million in the year-earlier quarter. Net income increased 21.2% to US$89.8 million from US$74.2 million in the year-earlier quarter. Revenues were US$2:61 billion, up 27.8% from US$2.04 billion the year before. Operating income was US$140.4 million versus US$130.2 million in the prior-year quarter, an increase of 7.9%. Direct operating expenses rose 29.8% to US$2.26 billion from US$1.74 billion in the comparable period the year before. Indirect operating expenses increased 21.9% to US$210.2 million from US$172.4 million in the equivalent prior-year period.

Prospects: Our evaluation of Quanta Services Inc. as of Jan. 14, 2018 is the result of our systematic analysis on three basic characteristics: earnings strength, relative valuation, and recent stock price movement. The company has generated a negative trend in earnings per share over the past 5 quarters and while recent estimates for the company have been mixed, PWR has posted better than expected results. Based on operating earnings yield, the company is about fairly valued when compared to all of the companies in our coverage universe. Share price changes over the past year indicates that PWR will perform well over the near term.

Financial Data

(US$ in Thousands)	9 Mos	6 Mos	3 Mos	12/31/2016	12/31/2015	12/31/2014	12/31/2013	12/31/2012
Earnings Per Share	1.84	1.76	1.46	1.26	1.59	1.35	1.87	1.44
Cash Flow Per Share	2.28	0.75	1.14	2.42	3.17	1.41	2.08	0.78
Tang Book Value Per Share	10.02	11.19	10.84	10.24	8.31	10.65	10.38	9.59
Income Statement								
Total Revenue	6,987,851	4,378,544	2,178,170	7,651,319	7,572,436	7,851,250	6,522,842	5,920,269
EBITDA	480,300	284,499	124,908	523,014	433,320	668,480	687,408	622,762
Depn & Amortn	158,821	101,077	49,595	201,885	197,648	194,007	161,615	157,991
Income Before Taxes	307,832	175,637	71,635	308,665	229,141	473,449	526,505	462,496
Income Taxes	105,183	62,837	22,592	107,246	97,472	157,408	217,940	158,859
Net Income	201,417	112,104	48,267	198,383	310,907	296,714	401,921	306,629
Average Shares	158,620	156,165	155,168	157,288	195,120	219,690	214,978	212,835
Balance Sheet								
Current Assets	2,948,239	2,617,199	2,474,913	2,288,745	2,277,519	2,553,976	2,313,318	2,201,727
Total Assets	6,640,246	5,753,344	5,543,053	5,354,059	5,213,543	6,312,024	5,793,245	5,140,757
Current Liabilities	1,592,492	1,286,016	1,264,738	1,205,228	1,203,744	1,137,325	1,043,520	881,179
Long-Term Obligations	760,208	483,638	419,310	353,562	475,364	72,489	...	...
Total Liabilities	2,912,716	2,246,621	2,146,710	2,014,632	2,128,049	1,797,551	1,559,057	1,374,209
Stockholders' Equity	3,727,530	3,506,723	3,396,343	3,339,427	3,085,494	4,514,473	4,234,188	3,766,548
Shares Outstanding	151,206	152,476	148,109	151,226	159,783	218,145	216,442	213,179
Statistical Record								
Return on Assets %	4.77	4.95	4.17	3.74	5.40	4.90	7.35	6.22
Return on Equity %	8.26	8.15	6.89	6.16	8.18	6.78	10.05	8.56
EBITDA Margin %	6.87	6.50	5.73	6.84	5.72	8.51	10.54	10.52
Net Margin %	2.88	2.56	2.22	2.59	4.11	3.78	6.16	5.18
Asset Turnover	1.50	1.54	1.50	1.44	1.31	1.30	1.19	1.20
Current Ratio	1.85	2.04	1.96	1.90	1.89	2.25	2.22	2.50
Debt to Equity	0.20	0.14	0.12	0.11	0.15	0.02	...	...
Price Range	38.47-27.61	38.47-23.04	38.47-21.72	35.67-17.29	30.41-18.74	37.20-25.53	31.56-25.74	27.60-20.34
P/E Ratio	20.91-15.01	21.86-13.09	26.35-14.88	28.31-13.72	19.13-11.79	27.56-18.91	16.88-13.76	19.17-14.13

Address: 2800 Post Oak Boulevard, Suite 2600, Houston, TX 77056 **Telephone:** 713-629-7600	**Web Site:** www.quantaservices.com **Officers:** Earl C. (Duke) Austin - President, Chief Executive Officer, Chief Operating Officer, Division Officer Randall C. Wisenbaker - Executive Vice President	**Auditors:** PricewaterhouseCoopers LLP **Investor Contact:** 713-341-7260 **Transfer Agents:** American Stock Transfer & Trust Company, New York, NY

QUEST DIAGNOSTICS, INC.

Exchange	Symbol	Price	52Wk Range	Yield	P/E
NYS	DGX	$98.49 (12/29/2017)	111.16-90.54	1.83	20.65

*7 Year Price Score 114.03 *NYSE Composite Index=100   ***12 Month Price Score 90.73**

Interim Earnings (Per Share)

Qtr.	Mar	Jun	Sep	Dec
2014	0.71	0.92	0.88	1.30
2015	0.42	0.81	2.35	1.29
2016	0.70	1.37	1.34	1.09
2017	1.16	1.37	1.15	...

Interim Dividends (Per Share)

Amt	Decl	Ex	Rec	Pay
0.45Q	02/21/2017	04/03/2017	04/05/2017	04/19/2017
0.45Q	05/16/2017	07/06/2017	07/10/2017	07/24/2017
0.45Q	08/18/2017	10/02/2017	10/03/2017	10/18/2017
0.45Q	11/29/2017	01/08/2018	01/09/2018	01/24/2018

Indicated Div: $1.80

Valuation Analysis

		Institutional Holding	
Forecast EPS	$5.65	No of Institutions	
	(01/18/2018)	916	
Market Cap	$13.4 Billion	Shares	
Book Value	$4.8 Billion	165,086,368	
Price/Book	2.79	% Held	
Price/Sales	1.75	93.41	

Business Summary: Diagnostic & Health Related Services (MIC: 4.2.2 SIC: 8071 NAIC: 621511)

Quest Diagnostics is a provider of diagnostic information services. Co. is comprised of two businesses: Diagnostic Information Services and Diagnostic Solutions. Co.'s Diagnostic Information Services business develops and delivers diagnostic testing information and services, providing insights that empower and enable a range of customers, including patients, clinicians, hospitals, IDNs, health plans, employers and accountable care organizations. Co.'s Diagnostic Solutions group includes its risk assessment services business, which provides solutions for insurers, and its healthcare information technology businesses, which provides solutions for healthcare providers.

Recent Developments: For the quarter ended Sep 30 2017, net income decreased 14.6% to US$175.0 million from US$205.0 million in the year-earlier quarter. Revenues were US$1.93 billion, up 2.4% from US$1.89 billion the year before. Operating income was US$298.0 million versus US$322.0 million in the prior-year quarter, a decrease of 7.5%. Direct operating expenses rose 2.9% to US$1.19 billion from US$1.16 billion in the comparable period the year before. Indirect operating expenses increased 9.1% to US$443.0 million from US$406.0 million in the equivalent prior-year period.

Prospects: Our evaluation of Quest Diagnostics Inc. as of Jan. 14, 2018 is the result of our systematic analysis on three basic characteristics: earnings strength, relative valuation, and recent stock price movement. The company has generated a negative trend in earnings per share over the past 5 quarters and while recent estimates for the company have been mixed, DGX has posted better than expected results. Based on operating earnings yield, the company is undervalued when compared to all of the companies in our coverage universe. Share price changes over the past year indicates that DGX will perform poorly over the near term.

Financial Data

(US$ in Thousands)	9 Mos	6 Mos	3 Mos	12/31/2016	12/31/2015	12/31/2014	12/31/2013	12/31/2012
Earnings Per Share	4.77	4.96	4.96	4.51	4.87	3.81	5.54	3.46
Cash Flow Per Share	8.44	7.99	8.19	7.61	5.63	6.47	4.29	7.47
Dividends Per Share	1.350	1.700	1.650	1.580	1.470	1.290	1.200	0.680
Dividend Payout %	28.30	34.27	33.27	35.03	30.18	33.86	21.66	19.65
Income Statement								
Total Revenue	5,773,000	3,842,000	1,899,000	7,515,000	7,493,000	7,435,000	7,146,000	7,382,562
EBITDA	1,105,000	740,000	361,000	1,301,000	1,337,000	1,081,000	1,562,000	1,488,506
Depn & Amortn	197,000	128,000	79,000	72,000	81,000	94,000	79,000	281,047
Income Before Taxes	796,000	538,000	246,000	1,086,000	1,103,000	823,000	1,324,000	1,042,770
Income Taxes	264,000	172,000	78,000	429,000	373,000	262,000	500,000	401,897
Net Income	518,000	357,000	164,000	645,000	709,000	556,000	849,000	555,721
Average Shares	140,000	140,000	141,000	142,000	145,000	145,000	153,000	160,065
Balance Sheet								
Current Assets	1,544,000	1,500,000	1,558,000	1,531,000	1,501,000	1,603,000	1,383,000	1,560,997
Total Assets	10,439,000	10,171,000	10,109,000	10,100,000	9,962,000	9,877,000	8,948,000	9,283,863
Current Liabilities	1,052,000	917,000	985,000	981,000	1,173,000	1,709,000	1,132,000	1,047,603
Long-Term Obligations	3,759,000	3,732,000	3,725,000	3,728,000	3,492,000	3,244,000	3,120,000	3,354,173
Total Liabilities	5,645,000	5,474,000	5,479,000	5,472,000	5,278,000	5,576,000	5,000,000	5,120,816
Stockholders' Equity	4,794,000	4,697,000	4,630,000	4,628,000	4,684,000	4,301,000	3,948,000	4,163,047
Shares Outstanding	136,000	136,000	137,000	137,000	143,000	144,000	144,000	158,331
Statistical Record								
Return on Assets %	6.53	6.94	6.99	6.41	7.15	5.91	9.31	5.96
Return on Equity %	14.23	15.25	15.24	13.82	15.78	13.48	20.93	14.11
EBITDA Margin %	19.14	19.26	19.01	17.31	17.84	14.54	21.86	20.16
Net Margin %	8.97	9.29	8.64	8.58	9.46	7.48	11.88	7.53
Asset Turnover	0.74	0.75	0.75	0.75	0.76	0.79	0.78	0.79
Current Ratio	1.47	1.64	1.58	1.56	1.28	0.94	1.22	1.49
Debt to Equity	0.78	0.79	0.80	0.81	0.75	0.75	0.79	0.81
Price Range	111.16-79.93	111.16-79.93	99.74-71.43	92.60-60.54	79.60-60.51	68.10-50.80	63.70-52.79	64.68-54.62
P/E Ratio	23.30-16.76	22.41-16.11	20.11-14.40	20.53-13.42	16.34-12.43	17.87-13.33	11.50-9.53	18.69-15.79
Average Yield %	1.37	1.48	1.93	2.01	2.08	2.18	2.23	1.15

Address: Three Giralda Farms, Madison, NJ 07940	**Web Site:** www.QuestDiagnostics.com
Telephone: 973-520-2700	**Officers:** Daniel C. Stanzione - Chairman Stephen H. Rusckowski - President, Chief Executive Officer

Auditors: PricewaterhouseCoopers LLP
Investor Contact: 973-520-2900
Transfer Agents: Computershare, Providence, RI

RALPH LAUREN CORP

Exchange	Symbol	Price	52Wk Range	Yield	P/E
NYS	RL	$103.69 (12/29/2017)	103.69-66.11	1.93	103.69

*7 Year Price Score 48.78 *NYSE Composite Index=100 *12 Month Price Score 107.21

TRADING VOLUME (thousand shares)

Interim Earnings (Per Share)

Qtr.	Jun	Sep	Dec	Mar
2014-15	1.80	2.25	2.41	1.42
2015-16	0.73	1.86	1.54	0.51
2016-17	(0.27)	0.55	0.98	(2.45)
2017-18	0.72	1.75	...	...

Interim Dividends (Per Share)

Amt	Decl	Ex	Rec	Pay
0.50Q	03/10/2017	03/29/2017	03/31/2017	04/13/2017
0.50Q	06/16/2017	06/28/2017	06/30/2017	07/14/2017
0.50Q	09/15/2017	09/28/2017	09/29/2017	10/13/2017
0.50Q	12/14/2017	12/28/2017	12/29/2017	01/12/2018

Indicated Div: $2.00

Valuation Analysis / **Institutional Holding**

Forecast EPS	$5.61	No of Institutions	579
(01/18/2018)			
Market Cap	$8.4 Billion	Shares	71,433,336
Book Value	$3.5 Billion	% Held	N/A
Price/Book	2.40		
Price/Sales	1.34		

Business Summary: Apparel, Footwear & Accessories (MIC: 1.4.2 SIC: 2329 NAIC: 315211)

Ralph Lauren designs, markets, and distributes lifestyle products, including apparel, accessories, home furnishings, and other licensed product categories. Co.'s brand names include Ralph Lauren, Ralph Lauren Collection, Ralph Lauren Purple Label, Polo Ralph Lauren, Double RL, Lauren Ralph Lauren, Polo Ralph Lauren Children, Chaps, and Club Monaco, among others. At Apr 1 2017, Co. sold directly to customers via its 466 retail stores, 619 concession-based shop-within-shops, and through its various e-commerce sites; and its international licensing partners operated 105 Ralph Lauren stores, 22 Ralph Lauren concession shops, and 136 Club Monaco stores and shops.

Recent Developments: For the quarter ended Sep 30 2017, net income increased 214.7% to US$143.8 million from US$45.7 million in the year-earlier quarter. Revenues were US$1.66 billion, down 8.6% from US$1.82 billion the year before. Operating income was US$193.3 million versus US$76.3 million in the prior-year quarter, an increase of 153.3%. Direct operating expenses declined 22.9% to US$668.4 million from US$866.4 million in the comparable period the year before. Indirect operating expenses decreased 8.6% to US$802.5 million from US$877.9 million in the equivalent prior-year period.

Prospects: Our evaluation of Ralph Lauren Corp. as of Jan. 14, 2018 is the result of our systematic analysis on three basic characteristics: earnings strength, relative valuation, and recent stock price movement. The company has enjoyed a very positive trend in earnings per share over the past 5 quarters. However, while recent estimates for the company have been mixed, RL has posted better than expected results. Based on operating earnings yield, the company is undervalued when compared to all of the companies in our coverage universe. Share price changes over the past year indicates that RL will perform poorly over the near term.

Financial Data

(US$ in Thousands)	6 Mos	3 Mos	04/01/2017	04/02/2016	03/28/2015	03/29/2014	03/30/2013	03/31/2012
Earnings Per Share	1.00	(0.20)	(1.20)	4.62	7.88	8.43	8.00	7.13
Cash Flow Per Share	14.17	12.79	11.55	11.63	10.16	10.03	11.19	9.58
Tang Book Value Per Share	29.14	27.33	26.85	31.15	31.53	31.24	27.38	24.70
Dividends Per Share	2.000	2.000	2.000	2.000	1.850	1.700	1.600	0.800
Dividend Payout %	200.00	...	...	43.29	23.48	20.17	20.00	11.22
Income Statement								
Total Revenue	3,011,300	1,347,100	6,652,800	7,405,000	7,620,000	7,450,000	6,944,800	6,859,500
EBITDA	432,100	96,400	(69,600)	602,000	1,034,000	1,157,000	1,142,000	1,066,800
Depn & Amortn	146,700	6,000	24,100	24,000	25,000	35,000	26,800	28,900
Income Before Taxes	280,100	87,700	(99,700)	563,000	998,000	1,105,000	1,098,800	1,024,400
Income Taxes	74,700	27,300	(5,600)	156,000	285,000	320,000	339,300	334,100
Net Income	203,300	59,500	(99,300)	396,000	702,000	776,000	750,000	681,000
Average Shares	82,300	82,500	82,700	85,900	89,100	92,000	93,700	95,500
Balance Sheet								
Current Assets	3,324,400	3,086,700	2,954,500	3,053,000	3,324,000	3,329,000	2,962,800	2,899,900
Total Assets	6,028,300	5,814,000	5,652,000	6,213,000	6,106,000	6,090,000	5,418,200	5,416,400
Current Liabilities	1,590,100	1,216,900	1,159,900	1,198,000	1,186,000	970,000	1,121,300	946,200
Long-Term Obligations	534,400	837,100	839,100	863,000	536,000	555,000	38,400	312,700
Total Liabilities	2,518,700	2,453,900	2,352,400	2,469,000	2,215,000	2,056,000	1,633,600	1,763,900
Stockholders' Equity	3,509,600	3,360,100	3,299,600	3,744,000	3,891,000	4,034,000	3,784,600	3,652,500
Shares Outstanding	81,300	81,300	81,000	82,900	86,300	88,700	90,900	92,700
Statistical Record								
Return on Assets %	1.34	N.M.	N.M.	6.33	11.54	13.52	13.88	13.14
Return on Equity %	2.28	N.M.	N.M.	10.21	17.76	19.90	20.22	19.63
EBITDA Margin %	14.35	7.16	N.M.	8.13	13.57	15.53	16.44	15.55
Net Margin %	6.75	4.42	N.M.	5.35	9.21	10.42	10.80	9.93
Asset Turnover	1.04	1.08	1.12	1.18	1.25	1.30	1.29	1.32
Current Ratio	2.09	2.54	2.55	2.55	2.80	3.43	2.64	3.06
Debt to Equity	0.15	0.25	0.25	0.23	0.14	0.14	0.01	0.09
Price Range	113.68-66.11	113.68-66.11	113.68-75.98	140.26-83.18	186.73-127.66	189.56-148.71	178.06-136.60	179.87-114.16
P/E Ratio	113.68-66.11	...	...	30.36-18.00	23.70-16.20	22.49-17.64	22.26-17.07	25.23-16.01
Average Yield %	2.34	2.22	2.12	1.70	1.15	1.04	1.01	0.56

Address: 650 Madison Avenue, New York, NY 10022	**Web Site:** www.RalphLauren.com **Officers:** Ralph Lauren - Executive Chairman, Chairman, Chief Executive Officer, Chief Creative Officer David R. Lauren - Vice-Chairman, Chief Innovation Officer, Executive Vice President	**Auditors:** Ernst & Young LLP **Transfer Agents:** The Bank of New York Mellon, Jersey City, NJ
Telephone: 212-318-7000		

RANGE RESOURCES CORP

Exchange	Symbol	Price	52Wk Range	Yield	P/E
NYS	RRC	$17.06 (12/29/2017)	35.71-15.63	0.47	N/A

*7 Year Price Score 33.84   *NYSE Composite Index=100   ***12 Month Price Score 70.73**

Interim Earnings (Per Share)

Qtr.	Mar	Jun	Sep	Dec
2014	0.20	1.04	0.86	1.69
2015	0.16	(0.71)	(1.81)	(1.93)
2016	(0.55)	(1.35)	(0.23)	(0.66)
2017	0.69	0.28	(0.52)	...

Interim Dividends (Per Share)

Amt	Decl	Ex	Rec	Pay
0.02Q	03/01/2017	03/13/2017	03/15/2017	03/31/2017
0.02Q	06/01/2017	06/13/2017	06/15/2017	06/30/2017
0.02Q	09/01/2017	09/14/2017	09/15/2017	09/29/2017
0.02Q	12/01/2017	12/14/2017	12/15/2017	12/29/2017

Indicated Div: $0.08

Valuation Analysis   **Institutional Holding**

Forecast EPS	$0.54	No of Institutions
	(01/18/2018)	668
Market Cap	$4.2 Billion	Shares
Book Value	$5.5 Billion	301,019,520
Price/Book	0.76	% Held
Price/Sales	1.94	97.94

Business Summary: Production & Extraction (MIC: 9.1.1 SIC: 1311 NAIC: 211111)

Range Resources is a natural gas, natural gas liquids and oil company, engaged in the exploration, development and acquisition of natural gas and oil properties. Co.'s properties in the Appalachian Region are located in the Appalachian Basin in the northeastern U.S., principally in Pennsylvania. Co.'s reserves are primarily in the Marcellus Shale formation, the Utica/Point Pleasant, Medina and Upper Devonian formations. Co.'s other operations include drilling, production and field operations in the Texas Panhandle, the Anadarko Basin of western Oklahoma, the Nemaha Uplift of Northern Oklahoma and Kansas. As of Dec 31 2016, Co. had total proved reserve of 12.1 trillion cubic feet equivalent.

Recent Developments: For the quarter ended Sep 30 2017, net loss amounted to US$127.7 million versus a net loss of US$42.0 million in the year-earlier quarter. Revenues were US$482.2 million, up 16.7% from US$413.2 million the year before. Direct operating expenses rose 41.3% to US$300.3 million from US$212.5 million in the comparable period the year before. Indirect operating expenses increased 48.8% to US$381.6 million from US$256.4 million in the equivalent prior-year period.

Prospects: Our evaluation of Range Resources Corp. as of Jan. 14, 2018 is the result of our systematic analysis on three basic characteristics: earnings strength, relative valuation, and recent stock price movement. The company has suffered a very negative trend in earnings per share over the past 5 quarters and while recent estimates for the company have been mixed, RRC has posted better than expected results. Based on operating earnings yield, the company is overvalued when compared to all of the companies in our coverage universe. Share price changes over the past year indicates that RRC will perform very poorly over the near term.

Financial Data

(US$ in Thousands)	9 Mos	6 Mos	3 Mos	12/31/2016	12/31/2015	12/31/2014	12/31/2013	12/31/2012
Earnings Per Share	(0.21)	0.08	(1.55)	(2.75)	(4.29)	3.79	0.70	0.08
Cash Flow Per Share	3.20	2.56	2.15	2.03	4.11	5.83	4.63	4.05
Tang Book Value Per Share	15.70	16.18	15.87	15.19	16.30	20.50	14.78	14.51
Dividends Per Share	0.080	0.080	0.080	0.080	0.160	0.160	0.160	0.160
Dividend Payout %	...	100.00	...	...	...	4.22	22.86	200.00
Income Statement								
Total Revenue	1,931,998	1,449,766	776,655	1,099,939	1,598,068	2,711,695	1,862,719	1,457,704
EBITDA	884,158	809,616	480,738	(625,525)	(874,023)	1,212,762	339,336	207,054
Depn & Amortn	529,937	304,882	151,131	8,400	11,900	12,900	13,200	13,200
Income Before Taxes	210,015	409,707	282,506	(802,138)	(1,052,362)	1,030,885	149,579	25,056
Income Taxes	98,054	170,046	112,395	(280,750)	(338,677)	396,503	33,857	12,054
Net Income	111,961	239,661	170,111	(521,388)	(713,685)	634,382	115,722	13,002
Average Shares	245,244	245,335	244,803	189,868	166,389	164,403	161,407	160,307
Balance Sheet								
Current Assets	337,250	360,614	297,537	281,883	439,074	570,292	248,301	327,614
Total Assets	11,637,739	11,621,336	11,421,745	11,282,245	6,900,031	8,746,780	7,299,086	6,728,735
Current Liabilities	671,366	596,992	631,080	702,653	351,720	755,264	495,561	455,143
Long-Term Obligations	3,981,962	3,848,589	3,738,795	3,773,517	2,651,303	3,073,000	3,140,516	2,878,185
Total Liabilities	6,100,259	5,959,445	5,839,269	5,873,877	4,140,373	5,289,351	4,884,634	4,371,343
Stockholders' Equity	5,537,480	5,661,891	5,582,476	5,408,368	2,759,658	3,457,429	2,414,452	2,357,392
Shares Outstanding	248,123	248,115	247,536	247,144	169,316	168,628	163,342	162,514
Statistical Record								
Return on Assets %	N.M.	0.39	N.M.	N.M.	N.M.	7.91	1.65	0.21
Return on Equity %	N.M.	0.86	N.M.	N.M.	N.M.	21.61	4.85	0.55
EBITDA Margin %	45.76	55.84	61.90	N.M.	N.M.	44.72	18.22	14.20
Net Margin %	5.80	16.53	21.90	N.M.	N.M.	23.39	6.21	0.89
Asset Turnover	0.19	0.24	0.17	0.12	0.20	0.34	0.27	0.23
Current Ratio	0.50	0.60	0.47	0.40	1.25	0.76	0.50	0.72
Debt to Equity	0.72	0.68	0.67	0.70	0.96	0.89	1.30	1.22
Price Range	39.41-16.58	44.75-21.22	46.45-26.80	46.45-20.45	64.75-21.17	93.70-52.28	84.31-62.05	73.28-54.02
P/E Ratio	...	559.38-265.25	...	...	...	24.72-13.79	120.44-88.64	916.00-675.25
Average Yield %	0.29	0.24	0.22	0.22	0.37	0.20	0.21	0.25

Address: 100 Throckmorton Street, Suite 1200, Fort Worth, TX 76102 **Telephone:** 817-870-2601	**Web Site:** www.rangeresources.com **Officers:** Jeffrey L. (Jeff) Ventura - Chairman, President, Chief Executive Officer, Chief Operating Officer Mark S. Scucchi - Vice President, Treasurer	**Auditors:** Ernst & Young LLP **Investor Contact:** 817-870-2601 **Transfer Agents:** Computershare Investor Services, LLC, Cleveland, OH

RAYMOND JAMES FINANCIAL, INC.

Exchange	Symbol	Price	52Wk Range	Yield	P/E
NYS	RJF	$89.30 (12/29/2017)	90.64-69.68	1.12	20.62

*7 Year Price Score 122.56 *NYSE Composite Index=100 *12 Month Price Score 103.04

Interim Earnings (Per Share)

Qtr.	Dec	Mar	Jun	Sep
2012-13	0.61	0.56	0.59	0.82
2013-14	0.81	0.72	0.85	0.94
2014-15	0.87	0.77	0.91	0.88
2015-16	0.73	0.87	0.87	1.18
2016-17	1.00	0.77	1.24	1.31

Interim Dividends (Per Share)

Amt	Decl	Ex	Rec	Pay
0.22Q	02/17/2017	03/30/2017	04/03/2017	04/17/2017
0.22Q	05/17/2017	06/29/2017	07/03/2017	07/17/2017
0.22Q	08/23/2017	09/29/2017	10/02/2017	10/16/2017
0.25Q	11/29/2017	01/02/2018	01/03/2018	01/17/2018

Indicated Div: $1.00

Valuation Analysis

		Institutional Holding	
Forecast EPS	$6.69	No of Institutions	
	(01/26/2018)	607	
Market Cap	$12.9 Billion	Shares	
Book Value	$5.6 Billion	126,943,720	
Price/Book	2.31	% Held	
Price/Sales	1.97	74.90	

Business Summary: Finance Intermediaries & Services (MIC: 5.5.1 SIC: 6211 NAIC: 523110)

Raymond James Financial is a financial holding company whose broker-dealer subsidiaries are engaged in various financial services businesses. The operating segments are: Private Client Group, which provides financial planning and securities transaction services to client accounts; Capital Markets, which conducts institutional sales, securities trading, equity research and investment banking, syndicate; Asset Management, which provides investment advisory and asset management services to individual and institutional investment portfolios, and sponsors mutual funds under the name Eagle; and Raymond James Bank, N.A. provides corporate loans, securities based loans and residential loans.

Recent Developments: For the year ended Sep 30 2017, net income increased 18.2% to US$638.9 million from US$540.7 million in the prior year. Revenues were US$6.52 billion, up 18.2% from US$5.52 billion the year before. Direct operating expenses rose 32.5% to US$153.8 million from US$116.1 million in the comparable period the year before. Indirect operating expenses increased 18.5% to US$5.44 billion from US$4.59 billion in the equivalent prior-year period.

Prospects: Our evaluation of Raymond James Financial Inc. as of Jan. 21, 2018 is the result of our systematic analysis on three basic characteristics: earnings strength, relative valuation, and recent stock price movement. The company has managed to produce a neutral trend in earnings per share over the past 5 quarters and while recent estimates for the company have been raised by analysts, RJF has posted better than expected results. Based on operating earnings yield, the company is undervalued when compared to all of the companies in our coverage universe. Share price changes over the past year indicates that RJF will perform in line with the market over the near term.

Financial Data
(US$ in Thousands)

	09/30/2017	09/30/2016	09/30/2015	09/30/2014	09/30/2013	09/30/2012	09/30/2011	09/30/2010
Earnings Per Share	4.33	3.65	3.43	3.32	2.58	2.20	2.19	1.83
Cash Flow Per Share	9.11	(3.65)	6.31	3.63	4.79	2.98	12.73	(8.56)
Tang Book Value Per Share	35.31	31.15	29.00	26.82	23.66	21.11	19.90	17.96
Dividends Per Share	0.880	0.800	0.720	0.640	0.560	0.520	0.520	0.440
Dividend Payout %	20.32	21.92	20.99	19.28	21.71	23.64	23.74	24.04
Income Statement								
Total Revenue	6,524,875	5,520,344	5,308,164	4,965,460	4,595,798	3,897,900	3,399,886	2,979,516
EBITDA	984,538	824,744	802,483	757,307	579,638	483,904	478,081	380,702
Depn & Amortn	56,560	47,373	25,771	41,359	(14,272)	15,983	27,336	24,558
Income Before Taxes	927,978	777,371	776,712	715,948	593,910	467,921	450,745	356,144
Income Taxes	289,111	271,293	296,034	267,797	197,033	175,656	182,894	133,625
Net Income	636,235	529,350	502,140	480,248	367,154	295,869	278,353	228,283
Average Shares	146,647	144,513	145,939	143,589	140,541	131,791	122,836	119,592
Balance Sheet								
Current Assets	12,249,371	11,515,382	9,427,793	8,496,359	10,560,162	8,694,956	8,961,474	9,243,879
Total Assets	34,883,456	31,593,733	26,479,684	23,325,652	23,186,122	21,160,265	18,006,995	17,883,081
Current Liabilities	26,737,453	24,142,242	19,930,688	17,157,683	17,930,339	16,069,177	14,383,200	12,408,785
Long-Term Obligations	2,452,652	2,301,575	1,762,898	1,734,713	1,257,446	1,410,806	711,950	2,877,428
Total Liabilities	29,301,743	26,679,637	21,957,653	19,184,416	19,523,198	17,891,325	15,419,376	15,580,265
Stockholders' Equity	5,581,713	4,914,096	4,522,031	4,141,236	3,662,924	3,268,940	2,587,619	2,302,816
Shares Outstanding	144,096	141,544	142,918	141,203	139,557	137,736	126,407	124,701
Statistical Record								
Return on Assets %	1.91	1.82	2.02	2.07	1.66	1.51	1.55	1.26
Return on Equity %	12.12	11.19	11.59	12.31	10.59	10.08	11.38	10.53
EBITDA Margin %	15.09	14.94	15.12	15.25	12.61	12.41	14.06	12.78
Net Margin %	9.75	9.59	9.46	9.67	7.99	7.59	8.19	7.66
Asset Turnover	0.20	0.19	0.21	0.21	0.21	0.20	0.19	0.17
Current Ratio	0.46	0.48	0.47	0.50	0.59	0.54	0.62	0.74
Debt to Equity	0.44	0.47	0.39	0.42	0.34	0.43	0.28	1.25
Price Range	85.37-57.41	59.32-40.43	61.29-48.56	56.07-40.04	48.12-36.54	38.59-24.11	39.46-24.42	31.12-22.11
P/E Ratio	19.72-13.26	16.25-11.08	17.87-14.16	16.89-12.06	18.65-14.16	17.54-10.96	18.02-11.15	17.01-12.08
Average Yield %	1.18	1.53	1.28	1.27	1.33	1.56	1.60	1.69

Address: 880 Carillon Parkway, St. Petersburg, FL 33716 Telephone: 727-567-1000	Web Site: www.raymondjames.com Officers: Paul C. Reilly - Chairman, Chief Executive Officer Francis S. Godbold - Vice-Chairman	Auditors: KPMG LLP Investor Contact: 727-567-5133 Transfer Agents: Computershare Inc., College Station, TX

RAYONIER INC.

Exchange	Symbol	Price	52Wk Range	Yield	P/E
NYS	RYN	$31.63 (12/29/2017)	31.78-27.03	3.16	29.84

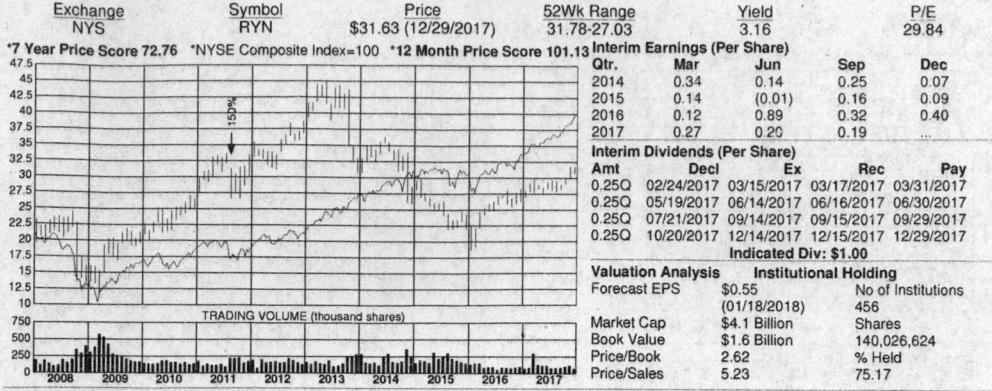

*7 Year Price Score 72.76   *NYSE Composite Index=100   *12 Month Price Score 101.13

Interim Earnings (Per Share)

Qtr.	Mar	Jun	Sep	Dec
2014	0.34	0.14	0.25	0.07
2015	0.14	(0.01)	0.16	0.09
2016	0.12	0.89	0.32	0.40
2017	0.27	0.20	0.19	...

Interim Dividends (Per Share)

Amt	Decl	Ex	Rec	Pay
0.25Q	02/24/2017	03/15/2017	03/17/2017	03/31/2017
0.25Q	05/19/2017	06/14/2017	06/16/2017	06/30/2017
0.25Q	07/21/2017	09/14/2017	09/15/2017	09/29/2017
0.25Q	10/20/2017	12/14/2017	12/15/2017	12/29/2017

Indicated Div: $1.00

Valuation Analysis / **Institutional Holding**

Forecast EPS	$0.55
	(01/18/2018)
Market Cap	$4.1 Billion
Book Value	$1.6 Billion
Price/Book	2.62
Price/Sales	5.23

No of Institutions	456
Shares	140,026,624
% Held	75.17

TRADING VOLUME (thousand shares)

Business Summary: REITs (MIC: 5.3.1 SIC: 6798 NAIC: 525930)

Rayonier is a timberland real estate investment trust. Co. has five business segments: The Southern Timber, Pacific Northwest Timber and New Zealand Timber, which reflect activities related to the harvesting of timber and other activities, such as recreational licenses; Real Estate, which reflects U.S. land sales comprised of: Improved Development, Unimproved Development, Rural, Non-Strategic/ Timberlands, and Large Dispositions; and Trading, which reflects the log trading activities that support Co.'s New Zealand operations. At Dec 31 2016, Co. owned, leased or managed approximately 2.7 million acres of timberlands located in the U.S. South, U.S. Pacific Northwest and New Zealand.

Recent Developments: For the quarter ended Sep 30 2017, net income decreased 29.1% to US$28.8 million from US$40.6 million in the year-earlier quarter. Revenues were US$177.9 million, up 3.8% from US$171.4 million the year before.

Prospects: Our evaluation of Rayonier Inc. as of Jan. 14, 2018 is the result of our systematic analysis on three basic characteristics: earnings strength, relative valuation, and recent stock price movement. The company has generated a negative trend in earnings per share over the past 5 quarters and while recent estimates for the company have been mixed, RYN has posted better than expected results. Based on operating earnings yield, the company is overvalued when compared to all of the companies in our coverage universe. Share price changes over the past year indicates that RYN will perform in line with the market over the near term.

Financial Data

(US$ in Thousands)	9 Mos	6 Mos	3 Mos	12/31/2016	12/31/2015	12/31/2014	12/31/2013	12/31/2012
Earnings Per Share	1.06	1.19	1.88	1.73	0.37	0.76	2.86	2.17
Cash Flow Per Share	1.76	1.98	1.67	1.66	1.41	2.50	4.34	3.62
Tang Book Value Per Share	12.09	12.19	12.12	11.49	10.49	11.74	13.16	11.66
Dividends Per Share	1.000	1.000	1.000	1.000	1.000	2.030	1.860	1.680
Dividend Payout %	94.34	84.03	53.19	57.80	270.27	267.11	65.03	77.42
Income Statement								
Total Revenue	559,178	381,232	186,512	788,278	544,874	603,521	1,707,822	1,571,000
EBITDA	135,775	96,387	49,377	372,970	195,499	264,622	636,770	585,435
Depn & Amortn	349	233	116	117,193	117,715	166,333	214,518	174,534
Income Before Taxes	111,476	79,630	41,364	222,834	43,082	44,842	380,864	366,526
Income Taxes	16,817	13,774	6,281	5,064	(859)	(9,601)	49,661	88,391
Net Income	84,691	60,003	33,843	211,972	46,165	99,337	371,896	278,685
Average Shares	128,965	129,088	123,922	122,812	125,900	131,038	130,105	128,702
Balance Sheet								
Current Assets	260,945	285,227	384,922	164,804	105,685	214,363	519,094	566,274
Total Assets	2,911,719	2,952,794	2,918,910	2,685,760	2,319,263	2,453,115	3,685,501	3,122,951
Current Liabilities	150,416	178,628	182,942	91,966	59,457	202,002	276,112	307,823
Long-Term Obligations	1,030,269	1,033,621	1,028,068	1,030,205	833,879	621,849	1,461,724	1,120,052
Total Liabilities	1,353,164	1,381,074	1,358,410	1,274,150	1,031,179	964,645	2,024,331	1,684,947
Stockholders' Equity	1,558,555	1,571,720	1,560,500	1,411,610	1,288,084	1,488,470	1,661,170	1,438,004
Shares Outstanding	128,916	128,897	128,760	122,904	122,770	126,773	126,257	123,332
Statistical Record								
Return on Assets %	4.76	5.29	8.81	8.45	1.93	3.24	10.92	9.76
Return on Equity %	9.11	10.16	16.43	15.66	3.33	6.31	24.00	20.13
EBITDA Margin %	24.28	25.28	26.47	47.31	35.88	43.85	37.29	37.27
Net Margin %	15.15	15.74	18.15	26.89	8.47	16.46	21.78	17.74
Asset Turnover	0.28	0.28	0.32	0.31	0.23	0.20	0.50	0.55
Current Ratio	1.73	1.60	2.10	1.79	1.78	1.06	1.88	1.84
Debt to Equity	0.66	0.66	0.66	0.73	0.65	0.42	0.88	0.78
Price Range	29.79-25.46	29.79-25.46	29.79-24.18	28.25-18.63	29.87-21.97	36.35-25.91	45.01-30.74	38.68-31.06
P/E Ratio	28.10-24.02	25.03-21.39	15.85-12.86	16.33-10.77	80.73-59.38	47.83-34.09	15.74-10.75	17.83-14.31
Average Yield %	3.57	3.63	3.74	3.98	3.97	6.20	4.60	4.83

Address: 1 Rayonier Way, Yulee, FL 32097
Telephone: 904-357-9100

Web Site: www.rayonier.com
Officers: Richard D. Kincaid - Chairman David L. Nunes - President, Chief Executive Officer, Chief Operating Officer

Auditors: Ernst & Young LLP
Investor Contact: 904-357-9177
Transfer Agents: Computershare, Providence, R.I.

RAYTHEON CO.

Exchange	Symbol	Price	52Wk Range	Yield	P/E	Div Achiever
NYS	RTN	$187.85 (12/29/2017)	191.38-142.90	1.70	25.25	12 Years

*7 Year Price Score 135.10 *NYSE Composite Index=100 *12 Month Price Score 105.13

TRADING VOLUME (thousand shares)

Interim Earnings (Per Share)

Qtr.	Mar	Jun	Sep	Dec
2014	1.89	1.76	1.65	1.88
2015	1.79	1.65	1.47	1.89
2016	1.43	2.38	1.79	1.84
2017	1.74	1.89	1.97	...

Interim Dividends (Per Share)

Amt	Decl	Ex	Rec	Pay
0.797Q	03/29/2017	04/10/2017	04/12/2017	05/11/2017
0.797Q	05/25/2017	06/30/2017	07/05/2017	08/03/2017
0.797Q	09/28/2017	10/11/2017	10/12/2017	11/09/2017
0.797Q	11/15/2017	01/02/2018	01/03/2018	02/01/2018

Indicated Div: $3.19 (Div. Reinv. Plan)

Valuation Analysis | **Institutional Holding**

Forecast EPS	$7.60	No of Institutions
	(01/17/2018)	1583
Market Cap	$54.3 Billion	Shares
Book Value	$10.9 Billion	277,640,736
Price/Book	5.00	% Held
Price/Sales	2.19	72.59

Business Summary: Defense (MIC: 7.1.2 SIC: 3812 NAIC: 334511)

Raytheon, together with its subsidiaries, is a technology company, engaged in defense and other government markets. Co. has five segments: Integrated Defense Systems, which is engages in integrated air and missile defense; large land- and sea-based radar solutions; command, control, communications, computers, cyber and intelligence solutions; Intelligence, Information and Services, which provides technical and services to intelligence, defense, federal and commercial customers; Missile Systems, which provides missile and combat systems; Space and Airborne Systems, which provides integrated sensor and communication systems for missions; and Forcepoint, which develops cybersecurity products.

Recent Developments: For the quarter ended Oct 1 2017, income from continuing operations increased 5.0% to US$568.0 million from US$541.0 million in the year-earlier quarter. Net income increased 4.6% to US$567.0 million from US$542.0 million in the year-earlier quarter. Revenues were US$6.28 billion, up 4.5% from US$6.01 billion the year before. Operating income was US$858.0 million versus US$830.0 million in the prior-year quarter, an increase of 3.4%. Direct operating expenses rose 4.8% to US$4.69 billion from US$4.47 billion in the comparable period the year before. Indirect operating expenses increased 3.7% to US$736.0 million from US$710.0 million in the equivalent prior-year period.

Prospects: Our evaluation of Raytheon Co. as of Jan. 14, 2018 is the result of our systematic analysis on three basic characteristics: earnings strength, relative valuation, and recent stock price movement. The company has produced a positive trend in earnings per share over the past 5 quarters and while recent estimates for the company have been mixed, RTN has posted better than expected results. Based on operating earnings yield, the company is about fairly valued when compared to all of the companies in our coverage universe. Share price changes over the past year indicates that RTN will perform well over the near term.

Financial Data

(US$ in Thousands)	9 Mos	6 Mos	3 Mos	12/31/2016	12/31/2015	12/31/2014	12/31/2013	12/31/2012
Earnings Per Share	7.44	7.26	7.75	7.44	6.80	7.18	6.16	5.65
Cash Flow Per Share	7.78	8.65	8.50	9.59	7.74	7.00	7.35	5.86
Dividends Per Share	3.060	3.060	2.930	3.600	2.615	1.815	2.200	2.000
Dividend Payout %	41.13	42.15	37.81	48.39	38.46	25.28	35.71	35.40
Income Statement								
Total Revenue	18,565,000	12,281,000	6,000,000	24,069,000	23,247,000	22,826,000	23,706,000	24,414,000
EBITDA	2,823,000	1,825,000	878,000	3,562,000	3,316,000	3,487,000	3,258,000	3,289,000
Depn & Amortn	401,000	263,000	130,000	316,000	307,000	301,000	303,000	318,000
Income Before Taxes	2,279,000	1,463,000	695,000	3,030,000	2,787,000	2,983,000	2,757,000	2,779,000
Income Taxes	667,000	419,000	198,000	857,000	733,000	790,000	808,000	878,000
Net Income	1,631,000	1,059,000	506,000	2,211,000	2,074,000	2,244,000	1,996,000	1,888,000
Average Shares	291,000	292,000	292,800	296,800	305,200	312,600	324,200	334,200
Balance Sheet								
Current Assets	10,778,000	10,937,000	10,515,000	10,678,000	9,812,000	10,292,000	9,816,000	9,246,000
Total Assets	30,278,000	30,229,000	29,869,000	30,052,000	29,281,000	27,900,000	25,967,000	26,686,000
Current Liabilities	6,492,000	6,587,000	6,307,000	6,427,000	6,126,000	5,930,000	5,810,000	5,902,000
Long-Term Obligations	4,749,000	4,747,000	5,086,000	5,335,000	5,330,000	5,330,000	4,734,000	4,731,000
Total Liabilities	19,421,000	19,414,000	19,485,000	19,986,000	19,153,000	18,375,000	14,932,000	18,660,000
Stockholders' Equity	10,857,000	10,815,000	10,384,000	10,066,000	10,128,000	9,525,000	11,035,000	8,026,000
Shares Outstanding	289,000	290,000	291,000	293,000	299,000	307,000	315,000	328,000
Statistical Record								
Return on Assets %	7.28	7.19	7.80	7.43	7.25	8.33	7.58	7.17
Return on Equity %	20.40	20.18	22.31	21.84	21.11	21.83	20.94	23.23
EBITDA Margin %	15.21	14.86	14.63	14.80	14.26	15.28	13.74	13.47
Net Margin %	8.79	8.62	8.43	9.19	8.92	9.83	8.42	7.73
Asset Turnover	0.83	0.83	0.83	0.81	0.81	0.85	0.90	0.93
Current Ratio	1.66	1.66	1.67	1.66	1.60	1.74	1.69	1.57
Debt to Equity	0.44	0.44	0.49	0.53	0.53	0.56	0.43	0.59
Price Range	186.58-132.97	164.26-132.97	156.97-124.22	150.54-117.62	127.95-95.57	110.47-88.13	91.04-52.67	59.28-47.99
P/E Ratio	25.08-17.87	22.63-18.32	20.25-16.03	20.23-15.81	18.82-14.05	15.39-12.27	14.78-8.55	10.49-8.49
Average Yield %	1.95	2.07	2.09	2.69	2.39	1.86	3.17	3.70

Address: 870 Winter Street, Waltham, MA 02451	**Web Site:** www.raytheon.com	**Auditors:** PricewaterhouseCoopers LLP
Telephone: 781-522-3000	**Officers:** Thomas Anthony Kennedy - Chairman, Chief Executive Officer, Executive Vice President, Chief Operating Officer, Vice President, Division Officer David C. Wajsgras - Senior Vice President, Vice President, Chief Financial Officer, Division Officer	**Investor Contact:** 877-786-7070 **Transfer Agents:** American Stock Transfer & Trust Co. Brooklyn, NY

REALOGY HOLDINGS CORP

Exchange	Symbol	Price	52Wk Range	Yield	P/E
NYS	RLGY	$26.50 (12/29/2017)	34.98-25.41	1.36	15.87

*7 Year Price Score N/A   *NYSE Composite Index=100   *12 Month Price Score 87.51

Interim Earnings (Per Share)

Qtr.	Mar	Jun	Sep	Dec
2014	(0.32)	0.46	0.68	0.14
2015	(0.22)	0.66	0.75	0.06
2016	(0.29)	0.63	0.73	0.40
2017	(0.20)	0.78	0.69	...

Interim Dividends (Per Share)

Amt	Decl	Ex	Rec	Pay
0.09Q	02/23/2017	03/07/2017	03/09/2017	03/23/2017
0.09Q	05/04/2017	05/15/2017	05/17/2017	05/31/2017
0.09Q	08/02/2017	08/14/2017	08/16/2017	08/30/2017
0.09Q	11/02/2017	11/15/2017	11/16/2017	11/30/2017

Indicated Div: $0.36

Valuation Analysis

		Institutional Holding	
Forecast EPS	$1.54	No of Institutions	
	(01/13/2018)	343	
Market Cap	$3.6 Billion	Shares	
Book Value	$2.5 Billion	156,221,632	
Price/Book	1.46	% Held	
Price/Sales	0.59	77.76	

Business Summary: Property, Real Estate & Development (MIC: 5.3.2 SIC: 6531 NAIC: 531210)

Realogy Holdings is a holding company. Through its subsidiaries, Co. is a provider of residential real estate services. Co. has four segments: real estate franchise services, which include brokerage brands such as Century 21®, Coldwell Banker®, Coldwell Banker Commercial®, and ERA®; Co.-owned real estate brokerage services, which operates real estate brokerage business under the Coldwell Banker®, Corcoran Group®, Sotheby's International Realty®, ZipRealty® and Citi Habitatssm brand names; relocation services, which is a provider of outsourced employee relocation services; and title and settlement services, which provides title and settlement (i.e., closing and escrow) services to customers.

Recent Developments: For the quarter ended Sep 30 2017, net income decreased 10.3% to US$96.0 million from US$107.0 million in the year-earlier quarter. Revenues were US$1.67 billion, up 1.8% from US$1.64 billion the year before.

Prospects: Our evaluation of Realogy Holdings Corp as of Jan. 14, 2018 is the result of our systematic analysis on three basic characteristics: earnings strength, relative valuation, and recent stock price movement. The company has generated a negative trend in earnings per share over the past 5 quarters and while recent estimates for the company have been mixed, RLGY has posted results that fell short of analysts expectations. Based on operating earnings yield, the company is undervalued when compared to all of the companies in our coverage universe. Share price changes over the past year indicates that RLGY will perform well over the near term.

Financial Data
(US$ in Millions)

	9 Mos	6 Mos	3 Mos	12/31/2016	12/31/2015	12/31/2014	12/31/2013	12/31/2012
Earnings Per Share	1.67	1.71	1.56	1.46	1.24	0.97	2.99	(14.41)
Cash Flow Per Share	4.56	4.91	4.60	4.05	3.71	2.90	3.38	(2.72)
Dividends Per Share	0.360	0.360	0.270	0.180	...	...	...	...
Dividend Payout %	21.56	21.05	17.31	12.33	...	...	...	...
Income Statement								
Total Revenue	4,670	2,996	1,203	5,810	5,706	5,328	5,289	4,672
EBITDA	441	243	9	612	59	566	523	30
Depn & Amortn	12	8	4	89	84	74	67	65
Income Before Taxes	302	149	(34)	349	282	225	175	(563)
Income Taxes	131	64	(9)	144	110	87	(242)	39
Net Income	176	81	(28)	213	184	143	438	(543)
Average Shares	138	138	139	145	148	147	146	37
Balance Sheet								
Current Assets	942	861	733	818	961	1,026	917	978
Total Assets	7,521	7,426	7,330	7,421	7,531	7,538	7,326	7,445
Current Liabilities	1,088	1,070	1,081	1,050	1,605	878	911	1,015
Long-Term Obligations	3,234	3,246	3,256	3,265	2,962	3,891	3,886	4,256
Total Liabilities	5,060	5,006	4,959	4,957	5,113	5,359	5,316	5,929
Stockholders' Equity	2,461	2,420	2,371	2,464	2,418	2,179	2,010	1,516
Shares Outstanding	135	136	138	140	146	146	146	145
Statistical Record								
Return on Assets %	3.11	3.24	3.08	2.84	2.44	1.92	5.93	N.M.
Return on Equity %	9.46	10.08	9.62	8.70	8.01	6.83	24.84	N.M.
EBITDA Margin %	9.44	8.11	0.75	10.53	10.46	10.62	9.89	0.64
Net Margin %	3.77	2.70	N.M.	3.67	3.22	2.68	8.28	N.M.
Asset Turnover	0.81	0.80	0.80	0.78	0.76	0.72	0.72	0.61
Current Ratio	0.87	0.80	0.68	0.78	0.60	1.17	1.01	0.96
Debt to Equity	1.31	1.34	1.37	1.33	1.22	1.79	1.93	2.81
Price Range	34.98-22.20	32.45-22.20	36.96-22.20	36.96-22.20	49.53-36.48	49.98-33.86	54.85-40.67	42.03-33.50
P/E Ratio	20.95-13.29	18.98-12.98	23.69-14.23	25.32-15.21	39.94-29.42	51.53-34.91	18.34-13.60	...
Average Yield %	1.24	1.31	0.96	0.61	...	...	...	...

Address: 175 Park Avenue, Madison, NJ 07940	Web Site: www.realogy.com	Auditors: PricewaterhouseCoopers LLP
Telephone: 973-407-2000	Officers: Richard A. Smith - Chairman, President, Chief Executive Officer Ryan M. Schneider - President, Chief Operating Officer, Incoming Chief Executive Officer	Investor Contact: 973-407-4669 Transfer Agents: Computershare Trust Company, N.A.

REALTY INCOME CORP

Exchange	Symbol	Price	52Wk Range	Yield	P/E	Div Acheiver
NYS	O	$57.02 (12/29/2017)	63.19-53.21	4.61	46.74	22 Years

*7 Year Price Score 95.89 *NSYE Composite Index=100 *12 Month Price Score 91.64

Interim Earnings (Per Share)

Qtr.	Mar	Jun	Sep	Dec
2014	0.23	0.23	0.26	0.32
2015	0.27	0.25	0.26	0.31
2016	0.25	0.27	0.27	0.33
2017	0.27	0.30	0.32	...

Interim Dividends (Per Share)

Amt	Decl	Ex	Rec	Pay
0.212M	10/10/2017	10/31/2017	11/01/2017	11/15/2017
0.212M	11/10/2017	11/30/2017	12/01/2017	12/15/2017
0.212M	12/12/2017	12/29/2017	01/02/2018	01/12/2018
0.219M	01/16/2018	01/31/2018	02/01/2018	02/15/2018

Indicated Div: $2.63

Valuation Analysis   Institutional Holding

Forecast EPS	$1.20 (01/26/2018)	No of Institutions	799
Market Cap	$16.1 Billion	Shares	241,374,496
Book Value	$7.4 Billion	% Held	68.25
Price/Book	2.18		
Price/Sales	13.47		

Business Summary: REITs (MIC: 5.3.1 SIC: 6798 NAIC: 525930)

Realty Income is a real estate investment trust that invests in commercial real estate. Co. focuses on in-house acquisition, portfolio management, asset management, real estate research, credit research, legal, finance and accounting, information technology, and capital markets. As of Dec 31, 2016, Co, owned a portfolio of 4,944 properties, located in 49 states and Puerto Rico, with over 83.0 million sq. ft. of leasable space; and with an average leasable space per property of approximately 16,800 sq. ft.; approximately 11,520 sq. ft. per retail property and 220,290 sq. ft. per industrial property.

Recent Developments: For the quarter ended Sep 30 2017, net income increased 14.1% to US$88.1 million from US$77.2 million in the year-earlier quarter. Revenues were US$306.9 million, up 10.7% from US$277.2 million the year before. Revenues from property income rose 10.3% to US$305.4 million from US$276.9 million in the corresponding quarter a year earlier.

Prospects: Our evaluation of Realty Income Corp. as of Jan. 21, 2018 is the result of our systematic analysis on three basic characteristics: earnings strength, relative valuation, and recent stock price movement. The company has enjoyed a very positive trend in earnings per share over the past 5 quarters. Because the company lacks sufficient analyst estimate data, we place greater weight on the historical EPS trend as the measure of earnings strength. Based on operating earnings yield, the company is overvalued when compared to all of the companies in our coverage universe. Share price changes over the past year indicates that O will perform well over the near term.

Financial Data

(US$ in Thousands)	9 Mos	6 Mos	3 Mos	12/31/2016	12/31/2015	12/31/2014	12/31/2013	12/31/2012
Earnings Per Share	1.22	1.17	1.14	1.13	1.09	1.04	1.06	0.86
Cash Flow Per Share	3.14	3.31	3.35	3.14	2.94	2.87	2.71	2.45
Tang Book Value Per Share	21.91	21.19	21.65	21.79	21.89	20.27	21.37	17.95
Dividends Per Share	2.507	2.475	2.439	2.403	2.279	2.193	2.178	1.778
Dividend Payout %	205.49	211.54	213.95	212.65	209.08	210.85	205.46	206.73
Income Statement								
Total Revenue	905,115	598,195	298,025	1,103,172	1,023,285	933,505	778,375	475,510
EBITDA	276,867	182,441	94,595	787,179	709,192	654,665	509,159	306,334
Depn & Amortn	15,880	10,659	4,513	467,440	421,168	382,064	327,245	158,933
Income Before Taxes	260,987	171,782	90,082	319,739	288,024	272,601	181,914	147,401
Income Taxes	2,621	1,488	1,047	3,262	3,169	3,461	2,734	1,430
Net Income	257,946	170,006	88,870	315,571	283,766	270,635	245,564	159,152
Average Shares	276,050	273,099	263,934	255,624	236,208	218,767	191,781	132,884
Balance Sheet								
Current Assets	130,187	132,484	148,267	114,004	121,972	68,238	49,580	26,907
Total Assets	13,701,419	13,574,116	13,422,186	13,152,871	11,865,870	11,012,622	9,924,441	5,443,363
Current Liabilities	153,051	173,879	144,523	262,007	220,135	213,357	181,243	120,230
Long-Term Obligations	5,792,276	5,993,219	5,428,720	5,839,605	4,841,486	4,930,947	4,166,840	2,883,868
Total Liabilities	6,346,990	6,572,710	6,387,243	6,386,067	5,334,274	5,399,221	4,538,994	3,030,569
Stockholders' Equity	7,354,429	7,001,406	7,034,943	6,766,804	6,531,596	5,613,401	5,385,447	2,412,794
Shares Outstanding	281,778	274,064	273,051	260,168	250,416	224,881	207,485	133,452
Statistical Record								
Return on Assets %	2.67	2.63	2.63	2.52	2.48	2.59	3.20	3.22
Return on Equity %	4.97	4.92	4.95	4.73	4.67	4.92	6.30	6.80
EBITDA Margin %	30.59	30.50	31.74	71.36	69.31	70.13	65.41	64.42
Net Margin %	28.50	28.42	29.82	28.61	27.73	28.99	31.55	33.47
Asset Turnover	0.09	0.09	0.09	0.09	0.09	0.09	0.10	0.10
Current Ratio	0.85	0.76	1.03	0.44	0.55	0.32	0.27	0.22
Debt to Equity	0.79	0.86	0.77	0.86	0.74	0.88	0.77	1.20
Price Range	66.93-53.21	72.14-53.21	72.14-53.49	72.14-51.17	55.14-43.38	49.57-37.33	55.09-36.68	42.96-34.52
P/E Ratio	54.86-43.61	61.66-45.48	63.28-46.92	63.84-45.28	50.59-39.80	47.66-35.89	51.97-34.60	49.95-40.14
Average Yield %	4.32	4.07	3.92	3.90	4.68	5.05	5.03	4.51

Address: 11995 El Camino Real, San Diego, CA 92130 **Telephone:** 858-284-5000	**Web Site:** www.realtyincome.com **Officers:** Sumit Roy - President, Chief Operating Officer, Chief Investment Officer, Executive Vice President John P. Case - President, Co-President, Chief Executive Officer, Executive Vice President, Chief Investment Officer	**Auditors:** KPMG LLP **Investor Contact:** 760-741-2111 **Transfer Agents:** Wells Fargo Shareowner Services, St. Paul, MN

RED HAT INC

Exchange	Symbol	Price	52Wk Range	Yield	P/E
NYS	RHT	$120.10 (12/29/2017)	129.44-70.12	N/A	65.27

*7 Year Price Score 119.31 **NYSE Composite Index=100 *12 Month Price Score 119.79

TRADING VOLUME (thousand shares)

Interim Earnings (Per Share)

Qtr.	May	Aug	Nov	Feb
2014-15	0.20	0.25	0.26	0.25
2015-16	0.26	0.28	0.25	0.29
2016-17	0.33	0.32	0.37	0.37
2017-18	0.40	0.53	0.54	...

Interim Dividends (Per Share)

No Dividends Paid

Valuation Analysis

		Institutional Holding	
Forecast EPS	$2.88	No of Institutions	
	(01/18/2018)	773	
Market Cap	$21.3 Billion	Shares	
Book Value	$1.4 Billion	198,771,040	
Price/Book	14.83	% Held	
Price/Sales	7.66	91.08	

Business Summary: Internet & Software (MIC: 6.3.2 SIC: 7372 NAIC: 511210)

Red Hat is a provider of open source software solutions, using a community-powered approach to develop and provide operating system, virtualization, management, middleware, cloud, mobile and storage technologies. Co.'s software offerings include: Red Hat Enterprise Linux, an operating system built with open source software components; and Red Hat JBoss Middleware, a suite of offerings used to develop, deploy and manage applications, integrate applications, data and devices, and automate business processes across hybrid cloud environments. Co.'s offerings also include other technologies, such as a realtime operating system, distributed computing, directory services and user authentication.

Recent Developments: For the quarter ended Nov 30 2017, net income increased 49.1% to US$101.3 million from US$67.9 million in the year-earlier quarter. Revenues were US$748.0 million, up 21.6% from US$615.3 million the year before. Operating income was US$118.4 million versus US$80.8 million in the prior-year quarter, an increase of 46.6%. Direct operating expenses rose 23.6% to US$111.8 million from US$90.5 million in the comparable period the year before. Indirect operating expenses increased 16.6% to US$517.8 million from US$444.0 million in the equivalent prior-year period.

Prospects: Our evaluation of Red Hat Inc. as of Jan. 14, 2018 is the result of our systematic analysis on three basic characteristics: earnings strength, relative valuation, and recent stock price movement. The company has produced a positive trend in earnings per share over the past 5 quarters and while recent estimates for the company have been raised by analysts, RHT has posted better than expected results. Based on operating earnings yield, the company is overvalued when compared to all of the companies in our coverage universe. Share price changes over the past year indicates that RHT will perform very well over the near term.

Financial Data

(US$ in Thousands)	9 Mos	6 Mos	3 Mos	02/28/2017	02/29/2016	02/28/2015	02/28/2014	02/28/2013
Earnings Per Share	1.84	1.67	1.46	1.39	1.07	0.95	0.93	0.77
Cash Flow Per Share	4.97	4.83	4.57	4.36	3.91	3.34	2.85	2.41
Tang Book Value Per Share	0.91	0.69	0.70	0.39	0.89	1.24	3.85	3.56
Income Statement								
Total Revenue	2,148,129	1,400,151	676,796	2,411,803	2,052,230	1,789,489	1,534,615	1,328,817
EBITDA	361,275	236,306	94,998	384,158	335,222	304,557	278,072	240,325
Depn & Amortn	23,728	15,985	7,976	54,077	48,909	48,001	45,169	38,818
Income Before Taxes	332,670	216,760	84,930	320,180	274,865	255,498	239,548	209,752
Income Taxes	61,315	46,711	11,740	66,477	75,500	75,297	61,256	59,548
Net Income	271,355	170,049	73,190	253,703	199,365	180,201	178,292	150,204
Average Shares	186,160	183,021	181,810	182,961	186,119	189,246	192,036	195,804
Balance Sheet								
Current Assets	2,504,710	2,332,363	2,301,649	2,315,702	1,872,433	1,970,239	1,571,182	1,368,749
Total Assets	4,759,484	4,639,384	4,512,436	4,535,185	4,155,099	3,802,985	3,106,619	2,813,660
Current Liabilities	1,825,046	1,795,826	1,791,380	1,891,073	1,559,177	1,334,692	1,148,086	985,712
Long-Term Obligations	762,367	756,743	751,173	745,633	723,942	715,402	...	...
Total Liabilities	3,326,344	3,239,037	3,206,892	3,287,865	2,820,667	2,514,647	1,555,454	1,293,499
Stockholders' Equity	1,433,140	1,400,347	1,305,544	1,247,320	1,334,432	1,288,338	1,551,165	1,520,161
Shares Outstanding	177,002	176,943	177,520	176,901	181,185	183,551	189,712	193,021
Statistical Record								
Return on Assets %	7.62	6.95	6.16	5.84	5.00	5.22	6.02	5.66
Return on Equity %	24.93	22.35	20.02	19.65	15.16	12.69	11.61	10.29
EBITDA Margin %	16.82	16.88	14.04	15.93	16.33	17.02	18.12	18.09
Net Margin %	12.63	12.15	10.81	10.52	9.71	10.07	11.62	11.30
Asset Turnover	0.63	0.61	0.58	0.56	0.51	0.52	0.52	0.50
Current Ratio	1.37	1.30	1.28	1.22	1.20	1.48	1.37	1.39
Debt to Equity	0.53	0.54	0.58	0.60	0.54	0.56	...	...
Price Range	129.24-68.71	107.50-68.71	89.66-68.71	84.86-65.35	83.65-60.93	71.09-48.19	59.93-42.35	61.95-47.41
P/E Ratio	70.24-37.34	64.37-41.14	61.41-47.06	61.05-47.01	78.18-56.94	74.83-50.73	64.44-45.54	80.45-61.57

Address: 100 East Davie Street, Raleigh, NC 27601
Telephone: 919-754-3700

Web Site: www.redhat.com
Officers: Narendra Kumar Gupta - Chairman James M. Whitehurst - President, Chief Executive Officer

Auditors: PricewaterhouseCoopers LLP
Investor Contact: 919-754-3700
Transfer Agents: Computershare, Providence, RI

REGAL BELOIT CORP

Exchange	Symbol	Price	52Wk Range	Yield	P/E	Div Acheiver
NYS	RBC	$76.60 (12/29/2017)	86.75-69.45	1.36	16.65	12 Years

*7 Year Price Score 88.64 *NYSE Composite Index=100 *12 Month Price Score 93.56

Interim Earnings (Per Share)

Qtr.	Mar	Jun	Sep	Dec
2014	0.96	1.24	1.05	(2.56)
2015	0.81	1.39	1.41	(0.43)
2016	0.93	1.26	1.32	1.01
2017	1.02	1.18	1.39	...

Interim Dividends (Per Share)

Amt	Decl	Ex	Rec	Pay
0.26Q	04/30/2017	06/28/2017	06/30/2017	07/14/2017
0.26Q	07/26/2017	09/28/2017	09/29/2017	10/13/2017
0.26Q	10/27/2017	12/28/2017	12/29/2017	01/12/2018
0.26Q	01/20/2018	03/28/2018	03/29/2018	04/13/2018

Indicated Div: $1.04

Valuation Analysis

		Institutional Holding	
Forecast EPS	$4.86	No of Institutions	373
	(01/20/2018)		
Market Cap	$3.4 Billion	Shares	51,313,040
Book Value	$2.3 Billion	% Held	92.32
Price/Book	1.50		
Price/Sales	1.03		

Business Summary: Electrical Equipment (MIC: 7.3.1 SIC: 3621 NAIC: 335312)

Regal Beloit is a manufacturer of electric motors, electrical motion controls, power generation and power transmission products. Co.'s segments are: Commercial and Industrial Systems, which designs, manufactures and sells primarily fractional, integral and large horsepower AC and DC motors and controls for commercial and industrial applications; Climate Solutions, which designs, manufactures and sells primarily fractional motors, electronic variable speed controls and blowers used in a variety of residential and light commercial air moving applications; and Power Transmission Solutions, which designs, manufactures and sells primarily mounted and unmounted bearings.

Recent Developments: For the quarter ended Sep 30 2017, net income increased 4.1% to US$63.6 million from US$61.1 million in the year-earlier quarter. Revenues were US$856.9 million, up 5.8% from US$809.6 million the year before. Operating income was US$94.0 million versus US$89.8 million in the prior-year quarter, an increase of 4.7%. Direct operating expenses rose 9.0% to US$629.9 million from US$577.9 million in the comparable period the year before. Indirect operating expenses decreased 6.3% to US$133.0 million from US$141.9 million in the equivalent prior-year period.

Prospects: Our evaluation of Regal Beloit Corp. as of Jan. 21, 2018 is the result of our systematic analysis on three basic characteristics: earnings strength, relative valuation, and recent stock price movement. The company has managed to produce a neutral trend in earnings per share over the past 5 quarters. However, while recent estimates for the company have been mixed, RBC has posted better than expected results. Based on operating earnings yield, the company is undervalued when compared to all of the companies in our coverage universe. Share price changes over the past year indicates that RBC will perform in line with the market over the near term.

Financial Data

(US$ in Thousands)	9 Mos	6 Mos	3 Mos	12/31/2016	01/02/2016	01/03/2015	12/28/2013	12/29/2012
Earnings Per Share	4.60	4.53	4.61	4.52	3.18	0.69	2.64	4.64
Cash Flow Per Share	7.80	9.27	9.64	9.86	8.55	6.52	6.80	8.44
Tang Book Value Per Share	2.52	1.00	N.M.	N.M.	N.M.	16.29	16.19	11.34
Dividends Per Share	1.000	0.980	0.960	0.950	0.910	0.860	0.790	0.750
Dividend Payout %	21.74	21.63	20.82	21.02	28.62	124.64	29.92	16.16
Income Statement								
Total Revenue	2,539,600	1,682,700	813,500	3,224,500	3,509,700	3,257,100	3,095,700	3,166,900
EBITDA	354,900	226,600	109,200	414,000	348,300	213,500	292,400	394,800
Depn & Amortn	103,100	68,800	34,400	93,400	95,500	92,000	84,400	82,000
Income Before Taxes	211,900	130,700	61,400	266,400	196,900	90,300	170,500	269,900
Income Taxes	46,400	28,800	13,800	57,100	48,400	54,200	44,500	69,600
Net Income	161,500	99,300	46,300	203,400	143,300	31,000	120,000	195,600
Average Shares	44,800	45,100	45,100	45,000	45,100	45,300	45,400	42,100
Balance Sheet								
Current Assets	1,630,200	1,643,100	1,615,400	1,532,000	1,635,200	1,652,000	1,725,900	1,539,900
Total Assets	4,464,000	4,483,000	4,444,400	4,358,500	4,591,700	3,407,600	3,643,500	3,569,100
Current Liabilities	734,900	732,800	714,000	701,600	612,800	561,300	700,900	533,900
Long-Term Obligations	1,113,800	1,199,500	1,269,100	1,310,900	1,715,600	625,400	609,000	754,700
Total Liabilities	2,194,900	2,277,200	2,311,800	2,319,700	2,654,400	1,473,200	1,587,300	1,615,700
Stockholders' Equity	2,269,100	2,205,800	2,132,600	2,038,800	1,937,300	1,934,400	2,056,200	1,953,400
Shares Outstanding	44,300	44,600	44,800	44,800	44,700	44,700	45,100	44,900
Statistical Record								
Return on Assets %	4.63	4.53	4.60	4.56	3.59	0.87	3.34	5.74
Return on Equity %	9.56	9.70	10.07	10.26	7.42	1.53	6.00	11.24
EBITDA Margin %	13.97	13.47	13.42	12.84	9.92	6.55	9.45	12.47
Net Margin %	6.36	5.90	5.69	6.31	4.08	0.95	3.88	6.18
Asset Turnover	0.74	0.72	0.71	0.72	0.88	0.91	0.86	0.93
Current Ratio	2.22	2.24	2.26	2.18	2.67	2.94	2.46	2.88
Debt to Equity	0.49	0.54	0.60	0.64	0.89	0.32	0.30	0.39
Price Range	86.75-56.90	83.10-54.51	76.25-51.81	75.10-49.38	80.95-55.46	80.02-63.13	84.67-62.35	75.00-50.97
P/E Ratio	18.86-12.37	18.34-12.03	16.54-11.24	16.62-10.92	25.46-17.44	115.97-91.49	32.07-23.62	16.16-10.98
Average Yield %	1.34	1.41	1.48	1.57	1.30	1.11		1.15

Address: 200 State Street, Beloit, WI 53511	Web Site: www.regal-beloit.com	Auditors: Deloitte & Touche LLP
	Officers: Mark J. Gliebe - Chairman, Chief Executive	Investor Contact: 608-364-8800
Telephone: 608-364-8800	Officer Jonathan J. Schlemmer - Chief Operating Officer	Transfer Agents: ComputerShare Investor Services, Providence, RI

REGAL ENTERTAINMENT GROUP

Exchange	Symbol	Price	52Wk Range	Yield	P/E
NYS	RGC	$23.01 (12/29/2017)	23.08-13.98	3.82	26.15

*7 Year Price Score 85.95   *NYSE Composite Index=100   *12 Month Price Score 93.60

Interim Earnings (Per Share)

Qtr.	Mar	Jun	Sep	Dec
2014	(0.01)	0.22	0.17	0.30
2015	0.15	0.34	0.14	0.35
2016	0.26	0.21	0.27	0.35
2017	0.31	0.15	0.07	...

Interim Dividends (Per Share)

Amt	Decl	Ex	Rec	Pay
0.22Q	02/09/2017	03/01/2017	03/03/2017	03/15/2017
0.22Q	04/26/2017	06/01/2017	06/05/2017	06/15/2017
0.22Q	07/26/2017	08/31/2017	09/05/2017	09/15/2017
0.22Q	10/24/2017	12/01/2017	12/04/2017	12/15/2017

Indicated Div: $0.88

Valuation Analysis

		Institutional Holding	
Forecast EPS	$0.89	No of Institutions	
	(01/18/2018)	408	
Market Cap	$3.6 Billion	Shares	
Book Value	N/A	146,831,232	
Price/Book	N/A	% Held	
Price/Sales	1.16	55.65	

TRADING VOLUME (thousand shares)

Business Summary: Entertainment (MIC: 2.3.2 SIC: 7832 NAIC: 512131)

Regal Entertainment is a holding company. Through its subsidiaries, Co. operates theatre circuits consisting of 7,267 screens in 561 theatres in 42 states along with Guam, Saipan, American Samoa and the District of Columbia as of Dec 31 2016. Co. operates its theatre circuit using its Regal Cinemas, United Artists, Edwards, Great Escape Theatres and Hollywood Theaters brands. Co. develops, acquires and operates multi-screen theatres primarily in mid-sized metropolitan markets and suburban growth areas of larger metropolitan markets throughout the U.S. Some of Co.'s theatres provide amenities such as wall-to-wall and floor-to-ceiling screens and Sony Digital Cinemaâ‚¬â€ž¢ 4K projection systems.

Recent Developments: For the quarter ended Sep 30 2017, net income decreased 73.0% to US$11.4 million from US$42.3 million in the year-earlier quarter. Revenues were US$716.0 million, down 11.8% from US$811.5 million the year before. Operating income was US$22.5 million versus US$87.2 million in the prior-year quarter, a decrease of 74.2%. Direct operating expenses declined 13.7% to US$264.9 million from US$306.9 million in the comparable period the year before. Indirect operating expenses increased 2.7% to US$428.6 million from US$417.4 million in the equivalent prior-year period.

Prospects: Our evaluation of Regal Entertainment Group as of Jan. 14, 2018 is the result of our systematic analysis on three basic characteristics: earnings strength, relative valuation, and recent stock price movement. The company has generated a negative trend in earnings per share over the past 5 quarters. However, while recent estimates for the company have been lowered by analysts, RGC has posted better than expected results. Based on operating earnings yield, the company is about fairly valued when compared to all of the companies in our coverage universe. Share price changes over the past year indicates that RGC will perform very poorly over the near term.

Financial Data

(US$ in Thousands)	9 Mos	6 Mos	3 Mos	12/31/2016	12/31/2015	01/01/2015	12/26/2013	12/27/2012
Earnings Per Share	0.88	1.08	1.14	1.09	0.98	0.68	1.01	0.93
Cash Flow Per Share	2.67	2.43	3.07	2.62	2.80	2.21	2.25	2.25
Dividends Per Share	0.880	0.880	0.880	0.880	0.880	1.880	0.840	1.840
Dividend Payout %	100.00	81.48	77.19	80.73	89.80	276.47	83.17	197.85
Income Statement								
Total Revenue	2,301,400	1,585,400	821,200	3,197,100	3,127,300	2,990,100	3,038,100	2,824,200
EBITDA	428,200	308,700	171,900	616,000	573,700	485,000	572,900	522,300
Depn & Amortn	190,000	126,200	62,100	235,600	221,800	212,000	204,500	186,200
Income Before Taxes	144,700	120,700	79,100	252,300	222,300	146,500	227,100	201,100
Income Taxes	61,300	48,700	30,700	111,200	100,100	73,400	107,000	91,200
Net Income	83,400	72,000	48,400	170,400	153,400	105,600	157,700	144,800
Average Shares	156,878	156,945	157,039	156,804	156,511	156,310	155,723	154,990
Balance Sheet								
Current Assets	319,000	386,500	514,300	446,900	438,200	341,400	465,100	257,800
Total Assets	2,672,200	2,748,400	2,686,100	2,645,700	2,632,300	2,539,500	2,704,700	2,209,500
Current Liabilities	378,100	434,700	521,900	510,000	551,300	477,000	506,400	387,500
Long-Term Obligations	2,427,000	2,431,800	2,284,300	2,288,800	2,315,000	2,333,600	2,280,900	1,973,200
Total Liabilities	3,527,500	3,583,500	3,512,400	3,484,800	3,510,100	3,434,300	3,418,100	2,906,300
Stockholders' Equity	(855,300)	(835,100)	(826,300)	(839,100)	(877,800)	(894,800)	(713,400)	(696,800)
Shares Outstanding	157,015	157,033	157,033	156,788	156,454	156,173	155,829	155,452
Statistical Record								
Return on Assets %	5.33	6.32	6.75	6.44	5.95	3.96	6.44	6.38
EBITDA Margin %	18.61	19.47	20.93	19.27	18.34	16.22	18.86	18.49
Net Margin %	3.62	4.54	5.89	5.33	4.91	3.53	5.19	5.13
Asset Turnover	1.21	1.21	1.22	1.21	1.21	1.12	1.24	1.24
Current Ratio	0.84	0.89	0.99	0.88	0.79	0.72	0.92	0.67
Price Range	24.45-13.98	24.45-20.14	24.45-19.57	24.45-16.68	24.28-17.69	23.09-18.20	19.72-13.73	15.84-11.58
P/E Ratio	27.78-15.89	22.64-18.65	21.45-17.17	22.43-15.30	24.78-18.05	33.96-26.76	19.52-13.59	17.03-12.45
Average Yield %	4.26	4.02	4.05	4.19	4.30	9.36	4.74	13.29

Address: 7132 Regal Lane, Knoxville, TN 37918	**Web Site:** www.regmovies.com	**Auditors:** KPMG LLP
Telephone: 865-922-1123	**Officers:** Amy E. Miles - Chairperson, Chief Executive Officer Gregory W. Dunn - President, Chief Operating Officer	**Investor Contact:** 866-734-2534
		Transfer Agents: Wells Fargo Bank Minnesota, St. Paul, MN

REGENCY CENTERS CORP

Exchange	Symbol	Price	52Wk Range	Yield	P/E
NYS	REG	$69.18 (12/29/2017)	71.70-58.96	3.06	76.02

*7 Year Price Score 90.09   *NYSE Composite Index=100   *12 Month Price Score 96.43

Interim Earnings (Per Share)

Qtr.	Mar	Jun	Sep	Dec
2014	0.21	0.28	0.52	0.80
2015	0.27	0.34	0.57	0.18
2016	0.49	0.35	0.05	0.54
2017	(0.26)	0.28	0.35	...

Interim Dividends (Per Share)

Amt	Decl	Ex	Rec	Pay
0.51Q	02/07/2017	02/22/2017	02/24/2017	03/01/2017
0.53Q	04/26/2017	05/18/2017	05/22/2017	05/31/2017
0.53Q	08/02/2017	08/14/2017	08/16/2017	08/30/2017
0.53Q	10/31/2017	11/14/2017	11/15/2017	11/29/2017

Indicated Div: $2.12

Valuation Analysis

		Institutional Holding	
Forecast EPS	$0.81	No of Institutions	
	(01/18/2018)	464	
Market Cap	$11.7 Billion	Shares	
Book Value	$6.6 Billion	194,794,976	
Price/Book	1.78	% Held	
Price/Sales	13.36	104.58	

Business Summary: REITs (MIC: 5.3.1 SIC: 6798 NAIC: 525930)

Regency Centers is a real estate investment trust and the general partner of the Regency Centers, L.P. (Operating Partnership). Co. engages in the ownership, management, leasing, acquisition, and development of retail shopping centers through the Operating Partnership, and has no other assets or liabilities other than through its investment in the Operating Partnership. As of Dec 31 2016, Co., the Operating Partnership, and their controlled subsidiaries on a consolidated basis owned 198 retail shopping centers and held partial interests in an additional 109 retail shopping centers through unconsolidated investments in real estate partnerships.

Recent Developments: For the quarter ended Sep 30 2017, income from continuing operations increased to US$63.5 million from US$1.5 million in the year-earlier quarter. Net income increased 472.1% to US$63.6 million from US$11.1 million in the year-earlier quarter. Revenues were US$262.1 million, up 71.6% from US$152.8 million the year before. Revenues from property income rose 74.9% to US$196.5 million from US$112.4 million in the corresponding quarter a year earlier.

Prospects: Our evaluation of Regency Centers Corp. as of Jan. 14, 2018 is the result of our systematic analysis on three basic characteristics: earnings strength, relative valuation, and recent stock price movement. The company has enjoyed a very positive trend in earnings per share over the past 5 quarters. Because the company lacks sufficient analyst estimate data, we place greater weight on the historical EPS trend as the measure of earnings strength. Based on operating earnings yield, the company is overvalued when compared to all of the companies in our coverage universe. Share price changes over the past year indicates that REG will perform well over the near term.

Financial Data

(US$ in Thousands)	9 Mos	6 Mos	3 Mos	12/31/2016	12/31/2015	12/31/2014	12/31/2013	12/31/2012
Earnings Per Share	0.91	0.61	0.68	1.42	1.36	1.80	1.40	(0.08)
Cash Flow Per Share	2.44	1.89	2.00	2.86	2.92	3.01	2.74	2.86
Tang Book Value Per Share	35.86	35.80	35.64	20.62	16.77	16.32	16.02	15.14
Dividends Per Share	2.070	2.040	2.010	2.000	1.940	1.880	1.850	1.850
Dividend Payout %	227.47	334.43	295.59	140.85	142.65	104.44	132.14	...
Income Statement								
Total Revenue	719,576	457,436	196,131	614,371	569,763	537,898	489,007	496,920
EBITDA	139,967	59,081	(4,248)	322,075	351,959	366,206	305,850	241,606
Depn & Amortn	(11,640)	(6,914)	(1,025)	168,210	154,908	155,211	144,305	139,555
Income Before Taxes	54,322	3,389	(30,422)	63,153	94,429	101,504	52,579	(10,078)
Income Taxes	...	296	50	...	...	(996)	...	13,224
Net Income	90,938	28,125	(21,367)	164,922	150,056	187,390	149,804	25,867
Average Shares	170,466	170,420	126,649	101,285	94,856	92,404	91,409	89,669
Balance Sheet								
Current Assets	173,794	230,073	164,685	37,446	102,008	180,922	143,204	78,851
Total Assets	11,118,745	11,192,344	11,135,972	4,488,906	4,191,074	4,197,170	3,913,516	3,853,458
Current Liabilities	322,714	296,588	283,774	138,936	164,515	181,197	147,045	127,185
Long-Term Obligations	3,522,130	3,508,026	3,407,226	1,642,420	1,872,478	2,021,357	1,854,697	1,941,891
Total Liabilities	4,523,283	4,500,058	4,404,623	1,897,605	2,136,965	2,290,578	2,070,162	2,122,693
Stockholders' Equity	6,595,462	6,692,286	6,731,349	2,591,301	2,054,109	1,906,592	1,843,354	1,730,765
Shares Outstanding	169,746	169,743	169,727	104,149	96,794	93,682	91,960	90,059
Statistical Record								
Return on Assets %	1.95	1.28	1.18	3.79	3.58	4.62	3.86	0.66
Return on Equity %	3.32	2.25	2.06	7.08	7.58	9.99	8.38	1.46
EBITDA Margin %	19.45	12.92	N.M.	52.42	61.77	68.08	62.55	48.62
Net Margin %	12.64	6.15	N.M.	26.84	26.34	34.84	30.63	5.21
Asset Turnover	0.11	0.10	0.09	0.14	0.14	0.13	0.13	0.13
Current Ratio	0.54	0.78	0.58	0.27	0.62	1.00	0.97	0.62
Debt to Equity	0.53	0.52	0.51	0.63	0.91	1.06	1.01	1.12
Price Range	77.49-58.96	85.30-58.96	85.30-62.58	85.30-65.38	69.90-57.09	64.96-45.97	59.20-45.88	50.52-36.69
P/E Ratio	85.15-64.79	139.84-96.66	125.44-92.03	60.07-46.04	51.40-41.98	36.09-25.54	42.29-32.77	...
Average Yield %	3.11	2.89	2.71	2.68	2.99	3.44	3.63	4.05

Address: One Independent Drive, Suite 114, Jacksonville, FL 32202
Telephone: 904-598-7000

Web Site: www.regencycenters.com
Officers: Martin E. Stein - Chairman, Chief Executive Officer Lisa Palmer - President, Executive Vice President, Senior Vice President, Chief Financial Officer

Auditors: KPMG LLP
Investor Contact: 904-598-7000
Transfer Agents: Broadridge Corporate Issuer Solutions, Inc. Philadelphia, PA

REGIONS FINANCIAL CORP

Exchange	Symbol	Price	52Wk Range	Yield	P/E
NYS	RF	$17.28 (12/29/2017)	17.49-13.17	2.08	18.00

*7 Year Price Score 123.42 *NYSE Composite Index=100 *12 Month Price Score 104.81

TRADING VOLUME (thousand shares)

Interim Earnings (Per Share)

Qtr.	Mar	Jun	Sep	Dec
2014	0.22	0.21	0.22	0.15
2015	0.16	0.20	0.18	0.21
2016	0.20	0.20	0.24	0.22
2017	0.24	0.25	0.25	...

Interim Dividends (Per Share)

Amt	Decl	Ex	Rec	Pay
0.065Q	02/09/2017	03/08/2017	03/10/2017	03/31/2017
0.07Q	04/20/2017	06/07/2017	06/09/2017	06/30/2017
0.09Q	07/27/2017	09/07/2017	09/08/2017	09/29/2017
0.09Q	10/19/2017	12/07/2017	12/08/2017	01/02/2018

Indicated Div: $0.36

Valuation Analysis / Institutional Holding

Valuation Analysis		Institutional Holding	
Forecast EPS	$1.00	No of Institutions	
	(01/18/2018)	928	
Market Cap	$20.1 Billion	Shares	
Book Value	$16.6 Billion	1,081,541,888	
Price/Book	1.21	% Held	
Price/Sales	3.36	67.51	

Business Summary: Banking (MIC: 5.1.1 SIC: 6021 NAIC: 522110)

Regions Financial is a financial holding company. Co. provides commercial, retail and mortgage banking services, as well as other financial services in the fields of asset management, wealth management, securities brokerage, insurance brokerage, trust services, merger and acquisition advisory services, and other specialty financing. At Dec 31 2016, Co. operated 1,906 Automated Teller Machines and 1,527 banking offices in Alabama, Arkansas, Florida, Georgia, Illinois, Indiana, Iowa, Kentucky, Louisiana, Mississippi, Missouri, North Carolina, South Carolina, Tennessee, and Texas. As of Dec 31 2016, Co. had total assets of $125.97 billion and total deposits of $99.04 billion.

Recent Developments: For the quarter ended Sep 30 2017, net income decreased 2.8% to US$311.0 million from US$320.0 million in the year-earlier quarter. Net interest income increased 6.5% to US$916.0 million from US$860.0 million in the year-earlier quarter. Provision for loan losses was US$76.0 million versus US$29.0 million in the prior-year quarter, an increase of 162.1%. Non-interest income fell 14.0% to US$515.0 million from US$599.0 million, while non-interest expense declined 5.7% to US$904.0 million.

Prospects: Our evaluation of Regions Financial Corp. as of Jan. 14, 2018 is the result of our systematic analysis on three basic characteristics: earnings strength, relative valuation, and recent stock price movement. The company has managed to produce a neutral trend in earnings per share over the past 5 quarters. However, while recent estimates for the company have been mixed, RF has posted results that fell short of analysts expectations. Based on operating earnings yield, the company is undervalued when compared to all of the companies in our coverage universe. Share price changes over the past year indicates that RF will perform poorly over the near term.

Financial Data
(US$ in Thousands)

	9 Mos	6 Mos	3 Mos	12/31/2016	12/31/2015	12/31/2014	12/31/2013	12/31/2012
Earnings Per Share	0.96	0.95	0.90	0.87	0.75	0.80	0.77	0.71
Cash Flow Per Share	1.85	1.65	1.57	1.55	1.19	1.52	2.72	1.76
Tang Book Value Per Share	8.91	8.86	8.68	8.56	8.20	7.94	7.19	6.84
Dividends Per Share	0.290	0.265	0.260	0.255	0.230	0.180	0.100	0.040
Dividend Payout %	30.21	27.89	28.89	29.31	30.67	22.50	12.99	5.63
Income Statement								
Interest Income	2,968,000	1,955,000	966,000	3,814,000	3,603,000	3,588,000	3,646,000	3,903,000
Interest Expense	271,000	174,000	85,000	313,000	268,000	309,000	384,000	603,000
Net Interest Income	2,697,000	1,781,000	881,000	3,501,000	3,335,000	3,279,000	3,262,000	3,300,000
Provision for Losses	194,000	118,000	70,000	262,000	241,000	69,000	138,000	213,000
Non-Interest Income	1,550,000	1,035,000	510,000	2,153,000	2,071,000	1,821,000	2,019,000	2,100,000
Non-Interest Expense	2,730,000	1,826,000	899,000	3,720,000	3,635,000	3,432,000	3,556,000	3,526,000
Income Before Taxes	1,323,000	872,000	422,000	1,672,000	1,530,000	1,599,000	1,587,000	1,661,000
Income Taxes	400,000	261,000	128,000	514,000	455,000	457,000	452,000	482,000
Net Income	928,000	617,000	301,000	1,163,000	1,062,000	1,155,000	1,122,000	1,120,000
Average Shares	1,193,000	1,212,000	1,224,000	1,261,000	1,334,000	1,387,000	1,410,000	1,387,000
Balance Sheet								
Net Loans & Leases	78,703,000	79,659,000	79,320,000	79,722,000	80,504,000	76,745,000	74,323,000	73,459,000
Total Assets	123,271,000	124,643,000	124,545,000	125,968,000	126,050,000	119,679,000	117,396,000	121,347,000
Total Deposits	97,591,000	98,093,000	99,424,000	99,035,000	98,430,000	94,200,000	92,453,000	95,474,000
Total Liabilities	106,647,000	107,750,000	107,823,000	109,304,000	109,206,000	102,690,000	101,628,000	105,848,000
Stockholders' Equity	16,624,000	16,893,000	16,722,000	16,664,000	16,844,000	16,989,000	15,768,000	15,499,000
Shares Outstanding	1,164,880	1,199,267	1,205,118	1,214,580	1,297,330	1,353,941	1,377,720	1,413,339
Statistical Record								
Return on Assets %	0.98	0.98	0.95	0.92	0.86	0.97	0.94	0.90
Return on Equity %	7.20	7.19	7.02	6.92	6.28	7.05	7.18	6.98
Net Interest Margin %	90.42	91.00	91.20	91.79	92.56	91.39	89.47	84.55
Efficiency Ratio %	59.16	61.23	60.91	62.34	64.06	63.45	62.77	58.74
Loans to Deposits	0.81	0.81	0.80	0.80	0.82	0.81	0.80	0.77
Price Range	15.91-9.87	15.91-8.02	15.91-7.60	14.64-7.08	10.80-8.70	11.30-9.06	10.42-7.13	7.65-4.34
P/E Ratio	16.57-10.28	16.75-8.44	17.68-8.44	16.83-8.14	14.40-11.60	14.13-11.33	13.53-9.26	10.77-6.11
Average Yield %	2.09	2.10	2.29	2.63	2.36	1.75	1.11	0.62

Address: 1900 Fifth Avenue North, Birmingham, AL 35203 **Telephone:** 205-581-7890	**Web Site:** www.regions.com **Officers:** O.B. Grayson Hall - Chairman, President, Chief Executive Officer, Chief Operating Officer, Head David J Turner - Senior Executive Vice President, Chief Financial Officer	**Auditors:** Ernst & Young LLP **Investor Contact:** 205-801-0265 **Transfer Agents:** Computershare Trust Company, N.A., Providence, RI

REINSURANCE GROUP OF AMERICA, INC.

Exchange	Symbol	Price	52Wk Range	Yield	P/E
NYS	RGA	$155.93 (12/29/2017)	164.17-122.13	1.28	12.83

*7 Year Price Score 126.91 *NYSE Composite Index=100 *12 Month Price Score 109.50

Interim Earnings (Per Share)

Qtr.	Mar	Jun	Sep	Dec
2014	1.92	2.84	2.28	2.75
2015	1.81	1.94	1.25	2.45
2016	1.17	3.64	3.07	2.92
2017	2.22	3.54	3.47	...

Interim Dividends (Per Share)

Amt	Decl	Ex	Rec	Pay
0.41Q	01/26/2017	02/07/2017	02/09/2017	03/02/2017
0.41Q	04/27/2017	05/05/2017	05/09/2017	05/30/2017
0.50Q	07/19/2017	08/04/2017	08/08/2017	08/29/2017
0.50Q	10/26/2017	11/06/2017	11/07/2017	11/28/2017

Indicated Div: $2.00

Valuation Analysis

		Institutional Holding	
Forecast EPS	$11.10 (01/18/2018)	No of Institutions	31
Market Cap	$10.0 Billion	Shares	784,655
Book Value	$8.1 Billion	% Held	
Price/Book	1.24	N/A	
Price/Sales	0.81		

TRADING VOLUME (thousand shares)

Business Summary: Life & Health (MIC: 5.2.2 SIC: 6311 NAIC: 524130)

Reinsurance Group of America is an insurance holding company. Through its subsidiaries, Co. is engaged in providing traditional reinsurance, which includes individual and group life and health, disability, and critical illness reinsurance. Co. also provides financial solutions, which includes longevity reinsurance, asset-intensive products, primarily annuities, and financial reinsurance. Co. has five geographic-based and business-based operational segments: U.S. and Latin America; Canada; Europe, Middle East and Africa; Asia Pacific; and Corporate and Other. Geographic-based operations are further segmented into traditional and financial solutions businesses.

Recent Developments: For the quarter ended Sep 30 2017, net income increased 14.5% to US$227.6 million from US$198.7 million in the year-earlier quarter. Revenues were US$3.15 billion, up 8.4% from US$2.90 billion the year before. Net premiums earned were US$2.49 billion versus US$2.25 billion in the prior-year quarter, an increase of 10.6%. Net investment income rose 13.7% to US$556.9 million from US$489.7 million a year ago.

Prospects: Our evaluation of Reinsurance Group of America Inc. as of Jan. 14, 2018 is the result of our systematic analysis on three basic characteristics: earnings strength, relative valuation, and recent stock price movement. The company has produced a positive trend in earnings per share over the past 5 quarters and while recent estimates for the company have been mixed, RGA has posted better than expected results. Based on operating earnings yield, the company is undervalued when compared to all of the companies in our coverage universe. Share price changes over the past year indicates that RGA will perform well over the near term.

Financial Data

(US$ in Thousands)	9 Mos	6 Mos	3 Mos	12/31/2016	12/31/2015	12/31/2014	12/31/2013	12/31/2012
Earnings Per Share	12.15	11.75	11.85	10.79	7.46	9.78	5.78	8.52
Cash Flow Per Share	24.04	23.70	23.53	22.74	31.38	33.74	24.02	26.70
Tang Book Value Per Share	125.79	123.60	115.24	110.31	94.09	102.13	83.87	93.47
Dividends Per Share	1.730	1.640	1.600	1.560	1.400	1.260	1.080	0.840
Dividend Payout %	14.24	13.96	13.50	14.46	18.77	12.88	18.69	9.86
Income Statement								
Premium Income	7,335,944	4,846,147	2,365,696	9,248,871	8,570,741	8,669,854	8,254,027	7,906,596
Total Revenue	9,283,326	6,138,016	3,008,740	11,521,511	10,418,178	10,904,194	10,318,353	9,840,911
Benefits & Claims	...	...	...	7,993,375	7,489,382	7,406,641	7,304,332	6,665,999
Income Before Taxes	887,321	547,159	207,844	1,043,946	744,795	1,008,533	635,254	919,223
Income Taxes	282,028	169,457	62,332	342,503	242,629	324,486	216,417	287,330
Net Income	605,293	377,702	145,512	701,443	502,166	684,047	418,837	631,893
Average Shares	65,653	65,608	65,671	64,989	67,292	69,962	72,461	74,153
Balance Sheet								
Total Assets	58,694,031	58,138,072	53,805,820	53,097,879	50,383,152	44,679,611	39,674,473	40,360,438
Total Liabilities	50,596,913	50,166,917	46,385,790	46,004,797	44,247,771	37,656,159	33,738,946	33,450,251
Stockholders' Equity	8,097,118	7,971,155	7,420,030	7,093,082	6,135,381	7,023,452	5,935,527	6,910,187
Shares Outstanding	64,368	64,491	64,388	64,302	65,204	68,772	70,768	73,927
Statistical Record								
Return on Assets %	1.40	1.37	1.45	1.35	1.06	1.62	1.05	1.74
Return on Equity %	9.89	9.86	10.90	10.58	7.63	10.56	6.52	9.66
Loss Ratio %	...	...	...	86.43	87.38	85.43	88.49	84.31
Net Margin %	6.52	6.15	4.84	6.09	4.82	6.27	4.06	6.42
Price Range	141.19-107.00	132.25-93.44	132.25-90.26	128.28-78.61	98.57-82.81	89.22-71.51	77.41-53.52	60.01-48.64
P/E Ratio	11.62-8.81	11.26-7.95	11.16-7.62	11.89-7.29	13.21-11.10	9.12-7.31	13.39-9.26	7.04-5.71
Average Yield %	1.37	1.39	1.45	1.55	1.53	1.58	1.65	1.52

Address: 16600 Swingley Ridge Road, Chesterfield, MO 63017
Telephone: 636-736-7000

Web Site: www.rgare.com
Officers: Anna Manning - President, Chief Executive Officer, Senior Executive Vice President Donna Haag Kinnaird - Chief Operating Officer

Auditors: Deloitte & Touche LLP
Investor Contact: 636-300-8828
Transfer Agents: Mellon Investor Services, L.L.C.

RELIANCE STEEL & ALUMINUM CO.

Exchange	Symbol	Price	52Wk Range	Yield	P/E
NYS	RS	$85.79 (12/29/2017)	87.62-69.11	2.10	16.89

*7 Year Price Score 94.63 *NYSE Composite Index=100 *12 Month Price Score 96.97

Interim Earnings (Per Share)

Qtr.	Mar	Jun	Sep	Dec
2014	1.11	1.22	1.21	1.18
2015	1.30	1.20	0.69	0.95
2016	1.27	1.38	0.68	0.84
2017	1.52	1.40	1.32	...

Interim Dividends (Per Share)

Amt	Decl	Ex	Rec	Pay
0.45Q	02/14/2017	03/08/2017	03/10/2017	03/24/2017
0.45Q	04/25/2017	05/24/2017	05/26/2017	06/16/2017
0.45Q	07/25/2017	08/16/2017	08/18/2017	09/08/2017
0.45Q	10/24/2017	11/16/2017	11/17/2017	12/08/2017

Indicated Div: $1.80

Valuation Analysis / Institutional Holding

Forecast EPS	$5.23	No of Institutions
(01/18/2018)		471
Market Cap	$6.3 Billion	Shares
Book Value	$4.4 Billion	71,979,928
Price/Book	1.42	% Held
Price/Sales	0.67	82.41

Business Summary: Non-Precious Metals (MIC: 8.2.2 SIC: 5051 NAIC: 423510)

Reliance Steel & Aluminum is a metals service center company. Co. provides metals processing services and distributes a line of metal products, including alloy, aluminum, brass, copper, carbon steel, stainless steel, titanium and specialty steel products to customers in a range of industries, including general manufacturing, non-residential construction, transportation, aerospace and defense, energy, electronics and semiconductor fabrication, and heavy industry. Co. also services the auto industry, primarily through its toll processing operations. As of Dec 31 2016, Co.'s network of metals service centers operated more than 300 locations in 39 states in the U.S. and in 12 other countries.

Recent Developments: For the quarter ended Sep 30 2017, net income increased 95.7% to US$99.0 million from US$50.6 million in the year-earlier quarter. Revenues were US$2.45 billion, up 12.1% from US$2.19 billion the year before. Operating income was US$158.7 million versus US$94.8 million in the prior-year quarter, an increase of 67.4%. Direct operating expenses rose 15.3% to US$1.76 billion from US$1.53 billion in the comparable period the year before. Indirect operating expenses decreased 5.9% to US$526.8 million from US$559.8 million in the equivalent prior-year period.

Prospects: Our evaluation of Reliance Steel & Aluminum Co. as of Jan. 14, 2018 is the result of our systematic analysis on three basic characteristics: earnings strength, relative valuation, and recent stock price movement. The company has generated a negative trend in earnings per share over the past 5 quarters. However, while recent estimates for the company have been mixed, RS has posted better than expected results. Based on operating earnings yield, the company is undervalued when compared to all of the companies in our coverage universe. Share price changes over the past year indicates that RS will perform poorly over the near term.

Financial Data

(US$ in Thousands)	9 Mos	6 Mos	3 Mos	12/31/2016	12/31/2015	12/31/2014	12/31/2013	12/31/2012
Earnings Per Share	5.08	4.44	4.42	4.16	4.16	4.73	4.14	5.33
Cash Flow Per Share	6.00	5.99	6.18	8.63	13.83	4.58	8.24	7.98
Tang Book Value Per Share	20.08	18.84	17.53	16.10	14.83	14.49	12.51	17.19
Dividends Per Share	1.775	1.750	1.700	1.650	1.600	1.400	1.260	0.800
Dividend Payout %	34.94	39.41	38.46	39.66	38.46	29.60	30.43	15.01
Income Statement								
Total Revenue	7,344,600	4,894,500	2,419,300	8,613,400	9,350,500	10,451,600	9,223,800	8,442,300
EBITDA	682,200	440,200	241,000	796,200	817,900	890,900	792,700	859,900
Depn & Amortn	164,200	83,500	55,200	222,000	218,500	213,800	192,400	151,500
Income Before Taxes	463,100	320,900	168,500	428,500	458,700	544,100	476,000	607,200
Income Taxes	145,900	102,700	55,100	120,100	142,500	170,000	153,600	201,100
Net Income	312,000	214,700	111,700	304,300	311,500	371,500	321,600	403,500
Average Shares	73,617	73,500	73,415	73,120	74,902	78,615	77,646	75,694
Balance Sheet								
Current Assets	3,169,100	3,144,400	3,025,600	2,688,500	2,554,200	3,121,100	2,738,900	2,277,400
Total Assets	7,846,900	7,831,200	7,724,400	7,411,300	7,121,600	7,836,600	7,341,000	5,857,700
Current Liabilities	781,200	747,800	766,000	656,000	989,700	662,800	573,400	578,200
Long-Term Obligations	1,896,000	1,990,100	1,951,900	1,846,700	1,427,900	2,222,300	2,072,500	1,123,800
Total Liabilities	3,432,000	3,500,100	3,479,300	3,262,500	3,207,500	3,737,600	3,466,400	2,299,300
Stockholders' Equity	4,414,900	4,331,100	4,245,100	4,148,800	3,914,100	4,099,000	3,874,600	3,558,400
Shares Outstanding	72,913	72,901	72,879	72,682	71,739	77,337	77,492	76,042
Statistical Record								
Return on Assets %	4.84	4.21	4.25	4.18	4.16	4.90	4.87	7.02
Return on Equity %	8.75	7.73	7.84	7.53	7.77	9.32	8.65	12.01
EBITDA Margin %	9.29	8.99	9.96	9.24	8.75	8.52	8.59	10.19
Net Margin %	4.25	4.39	4.62	3.53	3.33	3.55	3.49	4.78
Asset Turnover	1.22	1.18	1.16	1.18	1.25	1.38	1.40	1.47
Current Ratio	4.06	4.20	3.95	4.10	2.58	4.71	4.78	3.94
Debt to Equity	0.43	0.46	0.46	0.45	0.36	0.54	0.53	0.32
Price Range	87.62-66.87	87.62-66.87	87.62-66.87	86.34-51.75	66.33-52.37	76.12-57.14	75.84-62.10	62.10-44.98
P/E Ratio	17.25-13.16	19.73-15.06	19.82-15.13	20.75-12.44	15.94-12.59	16.09-12.08	18.32-15.00	11.65-8.44
Average Yield %	2.32	2.22	2.22	2.31	2.71	2.02	1.82	1.50

| Address: 350 South Grand Avenue, Suite 5100, Los Angeles, CA 90071 Telephone: 213-687-7700 | Web Site: www.rsac.com Officers: David H. Hannah - Chairman, Chief Executive Officer Gregg J. Mollins - President, Chief Executive Officer, Chief Operating Officer | Auditors: KPMG LLP Investor Contact: 213-576-2428 Transfer Agents: American Stock Transfer & Trust Company, Brooklyn, NY |

RENAISSANCERE HOLDINGS LTD.

Exchange	Symbol	Price	52Wk Range	Yield	P/E
NYS	RNR	$125.59 (12/29/2017)	150.35-123.88	1.02	N/A

*7 Year Price Score 109.80 *NYSE Composite Index=100 *12 Month Price Score 89.53

Interim Earnings (Per Share)

Qtr.	Mar	Jun	Sep	Dec
2014	3.56	2.95	1.70	4.34
2015	4.14	1.59	1.66	2.09
2016	2.95	3.22	3.56	1.72
2017	2.25	4.24	(12.75)	...

Interim Dividends (Per Share)

Amt	Decl	Ex	Rec	Pay
0.32Q	02/22/2017	03/13/2017	03/15/2017	03/31/2017
0.32Q	05/17/2017	06/13/2017	06/15/2017	06/30/2017
0.32Q	08/02/2017	09/14/2017	09/15/2017	09/29/2017
0.32Q	11/10/2017	12/14/2017	12/15/2017	12/29/2017

Indicated Div: $1.28

Valuation Analysis

Forecast EPS	N/A
Market Cap	$5.0 Billion
Book Value	$4.4 Billion
Price/Book	1.14
Price/Sales	2.56

Institutional Holding

No of Institutions	455
Shares	51,338,240
% Held	75.82

TRADING VOLUME (thousand shares)

Business Summary: General Insurance (MIC: 5.2.1 SIC: 6331 NAIC: 524126)

RenaissanceRe Holdings is a holding company. Together with its wholly owned and majority-owned subsidiaries and DaVinciRe Holdings Ltd, Co. is a global provider of reinsurance and insurance coverages and related services. Co.'s business consists of the following reportable segments: Property, which is comprised of catastrophe and other property reinsurance and insurance written on behalf of Co.'s operating subsidiaries and certain joint ventures managed by its ventures unit; and Casualty and Specialty, which is comprised of casualty and specialty reinsurance and insurance written on behalf of Co.'s operating subsidiaries and certain joint ventures managed by its ventures unit.

Recent Developments: For the quarter ended Sep 30 2017, net loss amounted to US$703.5 million versus net income of US$188.1 million in the year-earlier quarter. Revenues were US$634.7 million, up 43.5% from US$442.5 million the year before. Net premiums earned were US$547.8 million versus US$346.5 million in the prior-year quarter, an increase of 58.1%. Net investment income fell 21.7% to US$40.3 million from US$51.4 million a year ago.

Prospects: Our evaluation of RenaissanceRe Holdings Ltd. as of July 19, 2015 is the result of our systematic analysis on three basic characteristics: earnings strength, relative valuation, and recent stock price movement. The company has enjoyed a very positive trend in earnings per share over the past 5 quarters. However, while recent estimates for the company have been mixed, RNR has posted better than expected results. Based on operating earnings yield, the company is undervalued when compared to all of the companies in our coverage universe. Share price changes over the past year indicates that RNR will perform poorly over the near term.

Financial Data

(US$ in Thousands)	9 Mos	6 Mos	3 Mos	12/31/2016	12/31/2015	12/31/2014	12/31/2013	12/31/2012
Earnings Per Share	(4.54)	11.77	10.75	11.43	9.28	12.60	14.87	11.23
Cash Flow Per Share	18.22	17.37	17.34	11.34	9.61	16.76	18.36	14.63
Tang Book Value Per Share	93.89	106.97	103.29	102.35	93.06	89.95	80.10	67.95
Dividends Per Share	1.270	1.260	1.250	1.240	1.200	1.160	1.120	1.080
Dividend Payout %	...	10.71	11.63	10.85	12.93	9.21	7.53	9.62
Income Statement								
Premium Income	1,296,102	748,310	366,045	1,403,430	1,400,551	1,062,416	1,114,626	1,069,355
Total Revenue	1,612,386	977,651	472,066	1,727,837	1,515,102	1,260,077	1,380,482	1,405,934
Income Before Taxes	(371,609)	350,862	132,608	630,388	496,376	686,864	841,038	748,091
Income Taxes	(14,739)	4,238	334	340	(45,866)	608	1,692	1,429
Net Income	(224,532)	274,685	97,947	502,962	431,192	532,718	690,624	600,909
Average Shares	39,591	40,024	40,623	41,559	43,526	39,968	44,128	49,603
Balance Sheet								
Total Assets	15,044,924	13,705,680	13,319,627	12,352,082	11,560,871	8,203,550	8,179,131	7,928,628
Total Liabilities	10,641,912	8,750,425	8,458,790	7,485,505	6,828,687	4,337,835	4,274,747	4,425,563
Stockholders' Equity	4,403,012	4,955,255	4,860,837	4,866,577	4,732,184	3,865,715	3,904,384	3,503,065
Shares Outstanding	40,029	40,282	40,785	41,187	43,701	38,441	43,646	45,542
Statistical Record								
Return on Assets %	N.M.	3.83	3.67	4.20	4.36	6.50	8.58	7.65
Return on Equity %	N.M.	10.40	9.71	10.45	10.03	13.71	18.65	16.86
Net Margin %	(13.93)	28.10	20.75	29.11	28.46	42.28	50.03	42.74
Price Range	150.35-118.06	150.35-115.08	150.35-109.70	136.45-108.93	115.47-94.50	108.42-89.80	97.34-80.20	82.76-71.69
P/E Ratio	...	12.77-9.78	13.99-10.20	11.94-9.53	12.44-10.18	8.60-7.13	6.55-5.39	7.37-6.38
Average Yield %	0.92	0.95	0.99	1.05	1.15	1.16	1.26	1.42

Address: Renaissance House, 12 Crow Lane, Pembroke, HM 19	Web Site: www.renre.com	Auditors: Ernst & Young Ltd.
Telephone: 441-295-4513	Officers: Kevin J. O'Donnell - President, Chief Executive Officer, Executive Vice President, Global Chief Underwriting Officer Ross A. Curtis - Senior Vice President, Group Chief Underwriting Officer	Investor Contact: 441-295-4513
Fax: 441-295-9453		Transfer Agents: Computershare Shareowner Services LLC, Jersey City, NJ

REPUBLIC SERVICES INC

Exchange	Symbol	Price	52Wk Range	Yield	P/E	Div Achiever
NYS	RSG	$67.61 (12/29/2017)	67.61-56.42	2.04	28.65	13 Years

*7 Year Price Score 122.83 *NYSE Composite Index=100   *12 Month Price Score 96.68

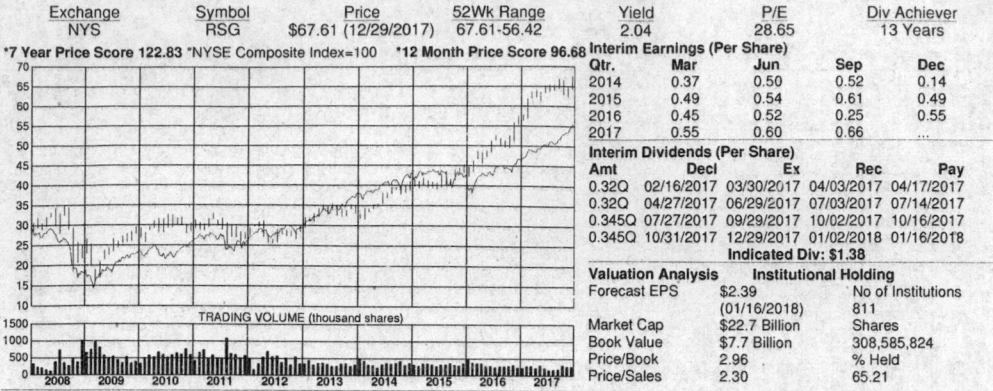

Interim Earnings (Per Share)

Qtr.	Mar	Jun	Sep	Dec
2014	0.37	0.50	0.52	0.14
2015	0.49	0.54	0.61	0.49
2016	0.45	0.52	0.25	0.55
2017	0.55	0.60	0.66	...

Interim Dividends (Per Share)

Amt	Decl	Ex	Rec	Pay
0.32Q	02/16/2017	03/30/2017	04/03/2017	04/17/2017
0.32Q	04/27/2017	06/29/2017	07/03/2017	07/14/2017
0.345Q	07/27/2017	09/29/2017	10/02/2017	10/16/2017
0.345Q	10/31/2017	12/29/2017	01/02/2018	01/16/2018

Indicated Div: $1.38

Valuation Analysis

		Institutional Holding	
Forecast EPS	$2.39	No of Institutions	
	(01/16/2018)	811	
Market Cap	$22.7 Billion	Shares	
Book Value	$7.7 Billion	308,585,824	
Price/Book	2.96	% Held	
Price/Sales	2.30	65.21	

Business Summary: Sanitation Services (MIC: 7.5.3 SIC: 4953 NAIC: 562219)

Republic Services is a provider of non-hazardous solid waste collection, transfer, disposal, recycling, and energy services. As of Dec 31 2016, Co. operated in 39 states and Puerto Rico through 333 collection operations, 204 transfer stations, 192 active landfills, 64 recycling centers, seven treatment, recovery and disposal facilities, and 10 salt water disposal wells. Co. also operated 71 landfill gas and renewable energy projects and had post-closure responsibility for 124 closed landfills. Co. provides residential, small-container commercial, and large-container industrial solid waste collection services.

Recent Developments:
For the quarter ended Sep 30 2017, net income increased 160.6% to US$223.3 million from US$85.7 million in the year-earlier quarter. Revenues were US$2.56 billion, up 6.3% from US$2.41 billion the year before. Operating income was US$448.1 million versus US$417.9 million in the prior-year quarter, an increase of 7.2%. Direct operating expenses rose 7.0% to US$1.58 billion from US$1.48 billion in the comparable period the year before. Indirect operating expenses increased 3.7% to US$533.8 million from US$514.7 million in the equivalent prior-year period.

Prospects:
Our evaluation of Republic Services Inc. as of Jan. 14, 2018 is the result of our systematic analysis on three basic characteristics: earnings strength, relative valuation, and recent stock price movement. The company has managed to produce a neutral trend in earnings per share over the past 5 quarters and while recent estimates for the company have been mixed, RSG has posted better than expected results. Based on operating earnings yield, the company is about fairly valued when compared to all of the companies in our coverage universe. Share price changes over the past year indicates that RSG will perform in line with the market over the near term.

Financial Data
(US$ in Thousands)

	9 Mos	6 Mos	3 Mos	12/31/2016	12/31/2015	12/31/2014	12/31/2013	12/31/2012
Earnings Per Share	2.36	1.95	1.87	1.78	2.13	1.53	1.62	1.55
Cash Flow Per Share	5.56	5.57	5.47	5.37	4.80	4.29	4.28	4.11
Dividends Per Share	1.305	1.280	1.260	1.240	1.160	1.080	0.990	0.910
Dividend Payout %	55.30	65.64	67.38	69.66	54.46	70.59	61.11	58.71
Income Statement								
Total Revenue	7,481,500	4,919,500	2,392,800	9,387,700	9,115,000	8,788,300	8,417,200	8,118,300
EBITDA	2,091,500	1,362,100	620,400	2,261,100	2,458,700	2,071,900	2,017,200	2,138,300
Depn & Amortn	828,900	548,100	232,200	919,800	898,700	838,500	806,700	926,900
Income Before Taxes	994,600	635,700	299,100	970,900	1,195,900	885,300	851,200	823,900
Income Taxes	371,900	238,500	108,400	351,600	445,500	337,400	262,100	251,800
Net Income	614,000	390,700	187,800	612,600	749,900	547,600	588,900	571,800
Average Shares	338,500	340,000	341,900	344,400	351,400	358,100	363,400	368,020
Balance Sheet								
Current Assets	1,396,700	1,292,800	1,234,400	1,284,500	1,230,300	1,391,000	1,421,900	1,231,300
Total Assets	20,948,600	20,761,100	20,595,800	20,629,600	20,577,200	20,094,000	19,949,200	19,616,900
Current Liabilities	2,591,500	2,543,000	1,777,200	1,812,000	1,834,800	1,826,000	1,717,100	1,695,000
Long-Term Obligations	7,152,000	7,075,700	7,663,900	7,653,100	7,568,700	7,050,800	7,002,400	7,051,100
Total Liabilities	13,276,600	13,098,200	12,912,500	12,938,300	12,803,100	12,348,700	12,045,700	11,913,600
Stockholders' Equity	7,672,000	7,662,900	7,683,300	7,691,300	7,774,100	7,745,300	7,903,500	7,703,300
Shares Outstanding	335,400	337,000	338,800	339,400	345,600	352,700	360,400	361,100
Statistical Record								
Return on Assets %	3.86	3.22	3.13	2.97	3.69	2.74	2.98	2.91
Return on Equity %	10.49	8.64	8.33	7.90	9.66	7.00	7.55	7.41
EBITDA Margin %	27.96	27.69	25.93	24.09	26.97	23.58	23.97	26.34
Net Margin %	8.21	7.94	7.85	6.53	8.23	6.23	7.00	7.04
Asset Turnover	0.47	0.47	0.46	0.45	0.45	0.44	0.43	0.41
Current Ratio	0.54	0.51	0.69	0.71	0.67	0.76	0.83	0.73
Debt to Equity	0.93	0.92	1.00	1.00	0.97	0.91	0.89	0.92
Price Range	66.94-49.49	65.11-49.49	63.69-45.62	57.50-42.20	45.25-39.04	40.89-31.53	35.44-29.33	31.14-25.39
P/E Ratio	28.36-20.97	33.39-25.38	34.06-24.40	32.30-23.71	21.24-18.33	26.73-20.61	21.88-18.10	20.09-16.38
Average Yield %	2.16	2.25	2.37	2.50	2.80	2.95	2.98	3.23

Address: 18500 North Allied Way, Phoenix, AZ 85054 **Telephone:** 480-627-2700	**Web Site:** www.republicservices.com **Officers:** Ramon A. Rodriguez - Chairman Donald W. Slager - President, Chief Executive Officer	**Auditors:** Ernst & Young LLP **Transfer Agents:** Wachovia Corp., Charlotte, NC

RESMED INC.

Exchange	Symbol	Price	52Wk Range	Yield	P/E
NYS	RMD	$84.69 (12/29/2017)	86.44-61.87	1.65	34.29

*7 Year Price Score 115.22 *NYSE Composite Index=100 *12 Month Price Score 105.92

TRADING VOLUME (thousand shares)

Interim Earnings (Per Share)

Qtr.	Sep	Dec	Mar	Jun
2014-15	0.58	0.64	0.64	0.61
2015-16	0.57	0.64	0.63	0.66
2016-17	0.54	0.54	0.62	0.71
2017-18	0.60	...	...	...

Interim Dividends (Per Share)

Amt	Decl	Ex	Rec	Pay
0.33Q	01/23/2017	02/07/2017	02/09/2017	03/16/2017
0.33Q	04/27/2017	05/09/2017	05/11/2017	06/15/2017
0.35Q	08/01/2017	08/15/2017	08/17/2017	09/21/2017
0.35Q	10/26/2017	11/08/2017	11/09/2017	12/14/2017

Indicated Div: $1.40

Valuation Analysis

		Institutional Holding	
Forecast EPS	$3.01 (01/18/2018)	No of Institutions	524
Market Cap	$12.0 Billion	Shares	109,385,416
Book Value	$2.0 Billion	% Held	54.68
Price/Book	5.88		
Price/Sales	5.67		

Business Summary: Medical Instruments & Equipment (MIC: 4.3.1 SIC: 3841 NAIC: 339112)

ResMed is a holding company. Through its operating subsidiaries, Co. is engaged in the development, manufacturing, distribution and marketing of medical devices and cloud-based software applications that diagnose, treat and manage respiratory disorders including sleep disordered breathing (SDB), chronic obstructive pulmonary disease, neuromuscular disease and other chronic diseases. SDB includes obstructive sleep apnea, and other respiratory disorders that occur during sleep. Co.'s portfolio of products includes devices, diagnostic products, mask systems, headgear and other accessories, dental devices, portable oxygen concentrators and cloud-based software informatics solutions.

Recent Developments: For the quarter ended Sep 30 2017, net income increased 13.2% to US$86.1 million from US$76.1 million in the year-earlier quarter. Revenues were US$523.7 million, up 12.5% from US$465.5 million the year before. Operating income was US$112.6 million versus US$94.1 million in the prior-year quarter, an increase of 19.6%. Direct operating expenses rose 11.1% to US$218.1 million from US$196.3 million in the comparable period the year before. Indirect operating expenses increased 10.3% to US$193.0 million from US$175.0 million in the equivalent prior-year period.

Prospects: Our evaluation of ResMed Inc. as of Jan. 14, 2018 is the result of our systematic analysis on three basic characteristics: earnings strength, relative valuation, and recent stock price movement. The company has managed to produce a neutral trend in earnings per share over the past 5 quarters and while recent estimates for the company have been mixed, RMD has posted better than expected results. Based on operating earnings yield, the company is about fairly valued when compared to all of the companies in our coverage universe. Share price changes over the past year indicates that RMD will perform well over the near term.

Financial Data
(US$ in Thousands)

	3 Mos	06/30/2017	06/30/2016	06/30/2015	06/30/2014	06/30/2013	06/30/2012	06/30/2011
Earnings Per Share	2.47	2.40	2.49	2.47	2.39	2.10	1.71	1.44
Cash Flow Per Share	2.97	2.93	3.90	2.73	2.77	2.82	2.62	1.86
Tang Book Value Per Share	5.10	4.46	2.39	9.08	10.15	9.06	9.13	9.54
Dividends Per Share	1.340	1.320	1.200	1.120	1.000	0.680	...	...
Dividend Payout %	54.25	55.00	48.19	45.34	41.84	32.38	...	...
Income Statement								
Total Revenue	523,659	2,066,737	1,838,713	1,678,912	1,554,973	1,514,457	1,368,515	1,243,148
EBITDA	123,183	476,472	457,835	424,154	415,704	362,775	316,839	287,810
Depn & Amortn	11,783	46,578	23,923	8,668	9,733	10,142	13,974	10,146
Income Before Taxes	108,485	418,743	439,566	435,916	431,078	385,119	331,945	303,707
Income Taxes	22,360	76,459	87,157	83,030	85,805	77,986	77,095	76,721
Net Income	86,125	342,284	352,409	352,886	345,273	307,133	254,850	226,986
Average Shares	143,480	142,453	141,669	142,687	144,359	146,410	149,316	157,195
Balance Sheet								
Current Assets	1,657,946	1,644,003	1,419,719	1,444,182	1,556,209	1,448,849	1,361,151	1,292,452
Total Assets	3,489,617	3,468,487	3,258,935	2,184,260	2,360,962	2,210,721	2,137,869	2,068,922
Current Liabilities	351,585	360,126	638,551	267,259	269,558	574,049	252,852	208,840
Long-Term Obligations	1,018,871	1,078,611	875,000	300,594	300,770	769	250,783	100,000
Total Liabilities	1,440,089	1,508,221	1,564,104	596,953	602,714	600,205	530,242	338,185
Stockholders' Equity	2,049,528	1,960,266	1,694,831	1,587,307	1,758,248	1,610,516	1,607,627	1,730,737
Shares Outstanding	142,263	142,174	140,660	140,474	140,304	142,013	142,021	151,668
Statistical Record								
Return on Assets %	10.34	10.18	12.91	15.53	15.10	14.13	12.08	12.29
Return on Equity %	18.44	18.73	21.42	21.10	20.50	19.09	15.23	15.04
EBITDA Margin %	23.52	23.05	24.90	25.26	26.73	23.95	23.15	23.15
Net Margin %	16.45	16.56	19.17	21.02	22.20	20.28	18.62	18.26
Asset Turnover	0.62	0.61	0.67	0.74	0.68	0.70	0.65	0.67
Current Ratio	4.72	4.57	2.22	5.40	5.77	2.52	5.38	6.19
Debt to Equity	0.50	0.55	0.52	0.19	0.17	N.M.	0.16	0.06
Price Range	81.38-57.34	78.91-57.34	64.08-49.43	74.82-46.25	57.11-42.03	51.17-30.63	35.01-23.46	35.61-29.62
P/E Ratio	32.95-23.21	32.88-23.89	25.73-19.85	30.29-18.72	23.90-17.59	24.37-14.59	20.47-13.72	24.73-20.57
Average Yield %	1.93	1.97	2.13	1.94	2.06	1.62	...	...

Address: 9001 Spectrum Center Blvd., San Diego, CA 92123 **Telephone:** 858-836-5000	**Web Site:** www.resmed.com **Officers:** Peter C. Farrell - Chairman, President, Chief Executive Officer Robert Andrew Douglas - President, Chief Operating Officer, Region Officer, Office of the Chief Executive Officer	**Auditors:** KPMG LLP **Investor Contact:** 858-836-5971 **Transfer Agents:** Computershare Trust Company N.A., Canton, MA

RETAIL PROPERTIES OF AMERICA INC

Exchange	Symbol	Price	52Wk Range	Yield	P/E
NYS	RPAI	$13.44 (12/29/2017)	15.69-11.83	4.93	21.00

*7 Year Price Score N/A   *NYSE Composite Index=100   *12 Month Price Score 90.45

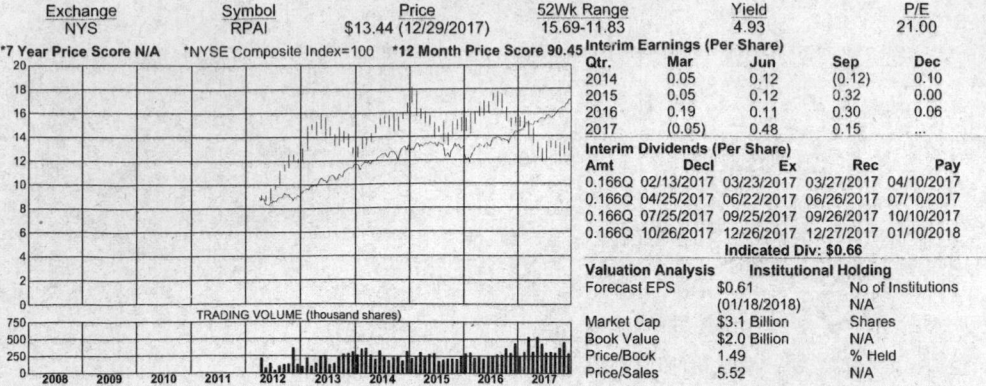

Interim Earnings (Per Share)

Qtr.	Mar	Jun	Sep	Dec
2014	0.05	0.12	(0.12)	0.10
2015	0.05	0.12	0.32	0.00
2016	0.19	0.11	0.30	0.06
2017	(0.05)	0.48	0.15	...

Interim Dividends (Per Share)

Amt	Decl	Ex	Rec	Pay
0.166Q	02/13/2017	03/23/2017	03/27/2017	04/10/2017
0.166Q	04/25/2017	06/22/2017	06/26/2017	07/10/2017
0.166Q	07/25/2017	09/25/2017	09/26/2017	10/10/2017
0.166Q	10/26/2017	12/26/2017	12/27/2017	01/10/2018

Indicated Div: $0.66

Valuation Analysis   **Institutional Holding**

Forecast EPS	$0.61	No of Institutions
	(01/18/2018)	N/A
Market Cap	$3.1 Billion	Shares
Book Value	$2.0 Billion	N/A
Price/Book	1.49	% Held
Price/Sales	5.52	N/A

TRADING VOLUME (thousand shares)

Business Summary: REITs (MIC: 5.3.1 SIC: 6798 NAIC: 525930)

Retail Properties of America is a real estate investment trust that owns and operates shopping centers in the U.S. As of Dec 31 2016, Co. owned 156 retail operating properties. Co.'s retail operating portfolio includes neighborhood and community centers, power centers, and lifestyle centers and multi-tenant retail-focused mixed-use properties, as well as single-user retail properties. In addition to its operating portfolio, as of Dec 31 2016, Co. owned two properties where it has begun redevelopment activities.

Recent Developments: For the quarter ended Sep 30 2017, loss from continuing operations was US$37.2 million compared with income of US$6.1 million in the year-earlier quarter. Net income decreased 50.5% to US$35.9 million from US$72.5 million in the year-earlier quarter. Revenues were US$130.5 million, down 9.7% from US$144.5 million the year before.

Prospects: Our evaluation of Retail Properties of America as of Jan. 14, 2018 is the result of our systematic analysis on three basic characteristics: earnings strength, relative valuation, and recent stock price movement. The company has enjoyed a very positive trend in earnings per share over the past 5 quarters. However, while recent estimates for the company have been lowered by analysts, RPAI has posted better than expected results. Based on operating earnings yield, the company is overvalued when compared to all of the companies in our coverage universe. Share price changes over the past year indicates that RPAI will perform in line with the market over the near term.

Financial Data
(US$ in Thousands)

	9 Mos	6 Mos	3 Mos	12/31/2016	12/31/2015	12/31/2014	12/31/2013	12/31/2012
Earnings Per Share	0.64	0.79	0.42	0.66	0.49	0.14	0.02	...
Cash Flow Per Share	1.05	1.12	1.14	1.11	1.12	1.08	1.02	0.76
Tang Book Value Per Share	8.45	8.54	8.28	8.49	8.50	8.72	9.22	9.75
Dividends Per Share	0.662	0.662	0.662	0.662	0.662	0.662	0.662	0.662
Dividend Payout %	103.52	83.86	157.74	100.38	135.20	473.21	3,312.50	...
Income Statement								
Total Revenue	411,551	281,032	143,693	583,143	603,960	600,614	551,223	567,023
EBITDA	50,001	64,258	42,026	384,260	373,360	357,412	345,909	401,037
Depn & Amortn	11,231	9,420	6,758	237,420	230,590	220,892	240,713	229,800
Income Before Taxes	(89,307)	(52,129)	(50,264)	37,110	3,832	2,685	(41,609)	(7,928)
Net Income	141,567	105,663	(9,100)	166,817	125,096	43,300	13,626	(447)
Average Shares	230,104	234,818	236,294	236,951	236,382	236,187	234,134	220,464
Balance Sheet								
Current Assets	102,148	99,591	111,979	132,060	134,228	198,305	139,008	223,500
Total Assets	4,069,093	4,264,323	4,466,617	4,452,973	4,621,251	4,803,860	4,877,576	5,237,427
Current Liabilities	114,250	103,411	97,546	122,307	109,097	100,316	93,595	112,183
Long-Term Obligations	1,717,609	1,879,234	2,077,702	1,997,925	2,166,238	2,334,465	2,299,633	2,592,089
Total Liabilities	2,020,155	2,161,846	2,364,136	2,300,887	2,465,914	2,615,979	2,570,236	2,863,168
Stockholders' Equity	2,048,938	2,102,477	2,102,481	2,152,086	2,155,337	2,187,881	2,307,340	2,374,259
Shares Outstanding	227,496	230,943	236,888	236,770	237,267	236,602	236,302	230,643
Statistical Record								
Return on Assets %	3.73	4.38	2.41	3.67	2.65	0.89	0.27	N.M.
Return on Equity %	7.56	9.24	5.17	7.72	5.76	1.93	0.58	N.M.
EBITDA Margin %	12.15	22.87	29.25	65.89	61.82	59.51	62.75	70.73
Net Margin %	34.40	37.60	N.M.	28.61	20.71	7.21	2.47	N.M.
Asset Turnover	0.13	0.13	0.13	0.13	0.13	0.12	0.11	0.10
Current Ratio	0.89	0.96	1.15	1.08	1.23	1.98	1.49	1.99
Debt to Equity	0.84	0.89	0.99	0.93	1.01	1.07	1.00	1.09
Price Range	16.80-11.83	17.74-11.83	17.74-13.94	17.74-14.16	18.21-13.19	16.87-12.30	16.03-11.94	12.56-8.64
P/E Ratio	26.25-18.48	22.46-14.97	42.24-33.19	26.88-21.45	37.16-26.92	120.50-87.86	801.50-597.00	...
Average Yield %	4.69	4.38	4.17	4.16	4.34	4.48	4.70	6.26

Address: 2021 Spring Road, Suite 200, Oak Brook, IL 60523 Telephone: 630-634-4200	Web Site: www.rpai.com Officers: Gerald M. Gorski - Chairman Michael P. Fitzmaurice - Senior Vice President	Auditors: Deloitte & Touche LLP Transfer Agents: Registrar & Transfer Company, Cranford, NJ

RITE AID CORP

Exchange	Symbol	Price	52Wk Range	Yield	P/E
NYS	RAD	$1.97 (12/29/2017)	8.70-1.43	N/A	13.13

*7 Year Price Score 61.22 *NYSE Composite Index=100   *12 Month Price Score 49.56

Interim Earnings (Per Share)

Qtr.	May	Aug	Nov	Feb
2014-15	0.04	0.13	0.10	1.81
2015-16	0.02	0.02	0.06	0.06
2016-17	0.00	0.01	0.01	(0.02)
2017-18	(0.07)	0.16	0.08	...

Interim Dividends (Per Share)

No Dividends Paid

Valuation Analysis / **Institutional Holding**

Forecast EPS	$-0.06	No of Institutions
	(01/16/2018)	547
Market Cap	$2.1 Billion	Shares
Book Value	$825.1 Million	637,120,192
Price/Book	2.55	% Held
Price/Sales	0.07	68.85

TRADING VOLUME (thousand shares)

Business Summary: Retail - Food & Beverage, Drug & Tobacco (MIC: 2.1.2 SIC: 5912 NAIC: 446110)

Rite Aid is a pharmacy retail healthcare company. Co. operates through its two reportable segments: Retail Pharmacy, which sells brand and generic prescription drugs, as well as an assortment of front-end products including health and beauty aids, personal care products, seasonal merchandise, and a private brand product line; and Pharmacy Services, which provides pharmacy benefit management (PBM) options through its EnvisionRxOption and MedTrak PBMs, as well as mail-order and specialty pharmacy services and cash pay infertility discount drug program via Design Rx, among others. As of Mar 4 2017, Co. operated 4,536 stores in 31 states across the country and in the District of Columbia.

Recent Developments: For the quarter ended Sep 2 2017, net income increased to US$170.7 million from US$14.8 million in the year-earlier quarter. Revenues were US$7.68 billion, down 4.4% from US$8.03 billion the year before. Direct operating expenses declined 3.6% to US$5.89 billion from US$6.11 billion in the comparable period the year before. Indirect operating expenses decreased 20.2% to US$1.51 billion from US$1.89 billion in the equivalent prior-year period.

Prospects: Our evaluation of Rite Aid Corp. as of Jan. 14, 2018 is the result of our systematic analysis on three basic characteristics: earnings strength, relative valuation, and recent stock price movement. The company has enjoyed a very positive trend in earnings per share over the past 5 quarters. Because the company lacks sufficient analyst estimate data, we place greater weight on the historical EPS trend as the measure of earnings strength. Based on operating earnings yield, the company is overvalued when compared to all of the companies in our coverage universe. Share price changes over the past year indicates that RAD will perform very poorly over the near term.

Financial Data

(US$ in Thousands)	9 Mos	6 Mos	3 Mos	03/04/2017	02/27/2016	02/28/2015	03/01/2014	03/02/2013
Earnings Per Share	0.15	0.08	(0.07)	...	0.16	2.08	0.23	0.12
Cash Flow Per Share	0.46	0.49	0.15	0.21	0.98	0.67	0.76	0.92
Income Statement								
Total Revenue	16,134,704	15,460,356	7,781,453	32,845,073	30,736,657	26,528,377	25,526,413	25,392,263
EBITDA	668,022	662,547	141,471	826,517	1,050,374	1,122,955	959,412	809,300
Depn & Amortn	292,448	274,104	142,092	346,081	322,396	298,523	284,603	286,374
Income Before Taxes	223,409	167,245	(110,558)	48,445	278,404	426,820	250,218	7,505
Income Taxes	89,268	71,878	(35,209)	44,392	112,939	(1,682,353)	804	(110,600)
Net Income	176,398	95,367	(75,349)	4,053	165,465	2,109,173	249,414	118,105
Average Shares	1,055,869	1,067,216	1,046,826	1,060,826	1,042,362	1,017,861	979,092	907,259
Balance Sheet								
Current Assets	5,929,445	5,181,369	4,977,567	5,065,288	4,550,727	4,221,758	4,285,125	4,409,047
Total Assets	11,340,614	11,498,308	11,460,138	11,593,752	11,277,010	8,863,252	6,944,871	7,078,719
Current Liabilities	6,905,915	2,981,211	3,008,695	3,005,248	2,996,895	2,485,000	2,507,452	2,578,270
Long-Term Obligations	3,017,354	7,120,439	7,217,807	7,307,358	6,967,288	5,544,567	5,707,969	5,996,220
Total Liabilities	10,515,470	10,764,698	10,899,510	10,899,510	10,979,682	10,695,582	8,806,196	9,058,573	9,538,153
Stockholders' Equity	825,144	733,610	560,628	614,070	581,428	57,056	(2,113,702)	(2,459,434)
Shares Outstanding	1,067,887	1,062,411	1,053,685	1,053,690	1,047,754	988,558	971,331	904,268
Statistical Record								
Return on Assets %	1.35	0.77	N.M.	0.03	1.65	26.76	3.57	1.64
Return on Equity %	21.11	13.22	N.M.	0.67	51.97	...	...	...
EBITDA Margin %	4.14	4.29	1.82	2.52	3.42	4.23	3.76	3.19
Net Margin %	1.09	0.62	N.M.	0.01	0.54	7.95	0.98	0.47
Asset Turnover	2.55	2.78	2.86	2.83	3.06	3.37	3.65	3.53
Current Ratio	0.86	1.74	1.65	1.69	1.52	1.70	1.71	1.71
Debt to Equity	3.66	9.71	12.87	11.90	11.98	97.18	...	...
Price Range	8.70-1.43	8.70-2.22	8.70-3.41	8.70-5.25	9.32-6.05	8.50-4.51	6.74-1.65	2.05-0.97
P/E Ratio	58.00-9.53	108.75-27.75	...	N.M.	58.25-37.81	4.09-2.17	29.30-7.17	17.08-8.07

Address: 30 Hunter Lane, Camp Hill, PA 17011
Telephone: 717-761-2633
Fax: 717-975-5905

Web Site: www.riteaid.com
Officers: John T. Standley - Chairman, President, Chief Executive Officer, Chief Operating Officer
Kermit R. Crawford - President, Chief Operating Officer

Auditors: DELOITTE & TOUCHE LLP
Investor Contact: 717-214-8867
Transfer Agents: American Stock Transfer & Trust Company, Brooklyn, NY

RLI CORP.

*7 Year Price Score 96.67   *NYSE Composite Index=100   *12 Month Price Score 97.49

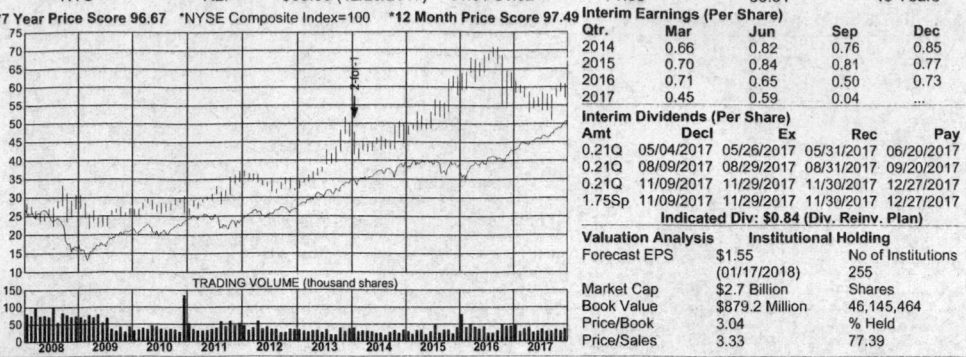

Interim Earnings (Per Share)

Qtr.	Mar	Jun	Sep	Dec
2014	0.66	0.82	0.76	0.85
2015	0.70	0.84	0.81	0.77
2016	0.71	0.65	0.50	0.73
2017	0.45	0.59	0.04	...

Interim Dividends (Per Share)

Amt	Decl	Ex	Rec	Pay
0.21Q	05/04/2017	05/26/2017	05/31/2017	06/20/2017
0.21Q	08/09/2017	08/29/2017	08/31/2017	09/20/2017
0.21Q	11/09/2017	11/29/2017	11/30/2017	12/27/2017
1.75Sp	11/09/2017	11/29/2017	11/30/2017	12/27/2017

Indicated Div: $0.84 (Div. Reinv. Plan)

Valuation Analysis — **Institutional Holding**

Forecast EPS	$1.55	No of Institutions
	(01/17/2018)	255
Market Cap	$2.7 Billion	Shares
Book Value	$879.2 Million	46,145,464
Price/Book	3.04	% Held
Price/Sales	3.33	77.39

Business Summary: General Insurance (MIC: 5.2.1 SIC: 6331 NAIC: 524126)

RLI is an insurance holding company. Through its subsidiaries, Co. is engaged in underwriting selected property and casualty insurance. Co. has three segments: casualty, which includes commerical and personal umbrella, general liability, commercial transportation, professional services, small commercial, executive products, medical professional liability, and other casualty; property, which includes commercial property, marine, specialty personal, property reinsurance, and crop reinsurance; and surety; which includes miscellaneous surety coverage, commercial surety bonds, bonds for small-to-medium sized contractors, and energy surety coverages.

Recent Developments: For the quarter ended Sep 30 2017, net income decreased 92.2% to US$1.7 million from US$22.3 million in the year-earlier quarter. Revenues were US$196.2 million, down 4.9% from US$206.4 million the year before. Net premiums earned were US$182.0 million versus US$183.6 million in the prior-year quarter, a decrease of 0.9%. Net investment income rose 5.1% to US$14.2 million from US$13.5 million a year ago.

Prospects: Our evaluation of RLI Corp. as of Jan. 14, 2018 is the result of our systematic analysis on three basic characteristics: earnings strength, relative valuation, and recent stock price movement. The company has generated a negative trend in earnings per share over the past 5 quarters and while recent estimates for the company have been mixed, RLI has posted better than expected results. Based on operating earnings yield, the company is about fairly valued when compared to all of the companies in our coverage universe. Share price changes over the past year indicates that RLI will perform poorly over the near term.

Financial Data

(US$ in Thousands)	9 Mos	6 Mos	3 Mos	12/31/2016	12/31/2015	12/31/2014	12/31/2013	12/31/2012
Earnings Per Share	1.81	2.27	2.33	2.59	3.12	3.09	2.90	2.40
Cash Flow Per Share	4.48	4.08	3.74	3.97	3.52	2.86	3.16	0.85
Tang Book Value Per Share	18.60	18.55	17.82	17.28	17.27	17.92	17.54	16.94
Dividends Per Share	2.820	2.810	2.800	2.790	2.750	3.710	2.170	3.130
Dividend Payout %	155.80	123.79	120.17	107.72	88.14	120.06	74.83	130.69
Income Statement								
Premium Income	549,641	367,616	183,285	728,608	700,161	687,375	630,802	576,571
Total Revenue	589,371	393,124	196,914	816,328	794,634	775,165	705,601	660,774
Benefits & Claims	306,927	183,737	93,390	349,778	299,045	296,609	259,801	271,645
Income Before Taxes	44,213	48,735	21,505	146,249	185,768	177,149	164,751	133,879
Income Taxes	11,847	14,443	6,615	42,162	59,138	54,042	49,411	39,386
Net Income	47,770	46,036	19,828	114,920	137,544	135,445	126,255	103,346
Average Shares	44,515	44,519	44,502	44,432	44,131	43,819	43,514	43,160
Balance Sheet								
Total Assets	2,956,520	2,881,582	2,777,518	2,777,633	2,736,579	2,775,542	2,740,310	2,644,632
Total Liabilities	2,077,364	2,003,848	1,929,643	1,954,061	1,913,110	1,930,480	1,911,344	1,848,269
Stockholders' Equity	879,156	877,734	847,875	823,572	823,469	845,062	828,966	796,363
Shares Outstanding	44,059	44,046	43,969	43,944	43,544	43,102	42,982	42,525
Statistical Record								
Return on Assets %	2.72	3.48	3.73	4.16	4.99	4.91	4.69	3.86
Return on Equity %	8.88	11.22	12.02	13.92	16.49	16.18	15.54	12.76
Loss Ratio %	55.84	49.98	50.95	48.01	42.71	43.15	41.19	47.11
Net Margin %	8.11	11.71	10.07	14.08	17.31	17.47	17.89	15.64
Price Range	68.82-51.02	71.00-53.01	71.00-54.60	71.00-54.60	63.02-46.91	50.54-40.31	51.77-32.33	37.22-31.05
P/E Ratio	38.02-28.19	31.28-23.35	30.47-23.43	27.41-21.08	20.20-15.04	16.36-13.05	17.85-11.15	15.51-12.94
Average Yield %	4.85	4.56	4.39	4.31	5.14	8.25	5.42	9.18

Address: 9025 North Lindbergh Drive, Peoria, IL 61615 Telephone: 309-692-1000 Fax: 309-692-1068	Web Site: www.rlicorp.com Officers: Jonathan E. Michael - Chairman, President, Chief Executive Officer Aaron H. Jacoby - Vice President	Auditors: KPMG LLP Investor Contact: 309-693-5880 Transfer Agents: Wells Fargo Shareholder Services, St. Paul, MN

ROBERT HALF INTERNATIONAL INC.

Exchange	Symbol	Price	52Wk Range	Yield	P/E	Div Achiever
NYS	RHI	$55.54 (12/29/2017)	57.04-43.24	1.73	21.78	12 Years

*7 Year Price Score 93.55   *NYSE Composite Index=100   *12 Month Price Score 105.80

Interim Earnings (Per Share)

Qtr.	Mar	Jun	Sep	Dec
2014	0.45	0.55	0.63	0.63
2015	0.58	0.67	0.73	0.71
2016	0.64	0.71	0.71	0.61
2017	0.62	0.64	0.68	...

Interim Dividends (Per Share)

Amt	Decl	Ex	Rec	Pay
0.24Q	02/08/2017	02/22/2017	02/24/2017	03/15/2017
0.24Q	05/03/2017	05/23/2017	05/25/2017	06/15/2017
0.24Q	08/01/2017	08/23/2017	08/25/2017	09/15/2017
0.24Q	10/31/2017	11/22/2017	11/24/2017	12/15/2017

Indicated Div: $0.96

Valuation Analysis

		Institutional Holding	
Forecast EPS	$2.57 (01/17/2018)	No of Institutions	629
Market Cap	$7.0 Billion	Shares	135,858,288
Book Value	$1.1 Billion	% Held	85.18
Price/Book	6.11		
Price/Sales	1.34		

Business Summary: Business Services (MIC: 7.5.2 SIC: 7363 NAIC: 561320)

Robert Half International provides staffing and risk consulting services. Co.'s Accountemps, Robert Half Finance & Accounting, and Robert Half Management Resources divisions provide personnel in the fields of accounting and finance. Co.'s OfficeTeam division provides temporary administrative support personnel. Co.'s Robert Half Technology division provides project and technology personnel. Co.'s Robert Half Legal division provides staffing of lawyers, paralegals and legal support personnel. The Creative Group provides interactive, design, marketing, advertising and public relations professionals. Protiviti employs personnel focusing on risk, advisory and transactional services.

Recent Developments: For the quarter ended Sep 30 2017, net income decreased 6.5% to US$84.7 million from US$90.6 million in the year-earlier quarter. Revenues were US$1.32 billion, down 1.0% from US$1.34 billion the year before. Direct operating expenses declined 1.0% to US$778.3 million from US$786.0 million in the comparable period the year before. Indirect operating expenses increased 2.0% to US$414.1 million from US$406.2 million in the equivalent prior-year period.

Prospects: Our evaluation of Robert Half International Inc. as of Jan. 14, 2018 is the result of our systematic analysis on three basic characteristics: earnings strength, relative valuation, and recent stock price movement. The company has managed to produce a neutral trend in earnings per share over the past 5 quarters. However, while recent estimates for the company have been mixed, RHI has posted results that fell short of analysts expectations. Based on operating earnings yield, the company is about fairly valued when compared to all of the companies in our coverage universe. Share price changes over the past year indicates that RHI will perform poorly over the near term.

Financial Data

(US$ in Thousands)	9 Mos	6 Mos	3 Mos	12/31/2016	12/31/2015	12/31/2014	12/31/2013	12/31/2012
Earnings Per Share	2.55	2.58	2.65	2.67	2.69	2.26	1.83	1.50
Cash Flow Per Share	3.80	3.96	3.88	3.44	3.33	2.54	2.27	2.09
Tang Book Value Per Share	7.36	7.04	6.82	6.83	6.03	5.77	5.22	4.58
Dividends Per Share	0.940	0.920	0.900	0.880	0.800	0.720	0.640	0.600
Dividend Payout %	36.86	35.66	33.96	32.96	29.74	31.86	34.97	40.00
Income Statement								
Total Revenue	3,920,507	2,595,798	1,287,370	5,250,399	5,094,933	4,695,014	4,245,895	4,111,213
EBITDA	436,433	288,141	141,478	617,537	633,945	546,306	445,349	391,772
Depn & Amortn	49,063	32,511	16,200	64,315	53,465	49,681	48,772	48,724
Income Before Taxes	388,478	256,208	125,501	554,110	581,030	497,349	397,579	344,245
Income Taxes	144,941	97,371	46,980	210,721	223,234	191,421	145,384	134,303
Net Income	243,537	158,837	78,521	343,389	357,796	305,928	252,195	209,942
Average Shares	124,200	125,104	126,418	128,766	132,930	135,541	137,589	139,409
Balance Sheet								
Current Assets	1,437,323	1,347,106	1,295,922	1,284,234	1,343,681	1,323,283	1,172,528	1,064,685
Total Assets	1,932,852	1,836,138	1,775,210	1,777,971	1,702,960	1,647,267	1,490,271	1,381,271
Current Liabilities	778,348	719,443	682,600	679,896	655,549	623,362	535,853	501,637
Long-Term Obligations	704	750	795	840	1,007	1,159	1,300	1,428
Total Liabilities	793,034	731,754	694,267	691,372	699,179	667,409	570,628	539,260
Stockholders' Equity	1,139,818	1,104,384	1,080,943	1,086,599	1,003,781	979,858	919,643	842,011
Shares Outstanding	125,346	126,184	127,179	127,796	131,156	135,134	137,466	139,438
Statistical Record								
Return on Assets %	16.89	18.08	19.23	19.68	21.36	19.50	17.57	15.55
Return on Equity %	28.76	30.10	31.84	32.76	36.07	32.21	28.63	25.49
EBITDA Margin %	11.13	11.10	10.99	11.76	12.44	11.64	10.49	9.53
Net Margin %	6.21	6.12	6.10	6.54	7.02	6.52	5.94	5.11
Asset Turnover	2.73	2.87	2.97	3.01	3.04	2.99	2.96	3.04
Current Ratio	1.85	1.87	1.90	1.89	2.05	2.12	2.19	2.12
Price Range	50.91-36.70	50.91-36.49	50.91-34.57	49.24-34.57	63.00-44.95	58.99-39.17	42.10-31.33	31.82-25.24
P/E Ratio	19.96-14.39	19.73-14.14	19.21-13.05	18.44-12.95	23.42-16.71	26.10-17.33	23.01-17.12	21.21-16.83
Average Yield %	2.04	2.09	2.12	2.15	1.45	1.52	1.76	2.12

Address: 2884 Sand Hill Road, Suite 200, Menlo Park, CA 94025 **Telephone:** 650-234-6000	**Web Site:** www.rhi.com **Officers:** Harold M. Messmer - Chairman, President, Chief Executive Officer M. Keith Waddell - Vice-Chairman, President, Chief Financial Officer, Treasurer	**Auditors:** PricewaterhouseCoopers LLP **Transfer Agents:** Computershare Trust Company, N.A., Canton, MA

ROCKWELL COLLINS INC

Exchange	Symbol	Price	52Wk Range	Yield	P/E
NYS	COL	$135.62 (12/29/2017)	136.02-89.21	0.97	28.31

*7 Year Price Score 113.09 *NYSE Composite Index=100 *12 Month Price Score 111.74

Interim Earnings (Per Share)

Qtr.	Dec	Mar	Jun	Sep
2012-13	0.94	1.17	1.20	1.28
2013-14	0.96	1.08	1.15	1.23
2014-15	1.24	1.17	1.33	1.38
2015-16	1.02	1.29	1.63	1.58
2016-17	1.10	1.27	1.12	1.31

Interim Dividends (Per Share)

Amt	Decl	Ex	Rec	Pay
0.33Q	01/31/2017	02/09/2017	02/13/2017	03/06/2017
0.33Q	04/19/2017	05/11/2017	05/15/2017	06/05/2017
0.33Q	08/01/2017	08/10/2017	08/14/2017	09/05/2017
0.33Q	10/31/2017	11/10/2017	11/13/2017	12/04/2017

Indicated Div: $1.32

Valuation Analysis

		Institutional Holding	
Forecast EPS	$7.09 (01/18/2018)	No of Institutions	954
Market Cap	$22.1 Billion	Shares	142,396,832
Book Value	$6.0 Billion	% Held	69.71
Price/Book	3.66		
Price/Sales	3.24		

Business Summary: Aerospace (MIC: 7.1.1 SIC: 3728 NAIC: 336413)

Rockwell Collins designs, produces and supports communications and aviation systems for commercial and military customers and provides information management services through voice and data communication networks and solutions worldwide. Co. also provides a range of services and support to its customers through a network of service centers, including equipment repair and overhaul, service parts, field service engineering, training, technical information services and aftermarket used equipment sales. As of Sept 30 2017, Co. served customer through its Interior Systems, Commercial Systems, Government Systems and Information Management Services operating segments.

Recent Developments: For the year ended Sep 30 2017, income from continuing operations decreased 3.0% to US$705.0 million from US$727.0 million a year earlier. Net income decreased 3.2% to US$705.0 million from US$728.0 million in the prior year. Revenues were US$6.82 billion, up 29.7% from US$5.26 billion the year before. Direct operating expenses rose 33.7% to US$4.87 billion from US$3.64 billion in the comparable period the year before. Indirect operating expenses increased 48.0% to US$1.04 billion from US$702.0 million in the equivalent prior-year period.

Prospects: Our evaluation of Rockwell Collins Inc. as of Jan. 14, 2018 is the result of our systematic analysis on three basic characteristics: earnings strength, relative valuation, and recent stock price movement. The company has enjoyed a very positive trend in earnings per share over the past 5 quarters and while recent estimates for the company have been mixed, COL has posted results that were in line with analysts expectations. Based on operating earnings yield, the company is undervalued when compared to all of the companies in our coverage universe. Share price changes over the past year indicates that COL will perform very well over the near term.

Financial Data

(US$ in Millions)	09/30/2017	09/30/2016	09/30/2015	09/30/2014	09/30/2013	09/30/2012	09/30/2011	09/30/2010
Earnings Per Share	4.79	5.51	5.13	4.42	4.58	4.15	4.06	3.52
Cash Flow Per Share	8.69	5.53	5.66	4.89	4.52	3.67	4.26	4.53
Tang Book Value Per Share	N.M.	N.M.	N.M.	N.M.	4.08	1.32	2.84	2.61
Dividends Per Share	1.320	1.320	1.260	1.200	1.200	1.080	0.960	0.960
Dividend Payout %	27.56	23.96	24.56	27.15	26.20	26.02	23.65	27.27
Income Statement								
Total Revenue	6,822	5,259	5,244	4,979	4,610	4,726	4,806	4,665
EBITDA	1,286	1,143	1,172	1,075	1,061	1,044	997	957
Depn & Amortn	168	144	152	141	180	174	141	149
Income Before Taxes	931	935	959	875	855	846	842	792
Income Taxes	226	208	268	264	236	248	240	241
Net Income	705	728	686	604	632	609	634	561
Average Shares	147	132	133	136	138	146	156	159
Balance Sheet								
Current Assets	4,760	3,490	3,233	3,204	3,094	2,787	2,889	2,689
Total Assets	17,997	7,707	7,389	7,063	5,400	5,314	5,389	5,064
Current Liabilities	3,069	2,346	2,144	2,198	1,981	1,440	1,495	1,452
Long-Term Obligations	6,676	1,382	1,680	1,663	563	779	528	525
Total Liabilities	11,954	5,629	5,514	5,179	3,782	4,055	3,866	3,582
Stockholders' Equity	6,043	2,078	1,875	1,884	1,618	1,259	1,523	1,482
Shares Outstanding	162	130	131	134	135	142	153	156
Statistical Record								
Return on Assets %	5.49	9.62	9.49	9.69	11.80	11.35	12.13	11.56
Return on Equity %	17.36	36.73	36.50	34.49	43.93	43.66	42.20	40.45
EBITDA Margin %	18.85	21.73	22.35	21.59	23.02	22.09	20.74	20.51
Net Margin %	10.33	13.84	13.08	12.13	13.71	12.89	13.19	12.03
Asset Turnover	0.53	0.69	0.73	0.80	0.86	0.88	0.92	0.96
Current Ratio	1.55	1.49	1.51	1.46	1.56	1.94	1.93	1.85
Debt to Equity	1.10	0.67	0.90	0.88	0.35	0.62	0.35	0.35
Price Range	131.35-79.21	94.44-78.30	99.00-73.48	83.47-65.90	74.69-52.59	59.96-46.92	67.20-44.89	67.84-48.15
P/E Ratio	27.42-16.54	17.14-14.21	19.30-14.32	18.88-14.91	16.31-11.48	14.45-11.31	16.55-11.06	19.27-13.68
Average Yield %	1.30	1.51	1.43	1.57	1.91	2.01	1.62	1.69

Address: 400 Collins Road N.E., Cedar Rapids, IA 52498 **Telephone:** 319-295-1000	**Web Site:** www.rockwellcollins.com **Officers:** Robert K. Ortberg - Chairman, President, Chief Executive Officer, Executive Vice President, Division Officer Patrick E. Allen - Chief Financial Officer, Senior Vice President	**Auditors:** DELOITTE & TOUCHE LLP **Investor Contact:** 319-295-7575 **Transfer Agents:** Wells Fargo Shareowner Services, St. Paul, MN

ROCKWELL AUTOMATION, INC.

Exchange	Symbol	Price	52Wk Range	Yield	P/E
NYS	ROK	$196.35 (12/29/2017)	200.83-137.74	1.70	30.92

*7 Year Price Score 120.26 *NYSE Composite Index=100 *12 Month Price Score 109.70

Interim Earnings (Per Share)

Qtr.	Dec	Mar	Jun	Sep
2012-13	1.14	1.24	1.45	1.53
2013-14	1.41	1.28	1.43	1.79
2014-15	1.56	1.51	1.52	1.49
2015-16	1.40	1.28	1.46	1.43
2016-17	1.65	1.45	1.67	1.58

Interim Dividends (Per Share)

Amt	Decl	Ex	Rec	Pay
0.76Q	02/08/2017	02/16/2017	02/21/2017	03/10/2017
0.76Q	04/05/2017	05/11/2017	05/15/2017	06/12/2017
0.76Q	06/07/2017	08/10/2017	08/14/2017	09/11/2017
0.835Q	11/01/2017	11/10/2017	11/13/2017	12/11/2017
		Indicated Div: $3.34		

Valuation Analysis **Institutional Holding**

Forecast EPS	$7.40 (01/18/2018)	No of Institutions	983
Market Cap	$25.2 Billion	Shares	117,929,088
Book Value	$2.7 Billion	% Held	71.50
Price/Book	9.47		
Price/Sales	3.99		

Business Summary: Electrical Equipment (MIC: 7.3.1 SIC: 3829 NAIC: 334519)

Rockwell Automation is a provider of industrial automation and information. As of Sept 30 2017, Co. operated two operating segments: Architecture & Software and Control Products & Solutions. Co.'s Architecture & Software segment contains all of the hardware, software and communication components of Co.'s integrated control and information architecture which are of controlling the customer's industrial processes and connecting with their business enterprise. Co.'s Control Products & Solutions segment combines a portfolio of motor control and industrial control products, application knowledge and project management capabilities.

Recent Developments: For the year ended Sep 30 2017, net income increased 13.2% to US$825.7 million from US$729.7 million in the prior year. Revenues were US$6.31 billion, up 7.3% from US$5.88 billion the year before. Direct operating expenses rose 8.3% to US$3.69 billion from US$3.40 billion in the comparable period the year before. Indirect operating expenses increased 3.5% to US$1.59 billion from US$1.53 billion in the equivalent prior-year period.

Prospects: Our evaluation of Rockwell Automation Inc. as of Jan. 14, 2018 is the result of our systematic analysis on three basic characteristics: earnings strength, relative valuation, and recent stock price movement. The company has generated a negative trend in earnings per share over the past 5 quarters and while recent estimates for the company have been mixed, ROK has posted results that fell short of analysts expectations. Based on operating earnings yield, the company is about fairly valued when compared to all of the companies in our coverage universe. Share price changes over the past year indicates that ROK will perform well over the near term.

Financial Data
(US$ in Thousands)

	09/30/2017	09/30/2016	09/30/2015	09/30/2014	09/30/2013	09/30/2012	09/30/2011	09/30/2010
Earnings Per Share	6.35	5.56	6.09	5.91	5.36	5.13	4.80	3.22
Cash Flow Per Share	8.05	7.26	8.83	7.49	7.29	5.07	4.51	3.48
Tang Book Value Per Share	10.50	5.14	7.54	9.96	9.72	4.96	4.07	2.33
Dividends Per Share	3.040	2.900	2.600	2.320	1.980	1.745	1.475	1.220
Dividend Payout %	47.87	52.16	42.69	39.26	36.94	34.02	30.73	37.89
Income Statement								
Total Revenue	6,311,300	5,879,500	6,307,900	6,623,500	6,351,900	6,259,400	6,000,400	4,857,000
EBITDA	1,262,900	1,173,900	1,343,000	1,336,500	1,177,200	1,156,800	1,052,400	727,000
Depn & Amortn	168,900	172,200	162,500	152,500	145,200	138,600	131,300	127,300
Income Before Taxes	1,037,400	943,100	1,127,500	1,134,200	980,900	965,900	867,600	544,200
Income Taxes	211,700	213,400	299,900	307,400	224,600	228,900	170,500	103,800
Net Income	825,700	729,700	827,600	826,800	756,300	737,000	697,800	464,300
Average Shares	129,900	131,100	135,700	139,700	140,900	143,400	145,200	144,000
Balance Sheet								
Current Assets	4,420,700	4,185,000	4,048,000	3,934,200	3,679,900	3,387,500	3,075,100	2,586,600
Total Assets	7,161,700	7,101,200	6,404,700	6,229,500	5,844,600	5,636,500	5,284,900	4,748,300
Current Liabilities	2,145,800	1,975,900	1,327,700	1,692,100	1,544,700	1,531,600	1,329,900	1,222,300
Long-Term Obligations	1,243,400	1,516,300	1,500,900	905,600	905,100	905,000	905,000	904,900
Total Liabilities	4,498,100	5,111,100	4,147,900	3,571,400	3,259,100	3,784,800	3,536,900	3,287,900
Stockholders' Equity	2,663,600	1,990,100	2,256,800	2,658,100	2,585,500	1,851,700	1,748,000	1,460,400
Shares Outstanding	128,400	128,500	132,400	136,700	138,900	139,800	141,900	141,700
Statistical Record								
Return on Assets %	11.58	10.78	13.10	13.70	13.17	13.46	13.91	10.26
Return on Equity %	35.49	34.27	33.68	31.54	34.09	40.84	43.50	33.44
EBITDA Margin %	20.01	19.97	21.29	20.18	18.53	18.48	17.54	14.97
Net Margin %	13.08	12.41	13.12	12.48	11.91	11.77	11.63	9.56
Asset Turnover	0.88	0.87	1.00	1.10	1.11	1.14	1.20	1.07
Current Ratio	2.06	2.12	3.05	2.33	2.38	2.21	2.31	2.12
Debt to Equity	0.47	0.76	0.67	0.34	0.35	0.49	0.52	0.62
Price Range	178.21-115.20	122.34-89.71	126.89-98.60	127.83-104.39	109.13-68.73	84.55-54.55	97.84-51.54	62.83-40.28
P/E Ratio	28.06-18.14	22.00-16.13	20.84-16.19	21.63-17.66	20.36-12.82	16.48-10.63	20.38-10.74	19.51-12.51
Average Yield %	2.02	2.65	2.28	1.97	2.27	2.39	1.95	2.36

Address: 1201 South Second Street, Milwaukee, WI 53204 Telephone: 414-382-2000	Web Site: www.rockwellautomation.com Officers: Keith D. Nosbusch - Chairman, President, Chief Executive Officer Blake D. Moret - President, Chief Executive Officer, Senior Vice President	Auditors: DELOITTE & TOUCHE LLP Investor Contact: 414-382-8510 Transfer Agents: Wells Fargo Shareowner Services, St. Paul, MN

ROLLINS, INC.

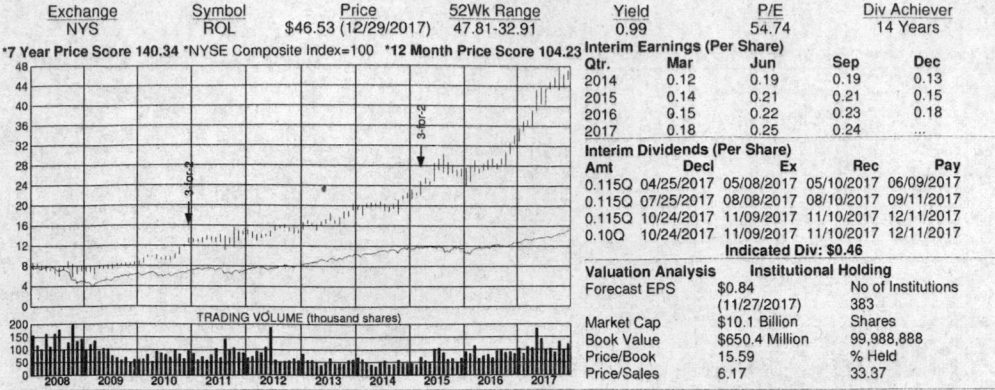

Exchange	Symbol	Price	52Wk Range	Yield	P/E	Div Achiever
NYS	ROL	$46.53 (12/29/2017)	47.81-32.91	0.99	54.74	14 Years

*7 Year Price Score 140.34 *NYSE Composite Index=100 *12 Month Price Score 104.23

Interim Earnings (Per Share)

Qtr.	Mar	Jun	Sep	Dec
2014	0.12	0.19	0.19	0.13
2015	0.14	0.21	0.21	0.15
2016	0.15	0.22	0.23	0.18
2017	0.18	0.25	0.24	...

Interim Dividends (Per Share)

Amt	Decl	Ex	Rec	Pay
0.115Q	04/25/2017	05/08/2017	05/10/2017	06/09/2017
0.115Q	07/25/2017	08/08/2017	08/10/2017	09/11/2017
0.115Q	10/24/2017	11/09/2017	11/10/2017	12/11/2017
0.10Q	10/24/2017	11/09/2017	11/10/2017	12/11/2017

Indicated Div: $0.46

Valuation Analysis / **Institutional Holding**

Forecast EPS	$0.84	No of Institutions
	(11/27/2017)	383
Market Cap	$10.1 Billion	Shares
Book Value	$650.4 Million	99,988,888
Price/Book	15.59	% Held
Price/Sales	6.17	33.37

Business Summary: Business Services (MIC: 7.5.2 SIC: 7342 NAIC: 561710)

Rollins provides pest and termite control services via its subsidiaries in North America, Australia, and Europe with international franchises in Central America, the Caribbean, the Middle East, Asia, the Mediterranean, Europe, Africa, Canada, Australia, and Mexico. Co.'s subsidiary, Orkin, LLC, provides pest control services and protection against termite damage, rodents and insects to homes and businesses. Co.'s other subsidiaries include Orkin Canada, a pest control provider in Canada; Western Pest Services, which is primarily a commercial pest control service company; and The Industrial Fumigant Company, which is a provider of pest management and sanitation services and products.

Recent Developments: For the quarter ended Sep 30 2017, net income increased 3.6% to US$51.4 million from US$49.7 million in the year-earlier quarter. Revenues were US$450.4 million, up 6.2% from US$424.0 million the year before. Direct operating expenses rose 6.4% to US$218.8 million from US$205.6 million in the comparable period the year before. Indirect operating expenses increased 7.7% to US$149.1 million from US$138.4 million in the equivalent prior-year period.

Prospects: Our evaluation of Rollins Inc. as of Jan. 14, 2018 is the result of our systematic analysis on three basic characteristics: earnings strength, relative valuation, and recent stock price movement. The company has produced a positive trend in earnings per share over the past 5 quarters and while recent estimates for the company have remained steady, ROL has posted results that fell short of analysts expectations. Based on operating earnings yield, the company is overvalued when compared to all of the companies in our coverage universe. Share price changes over the past year indicates that ROL will perform very well over the near term.

Financial Data

(US$ in Thousands)	9 Mos	6 Mos	3 Mos	12/31/2016	12/31/2015	12/31/2014	12/31/2013	12/31/2012
Earnings Per Share	0.85	0.84	0.81	0.77	0.70	0.63	0.56	0.51
Cash Flow Per Share	1.18	1.15	1.12	1.04	0.90	0.89	0.74	0.64
Tang Book Value Per Share	0.41	0.93	0.77	0.69	0.62	0.34	0.45	0.00
Dividends Per Share	0.545	0.530	0.515	0.500	0.420	0.347	0.300	0.293
Dividend Payout %	64.12	63.10	63.58	64.94	60.00	55.32	53.57	57.89
Income Statement								
Total Revenue	1,259,244	808,802	375,247	1,573,477	1,485,305	1,411,566	1,337,374	1,270,909
EBITDA	267,246	170,451	70,956	285,176	262,418	235,857	205,636	191,868
Depn & Amortn	41,630	27,317	13,771	24,700	19,400	16,627	14,415	15,212
Income Before Taxes	225,958	143,397	57,258	260,636	243,178	219,484	191,606	176,642
Income Taxes	80,569	49,438	16,988	93,267	91,029	81,820	68,276	65,310
Net Income	145,389	93,959	40,270	167,369	152,149	137,664	123,330	111,332
Average Shares	217,988	218,002	217,971	218,244	218,583	218,694	219,121	219,459
Balance Sheet								
Current Assets	282,926	361,626	305,755	290,171	313,879	283,958	274,442	205,992
Total Assets	1,046,527	980,526	924,865	916,538	852,431	808,162	739,217	692,506
Current Liabilities	308,786	287,097	267,515	276,991	252,986	252,679	235,792	228,416
Total Liabilities	396,088	363,064	341,314	347,993	328,402	345,486	300,962	337,550
Stockholders' Equity	650,439	617,462	583,551	568,545	524,029	462,676	438,255	354,956
Shares Outstanding	217,975	217,991	218,008	217,791	218,753	218,482	218,796	219,022
Statistical Record								
Return on Assets %	18.64	19.26	19.55	18.87	18.32	17.79	17.23	16.59
Return on Equity %	29.95	30.89	31.23	30.55	30.84	30.56	31.10	32.71
EBITDA Margin %	21.22	21.07	18.91	18.12	17.67	16.71	15.38	15.10
Net Margin %	11.55	11.62	10.73	10.64	10.24	9.75	9.22	8.76
Asset Turnover	1.67	1.72	1.78	1.77	1.79	1.82	1.87	1.89
Current Ratio	0.92	1.26	1.14	1.05	1.24	1.12	1.16	0.90
Price Range	46.14-28.12	43.66-27.39	37.13-26.54	34.09-24.08	30.35-21.27	22.53-18.10	20.26-14.69	16.19-12.97
P/E Ratio	54.28-33.08	51.98-32.61	45.84-32.77	44.27-31.27	43.36-30.39	35.76-28.73	36.18-26.24	31.75-25.44
Average Yield %	1.45	1.56	1.68	1.75	1.62	1.72	1.75	1.99

Address: 2170 Piedmont Road, N.E., Atlanta, GA 30324 **Telephone:** 404-888-2000	**Web Site:** www.rollins.com **Officers:** R. Randall Rollins - Chairman Gary W. Rollins - Vice-Chairman, President, Chief Executive Officer, Chief Operating Officer	**Auditors:** GRANT THORNTON LLP **Investor Contact:** 404-888-2000 **Transfer Agents:** American Stock Transfer and Trust, Brooklyn, NY

ROPER TECHNOLOGIES INC

Exchange	Symbol	Price	52Wk Range	Yield	P/E	Div Acheiver
NYS	ROP	$259.00 (12/29/2017)	267.21-184.93	0.64	37.59	24 Years

*7 Year Price Score 121.83 *NYSE Composite Index=100 *12 Month Price Score 107.03

Interim Earnings (Per Share)

Qtr.	Mar	Jun	Sep	Dec
2014	1.46	1.56	1.54	1.84
2015	1.54	1.69	1.58	2.05
2016	1.48	1.54	1.63	1.78
2017	1.53	1.74	1.84	...

Interim Dividends (Per Share)

Amt	Decl	Ex	Rec	Pay
0.35Q	03/14/2017	04/05/2017	04/07/2017	04/21/2017
0.35Q	06/12/2017	07/05/2017	07/07/2017	07/21/2017
0.35Q	09/25/2017	10/05/2017	10/06/2017	10/20/2017
0.412Q	12/18/2017	01/08/2018	01/09/2018	01/23/2018

Indicated Div: $1.65

Valuation Analysis		Institutional Holding	
Forecast EPS	$9.32 (01/20/2018)	No of Institutions	830
Market Cap	$26.5 Billion	Shares	118,006,056
Book Value	$6.5 Billion	% Held	93.85
Price/Book	4.10		
Price/Sales	6.04		

Business Summary: Electrical Equipment (MIC: 7.3.1 SIC: 3823 NAIC: 334513)

Roper Technologies designs and develops software (both license and software-as-a-service) and engineered products and solutions. Co. has four segments: Medical and Scientific Imaging, which provides products and software in medical applications, and digital imaging products; Radio Frequency Technology, which provides radio frequency identification communication technology and software solutions; Industrial Technology, which produces fluid handling pumps, materials analysis equipment and consumables, and leak testing equipment, among others; and Energy Systems and Controls, which produces control systems, fluid properties testing equipment, and industrial valves and controls, among others.

Recent Developments: For the quarter ended Sep 30 2017, net income increased 13.9% to US$190.3 million from US$167.1 million in the year-earlier quarter. Revenues were US$1.16 billion, up 22.7% from US$945.1 million the year before. Operating income was US$310.7 million versus US$267.4 million in the prior-year quarter, an increase of 16.2%. Direct operating expenses rose 18.2% to US$433.5 million from US$366.7 million in the comparable period the year before. Indirect operating expenses increased 33.6% to US$415.7 million from US$311.1 million in the equivalent prior-year period.

Prospects: Our evaluation of Roper Technologies Inc. as of Jan. 21, 2018 is the result of our systematic analysis on three basic characteristics: earnings strength, relative valuation, and recent stock price movement. The company has produced a positive trend in earnings per share over the past 5 quarters and while recent estimates for the company have been mixed, ROP has posted better than expected results. Based on operating earnings yield, the company is about fairly valued when compared to all of the companies in our coverage universe. Share price changes over the past year indicates that ROP will perform well over the near term.

Financial Data

(US$ in Thousands)	9 Mos	6 Mos	3 Mos	12/31/2016	12/31/2015	12/31/2014	12/31/2013	12/31/2012
Earnings Per Share	6.89	6.68	6.48	6.43	6.85	6.40	5.37	4.86
Cash Flow Per Share	11.11	11.14	11.14	9.49	9.23	8.41	8.10	6.92
Dividends Per Share	1.350	1.300	1.250	1.200	1.000	0.800	0.495	0.715
Dividend Payout %	19.59	19.46	19.29	18.66	14.60	12.50	9.22	14.71
Income Statement								
Total Revenue	3,380,888	2,220,976	1,086,305	3,789,925	3,582,395	3,549,494	3,238,128	2,993,489
EBITDA	1,095,505	709,264	332,028	1,292,664	1,290,831	1,197,377	1,031,359	908,954
Depn & Amortn	226,981	150,828	74,819	240,453	204,261	197,284	189,190	154,748
Income Before Taxes	731,323	466,758	211,344	940,652	1,002,345	921,456	754,130	686,681
Income Taxes	203,423	129,131	53,273	282,007	306,278	275,423	215,837	203,321
Net Income	527,900	337,627	158,071	658,645	696,067	646,033	538,293	483,360
Average Shares	103,680	103,409	103,078	102,464	101,597	100,884	100,209	99,558
Balance Sheet								
Current Assets	1,692,056	1,701,111	1,712,623	1,776,501	1,618,047	1,512,105	1,373,337	1,245,542
Total Assets	14,246,673	14,213,288	14,230,054	14,324,927	10,168,365	8,412,934	8,184,981	7,071,104
Current Liabilities	1,576,728	1,498,496	1,538,538	1,445,272	720,128	627,947	643,091	1,086,210
Long-Term Obligations	4,932,721	5,241,103	5,439,700	5,808,561	3,264,417	2,203,031	2,453,836	1,503,107
Total Liabilities	7,787,689	8,012,802	8,259,264	8,536,062	4,869,418	3,657,574	3,971,931	3,383,378
Stockholders' Equity	6,458,984	6,200,486	5,970,790	5,788,865	5,298,947	4,755,360	4,213,050	3,687,726
Shares Outstanding	102,362	102,219	102,031	101,672	100,870	100,126	99,312	98,604
Statistical Record								
Return on Assets %	5.74	5.60	5.44	5.36	7.49	7.78	7.06	7.78
Return on Equity %	11.67	11.69	11.66	11.85	13.85	14.41	13.63	14.01
EBITDA Margin %	32.40	31.93	30.56	34.11	36.03	33.73	31.85	30.36
Net Margin %	15.61	15.20	14.55	17.38	19.43	18.20	16.62	16.15
Asset Turnover	0.36	0.34	0.32	0.31	0.39	0.43	0.42	0.48
Current Ratio	1.07	1.14	1.11	1.23	2.25	2.41	2.14	1.15
Debt to Equity	0.76	0.85	0.91	1.00	0.62	0.46	0.58	0.41
Price Range	246.56-167.91	235.25-163.33	213.93-163.33	189.79-158.89	194.83-145.75	160.48-128.99	138.68-111.48	113.14-88.02
P/E Ratio	35.79-24.37	35.22-24.45	33.01-25.21	29.52-24.71	28.44-21.28	25.07-20.15	25.82-20.76	23.28-18.11
Average Yield %	0.65	0.67	0.69	0.68	0.58	0.56	0.39	0.70

Address: 6901 Professional Parkway East, Suite 200, Sarasota, FL 34240 **Telephone:** 941-556-2601	**Web Site:** www.roperind.com **Officers:** Brian D. Jellison - Chairman, President, Chief Executive Officer Laurence Neil Hunn - Executive Vice President	**Auditors:** PricewaterhouseCoopers LLP **Investor Contact:** 941-556-2601 **Transfer Agents:** American Stock Transfer & Trust Company, New York, NY

ROWAN COMPANIES PLC

Exchange	Symbol	Price	52Wk Range	Yield	P/E
NYS	RDC	$15.66 (12/29/2017)	20.19-9.04	N/A	N/A

*7 Year Price Score 41.79 *NYSE Composite Index=100 *12 Month Price Score 97.74

Interim Earnings (Per Share)

Qtr.	Mar	Jun	Sep	Dec
2014	0.48	0.26	0.96	(2.63)
2015	0.93	0.68	(1.92)	1.00
2016	0.98	1.72	0.04	(0.18)
2017	0.07	(0.23)	(0.17)	...

Interim Dividends (Per Share)

Dividend Payment Suspended

Valuation Analysis   Institutional Holding

Forecast EPS	N/A	No of Institutions
		403
Market Cap	$2.0 Billion	Shares
Book Value	$5.3 Billion	161,357,664
Price/Book	0.37	% Held
Price/Sales	1.48	N/A

Business Summary: Equipment & Services (MIC: 9.1.3 SIC: 1381 NAIC: 213111)

Rowan Companies is a provider of offshore contract drilling services to the international oil and gas industry. As of Dec 31 2016, Co.'s fleet consisted of 29 mobile offshore drilling units, including 25 self-elevating jack-up rigs and four ultra-deepwater drillships. Co.'s fleet operates worldwide, including the U.S. Gulf of Mexico, the U.K. and Norwegian sectors of the North Sea, the Middle East and Trinidad. Co.'s ultra-deepwater drillships are self-propelled vessels equipped with computer-controlled dynamic-positioning systems, which allow them to maintain position without anchors through the use of their onboard propulsion and station-keeping systems.

Recent Developments: For the quarter ended Sep 30 2017, net loss amounted to US$20.9 million versus net income of US$5.5 million in the year-earlier quarter. Revenues were US$291.6 million, down 23.1% from US$379.4 million the year before. Operating loss was US$7.0 million versus an income of US$33.6 million in the prior-year quarter. Direct operating expenses declined 10.0% to US$167.4 million from US$186.0 million in the comparable period the year before. Indirect operating expenses decreased 17.9% to US$131.2 million from US$159.8 million in the equivalent prior-year period.

Prospects: Our evaluation of Rowan Cos. Plc as of Sep. 17, 2017 is the result of our systematic analysis on three basic characteristics: earnings strength, relative valuation, and recent stock price movement. The company has managed to produce a neutral trend in earnings per share over the past 5 quarters. Because the company lacks sufficient analyst estimate data, we place greater weight on the historical EPS trend as the measure of earnings strength. Based on operating earnings yield, the company is overvalued when compared to all of the companies in our coverage universe. Share price changes over the past year indicates that RDC will perform very poorly over the near term.

Financial Data
(US$ in Thousands)

	9 Mos	6 Mos	3 Mos	12/31/2016	12/31/2015	12/31/2014	12/31/2013	12/31/2012
Earnings Per Share	(0.51)	(0.30)	1.65	2.55	0.75	(0.93)	2.03	1.46
Cash Flow Per Share	3.59	5.15	6.54	7.17	8.01	3.41	5.05	3.19
Tang Book Value Per Share	41.95	42.08	42.28	40.75	38.24	37.65	39.39	36.48
Income Statement								
Total Revenue	986,100	694,500	374,300	1,843,200	2,137,018	1,824,383	1,579,284	1,392,607
EBITDA	402,100	306,600	176,700	880,200	694,633	155,107	600,463	481,342
Depn & Amortn	304,000	200,600	99,100	402,900	392,735	322,641	271,008	247,900
Income Before Taxes	(10,000)	32,700	40,000	325,600	157,710	(269,607)	261,239	183,470
Income Taxes	29,300	51,100	29,700	5,000	64,399	(150,732)	8,663	(19,829)
Net Income	(39,300)	(18,400)	10,300	320,600	93,311	(114,852)	252,576	180,602
Average Shares	126,200	126,300	127,400	126,300	125,203	124,067	124,468	123,872
Balance Sheet								
Current Assets	1,488,600	1,484,800	1,514,900	1,580,300	921,275	941,096	1,528,878	1,552,550
Total Assets	8,373,200	8,456,100	8,553,300	8,675,600	8,347,267	8,411,192	7,975,761	7,699,487
Current Liabilities	256,600	297,200	339,600	483,800	328,671	333,221	354,584	294,094
Long-Term Obligations	2,510,200	2,516,600	2,552,500	2,553,400	2,692,419	2,807,324	2,008,700	2,009,598
Total Liabilities	3,078,500	3,146,000	3,221,500	3,561,700	3,574,808	3,719,793	3,082,000	3,167,763
Stockholders' Equity	5,294,700	5,310,100	5,331,800	5,113,900	4,772,459	4,691,399	4,893,761	4,531,724
Shares Outstanding	126,200	126,200	126,100	125,500	124,817	124,593	124,235	124,211
Statistical Record								
Return on Assets %	N.M.	N.M.	2.46	3.76	1.11	N.M.	3.22	2.52
Return on Equity %	N.M.	N.M.	4.07	6.47	1.97	N.M.	5.36	4.07
EBITDA Margin %	40.78	44.15	47.21	47.75	32.50	8.50	38.02	34.56
Net Margin %	N.M.	N.M.	2.75	17.39	4.37	N.M.	15.99	12.97
Asset Turnover	0.16	0.17	0.20	0.22	0.26	0.22	0.20	0.19
Current Ratio	5.80	5.00	4.46	3.27	2.80	2.82	4.31	5.28
Debt to Equity	0.47	0.47	0.48	0.50	0.56	0.60	0.41	0.44
Price Range	20.90-9.04	20.90-10.24	20.90-12.46	20.90-11.23	24.88-15.15	35.36-19.81	38.30-30.50	38.78-28.99
P/E Ratio	...	12.67-7.55	8.20-4.40	33.17-20.20	...	18.87-15.02	26.56-19.86	

Address: 2800 Post Oak Boulevard, Suite 5450, Houston, TX 77056-6189	**Web Site:** www.rowancompanies.com	**Auditors:** Deloitte & Touche LLP
Telephone: 713-621-7800	**Officers:** Thomas Peter Burke - President, Chief Executive Officer, Chief Operating Officer Stephen M. Butz - Executive Vice President, Chief Financial Officer, Treasurer	**Investor Contact:** 713-960-7517
Fax: 713-960-7660		**Transfer Agents:** Computershare Trust Company, N.A., Providence

ROYAL CARIBBEAN CRUISES LTD

Exchange	Symbol	Price	52Wk Range	Yield	P/E
NYS	RCL	$119.28 (12/29/2017)	129.23-83.87	2.01	16.12

*7 Year Price Score 140.31 *NYSE Composite Index=100 *12 Month Price Score 105.87

TRADING VOLUME (thousand shares)

Interim Earnings (Per Share)

Qtr.	Mar	Jun	Sep	Dec
2014	0.12	0.62	2.19	0.50
2015	0.20	0.84	1.03	0.94
2016	0.46	1.06	3.21	1.21
2017	0.99	1.71	3.49	...

Interim Dividends (Per Share)

Amt	Decl	Ex	Rec	Pay
0.48Q	02/07/2017	03/03/2017	03/07/2017	04/05/2017
0.48Q	05/03/2017	05/31/2017	06/02/2017	07/05/2017
0.60Q	09/06/2017	09/21/2017	09/22/2017	10/11/2017
0.60Q	12/05/2017	12/20/2017	12/21/2017	01/05/2018

Indicated Div: $2.40

Valuation Analysis

		Institutional Holding	
Forecast EPS	N/A	No of Institutions	763
Market Cap	$25.5 Billion	Shares	177,175,360
Book Value	$10.4 Billion	% Held	50.11
Price/Book	2.45		
Price/Sales	2.94		

Business Summary: Hotels, Restaurants & Travel (MIC: 2.2.1 SIC: 4489 NAIC: 487210)

Royal Caribbean Cruises is a cruise company. Co. owns and operates three cruise brands: Royal Caribbean International, Celebrity Cruises, and Azamara Club Cruises. Co. also owns a 50.0% joint venture interest in the German brand TUI Cruises, a 49.0% interest in the Spanish brand Pullmantur and a minority interest in the Chinese brand SkySea Cruises. Together, these brands operated a combined 49 ships in the cruise vacation industry as of Dec 31 2016, operating on a selection of worldwide itineraries that call on approximately 535 destinations on all seven continents. Co.'s cruise brands provide a range of onboard services, amenities and activities.

Recent Developments: For the quarter ended Sep 30 2017, net income increased 8.6% to US$752.8 million from US$693.3 million in the year-earlier quarter. Revenues were US$2.57 billion, up 0.2% from US$2.56 billion the year before. Operating income was US$737.5 million versus US$735.0 million in the prior-year quarter, an increase of 0.3%. Direct operating expenses declined 1.6% to US$1.32 billion from US$1.34 billion in the comparable period the year before. Indirect operating expenses increased 5.1% to US$513.8 million from US$488.7 million in the equivalent prior-year period.

Prospects: Our evaluation of Royal Caribbean Cruises Ltd. as of Aug. 2, 2015 is the result of our systematic analysis on three basic characteristics: earnings strength, relative valuation, and recent stock price movement. The company has generated a negative trend in earnings per share over the past 5 quarters and while recent estimates for the company have been mixed, RCL has posted better than expected results. Based on operating earnings yield, the company is about fairly valued when compared to all of the companies in our coverage universe. Share price changes over the past year indicates that RCL will perform very poorly over the near term.

Financial Data

(US$ in Thousands)	9 Mos	6 Mos	3 Mos	12/31/2016	12/31/2015	12/31/2014	12/31/2013	12/31/2012
Earnings Per Share	7.40	7.12	6.47	5.93	3.02	3.43	2.14	0.08
Cash Flow Per Share	13.84	13.51	13.20	11.65	8.87	7.87	6.43	6.32
Tang Book Value Per Share	47.40	43.68	41.75	41.16	35.67	35.86	37.96	36.00
Dividends Per Share	2.040	1.920	1.815	1.710	1.350	1.100	0.740	0.440
Dividend Payout %	27.57	26.97	28.05	28.84	44.70	32.07	34.58	550.00
Income Statement								
Total Revenue	6,773,378	4,203,834	2,008,560	8,496,401	8,299,074	8,073,855	7,959,894	7,688,024
EBITDA	1,467,723	719,934	290,167	2,517,612	1,758,491	1,784,546	1,546,927	1,083,234
Depn & Amortn	37,562	26,035	13,256	947,710	827,008	772,445	754,711	730,493
Income Before Taxes	1,216,735	549,013	202,846	1,283,388	665,783	764,146	473,692	18,287
Net Income	1,337,094	584,252	214,726	1,283,388	665,783	764,146	473,692	18,287
Average Shares	215,824	216,062	215,813	216,316	220,689	223,044	220,941	219,457
Balance Sheet								
Current Assets	798,152	767,641	756,689	748,305	837,022	801,083	956,374	888,060
Total Assets	22,099,314	22,024,168	22,017,257	22,310,324	20,921,855	20,713,190	20,072,947	19,827,930
Current Liabilities	5,057,112	5,285,953	5,271,742	4,441,601	4,292,827	3,849,247	4,267,010	4,066,151
Long-Term Obligations	6,076,499	6,478,806	6,841,403	8,101,701	7,767,378	7,644,318	6,511,426	6,970,464
Total Liabilities	11,663,826	12,340,760	12,750,427	13,188,912	12,858,816	12,428,831	11,264,682	11,519,181
Stockholders' Equity	10,435,488	9,683,408	9,266,830	9,121,412	8,063,039	8,284,359	8,808,265	8,308,749
Shares Outstanding	214,074	215,096	215,060	214,594	217,993	219,297	220,473	218,771
Statistical Record								
Return on Assets %	7.17	6.92	6.51	5.92	3.20	3.75	2.37	0.09
Return on Equity %	16.63	17.26	16.31	14.90	8.15	8.94	5.53	0.22
EBITDA Margin %	21.67	17.13	14.45	29.63	21.19	22.10	19.43	14.09
Net Margin %	19.74	13.90	10.69	15.11	8.02	9.46	5.95	0.24
Asset Turnover	0.39	0.39	0.40	0.39	0.40	0.40	0.40	0.39
Current Ratio	0.16	0.15	0.14	0.17	0.19	0.21	0.22	0.22
Debt to Equity	0.58	0.67	0.74	0.89	0.96	0.92	0.74	0.84
Price Range	124.46-68.05	113.91-65.48	100.32-65.48	101.21-65.48	102.73-66.69	83.56-46.06	47.44-31.82	35.53-22.46
P/E Ratio	16.82-9.20	16.00-9.20	15.51-10.12	17.07-11.04	34.02-22.08	24.36-13.43	22.17-14.87	444.13-280.75
Average Yield %	2.12	2.14	2.19	2.25	1.59	1.86	1.98	1.54

Address: 1050 Caribbean Way, Miami, FL 33132
Telephone: 305-539-6000

Web Site: www.royalcaribbean.com
Officers: Richard D. Fain - Chairman, Chief Executive Officer Adam M. Goldstein - President, Chief Operating Officer, Division Officer

Auditors: PricewaterhouseCoopers LLP
Investor Contact: 305-982-2625
Transfer Agents: American Stock Transfer and Trust Company, Brooklyn, NY

RPC, INC.

Exchange	Symbol	Price	52Wk Range	Yield	P/E
NYS	RES	$25.53 (12/29/2017)	26.73-16.83	1.10	67.18

*7 Year Price Score 105.57 *NYSE Composite Index=100 *12 Month Price Score 111.26

Interim Earnings (Per Share)

Qtr.	Mar	Jun	Sep	Dec
2014	0.18	0.29	0.30	0.37
2015	0.04	(0.16)	(0.16)	(0.18)
2016	(0.15)	(0.23)	(0.18)	(0.10)
2017	0.02	0.20	0.26	

Interim Dividends (Per Share)

Amt	Decl	Ex	Rec	Pay
0.05Q	10/26/2016	11/08/2016	11/10/2016	12/09/2016
0.06Q	07/26/2017	08/08/2017	08/10/2017	09/11/2017
0.07Q	10/25/2017	11/09/2017	11/10/2017	12/11/2017
0.07Q	10/25/2017	11/09/2017	11/10/2017	12/11/2017

Indicated Div: $0.28

Valuation Analysis		Institutional Holding	
Forecast EPS	$0.81	No of Institutions	
	(01/17/2018)	325	
Market Cap	$5.5 Billion	Shares	
Book Value	$881.9 Million	90,495,704	
Price/Book	6.27	% Held	
Price/Sales	3.98	21.80	

Business Summary: Equipment & Services (MIC: 9.1.3 SIC: 1389 NAIC: 213112)

RPC is a holding company for several oilfield services companies. Co. provides oilfield services and equipment to oil and gas companies engaged in the exploration, production and development of oil and gas properties throughout the U.S., including the southwest, mid-continent, Gulf of Mexico, Rocky Mountain and Appalachian regions, and in selected international markets. The services and equipment provided include: Technical Services, such as pressure pumping services, coiled tubing services, snubbing services, nitrogen services, and firefighting and well control; and Support Services, such as the rental of drill pipe and other oilfield equipment and oilfield training and consulting.

Recent Developments: For the quarter ended Sep 30 2017, net income amounted to US$57.3 million versus a net loss of US$38.9 million in the year-earlier quarter. Revenues were US$471.0 million, up 167.8% from US$175.9 million the year before. Operating income was US$97.4 million versus a loss of US$56.4 million in the prior-year quarter. Direct operating expenses rose 101.1% to US$294.8 million from US$146.6 million in the comparable period the year before. Indirect operating expenses decreased 8.0% to US$78.8 million from US$85.7 million in the equivalent prior-year period.

Prospects: Our evaluation of RPC Inc. as of Jan. 14, 2018 is the result of our systematic analysis on three basic characteristics: earnings strength, relative valuation, and recent stock price movement. The company has enjoyed a very positive trend in earnings per share over the past 5 quarters and while recent estimates for the company have been mixed, RES has posted results that fell short of analysts expectations. Based on operating earnings yield, the company is about fairly valued when compared to all of the companies in our coverage universe. Share price changes over the past year indicates that RES will perform well over the near term.

Financial Data

(US$ in Thousands)	9 Mos	6 Mos	3 Mos	12/31/2016	12/31/2015	12/31/2014	12/31/2013	12/31/2012
Earnings Per Share	0.38	(0.06)	(0.49)	(0.66)	(0.47)	1.14	0.77	1.27
Cash Flow Per Share	0.54	0.18	0.17	0.47	2.22	1.50	1.70	2.59
Tang Book Value Per Share	3.92	3.76	3.56	3.56	4.24	4.83	4.28	3.98
Dividends Per Share	0.110	0.050	0.050	0.050	0.155	0.420	0.400	0.520
Dividend Payout %	28.95	...	...	...	...	36.84	51.95	40.94
Income Statement								
Total Revenue	1,167,928	696.929	298,119	728,974	1,263,840	2,337,413	1,861,489	1,945,023
EBITDA	296,398	158,177	47,198	(18,546)	123,308	634,198	493,073	659,465
Depn & Amortn	127,679	87,379	45,412	220,600	274,400	233,400	215,400	214,900
Income Before Taxes	169,425	71,121	1,812	(239,360)	(153,041)	399,386	276,270	442,619
Income Taxes	64,617	23,647	(1,822)	(98,114)	(53,480)	154,193	109,375	168,183
Net Income	104,808	47,474	3,634	(141,246)	(99,561)	245,193	166,895	274.436
Average Shares	214,129	214,594	214,671	214,227	213,632	215,889	216,733	216,796
Balance Sheet								
Current Assets	642,440	601,678	524,653	479,057	492,208	851,628	604,925	567,827
Total Assets	1,148,626	1,105,885	1,049,054	1,035,452	1,237,094	1,759,358	1,383,860	1,367,163
Current Liabilities	164,363	148,344	124,770	101,468	107,464	239,012	168,052	164,511
Long-Term Obligations	...	...	...	...	...	224,500	53,300	107,000
Total Liabilities	266,773	257,574	241,446	228,653	284,813	680,976	415,158	467,931
Stockholders' Equity	881,853	848,311	807,608	806,799	952,281	1,078,382	968,702	899,232
Shares Outstanding	216,585	217,352	217,780	217,489	216,991	216,539	218,985	220,144
Statistical Record								
Return on Assets %	7.60	N.M.	N.M.	N.M.	N.M.	15.60	12.13	20.23
Return on Equity %	9.73	N.M.	N.M.	N.M.	N.M.	23.96	17.87	32.94
EBITDA Margin %	25.38	22.70	15.83	N.M.	9.76	27.13	26.49	33.91
Net Margin %	8.97	6.81	1.22	N.M.	N.M.	10.49	8.97	14.11
Asset Turnover	1.26	1.00	0.76	0.64	0.84	1.49	1.35	1.43
Current Ratio	3.91	4.06	4.20	4.72	4.58	3.56	3.60	3.45
Debt to Equity	...	...	...	...	...	0.21	0.06	0.12
Price Range	24.79-16.71	22.42-13.73	22.42-13.30	21.63-10.35	16.27-8.54	24.91-11.86	18.56-12.24	14.45-8.96
P/E Ratio	65.24-43.97	...	...	...	...	21.85-10.40	24.10-15.90	11.38-7.06
Average Yield %	0.56	0.27	0.29	0.33	1.22	2.15	2.62	4.36

Address: 2801 Buford Highway, Suite 520, Atlanta, GA 30329	Web Site: www.rpc.net	Auditors: GRANT THORNTON LLP
Telephone: 404-321-2140	Officers: R. Randall Rollins - Chairman Richard A. Hubbell - President, Chief Executive Officer	Investor Contact: 404-321-2140
		Transfer Agents: American Stock Transfer & Trust Company, Brooklyn, NY

RPM INTERNATIONAL INC (DE)

Exchange	Symbol	Price	52Wk Range	Yield	P/E	Div Achiever
NYS	RPM	$52.42 (12/29/2017)	56.26-48.31	2.44	20.16	43 Years

*7 Year Price Score 104.59 *NYSE Composite Index=100 *12 Month Price Score 93.75

Interim Earnings (Per Share)

Qtr.	Aug	Nov	Feb	May
2014-15	0.73	0.52	(0.44)	0.94
2015-16	0.74	0.62	0.14	1.13
2016-17	0.83	(0.54)	0.09	0.95
2017-18	0.86	0.70	...	...

Interim Dividends (Per Share)

Amt	Decl	Ex	Rec	Pay
0.30Q	04/04/2017	04/11/2017	04/14/2017	04/28/2017
0.30Q	07/05/2017	07/13/2017	07/17/2017	07/31/2017
0.32Q	10/05/2017	10/13/2017	10/16/2017	10/31/2017
0.32Q	01/03/2018	01/16/2018	01/17/2018	01/31/2018

Indicated Div: $1.28 (Div. Reinv. Plan)

Valuation Analysis — **Institutional Holding**

Forecast EPS	$3.02	No of Institutions 602
	(01/18/2018)	
Market Cap	$7.0 Billion	Shares
Book Value	$1.6 Billion	124,295,112
Price/Book	4.36	% Held
Price/Sales	1.35	67.27

Business Summary: Specialty Chemicals (MIC: 8.3.2 SIC: 2851 NAIC: 325510)

RPM International, through its subsidiaries, manufactures, markets and sells various chemical product lines including paints, protective coatings, roofing systems, sealants and adhesives, focusing on the maintenance and improvement needs of the industrial, specialty and consumer markets. Co.'s family of products includes those marketed under brand names such as API, Betumat, Carboline, CAVE, DAP, Day-Glo, Dri-Eaz, Dryvit, Euclid, EUCO, Fibergrate, Fibregrid, Fibrecrete, Flecto, Flowcrete, Grupo PV, Hummervoll, illbruck, Mohawk, Prime Resins, and Rust-Oleum, among others. As May 31 2017, Co.'s subsidiaries marketed products in approximately 168 countries and territories.

Recent Developments: For the quarter ended Nov 30 2017, net income amounted to US$95.9 million versus a net loss of US$70.3 million in the year-earlier quarter. Revenues were US$1.32 billion, up 10.5% from US$1.19 billion the year before. Direct operating expenses rose 14.2% to US$764.4 million from US$669.1 million in the comparable period the year before. Indirect operating expenses decreased 31.0% to US$419.6 million from US$607.8 million in the equivalent prior-year period.

Prospects: Our evaluation of RPM Inc. as of Jan. 14, 2018 is the result of our systematic analysis on three basic characteristics: earnings strength, relative valuation, and recent stock price movement. The company has produced a positive trend in earnings per share over the past 5 quarters and while recent estimates for the company have been raised by analysts, RPM has posted better than expected results. Based on operating earnings yield, the company is undervalued when compared to all of the companies in our coverage universe. Share price changes over the past year indicates that RPM will perform in line with the market over the near term.

Financial Data
(US$ in Thousands)

	6 Mos	3 Mos	05/31/2017	05/31/2016	05/31/2015	05/31/2014	05/31/2013	05/31/2012
Earnings Per Share	2.60	1.36	1.36	2.63	1.78	2.18	0.74	1.65
Cash Flow Per Share	2.61	2.69	2.96	3.66	2.54	2.15	2.86	2.30
Dividends Per Share	1.220	1.200	1.175	1.085	1.020	0.945	0.890	0.855
Dividend Payout %	46.92	88.24	86.40	41.25	57.30	43.35	120.27	51.82
Income Statement								
Total Revenue	2,660,810	1,345,394	4,958,175	4,813,649	4,594,550	4,376,353	4,078,655	3,777,416
EBITDA	378,557	212,266	449,424	674,326	625,629	582,966	378,009	460,563
Depn & Amortn	63,631	31,376	113,770	107,232	95,088	86,743	83,415	73,339
Income Before Taxes	263,948	155,011	243,320	481,386	451,230	421,599	221,562	320,210
Income Taxes	51,704	38,381	59,662	126,008	224,925	118,503	67,040	94,526
Net Income	211,879	116,416	181,823	354,725	239,484	291,660	98,603	215,936
Average Shares	135,592	135,720	135,165	136,716	134,893	132,288	128,956	128,717
Balance Sheet								
Current Assets	2,395,056	2,362,948	2,397,436	2,138,342	2,099,846	2,062,295	1,886,272	1,811,337
Total Assets	5,144,671	5,108,916	5,090,449	4,776,041	4,694,240	4,378,365	4,115,526	3,560,020
Current Liabilities	1,074,993	1,095,147	1,235,394	1,002,191	903,236	937,086	928,030	759,792
Long-Term Obligations	1,883,272	1,868,229	1,836,437	1,646,332	1,654,037	1,345,965	1,369,176	1,112,952
Total Liabilities	3,537,918	3,549,805	3,654,388	3,403,706	3,402,848	2,995,521	2,914,668	2,376,364
Stockholders' Equity	1,606,753	1,559,111	1,436,061	1,372,335	1,291,392	1,382,844	1,200,858	1,183,656
Shares Outstanding	133,666	133,537	133,563	132,944	133,203	133,273	132,596	131,555
Statistical Record								
Return on Assets %	7.26	3.77	3.69	7.47	5.28	6.87	2.57	6.09
Return on Equity %	24.37	12.39	12.95	26.56	17.91	22.58	8.27	17.60
EBITDA Margin %	14.23	15.78	9.06	14.01	13.62	13.32	9.27	12.19
Net Margin %	7.96	8.65	3.67	7.37	5.21	6.66	2.42	5.72
Asset Turnover	1.07	1.03	1.01	1.01	1.01	1.03	1.06	1.06
Current Ratio	2.23	2.16	1.94	2.13	2.32	2.20	2.03	2.38
Debt to Equity	1.17	1.20	1.28	1.20	1.28	0.97	1.14	0.94
Price Range	56.26-48.31	56.26-46.29	56.26-46.29	51.45-37.38	51.82-40.22	44.14-31.20	34.03-25.07	26.93-17.40
P/E Ratio	21.64-18.58	41.37-34.04	41.37-34.04	19.56-14.21	29.11-22.60	20.25-14.31	45.99-33.88	16.32-10.55
Average Yield %	2.32	2.28	2.25	2.38	2.17	2.46	3.06	3.72

Address: P.O. Box 777, 2628 Pearl Road, Medina, OH 44258	**Web Site:** www.rpminc.com	**Auditors:** DELOITTE & TOUCHE LLP
Telephone: 330-273-5090	**Officers:** Frank C. Sullivan - Chairman, Chief Executive Officer Ronald A. Rice - President, Chief Operating Officer	**Investor Contact:** 800-776-4488
Fax: 330-225-8743		**Transfer Agents:** Wells Fargo Bank, N.A., St. Paul, MN

RSP PERMIAN INC

Exchange	Symbol	Price	52Wk Range	Yield	P/E
NYS	RSPP	$40.68 (12/29/2017)	46.11-29.37	N/A	64.57

*7 Year Price Score N/A   *NYSE Composite Index=100   *12 Month Price Score 95.38

TRADING VOLUME (thousand shares)

Interim Earnings (Per Share)

Qtr.	Mar	Jun	Sep	Dec
2014	(2.03)	0.11	0.43	1.27
2015	(0.01)	(0.07)	0.10	(0.24)
2016	(0.17)	(0.10)	0.01	0.03
2017	0.26	0.20	0.14	...

Interim Dividends (Per Share)

No Dividends Paid

Valuation Analysis | Institutional Holding

Forecast EPS	$0.83	No of Institutions
	(01/18/2018)	304
Market Cap	$6.5 Billion	Shares
Book Value	$4.2 Billion	144,401,312
Price/Book	1.54	% Held
Price/Sales	9.52	69.23

Business Summary: Production & Extraction (MIC: 9.1.1 SIC: 1311 NAIC: 211111)

RSP Permian is an independent oil and natural gas company focused on the acquisition, exploration, development and production of unconventional oil and natural gas reserves in the Permian Basin of West Texas. Co. designs and manages the well development and supervises operation and maintenance activities on a day-to-day basis. Independent contractors engaged by Co. provides all the equipment and personnel associated with these activities. As of Dec 31 2016, Co. had total proved reserves of 236.9 million barrels of oil equivalent, consisting of 164.7 million barrels of oil, 176.79 billion cubic feet of natural gas, and 42.7 million barrels of natural gas liquids.

Recent Developments: For the quarter ended Sep 30 2017, net income increased to US$21.3 million from US$985,000 in the year-earlier quarter. Revenues were US$201.7 million, up 115.4% from US$93.6 million the year before. Operating income was US$67.1 million versus US$13.2 million in the prior-year quarter, an increase of 406.3%. Direct operating expenses rose 132.8% to US$46.7 million from US$20.0 million in the comparable period the year before. Indirect operating expenses increased 45.7% to US$87.9 million from US$60.3 million in the equivalent prior-year period.

Prospects: Our evaluation of RSP Permian Inc. as of Jan. 14, 2018 is the result of our systematic analysis on three basic characteristics: earnings strength, relative valuation, and recent stock price movement. The company has generated a negative trend in earnings per share over the past 5 quarters and while recent estimates for the company have been raised by analysts, RSPP has posted better than expected results. Based on operating earnings yield, the company is overvalued when compared to all of the companies in our coverage universe. Share price changes over the past year indicates that RSPP will perform very poorly over the near term.

Financial Data
(US$ in Thousands)

	9 Mos	6 Mos	3 Mos	12/31/2016	12/31/2015	12/31/2014	12/31/2013	12/31/2012
Earnings Per Share	0.63	0.50	0.20	(0.23)	(0.21)	0.03	...	0.72
Cash Flow Per Share	2.49	2.09	1.69	1.54	2.52	3.10	...	2.27
Tang Book Value Per Share	26.34	26.18	25.96	24.07	18.44	17.02	0.01	...
Income Statement								
Total Revenue	554,685	353,031	169,931	353,857	283,992	281,925	...	104,427
EBITDA	190,563	270,772	74,249	203,527	167,640	262,179	...	87,390
Depn & Amortn	3,106	129,872	1,019	194,360	154,039	87,844	...	48,347
Income Before Taxes	127,172	102,168	54,006	(43,557)	(29,937)	160,304	...	35,569
Income Taxes	35,822	32,144	15,072	(18,706)	(11,683)	157,806	...	(339)
Net Income	91,350	70,024	38,934	(24,851)	(18,254)	2,498	...	35,908
Average Shares	157,837	157,827	147,005	107,324	86,770	71,898	...	31,933
Balance Sheet								
Current Assets	168,790	129,152	146,077	776,262	187,540	173,742	...	82,356
Total Assets	6,236,835	5,859,073	5,725,874	4,996,427	2,979,571	2,289,947	10.00	513,238
Current Liabilities	200,263	138,949	113,169	108,269	77,402	130,041	...	28,165
Long-Term Obligations	1,478,500	1,190,965	1,132,358	1,132,275	698,650	500,000	...	111,586
Total Liabilities	2,059,651	1,707,526	1,609,447	1,579,699	1,120,987	964,176	...	159,395
Stockholders' Equity	4,177,184	4,151,547	4,116,427	3,416,728	1,858,584	1,325,771	10.00	353,843
Shares Outstanding	158,576	158,589	158,589	141,923	100,807	77,903	1,000.00	...
Statistical Record								
Return on Assets %	2.01	1.65	0.73	N.M.	N.M.	...	...	7.88
Return on Equity %	3.08	2.42	1.06	N.M.	N.M.	...	...	10.66
EBITDA Margin %	34.36	76.70	43.69	57.52	59.03	93.00	...	83.69
Net Margin %	16.47	19.84	22.91	N.M.	N.M.	0.89	...	34.39
Asset Turnover	0.15	0.13	0.11	0.09	0.11	...	...	0.23
Current Ratio	0.84	0.93	1.29	7.17	2.42	1.34	...	2.92
Debt to Equity	0.35	0.29	0.28	0.33	0.38	0.38	...	0.32
Price Range	46.11-29.37	46.11-30.49	46.11-27.59	45.67-18.29	30.54-19.23	32.88-19.59	...	...
P/E Ratio	73.19-46.62	92.22-60.98	230.55-137.95	...	...	N.M.	...	...

Address: 3141 Hood Street, Suite 500, Dallas, TX 75219	**Web Site:** www.rsppermian.com	**Auditors:** GRANT THORNTON LLP
Telephone: 214-252-2700	**Officers:** Michael K. Grimm - Chairman Steven D. Gray - Chief Executive Officer	**Investor Contact:** 214-252-2700
		Transfer Agents: American Stock Transfer & Trust Company, LLC

RYDER SYSTEM, INC.

Exchange	Symbol	Price	52Wk Range	Yield	P/E	Div Achiever
NYS	R	$84.17 (12/29/2017)	85.02-63.04	2.19	22.87	12 Years

*7 Year Price Score 88.97 ***NYSE Composite Index=100** ***12 Month Price Score 100.98**

Interim Earnings (Per Share)

Qtr.	Mar	Jun	Sep	Dec
2014	0.90	1.41	1.57	0.22
2015	0.99	1.59	1.69	1.43
2016	1.04	1.38	1.59	0.90
2017	0.71	0.96	1.11	...

Interim Dividends (Per Share)

Amt	Decl	Ex	Rec	Pay
0.44Q	02/10/2017	02/16/2017	02/21/2017	03/17/2017
0.44Q	05/05/2017	05/18/2017	05/22/2017	06/16/2017
0.46Q	07/14/2017	08/17/2017	08/21/2017	09/15/2017
0.46Q	10/06/2017	11/17/2017	11/20/2017	12/15/2017

Indicated Div: $1.84 (Div. Reinv. Plan)

Valuation Analysis

		Institutional Holding	
Forecast EPS	$4.53	No of Institutions	
	(01/18/2018)	481	
Market Cap	$4.5 Billion	Shares	
Book Value	$2.2 Billion	63,261,756	
Price/Book	2.05	% Held	
Price/Sales	0.63	91.44	

Business Summary: Trucking (MIC: 7.4.1 SIC: 7513 NAIC: 532120)

Ryder System is engaged in transportation and supply chain management solutions. Co. operates in three business segments: Fleet Management Solutions, which provides full service leasing, commercial rental, contract maintenance, and contract-related maintenance of trucks, tractors and trailers to customers principally in the U.S., Canada and the U.K.; Dedicated Transportation Solutions, which provides vehicles and drivers as part of a dedicated transportation solution in the U.S.; and Supply Chain Solutions, which provides supply chain solutions including distribution and transportation services in North America and Asia.

Recent Developments: For the quarter ended Sep 30 2017, income from continuing operations decreased 30.8% to US$58.9 million from US$85.1 million in the year-earlier quarter. Net income decreased 30.8% to US$58.6 million from US$84.8 million in the year-earlier quarter. Revenues were US$1.85 billion, up 7.2% from US$1.72 billion the year before. Direct operating expenses rose 10.6% to US$1.47 billion from US$1.33 billion in the comparable period the year before. Indirect operating expenses increased 7.9% to US$279.5 million from US$259.1 million in the equivalent prior-year period.

Prospects: Our evaluation of Ryder System Inc. as of Jan. 14, 2018 is the result of our systematic analysis on three basic characteristics: earnings strength, relative valuation, and recent stock price movement. The company has enjoyed a very positive trend in earnings per share over the past 5 quarters and while recent estimates for the company have been raised by analysts, R has posted better than expected results. Based on operating earnings yield, the company is undervalued when compared to all of the companies in our coverage universe. Share price changes over the past year indicates that R will perform poorly over the near term.

Financial Data

(US$ in Thousands)	9 Mos	6 Mos	3 Mos	12/31/2016	12/31/2015	12/31/2014	12/31/2013	12/31/2012
Earnings Per Share	3.68	4.16	4.58	4.90	5.71	4.11	4.53	4.09
Cash Flow Per Share	30.20	29.81	29.60	30.12	27.30	26.08	23.70	22.42
Tang Book Value Per Share	32.78	31.57	30.73	30.25	28.84	25.64	27.01	19.52
Dividends Per Share	1.780	1.760	1.730	1.700	1.560	1.420	1.300	1.200
Dividend Payout %	48.37	42.31	37.77	34.69	27.32	34.55	28.70	29.34
Income Statement								
Total Revenue	5,389,906	3,541,377	1,748,163	6,786,984	6,571,893	6,638,774	6,419,285	6,256,967
EBITDA	1,300,287	848,464	414,890	642,224	703,649	1,520,883	1,463,232	1,383,351
Depn & Amortn	960,705	638,078	320,048	88,000	84,000	1,040,259	957,141	939,677
Income Before Taxes	234,991	140,648	59,956	406,381	469,215	338,549	368,895	303,117
Income Taxes	86,456	51,026	21,677	141,741	163,226	118,090	125,699	102,218
Net Income	147,588	88,965	38,149	262,477	304,768	218,575	237,792	209,979
Average Shares	52,776	52,907	53,396	53,361	53,260	53,036	52,071	50,740
Balance Sheet								
Current Assets	1,252,580	1,176,688	1,113,340	1,101,557	1,098,302	1,076,197	1,062,493	1,040,237
Total Assets	11,258,974	11,124,784	10,973,807	10,902,454	10,967,809	9,675,986	9,103,782	8,318,979
Current Liabilities	1,230,329	1,617,364	1,977,799	1,744,069	1,680,255	1,093,591	1,231,139	1,272,665
Long-Term Obligations	5,205,284	4,795,992	4,353,110	4,599,864	4,883,326	4,500,275	3,929,987	3,452,821
Total Liabilities	9,083,910	9,018,685	8,894,011	8,850,179	8,980,698	7,856,512	7,207,068	6,851,492
Stockholders' Equity	2,175,064	2,106,099	2,079,796	2,052,275	1,987,111	1,819,474	1,896,714	1,467,487
Shares Outstanding	52,947	52,983	53,560	53,463	53,490	53,039	53,335	51,371
Statistical Record								
Return on Assets %	1.75	1.99	2.22	2.39	2.95	2.33	2.73	2.63
Return on Equity %	9.16	10.69	11.87	12.96	16.01	11.76	14.14	15.03
EBITDA Margin %	24.12	23.96	23.73	9.46	10.71	22.91	22.79	22.11
Net Margin %	2.74	2.51	2.18	3.87	4.64	3.29	3.70	3.36
Asset Turnover	0.64	0.63	0.63	0.62	0.64	0.71	0.74	0.78
Current Ratio	1.02	0.73	0.56	0.63	0.65	0.98	0.86	0.82
Debt to Equity	2.39	2.28	2.09	2.24	2.46	2.47	2.07	2.35
Price Range	84.69-62.56	84.69-60.54	84.69-57.17	84.69-47.79	99.58-54.03	95.52-68.76	73.78-49.93	57.18-33.40
P/E Ratio	23.01-17.00	20.36-14.55	18.49-12.48	17.28-9.75	17.44-9.46	23.24-16.73	16.29-11.02	13.98-8.17
Average Yield %	2.42	2.48	2.46	2.59	1.85	1.69	2.14	2.63

Address: 11690 N.W. 105th Street, Miami, FL 33178	Web Site: www.ryder.com	Auditors: PricewaterhouseCoopers LLP
Telephone: 305-500-3726	Officers: Robert E. Sanchez - Chairman, President, Chief Executive Officer, Chief Operating Officer, Division Officer Robert D. Fatovic - Executive Vice President, Chief Legal Officer, Corporate Secretary	Investor Contact: 305-500-4053 Transfer Agents: Wells Fargo Bank, N.A., St. Paul, MN

S&P GLOBAL INC

Exchange	Symbol	Price	52Wk Range	Yield	P/E	Div Acheiver
NYS	SPGI	$169.40 (12/29/2017)	172.57-108.39	0.97	24.88	43 Years

*7 Year Price Score 135.70 *NYSE Composite Index=100 *12 Month Price Score 107.65

Interim Earnings (Per Share)

Qtr.	Mar	Jun	Sep	Dec
2014	0.89	1.06	0.69	(3.06)
2015	1.10	1.28	0.92	0.91
2016	1.10	1.44	3.36	2.05
2017	1.53	1.62	1.61	...

Interim Dividends (Per Share)

Amt	Decl	Ex	Rec	Pay
0.41Q	01/25/2017	02/22/2017	02/24/2017	03/10/2017
0.41Q	04/26/2017	05/24/2017	05/26/2017	06/12/2017
0.41Q	06/27/2017	08/24/2017	08/28/2017	09/12/2017
0.41Q	11/02/2017	11/27/2017	11/28/2017	12/12/2017

Indicated Div: $1.64 (Div. Reinv. Plan)

Valuation Analysis — **Institutional Holding**

Valuation Analysis		Institutional Holding	
Forecast EPS	$6.66	No of Institutions	
	(01/26/2018)	1070	
Market Cap	$43.2 Billion	Shares	
Book Value	$839.0 Million	273,244,416	
Price/Book	51.49	% Held	
Price/Sales	7.35	80.50	

Business Summary: Credit & Lending (MIC: 5.4.1 SIC: 7323 NAIC: 561450)

S&P Global provides transparent and independent ratings, benchmarks, analytics and data to the capital and commodity markets worldwide. The capital markets include asset managers, investment banks, commercial banks, insurance companies, exchanges, and issuers; and the commodity markets include producers, traders and intermediaries within energy, metals, petrochemicals and agriculture. Co. has three segments: Ratings, which provides credit ratings, research and analytics to investors, issuers and other market participants; Market and Commodities Intelligence, which provides multi-asset-class data, research and analytical capabilities; and S&P Dow Jones Indices, which is an index provider.

Recent Developments: For the quarter ended Sep 30 2017, net income decreased 51.0% to US$452.0 million from US$923.0 million in the year-earlier quarter. Revenues were US$1.51 billion, up 5.1% from US$1.44 billion the year before. Operating income was US$658.0 million versus US$1.35 billion in the prior-year quarter, a decrease of 51.2%. Direct operating expenses declined 2.3% to US$421.0 million from US$431.0 million in the comparable period the year before. Indirect operating expenses amounted to US$434.0 million compared with an income of US$340.0 million in the equivalent prior-year period.

Prospects: Our evaluation of S&P Global Inc. as of Jan. 21, 2018 is the result of our systematic analysis on three basic characteristics: earnings strength, relative valuation, and recent stock price movement. The company has managed to produce a neutral trend in earnings per share over the past 5 quarters and while recent estimates for the company have been raised by analysts, SPGI has posted better than expected results. Based on operating earnings yield, the company is about fairly valued when compared to all of the companies in our coverage universe. Share price changes over the past year indicates that SPGI will perform very well over the near term.

Financial Data

(US$ in Thousands)	9 Mos	6 Mos	3 Mos	12/31/2016	12/31/2015	12/31/2014	12/31/2013	12/31/2012
Earnings Per Share	6.81	8.56	8.38	7.94	4.21	(0.42)	4.91	1.53
Cash Flow Per Share	5.86	6.09	6.52	5.56	0.72	4.45	2.97	2.67
Dividends Per Share	1.590	1.540	1.490	1.440	1.320	1.200	1.120	3.520
Dividend Payout %	23.35	17.99	17.78	18.14	31.35	...	22.81	230.07
Income Statement								
Total Revenue	4,475,000	2,962,000	1,453,000	5,661,000	5,313,000	5,051,000	4,875,000	4,450,000
EBITDA	2,116,000	1,412,000	691,000	3,550,000	2,074,000	247,000	1,542,000	1,352,000
Depn & Amortn	134,000	88,000	43,000	181,000	157,000	134,000	137,000	141,000
Income Before Taxes	1,872,000	1,250,000	611,000	3,188,000	1,815,000	54,000	1,346,000	1,130,000
Income Taxes	533,000	363,000	181,000	960,000	547,000	245,000	443,000	404,000
Net Income	1,234,000	820,000	399,000	2,106,000	1,156,000	(115,000)	1,376,000	437,000
Average Shares	257,900	259,900	260,800	265,200	274,600	271,500	279,800	284,600
Balance Sheet								
Current Assets	3,653,000	3,723,000	3,663,000	3,671,000	3,296,000	3,966,000	2,936,000	3,899,000
Total Assets	8,714,000	8,791,000	8,654,000	8,669,000	8,183,000	6,771,000	6,061,000	7,052,000
Current Liabilities	2,408,000	2,362,000	2,469,000	2,611,000	2,908,000	3,967,000	2,372,000	3,667,000
Long-Term Obligations	3,568,000	3,566,000	3,565,000	3,564,000	3,468,000	799,000	799,000	799,000
Total Liabilities	7,875,000	7,772,000	7,865,000	8,019,000	7,989,000	6,283,000	4,760,000	6,285,000
Stockholders' Equity	839,000	1,019,000	789,000	650,000	194,000	488,000	1,301,000	767,000
Shares Outstanding	255,000	257,000	257,800	258,300	265,200	272,000	271,000	279,000
Statistical Record								
Return on Assets %	20.37	26.33	26.14	24.93	15.46	N.M.	20.99	6.47
Return on Equity %	272.25	322.44	437.39	497.69	339.00	N.M.	133.08	38.31
EBITDA Margin %	47.28	47.67	47.56	62.71	39.04	4.89	31.63	30.38
Net Margin %	27.58	27.68	27.46	37.20	21.76	N.M.	28.23	9.82
Asset Turnover	0.68	0.68	0.68	0.67	0.71	0.79	0.74	0.66
Current Ratio	1.52	1.58	1.48	1.41	1.13	1.00	1.24	1.06
Debt to Equity	4.25	3.50	4.52	5.48	17.88	1.64	0.61	1.04
Price Range	156.82-107.54	149.40-106.17	132.59-96.38	127.56-80.77	108.59-85.40	93.71-71.98	78.20-42.67	56.65-42.40
P/E Ratio	23.03-15.79	17.45-12.40	15.82-11.50	16.07-10.17	25.79-20.29	...	15.93-8.69	37.03-27.71
Average Yield %	1.19	1.23	1.27	1.32	1.33	1.47	1.89	7.17

Address: 55 Water Street, New York, NY 10041
Telephone: 212-438-1000

Web Site: www.spglobal.com
Officers: Douglas L. Peterson - President, Chief Executive Officer, Division Officer Paul Sheard - Executive Vice President, Chief Economist

Auditors: Ernst & Young LLP
Investor Contact: 866-436-8502
Transfer Agents: ComputerShare, College Station, TX

SALESFORCE.COM INC

Exchange	Symbol	Price	52Wk Range	Yield	P/E
NYS	CRM	$102.23 (12/29/2017)	108.80-70.54	N/A	10223.00

*7 Year Price Score 121.13 ***NYSE Composite Index=100** ***12 Month Price Score 108.87**

TRADING VOLUME (thousand shares)

Interim Earnings (Per Share)

Qtr.	Apr	Jul	Oct	Jan
2014-15	(0.16)	(0.10)	(0.06)	(0.10)
2015-16	0.01	0.00	(0.04)	(0.04)
2016-17	0.06	0.33	(0.05)	(0.07)
2017-18	(0.01)	0.02	0.07	...

Interim Dividends (Per Share)

No Dividends Paid

Valuation Analysis

		Institutional Holding	
Forecast EPS	$1.33	No of Institutions	
	(01/18/2018)	1142	
Market Cap	$73.8 Billion	Shares	
Book Value	$8.8 Billion	687,376,960	
Price/Book	8.35	% Held	
Price/Sales	7.44	97.37	

Business Summary: Internet & Software (MIC: 6.3.2 SIC: 7372 NAIC: 511210)

Salesforce.Com is a provider of enterprise cloud computing solutions. Co.'s service offerings include, among others: Sales Cloud, which enables companies to store data, monitor leads and progress, forecast opportunities, gain insights through relationship intelligence and collaborate around sale on desktop and mobile devices; Service Cloud, which enables companies to deliver more personalized customer service and support; Marketing Cloud, which enables companies to plan and personalize one-to-one customer interactions; and Analytics Cloud, which is an app for business intelligence and it enables companies to deploy sales, service, marketing and custom analytics apps using any data source.

Recent Developments: For the quarter ended Oct 31 2017, net income amounted to US$51.4 million versus a net loss of US$37.3 million in the year-earlier quarter. Revenues were US$2.68 billion, up 24.9% from US$2.14 billion the year before. Operating income was US$116.0 million versus US$3.0 million in the prior-year quarter, an increase of. Direct operating expenses rose 22.0% to US$714.5 million from US$585.5 million in the comparable period the year before. Indirect operating expenses increased 18.8% to US$1.85 billion from US$1.56 billion in the equivalent prior-year period.

Prospects: Our evaluation of Salesforce.com Inc. as of Jan. 14, 2018 is the result of our systematic analysis on three basic characteristics: earnings strength, relative valuation, and recent stock price movement. The company has produced a positive trend in earnings per share over the past 5 quarters and while recent estimates for the company have remained steady, CRM has posted better than expected results. Based on operating earnings yield, the company is overvalued when compared to all of the companies in our coverage universe. Share price changes over the past year indicates that CRM will perform well over the near term.

Financial Data

(US$ in Thousands)	9 Mos	6 Mos	3 Mos	01/31/2017	01/31/2016	01/31/2015	01/31/2014	01/31/2013
Earnings Per Share	0.01	(0.11)	0.20	0.26	(0.07)	(0.42)	(0.39)	(0.48)
Cash Flow Per Share	3.34	3.40	3.31	3.14	2.44	1.88	1.46	1.30
Tang Book Value Per Share	0.67	0.03	N.M.	N.M.	0.74	N.M.	N.M.	0.98
Income Statement								
Total Revenue	7,629,009	4,949,168	2,387,579	8,391,984	6,667,216	5,373,586	4,071,003	3,050,195
EBITDA	786,992	449,400	195,545	437,171	438,764	106,752	(94,824)	4,254
Depn & Amortn	632,152	412,480	201,959	322,800	302,000	246,600	185,900	101,100
Income Before Taxes	113,891	7,490	(22,963)	25,383	64,279	(213,085)	(357,935)	(127,794)
Income Taxes	53,968	(1,039)	(13,756)	(154,249)	111,705	49,603	(125,760)	142,651
Net Income	59,923	8,529	(9,207)	179,632	(47,426)	(262,688)	(232,175)	(270,445)
Average Shares	738,106	729,386	706,174	700,217	661,647	624,148	597,613	564,896
Balance Sheet								
Current Assets	5,946,170	5,811,341	5,404,491	5,996,827	4,347,327	3,550,072	2,680,252	2,015,880
Total Assets	17,490,036	17,418,803	17,058,930	17,584,923	12,770,772	10,692,982	9,152,930	5,528,956
Current Liabilities	7,216,444	7,526,185	7,625,863	7,258,353	5,617,005	4,390,103	3,980,188	2,917,624
Long-Term Obligations	696,555	696,199	695,845	2,008,391	1,293,947	1,370,692	1,301,930	...
Total Liabilities	8,649,869	8,967,489	9,124,442	10,084,796	7,767,903	6,717,799	6,087,715	3,157,711
Stockholders' Equity	8,840,167	8,451,314	7,934,488	7,500,127	5,002,869	3,975,183	3,065,215	2,371,245
Shares Outstanding	722,300	718,700	712,200	707,460	670,929	650,596	610,143	585,626
Statistical Record								
Return on Assets %	0.05	N.M.	0.88	1.18	N.M.	N.M.	N.M.	N.M.
Return on Equity %	0.11	N.M.	1.95	2.87	N.M.	N.M.	N.M.	N.M.
EBITDA Margin %	10.32	9.08	8.19	5.21	6.58	1.99	N.M.	0.14
Net Margin %	0.79	0.17	N.M.	2.14	N.M.	N.M.	N.M.	N.M.
Asset Turnover	0.62	0.59	0.59	0.55	0.57	0.54	0.55	0.63
Current Ratio	0.82	0.77	0.71	0.83	0.77	0.81	0.67	0.69
Debt to Equity	0.08	0.08	0.09	0.27	0.26	0.34	0.42	...
Price Range	102.34-68.41	91.39-68.41	86.12-68.41	83.77-54.05	82.14-57.28	66.22-49.13	61.14-36.75	44.52-29.20
P/E Ratio	N.M.			430.60-342.05	322.19-207.88	...	...	...

Address: The Landmark @ One Market, Suite 300, San Francisco, CA 94105	Web Site: www.salesforce.com	Auditors: Ernst & Young LLP
	Officers: Marc Benioff - Chairman, Chief Executive Officer Keith G. Block - Co-Vice Chairman, President, Chief Operating Officer	Investor Contact: 415-536-6250
Telephone: 415-901-7000		Transfer Agents: Computershare, Providence, RI

SALLY BEAUTY HOLDINGS INC

Exchange	Symbol	Price	52Wk Range	Yield	P/E
NYS	SBH	$18.76 (12/29/2017)	26.80-15.14	N/A	12.03

*7 Year Price Score 62.06   *NYSE Composite Index=100   *12 Month Price Score 80.66

Interim Earnings (Per Share)

Qtr.	Dec	Mar	Jun	Sep
2012-13	0.32	0.36	0.42	0.38
2013-14	0.35	0.35	0.42	0.40
2014-15	0.35	0.39	0.39	0.36
2015-16	0.28	0.41	0.46	0.36
2016-17	0.39	0.41	0.49	0.28

Interim Dividends (Per Share)
No Dividends Paid

Valuation Analysis | Institutional Holding

Forecast EPS	$1.95	No of Institutions
	(01/18/2018)	336
Market Cap	$2.4 Billion	Shares
Book Value	N/A	174,398,224
Price/Book	N/A	% Held
Price/Sales	0.62	93.12

Business Summary: Retail - Specialty (MIC: 2.1.3 SIC: 5999 NAIC: 446120)

Sally Beauty Holdings is a holding company. Through its subsidiaries, Co. is an international retailer and distributor of beauty supplies with operations primarily in North America, South America and Europe. Co. has two segments: Sally Beauty Supply, a retailer of beauty supplies providing beauty supplies to both retail consumers and salon professionals; and Beauty Systems Group (BSG), including its franchise-based business Armstrong McCall, a beauty supply distributor. As of Sep 30 2017, Sally Beauty Supply had 3,763 company-operated retail stores (generally under the Sally Beauty banner) while BSG had 1,200 company-operated retail stores (generally under the CosmoProf banner).

Recent Developments: For the year ended Sep 30 2017, net income decreased 3.5% to US$215.1 million from US$222.9 million in the prior year. Revenues were US$3.94 billion, down 0.4% from US$3.95 billion the year before. Operating income was US$478.6 million versus US$498.3 million in the prior year, a decrease of 4.0%. Direct operating expenses declined 0.8% to US$1.97 billion from US$1.99 billion in the comparable period the year before. Indirect operating expenses increased 1.4% to US$1.49 billion from US$1.47 billion in the equivalent prior-year period.

Prospects: Our evaluation of Sally Beauty Holdings Inc. as of Jan. 14, 2018 is the result of our systematic analysis on three basic characteristics: earnings strength, relative valuation, and recent stock price movement. The company has generated a negative trend in earnings per share over the past 5 quarters and while recent estimates for the company have been raised by analysts, SBH has posted results that fell short of analysts expectations. Based on operating earnings yield, the company is undervalued when compared to all of the companies in our coverage universe. Share price changes over the past year indicates that SBH will perform very poorly over the near term.

Financial Data

(US$ in Thousands)	09/30/2017	09/30/2016	09/30/2015	09/30/2014	09/30/2013	09/30/2012	09/30/2011	09/30/2010
Earnings Per Share	1.56	1.50	1.49	1.51	1.48	1.24	1.14	0.78
Cash Flow Per Share	2.50	2.38	1.92	1.98	1.81	1.62	1.59	1.19
Income Statement								
Total Revenue	3,938,317	3,952,618	3,834,343	3,753,498	3,622,216	3,523,644	3,269,131	2,916,090
EBITDA	577,797	584,597	570,426	572,096	579,762	550,355	495,769	383,330
Depn & Amortn	99,200	86,300	75,100	65,100	59,400	51,000	47,300	42,400
Income Before Taxes	345,698	354,060	378,484	390,679	412,667	360,943	335,939	227,948
Income Taxes	130,622	131,118	143,397	144,686	151,516	127,879	122,214	84,120
Net Income	215,076	222,942	235,087	245,993	261,151	233,064	213,725	143,828
Average Shares	138,176	148,803	158,226	163,419	176,159	188,610	188,093	184,088
Balance Sheet								
Current Assets	1,170,503	1,172,827	1,187,102	1,104,149	1,015,817	1,163,907	879,148	794,775
Total Assets	2,123,093	2,132,063	2,094,351	2,029,973	1,950,086	2,065,800	1,728,600	1,589,412
Current Liabilities	574,565	488,665	491,699	463,537	542,653	477,388	460,006	407,652
Long-Term Obligations	1,771,853	1,783,294	1,786,839	1,810,667	1,612,685	1,615,322	1,410,111	1,559,591
Total Liabilities	2,486,709	2,408,229	2,392,172	2,377,026	2,253,565	2,180,885	1,947,582	2,049,738
Stockholders' Equity	(363,616)	(276,166)	(297,821)	(347,053)	(303,479)	(115,085)	(218,982)	(460,326)
Shares Outstanding	129,585	144,571	151,452	154,668	164,425	180,241	184,057	182,230
Statistical Record								
Return on Assets %	10.11	10.52	11.40	12.36	13.01	12.25	12.88	9.34
EBITDA Margin %	14.67	14.79	14.88	15.24	16.01	15.62	15.17	13.15
Net Margin %	5.46	5.64	6.13	6.55	7.21	6.61	6.54	4.93
Asset Turnover	1.85	1.87	1.86	1.89	1.80	1.85	1.97	1.89
Current Ratio	2.04	2.40	2.41	2.38	1.87	2.44	1.91	1.95
Price Range	29.12-17.38	32.75-22.13	34.88-23.44	30.67-24.14	31.57-22.76	28.07-16.28	18.47-11.01	11.70-6.75
P/E Ratio	18.67-11.14	21.83-14.75	23.41-15.73	20.31-15.99	21.33-15.38	22.64-13.13	16.20-9.66	15.00-8.65

Address: 3001 Colorado Boulevard, Denton, TX 76210 **Telephone:** 940-898-7500	**Web Site:** www.sallybeautyholdings.com **Officers:** Gary G. Winterhalter - Chairman, President, Chief Executive Officer Christian A. Brickman - President, Chief Executive Officer, Chief Operating Officer	**Auditors:** KPMG LLP **Investor Contact:** 940-297-3877 **Transfer Agents:** Computershare Trust Company N.A., Providence, RI

SANTANDER CONSUMER USA HOLDINGS INC

	Exchange	Symbol	Price	52Wk Range	Yield	P/E
	NYS	SC	$18.62 (12/29/2017)	18.62-11.17	0.64	10.01

*7 Year Price Score N/A   *NYSE Composite Index=100   *12 Month Price Score 114.57

Interim Earnings (Per Share)

Qtr.	Mar	Jun	Sep	Dec
2014	0.23	0.69	0.54	0.69
2015	0.81	0.79	0.62	0.08
2016	0.56	0.79	0.59	0.17
2017	0.40	0.74	0.55	...

Interim Dividends (Per Share)

Amt	Decl	Ex	Rec	Pay
0.15Q	05/01/2014	05/08/2014	05/12/2014	05/30/2014
0.03Q	10/27/2017	11/06/2017	11/07/2017	11/17/2017
		Indicated Div: $0.12		

Valuation Analysis   **Institutional Holding**

Forecast EPS	$1.97	No of Institutions
	(01/18/2018)	214
Market Cap	$6.7 Billion	Shares
Book Value	$5.9 Billion	341,030,912
Price/Book	1.14	% Held
Price/Sales	1.00	N/A

Business Summary: Credit & Lending (MIC: 5.4.1 SIC: 6141 NAIC: 522298)

Santander Consumer USA Holdings is a holding company. Through its subsidiaries, Co. is a consumer finance company focused on vehicle finance and third-party servicing. Co.'s primary business is the indirect origination and securitization of retail installment contracts, principally through manufacturer-franchised dealers in connection with their sale of new and used vehicles to retail consumers. Co. also originates vehicle loans through a web-based direct lending program, purchases vehicle retail installment contracts from other lenders, and services automobile and recreational and marine vehicle portfolios for other lenders.

Recent Developments: For the quarter ended Sep 30 2017, net income decreased 6.6% to US$199.4 million from US$213.5 million in the year-earlier quarter. Net interest income decreased 10.1% to US$1.06 billion from US$1.18 billion in the year-earlier quarter. Provision for loan losses was US$536.4 million versus US$610.4 million in the prior-year quarter, a decrease of 12.1%. Non-interest income rose 120.9% to US$58.9 million from US$26.7 million, while non-interest expense advanced 4.5% to US$303.8 million.

Prospects: Our evaluation of Santander Consumer USA Holdings Inc as of Jan. 14, 2018 is the result of our systematic analysis on three basic characteristics: earnings strength, relative valuation, and recent stock price movement. The company has enjoyed a very positive trend in earnings per share over the past 5 quarters. However, while recent estimates for the company have been mixed, SC has posted better than expected results. Based on operating earnings yield, the company is undervalued when compared to all of the companies in our coverage universe. Share price changes over the past year indicates that SC will perform in line with the market over the near term.

Financial Data
(US$ in Thousands)

	9 Mos	6 Mos	3 Mos	12/31/2016	12/31/2015	12/31/2014	12/31/2013	12/31/2012
Earnings Per Share	1.86	1.90	1.95	2.13	2.31	2.15	2.01	2.07
Cash Flow Per Share	15.19	14.95	14.71	12.45	10.98	11.18	6.13	4.16
Tang Book Value Per Share	16.07	15.50	14.78	14.30	12.01	9.83	7.38	5.99
Dividends Per Share	...	...	...	...	...	0.150	0.840	2.120
Dividend Payout %	...	...	...	...	...	6.98	41.79	102.42
Income Statement								
Total Revenue	5,086,163	3,377,840	1,686,724	6,623,142	6,697,184	6,127,331	4,245,587	3,244,191
Income Before Taxes	847,309	569,536	221,428	1,160,711	1,285,325	1,209,988	1,085,088	1,188,549
Income Taxes	239,819	161,434	78,001	394,245	458,032	443,639	389,418	453,615
Net Income	607,490	408,102	143,427	766,466	827,293	766,349	697,491	715,003
Average Shares	360,460	359,828	360,616	359,078	358,887	355,722	346,177	346,164
Balance Sheet								
Total Assets	38,765,557	39,507,482	39,061,940	38,539,104	36,570,373	32,342,176	26,401,896	18,741,644
Total Liabilities	32,880,323	33,828,749	33,642,942	33,300,485	32,145,410	28,783,827	23,715,064	16,542,110
Stockholders' Equity	5,885,234	5,678,733	5,418,998	5,238,619	4,424,963	3,558,349	2,686,832	2,199,534
Shares Outstanding	359,750	359,539	359,394	358,907	357,945	348,977	346,760	346,164
Statistical Record								
Return on Assets %	1.73	1.75	1.82	2.04	2.40	2.61	3.09	3.74
Return on Equity %	12.16	12.94	14.02	15.82	20.73	24.54	28.55	32.29
Net Margin %	11.94	12.08	8.50	11.57	12.35	12.51	16.43	22.04
Asset Turnover	0.17	0.17	0.17	0.18	0.19	0.21	0.19	0.17
Price Range	15.37-10.93	14.97-9.90	14.97-9.69	15.85-8.87	26.52-15.15	25.90-16.85	...	...
P/E Ratio	8.26-5.88	7.88-5.21	7.68-4.97	7.44-4.16	11.48-6.56	12.05-7.84	...	...
Average Yield %	...	...	...	...	...	0.73	...	...

Address: 1601 Elm Street, Suite 800, Dallas, TX 75201 **Telephone:** 214-634-1110	**Web Site:** www.santanderconsumerusa.com **Officers:** William J. Rainer - Chairman Sandra M. Broderick - Division Officer	**Auditors:** PricewaterhouseCoopers LLP **Transfer Agents:** Computershare Trust Company, N.A.

SCANA CORP

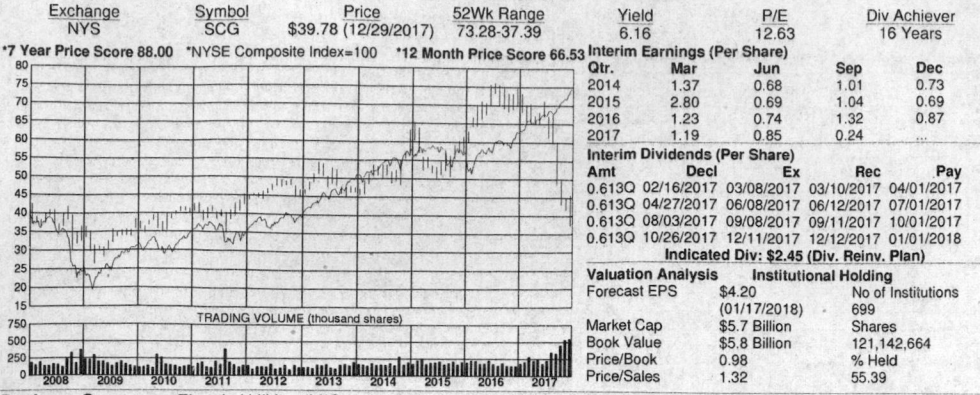

Exchange	Symbol	Price	52Wk Range	Yield	P/E	Div Achiever
NYS	SCG	$39.78 (12/29/2017)	73.28-37.39	6.16	12.63	16 Years

*7 Year Price Score 88.00   *NYSE Composite Index=100   *12 Month Price Score 66.53

Interim Earnings (Per Share)

Qtr.	Mar	Jun	Sep	Dec
2014	1.37	0.68	1.01	0.73
2015	2.80	0.69	1.04	0.69
2016	1.23	0.74	1.32	0.87
2017	1.19	0.85	0.24	...

Interim Dividends (Per Share)

Amt	Decl	Ex	Rec	Pay
0.613Q	02/16/2017	03/08/2017	03/10/2017	04/01/2017
0.613Q	04/27/2017	06/08/2017	06/12/2017	07/01/2017
0.613Q	08/03/2017	09/08/2017	09/11/2017	10/01/2017
0.613Q	10/26/2017	12/11/2017	12/12/2017	01/01/2018

Indicated Div: $2.45 (Div. Reinv. Plan)

Valuation Analysis   **Institutional Holding**

Forecast EPS	$4.20 (01/17/2018)	No of Institutions	699
Market Cap	$5.7 Billion	Shares	121,142,664
Book Value	$5.8 Billion	% Held	55.39
Price/Book	0.98		
Price/Sales	1.32		

Business Summary: Electric Utilities (MIC: 3.1.1 SIC: 4931 NAIC: 221122)

SCANA is a holding company. Through its regulated subsidiaries, Co. is engaged in the generation, transmission, distribution and sale of electricity in South Carolina and in the purchase, transmission and sale of natural gas in North Carolina and South Carolina. Through nonregulated subsidiary, Co. markets natural gas to retail customers in Georgia and to wholesale customers in the southeast. A service company subsidiary of Co. provides primarily administrative and management services to Co. and its subsidiaries. As of Dec 31 2016, Co. distributed electricity to approximately 709,000 customers and the purchase, sale and transportation of natural gas to approximately 358,000 customers.

Recent Developments:
For the quarter ended Sep 30 2017, net income decreased 82.0% to US$34.0 million from US$189.0 million in the year-earlier quarter. Revenues were US$1.08 billion, down 1.6% from US$1.09 billion the year before. Operating income was US$120.0 million versus US$348.0 million in the prior-year quarter, a decrease of 65.5%. Direct operating expenses declined 0.5% to US$583.0 million from US$586.0 million in the comparable period the year before. Indirect operating expenses increased 134.6% to US$373.0 million from US$159.0 million in the equivalent prior-year period.

Prospects:
Our evaluation of SCANA Corp. as of Jan. 14, 2018 is the result of our systematic analysis on three basic characteristics: earnings strength, relative valuation, and recent stock price movement. The company has managed to produce a neutral trend in earnings per share over the past 5 quarters. However, while recent estimates for the company have been mixed, SCG has posted results that fell short of analysts expectations. Based on operating earnings yield, the company is undervalued when compared to all of the companies in our coverage universe. Share price changes over the past year indicates that SCG will perform poorly over the near term.

Financial Data

(US$ in Thousands)	9 Mos	6 Mos	3 Mos	12/31/2016	12/31/2015	12/31/2014	12/31/2013	12/31/2012
Earnings Per Share	3.15	4.23	4.12	4.16	5.22	3.79	3.39	3.15
Cash Flow Per Share	9.37	9.26	9.38	7.62	7.41	5.14	7.57	6.38
Tang Book Value Per Share	40.47	40.85	40.63	38.59	36.62	33.48	31.45	29.73
Dividends Per Share	2.413	2.375	2.337	2.300	2.180	2.100	2.030	1.980
Dividend Payout %	76.59	56.15	56.74	55.29	41.76	55.41	59.88	62.86
Income Statement								
Total Revenue	3,249,000	2,173,000	1,173,000	4,227,000	4,380,000	4,951,000	4,495,000	4,176,000
EBITDA	769,000	617,000	346,000	1,652,000	1,868,000	1,546,000	1,441,000	1,309,000
Depn & Amortn	31,000	19,000	14,000	446,000	414,000	448,000	450,000	412,000
Income Before Taxes	468,000	423,000	245,000	864,000	1,136,000	786,000	694,000	602,000
Income Taxes	142,000	131,000	74,000	269,000	390,000	248,000	223,000	182,000
Net Income	326,000	292,000	171,000	595,000	746,000	538,000	471,000	420,000
Average Shares	143,000	142,900	142,900	142,900	142,900	141,900	139,100	133,300
Balance Sheet								
Current Assets	2,164,000	1,186,000	1,047,000	1,506,000	1,378,000	2,145,000	1,421,000	1,527,000
Total Assets	20,019,000	19,056,000	18,458,000	18,707,000	17,146,000	16,852,000	15,164,000	14,616,000
Current Liabilities	2,451,000	2,183,000	1,661,000	2,065,000	1,952,000	2,533,000	1,442,000	1,811,000
Long-Term Obligations	6,455,000	6,455,000	6,466,000	6,473,000	5,882,000	5,531,000	5,395,000	4,949,000
Total Liabilities	14,232,000	13,218,000	12,652,000	12,982,000	11,703,000	11,865,000	10,500,000	10,462,000
Stockholders' Equity	5,787,000	5,838,000	5,806,000	5,725,000	5,443,000	4,987,000	4,664,000	4,154,000
Shares Outstanding	143,000	142,900	142,900	142,900	142,900	142,700	141,000	132,000
Statistical Record								
Return on Assets %	2.34	3.29	3.29	3.31	4.39	3.36	3.16	2.98
Return on Equity %	7.85	10.61	10.38	10.63	14.30	11.15	10.68	10.42
EBITDA Margin %	23.67	28.39	29.50	39.08	42.65	31.23	32.06	31.35
Net Margin %	10.03	13.44	14.58	14.08	17.03	10.87	10.48	10.06
Asset Turnover	0.22	0.24	0.24	0.24	0.26	0.31	0.30	0.30
Current Ratio	0.88	0.54	0.63	0.73	0.71	0.85	0.99	0.84
Debt to Equity	1.12	1.11	1.11	1.13	1.08	1.11	1.16	1.19
Price Range	74.69-48.49	76.12-64.88	76.12-65.35	76.12-60.08	65.36-50.00	63.18-45.67	54.20-44.86	49.65-43.71
P/E Ratio	23.71-15.39	18.00-15.34	18.48-15.86	18.30-14.44	12.52-9.58	16.67-12.05	15.99-13.23	15.76-13.88
Average Yield %	3.59	3.38	3.30	3.29	3.90	4.06	4.16	4.24

Address: 100 SCANA Parkway, Cayce, SC 29033

Telephone: 803-217-9000

Web Site: www.scana.com

Officers: Kevin B. Marsh - Chairman, President, Chief Executive Officer, Chief Operating Officer Jimmy E. Addison - Executive Vice President, Senior Vice President, Chief Financial Officer

Auditors: Deloitte & Touche LLP

Investor Contact: 803-217-7512

Transfer Agents: SCANA Corporation, Columbia, SC

SCHLUMBERGER LTD

Exchange	Symbol	Price	52Wk Range	Yield	P/E
NYS	SLB	$67.39 (12/29/2017)	87.48-61.31	2.97	168.47

*7 Year Price Score 69.43 *NYSE Composite Index=100 *12 Month Price Score 85.45

Interim Earnings (Per Share)

Qtr.	Mar	Jun	Sep	Dec
2014	1.21	1.21	1.49	0.25
2015	0.76	0.88	0.78	(0.79)
2016	0.40	(1.56)	0.13	(0.14)
2017	0.20	(0.05)	0.39	...

Interim Dividends (Per Share)

Amt	Decl	Ex	Rec	Pay
0.50Q	01/19/2017	02/13/2017	02/15/2017	04/17/2017
0.50Q	04/20/2017	05/30/2017	06/01/2017	07/14/2017
0.50Q	07/19/2017	09/01/2017	09/06/2017	10/13/2017
0.50Q	10/18/2017	12/05/2017	12/06/2017	01/12/2018

Indicated Div: $2.00

Valuation Analysis

		Institutional Holding	
Forecast EPS	$1.46 (01/18/2018)	No of Institutions	2266
Market Cap	$93.4 Billion	Shares	1,311,667,712
Book Value	$39.6 Billion	% Held	74.32
Price/Book	2.36		
Price/Sales	3.16		

Business Summary: Equipment & Services (MIC: 9.1.3 SIC: 1389 NAIC: 213112)

Schlumberger is a provider of technology for reservoir characterization, drilling, production and processing to the oil and gas industry. Co. operates in the oilfield service markets, managing its business through four Groups: Reservoir Characterization, which include WesternGeco®, Wireline, Testing and Process; Drilling, which comprises Bits and Drilling Tools, M-I SWACO®, Drilling and Measurements, Land Rigs and Integrated Drilling Services; Production, which includes Well Services, Completions, Artificial Lift, Integrated Production Services and Schlumberger Production Management; and Cameron, which includes OneSubsea®, Surface Systems, Drilling Systems, and Valves and Measurement.

Recent Developments: For the quarter ended Sep 30 2017, net income increased 192.6% to US$556.0 million from US$190.0 million in the year-earlier quarter. Revenues were US$7.97 billion, up 12.7% from US$7.07 billion the year before. Direct operating expenses rose 8.0% to US$6.80 billion from US$6.29 billion in the comparable period the year before. Indirect operating expenses decreased 14.9% to US$495.0 million from US$582.0 million in the equivalent prior-year period.

Prospects: Our evaluation of Schlumberger Ltd. as of Jan. 14, 2018 is the result of our systematic analysis on three basic characteristics: earnings strength, relative valuation, and recent stock price movement. The company has produced a positive trend in earnings per share over the past 5 quarters. However, while recent estimates for the company have been mixed, SLB has posted better than expected results. Based on operating earnings yield, the company is overvalued when compared to all of the companies in our coverage universe. Share price changes over the past year indicates that SLB will perform very poorly over the near term.

Financial Data

(US$ in Thousands)	9 Mos	6 Mos	3 Mos	12/31/2016	12/31/2015	12/31/2014	12/31/2013	12/31/2012
Earnings Per Share	0.40	0.14	(1.37)	(1.24)	1.63	4.16	5.05	4.10
Cash Flow Per Share	3.92	3.56	4.10	4.60	6.95	8.64	7.40	5.11
Tang Book Value Per Share	3.55	3.49	4.19	4.48	12.30	13.89	15.34	11.57
Dividends Per Share	2.000	2.000	2.000	2.000	2.000	1.600	1.250	1.100
Dividend Payout %	500.00	1,428.57	...	...	122.70	38.46	24.75	26.83
Income Statement								
Total Revenue	22,433,000	14,464,000	6,940,000	28,010,000	35,711,000	48,871,000	46,459,000	42,321,000
EBITDA	3,245,000	1,837,000	1,086,000	1,365,000	6,427,000	11,208,000	12,182,000	10,431,000
Depn & Amortn	1,796,000	1,205,000	613,000	2,700,000	3,200,000	3,200,000	3,100,000	2,900,000
Income Before Taxes	1,027,000	351,000	334,000	(1,905,000)	2,881,000	7,639,000	8,691,000	7,191,000
Income Taxes	269,000	148,000	50,000	(278,000)	746,000	1,928,000	1,848,000	1,723,000
Net Income	749,000	205,000	279,000	(1,687,000)	2,072,000	5,438,000	6,732,000	5,490,000
Average Shares	1,392,000	1,387,000	1,402,000	1,357,000	1,275,000	1,308,000	1,333,000	1,339,000
Balance Sheet								
Current Assets	19,914,000	21,273,000	21,883,000	23,927,000	26,912,000	24,694,000	26,225,000	24,156,000
Total Assets	73,569,000	74,862,000	76,175,000	77,956,000	68,005,000	66,904,000	67,100,000	61,547,000
Current Liabilities	13,014,000	13,527,000	13,776,000	15,059,000	14,121,000	14,176,000	13,525,000	12,368,000
Long-Term Obligations	15,871,000	16,600,000	16,538,000	16,463,000	14,442,000	10,565,000	10,393,000	9,509,000
Total Liabilities	33,996,000	35,342,000	35,569,000	36,878,000	32,372,000	29,054,000	27,631,000	26,796,000
Stockholders' Equity	39,573,000	39,520,000	40,606,000	41,078,000	35,633,000	37,850,000	39,469,000	34,751,000
Shares Outstanding	1,385,261	1,384,524	1,389,476	1,391,475	1,256,367	1,275,312	1,307,330	1,328,255
Statistical Record								
Return on Assets %	0.71	0.23	N.M.	N.M.	3.07	8.12	10.47	9.38
Return on Equity %	1.33	0.43	N.M.	N.M.	5.64	14.07	18.14	16.59
EBITDA Margin %	14.47	12.70	15.65	4.87	18.00	22.93	26.22	24.65
Net Margin %	3.34	1.42	4.02	N.M.	5.80	11.13	14.49	12.97
Asset Turnover	0.38	0.37	0.39	0.38	0.53	0.73	0.72	0.72
Current Ratio	1.53	1.57	1.59	1.59	1.91	1.74	1.94	1.95
Debt to Equity	0.40	0.42	0.41	0.40	0.41	0.28	0.26	0.27
Price Range	87.48-62.88	87.48-65.25	87.48-72.01	86.38-61.06	94.61-67.34	117.95-79.90	94.46-69.30	79.85-59.67
P/E Ratio	218.70-157.20	624.86-466.07	...	...	58.04-41.31	28.35-19.21	18.70-13.72	19.48-14.55
Average Yield %	2.65	2.54	2.50	2.59	2.44	1.62	1.55	1.55

Address: 42 Rue Saint-Dominique, Paris, 75007	**Web Site:** www.slb.com	**Auditors:** PricewaterhouseCoopers LLP
Telephone: 713-513-2000	**Officers:** Paal Kibsgaard - Chairman, Chief Executive Officer Patrick Schorn - President, Division Officer	**Investor Contact:** 713-375-3535
		Transfer Agents: Computershare Trust Company, N.A., Providence, RI

SCHWAB (CHARLES) CORP (THE)

Exchange	Symbol	Price	52Wk Range	Yield	P/E
NYS	SCHW	$51.37 (12/29/2017)	52.28-37.53	0.78	32.93

*7 Year Price Score 129.71 *NYSE Composite Index=100 *12 Month Price Score 108.03

Interim Earnings (Per Share)

Qtr.	Mar	Jun	Sep	Dec
2014	0.24	0.23	0.24	0.25
2015	0.22	0.25	0.28	0.29
2016	0.29	0.30	0.35	0.36
2017	0.39	0.39	0.42	...

Interim Dividends (Per Share)

Amt.	Decl	Ex	Rec	Pay
0.08Q	04/20/2017	05/10/2017	05/12/2017	05/26/2017
0.08Q	07/20/2017	08/09/2017	08/11/2017	08/25/2017
0.08Q	10/19/2017	11/09/2017	11/10/2017	11/24/2017
0.10Q	01/25/2018	02/08/2018	02/09/2018	02/23/2018

Indicated Div: $0.40

Valuation Analysis / **Institutional Holding**

Forecast EPS	$2.40	No of Institutions	
	(01/25/2018)	1243	
Market Cap	$68.8 Billion	Shares	
Book Value	$18.0 Billion	1,250,793,216	
Price/Book	3.82	% Held	
Price/Sales	7.99	81.41	

Business Summary: Finance Intermediaries & Services (MIC: 5.5.1 SIC: 6211 NAIC: 523120)

Charles Schwab is a savings and loan holding company. Co. is engaged, through its subsidiaries, in wealth management, securities brokerage, banking, money management and financial advisory services. Co. provides financial services to individuals and institutional clients in two segments: Investor Services, which provides retail brokerage and banking services, retirement plan services, and other corporate brokerage services; and Advisor Services, which provides custodial, trading, and support services as well as retirement business services.

Recent Developments: For the quarter ended Sep 30 2017, net income increased 22.9% to US$618.0 million from US$503.0 million in the year-earlier quarter. Revenues were US$2.17 billion, up 13.1% from US$1.91 billion the year before. Indirect operating expenses increased 8.9% to US$1.22 billion from US$1.12 billion in the equivalent prior-year period.

Prospects: Our evaluation of Schwab (Charles) Corp. as of Jan. 21, 2018 is the result of our systematic analysis on three basic characteristics: earnings strength, relative valuation, and recent stock price movement. The company has managed to produce a neutral trend in earnings per share over the past 5 quarters and while recent estimates for the company have been raised by analysts, SCHW has posted better than expected results. Based on operating earnings yield, the company is about fairly valued when compared to all of the companies in our coverage universe. Share price changes over the past year indicates that SCHW will perform poorly over the near term.

Financial Data
(US$ in Thousands)

	9 Mos	6 Mos	3 Mos	12/31/2016	12/31/2015	12/31/2014	12/31/2013	12/31/2012
Earnings Per Share	1.56	1.49	1.40	1.31	1.03	0.95	0.78	0.69
Cash Flow Per Share	2.63	1.23	2.02	2.01	0.95	1.80	1.29	0.99
Tang Book Value Per Share	10.37	9.98	9.60	9.20	7.98	7.23	6.18	5 62
Dividends Per Share	0.310	0.300	0.290	0.270	0.240	0.240	0.240	0.240
Dividend Payout %	19.87	20.13	20.71	20.61	23.30	25.26	30.77	34.78
Income Statement								
Total Revenue	6,599,000	4,340,000	2,136,000	7,649,000	6,512,000	6,160,000	5,540,000	5,033,000
EBITDA	2,937,000	1,900,000	915,000	3,227,000	2,503,000	2,314,000	1,907,000	1,646,000
Depn & Amortn	240,000	148,000	72,000	234,000	224,000	199,000	202,000	196,000
Income Before Taxes	2,697,000	1,752,000	843,000	2,993,000	2,279,000	2,115,000	1,705,000	1,450,000
Income Taxes	940,000	613,000	279,000	1,104,000	832,000	794,000	634,000	522,000
Net Income	1,757,000	1,139,000	564,000	1,889,000	1,447,000	1,321,000	1,071,000	928,000
Average Shares	1,353,000	1,351,000	1,351,000	1,334,000	1,327,000	1,315,000	1,293,000	1,275,000
Balance Sheet								
Current Assets	31,379,000	28,478,000	26,925,000	51,334,000	50,004,000	48,798,000	46,258,000	55,559,000
Total Assets	230,714,000	220,601,000	227,061,000	223,383,000	183,718,000	154,642,000	143,642,000	133,637,000
Current Liabilities	207,170,000	197,573,000	204,399,000	201,755,000	165,275,000	139,124,000	129,772,000	120,775,000
Long-Term Obligations	3,268,000	3,518,000	3,518,000	2,876,000	2,890,000	1,899,000	1,903,000	1,632,000
Total Liabilities	212,687,000	203,112,000	210,079,000	206,962,000	170,316,000	142,839,000	133,261,000	124,048,000
Stockholders' Equity	18,027,000	17,489,000	16,982,000	16,421,000	13,402,000	11,803,000	10,381,000	9,589,000
Shares Outstanding	1,340,029	1,338,203	1,336,856	1,332,749	1,320,337	1,310,722	1,296,886	1,277,529
Statistical Record								
Return on Assets %	1.04	1.03	0.98	0.93	0.86	0.89	0.77	0.76
Return on Equity %	13.61	13.33	12.96	12.63	11.48	11.91	10.73	10.70
EBITDA Margin %	44.51	43.78	42.84	42.19	38.44	37.56	34.42	32.70
Net Margin %	26.63	26.24	26.40	24.70	22.22	21.44	19.33	18.44
Asset Turnover	0.04	0.04	0.04	0.04	0.04	0.04	0.04	0.04
Current Ratio	0.15	0.14	0.13	0.25	0.30	0.35	0.36	0.46
Debt to Equity	0.18	0.20	0.21	0.18	0.22	0.16	0.18	0.17
Price Range	44.04-30.90	43.53-24.34	43.53-24.05	40.47-22.22	35.42-25.96	30.78-23.65	26.00-14.36	15.38-11.61
P/E Ratio	28.23-19.81	29.21-16.34	31.09-17.18	30.89-16.96	34.39-25.20	32.40-24.89	33.33-18.41	22.29-16.83
Average Yield %	0.78	0.82	0.86	0.90	0.77	0.88	1.19	1.81

Address: 211 Main Street, San Francisco, CA 94105	**Web Site:** www.aboutschwab.com	**Auditors:** Deloitte & Touche LLP
Telephone: 415-667-7000	**Officers:** Charles R. Schwab - Chairman Walter W. Bettinger - President, Chief Executive Officer	**Investor Contact:** 415-667-1841
Fax: 415-627-8894		**Transfer Agents:** Wells Fargo Bank, N.A., St. Paul, MN

SCIENCE APPLICATIONS INTERNATIONAL CORP

Exchange	Symbol	Price	52Wk Range	Yield	P/E
NYS	SAIC	$76.57 (12/29/2017)	89.24-61.06	1.62	20.98

*7 Year Price Score N/A   *NYSE Composite Index=100   *12 Month Price Score 92.66

Interim Earnings (Per Share)

Qtr.	Apr	Jul	Oct	Jan
2014-15	0.69	0.70	0.77	0.76
2015-16	0.69	0.46	0.72	0.60
2016-17	0.71	0.81	0.91	0.79
2017-18	1.08	0.80	0.98	...

Interim Dividends (Per Share)

Amt	Decl	Ex	Rec	Pay
0.31Q	03/30/2017	04/11/2017	04/14/2017	04/28/2017
0.31Q	06/12/2017	07/12/2017	07/14/2017	07/28/2017
0.31Q	10/04/2017	10/12/2017	10/13/2017	10/27/2017
0.31Q	12/14/2017	01/11/2018	01/12/2018	01/26/2018

Indicated Div: $1.24 (Div. Reinv. Plan)

Valuation Analysis

Forecast EPS	$3.70 (01/17/2018)	No of Institutions 317
Market Cap	$3.3 Billion	Shares
Book Value	$322.0 Million	32,603,738
Price/Book	10.23	% Held
Price/Sales	0.76	N/A

Institutional Holding

TRADING VOLUME (thousand shares)

Business Summary: IT Services (MIC: 6.3.1 SIC: 7373 NAIC: 541512)

Science Applications International is a provider of technical, engineering and enterprise information technology (IT) services primarily to the U.S. government. Co. provides engineering, systems integration and information technology offerings for government projects. Co.'s offerings include: engineering; technology and equipment platform integration; maintenance of ground and maritime systems; logistics; training and simulation; operation and program support services; and end-to-end services spanning the design, development, integration, deployment, management and operations, sustainment and security of its customers' entire IT infrastructure.

Recent Developments: For the quarter ended Nov 3 2017, net income increased 2.4% to US$43.0 million from US$42.0 million in the year-earlier quarter. Revenues were US$1.15 billion, up 2.8% from US$1.11 billion the year before. Operating income was US$72.0 million versus US$74.0 million in the prior-year quarter, a decrease of 2.7%. Direct operating expenses rose 3.6% to US$1.04 billion from US$1.00 billion in the comparable period the year before. Indirect operating expenses decreased 7.5% to US$37.0 million from US$40.0 million in the equivalent prior-year period.

Prospects: Our evaluation of Science Applications International Corp. as of Jan. 14, 2018 is the result of our systematic analysis on three basic characteristics: earnings strength, relative valuation, and recent stock price movement. The company has generated a negative trend in earnings per share over the past 5 quarters. However, while recent estimates for the company have been mixed, SAIC has posted better than expected results. Based on operating earnings yield, the company is undervalued when compared to all of the companies in our coverage universe. Share price changes over the past year indicates that SAIC will perform poorly over the near term.

Financial Data
(US$ in Thousands)

	9 Mos	6 Mos	3 Mos	02/03/2017	01/29/2016	01/30/2015	01/31/2014	01/31/2013
Earnings Per Share	3.65	3.58	3.59	3.22	2.47	2.91	2.27	...
Cash Flow Per Share	4.51	6.15	7.46	6.04	4.95	5.92	3.77	...
Dividends Per Share	1.240	1.240	1.240	1.240	1.210	1.120	0.560	...
Dividend Payout %	33.97	34.64	34.54	38.51	48.99	38.49	24.67	...
Income Statement								
Total Revenue	3,326,000	2,181,000	1,103,000	4,450,000	4,315,000	3,885,000	4,121,000	4,781,000
EBITDA	228,000	144,000	73,000	296,000	253,000	259,000	196,000	294,000
Depn & Amortn	33,000	22,000	10,000	24,000	26,000	19,000	13,000	13,000
Income Before Taxes	163,000	101,000	52,000	220,000	183,000	223,000	176,000	281,000
Income Taxes	35,000	16,000	3,000	72,000	66,000	82,000	63,000	99,000
Net Income	128,000	85,000	49,000	148,000	117,000	141,000	113,000	182,000
Average Shares	44,200	44,700	45,500	45,900	47,400	48,500	49,700	...
Balance Sheet								
Current Assets	976,000	892,000	917,000	901,000	952,000	943,000	994,000	835,000
Total Assets	2,101,000	2,019,000	2,050,000	2,042,000	2,122,000	1,398,000	1,447,000	1,271,000
Current Liabilities	730,000	634,000	647,000	615,000	688,000	577,000	564,000	664,000
Long-Term Obligations	994,000	1,006,000	1,014,000	1,022,000	1,013,000	457,000	489,000	1,000
Total Liabilities	1,779,000	1,694,000	1,714,000	1,688,000	1,742,000	1,053,000	1,070,000	675,000
Stockholders' Equity	322,000	325,000	336,000	354,000	380,000	345,000	377,000	596,000
Shares Outstanding	43,000	44,000	44,000	44,000	45,000	46,000	49,000	...
Statistical Record								
Return on Assets %	7.77	7.98	7.84	6.99	6.67	9.94	8.31	13.74
Return on Equity %	48.31	47.38	46.72	39.67	32.36	39.17	23.23	28.99
EBITDA Margin %	6.86	6.60	6.62	6.65	5.86	6.67	4.76	6.15
Net Margin %	3.85	3.90	4.44	3.33	2.71	3.63	2.74	3.81
Asset Turnover	2.06	2.12	2.07	2.10	2.46	2.74	3.03	3.61
Current Ratio	1.34	1.41	1.42	1.47	1.38	1.63	1.76	1.26
Debt to Equity	3.09	3.10	3.02	2.89	2.67	1.32	1.30	N.M.
Price Range	89.24-61.06	89.24-60.10	89.24-51.45	88.65-40.50	55.70-39.89	52.13-34.65	39.03-30.94	...
P/E Ratio	24.45-16.73	24.93-16.79	24.86-14.33	27.53-12.58	22.55-16.15	17.91-11.91	17.19-13.63	...
Average Yield %	1.63	1.64	1.73	1.97	2.46	2.58	1.60	...

Address: 12010 Sunset Hills Rd., Reston, VA 20190 Telephone: 703-676-4300	Web Site: www.saic.com Officers: Edward J. Sanderson - Chairman Anthony J. Moraco - Chief Executive Officer, Division Officer, Holding/Parent Company Officer	Auditors: Deloitte & Touche LLP

SCOTTS MIRACLE-GRO CO (THE)

Exchange	Symbol	Price	52Wk Range	Yield	P/E
NYS	SMG	$106.99 (12/29/2017)	106.99-83.37	1.98	29.47

*7 Year Price Score 117.76 *NYSE Composite Index=100 *12 Month Price Score 100.87

Interim Earnings (Per Share)

Qtr.	Dec	Mar	Jun	Sep
2012-13	(1.10)	1.60	2.37	(0.32)
2013-14	(1.06)	2.00	1.95	(0.25)
2014-15	(1.23)	2.01	2.14	(0.38)
2015-16	(1.32)	3.38	3.44	(0.41)
2016-17	(1.09)	2.73	2.53	(0.53)

Interim Dividends (Per Share)

Amt	Decl	Ex	Rec	Pay
0.50Q	01/27/2017	02/22/2017	02/24/2017	03/10/2017
0.50Q	05/01/2017	05/24/2017	05/26/2017	06/09/2017
0.53Q	08/01/2017	08/23/2017	08/25/2017	09/08/2017
0.53Q	11/01/2017	11/22/2017	11/24/2017	12/08/2017

Indicated Div: $2.12

Valuation Analysis

		Institutional Holding	
Forecast EPS	$4.30		
	(01/17/2018)	No of Institutions	461
Market Cap	$6.2 Billion	Shares	
Book Value	$648.8 Million		49,915,360
Price/Book	9.58	% Held	
Price/Sales	2.35		72.46

Business Summary: Agricultural Chemicals (MIC: 8.3.3 SIC: 2879 NAIC: 325320)

Scotts Miracle-Gro provides consumer lawn and garden products in the following categories: lawn care, which includes lawn fertilizer products, grass seed products, and lawn-related weed, pest and disease control products as well as spreaders and outdoor cleaners; gardening and landscape, which includes water-soluble plant foods, continuous-release plant foods, potting mixes and garden soils, mulch and decorative groundcover products, plant-related pest and disease control products, organic garden products, live goods and seeding solutions as well as hydroponic gardening products; and controls, which includes insect control products, rodent control products and weed control products.

Recent Developments: For the year ended Sep 30 2017, income from continuing operations decreased 19.4% to US$198.3 million from US$246.1 million a year earlier. Net income decreased 30.5% to US$218.8 million from US$314.8 million in the prior year. Revenues were US$2.64 billion, up 5.4% from US$2.51 billion the year before. Operating income was US$433.4 million versus US$447.6 million in the prior year, a decrease of 3.2%. Direct operating expenses rose 4.0% to US$1.67 billion from US$1.61 billion in the comparable period the year before. Indirect operating expenses increased 19.1% to US$539.2 million from US$452.7 million in the equivalent prior-year period.

Prospects: Our evaluation of Scotts Co. as of Jan. 14, 2018 is the result of our systematic analysis on three basic characteristics: earnings strength, relative valuation, and recent stock price movement. The company has managed to produce a neutral trend in earnings per share over the past 5 quarters and while recent estimates for the company have been raised by analysts, SMG has posted better than expected results. Based on operating earnings yield, the company is about fairly valued when compared to all of the companies in our coverage universe. Share price changes over the past year indicates that SMG will perform in line with the market over the near term.

Financial Data

(US$ in Thousands)	09/30/2017	09/30/2016	09/30/2015	09/30/2014	09/30/2013	09/30/2012	09/30/2011	09/30/2010
Earnings Per Share	3.63	5.09	2.57	2.65	2.57	1.71	2.54	3.02
Cash Flow Per Share	5.96	3.87	4.04	3.91	5.54	2.51	1.89	4.46
Tang Book Value Per Share	N.M.	N.M.	N.M.	N.M.	1.79	N.M.	N.M.	0.95
Dividends Per Share	2.030	1.910	1.820	3.763	1.413	1.225	1.050	0.625
Dividend Payout %	55.92	37.52	70.82	141.98	54.96	71.64	41.34	20.70
Income Statement								
Total Revenue	2,642,100	2,836,100	3,016,500	2,841,300	2,816,500	2,826,100	2,835,700	3,139,900
EBITDA	505,700	533,500	378,200	378,500	387,500	314,200	316,100	453,800
Depn & Amortn	95,700	86,900	83,600	74,600	74,300	70,600	70,300	69,200
Income Before Taxes	343,900	384,900	244,100	256,600	254,000	181,800	194,800	337,800
Income Taxes	116,600	139,400	85,400	91,200	92,800	68,600	72,900	125,400
Net Income	218,300	315,300	159,800	166,500	161,100	106,500	167,900	204,100
Average Shares	60,200	62,000	62,200	62,700	62,600	62,100	66,200	67,600
Balance Sheet								
Current Assets	881,700	991,700	948,600	935,000	881,000	1,000,000	992,500	1,037,600
Total Assets	2,747,000	2,808,800	2,527,200	2,058,300	1,937,200	2,074,400	2,052,200	2,164,000
Current Liabilities	544,500	593,100	613,100	544,700	509,800	433,600	468,600	723,900
Long-Term Obligations	1,258,000	1,131,100	1,028,500	692,400	478,100	781,100	791,800	436,700
Total Liabilities	2,098,200	2,093,600	1,906,500	1,504,600	1,226,700	1,472,500	1,492,400	1,399,500
Stockholders' Equity	648,800	715,200	620,700	553,700	710,500	601,900	559,800	764,500
Shares Outstanding	58,100	60,300	61,400	60,700	62,000	61,300	60,800	65,000
Statistical Record								
Return on Assets %	7.86	11.79	6.97	8.33	8.03	5.15	7.96	9.31
Return on Equity %	32.01	47.08	27.21	26.34	24.55	18.29	25.36	30.26
EBITDA Margin %	19.14	18.81	12.54	13.32	13.76	11.12	11.15	14.45
Net Margin %	8.26	11.12	5.30	5.86	5.72	3.77	5.92	6.50
Asset Turnover	0.95	1.06	1.32	1.42	1.40	1.37	1.35	1.43
Current Ratio	1.62	1.67	1.55	1.72	1.73	2.31	2.12	1.43
Debt to Equity	1.94	1.58	1.66	1.25	0.67	1.30	1.41	0.57
Price Range	97.37-82.95	83.62-60.82	68.99-54.71	63.30-53.09	55.66-39.77	55.00-38.17	60.27-40.41	51.87-37.84
P/E Ratio	26.82-22.85	16.43-11.95	26.84-21.29	23.89-20.03	21.66-15.47	32.16-22.32	23.73-15.91	17.18-12.53
Average Yield %	2.21	2.70	2.92	6.44	3.03	2.69	2.01	1.42

Address: 14111 Scottslawn Road, Marysville, OH 43041 **Telephone:** 937-644-0011 **Fax:** 937-644-7614	**Web Site:** www.scotts.com **Officers:** James Hagedorn - Chairman, Chief Executive Officer Michael C. Lukemire - President, Chief Operating Officer, Region Officer	**Auditors:** DELOITTE & TOUCHE LLP **Investor Contact:** 937-644-0011 **Transfer Agents:** Wells Fargo Shareowner Services

628

SEALED AIR CORP

Exchange	Symbol	Price	52Wk Range	Yield	P/E
NYS	SEE	$49.30 (12/29/2017)	50.22-41.72	1.30	9.39

*7 Year Price Score 104.30 *NYSE Composite Index=100 *12 Month Price Score 97.97

Interim Earnings (Per Share)

Qtr.	Mar	Jun	Sep	Dec
2014	0.33	0.28	0.28	0.32
2015	0.46	0.13	0.42	0.61
2016	0.46	0.25	0.83	0.87
2017	(0.22)	0.45	4.15	...

Interim Dividends (Per Share)

Amt	Decl	Ex	Rec	Pay
0.16Q	02/15/2017	03/01/2017	03/03/2017	03/17/2017
0.16Q	05/18/2017	05/31/2017	06/02/2017	06/16/2017
0.16Q	07/07/2017	08/30/2017	09/01/2017	09/15/2017
0.16Q	10/05/2017	11/30/2017	12/01/2017	12/15/2017

Indicated Div: $0.64

Valuation Analysis / **Institutional Holding**

Forecast EPS	$1.80 (01/18/2018)	No of Institutions	653
Market Cap	$8.9 Billion	Shares	207,223,360
Book Value	$760.6 Million	% Held	91.25
Price/Book	11.69		
Price/Sales	1.79		

TRADING VOLUME (thousand shares)

Business Summary: Containers & Packaging (MIC: 8.1.3 SIC: 2671 NAIC: 322221)

Sealed Air is engaged in food safety and security, facility hygiene and product protection. Co. has three reportable segments: Food Care, which provides a range of integrated system solutions that improve the management of contamination risk and facility hygiene, extend product shelf life through packaging technologies, and improve merchandising, ease-of-use, and back-of-house preparation processes; Diversey Care, which provides Diversey®-branded system solutions for facility hygiene, food safety and security, and infection control; and Product Care, which provides tailored packaging solutions. Co.'s other category include its Medical Applications, which sells medical applications product.

Recent Developments: For the quarter ended Sep 30 2017, income from continuing operations decreased 2.2% to US$62.4 million from US$63.8 million in the year-earlier quarter. Net income increased 382.2% to US$787.4 million from US$163.3 million in the year-earlier quarter. Revenues were US$1.13 billion, up 6.2% from US$1.07 billion the year before. Operating income was US$160.1 million versus US$167.1 million in the prior-year quarter, a decrease of 4.2%. Direct operating expenses rose 8.6% to US$769.2 million from US$708.4 million in the comparable period the year before. Indirect operating expenses increased 6.5% to US$202.0 million from US$189.6 million in the equivalent prior-year period.

Prospects: Our evaluation of Sealed Air Corp. as of Jan. 14, 2018 is the result of our systematic analysis on three basic characteristics: earnings strength, relative valuation, and recent stock price movement. The company has generated a negative trend in earnings per share over the past 5 quarters and while recent estimates for the company have been mixed, SEE has posted results that fell short of analysts expectations. Based on operating earnings yield, the company is about fairly valued when compared to all of the companies in our coverage universe. Share price changes over the past year indicates that SEE will perform poorly over the near term.

Financial Data

(US$ in Thousands)	9 Mos	6 Mos	3 Mos	12/31/2016	12/31/2015	12/31/2014	12/31/2013	12/31/2012
Earnings Per Share	5.25	1.93	1.73	2.46	1.62	1.20	0.58	(7.31)
Cash Flow Per Share	4.11	4.50	4.76	4.65	4.75	(0.96)	3.21	2.09
Dividends Per Share	0.640	0.640	0.640	0.610	0.520	0.520	0.520	0.520
Dividend Payout %	12.19	33.16	36.99	24.80	32.10	43.33	89.66	...
Income Statement								
Total Revenue	3,233,800	2,102,500	1,032,200	6,778,300	7,031,500	7,750,500	7,690,800	7,648,100
EBITDA	502,800	316,200	158,300	981,400	853,400	806,100	810,200	(1,197,900)
Depn & Amortn	85,100	54,700	29,100	215,400	213,300	266,700	283,400	304,000
Income Before Taxes	274,300	167,200	82,600	565,900	425,900	267,200	176,800	(1,874,600)
Income Taxes	236,500	192,500	136,400	79,500	90,500	9,100	84,000	(261,900)
Net Income	848,400	44,600	(43,200)	486,400	335,400	258,100	124,200	(1,410,300)
Average Shares	188,900	194,800	195,700	197,200	206,700	213,900	213,500	192,800
Balance Sheet								
Current Assets	2,575,700	4,446,900	4,287,500	2,215,300	2,215,600	2,691,600	3,417,700	3,222,400
Total Assets	5,939,400	7,626,900	7,421,200	7,389,100	7,426,000	8,041,700	9,134,200	9,437,200
Current Liabilities	1,516,900	3,070,000	2,661,600	2,118,900	1,807,100	1,730,900	2,700,800	2,333,600
Long-Term Obligations	3,219,400	3,790,100	3,762,700	3,938,300	4,302,700	4,282,500	4,116,400	4,540,800
Total Liabilities	5,178,800	7,287,400	6,826,400	6,779,400	6,898,900	6,878,900	7,745,100	7,993,400
Stockholders' Equity	760,600	339,500	594,800	609,700	527,100	1,162,800	1,389,100	1,443,800
Shares Outstanding	180,394	190,037	195,824	193,482	196,013	210,531	196,198	194,557
Statistical Record								
Return on Assets %	14.81	5.00	4.56	6.55	4.34	3.01	1.34	N.M.
Return on Equity %	152.75	81.81	58.97	85.34	39.69	20.23	8.77	N.M.
EBITDA Margin %	15.55	15.04	15.34	14.48	12.14	10.40	10.53	N.M.
Net Margin %	26.24	2.12	N.M.	7.18	4.77	3.33	1.61	N.M.
Asset Turnover	0.74	0.73	0.83	0.91	0.91	0.90	0.83	0.73
Current Ratio	1.70	1.45	1.61	1.05	1.23	1.56	1.27	1.38
Debt to Equity	4.23	11.16	6.33	6.46	8.16	3.68	2.96	3.15
Price Range	50.22-41.72	50.22-42.30	52.68-42.45	52.68-38.36	55.40-39.42	43.47-29.86	34.13-17.51	21.04-13.11
P/E Ratio	9.57-7.95	26.02-21.92	30.45-24.54	21.41-15.59	34.20-24.33	36.23-24.88	58.84-30.19	...
Average Yield %	1.41	1.39	1.36	1.32	1.09	1.51	2.03	3.06

Address: 2415 Cascade Pointe Boulevard, Charlotte, NC 28208	**Web Site:** www.sealedair.com	**Auditors:** Ernst & Young LLP
Telephone: 980 221-3235	**Officers:** William J. Marino - Chairman Edward L. (Ted) Doheny - President, Chief Executive Officer - Designate, Chief Operating Officer	**Investor Contact:** 201-791-7600
Fax: 201-703-4205		**Transfer Agents:** ComputerShare Investor Services, Providence, RI

SEMPRA ENERGY

*7 Year Price Score 99.40 *NYSE Composite Index=100 *12 Month Price Score 97.47

Interim Earnings (Per Share)

Qtr.	Mar	Jun	Sep	Dec
2014	0.99	1.08	1.39	1.18
2015	1.74	1.17	0.99	1.46
2016	1.27	0.06	2.46	1.53
2017	1.75	1.03	0.22	...

Interim Dividends (Per Share)

Amt	Decl	Ex	Rec	Pay
0.823Q	02/23/2017	03/21/2017	03/23/2017	04/15/2017
0.823Q	06/21/2017	07/05/2017	07/07/2017	07/15/2017
0.823Q	09/08/2017	09/21/2017	09/22/2017	10/15/2017
0.823Q	12/15/2017	12/28/2017	12/29/2017	01/15/2018

Indicated Div: $3.29

Valuation Analysis / **Institutional Holding**

Forecast EPS	$5.26
	(01/18/2018)
Market Cap	$26.8 Billion
Book Value	$13.3 Billion
Price/Book	2.02
Price/Sales	2.41

No of Institutions	880
Shares	249,894,544
% Held	69.69

TRADING VOLUME (thousand shares)

Business Summary: Electric Utilities (MIC: 3.1.1 SIC: 4932 NAIC: 221210)

Sempra Energy is a holding company. Co.'s principal operating units are: Sempra Utilities, which includes Co.'s San Diego Gas & Electric Company, Southern California Gas Company and Sempra South American Utilities reportable segments; as well as Sempra Infrastructure, which includes Co.'s Sempra Mexico, Sempra Renewables and Sempra liquefied natural gas (LNG) & Midstream reportable segments. Sempra LNG & Midstream develops and, invests in liquefied natural gas (LNG)-related infrastructure in North America, develops and operates natural gas storage facilities in Alabama and Mississippi and owns a 50.2% interest in a liquefaction project in Louisiana.

Recent Developments: For the quarter ended Sep 30 2017, net income decreased 85.8% to US$102.0 million from US$719.0 million in the year-earlier quarter. Revenues were US$2.68 billion, up 5.7% from US$2.54 billion the year before. Direct operating expenses rose 4.8% to US$1.72 billion from US$1.64 billion in the comparable period the year before. Indirect operating expenses increased 92.7% to US$842.0 million from US$437.0 million in the equivalent prior-year period.

Prospects: Our evaluation of Sempra Energy as of Jan. 14, 2018 is the result of our systematic analysis on three basic characteristics: earnings strength, relative valuation, and recent stock price movement. The company has generated a negative trend in earnings per share over the past 5 quarters. However, while recent estimates for the company have been mixed, SRE has posted results that fell short of analysts expectations. Based on operating earnings yield, the company is undervalued when compared to all of the companies in our coverage universe. Share price changes over the past year indicates that SRE will perform very well over the near term.

Financial Data

(US$ in Thousands)	9 Mos	6 Mos	3 Mos	12/31/2016	12/31/2015	12/31/2014	12/31/2013	12/31/2012
Earnings Per Share	4.53	6.77	5.80	5.46	5.37	4.63	4.01	3.48
Cash Flow Per Share	13.26	13.23	10.87	9.24	11.70	8.79	7.32	8.34
Tang Book Value Per Share	41.18	41.48	41.20	40.13	42.63	40.51	39.10	36.04
Dividends Per Share	3.223	2.333	3.087	3.020	2.800	2.640	2.520	2.400
Dividend Payout %	71.14	34.45	53.23	55.31	52.14	57.02	62.84	68.97
Income Statement								
Total Revenue	8,243,000	5,564,000	3,031,000	10,183,000	10,231,000	11,035,000	10,557,000	9,647,000
EBITDA	2,585,000	2,077,000	1,201,000	3,042,000	3,379,000	3,125,000	3,046,000	2,820,000
Depn & Amortn	1,106,000	728,000	360,000	1,312,000	1,250,000	1,156,000	1,113,000	1,090,000
Income Before Taxes	1,154,000	1,149,000	752,000	1,207,000	1,600,000	1,443,000	1,399,000	1,262,000
Income Taxes	378,000	462,000	295,000	389,000	341,000	300,000	366,000	59,000
Net Income	758,000	701,000	441,000	1,371,000	1,350,000	1,162,000	1,009,000	865,000
Average Shares	253,364	252,822	252,246	251,155	250,923	250,655	249,332	246,693
Balance Sheet								
Current Assets	2,878,000	2,767,000	2,953,000	3,110,000	2,891,000	4,184,000	3,997,000	3,695,000
Total Assets	50,129,000	49,376,000	48,284,000	47,786,000	41,150,000	39,732,000	37,244,000	36,499,000
Current Liabilities	7,194,000	6,063,000	5,812,000	5,927,000	4,612,000	5,069,000	4,369,000	4,258,000
Long-Term Obligations	14,803,000	15,000,000	14,409,000	14,429,000	13,134,000	12,167,000	11,253,000	11,621,000
Total Liabilities	36,864,000	36,044,000	35,020,000	34,835,000	29,341,000	28,406,000	26,236,000	26,217,000
Stockholders' Equity	13,265,000	13,332,000	13,264,000	12,951,000	11,809,000	11,326,000	11,008,000	10,282,000
Shares Outstanding	251,000	251,000	251,000	250,152	248,298	246,330	244,461	242,368
Statistical Record								
Return on Assets %	2.38	3.69	3.24	3.07	3.34	3.02	2.74	2.47
Return on Equity %	8.88	13.55	11.57	11.04	11.67	10.41	9.48	8.57
EBITDA Margin %	31.36	37.33	39.62	29.87	33.03	28.32	28.85	29.23
Net Margin %	9.20	12.60	14.55	13.46	13.20	10.53	9.56	8.97
Asset Turnover	0.23	0.24	0.24	0.23	0.25	0.29	0.29	0.28
Current Ratio	0.40	0.46	0.51	0.52	0.63	0.83	0.91	0.87
Debt to Equity	1.12	1.13	1.09	1.11	1.11	1.07	1.02	1.13
Price Range	120.06-94.74	117.50-94.74	114.50-94.74	114.50-87.00	115.08-90.09	115.85-88.44	92.10-70.84	72.74-54.83
P/E Ratio	26.50-20.91	17.36-13.99	19.74-16.33	20.97-15.93	21.43-16.78	25.02-19.10	22.97-17.67	20.90-15.76
Average Yield %	2.95	2.17	2.92	2.92	2.71	2.61	3.04	3.71

Address: 488 8th Avenue, San Diego, CA 92101
Telephone: 619-696-2000

Web Site: www.sempra.com
Officers: Debra L. Reed - Chairman, President, Chief Executive Officer, Executive Vice President Jeffrey Walker Martin - Chief Financial Officer, Executive Vice President

Auditors: Deloitte & Touche LLP
Transfer Agents: American Stock Transfer & Trust Company, LLC, Brooklyn, NY

SENSIENT TECHNOLOGIES CORP.

Exchange	Symbol	Price	52Wk Range	Yield	P/E	Div Achiever
NYS	SXT	$73.15 (12/29/2017)	83.35-71.84	1.80	30.10	11 Years

*7 Year Price Score 111.67 *NYSE Composite Index=100 *12 Month Price Score 91.52

Interim Earnings (Per Share)

Qtr.	Mar	Jun	Sep	Dec
2014	(0.04)	0.59	0.44	0.53
2015	0.64	0.63	0.60	0.43
2016	0.69	0.63	0.79	0.71
2017	0.30	0.69	0.73	...

Interim Dividends (Per Share)

Amt	Decl	Ex	Rec	Pay
0.30Q	01/24/2017	02/03/2017	02/07/2017	03/01/2017
0.30Q	04/28/2017	05/10/2017	05/12/2017	06/01/2017
0.30Q	07/20/2017	08/02/2017	08/04/2017	09/01/2017
0.33Q	10/19/2017	11/03/2017	11/06/2017	12/01/2017

Indicated Div: $1.32

Valuation Analysis / Institutional Holding

Valuation Analysis		Institutional Holding	
Forecast EPS	$3.40	No of Institutions	
	(01/18/2018)	350	
Market Cap	$3.2 Billion	Shares	
Book Value	$879.5 Million	57,592,024	
Price/Book	3.62	% Held	
Price/Sales	2.33	86.09	

Business Summary: Specialty Chemicals (MIC: 8.3.2 SIC: 2816 NAIC: 325131)

Sensient Technologies is a manufacturer and marketer of colors, flavors and fragrances. Co.'s three reportable segments are: the Flavors & Fragrances Group, which is a developer, manufacturer and supplier of flavor and fragrance systems for the food, beverage, personal care and household-products industries; Color Group, which provides natural and synthetic color systems for use in foods, beverages and pharmaceuticals; colors and other ingredients for cosmetic; and Asia Pacific Group, which provides a range of products from its Flavors & Fragrances Group and Color Group, as well as products developed by regional technical teams.

Recent Developments: For the quarter ended Sep 30 2017, income from continuing operations decreased 9.6% to US$32.2 million from US$35.6 million in the year-earlier quarter. Net income decreased 9.6% to US$32.2 million from US$35.6 million in the year-earlier quarter. Revenues were US$353.5 million, up 1.1% from US$349.7 million the year before. Operating income was US$52.0 million versus US$51.2 million in the prior-year quarter, an increase of 1.7%. Direct operating expenses rose 1.6% to US$230.8 million from US$227.1 million in the comparable period the year before. Indirect operating expenses decreased 1.0% to US$70.7 million from US$71.4 million in the equivalent prior-year period.

Prospects: Our evaluation of Sensient Technologies Corp. as of Jan. 14, 2018 is the result of our systematic analysis on three basic characteristics: earnings strength, relative valuation, and recent stock price movement. The company has managed to produce a neutral trend in earnings per share over the past 5 quarters. However, while recent estimates for the company have been lowered by analysts, SXT has posted better than expected results. Based on operating earnings yield, the company is undervalued when compared to all of the companies in our coverage universe. Share price changes over the past year indicates that SXT will perform well over the near term.

Financial Data

(US$ in Thousands)	9 Mos	6 Mos	3 Mos	12/31/2016	12/31/2015	12/31/2014	12/31/2013	12/31/2012
Earnings Per Share	2.43	2.49	2.43	2.82	2.31	1.51	2.27	2.49
Cash Flow Per Share	4.20	4.19	4.84	4.98	2.79	3.90	3.09	2.80
Tang Book Value Per Share	10.69	10.84	10.26	10.04	9.74	12.95	15.54	13.91
Dividends Per Share	1.200	1.170	1.140	1.110	1.040	0.980	0.910	0.870
Dividend Payout %	49.38	46.99	46.91	39.36	45.02	64.90	40.09	34.94
Income Statement								
Total Revenue	1,033,391	679,872	341,397	1,383,210	1,375,964	1,447,821	1,467,550	1,459,050
EBITDA	157,053	92,853	36,178	231,323	213,035	180,890	223,078	238,200
Depn & Amortn	36,626	24,436	12,141	45,714	46,694	50,225	50,716	46,992
Income Before Taxes	105,953	58,889	19,226	167,285	149,396	114,598	156,215	174,307
Income Taxes	29,774	14,923	6,034	44,372	42,149	32,827	42,920	50,399
Net Income	76,179	43,966	13,192	126,256	106,785	73,646	113,295	123,908
Average Shares	43,864	44,290	44,479	44,843	46,204	48,819	49,934	49,822
Balance Sheet								
Current Assets	754,327	726,681	699,729	717,061	753,343	759,389	789,825	751,354
Total Assets	1,738,865	1,698,333	1,651,202	1,667,860	1,711,437	1,765,206	1,870,734	1,776,643
Current Liabilities	210,211	188,543	191,084	213,675	212,922	224,905	222,893	204,236
Long-Term Obligations	607,395	586,940	572,200	582,780	613,877	451,011	348,124	333,979
Total Liabilities	859,333	814,618	801,367	832,119	866,310	718,271	628,050	622,745
Stockholders' Equity	879,532	883,715	849,835	835,741	845,127	1,046,935	1,242,684	1,153,898
Shares Outstanding	43,475	43,866	44,258	44,238	44,780	47,424	49,849	49,690
Statistical Record								
Return on Assets %	6.19	6.50	6.38	7.45	6.14	4.05	6.21	7.20
Return on Equity %	12.23	12.71	12.61	14.98	11.29	6.43	9.45	11.22
EBITDA Margin %	15.20	13.66	10.60	16.72	15.48	12.49	15.20	16.33
Net Margin %	7.37	6.47	3.86	9.13	7.76	5.09	7.72	8.49
Asset Turnover	0.78	0.80	0.81	0.82	0.79	0.80	0.80	0.85
Current Ratio	3.59	3.85	3.66	3.36	3.54	3.38	3.54	3.68
Debt to Equity	0.69	0.66	0.67	0.70	0.73	0.43	0.28	0.29
Price Range	83.35-71.37	83.35-68.89	83.11-63.27	83.11-53.92	70.25-57.39	62.98-46.74	53.32-35.56	40.92-33.81
P/E Ratio	34.30-29.37	33.47-27.67	34.20-26.04	29.47-19.12	30.41-24.84	41.71-30.95	23.49-15.67	16.43-13.58
Average Yield %	1.54	1.52	1.54	1.61	1.60	1.80	2.13	2.37

Address: 777 East Wisconsin Avenue, Milwaukee, WI 53202-5304 Telephone: 414-271-6755 Fax: 414-347-4795	Web Site: www.sensient.com Officers: Paul Manning - President, Chief Executive Officer, Division Officer Stephen J. Rolfs - Senior Vice President, Vice President, Chief Financial Officer	Auditors: Ernst & Young LLP Investor Contact: 414-347-3779 Transfer Agents: Wells Fargo Bank Minnesota, N.A., St. Paul, MN

SERVICE CORP. INTERNATIONAL

Exchange	Symbol	Price	52Wk Range	Yield	P/E
NYS	SCI	$37.32 (12/29/2017)	38.00-28.81	1.61	19.64

*7 Year Price Score 123.76 ***NYSE Composite Index=100** ***12 Month Price Score 104.10**

Interim Earnings (Per Share)

Qtr.	Mar	Jun	Sep	Dec
2014	0.19	0.12	0.08	0.42
2015	0.30	0.25	0.23	0.36
2016	0.24	0.08	0.24	0.34
2017	0.91	0.36	0.29	

Interim Dividends (Per Share)

Amt	Decl	Ex	Rec	Pay
0.13Q	02/08/2017	03/13/2017	03/15/2017	03/31/2017
0.15Q	05/10/2017	06/13/2017	06/15/2017	06/30/2017
0.15Q	08/07/2017	09/14/2017	09/15/2017	09/29/2017
0.15Q	11/08/2017	12/14/2017	12/15/2017	12/29/2017

Indicated Div: $0.60

Valuation Analysis		Institutional Holding	
Forecast EPS	$1.51	No of Institutions	
	(01/18/2018)	447	
Market Cap	$7.0 Billion	Shares	
Book Value	$1.2 Billion	184,783,712	
Price/Book	5.66	% Held	
Price/Sales	2.27	80.35	

Business Summary: Miscellaneous Consumer Services (MIC: 2.2.3 SIC: 7261 NAIC: 812210)

Service Corporation International provides deathcare products and services. Co.'s funeral service and cemetery operations consist of funeral service locations, cemeteries, funeral/cemetery combination locations, crematoria, and other related businesses. Funeral service locations provide services related to funerals and cremations, including the use of funeral home facilities and motor vehicles, arranging and directing services, removal, preparation, embalming, cremations, memorialization, and catering. Co.'s cemeteries provide cemetery property interment rights, including developed lots, lawn crypts, mausoleum spaces, niches, and other cremation memorialization and interment options.

Recent Developments: For the quarter ended Sep 30 2017, net income increased 18.1% to US$56.1 million from US$47.5 million in the year-earlier quarter. Revenues were US$731.3 million, up 1.4% from US$721.5 million the year before. Operating income was US$109.1 million versus US$114.4 million in the prior-year quarter, a decrease of 4.7%. Direct operating expenses rose 0.2% to US$581.6 million from US$580.7 million in the comparable period the year before. Indirect operating expenses increased 54.2% to US$40.6 million from US$26.4 million in the equivalent prior-year period.

Prospects: Our evaluation of Service Corp. International as of Jan. 14, 2018 is the result of our systematic analysis on three basic characteristics: earnings strength, relative valuation, and recent stock price movement. The company has generated a negative trend in earnings per share over the past 5 quarters and while recent estimates for the company have remained steady, SCI has posted better than expected results. Based on operating earnings yield, the company is about fairly valued when compared to all of the companies in our coverage universe. Share price changes over the past year indicates that SCI will perform well over the near term.

Financial Data
(US$ in Thousands)

	9 Mos	6 Mos	3 Mos	12/31/2016	12/31/2015	12/31/2014	12/31/2013	12/31/2012
Earnings Per Share	1.90	1.85	1.57	0.90	1.14	0.81	0.67	0.70
Cash Flow Per Share	2.64	2.46	2.48	2.39	2.36	1.51	1.82	1.71
Dividends Per Share	0.560	0.540	0.520	0.510	0.440	0.340	0.270	0.280
Dividend Payout %	29.47	29.19	33.12	56.67	38.60	41.98	40.30	40.00
Income Statement								
Total Revenue	2,282,298	1,550,952	777,710	3,031,137	2,986,380	2,994,012	2,556,382	2,410,481
EBITDA	463,895	330,291	138,161	572,619	606,869	671,628	453,386	450,118
Depn & Amortn	71,800	47,528	22,158	178,189	172,915	167,185	138,198	137,660
Income Before Taxes	266,622	200,044	98,526	326,658	370,351	402,600	245,719	245,683
Income Taxes	(32,830)	(43,267)	(76,223)	149,353	135,027	225,980	96,615	91,548
Net Income	299,347	243,183	174,702	177,038	233,772	172,469	143,848	152,546
Average Shares	192,243	192,138	192,867	196,042	204,450	214,200	216,014	219,066
Balance Sheet								
Current Assets	404,883	354,869	390,757	354,396	308,409	396,856	393,747	286,199
Total Assets	12,625,198	12,388,284	12,259,166	12,038,149	11,718,888	11,923,644	12,906,070	9,683,568
Current Liabilities	579,729	524,349	612,990	537,870	519,396	552,008	642,584	412,104
Long-Term Obligations	3,292,816	3,290,944	3,224,653	3,196,616	3,071,738	2,963,794	3,155,548	1,916,621
Total Liabilities	11,386,520	11,183,587	11,077,997	10,945,436	10,534,196	10,554,918	11,491,840	8,340,541
Stockholders' Equity	1,238,678	1,204,697	1,181,169	1,092,713	1,184,692	1,368,726	1,414,230	1,343,027
Shares Outstanding	187,746	187,315	187,949	189,405	195,772	204,866	212,316	211,046
Statistical Record								
Return on Assets %	2.96	2.94	2.53	1.49	1.98	1.39	1.27	1.60
Return on Equity %	31.44	30.17	25.72	15.50	18.31	12.39	10.43	11.12
EBITDA Margin %	20.33	21.30	17.77	18.89	20.32	22.43	17.74	18.67
Net Margin %	13.12	15.68	22.46	5.84	7.83	5.76	5.63	6.33
Asset Turnover	0.25	0.25	0.25	0.25	0.25	0.24	0.23	0.25
Current Ratio	0.70	0.68	0.64	0.66	0.59	0.72	0.61	0.69
Debt to Equity	2.66	2.73	2.73	2.93	2.59	2.17	2.23	1.43
Price Range	35.80-24.90	33.45-24.90	31.75-24.49	28.67-21.65	31.94-22.29	23.22-16.82	19.24-13.81	14.54-10.55
P/E Ratio	18.84-13.11	18.08-13.46	20.22-15.60	31.86-24.06	28.02-19.55	28.67-20.77	28.72-20.61	20.77-15.07
Average Yield %	1.82	1.87	1.89	1.96	1.61	1.67	1.56	2.26

Address: 1929 Allen Parkway, Houston, TX 77019 **Telephone:** 713-522-5141	**Web Site:** www.sci-corp.com **Officers:** Thomas L. (Tom) Ryan - Chairman, President, Chief Executive Officer Michael R. Webb - President, Executive Vice President, Chief Operating Officer	**Auditors:** PricewaterhouseCoopers LLP **Transfer Agents:** Computershare Shareowner Services, Providence, RI

SERVICEMASTER GLOBAL HOLDINGS, INC

Exchange	Symbol	Price	52Wk Range	Yield	P/E
NYS	SERV	$51.27 (12/29/2017)	52.32-36.45	N/A	29.47

*7 Year Price Score N/A   *NYSE Composite Index=100   *12 Month Price Score 108.68

Interim Earnings (Per Share)

Qtr.	Mar	Jun	Sep	Dec
2014	(1.23)	0.44	(0.03)	0.22
2015	0.20	0.49	0.36	0.12
2016	0.28	0.11	0.51	0.23
2017	0.29	0.63	0.59	...

Interim Dividends (Per Share)

No Dividends Paid

Valuation Analysis		Institutional Holding	
Forecast EPS	$2.10	No of Institutions	297
	(01/01/2018)		
Market Cap	$6.9 Billion	Shares	155,476,224
Book Value	$852.0 Million		
Price/Book	8.13	% Held	
Price/Sales	2.40	N/A	

TRADING VOLUME (thousand shares)

Business Summary: Miscellaneous Consumer Services (MIC: 2.2.3 SIC: 8741 NAIC: 551112)

ServiceMaster Global Holdings is holding company. Co. is a provider of residential and commercial services, operating through a service network and franchised and licensed agreements. Co.'s portfolio of brands includes Terminix (termite and pest control), American Home Shield (home warranties), ServiceMaster Restore (disaster restoration), ServiceMaster Clean (janitorial), Merry Maids (residential cleaning), Furniture Medic (cabinet and wood furniture repair) and AmeriSpec (home inspection). Co. operates in three segments: Terminix, American Home Shield, and the Franchise Services Group (which includes ServiceMaster Restore, ServiceMaster Clean, Merry Maids, Furniture Medic and AmeriSpec).

Recent Developments: For the quarter ended Sep 30 2017, income from continuing operations increased 14.3% to US$80.0 million from US$70.0 million in the year-earlier quarter. Net income increased 14.3% to US$80.0 million from US$70.0 million in the year-earlier quarter. Revenues were US$797.0 million, up 5.1% from US$758.0 million the year before. Direct operating expenses rose 4.8% to US$419.0 million from US$400.0 million in the comparable period the year before. Indirect operating expenses increased 10.4% to US$223.0 million from US$202.0 million in the equivalent prior-year period.

Prospects: Our evaluation of ServiceMaster Global Holding as of Jan. 14, 2018 is the result of our systematic analysis on three basic characteristics: earnings strength, relative valuation, and recent stock price movement. The company has managed to produce a neutral trend in earnings per share over the past 5 quarters and while recent estimates for the company have been raised by analysts, SERV has posted better than expected results. Based on operating earnings yield, the company is about fairly valued when compared to all of the companies in our coverage universe. Share price changes over the past year indicates that SERV will perform well over the near term.

Financial Data (US$ in Millions)	9 Mos	6 Mos	3 Mos	12/31/2016	12/31/2015	12/31/2014	12/31/2013	12/31/2012
Earnings Per Share	1.74	1.66	1.14	1.13	1.17	(0.50)	(5.49)	(7.77)
Cash Flow Per Share	3.35	2.55	2.57	2.40	2.49	2.24	2.26	1.13
Income Statement								
Total Revenue	2,246	1,450	643	2,746	2,594	2,457	2,293	2,214
EBITDA	503	327	125	449	475	344	373	254
Depn & Amortn	80	54	26	61	47	48	48	42
Income Before Taxes	313	199	62	241	270	84	86	(26)
Income Taxes	109	76	24	85	107	40	43	(8)
Net Income	204	124	39	155	160	(57)	(507)	(714)
Average Shares	135	135	136	137	136	113	92	92
Balance Sheet								
Current Assets	1,259	1,140	1,003	998	933	1,044	1,213	1,085
Total Assets	5,647	5,541	5,402	5,386	5,098	5,134	5,905	6,415
Current Liabilities	1,227	1,219	1,134	1,042	955	905	972	899
Long-Term Obligations	2,654	2,678	2,694	2,772	2,698	3,017	3,867	3,881
Total Liabilities	4,794	4,800	4,718	4,700	4,553	4,775	5,882	5,880
Stockholders' Equity	852	741	685	686	545	359	23	535
Shares Outstanding	135	133	134	135	135	134	98	98
Statistical Record								
Return on Assets %	4.29	4.09	2.95	2.95	3.13	N.M.	N.M.	...
Return on Equity %	31.56	33.68	24.47	25.11	35.40	N.M.	N.M.	...
EBITDA Margin %	22.40	22.55	19.44	16.35	18.31	14.00	16.27	11.47
Net Margin %	9.08	8.55	6.07	5.64	6.17	N.M.	N.M.	N.M.
Asset Turnover	0.53	0.52	0.53	0.52	0.51	0.45	0.37	...
Current Ratio	1.03	0.94	0.88	0.96	0.98	1.15	1.25	1.21
Debt to Equity	3.12	3.61	3.93	4.04	4.95	8.40	168.13	7.25
Price Range	48.33-32.75	42.15-32.75	41.75-32.75	42.21-32.75	39.65-26.03	27.30-17.57	...	...
P/E Ratio	27.78-18.82	25.39-19.73	36.62-28.73	37.35-28.98	33.89-22.25	...	...	...

Address: 860 Ridge Lake Boulevard, Memphis, TN 38120	Web Site: www.servicemaster.com	Auditors: Deloitte & Touche LLP
Telephone: 901-597-1400	Officers: Anthony D. (Tony) DiLucente - Senior Vice President, Chief Financial Officer Mark J. Barry - President, Division Officer	Transfer Agents: Computershare Trust Company, N.A.

SERVICENOW INC

Exchange	Symbol	Price	52Wk Range	Yield	P/E
NYS	NOW	$130.39 (12/29/2017)	130.69-75.66	N/A	N/A

*7 Year Price Score N/A   *NYSE Composite Index=100   ***12 Month Price Score 111.05**

Interim Earnings (Per Share)

Qtr.	Mar	Jun	Sep	Dec
2014	(0.30)	(0.35)	(0.28)	(0.30)
2015	(0.38)	(0.40)	(0.26)	(0.23)
2016	(2.06)	(0.30)	(0.22)	(0.19)
2017	(0.24)	(0.33)	(0.14)	...

Interim Dividends (Per Share)

No Dividends Paid

Valuation Analysis / Institutional Holding

Valuation Analysis		Institutional Holding	
Forecast EPS	$1.20	No of Institutions	
	(01/26/2018)	514	
Market Cap	$22.5 Billion	Shares	
Book Value	$551.4 Million	186,469,248	
Price/Book	40.84	% Held	
Price/Sales	12.71	92.98	

Business Summary: IT Services (MIC: 6.3.1 SIC: 7372 NAIC: 511210)

ServiceNow provides enterprise cloud computing solutions that define, structure, manage and automate services for global enterprises. Co. markets its services to enterprises in a variety of industries, including financial services, consumer products, information technology services, health care, government, education and technology. Co. sells its subscription services primarily through direct sales and, to a lesser extent, through indirect channel sales. Co. also provides a portfolio of professional services to customers through its professional services and a network of partners.

Recent Developments: For the quarter ended Sep 30 2017, net loss amounted to US$24.2 million versus a net loss of US$36.3 million in the year-earlier quarter. Revenues were US$498.2 million, up 39.3% from US$357.7 million the year before. Operating loss was US$7.1 million versus a loss of US$26.8 million in the prior-year quarter. Direct operating expenses rose 23.8% to US$127.3 million from US$102.8 million in the comparable period the year before. Indirect operating expenses increased 34.2% to US$377.9 million from US$281.6 million in the equivalent prior-year period.

Prospects: Our evaluation of ServiceNow Inc as of Jan. 21, 2018 is the result of our systematic analysis on three basic characteristics: earnings strength, relative valuation, and recent stock price movement. The company has produced a positive trend in earnings per share over the past 5 quarters and while recent estimates for the company have remained steady, NOW has posted better than expected results. Based on operating earnings yield, the company is overvalued when compared to all of the companies in our coverage universe. Share price changes over the past year indicates that NOW will perform well over the near term.

Financial Data

(US$ in Thousands)	9 Mos	6 Mos	3 Mos	12/31/2016	12/31/2015	12/31/2014	12/31/2013	12/31/2012
Earnings Per Share	(0.90)	(0.98)	(0.95)	(2.75)	(1.27)	(1.23)	(0.54)	(0.51)
Cash Flow Per Share	3.44	3.20	1.59	0.97	2.02	0.96	0.60	0.66
Tang Book Value Per Share	2.17	1.79	1.55	1.42	2.91	2.13	2.71	1.93
Income Statement								
Total Revenue	1,386,656	888,486	416,783	1,390,513	1,005,480	682,563	424,650	243,712
EBITDA	87,678	27,520	13,713	(339,908)	(106,065)	(109,735)	(43,667)	(24,084)
Depn & Amortn	186,240	114,908	56,203	82,900	60,300	42,100	22,600	13,500
Income Before Taxes	(124,124)	(101,356)	(43,452)	(450,051)	(193,012)	(175,540)	(71,197)	(35,980)
Income Taxes	(2,801)	(4,221)	(2,790)	1,753	5,414	3,847	2,511	1,368
Net Income	(121,323)	(97,135)	(40,662)	(451,804)	(198,426)	(179,387)	(73,708)	(37,348)
Average Shares	171,883	170,419	168,742	164,533	155,706	145,355	135,415	73,908
Balance Sheet								
Current Assets	2,127,492	2,111,027	1,396,255	1,342,535	1,085,635	906,986	797,749	422,089
Total Assets	3,069,515	2,924,406	2,170,263	2,033,767	1,807,052	1,425,079	1,168,476	478,114
Current Liabilities	1,280,651	1,217,290	1,139,805	1,071,498	731,636	506,997	328,088	211,627
Long-Term Obligations	1,156,629	1,140,063	516,490	507,812	474,534	443,764	414,777	...
Total Liabilities	2,518,124	2,441,980	1,742,924	1,646,806	1,240,238	996,404	774,217	234,709
Stockholders' Equity	551,391	482,426	427,339	386,961	566,814	428,675	394,259	243,405
Shares Outstanding	172,706	170,712	169,721	167,430	160,785	149,509	140,354	126,367
Statistical Record								
EBITDA Margin %	6.32	3.10	3.29	N.M.	N.M.	N.M.	N.M.	N.M.
Asset Turnover	0.73	0.70	0.74	0.72	0.62	0.53	0.52	0.77
Current Ratio	1.66	1.73	1.22	1.25	1.48	1.79	2.43	1.99
Debt to Equity	2.10	2.36	1.21	1.31	0.84	1.04	1.05	...
Price Range	117.78-74.34	109.68-65.01	93.97-61.18	87.91-47.14	89.99-63.63	70.81-46.42	58.37-26.07	40.37-23.74

Address: 2225 Lawson Lane, Santa Clara, CA 95054 Telephone: 408-501-8550	Web Site: www.servicenow.com Officers: Frank Slootman - Chairman, President, Chief Executive Officer John J. Donahoe - President, Chief Executive Officer	Auditors: PricewaterhouseCoopers LLP Investor Contact: 408-961-2349 Transfer Agents: Computershare Trust Company, N.A

SHERWIN-WILLIAMS CO (THE)

Exchange	Symbol	Price	52Wk Range	Yield	P/E	Div Achiever
NYS	SHW	$410.04 (12/29/2017)	414.34-274.54	0.83	36.10	37 Years

*7 Year Price Score 126.33 *NYSE Composite Index=100 *12 Month Price Score 109.45

TRADING VOLUME (thousand shares)

Interim Earnings (Per Share)

Qtr.	Mar	Jun	Sep	Dec
2014	1.14	2.94	3.35	1.39
2015	1.38	3.70	3.97	2.12
2016	1.57	3.99	4.08	2.14
2017	2.53	3.36	3.33	...

Interim Dividends (Per Share)

Amt	Decl	Ex	Rec	Pay
0.85Q	02/15/2017	02/23/2017	02/27/2017	03/10/2017
0.85Q	04/19/2017	05/17/2017	05/19/2017	06/02/2017
0.85Q	07/19/2017	08/16/2017	08/18/2017	09/08/2017
0.85Q	10/18/2017	11/16/2017	11/17/2017	12/08/2017

Indicated Div: $3.40 (Div. Reinv. Plan)

Valuation Analysis

		Institutional Holding	
Forecast EPS	$14.97	No of Institutions	
	(01/18/2018)	1066	
Market Cap	$38.3 Billion	Shares	
Book Value	$2.7 Billion	95,109,424	
Price/Book	13.99	% Held	
Price/Sales	2.78	70.75	

Business Summary: Specialty Chemicals (MIC: 8.3.2 SIC: 5231 NAIC: 444120)

Sherwin-Williams is engaged in the development, manufacture, distribution and sale of paint, coatings and related products to professional, industrial, commercial and retail customers primarily in North and South America with additional operations in the Caribbean region, Europe and Asia. Co. has four reportable operating segments: Paint Stores Group, Consumer Group, Global Finishes Group and Latin America Coatings Group. As of Dec 31 2016, there were 4,180 Co.-operated specialty paint stores in the Paint Stores Group; 288 Co.-operated branches in the Global Finishes Group; and 339 Co.-operated stores in the Latin America Coatings Group.

Recent Developments: For the quarter ended Sep 30 2017, income from continuing operations decreased 18.1% to US$316.6 million from US$386.7 million in the year-earlier quarter. Net income decreased 18.1% to US$316.6 million from US$386.7 million in the year-earlier quarter. Revenues were US$4.51 billion, up 37.4% from US$3.28 billion the year before. Direct operating expenses rose 58.5% to US$2.60 billion from US$1.64 billion in the comparable period the year before. Indirect operating expenses increased 31.6% to US$1.39 billion from US$1.06 billion in the equivalent prior-year period.

Prospects: Our evaluation of Sherwin-Williams Co. as of Jan. 14, 2018 is the result of our systematic analysis on three basic characteristics: earnings strength, relative valuation, and recent stock price movement. The company has produced a positive trend in earnings per share over the past 5 quarters and while recent estimates for the company have been raised by analysts, SHW has posted better than expected results. Based on operating earnings yield, the company is about fairly valued when compared to all of the companies in our coverage universe. Share price changes over the past year indicates that SHW will perform well over the near term.

Financial Data

(US$ in Thousands)	9 Mos	6 Mos	3 Mos	12/31/2016	12/31/2015	12/31/2014	12/31/2013	12/31/2012
Earnings Per Share	11.36	12.11	12.74	11.99	11.16	8.78	7.26	6.02
Cash Flow Per Share	17.22	14.91	17.51	14.21	15.70	11.24	10.74	8.71
Tang Book Value Per Share	N.M.	N.M.	7.33	5.34	N.M.	N.M.	2.42	1.81
Dividends Per Share	3.390	3.380	3.370	3.360	2.680	2.200	2.000	1.560
Dividend Payout %	29.84	27.91	26.45	28.02	24.01	25.06	27.55	25.91
Income Statement								
Total Revenue	11,004,224	6,497,204	2,761,387	11,855,602	11,339,304	11,129,533	10,185,532	9,534,462
EBITDA	1,811,535	1,062,932	382,781	1,942,072	1,807,920	1,518,381	1,333,224	1,126,386
Depn & Amortn	401,007	169,271	51,761	197,711	198,562	198,945	187,794	179,202
Income Before Taxes	1,243,330	815,608	306,605	1,595,233	1,548,966	1,258,226	1,085,958	907,309
Income Taxes	326,921	215,805	67,453	462,530	495,117	392,339	333,397	276,275
Net Income	874,869	558,263	239,152	1,132,703	1,053,849	865,887	752,561	631,034
Average Shares	95,207	94,968	94,541	94,488	94,024	98,075	103,048	103,930
Balance Sheet								
Current Assets	4,683,904	4,854,001	3,876,664	3,627,298	2,658,874	2,566,780	3,158,717	3,149,238
Total Assets	20,779,657	20,717,398	6,988,903	6,752,521	5,791,855	5,706,052	6,382,507	6,234,737
Current Liabilities	4,371,661	4,151,913	2,939,002	2,829,179	2,141,859	2,680,666	2,528,557	1,876,436
Long-Term Obligations	10,083,828	10,751,284	1,211,512	1,211,326	1,920,196	1,122,715	1,122,373	1,632,165
Total Liabilities	18,038,668	18,326,138	4,923,553	4,874,080	4,923,945	4,709,582	4,607,972	4,442,933
Stockholders' Equity	2,740,989	2,391,260	2,065,350	1,878,441	867,910	996,470	1,774,535	1,791,804
Shares Outstanding	93,513	93,410	93,128	93,013	92,246	94,704	100,129	103,270
Statistical Record								
Return on Assets %	7.78	8.38	18.53	18.01	18.33	14.33	11.93	10.98
Return on Equity %	49.69	63.11	78.73	82.26	113.05	62.50	42.20	38.04
EBITDA Margin %	16.46	16.36	13.86	16.38	15.94	13.64	13.09	11.81
Net Margin %	7.95	8.59	8.66	9.55	9.29	7.78	7.39	6.62
Asset Turnover	1.00	0.92	1.85	1.89	1.97	1.84	1.61	1.66
Current Ratio	1.07	1.17	1.32	1.28	1.24	0.96	1.25	1.68
Debt to Equity	3.68	4.50	0.59	0.64	2.21	1.13	0.63	0.91
Price Range	361.03-240.63	361.03-240.63	315.36-240.63	312.10-239.35	292.44-218.94	264.93-175.60	195.07-153.82	158.59-91.00
P/E Ratio	31.78-21.18	29.81-19.87	24.75-18.89	26.03-19.96	26.20-19.62	30.17-20.00	26.87-21.19	26.34-15.12
Average Yield %	1.09	1.13	1.17	1.21	0.99	1.04	1.13	1.22

Address: 101 West Prospect Avenue, Cleveland, OH 44115-1075	**Web Site:** www.sherwin.com	**Auditors:** Ernst & Young LLP
Telephone: 216-566-2000	**Officers:** John G. Morikis - Chairman, President, President (frmr), Chief Executive Officer, Chief Operating Officer Allen J. Mistysyn - Senior Vice President, Vice President, Chief Financial Officer, Corporate Controller	**Investor Contact:** 216-566-2244
Fax: 216-566-3310		**Transfer Agents:** Wells Fargo Shareowner Services, St. Paul, MN

SIGNET JEWELERS LTD

Exchange	Symbol	Price	52Wk Range	Yield	P/E
NYS	SIG	$56.55 (12/29/2017)	95.63-47.88	2.19	9.33

*7 Year Price Score 63.12 *NYSE Composite Index=100 *12 Month Price Score 85.80

TRADING VOLUME (thousand shares)

Interim Earnings (Per Share)

Qtr.	Apr	Jul	Oct	Jan
2014-15	1.20	0.72	(0.02)	2.84
2015-16	1.48	0.78	0.19	3.42
2016-17	1.87	1.06	0.20	3.90
2017-18	1.03	1.33	(0.20)	...

Interim Dividends (Per Share)

Amt	Decl	Ex	Rec	Pay
0.31Q	03/09/2017	04/26/2017	04/28/2017	05/31/2017
0.31Q	05/25/2017	07/26/2017	07/28/2017	08/30/2017
0.31Q	08/24/2017	10/26/2017	10/27/2017	11/30/2017
0.31Q	01/10/2018	02/01/2018	02/02/2018	03/02/2018

Indicated Div: $1.24

Valuation Analysis / Institutional Holding

Forecast EPS N/A

No of Institutions 448

Market Cap	$3.4 Billion	Shares	96,620,288
Book Value	$2.8 Billion	% Held	
Price/Book	1.24		
Price/Sales	0.55	N/A	

Business Summary: Retail - Specialty (MIC: 2.1.3 SIC: 5944 NAIC: 448310)

Signet Jewelers is a holding company. Through its subsidiaries, Co. is a retailer of diamond jewelry. Co. operates retail jewelry stores in a variety of real estate formats including mall-based, free-standing, strip center and outlet store locations. At Jan 28 2017, the Sterling Jewelers division operated 1,588 stores in all 50 U.S. states; the Zale division, which consists of two segments: Zale Jewelry, which operated 970 jewelry stores in shopping malls in North America, and Piercing Pagoda, which operated 616 mall-based kiosks in the U.S. and Puerto Rico; and the U.K. Jewelry division operated 508 stores in shopping malls and off-mall locations principally as H.Samuel and Ernest Jones.

Recent Developments: For the quarter ended Oct 28 2017, net loss amounted to US$3.9 million versus net income of US$17.0 million in the year-earlier quarter. Revenues were US$1.16 billion, down 2.5% from US$1.19 billion the year before. Operating income was US$5.5 million versus US$32.1 million in the prior-year quarter, a decrease of 82.9%. Direct operating expenses declined 0.0% to US$835.8 million from US$836.2 million in the comparable period the year before. Indirect operating expenses decreased 0.7% to US$315.6 million from US$317.9 million in the equivalent prior-year period.

Prospects: Our evaluation of Signet Jewelers Limited as of Sep. 17, 2017 is the result of our systematic analysis on three basic characteristics: earnings strength, relative valuation, and recent stock price movement. The company has managed to produce a neutral trend in earnings per share over the past 5 quarters and while recent estimates for the company have been raised by analysts, SIG has posted better than expected results. Based on operating earnings yield, the company is undervalued when compared to all of the companies in our coverage universe. Share price changes over the past year indicates that SIG will perform very poorly over the near term.

Financial Data

(US$ in Thousands)	9 Mos	6 Mos	3 Mos	01/28/2017	01/30/2016	01/31/2015	02/01/2014	02/02/2013
Earnings Per Share	6.06	6.46	6.19	7.08	5.87	4.75	4.56	4.35
Cash Flow Per Share	29.95	12.21	9.11	9.13	5.59	3.55	2.94	3.74
Tang Book Value Per Share	24.41	30.77	32.57	31.73	26.67	22.97	31.62	28.32
Dividends Per Share	1.190	1.140	1.090	1.040	0.880	0.720	0.600	0.480
Dividend Payout %	19.64	17.65	17.61	14.69	14.99	15.16	13.16	11.03
Income Statement								
Total Revenue	3,959,900	2,803,000	1,403,400	6,408,400	6,550,200	5,736,300	4,209,200	3,983,400
EBITDA	248,800	243,400	111,300	655,700	865,100	716,700	680,700	659,900
Depn & Amortn	(7,600)	(7,500)	(4,000)	175,000	161,400	140,100	110,200	99,400
Income Before Taxes	213,700	224,800	102,700	713,800	657,800	540,600	566,500	556,900
Income Taxes	45,700	52,900	24,200	170,600	189,900	159,300	198,500	197,000
Net Income	168,000	171,900	78,500	543,200	467,900	381,300	368,000	359,900
Average Shares	60,100	70,500	68,200	76,700	79,700	80,200	80,700	82,800
Balance Sheet								
Current Assets	3,462,200	4,342,800	4,507,800	4,642,600	4,589,900	4,407,300	3,257,600	3,032,900
Total Assets	5,800,700	6,313,800	6,465,200	6,597,800	6,474,400	6,327,600	4,029,200	3,715,800
Current Liabilities	1,317,500	1,810,000	1,015,900	1,203,700	1,152,900	1,338,300	900,700	868,700
Long-Term Obligations	696,800	705,300	1,311,600	1,317,900	1,328,700	1,363,800	...	...
Total Liabilities	3,048,600	3,524,500	3,309,500	3,495,700	3,413,700	3,517,200	1,466,100	1,385,900
Stockholders' Equity	2,752,100	2,789,300	3,155,700	3,102,100	3,060,700	2,810,400	2,563,100	2,329,900
Shares Outstanding	60,400	60,300	68,400	68,300	79,400	80,300	80,200	81,400
Statistical Record								
Return on Assets %	7.58	7.71	7.37	8.33	7.33	7.38	9.53	9.66
Return on Equity %	16.64	17.16	15.19	17.68	15.98	14.23	15.08	15.36
EBITDA Margin %	6.28	8.68	7.93	10.23	13.21	12.49	16.17	16.57
Net Margin %	4.24	6.13	5.59	8.48	7.14	6.65	8.74	9.03
Asset Turnover	1.01	0.99	0.97	0.98	1.03	1.11	1.09	1.07
Current Ratio	2.63	2.40	4.44	3.86	3.98	3.29	3.62	3.49
Debt to Equity	0.25	0.25	0.42	0.42	0.43	0.49	...	...
Price Range	98.72-47.88	98.72-47.88	109.48-63.25	124.03-73.16	150.94-113.39	132.12-75.28	80.86-59.64	63.43-41.27
P/E Ratio	16.29-7.90	15.28-7.41	17.69-10.22	17.52-10.33	25.71-19.32	27.81-15.85	17.73-13.08	14.58-9.49
Average Yield %	1.70	1.52	1.30	1.11	0.68	0.65	0.64	0.98

Address: Clarendon House, 2 Church Street, Hamilton, HM11	Web Site: www.signetjewelers.com	Auditors: KPMG LLP
Telephone: 441-296-5872	Officers: H. Todd Stitzer - Chairman Sebastian Hobbs - President, Chief Customer Officer	Investor Contact: 440-207-3179700
		Transfer Agents: Capita Registrars, Kent, United Kingdom

SIMON PROPERTY GROUP, INC.

Exchange	Symbol	Price	52Wk Range	Yield	P/E
NYS	SPG	$171.74 (12/29/2017)	186.83-152.26	4.16	30.29

*7 Year Price Score 81.57 *NYSE Composite Index=100 *12 Month Price Score 92.46

Interim Earnings (Per Share)

Qtr.	Mar	Jun	Sep	Dec
2014	1.10	1.31	0.81	1.30
2015	1.16	1.52	1.36	1.84
2016	1.55	1.45	1.61	1.26
2017	1.53	1.23	1.65	...

Interim Dividends (Per Share)

Amt	Decl	Ex	Rec	Pay
1.75Q	01/31/2017	02/10/2017	02/14/2017	02/28/2017
1.75Q	04/26/2017	05/15/2017	05/17/2017	05/31/2017
1.80Q	08/01/2017	08/15/2017	08/17/2017	08/31/2017
1.85Q	10/27/2017	11/15/2017	11/16/2017	11/30/2017

Indicated Div: $7.15

Valuation Analysis | **Institutional Holding**

Forecast EPS	$6.39	No of Institutions
	(01/17/2018)	984
Market Cap	$54.9 Billion	Shares
Book Value	$3.9 Billion	397,559,808
Price/Book	14.19	% Held
Price/Sales	9.92	96.18

Business Summary: REITs (MIC: 5.3.1 SIC: 6798 NAIC: 525930)

Simon Property Group is a self-administered and self-managed real estate investment trust. Co. owns, develops and manages retail real estate properties, which consist primarily of malls, Premium Outlets®, and The Mills®. As of Dec 31 2016, Co. owned or held an interest in 206 income-producing properties in the U.S., which consisted of 108 malls, 67 Premium Outlets, 14 Mills, four lifestyle centers, and 13 other retail properties in 37 states and Puerto Rico. Internationally, as of Dec 31 2016, Co. had ownership interests in nine Premium Outlets in Japan, three Premium Outlets in South Korea, two Premium Outlets in Canada, one Premium Outlet in Mexico, and one Premium Outlet in Malaysia.

Recent Developments: For the quarter ended Sep 30 2017, net income increased 0.8% to US$592.6 million from US$587.9 million in the year-earlier quarter. Revenues were US$1.40 billion, up 3.4% from US$1.36 billion the year before. Revenues from property income rose 1.9% to US$1.28 billion from US$1.26 billion in the corresponding quarter a year earlier.

Prospects: Our evaluation of Simon Property Group Inc. as of Jan. 14, 2018 is the result of our systematic analysis on three basic characteristics: earnings strength, relative valuation, and recent stock price movement. The company has enjoyed a very positive trend in earnings per share over the past 5 quarters. Because the company lacks sufficient analyst estimate data, we place greater weight on the historical EPS trend as the measure of earnings strength. Based on operating earnings yield, the company is about fairly valued when compared to all of the companies in our coverage universe. Share price changes over the past year indicates that SPG will perform in line with the market over the near term

Financial Data
(US$ in Thousands)

	9 Mos	6 Mos	3 Mos	12/31/2016	12/31/2015	12/31/2014	12/31/2013	12/31/2012
Earnings Per Share	5.67	5.63	5.85	5.87	5.88	4.52	4.24	4.72
Cash Flow Per Share	11.45	11.20	10.99	10.76	9.75	8.79	8.71	8.27
Tang Book Value Per Share	11.97	12.09	13.55	13.16	13.50	15.33	17.98	17.87
Dividends Per Share	6.950	6.800	6.650	6.500	6.050	5.150	4.650	4.100
Dividend Payout %	122.57	120.78	113.68	110.73	102.89	113.94	109.67	86.86
Income Statement								
Total Revenue	4,110,948	2,707,311	1,345,763	5,435,229	5,266,103	4,870,818	5,170,138	4,880,084
EBITDA	2,919,624	1,907,339	1,015,941	3,966,872	4,017,480	3,673,776	3,816,420	4,016,054
Depn & Amortn	1,012,335	675,608	335,749	1,327,946	1,239,214	1,285,784	1,332,950	1,301,304
Income Before Taxes	1,302,881	826,358	481,990	1,781,372	1,854,569	1,395,391	1,346,331	1,587,725
Net Income	1,376,012	861,395	478,570	1,838,896	1,827,720	1,408,588	1,319,641	1,434,496
Average Shares	310,853	311,579	312,809	312,690	310,102	310,731	310,255	303,138
Balance Sheet								
Current Assets	1,195,022	1,128,694	1,135,000	1,224,678	1,325,739	1,192,479	2,298,345	1,705,819
Total Assets	31,032,410	30,965,966	30,946,093	31,103,578	30,650,673	29,532,330	33,324,574	32,586,606
Current Liabilities	1,290,382	1,205,267	1,081,185	2,573,760	2,692,345	2,426,844	2,465,704	2,098,916
Long-Term Obligations	23,410,357	23,422,685	23,149,053	22,977,104	22,502,173	20,852,993	23,588,531	23,113,007
Total Liabilities	27,160,536	27,054,872	26,671,979	26,655,368	26,153,672	24,413,616	27,284,683	26,497,997
Stockholders' Equity	3,871,874	3,911,094	4,274,114	4,448,210	4,497,001	5,118,714	6,039,891	6,088,609
Shares Outstanding	319,955	319,937	312,202	313,074	309,420	310,787	310,608	309,903
Statistical Record								
Return on Assets %	5.65	5.65	5.89	5.94	6.07	4.48	4.00	4.87
Return on Equity %	40.91	40.56	40.70	41.00	38.02	25.25	21.76	26.00
EBITDA Margin %	71.02	70.45	75.49	72.98	76.29	75.42	73.82	82.29
Net Margin %	33.47	31.82	35.56	33.83	34.71	28.92	25.52	29.39
Asset Turnover	0.18	0.18	0.17	0.18	0.18	0.15	0.16	0.17
Current Ratio	0.93	0.94	1.05	0.48	0.49	0.49	0.93	0.81
Debt to Equity	6.05	5.99	5.42	5.17	5.00	4.07	3.91	3.80
Price Range	207.01-152.26	227.60-152.26	227.60-165.40	227.60-174.20	206.19-171.00	187.46-141.62	169.56-134.02	153.76-119.15
P/E Ratio	36.51-26.85	40.43-27.04	38.91-28.27	38.77-29.68	35.07-29.08	41.47-31.33	39.99-31.61	32.58-25.24
Average Yield %	4.04	4.04	3.38	3.45	3.25	3.21	3.13	2.92

Address: 225 West Washington Street, Indianapolis, IN 46204 **Telephone:** 317-636-1600 **Fax:** 317-685-7336	**Web Site:** www.simon.com **Officers:** David Simon - Chairman, Chief Executive Officer Herbert Simon - Chairman Emeritus, Chairman	**Auditors:** Ernst & Young LLP **Investor Contact:** 800-461-3439 **Transfer Agents:** Computershare, Pittsburgh, PA

SIX FLAGS ENTERTAINMENT CORP

Exchange	Symbol	Price	52Wk Range	Yield	P/E
NYS	SIX	$66.57 (12/29/2017)	67.58-51.90	4.21	31.85

*7 Year Price Score 117.46 *NYSE Composite Index=100 *12 Month Price Score 102.28

TRADING VOLUME (thousand shares)

Interim Earnings (Per Share)

Qtr.	Mar	Jun	Sep	Dec
2014	(0.64)	0.67	1.08	(0.36)
2015	(0.75)	0.67	1.64	0.00
2016	(0.51)	0.64	1.09	0.02
2017	(0.63)	0.59	2.11	...

Interim Dividends (Per Share)

Amt	Decl	Ex	Rec	Pay
0.64Q	02/09/2017	02/27/2017	03/01/2017	03/13/2017
0.64Q	05/04/2017	05/23/2017	05/25/2017	06/12/2017
0.64Q	08/17/2017	08/29/2017	08/31/2017	09/11/2017
0.70Q	11/08/2017	11/29/2017	11/30/2017	12/11/2017

Indicated Div: $2.80

Valuation Analysis / Institutional Holding

Valuation Analysis		Institutional Holding	
Forecast EPS	$2.13	No of Institutions	
	(01/26/2018)	394	
Market Cap	$5.6 Billion	Shares	
Book Value	N/A	109,710,208	
Price/Book	N/A	% Held	
Price/Sales	4.15	N/A	

Business Summary: Sporting & Recreational (MIC: 2.2.4 SIC: 7996 NAIC: 713110)

Six Flags Entertainment is a regional theme park operator. As of Dec 31 2016, Co. has 18 regional theme and water parks, 16 are located in the U.S., one is located in Mexico City and one is located in Montreal, Canada. Co.'s parks generally provides a range selection of thrill rides, water attractions, themed areas, concerts and shows, restaurants, game venues and retail outlets. During 2016, Co.'s parks offered approximately 830 rides, including over 135 roller coasters. Co. has certain rights to use the Hanna-Barbera and Cartoon Network characters, including Yogi Bear, Scooby-Doo, The Flintstones and others.

Recent Developments: For the quarter ended Sep 30 2017, net income increased 65.1% to US$200.9 million from US$121.7 million in the year-earlier quarter. Revenues were US$580.4 million, up 4.1% from US$557.6 million the year before. Direct operating expenses rose 8.8% to US$212.6 million from US$195.4 million in the comparable period the year before. Indirect operating expenses decreased 74.1% to US$42.1 million from US$162.3 million in the equivalent prior-year period.

Prospects: Our evaluation of Six Flags Entertainment Corp. as of Jan. 21, 2018 is the result of our systematic analysis on three basic characteristics: earnings strength, relative valuation, and recent stock price movement. The company has produced a positive trend in earnings per share over the past 5 quarters and while recent estimates for the company have been mixed, SIX has posted better than expected results. Based on operating earnings yield, the company is about fairly valued when compared to all of the companies in our coverage universe. Share price changes over the past year indicates that SIX will perform in line with the market over the near term.

Financial Data
(US$ in Thousands)

	9 Mos	6 Mos	3 Mos	12/31/2016	12/31/2015	12/31/2014	12/31/2013	12/31/2012
Earnings Per Share	2.09	1.07	1.12	1.25	1.58	0.77	1.18	3.19
Cash Flow Per Share	5.54	5.25	5.00	5.00	5.06	4.15	3.80	3.44
Dividends Per Share	2.560	2.500	2.440	2.380	2.140	1.930	1.820	1.350
Dividend Payout %	122.49	233.64	217.86	190.40	135.44	250.65	154.24	42.32
Income Statement								
Total Revenue	1,102,318	521,900	99,528	1,319,398	1,263,938	1,175,793	1,109,930	1,070,332
EBITDA	470,619	116,048	(46,232)	419,428	443,915	338,049	391,752	392,855
Depn & Amortn	84,600	55,345	27,906	104,290	104,788	105,449	113,682	132,397
Income Before Taxes	312,141	12,546	(95,139)	233,266	263,224	160,011	203,925	213,834
Income Taxes	97,128	(1,537)	(37,591)	76,539	70,369	46,522	47,601	(172,228)
Net Income	175,803	(5,522)	(57,548)	118,302	154,690	76,022	118,552	354,009
Average Shares	85,876	88,832	91,151	94,398	97,981	98,139	100,371	110,936
Balance Sheet								
Current Assets	275,012	279,162	184,697	278,791	227,977	300,924	353,858	763,474
Total Assets	2,528,288	2,543,687	2,429,379	2,487,672	2,428,440	2,534,919	2,607,814	3,056,391
Current Liabilities	345,290	429,630	393,354	315,952	272,058	231,671	216,810	181,863
Long-Term Obligations	2,020,184	2,019,190	1,625,449	1,624,487	1,498,022	1,389,215	1,394,334	1,398,966
Total Liabilities	3,101,315	3,098,421	2,614,216	2,674,162	2,404,224	2,311,024	2,234,477	2,164,172
Stockholders' Equity	(573,027)	(554,734)	(184,837)	(186,490)	24,216	223,895	373,337	892,219
Shares Outstanding	83,737	85,563	91,256	90,849	91,550	92,937	94,857	107,637
Statistical Record								
Return on Assets %	6.86	3.85	4.47	4.80	6.23	2.96	4.19	12.38
Return on Equity %	...	...	...	...	124.69	25.46	18.74	42.65
EBITDA Margin %	42.69	22.24	N.M.	31.79	35.12	28.75	35.30	36.70
Net Margin %	15.95	N.M.	N.M.	8.97	12.24	6.47	10.68	33.07
Asset Turnover	0.52	0.51	0.54	0.54	0.51	0.46	0.39	0.37
Current Ratio	0.80	0.65	0.47	0.88	0.84	1.30	1.63	4.20
Debt to Equity	...	...	...	...	61.86	6.20	3.73	1.57
Price Range	64.88-50.68	64.88-48.06	61.79-48.06	61.33-46.74	54.96-42.34	43.24-33.15	39.98-30.55	32.42-20.43
P/E Ratio	31.04-24.25	60.64-44.92	55.17-42.91	49.06-37.39	34.78-26.80	56.16-43.05	33.88-25.89	10.16-6.40
Average Yield %	4.41	4.35	4.29	4.34	4.49	4.94	5.14	5.15

Address: 924 Avenue J East, Grand Prairie, TX 75050 **Telephone:** 972-595-5000	**Web Site:** www.sixflags.com **Officers:** James W.P. Reid-Anderson - Executive Chairman, Chairman, President, Chief Executive Officer Brett Petit - Senior Vice President	**Auditors:** KPMG LLP **Investor Contact:** 972-595-5000 **Transfer Agents:** Computershare

SKECHERS USA INC

Exchange	Symbol	Price	52Wk Range	Yield	P/E
NYS	SKX	$37.84 (12/29/2017)	38.66-22.54	N/A	23.50

*7 Year Price Score 124.30 *NYSE Composite Index=100 *12 Month Price Score 116.86

TRADING VOLUME (thousand shares)

Interim Earnings (Per Share)

Qtr.	Mar	Jun	Sep	Dec
2014	0.20	0.23	0.33	0.14
2015	0.37	0.52	0.43	0.19
2016	0.63	0.48	0.42	0.04
2017	0.60	0.38	0.59	...

Interim Dividends (Per Share)

Amt	Decl	Ex	Rec	Pay
200%	08/21/2015	10/16/2015	10/02/2015	10/15/2015

Valuation Analysis — **Institutional Holding**

Forecast EPS	$1.71	No of Institutions
	(01/18/2018)	388
Market Cap	$5.9 Billion	Shares
Book Value	$1.9 Billion	130,007,800
Price/Book	3.13	% Held
Price/Sales	1.48	76.25

Business Summary: Apparel, Footwear & Accessories (MIC: 1.4.2 SIC: 3149 NAIC: 316219)

Skechers U.S.A. designs and markets Skechers-branded lifestyle footwear for men, women and children, and performance footwear for men and women under the Skechers GO brand name. Co.'s brands are sold through department and specialty stores, athletic and independent retailers, boutiques and internet retailers. In addition to wholesale distribution, Co.'s footwear is available at its e-commerce website and its own retail stores. As of Feb 1 2017, Co. owned and operated 117 concept stores, 163 factory outlet stores and 134 warehouse outlet stores in the U.S., and 101 concept stores, 51 factory outlet stores, and five warehouse outlet stores internationally.

Recent Developments: For the quarter ended Sep 30 2017, net income increased 39.6% to US$106.8 million from US$76.5 million in the year-earlier quarter. Revenues were US$1.10 billion, up 16.1% from US$945.4 million the year before. Operating income was US$116.5 million versus US$103.4 million in the prior-year quarter, an increase of 12.7%. Direct operating expenses rose 12.2% to US$574.8 million from US$512.4 million in the comparable period the year before. Indirect operating expenses increased 23.3% to US$406.4 million from US$329.6 million in the equivalent prior-year period.

Prospects: Our evaluation of Skechers U.S.A Inc as of Jan. 14, 2018 is the result of our systematic analysis on three basic characteristics: earnings strength, relative valuation, and recent stock price movement. The company has enjoyed a very positive trend in earnings per share over the past 5 quarters and while recent estimates for the company have been raised by analysts, SKX has posted better than expected results. Based on operating earnings yield, the company is about fairly valued when compared to all of the companies in our coverage universe. Share price changes over the past year indicates that SKX will perform poorly over the near term.

Financial Data

(US$ in Thousands)	9 Mos	6 Mos	3 Mos	12/31/2016	12/31/2015	12/31/2014	12/31/2013	12/31/2012
Earnings Per Share	1.61	1.44	1.54	1.57	1.50	0.91	0.36	0.06
Cash Flow Per Share	1.89	1.85	1.99	2.34	1.52	1.08	0.66	(0.02)
Tang Book Value Per Share	12.08	11.42	10.99	10.35	8.64	7.05	6.12	5.78
Income Statement								
Total Revenue	3,203,939	2,106,193	1,077,038	3,577,196	3,159,068	2,386,668	1,854,095	1,567,425
EBITDA	343,206	220,969	128,573	443,750	344,030	252,466	137,761	66,880
Depn & Amortn	10,474	6,878	3,454	79,182	527	49,457	44,497	43,642
Income Before Taxes	329,411	211,551	124,042	359,484	333,497	191,380	82,215	10,473
Income Taxes	42,546	31,516	17,407	74,125	72,450	39,184	21,347	(39)
Net Income	245,840	153,530	93,995	243,493	231,912	138,811	54,788	9,512
Average Shares	156,741	156,174	155,927	155,084	154,200	153,078	151,689	149,826
Balance Sheet								
Current Assets	2,074,358	1,995,008	1,826,297	1,827,766	1,570,467	1,285,014	1,014,928	940,312
Total Assets	2,693,260	2,609,290	2,405,711	2,393,670	2,047,408	1,674,918	1,408,570	1,340,220
Current Liabilities	598,982	635,610	513,583	621,730	577,013	505,737	310,422	292,541
Long-Term Obligations	71,390	68,271	68,775	67,159	68,942	15,081	116,488	128,517
Total Liabilities	810,456	830,193	698,555	790,037	719,852	599,669	478,248	464,251
Stockholders' Equity	1,882,804	1,779,097	1,707,156	1,603,633	1,327,556	1,075,249	930,322	875,969
Shares Outstanding	155,844	155,804	155,380	154,931	153,602	152,271	151,674	150,885
Statistical Record								
Return on Assets %	10.26	9.19	10.72	10.94	12.46	9.00	3.99	0.72
Return on Equity %	14.52	13.64	15.25	16.57	19.30	13.84	6.07	1.10
EBITDA Margin %	10.71	10.49	11.94	12.40	10.89	10.58	7.43	4.27
Net Margin %	7.67	7.29	8.73	6.81	7.34	5.82	2.95	0.61
Asset Turnover	1.61	1.56	1.64	1.63	1.70	1.55	1.35	1.19
Current Ratio	3.46	3.14	3.56	2.94	2.72	2.54	3.27	3.21
Debt to Equity	0.04	0.04	0.04	0.04	0.05	0.01	0.13	0.15
Price Range	29.96-18.98	32.58-18.98	34.06-18.98	34.06-18.98	53.43-18.42	21.36-8.97	11.46-5.80	7.42-3.82
P/E Ratio	18.61-11.79	22.62-13.18	22.12-12.32	21.69-12.09	35.62-12.28	23.48-9.85	31.82-16.11	123.61-63.67

Address: 228 Manhattan Beach Blvd., Manhattan Beach, CA 90266 **Telephone:** 310-318-3100	**Web Site:** www.skechers.com **Officers:** Robert Greenberg - Chairman, Chief Executive Officer Michael Greenberg - President	**Auditors:** BDO USA, LLP **Investor Contact:** 310-829-5400 **Transfer Agents:** American Stock Transfer & Trust Company, Brooklyn, NY

SJW GROUP

Exchange	Symbol	Price	52Wk Range	Yield	P/E	Div Achiever
NYS	SJW	$63.83 (12/29/2017)	68.13-45.74	1.36	23.73	49 Years

*7 Year Price Score 129.62 *NYSE Composite Index=100 *12 Month Price Score 112.00

Interim Earnings (Per Share)

Qtr.	Mar	Jun	Sep	Dec
2014	0.04	0.34	1.88	0.28
2015	0.23	0.36	0.46	0.79
2016	0.16	0.82	0.92	0.67
2017	0.18	0.90	0.94	...

Interim Dividends (Per Share)

Amt	Decl	Ex	Rec	Pay
0.218Q	04/26/2017	05/04/2017	05/08/2017	06/01/2017
0.218Q	07/26/2017	08/03/2017	08/07/2017	09/01/2017
0.218Q	10/25/2017	11/03/2017	11/06/2017	12/01/2017
0.17Q	11/16/2017	11/28/2017	11/29/2017	12/11/2017

Indicated Div: $0.87

Valuation Analysis — **Institutional Holding**

Forecast EPS	$2.48	No of Institutions	
	(10/14/2017)	190	
Market Cap	$1.3 Billion	Shares	
Book Value	$452.5 Million	13,010,451	
Price/Book	2.89	% Held	
Price/Sales	3.49	56.55	

TRADING VOLUME (thousand shares)

Business Summary: Water Utilities (MIC: 3.2.1 SIC: 4941 NAIC: 221310)

SJW is a holding company with four subsidiaries: San Jose Water Company, is a public utility in the business of providing water service to approximately 229,000 connections that serve a population of approximately 1.0 million people in an area; SJWTX, Inc., which providing water service to approximately 13,000 connections that serve approximately 39,000 people; SJW Land Company, which owns and operates commercial buildings in the states of California and Tennessee; and Texas Water Alliance Limited, is undertaking activities to develop a water supply project in Texas.

Recent Developments: For the quarter ended Sep 30 2017, net income increased 3.1% to US$19.5 million from US$19.0 million in the year-earlier quarter. Revenues were US$124.6 million, up 10.9% from US$112.3 million the year before. Operating income was US$38.2 million versus US$36.3 million in the prior-year quarter, an increase of 5.2%. Direct operating expenses rose 17.7% to US$53.0 million from US$45.0 million in the comparable period the year before. Indirect operating expenses increased 7.7% to US$33.4 million from US$31.0 million in the equivalent prior-year period.

Prospects: Our evaluation of SJW Group as of Jan. 14, 2018 is the result of our systematic analysis on three basic characteristics: earnings strength, relative valuation, and recent stock price movement. The company has produced a positive trend in earnings per share over the past 5 quarters. Because the company lacks sufficient analyst estimate data, we place greater weight on the historical EPS trend as the measure of earnings strength. Based on operating earnings yield, the company is about fairly valued when compared to all of the companies in our coverage universe. Share price changes over the past year indicates that SJW will perform very well over the near term.

Financial Data

(US$ in Thousands)	9 Mos	6 Mos	3 Mos	12/31/2016	12/31/2015	12/31/2014	12/31/2013	12/31/2012
Earnings Per Share	2.69	2.67	2.59	2.57	1.85	2.54	1.12	1.18
Cash Flow Per Share	6.12	5.67	5.38	5.57	4.78	3.26	3.21	3.98
Tang Book Value Per Share	22.05	21.27	20.56	20.61	18.83	17.75	15.92	14.71
Dividends Per Share	0.855	0.840	0.825	0.810	0.780	0.750	0.730	0.710
Dividend Payout %	31.78	31.46	31.85	31.52	42.16	29.53	65.18	60.17
Income Statement								
Total Revenue	295,696	171,118	69,045	339,706	305,082	319,668	276,869	261,547
EBITDA	124,421	73,752	23,415	150,878	121,573	132,989	89,057	89,050
Depn & Amortn	36,217	24,152	12,119	42,659	38,233	35,424	32,616	31,005
Income Before Taxes	70,850	37,787	5,239	86,381	61,154	76,777	36,519	37,860
Income Taxes	27,055	13,532	1,568	33,542	23,272	24,971	14,135	15,542
Net Income	41,899	22,359	3,671	52,839	37,882	51,806	22,384	22,318
Average Shares	20,697	20,673	20,655	20,588	20,515	20,416	19,971	18,839
Balance Sheet								
Current Assets	87,121	72,892	73,736	99,611	73,376	68,093	39,652	42,911
Total Assets	1,511,570	1,471,186	1,435,777	1,443,376	1,340,963	1,269,304	1,109,986	1,087,499
Current Liabilities	93,418	70,396	50,780	63,573	79,623	44,694	59,195	49,107
Long-Term Obligations	431,009	430,926	433,388	433,335	380,825	384,365	334,997	335,598
Total Liabilities	1,059,099	1,035,076	1,014,377	1,021,730	957,180	909,149	788,811	812,895
Stockholders' Equity	452,471	436,110	421,400	421,646	383,783	360,155	321,175	274,604
Shares Outstanding	20,520	20,506	20,498	20,456	20,381	20,286	20,169	18,670
Statistical Record								
Return on Assets %	3.75	3.84	3.81	3.79	2.90	4.35	2.04	2.09
Return on Equity %	12.88	13.23	13.19	13.08	10.18	15.21	7.51	8.26
EBITDA Margin %	42.08	43.10	33.91	44.41	39.85	41.60	32.17	34.05
Net Margin %	14.17	13.07	5.32	15.55	12.42	16.21	8.08	8.53
Asset Turnover	0.25	0.25	0.25	0.24	0.23	0.27	0.25	0.25
Current Ratio	0.93	1.04	1.45	1.57	0.92	1.52	0.67	0.87
Debt to Equity	0.95	0.99	1.03	1.03	0.99	1.07	1.04	1.22
Price Range	57.43-42.19	56.69-38.13	56.69-32.66	56.69-29.35	35.60-27.64	32.87-25.64	30.03-24.58	26.62-22.69
P/E Ratio	21.35-15.68	21.23-14.28	21.89-12.61	22.06-11.42	19.24-14.94	12.94-10.09	26.81-21.95	22.56-19.23
Average Yield %	1.69	1.76	1.87	2.01	2.53	2.65	2.69	2.96

Address: 110 West Taylor Street, San Jose, CA 95110 **Telephone:** 408-279-7800	**Web Site:** www.sjwcorp.com **Officers:** W. Richard Roth - Chairman, President, Chief Executive Officer James P. Lynch - Chief Financial Officer, Treasurer	**Auditors:** KPMG LLP **Investor Contact:** 800-250-5147 **Transfer Agents:** American Stock Transfer & Trust Company, LLC, Brooklyn, NY

SL GREEN REALTY CORP

Exchange	Symbol	Price	52Wk Range	Yield	P/E
NYS	SLG	$100.93 (12/29/2017)	113.75-94.15	3.22	97.99

*7 Year Price Score 84.61   *NYSE Composite Index=100   *12 Month Price Score 90.72

Interim Earnings (Per Share)

Qtr.	Mar	Jun	Sep	Dec
2014	1.53	2.46	0.68	0.54
2015	0.44	(0.39)	1.64	1.02
2016	0.23	1.33	0.34	0.44
2017	0.11	0.08	0.40	...

Interim Dividends (Per Share)

Amt	Decl	Ex	Rec	Pay
0.775Q	03/23/2017	03/29/2017	03/31/2017	04/17/2017
0.775Q	06/16/2017	06/28/2017	06/30/2017	07/17/2017
0.775Q	09/19/2017	09/29/2017	10/02/2017	10/16/2017
0.813Q	12/01/2017	12/29/2017	01/02/2018	01/16/2018

Indicated Div: $3.25

Valuation Analysis / Institutional Holding

Forecast EPS	$1.13	No of Institutions	496
(01/18/2018)			
Market Cap	$9.8 Billion	Shares	140,255,088
Book Value	$7.1 Billion	% Held	104.33
Price/Book	1.38		
Price/Sales	6.45		

Business Summary: REITs (MIC: 5.3.1 SIC: 6798 NAIC: 525930)

SL Green Realty is a self-managed real estate investment trust, with in-house capabilities in property management, acquisitions and dispositions, financing, development and redevelopment, construction and leasing. As of Dec 31 2016, Co. owned interests in properties in the New York Metropolitan area, primarily in midtown Manhattan. Co.'s investments in the New York Metropolitan area also include investments in Brooklyn, Long Island, Westchester County, Connecticut and New Jersey. As of Dec 31 2016, Co. had 65 consolidated commercial properties and 23 unconsolidated commercial properties; and three consolidated residential properties and 18 unconsolidated residential properties.

Recent Developments: For the quarter ended Sep 30 2017, net income increased 5.7% to US$45.8 million from US$43.3 million in the year-earlier quarter. Revenues were US$374.6 million, down 10.1% from US$416.7 million the year before. Revenues from property income fell 4.5% to US$319.5 million from US$334.6 million in the corresponding quarter a year earlier.

Prospects: Our evaluation of SL Green Realty Corp. as of Jan. 14, 2018 is the result of our systematic analysis on three basic characteristics: earnings strength, relative valuation, and recent stock price movement. The company has generated a negative trend in earnings per share over the past 5 quarters. Because the company lacks sufficient analyst estimate data, we place greater weight on the historical EPS trend as the measure of earnings strength. Based on operating earnings yield, the company is overvalued when compared to all of the companies in our coverage universe. Share price changes over the past year indicates that SLG will perform well over the near term.

Financial Data
(US$ in Thousands)

	9 Mos	6 Mos	3 Mos	12/31/2016	12/31/2015	12/31/2014	12/31/2013	12/31/2012
Earnings Per Share	1.03	0.97	2.22	2.34	2.70	5.20	1.10	1.74
Cash Flow Per Share	5.55	5.76	6.05	6.32	5.30	5.12	4.19	3.95
Tang Book Value Per Share	70.79	70.56	72.87	73.63	73.50	69.73	66.88	66.49
Dividends Per Share	3.100	3.045	2.990	2.935	2.520	2.100	1.490	1.080
Dividend Payout %	300.97	313.92	134.68	125.43	93.33	40.38	135.45	62.07
Income Statement								
Total Revenue	1,150,131	775,531	377,381	1,863,981	1,662,829	1,519,978	1,469,077	1,400,255
EBITDA	310,650	204,329	110,895	1,327,727	1,121,708	870,139	760,751	717,855
Depn & Amortn	85,336	85,336	56,272	783,500	523,800	338,800	309,400	306,800
Income Before Taxes	29,202	(11,485)	(10,999)	223,028	274,038	213,939	121,136	80,486
Net Income	69,655	27,048	15,089	249,896	284,084	518,056	135,371	196,405
Average Shares	102,570	104,732	105,554	104,881	103,734	99,696	95,266	92,873
Balance Sheet								
Current Assets	850,578	870,159	1,093,521	966,884	1,107,032	914,062	836,223	744,306
Total Assets	15,109,870	15,309,707	15,877,271	15,857,787	19,857,941	17,096,587	14,959,001	14,387,754
Current Liabilities	684,178	753,682	758,446	380,410	554,909	441,887	374,074	317,459
Long-Term Obligations	6,467,716	6,418,734	6,621,790	6,523,798	10,447,108	8,199,609	6,967,579	6,557,938
Total Liabilities	7,990,100	8,072,110	8,312,000	8,231,302	12,287,960	10,088,098	8,384,046	7,918,402
Stockholders' Equity	7,119,770	7,237,597	7,565,271	7,626,485	7,569,981	7,008,489	6,574,955	6,469,352
Shares Outstanding	97,446	99,422	100,776	100,562	99,975	97,325	94,993	91,249
Statistical Record								
Return on Assets %	0.76	0.69	1.34	1.40	1.54	3.23	0.92	1.41
Return on Equity %	1.60	1.52	3.14	3.28	3.90	7.63	2.08	3.15
EBITDA Margin %	27.01	26.35	29.39	71.23	67.46	57.25	51.78	51.27
Net Margin %	6.06	3.49	4.00	13.41	17.08	34.08	9.21	14.03
Asset Turnover	0.10	0.10	0.10	0.10	0.09	0.09	0.10	0.10
Current Ratio	1.24	1.15	1.44	2.54	1.99	2.07	2.24	2.34
Debt to Equity	0.91	0.89	0.88	0.86	1.38	1.17	1.06	1.01
Price Range	113.75-94.23	119.20-94.23	119.20-94.23	119.20-80.54	134.00-100.95	123.10-90.96	98.15-76.65	85.14-68.16
P/E Ratio	110.44-91.49	122.89-97.14	53.69-42.45	50.94-34.42	49.63-37.39	23.67-17.49	89.23-69.68	48.93-39.17
Average Yield %	2.96	2.82	2.79	2.83	2.12	1.97	1.69	1.40

Address: 420 Lexington Avenue, New York, NY 10170 **Telephone:** 212-594-2700	**Web Site:** www.slgreen.com **Officers:** Stephen L. Green - Chairman Andrew Mathias - President	**Auditors:** Ernst & Young LLP **Transfer Agents:** Computershare Shareowner Services, Providence, RI

SM ENERGY CO.

Exchange	Symbol	Price	52Wk Range	Yield	P/E
NYS	SM	$22.06 (12/29/2017)	36.08-12.79	0.45	N/A

*7 Year Price Score 31.94   ***NYSE Composite Index=100**   ***12 Month Price Score 94.06**

Interim Earnings (Per Share)

Qtr.	Mar	Jun	Sep	Dec
2014	0.96	0.88	3.05	4.89
2015	(0.79)	(0.85)	0.05	(5.02)
2016	(5.10)	(2.48)	(0.52)	(2.12)
2017	0.67	(1.08)	(0.80)	...

Interim Dividends (Per Share)

Amt	Decl	Ex	Rec	Pay
0.05S	03/30/2016	04/20/2016	04/22/2016	05/04/2016
0.05S	09/23/2016	10/19/2016	10/21/2016	11/02/2016
0.05S	03/29/2017	04/19/2017	04/21/2017	05/03/2017
0.05S	09/27/2017	10/19/2017	10/20/2017	11/01/2017

Indicated Div: $0.10

Valuation Analysis / Institutional Holding

Forecast EPS	$-0.90	No of Institutions
	(01/18/2018)	411
Market Cap	$2.5 Billion	Shares
Book Value	$2.4 Billion	132,699,120
Price/Book	1.02	% Held
Price/Sales	2.11	N/A

Business Summary: Production & Extraction (MIC: 9.1.1 SIC: 1311 NAIC: 211111)

SM Energy is an independent energy company engaged in the acquisition, exploration, development, and production of crude oil and condensate, natural gas, and natural gas liquids in onshore North America. Co.'s operations are concentrated in three onshore operating areas in the U.S.: the South Texas & Gulf Coast Region; the Permian Region; and the Rocky Mountain Region. As of Dec 31 2016, Co. had total proved reserves of 395.8 million barrels of oil equivalent, consisting of 104.9 million barrels of oil, 1,111.10 billion cubic feet of natural gas, and 105.7 million barrels of natural gas liquids.

Recent Developments: For the quarter ended Sep 30 2017, net loss amounted to US$89.1 million versus a net loss of US$40.9 million in the year-earlier quarter. Revenues were US$295.4 million, down 16.2% from US$352.7 million the year before. Operating loss was US$85.6 million versus a loss of US$17.7 million in the prior-year quarter. Direct operating expenses declined 25.8% to US$257.3 million from US$346.5 million in the comparable period the year before. Indirect operating expenses increased 419.3% to US$123.7 million from US$23.8 million in the equivalent prior-year period.

Prospects: Our evaluation of SM Energy Co. as of Jan. 14, 2018 is the result of our systematic analysis on three basic characteristics: earnings strength, relative valuation, and recent stock price movement. The company has suffered a very negative trend in earnings per share over the past 5 quarters. Because the company lacks sufficient analyst estimate data, we place greater weight on the historical EPS trend as the measure of earnings strength. Based on operating earnings yield, the company is overvalued when compared to all of the companies in our coverage universe. Share price changes over the past year indicates that SM will perform very poorly over the near term.

Financial Data

(US$ in Thousands)	9 Mos	6 Mos	3 Mos	12/31/2016	12/31/2015	12/31/2014	12/31/2013	12/31/2012
Earnings Per Share	(3.33)	(3.05)	(4.45)	(9.90)	(6.61)	9.79	2.51	(0.83)
Cash Flow Per Share	4.56	4.84	5.12	7.20	14.45	21.67	20.09	14.12
Tang Book Value Per Share	21.61	22.45	23.51	22.44	27.21	33.89	23.96	21.37
Dividends Per Share	0.100	0.100	0.100	0.100	0.100	0.100	0.100	0.100
Dividend Payout %	...	...	...	...	...	1.02	3.98	...
Income Statement								
Total Revenue	788,838	493,459	372,738	1,217,450	1,556,965	2,522,307	2,293,374	1,505,102
EBITDA	(52,293)	28,199	170,839	(242,548)	334,007	1,936,931	1,196,517	714,629
Depn & Amortn	12,478	8,679	4,946	800,683	928,719	773,678	828,262	734,646
Income Before Taxes	(200,410)	(72,028)	118,940	(1,201,916)	(722,861)	1,064,699	278,611	(83,517)
Income Taxes	(65,825)	(26,555)	44,506	(444,172)	(275,151)	398,648	107,676	(29,268)
Net Income	(134,585)	(45,473)	74,434	(757,744)	(447,710)	666,051	170,935	(54,249)
Average Shares	111,575	111,277	111,329	76,568	67,723	68,044	67,998	65,138
Balance Sheet								
Current Assets	668,912	769,317	849,546	224,642	518,989	745,043	647,501	340,564
Total Assets	6,178,926	6,212,605	6,399,708	6,393,511	5,621,643	6,516,700	4,705,165	4,199,529
Current Liabilities	436,676	347,772	353,485	415,172	302,525	784,660	639,131	541,546
Long-Term Obligations	2,905,358	2,901,948	2,898,603	2,897,575	2,517,970	2,366,000	1,600,000	1,440,000
Total Liabilities	3,766,885	3,710,777	3,784,193	3,896,378	3,769,242	4,230,045	3,098,344	2,785,063
Stockholders' Equity	2,412,041	2,501,828	2,615,515	2,497,133	1,852,401	2,286,655	1,606,821	1,414,466
Shares Outstanding	111,624	111,453	111,258	111,257	68,075	67,463	67,056	66,195
Statistical Record								
Return on Assets %	N.M.	N.M.	N.M.	N.M.	N.M.	11.87	3.84	N.M.
Return on Equity %	N.M.	N.M.	N.M.	N.M.	N.M.	34.21	11.32	N.M.
EBITDA Margin %	N.M.	5.71	45.83	N.M.	21.45	76.79	52.17	47.48
Net Margin %	N.M.	N.M.	19.97	N.M.	N.M.	26.41	7.45	N.M.
Asset Turnover	0.20	0.22	0.25	0.20	0.26	0.45	0.52	0.38
Current Ratio	1.53	2.21	2.40	0.54	1.72	0.95	1.01	0.63
Debt to Equity	1.20	1.16	1.11	1.16	1.36	1.03	1.00	1.02
Price Range	41.27-12.79	41.27-14.10	41.27-17.32	41.27-7.60	59.01-18.22	89.58-30.17	91.98-52.21	83.35-41.80
P/E Ratio	...	...	...	...	...	9.15-3.08	36.65-20.80	...
Average Yield %	0.40	0.35	0.32	0.36	0.25	0.14	0.15	0.17

Address: 1775 Sherman Street, Suite 1200, Denver, CO 80203
Telephone: 303-861-8140
Fax: 303-861-0934

Web Site: www.sm-energy.com
Officers: William D. Sullivan - Chairman Javan D. Ottoson - President, Chief Executive Officer, Executive Vice President, Chief Operating Officer

Auditors: Ernst & Young LLP
Investor Contact: 303-861-8140
Transfer Agents: Computershare Trust Company NA, Golden, Co

SMITH (A O) CORP

Exchange	Symbol	Price	52Wk Range	Yield	P/E	Div Achiever
NYS	AOS	$61.28 (12/29/2017)	63.42-47.19	0.91	30.04	24 Years

*7 Year Price Score 150.93 *NYSE Composite Index=100 *12 Month Price Score 104.63

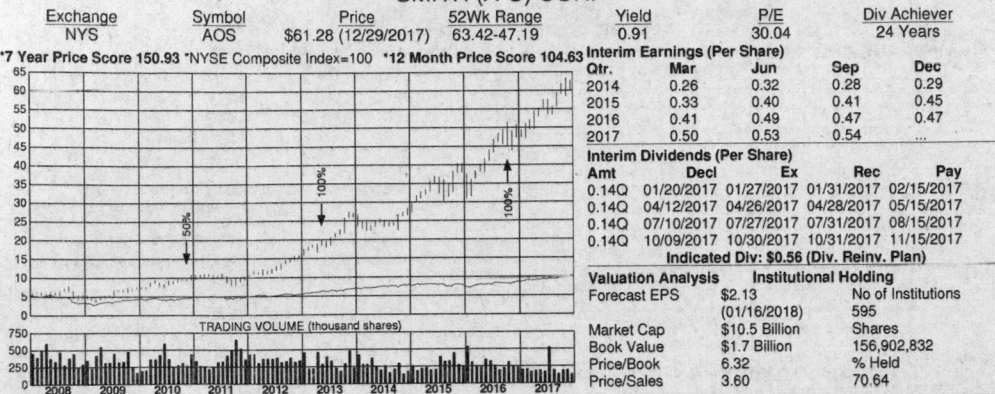

Interim Earnings (Per Share)

Qtr.	Mar	Jun	Sep	Dec
2014	0.26	0.32	0.28	0.29
2015	0.33	0.40	0.41	0.45
2016	0.41	0.49	0.47	0.47
2017	0.50	0.53	0.54	...

Interim Dividends (Per Share)

Amt	Decl	Ex	Rec	Pay
0.14Q	01/20/2017	01/27/2017	01/31/2017	02/15/2017
0.14Q	04/12/2017	04/26/2017	04/28/2017	05/15/2017
0.14Q	07/10/2017	07/27/2017	07/31/2017	08/15/2017
0.14Q	10/09/2017	10/30/2017	10/31/2017	11/15/2017

Indicated Div: $0.56 (Div. Reinv. Plan)

Valuation Analysis		Institutional Holding	
Forecast EPS	$2.13	No of Institutions	
	(01/16/2018)	595	
Market Cap	$10.5 Billion	Shares	
Book Value	$1.7 Billion	156,902,832	
Price/Book	6.32	% Held	
Price/Sales	3.60	70.64	

Business Summary: Household Appliances, Electronics & Goods (MIC: 1.5.1 SIC: 3639 NAIC: 335228)

A.O. Smith is comprised of two reporting segments: North America and Rest of World. The Rest of World segment is primarily comprised of China, Europe and India. Both segments manufacture and market lines of residential and commercial gas, gas tankless and electric water heaters, as well as water treatment products. Both segments primarily manufacture and market in their respective regions of the world. The North America segment also manufactures and globally markets specialty commercial water heating equipment, condensing and non-condensing boilers and water systems tanks. Co. also manufactures and markets in-home air purification products in China.

Recent Developments: For the quarter ended Sep 30 2017, net income increased 12.6% to US$93.7 million from US$83.2 million in the year-earlier quarter. Revenues were US$749.9 million, up 9.7% from US$683.9 million the year before. Direct operating expenses rose 10.6% to US$443.2 million from US$400.6 million in the comparable period the year before. Indirect operating expenses increased 6.2% to US$175.1 million from US$164.9 million in the equivalent prior-year period.

Prospects: Our evaluation of Smith (A.O.) Corp. as of Jan. 14, 2018 is the result of our systematic analysis on three basic characteristics: earnings strength, relative valuation, and recent stock price movement. The company has managed to produce a neutral trend in earnings per share over the past 5 quarters and while recent estimates for the company have been mixed, AOS has posted better than expected results. Based on operating earnings yield, the company is about fairly valued when compared to all of the companies in our coverage universe. Share price changes over the past year indicates that AOS will perform well over the near term.

Financial Data

(US$ in Thousands)	9 Mos	6 Mos	3 Mos	12/31/2016	12/31/2015	12/31/2014	12/31/2013	12/31/2012
Earnings Per Share	2.04	1.97	1.93	1.85	1.58	1.14	0.92	0.85
Cash Flow Per Share	1.93	2.11	2.36	2.55	1.94	1.46	1.52	0.78
Tang Book Value Per Share	4.87	4.74	4.45	4.13	4.15	3.60	3.13	2.27
Dividends Per Share	0.540	0.520	0.500	0.480	0.380	0.300	0.230	0.180
Dividend Payout %	26.47	26.40	25.91	25.95	24.05	26.32	25.14	21.11
Income Statement								
Total Revenue	2,228,100	1,478,200	740,000	2,685,900	2,536,500	2,356,000	2,153,800	1,939,300
EBITDA	439,100	287,400	139,500	534,900	472,900	352,200	301,800	297,600
Depn & Amortn	51,900	34,300	16,900	65,100	63,000	59,800	59,700	54,600
Income Before Taxes	380,000	248,400	120,400	462,500	402,500	286,700	236,400	233,800
Income Taxes	106,200	68,300	32,700	136,000	119,600	78,900	66,700	71,200
Net Income	273,800	180,100	87,700	326,500	282,900	207,800	169,700	158,700
Average Shares	174,355	174,889	175,419	176,825	179,009	181,973	185,575	186,216
Balance Sheet								
Current Assets	1,698,100	1,640,300	1,605,500	1,562,000	1,455,300	1,319,000	1,205,600	1,107,200
Total Assets	3,104,600	2,984,000	2,940,200	2,891,000	2,646,500	2,515,300	2,391,500	2,265,200
Current Liabilities	731,700	705,800	720,500	765,600	653,200	605,200	590,900	499,000
Long-Term Obligations	442,200	367,700	362,200	316,400	236,100	210,100	177,700	225,100
Total Liabilities	1,438,700	1,370,300	1,373,800	1,375,700	1,204,200	1,134,000	1,062,800	1,071,100
Stockholders' Equity	1,665,900	1,613,700	1,566,400	1,515,300	1,442,300	1,381,300	1,328,700	1,194,100
Shares Outstanding	171,929	172,538	173,035	173,441	175,896	178,799	182,478	184,853
Statistical Record								
Return on Assets %	12.03	12.23	12.19	11.76	10.96	8.47	7.29	6.86
Return on Equity %	22.34	22.36	22.38	22.02	20.04	15.34	13.45	13.88
EBITDA Margin %	19.71	19.44	18.85	19.92	18.64	14.95	14.01	15.35
Net Margin %	12.29	12.18	11.85	12.16	11.15	8.82	7.88	8.18
Asset Turnover	0.99	1.01	1.00	0.97	0.98	0.96	0.93	0.84
Current Ratio	2.32	2.32	2.23	2.04	2.23	2.18	2.04	2.22
Debt to Equity	0.27	0.23	0.23	0.21	0.16	0.15	0.13	0.19
Price Range	59.55-43.81	57.52-43.27	52.17-38.08	51.41-31.03	40.43-27.11	28.40-22.34	27.44-15.77	15.90-10.26
P/E Ratio	29.19-21.48	29.20-21.96	27.03-19.73	27.79-16.77	25.59-17.16	24.91-19.60	29.83-17.14	18.70-12.07
Average Yield %	1.04	1.05	1.08	1.13	1.11	1.21	1.11	1.42

Address: 11270 West Park Place, Milwaukee, WI 53224-9508	Web Site: www.aosmith.com	Auditors: Ernst & Young LLP
Telephone: 414-359-4000	Officers: Ajita G. Rajendra - Chairman, President, Chief Executive Officer, Chief Operating Officer, Executive Vice President, Senior Vice President, Division Officer Kevin J. Wheeler - President, Chief Operating Officer, Senior Vice President, Region Officer	Investor Contact: 414-359-4130
Fax: 414-359-4115		Transfer Agents: Wells Fargo Shareowner Services, N.A., St. Paul, MN

SOTHEBY'S

Exchange	Symbol	Price	52Wk Range	Yield	P/E
NYS	BID	$51.60 (12/29/2017)	57.70-38.72	N/A	27.16

7 Year Price Score 95.56   *NYSE Composite Index=100   *12 Month Price Score 97.66

Interim Earnings (Per Share)

Qtr.	Mar	Jun	Sep	Dec
2014	(0.09)	1.11	(0.40)	1.07
2015	0.07	0.96	(0.26)	(0.16)
2016	(0.41)	1.52	(0.99)	1.13
2017	(0.21)	1.43	(0.45)	...

Interim Dividends (Per Share)

Dividend Payment Suspended

Valuation Analysis		Institutional Holding	
Forecast EPS	$2.12	No of Institutions	
	(11/28/2017)	343	
Market Cap	$2.7 Billion	Shares	
Book Value	$519.8 Million	68,745,240	
Price/Book	5.21	% Held	
Price/Sales	2.76	105.86	

Business Summary: Miscellaneous Consumer Services (MIC: 2.2.3 SIC: 7389 NAIC: 453920)

Sotheby's is a global art business whose operations are organized under two segments: Agency and Finance. The Agency segment matches buyers and sellers of authenticated fine art, decorative art, jewelry, wine and collectibles (collectively, art or works of art or artwork or property) through the auction or private sale process. Agency segment activities also include the sale of artworks that are principally acquired incidental to the auction process and the activities of RM Sotheby's, an equity investee that operates as an auction house for investment-quality automobiles. The Finance segment provides art-related financing activities by making loans that are secured by works of art.

Recent Developments: For the quarter ended Sep 30 2017, net loss amounted to US$23.5 million versus a net loss of US$54.5 million in the year-earlier quarter. Revenues were US$171.4 million, up 87.3% from US$91.5 million the year before. Operating loss was US$39.8 million versus a loss of US$66.9 million in the prior-year quarter. Direct operating expenses rose 142.7% to US$95.1 million from US$39.2 million in the comparable period the year before. Indirect operating expenses decreased 2.6% to US$116.1 million from US$119.2 million in the equivalent prior-year period.

Prospects: Our evaluation of Sotheby's Holdings Inc. as of Jan. 14, 2018 is the result of our systematic analysis on three basic characteristics: earnings strength, relative valuation, and recent stock price movement. The company has managed to produce a neutral trend in earnings per share over the past 5 quarters and while recent estimates for the company have been raised by analysts, BID has posted better than expected results. Based on operating earnings yield, the company is about fairly valued when compared to all of the companies in our coverage universe. Share price changes over the past year indicates that BID will perform well over the near term.

Financial Data

(US$ in Thousands)	9 Mos	6 Mos	3 Mos	12/31/2016	12/31/2015	12/31/2014	12/31/2013	12/31/2012
Earnings Per Share	1.90	1.36	1.45	1.27	0.63	1.68	1.88	1.57
Cash Flow Per Share	3.51	4.97	8.38	2.77	2.28	0.64	3.47	(0.96)
Tang Book Value Per Share	8.71	9.12	8.00	8.34	12.05	12.51	16.27	14.43
Dividends Per Share	...	...	...	...	0.400	4.740	0.200	0.520
Dividend Payout %	...	...	...	...	63.49	282.14	10.64	33.12
Income Statement								
Total Revenue	673,829	502,435	187,537	805,377	961,494	938,053	853,678	768,492
EBITDA	66,399	103,912	(11,500)	145,650	219,768	246,927	245,004	220,215
Depn & Amortn	1,240	827	414	19,900	19,500	20,600	19,400	17,900
Income Before Taxes	42,889	88,604	(19,290)	96,734	169,299	193,021	185,693	159,436
Income Taxes	2,848	24,176	(7,292)	25,957	131,145	75,761	55,702	51,395
Net Income	42,087	65,566	(11,325)	74,112	43,727	117,795	130,006	108,292
Average Shares	52,532	53,054	53,016	57,653	68,121	69,606	69,175	68,527
Balance Sheet								
Current Assets	966,430	1,669,682	1,254,427	1,268,853	2,109,739	2,039,522	1,972,273	1,671,123
Total Assets	2,146,675	2,840,378	2,416,996	2,504,426	3,274,129	3,134,820	2,893,546	2,575,095
Current Liabilities	557,604	1,120,001	699,437	742,975	1,197,583	1,429,207	1,142,489	964,879
Long-Term Obligations	991,190	1,095,262	1,145,842	1,163,941	1,156,267	745,000	515,148	515,197
Total Liabilities	1,626,839	2,297,422	1,926,797	1,999,008	2,467,702	2,257,123	1,754,228	1,582,269
Stockholders' Equity	519,836	542,956	490,199	505,418	806,427	877,697	1,139,318	992,826
Shares Outstanding	52,503	52,670	53,411	52,971	65,791	68,991	69,131	67,779
Statistical Record								
Return on Assets %	4.78	2.71	3.67	2.56	1.36	3.91	4.75	4.34
Return on Equity %	20.79	13.76	15.99	11.27	5.19	11.68	12.19	11.39
EBITDA Margin %	9.85	20.68	N.M.	18.08	22.86	26.32	28.70	28.66
Net Margin %	6.25	13.05	N.M.	9.20	4.55	12.56	15.23	14.09
Asset Turnover	0.44	0.32	0.37	0.28	0.30	0.31	0.31	0.31
Current Ratio	1.73	1.49	1.79	1.71	1.76	1.43	1.73	1.73
Debt to Equity	1.91	2.02	2.34	2.30	1.43	0.85	0.45	0.52
Price Range	57.70-34.52	55.42-26.56	48.54-25.54	41.65-19.13	46.93-25.76	53.51-35.30	53.20-33.03	40.51-27.74
P/E Ratio	30.37-18.17	40.75-19.53	33.48-17.61	32.80-15.06	74.49-40.89	31.85-21.01	28.30-17.57	25.80-17.67
Average Yield %	...	...	...	...	1.03	11.32	0.47	1.56

Address: 1334 York Avenue, New York, NY 10021 **Telephone:** 212-606-7000	**Web Site:** www.sothebys.com **Officers:** Domenico De Sole - Chairman The Duke of Devonshire - Deputy Chairman	**Auditors:** Deloitte & Touche LLP **Investor Contact:** 800-700-6321 **Transfer Agents:** BNY Mellon Shareowner Services, Pittsburg, PA

SMUCKER (J.M.) CO.

Exchange	Symbol	Price	52Wk Range	Yield	P/E	Div Acheiver
NYS	SJM	$124.24 (12/29/2017)	141.92-99.99	2.51	N/A	19 Years

*7 Year Price Score 91.71   *NYSE Composite Index=100   *12 Month Price Score 88.87

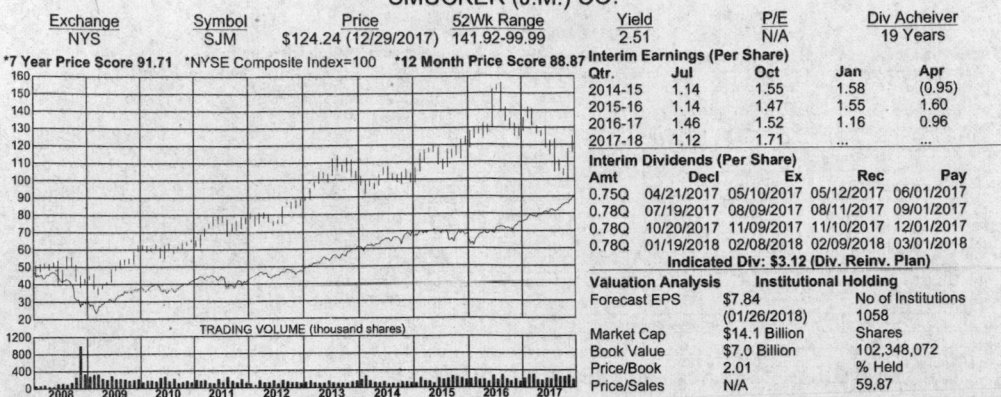

Interim Earnings (Per Share)

Qtr.	Jul	Oct	Jan	Apr
2014-15	1.14	1.55	1.58	(0.95)
2015-16	1.14	1.47	1.55	1.60
2016-17	1.46	1.52	1.16	0.96
2017-18	1.12	1.71	...	...

Interim Dividends (Per Share)

Amt	Decl	Ex	Rec	Pay
0.75Q	04/21/2017	05/10/2017	05/12/2017	06/01/2017
0.78Q	07/19/2017	08/09/2017	08/11/2017	09/01/2017
0.78Q	10/20/2017	11/09/2017	11/10/2017	12/01/2017
0.78Q	01/19/2018	02/08/2018	02/09/2018	03/01/2018

Indicated Div: $3.12 (Div. Reinv. Plan)

Valuation Analysis

		Institutional Holding	
Forecast EPS	$7.84 (01/26/2018)	No of Institutions	1058
Market Cap	$14.1 Billion	Shares	102,348,072
Book Value	$7.0 Billion	% Held	59.87
Price/Book	2.01		
Price/Sales	N/A		

Business Summary: Food (MIC: 1.2.1 SIC: 2033 NAIC: 311421)

Smucker (J.M.) manufactures and markets food and beverage products. Co.'s principal products are coffee, pet food, pet snacks, peanut butter, fruit spreads, shortening and oils, baking mixes and ready-to-spread frostings, frozen sandwiches, flour and baking ingredients, juices and beverages, and portion control products. Co. has three segments: U.S. Retail Coffee, U.S. Retail Consumer Foods, and U.S. Retail Pet Foods. The U.S. Retail Coffee segment primarily includes the domestic sales of Folgers, Dunkin' Donuts®, and Cafe Bustelo® branded coffee; and the U.S. Retail Consumer Foods segment primarily includes domestic sales of Jif®, Smucker's®, Crisco®, and Pillsbury® branded products.

Recent Developments: For the quarter ended Oct 31 2017, net income increased 9.8% to US$194.6 million from US$177.3 million in the year-earlier quarter. Revenues were US$1.92 billion, up 0.5% from US$1.91 billion the year before. Operating income was US$330.7 million versus US$303.3 million in the prior-year quarter, an increase of 9.0%. Direct operating expenses was unchanged at US$1.17 billion versus the comparable period the year before. Indirect operating expenses decreased 3.5% to US$424.3 million from US$439.6 million in the equivalent prior-year period.

Prospects: Our evaluation of Smucker (J.M.) Co. as of Jan. 21, 2018 is the result of our systematic analysis on three basic characteristics: earnings strength, relative valuation, and recent stock price movement. The company has enjoyed a very positive trend in earnings per share over the past 5 quarters. However, while recent estimates for the company have been mixed, SJM has posted better than expected results. Based on operating earnings yield, the company is undervalued when compared to all of the companies in our coverage universe. Share price changes over the past year indicates that SJM will perform very poorly over the near term.

Financial Data

(US$ in Thousands)	6 Mos	3 Mos	04/30/2017	04/30/2016	04/30/2015	04/30/2014	04/30/2013	04/30/2012
Earnings Per Share	...	4.76	5.10	5.76	3.33	5.42	5.00	4.06
Cash Flow Per Share	...	9.96	9.17	12.23	7.12	8.27	7.93	6.50
Dividends Per Share	3.030	3.000	2.920	2.650	2.500	2.260	2.040	1.880
Dividend Payout %	...	63.03	57.25	46.01	75.08	41.70	40.80	46.31
Income Statement								
Total Revenue	3,672,500	1,748,900	7,392,300	7,811,200	5,692,700	5,610,600	5,897,700	5,525,782
EBITDA	772,600	337,000	1,253,200	1,370,700	760,400	1,086,600	1,064,800	939,886
Depn & Amortn	208,200	106,000	211,700	221,700	157,500	157,500	154,100	158,936
Income Before Taxes	480,800	189,000	878,400	977,900	523,000	849,700	817,300	701,158
Income Taxes	159,400	62,200	286,100	289,200	178,100	284,500	273,100	241,414
Net Income	321,400	126,800	592,300	688,700	344,900	565,200	544,200	459,744
Average Shares	113,000	113,000	115,578	118,959	103,043	103,518	107,904	112,262
Balance Sheet								
Current Assets	1,785,800	1,692,100	1,641,800	1,573,400	2,052,300	1,539,100	1,595,200	1,643,465
Total Assets	15,702,000	15,641,600	15,639,700	15,984,100	16,882,600	9,072,100	9,031,800	9,115,226
Current Liabilities	1,854,500	1,750,900	1,832,600	1,213,000	1,022,600	891,000	596,800	616,972
Long-Term Obligations	4,294,100	4,444,800	4,445,500	5,146,000	5,944,900	1,879,800	1,967,800	2,020,543
Total Liabilities	8,665,700	8,709,700	8,789,500	8,975,600	9,795,700	4,042,500	3,883,000	3,951,840
Stockholders' Equity	7,036,300	6,931,900	6,850,200	7,008,500	7,086,900	5,029,600	5,148,800	5,163,386
Shares Outstanding	113,600	113,600	113,439	116,306	119,577	101,697	106,486	110,284
Statistical Record								
Return on Assets %	...	3.46	3.75	4.18	2.66	6.24	6.00	5.26
Return on Equity %	...	7.83	8.55	9.75	5.69	11.11	10.55	8.77
EBITDA Margin %	21.04	19.27	16.95	17.55	13.36	19.37	18.05	17.01
Net Margin %	8.75	7.25	8.01	8.82	6.06	10.07	9.23	8.32
Asset Turnover	...	0.46	0.47	0.47	0.44	0.62	0.65	0.63
Current Ratio	0.96	0.97	0.90	1.30	2.01	1.73	2.67	2.66
Debt to Equity	0.61	0.64	0.65	0.73	0.84	0.37	0.38	0.39
Price Range	141.92-101.91	156.23-114.41	156.23-124.74	132.52-105.59	118.20-96.45	114.36-91.81	105.00-73.65	81.44-67.68
P/E Ratio	...	32.82-24.04	30.63-24.46	23.01-18.33	35.50-28.96	21.10-16.94	21.00-14.73	20.06-16.67
Average Yield %	2.44	2.27	2.14	2.23	2.38	2.19	2.38	2.46

Address: One Strawberry Lane, Orrville, OH 44667-0280
Telephone: 330-682-3000

Web Site: www.jmsmucker.com
Officers: Richard K. Smucker - Executive Chairman, Executive Chairman (frmr), President, Chief Executive Officer, Co-Chief Executive Officer Mark R. Belgya - Vice-Chairman, Senior Vice President, Chief Financial Officer

Auditors: Ernst & Young LLP
Investor Contact: 330-684-3838
Transfer Agents: Computershare, Louisville, KY

645

SNAP-ON, INC.

Exchange	Symbol	Price	52Wk Range	Yield	P/E
NYS	SNA	$174.30 (12/29/2017)	181.53-141.51	1.88	17.90

*7 Year Price Score 110.15 *NYSE Composite Index=100 *12 Month Price Score 96.79

TRADING VOLUME (thousand shares)

Interim Earnings (Per Share)

Qtr.	Mar	Jun	Sep	Dec
2014	1.62	1.80	1.76	1.96
2015	1.87	2.03	1.98	2.22
2016	2.16	2.36	2.22	2.46
2017	2.39	2.60	2.29	...

Interim Dividends (Per Share)

Amt	Decl	Ex	Rec	Pay
0.71Q	02/09/2017	02/22/2017	02/24/2017	03/10/2017
0.71Q	04/27/2017	05/17/2017	05/19/2017	06/09/2017
0.71Q	08/03/2017	08/16/2017	08/18/2017	09/08/2017
0.82Q	11/06/2017	11/16/2017	11/17/2017	12/08/2017

Indicated Div: $3.28

Valuation Analysis

		Institutional Holding	
Forecast EPS	$10.09	No of Institutions	
	(01/11/2018)	786	
Market Cap	$9.9 Billion	Shares	
Book Value	$2.9 Billion	68,248,336	
Price/Book	3.40	% Held	
Price/Sales	2.54	84.10	

Business Summary: Industrial Machinery & Equipment (MIC: 7.2.1 SIC: 3429 NAIC: 332510)

Snap-on is a manufacturer and marketer of tools, equipment, diagnostics, repair information and systems solutions. Products and services include hand and power tools, tool storage, diagnostic software, information and management systems, shop equipment and solutions for vehicle dealerships and repair centers, as well as for the aviation and aerospace, agriculture, construction, government and military, mining, natural resources, power generation and technical education industries. Co. also provides financing programs to facilitate the sales of its products. Co.'s segments are: Commercial & Industrial Group; Snap-on Tools Group; Repair Systems & Information Group; and Financial Services.

Recent Developments: For the quarter ended Sep 30 2017, net income increased 1.4% to US$137.1 million from US$135.2 million in the year-earlier quarter. Revenues were US$982.8 million, up 8.5% from US$905.7 million the year before. Operating income was US$209.1 million versus US$208.2 million in the prior-year quarter, an increase of 0.4%. Direct operating expenses rose 9.7% to US$478.2 million from US$436.0 million in the comparable period the year before. Indirect operating expenses increased 13.0% to US$295.5 million from US$261.5 million in the equivalent prior-year period.

Prospects: Our evaluation of Snap-On Inc. as of Jan. 14, 2018 is the result of our systematic analysis on three basic characteristics: earnings strength, relative valuation, and recent stock price movement. The company has managed to produce a neutral trend in earnings per share over the past 5 quarters and while recent estimates for the company have remained steady, SNA has posted better than expected results. Based on operating earnings yield, the company is undervalued when compared to all of the companies in our coverage universe. Share price changes over the past year indicates that SNA will perform very poorly over the near term.

Financial Data

(US$ in Thousands)	9 Mos	6 Mos	3 Mos	12/31/2016	01/02/2016	01/03/2015	12/28/2013	12/29/2012
Earnings Per Share	9.74	9.67	9.43	9.20	8.10	7.14	5.93	5.20
Cash Flow Per Share	10.06	10.24	10.82	9.94	8.57	6.74	6.76	5.67
Tang Book Value Per Share	30.51	29.51	28.43	26.52	24.58	20.54	18.65	13.86
Dividends Per Share	2.840	2.740	2.640	2.540	2.200	1.850	1.580	1.400
Dividend Payout %	29.16	28.34	28.00	27.61	27.16	25.91	26.64	26.92
Income Statement								
Total Revenue	2,945,800	1,963,000	963,900	3,711,800	3,593,100	3,492,600	3,237,500	3,099,200
EBITDA	732,900	502,400	243,300	938,600	844,400	762,800	658,500	592,100
Depn & Amortn	69,400	45,900	23,100	85,600	82,500	79,500	76,700	76,700
Income Before Taxes	624,900	431,000	207,600	801,400	710,500	630,900	526,200	460,200
Income Taxes	187,100	129,900	62,600	244,300	221,200	199,500	166,700	148,200
Net Income	428,200	294,800	141,600	546,400	478,700	421,900	350,300	306,100
Average Shares	58,255	59,013	59,324	59,400	59,100	59,100	59,100	58,900
Balance Sheet								
Current Assets	2,145,900	2,034,100	1,974,100	1,884,000	1,898,700	1,858,600	1,796,200	1,669,000
Total Assets	5,256,200	5,067,100	4,877,800	4,723,200	4,486,900	4,310,100	4,110,000	3,902,300
Current Liabilities	1,222,800	1,073,800	971,500	989,500	670,500	718,700	715,400	589,200
Long-Term Obligations	755,000	755,600	755,400	708,800	861,700	862,700	858,900	970,400
Total Liabilities	2,334,400	2,212,200	2,130,100	2,106,000	2,074,200	2,102,300	1,996,800	2,100,200
Stockholders' Equity	2,921,800	2,854,900	2,747,700	2,617,200	2,412,700	2,207,800	2,113,200	1,802,100
Shares Outstanding	57,006	57,584	57,949	57,949	58,086	58,113	58,115	58,254
Statistical Record								
Return on Assets %	11.66	11.97	12.02	11.90	10.91	9.86	8.77	8.10
Return on Equity %	20.55	21.06	21.26	21.79	20.78	19.21	17.94	18.42
EBITDA Margin %	24.88	25.59	25.24	25.29	23.50	21.84	20.34	19.10
Net Margin %	14.54	15.02	14.69	14.72	13.32	12.08	10.82	9.88
Asset Turnover	0.79	0.80	0.81	0.81	0.82	0.82	0.81	0.82
Current Ratio	1.75	1.89	2.03	1.90	2.83	2.59	2.51	2.83
Debt to Equity	0.26	0.26	0.27	0.27	0.36	0.39	0.41	0.54
Price Range	181.53-141.51	181.53-145.97	181.53-145.97	176.20-135.41	174.09-131.45	139.35-97.23	108.88-77.06	80.03-50.62
P/E Ratio	18.64-14.53	18.77-15.10	19.25-15.48	19.15-14.72	21.49-16.23	19.52-13.62	18.36-12.99	15.39-9.73
Average Yield %	1.75	1.68	1.63	1.61	1.41	1.55	1.72	2.12

Address: 2801 80th Street, Kenosha, WI 53143	**Web Site:** www.snapon.com	**Auditors:** Deloitte & Touche LLP
Telephone: 262-656-5200	**Officers:** Nicholas T. Pinchuk - Chairman, President, Chief Executive Officer Aldo John Pagliari - Senior	**Investor Contact:** 262-656-6121
Fax: 262-656-5577	Vice President, Chief Financial Officer	**Transfer Agents:** Computershare Trust Company, N.A., Providence, RI

SONIC AUTOMOTIVE, INC.

Exchange	Symbol	Price	52Wk Range	Yield	P/E
NYS	SAH	$18.45 (12/29/2017)	25.95-16.40	1.08	11.98

*7 Year Price Score 78.31 *NYSE Composite Index=100 *12 Month Price Score 95.42

Interim Earnings (Per Share)

Qtr.	Mar	Jun	Sep	Dec
2014	0.36	0.51	0.47	0.50
2015	0.27	0.29	0.52	0.62
2016	0.31	0.50	0.40	0.84
2017	(0.01)	0.27	0.44	...

Interim Dividends (Per Share)

Amt	Decl	Ex	Rec	Pay
0.05Q	02/21/2017	03/13/2017	03/15/2017	04/14/2017
0.05Q	04/26/2017	06/13/2017	06/15/2017	07/14/2017
0.05Q	07/28/2017	09/14/2017	09/15/2017	10/13/2017
0.05Q	10/24/2017	12/14/2017	12/15/2017	01/12/2018

Indicated Div: $0.20

Valuation Analysis — **Institutional Holding**

Forecast EPS	$1.84 (01/01/2018)	No of Institutions	222
Market Cap	$575.0 Million	Shares	37,112,736
Book Value	$723.0 Million	% Held	63.79
Price/Book	0.80		
Price/Sales	0.06		

Business Summary: Retail - Automotive (MIC: 2.1.4 SIC: 5511 NAIC: 441110)

Sonic Automotive is an automotive retailer. As of Dec 31 2016, Co. operated 116 franchises in 13 states (representing 25 different brands of cars and light trucks), 18 collision repair centers, 107 franchised dealership stores and five EchoPark® stores. Co. has two segments: Franchised Dealerships, which is comprised of retail automotive franchises that sell new vehicles and buy and sell used vehicles, sell replacement parts, perform vehicle repair and maintenance services, and arrange finance and insurance products; and EchoPark®, which is comprised of stand-alone retail locations that provide customers an opportunity to search, buy, service, finance and sell pre-owned vehicles.

Recent Developments: For the quarter ended Sep 30 2017, income from continuing operations increased 4.0% to US$19.7 million from US$19.0 million in the year-earlier quarter. Net income increased 7.3% to US$19.4 million from US$18.1 million in the year-earlier quarter. Revenues were US$2.51 billion, down 2.0% from US$2.56 billion the year before. Operating income was US$55.8 million versus US$50.9 million in the prior-year quarter, an increase of 9.5%. Direct operating expenses declined 2.5% to US$2.14 billion from US$2.20 billion in the comparable period the year before. Indirect operating expenses decreased 0.4% to US$306.9 million from US$308.2 million in the equivalent prior-year period.

Prospects: Our evaluation of Sonic Automotive Inc. as of Jan. 14, 2018 is the result of our systematic analysis on three basic characteristics: earnings strength, relative valuation, and recent stock price movement. The company has enjoyed a very positive trend in earnings per share over the past 5 quarters and while recent estimates for the company have been mixed, SAH has posted results that were in line with analysts expectations. Based on operating earnings yield, the company is undervalued when compared to all of the companies in our coverage universe. Share price changes over the past year indicates that SAH will perform poorly over the near term.

Financial Data
(US$ in Thousands)

	9 Mos	6 Mos	3 Mos	12/31/2016	12/31/2015	12/31/2014	12/31/2013	12/31/2012
Earnings Per Share	1.54	1.50	1.73	2.04	1.70	1.84	1.53	1.53
Cash Flow Per Share	3.75	4.54	4.29	4.73	1.38	3.09	2.41	(1.25)
Tang Book Value Per Share	3.78	3.69	3.78	3.86	3.54	2.10	0.94	0.03
Dividends Per Share	0.200	0.200	0.200	0.200	0.113	0.100	0.100	0.100
Dividend Payout %	12.99	13.33	11.56	9.80	6.62	5.43	6.54	6.54
Income Statement								
Total Revenue	7,199,269	4,693,568	2,287,822	9,731,779	9,624,299	9,197,099	8,843,168	8,365,468
EBITDA	122,319	65,742	22,779	314,159	289,522	295,331	264,744	279,127
Depn & Amortn	2,428	1,617	831	81,125	72,130	61,621	58,284	58,350
Income Before Taxes	54,278	20,422	152	155,212	145,156	161,727	129,021	141,233
Income Taxes	22,254	8,128	172	60,696	57,065	63,168	44,343	49,972
Net Income	31,031	11,591	(541)	93,193	86,311	97,217	81,618	89,101
Average Shares	43,811	44,810	44,791	45,948	50,883	52,563	52,941	60,406
Balance Sheet								
Current Assets	1,832,776	1,960,160	1,946,335	2,031,044	2,083,112	1,768,959	1,732,185	1,611,033
Total Assets	3,614,569	3,645,156	3,607,635	3,639,336	3,562,381	3,183,135	3,051,170	2,776,722
Current Liabilities	1,731,746	1,904,884	1,847,979	1,936,880	1,914,621	1,647,006	1,594,536	1,524,155
Long-Term Obligations	1,016,390	887,327	897,352	839,675	781,145	742,610	730,157	610,798
Total Liabilities	2,891,595	2,931,746	2,885,357	2,914,172	2,833,333	2,516,417	2,437,531	2,250,177
Stockholders' Equity	722,974	713,410	722,278	725,164	729,048	666,718	613,639	526,545
Shares Outstanding	31,166	43,861	44,978	44,733	49,940	50,919	52,713	53,239
Statistical Record								
Return on Assets %	1.95	1.88	2.22	2.58	2.56	3.12	2.80	3.47
Return on Equity %	9.75	9.70	11.24	12.78	12.37	15.19	14.32	16.94
EBITDA Margin %	1.70	1.40	1.00	3.23	3.01	3.21	2.99	3.34
Net Margin %	0.43	0.25	N.M.	0.96	0.90	1.06	0.92	1.07
Asset Turnover	2.77	2.74	2.78	2.70	2.85	2.95	3.03	3.26
Current Ratio	1.06	1.03	1.05	1.05	1.09	1.07	1.09	1.06
Debt to Equity	1.41	1.24	1.24	1.16	1.07	1.11	1.19	1.16
Price Range	25.95-16.40	25.95-16.68	25.95-16.15	24.00-15.91	27.04-20.35	27.81-21.33	25.15-20.11	20.89-12.16
P/E Ratio	16.85-10.65	17.30-11.12	15.00-9.34	11.76-7.80	15.91-11.97	15.11-11.59	16.44-13.14	13.65-7.95
Average Yield %	1.00	1.01	1.03	1.09	0.47	0.41	0.44	0.58

Address: 4401 Colwick Road, Charlotte, NC 28211
Telephone: 704-566-2400
Fax: 704-536-5116

Web Site: www.sonicautomotive.com
Officers: O. Bruton Smith - Executive Chairman, Chairman, Chief Executive Officer David Bruton Smith - Vice-Chairman, Executive Vice President

Auditors: KPMG LLP
Investor Contact: 888-766-4218
Transfer Agents: American Stock Transfer & Trust Company, New York, NY

SONOCO PRODUCTS CO.

Exchange	Symbol	Price	52Wk Range	Yield	P/E	Div Achiever
NYS	SON	$53.14 (12/29/2017)	55.45-47.15	2.94	19.54	33 Years

*7 Year Price Score 99.51   ***NYSE Composite Index=100**   ***12 Month Price Score 96.57**

Interim Earnings (Per Share)

Qtr.	Mar	Jun	Sep	Dec
2014	0.50	0.59	0.69	0.53
2015	0.86	0.63	0.43	0.54
2016	0.59	0.55	0.64	1.03
2017	0.54	0.43	0.72	...

Interim Dividends (Per Share)

Amt	Decl	Ex	Rec	Pay
0.37Q	02/08/2017	02/17/2017	02/22/2017	03/10/2017
0.39Q	04/19/2017	05/10/2017	05/12/2017	06/09/2017
0.39Q	07/19/2017	08/09/2017	08/11/2017	09/08/2017
0.39Q	10/16/2017	11/09/2017	11/10/2017	12/08/2017

Indicated Div: $1.56 (Div. Reinv. Plan)

Valuation Analysis   **Institutional Holding**

Forecast EPS	$2.79	No of Institutions
	(01/18/2018)	504
Market Cap	$5.3 Billion	Shares
Book Value	$1.7 Billion	94,067,216
Price/Book	3.05	% Held
Price/Sales	1.08	69.34

Business Summary: Containers & Packaging (MIC: 8.1.3 SIC: 2671 NAIC: 322221)

Sonoco Products is a manufacturer of industrial and consumer packaging products and a provider of packaging services. Co. has four segments: Consumer Packaging, which include round composite cans, shaped rigid paperboard containers, fiber caulk/adhesive tubes, and peelable membrane easy-open closures for composite and metal cans; Paper and Industrial Converted Products, which include Recycled paperboard, chipboard, tubeboard, and lightweight corestock; Display and Packaging, which include printed backer cards, thermoformed blisters and heat sealing equipment; and Protective Solutions, which include custom-engineered, paperboard-based and expanded foam protective packaging and components.

Recent Developments: For the quarter ended Oct 1 2017, net income increased 11.3% to US$73.4 million from US$66.0 million in the year-earlier quarter. Revenues were US$1.32 billion, up 9.6% from US$1.21 billion the year before. Operating income was US$120.1 million versus US$104.8 million in the prior-year quarter, an increase of 14.5%. Direct operating expenses rose 10.3% to US$1.07 billion from US$973.4 million in the comparable period the year before. Indirect operating expenses increased 0.2% to US$130.8 million from US$130.5 million in the equivalent prior-year period.

Prospects: Our evaluation of Sonoco Products Co. as of Jan. 14, 2018 is the result of our systematic analysis on three basic characteristics: earnings strength, relative valuation, and recent stock price movement. The company has enjoyed a very positive trend in earnings per share over the past 5 quarters and while recent estimates for the company have been mixed, SON has posted better than expected results. Based on operating earnings yield, the company is undervalued when compared to all of the companies in our coverage universe. Share price changes over the past year indicates that SON will perform in line with the market over the near term.

Financial Data

(US$ in Thousands)	9 Mos	6 Mos	3 Mos	12/31/2016	12/31/2015	12/31/2014	12/31/2013	12/31/2012
Earnings Per Share	2.72	2.64	2.76	2.81	2.44	2.32	2.12	1.91
Cash Flow Per Share	3.31	3.16	3.99	3.93	4.46	4.09	5.25	3.96
Tang Book Value Per Share	1.50	2.07	1.56	2.17	1.26	0.43	3.60	1.01
Dividends Per Share	1.520	1.500	1.480	1.460	1.370	1.270	1.230	1.190
Dividend Payout %	55.88	56.82	53.62	51.96	56.15	54.74	58.02	62.30
Income Statement								
Total Revenue	3,737,632	2,412,998	1,172,324	4,782,877	4,964,369	5,014,534	4,848,092	4,786,129
EBITDA	439,955	264,392	138,981	666,129	562,432	561,422	530,695	518,964
Depn & Amortn	159,130	103,649	49,008	173,295	179,888	169,911	169,400	171,905
Income Before Taxes	242,328	135,893	77,915	441,277	327,946	339,120	304,569	287,074
Income Taxes	78,251	42,706	25,539	164,631	87,738	108,922	96,203	103,759
Net Income	169,670	96,858	53,733	286,434	250,136	239,165	219,113	196,010
Average Shares	100,684	100,717	100,980	101,782	102,392	103,172	103,248	102,573
Balance Sheet								
Current Assets	1,575,325	1,464,977	1,391,295	1,348,768	1,307,378	1,390,283	1,378,474	1,499,896
Total Assets	4,569,628	4,292,743	4,190,405	3,923,203	4,020,269	4,209,996	3,979,291	4,176,065
Current Liabilities	991,168	906,107	882,400	802,616	922,516	905,445	867,225	1,044,235
Long-Term Obligations	1,300,191	1,190,646	1,177,188	1,020,698	1,021,854	1,200,885	946,257	1,099,454
Total Liabilities	2,837,455	2,634,948	2,605,162	2,390,845	2,507,340	2,702,873	2,268,554	2,687,079
Stockholders' Equity	1,732,173	1,657,795	1,585,243	1,532,358	1,512,929	1,507,123	1,710,737	1,488,986
Shares Outstanding	99,398	99,396	99,384	99,193	100,944	100,603	102,147	100,847
Statistical Record								
Return on Assets %	6.37	6.47	6.80	7.19	6.08	5.84	5.37	4.79
Return on Equity %	16.65	16.64	17.80	18.76	16.57	14.86	13.70	13.48
EBITDA Margin %	11.77	10.96	11.86	13.93	11.33	11.20	10.95	10.84
Net Margin %	4.54	4.01	4.58	5.99	5.04	4.77	4.52	4.10
Asset Turnover	1.13	1.15	1.15	1.20	1.21	1.22	1.19	1.17
Current Ratio	1.59	1.62	1.58	1.68	1.42	1.54	1.59	1.44
Debt to Equity	0.75	0.72	0.74	0.67	0.68	0.80	0.55	0.74
Price Range	55.25-47.15	55.25-49.42	55.25-45.56	55.25-37.01	47.44-37.26	44.50-37.55	41.72-29.73	34.49-29.20
P/E Ratio	20.31-17.33	20.93-18.72	20.02-16.51	19.66-13.17	19.44-15.27	19.18-16.19	19.68-14.02	18.06-15.29
Average Yield %	2.94	2.87	2.89	3.01	3.18	3.06	3.39	3.80

Address: 1 N. Second St., Hartsville, SC 29550	Web Site: www.sonoco.com	Auditors: PricewaterhouseCoopers, LLP
Telephone: 843-383-7000	**Officers:** Harris E. DeLoach - Chairman, Chief Executive Officer Mancil Jack Sanders - President, Chief Operating Officer, Chief Executive Officer	**Investor Contact:** 843-339-6018
Fax: 843-383-7008		**Transfer Agents:** Continental Stock Transfer & Trust Company, New York, NY

SOUTH JERSEY INDUSTRIES, INC.

Exchange	Symbol	Price	52Wk Range	Yield	P/E	Div Achiever
NYS	SJI	$31.23 (12/29/2017)	38.12-30.78	3.59	63.73	17 Years

*7 Year Price Score 94.97 *NYSE Composite Index=100 *12 Month Price Score 89.19

Interim Earnings (Per Share)

Qtr.	Mar	Jun	Sep	Dec
2014	0.73	0.14	(0.07)	0.66
2015	0.79	0.19	(0.18)	0.74
2016	0.95	(0.06)	0.12	0.59
2017	0.47	(0.10)	(0.47)	...

Interim Dividends (Per Share)

Amt	Decl	Ex	Rec	Pay
0.273Q	02/13/2017	03/15/2017	03/17/2017	04/04/2017
0.273Q	04/24/2017	06/07/2017	06/09/2017	07/05/2017
0.273Q	08/30/2017	09/08/2017	09/11/2017	10/03/2017
0.28Q	11/20/2017	12/08/2017	12/11/2017	12/27/2017

Indicated Div: $1.12 (Div. Reinv. Plan)

Valuation Analysis

		Institutional Holding	
Forecast EPS	$1.14 (01/16/2018)	No of Institutions	297
Market Cap	$2.5 Billion	Shares	70,368,576
Book Value	$1.2 Billion	% Held	66.45
Price/Book	2.03		
Price/Sales	2.02		

Business Summary: Gas Utilities (MIC: 3.3.1 SIC: 4924 NAIC: 221210)

South Jersey Industries is a holding company. Co. operates via its subsidiaries: South Jersey Gas Co., which is a regulated natural gas utility; South Jersey Energy Co., which acquires and markets natural gas and electricity to retail end users; South Jersey Resources Group, LLC, which markets natural gas storage assets; South Jersey Exploration, LLC, which owns oil, gas and mineral rights in the Marcellus Shale region of Pennsylvania; Marina Energy, LLC, which develops and operates energy-related projects; South Jersey Energy Service Plus, LLC, which services residential and small commercial HVAC systems; and SJI Midstream, LLC, which invests in infrastructure and other midstream projects.

Recent Developments: For the quarter ended Sep 30 2017, loss from continuing operations was US$37.5 million compared with income of US$9.7 million in the year-earlier quarter. Net loss amounted to US$37.6 million versus net income of US$9.6 million in the year-earlier quarter. Revenues were US$227.1 million, up 3.7% from US$219.1 million the year before. Operating loss was US$55.3 million versus an income of US$12.6 million in the prior-year quarter. Direct operating expenses rose 40.7% to US$256.0 million from US$181.9 million in the comparable period the year before. Indirect operating expenses increased 7.6% to US$26.4 million from US$24.6 million in the equivalent prior-year period.

Prospects: Our evaluation of South Jersey Industries Inc. as of Jan. 14, 2018 is the result of our systematic analysis on three basic characteristics: earnings strength, relative valuation, and recent stock price movement. The company has generated a negative trend in earnings per share over the past 5 quarters. However, while recent estimates for the company have been lowered by analysts, SJI has posted results that fell short of analysts expectations. Based on operating earnings yield, the company is about fairly valued when compared to all of the companies in our coverage universe. Share price changes over the past year indicates that SJI will perform very well over the near term.

Financial Data

(US$ in Thousands)	9 Mos	6 Mos	3 Mos	12/31/2016	12/31/2015	12/31/2014	12/31/2013	12/31/2012
Earnings Per Share	0.49	1.08	1.12	1.56	1.53	1.46	1.27	1.49
Cash Flow Per Share	2.42	2.86	3.06	3.42	2.72	2.43	2.49	1.91
Tang Book Value Per Share	15.10	15.83	16.19	15.96	14.19	13.65	12.64	11.63
Dividends Per Share	1.090	1.081	1.073	1.064	1.018	0.960	0.900	0.825
Dividend Payout %	222.45	100.12	95.76	68.19	66.50	65.75	70.59	55.56
Income Statement								
Total Revenue	897,330	670,203	425,829	1,036,500	959,568	886,996	731,421	706,280
EBITDA	91,895	119,983	97,674	289,654	238,855	202,426	130,252	162,338
Depn & Amortn	73,793	48,879	24,323	90,389	72,451	63,004	49,637	41,336
Income Before Taxes	(20,189)	43,380	56,606	167,816	134,782	109,862	61,790	102,016
Income Taxes	(8,439)	16,326	21,870	54,151	1,360	4,449	(19,014)	11,479
Net Income	(7,535)	30,058	37,717	118,810	105,107	97,046	81,593	91,608
Average Shares	79,549	79,549	79,641	76,475	68,931	66,428	64,092	61,648
Balance Sheet								
Current Assets	323,463	356,462	436,628	473,313	431,274	566,697	482,898	394,837
Total Assets	3,740,066	3,741,860	3,747,352	3,730,567	3,480,900	3,349,425	2,924,855	2,631,440
Current Liabilities	684,170	734,119	681,023	952,624	832,974	850,185	764,973	651,844
Long-Term Obligations	1,180,319	1,066,680	1,079,298	808,005	1,006,394	859,491	680,400	601,400
Total Liabilities	2,518,716	2,462,611	2,439,454	2,441,327	2,443,361	2,416,993	2,097,855	1,895,226
Stockholders' Equity	1,221,350	1,279,249	1,307,898	1,289,240	1,037,539	932,432	827,000	736,214
Shares Outstanding	79,549	79,549	79,547	79,478	70,965	68,334	65,430	63,306
Statistical Record								
Return on Assets %	1.05	2.36	2.44	3.29	3.08	3.09	2.94	3.74
Return on Equity %	3.09	6.70	7.37	10.18	10.67	11.03	10.44	13.43
EBITDA Margin %	10.24	17.90	22.94	27.95	24.89	22.82	17.81	22.98
Net Margin %	N.M.	4.48	8.86	11.46	10.95	10.94	11.16	12.97
Asset Turnover	0.34	0.34	0.31	0.29	0.28	0.28	0.26	0.29
Current Ratio	0.47	0.49	0.64	0.50	0.52	0.67	0.63	0.61
Debt to Equity	0.97	0.83	0.83	0.63	0.97	0.92	0.82	0.82
Price Range	38.12-27.52	38.12-27.52	35.75-26.73	34.68-22.63	30.30-12.96	30.61-26.00	31.13-25.16	28.47-23.18
P/E Ratio	77.80-56.16	35.30-25.48	31.92-23.87	22.23-14.51	19.80-8.47	20.97-17.81	24.51-19.81	19.10-15.55
Average Yield %	3.21	3.29	3.46	3.66	3.94	3.41	3.43	3.23

Address: 1 South Jersey Plaza, Folsom, NJ 08037	Web Site: www.sjiindustries.com	Auditors: Deloitte & Touche LLP
Telephone: 609-561-9000	Officers: Walter M. Higgins - Chairman Michael J. Renna - President, Vice President, Chief Operating Officer, Chief Executive Officer	Investor Contact: 609-561-9000Ext.42 Transfer Agents: Computershare, Canton, MA

SOUTHERN COMPANY (THE)

Exchange	Symbol	Price	52Wk Range	Yield	P/E	Div Achiever
NYS	SO	$48.09 (12/29/2017)	53.25-46.78	4.82	89.06	15 Years

*7 Year Price Score 85.25 *NYSE Composite Index=100 *12 Month Price Score 96.72

Interim Earnings (Per Share)

Qtr.	Mar	Jun	Sep	Dec
2014	0.39	0.68	0.80	0.31
2015	0.56	0.69	1.05	0.29
2016	0.53	0.65	1.16	0.19
2017	0.66	(1.37)	1.06	...

Interim Dividends (Per Share)

Amt	Decl	Ex	Rec	Pay
0.56Q	01/13/2017	02/16/2017	02/21/2017	03/06/2017
0.58Q	04/17/2017	05/11/2017	05/15/2017	06/06/2017
0.58Q	07/17/2017	08/17/2017	08/21/2017	09/06/2017
0.58Q	10/16/2017	11/17/2017	11/20/2017	12/06/2017

Indicated Div: $2.32 (Div. Reinv. Plan)

Valuation Analysis — Institutional Holding

Forecast EPS	$2.96	No of Institutions
(01/18/2018)		1572
Market Cap	$48.3 Billion	Shares
Book Value	$24.9 Billion	648,801,024
Price/Book	1.94	% Held
Price/Sales	2.14	49.30

Business Summary: Electric Utilities (MIC: 3.1.1 SIC: 4911 NAIC: 221119)

Southern is a holding company. Through its subsidiaries, Alabama Power Company, Georgia Power Company, Gulf Power Company and Mississippi Power Company, each of which is an operating public utility company, Co. supplies electric service in the states of Alabama, Georgia, Florida, and Mississippi. In addition, Co. owns all of the common stock of Southern Power Company, which is also an operating public utility company that constructs, acquires, owns, and manages generation assets, including renewable energy projects, and sells electricity at market-based rates in the wholesale market.

Recent Developments: For the quarter ended Sep 30 2017, net income decreased 5.8% to US$1.11 billion from US$1.18 billion in the year-earlier quarter. Revenues were US$6.20 billion, down 1.0% from US$6.26 billion the year before. Operating income was US$2.05 billion versus US$1.92 billion in the prior-year quarter, an increase of 6.7%. Direct operating expenses declined 6.2% to US$3.05 billion from US$3.26 billion in the comparable period the year before. Indirect operating expenses increased 1.1% to US$1.10 billion from US$1.09 billion in the equivalent prior-year period.

Prospects: Our evaluation of Southern Company as of Jan. 14, 2018 is the result of our systematic analysis on three basic characteristics: earnings strength, relative valuation, and recent stock price movement. The company has generated a negative trend in earnings per share over the past 5 quarters. However, while recent estimates for the company have been mixed, SO has posted better than expected results. Based on operating earnings yield, the company is undervalued when compared to all of the companies in our coverage universe. Share price changes over the past year indicates that SO will perform very well over the near term.

Financial Data

(US$ in Thousands)	9 Mos	6 Mos	3 Mos	12/31/2016	12/31/2015	12/31/2014	12/31/2013	12/31/2012
Earnings Per Share	0.54	0.64	2.66	2.55	2.59	2.18	1.87	2.67
Cash Flow Per Share	5.87	5.53	4.96	5.13	6.89	6.48	6.95	5.61
Tang Book Value Per Share	17.67	16.77	18.75	17.83	22.72	22.39	21.85	21.52
Dividends Per Share	2.280	2.260	2.240	2.223	2.152	2.083	2.013	1.942
Dividend Payout %	422.22	353.13	84.21	87.16	83.11	95.53	107.62	72.75
Income Statement								
Total Revenue	17,403,000	11,202,000	5,771,000	19,896,000	17,489,000	18,467,000	17,087,000	16,537,000
EBITDA	4,456,000	1,499,000	2,180,000	7,240,000	6,841,000	6,117,000	5,662,000	6,713,000
Depn & Amortn	2,564,000	1,683,000	823,000	2,502,000	2,395,000	2,293,000	2,298,000	2,145,000
Income Before Taxes	644,000	(1,024,000)	941,000	3,421,000	3,629,000	3,008,000	2,559,000	3,749,000
Income Taxes	317,000	(273,000)	315,000	951,000	1,194,000	977,000	849,000	1,334,000
Net Income	379,000	(701,000)	669,000	2,493,000	2,421,000	2,031,000	1,710,000	2,415,000
Average Shares	1,010,000	1,005,000	1,000,000	958,000	914,000	901,000	881,000	879,000
Balance Sheet								
Current Assets	9,202,000	8,837,000	8,427,000	9,722,000	6,526,000	6,370,000	5,599,000	6,162,000
Total Assets	110,315,000	108,684,000	109,760,000	109,697,000	78,318,000	70,923,000	64,546,000	63,149,000
Current Liabilities	12,603,000	12,751,000	12,284,000	12,917,000	9,129,000	8,967,000	5,536,000	7,014,000
Long-Term Obligations	44,042,000	43,885,000	42,786,000	42,629,000	24,688,000	20,841,000	21,344,000	19,274,000
Total Liabilities	85,410,000	84,732,000	83,939,000	84,212,000	56,999,000	49,622,000	44,407,000	43,770,000
Stockholders' Equity	24,905,000	23,952,000	25,821,000	25,485,000	21,319,000	21,301,000	20,139,000	19,379,000
Shares Outstanding	1,003,627	999,100	994,100	990,394	911,721	907,777	887,086	867,768
Statistical Record								
Return on Assets %	0.56	0.67	2.83	2.64	3.24	3.00	2.68	3.93
Return on Equity %	2.44	2.88	11.27	10.62	11.36	9.30	8.65	12.66
EBITDA Margin %	25.60	13.38	37.78	36.39	39.12	33.12	33.14	40.59
Net Margin %	2.18	N.M.	11.59	12.53	13.84	11.00	10.01	14.60
Asset Turnover	0.21	0.23	0.23	0.21	0.23	0.27	0.27	0.27
Current Ratio	0.73	0.69	0.69	0.75	0.71	0.71	1.01	0.88
Debt to Equity	1.77	1.83	1.66	1.67	1.16	0.98	1.06	0.99
Price Range	51.71-46.59	54.54-46.59	54.54-46.59	54.54-46.45	52.79-41.61	50.88-40.40	48.65-40.12	48.42-42.03
P/E Ratio	95.76-86.28	85.22-72.80	20.50-17.52	21.39-18.22	20.38-16.07	23.34-18.53	26.02-21.45	18.13-15.74
Average Yield %	4.62	4.49	4.44	4.44	4.43	4.78	4.70	4.28

Address: 30 Ivan Allen Jr. Boulevard,	Web Site: www.southerncompany.com	Auditors: Deloitte & Touche LLP
N.W., Atlanta, GA 30308	Officers: Thomas A. Fanning - Chairman, President,	Transfer Agents: ComputerShare,
Telephone: 404-506-5000	Chief Executive Officer, Chief Operating Officer,	College Station, TX
Fax: 404-506-0455	Executive Vice President W. Paul Bowers - Executive	
	Vice President	

SOUTHERN COPPER CORP

Exchange	Symbol	Price	52Wk Range	Yield	P/E
NYS	SCCO	$47.45 (12/29/2017)	47.63-32.38	1.24	30.81

*7 Year Price Score 94.02   *NYSE Composite Index=100   *12 Month Price Score 107.85

Interim Earnings (Per Share)

Qtr.	Mar	Jun	Sep	Dec
2014	0.39	0.40	0.39	0.43
2015	0.35	0.37	0.12	0.08
2016	0.24	0.29	0.26	0.22
2017	0.41	0.39	0.52	...

Interim Dividends (Per Share)

Amt	Decl	Ex	Rec	Pay
0.08Q	01/26/2017	02/10/2017	02/14/2017	02/28/2017
0.12Q	04/27/2017	05/15/2017	05/17/2017	05/31/2017
0.14Q	07/20/2017	08/07/2017	08/09/2017	08/23/2017
0.25Q	10/19/2017	11/07/2017	11/08/2017	11/22/2017

Indicated Div: $0.59

Valuation Analysis   **Institutional Holding**

Forecast EPS	$1.87	No of Institutions
	(01/18/2018)	381
Market Cap	$36.7 Billion	Shares
Book Value	$6.6 Billion	63,281,872
Price/Book	5.57	% Held
Price/Sales	5.93	N/A

Business Summary: Mining (MIC: 8.2.4 SIC: 1021 NAIC: 212234)

Southern Copper produces copper, molybdenum, zinc and silver. Co.'s mining, smelting and refining facilities are located in Peru and Mexico and Co. conducts its exploration activities in those countries and in Argentina, Chile and Ecuador. Co.'s Peruvian copper operations involve mining, milling and flotation of copper ore to produce copper concentrates and molybdenum concentrates; the smelting of copper concentrates to produce blister and anode copper; and the refining of anode copper to produce copper cathodes. Co.'s Mexican operations are conducted via its Minera Mexico S.A. de C.V. subsidiary, which engages in the mining and processing of copper, molybdenum, zinc, silver, gold and lead.

Recent Developments: For the quarter ended Sep 30 2017, net income increased 103.2% to US$402.8 million from US$198.2 million in the year-earlier quarter. Revenues were US$1.68 billion, up 19.7% from US$1.40 billion the year before. Operating income was US$692.6 million versus US$362.4 million in the prior-year quarter, an increase of 91.1%. Direct operating expenses declined 6.0% to US$781.5 million from US$831.4 million in the comparable period the year before. Indirect operating expenses decreased 2.2% to US$202.4 million from US$206.9 million in the equivalent prior-year period.

Prospects: Our evaluation of Southern Copper Corp. as of Jan. 14, 2018 is the result of our systematic analysis on three basic characteristics: earnings strength, relative valuation, and recent stock price movement. The company has enjoyed a very positive trend in earnings per share over the past 5 quarters and while recent estimates for the company have been raised by analysts, SCCO has posted better than expected results. Based on operating earnings yield, the company is about fairly valued when compared to all of the companies in our coverage universe. Share price changes over the past year indicates that SCCO will perform poorly over the near term.

Financial Data

(US$ in Thousands)	9 Mos	6 Mos	3 Mos	12/31/2016	12/31/2015	12/31/2014	12/31/2013	12/31/2012
Earnings Per Share	1.54	1.28	1.18	1.00	0.93	1.61	1.92	2.28
Cash Flow Per Share	2.03	1.86	1.75	1.19	1.11	1.64	2.20	2.36
Tang Book Value Per Share	8.33	7.95	7.67	7.35	6.60	7.06	6.13	5.26
Dividends Per Share	0.390	0.300	0.230	0.180	0.340	0.460	0.680	3.710
Dividend Payout %	25.32	23.44	19.49	18.00	36.56	28.57	35.42	162.72
Income Statement								
Total Revenue	4,790,200	3,113,800	1,583,900	5,379,800	5,045,900	5,787,694	5,952,943	6,669,266
EBITDA	2,284,300	1,428,800	728,600	2,178,700	1,892,700	2,634,999	2,942,818	3,164,216
Depn & Amortn	493,800	324,600	153,400	639,100	503,600	443,000	393,600	33,500
Income Before Taxes	1,559,100	942,600	485,300	1,256,000	1,189,200	2,068,706	2,372,598	2,973,542
Income Taxes	556,600	336,600	176,200	501,100	464,900	754,629	769,300	1,080,872
Net Income	1,016,000	614,100	314,400	776,500	736,400	1,332,973	1,618,517	1,934,632
Average Shares	773,000	773,000	773,000	773,600	794,700	828,199	842,668	848,346
Balance Sheet								
Current Assets	2,952,400	2,644,700	2,773,800	2,566,100	2,484,200	2,489,789	3,416,050	4,287,959
Total Assets	13,982,400	13,515,300	13,523,000	13,234,300	12,593,200	11,551,910	11,210,422	10,383,749
Current Liabilities	979,800	800,800	989,500	999,000	920,200	1,150,905	783,584	857,135
Long-Term Obligations	5,956,300	5,955,600	5,954,900	5,954,200	5,951,500	4,006,000	4,204,900	4,203,900
Total Liabilities	7,392,900	7,223,000	7,438,300	7,402,000	7,330,300	5,747,450	5,676,760	5,618,609
Stockholders' Equity	6,589,500	6,292,300	6,084,700	5,832,300	5,262,900	5,804,460	5,533,662	4,765,140
Shares Outstanding	773,028	773,027	773,016	773,016	773,707	806,690	884,596	884,596
Statistical Record								
Return on Assets %	8.78	7.48	6.88	6.00	6.10	11.71	14.99	20.92
Return on Equity %	19.34	16.60	15.81	13.96	13.31	23.51	31.43	43.95
EBITDA Margin %	47.69	45.89	46.00	40.50	37.51	45.53	49.43	47.44
Net Margin %	21.21	19.72	19.85	14.43	14.59	23.03	27.19	29.01
Asset Turnover	0.46	0.45	0.43	0.42	0.42	0.51	0.55	0.72
Current Ratio	3.01	3.30	2.80	2.57	2.70	2.16	4.36	5.00
Debt to Equity	0.90	0.95	0.98	1.02	1.13	0.69	0.76	0.88
Price Range	41.77-26.01	39.10-25.20	39.10-25.20	34.98-22.29	33.14-24.40	33.54-26.08	41.96-24.78	38.94-28.16
P/E Ratio	27.12-16.89	30.55-19.69	33.14-21.36	34.98-22.29	35.63-26.24	20.83-16.20	21.85-12.91	17.08-12.35
Average Yield %	1.11	0.94	0.77	0.66	1.19	1.53	2.17	11.20

Address: 1440 East Missouri Avenue, Suite 160, Phoenix, AZ 85014	**Web Site:** www.southerncoppercorp.com	**Auditors:** Galaz, Yamazaki, Ruiz Urquiza, S.C.
Telephone: 602-264-1375	**Officers:** German Larrea Mota Velasco - Chairman Oscar Gonzalez Rocha - President, Chief Executive Officer	**Investor Contact:** 602-264-1375
Fax: 602-264-1397		**Transfer Agents:** Computershare, Jersey City, NJ

SOUTHWEST AIRLINES CO

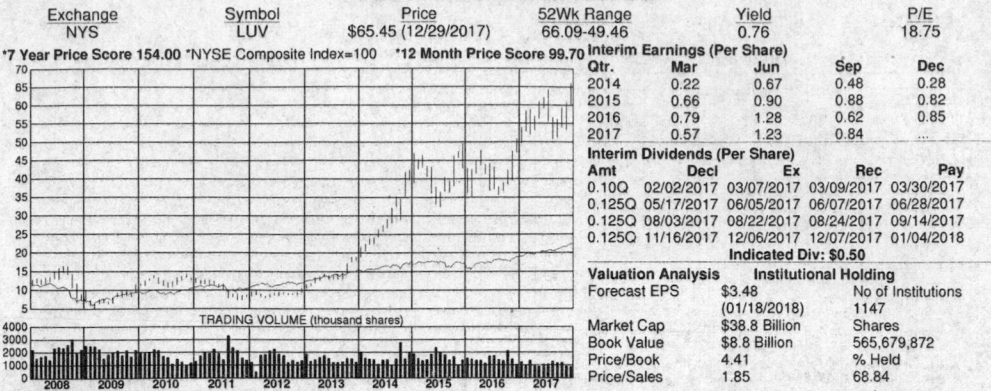

Exchange	Symbol	Price	52Wk Range	Yield	P/E
NYS	LUV	$65.45 (12/29/2017)	66.09-49.46	0.76	18.75

*7 Year Price Score 154.00 *NYSE Composite Index=100 *12 Month Price Score 99.70

Interim Earnings (Per Share)

Qtr.	Mar	Jun	Sep	Dec
2014	0.22	0.67	0.48	0.28
2015	0.66	0.90	0.88	0.82
2016	0.79	1.28	0.62	0.85
2017	0.57	1.23	0.84	...

Interim Dividends (Per Share)

Amt	Decl	Ex	Rec	Pay
0.10Q	02/02/2017	03/07/2017	03/09/2017	03/30/2017
0.125Q	05/17/2017	06/05/2017	06/07/2017	06/28/2017
0.125Q	08/03/2017	08/22/2017	08/24/2017	09/14/2017
0.125Q	11/16/2017	12/06/2017	12/07/2017	01/04/2018

Indicated Div: $0.50

Valuation Analysis — **Institutional Holding**

Forecast EPS	$3.48	No of Institutions
(01/18/2018)		1147
Market Cap	$38.8 Billion	Shares
Book Value	$8.8 Billion	565,679,872
Price/Book	4.41	% Held
Price/Sales	1.85	68.84

TRADING VOLUME (thousand shares)

Business Summary: Airlines/Air Freight (MIC: 7.4.4 SIC: 4512 NAIC: 481111)

Southwest Airlines operates Southwest Airlines, a passenger airline that provides scheduled air transportation in the U.S. and near-international markets. At Dec 31 2016, Co. operated a total of 723 Boeing 737 aircraft and served 101 destinations in 40 states, the District of Columbia, the Commonwealth of Puerto Rico, and eight near-international countries: Mexico, Jamaica, The Bahamas, Aruba, Dominican Republic, Costa Rica, Belize, and Cuba. Co. complements its short-haul routes with long-haul nonstop service between markets such as Los Angeles and Nashville, Las Vegas and Orlando, San Diego and Baltimore, Houston and New York LaGuardia, and Oakland and Baltimore.

Recent Developments: For the quarter ended Sep 30 2017, net income increased 29.6% to US$503.0 million from US$388.0 million in the year-earlier quarter. Revenues were US$5.27 billion, up 2.6% from US$5.14 billion the year before. Operating income was US$834.0 million versus US$695.0 million in the prior-year quarter, an increase of 20.0%. Direct operating expenses rose 5.1% to US$1.64 billion from US$1.56 billion in the comparable period the year before. Indirect operating expenses decreased 3.0% to US$2.80 billion from US$2.88 billion in the equivalent prior-year period.

Prospects: Our evaluation of Southwest Airlines Co as of Jan. 14, 2018 is the result of our systematic analysis on three basic characteristics: earnings strength, relative valuation, and recent stock price movement. The company has produced a positive trend in earnings per share over the past 5 quarters. However, while recent estimates for the company have been mixed, LUV has posted better than expected results. Based on operating earnings yield, the company is undervalued when compared to all of the companies in our coverage universe. Share price changes over the past year indicates that LUV will perform well over the near term.

Financial Data

(US$ in Thousands)	9 Mos	6 Mos	3 Mos	12/31/2016	12/31/2015	12/31/2014	12/31/2013	12/31/2012
Earnings Per Share	3.49	3.27	3.32	3.55	3.27	1.64	1.05	0.56
Cash Flow Per Share	6.83	6.52	7.02	6.83	4.90	4.22	3.49	2.74
Tang Book Value Per Share	12.49	11.93	11.26	11.45	9.15	8.06	8.85	8.06
Dividends Per Share	0.450	0.425	0.400	0.375	0.285	0.220	0.130	0.035
Dividend Payout %	12.89	13.00	12.05	10.56	8.72	13.41	12.38	6.16
Income Statement								
Total Revenue	15,897,000	10,627,000	4,883,000	20,425,000	19,820,000	18,605,000	17,699,000	17,088,000
EBITDA	3,474,000	2,378,000	882,000	4,819,000	4,575,000	2,854,000	2,177,000	1,636,000
Depn & Amortn	939,000	637,000	318,000	1,221,000	1,015,000	938,000	867,000	832,000
Income Before Taxes	2,513,000	1,723,000	553,000	3,547,000	3,479,000	1,816,000	1,209,000	685,000
Income Taxes	913,000	626,000	202,000	1,303,000	1,298,000	680,000	455,000	264,000
Net Income	1,600,000	1,097,000	351,000	2,244,000	2,181,000	1,136,000	754,000	421,000
Average Shares	598,000	605,000	614,000	633,000	669,000	696,000	718,000	757,000
Balance Sheet								
Current Assets	4,280,000	4,343,000	4,658,000	4,498,000	4,024,000	4,404,000	4,456,000	4,227,000
Total Assets	24,249,000	23,921,000	23,763,000	23,286,000	21,312,000	20,200,000	19,345,000	18,596,000
Current Liabilities	6,965,000	7,097,000	7,458,000	6,844,000	7,406,000	5,923,000	5,676,000	4,650,000
Long-Term Obligations	2,763,000	2,788,000	2,781,000	2,821,000	2,541,000	2,434,000	2,191,000	2,883,000
Total Liabilities	15,449,000	15,391,000	15,559,000	14,845,000	13,954,000	13,425,000	12,009,000	11,604,000
Stockholders' Equity	8,800,000	8,530,000	8,204,000	8,441,000	7,358,000	6,775,000	7,336,000	6,992,000
Shares Outstanding	593,387	598,565	604,662	615,160	647,601	675,594	700,474	730,319
Statistical Record								
Return on Assets %	8.97	8.66	9.05	10.04	10.51	5.75	3.97	2.29
Return on Equity %	25.19	24.55	26.51	28.33	30.86	16.10	10.52	6.05
EBITDA Margin %	21.85	22.38	18.06	23.59	23.08	15.34	12.30	9.57
Net Margin %	10.06	10.32	7.19	10.99	11.00	6.11	4.26	2.46
Asset Turnover	0.89	0.90	0.89	0.91	0.95	0.94	0.93	0.93
Current Ratio	0.61	0.61	0.62	0.66	0.54	0.74	0.79	0.91
Debt to Equity	0.31	0.33	0.34	0.33	0.35	0.36	0.30	0.41
Price Range	64.24-38.40	62.14-35.54	58.88-35.54	50.89-34.72	49.58-32.36	42.32-18.84	18.95-10.24	10.56-7.88
P/E Ratio	18.41-11.00	19.00-10.87	17.73-10.70	14.34-9.78	15.16-9.90	25.80-11.49	18.05-9.75	18.86-14.07
Average Yield %	0.85	0.87	0.89	0.90	0.70	0.76	0.92	0.39

Address: P.O. Box 36611, Dallas, TX 75235-1611	**Web Site:** www.southwest.com	**Auditors:** Ernst & Young LLP
Telephone: 214-792-4000	**Officers:** Gary C. Kelly - Chairman, President, Chief Executive Officer Ron Ricks - Vice-Chairman, Executive Vice President, Chief Regulatory Officer, Executive Vice President (frmr), Corporate Secretary	**Investor Contact:** 214-792-4415
Fax: 214-792-5015		**Transfer Agents:** Wells Fargo Shareowner Services, Mendota Heights, MN

SOUTHWEST GAS HOLDINGS INC

Exchange	Symbol	Price	52Wk Range	Yield	P/E	Div Achiever
NYS	SWX	$80.48 (12/29/2017)	86.27-72.83	2.46	23.74	10 Years

*7 Year Price Score 113.34 *NYSE Composite Index=100 *12 Month Price Score 96.73

Interim Earnings (Per Share)

Qtr.	Mar	Jun	Sep	Dec
2014	1.51	0.21	0.04	1.25
2015	1.53	0.10	(0.10)	1.39
2016	1.58	0.19	0.05	1.36
2017	1.45	0.37	0.21	...

Interim Dividends (Per Share)

Amt	Decl	Ex	Rec	Pay
0.495Q	02/23/2017	05/11/2017	05/15/2017	06/01/2017
0.495Q	05/03/2017	08/11/2017	08/15/2017	09/01/2017
0.495Q	09/26/2017	11/14/2017	11/15/2017	12/01/2017
0.495Q	11/13/2017	02/14/2018	02/15/2018	03/01/2018

Indicated Div: $1.98 (Div. Reinv. Plan)

Valuation Analysis		Institutional Holding	
Forecast EPS	$3.40 (01/16/2018)	No of Institutions	360
Market Cap	$3.8 Billion	Shares	45,744,352
Book Value	$1.7 Billion	% Held	77.03
Price/Book	2.24		
Price/Sales	1.57		

TRADING VOLUME (thousand shares)

Business Summary: Gas Utilities (MIC: 3.3.1 SIC: 4923 NAIC: 221210)

Southwest Gas Holdings is a holding company. Through its subsidiaries, Co. operates two business segments: natural gas operations (Southwest) and construction services (Centuri). Southwest focuses on the business of purchasing, distributing, and transporting natural gas. As of Dec 31 2016, Southwest purchased and distributed or transported natural gas to 2.0 million residential, commercial, and industrial customers in portions of Arizona, Nevada, and California. Co.'s 96.6% subsidiary, Centuri Construction Group Inc., provides installation, replacement, repair, and maintenance of energy distribution systems, and developing industrial construction solutions for energy services utilities.

Recent Developments: For the quarter ended Sep 30 2017, net income increased 258.4% to US$10.4 million from US$2.9 million in the year-earlier quarter. Revenues were US$593.2 million, up 9.8% from US$540.0 million the year before. Operating income was US$30.1 million versus US$15.5 million in the prior-year quarter, an increase of 93.9%. Direct operating expenses rose 14.3% to US$388.2 million from US$339.7 million in the comparable period the year before. Indirect operating expenses decreased 5.4% to US$174.9 million from US$184.8 million in the equivalent prior-year period.

Prospects: Our evaluation of Southwest Gas Holdings Inc. as of Jan. 14, 2018 is the result of our systematic analysis on three basic characteristics: earnings strength, relative valuation, and recent stock price movement. The company has produced a positive trend in earnings per share over the past 5 quarters. However, while recent estimates for the company have been mixed, SWX has posted better than expected results. Based on operating earnings yield, the company is undervalued when compared to all of the companies in our coverage universe. Share price changes over the past year indicates that SWX will perform well over the near term.

Financial Data

(US$ in Thousands)	9 Mos	6 Mos	3 Mos	12/31/2016	12/31/2015	12/31/2014	12/31/2013	12/31/2012
Earnings Per Share	3.39	3.23	3.05	3.18	2.92	3.01	3.11	2.86
Cash Flow Per Share	8.86	8.02	9.42	12.57	11.64	7.45	7.47	8.35
Tang Book Value Per Share	32.85	33.06	33.11	32.09	30.99	28.92	30.51	28.39
Dividends Per Share	1.890	1.845	1.800	1.755	1.580	1.425	1.285	1.150
Dividend Payout %	55.75	57.12	59.02	55.19	54.11	47.34	41.32	40.21
Income Statement								
Total Revenue	1,808,359	1,215,206	654,737	2,460,490	2,463,625	2,121,707	1,950,782	1,927,778
EBITDA	386,982	299,372	194,795	515,013	486,953	483,348	471,337	457,623
Depn & Amortn	189,089	130,560	72,478	214,037	201,233	194,360	185,283	182,612
Income Before Taxes	142,880	131,443	104,167	229,165	216,014	219,521	222,815	207,915
Income Taxes	47,411	44,317	35,638	78,468	79,902	78,373	77,942	75,276
Net Income	97,376	87,172	69,308	152,041	138,317	141,126	145,320	133,331
Average Shares	47,986	47,884	47,864	47,814	47,383	46,944	46,758	46,555
Balance Sheet								
Current Assets	538,918	483,585	454,404	533,307	558,174	606,783	494,672	458,417
Total Assets	5,855,070	5,665,239	5,551,913	5,581,126	5,358,685	5,214,515	4,565,174	4,488,057
Current Liabilities	656,406	490,035	496,828	628,375	535,045	470,117	434,164	535,129
Long-Term Obligations	1,731,981	1,685,698	1,564,132	1,549,983	1,551,204	1,637,592	1,381,327	1,268,373
Total Liabilities	4,139,379	3,948,671	3,836,532	3,917,636	3,764,277	3,725,992	3,150,651	3,177,878
Stockholders' Equity	1,715,691	1,716,568	1,715,381	1,663,490	1,594,408	1,488,523	1,414,523	1,310,179
Shares Outstanding	47,731	47,583	47,548	47,482	47,377	46,523	46,356	46,147
Statistical Record								
Return on Assets %	2.85	2.81	2.69	2.77	2.62	2.89	3.21	3.03
Return on Equity %	9.73	9.21	8.66	9.31	8.97	9.72	10.67	10.49
EBITDA Margin %	21.40	24.64	29.75	20.93	19.77	22.78	24.16	23.74
Net Margin %	5.38	7.17	10.59	6.18	5.61	6.65	7.45	6.92
Asset Turnover	0.43	0.43	0.44	0.45	0.47	0.43	0.43	0.44
Current Ratio	0.82	0.99	0.91	0.85	1.04	1.29	1.14	0.86
Debt to Equity	1.01	0.98	0.91	0.93	0.97	1.10	0.98	0.97
Price Range	86.27-64.35	86.27-64.35	86.27-62.88	78.83-53.86	63.38-50.78	64.04-47.62	55.91-42.24	45.94-39.52
P/E Ratio	25.45-18.98	26.71-19.92	28.29-20.62	24.79-16.94	21.71-17.39	21.28-15.82	17.98-13.58	16.06-13.82
Average Yield %	2.15	2.45	2.41	2.64	2.77	2.55	2.62	2.69

Address: 5241 Spring Mountain Road, Post Office Box 98510, Las Vegas, NV 89193-8510 **Telephone:** 702-876-7237 **Fax:** 702-873-3820	**Web Site:** www.swgas.com **Officers:** Michael J. Melarkey - Chairman John P. Hester - President, Chief Executive Officer, Executive Vice President, Senior Vice President	**Auditors:** PricewaterhouseCoopers LLP **Investor Contact:** 702-876-7237 **Transfer Agents:** Wells Fargo Shareowner Services, St. Paul, MN

SOUTHWESTERN ENERGY COMPANY

Exchange	Symbol	Price	52Wk Range	Yield	P/E
NYS	SWN	$5.58 (12/29/2017)	10.32-5.05	N/A	6.89

*7 Year Price Score 19.87   *NYSE Composite Index=100   *12 Month Price Score 83.02

Interim Earnings (Per Share)

Qtr.	Mar	Jun	Sep	Dec
2014	0.55	0.59	0.60	0.88
2015	0.12	(2.13)	(4.62)	(5.60)
2016	(3.03)	(1.61)	(1.52)	(0.30)
2017	0.57	0.45	0.09	...

Interim Dividends (Per Share)

No Dividends Paid

Valuation Analysis   Institutional Holding

Forecast EPS	$0.44	No of Institutions
	(01/18/2018)	655
Market Cap	$2.8 Billion	Shares
Book Value	$1.7 Billion	537,344,768
Price/Book	1.72	% Held
Price/Sales	0.92	93.29

TRADING VOLUME (thousand shares)

Business Summary: Production & Extraction (MIC: 9.1.1 SIC: 1311 NAIC: 211111)

Southwestern Energy is a holding company and an independent natural gas and oil company. Co.'s primary business is the exploration for and production of natural gas and oil, with its operations principally focused within the U.S. on development of unconventional natural gas reservoirs located in Pennsylvania, West Virginia and Arkansas. Through its affiliated midstream subsidiaries, Co. is engaged in natural gas gathering activities in Arkansas and Louisiana. As of Dec 31 2016, Co. had total estimated proved reserves of 5.25 trillion cubic feet equivalent, comprised of 4.87 trillion cubic feet of natural gas, 10.5 million barrels (MMBbls) of oil and 53.9 MMBbls of natural gas liquids.

Recent Developments: For the quarter ended Sep 30 2017, net income amounted to US$77.0 million versus a net loss of US$708.0 million in the year-earlier quarter. Revenues were US$737.0 million, up 13.2% from US$651.0 million the year before. Operating income was US$110.0 million versus a loss of US$725.0 million in the prior-year quarter. Direct operating expenses rose 8.8% to US$406.0 million from US$373.0 million in the comparable period the year before. Indirect operating expenses decreased 78.0% to US$221.0 million from US$1.00 billion in the equivalent prior-year period.

Prospects: Our evaluation of Southwestern Energy Company as of Jan. 14, 2018 is the result of our systematic analysis on three basic characteristics: earnings strength, relative valuation, and recent stock price movement. The company has suffered a very negative trend in earnings per share over the past 5 quarters. However, while recent estimates for the company have been mixed, SWN has posted results that fell short of analysts expectations. Based on operating earnings yield, the company is undervalued when compared to all of the companies in our coverage universe. Share price changes over the past year indicates that SWN will perform poorly over the near term.

Financial Data

(US$ in Thousands)	9 Mos	6 Mos	3 Mos	12/31/2016	12/31/2015	12/31/2014	12/31/2013	12/31/2012
Earnings Per Share	0.81	(0.80)	(2.86)	(6.32)	(12.25)	2.62	2.00	(2.03)
Cash Flow Per Share	1.90	1.84	1.46	1.14	4.15	6.64	5.45	4.73
Tang Book Value Per Share	3.24	3.13	2.54	1.85	5.85	13.15	10.26	8.65
Income Statement								
Total Revenue	2,394,000	1,657,000	846,000	2,436,000	3,133,000	4,038,000	3,371,145	2,715,043
EBITDA	802,000	705,000	385,000	(2,134,000)	(5,360,000)	2,460,000	2,022,524	(299,836)
Depn & Amortn	7,000	4,000	2,000	450,000	1,145,000	952,000	790,553	814,710
Income Before Taxes	698,000	635,000	351,000	(2,672,000)	(6,561,000)	1,449,000	1,190,377	(1,150,203)
Income Taxes	(14,000)	...	...	(29,000)	(2,005,000)	525,000	486,874	(443,139)
Net Income	712,000	635,000	351,000	(2,643,000)	(4,556,000)	924,000	703,503	(707,064)
Average Shares	502,290	498,224	494,494	435,337	380,521	352,410	350,465	348,610
Balance Sheet								
Current Assets	1,476,000	1,579,000	1,789,000	1,872,000	393,000	1,115,000	644,175	808,912
Total Assets	7,202,000	7,150,000	7,196,000	7,076,000	8,110,000	14,925,000	8,047,726	6,737,527
Current Liabilities	784,000	821,000	1,121,000	1,064,000	707,000	5,428,000	688,011	767,771
Long-Term Obligations	4,396,000	4,341,000	4,364,000	4,612,000	4,728,000	2,466,000	1,950,096	1,668,273
Total Liabilities	5,550,000	5,577,000	5,918,000	6,159,000	5,828,000	10,263,000	4,425,696	3,701,655
Stockholders' Equity	1,652,000	1,573,000	1,278,000	917,000	2,282,000	4,662,000	3,622,030	3,035,872
Shares Outstanding	509,111	502,546	502,466	495,217	390,091	354,477	352,928	351,035
Statistical Record								
Return on Assets %	7.12	N.M.	N.M.	N.M.	N.M.	8.04	9.52	N.M.
Return on Equity %	36.18	N.M.	N.M.	N.M.	N.M.	22.31	21.13	N.M.
EBITDA Margin %	33.50	42.55	45.51	N.M.	N.M.	60.92	60.00	N.M.
Net Margin %	29.74	38.32	41.49	N.M.	N.M.	22.88	20.87	N.M.
Asset Turnover	0.44	0.41	0.34	0.32	0.27	0.35	0.46	0.37
Current Ratio	1.88	1.92	1.60	1.76	0.56	0.21	0.94	1.05
Debt to Equity	2.66	2.76	3.41	5.03	2.07	0.53	0.54	0.55
Price Range	14.07-5.13	15.44-5.50	15.44-7.35	15.44-5.62	29.25-5.15	48.93-27.24	40.18-32.09	36.60-25.82
P/E Ratio	17.37-6.33	...	...	...	...	18.68-10.40	20.09-16.05	...

Address: 10000 Energy Drive, Spring, TX 77389 Telephone: 832-796-1000	Web Site: www.swn.com Officers: William J. Way - President, Executive Vice President, Chief Operating Officer Mark K. Boling - Executive Vice President, Secretary, General Counsel, Division Officer	Auditors: PricewaterhouseCoopers LLP Investor Contact: 281-.61-8.4847 Transfer Agents: Computershare Trust Company, N.A, Providence, RI

SPECTRUM BRANDS HOLDINGS INC

Exchange	Symbol	Price	52Wk Range	Yield	P/E
NYS	SPB	$112.40 (12/29/2017)	145.07-99.35	1.49	22.39

*7 Year Price Score 123.55 *NYSE Composite Index=100 *12 Month Price Score 84.34

Interim Earnings (Per Share)

Qtr.	Dec	Mar	Jun	Sep
2012-13	(0.26)	(0.79)	0.69	(0.70)
2013-14	1.04	0.64	1.47	0.88
2014-15	0.94	0.52	0.79	0.40
2015-16	1.24	1.26	1.71	1.48
2016-17	1.10	1.00	1.31	1.62

Interim Dividends (Per Share)

Amt	Decl	Ex	Rec	Pay
0.42Q	01/24/2017	02/10/2017	02/14/2017	03/07/2017
0.42Q	04/25/2017	05/12/2017	05/16/2017	06/13/2017
0.42Q	07/25/2017	08/11/2017	08/15/2017	09/12/2017
0.42Q	11/14/2017	11/27/2017	11/28/2017	12/19/2017

Indicated Div: $1.68

Valuation Analysis / **Institutional Holding**

Forecast EPS	$6.15 (01/26/2018)	No of Institutions N/A
Market Cap	$6.5 Billion	Shares N/A
Book Value	$1.8 Billion	% Held N/A
Price/Book	3.52	
Price/Sales	1.29	

Business Summary: Household & Personal Products (MIC: 1.7.1 SIC: 3691 NAIC: 335911)

Spectrum Brands Holdings is a branded consumer products company. Co. manages the business in five product-focused segments: Global Batteries and Appliances, which consists of consumer batteries, small appliances and personal care products; Hardware & Home Improvement, which includes security, plumbing and hardware products; Global Pet Supplies, which includes aquatics, companion animal and wet and dry pet food products; Home and Garden, which includes controls, household, and repellents products; and Global Auto Care, which includes appearance, performance, and A/C recharge products that include do-it-yourself automotive air conditioner recharge products.

Recent Developments: For the year ended Sep 30 2017, net income decreased 16.9% to US$297.1 million in the prior year. Revenues were US$5.01 billion, down 0.6% from US$5.04 billion the year before. Operating income was US$561.4 million versus US$656.2 million in the prior year, a decrease of 14.4%. Direct operating expenses rose 0.4% to US$3.13 billion from US$3.12 billion in the comparable period the year before. Indirect operating expenses increased 3.9% to US$1.31 billion from US$1.26 billion in the equivalent prior-year period.

Prospects: Our evaluation of Spectrum Brands Holdings Inc. as of Jan. 21, 2018 is the result of our systematic analysis on three basic characteristics: earnings strength, relative valuation, and recent stock price movement. The company has enjoyed a very positive trend in earnings per share over the past 5 quarters. However, while recent estimates for the company have been lowered by analysts, SPB has posted results that fell short of analysts expectations. Based on operating earnings yield, the company is undervalued when compared to all of the companies in our coverage universe. Share price changes over the past year indicates that SPB will perform very poorly over the near term.

Financial Data
(US$ in Thousands)

	09/30/2017	09/30/2016	09/30/2015	09/30/2014	09/30/2013	09/30/2012	09/30/2011	09/30/2010
Earnings Per Share	5.02	5.99	2.66	4.02	(1.06)	0.91	(1.47)	(5.28)
Cash Flow Per Share	11.35	10.34	7.99	8.22	4.93	4.92	4.45	1.59
Dividends Per Share	1.640	1.470	1.290	1.150	0.750	1.000	...	...
Dividend Payout %	32.67	24.54	48.50	28.61	...	109.89	...	...
Income Statement								
Total Revenue	5,007,400	5,039,700	4,690,400	4,429,109	4,085,581	3,252,435	3,186,916	2,567,011
EBITDA	659,200	830,600	635,200	633,277	487,564	405,484	330,213	253,574
Depn & Amortn	103,500	183,000	170,000	157,630	139,893	104,616	104,760	100,742
Income Before Taxes	344,600	397,600	193,300	273,529	(27,954)	108,957	17,124	(124,183)
Income Taxes	47,500	40,000	43,900	59,023	27,359	60,385	92,295	63,189
Net Income	295,800	357,100	148,900	214,092	(55,246)	48,572	(75,171)	(190,107)
Average Shares	59,000	59,600	55,900	53,261	52,034	53,309	51,092	36,000
Balance Sheet								
Current Assets	1,607,100	1,632,900	1,732,200	1,434,626	1,482,905	1,061,427	1,048,289	1,199,712
Total Assets	7,419,700	7,069,100	7,298,000	5,513,029	5,626,673	3,751,649	3,626,706	3,873,604
Current Liabilities	1,113,400	1,095,600	1,031,500	915,704	952,370	610,631	606,912	662,772
Long-Term Obligations	3,804,000	3,456,200	3,937,200	2,894,137	3,115,942	1,652,886	1,535,522	1,723,057
Total Liabilities	5,581,800	5,269,000	5,734,900	4,469,627	4,729,652	2,762,554	2,608,209	2,827,225
Stockholders' Equity	1,837,900	1,800,100	1,563,100	1,043,402	897,021	989,095	1,018,497	1,046,379
Shares Outstanding	57,600	59,400	59,400	52,713	52,210	51,483	52,226	51,020
Statistical Record								
Return on Assets %	4.08	4.96	2.32	3.84	N.M.	1.31	N.M.	N.M.
Return on Equity %	16.26	21.18	11.43	22.07	N.M.	4.83	N.M.	N.M.
EBITDA Margin %	13.16	16.48	13.54	14.30	11.93	12.47	10.36	9.88
Net Margin %	5.91	7.09	3.17	4.83	N.M.	1.49	N.M.	N.M.
Asset Turnover	0.69	0.70	0.73	0.80	0.87	0.88	0.85	0.74
Current Ratio	1.44	1.49	1.68	1.57	1.56	1.74	1.73	1.81
Debt to Equity	2.07	1.92	2.52	2.77	3.47	1.67	1.51	1.65
Price Range	145.07-103.06	137.69-89.60	105.95-83.68	90.53-62.76	67.64-40.24	42.12-22.17	36.00-20.70	29.51-23.21
P/E Ratio	28.90-20.53	22.99-14.96	39.83-31.46	22.52-15.61	...	46.29-24.36	...	...
Average Yield %	1.29	1.27	1.35	1.42	1.38	3.14	...	...

Address: 3001 Deming Way, Middleton, WI 53562 Telephone: 608-275-3340	Web Site: www.spectrumbrands.com Officers: David M. Maura - Chairman Andreas Rouve - President, Chief Executive Officer, Chief Operating Officer, Region Officer	Auditors: KPMG LLP Investor Contact: 608-275-3340 Transfer Agents: Computershare Shareowner Services, Jersey City, NJ

SPIRIT AEROSYSTEMS HOLDINGS INC

Exchange	Symbol	Price	52Wk Range	Yield	P/E
NYS	SPR	$87.25 (12/29/2017)	87.25-52.96	0.46	30.61

*7 Year Price Score 136.50 *NYSE Composite Index=100 *12 Month Price Score 118.54

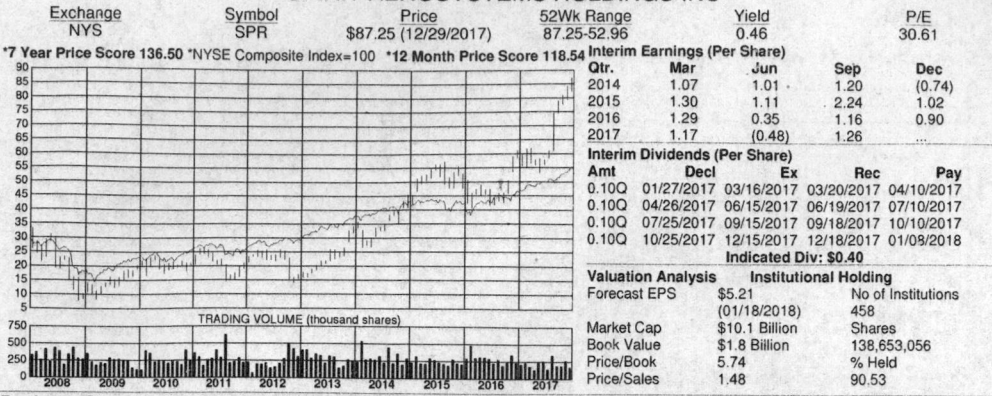

Interim Earnings (Per Share)

Qtr.	Mar	Jun	Sep	Dec
2014	1.07	1.01	1.20	(0.74)
2015	1.30	1.11	2.24	1.02
2016	1.29	0.35	1.16	0.90
2017	1.17	(0.48)	1.26	...

Interim Dividends (Per Share)

Amt	Decl	Ex	Rec	Pay
0.10Q	01/27/2017	03/16/2017	03/20/2017	04/10/2017
0.10Q	04/26/2017	06/15/2017	06/19/2017	07/10/2017
0.10Q	07/25/2017	09/15/2017	09/18/2017	10/10/2017
0.10Q	10/25/2017	12/15/2017	12/18/2017	01/08/2018

Indicated Div: $0.40

Valuation Analysis | **Institutional Holding**

Forecast EPS	$5.21 (01/18/2018)	No of Institutions 458
Market Cap	$10.1 Billion	Shares
Book Value	$1.8 Billion	138,653,056
Price/Book	5.74	% Held
Price/Sales	1.48	90.53

TRADING VOLUME (thousand shares)

Business Summary: Aerospace (MIC: 7.1.1 SIC: 3728 NAIC: 336413)

Spirit AeroSystems Holdings provides manufacturing and design expertise in a range of products and services for aircraft original equipment manufacturers. Co. has three segments: Fuselage Systems, which includes forward, mid and rear fuselage sections and systems; Propulsion Systems, which includes nacelles, struts/pylons and engine structural components; and Wing Systems, which includes wings, wing components, flight control surfaces and other miscellaneous structural parts. In addition to providing aerostructures for commercial aircraft, Co. designs, engineers and manufactures structural components for military aircraft such as Rotorcraft.

Recent Developments: For the quarter ended Sep 28 2017, net income increased 1.4% to US$147.2 million from US$145.1 million in the year-earlier quarter. Revenues were US$1.75 billion, up 2.2% from US$1.71 billion the year before. Operating income was US$211.4 million versus US$214.4 million in the prior-year quarter, a decrease of 1.4%. Direct operating expenses rose 2.7% to US$1.48 billion from US$1.44 billion in the comparable period the year before. Indirect operating expenses increased 1.2% to US$58.3 million from US$57.6 million in the equivalent prior-year period.

Prospects: Our evaluation of Spirit AeroSystems Holdings Inc. as of Jan. 14, 2018 is the result of our systematic analysis on three basic characteristics: earnings strength, relative valuation, and recent stock price movement. The company has produced a positive trend in earnings per share over the past 5 quarters. However, while recent estimates for the company have been mixed, SPR has posted results that were in line with analysts expectations. Based on operating earnings yield, the company is undervalued when compared to all of the companies in our coverage universe. Share price changes over the past year indicates that SPR will perform in line with the market over the near term.

Financial Data

(US$ in Thousands)	9 Mos	6 Mos	3 Mos	12/31/2016	12/31/2015	12/31/2014	12/31/2013	12/31/2012
Earnings Per Share	2.85	2.75	3.58	3.70	5.66	2.53	(4.40)	0.24
Cash Flow Per Share	6.62	6.28	6.15	5.67	9.32	2.58	1.84	3.86
Tang Book Value Per Share	15.12	15.21	16.36	15.82	15.59	11.45	10.17	13.80
Dividends Per Share	0.400	0.300	0.200	0.100	...	...	...	...
Dividend Payout %	14.04	10.91	5.59	2.70	...	...	...	...
Income Statement								
Total Revenue	5,268,400	3,520,200	1,694,100	6,792,900	6,643,900	6,799,200	5,961,000	5,397,700
EBITDA	346,000	134,200	216,000	732,800	875,600	368,200	(341,400)	112,700
Depn & Amortn	3,600	3,200	1,900	18,600	16,900	18,300	19,600	18,600
Income Before Taxes	316,700	113,800	205,600	660,500	808,100	262,400	(430,800)	11,400
Income Taxes	84,900	29,000	64,000	192,100	20,600	(95,900)	191,100	(24,100)
Net Income	232,100	84,900	141,700	469,700	788,700	358,800	(621,400)	34,800
Average Shares	117,000	118,200	120,700	127,000	139,400	141,600	141,300	142,700
Balance Sheet								
Current Assets	3,012,000	2,957,800	2,998,100	2,910,400	3,299,100	3,052,100	2,944,200	3,355,400
Total Assets	5,537,200	5,462,500	5,469,200	5,405,200	5,777,500	5,162,700	5,107,200	5,415,300
Current Liabilities	1,936,000	1,837,700	1,601,600	1,544,200	1,459,000	1,258,800	1,335,600	1,067,000
Long-Term Obligations	1,060,900	1,060,600	1,063,900	1,060,000	1,097,600	1,144,100	1,150,500	1,165,900
Total Liabilities	3,778,300	3,651,200	3,484,800	3,476,900	3,658,000	3,541,200	3,626,700	3,418,900
Stockholders' Equity	1,758,900	1,811,300	1,984,400	1,928,300	2,119,500	1,621,500	1,480,500	1,996,400
Shares Outstanding	115,624	118,346	120,637	121,642	135,617	141,089	144,798	143,697
Statistical Record								
Return on Assets %	6.24	6.07	7.81	8.38	14.42	6.99	N.M.	0.66
Return on Equity %	19.08	17.75	21.43	23.14	42.17	23.13	N.M.	1.75
EBITDA Margin %	6.57	3.81	12.75	10.79	13.18	5.42	N.M.	2.09
Net Margin %	4.41	2.41	8.36	6.91	11.87	5.28	N.M.	0.64
Asset Turnover	1.25	1.22	1.21	1.21	1.21	1.32	1.13	1.03
Current Ratio	1.56	1.61	1.87	1.88	2.26	2.42	2.20	3.14
Debt to Equity	0.60	0.59	0.54	0.55	0.52	0.71	0.78	0.58
Price Range	78.90-44.08	61.98-41.61	61.98-41.61	61.26-40.50	57.16-41.89	45.32-26.51	34.18-15.94	25.85-14.04
P/E Ratio	27.68-15.47	22.54-15.13	17.31-11.62	16.56-10.95	10.10-7.40	17.91-10.48	...	107.71-58.50
Average Yield %	0.67	0.58	0.40	0.21	...	...	...	...

Address: 3801 South Oliver, Wichita, KS 67210 **Telephone:** 316-526-9000	**Web Site:** www.spiritaero.com **Officers:** Robert D. Johnson - Chairman Thomas C. Gentile - President, Chief Executive Officer, Executive Vice President, Chief Operating Officer	**Auditors:** Ernst & Young LLP **Investor Contact:** 316-523-7040 **Transfer Agents:** Computershare, Pittsburgh, PA

SPIRE INC

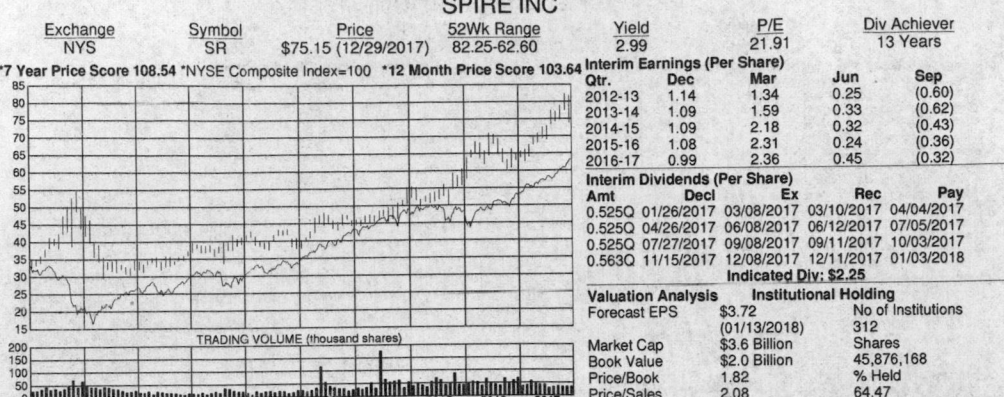

Exchange	Symbol	Price	52Wk Range	Yield	P/E	Div Achiever
NYS	SR	$75.15 (12/29/2017)	82.25-62.60	2.99	21.91	13 Years

*7 Year Price Score 108.54 *NYSE Composite Index=100 *12 Month Price Score 103.64

Interim Earnings (Per Share)

Qtr.	Dec	Mar	Jun	Sep
2012-13	1.14	1.34	0.25	(0.60)
2013-14	1.09	1.59	0.33	(0.62)
2014-15	1.09	2.18	0.32	(0.43)
2015-16	1.08	2.31	0.24	(0.36)
2016-17	0.99	2.36	0.45	(0.32)

Interim Dividends (Per Share)

Amt	Decl	Ex	Rec	Pay
0.525Q	01/26/2017	03/08/2017	03/10/2017	04/04/2017
0.525Q	04/26/2017	06/08/2017	06/12/2017	07/05/2017
0.525Q	07/27/2017	09/08/2017	09/11/2017	10/03/2017
0.563Q	11/15/2017	12/08/2017	12/11/2017	01/03/2018

Indicated Div: $2.25

Valuation Analysis

		Institutional Holding	
Forecast EPS	$3.72	No of Institutions	
	(01/13/2018)	312	
Market Cap	$3.6 Billion	Shares	
Book Value	$2.0 Billion	45,876,168	
Price/Book	1.82	% Held	
Price/Sales	2.08	64.47	

Business Summary: Gas Utilities (MIC: 3.3.1 SIC: 4924 NAIC: 221210)

Spire is a public utility holding company. Co. operates two business segments: Gas Utility and Gas Marketing. Co.'s Gas Utility segment includes the operations of Co.'s subsidiaries: Spire Missouri Inc., which is engaged in the purchase, retail distribution and sale of natural gas; Spire Alabama Inc., which is engaged in the purchase, retail distribution and sale of natural gas; and Spire Gulf Inc. and Spire Mississippi Inc., which is engaged the purchase, retail distribution and sale of natural gas; gas marketing. Co.'s Gas Marketing segment includes Co.'s subsidiary, Spire Marketing Inc., which is engaged in the marketing of natural gas and related activities on a non-regulated basis.

Recent Developments: For the year ended Sep 30 2017, net income increased 12.1% to US$161.6 million from US$144.2 million in the prior year. Revenues were US$1.74 billion, up 13.2% from US$1.54 billion the year before. Operating income was US$321.7 million versus US$282.3 million in the prior year, an increase of 14.0%. Direct operating expenses rose 11.9% to US$1.11 billion from US$994.9 million in the comparable period the year before. Indirect operating expenses increased 17.6% to US$305.7 million from US$259.9 million in the equivalent prior-year period.

Prospects: Our evaluation of Spire Inc. as of Jan. 14, 2018 is the result of our systematic analysis on three basic characteristics: earnings strength, relative valuation, and recent stock price movement. The company has managed to produce a neutral trend in earnings per share over the past 5 quarters and while recent estimates for the company have remained steady, SR has posted better than expected results. Based on operating earnings yield, the company is undervalued when compared to all of the companies in our coverage universe. Share price changes over the past year indicates that SR will perform very well over the near term.

Financial Data

(US$ in Thousands)	09/30/2017	09/30/2016	09/30/2015	09/30/2014	09/30/2013	09/30/2012	09/30/2011	09/30/2010
Earnings Per Share	3.43	3.24	3.16	2.35	2.02	2.79	2.86	2.43
Cash Flow Per Share	6.15	7.42	7.46	3.42	6.33	5.74	7.57	4.86
Tang Book Value Per Share	16.98	13.22	14.48	13.21	24.44	26.69	25.56	24.02
Dividends Per Share	2.100	1.960	1.840	1.760	1.700	1.660	1.620	1.580
Dividend Payout %	61.22	60.49	58.23	74.89	84.16	59.50	56.64	65.02
Income Statement								
Total Revenue	1,740,700	1,537,300	1,976,400	1,627,200	1,017,019	1,125,475	1,603,307	1,735,029
EBITDA	482,400	428,200	404,300	246,400	147,133	153,904	157,052	144,151
Depn & Amortn	154,100	137,500	130,800	83,300	49,283	41,339	39,764	37,908
Income Before Taxes	239,200	213,500	198,900	116,900	70,336	88,929	93,007	81,134
Income Taxes	77,600	69,300	62,000	32,300	17,578	26,289	29,182	27,094
Net Income	161,600	144,200	136,900	84,600	52,758	62,640	63,825	54,040
Average Shares	47,000	44,300	43,300	35,900	25,952	22,340	22,171	22,039
Balance Sheet								
Current Assets	725,500	569,600	530,100	604,900	475,880	343,016	369,134	414,195
Total Assets	6,546,700	6,077,400	5,290,200	5,074,000	3,125,386	1,880,262	1,783,082	1,840,196
Current Liabilities	1,097,900	1,161,300	853,800	782,800	353,178	252,124	231,934	333,924
Long-Term Obligations	1,995,000	1,833,700	1,771,500	1,851,000	912,712	339,416	364,357	364,298
Total Liabilities	4,555,400	4,309,200	3,716,600	3,565,600	2,079,104	1,278,651	1,209,751	1,304,619
Stockholders' Equity	1,991,300	1,768,200	1,573,600	1,508,400	1,046,282	601,611	573,331	535,577
Shares Outstanding	48,263	45,650	43,335	43,183	32,696	22,539	22,430	22,292
Statistical Record								
Return on Assets %	2.56	2.53	2.64	2.06	2.11	3.41	3.52	3.00
Return on Equity %	8.60	8.61	8.88	6.62	6.40	10.63	11.51	10.27
EBITDA Margin %	27.71	27.85	20.46	15.14	14.47	13.67	9.80	8.31
Net Margin %	9.28	9.38	6.93	5.20	5.19	5.57	3.98	3.11
Asset Turnover	0.28	0.27	0.38	0.40	0.41	0.61	0.89	0.96
Current Ratio	0.66	0.49	0.62	0.77	1.35	1.36	1.59	1.24
Debt to Equity	1.00	1.04	1.13	1.23	0.87	0.56	0.64	0.68
Price Range	77.40-59.97	70.84-54.53	56.02-46.15	49.56-44.24	48.16-37.70	43.27-37.37	39.74-33.52	35.90-30.34
P/E Ratio	22.57-17.48	21.86-16.83	17.73-14.60	21.09-18.83	23.84-18.66	15.51-13.39	13.90-11.72	14.77-12.49
Average Yield %	3.09	3.09	3.54	3.78	3.96	4.12	4.35	4.74

Address: 700 Market Street, St. Louis, MO 63101	Web Site: www.spireenergy.com	Auditors: DELOITTE & TOUCHE LLP
Telephone: 314-342-0500	Officers: Edward L. Glotzbach - Chairman Suzanne Sitherwood - President, Chief Executive Officer	Investor Contact: 314-342-0878
		Transfer Agents: Computershare Trust Company, N.A., Providence, RI

SPIRIT AIRLINES INC

Exchange	Symbol	Price	52Wk Range	Yield	P/E
NYS	SAVE	$44.99 (12/27/2017)	59.74-32.09	N/A	14.24

*7 Year Price Score N/A   *NYSE Composite Index=100   *12 Month Price Score 83.22

TRADING VOLUME (thousand shares)

Interim Earnings (Per Share)

Qtr.	Mar	Jun	Sep	Dec
2014	0.51	0.88	0.91	0.77
2015	0.94	1.05	1.35	1.04
2016	0.86	1.03	1.17	0.71
2017	0.46	1.12	0.87	...

Interim Dividends (Per Share)

No Dividends Paid

Valuation Analysis / Institutional Holding

Valuation Analysis		Institutional Holding	
Forecast EPS	$3.30	No of Institutions	
	(01/27/2018)	348	
Market Cap	$3.1 Billion	Shares	
Book Value	$1.6 Billion	74,578,080	
Price/Book	1.99	% Held	
Price/Sales	1.22	93.66	

Business Summary: Airlines/Air Freight (MIC: 7.4.4 SIC: 4512 NAIC: 481111)

Spirit Airlines is an airline that provides customers low, unbundled base fares with a range of optional services. Co. provides customers its Bare Fares, which are unbundled base fares that remove components typically included in the price of an airline ticket. Co. then gives customers Frill Control, which provides customers the freedom to save by paying only for the options they choose such as bags, advance seat assignments and refreshments. As of Dec 31 2016, Co.'s all-Airbus Fit Fleet operated more than 420 daily flights to 59 destinations in the U.S., Caribbean and Latin America; and its route network included 200 markets.

Recent Developments: For the quarter ended Sep 30 2017, net income decreased 26.0% to US$60.2 million from US$81.4 million in the year-earlier quarter. Revenues were US$687.2 million, up 10.6% from US$621.3 million the year before. Operating income was US$104.1 million versus US$135.2 million in the prior-year quarter, a decrease of 23.0%. Direct operating expenses rose 18.5% to US$315.8 million from US$266.6 million in the comparable period the year before. Indirect operating expenses increased 21.7% to US$267.3 million from US$219.5 million in the equivalent prior-year period.

Prospects: Our evaluation of Spirit Airlines Inc as of Jan. 21, 2018 is the result of our systematic analysis on three basic characteristics: earnings strength, relative valuation, and recent stock price movement. The company has produced a positive trend in earnings per share over the past 5 quarters and while recent estimates for the company have been raised by analysts, SAVE has posted better than expected results. Based on operating earnings yield, the company is undervalued when compared to all of the companies in our coverage universe. Share price changes over the past year indicates that SAVE will perform very poorly over the near term.

Financial Data
(US$ in Thousands)

	9 Mos	6 Mos	3 Mos	12/31/2016	12/31/2015	12/31/2014	12/31/2013	12/31/2012
Earnings Per Share	3.16	3.46	3.37	3.76	4.38	3.08	2.42	1.49
Cash Flow Per Share	6.06	6.29	5.62	6.72	6.55	3.58	2.69	1.57
Tang Book Value Per Share	22.64	21.74	20.59	20.12	17.13	13.78	10.60	8.04
Income Statement								
Total Revenue	1,980,659	1,293,428	591,746	2,321,956	2,141,463	1,931,580	1,654,385	1,318,388
EBITDA	302,439	196,795	62,753	550,001	584,180	399,444	313,398	188,085
Depn & Amortn	6,415	4,761	3,351	106,868	75,073	46,786	31,389	14,426
Income Before Taxes	270,658	175,878	51,822	419,460	502,403	352,994	282,410	174,584
Income Taxes	100,390	65,800	19,887	154,581	185,183	127,530	105,492	66,124
Net Income	170,268	110,078	31,935	264,879	317,220	225,464	176,918	108,460
Average Shares	69,458	69,561	69,592	70,508	72,426	73,294	72,999	72,590
Balance Sheet								
Current Assets	1,244,740	1,230,504	1,146,531	975,845	1,026,340	731,141	649,075	547,357
Total Assets	3,870,942	3,674,345	3,438,614	3,151,927	2,530,545	1,602.981	1,180,765	919,884
Current Liabilities	662,984	685,830	673,174	531,950	466,240	365,624	335,993	276,894
Long-Term Obligations	1,214,138	1,089,159	991,722	897,400	596,700	135,800	...	...
Total Liabilities	2,300,406	2,166,112	2,010,268	1,757,361	1,305,242	599,889	411,648	337,349
Stockholders' Equity	1,570,536	1,508,233	1,428,346	1,394,607	1,225,310	1,003,075	769,117	582,535
Shares Outstanding	69,373	69,369	69,369	69,326	71,541	72,775	72,566	72,470
Statistical Record								
Return on Assets %	6.25	7.16	7.57	9.30	15.35	16.20	16.84	12.99
Return on Equity %	15.01	17.09	17.36	20.17	28.47	25.44	26.18	20.62
EBITDA Margin %	15.27	15.21	10.60	23.69	27.28	20.68	18.94	14.27
Net Margin %	8.60	8.51	5.40	11.41	14.81	11.67	10.69	8.23
Asset Turnover	0.73	0.74	0.77	0.82	1.04	1.39	1.58	1.58
Current Ratio	1.88	1.79	1.70	1.83	2.20	2.00	1.93	1.98
Debt to Equity	0.77	0.72	0.69	0.64	0.49	0.14	...	...
Price Range	59.74-32.09	59.74-37.23	59.50-37.23	59.50-36.53	82.03-33.57	84.47-44.76	46.45-17.50	24.11-14.19
P/E Ratio	18.91-10.16	17.27-10.76	17.66-11.05	15.82-9.72	18.73-7.66	27.43-14.53	19.19-7.23	16.18-9.52

Address: 2800 Executive Way, Miramar, FL 33025 **Telephone:** 954-447-7920	**Web Site:** www.spirit.com **Officers:** H. McIntyre (Mac) Gardner - Chairman Robert L. Fornaro - President, Chief Executive Officer	**Auditors:** Ernst & Young LLP **Investor Contact:** 954-447-7920 **Transfer Agents:** Wells Fargo Shareholder Services

SPIRIT REALTY CAPITAL INC

Exchange	Symbol	Price	52Wk Range	Yield	P/E
NYS	SRC	$8.58 (12/29/2017)	11.27-6.71	8.39	95.33

*7 Year Price Score N/A   *NYSE Composite Index=100   *12 Month Price Score 89.60

TRADING VOLUME (thousand shares)

Interim Earnings (Per Share)

Qtr.	Mar	Jun	Sep	Dec
2014	0.04	(0.24)	0.02	0.09
2015	0.06	0.14	0.04	0.02
2016	0.06	0.10	0.06	0.00
2017	0.03	0.05	0.01	...

Interim Dividends (Per Share)

Amt	Decl	Ex	Rec	Pay
0.18Q	03/15/2017	03/29/2017	03/31/2017	04/14/2017
0.18Q	06/15/2017	06/28/2017	06/30/2017	07/14/2017
0.18Q	09/15/2017	09/28/2017	09/29/2017	10/13/2017
0.18Q	12/08/2017	12/28/2017	12/29/2017	01/12/2018

Indicated Div: $0.72

Valuation Analysis

		Institutional Holding	
Forecast EPS	$0.15	No of Institutions	
	(01/18/2018).	N/A	
Market Cap	$3.9 Billion	Shares	
Book Value	$3.3 Billion	N/A	
Price/Book	1.20	% Held	
Price/Sales	5.78	N/A	

Business Summary: REITs (MIC: 5.3.1 SIC: 6512 NAIC: 531120)

Spirit Realty Capital is a self-administered and self-managed real estate investment trust with in-house capabilities, including acquisition, portfolio management, asset management, credit research, real estate research, legal, finance and accounting and capital markets. Co. primarily invests in single-tenant, operationally essential real estate throughout the U.S., with business operations within mainly retail, but also office and industrial property types. Co.'s operations are carried out through an operating partnership, Spirit Realty, L.P. As of Dec 31 2016, Co.'s real estate portfolio consisted of 2,541 owned properties located in 49 states as well as in the U.S. Virgin Islands.

Recent Developments: For the quarter ended Sep 30 2017, net income decreased 80.6% to US$5.3 million from US$27.4 million in the year-earlier quarter. Revenues were US$169.6 million, down 1.7% from US$172.5 million the year before. Revenues from property income fell 0.6% to US$165.0 million from US$165.9 million in the corresponding quarter a year earlier.

Prospects: Our evaluation of Spirit Realty Capital Inc as of Jan. 14, 2018 is the result of our systematic analysis on three basic characteristics: earnings strength, relative valuation, and recent stock price movement. The company has managed to produce a neutral trend in earnings per share over the past 5 quarters and while recent estimates for the company have been mixed, SRC has posted results that fell short of analysts expectations. Based on operating earnings yield, the company is about fairly valued when compared to all of the companies in our coverage universe. Share price changes over the past year indicates that SRC will perform in line with the market over the near term.

Financial Data
(US$ in Thousands)

	9 Mos	6 Mos	3 Mos	12/31/2016	12/31/2015	12/31/2014	12/31/2013	12/31/2012
Earnings Per Share	0.09	0.14	0.19	0.21	0.26	(0.09)	...	0.12
Cash Flow Per Share	0.86	0.79	0.76	0.77	0.86	0.57	0.54	0.56
Tang Book Value Per Share	5.65	5.77	5.98	6.12	6.05	5.92	5.96	5.16
Dividends Per Share	0.720	0.715	0.710	0.705	0.685	0.669	0.302	...
Dividend Payout %	800.00	510.71	373.68	335.71	263.46	...	...	...
Income Statement								
Total Revenue	503,607	334,057	165,422	685,974	667,335	602,871	419,467	282,852
EBITDA	160,645	109,551	48,862	520,195	519,458	422,864	332,359	214,751
Depn & Amortn	16,937	11,127	5,462	277,563	270,892	253,016	185,151	82,588
Income Before Taxes	1,579	4,975	(3,223)	46,046	25,665	(50,222)	(32,059)	24,200
Income Taxes	419	430	165	965	601	673	1,113	...
Net Income	41,357	36,035	12,829	97,446	114,730	(33,799)	1,677	25,397
Average Shares	456,671	479,102	482,609	469,246	432,545	386,809	255,020	210,077
Balance Sheet								
Current Assets	11,947	11,246	9,309	10,059	21,790	176,181	66,588	93,772
Total Assets	7,434,787	7,519,323	7,588,796	7,677,971	7,918,996	8,017,001	7,231,045	3,289,536
Current Liabilities	149,858	147,036	146,836	148,915	142,475	123,298	114,679	30,172
Long-Term Obligations	3,863,145	3,846,623	3,657,857	3,664,628	4,092,787	4,369,634	3,778,218	1,757,322
Total Liabilities	4,175,622	4,163,490	3,979,954	3,995,863	4,429,165	4,698,900	4,113,011	1,922,109
Stockholders' Equity	3,259,165	3,355,833	3,608,842	3,682,108	3,489,831	3,318,101	3,118,034	1,367,427
Shares Outstanding	455,900	457,902	484,026	483,624	441,819	411,350	370,363	208,597
Statistical Record								
Return on Assets %	0.56	0.84	1.18	1.25	1.44	N.M.	0.03	0.75
Return on Equity %	1.21	1.80	2.57	2.71	3.37	N.M.	0.07	1.78
EBITDA Margin %	31.90	32.79	29.54	75.83	77.84	70.14	79.23	75.92
Net Margin %	8.21	10.79	7.76	14.21	17.19	N.M.	0.40	8.98
Asset Turnover	0.09	0.09	0.09	0.09	0.08	0.08	0.08	0.08
Current Ratio	0.08	0.08	0.06	0.07	0.15	1.43	0.58	3.11
Debt to Equity	1.19	1.15	1.01	1.00	1.17	1.32	1.21	1.29
Price Range	13.33-6.71	13.88-6.71	13.88-9.99	13.88-9.10	12.99-9.04	12.02-9.83	22.75-8.44	17.78-15.00
P/E Ratio	148.11-74.56	99.14-47.93	73.05-52.58	66.10-43.33	49.96-34.77		N.M.	148.17-125.00
Average Yield %	7.46	6.55	6.05	6.04	6.35	5.96	2.01	...

Address: 2727 North Harwood Street, Suite 300, Dallas, TX 75201 **Telephone:** 972-476-1900	**Web Site:** www.spiritrealty.com **Officers:** Richard I. Gilchrist - Chairman Jackson Hsieh - President, Chief Operating Officer, Chief Executive Officer	**Auditors:** Ernst & Young LLP **Investor Contact:** 480-606-0820

SPRINT CORP

*7 Year Price Score N/A   *NYSE Composite Index=100   *12 Month Price Score 70.58

Interim Earnings (Per Share)

Qtr.	Jun	Sep	Dec	Mar
2014-15	0.01	(0.19)	(0.60)	(0.06)
2015-16	(0.01)	(0.15)	(0.21)	(0.14)
2016-17	(0.08)	(0.04)	(0.12)	(0.07)
2017-18	0.05	(0.01)	...	...

Interim Dividends (Per Share)

No Dividends Paid

Valuation Analysis		Institutional Holding	
Forecast EPS	$-0.01	No of Institutions	
	(01/26/2018)	662	
Market Cap	$23.6 Billion	Shares	
Book Value	$19.0 Billion	814,329,984	
Price/Book	1.24	% Held	
Price/Sales	0.71	N/A	

TRADING VOLUME (thousand shares)

2008 2009 2010 2011 2012 2013 2014 2015 2016 2017

Business Summary: Services (MIC: 6.1.2 SIC: 4813 NAIC: 517110)

Sprint is a holding company. Through its subsidiaries, Co. is a communications company providing wireless and wireline communications products and services to consumers, businesses, government subscribers, and resellers. Co. has two segments: Wireless, which provides wireless services on a postpaid and prepaid payment basis to retail subscribers and also on a wholesale basis, including the sale of wireless services that utilize Co.'s network but are sold under the wholesaler's brand; and Wireline, which provides wireline voice and data communication services to other communications companies and business subscribers, as well as voice, data and internet protocol communication services.

Recent Developments: For the quarter ended Sep 30 2017, net loss amounted to US$48.0 million versus a net loss of US$142.0 million in the year-earlier quarter. Revenues were US$7.93 billion, down 3.9% from US$8.25 billion the year before. Operating income was US$601.0 million versus US$622.0 million in the prior-year quarter, a decrease of 3.4%. Direct operating expenses declined 18.2% to US$3.10 billion from US$3.79 billion in the comparable period the year before. Indirect operating expenses increased 10.3% to US$4.22 billion from US$3.83 billion in the equivalent prior-year period.

Prospects: Our evaluation of Sprint Corp as of Jan. 21, 2018 is the result of our systematic analysis on three basic characteristics: earnings strength, relative valuation, and recent stock price movement. The company has enjoyed a very positive trend in earnings per share over the past 5 quarters. Because the company lacks sufficient analyst estimate data, we place greater weight on the historical EPS trend as the measure of earnings strength. Based on operating earnings yield, the company is overvalued when compared to all of the companies in our coverage universe. Share price changes over the past year indicates that S will perform poorly over the near term.

Financial Data
(US$ in Thousands)

	6 Mos	3 Mos	03/31/2017	03/31/2016	03/31/2015	03/31/2014	12/31/2013	12/31/2012
Earnings Per Share	(0.15)	(0.18)	(0.30)	(0.50)	(0.85)	(0.04)	(0.54)	...
Cash Flow Per Share	1.29	1.23	1.05	0.98	0.62	0.54	(0.02)	...
Tang Book Value Per Share	N.M.	N.M.	N.M.	N.M.	N.M.	N.M.	N.M.	1,001.29
Income Statement								
Total Revenue	16,084,000	8,157,000	33,347,000	32,180,000	34,532,000	8,875,000	16,891,000	...
EBITDA	5,382,000	2,891,000	8,822,000	6,122,000	1,929,000	1,289,000	1,129,000	(23,000)
Depn & Amortn	3,626,000	1,780,000	7,098,000	5,794,000	3,797,000	868,000	2,026,000	...
Income Before Taxes	548,000	498,000	(771,000)	(1,854,000)	(3,919,000)	(95,000)	(1,815,000)	(23,000)
Income Taxes	390,000	292,000	435,000	141,000	(574,000)	56,000	45,000	4,000
Net Income	158,000	206,000	(1,206,000)	(1,995,000)	(3,345,000)	(151,000)	(1,860,000)	(27,000)
Average Shares	3,998,000	4,076,000	3,981,000	3,969,000	3,953,000	3,949,000	3,475,000	...
Balance Sheet								
Current Assets	11,935,000	12,496,000	14,117,000	6,833,000	9,777,000	11,579,000	13,058,000	11,000
Total Assets	82,466,000	83,324,000	85,123,000	78,975,000	83,030,000	84,689,000	86,095,000	3,115,000
Current Liabilities	10,897,000	11,571,000	12,458,000	11,963,000	10,940,000	9,698,000	10,669,000	4,000
Long-Term Obligations	34,236,000	34,459,000	35,878,000	29,268,000	32,531,000	31,787,000	32,017,000	...
Total Liabilities	63,446,000	64,309,000	66,315,000	59,192,000	61,320,000	59,377,000	60,511,000	5,000
Stockholders' Equity	19,020,000	19,015,000	18,808,000	19,783,000	21,710,000	25,312,000	25,584,000	3,110,000
Shares Outstanding	3,999,000	3,996,000	3,989,000	3,974,000	3,966,000	3,941,000	3,934,000	3,106
Statistical Record								
EBITDA Margin %	33.46	35.44	26.46	19.02	5.59	14.52	6.68	...
Net Margin %	0.98	2.53	N.M.	N.M.	N.M.	N.M.	N.M.	...
Asset Turnover	0.41	0.41	0.41	0.40	0.41	0.42	0.38	...
Current Ratio	1.10	1.08	1.13	0.57	0.89	1.19	1.22	2.75
Debt to Equity	1.80	1.81	1.91	1.48	1.50	1.26	1.25	...
Price Range	9.43-5.95	9.43-4.45	9.43-3.40	5.30-2.45	9.71-3.81	10.75-7.69	10.79-5.74	...

Address: 6200 Sprint Parkway, Overland Park, KS 66251
Telephone: 855-848-3280

Web Site: www.sprint.com
Officers: Raul Marcelo Claure - President, Chief Executive Officer, Associate/Affiliate Company Officer Nestor Cano - Chief Operating Officer

Auditors: DELOITTE & TOUCHE LLP

SQUARE INC

Exchange	Symbol	Price	52Wk Range	Yield	P/E
NYS	SQ	$34.67 (12/29/2017)	48.86-13.81	N/A	N/A

*7 Year Price Score N/A   *NYSE Composite Index=100   *12 Month Price Score 149.45

TRADING VOLUME (thousand shares)

Interim Earnings (Per Share)

Qtr.	Mar	Jun	Sep	Dec
2015	(0.33)	(0.20)	(0.35)	(0.36)
2016	(0.29)	(0.08)	(0.09)	(0.04)
2017	(0.04)	(0.04)	(0.04)	...

Interim Dividends (Per Share)

No Dividends Paid

Valuation Analysis   **Institutional Holding**

Forecast EPS	$0.26	No of Institutions
	(01/17/2018)	380
Market Cap	$13.4 Billion	Shares
Book Value	$732.9 Million	220,850,144
Price/Book	18.34	% Held
Price/Sales	6.56	N/A

Business Summary: IT Services (MIC: 6.3.1 SIC: 7372 NAIC: 511210)

Square is a commerce ecosystem that combines software with hardware to enable sellers to turn mobile devices and computing devices into payment and point-of-sale solutions. Co.'s products and services including: Managed Payments Solutions, which sellers can accept payments in person via the swipe, dip, or tap of a card, online; In-person/card present payments, which its custom-designed hardware can process all card payment forms, including magnetic stripe; Square Cash, which is an personal finance app that allows anyone to send and receive money electronically; and Square Point of Sale, which includes Square Dashboard, Co.'s cloud-based reporting and analytics tool.

Recent Developments: For the quarter ended Sep 30 2017, net loss amounted to US$16.1 million versus a net loss of US$32.3 million in the year-earlier quarter. Revenues were US$585.2 million, up 33.3% from US$439.0 million the year before. Operating loss was US$14.9 million versus a loss of US$32.0 million in the prior-year quarter. Direct operating expenses rose 27.0% to US$366.5 million from US$288.7 million in the comparable period the year before. Indirect operating expenses increased 28.1% to US$233.5 million from US$182.3 million in the equivalent prior-year period.

Prospects: Our evaluation of Square Inc as of Jan. 14, 2018 is the result of our systematic analysis on three basic characteristics: earnings strength, relative valuation, and recent stock price movement. The company has managed to produce a neutral trend in earnings per share over the past 5 quarters and while recent estimates for the company have remained steady, SQ has posted better than expected results. Based on operating earnings yield, the company is overvalued when compared to all of the companies in our coverage universe. Share price changes over the past year indicates that SQ will perform very well over the near term.

Financial Data
(US$ in Thousands)

	9 Mos	6 Mos	3 Mos	12/31/2016	12/31/2015	12/31/2014	12/31/2013	12/31/2012
Earnings Per Share	(0.16)	(0.21)	(0.25)	(0.50)	(1.24)	(1.08)	(0.82)	(0.71)
Cash Flow Per Share	0.29	0.40	0.23	0.07	0.16	(0.77)	(0.47)	(0.36)
Tang Book Value Per Share	1.70	1.64	1.48	1.37	1.27	...	...	...
Income Statement								
Total Revenue	1,598,218	1,013,059	461,554	1,708,721	1,267,118	850,192	552,433	203,449
EBITDA	(19,309)	(11,642)	(6,169)	(141,753)	(154,808)	(135,095)	(95,792)	(81,694)
Depn & Amortn	27,507	18,429	8,412	28,700	20,100	16,500	8,200	3,500
Income Before Taxes	(46,816)	(30,071)	(14,581)	(169,673)	(176,071)	(152,653)	(103,980)	(85,199)
Income Taxes	334	981	509	1,917	3,746	1,440	513	...
Net Income	(47,150)	(31,052)	(15,090)	(171,590)	(179,817)	(154,093)	(104,493)	(85,199)
Average Shares	383,951	376,357	366,737	341,555	170,498	142,042	127,845	119,220
Balance Sheet								
Current Assets	1,686,877	1,437,917	1,343,355	1,001,425	705,563	409,867	253,802	...
Total Assets	2,083,852	1,741,714	1,591,113	1,211,362	894,772	541,888	318,341	...
Current Liabilities	930,679	624,928	554,896	577,464	334,202	191,106	129,741	...
Long-Term Obligations	354,237	349,960	345,739	...	...	30,000	...	...
Total Liabilities	1,350,943	1,037,970	963,180	635,209	386,724	268,216	156,047	...
Stockholders' Equity	732,909	703,744	627,933	576,153	508,048	273,672	162,294	...
Shares Outstanding	387,802	382,620	373,365	364,547	334,949	154,603	138,017	132,969
Statistical Record								
Asset Turnover	1.31	1.42	1.41	1.62	1.76	1.98	...	...
Current Ratio	1.81	2.30	2.42	1.73	2.11	2.14	1.96	...
Debt to Equity	0.48	0.50	0.55	...	...	0.11	...	...
Price Range	28.81-10.93	24.78-8.94	17.93-8.62	15.48-8.37	13.09-11.90	...	...	...

Address: 1455 Market Street, Suite 600, San Francisco, CA 94103 **Telephone:** 415-375-3176	**Web Site:** www.squareup.com **Officers:** Jack Dorsey - Chairman, President, Chief Executive Officer Hillary Smith - General Counsel	**Auditors:** KPMG LLP **Transfer Agents:** American Stock Transfer & Trust Company, LLC, Brooklyn, NY

STANLEY BLACK & DECKER INC

Exchange	Symbol	Price	52Wk Range	Yield	P/E	Div Achiever
NYS	SWK	$169.69 (12/29/2017)	170.03-115.75	1.49	21.45	49 Years

*7 Year Price Score 117.98 *NYSE Composite Index=100 *12 Month Price Score 110.06

Interim Earnings (Per Share)

Qtr.	Mar	Jun	Sep	Dec
2014	1.02	1.36	1.47	0.91
2015	1.04	1.49	1.52	1.76
2016	1.28	1.84	1.68	1.70
2017	2.59	1.82	1.80	...

Interim Dividends (Per Share)

Amt	Decl	Ex	Rec	Pay
0.58Q	02/15/2017	02/27/2017	03/01/2017	03/21/2017
0.58Q	04/20/2017	06/05/2017	06/07/2017	06/20/2017
0.63Q	07/19/2017	08/30/2017	09/01/2017	09/19/2017
0.63Q	10/18/2017	11/30/2017	12/01/2017	12/19/2017

Indicated Div: $2.52

Valuation Analysis

Forecast EPS	$7.40 (01/18/2018)
Market Cap	$26.0 Billion
Book Value	$8.0 Billion
Price/Book	3.25
Price/Sales	2.12

Institutional Holding

No of Institutions	961
Shares	154,119,264
% Held	N/A

TRADING VOLUME (thousand shares)

Business Summary: Industrial Machinery & Equipment (MIC: 7.2.1 SIC: 3423 NAIC: 332212)

Stanley Black & Decker is a provider of hand tools, power tools and related accessories, mechanical access solutions (for example, automatic doors and commercial locking systems), electronic security and monitoring systems, healthcare solutions, engineered fastening systems and products and services for various industrial applications. Co. has three segments: Tools & Storage, which is comprised of the Power Tools and Hand Tools, Accessories & Storage businesses; Security, which is comprised of the Convergent Security Solutions and the Mechanical Access Solutions businesses; and Industrial, which is comprised of the Engineered Fastening and Infrastructure businesses.

Recent Developments: For the quarter ended Sep 30 2017, net income increased 10.1% to US$274.2 million from US$249.0 million in the year-earlier quarter. Revenues were US$3.30 billion, up 14.5% from US$2.88 billion the year before. Direct operating expenses rose 13.8% to US$2.05 billion from US$1.80 billion in the comparable period the year before. Indirect operating expenses increased 18.7% to US$898.1 million from US$756.4 million in the equivalent prior-year period.

Prospects: Our evaluation of Stanley Black & Decker, Inc. as of Jan. 14, 2018 is the result of our systematic analysis on three basic characteristics: earnings strength, relative valuation, and recent stock price movement. The company has enjoyed a very positive trend in earnings per share over the past 5 quarters and while recent estimates for the company have been mixed, SWK has posted better than expected results. Based on operating earnings yield, the company is about fairly valued when compared to all of the companies in our coverage universe. Share price changes over the past year indicates that SWK will perform well over the near term.

Financial Data

(US$ in Thousands)	9 Mos	6 Mos	3 Mos	12/31/2016	01/02/2016	01/03/2015	12/28/2013	12/29/2012
Earnings Per Share	7.91	7.79	7.81	6.51	5.79	4.76	3.09	5.30
Cash Flow Per Share	8.70	7.98	9.60	10.20	8.00	8.17	5.61	5.94
Dividends Per Share	2.370	2.320	2.290	2.260	2.140	2.040	1.980	1.800
Dividend Payout %	29.96	29.78	29.32	34.72	36.96	42.86	64.08	33.96
Income Statement								
Total Revenue	9,333,700	6,035,100	2,805,600	11,406,900	11,171,800	11,338,600	11,001,200	10,190,500
EBITDA	1,440,100	995,100	549,000	1,805,400	1,730,000	1,698,200	1,175,500	1,107,000
Depn & Amortn	119,900	75,800	33,700	408,000	414,000	449,800	441,300	445,300
Income Before Taxes	1,184,300	830,300	472,600	1,226,100	1,150,800	1,084,800	586,600	527,600
Income Taxes	239,800	160,000	79,500	261,200	248,600	227,100	69,300	78,900
Net Income	944,500	670,300	393,100	965,300	883,700	760,900	490,300	883,800
Average Shares	152,622	152,226	151,526	148,207	152,706	159,737	158,776	166,701
Balance Sheet								
Current Assets	5,028,700	4,839,100	4,368,300	4,788,500	3,662,100	3,948,800	3,968,700	4,098,300
Total Assets	19,773,200	19,312,300	18,662,100	15,634,900	15,172,300	15,849,100	16,535,100	15,844,000
Current Liabilities	4,002,200	3,866,900	4,214,400	2,807,500	2,802,600	2,832,000	3,221,000	3,073,400
Long-Term Obligations	3,818,000	3,817,400	3,815,600	3,815,800	3,836,600	3,839,800	3,799,400	3,526,500
Total Liabilities	11,757,500	11,612,300	11,850,600	9,267,900	9,360,700	9,420,000	9,735,900	9,176,900
Stockholders' Equity	8,015,700	7,700,000	6,811,500	6,367,000	5,811,600	6,429,100	6,799,200	6,667,100
Shares Outstanding	153,351	153,152	152,973	152,559	153,944	157,125	155,479	159,952
Statistical Record								
Return on Assets %	6.76	6.70	6.82	6.28	5.71	4.62	3.04	5.57
Return on Equity %	17.08	17.40	18.73	15.90	14.48	11.32	7.30	12.97
EBITDA Margin %	15.43	16.49	19.57	15.83	15.49	14.98	10.69	10.86
Net Margin %	10.12	11.11	14.01	8.46	7.91	6.71	4.46	8.67
Asset Turnover	0.69	0.68	0.67	0.74	0.72	0.69	0.68	0.64
Current Ratio	1.26	1.25	1.04	1.71	1.31	1.39	1.23	1.33
Debt to Equity	0.48	0.50	0.56	0.60	0.66	0.60	0.56	0.53
Price Range	152.30-113.49	143.05-111.40	132.87-104.24	125.78-90.14	110.17-90.51	97.36-75.64	92.36-73.97	81.34-59.25
P/E Ratio	19.25-14.35	18.36-14.30	17.01-13.35	19.32-13.85	19.03-15.63	20.45-15.89	29.89-23.94	15.35-11.18
Average Yield %	1.80	1.85	1.92	2.01	2.11	2.35	2.45	2.55

Address: 1000 Stanley Drive, New Britain, CT 06053	**Web Site:** www.stanleyblackanddecker.com	**Auditors:** Ernst & Young LLP
Telephone: 860-225-5111	**Officers:** John F. Lundgren - Chairman, President, Chief Executive Officer Janet M. Link - Senior Vice President, General Counsel, Secretary	**Transfer Agents:** Computershare Investor Services, Canton, MA
Fax: 860-827-3895		

STARWOOD PROPERTY TRUST INC.

Exchange	Symbol	Price	52Wk Range	Yield	P/E
NYS	STWD	$21.35 (12/29/2017)	22.97-21.32	8.99	12.86

*7 Year Price Score 77.22 *NYSE Composite Index=100 *12 Month Price Score 91.85

Interim Earnings (Per Share)

Qtr.	Mar	Jun	Sep	Dec
2014	0.60	0.52	0.73	0.37
2015	0.52	0.49	0.49	0.40
2016	0.11	0.47	0.44	0.50
2017	0.39	0.44	0.33	...

Interim Dividends (Per Share)

Amt	Decl	Ex	Rec	Pay
0.48Q	02/23/2017	03/29/2017	03/31/2017	04/14/2017
0.48Q	05/09/2017	06/28/2017	06/30/2017	07/14/2017
0.48Q	08/09/2017	09/28/2017	09/29/2017	10/13/2017
0.48Q	11/08/2017	12/28/2017	12/29/2017	01/15/2018

Indicated Div: $1.92

Valuation Analysis

		Institutional Holding	
Forecast EPS	$2.20	No of Institutions	451
	(01/26/2018)		
Market Cap	$5.6 Billion	Shares	
Book Value	$4.5 Billion	211,104,144	
Price/Book	1.24	% Held	
Price/Sales	6.78	89.80	

Business Summary: REITs (MIC: 5.3.1 SIC: 6798 NAIC: 525930)

Starwood Property Trust is a holding company. Co. conducts its operations as a real estate investment trust. Co. originates, acquires, finances and manages commercial mortgage loans and other commercial real estate debt investments, commercial mortgage-backed securities, and other commercial real estate investments in both the U.S. and Europe. Co.'s target assets include commercial real estate mortgage loans, other commercial real estate-related debt investments, residential mortgage-backed securities, certain residential mortgage loans, distressed or non-performing commercial loans, commercial properties subject to net leases and equity interests in commercial real estate.

Recent Developments: For the quarter ended Sep 30 2017, net income decreased 12.3% to US$92.8 million from US$105.8 million in the year-earlier quarter. Revenues were US$226.8 million, up 10.8% from US$204.7 million the year before. Revenues from property income rose 51.4% to US$60.2 million from US$39.7 million in the corresponding quarter a year earlier.

Prospects: Our evaluation of Starwood Properties Trust Inc. as of Jan. 21, 2018 is the result of our systematic analysis on three basic characteristics: earnings strength, relative valuation, and recent stock price movement. The company has generated a negative trend in earnings per share over the past 5 quarters and while recent estimates for the company have remained steady, STWD has posted better than expected results. Based on operating earnings yield, the company is undervalued when compared to all of the companies in our coverage universe. Share price changes over the past year indicates that STWD will perform in line with the market over the near term.

Financial Data

(US$ in Thousands)	9 Mos	6 Mos	3 Mos	12/31/2016	12/31/2015	12/31/2014	12/31/2013	12/31/2012
Earnings Per Share	1.66	1.77	1.80	1.50	1.91	2.24	1.82	1.76
Cash Flow Per Share	0.51	0.24	0.89	2.33	2.62	1.03	1.96	2.33
Tang Book Value Per Share	16.01	16.06	15.98	16.05	15.99	16.00	20.28	20.07
Dividends Per Share	1.920	1.920	1.920	1.920	1.920	1.920	1.820	1.860
Dividend Payout %	115.66	108.47	106.67	128.00	100.52	85.71	100.00	105.68
Income Statement								
Total Revenue	637,056	410,289	198,720	784,667	735,877	702,875	565,695	306,980
EBITDA	330,133	231,456	100,874	453,700	505,396	548,394	357,077	210,374
Depn & Amortn	(7,038)	(3,100)	(997)	99,428	62,681	42,141	31,535	5,669
Income Before Taxes	337,171	234,556	101,871	354,272	442,715	506,253	325,542	204,705
Income Taxes	18,285	8,469	(983)	8,344	17,206	24,096	24,053	1,023
Net Income	308,166	219,738	102,358	365,186	450,697	495,021	305,030	201,195
Average Shares	262,437	262,851	262,441	241,794	234,142	218,781	167,322	114,633
Balance Sheet								
Current Assets	503,483	338,539	295,293	768,340	471,289	370,621	432,078	214,447
Total Assets	62,706,268	64,542,945	70,478,741	77,256,266	85,738,138	116,099,297	110,770,575	4,324,373
Current Liabilities	382,335	328,449	305,017	364,931	317,903	298,932	357,530	112,259
Long-Term Obligations	7,633,418	6,790,009	6,483,301	6,200,670	5,432,278	4,685,252	3,436,649	1,393,705
Total Liabilities	58,209,476	60,025,782	65,977,132	72,733,992	81,597,822	112,238,441	106,488,047	1,605,027
Stockholders' Equity	4,496,792	4,517,163	4,501,609	4,522,274	4,140,316	3,860,856	4,282,528	2,719,346
Shares Outstanding	260,799	260,554	260,227	259,286	237,490	223,538	195,513	135,499
Statistical Record								
Return on Assets %	0.59	0.58	0.53	0.45	0.45	0.44	0.53	5.48
Return on Equity %	10.03	10.42	10.31	8.41	11.27	12.16	8.71	8.96
EBITDA Margin %	51.82	56.41	50.76	57.82	68.68	78.02	63.12	68.53
Net Margin %	48.37	53.56	51.51	46.54	61.25	70.43	53.92	65.54
Asset Turnover	0.01	0.01	0.01	0.01	0.01	0.01	0.01	0.08
Current Ratio	1.32	1.03	0.97	2.11	1.48	1.24	1.21	1.91
Debt to Equity	1.70	1.50	1.44	1.37	1.31	1.21	0.80	0.51
Price Range	22.97-21.30	23.30-20.39	23.30-18.39	23.30-16.93	24.67-19.74	30.67-21.78	28.55-22.96	24.35-18.57
P/E Ratio	13.84-12.83	13.16-11.52	12.94-10.22	15.53-11.29	12.92-10.34	13.69-9.72	15.69-12.62	13.84-10.55
Average Yield %	8.63	8.62	8.21	9.28	8.54	8.01	7.01	8.63

Address: 591 West Putnam Avenue, Greenwich, CT 06830	**Web Site:** www.starwoodpropertytrust.com	**Auditors:** Deloitte & Touche LLP
Telephone: 203-422-7700	**Officers:** Barry S. Sternlicht - Chairman, Chief Executive Officer Jeffrey F. DiModica - President	**Investor Contact:** 202-422-7700
		Transfer Agents: American Stock Transfer & Trust Company, LLC

663

STATE STREET CORP.

Exchange	Symbol	Price	52Wk Range	Yield	P/E
NYS	STT	$97.61 (12/29/2017)	99.29-75.97	1.72	16.92

*7 Year Price Score 107.68 *NYSE Composite Index=100 *12 Month Price Score 102.31

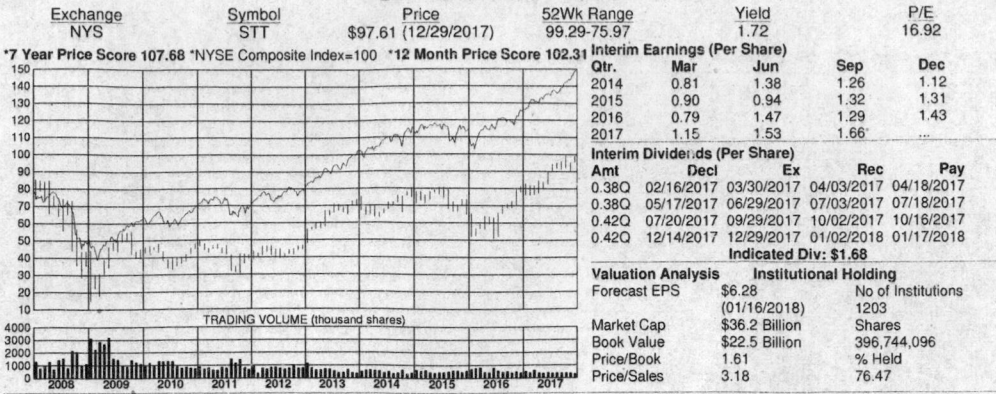

Interim Earnings (Per Share)

Qtr.	Mar	Jun	Sep	Dec
2014	0.81	1.38	1.26	1.12
2015	0.90	0.94	1.32	1.31
2016	0.79	1.47	1.29	1.43
2017	1.15	1.53	1.66˙	...

Interim Dividends (Per Share)

Amt	Decl	Ex	Rec	Pay
0.38Q	02/16/2017	03/30/2017	04/03/2017	04/18/2017
0.38Q	05/17/2017	06/29/2017	07/03/2017	07/18/2017
0.42Q	07/20/2017	09/29/2017	10/02/2017	10/16/2017
0.42Q	12/14/2017	12/29/2017	01/02/2018	01/17/2018

Indicated Div: $1.68

Valuation Analysis   **Institutional Holding**

Forecast EPS	$6.28	No of Institutions
	(01/16/2018)	1203
Market Cap	$36.2 Billion	Shares
Book Value	$22.5 Billion	396,744,096
Price/Book	1.61	% Held
Price/Sales	3.18	76.47

TRADING VOLUME (thousand shares)

Business Summary: Banking (MIC: 5.1.1 SIC: 6022 NAIC: 522110)

State Street is a financial holding company. Through its subsidiaries, Co. provides financial products and services to institutional investors. Co. has two lines of business: Investment Servicing, which provides, among others, custody, product- and participant-level accounting, daily pricing and administration, master trust and master custody, record-keeping, cash management, foreign exchange, brokerage and other trading services; and Investment Management, which provides investment management, investment research and investment advisory services to corporations, public funds and other investors. At Dec 31 2016, Co. had total assets of $242.70 billion and total deposits of $187.16 billion.

Recent Developments: For the quarter ended Sep 30 2017, net income increased 21.7% to US$685.0 million from US$563.0 million in the year-earlier quarter. Net interest income increased 12.3% to US$603.0 million from US$537.0 million in the year-earlier quarter. Non-interest income rose 7.7% to US$2.24 billion from US$2.08 billion, while non-interest expense advanced 1.9% to US$2.02 billion.

Prospects: Our evaluation of State Street Corp. as of Jan. 14, 2018 is the result of our systematic analysis on three basic characteristics: earnings strength, relative valuation, and recent stock price movement. The company has produced a positive trend in earnings per share over the past 5 quarters and while recent estimates for the company have been raised by analysts, STT has posted better than expected results. Based on operating earnings yield, the company is undervalued when compared to all of the companies in our coverage universe. Share price changes over the past year indicates that STT will perform in line with the market over the near term.

Financial Data

(US$ in Thousands)	9 Mos	6 Mos	3 Mos	12/31/2016	12/31/2015	12/31/2014	12/31/2013	12/31/2012
Earnings Per Share	5.77	5.40	5.34	4.97	4.47	4.57	4.62	4.20
Cash Flow Per Share	5.02	3.40	7.73	5.83	(3.44)	(1.32)	(4.42)	3.84
Tang Book Value Per Share	31.40	30.03	27.99	27.38	27.43	28.09	26.47	25.87
Dividends Per Share	1.560	1.520	1.480	1.440	1.320	1.160	1.040	0.960
Dividend Payout %	27.04	28.15	27.72	28.97	29.53	25.38	22.51	22.86
Income Statement								
Interest Income	2,111,000	1,350,000	650,000	2,512,000	2,488,000	2,652,000	2,714,000	3,014,000
Interest Expense	423,000	265,000	140,000	428,000	400,000	392,000	411,000	476,000
Net Interest Income	1,688,000	1,085,000	510,000	2,084,000	2,088,000	2,260,000	2,303,000	2,538,000
Provision for Losses	4,000	1,000	(2,000)	10,000	12,000	10,000	6,000	(3,000)
Non-Interest Income	6,636,000	4,393,000	2,158,000	8,123,000	8,272,000	8,035,000	7,581,000	7,111,000
Non-Interest Expense	6,138,000	4,117,000	2,086,000	8,077,000	8,050,000	7,827,000	7,192,000	6,886,000
Income Before Taxes	2,182,000	1,360,000	584,000	2,120,000	2,298,000	2,458,000	2,686,000	2,766,000
Income Taxes	375,000	238,000	82,000	(22,000)	318,000	421,000	550,000	705,000
Net Income	1,807,000	1,122,000	502,000	2,143,000	1,980,000	2,037,000	2,136,000	2,061,000
Average Shares	378,518	380,915	386,417	396,090	413,638	432,007	455,155	481,129
Balance Sheet								
Net Loans & Leases	23,581,000	24,307,000	22,486,000	19,704,000	18,753,000	18,161,000	13,458,000	12,285,000
Total Assets	235,986,000	238,274,000	236,802,000	242,698,000	245,192,000	274,119,000	243,291,000	222,582,000
Total Deposits	179,263,000	181,416,000	183,465,000	187,163,000	191,627,000	209,040,000	182,268,000	164,181,000
Total Liabilities	213,489,000	216,206,000	215,508,000	221,479,000	224,089,000	252,646,000	222,913,000	201,713,000
Stockholders' Equity	22,497,000	22,068,000	21,294,000	21,219,000	21,103,000	21,473,000	20,378,000	20,869,000
Shares Outstanding	370,840	374,106	376,359	381,939	399,651	415,195	434,128	458,662
Statistical Record								
Return on Assets %	0.98	0.92	0.95	0.88	0.76	0.79	0.92	0.94
Return on Equity %	10.75	10.32	10.64	10.10	9.30	9.73	10.36	10.21
Net Interest Margin %	79.24	82.14	78.46	82.96	83.92	85.22	84.86	84.21
Efficiency Ratio %	67.28	69.20	74.29	75.95	74.81	73.24	69.86	68.01
Loans to Deposits	0.13	0.13	0.12	0.11	0.10	0.09	0.07	0.07
Price Range	95.95-68.63	89.73-52.04	82.93-50.79	81.44-50.79	80.84-64.73	80.33-63.19	73.39-47.01	47.01-38.78
P/E Ratio	16.63-11.89	16.62-9.64	15.53-9.51	16.39-10.22	18.09-14.48	17.58-13.83	15.89-10.18	11.19-9.23
Average Yield %	1.89	2.01	2.12	2.24	1.78	1.65	1.62	2.22

Address: One Lincoln Street, Boston, MA 02111 Telephone: 617-786-3000	Web Site: www.statestreet.com Officers: Joseph L. Hooley - Chairman, Chief Executive Officer, President, Chief Operating Officer Ronald P. O'Hanley - Vice-Chairman, President, Chief Executive Officer, Chief Operating Officer	Auditors: Ernst & Young LLP Investor Contact: 617-664-3477 Transfer Agents: American Stock Transfer & Trust Company, LLC, Brooklyn, NY

STEPAN CO.

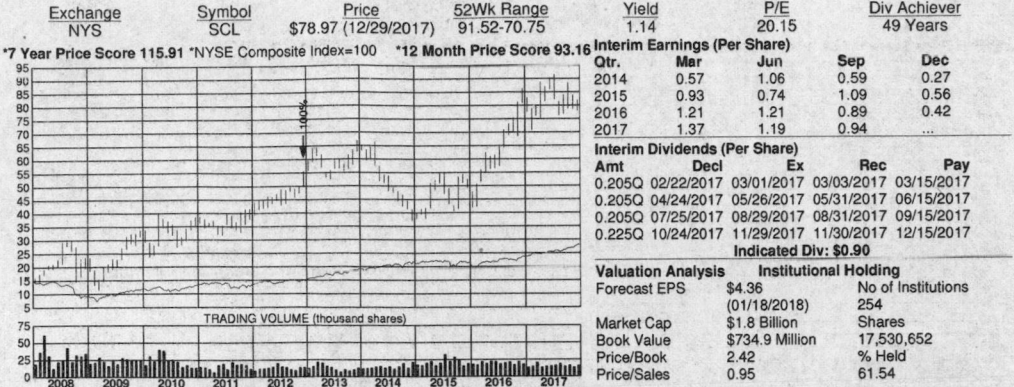

Exchange	Symbol	Price	52Wk Range	Yield	P/E	Div Achiever	
NYS	SCL	$78.97 (12/29/2017)	91.52-70.75	1.14	20.15	49 Years	

*7 Year Price Score 115.91 *NYSE Composite Index=100 *12 Month Price Score 93.16

Interim Earnings (Per Share)

Qtr.	Mar	Jun	Sep	Dec
2014	0.57	1.06	0.59	0.27
2015	0.93	0.74	1.09	0.56
2016	1.21	1.21	0.89	0.42
2017	1.37	1.19	0.94	...

Interim Dividends (Per Share)

Amt	Decl	Ex	Rec	Pay
0.205Q	02/22/2017	03/01/2017	03/03/2017	03/15/2017
0.205Q	04/24/2017	05/26/2017	05/31/2017	06/15/2017
0.205Q	07/25/2017	08/29/2017	08/31/2017	09/15/2017
0.225Q	10/24/2017	11/29/2017	11/30/2017	12/15/2017

Indicated Div: $0.90

Valuation Analysis

		Institutional Holding	
Forecast EPS	$4.36 (01/18/2018)	No of Institutions	254
Market Cap	$1.8 Billion	Shares	17,530,652
Book Value	$734.9 Million	% Held	61.54
Price/Book	2.42		
Price/Sales	0.95		

Business Summary: Specialty Chemicals (MIC: 8.3.2 SIC: 2843 NAIC: 325613)

Stepan is engaged in the production of specialty and intermediate chemicals, which are sold to other manufacturers for use in a variety of end products. Co. has three reportable segments: surfactants, polymers and specialty products. Surfactants are used in a variety of consumer and industrial cleaning compounds as well as in agricultural products, lubricating ingredients, oil field chemicals and other applications. Polymers are used primarily in plastics, building materials, refrigeration systems and coatings, adhesives, sealants and elastomers applications. Specialty products are used in food, flavoring, nutritional supplement and pharmaceutical applications.

Recent Developments: For the quarter ended Sep 30 2017, net income increased 2.3% to US$21.9 million from US$21.4 million in the year-earlier quarter. Revenues were US$487.8 million, up 9.6% from US$445.0 million the year before. Operating income was US$30.3 million versus US$28.7 million in the prior-year quarter, an increase of 5.5%. Direct operating expenses rose 14.0% to US$412.2 million from US$361.6 million in the comparable period the year before. Indirect operating expenses decreased 17.1% to US$45.3 million from US$54.7 million in the equivalent prior-year period.

Prospects: Our evaluation of Stepan Co. as of Jan. 14, 2018 is the result of our systematic analysis on three basic characteristics: earnings strength, relative valuation, and recent stock price movement. The company has managed to produce a neutral trend in earnings per share over the past 5 quarters and while recent estimates for the company have remained steady, SCL has posted results that fell short of analysts expectations. Based on operating earnings yield, the company is undervalued when compared to all of the companies in our coverage universe. Share price changes over the past year indicates that SCL will perform well over the near term.

Financial Data

(US$ in Thousands)	9 Mos	6 Mos	3 Mos	12/31/2016	12/31/2015	12/31/2014	12/31/2013	12/31/2012
Earnings Per Share	3.92	3.87	3.89	3.73	3.32	2.49	3.18	3.49
Cash Flow Per Share	9.54	8.61	9.50	9.28	8.06	3.60	6.64	5.11
Tang Book Value Per Share	30.61	29.37	27.85	26.17	23.69	22.61	23.15	21.01
Dividends Per Share	0.820	0.805	0.790	0.775	0.730	0.690	0.650	0.580
Dividend Payout %	20.92	20.80	20.31	20.78	21.99	27.71	20.44	16.62
Income Statement								
Total Revenue	1,451,184	963,370	468,269	1,766,166	1,776,167	1,927,213	1,880,786	1,803,737
EBITDA	176,444	124,977	66,029	201,988	191,359	155,788	167,724	181,339
Depn & Amortn	57,121	37,729	18,707	74,967	66,985	63,804	56,400	51,294
Income Before Taxes	110,705	81,393	44,330	113,816	109,841	80,543	100,966	120,446
Income Taxes	29,044	21,585	12,418	27,618	26,819	18,454	23,293	36,035
Net Income	81,694	59,795	31,913	86,191	75,968	57,101	72,828	79,396
Average Shares	23,374	23,391	23,331	23,094	22,858	22,917	22,924	22,730
Balance Sheet								
Current Assets	765,659	733,429	699,602	685,541	619,573	575,556	608,550	523,078
Total Assets	1,442,831	1,406,739	1,370,432	1,353,890	1,239,661	1,162,014	1,167,202	985,478
Current Liabilities	289,970	274,392	271,610	297,265	243,244	249,513	268,993	247,167
Long-Term Obligations	283,261	283,222	288,898	288,859	313,817	246,897	235,246	149,564
Total Liabilities	707,898	699,398	697,199	719,286	682,677	626,468	614,916	506,493
Stockholders' Equity	734,933	707,341	673,233	634,604	556,984	535,546	552,286	478,985
Shares Outstanding	22,521	22,535	22,468	22,424	22,280	22,255	22,332	21,965
Statistical Record								
Return on Assets %	6.63	6.67	6.88	6.63	6.33	4.90	6.77	8.39
Return on Equity %	13.39	13.64	14.27	14.43	13.91	10.50	14.12	17.99
EBITDA Margin %	12.16	12.97	14.10	11.44	10.77	8.08	8.92	10.05
Net Margin %	5.63	6.21	6.82	4.88	4.28	2.96	3.87	4.40
Asset Turnover	1.35	1.35	1.36	1.36	1.48	1.65	1.75	1.91
Current Ratio	2.64	2.67	2.58	2.31	2.55	2.31	2.26	2.12
Debt to Equity	0.39	0.40	0.43	0.46	0.56	0.46	0.43	0.31
Price Range	91.52-68.50	90.21-57.33	86.38-54.74	86.38-41.88	55.18-37.74	66.47-37.02	66.85-52.58	55.54-39.17
P/E Ratio	23.35-17.47	23.31-14.81	22.21-14.07	23.16-11.23	16.62-11.37	26.69-14.87	21.02-16.53	15.91-11.22
Average Yield %	1.02	1.05	1.13	1.23	1.57	1.31	1.10	1.26

Address: Edens & Winnetka Road, Northfield, IL 60093	**Web Site:** www.stepan.com	**Auditors:** Deloitte & Touche LLP
Telephone: 847-446-7500	**Officers:** F. Quinn Stepan - Chairman, President, Chief Executive Officer Frank Pacholec - Vice President, Vice President (frmr)	**Investor Contact:** 847-446-7500 **Transfer Agents:** Computershare Investor Services, LLC, Chicago, IL

STERIS PLC

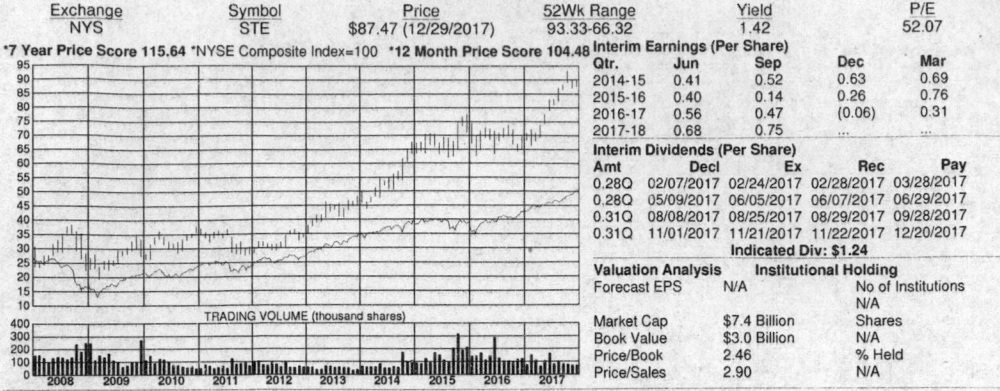

Exchange	Symbol	Price	52Wk Range	Yield	P/E
NYS	STE	$87.47 (12/29/2017)	93.33-66.32	1.42	52.07

*7 Year Price Score 115.64 *NYSE Composite Index=100 *12 Month Price Score 104.48

Interim Earnings (Per Share)

Qtr.	Jun	Sep	Dec	Mar
2014-15	0.41	0.52	0.63	0.69
2015-16	0.40	0.14	0.26	0.76
2016-17	0.56	0.47	(0.06)	0.31
2017-18	0.68	0.75	...	...

Interim Dividends (Per Share)

Amt	Decl	Ex	Rec	Pay
0.28Q	02/07/2017	02/24/2017	02/28/2017	03/28/2017
0.28Q	05/09/2017	06/05/2017	06/07/2017	06/29/2017
0.31Q	08/08/2017	08/25/2017	08/29/2017	09/28/2017
0.31Q	11/01/2017	11/21/2017	11/22/2017	12/20/2017

Indicated Div: $1.24

Valuation Analysis — **Institutional Holding**

Forecast EPS	N/A	No of Institutions N/A
Market Cap	$7.4 Billion	Shares
Book Value	$3.0 Billion	N/A
Price/Book	2.46	% Held
Price/Sales	2.90	N/A

Business Summary: Medical Instruments & Equipment (MIC: 4.3.1 SIC: 3842 NAIC: 339113)

STERIS is a provider of infection prevention and other procedural products and services. Co. has four segments: Healthcare Products, which provides infection prevention and procedural solutions, including capital equipment and related maintenance and installation services, as well as consumables; Healthcare Specialty Services, which provides a range of services for healthcare providers including hospital sterilization services and instrument and scope repairs; Life Sciences, which provides capital equipment and consumable products, and equipment maintenance and specialty services; and Applied Sterilization Technologies, which provides contract sterilization and laboratory services.

Recent Developments: For the quarter ended Sep 30 2017, net income increased 60.3% to US$64.4 million from US$40.2 million in the year-earlier quarter. Revenues were US$634.2 million, down 1.9% from US$646.4 million the year before. Operating income was US$99.4 million versus US$69.6 million in the prior-year quarter, an increase of 42.9%. Direct operating expenses declined 7.8% to US$367.4 million from US$398.5 million in the comparable period the year before. Indirect operating expenses decreased 6.2% to US$167.4 million from US$178.3 million in the equivalent prior-year period.

Prospects: Our evaluation of Steris PLC as of Sep. 17, 2017 is the result of our systematic analysis on three basic characteristics: earnings strength, relative valuation, and recent stock price movement. The company has enjoyed a very positive trend in earnings per share over the past 5 quarters and while recent estimates for the company have remained steady, STE has posted better than expected results. Based on operating earnings yield, the company is about fairly valued when compared to all of the companies in our coverage universe. Share price changes over the past year indicates that STE will perform in line with the market over the near term.

Financial Data
(US$ in Thousands)	6 Mos	3 Mos	03/31/2017	03/31/2016	03/31/2015	03/31/2014	03/31/2013	03/31/2012
Earnings Per Share	1.68	1.40	1.28	1.56	2.25	2.17	2.72	2.31
Cash Flow Per Share	5.32	4.99	4.96	3.59	4.14	3.56	3.91	2.55
Tang Book Value Per Share	N.M.	N.M.	N.M.	N.M.	3.54	4.93	4.09	8.38
Dividends Per Share	1.150	1.120	1.090	0.980	0.900	0.820	0.740	0.660
Dividend Payout %	68.45	80.00	85.16	62.82	40.00	37.79	27.21	28.57
Income Statement								
Total Revenue	1,242,123	607,964	2,612,756	2,238,764	1,850,263	1,622,252	1,501,902	1,406,810
EBITDA	274,858	129,906	347,131	306,885	288,692	263,844	297,914	275,296
Depn & Amortn	89,199	43,651	119,536	93,958	61,481	57,037	55,085	52,980
Income Before Taxes	161,601	74,254	184,646	171,884	208,820	188,376	227,098	211,108
Income Taxes	38,942	16,039	74,015	60,299	73,756	58,934	67,121	74,993
Net Income	122,536	58,077	109,965	110,763	135,064	129,442	159,977	136,115
Average Shares	85,869	85,720	86,094	71,184	60,045	59,745	58,844	58,963
Balance Sheet								
Current Assets	1,027,235	1,029,983	1,017,802	972,525	720,432	674,745	613,940	651,883
Total Assets	5,120,276	5,056,147	4,924,455	5,346,416	2,099,466	1,887,162	1,761,109	1,405,696
Current Liabilities	367,470	353,623	381,583	400,606	283,331	254,506	218,837	278,395
Long-Term Obligations	1,445,297	1,496,467	1,478,361	1,567,796	623,250	493,480	492,290	210,000
Total Liabilities	2,090,283	2,128,481	2,125,853	2,323,382	1,027,834	848,457	816,167	584,295
Stockholders' Equity	3,029,993	2,927,666	2,798,602	3,023,034	1,071,632	1,038,705	944,942	821,401
Shares Outstanding	85,123	85,220	84,948	85,920	59,675	58,968	58,759	57,733
Statistical Record								
Return on Assets %	2.78	2.31	2.14	2.97	6.78	7.10	10.10	9.59
Return on Equity %	4.77	4.01	3.78	5.40	12.80	13.05	18.11	16.87
EBITDA Margin %	22.13	21.37	13.29	13.71	15.60	16.26	19.84	19.57
Net Margin %	9.87	9.55	4.21	4.95	7.30	7.98	10.65	9.68
Asset Turnover	0.50	0.50	0.51	0.60	0.93	0.89	0.95	0.99
Current Ratio	2.80	2.91	2.67	2.43	2.54	2.65	2.81	2.34
Debt to Equity	0.48	0.51	0.53	0.52	0.58	0.48	0.52	0.26
Price Range	88.40-64.40	83.11-64.40	73.90-63.28	77.73-61.96	70.38-47.64	49.76-39.02	41.61-29.01	36.72-27.38
P/E Ratio	52.62-38.33	59.36-46.00	57.73-49.44	49.83-39.72	31.28-21.17	22.93-17.98	15.30-10.67	15.90-11.85
Average Yield %	1.54	1.58	1.57	1.43	1.54	1.83	1.24	2.08

Address: Chancery House,, 190 Waterside Road,, Hamilton Industrial Park, Leicester, 44060-1834
Telephone: 116-276-8636

Web Site: www.steris.com
Officers: John P. Wareham - Chairman Walter M. Rosebrough - President, Chief Executive Officer

Auditors: Ernst & Young LLP
Investor Contact: 440-392-7245
Transfer Agents: Computershare, Providence, RI

STORE CAPITAL CORP

Exchange	Symbol	Price	52Wk Range	Yield	P/E
NYS	STOR	$26.04 (12/29/2017)	26.37-19.77	4.76	29.26

*7 Year Price Score N/A *NYSE Composite Index=100 *12 Month Price Score 100.30

Interim Earnings (Per Share)

Qtr.	Mar	Jun	Sep	Dec
2014	0.15	0.15	0.13	0.19
2015	0.15	0.17	0.18	0.18
2016	0.18	0.21	0.24	0.20
2017	0.19	0.35	0.15	...

Interim Dividends (Per Share)

Amt	Decl	Ex	Rec	Pay
0.29Q	03/15/2017	03/29/2017	03/31/2017	04/17/2017
0.29Q	06/13/2017	06/28/2017	06/30/2017	07/17/2017
0.31Q	09/12/2017	09/28/2017	09/29/2017	10/16/2017
0.31Q	12/15/2017	12/28/2017	12/29/2017	01/16/2018

Indicated Div: $1.24

Valuation Analysis

		Institutional Holding	
Forecast EPS	$0.91	No of Institutions	
	(01/11/2018)	277	
Market Cap	$4.9 Billion	Shares	
Book Value	$3.1 Billion	195,319,696	
Price/Book	1.60	% Held	
Price/Sales	11.38	N/A	

Business Summary: REITs (MIC: 5.3.1 SIC: 6798 NAIC: 525930)

STORE Capital is an internally managed net-lease real estate investment trust that is engaged in the acquisition, investment and management of Single Tenant Operational Real Estate. As of Dec 31 2016, Co. owned a portfolio that consisted of investments in 1,660 property locations operated by 360 customers across 48 states. Co.'s customers operate across a range of industries within the service, retail and manufacturing sectors, with restaurants, early childhood education centers, movie theaters, health clubs and furniture stores representing the key industries in Co.'s portfolio. From time to time, Co. also provides mortgage financing to its customers.

Recent Developments: For the quarter ended Sep 30 2017, net income decreased 21.4% to US$28.6 million from US$36.3 million in the year-earlier quarter. Revenues were US$110.5 million, up 14.0% from US$97.0 million the year before. Revenues from property income rose 13.4% to US$104.0 million from US$91.8 million in the corresponding quarter a year earlier.

Prospects: Our evaluation of STORE Capital Corp as of Jan. 14, 2018 is the result of our systematic analysis on three basic characteristics: earnings strength, relative valuation, and recent stock price movement. The company has managed to produce a neutral trend in earnings per share over the past 5 quarters. However, while recent estimates for the company have been mixed, STOR has posted results that fell short of analysts expectations. Based on operating earnings yield, the company is about fairly valued when compared to all of the companies in our coverage universe. Share price changes over the past year indicates that STOR will perform well over the near term.

Financial Data
(US$ in Thousands)

	9 Mos	6 Mos	3 Mos	12/31/2016	12/31/2015	12/31/2014	12/31/2013	12/31/2012
Earnings Per Share	0.89	0.98	0.84	0.82	0.68	0.61	0.52	0.30
Cash Flow Per Share	1.54	1.60	1.64	1.65	1.52	1.38	1.10	0.82
Tang Book Value Per Share	16.28	16.43	15.97	15.58	14.62	13.74	12.29	11.76
Dividends Per Share	1.180	1.160	1.140	1.120	1.040	0.114	...	...
Dividend Payout %	132.58	118.37	135.71	136.59	152.94	18.67	...	...
Income Statement								
Total Revenue	332,723	222,179	107,971	376,343	284,762	190,441	108,904	40,610
EBITDA	191,531	131,787	61,320	349,550	264,361	177,110	97,991	32,458
Depn & Amortn	14,007	7,958	3,883	133,907	99,857	66,465	36,338	13,619
Income Before Taxes	85,586	63,270	27,797	110,463	82,722	42,686	22,473	7,367
Income Taxes	334	253	106	358	274	180	155	70
Net Income	121,030	92,450	31,390	123,325	83,770	48,139	26,313	8,176
Average Shares	190,043	172,661	160,810	149,124	122,207	78,454	49,893	27,338
Balance Sheet								
Current Assets	34,986	468,510	103,301	54,200	67,115	136,313	61,814	64,752
Total Assets	5,614,717	5,736,390	5,372,229	4,941,668	3,911,388	2,913,612	1,786,100	979,833
Current Liabilities	127,792	101,720	106,886	94,209	246,670	43,609	20,481	175,477
Long-Term Obligations	2,393,719	2,513,215	2,528,364	2,303,671	1,597,505	1,284,151	991,577	306,581
Total Liabilities	2,521,511	2,614,935	2,635,250	2,458,413	1,851,595	1,330,928	1,012,186	482,919
Stockholders' Equity	3,093,206	3,121,455	2,736,979	2,483,255	2,059,793	1,582,684	773,914	496,914
Shares Outstanding	190,013	190,017	171,378	159,341	140,858	115,212	62,966	42,247
Statistical Record								
Return on Assets %	2.98	3.13	2.73	2.78	2.45	2.05	1.90	...
Return on Equity %	5.56	5.89	5.43	5.41	4.60	4.09	4.14	...
EBITDA Margin %	57.56	59.32	56.79	92.88	92.84	93.00	89.98	79.93
Net Margin %	36.38	41.61	29.07	32.77	29.42	25.28	24.16	20.13
Asset Turnover	0.08	0.08	0.08	0.08	0.08	0.08	0.08	...
Current Ratio	0.27	4.61	0.97	0.58	0.27	3.13	3.02	0.37
Debt to Equity	0.77	0.81	0.92	0.93	0.78	0.81	1.28	0.62
Price Range	29.47-19.77	31.19-19.77	31.19-22.48	31.19-22.38	23.77-19.79	22.04-19.50	...	...
P/E Ratio	33.11-22.21	31.83-20.17	37.13-26.76	38.04-27.29	34.96-29.10	36.13-31.97	...	...
Average Yield %	4.89	4.55	4.29	4.21	4.77	0.55	...	...

Address: 8377 East Hartford Drive, Suite 100, Scottsdale, AZ 85255
Telephone: 480-256-1100

Web Site: www.storecapital.com
Officers: Morton H. Fleischer - Chairman Christopher H. Volk - President, Chief Executive Officer

Auditors: Ernst & Young LLP
Transfer Agents: American Stock Transfer & Trust Company, LLC

667

STRYKER CORP

Exchange	Symbol	Price	52Wk Range	Yield	P/E	Div Achiever
NYS	SYK	$154.84 (12/29/2017)	159.74-117.75	1.21	33.09	24 Years

*7 Year Price Score 126.52 *NYSE Composite Index=100 *12 Month Price Score 104.03

Interim Earnings (Per Share)

Qtr.	Mar	Jun	Sep	Dec
2014	0.18	0.33	0.16	0.67
2015	0.58	1.03	0.79	1.38
2016	1.07	1.00	0.94	1.34
2017	1.17	1.03	1.14	...

Interim Dividends (Per Share)

Amt	Decl	Ex	Rec	Pay
0.425Q	02/08/2017	03/29/2017	03/31/2017	04/28/2017
0.425Q	05/02/2017	06/28/2017	06/30/2017	07/31/2017
0.425Q	08/01/2017	09/28/2017	09/29/2017	10/31/2017
0.47Q	12/06/2017	12/28/2017	12/29/2017	01/31/2018

Indicated Div: $1.88

Valuation Analysis / **Institutional Holding**

Forecast EPS	$6.48 (01/18/2018)	No of Institutions 1433
Market Cap	$57.9 Billion	Shares
Book Value	$10.4 Billion	338,990,336
Price/Book	5.55	% Held
Price/Sales	4.77	69.99

Business Summary: Medical Instruments & Equipment (MIC: 4.3.1 SIC: 3841 NAIC: 339112)

Stryker is a medical technology company. Co. segregates its operations into three reportable business segments, Orthopaedics, MedSurg, and Neurotechnology and Spine. The Orthopaedics segment includes reconstructive (hip and knee) and trauma implant systems and other related products. The MedSurg segment includes surgical equipment and surgical navigation systems; endoscopic and communications systems; patient handling, emergency medical equipment, intensive care disposable products and reprocessed and remanufactured medical devices and other related products. The Neurotechnology and Spine segment includes neurovascular products, spinal implant systems and other related products.

Recent Developments: For the quarter ended Sep 30 2017, net income increased 22.3% to US$434.0 million from US$355.0 million in the year-earlier quarter. Revenues were US$3.01 billion, up 6.1% from US$2.83 billion the year before. Operating income was US$523.0 million versus US$486.0 million in the prior-year quarter, an increase of 7.6%. Direct operating expenses rose 6.7% to US$1.02 billion from US$960.0 million in the comparable period the year before. Indirect operating expenses increased 5.2% to US$1.46 billion from US$1.39 billion in the equivalent prior-year period.

Prospects: Our evaluation of Stryker Corp. as of Jan. 14, 2018 is the result of our systematic analysis on three basic characteristics: earnings strength, relative valuation, and recent stock price movement. The company has managed to produce a neutral trend in earnings per share over the past 5 quarters and while recent estimates for the company have been raised by analysts, SYK has posted better than expected results. Based on operating earnings yield, the company is about fairly valued when compared to all of the companies in our coverage universe. Share price changes over the past year indicates that SYK will perform well over the near term.

Financial Data

(US$ in Thousands)	9 Mos	6 Mos	3 Mos	12/31/2016	12/31/2015	12/31/2014	12/31/2013	12/31/2012
Earnings Per Share	4.68	4.48	4.45	4.35	3.78	1.34	2.63	3.39
Cash Flow Per Share	4.08	5.19	4.71	4.83	2.39	4.71	4.98	4.34
Tang Book Value Per Share	N.M.	0.49	N.M.	N.M.	6.92	6.33	8.50	13.24
Dividends Per Share	1.700	1.655	1.610	1.565	1.415	1.260	1.100	0.902
Dividend Payout %	36.32	36.94	36.18	35.98	37.43	94.03	41.83	26.62
Income Statement								
Total Revenue	8,973,000	5,967,000	2,955,000	11,325,000	9,946,000	9,675,000	9,021,000	8,657,000
EBITDA	1,887,000	1,253,000	649,000	2,467,000	2,132,000	1,538,000	1,519,000	1,982,000
Depn & Amortn	473,000	310,000	150,000	546,000	397,000	378,000	307,000	277,000
Income Before Taxes	1,414,000	943,000	499,000	1,921,000	1,735,000	1,160,000	1,212,000	1,705,000
Income Taxes	145,000	108,000	55,000	274,000	296,000	645,000	206,000	407,000
Net Income	1,269,000	835,000	444,000	1,647,000	1,439,000	515,000	1,006,000	1,298,000
Average Shares	380,200	379,800	379,300	378,500	380,900	382,800	382,100	383,000
Balance Sheet								
Current Assets	7,710,000	8,478,000	7,889,000	7,861,000	7,944,000	9,673,000	8,335,000	8,148,000
Total Assets	21,485,000	21,292,000	20,517,000	20,435,000	16,247,000	17,713,000	15,743,000	13,206,000
Current Liabilities	3,258,000	3,552,000	2,554,000	3,148,000	3,503,000	4,464,000	2,657,000	1,876,000
Long-Term Obligations	6,593,000	6,592,000	7,184,000	6,686,000	3,253,000	3,246,000	2,739,000	1,746,000
Total Liabilities	11,060,000	11,257,000	10,813,000	10,885,000	7,736,000	9,118,000	6,696,000	4,609,000
Stockholders' Equity	10,425,000	10,035,000	9,704,000	9,550,000	8,511,000	8,595,000	9,047,000	8,597,000
Shares Outstanding	374,000	374,063	374,000	375,000	373,000	378,000	378,000	380,000
Statistical Record								
Return on Assets %	8.54	8.13	8.41	8.96	8.47	3.08	6.95	10.11
Return on Equity %	18.01	17.77	18.25	18.19	16.82	5.84	11.40	15.90
EBITDA Margin %	21.03	21.00	21.96	21.78	21.44	15.90	16.84	22.89
Net Margin %	14.14	13.99	15.03	14.54	14.47	5.32	11.15	14.99
Asset Turnover	0.58	0.57	0.59	0.62	0.59	0.58	0.62	0.67
Current Ratio	2.37	2.39	3.09	2.50	2.27	2.17	3.14	4.34
Debt to Equity	0.63	0.66	0.74	0.70	0.38	0.38	0.30	0.20
Price Range	147.87-106.68	144.70-106.68	132.83-106.68	122.82-87.53	104.53-90.07	96.61-74.63	75.39-54.82	56.57-49.84
P/E Ratio	31.60-22.79	32.30-23.81	29.85-23.97	28.23-20.12	27.65-23.83	72.10-55.69	28.67-20.84	16.69-14.70
Average Yield %	1.30	1.34	1.37	1.42	1.48	1.52	1.62	1.68

Address: 2825 Airview Boulevard, Kalamazoo, MI 49002 **Telephone:** 269-385-2600 **Fax:** 269-385-1062	**Web Site:** www.stryker.com **Officers:** Kevin A. Lobo - Chairman, President, Chief Executive Officer Katherine Ann Owen - Vice President	**Auditors:** Ernst & Young LLP **Investor Contact:** 269-385-2600 **Transfer Agents:** American Stock Transfer & Trust Company, LLC, New York, NY

SUN COMMUNITIES INC

Exchange	Symbol	Price	52Wk Range	Yield	P/E
NYS	SUI	$92.78 (12/29/2017)	95.60-76.13	2.89	128.86

*7 Year Price Score 117.78 *NYSE Composite Index=100 *12 Month Price Score 101.68

Interim Earnings (Per Share)

Qtr.	Mar	Jun	Sep	Dec
2014	0.21	0.12	0.54	(0.35)
2015	0.13	0.23	0.54	1.62
2016	0.14	(0.12)	0.27	(0.04)
2017	0.29	0.16	0.31	...

Interim Dividends (Per Share)

Amt	Decl	Ex	Rec	Pay
0.67Q	03/03/2017	03/29/2017	03/31/2017	04/17/2017
0.67Q	05/22/2017	06/28/2017	06/30/2017	07/17/2017
0.67Q	09/05/2017	09/28/2017	09/29/2017	10/16/2017
0.67Q	12/11/2017	12/28/2017	12/29/2017	01/16/2018

Indicated Div: $2.68

Valuation Analysis

Forecast EPS	$0.95 (01/11/2018)
Market Cap	$7.4 Billion
Book Value	$2.7 Billion
Price/Book	2.69
Price/Sales	7.67

Institutional Holding

No of Institutions	361
Shares	87,745,016
% Held	96.47

TRADING VOLUME (thousand shares)

Business Summary: REITs (MIC: 5.3.1 SIC: 6798 NAIC: 525930)

Sun Communities is a self-administered and self-managed real estate investment trust. Co. is in the business of acquiring, operating, developing and expanding manufactured housing and recreational vehicle (RV) communities. Co. leases individual parcels of land with utility access for placement of manufactured homes and RVs to its customers. Co., through its subsidiary, Sun Home Services, Inc. (SHS), is engaged in the marketing, selling, and leasing of new and pre-owned homes to residents in Co.'s communities. At Dec 31 2016, Co. owned, operated or had an interest in a portfolio of 341 properties in 29 states and Ontario, Canada, while SHS had 10,733 occupied leased homes in its portfolio.

Recent Developments: For the quarter ended Sep 30 2017, net income increased 24.7% to US$29.0 million from US$23.2 million in the year-earlier quarter. Revenues were US$268.2 million, up 7.4% from US$249.7 million the year before. Revenues from property income rose 7.5% to US$211.0 million from US$196.4 million in the corresponding quarter a year earlier.

Prospects: Our evaluation of Sun Communities Inc. as of Jan. 14, 2018 is the result of our systematic analysis on three basic characteristics: earnings strength, relative valuation, and recent stock price movement. The company has managed to produce a neutral trend in earnings per share over the past 5 quarters. Because the company lacks sufficient analyst estimate data, we place greater weight on the historical EPS trend as the measure of earnings strength. Based on operating earnings yield, the company is overvalued when compared to all of the companies in our coverage universe. Share price changes over the past year indicates that SUI will perform very well over the near term.

Financial Data

(US$ in Thousands)	9 Mos	6 Mos	3 Mos	12/31/2016	12/31/2015	12/31/2014	12/31/2013	12/31/2012
Earnings Per Share	0.72	0.68	0.40	0.26	2.52	0.54	0.31	0.18
Cash Flow Per Share	3.47	3.52	3.55	3.61	3.39	3.23	3.30	3.19
Tang Book Value Per Share	34.53	34.62	32.01	32.27	26.35	18.36	10.53	6.47
Dividends Per Share	2.660	2.640	2.620	2.600	2.600	2.600	2.520	2.520
Dividend Payout %	369.44	388.24	655.00	1,000.00	103.17	481.48	812.90	1,400.00
Income Statement								
Total Revenue	740,544	472,299	234,400	833,778	674,731	471,675	415,222	339,616
EBITDA	358,710	232,764	120,295	154,169	435,978	241,255	202,632	163,630
Depn & Amortn	189,719	125,487	62,766	600	160,969	132,059	107,923	88,106
Income Before Taxes	70,865	42,026	25,423	31,254	164,131	32,215	18,132	4,344
Income Taxes	(612)	(493)	(122)	283	1,158	219	234	249
Net Income	67,298	40,116	24,457	31,321	160,419	31,444	19,430	8,313
Average Shares	78,808	75,154	73,120	66,321	53,702	41,805	34,747	27,272
Balance Sheet								
Current Assets	308,949	377,727	133,254	8,164	45,086	83,459	4,753	29,508
Total Assets	6,157,836	6,178,713	5,902,447	5,870,776	4,190,551	2,937,692	1,999,236	1,754,117
Current Liabilities	3,014,044	3,028,598	2,969,078	100,095	25,000	5,794	181,383	29,781
Long-Term Obligations	45,903	46,338	224,231	3,009,947	2,320,049	1,826,293	1,311,437	1,423,720
Total Liabilities	3,418,530	3,444,234	3,542,088	3,508,221	2,651,944	2,045,953	1,618,729	1,561,595
Stockholders' Equity	2,739,306	2,734,479	2,360,359	2,362,555	1,538,607	891,739	380,507	192,522
Shares Outstanding	79,341	78,987	73,739	73,206	58,395	48,573	36,140	29,755
Statistical Record								
Return on Assets %	1.15	1.07	0.85	0.62	4.50	1.27	1.04	0.53
Return on Equity %	2.69	2.66	2.08	1.60	13.20	4.94	6.78	25.16
EBITDA Margin %	48.44	49.28	51.32	18.49	64.62	51.15	48.80	48.18
Net Margin %	9.09	8.49	10.43	3.76	23.78	6.67	4.68	2.45
Asset Turnover	0.16	0.16	0.17	0.17	0.19	0.19	0.22	0.22
Current Ratio	0.10	0.12	0.04	0.08	1.80	14.40	0.03	0.99
Debt to Equity	0.02	0.02	0.09	1.27	1.51	2.05	3.45	7.40
Price Range	91.14-70.51	91.05-70.51	83.52-67.21	81.55-63.81	71.27-60.46	63.97-41.98	56.89-39.87	47.29-36.16
P/E Ratio	126.58-97.93	133.90-103.69	208.80-168.02	313.65-245.42	28.28-23.99	118.46-77.74	183.52-128.61	262.72-200.89
Average Yield %	3.24	3.32	3.47	3.58	3.93	5.15	5.45	5.94

Address: 27777 Franklin Rd., Suite 200, Southfield, MI 48034 **Telephone:** 248-208-2500	**Web Site:** www.suncommunities.com **Officers:** Gary A. Shiffman - Chairman, President, Chief Executive Officer John B. McLaren - President, Executive Vice President, Chief Operating Officer	**Auditors:** GRANT THORNTON LLP **Investor Contact:** 248-208-2500 **Transfer Agents:** Computershare Trust Company, N.A., Providence, RI

SUNTRUST BANKS, INC.

Exchange	Symbol	Price	52Wk Range	Yield	P/E
NYS	STI	$64.59 (12/29/2017)	66.03-52.30	2.48	16.56

*7 Year Price Score 120.98 *NYSE Composite Index=100 *12 Month Price Score 100.82

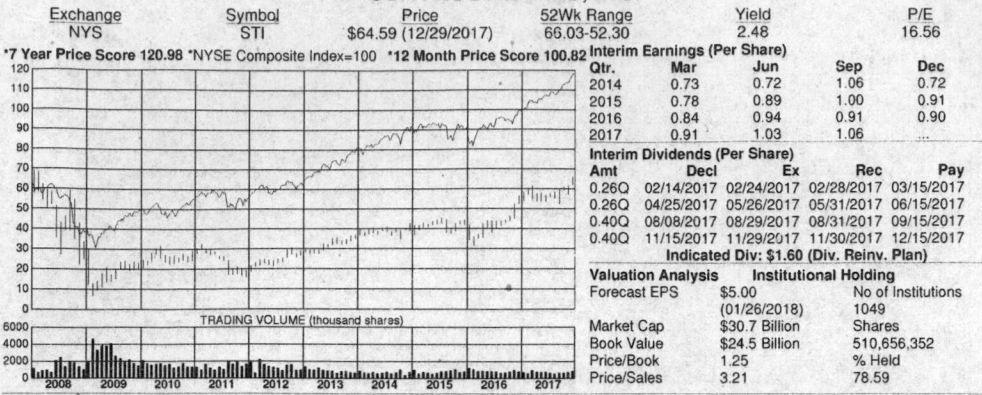

Interim Earnings (Per Share)

Qtr.	Mar	Jun	Sep	Dec
2014	0.73	0.72	1.06	0.72
2015	0.78	0.89	1.00	0.91
2016	0.84	0.94	0.91	0.90
2017	0.91	1.03	1.06	...

Interim Dividends (Per Share)

Amt	Decl	Ex	Rec	Pay
0.26Q	02/14/2017	02/24/2017	02/28/2017	03/15/2017
0.26Q	04/25/2017	05/26/2017	05/31/2017	06/15/2017
0.40Q	08/08/2017	08/29/2017	08/31/2017	09/15/2017
0.40Q	11/15/2017	11/29/2017	11/30/2017	12/15/2017

Indicated Div: $1.60 (Div. Reinv. Plan)

Valuation Analysis

Institutional Holding	
Forecast EPS	$5.00
(01/26/2018)	No of Institutions 1049
Market Cap	$30.7 Billion
Book Value	$24.5 Billion — Shares 510,656,352
Price/Book	1.25 — % Held 78.59
Price/Sales	3.21

TRADING VOLUME (thousand shares)

Business Summary: Banking (MIC: 5.1.1 SIC: 6021 NAIC: 522110)

SunTrust Banks is a financial holding company. Through its subsidiary, SunTrust Bank (the Bank), Co. provides a line of financial services for consumers, businesses, corporations, and institutions, and not-for-profit entities, both through its branches. In addition to deposit, credit, mortgage banking, and trust and investment services provided by the Bank, other subsidiaries of Co. provide asset and wealth management, securities brokerage, and capital market services. Co. operates three business segments: Consumer Banking and Private Wealth Management, Wholesale Banking, and Mortgage Banking. As of Dec 31 2016, Co. had total assets of $205.00 billion and total deposits of $160.00 billion.

Recent Developments: For the quarter ended Sep 30 2017, net income increased 13.4% to US$540.0 million from US$476.0 million in the year-earlier quarter. Net interest income increased 9.3% to US$1.43 billion from US$1.31 billion in the year-earlier quarter. Provision for loan losses was US$120.0 million versus US$97.0 million in the prior-year quarter, an increase of 23.7%. Non-interest income fell 4.8% to US$846.0 million from US$889.0 million, while non-interest expense declined 1.3% to US$1.39 billion.

Prospects: Our evaluation of SunTrust Banks Inc. as of Jan. 21, 2018 is the result of our systematic analysis on three basic characteristics: earnings strength, relative valuation, and recent stock price movement. The company has enjoyed a very positive trend in earnings per share over the past 5 quarters. Because the company lacks sufficient analyst estimate data, we place greater weight on the historical EPS trend as the measure of earnings strength. Based on operating earnings yield, the company is undervalued when compared to all of the companies in our coverage universe. Share price changes over the past year indicates that STI will perform in line with the market over the near term.

Financial Data

(US$ in Thousands)	9 Mos	6 Mos	3 Mos	12/31/2016	12/31/2015	12/31/2014	12/31/2013	12/31/2012
Earnings Per Share	3.90	3.75	3.66	3.60	3.58	3.23	2.41	3.59
Cash Flow Per Share	4.16	4.83	3.40	(1.36)	6.79	(2.24)	7.88	3.75
Tang Book Value Per Share	30.47	30.05	29.22	29.31	28.60	27.12	24.24	24.00
Dividends Per Share	1.180	1.040	1.020	1.000	0.920	0.700	0.350	0.200
Dividend Payout %	30.26	27.73	27.87	27.78	25.70	21.67	14.52	5.57
Income Statement								
Interest Income	4,747,000	3,111,000	1,528,000	5,778,000	5,265,000	5,384,000	5,388,000	5,867,000
Interest Expense	548,000	342,000	162,000	557,000	501,000	544,000	535,000	765,000
Net Interest Income	4,199,000	2,769,000	1,366,000	5,221,000	4,764,000	4,840,000	4,853,000	5,102,000
Provision for Losses	330,000	209,000	119,000	444,000	165,000	342,000	553,000	1,395,000
Non-Interest Income	2,520,000	1,674,000	847,000	3,383,000	3,268,000	3,323,000	3,214,000	5,373,000
Non-Interest Expense	4,243,000	2,853,000	1,465,000	5,468,000	5,160,000	5,543,000	5,880,000	6,307,000
Income Before Taxes	2,146,000	1,381,000	629,000	2,692,000	2,707,000	2,278,000	1,634,000	2,757,000
Income Taxes	606,000	381,000	159,000	805,000	764,000	493,000	273,000	773,000
Net Income	1,533,000	995,000	468,000	1,878,000	1,933,000	1,774,000	1,344,000	1,958,000
Average Shares	483,640	482,913	496,002	503,466	520,586	533,391	539,093	538,061
Balance Sheet								
Net Loans & Leases	145,327,000	145,363,000	143,924,000	145,758,000	136,528,000	134,407,000	127,532,000	122,695,000
Total Assets	208,252,000	207,223,000	205,642,000	204,875,000	190,817,000	190,328,000	175,335,000	173,442,000
Total Deposits	162,737,000	159,873,000	162,853,000	160,398,000	149,830,000	140,567,000	129,759,000	132,316,000
Total Liabilities	183,730,000	182,746,000	182,158,000	181,257,000	167,380,000	167,323,000	153,913,000	152,457,000
Stockholders' Equity	24,522,000	24,477,000	23,484,000	23,618,000	23,437,000	23,005,000	21,422,000	20,985,000
Shares Outstanding	476,001	481,644	485,712	491,188	508,712	524,540	536,097	538,959
Statistical Record								
Return on Assets %	0.97	0.95	0.95	0.95	1.01	0.97	0.77	1.11
Return on Equity %	8.16	7.91	7.99	7.96	8.32	7.99	6.34	9.51
Net Interest Margin %	87.46	88.63	89.40	90.36	90.48	89.90	90.07	86.96
Efficiency Ratio %	56.07	57.59	61.68	59.69	60.47	63.66	68.36	56.11
Loans to Deposits	0.89	0.91	0.88	0.91	0.91	0.96	0.98	0.93
Price Range	61.39-43.77	61.39-39.50	61.39-35.35	56.39-31.36	45.35-36.71	42.69-34.73	36.81-27.12	30.31-18.52
P/E Ratio	15.74-11.22	16.37-10.53	16.77-9.66	15.66-8.71	12.67-10.25	13.22-10.75	15.27-11.25	8.44-5.16
Average Yield %	2.15	2.03	2.14	2.35	2.20	1.81	1.10	0.81

Address: 303 Peachtree Street, N.E., Atlanta, GA 30308 **Telephone:** 800-786-8787	**Web Site:** www.suntrust.com **Officers:** William H. Rogers - Chairman, President, Chief Executive Officer Jorge Arrieta - Executive Vice President, General Auditor	**Auditors:** Ernst & Young LLP **Investor Contact:** 877-930-8971 **Transfer Agents:** Computershare, Providence, RI

SUPERIOR ENERGY SERVICES, INC.

Exchange	Symbol	Price	52Wk Range	Yield	P/E
NYS	SPN	$9.63 (12/29/2017)	19.03-7.89	N/A	N/A

*7 Year Price Score 41.03   *NYSE Composite Index=100   *12 Month Price Score 72.60

Interim Earnings (Per Share)

Qtr.	Mar	Jun	Sep	Dec
2014	0.23	0.47	0.51	0.44
2015	(0.07)	(5.22)	(5.45)	(1.57)
2016	(0.57)	(3.11)	(0.78)	(1.39)
2017	(0.60)	(0.42)	(0.39)	...

Interim Dividends (Per Share)

Dividend Payment Suspended

Valuation Analysis   Institutional Holding

Forecast EPS	$-1.64	No of Institutions
	(01/26/2018)	435
Market Cap	$1.5 Billion	Shares
Book Value	$1.1 Billion	195,776,272
Price/Book	1.32	% Held
Price/Sales	0.85	95.04

TRADING VOLUME (thousand shares)

Business Summary: Equipment & Services (MIC: 9.1.3 SIC: 1389 NAIC: 213112)

Superior Energy Services provide a range of services and products to the energy industry. Co. serves major, national and independent oil and natural gas exploration and production companies. Co. reports its operating results in four business segments: Drilling Products and Services, which includes downhole drilling tools and surface rentals; Onshore Completion and Workover Services, which include pressure pumping, fluid handling and workover and maintenance services; Production Services, which include intervention services; and Technical Solutions, which include well containment systems, completion tools and services and end-of-life services.

Recent Developments: For the quarter ended Sep 30 2017, loss from continuing operations was US$57.2 million compared with a loss of US$113.9 million in the year-earlier quarter. Net loss amounted to US$59.0 million versus a net loss of US$118.0 million in the year-earlier quarter. Revenues were US$506.0 million, up 55.1% from US$326.2 million the year before. Operating loss was US$55.3 million versus a loss of US$142.0 million in the prior-year quarter. Direct operating expenses rose 42.7% to US$368.3 million from US$258.2 million in the comparable period the year before. Indirect operating expenses decreased 8.1% to US$193.1 million from US$210.1 million in the equivalent prior-year period.

Prospects: Our evaluation of Superior Energy Services Inc. as of Jan. 21, 2018 is the result of our systematic analysis on three basic characteristics: earnings strength, relative valuation, and recent stock price movement. The company has enjoyed a very positive trend in earnings per share over the past 5 quarters. Because the company lacks sufficient analyst estimate data, we place greater weight on the historical EPS trend as the measure of earnings strength. Based on operating earnings yield, the company is overvalued when compared to all of the companies in our coverage universe. Share price changes over the past year indicates that SPN will perform very poorly over the near term.

Financial Data

(US$ in Thousands)	9 Mos	6 Mos	3 Mos	12/31/2016	12/31/2015	12/31/2014	12/31/2013	12/31/2012
Earnings Per Share	(2.80)	(3.19)	(5.88)	(5.85)	(12.33)	1.65	(0.70)	2.42
Cash Flow Per Share	(0.20)	(0.13)	(0.29)	0.40	4.20	6.66	5.61	6.91
Tang Book Value Per Share	2.01	2.33	2.67	3.29	7.10	10.76	10.51	10.76
Dividends Per Share	...	...	...	0.080	0.320	0.320	0.080	...
Dividend Payout %	...	...	...	...	...	19.39	...	...
Income Statement								
Total Revenue	1,377,033	871,004	400,936	1,450,047	2,774,565	4,556,622	4,611,824	4,568,068
EBITDA	95,963	43,508	4,106	(520,688)	(1,378,365)	1,159,523	625,391	1,185,081
Depn & Amortn	331,151	222,400	114,281	486,900	584,100	620,600	593,000	480,000
Income Before Taxes	(311,867)	(226,475)	(134,425)	(1,100,341)	(2,059,783)	442,189	(71,585)	590,569
Income Taxes	(102,978)	(74,775)	(44,764)	(267,001)	(252,020)	161,399	39,833	225,020
Net Income	(214,514)	(155,465)	(91,659)	(886,899)	(1,854,718)	257,817	(111,418)	365,935
Average Shares	153,082	152,857	152,701	151,558	150,461	156,726	159,206	151,106
Balance Sheet								
Current Assets	797,668	788,014	812,863	781,551	1,295,125	1,728,811	1,476,429	1,460,357
Total Assets	3,211,131	3,285,930	3,378,711	3,470,255	4,914,244	7,377,389	7,411,307	7,802,886
Current Liabilities	400,984	380,572	368,788	344,534	448,576	712,047	639,400	772,065
Long-Term Obligations	1,281,714	1,287,156	1,286,210	1,284,600	1,588,263	1,627,842	1,646,535	1,814,500
Total Liabilities	2,096,376	2,122,461	2,166,013	2,166,335	2,703,432	3,297,651	3,279,863	3,571,807
Stockholders' Equity	1,114,755	1,163,469	1,212,698	1,303,920	2,210,812	4,079,738	4,131,444	4,231,079
Shares Outstanding	153,083	153,077	152,831	151,861	150,861	149,708	159,158	157,933
Statistical Record								
Return on Assets %	N.M.	N.M.	N.M.	N.M.	N.M.	3.49	N.M.	6.16
Return on Equity %	N.M.	N.M.	N.M.	N.M.	N.M.	6.28	N.M.	12.84
EBITDA Margin %	6.97	5.00	1.02	N.M.	N.M.	25.45	13.56	25.94
Net Margin %	N.M.	N.M.	N.M.	N.M.	N.M.	5.66	N.M.	8.01
Asset Turnover	0.51	0.43	0.35	0.34	0.45	0.62	0.61	0.77
Current Ratio	1.99	2.07	2.20	2.27	2.89	2.43	2.31	1.89
Debt to Equity	1.15	1.11	1.06	0.99	0.72	0.40	0.40	0.43
Price Range	19.03-8.12	19.03-9.37	19.50-12.57	19.50-8.59	26.28-12.59	36.69-17.19	28.86-20.72	30.87-17.89
P/E Ratio	...	...	...	...	...	22.24-10.42	...	12.76-7.39
Average Yield %	...	...	...	0.53	1.70	...	0.31	...

Address: 1001 Louisiana Street, Suite 2900, Houston, TX 77002	**Web Site:** www.superiorenergy.com	**Auditors:** KPMG LLP
Telephone: 713-654-2200	**Officers:** Terence E. Hall - Chairman, President, Chief Executive Officer David D. Dunlap - President, Chief Executive Officer	**Investor Contact:** 281-999-0047
		Transfer Agents: Jones, Walker, LLP

SUPERVALU INC

Exchange	Symbol	Price	52Wk Range	Yield	P/E
NYS	SVU	$21.60 (12/29/2017)	34.37-14.77	N/A	1.35

*7 Year Price Score 42.27 ***NYSE Composite Index=100** ***12 Month Price Score 72.82**

Interim Earnings (Per Share)

Qtr.	Jun	Aug	Nov	Feb
2014-15	1.19	0.77	2.10	1.05

Qtr.	Jun	Sep	Nov	Feb
2015-16	1.61	0.77	0.91	1.33
2016-17	1.19	0.84	(0.70)	15.68

Qtr.	Jun	Aug	Nov	Feb
2017-18	0.28	(0.65)	0.67	...

Interim Dividends (Per Share)

Dividend Payment Suspended

Valuation Analysis		Institutional Holding	
Forecast EPS	$2.47	No of Institutions	
	(01/26/2018)	392	
Market Cap	$820.8 Million	Shares	
Book Value	$400.0 Million	102,799,288	
Price/Book	2.05	% Held	
Price/Sales	N/A	90.27	

TRADING VOLUME (thousand shares)

Business Summary: Retail - Food & Beverage, Drug & Tobacco (MIC: 2.1.2 SIC: 5411 NAIC: 445110)

Supervalu is a public company grocery distributor to wholesale customers across the U.S. Co.'s business is classified by management into two reportable segments: Wholesale, which provides wholesale customers a range of food and non-food products, including national and regional brands, and Co.'s owns extensive lines of private label products; and Retail, which provides a range of nationally advertised brand name and private-label products, including grocery (both perishable and nonperishable), general merchandise, home, health and beauty care, and pharmacy.

Recent Developments: For the quarter ended Sep 9 2017, loss from continuing operations was US$25.0 million compared with income of US$12.0 million in the year-earlier quarter. Net loss amounted to US$25.0 million versus net income of US$32.0 million in the year-earlier quarter. Revenues were US$3.80 billion, up 35.5% from US$2.81 billion the year before. Operating loss was US$7.0 million versus an income of US$58.0 million in the prior-year quarter. Direct operating expenses rose 40.0% to US$3.37 billion from US$2.41 billion in the comparable period the year before. Indirect operating expenses increased 28.7% to US$435.0 million from US$338.0 million in the equivalent prior-year period.

Prospects: Our evaluation of SUPERVALU Inc. as of Jan. 21, 2018 is the result of our systematic analysis on three basic characteristics: earnings strength, relative valuation, and recent stock price movement. The company has managed to produce a neutral trend in earnings per share over the past 5 quarters and while recent estimates for the company have been raised by analysts, SVU has posted better than expected results. Based on operating earnings yield, the company is undervalued when compared to all of the companies in our coverage universe. Share price changes over the past year indicates that SVU will perform in line with the market over the near term.

Financial Data

(US$ in Thousands)	9 Mos	6 Mos	3 Mos	02/25/2017	02/27/2016	02/28/2015	02/22/2014	02/23/2013
Earnings Per Share	15.98	14.61	16.10	17.01	4.62	5.11	4.90	(48.37)
Cash Flow Per Share	...	3.76	6.08	9.56	11.32	10.81	0.52	29.73
Dividends Per Share	...	...	...	...	...	...	...	0.613
Income Statement								
Total Revenue	11,742,000	7,804,000	4,004,000	12,480,000	17,529,000	17,820,000	17,155,000	17,097,000
EBITDA	259,000	172,000	127,000	362,000	702,000	682,000	693,000	176,000
Depn & Amortn	160,000	112,000	60,000	179,000	248,000	258,000	275,000	333,000
Income Before Taxes	(4,000)	(14,000)	24,000	2,000	258,000	181,000	11,000	(426,000)
Income Taxes	(7,000)	1,000	14,000	(20,000)	85,000	58,000	5,000	(163,000)
Net Income	12,000	(14,000)	11,000	650,000	178,000	192,000	182,000	(1,466,000)
Average Shares	38,000	38,000	38,428	38,285	38,285	37,714	36,857	30,285
Balance Sheet								
Current Assets	2,025,000	2,004,000	1,551,000	1,541,000	1,635,000	1,700,000	1,543,000	2,970,000
Total Assets	4,467,000	4,395,000	3,595,000	3,580,000	4,370,000	4,485,000	4,374,000	11,034,000
Current Liabilities	1,634,000	1,657,000	1,242,000	1,229,000	1,572,000	1,533,000	1,491,000	4,350,000
Long-Term Obligations	1,872,000	1,775,000	1,461,000	1,449,000	2,400,000	2,693,000	2,732,000	2,815,000
Total Liabilities	4,067,000	4,025,000	3,205,000	3,204,000	4,811,000	5,131,000	5,112,000	12,449,000
Stockholders' Equity	400,000	370,000	390,000	376,000	(441,000)	(646,000)	(738,000)	(1,415,000)
Shares Outstanding	38,000	38,000	38,428	38,285	37,857	37,142	36,571	30,428
Statistical Record								
Return on Assets %	...	12.77	15.44	16.40	4.03	4.26	2.37	N.M.
Return on Equity %	...	5,081.82	...	...	...	...	...	...
EBITDA Margin %	2.21	2.20	3.17	2.90	4.00	3.83	4.04	1.03
Net Margin %	0.10	N.M.	0.27	5.21	1.02	1.08	1.06	N.M.
Asset Turnover	...	3.13	3.46	3.15	3.97	3.96	2.23	1.49
Current Ratio	1.24	1.21	1.25	1.25	1.04	1.11	1.03	0.68
Debt to Equity	4.68	4.80	3.75	3.85	...	...	...	...
Price Range	35.77-14.77	37.10-19.30	40.04-22.54	41.79-25.69	83.30-28.56	73.01-42.84	58.80-26.32	46.55-12.11
P/E Ratio	2.24-0.92	2.54-1.32	2.49-1.40	2.46-1.51	18.03-6.18	14.29-8.38	12.00-5.37	...
Average Yield %	...	...	...	...	...	...	...	2.30

Address: 11840 Valley View Road, Eden Prairie, MN 55344
Telephone: 952-828-4000

Web Site: www.supervalu.com
Officers: David W. Johnson - Interim Chief Accounting Officer Mark Gross - President, Chief Executive Officer

Auditors: KPMG LLP
Investor Contact: 952-828-4000
Transfer Agents: Wells Fargo Shareowner Services, St. Paul, MN

SYNCHRONY FINANCIAL

Exchange	Symbol	Price	52Wk Range	Yield	P/E
NYS	SYF	$38.61 (12/29/2017)	38.97-26.50	1.55	14.74

*7 Year Price Score N/A   *NYSE Composite Index=100   *12 Month Price Score 104.11

Interim Earnings (Per Share)

Qtr.	Mar	Jun	Sep	Dec
2014	0.00	0.67	0.70	0.62
2015	0.66	0.65	0.69	0.65
2016	0.70	0.58	0.73	0.70
2017	0.61	0.61	0.70	...

Interim Dividends (Per Share)

Amt	Decl	Ex	Rec	Pay
0.13Q	01/25/2017	02/02/2017	02/06/2017	02/16/2017
0.13Q	04/26/2017	05/04/2017	05/08/2017	05/18/2017
0.15Q	07/26/2017	08/03/2017	08/07/2017	08/17/2017
0.15Q	10/25/2017	11/03/2017	11/06/2017	11/16/2017

Indicated Div: $0.60

Valuation Analysis

Forecast EPS	$2.56 (01/18/2018)
Market Cap	$30.2 Billion
Book Value	$14.4 Billion
Price/Book	2.10
Price/Sales	1.85

Institutional Holding

No of Institutions	699
Shares	750,359,552
% Held	N/A

Business Summary: Banking (MIC: 5.1.1 SIC: 6141 NAIC: 522291)

Synchrony Financial is a savings and loan holding company. Co. provides a range of credit products through programs it has established with a group of national and regional retailers, local merchants, manufacturers, buying groups, industry associations and healthcare service providers. Co. provides its credit products primarily through its wholly-owned subsidiary, Synchrony Bank (the Bank). Through the Bank, Co. provides deposit products insured by the Federal Deposit Insurance Corporation, including certificates of deposit, individual retirement accounts, money market accounts and savings accounts. At Dec 31 2016, Co. had total assets of $90.21 billion and total deposits of $52.06 billion.

Recent Developments: For the quarter ended Sep 30 2017, net income decreased 8.1% to US$555.0 million from US$604.0 million in the year-earlier quarter. Net interest income increased 11.3% to US$3.88 billion from US$3.48 billion in the year-earlier quarter. Provision for loan losses was US$1.31 billion versus US$986.0 million in the prior-year quarter, an increase of 32.9%. Non-interest income fell 9.5% to US$76.0 million from US$84.0 million, while non-interest expense advanced 9.1% to US$1.76 billion.

Prospects: Our evaluation of Synchrony Financial as of Jan. 14, 2018 is the result of our systematic analysis on three basic characteristics: earnings strength, relative valuation, and recent stock price movement. The company has managed to produce a neutral trend in earnings per share over the past 5 quarters. However, while recent estimates for the company have been mixed, SYF has posted better than expected results. Based on operating earnings yield, the company is undervalued when compared to all of the companies in our coverage universe. Share price changes over the past year indicates that SYF will perform poorly over the near term.

Financial Data
(US$ in Millions)

	9 Mos	6 Mos	3 Mos	12/31/2016	12/31/2015	12/31/2014	12/31/2013	12/31/2012
Earnings Per Share	2.62	2.65	2.62	2.71	2.65	2.78	...	...
Cash Flow Per Share	10.77	9.17	8.70	8.21	7.42	7.05	...	...
Tang Book Value Per Share	16.15	15.78	15.47	15.34	13.14	10.81	...	...
Dividends Per Share	0.540	0.520	0.390	0.260	...	...	...	...
Dividend Payout %	20.61	19.62	14.89	9.59	...	...	...	...
Income Statement								
Total Revenue	12,342	8,033	4,006	15,122	13,620	12,727	11,813	10,793
Income Before Taxes	2,449	1,570	782	3,570	3,531	3,386	3,142	3,376
Income Taxes	899	575	283	1,319	1,317	1,277	1,163	1,257
Net Income	1,550	995	499	2,251	2,214	2,109	1,979	2,119
Average Shares	790	807	817	831	835	757	...	...
Balance Sheet								
Total Assets	92,548	91,140	89,050	90,207	84,135	75,707	59,085	53,462
Total Liabilities	78,146	76,808	74,687	76,011	71,531	65,229	53,125	48,880
Stockholders' Equity	14,402	14,332	14,363	14,196	12,604	10,478	5,960	4,582
Shares Outstanding	782	795	810	817	833	833	...	...
Statistical Record								
Return on Assets %	2.37	2.51	2.54	2.58	2.77	3.13	3.52	...
Return on Equity %	14.98	15.51	15.73	16.75	19.18	25.66	37.55	...
Net Margin %	12.56	12.39	12.46	14.89	16.26	16.57	16.75	19.63
Asset Turnover	0.18	0.18	0.18	0.17	0.17	0.19	0.21	...
Price Range	37.93-26.37	37.93-25.12	37.93-23.36	37.26-23.36	35.99-28.52	30.50-22.93	...	...
P/E Ratio	14.48-10.06	14.31-9.48	14.48-8.92	13.75-8.62	13.58-10.76	10.97-8.25	...	...
Average Yield %	1.70	1.67	1.26	0.89	...		...	...

Address: 777 Long Ridge Road, Stamford, CT 06902 **Telephone:** 203-585-2400	**Web Site:** www.synchronyfinancial.com **Officers:** Margaret M. Keane - President, Chief Executive Officer Brian D. Doubles - Executive Vice President, Chief Financial Officer, Treasurer, Division Officer	**Auditors:** KPMG LLP **Transfer Agents:** Computershare Trust Company, N.A.

SYNNEX CORP

Exchange	Symbol	Price	52Wk Range	Yield	P/E
NYS	SNX	$135.95 (12/29/2017)	137.33-103.37	1.03	18.45

*7 Year Price Score 137.87 *NYSE Composite Index=100 *12 Month Price Score 104.31

TRADING VOLUME (thousand shares)

Interim Earnings (Per Share)

Qtr.	Feb	May	Aug	Nov
2013-14	1.01	1.01	1.15	1.41
2014-15	1.16	1.30	1.21	1.56
2015-16	1.17	1.11	1.47	2.13
2016-17	1.54	1.83	1.87	...

Interim Dividends (Per Share)

Amt	Decl	Ex	Rec	Pay
0.25Q	03/27/2017	04/11/2017	04/14/2017	04/28/2017
0.25Q	06/22/2017	07/12/2017	07/14/2017	07/28/2017
0.30Q	09/25/2017	10/12/2017	10/13/2017	10/27/2017
0.35Q	01/09/2018	01/18/2018	01/19/2018	01/31/2018

Indicated Div: $1.40

Valuation Analysis

		Institutional Holding	
Forecast EPS	$10.41	No of Institutions	
	(01/18/2018)	321	
Market Cap	$5.4 Billion	Shares	
Book Value	$2.2 Billion	34,665,392	
Price/Book	2.43	% Held	
Price/Sales	0.34	74.40	

Business Summary: IT Services (MIC: 6.3.1 SIC: 5045 NAIC: 334119)

Synnex is a business process services company, providing a range of distribution, logistics and integration services for the technology industry and providing outsourced services focused on customer engagement strategy to a range of enterprises. Co. has two segments: Technology Solutions, which distributes a range of information technology systems and products and also provides systems design and integration solutions; and Concentrix, which provides a portfolio of strategic solutions and end-to-end global business outsourcing services focused on customer engagement strategy, process optimization, technology innovation, front and back-office automation and business transformation to clients.

Recent Developments: For the quarter ended Aug 31 2017, net income increased 28.0% to US$75.2 million from US$58.7 million in the year-earlier quarter. Revenues were US$4.28 billion, up 16.5% from US$3.67 billion the year before. Operating income was US$122.2 million versus US$98.0 million in the prior-year quarter, an increase of 24.7%. Direct operating expenses rose 16.7% to US$3.90 billion from US$3.34 billion in the comparable period the year before. Indirect operating expenses increased 10.9% to US$252.7 million from US$227.9 million in the equivalent prior-year period.

Prospects: Our evaluation of Synnex Corp. as of Jan. 14, 2018 is the result of our systematic analysis on three basic characteristics: earnings strength, relative valuation, and recent stock price movement. The company has generated a negative trend in earnings per share over the past 5 quarters and while recent estimates for the company have been raised by analysts, SNX has posted better than expected results. Based on operating earnings yield, the company is undervalued when compared to all of the companies in our coverage universe. Share price changes over the past year indicates that SNX will perform in line with the market over the near term.

Financial Data

(US$ in Thousands)	9 Mos	6 Mos	3 Mos	11/30/2016	11/30/2015	11/30/2014	11/30/2013	11/30/2012
Earnings Per Share	7.37	6.97	6.25	5.88	5.24	4.57	3.06	3.99
Cash Flow Per Share	(0.72)	(2.62)	(0.06)	8.29	16.48	(6.10)	0.97	6.62
Tang Book Value Per Share	35.39	34.49	32.10	30.17	34.04	29.51	32.22	30.06
Dividends Per Share	1.000	0.950	0.900	0.850	0.575	0.125	...	...
Dividend Payout %	13.57	13.63	14.40	14.46	10.97	2.74	...	...
Income Statement								
Total Revenue	11,733,823	7,457,137	3,520,869	14,061,837	13,338,397	13,839,590	10,845,164	10,285,507
EBITDA	409,488	265,233	120,896	450,860	457,001	401,168	279,629	284,113
Depn & Amortn	59,058	38,873	19,460	65,803	103,510	91,699	24,462	24,630
Income Before Taxes	323,532	209,216	93,254	356,064	327,195	284,282	238,052	236,553
Income Taxes	113,432	74,279	31,465	121,059	118,588	104,132	85,730	84,050
Net Income	210,100	134,937	61,789	234,946	208,525	180,034	152,237	151,376
Average Shares	39,748	39,711	39,705	39,530	39,352	38,845	37,800	37,908
Balance Sheet								
Current Assets	4,453,933	4,325,509	3,896,996	4,045,109	3,649,781	3,899,989	2,931,733	2,580,461
Total Assets	5,739,360	5,528,922	5,107,768	5,223,263	4,444,147	4,713,042	3,325,889	2,963,262
Current Liabilities	2,773,362	2,665,243	2,315,999	2,477,828	1,918,157	2,721,729	1,789,378	1,494,707
Long-Term Obligations	564,085	579,032	590,399	603,229	638,798	264,246	65,405	81,152
Total Liabilities	3,522,489	3,412,712	3,069,549	3,247,487	2,644,766	3,059,484	1,914,667	1,644,239
Stockholders' Equity	2,216,871	2,116,210	2,038,219	1,975,776	1,799,381	1,653,558	1,411,222	1,319,023
Shares Outstanding	39,576	39,544	39,519	39,477	39,189	38,924	37,210	36,628
Statistical Record								
Return on Assets %	5.59	5.59	5.39	4.85	4.55	4.48	4.84	5.21
Return on Equity %	14.26	13.98	12.97	12.41	12.08	11.75	11.15	12.19
EBITDA Margin %	3.49	3.56	3.43	3.21	3.43	2.90	2.58	2.76
Net Margin %	1.79	1.81	1.75	1.67	1.56	1.30	1.40	1.47
Asset Turnover	2.96	3.01	3.11	2.90	2.91	3.44	3.45	3.54
Current Ratio	1.61	1.62	1.68	1.63	1.90	1.43	1.64	1.73
Debt to Equity	0.25	0.27	0.29	0.31	0.36	0.16	0.05	0.06
Price Range	128.37-100.66	127.70-90.32	127.70-78.16	118.71-78.16	96.10-68.43	76.94-52.36	66.42-32.60	43.89-28.42
P/E Ratio	17.42-13.66	18.32-12.96	20.43-12.51	20.19-13.29	18.34-13.06	16.84-11.46	21.71-10.65	11.00-7.12
Average Yield %	0.87	0.87	0.87	0.89	0.72	0.19	...	...

Address: 44201 Nobel Drive, Fremont, CA 94538
Telephone: 510-656-3333

Web Site: www.synnex.com
Officers: Dwight A. Steffensen - Chairman Kevin M. Murai - President, Chief Executive Officer, Co-Chief Executive Officer

Auditors: KPMG LLP
Transfer Agents: Computershare Trust Company, Providence, RI

SYNOVUS FINANCIAL CORP.

Exchange	Symbol	Price	52Wk Range	Yield	P/E
NYS	SNV	$47.94 (12/29/2017)	50.13-39.11	1.25	19.41

*7 Year Price Score 133.68 *NYSE Composite Index=100 *12 Month Price Score 104.17

Interim Earnings (Per Share)

Qtr.	Mar	Jun	Sep	Dec
2014	0.35	0.32	0.32	0.37
2015	0.38	0.40	0.42	0.42
2016	0.39	0.46	0.51	0.53
2017	0.56	0.60	0.78	...

Interim Dividends (Per Share)

Amt	Decl	Ex	Rec	Pay
0.15Q	03/03/2017	03/14/2017	03/16/2017	04/03/2017
0.15Q	06/02/2017	06/13/2017	06/15/2017	07/03/2017
0.15Q	09/08/2017	09/20/2017	09/21/2017	10/02/2017
0.15Q	12/08/2017	12/20/2017	12/21/2017	01/02/2018

Indicated Div: $0.60 (Div. Reinv. Plan)

Valuation Analysis | **Institutional Holding**

Forecast EPS	$2.61 (01/18/2018)	No of Institutions 432
Market Cap	$5.7 Billion	Shares 180,172,096
Book Value	$3.0 Billion	% Held
Price/Book	1.91	80.93
Price/Sales	3.90	

Business Summary: Banking (MIC: 5.1.1 SIC: 6021 NAIC: 522110)

Synovus Financial is a financial services company and a bank holding company. Through its subsidiary bank, Synovus Bank, Co. provides financial services, including commercial and retail banking, financial management, insurance, and mortgage services to its customers in Georgia, Alabama, South Carolina, Florida, and Tennessee. In addition to its banking operations, Co., through other non-bank subsidiaries, also provides various other financial services such as portfolio management and investment banking, trust, asset management and financial planning services, as well as mortgage services. As of Dec 31 2016, Co. had total assets of $30.10 billion and total deposits of $24.65 billion.

Recent Developments: For the quarter ended Sep 30 2017, net income increased 50.2% to US$98.0 million from US$65.2 million in the year-earlier quarter. Net interest income increased 16.2% to US$262.6 million from US$226.0 million in the year-earlier quarter. Provision for loan losses was US$39.7 million versus US$5.7 million in the prior-year quarter, an increase of 599.8%. Non-interest income rose 98.7% to US$135.4 million from US$68.2 million, while non-interest expense advanced 10.6% to US$205.6 million.

Prospects: Our evaluation of Synovus Financial Corp. as of Jan. 14, 2018 is the result of our systematic analysis on three basic characteristics: earnings strength, relative valuation, and recent stock price movement. The company has enjoyed a very positive trend in earnings per share over the past 5 quarters and while recent estimates for the company have been mixed, SNV has posted better than expected results. Based on operating earnings yield, the company is undervalued when compared to all of the companies in our coverage universe. Share price changes over the past year indicates that SNV will perform in line with the market over the near term.

Financial Data

(US$ in Thousands)	9 Mos	6 Mos	3 Mos	12/31/2016	12/31/2015	12/31/2014	12/31/2013	12/31/2012
Earnings Per Share	2.47	2.20	2.06	1.89	1.62	1.33	0.91	5.95
Cash Flow Per Share	5.17	4.20	4.20	3.75	3.38	2.79	4.74	4.19
Tang Book Value Per Share	23.44	23.04	22.62	22.32	22.00	21.24	20.12	22.98
Dividends Per Share	0.570	0.540	0.510	0.480	0.420	0.240	0.280	0.280
Dividend Payout %	23.08	24.55	24.76	25.40	25.93	18.05	30.77	4.71
Income Statement								
Interest Income	855,563	557,911	272,401	1,022,803	945,962	928,692	929,014	1,004,140
Interest Expense	101,966	66,887	32,474	123,623	118,644	109,408	118,822	150,023
Net Interest Income	753,597	491,024	239,927	899,180	827,318	819,284	810,192	854,117
Provision for Losses	58,620	18,934	8,674	28,000	19,010	33,831	69,598	320,369
Non-Interest Income	275,974	140,539	71,839	273,194	267,920	260,537	253,242	309,285
Non-Interest Expense	594,780	389,133	197,388	755,923	717,655	743,431	741,208	811,556
Income Before Taxes	376,171	223,496	105,704	388,451	358,573	302,559	252,628	31,477
Income Taxes	130,303	75,635	33,847	141,667	132,491	107,310	93,245	(798,732)
Net Income	245,868	147,861	71,857	246,784	226,082	195,249	159,383	830,209
Average Shares	121,814	123,027	123,059	125,078	133,201	139,154	134,225	130,014
Balance Sheet								
Net Loans & Leases	24,268,930	24,182,417	24,004,954	23,604,633	22,177,069	20,839,988	19,760,923	19,178,975
Total Assets	31,642,123	30,687,966	30,679,589	30,104,002	28,792,653	27,051,231	26,201,604	26,760,012
Total Deposits	26,186,228	25,218,816	25,105,712	24,648,060	23,242,661	21,531,700	20,876,790	21,057,044
Total Liabilities	28,645,045	27,690,019	27,717,462	27,176,078	25,792,457	24,009,961	23,252,619	23,190,581
Stockholders' Equity	2,997,078	2,997,947	2,962,127	2,927,924	3,000,196	3,041,270	2,948,985	3,569,431
Shares Outstanding	119,566	121,661	122,321	122,266	129,547	136,122	138,907	112,368
Statistical Record								
Return on Assets %	1.02	0.94	0.89	0.84	0.81	0.73	0.60	3.07
Return on Equity %	10.65	9.47	9.00	8.30	7.48	6.52	4.89	25.89
Net Interest Margin %	88.21	87.95	88.08	87.91	87.46	88.22	87.21	85.06
Efficiency Ratio %	47.48	54.13	57.34	58.33	59.12	62.51	62.69	61.79
Loans to Deposits	0.93	0.96	0.96	0.96	0.95	0.97	0.95	0.91
Price Range	46.06-31.75	44.41-27.65	43.74-27.07	41.78-25.95	33.56-24.49	27.51-21.84	25.20-17.08	17.85-10.71
P/E Ratio	18.65-12.85	20.19-12.57	21.23-13.14	22.11-13.73	20.72-15.12	20.68-16.42	27.69-18.77	3.00-1.80
Average Yield %	1.39	1.42	1.46	1.51	1.42	0.99	1.33	1.92

Address: 1111 Bay Avenue, Suite 500, Columbus, GA 31901 Telephone: 706-649-2311	Web Site: www.synovus.com Officers: Kessel D. Stelling - Chairman, President, Chief Executive Officer Allen J. Gula - Executive Vice President, Chief Operating Officer	Auditors: KPMG LLP Investor Contact: 706-649-3555 Transfer Agents: American Stock Transfer & Trust Company, LLC., Brooklyn, NY

SYSCO CORP

Exchange	Symbol	Price	52Wk Range	Yield	P/E	Div Achiever
NYS	SYY	$60.73 (12/29/2017)	62.64-49.11	2.37	27.73	40 Years

*7 Year Price Score 108.54 *NYSE Composite Index=100 *12 Month Price Score 101.33

Interim Earnings (Per Share)

Qtr.	Sep	Dec	Mar	Jun
2014-15	0.47	0.27	0.30	0.12
2015-16	0.41	0.48	0.38	0.38
2016-17	0.58	0.50	0.44	0.56
2017-18	0.69	...	...	...

Interim Dividends (Per Share)

Amt	Decl	Ex	Rec	Pay
0.33Q	02/24/2017	04/05/2017	04/07/2017	04/28/2017
0.33Q	05/25/2017	07/05/2017	07/07/2017	07/28/2017
0.33Q	07/28/2017	10/05/2017	10/06/2017	10/27/2017
0.36Q	11/17/2017	01/04/2018	01/05/2018	01/26/2018

Indicated Div: $1.44 (Div. Reinv. Plan)

Valuation Analysis — **Institutional Holding**

Forecast EPS	$2.79	No of Institutions
(01/17/2018)		1467
Market Cap	$31.7 Billion	Shares
Book Value	$2.2 Billion	571,429,888
Price/Book	14.17	% Held
Price/Sales	0.57	74.73

TRADING VOLUME (thousand shares)

Business Summary: Retail - Food & Beverage, Drug & Tobacco (MIC: 2.1.2 SIC: 5141 NAIC: 424410)

Sysco is a distributor of food and related products primarily to the foodservice or food-away-from-home industry. Co.'s segments are: U.S. Foodservice Operations, which includes U.S. Broadline operations, custom-cut meat and seafood companies, FreshPoint and European Imports; International Foodservice Operations, which includes broadline operations that distribute a line of food products and non-food products to international customers; and SYGMA, which consists of operating companies that distribute a line of food products and non-food products to certain chain restaurant customer locations. Co.'s other segment consists of its hotel supply operations and Sysco Labs technology solutions.

Recent Developments: For the quarter ended Sep 30 2017, net income increased 13.5% to US$367.6 million from US$323.9 million in the year-earlier quarter. Revenues were US$14.65 billion, up 4.9% from US$13.97 billion the year before. Operating income was US$623.1 million versus US$566.8 million in the prior-year quarter, an increase of 9.9%. Direct operating expenses rose 5.1% to US$11.86 billion from US$11.28 billion in the comparable period the year before. Indirect operating expenses increased 2.1% to US$2.17 billion from US$2.13 billion in the equivalent prior-year period.

Prospects: Our evaluation of Sysco Corp. as of Jan. 14, 2018 is the result of our systematic analysis on three basic characteristics: earnings strength, relative valuation, and recent stock price movement. The company has enjoyed a very positive trend in earnings per share over the past 5 quarters and while recent estimates for the company have been raised by analysts, SYY has posted better than expected results. Based on operating earnings yield, the company is about fairly valued when compared to all of the companies in our coverage universe. Share price changes over the past year indicates that SYY will perform in line with the market over the near term.

Financial Data

(US$ in Thousands)	3 Mos	07/01/2017	07/02/2016	06/27/2015	06/28/2014	06/29/2013	06/30/2012	07/02/2011
Earnings Per Share	2.19	2.08	1.64	1.15	1.58	1.67	1.90	1.96
Cash Flow Per Share	3.81	4.02	3.32	2.63	2.55	2.57	2.40	1.87
Tang Book Value Per Share	N.M.	N.M.	2.06	5.29	5.36	5.29	4.96	5.01
Dividends Per Share	1.300	0.970	1.230	1.180	1.140	1.100	0.800	1.030
Dividend Payout %	59.36	46.63	75.00	102.61	72.15	65.87	42.11	52.55
Income Statement								
Total Revenue	14,650,424	55,371,139	50,366,919	48,680,752	46,516,712	44,411,233	42,380,939	39,323,489
EBITDA	634,532	2,834,508	2,347,853	1,758,754	2,093,165	2,149,450	2,282,298	2,319,721
Depn & Amortn	7,192	765,400	608,700	495,800	493,800	473,500	384,900	374,000
Income Before Taxes	546,456	1,766,230	1,433,007	1,008,147	1,475,624	1,547,455	1,784,002	1,827,454
Income Taxes	178,816	623,727	483,385	321,374	544,091	555,028	662,417	675,424
Net Income	367,640	1,142,503	949,622	686,773	931,533	992,427	1,121,585	1,152,030
Average Shares	533,063	548,545	577,391	596,849	590,216	592,675	588,991	588,691
Balance Sheet								
Current Assets	8,597,002	8,033,438	10,053,899	11,494,304	6,681,972	6,207,427	6,084,808	5,732,882
Total Assets	18,418,590	17,756,655	16,721,804	17,989,281	13,167,950	12,663,947	12,094,972	11,385,555
Current Liabilities	6,140,282	6,095,886	4,434,456	9,399,615	4,367,630	3,749,282	3,423,579	3,575,075
Long-Term Obligations	8,426,359	7,660,877	7,336,930	2,271,825	2,384,167	2,639,986	2,763,688	2,279,517
Total Liabilities	16,183,336	15,375,139	13,242,196	12,729,057	7,901,255	7,472,137	7,409,932	6,680,313
Stockholders' Equity	2,235,254	2,381,516	3,479,608	5,260,224	5,266,695	5,191,810	4,685,040	4,705,242
Shares Outstanding	521,661	530,039	559,597	594,317	586,124	586,106	585,946	591,577
Statistical Record								
Return on Assets %	6.51	6.65	5.38	4.42	7.23	8.04	9.58	10.65
Return on Equity %	45.14	39.09	21.38	13.08	17.86	20.15	23.95	27.08
EBITDA Margin %	4.33	5.12	4.66	3.61	4.50	4.84	5.39	5.90
Net Margin %	2.51	2.06	1.89	1.41	2.00	2.23	2.65	2.93
Asset Turnover	3.08	3.22	2.86	3.13	3.61	3.60	3.62	3.63
Current Ratio	1.40	1.32	2.27	1.22	1.53	1.66	1.78	1.60
Debt to Equity	3.77	3.22	2.11	0.43	0.45	0.51	0.59	0.48
Price Range	56.61-47.26	56.61-47.26	50.74-35.68	41.25-35.54	37.85-31.16	35.24-28.31	31.55-25.47	32.65-27.29
P/E Ratio	25.85-21.58	27.22-22.72	30.94-21.76	35.87-30.90	23.96-19.72	21.10-16.95	16.61-13.41	16.66-13.92
Average Yield %	2.47	1.85	2.88	3.09	3.26	3.44	2.79	3.50

Address: 1390 Enclave Parkway, Houston, TX 77077-2099	**Web Site:** www.sysco.com	**Auditors:** Ernst & Young LLP
Telephone: 281-584-1390	**Officers:** Jacquelyn M. Ward - Chairman Thomas L. Bene - President, Executive Vice President, Chief Operating Officer, Chief Commercial Officer, Chief Executive Officer	**Investor Contact:** 281-584-1308
Fax: 281-584-2880		**Transfer Agents:** American Stock Transfer & Trust Company, New York, NY

TABLEAU SOFTWARE INC

Exchange	Symbol	Price	52Wk Range	Yield	P/E
NYS	DATA	$69.20 (12/29/2017)	82.17-43.32	N/A	N/A

*7 Year Price Score N/A ***NYSE Composite Index=100** ***12 Month Price Score 109.70**

TRADING VOLUME (thousand shares)

Interim Earnings (Per Share)

Qtr.	Mar	Jun	Sep	Dec
2014	(0.09)	(0.07)	(0.07)	0.31
2015	(0.14)	(0.27)	(0.19)	(0.58)
2016	(0.62)	(0.64)	(0.40)	(0.27)
2017	(0.71)	(0.54)	(0.59)	...

Interim Dividends (Per Share)

No Dividends Paid

Valuation Analysis   Institutional Holding

Forecast EPS	$0.18	No of Institutions
	(01/18/2018)	321
Market Cap	$5.5 Billion	Shares
Book Value	$752.6 Million	70,181,296
Price/Book	7.33	% Held
Price/Sales	6.28	58.43

Business Summary: Internet & Software (MIC: 6.3.2 SIC: 7372 NAIC: 511210)

Tableau Software provides software products that enable a population of business users to engage with data, ask questions, and solve problems. Co. provides five products: Tableau Desktop, a self-service analytics product; Tableau Server, a business intelligence platform for organizations; Tableau Online, a hosted software-as-a-service version of Tableau Server; Tableau Public, a cloud-based platform for analyzing and sharing public data; and Vizable, an application used to analyze data on a tablet. Co.'s products are built on a foundation of proprietary technologies, such as VizQL, its Live Query Engine and In-Memory Data Engine, which work together to develop its Hybrid Data Architecture.

Recent Developments: For the quarter ended Sep 30 2017, net loss amounted to US$46.6 million versus a net loss of US$30.3 million in the year-earlier quarter. Revenues were US$214.9 million, up 4.3% from US$206.1 million the year before. Operating loss was US$49.0 million versus a loss of US$29.4 million in the prior-year quarter. Direct operating expenses rose 24.5% to US$29.9 million from US$24.0 million in the comparable period the year before. Indirect operating expenses increased 10.7% to US$234.0 million from US$211.4 million in the equivalent prior-year period.

Prospects: Our evaluation of Tableau Software, Inc. as of Jan. 14, 2018 is the result of our systematic analysis on three basic characteristics: earnings strength, relative valuation, and recent stock price movement. The company has suffered a very negative trend in earnings per share over the past 5 quarters and while recent estimates for the company have remained steady, DATA has posted results that fell short of analysts expectations. Based on operating earnings yield, the company is overvalued when compared to all of the companies in our coverage universe. Share price changes over the past year indicates that DATA will perform very well over the near term.

Financial Data

(US$ in Thousands)	9 Mos	6 Mos	3 Mos	12/31/2016	12/31/2015	12/31/2014	12/31/2013	12/31/2012
Earnings Per Share	(2.11)	(1.92)	(2.02)	(1.92)	(1.17)	0.08	0.12	...
Cash Flow Per Share	3.14	3.17	2.87	2.32	1.91	1.32	0.75	0.42
Tang Book Value Per Share	9.00	9.53	9.68	10.12	10.03	9.62	3.93	0.87
Income Statement								
Total Revenue	627,703	412,786	199,906	826,943	653,587	412,616	232,440	127,733
EBITDA	(138,353)	(69,310)	(38,854)	(94,427)	(27,107)	20,682	9,765	8,004
Depn & Amortn	162	23,837	13,435	43,000	23,700	13,500	6,900	3,800
Income Before Taxes	(138,515)	(93,147)	(52,289)	(137,427)	(50,807)	7,182	2,865	4,204
Income Taxes	5,207	4,022	2,358	7,022	32,893	1,309	(4,211)	2,777
Net Income	(143,722)	(97,169)	(54,647)	(144,449)	(83,700)	5,873	7,076	1,427
Average Shares	79,440	78,511	77,416	75,162	71,701	74,319	59,092	39,652
Balance Sheet								
Current Assets	1,113,781	1,150,784	1,113,018	1,151,624	944,739	810,261	332,181	76,161
Total Assets	1,319,298	1,271,077	1,239,518	1,287,199	1,030,711	865,662	354,927	86,992
Current Liabilities	488,135	426,420	397,799	428,721	272,601	180,274	104,289	51,930
Total Liabilities	566,696	501,807	469,645	495,351	296,766	193,656	110,267	57,018
Stockholders' Equity	752,602	769,270	769,873	791,848	733,945	672,006	244,660	29,974
Shares Outstanding	79,729	79,075	77,956	76,718	73,204	69,868	62,198	34,317
Statistical Record								
Return on Assets %	N.M.	N.M.	N.M.	N.M.	N.M.	0.96	3.20	2.06
Return on Equity %	N.M.	N.M.	N.M.	N.M.	N.M.	1.28	5.15	5.72
EBITDA Margin %	N.M.	N.M.	N.M.	N.M.	N.M.	5.01	4.20	6.27
Net Margin %	N.M.	N.M.	N.M.	N.M.	N.M.	1.42	3.04	1.12
Asset Turnover	0.71	0.73	0.75	0.71	0.69	0.68	1.05	1.84
Current Ratio	2.28	2.70	2.80	2.69	3.47	4.49	3.19	1.47
Price Range	75.97-41.67	66.50-41.67	62.22-41.67	94.30-37.22	128.74-77.58	100.28-54.13	74.75-48.53	...
P/E Ratio	...	...	...	...	...	1253.50-676.63	622.92-404.42	...

Address: 1621 North 34th Street,	Web Site: www.tableausoftware.com	Auditors: PricewaterhouseCoopers LLP
Seattle, WA 98103	Officers: Christian Chabot - Chairman, Chief	Transfer Agents: American Stock
Telephone: 206-633-3400	Executive Officer, Co-Founder Adam Selipsky -	Transfer & Trust Company
	President, Chief Executive Officer	

TAHOE RESOURCES INC.

Exchange	Symbol	Price	52Wk Range	Yield	P/E
NYS	TAHO	$4.79 (12/29/2017)	11.18-4.18	N/A	15.45

*7 Year Price Score 36.78   *NYSE Composite Index=100   *12 Month Price Score 61.42

Interim Earnings (Per Share)

Qtr.	Mar	Jun	Sep	Dec
2014	0.17	0.24	0.13	0.07
2015	0.22	(0.04)	0.06	(0.53)
2016	0.17	0.05	0.20	(0.01)
2017	0.24	0.11	(0.03)	...

Interim Dividends (Per Share)

Amt	Decl	Ex	Rec	Pay
0.02M	04/06/2017	04/18/2017	04/20/2017	04/27/2017
0.02M	05/04/2017	05/16/2017	05/18/2017	05/25/2017
0.02M	06/08/2017	06/20/2017	06/22/2017	06/29/2017
0.02M	07/06/2017	07/18/2017	07/20/2017	07/27/2017

Valuation Analysis   Institutional Holding

Forecast EPS	$0.32	No of Institutions
	(01/18/2018)	249
Market Cap	$1.5 Billion	Shares
Book Value	$2.6 Billion	212,435,376
Price/Book	0.57	% Held
Price/Sales	1.86	49.98

Business Summary: Precious Metals (MIC: 8.2.1 SIC: 1044 NAIC: 212222)

Tahoe Resources is engaged in the operation of mineral properties for the mining of precious metals and the acquisition, exploration and development of mineral interests in the Americas.

Recent Developments: For the quarter ended Sep 30 2017, net loss amounted to US$8.4 million versus net income of US$63.0 million in the year-earlier quarter. Revenues were US$155.2 million, down 33.9% from US$234.7 million the year before. Operating income was US$2.6 million versus US$99.4 million in the prior-year quarter, a decrease of 97.4%. Direct operating expenses rose 10.8% to US$136.4 million from US$123.1 million in the comparable period the year before. Indirect operating expenses increased 32.3% to US$16.2 million from US$12.2 million in the equivalent prior-year period.

Prospects: Our evaluation of Tahoe Resources Inc. as of Jan. 14, 2018 is the result of our systematic analysis on three basic characteristics: earnings strength, relative valuation, and recent stock movement. The company has suffered a very negative trend in earnings per share over the past 5 quarters and while recent estimates for the company have been mixed, TAHO has posted results that fell short of analysts expectations. Based on operating earnings yield, the company is undervalued when compared to all of the companies in our coverage universe. Share price changes over the past year indicates that TAHO will perform very poorly over the near term.

Financial Data
(US$ in Thousands)

	9 Mos	6 Mos	3 Mos	12/31/2016	12/31/2015	12/31/2014	12/31/2013	12/31/2012
Earnings Per Share	0.31	0.54	0.48	0.41	(0.35)	0.61	(0.45)	(0.65)
Cash Flow Per Share	...	...	...	0.86	0.80	0.81	(0.45)	(0.61)
Tang Book Value Per Share	8.09	8.13	8.09	7.90	7.06	5.95	5.30	5.71
Dividends Per Share	...	...	...	0.240	0.240	0.020	...	...
Dividend Payout %	...	...	...	58.54	...	3.28	...	...
Income Statement								
Total Revenue	615,823	460,622	251,046	784,503	519,721	350.265	...	...
EBITDA	...	...	129,945	75,355	(171,491)	74,242	(77,005)	(100,632)
Depn & Amortn	116,385	83,595	42,980	(137,021)	(84,945)	(47,088)	(13,029)	(6,869)
Income Before Taxes	...	...	85,899	208,732	(88,232)	115,690	(63,976)	(93,763)
Income Taxes	41,784	32,903	11,202	90,856	(16,321)	24,900	1,621	(310)
Net Income	99,803	108,183	74,697	117,876	(71,911)	90,790	(65,597)	(93,453)
Average Shares	313,161	312,869	312,025	289,988	207,810	147,992	145,842	144,634
Balance Sheet								
Current Assets	347,998	376,683	370,366	359,442	228,201	134,584	35,811	166,270
Total Assets	3,127,529	3,129,228	3,092,942	3,071,253	2,002,461	975,628	883,333	852,943
Current Liabilities	169,875	158,402	118,336	150,436	150,880	91,875	104,965	16,925
Long-Term Obligations	2,871	3,962	40,424	42,250	7,711	...	...	...
Total Liabilities	485,854	474,912	458,538	499,099	338,430	97,568	109,179	21,646
Stockholders' Equity	2,641,675	2,654,316	2,634,404	2,572,154	1,664,031	878,060	774,154	831,297
Shares Outstanding	312,775	312,619	311,919	311,362	227,401	147,644	146,094	145,565
Statistical Record								
Return on Assets %	3.25	5.61	6.07	4.63	N.M.	9.77	N.M.	N.M.
Return on Equity %	3.83	6.61	7.16	5.55	N.M.	10.99	N.M.	N.M.
EBITDA Margin %	...	...	51.76	9.61	N.M.	21.20	...	...
Net Margin %	16.21	23.49	29.75	15.03	N.M.	25.92	...	...
Asset Turnover	0.26	0.29	0.35	0.31	0.35	0.38	...	...
Current Ratio	2.05	2.38	3.13	2.39	1.51	1.46	0.34	9.82
Debt to Equity	N.M.	N.M.	0.02	0.02	N.M.	...	...	...
Price Range	12.83-4.41	16.62-7.17	16.62-7.17	16.62-6.83	15.34-7.47	27.31-11.43	19.45-12.05	24.00-12.02
P/E Ratio	41.39-14.23	30.78-13.28	34.63-14.94	40.54-16.66	...	44.77-18.74	...	...
Average Yield %	...	...	...	2.04	2.18	0.09	...	...

Address: 5310 Kietzke Lane, Suite 200, Reno, NV 89511
Telephone: 775-448-5800
Fax: 775-398-7020

Web Site: www.tahoeresourcesinc.com
Officers: C. Kevin McArthur - Executive Chairman, Chief Executive Officer, President, Vice-Chairman Ronald W. Clayton - President, Chief Operating Officer, Vice President

Auditors: Deloitte LLP
Investor Contact: 775-448-5807
Transfer Agents: Computershare Investor Services Inc., Vancouver, British Columbia, Canada

TANGER FACTORY OUTLET CENTERS, INC.

Exchange	Symbol	Price	52Wk Range	Yield	P/E	Div Achiever
NYS	SKT	$26.51 (12/29/2017)	37.17-22.19	5.17	42.76	23 Years

*7 Year Price Score 68.21 *NYSE Composite Index=100 *12 Month Price Score 82.09

Interim Earnings (Per Share)

Qtr.	Mar	Jun	Sep	Dec
2014	0.15	0.20	0.24	0.18
2015	0.36	0.26	0.46	1.12
2016	0.28	0.76	0.72	0.25
2017	0.23	0.31	(0.17)	

Interim Dividends (Per Share)

Amt	Decl	Ex	Rec	Pay
0.343Q	04/06/2017	04/26/2017	04/28/2017	05/15/2017
0.343Q	07/06/2017	07/27/2017	07/31/2017	08/15/2017
0.343Q	10/05/2017	10/30/2017	10/31/2017	11/15/2017
0.343Q	01/11/2018	01/30/2018	01/31/2018	02/15/2018

Indicated Div: $1.37 (Div. Reinv. Plan)

Valuation Analysis

		Institutional Holding	
Forecast EPS	$0.65	No of Institutions	
	(11/27/2017)	385	
Market Cap	$2.5 Billion	Shares	
Book Value	$578.3 Million	113,002,832	
Price/Book	4.33	% Held	
Price/Sales	5.15	99.38	

Business Summary: REITs (MIC: 5.3.1 SIC: 6798 NAIC: 525930)

Tanger Factory Outlet Centers, along with its subsidiaries owns and operates outlet centers in the U.S. and Canada. Co. is a self-administered and self-managed real estate investment trust, which, through its controlling interest in Tanger Properties Limited Partnership and subsidiaries, focuses on developing, acquiring, owning, operating and managing outlet shopping centers. As of Dec 31 2016, Co.'s consolidated portfolio consisted of 36 outlet centers. Co. also had partial ownership interests in eight unconsolidated outlet centers, including four outlet centers in Canada. Each of Co.'s outlet centers, except one joint venture property, carries the Tanger brand name.

Recent Developments: For the quarter ended Sep 30 2017, net loss amounted to US$16.0 million versus net income of US$72.8 million in the year-earlier quarter. Revenues were US$120.8 million, up 1.4% from US$119.1 million the year before. Revenues from property income rose 1.5% to US$118.3 million from US$116.5 million in the corresponding quarter a year earlier.

Prospects: Our evaluation of Tanger Factory Outlet Centers Inc. as of Jan. 14, 2018 is the result of our systematic analysis on three basic characteristics: earnings strength, relative valuation, and recent stock price movement. The company has managed to produce a neutral trend in earnings per share over the past 5 quarters. Because the company lacks sufficient analyst estimate data, we place greater weight on the historical EPS trend as the measure of earnings strength. Based on operating earnings yield, the company is about fairly valued when compared to all of the companies in our coverage universe. Share price changes over the past year indicates that SKT will perform poorly over the near term.

Financial Data

(US$ in Thousands)	9 Mos	6 Mos	3 Mos	12/31/2016	12/31/2015	12/31/2014	12/31/2013	12/31/2012
Earnings Per Share	0.62	1.51	1.96	2.01	2.20	0.77	1.13	0.57
Cash Flow Per Share	2.59	2.58	2.54	2.51	2.33	2.01	2.01	1.80
Tang Book Value Per Share	6.12	6.61	6.88	4.47	3.81	2.96	2.78	3.85
Dividends Per Share	1.335	1.317	1.300	1.260	1.305	0.945	0.885	0.830
Dividend Payout %	215.32	87.25	66.33	62.69	59.32	122.73	78.32	145.61
Income Statement								
Total Revenue	361,747	240,982	121,368	465,834	439,369	418,558	385,009	356,997
EBITDA	94,234	86,461	39,408	349,911	350,808	206,336	228,597	183,285
Depn & Amortn	5,110	3,685	1,725	96,813	85,900	80,100	74,700	73,700
Income Before Taxes	39,628	49,769	21,196	193,457	210,684	69,099	102,281	59,771
Net Income	36,507	51,726	22,336	193,744	211,200	74,011	107,557	53,228
Average Shares	93,923	95,030	95,311	95,345	94,759	93,839	94,247	92,661
Balance Sheet								
Current Assets	8,773	8,362	7,225	12,222	142,864	62,880	15,241	10,335
Total Assets	2,541,446	2,529,493	2,539,770	2,526,214	2,326,707	2,097,660	2,006,456	1,672,425
Current Liabilities	84,091	71,383	82,772	78,143	125,784	97,946	87,850	48,233
Long-Term Obligations	1,773,981	1,729,002	1,699,461	1,687,866	1,563,806	1,443,194	1,328,049	1,093,537
Total Liabilities	1,963,169	1,901,760	1,876,499	1,855,998	1,751,570	1,600,841	1,484,197	1,189,816
Stockholders' Equity	578,277	627,733	663,271	670,216	575,137	496,819	522,259	482,609
Shares Outstanding	94,528	94,958	96,456	96,095	95,880	95,509	94,505	94,061
Statistical Record								
Return on Assets %	2.37	5.90	7.99	7.96	9.55	3.61	5.85	3.22
Return on Equity %	9.70	23.09	30.29	31.03	39.40	14.53	21.41	11.26
EBITDA Margin %	26.05	35.88	32.47	75.11	79.84	49.30	59.37	51.34
Net Margin %	10.09	21.46	18.40	41.59	48.07	17.68	27.94	14.91
Asset Turnover	0.19	0.20	0.20	0.19	0.20	0.20	0.21	0.22
Current Ratio	0.10	0.12	0.09	0.16	1.14	0.64	0.17	0.21
Debt to Equity	3.07	2.75	2.56	2.52	2.72	2.90	2.54	2.27
Price Range	38.96-23.38	41.74-25.22	41.74-31.09	41.74-29.67	40.55-30.58	37.65-32.02	38.57-30.14	34.43-28.10
P/E Ratio	62.84-37.71	27.64-16.70	21.30-15.86	20.77-14.76	18.43-13.90	48.90-41.58	34.13-26.67	60.40-49.30
Average Yield %	4.34	3.81	3.81	3.47	3.79	2.70	2.64	2.63

Address: 3200 Northline Avenue, Suite 360, Greensboro, NC 27408 **Telephone:** 336-292-3010 **Fax:** 336-297-0931	**Web Site:** www.tangeroutlet.com **Officers:** Thomas J. Guerrieri - Vice President, Chief Accounting Officer, Controller Steven B. Tanger - President, Chief Executive Officer	**Auditors:** PricewaterhouseCoopers LLP **Investor Contact:** 336-834-6892 **Transfer Agents:** Computershare Trust Company, NA, Providence, RI

TAPESTRY INC

Exchange	Symbol	Price	52Wk Range	Yield	P/E
NYS	TPR	$44.23 (12/29/2017)	48.74-34.99	3.05	27.47

*7 Year Price Score 68.85 *NYSE Composite Index=100 *12 Month Price Score 95.46

Interim Earnings (Per Share)

Qtr.	Sep	Dec	Mar	Jun
2014-15	0.43	0.66	0.32	0.04
2015-16	0.35	0.61	0.40	0.29
2016-17	0.42	0.71	0.43	0.53
2017-18	(0.06)	...	...	...

Interim Dividends (Per Share)

Amt	Decl	Ex	Rec	Pay
0.338Q	02/17/2017	03/08/2017	03/10/2017	04/03/2017
0.338Q	05/19/2017	06/07/2017	06/09/2017	07/05/2017
0.338Q	08/15/2017	09/07/2017	09/08/2017	10/02/2017
0.338Q	11/15/2017	12/07/2017	12/08/2017	01/02/2018

Indicated Div: $1.35

Valuation Analysis

		Institutional Holding	
Forecast EPS	$2.38 (01/18/2018)	No of Institutions	956
Market Cap	$12.6 Billion	Shares	305,747,328
Book Value	$2.9 Billion		
Price/Book	4.28	% Held	83.44
Price/Sales	2.65		

Business Summary: Apparel, Footwear & Accessories (MIC: 1.4.2 SIC: 3171 NAIC: 316992)

Tapestry is a marketer of accessories and gifts for women and men. Co.'s product offerings include women's and men's bags, leather goods, footwear, jewelry, travel bags, sunwear, watches and fragrance. Co.'s segments include: North America, which includes sales to North American consumers through Co.-operated stores, including the Internet, and sales to wholesale customers and distributors; International, which includes sales to consumers through Co.-operated stores, concession shop-in-shops and through the Internet; and Stuart Weitzman, which includes sales generated by the Stuart Weitzman brand, through numerous department stores, within third party distributors and operated stores.

Recent Developments: For the quarter ended Sep 30 2017, net loss amounted to US$17.7 million versus net income of US$117.4 million in the year-earlier quarter. Revenues were US$1.29 billion, up 24.2% from US$1.04 billion the year before. Operating loss was US$21.8 million versus an income of US$165.9 million in the prior-year quarter. Direct operating expenses rose 62.4% to US$524.5 million from US$322.9 million in the comparable period the year before. Indirect operating expenses increased 43.3% to US$786.2 million from US$548.8 million in the equivalent prior-year period.

Prospects: Our evaluation of Tapestry Inc. as of Jan. 14, 2018 is the result of our systematic analysis on three basic characteristics: earnings strength, relative valuation, and recent stock price movement. The company has managed to produce a neutral trend in earnings per share over the past 5 quarters and while recent estimates for the company have been raised by analysts, TPR has posted better than expected results. Based on operating earnings yield, the company is undervalued when compared to all of the companies in our coverage universe. Share price changes over the past year indicates that TPR will perform poorly over the near term.

Financial Data

(US$ in Thousands)	3 Mos	07/01/2017	07/02/2016	06/27/2015	06/28/2014	06/29/2013	06/30/2012	07/02/2011
Earnings Per Share	1.61	2.09	1.65	1.45	2.79	3.61	3.53	2.92
Cash Flow Per Share	2.78	3.05	2.69	3.41	3.56	5.02	4.25	3.51
Tang Book Value Per Share	N.M.	7.74	6.58	6.13	7.47	7.29	5.64	4.41
Dividends Per Share	1.350	1.350	1.350	1.350	1.350	1.238	0.975	0.675
Dividend Payout %	83.85	64.59	81.82	93.10	48.39	34.28	27.62	23.12
Income Statement								
Total Revenue	1,288,900	4,488,300	4,491,800	4,191,600	4,806,226	5,075,390	4,763,180	4,158,507
EBITDA	43,700	1,000,200	864,100	809,800	1,309,434	1,681,144	1,637,852	1,425,294
Depn & Amortn	65,500	212,800	210,600	191,800	189,360	162,987	132,909	125,106
Income Before Taxes	(42,300)	759,000	626,600	611,600	1,122,255	1,520,526	1,505,663	1,301,219
Income Taxes	(24,600)	168,000	166,100	209,200	340,919	486,106	466,753	420,419
Net Income	(17,700)	591,000	460,500	402,400	781,336	1,034,420	1,038,910	880,800
Average Shares	286,700	282,800	279,300	277,200	280,379	286,307	294,129	301,558
Balance Sheet								
Current Assets	3,022,300	3,953,300	2,172,900	2,506,500	1,855,217	2,070,947	1,804,528	1,452,388
Total Assets	7,454,400	5,831,600	4,892,700	4,666,900	3,663,131	3,531,897	3,104,321	2,635,116
Current Liabilities	1,734,900	753,800	826,700	834,700	813,118	722,510	718,160	593,017
Long-Term Obligations	1,888,200	1,579,500	861,200	879,100	...	485	985	23,360
Total Liabilities	4,514,400	2,829,700	2,209,800	2,177,000	1,242,478	1,122,739	1,111,390	1,022,547
Stockholders' Equity	2,940,000	3,001,900	2,682,900	2,489,900	2,420,653	2,409,158	1,992,931	1,612,569
Shares Outstanding	284,200	281,900	278,500	276,600	274,361	281,902	285,118	288,514
Statistical Record								
Return on Assets %	7.57	11.05	9.48	9.69	21.78	31.26	36.30	34.62
Return on Equity %	16.09	20.85	17.52	16.43	32.44	47.13	57.79	56.66
EBITDA Margin %	3.39	22.28	19.24	19.32	27.24	33.12	34.39	34.27
Net Margin %	N.M.	13.17	10.25	9.60	16.26	20.38	21.81	21.18
Asset Turnover	0.79	0.84	0.92	1.01	1.34	1.53	1.66	1.63
Current Ratio	1.74	5.24	2.63	3.00	2.28	2.87	2.51	2.45
Debt to Equity	0.64	0.53	0.32	0.35	...	N.M.	N.M.	0.01
Price Range	48.74-34.24	47.34-34.24	42.00-27.44	43.56-33.00	59.55-34.02	62.60-46.50	79.03-45.96	65.99-34.37
P/E Ratio	30.27-21.27	22.65-16.38	25.45-16.63	30.04-22.76	21.34-12.19	17.34-12.88	22.39-13.02	22.60-11.77
Average Yield %	3.33	3.43	3.92	3.62	2.67	2.23	1.50	1.33

Address: 10 Hudson Yards, New York, NY 10001	Web Site: www.coach.com	Auditors: Deloitte & Touche LLP
Telephone: 212-594-1850	Officers: Jide James Zeitlin - Chairman Todd Kahn - President, Chief Administrative Officer, Executive Vice President, Senior Vice President, General Counsel, Secretary	Transfer Agents: Mellon Investor Services, Jersey City, NJ
Fax: 212-594-1682		

TARGET CORP

*7 Year Price Score 71.33   *NYSE Composite Index=100   *12 Month Price Score 97.43

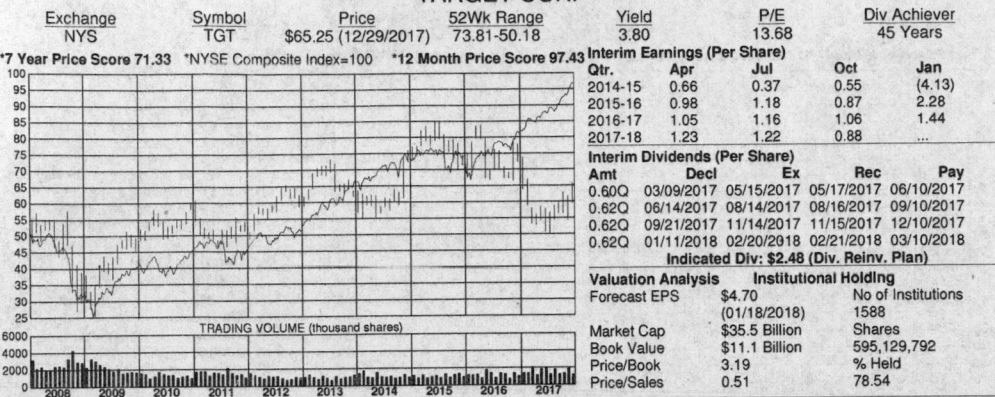

Interim Earnings (Per Share)

Qtr.	Apr	Jul	Oct	Jan
2014-15	0.66	0.37	0.55	(4.13)
2015-16	0.98	1.18	0.87	2.28
2016-17	1.05	1.16	1.06	1.44
2017-18	1.23	1.22	0.88	...

Interim Dividends (Per Share)

Amt	Decl	Ex	Rec	Pay
0.60Q	03/09/2017	05/15/2017	05/17/2017	06/10/2017
0.62Q	06/14/2017	08/14/2017	08/16/2017	09/10/2017
0.62Q	09/21/2017	11/14/2017	11/15/2017	12/10/2017
0.62Q	01/11/2018	02/20/2018	02/21/2018	03/10/2018

Indicated Div: $2.48 (Div. Reinv. Plan)

Valuation Analysis		Institutional Holding	
Forecast EPS	$4.70	No of Institutions	
	(01/18/2018)	1588	
Market Cap	$35.5 Billion	Shares	
Book Value	$11.1 Billion	595,129,792	
Price/Book	3.19	% Held	
Price/Sales	0.51	78.54	

Business Summary: Retail - General Merchandise/Department Stores (MIC: 2.1.1 SIC: 5331 NAIC: 452990)

Target sells a range of general merchandise and food. The majority of Co.'s general merchandise stores sell an edited food assortment, including perishables, dry grocery, dairy, and frozen items. Co.'s digital channels include a range of general merchandise, including items found in Co.'s stores, along with a complementary assortment such as additional sizes and colors sold only online. Co. also sells merchandise through periodic design and partnerships and provides in-store amenities such as Target Cafe and Target Photo, and leased or licensed departments such as Target Optical, Starbucks, and other food service offerings. As of Jan 28 2017, Co. had 1,802 stores in the U.S.

Recent Developments: For the quarter ended Oct 28 2017, income from continuing operations decreased 21.4% to US$478.0 million from US$608.0 million in the year-earlier quarter. Net income decreased 21.1% to US$480.0 million from US$608.0 million in the year-earlier quarter. Revenues were US$16.67 billion, up 1.4% from US$16.44 billion the year before. Operating income was US$869.0 million versus US$1.06 billion in the prior-year quarter, a decrease of 18.1%. Direct operating expenses rose 1.5% to US$11.71 billion from US$11.54 billion in the comparable period the year before. Indirect operating expenses increased 6.3% to US$4.09 billion from US$3.84 billion in the equivalent prior-year period.

Prospects: Our evaluation of Target Corp. as of Jan. 14, 2018 is the result of our systematic analysis on three basic characteristics: earnings strength, relative valuation, and recent stock price movement. The company has managed to produce a neutral trend in earnings per share over the past 5 quarters and while recent estimates for the company have been raised by analysts, TGT has posted better than expected results. Based on operating earnings yield, the company is undervalued when compared to all of the companies in our coverage universe. Share price changes over the past year indicates that TGT will perform very poorly over the near term.

Financial Data

(US$ in Millions)	9 Mos	6 Mos	3 Mos	01/28/2017	01/30/2016	01/31/2015	02/01/2014	02/02/2013
Earnings Per Share	4.77	4.95	4.89	4.70	5.31	(2.56)	3.07	4.52
Cash Flow Per Share	12.94	12.51	11.75	9.44	9.34	7.01	10.29	7.98
Tang Book Value Per Share	20.48	20.32	19.98	19.23	21.06	21.39	25.08	25.31
Dividends Per Share	2.420	2.400	2.360	2.320	2.160	1.900	1.580	1.320
Dividend Payout %	50.73	48.48	48.26	49.36	40.68	...	51.47	29.20
Income Statement								
Total Revenue	49,113	32,446	16,017	69,495	73,785	72,618	72,596	73,301
EBITDA	4,944	3,442	1,751	7,249	7,721	6,643	6,427	7,491
Depn & Amortn	1,784	1,151	573	2,280	2,191	2,108	2,198	2,120
Income Before Taxes	2,628	2,013	1,034	3,965	4,923	3,653	3,103	4,609
Income Taxes	802	664	357	1,296	1,602	1,204	1,132	1,610
Net Income	1,833	1,353	681	2,737	3,363	(1,636)	1,971	2,999
Average Shares	547	551	555	582	632	640	641	663
Balance Sheet								
Current Assets	14,709	11,620	11,739	11,990	14,130	14,087	11,573	16,388
Total Assets	40,708	37,366	37,218	37,431	40,262	41,404	44,553	48,163
Current Liabilities	15,376	12,729	12,392	12,708	12,622	11,736	12,777	14,031
Long-Term Obligations	11,277	10,892	11,086	11,031	11,945	12,705	12,622	14,654
Total Liabilities	29,571	26,268	26,197	26,478	27,305	27,407	28,322	31,605
Stockholders' Equity	11,137	11,098	11,021	10,953	12,957	13,997	16,231	16,558
Shares Outstanding	543	546	551	556	602	640	632	645
Statistical Record								
Return on Assets %	6.68	7.44	7.22	7.07	8.26	N.M.	4.26	6.23
Return on Equity %	23.87	24.50	23.64	22.96	25.02	N.M.	12.06	18.22
EBITDA Margin %	10.07	10.61	10.93	10.43	10.46	9.15	8.85	10.22
Net Margin %	3.73	4.17	4.25	3.94	4.56	N.M.	2.72	4.09
Asset Turnover	1.76	1.86	1.80	1.79	1.81	1.69	1.57	1.52
Current Ratio	0.96	0.91	0.95	0.94	1.12	1.20	0.91	1.17
Debt to Equity	1.01	0.98	1.01	1.01	0.92	0.91	0.78	0.89
Price Range	78.61-50.18	78.61-50.18	80.12-52.75	83.98-63.70	85.01-67.59	77.13-55.07	73.32-56.64	65.44-51.81
P/E Ratio	16.48-10.52	15.88-10.14	16.38-10.79	17.87-13.55	16.01-12.73	...	23.88-18.45	14.48-11.46
Average Yield %	3.99	3.76	3.46	3.16	2.77	3.03	2.38	2.21

Address: 1000 Nicollet Mall, Minneapolis, MN 55403
Telephone: 612-304-6073

Web Site: www.target.com
Officers: Brian C. Cornell - Chairman, Chief Executive Officer John J. Mulligan - Interim President, Interim Chief Executive Officer, Executive Vice President, Chief Financial Officer, Chief Operating Officer

Auditors: Ernst & Young LLP
Investor Contact: 800-775-3110
Transfer Agents: Mellon Investor Services, South Hackensack, N.J.

TARGA RESOURCES CORP

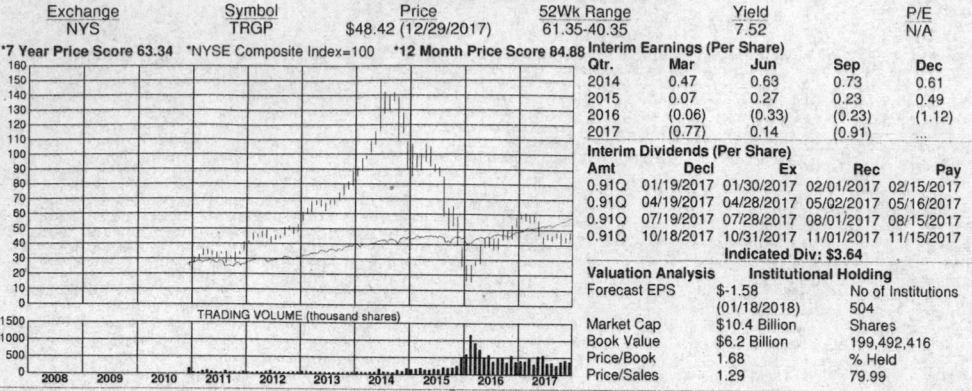

Exchange	Symbol	Price	52Wk Range	Yield	P/E
NYS	TRGP	$48.42 (12/29/2017)	61.35-40.35	7.52	N/A

*7 Year Price Score 63.34   *NYSE Composite Index=100   *12 Month Price Score 84.88

Interim Earnings (Per Share)

Qtr.	Mar	Jun	Sep	Dec
2014	0.47	0.63	0.73	0.61
2015	0.07	0.27	0.23	0.49
2016	(0.06)	(0.33)	(0.23)	(1.12)
2017	(0.77)	0.14	(0.91)	...

Interim Dividends (Per Share)

Amt	Decl	Ex	Rec	Pay
0.91Q	01/19/2017	01/30/2017	02/01/2017	02/15/2017
0.91Q	04/19/2017	04/28/2017	05/02/2017	05/16/2017
0.91Q	07/19/2017	07/28/2017	08/01/2017	08/15/2017
0.91Q	10/18/2017	10/31/2017	11/01/2017	11/15/2017

Indicated Div: $3.64

Valuation Analysis | **Institutional Holding**

Forecast EPS	$-1.58	No of Institutions	
	(01/18/2018)	504	
Market Cap	$10.4 Billion	Shares	
Book Value	$6.2 Billion		199,492,416
Price/Book	1.68	% Held	
Price/Sales	1.29		79.99

Business Summary: Refining & Marketing (MIC: 9.1.2 SIC: 4922 NAIC: 486210)

Targa Resources is a provider of midstream services and an independent midstream energy company. Co. operates two segments: Gathering and Processing, which consists of gathering, compressing, dehydrating, treating, conditioning, processing, and marketing natural gas and gathering crude oil; and Logistics and Marketing, which includes activities to convert mixed natural gas liquids (NGLs) into NGL products and provides certain services such as the fractionation, storage, terminaling, transportation, exporting, distribution and marketing of NGLs and NGL products, storing and terminaling of refined petroleum products and crude oil, as well as other natural gas supply and marketing activities.

Recent Developments: For the quarter ended Sep 30 2017, net loss amounted to US$155.1 million versus a net loss of US$3.2 million in the year-earlier quarter. Revenues were US$2.13 billion, up 29.0% from US$1.65 billion the year before. Operating loss was US$323.6 million versus an income of US$51.6 million in the prior-year quarter. Direct operating expenses rose 33.2% to US$1.82 billion from US$1.37 billion in the comparable period the year before. Indirect operating expenses increased 171.0% to US$636.8 million from US$235.0 million in the equivalent prior-year period.

Prospects: Our evaluation of Targa Resources Corp. as of Jan. 14, 2018 is the result of our systematic analysis on three basic characteristics: earnings strength, relative valuation, and recent stock price movement. The company has enjoyed a very positive trend in earnings per share over the past 5 quarters. Because the company lacks sufficient analyst estimate data, we place greater weight on the historical EPS trend as the measure of earnings strength. Based on operating earnings yield, the company is overvalued when compared to all of the companies in our coverage universe. Share price changes over the past year indicates that TRGP will perform very poorly over the near term.

Financial Data

(US$ in Thousands)	9 Mos	6 Mos	3 Mos	12/31/2016	12/31/2015	12/31/2014	12/31/2013	12/31/2012
Earnings Per Share	(2.66)	(1.98)	(2.45)	(1.80)	1.09	2.43	1.55	0.91
Cash Flow Per Share	3.75	4.15	4.77	5.41	19.34	18.14	9.20	10.42
Tang Book Value Per Share	17.32	19.22	16.68	19.36	N.M.	N.M.	N.M.	N.M.
Dividends Per Share	3.640	3.640	3.640	3.640	3.390	2.678	2.055	1.518
Dividend Payout %	...	...	...	...	311.01	110.19	132.58	166.76
Income Statement								
Total Revenue	6,112,100	3,980,300	2,112,600	6,690,900	6,658,600	8,616,500	6,556,000	5,885,700
EBITDA	(120,700)	73,000	39,300	610,300	663,000	982,900	656,600	530,900
Depn & Amortn	8,800	5,900	3,100	601,500	540,400	362,800	287,800	215,800
Income Before Taxes	(310,700)	(58,000)	(26,800)	(245,400)	(109,300)	473,000	234,700	194,300
Income Taxes	(132,300)	(34,900)	71,100	(100,600)	39,600	68,000	48,200	36,900
Net Income	(229,300)	(61,700)	(119,300)	(187,300)	58,300	102,300	65,100	38,100
Average Shares	215,600	205,000	191,800	154,400	53,600	42,100	42,100	41,800
Balance Sheet								
Current Assets	1,200,800	914,900	812,100	1,006,800	920,000	882,600	897,200	733,300
Total Assets	13,998,300	13,918,400	13,653,800	12,871,200	13,253,700	6,453,500	6,048,600	5,105,000
Current Liabilities	1,633,300	1,395,100	1,424,300	1,167,600	881,600	827,100	770,400	686,600
Long-Term Obligations	4,368,600	3,937,500	4,213,300	4,606,000	5,761,500	2,885,400	2,989,300	2,475,300
Total Liabilities	7,792,700	7,254,200	7,767,000	7,431,800	11,792,300	6,283,700	5,899,800	4,960,900
Stockholders' Equity	6,205,600	6,664,200	5,886,800	5,439,400	1,461,400	169,800	148,800	144,100
Shares Outstanding	215,632	215,575	196,639	184,720	56,020	42,143	42,162	42,294
Statistical Record								
Return on Assets %	N.M.	N.M.	N.M.	N.M.	0.59	1.64	1.17	0.85
Return on Equity %	N.M.	N.M.	N.M.	N.M.	7.15	64.22	44.45	25.15
EBITDA Margin %	N.M.	1.83	1.86	9.12	9.96	11.41	10.02	9.02
Net Margin %	N.M.	N.M.	N.M.	N.M.	0.88	1.19	0.99	0.65
Asset Turnover	0.60	0.57	0.55	0.51	0.68	1.38	1.18	1.31
Current Ratio	0.74	0.66	0.57	0.86	1.04	1.07	1.16	1.07
Debt to Equity	0.70	0.59	0.72	0.85	3.94	16.99	20.09	17.18
Price Range	61.35-40.68	61.35-36.88	61.35-27.52	58.20-15.43	107.22-25.74	150.62-85.34	88.46-52.84	52.84-39.62
P/E Ratio	...	...	...	...	98.37-23.61	61.98-35.12	57.07-34.09	58.07-43.54
Average Yield %	7.13	7.21	7.64	9.25	4.40	2.32	2.98	3.30

Address: 1000 Louisiana St., Suite 4300, Houston, TX 77002
Telephone: 713-584-1000
Fax: 713-584-1100

Web Site: www.targaresources.com
Officers: James W. Whalen - Executive Chairman, Advisor Joe Bob Perkins - President, Chief Executive Officer

Auditors: PricewaterhouseCoopers LLP
Investor Contact: 713-584-1000
Transfer Agents: Computershare Trust Company, N.A.

TAUBMAN CENTERS, INC.

Exchange	Symbol	Price	52Wk Range	Yield	P/E
NYS	TCO	$65.43 (12/29/2017)	76.17-46.30	3.82	62.31

*7 Year Price Score 67.76   *NYSE Composite Index=100   *12 Month Price Score 89.73

TRADING VOLUME (thousand shares)

Interim Earnings (Per Share)

Qtr.	Mar	Jun	Sep	Dec
2014	5.74	0.33	0.53	6.87
2015	0.47	0.37	0.50	0.42
2016	0.41	0.57	0.31	0.48
2017	0.28	0.22	0.07	...

Interim Dividends (Per Share)

Amt	Decl	Ex	Rec	Pay
0.625Q	03/02/2017	03/13/2017	03/15/2017	03/31/2017
0.625Q	06/01/2017	06/13/2017	06/15/2017	06/30/2017
0.625Q	09/01/2017	09/14/2017	09/15/2017	09/29/2017
0.625Q	12/04/2017	12/14/2017	12/15/2017	12/29/2017

Indicated Div: $2.50

Valuation Analysis

		Institutional Holding	
Forecast EPS	$0.86 (01/26/2018)	No of Institutions	354
Market Cap	$4.0 Billion	Shares	77,940,968
Book Value	$14.5 Million	% Held	104.85
Price/Book	274.87		
Price/Sales	6.37		

Business Summary: REITs (MIC: 5.3.1 SIC: 6798 NAIC: 525930)

Taubman Centers is a self-administered and self-managed real estate investment trust. The Taubman Realty Group Limited Partnership is a majority-owned partnership subsidiary of Co. that owns direct or indirect interests in all of Co.'s real estate properties. Co. owns, leases, acquires, disposes of, develops, expands, and manages regional shopping centers and interests therein. As of Dec 31 2016, Co. owned interests in 23 operating centers, which are located in Denver, Detroit, Honolulu, Kansas City, Los Angeles, Miami, Nashville, New York City, Orlando, Salt Lake City, San Francisco, San Juan, Sarasota, St. Louis, Tampa, Washington, D.C., Hanam, South Korea and Xi'an, China.

Recent Developments: For the quarter ended Sep 30 2017, income from continuing operations decreased 59.5% to US$14.3 million from US$35.2 million in the year-earlier quarter. Net income decreased 59.5% to US$14.3 million from US$35.2 million in the year-earlier quarter. Revenues were US$153.2 million, up 3.5% from US$148.0 million the year before. Revenues from property income rose 0.5% to US$88.1 million from US$87.7 million in the corresponding quarter a year earlier.

Prospects: Our evaluation of Taubman Centers Inc. as of Jan. 21, 2018 is the result of our systematic analysis on three basic characteristics: earnings strength, relative valuation, and recent stock price movement. The company has managed to produce a neutral trend in earnings per share over the past 5 quarters. Because the company lacks sufficient analyst estimate data, we place greater weight on the historical EPS trend as the measure of earnings strength. Based on operating earnings yield, the company is overvalued when compared to all of the companies in our coverage universe. Share price changes over the past year indicates that TCO will perform poorly over the near term.

Financial Data

(US$ in Thousands)	9 Mos	6 Mos	3 Mos	12/31/2016	12/31/2015	12/31/2014	12/31/2013	12/31/2012
Earnings Per Share	1.05	1.29	1.64	1.77	1.76	13.47	1.71	1.37
Cash Flow Per Share	4.34	4.72	5.29	5.04	5.01	5.75	5.84	5.40
Tang Book Value Per Share	0.24	0.63	1.05	1.19	1.87	5.03	...	...
Dividends Per Share	2.470	2.440	2.410	2.380	2.260	6.910	2.000	1.850
Dividend Payout %	235.24	189.15	146.95	134.46	128.41	51.30	116.96	135.04
Income Statement								
Total Revenue	456,981	303,759	149,083	612,557	557,172	679,129	767,154	747,974
EBITDA	230,981	156,812	76,106	337,347	299,983	312,736	412,835	391,803
Depn & Amortn	122,958	77,153	37,711	130,400	98,800	110,100	142,500	134,900
Income Before Taxes	27,949	27,367	12,849	120,662	138,142	111,833	140,312	114,287
Income Taxes	375	321	208	2,212	2,248	2,267	3,409	4,964
Net Income	54,092	43,369	23,525	132,613	134,127	893,013	132,590	106,174
Average Shares	60,710	61,001	61,053	60,829	62,161	64,921	64,575	61,376
Balance Sheet								
Current Assets	112,774	113,820	128,424	103,812	270,107	364,002	121,036	109,237
Total Assets	4,107,958	4,061,738	4,044,857	4,010,912	3,563,380	3,214,901	3,506,222	3,268,495
Current Liabilities	818,427	822,251	832,287	817,399	798,611	769,453	663,829	661,391
Long-Term Obligations	3,438,307	3,351,212	3,287,968	3,255,512	2,643,958	2,025,505	3,058,053	2,952,030
Total Liabilities	4,093,506	4,023,186	3,981,184	3,938,832	3,450,573	2,896,538	3,626,349	3,524,113
Stockholders' Equity	14,452	38,552	63,673	72,080	112,807	318,363	(120,127)	(255,618)
Shares Outstanding	60,712	60,706	60,685	60,430	60,233	63,324	63,101	63,310
Statistical Record								
Return on Assets %	2.21	2.65	3.22	3.49	3.96	26.57	3.91	3.21
Return on Equity %	180.56	161.32	158.75	143.06	62.22	900.96	...	...
EBITDA Margin %	50.54	51.62	51.05	55.07	53.84	46.05	53.81	52.38
Net Margin %	11.84	14.28	15.78	21.65	24.07	131.49	17.28	14.19
Asset Turnover	0.15	0.16	0.16	0.16	0.16	0.20	0.23	0.23
Current Ratio	0.14	0.14	0.15	0.13	0.34	0.47	0.18	0.17
Debt to Equity	237.91	86.93	51.64	45.17	23.44	6.36	...	...
Price Range	76.17-49.14	81.63-57.77	81.63-64.08	81.63-66.67	84.70-67.14	80.06-63.34	88.95-63.65	81.34-62.03
P/E Ratio	72.54-46.80	63.28-44.78	49.77-39.07	46.12-37.67	48.13-38.15	5.94-4.70	52.02-37.22	59.37-45.28
Average Yield %	3.82	3.47	3.33	3.27	3.03	9.43	2.68	2.46

Address: 200 East Long Lake Road, Suite 300, Bloomfield Hills, MI 48304-2324 Telephone: 248-258-6800	Web Site: www.taubman.com Officers: Robert S. Taubman - Chairman, President, Chief Executive Officer William S. Taubman - Chief Operating Officer	Auditors: KPMG LLP Investor Contact: 248-258-7367 Transfer Agents: Computershare, Providence, R.I.

TC PIPELINES, LP

Exchange	Symbol	Price	52Wk Range	Yield	P/E	Div Achiever
NYS	TCP	$53.10 (12/29/2017)	64.90-48.88	7.53	17.18	17 Years

*7 Year Price Score 85.28 ***NYSE Composite Index=100** ***12 Month Price Score 87.39**

Interim Earnings (Per Share)

Qtr.	Mar	Jun	Sep	Dec
2014	0.90	0.58	0.48	0.71
2015	0.88	0.66	0.70	(2.26)
2016	1.10	0.76	0.65	0.70
2017	1.05	0.73	0.61	...

Interim Dividends (Per Share)

Amt	Decl	Ex	Rec	Pay
0.94Q	01/23/2017	01/31/2017	02/02/2017	02/14/2017
0.94Q	04/25/2017	05/03/2017	05/05/2017	05/15/2017
1.00Q	07/20/2017	07/28/2017	08/01/2017	08/11/2017
1.00Q	10/24/2017	11/02/2017	11/03/2017	11/14/2017

Indicated Div: $4.00

Valuation Analysis		Institutional Holding	
Forecast EPS	$3.14	No of Institutions	
	(01/18/2018)	243	
Market Cap	$3.7 Billion	Shares	
Book Value	N/A	47,789,784	
Price/Book	N/A	% Held	
Price/Sales	9.70	61.79	

Business Summary: Equipment & Services (MIC: 9.1.3 SIC: 4922 NAIC: 486210)

TC PipeLines is engaged in acquiring, owning and participating in the management of energy infrastructure businesses in North America. As of Dec 31 2016, Co. had four wholly-owned pipelines and equity ownership interests in three natural gas interstate pipeline systems that are collectively designed to transport approximately 9.10 billion cubic feet per day of natural gas from producing regions and import facilities to market hubs and consuming markets primarily in the Western, Midwestern and Eastern U.S. All of Co.'s pipeline systems are operated by subsidiaries of TransCanada Corporation and its subsidiaries.

Recent Developments: For the quarter ended Sep 30 2017, net income decreased 8.3% to US$55.0 million from US$60.0 million in the year-earlier quarter. Revenues were US$100.0 million, down 2.9% from US$103.0 million the year before. Indirect operating expenses increased 4.7% to US$45.0 million from US$43.0 million in the equivalent prior-year period.

Prospects: Our evaluation of TC PipeLines L.P. as of Jan. 14, 2018 is the result of our systematic analysis on three basic characteristics: earnings strength, relative valuation, and recent stock price movement. The company has enjoyed a very positive trend in earnings per share over the past 5 quarters. However, while recent estimates for the company have been mixed, TCP has posted results that fell short of analysts expectations. Based on operating earnings yield, the company is undervalued when compared to all of the companies in our coverage universe. Share price changes over the past year indicates that TCP will perform poorly over the near term.

Financial Data

(US$ in Thousands)	9 Mos	6 Mos	3 Mos	12/31/2016	12/31/2015	12/31/2014	12/31/2013	12/31/2012
Earnings Per Share	3.09	3.13	3.16	3.21	(0.03)	2.67	2.13	2.51
Cash Flow Per Share	6.28	6.04	5.55	5.78	4.60	4.91	4.62	2.85
Dividends Per Share	3.820	3.760	3.710	3.660	3.460	3.300	3.180	3.100
Dividend Payout %	123.62	120.13	117.41	114.02	...	123.60	149.30	123.51
Income Statement								
Total Revenue	313,000	213,000	89,000	357,000	344,000	336,000	341,000	65,000
EBITDA	241,000	166,000	70,000	278,000	61,000	249,000	252,000	41,000
Depn & Amortn	75,000	51,000	22,000	86,000	85,000	86,000	86,000	11,000
Income Before Taxes	107,000	79,000	32,000	128,000	(77,000)	116,000	124,000	8,000
Income Taxes	1,000	1,000	...	...	...	...	...	...
Net Income	186,000	132,000	75,000	244,000	13,000	172,000	155,000	137,000
Average Shares	69,600	68,900	68,300	67,400	63,900	62,700	58,900	53,500
Balance Sheet								
Current Assets	121,000	100,000	107,000	102,000	81,000	68,000	69,000	12,000
Total Assets	3,591,000	3,516,000	3,166,000	3,158,000	3,133,000	3,349,000	3,443,000	1,998,000
Current Liabilities	108,000	130,000	66,000	66,000	59,000	291,000	55,000	11,000
Long-Term Obligations	2,427,000	2,333,000	1,786,000	1,835,000	1,896,000	1,446,000	1,575,000	685,000
Total Liabilities	2,675,000	2,602,000	1,880,000	1,929,000	1,982,000	1,997,000	2,094,000	697,000
Stockholders' Equity	...	...	64,000	83,000	...	...	...	...
Shares Outstanding	69,600	70,900	70,500	69,354	66,217	63,561	62,327	53,472
Statistical Record								
Return on Assets %	7.18	7.38	7.68	7.74	0.40	5.06	5.70	6.70
EBITDA Margin %	77.00	77.93	78.65	77.87	17.73	74.11	73.90	63.08
Net Margin %	59.42	61.97	84.27	68.35	3.78	51.19	45.45	210.77
Asset Turnover	0.11	0.11	0.11	0.11	0.11	0.10	0.13	0.03
Current Ratio	1.12	0.77	1.62	1.55	1.37	0.23	1.25	1.09
Debt to Equity	...	...	27.91	22.11	...	...	...	...
Price Range	64.90-47.64	64.90-47.64	64.90-47.53	59.99-35.44	72.53-41.48	76.59-45.52	52.18-40.36	47.58-38.50
P/E Ratio	21.00-15.42	20.73-15.22	20.54-15.04	18.69-11.04	...	28.69-17.05	24.50-18.95	18.96-15.34
Average Yield %	6.79	6.67	6.68	7.04	5.94	5.92	6.75	7.05

Address: 700 Louisiana Street, Suite 700, Houston, TX 77002-2761 **Telephone:** 877-290-2772	**Web Site:** www.tcpipelineslp.com **Officers:** Karl R. Johannson - Chairman, Holding/Parent Company Officer Brandon M. Anderson - President, Principal Executive Officer, Holding/Parent Company Officer	**Auditors:** KPMG LLP **Investor Contact:** 877-.29-0.2772 **Transfer Agents:** Computershare

TCF FINANCIAL CORP

Exchange	Symbol	Price	52Wk Range	Yield	P/E
NYS	TCF	$20.50 (12/29/2017)	20.85-14.76	1.46	17.98

*7 Year Price Score 92.53 *NYSE Composite Index=100 *12 Month Price Score 109.20

Interim Earnings (Per Share)

Qtr.	Mar	Jun	Sep	Dec
2014	0.24	0.29	0.29	0.11
2015	0.21	0.29	0.29	0.29
2016	0.26	0.31	0.31	0.27
2017	0.25	0.33	0.29	...

Interim Dividends (Per Share)

Amt	Decl	Ex	Rec	Pay
0.075Q	01/25/2017	02/13/2017	02/15/2017	03/01/2017
0.075Q	04/20/2017	05/11/2017	05/15/2017	06/01/2017
0.075Q	07/19/2017	08/11/2017	08/15/2017	09/01/2017
0.075Q	10/18/2017	11/14/2017	11/15/2017	12/01/2017

Indicated Div: $0.30 (Div. Reinv. Plan)

Valuation Analysis | **Institutional Holding**

Forecast EPS	$1.24 (01/24/2018)	No of Institutions	390
Market Cap	$3.5 Billion	Shares	173,544,128
Book Value	$2.6 Billion	% Held	81.69
Price/Book	1.37		
Price/Sales	2.48		

TRADING VOLUME (thousand shares)

Business Summary: Banking (MIC: 5.1.1 SIC: 6021 NAIC: 522110)

TCF Financial is a bank holding company. Through its subsidiary, TCF National Bank (TCF Bank), Co. provides retail banking products and commercial banking products. Co. also conducts commercial leasing and equipment finance business in all 50 states and, to a limited extent, in foreign countries; commercial inventory finance business in all 50 states and Canada and, to a limited extent, in other foreign countries and indirect auto finance business in all 50 states. Co.'s reportable segments are comprised of: Consumer Banking, Wholesale Banking and Enterprise Services. At Dec 31 2016, Co. had total assets of $21.44 billion and total deposits of $17.24 billion.

Recent Developments: For the quarter ended Sep 30 2017, net income increased 7.5% to US$60.5 million from US$56.3 million in the year-earlier quarter. Net interest income increased 10.4% to US$234.1 million from US$212.0 million in the year-earlier quarter. Provision for loan losses was US$14.5 million versus US$13.9 million in the prior-year quarter, an increase of 4.7%. Non-interest income fell 8.7% to US$109.2 million from US$119.7 million, while non-interest expense advanced 2.7% to US$235.0 million.

Prospects: Our evaluation of TCF Financial Corp. as of Jan. 21, 2018 is the result of our systematic analysis on three basic characteristics: earnings strength, relative valuation, and recent stock price movement. The company has produced a positive trend in earnings per share over the past 5 quarters and while recent estimates for the company have been raised by analysts, TCF has posted results that fell short of analysts expectations. Based on operating earnings yield, the company is undervalued when compared to all of the companies in our coverage universe. Share price changes over the past year indicates that TCF will perform very poorly over the near term.

Financial Data

(US$ in Thousands)	9 Mos	6 Mos	3 Mos	12/31/2016	12/31/2015	12/31/2014	12/31/2013	12/31/2012
Earnings Per Share	1.14	1.16	1.14	1.15	1.07	0.94	0.82	(1.37)
Cash Flow Per Share	0.10	(0.24)	0.06	1.73	2.19	1.91	2.55	3.12
Tang Book Value Per Share	12.12	11.88	11.56	11.34	10.61	9.75	8.87	8.41
Dividends Per Share	0.300	0.300	0.300	0.300	0.225	0.200	0.200	0.200
Dividend Payout %	26.32	25.86	26.32	26.09	21.03	21.28	24.39	...
Income Statement								
Interest Income	748,429	490,824	242,307	930,730	891,930	874,229	864,540	884,623
Interest Expense	65,051	41,549	20,193	82,624	71,542	58,600	61,916	104,604
Net Interest Income	683,378	449,275	222,114	848,106	820,388	815,629	802,624	780,019
Provision for Losses	46,184	31,639	12,193	65,874	52,944	95,737	118,368	247,443
Non-Interest Income	327,407	218,177	103,514	465,900	441,998	433,267	404,058	490,423
Non-Interest Expense	712,128	477,093	244,006	909,887	894,747	871,777	845,269	1,362,554
Income Before Taxes	252,473	158,720	69,429	338,245	314,695	281,382	243,045	(339,555)
Income Taxes	77,341	46,637	20,843	116,528	108,872	99,766	84,345	(132,858)
Net Income	167,238	106,710	46,278	212,124	197,123	174,187	151,668	(212,884)
Average Shares	169,240	168,857	168,529	167,807	166,241	164,084	161,926	159,268
Balance Sheet								
Net Loans & Leases	19,075,011	18,373,488	18,420,359	17,952,390	17,437,570	16,369,743	15,674,477	15,168,885
Total Assets	23,005,038	22,054,651	21,836,568	21,441,326	20,691,704	19,394,611	18,379,840	18,225,917
Total Deposits	18,107,486	17,518,804	17,465,590	17,242,522	16,719,989	15,449,882	14,432,776	14,050,786
Total Liabilities	20,428,430	19,527,586	19,372,456	19,013,843	18,400,788	17,272,962	16,426,872	16,362,544
Stockholders' Equity	2,576,608	2,527,065	2,464,112	2,427,483	2,290,916	2,121,649	1,952,968	1,863,373
Shares Outstanding	171,833	171,489	170,941	170,991	169,844	167,461	165,122	163,386
Statistical Record								
Return on Assets %	0.99	0.99	0.97	1.00	0.98	0.92	0.83	N.M.
Return on Equity %	8.68	8.65	8.75	8.97	8.93	8.55	7.95	N.M.
Net Interest Margin %	90.88	91.41	91.67	91.12	91.98	93.30	92.84	88.18
Efficiency Ratio %	64.07	64.18	70.56	65.15	67.08	66.68	66.63	99.09
Loans to Deposits	1.05	1.05	1.05	1.04	1.04	1.06	1.09	1.08
Price Range	19.91-13.80	19.91-11.92	19.91-11.72	19.91-10.47	17.16-13.95	17.19-14.26	16.45-12.15	12.44-9.85
P/E Ratio	17.46-12.11	17.16-10.28	17.46-10.28	17.31-9.10	16.04-13.04	18.29-15.17	20.06-14.82	...
Average Yield %	1.82	1.87	1.96	2.16	1.44	1.26	1.37	1.77

Address: 200 Lake Street East, Wayzata, MN 55391-1693
Telephone: 952-745-2760

Web Site: www.tcfbank.com
Officers: Craig R. Dahl - Vice-Chairman, President, Chief Executive Officer, Executive Vice President
Thomas F. Jasper - Vice-Chairman, Chief Operating Officer, Executive Vice President, Chief Financial Officer

Auditors: KPMG LLP
Investor Contact: 952-745-2756
Transfer Agents: Computershare Trust Company, N.A., Providence, RI

TE CONNECTIVITY LTD

Exchange	Symbol	Price	52Wk Range	Yield	P/E
NYS	TEL	$95.04 (12/29/2017)	96.23-67.31	1.68	20.22

*7 Year Price Score 115.48 *NYSE Composite Index=100 *12 Month Price Score 109.90

TRADING VOLUME (thousand shares)

Interim Earnings (Per Share)

Qtr.	Dec	Mar	Jun	Sep
2012-13	0.65	0.65	0.80	0.92
2013-14	0.84	0.87	0.97	1.59
2014-15	1.14	1.45	0.75	2.55
2015-16	0.91	1.03	2.35	1.23
2016-17	1.14	1.13	1.22	1.22

Interim Dividends (Per Share)

Amt	Decl	Ex	Rec	Pay
0.37Q	02/14/2017	02/22/2017	02/24/2017	03/10/2017
0.40Q	05/08/2017	05/24/2017	05/26/2017	06/09/2017
0.40Q	08/09/2017	08/23/2017	08/25/2017	09/08/2017
0.40Q	11/09/2017	11/22/2017	11/24/2017	12/08/2017

Indicated Div: $1.60

Valuation Analysis

Forecast EPS: N/A

Market Cap: $33.4 Billion
Book Value: $9.8 Billion
Price/Book: 3.43
Price/Sales: 2.55

Institutional Holding

No of Institutions: 863
Shares: 367,359,072
% Held: N/A

Business Summary: Electrical Equipment (MIC: 7.3.1 SIC: 5065 NAIC: 334111)

TE Connectivity operates three segments: Transportation Solutions, which engages in connectivity and sensor technologies, focusing on terminals and connector systems and components, sensors, relays, application tooling, and wire and heat shrink tubing; Industrial Solutions, which supplies products that connect and distribute power, data and signals, focusing on terminals and connector systems and components, heat shrink tubing, relays, and wire and cable; and Communications Solutions, which supplies electronics for the data and devices and appliances markets, focusing on terminals and connector systems and components, undersea telecommunication systems, heat shrink tubing, and antennas.

Recent Developments:
For the year ended Sep 30 2017, income from continuing operations decreased 13.8% to US$1.67 billion from US$1.94 billion a year earlier. Net income decreased 16.2% to US$1.68 billion from US$2.01 billion in the prior year. Revenues were US$13.11 billion, up 7.1% from US$12.24 billion the year before. Operating income was US$2.05 billion versus US$1.90 billion in the prior year, an increase of 7.6%. Direct operating expenses rose 5.6% to US$8.66 billion from US$8.21 billion in the comparable period the year before. Indirect operating expenses increased 12.8% to US$2.40 billion from US$2.13 billion in the equivalent prior-year period.

Prospects:
Our evaluation of TE Connectivity Ltd. as of Sep. 17, 2017 is the result of our systematic analysis on three basic characteristics: earnings strength, relative valuation, and recent stock price movement. The company has generated a negative trend in earnings per share over the past 5 quarters and while recent estimates for the company have remained steady, TEL has posted better than expected results. Based on operating earnings yield, the company is undervalued when compared to all of the companies in our coverage universe. Share price changes over the past year indicates that TEL will perform well over the near term.

Financial Data

(US$ in Millions)	09/30/2017	09/30/2016	09/25/2015	09/26/2014	09/27/2013	09/28/2012	09/30/2011	09/24/2010
Earnings Per Share	4.70	5.44	5.89	4.27	3.02	2.59	2.81	2.41
Cash Flow Per Share	6.54	5.17	4.74	5.09	4.91	4.58	4.00	3.72
Tang Book Value Per Share	6.42	3.14	8.14	7.56	6.83	5.47	7.63	7.77
Dividends Per Share	1.540	1.400	1.240	1.080	0.920	0.780	0.680	0.640
Dividend Payout %	32.77	25.74	21.05	25.29	30.46	30.12	24.20	26.56
Income Statement								
Total Revenue	13,113	12,238	12,233	13,912	13,280	13,282	14,312	12,070
EBITDA	2,504	1,706	2,157	2,610	1,869	2,070	2,274	2,182
Depn & Amortn	466	436	463	502	496	502	506	489
Income Before Taxes	1,928	1,162	1,575	1,996	1,248	1,415	1,629	1,558
Income Taxes	255	(779)	337	207	(29)	249	376	493
Net Income	1,683	2,009	2,420	1,781	1,276	1,112	1,245	1,103
Average Shares	358	369	411	417	423	430	443	457
Balance Sheet								
Current Assets	5,926	4,775	7,887	7,544	6,309	6,503	6,632	6,731
Total Assets	19,403	17,608	20,608	20,152	18,461	19,306	17,723	16,992
Current Liabilities	3,847	3,066	3,577	3,954	3,924	4,004	3,401	3,460
Long-Term Obligations	3,634	3,739	3,403	3,281	2,303	2,696	2,668	2,307
Total Liabilities	9,652	9,123	11,023	11,145	10,081	11,335	10,249	9,944
Stockholders' Equity	9,751	8,485	9,585	9,007	8,380	7,971	7,474	7,048
Shares Outstanding	351	355	393	407	411	422	423	443
Statistical Record								
Return on Assets %	9.09	10.34	11.91	9.25	6.78	6.02	7.06	6.66
Return on Equity %	18.46	21.88	26.10	20.54	15.65	14.44	16.87	15.73
EBITDA Margin %	19.10	13.94	17.63	18.76	14.07	15.59	15.89	18.08
Net Margin %	12.83	16.42	19.78	12.80	9.61	8.37	8.70	9.14
Asset Turnover	0.71	0.63	0.60	0.72	0.71	0.72	0.81	0.73
Current Ratio	1.54	1.56	2.20	1.91	1.61	1.62	1.95	1.95
Debt to Equity	0.37	0.44	0.36	0.36	0.27	0.34	0.36	0.33
Price Range	83.22-61.03	67.61-52.27	73.42-51.47	64.97-49.91	53.54-32.03	37.30-27.25	38.51-27.86	32.85-21.12
P/E Ratio	17.71-12.99	12.43-9.61	12.47-8.74	15.22-11.69	17.73-10.61	14.40-10.52	13.70-9.91	13.63-8.76
Average Yield %	2.08	2.30	1.92	1.86	2.18	2.31	2.01	2.46

Address: Rheinstrasse 20, Schaffhausen, CH-8200	Web Site: www.te.com	Auditors: Deloitte†& Touche†LLP
Telephone: 526-336-661	Officers: Thomas J. Lynch - Executive Chairman, Chairman, Chief Executive Officer, Division Officer Terrence R. Curtin - President, Chief Executive Officer, Executive Vice President, Vice President, Chief Financial Officer, Corporate Controller, Division Officer	Investor Contact: 610-893-9551 Transfer Agents: Computershare Shareowner Services LLC, Jersey City, NJ

TELEDYNE TECHNOLOGIES INC

Exchange	Symbol	Price	52Wk Range	Yield	P/E
NYS	TDY	$181.15 (12/29/2017)	186.24-121.11	N/A	30.86

*7 Year Price Score 124.68 *NYSE Composite Index=100 *12 Month Price Score 117.71

Interim Earnings (Per Share)

Qtr.	Mar	Jun	Sep	Dec
2014	1.20	1.47	1.47	1.62
2015	1.20	1.34	1.34	1.56
2016	1.10	1.31	.1.46	1.47
2017	0.84	1.66	1.90	...

Interim Dividends (Per Share)

No Dividends Paid

Valuation Analysis

		Institutional Holding	
Forecast EPS	$6.15	No of Institutions	
	(01/16/2018)	371	
Market Cap	$6.4 Billion	Shares	
Book Value	$1.9 Billion	40,858,648	
Price/Book	3.46	% Held	
Price/Sales	2.61	84.42	

TRADING VOLUME (thousand shares)

Business Summary: Electronic Instruments & Related Products (MIC: 6.2.3 SIC: 3812 NAIC: 334511)

Teledyne Technologies provides technologies for industrial markets. Co. has four segments: Instrumentation; which provides monitoring and control instruments for marine, environmental, industrial and other applications, as well as electronic test and measurement equipment; Digital Imaging, which includes sensors, cameras and systems, as well as micro electro mechanical systems; Aerospace and Defense Electronics, which provide electronic components and subsystems and communications products; and Engineered Systems, which provide systems engineering and integration, technology development, as well as manufacturing solutions for defense, space, environmental and energy applications.

Recent Developments: For the quarter ended Oct 1 2017, net income increased 32.7% to US$69.0 million from US$52.0 million in the year-earlier quarter. Revenues were US$662.2 million, up 25.7% from US$526.8 million the year before. Operating income was US$92.9 million versus US$68.8 million in the prior-year quarter, an increase of 35.0%. Direct operating expenses rose 28.0% to US$405.8 million from US$317.0 million in the comparable period the year before. Indirect operating expenses increased 16.0% to US$163.5 million from US$141.0 million in the equivalent prior-year period.

Prospects: Our evaluation of Teledyne Technologies Inc. as of Jan. 14, 2018 is the result of our systematic analysis on three basic characteristics: earnings strength, relative valuation, and recent stock price movement. The company has generated a negative trend in earnings per share over the past 5 quarters and while recent estimates for the company have remained steady, TDY has posted better than expected results. Based on operating earnings yield, the company is about fairly valued when compared to all of the companies in our coverage universe. Share price changes over the past year indicates that TDY will perform well over the near term.

Financial Data
(US$ in Thousands)

	9 Mos	6 Mos	3 Mos	01/01/2017	01/03/2016	12/28/2014	12/29/2013	12/30/2012
Earnings Per Share	5.87	5.43	5.08	5.37	5.44	5.75	4.87	4.39
Cash Flow Per Share	8.91	8.66	8.58	9.19	5.86	7.78	5.49	5.18
Tang Book Value Per Share	N.M.	N.M.	N.M.	3.60	N.M.	N.M.	4.34	N.M.
Income Statement								
Total Revenue	1,899,400	1,237,200	566,100	2,149,900	2,298,100	2,394,000	2,338,600	2,127,300
EBITDA	311,600	190,300	71,600	322,100	340,400	363,400	304,000	294,900
Depn & Amortn	87,400	56,000	22,800	57,600	58,300	62,300	59,600	48,900
Income Before Taxes	198,700	117,000	40,600	241,300	258,200	282,100	224,000	228,200
Income Taxes	39,100	26,400	10,100	50,400	62,700	66,500	39,500	65,400
Net Income	159,600	90,600	30,500	190,900	195,800	217,700	185,000	164,100
Average Shares	36,400	36,200	36,100	35,500	35,300	37,900	38,000	37,400
Balance Sheet								
Current Assets	1,041,000	1,038,700	985,100	846,200	828,200	941,700	799,100	744,800
Total Assets	3,847,500	3,780,100	3,673,000	2,774,400	2,718,500	2,862,200	2,751,100	2,406,400
Current Liabilities	525,100	619,800	599,600	501,800	393,600	539,000	418,100	407,300
Long-Term Obligations	1,193,200	1,153,500	1,209,600	515,800	762,900	618,900	549,000	556,200
Total Liabilities	1,994,100	2,048,600	2,068,900	1,220,000	1,374,400	1,434,900	1,279,400	1,258,600
Stockholders' Equity	1,853,400	1,731,500	1,604,100	1,554,400	1,344,100	1,427,300	1,471,700	1,147,800
Shares Outstanding	35,436	35,331	35,238	35,110	34,514	36,655	37,571	37,162
Statistical Record								
Return on Assets %	6.40	5.96	5.65	6.97	6.90	7.78	7.19	7.78
Return on Equity %	12.51	12.19	11.96	13.21	13.90	15.06	14.16	15.47
EBITDA Margin %	16.41	15.38	12.65	14.98	14.81	15.18	13.00	13.86
Net Margin %	8.40	7.32	5.39	8.88	8.52	9.09	7.91	7.71
Asset Turnover	0.74	0.71	0.68	0.78	0.81	0.86	0.91	1.01
Current Ratio	1.98	1.68	1.64	1.69	2.10	1.75	1.91	1.83
Debt to Equity	0.64	0.67	0.75	0.33	0.57	0.43	0.37	0.48
Price Range	161.03-102.63	135.76-97.28	135.24-86.08	128.89-76.61	111.48-83.47	108.50-88.48	92.99-65.07	65.76-54.85
P/E Ratio	27.43-17.48	25.00-17.92	26.62-16.94	24.00-14.27	20.49-15.34	18.87-15.39	19.09-13.36	14.98-12.49

Address: 1049 Camino Dos Rios, Thousand Oaks, CA 91360-2362	**Web Site:** www.teledyne.com	**Auditors:** Deloitte & Touche LLP
Telephone: 805-373-4545	**Officers:** Robert Mehrabian - Chairman, President, Chief Executive Officer Susan L. Main - Senior Vice President, Chief Financial Officer, Vice President, Controller	**Investor Contact:** 805-373-4542
Fax: 805-373-4775		**Transfer Agents:** Computershare, Jersey City, NJ

TELEFLEX INCORPORATED

Exchange	Symbol	Price	52Wk Range	Yield	P/E
NYS	TFX	$248.82 (12/29/2017)	270.19-158.86	0.55	45.49

*7 Year Price Score 143.64 *NYSE Composite Index=100 *12 Month Price Score 113.96

Interim Earnings (Per Share)

Qtr.	Mar	Jun	Sep	Dec
2014	0.76	1.02	1.18	1.08
2015	0.81	0.93	1.25	2.10
2016	1.04	1.26	1.40	1.29
2017	0.86	1.67	1.65	...

Interim Dividends (Per Share)

Amt	Decl	Ex	Rec	Pay
0.34Q	02/23/2017	03/01/2017	03/03/2017	03/15/2017
0.34Q	05/08/2017	05/16/2017	05/18/2017	06/15/2017
0.34Q	08/03/2017	08/11/2017	08/15/2017	09/15/2017
0.34Q	10/31/2017	11/14/2017	11/15/2017	12/15/2017

Indicated Div: $1.36 (Div. Reinv. Plan)

Valuation Analysis   **Institutional Holding**

Forecast EPS	$8.35 (01/18/2018)	No of Institutions	532
Market Cap	$11.2 Billion	Shares	
Book Value	$2.5 Billion		52,580,140
Price/Book	4.53	% Held	
Price/Sales	5.43		94.56

TRADING VOLUME (thousand shares)

Business Summary: Medical Instruments & Equipment (MIC: 4.3.1 SIC: 3841 NAIC: 339112)

Teleflex is a provider of medical technology products. Co. designs, develops, manufactures and supplies single-use medical devices used by hospitals and healthcare providers for common diagnostic and therapeutic procedures in critical care and surgical applications. Co. has six segments: Vascular North America; Anesthesia North America; Surgical North America; Europe, the Middle East and Africa; Asia; and OEM. All of Co.'s segments, other than the OEM segment, design, manufacture and distribute medical devices used in critical care, surgical applications and cardiac care. Co.'s OEM segment designs, manufactures and supplies devices and instruments for other medical device manufacturers.

Recent Developments: For the quarter ended Oct 1 2017, income from continuing operations increased 19.9% to US$79.4 million from US$66.2 million in the year-earlier quarter. Net income increased 16.1% to US$77.0 million from US$66.3 million in the year-earlier quarter. Revenues were US$534.7 million, up 17.4% from US$455.6 million the year before. Operating income was US$110.4 million versus US$86.5 million in the prior-year quarter, an increase of 27.6%. Direct operating expenses rose 11.9% to US$239.5 million from US$214.0 million in the comparable period the year before. Indirect operating expenses increased 19.2% to US$184.9 million from US$155.1 million in the equivalent prior-year period.

Prospects: Our evaluation of Teleflex Inc. as of Jan. 14, 2018 is the result of our systematic analysis on three basic characteristics: earnings strength, relative valuation, and recent stock price movement. The company has generated a negative trend in earnings per share over the past 5 quarters. However, while recent estimates for the company have been lowered by analysts, TFX has posted better than expected results. Based on operating earnings yield, the company is overvalued when compared to all of the companies in our coverage universe. Share price changes over the past year indicates that TFX will perform very well over the near term.

Financial Data

(US$ in Thousands)	9 Mos	6 Mos	3 Mos	12/31/2016	12/31/2015	12/31/2014	12/31/2013	12/31/2012
Earnings Per Share	5.47	5.22	4.81	4.98	5.10	4.04	3.45	(4.65)
Cash Flow Per Share	9.52	9.49	9.68	9.45	7.30	7.02	5.59	4.73
Dividends Per Share	1.360	1.360	1.360	1.360	1.360	1.360	1.360	1.360
Dividend Payout %	24.86	26.05	28.27	27.31	26.67	33.66	39.42	...
Income Statement								
Total Revenue	1,551,197	1,016,494	487,881	1,868,027	1,809,690	1,839,832	1,696,271	1,551,009
EBITDA	386,088	237,712	89,608	418,098	413,830	395,995	324,987	(16,907)
Depn & Amortn	110,306	72,284	34,371	117,906	108,393	111,133	92,976	80,468
Income Before Taxes	217,514	128,138	37,680	245,725	244,646	220,110	175,730	(165,369)
Income Taxes	19,404	9,426	(2,669)	8,074	7,838	28,650	23,547	16,413
Net Income	195,188	118,173	40,170	237,377	244,863	187,679	150,881	(190,057)
Average Shares	46,587	46,818	46,615	47,646	48,058	46,470	43,693	40,859
Balance Sheet								
Current Assets	1,766,751	1,407,618	1,395,127	1,183,393	1,006,431	1,053,209	1,200,554	1,069,079
Total Assets	5,680,733	5,290,024	5,232,436	3,891,213	3,878,516	3,977,255	4,209,007	3,739,497
Current Liabilities	374,645	376,051	392,358	427,646	666,712	634,899	635,120	274,405
Long-Term Obligations	2,172,805	1,887,716	1,957,797	850,252	646,000	700,000	930,000	965,280
Total Liabilities	3,208,256	2,931,495	3,013,532	1,751,872	1,869,244	2,065,946	2,295,480	1,960,547
Stockholders' Equity	2,472,477	2,358,529	2,218,904	2,139,341	2,009,272	1,911,309	1,913,527	1,778,950
Shares Outstanding	45,049	45,037	46,795	44,073	41,609	41,439	41,179	40,972
Statistical Record								
Return on Assets %	5.29	5.29	4.94	6.09	6.23	4.59	3.80	N.M.
Return on Equity %	11.04	10.97	10.57	11.41	12.49	9.81	8.17	N.M.
EBITDA Margin %	24.89	23.39	18.37	22.38	22.87	21.52	19.16	N.M.
Net Margin %	12.58	11.63	8.23	12.71	13.53	10.20	8.89	N.M.
Asset Turnover	0.43	0.43	0.42	0.48	0.46	0.45	0.43	0.40
Current Ratio	4.72	3.74	3.56	2.77	1.51	1.66	1.89	3.90
Debt to Equity	0.88	0.80	0.88	0.40	0.32	0.37	0.49	0.54
Price Range	242.56-139.41	210.37-139.41	197.10-139.41	188.35-126.00	140.26-109.41	119.15-90.94	98.82-71.31	71.38-57.73
P/E Ratio	44.34-25.49	40.30-26.71	40.98-28.98	37.82-25.30	27.50-21.45	29.49-22.51	28.64-20.67	...
Average Yield %	0.72	0.76	0.80	0.85	1.07	1.28	1.66	2.13

Address: 550 East Swedesford Road, Suite 400, Wayne, PA 19087
Telephone: 610-225-6800

Web Site: www.teleflex.com
Officers: Liam Kelly - President, Executive Vice President, Chief Operating Officer, Division Officer Thomas E. Powell - Executive Vice President, Senior Vice President, Chief Financial Officer

Auditors: PricewaterhouseCoopers LLP
Investor Contact: 610-948-2836
Transfer Agents: American Stock Transfer & Trust Company, New York, NY

TELEPHONE & DATA SYSTEMS INC

Exchange	Symbol	Price	52Wk Range	Yield	P/E	Div Achiever
NYS	TDS	$27.80 (12/29/2017)	32.75-24.81	2.23	N/A	42 Years

*7 Year Price Score 83.43 *NYSE Composite Index=100 *12 Month Price Score 90.40

Interim Earnings (Per Share)

Qtr.	Mar	Jun	Sep	Dec
2014	0.16	(0.20)	(1.07)	(0.16)
2015	1.33	0.21	0.46	(0.01)
2016	0.07	0.25	0.11	(0.05)
2017	0.33	0.09	(1.64)	...

Interim Dividends (Per Share)

Amt	Decl	Ex	Rec	Pay
0.155Q	02/24/2017	03/15/2017	03/17/2017	03/31/2017
0.155Q	05/26/2017	06/14/2017	06/16/2017	06/30/2017
0.155Q	08/16/2017	09/14/2017	09/15/2017	09/29/2017
0.155Q	11/29/2017	12/14/2017	12/15/2017	12/28/2017

Indicated Div: $0.62

Valuation Analysis

		Institutional Holding	
Forecast EPS	$-1.31 (01/05/2018)	No of Institutions	360
Market Cap	$3.1 Billion	Shares	114,972,736
Book Value	$4.0 Billion	% Held	
Price/Book	0.77	N/A	
Price/Sales	0.62		

TRADING VOLUME (thousand shares)

Business Summary: Services (MIC: 6.1.2 SIC: 4813 NAIC: 517110)

Telephone and Data Systems is a telecommunications company. Co. provided communications services to approximately 5.0 million wireless customers and 1.2 million wireline and cable connections at Dec 31 2016. Co. conducts its wireless operations through its subsidiary, United States Cellular Corp. Co. provides broadband, video, voice and hosted and managed services, through its subsidiary, TDS Telecommunications Corporation. Co. has four business segments comprised of: U.S. Cellular, which provides a range of wireless devices such as handsets, tablets, mobile hotspots, home phones and routers; and TDS Telecom's Wireline, Cable, and Hosted and Managed Services operations.

Recent Developments: For the quarter ended Sep 30 2017, net loss amounted to US$231.0 million versus net income of US$16.0 million in the year-earlier quarter. Revenues were US$1.25 billion, down 4.8% from US$1.31 billion the year before. Operating loss was US$232.0 million versus an income of US$33.0 million in the prior-year quarter. Direct operating expenses declined 6.5% to US$585.0 million from US$626.0 million in the comparable period the year before. Indirect operating expenses increased 37.1% to US$898.0 million from US$655.0 million in the equivalent prior-year period.

Prospects: Our evaluation of Telephone and Data Systems Inc. as of Jan. 14, 2018 is the result of our systematic analysis on three basic characteristics: earnings strength, relative valuation, and recent stock price movement. The company has suffered a very negative trend in earnings per share over the past 5 quarters. Because the company lacks sufficient analyst estimate data, we place greater weight on the historical EPS trend as the measure of earnings strength. Based on operating earnings yield, the company is overvalued when compared to all of the companies in our coverage universe. Share price changes over the past year indicates that TDS will perform in line with the market over the near term.

Financial Data

(US$ in Thousands)	9 Mos	6 Mos	3 Mos	12/31/2016	12/31/2015	12/31/2014	12/31/2013	12/31/2012
Earnings Per Share	(1.27)	0.48	0.64	0.39	1.98	(1.26)	1.29	0.75
Cash Flow Per Share	6.89	6.67	6.12	7.09	7.27	3.64	4.56	10.14
Tang Book Value Per Share	8.75	8.02	11.15	10.97	11.25	12.91	15.29	15.52
Dividends Per Share	0.613	0.606	0.599	0.592	0.564	0.536	0.510	0.490
Dividend Payout %	...	126.25	93.59	151.79	28.48	...	39.53	65.33
Income Statement								
Total Revenue	3,736,000	2,485,000	1,238,000	5,104,000	5,176,241	5,009,438	4,901,236	5,345,277
EBITDA	510,000	533,000	294,000	880,000	1,207,962	607,851	1,234,269	966,165
Depn & Amortn	632,000	422,000	211,000	820,000	810,500	797,600	984,400	785,300
Income Before Taxes	(238,000)	34,000	45,000	(48,000)	294,526	(284,189)	160,150	103,368
Income Taxes	39,000	44,000	34,000	40,000	171,992	(4,932)	126,043	73,582
Net Income	(134,000)	47,000	37,000	43,000	219,037	(136,355)	141,927	81,861
Average Shares	111,000	112,000	112,000	111,000	109,910	108,485	109,132	108,937
Balance Sheet								
Current Assets	2,004,000	1,924,000	2,025,000	2,059,000	2,158,343	1,766,955	2,087,337	1,763,437
Total Assets	9,210,000	9,378,000	9,349,000	9,446,000	9,422,462	8,906,939	8,904,147	8,623,900
Current Liabilities	829,000	786,000	738,000	887,000	944,384	1,063,256	1,191,756	924,608
Long-Term Obligations	2,443,000	2,428,000	2,431,000	2,433,000	2,439,827	1,993,586	1,720,074	1,721,571
Total Liabilities	5,227,000	5,211,000	5,173,000	5,301,000	5,296,088	4,979,837	4,785,486	4,611,539
Stockholders' Equity	3,983,000	4,167,000	4,176,000	4,145,000	4,126,374	3,927,102	4,118,661	4,012,361
Shares Outstanding	111,000	111,000	110,000	110,000	108,966	107,899	108,757	108,031
Statistical Record								
Return on Assets %	N.M.	0.57	0.77	0.45	2.39	N.M.	1.62	0.97
Return on Equity %	N.M.	1.30	1.73	1.04	-5.44	N.M.	3.49	2.05
EBITDA Margin %	13.65	21.45	23.75	17.24	23.34	12.13	25.18	18.08
Net Margin %	N.M.	1.89	2.99	0.84	4.23	N.M.	2.90	1.53
Asset Turnover	0.54	0.54	0.54	0.54	0.56	0.56	0.56	0.63
Current Ratio	2.42	2.45	2.74	2.32	2.29	1.66	1.75	1.91
Debt to Equity	0.61	0.58	0.58	0.59	0.59	0.51	0.42	0.43
Price Range	32.75-25.04	32.75-25.04	32.75-25.04	31.75-20.99	30.56-23.25	27.84-22.23	31.38-20.71	28.61-19.42
P/E Ratio	...	68.23-52.17	51.17-39.13	81.41-53.82	15.43-11.74	...	24.33-16.05	38.15-25.89
Average Yield %	2.20	2.15	2.12	2.14	2.07	2.14	2.10	2.08

Address: 30 North LaSalle Street, Suite 4000, Chicago, IL 60602	Web Site: www.teldta.com	Auditors: PricewaterhouseCoopers LLP
Telephone: 312-630-1900	Officers: Walter C.D. Carlson - Chairman LeRoy T. Carlson - President, Chief Executive Officer	Investor Contact: 312-592-5341
Fax: 312-630-1908		Transfer Agents: Computershare Trust Company, N.A., College Station, TX

TEMPUR SEALY INTERNATIONAL, INC.

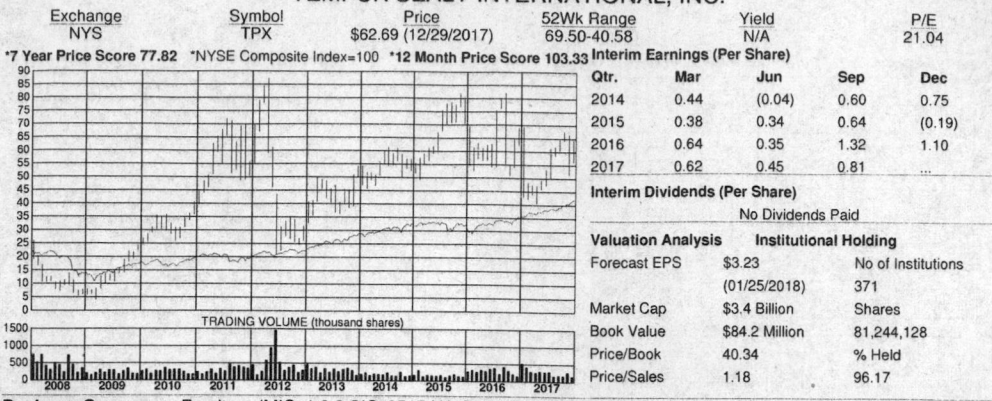

Exchange	Symbol	Price	52Wk Range	Yield	P/E
NYS	TPX	$62.69 (12/29/2017)	69.50-40.58	N/A	21.04

*7 Year Price Score 77.82 *NYSE Composite Index=100 *12 Month Price Score 103.33

Interim Earnings (Per Share)

Qtr.	Mar	Jun	Sep	Dec
2014	0.44	(0.04)	0.60	0.75
2015	0.38	0.34	0.64	(0.19)
2016	0.64	0.35	1.32	1.10
2017	0.62	0.45	0.81	...

Interim Dividends (Per Share)

No Dividends Paid

Valuation Analysis   **Institutional Holding**

Forecast EPS	$3.23	No of Institutions
	(01/25/2018)	371
Market Cap	$3.4 Billion	Shares
Book Value	$84.2 Million	81,244,128
Price/Book	40.34	% Held
Price/Sales	1.18	96.17

Business Summary: Furniture (MIC: 1.6.2 SIC: 2515 NAIC: 337910)

Tempur Sealy International develops, manufactures, markets, and distributes bedding products. Co.'s brand portfolio includes TEMPUR®, Tempur-Pedic®, Sealy®, Sealy Posturepedic® and Stearns & Foster®. Co.'s products are: Bedding, which includes mattresses, foundations and adjustable foundations; and Other, which includes pillows, mattress covers, sheets, cushions and various other comfort products. TEMPUR® and Tempur-Pedic® are registered trademarks of Co. Co. also owns various trademarks, trade names, service marks, logos and design marks, including Sealy®, Stearns & Foster® and Sealy Posturepedic®. Co. also licenses the Bassett® trade name in various territories.

Recent Developments: For the quarter ended Sep 30 2017, net income decreased 46.2% to US$41.2 million from US$76.6 million in the year-earlier quarter. Revenues were US$724.8 million, down 12.9% from US$832.4 million the year before. Operating income was US$94.6 million versus US$131.1 million in the prior-year quarter, a decrease of 27.8%. Direct operating expenses declined 12.3% to US$412.6 million from US$470.3 million in the comparable period the year before. Indirect operating expenses decreased 5.8% to US$217.6 million from US$231.0 million in the equivalent prior-year period.

Prospects: Our evaluation of Tempur-Sealy International Inc. as of Jan. 21, 2018 is the result of our systematic analysis on three basic characteristics: earnings strength, relative valuation, and recent stock price movement. The company has generated a negative trend in earnings per share over the past 5 quarters and while recent estimates for the company have been mixed, TPX has posted better than expected results. Based on operating earnings yield, the company is undervalued when compared to all of the companies in our coverage universe. Share price changes over the past year indicates that TPX will perform well over the near term.

Financial Data
(US$ in Thousands)

	9 Mos	6 Mos	3 Mos	12/31/2016	12/31/2015	12/31/2014	12/31/2013	12/31/2012
Earnings Per Share	2.98	3.49	3.39	3.38	1.17	1.75	1.28	1.70
Cash Flow Per Share	4.78	3.50	4.67	2.80	3.80	3.70	1.63	3.08
Income Statement								
Total Revenue	2,106,200	1,381,400	722,100	3,127,300	3,151,200	2,989,800	2,464,300	1,402,900
EBITDA	218,600	122,200	63,100	411,300	337,800	316,200	293,800	278,900
Depn & Amortn	10,100	3,700	(2,900)	56,100	53,500	57,700	59,400	30,900
Income Before Taxes	132,300	74,300	43,900	270,000	188,200	166,600	123,600	229,200
Income Taxes	48,000	27,700	14,600	86,800	125,400	64,900	49,100	122,400
Net Income	103,000	58,400	33,900	202,100	73,500	108,900	78,600	106,800
Average Shares	54,900	54,500	54,600	59,800	62,600	62,100	61,600	62,900
Balance Sheet								
Current Assets	657,300	647,600	640,800	671,500	809,100	766,400	727,500	821,100
Total Assets	2,735,300	2,711,200	2,680,300	2,702,600	2,655,500	2,662,600	2,729,900	1,313,000
Current Liabilities	610,600	537,600	550,700	545,500	713,000	538,300	441,500	212,100
Long-Term Obligations	1,686,700	1,793,200	1,789,800	1,817,800	1,273,300	1,535,900	1,796,900	1,025,000
Total Liabilities	2,651,100	2,689,400	2,698,100	2,717,800	2,365,300	2,459,900	2,611,300	1,290,700
Stockholders' Equity	84,200	21,800	(17,800)	(15,200)	290,200	202,700	118,600	22,300
Shares Outstanding	54,180	53,973	53,897	54,400	62,400	60,900	60,600	59,700
Statistical Record								
Return on Assets %	6.07	7.35	7.47	7.52	2.76	4.04	3.89	9.95
Return on Equity %	141.32	222.64	167.43	146.58	29.82	67.79	111.57	401.23
EBITDA Margin %	10.38	8.85	8.74	13.15	10.72	10.58	11.92	19.88
Net Margin %	4.89	4.23	4.69	6.46	2.33	3.64	3.19	7.61
Asset Turnover	1.05	1.10	1.19	1.16	1.19	1.11	1.22	1.31
Current Ratio	1.08	1.20	1.16	1.23	1.13	1.42	1.65	3.87
Debt to Equity	20.03	82.26	...	...	4.39	7.58	15.15	45.96
Price Range	69.50-40.58	82.04-40.58	82.04-42.20	82.04-50.94	81.89-49.17	61.34-45.64	54.19-31.49	87.26-21.02
P/E Ratio	23.32-13.62	23.51-11.63	24.20-12.45	24.27-15.07	69.99-42.03	35.05-26.08	42.34-24.60	51.33-12.36

Address: 1000 Tempur Way, Lexington, KY 40511
Telephone: 800-878-8889

Web Site: www.tempursealy.com
Officers: Scott L. Thompson - Chairman, President, Chief Executive Officer Robert B. Trussell - Vice-Chairman

Auditors: Ernst & Young LLP
Investor Contact: 800-805-3635
Transfer Agents: American Stock Transfer & Trust Company, LLC

TENET HEALTHCARE CORP.

Exchange	Symbol	Price	52Wk Range	Yield	P/E
NYS	THC	$15.16 (12/29/2017)	22.67-12.65	N/A	N/A

*7 Year Price Score 40.74 *NYSE Composite Index=100 *12 Month Price Score 77.59

TRADING VOLUME (thousand shares)

Interim Earnings (Per Share)

Qtr.	Mar	Jun	Sep	Dec
2014	(0.33)	(0.27)	0.09	0.62
2015	0.47	(0.61)	(0.29)	(0.98)
2016	(0.60)	(0.46)	(0.08)	(0.79)
2017	(0.53)	(0.55)	(3.64)	...

Interim Dividends (Per Share)

No Dividends Paid

Valuation Analysis   Institutional Holding

Forecast EPS	$0.65	No of Institutions
	(01/24/2018)	423
Market Cap	$1.5 Billion	Shares
Book Value	$24.0 Million	212,204,640
Price/Book	63.69	% Held
Price/Sales	0.08	N/A

Business Summary: Hospitals & Health Care Facilities (MIC: 4.2.1 SIC: 8062 NAIC: 622110)

Tenet Healthcare is a healthcare services company. As of Dec 31 2016, Co. operated 79 hospitals, 20 short-stay surgical hospitals, over 470 outpatient centers, nine facilities in the U.K. through its subsidiaries, partnerships and joint ventures, including USPI Holding Company, Inc. In addition, Co.'s Conifer Holdings, Inc. (Conifer) subsidiary provides healthcare business process services in the areas of hospital and physician revenue cycle management and care solutions to healthcare systems, as well as individual hospitals, physician practices, self-insured organizations, health plans and other entities. Co. has three segments: Hospital Operations and other; Ambulatory Care and Conifer.

Recent Developments: For the quarter ended Sep 30 2017, loss from continuing operations was US$288.0 million compared with income of US$79.0 million in the year-earlier quarter. Net loss amounted to US$289.0 million versus net income of US$80.0 million in the year-earlier quarter. Revenues were US$4.62 billion, down 5.2% from US$4.88 billion the year before. Operating income was US$51.0 million versus US$339.0 million in the prior-year quarter, a decrease of 85.0%. Indirect operating expenses increased 0.7% to US$4.57 billion from US$4.54 billion in the equivalent prior-year period.

Prospects: Our evaluation of Tenet Healthcare Corp. as of Jan. 21, 2018 is the result of our systematic analysis on three basic characteristics: earnings strength, relative valuation, and recent stock price movement. The company has suffered a very negative trend in earnings per share over the past 5 quarters. However, while recent estimates for the company have been mixed, THC has posted better than expected results. Based on operating earnings yield, the company is overvalued when compared to all of the companies in our coverage universe. Share price changes over the past year indicates that THC will perform very poorly over the near term.

Financial Data
(US$ in Millions)	9 Mos	6 Mos	3 Mos	12/31/2016	12/31/2015	12/31/2014	12/31/2013	12/31/2012
Earnings Per Share	(5.51)	(1.95)	(1.86)	(1.93)	(1.41)	0.12	(1.32)	1.30
Cash Flow Per Share	4.13	3.75	5.97	5.60	10.35	7.02	5.79	5.68
Income Statement								
Total Revenue	14,296	9,672	4,842	19,621	18,634	16,615	11,102	9,119
EBITDA	497	573	278	2,118	1,894	1,778	880	1,198
Depn & Amortn	33	22	11	891	838	877	564	452
Income Before Taxes	(325)	23	4	248	144	147	(158)	334
Income Taxes	(105)	(45)	(33)	67	68	49	(65)	125
Net Income	(475)	(108)	(53)	(192)	(140)	12	(134)	152
Average Shares	100	100	100	99	99	100	101	108
Balance Sheet								
Current Assets	5,309	5,382	5,052	5,257	5,171	4,717	3,710	2,681
Total Assets	23,208	24,341	24,510	24,701	23,682	18,141	16,130	9,044
Current Liabilities	4,139	4,337	3,767	4,034	4,308	3,577	2,928	1,763
Long-Term Obligations	14,741	15,012	15,071	15,064	14,383	11,695	10,690	5,158
Total Liabilities	23,184	23,968	24,080	24,284	22,991	17,490	15,375	7,901
Stockholders' Equity	24	373	430	417	691	651	755	1,143
Shares Outstanding	100	100	100	99	98	98	96	104
Statistical Record								
Return on Assets %	N.M.	N.M.	N.M.	N.M.	N.M.	0.07	N.M.	1.73
Return on Equity %	N.M.	N.M.	N.M.	N.M.	N.M.	1.71	N.M.	11.81
EBITDA Margin %	3.48	5.92	5.74	10.79	10.16	10.70	7.93	13.14
Net Margin %	N.M.	N.M.	N.M.	N.M.	N.M.	0.07	N.M.	1.67
Asset Turnover	0.80	0.80	0.80	0.81	0.89	0.97	0.88	1.04
Current Ratio	1.28	1.24	1.34	1.30	1.20	1.32	1.27	1.52
Debt to Equity	614.21	40.25	35.05	36.12	20.81	17.96	14.16	4.51
Price Range	23.82-12.65	31.60-14.38	32.61-14.38	32.61-14.38	60.78-27.23	63.27-38.75	49.25-32.47	33.50-17.56
P/E Ratio	...	...	...	...	...	527.25-322.92	...	25.77-13.51

Address: 1445 Ross Avenue, Suite 1400, Dallas, TX 75202 **Telephone:** 469-893-2200	**Web Site:** www.tenethealth.com **Officers:** Ronald A. (Ron) Rittenmeyer - Executive Chairman, Chief Executive Officer Keith B. Pitts - Vice-Chairman	**Auditors:** Deloitte & Touche LLP **Transfer Agents:** Computershare

TENNANT CO.

Exchange	Symbol	Price	52Wk Range	Yield	P/E	Div Achiever
NYS	TNC	$72.65 (12/29/2017)	76.30-60.40	1.16	106.84	44 Years

*7 Year Price Score 97.24 *NYSE Composite Index=100 *12 Month Price Score 89.22

Interim Earnings (Per Share)

Qtr.	Mar	Jun	Sep	Dec
2014	0.31	0.83	0.63	0.93
2015	0.27	0.79	(0.05)	0.73
2016	0.25	0.85	0.64	0.85
2017	(0.22)	(0.15)	0.20	...

Interim Dividends (Per Share)

Amt	Decl	Ex	Rec	Pay
0.21Q	02/15/2017	02/28/2017	03/02/2017	03/15/2017
0.21Q	04/26/2017	05/26/2017	05/31/2017	06/15/2017
0.21Q	08/17/2017	08/29/2017	08/31/2017	09/15/2017
0.21Q	11/09/2017	11/29/2017	11/30/2017	12/15/2017

Indicated Div: $0.84 (Div. Reinv. Plan)

Valuation Analysis		Institutional Holding	
Forecast EPS	$1.54	No of Institutions	
	(01/13/2018)	201	
Market Cap	$1.3 Billion	Shares	
Book Value	$294.3 Million	19,280,344	
Price/Book	4.40	% Held	
Price/Sales	1.39	84.07	

TRADING VOLUME (thousand shares)

Business Summary: Industrial Machinery & Equipment (MIC: 7.2.1 SIC: 3589 NAIC: 333319)

Tennant is engaged in designing, manufacturing and marketing solutions. Co. provides products and solutions consisting of mechanized cleaning equipment, detergent-free and other sustainable cleaning technologies, aftermarket parts and consumables, equipment maintenance and repair service, specialty surface coatings, and business solutions such as financing, rental and leasing programs, and machine-to-machine asset management solutions. Co. markets and sells the following brands: Tennant®, Nobles®, Green Machines™, Alfa Uma Empresa Tennant™, IRIS® and Orbio®. Co.'s Orbio Technologies Group markets and sells Orbio-branded products and solutions.

Recent Developments: For the quarter ended Sep 30 2017, net income decreased 68.7% to US$3.6 million from US$11.5 million in the year-earlier quarter. Revenues were US$261.9 million, up 30.9% from US$200.1 million the year before. Operating income was US$11.0 million versus US$16.3 million in the prior-year quarter, a decrease of 32.0%. Direct operating expenses rose 37.0% to US$157.3 million from US$114.8 million in the comparable period the year before. Indirect operating expenses increased 35.5% to US$93.6 million from US$69.0 million in the equivalent prior-year period.

Prospects: Our evaluation of Tennant Co. as of Jan. 14, 2018 is the result of our systematic analysis on three basic characteristics: earnings strength, relative valuation, and recent stock price movement. The company has generated a negative trend in earnings per share over the past 5 quarters and while recent estimates for the company have remained steady, TNC has posted results that fell short of analysts expectations. Based on operating earnings yield, the company is overvalued when compared to all of the companies in our coverage universe. Share price changes over the past year indicates that TNC will perform very poorly over the near term.

Financial Data

(US$ in Thousands)	9 Mos	6 Mos	3 Mos	12/31/2016	12/31/2015	12/31/2014	12/31/2013	12/31/2012
Earnings Per Share	0.68	1.12	2.12	2.59	1.74	2.70	2.14	2.18
Cash Flow Per Share	3.20	2.43	3.03	3.29	2.51	3.26	3.27	2.56
Tang Book Value Per Share	N.M.	N.M.	13.87	14.19	13.09	13.40	12.22	10.50
Dividends Per Share	0.840	0.830	0.820	0.810	0.800	0.780	0.720	0.690
Dividend Payout %	123.53	74.11	38.68	31.27	45.98	28.89	33.64	31.65
Income Statement								
Total Revenue	723,771	461,850	191,059	808,572	811,799	821,983	752,011	738,980
EBITDA	45,354	20,080	906	85,331	68,115	88,652	78,935	79,410
Depn & Amortn	30,841	15,289	4,737	17,891	16,550	17,694	17,686	18,072
Income Before Taxes	(2,632)	(6,959)	(4,541)	66,491	50,424	69,538	59,878	59,890
Income Taxes	385	(346)	(584)	19,877	18,336	18,887	19,647	18,306
Net Income	(2,989)	(6,548)	(3,957)	46,614	32,088	50,651	40,231	41,584
Average Shares	18,171	17,693	17,596	17,976	18,493	18,740	18,833	19,102
Balance Sheet								
Current Assets	423,673	426,647	287,788	297,922	293,644	347,089	315,296	273,446
Total Assets	1,002,798	997,211	467,147	470,037	432,295	486,932	456,306	420,760
Current Liabilities	202,910	194,610	120,233	132,829	133,216	145,630	131,526	121,694
Long-Term Obligations	383,252	405,716	45,013	32,735	21,194	24,571	28,000	30,281
Total Liabilities	708,485	713,056	190,595	191,494	180,088	206,281	192,460	185,706
Stockholders' Equity	294,313	284,155	276,552	278,543	252,207	280,651	263,846	235,054
Shares Outstanding	17,840	17,823	17,754	17,688	17,744	18,415	18,491	18,464
Statistical Record								
Return on Assets %	1.70	2.84	8.69	10.30	6.98	10.74	9.17	9.82
Return on Equity %	4.37	7.45	14.47	17.52	12.04	18.60	16.13	18.19
EBITDA Margin %	6.27	4.35	0.47	10.55	8.39	10.79	10.50	10.75
Net Margin %	N.M.	N.M.	N.M.	5.76	3.95	6.16	5.35	5.63
Asset Turnover	1.29	1.22	1.86	1.79	1.77	1.74	1.71	1.74
Current Ratio	2.09	2.19	2.39	2.24	2.20	2.38	2.40	2.25
Debt to Equity	1.30	1.43	0.16	0.12	0.08	0.09	0.11	0.13
Price Range	76.50-60.40	76.50-52.88	76.50-50.26	76.50-46.54	72.17-54.49	76.52-58.21	68.70-43.95	48.45-35.30
P/E Ratio	112.50-88.82	68.30-47.21	36.08-23.71	29.54-17.97	41.48-31.32	28.34-21.56	32.10-20.54	22.22-16.19
Average Yield %	1.21	1.21	1.29	1.37	1.28	1.15	1.35	1.67

Address: 701 North Lilac Drive, P.O. Box 1452, Minneapolis, MN 55440 **Telephone:** 763-540-1200	**Web Site:** www.tennantco.com **Officers:** H. Chris Killingstad - President, Chief Executive Officer David W. Huml - Senior Vice President	**Auditors:** KPMG LLP **Investor Contact:** 763-540-1204 **Transfer Agents:** Wells Fargo Bank, N.A., St. Paul, MN

TENNECO INC

Exchange	Symbol	Price	52Wk Range	Yield	P/E
NYS	TEN	$58.54 (12/29/2017)	68.71-51.74	1.71	16.97

*7 Year Price Score 96.72 *NYSE Composite Index=100 *12 Month Price Score 90.86

Interim Earnings (Per Share)

Qtr.	Mar	Jun	Sep	Dec
2014	0.75	1.32	1.27	0.33
2015	0.80	1.26	0.88	1.17
2016	0.99	1.49	3.24	0.77
2017	1.16	(0.05)	1.57	...

Interim Dividends (Per Share)

Amt	Decl	Ex	Rec	Pay
0.25Q	02/01/2017	03/03/2017	03/07/2017	03/23/2017
0.25Q	05/17/2017	06/05/2017	06/07/2017	06/23/2017
0.25Q	07/12/2017	09/06/2017	09/07/2017	09/26/2017
0.25Q	10/11/2017	12/01/2017	12/04/2017	12/20/2017

Indicated Div: $1.00

Valuation Analysis **Institutional Holding**

Forecast EPS	$6.68	No of Institutions
	(01/13/2018)	400
Market Cap	$3.0 Billion	Shares
Book Value	$647.0 Million	57,520,416
Price/Book	4.71	% Held
Price/Sales	0.34	86.46

Business Summary: Auto Parts (MIC: 1.8.2 SIC: 3714 NAIC: 336330)

Tenneco is a producer of clean air and ride performance products and systems for light vehicle, commercial truck and off-highway applications. Co. serves both original equipment manufacturers and replacement markets. As a parts supplier, Co. produces individual component parts for vehicles as well as groups of components that are combined as modules or systems within vehicles. Co. has six operating segments: North America Clean Air, North America Ride Performance, Europe, South America and India Clean Air, Europe, South America and India Ride Performance, Asia Pacific Clean Air and Asia Pacific Ride Performance.

Recent Developments: For the quarter ended Sep 30 2017, net income decreased 49.5% to US$99.0 million from US$196.0 million in the year-earlier quarter. Revenues were US$2.27 billion, up 8.5% from US$2.10 billion the year before. Direct operating expenses rose 9.8% to US$1.91 billion from US$1.74 billion in the comparable period the year before. Indirect operating expenses increased 11.3% to US$226.0 million from US$203.0 million in the equivalent prior-year period.

Prospects: Our evaluation of Tenneco Automotive Inc. as of Jan. 14, 2018 is the result of our systematic analysis on three basic characteristics: earnings strength, relative valuation, and recent stock price movement. The company has generated a negative trend in earnings per share over the past 5 quarters. However, while recent estimates for the company have been mixed, TEN has posted better than expected results. Based on operating earnings yield, the company is undervalued when compared to all of the companies in our coverage universe. Share price changes over the past year indicates that TEN will perform very poorly over the near term.

Financial Data
(US$ in Thousands)

	9 Mos	6 Mos	3 Mos	12/31/2016	12/31/2015	12/31/2014	12/31/2013	12/31/2012
Earnings Per Share	3.45	5.12	6.66	6.44	4.11	3.66	2.97	4.50
Cash Flow Per Share	7.87	9.33	9.45	8.72	8.66	5.61	8.32	6.07
Tang Book Value Per Share	10.97	10.09	10.73	9.44	6.09	6.63	5.49	2.30
Dividends Per Share	0.750	0.500	0.250	...	...	...	...	...
Dividend Payout %	21.74	9.77	3.75	...	...	...	...	...
Income Statement								
Total Revenue	6,883,000	4,609,000	2,292,000	8,599,000	8,209,000	8,420,000	7,964,000	7,363,000
EBITDA	447,000	255,000	179,000	740,000	722,000	700,000	629,000	633,000
Depn & Amortn	165,000	107,000	52,000	212,000	203,000	208,000	205,000	205,000
Income Before Taxes	228,000	113,000	112,000	436,000	452,000	401,000	344,000	323,000
Income Taxes	41,000	25,000	34,000	3,000	149,000	131,000	122,000	19,000
Net Income	139,000	56,000	63,000	363,000	247,000	226,000	183,000	275,000
Average Shares	52,687	53,505	54,231	56,407	60,193	61,782	61,594	61,083
Balance Sheet								
Current Assets	2,961,000	2,962,000	2,856,000	2,602,000	2,311,000	2,426,000	2,290,000	2,124,000
Total Assets	4,935,000	4,881,000	4,637,000	4,342,000	3,967,000	4,010,000	3,830,000	3,608,000
Current Liabilities	2,232,000	2,294,000	2,077,000	1,970,000	1,794,000	1,799,000	1,838,000	1,649,000
Long-Term Obligations	1,573,000	1,490,000	1,406,000	1,294,000	1,124,000	1,069,000	1,019,000	1,067,000
Total Liabilities	4,288,000	4,266,000	3,981,000	3,754,000	3,534,000	3,513,000	3,397,000	3,362,000
Stockholders' Equity	647,000	615,000	656,000	588,000	433,000	497,000	433,000	246,000
Shares Outstanding	52,043	53,311	54,051	54,235	57,593	61,209	60,870	60,494
Statistical Record								
Return on Assets %	3.92	6.12	8.21	8.71	6.19	5.77	4.92	7.90
Return on Equity %	28.55	48.44	63.57	70.91	53.12	48.60	53.90	222.97
EBITDA Margin %	6.49	5.53	7.81	8.61	8.80	8.31	7.90	8.60
Net Margin %	2.02	1.22	2.75	4.22	3.01	2.68	2.30	3.73
Asset Turnover	1.94	1.94	1.95	2.06	2.06	2.15	2.14	2.11
Current Ratio	1.33	1.29	1.38	1.32	1.29	1.35	1.25	1.29
Debt to Equity	2.43	2.42	2.14	2.20	2.60	2.15	2.35	4.34
Price Range	68.71-51.74	68.71-45.38	68.71-44.79	66.52-35.59	61.53-42.24	68.60-47.93	57.53-34.57	39.76-24.72
P/E Ratio	19.92-15.00	13.42-8.86	10.32-6.73	10.33-5.53	14.97-10.28	18.74-13.10	19.37-11.64	8.84-5.49
Average Yield %	1.26	0.85	0.44	...	...	...	...	...

Address: 500 North Field Drive, Lake Forest, IL 60045
Telephone: 847-482-5000

Web Site: www.tenneco.com
Officers: Gregg M. Sherrill - Executive Chairman, Chairman, Chief Executive Officer Brian J. Kesseler - Chief Executive Officer, Chief Operating Officer

Auditors: PricewaterhouseCoopers LLP
Investor Contact: 847-482-5162
Transfer Agents: Wells Fargo Bank, N.A. Shareowner Services, Mendota Heights, MN

TERADATA CORP (DE)

Exchange	Symbol	Price	52Wk Range	Yield	P/E
NYS	TDC	$38.46 (12/29/2017)	39.20-27.26	N/A	78.49

*7 Year Price Score 55.32 *NYSE Composite Index=100 *12 Month Price Score 110.44

Interim Earnings (Per Share)

Qtr.	Mar	Jun	Sep	Dec
2014	0.37	0.60	0.60	0.76
2015	0.15	(1.87)	0.55	(0.37)
2016	(0.36)	0.49	0.37	0.44
2017	(0.02)	(0.03)	0.10	...

Interim Dividends (Per Share)

No Dividends Paid

Valuation Analysis | Institutional Holding

Forecast EPS	$1.28	No of Institutions
	(11/20/2017)	511
Market Cap	$4.6 Billion	Shares
Book Value	$719.0 Million	147,128,128
Price/Book	6.45	% Held
Price/Sales	2.15	89.34

Business Summary: IT Services (MIC: 6.3.1 SIC: 7372 NAIC: 511210)

Teradata is a provider of analytic solutions and services. Co.'s services include analytics solutions, ecosystem architecture consulting and hybrid cloud solutions. These solutions include software and hardware technology components such as data warehousing, data, and tools for data integration, data discovery, and business intelligence. Co.'s services help companies architect, manage, and integrate their ever-changing analytic ecosystem, and include technology and data architecture consulting, analytic business consulting, open source consulting, and as-a-service services in the cloud. Additionally, Co. provides a set of support services.

Recent Developments: For the quarter ended Sep 30 2017, net income decreased 73.5% to US$13.0 million from US$49.0 million in the year-earlier quarter. Revenues were US$526.0 million, down 4.7% from US$552.0 million the year before. Operating income was US$7.0 million versus US$89.0 million in the prior-year quarter, a decrease of 92.1%. Direct operating expenses rose 7.0% to US$276.0 million from US$258.0 million in the comparable period the year before. Indirect operating expenses increased 18.5% to US$243.0 million from US$205.0 million in the equivalent prior-year period.

Prospects: Our evaluation of Teradata Corp. as of Jan. 14, 2018 is the result of our systematic analysis on three basic characteristics: earnings strength, relative valuation, and recent stock price movement. The company has generated a negative trend in earnings per share over the past 5 quarters and while recent estimates for the company have remained steady, TDC has posted better than expected results. Based on operating earnings yield, the company is overvalued when compared to all of the companies in our coverage universe. Share price changes over the past year indicates that TDC will perform well over the near term.

Financial Data

(US$ in Millions)	9 Mos	6 Mos	3 Mos	12/31/2016	12/31/2015	12/31/2014	12/31/2013	12/31/2012
Earnings Per Share	0.49	0.76	1.28	0.95	(1.53)	2.33	2.27	2.44
Cash Flow Per Share	2.85	3.17	3.40	3.43	2.87	4.38	3.12	3.41
Tang Book Value Per Share	1.34	2.38	2.97	2.93	1.97	2.87	3.56	2.95
Income Statement								
Total Revenue	1,530	1,004	491	2,322	2,530	2,732	2,692	2,665
EBITDA	107	67	35	350	(6)	616	612	667
Depn & Amortn	103	70	36	117	129	122	104	89
Income Before Taxes	1	(5)	(2)	221	(144)	494	508	578
Income Taxes	(6)	1	...	96	70	127	131	159
Net Income	7	(6)	(2)	125	(214)	367	377	419
Average Shares	125	127	130	131	139	157	166	171
Balance Sheet								
Current Assets	1,508	1,548	1,704	1,621	1,734	1,572	1,563	1,534
Total Assets	2,307	2,338	2,483	2,413	2,530	3,132	3,096	3,066
Current Liabilities	936	792	835	729	953	995	776	806
Long-Term Obligations	493	508	523	538	570	195	248	274
Total Liabilities	1,588	1,466	1,529	1,442	1,681	1,425	1,239	1,287
Stockholders' Equity	719	872	954	971	849	1,707	1,857	1,779
Shares Outstanding	120	126	129	130	130	147	159	165
Statistical Record								
Return on Assets %	2.81	4.28	6.83	5.04	N.M.	11.79	12.24	14.71
Return on Equity %	7.87	11.64	19.34	13.70	N.M.	20.59	20.74	25.53
EBITDA Margin %	6.99	6.67	7.13	15.07	N.M.	22.55	22.73	25.03
Net Margin %	0.46	N.M.	N.M.	5.38	N.M.	13.43	14.00	15.72
Asset Turnover	0.93	0.92	0.92	0.94	0.89	0.88	0.87	0.94
Current Ratio	1.61	1.95	2.04	2.22	1.82	1.58	2.01	1.90
Debt to Equity	0.69	0.58	0.55	0.55	0.67	0.11	0.13	0.15
Price Range	33.79-26.42	32.74-24.78	32.74-24.40	32.62-22.60	46.98-25.58	49.19-39.54	69.34-39.52	80.62-47.37
P/E Ratio	68.96-53.92	43.08-32.61	25.58-19.06	34.34-23.79	...	21.11-16.97	30.55-17.41	33.04-19.41

Address: 10000 Innovation Drive, Dayton, OH 45342

Telephone: 866-548-8348

Web Site: www.teradata.com

Officers: James M. Ringler - Chairman Victor L. Lund - President, Chief Executive Officer

Auditors: PricewaterhouseCoopers LLP

Investor Contact: 937-242-4878

Transfer Agents: Computershare Shareowner Services

TERADYNE, INC.

Exchange	Symbol	Price	52Wk Range	Yield	P/E
NYS	TER	$41.87 (12/29/2017)	44.43-25.38	0.67	19.57

*7 Year Price Score 134.55 *NYSE Composite Index=100 *12 Month Price Score 113.95

TRADING VOLUME (thousand shares)

Interim Earnings (Per Share)

Qtr.	Mar	Jun	Sep	Dec
2014	0.00	0.47	0.38	(0.46)
2015	0.15	0.48	0.34	0.01
2016	0.24	(1.10)	0.31	0.33
2017	0.42	0.87	0.52	...

Interim Dividends (Per Share)

Amt	Decl	Ex	Rec	Pay
0.07Q	01/25/2017	02/22/2017	02/24/2017	03/20/2017
0.07Q	05/09/2017	05/30/2017	06/01/2017	06/23/2017
0.07Q	08/24/2017	09/06/2017	09/07/2017	09/29/2017
0.07Q	11/14/2017	11/28/2017	11/29/2017	12/21/2017

Indicated Div: $0.28

Valuation Analysis / Institutional Holding

Forecast EPS	$2.22	No of Institutions
	(01/13/2018)	585
Market Cap	$8.2 Billion	Shares
Book Value	$2.1 Billion	229,037,888
Price/Book	3.90	% Held
Price/Sales	4.04	110.59

Business Summary: Semiconductors (MIC: 6.2.4 SIC: 3825 NAIC: 334515)

Teradyne is a global supplier of automation equipment for test and industrial applications. Co. designs, develops, manufactures and sells automatic test systems used to test semiconductors, wireless products, data storage and electronics systems in the consumer electronics, wireless, automotive, industrial, computing, communications, and aerospace and defense industries. Co.'s automatic test equipment and industrial automation products and services include: semiconductor test systems; defense/aerospace test instrumentation and systems, storage test systems, and circuit-board test and inspection systems; industrial automation products; and wireless test systems.

Recent Developments: For the quarter ended Oct 1 2017, net income increased 62.1% to US$103.4 million from US$63.8 million in the year-earlier quarter. Revenues were US$503.4 million, up 22.6% from US$410.5 million the year before. Operating income was US$128.7 million versus US$56.5 million in the prior-year quarter, an increase of 127.8%. Direct operating expenses rose 13.9% to US$208.6 million from US$183.1 million in the comparable period the year before. Indirect operating expenses decreased 2.8% to US$166.1 million from US$170.9 million in the equivalent prior-year period.

Prospects: Our evaluation of Teradyne Inc. as of Jan. 14, 2018 is the result of our systematic analysis on three basic characteristics: earnings strength, relative valuation, and recent stock price movement. The company has generated a negative trend in earnings per share over the past 5 quarters and while recent estimates for the company have been mixed, TER has posted better than expected results. Based on operating earnings yield, the company is undervalued when compared to all of the companies in our coverage universe. Share price changes over the past year indicates that TER will perform very well over the near term.

Financial Data

(US$ in Thousands)	9 Mos	6 Mos	3 Mos	12/31/2016	12/31/2015	12/31/2014	12/31/2013	12/31/2012
Earnings Per Share	2.14	1.93	(0.04)	(0.21)	0.97	0.37	0.70	0.94
Cash Flow Per Share	2.61	2.05	1.79	2.19	1.95	2.43	1.40	2.16
Tang Book Value Per Share	9.02	8.67	7.99	7.56	6.08	7.46	7.15	5.91
Dividends Per Share	0.270	0.260	0.250	0.240	0.240	0.180	...	...
Dividend Payout %	12.62	13.47	...	...	24.74	48.65	...	...
Income Statement								
Total Revenue	1,657,191	1,153,814	456,913	1,753,250	1,639,578	1,647,824	1,427,933	1,656,750
EBITDA	512,839	357,878	121,111	56,729	385,017	240,251	320,359	415,868
Depn & Amortn	81,556	54,886	27,213	117,448	137,231	144,200	129,700	128,500
Income Before Taxes	426,329	298,893	92,016	(55,060)	253,124	95,376	201,922	265,976
Income Taxes	62,713	38,696	6,795	(11,639)	46,647	14,104	36,975	48,927
Net Income	363,616	260,197	85,221	(43,421)	206,477	81,272	164,947	217,049
Average Shares	200,775	201,529	201,936	202,578	213,321	222,550	235,599	230,246
Balance Sheet								
Current Assets	2,140,088	2,080,025	1,854,153	1,623,803	1,259,968	1,243,846	1,440,277	1,236,061
Total Assets	3,089,327	3,030,225	2,842,280	2,762,493	2,548,674	2,538,520	2,629,824	2,429,345
Current Liabilities	431,375	439,207	393,057	372,696	372,857	292,406	475,632	297,828
Long-Term Obligations	362,595	359,245	355,937	352,669	...	...	...	171,059
Total Liabilities	979,430	981,577	922,427	933,834	582,888	459,540	644,730	650,990
Stockholders' Equity	2,109,897	2,048,648	1,919,853	1,828,659	1,965,786	2,078,980	1,985,094	1,778,355
Shares Outstanding	196,711	197,999	199,596	199,177	203,641	216,613	191,731	187,908
Statistical Record								
Return on Assets %	15.76	14.36	N.M.	N.M.	8.12	3.14	6.52	9.37
Return on Equity %	22.09	20.58	N.M.	N.M.	10.21	4.00	8.77	13.18
EBITDA Margin %	30.95	31.02	26.51	3.24	23.48	14.58	22.44	25.10
Net Margin %	21.94	22.55	18.65	N.M.	12.59	4.93	11.55	13.10
Asset Turnover	0.75	0.72	0.66	0.66	0.64	0.64	0.56	0.72
Current Ratio	4.96	4.74	4.72	4.36	3.38	4.25	3.03	4.15
Debt to Equity	0.17	0.18	0.19	0.19	...	...	...	0.10
Price Range	37.29-20.95	36.35-19.17	31.10-18.17	26.25-17.55	21.48-16.78	20.72-16.16	18.56-14.30	17.39-13.05
P/E Ratio	17.43-9.79	18.83-9.93	...	...	22.14-17.30	56.00-43.68	26.51-20.43	18.50-13.88
Average Yield %	0.90	0.98	1.08	1.15	1.24	0.94	...	...

Address: 600 Riverpark Drive, North Reading, MA 01864 **Telephone:** 978-370-2700	**Web Site:** www.teradyne.com **Officers:** Mark E. Jagiela - President, Chief Executive Officer, Vice President, Division Officer Gregory R. Beecher - Vice President, Chief Financial Officer, Treasurer	**Auditors:** PricewaterhouseCoopers LLP **Investor Contact:** 978-370-2425 **Transfer Agents:** Broadridge Corporate Issue Services, Brentwood, NY

TEREX CORP.

Exchange	Symbol	Price	52Wk Range	Yield	P/E
NYS	TEX	$48.22 (12/29/2017)	48.59-29.57	0.66	N/A

*7 Year Price Score 103.00 *NYSE Composite Index=100 *12 Month Price Score 114.66

Interim Earnings (Per Share)

Qtr.	Mar	Jun	Sep	Dec
2014	0.30	1.21	0.56	0.72
2015	0.01	0.78	0.40	0.15
2016	(0.65)	0.59	0.89	(2.46)
2017	(0.04)	1.04	0.66	...

Interim Dividends (Per Share)

Amt	Decl	Ex	Rec	Pay
0.08Q	02/21/2017	03/08/2017	03/10/2017	03/20/2017
0.08Q	05/12/2017	06/07/2017	06/09/2017	06/19/2017
0.08Q	07/13/2017	08/07/2017	08/09/2017	09/19/2017
0.08Q	10/11/2017	11/08/2017	11/09/2017	12/19/2017

Indicated Div: $0.32

Valuation Analysis		Institutional Holding	
Forecast EPS	$1.30	No of Institutions	
	(01/13/2018)	443	
Market Cap	$4.0 Billion	Shares	
Book Value	$1.4 Billion	107,353,200	
Price/Book	2.92	% Held	
Price/Sales	0.94	91.37	

Business Summary: Industrial Machinery & Equipment (MIC: 7.2.1 SIC: 3537 NAIC: 333924)

Terex is a manufacturer of lifting and material processing products and services. Co. delivers lifecycle solutions to a range of industries, including the construction, infrastructure, manufacturing, shipping, transportation, refining, energy, utility, quarrying and mining industries. Co. has three business segments: Aerial Work Platforms, which provides aerial work platform equipment, telehandlers and light towers; Cranes, which provides mobile telescopic cranes, lattice boom crawler cranes, tower cranes, and utility equipment; and Materials Processing, which markets materials processing and specialty equipment, including crushers, washing systems, apron feeders, and recycling equipment.

Recent Developments: For the quarter ended Sep 30 2017, net income decreased 39.2% to US$59.2 million from US$97.3 million in the year-earlier quarter. Revenues were US$1.11 billion, up 5.2% from US$1.06 billion the year before. Operating income was US$64.2 million versus US$39.6 million in the prior-year quarter, an increase of 62.1%. Direct operating expenses rose 2.3% to US$892.2 million from US$872.5 million in the comparable period the year before. Indirect operating expenses increased 7.3% to US$154.8 million from US$144.3 million in the equivalent prior-year period.

Prospects: Our evaluation of Terex Corp. as of Jan. 14, 2018 is the result of our systematic analysis on three basic characteristics: earnings strength, relative valuation, and recent stock price movement. The company has produced a positive trend in earnings per share over the past 5 quarters and while recent estimates for the company have been mixed, TEX has posted better than expected results. Based on operating earnings yield, the company is about fairly valued when compared to all of the companies in our coverage universe. Share price changes over the past year indicates that TEX will perform very well over the near term.

Financial Data

(US$ in Thousands)	9 Mos	6 Mos	3 Mos	12/31/2016	12/31/2015	12/31/2014	12/31/2013	12/31/2012
Earnings Per Share	(0.80)	(0.57)	(1.02)	(1.63)	1.33	2.79	1.93	0.93
Cash Flow Per Share	2.50	2.34	2.85	3.39	1.98	3.74	1.70	2.64
Tang Book Value Per Share	13.08	13.95	14.25	11.49	5.61	5.21	4.55	2.62
Dividends Per Share	0.310	0.300	0.290	0.280	0.240	0.200	0.050	...
Dividend Payout %	...	...	...	...	18.05	7.17	2.59	.
Income Statement								
Total Revenue	3,299,800	2,188,600	1,006,900	4,443,100	6,543,100	7,308,900	7,084,000	7,348,400
EBITDA	182,100	94,400	(52,700)	(107,500)	430,600	527,500	523,600	421,400
Depn & Amortn	48,700	31,300	16,300	65,500	98,400	110,400	104,400	100,400
Income Before Taxes	86,600	29,900	(88,600)	(270,700)	226,600	297,200	291,300	155,600
Income Taxes	(5,100)	(5,200)	(28,300)	(77,400)	81,000	37,700	87,400	54,200
Net Income	155,400	96,200	(4,600)	(176,100)	145,900	319,000	226,000	105,800
Average Shares	90,000	97,100	105,200	107,900	109,600	114,200	117,000	113,900
Balance Sheet								
Current Assets	2,457,100	2,403,600	2,597,700	2,700,500	3,144,200	3,356,200	3,639,400	3,797,400
Total Assets	3,602,700	3,760,600	4,163,100	5,006,800	5,637,100	5,928,000	6,536,700	6,746,200
Current Liabilities	1,013,600	1,020,700	1,277,700	1,407,000	1,458,600	1,643,100	1,724,700	1,708,800
Long-Term Obligations	980,000	980,300	979,600	1,562,000	1,751,000	1,636,300	1,889,900	2,014,900
Total Liabilities	2,223,000	2,220,200	2,467,800	3,522,100	3,759,700	3,922,100	4,346,600	4,738,500
Stockholders' Equity	1,379,700	1,539,800	1,695,300	1,484,700	1,877,400	2,005,900	2,190,100	2,007,700
Shares Outstanding	83,600	89,900	99,300	105,000	107,700	105,400	109,900	109,900
Statistical Record								
Return on Assets %	N.M.	N.M.	N.M.	N.M.	2.52	5.12	3.40	1.53
Return on Equity %	N.M.	N.M.	N.M.	N.M.	7.51	15.20	10.77	5.39
EBITDA Margin %	5.52	4.31	N.M.	N.M.	6.58	7.22	7.39	5.73
Net Margin %	4.71	4.40	N.M.	N.M.	2.23	4.36	3.19	1.44
Asset Turnover	0.93	0.90	0.88	0.83	1.13	1.17	1.07	1.06
Current Ratio	2.42	2.35	2.03	1.92	2.16	2.04	2.11	2.22
Debt to Equity	0.71	0.64	0.58	1.05	0.93	0.82	0.86	1.00
Price Range	45.02-22.48	37.50-19.53	33.11-19.16	33.05-14.46	28.85-16.83	44.74-25.66	41.99-26.01	28.11-14.11
P/E Ratio	...	...	...	...	21.69-12.65	16.04-9.20	21.76-13.48	30.23-15.17
Average Yield %	0.94	1.03	1.10	1.18	1.03	0.54	0.15	...

Address: 200 Nyala Farm Road, Westport, CT 06880	Web Site: www.terex.com	Auditors: PricewaterhouseCoopers LLP
Telephone: 203-222-7170	Officers: John L. Garrison - President, Chief Executive Officer John D. Sheehan - Senior Vice President, Chief Financial Officer	Investor Contact: 203-222-5943
Fax: 203-222-7976		Transfer Agents: American Stock Transfer & Trust Company, New York, NY

TEGNA INC

Exchange NYS	Symbol TGNA	Price $14.08 (12/29/2017)	52Wk Range 16.92-11.78	Yield 1.99	P/E 29.96

*7 Year Price Score 89.51 ***NYSE Composite Index=100** ***12 Month Price Score 86.37**

Interim Earnings (Per Share)

Qtr.	Mar	Jun	Sep	Dec
2014	0.25	0.90	0.51	2.92
2015	0.49	0.50	0.38	0.63
2016	0.38	0.45	0.54	0.61
2017	0.27	(0.60)	0.19	...

Interim Dividends (Per Share)

Amt	Decl	Ex	Rec	Pay
0.00Q	05/04/2017	06/01/2017	05/18/2017	05/31/2017
0.07Q	05/30/2017	06/07/2017	06/09/2017	07/03/2017
0.07Q	07/25/2017	09/07/2017	09/08/2017	10/02/2017
0.07Q	11/02/2017	12/07/2017	12/08/2017	01/02/2018

Indicated Div: $0.28 (Div. Reinv. Plan)

Valuation Analysis

		Institutional Holding	
Forecast EPS	$1.05 (01/17/2018)	No of Institutions	625
Market Cap	$3.0 Billion	Shares	250,350,848
Book Value	$705.9 Million	% Held	83.11
Price/Book	4.29		
Price/Sales	1.16		

TRADING VOLUME (thousand shares)

Business Summary: Radio & Television (MIC: 2.3.1 SIC: 2711 NAIC: 511110)

Tegna is involved in media and digital businesses that provide content and brands. Co. operates two reportable segments: Media, which includes 46 television stations operating in 38 markets, provides core advertising which includes local and national non-political advertising, political advertising, retransmission, digital which encompass digital marketing services and advertising on the stations' websites and tablet and mobile products; and Digital, which is comprised of three business units including; Cars.com, CareerBuilder, and G/O Digital businesses that operate in the automotive and human capital solutions industries.

Recent Developments: For the quarter ended Sep 30 2017, income from continuing operations decreased 33.9% to US$50.8 million from US$76.7 million in the year-earlier quarter. Net income decreased 70.1% to US$40.0 million from US$133.4 million in the year-earlier quarter. Revenues were US$464.3 million, down 10.7% from US$519.6 million the year before. Operating income was US$116.9 million versus US$185.9 million in the prior-year quarter, a decrease of 37.1%. Direct operating expenses rose 17.4% to US$235.5 million from US$200.5 million in the comparable period the year before. Indirect operating expenses decreased 16.0% to US$111.9 million from US$133.3 million in the equivalent prior-year period.

Prospects: Our evaluation of Tegna Inc. as of Jan. 14, 2018 is the result of our systematic analysis on three basic characteristics: earnings strength, relative valuation, and recent stock price movement. The company has generated a negative trend in earnings per share over the past 5 quarters and while recent estimates for the company have been mixed, TGNA has posted better than expected results. Based on operating earnings yield, the company is undervalued when compared to all of the companies in our coverage universe. Share price changes over the past year indicates that TGNA will perform very poorly over the near term.

Financial Data

(US$ in Thousands)	9 Mos	6 Mos	3 Mos	12/31/2016	12/31/2015	12/28/2014	12/29/2013	12/30/2012
Earnings Per Share	0.47	0.82	1.87	1.99	2.00	4.58	1.66	1.79
Cash Flow Per Share	2.69	3.22	3.24	3.15	2.71	3.64	2.24	3.20
Dividends Per Share	0.420	0.490	0.560	0.560	0.680	0.800	0.800	0.800
Dividend Payout %	89.36	59.76	29.95	28.14	34.00	17.47	48.19	44.69
Income Statement								
Total Revenue	1,412,703	948,439	778,471	3,341,198	3,050,945	6,008,174	5,161,362	5,353,197
EBITDA	421,092	287,321	201,472	1,156,125	1,163,873	1,727,709	880,925	992,528
Depn & Amortn	57,893	37,312	52,105	204,490	262,244	265,724	189,572	194,039
Income Before Taxes	201,086	139,751	93,951	719,622	628,000	1,188,741	515,289	648,020
Income Taxes	54,855	43,408	28,583	216,979	202,314	225,600	113,200	195,400
Net Income	(29,881)	(72,638)	57,714	436,697	459,522	1,062,171	388,680	424,280
Average Shares	218,095	217,812	217,569	219,681	229,721	231,907	234,189	236,690
Balance Sheet								
Current Assets	866,730	1,266,281	752,255	790,688	805,159	1,480,465	1,923,485	1,072,720
Total Assets	5,243,056	5,647,732	8,465,011	8,542,725	8,537,758	11,205,455	9,240,706	6,379,886
Current Liabilities	632,599	508,328	608,678	619,181	606,783	1,127,936	1,007,192	934,516
Long-Term Obligations	3,035,166	3,345,986	3,965,842	4,042,749	4,200,816	4,488,028	3,707,010	1,432,100
Total Liabilities	4,537,181	4,998,647	6,175,874	6,271,307	6,345,787	7,950,541	6,547,608	4,029,272
Stockholders' Equity	705,875	649,085	2,289,137	2,271,418	2,191,971	3,254,914	2,693,098	2,350,614
Shares Outstanding	215,205	215,115	214,789	214,487	219,754	226,739	227,568	230,042
Statistical Record								
Return on Assets %	1.48	2.54	4.83	5.10	4.62	10.42	4.99	6.42
Return on Equity %	7.10	12.80	18.39	19.51	16.74	35.81	15.45	17.84
EBITDA Margin %	29.81	30.29	25.88	34.60	38.15	28.76	17.07	18.54
Net Margin %	N.M.	N.M.	7.41	13.07	15.06	17.68	7.53	7.93
Asset Turnover	0.38	0.43	0.39	0.39	0.31	0.59	0.66	0.81
Current Ratio	1.37	2.49	1.24	1.28	1.33	1.31	1.91	1.15
Debt to Equity	4.30	5.15	1.73	1.78	1.92	1.38	1.38	0.61
Price Range	16.92-11.55	16.92-11.55	16.92-11.55	16.35-11.55	21.12-14.00	17.70-13.29	15.01-9.23	9.72-6.32
P/E Ratio	36.00-24.56	20.63-14.08	9.05-6.17	8.22-5.80	10.56-7.00	3.87-2.90	9.04-5.56	5.43-3.53
Average Yield %	2.91	3.35	3.88	3.89	3.91	5.21	6.63	10.12

Address: 7950 Jones Branch Drive, McLean, VA 22107-0150
Telephone: 703-873-6600

Web Site: www.gannett.com
Officers: Marjorie Magner - Chairman David T. (Dave) Lougee - President, Chief Executive Officer, Division Officer

Auditors: Ernst & Young LLP
Investor Contact: 703-854-6917
Transfer Agents: Wells Fargo Bank, N.A., St Paul, MN

TEXTRON INC

Exchange	Symbol	Price	52Wk Range	Yield	P/E
NYS	TXT	$56.59 (12/29/2017)	57.18-45.37	0.14	24.39

*7 Year Price Score 110.74 *NYSE Composite Index=100 *12 Month Price Score 103.80

Interim Earnings (Per Share)

Qtr.	Mar	Jun	Sep	Dec
2014	0.30	0.51	0.57	0.76
2015	0.46	0.60	0.63	0.82
2016	0.55	0.65	1.55	0.78
2017	0.37	0.57	0.60	...

Interim Dividends (Per Share)

Amt	Decl	Ex	Rec	Pay
0.02Q	02/22/2017	03/08/2017	03/10/2017	04/01/2017
0.02Q	04/26/2017	06/07/2017	06/09/2017	07/01/2017
0.02Q	07/25/2017	09/14/2017	09/15/2017	10/01/2017
0.02Q	10/25/2017	12/14/2017	12/15/2017	01/01/2018

Indicated Div: $0.08

Valuation Analysis

		Institutional Holding	
Forecast EPS	$2.48 (01/18/2018)	No of Institutions	661
Market Cap	$14.9 Billion	Shares	251,212,224
Book Value	$5.8 Billion	% Held	80.73
Price/Book	2.56		
Price/Sales	1.06		

Business Summary: Aerospace (MIC: 7.1.1 SIC: 3721 NAIC: 336411)

Textron has five operating segments: Textron Aviation, which manufactures, sells and services Beechcraft and Cessna aircraft, and services the Hawker brand of business jets; Bell, which supplies military and commercial helicopters, tiltrotor aircraft, and related spare parts and services; Textron Systems, which produces unmanned aircraft systems, marine and land systems, weapons and sensors, simulation, training and other defense and aviation mission support products and services; Industrial, which designs and manufactures fuel systems and functional components, specialized vehicles and equipment, and tools and test equipment; as well as Finance, which is a commercial finance business.

Recent Developments: For the quarter ended Sep 30 2017, income from continuing operations decreased 46.8% to US$159.0 million from US$299.0 million in the year-earlier quarter. Net income decreased 62.2% to US$159.0 million from US$421.0 million in the year-earlier quarter. Revenues were US$3.48 billion, up 7.2% from US$3.25 billion the year before. Direct operating expenses rose 8.1% to US$2.88 billion from US$2.66 billion in the comparable period the year before. Indirect operating expenses decreased 16.4% to US$404.0 million from US$483.0 million in the equivalent prior-year period.

Prospects: Our evaluation of Textron Inc. as of Jan. 14, 2018 is the result of our systematic analysis on three basic characteristics: earnings strength, relative valuation, and recent stock price movement. The company has produced a positive trend in earnings per share over the past 5 quarters and while recent estimates for the company have been mixed, TXT has posted better than expected results. Based on operating earnings yield, the company is about fairly valued when compared to all of the companies in our coverage universe. Share price changes over the past year indicates that TXT will perform poorly over the near term.

Financial Data

(US$ in Millions)	9 Mos	6 Mos	3 Mos	12/31/2016	01/02/2016	01/03/2015	12/28/2013	12/29/2012
Earnings Per Share	2.32	3.27	3.35	3.53	2.50	2.13	1.75	2.00
Cash Flow Per Share	4.65	4.90	3.58	3.75	3.95	4.25	2.91	3.32
Tang Book Value Per Share	13.15	12.61	12.14	12.80	10.72	8.12	9.39	4.95
Dividends Per Share	0.080	0.080	0.080	0.080	0.080	0.080	0.080	0.080
Dividend Payout %	3.45	2.45	2.39	2.27	3.20	3.76	4.57	4.00
Income Statement								
Total Revenue	10,181	6,697	3,093	13,788	13,423	13,878	12,104	12,237
EBITDA	1,000	639	269	1,418	1,523	1,423	1,182	1,368
Depn & Amortn	332	218	106	368	383	379	335	315
Income Before Taxes	539	336	121	876	971	853	674	841
Income Taxes	127	83	21	33	273	248	176	260
Net Income	413	254	101	962	697	600	498	589
Average Shares	266	269	272	272	278	281	284	294
Balance Sheet								
Current Assets	7,374	7,186	7,126	7,053	6,478	6,273	5,572	5,389
Total Assets	15,875	15,775	15,703	15,358	14,708	14,605	12,944	13,033
Current Liabilities	4,041	4,005	4,023	3,893	3,792	3,638	3,003	3,512
Long-Term Obligations	3,919	3,642	3,653	3,317	3,348	3,866	3,179	3,453
Total Liabilities	10,057	10,093	10,121	9,784	9,744	10,333	8,560	10,042
Stockholders' Equity	5,818	5,682	5,582	5,574	4,964	4,272	4,384	2,991
Shares Outstanding	263	265	267	270	274	276	282	271
Statistical Record								
Return on Assets %	4.04	5.77	5.93	6.42	4.77	4.29	3.84	4.43
Return on Equity %	10.93	16.36	17.27	18.31	15.13	13.64	13.54	20.59
EBITDA Margin %	9.82	9.54	8.70	10.28	11.35	10.25	9.77	11.18
Net Margin %	4.06	3.79	3.27	6.98	5.19	4.32	4.11	4.81
Asset Turnover	0.90	0.89	0.89	0.92	0.92	0.99	0.93	0.92
Current Ratio	1.82	1.79	1.77	1.81	1.71	1.72	1.86	1.53
Debt to Equity	0.67	0.64	0.65	0.60	0.67	0.90	0.73	1.15
Price Range	53.96-37.77	50.30-35.71	50.30-34.32	49.04-31.11	46.86-37.00	44.23-32.28	37.29-24.79	28.89-18.34
P/E Ratio	23.26-16.28	15.38-10.92	15.01-10.24	13.89-8.81	18.74-14.80	20.77-15.15	21.31-14.17	14.45-9.17
Average Yield %	0.17	0.18	0.19	0.20	0.19	0.21	0.28	0.32

Address: 40 Westminster Street, Providence, RI 02903	Web Site: www.textron.com	Auditors: Ernst & Young LLP
Telephone: 401-421-2800	Officers: Scott C. Donnelly - Chairman, President, Chief Executive Officer Frank T. Connor - Executive Vice President, Chief Financial Officer	Investor Contact: 401-457-2288 Transfer Agents: American Stock Transfer & Trust Cmpany, LLC, Brooklyn, NY

THE GAP INC

Exchange	Symbol	Price	52Wk Range	Yield	P/E	Div Achiever
NYS	GPS	$34.06 (12/29/2017)	34.94-21.20	2.70	15.70	12 Years

*7 Year Price Score 65.44   *NYSE Composite Index=100   *12 Month Price Score 115.55

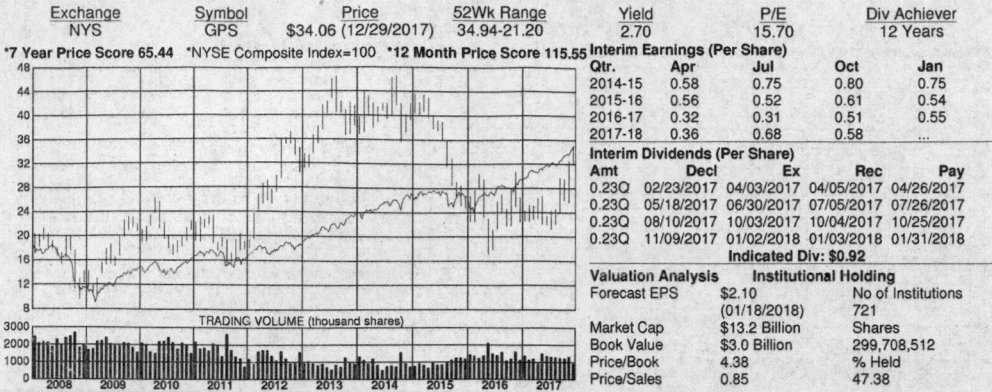

Interim Earnings (Per Share)

Qtr.	Apr	Jul	Oct	Jan
2014-15	0.58	0.75	0.80	0.75
2015-16	0.56	0.52	0.61	0.54
2016-17	0.32	0.31	0.51	0.55
2017-18	0.36	0.68	0.58	...

Interim Dividends (Per Share)

Amt	Decl	Ex	Rec	Pay
0.23Q	02/23/2017	04/03/2017	04/05/2017	04/26/2017
0.23Q	05/18/2017	06/30/2017	07/05/2017	07/26/2017
0.23Q	08/10/2017	10/03/2017	10/04/2017	10/25/2017
0.23Q	11/09/2017	01/02/2018	01/03/2018	01/31/2018

Indicated Div: $0.92

Valuation Analysis

Institutional Holding	
Forecast EPS	$2.10	No of Institutions
(01/18/2018)		721
Market Cap	$13.2 Billion	Shares
Book Value	$3.0 Billion	299,708,512
Price/Book	4.38	% Held
Price/Sales	0.85	47.38

Business Summary: Retail - Apparel and Accessories (MIC: 2.1.5 SIC: 5651 NAIC: 448140)

The Gap is a retailer providing apparel, accessories, and personal care products for men, women, and children under the Gap, Banana Republic, Old Navy, Athleta, and Intermix brands. Co. has stores in the U.S., Canada, the U.K., France, Ireland, Japan, Italy, China, Hong Kong, Taiwan, and Mexico, and has franchise agreements with unaffiliated franchisees to operate Gap, Banana Republic, and Old Navy stores throughout Asia, Australia, Europe, Latin America, the Middle East, and Africa. Under these agreements, third parties operate, or will operate, stores that sell apparel and related products under Co.'s brand names. At Jan. 28 2017, Co. had 3,659 Co.-operated and franchise store locations.

Recent Developments: For the quarter ended Oct 28 2017, net income increased 12.3% to US$229.0 million from US$204.0 million in the year-earlier quarter. Revenues were US$3.84 billion, up 1.1% from US$3.80 billion the year before. Operating income was US$378.0 million versus US$389.0 million in the prior-year quarter, a decrease of 2.8%. Direct operating expenses was unchanged at US$2.31 billion versus the comparable period the year before. Indirect operating expenses increased 3.9% to US$1.15 billion from US$1.10 billion in the equivalent prior-year period.

Prospects: Our evaluation of The Gap Inc. as of Jan. 14, 2018 is the result of our systematic analysis on three basic characteristics: earnings strength, relative valuation, and recent stock price movement. The company has managed to produce a neutral trend in earnings per share over the past 5 quarters and while recent estimates for the company have been mixed, GPS has posted better than expected results. Based on operating earnings yield, the company is undervalued when compared to all of the companies in our coverage universe. Share price changes over the past year indicates that GPS will perform well over the near term.

Financial Data

(US$ in Thousands)	9 Mos	6 Mos	3 Mos	01/28/2017	01/30/2016	01/31/2015	02/01/2014	02/02/2013
Earnings Per Share	2.17	2.10	1.73	1.69	2.23	2.87	2.74	2.33
Cash Flow Per Share	3.88	3.72	4.12	4.32	3.89	4.91	3.71	3.95
Tang Book Value Per Share	7.77	7.51	7.23	6.77	5.73	6.44	6.17	5.57
Dividends Per Share	0.920	0.920	0.920	0.920	0.920	0.880	0.700	0.500
Dividend Payout %	42.40	43.81	53.18	54.44	41.26	30.66	25.55	21.46
Income Statement								
Total Revenue	11,077,000	7,239,000	3,440,000	15,516,000	15,797,000	16,435,000	16,148,000	15,651,000
EBITDA	1,037,000	675,000	239,000	1,781,000	2,112,000	2,643,000	2,679,000	2,497,000
Depn & Amortn	(46,000)	(30,000)	(15,000)	590,000	588,000	560,000	530,000	555,000
Income Before Taxes	1,041,000	677,000	238,000	1,124,000	1,471,000	2,013,000	2,093,000	1,861,000
Income Taxes	398,000	263,000	95,000	448,000	551,000	751,000	813,000	726,000
Net Income	643,000	414,000	143,000	676,000	920,000	1,262,000	1,280,000	1,135,000
Average Shares	393,000	396,000	400,000	400,000	413,000	440,000	467,000	488,000
Balance Sheet								
Current Assets	4,483,000	4,258,000	4,119,000	4,315,000	3,985,000	4,317,000	4,430,000	4,132,000
Total Assets	7,895,000	7,617,000	7,411,000	7,610,000	7,473,000	7,690,000	7,849,000	7,470,000
Current Liabilities	2,596,000	2,399,000	2,302,000	2,453,000	2,535,000	2,234,000	2,445,000	2,344,000
Long-Term Obligations	1,248,000	1,248,000	1,248,000	1,248,000	1,310,000	1,332,000	1,369,000	1,246,000
Total Liabilities	4,871,000	4,672,000	4,549,000	4,706,000	4,928,000	4,707,000	4,787,000	4,576,000
Stockholders' Equity	3,024,000	2,945,000	2,862,000	2,904,000	2,545,000	2,983,000	3,062,000	2,894,000
Shares Outstanding	389,000	392,000	396,000	399,000	397,000	421,000	446,000	463,000
Statistical Record								
Return on Assets %	10.85	10.92	9.28	8.99	12.17	16.29	16.76	15.00
Return on Equity %	30.02	30.45	25.71	24.88	33.38	41.87	43.10	39.53
EBITDA Margin %	9.36	9.32	6.95	11.48	13.37	16.08	16.59	15.95
Net Margin %	5.80	5.72	4.16	4.36	5.82	7.68	7.93	7.25
Asset Turnover	1.95	2.01	2.08	2.06	2.09	2.12	2.11	2.07
Current Ratio	1.73	1.77	1.79	1.76	1.57	1.93	1.81	1.76
Debt to Equity	0.41	0.42	0.44	0.43	0.51	0.45	0.45	0.43
Price Range	30.71-21.20	30.71-21.20	30.71-17.09	30.71-17.09	43.45-22.45	46.59-35.74	46.48-31.22	37.27-21.52
P/E Ratio	14.15-9.77	14.62-10.10	17.75-9.88	18.17-10.11	19.48-10.07	16.23-12.45	16.96-11.39	16.00-9.24
Average Yield %	3.73	3.78	3.88	3.78	2.70	2.15	1.78	1.63

Address: Two Folsom Street, San Francisco, CA 94105
Telephone: 415-427-0100

Web Site: www.gapinc.com
Officers: Arthur L. Peck - President, Chief Executive Officer, Executive Vice-President, Division Officer, Region Officer, Division Officer Sebastian DiGrande - Executive Vice President, Chief Customer Officer

Auditors: Deloitte & Touche LLP
Investor Contact: 415-427-0100
Transfer Agents: Wells Fargo Bank, N.A., Mendota Heights, MN

THERMO FISHER SCIENTIFIC INC

Exchange	Symbol	Price	52Wk Range	Yield	P/E
NYS	TMO	$189.88 (12/29/2017)	200.37-140.98	0.32	32.24

*7 Year Price Score 123.97 ***NYSE Composite Index=100** ***12 Month Price Score 102.85**

TRADING VOLUME (thousand shares)

Interim Earnings (Per Share)

Qtr.	Mar	Jun	Sep	Dec
2014	1.36	0.69	1.17	1.49
2015	0.96	1.27	1.18	1.50
2016	1.01	1.30	1.19	1.59
2017	1.40	1.56	1.34	...

Interim Dividends (Per Share)

Amt	Decl	Ex	Rec	Pay
0.15Q	02/28/2017	03/13/2017	03/15/2017	04/17/2017
0.15Q	05/18/2017	06/13/2017	06/15/2017	07/17/2017
0.15Q	07/12/2017	09/14/2017	09/15/2017	10/16/2017
0.15Q	11/09/2017	12/14/2017	12/15/2017	01/15/2018

Indicated Div: $0.60

Valuation Analysis   **Institutional Holding**

Forecast EPS	$9.35	No of Institutions
	(01/18/2018)	1569
Market Cap	$76.1 Billion	Shares
Book Value	$24.7 Billion	428,075,296
Price/Book	3.08	% Held
Price/Sales	3.84	90.66

Business Summary: Biotechnology (MIC: 4.1.2 SIC: 3829 NAIC: 334519)

Thermo Fisher Scientific is a provider of analytical instruments, equipment, reagents and consumables, software and services for research, manufacturing, analysis, discovery and diagnostics. Markets served include pharmaceutical and biotech, academic and government, industrial and applied, as well as healthcare and diagnostics. Co. serves its customers through its five brands: Thermo Scientific, Applied Biosystems, Invitrogen, Fisher Scientific and Unity Lab Services. Co. has four business segments: Life Sciences Solutions, Analytical Instruments, Specialty Diagnostics and Laboratory Products and Services.

Recent Developments: For the quarter ended Sep 30 2017, income from continuing operations increased 12.8% to US$533.9 million from US$473.5 million in the year-earlier quarter. Net income increased 12.8% to US$533.9 million from US$473.5 million in the year-earlier quarter. Revenues were US$5.12 billion, up 13.9% from US$4.49 billion the year before. Operating income was US$636.2 million versus US$541.1 million in the prior-year quarter, an increase of 17.6%. Direct operating expenses rose 15.6% to US$2.82 billion from US$2.44 billion in the comparable period the year before. Indirect operating expenses increased 10.0% to US$1.66 billion from US$1.51 billion in the equivalent prior-year period.

Prospects: Our evaluation of Thermo Fisher Scientific Inc. as of Jan. 14, 2018 is the result of our systematic analysis on three basic characteristics: earnings strength, relative valuation, and recent stock price movement. The company has managed to produce a neutral trend in earnings per share over the past 5 quarters and while recent estimates for the company have been mixed, TMO has posted better than expected results. Based on operating earnings yield, the company is about fairly valued when compared to all of the companies in our coverage universe. Share price changes over the past year indicates that TMO will perform in line with the market over the near term.

Financial Data
(US$ in Thousands)

	9 Mos	6 Mos	3 Mos	12/31/2016	12/31/2015	12/31/2014	12/31/2013	12/31/2012
Earnings Per Share	5.89	5.74	5.48	5.09	4.92	4.71	3.48	3.21
Cash Flow Per Share	8.44	8.17	8.26	7.97	7.07	6.58	5.58	5.59
Dividends Per Share	0.600	0.600	0.600	0.600	0.600	0.600	0.600	0.540
Dividend Payout %	10.19	10.45	10.95	11.79	12.20	12.74	17.24	16.82
Income Statement								
Total Revenue	14,871,200	9,755,000	4,765,000	18,274,100	16,965,400	16,889,600	13,090,300	12,509,900
EBITDA	2,280,200	1,555,500	1,084,300	4,203,100	4,008,900	4,204,200	2,553,500	2,469,500
Depn & Amortn	306,100	194,300	464,500	1,758,000	1,688,200	1,684,800	999,900	983,700
Income Before Taxes	1,609,100	1,128,500	502,900	2,023,900	1,936,400	2,087,200	1,319,500	1,269,400
Income Taxes	(88,400)	(35,100)	(48,500)	(1,400)	(43,900)	191,700	40,400	11,000
Net Income	1,696,900	1,163,000	551,400	2,021,800	1,975,400	1,894,400	1,273,300	1,177,900
Average Shares	399,600	393,300	394,100	397,400	401,900	402,300	365,800	366,600
Balance Sheet								
Current Assets	8,844,000	7,452,500	7,248,100	7,021,000	5,741,200	6,539,800	9,880,700	4,834,800
Total Assets	55,985,300	46,513,700	46,213,600	45,907,500	40,889,000	42,852,100	31,863,400	27,444,600
Current Liabilities	7,031,300	5,075,800	5,302,900	4,865,800	4,147,300	5,349,800	3,126,000	2,093,300
Long-Term Obligations	19,230,400	15,255,700	15,188,400	15,372,400	11,473,900	12,351,600	9,499,600	7,031,200
Total Liabilities	31,283,500	24,122,100	24,418,400	24,368,200	19,538,800	22,304,000	15,007,300	11,979,900
Stockholders' Equity	24,701,800	22,391,600	21,795,200	21,539,300	21,350,200	20,548,100	16,856,100	15,464,700
Shares Outstanding	400,995	390,119	391,219	393,447	399,630	400,469	361,961	357,443
Statistical Record								
Return on Assets %	4.47	5.11	4.87	4.65	4.72	5.07	4.29	4.33
Return on Equity %	10.04	10.38	10.16	9.40	9.43	10.13	7.88	7.70
EBITDA Margin %	15.33	15.95	22.76	23.00	23.63	24.89	19.51	19.74
Net Margin %	11.41	11.92	11.57	11.06	11.64	11.22	9.73	9.42
Asset Turnover	0.38	0.43	0.42	0.42	0.41	0.45	0.44	0.46
Current Ratio	1.26	1.47	1.37	1.44	1.38	1.22	3.16	2.31
Debt to Equity	0.78	0.68	0.70	0.71	0.54	0.60	0.56	0.45
Price Range	194.04-139.63	176.44-139.63	161.05-139.63	159.56-121.94	143.03-118.13	129.29-109.63	111.35-63.78	65.28-45.95
P/E Ratio	32.94-23.71	30.74-24.33	29.39-25.48	31.35-23.96	29.07-24.01	27.45-23.28	32.00-18.33	20.34-14.31
Average Yield %	0.37	0.39	0.40	0.41	0.46	0.50	0.69	0.96

Address: 168 Third Avenue, Waltham, MA 02451	**Web Site:** www.thermofisher.com
Telephone: 781-622-1000	**Officers:** Jim P. Manzi - Chairman, Chairman (frmr) Marc N. Casper - President, Chief Executive Officer, Executive Vice President (frmr), Senior Vice President, Chief Operating Officer
Fax: 781-933-4476	

Auditors: PricewaterhouseCoopers LLP
Investor Contact: 781-622-1111
Transfer Agents: American Stock Transfer & Trust Company, LLC, Brooklyn, NY

THOR INDUSTRIES, INC.

Exchange	Symbol	Price	52Wk Range	Yield	P/E
NYS	THO	$150.72 (12/29/2017)	155.25-89.41	0.98	18.77

*7 Year Price Score 151.95 *NYSE Composite Index=100 *12 Month Price Score 122.37

TRADING VOLUME (thousand shares)

Interim Earnings (Per Share)

Qtr.	Oct	Jan	Apr	Jul
2014-15	0.73	0.54	1.17	1.30
2015-16	0.96	0.85	1.49	1.57
2016-17	1.49	1.23	2.11	2.26
2017-18	2.43	...	...	...

Interim Dividends (Per Share)

Amt	Decl	Ex	Rec	Pay
0.33Q	03/16/2017	03/28/2017	03/30/2017	04/13/2017
0.33Q	06/08/2017	06/21/2017	06/23/2017	07/12/2017
0.37Q	10/10/2017	10/23/2017	10/24/2017	11/07/2017
0.37Q	12/11/2017	12/22/2017	12/26/2017	01/09/2018

Indicated Div: $1.48

Valuation Analysis / Institutional Holding

Valuation Analysis		Institutional Holding	
Forecast EPS	$9.06	No of Institutions	
	(01/13/2018)	603	
Market Cap	$7.9 Billion	Shares	
Book Value	$1.7 Billion	58,123,496	
Price/Book	4.72	% Held	
Price/Sales	1.02	83.49	

Business Summary: Autos- Manufacturing (MIC: 1.8.1 SIC: 3716 NAIC: 336213)

Thor Industries, through its subsidiaries, manufactures a range of recreational vehicles and sells those vehicles in the U.S. and Canada. Co. has two reportable segments: towable recreational vehicles, which consists of the following operating segments that have been aggregated: Airstream (towable), Heartland (including Bison, CRV and DRV), Jayco (including Jayco towable, Starcraft and Highland Ridge), Keystone (including CrossRoads and Dutchmen) and KZ (including Livin' Lite); and motorized recreational vehicles, which consists of the following operating segments that have been aggregated: Airstream (motorized), Jayco (including Jayco motorized and Entegra Coach) and Thor Motor Coach.

Recent Developments: For the quarter ended Oct 31 2017, net income increased 63.1% to US$128.4 million from US$78.7 million in the year-earlier quarter. Revenues were US$2.23 billion, up 30.6% from US$1.71 billion the year before. Direct operating expenses rose 29.0% to US$1.90 billion from US$1.47 billion in the comparable period the year before. Indirect operating expenses increased 22.6% to US$147.8 million from US$120.5 million in the equivalent prior-year period.

Prospects: Our evaluation of Thor Industries Inc. as of Jan. 14, 2018 is the result of our systematic analysis on three basic characteristics: earnings strength, relative valuation, and recent stock price movement. The company has managed to produce a neutral trend in earnings per share over the past 5 quarters and while recent estimates for the company have been raised by analysts, THO has posted better than expected results. Based on operating earnings yield, the company is undervalued when compared to all of the companies in our coverage universe. Share price changes over the past year indicates that THO will perform well over the near term.

Financial Data

(US$ in Thousands)	3 Mos	07/31/2017	07/31/2016	07/31/2015	07/31/2014	07/31/2013	07/31/2012	07/31/2011
Earnings Per Share	8.03	7.09	4.88	3.74	3.35	2.88	2.26	1.92
Cash Flow Per Share	8.20	7.98	6.49	4.66	2.80	2.74	2.20	2.08
Tang Book Value Per Share	16.63	14.36	7.24	11.14	11.28	10.47	9.29	8.36
Dividends Per Share	1.360	1.320	1.200	1.080	1.920	2.220	0.600	0.400
Dividend Payout %	16.94	18.62	24.59	28.88	57.31	77.08	26.55	20.83
Income Statement								
Total Revenue	2,231,668	7,246,952	4,582,112	4,006,819	3,525,456	3,241,795	3,084,660	2,755,508
EBITDA	203,433	663,451	436,737	323,164	277,086	244,337	202,464	172,938
Depn & Amortn	15,311	98,258	52,575	31,381	25,834	24,987	24,978	24,009
Income Before Taxes	187,091	556,386	383,313	292,895	252,819	221,972	180,691	152,627
Income Taxes	58,685	182,132	125,291	90,886	77,303	70,296	58,952	46,354
Net Income	128,406	374,254	256,519	199,385	179,002	152,862	121,739	106,273
Average Shares	52,818	52,758	52,590	53,275	53,361	53,115	53,899	55,373
Balance Sheet								
Current Assets	1,317,588	1,180,167	1,016,858	775,841	844,049	830,704	684,886	623,767
Total Assets	2,709,966	2,557,931	2,325,464	1,503,248	1,408,718	1,328,268	1,243,054	1,198,070
Current Liabilities	877,385	781,046	651,662	378,335	370,715	361,672	311,090	278,598
Long-Term Obligations	90,000	145,000	360,000	...	...	...	...	...
Total Liabilities	1,025,861	981,391	1,060,242	438,061	431,021	435,654	392,227	361,796
Stockholders' Equity	1,684,105	1,576,540	1,265,222	1,065,187	977,697	892,614	850,827	836,274
Shares Outstanding	52,694	52,586	52,482	52,394	53,329	53,186	52,920	55,840
Statistical Record								
Return on Assets %	16.65	15.33	13.36	13.69	13.08	11.89	9.95	9.83
Return on Equity %	28.17	26.34	21.95	19.52	19.14	17.54	14.39	14.23
EBITDA Margin %	9.12	9.15	9.53	8.07	7.86	7.54	6.56	6.28
Net Margin %	5.75	5.16	5.60	4.98	5.08	4.72	3.95	3.86
Asset Turnover	3.05	2.97	2.39	2.75	2.58	2.52	2.52	2.55
Current Ratio	1.50	1.51	1.56	2.05	2.28	2.30	2.20	2.24
Debt to Equity	0.05	0.09	0.28	...	...	...	...	...
Price Range	136.22-74.53	115.42-74.53	76.54-48.06	64.38-50.03	64.16-49.03	55.27-27.22	34.47-18.00	37.71-23.24
P/E Ratio	16.96-9.28	16.28-10.51	15.68-9.85	17.21-13.38	19.15-14.64	19.19-9.45	15.25-7.96	19.64-12.10
Average Yield %	1.31	1.40	2.05	1.90	3.42	5.63	2.18	1.29

Address: 601 East Beardsley Ave., Elkhart, IN 46514-3305 **Telephone:** 574-970-7460	**Web Site:** www.thorindustries.com **Officers:** Peter B. Orthwein - Executive Chairman, Chairman, President, Chief Executive Officer Robert W. Martin - President, Chief Executive Officer, Chief Operating Officer, Division Officer	**Auditors:** DELOITTE & TOUCHE LLP **Transfer Agents:** Computershare Investor Services

3M CO

Exchange	Symbol	Price	52Wk Range	Yield	P/E	Div Achiever
NYS	MMM	$235.37 (12/29/2017)	243.14-174.18	2.00	26.30	58 Years

*7 Year Price Score 116.98 *NYSE Composite Index=100 *12 Month Price Score 108.56

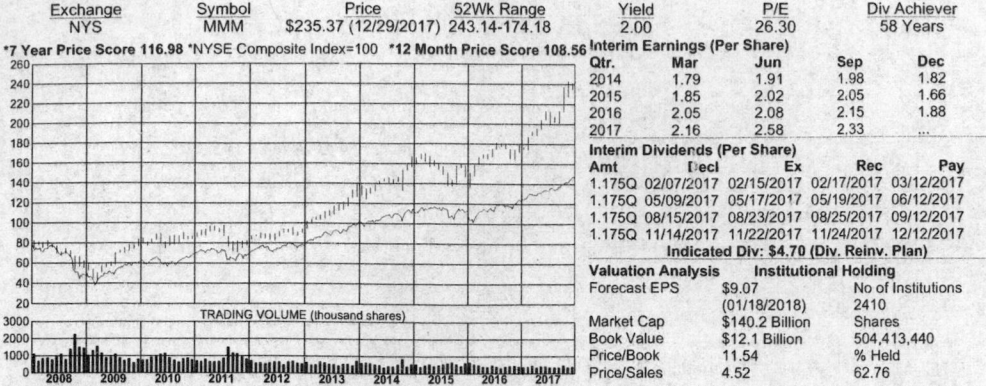

Interim Earnings (Per Share)
Qtr.	Mar	Jun	Sep	Dec
2014	1.79	1.91	1.98	1.82
2015	1.85	2.02	2.05	1.66
2016	2.05	2.08	2.15	1.88
2017	2.16	2.58	2.33	...

Interim Dividends (Per Share)
Amt	Decl	Ex	Rec	Pay
1.175Q	02/07/2017	02/15/2017	02/17/2017	03/12/2017
1.175Q	05/09/2017	05/17/2017	05/19/2017	06/12/2017
1.175Q	08/15/2017	08/23/2017	08/25/2017	09/12/2017
1.175Q	11/14/2017	11/22/2017	11/24/2017	12/12/2017

Indicated Div: $4.70 (Div. Reinv. Plan)

Valuation Analysis / Institutional Holding
Forecast EPS	$9.07	No of Institutions
(01/18/2018)		2410
Market Cap	$140.2 Billion	Shares
Book Value	$12.1 Billion	504,413,440
Price/Book	11.54	% Held
Price/Sales	4.52	62.76

Business Summary: Medical Instruments & Equipment (MIC: 4.3.1 SIC: 3841 NAIC: 339112)

3M is a technology company. Co. has five segments: Industrial, which provides tapes, coated, non-woven and bonded abrasives, and adhesives; Safety and Graphics, which provides personal protection products, traffic safety and security products and commercial graphics systems; Health Care, which provides medical and surgical supplies, skin health and infection prevention products and drug delivery systems; Electronics and Energy, which provides optical films solutions for electronic displays, packaging and interconnection devices, as well as insulating and splicing solutions; and Consumer, which provides sponges, scouring pads, cloths, consumer and office tapes.

Recent Developments: For the quarter ended Sep 30 2017, net income increased 7.7% to US$1.43 billion from US$1.33 billion in the year-earlier quarter. Revenues were US$8.17 billion, up 6.0% from US$7.71 billion the year before. Operating income was US$2.04 billion versus US$1.90 billion in the prior-year quarter, an increase of 7.2%. Direct operating expenses rose 5.1% to US$4.05 billion from US$3.85 billion in the comparable period the year before. Indirect operating expenses increased 6.5% to US$2.09 billion from US$1.96 billion in the equivalent prior-year period.

Prospects: Our evaluation of 3M Co as of Jan. 14, 2018 is the result of our systematic analysis on three basic characteristics: earnings strength, relative valuation, and recent stock price movement. The company has produced a positive trend in earnings per share over the past 5 quarters and while recent estimates for the company have been raised by analysts, MMM has posted better than expected results. Based on operating earnings yield, the company is about fairly valued when compared to all of the companies in our coverage universe. Share price changes over the past year indicates that MMM will perform well over the near term.

Financial Data
(US$ in Millions)

	9 Mos	6 Mos	3 Mos	12/31/2016	12/31/2015	12/31/2014	12/31/2013	12/31/2012
Earnings Per Share	8.95	8.77	8.27	8.16	7.58	7.49	6.72	6.32
Cash Flow Per Share	11.03	11.28	10.68	10.99	10.26	10.21	8.53	7.62
Tang Book Value Per Share	1.26	0.48	N.M.	N.M.	N.M.	7.28	12.77	12.03
Dividends Per Share	4.635	4.570	4.505	4.440	4.100	3.420	2.540	2.360
Dividend Payout %	51.79	52.11	54.47	54.41	54.09	45.66	37.80	37.34
Income Statement								
Total Revenue	23,667	15,495	7,685	30,109	30,274	31,821	30,871	29,904
EBITDA	7,194	4,776	2,212	8,697	8,381	8,543	8,037	7,771
Depn & Amortn	1,195	818	438	1,474	1,435	1,408	1,371	1,288
Income Before Taxes	5,876	3,879	1,737	7,053	6,823	7,026	6,562	6,351
Income Taxes	1,532	968	411	1,995	1,982	2,028	1,841	1,840
Net Income	4,335	2,906	1,323	5,050	4,833	4,956	4,659	4,444
Average Shares	612	612	612	618	637	662	693	703
Balance Sheet								
Current Assets	13,656	12,641	11,901	11,726	10,986	11,765	12,733	13,630
Total Assets	35,237	33,957	33,292	32,906	32,718	31,269	33,550	33,876
Current Liabilities	6,598	5,697	5,995	6,219	7,118	5,998	7,498	6,200
Long-Term Obligations	10,828	11,088	10,802	10,723	8,799	6,790	4,384	4,987
Total Liabilities	23,091	22,366	22,303	22,608	21,010	18,160	16,048	16,301
Stockholders' Equity	12,146	11,591	10,989	10,298	11,708	13,109	17,502	17,575
Shares Outstanding	595	596	597	596	609	635	663	687
Statistical Record								
Return on Assets %	15.85	16.04	15.38	15.35	15.11	15.29	13.82	13.53
Return on Equity %	45.47	45.90	44.87	45.77	38.95	32.38	26.56	26.86
EBITDA Margin %	30.40	30.82	28.78	28.89	27.68	26.85	26.03	25.99
Net Margin %	18.32	18.75	17.22	16.77	15.96	15.57	15.09	14.86
Asset Turnover	0.89	0.91	0.92	0.92	0.95	0.98	0.92	0.91
Current Ratio	2.07	2.22	1.99	1.89	1.54	1.96	1.70	2.20
Debt to Equity	0.89	0.96	0.98	1.04	0.75	0.52	0.25	0.28
Price Range	213.76-164.25	213.36-164.25	193.01-164.25	181.42-136.96	170.50-137.58	167.27-123.90	140.25-92.85	95.37-82.51
P/E Ratio	23.88-18.35	24.33-18.73	23.34-19.86	22.23-16.78	22.49-18.15	22.33-16.54	20.87-13.82	15.09-13.06
Average Yield %	2.43	2.49	2.56	2.64	2.62	2.40	2.23	2.65

Address: 3M Center, St. Paul, MN 55144
Telephone: 651-733-1110
Fax: 651-733-9973

Web Site: www.3M.com
Officers: Inge G. Thulin - Chairman, President, Executive Vice President, Chief Executive Officer, Chief Operating Officer Nicholas C. (Nick) Gangestad - Senior Vice President, Chief Financial Officer, Chief Accounting Officer

Auditors: PricewaterhouseCoopers LLP
Investor Contact: 651-737-8503
Transfer Agents: Wells Fargo Shareowner Services, St. Paul, MN

3D SYSTEMS CORP. (DE)

Exchange	Symbol	Price	52Wk Range	Yield	P/E
NYS	DDD	$8.64 (12/29/2017)	23.31-8.12	N/A	N/A

*7 Year Price Score 43.58 ***NYSE Composite Index=100** ***12 Month Price Score 58.15**

Interim Earnings (Per Share)

Qtr.	Mar	Jun	Sep	Dec
2014	0.05	0.02	0.03	0.02
2015	(0.12)	(0.12)	(0.29)	(5.32)
2016	(0.16)	(0.04)	(0.19)	0.04
2017	(0.09)	(0.08)	(0.34)	...

Interim Dividends (Per Share)

Amt	Decl	Ex	Rec	Pay
3-for-2	02/06/2013	02/25/2013	02/15/2013	02/22/2013

Valuation Analysis / Institutional Holding

Valuation Analysis		Institutional Holding	
Forecast EPS	$-0.04 (01/16/2018)	No of Institutions	339
Market Cap	$983.4 Million	Shares	84,126,080
Book Value	$617.7 Million		
Price/Book	1.59	% Held	54.20
Price/Sales	1.55		

TRADING VOLUME (thousand shares)

Business Summary: Computer Hardware & Equipment (MIC: 6.2.1 SIC: 7372 NAIC: 511210)

3D Systems is a holding company. Through its subsidiaries, Co. provides 3D printing solutions, including 3D printers, print materials, software, on demand manufacturing services and digital design tools. Co.'s solutions support applications in industries including healthcare, aerospace, automotive and durable goods. Co. provides a range of 3D printers, print materials, software, haptic devices, scanners and virtual surgical simulators. Co. provides a range of 3D printing technologies including Stereolithography, Selective Laser Sintering, Direct Metal Printing, MultiJet Printing and ColorJet Printing. Co. also provide digital design tools, including software, scanners and haptic devices.

Recent Developments: For the quarter ended Sep 30 2017, net loss amounted to US$37.3 million versus a net loss of US$21.4 million in the year-earlier quarter. Revenues were US$152.9 million, down 2.2% from US$156.4 million the year before. Operating loss was US$32.3 million versus a loss of US$22.0 million in the prior-year quarter. Direct operating expenses rose 8.0% to US$94.4 million from US$87.4 million in the comparable period the year before. Indirect operating expenses decreased 0.1% to US$90.9 million from US$91.0 million in the equivalent prior-year period.

Prospects: Our evaluation of 3D Systems Corp. as of Jan. 14, 2018 is the result of our systematic analysis on three basic characteristics: earnings strength, relative valuation, and recent stock price movement. The company has suffered a very negative trend in earnings per share over the past 5 quarters. Because the company lacks sufficient analyst estimate data, we place greater weight on the historical EPS trend as the measure of earnings strength. Based on operating earnings yield, the company is overvalued when compared to all of the companies in our coverage universe. Share price changes over the past year indicates that DDD will perform very poorly over the near term.

Financial Data
(US$ in Thousands)

	9 Mos	6 Mos	3 Mos	12/31/2016	12/31/2015	12/31/2014	12/31/2013	12/31/2012
Earnings Per Share	(0.47)	(0.32)	(0.28)	(0.35)	(5.85)	0.11	0.45	0.47
Cash Flow Per Share	0.33	0.40	0.52	0.51	(0.03)	0.47	0.26	0.65
Tang Book Value Per Share	2.49	2.70	2.63	2.88	2.77	4.05	4.08	1.47
Income Statement								
Total Revenue	468,805	315,898	156,431	632,965	666,163	653,652	513,400	353,633
EBITDA	(29,503)	(3,664)	(2,934)	(14,089)	(620,945)	41,042	90,607	69,012
Depn & Amortn	18,767	12,271	5,873	24,331	20,979	14,727	9,746	8,441
Income Before Taxes	(48,393)	(14,801)	(8,870)	(39,812)	(654,953)	17,387	64,006	43,279
Income Taxes	6,831	3,108	1,041	(547)	8,972	5,441	19,887	4,338
Net Income	(56,057)	(18,387)	(9,971)	(38,419)	(655,492)	11,637	44,107	38,941
Average Shares	111,697	111,398	111,289	111,189	111,969	108,023	98,393	81,723
Balance Sheet								
Current Assets	382,674	411,842	409,257	432,950	432,467	580,690	526,855	287,438
Total Assets	841,374	875,245	865,630	849,153	893,275	1,525,970	1,097,856	677,442
Current Liabilities	145,446	140,416	141,700	130,405	145,471	148,491	110,456	75,153
Long-Term Obligations	7,230	7,360	7,454	7,587	8,187	8,905	18,693	87,974
Total Liabilities	223,682	227,406	228,126	219,280	237,366	233,052	165,210	197,109
Stockholders' Equity	617,692	647,839	637,504	629,873	655,909	1,292,918	932,646	480,333
Shares Outstanding	113,816	113,881	113,788	113,615	112,223	111,524	103,218	89,250
Statistical Record								
Return on Assets %	N.M.	N.M.	N.M.	N.M.	N.M.	0.89	4.97	6.81
Return on Equity %	N.M.	N.M.	N.M.	N.M.	N.M.	1.05	6.24	10.57
EBITDA Margin %	N.M.	N.M.	N.M.	N.M.	N.M.	6.28	17.65	19.52
Net Margin %	N.M.	N.M.	N.M.	N.M.	N.M.	1.78	8.59	11.01
Asset Turnover	0.75	0.73	0.72	0.72	0.55	0.50	0.58	0.62
Current Ratio	2.63	2.93	2.89	3.32	2.97	3.91	4.77	3.82
Debt to Equity	0.01	0.01	0.01	0.01	0.01	0.01	0.02	0.18
Price Range	23.31-12.15	23.31-12.18	18.56-11.67	18.56-6.42	32.87-8.52	96.42-28.38	92.93-29.16	35.57-10.24
P/E Ratio	...	...	...	...	...	876.55-258.00	206.51-64.80	75.67-21.79

Address: 333 Three D Systems Circle, Rock Hill, SC 29730	Web Site: www.3DSystems.com	Auditors: BDO USA, LLP
Telephone: 803-326-3900	Officers: G. Walter Loewenbaum - Chairman Vyomesh I. Joshi - President, Chief Executive Officer	Investor Contact: 803-326-4010 Transfer Agents: U.S. Stock Transfer Corporation

TIFFANY & CO.

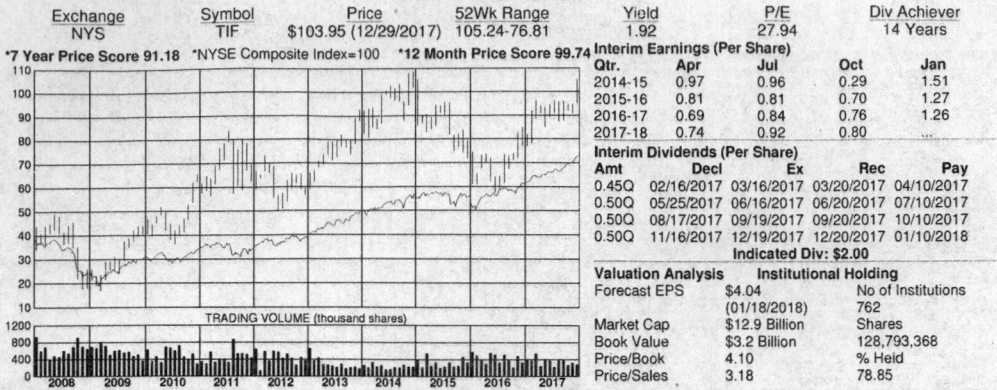

Exchange	Symbol	Price	52Wk Range	Yield	P/E	Div Achiever
NYS	TIF	$103.95 (12/29/2017)	105.24-76.81	1.92	27.94	14 Years

*7 Year Price Score 91.18   *NYSE Composite Index=100   *12 Month Price Score 99.74

Interim Earnings (Per Share)

Qtr.	Apr	Jul	Oct	Jan
2014-15	0.97	0.96	0.29	1.51
2015-16	0.81	0.81	0.70	1.27
2016-17	0.69	0.84	0.76	1.26
2017-18	0.74	0.92	0.80	...

Interim Dividends (Per Share)

Amt	Decl	Ex	Rec	Pay
0.45Q	02/16/2017	03/16/2017	03/20/2017	04/10/2017
0.50Q	05/25/2017	06/16/2017	06/20/2017	07/10/2017
0.50Q	08/17/2017	09/19/2017	09/20/2017	10/10/2017
0.50Q	11/16/2017	12/19/2017	12/20/2017	01/10/2018

Indicated Div: $2.00

Valuation Analysis   **Institutional Holding**

Forecast EPS	$4.04	No of Institutions
	(01/18/2018)	762
Market Cap	$12.9 Billion	Shares
Book Value	$3.2 Billion	128,793,368
Price/Book	4.10	% Held
Price/Sales	3.18	78.85

Business Summary: Retail - Specialty (MIC: 2.1.3 SIC: 5944 NAIC: 448310)

Tiffany & Co. is a holding company that operates through its subsidiary companies. Its principal subsidiary, Tiffany and Company, is a jeweler and specialty retailer. Through its subsidiaries, Co. designs and manufactures products and operates TIFFANY & CO. retail stores worldwide, and also sells its products through internet, catalog, business-to-business and wholesale operations. Co. also sells timepieces, leather goods, sterling silverware, china, crystal, stationery, fragrances and accessories. Co. has four reportable segments: (i) Americas, (ii) Asia-Pacific, (iii) Japan and (iv) Europe. As of Jan 31 2017, Co. operated a total of 313 TIFFANY & CO. stores.

Recent Developments: For the quarter ended Oct 31 2017, net income increased 5.4% to US$100.2 million from US$95.1 million in the year-earlier quarter. Revenues were US$976.2 million, up 2.8% from US$949.3 million the year before. Operating income was US$160.3 million versus US$155.2 million in the prior-year quarter, an increase of 3.3%. Direct operating expenses rose 2.2% to US$377.8 million from US$369.8 million in the comparable period the year before. Indirect operating expenses increased 3.3% to US$438.1 million from US$424.3 million in the equivalent prior-year period.

Prospects: Our evaluation of Tiffany & Co. as of Jan. 14, 2018 is the result of our systematic analysis on three basic characteristics: earnings strength, relative valuation, and recent stock price movement. The company has managed to produce a neutral trend in earnings per share over the past 5 quarters and while recent estimates for the company have been mixed, TIF has posted better than expected results. Based on operating earnings yield, the company is about fairly valued when compared to all of the companies in our coverage universe. Share price changes over the past year indicates that TIF will perform poorly over the near term.

Financial Data

(US$ in Thousands)	9 Mos	6 Mos	3 Mos	01/31/2017	01/31/2016	01/31/2015	01/31/2014	01/31/2013
Earnings Per Share	3.72	3.68	3.60	3.55	3.59	3.73	1.41	3.25
Cash Flow Per Share	5.87	6.29	5.91	5.60	6.33	4.76	1.21	2.58
Tang Book Value Per Share	25.37	25.24	24.53	24.20	22.96	21.92	21.20	20.47
Dividends Per Share	1.900	1.850	1.800	1.750	1.580	1.480	1.340	1.250
Dividend Payout %	51.08	50.27	50.00	49.30	44.01	39.68	95.04	38.46
Income Statement								
Total Revenue	2,835,400	1,859,300	899,600	4,001,800	4,104,900	4,249,913	4,031,130	3,794,249
EBITDA	481,200	322,800	143,600	925,100	955,200	983,201	488,972	861,663
Depn & Amortn	(6,100)	(4,100)	(2,000)	202,500	196,300	182,761	171,452	159,018
Income Before Taxes	459,100	308,700	136,100	676,600	709,900	737,537	254,866	643,576
Income Taxes	150,900	100,800	43,200	230,500	246,000	253,358	73,497	227,419
Net Income	308,200	207,900	92,900	446,100	463,900	484,179	181,369	416,157
Average Shares	125,000	125,100	125,300	125,500	129,100	129,918	128,867	127,934
Balance Sheet								
Current Assets	3,778,200	3,722,000	3,594,500	3,573,600	3,508,400	3,611,387	3,228,388	3,151,589
Total Assets	5,314,000	5,269,600	5,106,200	5,097,600	5,129,700	5,180,603	4,752,351	4,630,850
Current Liabilities	694,300	647,800	582,500	632,800	729,900	658,033	696,740	586,592
Long-Term Obligations	879,200	881,100	880,500	878,400	798,100	882,535	751,154	765,238
Total Liabilities	2,160,100	2,126,800	2,046,700	2,084,100	2,218,300	2,345,544	2,031,914	2,032,118
Stockholders' Equity	3,153,900	3,142,800	3,059,500	3,013,500	2,911,400	2,835,059	2,720,437	2,598,732
Shares Outstanding	124,300	124,500	124,700	124,500	126,800	129,326	128,312	126,934
Statistical Record								
Return on Assets %	8.91	8.89	8.81	8.70	9.00	9.75	3.87	9.44
Return on Equity %	15.37	15.22	15.04	15.02	16.15	17.43	6.82	16.78
EBITDA Margin %	16.97	17.36	15.96	23.12	23.27	23.13	12.13	22.71
Net Margin %	10.87	11.18	10.33	11.15	11.30	11.39	4.50	10.97
Asset Turnover	0.78	0.78	0.78	0.78	0.80	0.86	0.86	0.86
Current Ratio	5.44	5.75	6.17	5.65	4.81	5.49	4.63	5.37
Debt to Equity	0.28	0.28	0.29	0.29	0.27	0.31	0.28	0.29
Price Range	96.48-72.04	96.41-61.42	96.41-57.48	85.06-57.48	95.70-60.93	108.67-80.88	92.78-62.17	73.27-50.29
P/E Ratio	25.94-19.37	26.20-16.69	26.78-15.97	23.96-16.19	26.66-16.97	29.13-21.68	65.80-44.09	22.54-15.47
Average Yield %	2.16	2.24	2.39	2.49	1.88	1.54	1.73	2.04

Address: 727 Fifth Avenue, New York, NY 10022	Web Site: www.tiffany.com	Auditors: PricewaterhouseCoopers LLP
Telephone: 212-755-8000	Officers: Michael J. Kowalski - Chairman, Chief Executive Officer, Interim Chief Executive Officer Alessandro Bogliolo - Chief Executive Officer	Investor Contact: 212-230-5301
Fax: 212-605-4465		Transfer Agents: Computershare, Providence, RI

TIME WARNER INC

Exchange	Symbol	Price	52Wk Range	Yield	P/E
NYS	TWX	$91.47 (12/29/2017)	103.64-87.05	1.76	17.39

*7 Year Price Score 117.80 *NYSE Composite Index=100 *12 Month Price Score 88.49

Interim Earnings (Per Share)

Qtr.	Mar	Jun	Sep	Dec
2014	1.42	0.95	1.11	0.85
2015	1.15	1.16	1.26	1.06
2016	1.51	1.20	1.86	0.39
2017	1.80	1.34	1.73	...

Interim Dividends (Per Share)

Amt	Decl	Ex	Rec	Pay
0.403Q	04/27/2017	05/26/2017	05/31/2017	06/15/2017
0.403Q	06/30/2017	07/10/2017	07/10/2017	08/01/2017
0.403Q	09/29/2017	10/06/2017	10/10/2017	11/01/2017
0.403Q	12/18/2017	01/09/2018	01/10/2018	02/01/2018

Indicated Div: $1.61

Valuation Analysis

		Institutional Holding	
Forecast EPS	$6.23 (01/18/2018)	No of Institutions	1530
Market Cap	$71.3 Billion	Shares	870,693,312
Book Value	$27.3 Billion	% Held	
Price/Book	2.61	N/A	
Price/Sales	2.33		

Business Summary: Entertainment (MIC: 2.3.2 SIC: 7812 NAIC: 512110)

Time Warner is a media and entertainment company. Co. classifies its businesses into three reportable segments: Turner, consisting principally of cable networks and digital media properties operating more than 175 channels globally; Home Box Office, consisting premium pay television and OTT services domestically and premium pay, basic tier television and OTT services internationally, as well as home entertainment and content licensing; and Warner Bros., consisting principally of television, feature film, home video and videogame production and distribution. Co. also holds interests in companies that operate broadcast networks.

Recent Developments: For the quarter ended Sep 30 2017, income from continuing operations decreased 6.9% to US$1.37 billion from US$1.47 billion in the year-earlier quarter. Net income decreased 6.5% to US$1.37 billion from US$1.47 billion in the year-earlier quarter. Revenues were US$7.60 billion, up 6.0% from US$7.17 billion the year before. Operating income was US$2.25 billion versus US$2.01 billion in the prior-year quarter, an increase of 11.5%. Direct operating expenses rose 1.4% to US$3.93 billion from US$3.87 billion in the comparable period the year before. Indirect operating expenses increased 11.1% to US$1.42 billion from US$1.28 billion in the equivalent prior-year period.

Prospects: Our evaluation of Time Warner Inc. as of Jan. 14, 2018 is the result of our systematic analysis on three basic characteristics: earnings strength, relative valuation, and recent stock price movement. The company has generated a negative trend in earnings per share over the past 5 quarters. However, while recent estimates for the company have been mixed, TWX has posted better than expected results. Based on operating earnings yield, the company is undervalued when compared to all of the companies in our coverage universe. Share price changes over the past year indicates that TWX will perform in line with the market over the near term.

Financial Data

(US$ in Thousands)	9 Mos	6 Mos	3 Mos	12/31/2016	12/31/2015	12/31/2014	12/31/2013	12/31/2012
Earnings Per Share	5.26	5.39	5.25	4.96	4.62	4.34	3.92	3.09
Cash Flow Per Share	6.55	6.66	6.97	5.98	4.73	4.26	4.04	3.60
Dividends Per Share	1.610	1.610	1.610	1.610	1.400	1.270	1.150	1.040
Dividend Payout %	30.61	29.87	30.67	32.46	30.30	29.26	29.34	33.66
Income Statement								
Total Revenue	22,660,000	15,065,000	7,735,000	29,318,000	28,118,000	27,359,000	29,795,000	28,729,000
EBITDA	12,631,000	8,565,000	4,431,000	6,829,000	6,921,000	6,203,000	6,896,000	6,089,000
Depn & Amortn	6,381,000	4,555,000	2,203,000	190,000	189,000	202,000	251,000	248,000
Income Before Taxes	5,488,000	3,502,000	1,969,000	5,478,000	5,569,000	4,832,000	5,455,000	4,588,000
Income Taxes	1,472,000	922,000	470,000	1,281,000	1,651,000	785,000	1,749,000	1,526,000
Net Income	3,858,000	2,486,000	1,424,000	3,926,000	3,833,000	3,827,000	3,691,000	3,019,000
Average Shares	791,700	790,000	789,300	792,300	829,500	882,600	942,600	976,300
Balance Sheet								
Current Assets	14,608,000	13,404,000	12,908,000	13,485,000	12,513,000	13,180,000	12,844,000	13,288,000
Total Assets	68,343,000	66,096,000	65,649,000	65,966,000	63,848,000	63,259,000	67,994,000	68,304,000
Current Liabilities	9,851,000	8,839,000	8,162,000	9,703,000	8,002,000	9,204,000	8,383,000	9,829,000
Long-Term Obligations	21,898,000	21,843,000	22,402,000	22,392,000	23,594,000	21,376,000	20,099,000	19,122,000
Total Liabilities	41,076,000	40,109,000	40,224,000	41,631,000	40,229,000	38,783,000	38,090,000	38,427,000
Stockholders' Equity	27,267,000	25,987,000	25,425,000	24,335,000	23,619,000	24,476,000	29,904,000	29,877,000
Shares Outstanding	779,000	777,000	775,000	772,000	795,000	832,000	895,000	932,000
Statistical Record								
Return on Assets %	6.19	6.52	6.42	6.03	6.03	5.83	5.42	4.42
Return on Equity %	16.11	17.03	16.79	16.33	15.94	14.08	12.35	10.06
EBITDA Margin %	55.74	56.85	57.29	23.29	24.61	22.67	23.14	21.19
Net Margin %	17.03	16.50	18.41	13.39	13.63	13.99	12.39	10.51
Asset Turnover	0.46	0.46	0.46	0.45	0.44	0.42	0.44	0.42
Current Ratio	1.48	1.52	1.58	1.39	1.56	1.43	1.53	1.35
Debt to Equity	0.80	0.84	0.88	0.92	1.00	0.87	0.67	0.64
Price Range	103.22-78.57	100.41-73.54	98.96-69.21	96.74-60.07	91.01-63.41	87.36-58.98	67.41-45.86	46.27-32.37
P/E Ratio	19.62-14.94	18.63-13.64	18.85-13.18	19.50-12.11	19.70-13.73	20.13-13.59	17.20-11.70	14.97-10.47
Average Yield %	1.67	1.78	1.91	2.08	1.77	1.74	1.98	2.70

Address: One Time Warner Center, New York, NY 10019-8016	Web Site: www.timewarner.com	Auditors: Ernst & Young LLP
Telephone: 212-484-8000	Officers: Jeffrey L. Bewkes - Chairman, Chief Executive Officer Howard M. Averill - Executive Vice President, Chief Financial Officer	Investor Contact: 212-484-8920
Fax: 212-489-6183		Transfer Agents: Computershare Trust Company, N.A., Providence, RI

TIMKEN CO. (THE)

Exchange	Symbol	Price	52Wk Range	Yield	P/E
NYS	TKR	$49.15 (12/29/2017)	51.55-40.95	2.20	19.66

*7 Year Price Score 96.44   *NYSE Composite Index=100   *12 Month Price Score 98.16

Interim Earnings (Per Share)

Qtr.	Mar	Jun	Sep	Dec
2014	0.90	0.68	(0.24)	0.52
2015	(1.54)	0.43	0.75	(0.43)
2016	0.78	0.43	0.57	0.30
2017	0.48	1.04	0.68	...

Interim Dividends (Per Share)

Amt	Decl	Ex	Rec	Pay
0.26Q	02/10/2017	02/17/2017	02/22/2017	03/03/2017
0.27Q	05/09/2017	05/17/2017	05/19/2017	06/01/2017
0.27Q	08/08/2017	08/18/2017	08/22/2017	09/01/2017
0.27Q	11/03/2017	11/16/2017	11/17/2017	12/01/2017

Indicated Div: $1.08

Valuation Analysis   **Institutional Holding**

Forecast EPS	$2.63	No of Institutions
	(01/25/2018)	468
Market Cap	$3.8 Billion	Shares
Book Value	$1.4 Billion	74,595,168
Price/Book	2.68	% Held
Price/Sales	1.32	68.91

Business Summary: Industrial Machinery & Equipment (MIC: 7.2.1 SIC: 3562 NAIC: 332991)

Timken engineers, manufactures and markets bearings, transmissions, gearboxes, belts, chain, couplings and related products and provides a range of power system rebuild and repair services. Co.'s products include: tapered roller bearings, which can increase power density and can include customized geometries, engineered surfaces and specialized sealing solutions; spherical and cylindrical roller bearings, which used in gear drives, rolling mills and other industrial and infrastructure development applications; Carlisle® belts, which used in industrial, commercial and consumer applications; and Drives® roller chain, which are used in a range of mobile and industrial machinery applications.

Recent Developments: For the quarter ended Sep 30 2017, net income increased 59.1% to US$54.1 million from US$34.0 million in the year-earlier quarter. Revenues were US$771.4 million, up 17.3% from US$657.4 million the year before. Operating income was US$81.7 million versus US$57.1 million in the prior-year quarter, an increase of 43.1%. Direct operating expenses rose 13.7% to US$554.4 million from US$487.7 million in the comparable period the year before. Indirect operating expenses increased 20.2% to US$135.3 million from US$112.6 million in the equivalent prior-year period.

Prospects: Our evaluation of Timken Co. as of Jan. 21, 2018 is the result of our systematic analysis on three basic characteristics: earnings strength, relative valuation, and recent stock price movement. The company has enjoyed a very positive trend in earnings per share over the past 5 quarters and while recent estimates for the company have been mixed, TKR has posted better than expected results. Based on operating earnings yield, the company is undervalued when compared to all of the companies in our coverage universe. Share price changes over the past year indicates that TKR will perform poorly over the near term.

Financial Data

(US$ in Thousands)	9 Mos	6 Mos	3 Mos	12/31/2016	12/31/2015	12/31/2014	12/31/2013	12/31/2012
Earnings Per Share	2.50	2.08	1.61	1.92	(0.84)	1.87	2.74	5.07
Cash Flow Per Share	3.45	4.03	5.17	5.11	4.43	3.40	4.53	6.46
Tang Book Value Per Share	6.23	9.32	8.96	8.35	9.04	12.16	22.11	17.40
Dividends Per Share	1.060	1.050	1.040	1.040	1.030	1.000	0.920	0.920
Dividend Payout %	42.40	50.48	64.60	54.17	...	53.48	33.58	18.15
Income Statement								
Total Revenue	2,225,800	1,454,400	703,800	2,669,800	2,872,300	3,076,200	4,341,200	4,987,000
EBITDA	329,700	191,300	84,800	349,200	(64,300)	343,800	615,500	973,200
Depn & Amortn	102,500	48,700	23,900	95,500	94,600	115,500	175,900	179,000
Income Before Taxes	202,700	127,500	53,600	222,100	(189,600)	204,000	417,100	766,000
Income Taxes	28,500	7,400	15,500	69,200	(121,600)	54,700	154,100	270,100
Net Income	174,200	120,700	38,200	152,600	(70,800)	170,800	262,700	495,500
Average Shares	78,804	79,029	78,893	79,234	84,631	91,224	95,823	97,602
Balance Sheet								
Current Assets	1,474,300	1,659,500	1,270,700	1,204,000	1,206,400	1,481,900	1,937,500	2,174,100
Total Assets	3,363,600	3,238,500	2,815,600	2,758,300	2,785,300	3,001,400	4,477,900	4,244,700
Current Liabilities	568,700	537,900	498,400	452,700	505,300	533,800	980,100	667,900
Long-Term Obligations	959,800	947,100	600,100	635,000	580,600	522,100	206,600	455,100
Total Liabilities	1,940,600	1,851,500	1,494,500	1,483,400	1,460,800	1,425,200	1,841,300	2,012,500
Stockholders' Equity	1,423,000	1,387,000	1,321,100	1,274,900	1,324,500	1,576,200	2,636,600	2,232,200
Shares Outstanding	77,617	77,842	77,993	77,449	80,263	88,591	93,122	95,898
Statistical Record								
Return on Assets %	6.41	5.48	4.51	5.49	N.M.	4.57	6.02	11.50
Return on Equity %	14.36	12.16	9.57	11.71	N.M.	8.11	10.79	23.20
EBITDA Margin %	14.81	13.15	12.05	13.08	N.M.	11.18	14.18	19.51
Net Margin %	7.83	8.30	5.43	5.72	N.M.	5.55	6.05	9.94
Asset Turnover	0.93	0.92	0.95	0.96	0.99	0.82	1.00	1.16
Current Ratio	2.59	3.09	2.55	2.66	2.39	2.78	1.98	3.26
Debt to Equity	0.67	0.68	0.45	0.50	0.44	0.33	0.08	0.20
Price Range	49.70-32.00	49.50-30.00	45.65-28.97	40.95-23.41	43.50-26.46	49.73-37.75	45.26-33.98	41.01-25.02
P/E Ratio	19.88-12.80	23.80-14.42	28.35-17.99	21.33-12.19	...	26.59-20.19	16.52-12.40	8.09-4.93
Average Yield %	2.45	2.63	2.82	3.14	2.88	2.30	2.31	2.85

Address: 4500 Mount Pleasant Street N.W., North Canton, OH 44720-5450 **Telephone:** 234-262-3000	**Web Site:** www.timken.com **Officers:** John M. Timken - Chairman Richard G. Kyle - President, Group President, Chief Executive Officer, Chief Operating Officer	**Auditors:** Ernst & Young LLP **Investor Contact:** 330-471-7446 **Transfer Agents:** Wells Fargo Shareowner Services, Saint Paul, MN

TJX COMPANIES, INC.

Exchange	Symbol	Price	52Wk Range	Yield	P/E	Div Achiever
NYS	TJX	$76.46 (12/29/2017)	80.72-66.90	1.63	20.66	20 Years

*7 Year Price Score 101.90 *NYSE Composite Index=100 *12 Month Price Score 93.51

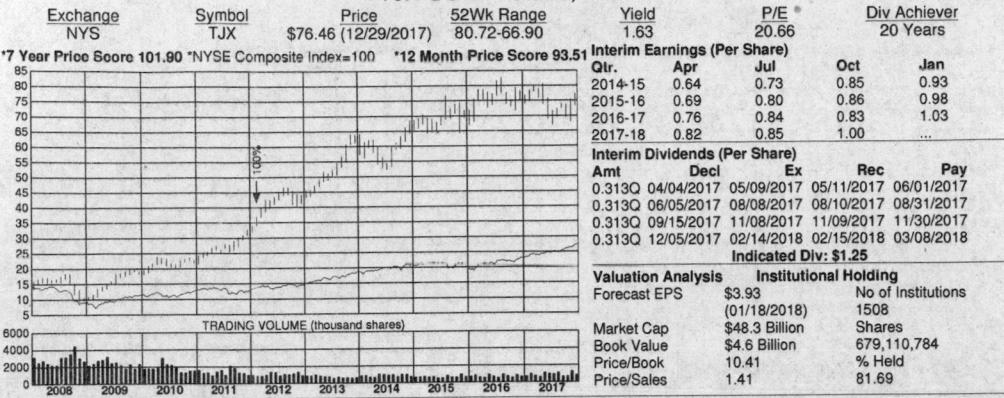

Interim Earnings (Per Share)

Qtr.	Apr	Jul	Oct	Jan
2014-15	0.64	0.73	0.85	0.93
2015-16	0.69	0.80	0.86	0.98
2016-17	0.76	0.84	0.83	1.03
2017-18	0.82	0.85	1.00	...

Interim Dividends (Per Share)

Amt	Decl	Ex	Rec	Pay
0.313Q	04/04/2017	05/09/2017	05/11/2017	06/01/2017
0.313Q	06/05/2017	08/08/2017	08/10/2017	08/31/2017
0.313Q	09/15/2017	11/08/2017	11/09/2017	11/30/2017
0.313Q	12/05/2017	02/14/2018	02/15/2018	03/08/2018

Indicated Div: $1.25

Valuation Analysis **Institutional Holding**

Forecast EPS	$3.93	No of Institutions
(01/18/2018)		1508
Market Cap	$48.3 Billion	Shares
Book Value	$4.6 Billion	679,110,784
Price/Book	10.41	% Held
Price/Sales	1.41	81.69

Business Summary: Retail - Apparel and Accessories (MIC: 2.1.5 SIC: 5651 NAIC: 448140)

TJX Companies is an apparel and home fashions retailer. Co. operates its business in four main segments. In the U.S., Co.'s two segments are comprised of Marmaxx (T.J. Maxx, Marshalls and tjmaxx.com) and HomeGoods. The TJX Canada segment operates Winners, HomeSense and Marshalls in Canada, and the TJX International segment operates T.K. Maxx, HomeSense and tkmaxx.com in Europe and Trade Secret in Australia. All of Co.'s stores, with the exception of HomeGoods and HomeSense, sell family apparel and home fashions. HomeGoods and HomeSense provide home fashions. As of Jan 28 2017, Co. operated a total of 2,800 stores in the U.S.; 418 stores in Canada; and 582 stores in Europe and Australia.

Recent Developments: For the quarter ended Oct 28 2017, net income increased 16.7% to US$641.4 million from US$549.8 million in the year-earlier quarter. Revenues were US$8.76 billion, up 5.7% from US$8.29 billion the year before. Direct operating expenses rose 5.2% to US$6.15 billion from US$5.84 billion in the comparable period the year before. Indirect operating expenses increased 8.3% to US$1.58 billion from US$1.46 billion in the equivalent prior-year period.

Prospects: Our evaluation of TJX Companies Inc. as of Jan. 14, 2018 is the result of our systematic analysis on three basic characteristics: earnings strength, relative valuation, and recent stock price movement. The company has enjoyed a very positive trend in earnings per share over the past 5 quarters and while recent estimates for the company have been mixed, TJX has posted better than expected results. Based on operating earnings yield, the company is undervalued when compared to all of the companies in our coverage universe. Share price changes over the past year indicates that TJX will perform poorly over the near term.

Financial Data

(US$ in Thousands)	9 Mos	6 Mos	3 Mos	01/28/2017	01/30/2016	01/31/2015	02/01/2014	02/02/2013
Earnings Per Share	3.70	3.53	3.52	3.46	3.33	3.15	2.94	2.55
Cash Flow Per Share	5.43	5.55	5.63	5.51	4.37	4.35	3.64	4.08
Tang Book Value Per Share	7.04	6.83	6.77	6.68	5.97	5.78	5.56	4.63
Dividends Per Share	1.145	1.093	1.040	0.990	0.805	0.670	0.550	0.440
Dividend Payout %	30.95	30.95	29.55	28.61	24.17	21.27	18.71	17.25
Income Statement								
Total Revenue	24,903,944	16,141,724	7,784,024	33,183,744	30,944,938	29,078,407	27,422,696	25,878,372
EBITDA	3,305,707	2,090,826	1,014,949	4,425,373	4,321,396	4,178,646	3,899,393	3,108,226
Depn & Amortn	534,000	347,100	172,600	658,796	616,696	588,975	548,823	1,700
Income Before Taxes	2,744,208	1,724,208	832,508	3,723,043	3,658,300	3,549,884	3,319,489	3,077,351
Income Taxes	1,013,536	634,972	296,229	1,424,809	1,380,642	1,334,756	1,182,093	1,170,664
Net Income	1,730,672	1,089,236	536,279	2,298,234	2,277,658	2,215,128	2,137,396	1,906,687
Average Shares	642,881	648,317	654,799	664,432	683,251	703,545	726,376	747,555
Balance Sheet								
Current Assets	8,390,034	7,567,781	7,548,500	7,750,774	6,772,560	6,715,061	6,067,998	5,711,543
Total Assets	13,877,695	12,935,615	12,763,481	12,883,808	11,499,482	11,128,381	10,201,022	9,511,855
Current Liabilities	5,467,981	4,656,533	4,605,392	4,757,656	4,402,230	3,929,634	3,517,843	3,760,596
Long-Term Obligations	2,229,855	2,229,103	2,228,351	2,403,831	1,709,268	1,684,597	1,274,216	774,552
Total Liabilities	9,232,087	8,394,811	8,209,958	8,373,209	7,192,407	6,864,151	5,971,129	5,845,918
Stockholders' Equity	4,645,608	4,540,804	4,553,523	4,510,599	4,307,075	4,264,230	4,229,893	3,665,937
Shares Outstanding	632,302	636,274	643,276	646,319	663,495	684,733	705,016	723,902
Statistical Record								
Return on Assets %	18.01	18.83	19.01	18.90	20.19	20.83	21.74	21.08
Return on Equity %	53.67	51.53	51.19	52.27	53.29	52.30	54.29	54.57
EBITDA Margin %	13.27	12.95	13.04	13.34	13.96	14.37	14.22	12.01
Net Margin %	6.95	6.75	6.89	6.93	7.36	7.62	7.79	7.37
Asset Turnover	2.57	2.76	2.73	2.73	2.74	2.73	2.79	2.86
Current Ratio	1.53	1.63	1.64	1.63	1.54	1.71	1.72	1.52
Debt to Equity	0.48	0.49	0.49	0.53	0.40	0.40	0.30	0.21
Price Range	80.72-66.90	82.87-66.90	82.87-71.80	82.87-67.91	76.78-64.21	68.60-52.23	64.05-43.58	46.64-34.04
P/E Ratio	21.82-18.08	23.48-18.95	23.54-20.40	23.95-19.63	23.06-19.28	21.78-16.58	21.79-14.82	18.29-13.35
Average Yield %	1.53	1.44	1.35	1.30	1.16	1.12	1.03	1.04

Address: 770 Cochituate Road, Framingham, MA 01701 **Telephone:** 508-390-1000 **Fax:** 508-390-2091	**Web Site:** www.tjx.com **Officers:** Carol Meyrowitz - Chairwoman, Chief Executive Officer Ernie L. Herrman - President, Chief Executive Officer	**Auditors:** PricewaterhouseCoopers LLP **Investor Contact:** 508-390-2323 **Transfer Agents:** Computershare, Providence, RI

TOLL BROTHERS INC.

Exchange	Symbol	Price	52Wk Range	Yield	P/E
NYS	TOL	$48.02 (12/29/2017)	50.66-30.90	0.67	15.15

*7 Year Price Score 97.08   *NYSE Composite Index=100   *12 Month Price Score 115.18

Interim Earnings (Per Share)

Qtr.	Jan	Apr	Jul	Oct
2012-13	0.03	0.14	0.26	0.54
2013-14	0.25	0.35	0.53	0.71
2014-15	0.44	0.37	0.36	0.79
2015-16	0.40	0.51	0.61	0.66
2016-17	0.42	0.73	0.87	1.16

Interim Dividends (Per Share)

Amt	Decl	Ex	Rec	Pay
0.08Q	02/21/2017	04/11/2017	04/14/2017	04/28/2017
0.08Q	06/20/2017	07/12/2017	07/14/2017	07/28/2017
0.08Q	09/19/2017	10/12/2017	10/13/2017	10/27/2017
0.08Q	12/13/2017	01/11/2018	01/12/2018	01/26/2018

Indicated Div: $0.32

Valuation Analysis

		Institutional Holding	
Forecast EPS	$3.77	No of Institutions	
(01/18/2018)		588	
Market Cap	$7.5 Billion	Shares	
Book Value	$4.5 Billion	168,724,800	
Price/Book	1.67	% Held	
Price/Sales	1.30	86.35	

TRADING VOLUME (thousand shares)

Business Summary: Builders (MIC: 2.2.5 SIC: 1531 NAIC: 236117)

Toll Brothers designs, builds, markets, sells and arranges financing for detached and attached homes in residential communities. Co. also builds and sells homes in urban infill markets through Toll Brothers City Living®. Co. is developing several land parcels for master planned communities. Co. also develops and operates for-rent apartments through joint ventures. Co. operates its own land development, architectural, engineering, mortgage, title, landscaping, security monitoring, lumber distribution, house component assembly, and manufacturing operations. In addition, Co. develops land for sale to other builders. Co. also develops, owns, and operates golf courses and country clubs.

Recent Developments: For the year ended Oct 31 2017, net income increased 40.1% to US$535.5 million from US$382.1 million in the prior year. Revenues were US$5.82 billion, up 12.5% from US$5.17 billion the year before. Operating income was US$644.9 million versus US$490.1 million in the prior year, an increase of 31.6%. Direct operating expenses rose 10.1% to US$4.56 billion from US$4.14 billion in the comparable period the year before. Indirect operating expenses increased 13.5% to US$607.8 million from US$535.4 million in the equivalent prior-year period.

Prospects: Our evaluation of Toll Brothers Inc. as of Jan. 14, 2018 is the result of our systematic analysis on three basic characteristics: earnings strength, relative valuation, and recent stock price movement. The company has generated a negative trend in earnings per share over the past 5 quarters and while recent estimates for the company have been raised by analysts, TOL has posted results that fell short of analysts expectations. Based on operating earnings yield, the company is undervalued when compared to all of the companies in our coverage universe. Share price changes over the past year indicates that TOL will perform well over the near term.

Financial Data
(US$ in Thousands)

	10/31/2017	10/31/2016	10/31/2015	10/31/2014	10/31/2013	10/31/2012	10/31/2011	10/31/2010
Earnings Per Share	3.17	2.18	1.97	1.84	0.97	2.86	0.24	(0.02)
Cash Flow Per Share	5.92	0.88	0.34	1.76	(3.36)	(1.01)	0.32	(0.88)
Tang Book Value Per Share	28.82	26.14	24.15	22.02	19.68	18.51	15.61	15.36
Dividends Per Share	0.240	...	...	...	...	...	...	...
Dividend Payout %	7.57	...	...	...	...	...	...	...
Income Statement								
Total Revenue	5,815,058	5,169,508	4,171,248	3,911,602	2,674,299	1,882,781	1,475,881	1,494,771
EBITDA	710,957	561,336	528,204	420,248	226,277	86,015	(26,929)	(132,692)
Depn & Amortn	18,700	15,500	15,700	22,999	25,210	22,586	23,142	20,044
Income Before Taxes	698,245	548,279	514,443	463,441	253,305	89,350	(28,172)	(140,657)
Income Taxes	278,816	206,932	172,395	164,550	97,091	(374,204)	(69,161)	(113,813)
Net Income	535,495	382,095	363,167	340,032	170,606	487,146	39,795	(3,374)
Average Shares	169,487	175,973	184,703	185,875	177,963	170,154	168,381	165,666
Balance Sheet								
Current Assets	7,996,764	8,186,386	8,141,760	7,357,425	5,793,960	5,384,411	4,576,395	4,681,148
Total Assets	9,445,225	9,736,789	9,206,515	8,416,902	6,827,459	6,181,044	5,055,246	5,171,555
Current Liabilities	1,688,111	1,726,136	1,188,196	1,156,619	984,631	800,229	807,758	901,574
Long-Term Obligations	3,220,024	3,775,451	3,790,240	3,399,586	2,503,664	2,252,944	1,654,937	1,710,968
Total Liabilities	4,914,031	5,507,497	4,983,958	4,562,526	3,494,472	3,059,344	2,468,893	2,616,102
Stockholders' Equity	4,531,194	4,229,292	4,222,557	3,854,376	3,332,987	3,121,700	2,586,353	2,555,453
Shares Outstanding	157,205	161,783	174,847	175,046	169,353	168,637	165,729	166,408
Statistical Record								
Return on Assets %	5.58	4.02	4.12	4.46	2.62	8.65	0.78	N.M.
Return on Equity %	12.23	9.02	8.99	9.46	5.29	17.02	1.55	N.M.
EBITDA Margin %	12.23	10.86	12.66	10.74	8.46	4.57	N.M.	N.M.
Net Margin %	9.21	7.39	8.71	8.69	6.38	25.87	2.70	N.M.
Asset Turnover	0.61	0.54	0.47	0.51	0.41	0.33	0.29	0.28
Current Ratio	4.74	4.74	6.85	6.36	5.88	6.73	5.67	5.19
Debt to Equity	0.71	0.89	0.90	0.88	0.75	0.72	0.64	0.67
Price Range	46.04-27.06	38.06-24.10	41.88-30.92	39.55-29.18	37.98-29.73	36.43-17.05	21.90-13.75	23.15-16.02
P/E Ratio	14.52-8.54	17.46-11.06	21.26-15.70	21.49-15.86	39.15-30.65	12.74-5.96	91.25-57.29	...
Average Yield %	0.66	...	...	...	...	...	...	...

Address: 250 Gibraltar Road, Horsham, PA 19044	Web Site: www.tollbrothers.com	Auditors: Ernst & Young LLP
Telephone: 215-938-8000	Officers: Robert I. Toll - Executive Chairman Richard T. Hartman - President, Chief Operating Officer	Investor Contact: 215-938-8312
Fax: 215-938-8023		Transfer Agents: American Stock Transfer and Trust Company, New York, NY

TOOTSIE ROLL INDUSTRIES INC

Exchange	Symbol	Price	52Wk Range	Yield	P/E	Div Achiever
NYS	TR	$36.40 (12/29/2017)	39.37-34.45	0.99	34.67	53 Years

*7 Year Price Score 101.50 *NYSE Composite Index=100   *12 Month Price Score 93.17

Interim Earnings (Per Share)

Qtr.	Mar	Jun	Sep	Dec
2014	0.15	0.14	0.40	0.27
2015	0.14	0.17	0.41	0.31
2016	0.16	0.17	0.45	0.27
2017	0.16	0.19	0.43	...

Interim Dividends (Per Share)

Amt	Decl	Ex	Rec	Pay
0.087Q	02/21/2017	03/03/2017	03/07/2017	03/28/2017
0.09Q	06/05/2017	06/15/2017	06/19/2017	07/10/2017
0.09Q	09/19/2017	09/29/2017	10/02/2017	10/12/2017
0.09Q	12/05/2017	12/15/2017	12/18/2017	01/02/2018

Indicated Div: $0.36

Valuation Analysis

Forecast EPS	N/A
Market Cap	$2.3 Billion
Book Value	$714.5 Million
Price/Book	3.20
Price/Sales	4.41

Institutional Holding

No of Institutions	234
Shares	16,809,048
% Held	23.24

TRADING VOLUME (thousand shares)

Business Summary: Food (MIC: 1.2.1 SIC: 2064 NAIC: 311340)

Tootsie Roll Industries and its consolidated subsidiaries are engaged in the manufacture and sale of confectionery products. This is the only industry segment in which Co. operates and is its only line of business. They are sold through candy and grocery brokers and by Co. itself to customers throughout the U.S. These customers include wholesale distributors of candy and groceries, supermarkets, variety stores, dollar stores, chain grocers, drug chains, discount chains, cooperative grocery associations, mass merchandisers, warehouse and membership club stores, vending machine operators, the U.S. military and fund-raising charitable organizations.

Recent Developments: For the quarter ended Sep 30 2017, net income decreased 6.0% to US$26.9 million from US$28.6 million in the year-earlier quarter. Revenues were US$183.0 million, down 1.8% from US$186.4 million the year before. Operating income was US$34.8 million versus US$39.3 million in the prior-year quarter, a decrease of 11.3%. Direct operating expenses rose 0.1% to US$115.1 million from US$115.0 million in the comparable period the year before. Indirect operating expenses increased 3.1% to US$33.1 million from US$32.1 million in the equivalent prior-year period.

Prospects: Our evaluation of Tootsie Roll Industries Inc. as of Jan. 14, 2018 is the result of our systematic analysis on three basic characteristics: earnings strength, relative valuation, and recent stock price movement. The company has managed to produce a neutral trend in earnings per share over the past 5 quarters. Because the company lacks sufficient analyst estimate data, we place greater weight on the historical EPS trend as the measure of earnings strength. Based on operating earnings yield, the company is about fairly valued when compared to all of the companies in our coverage universe. Share price changes over the past year indicates that TR will perform well over the near term.

Financial Data

(US$ in Thousands)	9 Mos	6 Mos	3 Mos	12/31/2016	12/31/2015	12/31/2014	12/31/2013	12/31/2012
Earnings Per Share	1.05	1.07	1.05	1.05	1.02	0.96	0.93	0.77
Cash Flow Per Share	1.11	1.35	1.50	1.53	1.40	1.34	1.69	1.49
Tang Book Value Per Share	7.41	7.20	7.22	7.27	6.97	6.74	6.68	5.95
Dividends Per Share	0.442	0.352	0.350	0.347	0.328	0.291	0.282	0.705
Dividend Payout %	42.04	32.96	33.19	33.09	32.19	30.25	30.24	91.86
Income Statement								
Total Revenue	393,266	210,251	104,455	521,100	540,112	543,525	543,383	549,870
EBITDA	71,269	31,692	14,747	115,514	111,621	110,569	104,155	93,707
Depn & Amortn	1,840	1,216	593	19,627	20,388	20,758	20,050	19,925
Income Before Taxes	69,429	30,476	14,154	97,912	92,578	91,294	85,458	75,014
Income Taxes	20,681	8,615	4,143	30,593	26,451	28,434	23,634	22,160
Net Income	48,879	21,946	10,051	67,510	66,089	63,298	60,849	52,004
Average Shares	62,986	63,270	63,605	64,106	65,182	66,177	65,163	68,098
Balance Sheet								
Current Assets	296,459	267,816	260,010	299,300	293,806	264,621	240,111	197,241
Total Assets	942,836	917,257	910,731	920,101	908,983	910,386	888,409	846,737
Current Liabilities	78,809	64,624	57,261	63,561	72,062	64,459	60,121	60,765
Long-Term Obligations	7,500	7,500	7,697	7,730	7,883	8,194	7,500	7,500
Total Liabilities	228,355	213,824	204,066	208,737	210,800	219,577	208,104	196,922
Stockholders' Equity	714,481	703,433	706,665	711,364	698,183	690,809	680,305	649,815
Shares Outstanding	62,879	63,236	63,512	63,694	64,549	65,666	64,679	67,473
Statistical Record								
Return on Assets %	7.13	7.49	7.49	7.36	7.27	7.04	7.01	6.08
Return on Equity %	9.40	9.75	9.64	9.55	9.52	9.23	9.15	7.88
EBITDA Margin %	18.12	15.07	14.12	22.17	20.67	20.34	19.17	17.04
Net Margin %	12.43	10.44	9.62	12.96	12.24	11.65	11.20	9.46
Asset Turnover	0.55	0.57	0.58	0.57	0.59	0.60	0.63	0.64
Current Ratio	3.76	4.14	4.54	4.71	4.08	4.11	3.99	3.25
Debt to Equity	0.01	0.01	0.01	0.01	0.01	0.01	0.01	0.01
Price Range	40.34-33.35	40.34-33.35	40.34-33.09	40.34-28.66	32.56-26.76	28.91-23.93	31.20-22.36	24.67-18.72
P/E Ratio	38.42-31.76	37.70-31.17	38.42-31.51	38.42-27.30	31.92-26.23	30.12-24.93	33.55-24.04	32.04-24.31
Average Yield %	1.20	0.96	0.96	1.00	1.09	1.10	1.03	3.35

Address: 7401 South Cicero Avenue, Chicago, IL 60629 **Telephone:** 773-838-3400 **Fax:** 773-838-3534	**Web Site:** www.tootsie.com **Officers:** Ellen R. Gordon - Chairwoman, Chief Executive Officer G. Howard Ember - Vice President	**Auditors:** PricewaterhouseCoopers LLP **Transfer Agents:** American Stock Transfer & Trust Company, Brooklyn, NY

TORCHMARK CORP

Exchange	Symbol	Price	52Wk Range	Yield	P/E	Div Achiever
NYS	TMK	$90.71 (12/29/2017)	91.16-73.00	0.66	19.34	11 Years

*7 Year Price Score 122.09 *NYSE Composite Index=100 ***12 Month Price Score 105.45**

TRADING VOLUME (thousand shares)

Interim Earnings (Per Share)

Qtr.	Mar	Jun	Sep	Dec
2014	0.99	0.98	1.00	1.12
2015	0.95	1.00	1.15	1.07
2016	1.01	1.13	1.25	1.11
2017	1.11	1.18	1.29	...

Interim Dividends (Per Share)

Amt	Decl	Ex	Rec	Pay
0.15Q	02/28/2017	03/30/2017	04/03/2017	05/01/2017
0.15Q	05/18/2017	06/30/2017	07/05/2017	08/01/2017
0.15Q	08/28/2017	10/05/2017	10/06/2017	11/01/2017
0.15Q	11/13/2017	01/04/2018	01/05/2018	02/01/2018

Indicated Div: $0.60 (Div. Reinv. Plan)

Valuation Analysis / Institutional Holding

Forecast EPS	$4.80	No of Institutions
	(01/18/2018)	620
Market Cap	$10.5 Billion	Shares
Book Value	$5.2 Billion	106,931,256
Price/Book	2.02	% Held
Price/Sales	2.57	67.16

Business Summary: Life & Health (MIC: 5.2.2 SIC: 6311 NAIC: 524113)

Torchmark is an insurance holding company for a group of insurance companies which market primarily individual life, and supplemental health insurance to middle income households. Co.'s segment comprised of Insurance, which consist of life, health, and annuities; and Investments, which consist of investment-grade securities. Life insurance products include traditional and interest-sensitive whole life insurance as well as term life insurance. Health insurance products are generally guaranteed-renewable and include Medicare Supplement, critical illness, accident, long-term care, and limited-benefit supplemental hospital and surgical coverages. Annuities include fixed-benefit contracts.

Recent Developments: For the quarter ended Sep 30 2017, income from continuing operations increased 8.1% to US$153.3 million from US$141.9 million in the year-earlier quarter. Net income increased 1.0% to US$153.3 million from US$151.9 million in the year-earlier quarter. Revenues were US$1.05 billion, up 5.7% from US$989.8 million the year before. Net premiums earned were US$819.2 million versus US$783.4 million in the prior-year quarter, an increase of 4.6%. Net investment income rose 5.5% to US$213.9 million from US$202.7 million a year ago.

Prospects: Our evaluation of Torchmark Corp. as of Jan. 14, 2018 is the result of our systematic analysis on three basic characteristics: earnings strength, relative valuation, and recent stock price movement. The company has produced a positive trend in earnings per share over the past 5 quarters and while recent estimates for the company have been mixed, TMK has posted better than expected results. Based on operating earnings yield, the company is undervalued when compared to all of the companies in our coverage universe. Share price changes over the past year indicates that TMK will perform in line with the market over the near term.

Financial Data
(US$ in Thousands)

	9 Mos	6 Mos	3 Mos	12/31/2016	12/31/2015	12/31/2014	12/31/2013	12/31/2012
Earnings Per Share	4.69	4.65	4.60	4.49	4.16	4.09	3.79	3.61
Cash Flow Per Share	13.05	13.14	12.92	11.62	8.95	6.61	8.13	6.49
Tang Book Value Per Share	40.97	39.67	36.70	34.95	29.53	33.27	24.84	27.73
Dividends Per Share	0.580	0.580	0.570	0.555	0.405	0.507	0.553	0.380
Dividend Payout %	12.37	12.47	12.39	12.36	9.74	12.39	14.61	10.54
Income Statement								
Premium Income	2,456,462	1,637,245	820,631	3,137,034	2,998,720	3,209,420	3,052,274	2,856,462
Total Revenue	3,098,674	2,052,659	1,023,581	3,934,629	3,766,065	3,964,296	3,771,938	3,589,516
Benefits & Claims	1,665,410	1,114,191	557,776	2,128,748	2,016,212	2,219,200	2,088,846	1,955,682
Income Before Taxes	614,277	393,667	191,741	772,235	766,187	778,468	763,126	765,993
Income Taxes	183,390	116,126	54,563	232,645	249,894	235,529	234,654	236,669
Net Income	427,148	273,814	133,541	549,779	527,100	542,939	528,472	529,324
Average Shares	118,442	119,096	120,429	122,367	126,757	132,640	139,563	146,847
Balance Sheet								
Total Assets	22,993,607	22,577,940	22,086,976	21,436,087	19,853,213	20,214,730	18,191,744	18,776,910
Total Liabilities	17,825,922	17,524,524	17,342,149	16,869,226	15,797,661	15,517,264	14,415,402	14,415,124
Stockholders' Equity	5,167,685	5,053,416	4,744,827	4,566,861	4,055,552	4,697,466	3,776,342	4,361,786
Shares Outstanding	115,359	116,258	117,267	118,031	122,369	127,930	134,252	141,353
Statistical Record								
Return on Assets %	2.50	2.54	2.62	2.66	2.63	2.83	2.86	2.94
Return on Equity %	10.97	11.30	12.24	12.72	12.04	12.81	12.99	12.29
Loss Ratio %	67.80	68.05	67.97	67.86	67.24	69.15	68.44	68.47
Net Margin %	13.78	13.34	13.05	13.97	14.00	13.70	14.01	14.75
Price Range	80.09-63.17	78.71-60.38	78.71-52.83	74.83-48.58	63.12-50.07	55.68-48.37	52.35-34.45	35.31-28.91
P/E Ratio	17.08-13.47	16.93-12.98	17.11-11.48	16.67-10.82	15.17-12.04	13.61-11.83	13.81-9.09	9.78-8.01
Average Yield %	0.78	0.82	0.86	0.91	0.71	0.96	1.25	1.15

Address: 3700 South Stonebridge Drive, McKinney, TX 75070 **Telephone:** 972-569-4000	**Web Site:** www.torchmarkcorp.com **Officers:** Gary L. Coleman - Co-Chairman, Co-Chief Executive Officer, Executive Vice President, Chief Financial Officer Larry M. Hutchison - Co-Chairman, Co-Chief Executive Officer, Executive Vice President, General Counsel	**Auditors:** Deloitte & Touche LLP **Investor Contact:** 972-569-3627 **Transfer Agents:** Wells Fargo Shareowner Services, St. Paul, MN

TORO COMPANY (THE)

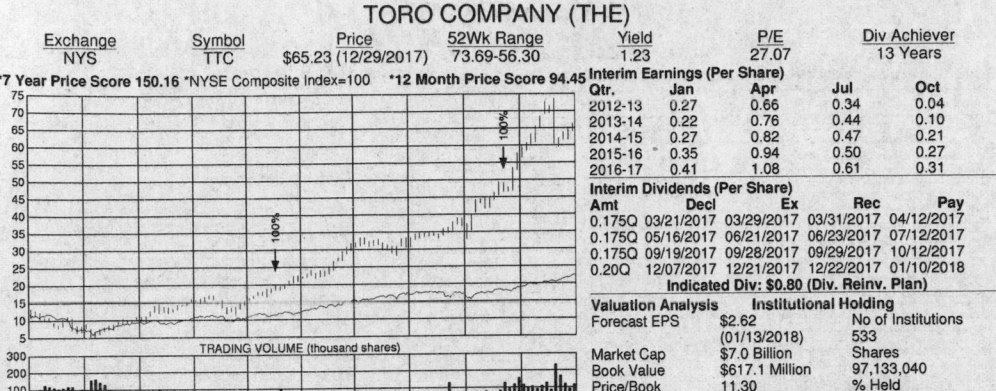

Exchange	Symbol	Price	52Wk Range	Yield	P/E	Div Achiever
NYS	TTC	$65.23 (12/29/2017)	73.69-56.30	1.23	27.07	13 Years

*7 Year Price Score 150.16 *NYSE Composite Index=100 *12 Month Price Score 94.45

Interim Earnings (Per Share)

Qtr.	Jan	Apr	Jul	Oct
2012-13	0.27	0.66	0.34	0.04
2013-14	0.22	0.76	0.44	0.10
2014-15	0.27	0.82	0.47	0.21
2015-16	0.35	0.94	0.50	0.27
2016-17	0.41	1.08	0.61	0.31

Interim Dividends (Per Share)

Amt	Decl	Ex	Rec	Pay
0.175Q	03/21/2017	03/29/2017	03/31/2017	04/12/2017
0.175Q	05/16/2017	06/21/2017	06/23/2017	07/12/2017
0.175Q	09/19/2017	09/28/2017	09/29/2017	10/12/2017
0.20Q	12/07/2017	12/21/2017	12/22/2017	01/10/2018

Indicated Div: $0.80 (Div. Reinv. Plan)

Valuation Analysis

		Institutional Holding	
Forecast EPS	$2.62 (01/13/2018)	No of Institutions	533
Market Cap	$7.0 Billion	Shares	97,133,040
Book Value	$617.1 Million	% Held	69.63
Price/Book	11.30		
Price/Sales	2.78		

Business Summary: Industrial Machinery & Equipment (MIC: 7.2.1 SIC: 3524 NAIC: 333112)

Toro designs, manufactures, and markets turf maintenance equipment and services, turf irrigation systems, landscaping equipment and lighting products, snow and ice management products, agricultural micro-irrigation systems, rental and construction equipment, and residential yard and snow thrower products. Co. has three segments: Professional, which consists of turf and landscape equipment, snow and ice management equipment, and irrigation products; Residential, which consists of walk power mowers, riding mowers, snow throwers, replacement parts, and home solutions products; and Distribution, which consists of its Co.-owned domestic distributorships.

Recent Developments: For the year ended Oct 31 2017, net income increased 15.9% to US$267.7 million from US$231.0 million in the prior year. Revenues were US$2.51 billion, up 4.7% from US$2.39 billion the year before. Operating income was US$355.1 million versus US$334.4 million in the prior year, an increase of 6.2%. Direct operating expenses rose 4.4% to US$1.58 billion from US$1.52 billion in the comparable period the year before. Indirect operating expenses increased 4.7% to US$565.7 million from US$540.2 million in the equivalent prior-year period.

Prospects: Our evaluation of Toro Co. as of Jan. 14, 2018 is the result of our systematic analysis on three basic characteristics: earnings strength, relative valuation, and recent stock price movement. The company has managed to produce a neutral trend in earnings per share over the past 5 quarters and while recent estimates for the company have been raised by analysts, TTC has posted better than expected results. Based on operating earnings yield, the company is about fairly valued when compared to all of the companies in our coverage universe. Share price changes over the past year indicates that TTC will perform in line with the market over the near term.

Financial Data

(US$ in Thousands)	10/31/2017	10/31/2016	10/31/2015	10/31/2014	10/31/2013	10/31/2012	10/31/2011	10/31/2010
Earnings Per Share	2.41	2.06	1.77	1.51	1.31	1.07	0.93	0.70
Cash Flow Per Share	3.33	3.29	2.13	1.62	1.92	1.56	0.91	1.47
Tang Book Value Per Share	2.88	2.28	1.35	2.63	2.10	1.62	1.18	1.33
Dividends Per Share	0.700	0.600	0.500	0.400	0.280	0.220	0.200	0.180
Dividend Payout %	29.05	29.13	28.17	26.49	21.37	20.56	21.62	25.81
Income Statement								
Total Revenue	2,505,176	2,392,175	2,390,875	2,172,691	2,041,431	1,958,690	1,883,953	1,690,378
EBITDA	415,657	392,736	351,263	311,280	283,586	253,226	228,581	196,834
Depn & Amortn	54,679	53,355	50,322	47,136	48,207	46,840	43,539	42,108
Income Before Taxes	343,224	320,872	282,678	249,183	219,616	190,266	169,144	138,669
Income Taxes	85,467	99,466	89,440	82,575	71,868	66,721	57,168	48,031
Net Income	267,717	230,994	201,591	173,870	154,845	129,541	117,658	93,237
Average Shares	111,252	111,987	113,514	115,256	118,210	121,236	127,188	133,748
Balance Sheet								
Current Assets	859,886	779,009	710,679	824,036	653,267	612,134	532,882	584,973
Total Assets	1,493,787	1,387,518	1,303,658	1,192,415	1,002,748	935,199	870,663	885,622
Current Liabilities	521,796	463,839	443,734	400,420	388,845	378,122	359,080	368,283
Long-Term Obligations	305,629	331,423	354,818	347,316	223,544	223,482	225,178	223,578
Total Liabilities	876,695	837,483	841,493	783,688	644,010	622,797	603,896	609,812
Stockholders' Equity	617,092	550,035	462,165	408,727	358,738	312,402	266,767	275,810
Shares Outstanding	106,882	108,427	109,301	111,356	113,577	116,532	118,412	125,579
Statistical Record								
Return on Assets %	18.58	17.12	16.15	15.84	15.98	14.31	13.40	10.61
Return on Equity %	45.88	45.52	46.30	45.31	46.14	44.61	43.37	31.55
EBITDA Margin %	16.59	16.42	14.69	14.33	13.89	12.93	12.13	11.64
Net Margin %	10.69	9.66	8.43	8.00	7.59	6.61	6.25	5.52
Asset Turnover	1.74	1.77	1.92	1.98	2.11	2.16	2.15	1.92
Current Ratio	1.65	1.68	1.60	2.06	1.68	1.62	1.48	1.59
Debt to Equity	0.50	0.60	0.77	0.85	0.62	0.72	0.84	0.81
Price Range	73.69-46.74	49.29-32.75	37.89-30.41	33.47-28.07	29.48-20.40	21.11-13.00	16.98-11.41	14.57-9.25
P/E Ratio	30.58-19.39	23.93-15.90	21.41-17.18	22.16-18.59	22.50-15.57	19.73-12.15	18.26-12.27	20.81-13.22
Average Yield %	1.12	1.41	1.48	1.29	1.18	1.18	1.36	1.47

Address: 8111 Lyndale Avenue South, Bloomington, MN 55420-1196	Web Site: www.thetorocompany.com	Auditors: KPMG LLP
Telephone: 952-888-8801	Officers: Richard M. Olson - Chairman, President, Chief Executive Officer, Chief Operating Officer, Vice President Renee J. Peterson - Chief Financial Officer, Vice President, Principal Financial Officer, Principal Accounting Officer, Chief Financial Officer, Vice President (frmr), Treasurer	Transfer Agents: Wells Fargo Shareowner Services, St. Paul, MN

TOTAL SYSTEM SERVICES, INC.

Exchange	Symbol	Price	52Wk Range	Yield	P/E
NYS	TSS	$79.09 (12/29/2017)	79.99-50.32	0.66	35.15

*7 Year Price Score 134.01 *NYSE Composite Index=100 *12 Month Price Score 113.90

Interim Earnings (Per Share)

Qtr.	Mar	Jun	Sep	Dec
2014	0.26	0.58	0.45	0.43
2015	0.42	0.45	0.65	0.45
2016	0.49	0.38	0.46	0.40
2017	0.57	0.62	0.66	...

Interim Dividends (Per Share)

Amt	Decl	Ex	Rec	Pay
0.10Q	03/08/2017	03/21/2017	03/23/2017	04/03/2017
0.10Q	06/07/2017	06/20/2017	06/22/2017	07/03/2017
0.13Q	07/25/2017	09/20/2017	09/21/2017	10/02/2017
0.13Q	12/11/2017	12/20/2017	12/21/2017	01/02/2018

Indicated Div: $0.52

Valuation Analysis   **Institutional Holding**

Forecast EPS	$3.34 No of Institutions
(01/18/2018)	656
Market Cap	$14.6 Billion Shares
Book Value	$2.4 Billion 176,013,312
Price/Book	6.18 % Held
Price/Sales	3.04 69.38

Business Summary: Business Services (MIC: 7.5.2 SIC: 7389 NAIC: 561499)

Total System Services is a payment solutions provider that provides payment processing services, merchant services and related payment services to financial and nonfinancial institutions. Co. has four operating segments: Merchant Services, which provides merchant services to merchant acquirers and merchants; North America Services, and International Services, through which Co. processes information via its cardholder systems to financial and nonfinancial institutions throughout the U.S. and internationally; and NetSpend, which provides general purpose reloadable prepaid debit cards, payroll cards, and alternative financial service solutions to underbanked and other consumers and businesses.

Recent Developments: For the quarter ended Sep 30 2017, net income increased 42.6% to US$124.7 million from US$87.4 million in the year-earlier quarter. Revenues were US$1.25 billion, up 8.8% from US$1.15 billion the year before. Operating income was US$199.7 million versus US$155.3 million in the prior-year quarter, an increase of 28.6%. Direct operating expenses rose 6.9% to US$898.5 million from US$840.3 million in the comparable period the year before. Indirect operating expenses decreased 1.2% to US$149.4 million from US$151.3 million in the equivalent prior-year period.

Prospects: Our evaluation of Total System Services Inc. as of Jan. 14, 2018 is the result of our systematic analysis on three basic characteristics: earnings strength, relative valuation, and recent stock price movement. The company has generated a negative trend in earnings per share over the past 5 quarters and while recent estimates for the company have been mixed, TSS has posted better than expected results. Based on operating earnings yield, the company is about fairly valued when compared to all of the companies in our coverage universe. Share price changes over the past year indicates that TSS will perform well over the near term.

Financial Data

(US$ in Thousands)	9 Mos	6 Mos	3 Mos	12/31/2016	12/31/2015	12/31/2014	12/31/2013	12/31/2012
Earnings Per Share	2.25	2.05	1.81	1.73	1.97	1.72	1.29	1.29
Cash Flow Per Share	4.45	4.24	4.54	3.92	3.29	3.04	2.42	2.43
Tang Book Value Per Share	N.M.	N.M.	N.M.	N.M.	N.M.	N.M.	N.M.	2.08
Dividends Per Share	0.430	0.400	0.400	0.400	0.400	0.400	0.400	0.400
Dividend Payout %	19.11	19.51	22.10	23.12	20.30	23.26	31.01	31.01
Income Statement								
Total Revenue	3,654,676	2,407,100	1,184,725	4,170,077	2,779,541	2,446,877	2,132,353	1,870,972
EBITDA	475,267	303,098	168,355	962,603	796,641	643,147	568,764	525,762
Depn & Amortn	3,924	2,612	1,302	387,866	260,502	250,218	212,845	170,908
Income Before Taxes	471,343	300,486	137,280	461,214	496,888	392,929	355,919	354,854
Income Taxes	153,917	99,289	43,082	161,175	151,364	129,761	112,369	115,102
Net Income	343,977	220,882	105,868	319,638	364,044	322,872	244,750	244,280
Average Shares	185,808	185,287	184,938	184,448	183,622	185,756	188,793	188,665
Balance Sheet								
Current Assets	998,838	1,027,008	1,050,811	1,022,689	882,902	690,553	653,933	574,726
Total Assets	6,218,890	6,277,014	6,350,680	6,366,177	3,908,300	3,733,581	3,686,568	2,023,838
Current Liabilities	971,680	943,180	452,258	420,353	339,218	296,513	297,215	230,519
Long-Term Obligations	2,394,283	2,564,068	3,229,137	3,313,276	1,383,634	1,405,106	1,435,751	192,014
Total Liabilities	3,862,130	4,012,478	4,205,950	4,266,257	2,065,282	2,040,819	2,105,491	598,628
Stockholders' Equity	2,356,760	2,264,536	2,144,730	2,099,920	1,843,018	1,692,762	1,581,077	1,425,210
Shares Outstanding	184,088	184,217	184,041	183,451	182,781	184,939	187,717	187,031
Statistical Record								
Return on Assets %	6.64	5.96	5.69	6.20	9.53	8.70	8.57	12.55
Return on Equity %	18.90	17.89	16.47	16.17	20.59	19.72	16.28	17.87
EBITDA Margin %	13.00	12.59	14.21	23.08	28.66	26.28	26.67	28.10
Net Margin %	9.41	9.18	8.94	7.67	13.10	13.20	11.48	13.06
Asset Turnover	0.76	0.73	0.78	0.81	0.73	0.66	0.75	0.96
Current Ratio	1.03	1.09	2.32	2.43	2.60	2.33	2.20	2.49
Debt to Equity	1.02	1.13	1.51	1.58	0.75	0.83	0.91	0.13
Price Range	70.04-46.77	59.64-46.58	56.43-46.58	56.43-37.96	56.37-33.27	34.41-28.70	33.30-21.42	24.39-19.40
P/E Ratio	31.13-20.79	29.09-22.72	31.18-25.73	32.62-21.94	28.61-16.89	20.01-16.69	25.81-16.60	18.91-15.04
Average Yield %	0.77	0.76	0.78	0.82	0.91	1.28	1.51	1.76

Address: One TSYS Way, Columbus, GA 31902	Web Site: www.tsys.com	Auditors: KPMG LLP
Telephone: 706-644-6081	Officers: M. Troy Woods - Chairman, President, Chief Executive Officer, Chief Operating Officer	Investor Contact: 706-644-6081
Fax: 706-649-2456	Kathleen Moates - Senior Deputy General Counsel	Transfer Agents: American Stock Transfer & Trust Company, LLC, Brookly, NY

TRANSOCEAN LTD

Exchange	Symbol	Price	52Wk Range	Yield	P/E
NYS	RIG	$10.68 (12/29/2017)	15.84-7.28	N/A	N/A

*7 Year Price Score 25.12   ***NYSE Composite Index=100**   ***12 Month Price Score 90.95**

Interim Earnings (Per Share)

Qtr.	Mar	Jun	Sep	Dec
2014	1.25	1.61	(6.12)	(2.05)
2015	(1.33)	0.93	0.88	1.67
2016	0.68	0.21	0.62	0.59
2017	0.23	(4.32)	(3.62)	...

Interim Dividends (Per Share)

Amt	Decl	Ex	Rec	Pay
0.75Q	11/04/2014	11/12/2014	11/14/2014	12/17/2014
0.75Q	02/06/2015	02/18/2015	02/20/2015	03/18/2015
0.15Q	05/15/2015	05/27/2015	05/29/2015	06/17/2015
0.15Q	08/14/2015	08/21/2015	08/25/2015	09/23/2015

Valuation Analysis

		Institutional Holding	
Forecast EPS	N/A	No of Institutions	668
Market Cap	$4.2 Billion	Shares	344,814,016
Book Value	$12.8 Billion	% Held	66.45
Price/Book	0.33		
Price/Sales	1.26		

Business Summary: Equipment & Services (MIC: 9.1.3 SIC: 1389 NAIC: 213112)

Transocean is a provider of offshore contract drilling services for oil and gas wells. Co. contracts its drilling rigs, related equipment and work crews predominantly on a dayrate basis to drill oil and gas wells. Co. focuses on deepwater and harsh environment drilling services. At Dec 31 2016, Co. owned or had partial ownership interests in and operated 56 mobile offshore drilling units, including 30 ultra-deepwater floaters, seven harsh environment floaters, three deepwater floaters, six midwater floaters and 10 high-specification jackups. At Dec 31 2016, Co. had four ultra-deepwater drillships and five high-specification jackups under construction or under contract to be constructed.

Recent Developments: For the quarter ended Sep 30 2017, net loss amounted to US$1.41 billion versus net income of US$236.0 million in the year-earlier quarter. Revenues were US$808.0 million, down 10.8% from US$906.0 million the year before. Operating loss was US$1.15 billion versus an income of US$229.0 million in the prior-year quarter. Direct operating expenses declined 21.0% to US$323.0 million from US$409.0 million in the comparable period the year before. Indirect operating expenses increased 508.2% to US$1.63 billion from US$268.0 million in the equivalent prior-year period.

Prospects: Our evaluation of Transocean Ltd. as of Aug. 2, 2015 is the result of our systematic analysis on three basic characteristics: earnings strength, relative valuation, and recent stock price movement. The company has suffered a very negative trend in earnings per share over the past 5 quarters. Because the company lacks sufficient analyst estimate data, we place greater weight on the historical EPS trend as the measure of earnings strength. Based on operating earnings yield, the company is undervalued when compared to all of the companies in our coverage universe. Share price changes over the past year indicates that RIG will perform in line with the market over the near term.

Financial Data
(US$ in Millions)

	9 Mos	6 Mos	3 Mos	12/31/2016	12/31/2015	12/31/2014	12/31/2013	12/31/2012
Earnings Per Share	(7.12)	(2.88)	1.65	2.08	2.16	(5.29)	3.87	(0.62)
Cash Flow Per Share	3.89	4.03	3.75	5.19	9.49	6.13	5.33	7.59
Tang Book Value Per Share	32.72	36.31	40.67	40.58	39.83	37.74	37.99	35.49
Income Statement								
Total Revenue	2,344	1,536	785	4,161	7,386	9,174	9,484	9,196
EBITDA	(1,910)	(967)	408	2,216	2,388	(232)	3,290	1,491
Depn & Amortn	648	451	232	893	948	1,124	1,094	(42)
Income Before Taxes	(2,892)	(1,661)	55	934	1,030	(1,800)	1,664	866
Income Taxes	103	(77)	(40)	107	206	146	258	50
Net Income	(3,016)	(1,599)	91	778	791	(1,913)	1,407	(219)
Average Shares	391	391	390	367	363	362	360	356
Balance Sheet								
Current Assets	4,451	4,286	5,071	5,098	4,785	6,001	6,772	8,647
Total Assets	22,441	23,847	26,717	26,889	26,329	28,413	32,546	34,255
Current Liabilities	1,885	1,858	2,547	1,985	2,669	3,770	3,554	5,463
Long-Term Obligations	6,501	6,525	6,937	7,740	7,397	9,059	10,379	11,092
Total Liabilities	9,642	9,642	10,817	11,087	11,831	14,742	15,855	18,510
Stockholders' Equity	12,799	14,205	15,900	15,802	14,498	13,671	16,691	15,745
Shares Outstanding	391	391	390	389	364	362	360	359
Statistical Record								
Return on Assets %	N.M.	N.M.	2.34	2.92	2.89	N.M.	4.21	N.M.
Return on Equity %	N.M.	N.M.	4.04	5.12	5.62	N.M.	8.68	N.M.
EBITDA Margin %	N.M.	N.M.	51.97	53.26	32.33	N.M.	34.69	16.21
Net Margin %	N.M.	N.M.	11.59	18.70	10.71	N.M.	14.84	N.M.
Asset Turnover	0.14	0.14	0.14	0.16	0.27	0.30	0.28	0.26
Current Ratio	2.36	2.31	1.99	2.57	1.79	1.59	1.91	1.58
Debt to Equity	0.51	0.46	0.44	0.49	0.51	0.66	0.62	0.70
Price Range	15.84-7.28	15.84-7.79	15.84-8.41	15.54-8.20	21.39-11.60	49.42-16.25	59.30-44.38	58.70-38.97
P/E Ratio	...	9.60-5.10	7.47-3.94	9.90-5.37		15.32-11.47		...

Address: Turmstrasse 30, Zug, 6300	**Web Site:** www.deepwater.com	**Auditors:** Ernst & Young LLP
Telephone: 417-490-500	**Officers:** Merrill A. (Pete) Miller - Chairman Jeremy D. Thigpen - President, Chief Executive Officer	**Investor Contact:** 713-232-7551 **Transfer Agents:** Computershare Shareowner Services LLC, Pittsburgh, PA

TRANSUNION

Exchange	Symbol	Price	52Wk Range	Yield	P/E
NYS	TRU	$54.96 (12/29/2017)	56.21-30.96	N/A	42.60

*7 Year Price Score N/A ***NYSE Composite Index=100** ***12 Month Price Score 118.25**

TRADING VOLUME (thousand shares)

Interim Earnings (Per Share)

Qtr.	Mar	Jun	Sep	Dec
2015	(0.04)	(0.02)	(0.02)	0.12
2016	0.07	0.09	0.22	0.26
2017	0.33	0.34	0.36	...

Interim Dividends (Per Share)

No Dividends Paid

Valuation Analysis		Institutional Holding	
Forecast EPS	$1.86	No of Institutions	
	(01/24/2018)	285	
Market Cap	$10.0 Billion	Shares	
Book Value	$1.5 Billion	191,665,008	
Price/Book	6.88	% Held	
Price/Sales	5.38	N/A	

Business Summary: Miscellaneous Consumer Services (MIC: 2.2.3 SIC: 7323 NAIC: 561450)

TransUnion is a global risk and information solutions provider to businesses and consumers. Co. has three reportable segments: U.S. Information Services (USIS), which provide consumer reports, risk scores, analytical services and decisioning capabilities to businesses through three delivery platforms, online data services, marketing services and decision services; International, which provides services similar to Co.'s USIS segment to businesses in select regions outside the U.S.; and Consumer Interactive, which provides solutions that help consumers manage their personal finances and take precautions against identity theft through both direct and indirect channels.

Recent Developments: For the quarter ended Sep 30 2017, net income increased 61.6% to US$71.9 million from US$44.5 million in the year-earlier quarter. Revenues were US$498.0 million, up 13.8% from US$437.6 million the year before. Operating income was US$126.6 million versus US$95.8 million in the prior-year quarter, an increase of 32.2%. Direct operating expenses rose 19.6% to US$169.3 million from US$141.5 million in the comparable period the year before. Indirect operating expenses increased 0.9% to US$202.1 million from US$200.3 million in the equivalent prior-year period.

Prospects: Our evaluation of TransUnion as of Jan. 21, 2018 is the result of our systematic analysis on three basic characteristics: earnings strength, relative valuation, and recent stock price movement. The company has generated a negative trend in earnings per share over the past 5 quarters and while recent estimates for the company have been mixed, TRU has posted better than expected results. Based on operating earnings yield, the company is about fairly valued when compared to all of the companies in our coverage universe. Share price changes over the past year indicates that TRU will perform very well over the near term.

Financial Data
(US$ in Thousands)

	9 Mos	6 Mos	3 Mos	12/31/2016	12/31/2015	12/31/2014	12/31/2013	12/31/2012
Earnings Per Share	1.29	1.15	0.90	0.65	0.04	(0.08)	(0.24)	(0.06)
Cash Flow Per Share	2.54	2.28	2.27	2.13	1.87	1.05	0.98	0.37
Income Statement								
Total Revenue	1,427,700	929,700	455,000	1,704,900	1,506,800	1,304,700	1,183,200	767,000
EBITDA	330,100	207,400	95,200	345,400	208,500	229,100	200,300	145,600
Depn & Amortn	2,500	1,600	700	67,700	60,300	56,700	44,000	26,700
Income Before Taxes	266,000	164,400	74,300	196,800	17,800	(14,300)	(39,600)	(5,300)
Income Taxes	68,700	36,300	11,500	74,000	11,300	2,600	2,300	6,600
Net Income	196,000	127,300	62,300	120,600	5,900	(12,500)	(35,100)	(8,800)
Average Shares	189,200	189,300	190,300	184,600	166,800	147,296	146,496	146,230
Balance Sheet								
Current Assets	689,000	550,300	513,700	550,000	427,500	401,000	349,700	400,600
Total Assets	4,882,500	4,756,600	4,753,800	4,781,200	4,446,700	4,665,800	4,492,300	4,378,800
Current Liabilities	375,300	394,200	381,500	373,300	296,000	329,900	247,600	218,300
Long-Term Obligations	2,352,100	2,297,300	2,309,300	2,325,200	2,164,600	2,865,900	2,853,100	2,670,300
Total Liabilities	3,426,400	3,385,700	3,386,200	3,418,400	3,215,300	4,078,700	3,864,400	3,676,000
Stockholders' Equity	1,456,100	1,370,900	1,367,600	1,362,800	1,231,400	587,100	627,900	702,800
Shares Outstanding	182,400	181,900	182,600	183,200	182,300	147,829	146,896	146,763
Statistical Record								
Return on Assets %	5.09	4.60	3.59	2.61	0.13	N.M.	N.M.	...
Return on Equity %	17.78	16.63	13.07	9.27	0.65	N.M.	N.M.	...
EBITDA Margin %	23.12	22.31	20.92	20.26	13.84	17.56	16.93	18.98
Net Margin %	13.73	13.69	13.69	7.07	0.39	N.M.	N.M.	N.M.
Asset Turnover	0.39	0.38	0.37	0.37	0.33	0.28	0.27	...
Current Ratio	1.84	1.40	1.35	1.47	1.44	1.22	1.41	1.84
Debt to Equity	1.62	1.68	1.69	1.71	1.76	4.88	4.54	3.80
Price Range	49.39-29.29	44.44-29.29	38.51-26.67	35.43-20.98	27.98-23.19	...	...	...
P/E Ratio	38.29-22.71	38.64-25.47	42.79-29.63	54.51-32.28	699.50-579.75	...	...	...

Address: 555 West Adams, Chicago, IL 60661 Telephone: 312-985-2000	Web Site: www.transunion.com Officers: Leo F. Mullin - Chairman Todd M. Cello - Executive Vice President, Chief Financial Officer	Auditors: Ernst & Young LLP Transfer Agents: American Stock Transfer & Trust Company, LLC

TRAVELERS COMPANIES INC (THE)

Exchange	Symbol	Price	52Wk Range	Yield	P/E	Div Achiever
NYS	TRV	$135.64 (12/29/2017)	136.36-115.18	2.12	15.75	11 Years

*7 Year Price Score 106.72 *NYSE Composite Index=100 *12 Month Price Score 100.92

Interim Earnings (Per Share)

Qtr.	Mar	Jun	Sep	Dec
2014	2.95	1.95	2.69	3.10
2015	2.55	2.53	2.97	2.84
2016	2.30	2.24	2.45	3.28
2017	2.17	2.11	1.05	...

Interim Dividends (Per Share)

Amt	Decl	Ex	Rec	Pay
0.67Q	01/24/2017	03/08/2017	03/10/2017	03/31/2017
0.72Q	04/20/2017	06/07/2017	06/09/2017	06/30/2017
0.72Q	07/20/2017	09/07/2017	09/08/2017	09/29/2017
0.72Q	10/19/2017	12/08/2017	12/11/2017	12/29/2017

Indicated Div: $2.88 (Div. Reinv. Plan)

Valuation Analysis		Institutional Holding	
Forecast EPS	$6.50 (01/18/2018)	No of Institutions	1432
Market Cap	$37.1 Billion	Shares	305,439,200
Book Value	$23.7 Billion	% Held	N/A
Price/Book	1.56		
Price/Sales	1.30		

Business Summary: General Insurance (MIC: 5.2.1 SIC: 6331 NAIC: 524126)

Travelers Companies is a holding company. Through its subsidiaries, Co. provides a range of commercial and personal property and casualty insurance products and services. Co.'s segments include: Business and International Insurance, which provides a range of property and casualty insurance and insurance related services to its clients; Bond & Specialty Insurance, which provides surety, fidelity, management liability, professional liability, and other property and casualty coverages and related risk management services to a range of primarily domestic customers; and Personal Insurance, which writes a range of property and casualty insurance covering individuals' personal risks.

Recent Developments: For the quarter ended Sep 30 2017, net income decreased 59.1% to US$293.0 million from US$716.0 million in the year-earlier quarter. Revenues were US$7.33 billion, up 5.2% from US$6.96 billion the year before. Net premiums earned were US$6.52 billion versus US$6.21 billion in the prior-year quarter, an increase of 5.1%. Net investment income rose 1.0% to US$588.0 million from US$582.0 million a year ago.

Prospects: Our evaluation of The Travelers Companies Inc. as of Jan. 14, 2018 is the result of our systematic analysis on three basic characteristics: earnings strength, relative valuation, and recent stock price movement. The company has generated a negative trend in earnings per share over the past 5 quarters. However, while recent estimates for the company have been mixed, TRV has posted better than expected results. Based on operating earnings yield, the company is undervalued when compared to all of the companies in our coverage universe. Share price changes over the past year indicates that TRV will perform well over the near term.

Financial Data

(US$ in Thousands)	9 Mos	6 Mos	3 Mos	12/31/2016	12/31/2015	12/31/2014	12/31/2013	12/31/2012
Earnings Per Share	8.61	10.01	10.14	10.28	10.88	10.70	9.74	6.30
Cash Flow Per Share	15.92	16.19	14.76	14.55	11.06	10.90	10.31	8.34
Tang Book Value Per Share	71.05	72.51	70.73	69.29	66.73	64.93	58.87	57.39
Dividends Per Share	2.780	2.730	2.680	2.620	2.380	2.150	1.960	1.790
Dividend Payout %	32.29	27.27	26.43	25.49	21.88	20.09	20.12	28.41
Income Statement								
Premium Income	19,057,000	12,534,000	6,183,000	24,534,000	23,874,000	23,713,000	22,637,000	22,357,000
Total Revenue	21,451,000	14,126,000	6,942,000	27,625,000	26,800,000	27,162,000	26,191,000	25,740,000
Benefits & Claims	13,125,000	8,319,000	4,094,000	15,070,000	13,723,000	13,870,000	13,307,000	14,676,000
Income Before Taxes	1,870,000	1,550,000	760,000	4,053,000	4,740,000	5,089,000	4,945,000	3,166,000
Income Taxes	365,000	338,000	143,000	1,039,000	1,301,000	1,397,000	1,272,000	693,000
Net Income	1,505,000	1,212,000	617,000	3,014,000	3,439,000	3,692,000	3,673,000	2,473,000
Average Shares	276,600	280,000	282,400	291,000	313,900	342,500	374,300	389,800
Balance Sheet								
Total Assets	104,311,000	102,669,000	101,246,000	100,245,000	100,184,000	103,078,000	103,812,000	104,938,000
Total Liabilities	80,573,000	78,811,000	77,634,000	77,024,000	76,586,000	78,242,000	79,016,000	79,533,000
Stockholders' Equity	23,738,000	23,858,000	23,612,000	23,221,000	23,598,000	24,836,000	24,796,000	25,405,000
Shares Outstanding	273,700	275,900	279,400	279,600	295,900	322,200	353,500	377,400
Statistical Record								
Return on Assets %	2.36	2.80	2.90	3.00	3.38	3.57	3.52	2.35
Return on Equity %	10.16	11.82	12.31	12.84	14.20	14.88	14.63	9.89
Loss Ratio %	68.87	66.37	66.21	61.42	57.48	58.49	58.78	65.64
Net Margin %	7.02	8.58	8.89	10.91	12.83	13.59	14.02	9.61
Price Range	130.15-104.67	129.44-104.67	124.99-104.67	122.57-102.08	115.83-96.14	106.95-80.26	90.99-71.82	74.33-56.87
P/E Ratio	15.12-12.16	12.93-10.46	12.33-10.32	11.92-9.93	10.65-8.84	10.00-7.50	9.34-7.37	11.80-9.03
Average Yield %	2.31	2.30	2.31	2.31	2.25	2.33	2.35	2.78

Address: 485 Lexington Avenue, New York, NY 10017 **Telephone:** 917-778-6000	**Web Site:** www.travelers.com **Officers:** Alan D. Schnitzer - Chairman, Vice-Chairman, Chief Executive Officer, Chief Executive Officer - Designate, Executive Vice President, Chief Legal Officer Avrohom J. Kess - Vice-Chairman, Chief Legal Officer	**Auditors:** KPMG LLP **Investor Contact:** 917-778-9844 **Transfer Agents:** Wells Fargo Bank, N.A. Shareowner Services, St. Paul, MN

TREEHOUSE FOODS INC

Exchange	Symbol	Price	52Wk Range	Yield	P/E
NYS	THS	$49.46 (12/29/2017)	89.94-41.87	N/A	N/A

*7 Year Price Score 81.01   *NYSE Composite Index=100   *12 Month Price Score 65.15

Interim Earnings (Per Share)

Qtr.	Mar	Jun	Sep	Dec
2014	0.38	0.57	0.47	0.80
2015	0.41	0.72	0.65	0.85
2016	(0.06)	0.27	0.65	(4.98)
2017	0.49	(0.60)	0.50	...

Interim Dividends (Per Share)

No Dividends Paid

Valuation Analysis   **Institutional Holding**

Forecast EPS	$2.74	No of Institutions
	(01/18/2018)	417
Market Cap	$2.8 Billion	Shares
Book Value	$2.6 Billion	78,920,240
Price/Book	1.09	% Held
Price/Sales	0.44	100.89

Business Summary: Food (MIC: 1.2.1 SIC: 2033 NAIC: 311421)

TreeHouse Foods is a consumer packaged food and beverage manufacturer operating across the U.S., Canada, and Italy. Co.'s operating segments are: North American Retail Grocery, which sells branded and private label products, such as non-dairy powdered creamers, sweeteners, condensed, ready to serve, and powdered soups, broths and gravies, and refrigerated salad dressings and sauces, among others; Food Away From Home, which sells aseptic products, ready-to-eat and hot cereals, pasta, retail bakery products, and cookies, crackers, pretzels, and candy, among others; and Industrial and Export, which include Co.'s co-pack business and non-dairy powdered creamer sales to industrial customers.

Recent Developments: For the quarter ended Sep 30 2017, net income decreased 23.0% to US$28.8 million from US$37.4 million in the year-earlier quarter. Revenues were US$1.55 billion, down 2.4% from US$1.59 billion the year before. Operating income was US$57.8 million versus US$77.6 million in the prior-year quarter, a decrease of 25.5%. Direct operating expenses declined 1.0% to US$1.29 billion from US$1.30 billion in the comparable period the year before. Indirect operating expenses decreased 2.7% to US$202.3 million from US$208.0 million in the equivalent prior-year period.

Prospects: Our evaluation of TreeHouse Foods Inc. as of Jan. 14, 2018 is the result of our systematic analysis on three basic characteristics: earnings strength, relative valuation, and recent stock price movement. The company has generated a negative trend in earnings per share over the past 5 quarters and while recent estimates for the company have been mixed, THS has posted results that fell short of analysts expectations. Based on operating earnings yield, the company is undervalued when compared to all of the companies in our coverage universe. Share price changes over the past year indicates that THS will perform poorly over the near term.

Financial Data
(US$ in Thousands)

	9 Mos	6 Mos	3 Mos	12/31/2016	12/31/2015	12/31/2014	12/31/2013	12/31/2012
Earnings Per Share	(4.59)	(4.44)	(3.57)	(4.10)	2.63	2.23	2.33	2.38
Cash Flow Per Share	7.81	9.98	7.85	8.57	6.63	5.39	5.95	5.64
Income Statement								
Total Revenue	4,607,200	3,058,400	1,536,200	6,175,088	3,206,405	2,946,102	2,293,927	2,182,125
EBITDA	230,600	185,100	141,000	98,007	275,271	240,916	245,329	239,875
Depn & Amortn	127,400	143,000	74,400	178,400	61,500	63,300	73,300	64,700
Income Before Taxes	13,800	(16,300)	39,700	(195,363)	171,264	136,570	124,910	124,209
Income Taxes	(9,000)	(10,300)	11,500	33,231	56,354	46,690	37,922	35,846
Net Income	22,800	(6,000)	28,200	(228,594)	114,910	89,880	86,988	88,363
Average Shares	57,700	57,000	57,600	55,717	43,709	40,238	37,396	37,118
Balance Sheet								
Current Assets	1,825,100	1,627,900	1,523,900	1,560,749	847,203	949,436	649,689	588,411
Total Assets	6,685,600	6,509,900	6,475,000	6,545,822	3,702,796	3,903,004	2,721,054	2,525,873
Current Liabilities	845,900	783,000	628,800	693,194	275,473	311,233	240,364	187,030
Long-Term Obligations	2,620,400	2,568,400	2,677,100	2,724,760	1,221,741	1,445,488	938,945	898,100*
Total Liabilities	4,088,300	3,967,000	3,926,400	4,042,498	1,847,937	2,143,747	1,447,936	1,346,618
Stockholders' Equity	2,597,300	2,542,900	2,548,600	2,503,324	1,854,859	1,759,257	1,273,118	1,179,255
Shares Outstanding	57,200	57,200	56,921	56,759	43,125	42,662	36,493	36,196
Statistical Record								
Return on Assets %	N.M.	N.M.	N.M.	N.M.	3.02	2.71	3.32	3.57
Return on Equity %	N.M.	N.M.	N.M.	N.M.	6.36	5.93	7.09	7.82
EBITDA Margin %	5.01	6.05	9.18	1.59	8.59	8.18	10.69	10.99
Net Margin %	0.49	N.M.	1.84	N.M.	3.58	3.05	3.79	4.05
Asset Turnover	0.94	0.96	0.97	1.20	0.84	0.89	0.87	0.88
Current Ratio	2.16	2.08	2.42	2.25	3.08	3.05	2.70	3.15
Debt to Equity	1.01	1.01	1.05	1.09	0.66	0.82	0.74	0.76
Price Range	89.94-63.34	104.35-63.34	104.35-63.34	104.35-63.34	92.90-69.44	87.95-63.59	75.19-52.13	65.52-48.42
P/E Ratio	...	...	...	...	35.32-26.40	39.44-28.52	32.27-22.37	27.53-20.34

Address: 2021 Spring Road, Suite 600, Oak Brook, IL 60523 **Telephone:** 708-483-1300	**Web Site:** www.treehousefoods.com **Officers:** Sam K. Reed - Chairman, President, Chief Executive Officer Matthew J. Foulston - Executive Vice President, Chief Financial Officer	**Auditors:** Deloitte & Touche LLP **Transfer Agents:** BNY Mellon Shareowner Services, South Hackensack, NJ

TRI POINTE GROUP INC

Exchange	Symbol	Price	52Wk Range	Yield	P/E
NYS	TPH	$17.92 (12/29/2017)	18.44-11.37	N/A	16.29

*7 Year Price Score N/A *NYSE Composite Index=100 *12 Month Price Score 120.57

Interim Earnings (Per Share)

Qtr.	Mar	Jun	Sep	Dec
2014	0.14	0.19	0.07	0.27
2015	0.09	0.34	0.31	0.53
2016	0.18	0.46	0.22	0.36
2017	0.05	0.21	0.48	...

Interim Dividends (Per Share)

No Dividends Paid

Valuation Analysis | **Institutional Holding**

Forecast EPS	$1.37	No of Institutions
	(01/18/2018)	273
Market Cap	$2.7 Billion	Shares
Book Value	$1.8 Billion	192,417,072
Price/Book	1.46	% Held
Price/Sales	1.10	69.28

TRADING VOLUME (thousand shares)

Business Summary: Builders (MIC: 2.2.5 SIC: 1531 NAIC: 236117)

TRI Pointe Group is engaged in the design, construction and sale of single-family detached and attached homes. As of Dec 31 2016, Co. had a portfolio of six homebuilding brands operating in 10 markets across eight states: Maracay Homes in Arizona, Pardee Homes in California and Nevada, Quadrant Homes in Washington, Trendmaker Homes in Texas, TRI Pointe Homes in California and Colorado and Winchester Homes in Maryland and Virginia. As of the same date, Co.'s operations consisted of 124 active selling communities and 28,309 lots owned or controlled. Co.'s operations are organized in two principal businesses: homebuilding and financial services.

Recent Developments: For the quarter ended Sep 30 2017, net income increased 105.7% to US$72.3 million from US$35.1 million in the year-earlier quarter. Revenues were US$717.7 million, up 23.3% from US$582.0 million the year before. Direct operating expenses rose 15.0% to US$534.5 million from US$464.6 million in the comparable period the year before. Indirect operating expenses increased 4.8% to US$66.2 million from US$63.2 million in the equivalent prior-year period.

Prospects: Our evaluation of Tri Pointe Group Inc as of Jan. 14, 2018 is the result of our systematic analysis on three basic characteristics: earnings strength, relative valuation, and recent stock price movement. The company has enjoyed a very positive trend in earnings per share over the past 5 quarters and while recent estimates for the company have been raised by analysts, TPH has posted better than expected results. Based on operating earnings yield, the company is undervalued when compared to all of the companies in our coverage universe. Share price changes over the past year indicates that TPH will perform in line with the market over the near term.

Financial Data

(US$ in Thousands)	9 Mos	6 Mos	3 Mos	12/31/2016	12/31/2015	12/31/2014	12/31/2013	12/31/2012
Earnings Per Share	1.10	0.84	1.09	1.21	1.27	0.58	0.50	...
Cash Flow Per Share	(0.71)	(1.24)	(0.82)	(0.98)	0.19	(0.78)	(7.16)	...
Tang Book Value Per Share	11.18	10.68	10.55	10.51	9.29	8.00	10.20	4.72
Income Statement								
Total Revenue	1,681,752	964,017	393,391	2,403,922	2,400,149	1,703,616	257,955	78,550
EBITDA	190,207	69,270	16,268	312,937	336,778	148,301	28,990	2,937
Depn & Amortn	11,631	7,744	3,841	15,699	20,209	20,049	3,237	431
Income Before Taxes	178,576	61,526	12,427	297,238	316,569	128,252	25,753	2,506
Income Taxes	69,824	23,712	4,614	106,094	112,079	43,767	10,379	...
Net Income	113,171	40,907	8,193	195,171	205,461	84,197	15,374	2,506
Average Shares	152,129	156,140	159,390	161,381	162,319	145,531	30,797	...
Balance Sheet								
Current Assets	3,659,064	3,513,871	3,362,715	3,325,007	2,908,125	2,628,751	497,211	214,455
Total Assets	3,896,066	3,751,997	3,599,716	3,564,640	3,138,071	2,913,524	506,035	217,516
Current Liabilities	167,605	141,654	156,075	125,901	125,409	135,272	45,617	10,995
Long-Term Obligations	1,669,558	1,617,861	1,419,914	1,382,033	1,172,947	1,171,691	138,112	57,368
Total Liabilities	2,053,637	1,974,043	1,760,542	1,735,193	1,473,388	1,459,344	183,729	68,363
Stockholders' Equity	1,842,429	1,777,954	1,839,174	1,829,447	1,664,683	1,454,180	322,306	149,153
Shares Outstanding	150,429	151,320	159,047	158,626	161,813	161,355	31,597	31,597
Statistical Record								
Return on Assets %	4.63	3.77	5.12	5.81	6.79	4.92	4.25	1.61
Return on Equity %	9.43	7.56	9.89	11.14	13.18	9.48	6.52	2.16
EBITDA Margin %	11.31	7.19	4.14	13.02	14.03	8.71	11.24	3.74
Net Margin %	6.73	4.24	2.08	8.12	8.56	4.94	5.96	3.19
Asset Turnover	0.66	0.65	0.69	0.72	0.79	1.00	0.71	0.50
Current Ratio	21.83	24.81	21.55	26.41	23.19	19.43	10.90	19.50
Debt to Equity	0.91	0.91	0.77	0.76	0.70	0.81	0.43	0.38
Price Range	14.08-10.52	14.07-10.52	14.07-10.52	14.07-9.05	16.05-12.50	19.93-12.73	20.51-13.66	...
P/E Ratio	12.80-9.56	16.75-12.52	12.91-9.65	11.63-7.48	12.64-9.84	34.36-21.95	41.02-27.32	...

Address: 19540 Jamboree Road, Suite 300, Irvine, CA 92612	**Web Site:** www.TRIPointeGroup.com	**Auditors:** Ernst & Young LLP
Telephone: 949-438-1400	**Officers:** Steven J. Gilbert - Chairman Thomas J. Mitchell - President, Chief Operating Officer, Secretary	**Investor Contact:** 949-478-8696
		Transfer Agents: American Stock Transfer & Trust Company, LLC

TRIBUNE MEDIA CO

Exchange	Symbol	Price	52Wk Range	Yield	P/E
NYS	TRCO	$42.47 (12/29/2017)	42.56-28.33	2.35	N/A

*7 Year Price Score N/A *NYSE Composite Index=100 *12 Month Price Score 100.16

Interim Earnings (Per Share)

Qtr.	Mar	Jun	Sep	Dec
2014	0.41	0.83	0.38	3.14
2015	0.37	(0.04)	0.29	(4.01)
2016	0.12	(1.76)	1.61	0.21
2017	(0.99)	(0.35)	(0.21)	...

Interim Dividends (Per Share)

Amt	Decl	Ex	Rec	Pay
0.25Q	02/14/2017	03/09/2017	03/13/2017	03/27/2017
0.25Q	05/05/2017	05/18/2017	05/22/2017	06/06/2017
0.25Q	08/02/2017	08/17/2017	08/21/2017	09/05/2017
0.25Q	10/26/2017	11/17/2017	11/20/2017	12/05/2017

Indicated Div: $1.00

Valuation Analysis / Institutional Holding

Forecast EPS	$1.16	No of Institutions
	(01/18/2018)	303
Market Cap	$3.7 Billion	Shares
Book Value	$2.9 Billion	91,139,728
Price/Book	1.29	% Held
Price/Sales	2.13	N/A

TRADING VOLUME (thousand shares)

Business Summary: Radio & Television (MIC: 2.3.1 SIC: 4833 NAIC: 515120)

Tribune Media is a holding company. Through its subsidiaries, Co. is a diversified media and entertainment company. Co.'s reportable segment, Television and Entertainment, provides audiences with news, entertainment and sports programming, including content produced by Tribune Studios and its production partners, on Tribune Broadcasting's 42 local television stations as of Dec 31 2016 and their websites, a national general entertainment cable network (WGN America), a radio station and other digital assets. Co. also holds a variety of investments in cable and digital assets, including equity investments in Television Food Network, G.P. and CareerBuilder, LLC.

Recent Developments: For the quarter ended Sep 30 2017, loss from continuing operations was US$18.7 million compared with income of US$153.8 million in the year-earlier quarter. Net loss amounted to US$18.7 million versus net income of US$145.8 million in the year-earlier quarter. Revenues were US$450.5 million, down 4.1% from US$470.0 million the year before. Operating loss was US$23.7 million versus an income of US$234.2 million in the prior-year quarter. Direct operating expenses rose 19.7% to US$297.5 million from US$248.6 million in the comparable period the year before. Indirect operating expenses amounted to US$176.7 million compared with an income of US$12.8 million in the equivalent prior-year period.

Prospects: Our evaluation of Tribune Media Company as of Jan. 14, 2018 is the result of our systematic analysis on three basic characteristics: earnings strength, relative valuation, and recent stock price movement. The company has generated a negative trend in earnings per share over the past 5 quarters and while recent estimates for the company have been mixed, TRCO has posted results that fell short of analysts expectations. Based on operating earnings yield, the company is overvalued when compared to all of the companies in our coverage universe. Share price changes over the past year indicates that TRCO will perform very well over the near term.

Financial Data

(US$ in Thousands)	9 Mos	6 Mos	3 Mos	12/31/2016	12/31/2015	12/28/2014	12/29/2013	12/30/2007
Earnings Per Share	(1.34)	0.48	(0.93)	0.16	(3.38)	4.75	2.41	...
Cash Flow Per Share	3.08	1.90	2.74	3.14	0.27	3.92	4.08	...
Dividends Per Share	6.770	6.770	6.770	1.000	7.480	...	...	...
Dividend Payout %	...	1,410.42	...	625.00	...	...	...	...
Income Statement								
Total Revenue	1,359,960	909,427	439,910	1,947,930	2,010,460	1,949,359	1,147,240	5,062,984
EBITDA	(39,331)	(77,085)	(94,002)	511,214	(205,835)	691,963	160,800	746,595
Depn & Amortn	173,401	115,377	57,608	72,409	74,289	29,000	8,000	228,070
Income Before Taxes	(330,184)	(270,352)	(189,863)	286,086	(444,554)	505,097	113,666	(63,115)
Income Taxes	(81,606)	(61,519)	(51,614)	347,202	22,323	278,699	95,965	(18,234)
Net Income	(134,683)	(115,996)	(85,594)	14,246	(319,918)	476,663	241,555	86,945
Average Shares	87,257	87,058	86,632	90,636	94,686	96,923	88,151	...
Balance Sheet								
Current Assets	1,206,041	946,127	937,054	1,296,300	1,021,945	2,160,823	1,735,280	1,385,023
Total Assets	8,174,081	8,045,275	8,151,981	9,401,051	9,758,535	11,396,455	11,476,009	13,149,719
Current Liabilities	686,808	475,206	497,321	550,853	547,417	684,180	798,837	2,189,966
Long-Term Obligations	2,917,454	3,010,784	3,014,397	3,391,627	3,452,544	3,490,897	3,760,475	11,840,206
Total Liabilities	5,291,939	5,129,115	5,200,330	5,861,285	5,932,337	6,201,024	6,550,448	16,663,659
Stockholders' Equity	2,882,142	2,916,160	2,951,651	3,539,766	3,826,198	5,195,431	4,925,561	(3,513,940)
Shares Outstanding	87,305	87,187	86,882	86,319	92,350	97,170	93,119	...
Statistical Record								
Return on Assets %	N.M.	0.56	N.M.	0.15	N.M.	4.18	...	0.66
Return on Equity %	N.M.	1.50	N.M.	0.39	N.M.	9.45	...	21.64
EBITDA Margin %	N.M.	N.M.	N.M.	26.24	N.M.	35.50	14.02	14.75
Net Margin %	N.M.	N.M.	N.M.	0.73	N.M.	24.45	21.06	1.72
Asset Turnover	0.20	0.21	0.21	0.20	0.19	0.17	...	0.38
Current Ratio	1.76	1.99	1.88	2.35	1.87	3.16	2.17	0.63
Debt to Equity	1.01	1.03	1.02	0.96	0.90	0.67	0.76	...
Price Range	42.40-28.33	42.40-28.33	40.38-28.33	40.38-27.36	70.16-33.54	89.34-56.70	77.60-48.67	...
P/E Ratio	...	88.33-59.02	...	252.38-171.00	...	18.81-11.94	32.20-20.20	...
Average Yield %	18.31	18.64	18.70	2.76	15.04	...	...	...

Address: 515 North State Street, Chicago, IL 60654	**Web Site:** www.tribune.com	**Auditors:** PricewaterhouseCoopers LLP
Telephone: 212-210-2786	**Officers:** Peter M. Kern - Interim Chief Executive Officer Gerald A. Spector - Executive Vice President, Chief Administrative Officer	**Investor Contact:** 212-210-2786
		Transfer Agents: EquiServe Trust Company, Providence, RI

TRINITY INDUSTRIES, INC.

Exchange	Symbol	Price	52Wk Range	Yield	P/E
NYS	TRN	$37.46 (12/29/2017)	37.88-25.49	1.39	24.97

*7 Year Price Score 95.51 *NYSE Composite Index=100 *12 Month Price Score 113.13

Interim Earnings (Per Share)

Qtr.	Mar	Jun	Sep	Dec
2014	1.43	1.01	0.90	0.86
2015	1.13	1.33	1.31	1.30
2016	0.64	0.62	0.55	0.44
2017	0.30	0.33	0.43	...

Interim Dividends (Per Share)

Amt	Decl	Ex	Rec	Pay
0.11Q	03/08/2017	04/11/2017	04/14/2017	04/28/2017
0.13Q	05/01/2017	07/12/2017	07/14/2017	07/31/2017
0.13Q	09/06/2017	10/12/2017	10/13/2017	10/31/2017
0.13Q	12/12/2017	01/11/2018	01/12/2018	01/31/2018

Indicated Div: $0.52

Valuation Analysis

		Institutional Holding	
Forecast EPS	$1.49	No of Institutions	
	(01/26/2018)	520	
Market Cap	$5.7 Billion	Shares	
Book Value	$4.0 Billion	153,127,440	
Price/Book	1.43	% Held	
Price/Sales	1.47	75.07	

Business Summary: Industrial Machinery & Equipment (MIC: 7.2.1 SIC: 3743 NAIC: 336510)

Trinity Industries is an industrial company that owns a range of businesses providing products and services to the energy, chemical, agriculture, transportation, and construction sectors. Co. manufactures and sells a variety of products and services principally including: railcars and railcar parts; parts and steel components; the leasing, management, and maintenance of railcars; highway products; construction aggregates; inland barges; structural wind towers; and trench shields and shoring products. Co. serves its customers through five business groups: Rail Group, Railcar Leasing and Management Services Group, Construction Products Group, Inland Barge Group, and Energy Equipment Group.

Recent Developments: For the quarter ended Sep 30 2017, net income decreased 24.2% to US$67.9 million from US$89.6 million in the year-earlier quarter. Revenues were US$973.6 million, down 12.4% from US$1.11 billion the year before. Operating income was US$153.0 million versus US$183.6 million in the prior-year quarter, a decrease of 16.7%. Direct operating expenses declined 12.7% to US$722.2 million from US$827.3 million in the comparable period the year before. Indirect operating expenses decreased 2.4% to US$98.4 million from US$100.8 million in the equivalent prior-year period.

Prospects: Our evaluation of Trinity Industries Inc. as of Jan. 21, 2018 is the result of our systematic analysis on three basic characteristics: earnings strength, relative valuation, and recent stock price movement. The company has enjoyed a very positive trend in earnings per share over the past 5 quarters. However, while recent estimates for the company have been mixed, TRN has posted better than expected results. Based on operating earnings yield, the company is about fairly valued when compared to all of the companies in our coverage universe. Share price changes over the past year indicates that TRN will perform well over the near term.

Financial Data

(US$ in Thousands)	9 Mos	6 Mos	3 Mos	12/31/2016	12/31/2015	12/31/2014	12/31/2013	12/31/2012
Earnings Per Share	1.50	1.62	1.91	2.25	5.08	4.19	2.38	1.60
Cash Flow Per Share	5.31	6.30	6.89	7.33	6.26	5.43	4.33	3.40
Tang Book Value Per Share	21.20	20.98	21.06	20.79	18.97	14.28	13.72	11.46
Dividends Per Share	0.460	0.440	0.440	0.440	0.420	0.350	0.250	0.200
Dividend Payout %	30.67	27.16	23.04	19.56	8.27	8.35	10.53	12.54
Income Statement								
Total Revenue	2,756,400	1,782,800	877,300	4,588,300	6,392,700	6,170,000	4,365,300	3,811,900
EBITDA	622,300	397,000	188,600	899,500	1,586,800	1,385,600	904,700	772,800
Depn & Amortn	220,700	146,500	72,800	156,200	142,300	130,000	129,000	193,700
Income Before Taxes	271,200	163,800	72,500	566,800	1,252,000	1,064,100	590,500	385,900
Income Taxes	97,800	58,100	20,800	202,100	426,000	354,800	204,400	134,000
Net Income	164,000	97,100	46,000	343,600	796,500	678,200	375,500	255,200
Average Shares	151,300	151,000	150,600	148,600	152,200	156,700	153,000	155,000
Balance Sheet								
Current Assets	2,266,800	2,149,700	1,867,600	1,944,700	2,278,800	2,495,200	1,765,600	1,630,700
Total Assets	9,564,900	9,452,100	9,143,400	9,125,300	8,885,900	8,733,800	7,313,400	6,669,900
Current Liabilities	612,700	579,500	555,000	582,200	746,400	1,005,000	783,700	771,300
Long-Term Obligations	3,276,400	3,270,000	3,036,000	3,056,600	3,195,400	3,553,000	2,989,800	3,055,000
Total Liabilities	5,577,000	5,522,400	5,186,300	5,206,800	5,232,000	5,737,900	4,911,300	4,616,900
Stockholders' Equity	3,987,900	3,929,700	3,957,100	3,918,500	3,653,900	2,995,900	2,402,100	2,053,000
Shares Outstanding	151,783	151,300	152,100	152,200	152,900	155,600	154,800	158,200
Statistical Record								
Return on Assets %	2.48	2.69	3.24	3.80	9.04	8.45	5.37	3.98
Return on Equity %	5.90	6.45	7.62	9.05	23.96	25.13	16.86	13.00
EBITDA Margin %	22.58	22.27	21.50	19.60	24.82	22.46	20.72	20.27
Net Margin %	5.95	5.45	5.24	7.49	12.46	10.99	8.60	6.69
Asset Turnover	0.41	0.43	0.47	0.51	0.73	0.77	0.62	0.59
Current Ratio	3.70	3.71	3.37	3.34	3.05	2.48	2.25	2.11
Debt to Equity	0.82	0.83	0.77	0.78	0.87	1.19	1.24	1.49
Price Range	31.90-21.01	29.24-18.57	29.24-16.73	29.24-15.64	36.80-22.37	50.30-26.57	28.32-17.65	18.02-10.93
P/E Ratio	21.27-14.01	18.05-11.46	15.31-8.76	13.00-6.95	7.24-4.40	12.00-6.34	11.90-7.41	11.27-6.83
Average Yield %	1.70	1.72	1.87	2.04	1.48	0.93	1.16	1.33

Address: 2525 N. Stemmons Freeway, Dallas, TX 75207-2401 **Telephone:** 214-631-4420 **Fax:** 214-589-8501	**Web Site:** www.trin.net **Officers:** Timothy R. Wallace - Chairman, President, Chief Executive Officer William A. McWhirter - Senior Vice President, Division Officer	**Auditors:** Ernst & Young LLP **Investor Contact:** 214-589-8909 **Transfer Agents:** American Stock Transfer & Trust Company

TRANSDIGM GROUP INC

Exchange	Symbol	Price	52Wk Range	Yield	P/E
NYS	TDG	$274.62 (12/29/2017)	287.60-210.04	N/A	34.85

*7 Year Price Score 111.03 *NYSE Composite Index=100 *12 Month Price Score 100.51

TRADING VOLUME (thousand shares)

Interim Earnings (Per Share)

Qtr.	Dec	Mar	Jun	Sep
2012-13	0.66	1.25	0.71	(0.23)
2013-14	1.44	1.49	(1.66)	1.90
2014-15	1.63	1.96	1.75	2.50
2015-16	1.97	2.47	2.52	3.44
2016-17	0.41	2.78	3.08	1.65

Interim Dividends (Per Share)

Amt	Decl	Ex	Rec	Pay
22.00U	07/03/2013	07/11/2013	07/15/2013	07/25/2013
25.00U	06/04/2014	06/12/2014	06/16/2014	06/26/2014
24.00U	10/14/2016	10/20/2016	10/24/2016	11/01/2016
22.00U	08/23/2017	08/31/2017	09/05/2017	09/12/2017

Valuation Analysis / Institutional Holding

Forecast EPS	$13.40 (01/18/2018)	No of Institutions	527
Market Cap	$14.3 Billion	Shares	68,396,448
Book Value	N/A	% Held	99.30
Price/Book	N/A		
Price/Sales	4.07		

Business Summary: Aerospace (MIC: 7.1.1 SIC: 3728 NAIC: 336412)

TransDigm Group is a holding company. Through its subsidiaries, Co. designs, produces and supplies engineered aircraft components for use on commercial and military aircraft. Co.'s segments are: power & control, which include operations that primarily develop, produce and market systems and components that mainly provide power to or control power of the aircraft; airframe, which includes operations that primarily develop, produce and market systems and components that are used in non-power airframe applications utilizing airframe and cabin structure technologies; and non-aviation, which includes operations that primarily develop, produce and market products for non-aviation markets.

Recent Developments: For the year ended Sep 30 2017, income from continuing operations increased 7.2% to US$628.5 million from US$586.4 million a year earlier. Net income increased 1.8% to US$596.9 million from US$586.4 million in the prior year. Revenues were US$3.50 billion, up 10.5% from US$3.17 billion the year before. Operating income was US$1.48 billion versus US$1.27 billion in the prior year, an increase of 16.7%. Direct operating expenses rose 5.3% to US$1.52 billion from US$1.44 billion in the comparable period the year before. Indirect operating expenses increased 9.7% to US$504.8 million from US$460.3 million in the equivalent prior-year period.

Prospects: Our evaluation of Transdigm Group Inc. as of Jan. 14, 2018 is the result of our systematic analysis on three basic characteristics: earnings strength, relative valuation, and recent stock price movement. The company has managed to produce a neutral trend in earnings per share over the past 5 quarters and while recent estimates for the company have been raised by analysts, TDG has posted better than expected results. Based on operating earnings yield, the company is about fairly valued when compared to all of the companies in our coverage universe. Share price changes over the past year indicates that TDG will perform in line with the market over the near term.

Financial Data
(US$ in Thousands)

	09/30/2017	09/30/2016	09/30/2015	09/30/2014	09/30/2013	09/30/2012	09/30/2011	09/30/2010
Earnings Per Share	7.88	10.39	7.84	3.16	2.39	5.97	3.17	2.52
Cash Flow Per Share	14.20	11.88	9.20	9.50	8.54	7.66	4.89	3.73
Dividends Per Share	46.000	...	...	25.000	34.850	...	...	7.650
Dividend Payout %	583.76	...	...	791.14	1,458.16	...	...	303.57
Income Statement								
Total Revenue	3,504,286	3,171,411	2,707,115	2,372,906	1,924,400	1,700,208	1,206,021	827,654
EBITDA	1,580,182	1,372,866	1,149,272	892,583	792,689	768,002	475,141	393,234
Depn & Amortn	140,163	120,900	93,663	96,385	73,515	68,227	60,460	30,165
Income Before Taxes	837,430	768,116	636,824	448,510	448,489	487,869	229,425	250,835
Income Taxes	208,889	181,702	189,612	141,600	145,700	162,900	77,200	87,390
Net Income	596,887	586,414	447,212	306,910	302,789	324,969	172,134	163,445
Average Shares	55,530	56,157	56,606	56,993	55,080	53,882	53,333	52,923
Balance Sheet								
Current Assets	2,133,552	2,930,697	1,831,962	1,689,576	1,320,495	1,050,531	870,292	583,508
Total Assets	9,975,661	10,726,277	8,427,050	6,756,848	6,148,879	5,459,617	4,513,636	2,677,818
Current Liabilities	870,994	752,603	658,215	585,907	322,500	233,915	206,859	113,012
Long-Term Obligations	11,393,620	9,943,191	8,183,502	7,233,836	5,700,193	3,598,625	3,122,875	1,771,646
Total Liabilities	12,926,865	11,377,767	9,465,356	8,312,947	6,485,260	4,240,783	3,702,687	2,084,839
Stockholders' Equity	(2,951,204)	(651,490)	(1,038,306)	(1,556,099)	(336,381)	1,218,834	810,949	592,979
Shares Outstanding	51,934	53,334	53,684	52,417	52,667	51,651	50,335	49,434
Statistical Record								
Return on Assets %	5.77	6.11	5.89	4.76	5.22	6.50	4.79	6.37
Return on Equity %	...	...	...	...	...	68.62	31.93	24.52	23.15
EBITDA Margin %	45.09	43.29	42.45	37.62	41.19	45.17	39.40	47.51
Net Margin %	17.03	18.49	16.52	12.93	15.73	19.11	14.27	19.75
Asset Turnover	0.34	0.33	0.36	0.37	0.33	0.34	0.34	0.32
Current Ratio	2.45	3.89	2.78	2.88	4.09	4.49	4.21	5.16
Debt to Equity	...	...	...	...	...	2.95	3.85	2.99
Price Range	289.86-210.04	291.81-187.29	244.35-171.82	197.00-137.86	162.48-125.52	145.61-77.38	93.94-61.00	63.56-39.18
P/E Ratio	36.78-26.65	28.09-18.03	31.17-21.92	62.34-43.63	67.98-52.52	24.39-12.96	29.63-19.24	25.22-15.55
Average Yield %	17.93	...	...	14.67	24.38	...	...	14.92

Address: 1301 East 9th Street, Suite 3000, Cleveland, OH 44114	Web Site: www.transdigm.com	Auditors: Ernst & Young LLP
Telephone: 216-706-2960	Officers: W. Nicholas Howley - Chairman, Chief Executive Officer Robert S. Henderson - Vice-Chairman, Executive Vice President, Division Officer	Investor Contact: 216-706-2945 Transfer Agents: Computershare, Providence, RI

TUPPERWARE BRANDS CORP

Exchange	Symbol	Price	52Wk Range	Yield	P/E
NYS	TUP	$62.70 (12/29/2017)	73.52-53.86	4.34	22.80

*7 Year Price Score 75.33 *NYSE Composite Index=100 *12 Month Price Score 92.35

Interim Earnings (Per Share)

Qtr.	Mar	Jun	Sep	Dec
2014	1.02	0.93	0.63	1.61
2015	0.59	1.23	0.72	1.15
2016	0.86	1.03	0.96	1.56
2017	0.93	(0.35)	0.61	...

Interim Dividends (Per Share)

Amt	Decl	Ex	Rec	Pay
0.68Q	02/01/2017	03/16/2017	03/20/2017	04/06/2017
0.68Q	05/24/2017	06/16/2017	06/20/2017	07/06/2017
0.68Q	08/14/2017	09/19/2017	09/20/2017	10/05/2017
0.68Q	11/02/2017	12/19/2017	12/20/2017	01/05/2018

Indicated Div: $2.72

Valuation Analysis

		Institutional Holding	
Forecast EPS	$4.75	No of Institutions	563
	(01/05/2018)		
Market Cap	$3.2 Billion	Shares	59,882,416
Book Value	$236.5 Million	% Held	76.23
Price/Book	13.49		
Price/Sales	1.41		

Business Summary: Plastics (MIC: 8.4.2 SIC: 3089 NAIC: 326199)

Tupperware Brands manufactures and sells Tupperware® products and cosmetics and personal care products under trade names such as Avroy Shlain®, BeautiControl®, Fuller®, NaturCare®, Nutrimetics® and Nuvo® brands. Co. operates in three geographic regions: Europe (Europe, Africa and the Middle East), Asia Pacific and the Americas. The Tupperware product line consists of preparation, storage, and serving solutions for the kitchen and home, and cookware, knives, microwave products, microfiber textiles, and water-filtration related items. Co. also manufactures and distributes skin and hair care products, cosmetics, bath and body care, toiletries, fragrances, jewelry and nutritional products.

Recent Developments: For the quarter ended Sep 30 2017, net income decreased 35.7% to US$31.4 million from US$48.8 million in the year-earlier quarter. Revenues were US$539.5 million, up 3.4% from US$521.8 million the year before. Operating income was US$68.0 million versus US$91.0 million in the prior-year quarter, a decrease of 25.3%. Direct operating expenses rose 8.5% to US$182.7 million from US$168.4 million in the comparable period the year before. Indirect operating expenses increased 10.1% to US$288.8 million from US$262.4 million in the equivalent prior-year period.

Prospects: Our evaluation of Tupperware Corp. as of Jan. 14, 2018 is the result of our systematic analysis on three basic characteristics: earnings strength, relative valuation, and recent stock price movement. The company has generated a negative trend in earnings per share over the past 5 quarters and while recent estimates for the company have been mixed, TUP has posted better than expected results. Based on operating earnings yield, the company is undervalued when compared to all of the companies in our coverage universe. Share price changes over the past year indicates that TUP will perform in line with the market over the near term.

Financial Data

(US$ in Thousands)	9 Mos	6 Mos	3 Mos	12/31/2016	12/26/2015	12/27/2014	12/28/2013	12/29/2012
Earnings Per Share	2.75	3.10	4.48	4.41	3.69	4.20	5.17	3.42
Cash Flow Per Share	4.46	4.35	4.51	4.65	4.54	5.65	6.25	5.42
Tang Book Value Per Share	1.75	1.65	1.11	0.25	N.M.	N.M.	N.M.	2.64
Dividends Per Share	2.720	2.720	2.720	2.720	2.720	2.720	2.480	1.440
Dividend Payout %	98.91	87.74	60.71	61.68	73.71	64.76	47.97	42.11
Income Statement								
Total Revenue	1,667,200	1,127,700	554,800	2,213,100	2,283,800	2,606,100	2,671,600	2,583,800
EBITDA	141,000	73,800	75,400	396,600	357,300	393,400	448,000	352,800
Depn & Amortn	400	300	100	49,900	52,200	51,700	50,000	47,600
Income Before Taxes	107,900	51,500	64,200	301,300	259,900	298,200	360,400	272,800
Income Taxes	46,800	21,800	16,800	77,700	74,100	83,800	86,200	79,800
Net Income	61,100	29,700	47,400	223,600	185,800	214,400	274,200	193,000
Average Shares	51,300	50,800	51,000	50,700	50,400	51,000	53,100	56,400
Balance Sheet								
Current Assets	623,600	609,500	602,700	545,300	550,500	753,600	779,000	766,500
Total Assets	1,708,500	1,660,700	1,677,600	1,587,800	1,598,200	1,783,100	1,843,900	1,821,800
Current Liabilities	635,100	595,700	585,100	547,600	614,000	747,400	737,500	694,500
Long-Term Obligations	605,300	605,300	605,900	606,000	608,200	615,200	619,900	414,400
Total Liabilities	1,472,000	1,427,000	1,409,900	1,375,000	1,437,200	1,597,300	1,591,000	1,342,700
Stockholders' Equity	236,500	233,700	267,700	212,800	161,000	185,800	252,900	479,100
Shares Outstanding	50,880	50,879	50,712	50,637	50,436	49,682	50,324	54,059
Statistical Record								
Return on Assets %	8.33	9.57	13.65	13.81	11.02	11.85	15.00	10.56
Return on Equity %	65.74	76.49	104.09	117.70	107.45	98.01	75.12	39.50
EBITDA Margin %	8.46	6.54	13.59	17.92	15.64	15.10	16.77	13.65
Net Margin %	3.66	2.63	8.54	10.10	8.14	8.23	10.26	7.47
Asset Turnover	1.35	1.37	1.34	1.37	1.35	1.44	1.46	1.41
Current Ratio	0.98	1.02	1.03	1.00	0.90	1.01	1.06	1.10
Debt to Equity	2.56	2.59	2.26	2.85	3.78	3.31	2.45	0.86
Price Range	73.52-52.62	73.52-52.62	66.72-50.96	66.72-43.97	72.68-48.42	95.54-59.64	96.00-64.00	66.56-51.16
P/E Ratio	26.73-19.13	23.72-16.97	14.89-11.38	15.13-9.97	19.70-13.12	22.75-14.20	18.57-12.38	19.46-14.96
Average Yield %	4.37	4.34	4.58	4.72	4.40	3.53	3.01	2.47

Address: 14901 South Orange Blossom Trail, Orlando, FL 32837 Telephone: 407-826-5050	Web Site: www.tupperwarebrands.com Officers: E. V. Goings - Chairman, Chief Executive Officer Asha Gupta - Region Officer	Auditors: PricewaterhouseCoopers LLP Investor Contact: 407-826-4475 Transfer Agents: Wells Fargo Bank, N.A., South St. Paul, MN

TWITTER INC

Exchange	Symbol	Price	52Wk Range	Yield	P/E
NYS	TWTR	$24.01 (12/29/2017)	25.20-14.29	N/A	N/A

*7 Year Price Score N/A   ***NYSE Composite Index=100**   ***12 Month Price Score 114.43**

Interim Earnings (Per Share)

Qtr.	Mar	Jun	Sep	Dec
2014	(0.23)	(0.24)	(0.29)	(0.20)
2015	(0.25)	(0.21)	(0.20)	(0.13)
2016	(0.12)	(0.15)	(0.15)	(0.23)
2017	(0.09)	(0.16)	(0.03)	...

Interim Dividends (Per Share)

No Dividends Paid

Valuation Analysis   **Institutional Holding**

Valuation Analysis		Institutional Holding	
Forecast EPS	$0.39	No of Institutions	
	(01/18/2018)	637	
Market Cap	$17.8 Billion	Shares	
Book Value	$4.8 Billion	416,845,472	
Price/Book	3.69	% Held	
Price/Sales	7.33	90.26	

TRADING VOLUME (thousand shares)

Business Summary: Internet & Software (MIC: 6.3.2 SIC: 7371 NAIC: 541511)

Twitter provides products and services for users, advertisers, developers and platform and data partners. Co.'s products and services for users include its Twitter platform for public self-expression and conversation in real time and its Periscope mobile application. Co.'s products and services for advertisers include Promoted Product for advertisers as well as MoPub mobile-focused advertising exchange and its Twitter Audience Platform. Co.'s products for developers include a set of tools, public application program interfaces (API) and embeddable widgets. Co.'s products for data partners include subscription access to its public data feed beyond its public API.

Recent Developments: For the quarter ended Sep 30 2017, net loss amounted to US$21.1 million versus a net loss of US$102.9 million in the year-earlier quarter. Revenues were US$589.6 million, down 4.3% from US$615.9 million the year before. Operating income was US$7.3 million versus a loss of US$78.1 million in the prior-year quarter. Direct operating expenses declined 6.7% to US$210.0 million from US$225.2 million in the comparable period the year before. Indirect operating expenses decreased 20.6% to US$372.3 million from US$468.9 million in the equivalent prior-year period.

Prospects: Our evaluation of Twitter Inc as of Jan. 14, 2018 is the result of our systematic analysis on three basic characteristics: earnings strength, relative valuation, and recent stock price movement. The company has enjoyed a very positive trend in earnings per share over the past 5 quarters and while recent estimates for the company have remained steady, TWTR has posted better than expected results. Based on operating earnings yield, the company is overvalued when compared to all of the companies in our coverage universe. Share price changes over the past year indicates that TWTR will perform very poorly over the near term.

Financial Data

(US$ in Thousands)	9 Mos	6 Mos	3 Mos	12/31/2016	12/31/2015	12/31/2014	12/31/2013	12/31/2012
Earnings Per Share	(0.51)	(0.63)	(0.62)	(0.65)	(0.79)	(0.96)	(6.82)	(0.68)
Cash Flow Per Share	1.13	1.07	1.11	1.08	0.58	0.14	0.01	(0.24)
Tang Book Value Per Share	4.83	4.72	4.70	4.61	4.47	4.51	4.40	4.39
Income Statement								
Total Revenue	1,711,739	1,122,106	548,251	2,529,619	2,218,032	1,403,002	1,329,780	316,933
EBITDA	(50,790)	(80,346)	(13,708)	(8,066)	(177,927)	(372,766)	(1,091,056)	(22,884)
Depn & Amortn	59,644	39,289	19,248	332,800	257,200	171,600	188,800	53,800
Income Before Taxes	(188,971)	(171,440)	(58,365)	(440,834)	(533,305)	(578,351)	(1,294,292)	(79,170)
Income Taxes	10,171	6,607	3,194	16,039	(12,274)	(531)	(3,646)	229
Net Income	(199,142)	(178,047)	(61,559)	(456,873)	(521,031)	(577,820)	(1,290,646)	(79,399)
Average Shares	736,515	730,069	722,048	702,135	662,424	604,990	379,020	117,401
Balance Sheet								
Current Assets	5,002,422	4,840,102	4,695,332	4,652,196	4,381,792	4,255,853	5,149,358	554,466
Total Assets	7,075,789	6,963,098	6,892,742	6,870,365	6,442,439	5,583,082	6,732,480	831,568
Current Liabilities	481,202	494,578	488,992	584,021	506,039	393,794	450,860	109,879
Long-Term Obligations	1,690,554	1,665,878	1,638,110	1,605,804	1,514,790	1,494,970	221,040	65,732
Total Liabilities	2,246,383	2,234,202	2,202,366	2,265,430	2,074,392	1,956,679	832,468	207,204
Stockholders' Equity	4,829,406	4,728,896	4,690,376	4,604,935	4,368,047	3,626,403	5,900,012	624,364
Shares Outstanding	741,907	736,470	729,745	721,572	694,132	642,385	1,139,844	125,597
Statistical Record								
Asset Turnover	0.35	0.36	0.37	0.38	0.37	0.23	0.35	0.41
Current Ratio	10.40	9.79	9.60	7.97	8.66	10.81	11.42	5.05
Debt to Equity	0.35	0.35	0.35	0.35	0.35	0.41	0.04	0.11
Price Range	24.87-14.29	24.87-14.29	24.87-14.01	24.87-14.01	52.87-22.14	69.00-30.50	73.31-39.06	...

Address: 1355 Market Street, Suite 900, San Francisco, CA 94103
Telephone: 415-222-9670

Web Site: www.twitter.com
Officers: Omid R. Kordestani - Executive Chairman Jack Dorsey - Chairman, Chief Executive Officer, Interim Chief Executive Officer

Auditors: PricewaterhouseCoopers LLP
Transfer Agents: Computershare Trust Company, N.A., Canton, MA

TYLER TECHNOLOGIES, INC.

Exchange	Symbol	Price	52Wk Range	Yield	P/E
NYS	TYL	$177.05 (12/29/2017)	184.11-144.77	N/A	45.17

*7 Year Price Score 132.28 *NYSE Composite Index=100 *12 Month Price Score 100.68

Interim Earnings (Per Share)

Qtr.	Mar	Jun	Sep	Dec
2014	0.33	0.42	0.48	0.43
2015	0.48	0.52	0.55	0.21
2016	0.44	0.49	0.58	1.31
2017	0.83	0.81	0.97	...

Interim Dividends (Per Share)

No Dividends Paid

Valuation Analysis		Institutional Holding	
Forecast EPS	$3.90	No of Institutions	
	(01/17/2018)	372	
Market Cap	$6.6 Billion	Shares	
Book Value	$1.1 Billion	45,039,796	
Price/Book	6.17	% Held	
Price/Sales	8.15	98.79	

TRADING VOLUME (thousand shares)

Business Summary: Internet & Software (MIC: 6.3.2 SIC: 7372 NAIC: 511210)

Tyler Technologies provides integrated information management solutions and services for the public sector, with a focus on local governments. Co. has two segments. The Enterprise Software Solutions segment provides municipal and county governments and schools with software systems and services to meet their information technology and automation needs for functions such as financial management and courts and justice processes. The Appraisal and Tax segment provides systems and software that automate the appraisal and assessment of real and personal property as well as property appraisal outsourcing services for local governments and taxing authorities.

Recent Developments: For the quarter ended Sep 30 2017, net income increased 8.0% to US$38.3 million from US$35.4 million in the year-earlier quarter. Revenues were US$214.1 million, up 10.1% from US$194.5 million the year before. Operating income was US$43.4 million versus US$36.9 million in the prior-year quarter, an increase of 17.6%. Direct operating expenses rose 9.6% to US$110.7 million from US$101.0 million in the comparable period the year before. Indirect operating expenses increased 6.1% to US$60.0 million from US$56.5 million in the equivalent prior-year period.

Prospects: Our evaluation of Tyler Technologies Inc. as of Jan. 14, 2018 is the result of our systematic analysis on three basic characteristics: earnings strength, relative valuation, and recent stock price movement. The company has generated a negative trend in earnings per share over the past 5 quarters and while recent estimates for the company have remained steady, TYL has posted better than expected results. Based on operating earnings yield, the company is overvalued when compared to all of the companies in our coverage universe. Share price changes over the past year indicates that TYL will perform well over the near term.

Financial Data
(US$ in Thousands)

	9 Mos	6 Mos	3 Mos	12/31/2016	12/31/2015	12/31/2014	12/31/2013	12/31/2012
Earnings Per Share	3.92	3.53	3.21	2.82	1.77	1.66	1.13	1.00
Cash Flow Per Share	5.70	5.04	5.42	5.25	2.61	3.74	2.07	1.93
Tang Book Value Per Share	4.72	3.03	1.57	N.M.	N.M.	5.32	2.63	N.M.
Income Statement								
Total Revenue	622,811	408,665	199,542	756,043	591,022	493,101	416,643	363,304
EBITDA	126,868	79,854	39,417	156,438	123,429	106,913	76,736	63,747
Depn & Amortn	10,413	6,921	3,458	27,131	15,005	12,446	10,917	9,879
Income Before Taxes	116,455	72,933	35,959	129,307	108,424	94,467	65,819	53,868
Income Taxes	14,308	9,049	3,653	19,450	43,555	35,527	26,718	20,874
Net Income	102,147	63,884	32,306	109,857	64,869	58,940	39,101	32,994
Average Shares	39,342	39,201	38,932	38,961	36,552	35,401	34,590	32,916
Balance Sheet								
Current Assets	399,721	352,278	271,575	282,960	268,215	346,710	217,235	122,757
Total Assets	1,493,118	1,438,509	1,355,681	1,357,945	1,356,570	573,982	444,488	338,315
Current Liabilities	359,309	359,582	322,245	361,501	337,572	232,839	192,110	169,795
Long-Term Obligations	...	...	...	10,000	66,000	...	...	18,000
Total Liabilities	415,340	420,907	388,844	442,420	497,713	237,009	198,169	193,016
Stockholders' Equity	1,077,778	1,017,602	966,837	915,525	858,857	336,973	246,319	145,299
Shares Outstanding	37,551	37,285	37,061	36,766	36,774	33,469	32,838	31,331
Statistical Record								
Return on Assets %	10.81	9.66	9.36	8.07	6.72	11.57	9.99	...
Return on Equity %	15.69	14.92	14.22	12.35	10.85	20.21	19.97	...
EBITDA Margin %	20.37	19.54	19.75	20.69	20.88	21.68	18.42	17.55
Net Margin %	16.40	15.63	16.19	14.53	10.98	11.95	9.38	9.08
Asset Turnover	0.57	0.56	0.58	0.56	0.61	0.97	1.06	...
Current Ratio	1.11	0.98	0.84	0.78	0.79	1.49	1.13	0.72
Debt to Equity	...	...	...	0.01	0.08	...	...	0.12
Price Range	181.33-141.13	177.15-141.13	175.47-128.61	175.47-119.50	180.61-104.17	114.09-76.00	104.62-48.44	49.00-30.34
P/E Ratio	46.26-36.00	50.18-39.98	54.66-40.07	62.22-42.38	102.04-58.85	68.73-45.78	92.58-42.87	49.00-30.34

Address: 5101 Tennyson Parkway, Plano, TX 75024 Telephone: 972-713-3700	Web Site: www.tylertech.com Officers: John M. Yeaman - Chairman John S. Marr - President, Chief Executive Officer	Auditors: Ernst & Young LLP Investor Contact: 972-713-3720 Transfer Agents: American Stock Transfer & Company, New York, NY

TYSON FOODS INC

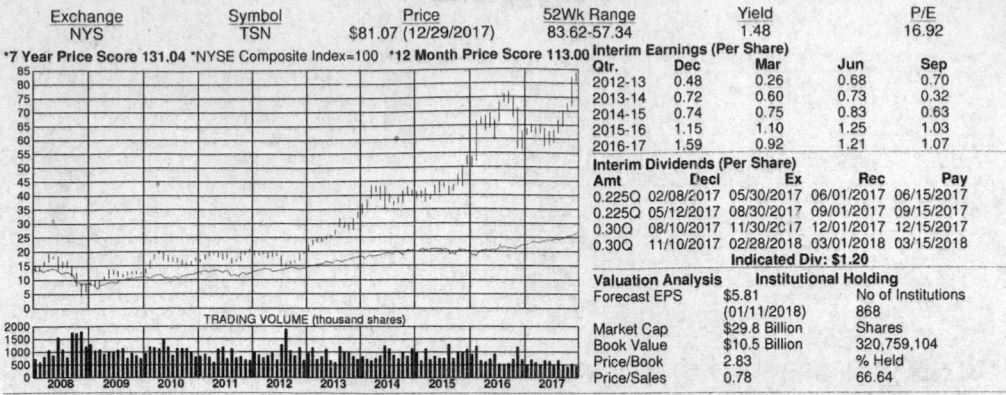

Exchange	Symbol	Price	52Wk Range	Yield	P/E
NYS	TSN	$81.07 (12/29/2017)	83.62-57.34	1.48	16.92

*7 Year Price Score 131.04 *NYSE Composite Index=100 *12 Month Price Score 113.00

Interim Earnings (Per Share)

Qtr.	Dec	Mar	Jun	Sep
2012-13	0.48	0.26	0.68	0.70
2013-14	0.72	0.60	0.73	0.32
2014-15	0.74	0.75	0.83	0.63
2015-16	1.15	1.10	1.25	1.03
2016-17	1.59	0.92	1.21	1.07

Interim Dividends (Per Share)

Amt	Decl	Ex	Rec	Pay
0.225Q	02/08/2017	05/30/2017	06/01/2017	06/15/2017
0.225Q	05/12/2017	08/30/2017	09/01/2017	09/15/2017
0.30Q	08/10/2017	11/30/2017	12/01/2017	12/15/2017
0.30Q	11/10/2017	02/28/2018	03/01/2018	03/15/2018

Indicated Div: $1.20

Valuation Analysis / Institutional Holding

Forecast EPS	$5.81	No of Institutions
	(01/11/2018)	868
Market Cap	$29.8 Billion	Shares
Book Value	$10.5 Billion	320,759,104
Price/Book	2.83	% Held
Price/Sales	0.78	66.64

Business Summary: Food (MIC: 1.2.1 SIC: 2015 NAIC: 311615)

Tyson Foods operates a vertically-integrated chicken production process. Co.'s operations consist of breeding stock, contract growers, feed production, processing, further-processing, marketing and transportation of chicken and related allied products, including animal and pet food ingredients. Through its subsidiary, Cobb-Vantress, Inc., Co. is engaged in poultry breeding stock suppliers. Co. also process live fed cattle and hogs and fabricate dressed beef and pork carcasses into primal and sub-primal meat cuts, case ready beef and pork and fully-cooked meats. Co. produces a range of fresh, frozen and refrigerated food products. Co.'s segments are beef, pork, chicken, and prepared foods.

Recent Developments: For the year ended Sep 30 2017, net income increased 0.3% to US$1.78 billion from US$1.77 billion in the prior year. Revenues were US$38.26 billion, up 3.7% from US$36.88 billion the year before. Operating income was US$2.93 billion versus US$2.83 billion in the prior year, an increase of 3.5%. Direct operating expenses rose 3.1% to US$33.18 billion from US$32.18 billion in the comparable period the year before. Indirect operating expenses increased 15.5% to US$2.15 billion from US$1.86 billion in the equivalent prior-year period.

Prospects: Our evaluation of Tyson Foods Inc. as of Jan. 14, 2018 is the result of our systematic analysis on three basic characteristics: earnings strength, relative valuation, and recent stock price movement. The company has managed to produce a neutral trend in earnings per share over the past 5 quarters and while recent estimates for the company have been raised by analysts, TSN has posted better than expected results. Based on operating earnings yield, the company is undervalued when compared to all of the companies in our coverage universe. Share price changes over the past year indicates that TSN will perform very well over the near term.

Financial Data

(US$ in Thousands)	09/30/2017	10/01/2016	10/03/2015	09/27/2014	09/28/2013	09/29/2012	10/01/2011	10/02/2010
Earnings Per Share	4.79	4.53	2.95	2.37	2.12	1.58	1.97	2.06
Cash Flow Per Share	7.12	7.07	6.24	3.34	3.74	3.28	2.81	3.85
Tang Book Value Per Share	N.M.	N.M.	N.M.	N.M.	12.10	11.12	9.77	8.24
Dividends Per Share	0.900	0.600	0.400	0.300	0.300	0.160	0.160	0.160
Dividend Payout %	18.79	13.25	13.56	12.66	14.15	10.13	8.12	7.77
Income Statement								
Total Revenue	38,260,000	36,881,000	41,373,000	37,580,000	34,374,000	33,278,000	32,266,000	28,430,000
EBITDA	3,542,000	3,458,000	2,814,000	1,871,000	1,869,000	1,714,000	1,738,000	1,952,000
Depn & Amortn	642,000	617,000	609,000	494,000	474,000	443,000	433,000	416,000
Income Before Taxes	2,628,000	2,598,000	1,921,000	1,252,000	1,257,000	927,000	1,074,000	1,203,000
Income Taxes	850,000	826,000	697,000	396,000	409,000	351,000	341,000	438,000
Net Income	1,774,000	1,768,000	1,220,000	864,000	778,000	583,000	750,000	780,000
Average Shares	370,000	390,000	413,000	364,000	367,000	370,000	380,000	379,000
Balance Sheet								
Current Assets	6,258,000	4,888,000	5,381,000	6,221,000	5,604,000	5,403,000	4,780,000	4,618,000
Total Assets	28,066,000	22,373,000	23,004,000	23,956,000	12,177,000	11,896,000	11,071,000	10,752,000
Current Liabilities	4,032,000	2,762,000	3,535,000	3,797,000	3,010,000	2,830,000	2,374,000	2,545,000
Long-Term Obligations	9,297,000	6,200,000	6,010,000	7,535,000	1,895,000	1,917,000	2,112,000	2,135,000
Total Liabilities	17,525,000	12,765,000	13,313,000	15,066,000	5,976,000	5,884,000	5,414,000	5,586,000
Stockholders' Equity	10,541,000	9,608,000	9,691,000	8,890,000	6,201,000	6,012,000	5,657,000	5,166,000
Shares Outstanding	368,000	361,000	369,000	376,000	344,000	359,000	370,000	377,000
Statistical Record								
Return on Assets %	7.05	7.81	5.11	4.80	6.48	5.09	6.89	7.33
Return on Equity %	17.66	18.37	12.92	11.48	12.78	10.02	13.90	16.44
EBITDA Margin %	9.26	9.38	6.80	4.98	5.44	5.15	5.39	6.87
Net Margin %	4.64	4.79	2.95	2.30	2.26	1.75	2.32	2.74
Asset Turnover	1.52	1.63	1.73	2.09	2.86	2.91	2.97	2.67
Current Ratio	1.55	1.77	1.52	1.64	1.86	1.91	2.01	1.81
Debt to Equity	0.88	0.65	0.62	0.85	0.31	0.32	0.37	0.41
Price Range	75.10-56.17	76.76-43.10	45.01-37.12	44.01-27.56	31.83-16.02	20.91-14.17	19.92-14.84	20.40-12.02
P/E Ratio	15.68-11.73	16.94-9.51	15.26-12.58	18.57-11.63	15.01-7.56	13.23-8.97	10.11-7.53	9.90-5.83
Average Yield %	1.42	0.97	0.97	0.82	1.27	0.87	0.91	1.00

Address: 2200 West Don Tyson Parkway, Springdale, AR 72762-6999
Telephone: 479-290-4000
Fax: 479-290-7984

Web Site: www.tyson.com
Officers: John Tyson - Chairman Thomas P. (Tom) Hayes - President, Chief Executive Officer

Auditors: PricewaterhouseCoopers LLP
Investor Contact: 479-290-4235
Transfer Agents: Computershare, Inc., Providence, RI

UDR INC

Exchange	Symbol	Price	52Wk Range	Yield	P/E
NYS	UDR	$38.52 (12/29/2017)	40.49-34.48	3.22	36.34

*7 Year Price Score 98.90   ***NYSE Composite Index=100**   ***12 Month Price Score 96.90**

Interim Earnings (Per Share)

Qtr.	Mar	Jun	Sep	Dec
2014	0.07	0.12	0.16	0.25
2015	0.28	0.33	0.05	0.63
2016	0.04	0.06	0.10	0.88
2017	0.09	0.03	0.06	...

Interim Dividends (Per Share)

Amt	Decl	Ex	Rec	Pay
0.31Q	03/23/2017	04/06/2017	04/10/2017	05/01/2017
0.31Q	06/22/2017	07/06/2017	07/10/2017	07/31/2017
0.31Q	09/21/2017	10/06/2017	10/10/2017	10/31/2017
0.31Q	12/14/2017	01/09/2018	01/10/2018	01/31/2018

Indicated Div: $1.24

Valuation Analysis / Institutional Holding

Valuation Analysis		Institutional Holding	
Forecast EPS	$0.27 (01/18/2018)	No of Institutions	502
Market Cap	$10.3 Billion	Shares	349,226,816
Book Value	$2.8 Billion	% Held	N/A
Price/Book	3.62		
Price/Sales	10.46		

TRADING VOLUME (thousand shares)

Business Summary: REITs (MIC: 5.3.1 SIC: 6798 NAIC: 525930)

UDR is a real estate investment trust that owns, operates, acquires, renovates, develops, redevelops, and manages multifamily apartment communities generally located in markets located throughout the U.S. Co. reports in two segments: Same-Store Communities and Non-Mature Communities/Other. As of Dec 31 2016, Co.'s consolidated real estate portfolio included 127 communities located in 18 markets, with a total of 39,454 completed apartment homes, which are held through its subsidiaries. In addition, Co. had an ownership interest in 27 communities containing 6,849 apartment homes through unconsolidated joint ventures or partnerships as of Dec 31 2017.

Recent Developments:
For the quarter ended Sep 30 2017, income from continuing operations decreased 40.4% to US$17.6 million from US$29.5 million in the year-earlier quarter. Net income decreased 40.4% to US$17.6 million from US$29.5 million in the year-earlier quarter. Revenues were US$251.1 million, up 3.2% from US$243.3 million the year before. Revenues from property income rose 3.3% to US$248.3 million from US$240.3 million in the corresponding quarter a year earlier.

Prospects:
Our evaluation of UDR Inc. as of Jan. 14, 2018 is the result of our systematic analysis on three basic characteristics: earnings strength, relative valuation, and recent stock price movement. The company has managed to produce a neutral trend in earnings per share over the past 5 quarters. Because the company lacks sufficient analyst estimate data, we place greater weight on the historical EPS trend as the measure of earnings strength. Based on operating earnings yield, the company is overvalued when compared to all of the companies in our coverage universe. Share price changes over the past year indicates that UDR will perform very well over the near term.

Financial Data
(US$ in Thousands)

	9 Mos	6 Mos	3 Mos	12/31/2016	12/31/2015	12/31/2014	12/31/2013	12/31/2012
Earnings Per Share	1.06	1.10	1.13	1.08	1.29	0.59	0.16	0.85
Cash Flow Per Share	2.03	2.06	2.04	2.02	1.67	1.56	1.36	1.32
Tang Book Value Per Share	10.46	10.64	11.18	11.40	10.90	10.54	11.03	11.78
Dividends Per Share	1.210	1.195	1.180	1.163	1.093	1.015	0.925	0.875
Dividend Payout %	114.15	108.64	104.42	107.64	84.69	172.03	578.13	102.94
Income Statement								
Total Revenue	742,911	491,820	243,841	959,861	894,638	818,046	758,926	729,363
EBITDA	472,692	315,205	155,529	613,658	558,885	490,693	465,151	472,016
Depn & Amortn	335,485	223,490	110,019	439,036	399,294	363,929	348,231	367,404
Income Before Taxes	44,130	28,252	15,398	53,521	39,267	8,168	(4,544)	(34,457)
Income Taxes	825	698	332	(3,774)	(3,886)	(15,098)	(7,299)	...
Net Income	52,314	36,124	25,967	292,718	340,383	154,334	44,812	212,177
Average Shares	269,062	268,859	268,688	267,311	263,752	253,445	249,969	238,851
Balance Sheet								
Current Assets	22,201	21,013	22,217	22,106	27,540	37,564	53,045	35,676
Total Assets	7,760,705	7,767,934	7,735,911	7,679,584	7,663,844	6,846,534	6,807,722	6,888,509
Current Liabilities	285,611	267,021	253,930	271,654	246,002	244,999	253,918	261,926
Long-Term Obligations	3,679,011	3,634,648	3,537,292	3,401,478	3,570,795	3,583,105	3,523,703	3,409,333
Total Liabilities	4,915,682	4,875,319	4,699,746	4,586,474	4,764,089	4,111,437	3,996,074	3,895,593
Stockholders' Equity	2,845,023	2,892,615	3,036,165	3,093,110	2,899,755	2,735,097	2,811,648	2,992,916
Shares Outstanding	267,599	267,557	267,398	267,259	261,844	255,114	250,749	250,139
Statistical Record								
Return on Assets %	3.76	3.91	4.02	3.81	4.69	2.26	0.65	3.11
Return on Equity %	10.05	10.29	10.26	9.74	12.08	5.56	1.54	7.97
EBITDA Margin %	63.63	64.09	63.78	63.93	62.47	59.98	61.29	64.72
Net Margin %	7.04	7.34	10.65	30.50	38.05	18.87	5.90	29.09
Asset Turnover	0.13	0.13	0.13	0.12	0.12	0.12	0.11	0.11
Current Ratio	0.08	0.08	0.09	0.08	0.11	0.15	0.21	0.14
Debt to Equity	1.29	1.26	1.17	1.10	1.23	1.31	1.25	1.14
Price Range	40.49-33.11	40.49-33.11	38.56-33.11	38.56-33.11	37.89-30.82	31.74-23.27	26.82-22.24	27.06-22.51
P/E Ratio	38.20-31.24	36.81-30.10	34.12-29.30	35.70-30.66	29.37-23.89	53.80-39.44	167.63-139.00	31.84-26.48
Average Yield %	3.30	3.31	3.32	3.27	3.24	3.66	3.80	3.47

Address: 1745 Shea Center Drive, Suite 200, Highlands Ranch, CO 80129
Telephone: 720-283-6120

Web Site: www.udrt.com
Officers: Joseph D. Fisher - Senior Vice President, Chief Financial Officer Tracy L. Hofmeister - Vice President, Controller, Interim Principal Accounting Officer

Auditors: Ernst & Young LLP
Investor Contact: 720-348-7762
Transfer Agents: Wells Fargo Shareowner Services, Saint Paul, MN

UGI CORP.

Exchange	Symbol	Price	52Wk Range	Yield	P/E	Div Achiever
NYS	UGI	$46.95 (12/29/2017)	51.68-45.31	2.13	19.09	29 Years

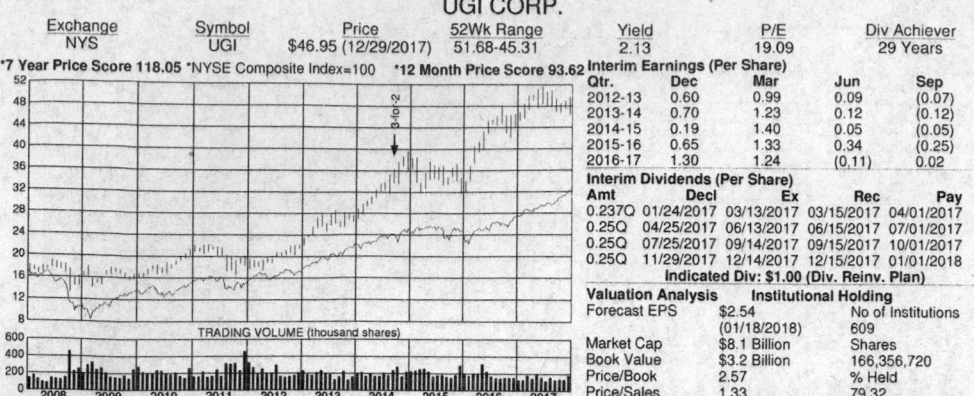

*7 Year Price Score 118.05 *NYSE Composite Index=100 *12 Month Price Score 93.62

Interim Earnings (Per Share)

Qtr.	Dec	Mar	Jun	Sep
2012-13	0.60	0.99	0.09	(0.07)
2013-14	0.70	1.23	0.12	(0.12)
2014-15	0.19	1.40	0.05	(0.05)
2015-16	0.65	1.33	0.34	(0.25)
2016-17	1.30	1.24	(0.11)	0.02

Interim Dividends (Per Share)

Amt	Decl	Ex	Rec	Pay
0.237Q	01/24/2017	03/13/2017	03/15/2017	04/01/2017
0.25Q	04/25/2017	06/13/2017	06/15/2017	07/01/2017
0.25Q	07/25/2017	09/14/2017	09/15/2017	10/01/2017
0.25Q	11/29/2017	12/14/2017	12/15/2017	01/01/2018

Indicated Div: $1.00 (Div. Reinv. Plan)

Valuation Analysis   **Institutional Holding**

Forecast EPS	$2.54	No of Institutions
	(01/18/2018)	609
Market Cap	$8.1 Billion	Shares
Book Value	$3.2 Billion	166,356,720
Price/Book	2.57	% Held
Price/Sales	1.33	79.32

Business Summary: Gas Utilities (MIC: 3.3.1 SIC: 4932 NAIC: 221210)

UGI is a holding company that, through its subsidiaries and affiliates, distributes, stores, transports and markets energy products and related services. In the U.S., Co. is the general partner and own limited partner interests in a retail propane marketing and distribution business; own and operate natural gas and electric distribution utilities; own all or a portion of electricity generation facilities; and own and operate an energy marketing, midstream infrastructure, storage, natural gas gathering, natural gas production and energy services business. Internationally, Co. markets and distributes propane and other liquefied petroleum gases in Europe.

Recent Developments: For the year ended Sep 30 2017, net income increased 7.2% to US$523.8 million from US$488.8 million in the prior year. Revenues were US$6.12 billion, up 7.7% from US$5.69 billion the year before. Operating income was US$1.00 billion versus US$988.0 million in the prior year, an increase of 1.6%. Direct operating expenses rose 16.3% to US$2.85 billion from US$2.45 billion in the comparable period the year before. Indirect operating expenses increased 0.9% to US$2.26 billion from US$2.24 billion in the equivalent prior-year period.

Prospects: Our evaluation of UGI Corp. as of Jan. 14, 2018 is the result of our systematic analysis on three basic characteristics: earnings strength, relative valuation, and recent stock price movement. The company has managed to produce a neutral trend in earnings per share over the past 5 quarters and while recent estimates for the company have been raised by analysts, UGI has posted better than expected results. Based on operating earnings yield, the company is undervalued when compared to all of the companies in our coverage universe. Share price changes over the past year indicates that UGI will perform well over the near term.

Financial Data

(US$ in Thousands)	09/30/2017	09/30/2016	09/30/2015	09/30/2014	09/30/2013	09/30/2012	09/30/2011	09/30/2010
Earnings Per Share	2.46	2.08	1.60	1.92	1.61	1.17	1.37	1.57
Cash Flow Per Share	5.55	5.58	6.72	5.82	4.69	4.18	3.31	3.64
Tang Book Value Per Share	N.M.	N.M.	N.M.	N.M.	N.M.	N.M.	1.60	0.67
Dividends Per Share	0.975	0.930	0.890	0.791	0.737	0.707	0.680	0.600
Dividend Payout %	39.63	44.71	55.63	41.19	45.85	60.23	49.52	38.14
Income Statement								
Total Revenue	6,120,700	5,685,700	6,691,100	8,277,300	7,194,700	6,519,200	6,091,300	5,591,400
EBITDA	1,276,200	1,277,500	1,148,500	1,307,700	1,130,300	769,800	776,800	843,900
Depn & Amortn	357,300	338,600	313,200	305,700	301,400	264,200	201,200	187,600
Income Before Taxes	697,100	710,200	594,200	767,900	590,800	286,500	439,900	525,400
Income Taxes	177,600	221,200	179,000	235,200	162,800	99,600	130,800	167,600
Net Income	436,600	364,700	281,000	337,200	278,100	199,400	232,900	261,000
Average Shares	177,159	175,572	175,667	175,231	173,281	170,148	169,416	165,766
Balance Sheet								
Current Assets	1,697,500	1,423,800	1,459,800	1,663,000	1,627,300	1,504,500	1,306,100	1,220,100
Total Assets	11,582,200	10,847,200	10,546,600	10,093,000	10,008,800	9,709,700	6,663,300	6,374,300
Current Liabilities	1,690,100	1,442,000	1,678,900	1,430,900	1,424,900	1,487,000	1,077,900	1,674,700
Long-Term Obligations	3,994,600	3,766,000	3,441,800	3,433,600	3,542,200	3,347,600	2,110,300	1,432,200
Total Liabilities	8,418,900	7,996,300	7,854,600	7,433,900	7,516,300	7,476,600	4,685,600	4,549,800
Stockholders' Equity	3,163,300	2,850,900	2,692,000	2,659,100	2,492,500	2,233,100	1,977,700	1,824,500
Shares Outstanding	173,143	172,960	172,388	172,273	171,643	168,930	167,754	165,560
Statistical Record								
Return on Assets %	3.89	3.40	2.72	3.35	2.82	2.43	3.57	4.20
Return on Equity %	14.52	13.12	10.50	13.09	11.77	9.45	12.25	15.28
EBITDA Margin %	20.85	22.47	17.16	15.80	15.71	11.81	12.75	15.09
Net Margin %	7.13	6.41	4.20	4.07	3.87	3.06	3.82	4.67
Asset Turnover	0.55	0.53	0.65	0.82	0.73	0.79	0.93	0.90
Current Ratio	1.00	0.99	0.87	1.16	1.14	1.01	1.21	0.73
Debt to Equity	1.26	1.32	1.28	1.29	1.42	1.50	1.07	0.78
Price Range	51.68-42.07	48.05-31.67	39.60-31.78	36.33-25.50	28.69-20.33	21.17-16.59	22.20-17.29	19.19-15.57
P/E Ratio	21.01-17.10	23.10-15.23	24.75-19.86	18.92-13.28	17.82-12.63	18.09-14.18	16.20-12.62	12.23-9.92
Average Yield %	2.04	2.34	2.52	2.61	2.99	3.68	3.30	3.48

Address: 460 North Gulph Road, King of Prussia, PA 19406
Telephone: 610-337-1000

Web Site: www.ugicorp.com
Officers: Marvin O. Schlanger - Chairman John L. Walsh - President, Chief Executive Officer, Chief Operating Officer

Auditors: Ernst & Young LLP
Investor Contact: 610-337-1000
Transfer Agents: ComputerShare Investor Services, Providence, RI

UNDER ARMOUR INC

Exchange	Symbol	Price	52Wk Range	Yield	P/E
NYS	UAA	$13.32 (12/29/2017)	27.32-10.59	N/A	41.63

*7 Year Price Score N/A   ***NYSE Composite Index=100**   ***12 Month Price Score 66.50**

Interim Earnings (Per Share)

Qtr.	Mar	Jun	Sep	Dec
2014	0.03	0.04	0.20	0.20
2015	0.03	0.04	0.23	0.23
2016	0.04	(0.12)	0.29	0.24
2017	(0.01)	(0.03)	0.12	...

Interim Dividends (Per Share)

No Dividends Paid

Valuation Analysis   Institutional Holding

Forecast EPS	$0.19	No of Institutions
	(01/18/2018)	644
Market Cap	$5.9 Billion	Shares
Book Value	$2.1 Billion	153,908,320
Price/Book	2.80	% Held
Price/Sales	1.20	135.23

TRADING VOLUME (thousand shares)

Business Summary: Apparel, Footwear & Accessories (MIC: 1.4.2 SIC: 5136 NAIC: 448110)

Under Armour is engaged in the development, marketing and distribution of apparel, footwear and accessories for men, women and youth. Co.'s apparel is provided in a range of styles and fits. Co. markets its apparel for consumers to choose HEATGEAR® when it is hot, COLDGEAR® when it is cold and ALLSEASONGEAR® between the extremes. Co.'s footwear offerings include frunning, basketball, cleated, slides and performance training, and outdoor footwear. Co.'s accessories primarily include the sale of gloves, bags and headwear. Co. also has agreements with its licensees to develop Under Armour apparel and accessories.

Recent Developments: For the quarter ended Sep 30 2017, net income decreased 57.7% to US$54.2 million from US$128.2 million in the year-earlier quarter. Revenues were US$1.41 billion, down 4.5% from US$1.47 billion the year before. Operating income was US$62.2 million versus US$199.3 million in the prior-year quarter, a decrease of 68.8%. Direct operating expenses declined 1.6% to US$760.3 million from US$772.9 million in the comparable period the year before. Indirect operating expenses increased 16.8% to US$583.2 million from US$499.3 million in the equivalent prior-year period.

Prospects: Our evaluation of Under Armour Inc. as of Jan. 14, 2018 is the result of our systematic analysis on three basic characteristics: earnings strength, relative valuation, and recent stock price movement. The company has suffered a very negative trend in earnings per share over the past 5 quarters and while recent estimates for the company have been mixed, UAA has posted better than expected results. Based on operating earnings yield, the company is overvalued when compared to all of the companies in our coverage universe. Share price changes over the past year indicates that UAA will perform very poorly over the near term.

Financial Data

(US$ in Thousands)	9 Mos	6 Mos	3 Mos	12/31/2016	12/31/2015	12/31/2014	12/31/2013	12/31/2012
Earnings Per Share	0.32	0.49	0.40	0.45	0.53	0.47	0.38	0.30
Cash Flow Per Share	1.68	1.78	1.00	0.70	(0.10)	0.51	0.28	0.48
Tang Book Value Per Share	3.38	3.14	3.15	3.20	2.33	2.81	2.14	1.94
Income Statement								
Total Revenue	3,611,192	2,205,576	1,117,331	4,825,335	3,963,313	3,084,370	2,332,051	1,834,921
EBITDA	63,738	2,565	10,169	545,416	488,413	411,145	312,226	248,422
Depn & Amortn	190	127	63	130,700	87,100	63,600	48,300	39,800
Income Before Taxes	38,311	(13,224)	2,286	388,282	386,685	342,210	260,993	203,439
Income Taxes	(1,349)	1,357	4,558	131,303	154,112	134,168	98,663	74,661
Net Income	39,660	(14,581)	(2,272)	256,979	232,573	208,042	162,330	128,778
Average Shares	222,848	219,168	439,360	444,848	441,736	438,760	431,916	425,520
Balance Sheet								
Current Assets	2,456,842	2,166,470	1,906,028	1,965,153	1,498,763	1,549,399	1,128,811	903,598
Total Assets	4,130,365	3,894,244	3,577,160	3,644,331	2,868,900	2,095,083	1,577,741	1,157,083
Current Liabilities	1,100,426	936,539	627,539	685,816	478,810	421,627	426,630	252,228
Long-Term Obligations	771,382	777,717	784,052	790,388	627,000	255,250	47,951	52,757
Total Liabilities	2,029,669	1,870,473	1,557,127	1,613,431	1,200,678	744,783	524,387	340,161
Stockholders' Equity	2,100,696	2,023,771	2,020,033	2,030,900	1,668,222	1,350,300	1,053,354	816,922
Shares Outstanding	441,629	440,922	440,266	438,438	432,192	427,791	423,257	419,044
Statistical Record								
Return on Assets %	3.66	5.92	6.93	7.87	9.37	11.33	11.87	12.37
Return on Equity %	7.10	11.43	12.52	13.86	15.41	17.31	17.36	17.67
EBITDA Margin %	1.77	0.12	0.91	11.30	12.32	13.33	13.39	13.54
Net Margin %	1.10	N.M.	N.M.	5.33	5.87	6.75	6.96	7.02
Asset Turnover	1.26	1.36	1.44	1.48	1.60	1.68	1.71	1.76
Current Ratio	2.23	2.31	3.04	2.87	3.13	3.67	2.65	3.58
Debt to Equity	0.37	0.38	0.39	0.39	0.38	0.19	0.05	0.06
Price Range	34.05-15.02	39.28-17.44	45.73-17.44	45.73-23.75	...	...	...	...
P/E Ratio	106.41-46.94	80.16-35.59	114.32-43.60	101.62-52.78	...	...	...	...

Address: 1020 Hull Street, Baltimore, MD 21230
Telephone: 410-454-6428

Web Site: www.underarmour.com
Officers: Kevin A. Plank - Chairman, President, Chief Executive Officer Patrik Frisk - President, Chief Operating Officer

Auditors: PricewaterhouseCoopers LLP
Transfer Agents: American Stock Transfer & Trust Company, New York, NY

UNION PACIFIC CORP

Exchange	Symbol	Price	52Wk Range	Yield	P/E	Div Achiever
NYS	UNP	$134.10 (12/29/2017)	136.32-101.40	1.98	23.69	10 Years

*7 Year Price Score 104.52 *NYSE Composite Index=100 *12 Month Price Score 106.62

Interim Earnings (Per Share)

Qtr.	Mar	Jun	Sep	Dec
2014	1.19	1.43	1.53	1.61
2015	1.30	1.38	1.50	1.31
2016	1.16	1.17	1.36	1.39
2017	1.32	1.45	1.50	...

Interim Dividends (Per Share)

Amt	Decl	Ex	Rec	Pay
0.605Q	02/02/2017	02/24/2017	02/28/2017	03/31/2017
0.605Q	05/11/2017	05/26/2017	05/31/2017	06/30/2017
0.605Q	07/27/2017	08/29/2017	08/31/2017	09/29/2017
0.665Q	11/16/2017	11/29/2017	11/30/2017	12/28/2017

Indicated Div: $2.66

Valuation Analysis — Institutional Holding

Forecast EPS	$5.81	No of Institutions
	(01/18/2018)	1989
Market Cap	$105.9 Billion	Shares
Book Value	$19.2 Billion	719,648,448
Price/Book	5.53	% Held
Price/Sales	5.05	74.39

TRADING VOLUME (thousand shares)

Business Summary: Rail (MIC: 7.4.3 SIC: 4011 NAIC: 482111)

Union Pacific, through its operating subsidiary, Union Pacific Railroad Company, is a Class I railroad operating in the U.S. As of Dec 31 2016, Co.'s network included 32,070 route miles, linking Pacific Coast and Gulf Coast ports with the Midwest and eastern U.S. gateways and providing several corridors to key Mexican gateways. Co. serves the western two-thirds of the country and maintains coordinated schedules with other rail carriers to move freight to and from the Atlantic Coast, the Pacific Coast, the Southeast, the Southwest, Canada, and Mexico. Co.'s six commodity groups includes agricultural, automotive, chemicals, coal, industrial products and intermodal.

Recent Developments: For the quarter ended Sep 30 2017, net income increased 5.6% to US$1.19 billion from US$1.13 billion in the year-earlier quarter. Revenues were US$5.41 billion, up 4.5% from US$5.17 billion the year before. Operating income was US$2.01 billion versus US$1.96 billion in the prior-year quarter, an increase of 2.7%. Direct operating expenses rose 8.1% to US$1.34 billion from US$1.24 billion in the comparable period the year before. Indirect operating expenses increased 4.2% to US$2.06 billion from US$1.97 billion in the equivalent prior-year period.

Prospects: Our evaluation of Union Pacific Corp. as of Jan. 14, 2018 is the result of our systematic analysis on three basic characteristics: earnings strength, relative valuation, and recent stock price movement. The company has managed to produce a neutral trend in earnings per share over the past 5 quarters and while recent estimates for the company have been raised by analysts, UNP has posted better than expected results. Based on operating earnings yield, the company is about fairly valued when compared to all of the companies in our coverage universe. Share price changes over the past year indicates that UNP will perform poorly over the near term.

Financial Data

(US$ in Thousands)	9 Mos	6 Mos	3 Mos	12/31/2016	12/31/2015	12/31/2014	12/31/2013	12/31/2012
Earnings Per Share	5.66	5.52	5.24	5.07	5.49	5.75	4.71	4.13
Cash Flow Per Share	9.38	9.28	8.92	9.02	8.48	8.23	7.36	6.49
Tang Book Value Per Share	24.25	24.47	24.37	24.43	24.38	23.99	23.27	21.17
Dividends Per Share	2.420	2.365	2.310	2.255	2.200	1.910	1.480	1.245
Dividend Payout %	42.76	42.84	44.08	44.48	40.07	33.22	31.42	30.11
Income Statement								
Total Revenue	15,790,000	10,382,000	5,132,000	19,941,000	21,813,000	23,988,000	21,963,000	20,926,000
EBITDA	7,634,000	4,947,000	2,378,000	9,491,000	10,285,000	10,804,000	9,347,000	8,610,000
Depn & Amortn	1,573,000	1,045,000	520,000	2,038,000	2,012,000	1,904,000	1,777,000	1,760,000
Income Before Taxes	5,540,000	3,557,000	1,688,000	6,766,000	7,656,000	8,343,000	7,048,000	6,318,000
Income Taxes	2,106,000	1,317,000	616,000	2,533,000	2,884,000	3,163,000	2,660,000	2,375,000
Net Income	3,434,000	2,240,000	1,072,000	4,233,000	4,772,000	5,180,000	4,388,000	3,943,000
Average Shares	797,600	807,200	814,800	835,400	869,400	901,100	931,600	953,000
Balance Sheet								
Current Assets	4,449,000	3,869,000	3,588,000	3,596,000	4,130,000	4,679,000	3,990,000	3,614,000
Total Assets	57,397,000	56,478,000	55,900,000	55,718,000	54,600,000	52,716,000	49,731,000	47,153,000
Current Liabilities	3,831,000	3,406,000	3,848,000	3,640,000	3,206,000	3,765,000	3,791,000	3,119,000
Long-Term Obligations	15,930,000	15,229,000	14,310,000	14,249,000	13,607,000	11,018,000	8,872,000	8,801,000
Total Liabilities	38,246,000	36,863,000	36,177,000	35,786,000	33,898,000	31,527,000	28,506,000	27,276,000
Stockholders' Equity	19,151,000	19,615,000	19,723,000	19,932,000	20,702,000	21,189,000	21,225,000	19,877,000
Shares Outstanding	789,834	801,484	809,169	815,824	849,211	883,366	912,001	938,930
Statistical Record								
Return on Assets %	8.05	8.05	7.75	7.65	8.89	10.11	9.06	8.53
Return on Equity %	23.22	22.55	21.52	20.78	22.78	24.43	21.35	20.45
EBITDA Margin %	48.35	47.65	46.34	47.60	47.15	45.04	42.56	41.14
Net Margin %	21.75	21.58	20.89	21.23	21.88	21.59	19.98	18.84
Asset Turnover	0.37	0.37	0.36	0.36	0.41	0.47	0.45	0.45
Current Ratio	1.16	1.14	0.93	0.99	1.29	1.24	1.05	1.16
Debt to Equity	0.83	0.78	0.73	0.71	0.66	0.52	0.42	0.44
Price Range	116.64-87.89	113.53-87.16	110.42-78.00	106.33-68.79	123.83-75.43	123.31-82.58	84.00-62.86	64.22-52.49
P/E Ratio	20.61-15.53	20.57-15.79	21.07-14.89	20.97-13.57	22.56-13.74	21.45-14.36	17.83-13.35	15.55-12.71
Average Yield %	2.30	2.32	2.42	2.55	2.21	1.89	1.96	2.13

Address: 1400 Douglas Street, Omaha, NE 68179 Telephone: 402-544-5000	Web Site: www.up.com Officers: Lance M. Fritz - Chairman, President, Chief Executive Officer Sherrye L. Hutcherson - Senior Vice President, Chief Human Resources Officer	Auditors: Deloitte & Touche LLP Investor Contact: 187-754-77261 Transfer Agents: Computershare Investor Services, LLC, Providence, RI

UNITED CONTINENTAL HOLDINGS INC

Exchange	Symbol	Price	52Wk Range	Yield	P/E
NYS	UAL	$67.40 (12/29/2017)	82.03-57.20	N/A	10.58

*7 Year Price Score 124.48 *NYSE Composite Index=100   *12 Month Price Score 85.41

TRADING VOLUME (thousand shares)

Interim Earnings (Per Share)

Qtr.	Mar	Jun	Sep	Dec
2014	(1.66)	2.01	2.37	0.09
2015	1.32	3.14	12.82	2.32
2016	0.88	1.78	3.01	1.28
2017	0.31	2.66	2.12	...

Interim Dividends (Per Share)

No Dividends Paid

Valuation Analysis   Institutional Holding

Forecast EPS	$7.43	No of Institutions
	(01/26/2018)	790
Market Cap	$20.0 Billion	Shares
Book Value	$9.0 Billion	340,591,552
Price/Book	2.23	% Held
Price/Sales	0.53	N/A

Business Summary: Airlines/Air Freight (MIC: 7.4.4 SIC: 4512 NAIC: 481111)

United Continental Holdings is a holding company and its principal, wholly-owned subsidiary is United Airlines, Inc. (United). Co. is engaged in the transportation of people and cargo through its mainline and its regional operations. As of Dec 31 2016, Co., through United and its regional carriers, operated more than 4,500 flights a day to 339 airports across five continents from its hubs. Co. also has contractual relationships with various regional carriers to provide regional jet and turboprop service branded as United Express. Including aircraft operated by United's regional carriers, United's fleet consisted of 1,231 aircraft as of Dec 31 2016.

Recent Developments: For the quarter ended Sep 30 2017, net income decreased 34.0% to US$637.0 million from US$965.0 million in the year-earlier quarter. Revenues were US$9.88 billion, down 0.4% from US$9.91 billion the year before. Operating income was US$1.09 billion versus US$1.62 billion in the prior-year quarter, a decrease of 32.8%. Direct operating expenses rose 6.5% to US$3.56 billion from US$3.34 billion in the comparable period the year before. Indirect operating expenses increased 5.7% to US$5.23 billion from US$4.95 billion in the equivalent prior-year period.

Prospects: Our evaluation of United Continental Holdings Inc. as of Jan. 21, 2018 is the result of our systematic analysis on three basic characteristics: earnings strength, relative valuation, and recent stock price movement. The company has generated a negative trend in earnings per share over the past 5 quarters and while recent estimates for the company have been raised by analysts, UAL has posted better than expected results. Based on operating earnings yield, the company is undervalued when compared to all of the companies in our coverage universe. Share price changes over the past year indicates that UAL will perform very poorly over the near term.

Financial Data
(US$ in Thousands)	9 Mos	6 Mos	3 Mos	12/31/2016	12/31/2015	12/31/2014	12/31/2013	12/31/2012
Earnings Per Share	6.37	7.26	6.38	6.85	19.47	2.93	1.53	(2.18)
Cash Flow Per Share	11.15	12.72	15.59	16.75	15.94	7.10	4.15	2.82
Tang Book Value Per Share	3.00	2.42	1.01	1.60	0.84	N.M.	N.M.	N.M.
Income Statement								
Total Revenue	28,298,000	18,420,000	8,420,000	36,556,000	37,864,000	38,901,000	38,279,000	37,152,000
EBITDA	4,376,000	2,713,000	779,000	4,427,000	4,907,000	1,870,000	1,324,000	132,000
Depn & Amortn	1,610,000	1,054,000	518,000	108,000	93,000	81,000	72,000	81,000
Income Before Taxes	2,399,000	1,419,000	145,000	3,819,000	4,219,000	1,128,000	539,000	(724,000)
Income Taxes	848,000	505,000	49,000	1,556,000	(3,121,000)	(4,000)	(32,000)	(1,000)
Net Income	1,551,000	914,000	96,000	2,263,000	7,340,000	1,132,000	571,000	(723,000)
Average Shares	300,600	307,700	314,600	330,300	377,000	390,000	390,000	331,000
Balance Sheet								
Current Assets	7,877,000	8,248,000	7,724,000	7,309,000	7,828,000	8,138,000	8,702,000	10,049,000
Total Assets	42,565,000	42,307,000	41,445,000	40,140,000	40,861,000	37,353,000	36,812,000	37,628,000
Current Liabilities	13,087,000	13,596,000	12,662,000	12,286,000	12,414,000	12,508,000	12,107,000	12,818,000
Long-Term Obligations	12,302,000	11,612,000	12,014,000	10,740,000	10,400,000	10,692,000	10,924,000	11,232,000
Total Liabilities	33,595,000	33,453,000	32,996,000	31,481,000	31,895,000	34,957,000	33,828,000	37,147,000
Stockholders' Equity	8,970,000	8,854,000	8,449,000	8,659,000	8,966,000	2,396,000	2,984,000	481,000
Shares Outstanding	296,252	305,010	311,130	314,612	364,609	374,525	362,283	332,472
Statistical Record								
Return on Assets %	4.70	5.50	5.00	5.57	18.77	3.05	1.53	N.M.
Return on Equity %	22.38	27.36	25.12	25.61	129.20	42.08	32.96	N.M.
EBITDA Margin %	15.46	14.73	9.25	12.11	12.96	4.81	3.46	0.36
Net Margin %	5.48	4.96	1.14	6.19	19.39	2.91	1.49	N.M.
Asset Turnover	0.90	0.90	0.90	0.90	0.97	1.05	1.03	0.98
Current Ratio	0.60	0.61	0.61	0.59	0.63	0.65	0.72	0.78
Debt to Equity	1.37	1.31	1.42	1.24	1.16	4.46	3.66	23.35
Price Range	82.03-52.47	82.03-39.31	76.05-37.75	76.05-37.75	73.62-50.78	66.89-37.73	39.83-23.38	25.17-17.48
P/E Ratio	12.88-8.24	11.30-5.41	11.92-5.92	11.10-5.51	3.78-2.61	22.83-12.88	26.03-15.28	...

Address: 233 South Wacker Drive, Chicago, IL 60606 Telephone: 872-825-4000	Web Site: www.unitedcontinentalholdings.com Officers: J. Scott Kirby - President Oscar Munoz - Chief Executive Officer, President, President (frmr-frmr), Chief Executive Officer (frmr)	Auditors: Ernst & Young LLP Investor Contact: 312-997-8610 Transfer Agents: ComputerShare Investor Services, Chicago, IL

UNITED PARCEL SERVICE INC

Exchange	Symbol	Price	52Wk Range	Yield	P/E
NYS	UPS	$119.15 (12/29/2017)	123.72-102.87	2.79	29.13

*7 Year Price Score 93.72   *NYSE Composite Index=100   ***12 Month Price Score 99.89**

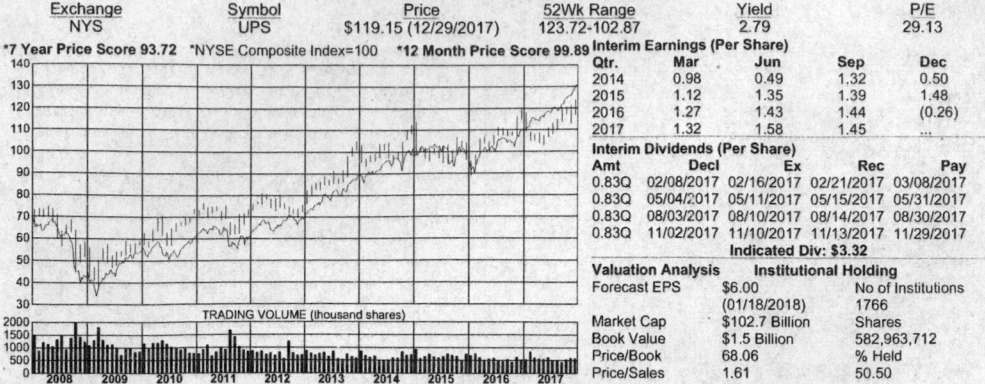

Interim Earnings (Per Share)

Qtr.	Mar	Jun	Sep	Dec
2014	0.98	0.49	1.32	0.50
2015	1.12	1.35	1.39	1.48
2016	1.27	1.43	1.44	(0.26)
2017	1.32	1.58	1.45	...

Interim Dividends (Per Share)

Amt	Decl	Ex	Rec	Pay
0.83Q	02/08/2017	02/16/2017	02/21/2017	03/08/2017
0.83Q	05/04/2017	05/11/2017	05/15/2017	05/31/2017
0.83Q	08/03/2017	08/10/2017	08/14/2017	08/30/2017
0.83Q	11/02/2017	11/10/2017	11/13/2017	11/29/2017

Indicated Div: $3.32

Valuation Analysis — **Institutional Holding**

Forecast EPS	$6.00	No of Institutions
	(01/18/2018)	1766
Market Cap	$102.7 Billion	Shares
Book Value	$1.5 Billion	582,963,712
Price/Book	68.06	% Held
Price/Sales	1.61	50.50

Business Summary: Airlines/Air Freight (MIC: 7.4.4 SIC: 4215 NAIC: 492110)

United Parcel Service focuses its operations in the field of transportation services, primarily domestic and international letter and package delivery. Co. reports its operations in three segments: U.S. Domestic Package operations, which include the time-definite delivery of letters, documents and packages throughout the U.S.; International Package operations, which include shipments wholly outside the U.S., as well as shipments with either origin or destination outside the U.S.; and Supply Chain & Freight operations, which includes Co.'s Forwarding, Logistics, Coyote, Marken, UPS Mail Innovations, UPS Freight and other aggregated business units.

Recent Developments: For the quarter ended Sep 30 2017, net income decreased 0.5% to US$1.26 billion from US$1.27 billion in the year-earlier quarter. Revenues were US$15.98 billion, up 7.0% from US$14.93 billion the year before. Operating income was US$2.04 billion versus US$2.03 billion in the prior-year quarter, an increase of 0.0%. Direct operating expenses rose 17.4% to US$3.69 billion from US$3.14 billion in the comparable period the year before. Indirect operating expenses increased 5.1% to US$10.26 billion from US$9.76 billion in the equivalent prior-year period.

Prospects: Our evaluation of United Parcel Service Inc. as of Jan. 14, 2018 is the result of our systematic analysis on three basic characteristics: earnings strength, relative valuation, and recent stock price movement. The company has managed to produce a neutral trend in earnings per share over the past 5 quarters and while recent estimates for the company have been mixed, UPS has posted better than expected results. Based on operating earnings yield, the company is undervalued when compared to all of the companies in our coverage universe. Share price changes over the past year indicates that UPS will perform poorly over the near term.

Financial Data
(US$ in Millions)

	9 Mos	6 Mos	3 Mos	12/31/2016	12/31/2015	12/31/2014	12/31/2013	12/31/2012
Earnings Per Share	4.09	4.08	3.93	3.87	5.35	3.28	4.61	0.83
Cash Flow Per Share	6.40	5.05	4.62	7.31	8.25	6.25	7.77	7.50
Tang Book Value Per Share	N.M.	N.M.	N.M.	N.M.	N.M.	N.M.	3.80	1.97
Dividends Per Share	3.270	3.220	3.170	3.120	2.920	2.680	2.480	2.280
Dividend Payout %	79.95	78.92	80.66	80.62	54.58	81.71	53.80	274.70
Income Statement								
Total Revenue	47,043	31,065	15,315	60,906	58,363	58,232	55,438	54,127
EBITDA	7,772	5,145	2,353	7,741	9,767	6,913	8,921	3,225
Depn & Amortn	1,688	1,116	554	2,224	2,084	1,923	1,867	1,858
Income Before Taxes	5,760	3,816	1,697	5,136	7,342	4,637	6,674	974
Income Taxes	1,954	1,274	539	1,705	2,498	1,605	2,302	167
Net Income	3,806	2,542	1,158	3,431	4,844	3,032	4,372	807
Average Shares	874	876	879	887	906	924	948	969
Balance Sheet								
Current Assets	12,910	12,394	11,494	13,849	13,208	11,808	13,387	15,591
Total Assets	41,356	39,724	38,380	40,377	38,311	35,471	36,212	38,863
Current Liabilities	12,167	11,082	11,406	11,730	10,696	8,639	7,131	8,390
Long-Term Obligations	14,355	14,257	12,938	12,394	11,316	9,864	10,824	11,089
Total Liabilities	39,847	38,480	37,845	39,972	35,841	33,330	29,738	34,210
Stockholders' Equity	1,509	1,244	535	405	2,470	2,141	6,474	4,653
Shares Outstanding	862	865	868	868	886	905	923	953
Statistical Record								
Return on Assets %	8.95	9.15	8.92	8.70	13.13	8.46	11.65	2.19
Return on Equity %	167.78	184.65	231.15	238.03	210.11	70.39	78.58	13.77
EBITDA Margin %	16.52	16.56	15.36	12.71	16.73	11.87	16.09	5.96
Net Margin %	8.09	8.18	7.56	5.63	8.30	5.21	7.89	1.49
Asset Turnover	1.61	1.61	1.59	1.54	1.58	1.62	1.48	1.47
Current Ratio	1.06	1.12	1.01	1.18	1.23	1.37	1.88	1.86
Debt to Equity	9.51	11.46	24.18	30.60	4.58	4.61	1.67	2.38
Price Range	120.16-102.87	120.16-102.87	120.16-100.66	120.16-88.70	114.25-94.46	112.45-93.62	105.08-73.73	81.11-70.02
P/E Ratio	29.38-25.15	29.45-25.21	30.58-25.61	31.05-22.92	21.36-17.66	34.28-28.54	22.79-15.99	97.72-84.36
Average Yield %	2.96	2.94	2.91	2.95	2.90	2.66	2.80	3.01

Address: 55 Glenlake Parkway N.E.,	Web Site: www.ups.com	Auditors: Deloitte & Touche LLP
Atlanta, GA 30328	Officers: David P. Abney - Chairman, Chief	Investor Contact: 404-828-6059
Telephone: 404-828-6000	Executive Officer, Senior Vice President, Chief	Transfer Agents: Computershare
	Operating Officer Richard N. Peretz - Senior Vice	Shareowner Services, Pittsburgh, PA
	President, Chief Financial Officer, Treasurer	

UNITED RENTALS INC

Exchange	Symbol	Price	52Wk Range	Yield	P/E
NYS	URI	$171.91 (12/29/2017)	173.33-101.62	N/A	24.42

*7 Year Price Score 138.81 *NYSE Composite Index=100 *12 Month Price Score 117.64

Interim Earnings (Per Share)

Qtr.	Mar	Jun	Sep	Dec
2014	0.56	0.90	1.84	1.86
2015	1.16	0.88	2.25	1.80
2016	1.01	1.52	2.16	1.79
2017	1.27	1.65	2.33	...

Interim Dividends (Per Share)

No Dividends Paid

Valuation Analysis　**Institutional Holding**

Forecast EPS	$10.56	No of Institutions
	(01/19/2018)	N/A
Market Cap	$14.5 Billion	Shares
Book Value	$2.2 Billion	N/A
Price/Book	6.58	% Held
Price/Sales	2.33	N/A

TRADING VOLUME (thousand shares)

Business Summary: Construction Services (MIC: 7.5.4 SIC: 7359 NAIC: 532412)

United Rentals is an equipment rental company and operates throughout the U.S. and Canada. The types of equipment that Co. provides include general construction and industrial equipment, aerial work platforms, trench safety equipment, power and heating, ventilating and air conditioning equipment; pumps; and general tools and light equipment. Co.'s segments are: general rentals, which includes the rental of construction, aerial and industrial equipment, general tools and light equipment, and related services and activities; and trench, power and pump, which includes the rental of specialty construction products and related services.

Recent Developments: For the quarter ended Sep 30 2017, net income increased 6.4% to US$199.0 million from US$187.0 million in the year-earlier quarter. Revenues were US$1.77 billion, up 17.1% from US$1.51 billion the year before. Operating income was US$448.0 million versus US$412.0 million in the prior-year quarter, an increase of 8.7%. Direct operating expenses rose 16.5% to US$993.0 million from US$852.0 million in the comparable period the year before. Indirect operating expenses increased 33.2% to US$325.0 million from US$244.0 million in the equivalent prior-year period.

Prospects: Our evaluation of United Rentals Inc. as of Jan. 21, 2018 is the result of our systematic analysis on three basic characteristics: earnings strength, relative valuation, and recent stock price movement. The company has produced a positive trend in earnings per share over the past 5 quarters and while recent estimates for the company have been raised by analysts, URI has posted better than expected results. Based on operating earnings yield, the company is undervalued when compared to all of the companies in our coverage universe. Share price changes over the past year indicates that URI will perform in line with the market over the near term.

Financial Data (US$ in Thousands)	9 Mos	6 Mos	3 Mos	12/31/2016	12/31/2015	12/31/2014	12/31/2013	12/31/2012
Earnings Per Share	7.04	6.87	6.74	6.45	6.07	5.15	3.64	0.79
Cash Flow Per Share	24.67	24.14	23.35	22.33	20.96	18.47	16.60	8.67
Income Statement								
Total Revenue	4,719,000	2,953,000	1,356,000	5,762,000	5,817,000	5,685,000	4,955,000	4,117,000
EBITDA	1,860,000	1,115,000	505,000	2,410,000	2,506,000	2,326,000	1,935,000	1,303,000
Depn & Amortn	810,000	518,000	250,000	990,000	976,000	921,000	852,000	699,000
Income Before Taxes	712,000	390,000	161,000	909,000	963,000	850,000	605,000	88,000
Income Taxes	263,000	140,000	52,000	343,000	378,000	310,000	218,000	13,000
Net Income	449,000	250,000	109,000	566,000	585,000	540,000	387,000	75,000
Average Shares	85,592	85,408	85,377	87,775	96,379	104,956	106,291	94,848
Balance Sheet								
Current Assets	1,639,000	1,483,000	1,320,000	1,361,000	1,294,000	1,546,000	1,362,000	1,343,000
Total Assets	13,744,000	13,284,000	11,822,000	11,988,000	12,083,000	12,467,000	11,231,000	11,026,000
Current Liabilities	1,773,000	1,744,000	1,317,000	1,184,000	1,233,000	1,478,000	1,286,000	1,351,000
Long-Term Obligations	7,677,000	7,571,000	6,772,000	7,193,000	7,555,000	7,434,000	6,569,000	6,734,000
Total Liabilities	11,533,000	11,336,000	10,069,000	10,340,000	10,607,000	10,669,000	9,383,000	9,452,000
Stockholders' Equity	2,211,000	1,948,000	1,753,000	1,648,000	1,476,000	1,798,000	1,848,000	1,574,000
Shares Outstanding	84,571	84,538	84,507	84,222	91,776	97,877	93,288	92,984
Statistical Record								
Return on Assets %	4.63	4.64	4.94	4.69	4.77	4.56	3.48	0.99
Return on Equity %	32.11	34.20	35.83	36.14	35.74	29.62	22.62	8.92
EBITDA Margin %	39.42	37.76	37.24	41.83	43.08	40.91	39.05	31.65
Net Margin %	9.51	8.47	8.04	9.82	10.06	9.50	7.81	1.82
Asset Turnover	0.48	0.47	0.49	0.48	0.47	0.48	0.45	0.54
Current Ratio	0.92	0.85	1.00	1.15	1.05	1.05	1.06	0.99
Debt to Equity	3.47	3.89	3.86	4.36	5.12	4.13	3.55	4.28
Price Range		138.74-70.92	133.36-63.47	133.36-57.95	109.12-43.34	105.13-59.48	119.02-74.46	77.95-45.52	46.82-27.23
P/E Ratio		19.71-10.07	19.41-9.24	19.79-8.60	16.92-6.72	17.32-9.80	23.11-14.46	21.41-12.51	59.27-34.47

Address: 100 First Stamford Place, Suite 700, Stamford, CT 06902 **Telephone:** 203-622-3131	**Web Site:** www.unitedrentals.com **Officers:** Jenne K. Britell - Chairman Michael J. (Mike) Kneeland - President, Chief Executive Officer	**Auditors:** Ernst & Young LLP **Investor Contact:** 203-618-7318 **Transfer Agents:** American Stock Transfer & Trust Company, New York, NY

731

UNITED STATES STEEL CORP.

Exchange	Symbol	Price	52Wk Range	Yield	P/E
NYS	X	$35.19 (12/29/2017)	41.57-19.17	0.57	51.00

*7 Year Price Score 85.16 *NYSE Composite Index=100 *12 Month Price Score 100.81

Interim Earnings (Per Share)

Qtr.	Mar	Jun	Sep	Dec
2014	0.34	(0.12)	(1.42)	1.88
2015	(0.52)	(1.79)	(1.18)	(7.75)
2016	(2.32)	(0.32)	0.32	(0.59)
2017	(1.03)	1.48	0.83	...

Interim Dividends (Per Share)

Amt	Decl	Ex	Rec	Pay
0.05Q	01/31/2017	02/08/2017	02/10/2017	03/10/2017
0.05Q	04/25/2017	05/08/2017	05/10/2017	06/09/2017
0.05Q	07/25/2017	08/07/2017	08/09/2017	09/08/2017
0.05Q	10/31/2017	11/09/2017	11/10/2017	12/08/2017

Indicated Div: $0.20

Valuation Analysis

		Institutional Holding	
Forecast EPS	$1.76	No of Institutions	
	(01/18/2018)	592	
Market Cap	$6.2 Billion	Shares	
Book Value	$2.8 Billion	138,740,352	
Price/Book	2.19	% Held	
Price/Sales	0.52	77.12	

Business Summary: Non-Precious Metals (MIC: 8.2.2 SIC: 3312 NAIC: 331111)

United States Steel is a steel producer of flat-rolled and tubular products with major production operations in North America and Europe. Co. has three reportable operating segments: Flat-Rolled Products, which includes the production of slabs, strip mill plates, sheets and tin mill products, as well as all iron ore and coke production facilities; U. S. Steel Europe, which produces and sells slabs, sheet, strip mill plate, tin mill products and spiral welded pipe; and Tubular Products, which produces and sells seamless and electric resistance welded (welded) steel casing and tubing, standard and line pipe and mechanical tubing and serve customers in the oil, gas and petrochemical markets.

Recent Developments: For the quarter ended Sep 30 2017, net income increased 188.2% to US$147.0 million from US$51.0 million in the year-earlier quarter. Revenues were US$3.25 billion, up 20.9% from US$2.69 billion the year before. Operating income was US$245.0 million versus US$132.0 million in the prior-year quarter, an increase of 85.6%. Direct operating expenses rose 19.9% to US$2.83 billion from US$2.36 billion in the comparable period the year before. Indirect operating expenses decreased 10.3% to US$174.0 million from US$194.0 million in the equivalent prior-year period.

Prospects: Our evaluation of United States Steel Corp. as of Jan. 14, 2018 is the result of our systematic analysis on three basic characteristics: earnings strength, relative valuation, and recent stock price movement. The company has suffered a very negative trend in earnings per share over the past 5 quarters and while recent estimates for the company have been raised by analysts, X has posted better than expected results. Based on operating earnings yield, the company is undervalued when compared to all of the companies in our coverage universe. Share price changes over the past year indicates that X will perform very poorly over the near term.

Financial Data

(US$ in Millions)	9 Mos	6 Mos	3 Mos	12/31/2016	12/31/2015	12/31/2014	12/31/2013	12/31/2012
Earnings Per Share	0.69	0.18	(1.62)	(2.81)	(11.24)	0.69	(11.56)	(0.86)
Cash Flow Per Share	3.95	3.75	2.75	4.63	2.46	10.28	2.86	7.85
Tang Book Value Per Share	15.08	13.62	11.45	12.08	15.31	24.68	21.24	9.72
Dividends Per Share	0.200	0.200	0.200	0.200	0.200	0.200	0.200	0.200
Dividend Payout %	28.99	111.11	...	...	...	28.99	...	...
Income Statement								
Total Revenue	9,117	5,869	2,725	10,261	11,574	17,507	17,424	19,328
EBITDA	754	452	35	218	(739)	877	(1,325)	730
Depn & Amortn	376	258	137	507	547	627	684	661
Income Before Taxes	181	64	(165)	(514)	(1,497)	28	(2,272)	(138)
Income Taxes	3	3	19	24	183	68	(560)	131
Net Income	228	81	(180)	(440)	(1,642)	102	(1,672)	(124)
Average Shares	176	176	174	156	146	152	144	144
Balance Sheet								
Current Assets	5,001	4,723	4,478	4,356	3,917	6,431	6,078	5,374
Total Assets	9,878	9,580	9,186	9,160	9,190	12,314	13,143	15,217
Current Liabilities	2,652	2,751	2,718	2,331	2,148	3,569	3,245	2,990
Long-Term Obligations	2,896	2,752	2,752	2,981	3,116	3,120	3,616	3,936
Total Liabilities	7,071	7,026	7,013	6,886	6,754	8,515	9,795	11,740
Stockholders' Equity	2,807	2,554	2,173	2,274	2,436	3,799	3,348	3,477
Shares Outstanding	174	174	174	173	146	145	144	144
Statistical Record								
Return on Assets %	1.27	0.29	N.M.	N.M.	N.M.	0.80	N.M.	N.M.
Return on Equity %	4.55	1.21	N.M.	N.M.	N.M.	2.85	N.M.	N.M.
EBITDA Margin %	8.27	7.70	1.28	2.12	N.M.	5.01	N.M.	3.78
Net Margin %	2.50	1.38	N.M.	N.M.	N.M.	0.58	N.M.	N.M.
Asset Turnover	1.22	1.21	1.17	1.12	1.08	1.38	1.23	1.23
Current Ratio	1.89	1.72	1.65	1.87	1.82	1.80	1.87	1.80
Debt to Equity	1.03	1.08	1.27	1.31	1.28	0.82	1.08	1.13
Price Range	41.57-16.42	41.57-15.91	41.57-13.25	37.49-6.67	27.33-7.09	46.00-22.73	30.09-16.18	32.25-17.89
P/E Ratio	60.25-23.80	230.94-88.39	...	...	...	66.67-32.94	...	...
Average Yield %	0.73	0.75	0.81	1.08	1.07	0.66	0.95	0.85

Address: 600 Grant Street, Pittsburgh, PA 15219-2800
Telephone: 412-433-1121
Fax: 412-433-4818

Web Site: www.ussteel.com
Officers: David B. Burritt - President, Chief Executive Officer, Chief Operating Officer, Chief Financial Officer, Executive Vice President Kevin P. Bradley - Executive Vice President, Chief Financial Officer

Auditors: PricewaterhouseCoopers LLP
Investor Contact: 412-433-1121
Transfer Agents: Wells Fargo Bank Shareowner Services, St. Paul, MN

UNITEDHEALTH GROUP INC

Exchange	Symbol	Price	52Wk Range	Yield	P/E
NYS	UNH	$220.46 (12/29/2017)	228.17-157.62	1.36	25.05

*7 Year Price Score 148.36 *NYSE Composite Index=100 *12 Month Price Score 111.68

TRADING VOLUME (thousand shares)

Interim Earnings (Per Share)

Qtr.	Mar	Jun	Sep	Dec
2014	1.10	1.42	1.63	1.55
2015	1.46	1.64	1.65	1.26
2016	1.67	1.81	2.03	1.74
2017	2.23	2.32	2.51	...

Interim Dividends (Per Share)

Amt	Decl	Ex	Rec	Pay
0.625Q	02/09/2017	03/08/2017	03/10/2017	03/21/2017
0.75Q	06/07/2017	06/15/2017	06/19/2017	06/27/2017
0.75Q	08/16/2017	09/07/2017	09/08/2017	09/19/2017
0.75Q	11/08/2017	11/30/2017	12/01/2017	12/12/2017

Indicated Div: $3.00

Valuation Analysis

		Institutional Holding	
Forecast EPS	$12.48 (01/18/2018)	No of Institutions	2015
Market Cap	$213.6 Billion	Shares	1,014,280,128
Book Value	$45.3 Billion	% Held	82.41
Price/Book	4.72		
Price/Sales	1.09		

Business Summary: Life & Health (MIC: 5.2.2 SIC: 6324 NAIC: 524114)

UnitedHealth Group is a health and well-being company. Co. has four reportable segments across its two business platforms, UnitedHealthcare and Optum: UnitedHealthcare, which provides health care benefits to an array of customers and markets through its UnitedHealthcare Employer & Individual, UnitedHealthcare Medicare & Retirement, UnitedHealthcare Community & State and UnitedHealthcare Global; OptumHealth, which serves the physical, emotional and health-related financial needs of individuals; OptumInsight, which provides services, technology and health care expertise to main participants in the health care industry; and OptumRx, which provides pharmacy care services and programs.

Recent Developments: For the quarter ended Sep 30 2017, net income increased 29.5% to US$2.56 billion from US$1.98 billion in the year-earlier quarter. Revenues were US$50.32 billion, up 8.7% from US$46.29 billion the year before. Net premiums earned were US$39.55 billion versus US$36.14 billion in the prior-year quarter, an increase of 9.4%.

Prospects: Our evaluation of UnitedHealth Group Inc. as of Jan. 14, 2018 is the result of our systematic analysis on three basic characteristics: earnings strength, relative valuation, and recent stock price movement. The company has managed to produce a neutral trend in earnings per share over the past 5 quarters and while recent estimates for the company have been mixed, UNH has posted better than expected results. Based on operating earnings yield, the company is about fairly valued when compared to all of the companies in our coverage universe. Share price changes over the past year indicates that UNH will perform well over the near term.

Financial Data
(US$ in Thousands)

	9 Mos	6 Mos	3 Mos	12/31/2016	12/31/2015	12/31/2014	12/31/2013	12/31/2012
Earnings Per Share	8.80	8.32	7.81	7.25	6.01	5.70	5.50	5.28
Cash Flow Per Share	15.25	14.96	14.60	10.26	10.22	8.28	6.95	6.95
Dividends Per Share	2.750	2.625	2.500	2.375	1.875	1.405	1.053	0.800
Dividend Payout %	31.25	31.55	32.01	32.76	31.20	24.65	19.14	15.15
Income Statement								
Total Revenue	149,098,000	98,776,000	48,723,000	184,840,000	157,107,000	130,474,000	122,489,000	110,618,000
Income Before Taxes	10,354,000	6,560,000	3,130,000	11,863,000	10,231,000	9,656,000	8,915,000	8,622,000
Income Taxes	3,252,000	2,019,000	939,000	4,790,000	4,363,000	4,037,000	3,242,000	3,096,000
Net Income	6,941,000	4,456,000	2,172,000	7,017,000	5,813,000	5,619,000	5,625,000	5,526,000
Average Shares	989,000	985,000	975,000	968,000	967,000	986,000	1,023,000	1,046,000
Balance Sheet								
Total Assets	140,432,000	138,097,000	137,157,000	122,810,000	111,383,000	86,382,000	81,882,000	80,885,000
Total Liabilities	95,134,000	94,936,000	95,254,000	84,536,000	77,553,000	53,928,000	49,733,000	49,707,000
Stockholders' Equity	45,298,000	43,161,000	41,903,000	38,274,000	33,830,000	32,454,000	32,149,000	31,178,000
Shares Outstanding	969,000	965,000	965,000	952,000	953,000	954,000	988,000	1,019,000
Statistical Record								
Return on Assets %	6.53	6.29	5.94	5.98	5.88	6.68	6.91	7.41
Return on Equity %	20.80	20.39	19.66	19.41	17.54	17.40	17.76	18.53
Net Margin %	4.66	4.51	4.46	3.80	3.70	4.31	4.59	5.00
Price Range	199.75-133.92	186.50-133.62	171.78-125.68	163.94-109.23	125.86-98.92	103.04-69.74	75.30-51.40	60.26-50.35
P/E Ratio	22.70-15.22	22.42-16.06	21.99-16.09	22.61-15.07	20.94-16.46	18.08-12.24	13.69-9.35	11.41-9.54
Average Yield %	1.61	1.67	1.71	1.75	1.61	1.68	1.61	1.45

Address: UnitedHealth Group Center, 9900 Bren Road East, Minnetonka, MN 55343 **Telephone:** 952-936-1300	**Web Site:** www.unitedhealthgroup.com **Officers:** Stephen J. Hemsley - Executive Chairman, President, Chief Executive Officer, Chief Operating Officer, Senior Executive Vice President John F. Rex - Executive Vice President, Chief Financial Officer	**Auditors:** Deloitte & Touche LLP **Investor Contact:** 800-328-5979 **Transfer Agents:** Wells Fargo Shareowner Services, St. Paul, MN

UNITED STATES CELLULAR CORP

Exchange	Symbol	Price	52Wk Range	Yield	P/E
NYS	USM	$37.63 (12/29/2017)	45.67-32.95	N/A	N/A

*7 Year Price Score 75.15 ***NYSE Composite Index=100** ***12 Month Price Score 88.05**

Interim Earnings (Per Share)

Qtr.	Mar	Jun	Sep	Dec
2014	0.23	(0.22)	(0.26)	(0.26)
2015	1.89	0.23	0.75	(0.02)
2016	0.10	0.32	0.20	(0.07)
2017	0.31	0.14	(3.51)	...

Interim Dividends (Per Share)

Dividend Payment Suspended

Valuation Analysis

		Institutional Holding	
Forecast EPS	$-3.18	No of Institutions	
	(01/06/2018)	165	
Market Cap	$3.2 Billion	Shares	
Book Value	$3.4 Billion	14,479,286	
Price/Book	0.94	% Held	
Price/Sales	0.83	14.61	

Business Summary: Services (MIC: 6.1.2 SIC: 4812 NAIC: 517212)

United States Cellular provides wireless telecommunications services. Co.'s postpaid customers are able to choose from a variety of national plans with voice, messaging and data usage options and pricing. Co. provides Shared Connect data plans which allow customers to share data usage among all users and devices connected to the plan. Co. also provides monthly prepaid service plans, which provide customers unlimited voice and unlimited messaging with a specified amount of high-speed data and unlimited data at lower speeds once the high-speed data limit is reached. Co. provides a range of wireless devices such as handsets, modems, mobile hotspots, home phone and tablets.

Recent Developments: For the quarter ended Sep 30 2017, net loss amounted to US$298.0 million versus net income of US$18.0 million in the year-earlier quarter. Revenues were US$963.0 million, down 5.9% from US$1.02 billion the year before. Operating loss was US$360.0 million versus an income of US$22.0 million in the prior-year quarter. Direct operating expenses declined 6.3% to US$446.0 million from US$476.0 million in the comparable period the year before. Indirect operating expenses increased 67.0% to US$877.0 million from US$525.0 million in the equivalent prior-year period.

Prospects: Our evaluation of United States Cellular Corp. as of Jan. 14, 2018 is the result of our systematic analysis on three basic characteristics: earnings strength, relative valuation, and recent stock price movement. The company has managed to produce a neutral trend in earnings per share over the past 5 quarters. Because the company lacks sufficient analyst estimate data, we place greater weight on the historical EPS trend as the measure of earnings strength. Based on operating earnings yield, the company is overvalued when compared to all of the companies in our coverage universe. Share price changes over the past year indicates that USM will perform poorly over the near term.

Financial Data

(US$ in Thousands)	9 Mos	6 Mos	3 Mos	12/31/2016	12/31/2015	12/31/2014	12/31/2013	12/31/2012
Earnings Per Share	(3.13)	0.58	0.76	0.56	2.84	(0.51)	1.65	1.31
Cash Flow Per Share	5.65	5.41	4.69	5.88	6.59	2.05	3.46	10.60
Tang Book Value Per Share	13.76	12.82	16.55	16.21	16.08	17.70	19.03	22.04
Dividends Per Share	...	...	...	...	...	...	5.750	...
Dividend Payout %	...	...	...	...	...	...	348.48	...
Income Statement								
Total Revenue	2,862,000	1,899,000	936,000	3,939,000	3,996,853	3,892,747	3,918,836	4,452,084
EBITDA	160,000	365,000	206,000	605,000	908,908	449,970	956,809	751,138
Depn & Amortn	460,000	307,000	153,000	607,000	595,500	593,200	791,100	597,700
Income Before Taxes	(379,000)	7,000	28,000	(58,000)	263,546	(188,468)	125,707	114,689
Income Taxes	(19,000)	33,000	33,000	33,000	156,334	(11,782)	113,134	63,977
Net Income	(261,000)	38,000	26,000	48,000	241,347	(42,812)	140,038	111,006
Average Shares	85,000	86,000	86,000	85,000	84,891	84,213	84,730	85,067
Balance Sheet								
Current Assets	1,504,000	1,440,000	1,524,000	1,558,000	1,671,642	1,279,175	1,401,191	1,196,476
Total Assets	6,780,000	7,077,000	7,024,000	7,110,000	7,059,978	6,487,268	6,445,708	6,587,450
Current Liabilities	673,000	651,000	587,000	718,000	747,938	856,894	1,006,173	754,999
Long-Term Obligations	1,626,000	1,613,000	1,616,000	1,618,000	1,628,507	1,151,819	878,032	878,858
Total Liabilities	3,385,000	3,391,000	3,354,000	3,476,000	3,499,465	3,185,277	3,054,502	2,853,595
Stockholders' Equity	3,395,000	3,686,000	3,670,000	3,634,000	3,560,513	3,301,991	3,391,206	3,733,855
Shares Outstanding	85,000	85,000	84,884	85,000	84,359	84,080	84,205	84,168
Statistical Record								
Return on Assets %	N.M.	0.71	0.92	0.68	3.56	N.M.	2.15	1.71
Return on Equity %	N.M.	1.37	1.79	1.33	7.03	N.M.	3.93	3.01
EBITDA Margin %	5.59	19.22	22.01	15.36	22.74	11.56	24.42	16.87
Net Margin %	N.M.	2.00	2.78	1.22	6.04	N.M.	3.57	2.49
Asset Turnover	0.56	0.55	0.56	0.55	0.59	0.60	0.60	0.69
Current Ratio	2.23	2.21	2.60	2.17	2.24	1.49	1.39	1.58
Debt to Equity	0.48	0.44	0.44	0.45	0.46	0.35	0.26	0.24
Price Range	45.67-33.97	45.67-33.97	45.87-33.97	45.87-33.97	43.36-34.42	44.45-31.93	48.80-32.62	47.61-33.76
P/E Ratio	...	78.74-58.57	60.36-44.70	81.91-60.66	15.27-12.12	...	29.58-19.77	36.34-25.77
Average Yield %	...	...	...	...	...	...	14.35	...

Address: 8410 West Bryn Mawr,	Web Site: www.uscellular.com	Auditors: PricewaterhouseCoopers LLP
Chicago, IL 60631	Officers: LeRoy T. Carlson - Chairman Kenneth R.	Investor Contact: 312-592-5341
Telephone: 773-399-8900	Meyers - President, Chief Executive Officer, Vice President, Assistant Treasurer	Transfer Agents: Computershare Trust Company, N.A., TX

US BANCORP (DE)

Exchange	Symbol	Price	52Wk Range	Yield	P/E
NYS	USB	$53.58 (12/29/2017)	56.41-49.69	2.24	15.95

*7 Year Price Score 105.42 *NYSE Composite Index=100 *12 Month Price Score 96.61

Interim Earnings (Per Share)

Qtr.	Mar	Jun	Sep	Dec
2014	0.73	0.78	0.78	0.79
2015	0.76	0.80	0.81	0.80
2016	0.76	0.83	0.84	0.81
2017	0.82	0.85	0.88	...

Interim Dividends (Per Share)

Amt	Decl	Ex	Rec	Pay
0.28Q	03/21/2017	03/29/2017	03/31/2017	04/17/2017
0.28Q	06/20/2017	06/28/2017	06/30/2017	07/17/2017
0.30Q	09/19/2017	09/28/2017	09/29/2017	10/16/2017
0.30Q	12/19/2017	12/28/2017	12/29/2017	01/16/2018

Indicated Div: $1.20

Valuation Analysis

		Institutional Holding	
Forecast EPS	$4.08 (01/26/2018)	No of Institutions	1836
Market Cap	$89.3 Billion	Shares	1,483,525,504
Book Value	$48.7 Billion	% Held	68.38
Price/Book	1.83		
Price/Sales	3.78		

Business Summary: Banking (MIC: 5.1.1 SIC: 6021 NAIC: 522110)

U.S. Bancorp is a multi-state financial services holding company. Co. provides a range of financial services, including lending and depository services, cash management, capital markets, and trust and investment management services. Co. also engages in credit card services, merchant and automatic teller machine (ATM) processing, mortgage banking, insurance, brokerage and leasing. Banking and investment services are provided through a network of 3,106 banking offices principally operating in the Midwest and West regions of the U.S. At Dec 31 2016, Co. had total assets of $445.96 billion and deposits of $334.59 billion.

Recent Developments: For the quarter ended Sep 30 2017, net income increased 3.5% to US$1.57 billion from US$1.52 billion in the year-earlier quarter. Net interest income increased 8.4% to US$3.14 billion from US$2.89 billion in the year-earlier quarter. Provision for loan losses was US$360.0 million versus US$325.0 million in the prior-year quarter, an increase of 10.8%. Non-interest income fell 0.9% to US$2.42 billion from US$2.45 billion, while non-interest expense advanced 3.7% to US$3.04 billion.

Prospects: Our evaluation of U.S. Bancorp as of Jan. 21, 2018 is the result of our systematic analysis on three basic characteristics: earnings strength, relative valuation, and recent stock price movement. The company has enjoyed a very positive trend in earnings per share over the past 5 quarters and while recent estimates for the company have been raised by analysts, USB has posted better than expected results. Based on operating earnings yield, the company is undervalued when compared to all of the companies in our coverage universe. Share price changes over the past year indicates that USB will perform in line with the market over the near term.

Financial Data
(US$ in Thousands)

	9 Mos	6 Mos	3 Mos	12/31/2016	12/31/2015	12/31/2014	12/31/2013	12/31/2012
Earnings Per Share	3.36	3.32	3.30	3.24	3.16	3.08	3.00	2.84
Cash Flow Per Share	5.23	4.41	4.29	3.10	4.98	2.96	6.22	4.21
Tang Book Value Per Share	18.44	18.06	17.57	17.18	16.00	14.66	12.95	11.97
Dividends Per Share	1.140	1.120	1.095	1.070	1.010	0.965	0.885	0.780
Dividend Payout %	33.93	33.73	33.18	33.02	31.96	31.33	29.50	27.46
Income Statement								
Interest Income	10,645,000	6,931,000	3,400,000	13,167,000	12,402,000	12,228,000	12,285,000	12,883,000
Interest Expense	1,548,000	969,000	455,000	1,639,000	1,401,000	1,453,000	1,681,000	2,138,000
Net Interest Income	9,097,000	5,962,000	2,945,000	11,528,000	11,001,000	10,775,000	10,604,000	10,745,000
Provision for Losses	1,055,000	695,000	345,000	1,324,000	1,132,000	1,229,000	1,340,000	1,882,000
Non-Interest Income	7,170,000	4,748,000	2,329,000	9,577,000	9,092,000	9,164,000	8,774,000	9,319,000
Non-Interest Expense	9,006,000	5,967,000	2,944,000	11,676,000	10,931,000	10,715,000	10,274,000	10,456,000
Income Before Taxes	6,206,000	4,048,000	1,985,000	8,105,000	8,030,000	7,995,000	7,764,000	7,726,000
Income Taxes	1,639,000	1,050,000	499,000	2,161,000	2,097,000	2,087,000	2,032,000	2,236,000
Net Income	4,536,000	2,973,000	1,473,000	5,888,000	5,879,000	5,851,000	5,836,000	5,647,000
Average Shares	1,678,000	1,690,000	1,701,000	1,724,000	1,772,000	1,813,000	1,849,000	1,896,000
Balance Sheet								
Net Loans & Leases	278,568,000	277,088,000	272,499,000	274,220,000	260,170,000	248,604,000	234,253,000	226,881,000
Total Assets	459,227,000	463,844,000	449,522,000	445,964,000	421,853,000	402,529,000	364,021,000	353,855,000
Total Deposits	342,589,000	347,262,000	336,873,000	334,590,000	300,400,000	282,733,000	262,123,000	249,183,000
Total Liabilities	410,504,000	415,524,000	401,724,000	398,666,000	375,722,000	359,050,000	322,908,000	314,857,000
Stockholders' Equity	48,723,000	48,320,000	47,798,000	47,298,000	46,131,000	43,479,000	41,113,000	38,998,000
Shares Outstanding	1,666,767	1,678,937	1,691,774	1,696,912	1,745,190	1,785,866	1,824,748	1,869,431
Statistical Record								
Return on Assets %	1.32	1.32	1.36	1.35	1.43	1.53	1.63	1.62
Return on Equity %	12.47	12.44	12.64	12.57	13.12	13.83	14.57	15.43
Net Interest Margin %	84.41	85.44	86.62	87.55	88.70	88.12	86.32	83.40
Efficiency Ratio %	49.53	50.81	51.39	51.34	50.86	50.09	48.79	47.09
Loans to Deposits	0.81	0.80	0.81	0.82	0.87	0.88	0.89	0.91
Price Range	56.41-42.66	56.41-39.06	56.41-38.69	52.54-37.45	46.02-39.76	45.91-38.78	40.60-31.94	35.19-27.57
P/E Ratio	16.79-12.70	16.99-11.77	17.09-11.72	16.22-11.56	14.56-12.58	14.91-12.59	13.53-10.65	12.39-9.71
Average Yield %	2.23	2.30	2.37	2.49	2.33	2.30	2.47	2.45

Address: 800 Nicollet Mall, Minneapolis, MN 55402 **Telephone:** 651-466-3000	**Web Site:** www.usbank.com **Officers:** Jennie P. Carlson - Executive Vice President Andrew Cecere - Chairman, Vice-Chairman, President, Chief Executive Officer, Chief Operating Officer, Chief Financial Officer	**Auditors:** Ernst & Young LLP **Investor Contact:** 612-303-0778 **Transfer Agents:** Computershare, Providence, R.I.

735

UNITED TECHNOLOGIES CORP

Exchange	Symbol	Price	52Wk Range	Yield	P/E	Div Achiever
NYS	UTX	$127.57 (12/29/2017)	128.12-108.18	2.19	19.75	23 Years

*7 Year Price Score 92.31   *NYSE Composite Index=100   *12 Month Price Score 97.73

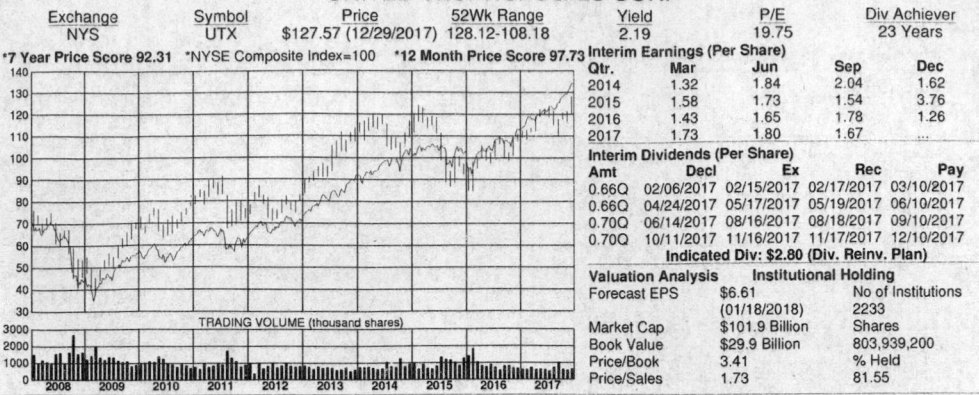

Interim Earnings (Per Share)

Qtr.	Mar	Jun	Sep	Dec
2014	1.32	1.84	2.04	1.62
2015	1.58	1.73	1.54	3.76
2016	1.43	1.65	1.78	1.26
2017	1.73	1.80	1.67	...

Interim Dividends (Per Share)

Amt	Decl	Ex	Rec	Pay
0.66Q	02/06/2017	02/15/2017	02/17/2017	03/10/2017
0.66Q	04/24/2017	05/17/2017	05/19/2017	06/10/2017
0.70Q	06/14/2017	08/16/2017	08/18/2017	09/10/2017
0.70Q	10/11/2017	11/16/2017	11/17/2017	12/10/2017

Indicated Div: $2.80 (Div. Reinv. Plan)

Valuation Analysis   **Institutional Holding**

Forecast EPS	$6.61	No of Institutions
	(01/18/2018)	2233
Market Cap	$101.9 Billion	Shares
Book Value	$29.9 Billion	803,939,200
Price/Book	3.41	% Held
Price/Sales	1.73	81.55

Business Summary: Aerospace (MIC: 7.1.1 SIC: 3724 NAIC: 336412)

United Technologies provides technology products and services to the building systems and aerospace industries. Co. has four segments: Otis, which designs, manufactures, sells and installs passenger and freight elevators; UTC Climate, Controls & Security, which provides heating, ventilating, air conditioning and refrigeration solutions; Pratt & Whitney, which supplies aircraft engines for the commercial, military, business jet and general aviation market; and UTC Aerospace Systems, which provides aerospace products and aftermarket service solutions for aircraft manufacturers, airlines, regional, business and general aviation markets, military, space and undersea operations.

Recent Developments: For the quarter ended Sep 30 2017, net income decreased 10.1% to US$1.33 billion from US$1.48 billion in the year-earlier quarter. Revenues were US$15.06 billion, up 4.9% from US$14.35 billion the year before. Operating income was US$2.16 billion versus US$2.25 billion in the prior-year quarter, a decrease of 3.9%. Direct operating expenses rose 6.8% to US$11.04 billion from US$10.34 billion in the comparable period the year before. Indirect operating expenses increased 5.4% to US$1.86 billion from US$1.76 billion in the equivalent prior-year period.

Prospects: Our evaluation of United Technologies Corp. as of Jan. 14, 2018 is the result of our systematic analysis on three basic characteristics: earnings strength, relative valuation, and recent stock price movement. The company has managed to produce a neutral trend in earnings per share over the past 5 quarters and while recent estimates for the company have been mixed, UTX has posted better than expected results. Based on operating earnings yield, the company is undervalued when compared to all of the companies in our coverage universe. Share price changes over the past year indicates that UTX will perform poorly over the near term.

Financial Data

(US$ in Millions)	9 Mos	6 Mos	3 Mos	12/31/2016	12/31/2015	12/31/2014	12/31/2013	12/31/2012
Earnings Per Share	6.46	6.57	6.42	6.12	8.61	6.82	6.25	5.66
Cash Flow Per Share	6.33	8.85	8.33	7.82	7.68	8.17	8.33	7.36
Dividends Per Share	2.680	2.640	2.640	2.620	2.560	2.360	2.195	2.030
Dividend Payout %	41.49	40.18	41.12	42.81	29.73	34.60	35.12	35 87
Income Statement								
Total Revenue	44,157	29,095	13,815	57,244	56,098	65,100	62,626	57,708
EBITDA	8,302	5,596	2,779	9,277	8,359	10,891	10,259	8,604
Depn & Amortn	1,582	1,039	512	1,105	1,068	1,122	1,050	920
Income Before Taxes	6,058	4,118	2,054	7,133	6,467	8,887	8,312	6,911
Income Taxes	1,624	1,118	586	1,697	2,111	2,264	2,238	1,711
Net Income	4,155	2,825	1,386	5,055	7,608	6,220	5,721	5,130
Average Shares	797	798	802	826	883	911	915	906
Balance Sheet								
Current Assets	32,963	32,829	29,305	28,550	26,706	29,758	29,442	29,610
Total Assets	96,352	94,793	90,373	89,706	87,484	91,289	90,594	89,409
Current Liabilities	25,249	23,919	23,726	21,906	22,618	22,895	22,800	23,786
Long-Term Obligations	24,063	23,883	20,898	21,697	19,320	17,872	19,741	21,597
Total Liabilities	66,471	66,351	62,779	62,127	60,126	60,076	58,728	63,495
Stockholders' Equity	29,881	28,442	27,594	27,579	27,358	31,213	31,866	25,914
Shares Outstanding	798	798	801	808	838	909	916	918
Statistical Record								
Return on Assets %	5.54	5.77	5.87	5.69	8.51	6.84	6.36	6.78
Return on Equity %	17.50	18.49	18.77	18.35	25.98	19.72	19.80	21.41
EBITDA Margin %	18.80	19.23	20.12	16.21	14.90	16.73	16.38	14.91
Net Margin %	9.41	9.71	10.03	8.83	13.56	9.55	9.14	8.89
Asset Turnover	0.63	0.63	0.64	0.64	0.63	0.72	0.70	0.76
Current Ratio	1.31	1.37	1.24	1.30	1.18	1.30	1.29	1.24
Debt to Equity	0.81	0.84	0.76	0.79	0.71	0.57	0.62	0.83
Price Range	123.71-98.67	122.50-98.67	113.68-97.21	110.98-84.66	124.11-86.82	120.09-99.17	113.80-82.01	86.89-70.88
P/E Ratio	19.15-15.27	18.65-15.02	17.71-15.14	18.13-13.83	14.41-10.08	17.61-14.54	18.21-13.12	15.35-12.52
Average Yield %	2.37	2.39	2.49	2.59	2.39	2.11	2.22	2.59

Address: 10 Farm Springs Road, Farmington, CT 06032 **Telephone:** 860-728-7000 **Fax:** 860-728-7028	**Web Site:** www.utc.com **Officers:** Gregory J. (Greg) Hayes - Chairman, President, Chief Executive Officer, Senior Vice President, Chief Financial Officer Akhil Johri - Executive Vice President, Chief Financial Officer	**Auditors:** PricewaterhouseCoopers LLP **Transfer Agents:** Computershare Trust Company, N. A., Canton, MA

UNIVAR INC

Exchange	Symbol	Price	52Wk Range	Yield	P/E
NYS	UNVR	$30.96 (12/29/2017)	32.81-26.99	N/A	134.61

*7 Year Price Score N/A   *NYSE Composite Index=100   *12 Month Price Score 94.86

TRADING VOLUME (thousand shares)

Interim Earnings (Per Share)

Qtr.	Mar	Jun	Sep	Dec
2014	(0.03)	0.20	0.46	(0.82)
2015	0.20	(0.12)	0.09	(0.03)
2016	0.10	0.29	(0.46)	(0.43)
2017	0.16	0.22	0.28	...

Interim Dividends (Per Share)

No Dividends Paid

Valuation Analysis

	Institutional Holding	
Forecast EPS	$0.94	No of Institutions
	(01/18/2018)	220
Market Cap	$4.4 Billion	Shares
Book Value	$1.1 Billion	143,204,240
Price/Book	4.10	% Held
Price/Sales	0.54	N/A

Business Summary: Specialty Chemicals (MIC: 8.3.2 SIC: 5169 NAIC: 325998)

Univar is a chemical and ingredients distributor and provider of specialty services. Co. purchases chemicals from chemical producers worldwide and warehouses, repackages, blends, dilutes, transports and sells those chemicals to more than 100,000 customer locations across approximately 150 countries. Co.'s operations are structured into four operating segments that represent the geographic areas under which it operates and manages its business: Univar USA; Univar Canada; Univar Europe and the Middle East and Africa; and Rest of World. The Rest of World segment includes developing businesses in Latin America (including Brazil and Mexico) and the Asia-Pacific region.

Recent Developments: For the quarter ended Sep 30 2017, net income amounted to US$38.9 million versus a net loss of US$63.0 million in the year-earlier quarter. Revenues were US$2.05 billion, up 2.5% from US$2.00 billion the year before. Operating income was US$90.9 million versus a loss of US$65.0 million in the prior-year quarter. Direct operating expenses rose 2.1% to US$1.59 billion from US$1.56 billion in the comparable period the year before. Indirect operating expenses decreased 27.7% to US$363.9 million from US$503.1 million in the equivalent prior-year period.

Prospects: Our evaluation of Univar Inc as of Jan. 14, 2018 is the result of our systematic analysis on three basic characteristics: earnings strength, relative valuation, and recent stock price movement. The company has produced a positive trend in earnings per share over the past 5 quarters. However, while recent estimates for the company have been mixed, UNVR has posted better than expected results. Based on operating earnings yield, the company is overvalued when compared to all of the companies in our coverage universe. Share price changes over the past year indicates that UNVR will perform poorly over the near term.

Financial Data
(US$ in Thousands)

	9 Mos	6 Mos	3 Mos	12/31/2016	12/31/2015	12/31/2014	12/31/2013	12/31/2012
Earnings Per Share	0.23	(0.51)	(0.44)	(0.50)	0.14	(0.20)	(0.83)	(2.01)
Cash Flow Per Share	1.84	2.28	2.19	3.25	2.98	1.27	2.91	0.16
Income Statement								
Total Revenue	6,294,500	4,245,800	1,998,800	8,073,700	8,981,800	10,373,900	10,324,600	9,747,100
EBITDA	326,400	208,200	97,900	232,600	370,200	348,200	330,500	258,000
Depn & Amortn	108,200	73,800	37,900	152,300	136,500	133,500	128,100	111,700
Income Before Taxes	108,200	62,800	24,200	(79,600)	26,700	(35,900)	(92,100)	(121,800)
Income Taxes	15,400	8,900	1,600	(11,200)	10,200	(15,800)	(9,800)	75,600
Net Income	92,800	53,900	22,600	(68,400)	16,500	(20,100)	(82,300)	(197,400)
Average Shares	141,400	141,300	140,800	137,800	120,100	99,718	99,299	98,355
Balance Sheet								
Current Assets	2,447,400	2,604,200	2,388,400	2,178,100	2,196,300	2,621,800	2,549,900	...
Total Assets	5,690,100	5,806,900	5,596,000	5,389,900	5,612,400	6,067,700	6,217,000	...
Current Liabilities	1,366,000	1,561,000	1,420,900	1,339,500	1,293,500	1,518,900	1,590,900	...
Long-Term Obligations	2,872,600	2,895,500	2,905,700	2,845,000	3,057,400	3,730,600	3,657,100	...
Total Liabilities	4,625,800	4,847,200	4,720,900	4,580,000	4,795,700	5,819,600	5,835,700	...
Stockholders' Equity	1,064,300	959,700	875,100	809,900	816,700	248,100	381,300	...
Shares Outstanding	140,800	140,600	140,200	138,800	138,000	100,190	99,956	99,781
Statistical Record								
Return on Assets %	0.60	N.M.	N.M.	N.M.	0.28	N.M.	...	...
Return on Equity %	3.49	N.M.	N.M.	N.M.	3.10	N.M.	...	...
EBITDA Margin %	5.19	4.90	4.90	2.88	4.12	3.36	3.20	2.65
Net Margin %	1.47	1.27	1.13	N.M.	0.18	N.M.	N.M.	N.M.
Asset Turnover	1.44	1.37	1.40	1.46	1.54	1.69	...	...
Current Ratio	1.79	1.67	1.68	1.63	1.70	1.73	1.60	...
Debt to Equity	2.70	3.02	3.32	3.51	3.74	15.04	9.59	...
Price Range	32.81-21.07	32.81-17.69	32.81-16.68	28.60-11.12	27.25-16.28	...	...	...
P/E Ratio	142.65-91.61	...	...	...	194.64-116.29	...	...	...

Address: 3075 Highland Parkway, Suite 200, Downers Grove, IL 60515 **Telephone:** 331-777-6000	**Web Site:** www.univar.com **Officers:** Stephen D. Newlin - Chairman, President, Chief Executive Officer David C. Jukes - Region Officer, President, Chief Operating Officer	**Auditors:** Ernst & Young LLP **Transfer Agents:** Wells Fargo Shareowner Services

UNIVERSAL CORP

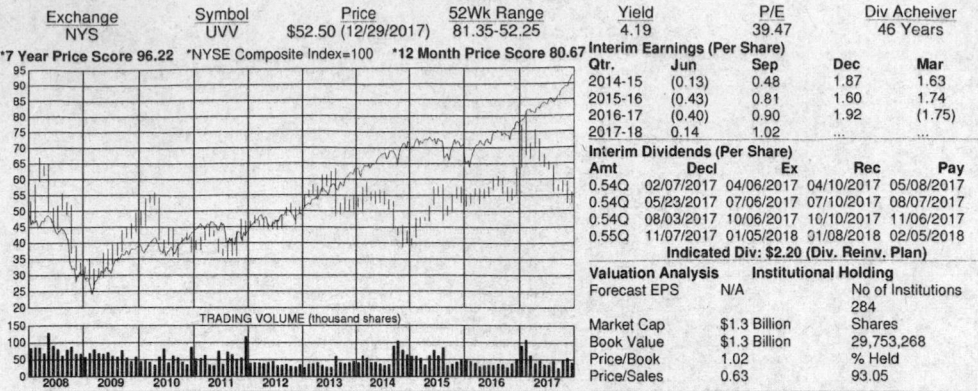

Exchange	Symbol	Price	52Wk Range	Yield	P/E	Div Acheiver
NYS	UVV	$52.50 (12/29/2017)	81.35-52.25	4.19	39.47	46 Years

*7 Year Price Score 96.22   *NYSE Composite Index=100   *12 Month Price Score 80.67

Interim Earnings (Per Share)

Qtr.	Jun	Sep	Dec	Mar
2014-15	(0.13)	0.48	1.87	1.63
2015-16	(0.43)	0.81	1.60	1.74
2016-17	(0.40)	0.90	1.92	(1.75)
2017-18	0.14	1.02	...	...

Interim Dividends (Per Share)

Amt	Decl	Ex	Rec	Pay
0.54Q	02/07/2017	04/06/2017	04/10/2017	05/08/2017
0.54Q	05/23/2017	07/06/2017	07/10/2017	08/07/2017
0.54Q	08/03/2017	10/06/2017	10/10/2017	11/06/2017
0.55Q	11/07/2017	01/05/2018	01/08/2018	02/05/2018

Indicated Div: $2.20 (Div. Reinv. Plan)

Valuation Analysis   **Institutional Holding**

Forecast EPS	N/A	No of Institutions
		284
Market Cap	$1.3 Billion	Shares
Book Value	$1.3 Billion	29,753,268
Price/Book	1.02	% Held
Price/Sales	0.63	93.05

Business Summary: Tobacco Products (MIC: 1.3.1 SIC: 5159 NAIC: 424590)

Universal is a holding company. Through its subsidiary, Co. is engaged in supplying leaf tobacco. Co. has the following segments: North America, South America, Africa, Europe, Asia, which are primarily involved in flue-cured and burley leaf tobacco operations for supply to cigarette manufacturers; Dark Air-Cured, which supplies dark air-cured tobacco to manufacturers of cigars, pipe tobacco, and smokeless tobacco products; Oriental, which supplies oriental tobacco to cigarette manufacturers; and Special Services, which provides laboratory services, including physical and chemical product testing, electronic nicotine delivery system and e-liquid testing, and smoke testing for customers.

Recent Developments: For the quarter ended Sep 30 2017, net income increased 6.8% to US$28.3 million from US$26.5 million in the year-earlier quarter. Revenues were US$488.2 million, up 6.9% from US$456.9 million the year before. Operating income was US$45.0 million versus US$43.3 million in the prior-year quarter, an increase of 3.8%. Direct operating expenses rose 7.1% to US$395.2 million from US$369.1 million in the comparable period the year before. Indirect operating expenses increased 8.1% to US$48.1 million from US$44.5 million in the equivalent prior-year period.

Prospects: Our evaluation of Universal Corp. as of Jan. 21, 2018 is the result of our systematic analysis on three basic characteristics: earnings strength, relative valuation, and recent stock price movement. The company has produced a positive trend in earnings per share over the past 5 quarters. Because the company lacks sufficient analyst estimate data, we place greater weight on the historical EPS trend as the measure of earnings strength. Based on operating earnings yield, the company is undervalued when compared to all of the companies in our coverage universe. Share price changes over the past year indicates that UVV will perform in line with the market over the near term.

Financial Data

(US$ in Thousands)	6 Mos	3 Mos	03/31/2017	03/31/2016	03/31/2015	03/31/2014	03/31/2013	03/31/2012
Earnings Per Share	1.33	1.21	0.88	3.92	4.06	5.25	4.66	3.25
Cash Flow Per Share	0.16	4.61	10.68	8.07	9.83	(0.15)	10.04	8.58
Tang Book Value Per Share	47.36	46.71	46.99	48.58	46.56	45.91	40.55	37.46
Dividends Per Share	2.150	2.140	2.130	2.090	2.050	2.010	1.970	1.930
Dividend Payout %	161.65	176.86	242.05	53.32	50.49	38.29	42.27	59.38
Income Statement								
Total Revenue	772,870	284,622	2,071,218	2,120,373	2,271,801	2,542,115	2,461,699	2,446,877
EBITDA	69,015	15,373	214,262	218,401	203,268	283,408	266,417	222,462
Depn & Amortn	17,485	8,818	35,911	36,754	35,394	37,257	43,408	42,158
Income Before Taxes	44,830	3,293	163,464	167,156	151,330	226,793	201,650	158,783
Income Taxes	13,435	(463)	56,732	54,430	38,006	75,535	66,366	61,159
Net Income	29,744	3,577	106,304	109,016	114,608	149,009	132,750	92,057
Average Shares	25,546	25,632	23,770	27,825	28,221	28,392	28,478	28,339
Balance Sheet								
Current Assets	1,571,853	1,539,302	1,561,399	1,638,546	1,634,610	1,673,247	1,745,973	1,690,629
Total Assets	2,139,510	2,104,988	2,123,405	2,232,797	2,198,473	2,270,907	2,306,155	2,266,919
Current Liabilities	280,912	258,986	267,996	246,270	270,913	454,977	622,597	392,708
Long-Term Obligations	368,909	368,821	368,733	370,000	370,000	240,000	181,250	392,500
Total Liabilities	851,129	822,929	836,916	818,575	835,748	892,677	1,047,584	1,083,468
Stockholders' Equity	1,288,381	1,282,059	1,286,489	1,414,222	1,362,725	1,378,230	1,258,571	1,183,451
Shares Outstanding	25,114	25,325	25,274	22,717	22,593	23,216	23,343	23,257
Statistical Record								
Return on Assets %	5.34	5.34	4.88	4.91	5.13	6.51	5.81	4.08
Return on Equity %	8.64	8.64	7.87	7.83	8.36	11.30	10.87	7.75
EBITDA Margin %	8.93	5.40	10.34	10.30	8.95	11.15	10.82	9.09
Net Margin %	3.85	1.26	5.13	5.14	5.04	5.86	5.39	3.76
Asset Turnover	0.96	0.95	0.95	0.95	1.02	1.11	1.08	1.09
Current Ratio	5.60	5.94	5.83	6.65	6.03	3.68	2.80	4.31
Debt to Equity	0.29	0.29	0.29	0.26	0.27	0.17	0.14	0.33
Price Range	81.35-53.15	81.35-53.15	81.35-52.33	58.41-46.80	56.82-38.53	63.36-48.43	58.36-44.03	48.60-35.11
P/E Ratio	61.17-39.96	67.23-43.93	92.44-59.47	14.90-11.94	14.00-9.49	12.07-9.22	12.52-9.45	14.95-10.80
Average Yield %	3.36	3.36	3.54	3.94	4.26	3.65	3.99	4.58

Address: 9201 Forest Hill Avenue, Richmond, VA 23235	Web Site: www.universalcorp.com	Auditors: Ernst & Young LLP
Telephone: 804-359-9311	Officers: George C. Freeman - Chairman, President, Chief Executive Officer, Principal Executive Officer, Principal Financial Officer Airton L. Hentschke - Senior Vice President, Chief Operating Officer	Investor Contact: 804-359-9311 Transfer Agents: Wells Fargo Bank, N.A., St. Paul, MN

UNIVERSAL HEALTH REALTY INCOME TRUST

Exchange	Symbol	Price	52Wk Range	Yield	P/E	Div Achiever
NYS	UHT	$75.11 (12/29/2017)	84.23-60.01	3.54	23.18	29 Years

*7 Year Price Score 111.74 *NYSE Composite Index=100 *12 Month Price Score 98.16

Interim Earnings (Per Share)

Qtr.	Mar	Jun	Sep	Dec
2014	0.29	0.26	2.18	1.25
2015	0.28	0.90	0.27	0.33
2016	0.33	0.34	0.28	0.33
2017	2.32	0.30	0.29	...

Interim Dividends (Per Share)

Amt	Decl	Ex	Rec	Pay
0.655Q	03/09/2017	03/16/2017	03/20/2017	03/31/2017
0.66Q	06/07/2017	06/15/2017	06/19/2017	06/30/2017
0.66Q	09/07/2017	09/15/2017	09/18/2017	09/29/2017
0.665Q	12/06/2017	12/15/2017	12/18/2017	12/29/2017

Indicated Div: $2.66 (Div. Reinv. Plan)

Valuation Analysis   **Institutional Holding**

Forecast EPS	N/A	No of Institutions
		208
Market Cap	$1.0 Billion	Shares
Book Value	$213.3 Million	10,179,211
Price/Book	4.84	% Held
Price/Sales	14.39	48.82

Business Summary: REITs (MIC: 5.3.1 SIC: 6798 NAIC: 525930)

Universal Health Realty Income Trust is real estate investment trust. Co. invests in health care and human service related facilities including acute care hospitals, rehabilitation hospitals, sub-acute facilities, surgery centers, free-standing emergency departments, childcare centers and medical office buildings (MOBs). As of Feb 28 2017, Co. had 67 real estate investments located in 20 states in the U.S. consisting of: six hospital facilities including three acute care, one rehabilitation and two sub-acute; 54 MOBs; three free-standing emergency departments; and, four preschool and childcare centers.

Recent Developments: For the quarter ended Sep 30 2017, net income increased 3.7% to US$4.0 million from US$3.8 million in the year-earlier quarter. Revenues were US$18.2 million, up 8.3% from US$16.8 million the year before.

Prospects: Our evaluation of Universal Health Realty Income Trust as of Jan. 14, 2018 is the result of our systematic analysis on three basic characteristics: earnings strength, relative valuation, and recent stock price movement. The company has produced a positive trend in earnings per share over the past 5 quarters. Because the company lacks sufficient analyst estimate data, we place greater weight on the historical EPS trend as the measure of earnings strength. Based on operating earnings yield, the company is overvalued when compared to all of the companies in our coverage universe. Share price changes over the past year indicates that UHT will perform very well over the near term.

Financial Data

(US$ in Thousands)	9 Mos	6 Mos	3 Mos	12/31/2016	12/31/2015	12/31/2014	12/31/2013	12/31/2012
Earnings Per Share	3.24	3.23	3.27	1.28	1.78	3.99	1.04	1.54
Cash Flow Per Share	3.27	3.02	3.03	3.02	2.87	2.54	2.47	2.42
Tang Book Value Per Share	13.95	13.79	14.07	12.31	13.15	13.64	11.26	11.93
Dividends Per Share	2.630	2.620	2.610	2.600	2.560	2.520	2.495	2.460
Dividend Payout %	81.17	81.11	79.82	203.13	143.82	63.16	239.90	159.74
Income Statement								
Total Revenue	54,089	35,895	17,750	67,081	63,950	59,786	54,280	53,950
EBITDA	45,138	39,057	33,092	44,897	51,352	78,162	36,956	44,439
Depn & Amortn	(126)	(100)	(68)	22,783	21,973	20,663	18,410	19,559
Income Before Taxes	37,596	34,020	30,485	12,759	21,155	49,123	11,074	17,112
Net Income	39,555	35,595	31,562	17,215	23,691	51,551	13,169	19,477
Average Shares	13,621	13,583	13,580	13,468	13,301	12,934	12,701	12,669
Balance Sheet								
Current Assets	15,593	24,689	23,393	11,542	10,302	10,166	8,700	7,872
Total Assets	498,978	499,825	502,379	524,750	458,901	428,866	373,145	383,038
Current Liabilities	177,320	183,414	170,463	626	504	545	491	539
Long-Term Obligations	83,464	90,649	103,004	315,717	252,704	213,155	199,987	197,936
Total Liabilities	285,671	290,778	288,275	333,473	263,859	224,285	207,515	205,367
Stockholders' Equity	213,307	209,047	214,104	191,277	195,042	204,581	165,630	177,671
Shares Outstanding	13,734	13,606	13,600	13,599	13,327	13,301	12,858	12,688
Statistical Record								
Return on Assets %	8.72	8.89	9.11	3.49	5.34	12.86	3.48	5.15
Return on Equity %	21.53	21.43	21.89	8.89	11.86	27.85	7.67	10.60
EBITDA Margin %	83.45	108.81	186.43	66.93	80.30	130.74	68.08	82.37
Net Margin %	73.13	99.16	177.81	25.66	37.05	86.23	24.26	36.10
Asset Turnover	0.14	0.14	0.14	0.14	0.14	0.15	0.14	0.14
Current Ratio	0.09	0.13	0.14	18.44	20.44	18.65	17.72	14.60
Debt to Equity	0.39	0.43	0.48	1.65	1.30	1.04	1.21	1.11
Price Range	84.23-55.17	79.68-55.17	66.64-52.27	65.59-47.26	56.87-43.54	49.13-40.06	58.85-38.52	50.61-37.77
P/E Ratio	26.00-17.03	24.67-17.08	20.38-15.98	51.24-36.92	31.95-24.46	12.31-10.04	56.59-37.04	32.86-24.53
Average Yield %	3.86	4.10	4.37	4.58	5.13	5.75	5.22	5.78

Address: Universal Corporate Center, 367 South Gulph Road, King of Prussia, PA 19406 **Telephone:** 610-265-0688 **Fax:** 610-768-3336	**Web Site:** www.uhrit.com **Officers:** Alan B. Miller - Chairman, President, Chief Executive Officer Charles F. Boyle - Vice President, Chief Financial Officer
Auditors: KPMG LLP **Transfer Agents:** Computershare, Providence, RI	

UNIVERSAL HEALTH SERVICES, INC.

Exchange	Symbol	Price	52Wk Range	Yield	P/E
NYS	UHS	$113.35 (12/29/2017)	126.65-95.77	0.35	15.57

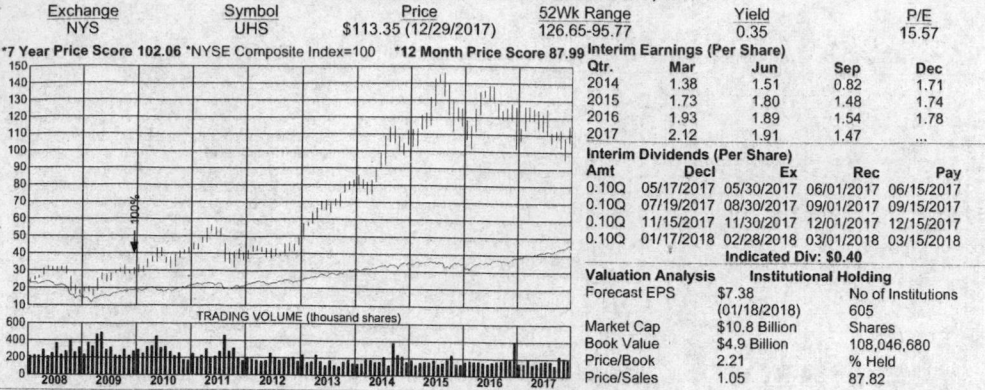

*7 Year Price Score 102.06 *NYSE Composite Index=100 *12 Month Price Score 87.99

Interim Earnings (Per Share)

Qtr.	Mar	Jun	Sep	Dec
2014	1.38	1.51	0.82	1.71
2015	1.73	1.80	1.48	1.74
2016	1.93	1.89	1.54	1.78
2017	2.12	1.91	1.47	...

Interim Dividends (Per Share)

Amt	Decl	Ex	Rec	Pay
0.10Q	05/17/2017	05/30/2017	06/01/2017	06/15/2017
0.10Q	07/19/2017	08/30/2017	09/01/2017	09/15/2017
0.10Q	11/15/2017	11/30/2017	12/01/2017	12/15/2017
0.10Q	01/17/2018	02/28/2018	03/01/2018	03/15/2018

Indicated Div: $0.40

Valuation Analysis

		Institutional Holding	
Forecast EPS	$7.38 (01/18/2018)	No of Institutions	605
Market Cap	$10.8 Billion	Shares	108,046,680
Book Value	$4.9 Billion	% Held	87.82
Price/Book	2.21		
Price/Sales	1.05		

Business Summary: Hospitals & Health Care Facilities (MIC: 4.2.1 SIC: 8062 NAIC: 622110)

Universal Health Services owns and operates, through its subsidiaries, acute care hospitals and outpatient facilities and behavioral health care facilities. Services provided by Co.'s hospitals include general and specialty surgery, internal medicine, obstetrics, emergency room care, radiology, oncology, diagnostic care, coronary care, pediatric services, pharmacy services and/or behavioral health services. As of Feb 28 2017, Co. owned and/or operated 319 inpatient facilities and 33 outpatient and other facilities including the following located in 37 states, Washington, D.C., the U.K., Puerto Rico and the U.S. Virgin Islands.

Recent Developments: For the quarter ended Sep 30 2017, net income decreased 7.6% to US$145.4 million from US$157.3 million in the year-earlier quarter. Revenues were US$2.54 billion, up 5.5% from US$2.41 billion the year before. Operating income was US$257.3 million versus US$277.6 million in the prior-year quarter, a decrease of 7.3%. Indirect operating expenses increased 7.1% to US$2.28 billion from US$2.13 billion in the equivalent prior-year period.

Prospects: Our evaluation of Universal Health Services Inc. as of Jan. 14, 2018 is the result of our systematic analysis on three basic characteristics: earnings strength, relative valuation, and recent stock price movement. The company has managed to produce a neutral trend in earnings per share over the past 5 quarters and while recent estimates for the company have been raised by analysts, UHS has posted results that fell short of analysts expectations. Based on operating earnings yield, the company is undervalued when compared to all of the companies in our coverage universe. Share price changes over the past year indicates that UHS will perform poorly over the near term.

Financial Data

(US$ in Thousands)	9 Mos	6 Mos	3 Mos	12/31/2016	12/31/2015	12/31/2014	12/31/2013	12/31/2012
Earnings Per Share	7.28	7.35	7.33	7.14	6.76	5.42	5.14	4.53
Cash Flow Per Share	11.20	10.61	13.53	13.22	10.33	10.48	9.02	8.40
Tang Book Value Per Share	11.00	10.55	9.81	7.75	6.65	4.51	2.04	N.M.
Dividends Per Share	0.400	0.400	0.400	0.400	0.400	0.300	0.200	0.600
Dividend Payout %	5.49	5.44	5.46	5.60	5.92	5.54	3.89	13.25
Income Statement								
Total Revenue	7,767,078	5,225,214	2,612,858	9,766,210	9,043,451	8,065,326	7,283,822	6,961,400
EBITDA	1,275,561	908,034	464,731	1,632,211	1,596,895	1,377,805	1,301,063	1,213,081
Depn & Amortn	334,127	223,910	110,798	350,800	337,500	314,500	285,600	270,500
Income Before Taxes	833,051	612,697	318,426	1,156,358	1,145,901	929,667	869,332	763,663
Income Taxes	286,774	211,782	107,899	409,187	395,203	324,671	315,309	274,616
Net Income	532,694	391,449	206,055	702,409	680,528	545,343	510,733	443,446
Average Shares	95,977	97,042	97,372	98,380	100,694	100,544	99,361	97,711
Balance Sheet								
Current Assets	1,755,187	1,763,160	1,732,074	1,681,371	1,718,304	1,615,138	1,432,329	1,407,496
Total Assets	10,639,360	10,552,487	10,448,259	10,317,802	9,634,113	8,974,443	8,311,723	8,200,843
Current Liabilities	1,397,497	1,322,229	1,517,427	1,317,373	1,100,406	1,182,827	1,059,888	894,058
Long-Term Obligations	3,927,396	3,988,912	3,772,515	4,030,230	3,387,303	3,210,215	3,209,762	3,727,431
Total Liabilities	5,774,148	5,739,633	5,712,297	5,784,582	5,384,466	5,238,497	5,061,744	5,487,498
Stockholders' Equity	4,865,212	4,812,854	4,735,962	4,533,220	4,249,647	3,735,946	3,249,979	2,713,345
Shares Outstanding	94,911	95,657	96,689	96,630	98,296	98,716	98,311	97,591
Statistical Record								
Return on Assets %	6.96	7.14	7.17	7.02	7.31	6.31	6.19	5.57
Return on Equity %	15.27	15.74	15.90	15.95	17.04	15.61	17.13	17.66
EBITDA Margin %	16.42	17.38	17.79	16.71	17.66	17.08	17.86	17.43
Net Margin %	6.86	7.49	7.89	7.19	7.53	6.76	7.01	6.37
Asset Turnover	1.01	1.01	0.99	0.98	0.97	0.93	0.88	0.88
Current Ratio	1.26	1.33	1.14	1.28	1.56	1.37	1.35	1.57
Debt to Equity	0.81	0.83	0.80	0.89	0.80	0.86	0.99	1.37
Price Range	128.06-101.55	138.28-101.55	138.74-101.55	138.74-101.55	146.24-102.53	114.84-74.35	83.12-48.35	49.46-36.82
P/E Ratio	17.59-13.95	18.81-13.82	18.93-13.85	19.43-14.22	21.63-15.17	21.19-13.72	16.17-9.41	10.92-8.13
Average Yield %	0.34	0.33	0.32	0.33	0.32	0.32	0.29	1.43

Address: Universal Corporate Center, 367 South Gulph Road, King of Prussia, PA 19406
Telephone: 610-768-3300

Web Site: www.uhsinc.com
Officers: Alan B. Miller - Chairman, Chief Executive Officer Marc D. Miller - President

Auditors: PriceWaterHouseCooper LLP
Investor Contact: 610-768-3300
Transfer Agents: Computershare, Canton, MA

UNUM GROUP

Exchange	Symbol	Price	52Wk Range	Yield	P/E
NYS	UNM	$54.89 (12/29/2017)	57.49-43.80	1.68	12.88

*7 Year Price Score 118.58 *NYSE Composite Index=100 *12 Month Price Score 106.12

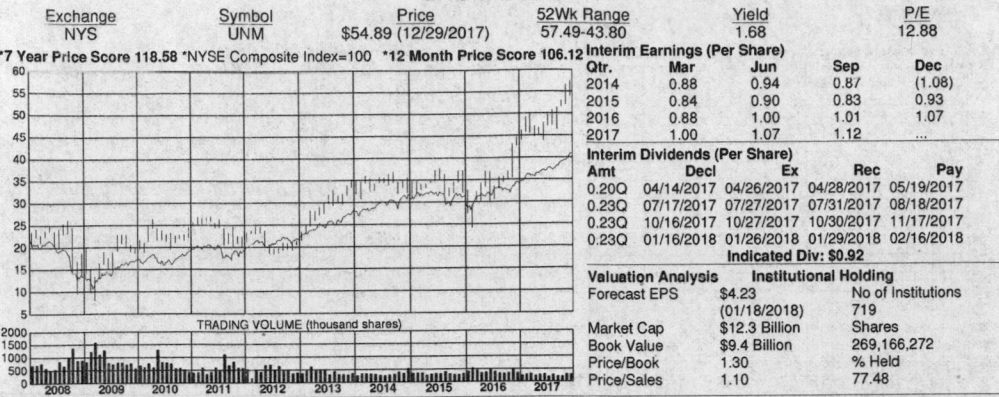

Interim Earnings (Per Share)

Qtr.	Mar	Jun	Sep	Dec
2014	0.88	0.94	0.87	(1.08)
2015	0.84	0.90	0.83	0.93
2016	0.88	1.00	1.01	1.07
2017	1.00	1.07	1.12	...

Interim Dividends (Per Share)

Amt	Decl	Ex	Rec	Pay
0.20Q	04/14/2017	04/26/2017	04/28/2017	05/19/2017
0.23Q	07/17/2017	07/27/2017	07/31/2017	08/18/2017
0.23Q	10/16/2017	10/27/2017	10/30/2017	11/17/2017
0.23Q	01/16/2018	01/26/2018	01/29/2018	02/16/2018

Indicated Div: $0.92

Valuation Analysis

		Institutional Holding	
Forecast EPS	$4.23	No of Institutions	
	(01/18/2018)	719	
Market Cap	$12.3 Billion	Shares	
Book Value	$9.4 Billion	269,166,272	
Price/Book	1.30	% Held	
Price/Sales	1.10	77.48	

Business Summary: Life & Health (MIC: 5.2.2 SIC: 6321 NAIC: 524114)

Unum Group is an insurance holding company. Through its subsidiaries, Co. provides products such as disability, life, accident, and other related services. Co.'s segments are: Unum U.S., which includes group disability insurance, group life and accidental death and dismemberment products, and supplemental and voluntary lines of business; Unum U.K., which includes group disability and life, and supplemental lines of business; and Colonial Life, which includes insurance for accident, sickness, and disability products, life products, and cancer and critical illness products. Other segment includes the Closed Block, which consists of individual disability, group and individual long-term care.

Recent Developments: For the quarter ended Sep 30 2017, net income increased 6.9% to US$252.3 million from US$236.0 million in the year-earlier quarter. Revenues were US$2.82 billion, up 2.0% from US$2.76 billion the year before. Net premiums earned were US$2.15 billion versus US$2.09 billion in the prior-year quarter, an increase of 3.1%. Net investment income fell 0.4% to US$609.0 million from US$611.4 million a year ago.

Prospects: Our evaluation of UNUM Group as of Jan. 14, 2018 is the result of our systematic analysis on three basic characteristics: earnings strength, relative valuation, and recent stock price movement. The company has produced a positive trend in earnings per share over the past 5 quarters and while recent estimates for the company have been raised by analysts, UNM has posted better than expected results. Based on operating earnings yield, the company is undervalued when compared to all of the companies in our coverage universe. Share price changes over the past year indicates that UNM will perform well over the near term.

Financial Data

(US$ in Thousands)	9 Mos	6 Mos	3 Mos	12/31/2016	12/31/2015	12/31/2014	12/31/2013	12/31/2012
Earnings Per Share	4.26	4.15	4.08	3.95	3.50	1.61	3.23	3.17
Cash Flow Per Share	5.45	5.26	4.93	4.73	5.23	4.79	3.90	4.89
Tang Book Value Per Share	40.60	39.71	38.44	37.56	35.00	33.11	32.53	31.13
Dividends Per Share	0.830	0.800	0.785	0.770	0.700	0.620	0.550	0.470
Dividend Payout %	19.48	19.28	19.24	19.49	20.00	38.51	17.03	14.83
Income Statement								
Premium Income	6,438,700	4,285,100	2,142,900	8,357,700	8,082,400	7,797,200	7,624,700	7,716,100
Total Revenue	8,447,600	5,628,500	2,806,500	11,046,500	10,731,300	10,509,700	10,353,800	10,515,400
Income Before Taxes	1,058,700	691,900	330,300	1,347,700	1,238,300	527,200	1,205,200	1,249,500
Income Taxes	331,400	216,900	100,400	416,300	371,200	113,800	347,100	355,100
Net Income	727,300	475,000	229,900	931,400	867,100	413,400	858,100	894,400
Average Shares	226,029	228,178	230,378	235,979	247,854	256,652	265,949	281,756
Balance Sheet								
Total Assets	63,805,700	63,381,600	62,524,700	61,941,500	60,589,700	62,497,100	59,403,600	62,236,100
Total Liabilities	54,357,100	54,065,000	53,417,300	52,973,500	51,925,800	53,944,700	50,744,500	53,623,500
Stockholders' Equity	9,448,600	9,316,600	9,107,400	8,968,000	8,663,900	8,552,400	8,659,100	8,612,600
Shares Outstanding	224,366	226,102	228,194	229,822	240,917	252,309	260,017	270,205
Statistical Record								
Return on Assets %	1.53	1.51	1.53	1.52	1.41	0.68	1.41	1.46
Return on Equity %	10.37	10.38	10.55	10.54	10.07	4.80	9.94	10.38
Net Margin %	8.61	8.44	8.19	8.43	8.08	3.93	8.29	8.51
Price Range	51.33-35.10	49.86-30.44	49.86-29.99	44.60-24.07	37.61-31.05	36.81-30.71	35.16-20.82	24.68-18.36
P/E Ratio	12.05-8.24	12.01-7.33	12.22-7.35	11.29-6.09	10.75-8.87	22.86-19.07	10.89-6.45	7.79-5.79
Average Yield %	1.83	1.92	2.04	2.25	2.04	1.81	1.90	2.24

Address: 1 Fountain Square, Chattanooga, TN 37402
Telephone: 423-294-1011

Web Site: www.unum.com
Officers: Danny Waxenberg - Senior Vice President, Chief Accounting Officer Kevin P. McCarthy - Executive Vice President, Chief Operating Officer, Region Officer

Auditors: Ernst & Young LLP
Transfer Agents: Computershare Trust Company, N.A., Providence, RI

URBAN EDGE PROPERTIES

Exchange	Symbol	Price	52Wk Range	Yield	P/E
NYS	UE	$25.49 (12/29/2017)	28.85-23.44	3.45	26.28

*7 Year Price Score N/A *NYSE Composite Index=100 *12 Month Price Score 92.52

TRADING VOLUME (thousand shares)

Interim Earnings (Per Share)

Qtr.	Mar	Jun	Sep	Dec
2014	0.18	0.18	0.14	0.16
2015	(0.12)	0.16	0.19	0.15
2016	0.19	0.34	0.19	0.19
2017	0.50	0.13	0.15	...

Interim Dividends (Per Share)

Amt	Decl	Ex	Rec	Pay
0.22Q	02/24/2017	03/13/2017	03/15/2017	03/31/2017
0.22Q	05/10/2017	06/13/2017	06/15/2017	06/30/2017
0.22Q	09/01/2017	09/14/2017	09/15/2017	09/29/2017
0.22Q	11/07/2017	12/14/2017	12/15/2017	12/29/2017

Indicated Div: $0.88 (Div. Reinv. Plan)

Valuation Analysis

		Institutional Holding	
Forecast EPS	$0.89 (11/20/2017)	No of Institutions	255
Market Cap	$2.9 Billion	Shares	122,130,576
Book Value	$927.9 Million	% Held	N/A
Price/Book	3.13		
Price/Sales	7.38		

Business Summary: REITs (MIC: 5.3.1 SIC: 6798 NAIC: 525930)

Urban Edge Properties is a real estate investment trust. Co. is focused on managing, developing, redeveloping, and acquiring retail real estate in urban communities, primarily in the New York metropolitan region. Urban Edge Properties LP is a Delaware limited partnership formed to serve as Co.'s majority-owned partnership subsidiary and to own, through affiliates, all of Co.'s real estate properties and other assets. As of Dec 31 2016, Co.'s portfolio consisted of 79 shopping centers, three malls and a warehouse park adjacent to one of its centers.

Recent Developments: For the quarter ended Sep 30 2017, net income decreased 6.6% to US$19.2 million from US$20.5 million in the year-earlier quarter. Revenues were US$94.1 million, up 17.7% from US$80.0 million the year before. Revenues from property income rose 17.7% to US$69.6 million from US$59.1 million in the corresponding quarter a year earlier.

Prospects: Our evaluation of Urban Edge Properties as of Jan. 21, 2018 is the result of our systematic analysis on three basic characteristics: earnings strength, relative valuation, and recent stock price movement. The company has suffered a very negative trend in earnings per share over the past 5 quarters. Because the company lacks sufficient analyst estimate data, we place greater weight on the historical EPS trend as the measure of earnings strength. Based on operating earnings yield, the company is about fairly valued when compared to all of the companies in our coverage universe. Share price changes over the past year indicates that UE will perform well over the near term.

Financial Data

(US$ in Thousands)	9 Mos	6 Mos	3 Mos	12/31/2016	12/31/2015	12/31/2014	12/31/2013	12/31/2012
Earnings Per Share	0.97	1.01	1.22	0.91	0.39	0.66	1.10	0.70
Cash Flow Per Share	1.37	1.48	1.43	1.38	1.39	...	...	...
Tang Book Value Per Share	7.35	5.39	4.17	4.30	4.07	2.13	...	...
Dividends Per Share	0.880	0.860	0.840	0.820	0.800	...	...	...
Dividend Payout %	90.72	85.15	68.85	90.11	205.13	...	...	...
Income Statement								
Total Revenue	309,666	215,565	126,064	325,976	322,945	315,676	362,995	304,233
EBITDA	125,283	93,902	66,870	200,868	151,206	168,991	214,979	168,488
Depn & Amortn	(4,667)	(2,656)	(1,172)	52,232	53,130	46,551	47,766	43,522
Income Before Taxes	89,753	70,279	55,055	97,434	42,642	67,515	111,435	71,214
Income Taxes	942	624	320	804	1,294	1,721	2,100	1,364
Net Income	81,347	64,169	50,586	90,815	38,785	65,772	109,314	69,837
Average Shares	111,260	104,260	100,093	99,794	99,278	99,245	99,248	99,248
Balance Sheet								
Current Assets	511,991	368,809	234,977	245,902	285,688	123,447	120,767	...
Total Assets	2,706,512	2,563,704	2,050,351	1,904,138	1,918,931	1,741,529	1,749,965	...
Current Liabilities	65,769	63,388	54,286	48,842	45,331	26,924	30,538	...
Long-Term Obligations	1,408,066	1,412,397	1,256,955	1,197,513	1,233,983	1,288,535	1,200,762	...
Total Liabilities	1,778,649	1,889,219	1,560,582	1,443,832	1,481,011	1,483,007	1,408,700	...
Stockholders' Equity	927,863	674,485	489,769	460,306	437,920	258,522	341,265	...
Shares Outstanding	113,817	107,564	99,826	99,754	99,290	104,964	...	...
Statistical Record								
Return on Assets %	4.35	4.59	6.20	4.74	...	3.77	...	...
Return on Equity %	14.49	18.18	26.48	20.17	...	21.93	...	...
EBITDA Margin %	40.46	43.56	53.05	61.62	46.82	53.53	59.22	55.38
Net Margin %	26.27	29.77	40.13	27.86	12.01	20.84	30.11	22.96
Asset Turnover	0.17	0.17	0.19	0.17	...	0.18	...	...
Current Ratio	7.78	5.82	4.33	5.03	6.30	4.59	3.95	...
Debt to Equity	1.52	2.09	2.57	2.60	2.82	4.98	3.52	...
Price Range	28.85-23.44	30.15-23.44	30.15-24.49	30.15-22.22	25.00-20.12	...	...	...
P/E Ratio	29.74-24.16	29.85-23.21	24.71-20.07	33.13-24.42	64.10-51.59	...	...	...
Average Yield %	3.39	3.18	3.07	3.08	3.52	...	...	...

Address: 888 Seventh Avenue, New York, NY 10019 **Telephone:** 212-956-2556	**Web Site:** www.uedge.com **Officers:** Jeffrey S. Olson - Chairman, President, Chief Executive Officer Robert Minutoli - Chief Operating Officer	**Auditors:** Deloitte & Touche LLP

URSTADT BIDDLE PROPERTIES INC

Exchange	Symbol	Price	52Wk Range	Yield	P/E	Div Achiever
NYS	UBA	$21.74 (12/29/2017)	24.29-18.41	4.97	27.17	18 Years

*7 Year Price Score 82.17   *NYSE Composite Index=100   *12 Month Price Score 99.62

Interim Earnings (Per Share)

Qtr.	Jan	Apr	Jul	Oct
2012-13	(0.02)	0.09	0.12	0.12
2013-14	0.46	0.08	0.11	0.77
2014-15	0.06	0.10	0.13	0.62
2015-16	0.08	0.12	0.13	0.16
2016-17	0.08	0.57	0.14	0.01

Interim Dividends (Per Share)

Amt	Decl	Ex	Rec	Pay
0.265Q	03/22/2017	03/30/2017	04/03/2017	04/17/2017
0.265Q	06/05/2017	06/28/2017	06/30/2017	07/14/2017
0.265Q	09/06/2017	10/05/2017	10/06/2017	10/20/2017
0.27Q	12/14/2017	01/04/2018	01/05/2018	01/19/2018

Indicated Div: $1.08

Valuation Analysis

		Institutional Holding	
Forecast EPS	$0.61	No of Institutions	
	(01/18/2018)	41	
Market Cap	$856.4 Million	Shares	
Book Value	$587.2 Million	917,172	
Price/Book	1.46	% Held	
Price/Sales	6.93	2.95	

Business Summary: REITs (MIC: 5.3.1 SIC: 6798 NAIC: 525930)

Urstadt Biddle Properties is a real estate investment trust engaged in the acquisition, ownership and management of commercial real estate. Co.'s sole business is the ownership of real estate investments, which consist principally of investments in income-producing properties, with primary emphasis on properties in the metropolitan New York tri-state area outside of the City of New York. At Oct 31 2016, Co. owned or had equity interests in 75 properties comprised of neighborhood and community shopping centers, office buildings, single tenant retail or restaurant properties and office/retail mixed use properties located in four states throughout the U.S.

Recent Developments: For the year ended Oct 31 2017, net income increased 60.2% to US$55.4 million from US$34.6 million in the prior year. Revenues were US$123.6 million, up 5.8% from US$116.8 million the year before. Revenues from property income rose 5.2% to US$119.5 million from US$113.6 million in the corresponding earlier year.

Prospects: Our evaluation of Urstadt Biddle Properties Inc. as of Jan. 14, 2018 is the result of our systematic analysis on three basic characteristics: earnings strength, relative valuation, and recent stock price movement. The company has suffered a very negative trend in earnings per share over the past 5 quarters. Because the company lacks sufficient analyst estimate data, we place greater weight on the historical EPS trend as the measure of earnings strength. Based on operating earnings yield, the company is undervalued when compared to all of the companies in our coverage universe. Share price changes over the past year indicates that UBA will perform very well over the near term.

Financial Data
(US$ in Thousands)

	10/31/2017	10/31/2016	10/31/2015	10/31/2014	10/31/2013	10/31/2012	10/31/2011	10/31/2010
Earnings Per Share	0.80	0.49	0.90	1.42	0.31	0.41	0.60	0.52
Cash Flow Per Share	1.67	1.70	1.49	1.64	1.66	1.86	1.68	1.78
Tang Book Value Per Share	10.08	10.08	9.42	8.40	7.84	9.09	11.41	11.69
Dividends Per Share	1.060	1.040	1.020	1.010	1.000	0.990	0.980	0.970
Dividend Payout %	132.50	212.24	113.33	71.13	322.58	241.46	163.33	186.54
Income Statement								
Total Revenue	123,560	116,792	115,312	102,328	94,245	91,295	91,011	85,149
EBITDA	73,778	68,352	63,576	80,837	53,352	53,875	53,862	49,896
Depn & Amortn	26,512	23,025	22,435	19,249	17,816	16,721	15,292	15,066
Income Before Taxes	34,641	32,586	27,894	51,487	27,787	28,898	31,556	27,641
Net Income	52,933	33,716	49,264	65,151	29,795	28,260	31,643	27,542
Average Shares	38,529	36,022	35,060	31,963	31,740	29,168	28,665	26,118
Balance Sheet								
Current Assets	30,612	28,185	31,167	95,513	25,515	164,614	29,043	37,972
Total Assets	996,713	931,324	861,075	819,005	650,026	724,243	576,264	557,053
Current Liabilities	4,200	4,977	3,438	1,622	1,450	1,632	893	1,397
Long-Term Obligations	301,071	281,016	283,207	245,697	175,496	154,836	159,985	129,802
Total Liabilities	409,483	332,291	320,297	343,962	204,112	239,725	177,843	153,399
Stockholders' Equity	587,230	599,033	540,778	475,043	445,914	484,518	398,421	403,654
Shares Outstanding	39,393	39,141	35,721	32,805	32,565	32,315	29,563	29,281
Statistical Record								
Return on Assets %	5.49	3.75	5.86	8.87	4.34	4.33	5.58	5.19
Return on Equity %	8.92	5.90	9.70	14.15	6.40	6.38	7.89	7.12
EBITDA Margin %	59.71	58.52	55.13	79.00	56.61	59.01	59.18	58.60
Net Margin %	42.84	28.87	42.72	63.67	31.61	30.95	34.77	32.35
Asset Turnover	0.13	0.13	0.14	0.14	0.14	0.14	0.16	0.16
Current Ratio	7.29	5.66	9.07	58.89	17.60	100.87	32.52	27.18
Debt to Equity	0.51	0.47	0.52	0.52	0.39	0.32	0.40	0.32
Price Range	24.33-18.41	25.13-18.57	24.22-17.43	22.08-18.13	23.05-18.12	20.78-15.61	20.05-15.31	19.55-13.72
P/E Ratio	30.41-23.01	51.29-37.90	26.91-19.37	15.55-12.77	74.35-58.45	50.68-38.07	33.42-25.52	37.60-26.38
Average Yield %	4.98	4.87	5.02	4.88	5.25	5.35	5.84

Address: 321 Railroad Avenue, Greenwich, CT 06830

Telephone: 203-863-8200

Web Site: www.ubproperties.com

Officers: Charles J. Urstadt - Chairman, Chief Executive Officer Willing L. Biddle - President, Chief Executive Officer, Chief Operating Officer

Auditors: PKF O'Connor Davies, LLP

Investor Contact: 203-863-8200

Transfer Agents: BNY Mellon Shareowner Services, Jersey City, N

US FOODS HOLDING CORP

Exchange	Symbol	Price	52Wk Range	Yield	P/E
NYS	USFD	$31.93 (12/29/2017)	31.93-25.77	N/A	27.06

*7 Year Price Score N/A   *NYSE Composite Index=100   *12 Month Price Score 98.47

TRADING VOLUME (thousand shares)

Interim Earnings (Per Share)

Qtr.	Mar	Jun	Sep	Dec
2015	0.04	0.97	0.03	(0.06)
2016	0.08	(0.07)	0.59	0.35
2017	0.12	0.29	0.42	...

Interim Dividends (Per Share)

No Dividends Paid

Valuation Analysis   Institutional Holding

Forecast EPS	$1.37	No of Institutions
	(01/18/2018)	264
Market Cap	$7.2 Billion	Shares
Book Value	$2.7 Billion	220,367,184
Price/Book	2.61	% Held
Price/Sales	0.30	N/A

Business Summary: Retail - Food & Beverage, Drug & Tobacco (MIC: 2.1.2 SIC: 5149 NAIC: 424490)

US Foods Holding is a holding company. Through its subsidiaries, Co. is engaged as a food company and a foodservice distributor. Co. supplies approximately 250,000 customer locations nationwide. They include independently owned single and multi-unit restaurants, regional restaurant concepts, national restaurant chains, hospitals, nursing homes, hotels and motels, country clubs, government and military organizations, colleges and universities, and retail locations. Co. provides approximately 400,000 fresh, frozen, and dry food stock-keeping units, as well as non-food items, sourced from over 5,000 suppliers.

Recent Developments: For the quarter ended Sep 30 2017, net income decreased 28.2% to US$95.6 million from US$133.0 million in the year-earlier quarter. Revenues were US$6.20 billion, up 6.2% from US$5.84 billion the year before. Operating income was US$190.0 million versus US$115.1 million in the prior-year quarter, an increase of 65.1%. Direct operating expenses rose 6.2% to US$5.11 billion from US$4.81 billion in the comparable period the year before. Indirect operating expenses decreased 1.0% to US$908.5 million from US$917.4 million in the equivalent prior-year period.

Prospects: Our evaluation of US Foods Holding Corp as of Jan. 14, 2018 is the result of our systematic analysis on three basic characteristics: earnings strength, relative valuation, and recent stock price movement. The company has generated a negative trend in earnings per share over the past 5 quarters and while recent estimates for the company have been raised by analysts, USFD has posted better than expected results. Based on operating earnings yield, the company is about fairly valued when compared to all of the companies in our coverage universe. Based price changes over the past year indicates that USFD will perform poorly over the near term.

Financial Data

(US$ in Thousands)	9 Mos	6 Mos	3 Mos	12/31/2016	01/02/2016	12/27/2014	12/28/2013
Earnings Per Share	1.18	1.35	0.99	1.03	0.98	(0.43)	(0.34)
Cash Flow Per Share	2.78	2.80	2.44	2.78	3.22	2.38	1.90
Income Statement							
Total Revenue	18,151,273	11,947,079	5,788,425	22,918,808	23,127,532	23,019,801	22,297,178
EBITDA	605,560	343,456	146,806	626,189	730,328	513,256	518,703
Depn & Amortn	213,433	141,358	70,282	266,000	253,000	261,000	240,000
Income Before Taxes	266,028	119,209	34,638	131,109	192,153	(36,946)	(27,384)
Income Taxes	78,203	26,935	7,822	(78,685)	24,635	35,968	29,822
Net Income	187,825	92,274	26,816	209,794	167,518	(72,914)	(57,206)
Average Shares	225,862	226,791	226,323	204,024	171,060	169,467	169,634
Balance Sheet							
Current Assets	3,134,171	3,021,523	2,993,671	2,789,171	3,060,433	2,820,099	...
Total Assets	9,358,234	9,208,096	9,177,596	8,944,450	9,239,359	9,022,538	...
Current Liabilities	2,246,250	2,213,066	2,095,207	1,969,285	1,802,823	1,825,587	...
Long-Term Obligations	3,596,647	3,623,397	3,772,270	3,705,751	4,682,149	4,661,697	...
Total Liabilities	6,613,050	6,574,638	6,603,214	6,406,800	7,327,741	7,357,822	...
Stockholders' Equity	2,745,184	2,633,458	2,574,382	2,537,650	1,911,618	1,664,716	...
Shares Outstanding	224,459	223,801	221,992	220,928	166,667	166,667	166,667
Statistical Record							
Return on Assets %	2.87	3.32	2.45	2.31	1.80	...	...
Return on Equity %	10.11	12.13	11.63	9.46	9.22	...	...
EBITDA Margin %	3.34	2.87	2.54	2.73	3.16	2.23	2.33
Net Margin %	1.03	0.77	0.46	0.92	0.72	N.M.	N.M.
Asset Turnover	2.58	2.58	2.54	2.53	2.49	...	...
Current Ratio	1.40	1.37	1.43	1.42	1.70	1.54	...
Debt to Equity	1.31	1.38	1.47	1.46	2.45	2.80	...
Price Range	30.57-22.38	30.57-22.38	27.98-22.38	27.48-22.38	...	...	...
P/E Ratio	25.91-18.97	22.64-16.58	28.26-22.61	26.68-21.73	...	...	...

Address: 9399 W. Higgins Road, Suite 500, Rosemont, IL 60018
Telephone: 847-720-8000

Web Site: www.usfoods.com
Officers: John C. Compton - Chairman Pietro Satriano - President, Chief Executive Officer

Auditors: Deloitte & Touche LLP
Transfer Agents: American Stock Transfer & Trust Company, LLC

USG CORP

Exchange	Symbol	Price	52Wk Range	Yield	P/E
NYS	USG	$38.56 (12/29/2017)	38.70-25.78	N/A	12.24

*7 Year Price Score 99.86   ***NYSE Composite Index=100**   ***12 Month Price Score 109.38**

Interim Earnings (Per Share)

Qtr.	Mar	Jun	Sep	Dec
2014	0.32	0.38	(0.09)	(0.37)
2015	0.16	0.54	0.52	5.52
2016	0.46	0.50	0.42	2.08
2017	0.37	0.24	0.46	...

Interim Dividends (Per Share)

No Dividends Paid

Valuation Analysis

		Institutional Holding	
Forecast EPS	$1.66 (01/18/2018)	No of Institutions	372
Market Cap	$5.5 Billion	Shares	
Book Value	$2.0 Billion		133,806,000
Price/Book	2.75	% Held	
Price/Sales	1.76		96.07

TRADING VOLUME (thousand shares)

Business Summary: Construction Materials (MIC: 8.5.1 SIC: 3275 NAIC: 327420)

USG, through its subsidiaries, is a manufacturer of building systems. Co.'s operations are organized into three segments: Gypsum, which manufactures and markets gypsum and related products in the U.S., Canada and Mexico; Ceilings, which manufactures and markets interior systems products in the U.S., Canada, Mexico, and Latin America; as well as USG Boral Building Products, which consists of its 50/50 joint ventures, USG Boral Building Products Pte. Limited and USG Boral Building Products Pty Limited, which manufactures and distributes products for wall, ceiling, floor lining and exterior systems that utilize gypsum wallboard, mineral fiber ceiling tiles, steel grid and joint compound.

Recent Developments: For the quarter ended Sep 30 2017, income from continuing operations increased 17.9% to US$66.0 million from US$56.0 million in the year-earlier quarter. Net income increased 6.5% to US$66.0 million from US$62.0 million in the year-earlier quarter. Revenues were US$795.0 million, up 3.7% from US$767.0 million the year before. Operating income was US$93.0 million versus US$97.0 million in the prior-year quarter, a decrease of 4.1%. Direct operating expenses rose 7.8% to US$632.0 million from US$586.0 million in the comparable period the year before. Indirect operating expenses decreased 16.7% to US$70.0 million from US$84.0 million in the equivalent prior-year period.

Prospects: Our evaluation of USG Corp. as of Jan. 14, 2018 is the result of our systematic analysis on three basic characteristics: earnings strength, relative valuation, and recent stock price movement. The company has produced a positive trend in earnings per share over the past 5 quarters and while recent estimates for the company have been mixed, USG has posted better than expected results. Based on operating earnings yield, the company is about fairly valued when compared to all of the companies in our coverage universe. Share price changes over the past year indicates that USG will perform in line with the market over the near term.

Financial Data

(US$ in Thousands)	9 Mos	6 Mos	3 Mos	12/31/2016	12/31/2015	12/31/2014	12/31/2013	12/31/2012
Earnings Per Share	3.15	3.11	3.37	3.46	6.73	0.25	0.42	(1.19)
Cash Flow Per Share	1.96	2.33	2.55	2.55	2.28	1.22	0.73	0.64
Tang Book Value Per Share	14.01	14.03	13.55	12.90	9.86	2.81	4.65	0.06
Income Statement								
Total Revenue	2,373,000	1,578,000	767,000	3,017,000	3,776,000	3,724,000	3,570,000	3,224,000
EBITDA	351,000	226,000	123,000	495,000	492,000	323,000	394,000	168,000
Depn & Amortn	98,000	65,000	33,000	129,000	130,000	134,000	135,000	136,000
Income Before Taxes	201,000	123,000	71,000	225,000	201,000	11,000	59,000	(170,000)
Income Taxes	76,000	49,000	29,000	63,000	(729,000)	7,000	11,000	12,000
Net Income	157,000	91,000	55,000	510,000	991,000	37,000	47,000	(126,000)
Average Shares	144,681	146,860	148,730	147,660	147,246	144,296	111,434	106,382
Balance Sheet								
Current Assets	935,000	949,000	953,000	949,000	1,400,000	1,152,000	1,700,000	1,327,000
Total Assets	3,892,000	3,887,000	3,912,000	3,869,000	4,736,000	3,994,000	4,121,000	3,723,000
Current Liabilities	394,000	379,000	869,000	422,000	991,000	563,000	568,000	551,000
Long-Term Obligations	1,077,000	1,077,000	584,000	1,083,000	1,675,000	2,205,000	2,292,000	2,305,000
Total Liabilities	1,910,000	1,919,000	1,936,000	1,983,000	3,300,000	3,587,000	3,483,000	3,717,000
Stockholders' Equity	1,982,000	1,968,000	1,976,000	1,886,000	1,436,000	407,000	638,000	6,000
Shares Outstanding	141,475	140,307	145,792	146,167	145,667	144,768	137,314	107,850
Statistical Record								
Return on Assets %	10.85	10.78	11.62	11.82	22.70	0.91	1.20	N.M.
Return on Equity %	25.70	26.03	28.51	30.62	107.54	7.08	14.60	N.M.
EBITDA Margin %	14.79	14.32	16.04	16.41	13.03	8.67	11.04	5.21
Net Margin %	6.62	5.77	7.17	16.90	26.24	0.99	1.32	N.M.
Asset Turnover	0.73	0.72	0.76	0.70	0.87	0.92	0.91	0.86
Current Ratio	2.37	2.50	1.10	2.25	1.41	2.05	2.99	2.41
Debt to Equity	0.54	0.55	0.30	0.57	1.17	5.42	3.59	384.17
Price Range	34.34-23.92	34.34-23.92	34.34-23.92	32.19-16.48	32.73-22.91	35.85-24.55	30.44-22.19	28.43-10.56
P/E Ratio	10.90-7.59	11.04-7.69	10.19-7.10	9.30-4.76	4.86-3.40	143.40-98.20	72.48-52.83	...

Address: 550 West Adams Street, Chicago, IL 60661-3676	Web Site: www.usg.com	Auditors: Deloitte & Touche LLP
Telephone: 312-436-4000	Officers: Jennifer F. Scanlon - President, Chief Executive Officer Matthew F. Hilzinger - Executive Vice President, Chief Financial Officer	Investor Contact: 312-436-6098 Transfer Agents: Computershare Trust Company, Providence, RI

VAIL RESORTS INC

Exchange	Symbol	Price	52Wk Range	Yield	P/E
NYS	MTN	$212.47 (12/29/2017)	236.71-160.98	1.98	36.26

*7 Year Price Score 163.48 *NYSE Composite Index=100 *12 Month Price Score 103.26

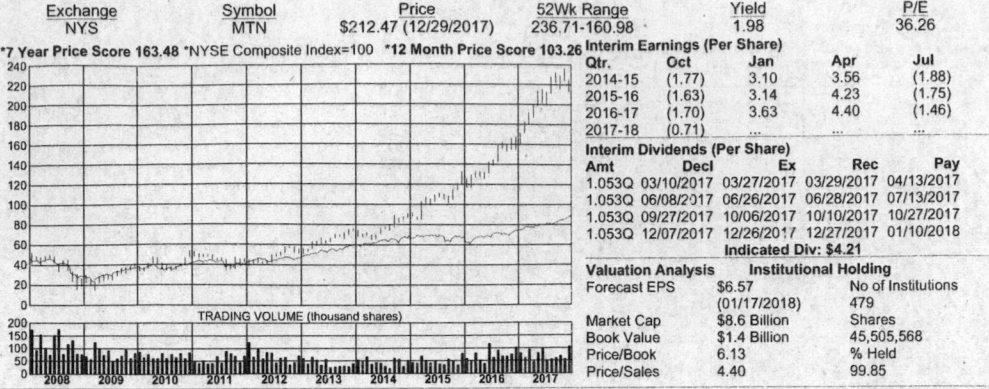

Interim Earnings (Per Share)

Qtr.	Oct	Jan	Apr	Jul
2014-15	(1.77)	3.10	3.56	(1.88)
2015-16	(1.63)	3.14	4.23	(1.75)
2016-17	(1.70)	3.63	4.40	(1.46)
2017-18	(0.71)	...	...	...

Interim Dividends (Per Share)

Amt	Decl	Ex	Rec	Pay
1.053Q	03/10/2017	03/27/2017	03/29/2017	04/13/2017
1.053Q	06/08/2017	06/26/2017	06/28/2017	07/13/2017
1.053Q	09/27/2017	10/06/2017	10/10/2017	10/27/2017
1.053Q	12/07/2017	12/26/2017	12/27/2017	01/10/2018

Indicated Div: $4.21

Valuation Analysis — **Institutional Holding**

Forecast EPS	$6.57	No of Institutions
	(01/17/2018)	479
Market Cap	$8.6 Billion	Shares
Book Value	$1.4 Billion	45,505,568
Price/Book	6.13	% Held
Price/Sales	4.40	99.85

Business Summary: Sporting & Recreational (MIC: 2.2.4 SIC: 7999 NAIC: 713990)

Vail Resorts is a holding company and operates through various subsidiaries. Co. operates in three segments: Mountain, which operates mountain resort properties and urban ski areas, as well as ancillary services, primarily including ski school, dining and retail/rental operations; Lodging, which owns and/or manages hotels under its RockResorts brand, other lodging properties, condominiums located in proximity to its mountain resorts, National Park Service concessionaire properties including Grand Teton Lodge Company, a resort ground transportation company, and mountain resort golf courses; and Real Estate, which owns, develops and sells real estate in and around its resort communities.

Recent Developments: For the quarter ended Oct 31 2017, net loss amounted to US$31.9 million versus a net loss of US$63.6 million in the year-earlier quarter. Revenues were US$220.9 million, up 23.9% from US$178.3 million the year before. Operating loss was US$103.7 million versus a loss of US$90.5 million in the prior-year quarter. Direct operating expenses rose 19.4% to US$218.6 million from US$183.1 million in the comparable period the year before. Indirect operating expenses increased 23.6% to US$105.9 million from US$85.7 million in the equivalent prior-year period.

Prospects: Our evaluation of Vail Resorts Inc. as of Jan. 14, 2018 is the result of our systematic analysis on three basic characteristics: earnings strength, relative valuation, and recent stock price movement. The company has managed to produce a neutral trend in earnings per share over the past 5 quarters. However, while recent estimates for the company have been lowered by analysts, MTN has posted better than expected results. Based on operating earnings yield, the company is about fairly valued when compared to all of the companies in our coverage universe. Share price changes over the past year indicates that MTN will perform very well over the near term.

Financial Data

(US$ in Thousands)	3 Mos	07/31/2017	07/31/2016	07/31/2015	07/31/2014	07/31/2013	07/31/2012	07/31/2011
Earnings Per Share	5.86	5.22	4.01	3.07	0.77	1.03	0.45	0.94
Cash Flow Per Share	13.93	11.64	11.73	8.36	6.81	6.20	5.14	7.42
Tang Book Value Per Share	N.M.	N.M.	6.23	6.08	8.98	9.84	12.38	13.05
Dividends Per Share	3.969	3.726	2.865	2.075	1.245	0.790	0.675	0.150
Dividend Payout %	67.73	71.38	71.45	67.59	161.69	76.70	150.00	15.96
Income Statement								
Total Revenue	220,850	1,907,218	1,601,286	1,399,924	1,254,646	1,120,797	1,024,394	1,167,046
EBITDA	(61,533)	581,455	440,502	343,747	243,407	227,504	184,300	204,119
Depn & Amortn	48,624	180,800	156,800	144,000	136,600	130,200	124,500	116,300
Income Before Taxes	(125,331)	346,566	241,336	148,506	42,810	58,338	26,214	54,178
Income Taxes	(93,404)	116,731	93,165	34,718	15,866	21,619	10,701	21,098
Net Income	(28,385)	210,553	149,754	114,754	28,478	37,743	16,453	34,489
Average Shares	40,211	40,366	37,312	37,406	37,057	36,733	36,673	36,754
Balance Sheet								
Current Assets	395,703	433,070	322,865	288,143	275,046	343,469	232,370	245,624
Total Assets	4,008,616	4,110,718	2,482,018	2,489,621	2,173,849	2,275,422	1,927,614	1,946,236
Current Liabilities	709,596	604,557	506,481	398,647	324,206	313,335	249,249	243,182
Long-Term Obligations	1,262,325	1,234,024	686,909	806,676	625,600	795,928	489,775	490,698
Total Liabilities	2,607,211	2,539,562	1,607,478	1,623,053	1,353,006	1,451,554	1,125,303	1,116,513
Stockholders' Equity	1,401,405	1,571,156	874,540	866,568	820,843	823,868	802,311	829,723
Shares Outstanding	40,406	40,081	36,179	36,513	36,203	35,954	35,582	36,070
Statistical Record								
Return on Assets %	6.17	6.39	6.01	4.92	1.28	1.80	0.85	1.78
Return on Equity %	17.87	17.22	17.16	13.60	3.46	4.64	2.01	4.26
EBITDA Margin %	N.M.	30.49	27.51	24.55	19.40	20.30	17.99	17.49
Net Margin %	N.M.	11.04	9.35	8.20	2.27	3.37	1.61	2.96
Asset Turnover	0.49	0.58	0.64	0.60	0.56	0.53	0.53	0.60
Current Ratio	0.56	0.72	0.64	0.72	0.85	1.10	0.93	1.01
Debt to Equity	0.90	0.79	0.79	0.93	0.76	0.97	0.61	0.59
Price Range	232.28-154.44	215.36-142.60	144.80-101.26	111.48-74.23	78.79-64.90	66.98-49.00	50.89-34.76	53.43-32.91
P/E Ratio	39.64-26.35	41.26-27.32	36.11-25.25	36.31-24.18	102.32-84.29	65.03-47.57	113.09-77.24	56.84-35.01
Average Yield %	2.04	2.10	2.32	2.23	1.75	1.37	1.57	0.33

Address: 390 Interlocken Crescent, Broomfield, CO 80021	**Web Site:** www.vailresorts.com	**Auditors:** PricewaterhouseCoopers LLP
Telephone: 303-404-1800	**Officers:** Robert A. Katz - Chairman, Chief Executive Officer Michael Z. Barkin - Executive Vice President, Vice President, Chief Financial Officer	**Investor Contact:** 303-404-1820
Fax: 303-404-6415		**Transfer Agents:** Wells Fargo Shareowner Services, Saint Paul, MN

VALERO ENERGY CORP

Exchange	Symbol	Price	52Wk Range	Yield	P/E
NYS	VLO	$91.91 (12/29/2017)	92.30-61.47	3.05	19.81

*7 Year Price Score 118.02 *NYSE Composite Index=100 *12 Month Price Score 113.69

Interim Earnings (Per Share)

Qtr.	Mar	Jun	Sep	Dec
2014	1.54	1.10	2.00	2.21
2015	1.87	2.66	2.79	0.69
2016	1.05	1.73	1.33	0.82
2017	0.68	1.23	1.91	...

Interim Dividends (Per Share)

Amt	Decl	Ex	Rec	Pay
0.70Q	01/26/2017	02/13/2017	02/15/2017	03/07/2017
0.70Q	05/03/2017	05/15/2017	05/17/2017	06/07/2017
0.70Q	07/20/2017	08/07/2017	08/09/2017	09/07/2017
0.70Q	11/01/2017	11/20/2017	11/21/2017	12/12/2017

Indicated Div: $2.80

Valuation Analysis

		Institutional Holding	
Forecast EPS	$4.88	No of Institutions	
	(01/18/2018)	1368	
Market Cap	$40.3 Billion	Shares	
Book Value	$20.4 Billion	449,344,576	
Price/Book	1.98	% Held	
Price/Sales	0.46	75.04	

Business Summary: Refining & Marketing (MIC: 9.1.2 SIC: 2911 NAIC: 324110)

Valero Energy is a petroleum refiner and ethanol producer. Co. sells its refined petroleum products in both the wholesale rack and bulk markets, and outlets carry the Valero®, Diamond Shamrock®, Shamrock®, Ultramar®, Beacon®, and Texaco® brand names in the U.S., Canada, the U.K., and Ireland. As of Dec 31 2016, Co. had two reportable segments: refining and ethanol. The refining segment includes Co.'s refining operations, the associated marketing activities, and logistics assets that support its refining operations. The ethanol segment includes Co.'s ethanol operations, the associated marketing activities, and logistics assets that support its ethanol operations.

Recent Developments: For the quarter ended Sep 30 2017, net income increased 33.8% to US$863.0 million from US$645.0 million in the year-earlier quarter. Revenues were US$23.56 billion, up 19.9% from US$19.65 billion the year before. Operating income was US$1.34 billion versus US$892.0 million in the prior-year quarter, an increase of 50.0%. Direct operating expenses rose 18.2% to US$21.94 billion from US$18.55 billion in the comparable period the year before. Indirect operating expenses increased 40.2% to US$286.0 million from US$204.0 million in the equivalent prior-year period.

Prospects: Our evaluation of Valero Energy Corp. as of Jan. 14, 2018 is the result of our systematic analysis on three basic characteristics: earnings strength, relative valuation, and recent stock price movement. The company has produced a positive trend in earnings per share over the past 5 quarters. However, while recent estimates for the company have been mixed, VLO has posted better than expected results. Based on operating earnings yield, the company is undervalued when compared to all of the companies in our coverage universe. Share price changes over the past year indicates that VLO will perform poorly over the near term.

Financial Data

(US$ in Thousands)	9 Mos	6 Mos	3 Mos	12/31/2016	12/31/2015	12/31/2014	12/31/2013	12/31/2012
Earnings Per Share	4.64	4.06	4.56	4.94	7.99	6.85	4.97	3.75
Cash Flow Per Share	10.98	10.46	11.54	10.43	11.29	8.06	10.27	9.56
Tang Book Value Per Share	46.51	45.07	44.34	44.35	43.39	40.20	36.04	32.28
Dividends Per Share	2.700	2.600	2.500	2.400	1.700	1.050	0.850	0.650
Dividend Payout %	58.19	64.04	54.82	48.58	21.28	15.33	17.10	17.33
Income Statement								
Total Revenue	67,588,000	44,026,000	21,772,000	75,659,000	87,804,000	130,844,000	138,074,000	139,250,000
EBITDA	4,292,000	2,440,000	1,054,000	4,928,000	7,704,000	7,149,000	5,547,000	5,119,000
Depn & Amortn	1,496,000	999,000	500,000	1,300,000	1,300,000	1,200,000	1,200,000	1,100,000
Income Before Taxes	2,442,000	1,201,000	433,000	3,182,000	5,971,000	5,552,000	3,982,000	3,706,000
Income Taxes	686,000	308,000	112,000	765,000	1,870,000	1,777,000	1,254,000	1,626,000
Net Income	1,694,000	853,000	305,000	2,289,000	3,990,000	3,630,000	2,720,000	2,083,000
Average Shares	441,000	446,000	451,000	464,000	500,000	530,000	548,000	556,000
Balance Sheet								
Current Assets	17,442,000	15,731,000	15,908,000	16,800,000	14,972,000	16,614,000	19,277,000	16,460,000
Total Assets	47,988,000	45,974,000	46,047,000	46,173,000	44,343,000	45,550,000	47,260,000	44,477,000
Current Liabilities	9,130,000	7,683,000	7,899,000	8,328,000	7,360,000	9,980,000	13,123,000	11,929,000
Long-Term Obligations	8,364,000	8,366,000	8,369,000	7,886,000	7,250,000	5,780,000	6,261,000	6,463,000
Total Liabilities	27,618,000	26,051,000	26,222,000	26,149,000	23,816,000	24,873,000	27,800,000	26,445,000
Stockholders' Equity	20,370,000	19,923,000	19,825,000	20,024,000	20,527,000	20,677,000	19,460,000	18,032,000
Shares Outstanding	437,966	442,003	447,162	451,501	473,039	514,298	535,569	552,095
Statistical Record								
Return on Assets %	4.37	4.01	4.65	5.04	8.88	7.82	5.93	4.76
Return on Equity %	10.13	9.05	10.37	11.26	19.37	18.09	14.51	12.06
EBITDA Margin %	6.35	5.54	4.84	6.51	8.77	5.46	4.02	3.68
Net Margin %	2.51	1.94	1.40	3.03	4.54	2.77	1.97	1.50
Asset Turnover	1.87	1.85	1.81	1.67	1.95	2.82	3.01	3.18
Current Ratio	1.91	2.05	2.01	2.02	2.03	1.66	1.47	1.38
Debt to Equity	0.41	0.42	0.42	0.39	0.35	0.28	0.32	0.36
Price Range	76.93-52.90	70.42-47.24	70.42-47.24	72.09-47.24	73.03-44.07	58.51-43.76	50.40-31.17	31.41-17.91
P/E Ratio	16.58-11.40	17.34-11.64	15.44-10.36	14.59-9.56	9.14-5.52	8.54-6.39	10.14-6.27	8.37-4.78
Average Yield %	4.12	4.22	4.20	4.09	2.76	2.05	2.20	2.65

Address: One Valero Way, San Antonio, TX 78249	Web Site: www.valero.com	Auditors: KPMG LLP
Telephone: 210-345-2000	Officers: Joseph W. Gorder - Chairman, President, Chief Executive Officer, Associate/Affiliate Company Officer, Executive Vice President, Chief Operating Officer, Chief Commercial Officer Michael S. Ciskowski - Executive Vice President, Chief Financial Officer	Investor Contact: 800-531-7911
Fax: 210-246-2646		Transfer Agents: ComputerShare Investor Services, Providence, RI

VALLEY NATIONAL BANCORP (NJ)

Exchange	Symbol	Price	52Wk Range	Yield	P/E
NYS	VLY	$11.22 (12/29/2017)	12.76-10.71	3.92	16.50

*7 Year Price Score 87.43   *NYSE Composite Index=100   ***12 Month Price Score 92.78**

Interim Earnings (Per Share)

Qtr.	Mar	Jun	Sep	Dec
2014	0.17	0.15	0.14	0.11
2015	0.13	0.14	0.15	0.01
2016	0.14	0.15	0.16	0.19
2017	0.17	0.18	0.14	...

Interim Dividends (Per Share)

Amt	Decl	Ex	Rec	Pay
0.11Q	03/01/2017	03/13/2017	03/15/2017	04/03/2017
0.11Q	05/25/2017	06/13/2017	06/15/2017	07/03/2017
0.11Q	08/22/2017	09/14/2017	09/15/2017	10/03/2017
0.11Q	11/28/2017	12/21/2017	12/22/2017	01/03/2018

Indicated Div: $0.44 (Div. Reinv. Plan)

Valuation Analysis

		Institutional Holding	
Forecast EPS	$0.67	No of Institutions	
	(01/01/2018)	344	
Market Cap	$3.0 Billion	Shares	
Book Value	$2.5 Billion	205,387,248	
Price/Book	1.17	% Held	
Price/Sales	3.18	55.59	

Business Summary: Banking (MIC: 5.1.1 SIC: 6021 NAIC: 522110)

Valley National Bancorp is a bank holding company. Through its subsidiary, Valley National Bank (the Bank), Co. provides commercial, retail, insurance and wealth management financial services products. The Bank provides banking services including automated teller machines, telephone and internet banking, remote deposit capture, overdraft facilities, drive-in and night deposit services, and safe deposit facilities. The Bank also provides international banking services including standby letters of credit, documentary letters of credit and related products, and certain ancillary services. As of Dec 31 2016, Co. had total assets of $22.86 billion and total deposits of $17.73 billion.

Recent Developments: For the quarter ended Sep 30 2017, net income decreased 7.5% to US$39.6 million from US$42.8 million in the year-earlier quarter. Net interest income increased 6.9% to US$164.9 million from US$154.1 million in the year-earlier quarter. Provision for loan losses was US$1.6 million versus US$5.8 million in the prior-year quarter, a decrease of 71.9%. Non-interest income rose 5.0% to US$26.1 million from US$24.9 million, while non-interest expense advanced 17.0% to US$132.6 million.

Prospects: Our evaluation of Valley National Bancorp as of Jan. 14, 2018 is the result of our systematic analysis on three basic characteristics: earnings strength, relative valuation, and recent stock price movement. The company has generated a negative trend in earnings per share over the past 5 quarters and while recent estimates for the company have been mixed, VLY has posted results that fell short of analysts expectations. Based on operating earnings yield, the company is undervalued when compared to all of the companies in our coverage universe. Share price changes over the past year indicates that VLY will perform in line with the market over the near term.

Financial Data

(US$ in Thousands)	9 Mos	6 Mos	3 Mos	12/31/2016	12/31/2015	12/31/2014	12/31/2013	12/31/2012
Earnings Per Share	0.68	0.70	0.67	0.63	0.42	0.56	0.66	0.73
Cash Flow Per Share	2.66	2.16	1.63	1.64	0.66	0.89	1.43	1.63
Tang Book Value Per Share	6.04	5.98	5.88	5.80	5.36	5.38	5.39	5.26
Dividends Per Share	0.440	0.440	0.440	0.440	0.440	0.440	0.598	0.652
Dividend Payout %	64.71	62.86	65.67	69.84	104.76	78.57	90.53	89.29
Income Statement								
Interest Income	621,913	410,263	199,116	766,923	707,023	636,603	616,097	671,193
Interest Expense	125,570	78,774	36,587	148,774	156,754	161,846	168,377	181,312
Net Interest Income	496,343	331,489	162,529	618,149	550,269	474,757	447,720	489,881
Provision for Losses	7,742	6,102	2,470	11,869	8,101	1,884	16,095	25,552
Non-Interest Income	75,837	49,749	25,059	103,225	83,802	77,616	128,653	120,946
Non-Interest Expense	372,756	240,191	120,952	476,125	499,075	403,255	381,338	374,900
Income Before Taxes	191,682	134,945	64,166	233,380	126,895	147,234	178,940	210,375
Income Taxes	55,873	38,785	18,071	65,234	-23,938	31,062	46,979	66,748
Net Income	135,809	96,160	46,095	168,146	102,957	116,172	131,961	143,627
Average Shares	264,936	264,778	264,546	255,268	234,437	205,716	199,309	197,354
Balance Sheet								
Net Loans & Leases	18,095,817	17,733,890	17,449,122	17,179,392	15,953,311	13,395,855	11,464,483	11,012,829
Total Assets	23,780,661	23,449,350	23,220,456	22,864,439	21,612,616	18,793,855	16,156,541	16,012,646
Total Deposits	17,312,766	17,250,018	17,331,141	17,730,708	16,253,551	14,034,116	11,319,262	11,264,018
Total Liabilities	21,242,677	21,025,449	20,821,915	20,487,283	19,405,525	16,930,838	14,615,501	14,510,269
Stockholders' Equity	2,537,984	2,423,901	2,398,541	2,377,156	2,207,091	1,863,017	1,541,040	1,502,377
Shares Outstanding	264,031	263,971	263,842	263,638	253,787	232,110	199,593	198,438
Statistical Record								
Return on Assets %	0.81	0.84	0.79	0.75	0.51	0.66	0.82	0.95
Return on Equity %	7.75	8.12	7.71	7.32	5.06	6.83	8.67	10.35
Net Interest Margin %	77.79	80.02	81.63	80.60	77.83	74.58	72.67	72.99
Efficiency Ratio %	55.76	50.56	53.95	54.72	63.11	56.46	51.20	47.33
Loans to Deposits	1.05	1.03	1.01	0.97	0.98	0.95	1.01	0.98
Price Range	12.76-9.46	12.76-8.86	12.76-8.55	11.97-8.31	11.14-9.05	10.80-9.21	10.65-8.85	12.59-8.72
P/E Ratio	18.76-13.91	18.23-12.66	19.04-12.76	19.00-13.19	26.52-21.55	19.29-16.45	16.14-13.41	17.25-11.95
Average Yield %	3.84	4.03	4.26	4.57	4.46	4.44	6.05	6.07

Address: 1455 Valley Road, Wayne, NJ 07470	**Web Site:** www.valleynationalbank.com	**Auditors:** KPMG LLP
Telephone: 973-305-8800	**Officers:** Gerald H. Lipkin - Chairman, Chief Executive Officer Rudy E. Schupp - President	**Investor Contact:** 973-305-8800
		Transfer Agents: American Stock & Transfer & Trust Company, Brooklyn, NY

VALMONT INDUSTRIES INC

Exchange	Symbol	Price	52Wk Range	Yield	P/E
NYS	VMI	$165.85 (12/29/2017)	172.85-136.05	0.90	19.81

*7 Year Price Score 92.88 ***NYSE Composite Index=100** ***12 Month Price Score 101.60**

Interim Earnings (Per Share)

Qtr.	Mar	Jun	Sep	Dec
2014	2.08	2.38	0.92	1.66
2015	1.28	1.19	0.52	(1.29)
2016	1.45	1.85	1.24	3.09
2017	1.72	2.01	1.55	...

Interim Dividends (Per Share)

Amt	Decl	Ex	Rec	Pay
0.375Q	03/06/2017	03/29/2017	03/31/2017	04/14/2017
0.375Q	06/05/2017	06/28/2017	06/30/2017	07/14/2017
0.375Q	09/05/2017	09/28/2017	09/29/2017	10/16/2017
0.375Q	12/04/2017	12/28/2017	12/29/2017	01/16/2018

Indicated Div: $1.50 (Div. Reinv. Plan)

Valuation Analysis

		Institutional Holding	
Forecast EPS	$6.99	No of Institutions	382
	(01/18/2018)		
Market Cap	$3.7 Billion	Shares	26,044,126
Book Value	$1.1 Billion	% Held	86.76
Price/Book	3.37		
Price/Sales	1.39		

Business Summary: Construction Materials (MIC: 8.5.1 SIC: 3499 NAIC: 332323)

Valmont Industries is a producer of fabricated metal products. Co. has five segments: Engineered Support Structures, which provides engineered metal, wood, and composite structures and components; Utility Support Structures, which provides engineered steel and concrete structures; Energy and Mining, which provides access systems applications, forged steel grinding media, on and off shore oil, gas, and wind energy structures; Coatings, which consists of galvanizing, anodizing and powder coating services; and Irrigation, which provides agricultural irrigation equipment and related parts and services for the agricultural industry as well as tubular products for industrial customers.

Recent Developments: For the quarter ended Sep 30 2017, net income increased 24.2% to US$36.7 million from US$29.5 million in the year-earlier quarter. Revenues were US$680.8 million, up 11.6% from US$610.2 million the year before. Operating income was US$59.9 million versus US$53.2 million in the prior-year quarter, an increase of 12.6%. Direct operating expenses rose 13.6% to US$517.2 million from US$455.2 million in the comparable period the year before. Indirect operating expenses increased 1.9% to US$103.7 million from US$101.8 million in the equivalent prior-year period.

Prospects: Our evaluation of Valmont Industries Inc. as of Jan. 14, 2018 is the result of our systematic analysis on three basic characteristics: earnings strength, relative valuation, and recent stock price movement. The company has managed to produce a neutral trend in earnings per share over the past 5 quarters and while recent estimates for the company have been mixed, VMI has posted results that fell short of analysts expectations. Based on operating earnings yield, the company is about fairly valued when compared to all of the companies in our coverage universe. Share price changes over the past year indicates that VMI will perform in line with the market over the near term.

Financial Data

(US$ in Thousands)	9 Mos	6 Mos	3 Mos	12/31/2016	12/26/2015	12/27/2014	12/28/2013	12/29/2012
Earnings Per Share	8.37	8.06	7.90	7.63	1.71	7.09	10.35	8.75
Cash Flow Per Share	10.05	9.22	7.77	9.56	11.72	6.79	14.92	7.47
Tang Book Value Per Share	28.04	21.25	23.77	21.22	18.00	25.37	37.33	31.75
Dividends Per Share	1.500	1.500	1.500	1.500	1.500	1.375	0.975	0.855
Dividend Payout %	17.92	18.61	18.99	19.66	87.72	19.39	9.42	9.77
Income Statement								
Total Revenue	2,030,989	1,350,210	637,473	2,521,676	2,618,924	3,123,143	3,304,211	3,029,541
EBITDA	267,899	185,713	86,528	344,175	225,476	404,255	552,878	452,861
Depn & Amortn	63,500	41,754	20,827	82,417	91,144	89,328	77,436	70,218
Income Before Taxes	174,292	123,731	55,324	220,454	93,007	284,183	449,417	359,290
Income Taxes	50,343	36,448	15,363	42,063	47,427	94,894	157,781	126,502
Net Income	119,851	84,643	38,979	173,232	40,117	183,976	278,489	234,072
Average Shares	22,751	22,740	22,660	22,709	23,405	25,719	26,899	26,764
Balance Sheet								
Current Assets	1,448,123	1,376,207	1,331,273	1,253,216	1,226,852	1,392,941	1,597,840	1,425,940
Total Assets	2,610,171	2,523,162	2,466,888	2,391,731	2,399,428	2,729,668	2,776,494	2,568,551
Current Liabilities	413,460	374,047	382,704	349,848	366,554	397,214	436,580	412,433
Long-Term Obligations	754,202	754,436	754,523	754,795	763,964	766,654	470,907	472,593
Total Liabilities	1,497,337	1,458,913	1,464,049	1,448,249	1,480,987	1,527,835	1,254,469	1,218,639
Stockholders' Equity	1,112,834	1,064,249	1,002,839	943,482	918,441	1,201,833	1,522,025	1,349,912
Shares Outstanding	22,607	27,900	22,584	22,520	22,857	24,229	26,824	26,674
Statistical Record								
Return on Assets %	7.61	7.44	7.37	7.11	1.57	6.70	10.45	9.63
Return on Equity %	18.30	18.10	18.54	18.31	3.79	13.55	19.45	18.80
EBITDA Margin %	13.19	13.75	13.57	13.65	8.61	12.94	16.73	14.95
Net Margin %	5.90	6.27	6.11	6.87	1.53	5.89	8.43	7.73
Asset Turnover	1.08	1.07	1.05	1.04	1.02	1.14	1.24	1.25
Current Ratio	3.50	3.68	3.48	3.58	3.35	3.51	3.66	3.46
Debt to Equity	0.68	0.71	0.75	0.80	0.83	0.64	0.31	0.35
Price Range	159.75-122.90	159.75-122.90	159.75-117.99	155.40-98.95	130.26-93.99	161.11-123.75	164.50-132.08	141.13-90.79
P/E Ratio	19.09-14.68	19.82-15.25	20.22-14.94	20.37-12.97	76.18-54.96	22.72-17.45	15.89-12.76	16.13-10.38
Average Yield %	1.02	1.06	1.09	1.17	1.29	0.95	0.67	0.70

Address: One Valmont Plaza, Omaha, NE 68154-5215	**Web Site:** www.valmont.com	**Auditors:** Deloitte & Touche LLP
Telephone: 402-963-1000	**Officers:** Mogens C. Bay - Executive Chairman, Chairman, President, Chief Executive Officer Stephen G. Kaniewski - President, Incoming Chief Executive Officer, Chief Operating Officer	**Investor Contact:** 402-963-1000
Fax: 402-963-1198		**Transfer Agents:** Wells Fargo Shareowner Services, Mendota Heights, MN

VALVOLINE INC

Exchange	Symbol	Price	52Wk Range	Yield	P/E
NYS	VVV	$25.06 (12/29/2017)	25.06-21.17	1.19	16.82

*7 Year Price Score N/A   *NYSE Composite Index=100   *12 Month Price Score 98.65

Interim Earnings (Per Share)

Qtr.	Dec	Mar	Jun	Sep
2015-16	0.32	0.34	0.44	0.11
2016-17	0.35	0.35	0.27	0.52

Interim Dividends (Per Share)

Amt	Decl	Ex	Rec	Pay
0.049Q	01/24/2017	02/27/2017	03/01/2017	03/15/2017
0.049Q	04/27/2017	05/30/2017	06/01/2017	06/15/2017
0.049Q	07/27/2017	08/30/2017	09/01/2017	09/15/2017
0.074Q	11/14/2017	11/30/2017	12/01/2017	12/15/2017

Indicated Div: $0.30

Valuation Analysis   **Institutional Holding**

Forecast EPS	$1.25	No of Institutions
	(01/18/2018)	360
Market Cap	$5.1 Billion	Shares
Book Value	N/A	192,816,336
Price/Book	N/A	% Held
Price/Sales	2.44	N/A

Business Summary: Specialty Chemicals (MIC: 8.3.2 SIC: 2992 NAIC: 324191)

Valvoline is a producer, marketer and supplier of engine and automotive maintenance products and services. Co.'s reportable segments are: Core North America, which sells Valvolineâ,,¢ and other branded and private label products in the U.S. and Canada to both retailers for consumers to perform their own automotive maintenance, as well as to installer customers who use Co.'s products to service vehicles; Quick Lubes; which services the passenger car and light truck quick lube market through two platforms: Co.-owned and franchised Valvoline Instant Oil Changesm stores and Express Careâ,,¢; and International, which sells Valvolineâ,,¢ and other branded products outside the U.S. and Canada.

Recent Developments: For the year ended Sep 30 2017, net income increased 11.4% to US$304.0 million from US$273.0 million in the prior year. Revenues were US$2.08 billion, up 8.0% from US$1.93 billion the year before. Operating income was US$532.0 million versus US$431.0 million in the prior year, an increase of 23.4%. Direct operating expenses rose 11.8% to US$1.31 billion from US$1.17 billion in the comparable period the year before. Indirect operating expenses decreased 25.5% to US$246.0 million from US$330.0 million in the equivalent prior-year period.

Prospects: Our evaluation of Valvoline Inc as of Jan. 14, 2018 is the result of our systematic analysis on three basic characteristics: earnings strength, relative valuation, and recent stock price movement. The company has generated a negative trend in earnings per share over the past 5 quarters and while recent estimates for the company have been mixed, VVV has posted better than expected results. Based on operating earnings yield, the company is undervalued when compared to all of the companies in our coverage universe. Share price changes over the past year indicates that VVV will perform in line with the market over the near term.

Financial Data
(US$ in Thousands)

	09/30/2017	09/30/2016	09/30/2015	09/30/2014	09/30/2013
Earnings Per Share	1.49	1.33	...	...	...
Cash Flow Per Share	(0.64)	1.51	...	...	...
Dividends Per Share	0.196	...	...	...	...
Dividend Payout %	13.15	...	...	...	...
Income Statement					
Total Revenue	2,084,000	1,929,000	1,966,900	2,041,300	1,996,200
EBITDA	574,000	468,000	334,400	301,200	415,700
Depn & Amortn	42,000	38,000	37,600	36,500	35,100
Income Before Taxes	490,000	421,000	296,800	264,720	380,600
Income Taxes	186,000	148,000	100,700	91,300	134,500
Net Income	304,000	273,000	196,100	173,400	246,100
Average Shares	204,000	205,000	...	...	...
Balance Sheet					
Current Assets	790,000	730,000	477,300	544,700	...
Total Assets	1,915,000	1,825,000	977,900	1,082,500	...
Current Liabilities	478,000	400,000	298,600	293,500	...
Long-Term Obligations	1,034,000	724,000	...	...	...
Total Liabilities	2,032,000	2,155,000	360,800	357,700	...
Stockholders' Equity	(117,000)	(330,000)	617,100	724,800	...
Shares Outstanding	203,000	205,000	...	...	...
Statistical Record					
Return on Assets %	16.26	19.43	19.04	...	...
Return on Equity %	...	189.66	29.23	...	...
EBITDA Margin %	27.54	24.26	17.00	14.76	20.82
Net Margin %	14.59	14.15	9.97	8.49	12.33
Asset Turnover	1.11	1.37	1.91	...	...
Current Ratio	1.65	1.83	1.60	1.86	...
Price Range	24.66-18.90	23.98-23.10	...	...	...
P/E Ratio	16.55-12.68	18.03-17.37	...	...	...
Average Yield %	0.87	...	...	...	...

Address: 100 Valvoline Way, Lexington, KY 40509 **Telephone:** 859-357-7777	**Web Site:** www.valvoline.com **Officers:** Stephen F. Kirk - Chairman Samuel J. Mitchell - President, Chief Executive Officer	**Auditors:** Ernst & Young LLP **Investor Contact:** 859-357-7777 **Transfer Agents:** Wells Fargo Shareowner Services

VARIAN MEDICAL SYSTEMS INC

Exchange	Symbol	Price	52Wk Range	Yield	P/E
NYS	VAR	$111.15 (12/29/2017)	112.42-76.57	N/A	41.47

*7 Year Price Score 106.37 *NYSE Composite Index=100 *12 Month Price Score 106.14

Interim Earnings (Per Share)

Qtr.	Dec	Mar	Jun	Sep
2012-13	0.86	1.02	1.03	1.08
2013-14	0.91	0.88	1.02	1.02
2014-15	0.92	1.05	1.13	0.99
2015-16	0.91	1.01	1.04	1.24
2016-17	0.22	0.60	0.98	0.89

Interim Dividends (Per Share)

No Dividends Paid

Valuation Analysis — **Institutional Holding**

Forecast EPS	$4.27	No of Institutions
	(01/18/2018)	815
Market Cap	$10.2 Billion	Shares
Book Value	$1.5 Billion	124,518,832
Price/Book	6.82	% Held
Price/Sales	3.82	81.85

TRADING VOLUME (thousand shares)

Business Summary: Medical Instruments & Equipment (MIC: 4.3.1 SIC: 3845 NAIC: 334510)

Varian Medical Systems is a manufacturer of medical devices and software for treating cancer and other medical conditions with radiotherapy, radiosurgery, proton therapy and brachytherapy. Co. has two segments: Oncology Systems, which designs, manufactures, sells and services hardware and software products for treating cancer with radiotherapy, and treatments such as fixed field intensity-modulated radiation therapy, image-guided radiation therapy, volumetric modulated arc therapy, stereotactic radiosurgery, stereotactic body radiotherapy and brachytherapy; and Imaging Components, which designs, manufactures, sells and services X-ray imaging components for use in a range of applications.

Recent Developments: For the year ended Sep 29 2017, income from continuing operations decreased 21.0% to US$257.1 million from US$325.3 million a year earlier. Net income decreased 37.8% to US$250.3 million from US$402.7 million in the prior year. Revenues were US$2.67 billion, up 1.8% from US$2.62 billion the year before. Operating income was US$341.9 million versus US$435.0 million in the prior year, a decrease of 21.4%. Direct operating expenses was unchanged at US$1.51 billion versus the comparable period the year before. Indirect operating expenses increased 20.0% to US$813.7 million from US$677.9 million in the equivalent prior-year period.

Prospects: Our evaluation of Varian Medical Systems Inc. as of Jan. 14, 2018 is the result of our systematic analysis on three basic characteristics: earnings strength, relative valuation, and recent stock price movement. The company has produced a positive trend in earnings per share over the past 5 quarters. However, while recent estimates for the company have been mixed, VAR has posted results that fell short of analysts expectations. Based on operating earnings yield, the company is about fairly valued when compared to all of the companies in our coverage universe. Share price changes over the past year indicates that VAR will perform very well over the near term.

Financial Data

(US$ in Thousands)	09/29/2017	09/30/2016	10/02/2015	09/26/2014	09/27/2013	09/28/2012	09/30/2011	10/01/2010
Earnings Per Share	2.68	4.19	4.09	3.83	3.98	3.76	3.36	2.91
Cash Flow Per Share	4.33	3.75	4.63	4.33	4.21	4.44	4.06	3.79
Tang Book Value Per Share	13.09	14.31	13.82	13.22	13.98	11.77	9.18	9.04
Income Statement								
Total Revenue	2,668,200	3,217,800	3,099,111	3,049,800	2,942,897	2,807,015	2,596,666	2,356,585
EBITDA	418,800	630,600	617,487	633,612	671,749	655,056	641,042	582,495
Depn & Amortn	76,900	79,800	68,520	62,457	62,859	60,982	52,591	48,293
Income Before Taxes	344,800	556,400	554,662	574,510	612,083	595,924	588,710	532,925
Income Taxes	87,700	153,700	142,644	170,807	173,835	168,875	180,084	165,444
Net Income	249,600	402,300	411,485	403,703	438,248	427,049	398,933	360,422
Average Shares	93,200	96,000	100,552	105,271	110,053	113,473	118,735	124,025
Balance Sheet								
Current Assets	2,190,300	2,616,000	2,525,045	2,494,165	2,704,783	2,170,515	1,854,617	1,681,344
Total Assets	3,179,400	3,816,000	3,600,748	3,357,290	3,468,474	2,878,726	2,498,761	2,323,952
Current Liabilities	1,550,100	1,614,000	1,382,904	1,201,654	1,160,579	1,236,531	1,125,912	903,541
Long-Term Obligations	...	287,500	337,500	387,500	450,000	6,250	6,250	17,869
Total Liabilities	1,684,400	2,075,500	1,889,148	1,740,870	1,754,627	1,368,950	1,254,870	1,048,585
Stockholders' Equity	1,495,000	1,740,500	1,711,600	1,616,420	1,713,847	1,509,776	1,243,891	1,275,367
Shares Outstanding	91,700	93,700	98,070	100,942	106,491	109,407	112,344	118,007
Statistical Record								
Return on Assets %	7.16	10.88	11.64	11.86	13.85	15.93	16.59	15.60
Return on Equity %	15.47	23.37	24.33	24.31	27.26	31.10	31.76	27.94
EBITDA Margin %	15.70	19.60	19.92	20.78	22.83	23.34	24.69	24.72
Net Margin %	9.35	12.50	13.28	13.24	14.89	15.21	15.36	15.29
Asset Turnover	0.76	0.87	0.88	0.90	0.93	1.05	1.08	1.02
Current Ratio	1.41	1.62	1.83	2.08	2.33	1.76	1.65	1.86
Debt to Equity	...	0.17	0.20	0.24	0.26	N.M.	0.01	0.01
Price Range	107.87-76.57	88.16-65.55	85.14-63.26	77.50-64.20	67.54-50.55	63.49-44.37	63.72-43.95	53.84-34.66
P/E Ratio	40.25-28.57	21.04-15.64	20.82-15.47	20.24-16.76	16.97-12.70	16.89-11.80	18.97-13.08	18.50-11.91

Address: 3100 Hansen Way, Palo Alto, CA 94304-1038	Web Site: www.varian.com	Auditors: PricewaterhouseCoopers LLP
Telephone: 650-493-4000	Officers: R. Andrew Eckert - Chairman Timothy E. Guertin - Vice-Chairman, President, Chief Executive Officer	Investor Contact: 650-424-5782
		Transfer Agents: Computershare Trust Company, N.A., Providence, RI

VECTOR GROUP LTD

Exchange	Symbol	Price	52Wk Range	Yield	P/E	Div Achiever
NYS	VGR	$22.38 (12/29/2017)	23.02-18.91	7.15	69.94	18 Years

*7 Year Price Score 97.28 *NYSE Composite Index=100 *12 Month Price Score 99.97

Interim Earnings (Per Share)

Qtr.	Mar	Jun	Sep	Dec
2014	0.02	0.07	0.12	0.10
2015	0.16	0.13	0.09	0.06
2016	0.15	0.18	0.17	0.03
2017	(0.03)	0.19	0.13	...

Interim Dividends (Per Share)

Amt	Decl	Ex	Rec	Pay
0.381Q	05/31/2017	06/16/2017	06/20/2017	06/29/2017
5%	08/30/2017	09/19/2017	09/20/2017	09/28/2017
0.381Q	08/30/2017	09/19/2017	09/20/2017	09/28/2017
0.40Q	11/29/2017	12/19/2017	12/20/2017	12/28/2017

Indicated Div: $1.60 (Div. Reinv. Plan)

Valuation Analysis

		Institutional Holding	
Forecast EPS	$0.66	No of Institutions	
	(10/21/2017)	286	
Market Cap	$3.0 Billion	Shares	
Book Value	N/A	78,075,296	
Price/Book	N/A	% Held	
Price/Sales	1.70	56.05	

TRADING VOLUME (thousand shares)

Business Summary: Tobacco Products (MIC: 1.3.1 SIC: 2111 NAIC: 312221)

Vector Group is a holding company. Co. is engaged in the manufacture and sale of cigarettes in the U.S. through its Liggett Group LLC and Vector Tobacco Inc. subsidiaries; and the real estate business through its New Valley LLC subsidiary (New Valley), which acquires or invests in additional real estate properties or projects. As of Dec 31 2016, New Valley owned 70.59% interest in Douglas Elliman Realty, LLC, which operates a residential brokerage company in New York. Co. has three segments: Tobacco, which consists of the manufacture and sale of cigarettes; E-Cigarettes, which includes the operations of its e-cigarette business; and Real Estate, which includes its investment in New Valley.

Recent Developments: For the quarter ended Sep 30 2017, net income decreased 20.3% to US$20.5 million from US$25.7 million in the year-earlier quarter. Revenues were US$484.6 million, up 5.6% from US$459.1 million the year before. Operating income was US$59.2 million versus US$69.4 million in the prior-year quarter, a decrease of 14.6%. Direct operating expenses rose 11.4% to US$338.1 million from US$303.4 million in the comparable period the year before. Indirect operating expenses increased 1.1% to US$87.3 million from US$86.3 million in the equivalent prior-year period.

Prospects: Our evaluation of Vector Group Ltd. as of Jan. 14, 2018 is the result of our systematic analysis on three basic characteristics: earnings strength, relative valuation, and recent stock price movement. The company has produced a positive trend in earnings per share over the past 5 quarters and while recent estimates for the company have remained steady, VGR has posted results that fell short of analysts expectations. Based on operating earnings yield, the company is overvalued when compared to all of the companies in our coverage universe. Share price changes over the past year indicates that VGR will perform well over the near term.

Financial Data

(US$ in Thousands)	9 Mos	6 Mos	3 Mos	12/31/2016	12/31/2015	12/31/2014	12/31/2013	12/31/2012
Earnings Per Share	0.32	0.36	0.35	0.52	0.44	0.30	0.34	0.27
Cash Flow Per Share	1.38	1.03	0.99	0.75	1.11	0.90	0.47	0.78
Dividends Per Share	1.524	1.506	1.488	1.469	1.399	1.333	1.269	1.209
Dividend Payout %	475.45	416.05	421.64	280.52	314.83	440.88	376.32	440.87
Income Statement								
Total Revenue	1,371,822	887,197	415,208	1,690,949	1,657,197	1,591,315	1,056,200	1,084,546
EBITDA	177,732	109,024	27,417	281,729	242,461	255,976	181,706	145,924
Depn & Amortn	...	...	...	20,782	20,423	17,843	11,063	10,608
Income Before Taxes	46,782	19,482	(17,059)	123,983	108,385	77,142	38,496	25,214
Income Taxes	22,517	16,045	(2,782)	49,163	41,233	33,251	24,795	23,095
Net Income	41,848	22,584	(4,227)	71,127	59,198	36,978	38,944	30,622
Average Shares	132,788	132,861	131,846	130,472	129,866	119,226	111,515	108,092
Balance Sheet								
Current Assets	699,932	716,523	660,452	705,463	583,739	857,846	588,311	639,056
Total Assets	1,409,904	1,420,286	1,387,072	1,404,035	1,310,756	1,573,392	1,260,159	1,086,731
Current Liabilities	268,202	241,113	191,088	196,148	216,292	270,095	405,005	195,159
Long-Term Obligations	1,175,910	1,158,877	1,143,771	1,132,943	886,249	860,711	540,766	586,946
Total Liabilities	1,812,624	1,788,139	1,730,104	1,736,035	1,516,803	1,630,419	1,355,195	1,165,983
Stockholders' Equity	(402,720)	(367,853)	(343,032)	(332,000)	(206,047)	(57,027)	(95,036)	(79,252)
Shares Outstanding	135,178	135,380	135,905	134,126	129,981	132,549	118,491	114,735
Statistical Record								
Return on Assets %	3.23	3.47	3.64	5.23	4.11	2.61	3.32	3.03
EBITDA Margin %	12.96	12.29	6.60	16.66	14.63	16.09	17.20	13.45
Net Margin %	3.05	2.55	N.M.	4.21	3.57	2.32	3.69	2.82
Asset Turnover	1.24	1.21	1.32	1.24	1.15	1.12	0.90	1.07
Current Ratio	2.61	2.97	3.46	3.60	2.70	3.18	1.45	3.27
Price Range	22.10-18.91	22.10-18.91	22.10-18.88	21.72-18.88	23.07-18.14	19.65-13.29	13.71-11.65	13.83-11.39
P/E Ratio	69.08-59.11	61.40-52.54	63.16-53.93	41.78-36.30	52.42-41.23	65.51-44.32	40.34-34.27	51.24-42.19
Average Yield %	7.46	7.34	7.35	7.28	6.88	7.68	9.89	9.42

Address: 4400 Biscayne Boulevard, Miami, FL 33137	**Web Site:** www.vectorgroupltd.com	**Auditors:** Deloitte & Touche LLP
Telephone: 305-579-8000	**Officers:** Bennett S. LeBow - Chairman Howard M. Lorber - President, Chief Executive Officer	**Investor Contact:** 212-687-8080
		Transfer Agents: American Stock Transfer & Trust Company, LLC, Brooklyn, NY

VECTREN CORP

Exchange	Symbol	Price	52Wk Range	Yield	P/E	Div Achiever
NYS	VVC	$65.02 (12/29/2017)	69.50-51.72	2.77	23.99	41 Years

*7 Year Price Score 118.18 *NYSE Composite Index=100 *12 Month Price Score 103.58

Interim Earnings (Per Share)

Qtr.	Mar	Jun	Sep	Dec
2014	0.62	0.14	0.57	0.68
2015	0.69	0.43	0.48	0.79
2016	0.58	0.39	0.74	0.84
2017	0.67	0.45	0.75	...

Interim Dividends (Per Share)

Amt	Decl	Ex	Rec	Pay
0.42Q	02/01/2017	02/13/2017	02/15/2017	03/01/2017
0.42Q	04/12/2017	05/11/2017	05/15/2017	06/01/2017
0.42Q	08/03/2017	08/11/2017	08/15/2017	09/01/2017
0.45Q	11/02/2017	11/14/2017	11/15/2017	12/01/2017

Indicated Div: $1.80 (Div. Reinv. Plan)

Valuation Analysis

		Institutional Holding	
Forecast EPS	$2.62 (01/12/2018)	No of Institutions	476
Market Cap	$5.4 Billion	Shares	68,338,728
Book Value	$1.8 Billion	% Held	57.29
Price/Book	2.96		
Price/Sales	2.04		

Business Summary: Electric Utilities (MIC: 3.1.1 SIC: 4932 NAIC: 221210)

Vectren is an energy holding company. Co.'s subsidiary, Vectren Utility Holdings, Inc., served as the intermediate holding company for three public utilities that provides natural gas distribution and transportation services and electric transmission and distribution services. Co., through Vectren Enterprises, Inc. subsidiary, is involved in nonutility activities in two primary business areas: infrastructure services, which provides underground pipeline construction and repair to utility infrastructure; and energy services, which assists schools, hospitals, governmental facilities, and other private institutions with reducing energy and maintenance costs through Energy Systems Group, LLC.

Recent Developments: For the quarter ended Sep 30 2017, net income increased 0.8% to US$61.9 million from US$61.4 million in the year-earlier quarter. Revenues were US$691.2 million, up 9.5% from US$631.0 million the year before. Operating income was US$107.5 million versus US$105.5 million in the prior-year quarter, an increase of 1.9%. Direct operating expenses rose 7.2% to US$204.2 million from US$190.5 million in the comparable period the year before. Indirect operating expenses increased 13.3% to US$379.5 million from US$335.0 million in the equivalent prior-year period.

Prospects: Our evaluation of Vectren Corp. as of Jan. 14, 2018 is the result of our systematic analysis on three basic characteristics: earnings strength, relative valuation, and recent stock price movement. The company has managed to produce a neutral trend in earnings per share over the past 5 quarters and while recent estimates for the company have remained steady, VVC has posted better than expected results. Based on operating earnings yield, the company is about fairly valued when compared to all of the companies in our coverage universe. Share price changes over the past year indicates that VVC will perform very well over the near term.

Financial Data

(US$ in Thousands)	9 Mos	6 Mos	3 Mos	12/31/2016	12/31/2015	12/31/2014	12/31/2013	12/31/2012
Earnings Per Share	2.71	2.70	2.64	2.55	2.39	2.02	1.66	1.94
Cash Flow Per Share	6.10	5.82	6.44	6.31	6.11	5.92	7.13	4.71
Tang Book Value Per Share	18.43	18.09	18.03	17.79	16.79	15.94	15.68	15.37
Dividends Per Share	1.680	1.660	1.640	1.620	1.540	1.460	1.425	1.405
Dividend Payout %	61.99	61.48	62.12	63.53	64.44	72.28	85.84	72.42
Income Statement								
Total Revenue	1,946,300	1,255,100	624,500	2,448,300	2,434,700	2,611,700	2,491,200	2,232,800
EBITDA	512,500	326,500	177,200	646,000	616,400	595,100	621,600	607,900
Depn & Amortn	205,700	136,100	67,800	260,000	256,300	273,400	277,800	254,600
Income Before Taxes	241,900	147,700	88,100	323,100	293,600	247,500	263,400	264,800
Income Taxes	86,100	54,000	32,200	111,300	95,700	81,100	67,100	82,500
Net Income	154,800	92,900	55,400	211,600	197,300	166,900	136,600	159,000
Average Shares	83,100	82,900	83,000	82,800	82,700	82,500	82,400	82,100
Balance Sheet								
Current Assets	613,500	559,600	525,100	678,800	659,400	686,400	630,400	678,400
Total Assets	6,061,800	5,871,500	5,712,600	5,800,700	5,409,900	5,162,300	5,102,600	5,089,100
Current Liabilities	872,100	804,400	675,300	828,400	527,800	762,700	510,500	794,300
Long-Term Obligations	1,639,100	1,590,400	1,590,200	1,589,900	1,722,800	1,407,300	1,777,100	1,553,400
Total Liabilities	4,238,400	4,076,700	3,922,200	4,032,600	3,726,100	3,555,700	3,548,300	3,563,000
Stockholders' Equity	1,823,400	1,794,800	1,790,400	1,768,100	1,683,800	1,606,600	1,554,300	1,526,100
Shares Outstanding	83,000	83,000	83,000	82,900	82,800	82,600	82,400	82,200
Statistical Record								
Return on Assets %	3.85	3.97	3.96	3.76	3.73	3.25	2.68	3.18
Return on Equity %	12.63	12.81	12.53	12.23	11.99	10.56	8.87	10.60
EBITDA Margin %	26.33	26.01	28.37	26.39	25.32	22.79	24.95	27.23
Net Margin %	7.95	7.40	8.87	8.64	8.10	6.39	5.48	7.12
Asset Turnover	0.45	0.46	0.45	0.44	0.46	0.51	0.49	0.45
Current Ratio	0.70	0.70	0.78	0.82	1.25	0.90	1.23	0.85
Debt to Equity	0.90	0.89	0.89	0.90	1.02	0.88	1.14	1.02
Price Range	68.11-47.14	62.51-47.14	58.61-47.14	53.15-39.71	49.31-38.39	48.12-34.89	37.56-29.40	30.27-27.62
P/E Ratio	25.13-17.39	23.15-17.46	22.20-17.86	20.84-15.57	20.63-16.06	23.82-17.27	22.63-17.71	15.60-14.24
Average Yield %	2.95	3.08	3.19	3.31	3.59	3.63	4.17	4.83

Address: One Vectren Square, Evansville, IN 47708
Telephone: 812-491-4000
Fax: 812-491-4149

Web Site: www.vectren.com
Officers: Carl L. Chapman - Chairman, President, Chief Executive Officer M. Susan Hardwick - Executive Vice President, Chief Financial Officer, Senior Vice President, Vice President, Controller, Assistant Treasurer

Auditors: Deloitte & Touche LLP
Investor Contact: 812-491-4080
Transfer Agents: Wells Fargo Shareowner Services, St. Paul, MN

VEEVA SYSTEMS INC

Exchange	Symbol	Price	52Wk Range	Yield	P/E
NYS	VEEV	$55.28 (12/29/2017)	66.82-41.35	N/A	64.28

*7 Year Price Score N/A   *NYSE Composite Index=100   *12 Month Price Score 99.87

Interim Earnings (Per Share)

Qtr.	Apr	Jul	Oct	Jan
2014-15	0.05	0.07	0.07	0.09
2015-16	0.09	0.09	0.07	0.13
2016-17	0.09	0.09	0.15	0.15
2017-18	0.24	0.25	0.22	...

Interim Dividends (Per Share)

No Dividends Paid

Valuation Analysis

	Institutional Holding	
Forecast EPS	$0.91	No of Institutions
	(01/18/2018)	420
Market Cap	$7.8 Billion	Shares
Book Value	$818.5 Million	106,885,256
Price/Book	9.54	% Held
Price/Sales	11.99	28.65

TRADING VOLUME (thousand shares)

2008 2009 2010 2011 2012 2013 2014 2015 2016 2017

Business Summary: IT Services (MIC: 6.3.1 SIC: 7372 NAIC: 511210)

Veeva Systems provides industry cloud solutions for the life sciences industry. Veeva Commercial Cloud is a suite of multichannel customer relationship management applications, master data management applications, territory allocation and alignment applications and customer reference and data and services. Veeva Vault is Co.'s enterprise content management platform and suite of applications for managing both commercial content and research and development content and data, including content and data from the clinical, regulatory and quality functions of life sciences companies.

Recent Developments: For the quarter ended July 31 2017, net income increased 192.1% to US$37.8 million from US$13.0 million in the year-earlier quarter. Revenues were US$166.6 million, up 26.8% from US$131.3 million the year before. Operating income was US$36.9 million versus US$23.8 million in the prior-year quarter, an increase of 54.9%. Direct operating expenses rose 19.5% to US$50.4 million from US$42.2 million in the comparable period the year before. Indirect operating expenses increased 21.4% to US$79.3 million from US$65.3 million in the equivalent prior-year period.

Prospects: Our evaluation of Veeva Systems Inc as of Jan. 14, 2018 is the result of our systematic analysis on three basic characteristics: earnings strength, relative valuation, and recent stock price movement. The company has generated a negative trend in earnings per share over the past 5 quarters and while recent estimates for the company have remained steady, VEEV has posted better than expected results. Based on operating earnings yield, the company is overvalued when compared to all of the companies in our coverage universe. Share price changes over the past year indicates that VEEV will perform well over the near term.

Financial Data

(US$ in Thousands)	9 Mos	6 Mos	3 Mos	01/31/2017	01/31/2016	01/31/2015	01/31/2014	01/31/2013
Earnings Per Share	0.86	0.79	0.63	0.47	0.38	0.28	0.15	0.11
Cash Flow Per Share	1.63	1.59	1.29	1.06	0.61	0.53	0.81	1.47
Tang Book Value Per Share	4.88	4.53	4.13	3.76	2.70	3.02	2.14	1.05
Income Statement								
Total Revenue	500,652	324,503	157,918	544,043	409,221	313,222	210,151	129,548
EBITDA	126,221	81,228	39,686	110,058	77,100	68,586	39,400	29,593
Depn & Amortn	5,507	3,542	1,756	4,900	3,100	1,400	900	500
Income Before Taxes	120,714	77,686	37,930	109,635	78,617	67,186	38,500	29,093
Income Taxes	12,454	3,819	1,907	40,831	24,157	26,803	14,885	10,310
Net Income	108,260	73,867	36,023	68,804	54,460	40,383	23,615	18,783
Average Shares	154,256	153,778	151,056	147,578	144,977	144,204	68,024	30,599
Balance Sheet								
Current Assets	846,069	833,355	789,112	711,865	500,964	501,837	353,732	86,890
Total Assets	1,046,216	1,035,870	995,663	917,700	705,799	544,890	370,308	89,820
Current Liabilities	214,350	255,578	269,046	246,784	186,279	135,523	86,617	54,289
Total Liabilities	227,748	269,267	286,759	264,722	200,550	138,057	90,212	55,854
Stockholders' Equity	818,468	766,603	708,904	652,978	505,249	406,833	280,096	33,966
Shares Outstanding	141,184	140,410	139,339	137,886	133,545	131,067	124,791	24,843
Statistical Record								
Return on Assets %	14.17	12.86	10.57	8.45	8.71	8.82	10.26	28.55
Return on Equity %	18.25	17.60	14.90	11.85	11.94	11.76	15.04	77.94
EBITDA Margin %	25.21	25.03	25.13	20.23	18.84	21.90	18.75	22.84
Net Margin %	21.62	22.76	22.81	12.65	13.31	12.89	11.24	14.50
Asset Turnover	0.71	0.68	0.67	0.67	0.65	0.68	0.91	1.97
Current Ratio	3.95	3.26	2.93	2.88	2.69	3.70	4.08	1.60
Price Range	66.82-37.54	66.82-37.31	53.62-26.71	47.36-20.61	32.69-22.83	37.80-17.87	46.24-31.00	...
P/E Ratio	77.70-43.65	84.58-47.23	85.11-42.40	100.77-43.85	86.03-60.08	135.00-63.82	308.27-206.67	...

Address: 4280 Hacienda Drive, Pleasanton, CA 94588 **Telephone:** 925-452-6500 **Fax:** 925-452-6504	**Web Site:** www.veeva.com **Officers:** Gordon Ritter - Chairman Matthew J. Wallach - President	**Auditors:** KPMG LLP **Transfer Agents:** American Stock Transfer & Trust Company, LLC, Brooklyn, NY

VENTAS INC

Exchange	Symbol	Price	52Wk Range	Yield	P/E
NYS	VTR	$60.01 (12/29/2017)	71.93-59.36	5.27	18.41

*7 Year Price Score 87.93 *NYSE Composite Index=100 *12 Month Price Score 91.94

Interim Earnings (Per Share)

Qtr.	Mar	Jun	Sep	Dec
2014	0.41	0.47	0.37	0.36
2015	0.37	0.45	0.07	0.37
2016	0.44	0.42	0.42	0.58
2017	0.55	0.42	1.71	...

Interim Dividends (Per Share)

Amt	Decl	Ex	Rec	Pay
0.775Q	02/10/2017	03/03/2017	03/07/2017	03/31/2017
0.775Q	05/18/2017	06/02/2017	06/06/2017	06/30/2017
0.775Q	08/30/2017	09/11/2017	09/12/2017	09/29/2017
0.79Q	12/11/2017	12/29/2017	01/02/2018	01/12/2018

Indicated Div: $3.16

Valuation Analysis

		Institutional Holding	
Forecast EPS	$3.15	No of Institutions	856
	(01/16/2018)		
Market Cap	$21.4 Billion	Shares	
Book Value	$10.7 Billion		405,070,304
Price/Book	1.99	% Held	
Price/Sales	6.01		96.39

Business Summary: REITs (MIC: 5.3.1 SIC: 6798 NAIC: 525930)

Ventas is a real estate investment trust, with a portfolio of seniors housing and healthcare properties located throughout the U.S., Canada and the U.K. Co.'s business segments include: triple-net leased properties, which acquires and owns seniors housing and healthcare properties throughout the U.S. and the U.K. and leases those properties to healthcare operating companies under triple-net or absolute-net leases that obligate the tenants to pay all property-related expenses; senior living operations, which invests in seniors housing communities throughout the U.S. and Canada; and office operations, which acquires, owns, develops, leases, and manages MOBs.

Recent Developments: For the quarter ended Sep 30 2017, income from continuing operations increased 4.3% to US$156.9 million from US$150.4 million in the year-earlier quarter. Net income increased 309.6% to US$615.2 million from US$150.2 million in the year-earlier quarter. Revenues were US$899.9 million, up 3.8% from US$867.1 million the year before. Revenues from property income rose 3.8% to US$866.8 million from US$835.0 million in the corresponding quarter a year earlier.

Prospects: Our evaluation of Ventas Inc. as of Jan. 14, 2018 is the result of our systematic analysis on three basic characteristics: earnings strength, relative valuation, and recent stock price movement. The company has managed to produce a neutral trend in earnings per share over the past 5 quarters. However, while recent estimates for the company have been lowered by analysts, VTR has posted better than expected results. Based on operating earnings yield, the company is about fairly valued when compared to all of the companies in our coverage universe. Share price changes over the past year indicates that VTR will perform very well over the near term.

Financial Data

(US$ in Thousands)	9 Mos	6 Mos	3 Mos	12/31/2016	12/31/2015	12/31/2014	12/31/2013	12/31/2012
Earnings Per Share	3.26	1.97	1.97	1.86	1.25	1.60	1.54	1.23
Cash Flow Per Share	4.08	4.08	4.04	3.96	4.21	4.27	4.08	3.39
Tang Book Value Per Share	27.21	26.21	26.41	27.16	26.02	28.08	28.91	29.73
Dividends Per Share	3.100	3.055	3.010	2.965	3.040	2.965	2.735	2.480
Dividend Payout %	95.09	155.08	152.79	159.41	243.20	185.31	177.60	201.63
Income Statement								
Total Revenue	2,678,861	1,778,933	883,443	3,443,522	3,286,398	3,075,746	2,810,053	2,485,299
EBITDA	779,349	517,947	255,866	1,827,193	1,673,771	1,634,643	1,550,817	1,281,227
Depn & Amortn	(5,097)	(4,265)	(2,555)	888,945	954,982	809,284	737,343	707,714
Income Before Taxes	448,201	299,836	149,617	518,508	351,675	448,517	478,990	280,112
Income Taxes	(13,119)	(5,304)	(3,145)	(31,343)	(39,284)	(8,732)	(11,828)	(6,282)
Net Income	963,916	349,958	198,127	649,231	417,843	475,767	453,509	362,800
Average Shares	359,333	358,311	357,572	348,390	334,007	296,677	295,110	294,488
Balance Sheet								
Current Assets	85,063	103,353	91,284	286,707	53,023	55,348	94,816	67,908
Total Assets	23,739,795	23,855,758	23,919,331	23,166,600	22,261,918	21,226,171	19,731,494	18,980,000
Current Liabilities	1,335,752	1,313,643	1,318,950	1,309,793	1,232,966	1,411,666	1,306,031	1,302,436
Long-Term Obligations	11,424,145	11,907,997	11,943,733	11,127,326	11,206,996	10,888,092	9,364,992	8,413,646
Total Liabilities	13,008,455	13,481,700	13,504,725	12,505,632	12,501,062	12,373,971	10,750,553	9,786,317
Stockholders' Equity	10,731,340	10,374,058	10,414,606	10,660,968	9,760,856	8,852,200	8,980,941	9,193,683
Shares Outstanding	356,163	356,134	354,863	354,124	334,342	298,471	294,189	291,866
Statistical Record								
Return on Assets %	4.97	3.08	3.02	2.85	1.92	2.32	2.34	2.00
Return on Equity %	11.04	7.05	6.97	6.34	4.49	5.34	4.99	3.90
EBITDA Margin %	29.09	29.12	28.96	53.06	50.93	53.15	55.19	51.55
Net Margin %	35.98	19.67	22.43	18.85	12.71	15.47	16.14	14.60
Asset Turnover	0.15	0.15	0.15	0.15	0.15	0.15	0.15	0.14
Current Ratio	0.06	0.08	0.07	0.22	0.04	0.04	0.07	0.05
Debt to Equity	1.06	1.15	1.15	1.04	1.15	1.23	1.04	0.92
Price Range	71.93-57.86	76.56-57.86	76.56-57.86	76.56-48.43	70.89-49.68	65.19-49.73	72.63-48.39	58.97-47.01
P/E Ratio	22.06-17.75	38.86-29.37	38.86-29.37	41.16-26.04	56.71-39.74	40.75-31.08	47.16-31.43	47.94-38.22
Average Yield %	4.77	4.61	4.56	4.59	5.14	5.23	4.64	4.65

Address: 353 N. Clark Street, Suite 3300, Chicago, IL 60654 **Telephone:** 877-483-6827	**Web Site:** www.ventasreit.com **Officers:** Debra A. Cafaro - Chairman, Chief Executive Officer Robert F. Probst - Executive Vice President, Chief Financial Officer, Acting Chief Accounting Officer	**Auditors:** KPMG LLP **Investor Contact:** 312-660-3848 **Transfer Agents:** Wells Fargo Shareowner Services, St. Paul, MN

VEREIT INC

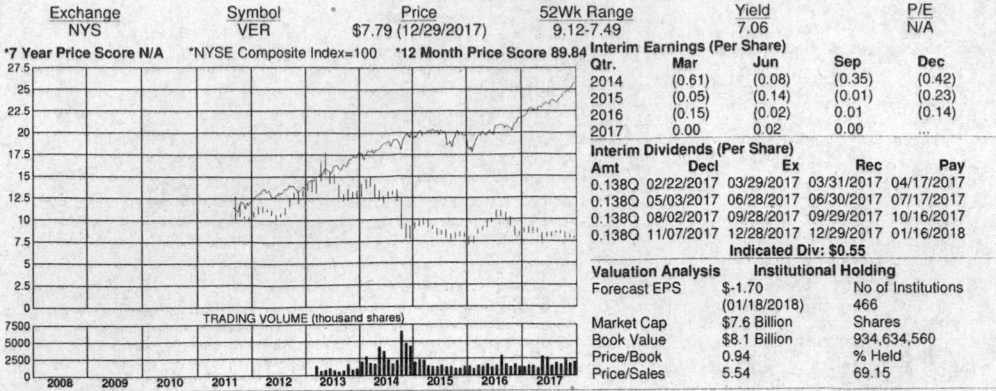

Exchange	Symbol	Price	52Wk Range	Yield	P/E
NYS	VER	$7.79 (12/29/2017)	9.12-7.49	7.06	N/A

*7 Year Price Score N/A   *NYSE Composite Index=100   *12 Month Price Score 89.84

Interim Earnings (Per Share)

Qtr.	Mar	Jun	Sep	Dec
2014	(0.61)	(0.08)	(0.35)	(0.42)
2015	(0.05)	(0.14)	(0.01)	(0.23)
2016	(0.15)	(0.02)	0.01	(0.14)
2017	0.00	0.02	0.00	...

Interim Dividends (Per Share)

Amt	Decl	Ex	Rec	Pay
0.138Q	02/22/2017	03/29/2017	03/31/2017	04/17/2017
0.138Q	05/03/2017	06/28/2017	06/30/2017	07/17/2017
0.138Q	08/02/2017	09/28/2017	09/29/2017	10/16/2017
0.138Q	11/07/2017	12/28/2017	12/29/2017	01/16/2018

Indicated Div: $0.55

Valuation Analysis   Institutional Holding

Forecast EPS	$-1.70	No of Institutions
	(01/18/2018)	466
Market Cap	$7.6 Billion	Shares
Book Value	$8.1 Billion	934,634,560
Price/Book	0.94	% Held
Price/Sales	5.54	69.15

TRADING VOLUME (thousand shares)

Business Summary: REITs (MIC: 5.3.1 SIC: 6798 NAIC: 525930)

VEREIT is a real estate operating company that operates two segments, its Real Estate Investment (REI) segment and its investment management segment, Cole Capital. Through its REI segment, Co. owns and manages a portfolio of retail, restaurant, office and industrial real estate properties. Through its Cole Capital segment, Co. is responsible for managing the affairs of certain non-traded real estate investment trusts on a day-to-day basis, identifying and making acquisitions and investments and recommending an approach for providing investors with liquidity. As of Dec 31 2016, Co. owned and managed a portfolio of 4,142 retail, restaurant, office and industrial real estate properties.

Recent Developments: For the quarter ended Sep 30 2017, net income decreased 45.5% to US$16.5 million from US$30.2 million in the year-earlier quarter. Revenues were US$333.7 million, down 8.0% from US$362.9 million the year before. Revenues from property income fell 7.5% to US$309.9 million from US$334.9 million in the corresponding quarter a year earlier.

Prospects: Our evaluation of VEREIT Inc. as of Jan. 14, 2018 is the result of our systematic analysis on three basic characteristics: earnings strength, relative valuation, and recent stock price movement. The company has generated a negative trend in earnings per share over the past 5 quarters. Because the company lacks sufficient analyst estimate data, we place greater weight on the historical EPS trend as the measure of earnings strength. Based on operating earnings yield, the company is overvalued when compared to all of the companies in our coverage universe. Share price changes over the past year indicates that VER will perform well over the near term.

Financial Data
(US$ in Thousands)

	9 Mos	6 Mos	3 Mos	12/31/2016	12/31/2015	12/31/2014	12/31/2013	12/31/2012
Earnings Per Share	(0.12)	(0.11)	(0.15)	(0.29)	(0.43)	(1.36)	(2.36)	(0.84)
Cash Flow Per Share	0.81	0.80	0.83	0.86	0.96	0.63	(0.04)	0.66
Tang Book Value Per Share	6.76	6.90	7.01	7.14	7.53	7.85	7.57	7.34
Dividends Per Share	0.550	0.550	0.550	0.550	0.275	1.076	0.907	0.884
Income Statement								
Total Revenue	1,018,687	684,959	348,029	1,454,823	1,556,017	1,579,257	240,496	16,822
EBITDA	855,288	583,150	282,749	909,616	865,146	448,900	(173,926)	6,874
Depn & Amortn	562,673	380,416	189,880	806,548	866,549	1,007,164	156,971	9,322
Income Before Taxes	73,543	55,370	19,126	(214,308)	(359,795)	(1,010,912)	(411,697)	(6,804)
Income Taxes	8,878	6,825	4,254	(3,701)	(36,303)	...	...	...
Net Income	63,940	47,846	14,438	(195,863)	(316,353)	(977,185)	(406,505)	(7,278)
Average Shares	974,167	998,093	973,849	931,422	903,360	793,150	174,052	9,150
Balance Sheet								
Current Assets	109,308	362,300	369,850	301,470	128,870	479,362	75,373	2,748
Total Assets	14,736,733	15,048,040	15,356,535	15,587,574	17,405,866	20,515,139	5,578,281	256,069
Current Liabilities	324,550	318,351	301,589	308,731	292,923	173,579	134,742	3,782
Long-Term Obligations	5,917,287	6,085,909	6,287,403	6,367,248	8,059,802	10,513,781	3,586,084	160,362
Total Liabilities	6,673,459	6,851,197	7,044,090	7,140,213	8,881,879	11,361,251	3,957,410	174,117
Stockholders' Equity	8,063,274	8,196,843	8,312,445	8,447,361	8,523,987	9,153,888	1,620,871	81,952
Shares Outstanding	974,245	974,250	974,238	974,146	904,884	905,530	202,344	11,157
Statistical Record								
EBITDA Margin %	83.96	85.14	81.24	62.52	55.60	28.42	N.M.	40.86
Net Margin %	6.28	6.99	4.15	N.M.	N.M.	N.M.	N.M.	N.M.
Asset Turnover	0.09	0.09	0.09	0.09	0.08	0.12	0.08	0.09
Current Ratio	0.34	1.14	1.23	0.98	0.44	2.76	0.56	0.73
Debt to Equity	0.73	0.74	0.76	0.75	0.95	1.15	2.21	1.96
Price Range	10.37-7.49	11.06-7.49	11.06-8.05	11.06-7.07	10.10-7.67	14.88-7.70	17.82-12.20	13.48-10.00
Average Yield %	6.43	6.08	5.89	6.00	3.13	8.72	6.44	7.69

Address: 2325 E. Camelback Road, Suite 1100, Phoenix, AZ 85016 **Telephone:** 800-606-3610	**Web Site:** www.ir.vereit.com **Officers:** Glenn J. Rufrano - Chief Executive Officer Michael J. Bartolotta - Executive Vice President, Chief Financial Officer, Treasurer	**Auditors:** Deloitte & Touche LLP **Investor Contact:** 800-606-3610 **Transfer Agents:** DST Systems, Inc.

VERIFONE SYSTEMS INC.

Exchange	Symbol	Price	52Wk Range	Yield	P/E
NYS	PAY	$17.71 (12/29/2017)	21.31-17.13	N/A	N/A

*7 Year Price Score 48.93 *NYSE Composite Index=100 *12 Month Price Score 90.20

TRADING VOLUME (thousand shares)

Interim Earnings (Per Share)

Qtr.	Jan	Apr	Jul	Oct
2012-13	0.11	(0.54)	(0.02)	(2.28)
2013-14	(0.15)	(0.22)	(0.26)	0.28
2014-15	0.12	0.15	0.08	0.32
2015-16	0.21	0.03	(0.28)	(0.04)
2016-17	(0.15)	(0.80)	(0.63)	0.03

Interim Dividends (Per Share)

No Dividends Paid

Valuation Analysis | Institutional Holding

Valuation Analysis		Institutional Holding	
Forecast EPS	$1.48	No of Institutions	
	(01/18/2018)	397	
Market Cap	$2.0 Billion	Shares	
Book Value	$754.6 Million	145,010,816	
Price/Book	2.64	% Held	
Price/Sales	1.06	93.00	

Business Summary: Electronic Instruments & Related Products (MIC: 6.2.3 SIC: 3578 NAIC: 334118)

VeriFone Systems is a holding company. Through its subsidiaries, Co. provides payments and commerce solutions at the point of sale (POS). Co. is engaged in designing, manufacturing, marketing and supplying a range of payment solutions and complementary services. Co.'s system solutions consist of POS electronic payment devices that run its operating systems, security and encryption software, and certified payment software, and that are designed to suit its clients' needs in a range of environments, including multilane and countertop implementations, self-service and unattended environments, in-vehicle and portable deployments, mobile point-of-sale solutions, as well as iPOS solutions.

Recent Developments: For the year ended Oct 31 2017, net loss amounted to US$175.3 million versus a net loss of US$9.7 million in the prior year. Revenues were US$1.87 billion, down 6.1% from US$1.99 billion the year before. Operating loss was US$112.4 million versus an income of US$32.8 million in the prior year. Direct operating expenses declined 3.3% to US$1.16 billion from US$1.20 billion in the comparable period the year before. Indirect operating expenses increased 8.4% to US$825.4 million from US$761.5 million in the equivalent prior-year period.

Prospects: Our evaluation of Verifone Systems Inc. as of Jan. 14, 2018 is the result of our systematic analysis on three basic characteristics: earnings strength, relative valuation, and recent stock price movement. The company has enjoyed a very positive trend in earnings per share over the past 5 quarters. However, while recent estimates for the company have been lowered by analysts, PAY has posted better than expected results. Based on operating earnings yield, the company is overvalued when compared to all of the companies in our coverage universe. Share price changes over the past year indicates that PAY will perform well over the near term.

Financial Data
(US$ in Thousands)

	10/31/2017	10/31/2016	10/31/2015	10/31/2014	10/31/2013	10/31/2012	10/31/2011	10/31/2010
Earnings Per Share	(1.55)	(0.08)	0.68	(0.34)	(2.73)	0.59	2.92	1.13
Cash Flow Per Share	1.48	1.74	2.19	1.78	2.18	2.03	1.89	1.83
Tang Book Value Per Share	N.M.	N.M.	N.M.	N.M.	N.M.	N.M.	3.49	N.M.
Income Statement								
Total Revenue	1,870,976	1,992,149	2,000,457	1,868,874	1,702,221	1,865,971	1,303,866	1,001,537
EBITDA	26,100	189,425	245,595	159,868	88,346	256,479	149,176	134,035
Depn & Amortn	135,722	153,034	141,192	157,280	150,960	129,695	31,829	28,724
Income Before Taxes	(142,819)	1,827	72,948	(39,884)	(106,958)	68,353	90,992	78,245
Income Taxes	32,500	11,527	(7,409)	(3,442)	188,043	2,050	(191,412)	(20,582)
Net Income	(173,829)	(9,281)	79,097	(38,130)	(296,055)	65,033	282,404	98,827
Average Shares	111,817	110,829	115,934	111,586	108,609	110,315	96,616	87,785
Balance Sheet								
Current Assets	718,655	757,427	782,264	785,572	824,992	1,135,443	1,160,448	761,091
Total Assets	2,322,170	2,494,807	2,473,062	2,702,243	2,993,720	3,490,607	2,313,561	1,075,326
Current Liabilities	542,253	538,799	541,241	492,414	587,664	570,390	703,280	259,806
Long-Term Obligations	762,044	859,896	760,241	851,040	943,325	1,252,701	211,756	468,231
Total Liabilities	1,567,577	1,681,076	1,573,558	1,668,453	1,879,114	2,182,812	1,119,368	869,301
Stockholders' Equity	754,593	813,731	899,504	1,033,790	1,114,606	1,307,795	1,194,193	206,025
Shares Outstanding	112,367	111,261	112,684	113,314	110,160	107,930	105,697	86,832
Statistical Record								
Return on Assets %	N.M.	N.M.	3.06	N.M.	N.M.	2.23	16.67	9.91
Return on Equity %	N.M.	N.M.	8.18	N.M.	N.M.	5.18	40.34	83.02
EBITDA Margin %	1.39	9.51	12.28	8.55	5.19	13.75	11.44	13.38
Net Margin %	N.M.	N.M.	3.95	N.M.	N.M.	3.49	21.66	9.87
Asset Turnover	0.78	0.80	0.77	0.66	0.53	0.64	0.77	1.00
Current Ratio	1.33	1.41	1.45	1.60	1.40	1.99	1.65	2.93
Debt to Equity	1.01	1.06	0.85	0.82	0.85	0.96	0.18	2.27
Price Range	21.31-15.41	31.11-15.04	38.93-26.20	37.53-22.41	35.94-15.75	54.45-27.85	56.84-31.12	33.83-13.26
P/E Ratio	...	...	57.25-38.53	...	...	92.29-47.20	19.47-10.66	29.94-11.73

Address: 88 West Plumeria Drive, San Jose, CA 95134
Telephone: 408-232-7800

Web Site: www.verifone.com
Officers: Alex W. (Pete) Hart - Chairman Paul Galant - Chief Executive Officer

Auditors: Ernst & Young LLP
Transfer Agents: Computershare, Canton, MA

Exchange	Symbol	Price	52Wk Range	Yield	P/E
NYS	VRTV	$28.90 (12/29/2017)	62.25-22.70	N/A	N/A

*7 Year Price Score N/A   *NYSE Composite Index=100   *12 Month Price Score 62.99

Interim Earnings (Per Share)

Qtr.	Mar	Jun	Sep	Dec
2014	0.00	0.36	(0.88)	(1.10)
2015	(0.14)	0.27	0.91	0.63
2016	0.21	0.49	0.34	0.26
2017	(0.14)	(0.58)	(0.91)	...

Interim Dividends (Per Share)

No Dividends Paid

Valuation Analysis   Institutional Holding

Forecast EPS	$-0.97	No of Institutions
	(01/17/2018)	218
Market Cap	$453.7 Million	Shares
Book Value	$535.7 Million	16,237,797
Price/Book	0.85	% Held
Price/Sales	0.05	N/A

TRADING VOLUME (thousand shares)

2008 2009 2010 2011 2012 2013 2014 2015 2016 2017

Business Summary: Industrial Machinery & Equipment (MIC: 7.2.1 SIC: 5111 NAIC: 424110)

Veritiv is a business to business distributor of print, publishing, packaging, and facility solutions. Additionally, Co. provides logistics and supply chain management solutions to its customers. Co.'s business is organized under four reportable segments: Print, which sells and distributes commercial printing, writing, copying, digital, format and specialty paper products, graphics consumables and graphics equipment; Publishing, which sells and distributes coated and uncoated commercial printing papers; Packaging, which provides standard as well as custom packaging solutions; and Facility Solutions, which sources and sells cleaning, break-room and other supplies such as towels, and wipers.

Recent Developments: For the quarter ended Sep 30 2017, net loss amounted to US$14.3 million versus net income of US$5.6 million in the year-earlier quarter. Revenues were US$2.12 billion, down 0.5% from US$2.13 billion the year before. Operating loss was US$10.5 million versus an income of US$23.0 million in the prior-year quarter. Direct operating expenses was unchanged at US$1.74 billion versus the comparable period the year before. Indirect operating expenses increased 8.6% to US$390.7 million from US$359.8 million in the equivalent prior-year period.

Prospects: Our evaluation of Veritiv Corp. as of Jan. 14, 2018 is the result of our systematic analysis on three basic characteristics: earnings strength, relative valuation, and recent stock price movement. The company has generated a negative trend in earnings per share over the past 5 quarters. Because the company lacks sufficient analyst estimate data, we place greater weight on the historical EPS trend as the measure of earnings strength. Based on operating earnings yield, the company is undervalued when compared to all of the companies in our coverage universe. Share price changes over the past year indicates that VRTV will perform very poorly over the near term.

Financial Data

(US$ in Thousands)	9 Mos	6 Mos	3 Mos	12/31/2016	12/31/2015	12/31/2014	12/31/2013	12/29/2012
Earnings Per Share	(1.37)	(0.12)	0.95	1.30	1.67	(1.62)	...	...
Cash Flow Per Share	3.99	0.86	1.59	8.75	7.06	0.41	...	...
Tang Book Value Per Share	23.06	30.17	30.29	29.97	28.11	26.50	13.77	...
Income Statement								
Total Revenue	6,140,300	4,023,500	1,994,600	8,326,600	8,717,700	7,406,500	4,089,100	4,123,300
EBITDA	(14,700)	(5,300)	3,400	119,600	122,900	25,300	62,100	69,700
Depn & Amortn	1,900	1,300	600	51,300	51,000	32,900	21,900	22,200
Income Before Taxes	(38,700)	(20,400)	(3,600)	40,800	44,900	(21,600)	12,800	19,200
Income Taxes	(13,100)	(9,100)	(1,400)	19,800	18,200	(2,100)	(228,500)	15,200
Net Income	(25,600)	(11,300)	(2,200)	21,000	26,700	(19,600)	242,400	5,100
Average Shares	15,700	15,700	15,690	16,150	16,000	12,080	...	...
Balance Sheet								
Current Assets	2,152,700	1,960,800	1,940,700	1,948,600	1,925,200	1,959,100	870,600	882,200
Total Assets	2,775,100	2,483,100	2,477,000	2,483,700	2,476,900	2,574,500	1,215,200	1,039,200
Current Liabilities	912,000	805,900	795,400	867,800	814,200	851,100	344,400	396,600
Long-Term Obligations	1,153,900	978,400	997,100	925,300	998,300	1,067,400	371,300	371,600
Total Liabilities	2,239,400	1,939,400	1,930,900	1,941,900	1,946,800	2,062,000	815,700	878,400
Stockholders' Equity	535,700	543,700	546,100	541,800	530,100	512,500	399,500	160,800
Shares Outstanding	15,700	15,700	15,700	15,700	16,000	16,000	25,800	...
Statistical Record								
Return on Assets %	N.M.	N.M.	0.63	0.84	1.06	N.M.	21.39	...
Return on Equity %	N.M.	N.M.	2.86	3.91	5.12	N.M.	86.05	...
EBITDA Margin %	N.M.	N.M.	0.17	1.44	1.41	0.34	1.52	1.69
Net Margin %	N.M.	N.M.	N.M.	0.25	0.31	N.M.	5.93	0.12
Asset Turnover	3.13	3.40	3.39	3.35	3.45	3.91	3.61	...
Current Ratio	2.36	2.43	2.44	2.25	2.36	2.30	2.53	2.22
Debt to Equity	2.15	1.80	1.83	1.71	1.88	2.08	0.93	2.31
Price Range	62.25-27.30	62.25-37.58	62.25-34.87	56.40-28.00	54.11-33.06	51.87-32.50	...	...
P/E Ratio	...	...	65.53-36.71	43.38-21.54	32.40-19.80	...	...	...

Address: 1000 Abernathy Road N.E., Building 400, Suite 1700, Atlanta, GA 30328 **Telephone:** 770-391-8200	**Web Site:** www.veritivcorp.com **Officers:** Mary A. Laschinger - Chairman, Chief Executive Officer, Holding/Parent Company Officer Stephen Joseph Smith - Senior Vice President, Chief Financial Officer	**Auditors:** Deloitte & Touche LLP **Transfer Agents:** Computershare Inc.

VERIZON COMMUNICATIONS INC

Exchange	Symbol	Price	52Wk Range	Yield	P/E	Div Achiever
NYS	VZ	$52.93 (12/29/2017)	54.64-42.89	4.46	13.57	12 Years

*7 Year Price Score 81.93   *NYSE Composite Index=100   *12 Month Price Score 96.98

Interim Earnings (Per Share)

Qtr.	Mar	Jun	Sep	Dec
2014	1.15	1.01	0.89	(0.61)
2015	1.02	1.04	0.99	1.32
2016	1.06	0.17	0.89	1.10
2017	0.84	1.07	0.89	...

Interim Dividends (Per Share)

Amt	Decl	Ex	Rec	Pay
0.578Q	03/03/2017	04/06/2017	04/10/2017	05/01/2017
0.578Q	06/01/2017	07/06/2017	07/10/2017	08/01/2017
0.59Q	09/07/2017	10/06/2017	10/10/2017	11/01/2017
0.59Q	12/07/2017	01/09/2018	01/10/2018	02/01/2018

Indicated Div: $2.36 (Div. Reinv. Plan)

Valuation Analysis — **Institutional Holding**

Forecast EPS	$3.76	No of Institutions
(01/18/2018)		2636
Market Cap	$215.9 Billion	Shares
Book Value	$26.8 Billion	3,108,184,576
Price/Book	8.04	% Held
Price/Sales	1.74	89.79

Business Summary: Services (MIC: 6.1.2 SIC: 4813 NAIC: 517110)

Verizon Communications is a holding company. Through its subsidiaries, Co. provides communications, information and entertainment products and services to consumers, businesses and governmental agencies. Co. operates in two segments: Wireless, which include wireless voice and data services and equipment sales, which are provided to consumer, business and government customers across the U.S.; and Wireline, which include voice, data and video communications products and enhanced services including broadband video and data, corporate networking solutions, data center and cloud services, security and managed network services and local and long distance voice services.

Recent Developments: For the quarter ended Sep 30 2017, net income decreased 0.3% to US$3.74 billion from US$3.75 billion in the year-earlier quarter. Revenues were US$31.72 billion, up 2.5% from US$30.94 billion the year before. Operating income was US$7.21 billion versus US$6.54 billion in the prior-year quarter, an increase of 10.2%. Direct operating expenses rose 3.1% to US$12.61 billion from US$12.23 billion in the comparable period the year before. Indirect operating expenses decreased 2.2% to US$11.90 billion from US$12.17 billion in the equivalent prior-year period.

Prospects: Our evaluation of Verizon Communications Inc. as of Jan. 14, 2018 is the result of our systematic analysis on three basic characteristics: earnings strength, relative valuation, and recent stock price movement. The company has enjoyed a very positive trend in earnings per share over the past 5 quarters. However, while recent estimates for the company have been mixed, VZ has posted better than expected results. Based on operating earnings yield, the company is undervalued when compared to all of the companies in our coverage universe. Share price changes over the past year indicates that VZ will perform in line with the market over the near term.

Financial Data
(US$ in Thousands)

	9 Mos	6 Mos	3 Mos	12/31/2016	12/31/2015	12/31/2014	12/31/2013	12/31/2012
Earnings Per Share	3.90	3.90	3.00	3.21	4.37	2.42	4.00	0.31
Cash Flow Per Share	5.46	4.85	4.16	5.55	9.53	7.71	13.54	11.01
Dividends Per Share	2.310	2.297	2.285	2.273	2.215	2.140	2.075	2.015
Dividend Payout %	59.23	58.91	76.17	70.79	50.69	88.43	51.88	650.00
Income Statement								
Total Revenue	92,079,000	60,362,000	29,814,000	125,980,000	131,620,000	127,079,000	120,550,000	115,846,000
EBITDA	33,686,000	22,740,000	10,380,000	39,628,000	47,454,000	33,263,000	46,757,000	27,007,000
Depn & Amortn	12,498,000	8,226,000	4,059,000	14,227,000	14,323,000	14,966,000	15,019,000	14,920,000
Income Before Taxes	17,731,000	12,198,000	5,203,000	21,084,000	28,326,000	13,490,000	29,135,000	9,573,000
Income Taxes	5,893,000	4,118,000	1,629,000	7,378,000	9,865,000	3,314,000	5,730,000	(660,000)
Net Income	11,432,000	7,812,000	3,450,000	13,127,000	17,879,000	9,625,000	11,497,000	875,000
Average Shares	4,089,000	4,087,000	4,087,000	4,086,000	4,093,000	3,981,000	2,874,000	2,862,000
Balance Sheet								
Current Assets	30,867,000	28,823,000	27,158,000	26,395,000	22,280,000	29,623,000	70,994,000	21,235,000
Total Assets	254,682,000	252,978,000	246,731,000	244,180,000	244,640,000	232,708,000	274,098,000	225,222,000
Current Liabilities	28,930,000	27,758,000	26,664,000	30,340,000	35,052,000	28,064,000	27,050,000	26,956,000
Long-Term Obligations	115,317,000	116,390,000	112,839,000	105,433,000	103,705,000	110,536,000	89,658,000	47,618,000
Total Liabilities	227,834,000	227,789,000	223,238,000	221,656,000	228,212,000	220,410,000	235,262,000	192,065,000
Stockholders' Equity	26,848,000	25,189,000	23,493,000	22,524,000	16,428,000	12,298,000	38,836,000	33,157,000
Shares Outstanding	4,079,441	4,079,408	4,079,370	4,076,684	4,073,175	4,154,964	2,862,000	2,858,569
Statistical Record								
Return on Assets %	6.45	6.57	4.99	5.36	7.49	3.80	4.61	0.38
Return on Equity %	67.33	71.69	58.23	67.22	124.48	37.65	31.94	2.52
EBITDA Margin %	36.58	37.67	34.82	31.46	36.05	26.18	38.79	23.31
Net Margin %	12.42	12.94	11.57	10.42	13.58	7.57	9.54	0.76
Asset Turnover	0.50	0.51	0.50	0.51	0.55	0.50	0.48	0.51
Current Ratio	1.07	1.04	1.02	0.87	0.64	1.06	2.62	0.79
Debt to Equity	4.30	4.62	4.80	4.68	6.31	8.99	2.31	1.44
Price Range	54.64-42.89	56.53-44.41	56.53-46.18	56.53-44.15	50.55-42.84	51.97-45.42	53.91-41.51	47.26-36.80
P/E Ratio	14.01-11.00	14.49-11.39	18.84-15.39	17.61-13.75	11.57-9.80	21.48-18.77	13.48-10.38	152.45-118.71
Average Yield %	4.77	4.58	4.44	4.42	4.70	4.40	4.27	4.78

Address: 1095 Avenue of the Americas, New York, NY 10036
Telephone: 212-395-1000

Web Site: www.verizon.com
Officers: Lowell C. McAdam - Chairman, President, Chief Executive Officer, Chief Operating Officer John G. Stratton - President, Executive Vice President, Chief Marketing Officer, Chief Operating Officer, Division Officer

Auditors: Ernst & Young LLP

VERSUM MATERIALS INC

Exchange	Symbol	Price	52Wk Range	Yield	P/E
NYS	VSM	$37.85 (12/29/2017)	42.50-26.78	0.53	21.51

*7 Year Price Score N/A   *NYSE Composite Index=100   *12 Month Price Score 107.95

TRADING VOLUME (thousand shares)

2008 2009 2010 2011 2012 2013 2014 2015 2016 2017

Interim Earnings (Per Share)

Qtr.	Dec	Mar	Jun	Sep
2015-16	0.60	0.49	0.44	0.41
2016-17	0.47	0.41	0.48	0.40

Interim Dividends (Per Share)

Amt	Decl	Ex	Rec	Pay
0.05Q	03/21/2017	04/03/2017	04/05/2017	04/19/2017
0.05Q	07/27/2017	08/03/2017	08/07/2017	08/21/2017
0.05Q	10/31/2017	11/10/2017	11/13/2017	11/27/2017

Indicated Div: $0.20

Valuation Analysis		Institutional Holding	
Forecast EPS	$2.11	No of Institutions	
	(01/17/2018)	437	
Market Cap	$4.1 Billion	Shares	
Book Value	N/A	106,968,968	
Price/Book	N/A	% Held	
Price/Sales	3.65	N/A	

Business Summary: Specialty Chemicals (MIC: 8.3.2 SIC: 2869 NAIC: 325998)

Versum Materials is a provider of solutions to the semiconductor and display industries with knowledge in the development, manufacturing, transportation and handling of specialty materials. Co. has two segments: Materials, which provides specialty materials focusing on Integrated Circuit and flat-panel display customers, including specialty process gas, cleaners and etchants, slurries, organosilanes and organometallics deposition films; and Delivery Systems and Services, which designs, manufactures, installs, operates, and maintains chemical and gas delivery and distribution systems enabling the use of specialty gases and chemicals delivered directly to Co.'s customers' manufacturing tools.

Recent Developments: For the year ended Sep 30 2017, net income decreased 9.1% to US$199.9 million from US$219.9 million in the prior year. Revenues were US$1.13 billion, up 16.2% from US$970.1 million the year before. Operating income was US$300.1 million versus US$278.9 million in the prior year, an increase of 7.6%. Direct operating expenses rose 18.1% to US$636.9 million from US$539.5 million in the comparable period the year before. Indirect operating expenses increased 25.2% to US$189.9 million from US$151.7 million in the equivalent prior-year period.

Prospects: Our evaluation of Versum Materials Inc. as of Jan. 14, 2018 is the result of our systematic analysis on three basic characteristics: earnings strength, relative valuation, and recent stock price movement. The company has generated a negative trend in earnings per share over the past 5 quarters and while recent estimates for the company have remained steady, VSM has posted results that fell short of analysts expectations. Based on operating earnings yield, the company is undervalued when compared to all of the companies in our coverage universe. Share price changes over the past year indicates that VSM will perform well over the near term.

Financial Data

(US$ in Thousands)	09/30/2017	09/30/2016	09/30/2015	09/30/2014	09/30/2013
Earnings Per Share	1.76	1.95	...	...	...
Cash Flow Per Share	2.41	2.32	...	...	...
Dividends Per Share	0.100	...	...	...	...
Dividend Payout %	5.68	...	...	...	...
Income Statement					
Total Revenue	1,126,900	970,100	1,009,300	942,500	852,800
EBITDA	338,500	348,300	270,100	209,500	(100)
Depn & Amortn	38,400	69,400	48,100	48,300	46,400
Income Before Taxes	252,700	278,500	221,900	160,900	(46,800)
Income Taxes	52,800	58,800	31,700	31,900	29,100
Net Income	193,000	212,000	184,100	123,600	(80,600)
Average Shares	109,400	108,700	...	...	...
Balance Sheet					
Current Assets	606,900	468,000	295,000	358,000	...
Total Assets	1,246,800	1,043,800	887,400	1,034,000	...
Current Liabilities	158,000	104,300	89,600	94,400	...
Long-Term Obligations	977,000	980,300	...	4,400	...
Total Liabilities	1,256,800	1,181,100	178,700	198,000	...
Stockholders' Equity	(10,000)	(137,300)	708,700	836,000	...
Shares Outstanding	108,815	108,675	...	...	...
Statistical Record					
Return on Assets %	16.85	21.90	19.16	...	...
Return on Equity %	...	74.00	23.84	...	...
EBITDA Margin %	30.04	35.90	26.76	22.23	N.M.
Net Margin %	17.13	21.85	18.24	13.11	N.M.
Asset Turnover	0.98	1.00	1.05	...	...
Current Ratio	3.84	4.49	3.29	3.79	...
Debt to Equity	...	...	...	0.01	...
Price Range	38.82-22.46	...	...	...	...
P/E Ratio	22.06-12.76	...	...	...	...
Average Yield %	0.33	...	...	...	...

Address: 8555 South River Parkway, Tempe, AZ 85284 **Telephone:** 602-282-1000	**Web Site:** www.versummaterials.com **Officers:** Guillermo Novo - President, Chief Executive Officer George G. Bitto - Senior Vice President, Chief Financial Officer	**Auditors:** KPMG LLP **Transfer Agents:** Broadridge Corporate Issuer Solutions, Inc.

VF CORP.

Exchange	Symbol	Price	52Wk Range	Yield	P/E	Div Achiever
NYS	VFC	$74.00 (12/29/2017)	74.61-48.32	2.49	31.22	44 Years

*7 Year Price Score 89.43 *NYSE Composite Index=100 *12 Month Price Score 113.33

Interim Earnings (Per Share)

Qtr.	Mar	Jun	Sep	Dec
2014	0.67	0.36	1.08	0.28
2015	0.67	0.40	1.07	0.72
2016	0.61	0.12	1.19	0.63
2017	0.50	0.27	0.97	...

Interim Dividends (Per Share)

Amt	Decl	Ex	Rec	Pay
0.42Q	02/17/2017	03/08/2017	03/10/2017	03/20/2017
0.42Q	04/28/2017	06/07/2017	06/09/2017	06/19/2017
0.42Q	07/24/2017	09/07/2017	09/08/2017	09/18/2017
0.46Q	10/19/2017	12/07/2017	12/08/2017	12/18/2017

Indicated Div: $1.84 (Div. Reinv. Plan)

Valuation Analysis — **Institutional Holding**

Forecast EPS	$3.03 (01/18/2018)	No of Institutions	1089
Market Cap	$29.2 Billion	Shares	449,962,176
Book Value	$3.9 Billion	% Held	99.54
Price/Book	7.41		
Price/Sales	2.48		

TRADING VOLUME (thousand shares)

Business Summary: Apparel, Footwear & Accessories (MIC: 1.4.2 SIC: 2329 NAIC: 315228)

VF is an apparel and footwear company. Co. designs, produces, procures, markets and distributes a range of products, including jeanswear, outerwear, footwear, backpacks, luggage, sportswear, and occupational and performance apparel. Products are marketed primarily under Co.-owned brand names. Co.'s products are marketed to consumers shopping in specialty stores, department stores, national chains, mass merchants and its own direct-to-consumer operations. Co. is organized by groupings of businesses called coalitions that consist of the following: Outdoor & Action Sports, Jeanswear, Imagewear, and Sportswear. As of Dec 31 2016, Co. operated 1,507 retail stores.

Recent Developments: For the quarter ended Sep 30 2017, income from continuing operations decreased 20.3% to US$386.8 million from US$485.2 million in the year-earlier quarter. Net income decreased 22.5% to US$386.1 million from US$498.5 million in the year-earlier quarter. Revenues were US$3.51 billion, up 5.4% from US$3.33 billion the year before. Operating income was US$483.9 million versus US$608.2 million in the prior-year quarter, a decrease of 20.4%. Direct operating expenses rose 3.5% to US$1.75 billion from US$1.69 billion in the comparable period the year before. Indirect operating expenses increased 24.0% to US$1.27 billion from US$1.03 billion in the equivalent prior-year period.

Prospects: Our evaluation of VF Corp. as of Jan. 14, 2018 is the result of our systematic analysis on three basic characteristics: earnings strength, relative valuation, and recent stock price movement. The company has enjoyed a very positive trend in earnings per share over the past 5 quarters and while recent estimates for the company have been mixed, VFC has posted better than expected results. Based on operating earnings yield, the company is about fairly valued when compared to all of the companies in our coverage universe. Share price changes over the past year indicates that VFC will perform well over the near term.

Financial Data

(US$ in Thousands)	9 Mos	6 Mos	3 Mos	12/31/2016	01/02/2016	01/03/2015	12/28/2013	12/29/2012
Earnings Per Share	2.37	2.59	2.44	2.54	2.85	2.38	2.71	2.42
Cash Flow Per Share	3.66	3.68	3.43	3.56	2.70	3.86	3.44	2.91
Tang Book Value Per Share	0.91	0.03	2.07	2.82	3.06	2.78	2.21	0.29
Dividends Per Share	1.680	1.630	1.580	1.530	1.330	1.107	0.915	0.757
Dividend Payout %	70.89	62.93	64.75	60.24	46.67	46.53	33.76	31.24
Income Statement								
Total Revenue	8,450,076	4,941,258	2,581,677	12,019,003	12,376,744	12,282,161	11,419,648	10,879,855
EBITDA	1,148,983	589,684	357,845	1,782,804	1,934,726	1,646,684	1,846,719	1,709,025
Depn & Amortn	207,590	131,908	66,438	281,577	272,075	214,504	203,597	196,898
Income Before Taxes	878,061	416,981	271,219	1,415,591	1,580,389	1,352,366	1,562,490	1,421,875
Income Taxes	161,753	87,437	56,540	243,064	348,796	304,861	352,371	335,737
Net Income	705,192	319,052	209,163	1,074,106	1,231,593	1,047,505	1,210,119	1,085,999
Average Shares	397,384	400,512	415,960	422,081	432,079	440,153	446,809	447,616
Balance Sheet								
Current Assets	5,627,427	3,897,650	4,092,150	4,293,098	4,163,136	4,185,854	3,882,982	3,449,583
Total Assets	10,874,921	9,173,728	9,246,278	9,739,287	9,639,542	9,980,140	10,315,443	9,633,021
Current Liabilities	3,821,395	2,431,143	1,835,859	1,785,400	1,941,713	1,620,241	1,568,001	1,732,212
Long-Term Obligations	2,144,221	2,111,623	2,051,482	2,039,180	1,401,820	1,423,581	1,426,829	1,429,166
Total Liabilities	6,937,501	5,529,389	4,873,221	4,798,366	4,254,704	4,349,258	4,238,405	4,507,396
Stockholders' Equity	3,937,420	3,644,339	4,373,057	4,940,921	5,384,838	5,630,882	6,077,038	5,125,625
Shares Outstanding	394,502	393,308	406,964	414,012	426,614	432,859	440,310	440,818
Statistical Record								
Return on Assets %	9.10	11.48	10.72	11.12	12.59	10.16	12.17	11.50
Return on Equity %	22.01	26.09	22.08	20.86	22.42	17.60	21.66	22.57
EBITDA Margin %	13.60	11.93	13.86	14.83	15.63	13.41	16.17	15.71
Net Margin %	8.35	6.46	8.10	8.94	9.95	8.53	10.60	9.98
Asset Turnover	1.10	1.25	1.24	1.24	1.27	1.19	1.15	1.15
Current Ratio	1.47	1.60	2.23	2.40	2.14	2.58	2.48	1.99
Debt to Equity	0.54	0.58	0.47	0.41	0.26	0.25	0.23	0.28
Price Range	63.95-48.32	65.12-48.32	65.24-48.32	66.75-53.07	77.61-61.81	75.46-55.99	62.08-36.44	42.22-31.75
P/E Ratio	26.98-20.39	25.14-18.66	26.74-19.80	26.28-20.89	27.23-21.69	31.71-23.53	22.91-13.44	17.44-13.12
Average Yield %	3.01	2.91	2.73	2.54	1.87	1.73	1.94	2.05

Address: 105 Corporate Center Boulevard, Greensboro, NC 27408
Telephone: 336-424-6000

Web Site: www.vfc.com
Officers: Steven E. Rendle - Chairman, President, Chief Executive Officer, Vice President, Division Officer, Chief Operating Officer Scott A. Roe - Vice President, Chief Financial Officer, Chief Accounting Officer, Controller

Auditors: PricewaterhouseCoopers LLP
Transfer Agents: Computershare Trust Company, N.A, Providence, RI

VISA INC

Exchange	Symbol	Price	52Wk Range	Yield	P/E
NYS	V	$114.02 (12/29/2017)	114.35-79.50	0.68	40.72

*7 Year Price Score 133.88 *NYSE Composite Index=100 *12 Month Price Score 107.72

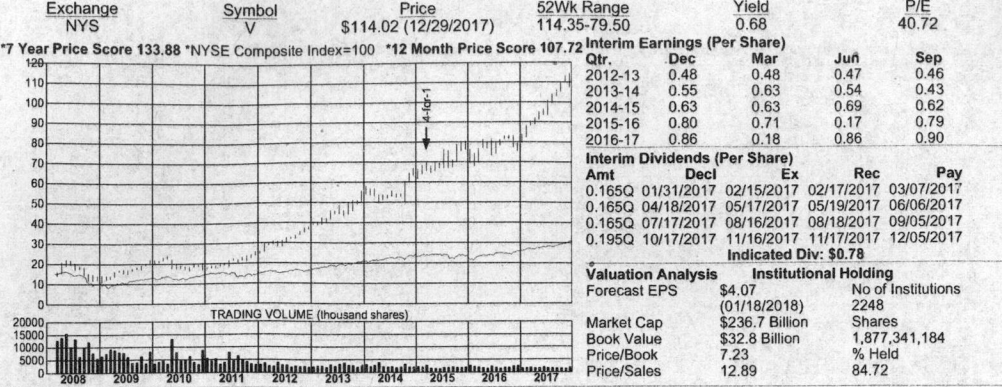

Interim Earnings (Per Share)

Qtr.	Dec	Mar	Jun	Sep
2012-13	0.48	0.48	0.47	0.46
2013-14	0.55	0.63	0.54	0.43
2014-15	0.63	0.63	0.69	0.62
2015-16	0.80	0.71	0.17	0.79
2016-17	0.86	0.18	0.86	0.90

Interim Dividends (Per Share)

Amt	Decl	Ex	Rec	Pay
0.165Q	01/31/2017	02/15/2017	02/17/2017	03/07/2017
0.165Q	04/18/2017	05/17/2017	05/19/2017	06/06/2017
0.165Q	07/17/2017	08/16/2017	08/18/2017	09/05/2017
0.195Q	10/17/2017	11/16/2017	11/17/2017	12/05/2017

Indicated Div: $0.78

Valuation Analysis

	Institutional Holding	
Forecast EPS	$4.07	No of Institutions
	(01/18/2018)	2248
Market Cap	$236.7 Billion	Shares
Book Value	$32.8 Billion	1,877,341,184
Price/Book	7.23	% Held
Price/Sales	12.89	84.72

Business Summary: Business Services (MIC: 7.5.2 SIC: 7389 NAIC: 561499)

Visa is a payments technology company that enables electronic payments across more than 200 countries and territories. Co. facilitates global commerce through the transfer of value and information among a network of consumers, merchants, financial institutions, businesses, strategic partners, and government entities. Co.'s transaction processing network, VisaNet, enables authorization, clearing, and settlement of payment transactions and allows Co. to provide its financial institution and merchant clients with a range of products, platforms, and services. Co. operates in a four party model, which includes card issuing financial institutions, acquirers, and merchants.

Recent Developments: For the year ended Sep 30 2017, net income increased 11.8% to US$6.70 billion from US$5.99 billion in the prior year. Revenues were US$18.36 billion, up 21.7% from US$15.08 billion the year before. Operating income was US$12.14 billion versus US$7.88 billion in the prior year, an increase of 54.1%. Indirect operating expenses decreased 13.7% to US$6.21 billion from US$7.20 billion in the equivalent prior-year period.

Prospects: Our evaluation of Visa Inc. as of Jan. 14, 2018 is the result of our systematic analysis on three basic characteristics: earnings strength, relative valuation, and recent stock price movement. The company has managed to produce a neutral trend in earnings per share over the past 5 quarters and while recent estimates for the company have been raised by analysts, V has posted better than expected results. Based on operating earnings yield, the company is about fairly valued when compared to all of the companies in our coverage universe. Share price changes over the past year indicates that V will perform well over the near term.

Financial Data

(US$ in Thousands)	09/30/2017	09/30/2016	09/30/2015	09/30/2014	09/30/2013	09/30/2012	09/30/2011	09/30/2010
Earnings Per Share	2.80	2.48	2.58	2.15	1.90	0.79	1.29	1.00
Cash Flow Per Share	4.38	2.56	2.96	2.34	0.95	1.54	1.17	0.80
Tang Book Value Per Share	N.M.	N.M.	3.00	1.39	1.23	1.40	1.03	0.62
Dividends Per Share	0.660	0.560	0.480	0.400	0.330	0.220	0.150	0.125
Dividend Payout %	23.57	22.58	18.60	18.56	17.39	27.85	11.63	12.47
Income Statement								
Total Revenue	18,358,000	15,082,000	13,880,000	12,702,000	11,778,000	10,421,000	9,188,000	8,065,000
EBITDA	12,757,000	8,891,000	9,426,000	8,093,000	7,585,000	2,426,000	5,897,000	4,956,000
Depn & Amortn	500,000	452,000	431,000	369,000	328,000	265,000	225,000	265,000
Income Before Taxes	11,694,000	8,012,000	8,995,000	7,724,000	7,257,000	2,207,000	5,656,000	4,645,000
Income Taxes	4,995,000	2,021,000	2,667,000	2,286,000	2,277,000	65,000	2,010,000	1,674,000
Net Income	6,699,000	5,991,000	6,328,000	5,438,000	4,980,000	2,144,000	3,650,000	2,966,000
Average Shares	2,395,000	2,414,000	2,457,000	2,524,000	2,624,000	2,712,000	2,828,000	2,956,000
Balance Sheet								
Current Assets	19,023,000	14,313,000	10,892,000	9,562,000	7,822,000	11,786,000	9,190,000	8,734,000
Total Assets	67,977,000	64,035,000	40,236,000	38,569,000	35,956,000	40,013,000	34,760,000	33,408,000
Current Liabilities	9,994,000	8,046,000	5,374,000	6,006,000	4,335,000	7,954,000	3,451,000	3,498,000
Long-Term Obligations	16,618,000	15,882,000	...	...	...	...	...	32,000
Total Liabilities	35,217,000	31,123,000	10,394,000	11,156,000	9,086,000	12,383,000	8,323,000	8,397,000
Stockholders' Equity	32,760,000	32,912,000	29,842,000	27,413,000	26,870,000	27,630,000	26,437,000	25,011,000
Shares Outstanding	2,076,000	2,133,000	2,215,000	3,048,000	3,120,000	3,244,000	3,248,000	3,340,000
Statistical Record								
Return on Assets %	10.15	11.46	16.06	14.59	13.11	5.72	10.71	9.03
Return on Equity %	20.40	19.04	22.10	20.04	18.28	7.91	14.19	12.31
EBITDA Margin %	69.49	58.95	67.91	63.71	64.40	23.28	64.18	61.45
Net Margin %	36.49	39.72	45.59	42.81	42.28	20.57	39.73	36.78
Asset Turnover	0.28	0.29	0.35	0.34	0.31	0.28	0.27	0.25
Current Ratio	1.90	1.78	2.03	1.59	1.80	1.48	2.66	2.50
Debt to Equity	0.51	0.48	...	...	...	...	...	N.M.
Price Range	106.21-75.43	83.36-67.77	76.38-50.06	58.25-45.63	49.71-34.00	33.75-21.07	23.21-16.73	24.15-16.37
P/E Ratio	37.93-26.94	33.61-27.33	29.60-19.40	27.09-21.22	26.16-17.89	42.72-26.66	17.99-12.97	24.15-16.37
Average Yield %	0.73	0.73	0.72	0.76	0.79	0.78	0.77	0.62

Address: P.O. Box 8999, San Francisco, CA 94128-8999 **Telephone:** 650-432-3200	**Web Site:** www.corporate.visa.com **Officers:** Ryan McInerney - President Alfred F. Kelly - Chief Executive Officer, Chief Executive Officer - Designate	**Auditors:** KPMG LLP **Investor Contact:** 650-432-7644 **Transfer Agents:** Wells Fargo Shareowner Services, St. Paul, MN

VISHAY INTERTECHNOLOGY, INC.

Exchange	Symbol	Price	52Wk Range	Yield	P/E
NYS	VSH	$20.75 (12/29/2017)	23.20-15.50	1.30	30.51

*7 Year Price Score 103.52 *NYSE Composite Index=100 *12 Month Price Score 113.68

Interim Earnings (Per Share)

Qtr.	Mar	Jun	Sep	Dec
2014	0.17	0.23	0.57	0.20
2015	0.20	0.17	(0.19)	(0.92)
2016	0.19	0.22	0.24	(0.33)
2017	0.24	0.36	0.41	...

Interim Dividends (Per Share)

Amt	Decl	Ex	Rec	Pay
0.063Q	02/16/2017	03/10/2017	03/14/2017	03/29/2017
0.063Q	05/23/2017	06/13/2017	06/15/2017	06/29/2017
0.063Q	08/22/2017	09/14/2017	09/15/2017	09/28/2017
0.068Q	11/15/2017	12/06/2017	12/07/2017	12/21/2017

Indicated Div: $0.27

Valuation Analysis

Forecast EPS	$1.42 (01/03/2018)
Market Cap	$3.0 Billion
Book Value	$1.6 Billion
Price/Book	1.87
Price/Sales	1.20

Institutional Holding

No of Institutions	396
Shares	198,330,912
% Held	98.20

Business Summary: Electrical Equipment (MIC: 7.3.1 SIC: 3679 NAIC: 334419)

Vishay Intertechnology is a manufacturer and supplier of discrete semiconductors and passive components. Semiconductors include MOSFETs, diodes, and optoelectronic components, which are used for various functions, including power control, power conversion, power management, signal switching, signal routing, signal blocking, signal amplification, data transfer, remote control, and circuit isolation. Passive components include resistive products, capacitors, and inductors, which are used to restrict current flow, suppress voltage increases, store and discharge energy, control alternating current and voltage, filter out unwanted electrical signals, and perform other functions.

Recent Developments: For the quarter ended Sep 30 2017, net income increased 76.5% to US$64.6 million from US$36.6 million in the year-earlier quarter. Revenues were US$677.9 million, up 14.5% from US$592.0 million the year before. Operating income was US$92.3 million versus US$57.2 million in the prior-year quarter, an increase of 61.3%. Direct operating expenses rose 11.5% to US$488.6 million from US$438.1 million in the comparable period the year before. Indirect operating expenses increased 0.3% to US$96.9 million from US$96.7 million in the equivalent prior-year period.

Prospects: Our evaluation of Vishay Intertechnology Inc. as of Jan. 14, 2018 is the result of our systematic analysis on three basic characteristics: earnings strength, relative valuation, and recent stock price movement. The company has produced a positive trend in earnings per share over the past 5 quarters and while recent estimates for the company have remained steady, VSH has posted better than expected results. Based on operating earnings yield, the company is undervalued when compared to all of the companies in our coverage universe. Share price changes over the past year indicates that VSH will perform well over the near term.

Financial Data
(US$ in Thousands)

	9 Mos	6 Mos	3 Mos	12/31/2016	12/31/2015	12/31/2014	12/31/2013	12/31/2012
Earnings Per Share	0.68	0.51	0.37	0.32	(0.73)	0.77	0.81	0.79
Cash Flow Per Share	2.26	2.25	2.18	2.01	1.66	2.01	2.02	1.92
Tang Book Value Per Share	9.62	10.25	9.52	9.18	9.36	10.13	11.54	10.15
Dividends Per Share	0.250	0.250	0.250	0.250	0.240	0.240	...	...
Dividend Payout %	36.76	49.02	67.57	78.13	...	31.17	...	...
Income Statement								
Total Revenue	1,929,033	1,251,150	606,258	2,323,431	2,300,488	2,493,282	2,370,979	2,230,097
EBITDA	349,863	217,600	96,181	260,096	250,368	347,465	350,033	338,816
Depn & Amortn	121,319	80,380	40,212	144,521	154,340	160,804	155,064	153,801
Income Before Taxes	212,339	126,151	50,442	94,216	74,740	167,143	176,405	170,037
Income Taxes	54,398	32,793	13,493	44,843	182,473	49,300	52,636	46,506
Net Income	157,313	92,909	36,719	48,792	(108,514)	117,629	122,980	122,738
Average Shares	156,701	155,300	154,876	150,697	147,700	153,716	151,417	155,844
Balance Sheet								
Current Assets	2,122,962	2,050,184	1,953,905	1,864,472	1,887,492	1,926,450	1,980,680	1,791,263
Total Assets	3,334,254	3,258,844	3,149,748	3,077,801	3,152,986	3,298,773	3,237,139	3,016,277
Current Liabilities	490,597	474,929	455,110	456,850	457,724	456,739	449,065	412,170
Long-Term Obligations	356,938	350,329	378,652	357,023	436,738	454,922	364,911	392,931
Total Liabilities	1,733,389	1,540,213	1,535,670	1,512,284	1,530,510	1,473,407	1,364,383	1,392,949
Stockholders' Equity	1,600,865	1,718,631	1,614,078	1,565,517	1,622,476	1,825,366	1,872,756	1,623,328
Shares Outstanding	144,003	146,254	146,176	145,976	147,590	147,453	147,331	143,272
Statistical Record								
Return on Assets %	3.35	2.55	1.83	1.56	N.M.	3.60	3.93	4.07
Return on Equity %	6.57	4.75	3.49	3.05	N.M.	6.36	7.04	7.59
EBITDA Margin %	18.14	17.39	15.86	11.19	10.88	13.94	14.76	15.19
Net Margin %	8.16	7.43	6.06	2.10	N.M.	4.72	5.19	5.50
Asset Turnover	0.77	0.76	0.75	0.74	0.71	0.76	0.76	0.74
Current Ratio	4.33	4.32	4.29	4.08	4.12	4.22	4.41	4.35
Debt to Equity	0.22	0.20	0.23	0.23	0.27	0.25	0.19	0.24
Price Range	18.80-13.75	17.35-11.72	16.90-11.56	16.60-10.28	14.59-9.30	16.17-12.68	15.32-10.28	12.74-8.18
P/E Ratio	27.65-20.22	34.02-22.98	45.68-31.24	51.88-32.13	...	21.00-16.47	18.91-12.69	16.13-10.35
Average Yield %	1.53	1.64	1.75	1.91	1.98	1.66	...	...

Address: 63 Lancaster Avenue, Malvern, PA 19355-2143 **Telephone:** 610-644-1300	**Web Site:** www.vishay.com **Officers:** Marc Zandman - Executive Chairman, Chief Business Development Officer Gerald Paul - President, Chief Executive Officer, Chief Technical Officer	**Auditors:** Ernst & Young LLP **Investor Contact:** 610-644-1300 **Transfer Agents:** American Stock Transfer & Trust Company, New York, NY

VISTA OUTDOOR INC

Exchange	Symbol	Price	52Wk Range	Yield	P/E
NYS	VSTO	$14.57 (12/29/2017)	39.34-13.25	N/A	N/A

*7 Year Price Score N/A   *NYSE Composite Index=100   *12 Month Price Score 68.04

TRADING VOLUME (thousand shares)

Interim Earnings (Per Share)

Qtr.	Jun	Sep	Dec	Mar
2014-15	0.64	0.53	(0.17)	0.25
2015-16	0.53	0.52	0.70	0.60
2016-17	0.48	1.22	(6.44)	(0.06)
2017-18	0.29	(2.01)	...	...

Interim Dividends (Per Share)

No Dividends Paid

Valuation Analysis

		Institutional Holding	
Forecast EPS	$0.57	No of Institutions	
	(01/25/2018)	223	
Market Cap	$834.5 Million	Shares	
Book Value	$1.2 Billion	70,304,712	
Price/Book	0.71	% Held	
Price/Sales	0.35	N/A	

Business Summary: Sporting & Recreational (MIC: 2.2.4 SIC: 3949 NAIC: 339920)

Vista Outdoor is a designer, manufacturer and marketer of consumer products in the outdoor sports and recreation markets. Co. operates in two segments, Outdoor Products, which product lines are action sports, archery/hunting accessories, camping, global eyewear and sport protection products, golf, hydration products, optics, shooting accessories, tactical products and water sports; and Shooting Sports, which designs, develops, produces, and sources ammunition and firearms for the hunting and sport shooting enthusiast markets, as well as ammunition for local law enforcement, the U.S. government and international markets.

Recent Developments: For the quarter ended Oct 1 2017, net loss amounted to US$114.7 million versus net income of US$73.2 million in the year-earlier quarter. Revenues were US$587.3 million, down 14.2% from US$684.3 million the year before. Operating loss was US$127.2 million versus an income of US$104.6 million in the prior-year quarter. Direct operating expenses rose 19.9% to US$608.1 million from US$507.1 million in the comparable period the year before. Indirect operating expenses increased 46.3% to US$106.4 million from US$72.7 million in the equivalent prior-year period.

Prospects: Our evaluation of Vista Outdoor Inc. as of Jan. 21, 2018 is the result of our systematic analysis on three basic characteristics: earnings strength, relative valuation, and recent stock price movement. The company has generated a negative trend in earnings per share over the past 5 quarters. However, while recent estimates for the company have been lowered by analysts, VSTO has posted better than expected results. Based on operating earnings yield, the company is undervalued when compared to all of the companies in our coverage universe. Share price changes over the past year indicates that VSTO will perform poorly over the near term.

Financial Data

(US$ in Thousands)	6 Mos	3 Mos	03/31/2017	03/31/2016	03/31/2015	03/31/2014	03/31/2013	03/31/2012
Earnings Per Share	(8.22)	(4.99)	(4.66)	2.35	1.25	...	...	...
Cash Flow Per Share	4.44	3.79	2.63	3.17	2.43	...	...	...
Tang Book Value Per Share	N.M.	N.M.	N.M.	N.M.	5.47	...	...	...
Income Statement								
Total Revenue	1,156,032	568,749	2,546,892	2,270,734	2,083,414	1,873,919	1,196,031	1,042,914
EBITDA	(40,585)	62,731	(113,245)	335,372	250,705	278,709	126,583	54,794
Depn & Amortn	47,250	23,390	93,779	72,614	66,551	44,902	25,128	24,490
Income Before Taxes	(112,797)	26,948	(250,694)	238,407	154,046	218,338	101,462	30,307
Income Taxes	(14,744)	10,296	23,760	91,370	74,518	85,081	36,770	19,647
Net Income	(98,053)	16,652	(274,454)	147,037	79,528	133,257	64,692	10,660
Average Shares	57,099	56,957	58,911	62,568	63,857	..	...	...
Balance Sheet								
Current Assets	1,103,031	1,095,802	1,109,847	1,049,664	1,065,061	849,674	415,529	...
Total Assets	2,810,266	2,961,307	2,976,747	2,942,634	2,573,124	2,457,658	797,812	...
Current Liabilities	363,970	321,985	346,389	368,901	307,912	332,627	214,577	...
Long-Term Obligations	1,012,941	1,075,175	1,089,252	652,787	332,500	1,014,911	...	...
Total Liabilities	1,636,723	1,690,674	1,731,682	1,282,467	924,360	1,586,927	265,912	...
Stockholders' Equity	1,173,543	1,270,633	1,245,065	1,660,167	1,648,764	870,731	531,900	...
Shares Outstanding	57,277	57,030	57,014	60,825	63,873	...	...	...
Statistical Record								
Return on Assets %	N.M.	N.M.	N.M.	5.32	...	8.19	...	...
Return on Equity %	N.M.	N.M.	N.M.	8.86	...	19.00	...	...
EBITDA Margin %	N.M.	11.03	N.M.	14.77	12.03	14.87	10.58	5.25
Net Margin %	N.M.	2.93	N.M.	6.48	3.82	7.11	5.41	1.02
Asset Turnover	0.75	0.78	0.86	0.82	...	1.15	...	...
Current Ratio	3.03	3.40	3.20	2.85	3.46	2.55	1.94	...
Debt to Equity	0.86	0.85	0.87	0.39	0.20	1.17	...	...
Price Range	41.05-18.42	51.80-18.42	52.69-19.99	52.87-41.78	45.64-34.03	...	...	...
P/E Ratio	...	...	...	22.50-17.78	36.51-27.22	...	...	...

Address: 262 N University Drive, Farmington, UT 84025
Telephone: 801-447-3000

Web Site: www.vistaoutdoor.com
Officers: Michael Callahan - Interim Chairman, Interim Chief Executive Officer Christopher T. Metz - Chief Executive Officer

Auditors: Deloitte & Touche LLP
Investor Contact: 801-447-3000
Transfer Agents: Computershare Trust Company, N.A.

VISTRA ENERGY CORP

Exchange	Symbol	Price	52Wk Range	Yield	P/E
NYS	VST	$18.32 (12/29/2017)	20.49-14.59	N/A	N/A

*7 Year Price Score N/A   *NYSE Composite Index=100   *12 Month Price Score 102.27

TRADING VOLUME (thousand shares)

Interim Earnings (Per Share)

Qtr.	Mar	Jun	Sep	Sep
2017	0.18	(0.06)	0.64	...

Interim Dividends (Per Share)

Amt	Decl	Ex	Rec	Pay
2.32U	12/08/2016	12/15/2016	12/19/2016	12/30/2016

Valuation Analysis

		Institutional Holding	
Forecast EPS	$1.16	No of Institutions	
	(01/25/2018)	195	
Market Cap	$7.8 Billion	Shares	
Book Value	$6.9 Billion	419,352,768	
Price/Book	1.13	% Held	
Price/Sales	N/A	N/A	

Business Summary: Electric Utilities (MIC: 3.1.1 SIC: 4911 NAIC: 221122)

Vistra Energy is a holding company. Co. is an energy company operating an integrated power business in Texas. Through its TXU Energy Retail Company LLC and Luminant subsidiaries, Co.'s operations consist of electricity solutions, including retail sales of electricity and related products to end users, power generation (including operations and maintenance and outage and project management) and sales of electricity in the wholesale marketplace, asset optimization and commodity risk management performed on an integrated basis for Co.'s retail and wholesale positions, and fuel logistics and management. Co. operates solely in the Electric Reliability Council of Texas, Inc. electricity market.

Recent Developments: For the quarter ended Sep 30 2017, net income increased 46.0% to US$273.0 million from US$187.0 million in the year-earlier quarter. Revenues were US$1.83 billion, up 8.5% from US$1.69 billion the year before. Direct operating expenses declined 4.1% to US$838.0 million from US$874.0 million in the comparable period the year before. Indirect operating expenses increased 208.5% to US$543.0 million from US$176.0 million in the equivalent prior-year period.

Prospects: On October 10, 2017, subsidiaries of Co. entered into a Settlement Agreement with Alcoa Corporation and Alcoa USA Corp. The terminated agreements were scheduled to terminate in 2038 absent the Settlement Agreement. The Alcoa Parties made a cash payment to the Vistra Parties in the amount of $237.5 million and transferred certain real property and related assets to the Vistra Parties, the Vistra Parties agreed to assume and be responsible for certain liabilities and asset retirement obligations related to Sandow Unit 4, the Three Oaks Mine and other property transferred from Alcoa and both parties released one another from any obligations and claims under the terminated agreements.

Financial Data

(US$ in Millions)	9 Mos	6 Mos	3 Mos	12/31/2016	12/31/2015	12/31/2014
Earnings Per Share	0.64	(0.06)	0.18	(0.38)	...	...
Cash Flow Per Share	...	1.93	0.97	0.77	...	...
Tang Book Value Per Share	5.10	4.24	3.99	3.47	...	...
Dividends Per Share	2.320	2.320	2.320	2.320	...	...
Income Statement						
Total Revenue	4,487	2,653	1,357	1,191	5,704	5,989
EBITDA	1,386	630	396	(120)	(3,501)	(5,646)
Depn & Amortn	621	437	226	54	767	1,154
Income Before Taxes	609	85	119	(233)	(5,556)	(8,549)
Income Taxes	284	33	41	(70)	(879)	(2,320)
Net Income	325	52	78	(163)	(4,677)	(6,229)
Average Shares	428	427	427	427	...	...
Balance Sheet						
Current Assets	2,440	2,397	2,185	2,473	3,450	...
Total Assets	15,000	14,784	14,715	15,167	15,658	...
Current Liabilities	1,119	1,008	981	1,504	2,812	...
Long-Term Obligations	4,540	4,531	4,541	4,577	3	...
Total Liabilities	8,065	8,126	8,035	8,570	38,542	...
Stockholders' Equity	6,935	6,658	6,680	6,597	(22,884)	...
Shares Outstanding	427	427	427	427	...	...
Statistical Record						
EBITDA Margin %	30.89	23.75	29.18	N.M.	N.M.	N.M.
Net Margin %	7.24	1.96	5.75	N.M.	N.M.	N.M.
Asset Turnover	...	...	...	0.31	...	...
Current Ratio	2.18	2.38	2.23	1.64	1.23	...
Debt to Equity	0.65	0.68	0.68	0.69	...	...
Price Range	18.70-13.60	17.95-13.60	17.95-13.60	16.40-13.60	...	...
Average Yield %	14.41	14.76	14.76	15.49	...	...

Address: 6555 Sierra Drive, Irving, TX 75039	Web Site: www.vistraenergy.com	Auditors: Deloitte & Touche LLP
Telephone: 214-812-4600	Officers: Cecily Small Gooch - Senior Vice President, Associate General Counsel, Chief Compliance Officer, Corporate Secretary	Investor Contact: 214-812-0046 Transfer Agents: American Stock Transfer & Trust Company, LLC, Hudson, Wisconsin

VMWARE INC

Exchange	Symbol	Price	52Wk Range	Yield	P/E
NYS	VMW	$125.32 (12/29/2017)	128.89-78.88	N/A	36.12

*7 Year Price Score 91.00   *NYSE Composite Index=100   ***12 Month Price Score 115.11**

Interim Earnings (Per Share)

Qtr.	Mar	Jun	Sep	Dec
2014	0.46	0.38	0.45	0.75
2015	0.45	0.40	0.60	0.88
2016	0.38	0.62	0.75	1.03
Qtr.	May	Aug	Nov	Jan
2017-18	0.56	0.81	1.07	...

Interim Dividends (Per Share)

No Dividends Paid

Valuation Analysis	Institutional Holding	
Forecast EPS	$5.14	No of Institutions
(01/25/2018)		662
Market Cap	$50.6 Billion	Shares
Book Value	$8.3 Billion	104,679,024
Price/Book	6.12	% Held
Price/Sales	N/A	22.08

Business Summary: Internet & Software (MIC: 6.3.2 SIC: 7372 NAIC: 511210)

VMware is a provider of virtualization and cloud infrastructure solutions. Co.'s virtualization infrastructure solutions are designed to deliver a software-defined data center, run on desktop computers and servers and support operating system and application environments, as well as networking and storage infrastructures. Co. has three product groups: Software-Defined Data Center, which are the basis for the private cloud environment; Hybrid Cloud Computing, which is comprised of VMware vCloud Air Network and VMware vCloud Air offerings; and End-User Computing solution that consists of VMware Workspace ONE, its digital workspace platform, which includes VMware AirWatch and VMware Horizon.

Recent Developments:
For the year ended Dec 31 2016, net income increased 19.0% to US$1.19 billion from US$997.0 million in the prior year. Revenues were US$7.09 billion, up 7.9% from US$6.57 billion the year before. Operating income was US$1.44 billion versus US$1.20 billion in the prior year, an increase of 20.2%. Direct operating expenses rose 3.4% to US$1.05 billion from US$1.02 billion in the comparable period the year before. Indirect operating expenses increased 5.6% to US$4.60 billion from US$4.36 billion in the equivalent prior-year period.

Prospects:
Our evaluation of VMware Inc. as of Jan. 21, 2018 is the result of our systematic analysis on three basic characteristics: earnings strength, relative valuation, and recent stock price movement. The company has enjoyed a very positive trend in earnings per share over the past 5 quarters and while recent estimates for the company have remained steady, VMW has posted better than expected results. Based on operating earnings yield, the company is about fairly valued when compared to all of the companies in our coverage universe. Share price changes over the past year indicates that VMW will perform very well over the near term.

Financial Data
(US$ in Thousands)	9 Mos	6 Mos	3 Mos	02/03/2017	12/31/2016	12/31/2015	12/31/2014	12/31/2013
Earnings Per Share	3.47	3.42	2.96	(0.02)	2.78	2.34	2.04	2.34
Cash Flow Per Share	...	...	...	9.48	5.65	4.48	5.07	5.91
Tang Book Value Per Share	8.82	9.41	8.72	8.97	8.69	7.84	6.68	7.39
Income Statement								
Total Revenue	5,612,000	3,636,000	1,736,000	496,000	7,093,000	6,571,000	6,035,000	5,207,000
EBITDA	1,175,000	843,000	350,000	(3,000)	1,714,000	1,429,000	1,262,000	1,292,000
Depn & Amortn	1,000	165,000	85,000	29,000	215,000	190,000	190,000	141,000
Income Before Taxes	1,133,000	665,000	258,000	(34,000)	1,473,000	1,213,000	1,048,000	1,147,000
Income Taxes	124,000	99,000	26,000	(26,000)	287,000	216,000	162,000	133,000
Net Income	1,009,000	566,000	232,000	(8,000)	1,186,000	997,000	886,000	1,014,000
Average Shares	413,013	412,768	414,018	408,625	423,994	426,547	434,513	433,415
Balance Sheet								
Current Assets	12,926,000	10,471,000	9,778,000	9,851,000	10,335,000	9,360,000	9,130,000	7,681,000
Total Assets	19,594,000	17,175,000	16,241,000	16,397,000	16,643,000	15,746,000	15,216,000	12,327,000
Current Liabilities	4,525,000	5,276,000	5,010,000	4,289,000	4,554,000	4,129,000	3,996,000	3,293,000
Long-Term Obligations	4,232,000	820,000	820,000	1,500,000	1,500,000	1,500,000	1,500,000	450,000
Total Liabilities	11,320,000	8,576,000	8,173,000	8,181,000	8,546,000	7,827,000	7,635,000	5,511,000
Stockholders' Equity	8,274,000	8,599,000	8,068,000	8,216,000	8,097,000	7,919,000	7,581,000	6,816,000
Shares Outstanding	403,819	409,651	408,409	410,060	408,351	421,947	429,359	430,349
Statistical Record								
Return on Assets %	...	...	...	N.M.	7.30	6.44	6.43	8.85
Return on Equity %	...	...	...	N.M.	14.77	12.86	12.31	16.15
EBITDA Margin %	20.94	23.18	20.16	N.M.	24.16	21.75	20.91	24.81
Net Margin %	17.98	15.57	13.36	N.M.	16.72	15.17	14.68	19.47
Asset Turnover	...	...	...	0.32	0.44	0.42	0.44	0.45
Current Ratio	2.86	1.98	1.95	2.30	2.27	2.27	2.28	2.33
Debt to Equity	0.51	0.10	0.10	0.18	0.19	0.19	0.20	0.07
Price Range	120.97-75.82	97.40-70.33	94.58-55.34	88.95-78.88	82.58-43.84	91.14-55.42	111.80-76.43	99.00-65.53
P/E Ratio	34.86-21.85	28.48-20.56	31.95-18.70	...	29.71-15.77	38.95-23.68	54.80-37.47	42.31-28.00

Address: 3401 Hillview Avenue, Palo Alto, CA 94304
Telephone: 650-427-5000

Web Site: www.vmware.com
Officers: Michael S. Dell - Chairman Michael S. Dell - Chairman

Auditors: PricewaterhouseCoopers LLP
Investor Contact: 650-427-2892
Transfer Agents: American Stock Transfer & Trust Co., New York, NY

VORNADO REALTY TRUST

Exchange	Symbol	Price	52Wk Range	Yield	P/E
NYS	VNO	$78.18 (12/29/2017)	89.58-72.38	3.22	18.88

*7 Year Price Score 86.62 *NYSE Composite Index=100 *12 Month Price Score 91.45

Interim Earnings (Per Share)

Qtr.	Mar	Jun	Sep	Dec
2014	0.33	0.41	0.69	2.72
2015	0.45	0.87	1.05	1.22
2016	(0.61)	1.16	0.35	3.43
2017	0.25	0.61	(0.15)	...

Interim Dividends (Per Share)

Amt	Decl	Ex	Rec	Pay
0.71Q	04/26/2017	05/04/2017	05/08/2017	05/19/2017
0.60Q	07/27/2017	08/03/2017	08/07/2017	08/18/2017
0.60Q	10/26/2017	11/03/2017	11/06/2017	11/20/2017
0.63Q	01/17/2018	01/26/2018	01/29/2018	02/15/2018

Indicated Div: $2.52

Valuation Analysis — **Institutional Holding**

Forecast EPS	$1.09 (01/18/2018)	No of Institutions 675
Market Cap	$14.8 Billion	Shares 224,471,824
Book Value	$4.6 Billion	% Held
Price/Book	3.25	91.41
Price/Sales	6.15	

Business Summary: REITs (MIC: 5.3.1 SIC: 6798 NAIC: 525930)

Vornado Realty Trust is a real estate investment trust. Co. conducts its business through, and substantially all of its interests in properties are held by, Vornado Realty L.P. Co. owns and operates office and retail properties in New York and Washington, DC/ Northern Virginia area. As of Dec 31 2016, Co. owned all or portions of, among others: office space in 36 properties, retail space in 70 properties, 12 residential properties and Hotel Pennsylvania in New York, a 32.4% interest in Alexander's, Inc. that owned seven properties in New York, office space and residential properties in Washington DC, theMart in Chicago, and a 70.0% controlling interest in an office complex in San Francisco.

Recent Developments: For the quarter ended Sep 30 2017, income from continuing operations decreased 50.8% to US$37.2 million from US$75.5 million in the year-earlier quarter. Net loss amounted to US$10.8 million versus net income of US$100.6 million in the year-earlier quarter. Revenues were US$528.8 million, up 5.2% from US$502.8 million the year before. Revenues from property income rose 4.9% to US$495.5 million from US$472.1 million in the corresponding quarter a year earlier.

Prospects: Our evaluation of Vornado Realty Trust as of Jan. 14, 2018 is the result of our systematic analysis on three basic characteristics: earnings strength, relative valuation, and recent stock price movement. The company has generated a negative trend in earnings per share over the past 5 quarters. Because the company lacks sufficient analyst estimate data, we place greater weight on the historical EPS trend as the measure of earnings strength. Based on operating earnings yield, the company is overvalued when compared to all of the companies in our coverage universe. Share price changes over the past year indicates that VNO will perform well over the near term.

Financial Data

(US$ in Thousands)	9 Mos	6 Mos	3 Mos	12/31/2016	12/31/2015	12/31/2014	12/31/2013	12/31/2012
Earnings Per Share	4.14	4.64	5.19	4.34	3.59	4.15	2.09	2.94
Cash Flow Per Share	5.74	5.25	5.42	5.28	3.57	6.05	5.57	4.43
Tang Book Value Per Share	17.73	30.09	29.68	29.97	27.54	27.63	27.58	28.06
Dividends Per Share	2.650	2.680	2.600	2.520	2.520	2.920	2.920	3.760
Dividend Payout %	64.01	57.76	50.10	58.06	70.19	70.36	139.71	127.89
Income Statement								
Total Revenue	1,547,900	1,246,887	620,848	2,506,202	2,502,267	2,635,940	2,760,909	2,766,457
EBITDA	428,069	326,215	151,423	1,761,684	1,499,334	1,377,389	1,324,381	900,561
Depn & Amortn	(35,446)	(24,391)	(11,459)	542,068	487,154	536,622	509,122	503,529
Income Before Taxes	223,578	167,817	71,911	841,275	661,022	400,282	369,708	(70,331)
Income Taxes	2,429	1,957	2,205	8,312	(84,695)	11,002	(6,406)	8,132
Net Income	183,084	195,982	63,881	906,917	760,434	864,852	475,971	617,260
Average Shares	190,847	190,444	190,372	190,173	189,564	188,690	187,709	186,530
Balance Sheet								
Current Assets	2,358,379	2,703,913	2,718,698	1,897,493	2,192,565	1,715,456	1,153,509	1,737,481
Total Assets	16,842,120	20,889,290	20,731,448	20,814,847	21,143,293	21,248,320	20,097,224	21,965,975
Current Liabilities	412,100	427,401	451,156	458,694	443,955	499,702	422,276	484,746
Long-Term Obligations	9,351,601	10,837,585	10,615,437	10,611,685	11,091,010	10,898,859	9,978,718	11,296,190
Total Liabilities	12,271,041	13,972,856	13,889,741	13,916,328	14,445,698	14,502,894	13,331,992	15,115,040
Stockholders' Equity	4,571,079	6,916,434	6,841,707	6,898,519	6,697,595	6,745,426	6,765,232	6,850,935
Shares Outstanding	189,877	189,465	189,343	189,100	188,576	187,887	187,284	186,734
Statistical Record								
Return on Assets %	4.51	4.56	5.12	4.31	3.59	4.18	2.26	2.90
Return on Equity %	15.62	14.15	15.93	13.30	11.31	12.80	6.99	9.00
EBITDA Margin %	27.65	26.16	24.39	70.29	59.92	52.25	47.97	32.55
Net Margin %	11.83	15.72	10.29	36.19	30.39	32.81	17.24	22.31
Asset Turnover	0.13	0.12	0.12	0.12	0.12	0.13	0.13	0.13
Current Ratio	5.72	6.33	6.03	4.14	4.94	3.43	2.73	3.58
Debt to Equity	2.05	1.57	1.55	1.54	1.66	1.62	1.48	1.65
Price Range	89.58-70.09	89.58-70.09	89.58-70.09	87.03-64.77	92.74-68.53	87.30-64.88	66.69-56.16	44.46-53.60
P/E Ratio	21.64-16.93	19.31-15.11	17.26-13.51	20.05-14.92	25.83-19.09	21.04-15.63	31.91-26.87	21.93-18.23
Average Yield %	3.34	3.31	3.21	3.23	3.09	3.86	4.68	6.30

Address: 888 Seventh Avenue, New York, NY 10019 **Telephone:** 212-894-7000	**Web Site:** www.vno.com **Officers:** Steven Roth - Chairman, Chief Executive Officer Joseph Macnow - Interim Chief Financial Officer, Executive Vice President, Chief Administrative Officer	**Auditors:** Deloitte & Touche LLP **Investor Contact:** 201-587-1000 **Transfer Agents:** American Stock Transfer & Trust Co., New York, NY

VOYA FINANCIAL INC

Exchange	Symbol	Price	52Wk Range	Yield	P/E
NYS	VOYA	$49.47 (12/29/2017)	52.07-34.18	0.08	N/A

*7 Year Price Score N/A   *NYSE Composite Index=100   *12 Month Price Score 107.56

Interim Earnings (Per Share)

Qtr.	Mar	Jun	Sep	Dec
2014	0.98	0.96	1.58	5.51
2015	0.77	1.24	0.18	(0.43)
2016	0.92	0.79	(1.24)	(2.64)
2017	(0.75)	0.89	0.81	...

Interim Dividends (Per Share)

Amt	Decl	Ex	Rec	Pay
0.01Q	02/02/2017	02/24/2017	02/28/2017	03/29/2017
0.01Q	04/28/2017	05/26/2017	05/31/2017	06/29/2017
0.01Q	07/27/2017	08/29/2017	08/31/2017	09/28/2017
0.01Q	10/26/2017	11/29/2017	11/30/2017	12/28/2017

Indicated Div: $0.04

Valuation Analysis

		Institutional Holding	
Forecast EPS	$2.72 (01/18/2018)	No of Institutions	420
Market Cap	$8.9 Billion	Shares	194,170,960
Book Value	$13.7 Billion	% Held	N/A
Price/Book	0.65		
Price/Sales	0.90		

Business Summary: Life & Health (MIC: 5.2.2 SIC: 6311 NAIC: 524210)

Voya Financial is a holding company. Through a number of direct and indirect subsidiaries, Co. is a retirement, investment and insurance company. Co.'s segments include: Retirement, which provides, among others, retirement services and products, providing tax-deferred; Investment Management, which provides domestic and international fixed income, equity, multi-asset and alternative investment products and solutions; Annuities, which provides fixed and indexed annuities, and other investment products and payout; Individual Life, which provides wealth protection and transfer opportunities; and Employee Benefits, which provides stop loss, voluntary employee-paid and disability products.

Recent Developments: For the quarter ended Sep 30 2017, net income amounted to US$214.0 million versus a net loss of US$236.5 million in the year-earlier quarter. Revenues were US$2.55 billion, up 0.9% from US$2.53 billion the year before. Net premiums earned were US$581.6 million versus US$726.7 million in the prior-year quarter, a decrease of 20.0%. Net investment income fell 5.1% to US$1.10 billion from US$1.16 billion a year ago.

Prospects: Our evaluation of Voya Financial Inc. as of Jan. 14, 2018 is the result of our systematic analysis on three basic characteristics: earnings strength, relative valuation, and recent stock price movement. The company has generated a negative trend in earnings per share over the past 5 quarters. However, while recent estimates for the company have been lowered by analysts, VOYA has posted results that fell short of analysts expectations. Based on operating earnings yield, the company is undervalued when compared to all of the companies in our coverage universe. Share price changes over the past year indicates that VOYA will perform very poorly over the near term.

Financial Data
(US$ in Thousands)

	9 Mos	6 Mos	3 Mos	12/31/2016	12/31/2015	12/31/2014	12/31/2013	12/31/2012
Earnings Per Share	(1.69)	(3.74)	(3.84)	(2.13)	1.80	9.02	2.38	2.06
Cash Flow Per Share	12.40	13.36	15.04	17.81	14.40	14.34	13.02	...
Tang Book Value Per Share	74.87	73.20	66.78	65.63	63.06	65.42	49.48	58.81
Dividends Per Share	0.040	0.040	0.040	0.040	0.040	0.040	0.020	...
Dividend Payout %	...	...	...	...	2.22	0.44	0.84	...
Income Statement								
Total Revenue	7,352,400	4,802,200	2,213,400	10,782,200	11,341,200	11,070,900	8,758,500	9,615,300
Income Before Taxes	309,800	71,700	(159,400)	(613,400)	584,500	785,200	758,100	606,000
Income Taxes	19,000	(5,100)	(17,000)	(214,700)	45,900	(1,752,200)	(32,500)	(5,200)
Net Income	172,300	23,700	(143,500)	(428,000)	408,300	2,299,700	600,500	473,000
Average Shares	182,400	187,700	191,700	200,800	227,400	255,100	251,800	...
Balance Sheet								
Total Assets	226,643,900	219,838,800	217,025,500	214,235,100	218,249,600	226,951,400	221,023,200	216,394,200
Total Liabilities	212,990,900	206,486,600	204,135,100	201,241,200	204,813,800	210,843,500	207,751,000	202,519,300
Stockholders' Equity	13,653,000	13,352,200	12,890,400	12,993,900	13,435,800	16,107,900	13,272,200	13,874,900
Shares Outstanding	179,746	179,692	189,926	194,639	209,095	241,875	261,675	230,000
Statistical Record								
Return on Assets %	N.M.	N.M.	N.M.	N.M.	0.18	1.03	0.27	0.22
Return on Equity %	N.M.	N.M.	N.M.	N.M.	2.76	15.65	4.42	3.60
Net Margin %	2.34	0.49	N.M.	N.M.	3.60	20.77	6.86	4.92
Asset Turnover	0.04	0.05	0.05	0.05	0.05	0.05	0.04	0.05
Price Range	42.93-28.82	42.93-23.47	42.93-23.38	41.00-23.38	48.14-36.04	43.07-33.11	35.89-20.67	...
P/E Ratio	...	...	...	...	26.74-20.02	4.77-3.67	15.08-8.68	...
Average Yield %	0.11	0.12	0.12	0.13	0.09	0.11	0.07	...

Address: 230 Park Avenue, New York, NY 10169 **Telephone:** 212-309-8200	**Web Site:** www.ing.us **Officers:** Rodney O. Martin - Chairman, Chief Executive Officer Alain M. Karaoglan - Executive Vice President, Chief Operating Officer	**Auditors:** Ernst & Young LLP **Transfer Agents:** Computershare Trust Company, N.A, Canton, MA

VULCAN MATERIALS CO (HOLDING COMPANY)

Exchange	Symbol	Price	52Wk Range	Yield	P/E
NYS	VMC	$128.37 (12/29/2017)	135.28-112.50	0.78	42.37

*7 Year Price Score 129.60 *NYSE Composite Index=100 *12 Month Price Score 94.61

TRADING VOLUME (thousand shares)

Interim Earnings (Per Share)

Qtr.	Mar	Jun	Sep	Dec
2014	0.41	0.35	0.50	0.28
2015	(0.30)	0.36	0.91	0.66
2016	0.14	0.91	1.04	1.00
2017	0.33	0.89	0.81	...

Interim Dividends (Per Share)

Amt	Decl	Ex	Rec	Pay
0.25Q	02/10/2017	02/22/2017	02/24/2017	03/10/2017
0.25Q	05/12/2017	05/22/2017	05/24/2017	06/09/2017
0.25Q	07/14/2017	08/21/2017	08/23/2017	09/08/2017
0.25Q	10/13/2017	11/21/2017	11/22/2017	12/08/2017

Indicated Div: $1.00 (Div. Reinv. Plan)

Valuation Analysis

		Institutional Holding	
Forecast EPS	$3.00	No of Institutions	785
	(01/18/2018)		
Market Cap	$17.0 Billion	Shares	157,032,432
Book Value	$4.7 Billion	% Held	88.33
Price/Book	3.62		
Price/Sales	4.49		

Business Summary: Mining (MIC: 8.2.4 SIC: 1429 NAIC: 212319)

Vulcan Materials is a supplier of construction aggregates (primarily crushed stone, sand and gravel) and a producer of asphalt mix and ready-mixed concrete. Co. has four operating (and reportable) segments: the Aggregates segment, which produces and sells aggregates (crushed stone, sand and gravel, sand, and other aggregates) and related products and services (transportation and other); the Asphalt Mix segment, which produces and sells asphalt mix in four states; the Concrete segment, which produces and sells ready-mixed concrete in six states, Washington D.C. and the Bahamas; and the Calcium segment, which consists of a Florida facility that mines, produces and sells calcium products.

Recent Developments: For the quarter ended Sep 30 2017, income from continuing operations decreased 24.1% to US$110.2 million from US$145.1 million in the year-earlier quarter. Net income decreased 23.5% to US$108.6 million from US$142.0 million in the year-earlier quarter. Revenues were US$1.09 billion, up 8.6% from US$1.01 billion the year before. Operating income was US$229.5 million versus US$227.1 million in the prior-year quarter, an increase of 1.1%. Direct operating expenses rose 12.1% to US$789.2 million from US$703.9 million in the comparable period the year before. Indirect operating expenses decreased 1.4% to US$76.0 million from US$77.1 million in the equivalent prior-year period.

Prospects: Our evaluation of Vulcan Materials Co. as of Jan. 14, 2018 is the result of our systematic analysis on three basic characteristics: earnings strength, relative valuation, and recent stock price movement. The company has produced a positive trend in earnings per share over the past 5 quarters and while recent estimates for the company have been mixed, VMC has posted results that were in line with analysts expectations. Based on operating earnings yield, the company is overvalued when compared to all of the companies in our coverage universe. Share price changes over the past year indicates that VMC will perform poorly over the near term.

Financial Data

(US$ in Thousands)	9 Mos	6 Mos	3 Mos	12/31/2016	12/31/2015	12/31/2014	12/31/2013	12/31/2012
Earnings Per Share	3.03	3.26	3.28	3.09	1.64	1.54	0.19	(0.41)
Cash Flow Per Share	5.27	5.27	5.25	4.83	3.78	1.98	2.74	1.83
Tang Book Value Per Share	5.66	5.04	4.47	5.35	4.45	2.45	1.22	N.M.
Dividends Per Share	0.950	0.900	0.850	0.800	0.400	0.220	0.040	0.040
Dividend Payout %	31.35	27.61	25.91	25.89	24.39	14.29	21.05	...
Income Statement								
Total Revenue	2,912,806	1,818,091	787,328	3,592,667	3,422,181	2,994,169	2,770,709	2,567,310
EBITDA	729,525	418,619	145,987	918,763	776,966	780,856	469,122	392,654
Depn & Amortn	227,974	148,339	71,563	238,237	228,866	239,611	271,180	301,146
Income Before Taxes	346,979	197,749	40,348	547,257	327,857	298,838	(3,703)	(120,418)
Income Taxes	81,557	42,477	(3,175)	124,851	94,943	91,692	(24,459)	(66,492)
Net Income	273,639	165,060	44,921	419,491	221,177	204,923	24,382	(52,593)
Average Shares	134,765	134,735	134,968	135,790	135,093	132,991	131,467	129,745
Balance Sheet								
Current Assets	1,746,972	2,184,812	1,157,762	1,137,182	1,084,591	920,469	951,496	984,972
Total Assets	9,439,334	9,869,943	8,744,324	8,471,475	8,301,632	8,061,902	8,259,143	8,126,599
Current Liabilities	413,699	925,793	360,898	372,244	353,479	451,878	299,135	436,411
Long-Term Obligations	2,809,966	2,809,293	2,329,248	1,982,751	1,980,334	1,855,447	2,522,243	2,526,401
Total Liabilities	4,754,200	5,267,839	4,223,563	3,898,999	3,847,444	3,885,203	4,321,037	4,365,537
Stockholders' Equity	4,685,134	4,602,104	4,520,761	4,572,476	4,454,188	4,176,699	3,938,106	3,761,062
Shares Outstanding	132,281	132,181	132,222	132,339	133,172	131,907	130,200	129,721
Statistical Record								
Return on Assets %	4.62	4.87	5.24	4.99	2.70	2.51	0.30	N.M.
Return on Equity %	8.94	9.73	9.96	9.27	5.13	5.05	0.63	N.M.
EBITDA Margin %	25.05	23.03	18.54	25.57	22.70	26.08	16.93	15.29
Net Margin %	9.39	9.08	5.71	11.68	6.46	6.84	0.88	N.M.
Asset Turnover	0.43	0.41	0.43	0.43	0.42	0.37	0.34	0.31
Current Ratio	4.22	2.36	3.21	3.05	3.07	2.04	3.18	2.26
Debt to Equity	0.60	0.61	0.52	0.43	0.44	0.44	0.64	0.67
Price Range	136.04-106.47	136.04-106.47	136.04-105.56	136.04-81.60	105.70-64.98	69.01-55.28	59.49-45.59	53.25-32.57
P/E Ratio	44.90-35.14	41.73-32.66	41.48-32.18	44.03-26.41	64.45-39.62	44.81-35.90	313.11-239.95	
Average Yield %	0.78	0.74	0.72	0.72	0.45	0.35	0.08	0.09

Address: 1200 Urban Center Drive, Birmingham, AL 35242 **Telephone:** 205-298-3000 **Fax:** 205-298-2963	**Web Site:** www.vulcanmaterials.com **Officers:** J. Thomas Hill - Chairman, President, Chief Executive Officer, Executive Vice President, Chief Operating Officer John R. McPherson - Executive Vice President, Senior Vice President, Chief Financial Officer, Chief Strategy Officer

Auditors: Deloitte & Touche LLP
Investor Contact: 205-298-3220
Transfer Agents: Computershare Shareowner Services LLC, Providence, RI

WABTEC CORP

Exchange	Symbol	Price	52Wk Range	Yield	P/E
NYS	WAB	$81.43 (12/29/2017)	92.51-69.70	0.59	30.84

*7 Year Price Score 96.34   *NYSE Composite Index=100   *12 Month Price Score 90.52

Interim Earnings (Per Share)

Qtr.	Mar	Jun	Sep	Dec
2014	0.83	0.91	0.93	0.95
2015	0.99	1.04	1.02	1.05
2016	1.02	1.00	0.91	0.42
2017	0.77	0.75	0.70	...

Interim Dividends (Per Share)

Amt	Decl	Ex	Rec	Pay
0.10Q	01/25/2017	02/08/2017	02/10/2017	02/24/2017
0.10Q	04/12/2017	05/10/2017	05/12/2017	05/26/2017
0.12Q	05/10/2017	08/10/2017	08/14/2017	08/28/2017
0.12Q	10/31/2017	11/10/2017	11/13/2017	11/27/2017

Indicated Div: $0.48

Valuation Analysis

		Institutional Holding	
Forecast EPS	$3.48	No of Institutions	
	(01/16/2018)	579	
Market Cap	$7.8 Billion	Shares	
Book Value	$2.7 Billion	127,796,240	
Price/Book	2.88	% Held	
Price/Sales	2.19	88.05	

Business Summary: Construction Services (MIC: 7.5.4 SIC: 3743 NAIC: 336510)

Westinghouse Air Brake Technologies is a provider of technology-based products and services for the rail industry. Co. has two segments: the Freight Segment, which manufactures and services components for new and existing locomotive and freight cars; supplies rail control and infrastructure products; overhauls locomotives; and provides heat exchangers and cooling systems for rail and other industrial markets; and the Transit Segment, which manufactures and services components for new and existing passenger transit vehicles; supplies rail control and infrastructure products; builds new commuter locomotives; and refurbishes passenger transit vehicles.

Recent Developments: For the quarter ended Sep 30 2017, net income decreased 17.0% to US$68.4 million from US$82.4 million in the year-earlier quarter. Revenues were US$957.9 million, up 41.8% from US$675.6 million the year before. Operating income was US$102.0 million versus US$120.1 million in the prior-year quarter, a decrease of 15.1%. Direct operating expenses rose 52.2% to US$704.7 million from US$463.1 million in the comparable period the year before. Indirect operating expenses increased 63.7% to US$151.2 million from US$92.4 million in the equivalent prior-year period.

Prospects: Our evaluation of Wabtec Corp. as of Jan. 14, 2018 is the result of our systematic analysis on three basic characteristics: earnings strength, relative valuation, and recent stock price movement. The company has enjoyed a very positive trend in earnings per share over the past 5 quarters and while recent estimates for the company have been raised by analysts, WAB has posted better than expected results. Based on operating earnings yield, the company is about fairly valued when compared to all of the companies in our coverage universe. Share price changes over the past year indicates that WAB will perform very poorly over the near term.

Financial Data

(US$ in Thousands)	9 Mos	6 Mos	3 Mos	12/31/2016	12/31/2015	12/31/2014	12/31/2013	12/31/2012
Earnings Per Share	2.64	2.85	3.10	3.34	4.10	3.62	3.01	2.60
Cash Flow Per Share	2.39	2.32	3.65	4.96	4.67	4.93	2.47	2.48
Tang Book Value Per Share	N.M.	N.M.	N.M.	N.M.	4.36	5.42	4.31	3.17
Dividends Per Share	0.420	0.400	0.380	0.360	0.280	0.200	0.130	0.080
Dividend Payout %	15.91	14.04	12.26	10.78	6.83	5.52	4.32	3.08
Income Statement								
Total Revenue	2,806,218	1,848,287	916,034	2,931,188	3,307,998	3,044,454	2,566,392	2,391,122
EBITDA	403,787	279,310	142,406	502,498	645,356	564,229	469,928	420,509
Depn & Amortn	76,970	51,051	25,229	47,100	43,100	38,800	33,500	28,900
Income Before Taxes	275,792	195,127	99,465	412,837	585,368	507,855	421,087	377,358
Income Taxes	64,776	52,030	27,461	99,433	186,740	156,175	128,852	125,626
Net Income	213,313	145,914	73,889	304,887	398,628	351,680	292,235	251,732
Average Shares	96,316	96,284	95,991	91,141	97,006	96,885	96,832	96,742
Balance Sheet								
Current Assets	2,277,125	2,344,809	2,166,233	2,867,631	1,612,448	1,637,864	1,333,047	1,092,938
Total Assets	6,449,650	6,438,740	6,030,899	6,581,018	3,300,335	3,303,841	2,821,997	2,351,542
Current Liabilities	1,465,440	1,482,099	1,471,407	1,446,639	664,776	738,802	579,400	553,059
Long-Term Obligations	1,824,156	1,934,604	1,782,624	1,762,967	695,294	520,403	450,288	317,853
Total Liabilities	3,731,948	3,871,883	3,679,308	4,375,041	1,600,728	1,496,599	1,236,738	1,074,712
Stockholders' Equity	2,717,702	2,566,857	2,351,591	2,205,977	1,699,607	1,807,242	1,585,259	1,276,830
Shares Outstanding	95,999	95,984	95,896	95,425	91,836	96,274	95,909	95,407
Statistical Record								
Return on Assets %	5.08	5.42	6.05	6.15	12.07	11.48	11.30	11.13
Return on Equity %	11.30	12.41	14.13	15.57	22.73	20.73	20.42	21.62
EBITDA Margin %	14.39	15.11	15.55	17.14	19.51	18.53	18.31	17.59
Net Margin %	7.60	7.89	8.07	10.40	12.05	11.55	11.39	10.53
Asset Turnover	0.72	0.67	0.65	0.59	1.00	0.99	0.99	1.06
Current Ratio	1.55	1.58	1.47	1.98	2.43	2.22	2.30	1.98
Debt to Equity	0.67	0.75	0.76	0.80	0.41	0.29	0.28	0.25
Price Range	92.51-69.70	91.50-66.25	88.48-66.25	88.12-60.58	102.39-68.89	91.24-70.82	74.27-43.77	44.34-34.40
P/E Ratio	35.04-26.40	32.11-23.25	28.54-21.37	26.38-18.14	24.97-16.80	25.20-19.56	24.67-14.54	17.06-13.23
Average Yield %	0.52	0.50	0.48	0.48	0.31	0.25	0.23	0.21

Address: 1001 Air Brake Avenue, Wilmerding, PA 15148	**Web Site:** www.wabtec.com	**Auditors:** Ernst & Young LLP
Telephone: 412-825-1000	**Officers:** Albert J. Neupaver - Chairman, Executive Chairman, Chairman (frmr), President, Chief Executive Officer Emilio A. Fernandez - Vice-Chairman	**Transfer Agents:** Wells Fargo Shareowner Services, St Paul, MN
Fax: 412-825-1019		

WAL-MART STORES INC

Exchange	Symbol	Price	52Wk Range	Yield	P/E	Div Achiever
NYS	WMT	$98.75 (12/29/2017)	99.62-65.66	2.07	26.26	41 Years

*7 Year Price Score 87.20 *NYSE Composite Index=100 *12 Month Price Score 114.60

Interim Earnings (Per Share)

Qtr.	Apr	Jul	Oct	Jan
2014-15	1.11	1.26	1.15	1.54
2015-16	1.03	1.08	1.03	1.44
2016-17	0.98	1.21	0.98	1.22
2017-18	1.00	0.96	0.58	...

Interim Dividends (Per Share)

Amt	Decl	Ex	Rec	Pay
0.51Q	02/21/2017	12/07/2017	12/08/2017	01/02/2018
0.51Q	02/21/2017	03/08/2017	03/10/2017	04/03/2017
0.51Q	02/21/2017	08/09/2017	08/11/2017	09/05/2017
0.51Q	02/21/2017	05/10/2017	05/12/2017	06/05/2017

Indicated Div: $2.04 (Div. Reinv. Plan)

Valuation Analysis / **Institutional Holding**

Forecast EPS	$4.43	No of Institutions
	(01/18/2018)	2265
Market Cap	$293.1 Billion	Shares
Book Value	$76.1 Billion	1,211,740,672
Price/Book	3.85	% Held
Price/Sales	0.59	27.91

Business Summary: Retail - General Merchandise/Department Stores (MIC: 2.1.1 SIC: 5331 NAIC: 452990)

Wal-Mart Stores operates retail and other stores in various formats. Co.'s operations comprise of three business segments: Walmart U.S., which is a merchandiser of consumer products, operating under the Walmart or Wal-Mart brands, as well as walmart.com., and operating retail stores in all 50 states, Washington D.C. and Puerto Rico.; Walmart International, which consists of operations in 27 countries outside of the U.S. and includes numerous formats divided into three categories: retail, wholesale and other; and Sam's Club, which operates membership-only warehouse clubs, as well as samsclub.com, in the U.S., and its members include both business owners and individual consumers.

Recent Developments: For the quarter ended Oct 31 2017, net income decreased 40.5% to US$1.90 billion from US$3.20 billion in the year-earlier quarter. Revenues were US$123.18 billion, up 4.2% from US$118.18 billion the year before. Operating income was US$4.76 billion versus US$5.12 billion in the prior-year quarter, a decrease of 6.9%. Direct operating expenses rose 4.6% to US$91.55 billion from US$87.48 billion in the comparable period the year before. Indirect operating expenses increased 5.1% to US$26.87 billion from US$25.58 billion in the equivalent prior-year period.

Prospects: Our evaluation of Wal-Mart Stores Inc. as of Jan. 14, 2018 is the result of our systematic analysis on three basic characteristics: earnings strength, relative valuation, and recent stock price movement. The company has produced a positive trend in earnings per share over the past 5 quarters and while recent estimates for the company have been mixed, WMT has posted better than expected results. Based on operating earnings yield, the company is undervalued when compared to all of the companies in our coverage universe. Share price changes over the past year indicates that WMT will perform well over the near term.

Financial Data

(US$ in Thousands)	9 Mos	6 Mos	3 Mos	01/31/2017	01/31/2016	01/31/2015	01/31/2014	01/31/2013
Earnings Per Share	3.76	4.16	4.41	4.38	4.57	5.05	4.88	5.02
Cash Flow Per Share	9.71	9.29	10.12	10.14	8.54	8.84	7.11	7.56
Tang Book Value Per Share	19.52	19.50	18.56	19.93	20.19	19.61	17.55	16.85
Dividends Per Share	2.030	2.020	2.010	2.000	1.960	1.920	1.880	1.590
Dividend Payout %	53.99	48.56	45.58	45.66	42.89	38.02	38.52	31.67
Income Statement								
Total Revenue	364,076,000	240,897,000	117,542,000	485,873,000	482,130,000	485,651,000	476,294,000	469,162,000
EBITDA	21,665,000	15,587,000	7,788,000	32,764,000	33,505,000	36,247,000	35,672,000	36,201,000
Depn & Amortn	7,827,000	5,169,000	2,551,000	10,000,000	9,400,000	9,100,000	8,800,000	8,400,000
Income Before Taxes	12,159,000	9,280,000	4,674,000	20,497,000	21,638,000	24,799,000	24,656,000	25,737,000
Income Taxes	3,999,000	3,024,000	1,522,000	6,204,000	6,558,000	7,985,000	8,105,000	7,981,000
Net Income	7,687,000	5,938,000	3,039,000	13,643,000	14,694,000	16,363,000	16,022,000	16,999,000
Average Shares	2,996,000	3,021,000	3,047,000	3,112,000	3,217,000	3,243,000	3,283,000	3,389,000
Balance Sheet								
Current Assets	65,368,000	56,763,000	57,336,000	57,689,000	60,239,000	63,278,000	61,185,000	59,940,000
Total Assets	209,414,000	201,566,000	199,718,000	198,825,000	199,581,000	203,706,000	204,751,000	203,105,000
Current Liabilities	80,435,000	72,811,000	74,193,000	66,928,000	64,619,000	65,272,000	69,345,000	71,818,000
Long-Term Obligations	40,906,000	40,469,000	40,025,000	42,018,000	44,030,000	43,692,000	44,559,000	41,417,000
Total Liabilities	133,269,000	125,177,000	126,027,000	121,027,000	119,035,000	122,312,000	128,496,000	126,762,000
Stockholders' Equity	76,145,000	76,389,000	73,691,000	77,798,000	80,546,000	81,394,000	76,255,000	76,343,000
Shares Outstanding	2,968,000	2,993,000	3,023,000	3,048,000	3,162,000	3,228,000	3,233,000	3,314,000
Statistical Record								
Return on Assets %	5.50	6.37	6.83	6.83	7.29	8.01	7.86	8.55
Return on Equity %	14.88	16.65	18.27	17.19	18.15	20.76	21.00	22.96
EBITDA Margin %	5.95	6.47	6.63	6.74	6.95	7.46	7.49	7.72
Net Margin %	2.11	2.46	2.59	2.81	3.05	3.37	3.36	3.62
Asset Turnover	2.38	2.45	2.45	2.43	2.39	2.38	2.34	2.36
Current Ratio	0.81	0.78	0.77	0.86	0.93	0.97	0.88	0.83
Debt to Equity	0.54	0.53	0.54	0.54	0.55	0.54	0.58	0.54
Price Range	88.65-65.66	80.26-65.66	75.44-63.15	74.30-63.15	87.33-56.42	90.47-72.66	81.21-68.76	77.15-57.36
P/E Ratio	23.58-17.46	19.29-15.78	17.11-14.32	16.96-14.42	19.11-12.35	17.91-14.39	16.64-14.09	15.37-11.43
Average Yield %	2.71	2.80	2.84	2.86	2.78	2.46	2.22	2.33

Address: 702 S.W. 8th Street, Bentonville, AR 72716 **Telephone:** 479-273-4000	**Web Site:** www.stock.walmart.com **Officers:** Gregory B. Penner - Chairman C. Douglas (Doug) McMillon - President, Chief Executive Officer, Executive Vice President, Division Officer

Auditors: Ernst & Young LLP
Investor Contact: 479-273-8446
Transfer Agents: Computershare Trust Company, N.A., Providence, RI

WASHINGTON PRIME GROUP

Exchange	Symbol	Price	52Wk Range	Yield	P/E
NYS	WPG	$7.12 (12/29/2017)	10.93-6.73	14.04	8.38

*7 Year Price Score N/A   *NYSE Composite Index=100   *12 Month Price Score 79.25

Interim Earnings (Per Share)

Qtr.	Mar	Jun	Sep	Dec
2014	0.22	0.45	0.21	0.22
2015	(0.07)	0.02	0.02	(0.53)
2016	0.05	0.10	0.01	0.14
2017	0.05	0.72	(0.06)	...

Interim Dividends (Per Share)

Amt	Decl	Ex	Rec	Pay
0.25Q	02/21/2017	03/06/2017	03/08/2017	03/15/2017
0.25Q	05/18/2017	05/30/2017	06/01/2017	06/15/2017
0.25Q	08/04/2017	08/30/2017	09/01/2017	09/15/2017
0.25Q	11/03/2017	11/30/2017	12/01/2017	12/15/2017

Indicated Div: $1.00

Valuation Analysis / Institutional Holding

Forecast EPS	$0.94 (01/23/2018)	No of Institutions	334
Market Cap	$1.3 Billion	Shares	195,188,976
Book Value	$1.1 Billion	% Held	
Price/Book	1.21	N/A	
Price/Sales	1.68		

Business Summary: REITs (MIC: 5.3.1 SIC: 6798 NAIC: 525930)

Washington Prime Group operates as a self-administered and self-managed real estate investment trust. Washington Prime Group, L.P. is Co.'s majority-owned partnership subsidiary that owns, develops, and manages, through its affiliates, all of Co.'s real estate properties and its other assets. Co. owns, develops and manages enclosed retail real estate properties and community centers. As of Dec 31 2016, Co.'s assets consisted of material interests in 114 shopping centers in the U.S., consisting of community centers and enclosed retail properties.

Recent Developments: For the quarter ended Sep 30 2017, loss from continuing operations was US$10.7 million compared with income of US$5.0 million in the year-earlier quarter. Net loss amounted to US$10.7 million versus net income of US$5.2 million in the year-earlier quarter. Revenues were US$179.3 million, down 14.6% from US$209.9 million the year before. Revenues from property income fell 14.8% to US$174.9 million from US$205.2 million in the corresponding quarter a year earlier.

Prospects: Our evaluation of Washington Prime Group as of Jan. 21, 2018 is the result of our systematic analysis on three basic characteristics: earnings strength, relative valuation, and recent stock price movement. The company has generated a negative trend in earnings per share over the past 5 quarters. Because the company lacks sufficient analyst estimate data, we place greater weight on the historical EPS trend as the measure of earnings strength. Based on operating earnings yield, the company is about fairly valued when compared to all of the companies in our coverage universe. Share price changes over the past year indicates that WPG will perform poorly over the near term.

Financial Data
(US$ in Thousands)

	9 Mos	6 Mos	3 Mos	12/31/2016	12/31/2015	12/31/2014	12/31/2013	12/31/2012
Earnings Per Share	0.85	0.92	0.30	0.29	(0.55)	1.10	1.00	0.84
Cash Flow Per Share	1.75	1.68	1.62	1.56	1.69	1.79	2.17	2.26
Tang Book Value Per Share	4.79	5.10	4.63	4.80	5.47	5.09	...	...
Dividends Per Share	1.000	1.000	1.000	1.000	1.000	0.500	...	...
Dividend Payout %	117.65	108.70	333.33	344.83	...	45.45	...	...
Income Statement								
Total Revenue	570,885	391,565	202,394	843,475	921,656	661,126	626,289	623,927
EBITDA	344,896	253,505	116,525	505,237	363,636	376,095	411,487	404,086
Depn & Amortn	199,982	132,884	66,994	285,632	329,895	198,934	184,467	189,715
Income Before Taxes	46,801	56,852	17,043	83,380	(106,188)	94,709	171,962	155,527
Income Taxes	2,996	2,548	2,026	2,232	849	1,215	196	165
Net Income	143,390	151,785	12,810	67,131	(85,297)	170,029	155,481	129,731
Average Shares	221,814	222,263	221,790	220,741	218,408	187,490	186,738	186,738
Balance Sheet								
Current Assets	138,447	169,526	191,091	159,320	207,856	178,384	86,978	...
Total Assets	4,553,440	4,618,800	5,017,039	5,107,466	5,479,484	3,528,003	3,002,658	...
Current Liabilities	276,958	271,665	290,961	327,591	383,995	209,312	192,324	...
Long-Term Obligations	2,998,908	3,000,523	3,484,633	3,506,404	3,668,476	2,348,864	918,614	...
Total Liabilities	3,461,087	3,468,288	3,956,766	4,014,023	4,263,490	2,738,952	1,437,489	...
Stockholders' Equity	1,092,353	1,150,512	1,060,273	1,093,443	1,215,994	789,051	1,565,169	...
Shares Outstanding	185,791	185,764	185,428	185,427	185,304	155,162	...	...
Statistical Record								
Return on Assets %	3.54	3.77	1.31	1.26	N.M.	5.21	...	...
Return on Equity %	15.71	16.19	6.10	5.80	N.M.	14.44	...	...
EBITDA Margin %	60.41	64.74	57.57	59.90	39.45	56.89	65.70	64.76
Net Margin %	25.12	38.76	6.33	7.96	N.M.	25.72	24.83	20.79
Asset Turnover	0.16	0.17	0.16	0.16	0.20	0.20	...	...
Current Ratio	0.50	0.62	0.66	0.49	0.54	0.85	0.45	...
Debt to Equity	2.75	2.61	3.29	3.21	3.02	2.98	0.59	...
Price Range	12.38-7.46	13.92-7.46	13.92-8.01	13.92-7.41	18.18-9.91	20.60-16.20	...	...
P/E Ratio	14.56-8.78	15.13-8.11	46.40-26.70	48.00-25.55	...	18.73-14.73	...	...
Average Yield %	10.83	9.73	9.28	9.33	7.15	2.75	...	...

Address: 180 East Broad Street, Columbus, OH 43215
Telephone: 614-621-9000

Web Site: www.wpglimcher.com
Officers: Louis G. Conforti - Interim Chief Executive Officer, Chief Executive Officer Mark E. Yale - Executive Vice President, Chief Financial Officer

Auditors: Ernst & Young LLP

WASTE MANAGEMENT; INC. (DE)

Exchange	Symbol	Price	52Wk Range	Yield	P/E	Div Achiever
NYS	WM	$86.30 (12/29/2017)	86.30-69.18	1.97	27.75	13 Years

*7 Year Price Score 120.26 *NYSE Composite Index=100 ***12 Month Price Score 103.45**

TRADING VOLUME (thousand shares)

Interim Earnings (Per Share)

Qtr.	Mar	Jun	Sep	Dec
2014	0.49	0.45	0.58	1.27
2015	(0.28)	0.60	0.74	0.60
2016	0.58	0.64	0.68	0.76
2017	0.67	0.81	0.87	...

Interim Dividends (Per Share)

Amt	Decl	Ex	Rec	Pay
0.425Q	02/27/2017	03/08/2017	03/10/2017	03/24/2017
0.425Q	05/11/2017	06/07/2017	06/09/2017	06/23/2017
0.425Q	08/24/2017	09/07/2017	09/08/2017	09/22/2017
0.425Q	11/06/2017	11/30/2017	12/01/2017	12/15/2017

Indicated Div: $1.70 (Div. Reinv. Plan)

Valuation Analysis — **Institutional Holding**

Forecast EPS	$3.20 (01/18/2018)	No of Institutions	1282
Market Cap	$37.5 Billion	Shares	
Book Value	$5.3 Billion		413,978,144
Price/Book	7.10	% Held	
Price/Sales	2.62		76.51

Business Summary: Sanitation Services (MIC: 7.5.3 SIC: 4953 NAIC: 562211)

Waste Management is a holding company. Through its subsidiaries, Co. is a provider of waste management environmental services. Co. partners with its residential, commercial, industrial and municipal customers and the communities it serves to manage and reduce waste at each stage from collection to disposal, while recovering resources and creating renewable energy. Co.'s Solid Waste business provides collection, transfer, disposal, and recycling and resource recovery services. Through its subsidiaries, Co. is also a developer, operator and owner of landfill gas-to-energy facilities. At Dec 31 2016, Co. owned or operated 243 solid waste landfills and five hazardous waste landfills.

Recent Developments: For the quarter ended Sep 30 2017, net income increased 27.6% to US$388.0 million from US$304.0 million in the year-earlier quarter. Revenues were US$3.72 billion, up 4.7% from US$3.55 billion the year before. Operating income was US$701.0 million versus US$560.0 million in the prior-year quarter, an increase of 25.2%. Direct operating expenses rose 3.9% to US$2.30 billion from US$2.22 billion in the comparable period the year before. Indirect operating expenses decreased 7.6% to US$713.0 million from US$772.0 million in the equivalent prior-year period.

Prospects: Our evaluation of Waste Management Inc. as of Jan. 14, 2018 is the result of our systematic analysis on three basic characteristics: earnings strength, relative valuation, and recent stock price movement. The company has managed to produce a neutral trend in earnings per share over the past 5 quarters and while recent estimates for the company have been mixed, WM has posted better than expected results. Based on operating earnings yield, the company is about fairly valued when compared to all of the companies in our coverage universe. Share price changes over the past year indicates that WM will perform in line with the market over the near term.

Financial Data
(US$ in Thousands)

	9 Mos	6 Mos	3 Mos	12/31/2016	12/31/2015	12/31/2014	12/31/2013	12/31/2012
Earnings Per Share	3.11	2.92	2.75	2.65	1.65	2.79	0.21	1.76
Cash Flow Per Share	7.18	6.88	6.74	6.66	5.52	5.04	5.25	4.94
Dividends Per Share	1.685	1.670	1.655	1.640	1.540	1.500	1.460	1.420
Dividend Payout %	54.18	57.19	60.18	61.89	93.33	53.76	695.24	80.68
Income Statement								
Total Revenue	10,833,000	7,117,000	3,440,000	13,609,000	12,961,000	13,996,000	13,983,000	13,649,000
EBITDA	2,514,000	1,664,000	886,000	3,015,773	2,652,000	3,484,000	2,258,000	3,061,000
Depn & Amortn	582,000	433,000	328,000	773,773	1,169,000	1,214,000	1,253,000	1,228,000
Income Before Taxes	1,660,000	1,049,000	466,000	1,866,000	1,098,000	1,804,000	528,000	1,349,000
Income Taxes	561,000	346,000	137,000	642,000	308,000	413,000	364,000	443,000
Net Income	1,046,000	660,000	298,000	1,182,000	753,000	1,298,000	98,000	817,000
Average Shares	440,800	444,400	444,100	446,500	455,900	465,600	469,800	464,400
Balance Sheet								
Current Assets	2,300,000	2,326,000	2,223,000	2,376,000	2,345,000	3,641,000	2,499,000	2,423,000
Total Assets	20,949,000	20,839,000	20,650,000	20,859,000	20,419,000	21,412,000	22,603,000	23,097,000
Current Liabilities	3,259,000	2,770,000	2,558,000	2,794,000	2,510,000	3,485,000	3,014,000	3,036,000
Long-Term Obligations	8,495,000	8,667,000	8,646,000	8,893,000	8,728,000	8,345,000	9,500,000	9,173,000
Total Liabilities	15,671,000	15,353,000	15,133,000	15,562,000	15,074,000	15,546,000	16,896,000	16,743,000
Stockholders' Equity	5,278,000	5,486,000	5,517,000	5,297,000	5,345,000	5,866,000	5,707,000	6,354,000
Shares Outstanding	434,205	439,711	441,905	439,315	447,177	458,537	464,320	464,220
Statistical Record								
Return on Assets %	6.62	6.24	5.90	5.71	3.60	5.90	0.43	3.57
Return on Equity %	25.97	24.26	22.61	22.15	13.43	22.43	1.63	13.12
EBITDA Margin %	23.21	23.38	25.76	22.16	20.46	24.89	16.15	22.43
Net Margin %	9.66	9.27	8.66	8.69	5.81	9.27	0.70	5.99
Asset Turnover	0.69	0.68	0.67	0.66	0.62	0.64	0.61	0.60
Current Ratio	0.71	0.84	0.87	0.85	0.93	1.04	0.83	0.80
Debt to Equity	1.61	1.58	1.57	1.68	1.63	1.42	1.66	1.44
Price Range	78.62-61.70	74.25-61.70	73.78-56.35	71.14-51.52	55.18-46.35	51.58-40.41	46.10-33.74	36.08-30.96
P/E Ratio	25.28-19.84	25.43-21.13	26.83-20.49	26.85-19.44	33.44-28.09	18.49-14.48	219.52-160.67	20.50-17.59
Average Yield %	2.35	2.42	2.51	2.65	2.98	3.33	3.60	4.22

Address: 1001 Fannin Street, Houston, TX 77002
Telephone: 713-512-6200
Fax: 713-512-6299

Web Site: www.wm.com
Officers: James C. Fish - President, Executive Vice President, Chief Executive Officer, Chief Financial Officer James E. Trevathan - Chief Operating Officer, Executive Vice President, Division Officer

Auditors: Ernst & Young LLP
Investor Contact: 713-265-1656
Transfer Agents: Computershare, Canton, MA

WATERS CORP.

Exchange	Symbol	Price	52Wk Range	Yield	P/E
NYS	WAT	$193.19 (12/29/2017)	200.27-135.49	N/A	28.49

*7 Year Price Score 117.98 *NYSE Composite Index=100 *12 Month Price Score 106.08

Interim Earnings (Per Share)

Qtr.	Mar	Jun	Sep	Dec
2014	0.82	1.13	1.34	1.78
2015	1.15	1.27	1.40	1.83
2016	1.15	1.57	1.53	2.15
2017	1.31	1.63	1.69	...

Interim Dividends (Per Share)

No Dividends Paid

Valuation Analysis — **Institutional Holding**

Forecast EPS	$7.42	No of Institutions
	(01/17/2018)	754
Market Cap	$15.4 Billion	Shares
Book Value	$2.6 Billion	91,248,640
Price/Book	5.84	% Held
Price/Sales	6.83	86.98

TRADING VOLUME (thousand shares)

Business Summary: Biotechnology (MIC: 4.1.2 SIC: 3826 NAIC: 334516)

Waters is a holding company. Co. is an analytical instrument manufacturer that primarily designs, manufactures, sells and services high performance liquid chromatography, ultra performance liquid chromatography and mass spectrometry technology systems and support products, including chromatography columns, other consumable products and post-warranty service plans. In addition, Co. designs, manufactures, sells and services thermal analysis, rheometry and calorimetry instruments through its TA® product line. Co. is also a developer and supplier of software-based products that interface with its instruments, as well as other suppliers' instruments.

Recent Developments: For the quarter ended Sep 30 2017, net income increased 9.0% to US$136.1 million from US$124.9 million in the year-earlier quarter. Revenues were US$565.6 million, up 7.4% from US$526.8 million the year before. Operating income was US$159.0 million versus US$151.7 million in the prior-year quarter, an increase of 4.8%. Direct operating expenses rose 8.0% to US$235.9 million from US$218.3 million in the comparable period the year before. Indirect operating expenses increased 8.9% to US$170.7 million from US$156.8 million in the equivalent prior-year period.

Prospects: Our evaluation of Waters Corp. as of Jan. 14, 2018 is the result of our systematic analysis on three basic characteristics: earnings strength, relative valuation, and recent stock price movement. The company has managed to produce a neutral trend in earnings per share over the past 5 quarters and while recent estimates for the company have been raised by analysts, WAT has posted better than expected results. Based on operating earnings yield, the company is about fairly valued when compared to all of the companies in our coverage universe. Share price changes over the past year indicates that WAT will perform well over the near term.

Financial Data (US$ in Thousands)	9 Mos	6 Mos	3 Mos	12/31/2016	12/31/2015	12/31/2014	12/31/2013	12/31/2012
Earnings Per Share	6.78	6.62	6.56	6.41	5.65	5.07	5.20	5.19
Cash Flow Per Share	8.51	8.30	8.04	7.77	6.80	6.07	5.68	5.10
Tang Book Value Per Share	25.72	24.34	22.87	21.78	18.21	15.72	13.84	10.77
Income Statement								
Total Revenue	1,621,803	1,056,219	497,969	2,167,423	2,042,332	1,989,344	1,904,218	1,843,641
EBITDA	509,937	325,059	141,819	720,788	657,438	612,139	595,463	580,321
Depn & Amortn	78,249	52,405	22,950	96,449	89,987	94,231	79,695	68,831
Income Before Taxes	415,359	261,559	113,487	600,114	541,919	490,740	490,105	487,625
Income Taxes	41,876	24,180	7,930	78,611	72,866	59,120	40,102	26,182
Net Income	373,483	237,379	105,557	521,503	469,053	431,620	450,003	461,443
Average Shares	80,521	80,756	80,769	81,417	83,087	85,151	86,546	88,979
Balance Sheet								
Current Assets	4,078,525	3,947,235	3,778,424	3,635,445	3,213,533	2,853,736	2,556,255	2,257,726
Total Assets	5,162,985	4,996,745	4,810,703	4,662,059	4,268,677	3,877,934	3,582,629	3,168,150
Current Liabilities	662,149	653,289	632,211	520,321	564,076	581,595	487,532	504,242
Long-Term Obligations	1,732,367	1,687,233	1,642,099	1,701,966	1,493,027	1,240,000	1,190,000	1,045,000
Total Liabilities	2,533,890	2,478,106	2,415,889	2,360,110	2,209,826	1,983,268	1,819,456	1,700,793
Stockholders' Equity	2,629,095	2,518,639	2,394,814	2,301,949	2,058,851	1,894,666	1,763,173	1,467,357
Shares Outstanding	79,522	79,811	80,001	80,023	81,472	83,147	84,819	86,390
Statistical Record								
Return on Assets %	11.25	11.36	11.61	11.65	11.52	11.57	13.33	15.62
Return on Equity %	22.42	22.99	23.71	23.85	23.73	23.60	27.86	34.16
EBITDA Margin %	31.44	30.78	28.48	33.26	32.19	30.77	31.27	31.48
Net Margin %	23.03	22.47	21.20	24.06	22.97	21.70	23.63	25.03
Asset Turnover	0.46	0.47	0.48	0.48	0.50	0.53	0.56	0.62
Current Ratio	6.16	6.04	5.98	6.99	5.70	4.91	5.24	4.48
Debt to Equity	0.66	0.67	0.69	0.74	0.73	0.65	0.67	0.71
Price Range	190.00-133.71	186.33-133.71	161.82-130.15	161.82-113.62	136.50-112.53	116.98-95.08	107.73-86.22	94.03-73.71
P/E Ratio	28.02-19.72	28.15-20.20	24.67-19.84	25.24-17.73	24.16-19.92	23.07-18.75	20.72-16.58	18.12-14.20

Address: 34 Maple Street, Milford, MA 01757	**Web Site:** www.waters.com	**Auditors:** PricewaterhouseCoopers LLP
Telephone: 508-478-2000	**Officers:** Christopher J. O'Connell - President, Chief Executive Officer Sherry L. Buck - Senior Vice President, Chief Financial Officer	**Investor Contact:** 508-482-2349
Fax: 508-872-1990		**Transfer Agents:** Computershare, Providence, RI

WATSCO INC.

Exchange	Symbol	Price	52Wk Range	Yield	P/E
NYS	WSO	$170.04 (12/29/2017)	171.38-135.45	2.94	31.31

*7 Year Price Score 114.21 *NYSE Composite Index=100 *12 Month Price Score 103.43

TRADING VOLUME (thousand shares)

Interim Earnings (Per Share)

Qtr.	Mar	Jun	Sep	Dec
2014	0.48	1.60	1.56	0.68
2015	0.65	1.85	1.64	0.74
2016	0.71	1.82	1.78	0.83
2017	0.71	2.07	1.82	...

Interim Dividends (Per Share)

Amt	Decl	Ex	Rec	Pay
1.05Q	04/03/2017	04/11/2017	04/14/2017	04/28/2017
1.25Q	07/03/2017	07/13/2017	07/17/2017	07/31/2017
1.25Q	10/02/2017	10/13/2017	10/16/2017	10/31/2017
1.25Q	01/02/2018	01/12/2018	01/16/2018	01/31/2018

Indicated Div: $5.00

Valuation Analysis

		Institutional Holding	
Forecast EPS	$5.60 (01/16/2018)	No of Institutions	410
Market Cap	$6.1 Billion	Shares	34,137,604
Book Value	$1.1 Billion	% Held	71.73
Price/Book	5.78		
Price/Sales	1.42		

Business Summary: Industrial Machinery & Equipment (MIC: 7.2.1 SIC: 5075 NAIC: 423730)

Watsco is a distributor of air conditioning, heating and refrigeration equipment and related parts and supplies. The products Co. distributes consist of: equipment, including residential ducted and ductless air conditioners, gas, electric and oil furnaces, commercial air conditioning and heating equipment and systems, and other equipment; parts, including replacement compressors, evaporator coils, motors and other component parts; and supplies, including thermostats, insulation material, refrigerants, ductwork, grills, registers, sheet metal, tools, copper tubing, concrete pads, tape, adhesives and other ancillary supplies.

Recent Developments: For the quarter ended Sep 30 2017, net income decreased 0.6% to US$80.0 million from US$80.5 million in the year-earlier quarter. Revenues were US$1.23 billion, down 0.9% from US$1.24 billion the year before. Operating income was US$114.5 million versus US$119.3 million in the prior-year quarter, a decrease of 4.1%. Direct operating expenses declined 0.6% to US$933.7 million from US$939.0 million in the comparable period the year before. Indirect operating expenses decreased 0.8% to US$181.4 million from US$182.9 million in the equivalent prior-year period.

Prospects: Our evaluation of Watsco Inc. as of Jan. 14, 2018 is the result of our systematic analysis on three basic characteristics: earnings strength, relative valuation, and recent stock price movement. The company has produced a positive trend in earnings per share over the past 5 quarters and while recent estimates for the company have been mixed, WSO has posted results that fell short of analysts expectations. Based on operating earnings yield, the company is about fairly valued when compared to all of the companies in our coverage universe. Share price changes over the past year indicates that WSO will perform in line with the market over the near term.

Financial Data

(US$ in Thousands)	9 Mos	6 Mos	3 Mos	12/31/2016	12/31/2015	12/31/2014	12/31/2013	12/31/2012
Earnings Per Share	5.43	5.39	5.14	5.15	4.90	4.32	3.68	2.70
Cash Flow Per Share	9.66	8.20	8.28	8.50	6.83	4.49	4.67	5.46
Tang Book Value Per Share	14.16	13.38	12.33	13.16	11.85	8.86	7.02	3.81
Dividends Per Share	4.400	4.000	3.800	3.600	2.800	2.000	1.150	7.480
Dividend Payout %	81.03	74.21	73.93	69.90	57.14	46.30	31.25	277.04
Income Statement								
Total Revenue	3,377,610	2,148,019	872,095	4,220,702	4,113,239	3,944,540	3,743,330	3,431,712
EBITDA	306,723	188,981	54,064	360,485	350,550	317,905	282,886	235,894
Depn & Amortn	16,509	10,934	5,365	14,853	13,802	12,158	11,677	10,986
Income Before Taxes	287,489	175,145	47,444	341,919	331,201	300,541	265,379	220,243
Income Taxes	82,855	50,530	13,676	105,936	104,677	91,839	77,660	62,642
Net Income	164,966	99,937	26,181	182,810	172,929	151,387	127,723	103,334
Average Shares	32,746	32,708	32,679	32,616	32,480	32,358	32,258	31,744
Balance Sheet								
Current Assets	1,438,941	1,451,741	1,300,501	1,240,156	1,181,265	1,157,335	1,021,102	1,015,451
Total Assets	2,148,219	2,154,418	1,935,279	1,874,649	1,788,442	1,791,067	1,669,531	1,682,055
Current Liabilities	460,399	424,436	378,898	314,888	270,301	287,022	243,506	282,358
Long-Term Obligations	285,045	379,544	280,597	235,642	245,814	303,885	230,557	316,196
Total Liabilities	1,096,080	1,135,753	956,943	868,821	831,132	907,107	829,135	933,841
Stockholders' Equity	1,052,139	1,018,665	978,336	1,005,828	957,310	883,960	840,396	748,214
Shares Outstanding	35,742	35,706	35,668	35,530	35,311	35,006	34,727	34,521
Statistical Record								
Return on Assets %	9.48	9.23	9.62	9.95	9.66	8.75	7.62	6.99
Return on Equity %	18.60	19.05	18.85	18.57	18.78	17.56	16.08	13.29
EBITDA Margin %	9.08	8.80	6.20	8.54	8.52	8.06	7.56	6.87
Net Margin %	4.88	4.65	3.00	4.33	4.20	3.84	3.41	3.01
Asset Turnover	2.09	2.06	2.23	2.30	2.30	2.28	2.23	2.32
Current Ratio	3.13	3.42	3.43	3.94	4.37	4.03	4.19	3.60
Debt to Equity	0.27	0.37	0.29	0.23	0.26	0.34	0.27	0.42
Price Range	161.07-130.88	159.03-130.88	159.03-129.00	159.03-108.09	131.89-104.92	108.20-85.53	97.47-74.13	80.12-66.22
P/E Ratio	29.66-24.10	29.50-24.28	30.94-25.10	30.88-20.99	26.92-21.41	25.05-19.80	26.49-20.14	29.67-24.53
Average Yield %	2.99	2.76	2.66	2.65	2.30	2.05	1.32	10.29

Address: 2665 South Bayshore Drive, Suite 901, Miami, FL 33133
Telephone: 305-714-4100

Web Site: www.watsco.com
Officers: Albert H. Nahmad - Chairman, President, Chief Executive Officer Aaron J. Nahmad - President, Vice President

Auditors: KPMG LLP
Investor Contact: 305-714-4100
Transfer Agents: American Stock Transfer & Trust Company, New York, NY

WAYFAIR INC

Exchange	Symbol	Price	52Wk Range	Yield	P/E
NYS	W	$80.27 (12/29/2017)	83.77-35.18	N/A	N/A

*7 Year Price Score N/A ***NYSE Composite Index=100** ***12 Month Price Score 111.47**

TRADING VOLUME (thousand shares)

Interim Earnings (Per Share)

Qtr.	Mar	Jun	Sep	Dec
2014	(0.85)	...	(0.71)	(0.71)
2015	(0.33)	(0.23)	(0.18)	(0.18)
2016	(0.49)	(0.57)	(0.72)	(0.52)
2017	(0.66)	(0.45)	(0.88)	...

Interim Dividends (Per Share)

No Dividends Paid

Valuation Analysis | **Institutional Holding**

Forecast EPS	$-1.93	No of Institutions
	(01/17/2018)	243
Market Cap	$7.0 Billion	Shares
Book Value	$3.0 Million	62,168,360
Price/Book	2322.66	% Held
Price/Sales	1.65	N/A

Business Summary: Retail - Furniture & Home Furnishings (MIC: 2.1.6 SIC: 5961 NAIC: 454111)

Wayfair is a holding company. Through its e-commerce business, Co. provides browsing, merchandising, and product discovery for products from approximately 8,000 products from over 10,000 suppliers. Co. provides five sites, including websites, mobile-optimized websites and mobile applications (collectively sites): Wayfair, Joss & Main, AllModern, DwellStudio, and Birch Lane. Wayfair is the only one of Co.'s sites that also operates internationally, operating as Wayfair.ca in Canada, Wayfair.co.uk in the U.K. and Wayfair.de in Germany. On its sites, Co. also feature certain products under its house brands, such as Three Postsâ‚¢ and Mercury Rowâ‚¢.

Recent Developments: For the quarter ended Sep 30 2017, net loss amounted to US$76.4 million versus a net loss of US$60.9 million in the year-earlier quarter. Revenues were US$1.20 billion, up 39.1% from US$861.5 million the year before. Operating loss was US$74.0 million versus a loss of US$61.6 million in the prior-year quarter. Direct operating expenses rose 39.1% to US$917.9 million from US$659.9 million in the comparable period the year before. Indirect operating expenses increased 34.6% to US$354.3 million from US$263.3 million in the equivalent prior-year period.

Prospects: Our evaluation of Wayfair Inc as of Jan. 14, 2018 is the result of our systematic analysis on three basic characteristics: earnings strength, relative valuation, and recent stock price movement. The company has managed to produce a neutral trend in earnings per share over the past 5 quarters. Because the company lacks sufficient analyst estimate data, we place greater weight on the historical EPS trend as the measure of earnings strength. Based on operating earnings yield, the company is overvalued when compared to all of the companies in our coverage universe. Share price changes over the past year indicates that W will perform very well over the near term.

Financial Data

(US$ in Thousands)	9 Mos	6 Mos	3 Mos	12/31/2016	12/31/2015	12/31/2014	12/31/2013	12/31/2012
Earnings Per Share	(2.51)	(2.35)	(2.47)	(2.29)	(0.92)	(2.97)	(0.99)	(0.80)
Cash Flow Per Share	0.80	0.70	0.79	0.74	1.61	0.08	0.83	0.10
Tang Book Value Per Share	N.M.	0.10	0.38	0.88	2.83	3.60	0.92	1.36
Income Statement								
Total Revenue	3,281,879	2,083,681	960,825	3,380,360	2,249,885	1,318,951	915,843	601,028
EBITDA	(104,741)	(54,031)	(35,930)	(139,861)	(46,141)	(126,493)	(2,686)	(12,427)
Depn & Amortn	62,574	39,100	20,100	54,600	32,491	21,780	13,039	8,812
Income Before Taxes	(171,172)	(94,980)	(56,329)	(193,767)	(77,348)	(147,923)	(15,480)	(21,005)
Income Taxes	671	434	210	608	95	175	46	50
Net Income	(171,843)	(95,414)	(56,539)	(194,375)	(77,443)	(148,098)	(15,526)	(21,055)
Average Shares	87,283	86,714	86,036	84,977	83,726	50,641	41,331	41,271
Balance Sheet								
Current Assets	776,595	417,246	432,362	477,091	492,323	486,868	163,127	140,124
Total Assets	1,138,140	751,478	742,123	761,683	694,581	555,523	196,300	163,577
Current Liabilities	650,249	598,547	566,584	557,220	397,026	232,592	145,009	98,093
Long-Term Obligations	410,675	82,725	41,542	28,900	...	...	...	...
Total Liabilities	1,135,111	739,538	705,661	682,299	452,036	249,984	145,953	98,570
Stockholders' Equity	3,029	11,940	36,462	79,384	242,545	305,539	50,347	65,007
Shares Outstanding	87,646	87,030	86,447	85,830	84,310	83,182	44,904	44,818
Statistical Record								
Asset Turnover	4.68	5.55	5.10	4.63	3.60	3.51	5.09	...
Current Ratio	1.19	0.70	0.76	0.86	1.24	2.09	1.12	1.43
Debt to Equity	135.58	6.93	1.14	0.36	...	...	...	...
Price Range	83.77-31.96	76.98-31.96	48.25-31.96	48.25-31.89	53.58-19.12	37.72-18.40	...	...

Address: 4 Copley Place, 7th Floor, Boston, MA 02116 **Telephone:** 617-532-6100	**Web Site:** www.wayfair.com **Officers:** Niraj Shah - Co-Chairman, Chief Executive Officer Enrique Colbert - Secretary, General Counsel	**Auditors:** Ernst & Young LLP **Transfer Agents:** Computershare Trust Company, N.A.

WEBSTER FINANCIAL CORP (WATERBURY, CONN)

Exchange	Symbol	Price	52Wk Range	Yield	P/E
NYS	WBS	$56.16 (12/29/2017)	58.39-44.50	1.85	22.20

*7 Year Price Score 127.67 *NYSE Composite Index=100 *12 Month Price Score 100.77

TRADING VOLUME (thousand shares)

Interim Earnings (Per Share)
Qtr.	Mar	Jun	Sep	Dec
2014	0.53	0.50	0.53	0.53
2015	0.52	0.55	0.54	0.55
2016	0.51	0.53	0.54	0.60
2017	0.62	0.64	0.67	...

Interim Dividends (Per Share)
Amt	Decl	Ex	Rec	Pay
0.25Q	01/31/2017	02/10/2017	02/14/2017	02/28/2017
0.26Q	04/24/2017	05/04/2017	05/08/2017	05/22/2017
0.26Q	07/24/2017	08/03/2017	08/07/2017	08/21/2017
0.26Q	10/24/2017	11/06/2017	11/07/2017	11/21/2017

Indicated Div: $1.04 (Div. Reinv. Plan)

Valuation Analysis
		Institutional Holding	
Forecast EPS	$2.60	No of Institutions	
	(01/12/2018)	383	
Market Cap	$5.2 Billion	Shares	
Book Value	$2.6 Billion	102,790,944	
Price/Book	1.96	% Held	
Price/Sales	4.48	90.55	

Business Summary: Banking (MIC: 5.1.1 SIC: 6021 NAIC: 522110)

Webster Financial is a bank holding company and financial holding company. Co., through Webster Bank, National Association, provides financial services to individuals, families, and businesses. Co. provides business and consumer banking, mortgage lending, financial planning, trust, and investment services through 175 banking offices, 350 ATMs, mobile banking, and its internet website. Investment services include securities-related services, and brokerage and investment advice. Co. also provides equipment financing, commercial real estate lending, and asset-based lending across the Northeast. At Dec 31 2016, Co. had total assets of $26.07 billion and total deposits of $19.30 billion.

Recent Developments: For the quarter ended Sep 30 2017, net income increased 24.5% to US$64.5 million from US$51.8 million in the year-earlier quarter. Net interest income increased 11.5% to US$200.9 million from US$180.2 million in the year-earlier quarter. Provision for loan losses was US$10.2 million versus US$14.3 million in the prior-year quarter, a decrease of 28.8%. Non-interest income fell 0.9% to US$65.8 million from US$66.4 million, while non-interest expense advanced 3.7% to US$161.8 million.

Prospects: Our evaluation of Webster Financial Corp. (CT) as of Jan. 14, 2018 is the result of our systematic analysis on three basic characteristics: earnings strength, relative valuation, and recent stock price movement. The company has managed to produce a neutral trend in earnings per share over the past 5 quarters. However, while recent estimates for the company have been mixed, WBS has posted better than expected results. Based on operating earnings yield, the company is about fairly valued when compared to all of the companies in our coverage universe. Share price changes over the past year indicates that WBS will perform poorly over the near term.

Financial Data
(US$ in Thousands)	9 Mos	6 Mos	3 Mos	12/31/2016	12/31/2015	12/31/2014	12/31/2013	12/31/2012
Earnings Per Share	2.53	2.40	2.29	2.16	2.15	2.08	1.86	1.86
Cash Flow Per Share	5.55	5.25	5.76	4.35	3.38	3.03	5.37	2.94
Tang Book Value Per Share	21.18	20.78	20.29	19.97	18.73	18.13	16.92	16.50
Dividends Per Share	1.020	1.010	1.000	0.980	0.890	0.750	0.550	0.350
Dividend Payout %	40.32	42.08	43.67	45.37	41.40	36.06	29.57	18.82
Income Statement								
Interest Income	677,490	446,469	219,680	821,913	760,040	718,941	687,640	693,502
Interest Expense	86,135	56,018	27,016	103,400	95,415	90,500	90,912	114,594
Net Interest Income	591,355	390,451	192,664	718,513	664,625	628,441	596,728	578,908
Provision for Losses	27,900	17,750	10,500	56,350	49,300	37,250	33,500	21,500
Non-Interest Income	193,439	127,593	63,042	264,478	239,545	202,108	191,050	192,758
Non-Interest Expense	490,026	328,203	163,784	623,191	554,554	502,138	498,059	501,804
Income Before Taxes	266,868	172,091	81,422	303,450	300,316	291,161	256,219	248,362
Income Taxes	81,322	51,041	21,951	96,323	93,976	91,409	76,670	74,665
Net Income	185,546	121,050	59,471	207,127	206,340	199,752	179,549	173,697
Average Shares	92,503	92,495	92,342	91,856	91,533	90,620	90,261	91,649
Balance Sheet								
Net Loans & Leases	17,277,473	17,113,507	16,924,090	16,899,845	15,533,836	13,808,713	12,568,005	11,959,200
Total Assets	26,350,182	26,174,930	26,002,916	26,072,529	24,677,820	22,533,010	20,852,999	20,146,765
Total Deposits	20,855,235	20,458,097	20,241,657	19,303,857	17,952,778	15,651,605	14,854,420	14,530,835
Total Liabilities	23,711,395	23,569,804	23,442,558	23,545,517	22,262,249	20,210,329	18,643,811	18,053,235
Stockholders' Equity	2,638,787	2,605,126	2,560,358	2,527,012	2,415,571	2,322,681	2,209,188	2,093,530
Shares Outstanding	91,915	92,051	91,981	91,752	91,561	90,381	89,959	84,963
Statistical Record								
Return on Assets %	0.94	0.90	0.86	0.81	0.87	0.92	0.88	0.89
Return on Equity %	9.44	9.07	8.78	8.36	8.71	8.82	8.35	8.79
Net Interest Margin %	86.96	87.21	87.70	87.42	87.45	87.41	86.78	83.48
Efficiency Ratio %	54.51	56.44	57.93	57.36	55.48	54.52	56.68	56.62
Loans to Deposits	0.83	0.84	0.84	0.88	0.87	0.88	0.85	0.82
Price Range	57.33-37.05	57.33-32.49	57.33-31.44	55.09-30.35	40.96-29.11	33.05-27.65	31.18-20.55	24.65-19.10
P/E Ratio	22.66-14.64	23.89-13.54	25.03-13.73	25.50-14.05	19.05-13.54	15.89-13.29	16.76-11.05	13.25-10.27
Average Yield %	2.04	2.17	2.32	2.55	2.43	2.46	2.17	1.62

Address: 145 Bank Street, Waterbury, CT 06702	**Web Site:** www.websterbank.com	**Auditors:** KPMG LLP
	Officers: James C. Smith - Chairman, President, Chief Executive Officer Joseph J. Savage - Executive Vice-Chairman, President, Executive Vice President	**Investor Contact:** 203-578-2202
Telephone: 203-578-2202		**Transfer Agents:** Computershare, Pittsburgh, PA

WEC ENERGY GROUP INC

Exchange	Symbol	Price	52Wk Range	Yield	P/E	Div Achiever
NYS	WEC	$66.43 (12/29/2017)	69.53-57.03	3.33	21.85	13 Years

*7 Year Price Score 103.07 *NYSE Composite Index=100 *12 Month Price Score 101.65

Interim Earnings (Per Share)

Qtr.	Mar	Jun	Sep	Dec
2014	0.91	0.58	0.56	0.54
2015	0.86	0.35	0.58	0.56
2016	1.09	0.57	0.68	0.61
2017	1.12	0.63	0.68	...

Interim Dividends (Per Share)

Amt	Decl	Ex	Rec	Pay
0.52Q	04/20/2017	05/10/2017	05/12/2017	06/01/2017
0.52Q	07/20/2017	08/10/2017	08/14/2017	09/01/2017
0.52Q	10/19/2017	11/13/2017	11/14/2017	12/01/2017
0.552Q	12/07/2017	02/13/2018	02/14/2018	03/01/2018

Indicated Div: $2.21 (Div. Reinv. Plan)

Valuation Analysis — **Institutional Holding**

Forecast EPS	$3.10 (01/18/2018)	No of Institutions 937
Market Cap	$21.0 Billion	Shares
Book Value	$9.2 Billion	272,813,824
Price/Book	2.27	% Held
Price/Sales	2.77	71.22

TRADING VOLUME (thousand shares)

Business Summary: Electric Utilities (MIC: 3.1.1 SIC: 4931 NAIC: 221112)

WEC Energy Group is a holding company. Co. has six segments: Wisconsin, which is engaged mainly in the generation of electricity and the distribution of electricity and natural gas in Wisconsin; Illinois, which is engaged mainly in the distribution of natural gas in Illinois; Other states, which is engaged mainly in the distribution of natural gas in Minnesota and Michigan; Electric transmission, which includes its approximate 60% ownership interest in American Transmission Company LLC, an electric transmission company; We Power, which is engaged in the ownership of electric power generating facilities for lease to its subsidiary, Wisconsin Electric Power Company; and corporate and other.

Recent Developments: For the quarter ended Sep 30 2017, net income decreased 0.7% to US$215.7 million from US$217.3 million in the year-earlier quarter. Revenues were US$1.66 billion, down 3.2% from US$1.71 billion the year before. Operating income was US$393.6 million versus US$399.0 million in the prior-year quarter, a decrease of 1.4%. Direct operating expenses declined 5.4% to US$1.01 billion from US$1.07 billion in the comparable period the year before. Indirect operating expenses increased 3.4% to US$249.5 million from US$241.3 million in the equivalent prior-year period.

Prospects: Our evaluation of WEC Energy Group Inc. as of Jan. 14, 2018 is the result of our systematic analysis on three basic characteristics: earnings strength, relative valuation, and recent stock price movement. The company has managed to produce a neutral trend in earnings per share over the past 5 quarters and while recent estimates for the company have been mixed, WEC has posted better than expected results. Based on operating earnings yield, the company is undervalued when compared to all of the companies in our coverage universe. Share price changes over the past year indicates that WEC will perform very well over the near term.

Financial Data

(US$ in Thousands)	9 Mos	6 Mos	3 Mos	12/31/2016	12/31/2015	12/31/2014	12/31/2013	12/31/2012
Earnings Per Share	3.04	3.04	2.98	2.96	2.34	2.59	2.51	2.35
Cash Flow Per Share	6.74	6.80	6.72	6.65	4.77	5.31	5.41	5.09
Tang Book Value Per Share	19.56	19.42	19.36	18.64	17.84	17.64	16.78	16.12
Dividends Per Share	2.055	2.030	2.005	1.980	1.743	1.560	1.445	1.200
Dividend Payout %	67.60	66.78	67.28	66.89	74.48	60.23	57.57	51.06
Income Statement								
Total Revenue	5,593,500	3,936,000	2,304,500	7,472,300	5,926,100	4,997,100	4,519,000	4,246,400
EBITDA	2,011,800	1,400,600	827,600	2,525,500	1,892,900	1,544,900	1,499,100	1,406,800
Depn & Amortn	593,500	392,300	194,600	762,600	583,500	419,400	400,200	371,700
Income Before Taxes	1,107,900	801,700	528,300	1,360,200	978,000	884,000	846,800	786,900
Income Taxes	458,800	329,100	213,300	566,500	433,800	361,700	337,900	306,300
Net Income	772,000	556,300	356,900	940,200	640,300	588,300	577,400	546,300
Average Shares	317,500	317,400	317,200	316,900	272,700	227,500	229,700	232,800
Balance Sheet								
Current Assets	1,823,300	1,779,700	1,855,300	2,168,700	2,206,800	1,535,400	1,551,100	1,313,900
Total Assets	31,013,000	30,559,600	30,016,600	30,123,200	29,355,200	15,163,400	14,769,400	14,285,000
Current Liabilities	3,026,100	2,787,300	2,054,600	2,431,600	2,709,000	1,668,700	1,496,400	1,443,300
Long-Term Obligations	8,785,800	8,799,700	9,143,600	9,158,200	9,124,100	4,186,400	4,363,200	4,453,800
Total Liabilities	21,787,300	21,376,400	20,860,600	21,163,000	20,670,000	10,713,300	10,506,000	10,119,500
Stockholders' Equity	9,225,700	9,183,200	9,156,000	8,960,200	8,685,200	4,450,100	4,263,400	4,165,500
Shares Outstanding	315,575	315,576	315,579	315,614	315,683	225,517	225,962	229,039
Statistical Record								
Return on Assets %	3.20	3.24	3.22	3.15	2.88	3.93	3.97	3.87
Return on Equity %	10.67	10.75	10.58	10.63	9.75	13.50	13.70	13.35
EBITDA Margin %	35.97	35.58	35.91	33.80	31.94	30.92	33.17	33.13
Net Margin %	13.80	14.13	15.49	12.58	10.80	11.77	12.78	12.87
Asset Turnover	0.25	0.25	0.26	0.25	0.27	0.33	0.31	0.30
Current Ratio	0.60	0.64	0.90	0.89	0.81	0.92	1.04	0.91
Debt to Equity	0.95	0.96	1.00	1.02	1.05	0.94	1.02	1.07
Price Range	67.04-54.58	65.82-54.58	65.82-54.58	65.82-51.31	57.47-44.97	55.23-40.31	44.94-36.85	41.28-33.92
P/E Ratio	22.05-17.95	21.65-17.95	22.09-18.32	22.24-17.33	24.56-19.22	21.32-15.56	17.90-14.68	17.57-14.43
Average Yield %	3.40	3.37	3.36	3.36	3.49	3.41	3.49	3.23

Address: 231 West Michigan Street, P.O. Box 1331, Milwaukee, WI 53201
Telephone: 414-221-2345
Fax: 414-221-2172

Web Site: www.wisconsinenergy.com
Officers: Gale E. Klappa - Chairman (frmr), Acting Chief Executive Officer, President, Chief Executive Officer Allen L. Leverett - President, Chief Executive Officer, Chief Operating Officer, Chief Financial Officer, Executive Vice President

Auditors: Deloitte & Touche LLP
Transfer Agents: Computershare Shareowner Services LLC, Providence, RI

WEINGARTEN REALTY INVESTORS

Exchange	Symbol	Price	52Wk Range	Yield	P/E
NYS	WRI	$32.87 (12/29/2017)	36.70-29.37	4.69	20.17

*7 Year Price Score 82.44 *NYSE Composite Index=100 *12 Month Price Score 93.49

Interim Earnings (Per Share)

Qtr.	Mar	Jun	Sep	Dec
2014	0.49	0.27	0.79	0.70
2015	0.36	0.20	0.35	0.37
2016	0.85	0.28	0.40	0.34
2017	0.24	0.49	0.56	...

Interim Dividends (Per Share)

Amt	Decl	Ex	Rec	Pay
0.385Q	04/24/2017	06/06/2017	06/08/2017	06/15/2017
0.385Q	07/27/2017	09/07/2017	09/08/2017	09/15/2017
0.385Q	10/24/2017	12/07/2017	12/08/2017	12/15/2017
0.75Q	12/11/2017	12/22/2017	12/26/2017	12/29/2017

Indicated Div: $1.54 (Div. Reinv. Plan)

Valuation Analysis		Institutional Holding	
Forecast EPS	$1.01 (01/18/2018)	No of Institutions	416
Market Cap	$4.2 Billion	Shares	155,193,744
Book Value	$1.6 Billion	% Held	89.02
Price/Book	2.62		
Price/Sales	7.32		

Business Summary: REITs (MIC: 5.3.1 SIC: 6798 NAIC: 525930)

Weingarten Realty Investors is a real estate investment trust, engaged in the ownership of shopping centers and other commercial real estate. Co.'s primary business is leasing space to tenants in the shopping centers Co. owns or leases. Co. also provides property management services. At Dec 31 2016, Co. owned or operated under long-term leases, either directly or through its interest in real estate joint ventures or partnerships, a total of 220 properties, which are located in 18 states. The portfolio of properties contains approximately 44.7 million square feet of gross leasable area. Co. also owned interests in 28 parcels of land held for development.

Recent Developments: For the quarter ended Sep 30 2017, income from continuing operations decreased 8.5% to US$35.9 million from US$39.2 million in the year-earlier quarter. Net income increased 21.4% to US$74.5 million from US$61.3 million in the year-earlier quarter. Revenues were US$144.1 million, up 4.0% from US$138.6 million the year before. Revenues from property income rose 3.4% to US$141.1 million from US$136.4 million in the corresponding quarter a year earlier.

Prospects: Our evaluation of Weingarten Realty Investors as of Jan. 14, 2018 is the result of our systematic analysis on three basic characteristics: earnings strength, relative valuation, and recent stock price movement. The company has produced a positive trend in earnings per share over the past 5 quarters. Because the company lacks sufficient analyst estimate data, we place greater weight on the historical EPS trend as the measure of earnings strength. Based on operating earnings yield, the company is about fairly valued when compared to all of the companies in our coverage universe. Share price changes over the past year indicates that WRI will perform in line with the market over the near term.

Financial Data

(US$ in Thousands)	9 Mos	6 Mos	3 Mos	12/31/2016	12/31/2015	12/31/2014	12/31/2013	12/31/2012
Earnings Per Share	1.63	1.47	1.26	1.87	1.29	2.25	1.50	0.90
Cash Flow Per Share	2.06	2.05	1.94	1.95	1.99	1.98	1.93	1.88
Tang Book Value Per Share	12.52	12.33	12.21	12.34	11.21	12.13	11.30	12.98
Dividends Per Share	1.520	1.500	1.480	1.460	1.380	1.550	1.220	1.160
Dividend Payout %	93.25	102.04	117.46	78.07	106.98	68.89	81.33	128.89
Income Statement								
Total Revenue	433,796	289,686	143,663	549,555	512,844	514,406	497,725	503,538
EBITDA	132,480	82,179	32,053	407,862	334,163	338,013	347,217	330,839
Depn & Amortn	2,105	1,421	768	165,097	148,590	154,257	150,147	147,251
Income Before Taxes	73,495	42,243	11,957	162,331	102,353	92,787	107,311	73,824
Income Taxes	(2,035)	(2,612)	(3,359)	6,856	52	(1,261)	7,051	79
Net Income	167,307	94,678	30,826	238,933	174,352	288,008	220,262	146,640
Average Shares	130,077	130,095	128,548	128,569	124,329	124,370	122,460	121,705
Balance Sheet								
Current Assets	140,705	96,985	94,498	110,723	106,950	100,970	173,927	99,144
Total Assets	4,313,190	4,346,757	4,352,091	4,426,928	3,901,945	3,814,094	4,223,929	4,184,784
Current Liabilities	119,094	104,393	90,728	116,859	112,205	112,479	108,535	119,699
Long-Term Obligations	2,214,319	2,291,474	2,323,447	2,323,447	2,356,528	2,113,277	1,938,188	2,204,030
Total Liabilities	2,704,849	2,762,779	2,783,865	2,846,992	2,512,483	2,328,908	2,845,754	2,607,654
Stockholders' Equity	1,608,341	1,583,978	1,568,226	1,579,936	1,389,462	1,485,186	1,378,175	1,577,130
Shares Outstanding	128,425	128,418	128,386	128,072	123,951	122,489	121,949	121,505
Statistical Record								
Return on Assets %	4.86	4.55	3.88	5.72	4.52	7.17	5.24	3.33
Return on Equity %	13.27	12.12	10.72	16.05	12.13	20.12	14.91	9.05
EBITDA Margin %	30.54	28.37	22.31	74.22	65.16	65.71	69.76	65.70
Net Margin %	38.57	32.68	21.46	43.48	34.00	55.99	44.25	29.12
Asset Turnover	0.13	0.14	0.13	0.13	0.13	0.13	0.12	0.11
Current Ratio	1.18	0.93	1.04	0.95	0.95	0.90	1.60	0.83
Debt to Equity	1.38	1.45	1.48	1.49	1.52	1.31	1.67	1.40
Price Range	38.98-29.37	43.44-29.37	43.44-31.37	43.44-32.48	38.41-30.43	36.96-27.27	35.84-26.77	28.85-21.56
P/E Ratio	23.91-18.02	29.55-19.98	34.48-24.90	23.23-17.37	29.78-23.59	16.43-12.19	23.89-17.85	32.06-23.96
Average Yield %	4.51	4.16	3.94	3.88	3.99	4.80	4.00	4.41

Address: 2600 Citadel Plaza Drive, P.O. Box 924133, Houston, TX 77292-4133 **Telephone:** 713-866-6000	**Web Site:** www.weingarten.com **Officers:** Stanford Alexander - Chairman Andrew M. Alexander - President, Chief Executive Officer	**Auditors:** Deloitte & Touche LLP **Investor Contact:** 713-866-6000 **Transfer Agents:** Computershare Trust Company, National Association, Canton, MA

WELBILT INC

Exchange	Symbol	Price	52Wk Range	Yield	P/E
NYS	WBT	$23.51 (12/29/2017)	23.51-18.25	N/A	36.73

*7 Year Price Score N/A   *NYSE Composite Index=100   *12 Month Price Score 103.30

TRADING VOLUME (thousand shares)

Interim Earnings (Per Share)

Qtr.	Mar	Jun	Sep	Dec
2015	0.10	0.27	0.30	0.48
2016	0.13	0.11	0.18	0.15
2017	0.04	0.21	0.24	...

Interim Dividends (Per Share)

No Dividends Paid

Valuation Analysis		Institutional Holding	
Forecast EPS	$0.76	No of Institutions	
	(01/09/2018)	248	
Market Cap	$3.3 Billion	Shares	
Book Value	$44.0 Million	134,412,560	
Price/Book	74.42	% Held	
Price/Sales	2.25	N/A	

Business Summary: Industrial Machinery & Equipment (MIC: 7.2.1 SIC: 3556 NAIC: 333294)

Welbilt is a commercial foodservice equipment company. Co. designs, manufactures and supplies food and beverage equipment for the commercial foodservice market. Co.'s portfolio of brands includes Clevelandâ,,¢, Convotherm®, Delfield®, fitKitchensm, Frymaster®, Garland®, Kolpak®, Lincolnâ,,¢, Manitowoc® Ice, Merco®, Merrychef® and Multiplex®. All of Co.'s products are supported by KitchenCare®, its aftermarket parts and repair service business. Co.'s products are used by commercial and institutional foodservice operators including restaurants, quick-service restaurant chains, hotels, caterers, supermarkets, convenience stores, business and industry, hospitals, schools and other institutions.

Recent Developments: For the quarter ended Sep 30 2017, net income increased 32.9% to US$33.1 million from US$24.9 million in the year-earlier quarter. Revenues were US$380.4 million, down 0.9% from US$384.0 million the year before. Operating income was US$70.3 million versus US$60.6 million in the prior-year quarter, an increase of 16.0%. Direct operating expenses declined 2.3% to US$236.5 million from US$242.0 million in the comparable period the year before. Indirect operating expenses decreased 9.6% to US$73.6 million from US$81.4 million in the equivalent prior-year period.

Prospects: Our evaluation of Welbilt Inc. as of Jan. 14, 2018 is the result of our systematic analysis on three basic characteristics: earnings strength, relative valuation, and recent stock price movement. The company has produced a positive trend in earnings per share over the past 5 quarters and while recent estimates for the company have been mixed, WBT has posted results that fell short of analysts expectations. Based on operating earnings yield, the company is about fairly valued when compared to all of the companies in our coverage universe. Share price changes over the past year indicates that WBT will perform in line with the market over the near term.

Financial Data

(US$ in Thousands)	9 Mos	6 Mos	3 Mos	12/31/2016	12/31/2015	12/31/2014	12/31/2013
Earnings Per Share	0.64	0.58	0.48	0.57	1.15	1.17	1.07
Cash Flow Per Share	0.98	0.87	0.68	0.88	1.04	1.46	1.47
Income Statement							
Total Revenue	1,079,500	699,100	328,000	1,456,600	1,570,100	1,581,300	1,541,800
EBITDA	187,400	107,300	43,400	238,600	232,900	224,900	239,800
Depn & Amortn	39,500	26,100	13,100	48,500	51,000	53,000	51,400
Income Before Taxes	82,000	37,000	7,100	104,800	196,300	187,200	204,600
Income Taxes	13,800	1,900	2,100	25,300	39,300	25,900	55,300
Net Income	68,200	35,100	5,000	79,500	157,100	159,800	146,100
Average Shares	140,885	140,661	140,431	139,714	137,016	137,016	137,016
Balance Sheet							
Current Assets	405,600	404,500	379,600	308,200	252,600	289,500	...
Total Assets	1,862,100	1,867,700	1,837,100	1,769,100	1,754,000	1,898,300	...
Current Liabilities	299,500	308,900	284,800	313,100	321,300	368,600	...
Long-Term Obligations	1,292,600	1,328,900	1,353,400	1,278,700	2,300	3,600	...
Total Liabilities	1,818,100	1,856,400	1,863,400	1,812,600	545,300	646,900	...
Stockholders' Equity	44,000	11,300	(26,300)	(43,500)	1,208,700	1,251,400	...
Shares Outstanding	139,272	138,974	138,878	138,562	137,016	...	...
Statistical Record							
Return on Assets %	4.87	4.43	3.63	4.50	8.60	...	...
Return on Equity %	...	...	...	13.61	12.77	...	...
EBITDA Margin %	17.36	15.35	13.23	16.38	14.83	14.22	15.55
Net Margin %	6.32	5.02	1.52	5.46	10.01	10.11	9.48
Asset Turnover	0.79	0.80	0.80	0.82	0.86	...	...
Current Ratio	1.35	1.31	1.33	0.98	0.79	0.79	...
Debt to Equity	29.38	117.60	...	...	N.M.	N.M.	...
Price Range	23.09-15.01	21.02-15.01	19.75-14.07	19.33-13.80	...	...	...
P/E Ratio	36.08-23.45	36.24-25.88	41.15-29.31	33.91-24.21	...	...	...

Address: 2227 Welbilt Boulevard, New Port Richey, FL 34655
Telephone: 727-375-7010

Web Site: www.manitowocfoodservice.com
Officers: Cynthia M. Egnotovich - Chairperson Hubertus M. Muehlhaeuser - President, Chief Executive Officer

Auditors: PricewaterhouseCoopers LLP
Transfer Agents: Computershare

WELLCARE HEALTH PLANS INC

Exchange	Symbol	Price	52Wk Range	Yield	P/E
NYS	WCG	$201.11 (12/29/2017)	212.99-136.63	N/A	25.23

*7 Year Price Score 157.34 *NYSE Composite Index=100 *12 Month Price Score 113.52

Interim Earnings (Per Share)

Qtr.	Mar	Jun	Sep	Dec
2014	1.00	(0.17)	0.44	0.17
2015	0.39	1.17	0.82	0.29
2016	0.83	2.04	1.54	1.00
2017	1.50	1.65	3.82	...

Interim Dividends (Per Share)

No Dividends Paid

Valuation Analysis		Institutional Holding	
Forecast EPS	$8.40	No of Institutions	
	(01/24/2018)	457	
Market Cap	$9.0 Billion	Shares	
Book Value	$2.3 Billion	56,043,324	
Price/Book	3.84	% Held	
Price/Sales	0.55	96.40	

Business Summary: Hospitals & Health Care Facilities (MIC: 4.2.1 SIC: 6324 NAIC: 524114)

WellCare Health Plans is a managed care company with a focus on government-sponsored managed care services. Co. manages its business in three reportable segments: Medicaid Health Plans, which includes plans for beneficiaries of Temporary Assistance for Needy Families, and other state-based programs that are not part of the Medicaid program; Medicare Health Plans, which provides eligible persons age 65 and over and some disabled persons with a variety of hospital, medical and prescription drug benefits; and Medicare Prescription Drug Plans (PDPs), which provides stand-alone Medicare Part D coverage to Medicare-eligible beneficiaries in its Medicare PDPs segment.

Recent Developments: For the quarter ended Sep 30 2017, net income increased 150.1% to US$171.6 million from US$68.6 million in the year-earlier quarter. Revenues were US$4.40 billion, up 22.8% from US$3.58 billion the year before. Net premiums earned were US$4.39 billion versus US$3.58 billion in the prior-year quarter, an increase of 22.7%.

Prospects: Our evaluation of WellCare Health Plans Inc. as of Jan. 21, 2018 is the result of our systematic analysis on three basic characteristics: earnings strength, relative valuation, and recent stock price movement. The company has generated a negative trend in earnings per share over the past 5 quarters and while recent estimates for the company have been mixed, WCG has posted better than expected results. Based on operating earnings yield, the company is about fairly valued when compared to all of the companies in our coverage universe. Share price changes over the past year indicates that WCG will perform in line with the market over the near term.

Financial Data

(US$ in Thousands)	9 Mos	6 Mos	3 Mos	12/31/2016	12/31/2015	12/31/2014	12/31/2013	12/31/2012
Earnings Per Share	7.97	5.69	6.08	5.43	2.67	1.44	3.98	4.22
Cash Flow Per Share	20.52	25.70	28.29	16.86	16.17	6.82	4.11	(0.71)
Tang Book Value Per Share	29.36	25.08	35.77	34.62	31.40	28.05	27.75	24.21
Income Statement								
Total Revenue	12,662,100	8,259,200	3,954,200	14,237,100	13,890,200	12,959,900	9,527,900	7,409,032
EBITDA	566,900	306,500	143,300	665,800	452,300	264,000	326,900	329,804
Depn & Amortn	84,600	53,200	23,900	77,200	62,000	46,800	36,700	29,243
Income Before Taxes	430,900	219,000	103,200	529,500	336,100	177,800	278,300	296,439
Income Taxes	140,000	76,500	35,900	287,400	217,500	114,100	103,000	111,711
Net Income	313,000	141,400	67,300	242,100	118,600	63,700	175,300	184,728
Average Shares	44,969	44,934	44,826	44,619	44,391	44,163	44,000	43,826
Balance Sheet								
Current Assets	6,761,400	6,346,900	7,268,500	5,119,600	4,268,500	3,526,300	2,692,700	2,100,710
Total Assets	9,128,500	8,513,100	8,342,600	6,152,800	5,193,600	4,495,000	3,450,700	2,675,516
Current Liabilities	5,289,000	4,826,700	5,013,000	3,055,000	2,441,600	1,935,700	1,237,100	1,113,426
Long-Term Obligations	1,181,600	1,180,800	1,180,100	997,600	912,100	900,000	600,000	120,000
Total Liabilities	6,795,100	6,360,800	6,278,900	4,152,700	3,465,300	2,899,100	1,932,800	1,352,352
Stockholders' Equity	2,333,400	2,152,300	2,063,700	2,000,100	1,728,300	1,595,900	1,517,900	1,323,164
Shares Outstanding	44,512	44,507	44,490	44,293	44,113	43,914	43,766	43,212
Statistical Record								
Return on Assets %	4.57	3.62	3.98	4.26	2.45	1.60	5.72	7.14
Return on Equity %	16.74	12.69	14.18	12.95	7.14	4.09	12.34	15.10
EBITDA Margin %	4.48	3.71	3.62	4.68	3.26	2.04	3.43	4.45
Net Margin %	2.47	1.71	1.70	1.70	0.85	0.49	1.84	2.49
Asset Turnover	2.07	2.18	2.14	2.50	2.87	3.26	3.11	2.86
Current Ratio	1.28	1.31	1.45	1.68	1.75	1.82	2.18	1.89
Debt to Equity	0.51	0.55	0.57	0.50	0.53	0.56	0.40	0.09
Price Range	183.87-113.51	183.60-104.23	148.67-88.00	141.40-70.06	98.51-72.85	84.25-56.64	74.76-45.78	74.24-45.90
P/E Ratio	23.07-14.24	32.27-18.32	24.45-14.47	26.04-12.90	36.90-27.28	58.51-39.33	18.78-11.50	17.59-10.88

Address: 8735 Henderson Road, Renaissance One, Tampa, FL 33634 Telephone: 813-290-6200	Web Site: www.wellcare.com Officers: Christian P. Michalik - Chairman Kenneth A. Burdick - President, Chief Executive Officer, Chief Operating Officer, Division Officer	Auditors: Deloitte & Touche LLP Investor Contact: 813-206-3916 Transfer Agents: Computershare Trust Company, N.A., Providence, RI

WELLS FARGO & CO.

Exchange	Symbol	Price	52Wk Range	Yield	P/E
NYS	WFC	$60.67 (12/29/2017)	61.61-49.58	2.57	15.68

*7 Year Price Score 96.94 ***NYSE Composite Index=100** ***12 Month Price Score 98.01**

TRADING VOLUME (thousand shares)

Interim Earnings (Per Share)

Qtr.	Mar	Jun	Sep	Dec
2014	1.05	1.01	1.02	1.02
2015	1.04	1.03	1.05	1.00
2016	0.99	1.01	1.03	0.96
2017	1.00	1.07	0.84	...

Interim Dividends (Per Share)

Amt	Decl	Ex	Rec	Pay
0.38Q	01/24/2017	02/01/2017	02/03/2017	03/01/2017
0.38Q	04/25/2017	05/03/2017	05/05/2017	06/01/2017
0.39Q	07/25/2017	08/02/2017	08/04/2017	09/01/2017
0.39Q	10/24/2017	11/02/2017	11/03/2017	12/01/2017

Indicated Div: $1.56 (Div. Reinv. Plan)

Valuation Analysis		Institutional Holding	
Forecast EPS	$4.87	No of Institutions	
	(01/18/2018)	2651	
Market Cap	$299.0 Billion	Shares	
Book Value	$205.9 Billion	4,534,640,640	
Price/Book	1.45	% Held	
Price/Sales	3.11	74.62	

Business Summary: Banking (MIC: 5.1.1 SIC: 6021 NAIC: 522110)

Wells Fargo is a financial holding company and a bank holding company.Co. has three operating segments: Community Banking; Wholesale Banking; and Wealth, Brokerage and Retirement. The Community Banking segment provides a line of financial products and services to consumers and businesses. The Wholesale Banking segment provides financial solutions to businesses across the U.S. and to financial institutions globally. The Wealth and Investment Management segment provides a range of personalized wealth management, investment and retirement products and services to clients across U.S. based businesses. At Dec 31 2016, Co. had total assets of $1.89 trillion and total deposits of $1.31 trillion.

Recent Developments: For the quarter ended Sep 30 2017, net income decreased 17.7% to US$4.65 billion from US$5.65 billion in the year-earlier quarter. Net interest income increased 4.4% to US$12.48 billion from US$11.95 billion in the year-earlier quarter. Provision for loan losses was US$717.0 million versus US$805.0 million in the prior-year quarter, a decrease of 10.9%. Non-interest income fell 8.9% to US$9.45 billion from US$10.38 billion, while non-interest expense advanced 8.2% to US$14.35 billion.

Prospects: Our evaluation of Wells Fargo & Co. as of Jan. 14, 2018 is the result of our systematic analysis on three basic characteristics: earnings strength, relative valuation, and recent stock price movement. The company has produced a positive trend in earnings per share over the past 5 quarters. Because the company lacks sufficient analyst estimate data, we place greater weight on the historical EPS trend as the measure of earnings strength. Based on operating earnings yield, the company is undervalued when compared to all of the companies in our coverage universe. Share price changes over the past year indicates that WFC will perform in line with the market over the near term.

Financial Data

(US$ in Thousands)	9 Mos	6 Mos	3 Mos	12/31/2016	12/31/2015	12/31/2014	12/31/2013	12/31/2012
Earnings Per Share	3.87	4.06	4.00	3.99	4.12	4.10	3.89	3.36
Cash Flow Per Share	4.68	2.24	1.61	0.03	2.88	3.35	10.90	11.04
Tang Book Value Per Share	27.83	27.49	26.47	26.17	25.21	23.42	20.10	18.81
Dividends Per Share	1.530	1.520	1.520	1.515	1.475	1.350	1.150	0.880
Dividend Payout %	39.53	37.44	38.00	37.97	35.80	32.93	29.56	26.19
Income Statement								
Interest Income	43,999,000	28,941,000	14,226,000	53,663,000	49,277,000	47,552,000	47,089,000	48,391,000
Interest Expense	6,740,000	4,158,000	1,926,000	5,909,000	3,976,000	4,025,000	4,289,000	5,161,000
Net Interest Income	37,259,000	24,783,000	12,300,000	47,754,000	45,301,000	43,527,000	42,800,000	43,230,000
Provision for Losses	1,877,000	1,160,000	605,000	3,770,000	2,442,000	1,395,000	2,309,000	7,217,000
Non-Interest Income	28,838,000	19,388,000	9,702,000	40,513,000	40,756,000	40,820,000	40,980,000	42,856,000
Non-Interest Expense	41,480,000	27,195,000	13,792,000	52,377,000	49,974,000	49,037,000	48,842,000	50,398,000
Income Before Taxes	22,536,000	15,678,000	7,605,000	32,120,000	33,641,000	33,915,000	32,629,000	28,471,000
Income Taxes	6,486,000	4,282,000	2,057,000	10,075,000	10,365,000	10,307,000	10,405,000	9,103,000
Net Income	15,863,000	11,267,000	5,457,000	21,938,000	22,894,000	23,057,000	21,878,000	18,897,000
Average Shares	4,996,799	5,037,699	5,070,399	5,108,329	5,209,799	5,324,399	5,371,199	5,351,499
Balance Sheet								
Net Loans & Leases	940,952,000	946,506,000	947,490,000	956,265,000	905,293,000	850,954,000	811,430,000	782,624,000
Total Assets	1,934,939,000	1,930,871,000	1,951,564,000	1,930,115,000	1,787,632,000	1,687,155,000	1,527,015,000	1,422,968,000
Total Deposits	1,306,706,000	1,305,830,000	1,325,444,000	1,306,079,000	1,223,312,000	1,168,310,000	1,079,177,000	1,002,835,000
Total Liabilities	1,729,010,000	1,725,641,000	1,750,064,000	1,730,534,000	1,594,634,000	1,502,761,000	1,356,873,000	1,265,414,000
Stockholders' Equity	205,929,000	205,230,000	201,500,000	199,581,000	192,998,000	184,394,000	170,142,000	157,554,000
Shares Outstanding	4,927,870	4,966,769	4,996,734	5,016,109	5,092,128	5,170,348	5,257,162	5,266,313
Statistical Record								
Return on Assets %	1.09	1.16	1.15	1.18	1.32	1.43	1.48	1.38
Return on Equity %	10.34	10.90	10.99	11.15	12.13	13.01	13.35	12.66
Net Interest Margin %	82.85	84.83	86.46	88.99	91.93	91.54	90.89	89.33
Efficiency Ratio %	58.29	55.28	57.64	55.62	55.51	55.49	55.46	55.23
Loans to Deposits	0.72	0.72	0.71	0.73	0.74	0.73	0.75	0.78
Price Range	59.73-43.75	59.73-43.75	59.73-43.75	57.29-43.75	58.52-50.02	55.71-44.23	45.54-34.18	36.13-28.43
P/E Ratio	15.43-11.30	14.71-10.78	14.93-10.94	14.36-10.96	14.20-12.14	13.59-10.79	11.71-8.79	10.75-8.46
Average Yield %	2.87	2.92	2.99	3.09	2.69	2.68	2.86	2.68

Address: 420 Montgomery Street, San Francisco, CA 94163 Telephone: 866-878-5865	Web Site: www.wellsfargo.com Officers: Timothy J. Sloan - President, Chief Executive Officer, Chief Operating Officer, Head, Senior Executive Vice President, Chief Financial Officer, Chief Administrative Officer John R. Shrewsberry - Senior Executive Vice President, Chief Financial Officer	Auditors: KPMG LLP Investor Contact: 415-371-2921 Transfer Agents: Wells Fargo Shareowners Services, St. Paul, MN

WELLTOWER INC

Exchange	Symbol	Price	52Wk Range	Yield	P/E	Div Achiever
NYS	HCN	$63.77 (12/29/2017)	77.66-63.27	5.46	25.61	13 Years

*7 Year Price Score 85.97 *NYSE Composite Index=100 *12 Month Price Score 89.68

Interim Earnings (Per Share)

Qtr.	Mar	Jun	Sep	Dec
2014	0.17	0.24	0.44	0.59
2015	0.56	0.89	0.52	0.37
2016	0.42	0.54	0.93	0.92
2017	0.86	0.51	0.20	...

Interim Dividends (Per Share)

Amt	Decl	Ex	Rec	Pay
0.87Q	01/26/2017	02/03/2017	02/07/2017	02/21/2017
0.87Q	04/27/2017	05/05/2017	05/09/2017	05/22/2017
0.87Q	07/27/2017	08/04/2017	08/08/2017	08/21/2017
0.87Q	10/26/2017	11/06/2017	11/07/2017	11/20/2017

Indicated Div: $3.48 (Div. Reinv. Plan)

Valuation Analysis

		Institutional Holding	
Forecast EPS	$2.03 (01/17/2018)	No of Institutions	949
Market Cap	$23.6 Billion	Shares	407,371,712
Book Value	$14.7 Billion	% Held	95.30
Price/Book	1.60		
Price/Sales	5.50		

Business Summary: REITs (MIC: 5.3.1 SIC: 6798 NAIC: 525930)

Welltower is a real estate investment trust. As of Dec 31 2016, Co.'s portfolio consisted a total of 1,313 properties that comprised of 631 triple-net properties (independent living facilities and independent supportive living facilities, continuing care retirement communities, assisted living facilities, care homes with and without nursing, Alzheimer's/dementia care facilities, long-term/post-acute care facilities and hospitals); 420 seniors housing properties (independent living facilities and independent supportive living facilities, assisted living facilities, care homes and Alzheimer's/dementia care facilities); and 262 outpatient medical properties (outpatient medical buildings).

Recent Developments: For the quarter ended Sep 30 2017, income from continuing operations decreased 54.4% to US$87.7 million from US$192.4 million in the year-earlier quarter. Net income decreased 74.8% to US$89.3 million from US$354.7 million in the year-earlier quarter. Revenues were US$1.09 billion, up 1.1% from US$1.08 billion the year before. Revenues from property income fell 13.8% to US$362.9 million from US$421.2 million in the corresponding quarter a year earlier.

Prospects: Our evaluation of Welltower Inc. as of Jan. 14, 2018 is the result of our systematic analysis on three basic characteristics: earnings strength, relative valuation, and recent stock price movement. The company has managed to produce a neutral trend in earnings per share over the past 5 quarters. Because the company lacks sufficient analyst estimate data, we place greater weight on the historical EPS trend as the measure of earnings strength. Based on operating earnings yield, the company is about fairly valued when compared to all of the companies in our coverage universe. Share price changes over the past year indicates that HCN will perform very well over the near term.

Financial Data

(US$ in Thousands)	9 Mos	6 Mos	3 Mos	12/31/2016	12/31/2015	12/31/2014	12/31/2013	12/31/2012
Earnings Per Share	2.49	3.22	3.25	2.81	2.34	1.45	0.28	0.98
Cash Flow Per Share	4.12	4.43	4.53	4.53	3.94	3.72	3.57	3.64
Tang Book Value Per Share	37.65	38.07	37.99	37.87	38.10	36.80	35.67	35.35
Dividends Per Share	3.470	3.460	3.450	3.440	3.300	3.180	3.060	2.960
Dividend Payout %	139.36	107.45	106.15	122.42	141.03	219.31	1,092.86	302.04
Income Statement								
Total Revenue	3,212,383	2,120,900	1,062,298	4,281,160	3,859,826	3,343,546	2,880,608	1,822,099
EBITDA	372,903	283,523	122,238	1,619,639	1,471,366	1,236,053	984,762	734,588
Depn & Amortn	12,275	7,837	3,369	910,386	835,249	851,840	882,517	548,935
Income Before Taxes	360,628	275,686	118,869	709,253	636,117	384,213	102,245	185,653
Income Taxes	(5,535)	(6,203)	2,245	(19,128)	6,451	(1,267)	7,491	7,612
Net Income	622,621	536,896	336,787	1,077,803	883,750	512,153	145,050	297,255
Average Shares	370,740	368,149	364,652	360,227	349,424	307,747	278,761	225,953
Balance Sheet								
Current Assets	295,311	487,641	423,137	949,798	818,252	553,423	231,601	1,141,421
Total Assets	28,180,379	27,975,786	27,767,277	28,865,184	29,023,845	25,014,296	23,083,957	19,549,109
Long-Term Obligations	11,521,592	11,379,946	11,454,185	12,358,245	12,967,686	10,828,013	10,652,014	8,531,899
Total Liabilities	13,450,454	13,146,954	13,131,074	14,058,791	14,433,285	11,839,143	11,669,374	9,254,308
Stockholders' Equity	14,729,925	14,828,832	14,636,203	14,806,393	14,590,560	13,175,153	11,414,583	10,294,801
Shares Outstanding	370,341	368,878	364,563	362,602	354,777	328,790	289,563	260,373
Statistical Record								
Return on Assets %	3.35	4.35	4.39	3.71	3.27	2.13	0.68	1.72
Return on Equity %	6.59	8.47	8.57	7.31	6.37	4.17	1.34	3.40
EBITDA Margin %	11.61	13.37	11.51	37.83	38.12	36.97	34.19	40.32
Net Margin %	19.38	25.31	31.70	25.18	22.90	15.32	5.04	16.31
Asset Turnover	0.15	0.15	0.15	0.15	0.14	0.14	0.14	0.11
Debt to Equity	0.78	0.77	0.78	0.83	0.89	0.82	0.93	0.83
Price Range	77.66-61.01	79.61-61.01	79.61-61.01	79.61-53.68	84.31-58.21	77.98-53.05	78.98-52.58	62.24-52.40
P/E Ratio	31.19-24.50	24.72-18.95	24.50-18.77	28.33-19.10	36.03-24.88	53.78-36.59	282.07-187.79	63.51-53.47
Average Yield %	4.96	4.88	4.90	4.94	4.68	4.97	4.75	5.16

Address: 4500 Dorr Street, Toledo, OH 43615 **Telephone:** 419-247-2800	**Web Site:** www.welltower.com **Officers:** Jeffrey H. Donahue - Chairman John Goodey - Executive Vice President, Chief Financial Officer	**Auditors:** Ernst & Young LLP **Transfer Agents:** Computershare, Providence, RI

WESCO INTERNATIONAL, INC.

Exchange	Symbol	Price	52Wk Range	Yield	P/E
NYS	WCC	$68.15 (12/29/2017)	74.45-49.60	N/A	17.61

*7 Year Price Score 75.65   *NYSE Composite Index=100   *12 Month Price Score 97.45

Interim Earnings (Per Share)

Qtr.	Mar	Jun	Sep	Dec
2014	0.97	1.29	1.52	1.40
2015	0.90	1.00	1.28	1.02
2016	0.77	1.02	(0.73)	0.97
2017	0.76	1.02	1.12	...

Interim Dividends (Per Share)

No Dividends Paid

Valuation Analysis		Institutional Holding	
Forecast EPS	$3.88	No of Institutions	
	(01/18/2018)	360	
Market Cap	$3.2 Billion	Shares	
Book Value	$2.1 Billion	54,271,572	
Price/Book	1.52	% Held	
Price/Sales	0.43	102.17	

TRADING VOLUME (thousand shares)

Business Summary: Electrical Equipment (MIC: 7.3.1 SIC: 5063 NAIC: 423610)

WESCO International is a distributor of products and provider of supply chain management and logistics services used primarily in industrial, construction, utility, and commercial, institutional and government markets. Co. is a provider of electrical, industrial, and communications maintenance, repair and operating and original equipment manufacturers products, construction materials, and supply chain management and logistics services. Co.'s primary product categories include general supplies, wire, cable and conduit, communications and security, electrical distribution and controls, lighting and sustainability, and automation, controls and motors.

Recent Developments: For the quarter ended Sep 30 2017, net income amounted to US$53.6 million versus a net loss of US$31.0 million in the year-earlier quarter. Revenues were US$2.00 billion, up 7.8% from US$1.86 billion the year before. Operating income was US$89.3 million versus US$92.6 million in the prior-year quarter, a decrease of 3.6%. Direct operating expenses rose 8.4% to US$1.61 billion from US$1.49 billion in the comparable period the year before. Indirect operating expenses increased 8.7% to US$296.1 million from US$272.5 million in the equivalent prior-year period.

Prospects: Our evaluation of Wesco International Inc. as of Jan. 14, 2018 is the result of our systematic analysis on three basic characteristics: earnings strength, relative valuation, and recent stock price movement. The company has managed to produce a neutral trend in earnings per share over the past 5 quarters and while recent estimates for the company have been raised by analysts, WCC has posted better than expected results. Based on operating earnings yield, the company is undervalued when compared to all of the companies in our coverage universe. Share price changes over the past year indicates that WCC will perform poorly over the near term.

Financial Data

(US$ in Thousands)	9 Mos	6 Mos	3 Mos	12/31/2016	12/31/2015	12/31/2014	12/31/2013	12/31/2012
Earnings Per Share	3.87	2.02	2.02	2.10	4.18	5.18	5.25	3.95
Cash Flow Per Share	3.46	4.73	5.53	6.79	6.52	5.65	7.14	6.58
Income Statement								
Total Revenue	5,682,375	3,682,215	1,772,591	7,336,017	7,518,487	7,889,626	7,513,342	6,579,301
EBITDA	287,204	181,880	83,054	225,226	391,542	484,717	483,658	343,801
Depn & Amortn	47,758	31,686	15,965	17,100	17,800	18,500	18,200	14,400
Income Before Taxes	188,599	116,657	50,368	131,551	303,910	384,153	379,851	281,639
Income Taxes	47,684	29,323	12,568	30,431	95,537	108,716	103,333	79,880
Net Income	140,918	87,238	37,729	101,588	210,687	275,906	276,430	201,777
Average Shares	47,804	48,776	49,401	48,333	50,373	53,258	52,650	51,133
Balance Sheet								
Current Assets	2,410,127	2,305,545	2,203,360	2,172,457	2,257,534	2,350,338	2,198,541	2,101,837
Total Assets	4,764,468	4,623,671	4,511,249	4,490,984	4,587,425	4,754,437	4,617,108	4,629,629
Current Liabilities	1,043,493	964,406	920,069	896,797	947,801	1,063,872	1,044,589	1,007,995
Long-Term Obligations	1,368,301	1,334,542	1,309,800	1,363,135	1,456,761	1,366,430	1,447,634	1,695,413
Total Liabilities	2,653,964	2,525,392	2,450,569	2,477,703	2,810,753	2,825,785	2,852,299	3,075,832
Stockholders' Equity	2,110,504	2,098,279	2,060,680	2,013,281	1,776,672	1,928,652	1,764,809	1,553,797
Shares Outstanding	46,999	47,972	48,773	48,611	42,173	44,489	44,267	44,061
Statistical Record								
Return on Assets %	4.02	2.21	2.24	2.23	4.51	5.89	5.98	5.22
Return on Equity %	9.17	5.09	5.22	5.35	11.37	14.94	16.66	13.88
EBITDA Margin %	5.05	4.94	4.69	3.07	5.21	6.14	6.44	5.23
Net Margin %	2.48	2.37	2.13	1.38	2.80	3.50	3.68	3.07
Asset Turnover	1.60	1.57	1.59	1.61	1.61	1.68	1.63	1.70
Current Ratio	2.31	2.39	2.39	2.42	2.38	2.21	2.10	2.09
Debt to Equity	0.65	0.64	0.64	0.68	0.82	0.71	0.82	1.09
Price Range	74.45-49.60	74.45-50.85	74.45-50.85	72.15-36.05	76.21-40.04	93.81-71.18	91.12-65.46	67.60-52.31
P/E Ratio	19.24-12.82	36.86-25.17	36.86-25.17	34.36-17.17	18.23-9.58	18.11-13.74	17.36-12.47	17.11-13.24

Address: 225 West Station Square Drive, Suite 700, Pittsburgh, PA 15219	Web Site: www.wesco.com	Auditors: PricewaterhouseCoopers LLP
Telephone: 412-454-2200	Officers: John J. Engel - Chairman, President, Chief Executive Officer Leslie J. Parrette - Senior Vice President	Transfer Agents: Computershare, Providence, RI

WEST PHARMACEUTICAL SERVICES, INC.

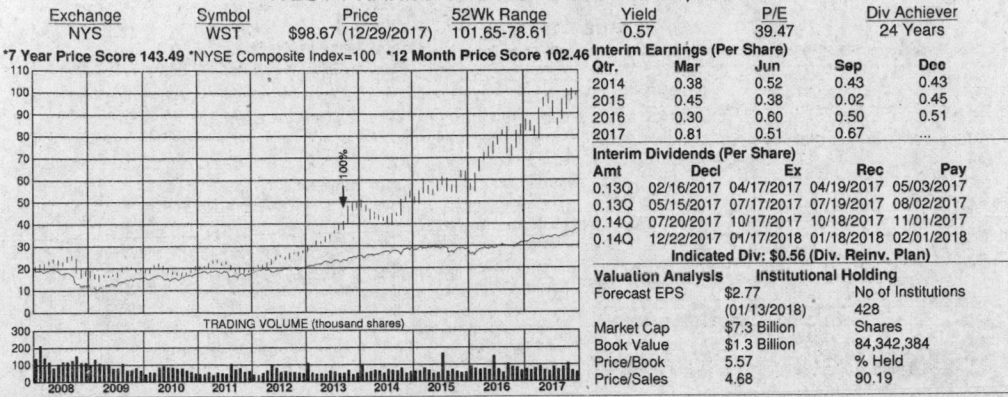

Exchange	Symbol	Price	52Wk Range	Yield	P/E	Div Achiever
NYS	WST	$98.67 (12/29/2017)	101.65-78.61	0.57	39.47	24 Years

*7 Year Price Score 143.49 *NYSE Composite Index=100 *12 Month Price Score 102.46

Interim Earnings (Per Share)

Qtr.	Mar	Jun	Sep	Dec
2014	0.38	0.52	0.43	0.43
2015	0.45	0.38	0.02	0.45
2016	0.30	0.60	0.50	0.51
2017	0.81	0.51	0.67	...

Interim Dividends (Per Share)

Amt	Decl	Ex	Rec	Pay
0.13Q	02/16/2017	04/17/2017	04/19/2017	05/03/2017
0.13Q	05/15/2017	07/17/2017	07/19/2017	08/02/2017
0.14Q	07/20/2017	10/17/2017	10/18/2017	11/01/2017
0.14Q	12/22/2017	01/17/2018	01/18/2018	02/01/2018

Indicated Div: $0.56 (Div. Reinv. Plan)

Valuation Analysis / **Institutional Holding**

Forecast EPS	$2.77 (01/13/2018)	No of Institutions	428
Market Cap	$7.3 Billion	Shares	84,342,384
Book Value	$1.3 Billion	% Held	90.19
Price/Book	5.57		
Price/Sales	4.68		

Business Summary: Rubber Products (MIC: 8.4.1 SIC: 3069 NAIC: 326299)

West Pharmaceutical Services is a manufacturer of packaging components and delivery systems for injectable drugs and healthcare products. Co.'s products include vial containment solutions, prefillable systems, self-injection platforms, cartridge systems and components, reconstitution and transfer systems, intradermal delivery solutions, specialty components, and contract manufacturing and analytical services. Proprietary Products segment provides proprietary packaging, containment and drug delivery products such as NovaPure® plungers. Contract-Manufactured Products segment includes a variety of custom contract-manufacturing and assembly solutions.

Recent Developments: For the quarter ended Sep 30 2017, net income increased 35.6% to US$51.0 million from US$37.6 million in the year-earlier quarter. Revenues were US$398.2 million, up 5.7% from US$376.7 million the year before. Operating income was US$63.9 million versus US$51.3 million in the prior-year quarter, an increase of 24.6%. Direct operating expenses rose 6.9% to US$273.2 million from US$255.6 million in the comparable period the year before. Indirect operating expenses decreased 12.5% to US$61.1 million from US$69.8 million in the equivalent prior-year period.

Prospects: Our evaluation of West Pharmaceutical Services Inc. as of Jan. 14, 2018 is the result of our systematic analysis on three basic characteristics: earnings strength, relative valuation, and recent stock price movement. The company has produced a positive trend in earnings per share over the past 5 quarters and while recent estimates for the company have remained steady, WST has posted better than expected results. Based on operating earnings yield, the company is about fairly valued when compared to all of the companies in our coverage universe. Share price changes over the past year indicates that WST will perform well over the near term.

Financial Data

(US$ in Thousands)	9 Mos	6 Mos	3 Mos	12/31/2016	12/31/2015	12/31/2014	12/31/2013	12/31/2012
Earnings Per Share	2.50	2.33	2.42	1.91	1.30	1.75	1.57	1.15
Cash Flow Per Share	3.42	3.33	3.23	2.99	2.95	2.58	3.17	2.75
Tang Book Value Per Share	15.98	15.05	14.17	13.56	12.20	11.31	10.60	8.25
Dividends Per Share	0.520	0.510	0.500	0.490	0.450	0.410	0.385	0.365
Dividend Payout %	20.80	21.89	20.66	25.65	34.62	23.43	24.52	31.74
Income Statement								
Total Revenue	1,183,500	785,300	387,700	1,509,100	1,399,800	1,421,400	1,368,400	1,266,400
EBITDA	239,700	150,800	84,600	284,900	214,700	266,800	243,200	196,300
Depn & Amortn	71,800	46,800	23,300	88,100	86,100	84,800	81,000	72,800
Income Before Taxes	163,100	100,200	59,500	189,800	116,100	169,000	147,100	108,600
Income Taxes	19,100	5,100	2,200	54,400	26,300	47,200	40,200	32,700
Net Income	150,700	99,700	60,900	143,600	95,600	127,100	112,300	80,700
Average Shares	75,900	75,800	74,900	75,000	73,800	72,800	71,400	71,800
Balance Sheet								
Current Assets	776,900	717,800	652,600	641,900	673,700	659,300	650,700	557,300
Total Assets	1,930,400	1,843,000	1,733,500	1,716,700	1,695,100	1,670,900	1,671,600	1,564,000
Current Liabilities	300,000	289,000	256,500	241,000	314,300	252,500	236,900	261,800
Long-Term Obligations	196,600	195,700	194,200	226,200	228,900	309,500	371,300	378,800
Total Liabilities	613,500	600,600	564,900	599,200	671,200	714,000	765,200	835,100
Stockholders' Equity	1,316,900	1,242,400	1,168,600	1,117,500	1,023,900	956,900	906,400	728,900
Shares Outstanding	74,300	74,002	73,553	73,100	72,300	71,300	70,200	68,600
Statistical Record								
Return on Assets %	10.36	9.94	10.72	8.39	5.68	7.61	6.94	5.43
Return on Equity %	15.44	15.00	16.26	13.38	9.65	13.64	13.73	11.63
EBITDA Margin %	20.25	19.20	21.82	18.88	15.34	18.77	17.77	15.50
Net Margin %	12.73	12.70	15.71	9.52	6.83	8.94	8.21	6.37
Asset Turnover	0.85	0.87	0.90	0.88	0.83	0.85	0.85	0.85
Current Ratio	2.59	2.48	2.54	2.66	2.14	2.61	2.75	2.13
Debt to Equity	0.15	0.16	0.17	0.20	0.22	0.32	0.41	0.52
Price Range	99.44-70.57	99.44-70.57	87.70-68.67	85.30-54.64	64.13-49.19	55.08-39.26	50.08-27.38	27.86-18.90
P/E Ratio	39.78-28.23	42.68-30.29	36.24-28.38	44.66-28.61	49.33-37.84	31.47-22.43	31.90-17.44	24.23-16.43
Average Yield %	0.60	0.61	0.64	0.67	0.79	0.90	1.04	1.54

Address: 530 Herman O. West Drive, Exton, PA 19341-0645 **Telephone:** 610-594-2900	**Web Site:** www.westpharma.com **Officers:** Eric M. Green - President, Chief Executive Officer Annette F. Favorite - Senior Vice President, Chief Human Resources Officer	**Auditors:** PricewaterhouseCoopers LLP **Investor Contact:** 610-594-3345 **Transfer Agents:** Broadbridge Corporate Issuer Solutions, Philadelphia, PA

WESTAR ENERGY INC

Exchange	Symbol	Price	52Wk Range	Yield	P/E	Div Achiever
NYS	WR	$52.80 (12/29/2017)	57.21-49.41	3.03	21.91	13 Years

*7 Year Price Score 108.56 *NYSE Composite Index=100 *12 Month Price Score 97.41

Interim Earnings (Per Share)

Qtr.	Mar	Jun	Sep	Dec
2014	0.52	0.40	1.10	0.31
2015	0.38	0.46	0.97	0.27
2016	0.46	0.51	1.08	0.38
2017	0.42	0.50	1.11	...

Interim Dividends (Per Share)

Amt	Decl	Ex	Rec	Pay
0.40Q	02/22/2017	03/07/2017	03/09/2017	04/03/2017
0.40Q	05/18/2017	06/07/2017	06/09/2017	07/03/2017
0.40Q	08/25/2017	09/07/2017	09/08/2017	10/02/2017
0.40Q	11/22/2017	12/07/2017	12/08/2017	01/02/2018

Indicated Div: $1.60 (Div. Reinv. Plan)

Valuation Analysis

Valuation Analysis		Institutional Holding	
Forecast EPS	$2.45	No of Institutions	
	(01/11/2018)	515	
Market Cap	$7.5 Billion	Shares	
Book Value	$3.9 Billion	138,991,552	
Price/Book	1.91	% Held	
Price/Sales	2.90	75.10	

TRADING VOLUME (thousand shares)

Business Summary: Electric Utilities (MIC: 3.1.1 SIC: 4931 NAIC: 221210)

Westar Energy is an electric utility in Kansas. As of Dec 31 2016, Co. provided electric generation, transmission and distribution services to approximately 704,000 customers in Kansas. Co. provides these services in central and northeastern Kansas, including the cities of Topeka, Lawrence, Manhattan, Salina and Hutchinson. Kansas Gas and Electric Company, Co.'s wholly owned subsidiary, provides these services in south-central and southeastern Kansas, including the city of Wichita. Co. also supplies electric energy at wholesale to municipalities and electric cooperatives in Kansas, and has contracts for the sale or purchase of wholesale electricity with other utilities.

Recent Developments: For the quarter ended Sep 30 2017, net income increased 1.4% to US$160.7 million from US$158.6 million in the year-earlier quarter. Revenues were US$794.3 million, up 3.9% from US$764.7 million the year before. Operating income was US$260.0 million versus US$270.6 million in the prior-year quarter, a decrease of 3.9%. Direct operating expenses rose 10.6% to US$332.2 million from US$300.4 million in the comparable period the year before. Indirect operating expenses increased 4.3% to US$202.1 million from US$193.7 million in the equivalent prior-year period.

Prospects: Our evaluation of Westar Energy Inc. as of Jan. 14, 2018 is the result of our systematic analysis on three basic characteristics: earnings strength, relative valuation, and recent stock price movement. The company has enjoyed a very positive trend in earnings per share over the past 5 quarters and while recent estimates for the company have been mixed, WR has posted better than expected results. Based on operating earnings yield, the company is undervalued when compared to all of the companies in our coverage universe. Share price changes over the past year indicates that WR will perform well over the near term.

Financial Data

(US$ in Thousands)	9 Mos	6 Mos	3 Mos	12/31/2016	12/31/2015	12/31/2014	12/31/2013	12/31/2012
Earnings Per Share	2.41	2.38	2.39	2.43	2.09	2.35	2.27	2.15
Cash Flow Per Share	6.12	6.02	5.76	5.77	5.18	6.34	5.51	4.72
Tang Book Value Per Share	27.65	26.92	26.79	26.84	25.87	25.02	23.88	22.89
Dividends Per Share	1.580	1.560	1.540	1.520	1.440	1.400	1.360	1.320
Dividend Payout %	65.56	65.55	64.44	62.55	68.90	59.57	59.91	61.40
Income Statement								
Total Revenue	1,976,222	1,181,895	572,574	2,562,087	2,459,164	2,601,703	2,370,654	2,261,470
EBITDA	576,809	303,231	138,084	1,024,166	918,498	920,513	856,651	832,735
Depn & Amortn	35,773	22,120	12,596	316,700	287,900	263,800	249,900	247,800
Income Before Taxes	412,804	196,337	84,393	545,740	453,796	473,595	424,584	408,598
Income Taxes	112,559	56,816	20,911	184,540	152,000	151,270	123,721	126,136
Net Income	290,032	131,726	59,661	346,577	291,929	313,259	292,520	275,146
Average Shares	142,516	142,596	142,695	142,474	139,278	132,824	128,298	126,898
Balance Sheet								
Current Assets	733,049	740,226	721,100	768,382	717,141	700,922	706,798	643,075
Total Assets	11,625,375	11,596,150	11,515,590	11,487,074	10,705,666	10,347,001	9,597,111	9,265,231
Current Liabilities	686,846	774,172	766,738	1,047,193	836,935	849,631	955,399	846,141
Long-Term Obligations	3,768,285	3,768,833	3,768,415	3,499,879	3,302,047	3,382,104	3,163,760	3,042,014
Total Liabilities	7,696,372	7,770,621	7,709,797	7,681,199	7,048,945	7,052,145	6,534,337	6,369,091
Stockholders' Equity	3,929,003	3,825,529	3,805,793	3,805,875	3,656,721	3,294,856	3,062,774	2,896,140
Shares Outstanding	142,094	142,093	142,047	141,791	141,353	131,687	128,254	126,503
Statistical Record								
Return on Assets %	3.01	3.02	3.05	3.11	2.77	3.14	3.10	3.06
Return on Equity %	8.90	9.05	9.11	9.26	8.40	9.85	9.82	9.65
EBITDA Margin %	29.19	25.66	24.12	39.97	37.35	35.38	36.14	36.82
Net Margin %	14.68	11.15	10.42	13.53	11.87	12.04	12.34	12.17
Asset Turnover	0.23	0.23	0.23	0.23	0.23	0.26	0.25	0.25
Current Ratio	1.07	0.96	0.94	0.73	0.86	0.82	0.74	0.76
Debt to Equity	0.96	0.99	0.99	0.92	0.90	1.03	1.03	1.05
Price Range	57.38-49.41	57.38-50.87	57.38-49.28	57.38-40.38	43.96-34.11	42.93-31.77	34.96-28.62	30.97-26.90
P/E Ratio	23.81-20.50	24.11-21.37	24.01-20.62	23.61-16.62	21.03-16.32	18.27-13.52	15.40-12.61	14.40-12.51
Average Yield %	2.94	2.84	2.81	2.90	3.73	3.89	4.28	4.58

Address: 818 South Kansas Avenue, Topeka, KS 66612	**Web Site:** www.WestarEnergy.com	**Auditors:** Deloitte & Touche LLP
Telephone: 785-575-6300	**Officers:** Charles Q. Chandler - Chairman Mark A. Ruelle - President, Chief Executive Officer, Chief Financial Officer	**Investor Contact:** 785-575-8227
		Transfer Agents: Continental Stock Transfer & Trust Company, New York, NY

WABCO HOLDINGS INC

Exchange	Symbol	Price	52Wk Range	Yield	P/E
NYS	WBC	$143.50 (12/29/2017)	155.08-104.21	N/A	25.95

*7 Year Price Score 111.56 *NYSE Composite Index=100 *12 Month Price Score 105.73

TRADING VOLUME (thousand shares)

Interim Earnings (Per Share)

Qtr.	Mar	Jun	Sep	Dec
2014	1.12	1.23	1.37	1.10
2015	1.22	1.12	0.67	1.70
2016	(0.24)	1.33	1.76	1.14
2017	1.48	1.61	1.30	...

Interim Dividends (Per Share)

No Dividends Paid

Valuation Analysis

		Institutional Holding	
Forecast EPS	$6.65	No of Institutions	
	(01/18/2018)	459	
Market Cap	$7.7 Billion	Shares	
Book Value	$951.5 Million	59,315,528	
Price/Book	8.09	% Held	
Price/Sales	2.50	91.05	

Business Summary: Construction Services (MIC: 7.5.4 SIC: 3711 NAIC: 336111)

WABCO engineers, develops, manufactures and sells systems controlling braking, stability, suspension, transmission automation, air compression and processing primarily for commercial vehicle. Co.'s key products include pneumatic anti-lock braking systems, electronic braking systems, electronic stability control, brake controls, automated manual transmission systems, and mechanical products such as air compressors and air control valves. Co. supplies commercial vehicle aftermarket distributors and service partners as well as fleet operators with replacement parts, fleet management solutions, diagnostic tools, training and other services. Co. provides remanufacturing services globally.

Recent Developments: For the quarter ended Sep 30 2017, net income decreased 25.9% to US$74.3 million from US$100.3 million in the year-earlier quarter. Revenues were US$827.8 million, up 22.6% from US$675.4 million the year before. Operating income was US$93.2 million versus US$87.8 million in the prior-year quarter, an increase of 6.2%. Direct operating expenses rose 25.3% to US$578.2 million from US$461.4 million in the comparable period the year before. Indirect operating expenses increased 23.9% to US$156.4 million from US$126.2 million in the equivalent prior-year period.

Prospects: Our evaluation of WABCO Holdings Inc. as of Jan. 14, 2018 is the result of our systematic analysis on three basic characteristics: earnings strength, relative valuation, and recent stock price movement. The company has managed to produce a neutral trend in earnings per share over the past 5 quarters and while recent estimates for the company have been raised by analysts, WBC has posted better than expected results. Based on operating earnings yield, the company is about fairly valued when compared to all of the companies in our coverage universe. Share price changes over the past year indicates that WBC will perform well over the near term.

Financial Data

(US$ in Thousands)	9 Mos	6 Mos	3 Mos	12/31/2016	12/31/2015	12/31/2014	12/31/2013	12/31/2012
Earnings Per Share	5.53	5.99	5.71	3.98	4.72	4.81	10.31	4.62
Cash Flow Per Share	6.40	6.30	6.75	7.26	6.84	5.25	10.66	5.59
Tang Book Value Per Share	6.83	6.26	5.13	4.10	6.10	5.86	11.85	4.23
Income Statement								
Total Revenue	2,370,100	1,542,300	747,300	2,810,000	2,627,500	2,851,000	2,720,500	2,477,400
EBITDA	374,800	258,500	127,800	455,000	369,200	434,400	703,500	396,400
Depn & Amortn	92,500	60,600	30,000	98,000	96,700	101,600	85,200	76,900
Income Before Taxes	270,700	190,000	93,900	344,300	265,400	333,000	623,200	318,000
Income Taxes	43,700	29,300	15,300	121,800	11,500	55,600	(21,000)	23,600
Net Income	237,800	167,900	80,700	223,000	275,200	291,500	653,200	302,000
Average Shares	53,866	54,158	54,513	55,981	58,274	60,546	63,382	65,323
Balance Sheet								
Current Assets	2,227,700	2,043,600	1,951,800	1,874,000	1,386,400	1,182,500	1,234,600	792,600
Total Assets	3,618,400	3,284,000	3,136,600	3,056,000	2,589,900	2,432,700	2,392,800	1,747,000
Current Liabilities	742,300	570,300	563,000	530,900	464,800	417,700	485,400	445,700
Long-Term Obligations	1,016,000	1,000,900	967,100	958,900	498,700	307,100	47,000	...
Total Liabilities	2,666,900	2,440,100	2,375,700	2,354,600	1,803,200	1,591,100	1,240,000	1,070,600
Stockholders' Equity	951,500	843,900	760,900	701,400	-786,700	841,600	1,152,800	676,400
Shares Outstanding	53,646	53,623	54,103	54,491	56,759	58,425	61,359	62,747
Statistical Record								
Return on Assets %	9.12	10.81	10.78	7.88	10.96	12.08	31.56	17.87
Return on Equity %	34.48	41.55	42.15	29.89	33.80	29.23	71.42	47.67
EBITDA Margin %	15.81	16.76	17.10	16.19	14.05	15.24	25.86	16.00
Net Margin %	10.03	10.89	10.80	7.94	10.47	10.22	24.01	12.19
Asset Turnover	0.93	0.96	0.98	0.99	1.05	1.18	1.31	1.47
Current Ratio	3.00	3.58	3.47	3.53	2.98	2.83	2.54	1.78
Debt to Equity	1.07	1.19	1.27	1.37	0.63	0.36	0.04	...
Price Range	150.98-96.60	127.51-87.00	117.70-87.00	113.91-84.83	133.21-94.54	110.68-84.36	93.41-62.66	65.19-44.66
P/E Ratio	27.30-17.47	21.29-14.52	20.61-15.24	28.62-21.31	28.22-20.03	23.01-17.54	9.06-6.08	14.11-9.67

Address: Chaussée de la Hulpe 166, Brussels, 48309-3511 Telephone: 266-398-00 Fax: 267-543-42	Web Site: www.wabco-auto.com Officers: Jacques R. Esculier - Chairman, Chief Executive Officer Sean Deason - Vice President, Assistant Secretary, Controller	Auditors: Ernst & Young Bedrijfsrevisoren BCVBA/ Reviseurs d'Entreprises SCCRL Investor Contact: 732-369-7477

WESTERN UNION CO

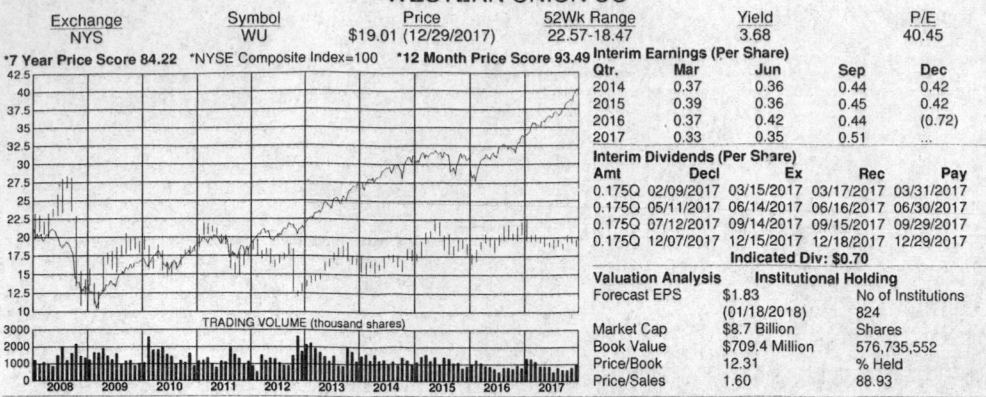

Exchange	Symbol	Price	52Wk Range	Yield	P/E
NYS	WU	$19.01 (12/29/2017)	22.57-18.47	3.68	40.45

*7 Year Price Score 84.22 ***NYSE Composite Index=100** ***12 Month Price Score 93.49**

Interim Earnings (Per Share)

Qtr.	Mar	Jun	Sep	Dec
2014	0.37	0.36	0.44	0.42
2015	0.39	0.36	0.45	0.42
2016	0.37	0.42	0.44	(0.72)
2017	0.33	0.35	0.51	...

Interim Dividends (Per Share)

Amt	Decl	Ex	Rec	Pay
0.175Q	02/09/2017	03/15/2017	03/17/2017	03/31/2017
0.175Q	05/11/2017	06/14/2017	06/16/2017	06/30/2017
0.175Q	07/12/2017	09/14/2017	09/15/2017	09/29/2017
0.175Q	12/07/2017	12/15/2017	12/18/2017	12/29/2017

Indicated Div: $0.70

Valuation Analysis

Forecast EPS	$1.83	**Institutional Holding**
	(01/18/2018)	No of Institutions: 824
Market Cap	$8.7 Billion	Shares
Book Value	$709.4 Million	576,735,552
Price/Book	12.31	% Held
Price/Sales	1.60	88.93

TRADING VOLUME (thousand shares)

Business Summary: Business Services (MIC: 7.5.2 SIC: 7389 NAIC: 522320)

Western Union is a holding company. Through its subsidiaries, Co. is engaged in money movement and payment services. Co.'s segments are consumer-to-consumer, which facilitates money transfers between two consumers, through a network of third-party agents; consumer-to-business, which facilitates bill payments from consumers to businesses and other organizations, including utilities, auto finance companies, mortgage servicers, financial service providers and government agencies; and business solutions, which facilitates payment and foreign exchange solutions, primarily cross-border, cross-currency transactions, for small and medium size enterprises and other organizations and individuals.

Recent Developments: For the quarter ended Sep 30 2017, net income increased 8.6% to US$235.6 million from US$216.9 million in the year-earlier quarter. Revenues were US$1.40 billion, up 2.0% from US$1.38 billion the year before. Operating income was US$271.6 million versus US$278.3 million in the prior-year quarter, a decrease of 2.4%. Direct operating expenses rose 2.2% to US$841.1 million from US$822.9 million in the comparable period the year before. Indirect operating expenses increased 5.6% to US$292.0 million from US$276.6 million in the equivalent prior-year period.

Prospects: Our evaluation of Western Union Co as of Jan. 14, 2018 is the result of our systematic analysis on three basic characteristics: earnings strength, relative valuation, and recent stock price movement. The company has produced a positive trend in earnings per share over the past 5 quarters and while recent estimates for the company have remained steady, WU has posted better than expected results. Based on operating earnings yield, the company is undervalued when compared to all of the companies in our coverage universe. Share price changes over the past year indicates that WU will perform poorly over the near term.

Financial Data

(US$ in Thousands)	9 Mos	6 Mos	3 Mos	12/31/2016	12/31/2015	12/31/2014	12/31/2013	12/31/2012
Earnings Per Share	0.47	0.40	0.47	0.51	1.62	1.59	1.43	1.69
Cash Flow Per Share	1.39	1.13	1.91	2.12	2.09	1.96	1.96	1.95
Dividends Per Share	0.685	0.670	0.655	0.640	0.620	0.500	0.500	0.425
Dividend Payout %	145.74	167.50	139.36	125.49	38.27	31.45	34.97	25.15
Income Statement								
Total Revenue	4,086,000	2,681,300	1,302,400	5,422,900	5,483,700	5,607,200	5,542,000	5,664,800
EBITDA	934,200	593,600	309,700	564,900	1,166,500	1,199,900	1,177,300	1,404,600
Depn & Amortn	197,100	131,600	66,400	74,200	67,700	66,600	64,200	61,700
Income Before Taxes	636,700	397,500	213,100	341,700	941,800	968,200	926,900	1,168,800
Income Taxes	72,900	69,300	51,400	88,500	104,000	115,800	128,500	142,900
Net Income	563,800	328,200	161,700	253,200	837,800	852,400	798,400	1,025,900
Average Shares	465,400	472,000	483,400	493,500	516,700	536,800	559,700	607,400
Balance Sheet								
Current Assets	1,034,700	1,059,200	1,323,300	1,004,400	1,399,300	1,846,200	2,157,000	1,849,000
Total Assets	9,873,600	9,408,200	9,486,000	9,419,600	9,458,900	9,890,400	10,121,300	9,465,700
Current Liabilities	1,305,000	1,372,600	1,686,200	1,622,800	1,090,700	1,071,700	1,200,100	1,157,100
Long-Term Obligations	3,283,400	3,182,400	3,180,900	2,786,100	3,225,600	3,720,400	4,213,000	4,029,200
Total Liabilities	9,164,200	8,747,000	8,735,700	8,517,400	8,054,000	8,590,000	9,016,600	8,525,100
Stockholders' Equity	709,400	661,200	750,300	902,200	1,404,900	1,300,400	1,104,700	940,600
Shares Outstanding	459,300	464,300	472,000	481,500	502,400	521,500	548,800	572,100
Statistical Record								
Return on Assets %	2.15	2.02	2.42	2.68	8.66	8.52	8.15	11.04
Return on Equity %	19.91	19.24	23.04	21.89	61.94	70.88	78.07	111.48
EBITDA Margin %	22.86	22.14	23.78	10.42	21.27	21.40	21.24	24.80
Net Margin %	13.80	12.24	12.42	4.67	15.28	15.20	14.41	18.11
Asset Turnover	0.56	0.58	0.57	0.57	0.57	0.56	0.57	0.61
Current Ratio	0.79	0.77	0.78	0.62	1.28	1.72	1.80	1.60
Debt to Equity	4.63	4.81	4.24	3.09	2.30	2.86	3.81	4.28
Price Range	22.57-18.47	22.57-18.78	22.57-18.11	22.14-16.44	22.56-16.96	18.58-15.15	19.37-13.36	19.73-11.95
P/E Ratio	48.02-39.30	56.42-46.95	48.02-38.53	43.41-32.24	13.93-10.47	11.69-9.53	13.55-9.34	11.67-7.07
Average Yield %	3.44	3.31	3.23	3.25	3.19	2.98	3.05	2.52

Address: 12500 East Belford Avenue, Englewood, CO 80112	Web Site: www.westernunion.com	Auditors: Ernst & Young LLP
Telephone: 866-405-5012	Officers: Hikmet Ersek - President, Chief Executive Officer Rajesh K. Agrawal - Executive Vice President, Chief Financial Officer, Acting Chief Financial Officer, Division Officer	Transfer Agents: Wells Fargo Bank, National Association, South St. Paul, MN

WESTLAKE CHEMICAL CORP

Exchange	Symbol	Price	52Wk Range	Yield	P/E	Div Achiever
NYS	WLK	$106.53 (12/29/2017)	106.53-57.29	0.79	23.11	12 Years

*7 Year Price Score 110.44 *NYSE Composite Index=100 *12 Month Price Score 124.35

Interim Earnings (Per Share)

Qtr.	Mar	Jun	Sep	Dec
2014	1.18	1.26	1.25	1.38
2015	1.10	1.54	1.39	0.84
2016	0.94	0.85	0.51	0.77
2017	1.06	1.17	1.61	...

Interim Dividends (Per Share)

Amt	Decl	Ex	Rec	Pay
0.191Q	02/17/2017	02/24/2017	02/28/2017	03/14/2017
0.191Q	05/19/2017	05/25/2017	05/30/2017	06/13/2017
0.21Q	08/18/2017	08/30/2017	09/01/2017	09/18/2017
0.21Q	11/17/2017	11/24/2017	11/27/2017	12/11/2017

Indicated Div: $0.84

Valuation Analysis / **Institutional Holding**

Forecast EPS	$5.55	No of Institutions
(01/18/2018)		337
Market Cap	$13.8 Billion	Shares
Book Value	$4.1 Billion	44,533,680
Price/Book	3.38	% Held
Price/Sales	1.77	27.99

Business Summary: Specialty Chemicals (MIC: 8.3.2 SIC: 2869 NAIC: 325211)

Westlake Chemical operates a manufacturer and marketer of basic chemicals, vinyls, polymers and building products. Co. operates in two operating segments: Olefins and Vinyls. The Olefins segment manufactures and markets polyethylene, styrene monomer and various ethylene co-products. The Vinyls segment manufactures and markets polyvinyl chloride (PVC), vinyl chloride monomer, ethylene dichloride, chlor-alkali (chlorine and caustic soda), chlorinated derivative products and ethylene. Co. also manufactures and sells products fabricated from PVC, including siding, pipe, fittings, profiles, trim, mouldings, fence and decking products, window and door components and film and sheet products.

Recent Developments: For the quarter ended Sep 30 2017, net income increased 213.0% to US$219.2 million from US$70.0 million in the year-earlier quarter. Revenues were US$2.11 billion, up 64.9% from US$1.28 billion the year before. Operating income was US$365.7 million versus US$46.6 million in the prior-year quarter, an increase of 685.5%. Direct operating expenses rose 49.6% to US$1.61 billion from US$1.08 billion in the comparable period the year before. Indirect operating expenses decreased 15.0% to US$132.3 million from US$155.6 million in the equivalent prior-year period.

Prospects: Our evaluation of Westlake Chemical Corp. as of Jan. 14, 2018 is the result of our systematic analysis on three basic characteristics: earnings strength, relative valuation, and recent stock price movement. The company has enjoyed a very positive trend in earnings per share over the past 5 quarters and while recent estimates for the company have been raised by analysts, WLK has posted better than expected results. Based on operating earnings yield, the company is undervalued when compared to all of the companies in our coverage universe. Share price changes over the past year indicates that WLK will perform well over the near term.

Financial Data

(US$ in Thousands)	9 Mos	6 Mos	3 Mos	12/31/2016	12/31/2015	12/31/2014	12/31/2013	12/31/2012
Earnings Per Share	4.61	3.51	3.19	3.06	4.86	5.07	4.54	2.88
Cash Flow Per Share	9.70	7.31	6.69	6.43	8.18	7.76	5.65	4.69
Tang Book Value Per Share	17.47	15.63	15.03	13.88	23.44	20.27	16.95	13.63
Dividends Per Share	0.782	0.762	0.753	0.744	0.693	0.582	0.412	2.136
Dividend Payout %	16.96	21.72	23.61	24.32	14.26	11.48	9.08	74.30
Income Statement								
Total Revenue	6,030,666	3,921,777	1,942,616	5,075,456	4,463,336	4,415,350	3,759,484	3,571,041
EBITDA	1,211,190	726,410	354,995	931,091	1,195,092	1,286,092	1,081,476	743,688
Depn & Amortn	338,016	219,463	114,626	305,273	209,271	174,173	129,222	120,924
Income Before Taxes	755,968	428,199	200,593	554,766	957,199	1,078,035	937,258	583,725
Income Taxes	232,690	124,071	55,883	138,520	298,396	398,902	331,747	199,614
Net Income	501,849	291,017	138,190	398,859	646,010	678,523	610,425	385,555
Average Shares	129,888	129,786	129,692	129,974	132,301	133,643	133,779	133,282
Balance Sheet								
Current Assets	2,699,533	2,377,635	2,251,288	2,408,316	2,175,189	2,011,287	1,649,082	1,751,413
Total Assets	11,244,125	10,885,707	10,724,830	10,890,253	5,575,252	5,213,990	4,060,909	3,412,196
Current Liabilities	1,170,276	1,030,921	943,431	1,183,083	522,642	537,180	404,858	398,510
Long-Term Obligations	3,349,402	3,489,900	3,601,642	3,678,654	764,115	763,997	763,879	763,761
Total Liabilities	7,175,351	7,044,870	7,065,634	7,366,624	2,309,374	2,302,479	1,642,306	1,539,940
Stockholders' Equity	4,068,774	3,840,837	3,659,196	3,523,629	3,265,878	2,911,511	2,418,603	1,872,256
Shares Outstanding	129,099	129,052	129,043	128,925	130,218	132,891	133,327	133,805
Statistical Record								
Return on Assets %	5.43	5.42	5.03	4.83	11.98	14.63	16.34	11.51
Return on Equity %	15.96	12.52	11.72	11.72	20.92	25.46	28.45	21.19
EBITDA Margin %	20.08	18.52	18.27	18.34	26.78	29.13	28.77	20.83
Net Margin %	8.32	7.42	7.11	7.86	14.47	15.37	16.24	10.80
Asset Turnover	0.70	0.83	0.73	0.61	0.83	0.95	1.01	1.07
Current Ratio	2.31	2.31	2.39	2.04	4.16	3.74	4.07	4.39
Debt to Equity	0.82	0.91	0.98	1.04	0.23	0.26	0.32	0.41
Price Range	83.55-49.84	67.34-41.21	67.21-39.88	59.17-39.88	78.59-49.82	97.96-53.67	61.03-39.31	40.05-20.43
P/E Ratio	18.12-10.81	19.19-11.74	21.07-12.50	19.34-13.03	16.17-10.25	19.32-10.59	13.44-8.66	13.90-7.09
Average Yield %	1.23	1.43	1.43	1.53	1.10	0.78	0.84	6.67

Address: 2801 Post Oak Boulevard, Suite 600, Houston, TX 77056	Web Site: www.westlake.com	Auditors: PricewaterhouseCoopers LLP
Telephone: 713-960-9111	Officers: James Chao - Chairman Albert Chao - President, Chief Executive Officer	Transfer Agents: American Stock Transfer & Trust Company, New York, NY

WESTROCK CO

Exchange	Symbol	Price	52Wk Range	Yield	P/E
NYS	WRK	$63.21 (12/29/2017)	64.42-49.34	2.72	22.82

*7 Year Price Score N/A   ***NYSE Composite Index=100**   ***12 Month Price Score 103.78**

Interim Earnings (Per Share)

Qtr.	Dec	Mar	Jun	Sep
2014-15	0.88	0.77	1.10	0.19
2015-16	(1.76)	0.22	0.36	(0.36)
2016-17	0.32	0.40	1.29	0.76

Interim Dividends (Per Share)

Amt	Decl	Ex	Rec	Pay
0.40Q	01/27/2017	02/08/2017	02/10/2017	02/20/2017
0.40Q	04/20/2017	05/03/2017	05/05/2017	05/15/2017
0.40Q	07/28/2017	08/09/2017	08/11/2017	08/21/2017
0.43Q	10/27/2017	11/09/2017	11/10/2017	11/20/2017

Indicated Div: $1.72

Valuation Analysis   Institutional Holding

Forecast EPS	$3.73	No of Institutions	
	(01/16/2018)	591	
Market Cap	$16.1 Billion	Shares	
Book Value	$10.3 Billion	250,059,632	
Price/Book	1.56	% Held	
Price/Sales	1.08	N/A	

Business Summary: Containers & Packaging (MIC: 8.1.3 SIC: 2653 NAIC: 322211)

WestRock is a provider of paper and packaging solutions for consumer and corrugated packaging markets. Co.'s segments include: Corrugated Packaging, in which Co. operates an integrated corrugated packaging system that manufactures containerboard, corrugated sheets, corrugated packaging and preprinted linerboard for sale to consumer and industrial products manufacturers and corrugated box manufacturers; Consumer Packaging, in which Co. operates integrated virgin and recycled fiber paperboard mills and consumer packaging converting operations; Land and Development, in which Co. develops and sells real estate primarily in the Charleston, SC region.

Recent Developments: For the year ended Sep 30 2017, income from continuing operations increased 351.3% to US$698.6 million from US$154.8 million a year earlier. Net income amounted to US$698.6 million versus a net loss of US$389.9 million in the prior year. Revenues were US$14.86 billion, up 4.9% from US$14.17 billion the year before. Operating income was US$835.0 million versus US$430.3 million in the prior year, an increase of 94.1%. Direct operating expenses rose 6.2% to US$12.12 billion from US$11.41 billion in the comparable period the year before. Indirect operating expenses decreased 18.2% to US$1.91 billion from US$2.33 billion in the equivalent prior-year period.

Prospects: Our evaluation of WestRock Co. as of Jan. 14, 2018 is the result of our systematic analysis on three basic characteristics: earnings strength, relative valuation, and recent stock price movement. The company has produced a positive trend in earnings per share over the past 5 quarters. Because the company lacks sufficient analyst estimate data, we place greater weight on the historical EPS trend as the measure of earnings strength. Based on operating earnings yield, the company is about fairly valued when compared to all of the companies in our coverage universe. Share price changes over the past year indicates that WRK will perform in line with the market over the near term.

Financial Data

(US$ in Thousands)	09/30/2017	09/30/2016	09/30/2015	09/30/2014	09/30/2013
Earnings Per Share	2.77	(1.54)	2.93	3.29	4.98
Cash Flow Per Share	7.54	6.63	7.06	8.02	7.17
Tang Book Value Per Share	5.83	9.37	9.36	12.07	...
Dividends Per Share	1.600	1.500	0.375	0.700	0.525
Dividend Payout %	57.76	...	12.80	21.28	10.54
Income Statement					
Total Revenue	14,859,700	14,171,800	11,381,300	9,895,100	9,545,400
EBITDA	1,952,200	1,340,500	1,477,700	1,338,500	1,274,300
Depn & Amortn	855,900	848,900	589,800	481,700	461,300
Income Before Taxes	818,600	234,900	755,200	761,500	706,100
Income Taxes	159,000	89,800	250,500	286,500	(21,800)
Net Income	708,200	(396,300)	507,100	479,700	727,300
Average Shares	255,700	257,900	173,300	146,000	146,100
Balance Sheet					
Current Assets	4,490,900	3,912,600	4,160,400	2,432,500	...
Total Assets	25,089,000	23,038,200	25,356,800	11,039,700	...
Current Liabilities	3,009,800	2,183,000	2,163,200	1,360,500	...
Long-Term Obligations	5,946,100	5,496,300	5,558,300	2,852,100	...
Total Liabilities	14,746,500	13,309,400	13,705,000	6,732,900	...
Stockholders' Equity	10,342,500	9,728,800	11,651,800	4,306,800	...
Shares Outstanding	254,500	251,000	257,000	140,000	...
Statistical Record					
Return on Assets %	2.94	N.M.	2.79	...	...
Return on Equity %	7.06	N.M.	6.36	...	...
EBITDA Margin %	13.14	9.46	12.98	13.53	13.35
Net Margin %	4.77	N.M.	4.46	4.85	7.62
Asset Turnover	0.62	0.58	0.63	...	...
Current Ratio	1.49	1.79	1.92	1.79	...
Debt to Equity	0.57	0.56	0.48	0.66	...
Price Range	59.73-45.05	51.93-27.01	58.62-45.07	...	...
P/E Ratio	21.56-16.26	...	20.01-15.38	...	...
Average Yield %	3.00	3.73	0.70	...	...

Address: 501 South 5th Street, Richmond, VA 23219-0501 **Telephone:** 804-444-1000	**Web Site:** www.westrock.com **Officers:** John A. Luke - Chairman Steven C. Voorhees - President, Chief Executive Officer	**Auditors:** Ernst & Young LLP

WESTWOOD HOLDINGS GROUP, INC.

Exchange	Symbol	Price	52Wk Range	Yield	P/E	Div Achiever
NYS	WHG	$66.21 (12/29/2017)	70.84-51.60	4.11	22.22	14 Years

*7 Year Price Score 92.79   *NYSE Composite Index=100   *12 Month Price Score 103.88

Interim Earnings (Per Share)

Qtr.	Mar	Jun	Sep	Dec
2014	0.75	1.14	0.92	0.72
2015	0.71	1.23	0.87	0.55
2016	0.44	0.69	0.72	0.93
2017	0.73	0.83	0.49	...

Interim Dividends (Per Share)

Amt	Decl	Ex	Rec	Pay
0.62Q	02/08/2017	03/08/2017	03/10/2017	04/03/2017
0.62Q	04/26/2017	06/07/2017	06/09/2017	07/03/2017
0.62Q	06/26/2017	09/07/2017	09/08/2017	10/02/2017
0.68Q	10/25/2017	12/07/2017	12/08/2017	01/02/2018

Indicated Div: $2.72

Valuation Analysis   Institutional Holding

Forecast EPS	N/A	No of Institutions
		113
Market Cap	$588.2 Million	Shares
Book Value	$155.4 Million	6,836,141
Price/Book	3.78	% Held
Price/Sales	4.49	66.27

Business Summary: Wealth Management (MIC: 5.5.2 SIC: 6282 NAIC: 523930)

Westwood Holdings Group is a holding company. Co. manages investment assets and provides services via its subsidiaries. Westwood Management Corp., Westwood Advisors, LLC and Westwood International Advisors Inc. provide investment advisory services to institutional clients, Westwood Funds®, other mutual funds, an Ireland-domiciled fund formed pursuant to the European Union's Undertakings for Collective Investment in Transferable Securities, individuals and Westwood Trust's clients, while Westwood Trust provides trust and custodial services and participation in self-sponsored common trust funds to institutions and individuals. At Dec 31 2016, Co. had assets under management of $21.24 billion.

Recent Developments: For the quarter ended Sep 30 2017, net income decreased 29.8% to US$4.1 million from US$5.9 million in the year-earlier quarter. Revenues were US$33.5 million, up 5.4% from US$31.8 million the year before. Indirect operating expenses increased 22.1% to US$27.7 million from US$22.7 million in the equivalent prior-year period.

Prospects: Our evaluation of Westwood Holdings Group Inc. as of Jan. 14, 2018 is the result of our systematic analysis on three basic characteristics: earnings strength, relative valuation, and recent stock price movement. The company has generated a negative trend in earnings per share over the past 5 quarters. Because the company lacks sufficient analyst estimate data, we place greater weight on the historical EPS trend as the measure of earnings strength. Based on operating earnings yield, the company is undervalued when compared to all of the companies in our coverage universe. Share price changes over the past year indicates that WHG will perform in line with the market over the near term.

Financial Data

(US$ in Thousands)	9 Mos	6 Mos	3 Mos	12/31/2016	12/31/2015	12/31/2014	12/31/2013	12/31/2012
Earnings Per Share	2.98	3.21	3.07	2.77	3.33	3.45	2.34	1.65
Cash Flow Per Share	5.85	5.34	4.97	5.94	7.12	3.53	2.96	1.92
Tang Book Value Per Share	12.19	10.59	10.89	11.07	9.67	11.47	9.00	7.61
Dividends Per Share	2.480	2.430	2.380	2.330	2.070	1.820	1.640	1.510
Dividend Payout %	83.22	75.70	77.52	84.12	62.16	52.75	70.09	91.52
Income Statement								
Total Revenue	99,871	66,379	32,623	123,021	130,936	113,241	91,825	77,495
EBITDA	26,276	19,812	8,500	36,939	44,816	42,974	29,038	20,847
Depn & Amortn	2,171	1,459	730	2,929	2,596	938	769	821
Income Before Taxes	24,105	18,353	7,770	34,010	42,220	42,036	28,269	20,026
Income Taxes	7,013	5,393	1,706	11,363	15,115	14,787	10,378	7,936
Net Income	17,092	12,960	6,064	22,647	27,105	27,249	17,891	12,090
Average Shares	8,420	8,316	8,311	8,165	8,149	7,906	7,643	7,338
Balance Sheet								
Current Assets	130,697	113,783	103,006	115,957	117,604	118,764	96,189	77,370
Total Assets	191,362	175,932	166,104	179,678	181,336	139,874	116,020	96,615
Current Liabilities	32,383	21,227	18,077	29,668	44,853	27,204	24,853	18,826
Total Liabilities	35,933	24,608	21,268	33,609	47,369	29,867	27,387	20,064
Stockholders' Equity	155,429	151,324	144,836	146,069	133,967	110,007	88,633	76,551
Shares Outstanding	8,884	9,801	8,888	8,810	8,630	8,308	8,176	8,031
Statistical Record								
Return on Assets %	13.66	15.64	15.24	12.51	16.88	21.30	16.83	12.88
Return on Equity %	16.65	18.29	18.40	16.13	22.22	27.44	21.66	16.37
EBITDA Margin %	26.31	29.85	26.06	30.03	34.23	37.95	31.62	26.90
Net Margin %	17.11	19.52	18.59	18.41	20.70	24.06	19.48	15.60
Asset Turnover	0.73	0.76	0.77	0.68	0.82	0.89	0.86	0.83
Current Ratio	4.04	5.36	5.70	3.91	2.62	4.37	3.87	4.11
Price Range	67.27-49.99	63.60-49.66	63.60-49.66	63.60-42.20	64.07-50.37	67.84-51.72	61.91-39.97	40.92-34.15
P/E Ratio	22.57-16.78	19.81-15.47	20.72-16.18	22.96-15.23	19.24-15.13	19.66-14.99	26.46-17.08	24.80-20.70
Average Yield %	4.34	4.39	4.27	4.30	3.55	3.09	3.47	3.97

Address: 200 Crescent Court, Suite 1200, Dallas, TX 75201
Telephone: 214-756-6900

Web Site: www.westwoodgroup.com
Officers: Richard M. Frank - Chairman Susan M. Byrne - Vice-Chairman, Chief Investment Officer

Auditors: Deloitte & Touche LLP
Investor Contact: 214-756-6900
Transfer Agents: American Stock Transfer & Trust Company, Brooklyn, NY

WEX INC

Exchange	Symbol	Price	52Wk Range	Yield	P/E
NYS	WEX	$141.23 (12/29/2017)	141.23-98.27	N/A	71.69

*7 Year Price Score 102.11 *NYSE Composite Index=100 *12 Month Price Score 108.31

Interim Earnings (Per Share)

Qtr.	Mar	Jun	Sep	Dec
2014	0.93	1.11	1.91	1.22
2015	0.57	0.68	0.83	0.54
2016	0.59	0.32	0.46	0.10
2017	0.68	0.40	0.79	...

Interim Dividends (Per Share)

No Dividends Paid

Valuation Analysis		Institutional Holding	
Forecast EPS	$5.36	No of Institutions	
	(01/17/2018)	322	
Market Cap	$6.1 Billion	Shares	
Book Value	$1.6 Billion	59,206,848	
Price/Book	3.73	% Held	
Price/Sales	5.01	N/A	

Business Summary: Miscellaneous Consumer Services (MIC: 2.2.3 SIC: 7389 NAIC: 561499)

Wex is a provider of corporate card payment solutions. Co. operates in three business segments: Fleet Solutions, which provides customers with fleet vehicle payment processing services specifically designed for the needs of commercial and government fleets; Travel and Corporate Solutions, which focuses on the complex payment environment of business-to-business payments, providing customers with payment processing solutions for their corporate payment and transaction monitoring needs; and Health and Employee Benefit Solutions, which is a provider of integrated software-as-a-service technologies and services for healthcare premium billing, payment and workflow management.

Recent Developments: For the quarter ended Sep 30 2017, net income increased 76.3% to US$33.9 million from US$19.2 million in the year-earlier quarter. Revenues were US$324.0 million, up 12.6% from US$287.8 million the year before. Operating income was US$63.7 million versus US$54.6 million in the prior-year quarter, an increase of 16.8%. Direct operating expenses rose 24.1% to US$1.1 million from US$859,000 in the comparable period the year before. Indirect operating expenses increased 11.6% to US$259.2 million from US$232.3 million in the equivalent prior-year period.

Prospects: Our evaluation of Wex Inc. as of Jan. 14, 2018 is the result of our systematic analysis on three basic characteristics: earnings strength, relative valuation, and recent stock price movement. The company has produced a positive trend in earnings per share over the past 5 quarters and while recent estimates for the company have been mixed, WEX has posted better than expected results. Based on operating earnings yield, the company is about fairly valued when compared to all of the companies in our coverage universe. Share price changes over the past year indicates that WEX will perform poorly over the near term.

Financial Data

(US$ in Thousands)	9 Mos	6 Mos	3 Mos	12/31/2016	12/31/2015	12/31/2014	12/31/2013	12/31/2012
Earnings Per Share	1.97	1.64	1.56	1.48	2.62	5.18	3.82	2.48
Cash Flow Per Share	(2.70)	(4.33)	(6.92)	(3.69)	11.48	7.62	1.02	1.84
Income Statement								
Total Revenue	919,243	595,241	291,357	1,018,460	854,637	817,647	717,463	623,151
EBITDA	145,965	84,381	50,413	241,137	273,613	378,456	300,895	260,025
Depn & Amortn	5,935	4,163	1,954	141,650	83,077	70,380	58,208	48,852
Income Before Taxes	123,336	70,906	43,611	87,101	184,908	301,639	238,400	206,183
Income Taxes	43,760	25,190	14,535	29,625	75,296	101,621	90,102	109,474
Net Income	80,462	46,491	29,401	60,637	111,317	202,211	149,208	96,922
Average Shares	43,101	43,060	43,119	40,914	38,843	39,000	39,103	39,092
Balance Sheet								
Current Assets	3,033,822	2,828,671	2,585,200	2,353,813	1,881,325	2,198,131	2,073,547	1,753,476
Total Assets	6,541,128	6,343,751	6,175,762	5,997,097	3,857,946	4,118,347	3,433,043	3,106,684
Current Liabilities	2,287,720	2,181,093	2,005,597	2,067,520	1,408,241	1,542,736	1,710,209	1,537,266
Long-Term Obligations	2,412,296	2,389,691	2,391,733	2,204,903	1,201,819	1,354,539	685,000	621,000
Total Liabilities	4,916,620	4,772,434	4,634,819	4,499,908	2,774,702	3,058,022	2,530,265	2,288,753
Stockholders' Equity	1,624,508	1,571,317	1,540,943	1,497,189	1,083,244	1,060,325	902,778	817,931
Shares Outstanding	42,921	42,915	42,899	42,841	38,746	38,897	38,987	38,908
Statistical Record								
Return on Assets %	1.33	1.35	1.30	1.23	2.79	5.36	4.56	3.59
Return on Equity %	5.48	5.30	5.04	4.69	10.39	20.60	17.34	12.66
EBITDA Margin %	15.88	14.18	17.30	23.68	32.02	46.29	41.94	41.73
Net Margin %	8.75	7.81	10.09	5.95	13.03	24.73	20.80	15.55
Asset Turnover	0.19	0.22	0.21	0.21	0.21	0.22	0.22	0.23
Current Ratio	1.33	1.30	1.29	1.14	1.34	1.42	1.21	1.14
Debt to Equity	1.48	1.52	1.55	1.47	1.11	1.28	0.76	0.76
Price Range	119.28-98.27	119.28-88.00	119.28-79.43	116.44-58.09	118.50-84.66	118.43-79.93	100.38-67.91	75.37-53.29
P/E Ratio	60.55-49.88	72.73-53.66	76.46-50.92	78.68-39.25	45.23-32.31	22.86-15.43	26.28-17.78	30.39-21.49

Address: 97 Darling Avenue, South Portland, ME 04106
Telephone: 207-773-8171

Web Site: www.wrightexpress.com
Officers: Melissa D. Smith - President, Chief Executive Officer, Region Officer Kenneth W. Janosick - Senior Vice President, General Manager

Auditors: Deloitte & Touche LLP
Investor Contact: 866-230-1633
Transfer Agents: American Stock Transfer & Trust Company, Brooklyn, NY

WEYERHAEUSER CO

Exchange	Symbol	Price	52Wk Range	Yield	P/E
NYS	WY	$35.26 (12/29/2017)	36.55-30.21	3.63	30.40

*7 Year Price Score 91.87 *NYSE Composite Index=100 *12 Month Price Score 100.23

Interim Earnings (Per Share)

Qtr.	Mar	Jun	Sep	Dec
2014	0.31	0.47	2.15	0.35
2015	0.17	0.26	0.35	0.12
2016	0.11	0.21	0.30	0.75
2017	0.21	0.03	0.17	...

Interim Dividends (Per Share)

Amt	Decl	Ex	Rec	Pay
0.31Q	02/10/2017	03/01/2017	03/03/2017	03/17/2017
0.31Q	05/18/2017	06/07/2017	06/09/2017	06/23/2017
0.31Q	08/24/2017	09/07/2017	09/08/2017	09/22/2017
0.32Q	11/09/2017	11/30/2017	12/01/2017	12/15/2017

Indicated Div: $1.28

Valuation Analysis

		Institutional Holding	
Forecast EPS	$1.18 (01/12/2018)	No of Institutions	1209
Market Cap	$26.6 Billion	Shares	690,060,032
Book Value	$9.0 Billion	% Held	88.32
Price/Book	2.94		
Price/Sales	3.81		

Business Summary: REITs (MIC: 5.3.1 SIC: 6798 NAIC: 525930)

Weyerhaeuser is a real estate investment trust. As of Dec. 31, 2016, Co. manages 13.1 million acres of private commercial timberlands where Co. owns 12.0 million of those acres and have leases on the other 1.1 million acres. In addition, Co. has renewable, long-term licenses on 13.9 million acres of Canadian timberlands. Co. has three segments: Timberlands, which include grade logs, fiber logs, timber, recreational leases and other products; Real Estate, Energy and Natural Resources, which maximizes the value of Co.'s timberland ownership through development of oil, natural gas, minerals and wind resources; and Wood Products, where Co. manufactures and distributes wood products.

Recent Developments: For the quarter ended Sep 30 2017, income from continuing operations decreased 19.8% to US$130.0 million from US$162.0 million in the year-earlier quarter. Net income decreased 42.7% to US$130.0 million from US$227.0 million in the year-earlier quarter. Revenues were US$1.87 billion, up 9.5% from US$1.71 billion the year before.

Prospects: Our evaluation of Weyerhaeuser Co. as of Jan. 14, 2018 is the result of our systematic analysis on three basic characteristics: earnings strength, relative valuation, and recent stock price movement. The company has enjoyed a very positive trend in earnings per share over the past 5 quarters and while recent estimates for the company have been mixed, WY has posted better than expected results. Based on operating earnings yield, the company is about fairly valued when compared to all of the companies in our coverage universe. Share price changes over the past year indicates that WY will perform well over the near term.

Financial Data

(US$ in Thousands)	9 Mos	6 Mos	3 Mos	12/31/2016	12/31/2015	12/31/2014	12/31/2013	12/31/2012
Earnings Per Share	1.16	1.29	1.47	1.39	0.89	3.18	0.95	0.71
Cash Flow Per Share	0.92	0.96	0.96	1.02	2.06	1.95	1.77	1.07
Tang Book Value Per Share	11.96	12.02	12.21	12.21	9.43	10.01	11.55	7.43
Dividends Per Share	1.240	1.240	1.240	1.240	1.200	1.020	0.810	0.620
Dividend Payout %	106.90	96.12	84.35	89.21	134.83	32.08	85.26	87.32
Income Statement								
Total Revenue	5,373,000	3,501,000	1,693,000	6,365,000	7,082,000	7,403,000	8,529,000	7,059,000
EBITDA	1,003,000	682,000	404,000	1,068,000	1,233,000	1,820,000	1,219,000	1,191,000
Depn & Amortn	394,000	262,000	133,000	198,000	314,000	500,000	472,000	456,000
Income Before Taxes	341,000	239,000	181,000	482,000	608,000	1,013,000	434,000	439,000
Income Taxes	31,000	58,000	24,000	89,000	(3,000)	185,000	(129,000)	55,000
Net Income	311,000	181,000	157,000	1,027,000	506,000	1,826,000	563,000	385,000
Average Shares	756,903	756,451	754,747	722,401	519,618	560,899	571,239	542,310
Balance Sheet								
Current Assets	1,517,000	2,088,000	1,465,000	1,622,000	2,174,000	3,033,000	2,326,000	2,140,000
Total Assets	18,402,000	18,990,000	19,001,000	19,243,000	12,486,000	13,457,000	14,498,000	12,592,000
Current Liabilities	1,023,000	1,524,000	1,022,000	1,206,000	875,000	918,000	1,128,000	1,230,000
Long-Term Obligations	6,444,000	6,447,000	6,774,000	6,840,000	5,402,000	5,402,000	5,407,000	3,951,000
Total Liabilities	9,357,000	9,900,000	9,786,000	10,063,000	7,617,000	8,153,000	7,703,000	8,522,000
Stockholders' Equity	9,045,000	9,090,000	9,215,000	9,180,000	4,869,000	5,304,000	6,795,000	4,070,000
Shares Outstanding	753,050	752,711	751,410	748,528	510,483	524,474	583,548	542,392
Statistical Record								
Return on Assets %	4.38	4.68	5.41	6.46	3.90	13.06	4.16	3.05
Return on Equity %	9.45	10.36	11.32	14.58	9.95	30.18	10.36	9.22
EBITDA Margin %	18.67	19.48	23.86	16.78	17.41	24.58	14.29	16.87
Net Margin %	5.79	5.17	9.27	16.14	7.14	24.67	6.60	5.45
Asset Turnover	0.35	0.33	0.33	0.40	0.55	0.53	0.63	0.56
Current Ratio	1.48	1.37	1.43	1.34	2.48	3.30	2.06	1.74
Debt to Equity	0.71	0.71	0.74	0.75	1.11	1.02	0.80	0.97
Price Range	34.96-28.64	34.96-28.64	34.19-26.77	33.12-22.22	36.69-26.87	36.64-27.72	32.60-26.65	28.52-18.69
P/E Ratio	30.14-24.69	27.10-22.20	23.26-18.21	23.83-15.99	41.22-30.19	11.52-8.72	34.32-28.05	40.17-26.32
Average Yield %	3.82	3.86	3.95	4.13	3.79	3.20	2.73	2.68

Address: 220 Occidental Avenue South, Seattle, WA 98104-7800 **Telephone:** 206-539-3000	**Web Site:** www.weyerhaeuser.com **Officers:** Rick R. Holley - Chairman Doyle R. Simons - President, Chief Executive Officer
Auditors: KPMG LLP **Investor Contact:** 253-924-2058 **Transfer Agents:** Computershare Investor Services, Canton, MA	

WGL HOLDINGS INC

Exchange	Symbol	Price	52Wk Range	Yield	P/E	Div Achiever
NYS	WGL	$85.84 (12/29/2017)	85.99-74.19	2.38	22.95	40 Years

*7 Year Price Score 122.61 *NYSE Composite Index=100 *12 Month Price Score 96.30

Interim Earnings (Per Share)

Qtr.	Dec	Mar	Jun	Sep
2012-13	1.01	1.73	(0.19)	(1.00)
2013-14	0.36	1.18	(0.23)	0.74
2014-15	1.28	1.63	(0.32)	0.03
2015-16	1.36	2.11	0.04	(0.21)
2016-17	1.13	2.39	0.16	0.06

Interim Dividends (Per Share)

Amt	Decl	Ex	Rec	Pay
0.51Q	02/01/2017	04/06/2017	04/10/2017	05/01/2017
0.51Q	05/11/2017	07/06/2017	07/10/2017	08/01/2017
0.51Q	09/21/2017	10/06/2017	10/10/2017	11/01/2017
0.51Q	11/22/2017	01/09/2018	01/10/2018	02/01/2018

Indicated Div: $2.04 (Div. Reinv. Plan)

Valuation Analysis

		Institutional Holding	
Forecast EPS	$3.68	No of Institutions	
	(01/11/2018)	391	
Market Cap	$4.4 Billion	Shares	
Book Value	$1.5 Billion	50,796,060	
Price/Book	2.87	% Held	
Price/Sales	1.87	63.85	

Business Summary: Gas Utilities (MIC: 3.3.1 SIC: 4924 NAIC: 221210)

WGL Holdings is a holding company. Through its wholly owned subsidiaries, Co. sells and delivers natural gas and provide energy-related products and services to customers. Co.'s segments include regulated utility, which is a regulated public utility that sells and delivers natural gas to retail customers; retail energy-marketing, which sells wind and other renewable energy credits and carbon offsets to retail customers; commercial energy systems, which focuses on energy efficient solutions for its customers; and midstream energy services, which focuses in the investment, management, development and optimization of natural gas storage and transportation midstream infrastructure projects.

Recent Developments: For the year ended Sep 30 2017, net income increased 5.6% to US$177.9 million from US$168.4 million in the prior year. Revenues were US$2.35 billion, unchanged from the year before. Operating income was US$341.0 million versus US$300.3 million in the prior year, an increase of 13.6%. Direct operating expenses declined 3.6% to US$1.71 billion from US$1.77 billion in the comparable period the year before. Indirect operating expenses increased 9.8% to US$306.7 million from US$279.2 million in the equivalent prior-year period.

Prospects: Our evaluation of WGL Holdings Inc. as of Jan. 14, 2018 is the result of our systematic analysis on three basic characteristics: earnings strength, relative valuation, and recent stock price movement. The company has generated a negative trend in earnings per share over the past 5 quarters and while recent estimates for the company have been raised by analysts, WGL has posted better than expected results. Based on operating earnings yield, the company is about fairly valued when compared to all of the companies in our coverage universe. Share price changes over the past year indicates that WGL will perform well over the near term.

Financial Data

(US$ in Thousands)	09/30/2017	09/30/2016	09/30/2015	09/30/2014	09/30/2013	09/30/2012	09/30/2011	09/30/2010
Earnings Per Share	3.74	3.31	2.62	2.05	1.55	2.71	2.28	2.16
Cash Flow Per Share	4.50	4.51	10.12	7.38	6.15	4.21	5.78	5.76
Tang Book Value Per Share	29.34	26.93	25.00	24.61	24.62	24.60	23.41	22.63
Dividends Per Share	1.995	1.900	1.805	1.720	1.640	1.575	1.530	1.490
Dividend Payout %	53.34	57.40	68.89	83.90	105.81	58.12	67.11	68.98
Income Statement								
Total Revenue	2,354,724	2,349,559	2,659,830	2,780,947	2,466,138	2,425,310	2,751,501	2,708,876
EBITDA	497,915	440,701	385,810	311,326	273,097	369,166	347,449	323,292
Depn & Amortn	155,083	135,759	124,384	112,268	104,731	98,251	101,383	98,464
Income Before Taxes	268,806	252,632	210,915	161,320	132,355	234,487	205,520	184,761
Income Taxes	111,159	98,074	83,804	57,254	52,292	93,349	87,150	73,556
Net Income	193,940	168,914	132,579	107,260	81,573	141,138	118,370	111,205
Average Shares	51,475	50,564	50,060	51,770	51,808	51,589	51,295	50,765
Balance Sheet								
Current Assets	985,889	843,474	781,383	835,515	820,011	832,761	724,733	717,265
Total Assets	6,626,009	6,058,705	5,294,201	4,856,499	4,260,060	4,110,947	3,809,034	3,643,894
Current Liabilities	1,488,988	1,026,926	982,914	1,020,285	950,077	757,015	576,740	544,051
Long-Term Obligations	1,430,861	1,444,300	944,201	679,228	524,067	589,202	587,213	592,875
Total Liabilities	5,095,146	4,654,971	4,022,781	3,581,750	2,957,342	2,813,218	2,578,146	2,462,326
Stockholders' Equity	1,530,863	1,403,734	1,271,420	1,274,749	1,302,718	1,297,729	1,230,888	1,181,568
Shares Outstanding	51,219	51,080	49,728	50,656	51,774	51,611	51,365	50,974
Statistical Record								
Return on Assets %	3.06	2.97	2.61	2.35	1.95	3.55	3.18	3.18
Return on Equity %	13.22	12.59	10.41	8.32	6.27	11.13	9.81	9.64
EBITDA Margin %	21.15	18.76	14.51	11.19	11.07	15.22	12.63	11.93
Net Margin %	8.24	7.19	4.98	3.86	3.31	5.82	4.30	4.11
Asset Turnover	0.37	0.41	0.52	0.61	0.59	0.61	0.74	0.77
Current Ratio	0.66	0.82	0.79	0.82	0.86	1.10	1.26	1.32
Debt to Equity	0.93	1.03	0.74	0.53	0.40	0.45	0.48	0.50
Price Range	85.99-58.69	73.33-57.67	58.57-42.12	45.40-35.88	46.80-36.85	44.70-37.34	41.60-35.06	37.78-31.27
P/E Ratio	22.99-15.69	22.15-17.42	22.35-16.08	22.15-17.50	30.19-23.77	16.49-13.78	18.25-15.38	17.49-14.48
Average Yield %	2.53	2.90	3.37	4.24	3.89	3.85	4.01	4.35

Address: 101 Constitution Ave., N.W., Washington, DC 20080 Telephone: 703-750-2000	Web Site: www.wglholdings.com Officers: Terry D. McCallister - Chairman, Chief Executive Officer Adrian P. Chapman - President, Chief Operating Officer	Auditors: DELOITTE & TOUCHE LLP Investor Contact: 202-624-6129 Transfer Agents: Computershare, Pittsburgh, PA

WHIRLPOOL CORP

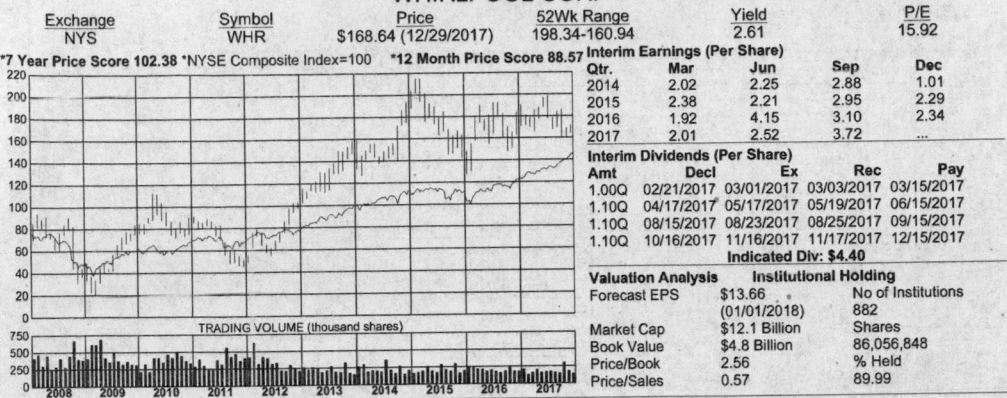

Exchange	Symbol	Price	52Wk Range	Yield	P/E
NYS	WHR	$168.64 (12/29/2017)	198.34-160.94	2.61	15.92

*7 Year Price Score 102.38 *NYSE Composite Index=100 *12 Month Price Score 88.57

Interim Earnings (Per Share)

Qtr.	Mar	Jun	Sep	Dec
2014	2.02	2.25	2.88	1.01
2015	2.38	2.21	2.95	2.29
2016	1.92	4.15	3.10	2.34
2017	2.01	2.52	3.72	...

Interim Dividends (Per Share)

Amt	Decl	Ex	Rec	Pay
1.00Q	02/21/2017	03/01/2017	03/03/2017	03/15/2017
1.10Q	04/17/2017	05/17/2017	05/19/2017	06/15/2017
1.10Q	08/15/2017	08/23/2017	08/25/2017	09/15/2017
1.10Q	10/16/2017	11/16/2017	11/17/2017	12/15/2017

Indicated Div: $4.40

Valuation Analysis

Forecast EPS	$13.66
	(01/01/2018)
Market Cap	$12.1 Billion
Book Value	$4.8 Billion
Price/Book	2.56
Price/Sales	0.57

Institutional Holding

No of Institutions	882
Shares	86,056,848
% Held	89.99

Business Summary: Household Appliances, Electronics & Goods (MIC: 1.5.1 SIC: 3639 NAIC: 335228)

Whirlpool manufactures and markets a line of home appliances and related products. Co.'s principal products are laundry appliances, refrigerators and freezers, cooking appliances, dishwashers, mixers and other small domestic appliances. Co. also produces hermetic compressors for refrigeration systems. Co. manufactures and markets products under brand names such as Whirlpool, KitchenAid, Maytag, Consul, Brastemp, Amana, Bauknecht, Jenn-Air, Indesit, and Hotpoint. Co.'s reportable segments consist of North America, Europe, Middle East and Africa, Latin America and Asia.

Recent Developments: For the quarter ended Sep 30 2017, net income increased 11.5% to US$272.0 million from US$244.0 million in the year-earlier quarter. Revenues were US$5.42 billion, up 3.2% from US$5.25 billion the year before. Operating income was US$331.0 million versus US$374.0 million in the prior-year quarter, a decrease of 11.5%. Direct operating expenses rose 4.5% to US$4.50 billion from US$4.31 billion in the comparable period the year before. Indirect operating expenses increased 3.2% to US$584.0 million from US$566.0 million in the equivalent prior-year period.

Prospects: Our evaluation of Whirlpool Corp. as of Jan. 14, 2018 is the result of our systematic analysis on three basic characteristics: earnings strength, relative valuation, and recent stock price movement. The company has produced a positive trend in earnings per share over the past 5 quarters. However, while recent estimates for the company have been lowered by analysts, WHR has posted results that fell short of analysts expectations. Based on operating earnings yield, the company is undervalued when compared to all of the companies in our coverage universe. Share price changes over the past year indicates that WHR will perform poorly over the near term.

Financial Data

(US$ in Thousands)	9 Mos	6 Mos	3 Mos	12/31/2016	12/31/2015	12/31/2014	12/31/2013	12/31/2012
Earnings Per Share	10.59	9.97	11.60	11.50	9.83	8.17	10.24	5.06
Cash Flow Per Share	18.45	19.14	19.10	15.76	15.57	18.89	15.91	8.89
Tang Book Value Per Share	N.M.	N.M.	N.M.	N.M.	N.M.	N.M.	19.35	10.34
Dividends Per Share	4.200	4.100	4.000	3.900	3.450	2.875	2.375	2.000
Dividend Payout %	39.66	41.12	34.48	33.91	35.10	35.19	23.19	39.53
Income Statement								
Total Revenue	15,551,000	10,133,000	4,786,000	20,718,000	20,891,000	19,872,000	18,769,000	18,143,000
EBITDA	921,000	891,000	281,000	2,009,000	1,953,000	1,748,000	1,789,000	1,420,000
Depn & Amortn	52,000	353,000	17,000	655,000	668,000	560,000	540,000	551,000
Income Before Taxes	678,000	410,000	198,000	1,114,000	1,031,000	881,000	917,000	558,000
Income Taxes	69,000	73,000	40,000	186,000	209,000	189,000	68,000	133,000
Net Income	618,000	342,000	153,000	888,000	783,000	650,000	827,000	401,000
Average Shares	74,000	75,100	76,000	77,200	79,700	79,600	80,800	79,300
Balance Sheet								
Current Assets	8,649,000	8,229,000	7,704,000	7,339,000	7,325,000	8,098,000	7,022,000	6,827,000
Total Assets	20,838,000	20,206,000	19,480,000	19,153,000	19,010,000	20,002,000	15,544,000	15,396,000
Current Liabilities	9,636,000	9,056,000	7,972,000	7,662,000	7,744,000	8,403,000	6,794,000	6,510,000
Long-Term Obligations	3,669,000	3,631,000	3,890,000	3,876,000	3,470,000	3,544,000	1,846,000	1,944,000
Total Liabilities	16,086,000	15,475,000	14,664,000	14,380,000	14,267,000	15,117,000	10,620,000	11,136,000
Stockholders' Equity	4,752,000	4,731,000	4,816,000	4,773,000	4,743,000	4,885,000	4,924,000	4,260,000
Shares Outstanding	72,000	73,000	74,000	74,465	77,221	77,956	77,417	78,407
Statistical Record								
Return on Assets %	3.89	3.78	4.55	4.64	4.01	3.66	5.35	2.62
Return on Equity %	16.36	15.83	18.61	18.61	16.27	13.25	18.01	9.48
EBITDA Margin %	5.92	8.79	5.87	9.70	9.35	8.80	9.53	7.83
Net Margin %	3.97	3.38	3.20	4.29	3.75	3.27	4.41	2.21
Asset Turnover	1.03	1.05	1.07	1.08	1.07	1.12	1.21	1.18
Current Ratio	0.90	0.91	0.97	0.96	0.95	0.96	1.03	1.05
Debt to Equity	0.77	0.77	0.81	0.81	0.73	0.73	0.37	0.46
Price Range	198.34-147.69	196.87-147.69	192.38-147.69	192.38-127.21	215.00-142.27	193.74-126.69	157.80-101.75	102.73-48.51
P/E Ratio	18.73-13.95	19.75-14.81	16.58-12.73	16.73-11.06	21.87-14.47	23.71-15.51	15.41-9.94	20.30-9.59
Average Yield %	2.38	2.33	2.30	2.33	1.93	1.88	1.86	2.69

Address: 2000 North M-63, Benton Harbor, MI 49022-2692	**Web Site:** www.whirlpoolcorp.com	**Auditors:** Ernst & Young LLP
Telephone: 269-923-5000	**Officers:** Jeff M. Fettig - Chairman, Chief Executive Officer Marc R. Bitzer - Vice-Chairman, President, Chief Operating Officer, Chief Executive Officer, Region Officer	**Investor Contact:** 269-923-2641 **Transfer Agents:** Computershare Trust Company, N.A., Providence, RI

WHITE MOUNTAINS INSURANCE GROUP, LTD.

Exchange	Symbol	Price	52Wk Range	Yield	P/E
NYS	WTM	$851.28 (12/29/2017)	947.00-839.51	0.12	6.18

*7 Year Price Score 107.11 *NYSE Composite Index=100 *12 Month Price Score 94.15

Interim Earnings (Per Share)

Qtr.	Mar	Jun	Sep	Dec
2014	15.48	15.53	8.45	11.71
2015	14.09	0.72	(10.01)	45.63
2016	2.34	66.79	18.80	(3.94)
2017	7.50	3.39	130.81	...

Interim Dividends (Per Share)

Amt	Decl	Ex	Rec	Pay
1.00A	02/27/2014	03/13/2014	03/17/2014	03/26/2014
1.00A	02/26/2015	03/12/2015	03/16/2015	03/25/2015
1.00A	02/26/2016	03/17/2016	03/21/2016	03/30/2016
1.00A	03/02/2017	03/16/2017	03/20/2017	03/29/2017

Indicated Div: $1.00

Valuation Analysis | **Institutional Holding**

Forecast EPS	N/A	No of Institutions 285
Market Cap	$3.2 Billion	Shares
Book Value	$3.5 Billion	4,017,924
Price/Book	0.92	% Held
Price/Sales	3.86	76.85

Business Summary: General Insurance (MIC: 5.2.1 SIC: 6331 NAIC: 524126)

White Mountains Insurance Group is an insurance holding company. Co.'s segments are OneBeacon, which is a specialty property and casualty insurance writer that provides insurance products through independent agencies, regional and national brokers, wholesalers and managing general agencies; HG Global/BAM, which consists of HG Global Ltd that provides 15%-of-par, first loss reinsurance protection for policies, and Build America Mutual Assurance Company, a mutual bond insurance company; and Other Operations, which consists of Co. and its intermediate holding companies, its wholly-owned investment management subsidiary and certain consolidated and unconsolidated private capital investments.

Recent Developments: For the quarter ended Sep 30 2017, income from continuing operations increased 275.8% to US$12.4 million from US$3.3 million in the year-earlier quarter. Net income increased 528.8% to US$551.5 million from US$87.7 million in the year-earlier quarter. Revenues were US$87.5 million, up 54.0% from US$56.8 million the year before. Net premiums earned were US$2.4 million versus US$3.4 million in the prior-year quarter, a decrease of 29.4%. Net investment income rose 27.1% to US$12.2 million from US$9.6 million a year ago.

Prospects: Our evaluation of White Mountains Insurance Group Ltd. as of Sep. 17, 2017 is the result of our systematic analysis on three basic characteristics: earnings strength, relative valuation, and recent stock price movement. The company has produced a positive trend in earnings per share over the past 5 quarters. Because the company lacks sufficient analyst estimate data, we place greater weight on the historical EPS trend as the measure of earnings strength. Based on operating earnings yield, the company is overvalued when compared to all of the companies in our coverage universe. Share price changes over the past year indicates that WTM will perform in line with the market over the near term.

Financial Data

(US$ in Thousands)	9 Mos	6 Mos	3 Mos	12/31/2016	12/31/2015	12/31/2014	12/31/2013	12/31/2012
Earnings Per Share	137.76	25.75	89.15	82.19	50.60	51.21	51.89	30.50
Cash Flow Per Share	18.76	11.74	(26.37)	(31.29)	30.23	19.71	(16.53)	(33.57)
Tang Book Value Per Share	914.94	786.98	781.19	777.29	629.03	606.43	632.29	593.20
Dividends Per Share	...	...	...	1.000	1.000	1.000	1.000	1.000
Dividend Payout %	...	...	...	1.22	1.98	1.95	1.93	3.28
Income Statement								
Premium Income	7,600	5,200	264,800	1,114,000	1,188,200	2,058,900	1,987,300	2,063,600
Total Revenue	259,800	178,900	385,900	1,360,700	1,808,600	2,510,200	2,317,400	2,435,700
Benefits & Claims	1,100	1,100	151,700	664,000	708,900	1,169,300	1,040,500	1,193,900
Income Before Taxes	2,600	1,000	37,900	(40,400)	154,900	301,700	344,900	262,800
Income Taxes	(5,300)	(1,300)	3,900	(45,400)	(700)	53,300	76,600	(15,700)
Net Income	604,700	49,800	34,300	412,500	297,600	312,700	321,800	207,400
Average Shares	4,243	4,514	4,512	4,953	5,811	6,026	6,109	6,708
Balance Sheet								
Total Assets	3,637,100	6,786,200	6,516,900	6,544,700	10,284,500	10,456,900	12,144,300	12,895,400
Total Liabilities	168,300	3,138,900	2,891,700	2,941,400	6,371,300	6,460,300	8,238,800	9,163,600
Stockholders' Equity	3,468,800	3,647,300	3,625,200	3,603,300	3,913,200	3,996,600	3,905,500	3,731,800
Shares Outstanding	3,749	4,571	4,572	4,563	5,623	5,986	6,176	6,290
Statistical Record								
Return on Assets %	11.21	1.56	5.13	4.89	2.87	2.77	2.57	1.53
Return on Equity %	16.25	2.88	11.71	10.95	7.52	7.91	8.43	5.29
Loss Ratio %	14.47	21.15	57.29	59.61	59.66	56.79	52.36	57.86
Net Margin %	232.76	27.84	8.89	30.32	16.45	12.46	13.89	8.52
Price Range	947.00-818.40	947.00-812.08	947.00-796.99	868.00-699.47	808.00-618.00	674.71-559.26	610.50-515.00	547.67-439.94
P/E Ratio	6.87-5.94	36.78-31.54	10.62-8.94	10.56-8.51	15.97-12.21	13.18-10.92	11.77-9.92	17.96-14.42
Average Yield %	...	...	...	0.12	0.14	0.16	0.17	0.20

Address: 14 Wesley Street, 5th Floor, Hamilton, HM 11 Telephone: 441-278-3160 Fax: 441-278-3170	Web Site: www.whitemountains.com Officers: Jess Brian Palmer - Vice President, Chief Accounting Officer Robert L. Seelig - Managing Director, General Counsel	Auditors: PricewaterhouseCoopers LLP Investor Contact: 203-458-5850 Transfer Agents: Computershare Trust Company, N.A., Providence, RI, United States

WHITING PETROLEUM CORP

Exchange	Symbol	Price	52Wk Range	Yield	P/E
NYS	WLL	$26.48 (12/29/2017)	52.40-16.00	N/A	N/A

*7 Year Price Score 15.15 ***NYSE Composite Index=100** ***12 Month Price Score 79.26**

TRADING VOLUME (thousand shares)

Interim Earnings (Per Share)

Qtr.	Mar	Jun	Sep	Dec
2014	3.64	5.04	5.28	(11.80)
2015	(2.52)	(2.92)	(36.56)	(1.36)
2016	(3.36)	(5.32)	(9.88)	(1.60)
2017	(0.96)	(0.72)	(3.16)	...

Interim Dividends (Per Share)

No Dividends Paid

Valuation Analysis / Institutional Holding

Valuation Analysis		Institutional Holding	
Forecast EPS	$-2.25	No of Institutions	
	(01/18/2018)	470	
Market Cap	$2.4 Billion	Shares	
Book Value	$4.7 Billion	351,170,304	
Price/Book	0.51	% Held	
Price/Sales	1.57	89.73	

Business Summary: Production & Extraction (MIC: 9.1.1 SIC: 1311 NAIC: 211111)

Whiting Petroleum is an independent oil and gas company engaged in the development, acquisition, exploration and production of crude oil, natural gas liquids and natural gas primarily in the Rocky Mountains and Permian Basin regions of the U.S. Co. sells its oil and gas production to end users, marketers and other purchasers that have access to nearby pipeline facilities. As of Dec 31 2016, Co. had estimated total proved reserves of 615.5 million barrels of oil equivalent, consisting of 394.8 million barrels of oil, 101.5 million barrels of natural gas liquids and 715.66 billion cubic feet of natural gas.

Recent Developments: For the quarter ended Sep 30 2017, net loss amounted to US$286.4 million versus a net loss of US$693.1 million in the year-earlier quarter. Revenues were US$324.2 million, up 2.7% from US$315.6 million the year before. Operating loss was US$481.0 million versus a loss of US$297.6 million in the prior-year quarter. Direct operating expenses rose 3.3% to US$118.1 million from US$114.4 million in the comparable period the year before. Indirect operating expenses increased 37.7% to US$687.0 million from US$498.8 million in the equivalent prior-year period.

Prospects: Our evaluation of Whiting Petroleum Corp. as of Jan. 14, 2018 is the result of our systematic analysis on three basic characteristics: earnings strength, relative valuation, and recent stock price movement. The company has suffered a very negative trend in earnings per share over the past 5 quarters. Because the company lacks sufficient analyst estimate data, we place greater weight on the historical EPS trend as the measure of earnings strength. Based on operating earnings yield, the company is overvalued when compared to all of the companies in our coverage universe. Share price changes over the past year indicates that WLL will perform very poorly over the near term.

Financial Data

(US$ in Thousands)	9 Mos	6 Mos	3 Mos	12/31/2016	12/31/2015	12/31/2014	12/31/2013	12/31/2012
Earnings Per Share	(6.44)	(13.16)	(17.76)	(21.28)	(45.40)	2.12	12.24	13.92
Cash Flow Per Share	5.81	6.39	6.94	9.42	21.51	59.45	59.01	47.53
Tang Book Value Per Share	52.00	55.08	55.75	56.81	93.08	115.51	129.06	117.15
Income Statement								
Total Revenue	1,007,023	682,832	371,317	1,284,982	2,050,798	3,085,097	2,828,385	2,173,452
EBITDA	(597,910)	(123,385)	(72,913)	(860,671)	(2,649,706)	320,051	689,507	740,893
Depn & Amortn	18,804	12,375	6,133	8,479	9,664	5,494	4,700	3,672
Income Before Taxes	(759,385)	(230,655)	(126,447)	(1,426,770)	(2,993,495)	143,915	571,871	662,011
Income Taxes	(320,001)	(77,703)	(39,476)	(87,646)	(774,227)	79,170	205,868	247,912
Net Income	(439,370)	(152,938)	(86,957)	(1,339,102)	(2,219,182)	64,807	366,055	414,189
Average Shares	90,698	90,683	90,652	62,967	48,868	30,629	29,897	29,757
Balance Sheet								
Current Assets	269,197	291,138	244,022	622,602	535,190	842,999	1,069,618	384,412
Total Assets	8,502,578	9,405,419	9,387,707	9,876,142	11,389,085	14,019,504	8,833,470	7,272,419
Current Liabilities	459,451	468,733	443,329	478,331	599,813	1,208,516	777,685	636,979
Long-Term Obligations	2,931,443	3,274,807	3,168,259	3,535,303	5,197,704	5,628,782	2,653,834	1,800,000
Total Liabilities	3,786,605	4,409,312	4,332,388	4,734,912	6,638,481	8,324,530	5,004,903	3,827,431
Stockholders' Equity	4,715,973	4,996,107	5,055,319	5,141,230	4,750,604	5,694,974	3,828,567	3,444,988
Shares Outstanding	90,698	90,698	90,674	90,503	51,036	41,722	29,664	29,407
Statistical Record								
Return on Assets %	N.M.	N.M.	N.M.	N.M.	N.M.	0.57	4.55	6.20
Return on Equity %	N.M.	N.M.	N.M.	N.M.	N.M.	1.36	10.07	12.78
EBITDA Margin %	N.M.	N.M.	N.M.	N.M.	N.M.	10.37	24.38	34.09
Net Margin %	N.M.	N.M.	N.M.	N.M.	N.M.	2.10	12.94	19.06
Asset Turnover	0.16	0.13	0.13	0.12	0.16	0.27	0.35	0.33
Current Ratio	0.59	0.62	0.55	1.30	0.89	0.70	1.38	0.60
Debt to Equity	0.62	0.66	0.63	0.69	1.09	0.99	0.69	0.52
Price Range	52.40-16.00	52.40-20.56	55.40-26.00	55.40-14.12	163.80-33.24	370.64-100.16	279.00-169.92	249.88-145.64
P/E Ratio	...	...	...	...	...	174.83-47.25	22.79-13.88	17.95-10.46

Address: 1700 Broadway, Suite 2300, Denver, CO 80290-2300	Web Site: www.whiting.com	Auditors: Deloitte & Touche LLP
Telephone: 303-837-1661	Officers: Sirikka R. Lohoefener - Controller, Treasurer Bradley J. Holly - President, Chief Executive Officer	Investor Contact: 303-390-4051
Fax: 303-861-4023		Transfer Agents: Computershare Trust Company, Inc.

WILEY (JOHN) & SONS INC.

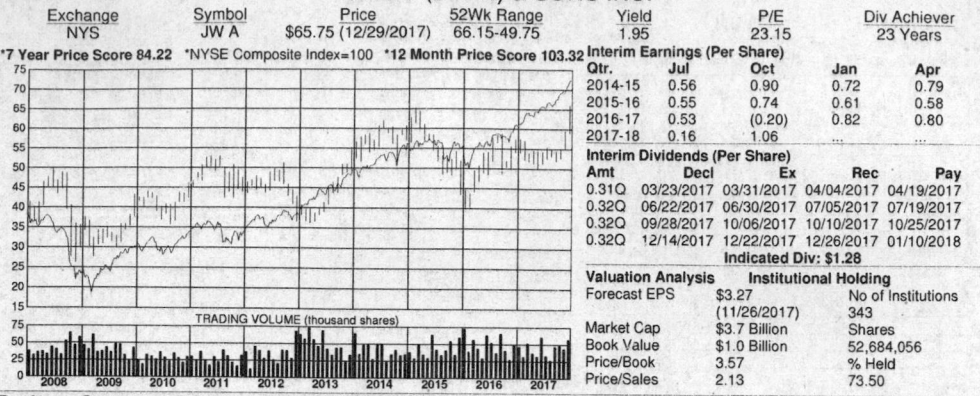

Exchange	Symbol	Price	52Wk Range	Yield	P/E	Div Achiever
NYS	JW A	$65.75 (12/29/2017)	66.15-49.75	1.95	23.15	23 Years

*7 Year Price Score 84.22 *NYSE Composite Index=100 *12 Month Price Score 103.32

Interim Earnings (Per Share)

Qtr.	Jul	Oct	Jan	Apr
2014-15	0.56	0.90	0.72	0.79
2015-16	0.55	0.74	0.61	0.58
2016-17	0.53	(0.20)	0.82	0.80
2017-18	0.16	1.06	...	...

Interim Dividends (Per Share)

Amt	Decl	Ex	Rec	Pay
0.31Q	03/23/2017	03/31/2017	04/04/2017	04/19/2017
0.32Q	06/22/2017	06/30/2017	07/05/2017	07/19/2017
0.32Q	09/28/2017	10/06/2017	10/10/2017	10/25/2017
0.32Q	12/14/2017	12/22/2017	12/26/2017	01/10/2018

Indicated Div: $1.28

Valuation Analysis

		Institutional Holding	
Forecast EPS	$3.27	No of Institutions	
	(11/26/2017)	343	
Market Cap	$3.7 Billion	Shares	
Book Value	$1.0 Billion	52,684,056	
Price/Book	3.57	% Held	
Price/Sales	2.13	73.50	

TRADING VOLUME (thousand shares)

Business Summary: Publishing (MIC: 2.3.3 SIC: 2731 NAIC: 511130)

John Wiley & Sons is a global research and learning company. Co. has three segments: Research segment, which provides scientific, technical, medical, and scholarly journals, as well as related content and services to libraries and individual researchers, among others; Publishing, which provides scientific, professional, and education books and related content in print and digital formats, test preparation services and course workflow tools, to libraries, corporations, students, professionals, and researchers; and Solutions, which provides online program management services for higher education institutions and learning, development, and assessment services for businesses and professionals.

Recent Developments: For the quarter ended Oct 31 2017, net income amounted to US$60.0 million versus a net loss of US$11.5 million in the year-earlier quarter. Revenues were US$451.7 million, up 6.1% from US$425.6 million the year before. Operating income was US$82.8 million versus US$47.6 million in the prior-year quarter, an increase of 73.7%. Direct operating expenses rose 7.4% to US$119.9 million from US$111.6 million in the comparable period the year before. Indirect operating expenses decreased 6.5% to US$249.1 million from US$266.4 million in the equivalent prior-year period.

Prospects: Our evaluation of Wiley (John) & Sons Inc. as of Jan. 14, 2018 is the result of our systematic analysis on three basic characteristics: earnings strength, relative valuation, and recent stock price movement. The company has generated a negative trend in earnings per share over the past 5 quarters and while recent estimates for the company have been raised by analysts, JW.A has posted better than expected results. Based on operating earnings yield, the company is undervalued when compared to all of the companies in our coverage universe. Share price changes over the past year indicates that JW.A will perform poorly over the near term.

Financial Data
(US$ in Thousands)

	6 Mos	3 Mos	04/30/2017	04/30/2016	04/30/2015	04/30/2014	04/30/2013	04/30/2012
Earnings Per Share	2.84	1.58	1.95	2.48	2.97	2.70	2.39	3.47
Cash Flow Per Share	6.15	6.48	5.49	6.02	6.05	5.94	5.67	6.29
Dividends Per Share	1.260	1.250	1.240	1.200	1.160	1.000	0.960	0.800
Dividend Payout %	44.37	79.11	63.59	48.39	39.06	37.04	40.17	23.05
Income Statement								
Total Revenue	863,175	411,444	1,718,530	1,727,037	1,822,440	1,775,195	1,760,778	1,782,742
EBITDA	170,542	50,167	322,926	304,777	352,767	309,665	295,385	365,305
Depn & Amortn	78,823	40,803	116,352	116,191	113,286	103,000	97,999	87,147
Income Before Taxes	85,572	6,096	191,116	174,793	225,461	195,534	186,922	272,095
Income Taxes	16,288	(3,140)	77,473	29,011	48,593	35,024	42,697	59,349
Net Income	69,284	9,236	113,643	145,782	176,868	160,510	144,225	212,746
Average Shares	56,875	57,709	58,199	58,734	59,594	59,514	60,224	61,272
Balance Sheet								
Current Assets	364,009	396,758	359,735	670,679	740,919	789,662	634,971	574,600
Total Assets	2,632,830	2,667,104	2,606,217	2,921,096	3,004,243	3,077,365	2,806,375	2,532,946
Current Liabilities	582,195	670,838	787,856	781,807	803,683	729,587	667,169	640,930
Long-Term Obligations	562,962	551,645	365,000	605,007	650,090	700,100	673,000	475,000
Total Liabilities	1,585,780	1,657,886	1,603,080	1,883,990	1,949,203	1,895,117	1,818,019	1,515,378
Stockholders' Equity	1,047,050	1,009,218	1,003,137	1,037,106	1,055,040	1,182,248	988,356	1,017,568
Shares Outstanding	56,866	57,089	57,167	57,564	58,838	59,052	58,670	59,515
Statistical Record								
Return on Assets %	5.96	3.40	4.11	4.91	5.82	5.46	5.40	8.55
Return on Equity %	16.11	9.07	11.14	13.90	15.81	14.79	14.38	21.26
EBITDA Margin %	19.76	12.19	18.79	17.65	19.36	17.44	16.78	20.49
Net Margin %	8.03	2.24	6.61	8.44	9.71	9.04	8.19	11.93
Asset Turnover	0.64	0.64	0.62	0.58	0.60	0.60	0.66	0.72
Current Ratio	0.63	0.59	0.46	0.86	0.92	1.08	0.95	0.90
Debt to Equity	0.54	0.55	0.36	0.58	0.62	0.59	0.68	0.47
Price Range	57.50-49.75	58.80-48.82	58.80-48.46	58.66-40.21	65.21-51.45	58.83-38.15	51.32-36.09	53.00-42.35
P/E Ratio	20.25-17.52	37.22-30.90	30.15-24.85	23.65-16.21	21.96-17.32	21.79-14.13	21.47-15.10	15.27-12.20
Average Yield %	2.35	2.33	2.31	2.40	1.97	2.04	2.23	1.68

Address: 111 River Street, Hoboken, NJ 07030
Telephone: 201-748-6000

Web Site: www.wiley.com
Officers: Matthew S. Kissner - Chairman, Interim Chief Executive Officer, Interim President Brian A. Napack - President, Chief Executive Officer

Auditors: KPMG LLP
Investor Contact: 201-748-6874
Transfer Agents: Registrar and Transfer Company, Cranford, NJ

WILLIAMS COS INC (THE)

Exchange	Symbol	Price	52Wk Range	Yield	P/E
NYS	WMB	$30.49 (12/29/2017)	32.42-27.02	3.94	53.49

*7 Year Price Score 68.08   *NYSE Composite Index=100   *12 Month Price Score 91.57

Interim Earnings (Per Share)

Qtr.	Mar	Jun	Sep	Dec
2014	0.20	0.15	2.22	0.24
2015	0.09	0.15	(0.05)	(0.95)
2016	(0.09)	(0.54)	0.08	(0.02)
2017	0.45	0.10	0.04	...

Interim Dividends (Per Share)

Amt	Decl	Ex	Rec	Pay
0.30Q	02/21/2017	03/08/2017	03/10/2017	03/27/2017
0.30Q	05/18/2017	06/07/2017	06/09/2017	06/26/2017
0.30Q	08/17/2017	09/07/2017	09/08/2017	09/25/2017
0.30Q	11/16/2017	12/07/2017	12/08/2017	12/26/2017

Indicated Div: $1.20 (Div. Reinv. Plan)

Valuation Analysis

		Institutional Holding	
Forecast EPS	$0.79	No of Institutions	
	(01/18/2018)	1062	
Market Cap	$25.2 Billion	Shares	
Book Value	$8.1 Billion	822,925,760	
Price/Book	3.11	% Held	
Price/Sales	3.15	92.20	

TRADING VOLUME (thousand shares)

Business Summary: Equipment & Services (MIC: 9.1.3 SIC: 4922 NAIC: 486210)

Williams Companies is an energy infrastructure company focused on connecting North America's hydrocarbon resource plays to markets for natural gas, natural gas liquids, and olefins. Co.'s operations are located in the U.S. As of Dec 31 2016, Co.'s interstate gas pipelines, midstream, and olefins production interests were largely held through Co.'s investment in Williams Partners L.P. Substantially all Co.'s operations are conducted through its subsidiaries. Co.'s business segments include Williams Partners, and Williams NGL & Petchem Services, and other, which include its Canadian construction services company.

Recent Developments: For the quarter ended Sep 30 2017, net income decreased 4.6% to US$125.0 million from US$131.0 million in the year-earlier quarter. Revenues were US$1.89 billion, down 0.7% from US$1.91 billion the year before. Operating income was US$277.0 million versus US$345.0 million in the prior-year quarter, a decrease of 19.7%. Direct operating expenses rose 5.7% to US$904.0 million from US$855.0 million in the comparable period the year before. Indirect operating expenses increased 0.7% to US$710.0 million from US$705.0 million in the equivalent prior-year period.

Prospects: Our evaluation of Williams Cos Inc. as of Jan. 14, 2018 is the result of our systematic analysis on three basic characteristics: earnings strength, relative valuation, and recent stock price movement. The company has suffered a very negative trend in earnings per share over the past 5 quarters. However, while recent estimates for the company have been mixed, WMB has posted results that fell short of analysts expectations. Based on operating earnings yield, the company is overvalued when compared to all of the companies in our coverage universe. Share price changes over the past year indicates that WMB will perform poorly over the near term.

Financial Data

(US$ in Thousands)	9 Mos	6 Mos	3 Mos	12/31/2016	12/31/2015	12/31/2014	12/31/2013	12/31/2012
Earnings Per Share	0.57	0.61	(0.03)	(0.57)	(0.76)	2.92	0.62	1.37
Cash Flow Per Share	4.14	4.20	4.23	4.87	3.57	2.94	3.25	2.95
Tang Book Value Per Share	N.M.	N.M.	N.M.	N.M.	N.M.	N.M.	3.77	3.52
Dividends Per Share	1.100	1.000	1.340	1.680	2.450	1.958	1.438	1.196
Dividend Payout %	192.98	163.93	...	...	...	67.04	231.85	87.32
Income Statement								
Total Revenue	5,803,000	3,912,000	1,988,000	7,499,000	7,360,000	7,637,000	6,860,000	7,486,000
EBITDA	1,545,000	1,227,000	800,000	1,814,000	378,000	2,610,000	2,208,000	2,399,000
Depn & Amortn	61,000	44,000	21,000	1,407,000	1,382,000	967,000	752,000	712,000
Income Before Taxes	666,000	632,000	499,000	(772,000)	(2,048,000)	896,000	946,000	1,178,000
Income Taxes	126,000	102,000	37,000	(25,000)	(399,000)	1,249,000	401,000	360,000
Net Income	487,000	454,000	373,000	(424,000)	(571,000)	2,114,000	430,000	859,000
Average Shares	829,368	828,575	826,476	750,673	749,271	723,641	687,185	625,486
Balance Sheet								
Current Assets	2,293,000	3,969,000	2,845,000	1,462,000	1,527,000	1,890,000	1,683,000	1,924,000
Total Assets	46,120,000	48,770,000	47,512,000	46,835,000	49,020,000	50,563,000	27,142,000	24,327,000
Current Liabilities	2,354,000	3,996,000	2,045,000	2,949,000	2,497,000	2,567,000	1,983,000	1,549,000
Long-Term Obligations	20,567,000	21,325,000	21,825,000	22,624,000	23,812,000	20,888,000	11,353,000	10,735,000
Total Liabilities	38,011,000	40,464,000	39,068,000	42,192,000	42,872,000	41,786,000	22,278,000	19,575,000
Stockholders' Equity	8,109,000	8,306,000	8,444,000	4,643,000	6,148,000	8,777,000	4,864,000	4,752,000
Shares Outstanding	826,000	826,000	826,000	750,000	749,000	747,000	683,000	681,000
Statistical Record								
Return on Assets %	1.01	1.03	0.03	N.M.	N.M.	5.44	1.67	4.20
Return on Equity %	7.28	7.61	0.20	N.M.	N.M.	30.99	8.94	26.18
EBITDA Margin %	26.62	31.37	40.24	24.19	5.14	34.18	32.19	32.05
Net Margin %	8.39	11.61	18.76	N.M.	N.M.	27.68	6.27	11.47
Asset Turnover	0.17	0.17	0.16	0.16	0.15	0.20	0.27	0.37
Current Ratio	0.97	0.99	1.39	0.50	0.61	0.74	0.85	1.24
Debt to Equity	2.54	2.57	2.58	4.87	3.87	2.38	2.33	2.26
Price Range	32.42-27.85	32.42-20.09	32.42-14.81	31.78-11.16	60.86-21.54	59.44-38.03	38.57-31.65	36.77-26.82
P/E Ratio	56.88-48.86	53.15-32.93	...	...	...	20.36-13.02	62.21-51.05	26.84-19.58
Average Yield %	3.69	3.47	5.09	7.14	5.37	4.00	4.05	3.79

Address: One Williams Center, Tulsa, OK 74172-0172
Telephone: 918-573-2000

Web Site: www.williams.com
Officers: Kathleen B. Cooper - Chairman Joshua II. De Rienzis - Vice President, Corporate Secretary

Auditors: Ernst & Young LLP
Transfer Agents: Computershare Trust Company, N.A., College Station, TX

WILLIAMS SONOMA INC

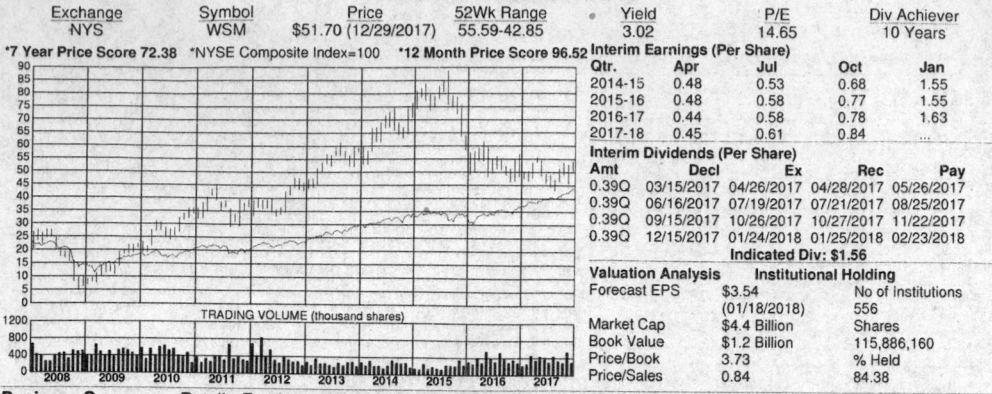

Exchange	Symbol	Price	52Wk Range	Yield	P/E	Div Achiever
NYS	WSM	$51.70 (12/29/2017)	55.59-42.85	3.02	14.65	10 Years

*7 Year Price Score 72.38   *NYSE Composite Index=100   *12 Month Price Score 96.52

Interim Earnings (Per Share)

Qtr.	Apr	Jul	Oct	Jan
2014-15	0.48	0.53	0.68	1.55
2015-16	0.48	0.58	0.77	1.55
2016-17	0.44	0.58	0.78	1.63
2017-18	0.45	0.61	0.84	...

Interim Dividends (Per Share)

Amt	Decl	Ex	Rec	Pay
0.39Q	03/15/2017	04/26/2017	04/28/2017	05/26/2017
0.39Q	06/16/2017	07/19/2017	07/21/2017	08/25/2017
0.39Q	09/15/2017	10/26/2017	10/27/2017	11/22/2017
0.39Q	12/15/2017	01/24/2018	01/25/2018	02/23/2018

Indicated Div: $1.56

Valuation Analysis | **Institutional Holding**

Forecast EPS	$3.54	No of Institutions
	(01/18/2018)	556
Market Cap	$4.4 Billion	Shares
Book Value	$1.2 Billion	115,886,160
Price/Book	3.73	% Held
Price/Sales	0.84	84.38

Business Summary: Retail - Furniture & Home Furnishings (MIC: 2.1.6 SIC: 5712 NAIC: 442110)

Williams-Sonoma is a retailer of products for the home. As of Jan 29 2017, the e-commerce channel had the following merchandising concepts: Williams Sonoma, Pottery Barn, Pottery Barn Kids, West Elm, PBteen, Williams Sonoma Home, Rejuvenation and Mark and Graham, which sell its products through its e-commerce websites and direct-mail catalogs. As of Jan 29 2017, Co. operated 629 stores comprising 583 stores in 43 states, Washington, D.C. and Puerto Rico, 26 stores in Canada, 19 stores in Australia and one store in the U.K. Co. also operates 66 franchised stores and/or e-commerce websites in a number of countries in the Middle East, the Philippines and Mexico.

Recent Developments: For the quarter ended Oct 29 2017, net income increased 2.8% to US$71.3 million from US$69.4 million in the year-earlier quarter. Revenues were US$1.30 billion, up 4.3% from US$1.25 billion the year before. Operating income was US$110.8 million versus US$110.0 million in the prior-year quarter, an increase of 0.8%. Direct operating expenses rose 5.7% to US$832.3 million from US$787.2 million in the comparable period the year before. Indirect operating expenses increased 2.3% to US$356.3 million from US$348.2 million in the equivalent prior-year period.

Prospects: Our evaluation of Williams-Sonoma Inc. as of Jan. 14, 2018 is the result of our systematic analysis on three basic characteristics: earnings strength, relative valuation, and recent stock price movement. The company has managed to produce a neutral trend in earnings per share over the past 5 quarters and while recent estimates for the company have been mixed, WSM has posted better than expected results. Based on operating earnings yield, the company is undervalued when compared to all of the companies in our coverage universe. Share price changes over the past year indicates that WSM will perform poorly over the near term.

Financial Data

(US$ in Thousands)	9 Mos	6 Mos	3 Mos	01/29/2017	01/31/2016	02/01/2015	02/02/2014	02/03/2013
Earnings Per Share	3.53	3.47	3.44	3.41	3.37	3.24	2.82	2.54
Cash Flow Per Share	6.07	6.09	6.34	5.94	6.01	4.94	4.71	3.61
Tang Book Value Per Share	13.88	13.86	13.93	14.29	13.38	13.33	13.35	13.39
Dividends Per Share	1.540	1.520	1.500	1.480	1.400	1.320	1.240	0.880
Dividend Payout %	43.63	43.80	43.60	43.40	41.54	40.74	43.97	34.65
Income Statement								
Total Revenue	3,612,449	2,313,113	1,111,507	5,083,812	4,976,090	4,698,719	4,387,889	4,042,870
EBITDA	371,357	131,378	55,997	620,582	631,673	640,119	576,511	516,922
Depn & Amortn	116,486	(12,680)	(6,477)	147,983	143,039	137,854	124,413	107,759
Income Before Taxes	253,897	143,678	62,577	471,911	488,007	502,203	452,682	409,956
Income Taxes	90,112	51,206	23,022	166,524	177,939	193,349	173,780	153,226
Net Income	163,785	92,472	39,555	305,387	310,068	308,854	278,902	256,730
Average Shares	85,384	86,848	87,710	89,462	92,102	95,200	98,765	101,051
Balance Sheet								
Current Assets	1,460,461	1,364,378	1,291,045	1,367,180	1,336,100	1,391,923	1,419,103	1,316,772
Total Assets	2,580,384	2,479,860	2,391,177	2,476,879	2,417,427	2,330,277	2,336,734	2,187,679
Current Liabilities	1,137,551	1,020,070	912,665	961,256	996,427	875,948	861,096	657,127
Long-Term Obligations	...	...	...	...	...	...	1,968	3,753
Total Liabilities	1,408,210	1,291,336	1,181,026	1,228,659	1,219,201	1,105,571	1,080,732	878,541
Stockholders' Equity	1,172,174	1,188,524	1,210,151	1,248,220	1,198,226	1,224,706	1,256,002	1,309,138
Shares Outstanding	84,478	85,742	86,883	87,325	89,563	91,891	94,049	97,734
Statistical Record								
Return on Assets %	12.25	12.63	13.04	12.51	13.10	13.27	12.36	11.89
Return on Equity %	26.45	26.16	25.73	25.03	25.66	24.97	21.81	19.70
EBITDA Margin %	10.28	5.68	5.04	12.21	12.69	13.62	13.14	12.79
Net Margin %	4.53	4.00	3.56	6.01	6.23	6.57	6.36	6.35
Asset Turnover	2.06	2.12	2.18	2.08	2.10	2.02	1.94	1.87
Current Ratio	1.28	1.34	1.41	1.42	1.34	1.59	1.65	2.00
Price Range	56.90-42.85	56.90-44.27	59.96-46.22	61.55-46.22	88.67-48.99	80.94-52.85	61.33-43.96	47.93-33.06
P/E Ratio	16.12-12.14	16.40-12.76	17.43-13.44	18.05-13.55	26.31-14.54	24.98-16.31	21.75-15.59	18.87-13.02
Average Yield %	3.11	3.03	2.92	2.80	1.87	1.88	1.96	2.28

Address: 3250 Van Ness Avenue, San Francisco, CA 94109	Web Site: www.williams-sonomainc.com	Auditors: DELOITTE & TOUCHE LLP
Telephone: 415-421-7900	Officers: Adrian D.P. Bellamy - Chairman Laura J. Alber - President, Chief Executive Officer	Transfer Agents: Wilson Sonsini Goodrich & Rosati Professional Corporation, Palo Alto, CA
Fax: 415-434-0881		

WORLDPAY INC

Exchange	Symbol	Price	52Wk Range	Yield	P/E
NYS	WP	$73.55 (12/29/2017)	75.87-59.88	N/A	51.08

*7 Year Price Score N/A   *NYSE Composite Index=100   *12 Month Price Score 103.40

TRADING VOLUME (thousand shares)

Interim Earnings (Per Share)

Qtr.	Mar	Jun	Sep	Dec
2014	0.18	(0.01)	0.20	0.35
2015	0.13	0.24	0.27	0.31
2016	0.25	0.38	0.41	0.28
2017	0.17	0.42	0.57	...

Interim Dividends (Per Share)

No Dividends Paid

Valuation Analysis

		Institutional Holding	
Forecast EPS	$3.35	No of Institutions	517
	(01/18/2018)		
Market Cap	$13.1 Billion	Shares	
Book Value	$558.2 Million		204,733,152
Price/Book	23.42	% Held	
Price/Sales	3.34		103.83

Business Summary: Business Services (MIC: 7.5.2 SIC: 7389 NAIC: 561499)

Vantiv is a holding company. Through its subsidiaries, Co. provides electronic payment processing services to merchants and financial institutions. Co. operates two segments: Merchant Services, which provides merchant acquiring and payment processing services to national merchants, regional and small-to-mid sized businesses; and Financial Institution Services, which provides card issuer processing, payment network processing, fraud protection, card production, prepaid program management, automated teller machine driving and network gateway and switching services that utilize Co.'s proprietary Jeanie debit payment network to a set of financial institutions.

Recent Developments: For the quarter ended Sep 30 2017, net income increased 22.9% to US$106.9 million from US$87.0 million in the year-earlier quarter. Revenues were US$1.03 billion, up 13.1% from US$914.0 million the year before. Operating income was US$168.9 million versus US$158.4 million in the prior-year quarter, an increase of 6.6%. Direct operating expenses rose 13.3% to US$479.5 million from US$423.4 million in the comparable period the year before. Indirect operating expenses increased 16.0% to US$385.4 million from US$332.2 million in the equivalent prior-year period.

Prospects: Our evaluation of Vantiv Inc as of Jan. 14, 2018 is the result of our systematic analysis on three basic characteristics: earnings strength, relative valuation, and recent stock price movement. The company has generated a negative trend in earnings per share over the past 5 quarters. However, while recent estimates for the company have been mixed, VNTV has posted better than expected results. Based on operating earnings yield, the company is about fairly valued when compared to all of the companies in our coverage universe. Share price changes over the past year indicates that VNTV will perform in line with the market over the near term.

Financial Data

(US$ in Thousands)	9 Mos	6 Mos	3 Mos	12/31/2016	12/31/2015	12/31/2014	12/31/2013	12/31/2012
Earnings Per Share	1.44	1.28	1.24	1.32	0.95	0.75	0.87	0.47
Cash Flow Per Share	4.74	5.30	4.87	4.27	5.23	4.18	3.46	2.51
Income Statement								
Total Revenue	2,960,731	1,926,966	928,202	3,578,991	3,159,938	2,577,203	2,108,077	1,863,239
EBITDA	432,609	235,232	77,472	602,758	479,742	384,868	389,602	252,883
Depn & Amortn	22,589	15,283	7,834	70,500	76,600	70,000	56,800	40,700
Income Before Taxes	312,579	161,029	40,468	422,724	297,406	235,167	291,900	157,611
Income Taxes	83,519	38,874	5,167	141,853	88,177	66,177	83,760	46,853
Net Income	189,780	97,662	28,885	213,208	147,946	125,292	133,572	57,610
Average Shares	162,882	162,510	197,496	162,115	200,934	199,170	206,027	122,747
Balance Sheet								
Current Assets	1,295,446	1,239,983	1,241,512	1,287,858	1,117,499	1,214,736	807,913	921,077
Total Assets	8,089,934	7,444,859	6,944,082	7,044,007	6,465,426	6,336,083	4,189,553	3,979,529
Current Liabilities	1,811,206	1,799,495	1,666,355	1,689,012	1,295,379	963,333	685,313	869,468
Long-Term Obligations	4,598,285	3,393,214	3,069,026	3,102,826	2,965,439	3,292,016	1,730,794	1,171,880
Total Liabilities	7,531,766	5,974,821	5,570,693	5,728,342	5,512,638	5,433,070	3,421,622	3,161,603
Stockholders' Equity	558,168	1,470,038	1,373,389	1,315,665	952,788	903,013	767,931	817,926
Shares Outstanding	177,759	197,537	197,074	196,177	190,531	188,497	190,581	211,484
Statistical Record								
Return on Assets %	3.29	3.05	3.04	3.15	2.31	2.38	3.27	1.54
Return on Equity %	26.11	16.70	17.06	18.75	15.94	15.00	16.85	7.97
EBITDA Margin %	14.61	12.21	8.35	16.84	15.18	14.93	18.48	13.57
Net Margin %	6.41	5.07	3.11	5.96	4.68	4.86	6.34	3.09
Asset Turnover	0.54	0.55	0.55	0.53	0.49	0.49	0.52	0.50
Current Ratio	0.72	0.69	0.75	0.76	0.86	1.26	1.18	1.06
Debt to Equity	8.24	2.31	2.23	2.36	3.11	3.65	2.25	1.43
Price Range	72.51-55.11	66.10-52.81	66.10-51.21	59.73-43.20	52.84-33.25	34.82-28.79	32.61-19.97	24.03-19.50
P/E Ratio	50.35-38.27	51.64-41.26	53.31-41.30	45.25-32.73	55.62-35.00	46.43-38.39	37.48-22.95	51.13-41.49

Address: 8500 Governor's Hill Drive, Symmes Township, OH 45249	**Web Site:** www.vantiv.com	**Auditors:** Deloitte & Touche LLP
	Officers: Jeffrey E. Stiefler - Chairman Charles D. Drucker - President, Chief Executive Officer	**Investor Contact:** 513-.90-0.4811
Telephone: 513-900-5250		**Transfer Agents:** American Stock Transfer & Trust Company, LLC

WORLD FUEL SERVICES CORP.

Exchange	Symbol	Price	52Wk Range	Yield	P/E
NYS	INT	$28.14 (12/29/2017)	47.25-26.45	0.85	80.40

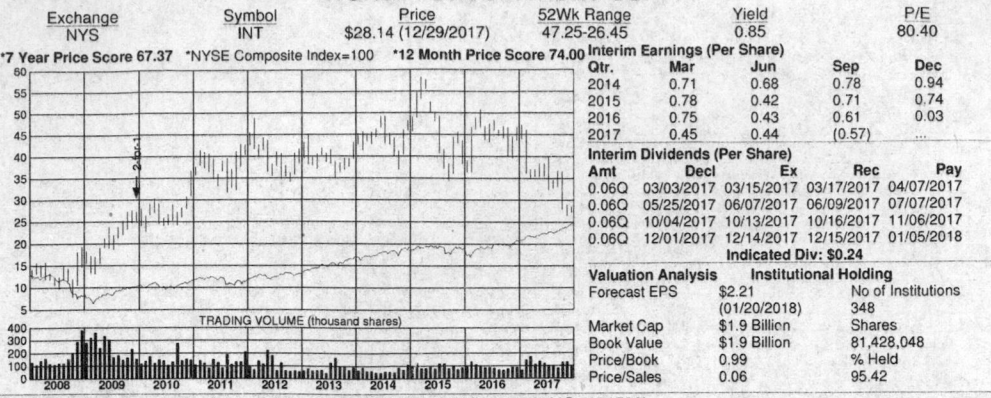

*7 Year Price Score 67.37 *NYSE Composite Index=100 *12 Month Price Score 74.00

Interim Earnings (Per Share)

Qtr.	Mar	Jun	Sep	Dec
2014	0.71	0.68	0.78	0.94
2015	0.78	0.42	0.71	0.74
2016	0.75	0.43	0.61	0.03
2017	0.45	0.44	(0.57)	...

Interim Dividends (Per Share)

Amt	Decl	Ex	Rec	Pay
0.06Q	03/03/2017	03/15/2017	03/17/2017	04/07/2017
0.06Q	05/25/2017	06/07/2017	06/09/2017	07/07/2017
0.06Q	10/04/2017	10/13/2017	10/16/2017	11/06/2017
0.06Q	12/01/2017	12/14/2017	12/15/2017	01/05/2018

Indicated Div: $0.24

Valuation Analysis / **Institutional Holding**

Forecast EPS	$2.21	No of Institutions
	(01/20/2018)	348
Market Cap	$1.9 Billion	Shares
Book Value	$1.9 Billion	81,428,048
Price/Book	0.99	% Held
Price/Sales	0.06	95.42

Business Summary: Equipment & Services (MIC: 9.1.3 SIC: 5172 NAIC: 424720)

World Fuel Services is a global energy management company involved in providing energy procurement advisory services, supply fulfillment and transaction and payment management solutions to commercial and industrial customers. Co. primarily contracts with third parties for the delivery and storage of fuel products, however, Co. also operates storage facilities and transportation assets. Co. operates in three reportable segments: aviation, which provides fuel and related products and services; marine, which products and services include fuel, lubricants and related products and services to a base of customers; and land, which provides fuel, lubricants, power and natural gas solutions.

Recent Developments: For the quarter ended Sep 30 2017, net loss amounted to US$37.9 million versus net income of US$43.0 million in the year-earlier quarter. Revenues were US$8.54 billion, up 15.4% from US$7.40 billion the year before. Operating income was US$61.3 million versus US$58.2 million in the prior-year quarter, an increase of 5.3%. Direct operating expenses rose 15.9% to US$8.30 billion from US$7.16 billion in the comparable period the year before. Indirect operating expenses increased 0.1% to US$178.6 million from US$178.4 million in the equivalent prior-year period.

Prospects: Our evaluation of World Fuel Services Corp. as of Jan. 21, 2018 is the result of our systematic analysis on three basic characteristics: earnings strength, relative valuation, and recent stock price movement. The company has enjoyed a very positive trend in earnings per share over the past 5 quarters. However, while recent estimates for the company have been mixed, INT has posted results that were in line with analysts expectations. Based on operating earnings yield, the company is undervalued when compared to all of the companies in our coverage universe. Share price changes over the past year indicates that INT will perform poorly over the near term.

Financial Data

(US$ in Thousands)	9 Mos	6 Mos	3 Mos	12/31/2016	12/31/2015	12/31/2014	12/31/2013	12/31/2012
Earnings Per Share	0.35	1.53	1.52	1.81	2.64	3.11	2.83	2.64
Cash Flow Per Share	0.44	2.34	2.97	2.95	6.37	2.00	3.71	2.04
Tang Book Value Per Share	15.04	15.90	15.48	9.44	12.41	11.83	12.24	12.12
Dividends Per Share	0.180	0.240	0.240	0.240	0.240	0.150	0.150	0.150
Dividend Payout %	51.43	15.69	15.79	13.26	9.09	4.82	5.30	5.68
Income Statement								
Total Revenue	24,823,400	16,280,400	8,194,300	27,015,800	30,379,700	43,386,389	41,561,947	38,945,338
EBITDA	222,000	140,800	71,400	223,800	284,300	325,088	285,952	277,292
Depn & Amortn	64,100	43,400	22,600	42,500	35,100	30,300	22,000	18,600
Income Before Taxes	115,600	70,900	36,100	142,100	219,300	269,551	246,665	239,595
Income Taxes	92,200	9,600	5,000	15,700	36,300	51,144	39,505	38,244
Net Income	22,800	61,400	31,300	126,500	186,900	221,747	203,075	189,345
Average Shares	68,200	68,700	69,200	69,800	70,700	71,323	71,800	71,817
Balance Sheet								
Current Assets	4,025,300	3,588,800	3,589,200	3,836,600	3,254,600	3,674,843	3,815,501	3,281,377
Total Assets	5,723,100	5,286,000	5,263,600	5,412,600	4,549,400	4,879,980	4,739,277	4,107,751
Current Liabilities	2,466,300	2,128,500	2,094,700	2,182,700	1,762,800	2,241,354	2,514,515	2,149,298
Long-Term Obligations	1,128,100	1,046,100	1,065,800	1,170,800	746,700	671,954	449,064	354,253
Total Liabilities	3,804,100	3,307,400	3,302,800	3,487,600	2,638,000	3,024,622	3,065,379	2,590,577
Stockholders' Equity	1,919,000	1,978,600	1,960,800	1,925,000	1,911,400	1,855,358	1,673,898	1,517,174
Shares Outstanding	67,700	68,600	69,600	69,900	70,788	72,082	71,883	72,147
Statistical Record								
Return on Assets %	0.46	2.12	2.19	2.53	3.96	4.61	4.59	4.84
Return on Equity %	1.29	5.43	5.41	6.58	9.92	12.57	12.73	13.25
EBITDA Margin %	0.89	0.86	0.87	0.83	0.94	0.75	0.69	0.71
Net Margin %	0.09	0.38	0.38	0.47	0.62	0.51	0.49	0.49
Asset Turnover	6.00	6.27	6.20	5.41	6.44	9.02	9.40	9.95
Current Ratio	1.63	1.69	1.71	1.76	1.85	1.64	1.52	1.53
Debt to Equity	0.59	0.53	0.54	0.61	0.39	0.36	0.27	0.23
Price Range	47.25-32.34	48.37-35.14	50.79-35.14	50.79-36.31	58.28-34.44	49.24-36.87	45.11-35.00	48.94-34.00
P/E Ratio	135.00-92.40	31.61-22.97	33.41-23.12	28.06-20.06	22.08-13.05	15.83-11.86	15.94-12.37	18.54-12.88
Average Yield %	0.46	0.57	0.54	0.53	0.51	0.34	0.38	0.38

Address: 9800 Northwest 41st Street, Miami, FL 33178	Web Site: www.wfscorp.com	Auditors: PricewaterhouseCoopers LLP
Telephone: 305-428-8000	**Officers:** Michael J. Kasbar - Chairman, President, Chief Operating Officer, Chief Executive Officer	**Investor Contact:** 305-428-8000
Fax: 305-392-5621	Jeffrey P. Smith - Executive Vice President, Chief Operating Officer	**Transfer Agents:** Wells Fargo Shareowner Services, St. Paul, MN

WORTHINGTON INDUSTRIES, INC.

Exchange	Symbol	Price	52Wk Range	Yield	P/E
NYS	WOR	$44.06 (12/29/2017)	53.14-39.65	1.91	16.14

*7 Year Price Score 111.81 *NYSE Composite Index=100 *12 Month Price Score 86.79

Interim Earnings (Per Share)

Qtr.	Aug	Nov	Feb	May
2014-15	0.63	0.43	(0.39)	0.43
2015-16	0.48	0.36	0.46	0.92
2016-17	1.02	0.72	0.55	0.86
2017-18	0.70	0.62	...	...

Interim Dividends (Per Share)

Amt	Decl	Ex	Rec	Pay
0.20Q	03/29/2017	06/13/2017	06/15/2017	06/29/2017
0.21Q	06/28/2017	09/14/2017	09/15/2017	09/29/2017
0.21Q	09/27/2017	12/14/2017	12/15/2017	12/29/2017
0.21Q	12/19/2017	03/14/2018	03/15/2018	03/29/2018

Indicated Div: $0.84

Valuation Analysis

		Institutional Holding	
Forecast EPS	$3.12 (01/16/2018)	No of Institutions	345
Market Cap	$2.7 Billion	Shares	42,317,840
Book Value	$919.3 Million	% Held	53.58
Price/Book	2.91		
Price/Sales	0.82		

TRADING VOLUME (thousand shares)

Business Summary: Non-Precious Metals (MIC: 8.2.2 SIC: 3312 NAIC: 331111)

Worthington Industries is a metals manufacturing company, focused on steel processing and manufactured metal products. Co. operates three segments: Steel Processing, which buys coils of steel from steel mills and mini-mills and processes them to customer specifications; Pressure Cylinders, which manufactures and sells filled and unfilled pressure cylinders, tanks, hand torches, and oil and gas equipment with accessories and related products for end-use market applications; and Engineered Cabs, which designs and manufactures open and enclosed cabs and operator stations and custom fabrications for mobile equipment, and provides complementary products such as machined structural components.

Recent Developments: For the quarter ended Nov 30 2017, net income decreased 16.5% to US$41.6 million from US$49.9 million in the year-earlier quarter. Revenues were US$871.3 million, up 19.7% from US$727.8 million the year before. Operating income was US$52.1 million versus US$43.0 million in the prior-year quarter, an increase of 20.9%. Direct operating expenses rose 20.9% to US$731.2 million from US$605.0 million in the comparable period the year before. Indirect operating expenses increased 10.4% to US$88.0 million from US$79.8 million in the equivalent prior-year period.

Prospects: Our evaluation of Worthington Industries Inc. as of Jan. 14, 2018 is the result of our systematic analysis on three basic characteristics: earnings strength, relative valuation, and recent stock price movement. The company has produced a positive trend in earnings per share over the past 5 quarters and while recent estimates for the company have been raised by analysts, WOR has posted results that fell short of analysts expectations. Based on operating earnings yield, the company is undervalued when compared to all of the companies in our coverage universe. Share price changes over the past year indicates that WOR will perform very poorly over the near term.

Financial Data

(US$ in Thousands)	6 Mos	3 Mos	05/31/2017	05/31/2016	05/31/2015	05/31/2014	05/31/2013	05/31/2012
Earnings Per Share	2.73	2.83	3.15	2.22	1.12	2.11	1.91	1.65
Cash Flow Per Share	4.65	4.77	5.38	6.60	3.23	3.32	3.94	2.49
Tang Book Value Per Share	5.42	5.71	9.89	7.33	6.10	6.73	6.74	6.48
Dividends Per Share	0.810	0.800	0.790	0.750	0.690	0.450	0.640	0.460
Dividend Payout %	29.67	28.27	25.08	33.78	61.61	21.33	33.51	27.88
Income Statement								
Total Revenue	1,719,503	848,237	3,014,108	2,819,714	3,384,234	3,126,426	2,612,244	2,534,701
EBITDA	147,601	67,938	290,153	202,205	126,018	215,060	186,596	154,573
Depn & Amortn	51,648	25,365	73,268	68,886	64,666	62,344	56,002	50,644
Income Before Taxes	77,108	33,766	187,089	101,649	25,552	126,045	106,676	84,432
Income Taxes	31,163	12,998	79,190	58,987	25,772	57,349	64,465	51,904
Net Income	84,937	45,534	204,515	143,715	76,785	151,300	136,442	115,595
Average Shares	63,468	64,590	64,874	64,755	68,483	71,664	71,314	70,252
Balance Sheet								
Current Assets	1,111,728	1,161,165	1,190,969	915,460	992,193	1,198,922	866,883	914,239
Total Assets	2,571,713	2,630,554	2,325,344	2,063,755	2,085,142	2,296,381	1,950,857	1,877,797
Current Liabilities	526,449	541,984	520,783	430,078	524,392	589,663	448,914	658,263
Long-Term Obligations	766,737	773,090	571,796	579,982	579,352	554,790	406,236	257,462
Total Liabilities	1,652,426	1,672,380	1,373,709	1,270,384	1,336,030	1,445,569	1,120,035	1,180,623
Stockholders' Equity	919,287	958,174	951,635	793,371	749,112	850,812	830,822	697,174
Shares Outstanding	60,755	62,144	62,802	61,533	64,141	67,408	69,752	67,906
Statistical Record								
Return on Assets %	7.52	7.67	9.32	6.91	3.50	7.12	7.13	6.50
Return on Equity %	19.66	20.34	23.44	18.58	9.60	17.99	17.86	16.62
EBITDA Margin %	8.58	8.01	9.63	7.17	3.72	6.88	7.14	6.10
Net Margin %	4.94	5.37	6.79	5.10	2.27	4.84	5.22	4.56
Asset Turnover	1.39	1.30	1.37	1.36	1.54	1.47	1.36	1.43
Current Ratio	2.11	2.14	2.29	2.13	1.89	2.03	1.93	1.39
Debt to Equity	0.83	0.81	0.60	0.73	0.77	0.65	0.49	0.37
Price Range	58.85-39.65	62.35-39.75	62.35-36.26	38.26-21.88	43.85-24.18	44.05-31.35	35.59-15.88	23.45-13.21
P/E Ratio	21.56-14.52	22.03-14.05	19.79-11.51	17.23-9.86	39.15-21.59	20.88-14.86	18.63-8.31	14.21-8.01
Average Yield %	1.71	1.66	1.70	2.48	2.02	1.19	2.54	2.58

Address: 200 Old Wilson Bridge Road, Columbus, OH 43085	**Web Site:** www.worthingtonindustries.com	**Auditors:** KPMG LLP
Telephone: 614-438-3210	**Officers:** John P. McConnell - Chairman, Chief Executive Officer Mark A. Russell - President, Chief Operating Officer	**Investor Contact:** 614-438-3077
Fax: 614-438-3256		**Transfer Agents:** Wells Fargo Shareowner Services, Saint Paul, MN

W.P. CAREY INC

Exchange	Symbol	Price	52Wk Range	Yield	P/E	Div Achiever
NYS	WPC	$68.90 (12/29/2017)	72.32-59.64	5.86	29.96	18 Years

*7 Year Price Score 88.91 *NYSE Composite Index=100 *12 Month Price Score 100.31

Interim Earnings (Per Share)

Qtr.	Mar	Jun	Sep	Dec
2014	1.25	0.64	0.27	0.29
2015	0.34	0.59	0.20	0.48
2016	0.54	0.48	1.03	0.44
2017	0.53	0.59	0.74	...

Interim Dividends (Per Share)

Amt	Decl	Ex	Rec	Pay
0.995Q	03/16/2017	03/29/2017	03/31/2017	04/17/2017
1.00Q	06/16/2017	06/28/2017	06/30/2017	07/14/2017
1.005Q	09/20/2017	09/29/2017	10/02/2017	10/16/2017
1.01Q	12/06/2017	12/28/2017	12/29/2017	01/16/2018

Indicated Div: $4.04 (Div. Reinv. Plan)

Valuation Analysis

		Institutional Holding	
Forecast EPS	$2.42	No of Institutions	
	(11/23/2017)	471	
Market Cap	$7.4 Billion	Shares	
Book Value	$3.2 Billion	62,369,348	
Price/Book	2.28	% Held	
Price/Sales	8.37	N/A	

TRADING VOLUME (thousand shares)

Business Summary: REITs (MIC: 5.3.1 SIC: 6798 NAIC: 525930)

W. P. Carey is a self-managed diversified REIT and an owner and manager of commercial real estate, primarily net leased to companies in the U.S. and Europe on a long-term basis. Co.'s owned real estate portfolio, which is diversified by property type, tenant, tenant industry, and geographic location, is comprised primarily of single-tenant industrial, office, retail, and warehouse facilities. In addition to managing its owned real estate portfolio, Co. manages a series of non-traded public and private investment programs through its investment management business. As of Dec 31 2016, Co. had 217 corporate tenants and owned 903 properties in 19 countries.

Recent Developments: For the quarter ended Sep 30 2017, income from continuing operations increased 1.9% to US$64.4 million from US$63.2 million in the year-earlier quarter. Net income decreased 25.5% to US$83.7 million from US$112.3 million in the year-earlier quarter. Revenues were US$210.8 million, down 6.4% from US$225.2 million the year before. Revenues from property income fell 1.9% to US$176.6 million from US$180.1 million in the corresponding quarter a year earlier.

Prospects: Our evaluation of W.P.Carey Inc. as of Jan. 14, 2018 is the result of our systematic analysis on three basic characteristics: earnings strength, relative valuation, and recent stock price movement. The company has produced a positive trend in earnings per share over the past 5 quarters. Because the company lacks sufficient analyst estimate data, we place greater weight on the historical EPS trend as the measure of earnings strength. Based on operating earnings yield, the company is about fairly valued when compared to all of the companies in our coverage universe. Share price changes over the past year indicates that WPC will perform very well over the near term.

Financial Data

(US$ in Thousands)	9 Mos	6 Mos	3 Mos	12/31/2016	12/31/2015	12/31/2014	12/31/2013	12/31/2012
Earnings Per Share	2.30	2.59	2.48	2.49	1.61	2.39	1.41	1.28
Cash Flow Per Share	4.98	4.91	4.80	4.84	4.52	4.04	3.03	1.70
Tang Book Value Per Share	24.18	24.30	13.21	13.34	13.09	14.82	12.38	14.03
Dividends Per Share	3.990	3.970	3.950	3.929	3.826	3.685	3.500	0.660
Dividend Payout %	173.48	153.28	159.27	157.80	237.65	154.18	248.23	51.56
Income Statement								
Total Revenue	651,341	440,587	219,059	941,533	938,383	906,193	489,851	373,995
EBITDA	305,545	202,067	97,196	590,646	663,573	655,391	297,355	121,448
Depn & Amortn	37,210	24,753	12,503	265,179	303,906	292,606	152,213	48,509
Income Before Taxes	142,961	93,122	42,736	142,058	165,341	184,663	42,506	23,762
Income Taxes	2,903	1,143	(1,305)	3,288	37,621	17,609	1,252	6,783
Net Income	202,080	121,802	57,484	267,747	172,258	239,826	98,876	62,132
Average Shares	108,143	107,783	107,764	107,073	106,507	99,827	69,708	48,078
Balance Sheet								
Current Assets	169,770	171,587	152,834	455,092	219,445	233,160	149,553	159,906
Total Assets	8,334,411	8,317,249	8,197,828	8,453,954	8,754,673	8,637,328	4,678,950	4,609,042
Current Liabilities	365,098	390,053	363,570	374,007	445,089	393,924	273,171	335,791
Long-Term Obligations	4,314,838	4,264,664	4,173,352	4,440,814	4,492,793	4,088,546	2,067,410	1,968,397
Total Liabilities	5,105,835	5,079,622	4,941,815	5,152,287	5,327,430	4,886,439	2,774,535	2,581,896
Stockholders' Equity	3,228,576	3,237,627	3,256,013	3,301,667	3,427,243	3,750,889	1,904,415	2,027,146
Shares Outstanding	106,897	106,866	106,511	106,294	104,448	104,040	68,266	68,485
Statistical Record								
Return on Assets %	2.97	3.30	3.17	3.10	1.98	3.60	2.13	2.04
Return on Equity %	7.55	8.54	8.05	7.94	4.80	8.48	5.03	4.57
EBITDA Margin %	46.91	45.86	44.37	62.73	70.71	72.32	60.70	32.47
Net Margin %	31.03	27.65	26.24	28.44	18.36	26.47	20.18	16.61
Asset Turnover	0.10	0.11	0.11	0.11	0.11	0.14	0.11	0.12
Current Ratio	0.46	0.44	0.42	1.22	0.49	0.59	0.55	0.48
Debt to Equity	1.34	1.32	1.28	1.35	1.31	1.09	1.09	0.97
Price Range	69.93-56.19	72.87-56.19	72.87-56.19	72.87-51.87	73.58-56.23	72.84-57.87	78.58-51.89	54.70-41.65
P/E Ratio	30.40-24.43	28.14-21.69	29.38-22.66	29.27-20.83	45.70-34.93	30.48-24.21	55.73-36.80	42.73-32.54
Average Yield %	6.28	6.24	6.22	6.28	6.01	5.71	5.39	1.41

Address: 50 Rockefeller Plaza, New York, NY 10020	Web Site: www.wpcarey.com	Auditors: PricewaterhouseCoopers LLP
Telephone: 212-492-8920	Officers: John J. Park - President, Chief Financial Officer, Managing Director Jason E. Fox - President, Chief Executive Officer, Global Head	Investor Contact: 212-492-8920
Fax: 212-492-1100		Transfer Agents: Computershare Shareowner Services, LLC, Pittsburgh, PA

WPX ENERGY, INC.

Exchange	Symbol	Price	52Wk Range	Yield	P/E
NYS	WPX	$14.07 (12/29/2017)	15.26-8.71	N/A	N/A

*7 Year Price Score N/A *NYSE Composite Index=100 *12 Month Price Score 102.13

Interim Earnings (Per Share)

Qtr.	Mar	Jun	Sep	Dec
2014	0.09	(0.66)	0.30	1.07
2015	0.32	(0.14)	(0.93)	(6.53)
2016	(0.06)	(0.68)	(0.72)	(0.51)
2017	0.22	0.18	(0.38)	...

Interim Dividends (Per Share)

No Dividends Paid

Valuation Analysis

		Institutional Holding	
Forecast EPS	$-0.46	No of Institutions	
	(01/18/2018)	456	
Market Cap	$5.6 Billion	Shares	
Book Value	$4.2 Billion	434,598,944	
Price/Book	1.35	% Held	
Price/Sales	4.72	N/A	

TRADING VOLUME (thousand shares)

Business Summary: Production & Extraction (MIC: 9.1.1 SIC: 1311 NAIC: 211111)

WPX Energy is an independent oil and natural gas exploration and production company engaged in the exploitation and development of properties. Co.'s principal areas of operation are the Delaware Basin in Texas and New Mexico, the Williston Basin in North Dakota, and the San Juan Basin in New Mexico and Colorado. As of Dec 31 2016, Co. had total estimated proved reserves of 346.4 million barrels of oil equivalent, which comprised of 51.0% crude oil, 35.0% natural gas and 14.0% natural gas liquids.

Recent Developments: For the quarter ended Sep 30 2017, loss from continuing operations was US$150.0 million compared with a loss of US$218.0 million in the year-earlier quarter. Net loss amounted to US$146.0 million versus a net loss of US$219.0 million in the year-earlier quarter. Revenues were US$224.0 million, down 10.8% from US$251.0 million the year before. Operating loss was US$67.0 million versus a loss of US$301.0 million in the prior-year quarter. Direct operating expenses declined 3.3% to US$87.0 million from US$90.0 million in the comparable period the year before. Indirect operating expenses decreased 55.8% to US$204.0 million from US$462.0 million in the equivalent prior-year period.

Prospects: Our evaluation of WPX Energy Inc. as of Jan. 14, 2018 is the result of our systematic analysis on three basic characteristics: earnings strength, relative valuation, and recent stock price movement. The company has produced a positive trend in earnings per share over the past 5 quarters. Because the company lacks sufficient analyst estimate data, we place greater weight on the historical EPS trend as the measure of earnings strength. Based on operating earnings yield, the company is overvalued when compared to all of the companies in our coverage universe. Share price changes over the past year indicates that WPX will perform very poorly over the near term.

Financial Data
(US$ in Millions)

	9 Mos	6 Mos	3 Mos	12/31/2016	12/31/2015	12/31/2014	12/31/2013	12/31/2012
Earnings Per Share	(0.49)	(0.83)	(1.69)	(2.05)	(7.42)	0.80	(5.91)	(1.12)
Cash Flow Per Share	0.96	0.80	0.69	0.83	3.46	5.28	3.17	3.98
Tang Book Value Per Share	9.87	10.23	10.04	9.38	11.60	21.20	20.44	26.43
Income Statement								
Total Revenue	1,098	874	461	693	1,888	3,493	2,761	3,189
EBITDA	183	258	179	(63)	(1,392)	1,226	(794)	721
Depn & Amortn	24	17	7	667	975	899	972	1,001
Income Before Taxes	18	148	125	(937)	(2,554)	204	(1,869)	(374)
Income Taxes	(2)	(22)	31	(325)	(915)	75	(655)	(111)
Net Income	22	168	92	(601)	(1,727)	164	(1,185)	(223)
Average Shares	398	423	410	313	234	206	200	198
Balance Sheet								
Current Assets	648	393	428	754	850	1,869	922	772
Total Assets	8,095	7,962	7,910	7,264	8,350	8,798	8,429	9,456
Current Liabilities	637	619	588	677	690	1,209	1,007	726
Long-Term Obligations	2,859	2,601	2,575	2,575	3,189	2,280	1,916	1,508
Total Liabilities	3,933	3,658	3,688	3,798	4,815	4,479	4,320	4,188
Stockholders' Equity	4,162	4,304	4,222	3,466	3,535	4,319	4,109	5,268
Shares Outstanding	398	398	397	344	275	203	201	199
Statistical Record								
Return on Assets %	N.M.	N.M.	N.M.	N.M.	N.M.	1.90	N.M.	N.M.
Return on Equity %	N.M.	N.M.	N.M.	N.M.	N.M.	3.89	N.M.	N.M.
EBITDA Margin %	16.67	29.52	38.83	N.M.	N.M.	35.10	N.M.	22.61
Net Margin %	2.00	19.22	19.96	N.M.	N.M.	4.70	N.M.	N.M.
Asset Turnover	0.15	0.15	0.12	0.09	0.22	0.41	0.31	0.32
Current Ratio	1.02	0.63	0.73	1.11	1.23	1.55	0.92	1.06
Debt to Equity	0.69	0.60	0.61	0.74	0.90	0.53	0.47	0.29
Price Range	15.54-8.71	15.54-8.71	15.54-6.34	15.54-3.56	14.55-5.16	26.62-10.27	23.45-14.19	19.67-13.37
P/E Ratio	...	...	...	...	...	33.27-12.84	...	...

Address: 3500 One Williams Center, Tulsa, OK 74172-0172	**Web Site:** www.wpxenergy.com	**Auditors:** Ernst & Young LLP
Telephone: 855-979-2012	**Officers:** Richard E. (Rick) Muncrief - Chairman, President, Chief Executive Officer Clay M. Gaspar - President, Senior Vice President, Chief Operating Officer	**Investor Contact:** 539-573-9360 **Transfer Agents:** Computershare Trust Company, N.A., Canton, MA

WYNDHAM WORLDWIDE CORP

Exchange	Symbol	Price	52Wk Range	Yield	P/E
NYS	WYN	$115.87 (12/29/2017)	116.66-75.93	2.00	20.80

*7 Year Price Score 113.71 *NYSE Composite Index=100 *12 Month Price Score 107.73

Interim Earnings (Per Share)

Qtr.	Mar	Jun	Sep	Dec
2014	0.69	1.20	1.64	0.67
2015	1.00	1.33	1.61	1.21
2016	0.84	1.39	1.78	1.52
2017	1.33	0.75	1.97	...

Interim Dividends (Per Share)

Amt	Decl	Ex	Rec	Pay
0.58Q	02/28/2017	03/15/2017	03/17/2017	03/30/2017
0.58Q	05/09/2017	05/24/2017	05/26/2017	06/09/2017
0.58Q	08/02/2017	08/23/2017	08/25/2017	09/08/2017
0.58Q	11/07/2017	11/24/2017	11/27/2017	12/11/2017

Indicated Div: $2.32

Valuation Analysis / Institutional Holding

Valuation Analysis		Institutional Holding	
Forecast EPS	$6.02	No of Institutions	726
	(01/18/2018)		
Market Cap	$11.7 Billion	Shares	113,126,640
Book Value	$624.0 Million	% Held	77.35
Price/Book	18.80		
Price/Sales	2.04		

TRADING VOLUME (thousand shares)

Business Summary: Hotels, Restaurants & Travel (MIC: 2.2.1 SIC: 7011 NAIC: 721110)

Wyndham Worldwide is a hospitality company. Co. has three segments: hotel group, which franchises in the upscale, upper midscale, midscale, economy and extended stay segments with a concentration in economy brands, and provides property management services; destination network, which provides vacation accommodations; and vacation ownership, which develops and markets Vacation Ownership Interests (VOIs) to individual consumers, provides consumer financing in connection with the sale of VOIs and provides property management services at resorts. Co.'s brands include Wyndham Hotels and Resorts, Days Inn, Super 8, Howard Johnson, Wingate by Wyndham, and Dolce Hotels and Resorts, among others.

Recent Developments: For the quarter ended Sep 30 2017, net income increased 3.0% to US$203.0 million from US$197.0 million in the year-earlier quarter. Revenues were US$1.63 billion, up 3.6% from US$1.57 billion the year before. Operating income was US$334.0 million versus US$336.0 million in the prior-year quarter, a decrease of 0.6%. Direct operating expenses rose 3.5% to US$771.0 million from US$745.0 million in the comparable period the year before. Indirect operating expenses increased 6.5% to US$524.0 million from US$492.0 million in the equivalent prior-year period.

Prospects: Our evaluation of Wyndham Worldwide Corp. as of Jan. 14, 2018 is the result of our systematic analysis on three basic characteristics: earnings strength, relative valuation, and recent stock price movement. The company has generated a negative trend in earnings per share over the past 5 quarters and while recent estimates for the company have been mixed, WYN has posted better than expected results. Based on operating earnings yield, the company is undervalued when compared to all of the companies in our coverage universe. Share price changes over the past year indicates that WYN will perform very well over the near term.

Financial Data
(US$ in Millions)

	9 Mos	6 Mos	3 Mos	12/31/2016	12/31/2015	12/31/2014	12/31/2013	12/31/2012
Earnings Per Share	5.57	5.38	6.02	5.53	5.14	4.18	3.21	2.75
Cash Flow Per Share	8.33	8.96	9.05	8.82	8.40	7.87	7.58	7.00
Dividends Per Share	2.240	2.160	2.080	2.000	1.680	1.400	1.160	0.920
Dividend Payout %	40.22	40.15	34.55	36.17	32.68	33.49	36.14	33.45
Income Statement								
Total Revenue	4,427	2,798	1,319	5,599	5,536	5,281	5,009	4,534
EBITDA	902	480	266	1,282	1,229	1,144	985	783
Depn & Amortn	197	128	63	214	197	196	180	31
Income Before Taxes	596	283	172	940	916	845	683	628
Income Taxes	173	64	31	328	304	316	250	229
Net Income	422	219	141	611	612	529	432	400
Average Shares	102	104	106	111	119	127	135	145
Balance Sheet								
Current Assets	2,039	2,258	2,302	1,812	1,869	1,867	1,940	1,866
Total Assets	10,261	10,348	10,343	9,819	9,716	9,679	9,741	9,463
Current Liabilities	2,121	2,384	2,349	2,032	1,957	1,859	1,790	1,931
Long-Term Obligations	5,667	5,534	5,482	5,283	4,955	4,792	4,608	4,018
Total Liabilities	9,637	9,761	9,681	9,105	8,766	8,424	8,118	7,533
Stockholders' Equity	624	587	662	714	950	1,255	1,623	1,930
Shares Outstanding	101	102	104	105	113	121	128	137
Statistical Record								
Return on Assets %	5.86	5.71	6.41	6.24	6.31	5.45	4.50	4.32
Return on Equity %	82.71	84.84	87.66	73.24	55.51	36.76	24.32	19.17
EBITDA Margin %	20.37	17.16	20.17	22.90	22.20	21.66	19.66	17.27
Net Margin %	9.53	7.83	10.69	10.91	11.05	10.02	8.62	8.82
Asset Turnover	0.57	0.56	0.55	0.57	0.57	0.54	0.52	0.49
Current Ratio	0.96	0.95	0.98	0.89	0.96	1.00	1.08	0.97
Debt to Equity	9.08	9.43	8.28	7.40	5.22	3.82	2.84	2.08
Price Range	105.41-63.32	105.27-63.32	85.79-63.32	80.79-61.63	94.11-70.18	86.77-68.62	73.69-53.21	55.04-36.87
P/E Ratio	18.92-11.37	19.57-11.77	14.25-10.52	14.61-11.14	18.31-13.65	20.76-16.42	22.96-16.58	20.01-13.41
Average Yield %	2.56	2.71	2.83	2.83	2.03	1.84	1.87	1.87

Address: 22 Sylvan Way, Parsippany, NJ 07054	**Web Site:** www.wyndhamworldwide.com	**Auditors:** Deloitte & Touche LLP
	Officers: Stephen P. Holmes - Chairman, Chief	**Investor Contact:** 973-753-5500
Telephone: 973-753-6000	Executive Officer David B. Wyshner - Chief Financial	**Transfer Agents:** Wells Fargo
Fax: 973-496-8906	Officer, Executive Vice President	Shareowner Services, St. Paul, MN

XEROX CORP

Exchange	Symbol	Price	52Wk Range	Yield	P/E
NYS	XRX	$29.15 (12/29/2017)	33.95-6.88	N/A	N/A

*7 Year Price Score 183.56 ***NYSE Composite Index=100** ***12 Month Price Score 139.49**

Interim Earnings (Per Share)

Qtr.	Mar	Jun	Sep	Dec
2014	0.92	0.88	0.88	0.56
2015	0.76	0.04	(0.16)	1.00
2016	0.12	0.60	0.68	(3.32)
2017	0.04	0.63	0.68	...

Interim Dividends (Per Share)

Amt	Decl	Ex	Rec	Pay
0.31Q	10/19/2016	12/13/2016	12/15/2016	01/31/2017
0.00Q	11/08/2016	01/03/2017	12/15/2016	12/31/2016
0.25Q	02/24/2017	03/29/2017	03/31/2017	04/28/2017
1-for-4	...	06/15/2017	...	...

Valuation Analysis **Institutional Holding**

Forecast EPS	$3.39	No of Institutions	
	(01/18/2018)	752	
Market Cap	$7.4 Billion	Shares	
Book Value	$5.6 Billion	450,322,656	
Price/Book	1.33	% Held	
Price/Sales	1.37	68.93	

Business Summary: Peripherals (MIC: 6.2.2 SIC: 3577 NAIC: 333315)

Xerox is a provider of digital print technology and related solutions. Co. operates in three main areas: Managed Document Services, which includes a continuum of solutions and services spanning from managing print to automating processes to managing content; Workplace Solutions, which is made up of two strategic product groups, Entry and Mid-Range, which share common technology, manufacturing and product platforms; and Graphic Communications, which are designed for customers in the graphic communications, enabling full-color, on-demand printing of a range of applications, including variable data for personalized content and one-to-one marketing.

Recent Developments: For the quarter ended Sep 30 2017, income from continuing operations increased 0.6% to US$179.0 million from US$178.0 million in the year-earlier quarter. Net income decreased 2.2% to US$182.0 million from US$186.0 million in the year-earlier quarter. Revenues were US$2.50 billion, down 5.0% from US$2.63 billion the year before. Direct operating expenses declined 5.4% to US$1.48 billion from US$1.56 billion in the comparable period the year before. Indirect operating expenses decreased 5.4% to US$854.0 million from US$903.0 million in the equivalent prior-year period.

Prospects: Our evaluation of Xerox Corp. as of Jan. 14, 2018 is the result of our systematic analysis on three basic characteristics: earnings strength, relative valuation, and recent stock price movement. The company has produced a positive trend in earnings per share over the past 5 quarters and while recent estimates for the company have remained steady, XRX has posted better than expected results. Based on operating earnings yield, the company is undervalued when compared to all of the companies in our coverage universe. Share price changes over the past year indicates that XRX will perform poorly over the near term.

Financial Data

(US$ in Thousands)	9 Mos	6 Mos	3 Mos	12/31/2016	12/31/2015	12/31/2014	12/31/2013	12/31/2012
Earnings Per Share	(1.97)	(1.97)	(2.00)	(1.96)	1.68	3.24	3.64	3.52
Cash Flow Per Share	2.46	5.43	4.84	4.31	6.05	7.15	7.75	7.90
Tang Book Value Per Share	5.39	4.56	4.14	2.79	N.M.	N.M.	N.M.	N.M.
Dividends Per Share	0.500	0.250	1.180	1.240	1.120	1.000	0.920	0.680
Dividend Payout %	...	...	...	...	66.67	30.86	25.27	19.32
Income Statement								
Total Revenue	7,518,000	5,021,000	2,454,000	10,771,000	18,045,000	19,540,000	21,435,000	22,390,000
EBITDA	567,000	328,000	65,000	1,078,000	1,344,000	2,212,000	2,470,000	2,822,000
Depn & Amortn	41,000	29,000	14,000	206,000	587,000	639,000	763,000	1,059,000
Income Before Taxes	344,000	177,000	(16,000)	568,000	412,000	1,206,000	1,312,000	1,348,000
Income Taxes	37,000	19,000	(24,000)	62,000	259,000	(23,000)	276,000	277,000
Net Income	385,000	206,000	16,000	(477,000)	474,000	969,000	1,159,000	1,195,000
Average Shares	263,385	263,210	256,142	255,994	269,056	299,640	318,381	332,296
Balance Sheet								
Current Assets	5,629,000	4,978,000	4,715,000	6,992,000	6,685,000	8,874,000	8,511,000	8,273,000
Total Assets	16,817,000	16,167,000	15,916,000	18,145,000	24,817,000	27,658,000	29,036,000	30,015,000
Current Liabilities	3,452,000	3,414,000	2,624,000	4,654,000	5,254,000	6,076,000	5,686,000	5,910,000
Long-Term Obligations	5,235,000	4,236,000	4,988,000	5,305,000	6,382,000	6,358,000	6,904,000	7,447,000
Total Liabilities	11,247,000	10,830,000	10,776,000	13,128,000	15,394,000	16,675,000	16,387,000	18,145,000
Stockholders' Equity	5,570,000	5,337,000	5,140,000	5,017,000	9,423,000	10,983,000	12,649,000	11,870,000
Shares Outstanding	254,586	254,170	254,146	253,593	253,209	279,186	297,080	305,943
Statistical Record								
Return on Assets %	N.M.	N.M.	N.M.	N.M.	1.81	3.42	3.93	3.96
Return on Equity %	N.M.	N.M.	N.M.	N.M.	4.65	8.20	9.45	9.89
EBITDA Margin %	7.54	6.53	2.65	10.01	7.45	11.32	11.52	12.60
Net Margin %	5.12	4.10	0.65	N.M.	2.63	4.96	5.41	5.34
Asset Turnover	0.26	0.35	0.44	0.50	0.69	0.69	0.73	0.74
Current Ratio	1.63	1.46	1.80	1.50	1.27	1.46	1.50	1.40
Debt to Equity	0.94	0.79	0.97	1.06	0.68	0.58	0.55	0.63
Price Range	33.95-5.74	29.29-5.74	7.54-5.74	7.41-5.72	9.22-6.12	9.43-6.78	8.06-4.49	5.77-4.10
P/E Ratio	...	...	...	...	5.49-3.64	2.91-2.09	2.21-1.23	1.64-1.17
Average Yield %	3.57	3.23	17.83	19.29	14.85	12.18	14.77	13.82

Address: P.O. Box 4505, 201 Merritt 7, Norwalk, CT 06851-1056	**Web Site:** www.xerox.com	**Auditors:** PricewaterhouseCoopers LLP
Telephone: 203-968-3000	**Officers:** Ashok Vemuri - Executive Vice President William F. Osbourn - Executive Vice President, Chief Financial Officer	**Transfer Agents:** Computershare Trust Company, N.A., Providence, RI

XL GROUP LTD

Exchange	Symbol	Price	52Wk Range	Yield	P/E
NYS	XL	$35.16 (12/29/2017)	46.66-35.06	2.50	N/A

*7 Year Price Score 101.34 *NYSE Composite Index=100 *12 Month Price Score 88.19

TRADING VOLUME (thousand shares)

Interim Earnings (Per Share)

Qtr.	Mar	Jun	Sep	Dec
2014	0.91	(1.03)	0.27	0.51
2015	0.14	3.11	0.09	0.75
2016	0.07	0.15	0.25	1.08
2017	0.57	1.14	(4.06)	...

Interim Dividends (Per Share)

Amt	Decl	Ex	Rec	Pay
0.22Q	02/17/2017	03/13/2017	03/15/2017	03/31/2017
0.22Q	05/18/2017	06/13/2017	06/15/2017	06/30/2017
0.22Q	08/02/2017	09/14/2017	09/15/2017	10/02/2017
0.22Q	10/26/2017	12/14/2017	12/15/2017	01/02/2018

Indicated Div: $0.88

Valuation Analysis		Institutional Holding	
Forecast EPS	N/A	No of Institutions	575
Market Cap	$9.0 Billion	Shares	
Book Value	$9.9 Billion		322,240,352
Price/Book	0.91	% Held	
Price/Sales	0.80	N/A	

Business Summary: General Insurance (MIC: 5.2.1 SIC: 6331 NAIC: 524126)

XL Group is a holding company. Through its subsidiaries, Co. is an insurance and reinsurance company providing property, casualty and specialty products to industrial, commercial and professional firms, insurance companies and other enterprises. Co. is organized into two operating segments: insurance, which include four business groups: Global Casualty, Global Energy, Property and Construction, Global Professional and Global Specialt, as well as four regions: Americas; Europe, Middle East & Africa; U.K. & Ireland; and Asia Pacific; and reinsurance, which provides casualty, property risk, property catastrophe, specialty, and other reinsurance lines on a global basis.

Recent Developments: For the quarter ended Sep 30 2017, net loss amounted to US$1.07 billion versus net income of US$128.7 million in the year-earlier quarter. Revenues were US$2.88 billion, up 11.4% from US$2.59 billion the year before. Net premiums earned were US$2.62 billion versus US$2.43 billion in the prior-year quarter, an increase of 7.7%. Net investment income fell 3.3% to US$202.8 million from US$209.8 million a year ago.

Prospects: Our evaluation of XL Group Ltd. as of Sep. 17, 2017 is the result of our systematic analysis on three basic characteristics: earnings strength, relative valuation, and recent stock price movement. The company has produced a positive trend in earnings per share over the past 5 quarters. However, while recent estimates for the company have been mixed, XL has posted better than expected results. Based on operating earnings yield, the company is undervalued when compared to all of the companies in our coverage universe. Share price changes over the past year indicates that XL will perform very well over the near term.

Financial Data

(US$ in Thousands)	9 Mos	6 Mos	3 Mos	12/31/2016	12/31/2015	12/31/2014	12/31/2013	12/31/2012
Earnings Per Share	(1.27)	3.04	2.05	1.56	4.15	0.69	3.63	2.10
Cash Flow Per Share	1.75	2.37	3.91	3.27	2.15	3.61	2.71	3.43
Tang Book Value Per Share	30.13	34.26	33.24	32.73	32.12	37.56	34.45	33.82
Income Statement								
Premium Income	7,660,610	5,039,708	2,522,791	9,777,934	8,226,425	5,895,070	6,309,521	6,090,441
Total Revenue	8,427,105	5,543,121	2,755,361	10,546,086	9,308,926	6,602,267	7,541,234	7,230,480
Benefits & Claims	6,179,262	3,112,539	1,583,456	6,072,835	4,766,200	3,258,393	3,731,464	3,765,482
Income Before Taxes	(629,213)	509,677	213,332	567,877	909,031	258,517	1,094,348	708,606
Income Taxes	(18,034)	42,098	13,092	42,129	(19,161)	96,897	77,505	34,028
Net Income	(589,226)	454,463	152,843	440,968	1,207,152	188,340	1,059,916	651,134
Average Shares	261,298	264,943	269,767	282,758	290,999	271,527	292,069	310,282
Balance Sheet								
Total Assets	63,790,208	62,382,250	61,024,619	58,434,102	58,682,938	45,046,819	45,652,887	45,387,779
Total Liabilities	53,850,361	51,301,698	50,049,735	47,495,590	47,005,859	35,013,067	35,655,254	34,877,707
Stockholders' Equity	9,939,847	11,080,552	10,974,884	10,938,512	11,677,079	10,033,752	9,997,633	10,510,072
Shares Outstanding	255,980	258,611	263,735	266,889	294,745	255,182	278,253	298,681
Statistical Record								
Return on Assets %	N.M.	1.34	0.94	0.75	2.33	0.42	2.33	1.44
Return on Equity %	N.M.	7.29	5.05	3.89	11.12	1.88	10.34	6.51
Loss Ratio %	80.66	61.76	62.77	62.11	57.94	55.27	59.14	61.83
Net Margin %	(6.99)	8.20	5.55	4.18	12.97	2.85	14.05	9.01
Price Range	46.66-33.21	44.20-32.18	41.19-30.67	39.18-30.67	40.41-34.37	36.30-27.96	33.03-25.06	25.76-19.06
P/E Ratio	...	14.54-10.59	20.09-14.96	25.12-19.66	9.74-8.28	52.61-40.52	9.10-6.90	12.27-9.08

Address: O'Hara House, One Bermudiana Road, Hamilton, HM 08
Telephone: 441-292-8515

Web Site: www.xlgroup.com
Officers: Eugene M. (Gene) McQuade - Chairman
Michael S. McGavick - Chief Executive Officer

Auditors: PricewaterhouseCoopers LLP
Investor Contact: 203-964-3470
Transfer Agents: Mellon Investor Services, New Jersey

XPO LOGISTICS, INC.

Exchange	Symbol	Price	52Wk Range	Yield	P/E
NYS	XPO	$91.59 (12/29/2017)	92.17-42.71	N/A	75.69

*7 Year Price Score 157.28 *NYSE Composite Index=100 *12 Month Price Score 126.11

Interim Earnings (Per Share)

Qtr.	Mar	Jun	Sep	Dec
2014	(0.70)	(0.28)	(0.23)	(0.87)
2015	(0.20)	(0.89)	(0.94)	(0.55)
2016	(0.21)	0.35	0.11	0.23
2017	0.16	0.38	0.44	...

Interim Dividends (Per Share)

No Dividends Paid

Valuation Analysis

		Institutional Holding	
Forecast EPS	$1.92	No of Institutions	
	(01/18/2018)	436	
Market Cap	$11.0 Billion	Shares	
Book Value	$3.3 Billion	148,810,896	
Price/Book	3.31	% Held	
Price/Sales	0.74	N/A	

TRADING VOLUME (thousand shares)

Business Summary: Airlines/Air Freight (MIC: 7.4.4 SIC: 4731 NAIC: 488510)

XPO Logistics is a transportation and logistics company. Co. has two segments: Transportation, which is a provider of freight brokerage provider, last mile logistics for heavy goods, less-than-truckload transportation, intermodal services and freight forwarder; and Logistics, which provide a range of contract logistics services, including engineered and customized solutions, warehousing and distribution, cold chain solutions and other inventory management solutions, including perform e-commerce fulfillment, warehousing, reverse logistics, storage, factory support, aftermarket support, manufacturing, distribution, packaging and labeling, as well as supply chain optimization services.

Recent Developments: For the quarter ended Sep 30 2017, net income increased 233.3% to US$71.0 million from US$21.3 million in the year-earlier quarter. Revenues were US$3.89 billion, up 4.7% from US$3.71 billion the year before. Operating income was US$186.8 million versus US$168.8 million in the prior-year quarter, an increase of 10.7%. Direct operating expenses rose 4.4% to US$3.30 billion from US$3.16 billion in the comparable period the year before. Indirect operating expenses increased 4.1% to US$398.9 million from US$383.2 million in the equivalent prior-year period.

Prospects: Our evaluation of XPO Logistics, Inc. as of Jan. 14, 2018 is the result of our systematic analysis on three basic characteristics: earnings strength, relative valuation, and recent stock price movement. The company has generated a negative trend in earnings per share over the past 5 quarters and while recent estimates for the company have been mixed, XPO has posted better than expected results. Based on operating earnings yield, the company is overvalued when compared to all of the companies in our coverage universe. Share price changes over the past year indicates that XPO will perform in line with the market over the near term.

Financial Data

(US$ in Thousands)	9 Mos	6 Mos	3 Mos	12/31/2016	12/31/2015	12/31/2014	12/31/2013	12/31/2012
Earnings Per Share	1.21	0.88	0.85	0.53	(2.65)	(2.00)	(2.26)	(1.49)
Cash Flow Per Share	6.34	4.96	5.69	5.66	0.98	(0.40)	(2.91)	(1.54)
Tang Book Value Per Share	N.M.	N.M.	N.M.	N.M.	N.M.	4.42	N.M.	6.90
Income Statement								
Total Revenue	11,186,900	7,299,800	3,539,500	14,619,400	7,623,200	2,356,600	702,303	278,591
EBITDA	913,000	571,800	248,100	933,900	137,200	(5,900)	(46,103)	(25,614)
Depn & Amortn	489,100	321,800	157,400	466,000	203,000	35,800	6,700	2,713
Income Before Taxes	201,500	100,100	15,100	106,800	(282,500)	(89,700)	(70,972)	(31,534)
Income Taxes	48,400	18,000	(9,800)	22,300	(90,900)	(26,100)	(22,442)	(11,195)
Net Income	135,700	73,200	21,300	69,000	(191,100)	(63,600)	(48,530)	(20,339)
Average Shares	129,800	124,700	124,400	122,800	92,800	53,600	22,752	15,694
Balance Sheet								
Current Assets	3,581,700	3,258,300	3,096,100	3,073,600	2,957,200	1,233,100	172,172	320,934
Total Assets	12,358,200	11,931,900	11,688,300	11,698,400	12,643,200	2,761,200	780,241	413,208
Current Liabilities	2,907,700	2,733,700	2,597,300	2,731,600	2,694,400	381,100	99,333	49,027
Long-Term Obligations	4,541,000	4,754,300	4,810,900	4,731,500	5,272,600	592,100	181,641	108,956
Total Liabilities	9,049,400	9,051,700	8,947,100	8,998,400	9,926,100	1,106,100	324,398	168,149
Stockholders' Equity	3,308,800	2,880,200	2,741,200	2,700,000	2,717,100	1,655,100	455,843	245,059
Shares Outstanding	119,600	112,500	111,622	111,087	109,523	77,421	30,538	17,957
Statistical Record								
Return on Assets %	1.34	0.97	0.93	0.57	N.M.	N.M.	N.M.	N.M.
Return on Equity %	5.49	4.21	4.13	2.54	N.M.	N.M.	N.M.	N.M.
EBITDA Margin %	8.16	7.83	7.01	6.39	1.80	N.M.	N.M.	N.M.
Net Margin %	1.21	1.00	0.60	0.47	N.M.	N.M.	N.M.	N.M.
Asset Turnover	1.20	1.21	1.20	1.20	0.99	1.33	1.18	1.03
Current Ratio	1.23	1.19	1.19	1.13	1.10	3.24	1.73	6.55
Debt to Equity	1.37	1.65	1.76	1.75	1.94	0.36	0.40	0.44
Price Range	67.78-32.17	64.76-24.43	52.54-23.30	49.35-19.56	50.56-21.62	42.48-23.24	26.45-15.82	19.02-11.35
P/E Ratio	56.02-26.59	73.59-27.76	61.81-27.41	93.11-36.91	...	...	...	...

Address: Five American Lane, Greenwich, CT 06831 **Telephone:** 855-976-6951	**Web Site:** www.xpologistics.com **Officers:** Bradley S. Jacobs - Chairman, Chief Executive Officer Karlis P. Kirsis - Senior Vice President, Corporate Counsel	**Auditors:** KPMG LLP **Investor Contact:** 855-976-4696 **Transfer Agents:** Computershare, Canton, MA

XYLEM INC.

Exchange	Symbol	Price	52Wk Range	Yield	P/E
NYS	XYL	$68.20 (12/29/2017)	69.34-47.00	1.06	39.65

*7 Year Price Score N/A   *NYSE Composite Index=100   *12 Month Price Score 112.34

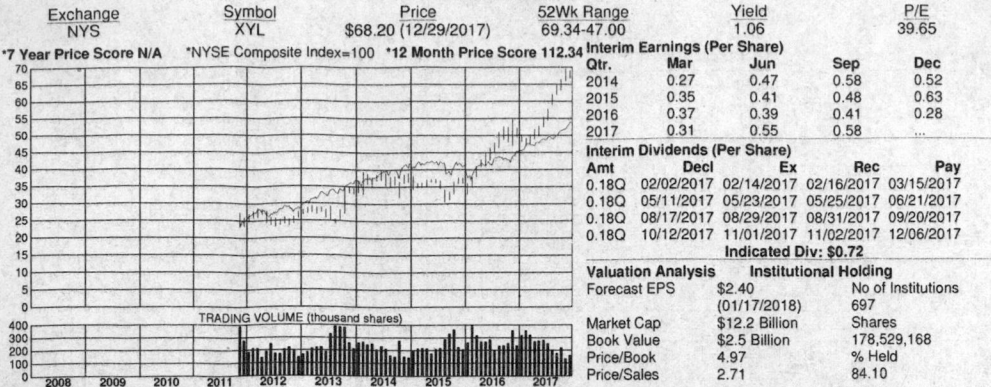

Interim Earnings (Per Share)

Qtr.	Mar	Jun	Sep	Dec
2014	0.27	0.47	0.58	0.52
2015	0.35	0.41	0.48	0.63
2016	0.37	0.39	0.41	0.28
2017	0.31	0.55	0.58	...

Interim Dividends (Per Share)

Amt	Decl	Ex	Rec	Pay
0.18Q	02/02/2017	02/14/2017	02/16/2017	03/15/2017
0.18Q	05/11/2017	05/23/2017	05/25/2017	06/21/2017
0.18Q	08/17/2017	08/29/2017	08/31/2017	09/20/2017
0.18Q	10/12/2017	11/01/2017	11/02/2017	12/06/2017

Indicated Div: $0.72

Valuation Analysis — **Institutional Holding**

Forecast EPS	$2.40	No of Institutions
	(01/17/2018)	697
Market Cap	$12.2 Billion	Shares
Book Value	$2.5 Billion	178,529,168
Price/Book	4.97	% Held
Price/Sales	2.71	84.10

Business Summary: Industrial Machinery & Equipment (MIC: 7.2.1 SIC: 3561 NAIC: 333911)

Xylem is a water technology company. Co. designs, manufactures and services engineered solutions ranging across a variety of applications. Co. has three reportable business segments: Water Infrastructure, which supports the process that collects water from a source and distributes it to users, and then returns the wastewater to the environment through three linked applications; Applied Water, which encompasses the uses of water and serves a set of end markets including: residential, commercial, industrial and agricultural; as well as Sensus, which develops technology solutions that enable use and conservation of water and energy resources.

Recent Developments: For the quarter ended Sep 30 2017, net income increased 42.5% to US$104.0 million from US$73.0 million in the year-earlier quarter. Revenues were US$1.20 billion, up 33.2% from US$897.0 million the year before. Operating income was US$152.0 million versus US$109.0 million in the prior-year quarter, an increase of 39.4%. Direct operating expenses rose 34.1% to US$724.0 million from US$540.0 million in the comparable period the year before. Indirect operating expenses increased 28.6% to US$319.0 million from US$248.0 million in the equivalent prior-year period.

Prospects: Our evaluation of Xylem Inc. as of Jan. 14, 2018 is the result of our systematic analysis on three basic characteristics: earnings strength, relative valuation, and recent stock price movement. The company has enjoyed a very positive trend in earnings per share over the past 5 quarters and while recent estimates for the company have remained steady, XYL has posted better than expected results. Based on operating earnings yield, the company is about fairly valued when compared to all of the companies in our coverage universe. Share price changes over the past year indicates that XYL will perform well over the near term.

Financial Data

(US$ in Millions)	9 Mos	6 Mos	3 Mos	12/31/2016	12/31/2015	12/31/2014	12/31/2013	12/31/2012
Earnings Per Share	1.72	1.55	1.39	1.45	1.87	1.83	1.22	1.59
Cash Flow Per Share	3.35	2.91	2.83	2.77	2.57	2.27	1.75	2.13
Tang Book Value Per Share	N.M.	N.M.	N.M.	N.M.	0.36	0.33	0.19	N.M.
Dividends Per Share	0.695	0.670	0.645	0.620	0.563	0.512	0.466	0.405
Dividend Payout %	40.40	43.21	46.38	42.73	30.12	27.98	38.16	25.46
Income Statement								
Total Revenue	3,430	2,235	1,071	3,771	3,653	3,916	3,837	3,791
EBITDA	558	348	149	495	544	568	449	533
Depn & Amortn	174	116	59	87	88	95	99	94
Income Before Taxes	322	191	70	340	403	421	298	388
Income Taxes	62	35	14	80	63	84	70	91
Net Income	260	155	56	260	340	337	228	297
Average Shares	180	180	180	180	181	184	186	186
Balance Sheet								
Current Assets	1,995	1,961	1,863	1,839	2,005	2,102	2,009	1,874
Total Assets	6,783	6,707	6,527	6,474	4,657	4,864	4,896	4,679
Current Liabilities	1,136	1,200	1,191	1,238	823	908	853	781
Long-Term Obligations	2,189	2,168	2,126	2,108	1,196	1,199	1,199	1,199
Total Liabilities	4,320	4,342	4,276	4,284	2,573	2,737	2,655	2,605
Stockholders' Equity	2,463	2,365	2,251	2,190	2,084	2,127	2,241	2,074
Shares Outstanding	179	179	179	179	178	182	184	185
Statistical Record								
Return on Assets %	5.36	4.88	4.23	4.66	7.14	6.91	4.76	6.53
Return on Equity %	13.22	12.25	11.34	12.13	16.15	15.43	10.57	15.19
EBITDA Margin %	16.27	15.57	13.91	13.13	14.89	14.50	11.70	14.06
Net Margin %	7.58	6.94	5.23	6.89	9.31	8.61	5.94	7.83
Asset Turnover	0.78	0.74	0.68	0.68	0.77	0.80	0.80	0.83
Current Ratio	1.76	1.63	1.56	1.49	2.44	2.31	2.36	2.40
Debt to Equity	0.89	0.92	0.94	0.96	0.57	0.56	0.54	0.58
Price Range	64.75-46.96	55.43-44.65	54.75-40.78	54.75-32.80	38.08-30.46	39.78-31.91	34.77-24.19	28.73-23.16
P/E Ratio	37.65-27.30	35.76-28.81	39.39-29.34	37.76-22.62	20.36-16.29	21.74-17.44	28.50-19.83	18.07-14.57
Average Yield %	1.32	1.34	1.34	1.38	1.59	1.39	1.63	1.57

Address: 1 International Drive, Rye Brook, NY 10573
Telephone: 914-323-5700
Fax: 914-323-5800

Web Site: www.xyleminc.com
Officers: Markos I. Tambakeras - Chairman Patrick K. Decker - President, Chief Executive Officer

Auditors: Deloitte & Touche LLP
Investor Contact: 914-323-5930
Transfer Agents: Wells Fargo Shareowner Services, St. Paul, MN

YUM! BRANDS INC

Exchange	Symbol	Price	52Wk Range	Yield	P/E	Div Acheiver
NYS	YUM	$81.61 (12/29/2017)	83.47-63.18	1.47	N/A	12 Years

*7 Year Price Score 104.13 *NYSE Composite Index=100 *12 Month Price Score 105.59

Interim Earnings (Per Share)

Qtr.	Mar	Jun	Sep	Dec
2015	0.81	0.53	0.95	0.63
2016	0.93	0.81	1.56	0.76
2017	0.77	0.58	1.18	...

Interim Dividends (Per Share)

Amt	Decl	Ex	Rec	Pay
0.30Q	12/21/2016	01/11/2017	01/13/2017	02/03/2017
0.30Q	03/24/2017	04/11/2017	04/14/2017	05/05/2017
0.30Q	05/19/2017	07/12/2017	07/14/2017	08/04/2017
0.30Q	10/23/2017	11/14/2017	11/15/2017	12/08/2017

Indicated Div: $1.20 (Div. Reinv. Plan)

Valuation Analysis		Institutional Holding	
Forecast EPS	$2.80	No of Institutions	
	(01/26/2018)	1247	
Market Cap	$27.7 Billion	Shares	
Book Value	N/A	324,409,856	
Price/Book	N/A	% Held	
Price/Sales	N/A	71.41	

TRADING VOLUME (thousand shares)

Business Summary: Hotels, Restaurants & Travel (MIC: 2.2.1 SIC: 5812 NAIC: 722211)

Yum! Brands, through its three concepts of KFC, Pizza Hut and Taco Bell (the Concepts), develops, operates, franchises and licenses a worldwide system of restaurants which prepare, package and sell a menu of food items. Most restaurants in each Concept provide consumers the ability to dine in and/or carry out food. In addition, Taco Bell and KFC provide a drive-thru option in several stores. Pizza Hut provides a drive-thru option on a limited basis. Pizza Hut typically provides delivery service, as does KFC on a more limited basis primarily in China. Co.'s registered trademarks and service marks include Kentucky Fried Chicken®, KFC®, Pizza Hut® and Taco Bell® marks.

Recent Developments: For the quarter ended Sep 30 2017, income from continuing operations increased 91.7% to US$418.0 million from US$218.0 million in the year-earlier quarter. Net income decreased 34.7% to US$418.0 million from US$640.0 million in the year-earlier quarter. Revenues were US$1.44 billion, down 5.4% from US$1.52 billion the year before. Operating income was US$643.0 million versus US$398.0 million in the prior-year quarter, an increase of 61.6%. Direct operating expenses declined 13.7% to US$717.0 million from US$831.0 million in the comparable period the year before. Indirect operating expenses decreased 73.7% to US$76.0 million from US$289.0 million in the equivalent prior-year period.

Prospects: Our evaluation of Yum! Brands Inc. as of Jan. 21, 2018 is the result of our systematic analysis on three basic characteristics: earnings strength, relative valuation, and recent stock price movement. The company has managed to produce a neutral trend in earnings per share over the past 5 quarters and while recent estimates for the company have been mixed, YUM has posted better than expected results. Based on operating earnings yield, the company is about fairly valued when compared to all of the companies in our coverage universe. Share price changes over the past year indicates that YUM will perform well over the near term.

Financial Data

(US$ in Millions)	9 Mos	6 Mos	3 Mos	12/31/2016	12/26/2015	12/27/2014	12/28/2013	12/29/2012
Earnings Per Share	...	...	...	4.04	2.92	2.32	2.36	3.38
Cash Flow Per Share	...	...	3.01		4.92	4.63	4.75	4.99
Tang Book Value Per Share	...	...	...	...	N.M.	1.22	1.44	0.95
Dividends Per Share	1.410	1.570	1.730	1.890	1.690	1.520	1.375	1.190
Dividend Payout %	...	...	...	46.78	57.88	65.52	58.26	35.21
Income Statement								
Total Revenue	4,301	2,865	1,417	6,366	13,105	13,279	13,084	13,633
EBITDA	1,699	1,006	526	1,919	2,592	2,229	2,458	2,876
Depn & Amortn	195	135	70	294	712	702	686	629
Income Before Taxes	1,182	658	347	1,318	1,746	1,397	1,525	2,098
Income Taxes	278	172	67	324	489	406	487	537
Net Income	904	486	280	1,619	1,293	1,051	1,091	1,597
Average Shares	353	358	364	400	443	453	461	473
Balance Sheet								
Current Assets	1,999	1,785	1,277	1,482	1,688	1,646	1,691	1,909
Total Assets	5,454	5,596	5,151	5,478	8,075	8,345	8,695	9,011
Current Liabilities	1,403	1,478	1,558	1,369	3,088	2,411	2,265	2,188
Long-Term Obligations	9,479	9,474	8,715	9,061	3,054	3,077	2,918	2,932
Total Liabilities	11,575	11,698	10,963	11,134	7,164	6,798	6,529	6,857
Stockholders' Equity	(6,121)	(6,102)	(5,812)	(5,656)	911	1,547	2,166	2,154
Shares Outstanding	339	345	350	355	420	434	443	451
Statistical Record								
Return on Assets %	...	...	...	23.51	15.79	12.37	12.36	17.95
Return on Equity %	...	...	...	...	105.50	56.77	50.65	80.53
EBITDA Margin %	39.50	35.11	37.12	30.14	19.78	16.79	18.79	21.10
Net Margin %	21.02	16.96	19.76	25.43	9.87	7.91	8.34	11.71
Asset Turnover	...	...	...	0.92	1.60	1.56	1.48	1.53
Current Ratio	1.42	1.21	0.82	1.08	0.55	0.68	0.75	0.87
Debt to Equity	...	...	...	...	3.35	1.99	1.35	1.36
Price Range	77.80-59.70	74.82-59.62	68.65-57.04	65.62-46.91	68.22-48.26	59.89-47.57	56.30-44.64	53.55-42.12
P/E Ratio				16.24-11.61	23.36-16.53	25.81-20.51	23.86-18.91	15.84-12.46
Average Yield %	2.07	2.40	2.76	3.18	2.93	2.85	2.74	2.46

Address: 1441 Gardiner Lane, Louisville, KY 40213 Telephone: 502-874-8300	Web Site: www.yum.com Officers: David C. Novak - Executive Chairman, Chairman, President, Chief Executive Officer Greg Creed - Chief Executive Officer, Division Officer	Auditors: KPMG LLP Investor Contact: 502-874-8006 Transfer Agents: American Stock Transfer & Trust Company, New York, NY

ZAYO GROUP HOLDINGS INC

Exchange	Symbol	Price	52Wk Range	Yield	P/E
NYS	ZAYO	$36.80 (12/29/2017)	37.07-29.92	N/A	99.46

*7 Year Price Score N/A   *NYSE Composite Index=100   *12 Month Price Score 100.12

TRADING VOLUME (thousand shares)

Interim Earnings (Per Share)

Qtr.	Sep	Dec	Mar	Jun
2014-15	(0.50)	0.02	(0.22)	0.03
2015-16	(0.06)	(0.04)	(0.08)	(0.12)
2016-17	0.06	0.08	0.11	0.09
2017-18	0.09	...	...	...

Interim Dividends (Per Share)

No Dividends Paid

Valuation Analysis		Institutional Holding	
Forecast EPS	$0.45	No of Institutions	
	(01/18/2018)	375	
Market Cap	$9.1 Billion	Shares	
Book Value	$1.5 Billion	218,054,256	
Price/Book	6.15	% Held	
Price/Sales	3.89	N/A	

Business Summary: Manufacturing (MIC: 6.1.1 SIC: 3669 NAIC: 334290)

Zayo Group Holdings is a holding company. Through its subsidiaries, Co. is a provider of bandwidth infrastructure in the U.S., Canada and Europe. Co. provides products and services through six segments: Fiber Solutions, which provides raw bandwidth infrastructure to customers; Transport, which provides lit bandwidth infrastructure solutions; Enterprise Networks, which provides communication solutions to medium and large enterprises; Zayo Colocation, which provides data center infrastructure solutions; Allstream, which provides Voice, SIP Trunking, Unified Communications and data services for businesses; and Other, which provides network and technical resources to customers.

Recent Developments: For the quarter ended Sep 30 2017, net income increased 47.8% to US$23.2 million from US$15.7 million in the year-earlier quarter. Revenues were US$643.5 million, up 27.5% from US$504.9 million the year before. Operating income was US$95.4 million versus US$87.0 million in the prior-year quarter, an increase of 9.7%. Direct operating expenses rose 35.6% to US$235.7 million from US$173.8 million in the comparable period the year before. Indirect operating expenses increased 28.0% to US$312.4 million from US$244.1 million in the equivalent prior-year period.

Prospects: Our evaluation of Zayo Group Holdings Inc as of Jan. 14, 2018 is the result of our systematic analysis on three basic characteristics: earnings strength, relative valuation, and recent stock price movement. The company has generated a negative trend in earnings per share over the past 5 quarters. However, while recent estimates for the company have been mixed, ZAYO has posted results that fell short of analysts expectations. Based on operating earnings yield, the company is overvalued when compared to all of the companies in our coverage universe. Share price changes over the past year indicates that ZAYO will perform well over the near term.

Financial Data

(US$ in Thousands)	3 Mos	06/30/2017	06/30/2016	06/30/2015	06/30/2014	06/30/2013	06/30/2012
Earnings Per Share	0.37	0.35	(0.31)	(0.66)	(0.80)	(0.61)	(0.01)
Cash Flow Per Share	3.84	3.73	2.93	2.57	2.54	1.82	0.75
Income Statement							
Total Revenue	643,500	2,199,800	1,721,700	1,347,100	1,123,187	1,004,354	375,526
EBITDA	69,400	872,500	592,900	401,300	353,305	312,774	138,051
Depn & Amortn	(32,800)	526,900	440,500	351,400	294,125	280,128	70,357
Income Before Taxes	28,600	104,100	(67,700)	(164,100)	(144,349)	(169,818)	16,974
Income Taxes	5,400	18,400	8,500	(8,800)	37,295	(24,205)	26,871
Net Income	23,200	85,700	(76,200)	(155,300)	(179,294)	(137,217)	(1,224)
Average Shares	248,000	246,800	243,300	235,422	223,000	223,000	223,000
Balance Sheet							
Current Assets	610,200	514,600	397,100	567,900	544,979	303,496	...
Total Assets	8,862,400	8,739,400	6,727,500	6,094,600	5,049,066	4,251,240	...
Current Liabilities	671,500	620,300	486,500	386,900	344,886	281,760	...
Long-Term Obligations	5,629,800	5,626,300	4,130,200	3,680,500	3,242,529	2,821,072	...
Total Liabilities	7,382,900	7,328,900	5,508,300	4,883,400	4,632,681	3,644,987	...
Stockholders' Equity	1,479,500	1,410,500	1,219,200	1,211,200	416,385	606,253	...
Shares Outstanding	247,361	246,471	242,649	243,008	223,000	223,000	223,000
Statistical Record							
Return on Assets %	1.19	1.11	N.M.	N.M.	N.M.	...	...
Return on Equity %	6.81	6.52	N.M.	N.M.	N.M.	...	...
EBITDA Margin %	10.78	39.66	34.44	29.79	31.46	31.14	36.76
Net Margin %	3.61	3.90	N.M.	N.M.	N.M.	N.M.	N.M.
Asset Turnover	0.30	0.28	0.27	0.24	0.24	...	...
Current Ratio	0.91	0.83	0.82	1.47	1.58	1.08	...
Debt to Equity	3.81	3.99	3.39	3.04	7.79	4.65	...
Price Range	35.55-29.71	35.22-27.56	29.43-21.89	32.03-22.00	...	...	...
P/E Ratio	96.08-80.30	100.63-78.74	...	...	...	...	...

Address: 1805 29th Street, Suite 2050, Boulder, CO 80301 **Telephone:** 303-381-4683	**Web Site:** www.zayo.com **Officers:** Daniel P. (Dan) Caruso - Chairman, Chief Executive Officer Matt Steinfort - Chief Financial Officer	**Auditors:** KPMG LLP **Transfer Agents:** American Stock Transfer & Trust Company LLC

ZIMMER BIOMET HOLDINGS INC

Exchange	Symbol	Price	52Wk Range	Yield	P/E
NYS	ZBH	$120.67 (12/29/2017)	132.61-103.33	0.80	37.83

*7 Year Price Score 100.96 *NYSE Composite Index=100 *12 Month Price Score 91.53

Interim Earnings (Per Share)

Qtr.	Mar	Jun	Sep	Dec
2014	1.29	1.03	0.96	0.90
2015	1.02	(0.91)	0.11	0.66
2016	0.52	(0.16)	0.78	0.34
2017	1.47	0.90	0.48	...

Interim Dividends (Per Share)

Amt	Decl	Ex	Rec	Pay
0.24Q	03/01/2017	03/29/2017	03/31/2017	04/28/2017
0.24Q	05/30/2017	06/21/2017	06/23/2017	07/28/2017
0.24Q	08/07/2017	09/21/2017	09/22/2017	10/27/2017
0.24Q	12/18/2017	12/28/2017	12/29/2017	01/29/2018

Indicated Div: $0.96

Valuation Analysis

		Institutional Holding	
Forecast EPS	$8.03 (01/17/2018)	No of Institutions	1207
Market Cap	$24.4 Billion	Shares	228,076,736
Book Value	$10.4 Billion	% Held	78.44
Price/Book	2.34		
Price/Sales	3.15		

TRADING VOLUME (thousand shares)

Business Summary: Medical Instruments & Equipment (MIC: 4.3.1 SIC: 3842 NAIC: 339113)

Zimmer Biomet Holdings is engaged in musculoskeletal healthcare. Co. designs, manufactures and markets orthopaedic reconstructive products; sports medicine, biologics, extremities and trauma products; office based technologies; spine, craniomaxillofacial and thoracic (CMF) products; dental implants; and related surgical products. Co. manages its operations through three geographic operating segments: the Americas; Europe, the Middle East and Africa; and Asia Pacific. Co.'s four product category operating segments are as follows: Americas Spine; Office Based Technologies; CMF; and Dental.

Recent Developments: For the quarter ended Sep 30 2017, net income decreased 37.4% to US$98.8 million from US$157.9 million in the year-earlier quarter. Revenues were US$1.82 billion, down 0.8% from US$1.83 billion the year before. Operating income was US$213.4 million versus US$195.5 million in the prior-year quarter, an increase of 9.2%. Direct operating expenses rose 4.5% to US$500.9 million from US$479.3 million in the comparable period the year before. Indirect operating expenses decreased 4.7% to US$1.10 billion from US$1.16 billion in the equivalent prior-year period.

Prospects: Our evaluation of Zimmer Biomet Holdings Inc. as of Jan. 14, 2018 is the result of our systematic analysis on three basic characteristics: earnings strength, relative valuation, and recent stock price movement. The company has generated a negative trend in earnings per share over the past 5 quarters. However, while recent estimates for the company have been mixed, ZBH has posted results that fell short of analysts expectations. Based on operating earnings yield, the company is undervalued when compared to all of the companies in our coverage universe. Share price changes over the past year indicates that ZBH will perform poorly over the near term.

Financial Data
(US$ in Thousands)

	9 Mos	6 Mos	3 Mos	12/31/2016	12/31/2015	12/31/2014	12/31/2013	12/31/2012
Earnings Per Share	3.19	3.49	2.43	1.51	0.77	4.19	4.43	4.29
Cash Flow Per Share	8.93	8.40	8.17	8.14	4.36	6.23	5.68	6.57
Tang Book Value Per Share	N.M.	N.M.	N.M.	N.M.	N.M.	20.05	17.54	14.85
Dividends Per Share	0.960	0.960	0.960	0.960	0.880	0.880	0.800	0.720
Dividend Payout %	30.09	27.51	39.51	63.58	114.29	21.00	18.06	16.78
Income Statement								
Total Revenue	5,749,800	3,931,700	1,977,300	7,683,900	5,997,800	4,673,300	4,623,400	4,471,700
EBITDA	1,287,300	925,700	499,600	1,787,200	1,142,800	1,263,700	1,298,200	1,313,400
Depn & Amortn	452,400	299,700	152,000	1,032,600	712,400	268,600	262,600	266,000
Income Before Taxes	588,800	461,600	265,200	399,600	153,200	943,900	981,100	990,100
Income Taxes	6,600	(21,800)	(34,100)	95,000	7,000	224,900	221,900	237,200
Net Income	582,400	483,600	299,400	305,900	147,000	720,100	761,000	755,000
Average Shares	204,000	203,700	203,100	202,400	189,800	171,700	171,800	176,000
Balance Sheet								
Current Assets	4,433,300	4,424,100	5,079,900	4,663,600	5,862,900	4,289,000	4,197,700	3,708,700
Total Assets	26,417,500	26,459,200	26,987,800	26,684,400	27,219,500	9,634,700	9,580,600	9,012,400
Current Liabilities	3,010,200	2,996,400	2,656,100	2,381,500	1,617,900	1,038,000	1,031,600	866,000
Long-Term Obligations	9,199,700	9,354,400	10,537,800	10,665,800	11,556,300	1,425,500	1,672,300	1,720,800
Total Liabilities	15,967,700	16,180,300	17,054,400	17,015,500	17,331,600	3,113,900	3,283,300	3,151,500
Stockholders' Equity	10,449,800	10,278,900	9,933,400	9,668,900	9,887,900	6,520,800	6,297,300	5,860,900
Shares Outstanding	202,400	202,100	201,600	200,600	202,700	169,700	169,800	171,600
Statistical Record								
Return on Assets %	2.44	2.72	1.86	1.13	0.80	7.50	8.19	8.59
Return on Equity %	6.46	7.18	5.07	3.12	1.79	11.24	12.52	13.25
EBITDA Margin %	22.39	23.54	25.27	23.26	19.05	27.04	28.08	29.37
Net Margin %	10.13	12.30	15.14	3.98	2.45	15.41	16.46	16.88
Asset Turnover	0.29	0.30	0.29	0.28	0.33	0.49	0.50	0.51
Current Ratio	1.47	1.48	1.91	1.96	3.62	4.13	4.07	4.28
Debt to Equity	0.88	0.91	1.06	1.10	1.17	0.22	0.27	0.29
Price Range	132.74-97.99	133.09-97.99	133.09-97.99	133.09-91.68	121.76-92.41	115.05-90.87	93.43-66.66	68.80-53.21
P/E Ratio	41.61-30.72	38.13-28.08	54.77-40.33	88.14-60.72	158.13-120.01	27.46-21.69	21.09-15.05	16.04-12.40
Average Yield %	0.82	0.81	0.82	0.85	0.81	0.87	1.00	1.15

Address: 345 East Main Street, Warsaw, IN 46580 **Telephone:** 574-267-6131	**Web Site:** www.zimmer.com **Officers:** Bryan C. Hanson - President, Chief Executive Officer Daniel P. Florin - Interim Chief Executive Officer, Senior Vice President, Chief Financial Officer	**Auditors:** PricewaterhouseCoopers LLP **Investor Contact:** 574-267-6131 **Transfer Agents:** American Stock Transfer & Trust Company LLC

ZOETIS INC

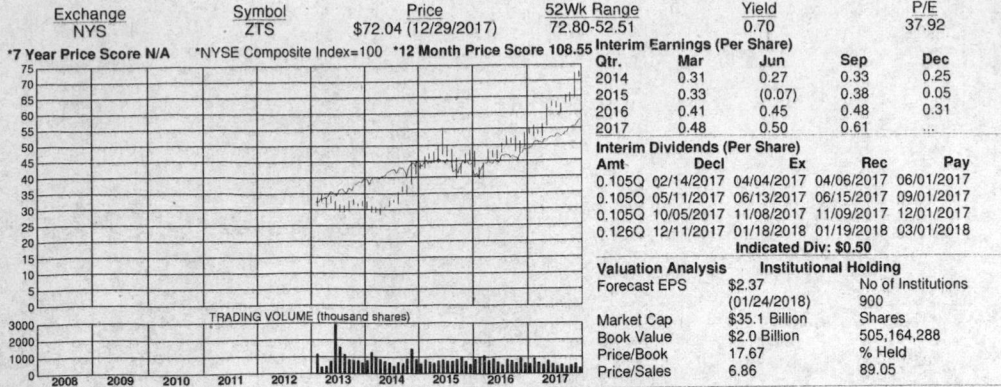

Exchange	Symbol	Price	52Wk Range	Yield	P/E
NYS	ZTS	$72.04 (12/29/2017)	72.80-52.51	0.70	37.92

*7 Year Price Score N/A   *NYSE Composite Index=100   *12 Month Price Score 108.55

Interim Earnings (Per Share)

Qtr.	Mar	Jun	Sep	Dec
2014	0.31	0.27	0.33	0.25
2015	0.33	(0.07)	0.38	0.05
2016	0.41	0.45	0.48	0.31
2017	0.48	0.50	0.61	...

Interim Dividends (Per Share)

Amt	Decl	Ex	Rec	Pay
0.105Q	02/14/2017	04/04/2017	04/06/2017	06/01/2017
0.105Q	05/11/2017	06/13/2017	06/15/2017	09/01/2017
0.105Q	10/05/2017	11/08/2017	11/09/2017	12/01/2017
0.126Q	12/11/2017	01/18/2018	01/19/2018	03/01/2018

Indicated Div: $0.50

Valuation Analysis		Institutional Holding	
Forecast EPS	$2.37	No of Institutions	
	(01/24/2018)	900	
Market Cap	$35.1 Billion	Shares	
Book Value	$2.0 Billion	505,164,288	
Price/Book	17.67	% Held	
Price/Sales	6.86	89.05	

Business Summary: Pharmaceuticals (MIC: 4.1.1 SIC: 2834 NAIC: 325412)

Zoetis engages in the discovery, development, manufacture and commercialization of animal health medicines and vaccines, with a focus on both livestock and companion animals. Co. organizes and operates its business in two segments: the U.S. and International. Co.'s main product categories are anti-infectives, vaccines, parasiticides, medicated feed additives, and other pharmaceutical products such as pain and sedation, oncology, antiemetic, allergy and dermatology, and reproductive products. Co.'s other product categories include nutritionals and agribusiness, as well as products and services in complementary areas, including biodevices, diagnostics and genetics.

Recent Developments: For the quarter ended Oct 1 2017, net income increased 24.9% to US$296.0 million from US$237.0 million in the year-earlier quarter. Revenues were US$1.35 billion, up 8.5% from US$1.24 billion the year before. Direct operating expenses rose 6.1% to US$435.0 million from US$410.0 million in the comparable period the year before. Indirect operating expenses decreased 1.1% to US$455.0 million from US$460.0 million in the equivalent prior-year period.

Prospects: Our evaluation of Zoetis Inc as of Jan. 21, 2018 is the result of our systematic analysis on three basic characteristics: earnings strength, relative valuation, and recent stock price movement. The company has enjoyed a very positive trend in earnings per share over the past 5 quarters and while recent estimates for the company have been mixed, ZTS has posted better than expected results. Based on operating earnings yield, the company is about fairly valued when compared to all of the companies in our coverage universe. Share price changes over the past year indicates that ZTS will perform well over the near term.

Financial Data

(US$ in Millions)	9 Mos	6 Mos	3 Mos	12/31/2016	12/31/2015	12/31/2014	12/31/2013	12/31/2012
Earnings Per Share	1.90	1.77	1.72	1.65	0.68	1.16	1.01	0.87
Cash Flow Per Share	2.09	1.68	1.59	1.43	1.33	1.25	1.36	0.91
Tang Book Value Per Share	N.M.	N.M.	N.M.	N.M.	N.M.	N.M.	N.M.	4.35
Dividends Per Share	0.410	0.410	0.390	0.380	0.332	0.288	0.195	...
Dividend Payout %	21.58	23.16	22.67	23.03	48.82	24.83	19.31	...
Income Statement								
Total Revenue	3,847	2,500	1,231	4,888	4,765	4,785	4,561	4,336
EBITDA	1,467	930	462	1,624	865	1,138	1,009	938
Depn & Amortn	247	166	84	230	196	201	206	197
Income Before Taxes	1,095	682	337	1,228	545	820	690	710
Income Taxes	313	196	98	409	206	233	187	274
Net Income	783	485	238	821	339	583	504	436
Average Shares	492	494	495	498	502	502	500	500
Balance Sheet								
Current Assets	4,894	3,584	3,383	3,390	3,830	3,465	3,357	2,864
Total Assets	9,288	7,802	7,649	7,649	7,913	6,607	6,558	6,262
Current Liabilities	1,746	1,784	1,730	1,117	1,781	1,086	1,415	1,123
Long-Term Obligations	4,952	3,719	3,718	4,468	4,463	3,643	3,642	509
Total Liabilities	7,299	6,087	6,040	6,162	6,845	5,296	5,618	2,236
Stockholders' Equity	1,989	1,715	1,609	1,487	1,068	1,311	940	4,026
Shares Outstanding	487	489	491	492	497	501	500	500
Statistical Record								
Return on Assets %	11.02	11.46	11.32	10.52	4.67	8.86	7.86	...
Return on Equity %	52.43	57.16	61.64	64.09	28.50	51.80	20.30	...
EBITDA Margin %	38.13	37.20	37.53	33.22	18.15	23.78	22.12	21.63
Net Margin %	20.35	19.40	19.33	16.80	7.11	12.18	11.05	10.06
Asset Turnover	0.60	0.66	0.66	0.63	0.66	0.73	0.71	...
Current Ratio	2.80	2.01	1.96	3.03	2.15	3.19	2.37	2.55
Debt to Equity	2.49	2.17	2.31	3.00	4.18	2.78	3.87	0.13
Price Range	65.40-47.25	63.51-47.25	55.98-45.42	53.78-39.33	55.38-39.65	44.93-28.40	34.64-29.15	...
P/E Ratio	34.42-24.87	35.88-26.69	32.55-26.41	32.59-23.84	81.44-58.31	38.73-24.48	34.30-28.86	...
Average Yield %	0.72	0.74	0.76	0.77	0.79	0.72	0.61	...

Address: 10 Sylvan Way, Parsippany, NJ 07054	Web Site: www.zoetis.com	Auditors: KPMG LLP
Telephone: 973-822-7000	Officers: Juan Ramon Alaix - Chief Executive Officer Glenn C. David - Executive Vice President, Senior Vice President, Chief Financial Officer, Acting Chief Financial Officer	Transfer Agents: Computershare Trust Company, N.A., College Station, TX

CONDENSED

STATISTICAL

TABULATION

The tab section consists of statistical highlights for all U.S. companies listed on the New York Stock Exchange.

Statistics for companies whose fiscal year ends prior to June 30 are listed under the prior calendar year. Statistics for companies whose fiscal year ends June 30 or after are listed under the current calendar year. Dividends and price ranges are on a calendar year basis.

Because of editorial constraints a column for fourth quarter results was not included. At fiscal year-end, full fiscal year per share earnings are listed and quarterly figures are eliminated. Quarterly per share earnings are inserted as the company reports in the current fiscal year.

NOTE: Figures listed under "Earnings Per Share" for investment companies are net asset value per share.

For abbreviations, see the blue section of the Handbook.

SYMBOL	COMPANY	NATURE OF BUSINESS	FISCAL YEAR-END	TOTAL REV. $MILL	NET INCOME $MILL	TOTAL ASSETS $MILL	NET STK EQUITY $MILL	NO OF INST	INST. HOLDINGS (SHARES)
DDD	3D Systems Corp. (DE)	Computer Hardware & Equipment	12/31/16	633.0	-38.4	849.2	629.9	331	84893957
MMM	3M Co	Medical Instruments & Equipment	12/31/16	30109.0	5050.0	32906.0	10298.0	2414	504737869
WBAI	500.com Ltd.	Sporting & Recreational	12/31/16	10.9	-203.0	2076.9	1709.5	45	5709986
WUBA	58.com Inc	IT Services	12/31/16	7592.1	-768.0	25326.0	17784.7	216	94041820
EGHT	8x8 Inc	Internet & Software	3/31/17	253.4	-4.8	333.9	288.6	235	81333019
ATEN	A10 Networks Inc	Internet & Software	12/31/16	230.0	-20.9	221.3	86.1	145	47491849
AAC	AAC Holdings Inc	Diagnostic & Health Related Service	12/31/16	279.8	-0.6	383.9	165.1	5	49166
AIR	AAR Corp	Aerospace	5/31/17	1767.6	56.5	1504.1	914.2	247	39655680
AAN	Aaron's Inc	Retail - Furniture & Home Furnishing	12/31/16	3207.7	139.3	2615.7	1481.6	352	88256226
ABB	ABB Ltd	Electrical Equipment	12/31/16	33828.0	1899.0	39499.0	13395.0	491	150402630
ABT	Abbott Laboratories	Medical Instruments & Equipment	12/31/16	20853.0	1400.0	52666.0	20538.0	2261	1520578290
ABBV	AbbVie Inc	Pharmaceuticals	12/31/16	25638.0	5953.0	66099.0	4636.0	2117	1256784588
ANF	Abercrombie & Fitch Co	Retail - Apparel and Accessories	1/28/17	3326.7	4.0	2295.8	1243.4	384	86678311
GCH	Aberdeen Greater China Fund Inc	Holding and other Investment Office	12/31/16	2.9	1.2	91.9	91.2	39	5255861
ACP	Aberdeen Income Credit Strategies	Finance Intermediaries & Services	10/31/16	24.5	19.1	289.9	191.3	34	3680077
JEQ	Aberdeen Japan Equity Fund Inc	Holding and other Investment Office	10/31/16	2.1	1.0	128.0	127.9	40	9412889
SGF	Aberdeen Singapore Fund Inc	Holding and other Investment Office	10/31/16	3.1	1.9	80.9	80.7	32	3712208
ABM	ABM Industries, Inc.	Sanitation Services	10/31/17	5453.6	3.8	3812.6	1375.7	280	73816175
AKR	Acadia Realty Trust	REITs	12/31/16	189.9	72.8	3996.0	1588.6	241	107150949
ACN	Accenture plc	Business Services	8/31/17	36765.5	3445.1	22689.9	8949.5	1399	553181872
ACCO	Acco Brands Corp	Office Equipment & Furniture	12/31/16	1557.1	95.5	2064.5	708.7	303	115247741
ATV	Acorn International Inc	Retail - Specialty	12/31/15	47.5	-40.2	240.7	178.3	10	290432
ATU	Actuant Corp	Industrial Machinery & Equipment	8/31/17	1095.8	-66.2	1517.0	500.5	271	79871103
AYI	Acuity Brands Inc (Holding Compan	Electrical Equipment	8/31/17	3505.1	321.7	2899.6	1665.6	582	55070514
GOLF	Acushnet Holdings Corp	Sporting & Recreational	12/31/16	1572.3	45.0	1736.2	735.9	103	34056405
ADX	Adams Diversified Equity Fund Inc	Holding and other Investment Office	12/31/16	28.3	18.9	1545.5	1513.5	128	24950572
PEO	Adams Natural Resources Fund Inc	Holding and other Investment Office	12/31/16	16.6	11.5	688.1	685.9	86	8033454
AGRO	Adecoagro SA	Agricultural Crop Production	12/31/16	988.8	2.0	1455.8	664.1	139	55965476
ADNT	Adient Plc	Auto Parts	9/30/17	16213.0	877.0	13170.0	4279.0	472	90291693
ADT	ADT Inc (DE)	Services							0
ATGE	Adtalem Global Education Inc	Educational Services	6/30/17	1809.8	122.3	2314.0	1669.0	366	73972247
AAP	Advance Auto Parts Inc	Retail - Automotive	12/31/16	9567.7	459.6	8315.0	2916.2	659	92430394
ADSW	Advanced Disposal Services Inc (D	Miscellaneous Consumer Services	12/31/16	1404.6	-30.4	3369.9	829.5	139	87342477
WMS	Advanced Drainage Systems Inc	Plastics	3/31/17	1257.3	32.9	1046.3	335.5	130	48246395
ASX	Advanced Semiconductor Engineeri	Semiconductors	12/31/16	274884.1	21680.3	357943.1	157355.2	198	104635229
ASIX	AdvanSix Inc	Plastics	12/31/16	1191.5	34.1	905.0	215.4	411	25193257
AAV	Advantage Oil & Gas Ltd	Production & Extraction	12/31/16	157.0	-15.7	1496.5	1208.3		0
AVK	Advent Claymore Convertible Secur	Holding and other Investment Office	10/31/17	26.8	16.0	583.7	353.4	79	6872844
AGC	Advent Claymore Convertible Secur	Holding and other Investment Office	10/31/17	14.2	6.8	315.3	184.1	52	10885456
LCM	Advent/Claymore Enhanced Growth	Holding and other Investment Office	10/31/17	5.4	2.1	124.9	86.8	37	3077788
ACM	AECOM	Construction Services	9/30/17	18203.4	339.4	14397.0	3996.1	415	149444875
ANW	Aegean Marine Petroleum Network	Equipment & Services	12/31/16	4076.2	51.9	1600.9	589.5	129	28732734
AEG	AEGON N.V.	Life & Health	12/31/16	46439.0	437.0	425425.0	24318.0	322	226000900
AER	Aercap Holdings NV	Aerospace	12/31/16	5152.1	1046.6	41620.5	8524.4	410	148523797
HIVE	Aerohive Networks Inc	Internet & Software	12/31/16	169.8	-36.9	136.5	28.7	106	30827956
AJRD	Aerojet Rocketdyne Holdings Inc	Defense	12/31/16	1761.3	18.0	2249.5	35.6	288	93780359
AES	AES Corp.	Electric Utilities	12/31/16	13586.0	-1130.0	36119.0	3576.0	727	769337191
AET	Aetna Inc.	Life & Health	12/31/16	63155.0	2271.0	69146.0	17881.0	1247	374823822
AMG	Affiliated Managers Group Inc.	Wealth Management	12/31/16	2194.6	472.8	8749.1	3619.6	695	67225504
AFL	AFLAC Inc	Life & Health	12/31/16	22559.0	2659.0	129819.0	20482.0	1322	337194911
MITT	AG Mortgage Investment Trust Inc	REITs	12/31/16	118.3	63.7	2628.6	655.9	149	22252284
AGCO	AGCO Corp.	Industrial Machinery & Equipment	12/31/16	7410.5	160.1	7168.4	2776.1	528	83333877
A	Agilent Technologies, Inc.	Medical Instruments & Equipment	10/31/17	4472.0	684.0	8426.0	4831.0	905	348603658
ATG PR	AGL Capital Trust II	Gas Utilities							0
AEM	Agnico Eagle Mines Ltd	Precious Metals	12/31/16	2138.2	158.8	7108.0	4492.5	424	149667477
ADC	Agree Realty Corp.	REITs	12/31/16	91.5	45.1	1111.9	683.0	254	30084712
AHC	AH Belo Corp	Publishing	12/31/16	260.0	-19.3	192.7	87.9	84	16084266
AL	Air Lease Corp	Miscellaneous Transportation Servic	12/31/16	1419.1	374.9	13975.6	3382.2	318	103700940
APD	Air Products & Chemicals Inc	Specialty Chemicals	9/30/17	8187.6	3000.4	18467.2	10086.2	1281	250711346
AYR	Aircastle Ltd.	Aerospace	12/31/16	773.0	151.5	7244.7	1834.3	199	55060474
AKS	AK Steel Holding Corp.	Non-Precious Metals	12/31/16	5882.5	-7.8	4036.0	-272.2	406	253240387
ALP PRQ	Alabama Power Co	Electric Utilities	12/31/16	5889.0	839.0	22516.0	6604.0		0
ALG	Alamo Group, Inc.	Construction Services	12/31/16	844.7	40.0	552.8	387.7	207	12086086
AGI	Alamos Gold Inc (New)	Precious Metals	12/31/16	482.2	-17.9	2492.2	1759.4	173	201092889
ALK	Alaska Air Group, Inc.	Airlines/Air Freight	12/31/16	5931.0	814.0	9962.0	2931.0	702	121537080
AIN	Albany International Corp	Industrial Machinery & Equipment	12/31/16	779.8	52.7	1263.4	507.5	228	35311902
ALB	Albemarle Corp.	Specialty Chemicals	12/31/16	2677.2	643.7	8161.2	3795.1	737	116892676
AA	Alcoa Corporation	Metal Products	12/31/16	9318.0	-400.0	16741.0	5654.0		0
ALEX	Alexander & Baldwin Inc (REIT)	REITs	12/31/16	387.5	-10.2	2156.3	1220.1		0
ALX	Alexander's Inc	REITs	12/31/16	226.9	86.5	1451.2	352.8	147	2154543
ARE	Alexandria Real Estate Equities Inc	REITs	12/31/16	921.7	-65.9	10354.9	4895.8	505	116630261
AQN	Algonquin Power & Utilities Corp	Water Utilities	12/31/16	1096.0	130.9	8249.5	1923.6	94	144695567
BABA	Alibaba Group Holding Ltd	Internet & Software	3/31/17	158273.0	43675.0	506812.0	281791.0	1235	1048714199
Y	Alleghany Corp	General Insurance	12/31/16	6131.0	456.9	23756.6	7939.9	454	16074163
ATI	Allegheny Technologies, Inc	Non-Precious Metals	12/31/16	3134.6	-640.9	5170.0	1355.2	436	151589940
ALLE	Allegion Plc	Services	12/31/16	2238.0	229.1	2247.4	113.3	472	96417414
AGN	Allergan PLC	Pharmaceuticals	12/31/16	14570.6	14973.4	128986.3	76192.7	1304	300640931
ALE	Allete Inc.	Electric Utilities	12/31/16	1339.7	155.3	4906.4	1893.0	366	50278173
AKP	Alliance California Municipal Income	Holding and other Investment Office	10/31/17	7.8	5.1	209.7	161.5	31	1617552
ADS	Alliance Data Systems Corp.	Business Services	12/31/16	7138.1	515.8	25514.1	1658.2	733	66885049

1st	2nd	3rd	2016	2015	2014	P/E RATIO		2016	2015	2014	AV. YLD %	AMOUNT	PAYABLE	PRICE RANGE 2016	
		-0.34	-0.35	-5.85	0.11	-		-						23.3 -	8.1
		2.33	8.16	7.58	7.49	29.8 -	21.3	4.44	4.10	3.42	2.2	1.360Y	32/4/39	243.1 -	174.2
			-0.49	-0.84	0.44									14.7 -	8.7
			-2.73	-1.07	0.13									79.2 -	28.0
	-0.01		-0.06	0.02	0.03									16.5 -	12.2
		-0.04	-0.32	-0.64	-0.74									9.8 -	6.1
		0.03	-0.03	0.48	0.41									12.6 -	6.0
	-0.66		1.37	0.24	1.83	32.1 -	23.0	0.30	0.30	0.30	0.8	0.0750Y	2/5/18	44.0 -	31.5
		0.35	1.91	1.86	1.08	24.9 -	14.1	0.10	0.09	0.09	0.3	0.030Y	32/4/39	47.5 -	26.9
	0.24		0.88	0.87	1.13	30.5 -	24.2	0.73	0.75	0.77	3.0			26.8 -	21.3
		0.34	0.94	2.92	1.49	61.1 -	41.5	1.04	0.96	0.88	2.1	0.280Y	32/4/39	57.5 -	39.0
		1.01	3.63	3.13	1.10	27.1 -	16.5	2.20	2.02	1.66	3.0	0.710Y	32/4/39	98.2 -	60.0
		0.15	0.51	0.71	0.69	37.3 -	17.4	0.80	0.80	0.80	6.3	0.20Y	12/11/17	19.0 -	8.9
			0.13	0.18	0.08	98.4 -	67.0	0.09	0.51	0.23	0.8	0.14460	1/8/18	12.8 -	8.7
			1.46	1.48	1.57	10.2 -	9.1	1.44	1.84	1.61	10.2	0.120	1/8/18	14.9 -	13.3
			0.08	0.05	0.04	119.2 -	92.0	0.31	0.07	0.15	3.7	0.4218C	1/8/18	9.5 -	7.4
			0.25	0.26	0.29	50.7 -	34.9	0.25	1.05	0.89	2.2	0.28350	1/8/18	12.7 -	8.7
		0.58	1.01	1.33	1.32	44.3 -	37.0	0.66	0.64	0.62	1.6	0.1750Y	32/4/39	44.8 -	37.4
		0.15	0.94	0.94	1.18	35.5 -	28.6	1.16	1.22	1.23	3.9	0.270Z	1/12/18	33.4 -	26.9
1.79			6.45	4.76	4.52			2.20	2.04	1.86		1.330	32/4/39		
		0.28	0.87	0.78	0.79	16.9 -	12.1	-						14.7 -	10.6
		-0.13		-0.51	-0.54									18.9 -	0.0
0.09			-1.78	0.32	2.26			0.04	0.04	0.04	0.2	0.040Y	10/16/17	28.9 -	22.3
1.70			6.63	5.09	4.05	36.2 -	23.6	0.52	0.52	0.52	0.3	0.130Y	32/4/39	239.9 -	156.4
		0.12	0.62	-0.74	0.23	34.3 -	25.1					0.120Y	12/15/17	21.3 -	15.6
			0.19	0.13	0.20	83.2 -	67.3	0.99	0.93	1.18	6.9	0.050	3/1/18	15.8 -	12.8
			0.41	0.37	0.50	50.2 -	43.2	1.14	1.38	1.89	5.9	0.10	3/1/18	20.6 -	17.7
		-0.05	0.02	0.14	0.02									-	
		2.17	-16.36									0.2750	2/15/18	-	
0.20			-0.05	2.14	2.07			0.36	0.36	0.34	1.0	0.180Y	32/4/39	45.9 -	31.4
		1.30	6.20	6.40	6.71	28.2 -	12.8	0.24	0.24	0.24	0.2	0.060Y	32/4/39	174.8 -	79.4
		0.04	-0.44											25.6 -	21.3
	0.29		0.27	-0.06	-0.07	94.1 -	67.4	0.20	0.08	1.68	0.9	0.070Y	12/15/17	25.4 -	18.2
		0.57	2.37	2.51	2.79	3.0 -	2.1	5.74	7.18	4.53	92.5			7.1 -	5.1
		0.68	1.12			41.3 -	19.1							46.3 -	21.4
		0.07	-0.09	0.12	0.09									9.2 -	3.8
			0.75	0.65	0.71	22.3 -	19.6	1.13	1.13	1.13	7.1	0.11640	1/31/18	16.7 -	14.7
			0.25	0.20	0.24	25.8 -	23.4	0.56	0.56	0.56	9.1	0.0470	1/31/18	6.5 -	5.8
			0.26	0.21	0.21	34.2 -	31.7	0.84	0.84	0.84	9.8	0.210	11/30/17	8.9 -	8.2
		0.64	0.62	-1.04	2.33	63.1 -	49.1	-						39.1 -	30.5
			1.11	0.73	0.37			0.08	0.08	0.05		0.020	12/13/17		
		0.08	0.15	0.27	0.29	42.1 -	31.9	0.26	0.24	0.22	4.7	0.39840Z	6/15/18	6.3 -	4.8
	1.67		5.52	5.72	4.54										
		-0.12	-0.73	-0.98	-0.85									6.3 -	3.1
		0.17	0.27	0.10	-0.92	132.3 -	65.9					0.030Y	5/28/04	35.7 -	17.8
		0.23	-1.71	0.44	1.06			0.44	0.40	0.20	3.9	0.130Y	32/4/39	11.9 -	10.2
		2.52	6.41	6.78	5.68	28.5 -	18.2	1.00	1.00	0.90	0.7	0.50Y	32/4/39	182.7 -	116.7
		2.22	8.57	9.28	8.01	24.1 -	16.5					0.30	32/4/39	206.5 -	141.3
		1.80	6.42	5.85	6.50	13.9 -	10.5	1.66	1.58	1.50	2.1	0.450Y	32/4/39	89.3 -	67.1
		1.17	1.80	0.01	3.37	10.9 -	9.5	1.90	2.27	2.40	10.2	0.4750Z	1/31/18	19.7 -	17.2
		0.76	1.96	3.06	4.36	38.5 -	29.6	0.52	0.48	0.44	0.8	0.150Y	32/4/39	75.5 -	58.0
		0.54	1.40	1.20	1.49	50.4 -	33.2	0.46	0.40	0.53	0.8	0.1490Y	32/4/39	70.6 -	46.5
		0.30	0.70	0.11	0.39	97.0 -	56.9	0.36	0.32	0.32	0.7	0.110	12/15/17	67.9 -	39.9
		0.42	1.97	2.16	1.24	26.7 -	22.8	1.92	1.85	1.74	4.0	0.520Z	1/3/18	52.7 -	44.8
		0.12	-0.90	-0.84	4.13			0.32	0.32	4.07	5.9	0.080Y	3/2/18	6.5 -	4.3
		0.90	3.44	2.34	2.38	14.0 -	10.1	0.23	0.17	0.13	0.6	0.10Y	32/4/39	48.3 -	34.6
0.70			2.89	5.88	4.61	57.0 -	46.5	2.53	3.20	3.02	1.7	1.10Y	32/4/39	164.6 -	134.3
		0.73	1.92	1.50	1.25			0.98	0.90	0.82		0.280Y	12/15/17		
		-0.02	-0.03	-2.86	-0.65			-				0.050Y	32/4/39	11.1 -	4.1
												0.31250Y	4/1/18	27.0 -	25.0
		1.42	3.46	3.76	3.42	34.5 -	20.9	0.36	0.32	0.28	0.4	0.110Y	1/29/18	119.3 -	72.2
		0.09	-0.07	-2.62	-0.02			0.02	0.01		0.2	0.010	10/31/17	11.5 -	6.0
		2.14	6.54	6.56	4.42	15.3 -	9.4	1.10	0.80	0.50	1.3	0.320	32/4/39	100.2 -	61.7
		0.47	1.64	1.79	1.30	39.8 -	26.8	0.68	0.67	0.63	1.3	0.170Y	1/8/18	65.3 -	43.9
		1.06	5.68	3.00	1.69	25.5 -	15.5	1.22	1.16	1.10	1.1	0.320Y	32/4/39	144.6 -	88.0
		0.60	-2.19											54.1 -	28.8
		0.13	-0.18	0.54	1.25			0.25			0.6	15.92G7Z	32/4/39	46.9 -	27.6
		3.97	16.91	15.04	13.29	26.1 -	23.2	16.00	14.00	13.00	3.8	4.50Z	2/15/18	441.0 -	392.6
		0.55	-1.99	1.63	1.01			3.23	3.05	2.88	2.7	0.43750Z	32/4/39	134.0 -	108.2
		0.15	0.44	0.42	0.31	32.6 -	19.0	0.55	0.49	0.37	4.7	0.31250	12/29/17	14.4 -	8.3
5.65			27.89	9.70	10.00	6.9 -	3.2	-						191.2 -	88.6
		-20.90	29.59	35.13	41.40	22.2 -	17.7					3.80360Y	6/15/09	656.2 -	523.2
		-1.12	-5.97	-3.53	-0.03			0.24	0.62	0.72	1.2	0.080Y	32/4/39	25.8 -	14.9
		0.94	2.39	1.59	1.80			0.48	0.40	0.32		0.160	12/29/17		
		-12.07	38.18	10.01	-7.42							13.750	32/4/39	-	
		0.88	3.14	2.92	2.90	25.6 -	19.8	2.08	2.02	1.96	2.9	0.560Y	3/1/18	80.5 -	62.2
			0.65	0.75	0.77	21.6 -	20.1	0.68	0.75	0.75	5.0	0.0421M	2/16/18	14.0 -	13.1
		4.20	7.34	8.85	7.87	36.0 -	28.7	0.52	-		0.2	0.570	32/4/39	264.6 -	210.4

SYMBOL	COMPANY	NATURE OF BUSINESS	FISCAL YEAR-END	TOTAL REV. $MILL	NET INCOME $MILL	TOTAL ASSETS $MILL	NET STK EQUITY $MILL	NO OF INST	INST. HOLDINGS (SHARES)
AOI	Alliance One International Inc	Tobacco Products	3/31/17	1714.8	-62.9	1971.9	203.5	108	16843096
AWF	AllianceBernstein Global High Inco	Holding and other Investment Office	3/31/17	82.6	70.7	1328.0	1195.9	137	18233088
AB	AllianceBernstein Holding LP	Wealth Management	12/31/16	239.4	216.6	1540.5		264	33415267
AFB	AllianceBernstein National Municipa	Holding and other Investment Office	10/31/17	26.4	18.9	697.7	521.6	75	5070630
LNT	Alliant Energy Corp	Electric Utilities	12/31/16	3320.0	381.7	13373.8	3862.0	623	192046816
NCV	AllianzGI Convertible & Income Fun	Holding and other Investment Office	2/28/17	72.0	64.3	968.9	962.2	83	14150265
NCZ	AllianzGI Convertible & Income Fun	Holding and other Investment Office	2/28/17	54.9	49.0	735.9	731.0	83	12059628
ACV	AllianzGI Diversified Income & Conv	Holding and other Investment Office	1/31/16	7.4	2.0	311.5	201.6		0
NIE	AllianzGI Equity & Convertible Inco	Holding and other Investment Office	1/31/17	17.5	11.2	597.8	596.9	74	5647596
NFJ	AllianzGI NFJ Dividend Interest & P	Holding and other Investment Office	1/31/17	46.5	32.8	1400.8	1395.1	121	24632551
ALSN	Allison Transmission Holdings Inc	Auto Parts	12/31/16	1840.2	214.9	4218.6	1080.3	371	247919373
ALL	Allstate Corp.	General Insurance	12/31/16	36534.0	1877.0	108610.0	20573.0	1287	373963906
ALLY	Ally Financial Inc	Credit & Lending	12/31/16	9835.0	1067.0	163728.0	13317.0	436	483579867
ALDW	Alon USA Partners LP	Refining & Marketing	12/31/16	1807.7	-4.4	695.6		45	3339523
AGD	Alpine Global Dynamic Dividend Fu	Holding and other Investment Office	10/31/16	10.2	8.7	127.1	125.0	40	3990771
AWP	Alpine Global Premier Properties Fu	Holding and other Investment Office	10/31/17	16.4	9.0	763.4	613.1	108	21198749
AOD	Alpine Total Dynamic Dividend Fun	Holding and other Investment Office	10/31/17	83.9	71.7	1105.8	1070.3	122	43887282
AYX	Alteryx Inc	Internet & Software	12/31/16	85.8	-24.3	111.4	21.6	96	16771389
ATUS	Altice USA Inc	Radio & Television	12/31/16	6017.2	-832.0	36474.2	2097.7	122	97568003
RESI	Altisource Residential Corp	REITs	12/31/16	56.8	-228.0	2284.8	863.1	143	45429660
MO	Altria Group Inc	Tobacco Products	12/31/16	25744.0	14239.0	45932.0	12770.0	2179	1593971080
ACH	Aluminum Corp of China Ltd.	Non-Precious Metals	12/31/16	144065.5	402.5	190076.9	38107.6	73	3053962
AMBR	Amber Road Inc	Internet & Software	12/31/16	73.2	-18.7	110.5	32.6	93	24266331
ABEV	Ambev SA	Beverages	12/31/16	45602.6	12546.6	83841.4	44825.0		0
AMC	AMC Entertainment Holdings Inc.	Entertainment	12/31/16	3235.8	111.7	8641.8	2010.7	239	67756695
AEE	Ameren Corp	Electric Utilities	12/31/16	6076.0	653.0	24699.0	7103.0	725	211445029
AMRC	Ameresco Inc	Construction Services	12/31/16	651.2	12.0	797.3	294.3	104	14117479
AMX	America Movil SAB de CV	Services	12/31/16	975412.5	8649.4	1515042.3	208915.2	479	297211050
AAT	American Assets Trust Inc	REITs	12/31/16	295.1	32.8	1936.9	809.6	218	57528135
AXL	American Axle & Manufacturing Hol	Auto Parts	12/31/16	3948.0	240.7	3448.1	530.0	321	135922291
ACC	American Campus Communities Inc	REITs	12/31/16	786.4	99.1	5865.9	3445.0	429	167634584
AEO	American Eagle Outfitters, Inc.	Retail - Apparel and Accessories	1/28/17	3609.9	212.4	1782.7	1204.6	504	209784509
AEP	American Electric Power Company,	Electric Utilities	12/31/16	16380.1	610.9	63467.7	17397.0	1219	424887458
AEL	American Equity Investment Life Ho	Life & Health	12/31/16	2220.3	83.2	56053.5	2291.6	330	102101146
AXP	American Express Co.	Credit & Lending	12/31/16	33823.0	5408.0	158893.0	20501.0	1884	895814257
AFG	American Financial Group Inc	General Insurance	12/31/16	6498.0	649.0	55072.0	4916.0	506	71580449
AMH	American Homes 4 Rent	REITs	12/31/16	878.9	6.7	8107.2	4192.9		0
AIG	American International Group Inc	General Insurance	12/31/16	52367.0	-849.0	498264.0	76300.0	1380	1002486942
AMID	American Midstream Partners LP	Equipment & Services	12/31/16	232.7	-3.5	1563.5	334.1	63	31602161
ARL	American Realty Investors, Inc.	Property, Real Estate & Developmen	12/31/16	119.7	-2.7	1174.9	121.9	22	135608
ARA	American Renal Associates Holding	Diagnostic & Health Related Service	12/31/16	749.8	-0.4	986.0	-33.5	70	30011624
AWR	American States Water Co	Water Utilities	12/31/16	436.1	59.7	1470.5	494.3	301	30318372
AMT	American Tower Corp (New)	REITs	12/31/16	5785.7	956.4	30879.1	6763.9	1289	484595288
AVD	American Vanguard Corp.	Agricultural Chemicals	12/31/16	312.1	12.8	430.0	282.2	186	28874339
AWK	American Water Works Co, Inc.	Water Utilities	12/31/16	3302.0	468.0	18482.0	5218.0	799	180744838
COLD	Americold Realty Trust	REITs							0
APU	AmeriGas Partners LP	Gas Utilities	9/30/17	2453.5	162.1	4059.3		313	27317815
AMP	Ameriprise Financial Inc	Wealth Management	12/31/16	11696.0	1314.0	139821.0	6292.0	1021	161693459
ABC	AmerisourceBergen Corp.	Pharmaceuticals	9/30/17	153143.8	364.5	35316.5	2064.5	1004	200651693
AME	AMETEK Inc	Electrical Equipment	12/31/16	3840.1	512.2	7100.7	3256.5	714	236537960
ANFI	Amira Nature Foods Ltd	Food	3/31/17	551.9	25.1	574.6	262.5	45	5224615
AMN	AMN Healthcare Services Inc	Diagnostic & Health Related Service	12/31/16	1902.2	105.8	1186.9	449.4	362	71482087
AP	Ampco-Pittsburgh Corp.	Industrial Machinery & Equipment	12/31/16	331.9	-79.8	565.9	147.9	95	7992323
APH	Amphenol Corp.	Electrical Equipment	12/31/16	6286.4	822.9	8498.7	3674.9	813	351268285
BETR	Amplify Snack Brands Inc	Food	12/31/16	270.8	27.3	838.2	51.7	126	80692554
AXR	AMREP Corp.	Business Services	4/30/17	42.4	-0.0	106.7	84.8	39	1796473
APC	Anadarko Petroleum Corp	Production & Extraction	12/31/16	7869.0	-3071.0	45564.0	12212.0	1252	634427062
ANDV	Andeavor	Refining & Marketing	12/31/16	24582.0	734.0	20398.0	5465.0	798	152280045
ANDX	Andeavor Logistics LP	Production & Extraction	12/31/16	1220.0	339.0	5860.0		214	77453354
AU	AngloGold Ashanti Ltd	Precious Metals	12/31/16	4085.0	63.0	7153.0	2715.0	237	198217708
BUD	Anheuser-Busch InBev SA/NV	Beverages	12/31/16	45517.0	1241.0	258381.0	71339.0	688	104065790
AXE	Anixter International Inc	Electrical Equipment	12/30/16	7622.8	120.5	4093.6	1292.2	312	40430540
NLY	Annaly Capital Management Inc	REITs	12/31/16	2339.3	1433.8	87905.0	12568.2	804	816225635
AMGP	Antero Midstream GP LP	Gas Utilities	12/31/16	16.9	9.7	17.4	10.3	89	120583870
AM	Antero Midstream Partners LP	Equipment & Services	12/31/16	590.2	219.8	2349.9		159	93133377
AR	Antero Resources Corp	Production & Extraction	12/31/16	1744.5	-848.8	14255.5	6262.6	355	522491390
ANTM	Anthem Inc	Life & Health	12/31/16	84863.0	2469.8	65083.1	25100.4	966	251982803
ANH	Anworth Mortgage Asset Corp.	REITs	12/31/16	108.7	22.5	5395.8	655.0	225	71336287
AON	Aon Plc	Brokers & Intermediaries	12/31/16	11627.0	1396.0	26615.0	5475.0	819	270453192
APA	Apache Corp	Production & Extraction	12/31/16	5354.0	-1405.0	22519.0	6238.0	1179	448157891
AIV	Apartment Investment & Manageme	REITs	12/31/16	995.9	430.4	6232.8	1793.9	483	205861127
ARI	Apollo Commercial Real Estate Fina	REITs	12/31/16	285.0	157.9	3483.0	1932.2	252	81605507
APO	Apollo Global Management LLC	Finance Intermediaries & Services	12/31/16	1970.4	402.8	5629.6	835.1	256	146250963
AFT	Apollo Senior Floating Rate Fund In	Holding and other Investment Office	12/31/16	28.1	19.4	448.0	281.3	54	5109149
AIF	Apollo Tactical Income Fund Inc	Holding and other Investment Office	12/31/16	29.6	21.7	409.6	248.4	33	4261516
APLE	Apple Hospitality REIT Inc	REITs	12/31/16	1041.0	144.7	4979.9	3517.1	229	134576274
AIT	Applied Industrial Technologies, Inc.	Industrial Machinery & Equipment	6/30/17	2593.7	133.9	1387.6	745.3	311	44915860
ATR	AptarGroup Inc.	Plastics	12/31/16	2330.9	205.6	2606.8	1174.0	455	81121442
APTV	Aptiv PLC	Auto Parts	12/31/16	16661.0	1257.0	12292.0	2401.0	719	272190879
WTR	Aqua America Inc	Water Utilities	12/31/16	819.9	234.2	6159.0	1850.1	572	115352005

T4

EARNINGS PER SHARE						P/E RATIO		DIVIDENDS PER SHARE			AV. YLD %	DIV. DECLARED		PRICE RANGE 2016	
QUARTERLY			ANNUAL												
1st	2nd	3rd	2016	2015	2014			2016	2015	2014		AMOUNT	PAYABLE		
	0.11		7.38	-1.70	-9.90	2.6	1.3					0.030Y	9/23/05	19.4	9.9
			0.89	1.00	1.14	14.7	13.8	1.11	1.44	1.58	8.7	0.00990	2/16/18	13.1	12.3
		0.46	2.23	1.89	1.86	11.8	9.2	1.75	1.93	1.89	7.4	0.510	11/16/17	26.3	20.6
			0.71	0.81	0.85	19.9	18.2	0.72	0.82	0.87	5.3	0.0458M	2/16/18	14.2	12.9
		0.73	1.64	1.68	1.73	27.5	22.5	1.18	1.10	1.02	2.9	0.0005F	32/4/18	45.2	36.9
			0.83	0.87	1.02	8.7	7.7	0.93	1.08	1.08	13.4	0.0650	2/1/18	7.3	6.4
			0.75	0.80	0.95	8.6	7.6	0.85	1.02	1.02	13.8	0.05750	2/1/18	6.5	5.7
			0.18			124.6	104.7	1.17			5.6	0.1670	2/1/18	22.4	18.8
			0.47	0.53	0.56	46.1	39.8	1.52	1.32	1.36	7.6	0.380	1/5/18	21.6	18.7
			0.38	0.41	0.49	35.8	33.6	1.65	1.80	1.80	12.5	0.2250	1/5/18	13.6	12.8
		0.75	1.27	1.03	1.25	34.7	25.8	0.60	0.60	0.51	1.6	0.150Y	32/4/39	44.1	32.8
		1.74	4.67	5.05	6.27	22.5	15.7	1.32	1.20	1.12	1.5	0.370Y	32/4/39	104.9	73.1
		0.63	2.15	-2.66	1.83	13.7	8.5	0.16			0.7	0.130Y	32/4/39	29.4	18.2
		0.47	-0.07	2.51	2.71			0.37	3.43	2.02	3.3	0.430	11/22/17	17.2	8.8
			0.70	0.80	0.70	15.7	12.8	0.78	0.77	0.64	7.7	0.0650	2/28/18	11.0	9.0
			0.17	0.14	0.22	40.4	30.1	0.60	0.60	0.60	9.8	0.050	2/28/18	6.9	5.1
			0.65	0.69	0.64	14.6	11.8	0.69	0.68	0.56	8.0	0.05750	2/28/18	9.5	7.7
		-0.06	-0.95	-0.76	-1.37									28.6	14.8
		-0.25	8320.00											34.3	17.9
		-0.80	-4.18	-0.81	3.34			0.75	1.83	2.03	5.9	0.150Z	1/12/18	15.6	10.6
		0.97	7.28	2.67	2.56	10.7	8.4	2.35	2.17	2.00	3.4	0.660Y	32/4/39	77.7	61.2
		0.09	0.02	0.01	-1.20	1172.5	516.5							23.4	10.3
		-0.08	-0.70	-1.07	-1.46									9.5	6.5
			0.79	0.78	0.76	8.8	6.4	0.59	0.62	0.72	9.9			7.0	5.1
		-0.33	1.13	1.06	0.66	30.8	9.7	0.80	0.80	0.60	3.6	0.20	12/18/17	34.8	11.0
		1.18	2.68	2.59	2.40	24.1	19.3	1.72	1.66	1.61	3.0	0.45750Y	32/4/39	64.5	51.7
		0.19	0.26	0.06	0.22	34.2	18.7							8.9	4.8
			0.13	0.52	0.67	148.0	93.5	14.53	11.13	4.78	90.9			19.2	12.2
		0.19	0.72	0.86	0.51	61.9	52.3	1.01	0.95	0.89	2.5	0.270Z	12/21/17	44.6	37.7
		0.75	3.06	3.02	1.85	6.9	4.4					0.020Y	12/29/08	21.2	13.6
		-0.01	0.75	1.02	0.58	68.6	53.6	1.66	1.58	1.50	3.6	0.440Z	32/4/39	51.4	40.2
		0.36	1.11	0.42	0.43	17.5	9.6	0.50	0.50	0.38	3.7	0.1250Y	32/4/39	19.4	10.6
		1.10	1.24	4.17	3.34	62.6	50.1	2.27	2.15	2.03	3.2	0.620Y	32/4/39	77.6	62.1
		0.63	0.97	2.72	1.58	33.2	23.0	0.24	0.22	0.20	0.9	0.260Y	32/4/39	32.2	22.3
		1.50	5.65	5.05	5.56	17.6	13.3	1.19	1.10	0.98	1.4	0.350Y	32/4/39	99.7	75.3
		0.13	7.33	3.94	4.97	14.9	11.7	2.15	2.03	1.91	2.2	0.350Y	32/4/39	109.1	85.9
		0.01	-0.14	-0.40	-0.34			0.20	0.20	0.20	0.9	0.36720Z	32/4/39	23.8	20.3
		-1.91	-0.78	1.65	5.20			1.28	0.81	0.50	2.0	0.220Y	32/4/39	67.2	58.1
		0.91	-1.11	-6.00	-8.58			1.71	1.89	1.85	12.1	0.41250	2/14/18	18.3	11.2
		0.59	-0.25	-0.21	2.28									14.5	0.0
		0.24	-0.28	0.83	0.73			1.30			7.8			23.1	10.0
		0.57	1.62	1.60	1.57	35.7	25.4	0.91	0.87	0.83	1.9	0.2550Y	32/4/39	57.9	41.2
		0.69	1.98	1.41	2.00	77.1	52.0	2.17	1.81	1.40	1.7	0.70Z	32/4/39	152.7	103.0
		0.14	0.44	-0.23	0.17	53.9	34.2	0.03	0.02	0.17	0.2	0.0150Y	1/10/18	23.7	15.1
		1.13	2.62	2.64	2.35	35.2	26.9	1.47	1.33	1.21	1.8	0.4150Y	32/4/39	92.3	70.6
		-0.62	1.77	1.91	2.82	28.2	23.8	3.72	3.60	3.44	8.2	0.950	32/4/39	49.9	42.1
		3.24	7.81	8.48	8.30	22.0	14.3	2.92	2.59	2.26	2.1	0.830Y	32/4/39	171.7	111.6
		0.23	6.32	-0.62	1.17	15.2	11.6	1.36	1.16	0.94	1.6	0.380Y	32/4/39	96.4	73.2
		0.66	2.19	2.45	2.37	33.3	22.5	0.36	0.36	0.33	0.6	0.090Y	32/4/39	72.9	49.2
	0.18		0.90	1.46	1.04									50.9	35.4
			0.57	2.15	1.68	0.69	23.7	16.5						18.3	12.4
			-0.18	-6.68	0.13	-0.11			0.45	0.72	0.72	3.0	0.090Y	4/28/17	91.0
			0.88	2.61	2.41	2.21	34.9	25.5	0.58	0.53	0.45	0.8	0.190Y	32/4/39	12.1
			0.01	0.36	0.13	0.06	33.7	13.7						7.3	0.0
	0.03		-1.27	1.43	-0.42						1.7		8/24/07	7.3	0.0
			-1.27	-5.90	-13.18	-3.47			0.20	1.08	0.99	0.4	0.93750Z	32/4/39	71.7
			3.54	6.12	12.36	6.44	18.8	12.3	2.10	1.85	1.10	2.2	0.590Y	32/4/39	115.4
			0.90	1.87	2.33	0.96	31.9	22.6	3.31	2.84	2.41	-6.5	1.0	2/14/18	59.7
				0.15	-0.20	-0.14	90.1	59.6							13.5	8.9
	0.76		0.71	4.96	5.54	177.5	146.8	1.70			1.5			126.0	104.3
		1.11	3.59	3.81	5.84	24.5	17.6					5.7	32/4/39	88.0	63.1
		0.31	1.39	0.42	-0.96	9.1	7.3	3.17	3.17	3.17	27.2	0.30Z	32/4/39	12.7	10.1
		0.02										0.0750	2/20/18	22.6	16.8
		0.33	1.24	0.76	0.05	28.6	20.8	0.97	0.67		3.0	0.3650	2/13/18	35.5	25.8
		-0.43	-2.88	3.43	2.57									26.2	17.6
		2.80	9.21	9.38	8.99	25.5	15.5	2.60	2.50	1.75	1.4	0.70Y	32/4/39	235.0	142.8
		0.11	0.17	0.08	0.18	37.2	30.2	0.60	0.60	0.56	10.4	0.150Z	1/29/18	6.3	5.1
		0.72	5.16	4.88	4.66			1.29	1.15	0.92		0.360	2/15/18		
		0.16	-3.71	-61.20	-14.06			1.00	1.00	0.95	2.1	0.250Y	32/4/39	63.8	38.4
		0.11	2.67	1.52	2.06	17.4	15.9	1.32	1.18	1.04	3.0	0.360Z	32/4/39	46.5	42.4
		0.54	1.74	1.54	1.72	11.3	9.7	1.84	1.78	1.60	10.1	0.50Z	1/31/18	19.6	16.8
		1.00	2.11	0.61	0.62	16.1	9.3	1.25	1.96	3.11	4.6	0.39840	12/15/17	34.0	19.7
			1.24	1.22	1.18	14.5	13.0	1.24	1.23	1.23	7.3	0.090	2/28/18	18.0	16.1
			1.50	1.48	1.50	11.1	10.3	1.52	1.56	1.66	9.4	0.10	2/28/18	16.7	15.5
		0.28	0.76	0.65	0.04	27.2	23.1	1.20	0.80		6.3	0.10Z	32/4/39	20.6	17.6
0.86			2.75	2.80	2.67	90.8	72.2	1.10	1.04	0.96	1.8	0.30Y	2/28/18	68.1	54.1
		0.83	3.17	3.09	2.85	28.4	22.6	1.22	1.14	1.09	1.5	0.320Y	32/4/39	90.1	71.6
		1.48	4.59	5.06	4.48			1.16	1.00	1.00		0.220	32/4/39		
		0.43	1.32	1.14	1.31	29.8	22.4	0.74	0.69	0.63	2.2	0.20470Y	32/4/39	39.3	29.5

SYMBOL	COMPANY	NATURE OF BUSINESS	FISCAL YEAR-END	TOTAL REV. $MILL	NET INCOME $MILL	TOTAL ASSETS $MILL	NET STK EQUITY $MILL	NO OF INST	INST. HOLDINGS (SHARES)
AQ	Aquantia Corp	Semiconductors	12/31/16	86.7	-0.4	65.7	19.6	-	0
WAAS	AquaVenture Holdings Ltd	Water Utilities	12/31/16	114.1	-20.5	536.7	367.5	73	9981572
ARMK	Aramark	Hotels, Restaurants & Travel	9/29/17	14604.4	373.9	11006.2	2459.1	382	256455741
ABR	Arbor Realty Trust Inc	REITs	12/31/16	213.2	74.6	2970.8	587.1	142	32774098
ARC	ARC Document Solutions, Inc.	Printing	12/31/16	406.3	-47.9	399.6	149.9	135	40661114
MT	ArcelorMittal SA	Non-Precious Metals	12/31/16	56791.0	1779.0	75142.0	30135.0	7	1197012
ARCH	Arch Coal Inc	Mining	12/31/16	575.7	33.4	2136.6	746.6	309	40438556
ADM	Archer Daniels Midland Co.	Food	12/31/16	62346.0	1279.0	39769.0	17173.0	1066	586332041
AROC	Archrock Inc	Equipment & Services	12/31/16	807.1	-54.6	2414.8	719.0	248	79200645
ARNC	Arconic Inc	Non-Precious Metals	12/31/16	12394.0	-941.0	20038.0	5115.0	1324	640169236
ARCO	Arcos Dorados Holdings Inc	Hotels, Restaurants & Travel	12/31/16	2928.6	78.8	1505.1	351.0	165	96398940
ARD	Ardagh Group SA	Containers & Packaging	12/31/16	6345.0	-55.0	10261.0	-2058.0	79	16440965
ASC	Ardmore Shipping Corp	Shipping	12/31/16	164.4	3.7	883.6	404.3	107	28736579
ACRE	Ares Commercial Real Estate Corp	REITs	12/31/16	82.0	40.3	1373.7	419.0	140	23791095
ARDC	Ares Dynamic Credit Allocation Fun	Finance Intermediaries & Services	10/31/16	39.5	28.5	594.1	391.8	54	8256306
ARES	Ares Management LP	Wealth Management	12/31/16	1199.2	111.8	5829.7	298.8	64	14372589
AGX	Argan Inc	Construction Services	1/31/17	675.0	70.3	644.2	291.6	237	13814009
ANET	Arista Networks Inc	Computer Hardware & Equipment	12/31/16	1129.2	184.2	1729.0	1107.8	402	44741232
AI	Arlington Asset Investment Corp	Credit & Lending	12/31/16	36.0	-41.3	4141.6	383.4	154	26876638
AHH	Armada Hoffler Properties Inc	REITs	12/31/16	258.4	28.1	982.5	148.1	194	40092490
ARR	ARMOUR Residential REIT Inc.	REITs	12/31/16	65.1	-45.5	7978.2	1092.1	191	31982046
AFI	Armstrong Flooring Inc	Plastics	12/31/16	1193.2	9.2	904.4	623.5	140	27256316
AWI	Armstrong World Industries Inc	Construction Materials	12/31/16	1234.5	104.7	1758.0	266.4	246	68750133
ARW	Arrow Electronics, Inc.	Electrical Equipment	12/31/16	23825.3	522.8	14206.4	4413.4	536	111276307
APAM	Artisan Partners Asset Management	Wealth Management	12/31/16	720.9	73.0	936.2	131.7	238	50048938
ASA	ASA Gold and Precious Metals Ltd	Holding and other Investment Office	11/30/16	1.2	-2.0	245.0	243.2	61	6664003
ABG	Asbury Automotive Group Inc	Retail - Automotive	12/31/16	6527.8	167.2	2336.1	279.7	253	27510228
AHP	Ashford Hospitality Prime Inc	REITs	12/31/16	405.9	19.3	1257.0	374.8	153	22559136
AHT	Ashford Hospitality Trust Inc	REITs	12/31/16	1492.0	-46.3	4891.5	791.6	230	93372662
ASH	Ashland Global Holdings Inc	Specialty Chemicals	9/30/17	3260.0	1.0	8618.0	3406.0		0
APB	Asia Pacific Fund, Inc. (The)	Holding and other Investment Office	3/31/17	4.7	2.3	135.2	134.1	40	7932618
GRR	Asia Tigers Fund, Inc. (The)	Holding and other Investment Office	10/31/16	1.1	0.3	40.2	39.9	27	1684946
ASPN	Aspen Aerogels Inc	Construction Materials	12/31/16	117.7	-12.0	134.7	115.6	65	18791937
AHL	Aspen Insurance Holdings Ltd	General Insurance	12/31/16	2938.5	203.3	12090.1	3646.9	344	67510721
ASB	Associated Banc-Corp	Banking	12/31/16	1144.5	200.3	29139.3	3091.3	346	138121513
AC	Associated Capital Group Inc	Brokers & Intermediaries	12/31/16	31.2	10.2	952.6	874.0	70	3690149
AIZ	Assurant Inc	Life & Health	12/31/16	7531.8	565.4	29709.1	4098.1	553	65347521
AGO	Assured Guaranty Ltd	General Insurance	12/31/16	1677.0	881.0	14151.0	6504.0	411	143575488
AZN	AstraZeneca Plc	Pharmaceuticals	12/31/16	23002.0	3499.0	62526.0	14854.0	634	395569020
HOME	At Home Group Inc	Furniture	1/28/17	765.6	27.1	1213.4	534.9	98	15450294
T	AT&T Inc	Services	12/31/16	163786.0	12976.0	403821.0	123135.0	2725	4220421418
ATTO	Atento SA	Services	12/31/16	1757.5	0.1	1377.6	430.9	37	70828666
ATH	Athene Holding Ltd	Life & Health	12/31/16	4107.0	805.0	86720.0	6905.0	294	98725517
ATKR	Atkore International Group Inc	Electrical Equipment	9/30/17	1503.9	84.6	1215.1	360.9	157	65607614
AT	Atlantic Power Corp	Electric Utilities	12/31/16	399.2	-122.4	1456.8	64.6	-	0
ATO	Atmos Energy Corp.	Gas Utilities	9/30/17	2759.7	396.4	10749.6	3898.7	554	96035674
AUO	AU Optronics Corp.	Electrical Equipment	12/31/16	329089.0	9965.1	405860.8	158448.1	169	74601741
ATHM	Autohome Inc	IT Services	12/31/16	5961.6	1227.9	9392.0	6360.4	218	53277407
ALV	Autoliv Inc.	Auto Parts	12/31/16	10073.6	567.1	8234.4	3677.2	397	41436851
AN	AutoNation, Inc.	Retail - Automotive	12/31/16	21609.0	430.5	10060.0	2310.3	442	94928242
AZO	AutoZone, Inc.	Retail - Automotive	8/26/17	10888.7	1280.9	9259.8	-1428.4	812	32676692
AVB	AvalonBay Communities, Inc.	REITs	12/31/16	2045.3	1034.0	17867.3	10171.4	685	162554263
AGR	Avangrid Inc	Electric Utilities	12/31/16	6018.0	630.0	31309.0	15109.0	258	44867236
AVY	Avery Dennison Corp	Containers & Packaging	12/31/16	6086.5	320.7	4396.4	925.5	736	104157414
AVH	Avianca Holdings SA	Airlines/Air Freight	12/31/16	4138.3	17.0	6351.3	1400.5	52	7549839
AVA	Avista Corp	Electric Utilities	12/31/16	1442.5	137.2	5309.8	1648.7	359	66431055
AVT	Avnet Inc	Electrical Equipment	7/1/17	17440.0	525.3	9699.6	5182.1	531	157688706
AVP	Avon Products, Inc.	Household & Personal Products	12/31/16	5717.7	-107.6	3418.9	-403.3	484	450355013
AVX	AVX Corp.	Electrical Equipment	3/31/17	1312.7	125.8	2477.4	2216.5	205	51033704
AXTA	Axalta Coating Systems Ltd	Miscellaneous Transportation Servic	12/31/16	4097.4	41.8	5854.8	1136.1	378	263552776
AXS	AXIS Capital Holdings Ltd	General Insurance	12/31/16	4005.7	513.4	20813.7	6272.4	425	89712589
AZUL	Azul SA	Airlines/Air Freight	12/31/16	6669.9	-126.3	8400.4	1002.0	70	31875018
AZRE	Azure Power Global Ltd	Electric Utilities	3/31/17	4183.0	-1172.6	57494.0	13222.1	22	11324018
AZZ	AZZ Inc	Business Services	2/28/17	858.9	60.9	977.8	529.8	221	27004467
BGS	B&G Foods Inc	Food	12/31/16	1391.3	109.4	3043.5	785.7	375	79395566
BW	Babcock & Wilcox Enterprises Inc	Industrial Machinery & Equipment	12/31/16	1578.3	-115.6	1529.1	552.1	168	33938981
BMI	Badger Meter Inc	Electronic Instruments & Related Pro	12/31/16	393.8	32.3	349.7	256.2	221	29136080
BHGE	Baker Hughes, A GE Company	Equipment & Services	12/31/16	13269.0	403.0	21721.0	14688.0	511	382199406
BLL	Ball Corp	Metal Products	12/31/16	9061.0	263.0	16173.0	3435.0	672	340964761
BANC	Banc Of California Inc	Banking	12/31/16	656.9	115.4	11029.9	980.2	244	69734111
BBVA	Banco Bilbao Vizcaya Argentaria S	Banking	12/31/16	42100.0	3475.0	731856.0	47364.0	335	219568341
BBD	Banco Bradesco SA	Banking	12/31/16	189109.1	17894.2	1192029.7	105302.4	302	938440697
BCH	Banco de Chile	Banking	12/31/16	2272341.0	575051.0	31357304.0	3307673.0	103	2614158
BLX	Banco Latinoamericano de Comerci	Banking	12/31/16	258.7	87.0	7180.8	1011.3	47	8981899
BMA	Banco Macro SA	Banking	12/31/16	37502.5	6540.8	154999.0	22105.9	196	22082814
BSMX	Banco Santander (Mexico) SA, Insti	Banking	12/31/16	101.1	16.5	1351.0	107.3	-	0
BSBR	Banco Santander Brasil SA	Banking	12/31/16	97919.5	7334.6	634393.2	84087.1	143	74392723
BSAC	Banco Santander Chile	Banking	12/31/16	2375942.0	476067.0	37030025.0	2908858.0	182	107086327
SAN	Banco Santander SA (Spain)	Banking	12/31/16	74765.0	6204.0	1339125.0	90938.0	424	224030242
CIB	BanColombia SA	Banking	12/31/16	20697855.0	2865328.0	196261044.0	21267583.0	196	58148284

	EARNINGS PER SHARE					P/E RATIO		DIVIDENDS PER SHARE			AV. YLD %	DIV. DECLARED		PRICE RANGE	
QUARTERLY			ANNUAL											2016	
1st	2nd	3rd	2016	2015	2014			2016	2015	2014		AMOUNT	PAYABLE		
		-0.21	-0.10	-6.64	-24.83	-		-				-		13.5 -	9.5
		-0.29	-0.28											-	
		0.26	1.16	0.96	0.63	37.7 -	28.5	0.38	0.34	0.23	1.0	0.1050Y	32/4/39	43.8 -	33.1
	0.21		0.83	0.90	1.70	10.6 -	8.8	0.62	0.58	0.52	7.6	0.53130Z	11/30/17	8.8 -	7.3
		-0.32	-1.04	2.04	0.15							- -		5.4 -	2.4
			1.86	-13.29	-3.00	17.7 -	10.7					0.3750Z	1/15/16	33.0 -	19.9
		2.83	1.31	-136.86	-26.30	71.2 -	46.5			0.10		0.350Y	12/15/17	93.2 -	60.9
		0.34	2.16	2.98	3.43	21.7 -	18.0	1.20	1.12	0.96	2.8	0.320Y	32/4/39	47.0 -	39.0
		-0.15	-0.80	-1.55	1.40	-		0.50	0.60	0.60	4.2	0.120Y	2/14/18	16.2 -	8.8
		0.22	-2.31	-0.93	0.63			0.09	-		0.4	0.060Y	32/4/39	30.6 -	19.2
		0.37	-0.25	-0.52								0.05950	1/2/15	-	
												0.140	11/30/17	-	
		0.12	1.23	0.07								0.110	8/31/16		
		0.39	1.41	1.20	0.85	10.0 -	9.0	1.04	1.00	1.00	7.8	0.270Z	1/16/18	14.2 -	12.8
			1.23	1.21	1.24	13.5 -	12.3	1.30	1.40	1.40	8.1	0.10750	3/30/18	16.6 -	15.2
		0.26	1.20	0.23	0.43	19.4 -	14.3	0.83	0.88	0.42	4.4	0.43750	32/4/39	23.3 -	17.2
		1.09	2.42	2.05	2.78	31.3 -	17.3	0.70	0.70	0.75	1.1	1.0Y	10/31/17	75.7 -	41.9
		1.68	2.50	1.67	1.29	97.4 -	35.3					-		243.6 -	88.2
		0.85	-1.79	-3.02	0.29			2.50	3.00	3.50	18.4	0.550Y	1/31/18	15.4 -	11.0
		0.17	0.85	0.75	0.37	18.6 -	15.0	0.72	0.68	0.64	5.2	0.190Z	1/4/18	15.9 -	12.7
		0.58	-1.67	-1.09	-4.32			3.02	1.65	4.80	12.2	0.16410Z	3/27/18	27.5 -	21.0
		-0.70	0.33	-		68.8 -	41.5							22.7 -	13.7
		0.92	1.87	1.68	1.14	32.4 -	20.7					8.557	32/4/39	60.5 -	38.8
		1.50	5.68	5.20	4.98	14.8 -	12.3					0.025	32/4/39	84.0 -	70.0
		0.61	1.57	1.86	-0.37	25.5 -	17.0	2.80	3.35	3.83	8.9	0.60	11/30/17	40.1 -	26.6
			-0.10	-0.09	-0.08							0.020	11/28/17		
		1.48	7.40	6.41	3.71	9.4 -	6.8					0.2250Y	32/4/39	69.5 -	50.1
		-0.09	0.55	-0.34	0.07	26.5 -	16.2	0.46	0.35	0.20	4.3	0.34380Z	1/16/18	14.6 -	8.9
		-0.40	-0.95	2.35	-0.75			0.48	0.48	0.48	7.3	0.2292GHZ	1/16/18	8.2 -	5.8
		-0.54	-0.46	4.48	3.00			1.56	1.46	1.36	2.5	0.2250Y	32/4/39	74.0 -	53.4
			0.20	0.23	-0.02	74.2 -	0.0	0.51	-		4.1	0.32B	1/5/18	14.8 -	0.0
			0.07	0.08	0.05	184.9 -	0.0	0.35	0.47	0.29	3.3	0.31850	1/8/18	12.9 -	0.0
		-0.13	-0.52	-0.28	-5.37							-		5.1 -	3.9
		-4.48	2.61	4.54	4.82							0.35160	32/4/39	-	
		0.41	1.26	1.19	1.16	21.0 -	16.9	0.45	0.41	0.37	1.8	0.33590Y	32/4/39	26.5 -	21.3
		0.06	0.41	0.00	-	95.7 -	79.0	0.10	-		0.3	0.10Y	1/10/18	39.3 -	32.4
		-1.05	9.13	2.05	6.44	11.6 -	9.6	2.03	1.37	1.06	2.1	0.560Y	32/4/39	106.3 -	87.7
		1.72	6.56	7.08	6.26			0.52	0.48	0.44		0.14250	32/4/39	-	
	0.38		2.76	2.23	0.98	12.8 -	9.7	1.37	1.38	1.40	4.3			35.4 -	26.7
		0.04	0.07	-0.01	-0.44	451.9 -	195.1	-						31.6 -	13.7
		0.49	2.10	2.37	1.19	20.5 -	15.6	1.92	1.88	1.84	5.0	0.50Y	32/4/39	43.0 -	32.9
			0.01	0.66	-0.61							0.34G	11/28/17	-	
		7.44	4.21	3.21	3.52							-		-	
		0.41	0.94	-0.08	-2.02	29.0 -	16.9							27.3 -	15.9
		-0.29	-1.02	-0.51	-1.47			-	0.09	0.27		0.030	12/31/15	3.6 -	2.3
		0.67	3.38	3.09	2.96	27.3 -	21.7	1.68	1.56	1.48	2.0	0.4850Y	32/4/39	92.3 -	73.2
			1.02	0.70	1.69	4.7 -	3.6	2.20	3.19	1.26	54.5	-		4.8 -	3.6
			10.58	8.57	6.64	6.3 -	2.4					-		67.0 -	25.5
		1.04	6.42	5.17	5.06	20.2 -	15.0	2.30	2.22	2.12	2.0	0.60Y	32/4/39	129.6 -	96.3
		1.00	4.15	3.89	3.52	13.6 -	9.3	-				-		56.3 -	38.7
10.00			40.70	36.03	31.57	19.5 -	12.1	-				-		793.7 -	493.1
		1.72	7.52	5.51	5.21	26.5 -	22.6	5.40	5.00	4.64	2.9	1.420Y	32/4/39	199.1 -	169.6
		0.32	2.04	1.05	1.70	26.0 -	18.5	1.73	-		3.8	0.4320	32/4/39	53.1 -	37.8
		1.20	3.54	2.95	2.60	33.1 -	19.8	1.60	1.46	1.34	1.8	0.450Y	32/4/39	117.1 -	70.1
			0.04	-0.14	0.13	254.7 -	161.3	0.12	0.52	0.29	1.6	-		10.2 -	6.5
		0.07	2.15	1.97	3.10	24.5 -	17.6	1.37	1.32	1.27	3.0	0.35750Y	32/4/39	52.7 -	37.9
0.47			3.80	4.12	3.89	12.5 -	9.5	0.68	0.64	0.60	1.7	0.180	32/4/39	47.6 -	35.9
		0.01	-0.29	-2.60	-0.88			-	0.24	0.24		0.060Y	32/4/39	5.9 -	1.9
	0.21		0.60	1.34	0.75	32.7 -	25.7	0.42	0.40	0.36	2.5	0.1150Y	11/16/17	19.6 -	15.4
		0.22	0.17	0.39	0.12									-	
		-5.61	5.08	6.04	7.29			1.43	1.22	1.10		0.34380	1/16/18	-	
			-0.55	-5.42	-0.35			-				-		28.9 -	20.3
			-1722.09	1046.00				-				-		-	
	0.32		2.96	2.52	2.32	22.2 -	14.7	0.60	0.58	0.56	1.1	0.170Y	2/20/18	65.7 -	43.5
		0.49	1.73	1.22	0.76	27.5 -	17.3	1.73	1.38	1.36	4.6	0.4650Y	1/30/18	47.5 -	29.9
		-2.48	-2.31	0.36								-		17.4 -	1.7
		0.27	1.11	0.90	1.03	46.5 -	31.2	0.43	0.39	0.37	1.0	0.130Y	32/4/39	51.6 -	34.6
		-0.24	-2.08	-								0.180Y	2/16/18	37.9 -	29.7
		0.13	0.81	1.00	1.65	53.0 -	44.2	0.26	0.26	0.26	0.7	0.10Y	32/4/39	42.9 -	35.8
		0.23	1.94	1.34	0.91	11.9 -	7.6	0.49	0.48	0.48	2.4	0.43750Y	12/15/17	23.1 -	14.7
			0.50	0.39	0.44	18.5 -	12.8	0.37	0.28	0.40	4.6	-		9.3 -	6.4
			2.80	2.83	2.40	4.2 -	2.8	0.98	0.91	0.72	10.1	-		11.7 -	7.9
			5.74	6.04	5.99	17.1 -	11.9	1560.15	1583.10	1482.31	1947.6			98.1 -	68.1
	0.44		2.22	2.66	2.75			-				0.3850	2/21/18	-	
														135.5 -	70.0
			2.43	2.06	1.96	4.4 -	2.8	11.28	4.45	2.39	127.2	-		10.8 -	6.9
		176.00	9.29	1.24	0.71	1.2 -	0.8	0.79	0.96	2.05	8.8	-		11.6 -	7.3
		0.54	2.53	2.38	3.02	12.7 -	8.4	567.70	555.94	423.12	2149.3	-		32.1 -	21.4
	0.11		0.41	0.40	0.48	17.0 -	13.0	0.35	0.70	1.07	5.5			7.0 -	5.3
			-3040.00	2680.00	2591.00	0.0 -	0.0	3500.05	3333.93	3088.70	8425.9	-		48.3 -	36.2

T7

SYMBOL	COMPANY	NATURE OF BUSINESS	FISCAL YEAR-END	TOTAL REV. $MILL	NET INCOME $MILL	TOTAL ASSETS $MILL	NET STK EQUITY $MILL	NO OF INST	INST. HOLDINGS (SHARES)
BXS	BancorpSouth Bank (Tupelo, MS)	Banking	12/31/16	762.2	132.7	14724.4	1723.9	258	74229469
BAC	Bank of America Corp.	Banking	12/31/16	93662.0	17906.0	2187702.0	266840.0	2533	8394949287
BOH	Bank of Hawaii Corp	Banking	12/31/16	655.2	181.5	16492.4	1161.5	403	46155816
BMO	Bank of Montreal (Quebec)	Banking	10/31/17	28086.0	5348.0	709580.0	44354.0	527	305709120
BK	Bank of New York Mellon Corp	Banking	12/31/16	15674.0	3547.0	333469.0	38811.0	1339	972558307
BNS	Bank of Nova Scotia Halifax	Banking	10/31/17	36047.0	7876.0	915273.0	60033.0	476	648222379
NTB	Bank Of NT Butterfield & Son Ltd (T	Banking	12/31/16	423.4	115.9	11103.5	710.7	-	0
BKU	BankUnited Inc.	Banking	12/31/16	1165.6	225.7	27880.2	2418.4	318	128437483
BCS	Barclays PLC	Banking	12/31/16	27747.0	2080.0	1213126.0	64873.0	341	118287556
MCI	Barings Corporate Investors	Holding and other Investment Office	12/31/16	28.2	22.2	321.9	281.6	54	2148124
BGH	Barings Global Short Duration High	Finance Intermediaries & Services	12/31/16	47.2	40.3	564.4	418.6	-	0
MPV	Barings Participation Investors	Holding and other Investment Office	12/31/16	12.8	10.3	155.8	136.6	37	1863217
BNED	Barnes & Noble Education Inc	Retail - Specialty	4/29/17	1874.4	5.4	1299.8	713.7	159	37117114
BKS	Barnes & Noble Inc	Retail - Specialty	4/29/17	3894.6	22.0	1932.9	574.3	282	61122271
B	Barnes Group Inc.	Industrial Machinery & Equipment	12/31/16	1230.8	135.6	2137.5	1168.4	347	61873502
CUDA	Barracuda Networks Inc	IT Services	2/28/17	352.6	10.2	464.8	6.4	203	43185571
BBG	Barrett (Bill) Corp	Production & Extraction	12/31/16	178.8	-170.4	1385.3	571.5	232	82952089
ABX	Barrick Gold Corp.	Precious Metals	12/31/16	8558.0	655.0	25264.0	7935.0	699	772535451
BAS	Basic Energy Services Inc	Equipment & Services	12/31/16	547.5	-123.4	768.2	414.4	188	32072446
BAX	Baxter International Inc	Medical Instruments & Equipment	12/31/16	10163.0	4965.0	15546.0	8290.0	1436	596948499
BTE	Baytex Energy Corp	Production & Extraction	12/31/16	602.0	-485.2	4594.1	1979.0	-	0
BBT	BB&T Corp.	Banking	12/31/16	11538.0	2426.0	219276.0	29881.0	1199	602160184
BFR	BBVA Banco Frances SA (Argentin	Banking	12/31/16	32103.6	3643.7	151752.7	16460.0	92	29785858
BBX	BBX Capital Corp (New)	Hotels, Restaurants & Travel	12/31/16	764.0	28.4	1436.1	454.6	58	30155460
BCE	BCE Inc	Services	12/31/16	21719.0	2894.0	50108.0	17540.0	626	502317846
BZH	Beazer Homes USA, Inc.	Builders	9/30/17	1916.3	31.8	2221.0	682.4	230	43495765
BDX	Becton, Dickinson & Co	Medical Instruments & Equipment	9/30/17	12093.0	1100.0	37734.0	12948.0	1494	249615403
BDC	Belden Inc	Electrical Equipment	12/31/16	2356.7	128.0	3806.8	1460.3	341	63559205
BXE	Bellatrix Exploration Ltd	Production & Extraction	12/31/16	199.6	-26.7	1453.7	863.4	76	30110086
T 28A	BellSouth Telecommunications, Inc.	Services	12/31/99	17478.0	2770.0	25295.0	8805.0	-	0
BEL	Belmond Ltd	Hotels, Restaurants & Travel	12/31/16	550.8	36.3	1524.1	686.4	208	112195876
BMS	Bemis Co Inc	Containers & Packaging	12/31/16	4004.4	236.2	3715.7	1259.7	515	97669668
BHE	Benchmark Electronics, Inc.	Electrical Equipment	12/31/16	2310.4	64.0	1998.7	1365.5	292	60112530
WRB	Berkley (WR) Corp	General Insurance	12/31/16	7654.2	601.9	23364.8	5047.2	526	121554660
BRK A	Berkshire Hathaway Inc	General Insurance	12/31/16	223604.0	24074.0	620854.0	283001.0	2495	1065685552
BHLB	Berkshire Hills Bancorp Inc	Banking	12/31/16	346.3	58.7	9162.5	1093.3	239	33554566
BERY	Berry Global Group Inc	Plastics	9/30/17	7095.0	340.0	8476.0	1012.0	421	134172602
BBY	Best Buy Inc	Retail - Appliances and Electronics	1/28/17	39403.0	1228.0	13856.0	4709.0	856	304347762
BSTI	BEST Inc	Trucking	12/31/16	8844.1	-1363.5	6295.9	2334.1	52	49185891
BHP	BHP Billiton Ltd.	Non-Precious Metals	6/30/17	38285.0	5890.0	117006.0	57258.0	573	66997831
BBL	BHP Billiton Plc	Production & Extraction	6/30/17	38285.0	5890.0	117006.0	57258.0	245	52670842
BIG	Big Lots, Inc.	Retail - General Merchandise/Depart	1/28/17	5200.4	152.8	1607.7	650.6	506	70295227
BH	Biglari Holdings Inc.	Holding and other Investment Office	12/31/16	850.1	99.5	1097.0	531.9	159	3416655
BIO	Bio-Rad Laboratories Inc	Biotechnology	12/31/16	2068.2	28.1	3850.5	2586.8	382	22645660
BIOA	BioAmber Inc	Specialty Chemicals	12/31/16	8.3	-22.5	161.3	48.5	46	15762329
BHVN	Biohaven Pharmaceutical Holding C	Pharmaceuticals	12/31/16	-	-63.7	27.0	-1.8	88	15362049
BITA	Bitauto Holdings Ltd	Internet & Software	12/31/16	5772.9	-541.3	29934.8	9543.5	111	21255747
BKH	Black Hills Corporation	Electric Utilities	12/31/16	1573.0	73.0	6515.4	1614.6	343	65247669
BKI	Black Knight Inc	Internet & Software	12/31/16	1026.0	45.8	3762.0	875.7	-	0
BSM	Black Stone Minerals LP	Production & Extraction	12/31/16	260.8	20.2	1128.8	54.0	80	23043106
BB	BlackBerry Ltd	Services	2/28/17	1309.0	-1206.0	3263.0	2057.0	452	337605743
BJZ	Blackrock California Municipal 2018	Holding and other Investment Office	12/31/16	2.7	2.2	96.2	96.1	18	962812
BFZ	BlackRock California Municipal Inco	Holding and other Investment Office	7/31/17	33.8	23.2	840.0	489.3	51	2640937
BHK	BlackRock Core Bond Trust	Holding and other Investment Office	8/31/17	50.0	40.8	1118.6	606.8	103	18619110
HYT	BlackRock Corporate High Yield Fu	Holding and other Investment Office	8/31/17	130.4	107.0	2215.2	1545.6	170	40494468
BTZ	BlackRock Credit Allocation Income	Holding and other Investment Office	10/31/17	106.1	86.8	2098.8	1598.0	146	54236180
DSU	BlackRock Debt Strategies Fund Inc	Holding and other Investment Office	2/28/17	55.9	45.7	1156.1	780.8	119	29141095
BGR	Blackrock Energy & Resources Trus	Holding and other Investment Office	12/31/16	13.4	8.0	494.6	487.1	89	6250689
CII	BlackRock Enhanced Capital & Inco	Holding and other Investment Office	12/31/16	11.7	5.6	677.5	665.2	92	9760890
BDJ	BlackRock Enhanced Equity Divide	Holding and other Investment Office	12/31/16	45.3	31.3	1773.9	1741.6	172	40992133
BOE	BlackRock Enhanced Global Divide	Holding and other Investment Office	12/31/16	20.5	10.7	943.3	929.9	116	21822494
EGF	BlackRock Enhanced Government	Holding and other Investment Office	12/31/16	3.7	2.6	114.1	90.1	24	5081590
BGY	BlackRock Enhanced International	Holding and other Investment Office	12/31/16	17.3	10.0	716.5	690.6	97	35349224
FRA	BlackRock Floating Rate Income Str	Holding and other Investment Office	8/31/17	38.7	28.3	834.4	556.0	104	11526726
BGT	BlackRock Floating Rate Income Tr	Holding and other Investment Office	10/31/17	23.8	17.2	521.1	342.9	68	6254971
BFO	BlackRock Florida Municipal 2020 T	Holding and other Investment Office	7/31/17	2.6	2.0	83.9	83.7	21	680513
BME	BlackRock Health Sciences Trust	Holding and other Investment Office	12/31/16	3.4	0.2	273.5	270.7	43	2957571
BLK	BlackRock Inc	Finance Intermediaries & Services	12/31/16	11155.0	3172.0	220177.0	29098.0	1346	156126501
BKT	BlackRock Income Trust Inc (The)	Holding and other Investment Office	8/31/16	22.8	18.0	622.6	444.9	87	38601176
BKN	BlackRock Investment Quality Muni	Holding and other Investment Office	4/30/17	18.7	13.6	423.0	264.6	57	1764576
BLW	Blackrock Limited Duration Income	Holding and other Investment Office	8/31/17	46.5	37.5	907.2	629.7	106	12320951
BTA	BlackRock Long-Term Municipal Ad	Holding and other Investment Office	4/30/17	12.4	9.0	277.6	164.7	39	3154079
BIT	BlackRock Multi-Sector Income Trust	Holding and other Investment Office	10/31/17	74.8	57.7	1271.4	765.9	75	13420879
MUI	BlackRock Muni Intermediate Durati	Holding and other Investment Office	4/30/17	36.2	24.8	931.3	580.9	92	9803813
MNE	BlackRock Muni New York Intermed	Holding and other Investment Office	7/31/17	3.8	2.4	103.9	65.1	26	616301
MUA	BlackRock MuniAssets Fund, Inc.	Holding and other Investment Office	4/30/17	29.8	25.3	576.4	505.3	63	2256158
BPK	Blackrock Municipal 2018 Term Tru	Holding and other Investment Office	12/31/16	6.9	5.7	243.3	239.2	52	2365069
BKK	BlackRock Municipal 2020 Term Tr	Holding and other Investment Office	4/30/17	13.2	11.0	332.2	315.8	59	2996905
BTT	BlackRock Municipal 2030 Target T	Holding and other Investment Office	7/31/17	88.3	63.4	2671.9	1679.8	86	9967696
BBK	Blackrock Municipal Bond Trust	Holding and other Investment Office	8/31/17	11.7	7.7	280.5	171.7	48	1167334

1st	2nd	3rd	EPS 2016	EPS 2015	EPS 2014	P/E High	P/E Low	Div 2016	Div 2015	Div 2014	Av Yld %	Div Amount	Payable	Price High 2016	Price Low 2016
		0.43	1.41	1.33	1.21	24.3	19.5	0.45	0.35	0.25	1.5	0.140Y	32/4/39	34.2	27.6
		0.48	1.50	1.31	0.36	19.9	14.7	0.25	0.20	0.12	1.0	1.750Y	32/4/39	29.9	22.1
		1.08	4.23	3.70	3.69	21.4	17.7	1.89	1.80	1.80	2.3	0.520Y	32/4/39	90.4	75.0
		2.05	6.92	6.57	6.41	15.0	9.7	3.40	3.24	3.08	4.0	0.2750	2/26/18	103.5	66.9
		0.94	3.15	2.71	2.15	17.5	13.9	0.72	0.68	0.66	1.4	0.3250Y	32/4/39	55.0	43.9
		1.66	5.77	5.67	5.66	14.7	9.4	2.88	2.72	2.56	4.1	0.30310	1/29/18	84.9	54.5
			1.18	1.23	1.65			0.40	0.50	0.50		0.320	11/27/17		
		0.62	2.09	2.35	1.95	19.6	14.6	0.84	0.63	1.05	2.4	0.210Y	32/4/39	40.9	30.5
			0.10	-0.02	-0.01	118.9	93.6	0.18	0.25	0.25	1.7			11.9	9.4
			1.12	1.04	1.23	14.5	13.1	1.20	1.20	1.20	7.8	0.30	1/12/18	16.2	14.6
			1.57	1.90	2.12	13.3	12.2	1.85	2.19	2.60	9.2	0.14821	4/2/18	20.8	19.2
			1.00	0.95	1.04	15.1	13.9	1.08	1.08	1.08	7.5	0.270	1/12/18	15.1	13.9
1.03				0.33	0.88									12.1	5.0
	-0.41	-0.49	0.21	-1.12				0.60			7.4	0.150Y	32/4/39	11.4	6.5
		0.65	2.48	2.19	2.12	29.2	18.5	0.51	0.48	0.45	0.9	0.140Y	12/8/17	72.4	45.9
		0.14	-0.08	-1.30	-0.10									27.8	19.5
		-0.39	-3.08	-10.10	0.31									7.4	2.8
		-0.01	0.56	-2.44	-2.50	47.9	24.2	0.08	0.14	0.20	0.4	0.030	12/15/17	26.8	13.6
		-0.53	-2.94	3403.46	-114.02									44.5	14.2
		0.45	9.01	1.76	4.56	7.3	4.9	0.51	1.27	2.05	0.9	0.160Y	32/4/39	66.0	44.4
		-0.04	-2.29	-5.72	-0.89				0.80	2.64		0.10	9/15/15	6.8	2.2
		0.74	2.77	2.56	2.75	18.2	15.0	1.15	1.05	0.95	2.5	0.35160Y	32/4/39	50.5	41.6
														25.5	15.3
		0.08	0.32	1.40	0.16	27.5	15.6	0.01			0.1	0.00750Y	1/22/18	8.8	5.0
		0.86	3.33	2.98	2.97	18.9	12.8	2.73	2.60	2.47	5.2	0.06671	2/12/18	62.8	42.5
		0.22	0.15	10.83	1.08	146.4	76.1					0.46880Y	7/15/15	22.0	11.4
		-0.75	4.49	3.35	5.99	50.8	36.7	2.64	2.40	2.18	1.4	0.750Y	32/4/39	228.2	164.8
		-0.18	2.65	1.54	1.69	32.6	24.4	0.20	0.20	0.20	0.3	1.68750Y	32/4/39	86.3	64.7
		-0.45	-0.12	-11.55	4.40									6.5	1.5
		0.08	0.35	0.16	-0.02							0.0250	11/4/08		
		0.61	2.48	2.44	1.89	20.8	16.5	1.16	1.12	1.08	2.5	0.30Y	32/4/39	51.6	41.0
		0.35	1.29	1.83	1.52	27.6	22.6							35.6	29.1
		1.26	4.68	3.87	4.86	15.6	13.4	1.51	0.47	1.43	2.2	0.57Y	32/4/39	73.0	62.5
		-2473.00	4645.00	4656.00	2092.00	20.4	16.3							299360.02	38100.0
		0.57	1.88	1.73	1.36	21.1	17.6	0.80	0.76	0.72	2.2	0.220Y	3/1/18	39.6	33.1
		0.79	1.89	0.70	0.51	32.2	25.1							60.8	47.5
		0.78	2.56	3.49	1.53	26.7	16.5	1.43	0.72	0.68	2.7	0.340Y	32/4/39	68.5	42.1
			-93.51	-89.21	-21.53									12.6	8.9
			-1.20	0.36	2.59			1.56	2.48	2.36	4.0			46.4	33.7
			-1.20	0.36	2.59			1.56	2.48	2.36	4.5			40.5	28.9
		0.10	2.80	2.06	2.16	21.3	16.6	0.76	0.51		1.5	0.250Y	32/4/39	59.5	46.5
		-20.09	81.28	-10.18	48.45	5.9	3.6							483.0	291.7
		0.91	0.95	3.85	3.05	285.6	192.5							271.3	182.9
		-0.16	-0.78	-1.52	-2.32									6.1	0.0
			-1.19	-5.05	-0.91										
			-8.31	-7.30	10.88									53.2	18.5
		0.50	1.37	-0.71	2.89	52.5	41.9	1.68	1.62	1.56	2.6	0.4750Y	32/4/39	71.9	57.4
			0.67	0.29		69.9	62.7							46.9	42.0
		0.16	0.26	-1.12	0.07	74.0	59.3	1.10	0.42		6.4	0.31250	11/24/17	19.2	15.4
		-0.52	-0.86	-0.58	-11.18									15.6	6.7
			0.34	0.36	0.40	45.0	0.0	0.33	0.38	0.54	2.3	0.0025M	2/1/18	15.3	0.0
			0.83	0.83	0.87	18.2	16.6	0.86	0.87	0.93	6.0	0.055M	2/1/18	15.1	13.8
			0.79	0.86	0.87	18.0	16.3	0.84	1.08	0.91	6.1	0.0650	1/9/18	14.3	12.9
			0.82	0.87	0.98	14.0	13.0	0.99	0.97	1.04	8.9	0.070	1/9/18	11.5	10.6
			0.88	0.96	0.99	15.5	14.4	0.92	0.97	0.97	6.9	0.0670	1/9/18	13.6	12.7
			0.78	0.87	0.90	15.2	14.4					0.06850	1/9/18	11.8	11.2
			0.27	0.29	0.25	54.9	45.7	1.00	1.50	2.76	7.4	0.07760	1/31/18	14.8	12.3
			0.13	0.11	0.40	126.3	105.2	1.15	1.20	1.20	7.7	0.08280	1/31/18	16.4	13.7
			0.17	0.17	0.04	54.5	47.9	0.56	0.56	0.56	6.4	0.04670	1/31/18	9.3	8.2
			0.15	0.11	0.00	92.4	78.3	1.05	1.16	1.24	8.1	0.0780	1/31/18	13.9	11.7
			0.36	0.41	0.49	38.0	36.2	0.53	0.62	0.66	4.0	0.0410	1/9/18	13.7	13.0
			0.09	0.08	0.00	74.6	60.8	0.52	0.59	0.66	8.4	0.0380	1/31/18	6.7	5.5
			0.76	0.81	0.87	19.5	18.0	0.75	0.81	0.89	5.3	0.0610	1/9/18	14.8	13.7
			0.74	0.78	0.99	19.9	18.3	0.70	0.81	0.84	5.0	0.05830	1/9/18	14.8	13.5
			0.46	0.42	0.47	33.0	0.0	0.38	0.44	0.61	2.6	0.026M	2/1/18	15.2	0.0
			0.02	-0.06	-0.01	1881.5	1617.0	3.00	6.70	4.20	8.5	0.20	1/31/18	37.6	32.3
		5.78	19.04	19.79	19.25	27.3	19.5	9.16	8.72	7.72	2.2	2.880Y	32/4/39	518.9	371.6
			0.28	0.32	0.35	22.9	21.7	0.34	0.40	0.43	5.4	0.02650	1/9/18	6.4	6.1
			0.88	0.90	0.94	17.9	15.9	0.91	0.95	0.96	6.1	0.062M	2/1/18	15.7	14.0
			1.32	1.16	1.26	12.3	11.5	1.30	1.29	1.22	8.2	0.07950	1/9/18	16.3	15.2
			0.68	0.69	0.71	18.4	16.4	0.70	0.72	0.74	5.9	0.0545M	2/1/18	12.5	11.2
			1.69	1.55	1.62	11.1	9.9	1.64	1.48	1.40	9.2	0.1317	1/9/18	18.7	16.7
			0.73	0.77	0.80	19.7	18.5	0.96	0.82	0.91	6.8	0.0495M	2/1/18	14.4	13.5
			0.64	0.68	0.69	22.2	20.7	0.66	0.69	0.73	4.8	0.0445M	2/1/18	14.2	13.2
			0.72	0.73	0.77	22.0	18.8	0.74	0.76	0.75	5.0	0.0545M	2/1/18	15.8	13.5
			0.36	0.41	0.61	42.0	40.9	0.37	0.60	0.68	2.5	0.005M	2/1/18	15.1	14.7
			0.57	0.90	0.74	27.9	26.2	0.56	0.67	0.81	3.6	0.0395M	2/1/18	15.9	14.9
			1.03	1.09	1.12	22.9	21.3	0.96	0.96	1.11	4.2	0.0718M	2/1/18	23.5	21.9
			0.89	0.90	0.97	18.4	16.3	0.91	0.98	1.05	5.9	0.0635M	2/1/18	16.3	14.5

SYMBOL	COMPANY	NATURE OF BUSINESS	FISCAL YEAR-END	TOTAL REV. $MILL	NET INCOME $MILL	TOTAL ASSETS $MILL	NET STK EQUITY $MILL	NO OF INST	INST. HOLDINGS (SHARES)
BAF	BlackRock Municipal Income Invest	Holding and other Investment Office	8/31/17	9.7	6.9	228.9	137.3	37	1160646
BBF	BlackRock Municipal Income Invest	Holding and other Investment Office	7/31/17	11.8	8.5	254.6	148.0	27	505628
BYM	BlackRock Municipal Income Qualit	Holding and other Investment Office	8/31/17	27.6	19.9	651.3	404.5	69	3019648
BFK	BlackRock Municipal Income Trust	Holding and other Investment Office	4/30/17	49.2	36.1	1060.2	638.0	70	4834609
MEN	BlackRock MuniEnhanced Fund Inc	Holding and other Investment Office	4/30/17	25.4	19.1	565.6	349.0	49	3829684
MUC	BlackRock MuniHoldings California	Holding and other Investment Office	7/31/17	41.0	28.4	1089.9	636.9	63	4950755
MUH	BlackRock MuniHoldings Fund II Inc	Holding and other Investment Office	4/30/17	13.1	9.8	279.5	175.6	43	1241444
MHD	BlackRock MuniHoldings Fund Inc	Holding and other Investment Office	4/30/17	18.1	13.4	386.4	238.7	38	1255257
MFL	BlackRock MuniHoldings Investmen	Holding and other Investment Office	8/31/17	41.0	29.4	968.7	564.4	63	5529568
MUJ	BlackRock MuniHoldings New Jerse	Holding and other Investment Office	7/31/17	32.2	23.3	794.1	469.4	42	2178921
MHN	BlackRock MuniHoldings New York	Holding and other Investment Office	8/31/17	30.7	21.3	783.1	464.8	47	2450442
MUE	BlackRock MuniHoldings Quality Fu	Holding and other Investment Office	7/31/17	23.0	16.8	519.3	319.4	53	3076412
MUS	BlackRock MuniHoldings Quality Fu	Holding and other Investment Office	4/30/17	13.4	9.8	299.1	181.6	35	2046649
MVT	BlackRock MuniVest Fund II Inc	Holding and other Investment Office	4/30/17	25.4	19.2	524.9	321.9	45	1043886
MYC	BlackRock MuniYield California Fun	Holding and other Investment Office	7/31/17	22.8	15.8	566.4	334.5	39	2535559
MCA	BlackRock MuniYield California Qua	Holding and other Investment Office	7/31/17	35.6	25.2	919.7	541.3	45	4128236
MYD	BlackRock MuniYield Fund Inc	Holding and other Investment Office	4/30/17	51.7	39.3	1112.5	687.9	73	4828324
MYF	BlackRock MuniYield Investment Fu	Holding and other Investment Office	7/31/17	16.0	11.9	348.3	204.4	35	1255643
MFT	BlackRock MuniYield Investment Q	Holding and other Investment Office	7/31/17	9.2	6.7	212.0	123.7	30	859880
MIY	BlackRock MuniYield Michigan Qual	Holding and other Investment Office	7/31/17	30.7	22.0	745.0	457.9	45	3287901
MYN	BlackRock MuniYield New York Qu	Holding and other Investment Office	7/31/17	36.3	25.4	929.0	564.2	55	2784640
MYJ	BlackRock MuniYield NJ Fund Inc	Holding and other Investment Office	7/31/17	16.1	11.7	389.7	228.3	26	1029673
MPA	BlackRock MuniYield Pennsylvania	Holding and other Investment Office	7/31/17	14.2	10.2	352.0	210.2	41	1079480
MQT	BlackRock MuniYield Quality Fund I	Holding and other Investment Office	4/30/17	22.1	16.4	503.2	308.7	52	3133404
MYI	BlackRock MuniYield Quality Fund I	Holding and other Investment Office	7/31/17	70.7	52.5	1602.5	985.6	90	8875488
MQY	BlackRock MuniYield Quality Fund I	Holding and other Investment Office	4/30/17	34.7	26.1	781.8	477.8	77	4819700
BNJ	Blackrock New Jersey Municipal Inc	Holding and other Investment Office	7/31/17	8.7	6.1	204.6	118.0	22	544788
BLH	Blackrock New York Municipal 2018	Holding and other Investment Office	12/31/16	1.2	0.8	54.2	54.1	13	266861
BQH	Blackrock New York Municipal Bond	Holding and other Investment Office	8/31/16	2.9	2.0	77.1	47.6	14	156551
BSE	BlackRock New York Municipal Inco	Holding and other Investment Office	8/31/17	6.1	4.1	160.1	98.1	28	801923
BNY	Blackrock New York Municipal Inco	Holding and other Investment Office	7/31/17	12.9	8.7	324.1	195.0	23	963169
BCX	Blackrock Resources & Commoditie	Holding and other Investment Office	12/31/15	35.4	24.6	834.4	827.0	112	39377069
BST	BlackRock Science & Technology T	Holding and other Investment Office	12/31/16	4.0	0.1	456.7	452.4	49	6627621
BSD	Blackrock Strategic Municipal Trust	Holding and other Investment Office	4/30/17	7.9	5.7	175.3	103.8	28	672979
BBN	BlackRock Taxable Municipal Bond	Holding and other Investment Office	7/31/17	110.7	90.5	2075.9	1339.1	118	8164927
BUI	BlackRock Utilities, Infrastructure &	Holding and other Investment Office	12/31/16	13.3	9.5	333.2	328.3	43	2027492
BGX	Blackstone / GSO Long-Short Credi	Holding and other Investment Office	12/31/16	23.1	17.8	361.2	215.2	44	4208244
BSL	Blackstone / GSO Senior Floating R	Holding and other Investment Office	12/31/16	25.5	18.9	427.5	268.2	43	3805912
BGB	Blackstone / GSO Strategic Credit F	Holding and other Investment Office	12/31/16	81.6	62.1	1255.5	749.9	84	20707077
BX	Blackstone Group LP (The)	Wealth Management	12/31/16	5125.8	103.2	26403.3		791	351689546
BXMT	Blackstone Mortgage Trust Inc	REITs	12/31/16	498.0	238.3	8812.6	2493.6	297	66644536
HRB	Block (H & R), Inc.	Miscellaneous Consumer Services	4/30/17	3036.3	408.9	2694.1	-60.9	686	262289158
APRN	Blue Apron Holdings Inc	Food	12/31/16	795.4	-54.9	273.4	61.5	87	17184399
BCRH	Blue Capital Reinsurance Holdings	General Insurance	12/31/16	42.6	14.3	204.7	183.3	70	7636886
BXG	Bluegreen Vacations Corp	Property, Real Estate & Developmen	12/31/16	662.7	75.0	1128.6	249.4	21	5044834
BXC	BlueLinx Holdings Inc	Construction Services	12/31/16	1881.0	16.1	444.1	-29.8	47	10526495
BWP	Boardwalk Pipeline Partners LP	Equipment & Services	12/31/16	1307.2	302.2	8637.8		250	258609529
BA	Boeing Co. (The)	Aerospace	12/31/16	94571.0	4895.0	89997.0	817.0	2177	513496669
BCC	Boise Cascade Co. (DE)	Construction Materials	12/31/16	3911.2	38.3	1439.2	580.0	244	45405392
BCEI	Bonanza Creek Energy Inc	Production & Extraction	12/31/16	195.3	-198.9	1134.5	19.1	138	21605632
BOOT	Boot Barn Holdings Inc	Retail - Apparel and Accessories	4/1/17	629.8	14.2	565.6	179.9	100	32644867
BAH	Booz Allen Hamilton Holding Corp.	Business Services	3/31/17	5804.3	252.5	3373.1	573.6	336	242061967
BWA	BorgWarner Inc	Auto Parts	12/31/16	9071.0	118.5	8834.7	3218.3	768	234341659
SAM	Boston Beer Co Inc (The)	Beverages	12/31/16	906.4	87.3	623.3	446.6	323	12492601
BXP	Boston Properties Inc	REITs	12/31/16	2550.8	512.8	18851.6	5786.3	655	187656155
BSX	Boston Scientific Corp.	Medical Instruments & Equipment	12/31/16	8386.0	347.0	18096.0	6733.0	833	1475348422
BIF	Boulder Growth & Income Fund Inc.	Holding and other Investment Office	11/30/16	24.3	9.0	1204.7	1153.1	103	18397392
BOX	Box Inc	Internet & Software	1/31/17	398.6	-151.8	493.7	74.7	223	90867095
BYD	Boyd Gaming Corp.	Hotels, Restaurants & Travel	12/31/16	2184.0	418.0	4670.8	-934.1	298	99058703
BPMP	BP Midstream Partners LP	Gas Utilities	12/31/16	103.0	45.9	87.6	73.9	2	5074579
BP	BP PLC	Production & Extraction	12/31/16	185474.0	115.0	263316.0	95286.0	1336	430588645
BPT	BP Prudhoe Bay Royalty Trust	Oil Royalty Traders	12/31/16	44.9	43.6	1.0	0.8	126	1034510
BRC	Brady Corp	Printing	7/31/17	1113.3	95.6	1050.2	700.1	261	50417125
BDN	Brandywine Realty Trust	REITs	12/31/16	525.5	40.2	4099.2	1866.3	356	234758231
BWG	BrandywineGLOBAL Global Income	Holding and other Investment Office	10/31/17	30.3	21.8	500.3	312.0	54	8071203
LND	Brasilagro Cia Brasileira De Proprie	Agricultural Crop Production	6/30/17	184.2	27.3	883.3	667.5		0
BAK	Braskem S A	Refining & Marketing	12/31/15	47283.0	3140.3	59961.3	2022.6	122	24173032
BRFS	BRF S.A.	Food	12/31/16	33732.9	-372.4	42944.9	11840.0	171	74452652
BPI	Bridgepoint Education, Inc.	Educational Services	12/31/16	527.1	-30.0	463.4	280.7	139	54920107
BGG	Briggs & Stratton Corp.	Industrial Machinery & Equipment	7/2/17	1786.1	56.6	1451.0	559.3	263	45873868
BFAM	Bright Horizons Family Solutions, In	Services	12/31/16	1569.8	94.8	2359.0	687.9		0
BEDU	Bright Scholar Education Holdings L	Educational Services	8/31/17	1328.4	172.0	2686.6	1416.1	44	13648628
EAT	Brinker International, Inc.	Hotels, Restaurants & Travel	6/28/17	3150.8	150.8	1413.7	-493.7	437	70933141
BCO	Brinks Co (The)	Business Services	12/31/16	3020.6	34.5	1994.8	337.1	397	57842604
BMY	Bristol-Myers Squibb Co.	Pharmaceuticals	12/31/16	19427.0	4457.0	33707.0	16177.0	2237	1406830645
BRS	Bristow Group Inc	Miscellaneous Transportation Servic	3/31/17	1400.5	-170.5	3113.8	1289.2	220	46848664
BTI	British American Tobacco Plc	Tobacco Products	12/31/16	14751.0	4648.0	39773.0	8182.0		0
BRX	Brixmor Property Group Inc	REITs	12/31/16	1275.8	275.6	9319.7	2922.9	347	335185282
BR	Broadridge Financial Solutions Inc	Finance Intermediaries & Services	6/30/17	4142.6	326.8	3149.8	1003.8	707	139445885
BKD	Brookdale Senior Living Inc	Hospitals & Health Care Facilities	12/31/16	4977.0	-404.4	9217.7	2078.0	356	211922510

1st	2nd	3rd	2016	2015	2014	P/E RATIO	2016	2015	2014	AV. YLD %	AMOUNT	PAYABLE	PRICE RANGE 2016
-	-	-	0.83	0.83	0.83	18.7 - 17.1	0.82	0.82	0.82	5.5	0.0685M	2/1/18	15.5 - 14.2
-	-	-	0.84	0.87	0.87	18.4 - 16.5	0.87	0.87	0.87	5.9	0.0665M	2/1/18	15.4 - 13.8
-	-	-	0.82	0.84	0.86	18.6 - 16.7	0.83	0.86	0.92	5.8	0.06M	2/1/18	15.2 - 13.7
-	-	-	0.87	0.88	0.93	16.9 - 15.4	0.90	0.91	0.91	6.3	0.065M	2/1/18	14.7 - 13.4
-	-	-	0.70	0.71	0.73	17.8 - 15.8	0.73	0.73	0.72	6.2	0.048M	2/1/18	12.5 - 11.1
-	-	-	0.77	0.78	0.82	19.7 - 17.9	0.80	0.82	0.86	5.5	0.0535M	2/1/18	15.2 - 13.8
-	-	-	0.91	0.93	0.95	17.9 - 16.0	0.94	0.97	1.09	6.1	0.0675M	2/1/18	16.3 - 14.5
-	-	-	1.00	1.03	1.04	18.2 - 15.9	1.06	1.06	1.10	6.2	0.0745M	2/1/18	18.2 - 15.9
-	-	-	0.86	0.89	0.89	17.7 - 16.2	0.86	0.86	0.86	5.8	0.0715M	2/1/18	15.3 - 13.9
-	-	-	0.84	0.84	0.86	17.8 - 16.6	0.87	0.89	0.89	6.0	0.0595M	2/1/18	14.9 - 13.9
-	-	-	0.75	0.80	0.83	19.4 - 17.7	0.71	0.82	0.87	5.1	0.0505M	2/1/18	14.5 - 13.3
-	-	-	0.78	0.80	0.82	18.3 - 16.5	0.81	0.83	0.85	5.9	0.064M	2/1/18	14.3 - 12.9
-	-	-	0.80	0.80	0.82	17.8 - 16.1	0.81	0.81	0.82	6.0	0.0635M	2/1/18	14.3 - 12.9
-	-	-	0.98	0.99	1.03	16.7 - 15.3	1.00	1.04	1.08	6.4	0.073M	2/1/18	16.4 - 15.0
-	-	-	0.86	0.87	0.91	18.8 - 16.8	1.01	0.90	0.95	6.6	0.062M	2/1/18	16.2 - 14.5
-	-	-	0.81	0.83	0.87	19.3 - 17.7	0.85	0.88	0.91	5.7	0.0585M	2/1/18	15.7 - 14.4
-	-	-	0.90	0.91	0.94	17.5 - 15.5	0.93	0.95	0.99	6.3	0.067Z	2/1/18	15.7 - 13.9
-	-	-	0.92	0.95	0.96	18.0 - 16.1	0.97	0.97	0.95	6.2	0.0695M	2/1/18	16.6 - 14.8
-	-	-	0.83	0.84	0.85	18.4 - 16.4	0.85	0.85	0.85	6.0	0.067M	2/1/18	15.3 - 13.6
-	-	-	0.79	0.83	0.86	18.1 - 16.8	0.83	0.86	0.90	6.0	0.057M	2/1/18	14.3 - 13.3
-	-	-	0.70	0.75	0.78	19.1 - 18.0	0.73	0.77	0.83	5.6	0.0475M	2/1/18	13.4 - 12.6
-	-	-	0.89	0.90	0.90	18.8 - 16.8	0.91	0.90	0.93	5.7	0.075M	2/1/18	16.8 - 15.0
-	-	-	0.80	0.81	0.87	18.6 - 17.2	0.83	0.88	0.89	5.8	0.0623M	2/1/18	14.9 - 13.8
-	-	-	0.79	0.91	0.83	17.5 - 15.7	0.82	0.85	0.84	6.3	0.054M	2/1/18	13.9 - 12.4
-	-	-	0.84	0.87	0.89	17.7 - 16.0	0.88	0.89	0.87	6.2	0.0585M	2/1/18	14.9 - 13.5
-	-	-	0.90	0.92	0.95	17.8 - 16.1	0.95	0.96	0.98	6.2	0.063M	2/1/18	16.0 - 14.4
-	-	-	0.86	0.86	0.88	18.6 - 16.5	0.90	0.85	0.90	5.9	0.0635M	2/1/18	16.0 - 14.2
-	-	-	0.23	0.25	0.35	65.2 - 0.0	0.23	0.33	0.37	1.8	0.0025M	2/1/18	15.0 - 0.0
-	-	-	0.71	0.74	0.79	21.8 - 0.0	0.73	0.79	0.80	5.1	0.059M	2/1/18	15.4 - 0.0
-	-	-	0.68	0.70	0.72	20.2 - 18.8	0.68	0.73	0.77	5.1	0.0465M	2/1/18	13.7 - 12.8
-	-	-	0.75	0.79	0.81	20.7 - 18.5	0.80	0.83	0.83	5.4	0.0505M	2/1/18	15.5 - 13.9
-	-	-		0.25	0.04			0.81	0.93		0.05160	1/31/18	9.8 - 7.8
-	-	-	0.00	0.03	-0.01		1.20	1.20	0.10	5.2	0.130	1/31/18	27.3 - 18.2
-	-	-	0.82	1.04	0.86	18.6 - 15.9	0.85	0.88	0.89	6.1	0.065M	2/1/18	15.2 - 13.0
-	-	-	1.63	1.63	1.59	14.7 - 13.2	1.58	1.58	1.58	6.9	0.13180	1/9/18	23.9 - 21.5
-	-	-	0.56	0.47	0.11	38.7 - 33.1	1.45	1.45	1.45	7.0	0.1210	1/31/18	21.6 - 18.6
-	-	-	1.40	1.22	0.94	11.9 - 11.2	1.43	1.27	1.20	8.9	0.1030	2/28/18	16.6 - 15.7
-	-	-		1.22	0.92		1.16	1.17	1.21	6.5	0.0970	2/28/18	18.5 - 17.0
-	-	-	1.39	1.48	1.17	11.8 - 11.0	1.34	1.37	1.28	8.4	0.1050	2/28/18	16.4 - 15.3
-	-	0.56	1.56	1.04	2.58	22.3 - 18.0	1.66	2.90	1.92	5.2	0.440	11/6/17	34.8 - 28.1
-	-	0.61	2.53	2.41	1.86	13.0 - 11.9	2.48	2.28	1.98	7.9	0.620Z	1/16/18	32.9 - 30.0
-	-0.74	-	1.49	1.71	1.72	21.1 - 13.5	0.80	0.80	0.80	3.1	0.240Y	32/4/39	31.5 - 20.1
-	-	-0.47	-0.84	-0.92	-0.88		-	-	-		-		10.0 - 3.0
-	-	-5.93	1.63	2.36	1.72		2.14	1.56	0.90		0.30	10/13/17	
-	-	749510.00	3040.00	-		0.0 - 0.0					0.15GY	1/23/18	18.3 - 13.0
-	-	0.62	1.77	-1.30	-1.60	6.2 - 3.6					0.1250Y	12/28/07	11.0 - 6.4
-	-	0.27	1.18	0.87	0.94	16.0 - 10.9	0.40	0.40	0.40	2.4	0.10	11/16/17	18.9 - 12.9
-	-	-	3.06	7.61	7.44	39.1 - 20.6	4.36	3.64	2.92	2.0	1.710Y	32/4/39	297.9 - 157.0
-	-	-	0.81	0.98	1.33	41.5 - 23.4	-	-	-		0.07GY	12/15/17	40.6 - 22.9
-	-	-	0.21	-4.04	-15.57	0.49	-	-	-		-		39.2 - 24.0
-	0.04	-	0.37	0.54	0.28	47.0 - 16.2	-	-	-		-		17.4 - 6.0
-	0.47	-	1.94	1.52	1.54	20.4 - 16.4	0.54	1.46	2.40	1.5	0.170Y	32/4/39	39.5 - 31.9
-	-	0.88	0.55	2.70	2.86	101.2 - 69.1	0.53	0.52	0.51	1.2	0.170Y	32/4/39	55.7 - 38.0
-	-	-	2.78	6.79	7.25	6.69	28.7 - 19.1	-	-		-		194.6 - 129.9
-	-	-	0.76	3.26	3.73	2.83	42.9 - 36.1	2.70	3.85	7.10	2.1	0.32810Z	32/4/39	139.9 - 117.7
-	-	-	0.20	0.25	-0.18	-0.09	119.2 - 87.5	-	-		-		29.8 - 21.9
-	-	-	0.08	0.03	0.03	138.6 - 111.6	0.49	0.33	0.44	5.0	0.0340	1/31/18	11.1 - 8.9
-	-	-0.32	-1.67	-11.48	-14.89		-	-	-		-		23.8 - 14.1
-	-	0.20	3.63	0.42	-0.48	9.9 - 5.3	-	-	-		0.050Y	1/15/18	35.8 - 19.3
-	-	-					-	-	-		0.1798GH	2/15/18	20.6 - 17.3
-	0.01	-	0.01	-0.35	0.20	4203.0 - 3331.0	2.38	2.38	2.34	6.5	-		42.0 - 33.3
-	-	-	2.04	5.86	10.60	16.1 - 7.7	2.04	5.86	10.60	9.5	1.23020	1/22/18	32.8 - 15.7
0.49	-	-	1.58	0.06	-0.89	25.2 - 20.2	0.81	0.80	0.78	2.2	0.20750Y	32/4/39	39.8 - 31.9
-	-	0.11	0.19	-0.21	0.00	97.8 - 82.8	0.62	0.60	0.60	3.6	0.180Z	32/4/39	18.6 - 15.7
-	-	-	0.92	1.09	1.43	14.9 - 13.0	1.30	1.90	1.77	10.0	0.07650	3/1/18	13.7 - 11.9
-	-	-	0.18	3.10	-0.23	24.2 - 0.0	1.36	-	0.09	44.8	-		4.3 - 0.0
-	-	-		3.95	1.09		-	1.11	1.12		-		32.6 - 19.0
-	-	0.33	-0.46	3.72	2.56		0.61	1.25	0.61	4.7	-		15.3 - 10.8
-	-	0.00	-0.65	-1.54	0.21		-	-	-		-		15.2 - 8.2
-0.36	-	-	0.60	1.00	0.59	42.9 - 33.5	0.54	0.50	0.48	2.3	0.140Y	4/3/18	25.7 - 20.1
-	-	0.51	1.55	1.50	1.07	61.1 - 43.9	-	-	-		-		94.7 - 68.0
-	-	1.05	-0.38	-0.43	-0.36		-	-	-		-		28.0 - 11.2
0.20	-	-	3.42	3.05	2.26	14.4 - 8.7	1.28	1.12	0.96	3.3	0.380Y	32/4/39	49.2 - 29.9
-	-	0.38	0.68	-0.24	-1.71	127.9 - 60.7	0.40	0.40	0.40	0.6	0.150Y	32/4/39	87.0 - 41.3
-	-	0.51	2.65	0.93	1.20	24.7 - 17.7	1.14	1.49	1.45	2.0	0.40Y	32/4/39	65.3 - 46.8
-	-0.88	-	-2.12	2.37	5.09		1.09	1.28	1.00	9.1	0.070Y	6/22/17	21.2 - 6.5
-	-	-	2.49	2.30	1.67	29.4 - 22.6	1.58	1.52	1.45	2.4	-		73.3 - 56.3
-	-	0.27	0.91	0.65	0.36	27.8 - 19.2	0.98	0.90	0.73	4.9	0.2750Z	32/4/39	25.3 - 17.5
0.42	-	-	2.53	2.32	2.12	36.2 - 26.0	1.20	1.08	0.84	1.6	0.3650Y	32/4/39	91.6 - 65.7
-	-	-2.22	-2.18	-2.48	-1.01		-	-	-		0.250Y	32/4/39	16.3 - 8.8

SYMBOL	COMPANY	NATURE OF BUSINESS	FISCAL YEAR-END	TOTAL REV. $MILL	NET INCOME $MILL	TOTAL ASSETS $MILL	NET STK EQUITY $MILL	NO OF INST	INST. HOLDINGS (SHARES)
BAM	Brookfield Asset Management Inc	Property, Real Estate & Developmen	12/31/16	24411.0	1651.0	159826.0	26453.0	521	579200913
BBU	Brookfield Business Partners LP	Construction Services	12/31/16	7960.0	-32.0	8193.0	1206.0	87	42413127
DTLA PR	Brookfield DTLA Fund Office Trust I	REITs	12/31/16	310.7	-18.8	2770.0	350.2	1	10000
INF	Brookfield Global Listed Infrastructu	Holding and other Investment Office	12/31/16	7.6	2.6	270.8	192.3	40	4013738
BIP	Brookfield Infrastructure Partners L	Electric Utilities	12/31/16	2115.0	360.0	21275.0	5013.0	299	143409200
RA	Brookfield Real Assets Income Fun	Holding and other Investment Office	12/31/16	6.6	5.5	1222.9	917.6	85	7710220
BEP	Brookfield Renewable Partners LP	Electric Utilities	12/31/16	2516.0	-36.0	27737.0	3448.0		0
BRO	Brown & Brown, Inc.	Brokers & Intermediaries	12/31/16	1766.6	257.5	5287.3	2360.2	391	129870542
BF B	Brown-Forman Corp	Beverages	4/30/17	2994.0	669.0	4625.0	1370.0	173	55848642
BRT	BRT Apartments Corp	REITs	9/30/17	105.8	13.6	993.9	166.0	46	4681616
BC	Brunswick Corp.	Leisure Equipment	12/31/16	4488.5	276.0	3284.7	1440.1	492	96782951
BT	BT Group Plc	Services	3/31/17	24062.0	1908.0	42372.0	8335.0	198	23651483
BPL	Buckeye Partners LP	Equipment & Services	12/31/16	3248.4	535.6	9421.1		525	114081164
BKE	Buckle, Inc. (The)	Retail - Apparel and Accessories	1/28/17	974.9	96.0	579.8	430.5	247	37281629
BBW	Build-A-Bear Workshop Inc	Retail - Specialty	12/31/16	364.2	1.4	199.6	99.1	124	16455616
BG	Bunge Ltd.	Food	12/31/16	42679.0	745.0	19188.0	7144.0	609	132620364
BURL	Burlington Stores Inc	Retail - Apparel and Accessories	1/28/17	5590.9	215.9	2574.5	-49.8	385	78677907
BWXT	BWX Technologies inc	Industrial Machinery & Equipment	12/31/16	1550.6	183.1	1579.8	150.0	378	111316764
BY	Byline Bancorp Inc	Banking	12/31/16	124.3	66.7	3295.8	382.7	73	6695166
CJ	C&J Energy Services Inc (New)	Equipment & Services	12/31/16	971.1	-944.3	1361.6	-298.6	139	66055972
GYB	Cabco Series 2004-101 Trust Gold	Holding and other Investment Office						3	75600
CABO	Cable One Inc	Radio & Television	12/31/16	819.6	98.9	1397.3	454.5	284	4704557
CBT	Cabot Corp.	Specialty Chemicals	9/30/17	2717.0	241.0	3314.0	1480.0	403	66258012
COG	Cabot Oil & Gas Corp.	Production & Extraction	12/31/16	1155.7	-417.1	5122.6	2567.7	734	507300448
CACI	CACI International Inc.	IT Services	6/30/17	4354.6	163.7	3911.1	1793.6	337	30364324
CADE	Cadence Bancorporation	Banking	12/31/16	423.7	65.8	9530.9	1080.5	70	7545832
CAE	CAE Inc	Aerospace	3/31/17	2704.5	251.5	5354.8	2020.8	206	155108405
CAI	CAI International Inc	Miscellaneous Transportation Servic	12/31/16	294.4	6.0	2055.9	457.5	147	14699006
CAA	CalAtlantic Group Inc	Builders	12/31/16	6476.7	484.7	8709.0	4207.6	455	132677361
CAL	Caleres Inc	Retail - Apparel and Accessories	1/28/17	2579.4	65.7	1475.3	613.1	245	51152915
CCC	Calgon Carbon Corp	Specialty Chemicals	12/31/16	514.2	13.8	775.2	381.1	255	68380595
CRC	California Resources Corp	Production & Extraction	12/31/16	1547.0	279.0	6354.0	-557.0	310	38038708
CWT	California Water Service Group (DE	Water Utilities	12/31/16	609.4	48.7	2411.7	659.5	278	40916487
CALX	Calix Inc	Manufacturing	12/31/16	458.8	-27.4	355.5	213.0	125	39035693
ELY	Callaway Golf Co (DE)	Leisure Equipment	12/31/16	871.2	189.9	801.3	598.9	320	102976731
CPE	Callon Petroleum Co. (DE)	Production & Extraction	12/31/16	200.9	-91.8	2267.6	1733.4	368	274378350
CPN	Calpine Corp	Electric Utilities	12/31/16	6716.0	92.0	19317.0	3268.0	437	342371174
CBM	Cambrex Corp	Pharmaceuticals	12/31/16	490.6	81.7	611.9	405.4	334	44207428
CPT	Camden Property Trust	REITs	12/31/16	891.0	819.8	6028.2	3014.9	493	110458182
CCJ	Cameco Corp.	Mining	12/31/16	2431.4	-61.6	8249.2	5258.4	402	248490709
CPB	Campbell Soup Co.	Food	7/31/17	7890.0	887.0	7726.0	1637.0	838	189686949
CWH	Camping World Holdings Inc	Retail - Automotive	12/31/16	3526.7	191.7	1563.8	-28.2	148	30665397
GOOS	Canada Goose Holdings Inc	Apparel, Footwear & Accessories	3/31/17	403.3	21.6	380.9	146.2	142	28238951
CM	Canadian Imperial Bank Of Comme	Banking	10/31/17	20896.0	4699.0	565264.0	31035.0	473	222387011
CNI	Canadian National Railway Co	Rail	12/31/16	12037.0	3640.0	37057.0	14841.0	776	483453244
CNQ	Canadian Natural Resources Ltd.	Production & Extraction	12/31/16	10523.0	-204.0	58648.0	26267.0	532	794510520
CP	Canadian Pacific Railway Ltd	Rail	12/31/16	6232.0	1599.0	19221.0	4626.0	540	123083591
CNNE	Cannae Holdings Inc	Property, Real Estate & Developmen	12/31/16	1178.4	-6.0	1464.8	897.4		0
CAJ	Canon, Inc.	Leisure Equipment	12/31/16	3401487.0	150650.0	5138529.0	2783129.0	235	16935770
CMD	Cantel Medical Corp	Medical Instruments & Equipment	7/31/17	770.2	71.4	786.4	523.9	305	43251173
COF	Capital One Financial Corp	Banking	12/31/16	27519.0	3751.0	357033.0	47514.0	1175	518119831
CSU	Capital Senior Living Corp.	Hospitals & Health Care Facilities	12/31/16	447.4	-28.0	1145.8	116.9	141	39779625
CIC	Capitol Investment Corp IV	Business Services	6/6/17		-0.0	0.3	0.0	1	460500
CMO	Capstead Mortgage Corp.	REITs	12/31/16	213.3	82.9	13576.9	1247.7	265	89171492
CRR	Carbo Ceramics Inc.	Equipment & Services	12/31/16	103.1	-80.1	723.5	616.6	230	29844670
CAH	Cardinal Health, Inc.	Pharmaceuticals	6/30/17	129976.0	1288.0	40112.0	6808.0	1047	340201607
CRCM	Care.com Inc	Services	12/31/16	161.8	7.0	155.2	114.6	128	29495426
CSL	Carlisle Companies Inc.	Rubber Products	12/31/16	3675.4	250.1	3965.8	2466.9	479	63951306
KMX	Carmax Inc.	Retail - Automotive	2/28/17	15875.1	627.0	16279.4	3108.6	681	238646208
CCL	Carnival Corp	Hotels, Restaurants & Travel	11/30/17	17510.0	2606.0	40778.0	24216.0	1056	487352307
CUK	Carnival Plc	Hotels, Restaurants & Travel	11/30/16	16389.0	2779.0	38936.0	22597.0	170	8669535
CRS	Carpenter Technology Corp.	Non-Precious Metals	6/30/17	1797.6	47.0	2878.1	1198.6	321	52870986
CSV	Carriage Services, Inc.	Miscellaneous Consumer Services	12/31/16	248.2	19.6	885.1	178.0	156	16638303
CARS	Cars.com Inc	IT Services	12/31/16	633.1	176.4	2547.3	2417.3	331	84990987
CARS	Cars.com Inc	IT Services	12/31/16	633.1	176.4	2547.3	2417.3	331	84990987
CRI	Carter's Inc	Apparel, Footwear & Accessories	12/31/16	3199.2	258.1	1946.6	788.1	484	61171499
CVNA	Carvana Co	Retail - Automotive	12/31/16	365.1	-93.1	335.8	135.0	102	20199842
CSLT	Castlight Health Inc	Internet & Software	12/31/16	101.7	-58.5	157.2	102.0	102	59710805
CTLT	Catalent Inc	Pharmaceuticals	6/30/17	2075.4	109.8	3454.3	723.5	321	154047923
CTT	Catchmark Timber Trust Inc	REITs	12/31/16	81.9	-11.1	709.8	381.1	156	31698420
CAT	Caterpillar Inc.	Construction Services	12/31/16	38537.0	-67.0	74704.0	13137.0	1797	514082954
CATO	Cato Corp.	Retail - Apparel and Accessories	1/28/17	956.6	47.2	606.3	383.9	216	25146566
CBZ	CBIZ Inc	Business Services	12/31/16	799.8	40.1	1118.6	480.0	183	56882055
CBL	CBL & Associates Properties Inc	REITs	12/31/16	1028.3	172.9	6104.0	1228.7	357	196281455
IGR	CBRE Clarion Global Real Estate In	Holding and other Investment Office	12/31/16	42.9	30.4	1103.8	1008.9	133	30461532
CBG	CBRE Group Inc	Property, Real Estate & Developmen	12/31/16	13071.6	572.0	10779.6	3014.5	699	399320851
CBS	CBS Corp	Radio & Television	12/31/16	13166.0	1261.0	24238.0	3689.0	1067	385480182
FUN	Cedar Fair LP	Sporting & Recreational	12/31/16	1288.7	177.7	1973.2		260	38291437
CDR	Cedar Realty Trust Inc	REITs	12/31/16	151.1	8.9	1233.5	580.7	214	104043290
CGI	Celadon Group, Inc.	Trucking	6/30/16	1065.4	24.8	1103.3	381.0	142	30904245

EARNINGS PER SHARE — QUARTERLY			ANNUAL			P/E RATIO		DIVIDENDS PER SHARE			AV. YLD %	DIV. DECLARED		PRICE RANGE 2016	
1st	2nd	3rd	2016	2015	2014			2016	2015	2014		AMOUNT	PAYABLE		
-	-	0.20	1.55	2.26	3.11	36.4 -	21.3	0.52	0.47	0.45	1.2	0.3546GH	12/29/17	56.4 -	32.9
-	-	-	0.06	-	-	-	-	-	-	-	-	0.06250	12/29/17	-	-
-	-	-	-	-	-	-	-	-	2.25	-	-	2.25GJ	1/4/16	30.0 -	0.0
-	-	0.18	0.28	0.38		78.3 -	69.9	1.40	1.40	2.06	10.4	0.08170	1/25/18	14.1 -	12.6
-	-	-0.04	1.13	0.69	0.45	-	-	-	-	-	-	0.31250	12/29/17	-	-
-	-	-	0.15	-	-	162.4 -	149.1	0.20	-	-	0.9	0.1990	1/25/18	24.4 -	22.4
-	0.03	-	-0.23	0.01	0.42	-	-	-	-	-	-	0.31250	1/31/18	-	-
-	-	0.53	1.82	1.70	1.41	28.5 -	22.7	0.50	0.45	0.41	1.1	0.150Y	32/4/39	51.9 -	41.3
-	0.62	-	2.61	1.61	1.53	26.4 -	16.8	0.66	0.60	0.55	1.3	1.7Y	32/4/39	68.8 -	44.0
-	-	-0.24	2.23	-0.17	-0.66	5.3 -	0.0	-	-	-	-	0.180Z	1/5/18	11.8 -	0.0
-	-	0.88	3.00	2.56	2.58	21.1 -	16.2	0.61	0.53	0.45	1.1	0.190Y	32/4/39	63.4 -	48.6
0.03	-	-	0.30	0.26	0.25	81.9 -	54.1	0.61	0.18	0.48	3.1	-	-	24.6 -	16.2
-	-	0.81	4.03	3.40	2.28	18.0 -	11.1	4.83	4.63	4.42	7.9	1.26250	32/4/39	72.6 -	44.6
-	-	0.41	3.06	3.38	3.39	8.1 -	4.5	1.94	3.66	2.02	10.6	1.757Y	1/26/18	24.6 -	13.7
-	-	0.09	0.09	1.59	0.81	159.4 -	81.7	-	-	-	-	-	-	14.4 -	7.3
-	-	0.59	5.01	5.07	3.17	-	-	-	-	-	-	1.21880Z	32/4/39	-	-
-	-	0.65	1.99	0.87	-0.39	61.8 -	40.3	-	-	-	-	-	-	123.0 -	80.3
-	-	0.46	1.76	1.22	0.27	35.5 -	22.3	0.36	0.32	0.40	0.7	0.110Y	32/4/39	62.5 -	39.2
-	-	0.32	3.27	-0.86	-	7.1 -	5.9	-	-	-	-	-	-	23.2 -	19.4
-	-	0.17	-7.98	-8.48	1.22	-	-	-	-	-	-	-	-	46.1 -	24.7
-	-	-	-	-	-	-	-	-	-	-	-	0.20760Z	11/15/17	23.5 -	0.0
-	-	5.48	17.14	15.16	7309.00	44.5 -	33.3	6.00	1.50	-	0.9	1.750Y	32/4/39	762.3 -	570.0
-	-	0.71	2.36	-5.27	3.03	27.2 -	21.5	1.04	0.88	0.84	1.8	0.3150Y	32/4/39	64.3 -	50.8
-	-	0.04	-0.91	-0.28	0.25	-	-	0.08	0.08	0.08	0.3	0.060Y	32/4/39	29.4 -	20.8
1.67	-	-	5.76	5.17	5.38	25.1 -	19.5	-	-	-	-	-	-	144.8 -	112.3
-	-	0.39	0.87	0.52	0.55	31.2 -	23.6	-	-	-	-	0.125GY	3/20/18	27.1 -	20.5
-	0.24	-	0.85	0.76	0.73	27.6 -	16.4	0.29	0.27	0.22	1.6	0.090	12/29/17	23.5 -	13.9
-	-	0.90	0.31	1.28	2.85	125.4 -	31.3	-	-	-	-	-	-	38.9 -	9.7
-	-	0.75	3.60	2.26	2.70	15.9 -	9.2	0.16	0.04	-	0.4	0.040Y	32/4/39	57.1 -	33.1
-	-	0.80	1.85	1.89	0.88	18.3 -	12.3	0.28	0.28	0.28	1.0	0.070Y	1/10/18	33.8 -	22.7
-	-	0.10	0.27	0.82	0.92	81.1 -	44.8	0.20	0.20	-	1.2	0.050Y	12/15/17	21.9 -	12.1
-	-	-3.11	6.76	-92.70	-37.50	3.4 -	1.0	-	0.30	-	-	0.010Y	10/15/15	23.2 -	6.5
-	-	0.70	1.01	0.94	1.19	45.1 -	32.2	0.69	0.67	0.65	1.8	0.180Y	32/4/39	45.6 -	32.5
-	-	-0.35	-0.56	-0.51	-0.41	-	-	-	-	-	-	-	-	7.7 -	4.7
-	-	0.03	1.98	0.17	0.20	7.7 -	5.1	0.04	0.04	0.04	0.3	0.010Y	12/13/17	15.3 -	10.1
-	-	0.08	-0.78	-3.77	0.65	-	-	-	-	-	-	1.250Y	12/29/17	16.1 -	9.5
-	-	0.63	0.26	0.64	2.31	58.2 -	36.9	-	-	-	-	-	-	15.1 -	9.6
-	-	0.52	2.48	1.76	1.81	25.0 -	17.2	-	-	-	-	14.7	5/3/07	62.0 -	42.6
-	-	0.38	9.05	2.76	3.27	10.6 -	8.7	7.25	2.80	2.64	8.3	0.750Z	32/4/39	95.7 -	79.1
-	-	-0.31	-0.16	0.16	0.47	-	-	0.40	0.40	0.40	3.4	0.10	1/15/18	17.4 -	8.1
0.91	-	-	1.81	2.21	2.59	35.3 -	24.9	1.25	1.25	1.25	2.3	0.350Y	32/4/39	63.8 -	45.1
-	-	0.68	0.09	-	-	524.3 -	295.1	0.08	-	-	0.2	0.136Y	12/29/17	47.2 -	26.6
-	0.33	-	0.26	0.14	-0.15	152.9 -	59.2	-	-	-	-	-	-	39.8 -	15.4
-	-	2.60	10.70	8.87	7.86	11.5 -	7.3	4.75	4.30	3.94	4.8	0.2750	1/29/18	123.5 -	77.6
-	-	1.27	4.67	4.39	3.85	23.0 -	14.4	1.50	1.25	1.00	1.7	0.4550	3/29/18	107.6 -	67.3
-	-	0.56	-0.19	-0.58	3.58	-	-	0.94	0.92	0.90	2.6	0.2750	1/1/18	46.7 -	27.8
-	-	3.50	10.63	8.40	8.46	21.9 -	13.3	1.85	1.40	1.40	1.0	0.56250	1/29/18	232.3 -	141.4
-	-	-	-0.09	-0.30	3.94	-	-	-	-	-	-	-	-	18.4 -	16.4
-	-	58.39	137.95	201.65	229.03	0.3 -	0.2	149.39	75.43	215.45	442.1	-	-	38.9 -	28.4
0.55	-	-	1.44	1.15	1.04	74.0 -	48.7	0.12	0.10	0.09	0.1	0.0850Y	1/31/18	106.5 -	70.2
-	-	2.14	6.89	7.07	7.59	14.6 -	11.2	1.60	1.50	1.20	1.9	0.3750Y	32/4/39	100.5 -	76.9
-	-	-0.28	-0.97	-0.50	-0.83	-	-	-	-	-	-	-	-	17.5 -	11.8
-0.02	-	-	-	-	-	-	-	-	-	-	-	-	-	-	-
-	-	0.13	0.70	0.97	1.33	16.2 -	12.3	0.95	1.14	1.36	9.4	0.46880Z	1/16/18	11.3 -	8.6
-	-	-6.69	-3.29	-4.76	2.41	-	-	-	0.63	1.26	-	0.10Y	11/16/15	16.3 -	6.0
0.36	-	-	4.32	3.62	3.38	19.4 -	12.7	1.61	1.41	1.25	2.2	0.46240Y	32/4/39	83.8 -	55.0
-	-	-0.01	0.10	-1.09	-2.77	205.9 -	83.6	-	-	-	-	-	-	20.6 -	8.4
-	-	1.37	3.82	4.82	3.82	30.3 -	24.2	1.30	1.10	0.94	1.3	0.370Y	32/4/39	115.9 -	92.4
-	-	0.81	3.03	2.73	2.16	25.3 -	18.3	-	-	-	-	-	-	76.8 -	55.4
-	-	1.83	3.72	2.26	1.59	18.7 -	14.0	1.35	1.10	1.00	2.1	0.450Y	32/4/39	69.5 -	52.1
-	-	1.83	3.72	2.26	1.59	18.8 -	13.8	1.35	1.10	1.00	2.2	-	-	70.1 -	51.2
0.49	-	-	0.23	1.11	2.47	229.7 -	150.7	0.72	0.72	0.72	1.7	0.180Y	32/4/39	52.8 -	34.7
-	-	0.17	1.12	1.12	0.85	25.7 -	20.8	0.15	0.10	0.10	0.6	0.0750Y	3/1/18	28.8 -	23.3
-	-	0.29	1.37	-	-	21.9 -	16.1	-	-	-	-	-	-	30.0 -	22.0
-	-	0.29	1.37	-	-	19.9 -	18.0	-	-	-	-	-	-	27.3 -	24.6
-	-	1.71	5.08	4.50	3.62	23.1 -	15.4	1.32	0.88	0.76	1.4	0.370Y	32/4/39	117.6 -	78.3
-	-	-0.29	-1.10	-0.42	-0.17	-	-	-	-	-	-	-	-	23.4 -	8.7
-	-	-0.14	-0.58	-0.85	-1.16	-	-	-	-	-	-	-	-	5.0 -	3.0
0.03	-	-	0.89	1.75	0.21	48.3 -	29.1	-	-	-	-	-	-	43.0 -	25.9
-	-	-0.10	-0.29	-0.21	0.02	-	-	0.53	0.50	0.47	4.5	0.1350Z	12/15/17	13.4 -	10.2
-	-	1.77	-0.11	3.50	5.88	-	-	3.08	2.94	2.60	2.7	0.780Y	32/4/39	158.4 -	91.4
-	-	0.11	2.39	2.15	1.86	13.1 -	5.3	1.20	1.20	0.20	6.4	0.330Y	1/2/18	31.2 -	12.6
-	-	0.18	0.75	0.65	0.58	23.0 -	17.0	-	-	-	-	-	-	17.3 -	12.8
-	-	-0.01	0.75	0.34	1.02	15.8 -	7.2	1.06	1.06	1.00	12.5	0.41410Z	12/29/17	11.9 -	5.4
-	-	-	0.26	0.27	0.30	30.8 -	27.5	0.60	0.57	0.54	7.8	0.050	1/31/18	8.0 -	7.1
-	-	-	-	-	-	-	-	-	-	-	-	-	-	44.2 -	30.0
-	-	0.58	1.69	1.63	1.45	26.2 -	17.8	-	-	-	-	-	-	69.5 -	54.5
-	-	1.46	2.81	2.89	5.27	24.7 -	19.4	0.66	0.60	0.54	1.1	0.180Y	32/4/39	72.3 -	61.6
-	-	3.38	3.14	1.99	1.86	23.0 -	19.6	3.33	3.08	2.85	5.0	0.890	12/15/17	6.8 -	4.7
-	-	-0.06	-0.08	0.09	0.18	-	-	0.20	0.20	0.20	3.6	0.40630Z	2/20/18	9.4 -	1.6
-	-0.06	-	0.88	1.52	1.29	10.7 -	1.8	0.08	0.08	0.08	1.4	0.020Y	4/21/17	-	-

SYMBOL	COMPANY	NATURE OF BUSINESS	FISCAL YEAR-END	TOTAL REV. $MILL	NET INCOME $MILL	TOTAL ASSETS $MILL	NET STK EQUITY $MILL	NO OF INST	INST. HOLDINGS (SHARES)
CE	Celanese Corp (DE)	Specialty Chemicals	12/31/16	5389.0	900.0	8357.0	2588.0	621	153189185
CLS	Celestica Inc	Electrical Equipment	12/31/16	6016.5	136.3	2822.3	1238.8	207	102650565
CEL	Cellcom Israel Ltd	Services	12/31/16	4027.0	148.0	6662.0	1322.0	50	9237160
CPAC	Cementos Pacasmayo SAA (Peru)	Construction Materials	12/31/16	1240.2	116.2	3320.6	1867.4	19	3806373
CX	Cemex S.A.B. de C.V.	Construction Materials	12/31/16	250909.0	14033.0	599728.0	167774.0	433	636130926
CVE	Cenovus Energy Inc.	Production & Extraction	12/31/16	12134.0	-545.0	25258.0	11590.0	358	741132931
CNC	Centene Corp	Hospitals & Health Care Facilities	12/31/16	40607.0	562.0	20197.0	5895.0	774	186521964
CEN	Center Coast MLP & Infrastructure	Finance Intermediaries & Services	11/30/16	1.1	-4.8	364.7	233.1	36	4515429
CNP	CenterPoint Energy, Inc	Electric Utilities	12/31/16	7528.0	432.0	21829.0	3460.0	746	408861734
EBR	Centrais Eletricas Brasileiras S.A.-E	Electric Utilities	12/31/16	60748.9	3584.5	170499.4	44203.5	69	12283025
CEE	Central & Eastern Europe Fund Inc	Holding and other Investment Office	10/31/17	6.5	4.0	209.8	199.4	37	4849745
CPF	Central Pacific Financial Corp	Banking	12/31/16	209.5	47.0	5384.2	504.6	205	45025045
CCS	Century Communities Inc	Construction Services	12/31/16	994.4	49.5	1007.5	473.6	154	21615804
CTL	CenturyLink Inc	Services	12/31/16	17470.0	626.0	47017.0	13399.0	975	528041477
CF	CF Industries Holdings Inc	Agricultural Chemicals	12/31/16	3685.0	-277.0	15131.0	3348.0	689	276995487
CGG	CGG	Equipment & Services	12/31/16	1196.9	-573.4	4861.5	1120.7	30	100806
GIB	CGI Group Inc	IT Services	9/30/17	10845.1	1035.2	11396.2	6202.6	270	191713410
ECOM	ChannelAdvisor Corp	IT Services	12/31/16	113.2	-8.0	139.2	87.0	118	25574428
CRL	Charles River Laboratories Internati	Biotechnology	12/31/16	1681.4	154.8	2711.8	836.8	470	61397965
CLDT	Chatham Lodging Trust	REITs	12/31/16	293.8	31.5	1303.0	676.7	187	40406991
CMCM	Cheetah Mobile Inc	Services	12/31/16	4564.6	-80.5	5541.1	3012.4	77	11181066
CHGG	Chegg Inc	Educational Services	12/31/16	254.1	-42.2	290.7	221.9	198	113960423
CHE	Chemed Corp	Diagnostic & Health Related Service	12/31/16	1576.9	108.7	880.1	524.1	373	21531169
CC	Chemours Co (The)	Specialty Chemicals	12/31/16	5400.0	7.0	6060.0	100.0	574	159043207
CHMI	Cherry Hill Mortgage Investment Co	REITs	12/31/16	42.3	24.8	792.9	154.2	100	7588604
CHK	Chesapeake Energy Corp.	Production & Extraction	12/31/16	7872.0	-4401.0	13028.0	-1460.0	774	684672806
CHKR	Chesapeake Granite Wash Trust	Oil Royalty Traders	12/31/16	12.4	12.5	31.9	31.9	-	0
CHSP	Chesapeake Lodging Trust	REITs	12/31/16	619.7	76.7	2035.4	1188.7	213	72027482
CPK	Chesapeake Utilities Corp.	Gas Utilities	12/31/16	498.9	44.7	1229.2	446.1	201	11576946
CVX	Chevron Corporation	Refining & Marketing	12/31/16	114472.0	-497.0	260078.0	145556.0	2765	1556319708
CBI	Chicago Bridge & Iron Co., N.V. (Ne	Construction Services	12/31/16	10679.6	-313.2	7839.4	1413.5	519	91960932
CHS	Chico's FAS Inc	Retail - Apparel and Accessories	1/28/17	2476.4	91.2	1109.0	609.2	378	159649172
CIM	Chimera Investment Corp	REITs	12/31/16	992.9	551.9	16684.9	3123.5	368	201514333
CO	China Cord Blood Corp	Diagnostic & Health Related Service	3/31/17	760.0	126.2	5182.9	1837.9	-	0
DL	China Distance Education Holdings	Educational Services	9/30/16	117.5	26.3	148.9	45.2	-	0
CEA	China Eastern Airlines Corp., Ltd.	Airlines/Air Freight	12/31/16	98560.0	4508.0	210051.0	47186.0	36	1307846
CHN	China Fund, Inc. (The)	Holding and other Investment Office	10/31/17	7.6	2.9	376.9	366.5	60	11969251
CGA	China Green Agriculture Inc	Agricultural Chemicals	6/30/17	285.2	25.2	455.7	397.5	31	1772546
LFC	China Life Insurance Co Ltd	Life & Health	12/31/16	546636.0	19127.0	2696951.0	303621.0	155	17841013
CHL	China Mobile Limited	Services	12/31/16	708421.0	108741.0	1520994.0	979021.0	465	95682714
BORN	China New Borun Corp	Beverages	12/31/16	2132.7	63.7	3150.6	1868.8	18	916809
COE	China Online Education Group	Educational Services	12/31/16	418.3	-514.8	775.5	-99.2	17	5433536
SNP	China Petroleum & Chemical Corp.	Production & Extraction	12/31/16	1930911.0	46672.0	1498609.0	710994.0	213	11732258
XRF	China Rapid Finance Ltd	Finance Intermediaries & Services	12/31/16	55.9	-33.4	58.5	14.0	35	8563343
ZNH	China Southern Airlines Co Ltd	Airlines/Air Freight	12/31/16	114792.0	5055.0	200461.0	43181.0	53	1221164
CHA	China Telecom Corp Ltd	Services	12/31/16	352285.0	18004.0	652368.0	315324.0	89	3522973
CHU	China Unicom (Hong Kong) Ltd	Services	12/31/16	274197.0	625.0	614154.0	227407.0	147	33305202
CYD	China Yuchai International Ltd.	Auto Parts	12/31/16	13664.8	515.7	18596.5	7683.8	98	11133001
ZX	China Zenix Auto International Ltd.	Auto Parts	12/31/16	2249.5	-25.9	3859.5	2537.6	12	3770269
CMG	Chipotle Mexican Grill Inc	Hotels, Restaurants & Travel	12/31/16	3904.4	22.9	2026.1	1402.5	761	29600882
CHH	Choice Hotels International, Inc.	Hotels, Restaurants & Travel	12/31/16	924.6	139.4	852.5	-311.3	247	32841193
CBK	Christopher & Banks Corp.	Retail - Apparel and Accessories	1/28/17	381.6	-17.8	134.6	71.3	113	21492952
CB	Chubb Ltd	General Insurance	12/31/16	31469.0	4135.0	159786.0	48275.0	1305	480370636
CHT	Chunghwa Telecom Co Ltd	Services	12/31/16	229991.0	40485.0	446915.0	360656.0	171	36232029
CHD	Church & Dwight Co Inc	Household & Personal Products	12/31/16	3493.1	459.0	4354.1	1977.9	937	237047645
CIEN	Ciena Corp	IT Services	10/31/17	2801.7	1262.0	3951.7	2136.3	480	182919902
CI	Cigna Corp	Life & Health	12/31/16	39668.0	1867.0	59360.0	13723.0	1085	262474405
XEC	Cimarex Energy Co	Production & Extraction	12/31/16	1257.3	-431.0	4681.7	2360.1	678	110470932
CBB	Cincinnati Bell Inc	Services	12/31/16	1185.8	102.1	1541.0	-121.7	219	62276324
CNK	Cinemark Holdings Inc	Entertainment	12/31/16	2918.8	255.1	4306.6	1261.8	418	130270201
CINR	Ciner Resources LP	Mining	12/31/16	475.2	41.4	413.1		36	1863704
CIR	Circor International Inc	Industrial Machinery & Equipment	12/31/16	590.3	10.1	820.8	404.4	188	19505445
CISN	Cision Ltd	IT Services	12/31/16		-0.7	325.9	313.8	54	29694663
CIT	CIT Group Inc	Banking	12/31/16	3093.7	-848.0	64170.2	10002.7	505	181806094
C	Citigroup Inc	Banking	12/31/16	82586.0	14912.0	1792077.0	225120.0	2163	2790900739
CFG	Citizens Financial Group Inc (New)	Banking	12/31/16	5763.0	1045.0	149520.0	19747.0	648	548783538
CIA	Citizens, Inc. (Austin, TX)	Life & Health	12/31/16	245.4	2.0	1583.7	249.1	76	13605703
CIO	City Office REIT Inc	REITs	12/31/16	72.5	-0.8	661.5	254.2	135	19392679
CVEO	Civeo Corp (Canada)	Business Services	12/31/16	397.2	-96.4	910.4	475.5	130	107373470
CIVI	Civitas Solutions Inc	Hospitals & Health Care Facilities	9/30/17	1474.5	6.3	1049.4	162.9	88	36054085
CLH	Clean Harbors Inc	Sanitation Services	12/31/16	2755.2	-39.9	3681.9	1084.2	355	66220550
CCO	Clear Channel Outdoor Holdings Inc	Advertising	12/31/16	2702.4	141.4	5718.8	-1082.7	146	39575664
CBA	ClearBridge American Energy MLP	Finance Intermediaries & Services	11/30/16	1.2	-22.9	806.1	584.7	-	0
CEM	ClearBridge Energy MLP Fund Inc	Holding and other Investment Office	11/30/16	-1.0	-32.8	1842.0	1148.3	104	18392621
EMO	ClearBridge Energy MLP Opportunit	Holding and other Investment Office	11/30/16	-1.4	-12.4	650.8	431.7	47	7350355
CTR	ClearBridge Energy MLP Total Retu	Holding and other Investment Office	11/30/16	2.3	-12.0	744.3	532.9	47	7526088
CLW	Clearwater Paper Corp	Paper & Forest Products	12/31/16	1734.8	49.6	1684.3	469.9	194	16672262
CLF	Cleveland-Cliffs Inc (New)	Mining	12/31/16	2109.0	174.1	1923.9	-1464.3	462	200162517
CLPR	Clipper Realty Inc	Property, Real Estate & Developmen	12/31/16	93.0	-3.7	905.2	-38.2	63	10165529
CLX	Clorox Co (The)	Household & Personal Products	6/30/17	5973.0	701.0	4573.0	542.0	1185	123042577

\<EPS 1st\>	\<EPS 2nd\>	\<EPS 3rd\>	\<Ann 2016\>	\<Ann 2015\>	\<Ann 2014\>	P/E RATIO	Div 2016	Div 2015	Div 2014	AV. YLD %	AMOUNT	PAYABLE	PRICE RANGE 2016
-	-	1.65	6.18	2.00	4.00	17.6 - 12.9	1.38	1.15	0.93	1.4	0.460Y	32/4/39	108.5 - 79.5
-	-	0.37	0.95	0.42	0.60	20.8 - 10.4							19.8 - 9.9
-	-	1.85	1.47	0.95	3.48						0.850	12/12/13	
-	-	-	0.21	0.38	0.33	62.8 - 0.0							13.2 - 0.0
-	-	-	0.33	0.03	-0.17	31.1 - 21.8							10.3 - 7.2
-	-	-0.06	-0.65	0.75	0.98		0.20	0.85	1.06	1.7	0.050	12/29/17	20.5 - 6.8
-	-	1.16	3.43	2.88	2.25	30.0 - 17.0							103.0 - 58.3
-	-	-	-0.24	-0.30	-0.24		1.25	1.25	1.46	11.2	0.10420	3/28/18	13.6 - 8.9
-	-	0.39	1.00	-1.61	1.42	30.4 - 24.6	1.03	0.99	0.95	3.7	0.27750Y	32/4/39	30.4 - 24.6
-	-	-0.58	2.62	-8.43	-4.60	2.8 - 1.4				0.31			7.2 - 3.5
-	-	-	0.42	0.43	0.43	59.9 - 47.0	0.49	0.97	2.49	2.2	0.56150	1/26/18	25.1 - 19.7
?	-	0.39	1.50	1.40	1.07	22.2 - 18.5	0.60	0.82	0.36	1.9	0.190Y	3/15/18	33.3 - 27.7
-	-	0.37	2.33	1.88	1.03	13.5 - 8.9							31.4 - 20.8
-	-	0.17	1.16	1.58	1.36	23.5 - 11.7	2.16	2.16	2.16	9.9	0.540Y	32/4/39	27.3 - 13.6
-	-	-0.37	-1.19	2.96	5.42		1.20	1.20	1.00	3.7	0.30Y	32/4/39	43.1 - 25.5
-	-	0.01	-27.57	-238.50	-208.64						1.2961E	12/27/05	15.2 - 0.0
-	-	0.92	3.42	3.04	2.69	20.4 - 13.4							69.7 - 46.0
-	-	-0.15	-0.31	-0.84	-1.40								15.0 - 8.4
-	-	1.08	3.23	3.13	2.66	36.6 - 23.7							118.1 - 76.5
-	-	0.36	0.81	0.86	2.30	29.3 - 23.2	1.38	1.20	0.93	6.7	0.110Z	2/23/18	23.8 - 18.8
-	-	-	-0.06	0.12	0.05								13.1 - 8.1
-	-	-0.11	-0.47	-0.68	-0.78								16.5 - 6.9
-	-	2.13	6.48	6.33	5.57	38.2 - 25.0	1.00	0.92	0.84	0.5	0.280Y	12/4/17	247.5 - 162.1
-	-	1.08	0.04	-0.50		1430.8 - 530.5	0.12	0.58		0.3	0.170	32/4/39	57.2 - 21.2
-	-	0.49	3.30	1.76	0.31	5.9 - 5.0	2.11	1.98	2.03	11.6	0.51250Y	1/16/18	19.4 - 16.6
-	-	-0.05	-6.45	-22.43	1.87			0.17	0.35		14.3750Y	32/4/39	7.2 - 3.5
-	-	0.10	-	-	-		0.42	1.52	2.40	17.3	0.06570	11/30/17	3.9 - 1.8
-	-	0.24	1.13	0.99	1.00	25.6 - 20.1	1.60	1.50	1.20	6.3	0.40Z	1/12/18	28.9 - 22.7
-	-	0.42	2.86	2.72	2.47	29.9 - 22.2	1.20	1.13	1.07	1.6	0.3250Y	32/4/39	85.5 - 63.4
-	-	1.03	-0.27	2.45	10.14		4.29	4.28	4.21	3.8	1.080Y	32/4/39	126.0 - 103.0
-	-	0.10	-3.05	-4.72	4.98		0.28	0.28	0.28	1.3	0.070Y	6/30/17	36.0 - 9.8
-	-	0.13	0.01	0.42	0.41	1496.0 - 715.0	0.31	0.30	0.24	2.9	0.08250Y	12/18/17	15.0 - 7.2
-	-	0.69	2.92	1.25	2.85	7.1 - 5.9	2.44	1.44	1.80	12.9	0.50Z	32/4/39	20.8 - 17.1
-	-	0.70	-1.25	1.36	1.60								
-	-	0.02	0.19	0.17	0.17	62.1 - 34.8	0.90		0.58	10.0	0.437	1/18/18	11.8 - 6.6
-	0.30	-	0.33	0.35	0.27	109.5 - 70.0	2.30			8.3			36.1 - 23.1
-	-	-	0.46	0.26	0.33	48.4 - 32.9	1.50	3.77	3.31	8.0	0.54930	1/4/18	22.3 - 15.2
0.13	-	-	0.67	0.93	0.81	2.1 - 1.8		0.10			0.1GY	1/31/15	1.4 - 1.2
-	0.43	-	0.66	1.22	1.14	26.9 - 20.1	1.77	2.00	1.33	11.4			17.8 - 13.3
-	-	-	5.31	5.30	5.35	11.0 - 9.2	10.33	10.59	11.33	19.3			58.5 - 48.9
-	-	0.42	2.48	5.01	3.08	0.6 - 0.4							1.6 - 1.1
-2.06	-	-	-3.03	-5.57	-1.71								21.4 - 0.0
-	0.22	-	0.39	0.27	0.40	216.7 - 179.0	12.34	17.88	21.48	16.0			84.5 - 69.8
-	-	-	-2.46	-2.05	-0.11								11.4 - 5.1
-	0.28	-	0.51	0.38	0.18	106.9 - 0.0	3.48	1.70	1.68	9.5			54.5 - 0.0
-	-	-					7.26	6.84	6.89	14.8			53.7 - 46.0
-	-	-	0.03	0.44	0.49	547.3 - 376.7							16.4 - 11.3
-	-	-	12.89	8.81	19.36						0.90	7/13/17	
-	-	0.29	-0.13	-0.14	0.38								2.1 - 1.1
-	-	0.69	0.77	15.10	14.13	644.3 - 349.0							496.1 - 268.7
-	-	0.84	2.46	2.22	2.10	32.0 - 21.7	0.83	0.79	0.75	1.3	0.2150Y	32/4/39	78.7 - 53.5
-	-	-0.05	-1.33	1.28	0.23						0.060Y	10/20/11	2.4 - 1.1
-	-	-0.15	8.87	8.62	8.42			2.66	2.70		0.710	32/4/39	
-	-	1.37	5.21	5.41	4.76	7.0 - 6.0	43.70	36.19	39.84	128.1			36.3 - 31.4
-	-	0.52	1.75	1.53	1.50	30.7 - 24.8	0.71	0.67	0.62	1.4	0.190Y	32/4/39	53.8 - 43.3
-	-	0.39	0.51	0.10	-0.38	53.9 - 38.4							27.5 - 19.6
-	-	2.21	7.19	8.04	7.83	29.4 - 18.9	0.04	0.04	0.04	0.0	0.040Y	32/4/39	211.7 - 135.7
-	-	0.96	-4.62	-25.92	5.78		0.40	0.64	0.62	0.4	0.080Y	32/4/39	142.5 - 91.3
-	-	-0.33	2.18	8.15	1.55	11.2 - 7.5					0.84380Y	1/2/18	24.4 - 16.4
-	-	0.33	2.19	1.87	1.66	20.4 - 14.7	1.08	1.00	1.00	2.8	0.290Y	32/4/39	44.6 - 32.3
-	-	0.46	2.08	2.58	2.23	15.5 - 11.3	2.26	2.17	2.10	8.3	0.5670	11/20/17	32.2 - 23.6
-	-	0.22	0.61	0.58	2.84	117.7 - 70.1	0.15	0.15	0.15	0.3	0.03750Y	12/12/17	71.8 - 42.8
-	-	-0.38	-0.07	-0.01									
-	-	1.61	-4.20	5.67	5.96		0.60	0.60	0.50	1.3	0.160Y	2/23/18	51.5 - 40.2
-	-	1.42	4.72	5.40	2.20	16.3 - 11.8	0.42	0.16	0.04	0.6	0.53130Y	32/4/39	77.1 - 55.7
-	-	0.68	1.97	1.55	1.55	21.6 - 16.3	0.46	0.40	0.10	1.3	0.220Y	2/15/18	42.6 - 32.1
-	-	0.07	0.04	-0.07	-0.13	263.3 - 148.8					0.05640	3/20/79	10.5 - 6.0
-	-	-0.12	-0.13	-0.53	-0.59		0.94	0.70	0.65	7.4	0.41410Z	1/25/18	13.8 - 11.5
-	-	-0.17	-0.90	-1.24	-1.77				0.26				3.6 - 1.6
-	-	0.20	0.25	0.08	-0.89	80.6 - 62.8							20.1 - 15.7
-	-	0.21	-0.69	0.76	-0.47								61.3 - 50.0
-	-	-0.17	0.39	-0.27	-0.03	15.9 - 9.1	2.10		0.49	45.1	0.08247Y	1/24/18	6.2 - 3.5
-	-	-	-0.39	-0.15	-0.29		0.80	1.22	1.21	9.0	0.20	3/1/18	10.5 - 7.1
-	-	-	-0.47	-0.16	-0.30		1.42	1.71	1.63	9.2	0.3550	3/1/18	17.7 - 12.2
-	-	-	-0.40	-0.18	-0.29		1.28	1.50	1.40	10.3	0.320	3/1/18	14.2 - 10.0
-	-	-	-0.31	-0.23	-0.24		1.16	1.40	1.33	9.2	0.290	3/1/18	14.1 - 10.5
-	-	0.05	2.90	2.97	-0.11	23.1 - 14.8							66.8 - 42.9
-	-	0.18	0.87	-5.13	-47.52	13.8 - 6.5			0.60		0.150Y	12/1/14	12.0 - 5.7
-	-	-0.04	-0.34	-0.12							0.0950Z	11/13/17	14.0 - 9.7
1.46	-	-	4.92	4.37	4.23	30.4 - 24.1	3.08	2.96	2.84	2.3	0.840Y	32/4/39	149.7 - 118.7

SYMBOL	COMPANY	NATURE OF BUSINESS	FISCAL YEAR-END	TOTAL REV. $MILL	NET INCOME $MILL	TOTAL ASSETS $MILL	NET STK EQUITY $MILL	NO OF INST	INST. HOLDINGS (SHARES)
CLD	Cloud Peak Energy Inc	Mining	12/31/16	800.4	21.8	1714.8	951.7	184	72177123
CLDR	Cloudera Inc	Internet & Software	1/31/17	261.0	-187.3	442.5	173.9	136	52135560
CMS	CMS Energy Corp	Electric Utilities	12/31/16	6399.0	551.0	21622.0	4253.0	686	314871791
CNA	CNA Financial Corp	General Insurance	12/31/16	9366.0	859.0	55233.0	11969.0	270	275884146
CNHI	CNH Industrial NV	Industrial Machinery & Equipment	12/31/16	24872.0	-252.0	45547.0	4444.0	168	310331239
CNO	CNO Financial Group Inc	Life & Health	12/31/16	3985.1	358.2	31975.2	4486.9	358	220657848
CEO	Cnooc Ltd.	Production & Extraction	12/31/16	146490.0	637.0	637681.0	382371.0	251	9748389
CNXM	CNX Midstream Partners LP	Equipment & Services	12/31/16	239.2	96.5	918.6	-	80	12448787
CNX	CNX Resources Corp	Mining	12/31/16	2026.4	-848.1	9184.0	3798.4	462	253328966
KO	Coca-Cola Co (The)	Beverages	12/31/16	41863.0	6527.0	87270.0	23062.0	2477	3283730557
CCE	Coca-Cola European Partners plc	Manufacturing	12/31/16	9133.0	549.0	18568.0	6461.0	-	0
KOF	Coca-Cola FEMSA SAB de CV	Beverages	12/31/16	177718.0	10070.0	279256.0	122137.0	164	19224643
CDE	Coeur Mining Inc	Precious Metals	12/31/16	665.8	55.4	1318.9	768.5	284	153013693
FOF	Cohen & Steers Closed-End Opport	Holding and other Investment Office	12/31/16	18.7	15.4	356.4	354.3	50	3479964
INB	Cohen & Steers Global Income Buil	Holding and other Investment Office	12/31/16	8.7	4.1	296.4	226.6	51	5847636
CNS	Cohen & Steers Inc	Wealth Management	12/31/16	349.9	92.9	333.7	265.8	202	25366235
UTF	Cohen & Steers Infrastructure Fund,	Holding and other Investment Office	12/31/16	102.2	58.8	2766.8	1876.7	160	21466972
LDP	Cohen & Steers Limited Duration Pr	Holding and other Investment Office	12/31/16	58.2	45.7	1051.1	733.8	57	6614203
MIE	Cohen & Steers MLP Income & Ene	Finance Intermediaries & Services	11/30/16	3.8	-4.6	424.4	318.1	44	5416971
RQI	Cohen & Steers Quality Income Re	Holding and other Investment Office	12/31/16	66.3	39.1	1929.0	1465.3	142	19413013
RNP	Cohen & Steers Reit & Preferred In	Holding and other Investment Office	12/31/16	66.2	48.9	1387.0	1034.6	98	9059151
PSF	Cohen & Steers Select Preferred & I	Holding and other Investment Office	12/31/16	27.2	21.8	445.5	311.2	43	1156431
RFI	Cohen & Steers Total Return Realty	Holding and other Investment Office	12/31/16	11.6	8.6	349.6	348.9	72	2821248
CFX	Colfax Corp	Industrial Machinery & Equipment	12/31/16	3647.0	128.1	6385.5	2896.9	311	97797343
CL	Colgate-Palmolive Co.	Household & Personal Products	12/31/16	15195.0	2441.0	12123.0	-243.0	1907	756960378
CLNS	Colony NorthStar Inc	REITs	12/31/16	398.5	42.3	850.6	184.1	430	468675052
CXP	Columbia Property Trust Inc	REITs	12/31/16	473.5	84.3	4299.8	2502.8	267	94554505
STK	Columbia Seligman Premium Techn	Holding and other Investment Office	12/31/16	2.2	-0.8	275.2	273.2	39	1339086
CCZ	Comcast Holdings Corp	Radio & Television	12/31/04	8586.0	986.0	41942.0	19912.0	7	411541
CMA	Comerica, Inc.	Banking	12/31/16	2960.0	477.0	72978.0	7796.0	736	177487228
FIX	Comfort Systems USA Inc	Construction Services	12/31/16	1634.3	64.9	708.5	376.6	250	46259604
CMC	Commercial Metals Co.	Non-Precious Metals	8/31/17	4569.7	46.3	2975.1	1400.8	331	129564373
CBU	Community Bank System Inc	Banking	12/31/16	440.8	103.8	8666.4	1198.1	240	43340299
CYH	Community Health Systems, Inc.	Hospitals & Health Care Facilities	12/31/16	18438.0	-1721.0	21944.0	1615.0	372	154903314
CHCT	Community Healthcare Trust Inc	REITs	12/31/16	25.2	2.7	251.5	194.0	113	16842654
CBD	Companhia Brasileira de Distribuica	Retail - General Merchandise/Depart	12/31/15	69220.0	265.0	47241.0	10354.0	-	0
SBS	Companhia de Saneamento Basico	Water Utilities	12/31/16	14098.2	2947.1	36745.0	15419.2	258	128632718
CIG	Companhia Energetica de Minas G	Electric Utilities	12/31/16	18773.0	334.0	42036.0	12930.0	216	106165288
ELP	Companhia Paranaense De Energia	Electric Utilities	12/31/16	13101.8	958.6	30434.2	14864.2	140	34172818
SID	Companhia Siderurgica Nacional	Non-Precious Metals	12/31/15	15331.9	1257.9	48650.0	7664.7	127	48927253
CCU	Compania Cervecerias Unidas S.A.	Beverages	12/31/16	1558897.7	118457.5	1871577.0	1077298.2	119	27832457
BVN	Compania de Minas Buenaventura	Precious Metals	12/31/16	1068.8	323.5	4266.4	2821.1	231	139102099
CODI	Compass Diversified Holdings	Miscellaneous Consumer Goods	12/31/16	978.3	54.7	1777.2	856.4	157	25191342
CMP	Compass Minerals International Inc	Mining	12/31/16	1138.0	162.7	2466.5	717.1	421	52102568
CRK	Comstock Resources Inc	Production & Extraction	12/31/16	175.7	-135.1	889.9	-271.3	155	19549785
CAG	Conagra Brands Inc	Food	5/28/17	7826.9	639.3	10096.3	3990.8	993	408798113
CXO	Concho Resources Inc	Production & Extraction	12/31/16	1635.0	-1462.4	12119.3	7622.7	588	161104127
CCM	Concord Medical Services Holdings	Diagnostic & Health Related Service	12/31/16	455.0	-265.1	3228.6	1166.2	20	26300419
CNDT	Conduent Inc	Business Services	12/31/16	6408.0	-983.0	7709.0	3430.0	335	186940359
COP	ConocoPhillips	Production & Extraction	12/31/16	24360.0	-3615.0	89772.0	34974.0	1993	1070641463
CCR	CONSOL Coal Resources LP	Mining	12/31/16	281.1	25.9	504.3	226.6	29	6944963
CEIX	CONSOL Energy Inc (New)	Mining	12/31/16	1230.9	41.5	2687.4	657.6	-	0
CEIX	CONSOL Energy Inc (New)	Mining	12/31/16	1230.9	41.5	2687.4	657.6	-	0
ED	Consolidated Edison Inc	Electric Utilities	12/31/16	12075.0	1245.0	48255.0	14298.0	1115	214131320
STZ	Constellation Brands Inc	Beverages	2/28/17	7331.5	1535.1	18602.4	6891.2	1058	186934826
CSTM	Constellium N.V.	Non-Precious Metals	12/31/16	4743.0	-4.0	3787.0	-579.0	-	0
CMS PRB	Consumers Energy Co.	Electric Utilities	12/31/16	6064.0	616.0	19946.0	5939.0	-	0
TCS	Container Store Group, Inc	Retail - Furniture & Home Furnishing	4/1/17	819.9	15.0	761.8	221.8	119	41534805
CBPX	Continental Building Products Inc	Construction Materials	12/31/16	461.4	44.0	634.7	309.0	190	40528551
CLR	Continental Resources Inc.	Production & Extraction	12/31/16	1980.3	-399.7	13811.8	4302.0	506	95826869
VLRS	Controladora Vuela Compania De A	Airlines/Air Freight	12/31/16	23512.5	3519.5	21781.8	10794.1	-	0
CVG	Convergys Corp	IT Services	12/31/16	2913.6	143.0	2371.8	1315.9	383	117272858
COO	Cooper Companies, Inc. (The)	Medical Instruments & Equipment	10/31/17	2139.0	372.9	4858.7	3175.7	622	60401741
CTB	Cooper Tire & Rubber Co.	Auto Parts	12/31/16	2924.9	248.4	2619.4	1076.0	350	75476792
CPS	Cooper-Standard Holdings Inc	Auto Parts	12/31/16	3472.9	139.0	2491.7	697.4	246	19032263
CPA	Copa Holdings S.A.	Airlines/Air Freight	12/31/16	2221.8	334.5	3846.1	1842.3	343	34910840
CLB	Core Laboratories N.V. (Netherland	Equipment & Services	12/31/16	594.7	63.9	573.1	151.4	514	59406303
CXW	CoreCivic Inc	REITs	12/31/16	1849.8	219.9	3271.6	1459.0	399	127653166
CLGX	CoreLogic Inc.	Business Services	12/31/16	1952.6	106.6	3907.5	1003.0	312	84864483
CORR	CorEnergy Infrastructure Trust Inc	REITs	12/31/16	89.3	-29.7	650.7	406.5	144	10611448
COR	CoreSite Realty Corp	REITs	12/31/16	400.4	58.7	1451.3	435.7	381	40022337
GLW	Corning Inc	Electrical Equipment	12/31/16	9390.0	3695.0	27899.0	17893.0	1462	853723886
CCT	Corporate Capital Trust Inc	Finance Intermediaries & Services	12/31/16	386.5	210.1	4430.7	2759.3	-	0
OFC	Corporate Office Properties Trust	REITs	12/31/16	574.3	11.4	3780.9	1523.1	355	126302136
CZZ	Cosan Ltd	Refining & Marketing	12/31/16	12518.1	277.8	50469.8	6272.5	173	81171949
CMRE	Costamare Inc	Shipping	12/31/16	468.2	81.7	2558.4	1074.4	149	29185989
COTV	Cotiviti Holdings Inc	Business Services	12/31/16	625.2	48.9	2002.3	939.3	169	80912439
COT	Cott Corp.	Beverages	12/31/16	3235.9	-77.8	3939.7	868.5	177	125418853
COTY	Coty, Inc.	Household & Personal Products	6/30/17	7650.3	-422.2	22548.2	9314.7	400	548036963
CUZ	Cousins Properties Inc	REITs	12/31/16	259.2	79.1	4171.6	2455.6	342	516273457

Stock data table (EPS = Earnings Per Share; quarterly 1st/2nd/3rd and annual 2016/2015/2014). P/E Ratio, Dividends Per Share (2016/2015/2014), Average Yield %, Dividend Declared (Amount, Payable), and 2016 Price Range (high – low).

1st	2nd	3rd	2016	2015	2014	P/E RATIO	Div 2016	Div 2015	Div 2014	AV. YLD %	AMOUNT	PAYABLE	PRICE RANGE 2016
		0.03	0.35	-3.36	1.29	17.9 - 8.2							6.3 - 2.9
		-0.40	-6.21										23.0 - 14.6
		0.61	1.98	1.89	1.74	25.5 - 21.0	1.24	1.16	1.08	2.7	0.33250Y	32/4/39	50.5 - 41.5
		0.53	3.17	1.77	2.55	17.3 - 12.7	3.00	3.00	2.00	6.3	0.30Y	32/4/39	55.0 - 40.2
	0.17		-0.18	0.19	0.52		0.15	0.21	0.28		0.110	5/2/17	
		0.59	2.01	1.39	0.24	12.7 - 9.3	0.31	0.27	0.24	1.4	0.090Y	12/26/17	25.5 - 18.7
		0.01	0.45	1.35		18274.0 - 0.0	28.08	41.50	41.02	37.0			182.7 - 0.0
		0.43	1.58	1.20		15.7 - 9.9	1.00	0.88		5.1	0.31330	2/14/18	24.8 - 15.6
		-0.11	-3.70	-1.64	0.70		0.01	0.14	0.25	0.1	0.010Y	32/4/39	16.3 - 11.4
		0.33	1.49	1.67	1.60	31.8 - 27.1	1.40	1.32	1.22	3.2	0.370Y	32/4/39	47.4 - 40.4
	0.61		1.42	0.13	0.12						0.210	12/4/17	
			4.85			18.7 - 12.4	32.53	30.79	28.84	43.8			90.9 - 59.9
		-0.09	0.34	-2.83	-11.28	35.4 - 19.9							12.0 - 6.8
			0.60		0.69		1.04	1.04	1.04	8.1	0.0870	3/29/18	13.4 - 11.8
			0.18	0.17	0.22	55.3 - 47.8	0.92	1.12	1.12	9.7	0.0690	3/29/18	9.9 - 8.6
		0.53	2.00	1.41	1.65	23.8 - 16.6	1.54	1.50	1.88	3.9	1.7Y	12/13/17	47.7 - 33.3
			0.69	0.68	0.72	34.8 - 28.1	2.03	1.60	1.48	9.0	0.1550	3/29/18	24.0 - 19.4
			1.59	1.68	1.77	17.1 - 15.4	1.88	1.87	2.17	7.2	0.1560	3/29/18	27.2 - 24.5
			-0.17	0.06	-0.01		1.17	1.32	1.26	11.0	0.0770	3/29/18	11.9 - 8.9
			0.36	0.29	0.31	36.8 - 33.3	0.96	0.96	0.76	7.6	0.080	3/29/18	13.3 - 12.0
			1.03	0.91	0.96	21.3 - 18.3	1.48	1.48	1.29	7.2	0.1240	3/29/18	21.9 - 18.9
			1.82	1.96	2.07	16.0 - 14.2	2.45	2.19	2.56	8.9	0.1720	3/29/18	29.1 - 25.8
			0.33	0.28	0.28	39.4 - 36.5	0.96	1.30	1.30	7.6	0.080	3/29/18	13.0 - 12.1
		0.37	1.04	1.34	3.02	41.5 - 33.5							43.2 - 34.9
		0.68	2.72	1.52	2.36	28.4 - 23.7	1.55	1.50	1.42	2.1	0.40Y	32/4/39	77.2 - 64.5
		0.00	0.21	0.60	0.10	70.0 - 54.3	0.40	0.40	0.10	3.0	0.5591GZ	32/4/39	14.7 - 11.4
		0.84	0.68	0.36	0.74	34.5 - 30.3	1.20	1.20	1.20	5.4	0.20Y	32/4/39	23.4 - 20.6
			-0.05	-0.04	-0.07		1.85	1.85	1.85	8.5	0.78067	1/23/18	24.4 - 18.3
											0.39460Z	1/16/18	63.2 - 0.0
		1.26	2.68	2.84	3.16	32.7 - 24.1	0.89	0.83	0.79	1.2	0.30Y	32/4/39	87.7 - 64.5
		0.59	1.72	1.30	0.61	26.0 - 18.8	0.28	0.25	0.23	0.8	0.0750Y	11/21/17	44.6 - 32.3
0.31		0.47	1.20	0.97		49.2 - 36.3	0.48	0.48	0.48	2.5	0.120Y	32/4/39	23.1 - 17.1
		0.68	2.32	2.19	2.22	26.9 - 21.2	1.26	1.22	1.16	2.3	0.340Y	32/4/39	62.3 - 49.1
		-0.98	-15.54	1.37	0.82						0.25G7	32/4/39	10.3 - 4.0
		0.02	0.24	-0.31		119.9 - 89.3	1.52	0.52		6.0	0.3950Z	12/1/17	28.8 - 21.4
				0.94	4.51		1.04	0.92					25.5 - 17.0
			4.31	0.78	1.32	2.6 - 1.9	0.21	0.27	0.63	2.1			11.2 - 8.4
		0.82	0.07	1.96	2.49	52.9 - 27.1	0.55	0.41	3.01	20.9			3.7 - 1.9
				4.16	4.21		1.08	0.86	2.30	12.2			11.3 - 6.8
			0.93		-0.07			0.41	0.29				4.1 - 1.8
		65.02	320.59	326.95	287.52	0.1 - 0.1	200.03	198.49	242.47	773.7			29.6 - 20.5
		0.26	-1.27	-1.25	-0.30		0.03		0.03	0.2	0.02250	4/21/97	14.9 - 11.0
		0.10	0.51	2.61	5.38	35.9 - 31.7	1.44	1.44	1.44	8.5	0.45310	1/30/18	18.3 - 16.1
		0.94	4.79	4.69	6.44	17.5 - 12.5	2.78	2.64	2.40	4.0	0.720Y	32/4/39	83.6 - 60.1
		-1.67	-11.52	-113.55	-6.20						0.1250	12/15/14	13.1 - 4.1
	0.54		-1.56	-0.60	0.70		1.00	1.00	1.00	2.7	0.21250Y	32/4/39	41.5 - 32.4
		-0.77	-10.85	0.54	4.88								153.9 - 108.1
		0.20	-2.00	-0.58	0.92			6.35	9.79				4.9 - 3.3
		-0.09	-4.85										17.7 - 13.3
		0.34	-2.91	-3.58	5.51		1.00	2.94	2.84	2.1	0.2650Y	32/4/39	56.2 - 42.5
		0.07	0.83	0.99		23.6 - 16.0	2.05	0.48		13.0	0.51250	2/15/18	19.6 - 13.3
													39.5 - 19.6
													25.0 - 0.0
		1.48	4.12	4.05	3.71	21.8 - 17.6	2.68	2.60	2.52	3.3	0.7150Y	32/4/39	89.7 - 72.6
		2.44	5.18	4.17	9.83	44.1 - 28.3	1.24			0.7	0.470	32/4/39	228.6 - 146.8
		0.43	-0.04	-5.27	0.48								
							4.50	4.50	4.50	5.6	1.1250Y	1/1/18	106.0 - 0.0
-0.02			0.11	0.47	-2.87	60.8 - 32.4							6.7 - 3.6
		0.29	0.39	0.37		26.3 - 19.5							28.4 - 21.1
		0.03	-1.08	-0.96	2.64								53.4 - 30.0
			3.48	2.44	0.60	4.5 - 2.3							15.8 - 8.0
		0.35	1.40	1.61	1.13	19.0 - 14.5	0.35	0.31	0.27	1.5	0.10Y	32/4/39	26.6 - 20.3
		2.09	5.59	4.14	5.51	45.6 - 31.3	0.06	0.06	0.06	0.0	0.030Y	32/4/39	254.9 - 175.2
		1.18	4.51	3.69	3.42	9.9 - 7.1	0.42	0.42	0.42	1.1	0.1050Y	32/4/39	44.5 - 32.0
		1.32	7.42	6.08	2.39	17.1 - 13.1							126.7 - 97.4
		2.45	7.90	-5.13	8.15						0.750	12/15/17	
		0.48	1.46	2.68	5.77		2.20	2.20	2.00		0.550	2/16/18	
		0.35	1.87	1.88	1.66	18.7 - 11.6	2.04	2.16	2.04	7.3	0.420Z	32/4/39	35.0 - 21.8
		0.36	1.19	1.41	0.79	41.3 - 29.4							49.1 - 35.0
		0.57	2.14	0.79	1.05	18.0 - 14.8	3.00	2.75	2.57	8.5	0.750	2/28/18	38.6 - 31.8
		0.46	1.54	1.03	0.66	77.6 - 52.3	2.39	1.79	1.47	2.3	0.980Z	1/16/18	119.5 - 80.6
		0.39	3.23	1.00	1.73	10.1 - 7.5	0.54	0.48	0.40	1.9	0.1550Y	32/4/39	32.6 - 24.2
		0.17	0.69	0.69	0.73	27.5 - 23.2	0.80	0.80	0.80	4.6	0.10137	1/11/18	19.0 - 16.0
		0.21	-0.03	1.74	0.25		1.10	1.10	1.10	3.3	0.2750Z	32/4/39	35.8 - 29.0
		1.26	0.98	1.68	0.58						0.07560	5/26/17	
			0.79	1.68	1.38						0.54690	1/16/18	
		0.20	0.55	0.18	-0.40	81.1 - 56.2							44.6 - 30.9
		0.30	-0.61	-0.03	0.10		0.24	0.24	0.23	1.5	0.060	12/8/17	22.7 - 10.4
-0.03			0.44	0.64	-0.26	46.7 - 32.6	0.25	0.20	0.20	1.4	0.1250	32/4/39	20.5 - 14.4
		0.03	0.31	0.58	0.22	30.9 - 25.6	0.24	0.32	0.30	2.7	0.060Z	1/12/18	9.6 - 7.9

SYMBOL	COMPANY	NATURE OF BUSINESS	FISCAL YEAR-END	TOTAL REV. $MILL	NET INCOME $MILL	TOTAL ASSETS $MILL	NET STK EQUITY $MILL	NO OF INST	INST. HOLDINGS (SHARES)
CVA	Covanta Holding Corp	Electric Utilities	12/31/16	1699.0	-4.0	4284.0	469.0	347	145332168
CPL	CPFL Energia SA	Electric Utilities	12/31/16	19112.1	900.9	42171.0	7970.0	114	11956642
CR	Crane Co.	Industrial Machinery & Equipment	12/31/16	2748.0	122.8	3428.0	1133.8	443	51513508
CRD B	Crawford & Co.	Brokers & Intermediaries	12/31/16	1177.6	36.0	735.9	153.9	63	11712685
BAP	CrediCorp Ltd.	Banking	12/31/16	16758.7	3514.6	156435.2	19656.1	362	60749793
CS	Credit Suisse Group AG	Banking	12/31/16	20323.0	-2710.0	819861.0	41897.0	305	78799505
CPG	Crescent Point Energy Corp	Production & Extraction	12/31/16	1939.9	-932.7	16163.6	9591.2	188	219935915
CEQP	Crestwood Equity Partners LP	Equipment & Services	12/31/16	2520.5	-216.3	4443.9	-	175	56644665
CRH	CRH Plc	Construction Materials	12/31/16	27104.0	1243.0	31594.0	13895.0	198	32703698
CRT	Cross Timbers Royalty Trust	Oil Royalty Traders	12/31/16	7.6		11.4	9.9	54	702317
CAPL	CrossAmerica Partners LP	Equipment & Services	12/31/16	1869.8	10.7	932.0	0.0	67	12147395
CCI	Crown Castle International Corp (N	REITs	12/31/16	3921.2	357.0	22675.1	7557.1	940	446786481
CCK	Crown Holdings Inc	Metal Products	12/31/16	8284.0	496.0	9599.0	366.0	520	151677688
CRY	CryoLife, Inc.	Medical Instruments & Equipment	12/31/16	180.4	10.8	316.1	209.0	178	31910045
CSRA	CSRA Inc	Computer Hardware & Equipment	3/31/17	4993.0	304.0	4888.0	330.0	377	166515574
CSS	CSS Industries, Inc.	Printing	3/31/17	322.4	28.5	339.2	294.2	109	8611239
CTS	CTS Corp	Electrical Equipment	12/31/16	396.7	34.4	517.7	317.9	161	40075650
CUBE	CubeSmart	REITs	12/31/16	510.0	87.9	3475.0	1655.4	347	253592736
CUB	Cubic Corp	Electronic Instruments & Related Pro	9/30/17	1485.9	-11.2	1336.3	689.6	232	31585656
CFR	Cullen/Frost Bankers, Inc.	Banking	12/31/16	1138.1	304.3	30196.3	3002.5	469	66171974
CULP	Culp Inc	Textiles	4/30/17	309.5	22.3	205.6	148.6	112	13730870
CMI	Cummins, Inc.	Auto Parts	12/31/16	17509.0	1394.0	15011.0	6875.0	1261	166867725
CURO	CURO Group Holdings Corp	Finance Intermediaries & Services	12/31/16	828.6	65.4	780.8	40.9	-	0
CW	Curtiss-Wright Corp.	Industrial Machinery & Equipment	12/31/16	2108.9	187.3	3037.8	1291.2	342	45654203
SRF	Cushing Energy Income Fund	Holding and other Investment Office	11/30/16	0.5	-0.3	30.0	27.8	24	394451
SRV	Cushing MLP Total Return Fund	Holding and other Investment Office	11/30/16	0.8	-2.0	149.8	100.0	34	1931060
SZC	Cushing Renaissance Fund	Holding and other Investment Office	11/30/16	5.7	3.6	130.0	117.6	27	929622
CUBI	Customers Bancorp Inc	Banking	12/31/16	345.7	78.7	9382.7	855.9	219	30754405
CVI	CVR Energy Inc	Refining & Marketing	12/31/16	4782.4	24.7	4050.2	858.1	196	94511013
UAN	CVR Partners LP	Agricultural Crop Production	12/31/16	356.3	-26.9	1312.2	-	87	26058325
CVRR	CVR Refining LP	Refining & Marketing	12/31/16	4431.3	15.3	2331.9		98	20314139
CVS	CVS Health Corporation	Retail - Food & Beverage, Drug & To	12/31/16	177526.0	5317.0	94462.0	36830.0	2145	1039534771
CELP	Cypress Energy Partners LP	Equipment & Services	12/31/16	298.0	-4.7	167.5	-	12	81248
CYS	CYS Investments, Inc.	REITs	12/31/16	114.3	16.4	13245.3	1535.7	244	123412804
DAN	Dana Inc	Auto Parts	12/31/16	5826.0	640.0	4860.0	1157.0	363	169137775
DHR	Danaher Corp	Medical Instruments & Equipment	12/31/16	16882.4	2553.7	45295.3	23002.8	1549	614407654
DAC	Danaos Corp	Shipping	12/31/16	498.3	-366.2	3127.1	487.7	25	4060266
DQ	DAQO New Energy Corp	Semiconductors	12/31/16	229.1	43.5	656.7	270.1	49	3385412
DRI	Darden Restaurants, Inc.	Hotels, Restaurants & Travel	5/28/17	7170.2	479.1	5504.2	2101.7	847	144466720
DAR	Darling Ingredients Inc	Food	12/31/16	3398.1	102.3	4698.0	1973.0	367	200864756
DVA	DaVita Inc	Diagnostic & Health Related Service	12/31/16	14745.1	879.9	18741.3	4648.0	679	183834748
DCP	DCP Midstream LP	Equipment & Services	12/31/16	1497.0	312.0	5161.0	-	209	86159402
DCT	DCT Industrial Trust Inc	REITs	12/31/16	392.8	93.1	3808.1	1862.0	356	120192390
DDR	DDR Corp	REITs	12/31/16	1005.6	60.0	8197.5	3237.5	409	402389741
DF	Dean Foods Co.	Food	12/31/16	7710.2	119.9	2606.2	610.6	404	120486160
DECK	Deckers Outdoor Corp.	Apparel, Footwear & Accessories	3/31/17	1790.1	5.7	1191.8	954.3	377	39185718
DE	Deere & Co.	Industrial Machinery & Equipment	10/29/17	29737.7	2159.1	65786.3	9557.3	1486	271140765
DEX	Delaware Enhanced Global Dividen	Holding and other Investment Office	11/30/16	10.8	6.7	265.5	181.2	57	7538337
DDF	Delaware Investments Dividend & I	Holding and other Investment Office	11/30/16	4.9	3.2	130.0	88.7	35	1763860
DKL	Delek Logistics Partners LP	Equipment & Services	12/31/16	448.1	62.8	415.5	-	62	6442855
DK	Delek US Holdings Inc (New)	Refining & Marketing	12/31/16	4197.9	-153.7	2985.1	991.9	-	0
DVMT	Dell Technologies Inc	Computer Hardware & Equipment	2/3/17	61642.0	-1672.0	118206.0	13474.0	695	191848039
DVMT	Dell Technologies Inc - Common Cl	Internet & Software	2/3/17	3199.0	313.0	16414.0			0
DLPH	Delphi Technologies PLC	Manufacturing	12/31/16	4486.0	236.0	2899.0	1026.0		0
DAL	Delta Air Lines Inc (DE)	Airlines/Air Freight	12/31/16	39639.0	4373.0	51261.0	12287.0	1154	754060268
DEL	Deltic Timber Corp.	Paper & Forest Products	12/31/16	219.4	9.2	554.7	251.2	152	12520893
DLX	Deluxe Corp	Printing	12/31/16	1849.1	229.4	2184.3	881.0	467	55274214
DNR	Denbury Resources, Inc. (DE)	Production & Extraction	12/31/16	975.6	-976.2	4274.6	468.4	354	396264926
DESP	Despegar.com Corp	Hotels, Restaurants & Travel	12/31/16	411.2	17.8	353.7	-82.3	65	48790717
DB	Deutsche Bank AG	Banking	12/31/16	40942.0	-1402.0	1590546.0	64503.0	306	445690189
DHG	Deutsche High Income Opportunitie	Holding and other Investment Office	9/30/16	17.2	12.6	323.8	230.7	52	8093127
KMM	Deutsche Multi-Market Income Trus	Holding and other Investment Office	11/30/16	14.5	11.0	279.7	202.6	45	9320757
KTF	Deutsche Municipal Income Trust	Holding and other Investment Office	11/30/16	38.0	29.8	823.3	491.5	69	4176629
KST	Deutsche Strategic Income Trust	Holding and other Investment Office	11/30/16	3.9	2.7	76.7	54.9	31	2391832
KSM	Deutsche Strategic Municipal Incom	Holding and other Investment Office	11/30/16	11.7	8.9	229.9	136.0	36	703110
DVN	Devon Energy Corp.	Production & Extraction	12/31/16	12197.0	-3302.0	25913.0	5927.0	1182	511164718
DHX	DHI Group Inc	Internet & Software	12/31/16	227.0	-5.4	310.1	103.9	182	49842901
DHT	DHT Holdings Inc	Equipment & Services	12/31/16	356.0	9.3	1403.7	685.0	149	58625823
DEO	Diageo Plc	Beverages	6/30/17	12050.0	2662.0	28848.0	10313.0	942	99263726
DO	Diamond Offshore Drilling, Inc.	Equipment & Services	12/31/16	1600.3	-372.5	6371.9	3750.1	452	175420939
DRH	DiamondRock Hospitality Co.	REITs	12/31/16	896.6	114.8	3069.5	1836.8	319	311676378
DSX	Diana Shipping Inc	Shipping	12/31/16	114.3	-164.2	1668.7	1056.6	131	47895022
DKS	Dick's Sporting Goods, Inc	Retail - Specialty	1/28/17	7922.0	287.4	4058.3	1929.5	580	99600391
DBD	Diebold Nixdorf Inc	Computer Hardware & Equipment	12/31/16	3316.3	33.0	5270.3	591.4	386	114974567
DLR	Digital Realty Trust Inc	REITs	12/31/16	2142.2	426.2	12192.6	5096.0	833	242373187
DDS	Dillard's Inc.	Retail - General Merchandise/Depart	1/28/17	6418.0	169.2	3888.1	1717.4	306	35868658
DIN	DineEquity Inc	Retail - Food & Beverage, Drug & To	12/31/16	634.0	98.0	2278.6	252.8	247	21365387
DPLO	Diplomat Pharmacy Inc	Diagnostic & Health Related Service	12/31/16	4410.4	28.3	1107.9	613.4	212	61239090
DFS	Discover Financial Services	Credit & Lending	12/31/16	10497.0	2393.0	92308.0	11323.0	1075	391711510
DIS	Disney (Walt) Co. (The)	Entertainment	9/30/17	55137.0	8980.0	95789.0	41315.0	2557	1227775110

| EARNINGS PER SHARE | | | | | | P/E | DIVIDENDS | | | AV. | DIV. DECLARED | | PRICE RANGE |
| QUARTERLY | | | ANNUAL | | | RATIO | PER SHARE | | | YLD | | | 2016 |
1st	2nd	3rd	2016	2015	2014		2016	2015	2014	%	AMOUNT	PAYABLE	
-	-	0.11	-0.03	0.51	-0.01	-	1.00	1.00	0.86	6.7	0.250Y	1/5/18	17.1 - 13.2
-	-	-	0.87	0.83	0.92	20.2 - 12.2	0.36	-	1.83	2.2			17.6 - 10.7
-	-	1.13	2.07	3.89	3.23	43.7 - 34.6	1.32	1.32	1.26	1.7	0.330Y	32/4/39	90.5 - 71.5
-	-	0.22	0.67	-0.79	0.57	19.2 - 12.5	0.28	0.28	0.24	2.7	0.050Y	12/7/17	12.9 - 8.3
-	-	-	44.23	38.84	29.27	-					4.83540	11/24/17	
-	0.13	-	-1.32	-1.73	1.07		0.70	1.17	0.70	4.6			18.0 - 13.4
-	-	-0.50	-1.81	-1.82	1.21		0.50	2.11	2.76	4.9	0.030	2/15/18	18.3 - 6.4
-	-	-0.72	-3.55	-54.00	3.00		3.17			12.8	0.60	2/14/18	28.1 - 20.1
-	-	-	1.49	0.89	0.79	25.4 - 22.4	0.64	0.62	0.62	1.8	-		37.9 - 33.4
-	-	0.25	1.06	1.35	2.66	17.7 - 13.3	1.06	1.35	2.66	6.9	0.10710	2/14/18	18.8 - 14.1
-	-	0.09	0.22	0.35	-0.32	134.6 - 104.0	2.40	2.23	2.08	9.3	0.62750	2/12/18	29.6 - 22.9
-	-	0.21	0.95	4.42	1.04	120.0 - 88.8	3.61	3.35	0.82	3.6	1.050Y	32/4/39	114.0 - 84.4
-	-	1.32	3.56	2.82	2.79	17.2 - 14.7					-		61.2 - 52.5
-	-	0.04	0.32	0.14	0.25	74.5 - 45.6	-	0.12	0.12		0.030Y	12/18/15	23.9 - 14.6
-	0.46	-	0.53	-	-	63.5 - 51.9	0.20			0.6	0.10Y	32/4/39	33.7 - 27.5
-	0.33	-	1.87	1.80	1.99	16.1 - 12.6	0.74	0.63	0.60	2.8	0.20Y	12/15/17	30.1 - 23.5
-	-	0.29	1.03	0.21	0.78	27.4 - 18.8	0.16	0.16	0.16	0.7	0.040Y	2/2/18	28.3 - 19.4
-	-	0.21	0.45	0.42	0.14	65.9 - 51.0	0.90	0.69	0.55	3.5	0.30Z	32/4/39	29.6 - 22.9
-	-	-0.81	0.06	0.85	2.59	1050.0 - 670.0	0.27	0.27	0.24	0.5	0.1350Y	9/15/17	63.0 - 40.2
-	-	1.41	4.70	4.28	4.29	21.6 - 17.4	2.15	2.10	2.03	2.3	0.33590Y	32/4/39	101.4 - 81.6
-	0.32	-	1.36	1.21	1.41	27.2 - 20.2	0.66	0.62	0.18	2.1	0.090	1/16/18	37.0 - 27.4
-	-	2.71	8.23	7.84	9.02	21.9 - 16.7	4.00	3.51	2.81	2.5	1.080Y	32/4/39	180.3 - 137.4
-	-	-	1.69	0.46	-	8.4 - 8.1					-		14.2 - 13.7
-	-	1.43	4.15	3.05	2.31	29.9 - 20.1	0.52	0.52	0.52	0.5	0.150Y	32/4/39	124.2 - 83.4
-	-	-	-0.13	0.24	-0.25		0.94	0.58	-	10.6	0.040	1/31/18	10.0 - 7.8
-	-	-	-0.29	-8.83	-5.60		1.08	0.27	-	8.6	0.09030	1/31/18	15.0 - 10.2
-	-	-	-0.01	0.58	0.53		1.64	1.64	1.64	9.0	0.13670	1/31/18	20.3 - 16.5
-	-	0.13	2.31	1.96	1.55	15.7 - 10.8					0.39840Z	6/15/18	36.2 - 25.1
-	-	0.26	0.28	1.95	2.00	135.0 - 60.9	2.00	2.00	5.00	8.4	0.50Y	11/17/17	37.8 - 17.1
-	-	-0.28	-0.26	0.85	1.04		0.71	1.25	1.41	17.1	0.020	5/15/17	6.9 - 2.6
-	-	0.47	0.10	1.97	2.43	165.5 - 67.5	-	3.12	2.93		0.940	11/17/17	16.6 - 6.8
-	-	1.26	4.90	4.63	3.96	17.1 - 13.6	1.70	1.40	1.10	2.2	0.50Y	32/4/39	83.9 - 66.8
-	-	0.13	0.13	0.35	-1.72	108.1 - 43.1	1.63	1.63	1.10	19.4	0.210	2/14/18	14.1 - 5.6
-	-	0.54	-0.04	-0.17	2.50		1.01	1.10	1.24	12.2	0.46880Z	1/15/18	8.9 - 7.5
-	-	0.46	4.36	0.99	1.84	7.6 - 4.0	0.24	0.23	0.20	1.0	0.060Y	32/4/39	33.0 - 17.6
-	-	0.81	3.65	4.74	3.63	25.9 - 21.6	0.57	0.54	0.40	0.7	0.140Y	32/4/39	94.6 - 78.8
-	-	0.08	-3.34	1.07	-0.04						0.4650	11/19/08	
-	-	-	0.16	0.05	0.08	379.2 - 114.4							60.7 - 18.3
-	0.67	-	2.90	5.47	2.15	33.6 - 24.7	2.10	2.20	2.20	2.5	0.630Y	32/4/39	97.5 - 71.5
-	-	0.05	0.62	0.48	0.39	29.5 - 18.8					-		18.3 - 11.7
-	-	-1.14	4.29	1.25	3.33	16.9 - 12.6							72.4 - 53.9
-	-	-0.41	1.64	0.91	2.84	25.3 - 18.2	3.12	3.12	3.00	8.8	0.780	2/14/18	41.6 - 29.8
-	-	0.28	1.03	1.05	0.58	59.6 - 42.9	1.18	1.13	0.28	2.2	0.360Z	32/4/39	61.4 - 44.2
-	-	-0.02	0.10	-0.27	0.25	154.7 - 74.1	0.76	0.69	0.62	7.2	0.190Z	32/4/39	15.5 - 7.4
-	-	0.02	1.31	-0.09	-0.22	16.7 - 6.9	0.36	0.28	0.28	2.3	0.090Y	32/4/39	21.9 - 9.1
-	1.54	-	3.70	4.66	-0.08	21.7 - 12.2							80.3 - 45.0
-	-	1.97	4.81	5.77	8.63	33.0 - 21.6	2.40	2.40	2.22	2.0	0.60Y	32/4/39	158.8 - 104.1
-	-	-	0.42	0.57	0.59	29.0 - 24.3	0.83	0.90	0.90	7.3	0.05250	1/26/18	12.2 - 10.2
-	-	-	0.38	0.44	0.44	28.8 - 26.3	0.59	0.63	0.63	5.6	0.040	1/26/18	11.0 - 10.0
-	-	0.50	2.07	2.52	2.85	17.4 - 13.2	2.48	2.16	1.80	7.9	0.7250	2/12/18	36.0 - 27.3
-	-	1.29	-2.49	0.32	3.35	-	0.60	0.60	1.00	2.3	0.150Y	32/4/39	35.1 - 20.9
-	-	-	-2.72	-3.02	-								84.8 - 54.6
-	-	1.09	-	-	-								84.8 - 54.6
-	-	-	1.78	-	-						0.17G	2/14/18	
-	-	1.64	5.79	5.63	0.78	9.7 - 7.6	0.68	0.45	0.30	1.4	0.3050Y	32/4/39	56.4 - 44.0
-	-	0.20	0.76	0.21	1.55	125.0 - 87.3	0.40	0.40	0.40	0.5	0.10Y	12/18/17	95.0 - 66.4
-	-	0.59	4.65	4.36	3.96	16.5 - 14.4	1.20	1.20	1.15	1.7	0.30Y	32/4/39	76.8 - 67.0
-	-	0.00	-2.61	-12.57	1.81		-	0.19	0.25		0.06250	32/4/39	3.9 - 1.0
-	-	-	0.30	-1.49	-								
-	0.07	-	-1.21	-5.06	1.31								
-	-	-	0.83	0.96	1.08	18.3 - 17.3	0.77	1.02	1.05	5.2	0.0660	1/31/18	15.2 - 14.4
-	-	-	0.49	0.54	0.64	18.3 - 17.4	0.51	0.60	0.68	5.8	0.0350	1/31/18	9.0 - 8.5
-	-	-	0.75	0.82	0.83	18.3 - 15.7	0.84	0.86	0.85	6.5	0.0525M	1/31/18	13.7 - 11.8
-	-	-	0.62	0.69	0.83	20.2 - 0.0	0.65	0.95	0.96	5.3	0.0440	1/31/18	12.5 - 0.0
-	-	-	0.80	0.83	0.87	16.2 - 14.6	0.79	0.91	0.93	6.4	0.050	1/31/18	13.0 - 11.7
-	-	0.43	-6.52	-35.55	3.91		0.42	0.96	0.94	1.1	0.060Y	32/4/39	49.0 - 29.5
-	-	0.02	-0.11	-0.21	0.51								6.5 - 1.6
-	0.04	-	0.10	1.04	0.18						0.020	12/6/17	
-	-	-	0.89	0.95	0.89	164.1 - 117.2	2.29	2.09	2.00	1.8			146.0 - 104.3
-	-	0.08	-2.72	-2.00	2.81		-	0.50	3.50		0.1250Y	32/4/39	19.5 - 10.2
-	-	0.11	0.57	0.43	0.83	21.0 - 18.5	0.50	0.50	0.41	4.5	0.1250Z	1/12/18	11.9 - 10.6
-	-	-0.04	-2.11	-0.89	-0.19						0.55470	1/16/18	
-	-	0.35	2.83	2.84	2.69	19.6 - 8.6	0.55	0.50	0.50	1.4	0.170Y	32/4/39	55.3 - 24.4
-	-	-0.47	-0.48	1.12	1.76		0.96	1.15	1.15	4.0	0.10Y	32/4/39	31.6 - 16.1
-	-	-0.02	2.20	1.56	0.99	57.3 - 45.2	3.52	3.40	3.32	3.1	0.4923GHZ	32/4/39	126.0 - 99.4
-	-	0.50	6.91	7.79	7.10	11.4 - 6.8	0.26	0.24	0.22	0.5	0.10Y	32/4/39	78.9 - 46.9
-	-	-24.98	5.33	5.52	1.90	14.4 - 7.0	3.73	3.54	3.13	7.4	0.970Y	1/12/18	77.0 - 37.3
-	-	0.01	0.42	0.41	0.11	51.9 - 29.8							21.8 - 12.5
-	-	1.59	5.77	5.13	4.90	13.4 - 10.0	1.16	1.08	0.92	1.8	0.350Y	32/4/39	77.5 - 57.7
-	-	1.51	5.73	4.90	4.26	20.2 - 16.9	1.42	1.81	0.86	1.3	0.840Y	32/4/39	115.8 - 96.9

SYMBOL	COMPANY	NATURE OF BUSINESS	FISCAL YEAR-END	TOTAL REV. $MILL	NET INCOME $MILL	TOTAL ASSETS $MILL	NET STK EQUITY $MILL	NO OF INST	INST. HOLDINGS (SHARES)
DNI	Dividend & Income Fund	Holding and other Investment Office	12/31/16	4.9	2.6	179.1	151.0	46	3831533
DNP	DNP Select Income Fund Inc	Holding and other Investment Office	10/31/17	119.3	62.2	3890.0	2870.5	237	15480708
DLB	Dolby Laboratories Inc	Manufacturing	9/29/17	1081.5	201.8	2533.6	2136.7	390	61734996
DG	Dollar General Corp	Retail - General Merchandise/Depart	2/3/17	21986.6	1251.1	11672.3	5406.3	823	292289769
D	Dominion Energy Inc (New)	Electric Utilities	12/31/16	11737.0	2123.0	71610.0	14605.0	1448	512343445
DM	Dominion Energy Midstream Partne	Gas Utilities	12/31/16	441.3	347.5	7186.9		120	41594873
DPZ	Dominos Pizza Inc.	Hotels, Restaurants & Travel	1/1/17	2472.6	214.7	716.3	-1883.1	521	54785646
UFS	Domtar Corp	Paper & Forest Products	12/31/16	5098.0	128.0	5680.0	2676.0	-	0
DCI	Donaldson Co. Inc.	Industrial Machinery & Equipment	7/31/17	2371.9	232.8	1979.7	850.1	476	129041265
RRD	Donnelley (RR) & Sons Company	Printing	12/31/16	6895.7	-495.9	4284.7	-105.7	419	105512450
DFIN	Donnelley Financial Solutions Inc	Business Services	12/31/16	983.5	59.1	978.9	111.1	206	31337752
LPG	Dorian LPG Ltd.	Shipping	3/31/17	167.4	-1.4	1746.2	976.0	106	29035169
DSL	DoubleLine Income Solutions Fund	Holding and other Investment Office	9/30/17	228.8	177.8	3148.9	2214.0	157	26828841
DBL	Doubleline Opportunistic Credit Fun	Holding and other Investment Office	9/30/17	30.3	24.3	417.3	327.9	77	3869377
PLOW	Douglas Dynamics, Inc.	Industrial Machinery & Equipment	12/31/16	416.3	39.0	671.9	220.5	158	22502556
DEI	Douglas Emmett Inc	REITs	12/31/16	742.6	85.4	7613.7	1921.1	340	212095066
DOV	Dover Corp	Industrial Machinery & Equipment	12/31/16	6794.3	508.9	10116.0	3799.7	914	166456570
DDE	Dover Downs Gaming & Entertainm	Hotels, Restaurants & Travel	12/31/16	182.3	0.8	170.3	115.7	50	7750385
DVD	Dover Motorsports, Inc.	Sporting & Recreational	12/31/16	45.9	3.8	81.3	53.8	56	10490178
DWDP	DowDuPont Inc	Plastics	12/31/15	73836.0	8926.0			1580	1606466080
DPS	Dr Pepper Snapple Group Inc	Beverages	12/31/16	6440.0	847.0	9791.0	2134.0	829	202809618
RDY	Dr. Reddy's Laboratories Ltd.	Pharmaceuticals	3/31/16	154708.0	20013.0	207650.0	128336.0	191	28110782
DRD	DRDGold Ltd	Precious Metals	6/30/17	2339.9	13.7	2287.4	1302.4	57	8426644
DHF	Dreyfus High Yield Strategies Fund	Holding and other Investment Office	3/31/17	26.1	20.8	382.5	258.7	70	8873766
DMB	Dreyfus Municipal Bond Infrastructu	Holding and other Investment Office	2/28/17	17.3	12.5	370.1	326.5	35	3162453
DSM	Dreyfus Strategic Municipal Bond F	Holding and other Investment Office	11/30/16	29.2	24.4	589.7	495.5	76	4672379
LEO	Dreyfus Strategic Municipals Inc	Holding and other Investment Office	9/30/17	39.2	31.9	828.4	678.5	79	4652306
DRQ	Dril-Quip Inc	Equipment & Services	12/31/16	538.7	93.2	1461.4	1356.4	350	52062529
DS	Drive Shack Inc	Sporting & Recreational	12/31/16	298.9	77.1	1172.0	218.1	173	54099054
DST	DST Systems Inc (DE)	IT Services	12/31/16	1556.7	427.3	2771.8	1115.2	481	59318884
DSW	DSW Inc	Retail - Apparel and Accessories	1/28/17	2711.4	124.5	1428.5	937.5	322	82324555
DTE	DTE Energy Co	Electric Utilities	12/31/16	10630.0	868.0	32041.0	9011.0	808	152589494
DTF	DTF Tax-Free Income, Inc.	Holding and other Investment Office	10/31/17	7.6	4.6	199.1	133.7	35	883733
DCO	Ducommun Inc.	Aerospace	12/31/16	550.6	25.3	515.4	212.1	146	11362754
DPG	Duff & Phelps Global Utility Income	Holding and other Investment Office	10/31/17	32.3	15.4	933.2	662.7	64	6191110
DSE	Duff & Phelps Select Energy MLP F	Holding and other Investment Office	11/30/16	1.6	-2.7	274.9	192.9	-	0
DUC	Duff & Phelps Utility & Corporate Bo	Holding and other Investment Office	10/31/17	15.0	9.3	393.3	268.0	54	10718393
DUK	Duke Energy Corp	Electric Utilities	12/31/16	22743.0	2152.0	132761.0	41033.0	1656	534500781
DRE	Duke Realty Corp	REITs	12/31/16	902.2	312.1	6772.0	3465.8	573	402761999
DNB	Dun & Bradstreet Corp (DE)	Business Services	12/31/16	1703.7	97.4	2209.2	-1002.0	500	44564767
DXC	DXC Technology Co	IT Services	10/31/16	18112.0	-673.0	11208.0	992.0	757	241761612
DXC	DXC Technology Co	IT Services	10/31/16	18112.0	-673.0	11208.0	992.0	757	241761612
DY	Dycom Industries, Inc.	Construction Services	7/29/17	3066.9	157.2	1899.3	671.6	443	43892459
DLNG	Dynagas LNG Partners LP	Equipment & Services	12/31/16	169.9	66.9	1106.7		48	6465797
DYN	Dynegy Inc (New) (DE)	Electric Utilities	12/31/16	4318.0	-1240.0	13053.0	2042.0	281	190439882
DX	Dynex Capital, Inc.	REITs	12/31/16	91.9	43.1	3397.7	467.2	162	30630950
ELF	e.l.f. Beauty Inc	Household & Personal Products	12/31/16	229.6	5.3	414.7	140.9	127	42799014
EGIF	Eagle Growth & Income Opportuniti	Holding and other Investment Office	12/31/16	8.5	4.9	181.7	136.2	13	1646778
EXP	Eagle Materials inc	Construction Materials	3/31/17	1211.2	198.2	2247.1	1203.5	459	54584832
ECC	Eagle Point Credit Company Inc	Holding and other Investment Office	12/31/16	55.8	31.4	448.4	288.0	26	10618414
ESTE	Earthstone Energy Inc	Production & Extraction	12/31/16	42.3	-54.5	316.5	241.5	71	8707748
DEA	Easterly Government Properties Inc	REITs	12/31/16	104.6	3.4	1045.5	559.3	166	42193401
EGP	EastGroup Properties Inc	REITs	12/31/16	253.0	95.5	1825.8	637.7	308	42244840
EMN	Eastman Chemical Co	Plastics	12/31/16	9008.0	854.0	15457.0	4532.0	866	143159607
KODK	Eastman Kodak Co.	Leisure Equipment	12/31/16	1543.0	15.0	1776.0	83.0	198	53210549
ETN	Eaton Corp plc	Electrical Equipment	12/31/16	19747.0	1922.0	30419.0	14897.0	1087	375776975
EV	Eaton Vance Corp	Wealth Management	10/31/17	1529.0	282.1	2330.9	1011.4	517	108432640
EOI	Eaton Vance Enhanced Equity Inco	Holding and other Investment Office	9/30/17	10.5	4.4	570.4	566.8	70	4851197
EOS	Eaton Vance Enhanced Equity Inco	Holding and other Investment Office	12/31/16	8.4	1.2	654.0	651.1	88	7168544
EFF	Eaton Vance Floating Rate Income	Finance Intermediaries & Services	5/31/17	10.7	7.2	216.2	136.4	28	2029989
EFT	Eaton Vance Floating Rate Income	Holding and other Investment Office	5/31/17	49.5	34.5	979.7	620.8	98	14304271
EHT	Eaton Vance High Income 2021 Tar	Holding and other Investment Office	3/31/17	13.0	10.2	296.1	220.7	19	2756576
ETX	Eaton Vance Municipal Income 202	Holding and other Investment Office	1/31/17	13.4	9.4	349.1	216.4	37	2256332
EVN	Eaton Vance Municipal Income Trus	Holding and other Investment Office	11/30/16	25.2	18.2	533.9	321.9	54	2470614
EOT	Eaton Vance National Municipal Op	Holding and other Investment Office	3/31/17	18.6	15.5	378.2	330.2	46	1990169
ETJ	Eaton Vance Risk-Managed Diversif	Holding and other Investment Office	12/31/16	14.1	6.9	638.0	635.6	114	18659018
EFR	Eaton Vance Senior Floating Rate T	Holding and other Investment Office	10/31/17	44.7	33.1	879.8	656.3	94	8136749
EVF	Eaton Vance Senior Income Trust	Holding and other Investment Office	6/30/17	21.7	15.3	432.6	332.4	69	17214481
EVG	Eaton Vance Short Duration Diversif	Holding and other Investment Office	10/31/17	18.6	12.5	361.9	273.8	66	10289137
EVT	Eaton Vance Tax Advantaged Divid	Holding and other Investment Office	8/31/17	86.0	60.0	2073.8	1617.6	122	13285711
ETW	Eaton Vance Tax Managed Global	Holding and other Investment Office	12/31/16	30.2	17.4	1156.6	1139.6	138	23032100
ETG	Eaton Vance Tax-Advantage Global	Holding and other Investment Office	10/31/17	119.3	96.1	1859.9	1390.6	101	14836353
EXD	Eaton Vance Tax-Advantaged Bond	Holding and other Investment Office	12/31/16	2.7	0.8	125.5	124.2	30	2162090
ETO	Eaton Vance Tax-Advantaged Glob	Holding and other Investment Office	10/31/17	13.6	7.1	480.1	357.8	50	2079770
ETB	Eaton Vance Tax-Managed Buy-Wri	Holding and other Investment Office	12/31/16	8.9	4.7	385.6	382.9	63	4350998
ETV	Eaton Vance Tax-Managed Buy-Wri	Holding and other Investment Office	12/31/16	17.3	7.6	907.2	899.0	131	11312575
ETY	Eaton Vance Tax-Managed Diversifi	Holding and other Investment Office	10/31/17	33.8	15.0	1797.5	1787.8	146	34475500
EXG	Eaton Vance Tax-Managed Global	Holding and other Investment Office	10/31/17	55.6	25.8	2901.2	2833.8	185	49452096
ECT	ECA Marcellus Trust I	Oil Royalty Traders	12/31/16	4.7	3.5	57.1	55.8	33	624226
ECR	Eclipse Resources Corp	Production & Extraction	12/31/16	235.0	-203.8	1197.9	546.7	131	251328398

1st	2nd	3rd	2016	2015	2014	P/E Ratio	Div 2016	Div 2015	Div 2014	Av Yld %	Amount	Payable	Price Range 2016
-	-	-	0.25	0.31	0.34	55.3 - 47.4	1.00	1.63	1.63	8.0	0.150	12/28/17	13.8 - 11.9
-	-	-	0.27	0.29	0.35	42.7 - 38.2	0.78	0.78	0.78	7.1	0.0650	4/10/18	11.5 - 10.3
-	-	0.73	1.81	1.75	1.99	34.9 - 25.4	0.48	0.40	-	0.9	0.160Y	32/4/39	63.3 - 46.1
-	-	0.93	3.95	3.49	3.17	23.6 - 17.3	0.88	-	-	1.1	0.260Y	32/4/39	93.4 - 68.3
-	-	1.03	3.44	3.20	2.24	24.7 - 20.8	2.80	2.59	2.40	3.6	0.8350Y	32/4/39	84.9 - 71.7
-	-	0.33	1.30	1.08	0.15	26.5 - 19.7	0.92	0.70	-	3.0	0.3180	2/15/18	34.5 - 25.6
-	-	1.18	4.30	3.47	2.86	50.9 - 36.8	1.52	1.24	1.00	0.8	0.460Y	32/4/39	218.9 - 158.4
-	-	1.11	2.04	2.24	6.64	31.3 - 17.6	1.65	1.60	1.40	3.5	0.4150	32/4/39	63.9 - 35.8
0.46	-	-	1.42	1.49	1.76	35.1 - 29.1	0.69	0.67	0.57	1.5	0.180Y	32/4/39	49.9 - 41.3
-	-	-0.11	-7.09	2.19	1.77	-	0.14	3.12	3.12	1.2	0.140Y	3/1/18	18.3 - 7.3
-	-	0.16	1.80	-	-	14.7 - 10.3	-	-	-	-	-	-	26.4 - 18.4
-	-0.22	-	2.29	0.45	0.09	-	-	-	-	-	0.150	1/31/18	21.5 - 19.0
-	-	-	1.71	1.85	1.78	12.6 - 11.1	1.89	1.90	1.80	9.2	0.1670	1/31/18	26.0 - 22.1
-	-	-	1.81	2.21	1.83	14.4 - 12.2	2.53	2.49	2.00	10.6	0.240Y	12/29/17	42.5 - 28.6
-	-	0.40	1.70	1.94	1.77	25.0 - 16.9	0.94	0.89	0.87	2.7	0.250Z	32/4/39	41.4 - 36.5
-	-	0.15	0.55	0.39	0.30	75.3 - 66.3	0.89	0.85	0.81	2.3	0.470Y	32/4/39	101.4 - 76.3
-	-	1.14	3.25	5.46	4.59	31.2 - 23.5	1.72	1.64	1.55	2.0	0.020Y	12/10/12	1.2 - 0.9
-	-	-	0.02	0.06	-0.02	58.5 - 46.1	-	-	-	-	0.080Y	12/10/17	2.5 - 0.0
-	-	-0.06	0.10	0.14	0.09	24.5 - 0.0	0.05	0.05	0.05	2.4	0.38GY	12/15/17	73.3 - 64.7
-	-	0.32	-	3.76	-	-	-	-	-	-	-	-	-
-	-	1.11	4.54	3.97	3.56	21.8 - 18.6	2.12	1.92	1.64	2.3	0.580Y	32/4/39	98.9 - 84.5
-	-	-	116.98	129.75	126.04	0.4 - 0.3	18.62	16.62	13.48	47.8	-	-	46.7 - 30.1
-0.03	-	-	0.15	0.17	-0.12	43.6 - 19.1	4.87	0.16	1.13	120.8	-	-	6.5 - 2.9
-	-	-	0.30	0.32	0.36	12.0 - 10.8	0.35	0.36	0.40	10.1	0.02350	2/22/18	3.6 - 3.3
-	-	-	0.71	0.73	0.60	19.1 - 17.2	0.75	0.75	0.50	5.8	0.053M	2/1/18	13.5 - 12.2
-	-	-	0.50	0.52	0.52	17.7 - 16.1	0.50	0.50	0.57	5.9	0.0415M	1/31/18	8.8 - 8.1
-	-	-	0.53	0.55	0.55	17.3 - 15.9	0.52	0.53	0.59	5.9	0.035M	2/28/18	9.2 - 8.4
-	-	-0.78	2.47	4.98	5.19	27.2 - 14.7	-	-	-	-	-	-	67.1 - 36.2
-	-	-0.03	1.07	0.24	0.44	5.8 - 2.3	0.48	0.48	1.92	12.5	0.52340Z	1/31/18	6.3 - 2.5
-	-	0.79	6.41	4.92	7.33	9.8 - 7.9	0.66	0.60	0.60	1.1	0.180Y	32/4/39	62.6 - 50.6
-	-	0.05	1.54	1.69	1.65	14.6 - 10.2	0.80	0.75	0.38	4.1	0.20Y	12/29/17	22.5 - 15.7
-	-	1.51	4.83	4.05	5.10	24.0 - 20.1	3.06	2.84	2.69	2.9	0.88250Y	32/4/39	116.0 - 97.1
-	-	-	0.57	0.69	0.73	28.0 - 24.4	0.88	0.84	0.85	6.0	0.05M	3/29/18	16.0 - 13.9
-	-	0.41	2.24	-6.63	1.79	15.6 - 10.9	-	-	-	-	0.0750Y	3/4/11	35.0 - 24.4
-	-	-	0.67	0.70	0.92	25.8 - 22.7	1.40	1.40	1.40	8.6	0.350	3/29/18	17.3 - 15.2
-	-	-	-0.10	-0.15	-0.09	-	0.88	1.58	0.32	12.7	0.220	11/20/17	8.4 - 5.1
-	-	-	0.38	0.41	0.35	24.9 - 23.1	0.60	0.60	0.82	6.5	0.0350	3/29/18	9.5 - 8.8
-	-	1.36	3.11	4.05	2.66	29.3 - 24.6	3.36	3.24	3.15	4.0	0.890Y	32/4/39	91.1 - 76.5
-	-	0.46	0.88	1.77	0.60	34.3 - 27.3	0.73	0.89	0.68	2.6	0.857Z	32/4/39	30.1 - 24.0
-	-	1.45	2.65	4.64	7.99	47.3 - 38.0	1.93	1.85	1.76	1.7	0.50250Y	32/4/39	125.4 - 100.8
-	0.88	-	-	-	-	-	-	-	-	-	0.180Y	1/16/18	99.0 - 68.0
-	0.88	-	-	-	-	-	-	-	-	-	0.180Y	1/16/18	72.5 - 64.9
0.90	-	-	3.89	2.41	1.15	29.4 - 19.6	-	-	-	-	0.0228G	32/4/39	114.4 - 76.0
-	-	-	1.69	1.60	1.58	-	-	-	-	-	0.56250	2/12/18	-
-	-	-0.89	-9.78	0.22	-2.65	-	-	-	-	-	1.34380Y	11/1/17	12.5 - 5.9
-	-	0.15	0.69	0.14	0.34	10.7 - 9.6	0.84	0.96	1.00	12.0	0.47660Z	1/15/18	7.4 - 6.6
-	-	-	0.12	-39.47	1560.00	-709.00	-	-	-	-	-	-	29.6 - 18.9
-	-	-	0.69	0.35	-	25.2 - 23.1	1.13	0.55	-	6.7	0.0730	1/31/18	17.4 - 15.9
-	1.31	-	3.05	3.71	2.49	38.1 - 28.6	0.40	0.40	0.40	0.4	0.10Y	32/4/39	116.2 - 87.2
-	-	-	2.14	1.89	0.32	10.3 - 7.8	2.40	2.40	0.55	12.2	0.16150Y	3/29/18	22.0 - 16.8
-	-	0.07	-2.92	-8.43	-3.11	-	-	-	-	-	-	-	15.0 - 8.0
-	-	0.02	0.10	-0.08	-	220.9 - 192.5	0.92	0.54	-	4.5	0.260Y	12/21/17	22.1 - 19.3
-	-	0.46	2.93	1.49	1.52	32.4 - 23.6	2.44	2.34	2.22	2.9	0.640Z	12/29/17	95.0 - 69.1
-	-	2.22	5.75	5.66	4.97	16.2 - 13.2	1.89	1.66	1.45	2.3	0.560Y	32/4/39	93.4 - 75.9
-	-	-1.20	0.28	-1.91	-2.95	58.2 - 11.1	-	-	-	-	0.250Y	12/12/08	16.3 - 3.1
-	-	3.14	4.21	4.23	3.76	-	2.28	2.20	1.96	-	0.60	32/4/39	-
-	-	0.58	2.12	1.92	2.44	26.9 - 19.7	1.08	1.01	0.91	2.3	0.310Y	32/4/39	57.1 - 41.8
-	-	-	0.14	0.23	0.08	105.1 - 88.6	1.04	1.04	1.04	7.7	0.08640	1/31/18	14.7 - 12.4
-	-	-	0.03	0.13	-	512.7 - 429.3	1.05	1.05	1.05	7.3	0.08750	1/31/18	15.4 - 12.9
-	-	-	1.06	1.11	0.99	16.5 - 15.2	1.11	1.42	0.97	6.6	0.0720	1/31/18	17.4 - 16.1
-	-	-	0.91	0.88	0.89	16.9 - 15.4	0.90	0.89	0.97	6.0	0.0670	1/10/18	15.4 - 14.1
-	-	-	-	-	-	-	-	-	-	-	0.050	1/10/18	10.2 - 9.9
-	-	-	0.94	0.92	0.72	22.4 - 20.0	0.85	0.85	0.57	4.2	0.0709M	1/31/18	21.0 - 18.8
-	-	-	0.77	0.89	0.89	17.1 - 15.9	0.77	0.89	0.90	6.0	0.0541M	1/19/18	13.1 - 12.2
-	-	-	1.06	1.09	1.10	22.2 - 19.6	1.03	1.03	1.03	4.7	0.0859M	1/31/18	23.5 - 20.8
-	-	-	0.11	0.20	0.07	88.1 - 82.1	1.12	1.12	1.12	12.0	0.0760	1/31/18	9.7 - 9.0
-	-	-	0.96	0.94	0.93	16.2 - 14.6	0.94	0.94	0.99	6.3	0.070	1/10/18	15.6 - 14.0
-	-	-	0.42	0.40	0.41	16.6 - 15.1	0.41	0.40	0.44	6.1	0.030	1/10/18	7.0 - 6.3
-	-	-	0.72	0.78	0.80	20.1 - 19.0	1.08	1.08	1.08	7.7	0.07650	1/31/18	14.5 - 13.7
-	-	-	0.74	0.81	1.43	31.5 - 27.9	1.74	1.45	1.32	7.9	0.1450	1/31/18	23.3 - 20.7
-	-	-	0.16	0.18	0.23	75.2 - 63.7	1.17	1.17	1.17	10.3	0.0910	1/31/18	12.0 - 10.2
-	-	-	1.27	1.16	1.30	13.9 - 11.4	1.23	1.23	1.23	7.4	0.10250	1/31/18	17.6 - 14.4
-	-	-	0.09	0.09	0.09	132.3 - 113.9	1.16	1.16	1.40	10.2	0.290	12/29/17	11.9 - 10.3
-	-	-	0.82	1.00	1.55	31.8 - 25.5	2.16	3.13	2.35	9.1	0.180	1/31/18	26.1 - 20.9
-	-	-	0.19	0.20	0.17	90.5 - 84.7	1.30	1.30	1.30	7.8	0.1080	1/31/18	17.2 - 16.1
-	-	-	0.12	0.11	0.11	130.2 - 124.7	1.33	1.33	1.33	8.7	0.11080	1/31/18	15.6 - 15.0
-	-	-	0.12	0.21	0.32	102.3 - 85.8	1.01	1.01	1.01	8.9	0.08430	1/31/18	12.3 - 10.3
-	-	-	0.20	0.13	0.43	47.5 - 40.1	0.98	0.98	0.98	10.9	0.0760	1/31/18	9.5 - 8.0
-	-	0.07	0.20	0.28	1.00	14.0 - 10.0	0.19	0.40	1.18	8.5	0.0730	11/30/17	2.8 - 2.0
-	-	-0.06	-0.84	-4.46	-1.27	-	-	-	-	-	-	-	3.1 - 1.8

SYMBOL	COMPANY	NATURE OF BUSINESS	FISCAL YEAR-END	TOTAL REV. $MILL	NET INCOME $MILL	TOTAL ASSETS $MILL	NET STK EQUITY $MILL	NO OF INST	INST. HOLDINGS (SHARES)
ECL	Ecolab Inc	Specialty Chemicals	12/31/16	13152.8	1229.6	18330.2	6901.1	1202	272848490
EC	Ecopetrol SA	Refining & Marketing	12/31/16	18485561.0	2447881.0	20437924.0	42026858.0	149	53256039
EPC	Edgewell Personal Care Co	Household & Personal Products	9/30/17	2298.4	5.7	4188.8	1741.7	507	67467472
EIX	Edison International	Electric Utilities	12/31/16	11869.0	1311.0	51319.0	11996.0	859	308524966
EDR	Education Realty Trust Inc	REITs	12/31/16	289.0	44.9	2506.2	1800.0	315	112689604
EW	Edwards Lifesciences Corp	Medical Instruments & Equipment	12/31/16	2963.7	569.5	4510.0	2619.0	979	199133711
EHIC	eHi Car Services Ltd	Miscellaneous Consumer Services	12/31/16	2108.9	33.1	8161.0	3991.1	38	19760421
EE	El Paso Electric Company	Electric Utilities	12/31/16	886.9	96.8	3376.3	1074.4	274	50682659
EGO	Eldorado Gold Corp	Precious Metals	12/31/16	432.7	-344.2	4797.9	3482.7	260	445036308
ELVT	Elevate Credit Inc	Finance Intermediaries & Services	12/31/16	580.4	-22.4	570.2	13.6	56	21936107
ELLI	Ellie Mae Inc	Internet & Software	12/31/16	360.3	37.8	751.5	654.9	269	40411724
EFC	Ellington Financial LLC	Property, Real Estate & Developmen	12/31/16	80.2	35.8	2413.2	637.7	-	0
EARN	Ellington Residential Mortgaging Re	REITs	12/31/16	26.2	11.9	1429.1	141.7	78	9138984
AKO B	Embotelladora Andina S.A.	Beverages	12/31/16	1777459.3	90526.0	2199109.7	820605.6	26	912540
ERJ	Embraer SA	Aerospace	12/31/16	6217.5	166.1	11664.6	3848.8	250	118743988
EME	EMCOR Group, Inc.	Construction Services	12/31/16	7551.5	181.9	3894.2	1537.1	429	75399716
EEX	Emerald Expositions Events Inc	Services	12/31/16	323.7	22.2	1572.5	527.8	77	19230798
EMES	Emerge Energy Services LP	Equipment & Services	12/31/16	128.4	-72.8	249.9	6.9	67	14476135
EBS	Emergent BioSolutions Inc	Biotechnology	12/31/16	488.8	51.8	970.1	- 596.2	260	46242441
EMR	Emerson Electric Co.	Electrical Equipment	9/30/17	15264.0	1518.0	19589.0	8718.0	1831	574021938
ESRT	Empire State Realty Trust Inc	REITs	12/31/16	678.0	52.4	3891.0	1154.1	226	158346683
EIG	Employers Holdings Inc	General Insurance	12/31/16	779.8	106.7	3773.4	840.6	206	33186588
EDN	Empresa Distribuidora y Comerciali	Electric Utilities	12/31/16	13079.6	-1188.6	18933.5	361.8	47	4345091
ENBL	Enable Midstream Partners L.P.	Equipment & Services	12/31/16	2272.0	312.0	11212.0		107	79343928
EEQ	Enbridge Energy Management LLC	Equipment & Services	12/31/16	-121.9	-120.1	0.8	0.8	213	72810883
EEP	Enbridge Energy Partners, L.P.	Equipment & Services	12/31/16	4481.9	-67.7	18110.1	-	404	163255019
ENB	Enbridge Inc	Equipment & Services	12/31/16	34560.0	2069.0	85832.0	21386.0	964	1084394758
ECA	EnCana Corp	Production & Extraction	12/31/16	2918.0	-944.0	14653.0	6126.0	543	740372380
EHC	Encompass Health Corp	Hospitals & Health Care Facilities	12/31/16	3646.0	247.6	4681.9	735.9	455	122139770
EXK	Endeavour Silver Corp	Precious Metals	12/31/16	156.8	3.9	180.5	133.3	104	29950376
NDRO	Enduro Royalty Trust	Oil Royalty Traders	12/31/16	9.2	8.5	107.3	107.3	35	38902801
ENIA	Enel Americas SA	Electric Utilities	12/31/16	-	-	11261555.5	4150468.9	189	108820242
ENIC	Enel Chile SA	Electric Utilities	12/31/16	2136040.7	317561.1	5398711.0	2763391.3	122	65368988
EOCC	Enel Generacion Chile SA	Electric Utilities	12/31/16	1659727.3	472558.4	3399682.5	1700962.5	113	9225537
EGN	Energen Corp.	Production & Extraction	12/31/16	532.9	-167.5	4579.8	3120.6	454	112683272
ENR	Energizer Holdings Inc (New)	Household & Personal Products	9/30/17	1755.7	201.5	1823.6	85.1	376	65578840
TXU 19	Energy Future Holdings Corp	Electric Utilities	12/31/15	5370.0	-5342.0	23330.0	-25061.0	67	17905838
ETE	Energy Transfer Equity LP	Equipment & Services	12/31/16	37504.0	995.0	79011.0	33.0	490	581680832
ETP	Energy Transfer Partners LP (New)	Equipment & Services	12/31/16	9151.0	705.0	18849.0	300.0	92	13673686
ERF	Enerplus Corp	Production & Extraction	12/31/16	693.3	397.4	2638.8	1460.5	304	132606819
ENS	Enersys	Electrical Equipment	3/31/17	2367.1	160.2	2293.0	1103.5	376	51258152
EGL	Engility Holdings Inc (New)	Services	12/31/16	2076.4	-10.8	2198.6	691.6	181	37648889
E	ENI S.p.A.	Production & Extraction	12/31/16	56693.0	-1464.0	124545.0	53037.0	217	32471905
ENLC	EnLink Midstream LLC	Equipment & Services	12/31/16	4252.4	-460.0	10275.9	1880.9	161	62802653
ENLK	EnLink Midstream Partners LP	Refining & Marketing	12/31/16	4252.4	-565.2	9153.4	-	204	153926555
EBF	Ennis Inc	Printing	2/28/17	356.9	1.8	324.3	251.4	188	29010900
ENVA	Enova International Inc	Credit & Lending	12/31/16	745.6	34.6	977.9	241.7	183	37314107
NPO	EnPro Industries Inc	Industrial Machinery & Equipment	12/31/16	1187.7	-40.1	1546.4	358.5	250	25105530
ESV	Ensco plc	Equipment & Services	12/31/16	2776.4	890.2	14374.5	8250.6	570	395952183
ETM	Entercom Communications Corp	Radio & Television	12/31/16	460.2	38.1	1076.2	421.1	170	34761749
ETM	Entercom Communications Corp	Radio & Television	12/31/16	460.2	38.1	1076.2	421.1	170	34761749
EAI	Entergy Arkansas Inc	Electric Utilities	12/31/16	2086.6	167.2	9606.1	2284.7	-	0
ETR	Entergy Corp	Electric Utilities	12/31/16	10845.6	-564.5	45904.4	8285.0	825	179665287
ELC	Entergy Louisiana LLC (New)	Electric Utilities	12/31/16	4177.0	622.0	17701.3	5081.8	1	66887
EMP	Entergy Mississippi Inc	Electric Utilities	12/31/16	1094.6	109.2	3602.1	1115.2	-	0
EZT	Entergy Texas Inc	Electric Utilities	12/31/16	1615.6	107.5	4033.1	1069.0	-	0
EPD	Enterprise Products Partners L.P.	Equipment & Services	12/31/16	23022.3	2513.1	52194.0		1196	883190757
EVC	Entravision Communications Corp.	Radio & Television	12/31/16	258.5	20.4	517.9	183.5	178	67962476
ENV	Envestnet Inc	Internet & Software	12/31/16	578.2	-55.6	872.4	413.8	208	50314667
EVHC	Envision Healthcare Corp	Hospitals & Health Care Facilities	12/31/16	3696.0	-18.6	16708.9	6731.1		0
EVA	Enviva Partners LP	Paper & Forest Products	12/31/16	464.3	21.4	726.2		68	19385485
ENZ	Enzo Biochem, Inc.	Diagnostic & Health Related Service	7/31/17	107.8	-2.5	107.7	88.9	169	34716684
EOG	EOG Resources, Inc.	Production & Extraction	12/31/16	7650.6	-1096.7	29459.4	13981.6	1309	570081873
EPE	EP Energy Corp	Production & Extraction	12/31/16	767.0	-27.0	4761.0	606.0	118	180761323
EPAM	Epam Systems, Inc.	Internet & Software	12/31/16	1160.1	99.3	925.8	781.4	303	52294281
EPR	EPR Properties	REITs	12/31/16	493.2	225.0	4865.0	2185.9	474	86711665
EQT	EQT Corp	Production & Extraction	12/31/16	1608.3	-453.0	15472.9	5860.3	743	212908147
EQGP	EQT GP Holdings LP	Equipment & Services	12/31/16	735.6	234.2	3076.4		78	27482668
EQM	EQT Midstream Partners LP	Equipment & Services	12/31/16	735.6	538.0	3075.8		250	61629509
EFX	Equifax Inc	Business Services	12/31/16	3144.9	488.8	6664.0	2662.7	827	160813434
EQC	Equity Commonwealth	REITs	12/31/16	500.7	232.9	4526.1	3260.4	359	154095436
ELS	Equity Lifestyle Properties Inc	REITs	12/31/16	870.4	173.3	3479.0	1008.5	330	96826469
EQR	Equity Residential	REITs	12/31/16	2425.8	4292.2	20704.1	10229.1	752	450311108
EQS	Equus Total Return, Inc.	Holding and other Investment Office	12/31/16	0.7	-2.5	73.1	42.7	19	1399227
ERA	ERA Group Inc	Miscellaneous Transportation Servic	12/31/16	247.2	-8.0	955.2	468.4	125	20247078
EROS	Eros International Plc	Entertainment	3/31/17	253.0	3.8	1343.4	804.5	93	32681115
ESE	ESCO Technologies, Inc.	Industrial Machinery & Equipment	9/30/17	685.7	53.7	1260.4	671.9	226	31345375
ESNT	Essent Group Ltd	General Insurance	12/31/16	458.3	222.6	1883.0	1343.8	289	94674874
ESS	Essex Property Trust Inc	REITs	12/31/16	1294.0	415.0	12217.4	6192.2	581	78603374
ESL	Esterline Technologies Corp	Electronic Instruments & Related Pro	9/29/17	2002.2	117.4	3130.3	1836.6	321	35431840

T22

1st	2nd	3rd	2016	2015	2014	P/E		2016	2015	2014	AV. YLD %	AMOUNT	PAYABLE	2016	
		1.34	4.14	3.32	3.93	33.2	28.5	1.42	1.34	1.16	1.1	0.410Y	32/4/39	137.4	117.9
			59.50	-175.00	122.70	0.2	0.1		2639.93	5129.26				14.6	8.6
		0.95	2.99	-4.44	5.69	27.3	18.9							81.7	56.6
		1.43	3.97	3.10	4.89	20.8	15.9	1.98	1.73	1.48	2.5	0.6050Y	32/4/39	82.6	63.2
		-0.01	0.65	0.40	1.09	65.6	53.2	1.50	1.46	1.38	3.9	0.390Z	32/4/39	42.6	34.6
		0.79	2.61	2.25	3.74	46.0	34.3							120.2	89.5
			0.24	5.42	-17.91	50.8	37.1							12.2	8.9
		1.47	2.39	2.03	2.27	25.5	18.8	1.23	1.17	1:11	2.3	0.3350Y	12/29/17	60.9	44.9
		-0.01	-0.48	-2.15	0.14				0.02	0.02		0.020	3/16/17	5.1	1.1
		0.01	-4.34	-3.97										9.4	6.0
		0.41	1.15	0.72	0.50	99.1	70.3							114.0	80.9
		0.25	1.09	1.98	2.10	15.6	13.3	1.95	2.45	3.08	12.3	0.410	12/15/17	17.0	14.5
		0.48	1.31		1.77	11.9	9.2	1.65	2.00	2.20	11.7	0.370Z	1/25/18	15.7	12.0
		15.50	91.08	88.40	52.19	0.3	0.2	361.95	293.99	282.39	1406.9			30.6	21.5
	0.08		0.23	0.09	0.45	109.8	78.3	0.09	0.16	0.48	0.4			25.3	18.0
		1.09	2.97	2.72	2.52	28.2	20.3	0.32	0.32	0.32	0.5	0.080Y	32/4/39	83.6	60.4
		0.25	0.35	0.31	-0.13	67.7	55.7					0.070Y	2/23/18	23.7	19.5
		0.16	-2.92	-0.39	3.70				3.08	4.68		0.670	8/13/15	23.5	5.8
		0.68	1.13	1.41	0.88	42.3	25.0							47.8	28.3
		0.64	2.52	3.99	3.03	27.8	22.3	1.90	1.88	1.72	3.1	0.4850Y	32/4/39	70.0	56.1
		0.12	0.38	0.29	0.27	57.7	52.0	0.40	0.34	0.34	1.9	0.1050Y	32/4/39	21.9	19.8
		0.66	3.24	2.90	3.14	15.4	11.2	0.36	0.24	0.24	0.9	0.150Y	11/22/17	50.0	36.2
		-0.62	-1.33	1.27	-0.87									52.0	28.6
		0.24	0.69	-1.78	1.29	25.0	20.1	1.27	1.26	0.55	8.2	0.3180	11/21/17	17.3	13.9
		-0.02	-1.54	-7.26	0.41									24.7	12.3
		0.19	-1.08	-0.25	0.67			2.33	2.31	2.20	13.8	0.350	11/14/17	26.0	12.6
		0.47	1.93	-0.04	1.37	30.1	17.9	2.12	1.86	1.40	4.6	0.2685GH	3/1/18	58.1	34.5
		0.30	-1.07	-6.28	4.58			0.06	0.28	0.28	0.5	0.0150	12/29/17	18.0	8.1
		0.67	2.59	1.91	2.29	19.3	14.9	0.94	0.88	0.78	2.1	0.250Y	32/4/39	50.1	38.6
		0.01	0.03	-1.47	-0.74	212.0	66.0							6.4	2.0
		0.36	0.26	0.42	0.86	16.7	10.8	0.24	0.38	0.80	7.0	0.01840Z	2/14/18	4.3	2.8
				13.48	11.65			204.75	258.47	289.39	2053.8			11.2	8.0
		6.47				1.0	0.7	76.96			1403.4			6.2	4.5
			57.62	47.90	33.65	0.5	0.3	359.31	485.80	548.00	1529.3			27.4	18.8
		-0.19	-1.77	-12.43	7.75				0.08	0.47		0.020Y	32/4/39	59.4	46.8
		0.40	2.04	-0.06		29.3	20.2	1.00	0.25		2.0	0.290	32/4/39	59.8	41.1
		0.22	0.92	1.11	0.57	21.6	16.5	1.14	1.02	0.75	6.4	0.2950	32/4/39	19.9	15.2
		0.33	0.98	0.42	0.51	27.3	16.0	1.98	1.72	1.43	9.4	0.5650	11/14/17	26.7	15.7
		0.07	1.72	-7.39	1.44	7.5	3.8	0.16	0.64	1.17	1.6	0.010Y	2/15/18	12.9	6.5
	1.00		2.99	3.77	3.02	28.1	20.6	0.70	0.70	0.50	1.0	0.1750	32/4/39	84.0	61.5
		0.26	-0.29	-7.02	1.97									35.6	26.3
		1.10	-0.41	-2.44	0.36			1.14	1.35	1.69	3.6			34.1	29.5
		0.03	-2.56	-2.17	0.55			1.02	0.98	0.63	5.8	0.2590	2/14/18	20.1	15.3
		-0.02	-1.99	-4.66	0.59			1.56	1.53	1.46	9.2	0.390	2/13/18	19.4	14.6
		0.33	1.39	-1.72	0.50	15.2	11.0	0.70	0.70	0.53	3.9	0.17Y	2/9/18	21.1	15.4
		-0.10	1.03	1.33	3.38	16.0	10.9			3.71				16.4	11.3
		22.49	-1.86	-0.93	0.85			0.84	0.80		1.1	0.220	12/20/17	94.3	62.8
		-0.08	3.13	-6.88	-16.88			0.04	0.60	3.00		0.010	32/4/39		
		0.09	0.91	0.73	0.69	17.7	10.4	0.23			1.9	0.090Y	12/15/17	16.1	9.5
		0.09	0.91	0.73	0.69	13.0	11.4	0.23			2.1	0.090Y	12/15/17	11.9	10.4
								0.36			1.5	1.180Y	1/2/18	25.3	21.4
		2.21	-3.26	-0.99	5.22			3.42	3.34	3.32	4.4	0.890Y	32/4/39	87.4	70.4
								0.35			1.5	0.30470Z	3/1/18	25.1	21.3
								0.36			1.5	1.230Y	2/1/18	25.3	21.4
								1.41	1.41	0.76	5.5	0.35160Z	3/1/18	27.4	0.0
		0.28	1.20	1.26	1.47	24.9	19.9	1.59	1.51	1.43	6.0	0.4250	32/4/39	29.9	23.9
		1.71	0.22	0.28	0.30	35.2	23.2	0.13	0.11	0.10	2.2	0.050Y	12/29/17	7.8	5.1
		-0.03	-1.30	0.12	0.38									54.3	31.4
		0.23	-0.47	3.16	0.66							1.31250Y	7/3/17	72.5	24.8
		0.19	0.91	1.58		34.6	27.5	2.02	0.70		7.1	0.6150	11/29/17	31.4	25.0
-0.01			0.97	-0.05	-0.23	12.2	6.6							11.8	6.4
		0.17	-1.98	-8.29	5.32			0.67	0.67	0.51	0.7	0.16750Y	32/4/39	109.4	83.2
		-0.29	-0.11	-15.37	3.02									6.8	1.6
		0.77	1.87	1.62	1.40	58.3	34.0							108.9	63.7
		0.77	3.17	2.93	2.86	24.5	19.9	3.84	3.63	3.42	5.4	0.360Z	32/4/39	77.6	63.1
		0.13	-2.71	0.56	2.54			0.12	0.12	0.12	0.2	0.030Y	32/4/39	67.0	50.8
		0.25	0.80	0.39		38.5	30.6	0.57	0.15		2.1	0.2440	2/23/18	30.8	24.5
		1.28	5.21	4.70	3.52	15.9	12.5	3.05	2.50	2.02	4.1	1.0250	2/14/18	82.7	65.1
		0.79	4.04	3.55	2.97	36.2	23.0	1.32	1.16	1.00	1.0	0.390Y	32/4/39	146.3	93.0
		0.25	1.62	0.56	-0.19	20.1	18.4			0.25		0.40630Z	2/15/18	32.5	29.8
		0.56	1.92	1.54	1.41	47.8	37.2	1.70	1.50	1.30	2.0	0.48750Z	32/4/39	91.7	71.3
		0.37	11.68	2.36	1.73	6.0	5.1	13.02	2.21	2.00	19.9	1.03620Z	32/4/39	70.4	59.9
			-0.19	-0.19	-0.20							0.1580	9/29/08	3.0	0.0
		-3.91	-0.39	0.42	0.84									17.4	8.1
			0.05	0.72	0.65										
		0.49	1.77	1.62	0.02	36.9	29.0	0.32	0.32	0.40	0.5	0.080Y	1/19/18	65.3	51.4
		0.82	2.41	1.72	1.03										
		1.21	6.27	3.49	2.06	43.0	35.4	6.40	5.76	5.11	2.6	1.750Z	32/4/39	269.4	221.7
		1.01	3.42	1.91	3.16	29.7	20.3					0.09	32/4/39	101.6	69.3

SYMBOL	COMPANY	NATURE OF BUSINESS	FISCAL YEAR-END	TOTAL REV. $MILL	NET INCOME $MILL	TOTAL ASSETS $MILL	NET STK EQUITY $MILL	NO OF INST	INST. HOLDINGS (SHARES)
ETH	Ethan Allen Interiors, Inc.	Retail - Furniture & Home Furnishing	6/30/17	763.4	36.2	568.2	400.7	234	35844222
EURN	Euronav NV	Shipping	12/31/16	684.3	204.0	3046.9	1888.0	90	35303452
EEA	European Equity Fund Inc (The)	Holding and other Investment Office	12/31/16	2.0	0.9	72.9	72.1	38	3673575
EVR	Evercore Inc	Finance Intermediaries & Services	12/31/16	1440.1	107.5	1662.3	527.3	388	43989125
RE	Everest Re Group Ltd	General Insurance	12/31/16	5794.3	996.3	21321.5	8075.4	624	47798109
EVRI	Everi Holdings Inc	Internet & Software	12/31/16	859.5	-249.5	1408.2	-107.8	192	77401149
ES	Eversource Energy	Electric Utilities	12/31/16	7639.1	942.3	32053.2	10711.7	129	24691983
EVTC	Evertec, Inc.	Business Services	12/31/16	389.5	75.0	885.7	104.7	182	63508699
EVH	Evolent Health Inc	Business Services	12/31/16	254.2	-159.7	1199.8	702.5	211	74836475
AQUA	Evoqua Water Technologies Corp	Industrial Machinery & Equipment	9/30/17	1247.4	2.2	1473.3	211.4	-	0
EXC	Exelon Corp	Electric Utilities	12/31/16	31360.0	1134.0	114904.0	25837.0	1212	880367576
EXPR	Express Inc	Retail - Apparel and Accessories	1/28/17	2192.5	57.4	1185.2	635.7	256	91519809
STAY	Extended Stay America Inc	Hotels, Restaurants & Travel	12/31/16	1270.6	69.9	4180.3	794.8	290	206562197
EXTN	Exterran Corp	Equipment & Services	12/31/16	1029.3	-227.9	1374.8	556.8	193	35864622
EXR	Extra Space Storage Inc	REITs	12/31/16	991.9	366.1	7091.4	2244.9	516	170565170
XOM	Exxon Mobil Corp	Production & Extraction	12/31/16	226094.0	7840.0	330314.0	167325.0	3057	2888509990
FN	Fabrinet	Manufacturing	6/30/17	1420.5	97.1	1033.1	681.6	272	44722146
FDS	FactSet Research Systems Inc.	Business Services	8/31/17	1221.2	258.3	1413.3	559.7	532	49302393
FICO	Fair Isaac Corp	Internet & Software	9/30/17	932.2	128.3	1255.6	426.5	365	38218174
FMSA	Fairmount Santrol Holdings Inc	Mining	12/31/16	535.0	-140.2	1202.9	251.0	219	176667109
SFUN	Fang Holdings Ltd	Internet & Software	12/31/16	916.4	-169.6	1614.8	487.1	130	209431627
FPI	Farmland Partners Inc	REITs	12/31/16	31.0	4.3	655.5	161.9	124	14445410
FBK	FB Financial Corp	Banking	12/31/16	265.2	40.6	3276.9	330.5	98	11064275
FFG	FBL Financial Group Inc	Life & Health	12/31/16	726.4	107.2	9566.1	1188.2	139	8237066
FCB	FCB Financial Holdings Inc	Banking	12/31/16	349.0	99.9	9090.1	982.4	208	45755312
AGM	Federal Agricultural Mortgage Corp	Credit & Lending	12/31/16	332.4	77.3	15606.0	643.4	163	8666176
FRT	Federal Realty Investment Trust (M	REITs	12/31/16	801.6	249.9	5423.3	1976.7	519	87018047
FSS	Federal Signal Corp.	Industrial Machinery & Equipment	12/31/16	707.9	43.8	643.2	394.1	234	64441185
FII	Federated Investors Inc (PA)	Wealth Management	12/31/16	1143.4	208.9	1155.1	594.8	443	118485455
FMN	Federated Premier Municipal Incom	Holding and other Investment Office	11/30/16	6.5	5.1	145.4	108.2	20	554603
FDX	FedEx Corp	Airlines/Air Freight	5/31/17	60319.0	2997.0	48552.0	16073.0	1662	242470521
RACE	Ferrari NV (New)	Autos- Manufacturing	12/31/16	3105.1	398.8	3849.6	325.0	296	60524477
FGP	Ferrellgas Partners LP	Gas Utilities	7/31/17	1930.3	-54.2	1610.0	-	129	7606556
FOE	Ferro Corp	Specialty Chemicals	12/31/16	1145.3	-20.8	1283.8	247.1	270	90342264
FCAU	Fiat Chrysler Automobiles NV	Autos- Manufacturing	12/31/16	111018.0	1803.0	104343.0	19168.0	273	505640774
FBR	Fibria Celulose SA	Paper & Forest Products	12/31/16	9614.8	1654.8	34440.3	13751.1	149	54263167
FNF	Fidelity National Financial Inc	General Insurance	12/31/16	9554.0	650.0	14463.0	5996.0	590	278914465
FNF	Fidelity National Financial Inc - FNF	General Insurance	12/31/15	9132.0	527.0	13931.0	5754.0	-	0
FIS	Fidelity National Information Service	Business Services	12/31/16	9241.0	568.0	26031.0	9741.0	883	350265208
FMO	Fiduciary / Claymore MLP Opportun	Holding and other Investment Office	11/30/16	3.2	-4.8	805.1	496.8	80	7239760
FAC	First Acceptance Corp	General Insurance	12/31/16	389.6	-29.3	400.1	72.5	39	8457934
FAF	First American Financial Corp	General Insurance	12/31/16	5575.8	343.0	8831.8	3008.2	402	105522801
FBP	First Bancorp	Banking	12/31/16	673.2	93.2	11922.5	1786.2	251	222526067
FCF	First Commonwealth Financial Corp	Banking	12/31/16	282.2	59.6	6684.0	749.9	224	81780491
FDC	First Data Corp (New)	IT Services	12/31/16	11584.0	420.0	40292.0	1220.0	477	515055057
FHN	First Horizon National Corp	Banking	12/31/16	1370.3	227.0	28555.2	2409.7	414	254445444
FR	First Industrial Realty Trust Inc	REITs	12/31/16	378.0	121.2	2793.3	1241.4	346	153527856
AG	First Majestic Silver Corp	Precious Metals	12/31/16	278.1	8.6	857.2	621.7	155	61768751
FRC	First Republic Bank (San Francisco,	Banking	12/31/16	2375.7	673.4	73277.8	6908.7	596	193582519
FEO	First Trust / Aberdeen Emerging Op	Holding and other Investment Office	12/31/16	4.9	3.4	90.1	83.7	31	1820528
FDEU	First Trust Dynamic Europe Equity I	Holding and other Investment Office	12/31/16	18.3	12.7	401.4	309.5	34	4937218
FIF	First Trust Energy Infrastructure Fu	Holding and other Investment Office	11/30/16	9.8	3.6	477.5	339.0	47	4727200
FFA	First Trust Enhanced Equity Income	Holding and other Investment Office	12/31/16	7.1	3.7	305.0	304.1	64	6384120
FSD	First Trust High Income Long/Short	Holding and other Investment Office	10/31/16	44.6	35.4	788.8	624.1	70	10021181
FPF	First Trust Intermediate Duration Pr	Finance Intermediaries & Services	10/31/16	144.0	117.5	2126.1	1459.9	86	11148351
FEI	First Trust MLP & Energy Income F	Finance Intermediaries & Services	10/31/16	11.5	-2.4	976.7	701.5	68	12308742
FMY	First Trust Mortgage Income Fund	Holding and other Investment Office	10/31/17	1.5	0.7	65.3	65.2	24	3091672
FPL	First Trust New Opportunities MLP	Finance Intermediaries & Services	10/31/16	5.2	21.6	418.3	307.9	52	5641900
FIV	First Trust Senior Floating Rate 202	Holding and other Investment Office	5/31/17	8.4	5.8	526.8	353.9	27	3399632
FCT	First Trust Senior Floating Rate Inco	Holding and other Investment Office	5/31/17	26.6	20.7	576.4	381.3	71	9596649
FGB	First Trust Specialty Finance and Fi	Holding and other Investment Office	11/30/16	11.2	9.5	125.6	97.8	34	1904984
FHY	First Trust Strategic High Income Fu	Holding and other Investment Office	10/31/16	11.7	9.0	159.1	115.3	38	2074312
FAM	First Trust/Aberdeen Global Opport	Holding and other Investment Office	12/31/16	17.3	12.6	291.9	208.5	56	5620536
FCFS	FirstCash Inc	Retail - Specialty	12/31/16	1088.4	60.1	2145.2	1450.0	274	53713307
FE	FirstEnergy Corp	Electric Utilities	12/31/16	14562.0	-6177.0	43148.0	6241.0	791	424286228
FIT	Fitbit Inc	Computer Hardware & Equipment	12/31/16	2169.5	-102.8	1820.2	998.5	259	143607570
OAKS	Five Oaks Investment Corp	REITs	12/31/16	77.0	-8.0	2299.6	142.5	46	7480778
FPH	Five Point Holdings LLC	Property, Real Estate & Developmen	12/31/16	39.4	-33.3	2114.6	242.9	57	48152229
FBC	Flagstar Bancorp, Inc.	Credit & Lending	12/31/16	904.0	171.0	14053.0	1336.0	182	63011614
DFP	Flaherty & Crumrine Dynamic Prefe	Finance Intermediaries & Services	11/30/16	43.8	35.3	711.9	462.2	52	1936146
PFD	Flaherty & Crumrine Preferred Inco	Holding and other Investment Office	11/30/16	15.2	12.1	224.2	146.5	36	621615
PFO	Flaherty & Crumrine Preferred Inco	Holding and other Investment Office	11/30/16	13.8	10.9	209.1	136.8	43	1179069
FFC	Flaherty & Crumrine Preferred Secu	Holding and other Investment Office	11/30/16	82.8	69.3	1250.4	814.8	100	6529346
FLC	Flaherty & Crumrine Total Return F	Holding and other Investment Office	11/30/16	19.9	15.8	302.1	196.9	39	1727625
FLT	FleetCor Technologies Inc	Business Services	12/31/16	1831.5	452.4	9626.7	3084.0	463	94961763
FND	Floor & Decor Holdings Inc	Construction Materials	12/29/16	1050.8	43.0	831.2	134.3	139	88972651
FTK	Flotek Industries Inc	Specialty Chemicals	12/31/16	262.8	-49.1	386.6	287.3	222	58567512
FLO	Flowers Foods, Inc.	Food	12/31/16	3926.9	163.8	2761.1	1210.1	407	170410803
FLS	Flowserve Corp	Industrial Machinery & Equipment	12/31/16	3991.5	145.1	4742.8	1648.2	621	155758964
FLR	Fluor Corp.	Construction Services	12/31/16	19036.5	281.4	9216.4	3125.2	763	138418005

T24

1st	2nd	3rd	2016	2015	2014	P/E RATIO	Div 2016	Div 2015	Div 2014	AV. YLD %	AMOUNT	PAYABLE	PRICE RANGE 2016
	0.54		2.00	1.27	1.47	18.7 - 13.5	0.59	0.46	0.39	2.0	0.190Y	4/25/18	37.4 - 26.9
			1.29	2.22	-0.39								
			0.11	0.09	0.09	89.8 - 70.6	0.08	0.17	0.11	0.9	0.03510	1/26/18	9.9 - 7.8
		1.04	2.43	0.98	2.08	37.9 - 27.9	1.27	1.15	1.03	1.6	0.40Y	12/8/17	92.2 - 67.8
		-15.73	23.68	22.10	25.91		4.70	4.00	3.20		1.30	32/4/39	
		-0.06	-3.78	-1.59	0.18								8.9 - 2.2
		0.82	2.96	2.76	2.58	22.2 - 18.3	1.78	1.67	1.57	2.9	0.4750Y	32/4/39	65.8 - 54.3
		0.08	1.01	1.11	0.86	18.9 - 12.9	0.40	0.40	0.40	2.4	0.10Y	9/8/17	19.1 - 13.0
		-0.18	-3.55	6.93	-53.83								27.4 - 10.5
			0.11	-0.85	-0.97	216.9 - 184.2							23.9 - 20.3
		0.85	1.22	2.54	1.88	34.7 - 27.5	1.26	1.24	1.24	3.4	0.32750Y	32/4/39	42.4 - 33.5
		0.08	1.38	0.81	1.37	8.4 - 3.9					0.567	12/23/10	11.6 - 5.3
		0.28	0.35	0.55	0.19	59.6 - 44.3	0.74	0.91	0.53	4.1	0.210	32/4/39	20.9 - 15.5
		0.09	-6.59	1.35									33.9 - 23.5
		0.74	2.91	1.56	1.53	30.2 - 24.6	2.93	2.24	1.81	3.7	0.780Z	32/4/39	87.9 - 71.6
		0.93	1.88	3.85	7.60	48.3 - 40.5	2.98	2.88	2.70	3.6	0.770Y	32/4/39	90.9 - 76.1
0.55			1.68	1.21	2.58								
1.77			8.19	5.71	4.92	25.0 - 19.0	1.88	1.66	1.48	1.1	0.560Y	32/4/39	204.9 - 155.5
		0.78	3.39	2.65	2.72	46.6 - 35.4	0.08	0.08	0.08	0.1	0.020Y	32/4/39	158.1 - 120.2
		0.15	-0.78	-0.57	1.03								13.0 - 2.5
		1.22	-1.81	-0.18	2.87			0.19	0.19				5.6 - 2.7
		0.01	0.09	0.08	-0.15	127.0 - 91.4	0.51	0.50	0.33	5.2	0.3750Y	1/2/18	11.4 - 8.2
		0.27	2.10	2.79	1.89	20.9 - 11.5	4.03	1.37	0.97	11.4			43.8 - 24.2
		1.08	4.28	4.53	4.39	18.5 - 14.1	3.68	3.60	1.40	5.3	0.440Y	12/29/17	79.0 - 60.1
		0.70	2.31	1.23	0.58	22.9 - 17.6							52.9 - 40.6
		1.71	5.97	4.19	3.37	13.4 - 9.0	1.04	0.64	0.56	1.6	0.3750Y	1/17/18	80.3 - 53.9
		1.47	3.50	3.03	2.41	41.5 - 34.4	3.84	3.62	3.30	2.9	0.3681GHZ	32/4/39	145.3 - 120.5
		0.21	0.71	1.00	1.00	32.5 - 18.5	0.28	0.25	0.09	1.6	0.070Y	12/5/17	23.1 - 13.2
		0.56	2.03	1.62	1.42	18.0 - 12.4	2.00	1.00	1.00	7.0	0.250Y	32/4/39	36.5 - 25.3
			0.81	0.87	0.89	18.6 - 16.7	0.86	0.88	0.90	6.0	0.061M	2/1/18	15.1 - 13.6
	2.84		6.51	3.65	6.75	38.6 - 28.2	1.00	0.80	0.60	0.5	0.50Y	32/4/39	251.1 - 183.6
		0.74	2.11	1.52	1.38						0.6350	5/2/17	
-0.49			-6.68	0.35	0.41		2.05	2.00	2.00	37.5	0.10	12/15/17	8.7 - 3.9
		0.27	-0.25	0.72	0.99						0.010Y	3/10/09	25.4 - 13.6
	0.75		1.18	0.22	0.46						7.8750	12/15/16	
			2.98	0.62	0.28	5.7 - 2.7	0.46	3.93		4.0			16.9 - 8.0
		0.62	2.34	1.89	0.75	17.4 - 10.3	0.88	0.80	0.37	2.7	0.270Y	32/4/39	40.6 - 24.2
				1.89	0.75			0.80	0.37		0.270Y	12/29/17	40.6 - 24.2
		0.18	1.72	2.19	2.35	56.2 - 44.8	1.04	1.04	0.96	1.2	0.290Y	32/4/39	96.6 - 77.0
		-0.14	-0.11	-0.26			1.72	1.71	1.68	12.3	0.43080	11/30/17	17.4 - 10.6
		0.05	-0.71	-0.05	0.68						0.0067	6/28/02	1.6 - 0.0
		0.19	3.09	2.62	2.15	18.5 - 11.9	1.20	1.00	0.84	2.6	0.380Y	32/4/39	57.0 - 36.8
		-0.05	0.43	0.10	1.87	16.3 - 10.8					0.14580	1/31/18	7.0 - 4.7
		0.22	0.67	0.56	0.48	22.9 - 18.1	0.28	0.28	0.28	2.1	0.080Y	2/16/18	15.3 - 12.1
		0.31	0.46	-7.70		41.5 - 32.2							19.1 - 14.8
		0.28	0.94	0.34	0.91	22.1 - 17.1	0.28	0.24	0.20	1.5	0.38750Y	32/4/39	20.8 - 16.1
		0.36	1.05	0.67	0.42	31.3 - 24.1	0.76	0.51	0.41	2.6	0.210Z	32/4/39	32.8 - 25.4
		-0.01	0.05	-0.84	-0.52	282.2 - 121.8							14.1 - 6.1
		1.14	3.93	3.18	3.07	26.8 - 22.0	0.63	0.59	0.54	0.7	0.170Y	32/4/39	105.2 - 86.6
			0.64	0.65	0.77	27.1 - 21.7	1.40	1.40	1.40	8.7	0.35C	12/29/17	17.4 - 13.9
			0.73	0.04		26.8 - 21.4	1.45	0.12		8.0	0.1210	2/15/18	19.6 - 15.6
			0.21	0.34	0.22	93.1 - 82.8	1.66	1.32	2.75	9.0	0.110	2/15/18	19.6 - 17.4
			0.19	0.20	0.24	86.2 - 71.3	0.95	0.94	0.92	6.4	0.2850	12/29/17	16.4 - 13.5
			1.00	1.11	1.31	17.3 - 16.1	1.06	1.26	1.31	6.3	0.1280	2/15/18	17.3 - 16.1
			1.94	1.96	1.85	12.9 - 11.4	1.95	2.11	1.91	8.1	0.15250	2/15/18	25.1 - 22.2
			-0.05	0.07	-0.03		1.42	1.38	1.33	9.1	0.11830	2/15/18	17.5 - 13.8
			-0.02	1.02	1.02		0.91	1.02	1.02	6.5	0.0650	2/15/18	14.5 - 0.0
			0.91	-0.22	-0.02	15.3 - 12.2	1.26	1.22	0.50	9.8	0.1050	2/15/18	13.9 - 11.1
											0.04170	2/15/18	10.3 - 9.0
			0.83	0.87	0.84	16.8 - 15.3	0.88	0.84	0.94	6.5	0.060	2/15/18	13.9 - 12.7
			0.66	0.64	0.65	12.6 - 9.3	0.70	0.69	0.69	9.8	0.1750	12/1/17	8.3 - 6.1
			1.09	1.24	1.38	12.7 - 11.3	1.20	1.36	1.44	9.1	0.080	2/15/18	13.8 - 12.3
			0.73	0.82	1.03	16.6 - 15.1	0.90	1.14	1.38	7.8	0.0750	2/15/18	12.1 - 11.0
		0.59	1.72	2.14	2.93	39.5 - 24.3	0.56			1.0	0.20	11/30/17	68.0 - 41.9
		0.89	-14.49	1.37	0.71		1.44	1.44	1.44	4.6	0.360Y	32/4/39	35.0 - 28.2
		-0.48	-0.47	0.75	0.63								8.1 - 5.0
		-0.23	-0.79	-0.21	0.03		2.05	1.35	1.50	42.9	0.18230	3/27/18	5.6 - 4.0
		-0.07	-0.89	-0.07									16.4 - 12.3
		0.70	2.66	2.24	-1.72	14.5 - 9.6					0.50Y	12/31/07	38.5 - 25.4
			1.84	1.79	1.76	14.8 - 12.8	1.92	1.92	1.97	7.5	0.1480	4/30/18	27.2 - 23.5
			1.09	1.10	1.12	14.6 - 12.7	1.08	1.08	1.16	7.2	0.0780	4/30/18	15.9 - 13.9
			0.88	0.90	0.92	14.7 - 12.6	0.88	0.88	0.95	7.3	0.0660	4/30/18	12.9 - 11.1
			1.58	1.61	1.64	14.1 - 12.1	1.63	1.63	1.68	7.8	0.1140	4/30/18	22.3 - 19.2
			1.60	1.65	1.67	14.0 - 12.4	1.63	1.63	1.72	7.6	0.1190	4/30/18	22.4 - 19.9
		2.18	4.75	3.85	4.24	40.7 - 27.6							193.4 - 131.3
		0.22	0.49	0.31	0.18	101.2 - 65.4							49.6 - 32.0
		-0.05	-0.88	-0.25	0.97								14.1 - 4.3
		-0.16	0.78	0.89	0.82	26.7 - 21.8	0.63	0.57	0.48	3.3	0.170Y	32/4/39	20.8 - 17.0
		0.36	1.11	2.00	3.76	46.7 - 33.9	0.76	0.72	0.64	1.7	0.190Y	32/4/39	51.9 - 37.6
		0.67	2.00	2.81	3.20	29.1 - 18.6	0.84	0.84	0.84	1.8	0.210Y	32/4/39	58.2 - 37.2

SYMBOL	COMPANY	NATURE OF BUSINESS	FISCAL YEAR-END	TOTAL REV. $MILL	NET INCOME $MILL	TOTAL ASSETS $MILL	NET STK EQUITY $MILL	NO OF INST	INST. HOLDINGS (SHARES)
FLY	Fly Leasing Ltd	Airlines/Air Freight	12/31/16	345.0	-29.1	3447.0	593.2	102	21069698
FMC	FMC Corp.	Agricultural Chemicals	12/31/16	3282.4	209.1	6139.3	1957.7	716	139440960
FNB	FNB Corp	Banking	12/31/16	880.7	170.9	21844.8	2571.6	403	285380640
FMX	Fomento Economico Mexicano, S.A	Beverages	12/31/16	399507.0	21140.0	545623.0	211904.0	331	129376694
FL	Foot Locker, Inc.	Retail - Apparel and Accessories	1/28/17	7766.0	664.0	3840.0	2710.0	732	143216019
F	Ford Motor Co. (DE)	Autos- Manufacturing	12/31/16	151800.0	4596.0	237951.0	29170.0	1505	2813441518
F 12A	Ford Motor Credit Company LLC	Credit & Lending	12/31/16	3825.0	1373.0	146089.0	12803.0	1	2
FELP	Foresight Energy LP	Mining	12/31/16	875.8	-178.8	1689.0		25	9072509
FCE A	Forest City Realty Trust Inc	REITs	12/31/16	929.5	-158.4	8228.6	3283.8	280	245918258
FOR	Forestar Group Inc (New)	Property, Real Estate & Developmen	12/31/16	197.3	58.6	733.2	560.7	232	39902207
FOR	Forestar Group Inc (New)	Property, Real Estate & Developmen	12/31/16	197.3	58.6	733.2	560.7	232	39902207
FTS	Fortis Inc	Electric Utilities	12/31/16	6838.0	585.0	47904.0	14597.0		0
FTV	Fortive Corp	Industrial Machinery & Equipment	12/31/16	6224.3	872.3	8189.8	2687.9	833	291598707
FTAI	Fortress Transportation & Infrastruct	Miscellaneous Transportation Servic	12/31/16	148.7	-20.1	1547.3	1053.8	77	21296185
FSM	Fortuna Silver Mines Inc	Precious Metals	12/31/16	210.3	17.9	562.9	423.2		0
FBHS	Fortune Brands Home & Security, In	Household Appliances, Electronics &	12/31/16	4984.9	413.2	5128.5	2361.5	603	159979855
FET	Forum Energy Technologies Inc	Equipment & Services	12/31/16	587.6	-82.0	1835.2	1235.2	193	112200969
FBM	Foundation Building Materials Inc	Construction Materials	12/31/16	1392.5	-28.4	1321.0	328.5	94	40733377
FCPT	Four Corners Property Trust Inc	REITs	12/31/16	124.0	156.8	937.2	465.0	253	59622935
FEDU	Four Seasons Education (Cayman)	Educational Services	2/28/17	203.2	17.7	296.1	165.7		0
FNV	Franco-Nevada Corp	Precious Metals	12/31/16	610.2	122.2	4221.6	4146.5		0
FI	Frank's International NV	Equipment & Services	12/31/16	487.5	-135.3	1588.1	1311.3	143	75733703
FC	Franklin Covey Co	Business Services	8/31/17	185.3	-7.2	210.7	85.1	75	8029433
FSB	Franklin Financial Network Inc	Banking	12/31/16	115.0	28.1	2943.2	270.3	126	8049310
BEN	Franklin Resources, Inc.	Wealth Management	9/30/17	6392.2	1696.7	17534.0	12620.0	842	296332659
FT	Franklin Universal Trust	Holding and other Investment Office	8/31/17	13.5	9.6	268.0	207.0	57	6647828
FCX	Freeport-McMoRan Inc	Non-Precious Metals	12/31/16	14830.0	-4315.0	37317.0	6051.0	1188	1160469526
FMS	Fresenius Medical Care AG & Co K	Diagnostic & Health Related Service	12/31/16	17910.8	1243.3	26933.9	10808.7	278	20698072
FDP	Fresh Del Monte Produce Inc.	Food	12/30/16	4011.5	225.1	2653.3	1791.8	234	37741622
FRO	Frontline Ltd	Equipment & Services	12/31/16	751.6	117.0	2966.3	1499.6	161	26701891
FSIC	FS Investment Corp	Finance Intermediaries & Services	12/31/16	422.8	207.3	4110.1	2297.4	217	88417077
FCN	FTI Consulting Inc.	Business Services	12/31/16	1810.4	85.5	2225.4	1207.4	282	49944595
FUL	Fuller (HB) Company	Specialty Chemicals	12/3/16	2094.6	124.1	2058.3	937.9	294	65799834
FF	FutureFuel Corp	Specialty Chemicals	12/31/16	253.2	56.3	529.0	332.8	151	23234512
GCV	Gabelli Convertible and Income Sec	Holding and other Investment Office	12/31/16	2.9	1.7	99.2	95.7	22	2485171
GDV	Gabelli Dividend & Income Trust	Holding and other Investment Office	12/31/16	53.6	29.5	2445.4	2597.7		0
GAB	Gabelli Equity Trust Inc (The)	Holding and other Investment Office	12/31/16	33.6	15.4	1698.7	1693.4	130	16670601
GGZ	Gabelli Global Small & Mid Cap Val	Holding and other Investment Office	12/31/16	2.5	0.8	130.1	128.0	52	2420828
GRX	Gabelli Healthcare & WellnessRx Tr	Holding and other Investment Office	12/31/16	3.3	-0.5	283.9	282.6	62	5648064
GGT	Gabelli Multimedia Trust Inc	Holding and other Investment Office	12/31/16	4.0	1.4	233.3	232.4	46	3459596
GUT	Gabelli Utility Trust	Holding and other Investment Office	12/31/16	8.8	4.8	340.8	337.8	54	2179734
GFA	Gafisa SA	Builders	12/31/15	2294.3	74.4	6760.3	3095.5		0
GCAP	GAIN Capital Holdings Inc	Finance Intermediaries & Services	12/31/16	411.8	35.3	1430.1	294.2	114	28745903
AJG	Gallagher (Arthur J.) & Co.	Brokers & Intermediaries	12/31/16	5594.8	414.4	11489.6	3596.6	719	184658378
GBL	GAMCO Investors Inc	Finance Intermediaries & Services	12/31/16	353.0	117.1	149.2	-166.6	116	8207926
GNT	GAMCO Natural Resources, Gold &	Holding and other Investment Office	12/31/16	2.4	0.3	167.0	149.0	37	3979356
GME	GameStop Corp	Retail - Appliances and Electronics	1/28/17	8607.9	353.2	4975.9	2254.1	533	130470814
GCI	Gannett Co Inc (New)	Publishing	12/25/16	3047.5	52.7	2844.7	856.8	273	111454050
GDI	Gardner Denver Holdings Inc	Manufacturing	12/31/16	1939.4	-36.6	4315.9	265.9	140	198143224
IT	Gartner Inc	IT Services	12/31/16	2444.5	193.6	2367.3	60.9	545	151730259
GLOG	GasLog Ltd	Equipment & Services	12/31/16	466.1	-21.5	4515.2	945.6		0
GLOP	GasLog Partners LP	Shipping	12/31/16	228.7	77.3	1489.1	642.4	88	17152868
GTES	Gates Industrial Corp PLC	Industrial Machinery & Equipment							0
GATX	GATX Corp	Miscellaneous Transportation Servic	12/31/16	1418.3	257.1	7105.4	1347.2	340	58321989
GZT	Gazit-Globe Ltd	Property, Real Estate & Developmen	12/31/16	4801.0	787.0	86887.0	8158.0	42	17790870
GCP	GCP Applied Technologies Inc	Specialty Chemicals	12/31/16	1355.8	72.8	1089.8	-142.7	206	65577243
GDL	GDL Fund (The)	Holding and other Investment Office	12/31/16	4.2	-6.6	415.5	216.8	58	11445462
GEGI 26	GE Global Insurance Holdings Corp	Brokers & Intermediaries	12/31/03	11621.0	656.0	52542.0	7943.0		0
GNK	Genco Shipping & Trading Ltd	Shipping	12/31/16	135.6	-217.8	1569.0	1029.7	91	21509602
GNRT	Gener8 Maritime Inc	Equipment & Services	12/31/16	404.6	67.3	2992.7	1437.4	93	75215125
GNRC	Generac Holdings Inc	Electrical Equipment	12/31/16	1444.5	98.8	1861.7	401.1	301	68534135
GAM	General American Investors Co., In	Holding and other Investment Office	12/31/16	21.5	8.2	1228.0	1212.7	106	9818813
BGC	General Cable Corp. (DE)	Electrical Equipment	12/31/16	3858.4	-93.8	2241.6	153.1	202	66554760
GD	General Dynamics Corp.	Aerospace	12/31/16	31353.0	2955.0	32872.0	10976.0	1441	304207270
GE	General Electric Co	Electrical Equipment	12/31/16	123693.0	8831.0	365183.0	75828.0	2950	6188738720
GIS	General Mills, Inc.	Food	5/28/17	15619.8	1657.5	21812.6	4327.9	1595	517270102
GM	General Motors Co	Autos- Manufacturing	12/31/16	166380.0	9427.0	221690.0	43836.0	1230	1174297182
GM 26	General Motors Financial Co Inc	Credit & Lending	12/31/16		754.0	87765.0	8693.0	52	9475070
GCO	Genesco Inc.	Retail - Apparel and Accessories	1/28/17	2868.3	97.4	1448.9	921.1	262	25052168
GWR	Genesee & Wyoming Inc.	Rail	12/31/16	2001.5	141.1	7635.0	2894.6	394	69785815
GEL	Genesis Energy L.P.	Equipment & Services	12/31/16	1712.5	113.2	5702.6		237	103300612
GEN	Genesis Healthcare Inc	Hospitals & Health Care Facilities	12/31/16	5732.4	-64.0	5779.2	-490.3	28	1463467
GNE	Genie Energy Ltd	Electric Utilities	12/31/16	212.1	-24.5	121.8	96.5	72	6209931
G	Genpact Ltd	Business Services	12/31/16	2570.8	269.7	2885.9	1286.6	300	189574738
GPC	Genuine Parts Co.	Auto Parts	12/31/16	15339.7	687.2	8859.4	3193.7	930	143645992
GNW	Genworth Financial, Inc. (Holding C	Life & Health	12/31/16	8369.0	-277.0	104658.0	12644.0	477	421788834
GEO	GEO Group Inc (The) (New)	REITs	12/31/16	2179.5	148.7	3749.4	975.1	354	134245603
GPRK	GeoPark Ltd	Production & Extraction	12/31/16	192.7	-49.1	640.5	105.8		0
GPE PRA	Georgia Power Co	Electric Utilities	12/31/16	8383.0	1347.0	34835.0	11622.0		0
GGB	Gerdau S.A.	Non-Precious Metals	12/31/16	37651.7	-2890.8	54635.1	24028.1	215	223886919

T26

EARNINGS PER SHARE						P/E RATIO		DIVIDENDS PER SHARE			AV. YLD %	DIV. DECLARED		PRICE RANGE 2016	
QUARTERLY			ANNUAL												
1st	2nd	3rd	2016	2015	2014			2016	2015	2014		AMOUNT	PAYABLE		
	0.09	-	-0.88	0.52	1.32	-		-	1.00	1.00	-	-		14.5 -	12.5
		0.41	1.56	3.66	2.29	61.2 -	36.6	0.66	0.66	0.60	0.9	0.1650Y	32/4/39	95.5 -	57.0
		0.23	0.78	0.86	0.80	20.9 -	15.5	0.48	0.48	0.48	3.4	0.45320Y	32/4/39	16.3 -	12.1
			1.05	0.88	0.83	98.4 -	70.7	24.17	21.99		26.4			103.3 -	74.2
		0.81	3.84	3.56	2.85	20.1 -	7.6	1.00	0.88	0.80	1.9	0.310Y	32/4/39	77.3 -	29.2
		0.39	1.15	1.84	0.80	11.5 -	9.2	0.85	0.60	0.50	7.2	0.136Y	32/4/39	13.2 -	10.6
		-0.07	-1.37	-0.25	0.54			-	1.28	0.38		0.06050	11/30/17	7.5 -	3.7
		0.02	-0.61	1.97	-0.04			0.34			1.4	0.140Y	12/29/17	26.2 -	20.4
		1.06	1.38	-6.22	0.38	16.3 -	0.0							22.5 -	0.0
		1.06	1.38	-6.22	0.38	12.1 -	0.0							16.8 -	0.0
		0.66	1.89	2.59	1.40	25.7 -	16.3	1.52	1.40	1.28	3.8	0.25620	3/1/18	48.6 -	30.7
		0.76	2.51			29.7 -	21.4	0.14			0.2	0.070Y	32/4/39	74.7 -	53.7
		0.04	-0.26	-0.18				1.32	0.48		8.0	0.330	11/27/17	20.0 -	13.5
		0.06	0.13	-0.08	0.12	69.8 -	31.2							9.1 -	4.0
		0.83	2.62	1.93	0.95	26.5 -	20.6	0.64	0.56	0.48	1.0	0.20Y	32/4/39	69.3 -	53.9
		-0.15	-0.90	-1.33	1.83									24.3 -	10.4
		0.03	-0.95	-0.26										17.2 -	11.3
		0.31	2.63	0.91		10.1 -	7.8	9.29			38.6	0.2750Z	1/12/18	26.6 -	20.4
		-	-2.21											10.1 -	8.3
		0.32	0.69	0.16	0.70	158.0 -	88.0	0.87	0.83	0.78	1.0	0.230	12/21/17	109.0 -	60.7
		0.01	-0.77	0.50	1.03			0.45	0.60	0.45		0.0750	9/15/17		
-0.17		-	0.47	0.66	1.07	47.0 -	33.9							22.1 -	15.9
		0.65	2.42	1.54	1.27	18.1 -	12.6							43.8 -	30.6
		0.73	2.94	3.29	3.79	16.1 -	13.5	0.72	1.10	0.48	1.7	0.230Y	32/4/39	47.3 -	39.7
		0.39	0.45	0.41		18.8 -	17.1	0.47	0.47	0.47	6.6	0.0320	2/15/18	7.3 -	6.7
		0.19	-3.16	-11.31	-1.26			-	0.57	1.25		0.050	32/4/39	19.3 -	11.2
		1.01	4.06	3.38	3.46	13.0 -	9.8	0.31	0.30	0.37	0.7			52.7 -	39.7
		0.23	4.33	1.17	2.53			0.55	0.50	0.50		0.150	12/8/17		
-0.11		-	0.75	1.29	-8.15			1.05	0.25			0.150	6/21/17		
		0.85	1.10	0.97		12.7 -	8.6	0.89	0.89	1.08	9.8	0.190	1/3/18	10.8 -	7.3
		0.85	2.05	1.58	1.44	22.1 -	15.6							45.2 -	31.9
		0.49	2.42	1.69	0.97	24.2 -	19.6	0.55	0.51	0.46	1.1	0.150Y	32/4/39	58.6 -	47.5
		0.08	1.29	1.06	1.22	12.7 -	10.0	2.53	0.24	0.48	17.6	0.060Y	12/17/18	16.4 -	12.8
		-	0.12	0.07	0.07	50.3 -	39.3	0.41	0.48	0.51	7.8	0.120	12/15/17	6.0 -	4.7
		0.36	0.30	0.41		65.0 -	55.8	1.32	1.24	1.18	6.1	0.110	3/22/18	23.4 -	20.1
		0.07	0.06	0.07		94.1 -	79.3	0.60	0.64	0.64	9.8	0.160	12/15/17	6.6 -	5.5
		0.10	-0.02	-0.07		135.3 -	106.5	0.12			1.0	0.34060	12/26/17	13.5 -	10.7
		-0.02	-0.03	0.01				0.52	0.51	0.62	5.1	0.130	12/15/17	10.9 -	9.5
		0.05	0.03	0.05		194.8 -	145.4	0.83	0.94	1.05	9.6	0.220	12/15/17	9.7 -	7.3
		0.11	0.13	0.13		65.4 -	57.5	0.60	0.60	0.60	8.7	0.050	3/22/18	7.2 -	6.3
	0.04		0.20	-0.11										22.2 -	6.0
		-0.04	0.67	0.22	0.71	14.9 -	8.4	0.21	0.20	0.20	3.0	0.060Y	12/21/17	10.0 -	5.6
		0.71	2.32	2.06	1.97	28.9 -	22.5	1.52	1.48	1.44	2.6	0.410Y	32/4/39	67.0 -	52.2
		0.55	3.92	3.24	4.28	8.2 -	7.1	0.06	0.28	0.50	0.2	0.020Y	1/10/18	32.0 -	27.8
		-	0.01	0.02	0.02	722.0 -	643.7	0.84	0.84	1.08	12.1	0.050	3/22/18	7.2 -	6.4
		0.59	3.78	3.47	2.99	7.0 -	4.2	1.44	1.32	1.10	6.7	0.380Y	32/4/39	26.5 -	16.0
		0.20	0.44	1.25		27.3 -	16.9	0.64	0.32		7.1	0.160Y	12/26/17	12.0 -	7.4
		0.13	-0.25	-2.35	-0.91									34.4 -	20.5
		-0.53	2.31	2.06	2.03	56.1 -	39.2							129.5 -	90.6
		0.03	-0.39	0.04	0.54			-	-	-		0.54690	1/2/18		
			2.17	2.38	0.75			1.91	1.78	0.58		0.53910Y	12/15/17		
		1.25	6.29	4.69	4.48	10.4 -	9.0	1.60	1.52	1.32	2.6	0.440Y	32/4/39	65.5 -	56.5
		1.89	3.96	3.45	0.39							0.350	1/2/18		
		9.21	1.02	0.57		33.4 -	25.1							34.0 -	25.6
		-0.36	-0.44	-0.26				0.64	0.64	0.80	6.4	0.10	12/15/17	10.4 -	9.7
		-0.90	-30.03	-29.60	-33.80							1.0Y	11/28/08		
		-0.81	0.81	2.06	-1.54							0.010Y	11/26/10		
		0.64	1.50	1.12	2.49	34.7 -	23.0					5.7Y	6/21/13	52.1 -	34.5
		0.30	0.48	0.32		121.8 -	103.7	3.18	1.15	3.50	9.3	0.37190Y	3/26/18	36.5 -	31.3
		-0.28	-1.89	-2.49	-12.86			0.72	0.54	0.72	3.8	0.180Y	12/29/17	30.1 -	15.4
		2.52	9.52	9.08	7.42	22.5 -	18.4	2.97	2.69	2.42	1.5	0.840Y	32/4/39	213.9 -	175.3
		0.21	0.89	-0.61	1.50	35.6 -	19.5	0.93	0.92	0.89	3.6	0.120Y	32/4/39	31.7 -	17.4
	0.74	-	2.77	1.97	2.83	22.8 -	18.1	1.78	1.67	1.55	3.1	0.490Y	32/4/39	63.2 -	50.1
		-2.03	6.00	5.91	1.65	7.7 -	5.4	1.52	1.38	1.20	4.0	0.380Y	32/4/39	46.5 -	32.4
		-8.56	4.11	4.12	3.92	15.4 -	5.1					0.3750Y	4/30/13	63.4 -	21.1
		0.80	2.42	3.89	4.58	32.8 -	25.9					1.250	10/1/15	79.5 -	62.6
		0.01	1.00	4.09	1.18	37.9 -	20.5	2.72	2.47	2.23	9.3	0.510	32/4/39	37.9 -	20.5
		-3.94	-0.82	-4.97	-0.02									4.7 -	0.7
		0.02	-1.14	-0.40	-1.31			0.24	0.12	0.06	3.8	0.15940	2/15/18	8.1 -	4.3
		0.38	1.28	1.09	0.85							0.060	32/4/39		
		1.08	4.59	4.63	4.61	21.9 -	17.5	2.63	2.46	2.30	2.9	0.6750Y	32/4/39	100.7 -	80.5
		0.21	-0.56	-1.24	-2.51									4.2 -	3.1
		0.31	1.33	1.25	1.32	25.7 -	17.3	1.73	1.67	0.41	6.1	0.470Z	10/30/17	34.1 -	23.1
		-	-0.82	-4.05	0.13										
								1.53	1.53	1.53	5.9	0.31250Z	4/1/18	29.3 -	0.0
		0.35	-1.70	-2.69	0.82			0.04	0.17	0.21	1.2			4.4 -	2.6

SYMBOL	COMPANY	NATURE OF BUSINESS	FISCAL YEAR-END	TOTAL REV. $MILL	NET INCOME $MILL	TOTAL ASSETS $MILL	NET STK EQUITY $MILL	NO OF INST	INST. HOLDINGS (SHARES)
GTY	Getty Realty Corp.	REITs	12/31/16	115.3	38.4	877.3	430.9	213	30437157
GGP	GGP Inc	REITs	12/31/16	2346.4	1288.4	22732.7	8635.8		0
GIG	GigCapital Inc	Business Services	10/11/17		-0.0	0.1	0.0	-	0
GIL	Gildan Activewear Inc	Apparel, Footwear & Accessories	1/1/17	2585.1	346.6	2990.1	2119.6	284	184375650
GKOS	Glaukos Corp	Medical Instruments & Equipment	12/31/16	114.4	4.5	134.4	117.3	173	37413490
GSK	GlaxoSmithKline Plc	Pharmaceuticals	12/31/16	27889.0	912.0	59081.0	1124.0	1077	307857761
BRSS	Global Brass & Copper Holdings Inc	Metal Products	12/31/16	1338.5	32.2	582.6	90.8	171	22972901
GMRE	Global Medical REIT Inc	REITs	12/31/16	8.2	-6.4	227.3	155.0	94	9538599
GNL	Global Net Lease Inc	REITs	12/31/16	214.2	47.1	2891.5	1347.8	161	55630123
GLP	Global Partners LP	Equipment & Services	12/31/16	8239.6	-199.4	2564.0		85	16296210
GPN	Global Payments Inc	Business Services	12/31/16	2202.9	124.9	10664.4	2630.8	618	180883823
GSL	Global Ship Lease, Inc.	Shipping	12/31/16	166.5	-65.1	776.3	328.9	-	0
GLOB	Globant SA	IT Services	12/31/16	322.9	35.9	284.7	208.5	128	25245719
GMED	Globus Medical Inc	Medical Instruments & Equipment	12/31/16	564.0	104.3	927.6	832.1		0
GMS	GMS Inc	Construction Materials	4/30/17	2319.1	48.9	1393.3	514.6	165	25495978
GNC	GNC Holdings Inc	Retail - Food & Beverage, Drug & To	12/31/16	2540.0	-286.3	2068.6	-95.0	213	49367754
GDDY	GoDaddy Inc	Internet & Software	12/31/16	1847.9	-16.5	3786.9	562.5	247	144167616
GOL	Gol Linhas Aereas Inteligentes SA	Airlines/Air Freight	12/31/16	9867.3	849.6	8404.4	-3650.0	78	14382816
GFI	Gold Fields Ltd.	Precious Metals	12/31/16	2749.5	10.9	6334.7	3067.0	239	358943228
GG	Goldcorp Inc	Precious Metals	12/31/16	3510.0	162.0	21497.0	13415.0	576	535413758
GSBD	Goldman Sachs BDC Inc	Finance Intermediaries & Services	12/31/16	125.1	76.2	1190.5	665.1	79	14980684
GS	Goldman Sachs Group Inc	Finance Intermediaries & Services	12/31/16	37712.0	7398.0	860165.0	86893.0	1727	341179320
GER	Goldman Sachs MLP Energy Renai	Finance Intermediaries & Services	11/30/16	5.1	-10.3	857.6	597.6		0
GMZ	Goldman Sachs MLP Income Oppor	Finance Intermediaries & Services	11/30/16	7.8	-3.9	656.8	454.6	57	9903489
GRC	Gorman-Rupp Company (The)	Industrial Machinery & Equipment	12/31/16	382.1	24.9	382.8	302.9	137	16531148
GPX	GP Strategies Corp.	Business Services	12/31/16	490.6	20.2	315.6	167.5	115	17135321
GRA	Grace (WR) & Co	Specialty Chemicals	12/31/16	1598.6	94.1	2911.8	368.8	373	65287282
GGG	Graco Inc	Industrial Machinery & Equipment	12/30/16	1329.3	40.7	1243.1	573.8	512	66790452
GHM	Graham Corp.	Industrial Machinery & Equipment	3/31/17	91.8	5.0	151.6	114.1	121	9724488
GHC	Graham Holdings Co.	Educational Services	12/31/16	2481.8	168.6	4432.7	2452.9	346	4810650
GWW	Grainger (W.W.) Inc.	Electrical Equipment	12/31/16	10137.2	605.9	5694.3	1797.9	839	59309810
GPT	Gramercy Property Trust	REITs	12/31/16	517.3	33.4	5603.5	2752.7	300	191289184
GRAM	Grana y Montero S.A.A. (Peru)	Construction Services	12/31/15	7832.4	88.2	8991.8	2654.6	46	25045105
GVA	Granite Construction Inc.	Construction Services	12/31/16	2514.6	57.1	1733.5	836.0	318	50895709
GPMT	Granite Point Mortgage Trust Inc	REITs	12/31/16	61.0	35.4	1495.6	428.0	62	6157956
GPMT	Granite Point Mortgage Trust Inc	REITs	12/31/16	61.0	35.4	1495.6	428.0	62	6157956
GRP U	Granite Real Estate Investment Tru	REITs	12/31/16	223.4	279.3	2911.6	1948.2		0
GPK	Graphic Packaging Holding Co	Containers & Packaging	12/31/16	4298.1	228.0	4603.4	1056.5	348	467363441
GTN	Gray Television Inc	Radio & Television	12/31/16	812.5	62.3	2783.3	492.9	230	69725019
AJX	Great Ajax Corp	REITs	12/31/16	70.3	27.8	957.4	272.3	82	14256696
GXP	Great Plains Energy Inc	Electric Utilities	12/31/16	2676.0	290.0	13570.0	6162.0	529	224218430
GWB	Great Western Bancorp Inc	Banking	9/30/17	497.7	144.8	11690.0	1755.0	217	69245951
GDOT	Green Dot Corp	Credit & Lending	12/31/16	718.8	41.6	1740.3	683.7	269	49681229
GBX	Greenbrier Companies Inc (The)	Rail	8/31/17	2169.2	116.1	2397.7	1018.1	325	38737343
GHL	Greenhill & Co Inc	Finance Intermediaries & Services	12/31/16	335.5	60.8	456.7	291.2	294	38685692
GEF	Greif Inc	Containers & Packaging	10/31/17	3638.2	118.6	3232.3	1042.4	300	29230566
GFF	Griffon Corp.	Construction Materials	9/30/17	1525.0	14.9	1873.5	398.8	180	37039281
GPI	Group 1 Automotive, Inc.	Retail - Automotive	12/31/16	10887.6	147.1	4461.9	930.2	286	32250646
GRUB	GrubHub Inc	Internet & Software	12/31/16	493.3	49.6	1197.5	972.1	274	111612939
PAC	Grupo Aeroportuario del Pacifico, S.	Airlines/Air Freight	12/31/16	11107.6	3281.9	36051.5	21353.0	128	6572335
ASR	Grupo Aeroportuario del Sureste SA	Airlines/Air Freight	12/31/16	9753.5	3629.3	29216.1	22754.0	139	14383944
AVAL	Grupo Aval Acciones Y Valores SA	Banking	12/31/16	17546970.0	2139866.0	24073721.0	15601553.0	63	76984941
SUPV	Grupo Supervielle SA	Banking	12/31/16	15358.1	1311.3	53206.0	6931.6	104	43746138
TV	Grupo Televisa SAB	Radio & Television	12/31/16	96287.4	3721.4	309054.1	83791.9	278	378576649
GTT	GTT Communications, Inc	Internet & Software	12/31/16	521.7	5.3	953.3	127.8	147	32217797
GSH	Guangshen Railway Co., Ltd.	Rail	12/31/16	17280.5	1158.3	32870.3	28054.1	43	1200972
GES	GUESS ?, Inc.	Retail - Apparel and Accessories	1/28/17	2209.4	22.8	1534.5	969.2	290	84704254
GGM	Guggenheim Credit Allocation Fund	Holding and other Investment Office	5/31/16	16.5	13.4	201.9	136.1	33	834454
GPM	Guggenheim Enhanced Equity Inco	Holding and other Investment Office	12/31/16	4.4	1.2	233.1	159.2	65	10019236
GOF	Guggenheim Strategic Opportunitie	Holding and other Investment Office	5/31/17	38.7	30.3	538.0	410.5	53	3499903
GBAB	Guggenheim Taxable Municipal Ma	Holding and other Investment Office	5/31/17	33.9	27.7	521.8	405.8	48	3963510
GWRE	Guidewire Software Inc	Internet & Software	7/31/17	514.3	21.2	1078.9	893.3	292	88107795
HAE	Haemonetics Corp.	Medical Instruments & Equipment	4/1/17	886.1	-26.3	1238.7	739.6	300	67555178
HK	Halcon Resources Corp	Production & Extraction	12/31/16	153.4	-479.2	1319.7	112.7	209	148425199
HAL	Halliburton Company	Equipment & Services	12/31/16	15887.0	-5763.0	27000.0	9409.0	1422	857990768
HYH	Halyard Health Inc	Medical Instruments & Equipment	12/31/16	1592.3	39.8	2071.8	1102.5	385	48330938
HBB	Hamilton Beach Brands Holding Co	Household Appliances, Electronics &	12/31/16	745.4	26.2	310.8	65.1	8	287430
HPS	Hancock John Preferred Income Fd	Holding and other Investment Office	7/31/17	57.4	45.2	928.8	616.7	60	4112521
HPF	Hancock John Preferred Income Fu	Holding and other Investment Office	7/31/17	43.4	34.0	705.1	465.6	56	1342508
HTD	Hancock John Tax-Advantaged Divi	Holding and other Investment Office	10/31/17	76.5	58.5	1366.0	934.9	100	7995450
HBI	HanesBrands Inc	Apparel, Footwear & Accessories	12/31/16	6028.2	539.4	6907.7	1223.9	845	397344129
HASI	Hannon Armstrong Sustainable Infr	REITs	12/31/16	81.2	14.7	1745.9	570.6	202	43494656
THG	Hanover Insurance Group Inc	General Insurance	12/31/16	4945.8	155.1	14220.4	2857.5	402	50121915
HOG	Harley-Davidson Inc	Autos- Manufacturing	12/31/16	5996.5	692.2	9890.2	1920.2	764	202446590
HMY	Harmony Gold Mining Co. Ltd.	Precious Metals	6/30/17	1416.0	17.0	2966.0	2234.0	143	119607949
HRS	Harris Corp.	Defense	6/30/17	5900.0	553.0	10090.0	2928.0	891	147066182
HSC	Harsco Corp.	Industrial Machinery & Equipment	12/31/16	1451.2	-85.7	1581.4	96.3	358	78872544
HHS	Harte Hanks Inc	Advertising	12/31/16	404.4	-130.9	213.4	2.7	120	29032953
HIG	Hartford Financial Services Group I	General Insurance	12/31/16	18300.0	896.0	223432.0	16903.0	944	421258956
HVT	Haverty Furniture Cos., Inc.	Retail - Furniture & Home Furnishing	12/31/16	821.6	28.4	454.5	281.9	177	20284687

| EARNINGS PER SHARE | | | | | | P/E RATIO | | DIVIDENDS PER SHARE | | | AV. YLD % | DIV. DECLARED | | PRICE RANGE 2016 | |
| QUARTERLY | | | ANNUAL | | | | | | | | | | | | |
1st	2nd	3rd	2016	2015	2014			2016	2015	2014		AMOUNT	PAYABLE		
-	-	0.24	1.12	1.11	0.69	26.6 -	20.6	1.03	1.15	0.96	3.9	0.320Z	1/4/18	29.8 -	23.1
-	-	0.23	1.34	1.43	0.69	19.4 -	14.2	1.06	0.71	0.63	4.6	0.39840Z	32/4/39	26.0 -	19.0
-	-	0.52	1.47	1.25	1.46	28.6 -	16.2	0.31	0.26	0.22	0.9	0.09350	12/11/17	42.0 -	23.8
-	-	0.04	0.12	-2.13	-5.29	435.3 -	204.2							52.2 -	24.5
-0.04	-	-	0.19	1.72	0.57	233.5 -	182.4	1.92	1.55	1.60	4.8			44.4 -	34.7
-	-	0.56	1.49	1.66	1.49	25.5 -	18.9	0.15	0.15	0.15	0.5	0.060	11/22/17	38.0 -	28.2
-	-	0.02	-0.68	-6.44	-1.64			0.74	1.02	0.09	8.2	0.46880Z	1/31/18	10.2 -	8.2
-	-	0.03	0.81	-0.03	-1.29	30.8 -	25.0	-	2.13	2.13		0.45310Y	1/16/18	25.0 -	20.2
-	-	0.44	-5.91	1.11	3.95			1.85	2.73	2.53	10.1	0.46250	32/4/39	21.6 -	16.1
-	-	0.71	0.81	2.06	1.69	128.7 -	87.0	0.02	0.04	0.04	0.0	0.010Y	32/4/39	104.3 -	70.5
-	-	0.15	-1.42	-0.67	0.10							0.54690	1/2/18	- -	
-	-	0.27	1.01	0.90	0.79									- -	
-	-	0.26	1.08	1.17	0.97	38.6 -	23.0							41.6 -	24.8
-	0.43	-	0.38	-0.43	-0.59	102.7 -	71.7							39.0 -	27.2
-	-	0.31	-4.12	2.60	2.81			0.80	0.72	0.64	10.2	0.20Y	12/30/16	11.4 -	3.4
-	-	0.17	-0.21	-0.81	-1.11									51.1 -	34.4
-	-	-	0.04	-0.21	-0.06	318.4 -	75.0							12.7 -	3.0
-	-	-	0.20	-0.45	-0.04	23.4 -	14.8	0.04	0.02	0.03	1.1			4.7 -	3.0
-	-	0.13	0.19	-5.03	-2.66	121.6 -	62.0	0.12	0.45	0.60	0.7	0.020	12/22/17	23.1 -	11.8
-	-	0.45	1.12	2.14	1.77	22.7 -	19.0	1.80	1.80	1.69	7.8	0.450	1/16/18	25.4 -	21.3
-	-	5.02	16.29	12.14	17.07	16.0 -	13.0	2.60	2.55	2.25	1.1	0.750Y	3/29/18	261.0 -	211.3
-	-	-	-0.13	0.09	0.05			0.64	1.33	0.32	8.9	0.160	11/29/17	8.8 -	5.4
-	-	-	-0.09	0.03				0.84	1.37	1.29	8.6	0.210	11/29/17	11.6 -	7.9
-	-	0.22	0.95	0.96	1.38	35.2 -	25.3	0.43	0.41	0.37	1.5	0.1250Y	32/4/39	33.5 -	24.1
-	-	0.19	1.21	1.09	1.43	25.7 -	18.7	-	-	-		0.025	2/1/89	31.1 -	22.6
-	-	0.70	1.33	1.99	3.63	57.6 -	49.9	0.51	-	-	0.7	0.210Y	32/4/39	76.6 -	66.4
-	-	0.43	0.24	1.95	1.22	190.1 -	115.7	0.44	0.40	0.37	1.2	0.13250Y	32/4/39	45.6 -	27.8
-	-	-	0.61	1.45	1.00	40.6 -	29.6	0.33	0.20	0.13	1.6	0.090Y	11/21/17	24.7 -	18.0
-	-	4.42	29.80	-17.87	195.03	20.5 -	17.3	4.84	9.10	10.20	0.8	1.330Y	32/4/39	610.1 -	515.0
-	-	2.79	9.87	11.58	11.45	26.2 -	15.8	4.83	4.59	4.17	2.4	1.280Y	32/4/39	258.2 -	156.3
-	-	0.32	0.19	-0.90	0.24	163.7 -	133.5	1.37	-	1.51	4.8	0.3750Z	1/12/18	31.1 -	25.4
-	-	-	0.13	0.45				-	0.76	0.81				6.9 -	2.2
-	-	1.14	1.42	1.52	0.64	46.9 -	32.2	0.52	0.52	0.52	1.0	0.130Y	32/4/39	66.7 -	45.7
-	-	0.27	0.52	-	-	37.1 -	33.6					0.380Z	1/18/18	19.3 -	17.4
-	-	0.27	0.52			36.2 -	0.0					0.380Z	1/18/18	18.8 -	0.0
-	-	-	-	-	-			2.43	2.30	2.21	5.6	0.2270	2/15/18	52.3 -	32.6
-	-	0.15	0.71	0.70	0.27	22.3 -	17.3	0.23	0.20	-	1.7	0.0750Y	32/4/39	15.8 -	12.3
-	-	0.21	0.86	0.57	0.82	20.2 -	11.7					0.030Y	10/15/08	17.4 -	10.1
-	-	0.38	1.65	1.68	0.40	8.9 -	7.7	0.99	0.64	-	7.2	0.45310Z	1/15/18	14.6 -	12.8
-	-	0.02	1.61	1.37	1.57	21.6 -	16.7	1.06	1.00	0.94	3.5	0.2750Y	32/4/39	34.7 -	26.9
-	-	0.59	2.14	1.90	1.81	21.2 -	15.6	0.56	0.36	1.76	1.4	0.20	2/21/18	45.4 -	33.5
-	-	0.26	0.80	0.72	0.90	80.8 -	29.5							64.6 -	23.6
0.83	-	-	5.73	5.93	3.44	9.5 -	7.0	0.81	0.60	0.15	1.8	0.230Y	2/16/18	54.2 -	40.3
-	-	-0.18	1.89	0.82	1.43	16.3 -	7.4	1.80	1.80	1.80	8.2	0.050Y	12/20/17	30.8 -	14.0
-	-	0.74	1.28	1.23	1.56	50.7 -	40.0	1.68	1.68	1.68	3.0	0.620Y	32/4/39	64.9 -	51.2
-	-	0.22	0.68	0.73	0.00	39.8 -	26.5	0.20	0.16	0.12	0.9	0.070Y	12/21/17	27.1 -	18.0
-	-	1.43	6.67	3.90	3.60	12.5 -	8.0	0.91	0.83	0.70	1.3	0.250Y	32/4/39	83.4 -	53.2
-	-	0.15	0.58	0.44	0.30	127.7 -	56.7							74.1 -	32.9
-	-	-	6.24	5.98	4.27	19.0 -	11.7	68.93	56.10	58.57	69.1			118.8 -	73.0
-	-	1.70	12.10	9.71	7.61	18.8 -	11.1	49.02	50.05	-	26.6			228.1 -	134.3
-	-	-	-	-	-			1175.51	2019.35	354.76	13947.3			9.2 -	7.5
-	-	-	-	-	-									30.1 -	13.4
-	-	-	1.20	3.52	1.74	22.7 -	14.6	1.54	1.58	-	6.5			27.3 -	17.5
-	-	-0.23	0.14	0.54	-0.85	335.4 -	166.1							47.0 -	23.3
-	-	0.13	0.16	0.15	0.09	208.8 -	152.9	3.48	2.16	3.52	12.1			33.4 -	24.5
-	-	-0.04	0.96	1.11	1.80	18.7 -	10.1	0.90	0.90	0.80	6.6	0.2250Y	1/3/18	17.9 -	9.7
-	-	-	2.02	1.95	1.64	11.9 -	10.7	2.18	2.16	1.46	9.5	0.18130	1/31/18	24.0 -	21.7
-	-	-	0.06	0.06	-0.06	149.8 -	132.2	0.96	0.96	0.96	11.4	0.240	12/29/17	9.0 -	7.9
-	-	-	1.40	1.28	1.44	15.6 -	14.0	2.19	2.19	2.19	10.5	0.18210	1/31/18	21.8 -	19.6
-	-	-	1.48	1.48	1.63	15.7 -	14.5	1.66	1.66	1.66	7.4	0.12570	1/31/18	23.2 -	21.4
-0.12	-	-	0.20	0.14	0.21	413.8 -	254.6							82.8 -	50.9
-	0.38	-	-1.09	0.32	0.67									59.0 -	36.9
-	-	2.82	-5.26	-633.60	100.17							14.3750	12/1/15	9.8 -	3.8
-	-	0.42	-6.69	-0.79	4.11			0.72	0.72	0.63	1.6	0.180Y	32/4/39	58.2 -	38.7
-	-	0.35	0.85	-9.15	0.58	57.2 -	41.8							48.6 -	35.5
-	-	0.31	1.92	1.41	-	20.8 -	13.0					0.085G	12/15/17	39.9 -	25.0
-	-	-	1.41	1.44	1.46	13.7 -	12.6	1.47	1.47	1.47	7.9	0.12220	1/31/18	19.4 -	17.7
-	-	-	1.59	1.64	1.64	14.2 -	12.7	1.68	1.68	1.68	7.8	0.140	1/31/18	22.6 -	20.3
-	-	-	1.44	1.38	1.54	18.4 -	16.5	1.47	1.45	1.35	5.8	0.1380	1/31/18	26.6 -	23.7
-	-	0.55	1.40	1.06	1.32	18.3 -	13.6	0.44	0.40	0.30	2.0	0.150Y	32/4/39	25.7 -	19.0
-	-	0.14	0.32	0.21	0.43	78.8 -	56.6	1.23	1.08	0.92	5.5	0.330Z	1/11/18	25.2 -	18.1
-	-	0.26	3.59	7.40	6.28	30.3 -	22.4	1.88	1.69	1.52	2.0	0.540Y	32/4/39	108.8 -	80.6
-	-	0.40	3.83	3.69	3.88	16.4 -	11.7	1.40	1.24	1.10	2.6	0.3650Y	32/4/39	62.9 -	44.8
0.03	-	-	0.15	-0.86	-0.27	19.9 -	10.6							3.0 -	1.6
1.32	-	-	2.59	3.11	4.95	55.8 -	38.6	2.00	1.88	1.68	1.7	0.570Y	32/4/39	144.5 -	100.0
-	-	0.16	-1.07	0.08	-0.31			0.05	0.82	0.82	0.3	0.05120Y	2/16/16	21.9 -	11.7
-	-	-0.04	-2.13	-2.77	0.38			0.09	0.34	0.34	7.6	0.0850Y	3/15/16	1.6 -	0.8
-	-	0.64	2.27	3.96	1.73	25.4 -	20.7	0.86	0.78	0.66	1.7	0.260Y	32/4/39	57.6 -	47.0
-	-	0.28	1.30	1.22	0.37	20.8 -	16.3	1.44	0.36	1.32	6.0	0.150Y	12/8/17	27.0 -	21.3

SYMBOL	COMPANY	NATURE OF BUSINESS	FISCAL YEAR-END	TOTAL REV. $MILL	NET INCOME $MILL	TOTAL ASSETS $MILL	NET STK EQUITY $MILL	NO OF INST	INST. HOLDINGS (SHARES)
HE	Hawaiian Electric Industries Inc	Electric Utilities	12/31/16	2380.7	250.1	12425.5	2101.0	366	66220344
HCHC	HC2 Holdings Inc	Business Services	12/31/16	1558.1	-94.5	2835.3	73.7	3	43552
HCA	HCA Healthcare Inc	Hospitals & Health Care Facilities	12/31/16	41490.0	2890.0	33758.0	-7302.0	745	309771572
HCI	HCI Group Inc	General Insurance	12/31/16	264.4	29.0	670.1	243.7	153	8818287
HCP	HCP Inc	REITs	12/31/16	2129.3	627.7	15759.3	5547.6	883	528724384
HDB	HDFC Bank Ltd	Banking	3/31/15	602121.8	107000.5	6070965.2	633156.9	455	161690207
HR	Healthcare Realty Trust, Inc.	REITs	12/31/16	411.6	85.6	3040.6	1653.4	318	146904138
HTA	Healthcare Trust Of America Inc	REITs	12/31/16	460.9	45.9	3747.8	1687.3	343	241271085
HL	Hecla Mining Co	Precious Metals	12/31/16	646.0	69.5	2371.7	1479.8	302	289727613
HEI	HEICO Corp	Aerospace	10/31/17	1524.8	186.0	2512.4	1161.1	309	26623267
HLX	Helix Energy Solutions Group Inc	Equipment & Services	12/31/16	487.6	-81.4	2246.9	1281.8	302	152366876
HP	Helmerich & Payne, Inc.	Equipment & Services	9/30/17	1804.7	-128.2	6440.0	4164.6	731	148505335
HLF	Herbalife Ltd	Household & Personal Products	12/31/16	4488.4	260.0	2565.4	196.3	328	107306610
HRI	Herc Holdings Inc	Miscellaneous Transportation Servic	12/31/16	1554.8	-19.7	3463.3	317.7	312	174833173
HTGC	Hercules Capital Inc	Holding and other Investment Office	12/31/16	158.7	100.3	1464.2	787.9	240	40320002
HRTG	Heritage Insurance Holdings Inc	General Insurance	12/31/16	439.0	33.9	1033.2	358.0	126	21899076
HT	Hersha Hospitality Trust	REITs	12/31/16	466.6	117.0	2155.5	835.4	241	62496710
HSY	Hershey Company (The)	Food	12/31/16	7440.2	720.0	5524.3	785.9	1040	137573694
HTZ	Hertz Global Holdings Inc (New)	Miscellaneous Transportation Servic	12/31/16	8803.0	-491.0	19155.0	1075.0	235	107325091
HES	Hess Corp	Production & Extraction	12/31/16	4844.0	-6132.0	28621.0	14534.0	784	340200919
HESM	Hess Midstream Partners LP	Oil Royalty Traders	12/31/16	509.8	206.3	2574.4	2238.1	52	15613435
HPE	Hewlett Packard Enterprise Co	IT Services	10/31/17	28871.0	344.0	61406.0	23466.0	820	1445371647
HXL	Hexcel Corp.	Plastics	12/31/16	2004.3	249.8	2400.6	1244.9	476	111071970
HF	HFF Inc	Property, Real Estate & Developmen	12/31/16	517.4	77.2	716.7	236.5	232	42580161
HCLP	Hi-Crush Partners LP	Mining	12/31/16	204.4	-81.0	529.3		142	41574773
HIW	Highwoods Properties, Inc.	REITs	12/31/16	665.6	524.3	4561.1	2136.4	373	120516630
HIL	Hill International Inc	Business Services	12/31/16	520.8	-18.8	401.2	88.4	89	32492823
HRC	Hill-Rom Holdings, Inc.	Medical Instruments & Equipment	9/30/17	2743.7	133.6	4528.7	1358.2	27	4651596
HI	Hillenbrand Inc	Industrial Machinery & Equipment	9/30/17	1590.2	126.2	1956.5	751.4	291	60780512
HTH	Hilltop Holdings, Inc.	Banking	12/31/16	1742.9	145.9	12738.1	1870.5	238	66629388
HGV	Hilton Grand Vacations Inc	Hotels, Restaurants & Travel	12/31/16	1583.0	168.0	2180.0	167.0	242	98446639
HGV	Hilton Grand Vacations Inc	Hotels, Restaurants & Travel	12/31/16	1583.0	168.0	2180.0	167.0	242	98446639
HLT	Hilton Worldwide Holdings Inc	Hotels, Restaurants & Travel	12/31/16	11663.0	348.0	26211.0	5899.0	497	382872931
HLT	Hilton Worldwide Holdings Inc	Hotels, Restaurants & Travel	12/31/16	11663.0	348.0	26211.0	5899.0	497	382872931
HNI	HNI Corp	Office Equipment & Furniture	12/31/16	2203.5	85.6	1330.2	500.6	240	47040764
HMLP	Hoegh LNG Partners LP	Shipping	12/31/16	91.1	41.4	810.5	364.8	49	13206808
HEP	Holly Energy Partners LP	Equipment & Services	12/31/16	402.0	147.6	1884.2		138	35792423
HFC	HollyFrontier Corp	Refining & Marketing	12/31/16	10535.7	-260.5	9435.7	4681.4	583	187330279
HD	Home Depot Inc	Retail - Hardware & Home Improvem	1/29/17	94595.0	7957.0	42966.0	4333.0	2492	1050071251
HMC	Honda Motor Co., Ltd.(Honda Giken	Autos- Manufacturing	3/31/17	13999200.0	616569.0	18958123.0	7295296.0	328	53891625
HON	Honeywell International Inc	Auto Parts	12/31/16	39302.0	4809.0	54146.0	19372.0	2030	710121804
HMN	Horace Mann Educators Corp.	General Insurance	12/31/16	1128.9	83.8	10576.8	1294.0	240	51170010
HZN	Horizon Global Corp	Auto Parts	12/31/16	649.2	-12.4	613.4	32.4	143	26367454
HRL	Hormel Foods Corp.	Food	10/29/17	9167.5	846.7	6975.9	4935.9	709	233288208
HOS	Hornbeck Offshore Services Inc	Equipment & Services	12/31/16	224.3	-63.8	2878.3	1403.0	154	35661645
DHI	Horton (DR) Inc	Builders	9/30/17	14091.0	1038.4	12184.6	7747.1	806	385096983
HST	Host Hotels & Resorts Inc	REITs	12/31/16	5430.0	762.0	11408.0	6994.0	715	972459516
HLI	Houlihan Lokey Inc	Wealth Management	3/31/17	872.1	108.3	1385.7	726.6	149	23909500
HOV	Hovnanian Enterprises, Inc.	Builders	10/31/17	2451.7	-332.2	1900.9	-460.4	195	63866102
HHC	Howard Hughes Corp	Property, Real Estate & Developmen	12/31/16	1035.0	202.3	6367.4	2567.7	314	43629131
HPQ	HP Inc	Computer Hardware & Equipment	10/31/17	52056.0	2526.0	32913.0	-3408.0	1390	1690873230
HRG	HRG Group Inc	Household & Personal Products	9/30/17	5008.5	106.0	35849.7	758.0	215	219061048
HSFC PR	HSBC Finance Corp	Credit & Lending	12/31/16	1414.0	-529.0	13882.0	5434.0		0
HSBC	HSBC Holdings Plc	Banking	12/31/16	77683.0	2479.0	2374986.0	175386.0	561	105313045
HUSI PR	HSBC USA, Inc.	Banking	12/31/16	5242.0	129.0	201301.0	20355.0	1	80000
HNP	Huaneng Power International Inc	Electric Utilities	12/31/16	113814.2	8814.3	309417.6	81521.5	109	2967253
HUBB	Hubbell Inc.	Electrical Equipment	12/31/16	3505.2	293.0	3525.0	1592.8	414	54677797
HUBS	HubSpot Inc	Internet & Software	12/31/16	271.0	-45.6	259.8	118.7	226	36711570
HBM	Hudbay Minerals Inc	Precious Metals	12/31/16	1128.7	-35.2	4456.6	1763.2	152	147760578
HPP	Hudson Pacific Properties Inc	REITs	12/31/16	639.6	28.0	6679.0	3113.5	261	176835432
HGT	Hugoton Royalty Trust (TX)	Oil Royalty Traders	12/31/16	2.7	1.9	28.1	26.9	112	6255956
HUM	Humana Inc.	Life & Health	12/31/16	54379.0	614.0	25396.0	10685.0	921	165962441
HII	Huntington Ingalls Industries, Inc.	Defense	12/31/16	7068.0	573.0	6352.0	1653.0	547	44605312
HUN	Huntsman Corp	Specialty Chemicals	12/31/16	9657.0	326.0	9189.0	1287.0	498	223039888
H	Hyatt Hotels Corp	Hotels, Restaurants & Travel	12/31/16	4429.0	204.0	7749.0	3903.0	252	47989995
HY	Hyster-Yale Materials Handling Inc	Autos- Manufacturing	12/31/16	2569.7	42.8	1287.1	463.8	181	9672938
IAG	IAMGold Corp	Precious Metals	12/31/16	987.1	52.6	3400.5	2221.7	239	293430644
IBN	ICICI Bank Ltd (India)	Banking	3/31/17	1133976.3	101883.8	9860426.6	1046320.0	435	759343018
IDA	Idacorp Inc	Electric Utilities	12/31/16	1262.0	198.3	6289.9	2153.9	351	54332906
IEX	IDEX Corporation	Industrial Machinery & Equipment	12/31/16	2113.0	271.1	3154.9	1543.9	471	88027531
IDT	IDT Corp	Services	7/31/17	1501.7	8.2	519.0	145.7	145	15621034
ITW	Illinois Tool Works, Inc.	Industrial Machinery & Equipment	12/31/16	13599.0	2035.0	15201.0	4254.0	1510	354575666
IMAX	IMAX Corp.	Entertainment	12/31/16	377.3	28.8	857.3	562.0	253	66913309
ICD	Independence Contract Drilling Inc	Equipment & Services	12/31/16	70.1	-22.2	302.1	257.3	92	31393783
IHC	Independence Holding Company	Life & Health	12/31/16	311.0	123.3	1134.5	436.6	77	3672058
IRT	Independence Realty Trust Inc	REITs	12/31/16	153.4	-9.8	1294.2	506.8	194	71551298
IFN	India Fund, Inc. (The)	Holding and other Investment Office	12/31/16	10.2	-0.1	734.5	689.7	128	11381856
IBA	Industrias Bachoco S.A.B. de C.V.	Food	12/31/16	52020.3	3946.6	45090.5	31662.3		0
INFY	Infosys Ltd.	IT Services	3/31/17	10208.0	2140.0	12854.0	10637.0	411	461069462
HIFR	InfraREIT Inc	REITs	12/31/16	172.1	-50.0	1876.7	688.0	163	40915894

T30

EARNINGS PER SHARE						P/E RATIO		DIVIDENDS PER SHARE			AV. YLD %	DIV. DECLARED		PRICE RANGE	
QUARTERLY			ANNUAL											2016	
1st	2nd	3rd	2016	2015	2014			2016	2015	2014		AMOUNT	PAYABLE		
-	-	0.55	2.29	1.50	1.64	16.7 -	13.9	1.24	1.24	1.24	3.7	0.310Y	32/4/39	38.4 -	31.8
-	-	-0.16	-2.83	-1.50	-0.72							8.57	8/27/13	7.1 -	4.3
-	-	1.15	7.30	4.99	4.16	12.4 -	10.2					2.7Y	32/4/39	90.5 -	74.2
-	-	-4.44	2.92	5.90	5.36	17.0 -	9.9	1.20	1.20	1.10	2.9	0.350Y	3/16/18	49.6 -	28.9
-	-	-0.02	1.34	-1.21	2.00	24.9 -	18.8	2.10	2.26	2.18	7.1	0.370Z	32/4/39	33.4 -	25.2
-	-	7.80	-	43.60	36.31									101.7 -	59.2
-	-	0.02	0.78	0.70	0.33	46.4 -	38.2	1.20	1.20	1.20	3.7	0.30Z	32/4/39	36.2 -	29.8
-	-	0.07	0.33	0.26	0.37	99.8 -	86.9	1.19	1.17	0.29	3.9	0.3050Z	32/4/39	32.9 -	28.7
-	-	0.00	0.18	-0.23	0.05	37.3 -	19.2	0.01	0.01	0.01	0.2	0.8750Y	1/2/18	6.7 -	3.5
-	-	0.42	1.47	1.26	1.15	52.9 -	32.9	0.10	0.09	0.30	0.2	0.070Y	32/4/39	77.8 -	48.4
-	-	0.02	-0.73	-3.58	1.85									9.7 -	4.9
-	-	-0.21	-0.54	3.87	6.46			2.76	2.75	2.44	4.7	0.70Y	32/4/39	81.1 -	42.3
-	-	0.66	3.02	3.97	3.40			-	-	0.30		0.30	32/4/39		
-	-	0.45	-0.70	9.00	-2.70									65.8 -	35.0
-	-	0.29	1.34	1.04	1.13	11.6 -	9.0	1.24	1.24	1.24	9.1	0.310	11/20/17	15.6 -	12.0
-	-	-0.34	1.14	3.05	1.82	16.3 -	8.2	0.23	0.05		1.7	0.060Y	12/15/17	18.6 -	9.3
-	-	-0.07	2.18	0.56	1.04	9.8 -	7.9	0.84	0.84	1.04	4.5	0.40630Z	1/16/18	21.5 -	17.3
-	-	1.28	3.34	2.32	3.77	34.7 -	30.8	2.40	2.24	2.04	2.2	0.5960Y	32/4/39	116.0 -	102.9
-	-	1.12	-5.85	3.00	-0.09									26.7 -	8.7
-	-	-2.02	-19.92	-10.78	7.53			1.00	1.00	1.00	2.1	1.0Y	32/4/39	62.8 -	38.1
-	-	0.27										0.32180	2/13/18	26.3 -	18.6
-	-	0.10	1.82	1.34		8.3 -	7.2	0.22			1.6	0.0750Y	32/4/39	15.1 -	13.1
-	-	0.76	2.65	2.44	2.12	24.1 -	18.8	0.43	0.40		0.8	0.1250Y	32/4/39	-63.8 -	49.8
-	-	0.54	1.99	2.18	1.61	24.4 -	13.1	1.80	1.80	1.83	5.1	1.757Y	2/21/18	48.6 -	26.1
-	-	0.32	-1.64	0.73	3.00				1.83	2.23		0.20	2/13/18	21.9 -	7.4
-	-	0.55	5.30	1.00	1.19	10.0 -	9.2	2.50	1.70	1.70	4.9	21.56250Z	32/4/39	53.2 -	48.9
-0.14	-	-	-0.36	0.14	-0.25									5.7 -	3.7
-	-	0.09	1.86	0.82	1.04	45.9 -	30.5	0.67	0.63	0.59	0.9	0.180Y	32/4/39	85.4 -	56.8
-	-	0.52	1.77	1.74	1.72	26.0 -	19.7	0.81	0.80	0.79	2.1	0.20750Y	12/29/17	46.0 -	34.9
-	-	0.31	1.48	2.09	1.17	20.5 -	14.8	0.06			0.2	0.070	2/28/18	30.3 -	21.9
-	-	0.43	1.70	-		25.1 -	14.7							42.7 -	25.0
-	-	0.43	1.70	-		15.0 -	15.0							25.6 -	25.6
-	-	0.55	1.05	4.26	2.04	78.3 -	52.8	0.84	0.42		1.3	0.150Y	12/29/17	82.2 -	55.4
-	-	0.55	1.05	4.26	2.04	53.9 -	53.9	0.84	0.42		1.5	0.150Y	12/29/17	56.6 -	56.6
-	-	0.84	1.88	2.32	1.35	29.7 -	17.5	1.09	1.04	0.99	2.6	0.2850Y	32/4/39	55.9 -	33.0
-	-	-	1.58	1.56	0.50			1.65	1.35	0.18		0.7899GH	2/15/18		
-	-	0.66	1.69	1.60	1.20	22.4 -	17.9	2.32	2.17	2.04	6.8	0.650	2/14/18	37.8 -	30.3
-	-	1.53	-1.48	3.90	1.42			1.32	1.31	3.26	4.1	0.330Y	32/4/39	51.6 -	23.9
-	-	1.84	5.46	4.71	3.76	34.9 -	24.5	2.36	1.88	1.56	1.5	0.890Y	32/4/39	190.4 -	133.5
115.04	-	-	191.16	282.66	318.54	0.2 -	0.1	88.05	88.63	79.67	294.4			34.4 -	27.2
-	-	1.75	6.20	6.04	5.33	25.2 -	18.7	2.45	2.15	1.87	1.8	0.7450Y	32/4/39	156.0 -	116.2
-	-	0.64	2.02	2.20	2.47	23.3 -	16.8	1.06	1.00	0.92	2.6	0.2750Y	12/29/17	47.1 -	34.0
-	-	0.27	-0.66	0.46										24.4 -	12.3
-	-	0.34	1.64	1.27	1.12	23.1 -	18.4	0.58	0.50	0.40	1.7	0.18750Y	32/4/39	37.9 -	30.1
-	-	-0.51	-1.76	1.84	2.41									8.4 -	1.5
-	-	0.76	2.36	2.03	1.50	21.8 -	11.7	0.32	0.25	0.14	0.9	0.1250Y	32/4/39	51.5 -	27.6
-	-	0.14	1.02	0.74	0.96	20.2 -	17.0	0.85	0.80	0.75	4.6	0.057Z	32/4/39	20.6 -	17.4
-	0.50	-	1.10	135.88	104.31	41.8 -	27.0	0.30			0.8	0.20Y	12/15/17	46.0 -	29.7
-	-	-2.28	-0.02	-0.11	1.87							0.47660Z	10/15/07	3.4 -	1.7
-	-	-	4.73	1.60	-0.60	27.9 -	22.3							131.8 -	105.3
-	-	0.41	1.43	2.48	2.62	15.7 -	10.2	0.50	0.67	0.61	2.7	0.13930Y	32/4/39	22.5 -	14.6
-	-	0.01	-0.99	-2.81	-0.51									20.1 -	14.3
-	-	-	-	-				0.86	1.59	1.59		0.39750Y	6/15/16		
-	-	-	0.07	0.64	0.69	738.0 -	567.6	2.55	2.50	2.45	5.6	0.50	6/15/18	51.7 -	39.7
-	-	-	-	-				0.49	1.02	1.01		0.40630Z	4/1/16		
0.04	-	-	0.58	0.94	0.76	54.5 -	42.1	17.18	13.65	13.71	63.6			31.6 -	24.4
-	-	1.47	5.24	4.77	5.48	26.2 -	21.0	2.59			2.2	0.770Y	32/4/39	137.5 -	109.9
-	-	-0.29	-1.29	-1.39	-4.20									93.0 -	47.9
-	-	0.17	-0.15	-1.41	0.34			0.02	0.02	0.02	0.2	0.010	9/29/17	11.8 -	4.7
-	-	0.07	0.25	-0.19	0.15	146.6 -	126.9	0.80	0.57	0.50	2.3	0.250Z	32/4/39	36.6 -	31.7
-	-	0.01	0.05	0.19	1.10	45.0 -	26.0	0.05	0.19	1.10	2.8	0.01080Z	1/16/18	2.3 -	1.3
-	-	3.44	4.07	8.44	7.36	64.1 -	48.0	0.87	1.15	1.11	0.4	0.40Y	32/4/39	260.9 -	195.2
-	-	3.27	12.14	8.36	6.86	20.8 -	15.3	2.10	1.70	1.00	1.0	0.720Y	32/4/39	252.0 -	185.2
-	-	0.60	1.36	0.38	1.31	24.6 -	14.1	0.50	0.50	0.50	1.9	0.1250Y	32/4/39	33.4 -	19.2
-	-	0.14	1.52	0.86	2.23	48.6 -	33.3							73.9 -	50.6
-	-	1.00	2.61	4.57	6.58	34.5 -	20.6	1.17	1.13	1.08	1.7	0.30250Y	12/15/17	90.0 -	53.7
-	-	0.07	0.12	-1.93	-0.55	72.8 -	28.3					0.1250	7/12/13	8.7 -	3.4
3.17	-	-	17.41	20.94	19.03	0.6 -	0.4	9.10	8.32	6.82	106.2			9.9 -	6.8
-	-	1.80	3.94	3.87	3.85	25.1 -	19.8	2.08	1.92	1.76	2.4	0.590Y	32/4/39	98.8 -	78.0
-	-	1.08	3.53	3.62	3.45	38.4 -	25.3	1.34	1.24	1.07	1.2	0.370Y	32/4/39	135.6 -	89.3
-0.08	-	-	1.03	3.63	0.82	19.7 -	9.9	0.75	2.03	0.59	5.0	0.19DY	12/29/17	20.3 -	10.2
-	-	1.85	5.70	5.13	7.28	29.7 -	21.3	2.40	2.07	1.81	1.7	0.780Y	32/4/39	169.3 -	121.6
-	-	-0.01	0.42	0.78	0.56	81.5 -	42.1							34.3 -	17.7
-	-	-0.16	-0.67	-0.33	-1.65									7.1 -	2.8
-	-	0.34	7.09	1.71	0.92	4.2 -	2.4	0.15	0.08	0.07	0.7	0.10Y	1/16/18	29.8 -	16.7
-	-	0.02	-0.19	0.78	0.14			0.72	0.72	0.72	7.4	0.060Z	1/15/18	10.6 -	8.7
-	-	-	0.01	0.08				1.71	1.82	1.86	6.5	0.0001B	1/8/18	28.8 -	21.1
-	-	0.59	6.58	6.36	6.55	10.3 -	7.0	14.97	17.75		26.5			67.6 -	46.2
-	-	0.35	0.90	0.88	0.77	18.0 -	15.1	0.97	1.49	0.98	6.4			16.2 -	13.6
-	-	0.35	1.14	0.31	-86.35	20.3 -	14.4	1.00	0.81		5.1	0.250Z	1/18/18	23.2 -	16.4

SYMBOL	COMPANY	NATURE OF BUSINESS	FISCAL YEAR-END	TOTAL REV. $MILL	NET INCOME $MILL	TOTAL ASSETS $MILL	NET STK EQUITY $MILL	NO OF INST	INST. HOLDINGS (SHARES)
ING	ING Groep NV	Banking	12/31/16	45988.0	4975.0	842216.0	47257.0	363	127766169
IR	Ingersoll-Rand Plc	Industrial Machinery & Equipment	12/31/16	13508.9	1476.2	17397.4	6643.8		0
NGVT	Ingevity Corp	Specialty Chemicals	12/31/16	908.3	35.2	832.8	127.0	300	44592482
INGR	Ingredion Inc	Food	12/31/16	5704.0	485.0	5782.0	2565.0	656	85192305
IIPR	Innovative Industrial Properties Inc	Property, Real Estate & Developmen	12/31/16	0.3	-4.4	63.3	60.4	26	308912
IPHI	Inphi Corp	Semiconductors	12/31/16	266.3	99.5	990.6	462.5	233	55302046
INSI	Insight Select Income Fund	Holding and other Investment Office	3/31/17	11.0	9.4	223.1	222.3	49	2654689
NSP	Insperity Inc	Business Services	12/31/16	2941.3	66.0	907.2	60.5	307	21924169
IBP	Installed Building Products Inc	Construction Services	12/31/16	863.0	38.4	462.1	154.0	185	24020957
INST	Instructure Inc	Internet & Software	12/31/16	110.9	-53.6	111.3	10.0	127	25354313
ITGR	Integer Holdings Corp	Medical Instruments & Equipment	12/30/16	1386.8	6.0	2832.5	725.2	257	37466901
I	Intelsat SA	Services	12/31/16	2188.0	990.2	12942.0	-3634.1		0
ICE	Intercontinental Exchange Inc	Finance Intermediaries & Services	12/31/16	5958.0	1422.0	82003.0	15717.0	854	575975538
IHG	InterContinental Hotels Group Plc	Hotels, Restaurants & Travel	12/31/16	1715.0	414.0	2927.0	-767.0	156	13237679
IBM	International Business Machines Co	IT Services	12/31/16	79919.0	11872.0	117470.0	18246.0	2558	716616938
IFF	International Flavors & Fragrances I	Specialty Chemicals	12/31/16	3116.3	405.0	4017.0	1626.2	668	89169519
IGT	International Game Technology PL	Entertainment	12/31/16	5153.9	211.3	15060.2	3068.7		0
IP	International Paper Co	Containers & Packaging	12/31/16	21079.0	904.0	33345.0	4341.0	1095	442807336
INSW	International Seaways Inc	Equipment & Services	12/31/16	398.3	-18.2	1662.5	1179.5	98	25451063
IPG	Interpublic Group of Companies Inc.	Advertising	12/31/16	7846.6	608.5	12485.2	2017.1	710	491061075
IPL PRD	Interstate Power & Light Co	Electric Utilities	12/31/16	1820.4	225.8	7304.7	2449.0		0
INXN	InterXion Holding NV	IT Services	12/31/16	421.8	39.9	1482.7	548.8	247	66876825
IPI	Intrepid Potash Inc	Agricultural Chemicals	12/31/16	210.9	-66.6	540.9	363.4	175	67871225
XON	Intrexon Corp	Biotechnology	12/31/16	190.9	-186.6	949.1	560.2		0
IVC	Invacare Corp	Medical Instruments & Equipment	12/31/16	1047.5	-42.9	903.7	422.4	201	54942658
VBF	Invesco Bond Fund	Holding and other Investment Office	2/28/17	10.7	9.5	230.1	227.5	46	2778852
VCV	Invesco California Value Municipal I	Holding and other Investment Office	2/28/17	44.3	33.4	1035.2	635.4	54	3865379
VTA	Invesco Dynamic Credit Opportuniti	Holding and other Investment Office	2/28/17	91.8	65.7	1619.0	981.8	105	26644005
IHIT	Invesco High Income 2023 Target T	Holding and other Investment Office	2/28/17	3.5	2.8	239.0	238.8	18	2467530
VLT	Invesco High Income Trust II	Holding and other Investment Office	2/28/17	10.9	8.8	182.4	132.8	36	2350387
IVZ	Invesco Ltd	Wealth Management	12/31/16	4734.4	854.2	25734.3	7503.8	773	410509083
IVR	Invesco Mortgage Capital Inc	REITs	12/31/16	454.5	254.4	15706.2	2241.6	267	84002152
OIA	Invesco Municipal Income Opportun	Holding and other Investment Office	2/28/17	23.0	19.4	419.4	353.3	62	3720453
VMO	Invesco Municipal Opportunity Trust	Holding and other Investment Office	2/28/17	70.6	52.4	1547.4	903.9	93	6197195
VKQ	Invesco Municipal Trust	Holding and other Investment Office	2/28/17	56.0	41.9	1236.3	740.3	95	6444790
VPV	Invesco Pennsylvania Value Munici	Holding and other Investment Office	2/28/17	22.8	16.6	540.3	329.7	51	4270000
IQI	Invesco Quality Municipal Income T	Holding and other Investment Office	2/29/12	23.1	19.8	524.2	443.1		0
VVR	Invesco Senior Income Trust	Holding and other Investment Office	2/28/17	72.2	52.1	1423.7	888.3	132	65066178
VGM	Invesco Trust for Investment Grade	Holding and other Investment Office	2/28/17	59.0	43.3	1294.3	752.9	100	5717823
VTN	Invesco Trust For Investment Grade	Holding and other Investment Office	2/28/17	19.8	14.0	478.9	280.5	43	1507028
IIM	Invesco Value Municipal Income Tr	Holding and other Investment Office	2/29/16	50.2	40.2	1203.6	786.8		0
ITG	Investment Technology Group Inc.	Finance Intermediaries & Services	12/31/16	469.1	-25.9	775.3	405.2	222	39172586
IRET	Investors Real Estate Trust	REITs	4/30/17	205.7	43.3	1474.5	560.9	190	77160530
NVTA	Invitae Corp	Diagnostic & Health Related Service	12/31/16	25.0	-100.3	130.7	99.1	104	39823698
INVH	Invitation Homes Inc	Property, Real Estate & Developmen	12/31/16	922.6	-78.2	9732.4	1957.4	210	332223660
IO	ION Geophysical Corp	Production & Extraction	12/31/16	172.8	-65.1	313.2	52.9	110	13380212
IQV	IQVIA Holdings Inc	Biotechnology	12/31/16	6878.0	115.0	21208.0	8633.0	548	215173685
IRM	Iron Mountain Inc (New)	REITs	12/31/16	3511.5	104.8	9486.8	1936.5	563	267203793
IRS	IRSA Inversiones y Representacion	Property, Real Estate & Developmen	6/30/17	74172.0	3030.0	231242.0	25864.0	74	14749885
ICL	Israel Chemicals Ltd	Agricultural Chemicals	12/31/16	5363.0	-122.0	8552.0	2574.0	81	83042338
STAR	iStar Inc	REITs	12/31/16	477.0	95.3	4825.5	1016.6	247	73835380
ITCB	Itau CorpBanca	Banking	12/31/16	1540565.0	14407.0	28909337.0	3184743.0	46	1637099
ITUB	Itau Unibanco Holding S.A.	Banking	12/31/16	237547.0	23263.0	1353241.0	122582.0	415	822230834
ITT	ITT Inc	Industrial Machinery & Equipment	12/31/16	2405.4	186.1	3601.7	1426.4	546	113701318
IVH	Ivy High Income Opportunities Fund	Finance Intermediaries & Services	9/30/17	31.2	25.0	404.2	270.6	31	2804887
JAX	J Alexander's Holdings Inc	Hotels, Restaurants & Travel	1/1/17	219.6	7.0	163.0	100.6	120	12817381
JILL	J.Jill Inc	Retail - Apparel and Accessories	1/28/17	639.1	24.1	567.6	121.0	96	14990754
JBL	Jabil Inc	Electrical Equipment	8/31/17	19063.1	129.1	11096.0	2353.5	504	211926214
JEC	Jacobs Engineering Group, Inc.	Construction Services	9/29/17	10022.8	293.7	7380.9	4428.4	736	131504944
JAG	Jagged Peak Energy Inc	Production & Extraction	12/31/16	76.5	-9.8	518.4	326.1	91	45611729
JHX	James Hardie Industries Plc	Construction Materials	3/31/17	1921.6	276.5	2012.7	-212.2	57	3744102
JHG	Janus Henderson Group Plc	Holding and other Investment Office	12/31/16	746.3	109.6	1616.2	1064.9	192	93682999
JOF	Japan Smaller Capitalization Fund I	Holding and other Investment Office	2/28/17	6.8	3.3	342.9	342.5	68	22241162
JBGS	JBG SMITH Properties	REITs	12/31/16	470.5	62.0	3660.6	2121.7	259	88485985
JBGS	JBG SMITH Properties	REITs	12/31/16	478.5	62.0	3660.6	2121.7	259	88485985
JELD	JELD-WEN Holding Inc	Manufacturing	12/31/16	3666.8	357.5	2516.3	192.9	175	48881459
JCAP	Jernigan Capital Inc	REITs	12/31/16	6.5	16.0	192.8	168.4	102	10179711
JT	Jianpu Technology Inc	Services	12/31/16	356.4	-182.1	134.5	52.6		0
JKS	JinkoSolar Holding Co., Ltd.	Semiconductors	12/31/16	21400.6	1826.7	26090.6	6460.7	112	8676617
JMP	JMP Group LLC	Finance Intermediaries & Services	12/31/16	169.4	2.9	1125.8	119.4		0
JBT	John Bean Technologies Corp	Industrial Machinery & Equipment	12/31/16	1350.5	67.6	1187.4	179.9	291	38801544
DECR 19	John Deere Capital Corp.	Credit & Lending	10/29/17	2227.0	328.4	35002.8	3656.7		0
BTO	John Hancock Financial Opportuniti	Holding and other Investment Office	12/31/16	18.3	9.3	761.8	651.4	81	4371512
HEQ	John Hancock Hedged Equity & Inc	Holding and other Investment Office	12/31/16	7.5	5.1	205.9	205.5	31	2210444
JHS	John Hancock Income Securities Tr	Holding and other Investment Office	10/31/17	11.9	8.7	291.4	181.4	36	3659242
HTY	John Hancock Investment Trust	Holding and other Investment Office	8/31/92	3.9	2.6	119.5	119.5		0
JHI	John Hancock Investors Trust	Holding and other Investment Office	10/31/17	14.2	11.1	253.5	163.7	52	987842
HPI	John Hancock Preferred Income Fu	Holding and other Investment Office	7/31/17	53.5	41.9	870.7	576.1	67	2150725
PDT	John Hancock Premium Dividend F	Holding and other Investment Office	10/31/17	70.9	53.6	1155.8	771.0	87	4797809
JNJ	Johnson & Johnson	Pharmaceuticals	1/1/17	71890.0	16540.0	141208.0	70418.0	3203	2284336143

| EARNINGS PER SHARE | | | | | | P/E RATIO | DIVIDENDS PER SHARE | | | AV. YLD % | DIV. DECLARED | | PRICE RANGE |
| QUARTERLY | | | ANNUAL | | | | | | | | | | 2016 |
1st	2nd	3rd	2016	2015	2014		2016	2015	2014		AMOUNT	PAYABLE	
-	-	-	1.28	1.27	0.06	14.7 - 10.8	0.53	0.31	0.12	3.1	0.39840Z	6/15/18	18.9 - 13.8
-	1.43	5.65	2.48	3.40			1.36	1.16	1.00		0.450	32/4/39	
-	-	0.79	0.83			95.9 - 63.0							79.6 - 52.3
-	-	2.26	6.55	5.51	4.74	21.6 - 17.4	1.90	1.74	1.68	1.5	0.60Y	32/4/39	141.7 - 114.1
-	-	0.09	-4.56								0.5375GHZ	1/16/18	32.3 - 15.5
-	-	-1.15	2.25	-0.35	-0.69	22.8 - 15.1							51.4 - 33.9
-	-	-	0.93	0.98	1.05	22.3 - 20.2	1.01	1.06	1.06	5.1	0.1367B	1/18/18	20.8 - 18.8
-	-	0.46	1.54	0.79	0.53	38.9 - 22.5	0.48	0.42	1.37	1.1	1.7Y	12/18/17	59.9 - 34.7
-	-	0.38	1.23	0.85	-0.20	62.9 - 32.7							77.4 - 40.3
-	-	-0.42	-1.92	-6.07	-7.50								36.4 - 19.8
-	-	0.43	0.19	-0.29	2.14	286.1 - 153.9							54.4 - 29.3
-	-	-	8.36	-36.68	1.99						0.71880	5/2/16	
-	-	0.62	2.37	2.28	1.71	30.4 - 23.7	0.68	0.58	0.52	1.1	0.20Y	32/4/39	72.1 - 56.2
-	-	-	1.94	5.13	1.56	32.7 - 24.2							63.5 - 47.0
-	-	2.92	12.38	13.42	11.90	14.7 - 11.3	5.50	5.00	4.25	3.5	1.50Y	32/4/39	181.9 - 139.7
-	-	1.39	5.05	5.16	5.06	30.8 - 22.8	2.40	2.06	1.72	1.8	0.690Y	32/4/39	155.4 - 115.3
-	-1.43	-	1.05	-0.39	0.49						0.20	12/12/17	
-	-	0.95	2.18	2.23	1.29	26.9 - 22.8	1.78	1.64	1.45	3.3	0.4750Y	32/4/39	58.7 - 49.6
-	-	-0.75	-0.62	4256.96	5238.24								
-	-	0.37	1.49	1.09	1.12	17.2 - 12.4	0.60	0.48	0.38	2.7	0.180Y	32/4/39	25.6 - 18.4
							1.27	1.27	1.27	5.0	0.31870Y	12/15/17	-27.3 - 0.0
-	-	-0.24	0.56	0.69	0.50						0.75G7	12/27/12	4.8 - 1.4
-	-	-0.02	-0.88	-6.94	0.13								26.2 - 11.3
-	-	-0.33	-1.58	-0.76	-0.83								
-	-	-0.57	-1.32	-0.81	-1.75		0.05	0.05	0.05	0.4	0.01140Y	1/16/18	17.9 - 10.4
-	-	0.84	0.85	0.86		24.2 - 21.7	0.95	1.38	1.18	4.9	0.0690	1/31/18	20.3 - 18.2
-	-	0.78	0.79	0.80		16.9 - 15.4	0.79	0.79	0.79	6.2	0.0535M	1/31/18	13.2 - 12.0
-	-	0.97	0.92	0.84		12.9 - 11.7	0.90	0.90	0.90	7.5	0.06250	1/31/18	12.5 - 11.4
-	-										0.050	1/31/18	10.2 - 9.5
-	-	1.14	1.18	1.28		13.3 - 12.4	1.24	1.29	1.37	8.4	0.0840	1/31/18	15.2 - 14.1
-	-	0.65	2.06	2.26	2.27		1.11	1.06	0.97		0.290	32/4/39	
-	-	0.43	1.98	0.67	-1.76	9.4 - 7.4	1.60	1.70	1.95	9.7	0.48440Z	1/25/18	18.6 - 14.6
-	-	-	0.42	0.40	0.42	19.5 - 17.1	0.39	0.40	0.42	5.0	0.0344M	1/31/18	8.2 - 7.2
-	-	-	0.85	0.83	0.83	15.7 - 14.4	0.85	0.79	0.84	6.6	0.0554M	1/31/18	13.4 - 12.2
-	-	-	0.83	0.80	0.80	15.7 - 14.6	0.82	0.81	0.83	6.5	0.0591M	1/31/18	13.0 - 12.1
-	-	-	0.81	0.78	0.81	15.6 - 14.7	0.78	0.88	0.90	6.3	0.0521M	1/31/18	12.6 - 11.9
-	-	-									0.0546M	1/31/18	13.0 - 12.1
-	-	-	0.31	0.32	0.31	15.4 - 13.9	0.32	0.32	0.36	7.0	0.01950	1/31/18	4.8 - 4.3
-	-	-	0.89	0.86	0.86	15.5 - 14.3	0.88	0.89	0.92	6.6	0.0636M	1/31/18	13.8 - 12.7
-	-	-	0.87	0.85	0.89	16.1 - 15.1	0.83	0.86	1.01	6.1	0.0583M	1/31/18	14.0 - 13.2
-	-	-	0.85	0.86	0.86	18.2 - 16.7	0.84	0.90	0.90	5.6	0.062M	1/31/18	15.4 - 14.2
-	-	-1.42	-0.79	2.63	1.40		0.28	0.21		1.4	0.070	12/15/17	23.9 - 17.9
-	0.05	-	0.49	0.11	-0.23	14.7 - 11.5	0.52	0.52	0.52	8.5	0.4187GHZ	1/2/18	7.2 - 5.6
-	-	-0.57	-3.02	-3.18	-56.14								11.5 - 7.9
-	-	-0.07	-0.32	-							0.080Y	32/4/39	24.1 - 20.0
-	-	0.41	-5.71	-2.29	-11.70								20.1 - 3.3
-	-	0.38	0.76	3.08	2.72	142.8 - 99.1							108.6 - 75.3
-	-	0.09	0.42	0.58	1.66	98.7 - 78.8	2.00	1.91	5.37	5.4	0.58750Y	32/4/39	41.4 - 33.1
0.06	-	-	-2.18	-0.07	-1.37			0.63	2.83				31.8 - 19.0
-	-	0.31	-0.10	0.40	0.36								
-	-	-0.48	0.55	-0.62	-0.40	22.9 - 20.3					0.56250Z	12/15/17	12.6 - 11.2
-	0.13	-	0.04	0.64	0.69	368.8 - 269.3	370.32	1224.66	295.28	2746.8			14.8 - 10.8
-	-	0.86	3.54	4.28	3.92	4.1 - 2.9	1.17	1.10	0.66	9.4			14.3 - 10.2
-	-	0.98	2.07	3.88	1.99	26.2 - 18.4	0.37	0.47	0.44	0.9	0.1280Y	32/4/39	54.3 - 38.0
-	-	-	1.57	1.62	1.67	10.2 - 9.2	1.60	1.96	1.85	10.4	0.10	1/31/18	16.0 - 14.5
-	-	-0.06	0.47	0.36		26.1 - 19.3							12.3 - 9.1
-	-	0.14											14.2 - 4.8
0.35	-	-	1.32	1.45	1.19	23.8 - 17.4	0.32	0.32	0.32	1.1	0.080Y	32/4/39	31.5 - 23.0
-	-	0.74	1.73	2.40	2.48	39.6 - 28.7					0.150Y	32/4/39	68.5 - 49.6
-	-	-0.07	-0.03										16.4 - 11.1
-	0.12	-	0.55	0.65	0.22	32.1 - 24.8	0.98	1.48	1.18	6.4			17.7 - 13.6
-	-	0.49	0.10	0.14	0.23						0.320	12/1/17	
-	-	-	0.06	0.06	0.05	228.9 - 162.0	0.88	0.13	0.20	7.6	0.0878B	12/21/17	13.7 - 9.7
-	-	-0.61	-107.00								0.2250Y	32/4/39	37.2 - 31.1
-	-	-0.61	-107.00								0.2250Y	32/4/39	37.2 - 31.8
-	-	0.47	-2.17	-15.88	-9.01								40.2 - 26.1
-	-	0.29	2.42	-0.69		10.1 - 7.7	1.40	1.05		6.6	0.350Z	1/12/18	24.5 - 18.6
-	-	-	-0.53	-0.57									8.4 - 4.9
-	-	1.10	14.03	5.35	3.86	2.1 - 1.0							29.9 - 14.1
-	-	-0.06	0.13	-0.01	0.57	55.5 - 40.3	0.39	0.49	0.23	6.8	0.030	4/13/18	7.2 - 5.2
-	-	0.80	2.27	1.88	1.03	52.8 - 36.1	0.40	0.37	0.36	0.4	0.10Y	12/29/17	119.8 - 81.8
-	-	-	0.50	0.10	0.35	79.2 - 63.5	1.48	1.33	1.18	4.1	0.37010	12/29/17	39.6 - 31.8
-	-	-	0.42	0.39	0.46	42.6 - 37.9	1.50	1.50	1.50	8.8	0.1564C	12/29/17	17.9 - 15.9
-	-	-	0.79	0.81	0.86	18.9 - 17.6	0.85	0.90	0.95	5.8	0.21810	12/29/17	14.9 - 13.9
-	-	-									1.0084B	12/18/17	10.2 - 8.3
-	-	-	1.32	1.41	1.58	14.3 - 12.5	1.39	1.49	1.64	7.9	0.3560	12/29/17	18.9 - 16.5
-	-	-	1.60	1.65	1.67	14.0 - 12.6	1.68	1.68	1.68	7.8	0.140	1/31/18	22.5 - 20.2
-	-	-	0.98	0.97	0.98	17.6 - 15.2	1.11	1.09	1.31	6.7	0.00750	1/31/18	17.3 - 14.9
-	-	1.37	5.93	5.48	5.70	24.2 - 18.8	3.15	2.95	2.76	2.4	0.840Y	32/4/39	143.6 - 111.8

SYMBOL	COMPANY	NATURE OF BUSINESS	FISCAL YEAR-END	TOTAL REV. $MILL	NET INCOME $MILL	TOTAL ASSETS $MILL	NET STK EQUITY $MILL	NO OF INST	INST. HOLDINGS (SHARES)
JCI	Johnson Controls International plc	Miscellaneous Consumer Goods	9/30/17	30172.0	1611.0	51884.0	20447.0	1130	999838729
JONE	Jones Energy Inc	Production & Extraction	12/31/16	127.8	-42.6	1886.7	527.2	117	81291255
JLL	Jones Lang LaSalle Inc	Property, Real Estate & Developmen	12/31/16	6803.8	318.2	7629.4	2789.7	486	50786196
JPM	JPMorgan Chase & Co	Banking	12/31/16	105486.0	24733.0	2490972.0	254190.0	3016	3249955999
JMEI	Jumei International Holding Ltd	Retail - Apparel and Accessories	12/31/16	6277.2	142.2	4746.1	3887.1	68	39603763
JNPR	Juniper Networks Inc	Peripherals	12/31/16	4990.1	592.7	9656.5	4962.5	736	411945346
JP	Jupai Holdings Ltd	Wealth Management	12/31/16	1127.7	207.6	2128.1	1500.6	14	712899
JE	Just Energy Group Inc	Electric Utilities	3/31/17	3757.1	446.4	1238.0	-149.3	-	0
LRN	K12 Inc	Educational Services	6/30/17	888.5	0.5	735.3	574.3	185	37601167
KAI	Kadant Inc	Industrial Machinery & Equipment	12/31/16	414.1	32.1	470.7	282.6	225	13835195
KDMN	Kadmon Holdings Inc	Pharmaceuticals	12/31/16	26.1	-208.8	62.6	-25.2	64	41092164
KAMN	Kaman Corp.	Industrial Machinery & Equipment	12/31/16	1808.4	58.9	1426.3	567.6	224	30739117
KSU	Kansas City Southern	Rail	12/31/16	2582.9	962.0	9198.7	4548.9	741	116436778
KS	KapStone Paper & Packaging Corp	Paper & Forest Products	12/31/16	3077.3	86.3	3255.9	904.3	301	102699523
KAR	KAR Auction Services Inc.	Retail - Automotive	12/31/16	3150.1	222.4	6557.6	1397.3	-	0
KED	Kayne Anderson Energy Developm	Holding and other Investment Office	11/30/16	1.8	-4.2	346.0	204.8	63	2802713
KYE	Kayne Anderson Energy Total Retur	Holding and other Investment Office	11/30/16	21.4	-2.0	669.0	475.9	77	7783387
KMF	Kayne Anderson Midstream / Energ	Holding and other Investment Office	11/30/16	17.8	-1.5	539.0	383.6	67	6350521
KYN	Kayne Anderson MLP Investment C	Holding and other Investment Office	11/30/16	11.4	-69.0	3923.6	2180.8	226	32925625
KB	KB Financial Group, Inc.	Banking	12/31/16	3444829.0	2143744.0	75673656.0	30998044.0	184	26573806
KBH	KB HOME	Builders	11/30/16	4368.5	180.6	5041.5	1926.3	393	102205657
KBR	KBR Inc	Construction Services	12/31/16	4268.0	-61.0	4144.0	757.0	354	190007503
FRAC	Keane Group Inc	Equipment & Services	12/31/16	420.6	-187.1	536.9	162.3	121	46162472
K	Kellogg Co	Food	12/31/16	13014.0	694.0	15111.0	1910.0	1005	458982325
KEM	KEMET Corp.	Electrical Equipment	3/31/17	757.8	48.0	734.5	154.7	240	47897739
KMPR	Kemper Corp. (DE)	General Insurance	12/31/16	2521.9	16.8	8210.5	1975.2	241	36798929
KMT	Kennametal Inc.	Industrial Machinery & Equipment	6/30/17	2058.4	49.1	2415.5	1017.3	408	97364099
KW	Kennedy-Wilson Holdings Inc	Property, Real Estate & Developmen	12/31/16	703.4	5.6	7659.1	1048.0	4	2975087
KEN	Kenon Holdings Ltd	Energy	12/31/16	1873.9	-411.9	5137.8	681.2	11	518494
KEG	Key Energy Services Inc (DE)	Equipment & Services	12/31/16	17.8	-10.2	658.0	242.6	133	34415118
KEY	KeyCorp	Banking	12/31/16	5390.0	791.0	136453.0	15240.0	970	1037924509
KEYS	Keysight Technologies Inc	Industrial Machinery & Equipment	10/31/17	3189.0	102.0	5933.0	2310.0	409	179484240
KRC	Kilroy Realty Corp	REITs	12/31/16	642.6	293.8	6706.6	3543.0	369	130190217
KRP	Kimbell Royalty Partners LP	Oil Royalty Traders	12/31/16	-	-0.0	0.0	0.0	23	3602704
KMB	Kimberly-Clark Corp.	Household & Personal Products	12/31/16	18202.0	2166.0	14602.0	-44.0	1796	333225366
KIM	Kimco Realty Corp	REITs	12/31/16	1170.8	378.8	11230.6	5256.1	627	472467902
KMI	Kinder Morgan Inc.	Equipment & Services	12/31/16	13058.0	708.0	80305.0	34431.0	1241	1646998649
KND	Kindred Healthcare Inc	Hospitals & Health Care Facilities	12/31/16	7219.5	-664.2	6112.7	812.6	271	95245186
KFS	Kingsway Financial Services Inc	General Insurance	12/31/16	176.6	0.8	501.0	62.4	29	9785542
KGC	Kinross Gold Corp.	Precious Metals	12/31/16	3472.0	-104.0	7979.3	4145.5	369	765415711
KEX	Kirby Corp.	Shipping	12/31/16	1770.7	141.4	4303.5	2409.3	370	74831851
KL	Kirkland Lake Gold Ltd	Precious Metals	12/31/16	406.7	42.1	1298.7	905.9	-	0
KRG	Kite Realty Group Trust	REITs	12/31/16	354.1	1.2	3656.4	1643.6	299	98407128
KKR	KKR & Co LP (DE)	Finance Intermediaries & Services	12/31/16	1908.1	309.3	39002.9	-	418	344429097
KIO	KKR Income Opportunities Fund	Finance Intermediaries & Services	10/31/16	31.3	24.6	393.4	269.5	39	3477131
KREF	KKR Real Estate Finance Trust Inc	REITs	12/31/16	48.6	31.2	6265.4	497.7	55	35260609
KMG	KMG Chemicals, Inc.	Specialty Chemicals	7/31/17	333.4	23.6	792.4	173.7	163	9751640
KNX	Knight-Swift Transportation Holding	Trucking	12/31/16	1118.0	93.9	1078.5	786.5	399	153084042
KNL	Knoll Inc	Office Equipment & Furniture	12/31/16	1164.3	82.1	858.6	309.2	233	56882410
KNOP	KNOT Offshore Partners LP	Equipment & Services	12/31/16	173.7	61.1	1292.3	521.7	56	14872563
KN	Knowles Corp	Electronic Instruments & Related Pro	12/31/16	859.3	-42.3	1515.1	1008.5	317	123072208
KSS	Kohl's Corp.	Retail - General Merchandise/Depart	1/28/17	18686.0	556.0	13574.0	5177.0	870	227753220
PHG	Koninklijke Philips NV	Household Appliances, Electronics &	12/31/16	24516.0	1448.0	32303.0	12601.0	392	75392075
KOP	Koppers Holdings Inc	Paper & Forest Products	12/31/16	1416.2	29.3	1087.5	30.4	256	24340223
KEP	Korea Electric Power Corp	Electric Utilities	12/31/16	60190384.0	7048581.0	177837042.0	71723693.0	192	107076005
KF	Korea Fund Inc (The)	Holding and other Investment Office	6/30/17	4.2	1.1	273.6	260.0	47	4594124
KFY	Korn/Ferry International (DE)	Business Services	4/30/17	1621.7	84.2	2062.9	1083.4	296	61045707
KOS	Kosmos Energy Ltd	Production & Extraction	12/31/16	385.4	-283.8	3341.5	1081.2	161	536761324
KRA	Kraton Corp	Plastics	12/31/16	1744.1	107.3	2906.6	457.9	217	35084292
KR	Kroger Co (The)	Retail - Food & Beverage, Drug & To	1/28/17	115337.0	1975.0	36505.0	6698.0	1109	904733936
KRO	Kronos Worldwide Inc	Specialty Chemicals	12/31/16	1364.3	43.3	1179.6	395.0	183	23067140
KT	KT Corp (Korea)	Services	12/31/16	22743665.0	711089.0	30587733.0	11441935.0	221	173308129
KYO	Kyocera Corp	Electrical Equipment	3/31/17	1422754.0	103843.0	3110470.0	2334219.0	111	2253468
LB	L Brands, Inc	Retail - Apparel and Accessories	1/28/17	12574.0	1158.0	8170.0	-729.0	703	265110091
LLL	L3 Technologies Inc	Aerospace	12/31/16	10511.0	710.0	11865.0	4553.0	843	85240935
LQ	La Quinta Holdings Inc	Hotels, Restaurants & Travel	12/31/16	1006.3	-1.3	2892.5	655.1	168	129106746
LZB	La-Z-Boy Inc.	Furniture	4/29/17	1520.1	85.9	888.9	589.9	292	51537694
LH	Laboratory Corporation of America	Diagnostic & Health Related Service	12/31/16	9641.8	732.1	14247.0	5505.8	983	119686430
LADR	Ladder Capital Corp	REITs	12/31/16	399.7	66.7	5578.3	971.4	144	55713546
LW	Lamb Weston Holdings Inc	Food	5/28/17	3168.0	326.9	2485.6	-647.2	514	128653358
LKB 04	Landesbank Baden-Wurttemberg	Banking	12/31/16	13453.0	10.0	243620.0	13081.0	-	0
LCI	Lannett Co., Inc.	Pharmaceuticals	6/30/17	633.3	-0.6	1603.3	561.1	205	34329681
LPI	Laredo Petroleum, Inc	Production & Extraction	12/31/16	454.9	-260.7	1782.3	180.6	216	350554941
LVS	Las Vegas Sands Corp	Hotels, Restaurants & Travel	12/31/16	11410.0	1670.0	20469.0	6177.0	791	345627178
LHO	LaSalle Hotel Properties	REITs	12/31/16	1227.6	252.8	3944.1	2558.1	355	148992986
LTM	LATAM Airlines Group SA	Airlines/Air Freight	12/31/16	8988.3	69.2	19198.2	4096.7	107	23409535
LDF	Latin American Discovery Fund, Inc.	Holding and other Investment Office	12/31/16	1.8	0.6	73.0	72.4	35	3962738
EL	Lauder (Estee) Cos., Inc. (The)	Household & Personal Products	6/30/17	11824.0	1249.0	11568.0	4384.0	955	237744187
LGI	Lazard Global Total Return & Incom	Holding and other Investment Office	12/31/16	6.4	3.9	177.2	151.0	39	3830753
LAZ	Lazard Ltd	Finance Intermediaries & Services	12/31/16	2383.7	387.7	4556.5	1236.0	421	109106436

T34

EARNINGS PER SHARE QUARTERLY			ANNUAL			P/E RATIO		DIVIDENDS PER SHARE			AV. YLD %	DIV. DECLARED		PRICE RANGE 2016	
1st	2nd	3rd	2016	2015	2014			2016	2015	2014		AMOUNT	PAYABLE		
-	-	0.59	-1.30	1.35	4.16	-		1.16	0.81	0.71	-	0.260	1/12/18		
-	-	-0.91	-1.04	-0.08	3.00							0.830Z	5/15/17	4.7 -	0.8
-	-	1.89	6.98	9.65	8.52	21.9 -	14.2	0.64	0.56	0.48	0.5	0.370Y	32/4/39	153.0 -	99.2
-	-	1.76	6.19	6.00	5.29	17.4 -	13.3	1.84	1.68	1.56	2.0	0.560Y	32/4/39	107.8 -	82.2
-	-	-	0.95	0.82	0.45	5.1 -	2.1							4.8 -	2.0
-	-	0.43	1.53	1.59	-0.73	20.2 -	15.9	0.40	0.40	0.20	1.4	0.10	32/4/39	30.9 -	24.4
0.04	-	-	1.03	0.16	0.06	27.6 -	0.0							28.4 -	0.0
-	-1.13	-	0.43	-3.07	0.94	20.0 -	9.6	0.50	0.58	0.84	7.9	0.53130	12/29/17	8.6 -	4.1
-0.21	-	-	0.23	0.29	0.50	90.9 -	65.7							20.9 -	15.1
-	-	1.17	2.88	3.10	2.56	39.4 -	19.8	0.74	0.66	0.57	0.9	0.210Y	2/8/18	113.6 -	57.0
-	-	-	-0.42	-9.74	-18.10									5.4 -	2.1
-	-	0.58	2.10	2.17	2.08	28.5 -	22.0	0.72	0.72	0.64	1.4	0.20Y	1/4/18	60.0 -	46.2
-	-	1.23	4.43	4.40	4.55	25.6 -	18.2	1.32	1.32	1.12	1.3	0.250Y	32/4/39	113.4	80.8
-	-	0.30	0.88	1.09	1.76	28.2 -	22.6	0.40	0.40	0.10	1.8	0.10Y	1/12/18	24.8 -	19.9
-	-	0.46	1.60	1.51	1.19	32.1 -	25.2	1.19	1.08	1.02	2.6	0.350Y	32/4/39	51.4 -	40.3
-	-	-	-0.39	-0.20	-0.15			1.92	2.12	2.04	10.8	0.40	1/12/18	20.4 -	14.4
-	-	-	-0.05	0.30	0.14			1.08	1.94	1.93	9.6	0.250	1/12/18	13.0 -	9.2
-	-	-	-0.07	0.30	-0.01			1.50	3.82	1.91	10.1	0.30	1/12/18	17.0 -	12.4
-	-	-	-0.61	-0.53	-0.76			2.20	2.63	2.52	11.8	0.07290	3/1/18	22.1 -	14.6
-	-	-1100.00	5559.00	4376.00	3611.00	0.0 -	0.0	968.55	765.23	500.96	2030.6			58.8 -	35.5
-	-	0.51	1.12	0.85	9.25	28.8 -	14.4	0.10	0.10	0.10	0.4	0.0250Y	32/4/39	32.3 -	16.1
-	-	0.32	-0.43	1.40	-8.66			0.32	0.32	0.32	1.9	0.080Y	32/4/39	21.1 -	13.6
-	-	0.04	-2.14	-	-									22.2 -	12.5
-	-	0.85	1.96	1.72	1.75	39.0 -	30.0	2.04	1.98	1.90	3.0	0.540Y	32/4/39	76.4 -	58.9
-	0.22	-	-1.17	-0.31	-1.52									27.1 -	6.2
-	-	0.92	0.33	1.65	2.12	213.5 -	111.2	0.96	0.96	0.96	2.0	0.240Y	32/4/39	70.5 -	36.7
0.48	-	-	-2.83	-4.71	1.99			0.80	0.72	0.72	2.0	0.20Y	32/4/39	49.0 -	31.7
-	-	-0.08	0.01	0.66	0.14	2250.0 -	1720.0	0.56	0.48	0.36	2.8	0.190Z	1/4/18	22.5 -	17.2
-	-	-	-7.67	1.36	8.76									37.5 -	8.7
-	-	-1.90	-0.51	-5.86	-1.16										
-	-	0.32	0.80	1.05	0.99	25.6 -	20.6	0.33	0.29	0.25	1.8	0.38280Y	32/4/39	20.4 -	16.5
-	-	-0.10	1.95	3.00	2.35	23.3 -	18.1							45.4 -	35.3
-	-	0.67	2.97	2.42	1.95	26.2 -	22.7	3.38	1.40	1.40	4.6	0.4250Z	32/4/39	77.9 -	67.5
-	-	0.01										0.360	2/14/18	20.6 -	0.0
-	-	1.60	5.99	2.77	4.04	22.5 -	18.3	3.68	3.52	3.36	3.0	1.0Y	32/4/39	135.0 -	109.9
-	-	0.24	0.79	2.00	0.89	33.0 -	21.9	1.03	0.97	0.92	5.0	0.32030Z	32/4/39	26.1 -	17.3
-	-	0.15	0.25	0.10	0.89	91.8 -	67.0	0.50	1.93	1.70	2.5	0.1250Y	32/4/39	22.9 -	16.8
-	-	-1.09	-7.65	-1.11	-1.36			0.48	0.48	0.48	5.7	18.750	32/4/39	11.7 -	5.6
-	-	-0.07	0.02	0.04	-0.75	428.0 -	0.0					0.080	6/30/09	8.6 -	0.0
-	-	0.05	-0.08	-0.86	-1.02							0.080	3/28/13	6.3 -	3.2
-	-	0.52	2.62	4.11	4.93	27.9 -	22.9					0.05	32/4/39	73.1 -	60.0
-	-	-	0.34	-0.04	-0.08	56.7 -	15.8					0.020	1/15/18	19.3 -	5.4
-	-	-0.01	0.01	0.18	-0.24	2421.0 -	1773.0	1.14	1.08	0.26	5.6	0.31750Z	1/12/18	24.2 -	17.7
-	-	0.30	0.59	1.01	1.16	35.9 -	26.8	0.64	1.58	2.03	3.4	0.40630	12/15/17	21.2 -	15.8
-	-	-	1.61	1.47	1.48	11.3 -	9.7	1.50	1.65	1.66	8.8	0.1250	4/30/18	18.2 -	15.6
-	-	0.32	1.61	1.95	-	14.2 -	12.3	1.22	0.73		5.8	0.370Z	1/12/18	22.9 -	19.8
0.46	-	-	1.57	1.03	-0.09	43.1 -	23.3	0.12	0.12	0.12	0.2	0.030Y	1/5/18	67.7 -	36.6
-	-	0.04	1.16	1.42	1.25	38.2 -	23.4					0.06GY	12/27/17	44.4 -	27.2
-	-	0.39	1.68	1.36	0.97	16.7 -	10.5	0.60	0.51	0.48	2.8	0.150Y	12/29/17	28.1 -	17.7
-	-	-	1.54	1.50	1.37			2.08	2.03	1.79		0.520	2/15/18		
-	-	0.17	-0.47	-2.69	-1.02									19.6 -	14.2
-	-	0.70	3.46	4.24	4.05	16.4 -	10.2	1.80	1.56	1.40	4.3	0.550Y	32/4/39	56.9 -	35.3
-	0.27	-	1.56	0.70	0.45	27.0 -	18.6	0.67	0.68	0.67	1.9			42.1 -	28.9
-	-	0.91	1.39	-3.51	-1.58	37.0 -	24.5	0.00	0.00	1.00	0.0	0.250Y	1/5/15	51.5 -	34.0
-	-	-2326.00	980.02	701.00	4290.00	0.0 -	0.0	1572.05	248.49	44.48	8461.7	0.08821	4/20/97	21.4 -	16.6
-	-	-	0.11	-0.02	-0.14	405.8 -	292.4	4.35	-	-	11.1	3.7989C	1/5/18	44.6 -	32.2
-	0.64	-	0.58	1.76	1.48	75.6 -	48.3	0.40	0.10	-	1.2	0.10Y	1/12/18	43.8 -	28.0
-	-	-0.16	-0.74	-0.18	0.72									50.7 -	26.5
-	-	-0.13	3.43	-0.34	0.07	14.8 -	7.7								
-	-	0.44	2.06	1.72	1.45	16.9 -	9.7	0.40	0.34	0.31	1.5	0.1250Y	32/4/39	34.9 -	19.9
-	-	0.64	0.37	-1.50	0.86	79.0 -	32.7	0.60	0.60	0.60	3.1	0.150Y	12/15/17	29.2 -	12.1
-	-	-435.00	2902.00	2258.09	4516.00	0.0 -	0.0	250.38		400.43	1591.7			18.6 -	13.8
-	71.81	-	-297.24	315.85	241.93	0.2 -	0.2	108.80	79.00	110.71	181.7			71.7 -	49.8
-	-	0.30	4.22	3.50	3.05	16.0 -	8.5	4.00	2.36	1.20	8.1	0.60Y	32/4/39	67.3 -	36.1
-	-	0.28	9.01	-2.93	7.56	22.1 -	16.2	2.80	2.60	2.40	1.6	0.750Y	32/4/39	199.1 -	145.7
-	-	0.11	-0.01	0.20	-2.67									18.5 -	13.1
-	0.47	-	1.55	1.34	1.02	21.8 -	15.2	0.36	0.28	0.20	1.3	0.120Y	12/20/17	33.8 -	23.6
-	-	1.74	7.02	4.34	5.91	23.4 -	18.4					0.0826L	6/30/00	163.9 -	129.1
-	-	0.28	1.06	1.42	0.86	14.2 -	12.2	1.28	2.23		9.2	0.3150Z	1/3/18	15.1 -	12.9
-	0.52	-	-	-	-							0.19130Y	3/2/18	56.9 -	36.3
0.35	-	-	1.20	4.04	1.62	24.4 -	12.6					0.0076	12/14/79	29.3 -	15.1
-	-	0.05	-1.16	-11.10	1.85									15.2 -	9.5
-	-	0.72	2.10	2.47	3.52	34.3 -	24.6	2.88	2.60	2.00	4.7	0.750Z	32/4/39	72.0 -	51.7
-	-	0.27	2.07	1.09	1.88	15.3 -	13.3	1.80	1.73	1.41	6.2	0.39370Z	32/4/39	31.6 -	27.6
-	-0.23	-	0.13	-0.40	-0.48	111.4 -	62.9							14.5 -	8.2
-	-	0.09	0.05	0.09	0.09	140.3 -	105.8	0.07	0.03	0.16	0.6	0.02250	1/10/18	12.6 -	9.5
1.14	-	-	2.96	2.82	3.06	43.8 -	26.1	1.14	0.92	0.78	1.1	0.380Y	32/4/39	129.6 -	77.3
-	-	-	0.40	0.39	0.37	46.0 -	34.5	0.95	1.11	1.25	5.9	0.11560	2/23/18	18.0 -	13.8
-	-	0.82	2.92	7.40	3.20			2.69	2.35	1.20		0.410	32/4/39		

SYMBOL	COMPANY	NATURE OF BUSINESS	FISCAL YEAR-END	TOTAL REV. $MILL	NET INCOME $MILL	TOTAL ASSETS $MILL	NET STK EQUITY $MILL	NO OF INST	INST. HOLDINGS (SHARES)
LOR	Lazard World Dividend & Income Fu	Holding and other Investment Office	12/31/16	4.9	3.4	89.7	76.8	32	3634107
LCII	LCI Industries	Auto Parts	12/31/16	1678.9	129.7	786.9	550.3	319	29486846
LFGR	Leaf Group Ltd	Internet & Software	12/31/16	113.5	-2.0	101.3	79.8		0
LEA	Lear Corp.	Auto Parts	12/31/16	18557.6	975.1	9900.6	3057.2	699	89563287
LEE	Lee Enterprises, Inc.	Publishing	9/24/17	566.9	27.5	620.9	-92.2	118	25395569
LGC U	Legacy Acquisition Corp	Business Services	12/31/16		-0.2	0.1	-0.1		0
LM	Legg Mason, Inc.	Wealth Management	3/31/17	2886.9	227.3	8290.4	3983.4	531	109455822
LEG	Leggett & Platt, Inc.	Furniture	12/31/16	3749.9	385.8	2984.1	1091.6	669	122535523
LEH 06	Lehman Brothers, Inc.	Finance Intermediaries & Services	11/30/02	12124.0	740.0	196219.0	3152.0		0
LDOS	Leidos Holdings Inc	IT Services	12/30/16	7043.0	244.0	9132.0	3135.0	531	154051800
LEJU	Leju Holdings Ltd	Property, Real Estate & Developmen	12/31/16	559.5	-9.8	575.9	408.5	33	5459869
LC	LendingClub Corp	Credit & Lending	12/31/16	1192.1	-146.0	5562.6	975.8	235	380317013
LEN	Lennar Corp	Builders	11/30/17	12646.4	810.5	18745.0	7872.3	728	232699612
LII	Lennox International Inc	Industrial Machinery & Equipment	12/31/16	3641.6	277.8	1760.3	37.6	443	37278187
LUK	Leucadia National Corp.	Agricultural Livestock	12/31/16	10062.6	130.0	45071.3	10253.1	652	306186021
LXP	Lexington Realty Trust	REITs	12/31/16	429.5	95.6	3441.5	1392.8	353	228358006
LPL	LG Display Co Ltd	Electrical Equipment	12/31/16	26504074.0	906713.0	24884336.0	12955997.0	164	33077449
USA	Liberty All-Star Equity Fund	Holding and other Investment Office	12/31/16	20.2	8.4	1209.9	1161.0	164	68316368
ASG	Liberty All-Star Growth Fund Inc.	Holding and other Investment Office	12/31/16	1.2	-0.4	140.2	126.5	48	3189856
LBRT	Liberty Oilfield Services Inc	Equipment & Services							0
LPT	Liberty Property Trust	REITs	12/31/16	746.7	356.8	5992.8	3003.4	503	180137615
LSI	Life Storage Inc	REITs	12/31/16	462.6	85.2	3858.0	2088.5	372	60527160
LITB	Lightinthebox Holding Co., Ltd.	Retail - Apparel and Accessories	12/31/16	292.5	-8.7	118.2	65.8	13	2997056
LLY	Lilly (Eli) & Co	Pharmaceuticals	12/31/16	21222.1	2737.6	38805.9	14007.7	1743	1014718397
LNC	Lincoln National Corp.	Life & Health	12/31/16	13330.0	1192.0	261627.0	14478.0	937	226360186
LNN	Lindsay Corp	Industrial Machinery & Equipment	8/31/17	518.0	23.2	506.0	270.1	229	15147427
LN	LINE Corporation	IT Services	12/31/16	140704.3	6762.8	256089.1	160833.6	71	8569709
LGF A	Lions Gate Entertainment Corp	Entertainment	3/31/17	3201.5	14.8	9196.9	2514.4	268	88244946
LAD	Lithia Motors Inc	Retail - Automotive	12/31/16	8678.2	197.1	3844.1	910.8	316	31917452
LAC	Lithium Americas Corp (New)	Mining	12/31/16	1.2	-27.7	45.3	42.4	-	0
LYV	Live Nation Entertainment Inc	Entertainment	12/31/16	8354.9	2.9	6764.3	1126.0	455	160687289
LYG	Lloyds Banking Group Plc	Banking	12/31/16	48313.0	2063.0	817793.0	48025.0	282	413547516
SCD	LMP Capital & Income Fund Inc	Holding and other Investment Office	11/30/16	13.1	9.0	363.1	275.8	43	5572076
LMI	Lockheed Martin Corp	Defense	12/31/16	47248.0	5302.0	47806.0	1511.0	1712	285251627
L	Loews Corp.	General Insurance	12/31/16	13105.0	654.0	76594.0	18163.0	675	269519102
LOMA	Loma Negra Compania Industrial Ar	Manufacturing	12/31/16	9874.4	491.2	8962.0	740.4	-	0
LPX	Louisiana-Pacific Corp	Paper & Forest Products	12/31/16	2233.4	149.8	2031.2	1195.7	444	166739703
LOW	Lowe's Companies Inc	Retail - Hardware & Home Improvem	2/3/17	65017.0	3093.0	34408.0	6434.0	1803	789063502
LXU	LSB Industries, Inc.	Specialty Chemicals	12/31/16	374.6	112.2	1270.4	637.5	182	24182454
LKSD	LSC Communications Inc	Printing	12/31/16	3654.0	106.0	1952.0	240.0	216	31892155
LTC	LTC Properties, Inc.	REITs	12/31/16	161.6	85.1	1394.9	740.0	305	40620729
LUB	Luby's, Inc.	Hotels, Restaurants & Travel	8/30/17	376.0	-23.3	226.5	144.1	80	14345059
LL	Lumber Liquidators Holdings Inc	Retail - Hardware & Home Improvem	12/31/16	960.6	-68.6	488.6	230.9	240	28592796
LXFR	Luxfer Holdings Plc	Industrial Machinery & Equipment	12/31/16	414.8	21.9	391.5	141.9	70	22863310
LXFT	Luxoft Holding, Inc.	IT Services	3/31/17	785.6	62.6	547.2	386.8	133	18945122
LDL	Lydall, Inc.	Industrial Machinery & Equipment	12/31/16	566.9	37.2	527.0	273.5	197	18002786
WLH	Lyon (William) Homes	Builders	12/31/16	1406.0	59.7	1998.2	697.1	174	33418835
LYB	LyondellBasell Industries NV	Diversified Chemicals	12/31/16	29183.0	3836.0	23442.0	6048.0	979	336219458
MTB	M & T Bank Corp	Banking	12/31/16	5721.9	1315.1	123449.2	16486.6	822	141890947
MTB PRA	M & T Capital Trust IV	Banking						3	104665
MDC	M.D.C. Holdings, Inc.	Builders	12/31/16	2326.8	103.2	2528.6	1320.1	329	51203160
MHO	M/I Homes Inc	Builders	12/31/16	1691.3	56.6	1548.5	654.2	224	31448653
MAC	Macerich Co (The)	REITs	12/31/16	1041.3	517.0	9958.1	4105.9	486	180967231
CLI	Mack Cali Realty Corp	REITs	12/31/16	613.4	117.2	4296.8	1527.2	344	115747111
MGU	Macquarie Global Infrastructure Tot	Holding and other Investment Office	11/30/16	18.9	11.2	411.5	287.7	59	5099545
MIC	Macquarie Infrastructure Corp	Business Services	12/31/16	1651.7	156.4	7559.3	2952.9	516	75103814
MFD	Macquarie/First Trust Global Infrastr	Holding and other Investment Office	11/30/16	12.3	9.6	157.0	108.3	34	1111854
M	Macy's Inc	Retail - General Merchandise/Depart	1/28/17	25778.0	619.0	19851.0	4323.0	883	323129665
MCN	Madison Covered Call & Equity Stra	Holding and other Investment Office	12/31/16	2.3	0.6	169.5	162.1	45	7665280
MSG	Madison Square Garden Co (The) (	Sporting & Recreational	6/30/17	1318.5	-72.7	3712.8	2408.2	294	18231689
MSP	Madison Strategic Sector Premium	Holding and other Investment Office	12/31/16	1.0	0.3	76.1	72.8	24	2535296
MMP	Magellan Midstream Partners LP	Equipment & Services	12/31/16	2205.4	802.8	6772.1		774	160226426
MGA	Magna International Inc	Auto Parts	12/31/16	36445.0	2031.0	22566.0	9768.0	535	246677617
MX	MagnaChip Semiconductor Corp	Semiconductors	12/31/16	688.0	-29.6	442.0	-72.1	100	31673444
MAIN	Main Street Capital Corp	Holding and other Investment Office	12/31/16	178.3	115.8	2080.3	1201.5	221	20107904
MMD	MainStay DefinedTerm Municipal O	Holding and other Investment Office	5/31/17	39.7	29.6	869.7	555.1		0
MNK	Mallinckrodt Plc	Pharmaceuticals	12/30/16	829.9	-153.2	15206.3	4984.3	475	112476650
MZF	Managed Duration Investment Grad	Holding and other Investment Office	7/31/17	6.6	5.3	160.7	160.3	32	3974825
MANU	Manchester United Plc	Entertainment	6/30/17	581.2	39.2	1534.3	477.6		0
MTW	Manitowoc Company Inc (The)	Construction Services	12/31/16	1613.1	-375.8	1517.8	590.5	328	141183634
MN	Manning & Napier Inc.	Wealth Management	12/31/16	248.9	9.3	220.6	162.9	98	9501392
MAN	ManpowerGroup	Business Services	12/31/16	19654.1	443.7	7574.2	2361.9	588	86710915
MFC	Manulife Financial Corp.	Life & Health	12/31/16	53337.0	2929.0	720681.0	42080.0	561	1033934093
MRO	Marathon Oil Corp.	Production & Extraction	12/31/16	4650.0	-2140.0	31094.0	17541.0	966	870093369
MPC	Marathon Petroleum Corp.	Refining & Marketing	12/31/16	63364.0	1174.0	44413.0	13557.0	1101	467621213
MMI	Marcus & Millichap Inc	Property, Real Estate & Developmen	12/31/16	717.4	64.7	394.0	258.9	144	19980045
MCS	Marcus Corp. (The)	Hotels, Restaurants & Travel	12/29/16	543.9	37.9	911.3	390.1	209	20892553
MRIN	Marin Software Inc	IT Services	12/31/16	99.9	-16.5	107.1	87.6	53	11099543
MPX	Marine Products Corp	Leisure Equipment	12/31/16	241.3	16.7	88.5	65.4	74	6001582
HZO	MarineMax Inc	Retail - Specialty	9/30/17	1052.3	23.5	640.0	302.2	189	29708572

1st	2nd	3rd	2016	2015	2014	P/E hi	P/E lo	2016	2015	2014	AV.YLD %	AMOUNT	PAYABLE	2016 hi	2016 lo
-	-	-	0.50	0.51	0.85	23.3 -	19.9	0.69	0.92	1.03	6.3	0.07410	2/23/18	11.6 -	10.0
-	-	1.26	5.20	3.02	2.56	25.3 -	16.9	1.40	2.00		1.3	0.550Y	12/1/17	131.8 -	87.7
-	-	-0.33	-0.10	-2.18	-14.26			-				-		10.1 -	6.3
-	-	3.96	13.33	9.59	8.23	13.6 -	9.9	1.20	1.00	0.80	0.8	0.50Y	32/4/39	180.9 -	132.1
-	-	0.11	0.64	0.43	0.13	5.0 -	2.7					0.190Y	10/1/08	3.2 -	1.8
-	-	-	-0.07					-				-		10.0 -	0.0
-	0.78	-	-0.25	2.04	2.33			0.80	0.64	0.52	2.1	0.280Y	32/4/39	42.1 -	30.7
-	-	0.60	2.76	2.28	0.68	19.6 -	15.8	1.34	1.26	1.22	2.7	0.360Y	32/4/39	54.0 -	43.5
-	-	0.53	2.35	3.27	1.94	27.8 -	20.6	14.92	1.28	0.64	26.7	0.320Y	32/4/39	65.2 -	48.3
-	-	-	-0.07	0.26	0.50			-	0.18			-		4.3 -	1.3
-	-	-0.02	-0.38	-0.01	-0.44									6.7 -	3.5
-	-	1.06	3.85	3.39	2.75	16.6 -	11.0	0.16	0.16	0.16	0.3	0.040Y	32/4/39	64.0 -	42.2
-	-	2.44	6.32	4.09	4.23	33.3 -	23.5	1.65	1.38	1.14	0.9	0.510Y	32/4/39	210.7 -	148.5
-	-	0.27	0.34	0.74	0.54	80.0 -	65.5	0.25	0.25	0.25	1.0	0.10Y	32/4/39	27.2 -	22.3
-	-	0.02	0.37	0.45	0.38	30.7 -	25.2	0.69	0.68	0.68	6.7	0.81250Z	2/15/18	11.4 -	9.3
1770.00	-	-	2534.00	2701.00	2527.00	0.0 -	0.0	246.60	250.23		1795.7			16.9 -	12.0
-	-	-	0.04	0.04	0.02	157.5 -	131.3	0.48	0.51	0.39	8.4	0.180	3/12/18	6.3 -	5.3
-	-	-	-0.02	-0.03	-0.04			0.36	0.77	0.33	7.4	0.120	3/12/18	5.6 -	4.2
-	-	0.40	2.43	1.60	1.47	18.6 -	15.5	1.90	1.90	1.90	4.6	0.40Z	32/4/39	45.3 -	37.6
-	-	0.76	1.96	3.16	2.67	46.5 -	36.0	3.70	3.20	2.72	4.6	1.0Z	32/4/39	91.1 -	70.6
-	-	-0.02	-0.07	-0.41	-0.30									3.1 -	1.8
-	-	0.53	2.58	2.26	2.23	34.1 -	28.9	2.04	2.00	1.96	2.5	0.56250Y	32/4/39	87.9 -	74.6
-	-	1.87	5.03	4.51	5.67	15.6 -	12.6	1.00	0.80	0.64	1.4	0.330Y	32/4/39	78.5 -	63.2
0.30	-	-	1.85	2.22	4.00	51.4 -	40.0	1.13	1.09	0.92	1.3	0.30Y	32/4/39	95.0 -	74.0
-0.63	-	-	31.48	-39.12	22.14	1.4 -	1.0							44.9 -	31.0
-	0.07	-	0.33	1.23	1.04	104.4 -	74.2	0.34	0.26	0.10	1.2	0.090Y	8/5/16	34.5 -	24.5
-	-	2.07	7.72	6.91	5.26	15.8 -	10.5	0.95	0.76	0.61	0.9	0.270Y	32/4/39	122.3 -	81.1
-	-	-	-0.45	-0.30	-0.05									10.7 -	2.9
-	-	0.53	-0.23	-0.33	-0.49			-				-		46.4 -	27.3
-	-	-	0.02	0.01	0.02	193.0 -	158.5	0.16	0.10	0.04	4.6	0.48440	7/15/15	3.9 -	3.2
-	-	-	0.50	0.58		29.4 -	26.7	1.24	1.12	1.12	8.8	0.310	12/29/17	14.7 -	13.4
-	-	3.24	17.49	11.46	11.21	18.5 -	14.3	6.77	6.15	5.49	2.4	2.0Y	32/4/39	322.8 -	250.9
-	-	0.46	1.93	0.72	1.55	26.2 -	23.4	0.25	0.25	0.25	0.5	0.06250Y	32/4/39	50.6 -	45.1
-	-	-	0.87	0.61	0.48	27.1 -	24.1					-		23.6 -	21.0
-	-	0.75	1.03	-0.62	-0.53	28.3 -	18.3					0.150Y	32/4/39	29.1 -	18.8
-	-	1.05	2.73	2.71	2.14	34.0 -	26.0	1.07	0.87	0.70	1.3	0.410Y	32/4/39	92.9 -	71.0
-	-	-0.91	2.54	-1.67	0.83	4.6 -	2.4					10.0Y	4/1/10	11.6 -	6.0
-	-	-0.07	3.23	-		9.0 -	4.3	0.25			1.2	0.260Y	3/2/18	28.9 -	13.7
-	-	0.52	2.21	1.94	1.99	23.8 -	19.6	2.19	2.07	2.04	4.6	0.190Z	3/30/18	52.6 -	43.3
-	-	-0.00	-0.35	-0.07	-0.12							0.10	9/25/00	4.2 -	2.4
-	-	-0.66	-2.51	-2.08	2.31									40.5 -	15.2
-	-	0.60	0.82	0.59	1.05			0.48	0.38	0.38		-			
-	-	0.73	2.06	1.91	1.59						1.00				
-	-	0.62	2.16	2.71	1.28	29.4 -	21.2					0.0194	9/15/82	63.6 -	45.7
-	-	0.71	1.55	1.48	1.34	19.4 -	10.7							30.0 -	16.7
-	-	2.67	9.13	9.59	7.99			3.33	3.04	2.70		0.90	12/12/17		
-	-	2.21	7.78	7.18	7.42	22.4 -	18.3	2.80	2.80	2.80	1.7	0.750Y	32/4/39	173.9 -	142.5
-	-	-	-									0.53130Z	12/16/13		
-	-	1.07	1.85	1.18	1.14	18.7 -	13.0	0.88	0.88	0.88	2.9	0.30Y	2/21/18	34.5 -	24.0
-	-	0.64	1.84	1.68	1.65	19.7 -	12.7					0.60940Y	9/15/17	36.3 -	23.3
-	-	0.12	3.52	3.08	10.45	20.7 -	15.0	2.75	6.63	2.51	4.5	0.740Z	32/4/39	72.7 -	52.7
-	-	0.39	1.30	-1.41	0.32	22.8 -	16.5	0.60	0.60	0.90	2.3	0.20Z	32/4/39	29.7 -	21.4
-	-	-	0.90	0.67	0.90	29.3 -	22.1	1.48	1.44	1.40	6.1	0.370	12/29/17	26.3 -	19.9
-	-	0.48	1.85	-1.39	16.10	44.8 -	34.5	4.89	2.24	3.89	6.5	1.420Y	32/4/39	82.8 -	63.9
-	-	-	1.13	1.44	1.23	12.8 -	10.2	1.20	1.40	1.40	9.3	0.30	12/1/17	14.4 -	11.6
-	-	0.12	3.22	4.22	3.86	11.1 -	5.4	1.39	1.19	0.95	5.5	0.37750Y	32/4/39	35.8 -	17.5
-	-	-	0.03	0.04	-0.02	273.7 -	247.7	0.72	0.72	0.72	9.2	0.180	12/29/17	8.2 -	7.4
-0.47	-	-	-3.12											229.7 -	167.5
-	-	-	0.06	0.07	-0.01	206.5 -	188.3	1.04	1.04	1.04	8.7	0.260	12/29/17	12.4 -	11.3
-	-	0.87	3.52	3.59	3.69	23.1 -	18.2	3.25	2.92	2.50	4.5	0.920	32/4/39	81.5 -	64.1
-	-	1.36	5.16	4.88	4.34	14.3 -	7.7	1.00	0.88	0.76	1.8	0.2750	12/8/17	73.7 -	39.6
-	-	0.15	-0.85	-2.47	-3.44									13.2 -	6.1
-	-	0.60	2.23	2.18	2.20	18.6 -	15.9	2.73	2.66	2.55	7.0	0.190	3/15/18	41.5 -	35.4
-	-	-	1.11	1.19	1.16	18.3 -	16.6	1.18	1.17	1.50	6.0	0.09M	3/29/18	20.4 -	18.4
-	-	0.66	-1.45	2.75	-4.92										
-	-	-	0.84	0.88	0.95	16.9 -	15.4	0.73	0.76	0.84	5.4	0.0450	1/31/18	14.2 -	12.9
-0.00	-	-	0.22	-0.55	0.15							0.090	1/5/18		
-	-	0.28	-10.92	1.84	4.20					0.32		0.080Y	12/10/15	40.9 -	21.6
-	-	0.10	0.62	0.90	0.67	13.0 -	4.9	0.64	0.72	0.72	13.4	0.080	2/1/18	8.1 -	3.0
-	-	2.04	6.27	5.40	5.30	20.8 -	14.3	1.72	1.60	0.98	1.6	0.930Y	32/4/39	130.4 -	89.8
-	-	0.54	1.41	1.05	1.80	19.5 -	11.8	0.74	0.67	0.57	3.4	0.30310	12/19/17	27.5 -	16.7
-	-	-0.70	-2.61	-3.26	4.46			0.20	0.68	0.80	1.4	0.050Y	32/4/39	18.2 -	10.8
-	-	1.77	2.21	5.26	4.39	30.2 -	21.6	1.36	1.14	0.92	2.5	0.460Y	32/4/39	66.8 -	47.7
-	-	0.39	1.66	1.69	1.27	19.6 -	14.1							32.6 -	23.4
-	-	0.39	1.36	0.84	0.92	25.4 -	17.9	0.45	0.21	0.35	1.5	0.11360Y	12/15/17	34.6 -	24.3
-	-	-1.34	-3.01	-6.37	-8.79									18.6 -	7.0
-	-	0.13	0.44	0.39	0.24	38.6 -	22.8	0.24	0.20	0.16	1.8	0.10Y	3/9/18	17.0 -	10.0
-	-	0.57	0.91	1.92	0.46	25.7 -	15.5							23.4 -	14.2

SYMBOL	COMPANY	NATURE OF BUSINESS	FISCAL YEAR-END	TOTAL REV. $MILL	NET INCOME $MILL	TOTAL ASSETS $MILL	NET STK EQUITY $MILL	NO OF INST	INST. HOLDINGS (SHARES)
MKL	Markel Corp (Holding Co)	General Insurance	12/31/16	5612.0	455.7	25875.3	8460.9	576	13428481
VAC	Marriott Vacations Worldwide Corp.	Hotels, Restaurants & Travel	12/30/16	1811.2	137.3	2391.4	907.8	339	24412567
MMC	Marsh & McLennan Companies Inc.	Brokers & Intermediaries	12/31/16	13211.0	1768.0	18190.0	6192.0	1013	541139297
MLM	Martin Marietta Materials, Inc.	Construction Materials	12/31/16	3818.7	425.4	7300.9	4140.0	701	70524109
MAS	Masco Corp.	Construction Materials	12/31/16	7357.0	491.0	5137.0	-298.0	811	358151279
DOOR	Masonite International Corp (New)	Construction Materials	1/1/17	1974.0	98.6	1475.9	646.9	207	33146719
MTZ	MasTec Inc. (FL)	Construction Services	12/31/16	5134.7	131.3	3183.1	1096.5	386	73657406
MA	Mastercard Inc	Business Services	12/31/16	10776.0	4059.0	18675.0	5656.0	1804	903756690
MTDR	Matador Resources Co	Production & Extraction	12/31/16	264.4	-97.4	1464.7	690.1	284	101109968
MTRN	Materion Corp	Metal Products	12/31/16	969.2	25.7	741.3	494.1	199	21690198
MATX	Matson Inc	Shipping	12/31/16	1941.6	80.5	2015.5	471.5	256	45913682
MLP	Maui Land & Pineapple Co., Inc.	Property, Real Estate & Developmen	12/31/16	47.4	21.8	38.9	17.7	87	5206688
MAXR	Maxar Technologies Ltd	Internet & Software	12/31/16	2063.8	139.6	3438.9	1158.7		0
MMS	MAXIMUS Inc.	Business Services	9/30/17	2451.0	209.4	1350.7	940.1	411	76515386
MXL	MaxLinear Inc	Semiconductors	12/31/16	387.8	61.3	422.7	352.4	244	67184722
MBI	MBIA Inc.	General Insurance	12/31/16	294.0	-338.0	11137.0	3227.0	314	147275312
MKC	McCormick & Co Inc	Food	11/30/17	4834.1	477.4	10385.8	2559.9	931	134715526
MDR	McDermott International Inc (Panam	Equipment & Services	12/31/16	2636.0	34.1	3222.2	1556.2	416	287148371
MCD	McDonald's Corp	Hotels, Restaurants & Travel	12/31/16	24621.9	4686.5	31023.9	-2204.3	2378	709583048
MUX	McEwen Mining Inc	Precious Metals	12/31/16	60.4	21.1	498.3	443.0	169	102407334
MCK	McKesson Corp	Pharmaceuticals	3/31/17	198533.0	5070.0	60969.0	11095.0	1285	230515653
MDU	MDU Resources Group Inc	Electric Utilities	12/31/16	4128.8	64.4	6284.5	2316.2	498	154129186
MTL	Mechel PAO	Non-Precious Metals	12/31/16	276009.0	7126.0	325465.0	-260274.0	92	23986286
MRT	MedEquities Realty Trust Inc	REITs	12/31/16	49.3	11.0	519.8	355.8	111	30622810
MPW	Medical Properties Trust Inc	REITs	12/31/16	541.1	225.0	6418.5	3248.4	459	352203829
MED	Medifast Inc	Household & Personal Products	12/31/16	274.5	17.8	121.2	96.0	228	13084698
MCC	Medley Capital Corp	Holding and other Investment Office	9/30/17	96.3	36.4	959.6	460.4	126	19881532
MDLY	Medley Management Inc	Finance Intermediaries & Services	12/31/16	76.0	1.0	122.4	-1.9	54	3453072
MD	Mednax; Inc.	Diagnostic & Health Related Service	12/31/16	3183.2	324.9	5339.4	2760.8	486	111287758
MDT	Medtronic PLC	Medical Instruments & Equipment	4/28/17	29710.0	4028.0	99816.0	50294.0	1428	1222777859
MRK	Merck & Co Inc	Pharmaceuticals	12/31/16	39807.0	3920.0	95377.0	40088.0	2573	2386860822
MCY	Mercury General Corp.	General Insurance	12/31/16	3227.7	73.0	4788.7	1752.4	283	35270747
MDP	Meredith Corp	Advertising	6/30/17	1713.4	188.9	2729.6	996.0	359	60614421
MTH	Meritage Homes Corp	Builders	12/31/16	3041.7	149.5	2888.7	1421.5	239	49326016
MTOR	Meritor Inc	Auto Parts	9/30/17	3347.0	324.0	2782.0	268.0	309	98796962
MTR	Mesa Royalty Trust	Oil Royalty Traders	12/31/16	1.4	1.2	4.0	3.4	27	210262
MSB	Mesabi Trust	Non-Precious Metals	1/31/17	10.7	9.6	14.2	10.2	62	2625045
MEI	Methode Electronics Inc	Electrical Equipment	4/29/17	816.5	92.9	704.0	541.1	307	40487076
MET	MetLife Inc	Life & Health	12/31/16	63476.0	800.0	898764.0	67309.0	1457	970902410
MCB	Metropolitan Bank Holding Corp	Banking	12/31/16	49.6	5.3	1220.3	109.5		0
MTD	Mettler-Toledo International, Inc.	Industrial Machinery & Equipment	12/31/16	2508.3	384.4	2166.8	434.9	659	31164803
MXE	Mexico Equity & Income Fund Inc (	Holding and other Investment Office	7/31/17	2.1	0.6	104.7	100.8	25	4412368
MXF	Mexico Fund; Inc.	Holding and other Investment Office	10/31/16	7.5	2.6	280.7	279.0	54	4298490
MFA	MFA Financial, Inc.	REITs	12/31/16	457.2	312.7	12484.0	3033.9	383	377338839
MFCB	MFC Bancorp Ltd (Cayman Islands)	Finance Intermediaries & Services	12/31/16	1131.7	-25.4	650.3	327.5	74	5238058
MCR	MFS Charter Income Trust	Holding and other Investment Office	11/30/16	28.7	24.0	584.4	477.1	79	24224714
MGF	MFS Government Markets Income	Holding and other Investment Office	11/30/16	6.4	5.1	192.2	174.4	51	22620039
CXE	MFS High Income Municipal Trust	Holding and other Investment Office	11/30/16	13.9	10.0	262.5	163.9	41	3436179
CMU	MFS High Yield Municipal Trust	Holding and other Investment Office	11/30/16	11.1	8.1	208.5	132.6	41	1344256
CIF	MFS Intermediate High Income Fun	Holding and other Investment Office	11/30/16	4.9	3.9	80.2	56.8	28	950103
MIN	MFS Intermediate Income Trust	Holding and other Investment Office	10/31/17	14.5	11.2	528.0	524.9	103	57188322
CXH	MFS Investment Grade Municipal Tr	Holding and other Investment Office	11/30/16	8.5	6.2	174.1	117.6	43	2845051
MMT	MFS Multimarket Income Trust	Holding and other Investment Office	10/31/17	26.7	21.4	583.3	471.5	114	25332795
MFM	MFS Municipal Income Trust	Holding and other Investment Office	10/31/17	21.8	16.2	427.2	416.8	65	5076361
MFV	MFS Special Value Trust	Holding and other Investment Office	10/31/17	2.0	1.4	43.1	42.8	16	268222
MTG	MGIC Investment Corp. (WI)	Credit & Lending	12/31/16	1062.5	342.5	5734.5	2548.8	433	404027591
MGP	MGM Growth Properties LLC	REITs	12/31/16	467.5	29.9	9506.7	1333.8	186	86648172
MGM	MGM Resorts International	Hotels, Restaurants & Travel	12/31/16	9455.1	1101.4	28173.3	6220.2	690	553077541
KORS	Michael Kors Holdings Ltd	Retail - Apparel and Accessories	4/1/17	4493.7	552.5	2409.6	1592.6	498	152488341
MFGP	Micro Focus International Plc	Internet & Software	4/30/17	1380.7	157.9	4646.0	1612.5	385	116331978
MFGP	Micro Focus International Plc	Internet & Software	4/30/17	1380.7	157.9	4646.0	1612.5	385	116331978
MAA	Mid-America Apartment Communiti	REITs	12/31/16	1125.3	212.2	11604.5	6413.9	542	123043604
MSL	MidSouth Bancorp, Inc.	Banking	12/31/16	98.1	9.4	1943.3	214.4	84	9777987
MPO	Midstates Petroleum Co Inc	Production & Extraction	12/31/16	48.5	9.9	760.9	561.8	100	47260078
MCRN	Milacron Holdings Corp	Industrial Machinery & Equipment	12/31/16	1166.7	30.5	1722.0	434.9	136	113268259
MLR	Miller Industries Inc. (TN)	Auto Parts	12/31/16	601.1	19.9	297.4	184.6	114	10633193
HIE	Miller/Howard High Income Equity F	Holding and other Investment Office	10/31/17	8.3	4.3	237.3	167.9	28	2020570
MTX	Minerals Technologies, Inc.	Specialty Chemicals	12/31/16	1638.0	133.4	2863.4	1006.5	312	41567473
MP PRD	Mississippi Power Co	Electric Utilities	12/31/16	1163.0	-48.0	8235.0	2976.0		0
MG	Mistras Group Inc	Business Services	12/31/16	404.2	9.6	469.4	270.6	107	22414312
MTU	Mitsubishi UFJ Financial Group Inc	Banking	3/31/17	4469277.0	202680.0	97185019.0	13985532.0	295	192722777
MIXT	MiX Telematics Ltd	Miscellaneous Transportation Servic	3/31/17	1540.1	121.5	1906.7	1444.5	50	6095048
MFG	Mizuho Financial Group Inc	Banking	3/31/17		362440.0	200456304.0	8261357.0	133	53692669
MBT	Mobile TeleSystems PJSC	Services	12/31/16	435692.0	48474.0	544470.0	139235.0	346	362122844
MODN	Model N, Inc	IT Services	9/30/17	131.2	-39.5	171.9	41.3	102	23320320
MOD	Modine Manufacturing Co	Auto Parts	3/31/17	1503.0	14.2	1449.5	414.0	191	48368475
MC	Moelis & Co	Finance Intermediaries & Services	12/31/16	613.4	38.4	598.8	211.8	201	31829969
MHK	Mohawk Industries, Inc.	Construction Materials	12/31/16	8959.1	930.4	10230.6	5776.5	742	72814883
MOH	Molina Healthcare Inc	Hospitals & Health Care Facilities	12/31/16	17782.0	52.0	7449.0	1649.0	354	69398006
TAP	Molson Coors Brewing Co.	Beverages	12/31/16	4885.0	1975.9	29341.5	11418.7	755	195792976

EARNINGS PER SHARE — QUARTERLY 1st	2nd	3rd	ANNUAL 2016	2015	2014	P/E RATIO	DIVIDENDS PER SHARE 2016	2015	2014	AV. YLD %	DIV. DECLARED AMOUNT	PAYABLE	PRICE RANGE 2016
		-18.82	31.27	41.74	22.27	30.7 - 28.5							1147.1 - 891.3
		1.47	4.83	3.82	2.33	29.4 - 16.7	1.25	1.05	0.25	1.1	0.40Y	1/4/18	142.1 - 80.7
		0.76	3.38	2.98	2.65	25.4 - 19.9	1.30	1.18	1.06	1.7	0.3750Y	32/4/39	86.0 - 67.4
		2.39	6.63	4.29	2.71	36.5 - 29.5	1.64	1.60	1.60	0.8	0.440Y	32/4/39	242.0 - 195.5
		0.46	1.47	1.02	2.38	30.1 - 21.7	0.39	0.36	0.33	1.1	0.1050Y	32/4/39	44.2 - 31.9
		1.00	3.17	-1.56	-1.26	26.6 - 18.4							84.2 - 58.4
		0.77	1.61	-0.98	1.35	31.5 - 21.4							50.7 - 34.5
		1.34	3.69	3.35	3.10	41.8 - 28.5	0.76	0.64	0.44	0.6	0.250Y	32/4/39	154.2 - 105.0
		0.15	-1.07	-8.34	1.56								31.4 - 20.3
		0.46	1.27	1.58	2.00	40.6 - 25.0	0.38	0.35	0.34	1.0	0.10Y	12/1/17	51.5 - 31.8
		0.79	1.85	2.34	1.63	20.0 - 12.3	0.74	0.70	0.66	2.4	0.20Y	3/1/18	36.9 - 22.8
		-0.03	1.15	0.36	0.94	23.8 - 0.0					0.1250	3/31/00	27.4 - 0.0
		0.41	3.74	3.84	1.31	22.8 - 0.0	1.48	1.48	1.30	2.5	0.370	12/29/17	85.4 - 0.0
		0.86	2.69	2.35	2.11	26.8 - 20.3	0.18	0.18	0.18	0.3	0.0450Y	32/4/39	72.0 - 54.7
		-0.14	0.91	-0.79	-0.19	35.4 - 22.7							32.2 - 20.7
		-2.17	-2.54	1.06	2.76						0.340Y	1/15/08	11.5 - 6.2
		0.85	3.69	3.11	3.34	28.7 - 24.3	1.72	1.60	1.48	1.7	0.520Y	32/4/39	105.9 - 89.8
		0.33	0.12	-0.08	-0.32	69.0 - 46.8					0.01670	7/1/00	8.3 - 5.6
		2.32	5.44	4.80	4.82	32.0 - 22.0	3.61	3.44	3.28	2.4	1.010Y	32/4/39	174.2 - 119.5
		-0.03	0.07	-0.07	-1.05	80.1 - 26.1	0.01	0.01		0.3	0.005D	2/14/18	5.6 - 1.8
	0.01		9.70	6.27	5.41	17.3 - 13.9	1.08	0.96	0.92	0.7	0.340Y	32/4/39	168.1 - 135.0
		0.45	0.33	-3.20	1.55	89.2 - 77.1	0.76	0.73	0.71	2.8	0.19750Y	32/4/39	29.4 - 25.4
			17.12	-276.65	-10.42	0.4 - 0.2							6.8 - 4.1
		0.17	-0.18	0.42	0.00		0.63	0.85	0.20	5.4	0.210Z	11/29/17	12.8 - 10.4
		0.21	0.86	0.63	0.29	16.5 - 14.1	0.91	0.88	0.84	6.9	0.240Z	32/4/39	14.2 - 12.2
		0.55	1.49	1.66	1.03	49.3 - 27.1	1.07	0.25		2.1	0.480Y	2/8/18	73.5 - 40.3
		0.18	0.97	1.27	1.58	8.2 - 5.2	1.12	1.27	1.48	17.0	0.40630Z	4/30/18	8.0 - 5.1
		0.03	0.02	0.46	0.24	505.0 - 277.5	0.80	0.60	0.20	11.2	0.20Y	12/6/17	10.1 - 5.5
		0.71	3.49	3.58	3.18	20.6 - 11.8							72.0 - 41.2
	1.48		2.48	2.41	3.02		1.52	1.22	1.12		0.460	32/4/39	
		-0.02	1.41	1.56	4.07	47.2 - 38.4	1.85	1.81	1.77	3.0	0.480Y	32/4/39	66.6 - 54.1
		0.84	1.32	1.35	3.23	48.6 - 39.3	2.48	2.47	2.46	4.4	0.6250Y	32/4/39	64.2 - 51.9
0.73			0.75	3.02	2.50	95.7 - 68.2	1.91	1.78	1.68	3.2	0.5450Y	32/4/39	71.8 - 51.1
		1.02	3.55	3.09	3.46	15.5 - 9.5							55.0 - 33.8
		0.51	6.23	0.64	2.51	4.3 - 2.1					0.10Y	12/8/08	26.8 - 12.8
		0.32	0.65	1.03	3.51	28.4 - 0.0	0.65	1.03	3.51	4.8	0.14790Z	4/30/18	18.4 - 0.0
		0.91	0.65	1.89	1.61	40.3 - 16.7	0.09	1.84	1.62	0.5	1.180	2/20/18	26.2 - 10.9
	0.64		2.20	2.57	2.51	21.7 - 16.9	0.36	0.36	0.30	0.9	0.110Y	1/26/18	47.8 - 37.1
		-0.08	0.63	4.57	5.42	88.5 - 70.5	1.58	1.48	1.33	3.2	0.40Y	32/4/39	55.7 - 44.4
		0.82	0.43	1.54		116.3 - 86.0							50.0 - 37.0
		3.99	14.22	12.48	11.44	48.5 - 29.2							689.1 - 414.5
			0.01	-0.09	0.01	1219.0 - 0.0	0.56	1.62	2.13	5.2	0.0480	12/28/17	12.2 - 0.0
			0.17	0.09	0.09	106.9 - 78.8	1.05	2.20	3.01	6.4	0.130	1/26/18	18.2 - 13.4
		0.15	0.80	0.80	0.81	11.1 - 9.7	0.80	0.80	0.80	9.6	0.20Z	32/4/39	8.9 - 7.8
	0.55		-2.00	-38.60	0.05								
			0.46	0.49	0.52	19.0 - 18.1	0.74	0.81	0.58	8.6	0.06160	1/31/18	8.8 - 8.3
			0.16	0.17	0.18	31.8 - 29.7	0.41	0.43	0.45	8.3	0.03070	1/31/18	5.1 - 4.8
			0.32	0.34	0.32	17.2 - 15.3	0.30	0.31	0.31	5.8	0.025M	1/31/18	5.5 - 4.9
			0.29	0.31	0.30	16.9 - 15.5	0.27	0.28	0.29	5.8	0.0215M	1/31/18	4.9 - 4.5
			0.19	0.20	0.21	15.9 - 13.4	0.26	0.24	0.23	9.4	0.0220	1/31/18	3.0 - 2.5
			0.11	0.12	0.15	40.1 - 37.3	0.42	0.45	0.48	9.8	0.03120	1/31/18	4.4 - 4.1
			0.53	0.55	0.55	19.5 - 17.8	0.49	0.51	0.53	5.0	0.038M	1/31/18	10.3 - 9.4
			0.34	0.36	0.39	18.5 - 17.4	0.53	0.57	0.55	8.6	0.04410	1/31/18	6.3 - 5.9
			0.41	0.42	0.41	18.0 - 16.3	0.38	0.39	0.41	5.4	0.0315M	1/31/18	7.4 - 6.7
			0.23	0.25	0.28	29.6 - 0.0	0.59	0.65	0.70	9.5	0.050	1/31/18	6.8 - 0.0
		0.32	0.86	2.60	0.64	18.0 - 11.5					0.0250Y	9/2/08	15.4 - 9.9
		0.18	0.52			60.9 - 47.7	1.04			3.7	0.420Y	1/16/18	31.7 - 24.8
		0.26	1.92	-0.82	-0.31	17.8 - 13.2					0.110	32/4/39	34.3 - 25.4
	1.32		4.44	4.28	3.22								
			0.77	0.61	0.89	46.6 - 37.9							35.9 - 29.1
			0.77	0.61	0.89	38.6 - 36.2							29.7 - 27.9
		1.00	2.69	4.41	1.97	41.0 - 34.9	3.28	3.08	2.92	3.2	0.92250Z	32/4/39	110.3 - 93.8
		0.05	0.58	0.90	1.58	27.0 - 19.1	0.36	0.36	0.35	2.7	1.0Y	1/15/18	15.7 - 11.1
		0.14	0.39	-232.74	10.10	54.8 - 28.4							21.4 - 11.1
		0.17	0.43	-0.65	-0.28	45.0 - 35.4							19.3 - 15.2
		0.39	1.75	1.41	1.31	16.5 - 13.5	0.68	0.64	0.60	2.6	0.180Y	12/11/17	28.9 - 23.6
			0.64	1.02		22.1 - 18.9	1.39	1.16		10.5	0.1160	3/29/18	14.1 - 12.1
		1.17	3.79	3.08	2.65	22.1 - 16.6	0.20	0.20	0.20	0.3	0.050Y	32/4/39	83.7 - 63.0
							1.31	1.31	1.31	7.5	1.31250	1/2/18	27.2 - 0.0
		-0.25	0.32	0.54	0.77	82.3 - 53.5							26.3 - 17.1
21.50			57.51	107.50	69.98	0.1 - 0.1	17.75	17.79	14.17	272.6			7.4 - 6.0
			0.23	0.19	0.20	56.3 - 24.9	2.83			33.7			12.9 - 5.7
4.66			33.50	31.64	19.64	0.1 - 0.1	15.30	13.83	12.15	423.5			3.9 - 3.4
		9.09	24.35	24.87	26.06	0.5 - 0.3	51.09	46.79	46.99	516.5			11.5 - 7.8
		-0.36	-1.21	-0.76	-0.86								16.5 - 8.4
	0.31		-0.03	0.45	2.72						0.10Y	12/5/08	23.6 - 10.3
		0.48	1.58	1.55	-0.19	31.5 - 21.3	3.29	1.00	1.40	8.3	0.370Y	11/20/17	49.8 - 33.6
		3.61	12.48	8.31	7.25	22.8 - 16.2							284.8 - 201.7
		-1.70	0.92	2.58	1.29	86.1 - 46.4							79.2 - 42.7
		1.29	9.26	1.93	2.76	11.0 - 8.3	1.64	1.64	1.48	1.8	0.410Y	32/4/39	101.6 - 76.5

SYMBOL	COMPANY	NATURE OF BUSINESS	FISCAL YEAR-END	TOTAL REV. $MILL	NET INCOME $MILL	TOTAL ASSETS $MILL	NET STK EQUITY $MILL	NO OF INST	INST. HOLDINGS (SHARES)
MNR	Monmouth Real Estate Investment	REITs	9/30/17	113.5	40.3	1443.0	712.9	232	57414709
MON	Monsanto Co	Agricultural Chemicals	8/31/17	14640.0	2260.0	21333.0	6438.0	1519	407855555
MCO	Moody's Corp.	Business Services	12/31/16	3604.2	266.6	5327.3	-1225.0	800	210318974
MOG A	Moog Inc	Industrial Machinery & Equipment	9/30/17	2497.5	141.3	3090.6	1214.3	279	36324912
MS	Morgan Stanley	Finance Intermediaries & Services	12/31/16	37949.0	5979.0	814949.0	76050.0	1363	1864482058
APF	Morgan Stanley Asia-Pacific Fund, I	Holding and other Investment Office	12/31/16	5.1	2.4	217.7	214.8	71	10383097
CAF	Morgan Stanley China A Share Fun	Holding and other Investment Office	12/31/16	10.6	2.1	456.6	454.7	81	9433956
MSD	Morgan Stanley Emerging Markets	Holding and other Investment Office	12/31/16	15.7	13.2	229.0	221.6	56	8662310
EDD	Morgan Stanley Emerging Markets	Holding and other Investment Office	10/31/17	58.8	42.4	851.0	585.0	87	17456428
MSF	Morgan Stanley Emerging Markets	Holding and other Investment Office	12/31/16	4.4	1.2	223.5	217.9	54	9314446
ICB	Morgan Stanley Funds - Income Se	Holding and other Investment Office	9/30/17	6.9	5.5	176.0	175.1	36	4761229
IIF	Morgan Stanley India Investment Fu	Holding and other Investment Office	12/31/16	4.9	-1.2	434.1	423.3	66	6884874
ICB	Morgan Stanley Trusts	Holding and other Investment Office	10/31/02	5.5	4.8	103.9	103.8		0
MOSC U	Mosaic Acquisition Corp	Business Services	8/15/17		-0.0	0.2	0.0	1	1179674
MOS	Mosaic Co (The)	Agricultural Chemicals	12/31/16	7162.8	297.8	16840.7	9584.6	759	324920311
MSI	Motorola Solutions Inc.	Manufacturing	12/31/16	6038.0	560.0	8463.0	-964.0	870	322726877
MOV	Movado Group, Inc.	Miscellaneous Consumer Goods	1/31/17	552.8	35.1	607.8	474.0	220	20570770
MPLX	MPLX LP	Equipment & Services	12/31/16	2590.0	256.0	16646.0	1000.0	342	268199241
MRC	MRC Global Inc	Industrial Machinery & Equipment	12/31/16	3041.0	-83.0	2164.0	1118.0	232	98682619
MSA	MSA Safety Inc	Office Equipment & Furniture	12/31/16	1149.5	91.9	1353.9	558.2	316	31821972
MSM	MSC Industrial Direct Co Inc	Industrial Machinery & Equipment	9/2/17	2887.7	231.4	2098.9	1225.1	432	53432254
MSCI	MSCI Inc	Publishing	12/31/16	1150.7	260.9	3082.6	317.6	464	100974993
MSGN	MSG Network Inc	Radio & Television	6/30/17	675.4	167.3	805.0	-944.2	265	67217912
MLI	Mueller Industries Inc	Industrial Machinery & Equipment	12/31/16	2055.6	99.7	1447.5	898.7	240	65795263
MWA	Mueller Water Products Inc	Industrial Machinery & Equipment	9/30/17	826.0	123.3	1258.3	488.4	306	153493139
MULE	MuleSoft Inc	IT Services	12/31/16	187.7	-49.6	202.9	40.1	134	30831711
MUR	Murphy Oil Corp	Production & Extraction	12/31/16	1874.1	-276.0	10295.9	4916.7	613	192468842
MUSA	Murphy USA Inc	Retail - General Merchandise/Depart	12/31/16	11594.6	221.5	2088.7	697.1		0
MVO	MV Oil Trust	Production & Extraction	12/31/16	5.5	4.6	19.5	19.5	39	1195616
MVC	MVC Capital Inc	Holding and other Investment Office	10/31/17	20.1	-5.6	403.4	279.5	88	13029217
MYE	Myers Industries Inc.	Plastics	12/31/16	558.1	1.1	381.7	93.0	195	32030296
MYOV	Myovant Sciences Ltd	Pharmaceuticals	3/31/17		-83.4	185.3	166.8	48	49555568
NBR	Nabors Industries Ltd	Production & Extraction	12/31/16	2007.1	-1029.7	8187.0	3247.0	587	341887592
NC	NACCO Industries Inc	Household Appliances, Electronics &	12/31/16	856.4	29.6	668.0	220.3	132	4185942
NTP	Nam Tai Property Inc	Property, Real Estate & Developmen	12/31/16	1.8	-9.5	248.8	236.3	68	11536247
NBHC	National Bank Holdings Corp	Banking	12/31/16	200.5	23.1	4573.0	536.2	159	31029452
NFG	National Fuel Gas Co. (NJ)	Gas Utilities	9/30/17	1579.9	283.5	6103.3	1703.7	509	74883976
NGG	National Grid plc	Electric Utilities	3/31/17	15035.0	7795.0	65840.0	20368.0	463	43571959
NHI	National Health Investors, Inc.	REITs	12/31/16	248.5	151.5	2403.6	1209.6	286	36835783
NOV	National Oilwell Varco Inc	Equipment & Services	12/31/16	7251.0	-2412.0	21140.0	13940.0	957	416146075
NPK	National Presto Industries, Inc.	Defense	12/31/16	341.9	44.6	417.6	350.2	191	5166057
NNN	National Retail Properties Inc	REITs	12/31/16	533.6	239.5	6334.2	3916.8	463	180139277
NSA	National Storage Affiliates Trust	REITs	12/31/16	199.0	18.0	1892.1	577.1	178	46759337
NW PRC	National Westminster Bank Plc	Banking	12/31/16	7637.0	-867.0	316476.0	15580.0		0
NSM	Nationstar Mortgage Holdings Inc	Credit & Lending	12/31/16	1915.0	19.0	19593.0	1677.0	157	101503502
NGS	Natural Gas Services Group Inc	Equipment & Services	12/31/16	71.7	6.5	293.5	233.0	129	13740277
NGVC	Natural Grocers By Vitamin Cottage	Retail - Food & Beverage, Drug & To	9/30/17	769.0	6.9	300.0	133.9	99	6554506
NRP	Natural Resources Partners L.P.	Mining	12/31/16	400.1	96.9	1444.7		94	11995075
NTZ	Natuzzi S.p.A.	Furniture	12/31/16	457.2	-6.1	347.2	149.0	23	10543811
NLS	Nautilus Inc	Leisure Equipment	12/31/16	406.0	34.2	333.1	160.9	220	44210572
NCI	Navigant Consulting, Inc.	Business Services	12/31/16	1034.5	58.1	1054.8	634.5	257	51862773
NVGS	Navigator Holdings Ltd.	Miscellaneous Transportation Servic	12/31/16	294.1	44.6	1724.8	956.5		0
NNA	Navios Maritime Acquisition Corp	Equipment & Services	12/31/16	290.2	62.9	1703.6	575.4	91	35473949
NM	Navios Maritime Holdings Inc	Shipping	12/31/16	441.6	-303.8	2752.9	678.3	114	31867297
NAP	Navios Maritime Midstream Partner	Shipping	12/31/16	91.8	24.9	475.8		27	2478265
NMM	Navios Maritime Partners LP	Shipping	12/31/16	190.5	-52.5	1268.6		97	27108066
NAV	Navistar International Corp.	Autos- Manufacturing	10/31/17	8570.0	30.0	6135.0	-4578.0	246	94901363
NCS	NCI Building Systems, Inc.	Metal Products	10/29/17	1770.3	54.7	1051.2	305.2	228	67690679
NCR	NCR Corp	Computer Hardware & Equipment	12/31/16	6543.0	270.0	7673.0	1542.0	594	142031109
NP	Neenah Inc	Paper & Forest Products	12/31/16	941.5	73.0	765.6	338.3	270	22630298
NNI	Nelnet Inc	Credit & Lending	12/31/16	1242.0	256.8	27180.1	2061.7	174	18897093
NPTN	NeoPhotonics Corp	Semiconductors	12/31/16	411.4	-0.2	390.9	225.4	140	42486847
NETS	Netshoes (Cayman) Ltd	Retail - Apparel and Accessories	12/31/16	1739.5	151.1	1113.7	123.6	39	18748751
NVRO	Nevro Corp	Medical Instruments & Equipment	12/31/16	228.5	-31.8	430.6	249.0	232	34984690
HYB	New America High Income Fund, In	Holding and other Investment Office	12/31/16	21.4	17.4	324.7	231.1	59	10974625
GF	New Germany Fund, Inc.	Holding and other Investment Office	12/31/16	4.9	1.9	264.3	235.8	49	10977074
IRL	New Ireland Fund Inc (The)	Holding and other Investment Office	10/31/17	0.9	-0.5	58.4	58.2	40	830130
NJR	New Jersey Resources Corp	Gas Utilities	9/30/17	2268.6	132.1	3928.5	1236.6	352	72820311
NEWM	New Media Investment Group Inc	Publishing	12/25/16	1255.4	31.6	1336.0	755.0	196	52542008
NMFC	New Mountain Finance Corp	Wealth Management	12/31/16	168.1	88.1	1656.0	938.6	156	34968203
EDU	New Oriental Education & Technolo	Educational Services	5/31/17	1799.5	274.5	2925.0	1680.9	353	134046333
NEWR	New Relic Inc	Internet & Software	3/31/17	263.5	-61.1	352.3	186.8	210	43283919
NRZ	New Residential Investment Corp	REITs	12/31/16	1257.2	504.5	18365.0	3260.1	364	192736128
SNR	New Senior Investment Group Inc	REITs	12/31/16	472.4	-72.2	2821.7	578.9	209	63709207
NWY	New York & Company Inc	Retail - Apparel and Accessories	1/28/17	929.1	-17.3	301.6	79.2	85	58100310
NYCB	New York Community Bancorp Inc.	Banking	12/31/16	1820.4	495.4	48926.6	6124.0	594	365910464
NYRT	New York REIT Inc	REITs	12/31/16	160.3	-82.5	2152.4	931.0	225	142161094
NYT	New York Times Co.	Publishing	12/25/16	1555.3	29.1	2185.4	847.8	322	152817842
NWL	Newell Brands Inc	Plastics	12/31/16	13264.0	527.8	33837.5	11348.8	934	535868656
NFX	Newfield Exploration Co	Production & Extraction	12/31/16	1472.0	-1230.0	4312.0	938.0	630	230030743

T40

EARNINGS PER SHARE						P/E RATIO		DIVIDENDS PER SHARE			AV. YLD %	DIV. DECLARED		PRICE RANGE	
QUARTERLY			ANNUAL											2016	
1st	2nd	3rd	2016	2015	2014			2016	2015	2014		AMOUNT	PAYABLE		
-	-	0.0/	0.50	0.43	0.40	36.4 -	27.6	0.64	0.60	0.60	4.1	0.38280Z	3/15/18	18.2 -	13.8
0.38	-	-	2.99	4.81	5.22	40.9 -	35.1	2.16	1.96	1.72	1.9	0.540Y	32/4/39	122.4 -	105.1
-	-	1.63	1.36	4.63	4.61	112.2 -	69.6	1.48	1.36	1.12	1.2	0.440Y	32/4/39	152.6 -	94.7
-	-	1.11	3.47	3.35	3.52	25.6 -	18.1	-	-	-	-	0.01480	10/5/88	88.9 -	63.0
-	-	0.93	2.92	2.90	1.60	18.4 -	13.9	0.70	0.55	0.35	1.5	0.250Y	32/4/39	53.9 -	40.7
-	-	-	0.17	0.16	0.15	108.2 -	80.3	0.15	0.14	1.22	0.9	0.1510	1/10/18	18.4 -	13.7
-	-	-	0.10	0.23	0.27	245.7 -	173.6	0.80	13.34	1.72	3.7	0.8323B	12/29/17	24.6 -	17.4
-	-	-	0.62	0.57	0.53	16.5 -	14.7	0.63	0.60	0.57	6.4	0.140	1/10/18	10.3 -	9.1
-	-	-	0.78	0.80	0.94	10.7 -	9.2	0.76	0.91	1.65	9.6	0.150	1/10/18	8.4 -	7.2
-	-	-	0.08	0.05	0.07	224.8 -	166.1	0.09	0.05	0.12	0.6	0.03210	1/10/18	18.0 -	13.3
-	-	-	0.71	0.67	0.64	25.9 -	0.0	1.13	0.81	0.70	6.3	0.04250	1/26/18	18.4 -	0.0
-	-	-	-0.08	-0.16	-0.08			1.14	0.04	-	3.4	0.3549B	1/10/18	36.8 -	25.6
-	-	-										0.04250	1/26/18	18.4 -	0.0
-	-	-0.01	-	-	-										
-	-	0.65	0.85	2.78	2.68	40.0 -	22.8	1.10	1.08	1.00	4.4	0.0250Y	32/4/39	34.0 -	19.4
-	-	1.25	3.24	3.02	5.29	29.2 -	23.9	1.70	1.43	1.30	2.0	0.520Y	32/4/39	94.5 -	77.3
-	-	0.75	1.90	2.02	1.97	17.2 -	11.1	0.44	0.40	0.26	1.7	0.130Y	12/15/17	32.7 -	21.1
-	-	0.29	-	1.22	1.55			2.03	1.70	1.34	5.8	0.60750	2/14/18	38.9 -	31.1
-	-	-0.03	-1.10	-3.38	1.40									22.0 -	14.3
-	-	0.83	2.42	1.87	2.33	35.5 -	27.3	1.31	1.27	1.23	1.7	0.56250Y	32/4/39	86.0 -	66.2
1.05	-	-	3.77	3.74	3.76	28.0 -	17.4	1.72	4.60	1.32	2.0	0.580Y	32/4/39	105.5 -	65.6
-	-	0.93	2.70	2.03	2.43	47.9 -	29.2	1.00	0.80	0.18	0.9	0.380	32/4/39	129.3 -	78.7
0.54	-	-	0.10	3.28	1.47	251.5 -	164.5							25.1 -	16.4
-	-	0.39	1.74	1.54	1.79	24.9 -	16.2	0.38	0.30	0.30	1.1	0.10Y	12/22/17	43.3 -	28.2
-	-	0.15	0.39	0.19	0.34	35.3 -	28.1	0.10	0.07	0.07	0.8	0.050Y	2/20/18	13.8 -	10.9
-	-	-0.19	-2.73	-3.57	-3.07									28.4 -	19.5
-	-	-0.38	-1.60	-13.03	5.03			1.20	1.40	1.33	4.5	0.250Y	32/4/39	32.2 -	22.6
-	-	1.90	5.59	4.02	5.26	14.5 -	10.9							81.0 -	61.0
-	-	0.23	0.40	1.27	3.40	22.2 -	12.0	0.40	1.27	3.40	6.6	0.220Z	1/25/18	8.9 -	4.8
-	-	-	0.85	0.41	0.07	12.9 -	10.0	0.71	0.54	0.54	7.3	0.150	1/8/18	11.0 -	8.5
-	-	0.11	0.03	0.57	-0.27	746.7 -	445.0	0.54	0.54	0.52	3.1	0.1350Y	1/2/18	22.4 -	13.4
-	-0.50	-	-0.04	-	-									-	
-	-	-0.52	-3.64	-1.29	-2.28			0.06	0.06	0.06	-	0.060	32/4/39	-	
-	-	1.23	4.32	3.13	-5.02	20.6 -	7.4	1.06	1.04	1.02	1.6	0.1650Y	32/4/39	88.8 -	31.9
-	-	0.40	-0.26	-0.32	-0.58			0.28	0.08	0.08	-	0.070	1/19/18	-	
-	-	0.26	0.79	0.14	0.22	46.7 -	38.3	0.22	0.20	0.20	0.7	0.090Y	3/15/18	36.9 -	30.3
-	-	0.69	-3.43	-4.50	3.52			1.60	1.56	1.52	2.8	0.4150Y	32/4/39	60.9 -	53.3
-	-	-	0.69	0.53	0.66	109.0 -	83.9							75.2 -	57.9
-	-	0.94	3.87	3.95	3.04	20.9 -	17.9	3.60	3.40	3.08	4.7	0.950Z	32/4/39	80.8 -	69.3
-	-	-0.07	-6.41	-1.99	5.82			0.61	1.84	1.64	1.7	0.050Y	32/4/39	41.7 -	29.9
-	-	1.19	6.39	5.83	3.82	18.9 -	14.4	5.05	4.05	5.05	4.8	4.56Y	3/15/17	120.5 -	92.0
-	-	0.35	1.38	1.20	1.24	33.4 -	26.6	1.78	1.71	1.65	4.3	0.4750Z	32/4/39	46.1 -	36.7
-	-	0.03	0.31	0.17	-	89.0 -	68.5	0.88	0.54	-	3.7	0.3333GHZ	12/29/17	27.6 -	21.2
-	-	-						1.54	1.27	1.18	5.9			26.6 -	25.5
-	-	0.07	0.19	0.37	2.45	106.2 -	78.7							20.2 -	14.9
-	-	0.04	0.50	0.79	1.11	64.1 -	45.6							32.0 -	22.8
-	-	0.03	0.51	0.72	0.60	26.8 -	9.5							13.7 -	4.8
-	-	1.48	7.78	-45.75	9.40	5.7 -	3.0	1.35	-	14.00	4.5	0.450	2/14/18	44.1 -	23.0
-	-	-0.34	-0.11	-0.30	-0.90									3.3 -	0.0
-	-	0.27	1.09	0.84	0.59	17.9 -	11.4					0.10Y	9/10/07	19.6 -	12.4
-	-	0.25	1.19	1.23	-0.75	21.6 -	12.3							25.8 -	14.6
-	-	-	0.80	1.76	1.52										
-	-0.41	-	0.40	0.56	0.08							0.050	12/12/17		
-	-0.34	-	-2.54	-1.42	-0.65							0.060	9/25/15		
-	0.10	-	1.19	1.33	0.13							0.42250	2/14/18		
-	-	-	-0.62	0.48	0.93							0.21250	11/13/15		
-	-	0.38	-1.19	-2.25	-7.60									45.3 -	22.9
-	-	0.25	0.70	0.24	0.15	29.4 -	18.9							20.6 -	13.3
-	-	0.77	1.71	-1.09	1.12	29.0 -	17.3							49.6 -	29.6
-	-	1.10	4.24	2.98	4.03	21.8 -	17.3	1.32	1.20	1.02	1.6	0.370Y	12/4/17	92.5 -	73.3
-	-	1.11	6.02	5.89	6.62	9.8 -	6.5	0.50	0.42	0.40	1.0	0.160Y	12/15/17	59.1 -	39.2
-	-	-0.42	0.00	0.09	-0.61									12.3 -	4.6
-	-	-	-21.14	-13.97	-22.63										
-	-	-0.21	-1.12	-2.54	-6.94									99.2 -	65.9
-	-	-	0.75	0.76	0.80	13.3 -	12.1	0.76	0.81	0.83	7.9	0.0550	2/28/18	10.0 -	9.1
-	-	-	0.12	0.13	0.21	166.4 -	109.0	1.18	1.23	4.34	7.1	0.1732B	1/26/18	20.0 -	13.1
-	-	-	-0.06	0.21	-0.04			2.22	1.13	0.37	16.7	0.289C	12/29/17	14.2 -	11.9
-	-	0.22	1.52	2.10	1.67	29.6 -	22.5	0.97	0.92	0.85	2.4	0.27250Y	32/4/39	45.0 -	34.3
-	-	-0.04	0.70	1.52	-0.10	24.9 -	17.0	1.34	1.29	0.54	9.2	0.370Y	11/16/17	17.4 -	11.9
-	-	0.31	1.60	0.55	1.10	9.3 -	8.5	1.36	1.36	1.48	9.5	0.340Y	12/28/17	14.9 -	13.6
0.81	-	-	1.43	1.23	1.37	65.7 -	30.3	0.40	-	0.35	0.6			94.0 -	43.3
-	-0.27	-	-1.39	-1.98	-2.58									60.0 -	29.8
-	-	0.73	2.12	1.32	2.53	8.6 -	7.1	1.84	1.75	0.38	11.0	0.50Z	32/4/39	18.3 -	15.2
-	-	-0.18	-0.88	-1.08	-0.70			1.04	0.75	0.23	10.9	0.260Z	12/22/17	10.8 -	7.5
-	-	0.01	-0.16	-0.27	0.04									2.9 -	1.3
-	-	0.21	1.01	-0.11	1.09	16.1 -	11.6	0.68	1.00	1.00	5.1	0.170Y	32/4/39	16.2 -	11.7
-	-	-	-0.50	-0.24	-0.56			0.38	0.46	0.31	4.5	2.A	1/26/18	10.1 -	3.9
-	-	0.20	0.18	0.38	0.20	111.1 -	72.5	0.16	0.16	0.16	0.9	0.040Y	32/4/39	20.0 -	13.1
-	-	0.48	1.25	1.29	1.35	43.9 -	22.4	0.76	0.76	0.66	1.7	0.230Y	32/4/39	54.9 -	28.0
-	-	0.44	-6.36	-21.18	6.52									43.7 -	24.5

T41

SYMBOL	COMPANY	NATURE OF BUSINESS	FISCAL YEAR-END	TOTAL REV. $MILL	NET INCOME $MILL	TOTAL ASSETS $MILL	NET STK EQUITY $MILL	NO OF INST	INST. HOLDINGS (SHARES)
NEU	NewMarket Corp	Specialty Chemicals	12/31/16	2049.5	243.4	1416.4	483.3	355	9252406
NEM	Newmont Mining Corp (Holding Co)	Mining	12/31/16	6711.0	-627.0	21031.0	10721.0	925	560930731
NR	Newpark Resources, Inc.	Equipment & Services	12/31/16	471.5	-40.7	798.2	500.5	247	110023950
NEXA	Nexa Resources SA	Metal Products	12/31/16	1912.8	93.2	6160.6	2848.0		0
NHF	NexPoint Credit Strategies Fund	Holding and other Investment Office	12/31/16	77.0	65.3	562.7	414.8	71	7741346
NXRT	NexPoint Residential Trust Inc	REITs	12/31/16	132.8	21.9	1035.4	231.5	135	13416804
NEE PRK	NextEra Energy Capital Holdings In	Electric Utilities							0
NEE	NextEra Energy Inc	Electric Utilities	12/31/16	16155.0	2912.0	89993.0	24341.0	1692	435791966
NEP	NextEra Energy Partners LP	Electric Utilities	12/31/16	715.0	82.0	7150.0	0.0	183	50787951
NGL	NGL Energy Partners LP	Refining & Marketing	3/31/17	13022.2	137.0	6320.4	63.9	134	78216238
NLSN	Nielsen Holdings PLC	Business Services	12/31/16	6309.0	502.0	15730.0	4102.0	503	426893524
NKE	NIKE Inc	Apparel, Footwear & Accessories	5/31/17	34350.0	4240.0	23259.0	12407.0	1774	1186172669
NINE	Nine Energy Service Inc	Equipment & Services							0
NI	NiSource Inc. (Holding Co.)	Equipment & Services	12/31/16	4492.5	331.5	18691.9	4071.2	665	332635535
NL	NL Industries, Inc.	Electrical Equipment	12/31/16	108.9	15.3	385.0	177.9	77	5625807
NOAH	Noah Holdings Ltd	Wealth Management	12/31/16	2513.6	643.8	5956.5	3662.8	103	28580365
NE	Noble Corp plc	Equipment & Services	12/31/16	2302.1	-929.6	11440.1	5758.7		0
NBL	Noble Energy Inc	Production & Extraction	12/31/16	3491.0	-998.0	21011.0	9288.0	780	512098568
NBLX	Noble Midstream Partners LP	Equipment & Services	12/31/16	160.7	85.5	369.4	271.5	94	17696324
NOK	Nokia Corp	Manufacturing	12/31/16	23614.0	-766.0	44901.0	20094.0	597	450215978
NOMD	Nomad Foods Ltd	Food	12/31/16	1927.7	36.4	4709.5	1902.5	177	135050283
NMR	Nomura Holdings Inc	Finance Intermediaries & Services	3/31/17	925702.0	239617.0	42852078.0	2789916.0	147	31819442
OSB	Norbord Inc	Paper & Forest Products	12/31/16	1766.0	183.0	1799.0	650.0		0
NAO	Nordic American Offshore Ltd (Ber	Equipment & Services	12/31/16	17.7	-32.2	374.9	234.2	86	7731379
NAT	Nordic American Tankers Ltd	Equipment & Services	12/31/16	357.5	-4.5	1349.9	871.0	204	30680568
JWN	Nordstrom, Inc.	Retail - General Merchandise/Depart	1/28/17	14757.0	354.0	7858.0	870.0	829	128107754
NSC	Norfolk Southern Corp.	Rail	12/31/16	9888.0	1668.0	34892.0	12409.0	1491	258135878
NOA	North American Energy Partners Inc	Equipment & Services	12/31/16	213.2	-0.4	350.1	159.0	56	12252915
NRT	North European Oil Royalty Trust	Oil Royalty Traders	10/31/17	7.8	7.0	2.1	0.1	55	1214946
NOC	Northrop Grumman Corp	Defense	12/31/16	24508.0	2200.0	25614.0	5259.0	1246	200746242
NRE	NorthStar Realty Europe Corp	REITs	12/31/16	151.2	-61.8	1845.4	593.4	181	43686094
NWN	Northwest Natural Gas Co.	Gas Utilities	12/31/16	676.0	58.9	3079.8	850.5	300	24849217
NWE	Northwestern Corp.	Electric Utilities	12/31/16	1257.2	164.2	5499.3	1676.2	352	59657273
NCLH	Norwegian Cruise Line Holdings Ltd	Hotels, Restaurants & Travel	12/31/16	4874.3	633.1	12973.9	4537.7	425	223776085
NVS	Novartis AG Basel	Pharmaceuticals	12/31/16	49436.0	6712.0	130124.0	74832.0	1290	298073735
NVO	Novo-Nordisk AS	Pharmaceuticals	12/31/16	111780.0	37925.0	97539.0	45269.0	677	175652634
DNOW	Now Inc	Equipment & Services	12/31/16	2107.0	-234.0	1603.0	1183.0	342	124474947
NQ	NQ Mobile Inc	IT Services	12/31/16	343.1	-127.6	853.6	385.8	65	11955604
NRG	NRG Energy Inc	Electric Utilities	12/31/16	12351.0	-774.0	30355.0	2041.0	591	371164448
NYLD	NRG Yield Inc	Electrical Equipment	12/31/16	1021.0	67.0	8383.0	1850.0	195	60220658
DCM	NTT DoCoMo Inc	Services	3/31/17	4584552.0	652538.0	7453074.0	5530629.0	183	25691355
NUS	NU Skin Enterprises, Inc.	Household & Personal Products	12/31/16	2207.8	143.1	1474.0	664.1	370	49581320
NUE	Nucor Corp.	Non-Precious Metals	12/31/16	16208.1	796.3	15223.5	7879.9	1053	319209004
NS	NuStar Energy LP	Refining & Marketing	12/31/16	1756.7	150.0	5030.5		290	60090746
NSH	NuStar GP Holdings LLC	Equipment & Services	12/31/16	56.1	55.1	274.6	243.8	113	32971177
JMLP	Nuveen All Cap Energy MLP Opport	Finance Intermediaries & Services	11/30/16	1	-0.6	168.0	121.8	28	1858106
NVG	Nuveen AMT-Free Municipal Credit	Holding and other Investment Office	10/31/16	141.2	104.2	5294.1	3370.2	196	20939167
NUW	Nuveen AMT-Free Municipal Value	Holding and other Investment Office	10/31/16	12.4	10.6	256.2	247.4	28	951726
NEA	Nuveen AMT-Free Quality Municipa	Holding and other Investment Office	10/31/16	102.0	73.6	6366.6	4037.2	207	38368146
NAZ	Nuveen Arizona Quality Municipal I	Holding and other Investment Office	2/28/17	11.1	7.8	259.0	165.1	24	623032
NBB	Nuveen Build America Bond Fund	Holding and other Investment Office	3/31/17	39.5	32.3	709.8	566.4	70	6331436
NBD	Nuveen Build America Bond Opport	Holding and other Investment Office	3/31/17	10.3	8.5	177.9	158.9		0
NKX	Nuveen California AMT-Free Qualit	Holding and other Investment Office	2/28/17	50.3	36.2	1170.9	732.6	58	3424786
NCB	Nuveen California Municipal Value	Holding and other Investment Office	2/29/16	3.1	2.7	56.9	56.7	13	146772
NCA	Nuveen California Municipal Value	Holding and other Investment Office	2/28/17	13.3	11.6	291.5	285.5	51	3059329
NAC	Nuveen California Quality Municipal	Holding and other Investment Office	2/28/17	127.7	93.9	3389.7	2221.6	84	8616963
NXC	Nuveen California Select Tax-Free I	Holding and other Investment Office	3/31/17	4.2	3.8	94.7	94.3	22	268560
NTC	Nuveen Connecticut Quality Munici	Holding and other Investment Office	5/31/17	12.6	8.3	331.4	205.5	51	2427408
JCE	Nuveen Core Equity Alpha Fund	Holding and other Investment Office	12/31/16	4.4	2.0	229.1	228.6	48	3677538
JQC	Nuveen Credit Strategies Income F	Holding and other Investment Office	7/31/17	103.2	70.7	2039.9	1265.4	154	47728388
JDD	Nuveen Diversified Dividend and In	Holding and other Investment Office	12/31/16	14.2	9.1	366.0	247.6	49	1978310
DIAX	Nuveen Dow 30SM Dynamic Overw	Holding and other Investment Office	12/31/16	15.1	9.8	608.6	597.2	70	6473827
JMF	Nuveen Energy MLP Total Return F	Holding and other Investment Office	11/30/16	2.5	-4.9	786.4	530.1	82	7285628
NEV	Nuveen Enhanced Municipal Value	Holding and other Investment Office	10/31/16	23.4	19.7	443.4	-388.8	47	2714463
JFR	Nuveen Floating Rate Income Fund	Holding and other Investment Office	7/31/17	57.5	40.6	1081.3	663.9	99	15331386
JRO	Nuveen Floating Rate Income Oppo	Holding and other Investment Office	7/31/17	41.7	29.6	755.3	465.2	89	8399846
NKG	Nuveen Georgia Quality Municipal I	Holding and other Investment Office	5/31/17	8.9	5.8	234.2	145.6	19	630669
JGH	Nuveen Global High Income Fund	Holding and other Investment Office	12/31/16	41.8	34.2	580.9	414.1	63	6402144
JHY	Nuveen High Income 2020 Target T	Finance Intermediaries & Services	12/31/16	11.9	10.0	177.1	133.5	22	2136266
JHA	Nuveen High Income December 20	Finance Intermediaries & Services	12/31/16	21.4	17.5	388.2	295.8		0
JHD	Nuveen High Income December 20	Finance Intermediaries & Services	12/31/16	12.4	10.1	365.0	274.8	39	4862306
NID	Nuveen Intermediate Duration Muni	Finance Intermediaries & Services	5/31/16	39.9	32.1	846.4	665.6	50	7694759
NIQ	Nuveen Intermediate Duration Quali	Holding and other Investment Office	5/31/17	8.8	6.5	240.1	182.7	33	2163017
NMY	Nuveen Maryland Quality Municipal	Holding and other Investment Office	5/31/17	21.3	14.2	571.7	342.4	54	3274139
NMT	Nuveen Massachusetts Quality Mun	Holding and other Investment Office	5/31/17	8.6	6.0	212.1	137.6	20	343314
NUM	Nuveen Michigan Quality Municipal	Holding and other Investment Office	2/28/17	20.5	14.3	509.0	314.3	56	1954448
NMS	Nuveen Minnesota Quality Municipa	Holding and other Investment Office	5/31/17	6.0	3.9	139.0	84.7	16	401483
NOM	Nuveen Missouri Quality Municipal I	Holding and other Investment Office	5/31/17	2.3	1.5	51.5	32.7	12	159110
JLS	Nuveen Mortgage Opportunity Term	Holding and other Investment Office	12/31/16	34.4	24.8	545.9	397.6	54	6150651
JMT	Nuveen Mortgage Opportunity Term	Holding and other Investment Office	12/31/16	10.4	7.3	164.3	117.6	27	2347771

EARNINGS PER SHARE						P/E RATIO		DIVIDENDS PER SHARE			AV. YLD %	DIV. DECLARED		PRICE RANGE 2016	
QUARTERLY			ANNUAL												
1st	2nd	3rd	2016	2015	2014			2016	2015	2014		AMOUNT	PAYABLE		
-	-	5.40	20.54	19.45	18.38	23.2 -	18.6	6.40	5.80	4.70	1.5	1.750Y	32/4/39	476.2 -	381.2
-	-	0.38	-1.18	0.43	1.02			0.13	0.10	0.23	0.4	0.0750Y	32/4/39	39.6 -	31.9
-	-	0.03	-0.49	-1.10	1.07									10.2 -	6.7
-	-	-	4.08	8.75	3.28	6.2 -	5.3	2.80	0.72	-	12.2	0.20	1/31/18	25.4 -	21.4
-	-	2.51	1.03	-0.51	-0.73	28.3 -	21.8	0.84	0.62	-	3.4	0.250Z	12/29/17	29.2 -	22.4
-	-	-	-	-	-							0.32810Z	3/1/18	26.0 -	22.3
-	-	1.79	6.25	6.06	5.60	25.5 -	18.9	3.48	3.08	2.90	2.5	0.98250Y	32/4/39	159.3 -	118.3
-	-	0.01	1.88	0.46	0.16	23.1 -	13.8	1.30	0.91	0.19	3.6	0.4050	2/14/18	43.4 -	25.9
-	-1.56	-	-2.35	-0.29	0.51			2.54	2.37	2.01	16.3	0.390	32/4/39	25.8 -	8.7
-	-	0.41	1.39	1.54	1.00			1.21	1.09	0.95		0.340	32/4/39	-	
-	0.46	-	2.16	1.85	1.49	30.0 -	23.5	0.62	0.54	0.47	1.1	0.20Y	32/4/39	64.8 -	50.8
-	-	0.04	1.02	0.90	1.67	27.0 -	21.4	0.64	0.83	1.02	2.5	0.1950Y	32/4/39	27.6 -	21.8
-	-	0.36	0.31	-0.49	0.59	49.5 -	17.4	-	-	-		0.1250Y	12/24/13	15.4 -	5.4
-	-	0.12	22.08	18.31	2.57	2.2 -	1.0	-	-	-				48.1 -	21.9
-	-	-0.40	-3.82	2.06	0.03			0.20	1.28	1.50		0.020Y	8/8/16		
-	-	-0.28	-2.32	-6.07	3.27			0.40	0.72	0.68	1.3	0.10Y	32/4/39	40.3 -	23.0
-	-	1.15	0.89	-	-	61.7 -	41.1					0.48830	2/12/18	54.9 -	36.6
-	-	-0.03	-0.13	0.63	0.85			0.26	0.14	0.37	4.6			6.5 -	4.5
-	-	-	0.20	-2.32	-										
15.77	-	-	35.52	60.03	55.81	0.2 -	0.1	22.72	14.94	13.60	378.0			6.8 -	5.3
-	-	1.50	2.13	-0.66	0.48	24.1 -	11.1	0.30	0.55	2.18	0.8	0.60	12/21/17	51.4 -	23.7
-	-	-	-1.54	-0.47	0.34							0.020	12/12/17		
-0.03	-	-	-0.05	1.29	-0.15			1.37	1.38	0.63		0.030	3/9/18		
-	-	0.67	3.15	3.72	3.71	15.9 -	12.2	6.33	1.32	1.20	14.1	0.370Y	32/4/39	50.0 -	38.3
-	-	1.75	5.62	5.10	6.39	26.0 -	19.0	2.36	2.36	2.22	1.9	0.720Y	32/4/39	145.9 -	107.0
-	-	-0.02	-0.01	-0.23	-0.03			0.08	0.08	0.08	1.6	0.020	1/5/18	7.4 -	0.0
-	-	0.20	0.67	1.26	1.96	12.1 -	9.1	0.78	1.43	2.09	11.3	0.220Z	11/29/17	8.1 -	6.1
-	-	3.68	12.19	10.39	9.75	25.5 -	18.6	3.50	3.10	2.71	1.3	1.10Y	32/4/39	310.5 -	227.0
-	-	-0.12	-1.07	-2.30	-			0.60	0.15	-	4.7	0.150Z	11/24/17	14.6 -	11.3
-	-	-0.30	2.12	1.96	2.16	32.6 -	26.8	1.87	1.86	1.85	3.0	0.47250Y	32/4/39	69.2 -	56.9
-	-	0.75	3.39	3.17	2.99	19.0 -	16.5	2.00	1.92	1.60	3.4	0.5250Y	32/4/39	64.3 -	56.1
-	-	1.74	2.78	1.86	1.62										
-	0.83	-	2.80	7.29	4.13	30.9 -	25.0	2.72	2.67	2.76	3.4			86.7 -	70.0
-	-	3.96	14.96	13.52	10.07	3.6 -	2.2	6.83	3.71	3.28	15.9			53.7 -	33.0
-	-	-0.08	-2.18	-4.68	1.06									22.7 -	9.9
-	-	-0.01	-0.26	-0.00	-0.19									4.4 -	3.3
-	-	0.53	-2.22	-19.46	0.23			0.23	0.58	0.54	1.1	0.030Y	32/4/39	29.5 -	12.3
-	-	0.56	0.58	0.40	0.59	34.4 -	27.0	0.94	0.63	1.42	5.2	0.2880Y	12/15/17	19.9 -	15.7
-	-	49.55	141.30	101.55	112.07	0.2 -	0.2	66.47	59.68	62.08	278.1			25.8 -	22.7
-	-	0.76	2.55	2.25	3.11	27.4 -	18.5	1.42	1.40	1.38	2.4	0.360Y	32/4/39	70.0 -	47.2
-	-	0.79	2.48	1.11	2.22	26.1 -	21.6	1.50	1.49	1.48	2.6	0.380Y	32/4/39	64.7 -	53.5
-	-	0.15	1.27	3.30	2.10	43.6 -	21.2	4.38	4.38	4.38	10.1	0.6563GH	3/15/18	55.3 -	26.9
-	-	0.26	1.28	1.68	1.44	24.3 -	10.9	2.18	2.18	2.18	9.2	0.5450	2/15/18	31.1 -	13.9
-	-	-	-0.05	-0.12	-0.32			1.03	1.37	1.00	11.1	0.2250	2/15/18	11.3 -	7.8
-	-	-	0.73	0.77	0.71	21.7 -	19.3	0.88	0.85	0.77	5.8	0.0725M	2/1/18	15.8 -	14.1
-	-	-	0.76	0.80	0.82	24.3 -	21.3	0.79	0.79	0.90	4.6	0.06M	2/1/18	18.5 -	16.2
-	-	-	0.72	0.77	0.79	19.7 -	18.0	0.76	0.80	0.82	5.6	0.058M	2/1/18	14.2 -	13.0
-	-	-	0.76	0.79	0.55	19.7 -	17.7	0.80	0.79	0.77	5.6	0.0495M	2/1/18	15.0 -	13.4
-	-	-	1.29	1.37	1.39	17.1 -	15.6	1.35	1.39	1.40	6.4	0.1030	2/1/18	22.1 -	20.1
-	-	-	1.27	1.37	1.40	18.1 -	16.2	1.31	1.37	1.35	6.0	0.09550	2/1/18	23.1 -	20.6
-	-	-	0.82	0.85	0.84	19.7 -	17.3	0.87	0.85	0.86	5.7	0.062M	2/1/18	16.2 -	14.2
-	-	-	0.82	0.84	0.83	22.4 -	0.0	1.04	0.90	0.78	6.1	0.054M	2/1/18	18.4 -	0.0
-	-	-	0.45	0.46	0.47	23.8 -	22.0	0.47	0.47	0.47	4.5	0.03M	2/1/18	10.7 -	9.9
-	-	-	0.88	0.87	0.84	17.7 -	15.9	0.93	0.93	0.89	6.3	0.0585M	2/1/18	15.6 -	14.0
-	-	-	0.64	0.66	0.67	25.3 -	22.9	0.67	0.80	0.93	4.4	0.0465M	2/1/18	16.2 -	14.7
-	-	-	0.67	0.70	0.60	18.7 -	17.7	0.68	0.68	0.69	5.5	0.041M	2/1/18	12.5 -	11.9
-	-	-	0.13	0.09	0.16	124.2 -	101.4	1.14	2.75	2.51	7.7	1.4197C	12/29/17	16.1 -	13.2
-	-	-	0.58	0.62	0.60	15.6 -	13.9	0.61	0.56	0.64	7.1	0.04750	2/1/18	9.1 -	8.1
-	-	-	0.46	0.46	0.48	28.5 -	24.5	1.08	1.08	1.03	8.7	0.2576C	12/29/17	13.1 -	11.3
-	-	-	0.27	0.25	0.18	69.8 -	0.0	1.04	1.06	-	12.5	0.2750	12/29/17	18.8 -	0.0
-	-	-	-0.12	-0.08	-0.32			1.35	1.34	1.28	10.8	0.30	2/15/18	14.4 -	9.9
-	-	-	0.85	0.93	0.96	17.8 -	16.0	0.95	0.97	0.96	6.6	0.065M	2/1/18	15.1 -	13.6
-	-	-	0.73	0.75	0.75	16.8 -	14.8	0.72	0.72	0.76	6.2	0.06750	2/1/18	12.2 -	10.8
-	-	-	0.77	0.79	-	16.6 -	13.8	0.76	0.76	0.79	6.5	0.07050	2/1/18	12.8 -	10.6
-	-	-	0.68	0.67	0.54	19.9 -	18.5	0.64	0.64	0.64	4.9	0.0405M	2/1/18	13.6 -	12.6
-	-	-	1.47	1.58	0.12	11.9 -	10.8	1.54	1.57	-	9.2	0.120	2/1/18	17.4 -	15.9
-	-	-	0.73	0.28	-	14.2 -	13.5	0.68	0.28	-	6.7	0.0470	2/1/18	10.4 -	9.9
-	-	-	0.60	0.04	-	17.2 -	16.4	0.61	-	-	6.1	0.03250	2/1/18	10.3 -	9.9
-	-	-	0.38	-	-	27.2 -	26.2	0.30	-	-	2.9	0.04150	2/1/18	10.4 -	10.0
-	-	-	0.68	0.69	0.69	20.1 -	18.5	0.68	0.68	0.67	5.1	0.05M	2/1/18	13.7 -	12.6
-	-	-	0.53	0.58	0.60	25.4 -	23.1	0.58	0.60	0.58	4.5	0.037M	2/1/18	13.4 -	12.2
-	-	-	0.67	0.68	0.60	19.7 -	18.3	0.67	0.67	0.67	5.2	0.0475M	2/1/18	13.2 -	12.3
-	-	-	0.69	0.65	0.58	21.7 -	0.0	0.71	0.68	0.68	5.1	0.05M	2/1/18	15.0 -	0.0
-	-	-	0.76	0.80	0.80	18.4 -	17.0	0.78	0.86	0.89	5.8	0.048M	2/1/18	14.0 -	12.9
-	-	-	0.80	0.74	-	21.3 -	0.0	0.81	0.48	-	5.2	0.060	2/1/18	17.0 -	0.0
-	-	-	0.72	0.62	0.65	24.4 -	0.0	0.73	0.73	0.73	5.9	0.053M	2/1/18	17.6 -	0.0
-	-	-	1.56	1.28	1.25	16.8 -	15.3	1.71	1.52	1.55	6.8	0.11350	2/1/18	26.3 -	23.8
-	-	-	-	1.20	1.22			1.67	1.53	1.56	6.9	0.11250	2/1/18	25.3 -	23.1

SYMBOL	COMPANY	NATURE OF BUSINESS	FISCAL YEAR-END	TOTAL REV. $MILL	NET INCOME $MILL	TOTAL ASSETS $MILL	NET STK EQUITY $MILL	NO OF INST	INST. HOLDINGS (SHARES)
JMM	Nuveen Multi-Market Income Fund	Holding and other Investment Office	6/30/17	4.9	3.7	112.1	77.1	27	4356205
NHA	Nuveen Municipal 2021 Target Ter	Finance Intermediaries & Services	5/31/17	3.5	2.2	114.5	83.6	12	842539
NZF	Nuveen Municipal Credit Income Fu	Holding and other Investment Office	10/31/16	109.2	80.6	3644.1	2321.8	157	16067628
NMZ	Nuveen Municipal High Income Opp	Holding and other Investment Office	10/31/15	54.2	45.6	793.6	684.1	68	4760958
NMI	Nuveen Municipal Income Fund, Inc	Holding and other Investment Office	10/31/16	4.9	4.2	101.5	96.5	28	395123
NUV	Nuveen Municipal Value Fund, Inc.	Holding and other Investment Office	10/31/16	94.4	83.3	2178.4	2150.4	213	28330977
NJV	Nuveen New Jersey Municipal Valu	Holding and other Investment Office	4/30/16	1.2	1.0	27.9	25.3	18	206924
NXJ	Nuveen New Jersey Quality Municip	Holding and other Investment Office	2/28/17	35.6	25.6	980.1	647.6	57	3692558
NRK	Nuveen New York AMT-Free Qualit	Holding and other Investment Office	2/28/17	34.4	23.8	2028.3	1244.7	92	8883789
NYV	Nuveen New York Municipal Value	Holding and other Investment Office	2/28/17	0.7	0.6	36.5	36.3	15	113636
NNY	Nuveen New York Municipal Value	Holding and other Investment Office	2/28/17	2.8	2.4	154.2	150.4	31	1088057
NAN	Nuveen New York Quality Municipal	Holding and other Investment Office	2/28/17	13.0	9.1	730.2	462.2	37	2491925
NXN	Nuveen New York Select Tax-Free I	Holding and other Investment Office	3/31/17	2.4	2.2	57.5	55.1	13	242749
NNC	Nuveen North Carolina Quality Muni	Holding and other Investment Office	5/31/17	14.1	8.8	409.9	246.0	49	1825833
NUO	Nuveen Ohio Quality Municipal Inco	Holding and other Investment Office	2/28/17	19.4	13.8	459.8	302.7	48	2211133
NPN	Nuveen Pennsylvania Municipal Val	Holding and other Investment Office	2/28/17	0.8	0.6	19.6	18.5	13	71048
NQP	Nuveen Pennsylvania Quality Munic	ETFs	2/28/17	31.8	22.5	914.4	558.4	69	3049594
JPT	Nuveen Preferred & Income 2022 T	Holding and other Investment Office	7/31/17	6.4	5.0	218.4	174.8	21	3008697
JPC	Nuveen Preferred & Income Opport	Holding and other Investment Office	7/31/17	89.7	70.0	1694.6	1122.8	164	20420432
JPS	Nuveen Preferred & Income Securiti	Holding and other Investment Office	7/31/17	184.3	143.8	3183.9	2118.5	190	25320016
JPI	Nuveen Preferred & Income Term F	Holding and other Investment Office	7/31/17	50.7	39.8	826.4	591.0	68	3534743
NAD	Nuveen Quality Municipal Income F	Holding and other Investment Office	10/31/16	63.8	45.3	5037.2	3179.2	203	25353404
JRI	Nuveen Real Asset Income & Growt	Holding and other Investment Office	12/31/15	15.5	11.6	246.3	168.8	66	6406243
JRS	Nuveen Real Estate Income Fund	Holding and other Investment Office	12/31/15	17.1	10.9	480.3	338.3	64	4474438
BXMX	Nuveen S&P 500 Buy-Write Income	Holding and other Investment Office	12/31/16	31.0	18.3	1428.1	1399.9	125	20460220
SPXX	Nuveen S&P 500 Dynamic Overwrit	Holding and other Investment Office	12/31/16	5.5	3.3	246.5	242.0	48	3562277
NIM	Nuveen Select Maturities Municipal	Holding and other Investment Office	3/31/17	4.7	4.0	128.5	128.0	50	1780198
NXQ	Nuveen Select Tax Free Income Po	Holding and other Investment Office	3/31/17	10.3	9.5	257.2	256.3	58	1961788
NXP	Nuveen Select Tax-Free Income Po	Holding and other Investment Office	3/31/17	10.0	9.3	251.1	248.5	64	1959994
NXR	Nuveen Select Tax-Free Income Po	Holding and other Investment Office	3/31/17	8.1	7.4	202.8	199.5	50	1657773
NSL	Nuveen Senior Income Fund	Holding and other Investment Office	7/31/17	25.0	17.9	442.3	269.1	76	10173254
JSD	Nuveen Short Duration Credit Oppo	Holding and other Investment Office	7/31/17	17.6	13.0	300.3	182.5	43	2681119
JTD	Nuveen Tax-Advantaged Dividend	Holding and other Investment Office	12/31/16	12.5	7.9	348.1	224.5	50	3129544
JTA	Nuveen Tax-Advantaged Total Retu	Holding and other Investment Office	12/31/16	9.8	6.5	257.9	176.1	45	3250838
NTX	Nuveen Texas Quality Municipal Inc	Holding and other Investment Office	2/28/17	9.3	6.4	232.3	151.9	34	428553
NPV	Nuveen Virginia Quality Municipal In	Holding and other Investment Office	5/31/17	15.4	10.3	404.5	259.8	38	1086786
NVR	NVR Inc.	Builders	12/31/16	5834.6	425.3	2643.9	1304.4	517	3906330
OAK	Oaktree Capital Group LLC	Wealth Management	12/31/16	1125.7	194.7	7649.1	805.9	229	37548672
OMP	Oasis Midstream Partners LP	Production & Extraction	12/31/16	120.9	40.1	450.0	331.7	29	6984592
OAS	Oasis Petroleum Inc.	Production & Extraction	12/31/16	704.7	-243.0	6178.6	2923.2	330	243972808
OBE	Obsidian Energy Ltd	Production & Extraction	12/31/16	575.0	-696.0	3339.0	2247.0	227	120665159
OXY	Occidental Petroleum Corp	Production & Extraction	12/31/16	10398.0	-574.0	43109.0	21497.0	1463	767348328
OII	Oceaneering International, Inc.	Equipment & Services	12/31/16	2271.6	24.6	3130.3	1516.6	432	123630706
OZM	Och-Ziff Capital Management Grou	Wealth Management	12/31/16	770.4	-124.7	1485.6	-181.9	133	93840971
OCIP	OCI Partners LP	Specialty Chemicals	12/31/16	258.2	-50.6	663.7		23	13228905
OCN	Ocwen Financial Corp.	Credit & Lending	12/31/16		-199.8	7655.7	653.0	216	78992373
OFG	OFG Bancorp	Banking	12/31/16	423.4	59.2	6501.8	920.4	204	56049985
OGE	OGE Energy Corp.	Electric Utilities	12/31/16	2259.2	338.2	9939.6	3443.8	523	164573381
OIBR C	Oi SA	Services	12/31/15	27353.8	-9159.3	99334.6	15455.9	27	3784018
OIS	Oil States International, Inc.	Equipment & Services	12/31/16	694.4	-46.4	1383.9	1204.3	308	69674360
ODC	Oil-Dri Corp. of America	Household & Personal Products	7/31/17	262.3	10.8	212.6	126.0	88	4239277
ORI	Old Republic International Corp.	General Insurance	12/31/16	5900.5	466.9	18591.6	4471.6	498	237704471
OLN	Olin Corp.	Diversified Chemicals	12/31/16	5550.6	-3.9	8762.6	2273.0	462	181381882
OMAM	OM Asset Management PLC	Finance Intermediaries & Services	12/31/16	663.5	126.4	1294.3	164.0	172	74561863
OHI	Omega Healthcare Investors, Inc.	REITs	12/31/16	900.8	366.4	8949.3	3858.7	574	185628458
OMC	Omnicom Group, Inc.	Advertising	12/31/16	15416.9	1148.6	23165.4	2162.0	987	306585113
OMN	Omnova Solutions Inc	Specialty Chemicals	11/30/16	759.9	-0.4	693.2	109.8	154	45019501
ASGN	On Assignment, Inc.	Business Services	12/31/16	2440.4	97.2	1752.7	868.9	297	57129098
ONDK	On Deck Capital Inc	Credit & Lending	12/31/16	291.3	-83.0	1064.1	259.5	108	62943555
OGS	ONE Gas, Inc.	Electric Utilities	12/31/16	1427.2	140.1	4942.8	1888.3	330	44550566
OLP	One Liberty Properties, Inc.	REITs	12/31/16	70.6	24.4	733.4	290.1	138	9296885
OMAD U	One Madison Corp	Business Services							0
OMF	OneMain Holdings Inc	Credit & Lending	12/31/16	3883.0	215.0	18123.0	3066.0	168	133665133
OKE	ONEOK Inc	Equipment & Services	12/31/16	8920.9	352.0	16138.8	188.7	982	309917390
OOMA	OOMA Inc	Internet & Software	1/31/17	104.5	-12.9	73.3	39.8	89	14333095
OPY	Oppenheimer Holdings Inc	Finance Intermediaries & Services	12/31/16	857.8	-1.2	2236.9	510.7	83	6940329
ORCL	Oracle Corp	Internet & Software	5/31/17	37728.0	9335.0	134991.0	53860.0	2306	2996717092
ORAN	Orange	Services	12/31/16	40872.0	2935.0	94668.0	30688.0	240	42430267
OA	Orbital ATK Inc	Defense	12/31/16	4455.0	293.0	5418.0	1806.0	561	60681559
ORC	Orchid Island Capital, Inc.	REITs	12/31/16	26.7	2.0	3138.7	332.8	86	16415183
OEC	Orion Engineered Carbons SA	Specialty Chemicals	12/31/16	1030.1	44.6	998.6	52.9	116	32793311
ORN	Orion Group Holdings Inc	Construction Services	12/31/16	578.2	-3.6	447.7	226.2	163	34886559
IX	Orix Corp. (Japan)	Credit & Lending	3/31/17	2683055.0	273239.0	11231895.0	2507698.0	165	5397354
ORA	Ormat Technologies Inc	Electric Utilities	12/31/16	662.6	93.9	2461.6	1078.4	265	27358557
OSK	Oshkosh Corp (New)	Autos- Manufacturing	9/30/17	6829.6	285.6	5098.9	2307.4	491	81746363
OR	Osisko Gold Royalties Ltd	Precious Metals	12/31/16	62.7	41.9	1416.3	1212.4		0
OUT	OUTFRONT Media Inc	REITs	12/31/16	1513.9	90.9	3738.5	1232.9	302	155784944
OSG	Overseas Shipholding Group Inc (N	Equipment & Services	12/31/16	462.4	-293.6	1030.5	254.3	53	1749228
OMI	Owens & Minor, Inc.	Medical Instruments & Equipment	12/31/16	9723.4	108.8	2717.8	960.0	404	74997385
OC	Owens Corning	Construction Materials	12/31/16	5677.0	393.0	7741.0	3849.0	515	131256773

EARNINGS PER SHARE — QUARTERLY			ANNUAL			P/E RATIO		DIVIDENDS PER SHARE			AV. YLD %	DIV. DECLARED		PRICE RANGE 2016	
1st	2nd	3rd	2016	2015	2014			2016	2015	2014		AMOUNT	PAYABLE		
-	-	-	0.41	0.47	0.40	18.8 -	0.0	0.48	0.28	-	6.5	0.0330	2/1/18	7.7 -	0.0
-	-	-	0.07			146.9 -	133.3	0.06			0.6	0.01750	2/1/18	10.3 -	9.3
-	-	-	0.72	0.83	0.72	21.5 -	19.2	0.87	0.78	0.72	5.9	0.07M	2/1/18	15.5 -	13.9
-	-	-		0.91	0.93				0.92	0.91		0.065M	2/1/18	13.9 -	12.7
-	-	-	0.50	0.51	0.50	26.0 -	22.4	0.51	0.51	0.55	4.3	0.039M	2/1/18	13.0 -	11.2
-	-	-	0.40	0.42	0.43	25.9 -	23.8	0.39	0.40	0.44	3.9	0.031M	2/1/18	10.4 -	9.5
-	-	-	0.62	0.62	0.65	27.2 -	0.0	0.81	0.81	0.83	5.5	0.0475M	2/1/18	16.9 -	0.0
-	-	-	0.79	0.67	0.71	17.7 -	16.4	0.82	0.77	0.68	6.0	0.058M	2/1/18	14.0 -	13.0
-	-	-	0.69	0.72	0.76	19.5 -	18.2	0.70	0.73	0.82	5.4	0.0475M	2/1/18	13.4 -	12.5
-	-	-	0.81	0.67	0.68	19.6 -	0.0	0.63	0.64	0.66	4.3	0.0425M	2/1/18	15.9 -	0.0
-	-	-	0.41	0.40	0.41	25.5 -	23.0	0.39	0.39	0.39	3.9	0.03M	2/1/18	10.4 -	9.4
-	-	-	0.65	0.71	0.67	22.3 -	20.4	0.79	0.77	0.76	5.7	0.0535M	2/1/18	14.5 -	13.2
-	-	-	0.57	0.56	0.60	25.1 -	23.1	0.55	0.57	0.63	4.0	0.042M	2/1/18	14.3 -	13.2
-	-	-	0.60	0.61	0.54	22.7 -	21.1	0.60	0.64	0.60	4.6	0.044M	2/1/18	13.6 -	12.7
-	-	-	0.81	0.85	0.76	19.1 -	17.8	0.83	0.93	0.99	5.6	0.052M	2/1/18	15.4 -	14.4
-	-	-	0.68	0.67	0.67	25.7 -	0.0	0.62	0.63	0.67	4.6	0.0455M	2/1/18	17.5 -	0.0
-	-	-	0.80	0.81	0.74	17.2 -	15.9	0.83	0.84	0.85	6.2	0.0535M	2/1/18	13.8 -	12.7
-	-	-										0.12750	2/1/18	26.1 -	24.8
-	-	-	0.77	0.80	0.79	13.9 -	12.5	0.80	0.77	0.76	7.8	0.0650	2/1/18	10.7 -	9.6
-	-	-	0.69	0.64	0.69	15.2 -	13.4	0.70	0.73	0.66	7.0	0.0620	2/1/18	10.5 -	9.2
-	-	-	1.86	1.96	1.98	13.8 -	12.5	2.13	1.94	2.46	8.6	0.14150	2/1/18	25.6 -	23.2
-	-	-	0.71	0.84	0.87	20.4 -	18.7	0.85	0.87	0.90	6.1	0.0575M	2/1/18	14.4 -	13.3
-	-	-		1.18	1.37				1.57	2.79		0.1060	2/1/18	18.8 -	15.9
-	-	-		0.38	0.37				0.96	0.90		0.250	12/29/17	11.6 -	10.7
-	-	-	0.18	0.17	0.17	80.4 -	70.8	0.93	1.00	1.00	6.8	0.22850	12/29/17	14.5 -	12.8
-	-	-	0.20	0.20	0.19	87.0 -	70.9	0.98	1.04	1.04	6.3	0.25250	12/29/17	17.4 -	14.2
-	-	-	0.32	0.34	0.36	32.7 -	30.1	0.33	0.34	0.34	3.3	0.026M	2/1/18	10.5 -	9.6
-	-	-	0.55	0.58	0.62	26.0 -	23.9	0.54	0.60	0.63	3.9	0.042M	2/1/18	14.3 -	13.2
-	-	-	0.58	0.60	0.66	26.0 -	23.8	0.56	0.61	0.64	3.9	0.0455M	2/1/18	15.1 -	13.8
-	-	-	0.58	0.60	0.64	26.7 -	24.0	0.56	0.61	0.63	3.8	0.0435M	2/1/18	15.5 -	13.9
-	-	-	0.45	0.45	0.44	15.9 -	14.1	0.42	0.42	0.44	6.2	0.03950	2/1/18	7.1 -	6.3
-	-	-	1.21	1.22	1.29	15.3 -	13.7	1.19	1.20	1.70	6.8	0.1060	2/1/18	18.5 -	16.5
-	-	-		0.53	0.66			1.24	1.29	1.22	7.8	0.310	12/29/17	17.6 -	14.0
-	-	-	0.47	0.47	0.49	29.7 -	24.4	1.01	1.09	1.03	7.9	0.2480	12/29/17	13.9 -	11.4
-	-	-		0.62	0.66			0.65	0.68	0.70	4.5	0.053M	2/1/18	14.8 -	0.0
-	-	-	0.66	0.72	0.71	20.3 -	19.1	0.68	0.75	0.73	5.2	0.046M	2/1/18	13.4 -	12.6
-	-	38.02	103.61	89.99	63.50	34.0 -	15.9	-	-	-		-		3525.7 -	1650.0
-	-	0.71	3.11	1.45	2.97	15.6 -	12.4	2.25	2.10	3.15	5.0	0.560	11/10/17	48.5 -	38.5
-	-	0.02						-	-	-		-		18.6 -	16.3
-	-	-0.18	-1.32	-0.31	5.05									16.2 -	7.0
-	-	-0.09	-1.39	-5.27	-3.51			-	0.03	0.56		0.010	10/15/15	2.7 -	0.8
-	-	0.25	-0.75	-10.23	0.79			3.02	2.97	2.88	4.7	0.770Y	32/4/39	73.7 -	58.0
-	-	-0.02	0.25	2.34	4.00	117.4 -	73.1	0.96	1.08	1.03	3.9	0.150Y	32/4/39	29.4 -	18.3
-	-	0.03	-0.73	0.14	0.80				0.87	1.72		0.020	11/20/17	3.9 -	2.2
-	-	-0.01	-0.58	0.61	1.48			0.38	0.74	1.76	4.5	0.080	12/8/17	10.2 -	0.0
-	-	-0.05	-1.61	-1.97	-3.60									5.9 -	2.2
-	-	0.00	1.03	-0.37	1.50	13.4 -	7.7	0.24	0.36	0.34	2.3	0.14580	4/2/18	13.8 -	7.9
-	-	0.92	1.69	1.36	1.98	22.0 -	19.3	1.13	1.02	0.93	3.2	0.33250Y	32/4/39	37.2 -	32.7
-	-	-		-12.55	-7.15									9.5 -	3.9
-	-	-0.30	-0.92	0.56	3.31									41.2 -	21.0
0.41	-	-	1.87	1.59	1.17	26.9 -	17.6	0.84	0.80	0.76	2.1	0.1730Y	32/4/39	50.3 -	32.8
-	0.17	-	1.62	1.48	1.44	13.2 -	11.2	0.75	0.74	0.73	3.8	1.7Y	32/4/39	21.5 -	18.1
-	0.31	-0.02	-0.01	1.33				0.80	0.80	0.80	2.5	0.20Y	32/4/39	37.1 -	26.0
-	0.17	1.05	1.29	0.43								0.090	12/29/17		-
-	-0.67	1.90	1.29	1.74		18.4 -	14.1	2.36	2.18	2.02	7.5	0.660Z	32/4/39	35.0 -	26.8
-	1.13	4.78	4.41	4.24		18.3 -	13.7	2.15	2.00	1.90	2.7	0.60Y	32/4/39	87.4 -	65.5
-	0.18	-0.01	-0.39	0.25								0.050	5/31/01	11.4 -	8.4
-	0.66	1.81	1.84	1.42		35.8 -	23.9							64.7 -	43.2
-	-0.06	-1.17	-0.02	-0.60										6.2 -	3.4
-	0.36	2.65	2.24	2.07		29.9 -	23.5	1.40	1.20	0.84	2.0	0.460Y	32/4/39	79.3 -	62.3
-	0.38	1.39	1.22	1.37		19.6 -	16.0	1.66	1.58	1.50	6.8	0.450Z	1/5/18	27.3 -	22.3
-	0.51	1.59	-1.89	4.38		20.5 -	13.9							32.6 -	22.0
-	0.43	1.66	1.16	1.49		35.4 -	28.6	2.46	2.43	2.13	4.6	0.770Y	32/4/39	58.8 -	47.4
-	-0.17	-1.38	-2.81	-1.18										12.6 -	7.6
-	0.57	-0.09	0.14	0.62				0.44	0.44	0.44	2.4	0.110	11/24/17	28.6 -	15.6
-	0.52	-	2.07	2.21	2.38	25.5 -	18.6	0.60	0.51	0.48	1.3	0.190Y	32/4/39	52.8 -	38.5
-	-	1.04	0.92	0.31		16.9 -	14.4	0.61	0.61	0.70	3.7			17.6 -	15.0
-	-	1.64	5.01	3.04	10.42	26.9 -	17.3	1.20	0.78	1.10	1.1	0.320Y	32/4/39	134.6 -	86.8
-	-	0.33	0.08	0.05	2.48	156.4 -	115.0	1.68	1.92	2.16	16.5	0.110Z	2/9/18	12.5 -	9.2
-	-	0.74	0.72	-1.11								0.19930	12/27/17		-
-	-	-0.18	-0.13	-0.29	0.25									11.0 -	5.2
-	60.89	-	198.52	179.21	142.77	0.5 -	0.4	286.77	114.45	62.73	357.6			89.4 -	73.8
-	0.38	1.87	2.43	1.18		35.1 -	27.6	0.52	0.26	0.21	0.9	0.080Y	12/5/17	65.5 -	51.6
0.74	-	2.91	2.90	3.61		31.6 -	21.5	0.74	0.68	0.15	1.0	0.240Y	32/4/39	92.1 -	62.5
-	0.05	0.40	0.32	36.40		43.6 -	24.9	0.16	0.13	0.03	1.2	0.050	1/15/18	17.5 -	9.9
-	0.36	0.66	-0.21	2.67		41.9 -	31.6	1.36	1.42	5.67	5.6	0.360Y	32/4/39	27.6 -	20.9
-	-0.07	-3.25										0.17970	5/13/16	5.5 -	2.0
-	0.18	1.76	1.65	1.00		21.0 -	10.3	1.02	1.01	1.00	3.4	0.25750Y	32/4/39	37.0 -	18.1
-	0.85	3.41	2.79	1.91		27.2 -	15.1	0.74	0.68	0.64	1.1	0.210Y	32/4/39	92.8 -	51.7

SYMBOL	COMPANY	NATURE OF BUSINESS	FISCAL YEAR-END	TOTAL REV. $MILL	NET INCOME $MILL	TOTAL ASSETS $MILL	NET STK EQUITY $MILL	NO OF INST	INST. HOLDINGS (SHARES)
OI	Owens-Illinois, Inc.	Containers & Packaging	12/31/16	6702.0	209.0	9135.0	254.0	506	190717495
OXM	Oxford Industries, Inc.	Apparel, Footwear & Accessories	1/28/17	1022.6	52.5	685.2	376.1	242	19341811
T 34D	Pacific Bell	Services	12/31/98	9406.0	1077.0	15093.0	3260.0		0
ROYT	Pacific Coast Oil Trust	Oil Royalty Traders	12/31/16	0.8	0.2	227.7	226.5	33	8184715
PKG	Packaging Corp of America	Containers & Packaging	12/31/16	5779.0	449.6	5777.0	1759.8	675	121718553
PAGS	PagSeguro Digital Ltd	Finance Intermediaries & Services							0
PANW	Palo Alto Networks, Inc	IT Services	7/31/17	1761.6	-216.6	3438.3	759.6	698	91892740
PAM	Pampa Energia SA	Electric Utilities	12/31/16	31295.0	-11.0	77277.0	11054.0		0
P	Pandora Media Inc	Internet & Software	12/31/16	1384.8	-343.0	1184.8	554.3	329	319795525
PHX	Panhandle Oil & Gas Inc	Production & Extraction	9/30/17	46.3	3.5	206.7	116.7	99	10695014
PAR	Par Technology Corp.	Electronic Instruments & Related Pro	12/31/16	229.7	1.8	124.5	69.6	58	4770843
PGRE	Paramount Group Inc	REITs	12/31/16	683.3	-9.9	8867.2	3990.0	178	162595310
PKE	Park Electrochemical Corp.	Electrical Equipment	2/26/17	114.6	9.3	308.6	182.8	139	19890797
PK	Park Hotels & Resorts Inc	REITs	12/31/16	2727.0	133.0	9834.0	3872.0	277	212309996
PK	Park Hotels & Resorts Inc	REITs	12/31/16	2727.0	133.0	9834.0	3872.0	277	212309996
PKD	Parker Drilling Co	Equipment & Services	12/31/16	427.0	-230.8	1103.6	339.1	182	106306817
PH	Parker Hannifin Corp	Industrial Machinery & Equipment	6/30/17	12029.3	983.4	15489.9	5261.6	930	125034341
PE	Parsley Energy Inc	Production & Extraction	12/31/16	457.8	-74.2	3938.8	2089.6	419	263981617
PRTY	Party City Holdco Inc	Retail - General Merchandise/Depart	12/31/16	2283.4	117.5	3394.0	1016.8	130	125124374
PAYC	Paycom Software Inc	Internet & Software	12/31/16	329.1	43.8	1078.6	116.5	260	55699997
PBF	PBF Energy Inc	Refining & Marketing	12/31/16	15920.4	170.8	7621.9	2025.0	305	132128178
PBFX	PBF Logistics LP	Refining & Marketing	12/31/16	187.3	87.3	748.1	-33.5	67	15987796
PCM	PCM Fund Inc	Holding and other Investment Office	6/30/17	14.8	11.3	194.2	117.4	29	995973
BTU	Peabody Energy Corp (New)	Mining	12/31/16	4715.3	-739.8	11777.7	330.2	414	138070681
PSO	Pearson Plc	Publishing	12/31/16	4552.0	-2337.0	10066.0	4344.0	125	29360571
PEB	Pebblebrook Hotel Trust	REITs	12/31/16	816.4	73.7	2809.3	1605.7	249	103794897
PBA	Pembina Pipeline Corp	Equipment & Services	12/31/16	4194.0	466.0	15017.0	8296.0	348	219748050
PGH	Pengrowth Energy Corp	Production & Extraction	12/31/16	487.4	-293.7	4101.3	1485.0	208	87418341
JCP	Penney (J.C.) Co.,Inc. (Holding Co.)	Retail - General Merchandise/Depart	1/28/17	12547.0	1.0	9314.0	1354.0	501	294326482
PEI	Pennsylvania Real Estate Investme	REITs	12/31/16	399.9	-11.3	2416.8	555.3	281	94206577
PFSI	Pennymac Financial Services Inc	Credit & Lending	12/31/16	1038.1	66.1	5133.9	347.3	106	25357092
PMT	Pennymac Mortgage Investment Tr	REITs	12/31/16	421.9	75.8	6357.5	1351.1		0
PAG	Penske Automotive Group Inc	Retail - Automotive	12/31/16	20118.5	342.9	8861.1	1750.9	337	100019131
PNR	Pentair PLC	Industrial Machinery & Equipment	12/31/16	4890.0	522.2	11534.8	4254.4	682	171751194
PEN	Penumbra Inc	Medical Instruments & Equipment	12/31/16	263.3	14.8	308.3	266.5	154	26036180
PFGC	Performance Food Group Co	Retail - Food & Beverage, Drug & To	7/1/17	16761.8	96.3	3804.1	925.5	181	90695461
PKI	PerkinElmer, Inc.	Biotechnology	1/1/17	2115.5	234.3	4276.7	2153.6	524	140375205
PBT	Permian Basin Royalty Trust	Oil Royalty Traders	12/31/16	21.1	19.3	4.4	0.6	111	5730449
PRGO	Perrigo Company plc	Pharmaceuticals	12/31/16	5280.6	-4012.8	13870.1	5958.1		0
PZE	Petrobras Argentina SA	Production & Extraction	12/31/16	21955.0	853.0	29097.0	12936.0		0
PTR	PetroChina Co Ltd	Production & Extraction	12/31/16	1616903.0	7900.0	2396950.0	1189319.0	207	5331482
PBR	Petroleo Brasileiro SA	Production & Extraction	12/31/16	81405.0	-4838.0	246983.0	76779.0	501	454709544
PQ	PetroQuest Energy Inc	Production & Extraction	12/31/16	66.7	-90.9	144.9	-251.1	104	12663511
PFE	Pfizer Inc	Pharmaceuticals	12/31/16	52824.0	7215.0	171615.0	59544.0	2847	5417055293
PCG	PG&E Corp (Holding Co)	Electric Utilities	12/31/16	17666.0	1407.0	68598.0	17940.0	872	486848080
PGTI	PGT Innovations Inc	Metal Products	12/31/16	458.5	23.7	436.6	132.5	181	56155204
GLT	PH Glatfelter Co	Paper & Forest Products	12/31/16	1610.9	21.6	1521.3	653.8	204	50050649
PHH	PHH Corp	Credit & Lending	12/31/16	622.0	-202.0	3175.0	1092.0	202	45121264
PM	Philip Morris International Inc	Tobacco Products	12/31/16	74953.0	6967.0	36851.0	-12688.0	2123	1333691288
PSX	Phillips 66	Refining & Marketing	12/31/16	85777.0	1555.0	51653.0	22390.0	1391	400595224
PSXP	Phillips 66 Partners LP	Equipment & Services	12/31/16	873.0	408.0	4109.0	-1.0	182	46017680
FENG	Phoenix New Media Ltd	Radio & Television	12/31/16	1444.9	80.6	3168.5	2165.8	60	14644907
DOC	Physicians Realty Trust	REITs	12/31/16	241.0	30.0	2888.1	1738.5	319	193851096
PDM	Piedmont Office Realty Trust Inc	REITs	12/31/16	555.7	107.9	4449.3	2177.0	279	139213034
PIR	Pier 1 Imports Inc.	Retail - Furniture & Home Furnishing	2/25/17	1828.4	30.1	843.1	292.0	273	80153751
PCQ	Pimco California Municipal Income	Holding and other Investment Office	12/31/16	21.4	17.8	448.7	408.5	27	871307
PCK	Pimco California Municipal Income	Holding and other Investment Office	12/31/16	23.7	19.7	481.1	430.6	33	1207754
PZC	Pimco California Municipal Income	Holding and other Investment Office	12/31/16	17.5	14.5	377.4	339.6	25	1007353
PTY	PIMCO Corporate & Income Opport	Holding and other Investment Office	7/31/17	99.0	87.9	1640.8	1378.7	110	6892688
PCN	PIMCO Corporate & Income Strateg	Holding and other Investment Office	7/31/15	32.9	28.2	760.1	739.1		0
PCI	PIMCO Dynamic Credit & Mortgage	Holding and other Investment Office	6/30/17	335.7	221.8	5935.7	3144.2	170	31018988
PDI	PIMCO Dynamic Income Fund	Holding and other Investment Office	6/30/16	223.6	177.0	2316.7	1222.5	111	7004767
PGP	PIMCO Global StocksPLUS & Inco	Holding and other Investment Office	6/30/17	15.8	12.3	182.6	119.5	35	617145
PHK	Pimco High Income Fund	Holding and other Investment Office	7/31/17	96.3	85.7	1180.0	986.9	119	8228749
PKO	PIMCO Income Opportunity Fund	Holding and other Investment Office	6/30/17	44.8	34.3	610.0	378.7	64	3205731
PFL	PIMCO Income Strategy Fund	Holding and other Investment Office	7/31/17	26.1	22.3	402.5	345.8	60	3935108
PFN	PIMCO Income Strategy Fund II	Holding and other Investment Office	7/31/17	54.8	47.5	794.6	704.8	91	11438066
PMF	Pimco Municipal Income Fund	Holding and other Investment Office	12/31/16	27.3	23.0	548.3	508.5	58	1368789
PML	Pimco Municipal Income Fund II	Holding and other Investment Office	12/31/16	57.4	48.4	1183.2	1094.5	91	5551900
PMX	Pimco Municipal Income Fund III	Holding and other Investment Office	12/31/16	29.9	25.3	579.3	538.4	51	1583728
PNI	Pimco New York Municipal Fund II	Holding and other Investment Office	12/31/16	9.7	7.9	216.3	197.8	18	406223
PNF	Pimco New York Municipal Income	Holding and other Investment Office	12/31/16	6.7	5.4	154.7	136.8	24	690661
PYN	Pimco New York Municipal Income	Holding and other Investment Office	12/31/16	4.1	3.2	91.0	83.0	16	212864
RCS	PIMCO Strategic Income Fund Inc	Holding and other Investment Office	6/30/17	34.5	29.5	1420.4	329.7	63	2735316
PF	Pinnacle Foods Inc.	Food	12/25/16	3127.9	211.1	6739.6	1948.0	402	129395007
PNW	Pinnacle West Capital Corp	Electric Utilities	12/31/16	3498.7	442.0	16004.3	4803.6	657	112214124
PES	Pioneer Energy Services Corp	Production & Extraction	12/31/16	277.1	-128.4	700.1	281.4	192	72890076
PHD	Pioneer Floating Rate Trust	Holding and other Investment Office	11/30/16	25.1	19.2	481.3	309.3	77	8596798
PHT	Pioneer High Income Trust	Holding and other Investment Office	3/31/17	34.1	27.9	444.0	312.8	71	6200673
MAV	Pioneer Municipal High Income Adv	Holding and other Investment Office	3/31/17	22.4	19.1	434.2	433.5	51	2437822

| EARNINGS PER SHARE | | | | | | P/E RATIO | DIVIDENDS PER SHARE | | | AV. YLD % | DIV. DECLARED | | PRICE RANGE 2016 |
| QUARTERLY | | | ANNUAL | | | | | | | | | | |
1st	2nd	3rd	2016	2015	2014		2016	2015	2014	%	AMOUNT	PAYABLE	2016
-	-	0.76	1.28	-0.47	0.45	20.1 - 14.0	-	-	-	-	0.59380 Y	2/15/08	25.7 - 17.9
-	-	0.06	1.85	2.78	2.75	41.0 - 28.2	1.00	0.84	0.72	1.7	0.270Y	2/2/18	75.8 - 52.1
-	-	0.04	0.01	0.26	1.40	221.0 - 111.0	0.01	0.26	1.40	0.6	0.02780Z	1/16/18	2.2 - 1.1
-	-	1.47	4.75	4.47	3.99	25.5 - 17.9	2.36	2.20	1.60	2.2	0.630Y	32/4/39	120.9 - 85.0
-0.70	-	-	-2.59	-2.02	-3.05	-	-	-	-	-	-		156.9 - 108.0
-	-	-	-0.01	2.28	0.51	-	-	-	-	-	-		71.1 - 36.0
-	-	-0.34	-1.49	-0.79	-0.15	-	-	-	-	-	-		13.6 - 4.5
-	-	0.07	-0.61	0.56	1.49	-	0.16	0.16	0.16	0.7	0.040Y	3/8/18	24.9 - 17.9
-	-	-0.10	0.11	-0.06	-0.24	104.7 - 50.0	-	-	-	-	-		11.5 - 5.5
-	-	-0.04	-0.05	-0.02	0.27	-	0.38	0.42	-	2.3	0.0950Z	32/4/39	17.5 - 15.2
-	-	0.04	0.89	0.96	-2.03	22.5 - 18.2	0.40	1.90	2.90	2.2	3.7Y	2/13/18	20.0 - 16.2
-	-	0.48	-	-	-	-	-	-	-	-	0.550Z	1/16/18	29.9 - 24.9
-	-	0.48	-	-	-	-	-	-	-	-	0.550Z	1/16/18	30.5 - 30.5
-	-	-0.15	-1.86	-0.78	0.19	-	-	-	-	-	1.81250Y	12/31/17	2.9 - 0.9
2.10	-	-	5.89	6.97	6.87	33.9 - 23.9	2.52	2.37	1.86	1.5	0.660Y	32/4/39	199.7 - 140.8
-	-	-0.05	-0.46	-0.45	0.42	-	-	-	-	-	-		36.9 - 23.9
-	-	0.08	0.98	0.09	0.59	17.3 - 10.0	-	-	-	-	-		16.9 - 9.8
-	-	0.24	0.74	0.36	0.11	115.7 - 59.4	-	-	-	-	-		85.6 - 43.9
-	-	2.85	1.74	1.65	-0.51	20.5 - 11.1	1.20	1.20	1.20	4.8	0.30Y	32/4/39	35.6 - 19.3
-	-	0.63	2.01	2.18	0.94	11.2 - 9.3	1.70	1.44	0.46	8.3	0.480	11/29/17	22.5 - 18.6
-	-	1.22	0.44	0.94		9.9 - 8.2	0.96	1.05	1.05	8.7	0.080	2/1/18	12.1 - 10.0
-	-	1.47	-40.45	-109.98	-44.10	-	-	0.07	5.10	-	-		39.5 - 23.0
-	-	-	-2.87	1.01	0.58	-	0.53	0.53	0.49	6.2	-		10.1 - 7.1
-	-	0.38	0.64	0.95	0.71	60.8 - 42.3	1.52	1.24	0.92	4.7	0.39840Z	1/12/18	38.9 - 27.1
-	-	0.22	1.01	1.02	1.06	45.7 - 30.4	1.90	1.80	1.72	5.0	0.2819GH	3/1/18	46.1 - 30.7
-	-0.02	-	-0.54	-2.02	-1.10	-	-	0.19	0.48	-	0.010Y	12/15/15	2.0 - 0.6
-	-	-0.41	-1.68	-2.53	-5.57	-	-	-	-	-	0.20Y	32/4/39	8.5 - 2.4
-	-	0.05	-0.40	-1.93	-0.44	-	0.84	0.84	0.80	6.6	0.4488GHZ	12/15/17	19.9 - 9.5
-	-	0.71	2.94	2.17	1.73	7.6 - 5.4	-	-	-	-	-		22.4 - 15.9
-	-	0.20	1.08	1.16	2.47	17.1 - 13.9	1.88	2.16	2.99	11.0	0.470Z	1/26/18	18.4 - 15.0
-	-	1.10	3.99	3.63	3.17	13.8 - 9.8	1.10	0.94	0.78	2.4	0.330Y	32/4/39	54.9 - 39.0
-	-	0.68	2.85	-0.42	1.11	-	1.34	-	-	-	0.350	32/4/39	-
-	-	0.01	0.44	0.08	-0.18	263.3 - 145.6	-	-	-	-	-		115.8 - 64.0
0.22	-	-	0.70	0.64	0.18	47.4 - 31.3	-	-	-	-	-		33.2 - 21.9
-	-	0.82	2.12	1.87	1.39	34.8 - 24.3	0.28	0.28	0.28	0.4	0.070Y	32/4/39	73.8 - 51.6
-	-	0.13	0.42	0.34	1.02	24.4 - 18.8	0.42	0.34	1.02	4.6	0.05960	2/14/18	10.2 - 7.9
-	-	0.31	-28.01	0.04	1.77	-	0.58	0.25	0.39	-	0.160	12/19/17	-
-	-	0.13	-	0.42	0.23	-	-	-	-	-	-		13.8 - 7.3
-	0.07	-	0.04	0.19	0.59	2034.0 - 1523.5	3.91	14.12	29.07	5.7	-		81.4 - 60.9
-	-	0.01	-0.37	-0.65	-0.56	-	-	-	0.41	-	-		11.5 - 7.7
-	-	-0.15	-5.24	-18.44	1.56	-	-	-	-	-	0.85940Y	1/15/16	4.4 - 1.6
-	-	0.47	1.17	1.11	1.42	31.8 - 26.6	1.20	1.12	1.04	3.5	0.340Y	32/4/39	37.2 - 31.1
-	-	1.07	2.78	1.79	3.06	25.7 - 16.0	1.93	1.82	1.82	3.0	0.530Y	32/4/39	71.6 - 44.5
-	-	0.12	0.47	0.47	0.33	36.0 - 21.4	-	-	-	-	-		16.9 - 10.1
-	-	0.27	0.49	1.47	1.57	51.1 - 34.0	0.50	0.48	0.44	2.5	0.130Y	2/1/18	25.1 - 16.7
-	-	-1.14	-3.77	-2.62	1.47	-	-	-	-	-	-		15.3 - 10.3
-	-	1.27	4.48	4.42	4.76	27.4 - 20.2	4.12	4.04	3.88	3.7	1.070Y	32/4/39	122.9 - 90.4
-	-	1.60	2.92	7.73	8.33	35.0 - 25.8	2.45	2.18	1.89	2.9	0.70Y	32/4/39	102.1 - 75.3
-	-	0.51	2.20	3.26	2.93	26.2 - 20.4	1.98	1.54	1.12	3.9	0.6780	2/13/18	57.6 - 44.9
-	-	0.13	0.14	0.13	0.43	57.8 - 17.6	-	-	-	-	-		8.1 - 2.5
-	-	0.07	0.22	0.15	-0.12	99.1 - 78.6	0.90	0.90	0.90	4.8	0.230	1/18/18	21.8 - 17.3
-	-	0.87	0.74	1.15	0.28	31.1 - 26.0	0.84	0.84	0.81	4.0	0.57Z	32/4/39	23.1 - 19.2
-	-	0.09	0.46	0.82	1.01	20.0 - 8.7	0.28	0.24	0.21	5.0	0.070Y	1/31/18	9.2 - 4.0
-	-	-	0.95	0.65	0.99	18.5 - 16.5	0.92	0.92	0.92	5.5	0.077M	2/1/18	17.6 - 15.7
-	-	-	0.62	0.38	0.68	16.8 - 14.9	0.61	0.65	0.73	6.1	0.035M	2/1/18	10.4 - 9.2
-	-	-	0.65	0.17	0.69	19.7 - 15.6	0.72	0.72	0.72	6.3	0.045M	2/1/18	12.8 - 10.2
-	-	-	1.30	0.68	1.14	13.2 - 11.0	1.59	2.21	3.40	9.8	0.130	2/1/18	17.2 - 14.3
-	-	-	-	0.73	0.99	-	-	1.70	2.30	-	0.11250	2/1/18	17.9 - 14.9
-	-	-	2.01	0.76	1.79	11.6 - 10.1	2.18	2.47	2.47	9.9	0.16410	2/1/18	23.4 - 20.3
-	-	-	3.87	0.80	3.70	8.1 - 7.2	5.24	4.19	3.52	17.7	0.22050	2/1/18	31.2 - 27.7
-	-	-	1.15	0.34	1.39	17.3 - 12.7	2.20	2.20	2.20	12.8	0.1220	2/1/18	19.9 - 14.6
-	-	-	0.74	0.21	0.84	13.4 - 9.9	1.26	1.46	1.46	14.8	0.08070	2/1/18	9.9 - 7.3
-	-	-	2.33	1.54	2.71	11.7 - 10.0	2.79	3.87	2.88	10.9	0.190	2/1/18	27.2 - 23.3
-	-	-	0.88	0.79	0.79	14.1 - 12.0	1.08	1.22	1.08	9.3	0.090	2/1/18	12.4 - 10.6
-	-	-	0.87	0.70	0.72	12.5 - 10.9	1.03	1.11	0.96	10.0	0.080	2/1/18	10.9 - 9.5
-	-	-	0.90	0.65	0.94	17.2 - 14.2	0.97	0.97	0.97	7.1	0.0597M	2/1/18	15.5 - 12.8
-	-	-	0.79	0.47	0.81	17.1 - 15.5	0.78	0.78	0.78	6.0	0.065M	2/1/18	13.5 - 12.3
-	-	-	0.77	0.20	0.75	15.7 - 14.3	0.75	0.75	0.79	6.4	0.0558M	2/1/18	12.1 - 11.0
-	-	-	0.72	0.43	0.75	18.0 - 15.5	0.80	0.80	0.80	6.7	0.0507M	2/1/18	12.9 - 11.1
-	-	-	0.70	0.47	0.67	19.3 - 17.0	0.68	0.68	0.68	5.3	0.057M	2/1/18	13.5 - 11.9
-	-	-	0.56	0.14	0.56	19.5 - 16.6	0.63	0.63	0.63	6.3	0.0423M	2/1/18	10.9 - 9.3
-	-	-	0.76	0.30	0.99	13.9 - 11.4	1.00	1.02	1.11	10.4	0.0720	2/1/18	10.6 - 8.6
-	-	0.39	1.79	1.81	2.13	37.0 - 29.5	1.08	0.98	0.89	1.9	0.3250Y	32/4/39	66.2 - 52.7
-	-	2.46	3.95	3.92	3.58	23.2 - 19.4	2.53	2.41	2.30	3.0	0.6950Y	32/4/39	91.8 - 76.4
-	-	-	-0.22	-1.96	-2.41	-0.60	-	-	-	-	-		7.2 - 1.7
-	-	-	0.77	0.76	0.75	16.2 - 14.8	0.72	0.69	0.80	6.0	0.060	1/5/18	12.4 - 11.4
-	-	-	1.19	1.36	1.50	8.7 - 8.1	1.34	1.61	1.65	13.5	0.0650	1/5/18	10.4 - 9.6
-	-	-	0.83	0.95	1.08	14.4 - 12.8	0.95	1.14	1.14	8.3	0.0525M	1/31/18	12.0 - 10.6

SYMBOL	COMPANY	NATURE OF BUSINESS	FISCAL YEAR-END	TOTAL REV. $MILL	NET INCOME $MILL	TOTAL ASSETS $MILL	NET STK EQUITY $MILL	NO OF INST	INST. HOLDINGS (SHARES)
MHI	Pioneer Municipal High Income Tru	Holding and other Investment Office	4/30/17	19.6	16.6	392.1	390.8	66	3796864
PXD	Pioneer Natural Resources Co	Production & Extraction	12/31/16	3824.0	-556.0	16459.0	10404.0	968	178923616
PJC	Piper Jaffray Companies	Finance Intermediaries & Services	12/31/16	747.3	-22.0	2125.5	759.3	260	13967106
PBI	Pitney Bowes Inc	Office Equipment & Furniture	12/31/16	3406.6	92.8	5837.1	-103.7	575	198783472
PBI 08	Pitney-Bowes Credit Corp	Credit & Lending	12/31/01	587.8	160.1	5721.0	1476.4	-	0
PJT	PJT Partners Inc	Finance Intermediaries & Services	12/31/16	499.4	-3.0	590.5	-8.6	-	0
PAA	Plains All American Pipeline LP	Equipment & Services	12/31/16	20182.0	726.0	24210.0		585	346759681
PAGP	Plains GP Holdings LP	Equipment & Services	12/31/16	20182.0	94.0	26103.0		308	132341924
PLNT	Planet Fitness Inc	Sporting & Recreational	12/31/16	378.2	21.5	1001.4	-130.8	229	104576809
PLT	Plantronics, Inc.	Manufacturing	3/31/17	881.2	82.6	1017.2	382.2	309	40756458
PAH	Platform Specialty Products Corp	Specialty Chemicals	12/31/16	3585.9	-73.7	10054.1	2736.1	256	287366924
AGS	PlayAGS Inc	Industrial Machinery & Equipment							
PHI	PLDT Inc	Services	12/31/16	165262.0	20006.0	475119.0	108175.0	106	20549113
PGEM	PLY Gem Holdings Inc	Construction Materials	12/31/16	1911.8	75.5	1257.7	4.1	146	21556047
PNC	PNC Financial Services Group (The	Banking	12/31/16	16423.0	3903.0	366380.0	45699.0	1469	470956455
PNM	PNM Resources Inc	Electric Utilities	12/31/16	1363.0	117.4	6471.1	1687.5	338	97323910
PII	Polaris Industries Inc.	Autos- Manufacturing	12/31/16	4516.6	212.9	3099.6	875.8	608	68823295
POL	PolyOne Corp.	Plastics	12/31/16	3339.8	165.2	2723.3	724.7	353	95827093
POR	Portland General Electric Co.	Electric Utilities	12/31/16	1923.0	193.0	7527.0	2344.0	379	110150957
PKX	POSCO (South Korea)	Non-Precious Metals	12/31/16	53083512.9	1363309.6	79762994.5	42373438.3	252	19980663
POST	Post Holdings Inc	Food	9/30/17	5225.8	48.3	11876.8	2780.0	358	77782093
PPDF	PPDAI Group Inc	Brokers & Intermediaries	12/31/16	1215.8	501.5	2147.3	772.2		0
PPG	PPG Industries Inc	Specialty Chemicals	12/31/16	14751.0	877.0	15769.0	4826.0	1106	228883845
PPL	PPL Corp	Electric Utilities	12/31/16	7517.0	1902.0	38315.0	9899.0	1067	585618580
PQG	PQ Group Holdings Inc	Chemicals	12/31/16	1064.2	-79.7	4259.7	1022.9	51	78965984
PX	Praxair Inc	Specialty Chemicals	12/31/16	10534.0	1500.0	19332.0	5021.0	1330	301133594
PDS	Precision Drilling Corp.	Production & Extraction	12/31/16	951.4	-155.6	4324.2	1962.1	222	157775431
APTS	Preferred Apartment Communities I	REITs	12/31/16	200.1	-9.5	2420.8	883.8	168	20694544
PBH	Prestige Brands Holdings Inc	Pharmaceuticals	3/31/17	882.1	69.4	3911.3	822.5	330	72904526
PVG	Pretium Resources Inc	Precious Metals	12/31/16		-80.4	1947.4	1107.0		0
PRI	Primerica Inc	Life & Health	12/31/16	1519.1	219.4	11438.9	1221.4	318	50813832
PGZ	Principal Real Estate Income Fund	Finance Intermediaries & Services	10/31/16	13.0	9.3	193.3	131.3		0
PRA	ProAssurance Corp	General Insurance	12/31/16	870.2	151.1	5065.2	1798.7	332	51357903
PG	Procter & Gamble Company (The)	Household & Personal Products	6/30/17	65058.0	15326.0	120406.0	55184.0	2857	1973679077
PGR	Progressive Corp. (OH)	General Insurance	12/31/16	23441.4	1031.0	33427.5	7957.1	847	556511531
PLD	Prologis Inc	REITs	12/31/16	2533.1	1209.9	30249.9	14991.1	59	10207956
PUMP	ProPetro Holding Corp	Equipment & Services	12/31/16	436.9	-53.1	541.4	221.0	137	50214307
PRO	Pros Holdings Inc	Internet & Software	12/31/16	153.3	-75.2	227.7	-3.4	148	33430648
PB	Prosperity Bancshares Inc.	Banking	12/31/16	794.2	274.5	22331.1	3642.3	347	68118035
PRLB	Proto Labs Inc	Manufacturing	12/31/16	298.1	42.7	414.2	379.8	256	32966535
PFS	Provident Financial Services Inc	Banking	12/31/16	357.7	87.8	9500.5	1251.8	222	53269923
PRU	Prudential Financial, Inc.	Life & Health	12/31/16	58779.0	4368.0	783962.0	45863.0	1253	339753401
GHY	Prudential Global Short Duration Hi	Finance Intermediaries & Services	7/31/17	52.9	39.7	986.7	678.2	77	14095448
PUK	Prudential Plc	Life & Health	12/31/16	72024.0	1921.0	470498.0	14666.0	248	25218223
ISD	Prudential Short Duration High Yield	Holding and other Investment Office	5/31/17	42.2	32.7	754.0	560.1	76	8727431
PSB	PS Business Parks Inc	REITs	12/31/16	387.4	128.0	2119.4	1613.3	287	25401516
PEG 31	PSEG Power LLC	Electric Utilities	12/31/16	4023.0	18.0	12193.0	5799.0	-	0
TLK	PT Telekomunikasi Indonesia (Pers	Services	12/31/16	116333000.0	19333000.0	79343000.0	84163000.0	227	58784252
PEG	Public Service Enterprise Group Inc	Electric Utilities	12/31/16	9061.0	887.0	40070.0	13130.0	1015	411738903
PSA	Public Storage	REITs	12/31/16	2560.5	1453.6	10130.3	9411.9	894	177392029
PHM	PulteGroup Inc	Builders	12/31/16	7668.5	602.7	10178.2	4659.4	707	302982462
PSTG	PURE Storage Inc	Internet & Software	1/31/17	728.0	-245.1	899.7	478.4	178	123009268
PCF	Putnam High Income Securities Fun	Holding and other Investment Office	8/31/17	5.4	3.9	124.7	123.6	54	6452040
PMM	Putnam Managed Municipal Income	Holding and other Investment Office	10/31/17	25.9	21.2	568.6	526.3	86	6532327
PIM	Putnam Master Intermediate Incom	Holding and other Investment Office	9/30/17	16.7	14.1	508.2	269.5	73	22650110
PMO	Putnam Municipal Opportunities Tru	Holding and other Investment Office	4/30/17	32.0	26.3	723.0	673.4	93	6981457
PPT	Putnam Premier Income Trust	Holding and other Investment Office	7/31/17	36.2	30.8	1294.5	596.6	130	38065658
PVH	PVH Corp	Apparel, Footwear & Accessories	1/29/17	8203.1	549.0	11067.9	4804.5	668	83251971
PZN	Pzena Investment Management Inc	Wealth Management	12/31/16	108.3	16.2	179.1	28.5	93	13465148
QTWO	Q2 Holdings Inc	Internet & Software	12/31/16	150.2	-36.4	201.0	100.2	175	40260101
QEP	QEP Resources Inc	Production & Extraction	12/31/16	1377.1	-1245.0	7245.4	3502.7	412	251000289
QGEN	Qiagen NV	Biotechnology	12/31/16	1338.0	80.4	4308.2	2607.1	320	159354888
QTS	QTS Realty Trust Inc	REITs	12/31/16	402.4	21.5	2086.5	834.5	249	61725076
QUAD	Quad/Graphics, Inc.	Printing	12/31/16	4329.5	44.9	2570.1	441.5	178	31001651
KWR	Quaker Chemical Corp.	Specialty Chemicals	12/31/16	746.7	61.4	692.0	402.8	247	14/92918
QCP	Quality Care Properties Inc	REITs	12/31/16	471.2	81.1	4789.4	3036.7	313	97906892
NX	Quanex Building Products Corp	Construction Materials	10/31/17	866.6	18.7	773.9	406.8	150	39926888
PWR	Quanta Services, Inc.	Construction Services	12/31/16	7651.3	198.4	5354.1	3339.4	650	183031068
QTM	Quantum Corp	Computer Hardware & Equipment	3/31/17	505.3	3.6	225.0	-116.0	167	72015018
QD	Qudian Inc	Finance Intermediaries & Services	12/31/16	1442.8	576.7	7117.6	2513.6		0
DGX	Quest Diagnostics, Inc.	Diagnostic & Health Related Service	12/31/16	7515.0	645.0	10100.0	4628.0	918	165162889
QHC	Quorum Health Corp	Hospitals & Health Care Facilities	12/31/16	2138.5	-347.7	1994.4	201.1	155	28501495
QUOT	Quotient Technology Inc	Internet & Software	12/31/16	275.2	-19.5	362.8	311.7	143	71772977
CTDD	Qwest Corp	Services	12/31/16	8910.0	1085.0	21149.0	8692.0	4	111435
RDN	Radian Group, Inc.	Credit & Lending	12/31/16	1238.5	308.3	5863.2	2872.3	352	237064400
RAS	RAIT Financial Trust	REITs	12/31/16	209.4	25.3	2406.8	454.0	171	68466468
RL	Ralph Lauren Corp	Apparel, Footwear & Accessories	4/1/17	6652.8	-99.3	5652.0	3299.6	581	71193005
RPT	Ramco-Gershenson Properties Trus	REITs	12/31/16	260.9	59.7	2061.5	870.7	238	95752200
RRC	Range Resources Corp	Production & Extraction	12/31/16	1099.9	-521.4	11282.2	5408.4	669	301761253
RNGR	Ranger Energy Services Inc	Production & Extraction	12/31/16	52.8	-5.0	135.7	112.6		0

T48

EPS 1st	EPS 2nd	EPS 3rd	EPS 2016	EPS 2015	EPS 2014	P/E high	P/E low	Div 2016	Div 2015	Div 2014	AV. YLD %	Amount	Payable	Price high	Price low
			0.83	0.91	1.05	14.9	13.7	0.84	1.08	1.14	7.1	0.0525M	1/31/18	12.4	11.4
		-0.13	-3.34	-1.83	6.38			0.08	0.08	0.08	0.0	0.040Y	32/4/39	198.9	127.9
		-3.91	-1.73	3.34	3.87							0.31250Y	12/15/17	86.8	53.0
		0.31	0.49	2.03	1.64	33.9	19.7	0.75	0.75	0.75	5.5	0.41880Z	32/4/39	16.6	9.6
		0.16	-0.17	-0.61				0.20			0.5	0.050Y	12/20/17	45.6	30.4
		-0.01	0.43	0.77	2.38	76.9	43.2	2.65	2.75	2.55	10.3	0.30	2/14/18	33.0	18.6
		0.03	0.94	1.41	1.25	37.2	20.8					0.30	2/14/18	35.0	19.6
		0.18	0.50	0.11		69.6	37.3	2.78			11.6	2.78G7	12/5/16	34.8	18.6
	0.59		1.96	2.63	2.59	29.3	21.1	0.60	0.60	0.40	1.2	0.150Y	32/4/39	57.5	41.4
		-0.24	-0.65	-1.52	-1.94									14.6	9.4
		42.72	92.33	101.85	157.51	0.4	0.3	106.49	151.70	182.97	327.5	0.8	10/14/94	38.3	27.7
		0.40	1.10	0.47	-0.46	18.0	13.4							19.8	14.8
		2.16	7.30	7.39	7.30	20.0	15.6	2.12	2.01	1.88	1.7	0.33590M	32/4/39	146.3	113.9
		0.92	1.46	0.20	1.45	31.2	22.9	0.88	0.80	0.74	2.2	0.2650Y	32/4/39	45.5	33.5
		1.28	3.27	6.75	6.65	40.9	24.1	2.20	2.12	1.92	2.3	0.580Y	32/4/39	133.7	78.8
		0.47	1.95	1.63	0.85	23.8	16.3	0.50	0.42	0.34	1.3	0.1750Y	32/4/39	46.5	31.8
		0.44	2.16	2.04	2.18	23.0	19.8	1.26	1.18	1.12	2.7	0.340Y	32/4/39	49.7	42.8
		10764.00	6627.00	1845.00	7432.00	0.0	0.0	2048.71	1983.43	1971.69	3081.6			79.2	50.6
		-0.93	-0.41	-2.33	-9.03							0.6250	2/15/18	88.4	76.2
		-0.09	-0.27											13.2	7.1
		2.36	3.28	5.14	7.51	36.2	29.0	1.56	1.42	1.31	1.4	0.450Y	32/4/39	118.7	95.3
		0.51	2.79	1.01	2.61	14.4	11.0	1.52	1.50	1.49	4.1	0.3950Y	32/4/39	40.1	30.8
		-0.03	-21.01											17.4	15.0
		1.45	5.21	5.35	5.73	30.0	22.2	3.00	2.86	2.60	2.3	0.8250Y	32/4/39	156.4	115.7
		-0.09	-0.53	-1.24	0.11				0.28	0.25		0.070	11/18/15	7.9	2.3
		-0.49	-2.11	-0.95	-0.31			0.82	0.73	0.66	4.9	0.250Z	1/16/18	21.9	12.4
	0.57		1.88	1.49	1.39	30.8	21.6							57.9	40.6
		-0.04	-0.47	0.00	-0.11									16.2	7.9
		1.46	4.59	3.70	3.29	22.9	15.2	0.70	0.64	0.48	0.8	0.20Y	32/4/39	105.3	70.0
			1.35	1.46	1.57	14.2	11.9	1.74	1.73	1.67	9.9	0.110	4/26/18	19.1	16.1
		0.54	2.83	-2.11	3.30	22.3	18.1	5.93	2.24	3.86	10.2	4.697Y	32/4/39	63.0	51.3
1.06			3.69	2.44	4.01	25.6	22.6	2.66	2.59	2.45	3.0	0.68960Y	32/4/39	94.4	83.5
		0.38	1.76	2.15	2.15	32.1	20.2	0.89	0.69	1.49	2.0	1.12470Z	32/4/39	56.5	35.5
		1.63	2.27	1.64	1.24	29.7	21.3	1.68	1.52	1.32	2.9	1.06750Z	32/4/39	67.4	48.4
		0.25	-1.72	-1.90										20.5	11.1
		-0.67	-2.47	-2.23	-1.27									29.9	20.6
		0.98	3.94	4.09	4.32	19.7	14.3	1.24	1.12	0.99	1.9	0.360Y	32/4/39	77.5	56.5
		0.49	1.61	1.77	1.60	65.7	30.5							105.8	49.1
		0.41	1.38	1.33	1.22	20.8	16.9	0.71	0.65	0.60	2.7	0.20Y	2/28/18	28.8	23.3
	5.09		9.71	12.17	3.23	12.1	10.2	2.80	2.44	2.17	2.6	0.750Y	32/4/39	117.2	98.7
			1.03	1.15	1.23	14.8	13.9	1.34	1.75	1.50	9.0	0.090	2/28/18	15.3	14.3
			0.75	1.01	0.87	67.8	51.1	1.00	0.78	0.70	2.2	0.42190Z	12/23/17	50.8	38.4
			1.06	1.20	1.22	15.1	13.9	1.36	1.59	1.60	8.9	0.09250	2/28/18	16.0	14.7
		0.66	2.31	2.52	4.19	59.5	47.8	3.00	2.20	4.75	2.4	0.3646GHZ	12/28/17	137.4	110.4
			195.98	157.38	147.78	0.2	0.1	11188.16	8775.90	10246.02	34803.6			36.1	28.2
		0.78	1.75	3.30	2.99	30.3	23.9	1.64	1.56	1.48	3.6	0.430Y	32/4/39	53.1	41.9
		1.61	6.81	6.07	5.25	33.9	28.8	7.30	6.50	5.60	3.4	0.31560Z	12/28/17	231.2	196.3
		0.58	1.75	1.36	1.26	19.7	10.5	0.36	0.33	0.23	1.4	0.090Y	32/4/39	34.4	18.5
		-0.20	-2.59	-6.56	-3.24									19.0	9.4
			0.35	0.35	0.36	26.3	23.3	0.37	0.37	0.43	4.2	0.02830Z	4/2/18	9.2	8.2
			0.43	0.45	0.45	18.0	16.6	0.44	0.44	0.46	5.9	0.0318MZ	4/2/18	7.7	7.1
			0.28	0.25	0.29	17.5	16.1	0.31	0.31	0.31	6.6	0.0260Z	4/2/18	4.9	4.5
			0.74	0.73	0.73	17.3	16.0	0.71	0.71	0.70	5.7	0.0461MZ	4/2/18	12.8	11.8
			0.31	0.28	0.32	18.0	15.9	0.31	0.31	0.31	5.9	0.0260Z	4/2/18	5.6	4.9
		3.05	6.89	5.27	1.74	20.0	12.4	0.15	0.15	0.15	0.1	0.03750Y	32/4/39	137.6	85.5
		0.17	0.58	0.50	0.53	20.9	14.5	0.41	0.41	0.35	4.0	0.030Y	11/22/17	12.1	8.4
		-0.14	-0.92	-0.67	-0.67									44.0	28.6
		-0.01	-5.62	-0.85	4.36				0.08	0.08		0.020Y	32/4/39	19.2	7.1
	0.06		0.34	0.56	0.50										
		0.13	0.46	0.53	0.51	132.7	102.4	1.44	1.28	1.16	2.7	0.390Z	1/5/18	61.0	47.1
		0.38	0.90	-13.40	0.38	31.1	20.4	1.20	1.20	1.20	5.2	0.30Y	12/1/17	28.0	18.4
		0.83	4.63	3.84	4.26	35.6	25.7	1.33	1.24	1.10	0.9	0.3550Y	1/31/18	164.8	125.5
		-0.36	0.87			22.6	15.5							19.6	13.5
		0.29	-0.05	0.47	0.78			0.16	0.16	0.16	0.8	0.040Y	12/29/17	24.1	18.5
		0.56	1.26	1.59	1.35	31.3	24.3							39.5	30.7
	-0.23		-2.24	0.48	-0.72									9.0	4.3
			1.90	-2.94	-0.51	18.4	6.0							34.9	11.5
		1.15	4.51	4.87	3.81	24.6	20.1	1.58	1.47	1.29	1.6	0.450Y	32/4/39	111.2	90.5
		-1.03	-12.24											9.4	2.7
		-0.12	-0.23	-0.32	-0.35									17.6	9.2
												0.42970Z	1/2/18	26.0	22.9
		0.30	1.37	1.22	4.16	16.4	11.6	0.01	0.01	0.01	0.1	0.00250Y	12/8/17	22.5	15.9
		-0.26	-0.01	0.08	-3.92			0.36	0.72	0.69	18.7	0.47660Z	1/16/18	3.8	0.3
	1.75		4.62	7.88	8.43	22.4	14.3	2.00	1.85	1.70	2.4	0.50Y	32/4/39	103.7	66.1
		0.33	0.66	0.73	-0.14	25.9	18.3	0.86	0.82	0.78	6.1	0.90630Z	1/2/18	17.1	12.1
		-0.52	-2.75	-4.29	3.79			0.08	0.16	0.16	0.3	0.020Y	32/4/39	35.7	15.6
		-0.42	-1.79											15.5	8.8

SYMBOL	COMPANY	NATURE OF BUSINESS	FISCAL YEAR-END	TOTAL REV. $MILL	NET INCOME $MILL	TOTAL ASSETS $MILL	NET STK EQUITY $MILL	NO OF INST	INST. HOLDINGS (SHARES)
RJF	Raymond James Financial, Inc.	Finance Intermediaries & Services	9/30/17	6524.9	636.2	34883.5	5581.7	607	126943717
RYAM	Rayonier Advanced Materials Inc	Specialty Chemicals	12/31/16	868.7	73.3	1421.9	211.7	242	47755552
RYN	Rayonier Inc.	REITs	12/31/16	788.3	212.0	2685.8	1411.6	459	140200299
RTN	Raytheon Co.	Defense	12/31/16	24069.0	2211.0	30052.0	10066.0	1580	278010451
RMAX	Re/Max Holdings Inc	Property, Real Estate & Developmen	12/31/16	176.3	22.7	437.2	463.8	173	20117425
RLGY	Realogy Holdings Corp	Property, Real Estate & Developmen	12/31/16	5810.0	213.0	7421.0	2464.0	346	156055919
O	Realty Income Corp	REITs	12/31/16	1103.2	315.6	13152.9	6766.8	799	241374503
RHT	Red Hat Inc	Internet & Software	2/28/17	2411.8	253.7	4535.2	1247.3	778	199074248
RLH	Red Lions Hotels Corp	Hotels, Restaurants & Travel	12/31/16	164.1	-4.7	344.5	155.3	86	18039985
RWT	Redwood Trust Inc	REITs	12/31/16	305.2	131.3	5483.5	1149.4	248	83304202
RBC	Regal Beloit Corp	Electrical Equipment	12/31/16	3224.5	203.4	4358.5	2038.8	373	51313042
RGC	Regal Entertainment Group	Entertainment	12/31/16	3197.1	170.4	2645.7	-839.1	411	145630838
RWGE U	Regalwood Global Energy Ltd	Business Services	9/27/17		-0.0	0.2	0.0		0
REG	Regency Centers Corp	REITs	12/31/16	614.4	164.9	4488.9	2591.3	464	194684683
RM	Regional Management Corp	Credit & Lending	12/31/16	240.5	24.0	712.2	207.5	105	11178067
RF	Regions Financial Corp	Banking	12/31/16	5967.0	1163.0	125968.0	16664.0	924	1081695663
RGS	Regis Corp.	Miscellaneous Consumer Services	6/30/17	1691.9	-16.1	1011.5	508.2	218	57757380
RGA	Reinsurance Group of America, Inc.	Life & Health	12/31/16	11521.5	701.4	53097.9	7093.1	31	786160
RS	Reliance Steel & Aluminum Co.	Non-Precious Metals	12/31/16	8613.4	304.3	7411.3	4148.8	474	71683725
RENX	RELX NV	Business Services	12/31/16		869.0	4413.0	4318.0	139	12569657
RELX	RELX PLC	Business Services	12/31/16			3170.0	3112.0	156	26818426
RNR	RenaissanceRe Holdings Ltd.	General Insurance	12/31/16	1727.8	503.0	12352.1	4866.6	452	51143693
SOL	ReneSola Ltd	Semiconductors	12/31/16	929.8	-34.7	1088.4	66.1		0
RENN	Renren Inc	Internet & Software	12/31/16	63.4	-185.4	1176.8	738.5	60	5470761
RSG	Republic Services Inc	Sanitation Services	12/31/16	9387.7	612.6	20629.6	7691.3	812	307540981
RMD	ResMed Inc.	Medical Instruments & Equipment	6/30/17	2066.7	342.3	3468.5	1960.3	521	109317368
REN	Resolute Energy Corp	Production & Extraction	12/31/16	164.5	-161.7	588.4	-75.7	159	25111548
RFP	Resolute Forest Products Inc	Paper & Forest Products	12/31/16	3545.0	-81.0	4277.0	1693.0	147	94166724
RSO	Resource Capital Corp	REITs	12/31/16	116.4	-30.4	2053.5	704.3	140	24817346
QSR	Restaurant Brands International Inc	Hotels, Restaurants & Travel	12/31/16	4145.3	615.6	19124.9	4999.5	329	185875775
RPAI	Retail Properties of America Inc	REITs	12/31/16	583.1	166.8	4453.0	2152.1		0
REVG	REV Group Inc	Auto Parts	10/31/17	2267.8	31.4	1254.4	572.4	98	16021034
REV	Revlon Inc	Household & Personal Products	12/31/16	2334.0	-21.9	3023.5	-614.8	128	14135644
REX	REX American Resources Corp	Refining & Marketing	1/31/17	453.8	32.3	454.0	340.4	181	7029396
REXR	Rexford Industrial Realty Inc	REITs	12/31/16	126.2	25.1	1515.0	939.3	206	90174934
RXN	Rexnord Corp (New)	Industrial Machinery & Equipment	3/31/17	1918.2	74.1	3539.3	1070.6	222	129092872
RH	RH	Retail - Furniture & Home Furnishing	1/28/17	2134.9	5.4	2192.5	919.9	266	31086963
RMP	Rice Midstream Partners LP	Production & Extraction	12/31/16	201.6	121.6	1399.2		107	79537316
RNG	RingCentral Inc	Internet & Software	12/31/16	379.7	-29.3	252.6	130.0	219	66306772
RIO	Rio Tinto Plc	Mining	12/31/16	33781.0	159.0	89263.0	39290.0	503	113626894
RBA	Ritchie Bros Auctioneers Inc	Business Services	12/31/16	566.4	91.8	1599.5	687.1	253	131627290
RAD	Rite Aid Corp	Retail - Food & Beverage, Drug & To	3/4/17	32845.1	4.1	11593.8	614.1	547	635302421
RIV	RiverNorth Opportunities Fund Inc	Finance Intermediaries & Services	10/31/16	3.6	2.6	74.3	74.0	14	342184
OPP	RiverNorth/DoubleLine Strategic Op	Holding and other Investment Office	6/30/17	12.2	8.7	292.9	220.8	20	1457733
RLI	RLI Corp.	General Insurance	12/31/16	816.3	114.9	2777.6	823.6	256	46183171
RLJ	RLJ Lodging Trust	REITs	12/31/16	1160.0	200.4	4023.4	2221.9	289	192277039
RRTS	Roadrunner Transportation System	Miscellaneous Transportation Servic	12/31/15	1995.0	48.0	1326.1	613.3	148	47509610
RHI	Robert Half International Inc.	Business Services	12/31/16	5250.4	343.4	1778.0	1086.6	627	136239611
ROK	Rockwell Automation, Inc.	Electrical Equipment	9/30/17	6311.3	825.7	7161.7	2663.6	987	117922868
COL	Rockwell Collins Inc	Aerospace	9/30/17	6822.0	705.0	17997.0	6043.0	957	142455512
RCI 14A	Rogers Cable Inc.	Radio & Television	12/31/06	3201.0	177.0	5245.0	419.0		0
RCI	Rogers Communications Inc.	Services	12/31/16	13702.0	835.0	28342.0	5269.0	354	289412403
ROG	Rogers Corp.	Plastics	12/31/16	656.3	48.3	1056.5	635.8	309	20096964
ROL	Rollins, Inc.	Business Services	12/31/16	1573.5	167.4	916.5	568.5	387	100005305
ROP	Roper Technologies Inc	Electrical Equipment	12/31/16	3789.9	658.6	14324.9	5788.9	830	118006053
RST	Rosetta Stone Inc	Internet & Software	12/31/16	194.1	-27.5	194.3	-1.7	126	23277311
RDC	Rowan Companies Plc	Equipment & Services	12/31/16	1843.2	320.6	8675.6	5113.9	404	160997355
RY	Royal Bank of Canada (Montreal, Q	Banking	10/31/17	50433.0	11428.0	1212853.0	73829.0	597	697508173
RBS	Royal Bank of Scotland Group Plc	Banking	12/31/16	15945.0	-5518.0	798656.0	48609.0	143	29205288
RCL	Royal Caribbean Cruises Ltd	Hotels, Restaurants & Travel	12/31/16	8496.4	1283.4	22310.3	9121.4	764	177724090
RDS A	Royal Dutch Shell Plc	Production & Extraction	12/31/16	240033.0	4575.0	411275.0	186646.0	1095	306817778
RGT	Royce Global Value Trust Inc	ETFs	12/31/16	2.3	0.7	109.4	100.2	60	3962115
RMT	Royce Micro-Cap Trust, Inc.	Holding and other Investment Office	12/31/16	5.1	1.0	409.3	363.7	91	12239296
RVT	Royce Value Trust, Inc.	Holding and other Investment Office	12/31/16	18.0	9.7	1368.8	1296.0	157	25128801
RES	RPC, Inc.	Equipment & Services	12/31/16	729.0	-141.2	1035.5	806.8	326	90061524
RPM	RPM International Inc (DE)	Specialty Chemicals	5/31/17	4958.2	181.8	5090.4	1436.1	604	124140017
RSPP	RSP Permian Inc	Production & Extraction	12/31/16	353.9	-24.9	4996.4	3416.7	305	144362808
RUBI	Rubicon Project Inc	Internet & Software	12/31/16	278.2	-18.1	519.8	299.5	150	36236558
RTEC	Rudolph Technologies, Inc.	Semiconductors	12/31/16	232.8	-37.0	338.7	293.7	260	38784244
RYB	RYB Education Inc	Educational Services	12/31/16	108.5	6.5	104.4	3.5	48	5729515
R	Ryder System, Inc.	Trucking	12/31/16	6787.0	262.5	10902.5	2052.3	482	63302948
RYI	Ryerson Holding Corp	Non-Precious Metals	12/31/16	2859.7	13.7	1558.7	-50.8	112	15699559
RHP	Ryman Hospitality Properties Inc	REITs	12/31/16	1149.2	159.4	2405.8	368.0	328	53319976
SPGI	S&P Global Inc	Credit & Lending	12/31/16	5661.0	2106.0	8669.0	650.0	1070	273244411
SBR	Sabine Royalty Trust	Oil Royalty Traders	12/31/16	30.0	27.5	5.2	4.4	94	1518984
SB	Safe Bulkers Inc	Shipping	12/31/16	109.8	-56.0	1173.8	578.5	91	23898292
SFE	Safeguard Scientifics, Inc.	Venture Capital	12/31/16		-22.3	231.8	169.8	148	27040256
SAFE	Safety, Income & Growth Inc	REITs	12/31/16	21.7	6.6	155.7	154.1	52	7424507
SAIL	SailPoint Technologies Holdings Inc	Services	12/31/16	132.4	-3.2	387.4	210.1		0
CRM	Salesforce.Com Inc	Internet & Software	1/31/17	8392.0	179.6	17584.9	7500.1	1148	687111300

1st	2nd	3rd	2016	2015	2014	P/E RATIO	Div 2016	Div 2015	Div 2014	AV. YLD %	AMOUNT	PAYABLE	PRICE RANGE 2016
		1.24	3.65	3.43	3.32	24.8 - 19.1	0.80	0.72	0.64	1.0	0.250Y	32/4/39	90.6 - 69.7
		0.28	1.55	1.30	0.75	13.4 - 7.9	0.28	0.28	0.14	1.9	2.0Y	2/15/18	20.7 - 12.2
		0.19	1.73	0.37	0.76	18.4 - 15.6	1.00	1.00	2.03	3.5	0.250Z	32/4/39	31.8 - 27.0
		1.97	7.44	6.80	7.18	25.7 - 19.2	3.60	2.62	1.81	2.1	0.79750Y	32/4/39	191.4 - 142.9
	0.42		1.29	1.30	1.10	52.1 - 35.9	0.60	2.00	0.25	1.0	0.180Y	11/29/17	67.2 - 46.3
		0.69	1.46	1.24	0.97	24.0 - 17.4	0.18			0.6	0.090Y	32/4/39	35.0 - 25.4
		0.32	1.13	1.09	1.04	55.9 - 47.1	2.40	2.28	2.19	4.2	0.2190Z	32/4/39	63.2 - 53.2
		0.54	1.07	0.95	0.93	121.0 - 65.5							129.4 - 70.1
		0.11	-0.23	0.13	0.12								10.0 - 6.2
		0.41	1.54	1.18	1.15	11.3 - 9.4	1.12	1.12	1.12	6.9	0.280Z	12/28/17	17.4 - 14.5
		1.39	4.52	3.18	0.69	19.2 - 15.4	0.95	0.91	0.86	1.2	0.260Y	32/4/39	86.8 - 69.5
		0.07	1.09	0.98	0.68	21.2 - 12.8	0.88	0.88	1.88	4.5	0.220Y	32/4/39	23.1 - 14.0
		0.35	1.42	1.36	1.80	50.5 - 41.5	2.00	1.94	1.88	3.1	0.530Z	32/4/39	71.7 - 59.0
		0.45	1.99	1.79	1.14	13.7 - 9.3							27.2 - 18.4
		0.25	0.87	0.75	0.80	20.1 - 15.1	0.26	0.23	0.18	1.8	0.39840Y	32/4/39	17.5 - 13.2
-0.49			-0.23	-0.62	-2.40				0.12		0.060Y	11/19/13	16.4 - 9.1
		3.47	10.79	7.46	9.78	15.2 - 11.3	1.56	1.40	1.26	1.2	0.50Y	32/4/39	164.2 - 122.1
		1.32	4.16	4.16	4.73	21.1 - 16.6	1.65	1.60	1.40	2.1	0.450Y	32/4/39	87.6 - 69.1
					0.45		0.35	0.83	0.88	1.7			23.3 - 16.4
					0.42		0.32	0.84	0.99	1.5			24.0 - 17.8
		-12.75	11.43	9.28	12.60		1.24	1.20	1.16		0.320	32/4/39	3.7 - 0.6
		-0.10	-0.17	-0.02	-0.17								11.4 - 6.0
		-0.02	-0.18	-0.22	0.06								67.6 - 56.4
		0.66	1.78	2.13	1.53	38.0 - 31.7	1.24	1.16	1.08	2.0	0.3450Y	32/4/39	86.4 - 61.9
	0.07		2.49	2.47	2.39	34.7 - 24.8	1.20	1.12	1.00	1.6	0.350Y	32/4/39	48.8 - 24.3
		-0.71	-10.33	-49.55	-1.50						20.31250Y	1/16/18	13.9 - 0.0
		0.26	-0.90	-2.78	-2.93		1.31	1.06	3.20	13.6	0.050Z	1/26/18	11.1 - 8.0
		0.41	-1.73	-0.43	1.36								
		0.37	1.45	0.50	-2.34	59.4 - 32.4	0.62	0.44	0.30	0.9	0.210Y	1/3/18	86.2 - 47.0
		0.15	0.66	0.49	0.14	23.8 - 17.9	0.66	0.66	0.66	4.9	0.16560Z	32/4/39	15.7 - 11.8
		0.00	0.58	0.43	0.03	56.1 - 40.9					0.050Y	2/28/18	32.5 - 23.8
		-0.61	-0.42	1.07	0.78						0.16740Y	10/8/13	35.4 - 15.9
		2.00	4.30	10.76	4.29	24.7 - 18.0							106.1 - 77.3
		0.01	0.36	0.03	0.02	87.6 - 59.8	0.54	0.51	0.48	2.0	0.36720Y	12/29/17	31.5 - 21.5
	0.23		0.66	0.80	0.30	39.7 - 30.5					0.71880Y	2/15/18	26.2 - 20.1
		0.56	2.16	2.20	0.45	49.0 - 11.6							105.8 - 25.1
		0.48	1.45	0.76	0.02	17.9 - 12.2	0.87	0.59		3.9	0.29170	2/14/18	26.0 - 17.8
		-0.07	-0.40	-0.46	-0.72								49.6 - 21.3
			2.55	-0.47	3.51	20.8 - 14.9	1.51	2.21	2.02	3.4			52.9 - 38.0
		0.09	0.85	1.27	0.85	53.8 - 29.2	0.66	0.60	0.54	1.9	0.170	12/20/17	45.8 - 24.9
		0.08	0.16	2.08	0.23	54.4 - 8.9					0.1150	32/4/39	8.7 - 1.4
		0.68				31.6 - 27.7	2.18			10.8	0.210	4/26/18	21.5 - 18.8
											0.150	3/29/18	19.6 - 18.1
		0.04	2.59	3.12	3.09	23.8 - 19.7	2.79	2.75	3.71	4.9	1.757Y	32/4/39	61.6 - 51.0
		0.01	1.61	1.68	1.06	15.5 - 12.0	1.32	1.32	1.04	6.1	0.48750Z	1/31/18	25.0 - 19.3
		0.21		1.23	1.32								11.7 - 6.1
		0.68	2.67	2.69	2.26	21.4 - 16.2	0.88	0.80	0.72	1.8	0.240Y	32/4/39	57.0 - 43.2
		1.67	5.56	6.09	5.91	36.1 - 24.8	2.90	2.60	2.32	1.7	0.8350Y	32/4/39	200.8 - 137.7
1.69			5.51	5.13	4.42	24.7 - 16.2	1.32	1.26	1.20	1.2	0.330	32/4/39	136.0 - 89.2
		0.91	1.62	2.67	2.56	43.0 - 23.8	1.92	1.92	1.83	3.5	0.480	4/3/18	69.6 - 38.5
		1.37	2.65	2.48	2.83	63.1 - 29.1					0.0075	2/12/92	167.2 - 77.0
		0.24	0.77	0.70	0.63	62.1 - 42.7	0.50	0.42	0.35	1.2	0.140Y	32/4/39	47.8 - 32.9
		1.84	6.43	6.85	6.40	41.6 - 28.8	1.20	1.00	0.80	0.5	0.41250Y	32/4/39	267.2 - 184.9
		-0.14	-1.25	-2.17	-3.47								13.5 - 7.6
		-0.17	2.55	0.75	-0.93						0.10	32/4/39	
		1.85	6.78	6.73	6.00	15.2 - 9.9	3.24	3.08	2.84	3.8	0.27810	2/23/18	102.8 - 67.2
			-0.59	-0.17	-0.30						0.53130	3/31/99	7.6 - 5.4
		3.49	5.93	3.02	3.43		1.71	1.35	1.10		0.60	32/4/39	
		0.49	0.58	0.30	2.36	115.0 - 87.8	3.76	3.76	3.72	6.7	- ·		66.7 - 51.0
			0.06	0.10	0.13	180.2 - 134.7	0.14			1.5	0.110	12/27/17	10.8 - 8.1
			0.03	0.03	0.12	316.0 - 267.9	0.64	1.26	2.90	7.3	0.20	12/27/17	9.5 - 8.0
			0.12	0.12	0.12	134.8 - 111.3	1.02	1.24	1.82	6.9	0.350	12/27/17	16.2 - 13.4
		0.26	-0.66	-0.47	1.14		0.05	0.16	0.42	0.2	0.10Y	32/4/39	26.7 - 16.8
	0.70		2.63	1.78	2.18	21.4 - 18.4	1.09	1.02	0.94	2.1	0.320Y	32/4/39	56.3 - 48.3
		0.14	-0.23	-0.21	0.03								46.1 - 29.4
		-2.11	-0.39	0.01	-0.70								8.9 - 1.7
		0.54	1.16	0.56	-0.14	23.9 - 18.1							27.8 - 21.1
			0.26	-0.22	-0.31	119.8 - 60.3							31.1 - 15.7
		1.11	4.90	5.71	4.11	17.4 - 12.9	1.70	1.56	1.42	2.2	0.460Y	32/4/39	85.0 - 63.0
		0.05	0.54	-0.02	-1.01	27.0 - 14.3							14.6 - 7.7
		0.46	3.11	2.16	2.17	22.7 - 18.7	3.00	2.70	2.20	4.7	0.80	1/16/18	70.7 - 58.1
		1.61	7.94	4.21	-0.42	21.7 - 13.7	1.44	1.32	1.20	1.0	0.410Y	1/16/18	172.6 - 108.4
		0.58	1.88	3.15	4.03	24.2 - 18.0	1.93	3.11	4.10	4.9	0.2270Z	1/30/18	45.5 - 33.9
	-0.07		-0.83	-0.74	0.06					0.22	0.50	1/30/18	
		-0.91	-1.09	-2.85	-0.25						0.02670	12/31/79	14.2 - 10.8
	-0.04										0.150Z	1/16/18	19.9 - 17.4
				-0.58	-0.74								15.8 - 13.0
		0.07	-0.07	-0.42	-0.39								108.8 - 70.5

T51

SYMBOL	COMPANY	NATURE OF BUSINESS	FISCAL YEAR-END	TOTAL REV. $MILL	NET INCOME $MILL	TOTAL ASSETS $MILL	NET STK EQUITY $MILL	NO OF INST	INST. HOLDINGS (SHARES)
SMM	Salient Midstream & MLP Fund	Holding and other Investment Office	11/30/16	8.2	2.0	352.2	254.6	48	5600546
SBH	Sally Beauty Holdings Inc	Retail - Specialty	9/30/17	3938.3	215.1	2123.1	-363.6	337	174604224
SJT	San Juan Basin Royalty Trust	Oil Royalty Traders	12/31/16	17.5	13.9	11.7	7.8	144	14125150
SN	Sanchez Energy Corp.	Production & Extraction	12/31/16	431.3	-257.0	1286.3	-696.1	212	56028981
SD	SandRidge Energy Inc	Production & Extraction	12/31/16	98.5	-334.0	1081.4	512.9	201	103607548
SDT	SandRidge Mississippian Trust I	Oil Royalty Traders	12/31/16	18.1	15.3	32.6	32.6	35	355495
SDR	SandRidge Mississippian Trust II	Oil Royalty Traders	12/31/16	20.4	16.1	122.0	122.0	26	410556
PER	SandRidge Permian Trust	Oil Royalty Traders	12/31/16	29.9	25.6	140.4	140.4	-	0
SNY	Sanofi	Pharmaceuticals	12/31/16	34708.0	4709.0	104672.0	57554.0	670	261732957
SC	Santander Consumer USA Holdings	Credit & Lending	12/31/16	6623.1	766.5	38539.1	5238.6	215	342586815
SOV PRC	Santander Holdings USA Inc.	Banking	12/31/16	10745.5	362.9	137370.5	19621.9	56	9131130
SAP	SAP SE	Internet & Software	12/31/16	22062.0	3646.0	44277.0	26376.0	496	54781272
SAR	Saratoga Investment Corp	Holding and other Investment Office	2/28/17	33.2	9.7	318.7	127.3	34	3041868
SSL	Sasol Ltd.	Production & Extraction	6/30/17	172407.0	20374.0	398939.0	211711.0	184	23530395
BFS PRD	Saul Centers Inc	REITs	12/31/16	217.1	45.3	1343.0	318.5	163	11910956
SCG	SCANA Corp	Electric Utilities	12/31/16	4227.0	595.0	18707.0	5725.0	695	121239260
SLB	Schlumberger Ltd	Equipment & Services	12/28/17	30664.0	-1505.0	71987.0	36842.0	2270	1310834176
SNDR	Schneider National Inc (WI)	Trucking	12/31/16	4045.7	156.9	3054.6	1186.5	132	37944004
SCHW	Schwab (Charles) Corp (The)	Finance Intermediaries & Services	12/31/16	7649.0	1889.0	223383.0	16421.0	1243	1250793234
SWM	Schweitzer-Mauduit International In	Paper & Forest Products	12/31/16	839.9	82.8	1173.7	508.3	240	32382214
SAIC	Science Applications International C	IT Services	2/3/17	4450.0	148.0	2042.0	354.0	315	32549157
SALT	Scorpio Bulkers Inc	Shipping	12/31/16	78.4	-124.8	1547.2	956.6	111	35301784
STNG	Scorpio Tankers Inc	Equipment & Services	12/31/16	522.7	-24.9	3230.2	1315.2	208	196572682
SMG	Scotts Miracle-Gro Co (The)	Agricultural Chemicals	9/30/17	2642.1	218.3	2747.0	648.8	464	49886599
SSP	Scripps (E.W.) Co (The)	Radio & Television	12/31/16	943.0	67.2	1728.4	945.9	235	76923209
SE	Sea Ltd	IT Services							0
SA	Seabridge Gold Inc	Precious Metals	12/31/16	-	-7.3	338.0	311.4	125	17678497
CKH	SEACOR Holdings Inc	Shipping	12/31/16	831.0	-215.9	2862.3	1060.9	208	21032444
SMHI	SEACOR Marine Holdings Inc	Miscellaneous Transportation Servic	12/31/16	215.6	-132.0	1015.1	544.6	106	16362264
SMHI	SEACOR Marine Holdings Inc	Miscellaneous Transportation Servic	12/31/16	215.6	-132.0	1015.1	544.6	106	16362264
SDRL	Seadrill Ltd	Production & Extraction	12/31/16	3169.0	-181.0	21666.0	9521.0	284	89667536
SDLP	Seadrill Partners LLC	Production & Extraction	12/31/16	1600.3	281.0	6780.7	-	68	9099954
SEE	Sealed Air Corp	Containers & Packaging	12/31/16	6778.3	486.4	7389.1	609.7	652	206659148
SSW	Seaspan Corp	Shipping	12/31/16	877.9	-139.0	5657.8	1747.2	163	26901211
SEAS	SeaWorld Entertainment Inc.	Sporting & Recreational	12/31/16	1344.3	-12.5	2378.8	461.2	183	90228907
WTTR	Select Energy Services Inc	Equipment & Services	12/31/16	302.4	-307.5	405.1	112.7	86	23727014
SEM	Select Medical Holdings Corp	Hospitals & Health Care Facilities	12/31/16	4286.0	115.4	4944.4	815.7	212	120020179
SEMG	SemGroup Corp	Equipment & Services	12/31/16	1332.2	2.1	3075.0	1446.0	234	82486953
SMI	Semiconductor Manufacturing Inter	Semiconductors	12/31/16	2914.2	376.6	10115.3	4150.7	55	7701523
SRE	Sempra Energy	Electric Utilities	12/31/16	10183.0	1371.0	47786.0	12951.0	883	249998268
SEND	SendGrid Inc	Internet & Software	12/31/16	79.9	-3.9	66.6	42.9	-	0
ST	Sensata Technologies Holding NV	Electrical Equipment	12/31/16	3202.3	262.4	6241.0	1942.0	349	216926473
SXT	Sensient Technologies Corp.	Specialty Chemicals	12/31/16	1383.2	126.3	1667.9	835.7	353	57592044
SQNS	Sequans Communications S A	Semiconductors	12/31/16	45.6	-24.8	65.1	8.9	47	29184252
SRG	Seritage Growth Properties	REITs	12/31/16	248.7	-51.6	2712.2	804.6	161	30950588
SCI	Service Corp. International	Miscellaneous Consumer Services	12/31/16	3031.1	177.0	12038.1	1092.7	449	185568048
SERV	ServiceMaster Global Holdings, Inc	Miscellaneous Consumer Services	12/31/16	2746.0	155.0	5386.0	686.0	296	155693919
NOW	ServiceNow Inc	IT Services	12/31/16	1390.5	-451.8	2033.8	387.0	514	186469246
SHAK	Shake Shack Inc	Hotels, Restaurants & Travel	12/28/16	268.5	12.4	538.2	152.2	181	33434738
SJR	Shaw Communications Inc	Radio & Television	8/31/17	4882.0	851.0	14373.0	6153.0	286	280972835
SHLX	Shell Midstream Partners LP	Equipment & Services	12/31/16	291.3	244.9	865.6	-	178	101909940
SHW	Sherwin-Williams Co (The)	Specialty Chemicals	12/31/16	11855.6	1132.7	6752.5	1878.4	1071	95277227
SHG	Shinhan Financial Group Co. Ltd.	Banking	12/31/16	20296675.0	2774778.0	295680324.0	31109698.0	143	11418901
SFL	Ship Finance International Ltd	Equipment & Services	12/31/16	413.0	146.4	2937.4	1134.1	237	39565491
SHOP	Shopify Inc	IT Services	12/31/16	389.3	-35.4	490.6	410.5	325	48354258
SSTK	Shutterstock Inc	Internet & Software	12/31/16	494.3	32.6	501.8	286.7	167	23485640
SBGL	Sibanye-Stillwater	Mining	12/31/16	31240.7	3701.6	41721.3	16679.7	136	87963573
SIG	Signet Jewelers Ltd	Retail - Specialty	1/28/17	6408.4	543.2	6597.8	3102.1	451	96723618
SBOW	SilverBow Resources Inc	Production & Extraction	12/31/16	101.5	-156.3	377.3	76.1	136	12291515
SPG	Simon Property Group, Inc.	REITs	12/31/16	5435.2	1838.9	31103.6	4448.2	981	397970906
SSD	Simpson Manufacturing Co., Inc. (D	Construction Materials	12/31/16	860.7	89.7	980.0	865.8	270	57873446
SHI	Sinopec Shanghai Petrochemical C	Refining & Marketing	12/31/16	77894.3	5955.6	34123.7	24750.0	73	1556867
SITE	SiteOne Landscape Supply Inc	Services	1/1/17	1648.2	30.6	742.6	148.8	186	46170741
SIX	Six Flags Entertainment Corp	Sporting & Recreational	12/31/16	1319.4	118.3	2487.7	-186.5	394	109710207
SJW	SJW Group	Water Utilities	12/31/16	339.7	52.8	1443.4	421.6	190	13001161
SKM	SK Telecom Co Ltd (South Korea)	Internet & Software	12/31/16	7091816.0	1675967.0	31297663.0	15971399.0	254	98261323
SKX	Skechers USA Inc	Apparel, Footwear & Accessories	12/31/16	3577.2	243.5	2393.7	1603.6	392	130527858
SLG	SL Green Realty Corp	REITs	12/31/16	1864.0	249.9	15857.8	7626.5	497	140162003
SM	SM Energy Co.	Production & Extraction	12/31/16	1217.5	-757.7	6393.5	2497.1	409	132708182
SFS	Smart & Final Stores Inc	Retail - Food & Beverage, Drug & To	1/1/17	4341.8	12.9	1952.4	552.2	116	78005553
SNN	Smith & Nephew Plc	Medical Instruments & Equipment	12/31/16	4669.0	784.0	7344.0	3958.0	254	32724948
AOS	Smith (A O) Corp	Household Appliances, Electronics &	12/31/16	2685.9	326.5	2891.0	1515.3	590	156842086
SJM	Smucker (J.M.) Co.	Food	4/30/17	7392.3	592.3	15639.7	6850.2	1058	102348069
SNAP	Snap Inc	Computer Hardware & Equipment	12/31/16	404.5	-514.6	1722.8	1518.9	331	227585785
SNA	Snap-On, Inc.	Industrial Machinery & Equipment	12/31/16	3711.8	546.4	4723.2	2617.2	785	68178006
SNH PRZ	SNH Capital Trust I	REITs							0
IPOA	Social Capital Hedosophia Holdings	Business Services	6/30/17	-	-0.0	0.4	0.0	49	45622796
SQM	Sociedad Quimica y Minera de Chil	Agricultural Chemicals	12/31/16	1939.3	278.3	4218.6	2246.1	299	39387460
SOGO	Sogou Inc	IT & Communications	12/31/16	660.4	56.1	524.8	166.3	-	0
SOI	Solaris Oilfield Infrastructure Inc	Industrial Machinery & Equipment	12/31/16	18.2	2.8	77.2	71.3	78	24637663

	QUARTERLY		ANNUAL			P/E RATIO		DIVIDENDS PER SHARE			AV. YLD %	DIV. DECLARED		PRICE RANGE 2016	
1st	2nd	3rd	2016	2015	2014			2016	2015	2014		AMOUNT	PAYABLE		
			0.11	0.09	-0.19	129.9	88.1	1.14	1.67	1.43	9.5	0.2440	11/29/17	14.3	9.7
		0.49	1.50	1.49	1.51	17.9	10.1							26.8	15.1
		0.32	0.30	0.36	1.28	28.6	21.0	0.33	0.36	1.28	4.5	0.06680	2/14/18	8.0	6.3
		-0.81	-4.63	-25.70	-1.06							0.81250Y	4/1/16	14.2	3.8
		-0.25	-17.61	-7.16	0.42							4.250Y	2/16/15	23.3	15.5
		0.05	0.54	1.24	1.53	3.4	1.5	0.54	1.24	1.53	39.1	0.04220Z	2/23/18	1.8	0.8
		0.05	0.40	1.14	2.01	4.3	1.9	0.40	1.14	2.02	28.9	0.0580Z	2/23/18	1.7	0.8
		0.12	0.54	1.90	2.55	7.3	3.6	0.54	1.97	2.54	18.5	0.1130Z	2/23/18	4.0	2.0
			3.63	3.25	3.30	13.9	10.9	4.38	4.28	4.17	9.5			50.6	39.5
		0.55	2.13	2.31	2.15	8.7	5.2				0.15	0.030	32/4/39	18.6	11.2
								1.83	1.83	1.83	9.6	0.45620Y	2/15/18	26.6	0.0
		0.82	3.04	2.56	2.74	38.3	28.4	0.82	0.77	0.72	0.8			116.4	86.3
			1.91	1.80	1.85	12.4	10.5	2.36	0.40	2.65	10.9	0.490Y	12/27/17	23.6	20.0
			21.66	48.70	48.27	1.6	1.3	14.15	16.87	17.85	47.7			34.2	27.1
		0.38	1.52	1.42	1.54			1.84	1.69	1.56		0.42970Z	1/15/18		
		0.24	4.16	5.22	3.79	17.6	9.0	2.30	2.18	2.10	3.8	0.61250Y	32/4/39	73.3	37.4
		0.39	-1.24	1.63	4.16			2.00	2.00	1.60	2.8	0.50	32/4/39	87.5	61.3
		0.21	1.00	0.91	0.86	29.0	18.4					0.050Y	1/8/18	29.0	18.4
		0.42	1.31	1.03	0.95	39.9	28.6	0.27	0.24	0.24	0.6	0.3720Y	32/4/39	52.3	37.5
		0.84	2.70	2.94	2.93	17.4	13.5	1.62	1.54	1.46	3.9	0.430Y	12/22/17	46.9	36.5
		0.98	2.47	2.91	2.27	36.1	24.7	1.21	1.12	0.56	1.6	0.310	32/4/39	89.2	61.1
			-2.22	-23.86	-10.20							0.46880Z	3/15/18		
-0.07			-0.15	1.20	0.30							0.51560Z	6/1/18		
		2.53	5.09	2.57	2.65	21.0	16.4	1.91	1.82	3.76	2.0	0.530Y	32/4/39	107.0	83.4
		-0.32	0.79	-1.06	0.18	29.9	17.7		1.03			0.15GY	9/10/08	23.6	14.0
														16.3	11.0
														17.5	8.7
		-0.03	-0.14	-0.18	-0.27										
		1.00	-12.76	-3.94	4.71							5.7Y	12/26/12	49.4	31.0
		-1.25	-7.47	-1.54										20.6	11.7
		-1.25	-7.47	-1.54										0.0	0.0
	-0.28		-0.36	-1.49	8.30						2.00	1.0	9/18/14		
		0.48	3.20	2.45	1.75			0.70	1.70	1.60		0.10	11/14/17		
		4.15	2.46	1.62	1.20	20.4	17.0	0.61	0.52	0.52	1.3	0.160Y	32/4/39	50.2	41.7
		0.42	-1.89	1.46	0.79							0.49220	1/30/18		
		0.64	-0.15	0.57	0.57			0.73	0.84	0.62	4.7	0.10	10/7/16	19.5	10.6
		0.04	-0.05											18.2	11.4
		0.14	0.87	0.99	0.91	22.4	14.0	0.00	0.10	0.40	0.0	0.10Y	3/11/15	19.4	12.2
		-0.25	0.04	0.69	0.68	1070.0	560.0	1.80	1.59	1.03	5.9	0.450Y	12/1/17	42.8	22.4
		0.00	0.08	0.10	0.00	113.9	57.0							9.1	4.6
		0.22	5.46	5.37	4.63	22.4	18.5	3.02	2.80	2.64	2.7	0.82250Y	32/4/39	122.2	100.8
			-0.52	-0.83	-2.50									24.0	18.0
		0.51	1.53	2.03	1.65									83.3	71.8
		0.73	2.82	2.31	1.51	29.6	25.5	1.11	1.04	0.98	1.4	0.330Y	32/4/39	4.6	1.7
		-0.20	-0.39	-0.46	-0.58									49.0	38.8
		0.31	-1.64	-0.71				1.00	0.50		2.3	0.250Z	1/11/18	38.0	28.8
		0.29	0.90	1.14	0.81	42.2	32.0	0.51	0.44	0.34	1.5	0.150Y	32/4/39	52.3	36.5
		0.59	1.13	1.17	-0.50	46.3	32.3							130.7	75.7
		-0.14	-2.75	-1.27	-1.23									46.5	30.6
		0.19	0.53	-0.65	0.07	87.7	57.7							30.3	20.2
		0.27	2.51	1.79	1.84	12.1	8.0	1.19	1.14	1.06	4.8	0.17440	4/2/18	33.9	25.3
		0.31	1.32	1.16	0.10	25.7	19.2	0.97	0.67		3.3	0.3330	2/14/18	414.3	274.5
		3.33	11.99	11.16	8.78	34.6	22.9	3.36	2.68	2.20	1.0	0.850Y	32/4/39	48.8	36.8
		-1055.00	5736.00	4789.00	4195.00	0.0	0.0	1191.31	935.99	651.73	2735.4				
0.32			1.50	1.88	1.24			1.80	1.74	1.63		0.350	12/29/17	150.8	42.8
		-0.09	-0.42	-0.30	-0.57									54.8	31.5
		0.14	0.91	0.54	0.61	60.2	34.6							10.4	4.3
			3.93	0.77	1.78	2.6	1.1	5.29	2.28	4.09	83.3				
		-0.20	5.87	4.75	4.56			0.88	0.72	0.60		0.310	32/4/39	33.8	0.0
		1.12	-15.61	-37.20	-6.47										
		1.65	5.87	5.88	4.52	31.8	25.9	6.50	6.05	5.15	3.9	1.04690Z	32/4/39	186.8	152.3
		0.59	1.86	1.38	1.29	32.8	21.6	0.68	0.60	0.41	1.5	0.210Y	1/25/18	60.9	40.2
0.18			0.55	0.30	-0.06	117.6	92.6	8.67		4.43	14.8			64.7	50.9
		0.41	-3.01	-1.04	-0.29									76.7	35.7
		2.11	1.25	1.58	0.77	54.1	41.5	2.38	2.14	1.93	4.0	0.70Y	32/4/39	67.6	51.9
		0.94	2.57	1.85	2.54	26.5	17.8	0.81	0.78	0.75	1.5	0.177Y	32/4/39	68.1	45.7
		-7086.00	23497.00	20988.00	25154.00	0.0	0.0	1095.37	1027.39	1041.26	4417.8			28.6	20.6
														38.7	22.5
		0.59	1.57	1.50	0.91	24.6	14.4							113.8	94.2
		0.40	2.34	2.70	5.20	48.6	40.2	2.94	2.52	2.10	2.8	0.40630Z	32/4/39	36.1	12.8
		-0.80	-9.90	-6.61	9.79			0.10	0.10	0.10	0.5	0.050Y	32/4/39	15.3	6.0
		0.07	0.17	0.50	0.52	89.7	35.3								
		0.14	0.88	0.46	0.56	43.8	34.0	0.63	0.60	0.78	1.8			38.5	29.9
		0.54	1.85	1.58	1.14	34.3	25.5	0.48	0.38	0.30	0.9	0.180Y	32/4/39	63.4	47.2
	1.71		5.76	3.33	5.42	24.6	17.4	2.65	2.50	2.26	2.2	0.780Y	32/4/39	141.9	100.0
		-0.36	-0.64	-0.51										27.1	11.8
		2.29	9.20	8.10	7.14	19.7	15.4	2.54	2.20	1.85	1.6	0.820Y	32/4/39	181.5	141.5
			-0.02												
		0.53	1.06	0.81	1.13	58.4	27.2	1.18	0.38	1.12	2.8			62.0	28.9
			0.11	-0.04	-0.41	125.9	100.0							13.9	11.0
		0.12	-0.23											21.7	10.0

T53

SYMBOL	COMPANY	NATURE OF BUSINESS	FISCAL YEAR-END	TOTAL REV. $MILL	NET INCOME $MILL	TOTAL ASSETS $MILL	NET STK EQUITY $MILL	NO OF INST	INST. HOLDINGS (SHARES)
SAH	Sonic Automotive, Inc.	Retail - Automotive	12/31/16	9731.8	93.2	3639.3	725.2	222	37140851
SON	Sonoco Products Co.	Containers & Packaging	12/31/16	4782.9	286.4	3923.2	1532.4	508	94046433
SNE	Sony Corp	Household Appliances, Electronics &	3/31/17	7603250.0	73289.0	17660556.0	2497246.0	370	89954020
BID	Sotheby's	Miscellaneous Consumer Services	12/31/16	805.4	74.1	2504.4	505.4	342	68730561
SOR	Source Capital, Inc.	Holding and other Investment Office	12/31/16	7.1	3.5	357.6	355.3	77	1574786
SJI	South Jersey Industries, Inc.	Gas Utilities	12/31/16	1036.5	118.8	3730.6	1289.2	296	70395980
SXE	Southcross Energy Partners LP	Gas Utilities	12/31/16	548.7	-94.9	1186.1			0
SO	Southern Company (The)	Electric Utilities	12/31/16	19896.0	2493.0	109697.0	25485.0	1569	648636224
SCCO	Southern Copper Corp	Mining	12/31/16	5379.8	776.5	13234.3	5832.3	383	65160666
LUV	Southwest Airlines Co	Airlines/Air Freight	12/31/16	20425.0	2244.0	23286.0	8441.0	1151	565531083
SWX	Southwest Gas Holdings Inc	Gas Utilities	12/31/16	2460.5	152.0	5581.1	1663.5	361	45779293
SWN	Southwestern Energy Company	Production & Extraction	12/31/16	2436.0	-2643.0	7076.0	917.0	654	536565416
SPA	Sparton Corp	Electrical Equipment	7/2/17	397.6	1.3	217.1	81.9	115	7681774
SPE	Special Opportunities Fund Inc	Holding and other Investment Office	12/31/16	8.0	5.4	189.1	188.0	43	6927018
SEP	Spectra Energy Partners LP	Equipment & Services	12/31/16	2533.0	1161.0	21606.0		312	71273008
SPB	Spectrum Brands Holdings Inc	Household & Personal Products	9/30/17	5007.4	295.8	7419.7	1837.9		0
TRK	Speedway Motorsports, Inc.	Sporting & Recreational	12/31/16	512.2	39.5	1498.1	797.8	119	11853985
SR	Spire Inc	Gas Utilities	9/30/17	1740.7	161.6	6546.7	1991.3	314	45881359
SPR	Spirit AeroSystems Holdings Inc	Aerospace	12/31/16	6792.9	469.7	5405.2	1928.3	460	138562331
SAVE	Spirit Airlines Inc	Airlines/Air Freight	12/31/16	2322.0	264.9	3151.9	1394.6	348	74578082
SRC	Spirit Realty Capital Inc (New)	REITs	12/31/16	686.0	97.4	7678.0	3682.1		0
SRLP	Sprague Resources LP	Equipment & Services	12/31/16	2390.0	10.2	1012.5		54	5393049
S	Sprint Corp (New)	Services	3/31/17	33347.0	-1206.0	85123.0	18808.0	662	814329959
SPXC	SPX Corp.	Industrial Machinery & Equipment	12/31/16	1472.3	-67.2	1912.5	191.6	333	50543575
FLOW	SPX Flow Inc	Industrial Machinery & Equipment	12/31/16	1996.0	-381.8	2603.2	760.7	203	41739381
SQ	Square Inc	IT Services	12/31/16	1708.7	-171.6	1211.4	576.2	394	221271157
JOE	St. Joe Co. (The)	Property, Real Estate & Developmen	12/31/16	95.7	15.9	1027.9	669.3	199	92708411
STAG	STAG Industrial Inc	REITs	12/31/16	250.2	34.5	2186.2	1027.0	267	88523333
SSI	Stage Stores Inc.	Retail - Apparel and Accessories	1/28/17	1442.7	-37.9	787.0	380.2	126	21090729
SMP	Standard Motor Products, Inc.	Auto Parts	12/31/16	1058.5	60.4	768.7	441.0	201	20852796
SXI	Standex International Corp.	Industrial Machinery & Equipment	6/30/17	755.3	46.5	867.7	408.7	199	14790983
SWK	Stanley Black & Decker Inc	Industrial Machinery & Equipment	12/31/16	11406.9	965.3	15634.9	6367.0	964	154043310
STN	Stantec Inc	Business Services	12/31/16	3098.4	130.5	4284.7	1975.7	1	6402
SGU	Star Group L.P.	Gas Utilities	9/30/17	1323.6	26.9	673.9		75	18698554
SCX	Starrett (LS) Co (The)	Industrial Machinery & Equipment	6/30/17	207.0	1.0	192.7	92.0	48	3006785
SRT	Startek, Inc.	Business Services	12/31/16	307.2	0.4	106.8	44.7	99	8519495
STWD	Starwood Property Trust Inc.	REITs	12/31/16	784.7	365.2	77256.3	4522.3	451	211104144
STT	State Street Corp.	Banking	12/31/16	10635.0	2143.0	242698.0	21219.0	1208	396450274
STO	Statoil ASA	Refining & Marketing	12/31/16	45873.0	-2922.0	104530.0	35072.0	311	181757808
SPLP	Steel Partners Holdings LP	Metal Products	12/31/16	1163.5	6.6	1967.1		29	7660179
SCS	Steelcase, Inc.	Office Equipment & Furniture	2/24/17	3032.4	124.6	1792.0	766.5	293	86034266
SCM	Stellus Capital Investment Corp	Finance Intermediaries & Services	12/31/16	39.5	17.3	379.9	170.9	58	4810543
SCL	Stepan Co.	Specialty Chemicals	12/31/16	1766.2	86.2	1353.9	634.6	253	17497880
STE	Steris Plc	Medical Instruments & Equipment	3/31/17	2612.8	110.0	4924.5	2798.6		0
STL	Sterling Bancorp (DE)	Banking	12/31/16	532.5	140.0	14178.4	1855.2	16	1276749
STC	Stewart Information Services Corp.	General Insurance	12/31/16	2006.6	55.5	1341.7	641.2	227	28766863
SF	Stifel Financial Corp	Finance Intermediaries & Services	12/31/16	2642.4	81.5	19129.4	2738.4	337	72822856
STM	STMicroelectronics NV	Semiconductors	12/31/16	6973.0	165.0	8008.0	4535.0	256	47760228
SGY	Stone Energy Corp	Production & Extraction	12/31/16	377.4	-590.6	1139.5	-637.3	155	24632937
EDF	Stone Harbor Emerging Markets Inc	Holding and other Investment Office	11/30/16	27.4	22.5	332.9	217.9		0
EDI	Stone Harbor Emerging Markets Tot	Finance Intermediaries & Services	11/30/16	7.8	6.0	206.2	134.0	29	1475131
STON	StoneMor Partners L P	Miscellaneous Consumer Services	12/31/16	326.2	-30.5	1787.0		92	11722039
SRI	Stoneridge Inc.	Auto Parts	12/31/16	696.0	77.5	394.5	178.3	185	27785267
STOR	STORE Capital Corp	REITs	12/31/16	376.3	123.3	4941.7	2483.3	278	195338425
SYK	Stryker Corp	Medical Instruments & Equipment	12/31/16	11325.0	1647.0	20435.0	9550.0	1438	339009796
RGR	Sturm, Ruger & Co., Inc.	Leisure Equipment	12/31/16	664.3	87.5	355.4	265.9	301	19538958
SPH	Suburban Propane Partners LP	Gas Utilities	9/30/17	1187.9	38.0	2171.3		206	19700582
SMFG	Sumitomo Mitsui Financial Group In	Banking	3/31/17	4061124.0	627870.0	191150981.0	10382282.0		0
INN	Summit Hotel Properties Inc	REITs	12/31/16	473.9	107.8	1718.5	1010.0	297	116720857
SUM	Summit Materials Inc	Mining	12/31/16	1626.1	46.1	2781.5	842.0	270	137015752
SMLP	Summit Midstream Partners LP	Equipment & Services	12/31/16	402.4	30.2	3115.2		89	38426481
SUI	Sun Communities Inc	REITs	12/31/16	833.8	31.3	5870.8	2362.6	359	87348807
SLF	Sun Life Financial Inc	Life & Health	12/31/16	28573.0	2581.0	258238.0	22368.0	376	282632747
SXC	SunCoke Energy Inc	Non-Precious Metals	12/31/16	1223.3	14.4	2120.9	311.1	209	67085562
SXCP	SunCoke Energy Partners LP	Metal Products	12/31/16	779.7	119.1	1696.0			0
SU	Suncor Energy Inc	Refining & Marketing	12/31/16	26968.0	445.0	88702.0	44630.0	772	1224818894
SUN	Sunoco LP	Equipment & Services	12/31/16	15698.0	-406.0	8701.0	2196.0	150	31218899
SHO	Sunstone Hotel Investors Inc	REITs	12/31/16	1189.3	134.2	3739.2	2482.8	295	309136418
STI 15	SunTrust Bank, Middle Georgia, N.	Banking							
STI	SunTrust Banks, Inc.	Banking	12/31/16	9161.0	1878.0	204875.0	23618.0	1049	510656348
SPN	Superior Energy Services, Inc.	Equipment & Services	12/31/16	1450.0	-886.9	3470.3	1303.9	435	195776279
SUP	Superior Industries International, Inc	Auto Parts	12/25/16	732.7	41.4	542.8	398.2	207	26171855
SVU	Supervalu Inc	Retail - Food & Beverage, Drug & To	2/25/17	12480.0	650.0	3580.0	376.0	392	102799286
SLD	Sutherland Asset Management Cor	REITs	12/31/16	171.5	49.2	2605.3	513.1	78	10506612
SWZ	Swiss Helvetia Fund Inc (The)	Holding and other Investment Office	12/31/16	8.1	4.2	328.4	327.9	68	15435242
SWCH	Switch Inc	Services	12/31/16	318.4	31.4	921.0	278.4		0
SYF	Synchrony Financial	Banking	12/31/16	15122.0	2251.0	90207.0	14196.0	711	751223557
SNX	Synnex Corp	IT Services	11/30/16	14061.8	234.9	5223.3	1975.8	317	34653223
SNV	Synovus Financial Corp.	Banking	12/31/16	1296.0	246.8	30104.0	2927.9	436	179768361
SYY	Sysco Corp	Retail - Food & Beverage, Drug & To	7/1/17	55371.1	1142.5	17756.7	2381.5	1470	570552185

EARNINGS PER SHARE QUARTERLY 1st	2nd	3rd	ANNUAL 2016	2015	2014	P/E RATIO	DIVIDENDS PER SHARE 2016	2015	2014	AV. YLD %	DIV. DECLARED AMOUNT	PAYABLE	PRICE RANGE 2016
-	-	0.44	2.04	1.70	1.84	12.7 - 8.0	0.20	0.11	0.10	1.0	0.050Y	32/4/39	25.9 - 16.4
-	-	0.72	2.81	2.44	2.32	19.7 - 16.8	1.46	1.37	1.27	2.8	0.390Y	32/4/39	55.5 - 47.1
-	101.35	-	117.49	-113.04	-124.99	0.4 - 0.2	9.98	12.47	24.56	26.8	-	-	48.3 - 28.3
-	-	-0.45	1.27	0.63	1.68	45.4 - 30.5	-	0.40	4.74		0.10Y	32/4/39	57.7 - 38.7
-	-	0.40	0.02	0.14		103.1 - 90.2	35.23	4.00	4.20	90.9	0.447Y	12/15/17	41.2 - 36.1
-	-	-0.47	1.56	1.53	1.46	24.4 - 19.7	1.06	1.02	0.96	3.1	0.280Y	32/4/39	38.1 - 30.8
-	-	-0.24	-1.48	-0.93	-0.93		-	1.60	1.60		0.40	11/13/15	4.6 - 1.4
-	-	1.06	2.55	2.59	2.18	20.9 - 18.3	2.22	2.15	2.08	4.5	0.580Y	32/4/39	53.3 - 46.8
-	-	0.52	1.00	0.93	1.61	47.6 - 32.4	0.18	0.34	0.46	0.5	0.30	32/4/39	47.6 - 32.4
-	-	0.84	3.55	3.27	1.64	18.6 - 13.9	0.38	0.28	0.22	0.7	0.1250Y	32/4/39	66.1 - 49.5
-	-	0.21	3.18	2.92	3.01	27.1 - 22.9	1.80	1.62	1.46	2.2	0.4950Y	32/4/39	86.3 - 72.8
-	-	0.09	-6.32	-12.25	2.62		-	-	-		0.00750	32/4/39	10.3 - 5.0
-0.29	-	-	-3.91	1.10	1.28						0.09070	10/5/05	24.0 - 17.2
-	-	-	0.63	0.41	0.22	25.6 - 0.0	0.81	1.19	1.48	5.4	0.27B	12/29/17	16.1 - 0.0
-	-	1.15	2.84	3.30	2.84	16.6 - 13.7	2.63	2.43	2.25	6.0	0.72620	11/29/17	47.1 - 38.8
-	-	1.31	5.99	2.66	4.02	24.2 - 16.6	1.47	1.29	1.15	1.2	0.420Y	32/4/39	145.1 - 99.3
-	-	0.22	0.96	-0.83	0.75	24.1 - 17.6	0.60	0.60	0.60	3.0	0.150Y	12/1/17	23.1 - 16.9
-	-	0.45	3.24	3.16	2.35	25.4 - 19.3	1.96	1.84	1.76	2.7	0.56250Y	32/4/39	82.3 - 62.6
-	-	1.26	3.70	5.66	2.53	23.6 - 14.3	0.10	-	-	0.2	0.10Y	32/4/39	87.3 - 53.0
-	-	0.87	3.76	4.38	3.08	15.9 - 8.5							59.7 - 32.1
-	-	0.01	0.21	0.26	-0.09	53.7 - 32.0	0.70	0.69	0.67	7.9	0.180Z	32/4/39	11.3 - 6.7
-	-	-0.68	0.38	3.65	5.84	79.2 - 61.1	2.16	1.92	1.56	8.2	0.63750	2/12/18	30.1 - 23.2
-	-0.01	-	-0.50	-0.85	-0.04								9.4 - 5.4
-	-	0.51	-2.02	-2.03	9.25		-	0.75	1.50		0.3750Y	7/1/15	32.0 - 22.2
-	-	0.30	-9.23	2.14									47.5 - 31.2
-	-	-0.04	-0.50	-1.24	-1.08								48.9 - 13.8
-	-	0.08	0.21	-0.02	4.40	93.1 - 77.9					0.160Y	9/28/07	19.6 - 16.4
-	-	0.20	0.29	-0.61	-0.28	99.4 - 78.6	1.39	1.37	1.29	5.2	0.42970Z	12/29/17	28.8 - 22.8
-	-	-0.64	0.12	0.96	0.51	37.3 - 12.6	0.58	0.53	0.47	26.3	0.050Y	12/13/17	4.5 - 1.5
-	-	0.57	2.62	1.99	1.85	20.7 - 15.5	0.68	0.60	0.52	1.4	0.190Y	12/1/17	54.1 - 40.6
1.10	-	-	4.08	4.27	3.35	26.7 - 20.9	0.54	0.46	0.38	0.6	0.180Y	2/23/18	108.8 - 85.3
-	-	1.80	6.51	5.79	4.76	26.1 - 17.8	2.26	2.14	2.04	1.6	0.630Y	32/4/39	170.0 - 115.8
-	-	0.40	1.22	1.65	1.74	30.3 - 18.3	0.45	0.42	0.37	1.5	0.1250	1/11/18	37.0 - 22.4
-	-	-0.24	0.70	0.59	0.57	16.2 - 12.9	0.40	0.36	0.34	3.9	0.110	2/6/18	11.4 - 9.0
0.06	-	-	-2.01	0.75	0.97		0.40	0.40	0.40	4.4	0.10Z	12/29/17	11.9 - 6.8
-	-	-0.07	0.02	-1.01	-0.35	722.0 - 403.5	-	-	-		0.250Y	11/27/06	14.4 - 8.1
-	-	0.33	1.50	1.91	2.24	15.3 - 14.2	1.92	1.92	1.92	8.7	0.480Z	32/4/39	23.0 - 21.3
-	-	1.66	4.97	4.47	4.57	20.0 - 15.3	1.44	1.32	1.16	1.6	0.420Y	32/4/39	99.3 - 76.0
-	0.44	-	-0.91	-11.80	6.87		0.69	6.73	10.51	3.7			21.4 - 16.3
-	-	0.27	0.25	4.98	-0.27	80.0 - 0.0	-	-	-		0.3750Z	12/15/17	20.0 - 0.0
-	-	0.22	1.36	0.68	0.69	13.2 - 9.2	0.45	0.42	0.40	2.9	0.12750Y	1/15/18	17.9 - 12.5
-	-	0.29	1.39	1.33	1.34	10.5 - 8.7	1.36	1.36	1.42	9.9	0.11330	4/13/18	14.6 - 12.1
-	-	0.94	3.73	3.32	2.49	24.5 - 19.0	0.78	0.73	0.69	1.0	0.2250Y	32/4/39	91.5 - 70.8
-	0.75	-	1.56	2.25	2.17		0.98	0.90	0.82		0.310	32/4/39	
-	-	0.33	1.07	0.60	0.20	24.3 - 19.8	0.28	0.28	0.07	1.2	0.070Y	2/20/18	26.1 - 21.1
-	-	0.46	1.85	-0.26	1.24	25.8 - 19.0	1.20	0.80	0.10	2.9	0.30Y	12/29/17	47.7 - 35.2
-	-	0.79	1.00	1.18	2.31	61.2 - 42.6					0.39060Y	12/15/17	61.2 - 42.6
-	-	-	0.19	0.12	0.14	130.4 - 56.8	0.24	0.34	0.34	1.4			24.8 - 10.8
-	-	0.06	-599.49	120.73	-204.28								50.5 - 17.4
-	-	-	1.42	2.24	2.05	12.2 - 10.4	2.16	2.16	2.16	13.4	0.180	4/26/18	17.3 - 14.7
-	-	-	0.63	1.96	1.69	26.5 - 22.3	1.81	1.81	1.81	11.6	0.15110Y	4/26/18	16.7 - 14.0
-	-	-	-0.94	-0.79	-0.40		2.31	2.58	2.43	28.3	0.330	5/15/17	11.4 - 5.9
-	-	0.28	2.74	0.81	-1.75	9.0 - 5.2							24.7 - 14.3
-	-	0.15	0.82	0.68	0.61	32.2 - 24.1	1.12	1.04	0.11	4.7	0.310	32/4/39	26.4 - 19.8
-	-	1.14	4.35	3.78	1.34	36.7 - 27.1	1.56	1.42	1.26	1.1	0.470Y	32/4/39	159.7 - 117.8
-	-	0.53	4.59	3.21	1.95	14.9 - 10.0	1.73	1.10	1.62	3.2	0.210Y	11/30/17	68.5 - 45.8
-	-	-0.48	0.24	1.38	1.56	133.1 - 95.5	3.55	3.52	3.50	13.9	0.60	2/13/18	31.9 - 22.9
171.14	-	-	616.83	448.86	560.68	0.0 - 0.0	30.73	25.02	25.20	397.5			8.8 - 7.0
-	-	0.17	1.00	1.24	0.05	19.2 - 14.5	0.55	0.47	0.46	3.4	0.0694GHZ	12/15/17	19.2 - 14.5
-	-	0.71	0.52	0.50		62.4 - 43.8							32.4 - 22.8
-	-	1.22	-0.71	-6.08	-0.93		2.30	2.27	2.04	10.3	0.5750	2/14/18	26.4 - 18.6
-	-	0.31	0.26	2.52	0.54	367.7 - 292.8	2.60	2.60	2.60	3.0	0.40630Z	32/4/39	95.6 - 76.1
-	-	1.32	4.03	3.55	2.86	13.1 - 8.1	1.62	1.51	1.44	3.8	0.23790	12/29/17	52.9 - 32.6
-	-	0.18	0.22	-0.34	-1.83	56.7 - 36.0	-	0.43	0.06		0.150	12/7/15	12.5 - 7.9
-	-	0.45	2.07	1.92	1.57	9.9 - 6.6	2.38	2.29	2.02	13.8	0.5940	3/1/18	20.4 - 13.7
-	-	0.78	0.28	-1.38	1.84	165.1 - 101.3	1.16	1.14	1.02	3.1	0.320	12/22/17	46.2 - 28.4
-	-	1.08	-5.26	1.11	0.85		3.27	2.68	2.05	11.1	0.82550	2/14/18	32.4 - 23.4
-	-	0.05	0.55	1.62	0.37	31.7 - 25.9	0.68	1.41	0.51	4.3	0.58HZ	1/16/18	17.4 - 14.2
-	-	1.06	3.60	3.58	3.23	18.3 - 14.5	1.00	0.92	0.70	1.7	0.36720Y	32/4/39	66.0 - 52.3
-	-	-0.39	-5.85	-12.33	1.65		0.08	0.32	0.32	0.7	0.080	32/4/39	19.0 - 7.9
-	-	-0.22	1.62	0.90	0.33	16.9 - 8.8	0.72	0.72	0.72	3.7	0.090Y	1/19/18	27.4 - 14.2
-	-	0.67	4.62	5.11	4.90	7.4 - 3.2					0.08750Y	32/4/39	34.4 - 14.8
-	-	0.37	1.85	-0.16	3.08	8.7 - 7.1	1.55	1.60	1.60	10.5	0.370Z	1/31/18	16.1 - 13.1
-	-	-	0.15	0.11	0.08	85.7 - 68.1	0.51	0.71	2.38	4.2	0.120	12/22/17	12.9 - 10.2
-	-	-	-	-	-	138.9 - 108.3	-	-	-		0.014GY	12/29/17	20.8 - 16.3
-	-	0.08	0.15	0.37		14.4 - 9.8	0.26	-	-	0.8	0.150Y	32/4/39	39.0 - 26.5
-	-	0.70	2.71	2.65	2.78	23.4 - 17.6	0.85	0.57	0.13	0.7	0.350Y	32/4/39	137.3 - 103.4
-	-	1.87	5.88	5.24	4.57	26.5 - 20.7	0.48	0.42	0.24	1.1	0.150Y	32/4/39	50.1 - 39.1
0.69	-	-	1.64	1.15	1.58	38.2 - 29.9	1.23	1.18	1.14	2.3	0.360Y	32/4/39	62.6 - 49.1

SYMBOL	COMPANY	NATURE OF BUSINESS	FISCAL YEAR-END	TOTAL REV. $MILL	NET INCOME $MILL	TOTAL ASSETS $MILL	NET STK EQUITY $MILL	NO OF INST	INST. HOLDINGS (SHARES)
SYX	Systemax, Inc.	Retail - Appliances and Electronics	12/31/17	1680.1	-32.6	566.1	214.4	120	11939638
DATA	Tableau Software Inc	Internet & Software	12/31/16	826.9	-144.4	1287.2	791.8	322	70185318
TAHO	Tahoe Resources Inc.	Precious Metals	12/31/16	784.5	117.9	3071.3	2572.2	251	210864191
TLRD	Tailored Brands Inc	Retail - Apparel and Accessories	1/28/17	3378.7	25.0	2097.9	-107.6	283	66688631
TWN	Taiwan Fund, Inc. (The)	Holding and other Investment Office	8/31/17	4.7	1.7	198.6	197.6	35	8803204
TSM	Taiwan Semiconductor Manufacturi	Semiconductors	12/31/16	947909.3	334247.2	1886455.3	1389248.3	864	1185196370
TAL	TAL Education Group	Educational Services	2/28/17	1043.1	116.9	1828.9	644.2	301	254456920
TEGP	Tallgrass Energy GP LP	Equipment & Services	12/31/16	605.1	26.8	3542.2		144	57307249
TEP	Tallgrass Energy Partners, LP	Equipment & Services	12/31/16	605.1	263.5	3019.0		176	46897476
SKT	Tanger Factory Outlet Centers, Inc.	REITs	12/31/16	465.8	193.7	2526.2	670.2	383	113081194
TPR	Tapestry Inc	Apparel, Footwear & Accessories	7/1/17	4488.3	591.0	5831.6	3001.9	952	307888698
TRGP	Targa Resources Corp	Refining & Marketing	12/31/16	6690.9	-187.3	12871.2	5439.4	505	199194244
TGT	Target Corp	Retail - General Merchandise/Depart	1/28/17	69495.0	2737.0	37431.0	10953.0	1589	595341194
TARO	Taro Pharmaceutical Industries Ltd.	Pharmaceuticals	3/31/17	879.4	456.4	2289.8	2067.5	170	7713827
TTM	Tata Motors Ltd	Autos- Manufacturing	3/31/17	2656495.1	61210.5	2666646.0	534197.0	363	95388013
TCO	Taubman Centers, Inc.	REITs	12/31/16	612.6	132.6	4010.9	72.1	354	77940970
TMHC	Taylor Morrison Home Corp	Builders	12/31/16	3550.0	52.6	4220.9	551.8	228	72778681
TCP	TC PipeLines, LP	Equipment & Services	12/31/16	357.0	244.0	3158.0	83.0	245	47832847
TCF	TCF Financial Corp	Banking	12/31/16	1396.6	212.1	21441.3	2427.5	390	173544120
TSI	TCW Strategic Income Fund Inc	Holding and other Investment Office	12/31/16	14.6	12.2	284.4	277.1	82	21005786
TEL	TE Connectivity Ltd	Electrical Equipment	9/30/17	13113.0	1683.0	19403.0	9751.0	869	367395166
TISI	Team Inc	Equipment & Services	12/31/16	1196.7	-12.7	1147.4	535.6	224	42315802
FTI	TechnipFMC plc	Services	12/31/16		-0.0	0.1	0.1		0
TECK	Teck Resources Ltd	Mining	12/31/16	9300.0	1040.0	35629.0	17442.0	405	441579712
TK	Teekay Corp	Equipment & Services	12/31/16	2328.6	-123.2	12814.8	899.4	178	30221096
TGP	Teekay LNG Partners LP	Equipment & Services	12/31/16	396.4	175.5	4315.5		144	36371078
TOO	Teekay Offshore Partners LP	Equipment & Services	12/31/16	1152.4	56.3	5718.6	285.0	108	76511433
TNK	Teekay Tankers Ltd	Equipment & Services	12/31/16	526.9	62.9	1932.4	920.6	160	59717454
TGNA	TEGNA Inc	Radio & Television	12/31/16	3341.2	436.7	8542.7	2271.4	625	250171888
TRC	Tejon Ranch Co	Property, Real Estate & Developmen	12/31/16	45.6	0.6	439.7	305.9	127	17863679
HQH	Tekla Healthcare Investors	Holding and other Investment Office	9/30/17	4.6	-6.3	1009.6	974.8	101	8363070
THQ	Tekla Healthcare Opportunities Fun	Finance Intermediaries & Services	9/30/17	23.8	7.1	1120.7	875.7	66	7800407
HQL	Tekla Life Sciences Investors	Holding and other Investment Office	9/30/17	1.7	-3.9	468.3	466.4	66	3285921
THW	Tekla World Healthcare Fund	Holding and other Investment Office	9/30/17	13.2	3.6	602.0	479.9	40	4242656
TDOC	Teladoc Inc	Diagnostic & Health Related Service	12/31/16	123.2	-74.2	303.7	230.9	215	69374918
TLRA	Telaria Inc	Advertising	12/31/16	166.8	-20.9	154.2	78.5	88	22422032
TEO	Telecom Argentina SA	Services	12/31/16	53323.0	3975.0	47914.0	19336.0	146	15592392
TI	Telecom Italia SpA	Radio & Television	12/31/16	19975.0	1808.0	70446.0	21207.0	119	19847258
TDY	Teledyne Technologies Inc	Electronic Instruments & Related Pro	1/1/17	2149.9	190.9	2774.4	1554.4	370	40874791
TFX	Teleflex Incorporated	Medical Instruments & Equipment	12/31/16	1868.0	237.4	3891.2	2139.3	536	52355281
VIV	Telefonica Brasil SA	Services	12/31/16	42508.5	4085.2	102066.3	69244.4	255	176913625
TEF	Telefonica SA	Services	12/31/16	52036.0	2369.0	123641.0	18157.0	322	53319872
TDS	Telephone & Data Systems Inc	Services	12/31/16	5104.0	43.0	9446.0	4145.0	361	114819593
TU	TELUS Corp	Services	12/31/16	12725.0	1223.0	27729.0	7917.0	324	336941714
TDF	Templeton Dragon Fund, Inc.	Holding and other Investment Office	12/31/16	18.4	9.2	655.7	654.8	93	20119075
EMF	Templeton Emerging Markets Fund	Holding and other Investment Office	8/31/17	6.6	2.8	321.5	321.0	63	6699095
TEI	Templeton Emerging Markets Inco	Holding and other Investment Office	12/31/16	14.1	12.1	589.2	584.1	117	15473794
GIM	Templeton Global Income Fund (DE	Holding and other Investment Office	12/31/16	16.0	13.8	1017.0	984.4	167	39631958
TPX	Tempur Sealy International, Inc.	Furniture	12/31/16	3127.3	202.1	2702.6	-15.2	371	81244125
TS	Tenaris SA	Equipment & Services	12/31/16	4293.6	55.3	14003.3	11287.4	273	120611860
THC	Tenet Healthcare Corp.	Hospitals & Health Care Facilities	12/31/16	19621.0	-192.0	24701.0	417.0	423	212204633
TNC	Tennant Co.	Industrial Machinery & Equipment	12/31/16	808.6	46.6	470.0	278.5	200	19289849
TEN	Tenneco Inc	Auto Parts	12/31/16	8599.0	363.0	4342.0	588.0	400	57651795
TVE	Tennessee Valley Authority	Electric Utilities	9/30/17	10739.0	685.0	50017.0	9133.0		0
TDC	Teradata Corp (DE)	IT Services	12/31/16	2322.0	125.0	2413.0	971.0	515	147634921
TER	Teradyne, Inc.	Semiconductors	12/31/16	1753.3	-43.4	2762.5	1828.7	587	228179876
TEX	Terex Corp	Industrial Machinery & Equipment	12/31/16	4443.1	-176.1	5006.8	1484.7	443	107297902
TX	Ternium S A	Non-Precious Metals	12/31/16	7224.0	595.6	8322.9	4391.3	184	43453702
TNH	Terra Nitrogen Co LP	Agricultural Chemicals	12/31/16	418.3	209.3	373.3		82	1094119
TRNO	Terreno Realty Corp	REITs	12/31/16	108.4	15.1	1279.0	811.8	196	58533198
TTI	TETRA Technologies, Inc.	Equipment & Services	12/31/16	694.8	-161.5	1315.5	233.5	221	133285489
TEVA	Teva Pharmaceutical Industries Ltd	Pharmaceuticals	12/31/16	21903.0	329.0	92890.0	33337.0	1047	627680034
TPL	Texas Pacific Land Trust	Property, Real Estate & Developmen	12/31/16	59.9	37.2	62.5	47.6	155	4911068
TGH	Textainer Group Holdings Ltd	Shipping	12/31/16	498.2	-50.7	4296.0	1127.7	146	16126639
TXT	Textron Inc	Aerospace	12/31/16	13788.0	962.0	15358.0	5574.0	663	251253205
GPS	The Gap Inc	Retail - Apparel and Accessories	1/28/17	15516.0	676.0	7610.0	2904.0	722	300617002
NWHM	The New Home Company Inc	Builders	12/31/16	694.5	21.0	419.1	244.5	90	13018293
TMO	Thermo Fisher Scientific Inc	Biotechnology	12/31/16	18274.1	2021.8	45907.5	21539.3	1569	428947078
THR	Thermon Group Holdings Inc	Electrical Equipment	3/31/17	264.1	14.6	454.1	307.9	120	39247588
TPRE	Third Point Reinsurance Ltd	General Insurance	12/31/16	689.0	27.6	3895.6	1414.1	157	84584058
TSLF	THL Credit Senior Loan Fund	Finance Intermediaries & Services	12/31/16	13.7	10.2	194.6	138.3	31	2108053
TRI	Thomson Reuters Corp	Publishing	12/31/16	11166.0	3098.0	27852.0	12773.0	447	207590979
THO	Thor Industries, Inc.	Autos- Manufacturing	7/31/17	7247.0	374.3	2557.9	1576.5	609	58451310
TDW	Tidewater Inc (New)	Equipment & Services	3/31/17	601.6	-660.1	4190.7	1634.9	220	31308730
TIER	Tier REIT Inc	REITs	12/31/16	242.8	-29.4	1552.5	618.5	191	31483316
TIF	Tiffany & Co	Retail - Specialty	1/31/17	4001.8	446.1	5097.6	3013.5	762	128819313
TLYS	Tilly's Inc	Retail - Apparel and Accessories	1/28/17	569.0	11.4	290.5	189.2	120	15068459
TSU	TIM Participacoes S.A.	Services	12/31/16	15617.4	750.4	34655.7	17187.5	166	80391850
TIME	Time Inc	Publishing	12/31/16	3076.0	-48.0	4305.0	1440.0	398	101819018
TWX	Time Warner Inc	Entertainment	12/31/16	29318.0	3926.0	65966.0	24335.0	1528	870352099

T56

| EARNINGS PER SHARE | | | | | | P/E RATIO | DIVIDENDS PER SHARE | | | AV. YLD % | DIV. DECLARED | | PRICE RANGE 2016 |
| QUARTERLY | | | ANNUAL | | | | PER SHARE | | | | | | |
1st	2nd	3rd	2016	2015	2014		2016	2015	2014	%	AMOUNT	PAYABLE	
-	-	-	-0.87	-2.69	-1.01	-	0.10	-	-	0.5	1.57Y	1/12/18	34.3 - 7.2
-	-	-0.59	-1.92	-1.17	0.08								82.2 - 43.3
-	-	-0.03	0.41	-0.35	0.61	36.1 - 10.2	0.24	0.24	0.02	3.0	0.020	32/4/39	14.8 - 4.2
-	-	0.75	-21.26	-0.01	1.70		0.72	0.72	0.72	4.7	0.180Y	12/22/17	24.9 - 9.4
-	-	-	0.12	0.07	0.08	182.6 - 0.0	-	2.63			0.660	1/9/18	21.9 - 0.0
-	-	3.47	12.89	11.68	9.81	3.3 - 2.3	24.45	17.90	11.97	68.4	-	● -	43.0 - 29.3
-	0.15	-	0.60	0.41	0.38	60.2 - 20.0	-	-					36.1 - 12.0
-	-	0.27	0.55	0.51	1.36	53.4 - 40.2	0.89	0.22		3.4	0.36750	2/14/18	29.4 - 22.1
-	-	1.96	2.23	1.91	1.36	24.6 - 18.7	2.90	2.19	1.43	6.0	0.9650	2/14/18	54.9 - 41.6
-	-	-0.17	2.01	2.20	0.77	18.5 - 11.0	1.26	1.30	0.94	4.5	0.34250Z	32/4/39	37.2 - 22.2
-0.06	-	-	1.65	1.45	2.79	29.5 - 21.2	1.35	1.35	1.35	3.2	0.33750Y	32/4/39	48.7 - 35.0
-	-	-0.91	-1.80	1.09	2.43		3.64	3.39	2.68	7.3	23.750	32/4/39	61.4 - 40.4
-	-	0.88	5.31	-2.56	3.07	13.9 - 9.5	2.16	1.90	1.58	3.7	0.620Y	32/4/39	73.8 - 50.2
-	2.15	-	12.62	11.31	8.14								
-	7.29	-	28.40	39.40	40.60	1.4 - 1.0	-	8.61	7.87				40.1 - 29.0
-	-	0.07	1.77	1.76	13.47	43.0 - 26.2	2.38	2.26	6.91	4.0	0.39060Z	32/4/39	76.2 - 46.3
-	-	0.45	1.69	1.85	2.17	14.5 - 11.0	-	-					24.6 - 18.6
-	-	0.61	3.21	-0.03	2.67	20.2 - 15.2	3.66	3.46	3.30	6.5	1.0	32/4/39	64.9 - 48.9
-	-	0.29	1.15	1.07	0.94	18.1 - 12.8	0.30	0.23	0.20	1.8	0.3048GHY	32/4/39	20.9 - 14.8
-	-	-	0.26	0.22	0.24	22.6 - 20.3	0.28	0.21	0.25	5.0	0.033C	1/12/18	5.9 - 5.3
-0.11	-	-	5.44	5.89	4.27		1.40	1.24	1.08		0.40Y	32/4/39	-
-	-	-2.80	-0.45	0.41	1.40		-	-			0.010	3/1/93	38.3 - 10.7
-	-	0.26	1932.42				-	-			0.13G	12/1/17	-
-	0.14	-	1.78	-4.29	0.63	19.3 - 8.4	0.10	0.20	0.90	0.4	0.46	12/29/17	34.4 - 14.9
-	-0.93	-	-1.62	1.13	-0.76		0.22	1.73	1.26		0.0550	2/14/18	-
-	-	-	1.69	2.21	2.30		-	-			0.140	2/9/18	-
0.20	-	-	-0.25	0.32	-0.22		0.44	2.18	2.15		0.53130	2/15/18	-
-	-0.22	-	0.40	1.35	0.66		0.18	0.24	0.12		0.030	11/24/17	-
-	-	0.19	1.99	2.00	4.58	8.5 - 5.9	0.56	0.68	0.80	3.9	0.070Y	32/4/39	16.9 - 11.8
-	-	-	0.03	0.14	0.27	● 839.3 - 623.0	-	-			0.0250	12/10/99	25.2 - 18.7
-	-	-0.17	-0.22	-0.24			3.10	2.61	2.13	12.8	0.520	12/29/17	26.2 - 21.7
-	-	-	0.18	0.11	-0.01	105.1 - 89.3	1.65	1.35	0.11	9.3	0.11250	1/31/18	18.9 - 16.1
-	-	-	-0.19	-0.25	-0.23		2.85	2.09	1.70	14.2	0.430	12/29/17	22.2 - 17.3
-	-	-	0.09	-0.02		169.8 - 145.8	1.40	0.23		9.8	0.11670	1/31/18	15.3 - 13.1
-	-	-0.55	-1.75	-2.91	-10.25		-	-					37.1 - 16.4
-	-	0.24	-0.40	-0.84	-0.46		-	-					5.0 - 1.9
-	-	0.89	4.10	3.51	3.79	9.7 - 4.4	9.51	3.36	5.28	34.8			39.7 - 18.0
-	-	-	0.08	0.00	0.07	131.1 - 98.0	-	-					10.5 - 7.8
-	-	1.90	5.37	5.44	5.75	34.7 - 22.6	-	-					186.2 - 121.1
-	-	1.65	4.98	5.10	4.04	54.3 - 31.9	1.36	1.36	1.36	0.6	0.340Y	32/4/39	270.2 - 158.9
-	-	-	2.27	2.15	4.12	7.4 - 5.9	1.84	3.35	2.73	12.3			16.7 - 13.4
-	-	0.15	0.42	0.51	0.61	27.7 - 22.2	0.73	0.89	0.73	6.9			11.6 - 9.3
-	-	-1.64	0.39	1.98	-1.26	84.0 - 63.6	0.59	0.56	0.54	2.1	0.1550Z	32/4/39	32.8 - 24.8
-	-	0.62	2.06	2.29	2.31	23.7 - 15.2	1.84	1.68	1.52	4.6	0.5050	1/2/18	48.8 - 31.4
-	-	-	0.27	0.30	0.49	83.6 - 61.4	1.69	4.01	4.31	8.5	1.366C	9/25/17	22.6 - 16.6
-	-	-	0.19	0.21	0.29	93.5 - 64.9	1.28	1.18	1.69	8.4	0.8687C	12/29/17	17.8 - 12.3
-	-	-	0.25	0.93	1.02	47.0 - 44.2	0.80	1.14	1.39	7.0	0.29530	12/29/17	11.8 - 11.0
-	-	-	0.10	0.33	0.35	67.5 - 63.9	0.30	0.64	0.62	4.5	0.01780Z	1/31/18	6.8 - 6.4
-	-	0.81	3.38	1.17	1.75	20.6 - 12.0	-	-			0.080Y	32/4/39	69.5 - 40.6
-	-	0.09	0.05	-0.07	0.98	743.4 - 519.4	0.86	0.90	0.90	2.8			37.2 - 26.0
-	-3.64	-	-1.93	-1.41	0.12		-	-			0.0267F	32/4/39	22.7 - 12.7
-	-	0.20	2.59	1.74	2.70	29.5 - 23.3	0.81	0.80	0.78	1.2	0.210Y	32/4/39	76.3 - 60.4
-	-	1.57	6.44	4.11	3.66	10.7 - 8.0	-	-			0.250Y	32/4/39	68.7 - 51.7
-	-	-					0.89	0.94	0.96	3.6	0.210Z	8/1/18	25.4 - 24.6
-	-	0.10	0.95	-1.53	2.33	41.3 - 28.7	-	-					39.2 - 27.3
-	-	0.52	-0.21	0.97	0.37		0.24	0.24	0.18	0.7	0.090Y	32/4/39	44.4 - 25.4
-	-	0.66	-1.63	1.33	2.79		0.28	0.24	0.20	0.7	0.080	32/4/39	48.6 - 29.6
-	-	0.05	0.30	0.00	-0.10	109.2 - 74.8	0.90	0.90	0.75	3.3	-		32.8 - 22.4
-	-	0.92	7.56	10.06	12.07	15.2 - 10.1	8.74	9.75	10.00	9.9	1.360	11/29/17	114.8 - 76.0
-	-	0.36	0.26	0.26	0.23	147.4 - 102.0	0.76	0.66	0.57	2.3	0.220Z	1/12/18	38.3 - 26.5
-	-	0.03	-1.85	-1.59	-2.16		-	-					5.2 - 1.9
-	-5.94	-	0.07	1.82	3.56	542.3 - 160.4	1.16	1.16	1.15	4.5	17.50	12/15/17	38.0 - 11.2
-	-	3.36	4.66	6.10	4.14	96.6 - 57.2	0.31	0.29	0.27	0.1	1.7Y	3/16/17	450.1 - 266.6
-	-0.16	-	-0.89	1.87	3.32		0.51	1.65	1.88		0.03D	8/30/16	-
-	-	0.60	3.53	2.50	2.13	16.2 - 12.9	0.08	0.08	0.08	0.2	0.020Y	32/4/39	57.2 - 45.4
-	-	0.58	2.23	2.87	2.74	15.7 - 9.5	0.92	0.88	0.70	3.6	0.230Y	32/4/39	34.9 - 21.2
-	-	0.21	1.01	1.28	0.30	12.8 - 9.9	-	-					12.9 - 10.0
-	-	1.34	5.09	4.92	4.71	39.4 - 27.7	0.60	0.60	0.60	0.3	0.150Y	32/4/39	200.4 - 141.0
-	0.15	-	0.71	1.52	0.80	33.6 - 22.5	-	-					23.9 - 16.0
-	-	0.52	0.26	-0.84	0.47		-	-					-
-	-	-	1.36	1.25			1.27	1.35	1.43	7.2	0.0960	1/31/18	18.6 - 16.4
-	-	0.46	4.13	1.60	2.35	13.3 - 10.2	1.36	1.34	1.32	3.0	0.3450	12/15/17	55.0 - 42.3
2.43	-	-	4.88	3.74	3.35	31.8 - 18.3	1.20	1.08	1.92	1.1	0.370Y	32/4/39	155.3 - 89.4
-	-0.81	-	-3.41	-1.34	2.82		0.75	1.00	1.00	6.4			29.2 - 0.7
-	-	-0.17	-0.62	-0.66	-0.36		0.72	0.36		3.9	0.180Z	12/29/17	20.6 - 16.1
-	-	0.80	3.59	3.73	1.41	29.3 - 21.4	1.58	1.48	1.34	1.7	0.50Y	32/4/39	105.2 - 76.8
-	-	0.30	0.27	0.50	0.65	61.1 - 30.0	-	-			1.7	2/20/18	16.5 - 8.1
-	-	0.13	0.31	0.86	0.64	62.7 - 39.7	0.89	0.66	1.64	5.4			19.4 - 12.3
-	-	0.14	-0.49	-8.32	0.80		0.76	0.76	0.19	4.9	0.040	12/15/17	19.6 - 10.0
-	-	1.73	4.96	4.62	4.34	20.9 - 17.6	1.61	1.40	1.27	1.6	0.40250Y	32/4/39	103.6 - 87.0

SYMBOL	COMPANY	NATURE OF BUSINESS	FISCAL YEAR-END	TOTAL REV. $MILL	NET INCOME $MILL	TOTAL ASSETS $MILL	NET STK EQUITY $MILL	NO OF INST	INST. HOLDINGS (SHARES)
TKR	Timken Co. (The)	Industrial Machinery & Equipment	12/31/16	2669.8	152.6	2758.3	1274.9	468	74595170
TMST	Timkensteel Corp	Metal Products	12/31/16	869.5	-105.5	1069.9	597.4	210	37398194
TWI	Titan International Inc	Industrial Machinery & Equipment	12/31/16	1265.5	-34.0	1263.0	293.9	218	69679608
TJX	TJX Companies, Inc.	Retail - Apparel and Accessories	1/28/17	33183.7	2298.2	12883.8	4510.6	1518	681460120
TOL	Toll Brothers Inc.	Builders	10/31/17	5815.1	535.5	9445.2	4531.2	594	168600948
TR	Tootsie Roll Industries Inc	Food	12/31/16	521.1	67.5	920.1	711.4	233	16801644
BLD	TopBuild Corp	Builders	12/31/16	1742.8	72.6	1690.1	972.5	281	39932647
TMK	Torchmark Corp	Life & Health	12/31/16	3934.6	549.8	21436.1	4566.9	627	107521472
TTC	Toro Company (The)	Industrial Machinery & Equipment	10/31/17	2505.2	267.7	1493.8	617.1	529	96705786
TD	Toronto Dominion Bank	Banking	10/31/17	45583.0	10203.0	1278995.0	74207.0	687	984153054
NDP	Tortoise Energy Independence Fun	Holding and other Investment Office	11/30/16	2.3	-1.8	319.3	246.1	36	2371269
TYG	Tortoise Energy Infrastructure Corp	Holding and other Investment Office	11/30/16	3.6	-38.0	2593.7	1412.3	197	18746933
NTG	Tortoise MLP Fund, Inc.	Holding and other Investment Office	11/30/16	0.4	-21.7	1514.4	904.9		0
TTP	Tortoise Pipeline & Energy Fund Inc	Holding and other Investment Office	11/30/15	9.3	2.2	286.0	197.4	46	2837149
TPZ	Tortoise Power & Energy Infrastruct	Holding and other Investment Office	11/30/15	9.4	6.1	198.3	147.6	48	1980669
TOT	Total SA	Production & Extraction	12/31/16	127925.0	6196.0	230978.0	98680.0	761	183906695
TSS	Total System Services, Inc.	Business Services	12/31/16	4170.1	319.6	6366.2	2099.9	656	176342669
TOWR	Tower International Inc	Auto Parts	12/31/16	1913.6	38.6	1162.5	207.8	167	20909518
TSQ	Townsquare Media Inc	Radio & Television	12/31/16	516.9	23.1	1080.7	389.3	95	10112927
TM	Toyota Motor Corp	Autos- Manufacturing	3/31/17	277597193.0	1831109.0	48750186.0	18000689.0	443	16095139
TPGE U	TPG Pace Energy Holdings Corp	Business Services	2/23/17		-0.0	0.4	-0.0	44	25779262
TPGH	TPG Pace Holdings Corp	Business Services	2/23/17		-0.0	0.5	-0.0	16	13158678
TRTX	TPG RE Finance Trust Inc	REITs	12/31/16	154.0	70.0	2665.6	970.7	51	15724679
TSLX	TPG Specialty Lending Inc	Credit & Lending	12/31/16	192.4	107.3	1675.5	952.2	115	38966720
TAC	TransAlta Corp.	Electric Utilities	12/31/16	2397.0	169.0	10996.0	3511.0	128	166972682
TRP	TransCanada Corp	Equipment & Services	12/31/16	12505.0	233.0	88051.0	25436.0	556	567760098
TCI	Transcontinental Realty Investors, I	Property, Real Estate & Developmen	12/31/16	118.5	0.0	1185.9	205.9	33	178863
TDG	TransDigm Group Inc	Aerospace	9/30/17	3504.3	596.9	9975.7	-2951.2	529	68400603
TLP	TransMontaigne Partners L.P.	Equipment & Services	12/31/16	164.9	44.1	689.7		103	12511927
RIG	Transocean Ltd	Equipment & Services	12/31/16	4161.0	778.0	26889.0	15802.0	668	345683710
TGS	Transportadora de Gas del Sur S.A.	Equipment & Services	12/31/16	7402.2	930.7	8931.3	2526.4		0
TRU	TransUnion	Miscellaneous Consumer Services	12/31/16	1704.9	120.6	4781.2	1362.8	285	191665001
TRV	Travelers Companies Inc (The)	General Insurance	12/31/16	27625.0	3014.0	100245.0	23221.0	1432	305803013
TVPT	Travelport Worldwide Ltd	Hotels, Restaurants & Travel	12/31/16	2351.4	16.8	2833.9	-359.9	228	128262226
TREC	Trecora Resources	Refining & Marketing	12/31/16	212.4	19.4	292.1	164.1	77	11355862
TG	Tredegar Corp.	Plastics	12/31/16	830.7	24.5	651.2	310.8	173	25219831
THS	TreeHouse Foods Inc	Food	12/31/16	6175.1	-226.6	6545.8	2503.3	414	78659604
TREX	Trex Co Inc	Metal Products	12/31/16	479.6	67.8	221.4	134.2	304	32184850
TPH	TRI Pointe Group Inc	Builders	12/31/16	2403.9	195.2	3564.6	1829.4	274	192203216
TY	Tri-Continental Corp.	Holding and other Investment Office	12/31/16	59.1	51.9	1523.0	1508.5	122	11764495
TCAP	Triangle Capital Corp	Holding and other Investment Office	12/31/16	113.7	68.9	1159.7	611.2	153	18049269
TRCO	Tribune Media Co	Radio & Television	12/31/16	1947.9	14.2	9401.1	3539.8	301	91304194
TNET	Trinet Group Inc.	Services	12/31/16	3060.3	61.4	2095.1	34.6	193	43307873
TRN	Trinity Industries, Inc.	Industrial Machinery & Equipment	12/31/16	4588.3	343.6	9125.3	3918.5	520	153127436
TSE	Trinseo SA	Synthetic Materials	12/31/16	3716.6	318.3	2409.5	445.1	268	44729590
GTS	Triple-S Management Corp	Life & Health	12/31/16	2984.8	17.4	2219.0	863.2	141	24049016
TPVG	TriplePoint Venture Growth BDC Co	Finance Intermediaries & Services	12/31/16	43.6	23.0	434.2	215.9	62	6441605
TRTN	Triton International Ltd	Business Services	12/31/16	845.1	-13.5	8713.6	1663.2	189	53727639
TGI	Triumph Group Inc.	Aerospace	3/31/17	3532.8	-43.0	4414.6	846.5	341	78218360
TROX	Tronox Ltd	Specialty Chemicals	12/31/16	2093.0	-59.0	4950.0	1017.0		0
TBI	TrueBlue Inc	Business Services	1/1/17	2750.6	-15.3	1130.4	525.2	258	46647643
TNP	Tsakos Energy Navigation Ltd	Equipment & Services	12/31/16	481.8	55.8	3277.6	1405.1	109	24759937
TUP	Tupperware Brands Corp	Plastics	12/31/16	2213.1	223.6	1587.8	212.8	564	59918080
TKC	Turkcell Iletisim Hizmetleri AS	Services	12/31/16	14285.6	1492.1	31600.2	16011.8	160	34009501
TPB	Turning Point Brands Inc	Tobacco Products	12/31/16	206.2	26.9	285.0	34.1	63	3641799
TRQ	Turquoise Hill Resources Ltd.	Precious Metals	12/31/16	1203.3	210.6	12460.2	8726.9	234	703707333
TPC	Tutor Perini Corp	Construction Services	12/31/16	4973.1	95.8	4038.6	1553.0	25	447716
TWLO	Twilio Inc	Internet & Software	12/31/16	277.3	-41.3	412.7	329.4	221	56407372
TWTR	Twitter Inc	Internet & Software	12/31/16	2529.6	-456.9	6870.4	4604.9	638	412109020
TWO	Two Harbors Investment Corp	REITs	12/31/16	741.1	353.3	20112.1	3401.1	417	288683461
TWO	Two Harbors Investment Corp	REITs	12/31/16	741.1	353.3	20112.1	3401.1	417	288683461
TYL	Tyler Technologies, Inc.	Internet & Software	12/31/16	756.0	109.9	1357.9	915.5	373	44972339
TSN	Tyson Foods Inc	Food	9/30/17	38260.0	1774.0	28066.0	10541.0	874	320052568
USPH	U.S. Physical Therapy, Inc.	Hospitals & Health Care Facilities	12/31/16	356.5	20.6	351.2	187.5	224	15174375
UBS	UBS Group AG	Holding and other Investment Office	12/31/16	35731.0	3204.0	935016.0	53620.0		0
UDR	UDR Inc	REITs	12/31/16	959.9	292.7	7679.6	3093.1	503	349657235
UGI	UGI Corp.	Gas Utilities	9/30/17	6120.7	436.6	11582.2	3163.3	615	166282714
UGP	Ultrapar Participacoes SA	Equipment & Services	12/31/16	77353.0	1561.6	24159.7	8527.6	139	32890526
UMH	UMH Properties Inc	REITs	12/31/16	99.2	11.5	680.4	317.0	150	21360467
UAA	Under Armour Inc	Apparel, Footwear & Accessories	12/31/16	4825.3	257.0	3644.3	2030.9	642	158736930
UFI	Unifi, Inc.	Textiles	6/25/17	647.3	32.9	571.5	360.8	182	17958200
UNF	Unifirst Corp	Business Services	8/26/17	1591.0	70.2	1819.1	1453.2	245	20522628
UN	Unilever N.V.	Household & Personal Products	12/31/16	52713.0	5184.0	56429.0	16354.0	686	182908890
UL	Unilever Plc	Household & Personal Products	12/31/16	52713.0	5184.0	56429.0	16354.0	728	118239177
UNP	Union Pacific Corp	Rail	12/31/16	19941.0	4233.0	55718.0	19932.0	1996	720650087
UIS	Unisys Corp.	IT Services	12/31/16	2820.7	-47.7	2021.6	-1631.0	260	96636263
UNT	Unit Corp.	Production & Extraction	12/31/16	602.2	-135.6	2479.3	1194.1	269	60725272
UAL	United Continental Holdings Inc	Airlines/Air Freight	12/31/16	36556.0	2263.0	40140.0	8659.0	790	340591540
UMC	United Microelectronics Corp	Semiconductors	12/31/16	147870.1	8315.7	386655.2	216579.9	159	188270604
UPS	United Parcel Service Inc	Airlines/Air Freight	12/31/16	60906.0	3431.0	40377.0	405.0	1774	583462287

T58

EARNINGS PER SHARE QUARTERLY			ANNUAL			P/E RATIO	DIVIDENDS PER SHARE			AV. YLD %	DIV. DECLARED		PRICE RANGE 2016
1st	2nd	3rd	2016	2015	2014		2016	2015	2014		AMOUNT	PAYABLE	
		0.68	1.92	-0.84	1.87	26.8 - 21.3	1.04	1.03	1.00	2.3	0.270Y	32/4/39	51.5 - 41.0
		-0.13	-2.39	-1.63	2.27			0.42	0.28		0.140Y	9/10/15	22.8 - 12.8
		-0.22	-0.81	-1.74	-1.50		0.02	0.02	0.02	0.2	0.0050Y	1/16/18	14.2 - 8.1
		1.00	3.33	3.15	2.94	24.2 - 20.1	0.81	0.67	0.55	1.1	0.31250Y	32/4/39	80.7 - 66.9
		0.87	2.18	1.97	1.84	23.2 - 14.2					0.080Y	32/4/39	50.7 - 30.9
		0.43	1.05	1.02	0.96	37.5 - 32.8	0.35	0.33	0.29	1.0	0.090Y	32/4/39	39.4 - 34.5
		0.88	1.92	2.09		39.5 - 18.8							75.8 - 36.1
		1.29	4.49	4.16	4.09	20.3 - 16.3	0.56	0.41	0.51	0.7	0.150Y	32/4/39	91.2 - 73.0
		0.61	2.06	1.77	1.51	35.8 - 27.3	0.60	0.50	0.40	0.9	0.20Y	32/4/39	73.7 - 56.3
		1.46	4.67	4.21	4.14	16.1 - 9.8	2.16	2.00	1.84	3.6	0.28130	1/31/18	75.0 - 45.7
			-0.12	-0.10	-0.12		1.75	1.75	1.75	12.2	0.43750	11/30/17	17.3 - 12.1
			-0.78	-0.62	-0.66		2.62	2.59	2.38	8.6	0.6550	11/30/17	37.0 - 24.7
			-0.46	-0.32	-0.54		1.69	1.69	1.69	9.0	0.42260	11/30/17	21.8 - 15.1
				0.22	0.08			1.95	1.63		0.40750	11/30/17	22.3 - 16.4
				0.88	0.81			2.86	1.50		0.1250	2/28/18	23.4 - 19.7
	0.79		2.52	2.16	1.86	22.6 - 19.2	2.70	2.70	3.16	5.2			57.0 - 48.5
		0.66	1.73	1.97	1.72	46.2 - 29.1	0.40	0.40	0.40	0.6	0.130Y	32/4/39	80.0 - 50.3
		0.72	1.82	9.06	1.01	18.2 - 11.6	0.41	0.10		1.6	0.120	2/28/18	33.0 - 21.1
		0.51	0.85	0.37	-1.41	15.1 - 8.2							12.8 - 7.0
202.84			735.36	687.66	574.92	0.2 - 0.1	448.34	351.14	255.11	390.1			128.3 - 103.8
		0.01											10.5 - 0.0
		0.35	2.09	2.23	-0.35	9.8 - 9.1	1.99	2.41		10.1	0.380Z	1/25/18	20.5 - 19.1
		0.41	1.83	1.18	1.68	11.8 - 10.0	1.56	1.56	1.53	7.7	0.390Y	1/12/18	21.6 - 18.3
			0.41	-0.09	0.52	20.4 - 12.4	0.16	0.72	0.72	2.4	0.33120	12/31/17	8.4 - 5.1
		0.70	0.16	-1.75	2.46	404.3 - 282.0	2.26	2.08	1.92	4.1	0.30630	2/28/18	64.7 - 45.1
		0.79	-0.10	-0.98	4.74						0.180	9/29/00	35.0 - 0.0
		3.08	10.39	7.84	3.16	27.7 - 20.2			25.00		22.7Y	32/4/39	287.6 - 210.0
		0.47	2.14	2.12	1.57	22.7 - 17.9	2.74	2.66	2.64	6.3	0.770	2/8/18	48.7 - 38.4
		-3.62	2.08	2.16	-5.29						0.150	32/4/39	
		-0.06	1.17	-0.22	0.13	20.3 - 8.1	0.41		0.85	2.5			23.7 - 9.5
		0.36	0.65	0.04	-0.08	86.5 - 47.6							56.2 - 31.0
		1.05	10.28	10.88	10.70	13.3 - 11.2	2.62	2.38	2.15	2.1	0.720Y	32/4/39	136.4 - 115.2
		0.04	0.14	0.13	0.98						0.0750	12/21/17	
		0.07	0.78	0.74	0.63	18.9 - 13.1							14.8 - 10.3
		0.25	0.75	-0.99	1.13	33.3 - 19.8	0.44	0.42	0.35	2.4	0.110Y	1/1/18	25.0 - 14.9
		0.50	-4.10	2.63	2.23								89.9 - 41.9
		0.68	2.29	1.52	1.27	51.4 - 27.4							117.8 - 62.7
		0.48	1.21	1.27	0.58	15.2 - 9.4							18.4 - 11.4
			0.90	0.81	0.73	30.1 - 24.6	0.91	0.81	0.75	3.7	0.095C	12/29/17	27.1 - 22.2
		0.36	1.62	2.16	2.08	12.4 - 5.7	1.89	2.36	2.56	11.9	0.39840Z	6/15/18	20.1 - 9.3
		-0.21	0.16	-3.38	4.75	266.0 - 177.1	1.00	7.48		2.6	0.250	32/4/39	42.6 - 28.3
		0.60	0.85	0.45	0.22	52.7 - 28.6							44.8 - 24.3
		0.43	2.25	5.08	4.19	16.8 - 11.3	0.44	0.42	0.35	1.5	0.130Y	32/4/39	37.9 - 25.5
		0.74	6.70	2.73	-1.55						0.360	1/23/18	
		0.91	0.71	2.02	2.41	40.7 - 21.4							28.9 - 15.2
		0.27	1.42	1.46	1.30	10.1 - 8.6	1.44	1.44	1.22	10.7	0.360	12/1/17	14.3 - 12.2
		0.75	-0.24	2.17	2.82		1.35		4.30		0.45D	12/22/17	
	-0.11		-21.29	4.68	3.91		0.16	0.16	0.16	0.6	0.040Y	12/15/17	34.5 - 19.8
		-2.07	-0.50	-2.75	-3.74						0.0450	12/1/17	
		0.51	-0.37	1.71	1.59						0.55470	1/30/18	29.3 - 19.6
0.25		0.47	1.69	0.32									
		0.61	4.41	3.69	4.20	16.7 - 12.2	2.72	2.72	2.72	4.3	0.680Y	32/4/39	73.5 - 53.9
		0.16	0.68	0.94	0.39	15.0 - 9.8		3.73					10.2 - 6.7
		0.38	1.49	1.10	-4.07	14.2 - 8.4					0.04GY	12/15/17	21.1 - 12.5
		0.03	0.10	0.16	0.02	48.3 - 24.7							4.8 - 2.5
		0.47	1.92	0.91	2.20	16.9 - 12.0					1.7Y	11/12/10	32.4 - 23.1
		-0.25	-0.78	-2.19	-1.58								34.9 - 23.2
		-0.03	-0.65	-0.79	-0.96								25.2 - 14.3
		0.52	2.02	2.70	0.92	8.5 - 7.0	1.86	2.08	2.08	11.6	0.3021GHZ	1/29/18	17.2 - 14.2
		0.52	2.02	2.70	0.92	8.3 - 0.0	1.86	2.08	2.08	14.3	0.3021GHZ	1/29/18	16.7 - 0.0
		0.97	2.82	1.77	1.66	65.3 - 51.3							184.1 - 144.8
		1.21	4.53	2.95	2.37	18.5 - 12.7	0.60	0.40	0.30	0.9	0.30Y	32/4/39	83.6 - 57.3
		0.41	1.64	1.77	1.62	47.5 - 34.7	0.68	0.60	0.48	1.0	0.20Z	12/8/17	78.0 - 56.9
	0.31		0.84	1.64	0.91						0.6060	5/10/17	
		0.06	1.08	1.29	0.59	37.5 - 31.9	1.16	1.09	1.01	3.1	0.310Z	32/4/39	40.5 - 34.5
		-0.11	2.08	1.60	1.92	24.8 - 21.8	0.93	0.89	0.79	1.9	0.250Y	32/4/39	51.7 - 45.3
		0.61	2.86	2.74	2.26	8.7 - 7.0	1.64	1.44	1.41	7.2			25.0 - 20.1
		-0.15	0.42	0.08	0.19	42.6 - 33.0	0.72	0.72	0.72	4.6	0.42190Z	3/15/18	17.9 - 13.8
		0.12	0.45	0.53	0.47	68.2 - 25.8							30.7 - 11.6
0.48			1.87	2.24	1.47	20.8 - 14.3					0.140	5/8/98	38.9 - 26.6
1.67			6.17	6.15	5.95	27.6 - 20.4	0.15	0.15	0.15	0.1	0.030Y	3/30/18	170.4 - 125.8
			1.82	1.72	1.79	33.7 - 22.1	1.26	1.20	1.13	2.3			61.4 - 40.3
			1.82	1.72	1.79	32.9 - 22.3	1.26	1.18	1.12	2.4			59.9 - 40.5
		1.50	5.07	5.49	5.75	26.9 - 20.0	2.25	2.20	1.91	2.0	0.6650Y	32/4/39	136.3 - 101.4
		-0.81	-0.95	-2.20	0.89						1.56250Y	12/1/13	15.2 - 7.0
		0.07	-2.71	-21.12	2.78								30.3 - 15.4
		2.12	6.85	19.47	2.93	12.0 - 8.4					2.15G7Y	32/4/39	82.0 - 57.2
		0.26	0.63	1.02	0.89	4.3 - 2.8	2.03	1.84	2.23	91.1			2.7 - 1.8
		1.45	3.87	5.35	3.28	32.0 - 26.6	3.12	2.92	2.68	2.8	0.830Y	32/4/39	123.7 - 102.9

SYMBOL	COMPANY	NATURE OF BUSINESS	FISCAL YEAR-END	TOTAL REV. $MILL	NET INCOME $MILL	TOTAL ASSETS $MILL	NET STK EQUITY $MILL	NO OF INST	INST. HOLDINGS (SHARES)
URI	United Rentals Inc	Construction Services	12/31/17	6641.0	1346.0	15030.0	3106.0	815	105792972
USM	United States Cellular Corp	Services	12/31/16	3939.0	48.0	7110.0	3634.0	165	14488299
X	United States Steel Corp.	Non-Precious Metals	12/31/16	10261.0	-440.0	9160.0	2274.0	591	138111248
UTX	United Technologies Corp	Aerospace	12/31/16	57244.0	5055.0	89706.0	27579.0	2236	804027471
UNH	UnitedHealth Group Inc	Life & Health	12/31/16	184840.0	7017.0	122810.0	38274.0	2028	1015675150
UTL	UNITIL Corp	Electric Utilities	12/31/16	383.4	27.1	1128.2	293.1	166	10406329
UNVR	Univar Inc	Specialty Chemicals	12/31/16	8073.7	-68.4	5389.9	809.9	221	143612292
UVV	Universal Corp	Tobacco Products	3/31/17	2071.2	106.3	2123.4	1286.5	284	29753267
UHT	Universal Health Realty Income Tru	REITs	12/31/16	67.1	17.2	524.8	191.3	208	10185081
UHS	Universal Health Services, Inc.	Hospitals & Health Care Facilities	12/31/16	9766.2	702.4	10317.8	4533.2	606	108050890
UVE	Universal Insurance Holdings Inc	General Insurance	12/31/16	685.3	99.4	1060.0	371.2	215	31474146
UTI	Universal Technical Institute, Inc.	Educational Services	9/30/17	324.3	-8.1	274.1	125.8	96	18397765
UNM	Unum Group	Life & Health	12/31/16	11046.5	931.4	61941.5	8968.0	725	269307091
UE	Urban Edge Properties	REITs	12/31/16	326.0	90.8	1904.1	460.3	255	122130572
UBA	Urstadt Biddle Properties Inc	REITs	10/31/17	123.6	52.9	996.7	587.2	40	919071
USB	US Bancorp (DE)	Banking	12/31/16	22744.0	5888.0	445964.0	47298.0	1836	1483525488
USFD	US Foods Holding Corp	Retail - Food & Beverage, Drug & To	12/31/16	22918.8	209.8	8944.4	2537.7	269	220007630
SLCA	US Silica Holdings, Inc.	Mining	12/31/16	559.6	-41.1	2073.2	1273.3	395	93259126
USAC	USA Compression Partners LP	Equipment & Services	12/31/16	265.9	12.9	1472.4		77	67038731
USNA	USANA Health Sciences Inc	Household & Personal Products	12/31/16	1006.1	100.0	470.6	325.3	213	11956822
USB PRI	USB Capital X	Banking						1	15070
USDP	USD Partners LP	Rail	12/31/16	111.1	24.2	306.0		36	7454869
USG	USG Corp	Construction Materials	12/31/16	3017.0	510.0	3869.0	1886.0	375	133518265
EGY	VAALCO Energy, Inc.	Production & Extraction	12/31/16	59.8	-26.5	81.0	-0.4	113	36924577
MTN	Vail Resorts Inc	Sporting & Recreational	7/31/17	1907.2	210.6	4110.7	1571.2	482	45573308
RIO 34	Vale Overseas Ltd	Finance Intermediaries & Services	12/31/05	84.1	0.0	1289.4	-0.0		0
VALE	Vale SA	Non-Precious Metals	12/31/16	27488.0	3982.0	99014.0	39042.0	531	1130465051
VALE	Vale SA	Non-Precious Metals	12/31/16	27488.0	3982.0	99014.0	39042.0	531	1130465051
VRX	Valeant Pharmaceuticals Internation	Pharmaceuticals	12/31/16	9674.0	-2409.0	43529.0	3152.0	446	186943919
VLO	Valero Energy Corp	Refining & Marketing	12/31/16	75659.0	2289.0	46173.0	20024.0	1377	449596134
VLP	Valero Energy Partners LP	Equipment & Services	12/31/16	362.6	188.8	971.9		112	21104827
VHI	Valhi, Inc.	Specialty Chemicals	12/31/16	1606.2	-15.9	2443.2	200.9	92	8888913
VR	Validus Holdings Ltd	General Insurance	12/31/16	2443.2	363.8	11349.8	3838.3	336	94767283
VLY	Valley National Bancorp (NJ)	Banking	12/31/16	870.1	168.1	22864.4	2377.2	344	205272150
VMI	Valmont Industries Inc	Construction Materials	12/31/16	2521.7	173.2	2391.7	943.5	385	26037664
VVV	Valvoline Inc	Specialty Chemicals	9/30/17	2084.0	304.0	1915.0	-117.0	359	192974850
VVV	Valvoline Inc	Specialty Chemicals	9/30/17	2084.0	304.0	1915.0	-117.0	359	192974850
VAR	Varian Medical Systems Inc	Medical Instruments & Equipment	9/29/17	2668.2	249.6	3179.4	1495.0	814	124077749
VGR	Vector Group Ltd	Tobacco Products	12/31/16	1690.9	71.1	1404.0	-332.0	285	78365362
VVC	Vectren Corp	Electric Utilities	12/31/16	2448.3	211.6	5800.7	1768.1	477	68393015
VVC 13	Vectren Utility Holdings Inc.	Electric Utilities	12/31/16	1377.8	173.6	5040.9	1624.0		0
VEC	Vectrus Inc	Services	12/31/16	1190.5	23.7	465.3	117.4	182	11376202
VEDL	Vedanta Ltd	Non-Precious Metals	3/31/17	807518.4	55122.1	1990296.0	605001.1	156	43817456
VEEV	Veeva Systems Inc	IT Services	1/31/17	544.0	68.8	917.7	653.0	421	106732018
VNTR	Venator Materials Plc	Manufacturing	12/31/16	2309.0	-87.0	2659.0	165.0	76	24785981
VTR	Ventas Inc	REITs	12/31/16	3443.5	649.2	23166.6	10661.0	861	405642806
VER	VEREIT Inc	REITs	12/31/16	1454.8	-195.9	15587.6	8447.4	467	934302746
PAY	VeriFone Systems Inc.	Electronic Instruments & Related Pro	10/31/17	1871.0	-173.8	2322.2	754.6	394	145042493
VRTV	Veritiv Corp	Industrial Machinery & Equipment	12/31/16	8326.6	21.0	2483.7	541.8	217	16269005
VZ	Verizon Communications Inc	Services	12/31/16	125980.0	13127.0	244180.0	22524.0	2640	3106074587
VET	Vermilion Energy Inc.	Production & Extraction	12/31/16	828.5	-160.1	4087.2	1578.5		0
VRS	Verso Corp	Paper & Forest Products	12/31/16	1224.0	-32.0	1855.0	770.0	86	55698899
VSM	Versum Materials Inc	Specialty Chemicals	9/30/17	1126.9	193.0	1246.8	-10.0	440	107406128
VFC	VF Corp.	Apparel, Footwear & Accessories	12/31/16	12019.0	1074.1	9739.3	4940.9	1096	449952494
VVI	Viad Corp.	Business Services	12/31/16	1205.0	42.3	869.8	357.4	214	22445013
VCO	Vina Concha y Toro S.A. (Chile)	Beverages	12/31/16	658447.6	47931.1	1015838.6	516209.5	37	496025
VNCE	Vince Holding Corp	Retail - Apparel and Accessories	1/28/17	268.2	-162.7	239.5	-14.0	62	7970851
VIPS	Vipshop Holdings Ltd	Retail - Apparel and Accessories	12/31/16	56591.3	2036.8	25094.5	5732.2	310	343155690
ZTR	Virtus Global Dividend & Income Fu	Holding and other Investment Office	12/31/16	14.0	7.8	468.0	345.1	61	6384068
VGI	Virtus Global Multi-Sector Income F	Holding and other Investment Office	11/30/16	14.6	10.5	259.6	187.2	35	2780726
ZF	Virtus Total Return Fund Inc	Holding and other Investment Office	12/31/16	8.4	3.5	312.3	228.3	71	5336695
V	Visa Inc	Business Services	9/30/17	18358.0	6699.0	67977.0	32760.0	2261	1879576602
VSH	Vishay Intertechnology, Inc.	Electrical Equipment	12/31/16	2323.4	48.8	3077.8	1565.5	397	196476391
VPG	Vishay Precision Group Inc.	Electronic Instruments & Related Pro	12/31/16	224.9	6.4	270.5	171.4	132	12409917
VSTO	Vista Outdoor Inc	Sporting & Recreational	3/31/17	2546.9	-274.5	2976.7	1245.1	223	70304713
VST	Vistra Energy Corp	Electric Utilities	12/31/16	1191.0	-163.0	15167.0	6597.0	195	419352766
VSI	Vitamin Shoppe Inc	Retail - Specialty	12/31/16	1289.2	25.0	734.2	440.0	200	27341615
VSLR	Vivint Solar Inc	Electrical Equipment	12/31/16	135.2	18.0	2126.4	556.3	92	108093178
VMW	VMware Inc	Internet & Software	2/3/17	496.0	-8.0	16397.0	8216.0	662	104679026
VOC	VOC Energy Trust	Oil Royalty Traders	12/31/16	5.7	4.8	85.5	85.5	43	1666574
VCRA	Vocera Communications, Inc.	Computer Hardware & Equipment	12/31/16	127.7	-17.3	182.1	103.4	165	35100926
VG	Vonage Holdings Corp	Services	12/31/16	955.6	17.9	940.4	441.3	292	217028699
VNO	Vornado Realty Trust	REITs	12/31/16	2506.2	906.9	20814.8	6898.5	676	224494922
VJET	voxeljet AG	Industrial Machinery & Equipment	12/31/16	22.3	11.3	62.1	51.4	42	1801897
IAE	VOYA Asia Pacific Dividend Equity I	Holding and other Investment Office	2/28/17	4.9	3.1	135.5	134.5	40	3530868
IHD	VOYA Emerging Markets High Divid	Holding and other Investment Office	2/28/17	5.9	3.5	177.1	175.7	37	6585698
VOYA	Voya Financial Inc	Life & Health	12/31/16	10782.2	-428.0	214235.1	12993.9	420	194005490
IGA	VOYA Global Advantage & Premiu	Holding and other Investment Office	2/28/17	5.3	3.2	215.2	213.3	53	4660430
IGD	VOYA Global Equity Dividend & Pre	Holding and other Investment Office	2/28/17	27.4	18.2	787.2	777.3	97	16983155
IDE	VOYA Infrastructure Industrials & M	Holding and other Investment Office	2/28/17	7.3	3.9	297.9	296.6	34	3482795

EARNINGS PER SHARE						P/E RATIO		DIVIDENDS PER SHARE			AV. YLD	DIV. DECLARED		PRICE RANGE	
QUARTERLY			ANNUAL					PER SHARE			%			2016	
1st	2nd	3rd	2016	2015	2014			2016	2015	2014		AMOUNT	PAYABLE		
-	-	2.33	6.45	6.07	5.15	26.9 -	15.8	-	-	-	-	-		173.3 -	101.6
-	-	-3.51	0.56	2.84	-0.51	81.6 -	58.8	-	-	-	-	5.75GY	32/4/39	45.7 -	33.0
-	-	0.83	-2.81	-11.24	0.69	-		0.20	0.20	0.20	0.7	0.050Y	32/4/39	41.6 -	19.2
-	-	1.67	6.12	8.61	6.82	20.9 -	17.7	2.62	2.56	2.36	2.2	0.70Y	32/4/39	128.1 -	108.2
-	-	2.51	7.25	6.01	5.70	31.5 -	21.7	2.38	1.88	1.41	1.3	0.750Y	32/4/39	228.2 -	157.6
-	-	0.16	1.94	1.89	1.79	27.1 -	22.3	1.42	1.40	1.38	3.0	0.360Y	11/29/17	52.5 -	43.2
-	-	0.28	-0.50	0.14	-0.20	-		-	-	-	-	-		32.8 -	27.0
-	1.02	-	3.92	4.06	5.25	20.8 -	13.3	2.09	2.05	2.01	3.3	0.550Y	32/4/39	81.3 -	52.3
-	-	0.29	1.28	1.78	3.99	65.8 -	46.9	2.60	2.56	2.52	3.6	0.6650Z	32/4/39	84.2 -	60.0
-	-	1.47	7.14	6.76	5.42	17.7 -	13.4	0.40	0.40	0.30	0.4	0.10Y	32/4/39	126.7 -	95.8
-	-	0.28	2.79	2.97	2.08	10.4 -	5.9	0.69	0.63	0.55	2.8	0.140Y	3/12/18	29.1 -	16.5
-	-	-0.21	-2.02	-0.38	0.08	-		0.04	0.32	0.40	1.2	0.020Y	3/31/16	3.9 -	2.4
-	-	1.12	3.95	3.50	1.61	14.6 -	11.1	0.77	0.70	0.62	1.6	0.230Y	32/4/39	57.5 -	43.8
-	-	0.15	0.91	0.39	-	31.7 -	25.8	0.82	0.80	-	3.2	0.220Z	32/4/39	28.9 -	23.4
-	-	0.14	0.49	0.90	1.42	49.6 -	37.6	1.04	1.02	1.01	4.9	0.39060Z	32/4/39	24.3 -	18.4
-	-	0.88	3.24	3.16	3.08	17.4 -	15.3	1.07	1.01	0.96	2.0	25.6250Y	32/4/39	56.4 -	49.7
-	-	0.42	1.03	0.98	-0.43	31.0 -	25.0	-	-	-	-	-		31.9 -	25.8
-	-	0.50	-0.63	0.22	2.23	-		0.25	0.44	0.50	0.7	0.06250Y	1/5/18	60.0 -	24.9
-	-	0.07	0.27	-3.15	0.60	73.1 -	54.5	2.10	2.08	1.98	12.5	0.5250	2/14/18	19.7 -	14.7
-	-	0.97	3.99	3.59	2.80	18.9 -	13.6	-	-	-	-	-		75.6 -	54.3
-	-	0.48	1.06	0.83	-0.29	15.9 -	8.7	1.25	1.11	-	10.2	0.3450	11/13/17	16.9 -	9.3
-	-	0.46	3.46	6.73	0.25	11.2 -	7.5	-	-	1.19	-	0.0250	32/4/39	38.7 -	25.8
-	-	-0.01	-0.45	-2.72	-1.36	-		-	-	-	-	0.001F	8/1/09	1.3 -	0.7
-0.71	-	-	4.01	3.07	0.77	59.0 -	40.1	2.87	2.08	1.25	1.4	1.0530Z	32/4/39	236.7 -	161.0
-	-	0.43	0.77	-2.35	0.13	15.9 -	10.1	0.04	0.25	0.67	0.4	-		12.2 -	7.8
-	-	0.43	0.77	-2.35	0.13	14.7 -	13.7	0.04	0.25	0.67	0.4	-		11.3 -	10.5
-	-	3.69	-6.94	-0.85	2.63	-		-	-	-	-	1.7	12/22/10	28.3 -	8.5
-	-	1.91	4.94	7.99	6.85	18.7 -	12.4	2.40	1.70	1.05	3.4	0.80Y	32/4/39	92.3 -	61.5
-	-	0.65	2.85	2.12	1.01	17.8 -	14.1	1.41	1.14	0.71	3.1	0.50750	2/13/18	50.8 -	40.2
-	-	0.13	-0.05	-0.39	0.16	-		0.08	0.08	0.11	2.3	0.020Y	12/22/17	7.2 -	2.2
-	-	-3.17	4.36	4.34	5.08	-		1.40	1.28	1.20	-	0.36250	12/15/17		
-	-	0.14	0.63	0.42	0.56	20.3 -	17.0	0.44	0.44	0.44	3.8	0.34380Y	32/4/39	12.8 -	10.7
-	-	1.55	7.63	1.71	7.09	22.7 -	17.8	1.50	1.50	1.38	1.0	-0.3750Y	32/4/39	172.8 -	136.1
-	-	0.27	1.33	-	-	18.8 -	15.9	-	-	-	-	0.07450Y	32/4/39	25.1 -	21.2
-	-	0.27	1.33	-	-	17.7 -	16.7	-	-	-	-	0.07450Y	32/4/39	23.5 -	22.2
-	-	0.98	4.19	4.09	3.83	26.8 -	18.3	-	-	-	-	0.0250	32/4/39	112.4 -	76.6
-	-	0.13	0.52	0.44	0.30	44.3 -	36.4	1.47	1.40	1.33	7.1	0.40Y	32/4/39	23.0 -	18.9
-	-	0.75	2.55	2.39	2.02	27.3 -	20.3	1.62	1.54	1.46	2.6	0.450Y	32/4/39	69.5 -	51.7
-	-	0.51	2.16	2.86	2.13	16.3 -	9.9	-	-	-	-	-		35.2 -	21.3
-	-	-	-42.21	-43.29	5.22	-		20.79	-	-	122.1	-		21.3 -	12.8
-	-	0.22	0.38	0.28	0.15	175.8 -	108.8	-	-	-	-	-		66.8 -	41.4
-	-	0.48	-	-	-	-		-	-	-	-	-			
-	-	1.71	1.86	1.25	1.60	38.7 -	31.9	2.96	3.04	2.96	4.6	0.790Z	32/4/39	71.9 -	59.4
-	-	0.00	-0.29	-0.43	-1.36	-		0.55	0.28	1.08	6.6	0.13960Z	32/4/39	9.1 -	7.5
-	-	-0.63	-0.08	0.68	-0.34	-		-	-	-	-	-		21.3 -	17.1
-	-	-0.91	1.30	1.67	-1.62	47.9 -	17.5	-	-	-	-	-		62.3 -	22.7
-	-	0.89	3.21	4.37	2.42	17.0 -	13.4	2.27	2.21	2.14	4.7	0.590Y	32/4/39	54.6 -	42.9
-	-	-0.32	-1.38	-1.98	2.51	-		2.58	2.58	2.58	6.3	0.2150	2/15/18	57.6 -	30.0
-	-	0.12	-0.93	-5.19	-6.62	-		-	-	-	-	0.030Y	11/25/08	17.6 -	3.4
-	-	0.48	1.95	-	-	21.8 -	13.7	-	-	-	-	0.050Y	32/4/39	42.5 -	26.8
-	-	0.97	2.54	2.85	2.38	29.4 -	19.0	1.53	1.33	1.11	2.6	0.460Y	32/4/39	74.6 -	48.3
-	-	2.19	2.09	1.32	2.58	29.4 -	20.5	0.40	0.40	1.90	0.8	0.10Y	1/2/18	61.4 -	42.9
-	-	-	64.16	66.66	50.06	0.6 -	0.0	440.89	358.67	296.00	1370.5	-		37.6 -	0.0
-	-2.00	-	1.40	9.30	-9.80	30.7 -	2.3	-	-	-	-	-		43.0 -	3.2
-	-	0.10	16.86	13.23	2.28	0.9 -	0.5	-	-	-	-	-		14.9 -	7.9
-	-	-	0.27	0.22	0.25	50.6 -	41.4	1.16	1.11	1.09	9.3	0.1130	2/20/18	13.7 -	11.2
-	-	-	0.93	0.91	1.23	20.3 -	16.7	1.87	2.02	1.62	11.0	0.1560	2/20/18	18.9 -	15.5
-	-	0.19	0.11	0.11	0.11	69.1 -	56.1	1.08	1.22	1.03	9.0	0.3610	1/9/18	13.1 -	10.7
-	-	0.86	2.48	2.58	2.15	46.1 -	32.1	0.56	0.48	0.40	0.6	0.1950Y	32/4/39	114.3 -	79.5
-	-	0.41	0.32	-0.73	0.77	72.5 -	48.4	0.25	0.24	0.24	1.4	0.06750	32/4/39	23.2 -	15.5
-	-	0.32	0.48	-0.96	0.28	58.1 -	31.7	-	-	-	-	-		27.9 -	15.2
-	-2.01	-	2.35	1.25	-	16.7 -	5.6	-	-	-	-	-		39.3 -	13.3
-	-	0.64	-0.38	-	-	-		2.32	-	-	13.6	2.32G7	32/4/39	20.5 -	14.6
-	-	-3.72	1.04	1.82	2.00	23.6 -	3.3	-	-	-	-	-		24.6 -	3.5
-	-	0.06	0.16	0.12	-0.35	37.8 -	16.6	-	-	-	-	-		6.0 -	2.6
-	-	1.07	2.78	2.34	2.04	46.4 -	28.4	-	-	-	-	-		128.9 -	78.9
-	-	0.11	0.28	0.47	1.85	21.1 -	11.6	0.28	0.47	1.85	7.0	0.110	2/14/18	5.9 -	3.2
-	-	-0.10	-0.64	-0.66	-1.12	-		-	-	-	-	-		31.9 -	18.3
-	-	0.04	0.08	0.10	0.09	129.0 -	72.3	-	-	-	-	-		10.3 -	5.8
-	-	-0.15	4.34	3.59	4.15	20.6 -	16.7	2.52	2.52	2.92	3.2	0.3974GHZ	32/4/39	89.6 -	72.4
-	-	-	-3.04	-2.58	-1.22	-		-	-	-	-	-		6.0 -	2.7
-	-	0.29	0.27	0.35	-	38.0 -	30.5	1.15	1.28	1.35	11.3	0.2050	1/16/18	11.0 -	8.8
-	-	0.20	0.30	0.34	-	47.9 -	37.7	1.04	1.15	1.30	11.8	0.1850	1/16/18	9.6 -	7.5
-	0.81	-2.13	1.80	9.02				0.04	0.04	0.04	0.1	0.010Y	32/4/39	52.1 -	34.2
-	-	0.17	0.17	0.19		60.9 -	57.9	1.12	1.12	1.12	10.4	0.2250	1/16/18	11.7 -	9.8
-	-	0.18	0.22	0.27		45.2 -	37.8	0.91	0.91	0.97	12.1	0.0610	2/15/18	8.1 -	6.8
-	-	0.23	0.26	0.48		76.0 -	56.6	1.54	1.62	1.62	10.2	0.290	1/16/18	17.5 -	13.0

T61

SYMBOL	COMPANY	NATURE OF BUSINESS	FISCAL YEAR-END	TOTAL REV. $MILL	NET INCOME $MILL	TOTAL ASSETS $MILL	NET STK EQUITY $MILL	NO OF INST	INST. HOLDINGS (SHARES)
IID	VOYA International High Dividend E	Holding and other Investment Office	2/28/17	2.1	1.4	57.6	57.0	16	365781
IRR	Voya Natural Resources Equity Inco	Holding and other Investment Office	2/28/17	3.6	1.7	156.6	156.0	44	4260864
PPR	VOYA Prime Rate Trust	Holding and other Investment Office	2/28/17	64.6	45.7	1274.7	857.1	136	51479333
VMC	Vulcan Materials Co (Holding Comp	Mining	12/31/16	3592.7	419.5	8471.5	4572.5	783	157487057
WTI	W & T Offshore Inc	Production & Extraction	12/31/16	400.0	-249.0	829.7	-659.0	171	80982378
WPC	W.P. Carey Inc	REITs	12/31/16	941.5	267.7	8454.0	3301.7	472	62484845
WNC	Wabash National Corp	Autos- Manufacturing	12/31/16	1845.4	119.4	898.7	472.4	339	92381533
WBC	WABCO Holdings Inc	Construction Services	12/31/16	2810.0	223.0	3056.0	701.4	461	59369507
WAB	Wabtec Corp	Construction Services	12/31/16	2931.2	304.9	6581.0	2206.0	578	127817823
WDR	Waddell & Reed Financial, Inc.	Finance Intermediaries & Services	12/31/16	1239.0	146.9	1406.3	844.0	345	105746317
WAGE	WageWorks Inc	Business Services	12/31/16	364.7	20.2	1343.4	408.1	304	49940059
WMT	Wal-Mart Stores Inc	Retail - General Merchandise/Depart	1/31/17	485873.0	13643.0	198825.0	77798.0	2282	1210177662
WD	Walker & Dunlop Inc	Business Services	12/31/16	575.3	113.9	3052.4	610.2	245	29274539
WAC	Walter Investment Management Cor	Credit & Lending	12/31/16	995.7	-529.2	16758.9	280.3	96	29409687
HCC	Warrior Met Coal Inc	Mining	12/31/16	297.6	-49.7	947.6	753.0	124	53235760
WPG	Washington Prime Group (New)	REITs	12/31/16	843.5	67.1	5107.5	1093.4	334	195188970
WRE	Washington Real Estate Investment	REITs	12/31/16	313.3	119.3	2253.6	1050.9	320	82518938
WCN	Waste Connections Inc (Canada)	Sanitation Services	12/31/16	3375.9	246.5	11193.1	5647.5	431	229724969
WM	Waste Management, Inc. (DE)	Sanitation Services	12/31/16	13609.0	1182.0	20859.0	5297.0	1288	414254294
WAT	Waters Corp.	Biotechnology	12/31/16	2167.4	521.5	4662.1	2301.9	752	91273255
WSO	Watsco Inc	Industrial Machinery & Equipment	12/31/16	4220.7	182.8	1874.6	1005.8	414	34173036
WTS	Watts Water Technologies Inc	Industrial Machinery & Equipment	12/31/16	1398.4	84.2	1800.3	736.3	295	33352310
W	Wayfair Inc	Retail - Furniture & Home Furnishing	12/31/16	3380.4	-194.4	761.7	79.4	243	62107359
WFT	Weatherford International Plc	Equipment & Services	12/31/16	5749.0	-3392.0	12664.0	2012.0	447	1197069390
WBS	Webster Financial Corp (Waterbury,	Banking	12/31/16	1086.4	207.1	26072.5	2527.0	382	103907845
WEC	WEC Energy Group Inc	Electric Utilities	12/31/16	7472.3	940.2	30123.2	8960.2	941	272860775
WTW	Weight Watchers International, Inc.	Miscellaneous Consumer Services	12/31/16	1164.9	67.7	1271.0	-1207.6	262	65934676
WRI	Weingarten Realty Investors	REITs	12/31/16	549.6	238.9	4426.9	1579.9	415	155437177
WMK	Weis Markets, Inc.	Retail - Food & Beverage, Drug & To	12/31/16	3136.7	87.2	1431.3	926.7	152	11126871
WBT	Welbilt Inc	Industrial Machinery & Equipment	12/31/16	1456.6	79.5	1769.1	-43.5	249	134575773
WCG	WellCare Health Plans Inc	Hospitals & Health Care Facilities	12/31/16	14237.1	242.1	6152.8	2000.1	457	56043025
WFC	Wells Fargo & Co.	Banking	12/31/16	94176.0	21938.0	1930115.0	199581.0	2658	4533245855
WSF	Wells Fargo Capital IV	Banking	-	-	-	-	-	-	-
EOD	Wells Fargo Global Dividend Opport	Holding and other Investment Office	10/31/17	17.7	13.8	352.1	303.7	51	11140112
WFE PRA	Wells Fargo Real Estate Investment	REITs	12/31/16	899.9	783.8	32398.4	32394.2	-	0
HCN	Welltower Inc	REITs	12/31/16	4281.2	1077.8	28865.2	14806.4	952	407756174
WAIR	Wesco Aircraft Holdings Inc.	Aerospace	9/30/17	1429.4	-237.3	1754.1	649.7	146	154373364
WCC	Wesco International, Inc.	Electrical Equipment	12/31/16	7336.0	101.6	4491.0	2013.3	364	54255167
WST	West Pharmaceutical Services, Inc.	Rubber Products	12/31/16	1509.1	143.6	1716.7	1117.5	430	84342729
WR	Westar Energy Inc	Electric Utilities	12/31/16	2562.1	346.6	11487.1	3805.9	514	139046386
WAL	Western Alliance Bancorporation	Banking	12/31/16	743.4	259.8	17200.8	1891.5	392	98861589
TLI	Western Asset Corporate Loan Fun	Holding and other Investment Office	9/30/17	9.6	7.1	178.8	113.0	42	3427010
EMD	Western Asset Emerging Markets D	Holding and other Investment Office	12/31/16	41.2	32.4	1336.2	1038.6	120	22848398
GDO	Western Asset Global Credit Define	Holding and other Investment Office	10/31/17	21.1	16.0	374.7	286.8	50	4077607
EHI	Western Asset Global High Income	Holding and other Investment Office	5/31/17	42.7	34.3	698.8	511.7	78	12100366
HIX	Western Asset High Income Fund II	Holding and other Investment Office	4/30/17	67.7	56.5	927.2	671.1	102	13309364
HIO	Western Asset High Income Opport	Holding and other Investment Office	9/30/17	51.5	44.8	747.3	730.5	119	41547026
HYI	Western Asset High Yield Defined	Holding and other Investment Office	5/31/17	22.6	20.0	393.5	385.8	-	0
PAI	Western Asset Income Fund	Holding and other Investment Office	12/31/16	7.7	6.6	138.5	138.3	32	761446
SBI	Western Asset Intermediate Muni F	Holding and other Investment Office	11/30/16	7.8	5.7	190.6	143.0	49	2409867
IGI	Western Asset Investment Grade D	Holding and other Investment Office	11/30/16	12.4	10.6	220.8	218.9	30	2186085
MMU	Western Asset Managed Municipals	Holding and other Investment Office	5/31/16	39.4	31.6	889.1	659.3	88	6644696
WMC	Western Asset Mortgage Capital Co	REITs	12/31/16	31.8	-25.0	3156.0	430.5	-	0
DMO	Western Asset Mortgage Defined O	Holding and other Investment Office	12/31/16	22.0	15.3	319.4	216.2	30	1173806
MHF	Western Asset Municipal High Inco	Holding and other Investment Office	10/31/17	8.1	6.9	173.0	171.5	52	2911057
MNP	Western Asset Municipal Partners F	Holding and other Investment Office	11/30/16	10.1	7.4	239.8	173.0	44	1581131
MTT	Western Asset Municipal Term Trus	Holding and other Investment Office	11/30/16	14.5	12.6	262.4	261.3	28	1202234
WEA	Western Asset Premier Bond Fund	Holding and other Investment Office	12/31/16	13.4	11.0	227.2	165.3	48	2179494
GFY	Western Asset Variable Rate Strate	Holding and other Investment Office	9/30/17	5.3	3.7	115.1	85.5	30	4832182
WIW	Western Asset/Claymore Inflation-Li	Holding and other Investment Office	11/30/16	30.8	21.0	1127.3	756.9	104	36798381
WIA	Western Asset/Claymore Inflation-Li	Holding and other Investment Office	11/30/17	12.5	7.9	545.1	369.1	68	17777457
WGP	Western Gas Equity Partners LP	Equipment & Services	12/31/16	1804.3	345.8	7736.1		140	40811251
WES	Western Gas Partners LP	Equipment & Services	12/31/16	1883.0	591.3	7733.0		-	0
WU	Western Union Co	Business Services	12/31/16	5422.9	253.2	9419.6	902.2	826	574272109
WLK	Westlake Chemical Corp	Specialty Chemicals	12/31/16	5075.5	398.9	10890.3	3523.6	340	44685137
WLKP	Westlake Chemical Partners LP	Specialty Chemicals	12/31/16	986.7	40.9	1555.2		64	15137387
WMLP	Westmoreland Resource Partners L	Mining	12/31/16	349.3	-31.6	386.9		13	25114
WBK	Westpac Banking Corp	Banking	9/30/17	37518.0	7990.0	851875.0	61288.0	198	22004330
WRK	WestRock Co	Containers & Packaging	9/30/17	14859.7	708.2	25089.0	10342.5	596	249777876
WHG	Westwood Holdings Group, Inc.	Wealth Management	12/31/16	123.0	22.6	179.7	146.1	113	6840314
WEX	Wex Inc	Miscellaneous Consumer Services	12/31/16	1018.5	60.6	5997.1	1497.2	324	59730912
WY	Weyerhaeuser Co	REITs	12/31/16	6365.0	1027.0	19243.0	9180.0	1208	690222714
WGL	WGL Holdings Inc	Gas Utilities	9/30/17	2354.7	193.9	6626.0	1530.9	398	50/91170
WPM	Wheaton Precious Metals Corp	Precious Metals	12/31/16	891.6	195.1	6153.3	4940.0	454	247243993
WHR	Whirlpool Corp	Household Appliances, Electronics &	12/31/16	20718.0	888.0	19153.0	4773.0	879	86254296
WTM	White Mountains Insurance Group,	General Insurance	12/31/16	1360.7	412.5	6544.7	3603.3	284	4017773
WSR	Whitestone REIT	REITs	12/31/16	104.4	7.9	855.2	255.7	149	21813932
WLL	Whiting Petroleum Corp	Production & Extraction	12/31/16	1285.0	-1339.1	9876.1	5141.2	468	348893490
WOW	WideOpenWest Inc	Services	12/31/16	1237.0	26.3	2770.8	-718.0	94	47185864
WRD	WildHorse Resource Development	Production & Extraction	12/31/16	127.3	-47.1	1442.3	1007.9	101	97086521

T62

EARNINGS PER SHARE						P/E RATIO	DIVIDENDS PER SHARE			AV. YLD %	DIV. DECLARED		PRICE RANGE 2016
1st	2nd	3rd	2016	2015	2014		2016	2015	2014		AMOUNT	PAYABLE	
-	-	-	0.20	0.22	0.25	39.3 - 32.4	0.83	0.83	0.88	11.5	0.0520	2/15/18	7.9 - 6.5
-	-	-	0.11	0.12	0.10	61.5 - 51.8	0.91	1.01	1.06	14.5	0.1620	1/16/18	6.8 - 5.7
-	-	-	0.32	0.33	0.40	17.5 - 15.7	0.33	0.35	0.41	6.2	0.0220	1/11/18	5.6 - 5.0
-	-	0.81	3.09	1.64	1.54	43.8 - 36.4	0.80	0.40	0.22	0.7	0.250Y	32/4/39	135.3 - 112.5
-	-	-0.01	-2.60	-13.76	-0.16				0.40		0.10Y	12/3/14	3.5 - 1.8
-	-	0.74	2.49	1.61	2.39	29.0 - 24.0	3.93	3.83	3.69	5.9	1.010Z	32/4/39	72.3 - 59.6
-	-	0.30	1.82	1.50	0.85	13.0 - 8.8	-	-			0.0750Y	1/25/18	23.8 - 16.0
-	-	1.30	3.98	4.72	4.81	39.0 - 26.2	-	-			0.070Y	32/4/39	155.1 - 104.2
-	-	0.70	3.34	4.10	3.62	27.7 - 20.9	0.36	0.28	0.20	0.5	0.120Y	32/4/39	92.5 - 69.7
-	-	0.45	1.78	2.94	3.71	12.8 - 9.2	1.84	1.72	1.36	9.8	0.250Y	2/1/18	22.7 - 16.5
-	-	0.24	0.54	0.63	0.50	148.5 - 106.4	-	-					80.2 - 57.5
-	-	0.58	4.57	5.05	4.88	21.8 - 14.4	1.96	1.92	1.88	2.5	0.510Y	32/4/39	99.6 - 65.7
-	-	1.06	3.65	2.65	1.58	15.3 - 8.3	-						55.8 - 30.3
-	-	-3.38	-14.71	-7.00	-2.93		-				0.22427Z	11/15/11	5.0 - 0.3
-	-	2.27	-13.15				-				11.217Y	11/22/17	29.9 - 15.5
-	-	-0.06	0.29	-0.55	1.10	37.7 - 23.2	1.00	1.00	0.50	11.8	0.42970Z	32/4/39	10.9 - 6.7
-	-	0.04	1.65	1.31	1.67	20.5 - 18.3	1.20	1.20	1.20	3.7	0.302	1/5/18	33.8 - 30.1
-	-	0.47	1.07	1.55	1.52	86.7 - 49.1	0.22	-		0.3	0.140	11/22/17	92.8 - 52.5
-	-	0.87	2.65	1.65	2.79	32.6 - 26.1	1.64	1.54	1.50	2.2	0.4250Y	32/4/39	86.3 - 69.2
-	-	1.69	6.41	5.65	5.07	31.2 - 21.1	-						200.3 - 135.5
-	-	1.82	5.15	4.90	4.32	33.3 - 26.3	3.60	2.80	2.00	2.4	1.250Y	32/4/39	171.4 - 135.4
-	-	0.77	2.44	-3.24	1.42	31.8 - 24.3	0.71	0.66	0.58	1.1	0.190Y	12/15/17	77.5 - 59.4
-	-	-0.88	-2.29	-0.92	-2.97		-						83.8 - 35.2
-	-	-0.26	-3.82	-2.55	-0.75		-						
-	-	0.67	2.16	2.15	2.08	27.0 - 20.6	0.98	0.89	0.75	1.9	0.40Y	32/4/39	58.4 - 44.5
-	-	0.68	2.96	2.34	2.59	23.5 - 19.3	1.98	1.74	1.56	3.1	0.55250Y	32/4/39	69.5 - 57.0
-	-	0.65	1.03	0.56	1.74	49.4 - 10.8	-	0.00	0.00		0.1750Y	10/11/13	50.9 - 11.1
-	-	0.56	1.87	1.29	2.25	19.6 - 15.7	1.46	1.38	1.55	4.5	0.757Z	32/4/39	36.7 - 29.4
-	-	0.16	3.24	2.21	2.05	20.9 - 10.5	1.20	1.20	1.20	2.4	0.30Y	11/20/17	67.8 - 34.0
-	-	0.24	0.57	1.15	1.17	41.2 - 32.0	-						23.5 - 18.3
-	-	3.82	5.43	2.67	1.44	39.2 - 25.2	-	-					213.0 - 136.6
-	-	0.84	3.99	4.12	4.10	15.4 - 12.4	1.51	1.48	1.35	2.7	0.390Y	32/4/39	61.6 - 49.6
-	-	-	0.62	0.68	0.78	10.5 - 8.9	0.58	0.72	0.72	9.6	0.16330	1/2/18	6.5 - 5.5
-	-	9.46	37.75	48.71	49.37	0.7 - 0.7	1.59	1.69	46.74	6.0	0.39840	12/29/17	27.3 - 25.5
-	-	0.20	2.81	2.34	1.45	27.6 - 22.5	3.44	3.30	3.18	4.9	0.81250Z	32/4/39	77.7 - 63.3
-	-	-2.32	0.93	-1.60	1.05	16.5 - 7.3	-						15.3 - 6.8
-	-	1.12	2.10	4.18	5.18	35.5 - 23.6	-						74.5 - 49.0
-	-	0.67	1.91	1.30	1.75	53.2 - 41.2	0.49	0.45	0.41	0.5	0.140Y	32/4/39	101.7 - 78.6
-	-	1.11	2.43	2.09	2.35	23.5 - 20.3	1.52	1.44	1.40	2.9	0.40Y	32/4/39	57.2 - 49.4
-	-	0.79	2.50	2.03	1.67	23.6 - 18.0	-				0.39060Z	1/2/18	59.0 - 45.0
-	-	-	0.71	0.80	0.78	17.0 - 14.5	0.87	0.87	0.87	7.8	0.0530	3/1/18	12.1 - 10.3
-	-	-	1.01	1.05	1.15	15.8 - 14.6	1.26	1.31	1.42	8.1	0.10	3/1/18	15.9 - 14.7
-	-	-	1.20	1.23	1.30	15.5 - 14.2	1.36	1.36	1.39	7.6	0.11350	3/1/18	18.6 - 17.0
-	-	-	0.97	0.99	1.06	10.7 - 10.1	1.16	1.16	1.16	11.4	0.06350	3/1/18	10.4 - 9.8
-	-	-	0.73	0.79	0.85	10.2 - 9.4	0.82	0.83	0.89	11.4	0.0460	3/1/18	7.5 - 6.9
-	-	-	0.39	0.41	0.43	13.4 - 12.6	-	0.43	0.44		0.02750	3/1/18	5.2 - 4.9
-	-	-	1.28	1.30	1.38	12.3 - 11.7	1.32	1.32	1.46	8.6	0.090	3/1/18	15.7 - 15.0
-	-	-	0.70	0.70	0.73	24.4 - 20.1	0.69	0.69	0.69	4.6	0.05750	3/1/18	17.1 - 14.0
-	-	-	0.41	0.42	0.46	24.3 - 22.7	0.48	0.48	0.48	5.0	0.034M	3/1/18	10.0 - 9.3
-	-	-	0.98	0.98	1.02	23.3 - 20.2	1.20	1.20	1.51	5.7	0.0850	3/1/18	22.9 - 19.8
-	-	-	0.74	0.78	0.79	19.6 - 18.1	0.78	0.78	0.78	5.6	0.063M	3/1/18	14.5 - 13.4
-	-	0.54	-0.61	-0.25	2.67		1.38	2.49	2.74	13.5	0.310	1/26/18	10.9 - 9.5
-	-	-	1.47	2.13	1.87	18.4 - 15.2	3.00	3.32	3.09	12.0	0.1789B	1/26/18	27.1 - 22.3
-	-	-	0.31	0.36	0.36	26.0 - 22.9	0.33	0.35	0.37	4.4	0.0255M	3/1/18	8.1 - 7.1
-	-	-	0.76	0.81	0.86	21.3 - 19.5	0.87	0.87	0.85	5.6	0.0625M	3/1/18	16.2 - 14.8
-	-	-	1.04	1.11	1.08	23.0 - 20.0	1.05	1.01	1.01	4.7	0.0840	3/1/18	23.9 - 20.8
-	-	-	0.93	1.00	1.04	15.5 - 14.0	1.03	1.08	1.08	7.5	0.06750	3/1/18	14.4 - 13.0
-	-	-	0.79	0.69	0.78	22.1 - 0.0	0.93	0.88	0.87	5.6	0.07750	3/1/18	17.4 - 0.0
-	-	-	0.34	0.25	0.38	33.6 - 32.2	0.40	0.37	0.44	3.6	0.0360	1/31/18	11.4 - 11.0
-	-	-	0.27	0.07	0.29	43.7 - 41.2	0.38	0.35	0.42	3.3	0.03450	1/31/18	11.8 - 11.1
-	-	0.44	1.53	0.39	1.02	31.0 -	1.71	1.40	1.04	4.1	0.54870	2/22/18	47.4 - 34.6
-	-	0.38	1.74	-1.95	2.12	37.9 - 24.7	3.29	2.95	2.55	6.0	0.920	2/13/18	66.0 - 42.9
-	-	0.51	0.51	1.62	1.59	44.3 - 36.2	0.64	0.62	0.50	3.3	0.1750Y	32/4/39	22.6 - 18.5
-	-	1.61	3.06	4.86	5.07	34.8 - 18.7	0.74	0.69	0.58	1.0	0.210Y	32/4/39	106.5 - 57.3
-	-	0.47	1.50	1.47	0.50	17.4 - 13.8	1.29	1.15	0.17	5.4	0.38640	2/23/18	26.1 - 20.6
-	-	-0.04	-1.51	-4.62	-0.58		0.73	0.60	-	20.0	0.11550	11/14/17	5.8 - 0.0
-	-	-	2.18	2.49	2.39	12.4 - 10.2	2.07	1.74	1.83	8.3			27.0 - 22.3
-	-	1.29	-1.54	2.93	3.29		1.50	0.38	0.70	2.7	0.430	32/4/39	64.4 - 49.3
-	-	0.49	2.77	3.33	3.45	25.6 - 18.6	2.33	2.07	1.82	3.9	0.680Y	32/4/39	70.8 - 51.6
-	-	0.79	1.48	2.62	5.18	95.4 - 66.4	-						141.2 - 98.3
-	-	0.17	1.39	0.89	3.18	26.3 - 21.7	1.24	1.20	1.02	3.7	0.320Z	32/4/39	36.5 - 30.2
-	-	0.16	3.31	2.62	2.05	26.0 - 22.4	1.90	1.80	1.72	2.3	0.510Y	32/4/39	86.0 - 74.2
-	-	0.15	0.45	-0.41	0.56	66.7 - 40.8	0.21	0.20	0.26	0.9	0.090	12/7/17	30.0 - 18.3
-	-	3.72	11.50	9.83	8.17	17.2 - 14.0	3.90	3.45	2.88	2.2	1.10Y	32/4/39	198.3 - 160.9
-	-	130.81	82.19	50.60	51.21		1.00	1.00	1.00		1.0	32/4/39	
-	-	0.07	0.26	0.24	0.32	57.3 - 42.9	1.24	1.14	1.14	9.3	0.0950Z	3/13/18	14.9 - 11.2
-	-	-3.16	-21.28	-45.40	2.12		-				1.56250Y	6/17/13	52.4 - 16.0
-	-	-0.02					-						18.4 - 8.8
-	-	-0.17	-0.11				-						18.5 - 10.6

SYMBOL	COMPANY	NATURE OF BUSINESS	FISCAL YEAR-END	TOTAL REV. $MILL	NET INCOME $MILL	TOTAL ASSETS $MILL	NET STK EQUITY $MILL	NO OF INST	INST. HOLDINGS (SHARES)
JW A	Wiley (John) & Sons Inc.	Publishing	4/30/17	1718.5	113.6	2606.2	1003.1	344	52836588
WG	Willbros Group Inc (DE)	Equipment & Services	12/31/16	731.7	-47.8	363.0	135.1	-	0
WMB	Williams Cos Inc (The)	Equipment & Services	12/31/16	7499.0	-424.0	46835.0	4643.0	1061	823017737
WPZ	Williams Partners LP (New)	Equipment & Services	12/31/16	7491.0	431.0	46265.0		17	5220536
WSM	Williams Sonoma Inc	Retail - Furniture & Home Furnishing	1/29/17	5083.8	305.4	2476.9	1248.2	558	115731843
WGO	Winnebago Industries, Inc.	Autos- Manufacturing	8/26/17	1547.1	71.3	902.5	441.7	295	33027575
WIT	Wipro Ltd	IT Services	3/31/17	550402.0	84895.0	793516.0	520304.0	177	124429862
WNS	WNS (Holdings) Ltd	IT Services	3/31/17	602.5	37.8	704.1	415.1	167	47757466
WWW	Wolverine World Wide, Inc.	Apparel, Footwear & Accessories	12/31/16	2494.6	87.7	2431.7	966.5	362	116739363
WF	Woori Bank (Korea)	Banking	12/31/01	7459439.0	705352.0	77849060.0		56	2193820
WK	Workiva Inc	Internet & Software	12/31/16	178.6	-44.0	143.1	-3.1	102	16217862
INT	World Fuel Services Corp.	Equipment & Services	12/31/16	27015.8	126.5	5412.6	1925.0	348	81428052
WWE	World Wrestling Entertainment Inc	Entertainment	12/31/16	729.2	33.8	600.9	239.7	225	45879608
WP	Worldpay Inc	Business Services	12/31/16	3579.0	213.2	7044.0	1315.7	520	205332643
WOR	Worthington Industries, Inc.	Non-Precious Metals	5/31/17	3014.1	204.5	2325.3	951.6	344	41768795
WPP	WPP Plc (New)	Advertising	12/31/16	14388.9	1400.1	34568.3	9324.5	293	12839140
WPX	WPX Energy, Inc.	Production & Extraction	12/31/16	693.0	-601.0	7264.0	3466.0	457	435821501
WYN	Wyndham Worldwide Corp	Hotels, Restaurants & Travel	12/31/16	5599.0	611.0	9819.0	714.0	726	113193926
XHR	Xenia Hotels & Resorts Inc	REITs	12/31/16	950.2	85.9	2860.3	1629.6	260	84643937
XRM	Xerium Technologies Inc	Industrial Machinery & Equipment	12/31/16	471.3	-21.6	541.9	-146.9	89	11953770
XRX	Xerox Corp	Peripherals	12/31/16	10771.0	-477.0	18145.0	5017.0	750	450154545
XIN	Xinyuan Real Estate Co Ltd	Property, Real Estate & Development	12/31/16	1561.6	73.0	4236.4	900.3	83	29516351
XL	XL Group Ltd	General Insurance	12/31/16	10546.1	441.0	58434.1	10938.5	575	322018411
XOXO	XO Group Inc	Internet & Software	12/31/16	152.1	12.1	210.2	174.5	177	27660900
XPO	XPO Logistics, Inc.	Airlines/Air Freight	12/31/16	14619.4	69.0	11698.4	2700.0	443	148887289
XYL	Xylem Inc.	Industrial Machinery & Equipment	12/31/16	3771.0	260.0	6474.0	2190.0	704	178979676
AUY	Yamana Gold Inc	Precious Metals	12/31/16	1787.7	-307.9	8801.7	4512.2	379	437603954
YELP	Yelp Inc	Internet & Software	12/31/16	713.1	-4.7	885.2	807.2	315	78576189
YEXT	Yext Inc	Services	1/31/17	124.3	-43.1	86.5	-7.1	71	25400346
YGE	Yingli Green Energy Holding Co Ltd	Semiconductors	12/31/16	8376.1	-2097.7	13499.8	-8348.4	76	5871565
YRD	Yirendai Ltd	Wealth Management	12/31/16	466.4	160.8	689.0	308.2	75	6607524
YPF	YPF SA	Refining & Marketing	12/31/16	210100.0	-28237.0	421139.0	118755.0	194	123624443
YUMC	Yum China Holdings Inc	Hotels, Restaurants & Travel	12/31/16	6752.0	502.0	3727.0	2377.0	669	353997528
YUM	Yum! Brands Inc	Hotels, Restaurants & Travel	12/31/16	6366.0	1619.0	5478.0	-5656.0	1247	324409860
YUME	YuMe Inc	Advertising	12/31/16	160.4	-7.7	137.4	97.2	79	17390144
ZAYO	Zayo Group Holdings Inc	Manufacturing	6/30/17	2199.8	85.7	8739.4	1410.5	375	219141336
ZEN	Zendesk Inc	Internet & Software	12/31/16	312.0	-103.8	475.3	299.4	213	111161527
ZBH	Zimmer Biomet Holdings Inc	Medical Instruments & Equipment	12/31/16	7683.9	305.9	26684.4	9568.9	1207	228127131
ZOES	Zoe's Kitchen Inc	Hotels, Restaurants & Travel	12/26/16	276.0	1.8	215.2	130.0	132	22109639
ZTS	Zoetis Inc	Pharmaceuticals	12/31/16	4888.0	821.0	7649.0	1487.0	900	505164290
ZTO	ZTO Express (Cayman) Inc	Shipping	12/31/16	9788.8	2053.9	23403.7	19745.0	134	124880660
ZYME	Zymeworks Inc	Pharmaceuticals	12/31/16	11.0	-33.8	94.0	67.9	15	1827787

| EARNINGS PER SHARE | | | | | | P/E RATIO | DIVIDENDS PER SHARE | | | AV. YLD | DIV. DECLARED | | PRICE RANGE |
| QUARTERLY | | | ANNUAL | | | | | | | | | | |
1st	2nd	3rd	2016	2015	2014		2016	2015	2014	%	AMOUNT	PAYABLE	2016
-	1.06	-	2.48	2.97	2.70	26.7 - 20.1	1.20	1.16	1.00	2.2	0.320Y	32/4/39	66.2 - 49.8
-	-	-0.54	-0.77	0.54	-1.62								3.7 - 1.1
-	-	0.04	-0.57	-0.76	2.92		1.68	2.45	1.96	5.7	0.30Y	32/4/39	32.4 - 27.0
-	-	0.27	-0.17	-3.27	1.01		3.40	3.40	2.20	8.6	0.60	2/9/18	42.2 - 35.0
-	-	0.84	3.37	3.24	2.82	16.5 - 12.7	1.40	1.32	1.24	2.8	0.390Y	32/4/39	55.6 - 42.9
0.57	-	-	1.68	1.52	1.64	34.5 - 14.6	0.40	0.36	-	1.1	0.10Y	1/24/18	58.0 - 24.5
-	7.85	-	36.18	35.13	31.66	0.2 - 0.1	5.95	4.95	3.98	112.6			6.4 - 4.5
-	0.18	-	1.12	1.10	0.79	37.1 - 24.0							41.6 - 26.9
-	-	0.24	0.89	1.20	1.30	35.9 - 23.6	0.24	0.24	0.24	0.9	0.060Y	2/1/18	31.9 - 21.0
													53.5 - 31.2
-	-	-0.34	-1.08	-1.09	-1.28								22.9 - 12.4
-	-	-0.57	1.81	2.64	3.11	26.1 - 14.6	0.24	0.24	0.15	0.7	0.060Y	32/4/39	47.3 - 26.4
-	-	0.28	0.44	0.32	-0.40	74.8 - 41.5	0.48	0.48	0.48	2.1	0.120Y	12/26/17	32.9 - 18.2
-	-	0.57	1.32	0.95	0.75	57.5 - 45.4							75.9 - 59.9
-	0.62	-	2.22	1.12	2.11	23.9 - 17.9	0.75	0.69	0.45	1.6	0.210Y	32/4/39	53.1 - 39.6
-	-	-	1.08	0.88	0.81	110.1 - 76.5	2.39	2.15	1.76	2.3	0.78130Y	1/31/18	118.9 - 82.6
-	-	-0.38	-2.05	-7.42	0.80								15.3 - 8.7
-	-	1.97	5.53	5.14	4.18	21.1 - 13.7	2.00	1.68	1.40	2.1	0.580Y	32/4/39	116.7 - 75.9
-	-	0.11	0.79	0.79	-	28.6 - 20.8	1.10	0.84	-	5.6	0.2750Z	1/12/18	22.6 - 16.5
-	-	0.07	-1.35	-0.28	-0.48						0.11250Y	12/17/07	7.5 - 3.8
-	-	0.68	-1.96	1.68	3.24		1.24	1.12	1.00	4.2	0.250Y	32/4/39	34.0 - 27.5
-	-	0.20	0.53	0.45	0.29	12.9 - 8.1	0.29	0.19	0.19	5.5			6.8 - 4.3
-	-	-4.06	1.56	4.15	0.69						0.220	32/4/39	20.8 - 16.3
-	-	0.13	0.47	0.21	0.02	44.3 - 34.6							92.2 - 42.7
-	-	0.44	0.53	-2.65	-2.00	173.9 - 80.6							
-	-	0.58	1.45	1.87	1.83	47.8 - 32.4	0.62	0.56	0.51	1.1	0.180Y	32/4/39	69.3 - 47.0
-	-	0.04	-0.33	-2.26	-1.69		0.02	0.06	0.13	0.6	0.0050	1/12/18	4.8 - 2.2
-	-	0.09	-0.06	-0.44	0.48								47.6 - 27.4
-	-	-0.19	-0.89	-0.61	-								14.8 - 11.4
-	-	-2.05	-11.54	-30.81	-7.49								3.1 - 1.7
-	-	-	1.35	0.44	-0.04	38.7 - 14.9							52.3 - 20.1
-	-	3.60	-72.13	11.68	22.95		1.65	0.66	0.71	7.4			26.2 - 16.9
-	-	0.53	1.36	-	-	31.6 - 19.0					0.1GY	12/21/17	43.0 - 25.9
-	-	1.18	4.04	2.92	2.32	20.7 - 15.6	1.89	1.69	1.52	2.6	0.360Y	32/4/39	83.5 - 63.2
-	-	0.00	-0.22	-0.49	-0.27						0.030Y	10/9/17	5.9 - 3.5
0.09	-	-	-0.31	-0.66	-0.80								37.1 - 29.9
-	-	-0.28	-1.11	-0.99	-1.26								35.6 - 22.1
-	-	0.48	1.51	0.77	4.19	87.8 - 68.4	0.96	0.88	0.88	0.8	0.240Y	32/4/39	132.6 - 103.3
-	-	0.01	0.09	0.06	-0.58	286.2 - 120.0							25.8 - 10.8
-	-	0.61	1.65	0.68	1.16	44.1 - 31.8	0.38	0.33	0.29	0.6	0.1260Y	32/4/39	72.8 - 52.5
-	-	-	2.91	2.15	0.68	6.1 - 3.9							17.6 - 11.2
-	-	-0.65	-2.65	-1.70	-1.77								18.6 - 0.0

This Page left intentionally blank